BUSINESS LAW

PRINCIPLES CASES
LEGAL ENVIRONMENT

TENTH EDITION

RONALD A. ANDERSON
Professor of Law and Government,
Drexel University
Member of the Pennsylvania
and Philadelphia Bars

IVAN FOX
Professor of Law and Chairman,
Business Law Department,
Pace University
Member of the New York Bar

DAVID P. TWOMEY
Professor of Law,
School of Management,
Boston College
Member of the Massachusetts
and Florida Bars

Copyright © 1989

by South-Western Publishing Co.
Cincinnati, Ohio

ISBN: 0-538-80234-0

Library of Congress Catalog Card Number: 87-63549

1 2 3 4 5 6 7 8 Ki 5 4 3 2 1 0 9 8

Printed in the United States of America

LA70JA
PUBLISHED BY
SOUTH-WESTERN PUBLISHING CO.
CINCINNATI   WEST CHICAGO, IL   CARROLLTON, TX   LIVERMORE, CA

ABOUT THE AUTHORS

Ronald A. Anderson, Professor of Law and Government, Drexel University, taught the subjects covered by this book for 40 years. He is the internationally renowned author of the definitive, 11-volume treatise on the Uniform Commercial Code and other well-respected professional works.

Professor Anderson was graduated from the University of Pennsylvania in 1933 and earned his *Juris Doctor* from that school in 1936. He is a member of the American Bar Association and is an active member of the legal community.

Ivan Fox, with Pace University since 1958, and currently Professor of Law and Chairman of the Business Law Department, is widely known for his work with the Fox-Lambers CPA Review Course and has lectured extensively to professional and banking groups on various business law topics.

Professor Fox was graduated from Pace University in 1954, earned his *Juris Doctor* from New York Law School in 1957, and received his LL.M. from New York University in 1963. He is a member of the New

York Bar and the New York State Bar Association.

David P. Twomey is Professor of Law at Boston College and is a nationally known labor arbitrator. He has written a great number of books and articles on labor law and business law topics, and he was elected to membership in the National Academy of Arbitrators in 1979.

Professor Twomey was graduated from Boston College in 1962 and earned his MBA at the University of Massachusetts at Amherst in 1963. After two years of business experience, he entered Boston College of Law and earned his *Juris Doctor* in 1968. He is a member of the Massachusetts, Florida, and Federal Bars. Professor Twomey joined the faculty of the Boston College School of Management in 1968 and was promoted to professor in 1978. He has a special interest in curriculum development, having recently served three terms as chairman of his school's Educational Policy Committee. He is chairman of the Business Law Department.

PREFACE

Our focus in preparing this Tenth Edition of BUSINESS LAW: PRINCIPLES, CASES, LEGAL ENVIRONMENT continues to be to create a flexible teaching tool with universally desirable qualities that can be adapted to each instructor's personal teaching philosophy. We have sought, in presenting a broad range of materials, to make this book (1) accurate, (2) understandable, (3) balanced, (4) life-oriented, and (5) thought provoking.

By *accurate*, we mean that we have done everything possible to insure that the content of the book is as up-to-date as modern publishing technology will permit. Accurate also means that new doctrines and minority trends have been identified. Accordingly, we have endeavored to make this book anticipatory as well as retrospective. In the process of so doing, we hope to emphasize the dynamic character of the law.

Understandable means that legalistic jargon and words of art must be translated into ordinary English. We have replaced linguistic provincialisms and obscure words with ordinary language that can be understood by the modern student.

Balanced means that from the myriad discrete legal topics that might have some significance for undergraduate students of business law, those with the greatest relevance have been selected. If all the volumes of professional treatises relating to business were added together, the number would exceed 1,000. The business law student is given one book. Obviously, careful choice is necessary to bring the great mass of the law down into a one-volume text for beginners. In addition, great care must be exercised to treat all portions of the student's book with the appropriate degree of intensity.

Life-oriented requires the book to be devoted to those areas that the undergraduate student of today will most likely meet in future years. Consequently, it means avoiding the unusual, the bizarre, the headline cases that have no real value for the business person. Above all, life-oriented brings out the interrelationship between the law and life: the law is shaped by the environment, and the law gives direction to the environment. For the purpose of curriculum compartmentalization, "law" is a separate subject but as far as life is concerned it is an inseparable part of living. The more the student can appreciate this interrelationship, the better will be the student's understanding both of law and of life.

Thought provoking means there are end-of-chapter materials that call for the student's developing skill in the analysis of data to identify basic questions, to apply existing principles to the solution of such basic questions, and to make intelligent decisions when there are no preexisting principles to govern the exact basic questions that are involved. This system not only brings the student back to the orientation of law to life but also assures the teaching of law a permanent place in the pattern of higher education.

The objectives set forth above have guided the writing of this book for more than a third of a century. Though our focus on these objectives has never wavered, the specific content of the book has evolved to keep pace with changing times. The early 1960s witnessed the integration of the Uniform Commercial Code in the Seventh Edition as a result of the growth in the number of states adopting the UCC. In subsequent years that coverage has been continually updated to keep pace with amendments to the UCC and other uniform and model acts. This modernizing is seen in the inclusion in this edition of the text and an analysis of the new UCC Article 2A, "Leases." Curriculum trends have us placing increasing emphasis upon environmental and regulatory topics.

THE LEGAL AND SOCIAL ENVIRONMENT OF BUSINESS

Part I of the book brings together various chapters relating to societal or public law that form the general background for individual business transactions. To borrow terms familiar to the economist, Part I deals with macro law while much of the balance of the book relates to micro law. It is important that the student see the background of macro law. It is also important that the student recognize that the legal environment of business is the sum total of the macro and micro areas.

More specifically, Part I deals with the regulatory environment in which business operates. The social forces behind the creation and evolution of the specific principles and substantive rules that govern disputes and transaction between individuals are explored. A comprehensive discussion of the federal and state court structure and the procedures involved in a lawsuit, from commencement to execution of the judgment, is included. The Constitution, as the foundation of the legal environment of business, is presented. The increasing role played by the administrative agencies in the government regulation of business is fully discussed.

This allocation of the indicated material to Part I is in harmony with the increased concern for an environmental approach to the teaching of business law. At the same time, this focusing on societal or public law is not made at the expense of the treatment of the areas of private law. There has been no lessening of attention to accuracy of content, clarity of expression, and thoroughness of subject matter coverage.

In addition to the topics discussed in Part I, other chapters throughout the book are appropriate for a course that focuses on public law. Although every chapter in the text possesses the potential for an environmental approach, some chapters lend themselves to this mode of teaching more readily than others. An outline of chapters emphasizing public law follows:

SUGGESTED LEGAL ENVIRONMENT OUTLINES

Chapters:

1. Law and Determination of Legal Rights
2. Ethics, Social Forces, and the Law

3. The Constitution as the Foundation of the Legal Environment
4. Government Regulation
45. Employment (Government Regulation of Employment)
51. Corporate Stock and Shareholders (Securities Regulation)
24. Personal Property (Protection of Trademarks, Copyrights, Patents, Computer Software and Chips)
5. The Legal Environment of International Trade
6. Administrative Agencies
7. Environmental Law and Community Planning
8. Consumer Protection
9. Crimes
10. Torts
39. Bankruptcy

(or)
Chapters:

1. Law and Determination of Legal Rights
2. Ethics, Social Forces, and the Law
3. The Constitution as the Foundation of the Legal Environment
4. Government Regulation
5. The Legal Environment of International Trade
6. Administrative Agencies
7. Environmental Law and Community Planning
8. Consumer Protection
9. Crimes
10. Torts
24. Personal Property (Protection of Trademarks, Copyrights, Patents, Computer Software and Chips)
39. Bankruptcy
45. Employment
51. Corporate Stock and Shareholders (Securities Regulation)

An introductory course that emphasizes societal or public law may include the chapters contained in either of the above outlines and other appropriate chapters selected for the course. An introductory course emphasizing private law may cover selected chapters from Part I, "The Legal and Social Environment of Business," and chapters on contracts, personal property, or agency. The instructor may choose to cover additional topics in this introductory course, depending upon the ability level of the students and the time allotted to the course at the institution. The remainder of the book may be covered in advanced courses.

PREPARATION FOR CPA EXAM

As was true in previous editions, this Tenth Edition includes material on topics essential to preparation for the business law section of the CPA exam. Topics generally tested on this exam (shown with relative weight expressed as a percentage) are:

The CPA and the Law (10%)
Business Organizations (20%)
Contracts (15%)
Debtor-Creditor Relationships (10%)
Government Regulation of Business (10%)
Uniform Commercial Code (25%)
Property (10%)

As this list suggests, the breadth and depth of CPA testing in the business law section necessitate inclusion of a great deal of material in any text purporting to prepare students for the exam. Adequate coverage of all these topics requires at least six semester hours. Consequently, this text is designed to accommodate a two-semester program in business law.

NEW TOPICS

New in this Tenth Edition are the chapters "Computers and the Law" and "Accountants' Liability and Malpractice." In Part 4, "Sales," coverage of international law is increased by discussion of pertinent sections of the United Nations Convention on Contracts for the International Sale of Goods. Chapter 42, Section 14, presents the law relating to "Disability of the Principal Under the Uniform Durable

Power of Attorney Act." Chapter 45 includes coverage of "Employer-Related Immigration Laws." Chapter 49 contains a new section, "Liability of Successor Corporations." The currently developing law relating to liability of corporate directors is presented in Chapter 52. The UCC appendix has been expanded to include the text of the new Article 2A, "Leases," and an appendix analyzing Article 2A has been added.

CASES

As in previous editions, this Tenth Edition contains ample cases — including case questions — integrated with the text of each chapter. Popular, precedent-setting cases have been retained while at the same time adding many new decisions (a substantial number of which have been decided since 1985).

FEATURES

An outline presented at the beginning of each chapter gives an overview of the topics covered. Points in the text have been enhanced by the use of illustrations. End-of-chapter summaries designed to assist students in assimilating the material are presented in each chapter.

A section on "Analysis of Court Opinions" is presented on pages vii-ix. This section includes a chart designed to assist students in identifying and analyzing ethical issues in the cases.

A glossary, a case index, and a subject index are included, as well as appendices "How to Find the Law," the "U.S. Constitution," and selected model or uniform business statutes.

ACKNOWLEDGMENTS

We thank the faculty and students who have provided valuable suggestions that have influenced this text. In particular we wish to thank the following reviewers: Kenneth A. Ackman, Miami-Dade Community College; John E. Adamson, Southwest Missouri State University; Dimitry Alexander, Miami-Dade Community College; Albert Clark, Southern University; J. Scott Kirkwood, Wingate College; Murray S. Levin, University of Kansas; Patrick A. Lyons, South Dakota State University; S. Alan Schlact, Kennesaw College; Roscoe Shain, Austin Peay State University; Gary L. Tidwell, College of Charleston; Marcus D. Williams, George Mason University; and John W. Yeargain, Southeastern Louisiana University.

STUDENT STUDY GUIDE

Accompanying this Tenth Edition is a student study guide authored by E. Clayton Hipp of Clemson University. The study guide contains highlights of each chapter in the text, a mix of questions and problems, and special exercises designed to demonstrate real-life application of legal rules and principles.

INSTRUCTOR'S MATERIALS

An instructor's manual prepared by Kim Tyler (of Shasta College) and the authors contains chapter outlines, lecture notes and teaching suggestions, case briefs, and answers to end-of-chapter questions and case questions. Transparencies and a printed test bank are available. The test questions are also available in an easy-to-use software package.

ANALYSIS OF COURT OPINIONS

Beginning with page 6, you will find opinions that were handed down by judges in actual cases. Some of these opinions show how the courts apply a rule of law that has been stated in the text. Other opinions extend or expand the rule stated in the text.

COMPONENTS OF A COURT OPINION

The information for each case is presented in three parts: (a) the heading, (b) the facts of the case, and (c) the opinion. In this explanation the first case, *Manrique v Fabbri*, p. 6, will be used as an example.

(a) HEADING. The heading of the case consists of the title and the source.

(1) Title. The title of the case usually consists of the names of the parties to the action. In the illustrative case Manrique, as plaintiff, sued Fabbri as defendant.

The title of an appealed case may not reveal who the plaintiff was in the original or lower court or who the defendant was. When the action is begun in the lower court, the first party named is the plaintiff and the second is the defendant. When the case is appealed, the name of the party who takes the appeal may appear first on the records of the higher court, so that if the defendant takes the appeal, the original order of the names of the parties is then reversed.

(2) Source. The second part of the heading gives the source of the opinion. *Manrique v Fabbri* was decided by the Florida Supreme Court and is found in "493 So 2d 437." This means that the opinion is found in the 493rd volume of the second series of the Southern (So) reporter[1] beginning at page 437.

(b) FACTS. The paragraph in smaller type following the heading is a summary of the facts of the case, which provides a background for an understanding and analysis of the opinion. Read the statement of facts. Keep in mind the principles of law that you

---

[1] See Appendix, "How to Find the Law," footnote 1, for sectional reporters.

studied in the chapter. Then read the opinion carefully to see how the court made its decision, what it decided, and whether it agrees with what you thought would be decided.

(c) OPINION. The opinion of the court includes the name of the judge, excerpts from the reasoning of the court, and the judgment.

(1) Judge. At the beginning of the opinion is the name of the judge who wrote it. The opinion in the first case was written by Judge Barkett.

The letter or letters following the name of the judge indicate the judge's rank or title. *J.* stands for Judge or Justice. (*JJ.* is the plural form.) Other abbreviations include *C.J.* for Chief Justice or Circuit Judge, *D.J.* for District Judge, *P.J.* for Presiding Judge or President Judge, and *C.* for Chancellor or Commissioner.

When a case is perfectly clear and obvious, the opinion will frequently be filed without naming the writing judge and will then have a heading of "memorandum" or "per curiam."

(2) Body of the Opinion. The material following the judge's name is quoted from the opinion of the court. Words enclosed in brackets [ ] did not appear in the original opinion but have been added to explain a legal term, to identify a party, or to clarify a statement. Ellipses (three or four periods) are used to indicate that something has been omitted that is not pertinent to the point of law with which we are concerned at this time.

Decisions vary in length from less than a page to more than a hundred pages, and opinions frequently involve several points of law. Each case in this book has been carefully edited so that the excerpts reprinted here will be convenient for student use.

Opinions do not follow a standard pattern of organization; but usually the well-written opinion will carefully examine the arguments presented by all parties and then explain why the court accepts or rejects those arguments in whole or in part. In this process the opinion may discuss the

opinion of the lower court, the decisions in similar cases in other courts, and material from other sources.[2]

(3) Judgment. The case is concluded with a statement of the court's decision. If the case has been appealed and if the court agrees with the lower court, the decision may simply be "Judgment affirmed" or a similar expression. If the appellate court disagrees, the decision may be expressed as "Judgment reversed." "Case remanded" means that the case is returned to the lower court to proceed further in harmony with the appellate court's decision. In lower court cases when the judgment is on a narrow issue, the judgment of the court may be limited to "Objection sustained" or "Objection dismissed."

A judge of the court who disagrees with the majority may file a dissenting opinion.

CHECKLIST FOR CASE STUDY

The questions in the following checklist will serve as a guide for the analysis of each case. It should be understood, however, that not every case will provide answers to all these questions.

(a) COURT. In what court was the action brought originally, and which court filed the opinion being studied?

(b) PARTIES. Who were the parties to the action? Were they the parties to the original transaction, or were they strangers such as creditors?

(c) PURPOSE OF THE ACTION. What was the relief or remedy sought in the action?

(d) ACTION APPEALED FROM. What was done in the lower court that the appellant deemed wrong and from which the appeal was taken?

(e) ARGUMENTS OF THE PARTIES. What were the arguments made by the respective parties?

(f) DECISION OF THE COURT. What did the court decide?

(g) BASIS FOR DECISION. On what author-

---

[2] See Appendix, "How to Find the Law."

ity or ground did the court base its decision? Was it common law, decision, statute, Restatement of the Law, text, logic, or the personal belief of the court?

(h) APPRAISAL OF THE DECISION. What social objectives are advanced by the deci-

sion? What social objectives are hindered or defeated by the decision? What ethical principles are involved in the case? Is the decision socially desirable? Is it practical in application? Does it give rise to any dangers?

BUSINESS ETHICS	
SELECTED ETHICAL PRINCIPLES OR ISSUES TO DISCUSS IN RELATION TO CASES	ELEMENTARY GUIDELINES FOR AN ETHICAL ANALYSIS OF CONTEMPLATED ACTION
1. INTEGRITY AND TRUTHFULNESS.	1. IDENTIFY THE ETHICAL PRINCIPLE(S) INVOLVED IN THE CASE.
2. PROMISE-KEEPING.	2. DEFINE THE PROBLEM FROM THE DECISION MAKER'S POINT OF VIEW.
3. LOYALTY.	
	3. IDENTIFY WHO COULD BE INJURED BY THE CONTEMPLATED ACTION.
4. FAIRNESS.	
5. DOING NO HARM.	4. DEFINE THE PROBLEM FROM THE OPPOSING POINT OF VIEW.
6. MAINTAINING CONFIDENTIALITY.	5. WOULD YOU (AS THE DECISION MAKER) BE WILLING TO TELL YOUR FAMILY, YOUR SUPERVISOR, YOUR CEO, AND THE BOARD OF DIRECTORS ABOUT THE ACTIONS PLANNED?
7. AVOIDING CONFLICT OF INTEREST.	
8. WHISTLEBLOWING.	6. WOULD YOU BE WILLING TO GO BEFORE A COMMUNITY MEETING, A CONGRESSIONAL HEARING, OR A PUBLIC FORUM TO DESCRIBE THE ACTION?
9. EFFICIENCY AND EFFECTIVENESS (CREATE NEW JOBS AND THE PRODUCTS NECESSARY FOR A HUMANE LIFE).	
	7. WITH MORAL COMMON SENSE AND FULL CONSIDERATION OF THE FACTS AND ALTERNATIVES, REACH A DECISION ABOUT WHETHER THE CONTEMPLATED ACTION SHOULD BE TAKEN.
10. INNOVATION.	

FIGURE 1
GUIDELINES TO BUSINESS ETHICS

CONTENTS

x

PART 1

THE LEGAL AND SOCIAL ENVIRONMENT OF BUSINESS

1

LAW AND DETERMINATION OF LEGAL RIGHTS

Why have law?

If you have ever been stuck in a traffic jam on a turnpike or crowded in a mob leaving a stadium, then you have been in a position to observe the need for order to keep things running smoothly and efficiently. What is true on a small scale for traffic jams and crowds is true on a large scale for society in general. The order, or pattern of rules, that society establishes to govern the conduct of individuals and the relationships among them we call law. Law is society's way of keeping things running smoothly and efficiently.

Stated another way, law is merely management at the societal level. You personally have objectives and make decisions to manage your life. Business people have objectives and make decisions to manage their businesses. Likewise, when society governs itself it determines its objectives and makes management decisions, albeit through a much more complex process. That which we call law is merely a particular aspect of the broad problem of management: the management of society.

In this text we will look generally at the process of managing society through the system of laws and enforcement agencies, and we will examine specifically those aspects of the system that deal with business. Perhaps the best place to start is with an explanation of the nature of law and legal rights.

A.   NATURE OF LAW AND LEGAL RIGHTS

Law consists of the body of principles that govern conduct and that can be enforced in courts or by administrative agencies. Much of the difficulty in seeking to understand the law is the result of regarding it as an absolute and exact science. The ideal of a definite body of law is not only attractive to the student but is dear to everyone. Long-revered is the maxim that "in the known certainty of the law lies the safety of all." The purpose of establishing our Constitution was to enable us to have a government of laws and not of people.

Actually, the certainty, the precision, and the logic of the law are very relative matters. In truth the law is an arbitrary set of rules that we have agreed upon to govern ourselves. Our reason for so doing is the quest for justice and the advancement of our social objectives.

§ 1:1   LEGAL RIGHTS

What are legal rights? Who has them? In answering these questions, we tend to make the mistake of thinking of the present as being characteristic of what was and what will be. But consider the evolution of the concept of the "rights of the human being" and the right of privacy.

(a) THE "RIGHTS OF THE HUMAN BEING" CONCEPT. Our belief in the American way of life and in the concepts on which our society or government is based should not ob-scure the fact that at one time there was no American way of life. While in the past many religious leaders, philosophers, and poets spoke of the rights and dignity of people, rulers laughed at such pretensions and held people tightly in a society based on status. A noble had the rights of a noble. A warrior had the rights of a warrior. A slave had very few rights at all. In each case, the law saw only status; rights attached not to the human being but to the status.

In the course of time, serfdom displaced slavery in much of the Western world. Eventually feudalism disappeared and, with the end of the Thirty Years War, the modern nation-state began to emerge. Surely one might say that in such a "new order," a human being had legal rights. But the person had rights not as a human being — only as a subject. Even when the English colonists settled in America, they brought with them not the rights of human beings but the rights of British subjects. Even when the colonies were within one year of war, the Second Continental Congress presented to King George III the Olive Branch Petition, which beseeched the king to recognize the colonists' rights as English subjects. For almost a year the destiny of the colonies hung in the balance with the colonists unable to decide between remaining loyal to the Crown, seeking to obtain recognition of their rights as English subjects (a "status" recognition), or doing something else.

Finally, the ill-advised policies of George III and the eloquence of Thomas Paine's *Common Sense* tipped the scales and the colonists spoke on July 4, 1776, not in terms of the rights of English subjects but in terms of the rights of people existing independently of any government. Had the American Revolution been lost, the Declaration of Independence would have gone rattling down the corridors of time with many other failures. But the American Revolution was won, and the new government that was established was based upon "human beings" as the building blocks rather than upon "subjects." Rights of human beings replaced the concept of rights of subjects. With this transition, the obligations of a monarch to faithful subjects were replaced by the rights of human beings existing without regard to will or authority of any kind. Since then, America has been going through additional stages of determining what is embraced by the concept of "rights of human beings."

(b) THE RIGHT OF PRIVACY. One legal right recognized by all Americans today is the right of privacy. Before 1890, however, this right did not exist in American law. Certainly those who wrote the Declaration of Independence and the Bill of Rights were conscious of rights. How can we explain that the law did not recognize a right of privacy until a full century later?

The answer is that at a particular time people worry about the problems that face them. Note the extent of the fears and concern of the framers of the Bill of Rights. The Fourth Amendment states, "The right of the people to be secure in their persons, houses, papers, and effects, against unreasonable searches and seizures, shall not be violated, and no Warrants shall issue, but upon probable cause, supported by Oath or affirmation, and particularly describing the place to be searched and the persons or things to be seized." The people of 1790 were afraid of a recurrence of the days of George III.

The framers of the Fourth Amendment declared what we today would regard as a segment of privacy — protection from police invasion of privacy. The people of 1790 just were not concerned with invasion of privacy by a private person. While a snooping person could be prosecuted to some extent under a Peeping Tom statute, this was a criminal liability. The victim could not sue for damages for invasion of privacy.

If we are honest in reviewing history, all that we can say is that modern people think highly of privacy and want it to be protected. Knowing that the law is responsive to the wishes of society, we can also say that the right is protected by government. But note that we should go no further than to say that it is a right that society wishes to protect at the present time. If circumstances arise in our national life of such a nature that the general welfare is opposed to the right of privacy we can expect that the "right" of privacy will be limited or modified. For example, although the right of privacy prevents a bank from giving out information about a customer's bank account, the federal government, acting under a 1969 statute, can require such information to see if income taxes are due or if money has been paid or received in criminal transactions.[1]

§ 1:2   WHAT IS THE LAW?

The expression, "a law," is ordinarily used in connection with a statute enacted by a state legislature or the Congress of the United States, such as an act of the federal Congress to provide old-age benefits. However, the statutes enacted by legislative bodies are not the only source of law.

Constitutional law includes the constitutions in force in the particular area or territory. In each state, two constitutions are in force — the state constitution and the national constitution.

Statutory law includes legislative acts declaring, commanding, or prohibiting something. Each state has its own legislature and the United States has the Congress: both of these bodies enact laws. In addition, every city, county, or other subdivision has some power to adopt ordinances which, within their sphere of operation, have the same binding effect as legislative acts.

Of great importance are **administrative regulations,** such as rules of the Securities and Exchange Commission and the National Labor Relations Board. The regulations promulgated by national and state administrative agencies generally have the force of statute and are therefore part of "the law."

---

[1] United States v Bisceglia, 420 US 141 (1975). But see § 36:4(a) of this book.

Law also includes principles that are expressed for the first time in court decisions. This is **case law**. For example, when a court decides a new question or problem, its decision becomes a **precedent,** which stands as the law for that particular problem in the future. This rule that a court decision becomes a precedent to be followed in similar cases is the doctrine of **stare decisis.**

Court decisions do not always deal with new problems or make new rules. In many cases, courts apply rules as they have been for many years — even centuries. These time-honored rules of the community are called the **common law**. Statutes will sometimes repeat or redeclare the common law rules. Many statutes depend upon the common law for definition of the terms in the statute.

Law also includes treaties made by the United States, and proclamations and orders of the President of the United States or of other public officials.

§ 1:3   Uniform State Laws

To secure uniformity as far as possible, the National Conference of Commissioners on Uniform State Laws, composed of representatives from all the states, has drafted statutes on various subjects for adoption by the states. The best example of such laws is the Uniform Commercial Code (UCC).[2] The UCC regulates the fields of sales of goods; commercial paper, such as checks; secured transactions in personal property; bulk transfers; and particular aspects of banking, letters of credit, warehouse receipts, bills of lading, and investment securities.

National uniformity has also been brought about in some areas of consumer protection by the adoption of the federal Consumer Credit Protection Act (CCPA), Title I of which is popularly known as the Truth in Lending Act.[3] A Uniform Consumer Credit Code (UCCC) has been proposed and is now before the states for adoption. To the extent that it is adopted, it will complement the Uniform Commercial Code.[4]

§ 1:4   Classifications of Law

Law is classified in many ways. For example, **substantive law,** which creates, defines, and regulates rights and liabilities, is contrasted with **procedural law,** which specifies the steps that must be followed in enforcing those rights and liabilities. Law

---

[2] The Code has been adopted in every state except Louisiana. It has also been adopted for Guam, the Virgin Islands, and the District of Columbia. Louisiana has adopted Articles 1, 3, 4, 5, 7, and 8 of the Code. In 1972, a group of Amendments to the Code was recommended. These have been adopted in Alabama, Alaska, Arizona, Arkansas, California, Colorado, Connecticut, Delaware, Florida, Georgia, Hawaii, Idaho, Illinois, Indiana, Iowa, Kansas, Kentucky, Maine, Maryland, Massachusetts, Michigan, Minnesota, Mississippi, Montana, Nebraska, Nevada, New Hampshire, New Jersey, New Mexico, New York, North Carolina, North Dakota, Ohio, Oklahoma, Oregon, Pennsylvania, Rhode Island, South Dakota, Tennessee, Texas, Utah, Virginia, Washington, West Virginia, Wisconsin, and Wyoming. The 1972 Amendments have also been adopted for Guam. The changes made by the 1972 Amendments to the UCC are confined mainly to Article 9 on secured transactions. In 1977, Article 8 of the Code, relating to investment securities, was amended. This amended version has been adopted in Arkansas, California, Colorado, Connecticut, Delaware, Florida, Hawaii, Idaho, Kansas, Kentucky, Maryland, Massachusetts, Michigan, Minnesota, Montana, Nevada,

New Hampshire, New Mexico, New York, North Dakota, Ohio, Oklahoma, Oregon, Rhode Island, South Dakota, Tennesse, Texas, Virginia, Washington, West Virginia, Wisconsin, and Wyoming. Article 2A on leases was promulgated recently; it has been adopted by Oklahoma.

Uniformity has also reached international scope. The United Nations Convention on Contracts for the International Sale of Goods (CIGS) applies to contracts made after January 1, 1988, between parties in the United States and those in the other nations that have thus far approved the Convention. The provisions of this Convention or international agreement have been strongly influenced by Article 2 of the Uniform Commercial Code.

[3] 15 United States Code § 1601 et seq., and 18 USC § 891 et seq.

[4] As of January, 1987, the 1968 version of the Uniform Consumer Credit Code has been adopted in Colorado, Indiana, Oklahoma, South Carolina, Utah, Wisconsin, and Wyoming. It has also been adopted for Guam. The 1968 version of the UCCC has been replaced by a 1974 version which has been adopted in Idaho, Iowa, Kansas, and Maine. In 1983, Idaho replaced the UCCC with the Idaho Credit Code.

may also be classified in terms of its origin, as coming from the Roman (or civil) codified law, the English common law of principles based on customs and usages of the community, or the law merchant. Law may be classified as to subject matter, such as the law of contracts, the law of real estate, and the law of wills.

Law is at times classified in terms of principles of law and principles of equity. At one time there were separate law courts and separate equity courts. Except in a few states, these courts have been combined so that one court applies principles of both law and equity. Even though administered by the same court, the two systems of principles remain distinct. That is, if the plaintiff seeks what historically would be equitable relief, the case is governed by equitable principles. If the plaintiff brings what historically would have been an action at law, the action is governed by law principles and not equity.[5] To illustrate the differ-

ence, consider the case of a homeowner making a contract to sell the home to a buyer. If the owner refuses to go through with the contract, the rules of law will permit the buyer to sue the owner for damages. But rules of equity will go further and will compel the owner to actually transfer the ownership of the house to the buyer. This equitable remedy is called specific performance.

B.   DETERMINATION OF LEGAL RIGHTS

Legal rights are meaningless unless they can be enforced. Government, therefore, provides a system by which the rights of the parties under the law can be determined and enforced. Generally the instrumentality of government by which this is accomplished is a court; the process involved is an action or a lawsuit. Administrative agencies have also been created to enforce law and to determine rights within

---

[5]   Gibbons v Stillwell, 149 Ill App 3d 411, 102 Ill Dec 864, 500 NE2d 965 (1986).

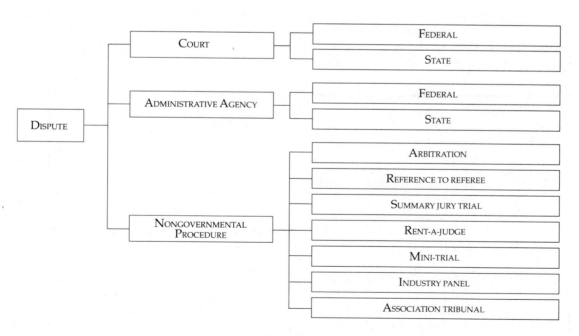

Figure 1-1
DISPUTE RESOLUTION PROCEDURES

certain areas. In addition, private agencies have developed as an out-of-court method of dispute resolution. Moreover, the parties may select the court in which a lawsuit may be brought and may specify the law to be applied.

§ 1:5   CONTRACT SELECTION OF LAW OR FORUM

The parties to a contract may to some extent control the determination of their legal rights by specifying (a) the law that should apply to the contract, and (b) the court in which any lawsuit should be brought.

(a) CHOICE OF LAW. In order to reduce the uncertainty of transactions or to further the convenience of the parties, it is customary for the modern contract to state that the contract should be governed by the law of a particular state or nation. This becomes important for an enterprise that does business in many states. Such an enterprise will typically specify that all contracts are governed by the law of the state in which the home office is located. For example, a life insurance company may issue policies to people all across the country. These policies will ordinarily state that they are governed by the law of the home office state. This means the le-gal staff of the insurance company need only concern itself with the law of one state rather than the law of 50 different states. As long as the state whose law is selected bears a reasonable relationship to the transaction, the designation by the contract will be followed.[6]

(b) CHOICE OF FORUM. The parties to a contract may specify that any lawsuit must be brought in the court of a particular state or country. This will generally be done for the convenience of the stronger party who will specify a local jurisdiction. If the choice is made in order to block lawsuits by the weaker party, the court selection provision will be held invalid. Thus, a provision that if a consumer in State A would bring a lawsuit against the manufacturer located in State B the suit must be brought in a distant State C is invalid as setting up an unconscionable barrier or hurdle to the bringing of the lawsuit. If, however, there is a reasonable relationship between the parties or the transaction and the jurisdiction of the court select-ed, the forum selection clause is valid and will be enforced. In the *Manrique* case the plaintiff claimed that he was not bound by the forum selection clause of the contract.

---

[6]   This concept is stated in the Uniform Commerical Code, § 1-105.

MANRIQUE v FABBRI

(Fla) 493 So 2d 437 (1986)

Fabbri made a contract to sell Florida land to Manrique. The contract specified that any lawsuit should be brought in the courts of the Nether-lands Antilles. A dispute arose and Manrique sued Fabbri in a Florida court. Fabbri raised the defense that suit could not be brought in Florida. An appeal was taken to the state supreme court.

BARKETT, J. . . . The Third District Court of Appeal has consistently held that contractual provisions requiring that future disputes be resolved in specified foreign jurisdictions are void as impermissible attempts to oust Florida of sub-ject matter jurisdiction. On the other hand, the Fourth District in *Maritime [Limited Partnership v. Greenman Advertising Associates, Inc.* (Fla App) 455 So 2d 1121]* has held that parties to a contract may agree to submit to the jurisdiction of a chosen forum provided that (1) the forum was not chosen because of one party's overwhelming bargaining power; (2) enforcement would not contravene public policy; (3) the purpose of such an agreement is not to transfer a local dispute to a remote and alien forum in order to inconvenience one or both of the parties.

In *Maritime*, the Fourth District relied upon and adopted the reasoning of the United States Supreme Court in *The Bremen v Zapata Off-Shore Co.*, 407 U.S. 1 (1972). In *Zapata*, a German corporation (Unterweser) contracted with Zapata, an American Corporation, to tow an oil rig across the Atlantic Ocean to Italy. The contract provided: "Any dispute arising must be treated before the London Court of Justice.' " The rig was damaged in transit and towed to Tampa. Zapata, notwithstanding such provision, instituted proceedings for damages against Unterweser in the United States District Court, Middle District of Florida. . . . The United States Supreme Court . . . held that forum selection clauses are prima facie valid and should be enforced unless enforcement is shown by the resisting party to be unreasonable under the circumstances. In *Zapata*, the Court rejected the same policy position adopted by the Third District in the case presently before us, saying:

> The argument that such clauses are improper because they tend to "oust" a court of jurisdiction is hardly more than a vestigial legal fiction. It appears to rest at core on historical judicial resistance to any attempt to reduce the power and business of a particular court and has little place in an era when all courts are overloaded and when businesses once essentially local now operate in world markets. It reflects something of a provincial attitude regarding the fairness of other tribunals. . . .

The Supreme Court gave compelling reasons why a freely negotiated private agreement unaffected by fraud, undue influence, or overweening bargaining power should be given full effect. It noted that at the very least such clauses represent efforts to eliminate uncertainty as to the nature, location, and outlook of the forum in which parties of differing nationalities might find themselves. Moreover, such clauses might be vital parts of agreements fixing monetary terms, with the consequences of the forum clause figuring prominently in the parties' calculations. The Court concluded:

> The correct approach would have been to enforce the forum clause specifically unless [the party] could clearly show that enforcement would be unreasonable and unjust, or that the clause was invalid for such reasons as fraud or overreaching.

The view articulated by the Court in *Zapata* enables freely contracting parties to conduct their interstate and international business affairs more efficiently. . . . Because the *Zapata* rule is based on a realistic assessment of modern commercial culture, and because the rule enhances contractual predictability within the culture, it is not surprising that it is rapidly becoming a majority view. . . .

We reject the position espoused by the Third District and adopt the view enunciated in *Zapata* and *Maritime*. Florida courts should recognize the legitimate expectations of contracting parties. The trial courts of this state can effectively protect a party by refusing to enforce those forum selection provisions which are unreasonable or result from unequal bargaining power. We hold that forum selection clauses should be enforced in the absence of a showing that enforcement would be unreasonable or unjust. . . .

We remand with directions that the matter be returned to the trial court for proceedings consistent herewith.

[Action remanded]

QUESTIONS

1. What did the court hold?
2. Are there any limits on the power to specify the court in which suits are to be brought?
3. Does the defendant have the burden of proving that a forum selection clause is reasonable?

§ 1:6   COURTS

A **court** is a tribunal established by government to hear and decide matters properly brought before it, to give redress to the injured or enforce punishment against wrongdoers, and to prevent wrongs. A **court of record** is one in which the proceedings are preserved in an official record. In a **court not of record** the proceedings are not officially recorded.

Each court is empowered to decide certain types or classes of cases. This power is called **jurisdiction**. A court may have original or appellate jurisdiction, or both. A court with **original jurisdiction** has the authority to hear a controversy when it is first brought into court. A court having **appellate jurisdiction,** on the other hand, has authority to review the judgment of an inferior court.

The jurisdiction of a court may be general, as distinguished from limited or special. A court having **general jurisdiction** has power to hear and decide all controversies involving legal rights and duties. A court of **limited** or **special jurisdiction** has authority to hear and decide only those cases that fall within a particular class, such as cases in which the amounts are below a specified sum.

Courts are frequently classified in terms of the nature of their jurisdiction. A **criminal court** is one that is established for the trial of crimes, which are regarded as offenses against the public. A **civil court,** on the other hand, is authorized to hear and decide issues involving private rights and duties and also noncriminal public matters. In like manner, courts are classified as equity courts, juvenile courts, probate courts, and courts of domestic relations, upon the basis of their limited jurisdiction.

Each court has inherent power to establish rules necessary to preserve order in the court or to transact the business of the court. An infraction of these rules or the disobedience to any other lawful order, as well as a willful act contrary to the dignity of the court or tending to pervert or obstruct justice, may be punished as **contempt of court.**

§ 1:7 ADMINISTRATIVE AGENCIES

The difficulties of courts' administering laws regulating business, labor, agriculture, public utilities, and other phases of the economy led Congress and the state legislatures to establish commissions or agencies of experts to make the rules and to pass judgment upon violations of the rules. Thus we find the Interstate Commerce Commission regulating interstate commerce and passing upon whether conduct of a carrier is a violation of its regulations. The Commission is a lawmaker, an executive that enforces the law, and a court that interprets and applies the law. This is also true of the Federal Trade Commission, the Securities and Exchange Commission, the National Labor Relations Board, and many other federal and state administrative agencies.

§ 1:8   PRIVATE PROCEDURES

Because of the rising costs, delays, and complexities of litigation, business people often seek to resolve disputes out of court.

(a) ARBITRATION. By the use of **arbitration,** a dispute is brought before one or more arbitrators (disinterested persons selected by the parties to the dispute) who make a decision that the parties have agreed in advance to accept as final. This procedure first reached an extensive use in the field of commercial contracts. Arbitration is encouraged as a means of avoiding expensive litigation and easing the workload of courts. Arbitration enables the parties to present the facts before trained experts familiar with the practices that form the background of the dispute.

A Uniform Arbitration Act has been adopted in a number of states.[7] Under this Act and similar statutes, the parties to a contract may agree in advance that all disputes arising thereunder will be submitted to arbitration. In some instances the contract will name the arbitrators for the duration of the contract.

The Federal Arbitration Act[8] declares that an arbitration clause in a contract relating to an interstate transaction is "valid, irrevocable, and enforceable."

In some states, by rule or statute, the arbitration of small claims is required. The losing party, however, may appeal from such compulsory arbitration to a court and the appeal will proceed just as though there never had been any prior arbitration. This is called **a trial** *de novo* and is required to preserve the constitutional right to a jury trial. As a practical matter, however, relatively few appeals are taken from the arbitration decision.

In the *Passage* case investors brought suit against stockbrokers, and the investors claimed that they were not required to arbitrate their claims.

---

[7] The 1955 version of the Uniform Arbitration Act has been adopted in Alaska, Arizona, Arkansas, Colorado, Delaware, Idaho, Illinois, Indiana, Iowa, Kansas, Maine, Maryland, Massachusetts, Michigan, Minnesota, Missouri, Montana, Nebraska, Nevada, New Mexico, North Carolina, North Dakota, Oklahoma, Pennsylvania, South Carolina, South Dakota, Tennessee, Texas, Utah, Vermont, Virginia, and Wyoming; and the District of Columbia. The earlier 1925 version of the Act is in force in Wisconsin.

[8] 9 USC § 1-14.

PASSAGE v PRUDENTIAL-BACHE SECURITIES, INC.

__ Mont __, 727 P2d 1298 (1986)

Larry Passage and others made investments through the broker G.T. Murray Co. The latter made the investments through its New York correspondent, Prudential-Bache Securities. Loss was sustained and Passage and the others sued the brokers to recover the loss. The brokers raised the defense that the papers that the customers had signed required them to submit their claims to arbitration and that accordingly the court could not act thereon. The lower court held that the arbitration clause was binding as to some of the claims. All parties appealed.

WEBER, J. . . . Did the District Court correctly determine that it had jurisdiction to order arbitration of the Passages' claims under the Federal Arbitration Act? . . .

This area of the law is undergoing rapid and comprehensive change as a result of recent U.S. Supreme Court decisions. That Court's decision in *Southland Corp. v. Keating* (1984), 465 U.S. 1, conclusively answers this question. In that case, Southland Corporation, the owner and franchisor of 7-Eleven convenience stores, was charged by 7-Eleven franchisees with fraud, oral misrepresentation, breach of contract, breach of fiduciary duty, and violation of state disclosure requirements in its franchise agreements. Southland Corporation appealed the decision of the California Court of Appeals that arbitration clauses in Southland's contracts with its franchisees were rendered void by California's Franchise Investment Law, which required judicial consideration of claims brought under it. The Supreme Court reversed. It held that, as interpreted, the California Franchise Investment Law conflicted with the Federal Arbitration Act and violated the Supremacy Clause [of the Constitution]. The Court reasoned:

> In enacting § 2 of the [F]ederal [Arbitration] Act, Congress declared a national policy favoring arbitration and withdrew the power of the states to require a judicial forum for the resolution of claims which the contracting parties agreed to resolve by arbitration. . . . Congress has thus mandated the enforcement of arbitration agreements.

In answer to the argument that claims brought in state court are not subject to the Arbitration Act, the Court [in *Southland*] stated:

> . . . it is clear beyond question that if this suit had been brought as a diversity action in a federal district court, the arbitration clause would have been enforceable. . . . We are unwilling to attribute to Congress the intent, in drawing on the comprehensive powers of the Commerce Clause, to create a right to enforce an arbitration contract and yet make the right dependent for its enforcement on the particular forum in which it is asserted. And since the overwhelming proportion of all civil litigation in this country is in the state courts, we cannot believe Congress intended to limit the Arbitration Act to disputes subject only to *federal*-court jurisdiction. Such an interpretation would frustrate congressional intent to place "[a]n arbitration agreement. . . . upon the same footing as other contracts, where it belongs." H.R. Rep. No. 96, 68th Cong., 1st Sess., 1 (1924).
>   In creating a substantive rule applicable in state as well as federal courts, Congress intended to foreclose state legislative attempts to undercut the enforceability of arbitration agreements.

Under *Southland*, a state court clearly has jurisdiction to order arbitration under the Federal Arbitration Act. . . .

The customer agreement forms signed by the Passages are one-page documents, but they contain a number of complex and technical agreements and promises on the parts of both parties. The arbitration clause, paragraph 14, is printed in the same typeface as the rest of the form. It is one of the longer provisions in the agreement. The Passages invested a significant amount of money with defendants, and there has been no suggestion that they require protection because they are in any way improvident persons.

The *Southland* opinion does not mandate that all arbitration clauses are enforceable:

We discern only two limitations on the enforceability of arbitration provisions governed by the Federal Arbitration Act: they must be part of a written maritime contract or a contract "evidencing a transaction involving commerce" and such clauses may be revoked upon "grounds as exist at law or in equity for the revocation of any contract."

The agreement between the Passages and Prudential clearly involves interstate commerce, since its object was purchase and sale of securities through a public stock exchange. . . .

There is nothing in the record to indicate that the arbitration clause in the client agreement form was not within the parties' reasonable expectations. Nor is there any evidence that the clause is oppressive or unconscionable. The federal caselaw demonstrates that arbitration clauses are common, and may be universal, in brokerage agreements. In *Southland*, which like the present case involved allegations of fraud and misrepresentation, the public policy of enforcement of arbitration clauses was forcefully stated. We conclude that . . . there is nothing in the record and no compelling law to prevent enforcement of the arbitration clause. . . .

[Judgment affirmed as to enforceability of the arbitration clause]

QUESTIONS

1. Who wanted the arbitration clause in the original agreements?
2. What law did the court apply?
3. What would have happened if the court had decided that arbitration was not required?

(b) REFERENCE TO THIRD PERSON. An out-of-court determination of disputes under construction contracts is often made under a term of the contract that any dispute shall be referred to the architect in charge of the construction and that the architect's decision shall be final.

Increasingly, other types of transactions provide for a third person or a committee to decide rights of persons. Thus, employees and an employer may have agreed as a term of the employment contract that claims of employees under retirement and pension plans shall be decided by a designated board or committee. The seller and buyer may have selected a third person to determine the price to be paid for goods. Ordinarily the parties agree that the decision of such a third person or board shall be final and that no appeal or review may be had in any court. In most cases, referral to a third person is used in situations that involve the determination of a particular fact in contrast to arbitration which seeks to end a dispute.

(c) ASSOCIATION TRIBUNALS. Many disputes never reach the law courts because both parties to the dispute belong to a group or association, and the tribunal created by the group or association disposes of the matter. Thus, a dispute between members of a labor union, a stockbrokers' exchange, or a church, may be heard by some board or committee within the association or group. Courts will review the action of such tribunals to determine that a fair and proper procedure was followed, but generally the courts will not go any further and will not examine the facts of the case to see if the association tribunal reached the same conclusion that the court would have reached.

Trade associations will commonly require their members to employ out-of-court methods of dispute settlement. Thus the National Association of Home Builders requires its member builders to employ arbitration. The National Automobile Dealers Association provides for panels to determine warranty claims of customers. The decision of such panels is final as to the dealer, but the consumer is allowed to bring a regular lawsuit if he or she loses before the panel.

(d) SUMMARY JURY TRIAL. This is in effect a dry run or mock trial in which the lawyers present their claims before a jury of six persons. The object is to get the reaction of a sample jury. No evidence is presented before this jury and it bases its opinion solely on what the lawyers state at this trial. The determination of the jury has no binding effect but it has value in that it gives the lawyers some idea of what a jury might think if there would be an actual trial. This has special value when the heart of a case is whether something is reasonable under all the circumstances. When the lawyers see how the sample jury reacts, the lawyers may moderate their positions and reach a settlement.

(e) RENT-A-JUDGE. Under this plan, the parties hire a judge to hear the case. In many states this is done by the parties' voluntarily choosing the judge as a "referee," with the judge acting under a statute authorizing the appointment of referees.[9] Under such a statute, the referee hears all the evidence just as though there were a regular trial and the judge's determination is binding on the parties unless reversed on appeal. In some jurisdictions, special provision is made for the parties to agree that the decision of the judge selected as referee shall be final.

(f) MINI-TRIAL. When only part of a case is really disputed, the parties may stay within the framework of the legal lawsuit but agree that only the disputed issues be submitted to a jury. For example, when

there is no real dispute over the liability of the defendant but the parties disagree as to the damages, the issue of damages alone may be submitted to the jury.

In some states, instead of submitting the matter to a regular jury, the attorneys will agree to hold a mini-trial. Under this system, the parties agree that a particular person, frequently a retired judge, should listen to the evidence on the disputed issues and decide the case. The agreement of the parties for the mini-trial may specify whether this decision is binding on the parties. As a practical matter, the evaluation of the case by a neutral will often bring the opposing parties together to reach a settlement.

(g) CONTRACT PROVISIONS. The parties' contract may pave the way for the settlement of future disputes by containing clauses requiring the parties to submit disputes to arbitration or to make use of one of the extralegal procedures described above. In addition, contracts may provide that no action may be taken until after the expiration of a specified cooling off period, or that the parties shall continue in the performance of their contract even though there is a dispute between them.

§ 1:9   DISPOSITION OF
              COMPLAINTS AND
              OMBUDSMEN

In contrast with the traditional and alternative procedures for resolving disputes are the procedures aimed at removing the ground for complaint before it develops into a dispute that requires resolution. For example, the complaint department in a department store will often be able to iron out the difficulty before the customer and the store are locked in an adversary position that could end in a lawsuit. Grievance committee procedures will often be effective to bring about an adjustment or removal of grounds for complaint. A statute may create a government official for the purpose of examining complaints. Such an official is often called an

---

[9]   See § 1:8(b)

ombudsman.[10] The few federal statutes that have created such an officer have not given the ombudsman any judicial power. Typically the ombudsman can only receive complaints, supervise the administration of the system, and make recommendations for improvements. Two of the federal statutes expressly declare that the creation of the office of ombudsman does not impair any right existing by law.[11] In addition, when the complaint involves a right that would require a jury trial at common law, the Seventh Amendment to the United States Constitution guarantees that right, and an ombudsman could not be given the power to decide such a matter. Moreover, the trend in America is to create special tribunals or administrative agencies rather than to give the ombudsman greater power.

C. COURT ORGANIZATION

Courts in the United States are organized in two distinct systems: the federal courts and the state courts. Although created under separate governments, the methods of operation and organization of these two systems are similar.

§ 1:10   PERSONNEL OF COURTS

Both the federal and state court systems require the assistance of many people. These include not only those in the direct employ of the court, but also those described as officers of the court and in many cases a jury as well.

   (a) OFFICERS OF THE COURT. The **judge** is the primary officer of the court. A judge is either elected or appointed. **Attorneys** or counselors at law are also officers of the court. They are usually selected by the parties to the controversy — but in some cases

by the judge — to present the issues of a case to the court.

   The **clerk** of the court is appointed in some of the higher courts but is usually elected to office in the lower courts. The principal duties of the clerks are to enter cases upon the court calendar, to keep an accurate record of the proceedings, to attest the same, and, in some instances, to approve bail bonds and to compute the amount of costs involved.

   The **sheriff** is the chief executive of a county. In addition to the duty of maintaining peace and order within the territorial limits of a county, the sheriff has many other duties in connection with the administration of justice in county courts of record: summoning witnesses, taking charge of the jury, preserving order in court, serving writs, carrying out judicial sales, and executing judgments. The **marshals** of the United States perform these duties in the federal courts. In county courts not of record, such as the courts of justices of the peace, these duties, when appropriate, are performed by a **constable.** Some of the duties of the sheriff are now performed by persons known as **court criers;** or by deputy sheriffs, known as **bailiffs.**

   (b) THE JURY. The **jury** is a body of citizens sworn by a court to try to determine by verdict the issues of fact submitted to them. A trial jury consists of not more than twelve persons. The first step in forming a jury is to make a **jury list.** This involves the preparation by the proper officers or board of a list of qualified persons from which a jury may be drawn.

   A certain number of persons drawn from the jury list constitute the **jury panel.** A trial jury is selected from members of the panel.

§ 1:11   FEDERAL COURTS

The Supreme Court of the United States is

---

[10]   This name is Swedish for "commissioner."
[11]   For example, see the Solid Waste Disposal Act of November 8, 1984, PL 98-616, § 703(a), 98 Stat 3225,

42 USC § 6917; and the Panama Canal Commission Act of September 17, 1979, PL 96-70, § 1113, 93 Stat 460, 22 USC § 3623.

the highest court in the federal system. The courts of appeals are intermediate courts. The district courts and special courts are the lower courts.

(a) SUPREME COURT OF THE UNITED STATES. The Supreme Court is the only court expressly established by the Constitution. Congress is authorized by the Constitution to create other federal courts.

The Supreme Court has original jurisdiction in all cases affecting ambassadors, other public ministers, and consuls, and in those cases in which a state is a party. Except as regulated by Congress, it has appellate jurisdiction in all cases that may be brought into the federal courts in accordance with the terms of the Constitution. The Supreme Court also has appellate jurisdiction in certain cases that have been decided by the supreme courts of the states. Thousands of cases are filed with this court each year.

(b) COURTS OF APPEALS. The United States, including the District of Columbia, is divided into 12 judicial circuits. Each of the circuits has a court of appeals. These courts are courts of record. There is also a court of appeals for the federal circuit. It has nationwide jurisdiction for certain subject areas such as patents and copyrights.

A court of appeals has appellate jurisdiction only and is empowered to review the final decisions of the district courts, except in cases that may be taken directly to the Supreme Court. The decisions of the courts of appeals are final in most cases. An appeal may be taken as a matter of right on certain constitutional questions. Otherwise, review depends on the discretion of the Supreme Court and, in some cases, of the court of appeals.

(c) DISTRICT COURTS. The United States, including the District of Columbia, is further divided into a number of judicial districts. Some states form a single district, whereas others are divided into two or more districts. District courts are also located in the territories.

The district courts have original jurisdiction in practically all cases that may be maintained in the federal courts. They are the trial courts for civil and criminal cases.

Civil cases that may be brought in these district courts are (a) civil suits brought by the United States; (b) actions brought by citizens of the same state claiming land under grants by different states; (c) proceedings under the bankruptcy, internal revenue, postal, copyright, and patent laws; (d) civil cases of admiralty and maritime jurisdiction; (e) actions against national banking associations; (f) cases between citizens of different states or between citizens of one state and a foreign state involving $10,000 or more; and (g) cases that arise under the federal Constitution, or laws and treaties made thereunder.

(d) OTHER FEDERAL COURTS. In addition to the Supreme Court, the courts of appeals, and the district courts, the following tribunals have been created by Congress to determine other matters as indicated by their titles: Court of International Trade, Claims Court, Tax Court, Court of Military Appeals, and the territorial courts.

§ 1:12   STATE COURTS

The system of courts in the various states is organized along lines similar to the federal court system, although differing in details, such as the number of courts, their names, and jurisdiction.

(a) STATE SUPREME COURT. The highest court in most states is known as the supreme court. In a few states it may have a different name, such as "Court of Appeals" in New York. The jurisdiction of a supreme court is ordinarily appellate, although in a few instances it is original. In some states the supreme court is required to render an opinion on certain questions that may be referred to it by the legislature or by the chief executive of the state. The decision of a state supreme court is final in all cases not involving the federal Constitution, laws, and treaties.

(b) INTERMEDIATE COURTS. In some states, intermediate courts have original jurisdiction in a few cases but, in the main, they have appellate jurisdiction of cases removed for review from the county or district courts. They are known as superior, circuit, or district appellate courts. As a general rule, their decisions may be reviewed by the highest state court.

(c) COUNTY AND DISTRICT COURTS. These courts of record have appellate jurisdiction of cases tried in the justice of the peace and police courts, as well as general original jurisdiction of criminal and civil cases. They also have jurisdiction of wills and guardianship matters, except when, as in some states, the jurisdiction of such cases has been given to special orphans', surrogate, or probate courts.

(d) OTHER STATE COURTS. In addition to the foregoing, the following, which are ordinarily not courts of record, have jurisdiction as indicated by their titles: city or municipal courts, police courts, traffic courts, small claims courts, and justice of the peace courts.

D. COURT PROCEDURE

Detailed laws specify how, when, and where a legal dispute can be brought to court. These rules of procedure are necessary in order to achieve an orderly, fair determination of litigation and in order to obtain, as far as humanly possible, the same decisions on the same facts. It is important to remember, however, that there is no uniform judicial procedure. While there are definite similarities, the law of each state may differ from that of the others. For the most part the uniform laws that have been adopted do not regulate matters of procedure.

§ 1:13   STEPS IN A LAWSUIT

The following are the steps in a lawsuit. Not every step is taken in every suit. The facts of a case may be such that the case ends before every possible step is taken.

The parties may not want to fight it out to the very end or to raise every possible point.

(a) COMMENCEMENT OF ACTION. An action is begun by filing a complaint with the clerk of the appropriate court. The complaint generally consists of a description of the acts complained of by the plaintiff and a request for some sort of reparation or relief.

(b) SERVICE OF PROCESS. The defendant must be served with **process** (a writ, notice, or summons; or the complaint itself) to give notice that the action is pending and to subject the defendant to the power of the court.

(c) PLEADINGS. After the plaintiff has filed a complaint and process has been served on the defendant, the defendant must make some reply, generally within 15 or 20 days. If the defendant fails to do so, the plaintiff ordinarily wins the case by default.

Before answering the plaintiff's complaint, the defendant may make certain preliminary objections, such as that the action was brought in the wrong court or that service was not properly made. If the objection is sustained, the case may be ended, depending upon the nature of the objection, or the plaintiff may be allowed to correct the mistake if that is possible. The defendant may also raise the objection, sometimes called a **motion to dismiss** or **demurrer**, that even if the plaintiff's complaint is accepted as true, the plaintiff is still not entitled to any relief.

If the defendant makes an objection that is overruled or dismissed, or if the defendant makes no objection, the defendant must file an **answer**, which either admits or denies some or all of the facts asserted by the plaintiff. For example, if the plaintiff declared that the defendant made a contract on a certain date, the defendant may either admit making the contract or deny having done so. An admission of having made the contract does not end the case, for the defendant may then be able to plead defenses, for example, that at a later date the plaintiff and defendant had agreed to set the contract aside.

Without regard to whether the defendant pleads such new matter, the defendant may generally assert a **counterclaim** or **cross complaint** against the plaintiff. Thus, the defendant may contend the plaintiff owes money or is liable for damages and that this liability should be offset against any claim the plaintiff may have.

After the defendant files an answer, the plaintiff may generally file preliminary objections to the answer. Just as the defendant could raise objections, the plaintiff may, in certain instances, argue that a counterclaim raised by the defendant could not be asserted in that action, that the answer is fatally defective in form, or that it is not legally sufficient. Again the court must pass upon the preliminary objections. When these are disposed of, the pleading stage is ordinarily over.

Generally, all of the pleadings in an action may raise only a few or perhaps one question of law, or a question of fact, or both. Thus, the whole case may depend on whether a letter admittedly written by the defendant amounted to an acceptance of the plaintiff's offer, thereby constituting a contract. If this question of law is answered in favor of the plaintiff, a judgment will be entered for the plaintiff; otherwise, for the defendant. By way of contrast, it may be that a certain letter would be an acceptance if it had been written by the defendant; but the defendant may deny having written it. Here the question is one of fact, and the judgment is entered for the plaintiff if it is determined that the facts happened as claimed by the plaintiff. Otherwise the judgment is entered for the defendant.

If the only questions involved are questions of law, the court will decide the case on the pleadings alone since there is no need for a trial to determine the facts. If questions of fact are involved, then there must be a trial to determine what the facts really were.

(d) PRETRIAL PROCEDURE. Many states and the federal courts have adopted other procedural steps that may be employed before the trial, with the purpose of eliminating the need for a trial, simplifying the issues to be tried, or giving the parties information needed for preparation for trial.

(1) Motion for Judgment on the Pleadings. After the pleadings are closed, many courts permit either party to move for a **judgment on the pleadings.** When such a motion is made, the court examines the record and may then enter a judgment according to the merits of the case as shown by the record.

(2) Motion for Summary Judgment. In most courts a party may shorten a lawsuit by bringing into court sworn statements and affidavits that show that a claim or defense of the adverse party is false or a sham. This procedure cannot be used when there is substantial dispute of fact concerning the matters to be proved by the use of the affidavits.

(3) Pretrial Conference. In many courts either party may request the court to call a **pretrial conference,** or the court may take the initiative in doing so. This conference is a discussion by a judge of the court and the attorneys in the case. The object of the conference is to eliminate matters that are not in dispute and to determine what issues remain for litigation. Some cases are settled at this stage.

(4) Discovery. The Federal Rules of Civil Procedure and similar rules in a large number of states now permit one party to inquire of the adverse party and of all witnesses about anything relating to the action. This includes asking the adverse party the names of witnesses; asking the adverse party and the witnesses what they know about the case; examining, inspecting, and photographing books, records, buildings, and machines; and making an examination of the physical or mental condition of a party when it has a bearing on the action. These procedures are classed as **discovery**.

(5) Depositions. Ordinarily a witness testifies in court at the time of the trial. In some instances it may be necessary or de-

sirable to take such testimony out of court before the time of the trial. It may be that the witness is aged or infirm or is about to leave the state or country and will not be present when the trial is held. In such case the interested party is permitted to have the testimony, called a **deposition**, of the witness taken outside of the court.

(e) DETERMINATION OF FACTS. A legal system must provide for someone to determine the facts of a case when the parties do not agree on the facts.

(1) The Trier of Facts. If the legal controversy is one that under the common law would have been tried by a jury, either party to the action has the constitutional right today to demand that the action be tried before a jury. If all parties agree, however, the case may be tried by the court or judge alone without a jury, and in some instances may be referred to a master or a referee appointed by the court to hear the matter.

In equity there is no constitutional right to a jury trial but a chancellor or equity judge may submit questions to a jury. There is the basic difference that in such cases the verdict or decision of the jury is only advisory to the chancellor; that is, the chancellor is not bound by the verdict. In contrast, the verdict of a jury in an action at law is binding on the court unless a basic error is present.

When new causes of action are created by statute, such as the right of an employee to obtain workers' compensation for an injury arising in the course of employment without regard to whether the employer was negligent, there is no constitutional right to a trial by jury. The trier of facts may accordingly be a judge without a jury, or a special administrative board or agency, such as a Workers' Compensation Board.

(2) Basis for Decision. The trier of fact, whether a jury, a judge, a referee, or a board, can only decide questions of fact on the basis of evidence presented before it. Each party offers evidence. The evidence usually consists of the answers of persons to questions in court. Their an-

swers are called **testimony**. The evidence may also include **real evidence,** that is, tangible things, such as papers, books, and records. It is immaterial whether the records are kept in ordinary ledger books or stored on computer tapes because a computer printout of data made for trial is admissible as evidence of the information contained in the computer.[12] In some cases, such as a damage action for improper construction of a building, the trier of fact may be taken to view the building so that a better understanding can be obtained.

The witness who testifies in court is usually a person who had some direct contact with the facts in the case, such as a person who saw the events occur or who heard one of the parties say something. In some instances, it is also proper to offer the testimony of persons who have no connection with the case when they have expert knowledge and their opinions as experts are desired.

A witness who refuses to appear in court may be ordered to do so by a **subpoena**, and may also be compelled to bring relevant papers to the court by a **subpoena duces tecum.** If the witness does not obey the subpoena, the witness may be arrested for contempt of court. In some states the names of the order upon the witness and the procedure for contempt have been changed, but the substance remains the same.

(f) CONDUCT OF THE TRIAL. The conduct of a trial will be discussed in terms of a jury trial. Generally a case is one of several assigned for trial on a certain day or during a certain trial period. When the case is called, the opposing counsel seat themselves at tables in front of the judge and the jury is selected. After the jury is sworn, the attorneys usually make **opening addresses** to the jury. Details vary in different jurisdictions, but the general pattern is that each attorney tells the jury what will be proven. When this step has been complet-

[12] See § 11:4.

ed, the presentation of the evidence by both sides begins.

The attorney for the plaintiff starts with the first witness and asks all the questions desired that are proper. This is called the **direct examination** of the witness, since it is made by the attorney calling the witness. After the direct examination has been finished, the opposing counsel asks the same witness other questions in an effort to disprove the prior answers. This is called **cross-examination.**

After the cross-examination has been completed, the attorney for the plaintiff may ask the same witness other questions to overcome the effect of the cross-examination. This is called **redirect examination.** This step in turn may be followed by further examination by the defendant's attorney, called **recross-examination.**

After the examination of the plaintiff's witness has been concluded, the plaintiff's second witness takes the witness stand and is subjected to an examination in the same way as the first. This continues until all of the plaintiff's witnesses have been called. Then the plaintiff "rests," and the defendant calls the first defense witness. The pattern of examination of witnesses is repeated except that now the defendant is calling the witnesses, and the defendant's attorney conducts the direct and redirect examination while the questioning by the plaintiff's attorney is cross- or recross-examination.

After the witnesses of both parties have been examined and all the evidence has been presented, each attorney makes another address, a **summation**, to the jury, which sums up the case and suggests that a particular verdict be returned by the jury.

(g) CHARGE TO THE JURY AND VERDICT. The summation by the attorneys is followed by a **charge** of the judge to the jury. This charge is a resumé of what has happened at the trial and an explanation of the applicable law. At its conclusion, the judge instructs the jury to retire and study the case in the light of the charge and then return a **verdict**. By such instructions, the judge leaves to the jury the problem of determining the facts but states the law that they must apply to such facts as they may find. The jury then retires to secret deliberation in the jury room.

(h) TAKING THE CASE FROM THE JURY AND ATTACKING THE VERDICT. At several points during the trial, or immediately after it, a party may take a step to end the case or to set aside the verdict the jury has returned.

(1) Voluntary Nonsuit. A plaintiff who is dissatisfied with the progress of the trial may wish to stop the trial and begin again at a later date. In most jurisdictions this can be done by taking a **voluntary nonsuit.**

(2) Compulsory Nonsuit. After the plaintiff has presented the testimony of all witnesses, the defendant may request the court to enter a nonsuit on the ground that the case presented by the plaintiff does not entitle the plaintiff to recover. This is called a **compulsory nonsuit.**

(3) Mistrial. When necessary to avoid great injustice, the trial court may declare that there has been a **mistrial** and thereby terminate the trial and postpone it to a later date. While either party may move the court to enter a mistrial, it is discretionary with the court whether it does so. A mistrial is commonly entered when the evidence has been of a highly prejudicial character and the trial judge does not believe that the jury can ignore it even when instructed to do so, or when a juror has been guilty of misconduct.

(4) Directed Verdict. After the presentation of all the evidence at the trial, either party may request the court to direct the jury to return a verdict in favor of the requesting party. When the plaintiff would not be entitled to recover even if all the testimony in the plaintiff's favor were believed, the defendant is entitled to have the court direct the jury to return a verdict for the defendant. The plaintiff is entitled to a directed verdict when, even if all the evidence on behalf of the defendant were believed, the jury would still be required to find for the plaintiff. In some states, the defendant may make a motion for a di-

rected verdict at the close of the plaintiff's proof.

(5) New Trial. After the verdict has been returned by the jury, a party may move for a new trial if not satisfied with the verdict or with the amount of damages awarded. If it is clear that the jury made a mistake or if material evidence that could not have been discovered before the trial becomes available later, the court will award a new trial and the case will be tried again before another jury.

(6) Judgment N.O.V. If the verdict returned by the jury is clearly wrong as a matter of law, the court may set aside the verdict and enter a judgment contrary to the verdict. This in some states is called a **judgment** *non obstante veredicto* (notwithstanding the verdict), or as it is abbreviated, a judgment n.o.v.

(i) JUDGMENT AND COSTS. The court enters a judgment conforming to the verdict unless a new trial has been granted, a mistrial declared after the return of the verdict, or a judgment n.o.v. entered. Generally whoever is the winning party will also be awarded costs in the action. In equity actions or those that had their origin in equity, and in certain statutory proceedings, the court has discretion to award costs to the winner or to divide them between the parties.

Costs ordinarily include the costs of filing papers with the court, the cost of having the sheriff or other officers of the court take official action, the statutory fees paid to the witnesses, the cost of a jury fee, if any, and the cost of printing the record when this is required on appeal. They do not include compensation for the time spent by the party in preparing the case or in being present at the trial, the time lost from work because of the case, or the fee paid to an attorney. Sometimes when a special statutory action is brought, the statute authorizes recovery of a small attorney's fee. Thus, a mechanics' lien statute may authorize the recovery of an attorney's fee of 10 percent of the amount recovered, or a ''reasonable attorney's fee.''

As a general rule, the costs that a party recovers represent only a small part of the total expenses actually sustained in the litigation.

(j) APPEAL. After a judgment has been entered, the party who is aggrieved thereby may appeal. This means that a party who wins the judgment but is not awarded as much as had been hoped, as well as a party who loses the case, may take an appeal.

The appellate court does not hear witnesses. It examines the record of the proceedings before the lower court, that is, the file of the case containing all the pleadings, the testimony of witnesses, and the judge's charge, to see if there was an error of law. To assist the court, the attorneys for the parties file arguments or briefs and generally make arguments orally before the court.

If the appellate court does not agree with the application of the law made by the lower court, it generally sets aside or modifies the action of the lower court and enters such judgment as it concludes the lower court should have entered. It may set aside the action of the lower court and send the case back to the lower court with directions to hold a new trial or with directions to enter a new judgment in accordance with the opinion that is filed by the appellate court.

(k) EXECUTION. After a judgment has been entered or after an appeal has been decided, the losing party generally will comply with the judgment of the court. If not, the winning party may then take steps to execute or carry out the judgment.

If the judgment is for the payment of a sum of money, the plaintiff may direct the sheriff or other judicial officer to sell as much of the property of the defendant as is necessary to pay the plaintiff's judgment and the costs of the proceedings and of the execution. Acting under this authorization, the sheriff may make a public sale of the defendant's property and apply the proceeds to the payment of the plaintiff's judgment. In most states the defendant is allowed a limited monetary exemption and an exemption for certain articles, such as personal clothing and tools of trade.

If the judgment is for the recovery of specific property, the judgment will direct the sheriff to deliver the property to the plaintiff.

If the judgment directs the defendant to do or to refrain from doing an act, it is commonly provided that failure to obey the order is a contempt of court punishable by fine or imprisonment.

§ 1:14 DECLARATORY JUDGMENT

In this century, a new court procedure for settling disputes, authorized by statute, has made its appearance. This is the **declaratory judgment** procedure. Under it a person, when confronted with the early stages of an actual controversy, may peti-tion the court to decide the question or declare the rights of the parties before loss is actually sustained. A copy of the petition is served on all parties. They may file answers. After all the pleadings have been filed, the court then decides the questions involved just as though a lawsuit had been brought.

§ 1:15 MOOTNESS AS A BAR TO COURT RELIEF

Courts have the power to determine controversies. Under declaratory judgment statutes, courts have the power to determine budding controversies that have not yet become full-blown disputes. Courts do not have the power to decide matters after the dispute has disappeared. When this occurs, the case is described as being moot. Just what this means was raised in the *Texas Employment* case.

TEXAS EMPLOYMENT COMMISSION V CAMARENA
(Tex App) 710 SW2d 665 (1986)

The Texas Unemployment Compensation Act of 1936 did not apply to farm workers. Robert Camarena and other farm workers brought a declaratory judgment action against the Texas Employment Commission. They claimed that the exemption of farm workers made by the Act of 1936 was unconstitutional. In 1985, the state legislature amended the compensation act by extending it to farm workers. This change did not become effective until January 1, 1986. In May and July, 1985, the lower court held that the exception of farm workers in the original act was unconstitutional. An appeal was taken by the Commission in July, 1985 claiming that the exception of farm workers was constitutional.

POWERS, J. . . . The Commission, its members, and the Attorney General contend the controversy has become moot on appeal. We sustain the contention.

We need not discuss at length the fundamental proposition that courts exist to determine actual and existing controversies and to enforce their determinations made in that connection. They do not sit to adjudicate controversies that are or become "moot" or abstract owing to the absence of a bona fide controversy or the absence of an existing fact or right necessary to their adjudication. . . . The mootness doctrine applies with full force to actions brought under the Uniform Declaratory Judgments Act, as the present actions were. . . .

A suit may fall within the mootness doctrine for any number of reasons.

Included among such reasons are two that apply in the present appeals: (1) an absence or discontinuance of any real or bona fide dispute between the litigants about the subject matter; and (2) a change in the basic law under which a pleaded controversy was or will be adjudicated. Either may result in the mootness of an appeal. An example of the first category occurs when a litigant unreservedly and voluntarily pays a disputed sum adjudged against him. . . . Another in that category exists when a real, actual, or bona fide controversy cannot arise until the happening of a contingency and there is no allegation or contention that it has in fact occurred. . . .

There exist several examples of the second category — a change in the basic law under which a pleaded controversy is required to be adjudicated. Mootness occurs in a suit to cancel an agency permit when a new statute brings all permits to an end, whether valid or not, and provides for issuance of new permits on surrender of the old. . . . A suit to enjoin an unconstitutional statute becomes moot when the Legislature enacts a new statute to the same effect that is conceded to be constitutional. . . . A suit to enjoin conduct prohibited by a statute becomes moot when the statute is amended in a way that requires judicial construction to determine whether the conduct falls within the proscription of the new statute. . . .

With these cases in mind, we turn to whether the controversy in the present appeals is moot insofar as it relates to the declaratory relief ordered in the trial-court judgments.

The judgments below declare that the Act, before its amendment by H.B. [House Bill] 32, was "unconstitutional and unenforceable" insofar as it purported to exclude "agricultural labor" from coverage. We hold the controversy to be moot in this regard. Whether the exclusion of "agricultural labor" was unconstitutional, as appellees contended, and whether the trial court erred in sustaining that contention, has been removed from the realm of legal controversy by H.B. 32, effective January 1, 1986. . . .

The sole argument advanced by appellees to avoid the mootness doctrine is a novel one. Appellees contend the judgments below should be considered by this Court, and affirmed on the merits, because they represent only a fragile and narrow political, as well as judicial, victory obtained by agricultural and ranch employees. In appellees' view, unless the judgments below be affirmed by this Court, as being free of the errors assigned by appellants, the Legislature next to convene will likely move to amend the Act in a way that erodes or even withdraws the coverage so narrowly won by agricultural and ranch workers in the 69th Legislature. In this connection, appellees refer to those parts of the trial-court judgments that purport to perpetuate the terms of H.B. 32 as constitutional minimums below which the Legislature may not fall in any future legislation on the subject.

We believe appellees' argument to be erroneous on several grounds. Among them are the following: (1) the argument erroneously imputes to the courts a power to decide a contingent and therefore a hypothetical case, or to decide a question not essential to any actual and existing controversy; (2) it erroneously presumes that a future Legislature will enact a statute that is unconstitutional; or (3) if it presumes a future enactment that is constitutional, it erroneously imputes to the courts a power to invalidate legislative acts merely because the courts find the acts to be unwise or bad policy. . . . We therefore reject appellees' argument. . . .

We hold the controversy to be moot. . . .
[Judgment reversed and action remanded]

QUESTIONS

1. What did the court decide?
2. What can make a case moot?
3. How does the *Texas Employment* case fit into the analysis made in your answer to Question #2?

§ 1:16   IMMUNITY FOR WRONG DECISION

The fact that a judge, jury, or arbitrator makes a wrong decision does not impose any liability upon the decision maker. If there is a crime involved, such as bribery, the wrongdoer may be prosecuted for that offense. However, there is no liability for merely making a wrong decision. For example, the fact that a judge does not know the law and makes a mistake does not entitle the loser to sue the judge. Even if the decision is later reversed on appeal, the winning party cannot go back and sue the judge. That is, the judge has immunity from liability while acting within the scope of judicial authority.[13]

[13]   Grane v Grane, 143 Ill App 3d 979, 98 Ill Dec 91, 493 NE2d 1112 (1986).

SUMMARY

Law consists of the pattern of rules established by society to govern conduct and relationships. These rules can be expressed as constitutional provisions, statutes, case decisions, and administrative regulations. Law can be further classified as substantive or procedural, and it can be described in terms of its historical origins, by the subject to which it relates, or in terms of law or equity.

Courts have been created to hear and resolve legal disputes. A specific court's power is defined by its jurisdiction, which may be original or appellate, general or special, and criminal or civil. The judge is the primary officer of a court. A jury may serve to determine issues of fact.

Courts in the United States are organized in two distinct systems, federal and state. The Supreme Court of the United States is the highest federal court. The United States courts of appeals are the intermediate courts and the United States district courts are the trial level courts. Most state court systems are similarly organized.

A lawsuit is begun by filing a complaint. The defendant named in the complaint must be served with process, that is, the defendant must be notified that an action has been commenced. The issues to be tried are developed through pleadings and pretrial procedures. Testimony and real evidence are presented at trial, where attorneys for the parties introduce evidence and examine the witnesses.

Because a formal trial can be time consuming and costly, the parties sometimes agree to an alternative method of resolving the dispute. Among common alternatives are arbitration, reference to a third person or association tribunal, the summary jury trial, the private judge/referee, and the mini-trial.

QUESTIONS AND CASE PROBLEMS

1. How can parties to a dispute avoid the expense of litigation?
2. What is the difference between original and appellate jurisdiction of a court?
3. What is the most significant uniform law?
4. On learning of the many steps of a lawsuit, Elaine exclaimed that all lawsuits must take a very long time. Is she correct?
5. Tenton owed Orlando $1,000. Orlando has a friend, Helen, who is a judge in the Court of International Trade. Orlando wants to sue Tenton in that court. May he do so?
6. Carolyn, Elwood, and Isabella are involved in a real estate development. The development is a failure, and Carolyn, Elwood, and Isabella want to have their rights determined. They could bring a lawsuit but they are afraid that the case is so complicated that a judge and jury not familiar with the problems of real estate development would not reach a proper result. What can they do?
7. Attorneys are, and at the same time are not, officers of the court. Explain this contradictory statement.
8. Ames brought an action against Jarvis Co. to recover damages resulting from a breach of contract. No process was served on the defendants, but Ames published notice of the action in the newspaper. Ames secured a judgment against the defendants. Later it was contended that the judgment was not valid. Do you agree? Why?
9. How does each of the following pretrial procedures contribute to the determination of legal disputes?

   (a) Motion for judgment on the pleadings
   (b) Motion for summary judgment
   (c) Pretrial conference
   (d) Discovery
10. A witness who is willing to testify concerning certain facts in a case lives in another state. How can the testimony be secured for use as evidence in the trial?
11. Briefly outline the steps in a trial beginning with the opening statements by the attorneys.
12. The right of privacy is a fundamental right that has always been recognized by American law. Appraise this statement.
13. The right to trial by jury is a fundamental procedure that must always be used whenever any issue of fact is to be determined. Appraise this statement.
14. Mostek Corporation, a Texas corporation, made a contract to sell computer-related products to the North American Foreign Trading Corporation, a New York corporation. North American used its own purchase order form on which appeared the statement that "any dispute arising out of this order shall be submitted to arbitration as provided in the terms set forth on the back of this order." Acting on the purchase order, Mostek delivered almost all of the goods but failed to deliver the final installment. North American then demanded that the matter be arbitrated. Mostek refused to do so. Was it required to arbitrate? [Re Mostek Corporation, 120 App Div 2d 383, 502 NYS2d 181]

2

ETHICS, SOCIAL FORCES, AND THE LAW

In Chapter 1, we defined *law* as a body of *enforceable* principles of conduct. In a democratic society, these principles of conduct are determined by the people. Laws represent an expression of the collective desires of the people to encourage conduct that is right, good, and just and to discourage conduct that is wrong, evil, or unjust. In this regard, the law has its underpinnings in ethics — the ethics of a society constitute a force that molds that society's law. Ethics in turn reflect social forces.

A. ETHICS AND LAW

To what extent do ethical values affect the law?

§ 2:1 WHAT ARE ETHICS?

Ethics are moral principles. More fully stated, ethics constitute the branch of philosophy dealing with values relating to human conduct, with respect to the goodness and the rightness of motives and actions. Thus far the matter is easy. The difficulty arises in defining *goodness*. The definition changes over time and with different societies. For example, the ancient Spartans believed that it was good that sickly infants be allowed to die. The England of two centuries ago believed it was good to punish some 250 offenses by death. Our society used to believe it was good for the marketplace to be governed by the rule of "Let the buyer beware." Gradually, public opinion regarded this as

24

not good; and much of modern law, with its protection of the consumer, is based on "Let the *seller* beware."

Consider the Founding Fathers who obtained our national independence and established our Constitution. We certainly respect, admire, and praise them. But they thought of "inalienable rights" as being the "rights of man" — white, free men over 21; women and slaves excluded. To them, labor unions were illegal conspiracies and employees could not strike or picket against their own employers. It was to take almost a century after they lived, a civil war, and a Constitutional amendment to delegalize the institution of slavery and abolish the concept that a slave was a thing or chattel owned by a master. It was to take the 20th century to give employees the right to unionize, strike, and picket and to recognize legal rights of women.[1]

Further study of history and of different societies will emphasize that goodness, and therefore ethics, does not have the same meaning at all times to all peoples.

§ 2:2   WHY ETHICAL CONCEPTS CHANGE

What makes the content of ethics change? This is important to a study of law because as ethical concepts change, so changes the law.

If we look closely at why one society or one generation believes something is bad although another society or generation thought it was good, we come to the conclusion that there are certain underlying currents that run through the pages of history. These currents are described in this chapter as social forces. Depending upon the importance attached to the different forces at different times, the content of the community's code of ethics changes. Thus, the underlying reason for changed ethics is

the change in the value placed upon the different social forces. To fully understand why society's evaluation of social forces changes requires a thorough study of practically every field of knowledge and necessarily lies beyond the scope of this book. It is sufficient for our purpose that we recognize that there are social forces, that these forces give rise to the ethical patterns of the day, that the evaluation of the social forces changes, and that with such changes there are corresponding changes in the field of ethics.

§ 2:3   ETHICS AND MODERN LAW

The social forces considered in this chapter give rise to our ethical concepts. These concepts in turn influence and give rise to the rules of law. The law existing at any one time is part of the social environment in which people live and work. The goals and objectives inspired by the environment will seek to advance certain social forces. Thus, there is an endless circle of interaction between social environment, social forces, ethics, and the law.

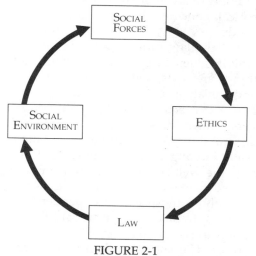

FIGURE 2-1
THE ENDLESS CIRCLE OF SOCIETAL INTERACTION

---

[1]   One quotation will be sufficient to show that our views of what is right or good today are much different from views in former years. In 1869, a woman lawyer was refused admission to the bar of the state of Illinois because she was a woman. On appeal the United States Supreme Court held that this was

proper. Bradley, J. stated that: "The paramount destiny and mission of woman are to fulfill the noble and benign office of wife and mother. This is the law of the Creator." (Bradwell v Illinois, 16 Wall 130 (1873), affirming 55 Ill 535).

By their very nature, ethical concepts are vague and general. The law, as opposed to broad ethical standards, must be more definite and stable in order to be capable of consistent enforcement. Notwithstanding this distinction between law and ethics, it is clear that there is a strong relation between them. Laws are made and remade as notions of justice change. A society's sense of justice is in turn influenced by its laws. The interactions are unquestionably complex, but a few observations can nonetheless be made.

(a) LAW AS THE CRYSTALLIZATION OF ETHICS. While all ethical values are not capable of expression as laws, certainly the more elemental ethical principles find their way into a society's legal framework. An ethical regard for the value of human life is crystallized in criminal codes detailing precisely defined degrees of offense — murder, manslaughter, negligent homicide. Similarly, an ethical obligation to look after the well-being of others takes the form of the parents' legally enforceable duty to care for their children. In these areas the law approaches the attainment of ethical values of society and locks the ethical concepts into binding rules of conduct.

But the law cannot equal the reach of ethical values, at least partly because some things are better left to individual choice and initiative. Criminal penalties for behavior that actively or negligently endangers human life stop short of imposing a general duty to intervene to save a life already in danger. Legal obligations to further the well-being of others are not extended to members of society generally, but only to those with a dependent relationship. In fact, it might be said that if a society's ethical codes constitute its concept of ideal behavior, then that society's law is its minimum standard of conduct.

(b) SOCIETAL ETHICS AS THE BLUEPRINT FOR FUTURE LAW. As we noted earlier, a society's ethical values change over time. The law similarly evolves to keep pace with changing technologies and values, though at a much more deliberate pace. Because of the close relationship between law and ethics, the ethical values of today's society can be regarded as a blueprint for the law of tomorrow.

(c) PARTICULAR APPLICATIONS. As you study business law, you will find many instances of established legal principles that became inadequate to serve society's changing notions of what was right or just. You will see that, as public sentiment against a particular law or legal principle grew, a legal system that was otherwise resistant to change found various ways to relieve the pressure. The change sometimes took the form of a judicial decision that found a new exception to an established rule or simply overturned an earlier decision. Or the change may have been manifested as a new statute or a constitutional amendment. Here are a few illustrations.

As we discussed in Chapter 1, there was not always a legally recognized right of privacy. The very rapid dissemination of information to great numbers of people made possible by the development of the modern newspaper, and much later by radio and television, created a need for enforceable protection against unwarranted intrusion upon private lives. Privacy is now a constitutionally protected right.[2]

Another example of changes in societal ethics resulting in changes in the law involves consumerism. As of 1776, the concept of what was "right" in the marketplace meant that everyone was equal. That was the year in which the Declaration of Independence proclaimed the political equality of everyone; and Adam Smith, in his *The Wealth of Nations*, declared that every person was the economic equal of every other person and should be allowed to move about in the marketplace freely and without restraint. But all this was before the rise of mass produc-

---

[2] Griswold v Connecticut, 381 US 479 (1965).

tion, modern distribution, and giant sellers. Beginning in the middle of this century, society began to feel that it was just not "right" to treat the consumer as the equal of the giant seller. The result, consumer protection laws, gave the consumer special protection because of such inequality. The Uniform Commercial Code placed special duties on merchants. Our American ideal of equality was modified in recognition of the fact that equality does not exist in the marketplace.

(d) IMPLICATIONS FOR BUSINESS. As the size, resources, and business patterns of society change, what seems right today may seem wrong in the future. While society's changing notions of what is right and just do not create binding obligations on businesses and business people, they do constitute a force that will help to mold future law. Businesses that act irresponsibly and with disregard for society's view of what is right will speed the transition from ethical concept to enforceable law. Business can only avoid society's tendency toward more stringent regulation and over-legalization by acting responsibly and in harmony with societal ethics. Today many companies have established codes of ethics as guides for their employees, requiring that company business be conducted not only in compliance with the law, but also in accordance with the highest standards of business integrity and honest dealings.

In the remainder of this chapter, we will examine some of the basic principles that this society regards as important in making its ethical decisions and its laws.

B. SOCIAL FORCES AND THE LAW

Every rule of law seeks some goal or objective. General objectives are the creation and maintenance of order, stability, and justice.

§ 2:4   SOCIAL FORCES

The desires or forces that motivate society in making its laws can be called social forces. These social forces influence the ethical concepts of society, which in turn produce society's laws.

The social forces and objectives of the law are, in effect, the opposite sides of the same coin. Because certain forces are pushing society, society seeks certain objectives. Asking what is the objective of a law is thus another way of asking what social force in society seeks that result. The sum of these societal drives gives us the ethical pattern or environment of society.

(a) PROTECTION OF THE STATE. A number of laws are designed to protect the existing governments, both state and national. Laws condemning treason, sedition, and subversive practices are examples of society taking measures to preserve governmental systems. Less dramatic are the laws that impose taxes to provide for the support of those governments.

Under the national social security system, a number is assigned to each person. The same number is used by other government programs and agencies, such as the Internal Revenue Service and various relief programs. The numbering system solves the problem of distinguishing between two persons with the same name. As the assigned numbers are shorter than the names of most people, the numbering system speeds up the process of storing and retrieving information. The use of the same identifying numbers by the various government programs makes it easier for the government to spot fraudulent claims. Various attacks, however, have been made on this numbering system on the ground that it is dehumanizing or violates religious principles. The *Bowen* case deals with a conflict between the plaintiff's religious beliefs and the governmental requirement of using a social security number in order to obtain financial assistance.

BOWEN V ROY

476 US ___, 90 L Ed 2d 735 (1986)

Federal law provides financial assistance to poor families through the food stamp program and the Aid to Families with Dependent Children. In order to obtain benefits under these programs, the federal law requires a recipient to give a social security number to any state welfare agency involved. Roy, an American Indian, was refused federal benefits for his two-year-old daughter because he would not furnish a social security number. He claimed that the use of a number was contrary to his religious belief, and that freedom of religion gave him the right to refuse to furnish a social security number. From a decision against him, he appealed.

BURGER, Ch. J. . . . Roy is a Native American descended from the Abenaki Tribe, and he asserts a religious belief that control over one's life is essential to spiritual purity and indispensable to "becoming a holy person." Based on recent conversations with an Abenaki chief, Roy believes that technology is "robbing the spirit of man." In order to prepare his daughter for greater spiritual power, therefore, Roy testified to his belief that he must keep her person and spirit unique and that the uniqueness of the [s]ocial [s]ecurity number as an identifier, coupled with the other uses of the number over which she has no control, will serve to "rob the spirit" of his daughter and prevent her from attaining greater spiritual power. . . .

Never to our knowledge has the Court interpreted the First Amendment to require the Government *itself* to behave in ways that the individual believes will further his or her spiritual development or that of his or her family. The Free Exercise Clause simply cannot be understood to require the Government to conduct its own internal affairs in ways that comport with the religious beliefs of particular citizens. Just as the Government may not insist that appellees engage in any set form of religious observance, so appellees may not demand that the Government join in their chosen religious practices by refraining from using a number to identify their daughter. "The Free Exercise Clause is written in terms of what the government cannot do to the individual, not in terms of what the individual can extract from the government." Sherbert v Verner, 374 US 398, 412 (1963) (Douglas, J., concurring). . . .

The statutory requirement that applicants provide a [s]ocial [s]ecurity number is wholly neutral in religious terms and uniformly applicable. There is no claim that there is any attempt by Congress to discriminate invidiously or any covert suppression of particular religious beliefs. . . . It may indeed confront some applicants for benefits with choices, but in no sense does it affirmatively compel appellees, by threat of sanctions, to refrain from religiously motivated conduct or to engage in conduct that they find objectionable for religious reasons. Rather, it is [Roy and his daughter] who seek benefits from the Government and who assert that, because of certain religious beliefs, they should be excused from compliance with a condition that is binding on all other persons who seek the same benefits from the Government.

This is far removed from the historical instances of religious persecution and intolerance that gave concern to those who drafted the Free Exercise Clause of the First Amendment. . . .

Governments today grant a broad range of benefits; inescapably at the same time the administration of complex programs requires certain conditions and restrictions. Although in some situations a mechanism for individual consideration will be created, a policy decision by a government that it wishes to treat all applicants alike and that it does not wish to become involved in case-by-case inquiries into the genuineness of each religious objection to such condition or restrictions is entitled to substantial deference. Moreover, legitimate interests are implicated in the need to avoid any appearance of favoring religious over nonreligious applicants. . . .

The [s]ocial [s]ecurity number requirement clearly promotes a legitimate and important public interest. No one can doubt that preventing fraud in these benefits programs is an important goal. . . .

[Judgment affirmed]

QUESTIONS

1. Does the court agree or disagree with the religious beliefs of Roy?
2. How does the decision affect Roy's religious freedom?
3. Who would be harmed if Roy were allowed to receive governmental benefits and still follow his beliefs?

(b) PROTECTION OF THE PERSON. At an early date, laws developed to protect the individual from being injured or killed. The field of criminal law is devoted to a large extent to the protection of the person. In addition, under civil law a suit can be brought to recover damages for the harm done by criminal acts. For example, a person who steals an automobile is subject to a penalty imposed by the state in the form of imprisonment or a fine, or both. In addition, the thief is liable to the owner for the money value of the automobile. Over the course of time, the protection of personal rights has broadened to include protection of reputation and privacy, and to protection of contracts and business relations from malicious interference by outsiders. The right to privacy is protected against news media seeking to learn and communicate what is happening.[3]

It is a federal offense to knowingly injure, intimidate, or interfere with anyone exercising a basic civil right (such as voting), taking part in any federal governmental program, or receiving federal assistance. Interference with attendance in a public school or college, with participation in any state or local governmental program, with service as a juror in a state court, or with the use of any public facility (common carrier, hotel, or restaurant) is prohibited when based on race, color, religion, or national origin discrimination.[4]

Protection of the person is expanding to protect economic interests. Laws prohibiting discrimination in employment, in furnishing hotel accommodations and transportation, and in commercial transactions in the sale of property are an extension of the concept of protecting the person. Because membership in a professional association, a labor union, or a trade or business group has economic importance to its

---

[3] Miller v National Broadcasting Co., 187 Cal App 3d 1463, 232 Cal Rptr 668 (1986).

[4] Civil Obedience Act of 1968, PL 90-284, 18 United States Code § 245.

members, an applicant can no longer be excluded arbitrarily from the membership, nor may a member be expelled without notice of the charges made and an opportunity to be heard.[5]

(c) PROTECTION OF PUBLIC HEALTH, SAFETY, AND MORALS. The law seeks to protect the public health, safety, and morals in many ways. Laws relating to quarantine, food inspection, and compulsory inocula-

___

[5]   Silver v New York Stock Exchange, 373 US 341 (1963); Cunningham v Burbank Board of Realtors, 262 Cal App 2d 211, 68 Cal Rptr 653 (1968).

tion protect the public health. Laws regulating highway speeds and laws requiring fire escapes or guard devices around moving parts of factory machinery are for the safety of the public. Laws prohibiting the sale of liquor to minors and those prohibiting obscenity protect the morals of the public.

In the *Tate* case, the system used to advance the objective of protecting the general welfare from traffic violators conflicted with the objective of protecting the person from unequal treatment under the law.

TATE V SHORT

401 US 395 (1971)

Texas provided that all motor vehicle traffic violations were to be punished by a fine. A person with money to pay the fine would never be imprisoned for a traffic violation. The law provided, however, that if a person who was fined did not have the money to pay the fine, that person could be imprisoned one day for every $5 of the fine. Tate was convicted for nine violations and fined a total of $425. He did not have any money. The court therefore ordered him imprisoned for 85 days. He claimed that this could not be done because it punished him for being poor and treated him differently than a defendant who had money to pay a fine. According to Tate, this deprived him of the protection to which he was entitled by equality before the law. Tate filed a petition for his release, naming Short, the local chief of police, as defendant. The state court rejected his claim and he appealed to the United States Supreme Court.

BRENNAN, J. . . . The Illinois statute involved in *Williams [v Illinois*, 399 US 235 (1970)] authorized both a fine and imprisonment. Williams was given the maximum sentence for petty theft for one year's imprisonment and a $500 fine, plus $5 in court costs. The judgment, as permitted by the Illinois statute, provided that if, when the one-year sentence expired, Williams did not pay the fine and court costs, he was to remain in jail a sufficient length of time to satisfy the total amount at the rate of $5 per day. We held that the Illinois statute as applied to Williams worked as an invidious discrimination solely because he was too poor to pay the fine, and therefore violated the Equal Protection Clause.

Although the instant case involves offenses punishable by fines only, petitioner's imprisonment for nonpayment constitutes precisely the same unconstitutional discrimination since, like Williams, petitioner was subjected to imprisonment solely because of his indigency. In *Morris v Schoonfield*, 399 US 508,

509 . . . (1970), four members of the Court anticipated the problem of this case and stated the view, which we now adopt, that "the same constitutional defect condemned in *Williams* also inheres in jailing an indigent for failing to make immediate payment of any fine, whether or not the fine is accompanied by a jail term and whether or not the jail term of the indigent extends beyond the maximum term that may be imposed on a person willing and able to pay a fine. In each case, the Constitution prohibits the State from imposing a fine as a sentence and then automatically converting it into a jail term solely because the defendant is indigent and cannot forthwith pay the fine in full."

Our opinion in *Williams* stated the premise of this conclusion in saying that "the Equal Protection Clause of the Fourteenth Amendment requires that the statutory ceiling placed on imprisonment for any substantive offense be the same for all defendants irrespective of their economic status." . . . Since Texas has legislated a "fines only" policy for traffic offenses, that statutory ceiling cannot, consistently with the Equal Protection Clause, limit the punishment to payment of the fine if one is able to pay it, yet convert the fine into a prison term for an indigent defendant without the means to pay his fine. Imprisonment in such a case is not imposed to further any penal objective of the State. It is imposed to augment the State's revenues but obviously does not serve that purpose: the defendant cannot pay because he is indigent and his imprisonment, rather than aiding collection of the revenue, saddles the State with the cost of feeding and housing him for the period of his imprisonment.

There are, however, other alternatives to which the State may constitutionally resort to serve its concededly valid interest in enforcing payment of fines. . . .

Several States have a procedure for paying fines in installments. . . .

This procedure has been widely endorsed as effective not only to collect the fine but also to save the expense of maintaining a prisoner and avoid the necessity of supporting his family under the state welfare program while he is confined.

[Judgment reversed]

QUESTIONS

1. What social force is advanced by the decision?
2. In the *Tate* case is the court concerned only with the person who will be jailed for lack of money to pay the fine?
3. Is payment of fine by installments a satisfactory solution for the situation of the defendant who does not have money to pay a fine?

(d) PROTECTION OF PROPERTY. Just as laws have developed to protect the individual's physical well-being, laws have developed to protect one's property from damage, destruction, and other harmful acts. As already noted, a thief who steals an automobile is civilly liable to the owner of the automobile for its value and is criminally responsible to the state.

(e) PROTECTION OF TITLE. Because of the importance of ownership of property, one of the objectives of the law has been to protect the title of the owner of property. Thus, if property is stolen, the true owner may recover it from the thief, and even from a person who purchased it in good faith from the thief.

(f) FREEDOM OF PERSONAL ACTION. In the Anglo-American stream of history, the desire for freedom from political domination gave rise to the American Revolution, and the desire for freedom from economic domination gave rise to the free enterprise philosophy. Today we find freedom as the dominant element in the constitutional provisions for the protection of freedom of religion, press, and speech, and also in such laws as those against trusts or business combinations in restraint of trade by others.

Freedom of action is also given to a patient who is competent to choose to die, so that person may refuse to take medical treatment that might prolong life.[6]

This right of freedom of personal action, however, cannot be exercised by one person in such a way that it interferes to an unreasonable extent with the rights of others. Freedom of speech, for example, does not mean freedom to speak or write a malicious, false statement about another person's character or reputation. In effect, this means that one person's freedom of speech must be balanced with another person's right to be free from defamation of character or reputation.

(g) FREEDOM OF USE OF PROPERTY. Freedom of action is often stated in terms of freedom of use of property. For example, the owner of an automobile is free to drive the car or not, to say who shall ride in it, to sell or give it away, and so on.

It must be remembered, however, that there are often restrictions on the use of property, such as speed laws governing the automobile, zoning laws regulating buildings, and antipollution laws restricting factories.

(h) ENFORCEMENT OF INTENT. When persons voluntarily enter into a transaction, the law usually seeks to enforce their in-

tent. This objective is closely related to the concept that the law seeks to protect the individual's freedom of action. For example, if a person provides by will for the distribution of property upon death, the law will generally allow the property to pass to the persons intended by the deceased owner. The law will likewise seek to carry out the intention of the parties to a business transaction.

In looking for the intent of the lawmaker in adopting a law, the court will go behind first appearances. For example, although ''intoxicating liquor'' does not ordinarily suggest cough medicine, a motorist will be held to have been driving under the influence of intoxicating liquor when the blood test shows twice the allowable maximum of alcohol in the blood in consequence of the motorist's taking cough syrup having a high alcohol content.[7]

The extent to which the intent of one person or of several persons will be carried out has certain limitations. Sometimes the intent is not effective unless it is manifested by a particular written formality. For example, a deceased person may have intended to leave property to a friend, but in most states that intent must be shown by a written will signed by the deceased owner. Likewise, in some cases the intent of the parties may not be carried out because the law regards the intent as illegal.

(i) PROTECTION FROM EXPLOITATION, FRAUD, AND OPPRESSION. Many rules of law have developed in the courts, and many statutes have been enacted, to protect certain groups or individuals from exploitation or oppression by others. Thus, in order to protect minors, persons under legal age, the law developed that minors could set aside contracts, subject to certain exceptions.

Persons who buy food that is packed in cans are given certain rights against the seller and the manufacturer. Since the contents of the cans are not visible, buyers of

---

[6]   Re Milton, 29 Ohio 3d 20, 505 NE2d 255 (1987).

[7]   Thornton v North Dakota State Highway Commissioners (ND) 399 NW2d 861 (1987).

such products need special protection from unscrupulous canners. The consumer is also protected by laws against adulteration and poisons in food, drugs, and household products. Laws prohibiting unfair competition and discrimination, both economic and social, are also designed to protect from oppression.

(j) Furtherance of Trade. Society seeks to further trade in a variety of ways, as by establishing a currency as a medium of payment; by recognizing and giving legal effect to installment sales; by adopting special rules for checks, notes, and similar instruments so that they can be widely used as credit devices and substitutes for money; and by enacting laws to mitigate the harmful effects of alternating periods of depression and inflation.

Laws that have been considered in connection with other objectives may also serve to further trade. For example, laws protecting against unfair competition have the objective of furthering trade, as well as the objective of protecting certain classes from oppression by others.

(k) Protection of Creditors. Society seeks to protect the rights of creditors and to protect them from dishonest or fraudulent acts of debtors. Initially, creditors are protected by the law that makes contracts binding and that provides machinery for the enforcement of contracts, and by the provision of the federal Constitution that prohibits states from impairing the obligation of contracts. Further, creditors may compel a debtor to come into bankruptcy. If the debtor has concealed property or transfers it to a friend in order to hide it from creditors, the law permits the creditors to claim the property for the payment of the debts due them.

(l) Rehabilitation of Debtors. Society has come to regard it as unsound that debtors should be ruined forever by the burden of their debts. Imprisonment for debt has been abolished. Bankruptcy laws have been adopted to provide the debtor with a means of starting a new economic life. In times of widespread depression, the same

objective has been served by special laws prohibiting the foreclosure of mortgages.

(m) Stability. Stability is particularly important in all business transactions. When you buy a house, for example, you not only want to know the exact meaning of the transaction under today's law, but you also want the transaction to have the same meaning in the future.

Because of the desire for stability, courts will ordinarily follow former decisions unless there is a strong reason to depart from them. Likewise, when no former case directly bears on the point involved, the court will strive to reach a decision that is a logical extension of some former decision or that follows a former decision by analogy, rather than to strike off on a fresh path to reach a decision unrelated to the past.

(n) Flexibility. If stability were always required, the cause of justice would often be defeated. The reason that originally gave rise to a rule of law may have ceased to exist.[8] Also, a rule may later appear unjust because it reflects a concept of justice that is outmoded or obsolete. For example, capital punishment, which one age believed just, has been seriously questioned by another age. We must not lose sight of the fact that the rule of law under question was created to further the sense of social justice existing at that time, and that our concepts of justice change.

Changes by legislative action are relatively easy to make. Furthermore, some statutes recognize the impossibility of laying down in advance a hard- and-fast rule that will do justice in all cases. The typical modern statute, particularly in the field of regulation of business, will often contain an "escape clause" by which a person can escape from the operation of the statute

---

[8]   "It is revolting to have no better reason for a rule of law than that it was laid down in the time of Henry IV. It is still more revolting if the grounds upon which it was laid down have vanished long since, and the rule simply persists from blind imitation of the past." Holmes, Collected Papers 187 (1920).

"The law must be stable, but it must not stand still." Roscoe Pound, *Introduction to the Philosophy of Law* (Connecticut: Yale University Press, 1922).

under certain circumstances. Thus, a rent control law may impose a rent ceiling — that is, a maximum above which landlords cannot charge. The same law may also authorize a greater charge when special circumstances make it just to allow such exception, as when the landlord has made expensive repairs to the property or when taxes have increased substantially.

The rule of law may be stated in terms of what a reasonable or prudent person would do. Thus, whether you are negligent in driving your automobile is determined in court by whether you exercised the degree of care that a prudent person would have exercised in the same situation. This is a vague and variable standard as to how you must drive your car, but it is the only standard that is practical. The alternative would be a detailed motor code specifying how you should drive your car under every situation that might arise; a code that obviously could not foresee every possibility and that certainly would be too long for any driver to remember.

Even constitutions are flexible to the extent that they can be changed by amendment or judicial construction. Constitutions state the procedures for their amendment. Making changes in constitutions is purposely made difficult to serve the objective of stability, but change can be made when the need for change is generally recognized by the people of the state or nation.

The social force of protecting the person is frequently the controlling factor in determining whether a court should adhere to the common law, thereby furthering stability; or whether it should change the law, thereby furthering flexibility. Thus, it will be seen that at many points the courts retain the common law when that will further the protection of the person. In other instances, the courts change the common law because a change will give the person greater protection. One court retained the common-law definition of *person* with the result that a reckless driver injuring a mother and killing her unborn child was not guilty of manslaughter with respect to the death of the unborn child, because such a child was not a *person* under the common law of crimes.[9] By this decision, the person of the defendant was protected because the common-law definition of *person* required him to be acquitted of the crime of manslaughter. However, in so doing, the court turned its back on protecting the person of the unborn child. Which person should the law protect? The social force of stability tipped the scales in favor of protecting the defendant.

(o) PRACTICAL EXPEDIENCY. Frequently the law is influenced by what is practical or expedient in the situation. Often the law will strive to make its rules fit the business practices of society. For example, a signature is frequently regarded by the law as including a stamping, printing, or typewriting of a name, in recognition of the business practice of "signing" letters and other instruments by mechanical means. A requirement of a handwritten signature would impose a burden on business that would not be practically expedient.

With the advent of the computer, the law of evidence has changed to allow a computer printout to be admitted in evidence as against the old law that records could not be produced in court unless the person who prepared them was present as a witness.[10]

§ 2:5   CONFLICTING OBJECTIVES

The specific objectives of the law sometimes conflict with each other. When this is true, the problem is one of social policy, which in turn means a weighing of social, economic, and moral forces to determine which objective should be furthered.

We find a conflict at times between the objective of the state seeking protection from the conduct of individuals or groups and the objective of freedom of action by

---

[9]   Meadows v Arkansas, 291 Ark 105, 722 SW2d 584 (1987).
[10]   See § 11:4.

those individuals and groups. For example, while protection of the freedom of the individual urges the utmost freedom of religious belief, society will impose limitations on religious freedom where it believes such freedom will cause harm to the public welfare. Hence, state laws requiring vaccination against smallpox were enforced as against the contention that this violated religious principles. Similarly, parents failing to provide medical care for a sick child will be held guilty of manslaughter if the child dies, even though the parents sincerely believed as a matter of religious principle that medical care was improper. In contrast, when the harm contemplated is not direct or acute, religious freedom will prevail, so that a compulsory child education law will not be enforced against Amish parents who as a matter of religion are opposed to state education.[11]

In the *Rasmussen* case the privacy interest of blood donors and the public welfare interest were in conflict with the interest of an AIDS victim seeking to learn the identity of the donors.

---

[11] Wisconsin v Yoder, 406 US 205 (1972) (high school student).

RASMUSSEN V SOUTH FLORIDA BLOOD SERVICE, INC.
(Fla) 500 So 2d 533 (1987)

Donald Rasmussen was hit by an automobile. In the hospital he was given a number of blood transfusions. Some time thereafter it was determined that he had AIDS. He filed a petition for a court order against the blood bank that had furnished the blood to the hospital. He wanted to learn the names and addresses of all blood donors so that he could determine if any had AIDS. He hoped by this to prove that he had contracted AIDS as the result of one of the transfusions in the hospital. He died from the AIDS and his estate continued the proceeding. The court of appeals certified the question to the state supreme court.

BARKETT, J. . . . The court must balance the competing interests that would be served by granting discovery or by denying it. . . .

The Supreme Court first recognized a right of privacy based on the United States Constitution in *Griswold v Connecticut*, 381 U.S. 479 (1965). This right of privacy has been described as "the most comprehensive of rights and the right most valued by civilized man." *Stanley v. Georgia*, 394 U.S. 557, 564 (1969). . . . In recent cases, the Court has discussed the privacy right as one of those fundamental rights that are " 'implicit in the concept of ordered liberty' such that 'neither liberty nor justice would exist if [they] were sacrificed.' " *Bowers v. Hardwick*, ___ U.S. ___, 106 S.Ct. 2841, 2844 (1986). . . .

In 1980, the voters of Florida amended our state constitution to include an express right of privacy. Art. V, § 23, Fla.Const. In approving the amendment, Florida became the fourth state to adopt a strong, freestanding right of privacy as a separate section of its state constitution, thus providing an explicit textual foundation for those privacy interests inherent in the concept of liberty which may not otherwise be protected by specific constitutional provisions.

Although the general concept of privacy encompasses an enormously broad and diverse field of personal action and belief, there can be no doubt that the

Florida amendment was intended to protect the right to determine whether or not sensitive information about oneself will be disclosed to others. . . .

It is now known that AIDS is a major health problem with calamitous potential. At present, there is no known cure and the mortality rate is high. As noted by the court below, medical researchers have identified a number of groups which have a high incidence of the disease and are labeled "high risk" groups. . . .

The [court order requested] gives petitioner access to the names and addresses of the blood donors with no restrictions on their use. There is nothing to prohibit petitioner from conducting an investigation without the knowledge of the persons in question. We cannot ignore, therefore, the consequences of disclosure to nonparties, including the possibility that a donor's co-workers, friends, employers, and others may be queried as to the donor's sexual preferences, drug use, or general life-style.

The threat posed by the disclosure of the donors' identities goes far beyond the immediate discomfort occasioned by third party probing into sensitive areas of the donors' lives. Disclosure of donor identities in any context involving AIDS could be extremely disruptive and even devastating to the individual donor. If the requested information is released, and petitioner queries the donors' friends and fellow employees, it will be functionally impossible to prevent occasional references to AIDS. As the district court recognized:

> AIDS is the modern day equivalent of leprosy. AIDS, or a suspicion of AIDS, can lead to discrimination in employment, education, housing and even medical treatment. . . .

We conclude, therefore, that the disclosure sought here implicates constitutionally protected privacy interests.

Our analysis of the interests to be served by denying discovery does not end with the effects of disclosure on the private lives of the fifty-one donors implicated in this case. Society has a vital interest in maintaining a strong volunteer blood supply, a task that has become more difficult with the emergence of AIDS. . . . [I]t is clearly "in the public interest to discourage any serious disincentive to volunteer blood donation." *Rasmussen*, 467 So.2d at 804. Because there is little doubt that the prospect of inquiry into one's private life and potential association with AIDS will deter blood donation, we conclude that society's interest in a strong and healthy blood supply will be furthered by the denial of discovery in this case.

In balancing the competing interests involved, we do not ignore Rasumussen's interest in obtaining the requested information. . . . However, we find that the discovery order requested here would do little to advance that interest. The probative value of the discovery sought by Rasmussen is dubious at best. The potential of significant harm to most, if not all, of the fifty-one unsuspecting donors in permitting such a fishing expedition is great and far outweighs the plaintiff's need under these circumstances. . . .

[Discovery refused]

QUESTIONS

1. What social forces were involved in the *Rasmussen* case?
2. Assume that Rasmussen had obtained the names and addresses of the do-

nors. If one of them had AIDS would that prove that Rasmussen had contracted AIDS from the blood transfusions?

As another example, the objective of protecting title may conflict with the objective of furthering trade. Consider again the example of the stolen property that was sold by the thief to one who purchased it for value and in good faith, without reason to know that the goods had been stolen. If we are to further the objective of protecting the title to the property, we will conclude that the owner can recover the property from the innocent purchaser. This rule, however, will discourage trade, for people will be less willing to buy goods if they run the risk that the goods were stolen and may have to be surrendered. If we instead think only of taking steps to encourage buying and selling, we will hold that the buyer takes a good title because the buyer acted in good faith and paid value. If we do this, we then destroy the title of the original owner and obviously abandon our objective of protecting title to property. As a general rule, American society has followed the objective of protecting title. In some instances, however, the objective of furthering trade is adopted by statute and the buyer is given good title, as in certain cases of commercial paper (notes, drafts, and checks) or of the purchaser from a regular dealer in other people's goods.

§ 2:6 LAW AS AN EVOLUTIONARY PROCESS

Law changes as society changes. Let us consider an example of this type of change. When the economy was patterned on a local community unit in which everyone knew each other and each other's product, the concept of "let the buyer beware" expressed a proper basis on which to conduct business. Much of the early law of the sale of goods was based on this view. In today's economy, however, with its interstate, na-

tional, and even international character, the buyer has little or no direct contact with the manufacturer or seller, and the packaging of articles makes their presale examination impossible. Under these circumstances, the consumer must rely on the integrity of others. Gradually, practices that were tolerated and even approved in an earlier era have been condemned, and the law has changed to protect the buyer.

Moreover, new principles of law are being developed to meet the new situations that arise. Every new invention and every new business practice introduces a number of situations for which there may be no existing rule of law. For example, how could there have been a law relating to stocks and bonds before those instruments came into existence? How could there have been a law with respect to the liability of radio and television broadcasters before such methods of communication were developed?

New inventions and new techniques for investigation have changed or produced new rules of law because it has become possible to prove facts that could not have been proven before. Thus, fingerprint identification, ballistics, and advanced chemical analysis techniques have made identification a certainty. The use of radar to determine speed is now commonplace. Within the last decade the development of the human leukocyte antigen test has made it possible to determine parentage with over 90% accuracy.[12]

§ 2:7 THE COURTS AND THE MAKING OF THE LAW

In the early days of our country, courts were thought to merely declare the law.

[12] Callison v Callison, (Okla) 687 P2d 106 (1984).

That is, they were to apply existing law to existing facts. They had no power to make new law.

Since the 1930s, it has been recognized and accepted that courts do make the law. Changing technology and cultural patterns produce new situations for which there is no law. A strict court will wait until the lawmaker passes a law. The liberal court will create a new rule to fill the gap. Similarly, the rule of law followed by a former court may appear outmoded in the light of the new technology and cultural pattern. Here the strict court will follow the former decision until the lawmaker makes a change. The liberal court will take charge and make the change by revising the earlier decision. As we moved through the last two decades, more and more courts adopted the liberal approach and their opinions openly recognized that they were making law to advance one or more of the social forces discussed in § 2:4.

The extent to which courts can make the law is, of course, limited by existing statutes and constitutions. These cannot be ignored by the courts. In many instances, however, the courts may reinterpret the statute or constitution so that the net result is the same as though they were amended.

When a court changes the prior law, the question arises whether the court should say that the law is changed from that date on or whether the court should state that the new rule goes back and should be applied to cases that arose before the new rule was declared.

If a new rule applies only to the future it is said to apply prospectively. If it is allowed to reach back into the past it is said to apply retrospectively. The fact that the judge has the power to state when the new rule of judge-made law should go into effect emphasizes the fact that the judge is in reality making the law.

The question of the timing of a change of law was involved in the *Adkins* case.

ADKINS V SKY BLUE, INC.

(Wyo) 701 P2d 549 (1985)

In 1971, the Supreme Court of Wyoming held that a bar selling liquor to a customer was not liable for the harm caused a third person because of the drunken driving of the bar's customer. In 1982, an intoxicated customer of a bar called "TV Lounge," owned by Sky Blue, Inc., drove his car into and permanently and severely crippled Leland Adkins. He brought a suit against Sky Blue. Thereafter, in 1983, the Wyoming Supreme Court reversed its 1971 decision and held that a bar could be held liable to the third person injured by the drunken driving of the customer of the bar. Adkins claimed that Sky Blue was liable because of the 1983 decision. Sky Blue claimed that the 1971 decision, under which it would not be liable, applied. The question was certified to the state supreme court.

Cardine, J. . . . [In] *Parsons v. Jow*, Wyo., 480 P2d 396 (1971), [the court held] there was no cause of action at common law against a vendor of liquor in favor of one injured by a vendee who becomes intoxicated — this for the reason that the proximate cause of injury was deemed to be the patron's consumption of liquor and not its sale. . . .

[In that case,] the Wyoming Supreme Court issued a clear pronouncement that it would not undertake to adopt a dramshop law [placing liability on vendors of liquor] by judicial decision but would leave that to the legislature. . . .

McClellan v. Tottenhoff, decided June 28, 1983, involved the sale of alcoholic beverage to a minor who became intoxicated and drove a car so as to fatally injure the plaintiff. Without prior warning or suggestion of what was to occur, the court . . . stated:

> The rule that there is no cause of action when a vendor sells liquor to a consumer who injures a third party was created by the courts. We see no reason to wait any longer for the legislature to abrogate it. Common law created by the judiciary can be abrogated by the judiciary.

The common law has served us well because it is flexible, able to grow and meet the requirements of changing conditions and a different society. There are times when change is necessary; but the doctrine of stare decisis is also important in an organized society. Change, therefore, should occur slowly, deliberately after much experience, and if possible so as not to affect vested rights or things in the past. Thus, it is said that:

> The courts may apply or effectuate common law principles in the light of altered or new conditions, and when the circumstances and conditions are different, in that the common law principles are unsuitable to new circumstances or conditions, the needs of society, or in conflict with public policy, the courts may make such changes or modifications as the situation requires. (Footnotes omitted.) 15A C.J.S. Common Law § 13.

Acknowledging that there ought to be an extreme reluctance to change the common law and recognizing the obvious benefits of the doctrine of stare decisis, yet on occasion it does become eminently clear that society has long passed beyond the point where an ancient doctrine remains viable. This court believed it had arrived at that place in deciding *McClellan v Tottenhoff*, supra — now the law of this state — and in stating.:

"We hereby overrule *Parsons v. Jow*, supra. . . ."

The rule of *McClellan v. Tottenhoff*, supra, became effective with the issuance of the court's opinion on June 28, 1983. The accident in which plaintiff was involved and which is the subject of this case, occurred May 5, 1982, more than a year prior to the court's pronouncement in *McClellan v Tottenhoff*. If the rule announced in *McClellan v. Tottenhoff*, supra, applies prospectively only — that is in the future, *henceforth* and from now on — then plaintiff's case is subject to the common-law rule of nonliability for sellers of intoxicating liquor as stated in *Parsons v. Jow*. And, as was held in *Parsons v. Jow*, it must be dismissed.

Initially it was held that a court issuing an overruling decision had merely discovered and announced existing law; since the overruling case did not create new law, but merely recognized what had always been the law, such law would operate both retrospectively and prospectively:

> "But the modern decisions, taking a more pragmatic view of the judicial function, have recognized the power of a court to hold that an overruling decision is operative prospectively only and is not even operative upon the rights of the parties to the overruling case. As a matter of constitutional law, retroactive operation of an overruling decision is neither required nor prohibited.". . .

Where an overruling decision announces a change in the common law, some guidelines are set forth in *Chevron Oil Company v. Huson*, 404 U.S. 97 (1971), for whether its operation should be retrospective or prospective only:

> In our cases dealing with the nonretroactivity question, we have generally considered three separate factors. First, the decision to be applied nonretroactively must establish a new principle of law, either by overruling clear past precedent on which litigants may have relied, . . . or by deciding an issue of first impression whose resolution was not clearly foreshadowed. . . . Second, it has been stressed that "we must. . . weigh the merits and demerits in each case by looking to the prior history of the rule in question, its purpose and effect, and whether retrospective operation will further or retard its operation." . . . Finally, we have weighed the inequity imposed by retroactive application, for "where a decision of this Court could produce substantial inequitable results if applied retroactively, there is ample basis in our cases for avoiding the 'injustice or hardship' by a holding of nonretroactivity." . . .

It has been repeatedly stated that where a decision might produce substantial inequitable results if applied retroactively, it is appropriate to avoid such hardship or injustice by providing for prospective operation only. Vendors of liquor in this state had no reason to suspect that this court would adopt a dramshop-type law placing liability on vendors of liquor. There were no cases following *Parsons v. Jow*, supra, suggesting an imminent change in the law. The court had given its firm assurance in *Parsons v. Jow*, supra, that this was a matter for the legislature. . . . Liquor vendors had no reason to obtain insurance or otherwise protect themselves against liability that did not exist. Insuring against this kind of broad liability is expensive, and they surely were justified in relying upon the pronouncement of this court in not purchasing insurance coverage.

The public policy of *McClellan v. Tottenhoff* and the purposes to be served by imposing civil liability upon vendors of liquor are to cause them (a) to exercise care in dispensing liquor, (b) to refuse liquor to intoxicated persons or refuse to sell in violation of law, and (c) to provide financial responsibility for negligence. Those purposes are not served or affected by retroactive operation of the law, for the incident complained of had already occurred — nothing could be done to change it. The stated public policy would not be promoted by holding the vendor retroactively liable for damages. . . .

There was no series of cases following *Parsons v. Jow* that suggested or even intimated that the court might overrule *Parsons v. Jow*. The vendors of liquor justifiably relied upon the law as we stated it to be. To hold now that a vendor of liquor, not liable for damages under the law existing at the time of the accident involved nevertheless, a year later, became liable because of a change in the law by an overruling case would be manifestly unfair. . . .

[The 1983 decision did not apply to accidents before its date]

QUESTIONS

1. Was the decision in the *Adkins* case inevitable?
2. Is the decision in the *Adkins* case just?
3. What social change forms the background for the legal change made by the *Adkins* case?

§ 2:8   LAW AS A SYNTHESIS

Many rules of law do not further one objective alone. Some rules are a combination of two or more objectives with each objective working toward the same result. In other instances, the objectives oppose each other, and the rule of law that emerges is a combination or synthesis of the different objectives.

Law as a synthesis may be illustrated by the law as it relates to a contract for the sale of a house. Originally such a contract could be oral; that is, merely spoken words with nothing in writing to prove that there was such a contract. Of course, there was the practical question of proof — that is, whether the jury would believe that there was such a contract — but no rule of law said that the contract had to be evidenced by a writing. This situation made it possible for a witness in court to swear falsely that Jones had agreed to sell Jones' house for a specified sum. Even though Jones had not made such an agreement, the jury might believe the false witness, and Jones would be required to give up the house on terms to which Jones had never agreed. To prevent such a miscarriage of justice, a statute was passed declaring that contracts for the sale of houses had to be evidenced by a writing.

This law ended the evil of persons lying that there was an oral agreement for the sale of a house, but was justice finally achieved? Not always, for cases arose in which Jones did in fact make an oral agreement to sell land to Smith. Smith would take possession of the land and would make valuable improvements at great expense and effort, and then Jones would have Smith thrown off the land. Smith would defend on the ground that Jones had orally agreed to sell the land. Jones would then say, "Where is the writing that the statute requires?" To this, Smith could only reply there was no writing. No writing meant no binding legal agreement; and therefore Smith lost the land, leaving Jones with the land and all the improvements that Smith had made. That certainly was not just.

Gradually, the courts developed the rule that even though the statute required a writing, the courts would enforce an oral contract for the sale of land when the buyer had gone into possession and made valuable improvements of such a nature that it would be difficult to determine what amount of money would be required to make up the loss to the buyer if the buyer were to be put off the land.

Thus, the law passed through three stages: (a) the original concept that all land contracts could be oral and did not require any written evidence. Because the perjury evil arose under that rule, the law swung to (b) the opposite rule that no such contract could be oral without any written evidence. This rule gave rise to the hardship case of the honest buyer under an oral contract who made extensive improvements. The law then swung back, not to the original rule, but to (c) a middle position, combining the writing requirement as to the ordinary transaction, but allowing oral contracts in special cases to prevent hardship.

This example is also interesting because it shows the way that the courts amend the law by decision. The flat requirement of the statute was eroded by decisions and by an exception created by the courts in the interest of furthering justice.

SUMMARY

A society's ethical code constitutes the foundation on which its laws are built. In contrast to ethics, however, the law must be more definite and stable in order to be enforceable. Nevertheless, a society's evolving ethical code can serve as a blueprint for the future form its laws will assume.

Some of the underlying principles that society regards as important in making its ethical decisions and formulating its laws include: protection of the state; protection of the person; protection of public health, safety, and morals; protection of property and title; freedom of personal action; freedom of use of property; enforcement of intent; protection from exploitation, fraud, and oppression; furtherance of trade; creditor protection; debtor rehabilitation; stability; flexibility; and practical expediency. These individual concerns sometimes conflict with one another and so as laws are created and evolve, society is continually seeking a proper balance or synthesis of its ultimate objectives.

Questions and Case Problems

1. What is the general purpose of the law?
2. What social force is involved in the rule that a professional association cannot arbitrarily exclude a person from membership?
3. Give an illustration of the social force of protection of title.
4. The social force in favor of freedom of personal action permits you to say anything you wish. Appraise the statement.
5. Does the law remain constant?
6. Of the specific objectives of the law, which do you consider to be the most important? Why?
7. (a) How can law be dynamic if stability is one of its specific objectives?
   (b) How do some statutes provide for built-in flexibility?
8. McCarthy owned a motor scooter. He obtained an insurance policy from the Foundation Reserve Insurance Company. This policy covered medical expenses when the insured was "struck by automobile." McCarthy rode his scooter into an automobile. The insurance company refused to pay his medical expenses on the ground that he had struck the automobile and had not been struck by an automobile. What social forces are involved in deciding the case?
9. The Reader's Digest Association published an article on truck hijacking. In the article it stated that John Doe, giving his actual name, had taken part in a truck hijacking eleven years before and had thereafter reformed. John Doe sued the Reader's Digest Association for damages. Reader's Digest Association raised the defense that it was not liable because the information was true. What was the theory on which John Doe sued? What social forces are involved? Is John's claim valid?

10. When O'Brien was prosecuted for burning his draft card, he raised the defense that the right of free speech gave him the privilege to express his disapproval of the draft and of the war in this manner. Was he correct? [United States v O'Brien, 391 US 367]
11. The city of Columbia, South Carolina, provided for the fluoridation of the city water supply. Hall claimed that this deprived him of his constitutional right to drink unfluoridated water, since there was no other water supply. Hall further attacked the validity of the plan on the ground that dental cavities are not contagious, and therefore a public health problem did not exist. Was he correct? [Hall v Bates, Mayor of Columbia, 247 SC 511, 148 SE2d 345]
12. The New York Social Services Law authorized the Social Services officials to replace necessary furniture and clothing of welfare recipients who lost such items by fire, flood, or other like catastrophe. Howard was on state welfare. Her clothing was stolen from her apartment by a burglar. She claimed that this was a catastrophe and that the Social Service official was required to replace the stolen clothing. Was she correct? [In re Howard, 28 NY2d 434, 271 NE2d 528]
13. The United States Congress has passed several laws aimed at preventing the sale of narcotics and harmful drugs. One of these laws makes it illegal for an unauthorized person to sell or supply marijuana or LSD. Judith Kuch was prosecuted for violating this Act. She admitted that she had transferred the substances covered by the Act and that she did not have a license as required by the Act. She claimed, however, that she was protected by religious free-

dom. She was, in fact, an ordained minister of the Neo-American Church and the substances were only used by her as part of the religious services in her church. Decide. [United States v Kuch (DC Dist Col) 288 F Supp 439,]

14. Pamela Korn, who lived in Connecticut, went to a local photographer, Marion Rennison, to have her picture taken. Without Korn's permission, Rennison gave Korn's picture to an advertiser who ran an ad in a newspaper using the picture. Korn was very much upset, particularly as the defendants had made money for themselves at the expense of her feelings. She claimed that she was humiliated and embarrassed and sued all the parties involved, claiming damages for an invasion of her privacy. They raised the defense that there was no right of privacy under Connecticut law because there was no statute declaring such right. Was this a valid defense? [Korn v Rennison, 21 Conn Supp 400, 156 A2d 476]

15. Norma Wons was admitted to the Jackson Memorial Hospital because of extreme internal bleeding. The doctors believed that without blood transfusions she would die. Norma's mind was not affected by her illness. She was 38 years of age. She refused to take the transfusion because of her religious belief. Her husband shared her religious belief. They had two boys, 12 and 14. The hospital sought a court order to authorize giving Norma the necessary transfusions without her consent. Should the court issue such authorization? [Wons v Public Health Trust of Dade County (Fla App) 500 So 2d 679]

3

THE CONSTITUTION AS THE FOUNDATION OF THE LEGAL ENVIRONMENT

A basic principle of the American Revolution was that there should be limits to governmental power. Americans saw the need for a central government but did not want that government to have unlimited power. Consequently, the document creating that central government, the Constitution of the United States, sets forth not only the structure and powers of government but also limitations on those powers. This Constitution, together with the constitutions of each of the states, forms the foundation of our legal environment.

A. THE FEDERAL SYSTEM

By creating a central government to coexist with the governments of the individual states, the U.S. Constitution created a federal system. In a **federal system,** a central government is given power to administer to national concerns while the individual states retain the power to administer to local concerns.

§ 3:1 WHAT A CONSTITUTION IS

The term *constitution* refers to either the

44

structure of the government and its relation to the people within its sphere of power or the written document setting forth that structure. When capitalized, the word refers to the written document that specifies the structure and powers of the United States national government and its relation to the people within the territory of the United States.

In speaking of the Constitution it is often necessary to distinguish between the written Constitution and the living Constitution. This is required because the Constitution has grown and changed as described in § 3:7.[1]

§ 3:2   THE BRANCHES OF GOVERNMENT

The written Constitution establishes a **tripartite** (three-part) division of government. That is, there is a **legislative branch** (Congress) to make the laws, an **executive branch** (the President) to execute the laws, and a **judicial branch** (courts) to interpret the laws. The national legislature or Congress is a **bicameral** (two-house) body consisting of a Senate and a House of Representatives. Members of the Senate are popularly elected for a term of six years. Members of the House of Representatives are popularly elected for a term of two years. The president is elected by an Electoral College whose membership is popularly elected. The president serves for a term of four years and is eligible for re-election for a second term. Judges of the United States are appointed by the president with the approval of the Senate and serve for life, subject to removal only by impeachment because of misconduct.

B.   THE STATES AND THE CONSTITUTION

The effect of the adoption of the Constitution was to take certain powers away from the states and to give them to the national government.

§ 3:3   DELEGATED AND SHARED POWERS

The national government possesses only the powers given by the states. These powers are set forth in the United States Constitution.

(a) DELEGATED POWERS. The powers given by the states to the national government are described as **delegated powers.** Some of these delegated powers are given exclusively to the national government. Thus, the national government alone may declare war or establish a currency.

(b) SHARED POWERS. Some of the powers delegated to the national government may still be exercised by the states. For example, the grant of power to the national government to impose taxes did not destroy the state power to tax. This is so even though both the national and state governments tax the same subject or base. Some of the shared powers may only be exercised by the states as long as there is no federal exercise. Thus, a state appliance safety law may apply until a federal law on the subject is adopted by Congress. Likewise, both the national government and a state may regulate navigation on navigable waterways within a state, subject to the supremacy of federal law.[2]

(c) PROHIBITED POWERS. The Constitution prohibits states from doing certain acts, even though the federal government is also similarly prohibited. Thus, neither states nor the national government may adopt *ex post facto* laws making criminal an act already committed that was not criminal when committed or increasing the penalty for an act already committed above the penalty in force at the time it was committed.

---

[1]   See generally, Anderson, *Government and Business* (4th ed) (South-Western Publishing Co., Cincinnati, Ohio, 1981).

[2]   Re Income Tax Cases, 157 Mich App 525, 403 NW2d 182 (1987).

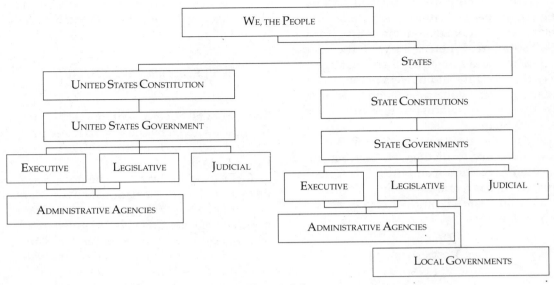

FIGURE 3-1
GOVERNMENTS OF THE UNITED STATES

§ 3:4   FEDERAL SUPREMACY

Federal law will bar state action both when there is a federal law regulating the particular subject and when the silence of Congress is seen as showing the congressional intent that there should be no regulation by anyone.

(a) EXPRESS FEDERAL REGULATION. The Constitution and statutes properly adopted by Congress are the supreme law of the land. They cancel out any conflicting state law.

This **federal supremacy** is expressly declared by the Constitution.[3] When there is a direct conflict between federal and state statutes, the decision as to which prevails is thus easy to make.

If there is no obvious conflict because the federal statute covers only part of the subject matter, the question arises whether a state law can regulate the areas not regulated by Congress or whether the partial regulation made by Congress **preempts** the field so as to prohibit state legislation.

(b) SILENCE OF CONGRESS. In some situations, the silence of Congress in failing to cover a particular phase of the subject, or in failing to have any law on the subject at all, is held to indicate that Congress does not want any law on the matter and that therefore no state law will be allowed to regulate the matter. When national uniformity is essential, it is generally held that the silence of Congress means that the subject has been preempted by Congress and that no state law on the subject may be adopted.[4]

C.   INTERPRETING AND AMENDING THE CONSTITUTION

The Constitution as we know it today has changed greatly from the Constitution as originally written. This change has been

---

[3]   US Const, Art VI, Cl 2. Michigan Canners and Freezers Ass'n., Inc. v Agricultural Marketing and Bargaining Board, 467 US 461 (1984).

[4]   Burbank v Lockheed Air Terminal, Inc. 411 US 624 (1972).

brought about by interpretation, amendment, and practice.

§ 3:5 CONFLICTING THEORIES

Within a very few years after the Constitution was adopted, conflict arose as to whether the Constitution was to be interpreted strictly, so as to give the federal government the least power possible, or broadly, so as to give the federal government the greatest power that the words would permit. These two views may be given the names of (a) the bedrock view and (b) the living document view.

By the bedrock view, the purpose of a constitution is to state certain fundamental principles for all time.[5] By the living document view, a constitution is merely a statement of goals and objectives and is intended to grow and change with time.

---

[5] Marbury v Madison, 1 (US) Cranch 137 (1803).

Whether the Constitution is to be liberally interpreted, under the living document view, or narrowly interpreted, under the bedrock view, has a direct effect upon the Constitution. For the last century, the Supreme Court has followed the living document view, which has resulted in strengthening the power of the federal government, permitting the rise of administrative agencies, and expanding the protection of human rights. If the Constitution had been strictly interpreted according to the bedrock theory, the central or federal government would have relatively little power today, administrative agencies would not be allowed, and many human rights would not be protected from governmental invasion. The living document view has given us the living constitution described in § 3:7. The living document view was first stated by the United States Supreme Court in the *McCulloch* case.

MCCULLOCH V MARYLAND
4 Wheat 316 (1819)

The first bank of the United States was chartered in 1791 and again in 1816. Hostile state legislation attempted to drive it out of existence. In 1818, Maryland adopted a law imposing a tax on bank notes issued by any bank not chartered by the state legislature. McCulloch, the cashier of the Baltimore branch of the National Bank, issued bank notes on which this tax had not been paid. Suit was brought by the State of Maryland against him to recover the statutory penalties imposed for violation of the statute.

MARSHALL, C. J. . . . The first question . . . is, has Congress power to incorporate a bank? . . .

This government of the Union . . . is acknowledged by all to be one of enumerated powers. . . .

Among the enumerated powers, we do not find that of establishing a bank or creating a corporation. . . . A constitution, to contain an accurate detail of all the subdivisions of which its great powers will admit, and of all the means by which they may be carried into execution, would partake of the prolixity of a legal code, and could scarcely be embraced by the human mind. It would probably never be understood by the public. Its nature, therefore, requires, that only its great outlines should be marked, its important objects designated, and the minor ingredients which compose those objects be deduced from the nature of the objects themselves. . . .

Although, among the enumerated powers of government, we do not find the word "bank" or "incorporation," we find the great powers to lay and collect taxes; to borrow money; to regulate commerce; to declare and conduct a war; and to raise and support armies and navies. The sword and the purse, all the external relations, and no inconsiderable portion of the industry of the nation, are intrusted to its government . . . A government, intrusted with such ample powers, on the due execution of which the happiness and prosperity of the nation so vitally depends, must also be intrusted with ample means for their execution. The power being given, it is the interest of the nation to facilitate its execution. It can never be their interest, and cannot be presumed to have been their intention, to clog and embarrass its execution by withholding the most appropriate means. Throughout this vast republic, . . . revenue is to be collected and expended, armies are to be marched and supported. The exigencies of the nation may require that the treasure raised in the North should be transported to the South, that raised in the East conveyed to the West, or that this order should be reversed. Is that construction of the Constitution to be preferred which would render these operations difficult, hazardous, and expensive? Can we adopt that construction (unless the words imperiously require it) which would impute to the framers of that instrument, when granting these powers for the public good, the intention of impeding their exercise by withholding a choice of means? If, indeed, such be the mandate of the Constitution, we have only to obey; but that instrument does not profess to enumerate the means by which the powers it confers may be executed; nor does it prohibit the creation of a corporation, if the existence of such a being be essential to the beneficial exercise of those powers. It is, then, the subject of fair inquiry, how far such means may be employed. . . .

The government which has a right to do an act, and has imposed on it the duty of performing that act, must, according to the dictates of reason, be allowed to select the means; and those who contend that it may not select any appropriate means, that one particular mode of effecting the object is excepted, take upon themselves the burden of establishing that exception. . . .

But the Constitution of the United States has not left the right of Congress to employ the necessary means, for the execution of the powers conferred on the government, to general reasoning. To its enumeration of powers is added that of making "all laws which shall be necessary and proper, for carrying into execution the foregoing powers, and all other powers vested by this Constitution, in the government of the United States, or in any department thereof."

. . . This provision is made in a constitution intended to endure for ages to come, and, consequently, to be adapted to the various crises of human affairs. To have prescribed the means by which government should, in all future time, execute its powers, would have been to change, entirely, the character of the instrument, and give it the properties of a legal code. It would have been an unwise attempt to provide, by immutable rules, for exigencies which, if foreseen at all, must have been seen dimly, and which can be best provided for as they occur. [The Court rejected the contention that "necessary" means "absolutely necessary."] . . . Sound construction of the Constitution must allow to the national legislature that discretion, with respect to the means by which the powers it confers are to be carried into execution, which will enable that body to perform the high duties assigned to it, in the manner most beneficial to the people. Let the end be legitimate, let it be within the scope of the Constitution, and all means which are appropriate, which are plainly adapted to that end, which are not prohibited, but consist with the letter and spirit of the Constitution, are constitutional.

. . . It can scarcely be necessary to say, that the existence of state banks can have no possible influence on the question. No trace is to be found in the Constitution of an intention to create a dependence of the government of the Union on those of the states, for the execution of the great powers assigned to it. . . . The choice of means implies a right to choose a national bank in preference to state banks, and Congress alone can make the election.

[Judgment against Maryland on the basis that, as Congress had authority to create a bank, a state law designed to harm that bank was unconstitutional, and therefore Maryland could not recover the penalty authorized by that state statute]

QUESTIONS

1. What section of the Constitution authorizes Congress to create a national bank?
2. Does the Court say that the creation of a national bank system is the best way to do the job?

Can we decide that we should adopt the bedrock view or the living document view? We cannot select one view to the exclusion of the other for the simple reason that we want both. Contradictory as this sounds, it is obvious that we want our Constitution to be durable. We do not want a set of New Year's resolutions that will be forgotten shortly. At the same time, we know that the world changes, and therefore we do not want a constitution that will hold us tied in a straightjacket of the past.

In terms of social forces that make the law, we are torn between our desire for stability and our desire for flexibility. We want a constitution that is stable. At the same time, we want one that is flexible. There is probably no one living today who believes that the Constitution should be either 100 percent stable or 100 percent flexible. Everyone wants both qualities, and the problem is how to reach a compromise. Some people will favor more change than others. That is why we have conflict.

It is essential that we recognize that our Constitution is in a sense torn between the conflicting desires of change and no change. To look only at the Constitution as it was written in 1787 and to ignore the stresses and strains of the change-no change conflict is misleading. If we do not see the conflict, we do not see the Constitution as it really is today. Even more important, we lack the understanding needed to meet the problems of tomorrow.

§ 3:6   AMENDING THE
             CONSTITUTION

The United States Constitution has been amended in three ways: (a) expressly, (b) by interpretation, and (c) by practice.

(a) CONSTITUTIONAL METHOD OF AMENDING. Article V of the Constitution sets forth the procedure to be followed for making amendments to the Constitution. Relatively few changes have been made to the Constitution by this formal amending process, although thousands of proposals for that purpose have been made.

(b) AMENDMENT BY JUDICIAL INTERPRETATION. The greatest change to the written Constitution has been made by the Supreme Court in "interpreting" the Constitution. Generally interpretation is used to apply the Constitution to a new situation that could not have been foreseen when the written Constitution was adopted.

(c) AMENDMENT BY PRACTICE. In practice, the letter of the Constitution is not always followed. Departure from the written Constitution began as early as 1793 when Washington refused to make treaties, as required by the Constitution, "by and with the consent of the Senate," and began the practice that has been followed since that time of the president's negotiating the treaty with the foreign country and then submitting it to the Senate for approval. Similarly, the Electoral College that was intended to exercise independent judgment in selecting the president now automatically elects the official candidate of the party that elected them to the Electoral College.

Other aspects of practice have added to the Constitution things that are not there. As written, the Constitution contemplates that Congress will originate and adopt laws. With the rise of the party system, which was not anticipated by the framers of the Constitution, the president has become the leader of the legislative program. This position of leadership has been strengthened greatly by modern media, beginning with Roosevelt's radio "fireside chats" of the thirties and broadening into television in later years.

§ 3:7   THE LIVING CONSTITUTION

The Constitution that has developed in the manner described in the preceding section is radically different from that which was written on paper. The living Constitution has the following characteristics:

(a) STRONG GOVERNMENT. The characteristic of the new Constitution is strong government. The concept of Adam Smith of *laissez faire* — of a "hands off" policy of government — has been largely forgotten. While freedom of the individual as a human being has expanded, business enterprises can now be regulated and the economy controlled.

(b) STRONG PRESIDENT. Instead of being merely an officer who carries out the laws, the president has become the political leader of a party, exerting a strong influence on the lawmaking process. If the president's political party is in control of both Houses of the Congress, the president acts as the leader of the lawmaking process.

(c) ECLIPSE OF THE STATES. Under the new Constitution, all governments have powers that they never possessed before, but the center of gravity has shifted from the states to the nation. When the Constitution was adopted in 1789, the federal government was to have only the very limited powers specified in Article I, § 8, of the Constitution. What regulation of business was permissible was to be imposed by the states. Today, the great bulk of the regulation of business is adopted by the federal government through Congress or its administrative agencies. As the American economy moved from the local community stage to the nationwide stage, the individual states were unable to provide effective regulation of business. It was inevitable that regulation would be drawn to the central government. Consequently, when we speak of government regulation of business, we ordinarily mean the national government, not the state or local governments.

(d) ADMINISTRATIVE AGENCIES. These were virtually unheard of in 1789 and no mention is made of them in the Constitution of 1789. The vast powers of the new Constitution are exercised to a very large degree by administrative agencies. They are in effect a fourth branch of the government not provided for in the written Constitution. More importantly, it is the administrative agencies that come in contact with the majority of business persons and citizens. The agencies are the "government" for most people.

In other words, the vast power of government to regulate business is not exercised directly by the legislatures, the courts, and the executive officers. But rather, this power is exercised by agencies. The members of the agencies — or the boards, commissions, or persons heading the agencies — are not elected by the voters, and their decisions are to a large degree not subject to effective review or reversal by the courts.

(e) HUMAN RIGHTS. The scope of human rights protected from governments has dramatically broadened. These rights are protected not merely from invasion by the federal government, but by any government. Most significant of all, unwritten rights are protected, although they are not guaranteed by any express constitutional provision.

The study of the evolution of the Constitution will serve as a guide to understanding the present; to foreseeing, even if dimly, the future; and to appreciating the problems that are involved. As people working in a business world, it is essential that we have this understanding. As citizens living and voting in an organized democratic society, it is our duty to ourselves and our nation to understand these problems so that we can intelligently take part in their solution.

D.   FEDERAL POWERS

The federal government possesses powers necessary to administer matters of national concern. Some of those powers are of particular interest to businesses.

§ 3:8   POWER TO REGULATE COMMERCE

The desire to protect commerce from restrictions and barriers set up by the individual states was a prime factor leading to the adoption of the Constitution of 1789. To protect commerce, Congress was given, by Article I, § 8, Clause 3, the power "to regulate Commerce with foreign Nations, and among the several States, and with the Indian Tribes."

Until 1937, the Supreme Court held that this provision only gave Congress the power to control or regulate that which crossed a state line, such as an interstate railway train or an interstate telegraph message.

(a) THE COMMERCE POWER BECOMES A GENERAL WELFARE POWER. In 1937, the Supreme Court began expanding the concept of interstate commerce so that by 1946 the power to regulate interstate commerce had become very broad. By that year, the power had expanded to the point that it gave authority to Congress to adopt regulatory laws that were "as broad as the economic needs of the nation."[6] By virtue of this broad interpretation, Congress can regulate manufacturing, agriculture, mining, stock exchanges, insurance, loan sharking,[7] monopolies, and conspiracies in restraint of trade. If desired, Congress can set standards, quotas, and priorities for industries.

The case that was the starting point in this transition of the commerce clause was the *Jones & Laughlin Steel Corporation* case.

[6]   American Power & Light Co. v Securities and Exchange Commission, 329 US 90 (1946).
[7]   Perez v United States, 402 US 146 (1971).

NLRB v JONES & LAUGHLIN STEEL CORP.
301 US 1 (1937)

The National Labor Relations Board found that Jones & Laughlin Steel Corporation had discharged ten employees at its Aliquippa, Pennsylvania plant because of their union activity and for the purpose of discouraging membership in the union. The board ordered these employees reinstated with full back pay and ordered that the employer cease

and desist from such conduct. When the employer failed to comply with
the board's order, the board petitioned the Court of Appeals to enforce
the order. The Court of Appeals denied the petition, holding that the
board's order lay beyond the range of federal power. The Supreme Court
granted certiorari.

HUGHES, C. J. . . . The scheme of the National Labor Relations Act . . . may
be briefly stated. The first section sets forth findings with respect to the injury to commerce resulting from the denial by employers of the right of employees to organize and from the refusal of employers to accept the procedure of collective bargaining. There follows a declaration that it is the policy
of the United States to eliminate these causes of obstruction to the free flow
of commerce. The Act then defines the terms it uses, including the terms
"commerce" and "affecting commerce." § 2. It creates the National Labor
Relations Board and prescribes its organization. §§ 3–6. It sets forth the right
of employees to self-organization and to bargain collectively through representatives of their own choosing. § 7. It defines "unfair labor practices." § 8.
It lays down rules as to the representation of employees for the purpose of
collective bargaining. § 9. The Board is empowered to prevent the described
unfair labor practices affecting commerce and the Act prescribes the procedure to that end. . . .

   . . . The respondent [Jones & Laughlin Steel Corp.] argues (1) that the Act
is in reality a regulation of labor relations and not of interstate
commerce; . . .

   The facts as to the nature and scope of the business of the Jones & Laughlin
Steel Corporation have been found by the Labor Board.

   [The Court discussed in detail the interstate organization of the employer
with various plants in different states.]

   Summarizing these operations, the Labor Board concluded that the works
in Pittsburgh and Aliquippa "might be likened to the heart of a self-contained,
highly integrated body. They draw in the raw materials from Michigan, Minnesota, West Virginia, Pennsylvania in part through arteries and by means
controlled by the respondent; they transform the materials and then pump
them out to all parts of the nation through the vast mechanism which the
respondent has elaborated."

   . . . The Scope of the Act. — The Act is challenged in its entirety as an attempt to regulate all industry, thus invading the reserved powers of the States
over their local concerns. . . .

   . . . The grant of authority to the Board does not purport to extend to the
relationship between all industrial employees and employers. Its terms do
not impose collective bargaining upon all industry regardless of effects upon
interstate or foreign commerce. It purports to reach only what may be
deemed to burden or obstruct that commerce and, thus qualified, it must be
construed as contemplating the exercise of control within constitutional
bounds. It is a familiar principle that acts which directly burden or obstruct
interstate or foreign commerce, or its free flow, are within the reach of the
congressional power. Acts having that effect are not rendered immune because they grow out of labor disputes. . . . It is the effect upon commerce,
not the source of the injury, which is the criterion. Whether or not particular
action does affect commerce in such a close and intimate fashion as to be

subject to federal control, and hence to lie within the authority conferred upon the Board, is left by the statute to be determined as individual cases arise. . . .

. . . Although activities may be intrastate in character when separately considered, if they have such a close and substantial relation to interstate commerce that their control is essential or appropriate to protect that commerce from burdens and obstructions, Congress cannot be denied the power to exercise that control.

. . . The stoppage of [respondent's] operations by industrial strife would have a most serious effect upon interstate commerce. In view of respondent's far-flung activities, it is idle to say that the effect would be indirect or remote. It is obvious that it would be immediate and might be catastrophic. We are asked to shut our eyes to the plainest facts of our national life and to deal with the question of direct and indirect effects in an intellectual vacuum. Because there may be but indirect and remote effects upon interstate commerce in connection with a host of local enterprises throughout the country, it does not follow that other industrial activities do not have such a close and intimate relation to interstate commerce as to make the presence of industrial strife a matter of the most urgent national concern. When industries organize themselves on a national scale, making their relation to interstate commerce the dominant factor in their activities, how can it be maintained that their industrial labor relations constitute a forbidden field into which Congress may not enter when it is necessary to protect interstate commerce from the paralyzing consequences of industrial war? We have often said that interstate commerce itself is a practical conception. It is equally true that interferences with that commerce must be appraised by a judgment that does not ignore actual experience.

Experience has abundantly demonstrated that the recognition of the right of employees to self-organization and to have representatives of their own choosing for the purpose of collective bargaining is often an essential condition of industrial peace. Refusal to confer and negotiate has been one of the most prolific causes of strife. . . . And of what avail is it to protect the facility of transportation, if interstate commerce is throttled with respect to the commodities to be transported!

. . . It is not necessary again to detail the facts as to respondent's enterprise. . . . [I]t presents in a most striking way the close and intimate relation which [an] industry may have to interstate commerce, and we have no doubt that Congress had constitutional authority. . . .

[The National Labor Relations Act was constitutional as applied to the respondent steel company and was within the scope of the power of Congress over interstate commerce]

QUESTIONS

1. What statute was involved in the *Jones & Laughlin Steel Corporation* case?
2. Was the decision of the Court inevitable?
3. Why was it important to hold that the labor relations were interstate commerce?

(b) THE COMMERCE POWER AS A LIMITATION ON STATES. The federal power to regulate commerce not only gives Congress the power to act but also prevents states from regulating commerce in any way that interferes with federal regulation or burdens interstate commerce. For example, if the federal government establishes safety device regulations for interstate carriers, a state cannot require different devices.

Because modern commerce is typically interstate in character, the silence of Congress, that is, the fact that Congress does not impose any regulation, is generally interpreted as excluding state action with respect to interstate commerce.

States may not use their tax power for the purpose of harming interstate commerce as such commerce is within the protection of the national government. For example, a state cannot impose a higher tax on goods imported from another state than it imposes on the same kind of goods produced in its own territory.[8]

The fact that a local law may have some effect upon out-of-state markets does not mean that the local law is unconstitutional as a burden on interstate commerce. This was the question involved in the *Commonwealth Edison Company* case.

---

[8] Johnson Brothers Wholesale Liquor Co. v Commissioner of Revenue, ___ Minn ___, 402 NW2d 791 (1987).

COMMONWEALTH EDISON CO. V MONTANA

453 US 609 (1981)

Montana imposed a severance tax on every ton of coal mined within the state. The tax varied depending upon the value of the coal and cost of production and could be as high as 30 percent of the price at which the coal was sold. Montana mine operators and some of the out-of-state customers claimed that this tax was unconstitutional as an improper burden on interstate commerce. From a decision sustaining the law, an appeal was taken to the United States Supreme Court.

MARSHALL, J. . . . In reviewing Commerce Clause challenges to state taxes, our goal has . . . been to "establish a consistent and rational method of inquiry" focusing on "the practical effect of a challenged tax." Mobil Oil Corp. v Commissioner of Taxes, 445 US 425, 443 (1980). . . . We conclude that the same "practical" analysis should apply in reviewing Commerce Clause challenges to state severance taxes.

In the first place, . . . we hold that a state severance tax is not immunized from Commerce Clause scrutiny by a claim that the tax is imposed on goods prior to their entry into the stream of interstate commerce. . . . We agree with appellants that the Montana tax must be evaluated under Complete Auto Transit's four-part test. Under that test, a state tax does not offend the Commerce Clause if it "is applied to an activity with a substantial nexus with the taxing State, is fairly apportioned, does not discriminate against interstate commerce, and is fairly related to services provided by the State." 430 US, at 279. . . .

Appellants assert that the Montana tax "discriminate[s] against interstate commerce" because 90% of Montana coal is shipped to other States under contracts that shift the tax burden primarily to non-Montana utility companies and thus to citizens of other States. But the Montana tax is computed at the same rate regardless of the final destination of the coal, and there is no suggestion here that the tax is administered in a manner that departs from this even-handed formula. We are not, therefore, confronted here with the type of differential tax treatment of interstate and intrastate commerce that the Court has found in other "discrimination" cases. . . .

The premise of our discrimination cases is that "[t]he very purpose of the Commerce Clause was to create an area of free trade among the several States." . . . Under such a regime, the borders between the States are essentially irrelevant. As the Court stated in West v Kansas Natural Gas Co., 221 US 229, 255 (1911), "in matters of foreign and interstate commerce there are no state lines." . . . Consequently, to accept appellants' theory and invalidate the Montana tax solely because most of Montana's coal is shipped across the very state borders that ordinarily are to be considered irrelevant would require a significant and, in our view, unwarranted departure from the rationale of our prior discrimination cases.

. . . [I]t is doubtful whether any legal test could adequately reflect the numerous and competing economic, geographic, demographic, social, and political considerations that must inform a decision about an acceptable rate or level of state taxation, and yet be reasonably capable of application in a wide variety of individual cases. But even apart from the difficulty of the judicial undertaking, the nature of the factfinding and judgment that would be required of the courts merely reinforces the conclusion that questions about the appropriate level of state taxes must be resolved through the political process. Under our federal system, the determination is to be made by state legislatures in the first instance and, if necessary, by Congress, when particular state taxes are thought to be contrary to federal interests. . . .

[Judgment affirmed]

QUESTIONS

1. Did the law in the *Commonwealth Edison* case have an effect on interstate commerce?
2. What is the legal significance of the facts, stated in your answer to Question #1?
3. Did the court approve the amount of the tax?

§ 3:9   THE FINANCIAL POWERS

The financial powers of the federal government include the powers to tax, borrow, spend, and coin money.

(a) THE TAXING POWER. The federal Constitution provides that "Congress shall have Power To lay and collect Taxes, Duties, Imposts and Excises, to pay the Debts and provide for the common Defense and general Welfare of the United States. . . ."[9] Subject to the express and implied limitations arising from the Constitution, the states may impose such taxes as they desire and as their own individual constitutions and statutes permit. In addition to express constitutional limitations, both na-

---

[9]   US Const, Art 1, § 8, Cl 1.

tional and local taxes are subject to the unwritten limitation that they be imposed for a public purpose.

The federal government is subject to certain limitations on the form of the taxes imposed by it. Capitation or poll taxes and all direct taxes must be apportioned among the states according to the census-determined population.[10] Today, direct taxes include taxes on real estate or personal property and taxes imposed on persons because of their ownership of property. Income taxes, to the extent that they tax the income from property, are direct, although by virtue of the Sixteenth Amendment their apportionment is no longer required.

All other taxes imposed by the federal government are regarded as indirect taxes. These include customs duties, taxes on consumption (such as gasoline and cigarette taxes), taxes on the exercise of a privilege (such as an amusement tax), taxes on the transmission of property upon death (such as estate taxes), taxes upon the privilege of making a gift, or taxes upon the privilege of employing workers (such as the federal employer's social security tax). In the case of a federal tax upon the exercise of a privilege, it is immaterial whether the privilege arises by virtue of a state or a federal law.

The only restriction upon the form of indirect federal taxes is that they be uniform throughout the continental United States and the incorporated territories. This requirement of uniformity does not prohibit a progressively graduated tax, wherein the greater the monetary value of the tax base, the greater the rate of tax. The requirement of uniformity also is not violated by a provision allowing credits against the federal tax for taxes paid to a state, even though the amount of the federal tax paid will vary from state to state, depending upon the existence of a state tax for which credit is allowable.

(b) The Borrowing Power. Congress is authorized "to borrow Money on the credit of the United States."[11] No limitation is prescribed to the purposes for which the United States can borrow.

Obligations of the United States issued to those lending money to the United States are binding, and Congress cannot attempt to repudiate them or to make them repayable in a less valuable currency than called for by the obligations without violating the legal rights of the holders.

The states have an inherent power to borrow money. State constitutions and statutes may impose a limit on the amount that can be borrowed. Frequently, these limitations are evaded by the creation of independent authorities or districts that borrow money by issuing bonds. The bonded indebtedness of such independent authorities and districts is not regarded as a debt of the state and therefore is not subject to the limitations applicable to state borrowing.

(c) The Spending Power. The federal government may use tax money and borrowed money ". . . to pay the Debts and provide for the common Defense and general Welfare of the United States."[12] From the earliest days of the Constitution there was disagreement over whether there was any limitation on the power of the United States to spend the money that it raised by taxation or borrowing. Madison claimed that the money of the United States could only be spent on a subject that could be directly regulated or legislated upon by Congress. Hamilton claimed that as long as the money was spent for a public purpose rather than a private purpose, it was immaterial whether Congress could legislate directly upon the object for which the money was spent.

This matter has become academic with the present interpretation of the commerce power as permitting federal regulation of anything. The situation can no longer arise in which Congress would be spending

---

[10] US Const, Art 1, § 9, Cl 4.

[11] US Const, Art 1, § 8, Cl 2.
[12] US Const, Art 1, § 8, Cl 1.

money for something that it could not regulate if it so chose.

(d) The Currency Power. The Constitution authorizes Congress "to coin Money, regulate the Value thereof" and "provide for the Punishment of counterfeiting the Securities and . . . Coin of the United States."[13] This federal power is made exclusive by prohibiting the states from coining money, emitting bills of credit, or making anything but gold and silver coins legal tender in payment of debts.[14]

The national government can determine what shall be legal tender and is not restricted to the use of metallic money but may issue paper money.[15] Congress can establish such base as it desires for paper currency and may change the base of existing currency.

§ 3:10   THE POWER TO OWN BUSINESSES

In a sense, government ownership of what would ordinarily be deemed private business represents the ultimate in the regulation of private business.

(a) Constitutionality of Government Ownership. Speaking generally, there is no constitutional barrier against state or federal government ownership and operation of businesses. It had formerly been assumed that there were certain purposes that were not public or for the general welfare. These purposes were clearly distinguished from those that were public or for the general welfare. It is impossible today to draw such a line between public and private and to prohibit a government from entering into any particular business on the ground that to do so is not in furtherance of a public purpose or does not advance the general welfare.

(b) Creation of New Business. The statement that the United States may constitutionally engage in business leads to the conclusion that it may constitutionally spend its money in order to create a new business or build new plants. There is no requirement that limits the national government to acquiring existing businesses and plants.

(c) Acquisition of Existing Businesses and Plants. The power to engage in and own businesses embraces the right to acquire existing businesses and plants by purchase or gift. The national government may also acquire the property by eminent domain if the owner will not voluntarily sell to the government at a price that is satisfactory to the government.

In the case of the United States, it is to be noted that the United States as a sovereign state may acquire land or any other property by any means. It may do so by war, purchase, or treaty.

(d) Sale and Distribution of Government Production. A government may sell or otherwise dispose of the products that the government-owned business manufactures. Congress is authorized to "dispose of and make all needful Rules and Regulations respecting the Territory or other Property belonging to the United States."[16] The power of a government to dispose of its property permits the government to compete with a private enterprise and to dispose of its products at any price it chooses without regard to whether the price is below cost or not. No constitutional privilege of the private business is violated by being underpriced by the national, a state, or local government.[17]

E.   CONSTITUTIONAL LIMITATIONS ON GOVERNMENT

The most significant limitations in the Constitution are found in the first ten amendments adopted in 1791 and in the post-Civ-

---

[13] US Const, Art 1, § 8, Cls 5,6.
[14] US Const, Art 1, § 10.
[15] Julliard v Greenman, 110 US 421 (1884).

[16] US Const, Art 4, § 3(2).
[17] Puget Sound Power & Light Co. v Seattle, 291 US 619 (1934).

il War amendments. Most state constitutions contain limitations similar to those of the national Constitution. The limitations discussed in the following sections are the limitations that are most important to the person and to business.

§ 3:11   Due Process

The most important limitation on the power of government is that found in the Fifth and Fourteenth Amendments to the Constitution. Those amendments prohibit the national government and the state governments, respectively, from depriving any person of life, liberty, or property without due process of law.

(a) Expansion of Due Process. By virtue of liberal interpretation of the Constitution, the **due process clause** is now held to be a guarantee of protection from unreasonable procedures[18] and unreasonable laws, and a guarantee of equal protection of the law, and a guarantee of protection of significant interests. The Supreme Court has extended the due process clause to protect the record or standing of a student.

Through judicial construction, due process of law affords the individual a wide protection. The guarantee, however, affords no protection when the matter is reasonably debatable. Therefore, due process of law does not bar the regulation of business, for any regulation that would have sufficient support to pass a legislature or the Congress would have sufficient claim to validity as to be debatable. The fact that many persons would deem the law unsound, unwise, hazardous, or un-American does not in itself make the law invalid under the due process clause.

As the due process concept is a limitation upon governmental action, it does not apply to transactions between private persons or to private employment or other nonpublic situations. In some cases, however, statutes, such as the federal Civil Rights Act and consumer protection laws, apply due process concepts to private transactions.

(b) Shortcut Procedures. Complaint has often been made of the delays of the law. Shortcut procedures are inspired by the legitimate desire to speed up litigation and to give everyone easy access to a day in court. However, procedures must not be so streamlined as to deprive defendants of reasonable notice and opportunity to be heard. In an era in which a defendant may be a resident or a business of a foreign state, statutes have generally been adopted to allow the plaintiff to sue a foreign defendant in the court where the plaintiff lives. Such state statutes are subject to the limitation that they can only be applied when the defendant has such a relationship, as by carrying on of business, within the state of the plaintiff that it is reasonable to require the defendant to appear in the plaintiff's state and defend an action in the courts of that state. Conversely, if the defendant does not have such a reasonable relation to the plaintiff's state, it is a denial of due process to require the defendant to go to the plaintiff's state.

§ 3:12   Equal Protection of the Law

The Constitution prohibits both the state and national governments from denying any person the equal protection of the laws.[19] This guarantee prohibits a government from treating one person differently from another when there is no reasonable ground for classifying them differently.

(a) Reasonable Classification. The equal protection clause does not require that all persons be protected or treated equally, and a law is valid even though it

---

[18] Mennonite Board of Missions v Adams, 462 US 792 (1983).

[19] US Const, Fourteenth Amendment as to the states; modern interpretation of due process clause of Fifth Amendment as to national government. Congress has adopted the Civil Rights Act to implement the concept of equal protection. Newport News Shipbuilding and Dry Dock Co. v EEOC, 462 US 669 (1983).

does not apply to everyone or everything. Whether a classification is reasonable depends on whether the nature of the classification made bears a reasonable relation to the evil to be remedied or to the object to be attained by the law. In determining this, the courts have been guided generally by considerations of historical treatment in the past and by the logic of the situation. The trend is to permit the classification to stand unless it is clear that the lawmaking body has been arbitrary or capricious.

(b) IMPROPER CLASSIFICATION. Laws that make distinctions in the regulation of business, the right to work, and the right to use or enjoy property on the basis of race, alienage, or religion are invalid. Also invalid are laws that impose restrictions on some but not all persons without any justification for the distinction.[20] A law prohibiting the ownership of land by aliens has been traditionally regarded as an exception to this rule. The danger of large alien holdings of land is considered such a social evil as to justify legislation directly prohibiting such holding, although it appears that in course of time this discrimination may be declared invalid.[21] A state statute taxing out-of-state insurance companies at a higher rate than in-state insurance companies violates the equal protection clause.[22]

The lawmaker may not discriminate on the basis of moral standards and cultural patterns. People cannot be deprived of the same treatment given to other persons because they do not have the same moral standards or cultural patterns as the lawmaker. Lawmakers cannot penalize people because they do not live, think, and dress the same as the lawmakers. In the *Moreno* case, the validity of an entitlement plan was challenged by those who did not receive the benefits.

---

[20] Carey v Brown, 447 US 445 (1980).

[21] The alien land laws have been declared unconstitutional by the supreme courts of California, Montana, and Oregon, as being in violation of the Fourteenth Amendment of the United States Constitution.

[22] Metropolitan Life Ins. Co. v Ward, 470 US 869 (1985).

UNITED STATES DEPARTMENT OF AGRICULTURE V MORENO

413 US 528 (1973)

The Federal Food Stamp Act provided for the distribution of food stamps to needy "households." In 1971, § 3(e) of the statute was amended to define households as limited to groups whose members were all related to each other. This was done because of Congressional dislike for the lifestyles of unrelated "hippies" who were living together in "hippie communes." Moreno and others applied for food stamps but were refused them because the relationship requirement was not satisfied. An action was brought to have the relationship requirement declared unconstitutional. The lower court held the statute unconstitutional and the Department of Agriculture appealed.

BRENNAN, J. . . . Appellees [the applicants for the food stamps] . . . consist of several groups of individuals who allege that, although they satisfy the income eligibility requirements for federal food assistance, they have nevertheless been excluded from the program solely because the persons in each group are not "all related to each other." Appellee Jacinta Moreno, for example, is a

56-year-old diabetic who lives with Ermina Sanchez and the latter's three children. They share common living expenses, and Mrs. Sanchez helps to care for appellee. Appellee's monthly income, derived from public assistance, is $75; Mrs. Sanchez receives $133 per month from public assistance. The household pay $135 per month for rent, gas, and electricity, of which appellee pays $50. Appelle spends $10 per month for transportation to a hospital for regular visits, and $5 per month for laundry. That leaves her $10 per month for food and other necessities. Despite her poverty, appellee has been denied federal food assistance solely because she is unrelated to the other members of her household. Moreover, although Mrs. Sanchez and her three children were permitted to purchase $108 worth of food stamps per month for $18, their participation in the program will be terminated if appellee Moreno continues to live with them.

Appellee Sheilah Hejny is married and has three children. Although the Hejnys are indigent, they took in a 20-year-old girl, who is unrelated to them, because "we felt she had emotional problems." The Hejnys receive $144 worth of food stamps each month for $14. If they allow the 20-year-old girl to continue to live with them, they will be denied food stamps by reason of § 3(e).

Appelle Victoria Keppler has a daughter with an acute hearing deficiency. The daughter requires special instruction in a school for the deaf. The school is located in an area in which the appellee could not ordinarily afford to live. Thus, in order to make the most of her limited resources, appellee agreed to share an apartment near the school with a woman who, like appellee, is on public assistance. Since appellee is not related to the woman, appellee's food stamps will be cut off if they continue to live together. . . .

In essence, appellees contend, and the District Court held, that the "unrelated person" provision of § 3(e) creates an irrational classification in violation of the equal protection component of the Due Process Clause of the Fifth Amendment. We agree.

Under traditional equal protection analysis, a legislative classification must be sustained if the classification itself is rationally related to a legitimate governmental interest. . . . The purposes of the Food Stamp Act were expressly set forth in the congressional "declaration of policy":

> It is hereby declared to be the policy of Congress . . . to safeguard the health and well-being of the Nation's population and raise levels of nutrition among low-income households. The Congress hereby finds that the limited food purchasing power of low-income households contributes to hunger and malnutrition among members of such households. The Congress further finds that increased utilization of food in establishing and maintaining adequate national levels of nutrition will promote the distribution in a beneficial manner of our agricultural abundances and will strengthen our agricultural economy, as well as result in more orderly marketing and distribution of food. To alleviate such hunger and malnutrition, a food stamp program is herein authorized which will permit low-income households to purchase a nutritionally adequate diet through normal channels of trade.

The challenged statutory classification (households of related persons versus households containing one or more unrelated persons) is clearly irrelevant to the stated purposes of the Act. As the District Court recognized, "the relationships among persons constituting one economic unit and sharing cooking facilities have nothing to do with their ability to stimulate the agricultural economy by purchasing farm surpluses, or with their personal nutritional requirements." . . .

[I]f it is to be sustained, the challenged classification must rationally further some legitimate governmental interest other than those specifically stated in the congressional "declaration of policy." . . . The legislative history indicates . . . that that amendment was intended to prevent so-called "hippies" and "hippie communes" from participating in the food stamp program. . . . The challenged classification clearly cannot be sustained by reference to this congressional purpose. For if the constitutional conception of "equal protection of the laws" means anything, it must at the very least mean that a bare congressional desire to harm a politically unpopular group cannot constitute a *legitimate* governmental interest. As a result, "a purpose to discriminate against hippies cannot, in and of itself and without reference to [some independent] considerations in the public interest, justify the 1971 amendment." . . .

The Government maintains that the challenged classification should nevertheless be upheld as rationally related to the clearly legitimate governmental interest in minimizing the fraud in the administration of the food stamp program. . . .

In practical effect, the challenged classification simply does not operate so as rationally to further the prevention of fraud. . . . Two *unrelated* persons living together . . . would constitute a single household ineligible for assistance. If financially feasible, however, these same two individuals can legally avoid the "unrelated person" exclusion simply by altering their living arrangements [by living apart]. . . . By so doing, they effectively create two separate "households," both of which are eligible for assistance. See Knowles v Butz, 358 F Supp 228 (ND Cal 1973).

Thus, in practical operation, the 1971 amendment excludes from participation in the food stamp program, *not* those persons who are "likely to abuse the program" but, rather, *only* those persons who are so desperately in need of aid that they cannot even afford to alter their living arrangements so as to retain their eligibility. Traditional equal protection analysis does not require that every classification be drawn with precise "mathematical nicety." Dandridge v Williams, 397 US [471] (1970). But the classification here in issue is not only "imprecise," it is wholly without any rational basis. The judgment of the District Court holding the "unrelated person" provision invalid under the Due Process Clause of the Fifth Amendment is therefore affirmed.

[Judgment affirmed]

QUESTIONS

1. Is there a constitutional right to receive food stamps?
2. Is it lawful for you to give presents to three of your four nephews and not give the fourth anything because you do not like the way he lives?
3. How would the *Moreno* case have been decided if there had been reason to believe that the excluded claimants were agitating to overthrow the government of the United States?

§ 3:13   PRIVILEGES AND IMMUNITIES

The federal Constitution declares that "The Citizens of each State shall be entitled to all Privileges and Immunities of Citizens in the several States."[23] This means that a person going into another state is entitled to make contracts, own property, and engage in business, to the same extent as the citizens of that state. Thus, a state cannot bar a traveler from another state from engaging in local business or from obtaining a hunting or fishing license merely because the traveler is not a resident. Likewise a law that requires an attorney to be a resident of the state is unconstitutional as a violation of this provision.[24]

§ 3:14   PROTECTION OF THE PERSON

The Constitution does not contain any express provision protecting "persons" from governmental action. Persons are expressly protected by the Constitution with respect to particular matters, such as freedom of speech, ownership of property, right to a jury trial, and so on. There is, however, no general provision declaring that the government shall not impair "rights of persons." There is not a word in the Constitution as to the inalienable rights that were so important on July 4, 1776.[25]

(a) RISE OF CONSTITUTIONAL PROTECTION OF THE PERSON. During the last four decades, the Supreme Court has been finding constitutional protection for a wide array of rights of the person that are not expressly protected by the Constitution, such as the right of privacy, the right to marry the person one chooses, protection from unreasonable zoning, protection of parental control, protection from durational residency requirements, protection from discrimination against poverty, and protection from sex discrimination.[26]

(b) DEMOCRACY AND THE PROTECTION OF THE PERSON. As the goal of a democracy is to promote the well-being and development of each individual, the concept of protecting a person and the goal of democracy would appear to be moving toward the same objective. This is ordinarily true but there may be a conflict between the democratic system of government and the protection of the person. We think of a democratic society as one in which the majority of the people govern. But is being governed by the majority sufficient for those who cherish the American ideal?

If we look closely at our individual and national desires, we see that the American way of life is not a society run by the will of the majority. Instead we find that the American way divides life into two zones. In one zone, the democratic concept is that the majority rules. In the other zone, that of the "person," not even the majority can interfere. To illustrate, the majority can declare by statute that before you marry you must have a health certificate. This is perfectly reasonable for the protection of the general health and welfare. But no one, not the majority, nor even the unanimous action of everyone in the United States, can command you to marry or not marry or choose your mate for you.

---

[23] US Const, Art IV, § 2, Cl 1.

[24] Supreme Court of New Hampshire v Piper, 470 US 274 (1985).

[25] The term *inalienable right* is employed in preference to *natural right, fundamental right,* or *basic right.* Apart from the question of scope or coverage, the adjective *inalienable* emphasizes the fact that the right is still possessed by the people, as opposed to the contention that people have surrendered or subordinated such rights to the will of society. The word *alien* is the term of the old common law for transferring title or ownership. Today we would say transfer and, instead of saying inalienable rights, would say nontransfer-

able rights. Inalienable rights of the people were therefore those that not only were possessed by the people, but ones they could not give up, even if they wanted to. Therefore they are still owned by everyone.

[26] In some cases, the courts have given the due process and equal protection clauses a liberal interpretation in order to find a protection of the person, thereby making up for the fact that there is no express constitutional guarantee of protection of the person. Davis v Passman, 442 US 228 (1979) (due process); Orr v Orr 440 US 268 (1979) (equal protection).

Most amazing is the fact that a relatively short time ago the second zone was unheard of and everything was thought to be in the zone that was controlled by the majority unless there was an express prohibition of such action by the Constitution.

Even more startling, the emergence of the second zone has taken place for the most part within your lifetime. The expansion of the second zone will have a profound effect on the rest of your life.

SUMMARY

The U.S. Constitution created the structure of our national government and gave it certain powers. It also placed limitations on those powers. It created a federal system, with a tripartite division of government and a bicameral national legislature.

Some governmental powers are possessed exclusively by the national government, while other powers are shared by both the states and the federal government. In areas of conflict, federal law is supreme.

The U.S. Constitution is not a detailed document. It takes much of its meaning from the way in which it is interpreted. In recent years, liberal interpretation has expanded the powers of the federal government.

Among the powers of the federal government that directly affect business are the power to regulate commerce; the power to tax, borrow, spend, and coin money; and the power to own and operate businesses. Among the limitations on government that are most important to business are the requirement of due process and the requirement of equal protection of the law.

The due process requirement stipulates that no person shall be deprived of life, liberty, or property without due process of law. The due process requirement applies to both the state and federal governments, but does not apply to private transactions.

The equal protection clause of the U.S. Constitution prohibits both the state and federal governments from treating one person differently than another unless there is a legitimate reason for doing so and unless the basis of classification is reasonable.

QUESTIONS AND CASE PROBLEMS

1. What are the characteristics of the Constitution as it is today?
2. Would a United States Constitutional amendment that deleted the present Article V and in its place provided that an amendment could be adopted by a majority of those voting at a presidential election be valid?
3. (a) Does equal protection prevent classification? (b) If not, when is classification proper?
4. A federal law is adopted providing that no one may operate a television station without a federal license. Is that statute constitutional?
5. Does the due process clause protect a business from being destroyed by taxation?

6. Perez was sued for damages arising from an automobile collision. A judgment was entered against Perez. He then filed a petition in bankruptcy. In due course, he was given a discharge in bankruptcy that discharged him from all debts, including the judgment. The state of Arizona then suspended Perez's automobile registration and operator's license pursuant to a state statute providing for such suspension whenever a judgment remained unpaid for 60 days, even though the judgment had been discharged in bankruptcy. Perez claimed that the state statute was unconstitutional and that the suspension of his licenses was therefore improper.

Was he correct? [Perez v Campbell, 402 US 637]

7. The home of the Crafts was supplied with gas by the city gas company. Because of some misunderstanding, the gas company believed that the Crafts were delinquent in paying their gas bill. The gas company had an informal complaint procedure for discussing such matters, but the Crafts had never been informed that such procedure was available. The gas company notified the Crafts that they were delinquent and that the company was shutting off the gas. The Crafts brought an action to enjoin the gas company from so doing on the theory that a termination without any hearing was a denial of due process. The lower courts held that the interest of the Crafts in receiving gas was not a property interest protected by the due process clause and that the procedures that the gas company followed satisfied the requirements of due process. The Crafts appealed. Were they correct in contending that they had been denied due process of law? [Memphis Light, Gas and Water Division v Craft, 436 US 1]

8. Gladys Boddie lived on welfare in Connecticut. She wanted to obtain a divorce but she did not have the $60 required to commence a divorce action. She claimed that the state requirement of the prepayment of such fees deprived her of her constitutional rights and that the statute was therefore invalid. Was she correct? [Boddie v Connecticut, 401 US 371]

9. The New York Civil Service law provided that only United States citizens could hold permanent civil service positions. Dougall was an alien who had lawfully entered and was lawfully residing in the United States. He held a job with the City of New York but was fired because of the state statute. He claimed that the statute was unconstitutional. Was he correct? [Sugarman v Dougall, 413 US 634]

10. A Tennessee statute required that the person be a resident of the state for one year and of the county for three months in order to register to vote in a state election. Blumstein moved into the state. He could not satisfy the residency requirements and therefore could not register to vote. He claimed that this deprived him of his constitutional right to vote and that therefore the residen-

cy requirements were invalid. The state claimed that the residency requirements were designed to insure that voters would be familiar with the issues involved in the elections and to give the voting officials time in which to verify any disputed claim to having a local residence. Were the residency requirements constitutional? [Dunn v Blumstein, 405 US 330]

11. The city of Philadelphia, Pennsylvania, made a contract with owners of land in New Jersey under which the city could dump solid waste on the land of the New Jersey owners. New Jersey adopted a statute prohibiting the depositing in New Jersey of solid waste originating in other states. There was no prohibition against depositing New Jersey solid wastes in New Jersey. Philadelphia and the owners of the New Jersey land claimed that the New Jersey statute was unconstitutional. Was the law unconstitutional? [Philadelphia v New Jersey, 437 US 617]

12. Heald was the executor of a deceased person who had lived in Washington, D.C. Heald refused to pay federal tax owed by the estate on the ground that the tax had been imposed by an act of Congress, but that, since residents of the District of Columbia had no vote in Congress, the tax law was necessarily adopted without their representation. In addition to having no voice in the adoption of the tax laws, the proceeds from taxes collected in the District were paid into the general treasury of the United States and were not maintained as a separate District of Columbia fund. Heald objected that the tax law was void as contrary to the Constitution because it amounted to taxation without representation. Decide. [Heald v District of Columbia, 259 US 114]

13. California owns the Belt Railroad that serves San Francisco Harbor and, through connections with other lines, handles interstate traffic. It is a common carrier and files tariffs with the Interstate Commerce Commission. A collective bargaining agreement was entered into between the state and the employees of the Belt Railroad. A number of employees later presented to the National Railroad Adjustment Board claims arising under the agreement. The board refused to exercise jurisdiction over the matter, on the theory that the Railway Labor Act did not apply to a state-owned railroad. The em-

ployees then brought an action against the board to compel it to exercise jurisdiction. Decide. [California v Taylor, 353 US 553]

14. Because of misconduct, Lopez and other public high school students were suspended for periods of up to ten days. A state statute authorized the principal of a public school to suspend a student for periods up to ten days without any hearing. A suit was brought by Lopez and others claiming that the statute was unconstitutional because it deprived them of due process by not giving them notice and a hearing to determine whether a suspension was justified. The lower court held the statute unconstitutional, and Goss and other school officials appealed. Was the state statute constitutional? [Goss v Lopez, 419 US 565]

15. The Robinsons lived in New York. They purchased an Audi automobile from a New York dealer. A year later they moved to Arizona. While driving through Oklahoma, their Audi was hit by another automobile. This resulted in a fire that severely injured the wife and children. Suit was brought on the theory that there was a design defect in the car. The suit was brought in Oklahoma against the manufacturer of the car, its distributor, and the dealer who had sold the car to the Robinsons. None of the defendants did business or had any connection or association with Oklahoma. The defendants claimed that it was a denial of due process for the state of Oklahoma, through its courts, to allow a suit to be brought against them. Were they correct? [World-Wide Volkswagen Corp. v Woodson, 444 US 286]

4

GOVERNMENT REGULATION

In Chapter 3, you saw that government can regulate business and much of our lives. Whether government should exercise this power comes down to a question of policy — whether we, the people, want government to do so. This in turn involves questions of economics, political science, the humanities, and related subjects. If society decides that there should be regulation by government, then questions arise as to what should be regulated and how. These questions involve important decisions for the welfare of society, because in every decision some social interest loses and some interest gains. Society must make the difficult decision of how it should manage it-

self. For the last century, the American people have called upon government to regulate more and more of their way of life. While there is some movement towards deregulation, the overwhelming pattern continues to be regulation of business by government.

A. POWER TO REGULATE BUSINESS

The states possess the power to adopt laws to protect the general welfare, health, safety, and morals of the people. This is called the **police power.** By virtue of their police power, states may regulate business in all of its aspects, so long as they do not impose an unreasonable burden on interstate commerce or any activity of the federal government. Local governments may also exercise this power to the extent each state permits. The federal government may impose upon any phase of business any regulation that is required by "the economic needs of the nation."[1]

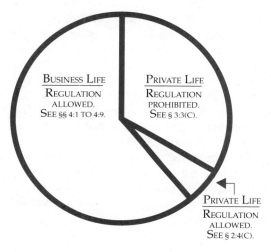

FIGURE 4-1
GOVERNMENT REGULATION OF AMERICAN LIFE

§ 4:1   REGULATION OF
            PRODUCTION,
            DISTRIBUTION, AND
            FINANCING

In order to protect the public from harm, government may prohibit false advertising and labeling, and it may establish health and purity standards for cosmetics, foods, and drugs. Without regard to the nature of the product, government may regulate business with respect to what materials may be used, the quantity of a product that may be produced or grown, and the price at which the finished product may be sold. Government may also engage in competi-

tion with private enterprises or own and operate an industry.

Regulation of production may take the form of providing encouragement or assistance for enterprises that would not prove attractive to private investors.[2]

Under its commerce power, the federal government may regulate all methods of interstate transportation and communication. A like power is exercised by each state over its intrastate traffic. The financing of business is directly affected by the national government, which creates a national currency and maintains a federal reserve bank system. State and other national laws may also affect financing by regulating financing contracts and documents, such as bills of lading and commercial paper.

The federal government may also establish standards for weights and measures. The Metric Conversion Act of 1975 declares that it is the policy of the United States to convert to the metric system. Various agencies have adopted regulations to carry out this policy.

§ 4:2   REGULATION OF
            COMPETITION

The federal government, and the states in varying degrees, prohibit unfair methods of competition. Frequently, a commission is established to determine whether a given practice comes within the general class of unfair methods of competition. In other instances, the statutes specifically define the practices condemned.

The Congress has declared "unlawful" all "unfair methods of competition" and has created a Federal Trade Commission to administer the law. The FTC has condemned harassing tactics, coercing by refusing to sell, boycotting, discriminating, disparaging of a competitor's products, enforcing payment wrongfully, cutting off or

---

[1]   American Power & Light Co. v SEC, 329 US 90 (1946).

[2]   Orphan Drug Act of January 4, 1983, PL 97–44, 96 Stat 2049, 21 USC §§ 301, 306 (encouraging development of drugs to fight diseases that are so rare that there is no commercial interest in developing drugs to prevent or treat them).

restricting the market, securing and using confidential information, spying on competitors, and inducing breach of customer contracts. The law also prohibits misrepresentation by appropriating business or corporate names, simulating trade or corporate names, appropriating trademarks, simulating the appearance of a competitor's goods, simulating a competitor's advertising, using deceptive brands or labels, and using false and misleading advertising.

A shift of emphasis is taking place in appraising methods of doing business. Instead of harm to competitors being the sole consideration, the effect upon the consumer is being given increasing recognition. Many practices that were condemned earlier only because they would harm a competitor by diverting customers are now condemned because such practices prevent the customer from getting full value for the money spent.

§ 4:3   REGULATION OF PRICES

Governments, both national and state, may regulate prices. This may be done directly by the lawmaker — that is, the Congress or the state legislature — or the power to do so may be delegated to an administrative officer or agency. This power extends to prices in any form. It includes not only what a buyer pays for goods purchased from a store, but also what a borrower pays as interest on a loan and what a tenant pays for rent.

(a) PROHIBITED PRICE DISCRIMINATION. The Clayton Act of 1914, applicable to interstate and foreign commerce, prohibits price discrimination between different buyers of commodities "where the effect of such discrimination may be substantially to lessen competition or tend to create a monopoly in any line of commerce."

The federal law prohibits the furnishing of advertising or other services that, when rendered to one purchaser but not another, will have the effect of granting the former a price discrimination or lower rate. It is made illegal for a seller to accept any fee or commission in connection with a sale, except for services actually rendered and unless the services are equally available to all on the same terms. The Clayton Act makes both the giving and the receiving of any illegal price discrimination a crime.

(b) PERMITTED PRICE DISCRIMINATION. Price discrimination is expressly permitted when it can be justified on the basis of: (1) difference in grade, quality, or quantity involved; (2) the cost of the transportation involved in performing the contract; (3) a good-faith effort to meet competition; (4) differences in methods or quantities; (5) deterioration of goods; or (6) a close-out sale of a particular line of goods. The Robinson-Patman Act of 1936 reaffirms the right of a seller to select customers and to refuse to deal with anyone as long as the refusal is in good faith and not for the purpose of restraining trade.

The meeting competition defense is available where the seller lowers the price for a general competitive area, as distinguished from doing so on an individual customer basis.[3]

§ 4:4   PREVENTION OF MONOPOLIES AND COMBINATIONS

To protect competitors and the public from monopolies and combinations in restraint of trade, the federal government and almost all of the states have enacted antitrust statutes.

(a) THE FEDERAL ANTITRUST ACT. The federal antitrust act, known as the Sherman Antitrust Act, is applicable to both sellers and buyers.[4] It provides that "[§ 1] Every contract, combination in the form of trust or otherwise, or conspiracy, in restraint of trade or commerce among the several states, or with foreign nations, is

---

[3]   Falls City Industries, Inc. v Vanco Beverages, Inc. 460 US 428 (1983).
[4]   This act has been amended by the Clayton Act, the Federal Trade Commission Act, the Shipping Act, and other legislation.

declared to be illegal. [§ 2] Every person who shall monopolize or attempt to monopolize, or combine or conspire with any other person or persons to monopolize any part of the trade or commerce among the several states, or with foreign nations, shall be deemed guilty of a felony."[5]

(b) PROHIBITED CONDUCT. Section 1 of the Sherman Act applies only when two or more persons agree or conspire to restrain trade. Under Section 2, one person or corporation may violate the law by monopolizing or attempting to monopolize interstate commerce. As discussed in the *Mandeville* case, the Sherman Act applies not only to buying and selling activities generally associated with trade and commerce, but also to manufacturing and production activities without regard to whether consumers, brokers, or manufacturers are involved.

[5] 15 United States Code, Ch. 1, §§ 1, 2.

MANDEVILLE ISLAND FARMS V AMERICAN CRYSTAL SUGAR CO.
334 US 219 (1948)

The raising of sugar beets is an important industry in California. Sugar refineries buy the beet crop of the farmers and make sugar from the beets. This sugar is then shipped out of California and sold in many states. In order to hold down the prices paid to the sugar beet farmers, the American Crystal Sugar Company and two other refiners agreed among themselves on the price that they would pay the farmers for sugar beets. Mandeville Island Farms was one of the farmers. It claimed that this price-fixing agreement between the sugar refiners violated the Sherman Antitrust Act. Mandeville sued American Crystal for treble (triple) damages as authorized by the federal statute. Judgment was entered for Mandeville, and American Crystal appealed.

RUTLEDGE, J. . . . The refiners controlled the seed supply and the only practical market for beets grown in northern California. When the new contracts were offered to the farmers, they had the choice of either signing or abandoning sugar-beet farming. . . . Because beet prices were determined for the three seasons with reference to the combined returns of the three refiners, the prices received by [the farmers] for those seasons were lower than if [American Crystal], the most efficient of the three, had based its prices on separate returns. . . .

[American Crystal] claimed that the growing, purchasing, and refining of sugar beets were local activities and not within the reach of the Sherman Act, which applied only to transactions in interstate commerce, and that no illegal practice occurred in the subsequent interstate distribution of the refined sugar.

. . . The broad form of [American Crystal]'s argument cannot be accepted. It is a reversion to conceptions formerly held but no longer effective to restrict either Congress' power, *Wickard v Filburn*, 317 US 111, or the scope of the Sherman Act's coverage. The artificial and mechanical separation of "production" and "manufacturing" from "commerce," without regard to their economic continuity, the effects of the former two upon the latter, and the varying methods by which the several processes are organized, related, and carried on in different industries, or indeed within a single industry, no longer suffices to put either production or manufacturing and refining processes beyond reach of Congress' authority or of the statute. . . . *Standard Oil Co. v United States*, 221 US 1. . . .

. . . The inquiry whether the restraint occurs in one phase or another, interstate or intrastate, of the total economic process is now merely a preliminary step. . . . The vital question becomes whether the effect is sufficiently substantial and adverse to Congress' paramount policy . . . to constitute a forbidden consequence. If so, the restraint must fall; and the injuries it inflicts upon others become remediable under the act's prescribed methods, including the treble damage provision.

. . . It is clear that the agreement is the sort of combination condemned by the act, even though the price fixing was by purchasers and the persons specially injured under the treble damage claim are sellers, not customers or consumers. . . .

. . . The statute does not confine its protection to consumers, or to purchasers, or to competitors, or to sellers. Nor does it immunize the outlawed acts because they are done by any of these. . . . The act is comprehensive in its terms and coverage, protecting all who are made victims of the forbidden practices by whomever they may be perpetrated. . . .

Nor is the amount of the nation's sugar industry which the California refiners control relevant, so long as control is exercised effectively in the area concerned, *Indiana Farmer's Guide v Prairie Farmer*, 293 US 218.

. . . Under the facts characterizing this industry's operation and the tightening of controls in this producing area by the new agreements and understandings, there can be no question that their restrictive consequences were projected substantially into the interstate distribution of the sugar. . . .

[Judgment affirmed]

QUESTIONS

1. Is the Sherman Antitrust Act limited to agreements between sellers that restrain trade?
2. Did American Crystal and other refiners intend to affect the price at which sugar was sold in the markets in other states?
3. Does the Sherman Antitrust Act apply to a combination of five manufacturers that agree to the price at which they will sell their furniture throughout the United States?

The Sherman Act does not deprive a city of the power to impose rent ceilings, as such a regulation does not involve concerted action.[6]

The fact that a manufacturer sells only through a particular distributor and refuses to sell through anyone else does not in itself constitute an illegal restraint of trade, even though other merchants are deprived of the benefit of selling the particular product.[7]

(c) BIGNESS. The Sherman Antitrust Act does not prohibit bigness. However, Sec-

---

[6]   Fisher v Berkley, 475 US 260 (1986).

[7]   Oakridge Investment, Inc. v Southern Energy Homes, Inc. (Okla App) 719 P2d 848 (1986).

tion 7 of the Clayton Act, as amended in 1950, provides that "no corporation . . . shall acquire the whole or any part of the assets of another corporation . . . , where in any line of commerce in any section of the country, the effect of such acquisition may be substantially to lessen competition, or to tend to create a monopoly."

(1) Premerger Notification. When large-size enterprises plan to merge, they must give written notice to the Federal Trade Commission and to the attorney in charge of the Antitrust Division of the Department of Justice and then wait a specified time to see if there is any objection to the proposed merger.[8]

[8] Antitrust Improvement Act of 1976, PL 94-435, 90 Stat 1383, § 201, 15 USC §§ 1311 et seq.

(2) Takeover laws. Antitrust laws are typically concerned with whether the combination or agreement is fair to society or to a particular class, such as consumers. Some legislation is aimed at protecting the various parties directly involved in the combining of different enterprises. There is concern that one enterprise may in effect be raiding another enterprise. Laws seeking to protect from unfairness in such situations have been adopted by Congress and four-fifths of the states. State laws are limited in effect because they can only operate within the area over which a state has control. In the *Edgar* case it was claimed that a state takeover law was unconstitutional because it went too far.

EDGAR V MITE CORP.
457 US 624 (1982)

An Illinois statute required a corporation seeking to buy out another corporation to file papers disclosing certain information. MITE Corporation, a Delaware corporation, offered to buy all the stock of the Chicago Rivet Company, an Illinois corporation. Edgar, the Illinois Secretary of State, sought an injunction to block MITE because it had not complied with the requirements of the Illinois statute. MITE claimed that the Illinois statute was unconstitutional because (1) it was in conflict with the federal Williams Act that amended the Securities and Exchange Act of 1934, and (2) it placed an unreasonable burden on interstate commerce. From a decision in favor of MITE, Edgar appealed.

WHITE, J. . . . The Williams Act, passed in 1968, was the congressional response to the increased use of cash tender offers in corporate acquisitions. . . . The Act imposes several requirements. First, it requires that upon the commencement of the tender offer, the offeror file with the SEC, publish or send to the shareholders of the target company, and furnish to the target company detailed information about the offer. The offeror must disclose information about its background and identity; the source of the funds to be used in making the purchase; the purpose of the purchase, including any plans to liquidate the company or make major changes in its corporate structure; and the extent of the offeror's holdings in the target company. . . .

There is no question that in imposing these requirements, Congress intended to protect investors. . . . But it is also crystal clear that a major aspect of the effort to protect the investor was to avoid favoring either management or the takeover bidder. . . . Congress disclaimed any "intention to provide a weapon for management to discourage takeover bids. . . ." Rondeau v Mosinee Paper Corp., [422 US 49,] 58, and expressly embraced a policy of neutrality. . . .

The Illinois Act requires a tender offeror to notify the Secretary of State and the target company of its intent to make a tender offer and the material terms of the offer 20 business days before the offer becomes effective.

. . . By providing the target company with additional time within which to take steps to combat the offer, the precommencement notification provisions furnish incumbent management with a powerful tool to combat tender offers, perhaps to the detriment of the stockholders who will not have an offer before them during this period. These consequences are precisely what Congress determined should be avoided, and for this reason, the precommencement notification provision frustrates the objectives of the Williams Act.

. . . The Commerce Clause permits only *incidental* regulation of interstate commerce by the states; direct regulation is prohibited. . . . The Illinois Act violates these principles for two reasons. First, it directly regulates and prevents, unless its terms are satisfied, interstate tender offers which in turn would generate interstate transactions. Second, the burden the Act imposes on interstate commerce is excessive in light of the local interests the Act purports to further.

. . . The Illinois Act . . . directly regulates transactions which take place across state lines, even if wholly outside the State of Illinois. A tender offer for securities of a publicly-held corporation is ordinarily communicated by the use of the mails or other means of interstate commerce to shareholders across the country and abroad. Securities are tendered and transactions closed by similar means. Thus, in this case, MITE Corporation, the tender offeror, is a Delaware corporation with principal offices in Connecticut. Chicago Rivet is a publicly-held Illinois corporation with shareholders scattered around the country, 27% of whom live in Illinois. Mite's offer to Chicago Rivet's shareholders, including those in Illinois, necessarily employed interstate facilities in communicating its offer, which, if accepted, would result in transactions occurring across state lines. These transactions would themselves be interstate commerce. Yet the Illinois law, unless complied with, sought to prevent Mite from making its offer and concluding interstate transactions not only with Chicago Rivet's stockholders living in Illinois, but also with those living in other states and having no connection with Illinois. Indeed, the Illinois law on its face would apply even if not a single one of Chicago Rivet's shareholders were a resident of Illinois, since the Act applies to every tender offer for a corporation meeting two of the following conditions: the corporation has its principal executive office in Illinois, is organized under Illinois laws, or has at least 10% of its stated capital and paid-in surplus represented in Illinois. . . . Thus the Act could be applied to regulate a tender offer which would not affect a single Illinois shareholder.

It is therefore apparent that the Illinois statute is a direct restraint on interstate commerce and that it has a sweeping extraterritorial effect. Furthermore, if Illinois may impose such regulations, so may other states; and interstate commerce in securities transactions generated by tender offers would be thoroughly stifled. . . .

Because the Illinois Act purports to regulate directly and to interdict interstate commerce, including commerce wholly outside the state, it must be held invalid.

. . . When a state statute regulates interstate commerce indirectly, the burden imposed on that commerce must not be excessive in relation to the local interests served by the statute. The most obvious burden the Illinois Act imposes on interstate commerce arises from the statute's previously-described nationwide reach which purports to give Illinois the power to determine whether a tender offer may proceed anywhere.

The effects of allowing the Illinois Secretary of State to block a nationwide tender offer are substantial. Shareholders are deprived of the opportunity to sell their shares at a premium. The reallocation of economic resources to their highest-valued use, a process which can improve efficiency and competition, is hindered. The incentive the tender offer mechanism provides incumbent management to perform well so that stock prices remain high is reduced. . . .

Appellant [Edgar] . . . contends that Illinois has an interest in regulating the internal affairs of a corporation incorporated under its laws. The internal affairs doctrine is a conflict of laws principle which recognizes that only one state should have the authority to regulate a corporation's internal affairs — matters peculiar to the relationships among or between the corporation and its current officers, directors, and shareholders — because otherwise a corporation could be faced with conflicting demands. See Restatement (Second) of Conflict of Laws, § 302, Comment b at 307-308 (1971). That doctrine is of little use to the state in this context. Tender offers contemplate transfers of stock by stockholders to a third party and do not themselves implicate the internal affairs of the target company. . . . Furthermore, the proposed justification is somewhat incredible since the Illinois Act applies to tender offers for any corporation for which 10% of the outstanding shares are held by Illinois residents, . . . The Act thus applies to corporations that are not incorporated in Illinois and have their principal place of business in other states. Illinois has no interest in regulating the internal affairs of foreign corporations.

We conclude with the Court of Appeals that the Illinois Act imposes a substantial burden on interstate commerce which outweighs its putative local benefits. It is accordingly invalid under the Commerce Clause.

[Judgment affirmed]

QUESTIONS

1. Was the Illinois Act intended to regulate commerce?
2. What is the attitude of the court to corporate takeovers?
3. The Illinois Act was valid as a regulation of internal affairs of Illinois corporations. Appraise this statement.

(d) PRICE FIXING. Agreements fixing prices, whether horizontally or vertically, violate the federal antitrust law. Thus, manufacturers cannot agree between themselves on the price at which they will sell (horizontal price fixing); likewise, a wholesaler cannot require a dealer to agree not to resell below a stated price (vertical price fixing).[9]

(e) EXCEPTIONS TO THE ANTITRUST LAW. By statute or decision, associations of exporters, marine insurance associations, farmers' cooperatives, and labor unions are exempt from the Sherman Antitrust Act with respect to agreements between their members. Certain pooling and revenue dividing agreements between carriers are exempt from the antitrust law when approved by the appropriate federal agency. The Newspaper Preservation Act of 1970 grants an antitrust exemption to operating agreements entered into by newspapers to prevent financial collapse. The Soft Drink Interbrand Competition Act[10] grants the soft drink industry a limited exemption when it is shown that, in fact, there is substantial competition in spite of the agreements.

The general approach of the Supreme Court of the United States to the trust problem has been that an agreement is not automatically or per se to be condemned as a restraint of interstate commerce merely because it creates a power or a potential to monopolize interstate commerce. It is only when the restraint imposed is unreasonable that the practice is unlawful.

(f) PUNISHMENT AND CIVIL REMEDY. A violation of either of the Sherman Act provisions stated in § 4:4(a) of this text is punishable by fine or imprisonment or both at the discretion of the court. The maximum fine for a corporation is $1,000,000. A natural person can be fined a maximum of $100,000 or imprisoned for a maximum

term of three years or both. In addition to this criminal penalty, the law provides for an injunction to stop the unlawful practices and permits suing the wrongdoers for damages.

(1) Individual Damage Suit. Any person or enterprise harmed may bring a separate action for treble damages (three times the damages actually sustained).

(2) Class Action Damage Suit by State Attorney General. When the effect of an antitrust violation is to raise prices, the attorney general of a state may bring a class action to recover damages on behalf of those who have paid the higher prices.[11] This action is called a *parens patriae* action, on the theory that the state is suing as the "parent" of its people.

§ 4:5   REGULATION OF
                    EMPLOYMENT

Basically, parties are free to make an employment contract on any terms they wish. By statute, certain limitations are imposed on this freedom of contract. Persons under a certain age cannot be employed at certain kinds of labor. Statutes commonly specify minimum wages and maximum hours that the employer must observe. A state may require employers to pay employees' wages for the time that they are away from work for the purpose of voting.

(a) FAIR LABOR STANDARDS ACT. By this statute, which is popularly known as the Wage and Hour Act, Congress provides that, subject to certain exceptions, persons working in interstate commerce or in an industry producing goods for interstate commerce cannot be paid less than a specified minimum wage. Furthermore, they cannot be employed for more than 40 hours a week unless they are paid time and a half for overtime.[12] The act prohibits the employment of children under the age of 14

---

[9] Vertical price-maintenance agreements were authorized by statutes in varying degrees from 1931 to 1975, but the Consumer Goods Pricing Act of 1975, PL 94–145, 89 Stat 801, abolished the immunity from the federal antitrust law that had been given to such agreements. Although the states may permit such agreements as long as interstate commerce is not involved, the area of intrastate commerce is so slight that for all practical purposes such agreements are now illegal.

[10] Act of July 9, 1980, PL 96–308, 94 Stat 939, 15 USC §§ 3501 et seq.

[11] Antitrust Improvement Act of 1976, PL 94–435, 90 Stat 1383, Title III, 15 USC §§ 1311 et seq.

[12] Fair Labor Standards Amendment of 1977, PL 95–151, 91 Stat 1245, 29 USC §§ 201 et seq.

years. It permits the employment of children between the ages of 14 and 16 years in all industries except mining and manufacturing under certain prescribed conditions. This act has been copied by a number of states in regulating those phases of industry not covered by the federal statute.

(b) FAIR EMPLOYMENT PRACTICES ACTS. With some exceptions, employers of 15 or more persons are forbidden to discriminate against any person because of race, religious creed, color, sex, national origin, or age with regard to compensation and other privileges or conditions of employment.[13] Special protection for migrant farm workers is provided by the Federal Migrant and Seasonal Agricultural Work Protection Act.[14]

(1) Sex Discrimination. An employer cannot discriminate on the basis of sex.[15] An employer may not hire on the basis of a stereotypical pattern of what is "woman's work" and what is "man's work." Women, therefore, cannot be excluded from working as bartenders, and men cannot be excluded from working as airline flight attendants. Indirect sex discrimination is also prohibited, as when the employer establishes height and weight specifications for job applicants; but such requirements have no bearing on the performance of the work, and their effect is to exclude women from the job.

The equality of the sexes is literally applied so that a law is unconstitutional when it gives to women a protection or an advantage that it does not give to men performing the same work. Likewise, it is a discriminatory labor practice to allow women seniority rights that are not available to men on the same terms, or to pro-

hibit women from working at jobs that involve the lifting of heavy weights. A standardized "compulsory pregnancy leave" regulation for public school teachers is unconstitutional. This is so because no consideration is given the fitness of the individual teacher to continue teaching; and there is no proof that pregnant teachers, as a class, are necessarily and universally unfit to teach.[16] The protection against sex discrimination is not limited to situations that are customarily regarded as employment. Thus, it is held that a law partnership violates the act if it refuses to invite an associate to become a partner because the associate is a woman.[17]

(2) Allowable Distinctions. The federal law does not require that every employee be treated the same as every other. It does not prohibit the testing or screening of applicants or employees for the purpose of determining whether a person is qualified to be hired, promoted, given a wage increase, or given special training. The Civil Rights Act has no effect upon the employer's right to establish compensation scales, to provide bonus pay and incentive pay, or to pay different rates in different geographic areas. The employer may also recognize seniority status, voluntarily or as a result of collective bargaining.

(3) Proof of discrimination. The claim that there has been improper discrimination against an applicant or employee is made in a court or before an administrative agency. The procedure is regulated by statute, and the claimant does not have any choice as to whether to go to court or to an agency.

Who has the burden of proof when the claimant brings a lawsuit or files a complaint with an administrative agency? This is a vital question because, as a practical matter, there will be many cases in which it is impossible to prove exactly what happened. In such cases, whoever has the bur-

---

[13] Federal Civil Rights Act of 1964, Title VII, as amended by the Equal Employment Opportunities Act of 1972 and 1986. TWA v Thurston, 469 US 111 (1985). With minor exceptions, the federal law prohibits age discrimination. In some states and cities, state statutes and local ordinances also prohibit age discrimination.

[14] Act of January 14, 1983, PL 97-470, 96 Stat 2583, 29 USC § 1801.

[15] Washington County v Gunther, 452 US 161 (1981).

[16] Cleveland Board of Education v La Fleur, 414 US 632 (1974).

[17] Hishon v King & Spalding, 467 US 69 (1984).

den of proving what did happen will lose, because it will not be possible to carry the burden of proof. In the *Johnson* case the court applied the federal rule as to the burden of proof.

Johnson v Bozeman School District No. 7
___ Mont ___, 734 P2d 209 (1987)

Dallas Johnson was a school teacher. He applied to the Bozeman School District for a teaching position. His application was rejected. He claimed that this was done because his wife was employed by the school district, and the school district had followed a rule against nepotism, or the hiring of a close relative of an employee. Dallas claimed that this discriminated against him, and he filed a complaint with the Montana Human Rights Commission. The Commission decided in his favor, and the school district appealed.

Turnage, C. J. . . . Donovan Miller was the personnel director for the School District from 1975 to 1980. Part of his job involved screening all applications for teaching in the School District. His procedure was to review the applications, assign each one a numerical rating, and then send those applications with the highest ratings to the principal of the school where an opening existed. The applicants were rated on a scale from "one to five;" a rating of "one" was superior and a rating of "five" was poor. Johnson's application was rated along with a large number of other applicants for the teaching position at Bozeman Junior High. Johnson was rated at "four." The other applicants all had higher ratings than Johnson.

The School District had never hired any one rated less than "two." Miller's policy was to send only those applications rated a "one" or "two" to the particular principal for review. . . .

Did the Human Rights Commission and the District Court err in finding that the School District discriminated against Johnson on the basis of his marital status?

At the time Johnson applied for a teaching position with the School District, the School District had a policy in effect which prevented spouses from teaching in the same school. The Human Rights Commission . . . concluded that Johnson had been unlawfully discriminated against, in violation of [Montana Statute] § 49-2-303(1)(a), MCA, which provides:

> It is an unlawful discriminatory practice for . . . an employer to refuse employment to a person, to bar him from employment, or to discriminate against him in compensation or in a term, condition, or privilege of employment because of his . . . *marital status* . . . [Emphasis added.]

. . . The parties have framed the question: "Which factor was primary in the rejection of Johnson's application — his rating or his marital status?" . . .

We have held that reference to federal case law is both appropriate and helpful in employment discrimination cases filed under the Montana Human

Rights Act, Title 49, MCA, because they closely parallel those of Title VII of the Federal Civil Rights Act of 1964, 42 U.S.C. § 2000e et seq.

In order to aid plaintiffs in proving their claims of employment discrimination, the United States Supreme Court articulated a three-stage test, which employs shifting burdens of proof. *McDonnell Douglas Corp. v. Green* (1973), 411 U.S. 792 (employer rejected the re-employment application of a black civil rights activist).

Under the first stage of the *McDonnell Douglas* test, the plaintiff bears the burden of establishing a prima facie case of discrimination. He must show the following:

(1) that he is a member of a *protected class;*
(2) that he applied for and was *qualified* for the job;
(3) that despite his qualifications he was *rejected;* and
(4) that, after his rejection, the *position remained open* and the employer continued to seek applications from persons of the *complainant's qualifications.*

This prima facie case creates a rebuttable presumption of discrimination.

Under the second stage of the *McDonnell Douglas* test, if the plaintiff has established his prima facie case, the burden then shifts to the employer "to articulate some legitimate, nondiscriminatory reason for the employee's rejection." The burden on the employer at this stage is merely one of production, not persuasion. "The defendant need not persuade the court that it was actually motivated by the proffered reasons. It is sufficient if the defendant's evidence raises a genuine issue of fact as to whether it discriminated against the plaintiff." . . . If the employer is able to demonstrate a *legitimate, nondiscriminatory reason* for not hiring the complainant, even though that may not have been the actual reason for the rejection, then the plaintiff's prima facie case of discrimination is rebutted.

Under the third stage, if the plaintiff's prima facie case is rebutted, he then has an opportunity to prove, by a preponderance of the evidence, that the legitimate reasons offered by the employer are only a *pretext for discrimination.* . . .

We have consistently used the *McDonnell Douglas* test as the appropriate method of proving an employment discrimination claim. . . . § 49-2-303(1)(a), MCA, is a "strongly worded directive from the legislature prohibiting employment discrimination and encouraging public employers to hire, promote, and dismiss employees solely on merit."

However, Johnson never reached the protection afforded by § 49-2-303(1)(a), MCA, because his qualifications never reached the minimum hiring standard used by the School District. The record reveals that the School District had never hired anyone with a three, four or five rating. Johnson's rating of four was based on poor college grades, supervisors' poor recommendations and inferior experience. He was under-qualified in contrast to the other applicants. Under the *McDonnell Douglas* test, Johnson needed to show that he was in a position to be considered for employment before he could invoke the protection of § 49-2-303(1)(a).

Johnson failed to prove that his marital status was the substantial factor in his rejection. . . . The record reveals that the School District's *substantial and motivating* factor in Johnson's rejection was his rating of "four," and not his marital status. As the School Superintendent testifed: "[Johnson] was screened out by his rating before you would even consider the nepotism policy. Even if the policy hadn't existed, obviously he would have been screened out." Under the test of *McDonnell Douglas*, the key element of a plaintiff's prima facie case is his qualifications for the job. Without adequate qualifications, the analysis ends. . . . The Bozeman School District set a qualification standard which Johnson failed to reach. Johnson has failed to establish the "qualified" element of his prima facie case, thereby precluding the need for the School District to rebut his evidence.

If, arguendo, Johnson had established his prima facie case, the School District in stage two of the *McDonnell Douglas* test produced enough evidence to raise a genuine issue of fact; thereby rebutting Johnson's prima facie case of discrimination, and carrying the analysis to the third stage of the test. At the third stage, Johnson must prove, by a preponderance of the evidence, that the reasons offered by the School District for his rejection are merely a pretext for discrimination. However, Johnson's claim also fails at this stage because the District Court's order, in discussing Johnson's rejection, stated: "this was not a mere pretext for hiring someone else."

We cannot allow Johnson's marital status to secure what his qualifications could not. As we held in *Snell*, 198 Mont. at 69, 643 P.2d at 848, "this Court has a responsibility to the employer as well as to the employee. Part of that responsibility consists in requiring adequate credible evidence of discrimination before subjecting an employer to the penalties associated with a finding of discrimination."

We hold that *McDonnell Douglas* defines the appropriate test in this case. However, both the Human Rights Commission and the District Court failed to apply the *McDonnell Douglas* test to the facts. . . .

[Judgment reversed]

QUESTIONS

1. Why did the Montana Supreme Court follow the rule declared by the United States Supreme Court?
2. Why did the court hold as it did?
3. Could the school district rule against nepotism have been adopted for any purpose other than discrimination against employees?

---

§ 4:6   REGULATION OF LABOR
              RELATIONS

Statutes generally declare the right of employees to form a union and require the employer to deal with the union as the bargaining representative of the employees. An employer cannot refuse in advance to bargain with the proper representative of the employees on the ground that the employer is afraid that improper

demands will be made by the representative.[18]

(a) MACHINERY TO ENFORCE COLLECTIVE BARGAINING. To protect the rights of workers to unionize and bargain collectively, the federal government created the National Labor Relations Board (NLRB). The NLRB determines the proper collective

[18] Skyline Corp. v NLRB (CA5 NLRB) 613 F2d 1328 (1980).

bargaining unit and eliminates unfair practices by which the employer and the union might interfere with employees' rights.

(b) SELECTION OF BARGAINING REPRESENTATIVE. Generally there is an election by secret ballot to select the bargaining representative of the employees within a particular collective bargaining unit.

(c) EXCLUSIVE AND EQUAL REPRESENTATION OF ALL EMPLOYEES. Any union selected by the majority of the workers within the unit is the exclusive representative of all the employees in the unit for the purpose of bargaining with respect to wages and hours or other conditions of employment. Whether or not all the workers are members of the representative union is immaterial for, in any case, this union is the exclusive representative of every employee. It is unlawful for any employee, whether a member or nonmember of the union, to attempt to make a contract directly with the employer. Except as to grievances, every worker must act through the representative union with respect to the contract of employment. At the same time, the union is required to represent all workers fairly, nonmembers as well as members. It is unlawful for the union, in bargaining with the employer, to discriminate in any way against any employee. It makes no difference whether a particular worker is a member of the representative union. The union cannot use its position as representative of all workers to further its interest as a union.

The fact that the representative of the bargaining unit must represent all employees fairly does not bar it from exercising independent judgment and from failing to prosecute an employee's grievance if the union honestly believes the grievance has no merit.[19]

(d) UNFAIR LABOR PRACTICES. The National Labor Relations Act prohibits certain practices as unfair and authorizes the NLRB to conduct proceedings to stop such practices.

(1) Unfair Employer Practices. The federal law declares that it is an unfair labor practice for an employer to interfere with unionization, to discriminate against any employee because of union activities, or to refuse to bargain collectively as to wages, hours, and other terms and conditions of employment.

(2) Unfair Union Practices. The federal law declares it to be an unfair labor practice for a union to interfere with employees in forming a union or in refraining from joining a union; to cause an employer to discriminate against an employee for belonging to another union or no union; to refuse to bargain collectively; and under certain circumstances to stop work or refuse to work on materials or to persuade others to stop work.

(3) Procedure for Enforcement. Under the National Labor Relations Act, the NLRB issues a complaint whenever it appears that an unfair labor practice has been committed. The complaint informs the respondent of the charges made and gives notice to appear at a hearing before an administrative law judge (ALJ). The ALJ conducts a hearing and sends a report to the parties and the five-member board in Washington, D.C. *recommending* either an order to cease and desist from an unfair labor practice or a dismissal of the complaint. Unless either party files timely exceptions to the ALJ's findings, the ALJ's recommended order becomes an order of the board. When exceptions are filed, the five-member board reviews the case and either finds the respondent guilty or not guilty. When the respondent is found guilty, the board issues a cease and desist order, which can be enforced by the U.S. Court of Appeals.

Proceeding before the NLRB is the only way of enforcing rights under the federal statute. A lawsuit cannot be brought in a state court.

(4) Constitutional Protection. Any employment practice that violates a constitutional right of a worker can be stopped by court action if not within the control of an administrative agency.

---

[19] Sanders v Youthcraft Coats and Suits, Inc. (CA8 Mo) 700 F2d 1226 (1983).

(e) UNION ORGANIZATION AND MANAGE-MENT. In order to insure the honest and democratic administration of unions, Congress adopted the Labor-Management Reporting and Disclosure Act of 1959. It regulates unions operating in or affecting interstate commerce. The act protects the rights of union members within their unions by guaranteeing equality, the right to vote on specified matters, and the right to information on union matters and contracts. It also protects members from interference with the enjoyment of these rights.

In the *United Steelworkers* case, the court was faced with the question of whether the election procedure of the union violated the federal statute.

UNITED STEELWORKERS OF AMERICA v USERY
429 US 305 (1977)

The Steelworkers union was run by officers elected from the members of the union. A rule of the union stated that a member was not eligible to be an officer unless the member had attended at least one-half of the regular meetings of the union in the preceding three years. When this rule was applied to a local branch of the union, Local 3489, the result was to disqualify 96.5% of the membership of the local union from holding office. This meant that only 23 members were eligible. Nine of these were already officers of the local. An election was held in the local to vote for new officers. The meeting-attendance rule was applied to determine who were eligible. W.J. Usery, the Secretary of Labor of the United States, claimed that the election was invalid because of the meeting-attendance eligibility requirement. He claimed that it violated the Labor-Management Reporting and Disclosure Act, § 401(e), 29 USC § 481(e), which declared that "Every member in good standing shall be eligible to be a candidate and hold office . . . subject to . . . reasonable qualifications uniformly imposed." The district court sustained the meeting-attendance rule as a reasonable qualification uniformly imposed. On appeal, the court of appeals held the rule invalid. The local then appealed to the Supreme Court.

BRENNAN, J. . . . [The] LMRDA [Labor-Management Reporting and Disclosure Act] does not render unions powerless to restrict candidacies for union office. The injunction in § 401(e) that "every member in good standing shall be eligible to be a candidate and to hold office" is made expressly "subject to . . . reasonable qualifications uniformly imposed." . . . But "Congress plainly did not intend that the authorization . . . of 'reasonable qualifications . . .' should be given a broad reach. The contrary is implicit in the legislative history of the section and its wording. . . ." The basic objective of Title IV of LMRDA is to guarantee "free and democratic" union elections modeled on "political elections in the country" where "the assumption is that voters will exercise common sense and judgment in casting their ballots."
. . . Thus, Title IV is not designed merely to protect the right of a union member to run for a particular office in a particular election." . . . Congress emphatically asserted a vital public interest in assuring free and democratic union elections that transcends the narrower interest of the complaining union

member." . . . The goal was to "protect the rights of rank-and-file members to participate fully in the operation of their union through processes of democratic self-government, and, through the election process, to keep the union leadership responsive to the membership." *Wirtz v Hotel Employees*, [291] US 492 at 497 [(1968)] . . .

Whether a particular qualification is "reasonable" within the meaning of § 402(e) must therefore "be measured in terms of its consistency with the Act's command to unions to conduct 'free and democratic' union elections." . . . Congress was not concerned only with corrupt union leadership. Congress chose the goal of "free and democratic" union elections as a preventive measure "to curb the possibility of abuse by benevolent as well as malevolent entrenched leadership." [The ability to attain these goals is] seriously impaired by candidacy qualifications which substantially deplete the ranks of those who might run in opposition to incumbents. . . .

. . . The antidemocratic effects of the meeting attendance rule outweigh the interests urged in its support. . . . An attendance requirement that results in the exclusion of 96.5% of the members from candidacy for union office hardly seems to be a "reasonable qualification" consistent with the goal of free and democratic elections. A requirement having that result obviously severely restricts the free choice of the membership in selecting their leaders. . . .

Petitioners next argue that the rule is reasonable within § 401(e) because it encourages attendance at union meetings, and assures more qualified officers by limiting election to those who have demonstrated an interest in union affairs, and are familiar with union problems. But the rule has plainly not served these goals. It has obviously done little to encourage attendance at meetings, which continue to attract only a handful of members. Even as to the more limited goal of encouraging the attendance of potential dissident candidates, very few members, as we have said, are likely to see themselves as such sufficiently far in advance of the election to be spurred to attendance by the rule.

As for assuring the election of knowledgeable and dedicated leaders, the election provisions of LMRDA express a congressional determination that the best means to this end is to leave the choice of leaders to the membership in open democratic elections, unfettered by arbitrary exclusions. Pursuing this goal by excluding the bulk of the membership from eligibility for office, and thus limiting the possibility of dissident candidacies, run directly counter to the basic premise of the statute. We therefore conclude that Congress, in guaranteeing every union member the opportunity to hold office, subject only to "reasonable qualifications," disabled unions from establishing eligibility qualifications as sharply restrictive of the openness of the union political process as is petitioners' attendance rule.

[Judgment affirmed]

Questions

1. What was the basis for the claim of the Secretary of Labor?
2. What was the object of Congress in adopting the statute involved in the *Steelworkers* case?

§ 4:7   SOCIAL SECURITY

Employees and employers are required to pay social security taxes. These taxes provide employees with four types of insurance protection — retirement benefits, disability benefits, life insurance benefits, and health insurance (Medicare).

The federal Social Security Act establishes a single federal program of aid for the needy aged, the blind, and the disabled. This is called the Supplemental Security Income program (SSI). Payments are administered directly by the Department of Health and Human Services.

The states also have plans of assistance for the unemployed, aged, and disabled. The federal law encourages the making of payments under state programs in addition to those received under the federal program. Such additional programs are called State Supplemental Payments (SSP). State plans typically establish an administrative board or agency with which claims for assistance are filed. If the board approves a claim, assistance is given to the applicant in the amount specified by the statute for the number of weeks or other period of time designated by the statute.

Unemployment compensation laws generally deny the payment of benefits when the employee was discharged for good cause, or abandoned work without cause, failed or refused to seek or accept an offer of suitable employment, or when the unemployment was the result of a labor dispute. A state may refuse to pay unemployment compensation to workers who financed the strike that caused their unemployment.[20]

B.   LIMITATIONS ON STATE POWER TO REGULATE

By virtue of their police power, the states may regulate business to prevent the sale of harmful products, to protect from fraud, and so on. The power of the states is subject to important limitations.

§ 4:8   CONSTITUTIONAL LIMITATIONS

A state law, although made under the police power, cannot (1) impose an unreasonable burden on or discriminate against interstate commerce, nor (2) invade a right that is protected by the federal Constitution.

§ 4:9   FEDERAL SUPREMACY

A state law cannot conflict with a federal law or regulation on the same subject matter. Moreover, when the federal government regulates a particular activity, state regulation is generally excluded even as to matters not covered by the federal regulation. That is, the federal government occupies or preempts the entire field even though every detail is not regulated.[21]

§ 4:10   STATE AND LOCAL GOVERNMENT AS MARKET PARTICIPANTS

When a state or local government, such as a city or county, enters the marketplace to buy or sell goods, whether produced by itself or others, it is not acting as a government. It is a market participant as contrasted with a government regulating the conduct of others. When a state or local government is a market participant, it is not subject to the limitations imposed upon state governments by the United States Constitution. The *White* case raised the question of whether a city was subject to limitations of the Commerce Clause when it was having a building constructed.

---

20   Baker v General Motors Corp. 478 US ___, 92 L Ed 2d 504 (1986) (workers contributed to union strike fund).

21   Alessi v Raybestos-Manhattan, Inc. 451 US 504 (1981).

WHITE V MASSACHUSETTS COUNCIL OF CONSTRUCTION EMPLOYERS, INC.
460 US 204 (1983)

> The mayor of Boston issued an executive order, that on all construction work done by the city of Boston, at least one-half of the work force had to be bona fide residents of Boston. An employer organization claimed that this requirement was a violation of the Commerce Clause of the United States Constitution. From a decision holding the executive order invalid, the mayor appealed.

REHNQUIST, J. . . . We were first asked in Hughes v Alexandria Scrap Corp., 426 US 794 (1976), to decide whether state and local governments are restrained by the Commerce Clause when they seek to effect commercial transactions not as "regulators" but as "market participants." In that case, the Maryland legislature, in an attempt to encourage the recycling of abandoned automobiles, offered a bounty for every Maryland-titled automobile converted into scrap if the scrap processor supplied documentation of ownership. An amendment to the Maryland statute imposed more exacting documentation requirements on out-of-state than in-state processors, who in turn demanded more exacting documentation from those who sold the junked automobiles for scrap. As a result, it became easier for those in possession of the automobiles to sell to in-state processors. "The practical effect was substantially the same as if Maryland had withdrawn altogether the availability of bounties on hulks delivered by unlicensed suppliers to licensed non-Maryland processors." 426 US, at 803, n13. In upholding the Maryland statute in the face of a Commerce Clause challenge, we said that "[n]othing in the purpose animating the Commerce Clause prohibits a State, in the absence of congressional action, from participating in the market and exercising the right to favor its own citizens over others." Id., at 810 (footnotes omitted). Because Maryland was participating in the market, rather than acting as a market regulator, we concluded that the Commerce Clause was not "intended to require independent justification," id., at 809, for the statutory bounty.

We faced the question again in Reeves, Inc. v Stake, 447 US 429 (1980), when confronted with a South Dakota policy to confine the sale of cement by a state operated cement plant to residents of South Dakota. We underscored the holding of Hughes v Alexandria Scrap Corp., saying:

> The basic distinction drawn in Alexandria Scrap between States as market participants and States as market regulators makes good sense and sound law. As that case explains, the Commerce Clause responds principally to state taxes and regulatory measures impeding free private trade in the national marketplace. There is no indication of a constitutional plan to limit the ability of the States themselves to operate freely in the free market. 447 US, at 436-437.

We concluded that South Dakota, "as a seller of cement, unquestionably fits the 'market participant' label" and applied the "general rule of Alexandria Scrap." Id., at 440.

Alexandria Scrap and Reeves, therefore, stand for the proposition that when a state or local government enters the market as a participant it is not subject to the restraints of the Commerce Clause. As we said in Reeves, in this kind of case there is "a single inquiry: whether the challenged 'program constituted direct state participation in the market.' " Id., at 436, n7. We reaffirm that principle now.

. . . The Supreme Judicial Court of Massachusetts expressed reservations as to the application of the "market participation" principle to the city here, reasoning that "the implementation of the mayor's order will have a significant impact on those firms which engage in specialized areas of construction and employ permanent works crews composed of out-of-state residents." 384 Mass, at ___, 425 NE2d, at 354. Even if this conclusion is factually correct, it is not relevant to the inquiry of whether the city is participating in the marketplace when it provides city funds for building construction. If the city is a market participant, then the Commerce Clause establishes no barrier to conditions such as these which the city demands for its participation. Impact on out-of-state residents figures in the equation only after it is decided that the city is regulating the market rather than participating in it, for only in the former case need it be determined whether any burden on interstate commerce is permitted by the Commerce Clause.

. . . We hold that on the record before us the application of the mayor's executive order to the contracts in question did not violate the Commerce Clause of the United States Constitution. Insofar as the city expended only its own funds in entering into construction contracts for public projects, it was a market participant and entitled to be treated as such under the rule of Hughes v Alexandria Scrap Corp., supra. . . .

[Judgment reversed and action remanded]

QUESTIONS

1. Did the court determine whether the mayor's order placed an unreasonable burden on interstate commerce?
2. Would it have made any difference if the mayor's order had required that all construction work performed in the city should be performed only by city residents?
3. In the situation in the *White* case, does it make any difference whose money is being used to pay for the work?

When a state or local government is a market participant, it is subject to all laws applicable to ordinary persons. For example, when a city owns and operates a mass transit system it is in the position of a private employer and therefore is subject to the federal minimum wage law.[22]

[22] Garcia v San Antonio Metropolitan Transit Authority, 469 US 528 (1985).

SUMMARY

Regulation by government has occurred primarily to protect one group from the improper conduct of another group. Until the middle third of this century, regulation of business was primarily directed at protecting competitors from misconduct of other competitors. Beginning with the middle third of this century, regulation has expanded in the interest of protecting consumers.

In the last one hundred years, the federal government has regulated advertising and food, drugs, and cosmetics. This protects consumers from false claims and from untested and possibly unsafe drugs. Unfair methods of competition are prohibited. Prices have been regulated both by the setting of the exact price or a maximum price and by prohibiting discrimination as to prices. Price discrimination between buyers is prohibited when the effect of such discrimination could tend to create a monopoly or lessen competition. Certain exceptions are made where the circumstances are such that the price discrimination does not have the purpose or result of harming someone else. The Sherman Antitrust Act prohibits conspiracies in restraint of trade and the monopolization of trade. A partial attempt to solve the problem of bigness is made by the Clayton Act in prohibiting mergers or the acquisition of the assets of another corporation when such conduct would tend to lessen competition or give rise to a monopoly. Violation of these statutes subjects the wrongdoer to criminal prosecution and suit, by persons harmed, for treble the damages. The application of these laws is modified to some extent by express exceptions and by the approach of the Supreme Court to antitrust cases. Employment has been regulated in a variety of ways. The federal Fair Labor Standards Act, also known as the Wage and Hour Act, requires that employees be paid not less than a specified minimum wage. Fair employment practice acts prohibit discrimination in employment because of race, religion, color, sex, or national origin. Discrimination because of age is partially prohibited. Special protection is afforded by statute to migrant farm workers. The right of employees to bargain collectively with their employer and the right to choose their representative for such purpose is guaranteed by the National Labor Relations Act. The representative selected by the employees to bargain on their behalf is required to represent all employees fairly and equally without regard to whether particular employees are members of the representative union. The National Labor Relations Act prohibits both employers and unions from committing specified acts that would violate the rights of employees. The enforcement of the National Labor Relations Act is entrusted to a general counsel and the National Labor Relations Board (NLRB). In order to protect union members from misconduct within their own unions, the federal Labor-Management Reporting and Disclosure Act imposes certain limitations on unions to insure that they are run in an honest and democratic manner. As an aspect of regulating the rewards of labor, the social security system under federal law provides for payment to workers retired because of age or disability. The federal Supplemental Security payment (SSI) will in some cases be added to or supplemented by payments made under state programs (SSP).

Many of the regulations imposed by the federal government are paralleled or copied by state laws making a similar regulation as to local matters. The action of the states is restricted by the limitations arising from the Constitution and by the doctrine of the supremacy of federal law.

Questions and Case Problems

1. Describe the objective of each of the following rules of law:

   (a) Horizontal price-fixing is illegal under the federal law without regard to whether the price fixed is fair and reasonable.

   (b) Farmers' and dairy farmers' cooperatives are exempt by statute from the operation of the Sherman Antitrust Act.

2. What government can regulate business?

3. The Danabo Corporation paid the workers in its Pennsylvania factory $.50 an hour more than workers doing the same work in its Mississippi factory. Was the Danabo Corporation guilty of unfair employment practices?

4. Hart is employed by the Bulldog Concrete Forms Company. Her employer refused to promote her because she belonged to a labor union. She claimed that the employer violated a fair employment practices act. Was she correct?

5. Cressler owns a factory. She refuses to obey the state safety laws on the ground that there is no constitutional provision that grants the state the power to make such laws. Does this justify Cressler's refusing to obey the state law?

6. Compare the power to regulate competition and the power to regulate prices.

7. What limitations are imposed upon the purchasing of the assets of an existing enterprise?

8. Jim Mandell applied to the Conestago Airlines for a job as an airflight attendant. His application was rejected on the ground that the airline was only employing female attendants because the passengers preferred them. Jim claimed that the airline was guilty of an unlawful discrimination in its employment practices. Was he correct?

9. The Hines Cosmetic Company sold beauty preparations nationally to beauty shops at a standard or fixed price schedule. Some of the shops were also supplied with a free demonstrator and with free advertising materials. The shops that were not so supplied claimed that the giving of the free services and materials was an unlawful price discrimination. Hines replied that there was no price discrimination because it charged everyone the same. What it was giving free was merely a promotional campaign that was not intended to discriminate against those who were not given anything free. Was Hines guilty of unlawful price discriminations?

10. A New Jersey statute provides that no rebates, allowances, concessions, or benefits shall be given, directly or indirectly, so as to permit any person to obtain motor fuel from a retail dealer below the posted price or at a net price lower than the posted price applicable at the time of the sale. An action was brought by Fried, a retail gasoline dealer, to prevent the enforcement of the statute. He claimed that it was invalid because it was discriminatory in that it related only to the sale of gasoline and that it denied due process by regulating the price. Was the law constitutional? [Fried v Kervick, 34 NJ 68, 167 A2d 380]

11. Moore ran a bakery in Santa Rosa, New Mexico. His business was wholly intrastate. Mead's Fine Bread Company, his competitor, engaged in an interstate business. Mead cut the price of bread in half in Santa Rosa but made no price cut in any other place in New Mexico or in any other state. As a result of this price cutting, Moore was driven out of business. Moore then sued Mead for damages for violation of the Clayton and Robinson-Patman Acts. Mead claimed that the price cutting was purely intrastate and therefore did not constitute a violation of federal statutes. Was Mead correct? [Moore v Mead's Fine Bread Co. 348 US 115]

12. The El Paso Natural Gas Company acquired the stock and assets of the Pacific Northwest Pipe Line Company. El Paso, although not a California enterprise, supplied over half of the natural gas used in California; all the other natural gas was supplied by California sources. No gas was sold in California by Pacific Northwest, although it was a strong, experienced company within the Northwest area and had attempted several times to enter the California market. United States claimed that the acquisition of Pacific by El Paso constituted a violation of § 7 of the Clayton Act, as amended, because the effect would be to remove competition be-

tween the two companies within California. The defense was raised that (a) California was not a "section" of the country within the Clayton Act, (b) the sale of natural gas was not a line of commerce, and (c) the acquisition did not lessen competition when there had not been any prior sales by Pacific within the area. Decide. [United States v El Paso Natural Gas Co. 376 US 651]

13. Copperweld Corp. purchased Regal Tube Co. Some time later the Independence Tube Corp. sued Copperweld and Regal for damages for conspiring in violation of the Sherman Antitrust Act. They denied liability for "conspiring" because Regal was the wholly owned subsidiary of Copperweld. Were they liable? [Copperweld Corp. v Independence Tube Corp. 467 US 752]

14. A federal statute prohibits importing fish into a state that prohibits such importation. Taylor ran a business in Maine of selling live baitfish. He imported from other states a large quantity of a kind of minnow that was not found in Maine. Maine prohibited the importation of live fish. He was prosecuted for violating the Maine statute. He claimed that the statute was unconstitutional as an interference with interstate commerce. The argument was made that the law was valid because there was a fear that the introduction of an alien fish might bring parasites in-

to the waters of Maine and might have a harmful effect on the wildlife of Maine. Was the statute constitutional? [Maine v Taylor, 477 US ___, 91 L Ed 2d 110]

15. The Duke Power Company established standards for promotion from one department to another. In order to be promoted from one department to another, an employee had to have a high school education and had to pass two aptitude tests. These tests were prepared by professional test preparers. Willie S. Griggs and other blacks were employed in the Labor Department of Duke. They applied for promotion out of the Labor Department. They could not get the necessary scores on the aptitude tests. They claimed that by requiring them to pass the tests, the employer was guilty of prohibited racial discrimination. Griggs and other employees brought a class action under Title VII of the federal Civil Rights Act of 1964. It was shown that the aptitude tests did not specifically test for any of the qualities needed in the department to which promotion was sought. It was also shown that white workers obtained better scores on the tests apparently because of their having a better public school education. Griggs claimed that Duke was guilty of unlawful discrimination. Was he correct? [Griggs v Duke Power Co. 401 US 424]

5

THE LEGAL ENVIRONMENT OF INTERNATIONAL TRADE

American business firms have become increasingly international in their orientation and operations. In world trade American businesses must compete with the business firms of other nations, including host-country firms. The success or failure of the American firms doing business in foreign countries may well depend on accurate information about the laws and customs of the host countries. In their domestic operations, American business firms compete against imports from other nations of the world. Such imported goods include Japanese automobiles, German steel, French wine, Taiwanese tex-

tiles, and Chilean copper. American business firms should be well aware of the business practices of foreign business firms in order to compete effectively, and also to ascertain if foreign firms are using unfair methods of competition in violation of American antitrust laws, antidumping laws, or international trade agreements.

Individuals from all over the world participate in the U.S. securities markets. Special problems exist in the regulation and enforcement of American securities laws involving financial institutions of countries with secrecy laws.

A. GENERAL PRINCIPLES

Nations enter into treaties and conferences to further international trade. The business world has developed certain forms of organizations for conducting that trade.

§ 5:1 THE LEGAL BACKGROUND

Because of the complexity and ever-changing character of the legal environment of international trade, this section will give consideration to certain underlying elements. Subsequent sections of this chapter will give particular attention to certain problems that are currently of international importance.

(a) WHAT LAW APPLIES. When there is a sale of goods within the United States there is typically one law. Some variation may be introduced when the transaction is between parties in different states but, for the most part, the law governing the transaction is the American law of contracts and the Uniform Commercial Code.[1] In contrast, when an international sale is made, it is necessary to determine whether it is the law of the exporter's state or the law of the importer's state that will govern. The parties to an international contract often resolve that question themselves as part of their contract, setting forth which state's law will govern should a dispute arise. Such agreement language is called a **choice-of-law clause**. As another alternative, the parties to the contract may agree to be bound to arbitrate any contractual dispute that may arise, according to dispute resolution procedures set forth in their contract.

In order to eliminate uncertainty, a number of treaties have been entered into by the major trading countries of the world so that when their citizens deal with each other, their rights and liabilities are determined by looking at the treaty. These treaties are discussed in § 5:2.

(b) CONFLICTING IDEOLOGIES. Law, for all peoples and at all times, is the result of the desire of the lawmaker to achieve certain goals. These are the social forces that make the law. In the eyes of the lawmaker, the attainment of these goals is proper and therefore ethical. This does not mean that we all can agree on what the international law should be, because different peoples have different ideas as to what is right. This affects our views as to ownership, trade, and dealings with foreign merchants. For example, a very large part of the world does not share the American dislike for trusts. Other countries do not have our antitrust laws, and therefore, their merchants can form a trust to create greater bargaining power in dealing with American and other foreign merchants.

Likewise, in a state in which all property is owned by the state, it necessarily follows that international trade with private persons in that state is eliminated.

(c) FINANCING INTERNATIONAL TRADE. There is no international currency. This creates problems as to what currency to use and how to make payment in international transactions. Centuries ago buyers used precious metals, jewels, or furs in payment. Today, the parties to an international transaction agree in their sales contract on the currency to be used to pay for the goods. They commonly require that the buyer furnish a letter of credit. By this, an issuer, typically a bank, agrees to pay the amounts of the drafts drawn against the buyer for the purchase price.[2] In trading with merchants in some countries, the foreign country itself will promise that the seller will be paid.

§ 5:2 INTERNATIONAL TRADE ORGANIZATIONS, CONFERENCES, AND TREATIES

A large number of organizations exist that affect the multinational markets for goods,

---

[1] The UCC is analyzed in Chapters 27 et seq. Contract law is set forth in Chapters 12 et seq.

[2] Orders to pay or drafts are commercial paper and are discussed in Chapter 32 et seq. The agreement of a bank to pay drafts is a letter of credit and is discussed in Chapter 38.

services, and investments. A world view of multinational trade includes the "industrialized world," which generally favors free trade; the "centrally planned world," with its trade often focusing on providing for unplanned shortages or disposing of unplanned surpluses; and the developing countries of the world, sometimes called the **"third world,"** who are not in favor of free trade and seek to use trade to structurally improve their own economies. A survey of major international organizations, conferences, and treaties follows.

(a) GATT. The **General Agreement on Tariffs and Trade (GATT)** is a multilateral treaty, subscribed to by eighty-eight governments, including the United States. These countries, together, account for more than four-fifths of world trade. The basic aim of the GATT is to liberalize world trade and place it on a secure basis, thereby contributing to economic growth and development of the world's peoples. Negotiations are conducted in rounds, like the Tokyo Round that started in 1973 and concluded in 1979. Although the GATT is a long and complicated document, it is based on the fundamental principles of trade without discrimination and protection through tariffs. The principle of trade without discrimination is embodied in its **most-favored nation** clause, which states that trade must be conducted on the basis of nondiscrimination. All contracting parties are bound to grant to each other treatment as favorable as they give to any country in the application and administration of import and export duties and charges. Thus, no country is to give special trading advantages to another: all are to be on an equal basis and share the benefits of any moves toward lower trade barriers. Exceptions to this basic rule are allowed in certain special circumstances involving regional trading arrangements, like the European Economic Community (the Common Market), and special preferences granted to developing countries. The second basic principle is that where protection is given for domestic industry, it should be extended essentially through the tariff, and not through other commercial measures. The aim of this rule is to make the extent of protection clear, and to make competition possible.

(b) CISG. The **United Nations Convention on Contracts for the International Sale of Goods (CISG)**[3] sets forth uniform rules to govern the formation of international sales contracts and the rights and obligations of the buyer and seller. The provisions of this Convention became effective on January 1, 1988, between the United States and the other nations that had approved it.[4] The provisions of the Convention or international agreement have been strongly influenced by Article 2 of the Uniform Commercial Code.

(c) UNCTAD. The **United Nations Conference on Trade and Development (UNCTAD)** represents the interests of the less-developed countries of the world. Its prime objective is the achievement of an international redistribution of income through trade. Through UNCTAD pressure, the developed countries of the world agreed to a system of preferences, with quota limits, for manufactured imports from the developing countries.

(d) EEC. The **European Economic Community (EEC)** was established in 1958 to remove trade and economic barriers between member countries and to unify their economic policies. The EEC's Treaty of Rome contains the governing principles of this regional trading group. This treaty was signed by the original six nations of Belgium, France, West Germany, Italy, Luxembourg, and the Netherlands. Membership in the EEC has expanded by the entry of Denmark, Ireland, Great Britain, Greece, Spain, and Portugal. It also has free trade agreements with other Western European countries such that Western Europe has become an industrial free trade area.

---

[3] 52 Fed. Reg. 6262 (1987).
[4] The contracting nations are currently Argentina, Austria, China, Egypt, Finland, France, Italy, Hungary, Lesotho, Mexico, Sweden, Syria, the United States, Yugoslavia, and Zambia. Ratification proceedings are presently under way in other countries.

(e) COMECON. The **Council of Mutual Economic Cooperation (COMECON)** was formed in 1949 to coordinate trade and other forms of economic relations among the centrally planned economies of Eastern Europe. The council includes the countries of Bulgaria, Czechoslovakia, East Germany, Hungary, Poland, Romania, and the USSR.

(f) REGIONAL TRADING GROUPS OF DEVELOPING COUNTRIES. In recent years numerous trading arrangements between groups of developing countries have been established.

(g) IMF-WORLD BANK. The **International Monetary Fund** (IMF) was created after World War II by a group of nations meeting in Bretton Woods, New Hampshire. The Articles of Agreement of the Fund state that the purpose is to "facilitate the expansion and balanced growth of international trade" and to "shorten the duration and lessen the disequilibrium in the international balance of payments of members." The Fund helps to achieve such purposes by administering a complex lending system through which a country can borrow money from other Fund members or from the Fund by means of **Special Drawing Rights (SDR)** sufficient to permit that country to maintain the stability of its currency's relationship to other world currencies. The Bretton Woods conference after World War II also set up the International Bank for Reconstruction and Development (World Bank) to facilitate the lending of money by capital surplus countries — such as the United States — to countries needing economic help and wanting foreign investments after the War.

(h) OPEC. The **Organization of Petroleum Exporting Countries (OPEC)** is a producer cartel or combination. Its two main goals have been to raise the taxes and royalties earned from crude oil production and to assume control from the major oil companies over production and exploration. Its early success in attaining these goals has led other nations who export raw materials to form similar cartels. For example,

copper- and bauxite-producing nations have formed cartels. More recently, an oversupply of oil combined with decreased demand have reduced the effectiveness of OPEC price structures.

§ 5:3   FORMS OF BUSINESS ORGANIZATIONS

The decision to participate in international business transactions and the extent of that participation depend on the financial position of the individual firm, production and marketing factors, and tax and legal considerations. A number of forms of business organizations exist for doing business abroad.

(a) EXPORT SALES. A direct sale to customers abroad by an American firm, with terms of payment commonly based on an irrevocable letter of credit, is an **export sale.** No foreign presence exists for the American firm in such an arrangement. The export is subject to a tariff by the foreign country, but the firm is not subject to local taxation by that country.

(b) AGENCY ARRANGEMENTS. A United States manufacturer may decide to make a limited entry into international business by appointing an agent to represent it in a foreign market. The agent will receive commission income for sales made on behalf of the U.S. principal. The appointment of a foreign agent, with authority to make contracts for a U.S. firm, commonly constitutes "doing business" in that country, and subjects the U.S. firm to local taxation.

(c) FOREIGN DISTRIBUTORSHIPS. A distributor takes title to goods and bears the financial and commercial risks for the subsequent sale of the goods. The decision to appoint a foreign distributor is often made to avoid a major financial investment by a U.S. firm or to avoid management of a foreign operation with its complicated local business, legal, and labor conditions. Care is required in designing an exclusive distributorship for an EEC country, lest it be in violation of EEC antitrust laws.

(d) LICENSING. American firms may select licensing as a means to do business in other countries. Licensing involves the transfer of technology rights in a product so that it may be produced by a different business organization in a foreign country in exchange for royalties and other payments as agreed. The technology being licensed may fall within the internationally recognized categories of patents, trademarks, and "know-how" (trade secrets and unpatented manufacturing processes outside the public domain). These intellectual property rights, which are legally enforceable, may be licensed separately or incorporated into a single, comprehensive licensing contract. Franchising, which involves granting permission to use a trademark, trade name, or copyright under specified conditions, is a form of licensing that is now very common in international business.

(e) Wholly Owned Subsidiaries. A firm seeking to maintain control and authority over its own operations, including the protection of its own technological expertise, may choose to do business abroad through a wholly owned subsidiary. In Europe the most common choice of foreign business organization, similar to the United States corporate form of business organization, is called the **société anonyme (S.A.)**. In German-speaking countries this form is called **Aktiengesellschaft (A.G.)**.

Corporations doing business in more than one country pose many taxation problems for the governments in the countries in which the firm does business. The United States has established tax treaties with many countries. These treaties grant relief to corporations from double taxation. Credit is normally given to U.S. corporations for taxes paid to foreign governments.

A potential for tax evasion by U.S. corporations exists by their selling goods to their overseas subsidiaries. Corporations may sell goods at less than the fair market value to avoid a U.S. tax on the full profit for such sales. By allowing the foreign subsidiaries located in countries with lower tax rates to make higher profits, the company as a whole would minimize its taxes. Section 482 of the Internal Revenue Code, however, allows the IRS to reallocate the income between the parent and its foreign subsidiary corporation. The parent corporation is insulated from such a reallocation if it can show, based on independent transactions with unrelated parties, that its charges were at arm's length.[5] In the *Du Pont* case, the IRS reallocation of income between the related corporations resulted in a $9 million tax deficiency for the parent corporation. In reading the decision, note the significance of tax considerations in the creation of the subsidiary corporation and its functioning.

---

[5]   United States Steel Corp. v Commissioner (CA2 NY) 617 F2d 942 (1980).

E. I. Du Pont de Nemours & Co. v United States
(US Ct of Cl) 608 F2d 445 (1979)

Early in 1959 Du Pont de Nemours (taxpayer or plaintiff), the American chemical company, created a wholly owned Swiss marketing and sales subsidiary for foreign sales — Du Pont International S.A. (DISA). Most of the Du Pont chemical products marketed abroad were first sold by taxpayer to DISA, which then arranged for resale to the ultimate consumer through independent distributors. The profits on these Du Pont sales were divided for income tax purposes between plaintiff and DISA via the mechanism of the prices plaintiff charged DISA. For 1959 and

1960 the Commissioner of Internal Revenue, acting under Section 482 of the Internal Revenue Code that gives authority to reallocate profits among commonly controlled enterprises, found these divisions of profits economically unrealistic. DISA was found to have been given too great a share. Accordingly, the Commissioner reallocated a substantial part of DISA's income to the taxpayer. This increased the latter's taxes for 1959 and 1960 by considerable sums. Du Pont contends that the prices it charged DISA were valid under the Treasury regulations implementing Section 482. From a judgment in the Commissioner's favor, Du Pont appealed.

DAVIS, J. . . .

I. Design, Objectives and Functioning of DISA

A. Du Pont first considered formation of an international sales subsidiary in 1957.

A decreasing volume of domestic sales, increasing profits on exports, and the recent formation of the Common Market in Europe convinced taxpayer's president of the need for such a subsidiary. . . .

Neither in the planning stage nor in actual operation was DISA a sham entity; nor can it be denied that it was intended to, and did, perform substantial commercial functions which taxpayer legitimately saw as needed in its foreign (primarily European) market. Nevertheless, we think it also undeniable that the tax advantages of such a foreign entity were also an important, though not the primary, consideration in DISA's creation and operation. During the planning stages, plaintiff's internal memoranda were replete with references to tax advantages, particularly in planning prices on Du Pont goods to be sold to the new entity. The tax strategy was simple. If Du Pont sold its goods to the new international subsidiary at prices below fair market value, that company, upon resale of the goods, would recognize the greater part of the total profit (*i.e.*, manufacturing and selling profits). Since this foreign subsidiary could be located in a country where its profits would be taxed at a much lower level than the parent Du Pont would be taxed here, the enterprise as a whole would minimize its taxes. . . .

Consistently with that aim, plaintiff's prices on its intercorporate sales to DISA were deliberately calculated to give the subsidiary the lion's share of the profits. Instead of allowing each individual producing department to value its goods economically and to set a realistic price, Du Pont left pricing on the sales to DISA with the Treasury and Legal Departments. Neither department was competent to set an economic value on goods sold to DISA, and no economic correlation of costs to prices was attempted. Rather, an official of the Treasury Department established a pricing system designed to leave DISA with 75 percent of the total profits. If the goods' cost was greater than DISA's selling price, the department would price the item at its cost *less* DISA's selling expense. This latter provision was designed to insulate DISA from any loss. On the whole, the pricing system was based solely on Treasury and Legal Department estimates of the greatest amount of profits that would be shifted to DISA without evoking IRS intervention. . . . It is not that there was anything "illegal" or immoral in Du Pont's plan; it is simply that that plan made it very difficult, perhaps impossible, to satisfy the controlling Treasury regulations under Section 482.

Section 482 gives the Secretary of the Treasury (or his delegate) discretion to allocate income between related corporations when necessary to "prevent evasion of taxes or clearly to reflect the income" of any of such corporations.

. . .

. . . the court concludes as a matter of law that plaintiff is not entitled to recover. . . .

QUESTIONS

1. Was DISA a sham corporation created for tax evasion purposes?
2. Explain the tax strategy behind the creation of DISA.
3. What is the source of the IRS's authority to reallocate the income of DISA to Du Pont?

(f) JOINT VENTURES. A U.S. manufacturer and a foreign entity may form a joint venture whereby the two firms agree to perform different functions for a common result. The responsibilities and liabilities of such operations are governed by contract. For example, Hughes Aircraft Co. formed a joint venture with two Japanese firms, C. Itoh & Co. and Mitsui, and successfully bid on a telecommunications space satellite system for the Japanese government.

B.   GOVERNMENTAL REGULATION

Nations regulate trade to protect the economic interests of their citizens or to protect themselves in international relations and transactions.

§ 5:4   ANTITRUST

As explained in Chapter 4, antitrust laws exist in the United States to protect the American consumer by assuring the benefits of competitive products from foreign competitors as well as domestic competitors. Competitors' private agreements designed to raise the price of imports or to exclude imports from our domestic markets in exchange for not competing in other countries are restraints of trade in violation of our antitrust laws. The antitrust laws also exist to protect American export and investment opportunities against privately imposed restrictions, whereby a group of competitors seeks to exclude another competitor from a particular foreign market. Antitrust laws also exist in other countries where American firms compete. These laws are usually not directed at breaking up cartels, but rather at regulating them in the national interest.

(a) JURISDICTION. In U.S. courts the U.S. antitrust laws have a broad extraterritorial reach. Our antitrust laws must be reconciled with the rights of other interested countries as embodied in such international law concepts as sovereign immunity and comity.

(1) The Effects Doctrine. Judge Learned Hand's decision in *United States v Alcoa*[6] established the **effects doctrine**. Under this doctrine, U.S. courts will assume jurisdiction and will apply the antitrust laws to conduct outside of the United States where the activity of the business firms outside the United States has a direct and substantial effect on U.S. commerce. This basic rule has been modified to require that the effect on U.S. commerce also be foreseeable.

(2) The "Jurisdictional Rule of Reason."

---

[6]   (CA2 NY) 148 F2d 416 (1945).

The "jurisdictional rule of reason" addresses the problems arising when conduct taking place outside of the United States has the requisite effect on United States commerce, but a foreign state also has a significant interest in regulating the conduct in question. The **"jurisdictional rule of reason"** balances the vital interests, including laws and policies, of the United States with the vital interests of the foreign country involved. This rule of reason is based on the principle of comity. **Comity** is a principle of international law that contemplates that the laws of all nations deserve the respect legitimately demanded by equal participants in international affairs.

(b) DEFENSES. Three defenses are commonly raised to the extraterritorial application of the U.S. antitrust laws. These defenses are also commonly raised to attack jurisdiction in other legal actions involving international law.

(1) Act of State Doctrine. The classic enunciation of the **act of state doctrine** is that:

> Every sovereign state is bound to respect the independence of every other sovereign state, and the courts of one country will not sit in judgment of another government's acts done within its own territory.[7]

The act of state doctrine is based on the judiciary's concern over its possible interference with the conduct of foreign rela-

tions, considering such matters political, not judicial, questions.[8]

(2) The Sovereign Compliance Doctrine. This doctrine allows a defendant to raise as an affirmative defense to an antitrust action the fact that the defendant's actions were compelled by a foreign state.[9] In order to establish this defense, compulsion by the government is required. The Japanese government uses informal and formal contacts within an industry to establish a consensus on a desired course of action. Such governmental action is not a defense for a U.S. firm, however, because the activity in question is not compulsory.

(3) The Sovereign Immunity Doctrine. This doctrine states that a foreign sovereign generally cannot be sued unless an exception to the Foreign Sovereign Immunities Act of 1976 applies.[10] The most important exception covers the commercial conduct of a foreign state.

The *Timberlane* decision discusses the factors considered by a U.S. court in deciding whether or not to take jurisdiction of a case concerning transactions that occurred outside its borders. This case is an example of the "jurisdictional rule of reason" test. The *Timberlane* court also considers a number of defenses to its assuming extraterritorial jurisdiction.

[7] Underhill v Hernandez, 108 US 250, 252 (1897).

[8] First City Bank v Banco National de Cuba, 406 US 759(1972).
[9] Mannington Mills, Inc. v Congoleum Corp. (CA3 Pa) 595 F2d 1287 (1979).
[10] *See* Verlinden B. V. v Central Bank of Nigeria, 461 US 574 (1983).

TIMBERLANE LUMBER CO. V BANK OF AMERICA

(CA9 Cal) 549 F2d 597 (1976)

The Timberlane Lumber Company, an Oregon partnership, brought an antitrust suit alleging violations of Sections 1 and 2 of the Sherman Act against the Bank of America, several employees of the Bank who worked for the Bank in Honduras, and others. Timberlane alleged that the defendants conspired to prevent Timberlane, through Honduras subsidiaries, from milling lumber in Honduras and exporting it to the United States, thus maintaining control of the Honduran lumber business in the hands of individuals financed and controlled by the Bank. The defendants contend that the action must be dismissed because of the act of state doctrine since a Honduran court approved certain of the challenged activities. Defendants also contend that the court lacked jurisdiction because these activities occurred in Honduras, and the court lacked subject matter jurisdiction under the effects doctrine. From a judgment in favor of Bank of America, Timberlane appealed.

CHOY, C. J. . . . The conspiracy sketched by Timberlane actually started before the plaintiffs entered the scene. The Lima family operated a lumber mill in Honduras, competing with Lamas and Casanova, [two Honduras corporations], in both of which the Bank [Bank of America Corporation] had significant financial interests. The Lima enterprise was also indebted to the Bank. By 1971, however, the Lima business was in financial trouble. Timberlane alleges that driving Lima under was the first step in the conspiracy which eventually crippled Timberlane's efforts, . . . [V]arious interests in the Lima assets, including its milling plant, passed to Lima's creditors: Casanova, the Bank, and the group of Lima employees who had not been paid the wages and severance pay due them. Under Honduran law, the employees' claim had priority.

Enter Timberlane, with a long history in the lumber business, in search of alternative sources of lumber for delivery to its distribution system on the East Coast of the United States. After study, it decided to try Honduras. . . . Timberlane became aware that the Lima plant might be available and began negotiating for its acquisition. . . .

Realizing that they were faced with better-financed and more vigorous competition from Timberlane and its Honduran subsidiaries, the defendants and others extended the anti-Lima conspiracy to disrupt Timberlane's efforts. The primary weapons employed by the conspirators were the claim still held by the Bank in the remaining assets of the Lima enterprise under the all-inclusive mortgage Lima had been forced to sign and another claim held by Casanova. Maya made a substantial cash offer for the Bank's interest in an effort to clear its title, but the Bank refused to sell. Instead, the Bank surreptitiously conveyed the mortgage to Casanova for questionable consideration, Casanova paying nothing and agreeing only to pay the Bank a portion of what it collected. Cassanova immediately assigned the Bank's claim and its own on similar terms to Caminals [a citizen of Spain, described as an agent or employee of the Bank], who promptly set out to disrupt the Timberlane operation.

Caminals is characterized as the "front man" in the campaign to drive Timberlane out of Honduras, with the Bank and other defendants intending and carrying responsibility for his actions. Having acquired the claims of Casanova and the Bank, Caminals went to court to enforce them, ignoring throughout Timberlane's offers to purchase or settle them. . . .

As a result of the conspiracy, Timberlane's complaint claimed damages then estimated in excess of $5,000,000. Plaintiffs also allege that there has been a direct and substantial effect on United States foreign commerce, and that defendants intended the results of the conspiracy, including the impact on United States commerce. . . .

The defendants argue — as the district court apparently held — that the injuries allegedly suffered by Timberlane resulted from acts of the Honduran government, principally in connection with the enforcement of the security interests in the Maya plant, which American courts cannot review. Such an application of the act of state doctrine seems to us to be erroneous. Even if the *coup de grace* to Timberlane's enterprise in Honduras was applied by official authorities, we do not agree that the doctrine necessarily shelters these defendants or requires dismissal of the Timberlane action.

The leading modern statement of the act of state doctrine appears in *Banco Nacional de Cuba v Sabbatino*, 376 U.S. 398 (1964). The Court concluded that the doctrine was not compelled by the nature of sovereignty, by international law, or by the text of the Constitution. Rather, it derives from the judiciary's concern for its possible interference with the conduct of foreign affairs by the political branches of the government:

> The doctrine as formulated in past decisions expresses the strong sense of the Judicial Branch that its engagement in the task of passing on the validity of foreign acts of state may hinder rather than further this country's pursuit of goals both for itself and for the community of nations as a whole in the international sphere.

The Court recognized that not every case is identical in its potential impact on our relations with other nations. . . .

A corollary to the act of state doctrine in the foreign trade antitrust field is the often-recognized principle that corporate conduct which is compelled by a foreign sovereign is also protected from antitrust liability, as if it were an act of the state itself. Thus, in *Interamerican Refining Corp. v Texaco Maracaibo, Inc.*, 307 F.Supp. 1291 (D.Del. 1970), a refusal by defendants to sell Venezuelan crude oil to plaintiff was held not to be an illegal restraint of trade because it was a complete defense that the Venezuelan government had imposed a boycott forbidding such sales. The court there observed that "[w]hen a nation compels a trade practice, firms there have no choice but to obey. Acts of business become effectively acts of the sovereign." . . .

On the basis of the foregoing analysis, we conclude that the court below erred in dismissing the instant suit. . . . Timberlane does not seek to name Honduras or any Honduran officer as a defendant or co-conspirator, nor does it challenge Honduran policy or sovereignty in any fashion that appears on its face to hold any threat to relations between Honduras and the United States. . . .

Under these circumstances, it is clear that the "act of state" doctrine does not require dismissal of the Timberlane action.

Extraterritorial Reach of the United States Antitrust Laws

There is no doubt that American antitrust laws extend over some conduct in other nations. . . .

That American law covers some conduct beyond this nation's borders does not mean that it embraces all, however. Extraterritorial application is understandably a matter of concern for the other countries involved. Those nations have sometimes resented and protested, as excessive intrusions into their own spheres, broad assertions of authority by American courts. . . .

It is the effect on American foreign commerce which is usually cited to support extraterritorial jurisdiction. *Alcoa [United States v Alcoa*, 148 F2d 416 (1945)] set the course, when Judge Hand declared,

> [I]t is settled law . . . that any state may impose liabilities, even upon persons not within its allegiance, for conduct outside its borders that has consequences within its borders which the state reprehends; and these liabilities other states will ordinarily recognize.

Despite its description as "settled law," *Alcoa's* assertion has been roundly disputed by many foreign commentators as being in conflict with international law, comity, and good judgment. Nonetheless, American courts have firmly concluded that there is some extraterritorial jurisdiction under the Sherman Act.

Even among American courts and commentators, however, there is no consensus on how far the jurisdiction should extend. The district court here concluded that a "direct and substantial effect" on United States foreign commerce was a prerequisite, without stating whether other factors were relevant or considered. . . .

[But] an effect on United States commerce, although necessary to the exercise of jurisdiction under the antitrust laws, is alone not a sufficient basis on which to determine whether American authority *should* be asserted in a given case as a matter of international comity and fairness.

What we prefer is an evaluation and balancing of the relevant considerations in each case — in the words of Kingman Brewster, a "jurisdictional rule of reason." . . .

The elements to be weighed include the degree of conflict with foreign law or policy, the nationality or allegiance of the parties and the locations or principal places of business of corporations, the extent to which enforcement by either state can be expected to achieve compliance, the relative significance of effects on the United States as compared with those elsewhere, the extent to which there is explicit purpose to harm or affect American commerce, the foreseeability of such effect, and the relative importance to the violations charged of conduct within the United States as compared with conduct abroad. . . .

We conclude, then, that the problem should be approached in three parts: Does the alleged restraint affect, or was it intended to affect, the foreign commerce of the United States? Is it of such a type and magnitude so as to be cognizable as a violation of the Sherman Act? As a matter of international comity and fairness, should the extraterritorial jurisdiction of the United States be asserted to cover it? The district court's judgment found only that the restraint involved in the instant suit did not produce a direct and substantial effect on American foreign commerce. That holding does not satisfy any of these inquiries.

The Sherman Act is not limited to trade restraints which have both a direct and substantial effect on our foreign commerce. Timberlane has alleged that the complained of activities were intended to, and did, affect the export of lumber from Honduras to the United States — the flow of United States foreign commerce, and as such they are within the jurisdiction of the federal courts under the Sherman Act. Moreover, the magnitude of the effect alleged would appear to be sufficient to state a claim.

The comity question is more complicated. From Timberlane's complaint it is evident that there are grounds for concern as to at least a few of the defendants, for some are identified as foreign citizens: Laureano Gutierrez Falls, Michael Casanova and the Casanova firms, of Honduras, and Patrick Byrne, of

Canada. Moreover, it is clear that most of the activity took place in Honduras, though the conspiracy may have been directed from San Francisco, and that the most direct economic effect was probably on Honduras. However, there has been no indication of any conflict with the law or policy of the Honduran government, nor any comprehensive analysis of the relative connections and interests of Honduras and the United States. Under these circumstances, the dismissal by the district court cannot be sustained on jurisdictional grounds.

[Dismissal vacated and action remanded]

QUESTIONS

1. Are the U.S. antitrust laws limited to transactions that take place within its territorial boundaries?
2. Did the act of state doctrine require the dismissal of the plaintiff's claim?
3. What are the relevant considerations to be used to determine whether or not to exercise jurisdiction in extraterritorial application of antitrust laws?

(c) LEGISLATION. In response to business uncertainty as to the applicability of the antitrust laws to international transactions, Congress passed the Foreign Trade Antitrust Improvements Act of 1982. This act, in essence, codified the effects doctrine by requiring a direct, substantial, and reasonably foreseeable effect on U.S. domestic commerce or exports by U.S. residents before business conduct abroad may come within the purview of the U.S. antitrust laws.[11]

(d) FOREIGN ANTITRUST LAWS. Because of the different attitudes of countries towards cartels and business combinations, antitrust laws vary among the countries of the world in content and application. Japan, for example, has stressed consumer protection against such practices as price fixing and false advertising. However, with regards to mergers, corporate interlocking directorates, stock ownership, and agreements among companies to control production, Japanese law is much less restrictive than American law.

Europe is a major market for American products, services, and investments. American firms doing business in Europe are subject to the competition laws of the EEC. The Treaty of Rome uses the term *competition* rather than *antitrust*. Articles 85 and 86 of the Treaty of Rome set forth the basic regulation on business behavior in the EEC.

Article 85 (1) expressly prohibits agreements and concerted practices that:

1. Even indirectly fix prices of purchases or sales, or fix any other trading conditions;
2. Limit or control production, markets, technical development, or investment;
3. Share markets or sources of supply;
4. Apply unequal terms to parties furnishing equivalent considerations, thereby placing them at a competitive disadvantage; or
5. Make a contract's formation turn upon acceptance of certain additional obligations that according to commercial usage, have no connection with the subject of such contracts.

Article 85(3) allows for an individual exemption if the agreement meets certain conditions such as: improves the production or distribution of goods or promotes technical or economic progress, and

---

[11] Public Law 97–290, 96 Stat. 1233, 15 USC 6(a).

reserves to consumers a fair share of the resulting economic benefits.

Article 86 provides that it is unlawful for one or more enterprises, having a dominant market position within at least a substantial part of the Common Market, to take improper advantage of such a position if trade between the member states may be affected thereby.

The *Windsurfing International, Inc.* case is a recent decision on EEC law relating to competition. This case relates to the use of licensing agreements to exclude other manufacturers from the German market and to restrict production of the products to Germany. The matter was heard before the Court of Justice of the European Communities, a court created by the Treaty of Rome to adjudicate controversies involving alleged violations of the EEC rules governing competition.

WINDSURFING INTERNATIONAL V EEC

1986 Com Mkt Rptr ¶ 14,271

Windsurfing International, Inc. (WSI), with home offices in Torrence, California, extended its sailboard operations to Europe and submitted a patent claim in Germany. A sailboard consists of a board and a rig (the rig consists of a mast, a sail, and spars). The sailboard makes it possible to combine the art of surfing with the sport of sailing. WSI's patent application, and the patent itself when later issued, applied only to the rig. Nevertheless, WSI, in its licensing agreements with German companies for the production and sale of the product, imposed conditions on the licensees that extended beyond the German patent protection of the rig. Following complaints from competitors, the Commission concluded that the licensing agreement clauses were intended and had the effect of excluding other sailboard manufacturers from the German market and retaining production in Germany in violation of Article 85(1) of the EEC Treaty. It fined WSI 50,000 ECUs (European Currency Unit, which at the time of the Court of Justice decision in 1986 was equal to 93 cents on one U.S. dollar). WSI disagreed with the findings and the fine, and appealed to the Court of Justice.

BAHLMANN, President of the Fourth Chamber. . . . The scope of the patent of invention granted to Windsurfing International in the Federal Republic of Germany in 1978, following a patent claims procedure begun in 1969, has always been a matter of dispute. It is again in dispute in these proceedings because Windsurfing International argues that the clauses at issue in its licensing agreements are linked to the exercise of its patent rights and must therefore enjoy the protection which the EEC Treaty affords to industrial property rights, while this is denied by the Commission. . . .

The decision whereby the German Patent Office granted the patent on March 31, 1978, indicates that the patent granted is for "a rig for a sailboard" capable of being "used not only for sailboards but also for ice yachts, sand yachts, surfboards, canoes, rowing boats or small sailing boats." It should also be pointed out, first, that the patent decision mentions the existence of other kinds of patented rigs and defines the novelty of the invention as residing in the fact that the rig makes it possible to beat to windward, and, secondly, that the description of the invention refers only to components of the rig. . . .

The clauses contained in the licensing agreements, insofar as they relate to parts of the sailboard not covered by the German patent or include the complete sailboard within their terms of reference, can therefore find no justification on grounds of the protection of an industrial property right.

Appraisal of licensing agreements in light of Article 85(1) of the EEC Treaty

A. *Restriction of competition*

It is therefore necessary to examine whether the clauses referred to in the contested decision were compatible with Article 85(1) of the Treaty. For that purpose it must first be determined whether those clauses had as their object or effect the prevention, restriction or distortion of competition with the Common Market. . . .

[One] clause at issue relates to the obligation on the licensees to sell the components covered by the German patent, and therefore in particular the rigs, only in conjunction with the boards approved by the licensor, or in other words as complete sailboards. . . .

Windsurfing International takes the view that . . . the sale of rigs to unlicensed manufacturers . . . would have enabled unlicensed manufacturers to combine the rigs with their boards, which would have constituted patent infringement. . . .

The Commission observes that the risk of a patent infringement by third parties can in no way justify the prohibition on the sale of rigs, which cannot in itself constitute a patent infringement, particularly in view of the fact that the risk of patent infringements is by no means precluded where licensees sell complete sailboards.

. . . [T]he patent must be regarded as confined to the rig. That being the case, it cannot be accepted that the obligation arbitrarily placed on the licensee to sell the patented product only in conjunction with a product outside the scope of the patent is indispensable to the exploitation of the patent. . . .

[A] clause at issue provides for the obligation on the licensees to restrict production of the licensed product to a specific manufacturing plant in the Federal Republic of Germany, together with Windsurfing International's right to terminate the agreement immediately should the licensees change their production site. . . .

Windsurfing International clearly cannot rely on the specific subject matter of the patent in order to gain the protection afforded by the patent in a country where there is no patent protection. Insofar as Windsurfing International prohibited its licensees from also manufacturing the product in a country where it had no patent protection and so marketing that product without paying a royalty, it limited freedom of competition by means of a clause that had nothing to do with the patent.

That conclusion is not in any way affected by the argument based on Windsurfing International's need to maintain quality controls over the products of its licensees. It should be pointed out that, as has been stated earlier, quality controls are permissible only with regard to the patented product itself and on the basis of objective criteria laid down in advance, and that those conditions are not met here. It should also be noted that a change of production site would not seem to have any great significance for the purposes of quality controls in a situation where, even in the Federal Republic of Germany, the manufacture of components is often farmed out to subcontractors.

Finally, as far as the transfer of production abroad is concerned, no great costs are involved, particularly where production is contracted out.

It must therefore be concluded that the clauses in the agreements prohibiting Windsurfing International's licensees from opting to start production in a Member State other than the Federal Republic of Germany satisfied, as far as their effect on competition was concerned, the conditions laid down in Article 85(1).

B. Obstacle to intra-Community trade

Windsurfing International further argues that even though certain clauses in the licensing agreements may have been of such a nature as to restrict competition, they could not have had any appreciable effect on trade between Member States.

That argument must be rejected. Article 85(1) of the Treaty does not require that each individual clause in an agreement should be capable of affecting intra-Community trade. Community law on competition applies to agreements between undertakings which may affect trade between Member States; only if the agreement as a whole is capable of affecting trade is it necessary to examine which are the clauses of the agreement that have as their object or effect a restriction or distortion of competition.

In a case such as the present one, in which there is no doubt as to the significance of the agreements at issue for trade between Member States, it is therefore unnecessary to examine whether each clause restricting competition, taken in isolation, may affect intra-Community trade. . . .

[The fine is set at ECU 25,000]

Questions

1. Did WSI contend that it was entitled to include the disputed clauses in the German licensing agreements because they were linked to the exercise of the patent rights?
2. Why was it a violation of Article 85(1) for WSI to require a clause restricting production of the WSI licensed product to Germany?
3. Did the Court of Justice agree with WSI that the individual clauses did not have any appreciable effect on trade between member states?

Firms drafting licensing agreements (like Windsurfing International) experienced significant concern that their agreements might be found to be in violation of Article 85(1). The EEC issued a Patent Licensing Regulation effective January 1, 1985, to help provide a clear framework for parties within the EEC in drafting patent licensing agreements so that violations of the Article 85(1) could be avoided. Under the regulation, clauses commonly found in patent license agreements are classified into three groups: (1) the "permitted list," which consists of clauses that may infringe Article 85(1), but are exempted under Article 85(3); (2) the "white list," which includes clauses that do not infringe Article 85(1); and (3) the "black list," which includes those clauses that restrict competition and will prevent granting of an exemption.

§ 5:5 SECURITIES REGULATION IN AN INTERNATIONAL ENVIRONMENT

Illegal conduct in the U.S. securities markets, whether this conduct is initiated in the United States or abroad, threatens the vital economic interests of the United States. Investigation and litigation concerning possible violations of the U.S. securities laws often have extraterritorial effects and may conflict with the laws of foreign countries.

(a) JURISDICTION. U.S. district courts have jurisdiction over violations of the antifraud provisions of the Securities Exchange Act where losses occur from sales to Americans living in the United States. This is true whether or not the actions occurred in this country, and where losses occur to Americans living abroad if the acts occurred in the United States. The antifraud provisions do not apply, however, to losses from sales of securities to foreigners outside the United States unless acts within the United States caused the losses.[12]

(b) IMPACT OF FOREIGN SECRECY LAWS ON SEC ENFORCEMENT. **Secrecy laws** are confidentiality laws applied to home-country banks. These laws prohibit the disclosure of business records or the identity of bank customers. **Blocking laws** prohibit the disclosure, copying, inspection, or removal of documents located in the territory of the enacting country in compliance with orders from foreign authorities. These laws impede, and indeed sometimes foreclose, the SEC's ability to properly police its securities markets.

The *Banca Della Suizzera* case demonstrates how the SEC, in certain circumstances, can obtain discovery from foreign financial institutions despite the existence of secrecy laws.

The SEC is not limited to litigation when a securities law enforcement investigation runs into secrecy or blocking laws. For example, the SEC may rely on the 1977 Treaty of Mutual Assistance in Criminal Matters between the United States and Switzerland.[13] While this treaty has served to deter the use of Swiss secrecy laws to conceal fraud in the U.S., its benefits for securities enforcement have been limited. It applies only where there is a dual criminality, that is, the conduct involved constitutes a criminal offense under the laws of both the United States and Switzerland.

---

[12] Fidenas v Honeywell Bull, S.A. (CA2 NY) 606 F2d 5 (1979).

[13] 27 UST 2021.

SEC v BANCA DELLA SUIZZERA ITALIANA
92 FRD 111 (DC NY 1981)

Banca Della Suizzera Italiana (BSI), a Swiss bank with an office in the United States, purchased certain call options and common stock of St. Joe Minerals Corporation (St. Joe), a New York corporation, immediately prior to the announcement on March 11, 1981 of a cash tender offer by Joseph Seagram & Sons Inc. for all St. Joe common stock at $45 per share. On March 10, 1981, when BSI acted, the stock traded at approximately $30 per share. On March 11, 1981 the stock moved sharply higher in price, and BSI instructed its broker to close out the purchases of the options and sell most of the shares of stock, resulting in an overnight profit of $2 million. The SEC noticed the undue activity in the options market, initiated suit against BSI and obtained a temporary restraining order, freezing the proceeds in BSI's bank account at a New York bank. The SEC, through the Departments of State and Justice, and the Swiss government sought without success to learn the identity of BSI's customers involved in the transactions, believing that the customers had used inside information in violation of the Securities Exchange Act of 1934. The SEC brought a motion to compel disclosure. BSI, a Swiss bank, contended that it might be subject to criminal liability under Swiss penal and banking laws if it disclosed the requested information.

POLLACK, D. J. . . . BSI claims that it may be subject to criminal liability under Swiss penal and banking law if it discloses the requested information. However, this Court finds the factors in § 40 of the Restatement of Foreign Relations* to tip decisively in favor of the SEC. Moreover, it holds BSI to be "in the position of one who deliberately courted legal impediments . . . and who thus cannot now be heard to assert its good faith after this expectation was realized." BSI acted in bad faith. It made deliberate use of Swiss nondisclosure law to evade in a commercial transaction for profit to it, the strictures of American securities law against insider trading. Whether acting solely as an agent or also as a principal (something which can only be clarified through disclosure of the requested information), BSI invaded American securities markets and profited in some measure thereby. It cannot rely on Swiss nondisclosure law to shield this activity.

The first of the § 40 factors is the vital national interest of each of the States. The strength of the United States interest in enforcing its securities laws to ensure the integrity of its financial markets cannot seriously be doubted. That interest is being continually thwarted by the use of foreign bank accounts. Congress, in enacting legislation on bank record-keeping, expressed its concern over the problem over a decade ago. . . .

The Swiss government, on the other hand, though made expressly aware of the litigation, has expressed no opposition. In response to BSI's lawyers' inquiries, the incumbent Swiss Federal Attorney General, Rudolf Gerber, said only that a foreign court could not change the rule that disclosure required the consent of the one who imparted the secret and that BSI might thus be subject to prosecution. The Swiss government did not "confiscate" the Bank records to prevent violations of its law. . . . NEITHER THE UNITED STATES NOR THE SWISS GOVERNMENT has suggested that discovery be halted. . . . The Court of Appeals in *United States v National City Bank*, 396 F2d 897 (2d cir. 1968), found the fact that the governments concerned had not intervened of great importance. It observed that "when foreign governments, including

---

*   § 40 reads as follows:
§ 40. Limitations on Exercise of Enforcement Jurisdiction. Where two states have jurisdiction to prescribe and enforce rules of law and the rules they may prescribe require inconsistent conduct upon the part of a person, each state is required by international law to consider, in good faith, moderating the exercise of its enforcement jurisdiction, in the light of such factors as
(a) vital national interests of each of the states,
(b) the extent and the nature of the hardship that inconsistent enforcement actions would impose upon the person,
(c) the extent to which the required conduct is to take place in the territory of the other state,
(d) the nationality of the person, and
(e) the extent to which enforcement by action of either state can reasonably be expected to achieve compliance with the rule prescribed by that state.

Germany, have considered their vital national interests threatened, they have not hesitated to make known their objections . . . to the issuing court." It is true that BSI may be subject to fines and its officers to imprisonment under Swiss law. However, this Court notes that there is some flexibility in the application of that law. Not only may the particular bank involved obtain waivers from its customers to avoid prosecution, but Article 34 of the Swiss Penal Code contains a "State of Necessity" exception that relieves a person of criminal liability for acts committed to protect one's own good, including one's fortune, from an immediate danger if one is not responsible for the danger and one cannot be expected to give up one's good.

Of course, given BSI's active part in the insider trading transactions alleged here, the Swiss government might well conclude — as this Court has — that BSI is responsible for the conflict it is in and that therefore the "State of Necessity" exception should not apply. However, that is certainly no cause for this Court to withhold its sanctions since the dilemma would be a result of BSI's bad faith. A party's good or bad faith is an important factor to consider, and this Court finds that BSI, which deposited the proceeds of these transactions in an American bank account in its name and which certainly profited in some measure from the challenged activity, undertook such transactions fully expecting to use foreign law to shield it from the reach of our laws. Such "deliberate courting" of foreign legal impediments will not be countenanced.

The last three of the § 40 Restatement of Foreign Relations Law factors — the place of performance, the nationality of the resisting party, and the extent to which enforcement can be expected to achieve compliance with the rule prescribed by that state — appear to be less important in this Circuit. . . .

It would be a travesty of justice to permit a foreign company to invade American markets, violate American laws if they were indeed violated, withdraw profits and resist accountability for itself and its principals for the illegality by claiming their anonymity under foreign law. . . .

[T]his decision shall constitute an order that BSI is directed to complete its answers to all of the demands in the SEC's First Interrogatories, pertaining to St. Joe.

[So ordered]

NOTE: Confronted with the judge's opinion and the possibility of substantial fines, BSI obtained a waiver of the secrecy laws from its customer and produced the requested information.

QUESTIONS

1. What are the dominant factors considered by a court when deciding on whether or not to issue a subpoena or discovery order to a foreign bank in a secrecy jurisdiction?
2. Did the court find that the Swiss interest in bank secrecy outweighed the U.S. interest?
3. Did BSI act in good faith?
4. Did the court give significant weight to BSI's potential liability under Swiss law?

§ 5:6   BARRIERS TO TRADE

A common barrier to the free movement of goods across borders is the tariff barrier. A wide range of nontariff barriers also restricts the free movement of goods, services, and investments. Governmental export controls used as elements of foreign policy have proven to be a major barrier to trade with certain countries.

(a) TARIFF BARRIERS. A **tariff** is an import or export duty or tax placed on goods as they move into or out of a country. Tariffs restrict foreign imports. The tariff raises the total cost and thus the price of the imported product in the domestic market, making the price of the domestically produced product, not subject to the tariff, more advantageous. Under the General Agreement on Tariff and Trade (GATT) seven rounds of negotiations have been pursued since 1948. One goal was the reduction of tariffs by its member nations.

(b) NONTARIFF BARRIERS. Nontariff barriers consist of a wide range of restrictions that inhibit the free movement of goods between countries. An import quota, such as the unilateral or bilateral limitation of the number of automobiles that can be imported from one country to another, is such a barrier. More subtle nontariff barriers exist in all countries. For example, Japan's complex customs procedures resulted in the restriction of the sale of U.S.-made aluminum baseball bats in Japan by requiring the individual uncrating and "destruction testing" of bats at the ports of entry. Government subsidies are also nontariff barriers to

trade. A major objective of the Tokyo Round of the GATT was to produce agreements on limiting the use of nontariff measures.

(c) EXPORT CONTROLS AS INSTRUMENTS OF FOREIGN POLICY. U.S. export controls have been used as instruments of foreign policy in recent years. For example, the United States has sought to deny goods and technology of strategic or military importance to unfriendly nations. The United States has also denied goods such as grain, technology, or machine parts to the Soviet Union to protest or to punish activities it considered violative of human rights or world peace.

The Export Administration Act of 1979[14] is the principal statute imposing export controls on goods and technical data. It empowers the president and the Department of Commerce to implement its directives. The system of export controls is implemented through a complicated licensing procedure designed to ensure that U.S. origin goods do not go to unauthorized locations.

The *Sensor* decision is an example of the international effects of the extraterritorial reach of President Reagan's June 1982 export controls under the Act. The extension of controls to certain foreign companies, owned by American companies, selling parts to be used in the Soviet Union's Siberia-to-Western Europe natural gas pipeline was challenged.

---

[14]   Pub. L. 96–72, 93 Stat 503, 50 USC § § 2401–20.

COMPAGNIE EUROPEENNE DES PETROLES V SENSOR NEDERLAND

District Court AT THE HAGUE, 22 ILM 66 (1983)

Sensor, a Netherlands business organization, wholly owned by Geosource, Inc. of Houston, Texas, made a contract with C.E.P. to deliver 2,400 strings of geophones to Rotterdam by September 20, 1982. The ultimate destination was identified as the U.S.S.R. Thereafter, in June of

> 1982, the president of the United States prohibited the shipment of equipment manufactured in foreign countries under license from U.S. firms. The president had a foreign policy objective of sanctioning the imposition of martial law in Poland. He was acting under regulations issued under the Export Administration Act of 1979. Sensor, in July and August of 1982, notified C.E.P. that as a subsidiary of an American corporation it had to respect the president's embargo. C.E.P. filed suit in district court of the Netherlands asking that Sensor be ordered to deliver the geophones forthwith or pay a fine for each day after October 18, 1982 that Sensor failed to deliver the geophones.

THE PRESIDENT OF THE DISTRICT COURT AT THE HAGUE. . . . Sensor has submitted that it is subject to the Export Administration Regulations and that by virtue of those Regulations it cannot fulfil its obligations towards C.E.P.

Under Section 11 of the Export Administration Act, any infringement of the regulation is punishable by a fine, by a term of imprisonment of up to ten years and by withdrawal of export licenses. . . .

It has been found that the contract between C.E.P. and Sensor is governed by Netherlands law. To what extent, therefore, is it necessary to take into account a measure under U.S. law that operates in restraint of trade?

In answering that question, the first consideration must be that that measure extends to the transaction between C.E.P. and Sensor simply and solely via the jurisdiction rule of [Export Administration Regulations] section (2)(iv).* The object of that rule is manifestly to endow the measure with effects vis-à-vis corporations located outside the United States which conclude contracts outside the United States with non-American corporations.

That is the situation that arises in the present case. What particularly merits attention is the fact that, under international law as commonly interpreted, Sensor Nederland B. V. has Netherlands nationality, having been organized in the Netherlands under Netherlands law and both its registered office and its real centre of administration being located within the Netherlands. In accordance with this interpretation, the Treaty of Friendship, Commerce and Navigation between the Kingdom of the Netherlands and the United States of America of March 27, 1956, provides in Article XXIII, third paragraph:

> Companies constituted under the applicable laws and regulations within the territories of either Party shall be deemed companies thereof and shall have their juridical status recognized within the territories of the other Party.

The circumstance that the trade embargo imposed by the American authorities has been endowed with extra-territorial effects as hereinbefore described raises the question as to whether the jurisdiction rule that brings about such effects is compatible with international law.

---

*   "(2) For the purposes of this § 385.2(c) only, the term "person subject to the jurisdiction of the United States" includes: . . .
"(i) Any person, wherever located, who is a citizen or resident of the United States;
"(ii) Any person actually within the United States;
"(iii) Any corporation organized under the laws of the United States or of any state, territory, possession, or district of the United States; or
"(iv) Any partnership, association, corporation, or other organization, wherever organized or doing business, that is owned or controlled by persons specified in paragraphs (i), (ii), or (iii) of this section."

The starting-point for answering such questions is the universally accepted rule of international law that in general it is not permissible for a State to exercise jurisdiction over acts performed outside its borders. Exceptions to this rule are, however, possible, for instance under the so-called "nationality principle" or the "protection principle." . . .

The American jurisdiction rule would not appear to be justified by the nationality principle in so far as that rule brings within its scope companies of other than U.S. nationality.

The position would be different if, in the first place, the criterion "owned or controlled by persons specified in paragraphs (i), (ii), or (iii) of this section" were intended to be a yardstick for the (U.S.) nationality of the corporation — which is possible — and, moreover, if that criterion were accepted in international law . . . but in general, according to the views held outside the United States, this has to be regarded as in itself dubious, and in the relations between the United States and the Netherlands it is out of the question, having regard to the treaty provision hereinbefore cited. . . . The consequence of this is that the nationality principle offers insufficient basis for the jurisdiction rule here at issue.

Under the protection principle, it is permissible for a State to exercise jurisdiction over acts — wheresoever and by whomsoever performed — that jeopardize the security or creditworthiness of that State or other State interests. Such other State interests do not include the foreign policy interest that the U.S. measure seeks to protect. The protection principle cannot therefore be invoked in support of the validity of the jurisdiction rule here at issue.

It is also of importance to examine whether the acts of exportation covered by the American embargo, in so far as they are performed outside the United States, have direct and illicit effects within the territory of the United States. If that is the case, then those acts can be regarded as having been performed within the United States and on that ground brought within the jurisdiction of the United States under generally accepted rules of international law.

It cannot, however, be seen how the export to Russia of goods not originating in the United States by a non-American exporter could have any direct and illicit effects within the United States. Via this route too, therefore, the jurisdiction rule cannot be brought into compatibility with international law. . . .

Under these circumstances the jurisdiction rule cannot have the consequence that the Netherlands courts will take the American embargo into account. . . .

Under the rules of Netherlands private international law, even where Netherlands law has to be applied to an international contract, as in the present case, the Netherlands courts are nevertheless, under certain circumstances, bound to accord priority over Netherlands law to the application of mandatory provisions of foreign law.

Among the circumstances under which the Netherlands courts are required to accord such priority is the situation in which the contract meets the condition of showing a sufficient nexus with the foreign country concerned. That condition is not fulfilled in the present case.

It follows from the foregoing that Sensor's reliance on the American embargo fails and that the claim, against which no defense other than that hereinbefore discussed has been adduced, must be allowed, Sensor being ordered to pay costs.

[Judgment for plaintiff]

QUESTIONS

1. State the issue before the court.
2. Under what authority did the President impose the trade embargo against the Soviet Union on June 22, 1982?
3. Does the nationality principle of jurisdiction bring the foreign subsidiary of a U.S. corporation within the scope of U.S. regulatory jurisdiction?
4. Discuss whether or not the export controls on goods to be used on the Soviet pipeline would have had a significant adverse economic impact on American industries.

§ 5:7   RELIEF MECHANISMS FOR ECONOMIC INJURY CAUSED BY FOREIGN TRADE

In the dynamic and profitable markets that the United States provides for foreign-produced goods, certain U.S. industries may suffer severe economic injury as a result of foreign competition. American law provides protection against unfair competition from foreigners' goods and provides certain economic relief for U.S. industries, communities, firms, and workers adversely affected by import competition.

(a) ANTIDUMPING LAWS AND EXPORT SUBSIDIES. Selling foreign goods in the United States at less than their fair value is called **dumping** and is prohibited under the Trade Agreement Act of 1979[15]. Proceedings in antidumping cases are conducted by two federal agencies, which separately examine two distinct components. The International Trade Administration (ITA) of the Department of Commerce investigates the matter of whether specified foreign goods are being sold in the U.S. at less than fair value (LTFV). The International Trade Commission (ITC) conducts proceedings to determine if there is an injury to a domestic industry as a result of such sales. Findings of both LTFV sales and injury must be present before remedial

action is taken. Remedial action might include the addition of duties to reflect the difference between the fair value of the goods and the price being charged in the U.S.

A settlement of the matter may be reached through a suspension agreement, whereby prices are revised to completely eliminate any LTFV sales, and other corrective measures are taken.

The 1979 Act also applies to subsidy practices by foreign countries selling subsidized goods in the United States at less than their fair value. Basically, countervailing duties are imposed when (1) the ITA determines that a subsidy from any source is being provided to a class of merchandise imported to the United States, and (2) the ITC determines that a domestic industry is materially injured, threatened with material injury, or that the establishment of an industry is materially injured, threatened with material injury, or that the establishment of an industry in the United States is materially retarded by reason of the subsidized importation. Judicial review of both ITA and ITC decisions is before the Court of International Trade.

(b) RELIEF FROM IMPORT INJURIES. Title II of the Trade Act of 1974[16] provides relief for U.S. industries, communities, firms, and workers when any one or more of them are

---

[15]   Pub. L. 96–39, § 106, 93 Stat 193.

[16]   Pub. L. 93–618, 88 Stat 1978, 19 USC § 2251–2298.

substantially adversely affected by import competition. The Department of Commerce, the Secretary of Labor, and the president have roles in determining eligibility. The relief provided may be import relief, such as the imposition of a duty or quota on the foreign goods. Workers found to be eligible may seek assistance in the form of readjustment allowances, job training, job search allowances, as well as certain unemployment compensation eligibility.

§ 5:8   EXPROPRIATION

A major concern of U.S. businesses that do business abroad is the risk of expropriation of financial assets by a host government. Firms involved in the extraction of natural resources, banking, communications, or defense-related industries are particularly susceptible to nationalization. Multinational corporations commonly have a staff of full-time political scientists and former Foreign Service officers studying the countries relevant to their operations to monitor and calculate risks of expropriation. Takeovers of American-owned businesses by foreign countries may be motivated by a short-term domestic political advantage, or by the desire to demonstrate political clout in world politics. Takeovers may also be motivated by longer-term considerations associated with planned development of the country's economy.

Treaty commitments, or provisions in other international agreements between the United States and the host country, may serve to narrow expropriation uncertainties. Treaties commonly contain provisions whereby property will not be expropriated except for public benefit and with the prompt payment of just compensation.

One practical way to investigate the risk of traumatic investment loss due to foreign expropriation of a firm's property is to purchase insurance through private companies such as Lloyd's of London. Commercial insurance is also available against such risks as host governments' arbitrary recall

of letters of credit and commercial losses due to embargoes.

The Overseas Private Investment Corporation (OPIC) is an agency of the United States under the policy control of the Secretary of State. OPIC supports private investments in less-developed, friendly countries. OPIC offers asset protection insurance against risk of loss to plant and equipment as well as losses of deposits in overseas bank accounts to companies that qualify on the basis of a "substantial U.S. interest" being involved.

§ 5:9   GOVERNMENT-ASSISTED
EXPORT PROGRAMS

Massive U.S. trade deficits and the recognition that U.S. exporters encounter strong competition from foreign, government-assisted enterprises that are aggressively structured to promote the export trade of the foreign country have led the U.S. government to take legislative action to bolster the export performance of U.S. firms.

(a) EXPORT TRADING COMPANY ACT. The Export Trading Company Act of 1982 (ETCA)[17] is designed to stimulate and promote additional U.S. exports by promoting the formation of U.S.-based export trading companies and by allowing banks to invest in these export trading companies. The act also clarified applicable antitrust restrictions and provided a limited exception from antitrust liability through a certificate of review process.

Trading companies exist in many European and East Asian countries. They are primary competitors of U.S. exporters. Japan's export trading companies, or *sogo shosha*, provide comprehensive export services, and may serve as models for U.S. trading companies created under the 1982 Act. For example a *sogo shosha* may participate in the purchase transaction of goods for export. It may then handle the paperwork and documents related to the export transaction. It may obtain insurance

[17]   Pub. L. 97–290, 96 Stat 1233 (1982).

coverage and provide warehousing and transportation services. Through access to or ownership of banks, the *sogo shosha* may extend credit or make loans or loan guarantees to buyers, sellers, and suppliers. It has expertise in marketing research relative to target export markets and expertise in foreign exchange and tariff requirements. By encouraging exporters to form trading companies with banking institutions (banks have been prohibited by law from engaging in commercial as opposed to banking activities), and specifically allowing and encouraging the bank-related firms to perform comprehensive export services, Congress believes that increased export activity will be generated.

(b) FOREIGN SALES CORPORATIONS. The **Foreign Sales Corporation** created by the Foreign Sales Corporation Act of 1984[18] replaces the Domestic International Sales Corporation (DISC) created by the Revenue Act of 1971, in response to complaints from several of the United States' major trading partners. These trading partners viewed certain DISC indefinite tax deferment rules as creating an illegal export subsidy in violation of the GATT.

The 1984 Act provides export incentives for U.S. firms that form Foreign Sales Corporations (FSC), so as to continue export incentives to U.S. firms without violating the GATT. In order to qualify for the tax incentives provided under the 1984 Act, an FSC subsidiary of an American firm must be organized under the laws of a U.S. possession (such as the Virgin Islands, Guam, but not Puerto Rico), or under the laws of an acceptable foreign country, that is, a country with an income tax treaty with the United States containing an exchange-of-information program. The FSC must satisfy certain other organizational requirements in order to be eligible for the tax incentives provided by the law.

(c) UNITED STATES EXPORT-IMPORT BANK (EXIMBANK). **Eximbank** is wholly owned

by the U.S. government. Its primary purpose is to facilitate U.S. exports by making direct loans in the form of dollar credits to foreign importers for the purchase of U.S. goods and services. Payments are then made directly to the U.S. exporter of goods and services. Such loans are made where private financial sources are unwilling to assume the political and economic risks existing in the country in question. Loans are also made by Eximbank to enable U.S. suppliers of goods and services to compete for major foreign contracts with foreign firms that have government-subsidized export financing.

(d) OTHER PROGRAMS. As stated previously, OPIC provides expropriation insurance for U.S. private investments in friendly, less-developed countries. The Commodity Credit Corporation (CCC) provides financing for agricultural exports. Also, the Small Business Administration has an export loan program.

§ 5:10 THE FOREIGN CORRUPT PRACTICES ACT

Legal restrictions on U.S. firms doing business abroad exist in connection with payments made to foreign government officials in the procurement of business from foreign governments. Passage of the Foreign Corrupt Practices Act of 1977[19] resulted from the bribery scandals connected to the Lockheed Aircraft Company's procurement of foreign government contracts. The act requires strict accounting standards and internal control procedures to prevent the hiding of improper payments to foreign officials. The act prohibits the offer, payment, or gift to foreign officials, or third parties who might have influence with foreign officials, to influence a decision on behalf of the firm making the payment. It provides for sanctions against the company of up to $1 million, and for fines and imprisonment for the employees in-

---

[18] Title VIII of the Tax Reform Act of 1984, Pub L 98–369, 98 Stat 678. See IRC § § 921 through 927.

[19] Pub. L. 95–213, 94 Stat 1494.

volved. The act does not apply, however, to payments to low-level officials to expedite performance of routine government services.

SUMMARY

In order to understand the international legal environment in which American firms do business, information on certain international trade treaties and organizations is necessary. The General Agreement on Tariffs and Trade, a multilateral treaty subscribed to by the United States and most of the industrialized countries of the world, is based on the principle of trade without discrimination. The United Nations Convention on Contracts for the International Sale of Goods, influenced by UCC Article 2, provides uniform rules for international sales contracts between parties in contracting nations. The European Economic Community is a regional trading group that includes most of Western Europe, making the area an industrial free-trade zone for its member countries and certain other developing countries. COMECON is a regional trading group of Eastern European countries and USSR.

American firms may choose to do business abroad by making export sales or contracting with a foreign distributor to take title to their goods and sell them abroad. Such methods generally do not result in foreign presence by the U.S. firms. American firms may also license their technology or trademarks for foreign use. An agency arrangement, or the organization of a foreign subsidiary, may be required to effectively participate in foreign markets. This results in foreign presence for the U.S. firm, subjecting the firm to taxation in the host country. However, tax treaties commonly resolve the matter of double taxation.

In choosing the form for doing business abroad, U.S. firms must be careful not to violate the antitrust laws of host countries. Anticompetitive foreign transactions may have an adverse impact on competition in U.S. domestic markets. U.S. antitrust laws have a broad extraterritorial reach. The U.S. courts apply a "jurisdictional rule of reason" weighing the interests of the United States with the interests of the foreign country involved in making a decision on whether or not to hear the case. Illegal conduct may occur in the U.S. securities markets, which are used by citizens of most nations of the world; and it is in no nation's interest to interfere with enforcement efforts to preserve the integrity of these markets. However, U.S. enforcement efforts run into foreign countries' secrecy and blocking laws that hinder effective enforcement.

Tariff and nontariff barriers exist to free trade. Additionally, the United States has used export controls as an instrument of foreign policy.

Relief exists for domestic firms threatened by unfair foreign competition through antidumping laws. Also, economic programs exist to assist industries, communities, and workers injured by import competition. Programs also exist to bolster the export performance of U.S. firms.

QUESTIONS AND CASE PROBLEMS

1. What social forces are affected by the extraterritorial application of U.S. antitrust laws?
2. How does the most favored nation clause of the GATT work to foster the principle of trade without discrimination?
3. How does the selling of subsidized foreign

goods in the United States adversely affect free trade?

4. Under an exclusive distributorship agreement made between Grundig, a German manufacturer of radios and televisions, and Consten, a distributor, Consten was appointed exclusive distributor in France of Grundig products. Consten agreed not to deliver any Grundig products directly or indirectly outside France. Grundig undertook not to deliver to anyone in France except Consten and, in addition, imposed restrictions upon its distributors in each of the member states of the EEC not to export to France. The commission contends that the distributor agreement that prevented other firms from importing Grundig products into France and prohibited Consten from reexporting such products to other countries violated Article 85, paragraph 1 of the Treaty of Rome. Consten and Grundig state that they are not competitors subject to Article 85(1) and their relationship did not impair trade. Decide. [Grundig v EEC, 1966 ECR 229]

5. Mirage Investments Corporation (MIC) planned a tender offer for the shares of Gulf States International Corp. (GSIC). Archer, an officer of MIC, placed purchase orders for GSIC stock through the New York office of the Bahamian Bank (BB) prior to the announcement of the tender offer, making a $300,000 profit when the tender offer was made public. The Bahamas is a secrecy jurisdiction; the bank informs the SEC that under its law it cannot disclose the name of the person for whom it purchased the stock. What, if anything, may the SEC do to discover whether or not the federal securities laws have been violated?

6. National Dynamics Corp. (ND), a large defense contractor, has been selected by the oil-rich African nation of Nirombia to build and deliver twenty ND-21 jet fighter planes at an average price of $16 million per plane. N.D.'s back orders are small, and it needs the contract to avoid layoffs of many hundreds of workers. At a meeting held in Nirombia to finalize the contract, the Prime Minister made it very clear to ND's senior representative that a .025 percent of the contract price "finder's fee" would be required to be deposited in his brother-in-law's account in Switzerland in order to finalize the contract. He pointed out that the contract was being made in Nirombia where American law did not apply. He stated that such a payment was an ordinary business custom in his country and on the African continent; and said such payment was offered by ND's European competitor if the contract were awarded to it. The Prime Minister laughed, saying "The percentage is so small you can consider it an entertainment expense if you want to." Advise National Dynamics.

7. Six major oil companies, four based in the United States and two in Western Europe, operate oil concessions in an African country. Five of these producers, concerned about the stability of their operations in this African country and seeking leverage in their dealings with that country, form a joint venture called Petro Supply Corp., incorporated in the Bahamas. The purpose of the joint venture is to arrange back-up commitments from other African sources of scarce low-sulphur oil, required by environmental standards in the United States and Europe. They agree to pool such oil on a pro-rata basis among the participants. The three American firms (A, B, and C) and the two European firms (D, in which the British government owns 50 percent of the stock, and E, in which the French government owns 50 percent of the stock) agree that the fourth American firm, Mesquite Petroleum of San Angelo, Texas, not be included in the joint venture because of its cutthroat pricing tactics in both the United States and Europe and the reckless takeover ventures of the corporate chairman. The U.S. Justice Department contends in a court action that the joint venture is a violation of the Sherman Act. The joint venture contends that the U.S. court has no jurisdiction over a Bahamian corporation seeking oil supplies outside of the United States; it contends that the ownership by the British and French governments entitles the venture to sovereign immunity; and it contends that a joint venture to share the large and unusual risks involved in producing low-sulphur oil in the African nation is a justifiable business reason for the joint venture. Decide.

8. Assume that prior to the formation of the European Economic Community the lowest cost source of supply for a certain product consumed in France was the United States. Explain the basis by which, after the EEC was formed, higher cost German producers

could have assumed the position formerly held by the U.S. sources of supply.

9. Brannan filed suit in a Texas state court alleging that he was the owner of two ranches in Mexico that had been expropriated by the Mexican government without payment to him. Mexico contended that Brannan's petition was barred by the doctrine of sovereign immunity. Brannan disagreed. Decide. [United Mexican States v Ashley (Sup Ct Tx) 556 SW2d 784]

10. Timken Roller Bearing Co. of Ohio (American Timken) owns 30 percent of the outstanding shares of British Timken, a foreign competitor. In 1928 American Timken and British Timken organized French Timken, and since that date have together owned all the stock of the French Company. Since 1928 American Timken, British Timken, and French Timken have continuously kept operative "business agreements" regulating the manufacture and sale of antifriction bearings by the three companies and providing for the use by the British and French corporations of the trademark "Timken." Under these agreements the contracting parties have (1) allocated trade territories among themselves; (2) fixed prices on products of one of the parties sold in the territory of the others; and (3) cooperated to protect each other's markets and to eliminate outside competition. The United States Department of Justice contends that American Timken has violated Sections 1 and 3 of the Sherman Act. American Timken contends that its actions were legal, since it was entitled to enter a joint venture with British Timken to form French Timken, and was legally entitled to license the trademark "Timken" to the British and French companies. Decide. [Timken Roller Bearing Co. v United States, 341 US 593]

11. Roland Staemphfli was employed as the chief financial officer of Honeywell Bull S.A. (HB), a Swiss computer company operating exclusively in Switzerland. Staemphfli purportedly arranged financing for HB in Switzerland through the issuance of promissory notes for DM 7,500,000. He had the assistance of Fidenas, a Bahamian company dealing in commercial paper. Unknown to Fidenas the HB notes were fraudulent, having been prepared and forged by Staemphfli, who lost all of the proceeds in a speculative investment. Staemphfli was convicted of criminal fraud. HB denied responsibility for the fraudulently issued notes when they came due. Fidenas' business deteriorated because of its involvement with the HB notes. It sued HB and others in the United States for violations of the U.S. securities laws. HB defended that the U.S. court did not have jurisdiction over the transactions in question. Decide. [Fidenas v Honeywell Bull, S.A. (CA2 NY) 606 F2d 5]

12. Marc Rich & Co., A.G., a Swiss commodities trading corporation, refused to comply with a grand jury subpoena requesting certain business records maintained in Switzerland relating to crude oil transactions and possible violations of U.S. income tax laws. Marc Rich contends that a U.S. court has no authority to require a foreign corporation to deliver to a U.S. court documents located abroad. The court disagreed and imposed fines, froze assets, and threatened to close a Marc Rich wholly owned subsidiary that does business in the state of New York. The fines amounted to $50,000 for each day the company failed to comply with the court's order. Marc Rich appeals the judge's decision. Decide. [Marc Rich v U.S. (CA2 NY) 707 F2d 633]

13. The United States Steel Corporation formed Orinoco Mining Company, a wholly owned corporation, to mine large deposits of iron ore that U.S. Steel had discovered in Venezuela. Orinoco, which was incorporated in Delaware, was subject to Venezuela's maximum tax of 50 percent on net income. Orinoco was also subject to U.S. income tax, but the U.S. foreign tax credit offset this amount. U.S. Steel Corp. purchased the ore from Orinoco in Venezuela. U.S. Steel formed Navios, Inc., a wholly owned subsidiary, to transport the ore for it. Navios, a Liberian corporation, was subject to a 2.5 percent Venezuelan excise tax and was exempt from U.S. income taxes. Although U.S. Steel was Navios' primary customer, it charged other customers the same price it charged U.S. Steel. U.S. Steel's investment in Navios was $50,000. In seven years Navios accumulated nearly $80 million in cash, but had not paid any dividends to U.S. Steel. The IRS used Internal Revenue Code Section 482 to allocate $52 million of Navios'

income to U.S. Steel, and U.S. Steel challenged this action, contending its charges to U.S. Steel were at arm's length and the same it charged other customers. Decide. [United States Steel Corp. v Commissioner (CA2 NY) 617 F2d 942]

14. On May 9, 1986 the Florida Citrus Mutual, which represents the U.S. concentrated orange juice industry, filed a petition with the ITA contending that Brazilian shipments of concentrated orange juice were selling at less than fair value (LTFV) and that increasing production and stock levels of the product in Brazil were undercutting the U.S. industry. The ITA required the importers to furnish necessary financial information to ascertain if the products were being sold at LTFV, and thereafter ruled that the juice was being sold at LTFV. On April 13, 1987 the ITC concluded that the imported products were injuring or threatening to injure the U.S. industry. The importers contend that they have paid the significant shipping costs and all import duties and, in our free trade economy, they must be allowed to sell their products at any price they deem appropriate even if it should turn out to be less than the fair value of the product. Decide. [Florida Citrus Mutual v. Citrosuco Paulista S.A. 4 ITR 519]

6

ADMINISTRATIVE AGENCIES

In Chapter 4, we discussed the ability of governments — federal, state, and local — to regulate many aspects of business. Early in this country's history all of this regulation was accomplished through direct application of the powers of the legislative, executive, and judicial branches of government. However, the pace of advancing technology began to outstrip this cumbersome tripartite government's ability to keep up with it. A new type of governmental structure, designed to be able to specialize in a particular field, began to emerge — the administrative agency.

A. NATURE OF THE ADMINISTRATIVE AGENCY

An **administrative agency** is a governmental body charged with administering and implementing legislation. An agency may be a department, independent establishment, commission, administration, authority, board, or bureau. Agencies exist on the federal and state levels.

§ 6:1   THE IMPORTANCE OF THE ADMINISTRATIVE AGENCY

In this new age of complex regulation, most people and businesses do not come into direct contact with the constitutional branches of government. Typically they deal with an administrative agency. To them, an agency is the government.

Large areas of the American economy are governed by federal administrative agencies created to carry out the general policies specified by Congress. A contract must be in harmony with the law declared by Congress and the courts and also with the regulations and decisions of the appropriate administrative agency. For example, a contract to market particular goods might not be prohibited by any statute or court decision, but it may still be condemned by the Federal Trade Commission as an unfair method of competition. A contract not in harmony with the guidelines of a specific commission, such as a contract of a carrier charging a higher or a lower rate than that approved by the Interstate Commerce Commission, is illegal. Other federal administrative agencies include the Federal Communications Commission, the Federal Maritime Commission, the Federal Power Commission, the National Labor Relations Board, and the Securities and Exchange Commission. The law governing these agencies is known as **administrative law**.

State administrative agencies may also affect business and the citizen, because state agencies may have jurisdiction over fair employment practices, workers' compensation claims, and the renting of homes and apartments.

§ 6:2   UNIQUENESS OF ADMINISTRATIVE AGENCIES

Federal and state governments alike are divided into three branches — executive, legislative, and judicial. Many of the offices in these branches are filled by persons who are elected. The judicial branch acts as a superguardian to prevent the executive and the legislative branches from exceeding the proper spheres of their power. In contrast to the situation in the tripartite structure, members of administrative agencies are ordinarily appointed (in the case of federal agencies, by the president of the United States with the consent of the Senate). The major agencies combine legislative, executive, and judicial powers; they may make the rules, police the community to see that the rules are obeyed, and sit in judgment to determine whether there have been violations of their rules.

In the *Withrow* case the challenge was made that it was unfair to have the same body both investigate and then decide the case.

WITHROW V LARKIN
421 US 35 (1975)

Doctors must obtain a license from the state in which they practice. These licenses are ordinarily issued by a licensing board that reviews the qualifications of each applicant. In addition, the statutes creating these licensing boards ordinarily give them the power to revoke a license when there is good reason to do so. The Wisconsin statute authorized the medical licensing board to investigate any case to see if there was cause for revoking a license. If it thought that the circumstances appeared sufficiently bad, the same board could then hold a hearing to see what should be done.

Duane Larkin was a doctor licensed under the laws of Wisconsin. The state medical licensing board conducted an investigation of Larkin. The board concluded that it should hold a hearing to determine whether Larkin's license should be suspended. Larkin claimed that his constitutional rights would be violated if the same body that had investigated the case against him would also act as judge to determine whether his license should be suspended. He brought a lawsuit against Harold Withrow and the other members of the licensing board to enjoin them from holding the hearing. An injunction was granted and Withrow and the other members of the board appealed.

WHITE, J. . . . Concededly, a "fair trial in a fair tribunal is a basic requirement of due process." *In re Murchison*, 349 US 133 . . . (1955) . . .

The contention that the combination of investigative and adjudicative functions necessarily creates an unconstitutional risk of bias in administrative adjudication has a . . . difficult burden of persuasion to carry. It must overcome a presumption of honesty and integrity in those serving as adjudicators: and it must convince that, under a realistic appraisal of psychological tendencies and human weakness, conferring investigative and adjudicative powers on the same individuals poses such a risk of actual bias or prejudgment that the practice must be forbidden if the guarantee of due process is to be adequately implemented.

Very similar claims have been squarely rejected in prior decisions of this Court. . . . *FTC v Cement Institute*, 333 US 683 (1948) . . .

More recently we have sustained against due process objection a system in which a [s]ocial [s]ecurity examiner has responsibility for developing the facts and making a decision as to disability claims, and observed that the challenge to this combination of functions "assumes too much and would bring down too many procedures designed, and working well, for a government structure of great and growing complexity." . . .

That is not to say that there is nothing to the argument that those who have investigated should not then adjudicate. The issue is substantial, it is not new, and legislators and others concerned with the operations of administrative agencies have given much attention to whether and to what extent distinctive administrative functions should be performed by the same persons. No single answer has been reached. Indeed, the growth, variety, and complexity of the administrative processes have made any one solution highly unlikely. Within the Federal Government itself, Congress has addressed the issue in several different ways, providing for varying degrees of separation from complete separation of functions to virtually none at all. For the generality of agencies, Congress has been content with § 5 of the Administrative Procedure Act, 5 USC § 554(d), which provides that no employee engaged in investigating or prosecuting may also participate or advise in the adjudicating function, but which also expressly exempts from this prohibition "the agency or a member or members of the body comprising the agency."

. . . The case law, both federal and state, generally rejects the idea that the combination [of] judging [and] investigating functions is a denial of due process. . . ." Similarly, our cases . . . offer no support for the bald proposition applied in this case by the District Court that agency members who participate in an investigation are disqualified from adjudicating. . . .

When the Board instituted its investigative procedures, it stated only that it would investigate whether proscribed conduct had occurred. Later in noticing the adversary hearing, it asserted only that it would determine if violations had been committed which would warrant suspension of appellee's license. Without doubt, the Board then anticipated that the proceeding would eventuate in an adjudication of the issue; but there was no more evidence of bias or the risk of bias or prejudgment than inhered in the very fact that the Board had investigated and would now adjudicate. Of course, we should be alert to the possibilities of bias that may lurk in the way particular procedures actually work in practice. The processes utilized by the Board, however, do not in themselves contain an unacceptable risk of bias. The investigative proceeding had been closed to the public, but appellee and his counsel were permitted to be present throughout; counsel actually attended the hearings and knew the facts presented to the Board. No specific foundation has been presented for suspecting that the Board had been prejudiced by its investigation or would be disabled from hearing and deciding on the basis of the evidence to be presented at the contested hearing. The mere exposure to evidence presented in nonadversary investigative procedures is insufficient in itself to impugn the fairness of the board members at a later adversary hearing. Without a showing to the contrary, state administrators, "are assumed to be men of conscience and intellectual discipline, capable of judging a particular controversy fairly on the basis of its own circumstances." *United States v Morgan*, 313 US 409, . . . (1941).

We are of the view, therefore, that the District Court was in error when it entered the restraining order against the Board's contested hearing and when it granted the preliminary injunction based on the untenable view that it would be unconstitutional for the Board to suspend appellee's license "at its own contested hearing on charges evolving from its own investigation. . . ."

[Judgment reversed]

QUESTIONS

1. Who objected to the combining of the functions of investigating and adjudicating?
2. What is the practical basis for this objection?
3. How does the decision in the *Withrow* case compare with the theory of American government?

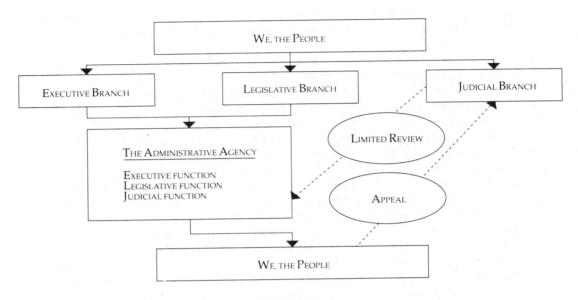

FIGURE 6-1
THE ADMINISTRATIVE CHAIN OF COMMAND

§ 6:3   AGENCY POWERS

An agency has only such powers as have been granted by the statute creating the agency.[1] However, as the technology and the economy have become more complicated, the powers given to agencies have broadened. The modern agency typically possesses legislative, executive, and judicial powers.

In order to meet the objection that the exercise of executive, legislative, and judicial powers by the same body is a potential threat to impartiality, some steps have been taken toward decentralizing the administrative functions. Thus, the prosecutorial power of the National Labor Relations Board was withdrawn from the board and entrusted to an independent General Counsel by the Labor-Management Relations Act of 1947. In a number of agencies, such as the Federal Trade Commission, the judicial function is assigned to administrative law judges.

§ 6:4   RIGHT TO KNOW

In order to avoid the evils of secret government, provision is made for public knowledge of the activity of administrative agencies. This is done through (a) open records, (b) open meetings, and (c) public announcement of agency guidelines. The more recently adopted statutes creating new agencies typically contain provisions regulating these matters. For most federal agencies not otherwise regulated, these matters are controlled by the Administrative Procedure Act (APA). A number of states have adopted statutes that copy the provisions of the APA.

(a) OPEN RECORDS. The Freedom of Information Act[2] provides that information contained in records of federal administrative agencies shall be made available upon proper request. Numerous exceptions to this right are made in order to prevent persons from obtaining information that is not necessary to their legitimate interests. The

---

[1]   Association for Retarded Citizens v Department of Developmental Services, 38 Cal 3d 384, 211 Cal Rptr 758, 696 P2d 150 (1985).

[2]   Added to the APA by Act of December 31, 1974, PL 93-579, 88 Stat 1897, as amended, 5 USC §§ 552 et seq.

state statutes typically exempt from disclosure information that would constitute an invasion of the privacy of others. However, freedom of information acts are broadly construed, and unless an exemption of particular papers is clearly given, the papers in question are subject to public inspection.[3]

(b) OPEN MEETINGS. The government, via the Sunshine Act of 1976, requires most of the meetings of the major administrative agencies to be open to the public.[4] The object of this statute is to enable the public to know what is being done and to prevent administrative misconduct by making an agency aware that the public is watching. The term *meeting*, as used in these statutes, is liberally construed so that it does not matter whether a particular governmental unit is meeting alone or is discussing matters with an outsider, such as a consultant or a real estate developer.

(c) PUBLIC ANNOUNCEMENT OF AGENCY GUIDELINES. In order to inform the public of the way in which administrative agencies operate, the APA, with certain exceptions, requires that each federal agency publish in the *Federal Register* a statement of the rules, principles, and procedures followed by the agency.[5]

B. LEGISLATIVE POWER OF AN AGENCY

An administrative agency has power to make laws that regulate a particular segment of life or industry.

§ 6:5   AN AGENCY'S REGULATIONS AS LAW

An agency may adopt regulations within the scope of its authority. If the regulation is not authorized by the law creating the agency, the regulation is invalid.[6]

There once was a great reluctance to accept the fact that agencies made law because of our constitutional doctrine that only the lawmaker, namely, the Congress or the state legislature, can make laws. It therefore seemed an improper transfer, or delegation, of power for the lawmaker to set up a separate body or agency and give it the power to make the laws.

The same forces that initially led society to create the administrative agencies caused society to clothe them with the power to make the laws. Practical expediency gradually prevailed in favor of the conclusion that if an agency should do a job, the agency must have sufficient power to do it.

In the early days of administrative regulation, the legislative character of the administrative rules was not clearly perceived. An agency's sphere of power was so narrow that the agency was, in effect, merely a thermostat. That is, the lawmaker told the agency when to do what, and all that the agency did was to act in the manner specified by such direction. For example, the cattle inspector was told to take certain steps when it was determined that cattle had hoof-and-mouth disease. Here it was clear that the lawmaker had set the standard, and the agency authority merely swung into action when the specified situation existed.

The next step in the growth of the administrative power was to authorize the cattle inspector to act upon the discovery of a contagious cattle disease. Thus, the inspector had to formulate a rule or guide as to which diseases were contagious. Here again, the discretionary and the legislative aspects of the agency's conduct were obscured by the belief that the field of science would define *contagious*, leaving no area of discretionary decision to the agency.

Today's health commission, an agency,

---

[3] Legislative Joint Auditing Committee v Woosley, 291 Ark 89, 722 SW2d 581 (1987).
[4] PL 94-409, 90 Stat 1241, 5 USC § 552.
[5] APA codified to 5 USC § 552, Act of September 13, 1976, PL 94-409, 90 Stat 1247. See § 6:7 for a description of the Federal Register.

[6] Bowen v American Hospital Ass'n, ___ US ___, 90 L Ed 2d 584 (1986).

is authorized to make such rules and regulations for the protection or improvement of the common health as it deems desirable. Its rules thus make up the health law. In regulating various economic aspects of national life, the agency is truly the lawmaker.

Gradually, the courts have come to recognize the authority of an agency, even though the lawmaker creating the agency did nothing more than state the goal or objective to be attained by the agency. Some courts still speak in terms of requiring a standard but then state that the fact that the standard is not precise has no significance when the standard is as precise as possible.[7]

It has been sufficient for a legislature to authorize an agency to grant licenses "as public interest, convenience, or necessity requires;" "to prohibit unfair methods of competition;" to regulate prices so that they, "in [the agency's] judgment, will be generally fair and equitable;" to prevent "profiteering;" "to prevent the existence of intercorporate holdings, which unduly or unnecessarily complicate the structure [or] unfairly or inequitably distribute voting power among security holders;" and to renegotiate government contracts to prevent "excessive profits."

The authority of an agency is not limited to the technology existing when the agency was created. To the contrary, the sphere in which an agency may act expands with new scientific developments. So it has been held that although community cable television (CATV) was developed after the Federal Communication Commission was created by the Federal Communications Act of 1934, the commission can regulate CATV. This power to regulate includes both the mechanical aspects of broadcasting and reception and also the content of the broadcast. Thus, the commission may require such systems to originate local programs (cablecasting) in order to serve the

local communities, in addition to their activity of transmitting programs from a distance.[8]

When the matter is a question of policy not specifically addressed by statute, the agency given the discretion to administer the statute may establish new policies covering such issues. This power is granted whether the lawmaker had intentionally left such matters to the discretion of the agency or had merely never foreseen the problem. In either case, the matter is one to be determined within the discretion of the agency, and a court will not review a policy decision that has been made by the agency.[9]

§ 6:6   PUBLIC PARTICIPATION IN ADOPTION OF REGULATIONS

In some instances, nongovernmental bodies or persons play a part in furnishing information or opinions that may ultimately affect the adoption of a rule by an agency. This pattern of public participation may be illustrated by the Federal Trade Commission practice, begun in 1919, of calling together members of each significant industry so that the members can discuss which trade practices are fair and which are not. The conclusions of these conferences are not automatically binding on the Federal Trade Commission. They do, however, serve as a valuable means of bringing to the commission detailed information regarding the conduct of the particular industry or business in question. Under the Federal Trade Commission practice, the rules of fair practice agreed to at a trade

---

[7]   Fort Gratiot Charter Township v Kettlewell, 150 Mich App 648, 389 NW2d 468 (1986).

[8]   United States v Midwest Video Corp. 406 US 649 (1972) (sustaining a Commission regulation that provided that "no CATV system having 3,500 or more subscribers shall carry the signal of any television broadcast station unless the system also operates to a significant extent as a local outlet by cablecasting and has available facilities for local production and presentation of programs other than automated services.")

[9]   Chevron, U.S.A., Inc. v National Resources Defense Council, Inc. 467 US 837 (1984).

conference may be approved or disapproved by the commission. When the rules are approved, a further distinction is made between those rules that are "affirmatively approved" by the commission and those that are merely "accepted as expressions of the trade." In the case of the former, the commission will enforce compliance by the members of the industry. In the case of the latter, the commission will accept the practices as fair trade practices but will not enforce compliance by persons not willing to comply. This technique of industry participation has recently been followed by several other major federal administrative agencies. In addition, the APA, with certain exceptions, requires that a federal agency planning to adopt a new regulation must give public notice of such intent. The agency must then hold a hearing at which members of the public may be present to express their views and make suggestions.[10]

§ 6:7   PUBLIC KNOWLEDGE OF REGULATIONS

When an agency adopts a regulation, a practical problem arises as to how to inform the public of its existence. Some regulations will have already attracted such public attention that the news media will give the desired publicity. The great mass of regulations, however, do not attract this attention. In order to provide publicity for all regulations, the Federal Register Act provides that an administrative regulation is not binding until it is printed in the *Federal Register*. This is a government publication, published five days a week, that lists all administrative regulations, all presidential proclamations and executive orders, and such other documents and classes of documents as the president or Congress may direct.

The Federal Register Act provides that the printing of an administrative regula-

tion in the *Federal Register* is sufficient to give notice of the contents of the regulation to any person subject thereto or affected thereby. This means that no one can claim ignorance of the published regulation as an excuse. This is so, even though the person in fact did not know that the regulation had been published in the *Register*.

C.   EXECUTIVE POWER OF THE AGENCY

The modern administrative agency has the power to execute the law and to bring proceedings against violators.

§ 6:8   EXECUTION OF THE LAW

The power of an agency to execute the law is, of course, confined to matters within an agency's jurisdiction. Within that sphere, an agency typically has the power to investigate, to require persons to appear as witnesses, to require witnesses to produce relevant papers and records, and to bring proceedings against violators of the law. In this connection, the phrase *the law* embraces regulations adopted by an agency as well as statutes and court decisions. Increasingly, agencies are required to file opinions and reports or to give explanations for their actions.

An agency may investigate in order to see if there is any violation of the law or of its rules generally, to determine whether there is need for the adoption of additional rules, to ascertain the facts with respect to a particular suspected or alleged violation, and to determine whether its decisions are being obeyed.

The federal Antitrust Civil Process Act is an example of the extent to which administrative investigation is authorized. The act authorizes the attorney general or the assistant attorney general in charge of the Antitrust Division of the Department of Justice to make a civil investigative demand (CID) upon any person believed to

---

[10]   APA codified to 5 USC §§ 553, 556, by Act of September 6, 1966 PL 89-554, 80 Stat 383, as amended.

have knowledge relevant to any civil anti-trust investigation. This might be in connection with an investigation before bringing a suit to enjoin a monopolistic practice or an investigation made upon receiving a premerger notification. The person so notified can be compelled to produce relevant documents, furnish written answers to written questions, or appear in person and give oral testimony.[11] Similar power to require the production of papers is possessed by the Federal Trade Commission, the Federal Maritime Commission, the National Science Foundation, the Treasury Department, the Department of Agriculture, the Department of the Army, the Department of Labor, and the Veterans Administration.

§ 6:9   CONSTITUTIONAL LIMITATIONS ON ADMINISTRATIVE INVESTIGATION

The Constitution does not impose any significant limitations on the power of an agency to conduct an investigation.

(a) INSPECTION OF PREMISES. In general, a person has the same protection against unreasonable search and seizure by an administrative officer as that person has against unreasonable search and seizure by a police officer.

In contrast, when the danger of concealment is great, a warrantless search can be validly made of the premises of a highly regulated business, such as one selling liquor or firearms. Likewise, when violation of the law is dangerous to health and safety, the law may authorize inspection of the workplace without giving advance notice or obtaining a search warrant when such a requirement could defeat the purpose of the inspection.

(b) AERIAL INSPECTION. A search warrant is never required when the subject matter can be seen from a public place. For example, when a police officer walking on the public pavement can look through an open window and see illegal weapons, a search warrant is not required to enter the premises and seize the weapons. Utilizing the airplane and helicopter, the eyes of the law can see from the air. May an agency gather information in this manner? It has been held that a police officer may do so,[12] and there is no reason to believe the same power is not possessed by an agency.

(c) PRODUCTION OF PAPERS. For the most part, the constitutional guarantee against unreasonable search and seizure does not afford much protection with regard to papers and records being investigated by an agency. That guarantee does not apply if there is not an actual seizure. For example, a subpoena to testify or to produce records cannot be opposed on the ground that it is a search and seizure, as the constitutional protection is limited to cases of actual physical search and seizure rather than the obtaining of information by compulsion.

The protection afforded by the guarantee against self-incrimination is likewise narrow. It cannot be invoked when a corporate employee or officer in control of corporate records is compelled to produce the records, even though that person would be incriminated by them. It cannot be invoked when a person is compelled to produce corporate records. Finally, it cannot be invoked if records that by law must be kept by the person subject to the administrative investigation are involved.

D.   JUDICIAL POWER OF THE AGENCY

The modern administrative agency possesses judicial powers.

---

[11] Antitrust Civil Process Act of 1962, as amended by the Antitrust Improvement Act of 1976, §§ 101, 102, PL 94-435, 90 Stat 1383, 15 USC § 1311 et seq.

[12] California v Ciraolo, 476 US ___, 90 L Ed 2d 210 (1986).

§ 6:10 THE AGENCY AS A SPECIALIZED COURT

An agency may be given power to sit as a court and to determine whether there have been any violations of the law or of its regulations. Thus, the National Labor Relations Board determines whether a prohibited labor practice has been performed; the Federal Trade Commission acts as a court to determine whether unfair competition exists, and so on.

At first glance, the conferring of such power seems contrary to American tradition. When an administrative agency sits as judge to determine whether one of its regulations has been violated, there is some question that the agency is not impartial, since it is trying the accused for violating agency law rather than "the law." There is also the objection that an agency is determining important rights but does so without a jury, which seems inconsistent with the long-established emphasis of our history upon the sanctity of trial by jury. In spite of these objections to an agency's exercise of judicial power, such exercise is now firmly established.

§ 6:11 PATTERN OF ADMINISTRATIVE PROCEDURE

At the beginning of the era of modern regulation of business, the power of agencies to adjudicate rested, to a large extent, in minor executives or police officers charged with the responsibility of enforcing laws applicable to limited fact situations. The example of the health officer empowered to condemn and destroy diseased cattle was typical. In view of the need for prompt action and because of the relative simplicity of the fact determination to be made, it was customary for such a person to exercise summary powers. Upon finding cattle believed to be diseased, the officer would destroy animals immediately, without delaying to find their true owner and without holding a formal hearing to determine whether the animals were in fact diseased.

Today, the exercise of summary powers is the exceptional case. Concepts of due process generally require that some notice be given those who will be adversely affected and that some form of hearing be held at which they may present their case.

(a) PRELIMINARY STEPS. It is commonly provided that either a private individual aggrieved by the conduct of another, or an agency, may file a written complaint. This complaint is then served on the alleged wrongdoer, who is given the opportunity to file an answer. There may be other phases of pleading between the parties and the agency, but eventually the matter comes before the agency to be heard. After a hearing, the agency makes a decision and enters an order either dismissing the complaint or directing the adverse party to do or not to do certain acts.

The complaint filing and prehearing stage of the procedure may be more detailed. In many of the modern administrative statutes, provision is made for an examination of the informal complaint by some branch of the agency to determine whether the case comes within the scope of the agency's authority. It is also commonly provided that an investigation be made by the agency to determine whether the facts are such as to warrant a hearing of the complaint. If it is decided that the complaint is within the jurisdiction of the agency and that the facts appear to justify it, a formal complaint is issued and served on the adverse party. An answer is then filed as stated above.

With the increasing complexity of the subjects regulated by administrative agencies, the trend is to require greater preliminary examination upon the basis of an informal complaint.

(b) THE ADMINISTRATIVE HEARING. In order to satisfy the requirements of due process, it is generally necessary for an agency to give notice and to hold a hearing at which all persons affected may be present. A significant difference between an agency's hearing and a court hearing is that, as found in the *Atlas* case, there is no right of trial by jury before an agency. For example, a workers' compensation board may decide a claim without any jury. The absence of a jury does not constitute a denial of due process. Similarly, there is no right to a jury trial in an action for violation of the Age Discrimination in Employment Act. An agency is ordinarily not subject to the rules of evidence.[13]

[13] New South Communications, Inc. v Answer Iowa, Inc. (Miss) 490 So 2d 1225 (1986).

ATLAS ROOFING COMPANY, INC. v OCCUPATIONAL SAFETY AND HEALTH REVIEW COMMISSION
430 US 442 (1977)

In order to protect factory and industrial workers from unnecessary hazards and unsafe working conditions, Congress adopted the Occupational Safety and Health Act of 1970 (OSHA). The Act is administered by the Occupational Safety and Health Administration (also known as OSHA). If one of the OSHA examiners finds a dangerous condition in a place of employment, the employer is ordered to eliminate the bad condition. If the employer does not do so, OSHA can impose a fine or civil penalty on the employer. In the *Atlas Roofing Company* case, the OSHA examiner decided that a condition in the Atlas Roofing Company was hazardous and ordered its correction. Atlas Roofing refused to do so. OSHA imposed a fine on Atlas. Atlas claimed that it was entitled to a jury trial on the question of whether there was a hazardous working condition and whether the company had violated the law. Atlas claimed that this right to trial by jury was guaranteed by the Seventh Amendment of the federal Constitution. That Amendment declares: "In suits at common law, where the value in controversy shall exceed twenty dollars, the right of trial by jury shall be preserved, . . ." The lower court decided against Atlas and it appealed.

WHITE, J. . . . The issue in this case is whether, consistent with the Seventh Amendment, Congress may create a new cause of action in the Government for civil penalties enforceable in an administrative agency where there is no jury trial. After extensive investigation, Congress concluded, in 1970, that work-related deaths and injuries had become a "drastic" national problem.

. . . Congress enacted the Occupational Safety and Health Act of 1970, . . . The Act created a new statutory duty to avoid maintaining unsafe or unhealthy working conditions, and empowers the Secretary of Labor to promulgate health and safety standards. Two new remedies were provided — permitting the Federal Government, proceeding before an administrative agency, (1) to obtain abatement orders requiring employers to correct unsafe working conditions and (2) to impose civil penalties on any employer maintaining any unsafe working condition. Each remedy exists whether or not an employee is actually injured or killed as a result of the condition, and existing state statutory and common law remedies for actual injury and death remain unaffected.

Under the Act, inspectors, representing the Secretary of Labor, are authorized to conduct reasonable safety and health inspections. . . . If a violation is discovered, the inspector, on behalf of the Secretary, issues a citation to the employer fixing a reasonable time for its abatement and, in his discretion, proposing a civil penalty. . . . Such proposed penalties may range from nothing for de minimis and nonserious violations, to not more than $1,000 for serious violations, to a maximum of $10,000 for willful or repeated violations, . . .

If the employer wishes to contest the penalty or the abatement order, he may do so by notifying the Secretary of Labor within 15 days, in which event the abatement order is automatically stayed. . . . An evidentiary hearing is then held before an administrative law judge of the Occupational Safety and Health Review Commission. The Commission consists of three members, appointed for six-year terms, each of whom is qualified to adjudicate contested citations and assess penalties "by reason of training, education or experience." . . . At this hearing the burden is on the Secretary to establish the elements of the alleged violation and the propriety of his proposed abatement order and proposed penalty; and the judge is empowered to affirm, modify, or vacate any or all of these items, giving due consideration in his penalty assessment to "the size of the business of the employer . . . , the gravity of the violation, the good faith of the employer, and the history of previous violations." . . . The judge's decision becomes the Commission's final and appealable order unless within 30 days a Commissioner directs that it be reviewed by the full Commission. . . .

If review is granted, the Commission's subsequent order directing abatement and the payment of any assessed penalty becomes final unless the employer timely petitions for judicial review in the appropriate court of appeals. . . . The Secretary similarly may seek review of Commission orders, . . . but, in either case, "the findings of the Commission with respect to questions of fact, if supported by substantial evidence on the record considered as a whole, shall be conclusive." . . . If the employer fails to pay the assessed penalty, the Secretary may commence a collection action in a federal district court in which neither the fact of the violation nor the propriety of the penalty assessed may be retried. . . . Thus, the penalty may be collected without the employer ever being entitled to a jury determination of the facts constituting the violation.

Congress has often created new statutory obligations, provided for civil penalties for their violation, and committed exclusively to an administrative agency the function of deciding whether a violation has in fact occurred. These statutory schemes have been sustained by this Court. *Helvering v Mitchell*, 303 US 391 . . . (1938) . . .

. . . It is apparent from the history of jury trial in civil matters that factfinding, which is the essential function of the jury in civil cases . . . was never the exclusive province of the jury under either the English or American legal systems at the time of the adoption of the Seventh Amendment; and the question whether a fact would be found by a jury turned to a considerable degree on the nature of the forum in which a litigant found himself. Critical factfinding was performed without juries in suits in equity, and there were no juries in admiralty. *Parsons v Bedford*, 3 Pet 433 . . . (1830) . . . neither was there in the military justice system. The jury was the factfinding mode in most suits in the common law courts, but it was not exclusively so: condemnation was a suit at common law but constitutionally could be tried without a jury. . . .

The Seventh Amendment was declaratory of the existing law, for it required only that jury trial in suits at common law was to be "preserved." It thus did not purport to require a jury trial where none was required before. . . .

The point is that the Seventh Amendment was never intended to establish the jury as the exclusive mechanism for factfinding in civil cases. It took the existing legal order as it found it, and there is little or no basis for concluding that the Amendment should now be interpreted to provide an impenetrable barrier to administrative factfinding under otherwise valid federal regulatory statutes. We cannot conclude that the Amendment rendered Congress powerless — when it concluded that remedies available in courts of law were inadequate to cope with a problem within Congress' power to regulate — to create new public rights and remedies by statute and commit their enforcement, if it chose, to a tribunal other than a court of law — such as an administrative agency — in which facts are not found by juries. . . .

Congress found the common law and other existing remedies for work injuries resulting from unsafe working conditions to be inadequate to protect the Nation's working men and women. It created a new cause of action, and remedies therefor, unknown to the common law, and placed their enforcement in a tribunal supplying speedy and expert resolutions of the issues involved. The Seventh Amendment is no bar to the creation of new rights or to their enforcement outside the regular courts of law.

[Judgment affirmed]

QUESTIONS

1. Who was the plaintiff in this case?
2. Who was the defendant in this case?
3. The right to trial by jury exists in all important cases. Appraise this statement.

Another significant difference between an administrative hearing and a judicial determination is that an agency may be authorized to make an initial determination without holding a hearing. If an agency's conclusion is challenged, the agency will then hold a hearing. A court, on the other hand, must have a trial before it makes a judgment. This has important practical consequences in that when a hearing is sought after an agency has acted, the objecting party has the burden of proof and the cost of going forward. The result is that fewer persons go to the trouble of seeking such a hearing. This, in turn, reduces the number of hearings and the amount of litigation in which

an agency becomes involved. Thus, from the government's standpoint, money and time are economized.

It is held that when the administrative action concerns only the individuals directly affected, rather than a class of persons or the community generally, it is necessary to have some form of hearing before an agency may make a judicial decision. Thus, it has been held that, as a civil service employee may only be removed for cause, it is a denial of due process for a statute to authorize an agency to remove the employee without a hearing. It is not sufficient that the employee is given the right to appeal such action. Because the employee has a significant interest in continued employment, there must be some pre-removal hearing to determine that there is no basic error in the administrative action.[14]

(c) Streamlined Procedure. Informal settlement and consent decrees are practical devices to cut across the procedures outlined above. In many instances, the alleged wrongdoer is willing to change upon being informally notified that a complaint has been made. It is, therefore, sound public relations, as well as expeditious handling of the matter, for an agency to inform the alleged wrongdoer of the charge made, prior to the filing of any formal complaint, in order to encourage a voluntary settlement. A matter that has already gone into the formal hearing stage may also be terminated by agreement, and a stipulation or consent decree may be filed setting forth the terms of the agreement.

A further modification of this general pattern is made in the case of the Interstate Commerce Commission. Complaints received by the commission are referred to the Bureau of Informal Cases, which endeavors to secure an amicable adjustment with the carrier. If this cannot be done, the complainant is notified that it will be necessary to file a formal complaint. At this stage of the proceedings, the parties can expedite the matter by agreeing that the case may be heard on the pleadings alone. In this event, the complainant files a pleading or memorandum to which the defendant files an answering memorandum. The plaintiff then files a reply or rebuttal memorandum. If the parties do not agree to this procedure, a hearing is held after the pleadings have been filed.

(d) Rehearing and Correction of Administrative Action. Under some statutes, an agency is given the power to rehear or correct a decision within a specified time after it has been made.[15]

§ 6:12   Punishment and Enforcement Powers of Agencies

Originally agencies were powerless to impose any punishment or to enforce their decisions. If the person regulated did not voluntarily comply with an agency's decision, the agency could only petition a court to order that person to obey.

Within the last few decades, agencies have been increasingly given the power to impose a penalty and to issue orders that are binding on the regulated person unless an appeal is taken to a court and the administrative decision reversed. As an illustration of the power to impose penalties, the Occupational Safety and Health Act of 1970 provides for the assessment of civil penalties against employers failing to put an end to dangerous working conditions when ordered to do so by the administrative agency created by that statute. Likewise, environmental protection statutes adopted by states commonly give the state agency the power to assess a penalty for a violation of the environmental protection regulations. As an illustration of the issuance of binding orders, the Federal Trade Commission can issue a cease and desist order to stop a practice that it decides is improper. This order to stop is binding unless reversed on an appeal.

In order to assure itself that a particular person is obeying the law, including the agency's regulations and orders, an administrative agency may require proof of compliance. At times, the question of compliance may be directly determined by an agency investigation either of a building or plant or by an examination of witnesses and documents. An agency may require the regulated person or enterprise to file reports in a specified form.[16] An agency may also hold a hearing or audit on the question of compliance and may require the filing of a detailed statement or plan of

---

[14]   Cleveland Board of Education v Loudermill, 470 US 532 (1985).

[15]   100 Friends of Oregon v Land Conservation and Development Commission, 301 Or 622, 724 P2d 805 (1986).

[16]   United States v Morton Salt Co. 338 US 632 (1950).

operation showing that the regulated person or enterprise is acting properly.

§ 6:13   EXHAUSTION OF ADMINISTRATIVE REMEDY

When the law creates an agency, all parties must follow the procedure specified by the law. While an appeal may be taken to a court, it cannot be taken until the agency has acted. This principle is stated as requiring that the parties exhaust the administrative remedy before they may go into court or take an appeal.[17]

As long as an agency is acting within the scope of its authority or jurisdiction, a party cannot appeal before the agency has made a final decision. The fact that the complaining party does not want the agency to decide the matter, or is afraid

that the agency will reach a wrong decision, is not ground for bypassing the agency by going to court before the agency has acted. Neither can an appeal be made before the agency has made a final decision.

§ 6:14   APPEAL FROM ADMINISTRATIVE ACTION

The statute creating the modern administrative agency typically provides for the taking of an appeal from the administrative decision to a particular court. The statute may state that a party in interest or any person aggrieved by the administrative action may appeal. This requires the appellant to have a legally-recognized right or interest that is harmed by the administrative action. The fact that a person or a group of citizens do not like the action of the agency does not entitle them to appeal. The *Health Central* case faced the question of who could appeal.

---

[17]   Park 'N Fly of San Francisco, Inc. v South San Francisco, 188 Cal App 3d 1201, 234 Cal Rptr 23 (1987).

HEALTH CENTRAL V COMMISSIONER OF INSURANCE
152 Mich App 336, 393 NW2d 625 (1986)

The Commissioner of Insurance of Michigan wanted Health Central and other health maintenance organizations (HMOs) to reveal the salaries paid to their doctors and to make such information public. The HMOs brought a suit for a declaratory judgment, hoping to establish that the Commissioner could not make such information public. The court decided against the Commissioner, and he appealed.

PER CURIAM, J. . . . This is a "reverse FOIA" [Freedom of Information Act] case, where the plaintiff seeks to prevent disclosure, rather than compel disclosure, of information contained in a government agency file. The FOIA requires disclosure of all public records and only authorizes nondisclosure, at the agency's discretion, under certain enumerated exceptions. Thus, the FOIA did not create any right to prevent disclosure, and "[a]ny asserted right by third parties to prohibit disclosure must have a basis independent of the FOIA." *Tobin v Civil Service Comm*, 416 Mich. 661, 668-669, 331 N.W.2d 184 (1982). "In effect, a reverse FOIA suit to prevent disclosure of information within an FOIA exemption must be evaluated as if the FOIA did not exist." 416 Mich. 670.

. . . The most egregious jurisdictional problem . . . is the question of standing of the plaintiffs to bring this suit. The plaintiff HMOs maintain that the disclosure of their employees' salaries would constitute a common-law invasion of privacy by the "public disclosure of embarrassing private facts". Following the abandonment at the show-cause hearing of the claim that the Commissioner could not obtain the salary information, the focus of both the plaintiffs and the trial court was upon the privacy interest of HMO employees, rather than upon the privacy interests of the named plaintiffs. Nonetheless, the Commissioner did not challenge the standing of the HMOs to assert their employees' rights of privacy either below or in this appeal.

The right of privacy is a personal right and cannot ordinarily be asserted by anyone other than the person whose privacy has been invaded. . . .

> The right of privacy is a personal right designed to protect persons from unwanted disclosure of personal information. It does not extend to protect corporations from disclosure of information acquired or maintained in the regular course of business. . . .

In *Human Rights Party*, 76 Mich.App. pp. 211-212, 256 N.W.2d 439, this Court considered whether the plaintiff political party had standing to assert violations of constitutional rights of state prison inmates. The Court, considering declaratory judgments under the APA, concluded that unless aggrieved prisoners were added to the suit by joinder, the plaintiff would be without standing to pursue the suit. In doing so, the Court cited *Wisconsin's Environmental Decade, Inc. v Public Service Comm of Wisconsin*, 69 Wis.2d 1, 9-10, 230 N.W.2d 243, 247-248 (1975), which considered the meaning of the terms "aggrieved" person, "directly affected" by the agency decision, and that the decision "directly affect the legal rights, duties or privileges" of the person seeking review. The Wisconsin Supreme Court, in turn, likened its own analysis to the two-pronged standing analysis outlined by the United States Supreme Court in *Ass'n of Data Processing Service Organizations v Camp*, 397 U.S. 150, 153, n. 7 (1970), and *Barlow v Collins*, 397 U.S. 159 (1970).

That analysis asks: (1) Does the challenged action cause the petitioner injury in fact? and (2) is the interest allegedly injured arguably within the zone of interests to be protected by the statute or constitutional guarantee in question. Justice Brennan, concurring in *Barlow, supra*, 397 U.S. 172-173, stated that the purpose of the injury in fact requirement is to bring concreteness and adverseness to a case. An interest meeting the second prong of the test could represent aesthetic, conservational, spiritual, recreational or economic values. The Michigan court rule for declaratory judgments, GCR 1963, 521, now MCR 2.605, is sufficiently similar to the "case" or "controversy" requirement of Article III of the United States Constitution to support our adoption of the federal test.

Accordingly, we find that plaintiff HMOs have failed to allege injuries that are more than merely conjectural. . . . Most importantly, the HMOs raise only the putative right of privacy of their employees and fail to show the existence of any injury to themselves of sufficient immediacy and ripeness to warrant judicial intervention. . . .

[Judgment reversed and action remanded]

QUESTIONS

1. Did the HMOs establish that they would be hurt by complying with the request of the insurance commissioner?

2. Why does the court describe the proceeding as a "reverse FOIA" case?
3. How would the case have been decided if the insurance commissioner requested the salary information on the basis that he would then be in the position to order the HMOs to pay larger salaries if he deemed that those paid were inadequate?

§ 6:15   FINALITY OF ADMINISTRATIVE DETERMINATION

Basic to the Anglo-American legal theory is the belief that no one, not even a branch of the government, is above the law. Thus, the growth of powers of the administrative agency was frequently accepted or tolerated on the theory that if the administrative agency went too far, the courts would review the administrative action. The typical modern statute provides that an appeal may be taken from the administrative action.

When the question that an agency decides is a question of law, the court on appeal will reverse the agency if the court disagrees with the decision. This concept is being eroded to some extent by modern technology. Thus, it is held that the court will accept the agency's interpretation of the statute when the statute relates to a technical matter. Here the court will tend to accept the agency's interpretation as long as it is reasonable, even though it is not the only interpretation that could have been made.[18]

In contrast with an agency's decision on matters of law, the controversy may turn on a question of fact or a mixed question of law and fact. In such cases, a court will accept the conclusion of an agency if it is supported by substantial evidence. A court will not reverse an agency's decision merely because the court would have made a different decision on the same facts.[19] As most disputes before an agency are based on questions of fact, the net result is that the decision of the agency will be final in most cases.

The greatest limitation upon court review of the administrative action is the rule that a decision involving discretion will not be reversed in the absence of an error of law; or a clear abuse of, or the arbitrary or capricious exercise of, discretion.

The courts reason that, since the members of the agencies were appointed because of expert ability, it would be absurd for the court, which is manifestly unqualified technically to make a decision in the matter, to step in and determine whether the agency made the proper choice. Courts will not do so unless the agency has clearly acted wrongly, arbitrarily, or capriciously. As a practical matter, the action of an agency is rarely found to be arbitrary or capricious. As long as an agency has followed the proper procedure, the fact that the court disagrees with the conclusion reached by the agency does not make that conclusion arbitrary or capricious. In areas in which economic or technical matters are involved, it is generally sufficient that the agency had a reasonable basis for the decision made. A court will not attempt to second-guess the agency as to complex criteria with which an administrative agency is intimately familiar. The judicial attitude is that, for protection from laws and regulations that are unwise, improvident, or out of harmony with a particular school of thought, the people must resort to the ballot box and not to the court.

No agency has unlimited funds or an unlimited staff. An agency must therefore exercise the discretion to choose which cases

[18] Chemical Mfrs, Ass'n. v Natural Resources Defense Council, Inc. 470 US 116 (1985).
[19] Service Employees International v State Educational Labor Relations Board, 153 Ill App 3d 744, 106 Ill Dec 112, 505 NE2d 418 (1987).

should be handled. Ordinarily the decision of an agency to do nothing about a particular complaint will not be reversed by a court.[20] That is, the courts will not override an agency's decision to do nothing. Exceptions are made, however, when it is obvious that the agency is refusing to act for an improper reason. If it is obvious that the agency wrongly believed that there was no authority to act; that the agency had taken a bribe to keep out; or that, on the basis of the facts, there was no logical explanation for the agency's refusal to act; then the court may override the decision.

§ 6:16   LIABILITY OF AGENCY

The decision of an agency may cause substantial loss to a business by increasing its operating costs or by making a decision that later is shown to be harmful to the economy. An agency is not liable for such loss when it had acted in good faith in the exercise of discretionary powers.[21]

---

[20]   Heckler v Chaney, 470 US 821 (1985).

[21]   Butz v Economou, 438 US 478 (1978).

SUMMARY

The administrative agency is unique because it combines the three functions that are kept separate under the traditional system: legislative, executive, and judicial. By virtue of legislative power, an agency adopts regulations that have the force of law, although the members of the agency were not elected by those who are subject to the regulations. By virtue of the executive power, an agency carries out and enforces the regulations, makes investigations, and requires the production of documents. By virtue of the judicial power, an agency acts as a court to determine whether there has been a violation of any regulation. To some extent, an agency is restricted by constitutional limitations in making inspection of premises and in requiring the production of papers. These limitations, however, have a very narrow application. The protection against unreasonable search and seizure and the protection against self-incrimination are so narrowed by judicial construction as to have little protective value. When an agency acts as a judge, it is not required that there be a jury trial or that the ordinary courtroom procedures be followed. Typically, an agency will give notice to the person claimed to be acting improperly, and a hearing will then be held before the agency. When the agency has determined that there has been a violation, the stopping of the violation may be ordered. Under some statutes, the agency may go further and impose a penalty upon the violator.

An appeal may be taken from any decision of the agency by a person harmed thereby. Only a person with a legally recognized interest can appeal from the agency ruling. No appeal can be taken until every step available before the agency has been taken; that is, the administrative remedy must first be exhausted.

As a practical matter, an appeal from the administrative action will ordinarily have little value. When the controversy turns on a determination of facts, a court will not reverse the decision of an agency because it disagrees with the conclusion that the agency drew from those facts. When an agency is given discretion to act, a court will never reverse the agency just because it disagrees with the choice that the agency made. In contrast, if an agency made a wrong decision as to a question of law, a court will generally reverse the agency when the court disagrees with the decision. In the absence of an error of law, an agency's decision will only be reversed if the court decides that the administrative action was arbitrary and capricious.

Protection from secret government is provided by the right to know what is contained in most administrative agency records; by the requirement that most agency meetings be open to the public; by the invitation to the public to take part in rule making; and by publicity, through publication in the *Federal Register*, to the guidelines followed by the agency and to regulations that have been adopted.

QUESTIONS AND CASE PROBLEMS

1. What social forces are affected by the principle that the same administrative agency may conduct an investigation to determine if there is reason to believe that there has been a violation, and then hold a hearing to determine whether in fact there was a violation?

2. Can an administrative agency make laws?

3. Pennington is a licensed physician. She is appointed State Health Administrator in 1984 under a statute adopted in 1960. The statute authorizes the Administrator to adopt regulations protecting from health hazards and disease. In 1985, certain candy manufacturers began using a new artificial sweetener, Doucetran. Tests conducted by Pennington convince her that Doucetran may cause cancer. She adopts a regulation prohibiting the use of Doucetran. The candy manufacturers claim that she cannot do this on the theory that she could only regulate those health hazards that were known in 1960 when the legislature adopted the statute. Are they correct?

4. There is a department in the federal government called the Department of Housing and Urban Development (HUD). It decides to hold a conference of leading building contractors for the purpose of deciding patterns of urban development that should be encouraged by HUD. Culpepper wants to attend the meeting. She is denied admission because she is neither a government official nor a building contractor. Is she entitled to attend the meeting?

5. Adams is appointed the state Price Control Administrator. By virtue of this position, he requires all sellers of goods and suppliers of services to keep records of the prices charged by them. He suspects that the Ace Overhead Garage Door Corporation is charging more than the prices permitted by law. To determine this, he notifies the company to produce the records that it was required to keep. It refuses to do so on the grounds that Adams does not have the authority to require the production of papers. Is this a valid defense?

6. Bell was employed by the Sinclair Radio Corporation. She was fired from her job and made a complaint to the National Labor Relations Board that she was fired because she belonged to a union. The examiner of the board held a hearing at which Bell produced evidence of an anti-union attitude of the employer. The employer produced evidence that Bell was fired because she was chronically late and did poor work. The examiner and the Labor Relations Board concluded that Bell was fired because of her union membership. Sinclair appealed. The court reached the conclusion that, had the court been the board, it would have held that the discharge of Bell was justified because it would not have believed the testimony of Bell's witnesses. Will the court reverse the decision of the National Labor Relations Board?

7. An agency created by an act of Congress
   (a) can be given only the power to carry out the terms of an act of Congress
   (b) can be given only executive power
   (c) can be given executive, legislative, and judicial powers
   Is any of these three alternatives correct? Explain.

8. Compare the procedure of a lawsuit with the procedure followed when an unfair labor practice complaint is made to the National Labor Relations Board.

9. The New York City charter authorizes the New York City Board of Health to adopt a health code and declares that it "shall have

the force and effect of law." The board adopted a code in 1964 that provided for the fluoridation of the public water supply. A suit was brought to enjoin the carrying out of this program on the ground that it was unconstitutional and that money could not be spent to carry out such a program in the absence of a statute authorizing such expenditure. It was also claimed that the fluoridation program was unconstitutional because there were other means of reducing tooth decay; fluoridation was discriminatory in that it benefited only children; it unlawfully imposed medication on the children without their consent; and fluoridation "is or may be" dangerous to health. Was the code provision valid? [Paduano v City of New York, 257 NYS2d 531]

10. The Federal Trade Commission directs the Essex Manufacturing Company to install safety devices in its factory. Essex claims that the commission's order can be ignored because the members of the commission were not elected by the voters, and therefore the commission cannot make an order that has the force of law. Is this defense valid?

11. The Congress of the United States adopted a law to provide insurance to protect the wheat farmers. The agency in charge of the program adopted regulations to govern applications for this insurance. These regulations were published in the *Federal Register*. Merrill applied for insurance but his application did not comply with the regulations. He claimed that he was not bound by the regulations because he never knew they had been adopted. Is he bound by the regulations? [Federal Crop Insurance Corp. v Merrill, 332 US 380]

12. The Occupational Safety and Health Act of 1970 authorizes the Secretary of Labor to adopt job safety standards to protect workers from harmful substances. The secretary is directed by the statute to adopt that standard "which most adequately assures, to the extent feasible, on the basis of the best available evidence" that no employee will suffer material impairment of health. Acting under this authorization, the secretary adopted a Cotton Dust Standard to protect workers exposed to cotton dust. This dust causes serious lung disease that disables about one out of twelve cotton factory workers. The cotton industry attacked the validity of the Cotton Dust Standard on the ground that the secretary, in adopting the standard, had not considered the cost to the cotton industry of complying with the standard (a cost of $656.5 million). Was the Cotton Dust Standard valid? [American Textile Manufacturers Institute, Inc. v Donovan, 452 US 490]

13. The Fair Labor Standards Act of 1938 (FLSA) authorizes the Secretary of Labor to issue a subpoena directing an employer to produce papers relating to hours and wages of employees. Acting in the name of the Secretary of Labor, Donovan, an employee of the Department of Labor, entered the lobby of Lone Steer Inc., a motel-restaurant, and served a subpoena on an employee of Lone Steer directing the production of papers relating to wages and hours of the employees. Lone Steer refused to comply with this subpoena, claimed that the administrative subpoena could not constitutionally be issued unless there first was a judicial subpoena issued by a court, and asserted that entering into the lobby to serve the administrative subpoena was an unreasonable search that violated the Fourth amendment of the Constitution. Was Lone Steer correct? [Donovan v Lone Steer, Inc. 464 US 408]

14. The planning commissioner and a real estate developer planned to meet to discuss the rezoning of certain land in order to permit the real estate developer to construct certain buildings that were not allowed under the then existing zoning law. A homeowners' association claimed that it had the right to be present at the meeting. This claim was objected to on the theory that the state's Open Meetings Act applied only to meetings of the specified governmental units and did not extend to a meeting between one of them and an outsider. Was this objection valid?

15. The Interstate Commerce Commission had to determine the valuation of the stock of a railroad and whether the stock should be split. The commission informed the parties that instead of having an oral hearing, it would dispose of the matter on the basis of the sworn written statements of the parties. Laird owned some of the stock of the railroad. He claimed that he had a right to an oral hearing. Was he correct? [Laird v ICC (CA3 ICC) 691 F2d 147]

7

ENVIRONMENTAL LAW AND COMMUNITY PLANNING

For the first two centuries of national existence, Americans looked upon their country as one of unlimited resources. To them, there was no need to conserve or protect these resources. The answer to any shortage problem was always very easy — just move westward where there was more of everything. As long as the open West was available, there was no need to talk of protecting the environment. In 1912, the territories of New Mexico and Arizona became the 47th and 48th states, and the United States then stretched from the Atlantic to the Pacific. Americans and American industry were thus locked into a land area that remained constant. While Hawaii and Alaska later became states, the geographical limits of the continental United States remained unchanged.

Increasing population and industrialization consumed national resources and created waste that threatened to destroy much of what was left. The result was that America had to begin to conserve resources and to stop pollution of the environment. The desire to protect people from the harmful effects of pollution and the desire to protect America from a shortage of resources led to the movement for environmental protection at the governmental level. At the private level, added impetus was given to the concept of community planning.

Underlying these trends was the basic policy decision to restrict freedom of enterprise and the freedom of the use of property and of personal action in the interst of the general welfare.

	ENVIRONMENTAL ISSUES	
	RESOURCE PROTECTION	COMMUNITY PLANNING
LEGAL BODY EXERCISING CONTROL	INTERNATIONAL GOVERNMENTS U.S. GOVERNMENT STATE GOVERNMENTS LOCAL GOVERNMENTS	STATE GOVERNMENTS LOCAL GOVERNMENTS
TYPE OF CONTROL AND DEVICES USED	DIRECT CONTROL THROUGH STATUTES AND ORDINANCES LIMITED OR INCIDENTAL STATE GOVERNMENTAL CONTROL THROUGH NUISANCE LAW AND RESTRICTIVE COVENANTS	DIRECT CONTROL THROUGH STATUTES, ORDINANCES, AND RESTRICTIVE COVENANTS

FIGURE 7-1
THE LEGAL ENVIRONMENT OF RESOURCE
PROTECTION AND COMMUNITY PLANNING

A.   PREVENTION OF POLLUTION

As America changed from a rural and agricultural society to an urban and industrial one, new laws were needed to prevent the pollution of the environment.

§ 7:1   STATUTORY ENVIRONMENTAL PROTECTION

Beginning with the National Environmental Policy Act of 1969 (NEPA), Congress has adopted a series of laws designed to prevent the pollution of the air and water and to reduce noise.[1] Congress has adopted other statutes designed to reduce the problem of waste disposal by encouraging recycling or reuse of various products.[2]

State legislatures have also been active in this area, and many states have laws that are similar to the federal laws. Statutes may require that before a permit may be issued for earth removal and similar operations requiring blasting, the contractor and the permit-issuing agency must agree on "satisfactory dust control provi-

---

[1] For example, see the Clean Air Act, 42 USC § 1857 et seq., the National Motor Vehicles Emissions Standards Act, 42 USC § 1857f-1 et seq., the Noise Control Acts of 1970 and 1972, 42 USC § 4901, the Water Pollution Control Act Amendments of 1972, 33 USC § 1251 et seq. The pollution of navigable waters had already been prohibited by the River and Harbor Appropriations Act of 1899.

[2] See for example, the Solid Waste Disposal Act, Act of October 20, 1965, 79 Stat 997, 42 USC §§ 3251 et seq., the Resource Recovery and Policy Act of 1970, Act of October 26, 1970, PL 91-512, 84 Stat 1227, 42 USC §§ 3251 et seq., the Resource Conservation and Recovery Act of 1976, Act of October 21, 1976, PL 94-580, 90 Stat 2795, 42 USC §§ 6901 et seq. These statutes have been amended many times.

sions."[3] A state law must not (a) conflict with a federal statute, nor (b) place an unreasonable burden on interstate commerce.

§ 7:2   WASTE CONTROL

Modern industries and life styles produce a large quantity of waste materials. Some of the industrial waste can be used to make by-products. Some can be used again or recycled. Some wastes are biodegradable.

In contrast, some waste materials remain and some are dangerous to life, both human and animal, and to vegetation and water supplies. The state and federal governments have adopted programs for protecting the nation and the public from harmful wastes.[4] A license may be required for the disposal of radioactive wastes. A state law providing for a spill fund to compensate persons for damage from hazardous waste disposal is valid.[5]

The Comprehensive Environmental Response, Compensation and Liability Act of

1980 (CERCL)[6] provides for the establishment of a national inventory of inactive hazardous waste sites and the creation of a multimillion-dollar Hazardous Waste Fund, commonly called "Superfund," to pay the cost of eliminating or containing the condemned waste sites.

§ 7:3   ENVIRONMENTAL IMPACT STATEMENTS

Environmental protection legislation typically requires that any activity that might have a significant effect upon the environment be supported by an environmental impact statement (EIS). Whenever any bill is proposed in Congress and whenever any federal action significantly affecting the quality of the human environment is considered, a statement must be prepared as to the environmental impact of the action. A number of states impose the same requirement on government officials and some require an environmental impact statement for any large private building construction.

In the *Chinese Staff* case the underlying question was what was included in the environment.

---

[3] Tebo v Board of Appeals of Shrewsbury, 22 Mass App 618, 495 NE2d 892 (1986).
[4] See for example, the Nuclear Waste Policy Act of 1982, Act of January 7, 1983, PL 97–425, 42 USC §§ 10101-10226.
[5] Exxon Corp. v Hunt, 475 US 355, (1986).

[6] Act of December 11, 1980, PL 96-510, 94 Stat 2767, 42 USC §§ 9601 et seq.

CHINESE STAFF AND WORKERS ASS'N. V NEW YORK

68 NY2d 359, 502 NE2d 176 (1986)

Henry Street Partners wished to build a high-rise luxury condominium on a vacant lot in the Chinatown section of New York City. The appropriate city agencies issued a permit allowing the construction of the building. The issuance of the permit was then attacked by a lawsuit brought by the Chinese Staff and Workers Association and others protesting on the ground that the proposed building would have a harmful effect on the Chinatown section by driving out the poorer residents and businesses. From a judgment against the objectors, they appealed.

ALEXANDER, J. . . . The regulations promulgated by the City of New York (Executive Order No. 91, Aug. 24, 1977, entitled City Environmental Quality Review [CEQR]) as authorized by and in implementation of the State Environmental Quality Review Act (ECL art. 8 [SEQRA]) require lead agencies to consider both the short- and long-term and primary and secondary effects of a proposed action in determining whether the action may have a significant effect on the environment so as to require the preparation of an Environmental Impact Statement (EIS). . . .

In reviewing administrative proceedings in general and SEQRA determinations in particular, we are limited to considering "whether a determination was made in violation of lawful procedure, was affected by an error of law or was arbitrary and capricious or an abuse of discretion." . . . The limited issue presented for our review is whether the respondents identified the relevant areas of environmental concern, took a "hard look" at them, and made a "reasoned elaboration" of the basis for their determination. . . .

The initial determination to be made under SEQRA and CEQR is whether an EIS is required, which in turn depends on whether an action may or will not have a significant effect on the environment. In making this initial environmental analysis, the lead agencies must study the same areas of environmental impacts as would be contained in an EIS, including both the short-term and long-term effects as well as the primary and secondary effects of an action on the environment. The threshold at which the requirement that an EIS be prepared is triggered is relatively low: it need only be demonstrated that the action may have a significant effect on the environment. . . .

The dispute here concerns the reach of the term "environment", which is defined [in the State Environmental Quality Review Act and the city regulations] as "the *physical conditions* which will be affected by a proposed action, *including* land, air, water, minerals, flora, fauna, noise, objects of historic or aesthetic significance, *existing patterns of population concentration, distribution, or growth, and existing community or neighborhood character*" [emphasis supplied]. Petitioners argue that the displacement of neighborhood residents and businesses caused by a proposed project is an environmental impact within the purview of SEQRA and CEQR, and the failure of respondents to consider these potential effects renders their environmental analysis invalid. Respondents contend that any impacts that are not either directly related to a primary physical impact or will not impinge upon the physical environment in a significant manner are outside the scope of the definition of "environment", and that the lead agencies were therefore not required to investigate the potential effects alleged by petitioners.

. . . It is clear from the express terms of the statute and the regulations that environment is broadly defined . . . and expressly includes as physical conditions such considerations as "existing patterns of population concentration, distribution, or growth, and existing community or neighborhood character". Thus, the impact that a project may have on population patterns or existing community character, with or without a separate impact on the physical environment, is a relevant concern in an environmental analysis since the statute includes these concerns as elements of the environment. That these factors might generally be regarded as social or economic is irrelevant in view of this explicit definition. By their express terms, therefore, both SEQRA and CEQR require a lead agency to consider more than impacts upon the physical environment in determining whether to require the preparation of an EIS. In sum, population patterns and neighborhood character are physical conditions of the environment under SEQRA and CEQR regardless of whether there is any impact on the physical environment (*see*, Ulasewicz, *Department of Environmen-*

tal Conservation and SEQRA: Upholding Its Mandates and Charting Parameters For The Elusive Socio-Economic Assessment, 46 Alb.L.Rev. 1255, 1266, 1282).

Turning to the specific allegations in this case, we conclude that under CEQR the potential displacement of local residents and businesses is an effect on population patterns and neighborhood character which must be considered in determining whether the requirement for an EIS is triggered. A significant effect on the environment may be found if a proposed project impairs "the character or quality of . . . existing community or neighborhood character" (CEQR 6[a][5]) or impacts upon "existing patterns of population concentration, distribution, or growth" (ECL 8-0105[6]; *see,* CEQR 6[a][10]). It is not relevant whether the proposed project may effect these concerns primarily or secondarily or in the short term or in the long term since the regulations expressly include all such effects (CEQR 1[g]).

The potential acceleration of the displacement of local residents and businesses is a secondary long-term effect on population patterns, community goals and neighborhood character such that CEQR requires these impacts on the environment to be considered in an environmental analysis. . . .

We do not decide whether these impacts will in fact flow from the construction of Henry Street Tower nor do we express any opinion on the merits of the proposed project. Our holding is limited to a determination that existing patterns of population concentration, distribution or growth and existing community or neighborhood character are physical conditions such that the regulations adopted by the City of New York pursuant to SEQRA require an agency to consider the potential long-term secondary displacement of residents and businesses in determining whether a proposed project may have a significant effect on the environment. Since respondents did not consider these potential effects on the environment in their environmental analysis, their determination does not comply with the statutory mandate and therefore is arbitrary and capricious. . . .

[Judgment reversed]

QUESTIONS

1. What was the basic controversy in the *Chinese Staff* case?
2. Which interpretation is adopted by the court? What reason does the court give for its position?
3. How did the court describe the action of issuing the permit for the construction of the high-rise building?

While an EIS must consider alternative methods, it is not required to discuss every alternative that could be imagined. It is only required to consider alternatives that are practical and feasible.[7]

When the law requires that an environmental impact statement be filed before a particular construction or improvement can be made, a court will prohibit the construction or improvement if no statement has been filed. It will also do so if a statement has been filed but is so deficient or poor that, in effect, it is no statement at all.

The duty of a federal agency does not end with its issuing an EIS. It has a continuing duty to gather relevant information, to

---

[7]   Bowman v City of Petaluma, 185 Cal App 3d 1065, 230 Cal Rptr 413 (1986).

evaluate such information, and to issue a revised or supplemental EIS if the new information indicates such course of action.

§ 7:4   REGULATION BY ADMINISTRATIVE AGENCIES

For the most part, the law against pollution is a matter of the adoption and enforcement of regulations by administrative agencies, such as the federal EPA (Environmental Protection Agency). Administrative agency control is likely to increase in the future because of the technical nature of the problems involved and because of the interrelationship of pollution problems and nonpollution problems.

§ 7:5   LITIGATION

A private person may bring a lawsuit to recover damages or obtain an injunction against a polluter if damages peculiar to such plaintiff can be shown. This requirement of harm to the plaintiff has to some extent been relaxed so that a person may sometimes sue without proving any harm different than that sustained by any other member of the general public. For example, federal statutes authorize a private suit by any person in a federal district court to stop a violation of the air, water, and noise pollution standards. Courts have been increasingly willing to recognize the right of organizations to sue on behalf of their members.

A private person does not always have the right to sue for violation of an environmental protection control. In some instances the right to sue is restricted to a particular government agency or to the attorney general of the United States.

It is reasonable to expect that courts will not take an active part in the solution of pollution problems. It is likely that on these technical problems they will defer to the decisions made or to be made by the appropriate administrative agency.[8] This is true particularly when the matter is merely a small segment of the total pollution problem or when jurisdiction by a court could hamper or disrupt the work of administrative agencies and study groups.[9]

§ 7:6   CRIMINAL LIABILITY

Knowingly doing an act prohibited by an environmental protection statute is generally a crime. For example, the dumping of hazardous wastes without a federal permit is a crime.

In a prosecution for such a crime, it is no defense that the defendant did not intend to violate the law or was not negligent. It is also no defense that the defendant operated a business in the customary way and did not produce a greater amount of pollution than other similar enterprises.

In the *Arizona Mines* case, the question was raised whether good intentions is a defense to a criminal prosecution for air pollution.

---

[8]   Boomer v Atlantic Cement Co. 26 NY2d 219, 309 NYS2d 312, 257 NE2d 870 (1970).
[9]   Ohio v Wyandotte Chemicals Corp. 401 US 493 (1971). (Ohio sought to enjoin Canada, Michigan, and Delaware corporations from dumping mercury into tributaries of Lake Erie, which allegedly polluted the lake used by parts of Ohio as a water supply. The Supreme Court refused to decide the case).

ARIZONA V ARIZONA MINES SUPPLY CO.
107 Ariz 199, 484 P2d 619 (1971)

Maricopa County, Arizona adopted an air pollution control regulation. The Arizona Mines Supply Company operated a mine within the county. It installed equipment in its mine in order to meet the standards of the regulation. In spite of these efforts, Arizona Mines polluted the air. It was prosecuted by Arizona for violating the regulation. It raised the defense that it was not guilty because it had not violated the regulation intentionally. To back up this argument, it showed that it had done its best to comply with the regulation by installing the special equipment. The prosecution objected to the admission of this evidence on the ground that it was sufficient to show that the defendant had violated the law. That is, the prosecution claimed that it was not necessary to show that the defendant had intentionally violated the law. The trial court admitted the evidence of the defendant's attempt to comply with the law. The prosecution claimed that this was wrong and filed a petition with the state supreme court to review the decision of the trial judge admitting such evidence.

UDALL, J. . . . [The defendant contends] that the State must prove knowledge or intent as a prerequisite to conviction. [The] Maricopa County Air Pollution Control Regulation . . . provides that: "No person shall cause, suffer, allow or permit the discharge into the atmosphere from any single source of emission whatsoever any air contaminants for a period or periods aggregating more than three minutes in any one hour which is:

a. As dark as or darker in shade than that designated as No. 2 on the Ringelmann Chart as published by the U.S. Bureau of Mines, or
b. Of an opacity equal to or greater than an air contaminant designated as No. 2 on the Ringelmann Chart."

Nowhere does this regulation (or the Air Pollution Act, for that matter) provide, either expressly or impliedly, that before the state may convict someone of "air pollution" it must first prove that the air contaminant was discharged knowingly or intentionally. Defendant argues that some degree of knowledge or intent is prerequisite to conviction. The State, on the other hand, contends that it need not prove intent or knowledge since this offense is more in the nature of "malum prohibitum."

After having carefully considered the apparent intent of legislature, . . . and the consequences of unabated air pollution to public health; we find that the state need not prove intent or knowledge on the part of the accused as a prerequisite to conviction. That the legislature may make the doing of an act or the neglect to do something a crime without requiring criminal intent is well-settled *Troutner v State*, 17 Ariz 506, 154 P 1048 (1916). . . .

"Whether a criminal intent or guilty knowledge is a necessary element of a statutory offense is a matter of construction to be determined from the language of the statute, *in view of its manifest purpose and design.* There are many instances in recent times where the legislature in the exercise of the police power has prohibited, under penalty, the performance of a specific act. *The doing of the inhibited act constitutes the crime,* and the moral turpitude or *purity of the motive* by which it was prompted *and knowledge or ignorance* of its criminal character *are immaterial circumstances* on the question of guilt. The only fact to be determined in these cases is whether the defendant did the act."

With regard to the introduction by a defendant of evidence of expenditures made in installing pollution control equipment and precautions taken to avoid pollution, such will not constitute a defense to prosecution and conviction, and are, therefore, inadmissible at trial. Evidence of "extenuating circumstances" may, however, be presented to the court *after verdict* in mitigation of the penalty to be imposed. " . . . *Although extenuating circumstances would be no legal bar to conviction, they would certainly be important factors in determining a penalty, and might even warrant granting of probation."* [Emphasis added.] *Fitzpatrick v Board of Examiners,* 96 Ariz 309 at 315, 394 P2d 423 at 427.

[Admission of evidence sustained for limited purpose of determining the penalty to be imposed after the guilt of the defendant was established]

QUESTIONS

1. Why did Arizona Mines Supply Company claim that it was not guilty of violating the regulation?
2. What is the Ringelmann chart?
3. What was the basis for the defense that knowledge or intent was necessary for conviction?

B. COMMUNITY PLANNING

In order to provide for the orderly growth of communities, some planning and control is necessary. Community planning may be classified as private (restrictive covenants) and public (zoning).

§ 7:7 RESTRICTIVE COVENANTS IN PRIVATE CONTRACTS

In the case of private planning, a real estate developer will take an undeveloped tract or area of land, map out on paper an "ideal" community, and then construct the buildings shown on the plan. These are then sold to private purchasers. The deeds to the buyers will contain **restrictive covenants** that obligate the buyers to observe certain limitations in the use of their property, the nature of buildings that will be maintained or constructed on the land, and so on. If a restrictive covenant is valid, it binds anyone becoming the owner of the land if the covenant is stated in a recorded deed or if the buyer has notice or knowledge of the restriction.[10] If a restrictive covenant violates a statute, rule of law, or public policy, it is not valid and will not be enforced.

A restrictive covenant will be given its ordinary meaning. If there is any uncertainty, the covenant will be construed strictly in favor of the free use of the land. When there is no uncertainty and no reason to depart from the meaning of the words of the covenant, a court will enforce those words. For example, a television satellite dish is a structure within the meaning of a restrictive covenant.[11]

In the *Sherwood Estates* case the protection of a pet came in conflict with the law of restrictive covenants.

[10] Hicks v Loveless (Tex App) 714 SW2d 30 (1986).
[11] Shoreline Estate Homeowners Ass'n. v Loucks, 84 Or App 302, 733 P2d 942 (1987).

SHERWOOD ESTATES HOMES ASS'N., INC. V McCONNELL
(Mo App) 714 SW2d 848 (1986)

The McConnells bought a home in the Sherwood Estates. The land was subject to a restrictive covenant that "no building, fence, or other structure" could be built on the land without the approval of the developer of the property. The McConnells built a dog pen in their yard. They claimed that approval was not required on the theory that the restrictive covenant did not apply because it showed an intent to restrict only major construction and not minor additions to the landscape. A lawsuit was brought to compel the McConnells to remove the dog pen because prior approval had not been obtained. From a judgment against the McConnells, they appealed.

PER CURIAM . . . The parties agree that appellant became a landowner within the development known as Sherwood Estates and that appellants knew of the restrictions applicable to the homesites therein. . . . Respondent [Association] contended that the dog pen violated the prohibition set forth in Restriction VII of its Declaration of Restrictions which reads as follows:

VII: Approval of Plans
No building, fence, wall or other structure shall be commenced, erected or maintained, nor shall any addition thereto or change or alterations therein be made, until plans and specifications, color scheme, plot plan and grading plan therefor, or other information satisfactory to the Company shall have been submitted to and approved in writing by the Company and a copy thereof as finally approved lodged with the Company. In so passing upon such plans, specifications and other requirements, the Company may take into consideration the suitability of the proposed building or other structure and the materials of which it is to be built, to the site upon which, it is proposed to erect same, the harmony thereof with the surroundings and the effect of the building or other structure as planned on the outlook from adjacent or neighboring property.

Respondent presented uncontroverted evidence that such a dog pen did not help property values and in fact lessened property values. The dog pen in question has concrete block flooring and is enclosed by fencing. The entire structure is housed inside the rear fenced yard of appellants. . . .

It is appellants' contention first that their dog pen is not within the term "other structure" and to so conclude this court would be following the rule in Missouri that the law favors the free use of real property and that restrictions on the use of land are to be strictly construed. . . .

In contrast, respondent contends appellants' dog pen is within the term "other structure" as found and contemplated by Restriction VII and argues such restrictions which are adopted for the purpose of a pleasant residential environment are properly recognized within our law . . .

A reading of the Declaration of Restrictions discloses the intent and purpose thereof is to maintain a harmonious residential area. In addition, the Declaration of Restrictions is intended to safeguard against the effects of any structure upon the surrounding area and dwellings already upon the land. It is also obvious that the protection of the value of the various properties is one of the main purposes of the Declaration.

A structure has been defined as
Any construction or any production or any piece of work artificially built up or composed of parts joined together in some definite manner. That which is built or constructed; an edifice or building of any kind. A combination of material, to form a construction for occupancy, use or ornamentation, whether installed on, above or below the surface of a parcel of land. Black's Law Dictionary 1276 (rev. 5th ed. 1969).

The evidence herein revealed that appellants' dog pen has a concrete block flooring. In addition, it is a manufactured fence type structure which can be assembled by the owner. According to appellants, it is portable and can be moved by two or more persons.

There is no doubt that appellants' dog pen falls within the definition of structure as that term is defined by Black's, *supra*. In addition, our courts have held that the term "structure: is not synonymous with the term "building". . . .

These modern times bear witness to the continual conflict between the unrestricted and free use of land so jealously guarded by our heritage, and the ever increasing closeness produced by residential expansion to serve the needs of our expanding population. The present case illustrates this conflict. One interest must prevail over the other when the two interest[s] collide. In the present case, the evidence is uncontroverted that Sherwood Estates was developed for residential use and to further that use the developing company set forth certain restrictions. There is no dispute that respondent herein is the proper substituted party for the developing company. It is likewise not in dispute that appellants acquired their property with full knowledge and acceptance of the restrictions. Enforcement of the restrictions by respondent is also not in dispute.

This court holds, and thus rules, that appellants' dog pen falls within the definition of the term "structure", Black's *supra*, and further, that their dog pen is a structure with the meaning and contemplation of the term "other structure" as that term is found and is made use of in Restriction VII. . . .

The judgment of the trial court is affirmed and appellants are hereby ordered to remove their dog pen from their property . . .

[Judgment affirmed]

QUESTIONS

1. If restrictive covenants are strictly construed in order to favor the free use of land, why didn't the court declare that there was nothing in the restrictive covenant prohibiting dog pens and that accordingly the pen should be allowed?

2. Assume that the McConnells had their house repainted. To do this the painting contractor erected rigid pipe and plank scaffolding that remained surrounding the house for about a month while the painting work was being done. Was this a violation of the restrictive covenant?

3. Assume that in the painting scaffolding case, the scaffolding was allowed to remain surrounding the building for a long time after the painting was finished. Would that be a violation of the covenant?

§ 7:8   PUBLIC ZONING

By **zoning**, a governmental unit, such as a city, adopts an ordinance imposing restrictions upon the use of the land. The object of zoning is to insure an orderly physical development of the regulated area. In effect, zoning is the same as the restrictive covenants with the difference being the source of authority. In most cases, zoning is based upon an ordinance of a local political subdivision, such as a municipality or a county. Restrictive covenants are created by agreement of the parties.

The zoning power permits any regulation that is conducive to advancing public health, welfare, and safety. The object of a particular zoning regulation may be to prevent high density of population. Some zoning ordinances may be conservation-inspired. Thus, the ordinance may prohibit the extraction of natural resources from any land within the zoned area.[12]

The fact that a house is designed for the landowner by an internationally known architect does not give the landowner the right to build the house when it violates the local zoning ordinance in a number of points.[13]

(a) NONCONFORMING USE. When the use of the land is in conflict with a zoning ordinance when the ordinance goes into effect, such use is described as a **nonconforming use**. For example, when a zoning ordinance is adopted that requires a setback of 25 feet from the boundary line, an existing building that has a 10-foot setback is a nonconforming use.

A nonconforming use has a constitutionally protected right to continue. If the nonconforming use is discontinued, however, it cannot be resumed. The right to a nonconforming use may thus be lost by abandonment. If the owner of a garage stops using it for a garage and uses it for storing goods, a return to the use of the property as a garage will be barred by abandonment.

(b) VARIANCE. The administrative agency charged with the enforcement of a zoning ordinance may grant a **variance**. This permits the owner of the land to use it in a specified manner inconsistent with the zoning ordinance.

The agency will ordinarily be reluctant to permit a variance when neighboring property owners object because, to the extent that variation is permitted, the basic plan of the zoning ordinance is defeated. Likewise, the allowance of an individual variation may result in such inequality as to be condemned by the courts as **spot zoning**. In addition, there is the consideration of practical expediency that if variances are readily granted, every property owner will request a variance and thus flood the agency with such requests. When the desired use of the land is in harmony with the general nature of the surrounding areas, it is probable that a zoning variance will be granted. A zoning variance will not be granted on the ground of hardship when the landowner created the hardship. Hardship may have been created by purchasing a lot that was too small to satisfy the zoning requirements or by selling portions of a tract, leaving the remaining part undersized.

It is unlikely that a variance from the zoning standard will be granted when the only reason advanced for the variance is that it would enable the owner to make more money.

For example, a variance would not be granted to an outdoor advertiser on the basis that a variance would permit the construction of outdoor billboards that would produce more money.[14]

§ 7:9   EMINENT DOMAIN

Eminent domain is the power of government to take private property for a public purpose. The power of eminent domain plays an important role in community planning because it is the means by which the land required for housing, redevelopment, and other projects may be acquired. Eminent domain has not become important in the area of environmental protection, although it is always present as a possible alternative on the theory that the op-

---

[12] American Aggregates Corp. v Highland Township, 151 Mich App 37, 390 NW2d 192 (1986).
[13] Burroughs v Town of Paradise Valley (App) 150 Ariz 570, 724 P2d 1239 (1986).

[14] Foster and Kleiser Outdoor Advertising, Inc. v University Furniture Galleries, Inc. (Ala Civ App) 500 So 2d 29 (1986).

erators of a government-owned plant would be more concerned than private owners with protection of the environment.

When property is taken by government through eminent domain, it must be taken for a public purpose and the government must pay the owner the fair value of the property taken. The taking of property for a private purpose is void as a deprivation of property without due process of law.

The fact that a zoning restriction may have the effect of preventing the landowner from making the most profitable use of the land, and may thereby lower the value of the land, does not constitute an eminent domain taking of the land and does not entitle the landowner to compensation.

C. NUISANCES

The common law, supplemented by statutes, prohibits conduct constituting a nuisance.

§ 7:10 DEFINITION OF NUISANCE

Conduct that unreasonably interferes with the enjoyment or use of land is a **nuisance**. This may be smoke from a chemical plant that damages the paint on neighboring houses. It may be noise, dirt, and vibration from the passing of heavy trucks. Some conduct is clearly so great an interference with others that it is easy to conclude that it constitutes a nuisance. Every interference is not a nuisance. Furthermore, it is frequently difficult to determine whether the interference is sufficiently great to be condemned as unreasonable and, therefore, as being a nuisance. The fact that the activity or business of the defendant is lawful and is conducted in a lawful manner does not establish that it is not a nuisance. It is the effect upon others that determines whether there is a nuisance. Thus, a landfill may be a nuisance even though operated by a city in a non-negligent manner and in accordance with the state's solid waste

disposal statutes.[15] The courts attempt to balance the social utility of the protection of a plaintiff with the social utility of the activity of the defendant. Thus, the mere fact that the plaintiff shows harm does not establish that the defendant's conduct is a nuisance, if the court believes that the conduct is socially desirable and, therefore, should be allowed to continue at the expense of the plaintiff's interest. For example, it has been held that smoke, fumes, and noise from public utilities and power plants were not nuisances, although they harmed the complaining plaintiffs. The courts believed that the interests of the community in the activity of the defendants outweighed the interests of the plaintiffs affected. Similarly, the proper use of land does not constitute a nuisance as to a neighbor, even though the neighbor does not like the use. In any case, to constitute a nuisance, the plaintiff must sustain a harm that goes beyond mere inconvenience or annoyance with the defendant's activity.[16] For example, when trees and underbrush on the landowner's land serve as a screen to hide the neighbor's backyard from public view, the neighbor has no legal ground for objecting to the landowner's removing such trees and underbrush even though the neighbor has lost the privacy that such trees and underbrush had given.

If conduct is held to constitute a nuisance, the persons affected may sue for monetary damages for the harm caused and may obtain an injunction or court order to stop the offending conduct.

(a) PRIVATE AND PUBLIC NUISANCES. When a nuisance affects only one or a few persons, it is called a **private nuisance**. When it affects the community or public at large it is called a **public nuisance**. At this point, the law of nuisance is very close to environmental protection, although there is a difference between the two. Environ-

---

[15] Wilhelm v Great Falls, ___ Mont ___, 732 P2d 1315 (1987).
[16] Crites v Sho-Me Dragways, Inc. (Mo App) 725 SW2d 90 (1987).

mental protection law is more concerned with harm to the environment and is less concerned with the social utility of the defendant's conduct than is the law of nuisance.

The existence of a statutory environmental protection procedure may bar or supersede the prior common law of nuisance.[17]

(b) CRIMINAL NUISANCE. Distinct from the nuisance that is harmful to other persons or to the enjoyment of the use of their land is the nuisance classified as such because it is a place where criminal acts repeatedly occur. Either by virtue of common-law principles or express provisions of statute, places conducting illegal gambling or the illegal sale of liquor or narcotics are declared to be nuisances.[18] The reason for this classification is one of practical expediency. In addition to prosecuting individuals involved in crime, the place may be shut down in the same way that any nuisance may be stopped.

(c) PERMANENT AND CONTINUING NUISANCES. A nuisance may be classified as (1) permanent or (2) continuing. The **permanent nuisance** consists of a single act that has caused permanent harm to the plaintiff. The **continuing nuisance** is a nuisance that is a series of related acts or a continuation of an activity, such as the emission of smoke from a factory.

(d) NUISANCES PER SE AND NUISANCES IN FACT. Nuisances may also be classified as nuisances per se and nuisances in fact. A **nuisance per se** is an act, occupation, or structure that is a nuisance at all times and under any circumstances. In contrast, a **nuisance in fact** is situational in that whether there is a nuisance depends upon the surrounding circumstances.[19] For example, the raising of pigs in a farming area is not a nuisance. The same activity in a large city would be a nuisance. It is, therefore, not a nuisance per se and could only be a nuisance in fact.

§ 7:11   THE TECHNOLOGICAL ENVIRONMENT OF THE LAW OF NUISANCE

As technology changes, new ways of manufacturing, new methods of transportation, and new ways of living develop. As the environment changes, corresponding changes are reflected in the law.

In the *Prah* case the ancient law of property rights was tested against the modern need for solar heating.

---

[17] Milwaukee v Illinois, 451 US 304 (1981).
[18] Colorado v Garner, ___ Colo ___, 732 P2d 1194 (1987).

[19] City of Sundown v Shewmake (Tex App) 691 SW2d 57 (1985).

PRAH V MARETTI

108 Wis 2d 223, 321 NW2d 182 (1982)

Prah bought one of two vacant lots. On his lot he built a house heated by solar energy. Maretti purchased the neighboring vacant lot and made plans to build a house on it. If Maretti built according to his plans, his house would interfere with the solar energy utilized by Prah's house. Prah requested Maretti to build his house a few feet further away from the boundary line. There was no evidence that Maretti would be harmed if he relocated his proposed house as requested. However, Maretti refused. His proposed location satisfied the zoning law and the restrictive covenant in his deed. Prah then sued to enjoin Maretti from building his house so as to interfere with the solar energy of Prah's house. From a decision against Prah, he appealed.

ABRAHAMSON, J. . . . The defendant asserts that he has a right to develop his property in compliance with statutes, ordinances and private covenants without regard to the effect of such development upon the plaintiff's access to sunlight. In essence, the defendant is asking this court to hold that the private nuisance doctrine is not applicable in the instant case and that his right to develop his land is a right which is *per se* superior to his neighbor's interest in access to sunlight. This position is expressed in the maxim "cujus est solum, ejus est usque ad coelum et ad infernos," that is the owner of land owns up to the sky and down to the center of the earth. The rights of the surface owner are, however, not unlimited.

The defendant is not completely correct in asserting that the common law did not protect a landowner's access to sunlight across adjoining property. At English common law a landowner could acquire a right to receive sunlight across adjoining land by both express agreement and under the judge-made doctrine of "ancient lights." Under the doctrine of ancient lights if the landowner had received sunlight across adjoining property for a specified period of time, the landowner was entitled to continue to receive unobstructed access to sunlight across the adjoining property. Under the doctrine the landowner acquired a negative prescriptive easement and could prevent the adjoining landowner from obstructing access to light.

Although American courts have not been as receptive to protecting a landowner's access to sunlight as the English courts, American courts have afforded some protection to a landowner's interest in access to sunlight. American courts honor express easements to sunlight. American courts initially enforced the English common law doctrine of ancient lights, but later every state which considered the doctrine repudiated it as inconsistent with the needs of a developing country. Indeed, for just that reason this court concluded that an easement to light and air over adjacent property could not be created or acquired by prescription and has been unwilling to recognize such as easement by implication.

Many jurisdictions in this country have protected a landowner from malicious obstruction of access to light (the spite fence cases) under the common law private nuisance doctrine. If an activity is motivated by malice it lacks utility and the harm it causes others outweighs any social values. This court was reluctant to protect a landowner's interest in sunlight even against a spite fence, only to be overruled by the legislature. Shortly after this court upheld a landowner's right to erect a useless and unsightly sixteen-foot spite fence four feet from his neighbor's windows, *Metzger v. Hochrein*, 107 Wis. 267, 83 N.W. 208 (1900), the legislature enacted a law specifically defining a spite fence as an actionable private nuisance. Thus a landowner's interest in sunlight has been protected in this country by common law private nuisance law at least in the narrow context of the modern American rule invalidating spite fences.

This court's reluctance in the nineteenth and early part of the twentieth century to provide broader protection for a landowner's access to sunlight was premised on three policy considerations. First, the right of landowners to use their property as they wished, as long as they did not cause physical damage to a neighbor, was jealously guarded.

Second, sunlight was valued only for aesthetic enjoyment or as illumination. Since artificial light could be used for illumination, loss of sunlight was at most a personal annoyance which was given little, if any, weight by society.

Third, society had a significant interest in not restricting or impeding land development. . . . These three policies are no longer fully accepted or applicable. They reflect factual circumstances and social priorities that are now obsolete.

First, society has increasingly regulated the use of land by the landowner for the general welfare.

Second, access to sunlight has taken on a new significance in recent years. In this case the plaintiff seeks to protect access to sunlight, not for aesthetic reasons or as a source of illumination but as a source of energy. Access to sunlight as an energy source is of significance both to the landowner who invests in solar collectors and to a society which has an interest in developing alternative sources of energy.

Third, the policy of favoring unhindered private development in an expanding economy is no longer in harmony with the realities of our society. The need for easy and rapid development is not as great today as it once was, while our perception of the value of sunlight as a source of energy has increased significantly.

Courts should not implement obsolete policies that have lost their vigor over the course of the years. The law of private nuisance is better suited to resolve landowners' disputes about property development in the 1980's than is a rigid rule which does not recognize a landowner's interest in access to sunlight. As we said in *Ballstadt v. Pagel*, 202 Wis. 484, 489, 232 N.W. 862 (1930), "What is regarded in law as constituting a nuisance in modern times would no doubt have been tolerated without question in former times." . . .

Yet the defendant would have us ignore the flexible private nuisance law as a means of resolving the dispute between the landowners in this case and would have us adopt an approach . . . of favoring the unrestricted development of land and of applying a rigid and inflexible rule protecting his right to build on his land and disregarding any interest of the plaintiff in the use and enjoyment of his land. This we refuse to do.

[Judgment reversed and action remanded]

Questions

1. Was the nuisance involved in the *Prah* case a public or private nuisance?
2. In its opinion the court states that the American courts have repudiated the doctrine of ancient lights as "inconsistent with the needs of a developing country." What does this statement tell you as to the nature and the development of the law?
3. In its opinion, the court states that, by using private nuisance law, it is departing from the narrow protection of a landowner's access to sunlight because that law is obsolete. What factors does the court give in support of this conclusion?

The *Prah* case is a departure from American property law. However, the movements in favor of environmental protection and fuel conservation will probably lead other courts to follow its conclusion in the next century.[20]

[20] The *Prah* case has been rejected in Sher v Herbert, 181 Cal App 3d 867, 226 Cal Rptr 698 (1986).

SUMMARY

America has awakened to the fact that resources are not unlimited and that the misuse of resources can be harmful to life. This realization has led to the adoption of numerous state and federal laws aimed at preventing the pollution of air, water, and earth. With the advent of the nuclear age, the problem of disposing of wastes in such a way as to avoid environmental pollution has become increasingly acute. A person violating an environmental protection law is subject to administrative agency action, civil suit, and criminal prosecution.

Community planning has both governmental and private aspects. With respect to government, community planning ordinarily takes the form of a zoning statute or ordinance that regulates the kind of use to which land may be put. When a zoning ordinance is adopted, there may be some spots in the zoned area that are being used in a manner that violates the zoning plan. Such a nonconforming use cannot be outlawed by the zoning ordinance. As the converse of allowing the nonconforming use to continue, the person wishing to use land in a way not permitted by the zoning ordinance may petition the zoning board or authority for a variance from the general zoning plan. Government may also take part in community planning by taking land by eminent domain for use for a public purpose. At the private level, community planning is made by means of restrictive convenants in the deeds given by the planning owner of a large tract to the purchasers of individual lots of the tract.

Traditional equity power authorizes enjoining (stopping) of nuisances. A public nuisance may also be stopped by direct government action.

QUESTIONS AND CASE PROBLEMS

1. "Smoke, fumes, and noise from public utilities and power plants are not to be condemned as nuisances merely because some harm is sustained from their activity by a particular plaintiff." Which of the objectives of the law listed in Chapter 2 are operative?
2. What is the purpose of an environmental impact statement?
3. The Federal Oil Company was loading a tanker with fuel oil. The loading hose snapped for some unknown reason and about one thousand gallons of oil poured into the ocean. The Federal Oil Company was prosecuted for water pollution. It raised the defense that it had exercised due care, was not at fault in any way, and had not intended to pollute the water. Is it guilty?
4. Annabel purchased a building in an area in the city that was zoned residential. She wanted to run a quick-printing shop in the building. She was informed that she could not do so because of the zoning regulation. She replied that she could do so because the deed that transferred ownership of the property to her did not contain any restriction prohibiting such use. Was she correct?
5. Magnolia City wanted to build a thruway from one side of the city to the other in order to facilitate thru traffic. To acquire the land for such a highway, it purchased various parcels of land from private owners. Thomp-

son refused to sell his land. The city tendered to Thompson the fair value of his land and demanded that he surrender the land to the city. Thompson claimed that the city could not require him to sell the land. Was Thompson correct?

6. What remedies does a homeowner have when smoke from a nearby factory causes the paint on the home to peel?

7. Carlotta owns a grocery store. It is located in an area that is later zoned as exclusively residential. Can Carlotta continue to run the grocery store after the adoption of the zoning regulation?

8. Mark divides a large tract of land into small lots. He then sells the lots. In the deed to each buyer is a provision stating that the buyer will not build a house closer than 6 feet to any boundary line of the lot. Madeline buys one of these lots and begins to build 2 feet from the boundary line. Her neighbor, Jason, protests that Madeline cannot do this because of the 6-foot restriction in her deed. Madeline replies that this restriction was made with Mark and that it has no effect between Jason and Madeline. Is Madeline correct?

9. A zoning ordinance of the city of Dallas, Texas, prohibited the use of property in a residential district for gasoline filling stations. Lombardo brought an action against the city to test the validity of the ordinance. He contended that the ordinance violated the rights of the owners of property in such districts. Do you agree with this contention? [Lombardo v City of Dallas, 124 Tex 1, 73 SW2d 475]

10. Shearing was a homeowner in Rochester. The city burned trash on a nearby tract of land. Fires burned continuously on open ground, not in an incinerator, at times within 800 yards of the plaintiff's house. The smoke and dirt from the fires settled on the house of the plaintiff and on those of other persons in the area. The plaintiff sued to stop the continuance of such burning and to recover damages for the harm done to his home. Decide. [Shearing v Rochester, 51 Misc 2d 436, 273 NYS2d 464]

11. The Belmar Drive-In Theatre Co. brought an action against the Illinois State Toll Highway Commission because the bright lights of the toll road station interfered with the showing of motion pictures at the drive-in.

Decide. [Belmar Drive-In Theatre Co. v Illinois State Toll Highway Commission, 34 Ill 2d 544, 216 NE2d 788]

12. The Stallcups lived in a rural section of the state. In front of their house ran a relatively unused, unimproved public county road. Wales Trucking Co. transported concrete pipe from the plant where it was made to a lake where the pipe was used to construct a water line to bring water to a nearby city. In the course of four months Wales made 825 trips over the road carrying from 58,000 to 72,000 pounds of pipe per trip and making the same number of empty return trips. The heavy use of the road by Wales cut up the dirt and made it like ashes. The Stallcups sued Wales for damages caused by the deposit of dust on their house and for the physical annoyance and discomfort caused by the dust. Wales defended on the ground that it had not been negligent and that its use of the road was not unlawful. Decide. [Wales Trucking Co. v Stallcup (Tex Civ App) 465 SE2d 44]

13. Gallagher owned a tract of land that was subject to the restriction that it be used "for residence only." He began to build a townhouse condominium on the land. The owners of the neighboring land, acting as the Don Cesar Property Owners Corporation, brought an action against Gallagher to prevent the construction of the condominium. Were they entitled to prevent the construction? [Don Cesar Property Owners Corp. v Gallagher (Fla App) 452 So 2d 1047]

14. A modular home is a home that is constructed in two or more parts. The parts are then moved to a particular tract of land where they are fastened together. When completed, the house is as immobile as, and has the same appearance as, an ordinary house that is constructed piece by piece. The modular home, however, costs less. The Town of Fishkill adopted a zoning ordinance that prohibited mobile homes unless they were placed in trailer parks. Did the ordinance apply to a modular home? [Kyritsis v Fenny, 310 NYS2d 702]

15. Patrick Bossenberry owned a house in a planned community area. Each lot in the area was limited by a restrictive covenant to use for a single family dwelling. The covenant defined *family* so as to require blood or marital relationship between most of the oc-

cupants. Bossenberry rented his building to Kay-Jan, Inc. Kay-Jan wanted to use the building as a care home for not more than six adult mentally retarded persons. The neighbors sought to enjoin this use as a breach of the covenant. A number of Michigan statutes had been adopted, advancing the public policy of providing care for mentally retarded persons. Could the neighbors prevent the use of the property as a care home for mentally retarded adults? [Craig v Bossenberry, 134 Mich App 543, 351 NW2d 596]

8

CONSUMER PROTECTION

In the last few decades, the consumer protection movement has made a substantial number of changes to traditional law.

A. GENERAL PRINCIPLES

Consumer protection began with the aim of protecting the person of limited means and limited knowledge. This is the opening wedge, but the movement has expanded so that today the objective is protecting everyone from being victimized. This is in keeping with the American concept of equality before the law. If protection is needed, it should be extended to everyone who needs it.

§ 8:1 EXPANSION OF PROTECTION

The consumer protection movement was started to protect poor, ignorant individuals. The social forces of protecting the person and protecting from fraud, exploitation, and oppression have expanded the category of protected consumers. Many

154

consumer protection statutes now define *consumer* as any person, partnership, corporation, bank, or government that uses goods or services. Thus, it has been held that *consumer* includes a collector paying nearly $100,000 for jade art objects, a glass manufacturer purchasing 3,000,000 gallons of diesel oil fuel, or the city of Boston purchasing insurance.[1]

In a few states, a limitation is imposed that a suit involving the consumer be of public interest or concern. Thus, a dispute between real estate brokers could not be brought within the consumer protection statute when the facts were so unusual that there was no general public interest in the outcome of the case. That is, it was not a situation that was likely to occur with many other consumers. Note that the fact that both the plaintiff and the defendant in the broker case were experienced business persons did not exclude either of them from the protection of the consumer protection statute.[2]

§ 8:2 WHO IS A DEFENDANT IN A CONSUMER PROTECTION SUIT?

The defendant in consumer protection situations is a person or an enterprise that regularly enters into the kind of transaction in which the injured consumer was involved. For example, it is the merchant seller, the finance company, the bank, the leasing company, the home repairers, and any others who enter regularly in a particular kind of transaction.

Society feels that such a business or enterprise, familiar with all the procedures and practices of that business, is likely to be able to victimize the consumer. Of course this argument is less convincing as we move away from the original image of the poor little consumer. Nevertheless, there is still the sound basis that the purpose of consumer protection is to clean up the business world, and therefore it is the defendant in business with which consumer protection is concerned.

§ 8:3 CONSUMER NEGLIGENCE

Consumer protection law is directed at protecting the consumer from the misconduct of others. Disclosure provisions are frequently imposed in order to give the consumer the information that the consumer would lack and would not have enough experience or bargaining power to demand. In a limited number of situations, the consumer is given the power to rescind a transaction if hindsight makes the consumer unhappy with the deal that had been made.

Consumer protection, however, does not protect a consumer from the consumer's own negligence. Thus, a consumer is bound by a contract even though the consumer signed without reading or understanding what it meant. Moreover, when the contract signed by the consumer clearly states one thing, the consumer cannot prove that the other contracting party had made statements contradicting what was stated in the signed contract.[3]

Consumers should exercise reasonable care and not blindly trust consumer protection law to rescue them from their own blunders.

§ 8:4 CONSUMER REMEDIES

The theoretical right of the consumer to sue or to assert a defense is often of little practical value to the consumer because of the small size of the amount involved and the high cost of litigation. Consumer protection legislation provides special remedies.

(a) GOVERNMENT AGENCY ACTION. The Uniform Consumer Credit Code (UCCC)

---

[1] Boston v Aetna Life Ins. Co. 399 Mass 569, 506 NE2d 106 (1987).
[2] Broten v May, ___ Wash App ___, 735 P2d 86 (1987).

[3] Heidt v Potamkin Chrysler-Plymouth, Inc. 181 Ga App 903, 354 SE2d 440 (1987).

provides for an administrator who will, in a sense, police business practices to insure conformity with the law. This is not regarded by some as an improvement and has been criticized because of the danger that the administrator may be creditor-oriented. As a consequence, the debtor might be deprived of protection in many cases when it is a question of policy or discretion as to what action, if any, should be taken by the administrator.

(b) ACTION BY ATTORNEY GENERAL. A number of states provide that the state attorney general may bring an action on behalf of a particular group of consumers to obtain cancellation of their contracts and restitution of whatever they had paid.

Many states permit the attorney general to bring an action to enjoin violation of the consumer protection statute. Consumer protection statutes commonly give the attorney general the authority to seek a voluntary stopping of improper practices before seeking to obtain an injunction from a court.

(c) ACTION BY CONSUMER. Some consumer protection statutes provide that a consumer who is harmed by a violation of the statutes may sue the enterprise that ac-

ted improperly. The consumer may sue to recover a specified penalty or may bring an action on behalf of consumers as a class. Consumer protection statutes are often designed to rely on private litigation as an aid to enforcement of the statutory provisions. The Consumer Product Safety Act of 1972 authorizes "any interested person" to bring a civil action to enforce a consumer product safety rule and certain orders of the Consumer Product Safety Commission. In some cases, however, the individual consumer cannot bring any action, and enforcement of the law is entrusted exclusively to an administrative agency.

In any case, a consumer who shows only that the defendant had broken a contract is not entitled to recover under a fair business practices or deceptive trade practices act. In addition, the plaintiff must show misconduct of the kind prohibited by the statutes.[4]

The *Varady* case illustrates the use of a statutory penalty in the Uniform Consumer Credit Code (UCCC) to induce private litigation as an enforcement aid.

---

[4]   Gross v Ideal Pool Corp. 181 Ga App 483, 352 SE2d 806 (1987).

VARADY v WHITE
42 Colo App 389, 661 P2d 284 (1982)

Robert White was an electronic technician. His wife Marilyn was a homemaker. The Whites owned a 90-acre tract of land, which they subdivided and sold as unimproved lots. The sixth lot was sold to Kenneth Varady. All sales were made partly on credit, with an unpaid balance being secured by some form of collateral agreement. The Whites failed to inform Varady of certain matters that the UCCC required them to disclose. Within three days after the transfer of ownership of the land to Varady, Varady notified the Whites that he was rescinding the transaction. The Whites refused to return Varady's money to him or to take back the land. Varady brought an action against the Whites. From a judgment in their favor, he appealed.

KELLY, J. . . . [UCCC] Section 5–2–104(1)(a) provides that a "consumer credit sale" is a sale of an interest in land in which "[c]redit is granted . . . by a person who *regularly* engages as a seller in *credit transactions of the same kind. . . ."* (emphasis added). Thus, in order to determine whether the disputed transaction is subject to the disclosure requirements of the UCCC, we must consider whether, as a matter of law, the prior transactions constituted "regular" credit transactions and whether they were of "the same kind" as the subject transaction.

Colorado's UCCC is based on the Federal Consumer Credit Protection Act (CCPA), 15 U.S.C.A. § 1601, et seq., and the intent of the CCPA "seems to have been to except from the Act only those lenders whose extensions of credit are an occasional, isolated, and incidental portion of their business." *Eby v Reb Realty, Inc.*, 495 F2d 646 (9th Cir. 1974). Thus, private homeowners who take back second mortgages upon selling their homes would normally not be required to comply with the disclosure requirements of the Act.

Although the Whites sold their own home and took a second mortgage, they had subdivided their 90-acre property and sold five unimproved lots in their subdivision prior to the sale to plaintiffs. Neither defendant had a real estate license or worked full time in the real estate business: Robert White was an electronic technician and Marilyn White was a housewife. However, the subdivision and the sale of lots is itself a business venture. After five separate sales of lots from a 90-acre tract, the Whites cannot claim ignorance of real estate transactions. Moreover, they sold more unimproved lots after the sale to plaintiffs. In *Eby, supra,* the realty firm was held to have engaged in "regular" credit transactions although it had sold only three parcels on credit within a time span of nineteen months. The Whites sold lots in September and October of 1974, and April, June, and July of 1976 before the sale to the Varadys. This constitutes "regular" credit transactions for purposes of § 5–2–104(1)(a), C.R.S. 1973.

Since the phrase "credit transactions of the same kind" is not included in the definition of a credit transaction under the CCPA, we must interpret this phrase without the aid of federal guidelines. While the Whites sold the Varadys improved land and the prior sales conveyed unimproved lots, the presence or absence of improvements is not a critical factor in determining whether transactions are of the same kind. All the sales consisted of an "interest in land" purchased primarily for a personal, family, or household use under § 5–2–104(1)(c), C.R.S. 1973.

The two sales in 1974 and the sale to the Varadys in 1976 involved second deeds of trust, while the other three sales in 1976 involved first deeds of trust. However, the Whites were the creditors in each of the transactions, so the form of the security interest is not determinative of this issue. Although these six transactions were not identical in each minute detail, we conclude, as a matter of law, that they were "credit transactions of the same kind." Therefore, since the Whites regularly engaged in credit transactions of the same kind, their sale to the Varadys was a "consumer credit sale" under § 5–2–104(1)(a), C.R.S. 1973.

Since the Varady-White transaction was a consumer credit sale of an interest in land, the debtors have rescission rights under § 5–5–204, C.R.S. 1973. This section permits the debtor to rescind the transaction "until midnight of the third business day following the consummation of the transaction or the delivery of the disclosures required under this section . . . whichever is later. . . ." When a debtor rescinds, § 5–5–204(2), C.R.S. 1973, affords him a number of rights. First, he is not liable for any credit service charge, and any security interest given by the debtor becomes void upon the rescission. Second, within ten days after receipt of a notice of rescission, the creditor must return to the debtor "the money or property given as earnest money, down payment, or otherwise," and must terminate any security interest created under the transaction. And third, upon the performance of the creditor's obligations, the debtor must tender the property to the creditor, and unless the creditor takes possession of the property within ten days after the tender by the debtor, the debtor may keep the property without paying for it.

Where, as here, the creditors have not made the disclosures required by the UCCC, the debtors are at liberty to rescind the contract at their pleasure. *Sosa v Fite*, 498 F2d 114 (5th Cir. 1974). Since the Varadys gave the Whites notice of their intent to rescind within three days of closing, and the Whites did not return the Varadys' payments and terminate their security interest within ten days of the notice of rescission, the Whites must return all money paid to them by the Varadys, and ownership of the property vests in the Varadys without their obligation to pay for it.

The Whites were subject to a statutory duty to inform the Varadys of their right to rescind the transaction. . . . Although the Whites did not act purposefully to deprive the Varadys of their rights, it is up to the creditor to avoid forfeiture by complying with the UCCC. The creditors' "lament of any inequity being visited upon them is utterly unpersuasive, for the power was completely theirs to prevent this parade of creditor horribles from ever occurring." *Sosa, supra.* In short, all the Whites had to do to avoid this result was to follow the law. . . .

[Judgment reversed]

QUESTIONS

1. Why did the court hold that the UCCC was applicable?
2. Was the answer to the first question inevitable?
3. What social forces are affected by this decision?

(d) SCOPE OF RELIEF. The consumer protection statutes only provide relief as to conduct condemned by such statutes. They afford no protection to a consumer against a mere breach of contract. Thus, the fact that the seller never delivers the goods purchased by the buyer does not by itself constitute a violation of a consumer protection statute. However, there may be other circumstances that, when combined with the nondelivery of the goods, will show that the seller has violated a consumer protection statute.

§ 8:5   CIVIL AND CRIMINAL PENALTIES

The seller or lender engaging in improper consumer practices may be subject to civil penalties and criminal punishment. In some instances the laws in question are the general laws applicable to improper conduct, while in other cases the laws are specifically aimed at the particular consumer practices.

An example of a violation of the general law is a contractor who falsely stated to a homeowner that certain repairs needed on the roof cost, with labor and materials, $650. In fact, they cost only $200, and the contractor was guilty of the crime of obtaining money by false pretenses.

Illustrative of specific consumer protection statutes, the Truth in Lending Act subjects the creditor to a separate claim for damages for each periodic statement that violates the disclosure requirements. Furthermore, consumer protection statutes of the disclosure type generally provide that the creditor cannot enforce the obligation of the debtor if the required information is not set forth in the contract.

B.   AREAS OF CONSUMER PROTECTION

The following sections discuss the more important areas of consumer protection.

§ 8:6   ADVERTISING

Statutes commonly prohibit fraudulent advertising, but most advertising regulations are entrusted to an administrative agency, such as the Federal Trade Commission (FTC). The FTC is authorized to issue orders to stop false or misleading advertising. Statutes prohibiting false advertising are liberally interpreted.

(a) DECEPTION. Under consumer protection statutes, deception, rather than fraud, is the significant element. There is a breach of such statutes even though there is no proof that the wrongdoer intended to defraud or deceive anyone.[5]

This is a shift of social point of view. That is, instead of basing the law in terms of fault of the actor, the law is concerned with the problem of the buyer, who is likely to be misled by statements made without regard to whether the defendant had any evil in-

---

[5]   Haag v Dry Basement, Inc. 11 Kan App 2d 649, 732 P2d 392 (1987).

tent. The good faith of an advertiser or the absence of intent to deceive is immaterial, as the purpose of false advertising legislation is to protect the consumer rather than to examine the advertiser's motives.

The net effect of the truth in advertising legislation is that a seller must make an accurate and substantially complete description of the product and the terms on which it is sold and must do so in a way that the buyer can be expected to understand.

At common law, a seller was not liable when the product did not live up to the opinion expressed by the seller to the buyer. The theory of the common law was that the buyer should recognize that the statement was merely the opinion of the seller and that the buyer should not rely thereon. In the realities of the marketplace, buyers do rely on sellers' opinions, and therefore, the unfair trade practices laws condemn false opinions of sellers that mislead buyers.

The FTC requires that an advertiser maintain a file containing the data claimed to support an advertising statement as to safety, performance, efficacy, quality, or comparative price of an advertised product. The FTC can require the advertiser to produce this material. If it is in the interest of the consumer, the commission can make this information public, except to the extent that it contains trade secrets or matter that is privileged.

The *Colgate-Palmolive* case involves action taken by the Federal Trade Commission to protect consumers from advertising that the commission thought was misleading.

FTC V COLGATE-PALMOLIVE CO.

380 US 374 (1965)

The Colgate-Palmolive Co. sells a shaving cream, Rapid Shave. To test the effectiveness of the cream, the company put it on sandpaper and then shaved the sandpaper. The company then wanted to run a commercial on television showing this test as proof that the product could soften even the toughness of sandpaper. When the actual test was telecast, the sandpaper looked like ordinary colored paper. In order to have something that really looked like sandpaper, the advertiser used a sheet of Plexiglass on which sand had been sprinkled. The Federal Trade Commission prohibited this commercial on the ground that it deceived the viewer. The advertiser claimed that there was no deception because the viewer was merely being given an accurate visual representation of the test that had actually been made. The FTC issued an order to stop the commercial. The court of appeals reversed this order. The case was then appealed to the U.S. Supreme Court.

WARREN, C. J. . . . The Commission found that the undisclosed use of a plexiglass substitute for sandpaper was [a] material misrepresentation that was a deceptive act separate and distinct from [any] misrepresentation concerning Rapid Shave's underlying qualities. Even if the sandpaper could be shaved just as depicted in the commercials, the Commission found that viewers had been misled into believing they had seen it done with their own eyes. As a result of these findings the Commission entered a cease-and-desist order against the respondents [Colgate and the advertiser]. . . .

. . . The Commission expressed the view that without this visible proof of Rapid Shave's moisturizing ability some viewers might not have been persuaded to buy the product. . . .

. . . When the Commission was created by Congress in 1914, it was directed by § 5 to prevent "unfair methods of competition in commerce." Congress amended the Act in 1938 to extend the Commission's jurisdiction to include "unfair or deceptive acts or practices in commerce" — a significant amendment showing Congress' concern for consumers as well as for competitors. It is important to note the generality of these standards of illegality. . . . *Federal Trade Comm'n v Motion Picture Advertising Service Co.* 344 US 392, 394.

This statutory scheme necessarily gives the Commission an influential role in interpreting § 5 and in applying it to the facts of particular cases arising out of unprecedented situations. Moreover, as an administrative agency which deals continually with cases in the area, the Commission is often in a better position than are courts to determine when a practice is "deceptive" within the meaning of the Act. . . . [Compare] *Federal Trade Comm'n v R. F. Kappel & Bro., Inc.* 291 US 301.

We accept the Commission's determination that the commercials involved in this case contained three representations to the public: (1) that sandpaper could be shaved by Rapid Shave; (2) that an experiment had been conducted which verified this claim; and (3) that the viewer was seeing this experiment . . . . For the purposes of our review, we can assume that the first two representations were true; the focus of our consideration is on the third, which was clearly false. The parties agree that § 5 prohibits the intentional misrepresentation of any fact which would constitute a material factor in a purchaser's decision whether to buy. They differ, however, in their conception of what "facts" constitute a "material factor" in a purchaser's decision to buy. Respondents submit, in effect, that the only material facts are those which deal with the substantive qualities of a product. The Commission, on the other hand, submits that the misrepresentation of *any* fact so long as it materially induces a purchaser's decision to buy is a deception prohibited by § 5.

The Commission's interpretation of what is a deceptive practice seems more in line with the decided cases than that of respondents. . . . *Federal Trade Comm'n v Algoma Lumber Co.* 291 US 67.

We agree with the Commission . . . that the undisclosed use of plexiglass in the present commercials was a material deceptive practice. . . . Respondents claim that it will be impractical to inform the viewing public that it is not seeing an actual test, experiment or demonstration, but we think it inconceivable that the ingenious advertising world will be unable, if it so desires, to conform to the Commission's insistence that the public be not misinformed. If, however, it becomes impossible or impractical to show simulated demonstrations on television in a truthful manner, this indicates that television is not a medium that lends itself to this type of commercial, not that the commercial must survive at all costs. . . .

[Judgment reversed]

QUESTIONS

1. Was Colgate-Palmolive being sued for damages for fraud?
2. Who was harmed by the commercial for Rapid Shave?
3. Was Colgate-Palmolive guilty of fraudulent selling practices?

(b) CORRECTIVE ADVERTISING. When an enterprise has made false and deceptive statements in advertising, the Federal Trade Commission may require that new advertising be made in which the former statements are contradicted and the truth stated. This corrective advertising required by the Federal Trade Commission is also called **retractive advertising.**

§ 8:7   SEALS OF APPROVAL

Many commodities are sold or advertised with a sticker or tag stating that the article has been approved or is guaranteed by some association or organization. Ordinarily, when a product is thus sold, it will, in fact, have been approved by some testing laboratory and will probably have proven adequate to meet ordinary consumer needs. A seller who sells with a seal of approval of a third person makes, in effect, a guarantee that the product has been so approved, so that such a seller is liable if the product was, in fact, not approved. In addition, the seller would ordinarily be liable for fraud if the statement is not true.

§ 8:8   LABELING

Closely related to the regulation of advertising is the regulation of labels and marking of products. Various federal statutes are designed to give the consumer accurate information about the product, while others require warnings as to dangers of use or misuse. Consumer protection regulations prohibit the use in the labeling or marking of products of such terms as *jumbo*, *giant*, or *full*, that tend to exaggerate and mislead.

§ 8:9   SELLING METHODS

Consumer protection statutes prohibit the use of improper and deceptive selling methods.[6] These statutes are liberally con-

---

[6] As to states adopting the Uniform Consumer Credit Code (UCCC) see § 1:3. The Uniform Consumer Sales Practices Act has been adopted in Kansas, Ohio, and Utah; a Uniform Deceptive Trade Practices Act (1966 revision) has been adopted in Colorado, Georgia, Hawaii, Minnesota, Nebraska, New Mexico, Ohio, and Oregon: the 1964 version of the Uniform Deceptive Trade Practices Act was adopted in Delaware, Illinois, Maine, and Oklahoma; and a Model Land Sales Practice Act has been adopted in Alaska, Connecticut, Florida, Hawaii, Idaho, Kansas, Minnesota, Montana, South Carolina, and Utah.

strued to protect consumers from improper practices.

(a) DISCLOSURE OF TRANSACTION TERMS. The federal law requires the disclosure of all interest charges, points or fees for granting loans, and similar charges. These charges must be set forth as an annual percentage rate so that the consumer can see just how much the transaction costs a year and can compare alternatives.[7]

If sellers advertise that they will sell or lease on credit, they cannot state merely the monthly installments that will be due. They must give the consumer additional information: (1) the total cash price; (2) the amount of the down payment required; (3) the number, amounts, and due dates of payments; and (4) the annual percentage rate of the credit charges.[8]

In various ways, consumer protection statutes seek to protect the consumer from surprise or unbargained-for terms and from unwanted contracts.

(1) More-Than-Four-Installments Rule. Whenever a consumer sale or contract provides for payment in more than four installments, it is subject to the Truth in Lending Act. This is so even though no service or finance charge is expressly added because of the installment pattern of paying.

When consumer credit is advertised as repayable in more than four installments and no finance charge is expressly imposed, the advertisement must "clearly and conspicuously" state that "the cost of credit is included in the price" quoted for the goods and services.

The *Mourning* case raised the question of whether an administrative regulation was valid when it required disclosure information whenever payment was made by the consumer in more than four installments.

---

[7]   Consumer Credit Protection Act (CCPA), 15 USC § § 1605, 1606, 1636; Regulation Z adopted by the Federal Reserve Board of Governors, § 226.5.
[8]   Regulation Z, § 1210, Consumer Leasing Act of 1976, 15 USC § 1667.

MOURNING V FAMILY PUBLICATION SERVICE, INC.
411 US 356 (1973)

When goods or services are sold on the installment plan, it is customary to charge the customer more than when the full price is paid at one time in cash. When there is a time price and a cash price, consumer protection statutes generally require that the consumer be informed of the two prices so that the consumer may make an intelligent choice. The Federal Reserve Board adopted a regulation called Regulation Z, stating that whenever a consumer paid for goods or services in more than four installments, the seller had to disclose the information specified in the Truth in Lending Act. Family Publications sold a magazine to Leila Mourning. Payment was to be made by her in 30 installments, but no extra charge was made over the cash price. Leila claimed that Family Publications violated Regulation Z because it did not disclose the information required by the Truth in Lending Act. Family Publications claimed that the more than four installments rule of Regulation Z was invalid and that the federal Truth in Lending Act could not apply to it, because it did not make any extra charge for the making of installment payments. The court of appeals held the regulation invalid and Mourning appealed.

BURGER, C. J. . . . Passage of the Truth in Lending Act in 1968 culminated several years of congressional study and debate as to the propriety and usefulness of imposing mandatory disclosure requirements on those who extend credit to consumers in the American market. By the time of passage, it had become abundantly clear that the use of consumer credit was expanding at an extremely rapid rate. . . .

The Truth in Lending Act was designed to remedy the problems which had developed. . . . This purpose was . . . "to assure a meaningful disclosure of credit terms so that the consumer will be able to compare more readily the various credit terms available to him and avoid the uninformed use of credit." . . .

. . . Congress determined to lay the structure of the Act broadly and to entrust its construction to an agency with the necessary experience and resources to monitor its operation. Section 105 delegated to the Federal Reserve Board broad authority to promulgate regulations necessary to render the Act effective. . . . In addition to granting to the Board the authority normally given to administrative agencies to promulgate regulations designed to "carry out the purposes" of the Act, Congress specifically stated: "These regulations may contain such classifications, differentiations, or other provisions, and may provide for such adjustments and exceptions for any class of transactions, as in the judgment of the Board are necessary or proper . . . to prevent circumvention or evasion [of the Act], or to facilitate compliance therewith." . . .

One means of circumventing the objectives of the Truth in Lending Act, as passed by Congress, was that of "burying" the cost of credit in the price of goods sold. Thus in many credit transactions in which creditors claimed that no finance charge had been imposed, the creditor merely assumed the cost of extending credit as an expense of doing business, to be recouped as part of the price charged in the transaction. Congress was well aware, from its extensive studies, of the possibility that merchants could use such devices to evade the disclosure requirements of the Act. The Committee hearings are replete with suggestions that such manipulation would render the Act a futile gesture in the case of goods normally sold by installment contract. Opponents of the bill contended that the reporting provisions would actually encourage merchants who had formerly segregated their credit costs not to do so. They predicted that the effect of the Act would thus be to reduce the amount of information available to the consumer, a result directly contrary to that which was intended. . . .

. . . The Board's objective in promulgating the [more than four installment] rule was to prevent the Act from fulfilling the prophecy which its opponents had forecast. . . .

That the approach taken may reflect what respondent views as an undue paternalistic concern for the consumer is beside the point. The statutory scheme is within the power granted to Congress under the Commerce Clause. It is not a function of the courts to speculate as to whether the statute is unwise or whether the evils sought to be remedied could better have been regulated in some other manner.

[Judgment reversed and remanded]

QUESTIONS

1. What is Regulation Z?
2. Does the court pass upon the wisdom of the disclosure requirement or of

the application of the more-than-four-installments rule?

3. What is the basis for selecting four installments rather than three or five?

(2) Contract on Two Sides. In order to be sure that disclosures required by federal law are seen by the consumer, special provision is made for the case when the terms of the transaction are printed on both the front and back of a sheet or contract. In such case, (a) both sides of the sheet must carry the warning: "NOTICE: see other side for important information," and (b) the page must be signed at the end of the second side. Conversely, the requirements of the federal law are not satisfied when there is no warning of "see other side" and the parties sign the contract on the face, or the first side, of the paper only.

(3) Particular Sales and Leases. The Motor Vehicle Information and Cost Savings Act requires the disclosure to the buyer of various elements in the cost of an automobile. The act prohibits selling an automobile without informing the buyer that the odometer has been reset below the true mileage. A buyer who is caused actual loss by odometer fraud may recover from the seller three times the actual loss or $1500, whichever is greater.[9] There is a breach of the federal statute when the seller has knowledge that the odometer has turned itself at 100,000 miles but the seller then states that the mileage is 20,073 miles instead of 120,073. The Consumer Leasing Act of 1976 requires that persons leasing automobiles and other durable goods to consumers make a full disclosure to the consumer of the details of the transaction.

(b) Home Solicited Sales. A sale of goods or services for $25 or more made to a buyer at home may be set aside within three days. This right may be exercised merely because the buyer does not want to go through with the contract. There is no requirement of proving any misconduct of the seller nor any defect in the goods or services.[10]

(c) Referral Sales. The technique of giving the buyer a price reduction for customers referred to the seller is theoretically lawful. In effect, it is merely paying the buyer a commission for the promotion of other sales. In actual practice, however, the referral sales technique is often accompanied by fraud or by exorbitant pricing, so that consumer protection laws variously condemn referral selling. As a result, the referral system of selling has been condemned as unconscionable under the UCC and is expressly prohibited by UCCC.

§ 8:10   THE CONSUMER CONTRACT

There are several ways that consumer contracts are affected by consumer protection legislation.

(a) Form of Contract. Consumer protection laws commonly regulate the form of the contract, requiring that certain items be specifically listed, that payments under the contract be itemized, and that the allocation to such items as principal, interest, and insurance be indicated. Generally, certain portions of the contract or all of the contract must be printed in type of a certain size, and a copy must be furnished to the buyer. Such statutory requirements are more demanding than the statute of frauds section of the UCC. It is frequently provided that the copy furnished the consumer must be completely

---

[9] Act of October 20, 1972, §§ 403, 409, PL 92–513, 86 Stat 947, 15 USC §§ 1901 et seq., as amended.

[10] Federal Trade Commission Regulation, 16 CFR § 429.1.

filled-in. Back-page disclaimers are void if the front page of the contract does not call attention to the presence of such terms.

(b) CONTRACT TERMS. Consumer protection legislation does not ordinarily affect the right of the parties to make a contract on such terms as they choose. It is customary, however, to prohibit the use of certain clauses that, it is believed, bear too harshly on the debtor or that have too great a potential for exploitive abuse by a creditor. For example, the UCCC prohibits provisions permitting a creditor to enter a judgment against a debtor without giving the debtor any chance to make a defense.[11]

The federal Warranty Disclosure Act of 1974 establishes disclosure standards for consumer goods warranties in order to make them understood by the consumer.[12]

The parties to a credit transaction may agree that payments should be made in installments but that if there is a default as to any installment, the creditor may declare the entire balance due at once. This cancels or destroys the schedule for payments by making the entire balance immediately due. Such *acceleration* of the debt can cause the debtor great hardship. Because of this, some statutes limit or prohibit the use of acceleration clauses.

(c) LIMITATION OF CREDIT. Various laws may limit the ability to borrow money or purchase on credit. In some states, it is prohibited to make "open-end" mortgages, by which the mortgage secures a specified debt and such additional loans as may thereafter be made. Consumer protection is also afforded in some states by placing a time limit on smaller loans.

(d) UNCONSCIONABILITY. To some extent, consumer protection has been provided under the UCC by those courts that hold that the "unconscionability" provision protects from "excessive" or "exorbi-

tant" prices when goods are sold on credit.[13]

§ 8:11   CREDIT CARDS

Today's credit card may be designed for a specific use, such as for travel and entertainment or for a particular group of commodities; or it may be a general-purpose card, covering the purchase of any kind of goods and services.

(a) UNSOLICITED CREDIT CARD. The unsolicited distribution of credit cards to persons who have not applied for them is prohibited.

(b) SURCHARGE PROHIBITED. A seller cannot add any charge to the purchase price because the buyer uses a credit card instead of paying with cash or a check.[14]

(c) UNAUTHORIZED USE. A cardholder is not liable for more than $50 for the unauthorized use of a credit card. In order to impose liability up to that amount, the issuer must show that (1) the credit card was an accepted card,[15] (2) the issuer had given the holder adequate notice of possible liability in such case, (3) the issuer had furnished the holder with a self-addressed, prestamped notification form to be mailed by the holder in the event of the loss or theft of the credit card, (4) the issuer had provided a method by which the user of the card could be identified as the person authorized to use it,[16] and (5) unauthorized use of the card had occurred

---

[11] UCCC § § 2.415, 3.407.

[12] Act of January 4, 1975, PL 93–637, 88 Stat 2183, 15 USC § 2301.

[13] UCC § 2–302(1).

[14] Truth in Lending Act Amendment of 1976, 15 USC § 1666f. Ironically, the same section permits a merchant to offer a discount to cash paying customers and not customers using a credit card.

[15] A credit card is "accepted" when "the card holder has requested and received or has signed or has used, or authorized another to use [it], for the purpose of obtaining money, property, labor, or services on credit." CCPA § 103(1). Transamerica Ins. Co. v Standard Oil Co. (ND) 325 NW2d 210 (1982).

[16] Regulation Z of the Board of Governors of the Federal Reserve § 226.13(d), as amended, provides that the identification may be "signature, photograph, or fingerprint on the credit card or by electronic or mechanical confirmation."

or might occur as a result of loss, theft, or some other event.

(d) Unauthorized Purpose Distinguished. There is an unauthorized use of a credit card only when it is used without the permission or approval of the cardholder. In contrast, the holder may authorize another person to use the card but to use it for a particular purpose, such as to buy a particular item. If the person uses the card for a purpose other than the one specified by the holder, there is still an authorized use of the card, even though it is for an unauthorized purpose. In such case, the cardholder is liable for all charges made on the card, even though they were not intended by the cardholder when the card was loaned.[17] The same rule is applied when an employer has cards issued to employees with the purpose of making employment-related purchases, but one of the employees uses the card for personal purposes.

§ 8:12   Payments

Consumer legislation may provide that when a consumer makes a payment on an open charge account, the payment must be applied toward payment of the earliest charges. The result is that, should there be a default at a later date, any right of repossession of the creditor is limited to the later, unpaid items. This outlaws a contract provision by which, upon the default of the buyer, the seller could assert the right to repossess all purchases that had been made at any prior time. Such a provision is outlawed by the UCCC and is probably unconscionable under the UCC.

§ 8:13   Preservation of Consumer Defense

Consumer protection laws generally prohibit a consumer from waiving or giving up any defense provided by law.

In the ordinary contract situation, when

goods or services purchased or leased by a consumer are not proper or are defective, the consumer is not required to pay the seller or lessor, or is only required to pay a reduced amount. With the modern expansion of credit transactions, sellers and lessors have used several techniques for getting paid without regard to whether the consumer had any complaint against them.

To prevent this, the Federal Trade Commission has adopted a regulation that requires that in every sale or lease of goods or services to a consumer, the contract of the consumer contain a clause giving the consumer the right to assert defenses. These defenses may be asserted not only against the seller or lessor but also against a third person, such as a bank or finance company, to which the seller or lessor transfers the collection rights. The commission regulation requires that the following notice be included in boldface type at least ten points in size:

> **NOTICE**
> **ANY HOLDER OF THIS CONSUMER CREDIT CONTRACT IS SUBJECT TO ALL CLAIMS AND DEFENSES WHICH THE DEBTOR COULD ASSERT AGAINST THE SELLER OF GOODS OR SERVICES OBTAINED PURSUANT HERETO OR WITH THE PROCEEDS HEREOF. RECOVERY HEREUNDER BY THE DEBTOR SHALL NOT EXCEED AMOUNTS PAID BY THE DEBTOR HEREUNDER.**

§ 8:14   Product Safety

The health and well-being of consumers is protected by a variety of statutes and rules of law, some of which antedate the modern consumer protection era.

States typically have laws governing the manufacture of various products and establishing product safety standards. The federal Consumer Product Safety Act provides for research and the setting of uniform standards for products in order to reduce health hazards; establishes civil and criminal penalties for the distribution of

---

[17] Michigan National Bank v Olson, 44 Wash App 898, 723 P2d 438 (1986).

unsafe products; recognizes the right of an aggrieved person to sue for monetary damages and to obtain an injunction against the distribution of unsafe products and creates a Consumer Product Safety Commission to administer the act.[18]

A consumer, as well as various non-consumers, may hold a seller or manufacturer liable for *damages* when the product causes harm as discussed in Chapter 30 of this book.

The federal Anti-Tampering Act[19] makes it a federal crime to tamper with consumer products.

§ 8:15 CREDIT, COLLECTION, AND BILLING METHODS

Various provisions have been made to protect consumers from discriminatory and improper credit and collection practices.

(a) CREDIT DISCRIMINATION. It is unlawful to discriminate against an applicant for credit on the basis of race, color, religion, national origin, sex, marital status, or age; because all or part of the applicant's income is obtained from a public assistance program; or because the applicant has in good faith exercised any right under the Consumer Credit Protection Act (CCPA). When a credit application is refused, the applicant must be furnished a written explanation why the application was rejected.

(b) CORRECTION OF ERRORS. When the consumer believes that an error has been made in billing by the issuer of a credit card, the consumer should send the creditor a written statement and explanation of the error. The creditor or card issuer must investigate and make a prompt written reply to the consumer.[20]

(c) IMPROPER COLLECTION METHODS. Unreasonable methods of debt collection

are often expressly prohibited by statute or are held by courts to constitute an unreasonable invasion of privacy.[21] Statutes generally prohibit sending bills in such form that they give the impression that a lawsuit has been begun against the consumer and that the bill is legal process or a warrant issued by the court. The CCPA prohibits the use of extortionate methods of loan collection. A creditor may be prohibited from informing the employer of the debtor that the latter owes money.

When the seller made telephone calls to the buyer and the buyer's relatives and made obscene, threatening, and malicious statements that caused the buyer to become physically ill, the seller was liable for the tort of intentional mental disturbance. (A tort is a private injury or wrong arising from a breach of duty created by law.) In order to give rise to such liability, the statements made must be more than mere insults, indignities, threats, and annoyances, and must be so shocking and outrageous as to exceed all reasonable bounds of decency.

A creditor is liable for unreasonably attempting to collect a bill that, in fact, has been paid. This liability can arise under general principles of tort law as distinguished from special consumer protection legislation.

A debt collection letter sent to the debtor's place of employment was found to be a violation of the Fair Debt Collection Practices Act when the words "final demand for payment" could be read through the envelope, and it was likely that the debtor would be embarrassed by the delivery of such a letter to the employer's address.[22] A state debt collection law was violated by a bank's threat to prosecute the depositors if they did not return to the bank money that had been paid to them by mistake.[23]

---

[18]   Act of October 27, 1972, PL 92–573, 86 Stat 1207, 15 USC § § 2051–2081.
[19]   Act of October 13, 1983, PL 98–127, 97 Stat 831, 13 USC § 1365.
[20]   Fair Credit Billing Act, Act of October 18, 1974, PL 93–495, 15 USC § 1601.

[21]   Fair Debt Collection Practices Act, Act of September 20, 1977, PL 95–109, 91 Stat 874, 15 USC § § 1692 et seq.
[22]   Kleczy v First Federal Credit Control, Inc. 21 Ohio App 3d 56, 486 NE2d 204 (1984).
[23]   Brown v Oaklawn Bank (Tex) 718 SW2d 678 (1986).

When a collection agency violates the Fair Debt Collection Practices Act, it is liable to the debtor for damages. It is no defense that the debtor in fact owed the money that the agency was seeking to collect.

§ 8:16   PROTECTION OF CREDIT STANDING AND REPUTATION

In many instances one party to a transaction wishes to know certain things about the other party. This situation arises when a person purchases on credit or applies for a loan, a job, or a policy of insurance. Between two and three thousand private credit bureaus gather such information on borrowers, buyers, and applicants and sell such information to interested persons.

The Fair Credit Reporting Act (FCRA) of 1970[24] seeks to protect consumers from various abuses that may arise. FCRA applies only to consumer credit, which is defined as credit for "personal, family, and household" use, and does not apply to business or commercial transactions.

(a) PRIVACY. A report on a person based on personal investigation and interviews, called an **investigative consumer report,** may not be made without informing the person investigated of the right to discover the results of the investigation.[25] Bureaus are not permitted to disclose information to persons not having a legitimate use for it. It is a federal crime to obtain or to furnish a bureau report for an improper purpose.

On request, a bureau must tell a consumer the names and addresses of persons to whom it has made a credit report during the previous six months. It must also tell, when requested, which employers were given such a report during the previous two years.

A store may not publicly display a list of named customers from whom it will not accept checks, as such action is an invasion of the privacy of those persons.

(b) PROTECTION FROM FALSE INFORMATION. Much of the information obtained by bureaus is based on statements made by persons, such as neighbors, when interviewed by the bureau's investigator. Sometimes the statements are incorrect. Quite often they are hearsay evidence and would not be admissible in a legal proceeding. Nevertheless, such statements may go on the records of the bureau without further verification and will be furnished to a client of the bureau, who will tend to regard them as accurate and true.

A person has a limited right to request an agency to disclose the nature and substance of the information possessed by the bureau. The right to know does not extend to medical information. It is not required that the bureau identify the persons giving information to its investigators. The bureau is not required to give the applicant a copy of, nor to permit the applicant to see, his/her file.

When a person claims that the information of the bureau is erroneous, the bureau must take steps within a reasonable time to determine the accuracy of the disputed item.

Adverse information obtained by investigation cannot be given to a client after three months unless verified to determine that it is still valid. Most legal proceedings cannot be reported by a bureau after seven years. A bankruptcy proceeding cannot be reported after ten years.

In the *Thompson* case, a person who was denied credit because of the mistake of a credit reporting agency brought suit against the agency. Was it liable? The court was faced with determining what standard of care should be required of a credit reporting agency.

---

[24]   Act of October 26, 1970, PL 91–508, 84 Stat 1128, 15 USC § § 1681 seq.
[25]   CCPA, § 606, 15 USC § 1681(d).

Thompson v San Antonio Retail Merchants Ass'n

(CA5 Tex) 682 F2d 509 (1982)

> The San Antonio Retail Merchants Association (SARMA) was a credit reporting agency. It was asked by one of its members to furnish information on William Douglas Thompson, III. It supplied information from a file that contained data on William III and also on William Daniel Thompson, Jr. The agency had jumbled information related to William Jr. into the file relating to William III, so that all information appeared to relate to William III. William Jr. had a bad credit standing, and SARMA gave a bad report on William III. Because of this report, he was denied credit by several enterprises and then sued SARMA for its negligence in confusing him with William Jr. From a judgment in his favor, SARMA appealed.

Per Curiam. SARMA provides a computerized credit reporting service to local business subscribers. This service depends heavily upon credit history information fed into SARMA's files by subscribers. A key mechanism used by SARMA to update its files is a computerized "automatic capturing" feature. A subscriber must feed certain identifying information from its own computer terminal into SARMA's central computer in order to gain access to the credit history of a particular consumer. When presented with this identifying information, SARMA's computer searches its records and displays on the subscriber's terminal the credit history file that most nearly matches the consumer. The decision whether to accept a given file as being that of a particular consumer is left completely to the terminal operator. When a subscriber does accept a given file as pertaining to a particular consumer, however, the computer automatically captures into the file any information input from the subscriber's terminal that the central file did not already have.

A disadvantage of an automatic capturing feature is that it may accept erroneous information fed in by subscribers, unless special auditing procedures are built into the system. In the instant case, SARMA failed to check the accuracy of a social security number obtained by its automatic capturing feature. The social security number is the single most important identifying factor for credit-reference purposes. As a result, the computer erroneously began to report the bad credit history of "William Daniel Thompson, Jr.," to subscribers inquiring about "William Douglas Thompson, III."

Under 15 U.S.C. § 1681o of the Fair Credit Reporting Act (Act), a "consumer reporting agency" is liable to "any consumer" for negligent failure to comply with "any requirement imposed" by the Act. In the instant case, the district court determined that SARMA was liable under section 1681o for negligent failure to comply with section 1681e(b) of the Act, which provides:

> When a consumer reporting agency *prepares* a consumer report, it shall follow *reasonable procedures* to assure *maximum possible accuracy* of information concerning the individual about whom the report relates.

15 U.S.C. § 1681e(b) (emphasis added).

Section 1681e(b) does not impose strict liability for any inaccurate credit report, but only a duty of reasonable care in preparation of the report. That duty extends to updating procedures, because "preparation" of a consumer report should be viewed as a continuing process and the obligation to insure accuracy arises with every addition of information. The standard of conduct by which the trier of fact must judge the adequacy of agency procedures is what a reasonably prudent person would do under the circumstances.

Applying the reasonable-person standard, the district court found two acts of negligence in SARMA's updating procedures. First, SARMA failed to exercise reasonable care in programming its computer to automatically capture information into a file without requiring any minimum number of "points of correspondence" between the consumer and the file or having an adequate auditing procedure to foster accuracy. Second, SARMA failed to employ reasonable procedures designed to learn the disparity in social security numbers for the two Thompsons when it revised file number 5867114 at Gulf's request.

With respect to the first act of negligence, George Zepeda, SARMA's manager, testified that SARMA's computer had no minimum number of points of correspondence to be satisfied before an inquiring subscriber could accept credit information. Moreover, SARMA had no way of knowing if the information supplied by the subscriber was correct. Although SARMA did conduct spot audits to verify social security numbers, it did not audit all subscribers. With respect to the second act of negligence, SARMA's verification process failed to uncover the erroneous social security number even though Gulf made a specific request for a "revision" to check the adverse credit history ascribed to the plaintiff. SARMA's manager, Mr. Zepeda, testified that what should have been done upon the request for a revision, was to pick up the phone and check with Gordon's and learn, among other things, the social security number for William Daniel Thompson, Jr. It was the manager's further testimony that the social security number is the single most important information in a consumer's credit file. In light of this evidence, this Court cannot conclude that the district court was clearly erroneous in finding negligent violation of section 1681e(b). *See Colletti v Credit Bureau Services, Inc.*, 644 F2d 1148, 1158 (5th Cir. 1981).

The district court's award of $10,000 in actual damages was based on humiliation and mental distress to the plaintiff. Even when there are no out-of-pocket expenses, humiliation and mental distress do constitute recoverable elements of damage under the Act. In the instant case, the amount of damages is a question of fact which may be reversed by this Court only if the district court's findings are clearly erroneous. . . .

[Judgment affirmed]

QUESTIONS

1. What justification was there for the improper reporting by SARMA?
2. What was the significance of the social security numbers?
3. Was the question of liability of SARMA affected by the fact that the report had been supplied by a computer?

§ 8:17 EXPANSION OF CONSUMER PROTECTION

Various state laws aimed at preventing fraudulent sales of corporate securities, commonly called blue sky laws, have been adopted. These statutes are discussed in Chapter 51 on corporate stock. Other statutes have been adopted to protect purchasers of real estate and buyers of services.

(a) REAL ESTATE DEVELOPMENT SALES. Anyone promoting the sale of a real estate development that is divided into fifty or more parcels of less than five acres each must file with the Secretary of Housing and Urban Development (HUD) a **development statement**. This statement must set forth significant details of the development, as required by the federal Land Sales Act.[26]

Anyone buying or renting one of the parcels in the subdivision must be given a **property report.** This is a condensed version of the development statement filed with the secretary of HUD. This report must be given to the prospective customer more than 48 hours before signing the contract to buy or lease.

If the development statement is not filed with the secretary, the sale or rental of the real estate development may not be promoted through the channels of interstate commerce nor by the use of the mail.

If the property report is given to the prospective buyer or tenant less than 48 hours before signing a contract to buy or lease, or after it has been signed, the contract may be avoided within 48 hours. If the property report is never received, the contract may be avoided, and there is no statutory limitation on the time in which to do so.

The federal statute prohibits imposing or receiving unauthorized payments in connection with a real estate settlement.

State statutes frequently require that particular enterprises selling property tell or disclose certain information to prospective buyers.[27]

(b) SERVICE CONTRACTS. The UCCC treats a consumer service contract the same as a consumer sale of goods if (1) payment is made in installments or a credit charge is made, and (2) the amount financed does not exceed $25,000. It defines *services* broadly as embracing work, specified privileges, and insurance provided by a noninsurer. The inclusion of *privileges* makes the UCCC apply to contracts calling for payment on the installment plan or including a financing charge for transportation, hotel and restaurant accommodations, education, entertainment, recreation, physical culture (such as athletic clubs or bodybuilding schools), hospital accommodations, funerals, and cemetery accommodations.

In some states, it is unlawful for a repair shop to make unauthorized repairs to an automobile and then to refuse to return the automobile to the customer until paid for such repairs.[28]

Some states have adopted statutes requiring that any present payments for future funeral services or goods must be deposited in a bank account or similar depository to be held for the benefit of the customer. A contract that does not provide for such deposit is void as being against public policy.

Consumer protection legislation commonly prohibits charging for services that, in fact, are not performed.

(c) FRANCHISES. In order to protect a prospective franchisee from deception, a Federal Trade Commission regulation requires that the franchisor give a prospective franchisee a disclosure statement ten days before the franchisee signs a contract or pays any money for a franchise. The disclosure statement provides detailed information relating to the franchisor's finances,

---

[26] Act of August 1, 1968, as amended, PL 90–448, 82 Stat 590, 15 USC § § 1701–1720.

[27] Tara Hills Condominium Ass'n. v Gaughan, ___ Minn App ___, 399 NW2d 638 (1987).

[28] Gonzalez v Tremont Body & Towing, Inc. (Fla App) 483 So 2d 503 (1986).

experience, size of operation, and involvement in litigation. The statement must set forth any restrictions imposed on the franchisee; any costs that must be paid initially or in the future; and the provisions for termination, cancellation, and renewal of the franchise. False statements as to sales, income, or profits are prohibited. Violation of the regulation is subject to a fine of $10,000.

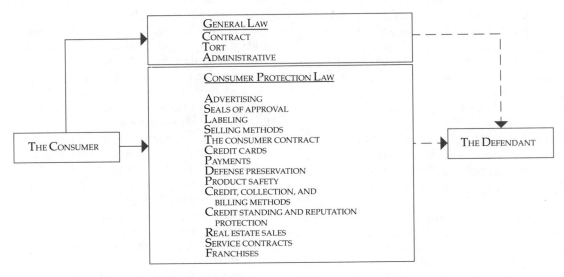

FIGURE 8-1
THE LEGAL ENVIRONMENT FOR THE CONSUMER

In the *Morris* case the franchisees claim that they were misled by the concealment of a material fact by the franchisor.

MORRIS V INTERNATIONAL YOGURT CO.
107 Wash 2d 314, 729 P2d 33 (1986)

The International Yogurt Company (IYC) had developed a unique mix for making frozen yogurt and related products. Morris and his wife purchased a franchise from the company. They were not told that the company would sell its yogurt mix to anyone and that a franchise was not required to obtain the mix. The franchise business of the Morrises was a failure, and they sold it at a loss after three years. They then sued the company for fraud and for violation of the state Franchise Investment Protection Act (FIPA) and the state Consumer Protection Act. From a decision against them, they appealed.

DURHAM, J. . . . The next issue we must consider is if IYC violated FIPA by failing to disclose to the Morrises that the yogurt mix was available to nonfranchisees. RCW [the Revised Code of Washington] 19.100.170 provides in part:

> It is unlawful for any person in connection with the offer, sale, or purchase of any franchise directly or indirectly:
> (2) To sell or offer to sell a franchise in this state by means of any written or oral communication which includes an untrue statement of a material fact or omits to state a material fact necessary in order to make the statements made in light of the circumstances under which they were made not misleading.

. . . Initially, we must determine when a fact is material under RCW 19.100.170(2). This provision is essentially the same as the antifraud provision in the Securities Act of Washington, RCW 21.20.010(2). For purposes of the latter provision, a "material fact" is " 'a fact to which a reasonable man would attach importance in determining his choice of action in the transaction in question.' " . . .

The next question is if IYC's failure to disclose to the Morrises that the yogurt mix was available to nonfranchisees was an omission of a material fact. In order to determine if a reasonable person would consider this fact important in purchasing the franchise, it is necessary to consider initially the importance of the yogurt mix itself to the potential franchisee.

The evidence in the record indicates that the yogurt mix was an essential element of the franchise. First, the franchise agreement placed particular emphasis on the fact that, in exchange for purchasing an IYC franchise, the franchisee would obtain the right to purchase and use a special yogurt mix. The agreement goes to considerable length in discussing the yogurt mix. Section 9 of the agreement states in part:

> The yogurt mix to be used in the preparation of all frozen yogurt sold at the Franchised Location is unique, and its formula and process for manufacture may be regarded as a trade secret. The right to purchase and use the mix is granted to Franchisee pursuant to this Agreement.

Thus, the agreement clearly indicates that the right to purchase this one-of-a-kind yogurt mix is a key feature of the franchise.

Section 9 of the agreement further provides that the franchisor will make the formula for the manufacture of the mix available to certain dairy manufacturers, which shall be regarded as approved sources from which the franchisee will purchase the mix. If the franchisee wishes to purchase the mix from a different manufacturer, he must request in writing that the franchisor disclose the formula and process for manufacture to that manufacturer. The agreement further states:

> Franchisor shall exercise its reasonable good business judgment in determing whether the formula and process should be disclosed to that manufacturer, *taking into consideration such factors as that manufacturer's ability to produce a mix of satisfactory quality, and that manufacturer's ability to adequately protect the formula and process from disclosure to unauthorized persons.*

(Italics ours.) By suggesting that IYC will limit access to the formula for the yogurt mix, this provision reinforces the fact that the mix is significant to IYC's product.

. . . In summary, the evidence as a whole indicates that the yogurt mix as well as the flavoring contributed to the distinctiveness of IYC's final product. . . . This yogurt mix was a major, essential element of IYC yogurt.

. . . IYC's failure to disclose to the Morrises the availability of the yogurt mix to nonfranchisees was an omission of a material fact. In deciding whether to purchase the franchise, a reasonable person reading the franchise agreement would have considered it important that the same yogurt mix was available to persons not purchasing the franchise. The fact that an essential component of the franchise's major product is unique and considered a trade secret is a far less value to the potential franchisee if that ingredient is generally available to all persons whether or not they have purchased the franchise. A person might not consider it worthwhile to invest in the franchise if he knew he could obtain the mix without paying the franchise fee. For these reasons, we conclude that IYC's failure to disclose to the Morrises the availability of the yogurt mix to nonfranchisees was an omission of a material fact necessary to make the statements IYC made not misleading, and therefore, was a violation of RCW 19.100.170(2).

. . . FIPA's provision on damages states that a person who sells a franchise in violation of the statute "shall be liable to the franchisee . . . who may sue at law or in equity for damages caused thereby". RCW 19.100.190(2). . . .

We hold . . . that in an action alleging the omission of a material fact in violation of RCW 19.100.170(2), proof of nondisclosure of a material fact establishes a presumption of reliance which the defendant may rebut by proving that the plaintiff would still have purchased the franchise even if the material fact had been disclosed. This case is remanded to the trial court to determine, in a manner consistent with this opinion, if IYC's failure to disclose to the Morrises the availability of the mix to nonfranchisees cause the Morrises to suffer damages.

. . . We reverse the Court of Appeals decision that IYC did not omit a material fact in violation of RCW 19.100.170(2) when it failed to disclose to the Morrises the availability of the yogurt mix to nonfranchisees. We remand the case to the trial court to decide if the Morrises may recover damages for IYC's violation of RCW 19.100.170(2), according to the principles in this opinion.

[Reversed on the issue of the effect of the omission and action remanded to determine damages]

QUESTIONS

1. Did the company expressly state that its unique yogurt mix would only be sold to franchisees?
2. Why does the court describe the availability of the yogurt mix to nonfranchisees as a material fact?
3. Why is the court concerned with "reliance" by the prospective franchise buyer?

SUMMARY

With the modern era of consumer protection, society has accepted the premise that

equality before the law, an essential part of the American way of life, is not appropriate to the marketplace where modern methods of marketing, packaging, and financing have reduced the ordinary consumer to a subordinate position. In order to protect the consumer from the hardship, fraud, and oppression that could result from being in such an inferior position, the law has, at many points, limited the freedom of action of the enterprise with which the consumer deals.

These consumer protection laws are directed at false and misleading advertising; misleading or false use of seals of approval and labels; the methods of selling — requiring the disclosure of terms, permitting consumer cancellation of home-solicited sales, and, in some states, prohibiting referral sales. The consumer is protected in a contract agreement by regulating its form, prohibiting unconscionable terms, and limiting the credit that can be extended to a consumer. Credit card protections include the prohibition of the unauthorized distribution of such cards and limited liability of the cardholder for the unauthorized use of a credit card. The application of payments; the preservation of consumer defenses, as against a transferee of the consumer's contract; product safety; the protection of credit standing and reputation; and, to some extent, real estate development sales, franchises, and service contracts are all included in consumer protection laws.

When a consumer protection statute is violated, an action may sometimes be brought by the consumer against the wrongdoer. More commonly, such action is brought by an administrative agency or by the attorney general of the state.

QUESTIONS AND CASE PROBLEMS

1. What is the object of each of the following rules of law:
   (a) Back-page disclaimers are void if the front page of the contract does not call attention to the presence of such terms.
   (b) A consumer's waiver of a statute designed for consumer protection is void, but the transaction otherwise binds the consumer.

2. Neil purchased a printing press from Guardian Press Company for $12,000, payment to be made in three installments of $4,000 each. Neil later sued Guardian for failing to make the disclosures specified by the federal Truth in Lending Act. Was Guardian required to make disclosures under the Act?

3. Cora telephoned from her home to the Nowlin Music Supply Company and ordered an electric guitar. The employee of Nowlin answering the phone stated that Cora's order was accepted and the guitar would be sent to Cora within a few days. That night, Cora saw an ad in the newspaper for the same guitar for $100 less than the Nowlin price. Cora wrote and mailed a letter the next day to the Nowlin Company stating that she canceled her order. May Cora do so?

4. What is the purpose of corrective advertising?

5. The Madison Home Appliance Store charged its credit card customers a price slightly higher than the price charged customers paying cash. It did this to offset the discount that it was required to allow the companies issuing the credit cards used by the customers. May Madison charge this higher price to credit card purchasers?

6. The Merit Breakfast Food Company sold its breakfast cereal in ordinary-sized packages. The packages, however, were labeled *jumbo* size. Merit was ordered to stop using this term by the Federal Trade Commission. Merit raised the defense that the term *jumbo* was not used with any intent to defraud, and therefore its use was not improper. Was this a valid defense?

7. Compare the sale of a television by a dealer for $400 payable in (a) cash, (b) two installments, and (c) eight installments.

8. Thomas was sent a credit card through the mail by a company that had taken his name and address from the telephone book. Because he never requested the card, Thomas left the card lying on his desk. A thief stole the card and used it to purchase merchandise in several stores in the name of Thomas. The issuer of the credit card claimed that Thomas was liable for the total amount of the

purchases made by the thief. Thomas claimed that he was not liable for any amount. The court decides that Thomas was liable for $50. Who is correct?

9. A federal statute prohibits the interstate shipment of deceptively or fraudulently labeled goods. Acting under the authority of this statute, federal officers seized a shipment of 95 barrels that were labeled *apple cider vinegar*. This vinegar had been made from dried apples that had been soaked in water. The government claimed that the label was false because *apple cider vinegar* meant to the average person that the vinegar had been made from fresh apples. The shipper claimed that as the barrels in fact contained vinegar that had been made from cider produced from apples, the labels were truthful in calling the contents by the name of *apple cider vinegar*. Was the shipper correct? [United States v 95 Barrels of Alleged Apple Cider Vinegar, 265 US 438]

10. Wilke was contemplating retiring. In response to an advertisement, he purchased from Coinway thirty coin-operated testing machines. He purchased these because Coinway's representative stated that, by placing these machines at different public places, Wilke could obtain supplemental income. This statement was made by the representative although he had no experience as to the cost of servicing such machines or their income-producing potential. The operational costs of the machines by Wilke exceeded the income. Wilke sued Coinway to rescind the contract for fraud. Coinway defended on the ground that the statements made were merely matters of opinion and did not constitute fraud. Was Wilke entitled to rescission? [Wilke v Coinway, Inc. 257 Cal App 2d 126, 64 Cal Rptr 845]

11. Greif obtained credit cards from Socony Mobil Oil Co. for himself and his wife. The card specified, "This card is valid unless expired or revoked. Named holder's approval of all purchases is presumed unless written notice of loss or theft is received." Later Greif returned his card to the company, stating that he was canceling it, but that he could not return the card in his wife's possession because they had separated. Subsequently Socony sued Greif for purchases made by the wife on the credit card in her possession. He defended on the ground that he had canceled the credit card contract. Decide. [Socony Mobil Oil Co. v Greif, 10 App Div 2d 119, 197 NYS2d 522]

12. To what extent may the holder of a credit card be held liable for purchases made with the card by a thief who has stolen the card?

13. A suit was brought against General Foods on the ground that it was violating the state law prohibiting false and deceptive advertising. It raised the defense that the plaintiffs failed to show that the public had been deceived by the advertising, that the public in fact had not relied on the advertising, and that there was no proof that anyone had sustained any damage because of the advertising. Were these valid defenses? [Committee on Children's Television, Inc. v General Foods Corp. 35 Cal 3d 197, 197 Cal Rptr 783, 783P2d 673 P2d 660]

14. The McNeils ran Hangman Ridge Training Stables, Inc. They owned all the stock in the corporation. They needed money and the Farmers Home Loan Administration agreed to give them a loan if property owned by the corporation was transferred to the McNeils as individuals and they gave the lender the mortgage on that land. The Safeco Title Insurance Company handled the transaction. The employee in charge told the parties that she was not an attorney. About a year later it was learned that the McNeils owed $3,500 in taxes because of the transaction. They claimed that the Safeco employee should have informed them that they should have obtained independent legal and tax advice. They claimed that because of this Safeco had violated the state consumer protection act. Were they correct? [Hangman Ridge Training Stables, Inc. v Safeco Ins. Co. 105 Wash 2d 778, 719 P2d 531]

15. The town of Newport obtained a corporate MasterCard. The card was given to the town clerk to use in purchasing fuel for the town hall. The town clerk used the card for personal restaurant, hotel, and gift shop debts. The town refused to pay the card charges on the ground that they were unauthorized. Was the town correct? [Master-Card v Town of Newport, 133 Wis App 2d 328, 396 NW2d 345]

9

CRIMES

Law sets the standards of conduct for all to follow. What happens when someone does not follow the law? There are two aspects to the problem. On the one hand, society wants to punish the wrongdoer and prevent others from repeating what was done. On the other hand, society, through the law, authorizes the victim to sue the wrongdoer for damages sustained by the victim. The first phase of punishment and prevention is governed by principles of criminal law, discussed in this chapter. The second phase is governed by the principles of tort law, discussed in the next chapter.

It is important to bear in mind that society has made a choice of having both criminal law and tort law, as contrasted with having only one and not the other. By having both, society rejects any argument that it is unfair to punish a wrongdoer twice for the one wrong.

A.   GENERAL PRINCIPLES

A **crime** is an offense against the sovereign, a breach of public duty. Most crimes have certain common characteristics. These are discussed in the following sections.

§ 9:1   CLASSIFICATION OF CRIMES

A crime may be classified according to the source of the criminal law, the seriousness of the offense, or the nature of the crime.

(a) SOURCE OF CRIMINAL LAW. Crimes are classified, in terms of their origin, as common-law and statutory crimes. Some offenses that are defined by statute are merely declaratory of the common law. Each state has its own criminal law, although a common pattern among the states may be observed.

(b) SERIOUSNESS OF OFFENSE. Crimes are classified in terms of their seriousness: as treason, felonies, and misdemeanors. **Treason** is defined by the Constitution of the United States, which states that "Treason against the United States, shall consist only in levying war against them, or in adhering to their enemies, giving them aid and comfort."[1] **Felonies** include the other more serious crimes, such as arson, murder, and robbery, which are punishable by confinement in prison or by death. Crimes not classified as treason nor felonies are **misdemeanors.** Reckless driving, weighing and measuring goods with uninspected scales and measuring devices, and disturbing the peace by illegal picketing are generally classified as misdemeanors. An act may be a felony in one state and a misdemeanor in another.

(c) NATURE OF CRIMES. Crimes are also classified in terms of the nature of the misconduct. **Crimes mala in se** are crimes that are inherently vicious or, in other words, that are naturally evil as measured by the standards of a civilized community. **Crimes mala prohibita** are acts that are only wrong because they are declared wrong by some statute.

§ 9:2   BASIS OF CRIMINAL LIABILITY

A crime generally consists of two elements (a) an act or omission, and (b) a mental state.

(a) MENTAL STATE. Mental state does not require an awareness or knowledge of guilt. In most crimes, it is sufficient that the defendant voluntarily did the act that is criminal, regardless of motive or intent. The lawmaker may make an act a crime, even though the actor has no knowledge that a law is being broken.[2] In some instances, a particular mental state is required, such as the necessity that a homicide be with *malice aforethought* in order to constitute murder. In some cases, it is the existence of a specific intent that differentiates one crime from other offenses. An assault with intent to kill is distinguished by that intent from an ordinary assault or from an assault with intent to rob.

(b) HARM TO OTHERS. Causing harm is typical of some crimes, such as murder or arson. Other crimes, however, are committed without harm to others. For example, a person may be guilty of the crime of speeding or reckless driving on the highway, although no one is hurt. In such case, it is the social judgment that the act condemned as a crime has such a potential for harm to others that the act should be prohibited before it does cause harm to others.

---

[1] US Const, Art 3, § 3, Cl 1.

[2] Colorado v Mendro, ___ Colo ___, 731 P2d 704 (1987) (contractor's trust fund statute).

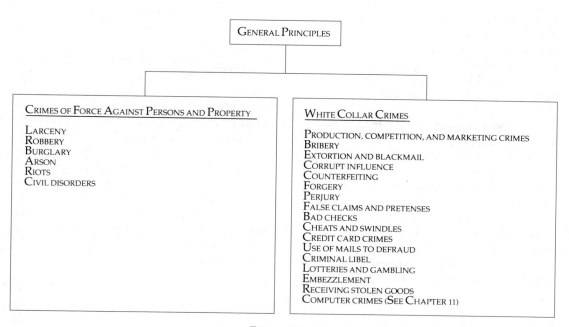

FIGURE 9-1
THE LAW OF CRIMES

§ 9:3   PARTIES TO A CRIME

Two or more parties may directly or indirectly commit or contribute to the commission of a crime. At common law, participants in the commission of a felony may be principals or accessories. The statutory trend is to simplify or abolish these distinctions and to treat everyone taking part in a crime as being guilty of the crime. Sometimes a distinction is made in terms of first degree, second degree, and so on, to distinguish between different degrees of conduct. At times, the statutory change is basically a change of name, as when the crime of harboring a known fugitive is created in place of accessory after the fact.

§ 9:4   RESPONSIBILITY FOR CRIMINAL ACTS

In some cases, particular persons are not held responsible for their criminal acts. In other cases, persons are held criminally responsible for acts committed by others.

(a) EMPLOYERS. An employer is liable for the crime committed by the employee when the employer directs or requires the commission of the crime. The fact that the employee is also guilty of a crime does not shield the employer, and both the employer and the employee carrying out the wrongful plan are guilty of crimes. Thus, an employer is guilty of a crime when the employer gives the employee money to bribe a building inspector to overlook violations of the fire code. The employee is also guilty of the crime of bribery when the employee pays the money to the inspector.

When the employer has not directed the commission of the crime, the employer is not liable for an employee's crime that is committed outside of the scope of the employment of the employee.

(b) CORPORATIONS. The modern tendency is to hold corporations criminally responsible for their acts. A corporation may also be held liable for crimes based upon the failure to act. Thus, a corporation may be held criminally responsible when an employee is killed because of the corporation's failure to install the safety devices required by law.

In some instances, the crime may be defined by statute in such a way that it requires, or is interpreted as requiring, a "living person" to commit the crime, in which case a corporation cannot be held criminally liable. Certain crimes, such as perjury, cannot be committed by corporations.

It is also usually held that crimes punishable only by imprisonment or corporal punishment cannot be committed by corporations. If the statute imposes a fine in addition to or in lieu of imprisonment or corporal punishment, a corporation may be convicted for the crime. Thus, a corporation may be fined for violating the federal antitrust law by conspiring to restrain interstate commerce.

(c) PERSONS UNDER INCAPACITY. Minors below a certain age, insane persons, and, to a limited extent, intoxicated persons are not responsible for their crimes. Intoxication generally does not relieve a person from criminal responsibility, unless a crime requires specific intent that cannot be formed because of intoxication. Generally the law applicable to persons under incapacity comes from the common law, although there is an increasing trend toward statutory regulation.[3]

§ 9:5　　ATTEMPTS AND CONSPIRACIES

Prior to the commission of an intended crime, there may be conduct that is itself a crime, such as an attempt or a conspiracy.

(a) ATTEMPTS. When the criminal fails to commit the crime intended, it may be that what has been done constitutes an **attempt**. Attempts are punished as distinct

crimes. It is, however, difficult to determine just what constitutes an attempt. Obviously, it is something less than committing the intended crime, but it must be more than merely preparing to commit that crime. Thus, the purchasing of a gun with which to kill the victim is not regarded as an attempt but as mere preparation, and ordinarily is not itself a crime. However, when the criminal points the gun at the door through which the victim is expected to leave the building, an attempt has been committed. The modern trend is to condemn as an attempt any conduct that has reached such a point that the potential for harm to others is unreasonably great. Thus, a person attempting to fire a gun at the victim is guilty of an attempt even though the gun may malfunction. Likewise, a robber pointing a gun at the victim and demanding money is guilty of an attempt even though the robber changes his mind and does not take any money.

(b) CONSPIRACIES. A **conspiracy** is an agreement between two or more persons to commit an unlawful act or to use unlawful means to achieve an otherwise lawful result. The crime is the agreement, and it is immaterial that nothing is done to carry out the agreement. Some statutes, however, require that there be some act done to carry out the conspiracy before the crime is committed.

(c) NUMBER OF OFFENSES. If the criminal actually commits the intended crime, there is no criminal attempt. There can only be an attempt when the intended crime is not committed.

In contrast with the concept of an attempt, a conspiracy is a separate crime. Consequently, the fact that the intended crime is actually committed does not erase the conspiracy. Defendants may thus be prosecuted both for having conspired to commit the crime and for having committed the crime intended. They may be prosecuted for the conspiracy, although the contemplated crime, in fact, is not committed.

---

[3]　See for example, Insanity Defense Reform Act of 1984, § 401, PL 98-473, 98 Stat 2057, 18 USC § 402.

§ 9:6 CRIMINAL FINES AND ADMINISTRATIVE PENALTIES COMPARED

The differences between a monetary penalty imposed by an administrative agency and a fine imposed by a court are very slight and largely theoretical. In both the administrative proceeding and the criminal court prosecution, the monetary penalty represents dollars paid by the defending party to the government. Both the fine and the penalty are imposed because the defending party failed to follow a standard of conduct required by the government.

A minor point of difference between court and agency fines is that in many jurisdictions the judges are elected, so that the judge imposing the fine is directly responsible to the voters. In contrast, members of an administrative agency are typically appointed by someone who was elected by the voters, and thus the control of the voters over the administrative personnel is "once removed."

Another minor difference is that courts and judges have for many centuries had the power to impose fines. The imposition of a monetary penalty by administrative agencies is less than a half-century old. Originally agencies were not given any such power. Then agencies were given the power to impose a penalty, but the penalty could not be collected or enforced unless the agency went to a court and obtained a court order directing the defending party to pay the penalty. The more recently created agencies have the power to make assessments for violation of the law and of their regulations, and these assessments are final and binding upon the defendant if no appeal is taken within a specified number of days. After the lapse of the specified time, the penalty can be collected as in the case of any other monetary judgment. The defendant cannot attack the penalty on the ground that it was improperly entered or excessive.

There are certain practical differences between the agency's monetary penalty and the court's fine. The administrative determination can be made without a jury. In contrast, most crimes that can be punished by the imposition of a substantial fine will be tried by a jury. Because a criminal conviction and fine is a stigma, or blot, on the reputation of the defendant, a jury is less likely to find a respectable businessperson guilty of a crime. Moreover, a judge does not like to treat a respected citizen as a criminal. Typically, these feelings are not shared by the members of an agency who will, therefore, be more likely to enforce the law and impose a substantial penalty in order to deter the defendant and others from violating the law.

In many instances, the administrative penalty will be significantly larger than fines imposed by a court. The reason is partly historical. The statute defining a particular crime and specifying the maximum fine ordinarily follows the pattern of an earlier statute that may be from the last century. What was then a large fine is today insignificant. Thus, a maximum fine inherited from the past may specify that the fine that can be imposed for armed robbery may not exceed $1,000. In contrast, the agency with power to impose a penalty is a creation of our time, and therefore any penalties are stated in terms of the modern purchasing power of the dollar. Thus, it is not unusual to authorize an agency to impose a penalty not to exceed $10,000. This difference in the maximum penalty may also be justified theoretically. For example, in the case of armed robbery there is but one victim of the crime, whereas in the case of the administrative agency, there may be many victims of the crime (i.e., factory pollution of the environment).

§ 9:7 INDEMNIFICATION OF CRIME VICTIM

Typically the victim of a crime does not benefit from the criminal prosecution and conviction of the wrongdoer. Any fine that is imposed upon the defendant is paid to the government and is not received in any way by the victim.

(a) STATUTORY ASSISTANCE. Several states have adopted statutes to provide a limited degree of indemnification to victims of crime in order to compensate them for the harm or loss sustained.[4] Under some criminal victim indemnification statutes, dependents of a deceased victim are entitled to recover the amount of the support that they were deprived of by the victim's death. The Victims of Crime Act of 1984 creates a federal Crime Victims Fund. This fund receives the fines paid into the federal courts and other moneys. From this fund, grants are made to the states to assist them in financing programs to provide indemnity to and assistance for victims of crime.[5] The Victim and Witness Protection Act of 1982 authorizes the sentencing judge in a federal district court to order, in certain cases, that the defendant make restitution to the victim or pay the victim the amount of medical expenses or loss of income caused by the crime.[6]

Mob violence statutes frequently impose liability for property damage upon the local government. The term *property* in such a statute generally applies to tangible property and does not authorize recovery for loss of profits or goodwill resulting from business interruption. The fact that the government was unable to prevent the harm or damage is not a defense to liability under such statutes.

(b) ACTION FOR DAMAGES. While the criminal prosecution of a wrongdoer does not financially benefit the victim of the crime, the victim is typically entitled to bring a civil action for damages against the wrongdoer for the harm sustained. The modern pattern of statutes creating business crimes is to give the victim the right to sue for damages. Thus, the wrongdoer violating the federal antitrust act or the Racketeer Influenced and Corrupt Organizations Act (RICO) is liable to the victim for three times the damages actually sustained. A number of states have adopted statutes following the pattern of RICO.

A damage suit may be brought under the federal act without proof of a "racketeering injury" or the prior conviction of the defendant.[7] In the *Banderas* case the question was whether the Florida RICO authorized a civil action for damages when (1) the misconduct was making a false claim for payment and (2) there was no proof that the defendant was related to organized crime.

---

[4] A Uniform Crime Victims Reparations Act has been adopted in Kansas, Louisiana, Montana, North Dakota, Ohio, and Texas.

[5] Act of October 12, 1984, PL 98-473, 98 Stat 2170, 18 USC § 1401 et seq.

[6] Act of October 12, 1982, PL 97-291, 96 Stat 1253, 18 USC § 3579.

[7] Sedima, S.P.R.L. v Imrex Co., Inc. 473 US 479 (1985).

BANDERAS v BANCO CENTRAL DEL ECUADOR

(Fla App) 461 So 2d 265 (1985)

The Banco Central administered a humanitarian plan for the government of Ecuador. Fernando Banderas and his wife presented false claims that were paid by the bank. After the fraud was discovered, the bank sued Banderas and his wife for damages for fraud and treble damages under the Florida version of RICO. Defendants asserted that they were not liable for RICO damages because there was not proof that they were related to organized crime and because the wrong committed by them was merely ordinary fraud. They had not used any racketeering methods. From a judgment in favor of the bank, the defendants appealed.

HENDRY, J. . . . Appellants raise . . . on appeal: 1) whether the civil damages provisions of RICO were improperly applied to these defendants because there was no showing that they were connected to organized crime; 2) whether the civil damages provisions were improperly applied to a mere "garden variety" fraud case.

The Florida RICO Act, promulgated in 1977, is nearly identical to the federal RICO statute, 18 U.S.C. §§ 1961-1968 (1970), passed as Title IX of the Organized Crime Control Act of 1970. Thus, we can also look to a wealth of material on the federal RICO statute for guidance on this issue. The legislative history shows that Congress was clearly concerned, during the drafting of this bill, with the constitutional problems associated with trying to limit the statute's target to "organized crime" only; that is, that the statute would not survive attacks on the grounds that it was unconstitutionally overbroad or that it created status crimes. Status crimes, related as they are to the old English bills of attainder, are especially disfavored. *Cf. Robinson v California*, 370 U.S. 660 (1962) (state cannot make drug addiction a crime); *Lanzetta v New Jersey*, 306 U.S. 451 (1939) (state cannot make being a "gangster" a crime). Secondly, Congress deliberately made the scope of the statute as broad as possible "to avoid opening loopholes through which the minions of organized crime might crawl to freedom." Congress chose the only course available to it which would effectuate the broad purpose of the statute without creating serious constitutional issues. It imposed enhanced sanctions for the types of activities which were characteristic of "organized crime". Thus, all persons who engage, over a period of time, in activities which Congress has defined as being "racketeering activities" are subject to criminal prosecution or civil litigation under RICO.

Against this background, it is now well established in the federal courts that it is not necessary to prove a nexus to organized crime in order to obtain damages in a private civil RICO suit.

Appellants' second argument, that the trial court permitted Central Bank to turn a "garden variety" fraud case into a treble damage civil RICO action is, paraphrasing Mr. Justice Cardozo, to spread the study of horticulture to unaccustomed fields. *United States v Constantine*, 296 U.S. 287, 299 (1935) (Cardozo, J., dissenting). We cannot accept appellants' argument. The statute makes no distinction between levels or degrees of fraudulent activity. *See* § 895.02(1)(a)16. Thus, courts are not in a position to decide whether certain frauds are "garden variety" subject only to simple compensatory and possible punitive damages, and whether other frauds are "exotic arrangements" meriting the full range of enhanced penalties available under RICO. Fraud is not so easily parsed.

Section 895.02(4) defines "pattern of racketeering activity" as:

[E]ngaging in at least two incidents of racketeering conduct that have the same or similar intents, results, accomplices, victims, or methods of commission or that otherwise are interrelated by distinguishing characteristics and are not isolated incidents, provided at least one of such incidents occurred within 5 years after a prior incident of racketeering conduct.

This case fits precisely within the parameters of the statute. This was not a technical securities or business fraud. This was a well-organized, ongoing, systematic, criminal scheme devised by appellants to defraud the government of Ecuador — their own government.

At some time prior to June, 1981, appellants and Florida Aviation Corp. [FAVCO] and Banla formed a conspiracy for the express purpose of carrying out this scheme. In furtherance of this scheme, these appellants created four fictitious "hospitals" in three different states [Florida, Texas and Missouri]. Appellants sent "statements," in medical terminology, on invoices which they caused to be printed in the names of these non-existent hospitals. They sent seventy of these statements over the course of thirteen months, which the Central Bank paid in good faith. The bank didn't realize there was a problem with the medical assistance program until the spring of 1982 when an employee at Southeast Bank noticed that the address listed for St. John's Hospital corresponded to a vacant lot. Appellants earned over $851,000.00 on a few dollars invested in printing a medical dictionary. Innocent banks were drawn into the scheme. As a result, there were also violations of the federal mail and wire fraud statutes. . . . [T]his case presents one version of precisely the sort of activity that should, without controversy, fall within the statute's application.

[Judgment affirmed]

QUESTIONS

1. What is the importance of not requiring a RICO plaintiff to prove that the defendant was connected to organized crime?
2. Did the case present a simple common-law fraud?
3. Is passing a bad check conduct that brings the wrongdoer under a RICO-type statute?

---

§ 9:8   SENTENCING

The problem of sentencing the convicted criminal is one of the most difficult problems in the administration of justice. The difficulty is that society is caught between conflicting social purposes. Uniformity and stability are desired. At the same time flexibility is desired in order to make the punishment fit both the crime and the criminal. For the earlier part of this century, the emphasis has been on flexibility in sentencing. This, however, has produced a very inconsistent pattern of sentencing. Various reform movements are underway to secure more uniform sentencing of criminals.[8]

(a) THE INDIGENT DEFENDANT. When a court imposes sentence, it cannot impose an alternative (1) fine or (2) imprisonment if the defendant does not have the money to pay the fine. For example, it is unconstitutional to sentence a defendant to "$30 or 30 days."[9]

[8]   The Sentencing Reform Act of October 12, 1984, Chapter 227, PL 98-473, 98 Stat 1987, 18 USC § § 3551 et seq. contains provisions designed to produce greater uniformity in sentencing. The Commissioners on Uniform Laws have proposed a Model Sentencing and Corrections Act.
[9]   Tate v Short, 401 US 395 (1971).

This conclusion is reached on the ground that such a sentence in the alternative discriminates on the basis of poverty by making the poor person, who cannot pay the fine, go to jail, while the rich person pays the fine and walks out of the court.

(b) WHITE COLLAR CRIMES. There is much criticism about the sentencing of white collar criminals on the ground that the penalties are not sufficiently large to serve either the purpose of punishing the defendant or of deterring others from committing similar crimes. It can be recognized that there is a reluctance on the part of judges to send an otherwise respectable person to jail. But one of the fundamentals of our American system is equality before the law; therefore no exception should be made because the defendant had a good standing or a good education. In some instances, the lawmaker is at fault in failing to provide punishments that fit the crime.

(c) FORFEITURE OF CRIME-RELATED PROPERTY. When a defendant is convicted of a crime, the court may also declare that the defendant's rights in any instrument of that crime are forfeited. When the forfeited property can only be used for a criminal purpose, as in the case of engraved plates used for making counterfeit money, there is no question of the right of the government to confiscate the property. This confiscation is allowable, even though this in effect increases the penalty imposed on the defendant.

Forfeiture is not limited to property that can only be used for crime. Thus, an automobile that is used to carry illegal merchandise may itself be seized by the government, even though it is obvious that the automobile could also be put to a lawful use.

As we move into the area of the white collar crimes, this problem of defining crime-related property becomes increasingly difficult because the property involved is not by itself criminal, or even potentially criminal, in character. Legislation in this area has been directed at depriving the wrongdoer of the gains obtained by the crime or of taking away the power to benefit from the crime. An example of the first type of legislation is the Sherman Antitrust Act, under which a defendant guilty of unlawfully acquiring the stock of competing corporations may be ordered by the court to sell or otherwise dispose of such shares. This is called a divestiture order. Illustrative of both the first and the second type of legislation is the federal RICO Act under which the court is required to enter an order against the defendant forfeiting any property acquired or used in exercising unlawful racketeering influence. Under RICO the fruits of the racketeering activity may be forfeited regardless of their nature.[10]

In the *Kravitz* case the defendant attacked the validity and application of the RICO forfeiture provisions.

[10] 4447 Corporation v Goldsmith, ___ Ind ___, 504 NE2d 559 (1987).

UNITED STATES V KRAVITZ

(CA3 Pa) 738 F2d 102 (1984)

Kravitz owned 100 percent of the stock of American Health Programs, Inc. (AHP). In order to obtain the Philadelphia Fraternal Order of Police as a customer for AHP, Kravitz paid money bribes to persons whom he thought were officers of that organization, but who, in fact, were federal undercover agents. He was prosecuted for violating RICO. He was convicted, and the court ordered the forfeiture of all of the shares of stock of AHP owned by Kravitz. He claimed that the court was not required to order the forfeiture and that the statute was unconstitutional as interpreted. From a decision against Kravitz, he appealed.

Gibbons, C. J. . . . Charles Kravitz appeals from a judgment of sentence imposed following his conviction for violations of the Racketeer Influenced and Corrupt Organizations Act, 18 U.S.C. § 1961 *et seq.* (1982) ("RICO"). He contends that his conviction should be set aside, and that in any event the court erred in ordering forfeiture of his interest as a stockholder in American Health Programs, Inc. (AHP). We hold that his objections to the RICO convictions are without merit, and that the forfeiture order was proper.

A primary question presented by this appeal is whether forfeiture under section 1963 is mandatory upon a finding that the appellant's property was used to promote racketeering. We conclude, as have all other courts to decide the question, that forfeiture is mandatory.

Several factors compel that conclusion. The first is the plain meaning of the language employed in section 1963(a), stating that "[w]hoever violates any provision of section 1962 . . . shall forfeit to the United States" the illegally used interest. As the Fifth Circuit pointed out in *United States v L'Noste*, 609 F2d 796 (CA5, 1980), although there are occasions where "shall" has been interpreted to vest discretionary, rather than mandatory, authority to act, the wording of the statute is the most persuasive evidence of Congressional intent. Nor does the legislative history ever discuss forfeiture in discretionary terms. The wording of the remaining penalties established under section 1963(a) also supports a mandatory interpretation of forfeiture: section 1963(a) states that a defendant "shall be fined not more than $25,000 or imprisoned not more than twenty years, *or both*" (emphasis added). Thus, where Congress intended for the penalty to be optional, as in the choice between fine or imprisonment, they specified that there was such a choice. The section's wording provides no choice regarding the imposition of forfeiture.

Moreover, a literal reading of section 1963(a) is consistent with RICO purposes. The criminal forfeiture provision was viewed as an innovative means of addressing the spread of organized crime that has infiltrated so many aspects of American society. Of foremost concern during Congressional hearings on RICO was the weakness of current efforts at curtailing the spread of organized crime to legitimate business endeavors. For instance, the Senate Judiciary Committee's report quoted the Attorney General's testimony that:

> While the prosecutions of organized crime leaders can seriously curtail the operations of the Cosa Nostra, as long as the flow of money continues, such prosecutions will only result in a compulsory retirement and promotion system as new people step forward to take the place of those convicted.

S.Rep. No. 91-617 91st Cong. 1st Sess. 78 (1969). The report stated that forfeiture as a penalty for the criminal offense — although disfavored throughout American history — was an innovative approach which could provide the linchpin in the renewed effort against organized crime:

> Title IX recognizes that present efforts to dislodge the forces of organized crime from legitimate fields of endeavor have proven unsuccessful. To remedy this failure, the proposed statute adopts the most direct route open to accomplish the desired objective. Where an organization is acquired or run by defined racketeering methods, then the persons involved can be legally separated from the organization, either by

the criminal law approach of fine, imprisonment and forfeiture, or through a civil law approach of equitable relief broad enough to do all that is necessary to free the channels of commerce from all illicit activity.

In light of RICO's central goal of inhibiting organized crime's infiltration of legitimate business, it is certainly not likely that forfeiture was viewed by its drafters as an optional penalty. At the least, a mandatory interpretation of section 1963(a)'s forfeiture would promote, rather than discourage, RICO's intended purpose. Indeed, it is consistent with RICO's own construction clause, Pub.L. No. 91-452, § 904(a), 84 Stat. 922, 947 (1970), which states that the statute "shall be liberally construed to effectuate its remedial purposes."

When Congress has opted to provide for discretionary forfeiture, it has done so expressly. Thus, under the Internal Revenue Laws there is district court discretion to remit or mitigate the forfeiture. 18 U.S.C. § 3617 (1982). The Organized Crime Control Act itself elsewhere contains a permissive, rather than mandatory, forfeiture provision. In establishing penalties for illegal gambling, Congress provided that "[a]ny property . . . used in violation of the provisions of this section may be seized and forfeited to the United States." 18 U.S.C. § 1955(d) (1982).

Finally, we note that where Congress did provide for the remission or mitigation of the forfeiture order, it vested that decisionmaking authority with the Attorney General, not the federal courts. Section 1963(c) explicitly incorporates "[a]ll the provisions of law relating to the . . . remission of mitigation of forfeitures for violation of the customs laws . . ."; it also imposes upon the Attorney General "[s]uch duties as are imposed upon the collector of customs . . . with respect to the disposition of property. . . ." Under the customs laws, it is the Attorney General who has the authority to grant remission or mitigation. Moreover, courts have uniformly held that the remission decision of the Attorney General is not open to judicial review. Therefore, since 1963(c) vests the Attorney General with the powers given to him under the customs laws, we conclude that any petition for remission or mitigation must be brought before the Attorney General, and that the federal courts have no authority to modify or review that decision.

Kravitz also challenges the forfeiture on eighth amendment grounds. He argues that forfeiture constitutes a disproportionate penalty because AHP's contract with the FOP expired prior to indictment. Since AHP was no longer providing services pursuant to the illegally secured contract, Kravitz would have us accept that the taint upon the property had dissipated, and thus that the order of forfeiture was cruel and unusual punishment, in violation of the eighth amendment.

Kravitz's eighth amendment argument completely ignores the nature of RICO's forfeiture provision. Forfeiture under RICO is an in personam penalty designed as part of the punishment for the criminal offense committed. It is simply incorrect that the termination of the criminal conduct bars the imposition of punishment. Although in personam forfeiture is not commonly used in our system of jurisprudence, it is nonetheless a legitimate weapon in the enforcement of our criminal laws and, as with any punishment for criminal conduct, may be imposed despite the cessation of the criminal conduct charged in the indictment.

[Judgment affirmed]

QUESTIONS

1. What kind of property was ordered forfeited?
2. Would you classify the property forfeited as an instrument of crime?
3. Is it material whether the forfeited property is acquired by means of crime?

B. WHITE COLLAR CRIMES

Those crimes that do not use, or threaten to use, force or violence or do not cause injury to persons or physical damage to property are called **white collar crimes.** Computer crimes, a type of white collar crimes, are discussed in Chapter 11 of this text. A particular defendant may be guilty of both a white collar crime and a traditional crime of the kind described in Part C of this chapter.

§ 9:9　CRIMES RELATED TO PRODUCTION, COMPETITION, AND MARKETING

The person or enterprise in business may be guilty of the various crimes relating to labor and employment practices, conspiracies and combinations in restraint of trade, price discrimination, and environmental pollution discussed in Chapters 4 and 7.

(a) IMPROPER USE OF INTERSTATE COMMERCE. The shipment of improper goods or the transmission of improper information in interstate commerce constitutes a crime under various federal statutes. Thus, it is a federal crime to send in interstate commerce a statement as part of a scheme to defraud; to send a blackmail or extortion threat; or to ship adulterated or misbranded foods, drugs, or cosmetics; or to ship into a state child-labor-made or convict-labor-made goods or intoxicating liquor when the sale of such goods is prohibited by the destination state.

(b) SECURITIES CRIMES. In order to protect the investing public, both state and federal laws have regulated the issuance and public sale of stocks and bonds.[11] Between 1933 and 1940, seven such regulatory statutes were adopted by Congress. As a practical matter, these federal statutes have largely displaced state statutes by virtue of the principle of federal preemption. Violation of these statutes is typically made a crime.

In the *Shafer* case the defendant claimed that he acted in good faith and that the securities statute did not apply to him.

[11]　See § 51:10.

NEW MEXICO V SHAFER
102 NM 629, 698 P2d 902 (1985)

New Mexico prohibits the sale of unregistered securities unless the sale is an isolated transaction. Shafer sold stock of SBS Development, Inc. It was a Texas corporation and its stock was not registered in New Mexico. Shafer was prosecuted for violating the New Mexico statute. He raised the defenses that (1) he had acted in good faith on the advice of an attorney, and (2) he came within the protection of the "isolated transaction" exception. He was convicted and appealed.

DONNELLY, C. J. . . . New Mexico follows the rule that good faith reliance on the advice of counsel is not a defense to a charge of selling unregistered securities. This is so because scienter is not an element of the crime of offering to sell or selling unregistered securities.

Reliance on an attorney's advice is not a defense to the crime of selling or offering to sell unregistered securities. Thus, the accuracy of the advice given to defendants by Texas counsel relying upon Texas law is irrelevant. The court in *State v. Sheets* [94 N.M. 356 (Ct. App.) (1980)], held that the sale of unregistered securities is not a crime requiring proof of specific intent. All that is required is a willful or purposeful act of offering to sell or selling an unregistered security. The state is only required to prove that the defendant acted intentionally in the sense that he was aware of what he was doing.

. . . (c) Defendants also requested a defense instruction that they believed they had engaged in sales or solicitations of securities only in Texas. The trial judge correctly denied the requested instruction. Defendants' understanding or belief concerning the propriety of their acts went to their knowledge or intent. Knowledge or intent is not an element of a charge of soliciting to sell or selling unregistered securities under New Mexico law. All that is necessary is a willful act of selling or offering to sell an unregistered security that is required to be registered in this state. Mistake of fact is not a defense.

(d) The trial court refused defendants' requested instruction that isolated transactions, pledges, and sales, where the number of securities holders does not exceed twenty-five, are exempt from the securities laws.

NMSA [New Mexico Statutes Annotated] 1978, Section 58-13-30 (Cum. Supp. 1982) states:

> Except as expressly provided in this section . . . Sections 58-13-4 through 58-13-28 NMSA 1978 do not apply to:
> A. any isolated transaction, whether effected through a broker-dealer or not; . . .
> G. any transaction executed by a bona fide pledgee without any purpose of evading the Securities Act of New Mexico;
> J. the issuance and sale by any corporation organized under the laws of this state of its securities at a time when the number of security holders does not, and will not, in consequence of the sale exceed twenty-five and:
> (1) the seller reasonably believes that all buyers are purchasing for investment; and
> (2) no commission or other remuneration is paid or given directly or indirectly for soliciting any prospective buyer . . .

Defendants initially contend that there was evidence that all of the transactions resulting in their convictions were isolated within the meaning of Section 58-13-30(A). An isolated transaction under this section is one that is "unique; occurring alone or once; sporadic, not likely to recur." *See State v. Sheets*, 94 N.M. at 365, 610 P.2d at 769 (quoting *Besser Co. v Bureau of Revenue*, 74 N.M. 377, 394 P.2d 141 (1964)). The record shows no isolated transaction regarding the sale or offer to sell securities. Instead the evidence shows that between June and December of 1982, over $150,000 worth of stock in the corporation was sold. Of the twenty-three sales of stock listed on the corporation's books, seven took place in New Mexico. . . .

The exemptions provided for in Section 58-13-30(J) (number of securities holders does not exceed twenty-five) require a sale by a corporation organized under the laws of this state. SBS Development, Inc. was organized under the laws of Texas. Thus, the instruction on this exemption under New Mexico law was properly refused. . . .

[Conviction affirmed]

QUESTIONS

1. What is the status in New Mexico of the defense that a lawyer informed the seller of stock that such a proposed sale would be lawful? Why?
2. Why does the New Mexico statute exempt the "isolated transaction" sale?
3. Assume that only one sale of the SBS Development stock had been made in New Mexico and that all other sales had been made in Texas. Would the defendant come within the protection of the "isolated transaction" exemption?

§ 9:10   BRIBERY

Bribery is the act of giving money, property, or any benefit to a particular person to influence that person's judgment in favor of the giver of the bribe. At common law, the crime was limited to doing such acts to influence a public official. In this century, the common-law concept has expanded to include commercial bribery. Thus, it is now a crime to pay a competitor's employee money in order to obtain secret information about the competitor.

The giving and the receiving of a bribe each constitutes a crime. In addition, the act of seeking to obtain a bribe may be a crime of solicitation of bribery. In some states, bribery is broadly defined to include solicitation of bribes.[12]

The crime of bribery is complete when the bribe has been paid or received. Whether the person paying the bribe obtains what was bargained for does not affect the guilt of either the giver or the receiver of the bribe.

§ 9:11   EXTORTION AND
                   BLACKMAIL

Extortion and blackmail are crimes by which the wrongdoer seeks to force the

victim to do some act, typically paying money, that the victim would not otherwise desire to do.

(a) EXTORTION. When a public officer, acting under the apparent authority of the office, makes an illegal demand, the officer has committed the crime of **extortion**. For example, if a health inspector threatens to close down a restaurant on a false charge of violation of the sanitation laws unless the restaurant pays the inspector a sum of money, the inspector has committed extortion. If the restaurant voluntarily offers the inspector the money to prevent the restaurant's being shut down because of actual violations of the sanitation laws, the crime committed would be **bribery**.

Modern statutes tend to ignore the "public officer" aspect of the common law and expand extortion to include any obtaining of something of value by threat. This might be in connection with loansharking or labor racketeering. In a number of states, statutes extend the extortion concept to include the making of "terroristic threats."[13]

(b) BLACKMAIL. In jurisdictions where extortion is limited to conduct of public officials, a non-official commits **blackmail** by making demands that would be extortion if

---

[12] Martinez v Texas (Tex App) 696 SW2d 930 (1985).

[13] Pennsylvania v Bunting, 284 Pa Super 444, 426 A2d 130 (1981).

made by a public official. Ordinarily, the concept of blackmail is used in the context of a threat to give publicity to some matter that would damage the victim's personal or business reputation.

§ 9:12   CORRUPT INFLUENCE

In harmony with changing concepts of right and wrong, society has increasingly outlawed practices on the ground that they exerted a corrupting influence on business transactions. To some extent, this objective of the law was attained by applying the criminal law of extortion, blackmail, and bribery to business situations. In time, the definitions of these crimes were expanded to include practices similar to the old crimes but not within the technical definition of such crimes. Thus, the crime of bribery was extended to include commercial bribery.

(a) IMPROPER POLITICAL INFLUENCE. In order to protect from the improper influencing of political or governmental action, various acts have been classified as crimes. For instance, it is a crime for the holder of a government office to be financially interested in or to receive money from an enterprise that is seeking to do business with the government. Such conflict of interests is likely to produce a result that is harmful to the public. Thus, lobbyists and foreign agents must register in Washington, D.C.,[14] and must adhere to statutes regulating the giving and receiving of contributions for political campaigns. Violation of these regulatory statutes is a crime.

(b) IMPROPER COMMERCIAL INFLUENCE. The protection from improper influence is extended to the commercial world by statutes making it a crime to engage in commercial bribery, to engage in loan sharking, to use gangster methods to influence legitimate business, or to run a legitimate business for the purpose of laundering gangster money.

Under federal statutes, it is a crime to obtain a benefit by means of a threat of economic or physical loss or harm, to use racketeering methods or money obtained from racketeering to acquire an interest in a legitimate business, or to travel in interstate commerce for the purpose of engaging in racketeering activities. A person convicted of such crimes is subject to punishment by fine, imprisonment, and the forfeiture of money obtained by the criminal conduct. The convicted defendant is also subject to civil liability to the victims of the crime.[15]

§ 9:13   COUNTERFEITING

It is a federal crime to make, to possess with intent to pass, or to pass counterfeit coins, bank notes, or obligations or other securities of the United States. Legislation has also been adopted against the passing of counterfeit foreign securities or notes of foreign banks.

The various states also have statutes prohibiting the making and passing of counterfeit coins and bank notes. These statutes often provide, as does the federal statute, a punishment for the mutilation of bank notes or the lightening or mutilation of coins.

§ 9:14   FORGERY

Forgery consists of the fraudulent making or material altering of an instrument, such as a check, that apparently creates or changes a legal liability of another person. The instrument must have some apparent legal efficacy in order to constitute forgery.

Ordinarily, forgery consists of signing another's name with intent to defraud. It may also consist of making an entire instrument or altering an existing one. It may result from signing a fictitious name or the

---

[14] Foreign Agents Registration Act, Act of June 8, 1938, 52 Stat 631, 22 USC § § 611 et seq., as amended.

[15] Act of June 25, 1948, 62 Stat 793, 18 USC § 1951; Travel Act of September 13, 1961, PL 87-228, 75 Stat 498, 18 USC § 1952; Racketeer Influenced and Corrupt Organizations Act of October 15, 1970, PL 91-452, 84 Stat 941, 18 USC § § 1961 et seq.

offender's own name with the intent to defraud.

When the nonowner of a credit card signs the owner's name on a credit card invoice without the owner's permission, such act is a forgery.

§ 9:15   PERJURY

Perjury consists of knowingly giving false testimony in a judicial proceeding after having been sworn or having affirmed to tell the truth.[16] By statute, knowingly making false answers on any form filed with a government is typically made perjury or is subjected to the same punishment as perjury. In some jurisdictions, the out-of-court offense is called false swearing.

§ 9:16   FALSE CLAIMS AND PRETENSES

Many statutes declare it a crime to make false claims or to obtain goods by false pretenses.

(a) FALSE CLAIMS. A statute may expressly declare that the making of a false claim is a crime.

The federal False Statement statute makes it a crime to knowingly and willfully make a false material statement as to any matter within the jurisdiction of any de-

partment or agency of the United States.[17] Thus, it is a crime for a contractor to make a false claim against the United States for payment for work that was never performed by the contractor. Other statutes indirectly regulate the matter by declaring that the signing of a false written claim constitutes perjury or is subject to the same punishment as perjury.

(b) OBTAINING GOODS BY FALSE PRETENSES. In almost all of the states, statutes are directed against obtaining money or goods by means of false pretenses. These statutes vary in detail and scope. Sometimes the statutes are directed against a particular form of deception, such as the using of a bad check. In any case, an intent to defraud is an essential element of obtaining property by false pretenses.[18]

The Trademark Counterfeiting Act of 1984[19] makes it a federal crime to deal in goods and services under a counterfeit mark.

False representations as to future profits or the identity of the defendant are other common forms of false pretenses.

In the *Barnes* case the defendant claimed that he was not guilty of the crime of obtaining property by false pretenses.

---

[16]   New York v Loizides, 479 NYS2d 663 (1984).

[17]   United States v Petullo (CA7 Ill) 709 F2d 1178 (1983).
[18]   Miller v Wyoming (Wyo) 732 P2d 1054 (1987).
[19]   Act of October 12, 1984, § 1502, PL 98–473, 98 Stat 2178, 18 USC § 113.

WEST VIRGINIA V BARNES

___ WVa _____, 354 SE2d 606 (1987)

Mary Jacobs was a tenant in New Martinsville Towers, a government-financed housing project. The rent of tenants was determined by their ability to pay. Barnes was in charge of the management of the Towers. He borrowed $7,800 from Jacobs on the basis that he was going to buy Easter clothes and other items for his family, and he would see to it that the rent of Jacobs was not raised and that she would be given a particular job. He did not have any authority to prevent an increase in the rent nor to obtain the job. The rent of Jacobs was thereafter increased, and she did not get the job. Barnes was prosecuted for obtaining money by false pretenses. He was convicted and appealed.

PER CURIAM . . . Where a person obtains a loan of money by means of a knowingly false representation or pretense relating to a past or existing fact, the person obtaining the loan may be convicted of the crime of obtaining money by false pretenses. The lender intends to pass both title to and possession of the loan proceeds. An intent to repay the loan is no defense to a prosecution for obtaining money by false pretenses.

The crime of obtaining money or property by false pretenses is complete when the fraud intended is consummated by obtaining title to and possession of the property by means of a knowingly false representation or pretense. The crime is not purged by ultimate restoration or payment to the victim. It is sufficient if the fraud of the accused has put the victim in such a position that [the victim] may eventually suffer loss. . . .

The appellant [Barnes] also argues that the State's case was fatally damaged when Ms. Jacobs testified that the money was loaned to the appellant so that he could buy Easter clothes and other items for his family. The appellant contends that this evidence indicates that the loan was not fraudulently induced by any promises to Ms. Jacobs and that he was, therefore, entitled to a judgment of acquittal.

While Ms. Jacobs did testify that the money was loaned to the appellant so that he could buy Easter clothes and other items for his family, she also testified that, in making the loan, she relied upon the appellant's promises that he would see that her rent was not raised and that she would get the job at the New Martinsville Towers. . . .

The essential elements of the crime of obtaining money or property by false pretenses, *W.Va.Code*, 61-3-24(a), as amended, are: (1) the intent to defraud; (2) actual fraud; (3) the false pretense was used to accomplish the objective; and (4) the fraud was accomplished by means of the false pretense, that is, the false pretense must be in some degree the cause, if not the controlling cause, which induced the owner to part with his or her property. In this case it is important to recognize that the false pretense need not be the sole inducing cause of the owner's parting with the property.

The types of promises made by the appellant in this case may constitute indictable false pretenses: "When one makes a promise to perform in the future with the intent to cheat, defraud or deceive, such promise constitutes a misrepresentation of an existing fact which is indictable as a 'false pretense' under W.Va.Code § 61-3-24 (1977)." Syl., *State v. Moore*, ___ W. Va. ___, 273 S.E.2d 821 (1980). . . .

[Judgment affirmed]

QUESTIONS

1. What defenses did Barnes raise?
2. What disposition did the court make of these defenses? Why?
3. Would it have made any difference if Barnes had actually repaid the money to Jacobs?

§ 9:17   BAD CHECKS

The use of a bad check is commonly made a crime by a statute directly aimed at the use of bad checks. In the absence of a bad check statute, the use of a bad check could generally be prosecuted under a false pretense statute.

Under a bad check statute it is a crime to use or pass a check with knowledge that there will not be sufficient funds in the bank to pay the check when it is presented for payment. Knowledge that the bad check will not be paid when surrendered to the bank is an essential element of the crime.[20]

The bad check statutes typically provide that if the check is not made good within a specified number of days after payment by the bank is refused, it is presumed that the defendant had acted with the intent to defraud.

§ 9:18   CHEATS AND SWINDLES

Various statutes are designed to protect the public from being deceived.

(a) FALSE WEIGHTS, MEASURES, AND LABELS. Cheating, defrauding, or misleading the public by use of false, improper, or inadequate weights, measures, and labels is a crime. Both the federal and state governments have adopted many statutes on this subject.

(b) SWINDLES AND CONFIDENCE GAMES. The act of a person who, intending to cheat and defraud, obtains money or property by trick, deception, fraud, or other device, is an act known as a **swindle** or **confidence game**. Bad stock and spurious works of art are frequently employed in swindling operations.

§ 9:19   CREDIT CARD CRIMES

It is a crime to steal a credit card and, in some states, to possess the credit card of another person without the consent of that person. The use of a credit card without the permission of the rightful cardholder constitutes the crime of obtaining goods or services by false pretenses or with the intent to defraud. Likewise, a person continuing to use a credit card with knowledge that it has been canceled is guilty of the crime of false pretenses.

When, without permission, the wrongdoer signs the name of the rightful cardholder on the slip for the credit card transaction, the wrongdoer commits the crime of forgery. The district attorney has the discretion to choose the particular crime for which to prosecute the wrongdoer.

The Credit Card Fraud Act of 1984[21] makes it a federal crime to obtain anything of value in excess of $1,000 in a year by means of a counterfeit credit card, to make or traffic in such cards, or to possess more than 15 counterfeit cards at one time.

§ 9:20 USE OF MAILS TO DEFRAUD

Congress has made it a crime to use the mails to further any scheme or artifice to defraud. To constitute this offense, there must be (a) a contemplated or organized scheme to defraud or to obtain money or property by false pretenses, and (b) the mailing or the causing of another to mail a letter, writing, or pamphlet for the purpose of executing or attempting to execute such scheme or artifice. Illustrations of schemes that come within the statute are false statements to secure credit, circulars announcing false cures, false statements to induce the sale of stock of a corporation, and false statements as to the origin of a fire and the value of destroyed goods for the purpose of securing indemnity from an insurance company. Federal law also makes it a crime to use a telegram or a telephone to defraud.

§ 9:21   CRIMINAL LIBEL

A person who falsely defames another without legal excuse or justification may be

---

[20] Missouri v Smiles (Mo App) 723 SW2d 65 (1986).

[21] Act of October 12, 1984 § 1029, PL 98-473, 98 Stat 2183, 18 USC § 1029.

subject to criminal liability as well as civil liability. Criminal libel is made a crime because of its tendency to cause a breach of the peace. Under some statutes, however, the offense appears to be based upon the tendency to injure another.

No publication or communication to third persons is required in the case of criminal libel. The offense is committed when the defendant communicates the libel directly to the person libeled as well as when it is made known to third persons.

The truth of the statement is a defense in civil libel. In order to constitute a defense to criminal libel, the prevailing view requires that a proper motive on the part of the accused be shown as well as proof that the statement was true.

In a number of states, **slander** (oral defamation) or particular kinds of slander have also been made criminal offenses by statutes.

§ 9:22 LOTTERIES AND GAMBLING

There are three elements to a **lottery**: (a) a payment of money or something of value for an opportunity to win, (b) a prize, (c) by lot or chance. If these elements are present, it is immaterial that the transaction appears to be a legitimate form of business or advertising, or that the transaction is called by some name other than a lottery, such as a raffle. The sending of a chain letter through the mail is generally a federal offense both as a mail fraud and as an illegal lottery, when the letter solicits contributions or payments.

In many states, government lotteries are legal.

Gambling is a crime under modern statutes. It is similar to a lottery in that there are the three elements of payment, chance, and prize. Equipment used in gambling is generally declared by law to be contraband and may be confiscated by the government. If the winner of an electronic video card game receives something of value as a prize, the game is an illegal gambling device.

§ 9:23   EMBEZZLEMENT

Embezzlement is the fraudulent conversion of another's property or money by a person to whom it has been entrusted, as in the case of an employee's conversion of the employer's money. Embezzlement is a statutory crime designed to cover the case of unlawful takings that are not larceny because the wrongdoer did not take the property from the possession of another, and which are not robbery because there is neither a taking nor the use of force or fear.

It is immaterial whether the defendant received the money or property from the victim or from a third person to deliver to the victim. Thus, an agent commits embezzlement when the agent receives and keeps payments from third persons, — payments the agent should have remitted to the principal. Generally, the fact that the defendant intends to return the property or money embezzled, or does in fact do so, is no defense.

Today, every jurisdiction has not only a general embezzlement statute but also various statutes applicable to particular situations, such as embezzlement by trustees, employees, and government officials.

§ 9:24 RECEIVING STOLEN GOODS

The crime of **receiving stolen goods** is the receiving of goods that have been stolen with knowledge of that fact, and with the intent to deprive the owner of them. It is immaterial that the receiver does not know the identity of the owner or of the thief.

C.   CRIMES OF FORCE AND CRIMES AGAINST PROPERTY

In contrast with the white collar crimes are those that involve the use of force, threat of force, or that cause injury to persons or damage to property.

§ 9:25   LARCENY

Larceny is the wrongful or fraudulent taking and carrying away of the personal property of another by any person with a fraudulent intent to deprive the owner of such property.[22] The place from which the property is taken is generally immaterial, although by statute the offense is sometimes subjected to a greater penalty when property is taken from a particular kind of building, such as a warehouse. Shoplifting is a common form of larceny. In many states, shoplifting is made a separate crime.

Although the term is broadly used in everyday speech, every unlawful taking is not a larceny. At common law, a defendant taking property of another with the intent to return it was not guilty of larceny. This has been changed in some states so that a person who "borrows" a car for a joyride is guilty of larceny, theft, or some other statutory offense.

Statutes in many states penalize as **larceny by trick** the use of any device or fraud by which the wrongdoer obtains the possession of, or title to, personal property from the true owner. In some states all forms of larceny and robbery are consolidated into a statutory crime of theft. At common law, there was no crime known as "theft."

§ 9:26   ROBBERY

Robbery is the taking of personal property from the presence of the victim by use of force or fear. In most states, there are aggravated forms of robbery, such as robbery with a deadly weapon. The crime of robbery may overlap the crime of larceny. When the unlawful taking is not by force or fear, as when the victim does not know that the property is being taken, the offense is larceny, but it cannot be robbery. In contrast, when the property is taken from the victim by use of force or fear, there is both robbery and larceny. In such

case, the prosecuting attorney will determine for which crime the defendant is to be prosecuted.

§ 9:27   BURGLARY

At common law, **burglary** was the breaking and entering in the nighttime of the dwelling house of another, with the intent to commit a felony therein.[23] While one often thinks of burglary as stealing property, any felony would satisfy the definition. The offense was aimed primarily at protecting the habitation and thus illustrates the social objective of protection of the person, in this case, the persons living or dwelling in the building.

Modern statutes have eliminated many of the elements of the common-law definition so that under some statutes, it is immaterial when or whether there is an entry to commit a felony. The elements of breaking and entering are frequently omitted. Under some statutes, the offense is aggravated and the penalty is increased in terms of the place where the offense is committed, such as a bank building, freight car, or warehouse. Related statutory offenses have been created, such as the crime of possessing burglar's tools.

§ 9:28   ARSON

At common law, **arson** was the willful and malicious burning of the dwelling house of another. As such, it was designed to protect human life, although the defendant was guilty if there was a burning of the building even though no one was actually hurt. In most states, arson is a felony so that if someone is killed in the resulting fire, the offense is murder by application of the felony-murder rule. A homicide, however unintended, occurring in the commission of a felony is automatically classified as murder. Statutes may expand the kind of property involved in arson. Thus, a stat-

---

[22]   North Carolina v Lively, 83 NC App 639, 351 SE2d 111 (1986).

[23]   North Carolina v White, 84 NC App 299, 352 SE2d 261 (1987).

ute may make it arson to burn a "structure" of such a nature that persons are commonly present.[24]

In virtually every state, a special offense of **burning to defraud** an insurer has been created by statute. Such burning is not arson when the defendant burns the defendant's own house in order to collect the insurance money.

§ 9:29   RIOTS AND CIVIL DISORDERS

Damage to property in the course of a riot or civil disorder is ordinarily a crime to the

[24]   Florida v Jones (Fla App) 501 So 2d 753 (1987).

same extent as though only one wrongdoer were involved. That is, there is a charge of larceny or arson, and so on, depending on the nature of the circumstances, without regard to whether one person or many are involved. In addition, the act of assembling as a riotous mob and engaging in civil disorders is generally some form of crime in itself, without regard to the destruction or theft of property, whether under common-law concepts of disturbing the peace or under modern antiriot statutes.

A statute may make it a crime to riot or to incite to riot. However, a statute relating to inciting must be carefully drawn to avoid infringing upon constitutionally protected free speech.

SUMMARY

When a person does not live up to the standards set by the law, society may regard the conduct of the defendant as so dangerous to the government, to people, to property, that it will prosecute the defendant for such misconduct. This punishable conduct, called crime, may be common law or statutory in origin. In a few states, there are only statutory crimes. Crimes are classified as treason, felony, and misdemeanor, with a felony being a crime that is punishable by imprisonment or death.

In terms of the parties taking part in a crime, there are principals in the first and second degree and accessories before and after the fact. The statutory trend is to abolish distinctions and to treat everyone taking part in a crime as being guilty of the crime.

Employers and corporations may be criminally responsible for their acts and the acts of their employees. Minors, the insane, and the intoxicated are held criminally responsible to a limited extent. This means that in some cases they will not be held responsible for a crime

when a normal, adult person would be held responsible.

Crimes are often classified in terms of whether force or violence is involved. The phrase *white collar crime* is frequently used in reference to crimes that do not involve force or violence. Some white collar crimes are linked with modern technology. When modern technology is involved, the criminal law frequently lags behind the technology because it takes time for the lawmaker to become aware that the white collar criminal has found a new way to commit a crime. White collar crimes embrace crimes relating to illegal methods of production, competition, and marketing, such as the illegal use of interstate transportation and communication. Other white collar crimes include crimes relating to securities, such as stocks and bonds; computer crimes; bribery; extortion; blackmail; and crimes relating to the exercise of improper influence in politics and in business. Counterfeiting; forgery; perjury; the making of false claims against the government, and the obtaining of goods or money by false pretenses; the use of bad checks; the use of false weights, measures and labels; swindles and confidence games; dealing in counterfeit credit cards and possessing more than 15 such cards at one time; using the mails to defraud; making defamatory statements about another; engaging in lotteries and gambling; embezzlement; and receiving stolen goods are also labeled white collar crimes.

In contrast with the foregoing crimes that are loosely called white collar crimes, are the crimes of force and violence. Most common of these are: larceny, robbery, burglary, arson, and burning to defraud an insurer. Taking part in a riot or civil disorder may be a crime in itself, in addition to the traditional forms of crime that may be committed in the course of the riot or disorder.

There is no uniform law of crimes. Each state and the federal government defines and punishes crimes as it chooses. While there is a tendency to follow a common pattern, there are many variations as to details between the law of different states and the federal law.

QUESTIONS AND CASE PROBLEMS

1. What is the objective of the rule of law that a person buying a gun with the intent to kill a neighbor is not guilty of attempted murder?
2. What is a crime that is malum in se?
3. Hunter was employed by the Watson Corporation. He was killed at work by an explosion caused by the gross negligence of the corporation. The corporation was prosecuted for manslaughter. It raised the defense that only people could commit manslaughter and that therefore it was not guilty. Was this defense valid?
4. Johnny took a radio from the Englehart Music Store without the knowledge of any clerk that he was removing it. He was then prosecuted for larceny. He claimed that he could only be prosecuted for shoplifting because larceny was a serious felony and all that he had done was to take merchandise from a store. Was this defense valid?
5. Garrison purchased goods that she knew had been stolen. When the police traced some stolen articles and discovered Garrison's activities, Garrison was prosecuted for embezzlement. Was she guilty?
6. Compare larceny, robbery, and embezzlement.
7. Gail drove her automobile after having had dinner and several drinks. She fell asleep at the wheel and ran over and killed a pedestrian. She was prosecuted for manslaughter and raised the defense that she did not intend to hurt anyone and because of the drinks did not know what she was doing. Was this a valid defense?
8. Koonce entered a gas station after it was closed for the night. By means of force, he removed the cash box from a soft drink vending machine. He was prosecuted for burglarizing a "warehouse." Was he guilty? [Koonce v Kentucky (Ky) 452 SW2d 822; Shumate v Kentucky (Ky) 433 SW2d 340]
9. Buckley took a credit card from the coat of its owner with the intent to never return it. He then purchased some goods at a department store and paid for them by presenting the credit card to the sales clerk and then signing the credit card slip with the name of the owner of the credit card. What crimes, if any, did Buckley commit? [Buckley v Indiana, 163 Ind App 113, 322 NE2d 113]
10. Berman organized Greatway Travel, Ltd. Greatway sold travel consultant franchises and promised that the franchisees would receive various discounts and assistance. None of these promises were ever kept because Greatway lost all its money through mismanagement. Berman was prosecuted for obtaining money by false pretenses. Was he guilty? [Berman v Maryland, 35 Md App 193, 370 A2d 580]
11. Lang and his wife lived in a trailer in a trailer park. Winhoven broke into the trailer in order to steal. He was prosecuted and convicted of breaking and entering "an occupied dwelling" with the intent to commit larceny. He raised the defense that he had not broken into an occupied dwelling but into a trailer. Was he correct? [Michigan v Winhoven, 65 Mich App 522, 237 NW2d 540]

12. Bryant was indicted for having knowingly received stolen property. He raised the defense that the money that he had received had been embezzled by the person from whom he had received it and that it was, therefore, not "stolen" property. Was he correct? [New Mexico v Bryant, 99 NM App 149, 655 P2d 161]

13. Skelton attempted to rob a general store. He used a small wooden toy pistol. The attempt failed and he was arrested. He was prosecuted for attempted armed robbery. Was he guilty? [Illinois v Skelton, 83 Ill 2d 58, 46 Ill Dec 571, 414 NE2d 455]

14. Jennings operated a courier service to collect and deliver money. The contract with his customers gave Jennings a day or so to deliver the money that had been collected. Instead of holding collections until delivered, Jennings made short-term investments with the money. He always made deliveries to the customers on time but kept the profit from the investments for himself. He was prosecuted for larceny. Was he guilty? [New York v Jennings, 69 NY2d 103, 512 NYS2d 652, 504 NE2d 1079]

15. Goodrich was convicted of an assault and battery. The sentencing judge ordered him to pay the past and future medical expenses the victim required because of the crime. The state law authorized the trial judge to enter an order of restitution "for injury to or loss of property, actual expenses incurred for treatment for injury to persons, and lost wages resulting from injury." The statute further provided: "the offender shall remain under the court's jurisdiction for a maximum term of ten years subsequent to the imposition of sentence. The portion of the sentence concerning restitution may be modified as to amount, terms and conditions during the next ten-year period." Goodrich claimed that the order to pay medical expenses that had not yet been incurred by the victim was invalid. Was he correct? [Washington v Goodrich, 47 Wash App 114, 733 P2d 1000]

10

TORTS

When a wrong has been done that has caused harm to someone, the law generally allows the injured person to recover monetary damages from the wrongdoer. When the wrong that has been done is the breaking of a contract, the right of the aggrieved person is governed by contract law. When there is no contract, the right of the ag-grieved person is typically governed by tort law.

A. GENERAL PRINCIPLES

In this chapter you will see many points at which there is a gradual expansion of the law of torts. This expansion is being made in response to what society thinks is right as it strives to promote the social forces described in Chapter 2.

§ 10:1 TORT AND CRIME DISTINGUISHED

A crime is a wrong arising from a violation of a public duty, whereas a **tort** is a wrong arising from a violation of a private duty. More practically stated, a crime is a wrong of such a serious nature that the state steps in to take some action to punish the wrongdoer and to deter others from committing the same wrong. Whenever the act that is punished as a crime causes harm to an identifiable person, that person may sue the wrongdoer for monetary damages to compensate for the harm. As to the person harmed, the wrongful act is called a tort; as to the government, (that same) wrongful act is a crime. If, however, a crime does not hurt an identifiable person, it is not a tort. For example, bribing a public official is a crime, but no individual person is harmed so that no tort is committed. Conversely, there may be a tort, even though there is no crime. For example, if I walk away with your coat wrongly but honestly thinking that it is mine, I have committed the tort of conversion. That is, I have committed an act wrongful to you. However, I have not committed any crime because I did not have the mental state necessary to constitute a crime such as larceny or theft.

§ 10:2 TORT AND BREACH OF CONTRACT DISTINGUISHED

The wrongs or injuries caused by a breach of contract arise from the violation of an obligation or duty created by the agreement of the parties. In contrast, a tort arises from the violation of an obligation or duty created by law. The same act may be both a breach of contract and a tort. For example, when an agent exchanges property instead of selling it as directed by the principal, the agent is liable for breach of contract and for the tort of conversion.

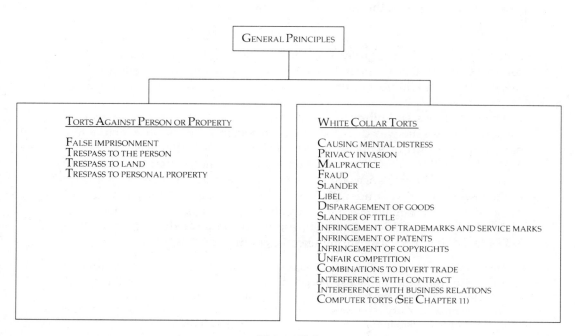

Figure 10-1
TORT LAW

§ 10:3   BASIS OF TORT LIABILITY

The mere fact that a person is hurt or harmed in some way does not mean that such person can sue and recover damages from the person causing the harm. There must exist a recognized basis for liability.

(a) DUTY. The mere fact that someone is hurt does not mean that someone must pay for the harm. Society does not want to go that far. In trying to state how far society will go, many courts speak in terms of a duty having been broken. That is, the plaintiff will not be allowed to recover from the defendant if the defendant did not break a duty that was owed to the plaintiff. There is a strong modern trend to ignore whether there is a duty. By this view, the court looks directly at the facts and considers whether there are interests involved that should be protected from harm. If the defendant has harmed such an interest, the defendant is required to pay for the damages.

In the *Donaca* case the defendant denied liability on the ground that there was no duty owed to the plaintiff.

DONACA V CURRY COUNTY
303 Or 30, 734 P2d 1339 (1987)

Donaca was riding his motorcycle on a county road. A private road intersected with the county road. Because of the tall grass growing at the intersection of the two roads, Donaca could not see an automobile coming down the private road and ran into it at the intersection. He claimed that the county was negligent in failing to cut the grass that obscured the intersection. The county raised the defense that it could not be negligent because it did not owe any duty to the plaintiff to cut the grass. The court of appeals sustained this defense and dismissed Donaca's complaint. He appealed.

LINDE, J. . . . "No duty" is only a defendant's way of denying legal liability for conduct that might be found in fact to have unreasonably caused a foreseeable risk of harm to an interest of the kind for which the plaintiff claims damages. . . .

The ambiguous and ultimately unhelpful role of "duty" in reaching a conclusion on this issue was discussed in a Wisconsin decision on which defendant and the Court of Appeals relied, *Walker v. Bignell*, 100 Wis.2d 256, 301 N.W.2d 447 (1981). The Wisconsin Supreme Court noted that the defendant county, under circumstances much like the present, had successfully argued in the lower court that "under the Wisconsin formulation of the elements of a cause of action in negligence, i.e., duty, breach, causation, and damage, the plaintiffs' action is defeated [at] the threshold for want of a duty to breach." *Id*. 301 N.W.2d at 451-52. The supreme court continued:

> This court on a number of occasions has discussed the somewhat elusive concept of 'duty.' [In two earlier opinions] this court repeated the words of Dean Prosser:
> "There is a duty if the court says there is a duty; the law, like the constitution, is what we make it. Duty is only a word with which we state our conclusion that there is or is not to be liability; it necessarily begs the essential question . . ."
> We find it unnecessary to ground our decision relative to the defendants' ulti-

mate liability upon the somewhat nebulous concept of duty. . . . Instead we prefer to declare directly that as a matter of public policy, municipalities should not be exposed to common law liability under the circumstances present in this case. Exposure to such liability would, we feel, place an unreasonable and unmanageable burden upon municipalities. . . .

There is nothing new in the observation that "duty" is only a conclusion embodying policies making a defendant civilly liable for failure to protect a plaintiff against an injury. . . . And, of course, negligence law itself like all law is a part of a state's public policy. Some courts and some theorists therefore have taken the further step that in the absence of statutory sources of public policy, a court should articulate and justify rules of law in terms of policy (described a bit self-servingly as "public" or "social" policy), in other words, adopt a legislative mode of making policy rather than a judicial search for policy made by others or for the implications of existing principles. This is what the Court of Appeals, quoting *Walker v. Bignell, supra,* did in this case.

We have not embraced freewheeling judicial "policy declarations" in other cases. . . .

We do not immunize counties from whatever responsibility for visibility of intersections they otherwise might have in order to relieve them of the cost of defending against unsuccessful claims. Nor are counties immune from liability that owners of private roads would face under identical circumstances merely because precautions are costly. . . .

The Court of Appeals let an argument against the cost of a "duty to control vegetation at intersections" lead it into a categorical "no duty" rule for uncontrolled intersections between public and private roads though not all roads. The rule illustrates the pitfalls of cost-based judicial generalizations. The risk of collisions at obstructed intersections and the cost of clearing the obstructions are empirical data. They can be expected to differ substantially from one location to another. One county road may carry many times the traffic of another. One private road may take many cars onto a county road daily, or during some seasons, more than some intersecting public roads do; another may hardly ever be used. Risks of collision will differ accordingly. The cost of controlling vegetation may differ from climate to climate, from county to county and from road to road. Of course there are no data of this kind in the record; the case was decided on plaintiff's complaint alone. The "no-duty" rule stated by the Court of Appeals will be taken to govern county roads throughout Oregon, regardless of particular circumstances; . . .

If there is an indication of legislative policy toward the problem of obstructed visibility at road intersections, it is found in ORS 368.256, which provides:

(1) Except as authorized by the county governing body, an owner or lawful occupant of land shall not allow: . . .

(b) Any structure, tree, drainage way, soil deposit or other natural or manmade thing on that land to present a danger to or create a hazard for the public traveling on a public road or facilities within the right of way of the public road by obstructing, hanging over or otherwise encroaching or threatening to encroach in any manner on a public road that is under county jurisdiction.

The county disputes plaintiff's claim that the county itself is meant to be included among landowners who may not allow obstructing plants or structures to endanger travel, and we agree that the statute does not literally cover this case. The statute does, however, show a public policy placing safety of the traveling public over the cost of removing dangerous obstructions, if that is the issue.

But the issue need not be seen in the all-or-nothing terms in which the Court of Appeals (and the Wisconsin court) cast it. Broadly phrased arguments over "duty" in common-law negligence tend to turn into a disputed rule of law what properly is a determination of the ordinary issues of negligence liability: whether defendant's conduct caused a foreseeable kind of harm to an interest protected against that kind of negligent invasion, and whether the conduct creating the risk of that kind of harm was unreasonable under the circumstances. The existence and magnitude of the risk at the intersection in question bear on the foreseeability of harm; the feasibility and cost of avoiding the risk bear on the reasonableness of defendant's conduct. Both clearly are empirical questions. We do not mean that they must in every case be submitted to a jury; in an extreme case a court can decide that no reasonable fact-finder could find the risk foreseeable or defendant's conduct to have fallen below acceptable standards. . . . The circuit court held that the complaint did not state ultimate facts sufficient to constitute a claim for relief, in other words, that the county would not be liable no matter how foreseeable (or actually known) a danger was created by uncontrolled grass obscuring the intersection and how easy it might have been for the county to remove that danger or warn against it. The Court of Appeals affirmed the dismissal of the complaint on grounds that the county was immune from liability — had "no duty" — under any circumstances encompassed within the complaint. That was erroneous.

[Judgment reversed and action remanded]

QUESTIONS

1. What is the attitude of the Oregon Supreme Court as to the usefulness of the concept of duty in deciding negligence cases?
2. What led the lower court to conclude that there was no duty on the county to cut the grass at intersections?
3. According to the Supreme Court of Oregon, what should be the analysis in a negligence case?

(b) VOLUNTARY ACT. The defendant must be guilty of a voluntary act or omission. Acts committed or omitted by one who is confronted with a sudden peril caused by another are considered involuntary acts.

(c) INTENT. Whether intent to do an unlawful act or intent to cause harm is required as a basis for tort liability depends upon the nature of the tort involved. Liability is imposed for some torts even though the person committing the tort acted without any intent to do wrong. Thus, a person going on neighboring land without consent of the landowner is liable for the tort of trespass, even though such action was caused by an honest mistake as to the location of the boundary line.

In other torts, the intent of the actor is an essential element. Thus, in the case of slander and interference with contracts, it is necessary for the plaintiff to show that the defendant intended to cause harm or at least had the intent to do an act that a reasonable person would anticipate was likely to cause harm.

(d) MOTIVE. As a general rule, motive is immaterial except as it may be evidence to show the existence of intent. In most instances, a legal right may be exercised even with bad motives, and an act that is unlawful is not made lawful by good motives.

(e) CAUSAL RELATIONSHIP. In order to put legal responsibility upon one as a wrongdoer, it is necessary to show that there was a relationship of cause and effect between the wrongful act and the harm sustained by the plaintiff. In some states, the wrongful act must have been the proximate (or immediate) cause of the plaintiff's harm. In many states, however, the requirement of a causal connection has been relaxed. In those states, it is now sufficient that the defendant's act or omission substantially contributes to the harm rather than being the sole and proximate cause.[1]

(1) Foreseeability. In many instances, the courts define a causal relationship in terms of foreseeability. That is, if it was reasonably foreseeable that the conduct of the defendant could cause harm to the plaintiff, there is a sufficient causal relationship between the defendant's conduct and the plaintiff's harm.

(2) Act of Third Person. The fact that the wrongful act of a third person takes effect between the time that the defendant acted or failed to act and the time the plaintiff is injured does not establish that the causative chain between the defendant's conduct and the plaintiff's harm has been broken. The action of a third person, therefore, does not insulate the defendant from liability for the plaintiff's harm. If the conduct of the third person was foreseeable, it does not relieve the defendant from liability to the plaintiff. To the contrary, both the defendant and the third person are liable to the plaintiff, and the question of division of

liability discussed in § 10:7 of this book then arises.

The fact that the plaintiff is harmed by a criminal act of a third person does not break the chain of liability when the defendant was under a duty to protect the plaintiff from the class of harm that was sustained. Thus, a multistory garage, operated on a park-it-yourself-and-lock basis, was liable to the plaintiff parking her car in the garage when she was robbed at gunpoint. The garage was negligent in failing to provide adequate security for the protection of its customers or to warn them that no security was provided.[2]

(f) LIABILITY FOR TORT OF EMPLOYEE OR CHILD. A person may be innocent of wrong, yet be held liable for the tort committed by another person. As will be discussed later in the chapters on agency, the tort of an employee or agent may, in some cases, impose liability upon the employer or principal.

A parent is ordinarily not liable for the tort committed by a child. That is, the mere fact that the person sued is the parent of the child committing the wrong does not impose liability on the parent.

There are several instances, however, in which a parent will be held liable. If the parent knows that the child has a dangerous characteristic, such as a disposition to set houses on fire, and does not take reasonable steps to prevent this, the parent will be held liable for the harm caused by the child. If the child is a reckless driver and the parent allows the child to use the parent's car, the parent is liable on the theory that the parent was negligent in entrusting the car to the child. In about half of the states, a parent supplying a family car is liable for any harm negligently caused by any member of the family while driving the car. In some states, any person lending an automobile is liable for the harm caused by the negligence of the person borrowing or renting the car. In some states, statutes

---

[1]   Domingue v Louisiana Department of Public Safety (La App) 490 So 2d 722 (1986).

[2]   Allright, Inc. v Pearson (Tex App) 711 SW2d 686 (1986).

make a parent liable for willful or malicious property damage caused by minor children. Such statutes generally specify a maximum limitation on such liability.

§ 10:4   LIABILITY-IMPOSING CONDUCT

Typically, American law imposes tort liability only when there is some fault on the part of the defendant. Thus, it is required that the defendant either intended to cause the harm of the plaintiff or that the defendant was negligent. In a number of instances, the law of this century has made exceptions to the concept that liability can only be based on fault and has imposed liability solely because the plaintiff has been harmed by the act of the defendant. Although there is a duty to act in good faith, there is no tort of bad faith.[3] Thus, a defendant who acts within legal or contract rights is not liable to the plaintiff on the theory that the defendant exercised those rights in bad faith.

§ 10:5   ABSOLUTE LIABILITY

In some areas of the law, liability for harm is imposed without regard to whether there was any fault on the part of the defendant; that is, without regard to whether there was any negligence or intention to cause harm. For example, in most states when a contractor blasts with dynamite and debris is hurled onto the land of another, the landowner may recover damages from the contractor even though the contractor was not negligent and did not intentionally cause the harm.

By this concept of absolute liability, society is saying that the activity is so dangerous to the public that liability must be imposed even though no fault is present. Yet society will not go so far as to say that the activity is so dangerous that it must be outlawed. Instead, the compromise is made to allow the activity to continue but to make the one who stands to benefit from the activity pay its injured victims regardless of the circumstances under which the injuries are inflicted.

(a) INDUSTRIAL ACTIVITY. Generally there is absolute liability for harm growing out of the storage of inflammable gas and explosives in the middle of a populated city; crop dusting when the chemical used is dangerous to life and the dusting is likely to be spread by the wind; and for factories emitting dangerous fumes, smoke, and soot in populated areas. However, the mere fact that activity is industrial in nature does not mean that strict liability is to be applied. Thus, drilling and operating a natural gas well is not an activity that results in strict liability.[4]

(b) CONSUMER PROTECTION. Pure food statutes may impose absolute liability upon the seller of foods in favor of the ultimate consumer who is harmed by them. Decisions and statutes governing product liability impose liability although the defendant is not negligent and intends no harm.[5]

(c) WILD ANIMALS. A person keeping a wild animal is absolutely liable for any harm caused by it. This liability is not affected by the fact that the animal was tamed and the owner had no reason to foresee that harm would occur.

(d) NO-FAULT LIABILITY. No-fault liability is another name for absolute liability. However called, the defendant is liable for harm caused the plaintiff by virtue of the fact that such harm was caused the plaintiff. Liability is imposed without regard to the absence of any fault or intention to harm on the part of the defendant.

No-fault liability is based on statutes. Typically, recovery on no-fault liability is less than the liability that would exist if fault of the defendant could be established. Generally the plaintiff is allowed to prove

---

[3]   North Century Kansas Produce Credit v Hansen, 240 Kan 671, 732 P2d 726 (1987).

[4]   Williams v Amoco Production Co. 241 Kan 102, 734 P2d 1113 (1987).
[5]   See Chapter 30 of this book.

such fault and recover a greater amount when serious injury or death has been caused.

No-fault liability is today associated with automobiles. A half century before the no-fault concept was applied to automobile liability, it became the basis for workers' compensation. Under such statutes, the worker is compensated when the employment-related harm is sustained, without any question being raised as to the presence or absence of fault on the part of the employer. The amount recovered by a worker is smaller than could be recovered if a common-law action could be prosecuted. The injured worker who is covered by workers' compensation is restricted to the recovery permitted by such law and does not have the choice of bringing a lawsuit to seek a larger recovery.

§ 10:6   NEGLIGENCE

The widest range of tort liability today arises in the field of **negligence,** which exists whenever the defendant has acted with less care than would be exercised by a reasonable person under the circumstances.[6] Such negligence must be causally related to the harm sustained by the plaintiff.

(a) THE "REASONABLE PERSON." The reasonable person whose behavior is made the standard is an imaginary person. In a given case that is tried before a jury, "reasonable" is what appears to the composite, or combined, minds of the jurors to be sensible or suitable under the circumstances.

This reasonable person is not any one of the jurors nor an average of the jurors. The law is not concerned with what the jurors would do in a like situation, for it is possible that they may be more careful or less careful than the abstract reasonable person.

(b) VARIABLE CHARACTER OF THE STANDARD. By definition, the standard is a variable standard for it does not tell you in advance what should be done. This is confusing to everyone, in the sense that the exact answer in any borderline case is unknown until the lawsuit is over. From the standpoint of society, however, this very flexibility is desirable because it is obviously impossible to foresee every possible variation in the facts that might arise and even more impossible to keep such a code of conduct up-to-date. Imagine how differently the reasonable person must act while driving today's automobile on today's superhighways than when driving a Model T on dirt roads three-quarters of a century ago.

(c) DEGREE OF CARE. The degree of care required of a person is that which an ordinarily prudent person would exercise under similar circumstances. It does not mean such a degree of care as would have prevented the harm from occurring, nor is it enough that it is just as much care as everyone else exercises. Nor is it sufficient that one has exercised the degree of care that is customary for persons in the same kind of work or business, or that one has employed the methods customarily used. If one is engaged in services requiring skill, the care, of course, must measure up to a higher standard. In any case, the degree of care exercised must be commensurate with the danger that would probably result if such care were lacking. In all cases, it is the diligence, care, and skill that can be reasonably expected under the circumstances. Whether one has exercised the degree of care that is required under the circumstances is a question that is determined by the jury.

(d) CONTRIBUTORY NEGLIGENCE. At common law, a plaintiff could not recover for injuries caused by another's negligence if the plaintiff's own negligence had contributed to the injury. The plaintiff guilty of contributory negligence was denied recovery without regard to whether the defendant was more negligent. The common law did not recognize comparative degrees of negligence, nor did it try to apportion the injury to the two parties in terms of the degree of their respective fault.

---

[6]   McCaskill v Welch (La App) 463 So 2d 942 (1985).

In order to avoid the harshness of the common-law rule as to contributory negligence, there developed a doctrine variously called the doctrine of last clear chance, the humanitarian doctrine, and the doctrine of discovered peril. Under this concept, although the plaintiff was negligent, the defendant was liable if the defendant had the last clear chance to avoid the injury. When the defendant had such opportunity but did not make use of it, the theory was that the plaintiff's negligence was not the cause of the harm sustained.

(e) COMPARATIVE NEGLIGENCE. In most states, the common-law rule as to contributory negligence has been rejected because it is regarded as unjust that the plaintiff who has been contributorily negligent should forfeit all rights even when the plaintiff's negligence was slight in comparison to the defendant's negligence. These states provide that there should be a comparing of the negligence of the plaintiff and the defendant with the result that the negligence of the plaintiff does not bar recovery but only reduces the plaintiff's recovery to the extent that the harm was caused by the plaintiff's fault. For example, if the jury decides that the plaintiff had sustained damages of $100,000 but that the plaintiff's own negligence was one-fourth the cause of the damage, the plaintiff would be allowed to recover $75,000. At common law, the plaintiff in such case would have recovered nothing.

In some states the comparative negligence concept is modified by ignoring the negligence of the plaintiff if it is slight and the negligence of the defendant is great or gross. At the other extreme, some states refuse to allow the plaintiff to recover anything if the negligence of the plaintiff was more than 50 percent of the cause of the harm.[7]

The trend of the law is to apply the concept of comparative fault to all actions, even though the defendant's alleged liability is based on warranty, strict tort, or absolute liability.

In the *Langley* case, the argument was made that the court should abolish the defense of contributory negligence and substitute the concept of comparative negligence.

---

[7]   North v Bunday, ___ Mont ___, 735 P2d 270 (1987).

LANGLEY V BOYTER
(App) 284 SC 162, 325 SE2d 550 (1984)

Robin Langley and James Boyter were driving automobiles in opposite directions on a two-lane highway. At a curve in the road the two cars collided. Each driver claimed that the other had crossed into the wrong lane. Langley sued Boyter for the damages sustained. Langley requested the judge to instruct the jury that any negligence on her part would merely reduce the amount that she could recover. The judge refused to do so and instructed the jury that any negligence on Langley's part barred her from recovering anything. The jury returned a verdict against Langley. A judgment was entered in favor of Boyter, and Langley appealed.

SANDERS, C. J. . . . To paraphrase John Locke, there is nothing less powerful than an idea whose time is gone. In our opinion, the doctrine of contributory negligence is an idea whose time is gone in South Carolina. It is extinct almost everywhere it once existed. It no longer exists in England, the country of its birth. It survives only in parts of this country, where it is threatened and endangered. Indeed, the doctrine of contributory negligence exists today as the Ivory-Billed Woodpecker of the common law.

The continued existence of the doctrine of contributory negligence as presently applied in South Carolina cannot be justified on any logical basis. It is contrary to the basic premise of our fault system to allow a defendant, who is at fault in causing an accident, to escape bearing any of its cost, while requiring a plaintiff, who is no more than equally at fault or even less at fault, to bear all of its cost. . . .

It is argued that the numerous exceptions to the doctrine of contributory negligence allow juries sufficient flexibility to do substantial justice, and even where no exception is applicable juries often ignore the doctrine when necessary to render justice.

In our opinion, the very fact courts and legislatures have had to craft so many exceptions to the doctrine of contributory negligence in order to produce justice supports an argument against its retention, particularly in view of the difficulties which have been encountered in applying these exceptions. The doctrine of comparative negligence presents a less difficult and easier to understand alternative.

While we agree that juries may often ignore the law because of its harshness, we view this proclivity as a compelling reason to abrogate the doctrine rather than retain it. There is something fundamentally wrong with a rule of law which is so contrary to the convictions of ordinary citizens that, when serving as jurors, they often refuse to enforce it in violation of their oaths. The disrespect for the law engendered by perpetuating such a rule is obvious.

The further argument is made that the doctrine of contributory negligence is a deterrent to carelessness. The fallacy of this argument was pointed out by Professor Prosser:

> The assumption that the speeding motorist is, or should be, meditating on the possible failure of a lawsuit for his possible injuries lacks all reality, and it is quite as reasonable to say that the rule promotes accidents by encouraging the negligent defendant.

We are of the opinion that the common law doctrine of contributory negligence should no longer be applied in South Carolina, and the doctrine of comparative negligence should be adopted in its place. There remains the question of which form of the doctrine of comparative negligence should be adopted.

The four leading versions of the doctrine are the slight-gross version, two modified versions, and the pure version.

Under the slight-gross version, if the defendant's negligence is gross and the plaintiff's negligence is slight, then the plaintiff may recover, with his damages reduced in proportion to his own negligence. This version has been adopted by statute in only two states and has not been looked on with favor by the commentators and courts. There appears to be very little difference in this version from the exception to the doctrine of contributory negligence already recognized in South Carolina which provides that a plaintiff guilty of simple contributory negligence is not barred from recovery against a defendant whose conduct is reckless.

The two modified versions of the doctrine of comparative negligence are similar to each other. One allows recovery by the plaintiff if his negligence was *not as great as* the negligence of the defendant. The other modified version allows the plaintiff to recover if his negligence is *not greater than* the defendant's negligence. In both versions, recovery is reduced by the amount of the plaintiff's negligence. The majority of the states have adopted one of these two versions. The recent trend in the states has been toward the latter version.

Under the pure version of comparative negligence, the plaintiff may recover even if his negligence is greater than that of the defendant, with his recovery diminished by the amount of his negligence. This version is recognized in a minority of the states. . . .

We choose the not-greater-than version of the doctrine for essentially two reasons. Unlike the pure version, it does not allow a plaintiff to recover when he has been the most at fault in causing an accident. But, unlike the not-as-great-as version, it does not allow a defendant to escape all responsibility for an accident which he was equally at fault in causing. Instead, the not-greater-than version of the doctrine strikes the reasonable balance of providing that parties equally at fault in causing an accident share equally in its cost.

In choosing this modified version of the doctrine over the pure version, we are also influenced by the conservative approach taken by our Supreme Court in abrogating doctrines of common law. . . .

[Reversed and remanded]

QUESTIONS

1. Assume that two cars collide at an intersection. The driver of car No. 1 sues the driver of car No. 2. The jury decides that driver No. 1 was 60 percent at fault and that driver No. 2 was 40 percent at fault. The total damages to car No. 1 amounted to $10,000. How much does car owner No. 1 recover in the action?
2. What social forces underlie the concept of comparative negligence?
3. What kind of comparative negligence doctrine is preferable?

(f) PROOF OF NEGLIGENCE. The plaintiff ordinarily has the burden of proving that the defendant did not exercise reasonable care. In some instances, however, it is sufficient for the plaintiff to prove that the injury was caused by something that was within the control of the defendant. If injury ordinarily results from a particular object only when there is negligence, the proof of the fact that injury resulted is held sufficient proof that the defendant was negligent. This is expressed by the maxim *res ipsa loquitur* (the occurrence or the thing speaks for itself).

This concept does not establish that the defendant was negligent but merely allows the jury to conclude or infer that the defendant was negligent. The defendant is not barred from proving lack of negligence or from explaining that the harm was caused by some act for which the defendant was not responsible; and the jury, if it believes the defendant's evidence, can refuse to infer negligence from the mere happening of the event and can conclude that the defendant was not negligent.

The burden of proving that the plaintiff was contributorily negligent is on the defendant, both under common law and under the comparative negligence concept.

(g) VIOLATION OF STATUTE. By the general rule, if harm is sustained while the defendant is violating a statute, the defendant is deemed negligent and is liable for the harm. Many courts narrow this concept so that the defendant is liable only if the statute is intended to protect against the kind of harm that was sustained because of the violation of the statute and if the plaintiff was a member of the class that the statute was designed to protect. For example, in a suit over a collision of the automobiles of the plaintiff and defendant, the fact that the defendant was driving without proper tags in violation of an automobile registration law will be ignored. This is because the purpose of the registration statute was not to describe negligent driving nor to protect other drivers from being negligently harmed.

(h) ASSUMPTION OF RISK. The plaintiff may have taken chances with a known danger. For example, the plaintiff may drive an automobile although its brakes are known to be bad. In such case, there is an assumption of risk by the plaintiff that harm may be sustained because of the defective brakes. At common law, the plaintiff who had assumed risk was barred from recovering from the defendant for the harm sustained by the plaintiff when the risk was realized. Early in this century, workers' compensation legislation abolished the defense of assumption of risk with respect to workers' compensation claims.

In many situations, there is little or no difference between contributory negligence and assumption of risk. In situations in which that is true, a comparative negligence or comparative fault statute has the effect of abolishing the common-law effect of assumption of risk, and requires a comparison of the fault of the respective parties, with a reduction of the plaintiff's recovery to the extent directed by the statute.[8]

§10:7 DIVISION OF LIABILITY

In some instances, when two or more de-

fendants have caused harm to the plaintiff, it is difficult or impossible to determine what damage was done by each of such wrongdoers or tortfeasors. For example, suppose automobile No. 1 strikes automobile No. 2, which is then struck by automobile No. 3. Ordinarily, it is impossible to determine how much of the damage to automobile No. 2 was caused by each of the cars. Similarly, a tract of farmland downriver may be harmed because two or more factories have dumped industrial wastes into the river. It is not possible to determine how much damage each of the factories has caused the farmland.

By the older view, a plaintiff was denied the right to recover from any of the wrongdoers in these situations. The courts followed the theory that a plaintiff is not entitled to recover from a defendant unless the plaintiff can prove what harm was caused by that defendant. The modern trend of the cases is to hold all the defendants jointly and severally (collectively and individually) liable for the total harm sustained by the plaintiff.

§ 10:8 WHO MAY SUE

Ordinarily the person who brings suit for a tort is the person whose property has been damaged or who has sustained personal injury.

In some torts, not only the immediate victim has the right to sue but also persons standing in certain relationships to the victim. Thus, under certain circumstances, one spouse can sue for an injury to the other spouse, or a parent can sue for an injury to the child. In a wrongful death action, members of the surviving group (typically the spouse, child, and parents of the person who has been killed) have a right to sue the wrongdoer for such death.

§ 10:9 IMMUNITY FROM LIABILITY

Basically, every person committing a tort is liable for damages for the harm caused thereby. However, certain persons and en-

---

[8] ITT Rayonier, Inc. v Puget Sound Freight Lines, 44 Wash App 368, 722 P2d 1310 (1986).

tities are not subject to tort liability. This is called **immunity from liability**.

Governments are generally immune from tort liability. This rule has been eroded by decision and in some instances by statutes, such as the Federal Tort Claims Act. Subject to certain exceptions, this act permits the recovery of damages from the United States for property damage, personal injury, or death-action claims arising from the negligent act or omission of any employee of the United States under such circumstances that the United States, "if a private person, would be liable to the claimant in accordance with the law of the place where the act or omission occurred." A fast-growing number of states have abolished governmental immunity although many still recognize it.

Very young children are immune from tort liability.

At the beginning of this century, charities were immune, and child and parent and spouses could not sue each other. These immunities are fast disappearing.[9]

B.   WHITE COLLAR TORTS

A classification of torts may be made, similar to that made in the law of crimes, between white collar torts and torts of force. Computer torts are discussed in Chapter 11.

§ 10:10   CAUSING OF MENTAL DISTRESS

When the defendant commits an act that by itself is a tort, there is ordinarily recovery for the mental distress that is caused thereby. At common law, if no tort was committed, the plaintiff could not recover for mental distress.

(a) INTENTIONALLY CAUSED MENTAL DISTRESS. With the turn of this century, and particularly in the last four decades, recov-

ery has been allowed in a number of cases in which no ordinary or traditional form of tort was committed. The common element in these cases was that the defendant had willfully subjected the plaintiff to unnecessary emotional disturbance.[10] This result was reached when an employee of a common carrier or hotel insulted a patron; an outrageous practical joke was played upon the plaintiff; the corpse of a close relative was concealed or mistreated, or interference was made with the burial; or statements were made to humiliate the plaintiff because of race, creed, or national origin.

The concept of liability for intentionally caused distress is applicable in a commercial setting, as when a collection agency uses harassing techniques to collect the debt owed by a consumer. Another example is when a manufacturer engages in a continuing campaign, including illegal electronic eavesdropping, to intimidate a critic of the defendant's product. In either case, the tort may be called the tort of outrageous conduct, or the tort of outrage. No distinction is made between causing mental distress or fear for the purpose of causing such distress or fear and coercing the victim into acting, or refraining from acting, in a particular way.

When there is liability for intentionally caused distress, there is also liability for any physical harm that is caused by the distress.

The fact that the plaintiff's rights have been violated and that the plaintiff was upset or made angry does not entitle the plaintiff to recover for emotional distress. For example, the fact that the plaintiff was wrongly denied the right to vote by the voting registrars does not in itself entitle the plaintiff to recover damages for outrageous conduct.[11]

(b) NEGLIGENTLY CAUSED MENTAL DISTRESS. In many jurisdictions, the concept of

---

[9]   Miller v Fallon County, ___ Mont ___, 721 P2d 342 (1986).

[10]   Midwest Buslines, Inc. v Johnson (Ark) 724 SW2d 453 (1987).
[11]   Santana v Registrars of Voters of Worcester, 398 Mass 862, 502 NE2d 132 (1986).

liability for distress has been expanded to impose liability for negligently caused distress.

In the *Schultz* case the plaintiff suffered a great emotional shock because of the negligence of the defendant. He claimed that he was entitled to damages for such emotional stress.

SCHULTZ V BARBERTON GLASS CO.
4 Ohio 3d 131, 447 NE2d 109 (1983)

A truck of the Barberton Glass Co. was transporting large sheets of glass down the highway. Elliot Schultz was driving his automobile some distance behind the truck. Because of the negligent way that the sheets of glass were fastened in the truck, a large sheet fell off the truck, shattered upon hitting the highway, and then bounced up and broke the windshield of the Schultz car. He was not injured but suffered great emotional shock. He sued Barberton to recover damages for such shock. Barberton denied liability on the ground that Schultz had not sustained any physical injury at the time or as the result of the shock. From a decision in favor of Barberton, Schultz appealed.

CELEBREZZE, C. J. . . . The issue raised in this appeal is whether a contemporaneous physical injury is a necessary condition precedent to liability for the negligent infliction of serious emotional distress. For the reasons which follow, we conclude that a contemporaneous physical injury is unnecessary.

In 1908, Ohio adopted the [impact] rule which requires the finding of contemporaneous physical injury before any recovery can be obtained for fright, shock, emotional distress, or mental suffering. *Miller v. Baltimore & Ohio S.W. R.R. Co., 78 Ohio St. 309, 85 N.E. 499 (1908).* The court reasoned that " . . . 'if the right of recovery in this class of cases should be once established, it would naturally result in a flood of litigation in cases where the injury complained of may be easily feigned without detection, and where the damages must rest upon mere conjecture or speculation. The difficulty which often exists in cases of alleged physical injury, in determining whether they exist, and if so, whether they were caused by the negligent act of the defendant, would not only be greatly increased, but a wide field would be opened for fictitious or speculative claims. To establish such a doctrine would be contrary to principles of public policy.' "

We find that the reasons set forth in *Miller* are no longer valid. The first concern that a flood of litigation would result if recovery were permitted has not materialized. Commentators and courts in other jurisdictions have concluded that this argument lacks merit. As stated in *Falzone v. Busch* (1965), 45 N.J. 559, 567, 214 A.2d 12, "there is no indication of an excessive number of actions of this type in other states which do not require an impact as a basis for recovery." . . .

Even if there may be a possibility of increased litigation, it is not a valid reason for denying a judicial forum. The Supreme Court of Pennsylvania, quoting Prosser, Intentional Infliction of Mental Suffering: A New Tort (1939), 37 Mich.L.Rev. 874, stated: " 'It is the business of the law to remedy wrongs that deserve it, even at the expense of a "flood of litigation"; and it is a pitiful confession of incompetence on the part of any court of justice to deny relief upon the ground that it will give the courts too much work to do.' " *Niederman v. Brodsky* (1970), 436 Pa. 401, 412, 261 A.2d 84. Even if the caseload increases, the "proper remedy" is an expansion of the judicial machinery, not a decrease in the availability of justice.

Therefore, we are not convinced that the problem of increased litigation is real or inevitable. Moreover, even if the caseload increases, we believe it is an unacceptable reason for denying justice.

A second reason for the physical injury requirement is the fear of fictitious injuries and fraudulent claims. . . .

The danger of illusory claims for mental distress is no greater than in cases of physical injury, especially when the injury is slight. The opportunity for fraud is as likely in such a case as one absent any physical injury. "The problem is one of adequate proof, and it is not necessary to deny a remedy in all cases because some claims may be false." Prosser, Law of Torts (4 Ed.1971) 327–328, Section 54.

We are not convinced that the fear of fraudulent claims is a valid reason to preclude the opportunity for recovery. The judicial system and evidentiary requirements have proven to be safeguards against fictitious claims in other personal injury cases and will function similarly in emotional distress cases.

The last argument urged by appellee for retaining the physical injury rule is that problems regarding the proof of emotional distress are insurmountable because damages must be based upon conjecture or speculation. . . .

Judges and juries will consider the credibility of witnesses and the genuineness of the proof as they do in other cases. In most instances, expert medical testimony will help establish the validity of the claim of serious emotional distress. Three medical doctors and a doctor of psychology testified, in the case *sub judice*, to the effect that appellant suffers from traumatic neurosis which was directly caused by the collision. Appellee did not offer expert testimony to the contrary.

Having carefully examined the arguments in support of the contemporaneous physical injury rule, it is clear that continued adherence to the rule makes little sense. Legal scholars who have considered the rule denying recovery in the absence of contemporaneous physical injury or impact are unanimous in condemning it as unjust and contrary to experience. The justifications for the doctrine are no longer valid and the reasons for abrogating it are strong. Consequently, the earlier cases upholding the doctrine are overruled.

Emotional injury can be as severe and debilitating as physical harm and is deserving of redress. "The gravity of appellant's injury and the inherent humanitarianism of our judicial process and its responsiveness to the current needs of justice dictate that appellant be afforded a *chance* to present [her] case to a jury. . . " An award of damages for emotional suffering is not new in Ohio. As previously indicated, damages have been allowed when a contemporaneous physical injury has been established. Recovery for emotional distress unaccompanied by a contemporaneous physical injury has been allowed under special circumstances. . . . Similarly, those injured by the negligent infliction of serious emotional distress should have the opportunity to recover damages.

For these reasons, we hold that a cause of action may be stated for the negligent infliction of serious emotional distress without a contemporaneous physical injury.

... We conclude that appellant has such a cause of action. ...

[Judgment reversed and action remanded]

QUESTIONS

1. What is the impact rule?
2. What is the rationale or underlying theory of the impact rule?
3. What is the justification for the impact rule?

(c) BYSTANDER RECOVERY. When a bystander is a spectator to the negligent conduct of the defendant, and the witnessing of such conduct causes serious and reasonably foreseeable emotional distress, the bystander may recover damages for such harm from the wrongdoer. Many courts limit this liability to spectators who are closely related to the person directly endangered by the defendant's conduct.

A few courts have eliminated the requirement that the bystander actually see the event that causes shock. Thus, the relative arriving shortly after the actual occurrence may recover damages for the emotional distress caused by the negligence of the defendant.[12]

§ 10:11   INVASION OF PRIVACY

As an aspect of protecting the person from unreasonable interference, the law has come to recognize a right of privacy. This right is most commonly invaded in one of the following ways: (a) invasion of physical privacy, as by planting a microphone in a person's home; (b) giving unnecessary publicity to personal matters of the plaintiff's life, such as financial status or past careers; (c) false public association of the plaintiff with some product or principle, such as indicating that the plaintiff endorses a product or is in favor of a particular law, when such is not the case; or (d)

commercially exploiting the plaintiff's name or picture as in using them in advertising without permission.

When a party has a legitimate business interest in making information known, such conduct is generally not regarded as an invasion of privacy. The conduct is protected by a privilege as long as good faith is exercised by the disclosing party.

§ 10:12   MALPRACTICE

Malpractice liability is a tort liability imposed for a poor or bad performance of a legal duty when the performance results in harm. Usually, it will be a poor performance because of negligence, as distinguished from harm that is intentionally caused. Typically, the duty of performance will be a duty that arises from a contract, and therefore the wrongdoer is guilty of both a breach of contract and a tort. Because of this interrelationship, the subject matter of malpractice will be considered in detail in Chapter 23.

§ 10:13   FRAUD

A person is entitled to be protected from fraud and may recover damages for harm caused by fraud. This protects the plaintiff from false statements made with knowledge of their falsity or with reckless indifference as to whether they were true or not.[13]

---

[12] Tommy's Elbow Room, Inc. v Kavorkian (Alaska) 727 P2d 1038 (1986).

[13] The concept of fraud is more fully analyzed in § 15:5 of this book.

In some instances, anti-fraud provisions have been adopted by consumer protection statutes. To illustrate, when the seller of a used car turns the odometer back with the intent to defraud, the seller is liable under the federal Motor Vehicle Information and Cost Savings Act to whomever purchases the automobile, without regard to whether the purchaser bought directly from that dealer or from an intermediate dealer.

Fraud is to be distinguished from racketeering. The fact that deceptive practices are used does not constitute racketeering activity within a RICO-type statute. Thus, a seller of a laundromat did not engage in racketeering activity when the seller created the false appearance of the profitable nature of the laundromat by stuffing the coinboxes with coins.[14]

§ 10:14 Defamation by Slander

A person is liable for defamation of another. Reputation is injured by **defamation**, which is a publication tending to cause one to lose the esteem of the community. **Slander** is a form of defamation consisting of the publication or communication to another of false, spoken words. Thus, a false statement by the manager of a business that the former manager had been fired for stealing is slander. The fact that language is offensive or derogatory does not in itself constitute slander.

(a) PRIVILEGE. Under certain circumstances, no liability arises when false statements are made, even though they cause damage. This absolute privilege exists in the case of publication by a public officer when the publication is within the officer's line of duty. The rule is deemed necessary to encourage public officers in the performance of their public duties.

Other circumstances may afford a qualified or conditional privilege. A communication made in good faith, upon a subject in which the party communicating has an interest or right, is privileged if made to a person having corresponding interest or right.[15] Thus, the owner of a watch may in good faith charge another person with the theft of the watch. A mercantile agency's credit report is conditionally privileged when made to an interested subscriber in good faith in the regular course of the agency's business. Also, when a client tells an attorney that a customer of the client owes money, such statement does not impose liability for defamation, even though it is wrong. The former employer of a job applicant has a qualified privilege to tell the prospective employer of the applicant why the former employer discharged the applicant.

Statements made in pleadings filed in court are protected by a privilege. In the *Defend* case, the controversy turned on whether this protection was an absolute or a conditional privilege.

---

[14] Waldschmidt v Crosa, 177 Ga App 707, 340 SE2d 664 (1986).

[15] Parry v George H. Brown & Associates, Inc. 46 Wash App 193, 730 P2d 95 (1986).

DEFEND V LASCELLES
149 Ill App 3d 630, 102 Ill Dec 819, 500 NE2d 712 (1986)

Lascelles and his wife were real estate developers. Defend and Johnson purchased homes constructed by them and later sued the Lascelles. Defend and Johnson claimed that in promoting the development, the defendants had committed mail and wire fraud and were guilty of violating the Racketeer Influenced and Corrupt Organizations Act (RICO). The defendants counterclaimed that the plaintiff's claim was made maliciously and that the defendants were entitled to damages for defamation. The plaintiffs replied that the statements in their complaint, although defamatory, were absolutely privileged. The court refused to dismiss the counterclaim and the plaintiffs appealed.

MORTHLAND, J. . . . We begin our analysis by recognizing the oft-stated principle in Illinois that anything said or written in a legal proceeding, including pleadings, is protected by an absolute privilege against defamation actions, subject only to the qualification that the words be relevant or pertinent to the matters in controversy. . . .

The privilege itself is steeped in public policy: it is uniformly recognized that the judicial system would best be served if persons with knowledge of relevant facts could report those facts to the court without fear of civil liability.

Plaintiff calls our attention to another view in this area which substitutes a different yardstick for the "relevant and pertinent" inquiry relied upon by many courts. That analysis provides for an absolute privilege when otherwise defamatory material is published in a judicial proceeding if the statements have "some relation" to the litigation. Specifically, section 587 of the Restatement (Second) of Torts states the following:

> A party to a private litigation or a private prosecutor or defendant in a criminal prosecution is *absolutely privileged* to publish defamatory matter concerning another in communications preliminary to a proposed judicial proceeding, or in the institution of or during the course and as a part of, a judicial proceeding in which he participates, if the matter has *some relation* to the proceeding. (Emphasis added.) Restatement (Second) of Torts § 587, at 248 (1977).

The Restatement standard has gained wide acceptance, becoming the majority rule today. At least two appellate courts in Illinois have heretofore embraced versions of the Restatement rule.

Clearly, then, depending upon the analysis employed, the threshold inquiry concerns whether the complained-of allegations are "relevant and pertinent" or bear "some relation" to the litigation. If so, pleadings in a judicial proceeding are absolutely privileged and cannot ordinarily form the basis of a defamation action. Defendants steadfastly maintain, though, that any pleading filed maliciously should not be granted an absolute privilege.

As a general principle, certain types of statements are deemed so privileged that the person making the statement should not be deterred from speaking by the threat of civil liability. In such a case an absolute privilege is granted, and no cause of action for defamation will lie against the person making the statement even if it is made with malice. This immunity afforded *absolutely* privileged matter is complete. It is not conditioned upon an honest or reasonable belief that the defamatory matter is true, or upon the absence of ill will on the part of the speaker. On the other hand, where only a *qualified* privilege is granted based upon a lesser concern for the freedom of the speaker, the person making the statement is immune from liability unless the privilege is abused or some element such as malice is present. When a qualified privilege is shown, the plaintiff has the burden of alleging and proving actual malice.

The law thus clearly allows for an absolute privilege where there exists a significant interest in protecting the type of speech involved. In such cases, malice alone on the part of the speaker will not defeat the privilege. Accordingly, the prevailing rule in the United States today is that libelous material contained in a pleading is absolutely privileged so long as it is pertinent, relevant, or bears some reasonable relation to the judicial proceeding, irrespective of whether it is false and malicious. . . .

The weight of authority in Illinois clearly favors recognition of an absolute privilege for statements made in a judicial proceeding based upon public policy. The defense of privilege or immunity in defamation cases rests upon the idea that "conduct which otherwise would be actionable is to escape liability because the defendant is acting in furtherance of some interest of social importance," an interest to be protected "even at the expense of uncompensated harm to the plaintiff's reputation." (Prosser, Torts § 114, at 776 (4th ed. 1971).) Further, comment *a* to section 587 of the Restatement explains:

> The privilege stated in this Section is based upon the public interest in according to all men the utmost freedom of access to the courts of justice for the settlement of their private disputes. . . . It protects a party to a private litigation . . . from liability for defamation *irrespective of his purpose in publishing the defamatory matter, of his belief in its truth or even his knowledge of its falsity.*" (Emphasis added.) Restatement (Second) of Torts § 587, comment *a*, at 249 (1977); see also *Bond v. Pecaut* (N.D.Ill. 1983), 561 F.Supp. 1037.

. . . We hold that otherwise defamatory statements made in a pleading filed in a judicial proceeding enjoy an absolute privilege if they are relevant, pertinent, or bear some relation to the subject in controversy. Whether or not the occasion gives rise to the privilege is solely a question of law for the court. If the complained-of statements are found not to reasonably relate to the issues, then the absolute privilege is no longer available, and a charge of malice will enter into consideration as if a qualified privilege were involved instead.

Under the precise question certified, then, we find that pleading a civil cause of action for violation of the applicable RICO provision is absolutely privileged from any counterclaim based on defamation so long as it has some relation to the matter in controversy. If such is the case, malicious intent in filing the pleading is irrelevant.

We note that our conclusion is in agreement with a recent pronouncement of the Ohio Supreme Court. In *Surace v. Wuliger* (1986), 25 Ohio St.3d 229, 495 N.E.2d 939, the Ohio court, relying on the absolute-privilege doctrine available in judicial proceedings, held that a party named as defendant in a civil RICO complaint could not sue for defamation. The court found that, as a matter of public policy, statements made in a written pleading are absolutely privileged only if "the allegedly defamatory statement bears some reasonable relation to the judicial proceeding in which it appears." 25 Ohio St.3d 229, 233, 495 N.E.2d 939, 943.

. . . Finally, defendants contend that granting an absolute privilege here will deprive them of a remedy at law for an injury to their reputation in violation of article I, section 12 of the Illinois Constitution of 1970 (Ill.Const.1970, art. I, § 12). That provision of our Constitution reads in full: "Every person shall find a certain remedy in the laws for all injuries and wrongs which he receives to his person, privacy, property or reputation. He shall obtain justice by law, freely, completely, and promptly." Ill.Const.1970, art. I, § 12.

Defendants' contention, however, is unsupported by case law. Persons defamed in pleadings or trial testimony may be left without legal redress, even if their reputations are damaged, because of the public policy favoring free and open administration of justice.

[Judgment reversed and action remanded]

QUESTIONS

1. What tests can be used by a court to determine whether statements in a pleading in court are privileged?
2. What is the difference between the tests given in your answer to Question 1?
3. Is it ever important whether statements in a pleading in court were made maliciously?

If a consumer makes false statements about a seller, such as that the consumer purchased a "lemon" from the automobile dealer, the consumer is liable for defamation. The fact that a person is a consumer does not give rise to any privilege to make false statements.

§ 10:15   DEFAMATION BY LIBEL

The reputation of a person or a business may be defamed by written statements. This is known as **libel**. Although the defaming statement is described as a writing, it may also be in print, picture, or in any other permanent, visual form. For example, to construct a gallows in front of another's residence is a libel. A written report falsely stating that an employee has falsified time work records is libelous.

§ 10:16   DISPARAGEMENT OF GOODS AND SLANDER OF TITLE

In the transaction of business, one is entitled to be free from the interference of malicious, false statements made by others as to the title or the quality of goods sold by the business. Actual damage must be proved by the plaintiff to have resulted from the false communications by the defendant to a third person. The plaintiff must show that as a consequence of the

statement, the third person had refrained from dealing with the plaintiff.

§ 10:17   INFRINGEMENT OF TRADEMARKS AND SERVICE MARKS

A **trademark** or **service mark** is a word, name, device, symbol, or any combination of these, used by a manufacturer or seller of goods or a provider of services, to distinguish those goods and services from those of other persons. When the mark of a particular person is used or substantially copied by another, it is said that the mark is infringed. The owner of the mark may sue for damages and enjoin its wrongful use.[16]

§ 10:18   INFRINGEMENT OF PATENTS

A grant of a **patent** entitles the patentee to prevent others from making, using, or selling a particular invention for a period of 17 years. Anyone so doing without the patentee's permission is guilty of a patent infringement. If the inventor does not have a patent or if the patent is invalid, anyone may copy the invention without liability.

An infringement occurs, even though all parts or features of an invention are not copied, if there is a substantial identity of names, operations, and result between the

[16]   § 24:3 of this book.

original and the new device. In the case of a process, however, all successive steps or their equivalent must be copied. In the case of a combination of an ingredient, the use of the same ingredient with others constitutes an infringement, except when the result is a compound essentially different in nature.

§ 10:19   INFRINGEMENT OF COPYRIGHTS

A wrong similar to the infringement of a patent is the infringement of a copyright. A copyright is the right given by statute to prevent others for a limited time from printing, copying, or publishing a production resulting from intellectual labor. The right exists for the life of the author and for fifty years thereafter.[17]

Infringement of a copyright in general consists of copying the form of expression of ideas or conceptions. There is no copyright in the idea or conception itself, but only in the particular way in which it is expressed. In order to constitute an infringement, the production need not be reproduced entirely nor be exactly the same as the original. Reproduction of a substantial part of the original, although paraphrased or otherwise altered, constitutes an infringement, but appropriation of only a word or single line does not.

One guilty of infringement of copyright is liable to the owner for damages, which are to be determined by the court. The owner is also entitled to an injunction to restrain further infringement.

§ 10:20   UNFAIR COMPETITION

Unfair competition is unlawful. The person injured thereby may sue for damages and an injunction to stop the practice, or may report the matter to the Federal Trade Commission or to an appropriate state agency.

It is unfair competition to imitate signs, storefronts, advertisements, and the packaging of goods of a competitor. Thus, when one adopts a box of distinctive size, shape, and color in which to market a product, and the package is imitated by a competitor, the latter is liable for unfair competition.

Every similarity to a competitor, however, is not necessarily unfair competition. For example, the term *downtown* is merely descriptive so that the Downtown Motel cannot obtain an injunction against the use of the name Downtown Motor Inn, because a name that is merely descriptive cannot be exclusively appropriated or adopted. As an exception, if the descriptive word has been used by a given business for such a long time as to be identified with the business in the public mind, a competitor cannot use that name.

The goodwill that is related to a trade name is an important business asset. There is a judicial trend in favor of protecting a trade name from a competitor's use of a similar name.

Historically the law as to unfair competition was only concerned with protecting competitors from unfair competition by their rivals. Under consumer protection statutes, most states now give protection to the consumer who is harmed by unfair competitive practices.

§ 10:21   COMBINATIONS TO DIVERT TRADE

Business relations may be harmed by a combination to keep third persons from dealing with another, who is the object of attack. Such a combination, resulting in injury, constitutes an actionable wrong known as conspiracy if the object is unlawful or if a lawful object is sought by unlawful means.

If the object of a combination is to further a lawful interest of the combination, no actionable wrong exists so long as lawful means are employed. For example, when employees are united in a strike,

---

[17]   Copyright Act of 1976, Act of October 19, 1976, § 302, PL 94-553, 90 Stat 2541, 2572, 17 USC § 302.

they may peacefully persuade others to withhold their patronage from the employer. On the other hand, all combinations to drive or keep away customers or prospective employees by violence, force, threats, or intimidation are actionable wrongs.

Labor laws prohibit some combinations as unfair labor practices, while other combinations to divert trade are condemned as illegal trusts.

§ 10:22 MALICIOUS INTERFERENCE WITH CONTRACT

The extent of tort law relating to interference with contracts and other economic relationships has increased greatly in recent years as the result of society's seeking to impose upon the marketplace higher ethical standards to prevent the oppression of victims of improper practices. In general terms, when the defendant interferes with and brings about the breach of the contract between a third person and the plaintiff, the circumstances may be such that the plaintiff has an action in tort against the defendant for interfering with contractual relations.[18]

As the tort in question is the malicious interfering with contract, it follows that there is no tort when the interference is not malicious but is done to safeguard or protect one's own financial or economic interest.[19]

However, the fact that the defendant is a competitor of the plaintiff does not constitute justification for the defendant's causing third persons to break their contracts with the plaintiff.

The fact that a contract is terminable at will does not deprive it of protection from interference. Likewise, it is immaterial that the contract could be ignored because not evidenced by a writing that satisfies the statute of frauds.

In addition to protecting existing contracts from deliberate interference, tort liability is imposed for acts intentionally committed to prevent the making of a contract.

§ 10:23 WRONGFUL INTERFERENCE WITH BUSINESS RELATIONS

One of the fundamental rights of an individual is to earn a living by working or by engaging in trade or business. A wrongful interference with this liberty is a tort.[20]

The right to conduct one's business is, nevertheless, subject to the rights of others. Hence, the injuries suffered by one in business through legitimate competition give no right to redress.

In the *Leigh* case, the party injured by a breach of contract claimed that the other party had broken the contract maliciously and had interfered with the aggrieved party's business relations.

[18]   Gross v Lowder Realty Better Homes and Gardens (Ala) 494 So 2d 590 (1986).
[19]   Genet Co. v Annheuser-Busch, Inc. (Fla App) 498 So 2d 683 (1986).

[20]   Tamiami Trail Tours, Inc. v Cotton (Fla App) 463 So 2d 1126 (1985).

LEIGH FURNITURE AND CARPET CO. V ISOM
(Utah) 657 P2d 293 (1982)

Leigh Furniture Company sold its furniture store to T. Richard Isom. The buyer made a down payment, and the balance was to be paid in ten annual installments. Thereafter Leigh, who was the key person of Leigh Furniture, was heard to complain that he lost by the contract and that he wanted to get out of it. Leigh, his wife, and his bookkeeper frequently went into the store now run by Isom and made remarks that drove customers away. In addition, Leigh failed to live up to the terms of the sales contract that required him to repair the furnace and to pay half of the heating bills. Leigh refused to accept the balance that was due under the contract and at the end of five years falsely claimed that the installments had not been made and that Isom had therefore broken the contract. Leigh sued Isom for the balance of the debt, and Isom counterclaimed for damages caused by Leigh's conduct. From a decision in favor of Isom, Leigh appealed.

Oaks, J. . . . The tort of intentional interference with prospective economic relations reaches beyond protection of an interest in an existing contract and protects a party's interest in prospective relationships of economic advantage not yet reduced to a formal contract. . . .

Influenced by the model of the intentional tort, many jurisdictions and the first *Restatement of Torts* define the tort of intentional interference with prospective economic relations as a prima facie tort, subject to proof of privilege as an affirmative defense. To recover, the plaintiff need only prove a prima facie case of liability, *i.e.*, that the defendant intentionally interfered with his prospective economic relations and caused him injury. As with other intentional torts, the burden of going forward then shifts to the defendant to demonstrate as an affirmative defense that under the circumstances his conduct, otherwise culpable, was justified and therefore privileged. . . .

We recognize a common-law cause of action for intentional interference with prospective economic relations, and adopt the Oregon definition of this tort. Under this definition, in order to recover damages, the plaintiff must prove (1) that the defendant intentionally interfered with the plaintiff's existing or potential economic relations, (2) for an improper purpose or by improper means, (3) causing injury to the plaintiff. Privilege is an affirmative defense, *Searle v. Johnson*, Utah, 646 P.2d 682 (1982), which does not become an issue unless "the acts charged would be tortious on the part of an unprivileged defendant." . . .

There was ample evidence that Isom had business relationships with various customers, suppliers, and potential business associates, and that Leigh, the former owner of the business, understood the value of those relationships. There was also substantial competent evidence that the Corporation, through Leigh, his wife, and his bookkeeper, intentionally interfered with and caused a termination of some of those relationships (actual or potential). Their frequent visits to Isom's store during business hours to confront him, question him, and make demands and inquiries regarding the manner in which he was conducting his business repeatedly interrupted sales activities, caused his customers to comment and complain, and more than once caused a customer to leave the store. Driving away an individual's existing or potential customers is the archetypal injury this cause of action was devised to remedy. . . .

Taken in isolation, each of the foregoing interferences with Isom's business might be justified as an overly zealous attempt to protect the Corporation's interests under its contract of sale. As such, none would establish the intentional interference element of this tort, though some might give rise to a cause of action for breach of specific provisions in the contract or of the duty of good faith performance which inheres in every contractual relation. Even in small groups, these acts might be explained as merely instances of aggressive or abrasive—though not illegal or tortious—tactics, excesses that occur in contractual and commercial relationships. But in total and in cumulative effect, as a course of action extending over a period of three and one-half years and culminating in the failure of Isom's business, the Leigh Corporation's acts cross the threshold beyond what is incidental and justifiable to what is tortious. The Corporation's acts provide sufficient evidence to establish two of the elements in the definition of this tort: an intentional interference with present or prospective economic relations that caused injury to the plaintiff. . . .

The evidence was also sufficient to support the verdict under the requirement that the intentional interference with prospective economic relations (in this case, Isom's relations with his customers, suppliers, and potential business associates) must have been for an improper purpose or by the use of improper means. . . .

[There was] substantial evidence from which the jury could have concluded that the Corporation breached its express and implied contractual duties for the purpose of ruining Isom's business and obtaining possession of the building in order to sell it more profitably elsewhere. By themselves, the Corporation's breaches would not satisfy the requirement of "improper means," but they could do so when coupled with the improper purpose of injuring Isom. In combination, a breach of contract and an intent to injure satisfy the improper means requirement for the cause of action for intentional interference with prospective economic relations.

[Judgment affirmed]

QUESTIONS

1. When will a court impose damages for interference with economic relations of another?
2. In order to prove the tort of intentional interference with prospective economic relations, must the plaintiff show a clear act of such interference?
3. Assume that you manufacture electric fans and by inventing a substantially superior fan you drive your competitors out of business. Can the competitors sue you for the loss that you caused them?

C. TORTS AGAINST PERSON OR PROPERTY

In contrast with the white collar torts, some torts involve the use of force against persons or property.

§ 10:24 TREPASS TO THE PERSON

Trepass to the person consists of any contact with the victim's person for which consent was not given. It thus includes what is technically described as a **battery.** It includes an **assault** in which the victim apprehends the commission of a battery but is in fact not touched. It also includes false imprisonment.

In some instances, as in cases of self-defense, a person will have a right to use force that would otherwise constitute an unlawful battery.

§ 10:25   FALSE IMPRISONMENT

False imprisonment is the intentional, unprivileged detaining of a person without that person's consent.[21] It may take the extreme form of kidnapping. At the other extreme, a shopper who is detained in a store manager's office and questioned as to shoplifting is the victim of false imprisonment where there is no reasonable ground for believing that the shopper is a thief. Likewise, a merchant is liable for false imprisonment when a person detained under suspicion of shoplifting is detained after it is determined that the person was innocent and the original suspicion was a mistake.[22] False imprisonment also includes detention under an official arrest when there is no legal justification for the arrest.

(a) DETENTION. Any detention at any place by any means for any duration of time is sufficient to satisfy the detention element of false imprisonment. Stone walls are not required to make a false imprisonment. If a robber holds a bank teller at gunpoint for the purpose of preventing the teller from attacking the other robbers or from escaping, there is a sufficient detention.

(b) CONSENT AND PRIVILEGE. By definition, no false imprisonment occurs when the person detained consents to it. For example, when a merchant without any justification detains a person on the suspicion of shoplifting, such detention is not a false imprisonment if the victim consents to it without any protest. If the merchant had reasonable grounds for believing that the victim was guilty of shoplifting, the action of the merchant was not false imprisonment, even though the victim was detained under protest and did not consent

to it. Statutes frequently give merchants a privilege to detain persons reasonably suspected of shoplifting.

§ 10:26   TRESPASS TO LAND

A **trespass to land** consists of any unpermitted entry below, on, across, or above land. This rule is modified to permit the proper flight of aircraft above the land so long as it does not interfere with a proper use of the land.

§ 10:27   TRESPASS TO PERSONAL PROPERTY

An illegal invasion of property rights with respect to property other than land constitutes a **trespass to personal property** whether done intentionally or negligently. When done in good faith and without negligence, there is no liability. This is in contrast with the case of trespass to land where good faith and absence of negligence is not a defense.

Negligent damage to personal property imposes liability for harm done. Intentional damage to personal property will impose liability for the damage done and also may justify exemplary or punitive damages.

A **conversion** occurs when personal property is taken by the wrongdoer and kept from its true owner or prior possessor. For example, a bank clerk commits conversion by unlawfully taking money from the bank. Conversion is the civil side of the crimes relating to stealing. The good faith of the converter, however, is not a defense to civil liability. Thus, an innocent buyer of stolen goods is liable for damages for converting them.

[21] Walker v Portland, 71 Or App 693, 693 P2d 1349 (1985).
[22] Latek v K Mart Corp. 224 Neb 807, 401 NW2d 503 (1987).

SUMMARY

Conduct that harms other people or their property is generally called a tort. The injured person may sue the wrongdoer to recover damages to compensate for the harm or loss caused. The conduct that is a tort may also be a crime and may sometimes be a breach of contract. Tort liability is generally imposed because of the fault of the wrongdoer; in some cases it is imposed when there is no fault. In any case, the harm-causing conduct of the defendant must be voluntary and must have a causal relationship to the harm sustained. Motive is not required to constitute a tort. In some cases, intent is an essential element of the tort. In others, it is not. Liability is imposed without fault in connection with industrial activity, consumer protection, wild animals, and certain areas of liability to workers or to victims of automobile collisions. Negligence is the failure to follow the degree of care that would be followed by a reasonably prudent person in order to avoid foreseeable harm. If the negligence of the plaintiff contributes to the plaintiff's harm, the recovery obtained by the plaintiff may be reduced proportionately or barred, depending upon the type of comparative negligence rule that is in force. In a minority of states, the common-law contributory negligence rule is still followed. Under this law, any negligence of the plaintiff bars all recovery. Negligence must be proven as a fact, although the plaintiff may be aided by the doctrine of "res ipsa loquitur," which permits an inference of negligence of the defendant when things cause harm and, in the experience of society, harm would not result in the absence of negligence. In most states, the violation of a statute is proof that the defendant was negligent, provided the statute is designed to protect from the kind of harm that has been sustained and the plaintiff is a member of the class that the statute sought to protect. In general, any person aggrieved or harmed by a tort can sue the defendant. In some instances a relative of the injured person will have a right to sue the defendant because of the harm caused. When there are two or more persons causing harm in such a way that it is not possible to determine how much harm was caused by each person, all the persons causing the harm are jointly and severally liable to the plaintiff by the modern trend.

While ordinarily any wrongdoer may be sued, some wrongdoers have a limited immunity, while others may be liable for the tortious acts of third persons. Governments may be immune from suit. To some extent, minors, parents of the aggrieved person, and the spouse of that person may be immune from suit. The trend of the law is to treat charities the same as other defendants and impose tort liability upon them.

Some specific torts include: the causing of mental distress of the victim or of a bystander, either intentionally or negligently; invasion of privacy; defamation by slander or libel; disparagement of goods and slander of title; infringement of trade and service marks, patents, and copyrights; unfair competition; combinations to divert trade; malicious interference with contracts; interference with business relations; trespass to person; false imprisonment; trespass to land and to personal property; and conversion.

QUESTIONS AND CASE PROBLEMS

1. What is the objective of each of the following rules of law?
   (a) In some areas of law, liability for harm exists without regard to whether there was any negligence or intention to cause harm.
   (b) Geographical and descriptive names cannot ordinarily be adopted as trademarks.
2. Is proof of a bad motive essential to imposing tort liability?
3. The Coleman Construction Company was constructing a highway. It was necessary to blast rock with dynamite. The corporation's employees did this with the greatest of care. In spite of their precautions, some flying fragments of rock damaged a neighboring house. The owner of the house sued the corporation for the damages. The corporation raised the defense that the owner was suing for tort damages and that such damages could not be imposed because the corpora-

tion had been free from fault. Was this defense valid?

4. Burnstein drove a car on a country road at 35 miles an hour. The maximum speed limit was 45 miles an hour. He struck and killed a cow that was crossing the road. The owner of the cow sued Burnstein for the value of the cow. Burnstein raised the defense that as there was no driving above the speed limit, there could be no liability for negligence. Was this defense valid?

5. The Brunswick Corporation manufactured and sold raincoats that it advertised to consumers as "waterproof" when in fact they were merely "water resistant." The Brunswick Corporation was sued for engaging in unfair competition. It raised the defense that it was not guilty because it was understood in the trade that "waterproof" meant only "water resistant," and therefore no unfair advantage was taken of any competitor. Was this defense valid?

6. Jessica Sorensen was a minor. She was riding in an automobile driven by her father, Paul. The car collided with another car. Jessica was injured. She sued her father for her injuries. He raised the defense that a child could not sue his/her father for negligence. Was he correct? [Sorensen v Sorensen (Mass) 369 Mass 350, 339 NE2d 907]

7. Henry Neiderman was walking with his small son. An automobile driven by Brodsky went out of control, ran up on the sidewalk, and struck a fire hydrant, a litter pole and basket, a newsstand, and Niederman's son. The car did not touch Niederman, but the shock and fright caused damage to his heart. He sued Brodsky for the harm that he sustained as the result of Brodsky's negligence. Brodsky defended on the ground that he was not liable because he had not touched Niederman. Was this a valid defense? [Niederman v Brodsky, 436 Pa 401, 261 A2d 84]

8. Carrigan, a district manager of Simples Time Recorder Company, was investigating complaints of mismanagement of the Jackson office of the company. He called at the home of Hooks, the secretary of that office. She expressed the opinion that part of the trouble was caused by stealing of parts and equipment by McCall, another employee. McCall was later discharged and sued Hooks for slander. Was she liable? [Hooks v McCall (Miss) 272 So 2d 925]

9. Giles, a guest at a Pick Hotel, wanted to remove his briefcase from the right-hand side of the front seat of his auto. To support himself while so doing, he placed his left hand on the center door pillar of the right-hand side of the car. The hotel bellboy closed the rear door of the car without noticing Giles' hand. One of Giles' fingers was smashed by the closing of the door and thereafter had to be amputated. Giles sued the Pick Hotels Corp. Was he entitled to recover? [Giles v Pick Hotels Corp. (CA6 Mich) 232 F2d 887]

10. A statute required that air vent shafts on hotel roofs have parapets at least 30 inches high. Edgar Hotel had parapets only 27 inches high. Nunneley was visiting a registered guest at the Edgar Hotel. She placed a mattress on top of a parapet. When she sat on the mattress, the parapet collapsed and she fell into the air shaft and was injured. She sued the hotel, claiming that its breach of the statute as to the height of the parapets constituted negligence. Decide. [Nunneley v Edgar Hotel, 36 Cal 2d 493, 225 P2d 497]

11. A, B, and C owned land. They did some construction work on their land that prevented the free flow of surface water and caused a flooding of land owned by D. D sued A for the damage caused his land by the flooding. A claimed that D could not hold him liable for any damage since D could not prove how much of the total damage had been caused by A, and how much by B and C, and that in any event, A could not be liable for more than 1/3 of the total damage sustained by D. Decide. [Thorson v Minot (ND) 153 NW2d 764]

12. Tom Lawrence took his automobile to Wayne Strand Pontiac-GMC, Inc., for repairs. Strand left the car on its lot with the key in the ignition. Two weeks later Lawrence's car was stolen. Ronald Williamson was driving his car and came into the vicinity of the stolen car just as the thieves abandoned it and ran away on foot. In order to avoid hitting the thieves, Williamson swerved. In so doing, he struck the abandoned car and was injured. He then sued Wayne Strand for damages. Was Strand liable for damages? [Williamson v Wayne Strand Pontiac-GMC, Inc. (Tex App) 658 SW2d 263]

13. Collete Bass worked in a building owned by Nooney Company. As part of her job she

was going from one floor to another when the elevator stopped moving. She was alone in the elevator for about an hour before she was rescued. The emergency phone in the elevator was dead. She sued the Nooney Company for the mental distress to which she was subjected. The Nooney Company claimed that it was not liable because there was no proof that it had been negligent. Bass claimed Nooney had the burden of proving that it was not negligent. Was she correct? [Bass v Nooney Co. (Mo) 646 SW2d 765]

14. Alexander Kriventsov lived with his nephew and with the nephew's parents and grandparents. They constituted a close family group. A San Rafael taxicab ran over and killed the nephew and fled from the scene of the accident. Alexander saw this and pursued and apprehended the fleeing cab. Alexander then sued the cab company for the emotional harm he had sustained in witnessing the death of his nephew. The company denied liability on the ground that the plaintiff was not the parent of the person who was killed. Can the uncle recover on the bystander theory? [Kriventsov v San Rafael Taxicabs, Inc. 186 Cal App 3d 1445, 229 Cal Rptr 768]

15. G. I. Joe's was a retail store. It displayed for sale shotguns and ammunition. These were not behind glass or any barrier and could be removed by anyone within the store. John Stillwell stole a shotgun and some shells from the store and later shot and killed Michael Kimbler. Kimbler's estate sued Stillwell and G. I. Joe's for damages caused by Michael's death. G. I. Joe's denied liability on the ground that the harm had been caused by the double criminal act of a third person, that of stealing and then subsequently killing, and G. I. Joe's was not the cause of the harm. Was this defense valid? [Kimbler v Stillwell, 303 Or 23, 734 P2d 1344]

11

COMPUTERS AND THE LAW

Traditional rules of law drawn from contract law, tort law, and criminal law may be applied to computers. New rules that apply only to computers may also be created.

A. GENERAL PRINCIPLES

The modern electronic computer has been in use for little over one-third of a century. In that time, changes in the design,

size, and capacity of computers have resulted in their widespread use.

§ 11:1 COMPUTERS AND THE ENVIRONMENT OF THE LAW

Computers are now part of the business environment. They have created new situations for which no prior law exists or the prior law is not adequate. In the last three decades, judges and lawmakers have been making new law to govern the new computer situations.[1]

The development of computer law is slow because the lawmaker and judge must become familiar with the computer and its problems.

In this chapter the word *computer*, unless otherwise indicated, is used to refer collectively to hardware, software, and data. Hardware refers to the tangible objects, including the piece of equipment commonly known as the computer and all auxiliary attachments, such as disk and tape drives, monitors, printers, and terminals. Software describes the programs or instructions that control the operation of the hardware. Data refers to information, other than operating software, that is contained within the memory of the computer during processing or stored on some magnetic medium.

---

[1]   Statutes that have an application to computers are discussed in other chapters of this book. As to computers, trade secrets, and copyright protection, see § 24:12; as to the Financial Privacy Act and the Fair Credit Reporting Act, see § 8:16 and § 36:4; and as to the Electronic Fund Transfers Act, see § 36:16.

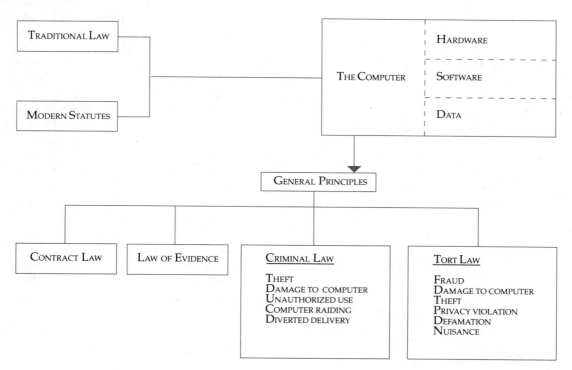

Figure 11-1
LAW AND THE COMPUTER

§ 11:2   MANAGEMENT AND THE COMPUTER

The law of computers relating to management is merely an extension of prior principles to new situations.

(a) NEGLIGENT USE OF THE COMPUTER. Management may be liable under ordinary negligence principles because of careless use of the computer. If management knows that its computer is not working properly but continues to use it without attempting to correct it, management may be held liable to third persons who are harmed by computer error.[2] Here the rules of law are the same as when management knowingly uses any other defective equipment. For example, a store making deliveries in a truck that is known to have bad brakes would be liable for negligence if the bad brakes led to a collision causing harm.

(b) PROTECTION OF THE COMPUTER. If the enterprise has a computer, management must take reasonable steps to maintain, protect, and insure the accuracy of the computer. The duty to maintain is the same as the duty to maintain the building or any other equipment of the enterprise. Management must exercise care in the selection of personnel operating the computer, for the purpose of protecting against computer crimes and torts and protecting customers of the enterprise from inaccuracy.

Under general principles of law, a breach of the foregoing duties can cause a court to impose liability on management. Again, there is the limitation that management has discretion to makes choices and that liability will not be imposed if the choice made by management with respect to the computer personnel or computer protection appeared reasonable under the circumstances.

§ 11:3   CONTRACT LAW AND THE COMPUTER

Contract law has not been affected by the computer, although contracts have been developed to govern computer-related transactions. Thus, the law for the sale of a computer is the same as the law governing the sale of a television set. When the customer asks the dealer for computer equipment that is compatible with an existing system, the law is the same as in any other case in which the buyer asks the seller to provide goods that will meet the particular needs of the buyer. For example, when a govern-

ment representative asked a seller for a tape suitable for use in the government's NCR-304 computer system, there arose an implied warranty, unless otherwise excluded, that the tape furnished by the seller was fit for that purpose.[3] When the seller knows that the buyer is purchasing a computer in order to produce a payroll on time and with reduced work hours, an implied warranty arises that the machine will perform as desired by the buyer.[4]

Because of the subject matter involved, contracts will apply to the sale or lease of computers, the sale or lease of software, the development of customized software, and the providing of services for maintenance and repair. There may be a contract for an outside organization to provide the computer services that will be needed by the enterprise. In connection with software, there will probably be special contract provisions imposing restrictions as to matters that are trade secrets or otherwise protected.

There is some indication that when a computer-related contract is made by experienced business enterprises, the contract will be interpreted very strictly. In such a case, it has been held that the customer was bound by fine-print provision of the contract on the theory that the customer knew from experience that such a clause would probably be in the contract.[5] Because of the consumer protection movement, it is unlikely that a court will take this approach with a small business purchasing its first computer or a person purchasing a computer for home use.

§ 11:4   THE COMPUTER AND THE LAW OF EVIDENCE

The law of evidence has changed drastical-

[2]   Swiss Air Transportation Co. v Benn, 467 NYS2d 341 (1983).

[3]   Appeals of Reeves v Soundcraft Corp. (ASBCA) 2 UCCRS 210 (1984).
[4]   Sperry Rand Corp. v Industrial Supply Corp. (CA5 Fla) 337 F2d 363 (1964); National Cash Register Co. v Adell Industries Inc. 57 Mich App 413, 225 NW2d 785 (1975).
[5]   AMF, Inc. v Computer Automation (SD Ohio) 573 F Supp 924 (1983).

ly in order to make it possible to admit evidence produced by the computer.

Computer printouts of "business records stored on electronic computing equipment are admissible in evidence if relevant and material, without the necessity of identifying, locating, and producing as witnesses the individuals who made the entries in the regular course of business if it is shown (1) that the electronic computing equipment is recognized as standard equipment, (2) the entries are made in the regular course of business at or reasonably near the time of the happening of the event recorded, and (3) the foundation testimony satisfies the court that the sources of information, method and time of preparation were such as to indicate its trustworthiness and justify its admission."[6]

(a) COMPUTER EVIDENCE FROM A PARTY TO LITIGATION. When a store sues its customer, can it prove what the customer owed by what the store's computer says? This question can arise in any contract setting, such as a suit for wages, commissions, or refunds. In the *Victory Memorial Hospital* case the defendant objected to the admission of the hospital computer's printout on the ground that the information that had been supplied to the computer as input was wrong.

[6] Prudential Ins. Co. v Kinney Plantation, Inc. (La App) 496 So 2d 1211 (1986).

VICTORY MEMORIAL HOSPITAL V RICE
143 Ill App 3d 621, 97 Ill Dec 635, 493 NE2d 117 (1986)

Michael Rice was treated for gunshot wounds at the Victory Memorial Hospital. He refused to pay the hospital bill because he claimed it was not correct. As proof of the amount owed to it, the hospital offered in evidence a computer printout of the services rendered the defendant and the amounts owed for them. The court refused to admit the printout on the ground that there was no proof that the printout represented what the defendant owed. Judgment was entered against the hospital, and the hospital appealed.

LINDBERG, J. . . . Plaintiff . . . argues that the trial court erred when it refused to admit the computerized bills into evidence as business records. In Illinois, business records supplied by a computer are admissible in evidence without testimony of the persons who made the entries in the regular course of business if it is shown that (1) the electronic computing equipment is recognized as standard; (2) the entries are made in the regular course of business at or reasonably near the time of the happening of the event recorded; and (3) the foundation testimony satisfies the court that the sources of information, method and time of preparation were such as to indicate its trustworthiness and justify its admission.

In the present case the court stated that there was insufficient proof that the items listed on the bills represented services actually performed on defendant. In other words, the court questioned the reliability and trustworthiness of the data before its entrance into the computer. The only method of verifying such information would have been to match the computerized bill against the original entry data. There was testimony that in order for the hospital to have produced all of the documents of original entry in the present case it would have been forced to inaugurate an extremely involved and time consuming retrieval process, especially since defendant had been hospitalized on several occasions and had been treated on an outpatient basis also. The record indicates that a hospital witness produced approximately 30 slips indicating certain laboratory tests that were done on defendant and the results of those tests. She matched them to the corresponding date and charge on the bill. The original slips in question were in five parts, the last part of which went to the data processing department to be entered into the computer by code number. In contrast to the other four portions of the slip, the part which went to the billing department contained only numbers which were fed into the computer by trained personnel. The trial court questioned the verification testimony because the slips produced by the witness were not the actual number coded slips which were used to enter the data. Since the five slips in each packet contained the same information, however, and since the slips produced could be matched to the corresponding date and charge on the bill, as to those tests, the supporting documentation verifying the trustworthiness of the input information was sufficient in our opinion to show that defendant had been given the service for which he was charged.

In view of the rationale supporting prior decisions in Illinois regarding the admissibility of computerized evidence, we also conclude that the proper foundation was presented to establish that the source of information and method of preparation indicated trustworthiness and supported admission of the entire computerized bill. By way of contrast to the extensive, knowledgeable testimony in the present case, the rejected foundation testimony in *Department of Mental Health v. Beil (1976)*, 44 Ill.App.3d 402, 2 Ill.Dec. 655, 357 N.E.2d 875 merely established that the entries were made in the regular course of business, and *In re Estate of Buddeke (1977)*, 49 Ill.App.3d 431, 7 Ill.Dec. 285, 364 N.E.2d 446, the hospital manager testified that she did not know anything about how the charges were fed into the computer. In *People v. Gauer (1972)*, 7 Ill.App.3d 512, 514, 288 N.E.2d 24 this court stated that considering the general use of electronic computing and recording equipment in the business world and the business world's reliance on the equipment, the scientific reliability of such machines can scarcely be questioned. The Illinois Supreme Court held in *Grand Liquor Co., Inc. v. Department of Revenue (1977)*, 67 Ill.2d 195, 10 Ill.Dec. 472, 367 N.E.2d 1238 that computer printouts are admissible pursuant to Supreme Court Rule 238 (87 Ill.2d R. 238) as long as the foundational tests set forth above, first expounded in the Mississippi case of *King v. State ex rel. Murdock Acceptance Corp (1969)*, 222 So.2d 393, were met. Although in *King* the court stressed that the trial court must be satisfied from the foundation testimony that the sources of information, method, and time of preparation were such as to indicate trustworthiness and justify admission, we are of the opinion that in the present case the trial court erred in not admitting the computerized bill into evidence as a business record based on the foundational evidence offered. The jury would still be free to accord the bills as much weight as in their opinion they deserved.

[Judgment reversed and action remanded]

QUESTIONS

1. Before the printout of a computer will be admitted in evidence, what must be shown?

2. What had been done by the hospital to support the admission of the computer printout into evidence?
3. Does the computer printout establish that the defendant owed the amount claimed by the plaintiff?

(b) COMPUTER EVIDENCE FROM A THIRD PERSON. Can the computer evidence generated by a third person be used to establish such facts as are shown thereby? This most frequently arises in a criminal prosecution in which a link in the chain of evidence against the defendant is the fact that a phone call was made from one particular place to another at a particular time. The computer-generated records of the telephone company have been admitted in evidence in such case to prove the making of the phone call.

(c) WEIGHT OF COMPUTER EVIDENCE. In all matters relating to evidence there are basically two steps: (1) Can the particular evidence be admitted in court and considered in deciding the case? (2) Assuming that the evidence can be admitted and considered, what weight is to be given to it? Must it be believed or can it be contradicted?

Computer evidence must meet these two challenges. Thus, the proper foundation must be established before the computer printout is admissible in court. After that, it is for the trier of fact to decide if the computer printout should be regarded as conclusive, inconclusive, or if it should be ignored.

B. CRIMINAL LAW AND THE COMPUTER

In some situations, the ordinary law of crimes fits the computer crime situation. In other situations, new law is required.

§ 11:5 WHAT IS A COMPUTER CRIME?

The term *computer crime* is frequently used. It has no established definition. Generally the phrase is used to refer to a crime that can only be committed by a person having some knowledge of the operation of a computer. Just as stealing an automobile requires knowledge of how to operate and drive a car, so the typical computer crime requires knowledge of how the computer works. This concept of a computer crime is satisfactory for the purpose of setting the stage, but it fails to tell us what law will be applied: the law of crimes or a new law relating to computers.

Some crimes may involve a computer without making direct use of one. In such case, the ordinary law of crimes will apply. For example, a person using the mail to falsely advertise a service as computerized is guilty of committing the federal crime of using the mails to defraud when such service was in fact not computerized.

The person dealing with the computer user may be guilty of a crime when the computer makes a mistake and such person takes advantage of the mistake without telling the computer user what has happened.[7]

The more serious and costly wrongs relating to computers do not fit into the ordinary definitions of crime. There is a definite trend of adopting statutes to declare new computer crimes. These statutes are strictly construed and only that conduct that is covered by the statute in question can be punished as the crime. The *Olson* case raised the question of whether the computer crime statute outlawed what the defendant did.

---

[7] Louisiana v Langford (La App) 467 So 2d 41 (1985).

WASHINGTON V OLSON

47 Wash App 514, 735 P2d 1362 (1987)

Information concerning the students at the University of Washington was stored in the university computer. Olson was an officer of the university police department. As such, he had authority to use the university computer. He obtained from the computer information on some of the coeds. This information was not in connection with any police investigation. He was tried and convicted of the statutory crime of computer trespass. He appealed.

GROSSE, J. . . . RCW [Revised Code of Washington] 9A.52.110 reads as follows:

Computer trespass in the first degree. (1) A person is guilty of computer trespass in the first degree if the person, without authorization, intentionally gains access to a computer system or electronic data base of another; and

(a) The access is made with the intent to commit another crime; or

(b) The violation involves a computer or data base maintained by a government agency.

(2) Computer trespass in the first degree is a class C felony.

RCW 9A.52.010(6) defines "access":

"Access" means to approach, instruct, communicate with, store data in, retrieve data from, or otherwise make use of any resources of a computer, directly or by electronic means. . . .

Olson's contention, both at trial and here on appeal, is that his conduct does not amount to unauthorized access either as a matter of fact or as a matter of law. We believe that the evidence at trial showed only unauthorized use of computer data which is not prohibited by this statute. Therefore, we reverse the conviction.

Our initial task is to determine what conduct is prohibited by RCW 9A.52.110; in other words, the legislative intent. Whenever we are faced with a question of statutory interpretation we look to the plain meaning of the words used in the statute. In subsection (1) of RCW 9A.52.110 the phrase "without authorization" modifies the phrase "intentionally gains access". Thus the unlawful act is unauthorized access. "Authorize" means "to endorse, empower, justify, or permit by or as if by some recognized or proper authority (as custom, evidence, personal right, or regulating power)". Webster's Third New International Dictionary 146 (1981). The testimony that Olson had an access code establishes that he was permitted to "approach, instruct, communicate with, store data in, retrieve data from, or otherwise make use of any resources of a computer, directly or by electronic means." RCW 9A.52.010(6).

In determining legislative intent, the title of an act bears consideration. The title of the act is "Computer Trespass"; Laws of 1984, ch. 273. Historically, a trespass was an intrusion or invasion into tangible property which interfered with the right of exclusive possession. In the context of computers, a trespass is an invasion or intrusion upon the data base. The general trespass statutes criminalize the entering and remaining upon premises when not licensed, invited, or privileged to enter or remain. By analogy, the computer trespass statute criminalizes the entry into the computer base, not the use of the information obtained. Of course, we can imagine situations where there are conditions attached to computer access. However, the facts of the instant case establish an unauthorized use of data, not a conditioned access.

The trial court reviewed stipulated police reports. Our review of these reports supports Olson's position that departmental policy prohibited certain uses of data but did not withdraw permission to "access" the computer. The pertinent provisions of the various reports are as follows:

The offense report: "There is no indication that any of this material is connected to any investigation being conducted by UWPD nor to any investigation we have conducted in the recent past."

A statement signed by Sergeant Franklin: "These inquiries were not part of any official inquiry by Officer Olson, but were solely for his own use for some sort of collection he called his Rogues Gallery."

Lieutenant Stegmeier's statement: "I advised him that this was a gross misuse of Departmental equipment and State information systems and a violation of departmental policy."

Sergeant Robert White's statement: "Information received on the ACCESS terminal is regarded as the official business of the UWPD and is not to be divulged outside the department without proper authority. This policy is contained in the UWPD Departmental Procedures Manual, section 14.03.00, Use of Teletype/Computer Systems."*

While the evidence shows that certain uses of retrieved data were against departmental policy, it did not show that permission to access the computer was conditioned on the uses made of the data. This is a critical distinction. In *State v. Clark*, 96 Wash.2d 686, 638 P.2d 572 (1982), defendant Clark was given permission to use Dennis Noll's car to run some errands and return at noon. Instead, he drove to Colorado with the car and was charged with taking a motor vehicle without the owner's permission. In holding that the facts described the offense of theft rather than taking and riding, the Supreme Court applied reasoning that is applicable to the instant case.

We think the appellant was clearly a bailee of Noll's vehicle since he was entrusted with the car to do certain errands and return. Also, the above theft statute clearly covers the appellant's conduct without having to interpret RCW 9A.56.-070(1) expansively. It would seem logical that RCW 9A.56.080(1) is intended only to prevent the initially unauthorized use of a vehicle. Otherwise, the theft statute and the joy riding statute would proscribe the same conduct, yet a defendant potentially could suffer a different penalty depending on which crime was charged. We do not believe such an overlap between RCW 9A.56.020 and RCW 9A.56.070(1) was intended by the legislature. If we were to accept the State's argument that exceeding the scope of permission is violative of RCW 9A.56.070(1), we would be forced to arrive at absurd results. For instance, if a person takes a car with the owner's permission, then exceeds that permission to some degree, we would be compelled to find him guilty even if he returns the car to the owner. We cannot believe the legislature intended such a result.

---

* The policy manual . . . does not condition access to the computer system on whether the information retrieved will be used for personal purposes.

Clark, at 691-92, 638 P.2d 572. The actus reus of the joy riding statute is the taking or driving away of the vehicle without permission. The actus reus of the computer trespass statute is accessing a computer without authorization. At the time Clark drove away the car he had permission. At the time Olson retrieved data he had authorization. It was the personal use of this data after access that was against departmental policy.

. . . Taken in a light most favorable to the prosecution, the police reports indicate, at most, a violation of departmental policy on the use of computer data. They do not establish unauthorized access beyond a reasonable doubt. . . .

[Conviction reversed]

QUESTIONS

1. What was the loophole in the statute that required the reversal of the conviction?
2. What should the statute have said to cover the situation that arose in the *Olson* case?
3. How do you explain the fact that the statute did not cover the situation in the *Olson* case?

§ 11:6   THE COMPUTER AS THE VICTIM

A traditional crime may be committed by stealing or intentionally damaging the computer.

(a) THEFT OF HARDWARE. When the computer is itself stolen, the ordinary law relating to theft crimes should apply. No reason can be found why a theft of a computer should not be subject to the same law as the theft of a typewriter or a desk. Whatever the crime would be by statute in the case of these other objects, the same crime is committed when a computer is the subject matter of the theft.

(b) THEFT OF SOFTWARE. When a thief takes software, either in the form of a program written on paper, or a program on a disk or tape, a situation arises that does not fit into the standard definitions of crimes. The thief commits larceny of the piece of paper or of the tape or disk, but the program is not something that can be stolen because it is not property within the traditional concept of what constitutes property for the purpose of crime.

The distinction between the program and the substance on which it is written or recorded is important. If the law ignores the program, the thief stealing the piece of paper or the disk or tape carrying the program is guilty only of petty larceny in most states. This is so because the value of the piece of paper or the disk or tape will be relatively small and thus bring the crime down to the category of petty larceny. In contrast, the program itself may have a value of thousands of dollars so that if the grade of larceny is determined by the value of the program, the thief is guilty of grand larceny, an offense that generally carries much more significant penalties and is typically a felony. In some states, the unauthorized taking of information may constitute a crime under a trade secrets protection statute. In a small number of states, larceny and theft statutes have been amended to make the theft of computer programs a felony.

(c) INTENTIONAL DAMAGE. The computer may be the "victim" of a crime when it is intentionally destroyed or harmed. In the most elementary form of damage, it could be harmed if smashed with an ax or destroyed in an explosion or a fire. In such cases, the wrongdoer may be seeking to do more than merely destroy or harm the computer. The intent may be to cause the computer's owner the financial loss of the computer and the destruction of the information that is stored in it.

When the wrongdoer has the purpose of destroying the software or the stored information, it is more likely that a more subtle way of committing the crime will be employed. In such case, the wrongdoer might gain access to the computer and then erase or alter the data in question. The wrongdoer might also achieve the desired purpose by interfering with the air-conditioning required by the computer, thereby causing it to malfunction. Or the wrongdoer may intentionally plant a "bug" or "virus" in software causing the program to malfunction or to give incorrect output. Such damage may be the work of an angry employee or ex-employee, or the work of a competitor. In the area of criminal law, it might be a person destroying the record of prior convictions.

Whatever attack is made upon the computer, whether physical or electrical, the question of criminal liability of the wrongdoer will in time give rise to new law. At present such misconduct will constitute the crime of malicious destruction of, or damage to, property. This is a minor crime and the penalty is typically so trivial compared to the dollar value of the damage done to the computer or its data bank that prosecution for such a crime is meaningless.[8] In the next decade statutes imposing substantial penalties for the destruction of or damage to hardware, software, and information stored in computers will probably be adopted.

§ 11:7 UNAUTHORIZED USE OF COMPUTER

The least serious of computer crimes is the unlawful use of someone else's computer. In some states the unlawful use of a computer is not a crime. Although the user is stealing the time of the computer, the wrongdoer is not regarded as committing the crime of larceny because the wrongdoer has no intent to deprive the owner permanently of the computer.

In some states the borrowing of another's automobile without the owner's permission is not a crime where there is no intention to deprive the owner permanently thereof. If following the common law, states will undoubtedly use the same approach in the case of the unauthorized use of a computer.[9] In other states, however, the borrowing of an automobile for a joyride is, by statute, made a crime. It can be anticipated that these states will also adopt laws making it a crime to use a computer without the consent of the owner. Federal legislation has entered the field with the statute described in § 11:8 of this book.

In the *Evans* case a statute creating crimes of larceny, embezzlement, and false pretenses in connection with computer time, services, or stored information was applied.

---

[9] The court in Indiana v McGraw, ___ Ind ___, 480 NE2d 552 (1985) followed this approach.

EVANS V VIRGINIA
226 Va 292, 308 SE2d 126 (1983)

The Central Fidelity Bank had a department that sold stocks and bonds, primarily to large institutions. Evans and Smith worked in this department as salesmen. At intervals the bank would make computer printouts of the names and addresses of its customers and maturity dates of their investments. Smith asked that an extra copy of this printout be made for him. Smith was given two extra copies. He gave one to Evans. Thereafter Evans and Smith resigned from the bank and went to work for a competing bank. Smith gave the computer printout of customers to the new employer. Evans and Smith were then prosecuted for petit (petty) larceny by embezzlement. They appealed.

GORDON, J. . . . According to an officer of Central Fidelity, a customer security list would be useful for many years to come, an invaluable sales tool to produce profits. Another officer testified that if a competitor obtained the information on a list, the competitor would be given an edge in the business.

Central Fidelity brought a civil suit under Code § 18.2-500 for injury to its trade or business, resulting in a favorable decree. The indictments involved in this appeal followed.

In *Lund v. Commonwealth*, 217 Va. 688, 232 S.E.2d 745 (1977), this Court held that the taking of computer time and services in the form of printouts could not constitute larceny because the subject matter of larceny must be goods and chattels. Computer time and services, reasoned the Court, were not goods or chattels.

In 1978 the General Assembly enacted Code § 18.2-98.1:

Computer time or services or data processing services or information or data stored in connection therewith is hereby defined to be property which may be the subject of larceny under § § 18.2-95 or 18.2-96, or embezzlement under § 18.2-111, or false pretenses under § 18.2-178.

Code § 18.2-111, under which Evans and Smith were prosecuted, makes a person guilty of larceny if he [does] "wrongfully and fraudulently use, dispose of, conceal or embezzle any . . . personal property, tangible or intangible, which he shall have received . . . by virtue of his . . . employment. . . ."

The indictments charged that Evans and Smith "unlawfully and feloniously did steal computer information or data stored in connection therewith, to-wit: a customer securities list."* . . .

The trial court instructed the jury that to convict it must find that the customer security list "was of some value." Code § 18.2-96 makes "simple larceny not from the person of another of goods and chattels of the value of less than $200" punishable as a misdemeanor.

The Commonwealth adduced no proof, says counsel, of the value of the list. Counsel therefore concludes that the evidence does not support the giving of the instruction. . . .

The petit larceny statute, Code § 18.2-96, does not require proof of any minimum value.

"At the common law, an article to be the subject of larceny must be of some value. It is sufficient, however, it is said, if it be worth less than the smallest coin known to the law." *Wolverton v. Commonwealth*, 75 Va. 909, 913 (1881).

---

* The trial did not proceed on the theory that the defendants embezzled a piece of paper. As observed by the trial judge, "there was never any indication, any observation, any allegation that this was a case involving the theft of paper."

Under settled Virginia law, no proof need be adduced to show that the subject of petit larceny has a specific value.

The evidence respecting the nature and use of the customer security list supplied proof that the list had value. The proof was augmented by testimony that the list was an invaluable sales tool, giving a competitor a valuable edge if the list fell into the competitor's hands.

Counsel argues that the intent to deprive the owner of his property is a necessary element of embezzlement. This element being lacking, he concludes the convictions must be reversed.

This Court in a recent case, however, described the elements of embezzlement:

> A person entrusted with possession of another's personalty who converts such property to his own use or benefit is guilty of the statutory offense of embezzlement. Code § 18.2-111.

C.D. Smith v. Commonwealth, 222 Va. 646, 649, 283 S.E.2d 209, 210 (1981). And Black's Law Dictionary 300 (5th ed. 1979), to which counsel referred us, gives this definition of the noun form of *to convert*:

> Unauthorized and wrongful exercise of dominion and control over another's personal property, to exclusion of or inconsistent with rights of the owner.

Proof was adduced that Evans and Smith converted the customer security list by exercising dominion and control inconsistent with the rights of Central Fidelity, the owner. The proof therefore justified the conviction of statutory embezzlement. . . .

[Conviction affirmed]

QUESTIONS

1. Is the decision in the Evans case in harmony with the common law?
2. Why was the prosecution for embezzlement?
3. Which of the two statutes quoted in the *Evans* case was the more essential to the prosecution?

§ 11:8   COMPUTER RAIDING

A more serious computer crime involves taking information from a computer without the consent of the owner of the information. Whether this is done by having the computer make a printout of stored information or by tapping into the data bank of the computer by some electronic means is not important. In many instances, the taking of information from the computer constitutes a crime of stealing trade secrets.

The Counterfeit Access Device and Computer Fraud and Abuse Act of 1984[10] makes it a federal crime to access a computer without authorization.

§ 11:9   DIVERTED DELIVERY BY COMPUTER

In many industries, deliveries are controlled by a computer. The person in charge of that computer or a criminal gaining access unlawfully to the computer may

[10] Act of October 12, 1984, § 2102, PL 98-473, Stat 2190, 18 USC § § 1030 et seq.

cause the computer to direct delivery to an improper place. That is, instead of shipping goods to the customers to whom they should go, the wrongdoer diverts the goods to a different place where they will be received either by the wrongdoer or by a confederate.

In precomputer days, written orders were sent from the sales department to the shipping department. The shipping department would then send the ordered goods to the proper places. If the person in the sales department or the person in the shipping department were dishonest, either one of them could divert the goods from the proper destination. Today this fraudulent diversion of goods may be effected by causing the computer to give false directions. Basically, the crime is the same as in the precomputer era. The computer is merely the new instrument by which the old crime is committed. The thing that gives this old crime a new social significance is the amazingly large dollar value of the theft accomplished by means of it. In one case, several hundred loaded freight cars were made to disappear. In another case, a loaded oil tanker was diverted to unload into a fleet of tank trucks operated by an accomplice of the computer operator.

The diverted delivery crime is not limited to goods and has embraced transferring money from a proper account to a wrong account. Here millions of dollars have been involved in a single crime.

The case of the diverted delivery computer crime does not require any new law because the appropriation of goods or money improperly delivered comes within the larceny-theft-embezzlement spectrum of crime. However, when a diverted delivery crime is effected by means of a computer, future statutes may classify the crime as aggravated larceny, and so on, in order to impose the more severe penalty that society feels is called for by the huge dollar values involved. This feeling of society has led to the Electronic Fund Transfers Act described in § 11:10.

§ 11:10   ELECTRONIC FUND
           TRANSFER CRIMES

The Electronic Fund Transfers Act (EFTA)[11] makes it a crime to use any counterfeit control device to obtain money or goods in excess of a specified amount through an electronic fund transfer system, to ship such devices or goods so obtained in interstate commerce, or to knowingly receive goods that have been obtained by means of the fraudulent use of the transfer system.

C.   TORT LAW AND THE COMPUTER

Tort law applies to the computer with respect to damage to the computer, fraud, theft, the protection of privacy, defamation, and nuisance.

§ 11:11   FRAUD

The basic principles of tort law for fraud are applicable in computer situations. For example, if false statements are knowingly made to induce the sale of a computer, the seller is liable for fraud damages to the same extent as though any other kind of goods were the subject of the sale.[12] If the wrongdoer feeds false information to the computer and then uses the printout to deceive the victim, the wrongdoer is subject to the ordinary tort law governing fraud.

§ 11:12   DAMAGE TO THE
               COMPUTER

Tort liability for damage to the computer arises in connection with damage to hardware and software.

(a) DAMAGE TO HARDWARE. Damage to hardware, including its destruction, will

---

[11] Act of October 10, 1978, § 916(n), PL 90-321, PL 95-630, 92 Stat 3738, 15 USC § 1693n.
[12] Computer Systems Engineering, Inc. v Qantel Corp. (CA1 Mass) 740 F2d 59 (1984).

impose tort liability under the same principles of law as would apply were it a typewriter, a car, a desk, or any other tangible property that was damaged or destroyed. The fact that the damage to the computer may cause a shutdown of the activities of the computer owner is significant in determining whether the defendant's act was done with such wantonness or reckless indifference to consequences as to authorize imposing punitive or exemplary damages upon the wrongdoer. Punitive or exemplary damages are those in excess of the amount needed to compensate the plaintiff for loss. Such damages are imposed to punish or make an example of the defendant.

(b) DAMAGE TO SOFTWARE. The defendant may have damaged the software, for example, by erasing a part of the computer's memory. Here the tort law aspect of liability and of recovery of punitive damages is the same as for any other kind of property. In states that follow the traditional definition of property, courts will probably hold that software is not property and therefore is not entitled to the protection that the tort law gives to property.

§ 11:13 THEFT OF THE COMPUTER

The civil or tort liability for the theft of a computer parallels the criminal law with respect to such theft. Thus, an actual taking away of the hardware constitutes the tort of conversion. For information on protection for computer programs, see § 24:12.

§ 11:14 THE COMPUTER AND THE PROTECTION OF PRIVACY

The law relating to the protection of privacy applies whether or not a computer is involved. That is, there is no change made or needed in the law of privacy because a computer had been used to invade the privacy in question.

(a) WHY IS THERE CONCERN OVER PROTECTION OF PRIVACY? There is much public concern over protection of privacy because of the efficiency of the computer. Consider the number of places that have some information about you. Every school you ever attended has some of your personal history. If you have applied for any kind of license, purchased goods on credit, obtained insurance, applied for a job, been treated by a doctor, or been admitted to a hospital, more of your life story is on paper. But this has never bothered you because, assuming that you had thought about it, you would have recognized that it would be practically impossible for anyone to assemble all the information about you from all the places where it is kept. Even assuming that the prying stranger would know where to inquire, the cost of going back into old files to dig up information would be prohibitive.

Now let us move forward into the computer age. By connecting separate computers into a network, it is possible to print out the story of your life within a matter of seconds. Thus, nothing that you did lies hidden away in dusty filing cabinets, and everything can be brought into the light within seconds.

When to this danger of efficiency we add the ability of an outsider to invade a computer by computer raiding and acquire its information, even without anyone knowing that this has been done, we have a terrifying product of: A [efficiency of the computer] times B [availability of information to unauthorized outsider].

(b) WHO IS LIABLE FOR COMPUTER INVASION OF PRIVACY? The person making public the information stored in the computer may be an authorized user of the computer or an outsider without authority who invades the computer and then makes public the private information obtained from the computer. In either case there is no problem in applying ordinary tort law to hold such person liable for tort damages for invasion of privacy.

Can management be held liable for the invasion of privacy? If the wrongdoer is an employee, it is possible that management will be liable for the employee's misconduct on the theory that management had not properly screened job applicants, or was negligent in supervising employees, or is liable for employee misconduct under the circumstances.[13] If the wrongdoer is an outsider, can management be held liable for the invasion of privacy? It may be argued that management could have prevented the invasion of privacy by maintaining a better security system over the computer. It can be claimed that because of the negligence of management, it was possible for the outsider to raid the computer and obtain the information that was thereafter made public.

As an analogy, in some states, if the owner of an automobile leaves it parked on the street with the ignition key in the car and a thief steals the car and runs into a third person, the third person may sue the car owner for the injury caused by the thief who drove the car. Other courts refuse to impose liability in such case.

Returning to the computer, a court that would impose liability on the negligent car owner could impose liability on the negligent protector of the computer for the harm caused by the thief who raided the computer and then injured the plaintiff by making public the information that had been private up to that point. Again, the area is one in which statutory regulation can be expected.

§ 11:15   DEFAMATION BY
              COMPUTER

A person's credit standing or reputation may be damaged because a computer contains erroneous information and the erroneous information is supplied to third persons. Will the data bank operator or service company be held liable to the person who is harmed? If the operator or the company had exercised reasonable care to prevent errors and to correct errors, it is probable that there will not be any liability on either the actual programmer (employee) operating the equipment or the management providing the computer service.

The supplier of the wrong information is liable for the damages caused thereby when the error was caused by its negligence. As the supplier is furnishing information to a limited group of subscribers, it is not protected by the guarantee of free speech.[14]

When negligence or an intent to harm is shown, the wrongdoer could be held liable for what may be called defamation by computer. It is likely that liability could be avoided by supplying the person to whom the information relates with a copy of any printout of information which the data bank supplies the third person, as this would tend to show good faith and due care on the part of the management of the data bank operation and a reasonable effort to keep the information accurate.

Liability for defamation by computer may arise under the federal Fair Credit Reporting Act of 1970 when the person affected is a consumer. The federal Credit Card Act of 1970 further protects from defamation by computer. These acts, which are not limited to situations involving computers, are discussed in Chapter 8 on consumer protection.

§ 11:16   THE COMPUTER AS A
              NUISANCE

The modern world generally looks upon the computer as a blessing. Whether it could be considered a nuisance was the issue in the *Page County Appliance Center* case. The court there considered whether interference with the conduct of a business because of radiation from a neighboring computer imposed liability on the user of the computer.

---

[13] The subject of employer liability for employee misconduct is discussed in Chapter 44 of this book.

[14] Dunn & Bradstreet, Inc. v Greenmoss Builders, 472 US 749 (1985).

PAGE COUNTY APPLIANCE CENTER, INC. V HONEYWELL, INC.

(Iowa) 347 NW2d 171 (1984)

> ITT Electronic Services, Inc. (ITT), a subsidiary of Honeywell, Inc., leased a Honeywell computer to the Central Travel Service. A nearby enterprise, the Page County Appliance Center, Inc. claimed that there was a radiation leakage from the computer that interfered with the reception of the display televisions in the store and that this caused a loss of sales. Appliance Center sued the travel agency, Honeywell, and its subsidiary. The defendants moved the trial court to enter a verdict in their favor. The court refused to do so. They appealed.

REYNOLDSON, C. J. . . . Appliance Center has owned and operated an appliance store in Shenandoah, Iowa, since 1953. In 1975 the store was acquired from his father by John Pearson, who sold televisions, stereos, and a variety of appliances. Before 1980 Pearson had no reception trouble with his display televisions. In early January 1980, however, ITT placed one of its computers with Central Travel Service in Shenandoah as part of a nationwide plan to lease computers to retail travel agents. Central Travel was separated by only one other business from the Appliance Center. [The] ITT computer was manufactured, installed, and maintained by Honeywell.

Thereafter many of Pearson's customers told him his display television pictures were bad; on two of the three channels available in Shenandoah he had a difficult time "getting a picture that was fit to watch." After unsuccessfully attempting several remedial measures, in late January 1980, he finally traced the interference to the operations of Central Travel's computer. Both defendants concede Pearson's problems were caused by radiation leaking from the Honeywell computer.

Appliance Center is alleging a "private nuisance," that is, an actionable interference with a person's interest in the private use and enjoyment of his or her property. *Larsen v. McDonald*, 212 N.W.2d 505, 508 (Iowa 1973). . . .

Principles governing our consideration of nuisance claims are well established. One's use of property should not unreasonably interfere with or disturb a neighbor's comfortable and reasonable use and enjoyment of his or her estate. A fair test of whether the operation of a lawful trade or industry constitutes a nuisance is the reasonableness of conducting it in the manner, at the place, and under the circumstances shown by the evidence. Each case turns on its own facts and ordinarily the ultimate issue is one of fact, not law. *Patz v. Famegg Products, Inc.*, 196 N.W.2d 557, (Iowa 1972). The existence of a nuisance is not affected by the intention of its creator not to injure anyone. . . .

When the alleged nuisance is claimed to be offensive to the person, courts apply the standard of "normal persons in a particular locality" to measure the existence of a nuisance. This normalcy standard also is applied where the use of property is claimed to be affected. "The plaintiff cannot, by devoting his own land to an unusually sensitive use, . . . make a nuisance out of conduct of the adjoining defendant which would otherwise be harmless." W. Prosser, *The Law of Torts* § 87, at 579 (4th ed. 1971).

In the case before us, ITT asserts the Appliance Center's display televisions constituted a hypersensitive use of its premises as a matter of law, and equates this situation to cases involving light thrown on outdoor theater screens in which light-throwing defendants have carried the day. Several of those cases are distinguishable both on facts and by the way the issue was raised.

We cannot equate the rare outdoor theater screen with the ubiquitous television that exists, in various numbers, in almost every home. Clearly, the presence of televisions on any premises is not such an abnormal condition that we can say, as a matter of law, that the owner has engaged in a *peculiarly* sensitive use of the property.

ITT's second contention asserts trial court should have directed a verdict in its favor because it did not participate in the creation or maintenance of the alleged nuisance. We have noted ITT was engaged in a multimillion dollar, national program to lease computers to travel agencies. It owned this computer and leased it to Central Travel. It was to ITT that the agency first turned when the effect of the computer radiation became apparent. ITT continued to collect its lease payments; the computer did not operate for the benefit of Crowell [owner of Central Travel Service] alone. The jury could have found ITT evidenced some measure of its responsibility, as owner of the computer, in contacting Honeywell and making belated inquiries regarding Appliance Center's problems both to Pearson and Crowell.

It is no ground for directed verdict that the computer was leased to Central Travel. "One is subject to liability for a nuisance caused by an activity, not only when he carries on the activity but also when he participates to a substantial extent in carrying it on." Restatement (Second) of Torts § 834 (1979). Even one who contracts out nuisance-causing work to independent contractors may have the duty, upon notice, "to take reasonably prompt and efficient means to suppress the nuisance." *Shannon v. Missouri Valley Limestone Co.*, 255 Iowa 528, 533, 122 N.W.2d 278, 281 (1963). A failure to act under circumstances in which one is under a duty to take positive action to prevent or abate the invasion of the private interest may make one liable, Restatement (Second) of Torts § 824, and this may include a lessor or licensor. *Id.* comment d.

An action for damages for nuisance need not be predicated on negligence. Nuisance ordinarily is considered as a condition, and not as an act or failure to act on the part of the responsible party. A person responsible for a harmful condition found to be a nuisance may be liable even though that person has used the highest possible degree of care to prevent or minimize the effect.

Where there is reasonable doubt whether one of several persons is substantially participating in carrying on an activity, the question is for the trier of fact. Restatement (Second) of Torts § 834 comment d. We hold such reasonable doubt existed on the record made in this case, and trial court did not err in refusing to direct a verdict on this ground.

[Judgment affirmed as to the matters set forth in the above excerpt from the opinion]

Questions

1. In the *Page County Appliance* case, who was negligent?
2. How does your answer to Question 1 affect the decision in the case?
3. Did the fact that the computer was leased have any significance?

SUMMARY

The law applicable to computers may be traditional rules of law or it may be new rules that apply only to computers. Many problems arise because the law has not yet caught up with the many new situations created by the computer. The law of contract has not been changed by the computer. In contrast, the law of evidence has changed to allow computer printouts to be admitted in evidence when the proper foundation is laid. That is, before they may be so admitted in favor of the computer user, it is necessary to establish that they were properly made by standard procedures using a standard computer. The law of torts has remained unchanged with respect to fraud, property damage, theft, defamation, privacy, and nuisance. However, a change must be made in some areas in order to protect the interests that modern society wishes protected. Statutory reform is required in order to expand the area of criminal law to meet the crimes in which computers are involved. The unauthorized user is covered by the criminal law of only a few states. Criminal conduct of diverting deliveries of goods and the transfer of funds, the theft of software, and computer raiding are made crimes to some extent by the federal Computer Access Device and Computer Fraud and Abuse Act of 1984 and the Electronic Fund Transfers Act of 1978.

QUESTIONS AND CASE PROBLEMS

1. What social forces are affected by allowing computer printouts to be introduced as evidence?
2. The Metro Supply Store sued Connors for the bill owed to it. At the trial Metro offers as evidence of the debt its computer printout showing the various purchases made by Connors and the balance due. Connors objects that this printout cannot be admitted in court. Is he correct?
3. The town of Janesville sues Leonard for back taxes. The town produces a computer printout showing the taxes that are due. Leonard claimed that he had paid the amounts shown to be due with money orders, but that over the course of time he has lost the money order receipts. The town objects to Leonard's testimony on the ground that it contradicts what the computer says, and the computer cannot be contradicted. Is Leonard's testimony admissible?
4. The Sixth Amendment of the United States Constitution guarantees that "in all criminal prosecutions, the accused shall enjoy the right . . . to be confronted with the witnesses against him . . ." Rankin is prosecuted for a criminal conspiracy. Part of the evidence offered against him is the computer records of the telephone company showing a number of calls made from Rankin's home to the meeting place of the other accused conspirators. Rankin claimed that the Sixth Amendment of the Constitution requires that the prosecution produce in court a witness who can testify on the basis of the witness's own observation that the phone calls in question were made as stated by the computer printout. Is he correct?
5. Ajax Corporation and Keystone Corporation are competitors. Ajax wants to learn the names and addresses of the customers of Keystone. Ajax bribes an employee of Keystone to make a computer printout of the desired information. Of what crime is Ajax guilty?
6. Hinkin steals a computer chip on which is stored information having commercial value of a million dollars. He is prosecuted for grand larceny. He raises the defense that he only committed petty larceny because the chip only costs $10, and by statute a larceny under $100 is petty larceny. Is he correct?
7. The Clayton factory controls a series of manufacturing operations by computers.

The large number of computers, concentrated in a small area, set up an electromagnetic field that interfered with the fine instruments used by the Scientific Testing Laboratories housed in a neighboring building. Scientific sues Clayton, claiming that the operation of Clayton's computers constitutes a nuisance. Clayton replies that it cannot be responsible for any side effects because it was not negligent. Clayton states that, therefore, there cannot be a nuisance. Is Clayton correct?

8. Taylor was employed by Hopkins Company. After he was fired he sought revenge against his former employer. He turned off the air-conditioning in the computer room. It was midsummer, and the heat during the night ruined the memory bank of the computer. Hopkins asked the district attorney to prosecute Taylor. For what crimes could Taylor be prosecuted?

9. Lund was a graduate student at a university. In working on his doctoral dissertation, he made use of the university computer and was assisted by the personnel of the computer facility. The value of the information he thus obtained was about $30,000. Lund had not been authorized to use the computer, and he was prosecuted for common-law grand larceny. Was he guilty? [Lund v Virginia, 217 Va 688, 232 SE2d 745]

10. Curtis advertised that he ran a computerized dating service. He promised that persons replying to his ad would be mailed forms and information about the computerized service. Actually he did not have a computer and did the matching by hand. He was prosecuted for using the mails to defraud. Was he guilty? [United States v Curtis (CA10 Okla) 537 F2d 1091]

11. Pompeii Estates was a builder. It constructed a house to which the Consolidated Edison Company supplied electricity. As the house was a newly constructed, unoccupied house, Pompeii wrote Consolidated Edison giving it an address where Pompeii could be reached. This address was never fed into the computer of Consolidated Edison. Consolidated Edison used the computer to determine when bills were not paid. When the bill for the empty Pompeii house was not paid, the computer directed the mailing of a notice to the empty house that the electricity would be shut off if the bill was not paid. Consolidated Edison did not send any notice to the address of Pompeii that it had in its files. Thereafter Consolidated shut off the electricity, which in turn shut off the heating system. Consequently, the pipes froze and burst, causing extensive damage to the house. Pompeii sued Consolidated Edison for the damage. Was Consolidated Edison liable? [Pompeii Estates, Inc. v Consolidated Edison Co. 91 Misc 2d 233, 397 NYS2d 577]

12. Schlicht had a bank account. The bank's computer made a mistake and showed that he had a balance of $9,000 more than he really had in his account. He withdrew the $9,000. When the bank learned of the mistake, he was prosecuted for the crime of theft. Was he guilty? [Colorado v Schlicht, ___ Colo App ___, 709 P2d 94 (1985)].

13. Dorothy Judd had a bank account in Citibank. Withdrawals could be made from a cash machine by use of a plastic card. She claimed that the bank had charged her account for $800 more than she had actually removed from it. She sued the bank for this amount. The bank defended by proving that its computers showed withdrawals on her account from a cash machine in the amount of $800. She produced evidence that at the times shown on the bank's computer printouts, she was at work and could not have made the withdrawals. The bank claimed that its computer printouts could not be contradicted. Was it correct? [Judd v Citibank, 435 NYS2d 210]

14. C.M. Brown and Associates was an insurance broker. Kimberlin was one of its salesmen. Brown gave a computer service company monthly reports of business. The computer service prepared a monthly statement from Brown's information. Brown then gave the monthly statement to the salesmen to show how much business they had produced and what commissions were owed to them. Kimberlin claimed that commissions were payable on both new policies written by him and on renewal of old policies that he had originally written. Brown claimed that commissions were only due on the new policies. Kimberlin sued Brown and offered in evidence the computer printout that had been received from Brown. He did not offer any evidence as to the way the computer printout had been

prepared. Brown claimed that the computer printout was therefore not admissible. Was Brown correct? [Kimberlin v C.M. Brown and Associates, Inc. (Mo App) 722 SW2d 90]

15. Hodgeson was prosecuted for manslaughter. The district attorney wanted to show that a phone call had been made from a certain telephone. In order to do this, the records of the telephone company were offered in evidence. The records consisted of a computer printout. Hodgeson objected to admitting this printout in evidence without producing in court the persons who had supplied the information that was stored in the computer. Should the printout be admitted? [Louisiana v Hodgeson (La) 305 So 2d 421]

PART 2

CONTRACTS

12

NATURE AND CLASSES OF CONTRACTS

Practically every personal business activity involves a contract: enrolling in college, purchasing a color television, renting an apartment. In each transaction relating to the acquisition of raw materials, their manufacture, and the distribution of the finished product by businesses, there are contracts that define the relationship and the rights and obligations of the parties.

A. NATURE OF CONTRACTS

As pervasive as contracts are in our lives, the legal language of contracts is not very familiar to most of us. For that reason, this introductory chapter is devoted primarily to the terminology or vocabulary that is needed to work with contract law.

In addition, this chapter deals with something called **quasi contracts**. These, as you might guess, are not true contracts. They lack some essential element that the law requires of a true contract. Nevertheless, society, through its laws, has created this special class of obligations that are enforced in a limited way.

251

§ 12:1   DEFINITION OF A CONTRACT

A **contract** is a binding agreement.[1] By one definition "a contract is a promise or a set of promises for the breach of which the law gives a remedy, or the performance of which the law in some way recognizes as a duty."[2] Contracts arise out of agreements; hence a contract may be defined as an agreement creating an obligation.

The substance of the definition of a contract is that by mutual agreement or assent the parties create enforceable duties or obligations. That is, each party is legally bound to do or to refrain from doing certain acts.

§ 12:2 ELEMENTS OF A CONTRACT

The elements of a contract are: (1) an agreement, (2) between competent parties, (3) based upon the genuine assent of the parties, (4) supported by consideration, (5) made for a lawful objective, and (6) in the form required by law, if any. These elements will be considered in the chapters that follow.

§ 12:3   SUBJECT MATTER OF CONTRACTS

The subject matter of a contract may relate to the performance of personal services, such as contracts of employment to work on an assembly line, to work as a secretary, to sing on television, or to build a house. The contract may provide for the transfer of ownership of property, such as a house (real property) or an automobile (personal property), from one person to another. A contract may also call for a combination of these things. For example,

[1]   The Uniform Commercial Code defines *contract* to mean "the total legal obligation which results from the parties' agreement as affected by [the Code] and any other applicable rules of law," UCC § 1-201(11).
[2]   Restatement, Contracts, 2d § 1.

a builder may contract to supply materials and do the work involved in installing the materials, or a person may contract to build a house and then transfer the house and the land to the buyer.

§ 12:4   PARTIES TO A CONTRACT

A person who makes a promise is the **promisor**, and the person to whom the promise is made is called the **promisee**. If the promise is binding, it imposes upon the promisor a duty or obligation, and the promisor may be called the **obligor**. The promisee who can claim the benefit of the obligation is also called the **obligee**. The parties to a contract are said to stand in privity with each other, and the relationship between them is termed **privity of contract**.

In written contracts, parties may be referred to by name. More often, however, they are given special names that serve better to identify each party. For example, the parties to a contract by which one person agrees that another may occupy a house upon the payment of money are called landlord and tenant, or lessor and lessee, and the contract between them is known as a lease. Other parties have their distinctive names, such as vendor and vendee, the parties to a sales contract; shipper and carrier, the parties to a transportation contract; and insurer and insured, the parties to an insurance policy.

A party to a contract may be an individual, a partnership, a corporation, or a government. A party to a contract may be an agent acting on behalf of another person. There may be one or more persons on each side of the contract. In some cases there are three-sided contracts, as in the case of a credit card transaction, which involves the company issuing the card, the holder of the card, and the business furnishing goods and services in reliance on the credit card.

In addition to the original parties to the

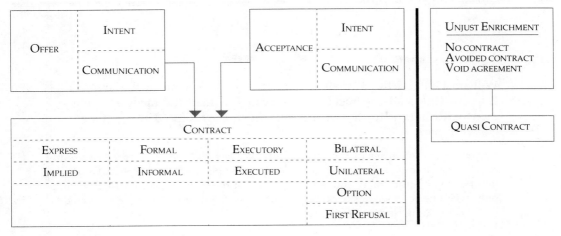

Figure 12-1
CONTRACTUAL LIABILITY

contract, other persons may have rights or duties with respect to it. For example, one party may to some extent assign rights under the contract to a third person. Also, the contract may have been made for the benefit of a third person, as in a life insurance contract, in which case the third person (the beneficiary) is permitted to enforce the contract.

§ 12:5 HOW A CONTRACT ARISES

A contract is based upon an agreement. An agreement arises when one person, the **offeror**, makes an offer and the person to whom the offer is made, the **offeree**, accepts.[3]

There must be both an offer and an acceptance. If either is lacking, there is no contract.

An offeror may make an offer to a particular person or it may be made to the public at large. The latter case arises, for example, when a reward is offered to the public for the return of lost property.

It is frequently said that a meeting of minds is essential to an agreement or a

contract. Modern courts do not stress the meeting of the minds, however, because in some situations the law finds an agreement, even though the minds of the parties have not in fact met. The real test is not whether a meeting of the minds occurred, but whether, under the circumstances, one party was reasonably entitled to believe that there was an offer and the other to believe that there was an acceptance.

§ 12:6   INTENT TO MAKE A BINDING AGREEMENT

Because a contract is based on the consent of the parties and is a legally binding agreement, it follows that the parties must have an intent to enter into an agreement that is binding. Sometimes the parties are in agreement, but their agreement does not produce a contract. Sometimes there is merely a preliminary agreement, but the parties never actually make a contract. It may be merely an agreement as to future plans or intentions without any contractual obligation to carry out those plans or intentions. In the *Bowman* case there was a dispute as to whether an agreement was a contract.

[3] Dura-wood Treating Company v Century Forest Industries, Inc. (CA5 Tex) 675 F2d 745 (1982).

BOWMAN V HILL
45 NC App 116, 262 SE2d 376 (1980)

William Hill and the Terrells owned two tracts of land in the town of Dayton. They sold one tract to Dr. Terry O. Bowman and made an agreement with him as to the second lot, which they kept. The agreement stated in part:

> . . . whereas the parties of the second part [*William Hill and the Terrells*] desire to construct a building adjacent to the building of the party of the first part [Dr. Bowman] at some future time; and WHEREAS, all of the parties are *desirous* of having one large inter-connecting parking lot located in front of the buildings and sidewalks connecting to said parking lots;
> WITNESSETH:
> That for the mutual considerations *expressed hereinabove*, the parties do contract as follows: . . . [emphasis added]

The agreement went on to provide that when the Hill-Terrell lot was paved for a parking lot, Bowman would pave a similar parking area on his tract. The Hill-Terrell lot was thereafter sold, and the buyer constructed a building where the parking lot would have been. Bowman sued Hill and Terrell for having broken their contract. The lower court held the defendants liable for breach of contract and they appealed.

HILL, J. . . . One of the elements of a valid contract is a promise, which has been defined as an assurance that a thing will or will not be done. "The mere expression of an intention or desire is not a promise, . . ."

> An apparent promise which, according to its terms, makes performance optional with the promisor no matter what may happen, or no matter what course of conduct in other respects he may pursue, is in fact no promise. Such an expression is often called an illusory promise. Williston, Contracts § 1A (3d ed 1957).

When we give the ordinary and usual meaning to the words of the contract — desire and desirous — it is apparent that they express a wish or request. Certainly, they do not carry the thrust of a promise to do or refrain from doing anything with regard to the remaining property. There is no expressed obligation to develop the property at anytime.

In the case of *Jones v Realty Co.*, 226 NC 303, 37 SE2d 906 (1946), the plaintiff sued to recover a sales commission for procuring a purchaser who was ready, willing, and able to buy land on terms set out in an agreement. The trial court interpreted the agreement between the parties to mean that the commission was to be paid "when" — and only when — "the deal is closed up." The deal never closed, and the Court said at p. 306 that,

> It can make no difference whether the event be called a contingency or the time of performance. Certainly, under either construction, the result would be the same; since, if the event does not befall, or a time coincident with the happening of the event does not arrive, in neither case may performance be exacted. Nor will it do to say that a promise to pay 'when the deal is closed up' is a promise to pay when it ought to be closed up according to the terms of the contract. Such is not the meaning of the words used. It is the event itself, and not the date of its expected or contem-

plated happening, that makes the promise to pay performable. *Amies v Wesnofske,*
255 NY 156, 174 NE 436, 73 ALR 918.

By the conveyance of the property . . . , the defendants served notice to the
plaintiff, and to all the world, that they would never develop the property, and
such conveyance and notice terminated the agreement, if any there was. . . .
[Judgment reversed]

QUESTIONS

1. Who were the defendants in this case?
2. Why didn't the plaintiff sue the purchaser of the second Hill-Terrell tract?
3. Did the purchaser of the second tract know of the agreement as to the parking lot?

§ 12:7   ADDITIONAL PRINTED MATTER

Frequently a contract is mailed or delivered
by one party to the other in an envelope that
contains additional printed matter. Similarly, when goods are purchased, the buyer often receives with the goods a manufacturer's
manual and various pamphlets. What effect
do all these papers have upon the contract?
The same question arises when a worker
gets a new job, and the employer hands the
new employee a handbook or a set of rules.
Is this material a part of the contract?

(a) INCORPORATION OF OTHER STATEMENT.
The contract itself may furnish the answer.
Sometimes the contract will expressly refer
to and incorporate into the contract the
terms of the other writing or printed statement. For example, a warehouse contract
may expressly state that it covers the "goods
of the customer," but instead of listing the
goods, the contract will continue by following the words "goods of the customer" with
the words "as set forth in Schedule A, which
is delivered to the customer with this contract." Frequently such a schedule will be
stapled or otherwise attached to the contract
itself. The contract may say that the customer will be charged at the rates set forth in the
approved tariff schedule posted on the
premises of the warehouse, and may continue with the words, "a copy of which is at-

tached hereto and made part of this
contract."

(b) EXCLUSION OF OTHER STATEMENT. As
the opposite of incorporation, the contract
may declare that there is no agreement
outside of the contract. This means that either there never was anything else or that
any prior agreement was merely a preliminary step that is finally canceled out or
erased. The contract in its final form is stated
in the writing. For example, the seller of
goods may state in the contract that no statements as to the goods have been made to the
buyer and that the written contract contains
all of the terms of the sale.

(c) REDUCTION OF CONTRACT TERMS. The
effect of accompanying or subsequently delivered printed matter may be to reduce the
terms of the written contract. That is, one
party may have had a better bargain under
the original contract. In this case, the accompanying matter will generally be ignored if it
is not shown that the party who would be
harmed had agreed that it be part of the
contract.

This is so because a contract, once made,
cannot be changed by unilateral action; that
is, by the action of one party or one side of
the contract without the agreement of the
other.

(d) EMPLOYEE'S HANDBOOK. It is a common practice for large employers to hand a
new employee a manual or handbook

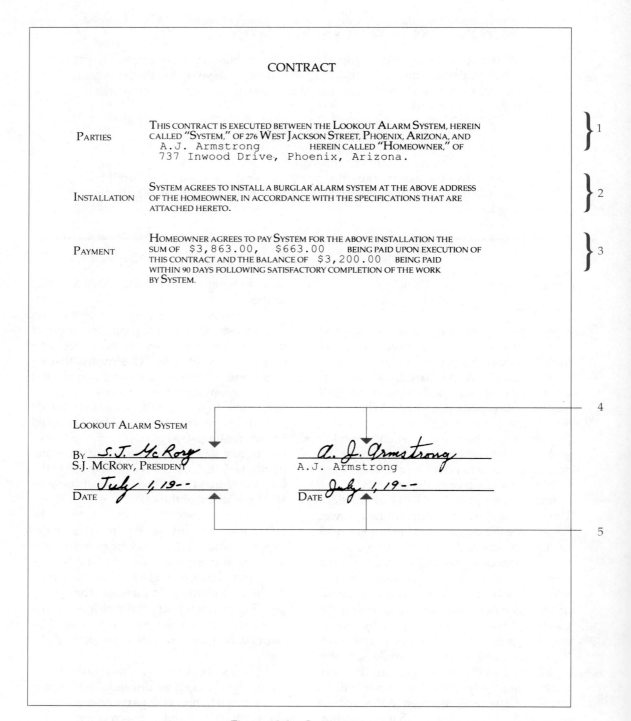

Figure 12-2   CONTRACT
Note that this contract includes the important items of information:
(1) the name and address of each party, (2) the promise or
consideration of the seller, (3) the promise or consideration of the
buyer, (4) the signatures of the two parties, (5) the date.

setting forth various matters relating to the employment. The question can then arise whether the statements in the handbook are binding terms of the employment contract or whether they are merely statements of the employer's existing policies or practices. If the handbook constitutes part of the contract, it cannot be changed by the action of the employer alone. If merely a statement of policies or practices, the terms of the handbook can be changed at will. Litigation frequently arises when the employee is fired or is denied pension rights, and the employee claims that this is a violation of the terms of the handbook.

Whether the handbook is part of the employment contract depends upon a question of the intent of the parties. If the handbook has been carefully written, it will specify whether it represents terms of the contract or merely policies. If this is not done by the handbook or other terms of the contract, it then becomes a question of fact as to what intent the parties had. This means that ordinarily the question is decided by the jury as a question of fact.

In the *Duldulao* case the court was faced with the question of whether an employees' handbook was part of the employment contract.

Duldulao v Saint Mary of Nazareth Hospital Center

115 Ill 2d 482, 106 Ill Dec 8, 505 NE2d 314 (1987)

Nora Duldulao went to work for the Saint Mary of Nazareth Hospital Center. She had been working five years when the hospital distributed a revised employees' handbook. The handbook stated that a permanent employee could not be discharged without prior written warnings to the employee and, ultimately, the making of a documented investigation. Six years later, there was a reorganization of the hospital staff, and Nora was discharged. There was no compliance with the handbook provisions. She sued the hospital for breach of the employment contract. From a judgment in favor of the hospital, Nora appealed. The appellate court reversed and remanded the action to the lower court. The hospital appealed.

MORAN, J. . . . The contractual status of employee handbooks has been the subject of a great deal of litigation in recent years. Several courts have rejected the notion that an employee handbook or manual can ever create binding contractual obligations. . . . However, the overwhelming majority of courts considering the issue have held that an employee handbook may, under proper circumstances, be contractually binding. . . .

Nearly all courts agree on the general rule, that an employment relationship without a fixed duration is terminable at will by either party. Those courts which hold that an employee handbook can never create enforceable job security rights appear to apply this general rule as a limit on the parties' freedom to contract. The majority of courts, however, interpret the general "employment-at-will rule" as a rule of construction, mandating only a presumption that a hiring without a fixed term is at will, a presumption which can be overcome by demonstrating that the parties contracted otherwise. We agree with the latter interpretation.

We find particularly persuasive the opinion of the Supreme Court of Minnesota in *Pine River State Bank v. Mettille* (Minn. 1983), 333 N.W.2d 622, which analyzed an employee handbook in terms of the traditional requirements for contract formation: offer, acceptance, and consideration. In *Pine River* an employee handbook was distributed to the plaintiff several months after he began working for defendant. The handbook contained a section entitled "Job Security" which described the generally secure nature of employment in the banking industry. The court held that this section of the handbook did not constitute an offer because it contained no definite promises. The handbook, however, also contained a section entitled "Disciplinary Policy," which stated that "[i]f an employee has violated a company policy, the following procedure will apply . . ." followed by a step-by-step process of progressive discipline ending with "[d]ischarge from employment for an employee whose conduct does not improve as a result of the previous action taken." The court held this to be a specific offer for a unilateral contract — the bank's promise in exchange for the employee's performance, *i.e.,* the employee's labor. By performing, the employee both accepted the contract and provided the necessary consideration, and thus the bank's dismissal of the plaintiff without the benefit of the progressive disciplinary procedures constituted a breach of the employment contract.

Following the reasoning in *Pine River,* we hold that an employee handbook or other policy statement creates enforceable contractual rights if the traditional requirements for contract formation are present. First, the language of the policy statement must contain a promise clear enough that an employee would reasonably believe that an offer has been made. Second, the statement must be disseminated to the employee in such a manner that the employee is aware of its contents and reasonably believes it to be an offer. Third, the employee must accept the offer by commencing or continuing to work after learning of the policy statement. When these conditions are present, then the employee's continued work constitutes consideration for the promises contained in the statement, and under traditional principles a valid contact is formed.

Applying the above principles to the case at bar it is apparent that the document entitled "Employee Handbook" created an enforceable right to the particular disciplinary procedures described therein. The amended handbook states that "[a]t the end of 90 calendar days since employment the employee becomes a permanent employee and termination comtemplated by the hospital *cannot occur* without proper notice and investigation." (Emphasis added.) It states that permanent employees *"are never* dismissed without prior written admonitions and/or an investigation that has been properly documented" (emphasis added), and that "three warning notices within a twelve-month period *are required* before an employee is dismissed, except in the case of immediate dismissal." (Emphasis added.) The reservation as to "immediate dismissal" does not detract from the definiteness of the offer, because that term is well defined. An "immediate dismissal" justifies dismissal "without notice for a grave and valid reason," and the list of examples of grave offenses includes such offenses as "Mistreatment of a patient," "Fighting on hospital premises," "Unauthorized Possession of Weapons," and "Reporting to work under the influence of intoxicants." The handbook also lists offenses which are specifically not subject to immediate dismissal, such as "Deliberate Violation of Instructions," "Unwillingness to Render Satisfactory Service," and "Unauthorized Absence." An employee reading the handbook would thus reasonably believe that, except in the case of a very serious offense, he or she would not be terminated without prior written warnings. Furthermore, the handbook creates rights even for probationary employees who may be terminated "without notice but for just cause."

Moreover, the handbook contains no disclaimers to negate the promises made. In fact, the introduction to the handbook states just the opposite, that the policies in the handbook "are designed to clarify your *rights* and duties as employees." (Emphasis added.) Thus, the handbook language is such that an employee would reasonably believe that after the expiration of the initial probationary period the progressive disciplinary procedure would be part of the employer's offer.

Finally, it is undisputed that defendant gave the handbook to plaintiff and intended that plaintiff become familiar with its contents. In fact, a significant part of plaintiff's duties as an employee consisted of instructing new employees on the contents of the handbook. There is no question but that plaintiff continued to work with knowledge of the handbook provisions. Under these circumstances the handbook's provisions became binding on the employer.

[Judgment affirmed with respect to the handbook's being part of the employment contract and action remanded 'for such further proceedings as are consistent with this opinion.']

Questions

1. When can the job security provisions of an employee's handbook be regarded as part of the employment contract?
2. Does it make any difference whether the employee's handbook is given to the employee at the time that the employee agrees to work for the employer or at a later date?
3. What social forces are advanced by recognizing the handbook as part of the employment contract?

B. Classes of Contracts

Contracts are classified with respect to their form, their binding character, and the extent to which they have been performed.

§ 12:8   Formal and Informal Contracts

Contracts can be classified as formal or informal contracts.

(a) FORMAL CONTRACTS. **Formal contracts** are enforced because the formality with which they are executed is considered sufficient to signify that the parties intend to be bound by their terms. Formal contracts include (1) contracts under seal, (2) contracts of record, and (3) negotiable instruments.

A **contract under seal** is executed by affixing a seal or making an impression upon the paper or upon some tenacious substance, such as wax, attached to the document. Although at common law an impression was necessary, the courts now treat various signs or marks to be the equivalent of a seal. Most states hold that there is a seal if a person's signature or a corporation's name is followed by a scroll or scrawl, the word *seal*, or the letters *L.S.* In some jurisdictions the body of the contract must recite that the parties are sealing the contract, in addition to their making a seal following their signatures.[4]

A contract under seal was binding at common law solely because of its formality. In many states, this has been changed by statute. The Uniform Commercial Code abolishes the law of seals for the sale of goods. In some states the law of seals has been abolished generally without regard to the nature of the transaction involved.

[4]   Lumbermen's Mutual Cas. Co. v Pattillo Constr. Co. 172 Ga App 452, 323 SE2d 649 (1984).

A **contract of record** is an agreement or obligation that has been recorded by a court. One form of contract of record arises when one acknowledges before a proper court the obligation to pay a certain sum unless a specified condition is met. For example, a party who has been arrested may be released on a promise to appear in court and may agree to pay a certain sum on failing to do so. An obligation of this kind is known as a **recognizance**.

Similarly, an agreement made with an administrative agency is binding because it has been so made. For example, when a business agrees with the Federal Trade Commission that the enterprise will stop a particular practice that the Commission regards as unlawful, the business is bound by its agreement and cannot thereafter reject it.

Negotiable instruments are contracts governed by the law of commercial paper. These special-purpose contracts must meet certain formal requirements in order to be enforceable.

(b) INFORMAL CONTRACTS. All other contracts are called **informal**, or **simple**, **contracts** without regard to whether they are oral or written. These contracts are enforceable, not because of the form of the transaction, but because they represent the agreement of the parties.

§ 12:9   EXPRESS AND IMPLIED
                    CONTRACTS

Simple contracts may be classified in terms of the way in which they are created, as express contracts or implied contracts.

(a) EXPRESS CONTRACTS. An **express con-** tract is one in which the agreement of the parties is manifested by their words, whether spoken or written.

(b) IMPLIED CONTRACTS. An **implied contract** (or, as sometimes stated, a contract implied in fact) is one in which the agreement is not shown by words, written or spoken, but by the acts and conduct of the parties. Such a contract arises, for example, when one person renders services under circumstances indicating that payment for them is expected, and the other person, knowing such circumstances, accepts the benefit of those services. Similarly, when an owner requests a professional roofer to make repairs to the roof of a building, an obligation arises to pay the reasonable value of such services, although no agreement has been made as to compensation.

In terms of effect, there is no difference between an implied contract and an express contract. The difference relates solely to the manner of proving the existence of the contract.

An implied contract cannot arise when there is an existing express contract on the same subject.[5] Likewise, no contract is implied when the relationship of the parties is such that by a reasonable interpretation, the performance of services or the supplying of goods was intended as a gift.

In *Novak's Estate*, the mother died, and her daughter claimed compensation for services she had rendered to her mother.

---

[5]   Clark-Fitzpatrick, Inc. v Long Island Railroad Co. 124 App Div 2d 534, 507 NYS2d 679 (1986).

NOVAK'S ESTATE
—— Minn App ——, 398 NW2d 653 (1987)

Clara Novak was sick. Her daughter Janie helped her in many ways. Clara died, and Janie then claimed that she was entitled to be paid for the services that she had rendered her mother. The court dismissed her claim, and she appealed.

Sedgwick, J. . . . Clara Novak suffered kidney failure in 1971. Dialysis treatment was required since November 1977. She died on June 23, 1984, just before her 71st birthday.

Clara Novak's will provided $2,000 to her church and the residue of her estate to be divided equally among her children. One daughter, Janie Novak, claims she is entitled to a greater share because she was the primary caretaker for her mother for at least six years. Janie's claim against the estate for $26,105.50 for her services was denied. Her siblings claim Janie was simply doing her part and that three other children also helped their mother.

Janie Novak claims she averaged two hours a day helping her mother. Janie became a licensed practical nurse at her mother's suggestion. She worked nights in order to help her mother during the day. She drove her mother to the Little Falls hospital 96 times for dialysis and made seven trips to the Hennepin County Medical Center. Janie also reports the loss of 16 days, 5 hours of vacation time on her mother's behalf. She incurred phone expense because of her mother's condition. She lived a quarter mile distance from her mother and was a frequent visitor. Appellant argued:

> Janie . . . provided nursing services on a daily basis in Clara's home. Janie would also check her mother's blood pressure and other vital signs, bathe her, do her hair, clip her toe and fingernails, massage her scalp, and attended to other hygiene needs. Janie would do her mother's shopping for her, pay her bills, provide her with transport to and from various business establishments, and otherwise attend to her mother's needs. After one of her mother's many hospitalizations, Janie kept her mother in her own home for a period of some three months, and personally attended to her mother's various medical ailments at the time. In short, Janie provided nursing services for her mother's well-being for a period in excess of thirteen years.

The family responded that Janie merely did her share; three other siblings also helped out. The trips for dialysis were thrice weekly and since other family members gave Clara rides, 96 trips over 6 years was not an unreasonable figure. The siblings state that Janie's son Jeffrey often made the dialysis trips rather than Janie. In 1978, Clara purchased a new car for the trips and paid for travel expenses. The family offered as evidence a number of checks, mostly for small amounts, payable to Janie Novak. From September 1983 to March 1984, another daughter took Clara in and cared for her. The family also points out that Clara's medical needs were satisfied by the Little Falls hospital, and that the medical services, such as blood pressure checks, temperature, etc., supplied by Janie were solely for her own peace of mind. She did not maintain records as a nurse would when providing professional services. . . .

The courts proceed on the premise that services provided between family/household member are gratuitous.

> The presumption of gratuity is dependent on the existence of a family relation and only arises when it is shown that the services rendered were of the type which members of a family usually and ordinarily render to each other by reason of family relation. The authorities stress the fact that the presence of those reciprocal duties within the family is essential to the creation of this presumption.

In re Estate of Tilghman, 240 Minn. 494, 495, 61 N.W.2d 743, 745 (1953). The presumption operates if the family relation exists. . . .

Appellant argues that "family" does not include a blood relation who lives independently from the person to whom the services were rendered, *i.e.,* a non-household member should not be saddled with the presumption. We believe the presumption properly applies to immediate family regardless of their residence. "Household" is simply a more inclusive term since it may include individuals residing with a family and participating in the exchange of services, but absent a blood tie. Whether or not family members reside in the same household, the question is the extent to which care furnished exceeds "reciprocal duties and mutual benefits." *Id.* at 499, 61 N.W.2d at 747. . . .

In re Estate of Beecham, 378 N.W.2d 800 (Minn.1985), represents the most recent analysis of the evidentiary presumption and its application. *Beecham* concerned a middle-aged woman, compelled to care for her husband's elderly and infirm parents two years after her marriage. The father died six months later, but the mother resided with the Beecham's for six and one-half years. The elderly Mrs. Beecham required constant care and could render no assistance to the household beside $600 a month for "room and board." She also left her familial caretakers only $1,500 from an estate of $166,000. The presumption of gratuity was overcome by this evidence and ceased to carry any evidentiary value. An implied contract was found in order to balance the equities.

> Those types of services are beyond services usually and ordinarily gratuitously rendered to family members. Particularly is that true when the fact is considered that Alice knew her in-laws a very short time before taking them into her home, had no blood relationship to them, and accepted the onus for her mother-in-law's extended care. Admittedly, neither the degree of kinship nor the length of family relationship is dispositive on the issue. However, they are relevant and when considered in the light of qualitative and quantitative care rendered, they lend support to the trial court's finding of the existence of an implied contract under the *Tilghman* analysis. Moreover, the absence of reciprocity of services between Alice and her mother-in-law is an important factor under the *Tilghman* analysis in the determination of whether the presumption has been overcome.

Id. at 804.

The evidentiary presumption arises where there is a family relationship, as evidenced by a close blood relation and/or a membership in a family's household. Once the "close" relationship is established where individuals are presumed to commonly share duties and provide services to other family members, the analysis shifts to an examination of whether the exchange of services was actually mutual and reciprocal. If one party rendered or received an obviously disproportionate share of services, the absence of mutuality may obviate the presumption.

The more distant the kinship or relationship, the easier it is to overcome the presumption since reciprocal benefits are more limited. A daughter-in-law (see *Beecham*) or a daughter with no parental contact for fifty years (*Tilghman*) will be able to avoid the presumption, while a child who has always been close to her parents will have a difficult task overcoming the presumption absent significant inequities. It must be remembered the presumption is an evidentiary device, and it is not an absolute bar to recovery.

In the present case, Janie Novak lived nearby and provided a number of services to her elderly, sick mother. Her care and assistance does not rise to the level in *Tilghman* and *Beecham* and does not appear to be disproportionate to the aid provided by her siblings. She also received one-sixth of the estate.

Even if she provided more services, while others did less (and perhaps other siblings did nothing), the balancing of the equities does not justify an interference with the testamentary plan of the deceased.

[Judgment affirmed]

QUESTIONS

1. What is the basis for the presumption applied by the court?
2. What is the distinction between family and household?
3. Did the facts of the case confirm or rebut the presumption of gratuity?

§ 12:10 VALID AND VOIDABLE CONTRACTS AND VOID AGREEMENTS

Contracts may be classified in terms of enforceability of validity.

(a) VALID CONTRACTS. A **valid contract** is an agreement that is binding and enforceable.

(b) VOIDABLE CONTRACTS. A **voidable contract** is an agreement that is otherwise binding and enforceable but, because of the circumstances surrounding its execution or the lack of capacity of one of the parties, it may be rejected at the option of one of the parties. For example, a person who has been forced to sign an agreement which that person would not have voluntarily signed may in some instances avoid the contract.

(c) VOID AGREEMENTS. A **void agreement** is without legal effect. An agreement that contemplates the performance of an act prohibited by law is usually incapable of enforcement; hence it is void. Likewise, it cannot be made binding by later approval or ratification.[6]

§ 12:11 EXECUTED AND EXECUTORY CONTRACTS

Contracts may be classified, in terms of the extent to which they have been performed, as executed contracts and executory contracts.

(a) EXECUTED CONTRACTS. An **executed contract** is one that has been completely performed. In other words, an executed contract is one under which nothing remains to be done by either party.[7] A contract may be executed at once, as in the case of a cash sale; or it may be executed or performed in the future.

(b) EXECUTORY CONTRACTS. In an **executory contract**, something remains to be done by one or both parties. For example, if a utility company agrees to furnish electricity to a customer for a specified period of time at a stipulated price, the contract is executory. If the entire price is paid in advance, the contract is still deemed executory; although, strictly speaking, it is executed on one side and executory on the other.

§ 12:12 BILATERAL AND UNILATERAL CONTRACTS

In making an offer, the offeror is, in effect, extending a promise to do something, such as to pay a sum of money, if the offeree will do what the offeror requests. Contracts are classified as bilateral or unilateral. Some bilateral contracts look ahead to the making of a later contract. Depending on their terms, these are called option contracts or first-refusal contracts.

---

[6] See § 16:1. Although the distinction between a void agreement and a voidable contract is clear in theory, there is frequently confusion because some courts describe a given transaction as void, while others regard it as merely voidable.

[7] Lockheed Missiles v Gilmore Industries, 135 Cal App 3d 556, 185 Cal Rptr 409 (1982).

(a) BILATERAL CONTRACT. If the offeror extends a promise and asks for a promise in return and if the offeree accepts the offer by making the promise, the contract is called a **bilateral contract**. One promise is given in exchange for another, and each party is bound by the obligation. For example, when the house painter offers to paint the owner's house for $1,000, and the owner promises to pay $1,000 for the job, there is an exchange of promises, and the agreement gives rise to a bilateral contract.

(b) UNILATERAL CONTRACT. In contrast, the offeror may offer to do something only when something is done by the offeree. As only one party is obligated to perform after the contract has been made, this kind of contract is called a unilateral contract. This is illustrated by the case of the reward for the return of lost property. The offeror does not wish to have promises by members of the public that they will try to return the property. The offeror wants the property and promises to pay anyone who returns the property. The offer of a unilateral contract calls for an act; a promise to do the act does not give rise to a contract.

(c) OPTION AND FIRST-REFUSAL CONTRACTS. The parties may make a contract that gives a right to one of the parties to enter into a second contract at a later date. If one party has an absolute right to enter into the later contract, the initial contract is called an **option contract.** Thus, a bilateral contract may be made today giving one of the parties the right to buy the other party's house for a specified amount. This is an option contract, as the party with the privilege has the freedom of choice, or option, to buy or not buy. If the option is exercised, the other party to the contract must follow the terms of the option and enter into the second contract. If the option is never exercised, no second contract ever arises, and the offer protected by the option contract merely expires.[8]

In contrast with an option contract, a contract may merely give a **right of first refusal**. This only imposes the duty to make the first offer to the party having the right of first refusal. For example, the homeowner could make a contract providing that, should the owner desire to sell at some future time, the other party to the contract could buy either at a fixed price or at a price matching a good-faith bid by a third person. Here the homeowner cannot be required to sell, but if the owner attempts to sell, an option immediately comes into existence by which the other party can buy or not buy.

The situation can arise in which it is a question as to whether there is a contract to sell, an option to buy, or a right of first refusal. In all cases, the question is determined by the intent of the parties.

§ 12:13   QUASI CONTRACTS

In some cases, the courts will pretend that there is a contract when in fact there is no contract. Such a make-believe contract is called a quasi contract.

(a) PREVENTION OF UNJUST ENRICHMENT. These quasi contracts are recognized in a limited number of situations in order to attain an equitable or just result.[9] These instances may be classified in terms of situations in which there is no contract between the parties; those in which there was a contract between the parties, but it has been avoided; and those in which there was an attempted contract, but for some reason the agreement is held illegal and therefore void.

(1) No Contract. In some cases the hoped for contract is never formed. The parties expect there will be a contract, but something happens that prevents their reaching a final agreement. Meanwhile, one or more of the parties may have jumped the gun and begun performing as though there were a contract.

---

[8]   Sutton Place Development Co. v Bank of Commerce and Industry, 149 Ill App 3d 513, 103 Ill Dec 122, 501 NE2d 143 (1986).

[9]   Perkins v Daughtery (Ky App) 722 SW2d 907 (1987).

When it is finally clear that there is no contract, a party who had rendered some performance will seek to be paid for what was done. The claim will be made that if payment is not made, the other party will be unjustly enriched. This was the claim made by the plaintiff in the *Dursteler* case.

DURSTELER V DURSTELER
108 Idaho App 230, 697 P2d 1244 (1985)

Michael and Dennis Dursteler were brothers. Michael and Mary, his wife, owned a mink ranch. They made an agreement to sell the ranch to Dennis and Gloria, his wife. Acting on the basis of the contemplated agreement, Dennis made a down payment of $10,000 and paid $850 for feed during a training period that was to end with the transfer of the title of the ranch to the buyers. During this time, Dennis also made farm building repairs of approximately $2,000. The transfer of title was not carried out. When Dennis sued for breach of the agreement, it was held that the agreement was too vague to be a contract and therefore could not be enforced. Dennis then sued Michael in quasi contract to recover the amount of all the payments made by him.

BURNETT, J. . . . We now examine the judge's decision to compel certain payments by the sellers to the purchasers. Having determined the contract to be unenforceable, the judge stated in his memorandum opinion that he "must attempt to place the parties, as nearly as possible, in the same position as they were at the time of the attempted making of the contract." This proposition, sounding in rescission, causes us some disquietude. Had a contract existed, and had the court found that the contract was rescinded, the court's duty would have been as the judge stated . . . . But here no enforceable contract existed. There was nothing to rescind.

We do not gainsay that authority exists for granting restitution to parties who have unsuccessfully attempted to form a contract. . . . But our concern is with the proper application of the remedy. We think the proper use of restitution, in a case such as this, is not to restore the parties' precontract positions but to assure that each party receives reasonable value for the benefits conferred on the other during the period of attempted performance of the contract.

Under the doctrine of unjust enrichment, parties to a contract that fails to materialize may be required to pay restitution for the value of benefits each has conferred and the other has unjustly retained. We believe this principle is applicable here. If a trial court reaches the right result, albeit upon an erroneous theory, its decision will be upheld upon the correct theory. Accordingly, our task is to determine whether the payments ordered by the district court can be upheld as restitution for unjust enrichment.

We turn first to the buyers' claims. As noted earlier, the buyers made a $10,000 down payment. They also paid, in round figures, $850 for feed, $140 for a welder and $668 for other expenses incurred while attempting to operate the ranch. The district judge further found, upon substantial evidence, that the buyers had furnished $2,000 in labor and materials to make necessary repairs on the roof of the ranch house and had provided other labor for nonspecific tasks, for which a fair wage would have been $1,200. Of these amounts, the buyers had been reimbursed $355, leaving a net claim of about $14,503. The court awarded this approximate sum.

Although such an award might have been appropriate for restoring the buyers to their pre-"contract" status quo, it was not entirely proper upon a theory of unjust enrichment. The measure of restitution for unjust enrichment is the benefit conferred which it would be unjust for the other party to retain. In *Gillette v. Storm Circle Ranch*, 101 Idaho 663, 619 P.2d 1116 (1980), our Supreme Court held that the measure of unjust enrichment is not necessarily the value of labor and materials provided. However, in *Hartwell Corp. v. Smith*, 107 Idaho 134, 686 P.2d 79 (Ct. App. 1984), we noted that while the value of labor and materials is not the measure, per se, of the benefit conferred, it may be competent evidence of the value.

Applying these rules to the buyers' claims, there is an obvious correlation between the $10,000 down payment and the resultant benefit conferred upon the sellers. The $850 paid for feed also produces a direct, equivalent benefit. The sum of these items is $10,850. After deducting the $355 reimbursed, the buyers' entitlement, so far as we can determine it on the present record, is $10,495.

However, the record does not permit us to determine the benefit derived by the sellers from the roof repairs. The district judge found that the repairs were necessary and that the buyers had furnished $2,000 in labor and materials. Those findings are not clearly erroneous and will not be set aside. But neither are they dispositive on a question of unjust enrichment. The benefit to the sellers must be ascertained. It may or may not be $2,000. Similarly, we are unable to determine whether the sellers derived a benefit, and to quantify the benefit, if any, resulting from the other items claimed by the purchasers — their miscellaneous expenditures, their labor for non-specific tasks and their purchase of a welder (the necessity of which was disputed). These items require further analysis and fact-finding in light of the standards governing recovery for unjust enrichment. A remand for this purpose is appropriate. . . .

[Action remanded]

QUESTIONS

1. What is the measure of the damages recovered in an action based on quasi contract?
2. When suit is brought on a quasi contract, does the court seek to put the parties back in the position they held before the transaction?
3. Did the appellate court make a final determination in the action? Explain.

The no contract case may arise in a situation where there is a mistake as to the subject matter of the contract. For example, a painter may begin painting the house of *A* because of a mistake as to the address of the building. *A* sees the work going on and realizes the painter is making a mistake. Nevertheless, *A* does not stop the painter.

When the painter finishes the work and presents a bill for painting, *A* then refuses to pay because there never was a contract. This is true because *A* never expressly agreed for the painting. Likewise, the conduct of *A* never caused the painter as a reasonable person to believe that *A* was entering into a contract. The painter just assumed that everything was all right.

In such case, the law deems it inequitable that *A* should have remained silent and then reaped the benefits of the painter's mistake. *A* will therefore be required to pay the painter the reasonable value of the painting. This liability is described as quasi-contractual.

(2) The Avoided Contract. In some situations, one party to the contract may be able to avoid it or set it aside. As will be seen in Chapter 14, the contract of a minor can be avoided. If the contract was for a necessary received by the minor, the minor must pay the reasonable value of what was received. The minor is not required to pay the contract price, but only the reasonable value of the benefit received. As the liability enforced against the minor is not based on the contract, it is called quasi-contractual.

For example, when the parties rescind or set aside their contract, a party who has already conferred a benefit on the other party before the contract was rescinded may recover in quasi contract for the value of such benefit. Thus, a contractor may recover for the value of an irrigation system installed on the defendant's land before the construction contract was set aside.[10]

(3) The Void Agreement. In some instances, the parties make a contract, one party receives the benefit of the contract, and then the benefited party seeks to avoid paying on the ground that the contract was void because of illegality. For example, governmental units, such as cities, must generally advertise for the lowest responsible bidder when a contract is to be made to obtain supplies or to construct buildings. In some instances, the city officials may improperly skip the advertising. This might be done either because of a corrupt purpose or because the officials honestly, but wrongly, believed that the particular contract came within an exception to the requirement of advertising. Whatever the reason, the city officials enter into a contract with a contractor without following the statutory procedures. The contractor fully performs the contract. When the contractor requests to be paid, the city officials refuse to live up to the contract on the ground that the contract violated the statutory requirements and therefore was illegal and void. In such cases, it will be held that, although the contract is void, the city must pay the reasonable value of what has been done. In this way, the contractor gets paid for what the contractor really did. The city is not required to pay for any more than it has actually received. The danger of the city's paying inflated prices, which was the evil that the advertising statute sought to avoid, does not arise, because the court does not require the city to pay the contract price but only the reasonable value of the benefit conferred upon the city.

(b) WHEN QUASI-CONTRACTUAL LIABILITY DOES NOT EXIST. While the objective of the quasi contract is to do justice, one must not jump to the conclusion that a quasi contract will arise every time there is an injustice. The mere fact that someone has benefited someone else and has not been paid will not necessarily give rise to a quasi contract.[11] For example, no quasi-contractual obligation arises when the plaintiff merely confers upon the defendant a benefit to which the defendant was already entitled.

(1) Unexpected Cost. The fact that performance of a contract proves more difficult or more expensive than had been expected does not entitle a party to extra compensation when there was no misrep-

---

[10] J & M Construction, Inc. v Southam (Utah) 722 P2d 779 (1986).

[11] Murdock-Bryant Construction Inc. v Pearson, 146 Ariz 48, 703 P2d 1197 (1985).

resentation as to the conditions that would be encountered or the events that would occur. Courts are particularly unwilling to allow extra compensation when the complaining party is experienced with the particular type of contract and the problems that are likely to be encountered. That is, the contractor is not entitled to quasi-contractual recovery for extra expense on the theory that the extra work had conferred a greater benefit than had been contemplated.

(2) Contract with Third Person. When a person has a binding contract with a third person, only that third person is required to pay for the performance made under the contract. Even though performance did benefit the defendant, the person cannot sue the defendant for quasi contract when the third person fails to make payment under the contract. For example, a subcontractor doing work that benefits the homeowner can only sue the contractor on the

contract between the subcontractor and the contractor. The subcontractor cannot sue the owner merely because the owner was benefited by the work done by the subcontractor. Likewise, when a distributor of tires is not paid by a dealer, the distributor cannot sue the customer who bought the tires from the dealer for the bill that the dealer should have paid the distributor.[12]

(3) No Unjust Enrichment. In order to recover in quasi contract, the plaintiff must prove that the defendant was enriched, the extent or dollar value of such enrichment, and that such enrichment was unjust. If the plaintiff cannot prove all these elements, there can be no recovery in quasi contract.

The *Green Quarries* case raised the question of when a benefit is unjust.

---

[12]   Kapral's Tire Service, Inc. v Aztek Tread Corp. 124 App Div 2d 1011, 508 NYS2d 777 (1986).

GREEN QUARRIES, INC. V RAASCH
(Mo App) 676 SW2d 261 (1984)

Ernie Raasch made a contract with Anchor Company to do some building on his land. Green Quarries, Inc., supplied rock and concrete for the construction work. Anchor did not pay Green Quarries and later went bankrupt. Green Quarries then sued Raasch on the theory that there was a quasi-contractual obligation to pay for the materials. Green Quarries did not make any statement as to whether Raasch had paid Anchor or Anchor's trustee in bankruptcy. From a judgment against Green Quarries, it appealed.

NUGENT, J. . . . The doctrine of quasi-contract, also known as a contract implied in law, is based primarily on the principle of unjust enrichment. Unlike a contract implied in fact, a contract implied in law is imposed, or created, without regard to the promise of the party to be bound. The duty which engenders a quasi-contractual obligation is most often based upon the principle of unjust enrichment. Unjust enrichment occurs where a benefit is conferred upon a person in circumstances in which retention by him of that benefit without paying its reasonable value would be unjust. Thus, quantum meruit [payment of a reasonable amount for labor and materials] is a remedy for the enforcement of a quasi-contractual obligation.

Courts generally recognize that the essential elements of quasi-contract or contract implied in law are: (1) a benefit conferred upon the defendant by the plaintiff; (2) appreciation by the defendant of the fact of such benefit; and (3) acceptance and retention by the defendant of that benefit under circumstances in which retention without payment would be inequitable. The most significant requirement is that the enrichment to the defendant be unjust, that retention of the benefit be inequitable.

In resolving the issue whether a landowner has been unjustly enriched by a subcontractor's improvements on the owner's real estate, the courts have repeatedly looked to whether the landowner has already paid the general contractor the amount due the general contractor under their express contract. If the owner has indeed paid the general contractor for the materials, the owner's retention of them without further payment has been found not to constitute unjust enrichment. Although the subcontractor may remain unpaid and thus suffer detriment, equity will not require the owner to pay twice. . . .

Green Quarries contends . . . that it was not required to plead or prove that the defendant owners never paid the general contractor. Plaintiff argues that payment is an affirmative defense to be pleaded and proved by the defendant owners. In a claim based on unjust enrichment, plaintiff's contention cannot be correct. Payment or non-payment by the owner is a factor which determines whether the petition alleges the most important element for a recovery based on quasi-contract — unjust enrichment. . . .

Non-payment by the owner to the general contractor must be pleaded by the subcontractor in order to state a claim based on unjust enrichment. Thus, plaintiff's petition must allege that the defendants did not pay Anchor. Because of the facts of the case at bar, however, plaintiff must also plead that the Raaschs have not made payment to the trustee in bankruptcy. Plaintiff alleges in its petition that Anchor filed for bankruptcy in May of 1980 and that in December of 1980, Anchor was adjudicated bankrupt. Thus, in order to constitute a claim for unjust enrichment, plaintiff must here allege that neither the trustee in bankruptcy nor the general contractor has been paid by the defendants.

[Judgment affirmed]

QUESTIONS

1. What was the fatal weakness in the plaintiff's case? Explain.
2. With respect to the point raised by your answer to Question 1, who had the burden of proof?
3. What is the practical effect on Green Quarries of the decision of the court?

(c) EXTENT OF RECOVERY. When recovery is allowed in quasi contract, the plaintiff recovers the reasonable value of the benefit conferred upon the defendant.[13]

The fact that the plaintiff may have sustained greater damages, or have been put to greater expense, is ignored. Thus, the plaintiff cannot recover lost profits or other kinds of damages that would be recovered in a suit for breach of a contract.

[13]   City of Damascus v Bivens, 291 Ark 600, 726 SW2d 677 (1987).

SUMMARY

A contract is an agreement of two or more parties that they intend to be binding (contractual intent). A contract arises when an offer is accepted with such intent. When more than one document is involved or more than one conversation is held, a question arises as to how much is to be regarded as part of the agreement of the parties. When a written contract is sent with additional printed matter, questions arise whether the additional matter is part of the contract or is excluded from the contract and whether it reduces or modifies the terms of the contract.

Contracts may be classified in a number of ways: as to parties, subject matter, form, manifestation, validity, and obligations. With respect to form, a contract may be formal, such as those under seal or those appearing on the records of courts or administrative agencies. The manifestation of the agreement distinguishes between agreements that are expressed by words, written or oral, and those that are expressed by or deduced from conduct. The question of validity requires distinguishing between contracts that are valid; those that are voidable; and those that are not contracts at all, but are merely void agreements. Contracts can be distinguished, on the basis of the obligations created, as executed contracts, in which everything has been performed, and executory contracts, in which something remains to be done. The bilateral contract is formed by exchanging a promise for a promise, and therefore each party has the obligation of thereafter rendering the promised performance. In the unilateral contract, which is the doing of an act in exchange for a promise, no performance is required of the offeree performing the act. The only obligation is that of the promisor.

In certain situations, the law regards it as unjust that a person should receive a benefit and not pay for it. In such case, the law of quasi contracts allows the performing person to recover the reasonable value of the benefit conferred upon the benefited person, even though there is no contract of any kind between them requiring any payment. The unjust enrichment, which quasi contract is designed to prevent, sometimes arises when there never was any contract between the persons involved or when there was a contract, but for some reason it was avoided or held that it was merely a void agreement. Quasi-contractual recovery is not allowed merely because someone loses money. It is not allowed merely because the cost of performance under a contract rises above that contemplated; because a person breaks a contract with the performing person to pay for services rendered under that contract; or if the performing party is unable to prove that there was any enrichment, the extent of such enrichment, or that any enrichment was unjust.

QUESTIONS AND CASE PROBLEMS

1. State the specific objective(s) of the law (from the list in Chapter 2, § 2:4) illustrated by the following quotation: "A person shall not be allowed to enrich himself unjustly at the expense of another."
   Note: As you study the various rules of law in this chapter and the chapters that follow, consider each rule in relationship to its social, economic, and moral background. Try to determine the particular objective(s) of each important rule. To the extent that you are able to analyze law as the product of society striving for justice, you will have a greater insight into the law itself, the world

in which you live, the field of business, and the human mind.

2. What is a contract?

3. Ackerman went to the phone book and sent letters to randomly selected names. The letter to each stated, "It is agreed that we will paint your house for a price based on the cost of our labor and paint plus an additional 10% for profit." He sent such a letter to Maria. Is there a contract between Ackerman and Maria?

4. Henry makes a written contract to paint Betty's house for $500. The reasonable value of such work is $1,000. Henry made the price low in the hope that Betty's neighbors would have him paint their houses. He painted Betty's house. He got no work from the neighbors. He then sent Betty a bill for $1,000 on the ground that an implied contract existed to pay him the reasonable value of his services. Was he entitled to recover $1,000?

5. Henry said to Hilda, "I want to buy your old automobile." She replied, "It's yours for $400." Henry replied, "I'll take it." Later Henry changed his mind and refused to take or pay for the car. When Hilda sued him for damages, he raised the defense that he had never made a contract with her because they had never expressly stated, "We hereby make a contract for the sale of the automobile." Henry claimed that in the absence of such an express declaration showing that they intended to make a contract, there could be no binding agreement to purchase the automobile. Was he correct?

6. The Acme Machinery Company installed a furnace in the home of Milton. Milton has not yet paid the balance due. Is the contract executed or executory?

7. Compare an implied contract and a quasi contract.

8. *A* made a contract to construct a house for *B*. Subsequently, *B* sued *A* for breach of contract. *A* raised the defense that the contract was not binding because it was not sealed. Is this a valid defense? [Cooper v G. E. Construction Co. 116 Ga App 690, 158 SE2d 305]

9. Carlos Esteban was nine years old when his parents were killed in an auto crash. Maria Pedrillo, a friend of the family, took Carlos into her home and raised him. Carlos was never adopted by Maria, but all the neighbors thought he was related to Maria. About twenty years later, Maria became

very sick and, after a long period, finally died. During this time she was dependent on Carlos, who ran the house, prepared her meals, and did whatever had to be done. Carlos kept an itemized list of what he had done. He gave a copy of this list to the executor of Maria's estate and demanded that he be paid the reasonable value of his services. Was he entitled to compensation for such services?

10. Dozier and his wife, daughter, and grandson lived in the house Dozier owned. At the request of the daughter and grandson, Paschall made some improvements to the house. Dozier did not authorize these, but he knew that the improvements were being made and did not object to them. Paschall sued Dozier for the reasonable value of the improvements. Dozier defended on the ground that he had not made any contract for such improvements. Was he obligated to pay for such improvements?

11. Harriet went away for the summer. In her absence, Landry, a housepainter, painted her house. Landry had a contract to paint a neighbor's house, but painted Harriet's house by mistake. The painting of Harriet's house was worth $1,000. When she returned from her vacation, Landry billed her for $1,000. She refused to pay. He claimed that she had a quasi-contractual liability for that amount. Was he correct?

12. William was a certified public accountant. He did all the accounting work for his wife, Frances. William and Frances were divorced but remained friendly. William continued to perform the accounting services as before for her and also for North Star Motors, a business operated by Frances' brother. When Frances sued William on a promissory note, he counterclaimed for compensation for his accounting services rendered to his ex-wife and her brother on the theory that an implied contract arose to pay him for such services. Was he entitled to recover on the counterclaim? [Ryan v Ryan (Del Super) 298 A2d 343]

13. Margrethe and Charles Pyeatte were married. They agreed that she would work so that he could go to law school and that when he finished law school, she would go back to school for her master's degree. After Charles was admitted to the Bar and before Margrethe went back to school, the two

were divorced. She sued Charles for breaking their contract. The court held that there was no contract because the agreement between them was too vague to be enforced. Margrethe then claimed that she was entitled to quasi contractual recovery of the money that she had paid for Charles' support and law school tuition. He denied liability. Was she entitled to recover for the money she spent for Charles' maintenance and law school tuition? [Pyeatte v Pyeatte (App) 135 Ariz 346, 661 P2d 196]

14. Carriage Way was a real estate development of approximately 80 houses and 132 apartments. The property owners were members of the Carriage Way Property Owners Association. Each year, the association would take care of certain open neighboring areas that were used by the property owners, including a nearby lake. The board of directors of the association would make an assessment or charge against the property owners to cover the cost of this work. The property owners paid these assessments for a number of years and then refused to pay any more. In spite of this refusal, the association continued to take care of the areas in question. The association then sued the property owners and claimed that they were liable for the benefit that had been conferred upon them. Were the owners liable? [Board of Directors of Carriage Way Property Owners Ass'n. v Western National Bank, 139 Ill App 3d 542, 94 Ill Dec 97, 487 NE2d 974]

15. Faith Cook went to work for M & W Distributors, a company owned by Heck's Inc. She was given an employee's handbook that listed a number of grounds for discharge of employees and gave the impression that an employee would not be discharged without cause. Some years later Cook was discharged. Her work record was excellent, and the letter terminating her employment stated merely that she was discharged "in the best interest of the company." She sued both Heck's and M & W. She claimed that by firing her for a reason not stated in the employees' handbook, her contract of employment had been broken. Was she correct? [Cook v Heck's Inc. ___ WVa ___, 342 SE2d 453]

13

━━━◆◆━━━

THE AGREEMENT

As described in Chapter 12, a contract consists of enforceable obligations that have been voluntarily assumed. Thus, one of the essential elements of a contract is an agreement. The importance of requiring an agreement is that it shows that the parties have voluntarily surrendered a part of their freedom of action — they have bound themselves to act in the manner specified in the contract. Because freedom of action is so essential to the American way of life, society is very careful to be sure that there is a proper agreement whenever any part of that freedom is surrendered. Therefore, it is necessary to show that there was an offer and that while the offer was still existing, it was accepted without any qualification. Only then can it be said that both parties have assented to the terms of the contract, and only then is each party bound by the obligations stated in the contract.

A.   REQUIREMENTS OF AN OFFER

An **offer** expresses the willingness of the offeror to enter into a contractual agreement regarding a particular subject. It is a promise that is conditional upon an act, a forbearance, or a return promise that is given in exchange for the promise or its performance.

§ 13:1 CONTRACTUAL INTENTION

To constitute an offer, the offeror must intend to create a legal obligation or must appear to intend to do so. This intent may be shown by conduct. For example, when one party signs a written contract and sends it to the other party, such action is an offer to enter into a contract on the terms of the writing.[1]

There is no contract when a social invitation is made or when an offer is made in jest or excitement because a reasonable person would not regard such an offer as indicating a willingness to enter into a binding agreement.

(a) INVITATION TO NEGOTIATE. The first statement made by one of two persons is not necessarily an offer. In many instances, there may be a preliminary discussion or an *invitation* by one party to the other to *negotiate* or to make an offer. Thus, an inquiry by a school as to whether a teacher wished to continue the following year was merely a survey or invitation to negotiate and was not an offer that could be accepted. Therefore, the teacher's positive response did not create a contract.[2]

The *Four Seasons Hotels* case turned on whether a letter between the parties showed contractual intent.

---

[1] Jaffe v Gibbons (App) 290 SC 468, 351 SE2d 343 (1986).

[2] Knipmeyer v Diocese of Alexandria (La App) 492 So 2d 550 (1986).

FOUR SEASONS HOTELS LIMITED v VINNIK AND JENKINS
130 App Div 2d 538, 515 NYS2d 1 (1987).

The 795 Fifth Avenue Corporation owned the Pierre Hotel in New York City. The Four Seasons Hotel wished to lease the Pierre Hotel from 795. However, 53 rooms of the hotel were owned by Daniel Vinnik and Dale Jenkins. Four Seasons began negotiation with them to lease their rooms. Finally, Four Seasons sent them a letter offering terms to which they agreed. Later Vinnik and Jenkins claimed that this letter did not constitute a binding contract. Four Seasons brought suit against them, claiming a breach of contract. Vinnick and Jenkins filed a motion to dismiss on the ground that there was no contract. This motion was overruled, and they appealed.

WALLACH, J. . . . Four Seasons, through its then chairman and president, Mr. Sharp, made contact with Vinnik and Jenkins, and entered into negotiations with them for a lease of their rooms. . . .

The proposal came in the form of a letter from Sharp to Vinnik, dated March 10, 1980. . . . The letter then stated . . . that if Four Seasons' revised proposal was accepted by 795 substantially as submitted, then

> We would agree to enter into a lease of the Suites with you at a rental structured so that in one form or another, as compared with the rental structure you have today, you will effectively receive $450,000 annually to be increased according to the C.P.I. We also will assume the payment of all other operating and maintenance costs. . . . The remaining terms and conditions of our lease with you for the Suites would be finalized after completion of our negotiations with 795 Fifth Avenue Corporation so that to the greatest extent possible the leases would be consistent with each other. . . .
>
> If you are in agreement with the proposals set out above, kindly sign the enclosed copy of this letter in the space indicated and return same to us.

Vinnik signed the letter on behalf of himself and Jenkins in the space indicated, a signature line above which were typed the words "Accepted and Agreed"; . . . When Four Seasons was awarded the Pierre contract, Vinnik and Jenkins refused to lease their rooms to it. . . .

The action [is based] on the theory that the March 10 letter is a contract to enter into a lease. . . .

There can be no contract absent a mutual intent to be bound. Whether such intent exists is a mixed question of law and fact. This means that the question is to be decided by the court if determinable from the language employed in the written instrument, and if not so determinable — if resort must be had to disputed evidence or inferences outside the written words of the instrument — then by the finder of the facts. . . .

In determining whether the parties intended to enter into a contract, an objective test is generally to be applied. "This means that the manifestation of a party's intention rather than the actual or real intention is ordinarily controlling, for a contract is an obligation attached, by the mere force of law, to certain acts of the parties, usually words, which ordinarily accompany and represent a known intent." (21 NY Jur2d, Contracts, § 29). In considering these manifestations of intent, the fact finder should not put disproportionate emphasis on any single act, phrase or other expression but, instead, on the totality of these, given the attendant circumstances, the situation of the parties, and the objectives they were striving to attain.

Relevant on any inquiry concerning contractual intent are signed writings. Sometimes a writing unequivocally reveals the parties' intent to form a binding contract; at other times its sense shows only an intent to continue negotiations. A writing can also indicate that the parties have, in piecemeal fashion, reached agreement on some terms but not on others, in which case there is a contract if the matters left open were not deemed material by the parties, and there is not a contract if the matters left open were deemed material. Definiteness is essential, but only as to material terms. A contract does not necessarily lack all effect merely because it expresses the idea that something is left to future agreement. Should the fact finder find that "the parties have completed their negotiations of what they regard as essential elements, and performance has begun on the good faith understanding that agreement on the unsettled matters will follow, the court will find and enforce a contract even though the parties have expressly left these other elements for future negotiation and agreement, if some objective method of determination is available, independent of either party's mere wish or desire. Such objective criteria may be found in the agreement itself, commercial practice or other usage and custom. If the contract can be rendered certain and complete, by reference to something certain, the court will fill in the gaps" (*Metro-Goldwyn-Mayer, Inc. v. Scheider*, 40 N.Y.2d 1069, 1070-1071, 392 N.Y.S.2d 252, 360 N.E.2d 930, quoting Fein, J. at Trial Term, 75 Misc.2d 418, 422). The writing, other writings, usage and custom, the parties' situation, objectives, acts and utterances — a wide array of facts and circumstances can be relevant, and is admissible, in deciding whether gaps in a purported agreement are material, and, if not, how they should be filled in. . . .

Turning to defendants' motion to dismiss . . . , the March 10 letter cannot be condemned as an agreement to agree simply because it does not contain most of the terms usually found in a formal lease. Rather, to be enforceable as a contract, the letter need contain only the terms deemed material by the parties to their bargain. From a mere inspection of the letter, it cannot be said as a matter of law that anything material was left open to be agreed upon thereafter. The method of payment, for example, was apparently of no concern to the parties, for this was to be worked out "in one form or another". And it does not unduly strain the ordinary significance of the word "finalize", given its context, to say that it indicates that negotiations on matters of substance had been completed, and that all that remained to be done was to prepare a formal lease consistent with the 795/Four Seasons lease to be entered into should Four Seasons be awarded the Pierre contract.

[Judgment affirmed]

QUESTIONS

1. What essential element of a contract was involved in the *Four Seasons* case?
2. Who determines whether the element stated in your answer to Question 1 exists?
3. In determining whether the element stated in your answer to Question 1 exists, does the court apply a subjective test or an objective test?

Ordinarily a seller sending out circulars or catalogs listing prices is not regarded as making an offer to sell at those prices, but as merely indicating a willingness to consider an offer made by a buyer on those terms. The reason for this rule is, in part, the practical consideration that since a seller does not have an unlimited supply of any commodity, the seller cannot possibly intend to make a contract with everyone who sees the circular. The same principle is applied to merchandise that is displayed with price tags in stores or store windows and to most advertisements. A For Sale advertisement in a newspaper is merely an invitation to negotiate and is not an offer that can be accepted by a reader of the paper, even though the seller in fact has only one of the particular item advertised.

The circumstances may be such, however, that even a newspaper advertisement constitutes an offer. Thus, the seller may make an offer when the advertisement states that specific items will be sold at a clearance sale at the prices listed and adds the words *first-come, first-served*.

Quotations of prices, even when sent on request, are, likewise, not offers in the absence of previous dealings between the parties or the existence of a trade custom that would give the recipient of the quotation reason to believe that an offer was being made. Whether a price quotation is to be treated as an offer or merely an invitation to negotiate is a question of the intent of the party making such quotations. Although sellers are not bound by quotations and price tags, they will, as a matter of goodwill, ordinarily make every effort to deliver the merchandise at those prices.[3]

In some instances, it is apparent that an invitation to negotiate and not an offer has been made. When construction work is done for the national government, for a state government, or for a political subdivision, statutes require that a printed statement of the work to be done be published and circulated. Contractors are invited to submit bids on the work, and the statute generally requires that the bid of the lowest responsible bidder be accepted. Such an invitation for bids is clearly an invitation to negotiate, both from its nature and from the fact that it does not specify the price to be paid for the work. The bid of each contractor is an offer, and there is no contract until the government accepts one of these bids. This procedure of advertising for bids is also commonly employed by private persons when a large construction project is involved.

In some cases, the fact that material terms are missing serves to indicate that the parties are merely negotiating and that an oral contract has not been made. When a letter or printed promotional matter of a party leaves many significant details to be worked out later, the letter or printed matter is merely an invitation to negotiate and is not an offer that may be accepted and a contract thereby formed.

(b) STATEMENT OF INTENTION. In some instances, a person may make a statement of intention but not intend to be bound by a contract. For example, when a lease does not expressly allow the tenant to terminate the lease in the case of a job transfer, the landlord might state that should the tenant be required to leave for that reason, the landlord would try to find a new tenant to take over the lease. This declaration of in-

tention does not give rise to a binding contract, and the landlord cannot be held liable for breach of contract should the landlord fail to obtain a new tenant or not even attempt to obtain a new tenant. Likewise, a statement in the handbook given to employees that "it is normal" for a particular class of employees to be reemployed after the expiration of their initial period of employment did not create any contract right requiring the employer to reemploy.[4]

(c) AGREEMENT TO MAKE A CONTRACT AT A FUTURE DATE. No contract arises when the parties merely agree that at a future date they shall consider making a contract or shall make a contract on terms to be agreed upon at that time. In such a case, neither party is under any obligation until the future contract is made. Similarly, there is no contract between the parties if essential terms are left open for future negotiation. Thus, a promise to pay a bonus or compensation to be decided upon after three months of business operation is not binding.

§ 13:2   DEFINITENESS

An offer, and the resulting contract, must be definite and certain.[5] If an offer is indefinite or vague or if an essential provision is lacking, no contract arises from an attempt to accept it. The reason is that the courts cannot tell what the parties are to do. Thus, an offer to conduct a business for such time as should be profitable is too vague to be a valid offer. The acceptance of such an offer does not result in a contract that can be enforced. Likewise, a promise to give an injured employee "suitable" employment that the employee is "able to do" is too vague to be a binding contract. A statement by a landlord to the tenant that "some day it [the rented land] will be your own" is too indefinite to be an offer, and

---

[3] Statutes prohibiting false or misleading advertising may also require adherence to advertised prices.

[4] Brumbach v Rensselaer Polytechnic Institute, 126 App Div 2d 841, 510 NYS2d 752 (1987).
[5] Seawell v Continental Cas. Co. 84 NC App 277, 352 SE2d 263 (1987).

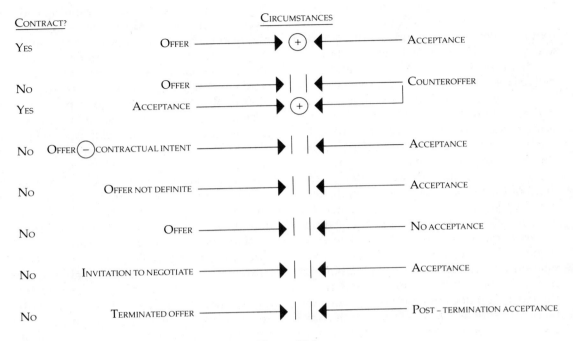

Figure 13-1
OFFER AND ACCEPTANCE

no contract for the sale of the land arises when the tenant agrees to the statement.

The law does not favor the destruction of contracts because that would go against the social force of carrying out the intent of the parties. Consequently, when it is claimed that a contract is too indefinite to be enforced, a court will do its best to find the intent of the parties and thereby reach the conclusion that the contract is not too indefinite.[6]

The question of how definite is *definite* was raised in the *Midland Hotel* case.

[6] Welsh v Northern Telecom, Inc. 85 NC App 310, 354 SE2d 746 (1987).

MIDLAND HOTEL v REUBEN H. DONNELLEY CORP.

149 Ill App 3d 53, 103 Ill Dec 742, 501 NE2d 1280 (1986)

Reuben Donnelley published a tourist guide to Chicago. The Midland Hotel made a contract with Donnelley to be listed in the guide. When the guide was published, Midland found that it was listed only under "Banquet Rooms" and not under "Hotels." Midland sued Donnelley for the profit that it claimed to have lost because it was not properly listed. The defendant raised the defense that the agreement between them was too vague to be enforced because it did not specify any particular listing of Midland, but merely stated that there would be "appropriate listing." Judgment was entered for Midland and Donnelley appealed.

SCARIANO, J. . . . Defendant, citing *Panko v. Advanced Appliance Service* (1977), 55 Ill. App.3d 301, 13 Ill.Dec. 308, 371 N.E.2d 3, argues that a contract in which it agreed simply to provide plaintiff with "appropriate" listings is too vague and ambiguous to be enforced. We disagree. Whether a contract is ambiguous is a question of law for the court. The primary object in construing a contract is to give effect to the intention of the parties, and a contract is sufficiently definite and certain if the court is able, from its terms and provisions and allowable extrinsic evidence to ascertain what the parties agreed to. Plaintiff is known as the "Midland *Hotel*," and defendant's offer was made in the hotel itself; [an executive officer of the plaintiff] testified that a few days after the *Guide* was issued, the representative of defendant with whom he had originally negotiated acknowledged that failure to list the Midland under "Hotels" "was a mistake and he was sorry it happened;" and when asked whether a hotel should be listed under "Hotels", Donnelley's district sales manager testified, "You would think they should be there." Defendant argues that there are numerous other listings for the Midland that would also be appropriate, such as "Ballrooms," "Cocktail Lounges," "Coffee Shops," etc. However, plaintiff does not claim that it should have been listed under these headings as well, or that the listing under "Banquet Rooms" that it did receive was inappropriate. It is not necessary that a contract provide for every collateral matter and every future contingency to be sufficiently definite to be enforceable. We conclude that an offer to list the Midland Hotel in the "appropriate" places is not so ambiguous as to render the contract unenforceable.

[Judgment affirmed on vagueness issue]

QUESTIONS

1. Is the term *appropriate listing* sufficiently definite to be enforced?
2. What social force is involved in cases raising the question of the definiteness of the agreement?
3. How could the controversy in the *Midland Hotel* case have been avoided?

(a) DEFINITE BY INCORPORATION. An offer and the resulting contract that by themselves may appear "too indefinite" may be made definite by reference to another writing. For example, a lease agreement that was too vague by itself was made definite because the parties agreed that the lease should follow the standard form with which both were familiar. An agreement may also be made definite by reference to the prior dealings of the parties and to trade practices.

(b) IMPLIED TERMS. Although an offer must be definite and certain, not all of its terms need be expressed. Some of the omitted terms may be implied by law. For example, an offer "to pay $50 for a watch" does not state the terms of payment. A court, however, would not condemn this provision as too vague, but would hold that it required that cash be paid and that the payment be made upon delivery of the watch. Likewise, terms may be implied from conduct. As an illustration, where the borrowed money was given to the borrower by a check on which there was written the word *loan*, the act of the borrower in indorsing the check constituted an agreement to repay the amount of the check.

(c) DIVISIBLE CONTRACTS. When the

agreement consists of two or more parts and calls for corresponding performances of each part by the parties, the agreement is a **divisible contract.** Thus, in a promise to buy several separate articles at different prices at the same time, the agreement may be regarded as separate or divisible promises for the articles. When a contract contains a number of provisions or performances to be rendered, the question arises whether the parties intended merely a group of separate, divisible contracts or whether it was to be a package deal so that complete performance by each party is essential.

(d) UNIMPORTANT, VAGUE DETAILS IGNORED. If a term of an agreement that is too vague is not important, it may sometimes be ignored. If the balance of the agreement is definite, there can then be a binding contract. For example, where the parties agreed that one of them would manage a motel that was being constructed for the other, and where it was agreed that the contract would begin to run before the completion of the construction, the management contract did not fail because it did not specify any date on which it was to commence. It was apparent that the exact date was not essential and could not be determined at the time when the contract was made.

(e) EXCEPTIONS TO DEFINITENESS. The law has come to recognize certain situations where the practical necessity of doing business makes it desirable to have a contract, yet the situation is such that it is either impossible or undesirable to adopt definite terms in advance. In these cases, the indefinite term is often tied to the concept of good-faith performance or to some independent factor that will be definitely ascertainable at some time in the future, for example, market price, cost to complete, or production requirements. Thus, the law recognizes binding contracts in the case of a contract to buy all requirements of the buyer from the seller and the contract of a producer to sell the entire production or output to a

given buyer. These are binding contracts although they do not state the exact quantity of goods that are to be bought or sold. Contracts are also binding although they run for an indefinite period of time; or require a buyer to pay the costs plus a percentage of costs as profit; or require one person to supply professional services as needed.

An agreement is not made too indefinite to be binding because it does not specify exact prices or quantities. When these relate to the future or future events, it is obvious that the agreement cannot be precise. In such case, an agreement is deemed sufficiently definite if it specifies a standard or formula by which the variable factors are to be determined.[7]

§ 13:3   COMMUNICATION OF OFFER TO THE OFFEREE

The offer must be communicated to the offeree. Otherwise the offeree cannot accept, even though knowledge of the offer has been indirectly acquired. Internal management communications of an enterprise that are not intended for outsiders or employees do not constitute offers and cannot be accepted by them. Sometimes, particularly in the case of unilateral contracts, the offeree performs the act called for by the offeror without knowing of the offer's existence. Such performance does not constitute an acceptance.[8] Thus, without knowing that a reward is offered for the arrest of a particular criminal, a person may arrest the criminal. In most states, if that person learns thereafter that a reward has been offered for the arrest, the reward cannot be recovered.[9]

7   Lessley v Hardage, 240 Kan 72, 727 P2d 440 (1986).
8   Richard D. Price, Jr., & Associates v East Peoria, 154 Ill App 3d 725, 107 Ill Dec 564, 507 NE2d 228 (1987).
9   With respect to the offeror, it should not make any difference as a practical matter whether the services were rendered with or without knowledge of the existence of the offer. Only a small number of states have adopted this view, however.

Not only must the offer be communicated, but it must be communicated by the offeror or at the offeror's direction.

B.   TERMINATION OF OFFER

An offer gives the offeree power to bind the offeror by contract. This power does not last forever, and the law specifies that under certain circumstances the power ends or is terminated.

Once the offer is terminated, the offeree cannot revive it. If an attempt is made to accept the offer after it has been terminated, this attempt is meaningless, unless the original offeror is willing to regard the late acceptance as a new offer, which the original offeror then accepts.

Offers may be terminated in any one of the following ways:

(1) revocation of the offer by the offeror,
(2) counteroffer by offeree,
(3) rejection of offer by offeree,
(4) lapse of time,
(5) death or disability of either party, and
(6) subsequent illegality.

§ 13:4   REVOCATION OF THE OFFER BY THE OFFEROR

Ordinarily the offeror can revoke the offer before it is accepted. If this is done, the offeree cannot create a contract by accepting the revoked offer. Thus, the bidder at an auction sale may withdraw (revoke) a bid (offer) before it is accepted. The auctioneer cannot thereafter accept that bid.

An ordinary offer may be revoked at any time before it is accepted, even though the offeror has expressly promised that the offer will be good for a stated period and that period has not yet expired. It may also be revoked even though the offeror has expressly promised to the offeree that the offer will not be revoked before a specified later date.

(a) WHAT CONSTITUTES A REVOCATION. No particular form or no particular words are required to constitute a revocation. Any words indicating the offeror's termination of the offer are sufficient. A notice sent to the offeree that the property which is the subject of the offer has been sold to a third person is a revocation of the offer. An order for goods by a customer, which is an offer to purchase at certain prices, is revoked by a notice to the seller of the cancellation of the order, provided such notice is communicated before the order is accepted.

(b) COMMUNICATION OF REVOCATION. A revocation of an offer is ordinarily effective only when it is made known to the offeree. Until it is communicated to the offeree, directly or indirectly, the offeree has reason to believe that there is still an offer which may be accepted; and the offeree may rely on this belief.

Except in a few states, a letter or telegram revoking an offer made to a particular offeree is not effective until received by the offeree. It is not a revocation at the time it is written by the offeror nor even when it is mailed or dispatched. A written revocation is effective, however, when it is delivered to the offeree's agent, or to the offeree's residence or place of business under such circumstances that the offeree may be reasonably expected to be aware of its receipt.

It is ordinarily held that there is a sufficient communication of the revocation when the offeree learns indirectly of the offeror's revocation. This is particularly true in a land sale, when the seller-offeror, after making an offer to sell the land to the offeree, sells the land to a third person, and the offeree indirectly learns of such sale and necessarily realizes that the seller cannot perform the original offer and therefore must be deemed to have revoked it.

If the offeree accepts an offer before it is effectively revoked, a valid contract is created. Thus, there may be a contract when the offeree mails or telegraphs an acceptance without knowing that a letter of revocation has already been mailed.

When an offer is made to the public, it may usually be revoked in the same manner in which it was made. For example, an offer of a reward that is made to the general public by an advertisement in a newspaper may be revoked in the same manner. A member of the public cannot recover the amount of the reward by thereafter performing the act for which the reward was originally offered. This exception is made to the rule requiring communication of revocation because it would be impossible for the offeror to communicate the fact that the offer was revoked to every member of the general public who knows of the offer. The public revocation of the public offer is effective, even though it is not seen by the person attempting to accept the original offer.

(c) OPTION CONTRACTS. An **option contract** is a binding promise to keep an offer open for a stated period of time or until a specified date. This requires that the promisor receive consideration, that is, something, such as a sum of money, as the price for the promise to keep the offer open. In other words, the option is a contract to refrain from revoking an offer.

When an option contract recites the giving of a specified consideration, but such consideration in fact was never paid, the option contract is merely an offer and may be revoked at any time prior to acceptance.[10]

(d) FIRM OFFERS. As another exception to the rule that an offer can be revoked at any time before acceptance, statutes in some states provide that an offeror cannot revoke an offer prior to its expiration when the offeror makes a **firm offer,** that is, an offer that states that it is to be irrevocable, or irrevocable for a stated period of time. Under the Uniform Commercial Code, this doctrine of firm offers applies to a merchant's signed, written offer to buy or sell goods, but with a maximum of three months on its period of irrevocability.[11]

(e) DETRIMENTAL RELIANCE. There is growing authority that when the offeror foresees that the offeree will rely on the offer's remaining open, the offeror is obligated to keep the offer open for a reasonable time.

The concept of detrimental reliance can thus prevent the revocation of an offer. This was the issue in the *Arango Construction* case.

---

[10] Hamilton Bancshares, Inc. v Leroy, 131 Ill App 3d 907, 87 Ill Dec 86, 476 NE2d 788 (1985).

[11] UCC § 2-205.

ARANGO CONSTRUCTION CO. V SUCCESS ROOFING, INC.

46 Wash App 314, 730 P2d 720 (1986)

Arango Construction Company wanted to do certain construction work for the United States government. In preparing its bid, Arango phoned Success Roofing to see what it would charge for doing the roofing work involved. Success offered to do the work for a specified price. Arango then made a bid to the government. Its bid was accepted. Thereafter Success notified Arango that it was withdrawing its bid to do the roofing work because it had made a significant mistake in its calculation. Arango claimed it could not do this because Arango had used the bid in making its own bid to the United States. Arango sued Success for damages caused by the revocation of its bid. From a judgment for Success, Arango appealed.

COLEMAN, J. . . . In contract law, construction bidding is treated as a unique category. Since construction bidding deadlines make the drafting of written agreements impossible, contractors must rely on oral bids. Therefore, the courts consider the subcontractor's oral bid an irrevocable offer until the general contractor has been awarded the prime contract; then the courts apply promissory estoppel to ensure that the subcontractor does not raise the bid. This concept was explained in J. Feinman, *Promissory Estoppel and Judicial Methods*, 97 Harv.L.Rev. 678, (1984).

> A recurrent example of the flexible approach to promise is found in the courts' treatment of construction bidding cases, which have repeatedly generated important promissory estoppel decision. In the typical case, a general contractor preparing to bid on a construction project receives bids on parts of the job from subcontractors and suppliers. The general then prepares its own bid on the basis of the lowest reliable subcontract bids. Subcontractors occasionally miscalculate, in part because they often compute their bids and telephone them to the general only hours before the general's bid is due. A subcontractor may also intentionally submit a low bid in the hope of receiving the contract and renegotiating the price. Conflict typically arises when, after the general has calculated and submitted its own bid and won the contract, a subcontractor notifies the general that the subcontractor has made an error or an intentionally low bid and refuses to perform.
>
> Under traditional contract analysis, the subcontractor could withdraw with impunity, because its bid was regarded as an offer, revocable until accepted, to enter into a bilateral contract. In the leading case of *Drennan v. Star Paving Co.*, [51 Cal.2d 409, 333 P.2d 757 (1958),] however, Justice Traynor held that the business context of the bid required that promissory estoppel apply to make the subcontractor's offer irrevocable until the general contractor had an opportunity to accept after being awarded the prime contract. The general's acceptance of the subcontractor's bid then created a traditional bilateral contract, for breach of which the subcontractor was required to pay as damages the difference between its bid and the higher price the general had to pay another subcontractor to perform the work. Cases since *Drennan* have held that promissory estoppel normally binds a subcontractor to the terms of its bid. Although the subcontractor does not make an explicit promise to keep its bid open, the court infers such a promise. . . .

This court has accepted the *Drennan* rationale in *Ferrer v. Taft Structural, Inc.*, 21 Wash.App. 832, 587 P.2d 177 (1978).

> This concept [promissory estoppel] applies readily to the unique situation of a subcontractor and a general contractor, as exists here. A subcontractor submits a bid to the general contractor, knowing the general cannot accept the bid as an offer immediately, but must first incorporate it into the general's offer to the prospective employer. The general contractor incorporates the bid in reliance upon the subcontractor to perform as promised, should the prospective employer accept the general's offer. Thus, the elements of predictable and justifiable reliance and change of position are satisfied. Numerous courts and authorities have opined that a subcontractor's bid upon which a general contractor relies should be deemed irrevocable for a reasonable time pursuant to the doctrine of promissory estoppel.
>
> Thus, had Taft refused to perform following the award of the contract to Halvorson, a breach of contract action based on Taft's original bid would have been appropriate.

(Citations omitted.) *Ferrer*, at 835, 587 P.2d 177.

Thus, as a matter of law, a subcontractor's bid is considered an irrevocable offer until the award of the prime contract; then, the general contractor's acceptance of the bid results in a bilateral contract. . . . Thus, if the subcontractor refuses to perform following the award of the contract, the general contractor may recover damages under the doctrine of promissory estoppel. *Ferrer*, at 835, 587 P.2d 177.

The *Ferrer* court listed the five elements of promissory estoppel:

> The prerequisites for an action based on promissory estoppel, a doctrine well recognized in this jurisdiction, have been stated as follows:
> (1) A promise which (2) the promisor should reasonably expect to cause the promisee to change his position and (3) which does cause the promisee to change his position (4) justifiably relying upon the promise, in such a manner that (5) injustice can be avoided only by enforcement of the promise.

(Citation omitted.) *Ferrer*, at 834, 587 P.2d 177.

Elements (1) through (3) are met in this case. Success's bid was a promise. Success could reasonably expect that promise to cause Arango to change position by including the Success bid in Arango's prime bid. Success confirmed its bid 2 days after it was given, and Arango informed Success that it would be including that bid in its prime bid to be submitted 13 days later. Arango did include Success's bid in its prime bid, thereby changing its position.

The only element of promissory estoppel in dispute is whether Arango justifiably relied on Success's bid. Success contends that as a prudent and experienced general contractor, Arango should have known that Success's bid was too low for the job involved. . . . Success had to present evidence supporting this assertion. Success, however, has submitted no evidence that Arango should have known. The only other bid found in the record was from Tin Benders. Its bid was for $38,500 . . . as compared to the $34,659 bid by Success. There is nothing in the record to support an inference that Arango knew or should have known that Success had made a mistake. . . .

The judgment of the trial court is reversed and the cause remanded with instruction to enter judgment in favor of Arango on its complaint for damages.

[Judgment reversed and action remanded]

QUESTIONS

1. Was the decision in the *Arango Construction* case in harmony with general contract law? Explain.
2. What social forces are advanced by the decision? Explain.
3. How could the problem in the *Arango Construction* case have been avoided?

---

§ 13:5   COUNTEROFFER BY OFFEREE

Ordinarily if *A* makes an offer, such as to sell a used automobile to *B* for $1,000, and *B* in reply makes an offer to buy at $750, the original offer is terminated. *B* is in effect saying, "I refuse your original offer, but in its place I make a different offer."

Such an offer by the offeree is known as a **counteroffer.**

The making of a counteroffer terminates the offeree's power to accept the offer unless the intent is manifested that the counteroffer should not have the effect of a rejection.[12]

[12] Thurmond v Wieser (Tex App) 699 SW2d 680 (1985).

Counteroffers are not limited to offers that directly contradict the original offers. Any departure from, or addition to, the original offer is a counteroffer, even though the original offer was silent as to the point added by the counteroffer. For example, when the offeree stated that the offer was accepted and added that time was of the essence, the acceptance was a counteroffer because the original offer had been silent on that point.

§ 13:6   REJECTION OF OFFER BY OFFEREE

If the offeree rejects the offer and communicates this rejection to the offeror, the offer is terminated, even though the period for which the offeror agreed to keep the offer open has not yet expired. It may be that the offeror is willing to renew the offer; but unless this is done, there is no longer any offer for the offeree to accept.

§ 13:7   LAPSE OF TIME

When the offer states that it is open until a particular date, the offer terminates on that date if it has not yet been accepted. This is particularly so where the offeror declares that the offer shall be void after the expiration of the specified time. Such limitations are strictly construed. When a specified time limitation is imposed on an option, the option cannot be exercised after the expiration of that time, without regard to whether the late exercise was made within what would have been held a reasonable time if no time period had been specified.[13] It has been held that the buyer's attempt to exercise an option one day late had no effect.

When the offeree attempts to accept after the deadline for acceptance has passed, the act of the offeree has no effect as an acceptance but instead is the making of a counteroffer. If the original offeror accepts this counteroffer, there is a contract.[14] If the counteroffer is not accepted, there is no contract.

If the offer does not specify a time, it will terminate after the lapse of a reasonable time. What constitutes a reasonable time depends upon the circumstances of each case; that is, upon the nature of the subject matter, the nature of the market in which it is sold, the time of the year, and other factors of supply and demand. If a commodity is perishable in nature or fluctuates greatly in value, the reasonable time will be much shorter than if the subject matter is a staple article. An offer to sell a harvested crop of tomatoes would expire within a very short time. When a seller purports to accept an offer after it has lapsed by the expiration of time, the seller's acceptance is merely a counteroffer and does not create a contract unless that offer is accepted by the buyer.

§ 13:8   DEATH OR DISABILITY OF EITHER PARTY

If either the offeror or the offeree dies or becomes insane before the offer is accepted, it is automatically terminated.

§ 13:9   SUBSEQUENT ILLEGALITY

If the performance of the contract becomes illegal after the offer is made, the offer is terminated. Thus, if an offer is made to sell alcoholic liquors but a law prohibiting such sales is enacted before the offer is accepted, the offer is terminated.

C.   ACCEPTANCE OF OFFER

Once the offeror expresses or appears to express a willingness to enter into a contractual agreement with the offeree, the latter may accept the offer. An *acceptance*

[13]   Watson v Hatch (Utah) 728 P2d 989 (1986).

[14]   Field v Alexander & Alexander, ___ Ind App ___, 503 NE2d 627 (1987).

is the assent of the offeree to the terms of the offer. No particular form of words or mode of expression is required, but there must be a clear expression that the offeree agrees to be bound by the terms of the offer.

§ 13:10   PRIVILEGE OF OFFEREE

Ordinarily the offeree may refuse to accept an offer. If there is no acceptance, by definition there is no contract. The fact that there had been a series of contracts between the parties and that one party's offer had always been accepted by the other does not create any legal obligation to continue to accept subsequent offers.

Certain partial exceptions exist to the privilege of the offeree to refuse to accept an offer.

(a) PLACES OF PUBLIC ACCOMMODATION AND PUBLIC UTILITIES. Places of public accommodation and public utilities are under a duty to serve any fit person. Consequently, when a fit person offers to register at a hotel, that is, offers to hire a room, the hotel has the obligation to accept the offer and to enter into a contract for the renting of the room. There is no duty to accept on the part of the hotel, however, unless the person is fit and the hotel has space available.

(b) ANTIDISCRIMINATION. When offers are solicited from members of the general public, an offer generally may not be rejected because of the race, nationality, religion, or color of the offeror. If the solicitor of the offer is willing to enter into a contract to rent, sell, or employ, antidiscrimination laws compel the solicitor to accept an offer from any otherwise-fit person.

(c) CONSUMER PROTECTION. Statutes and regulations designed to protect consumers from false advertising may require a seller to accept an offer from a customer to purchase advertised goods and may impose a penalty for an unjustified refusal.

§ 13:11   EFFECT OF ACCEPTANCE

When an offer has been accepted, a binding agreement or contract is created, assuming that all of the other elements of a contract are present. Thereafter, neither party can withdraw from or cancel the contract without the consent of the other party (or the existence of such facts as under the law justifies such unilateral action.) For example, when an enterprise conducts a prize contest, its offer to conduct the contest according to stated rules is accepted when an entrant sends in the entry form. The enterprise must then conduct the contest according to the announced contest rules because it is bound by a contract.[15]

§ 13:12   NATURE OF THE ACCEPTANCE

An acceptance is the offeree's manifestation of intent to enter into a binding agreement on the terms stated in the offer. In the absence of a contrary requirement in the offer, an acceptance may be indicated by an informal "OK," by a mere affirmative nod of the head, or, in the case of an offer of a unilateral contract, by performing the act called for. However, while the acceptance of an offer may be shown by conduct, it must be very clear that the offeree intended to accept the offer.

The acceptance must be absolute and unconditional. It must accept just what is offered. If the offeree changes any terms of the offer or adds any new term, there is no acceptance because the offeree does not agree to what was offered.

What constituted an acceptance was the question involved in the *Holman Erection Company* case.

---

[15]   First Texas Savings Ass'n. v Jergins (Tex App) 705 SW2d 390 (1986).

Holman Erection Co. v Orville E. Madsen & Sons, Inc.

—— Minn ——, 330 NW2d 693 (1983)

The city of Moorhead advertised for bids for the construction of a waste-water treatment facility. Orville E. Madsen submitted a bid. In the bid it listed Holman Erection Co. as the subcontractor for the steel work. The city awarded the contract to Madsen. Madsen then switched from Holman to another subcontractor in order to satisfy the contract provision that contractors should make an effort to comply with the federal Minority Business Enterprise (MBE) regulation. Holman then sued Madsen for breach of contract, claiming that its bid had been accepted by Madsen when it was included in Madsen's bid submitted to the city. From a judgment for Madsen, Holman appealed.

YETKA, J. . . . Appellant Holman argues that a binding contractual relationship was created between it and Madsen when Madsen utilized Holman's sub-bid in its general bid for the waste treatment plant project and listed Holman as a proposed subcontractor for steel erection work. Does the act of listing Holman in the general bid constitute an acceptance of Holman's offer to do the work when no other communication occurred after the offer and prior to the substitution of a different subcontractor? We think not.

To constitute an acceptance, Madsen's acts must be deemed a manifestation of assent when evaluated under an objective standard. The form of the assent, whether it be written, oral, or by conduct, is not relevant as long as objective standards are applied and the essential finding of mutual assent is made. The Restatement (Second) of Contracts § 19 (1979) provides:

> (1) The manifestation of assent may be made wholly or partly by written or spoken words or by other acts or by failure to act.
> (2) The conduct of a party is not effective as a manifestation of his assent unless he intends to engage in the conduct and knows or has reason to know that the other party may infer from his conduct that he assents. . . .

Holman argues that listing Holman as a subcontractor, as required by the awarding authority, constitutes an acceptance . . .

Appellant's argument flies in the face of a large body of precedent holding that no contract is formed by the listing of a subcontractor in a general contractor's bid. There is no case in Minnesota that deals precisely with the issue presented. This court has held, however, that the subcontractor may be bound to his bid as submitted to the general contractor by operation of promissory estoppel. . . .

In Minnesota, as well as most other jurisdictions, the subcontractor may be obligated to perform by application of promissory estoppel. The general, however, remains free to avoid the listed subcontractor and negotiate with other subcontractors. This one-sided arrangement seems, on its face, unfair. Why should one party be bound and other not? A close examination of the construction business and the nature of the bidding process, however, reveals several justifications for the unequal treatment of generals and subcontractors.

First, the reason a subcontractor is bound by its bid is the existence of justifiable reliance by the general on the subcontractor's price for specified work. The general makes his bid after gathering and evaluating a number of subcontract bids. Once the general wins the prime contract from the awarding authority, he is bound to his own bid. For the subcontractor to be able to refuse to perform would subject the general to a financial detriment.

In contrast, the subcontractor does not rely on the general and suffers no detriment. A subcontractor submits bids to all or most of the general contractors that it knows are bidding on a project. The subcontractor receives invitations to bid from some generals and submits bids to others without invitation. The time and expense involved in preparing the bid is not segregated to any particular general. The total cost is part of the overhead of doing business. The same bid is submitted to each general. Thus, whether or not any particular general wins the contract is of little or no concern to the subcontractor. The subcontractor engages in the same work and expense in preparing its bid regardless of who wins the general contract and whether the subcontractor wins the contract on which it bid. No further expense is incurred until a formal agreement is reached with the general and actual work commences. Clearly, the promissory estoppel concept is not applicable in this situation. . . . With no detrimental reliance, there can be no estoppel claim. Ample justification exists for binding the subcontractor and not binding the general. The two situations are very different.

Second, the nature of the bidding process compels allowing the general sufficient leeway to maintain its flexibility in executing subcontracts and selecting the subcontractors it will hire for a project. Typically, subcontractors submit their bids only a few hours before the general bid must be submitted to the awarding authority. The general's representatives take the bids over the telephone and hurriedly compile their own bid. This period of time is hectic and complex. The bids received consist of the contract price and a listing of work included. Specifics are left for future negotiation and clarification. . . .

The bidding process puts the subcontractor and the general in very different positions as to the content of the subcontract. The subcontractors have the luxury of preparing their bids on their own timetable, subject only to the deadline for submitting their bids to the general contractors. The same bid goes to all the general contractors and covers the same work. The generals, on the other hand, are dealing with all the various construction aspects of the project and with numerous potential subcontractors. They compile their bids, as the various subcontractor bids are received, within a few hours of the deadline for submission of the prime bid. Specifics are necessarily given less than thorough consideration and are left for future negotiations. Finally, the lowest dollar amount bidder is not always the one chosen to do the work or the one listed as the potential subcontractor. Reliability, quality of work, and capability to handle the job are all considerations weighed by the general in choosing subcontractors. MBE regulations requiring an effort to use a percentage of minority contractors are another potential consideration.

Binding general contractors to subcontractors because a particular bid was listed in the general bid or was utilized in making the bid would remove a considerable degree of needed flexibility. The present case illustrates the consequences quite well. Because the project involved was a public project, MBE regulations required that an effort be made to use minority contractors. When Madsen began to put the specifics of the project together, it was forced to juggle the subcontracts in order to comply with the MBE regulations. Van Knight, the subcontractor chosen instead of Holman, qualified as a minority business and offered to supply materials and supplies not included in Holman's bid. Despite a slightly higher cost, Madsen selected Van Knight as the steel erection subcontractor.

If Madsen was bound to the bids listed in its prime bid, there is a possibility that the contract would have been lost due to failure to comply with MBE regulations. The next highest qualifying bidder would then have been selected, to the awarding authority's greater expense and to Madsen's detriment. Such a result imposes a greater cost on the project and a loss to the general contractor. The result under the prevailing law in most jurisdictions, and which we adopt here, would not impose any additional expenses on the rejected subcontractor.

A decision in favor of the subcontractor on this issue would place Minnesota in a minority position as perhaps the sole state to hold that a contract is formed by the mere listing of a subcontractor in a general contractor's bid to the awarding authority. Although supplying some certainty and symmetry to the construction industry, such a decision would also impose a rigidity on the process and result in greater cost to awarding authorities and potential detriment to general contractors. If such a change is to take place, it is one properly brought before the legislature.

[Judgment affirmed]

QUESTIONS

1. Why does the court hold that there was no acceptance when the subcontractor's bid was listed in the general contractor's bid?
2. Does promissory estoppel bar the general contractor from rejecting a subcontractor's bid after being awarded the general contract?
3. How would the *Holman* case have been decided if there were no requirement of employing minority workers?

Where the offeree does not accept the offer exactly as made, the addition of any qualification coverts the "acceptance" into a counteroffer, and no contract arises unless such a counteroffer is accepted by the original offeror. The addition of new terms in the acceptance, however, does not always mean that the attempted acceptance fails. The acceptance is still unqualified if the new terms are merely those that (1) would be implied by law as part of the offer; (2) con-stitute a mere request; or (3) relate to a mere clerical detail.

§ 13:13   WHO MAY ACCEPT

An offer may be accepted only by the person to whom it is directed. If anyone else attempts to accept it, no agreement or contract with that person arises.

If the offer is directed, not to a specified individual, but to a particular class, it may be accepted by anyone within that class. If the offer is made to the public at large, it may be accepted by any member of the public at large who has knowledge of the existence of the offer.

When a person to whom an offer was not made attempts to accept it, the attempted acceptance has the effect of an offer. If the original offeror is willing to accept this offer, a binding contract arises. If the original offeror does not accept the new offer, there is no contract.

§ 13:14 MANNER OF ACCEPTANCE

The acceptance must conform to any conditions expressed in the offer concerning the manner of acceptance. When the offeror specifies that there must be a written acceptance, no contract arises when the offeree makes an oral acceptance. If the offeror calls for an acceptance by a specified date, a late acceptance has no effect. When an acceptance is required by return mail, it is usually held that the letter of acceptance must be mailed the same day that the offer was received by the offeree. If the offer specifies that the acceptance be made by the performance of an act by the offeree, the latter cannot accept by making a promise to do the act but must actually perform it.

When a person accepts services offered by another and it reasonably appears that compensation was expected, the acceptance of the services without any protest constitutes an acceptance of the offer, and a contract exists for the payment for such services.

When the offeror has specified a particular manner of acceptance, the offeree cannot accept in any other way. However, acceptance in some other way is effective (1) if the manner of acceptance specified was merely a suggested alternative and was not clearly the exclusive method of acceptance, or (2) if the offeror has proceeded on the basis that there had been an effective acceptance.

(a) SILENCE AS ACCEPTANCE. In most cases, the offeree's silence and failure to act cannot be regarded as an acceptance. Ordinarily the offeror is not permitted to frame an offer in such a way as to make the silence and inaction of the offeree operate as an acceptance.[16]

In the case of prior dealings between the parties, as in a record or book club, the offeree may have a duty to reject an offer expressly, and the offeree's silence may be regarded as an acceptance.

(b) UNORDERED GOODS AND TICKETS. When a seller writes to a person with whom the seller has not had any prior dealings that, unless notified to the contrary, specified merchandise will be sent to be paid for at stated prices, there is no acceptance if the recipient of the letter ignores the offer and does nothing. The silence of the person receiving the letter is not an acceptance, and the sender, as a reasonable person, should recognize that none was intended.

This rule applies to all kinds of goods, books, magazines, and tickets sent through the mail when they have not been ordered. The fact that the items are not returned does not mean that they have been accepted; that is, the offeree is neither required to pay for nor return the items. If desired, the recipient of the unordered goods may write "Return to Sender" on the unopened package and put the package back into the mail without any additional postage. This is not required, and the Postal Reorganization Act of 1970 provides that the person who receives unordered mailed merchandise from a commercial (noncharitable) sender has the right "to retain, use, discard, or dispose of it in any manner the recipient sees fit without any obligation whatsoever to the sender."[17] It provides further that any unordered merchandise that is mailed must have attached to it a clear and conspicuous statement of the recipient's rights to treat the goods in this manner.

[16] Club Chain of Manhattan, Ltd. v Christopher & Seventh Gourmet, Ltd. 74 App Div2d 277, 427 NYS2d 627 (1980).
[17] Federal Postal Reorganization Act § 3009.

§ 13:15 Communication of Acceptance

If the offeree accepts the offer, must the offeror be notified? The answer depends upon the nature of the offer.

If the offeror makes an offer of a unilateral contract, communication of acceptance is ordinarily not necessary. In such a case, the offeror calls for a completed or accomplished act. If that act is performed by the offeree with knowledge of the offer, the offer is accepted without any further action by way of notifying the offeror. As a practical matter, there will eventually be some notice to the offeror because the offeree who has performed the act will ask the offeror to pay for the performance that has been rendered.

If the offer pertains to a bilateral contract, an acceptance is not effective unless communicated.[18] The acceptance must be communicated directly to the offeror or the offeror's agent.

The *Rothenbuecher* case raised the question whether there was an acceptance when the offeree signed a written offer.

[18]   Rosin v First Bank of Oak Park, 126 Ill App 3d 230, 81 Ill Dec 443, 466 NE2d 1245 (1984).

Rothenbuecher v Tockstein
88 Ill App 3d 968, 411 NE2d 92 (1980)

Tockstein offered to purchase a duplex from Rothenbuecher. The written offer stated that it was "subject to the approval of the owner [Rothenbuecher] within one day." The offer was given by Tockstein to Rothenbuecher's real estate agent on July 9. On July 10, Rothenbuecher signed the written offer and gave it back to the agent. On July 11, Tockstein was notified that the offer had been signed. On July 13, Tockstein informed the real estate agent that the offer was withdrawn. Rothenbuecher then sued Tockstein for breach of contract. The lower court held that there was a binding contract. Tockstein appealed.

HARRISON, J. . . . The judgment . . . is challenged upon the grounds that (1) no valid contract of sale existed between the parties under the facts presented, . . . Judgment is reversed.

Defendant [Tockstein] signed her own name and the name of her mother, Hazel B. Jones to a form contract of sale supplied by an agent of Ira E. Berry, Incorporated, a realty company, for the purchase of a duplex located at 27 and 29 Coral in or near the city of Belleville, Illinois on the evening of July 9, 1979. The parties agree that as initially signed by her, the instrument constituted an offer to purchase the property for the sum of $80,500. In conjunction with the offer, Tockstein tendered a check in the amount of $500 . . . The instrument specified that the offer to purchase was made "subject to the approval of the owner . . . within . . . one day. It was to be transmitted to the seller by his sales agent, Barbara Olsson, an employee of the Ira E. Berry Company, who had shown the property to Tockstein. Rothenbuecher testified that he returned from a trip to the Bahama Islands on the afternoon of July 10, 1979 and was presented with the written offer that evening by another employee of the realtor at which time he assented by placing his signature at the bottom of the proposed contract. It appeared that no notice of Rothenbuecher's interest in accepting the offer was communicated to the defendant at any time on July 10. Although she expressed some doubt as to the accuracy of her memory concerning the specific date, Olsson's testimony indicated that actual notice of Rothenbuecher's interest was given to the prospective buyer by telephone on July 11. During their conversation the defendant requested that an additional clause be inserted in the proposal allowing a contractor to inspect the premises in order to assure that it met with buyer's approval. This inspection was accomplished on July 13. On July 15 the defendant informed Olsson by telephone that she no longer wished to purchase the property and withdrew her offer. Two days later plaintiff filed this claim seeking [to enforce the contract]. Physical delivery of the written acceptance signed by the seller was accomplished on July 23, 1979.

. . . The mutual assent necessary to the formation of a bilateral contract, such as the one here contemplated, requires the communicated expression of a promise to purchase and an acceptance in the form of a promise to sell. (*See generally* Restatement (Second) of Contracts §§ 1, 19 (1973).) The appellant argues that no valid contract was formed under the present circumstances. We agree with that conclusion because of certain facts regarding the terms of the offer, its retraction and Rothenbuecher's failure to timely communicate acceptance.

Tockstein signed an instrument prepared by the seller's agent, thus creating the offer with which we are concerned. That offer was conditioned on "approval" by the seller within a 24-hour period. We can find no other logical meaning in the term "approval" than acceptance of the tendered offer. If it were to stand for less than acceptance, it would merely amount to a promise to consider the terms advanced as a legitimate offer. Therefore, acceptance is required in the very terms of the offer by means of a promise to perform communicated within a day. It is the essence of a valid acceptance that it be objectively manifested by or on behalf of the offeree. Otherwise an offeree's assent could remain undisclosed and while he might find the terms of an offer agreeable, he could, for example, hold assent in reserve while other offers were entertained.

. . . The Restatement defines acceptance as "a manifestation of assent" requiring the offeree to ". . . complete every act essential to the making of the promise." (Restatement (Second) of Contracts § 52(1), (3) (1973).), and concludes that

> Unless the offer provides otherwise, (a) an acceptance made in a manner and by a medium invited by an offer is operative and completes the manifestation of mutual assent *as soon as put out of the offeree's possession*, without regard to whether it ever reaches the offeror; (Restatement (Second) of Contracts § 64(a) (1973).)
> [Emphasis added.]

As we have stated, it is without dispute that no communication of acceptance occurred on July 10 as the offer required and that no physical delivery of acceptance occurred until July 23, six days after this suit was instituted. At best, the signed agreement constituting a purported acceptance was given to the seller's agent on the evening of July 10. However, this was inadequate to communicate acceptance since it cannot be said that as a matter of legal effect this put the manifestation of assent out of the offeree's [Rothenbuecher's] possession. While still in the hands of his agent, and without notice to the offeror, the seller could have at any time during the period of the condition given instructions that his acceptance be revoked. (*See* Restatement (Second) of Contracts § 64(a), Comment e (1973).) The appellant withdrew her offer on July 15 and it is elementary that an offeree's power to accept is terminated by revocation of the offer (*Branch v Matteson* (1921), 298 Ill 387, 392, 131 NE 804); . . . And hence, under these facts no contract resulted between the parties. (Restatement (Second) of Contracts § 34(2) (1973).) There being no agreement to enforce, we find it necessary to reverse the judgment.

[Judgment reversed]

QUESTIONS

1. Did the owner intend to accept the offer?
2. On what ground did the court then hold that there was no contract?
3. How would the case have been decided if the offer had not contained any time limitation?

§ 13:16   ACCEPTANCE BY MAIL OR TELEGRAPH

When the offeree sends an acceptance by mail or telegraph, questions may arise as to the right to use such means of communication and the time the acceptance is effective.

(a) RIGHT TO USE MAIL OR TELEGRAPH. Express directions of the offeror, prior dealings between the parties, or custom of the trade may make it clear that only one method of acceptance is proper. For example, in negotiations with respect to property of rapidly fluctuating value, such as wheat or corporation stocks, an acceptance sent by mail may be too slow. When there is no indication that mail or telegraph is not a proper method, an acceptance may be made by either of those means without regard to the manner in which the offer was made. The trend of the modern decisions supports the following provision of the Uniform Commercial Code relating to sales of personal property: "Unless otherwise unambiguously indicated by the language or circumstances, an offer to make a sales contract shall be construed as inviting acceptance in any manner and by any medium reasonable in the circumstances."

(b) WHEN ACCEPTANCE BY MAIL OR TELEGRAPH IS EFFECTIVE. If the offeror does not specify otherwise, a mailed acceptance takes effect when the acceptance is properly mailed (the "mailbox rule"). Likewise, a telegraph acceptance takes effect when and where the telegram is dispatched or sent, unless the offeror specifies otherwise or unless custom or prior dealings indicate that acceptance by telegraph is improper. If the offeror specifies that an acceptance shall not be effective until received, there is no acceptance until the acceptance is received. Likewise, the "mailbox rule" does not apply when the offeror requires receipt of a payment to accompany an acceptance.[19]

The letter must be properly addressed to the offeror, and any other precaution that is ordinarily observed to insure safe transmission must be taken. If it is not mailed in this manner, the acceptance does not take effect when mailed, but only when received by the offeror.

The rule that a properly mailed acceptance takes effect at the time it is mailed is applied strictly. The rule applies even though the acceptance letter never reaches the offeror.

[19]   American Heritage Life Ins. Co. v Koch (Tex App) 721 SW2d 611 (1986).

(c) PROOF OF ACCEPTANCE BY MAIL OR TELEGRAPH. How can the time of mailing be established, or even the fact of mailing in the case of a destroyed or lost letter? A similar problem arises in the case of a telegraphic acceptance. In either case, the problem is not one of law but one of fact: a question of proving the case to the jury. The offeror may testify in court that an acceptance was never received or that an acceptance was sent after the offer had been revoked. The offeree may then testify that the acceptance letter was mailed at a particular time and place. The offeree's case will be strengthened if postal receipts for the mailing and delivery of a letter sent to the offeror can be produced, although these, of course, do not establish the contents of the letter. Ultimately, the case goes to the jury, or to the judge, if a jury trial has been waived, to determine whether the acceptance was made at a certain time and place as claimed by the offeree.

§ 13:17   ACCEPTANCE BY TELEPHONE

Ordinarily acceptance of an offer may be made by telephone unless the circumstances are such that by the intent of the parties or the law of the state, no acceptance can be made or contract arise in the absence of a writing.

A telephoned acceptance is effective when and where the acceptance is spoken into the phone.[20] Consequently, when an employee who lived in Kansas applied for a job to work in Missouri and the employer telephoned from Missouri to Kansas accepting the application, the employment contract was a Missouri contract because the acceptance by the employer was spoken into the phone in that state. Thus, the Kansas Workers' Compensation statute did not apply when the employee was subsequently injured.

§ 13:18   AUCTION SALES

At an auction sale the statements made by the auctioneer to draw forth bids are merely invitations to negotiate. Each bid is an offer, which is not accepted until the auctioneer indicates that a particular offer or bid is accepted. Usually this is done by the fall of the auctioneer's hammer, indicating that the highest bid made has been accepted. As a bid is merely an offer, the bidder may withdraw the bid at any time before it is accepted by the auctioneer.

Ordinarily the auctioneer may withdraw any article or all of the property from the sale if not satisfied with the amounts of the bids that are being made. Once a bid is accepted, however, the auctioneer cannot cancel the sale. In addition, if it had been announced that the sale was to be made "without reserve," the goods must be sold to the person making the highest bid, regardless of how low that may be.

[20]   O'Briant v Daniel Construction Co. 279 SC 254, 305 SE2d 241 (1983).

SUMMARY

As a contract arises when an offer is accepted, it is necessary to find that there was an offer and that it was accepted. If either element is missing, there is no contract.

An offer does not exist unless the offeror has contractual intent. This intent is lacking if the statement of the person is merely an invitation to negotiate, a statement of intention, or an agreement to agree at a later date. Newspaper ads, price quotations, and catalog prices are ordinarily merely invitations to negotiate and cannot be accepted. In addition to the contractual intent, an offer must be definite. If an offer is indefinite, its acceptance will not create a contract because it will be held that the resulting agreement is too vague to enforce. In some cases, an offer that is by itself too indefinite is made definite because some writing or standard is incorporated by reference and made part of the offer. In some cases, the offer is made definite by implying terms that were not stated. In other cases, the indefinite part of the offer is ignored when that part can be divided or separated from the balance of the offer. In other cases, the requirement of definiteness is ignored either because the matter that is not definite is unimportant or because there is an exception to the rule requiring definiteness. Assuming that there is in fact an offer that is made with contractual intent and that it is sufficiently definite, it still does not have the legal effect of an offer unless it is communicated to the offeree by or at the direction of the offeror.

In some cases, no contract arises because there is no offer that satisfies the requirements just stated. In other cases, there was an offer, but it was terminated before it was accepted. By definition, an attempted acceptance made after the offer has been terminated has no effect. The ordinary offer may be revoked at any time by the offeror. All that is required is the showing of intent to revoke and the communication of that intent to the offeree. The offeror's power to revoke is barred by the existence of an option contract under common law, a firm offer under the Uniform Commercial Code or local non-Code statute, and by the application of the doctrine of detrimental reliance by the offeree. An offer is also terminated by the rejection of the offer or making of a counteroffer;

by the lapse of the time stated in the offer, or of a reasonable time when none is stated; by the death or disability of either party; or by a change of law that makes illegal a contract based on the particular offer.

When the offer is accepted, a contract arises. Only the offeree can accept an offer and the acceptance must be of the offer exactly as made without any qualification or change. Ordinarily the offeree may accept or reject as the offeree chooses. Limitations on this freedom of action have been imposed by antidiscrimination and consumer protection laws.

The acceptance is any manifestation of intent to agree to the terms of the offer. Ordinarily silence or failure to act does not constitute acceptance, and the recipient of unordered goods and tickets may make any disposition thereof without such action constituting an acceptance. An acceptance does not exist until the words or conduct manifesting assent to the offer are communicated to the offeror. Acceptance by mail or telegraph takes effect at the time and place when or where the letter is mailed or the telegram dispatched. A telephoned acceptance is effective when and where spoken into the phone.

In an auction sale, the auctioneer asking for bids makes an invitation to negotiate, a person making a bid is making an offer, and the acceptance of the highest bid by the auctioneer is an acceptance of that offer and gives rise to a contract. When the auction sale is without reserve, the auctioneer must accept the highest bid. If not expressly made without reserve, the auctioneer may refuse to accept any of the bids.

Questions and Case Problems

1. What objective of the law (from the list in § 2:4) is illustrated by each of the following statements?

   (a) Economic life would be most uncertain if we did not have the assurance that contracts, once made, would be binding.

   (b) An offer is terminated by the lapse of a

   reasonable time, when no time has been stated.

2. The Hamilton store ran a newspaper ad stating that a certain television set was on sale for $400. Nora phoned the store to say that she wanted one of the sets. The store stated that it was sold out and could not fill her or-

der. She sued Hamilton for breach of contract. Was it liable?

3. The Croft Cement Works agreed to supply Grover with as much cement as Grover would buy at a specified price per unit. Was this a requirements contract?

4. Katherine mailed Paul an offer that stated that it was good for ten days. Two days later she mailed Paul another letter stating that the original offer was revoked. That evening Paul phoned Katherine to say that he accepted the offer. She said that he could not do so because she had mailed him a letter of revocation and that he would undoubtedly receive the letter of revocation in the next morning's mail. Was the offer revoked by Katherine?

5. When an offer is rejected by the offeree, can the offeree thereafter accept the offer if the offeror refuses to make a better offer?

6. Compare the communication of an offer, the communication of the revocation of an offer, and the communication of the acceptance of an offer.

7. The Lessack Auctioneers advertised an auction sale that was open to the public and was to be conducted with reserve. Gordon attended the auction and bid $100 for a work of art which was worth much more. No higher bid, however, was made but Lessack refused to sell the item for $100 and withdrew the item from the sale. Gordon claimed that as he was the highest bidder, Lessack was required to sell the item to him. Was he correct?

8. The Willis Music Co. advertised a television set at $22.50 in the Sunday newspaper. Ehrlich ordered a set, but the company refused to deliver it on the ground that the price in the newspaper ad was a mistake. Ehrlich sued the company. Was it liable? Reason? [Ehrlich v Willis Music Co. 93 Ohio App 246, 113 NE2d 252]

9. Hall, the owner of a tract of land, wanted to have an office building constructed on it. He advertised for bids for the construction of the building. Davis, a contractor, sent in a bid accompanied by a letter stating that he accepted Hall's offer and thanked him for the contract. Did Davis have a contract with Hall?

10. A dealer received a purchase order from a customer. In order to fill the order for the customer, the dealer ordered from the factory the goods called for by the buyer's pur-

chase order. The buyer thereafter canceled the order. Could the buyer do so? [Antonucci v Stevens Dodge, Inc. 73 Misc 2d 173, 340 NYS2d 979]

11. A owned land. He signed a contract agreeing to sell the land, but reserving the right to take the hay from the land until the following October. He gave the contract form to B, a broker. C, a prospective buyer, agreed to buy the land and signed the contract but crossed out the provision as to the hay crop. Was there a binding contract between A and C?

12. Soar was a professional football player in the National Football League. He claimed that a commissioner of the league had agreed that he would be included in the league's pension plan "if sufficient funds become available." Soar brought suit against the football league players' association to enforce this promise. Was he entitled to recover? [Soar v National Football League Players' Ass'n (CA1 RI) 550 F2d 1287]

13. A. H. Zehmer discussed selling a farm to Lucy. After a 40-minute discussion of a first draft of a contract, Zehmer and his wife, Ida, signed a second draft stating: "We hereby agree to sell to W. O. Lucy the Ferguson Farm complete for $50,000 title satisfactory to buyer." Lucy agreed to purchase the farm on these terms. Thereafter the Zehmers refused to transfer title to Lucy and claimed that they had made the contract for sale as a joke. Lucy brought an action to compel performance of the contract. The Zehmers claimed that there was no contract. Were they correct? [Lucy v Zehmer, 198 Va App 493, 84 SE2d 516]

14. Wheeler operated a gas service station which he leased from W.C. Cornitius, Inc. The lease ran for three years. Although the lease did not contain any provision for renewal, the lease was in fact renewed six times for successive three-year terms. The landlord refused to renew the lease for a seventh time. Wheeler brought suit to compel the landlord to accept his offer to renew the lease. Decide. [William C. Cornitius, Inc. v Wheeler, 276 Or 747, 556 P2d 666]

15. Cogdill made an offer to the Bank of Benton. The proper officer stated that he would "start the paperwork." Did Cogdill have a contract with the Bank of Benton? [Bank of Benton v Cogdill, 118 Ill App 3d 280, 73 Ill Dec 871, 454 NE2d 1120]

14

CONTRACTUAL CAPACITY

If society desired to treat all persons as equals, everyone would be able to make a contract and, conversely, all persons would be fully bound by their contracts. Such a rule of law would lay a trap for minors, intoxicated persons, and incompetents. They would enter into contracts and find themselves bound thereby, even though the contracts were unwise from the standpoint of their best interests. To prevent this, society departs from the concept of equality and declares that certain per- sons cannot make contracts that will bind them. Thus, minors, intoxicated persons, and insane persons may have the right to avoid their contracts. This is described technically as lacking contractual capacity.

A. GENERAL PRINCIPLES

It has already been stated that the parties to an agreement must have contractual ca- pacity. This chapter analyzes what contractual capacity means and who does not have such capacity.

§ 14:1   DEFINITION

Contractual capacity is the ability to understand that a contract is being made and to understand its general nature. The fact that a person does not understand the full legal meaning of a contract does not mean that contractual capacity is lacking.

If any party to a contract does not have contractual capacity, the contract is either void or voidable.

Some persons, such as minors, are deemed by the law to lack contractual capacity. Ordinarily, however, every party to a contract is presumed to have contractual capacity until the contrary is shown.[1] When there is evidence that a party has some illness, the question often arises whether that illness, or medication taken for it, had impaired the contractual capacity of the party.

§ 14:2   DOUBLE ASPECT OF CAPACITY

In order to give rise to a contract, all parties

to the agreement must have contractual capacity. This has both a negative and a positive aspect.

(a) NEGATIVE ASPECT OF CAPACITY. If capacity is lacking, the contract is voidable and in some instances, is void. As this chapter will show, many concepts of incapacity have been abolished. This is understandable in terms of the growing importance and recognition of the social force of protecting the person. That is, a person is not to be denied the capacity to make a binding contract unless there is some actual physical or mental disability that the law should recognize in order to protect that person. Incapacity based on discrimination against sex, alienage, or as punishment for crime is disappearing from the law.

(b) POSITIVE ASPECT OF CAPACITY. As to the positive aspect, contractual capacity is in most instances the equivalent of freedom of contract.[2] That is, persons with capacity to contract may make whatever contract they choose, and the law will not lightly nullify or reject their desires. This positive aspect of capacity was the basis for the decision in the *Sinclair Oil Corporation* case.

---

[1]   Kennedy v Bearden (La App) 471 So 2d 871 (1985).

[2]   Fidelity & Deposit Co. v Sun Life Ins. Co. 174 Ga App 214, 329 SE2d 517 (1985).

SINCLAIR OIL CORP. V COLUMBIA CAS. CO.
(Wyo) 682 P2d 975 (1984)

Sinclair Oil Corporation obtained a contract of insurance from the Columbia Casualty Company to protect it from liability to third persons. An accident occurred in the unloading of a tanker, and Sinclair was sued by the injured person for both compensatory and punitive damages.* Columbia claimed that the provision of the policy obligating it to pay punitive damages was invalid. Sinclair brought suit on the policy, and the question as to punitive damages was certified to the Wyoming Supreme Court.

BROWN, J. . . . Columbia contends that:

---

*   Authors' Note: Compensatory damages compensate the plaintiff for the loss sustained. Punitive damages are recovered from the defendant to punish for highly improper conduct. See § 22:8.

1) In Wyoming, punitive damages are imposed upon persons guilty of willful and wanton misconduct solely for purposes of punishment and deterrence, and not for purposes of compensation. These goals of punishment and deterrence are frustrated if the wrongdoer has the right to contract with an insurance company for payment of amounts imposed as punitive damages.

2) The trend and weight of authority among courts confronted with the factual and legal circumstances of this case is to hold that insurance coverage for punitive damages is contrary to public policy.

3) The interest of the people of the State of Wyoming in preventing frustration of the salutary goals of punishment and deterrence in punitive damages cases overrides the wrongdoers interest in freedom of contract. . . .

Succinctly, Columbia contends that there can be no punishment or deterrence if Sinclair is permitted to shift the financial burden of punitive damages to its insurance carrier. We are confronted here with competing policies, and we must therefore determine which is dominant. On the one hand, we have a policy regarding the purposes of punitive damages, and on the other hand, we have a policy with respect to freedom to contract for insurance coverage.

We have said that the purposes and justification for punitive damages is to publicly condemn some notorious action or inaction, to punish a defendant, and to serve as a warning and deterrent to others. Punitive damages are not allowed to compensate plaintiffs nor are they designed to be a windfall.

Courts unanimously recognize the basic right of persons, real and artificial, to freely enter into contracts. It was said in *Baltimore & Ohio Southwestern Railway Company v. Voigt*, 176 U.S. 498 (1900):

> The right of private contract is no small part of the liberty of the citizen, and that the usual and most important function of courts of justice is rather to maintain and enforce contracts, than to enable parties thereto to escape from their obligation on the pretext of public policy, unless it clearly appears that they contravene public right or the public welfare. It was well said by Sir George Jessel, M. R., in Printing & Co. v. Sampson, L. R. 19 Eq. 465: "It must not be forgotten that you are not to extend arbitrarily those rules which say that a given contract is void as being against public policy, because if there is one thing which more than another public policy requires it is that men of full age and competent understanding shall have the utmost liberty of contracting, and that their contracts, when entered into freely and voluntarily, shall be held sacred, and shall be enforced by courts of justice. Therefore, you have this paramount public policy to consider — that you are not lightly to interfere with this freedom of contract. . . ."

We will not invalidate a contract entered into freely by competent parties on the basis of public policy unless that policy is well settled, unambiguous and not in conflict with another public policy equally or more compelling.

Courts are not uniform in their determination of whether or not public policy precludes insuring against punitive damages. . . .

It is not necessary to determine which is the majority view nor are we concerned with the trend. We have never adopted a majority view solely to be aligned with a plurality nor have we detected a trend and jumped on the "band wagon." We adopt the position that most nearly comports with the jurisprudence of the State of Wyoming and appears to be the more rational.

[The court then analyzed the conflicting views and sustained the right to insure against liability for punitive damages.]

B.   Minors

At common law any person, male or female, under twenty-one years of age was a **minor** (or an infant). At common law, minority ended the day before the twenty-first birthday. The "day before the birthday" rule is still followed, but the age of majority has been reduced from twenty-one years to eighteen years in most states and to nineteen in a few.

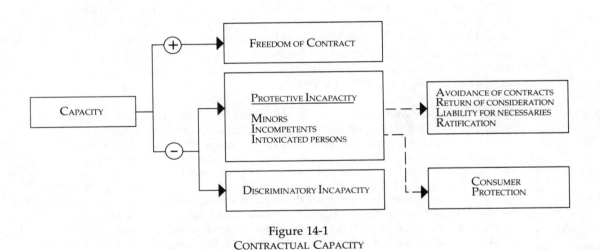

Figure 14-1
CONTRACTUAL CAPACITY

§ 14:3 MINOR'S POWER TO AVOID CONTRACTS

With exceptions that will be noted later, a contract made by a minor is voidable at the election of the minor. The minor may affirm or ratify the contract upon attaining majority by performing the contract or by giving an express statement of approval. Once the contract is affirmed, it can no longer be avoided.

(a) WHAT CONSTITUTES AVOIDANCE. Avoidance or disaffirmance of a contract by a minor may be accomplished by any ex-

pression of an intention to repudiate the contract. Any act inconsistent with the continuing validity of the contract is also a disaffirmance. Thus, when a minor sold property to *A* and later, on reaching majority, made a sale of the same property to *B*, the second sale was an avoidance of the first.

(b) TIME FOR AVOIDANCE. The minor can avoid a contract only during minority and for a reasonable time after attaining majority. After the lapse of such reasonable time, the contract is deemed ratified and cannot be avoided by the minor. A few states permit the former minor to avoid a wholly executory contract thereafter in the absence of an express affirmance.

(c) MINOR'S MISREPRESENTATION OF AGE. Generally the fact that the minor has misrepresented age does not affect the minor's power to avoid the contract. A few states hold that such fraud of the minor prevents the minor from avoiding the contract. A few states permit the minor to avoid the contract in such case, but require the minor to pay for any damage to the property received under the contract.

In any case, the other party to the contract may avoid it because of the minor's fraud.

§ 14:4   RESTITUTION BY MINOR AFTER AVOIDANCE

When a minor avoids a contract, the question arises as to what must be returned by the minor to the other contracting party.

(a) ORIGINAL CONSIDERATION INTACT. When a minor still has what was received from the other party, the minor, on avoiding the contract, must return it to the other party or offer to do so. That is, the minor must put things back to the original position, or as it is called, restore the **status quo ante.** If the minor who is able to return the consideration does not do so, the minor cannot avoid the contract. By virtue of this rule, when a contract is avoided, the minor must avoid all of it. Part of it cannot be kept.

(b) ORIGINAL CONSIDERATION DAMAGED OR DESTROYED. What happens if the minor cannot return what has been received because it has been spent, used, damaged, or destroyed? The minor's right to avoid the contract is not affected thereby. The minor can still avoid the contract and is only required to return what remains. The fact that nothing remains or that what remains is damaged does not bar the right to avoid the contract. In those states that follow the common-law rule, the minor can thus refuse to pay for what has been received under the contract or can get back what had been paid or given, even though the minor does not have anything to return or returns any property in a damaged condition. There is, however, a trend that would limit this rule.

In the *Star Chevrolet* case the dealer claimed a credit for the salvage value of the automobile purchased by the minor.

STAR CHEVROLET CO. V GREEN

(Miss) 473 So 2d 157 (1985)

Kevin Green purchased an automobile from Star Chevrolet Company. He later notified Star that he was a minor and was avoiding the contract. Star refused to take back the car and to refund the purchase price. Kevin continued to use the car. He was involved in a collision. His insurance paid his claim and he transferred the car to the insurance company. The company later sold the car for salvage for $1,500. Kevin sued Star for the price that he had paid for the car. Star claimed that it was entitled to a setoff of $1,500 for the salvage value of the car. The lower court refused to allow this setoff, and Star appealed.

SULLIVAN, J. . . . Upon disaffirmance of a minor's contract, he is required to return the consideration received by him if he still has such consideration in his possession, or if it is within his powers to do so. This requirement can be complied with not only by an actual return of the consideration but also by a tender or offer to return it.

From the time Kevin disaffirmed the contract in November, 1981, until suit was filed, Star Chevrolet refused to fully refund the purchase price unless the Camaro's blown head gasket was repaired. This position was erroneous as a matter of law. We held in *Johnson Motors v. Coleman* that depreciation, finance charges, insurance charges, etc. during the period the minor used the automobile were not recoverable by the dealer. 232 So.2d at 721. Likewise, Kevin's duty to tender the vehicle was not contingent upon its restoration to the condition at the time of sale. . . .

Appellant [Star] contends that Kevin's minority in this case has been converted from a shield for protection into a sword for attack. It is asserted that appellee would be unjustly enriched if in addition to the insurance recovery already received, he were awarded a judgment for the full purchase price of the vehicle. Appellant insists that the law requires that it be placed in status quo, either by offsetting the minor's insurance recovery against the judgment or by reducing the judgment in the amount of the salvage value of the vehicle.

Appellee asserts that the law does not require a minor to place the other party in status quo by returning the consideration when the minor, through his inexperience and youth, has lost, squandered or destroyed the consideration. . . .

Our sole focus is upon whether or not the consideration, i.e. the vehicle, remained in the minor's hands during disaffirmance of the contract, or whether it passed from the minor's hands by squandering, destruction or loss.

Before reaching the precise question at hand, some general principles warrant restatement. First, the right of a minor to disaffirm his contract is based upon sound public policy to protect the minor from his own improvidence and the overreaching of adults. It is the policy of the law to discourage adults from contracting with minors and the adult cannot complain if, as a consequence of his violation of this rule of conduct, he is injured by the minor's exercise of the right of disaffirmance, since this injury might have been avoided if the adult had declined to enter into the contract.

Second, if upon disaffirmance the minor has in his possession the specific property or any part of it which he received he must return it. Thus, where a minor repudiates an automobile sales contract while the vehicle is still in his hands, he must tender the vehicle in order for his purchase price to be refunded. As noted before, the seller may not deduct from the refunded purchase price allowances for use and depreciation.

Third, the general rule is that upon disaffirmance of a minor's contract, he is required to return the consideration only if it is still in his possession. The minor who disaffirms a contract is not obliged to return the consideration received by him or its equivalent where during his minority he has wasted, squandered, destroyed, used, or otherwise disposed of the consideration.

Finally, depreciation in the value of the vehicle due to the minor's misuse or neglect, short of [an] intentional or grossly negligent act amounting to an independent tort, is not allowable by way of recoupment. In other words, the minor is not liable for damages due to the very improvidence and indiscretion of infancy against which the law seeks to protect him. On the other hand, a minor may not use infancy, which is a shield for protection, as a sword for attack; such conduct by the minor amounts to fraud.

Turning to the facts of this case, the minor clearly had the consideration, i.e. the vehicle, in his possession when he first notified appellant of the disaffirmance of the contract. Had appellant offered the minor, as the law required, a full refund of his purchase price, the minor clearly would have been required to return the vehicle. Instead, the appellant did not, and while suit was pending the minor repaired the vehicle and began to use it. There is no hint in the record that the accident which destroyed the vehicle was the result of any deliberate design on the minor's part to fraudulently deprive appellant of that which would have placed him in status quo. For aught that appears in the record, the accident was caused by the carelessness and improvidence with which the law expects a minor to deal with his property. Disaffirmance at this point would have required the appellant to refund the full purchase price and the appellee, in turn, to return the damaged Camaro, since the law does not condition a minor's right to disaffirm a contract upon placing the other party in status quo, but only requires the return of whatever consideration remains in the minor's hands.

This case goes one step further. Prior to trial, the minor transferred title to the vehicle to the insurance company and used the proceeds to purchase another vehicle. The insuror obtained $1500 salvage value for the damaged Camaro. We are urged to offset the minor's recovery by the $1500 salvage value of the car on the ground that the minor had the duty to tender this consideration to appellant in order to receive a refund of the full purchase price.

We are persuaded that the appellant's contention is sound. The *Fisher v. Taylor Motor Co.*, 249 N.C. 617, 107 S.E.2d 94 (1959), in facts remarkably similar to the case *sub judice*, the Supreme Court of North Carolina allowed the defendant a setoff in the amount of the salvage value of the vehicle upon the principle that the minor would be liable for any tortious disposition of the property after disaffirmance and before surrender to those from whom it was obtained. Likewise, in this case we hold that the minor is liable, and the appellant is entitled to a setoff, for the salvage value of the consideration which he intentionally conveyed away. . . .

[Judgment reversed as to setoff claim]

QUESTIONS

1. What is the justification for the common-law rule on avoidance of contracts by minors?
2. What is the common-law rule as to the liability of a minor avoiding a contract for property that had been damaged?
3. Does the *Star Chevrolet* case follow the common-law rule stated in your answer to Question 2?

§ 14:5 RECOVERY OF PROPERTY BY MINOR UPON AVOIDANCE

When a minor avoids a contract, the other contracting party must return the money received from the minor. Any property received from the minor must also be returned. If the property has been sold to a third person who did not know of the minority of the original seller, the minor cannot get the property back, but in such cases the minor is entitled to recover the money value of the property or the money received by the other contracting party from the third person.

§ 14:6   CONTRACTS FOR NECESSARIES

A minor can avoid a contract for necessaries but must pay the reasonable value for furnished necessaries. This duty of the minor is called a quasi-contractual liability.[3] It is a duty that the law imposes upon the minor rather than one created by contract.

(a) WHAT CONSTITUTES NECESSARIES. Originally **necessaries** were limited to those things absolutely necessary for the sustenance and shelter of the minor. Thus limited, the term would extend only to the most simple foods, clothing, and lodging. In the course of time, the rule was relaxed to extend generally to things relating to the health, education, and comfort of the minor. Thus, the rental of a house used by a married minor is a necessary. Services reasonably necessary to obtaining employment by a minor have been held to be necessaries.

The rule has also been relaxed to hold that whether an item is a necessary in a particular case depends upon the financial and social status, or station in life, of the minor. As such, the rule does not treat all minors equally. For example, college education may be regarded as necessary for one minor but not for another, depending upon their respective family backgrounds.

Property other than food or clothing acquired by a minor is generally not regarded as a necessary. Although this rule is obviously sound in the case of jewelry and property used for pleasure, the same view is held even though the minor is self-supporting and uses the property in connection with work. Examples are tools of trade or an automobile used to go to and from work. The more recent decisions, however, hold that property used by a minor to earn a living is a necessary. Thus, it has been held that a tractor and farm equipment were necessaries for a married minor who supported a family by farming.

These changes have come about because, in this century, minors have taken a greater part in the business and working world, in many cases leaving the parental home to lead independent lives as young adults.

(b) CONTRACT WITH PARENT OR GUARDIAN. When a third person supplies the parents or guardian of a minor with goods or services that are needed by the minor, the minor is not liable for such necessaries. This is so because the contract of the third person is with the parent or guardian, not with a minor.[4]

(c) SETTLEMENT OF MINOR'S CLAIM. When a lawsuit is brought between persons with capacity, they may ordinarily settle the case on any terms they see fit. When a minor is a party or has an interest in the case, it is commonly provided that the court in which the action was brought must approve the settlement. This requirement is imposed in order to protect the interests of the minor. If the minor had an attorney, the court must consider whether it was reasonably necessary to employ an attorney on behalf of the minor, whether the contract with the attorney was fair and reasonable at the time it was entered into, and whether it was fair in relation to the amount of the legal services actually performed.[5]

§ 14:7 MINOR'S RATIFICATION OF VOIDABLE CONTRACT

A minor cannot avoid a contract after it has been ratified. The ratification cannot be canceled or set aside.

(a) WHAT CONSTITUTES RATIFICATION.

---

[3] See § 12:13 as to quasi-contractual liability generally.

[4] Hammond's Estate v Aetna Cas. Co. 141 Ill App 3d 963, 96 Ill Dec 270, 491 NE2d 84 (1986).

[5] Nixon v Bryson (Fla App) 488 So 2d 607 (1986).

Ratification consists of any words or conduct of the minor manifesting an intent to be bound by the terms of the contract. In the *Jones* case it was claimed by the defendant that the minor's use of the defendant's services after the minor attained majority constituted a ratification of the contract made while still a minor.

JONES V DRESSEL
(Colo) 623 P2d 370 (1981)

William Michael Jones, aged seventeen, signed a contract with Free Flight Sport Aviation, Inc. to provide air transportation in Colorado in connection with skydiving. The contract contained a clause declaring that Free Flight Aviation would not be liable for any damage or injury resulting from a flight. Jones thereafter became eighteen, which by Colorado law was the age of the majority. Ten months later Jones was injured in the crash of a Free Flight plane piloted by Dressel. He sued Dressel and Free Flight for damages on the ground that the crash had been caused by the negligence of Dressel. The defense was raised that the no-liability clause protected the defendants from any liability. Jones claimed that the clause was not binding because he had been a minor when the contract was made, and he avoided the contract, and therefore was not bound by the no-liability clause. Judgment was entered for the defendants. Jones appealed.

ERIKSON, J. . . . On November 17, 1973, the plaintiff, William Michael Jones, who was then seventeen years old, signed a contract with the defendant, Free Flight Sport Aviation, Inc. (Free Flight).* The contract allowed Jones to use Free Flight's recreational skydiving facilities, which included use of an airplane to ferry skydivers to the parachute jumping site. A covenant not to sue and a clause exempting Free Flight from liability were included in the contract:

2A. EXEMPTION FROM LIABILITY. The [plaintiff] exempts and releases the Corporation, its owners, officers, agents, servants, employees, and lessors from any and all liability, claims, demands or actions or causes of action whatsoever arising out of any damage, loss or injury to the [plaintiff] or the [plaintiff's] property while upon the premises or aircraft of the Corporation or while participating in any of the activities contemplated by this Agreement, whether such loss, damage, or injury results from the negligence of the Corporation, its officers, agents, servants, employees, or lessors or from some other cause.

The contract also contained an alternative provision which would have permitted Jones to use Free Flight's facilities at an increased cost, but without releasing Free Flight from liability for negligence.

On December 28, 1973, Jones attained the age of eighteen. Ten months later, on October 19, 1974, he suffered serious personal injuries in an airplane

---

* Even though Jones' mother had ratified the terms of this contract on November 16, 1973, it should be noted that the approval by a parent does not necessarily validate an infant child's contract. *See generally, Kaufman v. American Youth Hostels*, 13 Misc.2d 8, 174 N.Y.S.2d 580 (1957); *Fedor v. Mauwehu Council, Boy Scouts of America*, 21 Conn.Sup. 38, 143 A.2d 466 (1958).

crash which occurred shortly after takeoff from Littleton Airport. Free Flight furnished the airplane as part of its skydiving operation.

On November 21, 1975, nearly two years after attaining his majority, Jones filed suit against Free Flight alleging negligence and willful and wanton misconduct as the cause of the airplane crash. . . .

As a matter of public policy, the courts have protected minors from improvident and imprudent contractual commitments by declaring that the contract of a minor is voidable at the election of the minor after he attains his majority. A minor may disaffirm a contract made during his minority within a reasonable time after attaining his majority or he may, after becoming of legal age, by acts recognizing the contract, ratify it. . . .

Affirmance is not merely a matter of intent. It may be determined by the actions of a minor who accepts the benefits of a contract after reaching the age of majority, or who is silent or acquiesces in the contract for a considerable length of time. What act constitutes ratification or disaffirmance is ordinarily a question of law to be determined by the trial court. We agree that what constitutes a reasonable time for affirmance or disaffirmance is ordinarily a question of fact to be determined by the facts in a particular case. We conclude, however, that the trial court properly determined that Jones ratified the contract, as a matter of law, by accepting the benefits of the contract when he used Free Flight's facilities on October 19, 1974.

Thus, since Jones ratified the contract, the factual issue of whether his suit for personal injuries was filed within a reasonable time after attaining his majority and constituted disaffirmance of the contract, is not relevant. Accordingly, the entry of summary judgment on the issue of ratification was not error. . . .

[Judgment affirmed as to ratification]

QUESTIONS

1. In what ways may a minor ratify a contract?
2. Did Jones ratify his contract? Answer and explain.
3. Did Jones know when he took the flight in question that the contract contained a no-liability (exculpatory) clause?

The making of payments after attaining majority may constitute a ratification. Many courts, however, refuse to recognize payment as ratification in the absence of further evidence of an intent to ratify, an express statement of ratification, or an appreciation by the minor that such payment might constitute a ratification.

An acknowledgment by the minor that a contract had been made during minority, without an intent to be bound thereby, is not a ratification.

(b) FORM OF RATIFICATION. Generally no special form is required for ratification of a minor's voidable contract, although in some states a written ratification or declaration of intention is required.

(c) TIME FOR RATIFICATION. A minor can avoid a contract any time during minority and for a reasonable time thereafter but, of necessity, can only ratify a contract after attaining majority. The minor must have attained majority or the "ratification" would itself be regarded as voidable.

§ 14:8   CONTRACTS THAT MINORS CANNOT AVOID

Statutes in many states deprive a minor of the right to avoid an educational loan,[6] a contract for medical care, a contract made while running a business, a contract approved by a court, a contract made in performance of a legal duty, or a contract relating to bank accounts, insurance policies, or corporate stock. In most states, the contract of a veteran, although a minor, is binding, particularly a contract for the purchase of a home. In some states, by court decision, a minor who is nearly an adult, or who appears to be an adult, cannot avoid a contract, particularly when it is made in connection with a business or employment.

Some courts take an intermediate position with respect to employment contracts. These courts allow the minor to avoid the contract, but prohibit the minor from using any secret information obtained in the course of the employment or from competing with the former employer when the avoided contract contained a noncompetitive clause. It is also held that when a minor has settled a claim and received the amount specified in a release, the release is binding upon the minor and cannot be set aside when the minor attains majority.

As an exception to the right to disaffirm a contract during minority, a minor cannot fully avoid a conveyance for the transfer of land until majority is attained.

§ 14:9   LIABILITY OF THIRD PERSON FOR MINOR'S CONTRACT

The question arises whether parents are bound by the contract of their minor child. The question also arises whether a person

[6] A Uniform Minor Student Capacity to Borrow Act makes educational loans binding on minors in Arizona, Mississippi, North Dakota, Oklahoma, and Washington. This uniform act was reclassified as a model act by the Commissioners on Uniform Laws, indicating that it was recognized that uniformity was not important and that the matter was primarily local in character.

cosigning a minor's contract is bound if the contract is avoided.

(a) LIABILITY OF PARENT. Ordinarily a parent is not liable on a contract made by a minor child. The parent may be liable, however, if the child is acting as the agent of the parent in making the contract. Also, the parent is liable to a seller of necessaries for the reasonable value of the necessaries supplied by the seller to the child if the parent had deserted the child.

(b) LIABILITY OF COSIGNER. When the minor makes a contract, another person, such as a parent or a friend, may sign the contract along with the minor for the purpose of accommodating the minor by making the contract more attractive to the third person.

With respect to the other contracting party, the cosigner is bound independently of the minor. Consequently, if the minor avoids the contract, the cosigner remains bound by the contract. If the debt to the creditor is actually paid, the obligation of the cosigner is discharged.

If the minor avoids a sales contract but does not return the goods, the cosigner remains liable for the purchase price.

C.   OTHER PERSONS LACKING CAPACITY

While minors form the largest class of persons who are under an incapacity, there may be other persons who lack contractual capacity. These are persons who are incompetent or intoxicated, and in some cases are persons against whom society has discriminated.

§ 14:10   INCOMPETENTS

A person who is mentally deranged is generally called an **incompetent** and lacks capacity to make a contract. The cause of the incapacity is immaterial. It may be the result of insanity, senile dementia, imbecility, excessive use of drugs or alcohol, or a stroke. If the person is so mentally deranged as to be unable to understand that a contract is being made or the general nature of the contract, the person lacks contractual capacity.

An incompetent may have lucid intervals. If a contract is made during such an interval and is not affected by any delusion, the contract is valid and binding.

(a) EFFECT OF INCOMPETENCE. An incompetent person may ordinarily avoid a contract in the same manner as a minor.[7] Upon the removal of the disability, that is, upon becoming normal, the formerly incompetent person either can ratify or disaffirm the contract.

As in the case of minors, the other party to the contract has no right to disaffirm the contract merely because the incompetent has the right to do so.

(b) APPOINTMENT OF GUARDIAN. If a court appoints a guardian for the incompetent person, a contract made by the incompetent before that appointment may be ratified or disaffirmed by the guardian. If the incompetent person makes a contract after a guardian has been appointed, the contract is void and not merely voidable.

§ 14:11   INTOXICATED PERSONS

The capacity of a party to contract and the validity of the contract are not affected by the party's being drunk at the time of making the contract as long as the party knew

---

[7]   Palmer v Palmer (Fla App) 479 So 2d 221 (1985).

that a contract was being made. The fact that the contract was foolish and would not have been made if sober does not make the contract voidable unless it can be shown that the other party purposely caused the person to become drunk in order to induce the making of the contract.

If the degree of intoxication is such that a person does not know that a contract is being made, the contract is voidable by that person. The situation is the same as though the person were insane at the time and did not know what was being done. Upon becoming sober, the person may avoid or rescind the contract. An unreasonable delay in taking steps to set aside a known contract entered into while intoxicated, however, may bar the intoxicated person from asserting this right.

§ 14:12   PERSONS UNDER DISCRIMINATORY INCAPACITY

In the last century there were three classes of persons who were deemed under a common-law incapacity because society was discriminating against them. These were criminals convicted of a felony, aliens, and married women. By court decision, statute, or treaty, these incapacities have almost disappeared from the law. Except in time of war, alienage has no significance. Married women now have full contractual capacity except that in a few states a wife cannot make any promise to pay her husband's debt if he does not pay.

SUMMARY

An agreement that otherwise appears to be a contract may not be binding because a party thereto lacks contractual capacity. In such case, the contract is ordinarily voidable at the election of that party who lacks contractual capacity. In some cases the contract is void. Ordinarily contractual incapacity is the inability, for mental or physical reasons, to understand that a contract is being made and to understand its general terms and nature. This is typically the case when it is claimed that incapacity exists because of insanity or intoxication. The incapacity of minors arises because society is discriminating in favor of that class in order to protect them from unwise contracts.

Historically minors were persons under twenty-one years of age. In most states today the age of majority has been reduced to eighteen years. Typically a minor can avoid any contract. If the minor received anything from the other party, the minor, upon avoiding the contract, must return what had been received from the other party, if the minor still has it. If what was received has been destroyed, lost, or spent, the minor is not required to make any return or to pay damages for the value of what has not been returned. If what was received has been damaged, the minor must return such property but is not required to pay money for the damage sustained by the property. If the minor had originally transferred property to the other contracting party, as a minor buyer making a trade-in, the minor may recover such property upon avoiding the contract. This right to recover property exists only as long as the minor's former property is owned by the other contracting party. If the other contracting party has resold the property to a third person buying in good faith and for value, the minor cannot recover the property from such third person.

A minor can avoid contracts, which means that the minor cannot be required to pay the purchase price or perform any obligation of contracts. By statute and decision, however, exceptions have been made to this general rule and certain kinds of contracts may no longer be avoided by a minor. Examples include contracts of insurance, contracts to purchase stock, or contracts made by a minor running a busi-

ness. When a minor avoids a contract for a necessary, the minor must pay the reasonable value of any benefit received. At common law, a necessary was limited to the minimal needs of food, clothing, and shelter. The concept of a necessary has expanded so that it now embraces needs reasonably necessary for the minor's existence and employment, taking into consideration the social position and background of the minor. By this modern view, an automobile used in connection with the minor's work and the services of an employment agency are necessaries.

Only a minor is liable for the minor's contract. Parents of the minor are not liable on the contracts of the minor merely because they are the parents. Frequently, an adult will enter into the contract as a coparty of the minor. Such an adult, whether a parent or a non-relative, is liable on the contract made by such person and the minor without regard to whether the minor has avoided the contract. However, the cosigner is released if everything in its original condition is returned by the minor to the other contracting party.

The contract of an insane person is voidable to much the same extent as the contract of a minor, with the important distinction that if a guardian has been appointed for the insane person, a contract made by the insane person is void and not merely voidable.

An intoxicated person lacks contractual capacity to make a contract if the intoxication is such that the person does not understand that a contract is being made. Modern law abandons a former distinction between voluntary and involuntary intoxication.

QUESTIONS AND CASE PROBLEMS

1. (a) What is the objective of the rule of law that a minor who avoids a contract usually cannot recover property if the other party has transferred it to a third person who did not know of the minority and purchased the property for value?

   (b) How is the evolutionary nature of the law illustrated by the changes in the definition of a minor's necessaries?

2. What contracts of a minor can be avoided?

3. Michael was sixteen years old. He purchased a motorcycle to go on a summer camping

trip. After having driven the motorcycle approximately 5,000 miles and after having wrecked and repaired it once, he brought it back to the dealer who sold him the motorcycle and demanded the return of the full price paid. The dealer refused to take back the motorcycle or to return any part of the purchase price. Was the dealer required to take back the motorcycle and refund the purchase price?

4. Oscar Adams, age sixteen, purchased a radio from Braverman Brothers. The radio was stolen from Oscar. He then avoided the contract with Braverman. Braverman Brothers then demanded that Oscar's mother, Joyce, pay for the radio set. Was she liable?

5. Helen, age seventeen, wanted to buy a motorcycle. She did not have the money to pay cash but persuaded the dealer to sell a cycle to her on credit. He did so partly because she said that she was twenty-two. Helen showed the dealer an identification card that falsely stated that her age was twenty-two. Helen drove the motorcycle away. A few days later she damaged it and then returned it to the dealer and stated that she avoided the contract because she was a minor. The dealer said that she could not do so because (a) she had misrepresented her age and (b) the motorcycle was damaged. Can she avoid the contract?

6. Compare ratification by a minor of a contract when (a) the minor ratifies the contract while still a minor, and (b) the minor ratifies the contract a day after becoming an adult.

7. Martinson executed a note payable to Matz. At the time Martinson was drunk. The next day he was told that he signed the note. Five years later, Martinson's wife told Matz's attorney that Martinson would not pay the note because he was drunk at the time he executed the note. Matz brought suit on the note two years after that. Could he recover? [Matz v Martinson, 127 Minn 262, 149 NW 370]

8. On February 28, 1958, Alice Sosik signed a note promising to make certain payments to Conlon. She later sued to have the note set aside on the ground that she lacked mental capacity. A letter from a physician was presented that stated that he had examined her on July 3, 1959, and that she "is suffering from a chronic mental illness and is totally incapable of managing her affairs." Did the letter provide sufficient proof to allow her to set the note aside? [Sosik v Conlon, 91 RI 439, 164 A2d 696]

9. Stuhl was twenty years of age. At that time, twenty-one years was the age of majority. He gave a check to Eastern Airlines to pay for a flight ticket. By the time his check was dishonored by the bank for insufficient funds, Stuhl had already flown on the flight. Eastern Airlines then sued him on the check. He filed an answer in the lawsuit in which he stated that he was a minor when he bought the flight ticket and that he now disaffirmed the contract with Eastern Airlines for the flight. Could he avoid the contract? [Eastern Airlines, Inc. v Stuhl, 65 Misc 2d 901, 318 NYS2d 996, aff'd 68 Misc 2d 269, 327 NYS2d 752]

10. A, who appeared to be more than twenty-one years of age but made no statement regarding his age, purchased an automobile from B. He later informed B that he was a minor and avoided the contract. A gave as his explanation that there were certain defects in the car. B claimed that these defects were trivial. Assuming that the defects were trivial, could A avoid the contract?

11. Ellen purchased a refrigerator for her new apartment. Because she was not employed, the store did not want to sell it to her on credit unless her father, who had a good job, would sign a promissory note for the amount of the purchase price. Both Ellen and her father signed such a note. Six months later, the refrigerator was destroyed by a fire in the apartment house. Ellen and her father refused to make any more payments for the refrigerator. The store sued both of them for the balance of the purchase price. Were they liable?

12. Thomas Bell, a minor, went to work in the beauty parlor of Sam Pankas and agreed that when he left the employment, he would not work in or run a beauty parlor business within a ten-mile radius of downtown Pittsburgh, Pennsylvania, for a period of two years. Contrary to this provision, Bell and another employee of Pankas opened up a beauty shop three blocks from Pankas' shop and advertised themselves as former employees of Pankas. Pankas sued Bell to stop the breach of the non-competition or restrictive covenant. Bell claimed that he was not bound because he was a minor when he had agreed to the cov-

enant. Was he bound by the convenant? [Pankas v Bell, 413 Pa 494, 198 A2d 312]

13. Saccavino made a contract with Carl Gambardella, then fifteen years of age, and Carl's parents, that he would train Carl to be a horse rider and that he would receive, in return, a share of Carl's earnings from exhibitions and racing. When Saccavino sued on the contract years later, Carl claimed that it was void. Was he correct? [Saccavino v Gambardella, 22 Conn Supp 168, 164 A2d 304]

14. Mervin Hyland had done business with the First State Bank for almost ten years. In March he signed a note promising to repay the bank a loan that he had made. He was drunk at the time, but understood that he was signing a note. In May he paid the bank the interest due on the note. Some time later he claimed that he did not have to pay the note because he was intoxicated when he signed it. Was this a valid defense? [First State Bank v Hyland (SD) 399 NW2d 894]

15. Salvador Valencia was still in high school when his father gave him two truck-tractor semi-trailer rigs so that he could start his own trucking business. He did so, and some time later he took a truck to White for repairs and for the installation of a new engine. During all this time he was provided by his parents with board, room, clothing, medical needs, and education. He got into a dispute with White over the work and disaffirmed the contract. White claimed that Valencia was liable for the reasonable value of the benefit that he had received under the contract. Was Valencia right? [Valencia v White (App) 134 Ariz 139, 654 P2d 287]

15

GENUINENESS OF ASSENT

In order to protect the voluntary character of contractual agreements, special rules have been developed to meet the situation in which the apparent agreement does not reflect the true intentions of the parties. This situation might occur as a result of mistake, deception, or pressure. This chapter considers the scope of these factors and the remedies that are available to the contracting party who is the victim of such practices.

A. MISTAKE

The agreement of the parties may be affected by the fact that one or both of them made a mistake.

§ 15:1 UNILATERAL MISTAKE

A unilateral mistake as to a fact does not affect the contract. For example, a customer orders a water-resistant coat, mistakenly thinking that this means it is waterproof. The customer cannot get out of the contract on the basis of this one-sided or unilateral mistake of fact as to the quality of the coat.

As exceptions to the statement that a unilateral mistake of fact does not affect the contract, the agreement has no effect if it

Figure 15-1
ANY OF THESE FACTORS CAN CAUSE THE
AVOIDANCE OF A CONTRACT.

states that it shall be void if the fact is not as believed. The party making the mistake may also avoid the contract if the mistake is known, or should be known or recognized, by the other contracting party.

A unilateral mistake as to (a) expectations or (b) the law does not have any effect upon the contract. Thus, the fact that a signer of a contract would not have signed if the signer had understood the legal effect of the contract is not a defense.

A minority of states recognize unilateral mistake as a defense unless (1) the mistake is the result of inexcusable lack of due care, or (2) the other party has so changed position in reliance on the contract that rescission would be unconscionable.[1]

(a) MISTAKE AS TO NATURE OF PAPER. When a party makes a negligent mistake as to the nature of a paper, the party is bound according to its terms. For example, when the printed form for a corporation's loan application contained a guaranty by the president of the corporation of the corporate debt, the president signing the application without reading it was bound by this guaranty. This is true even though the president did not know that it was in the application and the application was headed merely "application for credit."

(b) MISTAKE AS TO TERMS OF PAPER. A person who has the ability and the opportunity to read a paper before signing is bound by its terms even though such person signed without reading. Such a signer cannot avoid liability on the ground that there had not been any explanation given of the terms of the writing.

A person unable to read or to understand the terms of a paper is bound by signing the paper without obtaining an explanation of it, unless the other contracting party knows, or has reason to know, of the signer's disability or educational limitation.

Even when a consumer is involved, a court will not permit a contracting party to escape contractual obligations by claiming not to have understood the meaning of the terms clearly expressed in the agreement.[2]

If the party justifiably relies on the explanation of the other party as to the content of the paper, the contract may be avoided when such statements are fraudulent. At one time, the law only regarded reliance on statements of the other party as to the content of a writing as justified when the other party was a lawyer. With the complexity of modern life and the detailed character of many printed forms, the law has come to regard as justifiable the reliance on the statements of the other party when the other party is an agent or salesperson who handles such forms continually and therefore has greater knowledge of their content than the casual customer.

(c) MISTAKE AS TO RELEASE. An insurance claimant is bound by a release given to the insurance company when there is a unilateral mistake as to its meaning resulting from carelessness in reading the release. When a release is given and accepted in good faith, it is initially immaterial that the releasor or both of the parties were

[1]   BMW of North America, Inc. v Krathen (Fla App) 471 So 2d 585 (1985).

[2]   Lanier v Associates Finance, Inc. 114 Ill 2d 1, 101 Ill Dec 852, 499 NE2d 440 (1986).

mistaken as to the seriousness or possible future consequences of a known injury or condition. If the release covers all claims "known or unknown," the courts following the common-law view hold the releasor bound even though there were other injuries of which the releasor was unaware because the effects of the unknown injuries had not yet appeared. Some courts depart from this and hold the release effective only with respect to the conditions or consequences that were known as of the time when the release was given.

§ 15:2   MUTUAL MISTAKE

When both parties make the same mistake of fact, the agreement is void. Thus, the contract is void if both parties mistakenly believe that the contract can be performed, when in fact, it is impossible to perform it. Assume that *A* meets *B* downtown and makes a contract to sell to *B* an automobile, which both believe is in *A's* garage. Actual-

ly the automobile was destroyed by fire an hour before the agreement was made. Since this fact is unknown to both parties, there is a mutual mistake as to the possibility of performing the contract, and the agreement is void.

When a sale is made of a business and both the seller and buyer believe that it is operating at a profit, there is a mutual mistake of fact when the business is actually running at a loss, and the agreement is therefore not binding. No contract arose when the seller stated the price was "fifty-six twenty" and meant $5,620.00 but the buyer thought that the seller was saying "$56.20" because the buyer had priced similar goods ranging in cost from $50 to $200.[3]

In the *Bailey* case the buyer bought a house and land without the seller or the buyer knowing the location of the eastern boundary of the land.

[3]   Konic International Corp. v Spokane Computer Services, Inc. 109 Idaho App 527, 708 P2d 932 (1985).

BAILEY V EWING
105 Idaho App 636, 671 P2d 1099 (1983)

Mary Ellen Erhardt owned a tract of land. After her death, her personal representative decided to sell the land. After discussion with an auctioneer, it was concluded that a better price could be obtained by selling the land as two parcels. At the auction sale, one parcel, described as lot five, was sold to Ewing. A week later, lot six and a 25-foot strip along its eastern boundary was sold to Bailey. Bailey claimed that the boundary line between lots five and six was further to the west than Ewing believed, with the result that both parties claimed ownership of a common strip of land. Bailey brought an action of ejectment to expel Ewing from the strip. Ewing counterclaimed by requesting a reformation of his deed to show that he owned the disputed strip. From a judgment in favor of Bailey, Ewing appealed.

SWANSTROM, J. . . . On October 1, 1977, Erhardt, as the personal representative of decedent Mary Ellen Erhardt, conducted an auction sale of decedent's real and personal property. . . .

On the day of the sale, Erhardt conducted a tour of lot five and the house situated on that lot. During the tour, he indicated to Ewing and other prospective purchasers that he thought the east boundary line of lot five was at or near some lilac bushes about thirteen feet east of the house. He stated several times that he was not sure of the actual location of the boundary line. In addition, the auctioneer mentioned, before bidding began, that nobody knew exactly where the property lines were. Two later surveys showed, in fact, that the boundary line between lots five and six was less than one foot east of the base of the house on lot five. The vertical plane of the true line passed through the eaves of the house. Domestic water and sewer lines serving the house were located along side the house beneath the surface of lot six.

A week after the auction, the personal representative sold the remaining parcel to Bailey, who had attended the auction. The personal representative later deeded lot five to Ewing, and lot six and the adjoining strip to Bailey. During his occupancy of the house on lot five, Ewing mowed the grass, trimmed the lilac bushes and otherwise acted as owner of the property between the house and the lilacs. In June of 1978, Ewing erected a fence just to the east of the lilac bushes. Bailey then caused a survey to be conducted and learned where the "true" line was. He asserted his claim to the strip of property between the bushes and the line, demanding that the fence be removed. After Ewing failed to remove the fence and relinquish the property, Bailey brought this action. Ewing counterclaimed and filed a third-party complaint, seeking reformation of his deed and of the deed to Bailey. He alleged mutual mistake, as well as fraud or misrepresentation on the part of the personal representative. The trial court found no fraud or misrepresentation had occurred. We do not question this finding and it is not material to our decision. The trial court also held that Ewing had made a unilateral mistake as to the location of the boundary line between lots five and six and was therefore not entitled to relief. We focus on this conclusion.

A mistake is an unintentional act or omission arising from ignorance, surprise, or misplaced confidence. The mistake must be material or, in other words, so substantial and fundamental as to defeat the object of the parties. A unilateral mistake is not normally grounds for relief for the mistaken party, whereas a mutual mistake is. A mutual mistake occurs when both parties, at the time of contracting, share a misconception about a basic assumption or vital fact upon which they based their bargain. Some courts require the parties to have the *same* misconception about the *same* basic assumption or vital fact. However, mutual mistake also has been defined to include situations in which the parties labor under *differing* misconceptions as to the *same* basic assumption or vital fact. RESTATEMENT (SECOND) CONTRACTS § 152, comment h (1981) [hereafter cited as Restatement]. We believe the Restatement presents the better view. The assumption or fact must be the same; otherwise two unilateral mistakes, instead of one mutual mistake, would result.

It is undisputed that Erhardt intended to sell the house with lot five and that he assumed the boundary line was located so as to allow him to sell the *whole* house. Erhardt believed the boundary line was somewhere east of its subsequently determined "true" location. Ewing shared this belief. Thus, both Ewing and Erhardt mistakenly believed that the boundary line was further east than it turned out to be. As a result of their ignorance concerning the true location, an act that neither of them intended occurred. Neither intended that the property sold as lot five would fail to include the whole house. Thus, there was an "unintentional act . . . arising from ignorance." We hold, therefore, that Ewing and Erhardt made a mutual mistake regarding the location of the boundary line between lots five and six.

[Judgment reversed and action remanded]

QUESTIONS

1. How is the mistake in the *Bailey* case classified and why?
2. How was the mistake classified by the trial court?
3. What was the significance of holding that the mistake was a mutual mistake of fact?

(a) MISTAKE AS TO EXPECTATIONS. A mutual mistake with respect to expectations ordinarily has no effect on the contract unless the realization of those expectations is made an express condition of the contract. This means that the mistake has no effect unless the contract says that it shall be void if the matter is not as believed.

(b) MISTAKE OF LAW. When the mutual or bilateral mistake is one of law, the contract generally is binding. Thus, even if both parties to a lease mistakenly believe that the leased premises can be used for boarding animals because they are unaware of a zoning regulation that prohibits such a use of the property, the tenant does not have a right to rescind the lease for mutual mistake of law. In the eyes of the law, the parties should have known what the zoning regulations allowed. A few courts have refused to follow this rule, and in several states statutes provide that a mutual mistake of law shall have the same effect as a mutual mistake of fact.

(c) COLLATERAL MATTERS. When a mutual mistake occurs as to a collateral matter, it has no effect on the contract. For example, where the plaintiff asks the fire insurer to issue a policy and both the insured and the insurance company wrongly believed that there was no other policy, the policy that was then issued was not void because of the mutual mistake that there was no other policy. That mistake related to a collateral matter.

B.   DECEPTION

One of the parties to a contract may have been misled by an innocent misrepresenta-tion, a failure to disclose information, or a fraudulent statement.

§ 15:3   INNOCENT MISREPRESENTATION

Suppose one party to a contract makes a statement of fact that is false but that is innocently made without intending to deceive the other party. Can the other party set aside the contract on the ground of being misled by the statement?

Equity will permit the rescission of the contract when the innocent misstatement of a material fact induces another to make the contract. If the deceived person is a defendant in an action *at law* for breach of contract, it is generally held that such innocent deception by the plaintiff cannot be asserted as a defense. There is a tendency, however, for the law courts to adopt the rule of equity. For example, it may be possible for an insurance company to avoid its policy because of an innocent misstatement of a material fact by the applicant. Contracts between persons standing in confidential relationships, such as guardian and ward, or parent and child, can be set aside for the same reason. Some courts go beyond this and permit the recovery of damages sustained because of the misrepresentation.

Modern law is increasingly concerned with the plight of the plaintiff and less concerned with whether the defendant was at fault. This is clearly seen in the case of warranties in the sale of goods.[4] Courts that take this approach see no difference

---

[4]   See Chapter 30.

between an intentional fraudulent statement and an innocent misrepresentation: the plaintiff is misled and harmed in either case.[5]

In some states, statutes have defined *fraud* so as to include innocent misrepresentation.

§ 15:4 NONDISCLOSURE

In contrast to innocent misrepresentation, nondisclosure by one party to a contract generally will not make a contract voidable by the other party. Under certain circumstances, however, nondisclosure will serve to make a contract voidable, especially when the nondisclosure consists of active concealment.

(a) GENERAL RULE OF NONLIABILITY. Ordinarily there is no duty on a party to a contract to volunteer information to the other. If *A* does not ask *B* any questions, *B*

is not under any duty to make a full statement of material facts. Consequently, the nondisclosure of information that is not asked for does not impose fraud liability nor impair the validity of a contract.

(b) EXCEPTIONS. In some instances, the failure to disclose information that was not requested is regarded as fraudulent, and the party to whom the information was not disclosed has the same remedies as though a known false statement were intentionally made.

(1) Unknown Defect or Condition. There is developing in the law a duty for one party who knows of a defect or condition to disclose that information to the other party where the defect or condition is obviously unknown to the other person and is of such a nature that it is unlikely that the other person would discover the truth or inquire about it.

In the *Reed* case, the buyer of a house claimed that she should have been told by the seller that five people had been murdered in the house.

---

[5] Yost v Rieve Enterprises, Inc. (Fla App) 461 So 2d 178 (1984).

REED V KING

145 Cal App 3d 261, 193 Cal Rptr 130 (1983)

Robert King sold his house to Doris Reed. She was not told that ten years before a woman and her four small children had been murdered in the house. Some time after the sale, Reed learned of the murders and sued to rescind the sale. She claimed that because of its bad reputation, the house was not worth what she had paid for it. From a judgment in favor of King, Reed appealed.

BLEASE, A. J. . . . The critical question is: does the seller have a duty to disclose here? Resolution of this question depends on the materiality of the fact of the murders.

In general, a seller of real property has a duty to disclose: "where the seller knows of facts *materially* affecting the value or desirability of the property which are known or accessible only to him and also knows that such facts are not known to, or within the reach of the diligent attention and observation of the buyer, the seller is under a duty to disclose them to the buyer. . . .

Whether information "is of sufficient materiality to affect the value or desirability of the property . . . depends on the facts of the particular case." Materiality "is a question of law, and is part of the concept of right to rely or justifiable reliance." Accordingly, the term is essentially a label affixed to a normative conclusion. Three considerations bear on this legal conclusion: the gravity of the harm inflicted by nondisclosure; the fairness of imposing a duty of discovery on the buyer as an alternative to compelling disclosure; and its impact on the stability of contracts if rescission is permitted.

Numerous cases have found non-disclosure of physical defects and legal impediments to use of real property are material.* However, to our knowledge, no prior real estate sale case has faced an issue of non-disclosure of the kind presented here. Should this variety of ill-repute be required to be disclosed? Is this a circumstance where "non-disclosure of the facts amounts to a failure to act in good faith and in accordance with reasonable standards of fair dealing[?]" (Rest.2d Contracts, § 161, subd. (b).)

The paramount argument against an affirmative conclusion is it permits the camel's nose of unrestrained irrationality admission to the tent. If such an "irrational" consideration is permitted as a basis of rescission the stability of all conveyances will be seriously undermined. Any fact that might disquiet the enjoyment of some segment of the buying public may be seized upon by a disgruntled purchaser to void a bargain. In our view, keeping this genie in the bottle is not as difficult a task as these arguments assume. We do not view a decision allowing Reed to survive a demurrer in these unusual circumstances as endorsing the materiality of facts predicating peripheral, insubstantial, or fancied harms.

The murder of innocents is highly unusual in its potential for so disturbing buyers they may be unable to reside in a home where it has occurred. This fact may foreseeably deprive a buyer of the intended use of the purchase. Murder is not such a common occurrence that *buyers* should be charged with anticipating and discovering this disquieting possibility. Accordingly, the fact is not one for which a duty of inquiry and discovery can sensibly be imposed upon the buyer.

Reed alleges the fact of the murders has a quantifiable effect on the market value of the premises. We cannot say this allegation is inherently wrong and, in the pleading posture of the case, we assume it to be true. If information known or accessible only to the seller has a significant and measurable effect on market value and, as is alleged here, the seller is aware of this effect, we see no principled basis for making the duty to disclose turn upon the character of the information. Physical usefulness is not and never has been the sole criterion of valuation. . . .

Reputation and history can have a significant effect on the value of reality. "George Washington slept here" is worth something, however physically inconsequential that consideration may be. Ill-repute or "bad will" conversely may depress the value of property.

---

* For example, the following have been held of sufficient materiality to require disclosure: the home sold was constructed on filled land (*Burkett v. J. A. Thompson & Son* (1957) 150 Cal.App.2d 523, 310 P2d 56); improvements were added without a building permit and in violation of zoning regulations (*Barder v. McClung* (1949) 93 Cal.App.2d 692, 209 P2d 808) or in violation of building codes (*Curran v. Heslov* (1953) 115 Cal.App.2d 476, 252 P2d 378); the structure was condemned (*Katz v. Department of Real Estate* (1979) 96 Cal.App.3d 895, 158 Cal.Rptr. 766); the structure was termite-infested (*Godfrey v. Steinpress* (1982) 128 Cal.App.3d 154, 180 Cal.Rptr. 95); there was water infiltration in the soil (*Barnhouse v. City of Pinole* (1982) 133 Cal.App.3d 171, 183 Cal.Rptr. 881); the correct amount of net income a piece of property would yield (*Ford v. Cournale* (1973) 36 Cal.App.3d 172, 111 Cal.Rptr.334.)

Whether Reed will be able to prove her allegation the decade-old multiple murder has a significant effect on market value we cannot determine. If she is able to do so by competent evidence she is entitled to a favorable ruling on the issues of materiality and duty to disclose.

[Judgment reversed]

QUESTIONS

1. How was the plaintiff harmed in the *Reed* case?
2. How does the *Reed* case compare with other nondisclosure cases?
3. Does this case stand for the proposition that a buyer can rescind a sales contract whenever the buyer learns of some fact that the seller had failed to volunteer to the buyer?

(2) Confidential Relationship. If *A* and *C* stand in a confidential relationship, such as that of attorney and client, *A* has a duty to reveal anything that is material to *C*'s interest when dealing with *C*. *A*'s silence has the same legal consequence as a knowingly made false statement that there was no material fact to be told to *C*.

As banks offer an increasingly wider range of services to their customers, situations can arise in which the relationship of the bank to its customer is such that the bank has a duty of disclosure that does not exist in the ordinary bank-customer case.[6] For example, many banks act as brokers to buy and sell stock for their depositors. Assume that such a bank also owns stock in its trust department. If it made a contract with a depositor to sell such stock, it would be under a duty to tell the depositor that it owned the stock and that it knew that the stock would soon be worthless because the corporation that had issued the stock was planning to go into bankruptcy.

The relationship between the buyer of a house and a financial institution lending the money to finance the purchase is not a confidential relationship, and therefore the lender is not under any duty to disclose information possessed by it.

(3) Fine Print. An intent to conceal may be present when a printed contract or document contains certain clauses in such fine print that it is reasonable to believe that the other contracting party will neither take the time nor even be able to read such provisions.

In some instances, legislatures have outlawed certain fine print contracts. Statutes commonly declare that insurance policies may not be printed in type of smaller size than designated by statute. Consumer protection statutes frequently require that particular clauses be set in large type. When a merchant selling goods under a written contract disclaims the obligation that goods be fit for their normal use, the Uniform Commercial Code requires the waiver to be set forth in "conspicuous" writing[7] that is defined as requiring "a term or clause . . . [to be] so written that a reasonable person against whom it is to operate ought to have noticed it. A printed heading in capitals . . . is conspicuous. Language in the body of a form is 'conspicuous' if it is in larger or other contrasting type or color . . . ."[8]

There is a growing trend to treat a fine print clause as not binding upon the party who would be harmed thereby, without considering whether fraud was involved. A provision freeing the other contracting

---

[6] Hooper v Barnett Bank (Fla App) 474 So 2d 1253 (1985).

[7] Uniform Commercial Code § 2-316(2).
[8] UCC § 1-201(10).

party from liability is not binding when it is printed in type that is so small that a person with normal vision would have difficulty in reading it.

(4) Active Concealment. Nondisclosure may be more than the passive failure to volunteer information. It may consist of a positive act of hiding information from the other party by physical concealment, or it may consist of furnishing the wrong information. Such conduct constitutes fraud.

§ 15:5   FRAUD

Fraud is (1) the making of a false statement of fact, (2) with knowledge of its falsity or with reckless indifference as to its truth, (3) with the intent that the listener rely thereon, (4) with the result that the listener does so rely, and (5) with the consequence that the listener is harmed.

A seller committed fraud when a car was sold as a "new" demonstrator but in fact had been damaged and repaired three times.[9]

(a) RELIANCE ON STATEMENT. The fact that a fraudulent statement has been made has no importance unless the other party relies on the statement's truth. Consequently, no fraud is shown when the victim has the same knowledge of the true facts as the alleged wrongdoer or the victim should have known such facts.[10] When the false statements have been made after a contract has been signed, it is obvious that the making of the contract was not induced by the statements, and that the other party to the contract had not relied thereon.

When the false statement is such that no reasonable person would believe it to be true, a person cannot claim fraud, even though the person in fact relied on the statement. Similarly, if the victim of the false statement could have easily determined that it was false, it will be held that there is no fraud liability. However, the

fraud victim is not barred from relief because every possible step was not taken to determine whether statements were true. The modern American economy depends upon a fast turnover of goods and this is only possible when there is reliance by buyers upon statements of sellers. Thus, the buyer of a used car is entitled to rely on the statement of the seller that the car had never been in a wreck and that it had nothing wrong with it. This is true, even though if the buyer had had the car raised on a lift, the buyer could have seen the wreck-caused damage to the car and thus learned that the statements of the seller were false.

(b) STATEMENT OF INTENTION OR PROMISE. A statement of intention or promise can constitute fraud when made by a person who does not intend to keep it. To illustrate, a customer purchases goods from a merchant on credit and agrees to pay for them in sixty days. If the customer does not intend to pay for the goods and does not do so, the customer is guilty of fraud by misrepresenting intention.[11]

The mere fact that the defendant has not performed a promise does not in itself establish that the defendant was guilty of fraud.[12] It must be shown that the person made the promise with the intention of not keeping it.

(c) STATEMENT OF OPINION OR VALUE. Ordinarily a misstatement of opinion or value is not regarded as fraudulent on the theory that the person hearing the statement recognizes or should recognize that it is merely the speaker's personal view and not a statement of fact.

If, however, the defendant, in making a statement as to the future, had knowledge not available to the plaintiff that showed that such expectations could not be realized, the statement as to the future expectations can be held fraudulent. Thus, a state-

---

[9]   Martin Chevrolet Sales, Inc. v Dover, ___ Ind App ___, 501 NE2d 1122 (1986).
[10]   Epperson v Roloff (Nev) 719 P2d 799 (1986).

[11]   Goldome Credit Corp. v Hardy (Ala Civ App) 503 So 2d 1227 (1987).
[12]   Lawrence v Underwood, 81 Or App 533, 726 P2d 1189 (1986).

ment that a business would make a stated profit in the future is actionable when the speaker knew that, on the basis of past events, such prediction was false. Likewise, a statement of opinion may be fraudulent when the speaker knows of past or present facts that make the opinion false.

In the *Master Abrasives* case a franchisee claimed that the sales pitch made by the franchisor was fraudulent.

MASTER ABRASIVES CORP. V WILLIAMS
(Ind App) 469 NE2d 1196 (1984)

Master Abrasives Corp. sold a dealership to Williams giving him the exclusive right to sell its products in twenty-two counties. Williams purchased the dealership because Robert F. Oldham, the vice president and national sales manager of Master, told him that there was the potential for earning $30,000 to $40,000 a year, and that the company had distributors who were currently earning that amount. Williams gave Master a down payment. Williams did not pay the balance. When Master sued him he raised the defense of fraud. From a decision in favor of Williams, Master appealed.

CONOVER, J. . . . On September 18, 1982, Master and Williams entered into a sale and distribution agreement whereby Williams paid Master $1,000 and executed a 90-day note in favor of Master for $2,000. Master was to grant Williams exclusive selling rights to its trademarked product for two territories containing a total of 22 counties, provide product education, and sales assistance. At the time of the agreement, Master Abrasive's product line included grinding wheels and grinding points, in various grits, used in metal fabrication applications.

Prior to signing the agreement, Robert F. Oldham (Oldham), controller, vice president, and national sales manager of Master represented to Williams there was a potential for earning $30,000 to $40,000 annually from a distributorship, and Master had distributors who were currently earning that amount.
. . .

Williams argues Oldham's statements concerning profit potential and ease of earning back the investment are sufficient to support a finding of fraud. We disagree. These statements are mere opinion. Williams had no right to rely thereon. The essential elements of actual fraud are a material representation of past or existing *facts*, which representations are false, made with a knowledge or reckless ignorance of this falsity, which causes a reliance upon these representations, to the detriment of the person so relying.

While Oldham's statements as to the profit potential of the franchise are not sufficient for a finding of fraud, his statements about existing distributorships and their profitability will support such a finding. Testimony by Williams showed he relied on Oldham's representation Master had distributors earning $30,000 per year from the distributorships. Testimony by Johnson, however, shows there were only two distributors at the time, one of them being Oldham, and the *total sales* by these distributors during 1982 was only $10,000 to $15,000. Using Oldham's estimated cost of sales percentage of 40%, this shows earnings of only $6,000 to $9,000 for all the distributorships combined. Such a discrepancy is a clear misrepresentation by Oldham of an existing material fact.

A purchaser may rely on statements of fact made by the seller which are not obviously false and where the buyer lacks facilities for ascertaining the truth, as where facts are peculiarly within the knowledge of the seller. Here, the profitability of existing distributorships could have been known only by the principals of Master or the distributors themselves. Thus Williams reasonably could have relied upon such representations. That they were false statements renders them fraudulent. . . .

[Judgment affirmed]

QUESTIONS

1. What distinction did the court make between statements as to the potential earnings of Williams and the actual earnings of other dealers?
2. How would the case have been decided if nothing had been said as to the earnings of the other dealers?
3. Was Williams entitled to rely on the statements made to him as to the earnings of other dealers? Explain.

(d) STATEMENT OF LAW. A misstatement of law is treated in the same manner as a misstatement of opinion or value. Ordinarily the listener is regarded as having an opportunity of knowing what the law is, an opportunity equal to that of the speaker, so that the listener is not entitled to rely on what the speaker says. When the speaker has expert knowledge of the law or claims to have such knowledge, however, the misstatement of law can be the basis for fraud liability.

(e) USE OF ASSUMED NAME. The use of an assumed name is not necessarily fraudulent or unlawful. It is only such when the user of the name uses the name of another person or makes up a name for the purpose of concealment to avoid arrest or to avoid creditors or to imitate a competitor and deceive customers.

In the absence of any intent to evade or deceive by the use of the assumed name, it is lawful for a person to go by any name, although other persons may refuse to enter into contracts unless the actual name is used. If a person makes a contract in an as-

sumed or fictitious name or in a trade name, such person is bound by the contract because that name was in fact used to identify that person.

A married woman has the right to retain her maiden name. Moreover, a married woman who has taken her husband's name may return to her maiden name if they are divorced.

(f) UNCONSCIONABILITY AND CONSUMER PROTECTION. In many states, greater protection than is allowed under the common-law doctrine of fraud is given by applying the concept of unconscionability or the specific provisions of a consumer protection statute. That is, relief is at times given the victim in deception and hardship cases, even though some of the elements required to impose fraud liability are not present.

C.   PRESSURE

What appears to be an agreement may not in fact be voluntary because one of the parties entered into it because of undue influence or physical or economic duress.

§ 15:6   UNDUE INFLUENCE

An aged parent may entrust all business affairs to a trusted child; an invalid may rely on a nurse; a client may follow implicitly whatever an attorney recommends. The relationship may be such that for practical purposes, the one person is helpless in the hands of the other. When such a confidential relationship exists, it is apparent that the parent, the invalid, or the client is not in fact exercising a free will in making a contract suggested by the child, nurse, or attorney, but is merely following the will of the other person. Because of the great possibility that the person dominating the other will take unfair advantage, the law presumes that the dominating person exerts **undue influence** upon the other person whenever the dominating person obtains any benefit from a contract made with the dominated person. The contract is then voidable and may be set aside by the dominated person unless the dominating person can prove that, at the time the contract was made, no unfair advantage had been taken.

The class of confidential relationships is not well-defined. It ordinarily includes the relationships of parent and child, guardian and ward, physician and patient, attorney and client, and any other relationship of trust and confidence in which one party exercises a control or influence over another.[13]

Whether undue influence exists is a difficult question for the court (ordinarily the jury) to determine. The law does not regard every influence as undue. Thus, nagging may drive a person to make a contract, but that is not ordinarily regarded as undue influence. Persuasion and argument are not in themselves undue influence.

An essential element of undue influence is that the person making the contract does not exercise free will. In the absence of a recognized type of confidential relationship, such as that between parent and child, the courts are likely to take the attitude that the person who claims to have been dominated was merely persuaded, and consequently, there was no undue influence.

§ 15:7   DURESS

A party may enter into a contract to avoid a threatened danger. The danger threatened may be a physical harm to person or property, called **physical duress;** or it may be a threat of financial loss, called **economic duress.**

(a) PHYSICAL DURESS. A person makes a contract under **duress** when there is such violence or threat of violence that the person is deprived of free will and makes the contract to avoid harm. The threatened harm may be directed at a near relative of the contracting party as well as against a contracting party. A contract is executed under duress when it is executed by parents under threat that their child will be prosecuted for a crime if they do not make the contract.[14] If a contract is made under duress, the resulting agreement is voidable at the victim's election.

Agreements made to bring an end to mass disorders or violence are ordinarily not binding contracts because they were obtained by duress.

(b) ECONOMIC DURESS. The economic pressure on a contracting party may be so great that it will be held to constitute duress. Economic duress occurs when the victim is threatened with irreparable loss for which adequate recovery could not be obtained by suing the wrongdoer.

In the *Rich & Whillock* case, the creditor reduced the amount of the bill that was owed when the debtor refused to pay anything if the full bill was demanded.

---

13 Misskelly v Rogers (Mo App) 721 SW2d 170 (1986).

14 Nebraska v Rodriquez, 20 Neb 808, 374 NW2d 1 (1985).

RICH & WHILLOCK, INC. V ASHTON DEVELOPMENT, INC.

157 Cal App 3d 1154, 204 Cal Rptr 86 (1984)

Ashton Development, Inc. and Bob Britton, Inc. were developing a tract of land. They made a contract with Rich & Whillock to perform grading and excavating work. Installment payments were made for this work as it progressed. When the project was completed, there was a balance due Rich & Whillock of approximately $72,000. Ashton and Britton offered to pay $50,000 and declared that it would be necessary to bring a lawsuit to get any more. Rich & Whillock informed Ashton and Britton that they would be forced into bankruptcy if they were not paid because they owed subcontractors, laborers, and suppliers of equipment in connection with the job. In order to avoid bankruptcy, Rich & Whillock accepted $50,000 and signed a release of any additional amount. Some time later Rich & Whillock sued Ashton and Britton for $22,000. The defendants raised the defense that this claim was barred by the release.

WEINER, A. J. . . . At the outset it is helpful to acknowledge the various policy considerations which are involved in cases involving economic duress. Typically, those claiming such coercion are attempting to avoid the consequences of a modification of an original contract or of a settlement and release agreement. On the one hand, courts are reluctant to set aside agreements because of the notion of freedom of contract and because of the desirability of having private dispute resolutions be final. On the other hand, there is an increasing recognition of the law's role in correcting inequitable or unequal exchanges between parties of disproportionate bargaining power and a greater willingness to not enforce agreements which were entered into under coercive circumstances.

California courts have recognized the economic duress doctrine in private sector cases for at least 50 years. The doctrine is equitably based and represents "but an expansion by courts of equity of the old commonlaw doctrine of duress." As it has evolved to the present day, the economic duress doctrine is not limited by early statutory and judicial expressions requiring an unlawful act in the nature of a tort or a crime. Instead, the doctrine now may come into play upon the doing of a wrongful act which is sufficiently coercive to cause a reasonably prudent person faced with no reasonable alternative to succumb to the perpetrator's pressure. The assertion of a claim known to be false or a bad faith threat to breach a contract or to withhold a payment may constitute a wrongful act for purposes of the economic duress doctrine. Further, a reasonably prudent person subject to such an act may have no reasonable alternative but to succumb when the only other alternative is bankruptcy or financial ruin. . . .

The underlying concern of the economic duress doctrine is the enforcement in the marketplace of certain minimal standards of business ethics. Hard bargaining, "efficient" breaches and reasonable settlements of good faith disputes are all acceptable, even desirable, in our economic system. That system can be viewed as a game in which everybody wins, to one degree or another, so long as everyone plays by the common rules. Those rules are not limited to precepts of rationality and self-interest. They include equitable notions of fairness and propriety which preclude the wrongful exploitation of business exigencies to obtain disproportionate exchanges of value. Such exchanges make a mockery of freedom of contract and undermine the proper functioning of our economic system. The economic duress doctrine serves as a last resort to correct these aberrations when conventional alternatives and remedies are unavailing. The necessity for the doctrine in cases such as this has been graphically described.

> Nowadays, a wait of even a few weeks in collecting on a contract claim is sometimes serious or fatal for an enterprise at a crisis in its history. The business of a creditor in financial straits is at the mercy of an unscrupulous debtor, who need only suggest that if the creditor does not care to settle on the debtor's own hard terms, he can sue. This situation, in which promptness in payment is vastly more important than even approximate justice in the settlement terms, is too common in modern business relations to be ignored by society and the courts.

Here, Britton and Ashton acted in bad faith when they refused to pay Rich & Whillock, Inc.'s final billing and offered instead to pay a compromise amount of $50,000. At the time of their bad faith breach and settlement offer, Britton, and through him, Ashton, knew Rich & Whillock, Inc. was a new company overextended to creditors and subcontractors and faced with imminent bankruptcy if not paid its final billing. Whillock and Rich strenuously protested Britton's and Ashton's coercive tactics, and succumbed to them only to avoid economic disaster to themselves and the adverse ripple effects of their bankruptcy on those to whom they were indebted. Under these circumstances, the trial court found the July 10 agreement and August 20 release were the products of economic duress. That finding is consistent with the legal principles discussed above and is supported by substantial evidence. Accordingly, the court correctly concluded Ashton Development, Inc. and Bob Britton, Inc. were liable for the $22,286.45 balance due under the contract.

[Judgment affirmed]

QUESTIONS

1. What did the court decide?
2. What is the basis for the court's decision?
3. What is the basis for the doctrine that the court applied?

Generally, a threat of economic loss or pressure caused by economic conditions does not constitute duress that makes a contract voidable. The fact that the plaintiff drove a hard bargain does not give rise to the defense of economic duress. When money is in fact owed a creditor, a threat by the creditor to sue the debtor to collect the amount owed does not constitute unlawful duress. It is merely a statement of what the law entitles the creditor to do.

There is some indication that in a consumer situation, duress may be given a broader meaning to include any pressure that, as a practical matter, does not leave the weaker party a choice. Thus, it has been held that a tenant may have acted under duress in agreeing to limit the liability of a furniture moving company when all of the tenant's furniture had been loaded on the moving van; it was 7 p.m.; and the movers then refused to drive the van to the new apartment until the tenants signed the limitation of liability.[15] In all cases, the economic pressure must have been exerted by the other contracting party. If merely produced by the victim's own financial condition, a contract entered into voluntarily cannot be avoided on the ground of duress.

§ 15:8   ADHESION CONTRACTS

Pressure on a contracting party may not be as extreme as physical duress or economic duress. It may still be sufficient to justify the conclusion that there was no genuine assent freely given and that, accordingly, the basic element of a voluntary agreement was lacking and that what appears to be a contract is merely a voidable transaction. Such a situation is frequently described as involving a **contract of adhesion.** Such a contract is one that is offered by a dominant party to a party with inferior bargaining power on a take-it-or-leave-it basis. The weaker person cannot go elsewhere to obtain the goods or services desired and therefore must deal on the terms dictated by the superior party or do without.

With the rise of the concept of unconscionability[16] and the adoption of consumer protection laws,[17] the need to apply the adhesion contract concept has diminished greatly. In most cases it is held that the concept is not applicable either because there is not a gross inequality of bargaining power or because the goods or services could be obtained elsewhere.[18]

D.   REMEDIES

When there is not a genuine agreement of the parties, the remedy may be a rescission of the contract, an action for damages, or an action for reformation of the contract.

Mistake, fraud, undue influence, and duress may make the agreement voidable or, in some instances, void. The following remedies are then available.

§ 15:9   RESCISSION

If the contract is voidable, it can be rescinded or set aside by the party who has been injured or of whom advantage has been taken. If not avoided, however, the contract is valid and binding. In no case can the other party, the wrongdoer, set aside the contract. If the agreement is void, neither party can enforce it and no act of avoidance is required by either party to set the contract aside.

§ 15:10   DAMAGES

If the other party was guilty of a wrong, such as fraud, as distinguished from making an innocent mistake, the injured party may sue for damages caused by such a wrong. In the case of the sale of goods, the aggrieved party may both rescind and recover damages; but in other contracts, the victim must choose one of these two remedies.[19] Thus, a buyer rescinding a contract for the sale of a house because of fraud cannot also recover damages for the fraud.

§ 15:11   REFORMATION OF CONTRACT BY COURT

At times a written contract does not correctly state the agreement already made by the parties. When this occurs either party can have the court correct or reform the writing to state the agreement actually

---

[15]   Peter Matthews, Ltd. v Robert Mabey, Inc. 117 App Div 2d 943, 499 NYS2d 254 (1986). (Note that other courts would have reached the same result by finding that under the circumstances the limitation of liability was unconscionable and not binding. As to unconscionability, generally, see § 17:5.)
[16]   See § 17:5 of this book.
[17]   See Chapter 8 of this book.
[18]   Cubic Corporation v Marty, 185 Cal App 3d 438, 229 Cal Rptr 828 (1986).

[19]   UCC § 2-721, Potomac Leasing Co. v Thrasher, 181 Ga App 883, 354 SE2d 210 (1987).

made. A court action for reformation may be necessary because a change of circumstances or the occurrence of certain events may cause the other party to refuse to voluntarily change the written contract. For example, if A obtains a collision insurance policy on an automobile, but through mistake the policy describes the wrong car, A can obtain a decree of court declaring that the policy covers the car that A and the insurance company intended to insure rather than the car wrongly identified in the policy. The insurance company would have gladly made the correction prior to any loss being sustained, but if the car A intended to insure has been damaged, court reformation would be necessary.

In the *Phil Bramsen* case the parties contracted in terms of a cost of living index that did not exist.

PHIL BRAMSEN DISTRIBUTOR, INC. V MASTRONI AND KUHSE
(App) 151 Ariz 194, 726 P2d 610 (1986)

Mastroni and Kuhse leased land to Phil Bramsen Distributor. The lease specified the amount of the rent and provided that such amount would be reset every five years according to the cost of living index prepared by the United States Department of Labor for the city of Phoenix. A dispute arose, and the lessee brought a suit to rescind the lease on the ground that there was no such cost of living index. The lessor counterclaimed, seeking a reformation of the lease. The lower court reformed the lease to refer to the Phoenix cost of living index prepared by the Bureau of Business and Economic Research at Arizona State University. The lessee appealed.

HATHAWAY, J. . . . Neither the Bureau of Labor Statistics (BLS) nor any other subdivision of the United States Government prepares a consumer price index (CPI) for Phoenix. . . .

After a trial to the court, judgment was entered . . . reforming the rent escalation clause by replacing the "consumer price index prepared by the United States Bureau of Labor Statistics" with the "consumer price index for Phoenix, Arizona." The court went on to hold that the metropolitan Phoeniz consumer price index prepared by the Bureau of Business and Economic Research, Arizona State University, would be used in the reformed escalation clause. . . .

Before reformation can be granted, a court must be presented with clear and convincing evidence that (1) a mutual mistake was made by the parties in drafting the instrument, and (2) that the minds of the parties had met on a definite intention before the instrument was drafted.

Appellants argue that in the current situation, there was no mutual mistake but rather a unilateral mistake on the part of the appellees. Their argument is based largely upon *Seattle First National Bank v. Earl*, 17 Wash.App. 830, 565 P.2d 1215 (1977). In that case, the parties entered into a 49-year lease agreement with an option for 20 additional years. The lessor suggested that the escalation clause be based on the cost of living index prepared for the City of Spokane, Washington. As in our case, there was no such cost of living index. Since the lessor had suggested the use of the cost of living index and the other party had accepted the lessor's analysis and opinion, the court held that the mistake was unilateral on the part of the lessor as opposed to mutual. The Washington court refused to reform the escalation clause. The same result does not necessarily hold true under the facts of the case at bench.

In the present case, the parties agreed to an escalation clause based on the rate of inflation. It was a mistake of fact that caused the clause to fail. The draftsman, Mastroni's attorney, inserted the term "cost of living index for the City of Phoenix prepared by the Bureau of Labor Statistics." There is no evidence that either appellees or appellants Bramsen had any independent knowledge of such an index or relied on anyone's word but the attorney's. Therefore, by mutual mistake the parties believed they had a workable formula. Appellants argue that because the attorney was Mastroni's agent, the mistake is still unilateral. Even if we were to agree that the drafter was Mastroni's agent, this argument fails. If a mutual mistake of the parties results from the mistake of the draftsman, it is immaterial, so far as reformation is concerned, which party employed him.

The parties clearly intended to have an escalation clause based on inflation. It was only the error of the scrivner that caused this escalation clause to be unenforceable and the trial court could have found that there was a mutual mistake.

Appellants also argue that there was no agreement by the parties to the lease concerning the escalation clause prior to the drafting of the lease. The parties did, however, agree that there would be an escalation clause based upon inflation. Therefore there was an agreement prior to the drafting of the lease. Appellants Bramsen also argue that the misrepresentation, albeit innocent, as to the existence of a consumer price index for Phoenix prepared by the BLS should preclude reformation of the contract. Any innocent representations did not go to the heart of the agreement, since appellants were prepared to accept an escalation clause based on the CPI for the City of Phoenix. The cases cited by Bramsen are inapposite. No equitable reason appears for refusing to reform the lease agreement. On the contrary, equity favors the reformation, otherwise appellant would receive an unconscionable windfall if allowed to enforce his lease at the current rental price. Additionally, the court correctly excluded evidence of fairness. Courts will not consider the adequacy of consideration unless unconscionable. This contract is not unconscionable.

Appellees argue that the trial court, rather than reforming the contract, could have interpreted the contract to encompass the CPI prepared by Arizona State University rather than the mythical one prepared by the BLS. We do not agree with appellees' argument. The language "cost of living index for Phoenix, Arizona . . . prepared by the Bureau of Labor Statistics" is not ambiguous. Therefore, rules of construction relative to ambiguous instruments are not applicable. If this escalation clause is to be enforced at all, it must be done through reformation of the contract. We see no equitable, legal or factual reasons for precluding the trial court from reforming this contract.

[Judgment as to reformation affirmed]

QUESTIONS

1. Why was reformation granted in the *Bramsen* case?
2. What was the significance of the fact that the improper description of the

> cost of living index was added to the written lease by the attorney for one of the lessors? Explain.
>
> 3. Did the court regard the lease provision relating to the cost of living index as ambiguous?

SUMMARY

The assent of a party to an agreement is not genuine or voluntary in certain cases of mistake, deception, or pressure. When this is so, the agreement of the parties does not give rise to a contract, and what appears to be a contract can be avoided by the victim of such circumstances or conduct.

As to mistake, it is necessary to distinguish between unilateral mistakes that are unknown to the other contracting party and those that are known. Mistakes that are unknown to the other party typically do not affect the binding character of the agreement. A unilateral mistake that the other contracting party has knowledge or reason to know makes the contract avoidable by the victim of the mistake.

The deception situation may be one of innocent misrepresentation, nondisclosure, or fraud. The innocent misrepresentation generally has no effect on the binding quality of an agreement, although there is a trend to recognize it as a ground for avoiding the contract. A few courts allow the recovery of damages. When one party to the contract knows of a fact that has a bearing on the transaction, the failure to volunteer information as to that fact to the other contracting party is called nondisclosure. The law ordinarily does not attach any significance to nondisclosure, deeming that it is preferable that the party lacking the knowledge ask questions of the party with knowledge, rather than imposing a duty on the party with knowledge to volunteer information. Thus, the agreement of the parties is not affected by the fact that one party did not disclose information to the other party. Contrary to this rule, there is a duty to volunteer information when a confidential relationship exists between the possessor of the knowledge and the other contracting party. A strong modern trend in the law imposes a duty to disclose or volunteer information relating to matters that are not likely to be inquired about by the other contracting party, such as a hidden defect or condition that a stranger is not likely to perceive and is not likely to inquire about.

When concealment goes beyond mere silence and consists of actively taking of steps to hide the truth, the conduct may be classified as fraud rather than nondisclosure. There is a growing trend to hold fine print clauses not binding on the theory that they are designed to hide the truth from the other contracting party. Consumer protection statutes often outlaw fine print clauses by requiring particular contracts or particular clauses in contracts to be printed in type of a specified size. Fraud is the making of a false statement, with knowledge of its falsity or reckless indifference as to its truth, with the intent that the other person rely thereon and such person does rely on such false statement and sustains harm or loss. Ordinarily the false statement cannot be a statement of intention or a promise, although it is fraud when the present, secret intention is contrary to the stated intention. Likewise, a statement of opinion, value, or law cannot ordinarily be the basis for fraud liability, although it can when the maker of the false statement claims to be an expert as to the particular subject matter and is making the statement as an expert. The use of an assumed name is not fraudulent when not done for the purpose of deceiving.

The free will of a person, essential to the voluntary character of a contract, may be lacking because the agreement had been obtained by pressure. This may range from undue influence, which is something more than nagging or continuous hounding; through the array of threats of extreme economic loss (called economic duress); to the threat of physical force that would cause serious personal injury or damage to property (called physical duress). The mere fact that one party to the contract has great bargaining power and offers the other party a printed contract on a take-it-or-leave-it basis (an adhesion contract) does not prove that the agreement was not voluntary. However, some courts have held that in such cases the agreement is not voluntary if the weaker party cannot obtain the desired goods or services elsewhere.

When the voluntary character of an agreement has been destroyed by mistake, deception, or pressure, the victim may avoid or rescind the contract or may ratify the contract and obtain money damages from the wrongdoer sufficient to put the victim in the position that the victim would have held had there been a voluntary agreement. In cases of fraud, some jurisdictions depart from this rule and limit the plaintiff to recovering the out-of-pocket expenses. All these remedies may be lost by delay. Rescission is also lost if the aggrieved party is not able to put things back the way they were before the contract was made (restore the status quo ante). When the mistake consists of an error in putting an oral contract in writing, either party may ask the court to reform or correct the writing so that it states the actual agreement of the parties.

QUESTIONS AND CASE PROBLEMS

1. Explain the objective of each of the following rules of law:
   (a) One party generally cannot set aside a contract because the other party failed to volunteer information that the complaining party would desire to know.
   (b) In certain close relationships that are regarded as confidential, it is presumed that a contract that benefits the dominating person was obtained by undue influence, and the dominating person has the burden of proving the contrary.
2. How is a contract affected by a unilateral mistake?
3. Lester purchased a used automobile from MacKintosh Motors. He asked the seller if the car had ever been in a wreck. The MacKintosh salesperson had never seen the car before that morning and knew nothing of its prior history, but quickly answered Lester's question by stating: "No. It has never been in a wreck." In fact, the auto had been seriously damaged in a wreck and, although repaired, was worth much less than the value it would have had if there had not been any wreck.

When Lester learned the truth, he sued MacKintosh Motors and the salesperson for damages for fraud. They raised the defense that the salesperson did not know that the statement was false and had not intended to deceive Lester. Did the conduct of the salesperson constitute fraud?

4. For convenience, Henry Hanschlagel wants to shorten and change his name. May he open a bank account using the name of *Henry Shaw* without his first obtaining a court order approving this change of name?
5. Yang and Richard make a contract for the sale of an automobile. They orally agree that the price Richard is to pay is $2,000 but when the written contract is typed, the amount is wrongly stated as $3,000 and this contract is signed before anyone notices the mistake. Yang then claims that the written contract is binding and that Richard is required to pay $3,000. He claims that he is only required to pay the originally agreed to amount of $2,000. Is he correct?
6. Compare (a) misrepresentation, (b) nondisclosure, and (c) fraud.

7. Mary purchased a home from the Mitchell Developers. She was told that the house was free from termites. Actually the house was infested with termites, and there was extensive termite damage in the house. This was known to Mitchell, and Mitchell had intentionally concealed the damage by paint and paper. When Mary learned of the actual termite condition, she sued Mitchell for damages for fraud and to set aside the contract. How will her claims be decided by the court?

8. If a buyer makes an arithmetic mistake in calculating the quantity of goods to purchase, what effect does such mistake have upon the contract to purchase the excessive amount?

9. The Browns were having a house built. The contractor purchased brick from the Georgia-Carolina Brick and Tile Co. The contract required the brick company to supply the entire quantity ordered from the same "run" or manufacturer's lot of brick. Bricks from two different runs were sent. The color for the two was not exactly the same. The representative of the brick company falsely stated to the Browns that when the bricks dried out, they would all be the same color. The representative knew that this was false. When the company was sued for fraud, it raised the defense that the statement of its representative was merely an opinion and therefore could not give rise to fraud liability. Was this defense valid? [Georgia-Carolina Brick & Tile Co. v Brown, 153 Ga App 747, 266 SE2d 531]

10. A claimed that B owed him money. A was under the impression that B did not have much money. On the basis of this impression, A made a settlement agreement with B for a nominal amount. When A later learned that B was in fact reasonably wealthy, A sought to set the agreement aside. Was A entitled to do so?

11. An agent of Thor Food Service Corp. was seeking to sell Makofske a combination refrigerator-freezer and food purchase plan. Makofske was married and had three children. After being informed of the eating habits of Makofske and his family, the agent stated that the cost of the freezer and food would be about $95 to $100 a month. Makofske carefully examined the agent's itemized estimate and made some changes to it. Makofske then signed the contract and purchased the refrigerator-freezer. The cost proved to be greater than the estimated $95 to $100 a month, and Makofske claimed that the contract had been obtained by fraud. Decide. [Thor Food Service Corp. v Makofske, 28 Misc 2d 872, 218 NYS2d 93]

12. On December 1, 1964, Neely, a senior in college, made a contract to play the following year for the Houston Oilers professional football team. It was agreed orally that the making of this contract would be kept secret so that Neely would appear to be eligible for a postseason college game. Neely then received a better offer from the Dallas Cowboys and after college went to play for them. Houston sought an injunction against Neely to prevent him from playing with the Dallas Cowboys. Neely claimed Houston could not enforce the contract because of its fraud in stating that the contract would be effective on January 2, 1965, and in filing the contract with the League Commissioner before that time. This violated the agreement to keep the execution of the contract secret so as to make him appear eligible for the post-season college football game. Was Neely's defense valid? [Houston Oilers, Inc. v Neely (CA10 Okla) 361 F2d 36]

13. In 1622, a fleet of Spanish treasure ships sank, 40 nautical miles off the Florida coast. In 1971, Treasure Salvors, Inc. located one of the wrecked ships, the Atocha. Treasure Salvors and the Department of State of Florida believed that the wreck was located on the Florida coastal strip. On this basis, the State of Florida and Treasure Salvors made successive annual contracts giving Treasure Salvors the right to search for sunken treasure of the wreck in return for its giving Florida 25 percent of everything that was found. In a subsequent lawsuit, it was determined that the wreck was not on Florida land. Treasure Salvors claimed that it was not bound by its contract with Florida. Was it correct? [Florida v Treasure Salvors, Inc. (CA5 Fla) 621 F2d 1340]

14. Sippy was thinking of buying the house of Christich. He noticed water marks on the ceiling, but the agent showing the house

stated that the roof had been repaired and was in good condition. Sippy was not told that the roof still leaked and that the repairs had not been able to stop the leaking. Sippy bought the house. Some time later, heavy rains caused water to leak into the house. Sippy claimed that Christich was guilty of fraud. Was he correct? [Sippy v Christich, 4 Kan App 2d 511, 609 P2d 204]

15. Pileggi owed money to Young. Young threatened to bring suit against Pileggi for the amount due. Pileggi feared the embarrassment of being sued and the possibility that he might be thrown into bankruptcy because of the suit. In order to avoid being sued, Pileggi executed a promissory note promising to pay to Young the amount due. He later asserted that the note was not binding because he had executed it under duress. Is this defense valid? [Young v Pileggi, 309 Pa Super 565, 455 A2d 1228]

16

CONSIDERATION

In Chapter 13, you saw that an agreement between the parties is one of the essential ingredients of a binding contract. The existence of an agreement ensures that the obligations created by the contract have been voluntarily assumed. Society will not, however, muster its resources to enforce every promise. As a condition for enforceability, society requires that a promise be supported by a consideration, that is, the promise must have been obtained in return for something else. Does it matter what is offered in return? Historically, it does not.

In the days of Adam Smith, the law left it to the contracting parties to determine what each party wanted as consideration. Whether that was too much or too little was no concern of the law. In the last few decades, this social desire for unrestricted bargaining freedom lost much of its appeal when it was seen that those with inferior economic power or education could not take care of themselves. In order to prevent consumer exploitation, consumer protection statutes and the concept of unconscionability have made the law examine the sufficiency or adequacy of the consideration. Going in the opposite direction, society has chosen to enforce promises made in certain situations even though no consideration at all was present. Thus, in some instances, no consideration is required to make a promise binding.

A.   GENERAL PRINCIPLES

One of the elements needed to make an agreement binding is consideration. This chapter discusses what this means.

§ 16:1   DEFINITION

Consideration is what a promisor demands and receives as the price for the promise.[1] Consideration is something to which the promisor is not otherwise entitled, which the promisor specifies as the price for the promise. It is not necessary that the promisor expressly use the word *consideration*.

Since consideration is the price paid for the promise, it is unimportant who pays that price as long as it has been agreed that it should be paid in that way. For example, consideration may be the extending of credit to a third person, as extending credit to the corporation of which the promisor is a stockholder. Likewise, when a bank lends money to a third person, such lending is consideration for the promise of its customer to repay the loan to the bank if it will loan the money to the third person.[2]

(a) NATURE OF CONTRACT. In a unilateral contract, the consideration for the promise is the doing of the act called for. The doing of the act in such case is also the acceptance of the offer of the promisor.

In a bilateral contract, which is an exchange of promises, each promise is the consideration for the other promise. When a lawsuit is brought for breaking a promise, it is the consideration for the broken promise to which attention is directed.

(b) AGREED EXCHANGE. Consideration is what is agreed to in return for the promise of the defendant. In most cases, this will directly benefit the defendant (the promisor) and will be some burden or detriment to the plaintiff (the promisee). For example, an employer who promises to pay wages sustains detriment by promising to pay the wages in exchange for the benefit of receiving the employee's promise to work. The important thing, however, is that what is received is what was asked for as the price of the promise.

As long as someone gives what was asked for by the promisor, the promisor's obligation is supported by consideration, even though the economic benefit of the promise is not received by the third person giving the consideration. Thus, when a third person comes to the financial aid of a debtor by making some promise *to* the creditor in exchange for some promise *from* the creditor, consideration exists. The contract is binding, even though the creditor's promise benefits the debtor rather than the third person. A promise guaranteeing a loan to a corporation is binding although the money loaned was all received by the corporation and nothing was received by the promisor.

§ 16:2   EFFECT OF ABSENCE OF CONSIDERATION

The absence of consideration makes a promise not binding. Thus, a person sued for breaking a promise will not be held liable when no consideration was received for the promise. For example, when the promise of an employee to refrain from competing with the employer is not supported by consideration, the promise is not binding, and the employee may compete with the employer. When a creditor promises the debtor that the debtor can have more time in which to pay the debt, the creditor is not bound by that promise because no consid-

---

[1]   Starr v Robinson, 181 Ga App 9, 351 SE2d 238 (1986).
[2]   Peterson Bank v Langendorf, 136 Ill App 3d 537, 90 Ill Dec 961, 483 NE2d 279 (1985).

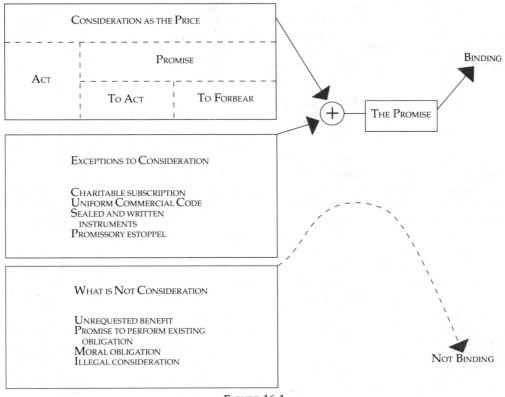

FIGURE 16-1
CONSIDERATION AND PROMISES

eration was given for it.[3] Likewise, an offer that is to be held open for a specified number of days may be revoked at any time when no consideration is given for the promise to keep the offer open.

(a) MORAL OBLIGATION. The fact that the promisor feels morally obligated to make the promise does not make the promise binding when there is no consideration for it. Thus, a promise to pay money to an investor because the promisor feels responsible for the investor's loss is not binding. There is no consideration for the promise, and the moral obligation of the promisor does not constitute or take the place of consideration.[4]

(b) LEGALITY DISTINGUISHED. While the absence of consideration ordinarily prevents enforcing a promise, the absence of consideration has no greater effect. That is, the agreement is not illegal because there was no consideration. Consequently, when a person keeps the promise, the performance rendered cannot be thereafter revoked on the ground that there was no consideration. To illustrate, a promise to make a gift cannot be enforced because there is no consideration for the promise, but once the gift is made, the donor cannot take the gift back because there was no consideration.

16:3   LEGALITY OF
            CONSIDERATION

The law will not permit persons to make contracts that violate the law. Accordingly,

---

[3] Howard v South Carolina National Bank, 288 SC App 432, 343 SE2d 41 (1986).
[4] Seller v Citizens & Southern National Bank, 177 Ga App 85, 338 SE2d 480 (1985).

a promise to do something that the law prohibits or a promise to refrain from doing something that the law requires is not valid consideration, and the contract is illegal. This subject is further discussed in Chapter 17.

§ 16:4   FAILURE OF CONSIDERATION

When a promise is given as consideration, the question arises as to whether the promisor will perform the promise.

(a) NONPERFORMANCE OF PROMISE. If the promise is not performed, the law describes the default as a "failure of consideration."[5]

(b) BAD BARGAIN DISTINGUISHED. When the promisor performs the promise, there is never a failure of consideration. The fact that it turns out that the consideration is disappointing does not mean that there has been a failure of consideration. That is, the fact that the contract proves to be a bad bargain for the promisor does not constitute a failure of consideration or affect the binding character of the contract.[6] For example, when one buys a store building in a real estate development, one obviously does so in the expectation of obtaining a large volume of trade by virtue of the location. It may be that this will not occur because of the continuing of earlier shopping habits of the public. While the buyer of the store building is disappointed, there has not been any failure of consideration with respect to the contract for the purchase of the store from the owner.

B.   WHAT CONSTITUTES CONSIDERATION

The sections that follow analyze certain common situations in which a lawsuit turned on whether the promisor received consideration for the promise sued upon.

§ 16:5   A PROMISE AS CONSIDERATION

In a bilateral contract, each party makes a promise to the other. The promise that one party makes is consideration for the promise made by the other.

The fact that parties appear to be in agreement does not mean that there is a promise. Thus, a statement that a proposed step would be "no problem" does not constitute a promise.[7]

(a) BINDING CHARACTER OF PROMISE. To constitute consideration, a promise must be binding; that is, it must impose a liability or create a duty. An unenforceable promise cannot be consideration. Suppose that a coal company promises to sell to a factory at a specific price all the coal which it orders, and that the factory agrees to pay that price for any coal which it orders from the coal company. The promise of the factory is not consideration because it does not obligate the factory to buy any coal from the coal company. If, however, the factory promises to purchase all the coal it requires for a specific period, and the coal dealer agrees to supply it at a specific price per ton, there is a valid contract.

(b) CONDITIONAL PROMISE. Can a conditional promise be consideration? Assume that an agreement states "buyer promises to buy, provided buyer can obtain financing." Is such a promise consideration for the seller's promise to sell, or is the buyer's promise not consideration because it does not impose any obligation on the buyer at the time that the promise is made?

The fact that a promise is conditional does not prevent it from being considera-

[5]   Alber v Standard Heating and Air Conditioning, Inc. (Ind App) 476 NE2d 507 (1985).
[6]   Perry v Welch (Tex App) 725 SW2d 347 (1987).

[7]   Cantrell v City Federal Sav. & Loan Ass'n. (Ala) 496 So 2d 746 (1986).

tion, even though, as a practical matter, it is unlikely that the condition would ever be satisfied.[8] Thus, the promise of a fire insurance company to pay the homeowner in case of fire is consideration for the payment of premiums by the homeowner, even though it is probable that there will never be a fire.

(c) CANCELLATION PROVISION. Although a promise must impose a binding obligation, it may authorize one or either party to terminate or cancel the agreement under certain circumstances or upon giving notice to the other party. The fact that the contract may be terminated in this manner

does not make the contract any less binding prior to such termination.

§ 16:6 PROMISE TO PERFORM EXISTING OBLIGATION

Ordinarily a promise to do what one is already under a legal obligation to do is not consideration. Similarly, a promise to refrain from doing what one has no legal right to do is not consideration. This preexisting duty or legal obligation can be based upon statute, upon general principles of law, upon responsibilities of an office held by the promisor, or upon a preexisting contract.

In the *Crookham & Vessels* case a promise was made to pay a subcontractor extra money because of difficulties encountered by the subcontractor.

---

[8] Charles Hester Enterprises, Inc. v Illinois Founders Ins. Co. 114 Ill 2d 278, 102 Ill Dec 306, 499 NE2d 1319 (1986).

CROOKHAM & VESSELS, INC. V LARRY MOYER TRUCKING, INC.

16 Ark App 214, 699 SW3d 414 (1985)

Crookham & Vessels had a contract to build an extension of railroad for the Little Rock Port Authority. They made a contract with Larry Moyer Trucking Co. to dig drainage ditches. The ditch walls collapsed because water would not drain off. This required that the ditches be dug over again. Larry Moyer refused to do this unless extra money was paid. Crookham & Vessels agreed to pay the additional compensation, but after the work was done they refused to pay it. Larry Moyer sued for the extra compensation promised. Judgment was entered in favor of Larry Moyer, and Crookham & Vessels appealed.

COOPER, J. . . . The appellant was the general contractor on a project to build an extension of a railroad for the Little Rock Port Authority. The appellee entered into a subcontract agreement with the appellant in January 1982 to do the excavation and dirt work on the project, which provided that the appellee would perform the work according to the plans and specifications provided by Garver & Garver, Inc. The problem in this case arose when the water would not drain out of the ditches the appellee constructed because the culverts through which they were to drain were clogged off of the jobsite. This caused the ditches to collapse, requiring the appellee to repeatedly have to redig the ditches. Larry Moyer, owner of the appellee, testified that, because of this problem, which began shortly after he started working, he told the appellant's representative, Alan McElhaney, that he would not continue to work without extra pay for redigging the ditches. He stated that McElhaney agreed to this.

The Port Authority's Invitation to Bid required each bidder to make an inspection of the jobsite, stating,

> Each Bidder should visit the site of the proposed work and fully acquaint himself with the existing conditions there relating to construction and labor, and should fully inform himself as to the facilities involved, and the difficulties and restrictions attending the performance of the Contract. . . . The Contractor by the execution of the Contract shall not be relieved of any obligation under it due to his failure to receive or examine any form or legal instrument or to visit the site and acquaint himself with the conditions there existing and the Owner will be justified in rejecting any claim based on facts regarding which he should have been on notice as a result thereof.

Moyer testified that the contract required him to make this inspection, that he did do so, and that there was nothing stopping him from inspecting the culverts. He also admitted that he was required under the contract's plans and specification to build the drainage ditches to meet the specifications and be up to grade at the time the project closed. Moyer acknowledged that that was precisely what he accomplished.

Under Arkansas law, there must be additional consideration when the parties to a contract enter into an additional contract. *Buchanan v. Thomas*, 230 Ark. 31, 320 S.W.2d 650 (1959); *Feldman v. Fox*, 112 Ark. 223, 164 S.W. 766 (1914). In *Buchanan*, the subcontractor sent a bid by wire to the contractor which, apparently through the error of the telegraph company, was transmitted as about twenty-five percent lower than the subcontractor's intended bid. Based on this lower bid, the contractor submitted his bid to the owner and informed the subcontractor that he intended to hold him to the lower bid. The subcontractor performed the work and alleged at trial that it was only done after the contractor agreed to pay him half of the difference between the two bids. The court found that the subcontractor had already contracted to do the work for the lower price, found there was no consideration for the oral modification of the contract, citing *Feldman*, and held that the subcontractor was not entitled to extra compensation. In *Feldman*, the court, in holding no consideration existed for a contract raising the price of crops that the seller was already obligated to sell to the buyer, stated:

> If no benefit is received by the obligee except what he was entitled to under the original contract, and the other party to the contract parts with nothing except what he was already bound for, there is no consideration for the additional contract concerning the subject matter of the original one. *Thompson v. Robinson*, 34 Ark. 44; 1 Brandt on Suretyship and Guaranty, § 387; I Page on Contracts, § 312.
>
> "Mere performance of an existing contract or a part thereof," says Mr. Page in the section cited above, "is of itself no consideration for a new promise to the party performing. . . . If, without legal justification, one party to a contract breaks it, or threatens to break it, and to induce performance on his part the adversary party promises to pay more than was provided for by the original contract, there is in principle no consideration for such promise, as the party who threatens to break the contract does, when he finally performs it, no more than he was bound in law to do."

112 Ark. at 226, 164 S.W. 766.

Here, the contract admittedly required the appellee to dig the ditches so that he met the specifications at the time the project was approved, and it is undisputed that that is what the appellee did. Where the work performed is covered under the terms of the contract, as here, there can be no recovery for it as extra work. *Baton Rouge Contracting Co. v. West Hatchie Drainage District of Tippah County*, 304 F.Supp. 580, 585 (N.D.Miss. 1969) (where contractor is able to complete a drainage canal in accordance with specifications, although plagued by slide-ins, he is not entitled to extra compensation for the extra work occasioned by the slide-ins). Here, as in *Baton Rouge*, the appellee had the duty to acquaint himself before bidding with the conditions, nature, and extent of the work to be performed, and the condition of the culverts in question could have been taken into account. In Arkansas, it is settled that "[i]nconvenience or the cost of compliance with the contract or other like thing cannot excuse a party from the performance of an absolute and unqualified undertaking to do that which is possible and lawful." *Polzin v. Beene*, 126 Ark. 46, 50, 189 S.W. 654, 655 (1916); *Hurley v. Horton*, 213 Ark. 564, 211 S.W.2d 655 (1948). *Accord, Baton Rouge*, 304 F.Supp. at 585 ("Where one agrees to do, for a fixed sum, a thing possible to be performed, he will not be excused or become entitled to additional compensation because unforeseen difficulties are encountered."). Here, the appellee did no more than was required by its contract; the unforeseen clogged culverts merely made it more difficult. The appellant has received no additional consideration for its alleged promise to pay extra, having gotten no more than it bargained for in the first place. Therefore, the jury verdict in the amount of $12,095.00 for the "extra ditching" must be overturned.

[Judgment reversed as to extra compensation claim]

QUESTIONS

1. Whose fault required the additional work?
2. Could the subcontractor have protected himself by examining the culverts before entering into the contract?
3. Was the amount of the extra compensation demanded by the subcontractor reasonable for the extra work done?

(a) COMPLETION OF CONTRACT. When a contractor refuses to complete a building unless the owner promises a payment or bonus in addition to the sum specified in the original contract, and the owner promises to make that payment, the question arises whether the owner's promise is binding. Most courts hold that the second promise of the owner is without consideration.

If the promise of the contractor is to do something that is neither expressly nor implicitly a part of the first contract, then the promise of the other party is binding. For example, if a bonus of $1,000 is promised in return for the promise of a contractor to complete the building at a date earlier than that specified in the original agreement, the promise to pay the bonus is binding. Similarly, when a cement subcontractor is obligated by contract to pour cement for the construction of a building on five working days during working hours, and then promises to pour round-the-clock, seven days a week, the subcontractor is promising a performance that was not already required. Thus, such promise constitutes consideration for the contractor's promise to make an additional payment to the subcontractor.[9]

(1) Good Faith Adjustment. There is a trend to enforce a second promise to pay a contractor a greater amount for the performance of the original contract when there are extraordinary circumstances caused by unforeseeable difficulties and when the additional amount promised the contractor is reasonable under the circumstances.

[9] Penn Compression Moulding, Inc. v Mar-Bal, Inc. 73 NC App 291, 326 SE2d 280 (1985).

When parties to a contract, in a good faith effort to meet the business realities of a situation, agree to a reduction of contract terms, there is some authority that the promise of the one party to accept the lesser performance of the other is binding. These cases have held that the promise is binding, even though technically the promise to render the lesser performance is not consideration because the obligor was already obligated to render the greater performance. Thus, a landlord's promise to reduce the rent was binding when the tenant could not pay the original rent, and the landlord preferred to have the building occupied even though receiving a smaller rental. A similar good faith adjustment to economic realities was made in the *Angel* case.

ANGEL V MURRAY
113 RI 482, 322 A 2d 630 (1974)

John Murray was director of finance of the city of Newport. A contract was made with Alfred Maher to remove trash. Later, Maher requested that the city council increase his compensation. Maher's costs were greater than had been anticipated because four hundred new dwelling units had been put into operation. The city council voted to pay Maher an additional $10,000 a year. After two such annual payments had been made, Angel and other citizens of the city sued Murray and Maher for a return of the $20,000. They held that Maher was already obligated by his contract to perform the work for the contract sum, and there was, accordingly, no consideration for the payment of the increased compensation. From a decision in favor of the plaintiffs, the city and Maher appealed.

ROBERTS, C. J. . . . It is generally held that a modification of a contract is itself a contract, which is unenforceable unless supported by consideration. . . . *Rose v Daniels*, 8 RI 381 (1866).

The preexisting duty rule is followed by most jurisdictions, . . .

The primary purpose of the preexisting duty rule is to prevent what has been referred to as the "hold-up game." . . . A classic example of the "hold-up game" is found in *Alaska Packers' Ass'n v Domenico*, 117 F 99 (9th Cir 1902). There 21 seamen entered into a written contract with Domenico to sail from San Francisco to Pyramid Harbor, Alaska. They were to work as sailors and fishermen out of Pyramid Harbor during the fishing season of 1900. The contract specified that each man would be paid $50 plus two cents for each red salmon he caught. Subsequent to their arrival at Pyramid Harbor, the men stopped work and demanded an additional $50. They threatened to return to

San Francisco if Domenico did not agree to their demand. Since it was impossible for Domencio to find other men, he agreed to pay the men an additional $50. After they returned to San Francisco, Domenico refused to pay the men an additional $50. The court found that the subsequent agreement to pay the men an additional $50 was not supported by consideration because the men had a preexisting duty to work on the ship under the original contract, and thus the subsequent agreement was unenforceable.

Another example of the "hold-up game" is found in the area of construction contracts. Frequently, a contractor will refuse to complete work under an unprofitable contract unless he is awarded additional compensation. The courts have generally held that a subsequent agreement to award additional compensation is unenforceable if the contractor is only performing work which would have been required of him under the original contract. . . .

These examples clearly illustrate that the courts will not enforce an agreement that has been procured by coercion or duress and will hold the parties to their original contract regardless of whether it is profitable or unprofitable. However, the courts have been reluctant to apply the preexisting duty rule when a party to a contract encounters unanticipated difficulties and the other party, not influenced by coercion or duress, voluntarily agrees to pay additional compensation for work already required to be performed under the contract. For example, the courts have found that the original contract was rescinded, . . . abandoned, . . . or waived.

Although the preexisting duty rule has served a useful purpose insofar as it deters parties from using coercion and duress to obtain additional compensation, it has been widely criticized as a general rule of law. . . . The modern trend appears to recognize the necessity that courts should enforce agreements modifying contracts when unexpected or unanticipated difficulties arise during the course of the performance of a contract, even though there is no consideration for the modification, as long as the parties agree voluntarily.

Under the Uniform Commercial Code, § 2-209(1), which has been adopted by 49 states, "an agreement modifying a contract [for the sale of goods] needs no consideration to be binding.". . . Although at first blush this section appears to validate modifications obtained by coercion and duress, the comments to this section indicate that a modification under this section must meet the test of good faith imposed by the Code, and a modification obtained by extortion without a legitimate commercial reason is unenforceable.

The modern trend away from a rigid application of the preexisting duty rule is reflected by § 89D(a) of the American Law Institute's Restatement Second of the Law of Contracts, which provides: "A promise modifying a duty under a contract not fully performed on either side is binding (a) if the modification is fair and equitable in view of circumstances not anticipated by the parties when the contract was made. . . ."

We believe that § 89D(a) is the proper rule of law and find it applicable to the facts of this case. It not only prohibits modifications obtained by coercion, duress, or extortion but also fulfills society's expectation that agreements entered into voluntarily will be enforced by the courts. . . .

Section 89D(a), of course, does not compel a modification of an unprofitable or unfair contract; it only enforces a modification if the parties voluntarily agree and if (1) the promise modifying the original contract was made before the contract was fully performed on either side, (2) the underlying circumstances which prompted the modification were unanticipated by the parties, and (3) the modification is fair and equitable.

The evidence, which is uncontradicted, reveals that in June of 1968 Maher requested the city council to pay him an additional $10,000 for the year beginning on July 1, 1968, and ending on June 30, 1969. This request was made at a public meeting of the city council, where Maher explained in detail his reasons for making the request. Thereafter, the city council voted to authorize the Mayor to sign an amendment to the 1964 contract which provided that Maher would receive an additional $10,000 per year for the duration of the contract. Under such circumstances we have no doubt that the city voluntarily agreed to modify the 1964 contract.

Having determined the voluntariness of this agreement, we turn our attention to the three criteria delineated above. First, the modification was made in June of 1968 at a time when the five-year contract which was made in 1964 had not been fully performed by either party. Second, although the 1964 contract provided that Maher collect all refuse generated within the city, it appears this contract was premised on Maher's past experience that the number of refuse-generating units would increase at a rate of 20 to 25 per year. Furthermore, the evidence is uncontradicted that the 1967–1968 increase of 400 units "went beyond any previous expectation." Clearly, the circumstances which prompted the city council to modify the 1964 contract were unanticipated. Third, although the evidence does not indicate what proportion of the total this increase comprised, the evidence does indicate that it was a "substantial" increase. In light of this, we cannot say that the council's agreement to pay Maher the $10,000 increase was not fair and equitable in the circumstances.

[Judgment reversed and action remanded]

QUESTIONS

1. What was the basis for the plaintiff's suit?
2. How would the *Angel* case have been decided under the common-law rule as to consideration?
3. Could the contract have been written in a way that would have avoided the problem involved in the *Angel* case?

(2) Contract for Sale of Goods. When the contract is for the sale of goods, any modification made by the parties to the contract is binding without regard to the existence of consideration for the modification.

(b) COMPROMISE AND RELEASE OF CLAIMS. The rule that doing or promising to do what one is bound to do is not consideration applies to a part payment made in satisfaction of an admitted debt. For example, if one person owes another $100, the promise of the latter to accept $50 in full payment is not binding and will not prevent the creditor from demanding the remainder later. The part payment made by the debtor was not consideration for the promise to release the balance of the claim.

If the debtor pays before the debt is due, there is consideration since on the day when the payment was made, the creditor was not entitled to demand any payment. Likewise, if the creditor accepts some article, even of slight value, in addition to the part payment, consideration exists and the agreement is held to be binding.

A debtor and creditor may have a bona fide dispute as to the amount owed or as to whether any amount is owed. In such case, payment by the debtor of less than the amount claimed by the creditor is consideration for the latter's agreement to release or settle the claim. It is generally regarded as sufficient if the claimant believes in the merit of the claim. Conversely, if the claimant knows that the claim does not have any merit and is merely pressing the claim in order to force the other party to make some payment to buy peace from the annoyance of a lawsuit, the settlement agreement based on the part payment is not binding.

(c) PART-PAYMENT CHECKS. The acceptance and cashing of a check for part of a debt releases the entire debt when the check bears a notation that it is intended as final or full payment and the total amount due is disputed or unliquidated. It probably has this same effect even though the debt is not disputed or unliquidated.[10] In some jurisdictions, this principle is applied without regard to the form of payment or whether the claim is disputed, it being required only that the part payment was in fact received and accepted as discharging the obligation. The California Civil Code § 1541, provides: "An obligation is extinguished by a release therefrom given to the debtor by the creditor upon a new consideration, or in writing, with or without new consideration."

(d) COMPOSITION OF CREDITORS. In a composition of creditors, the various creditors of one debtor mutually agree to accept a fractional part of their claims in full satisfaction thereof. Such agreements are binding and are supported by consideration. When creditors agree to extend the due date of their debts, the promise of each creditor to forbear is likewise consideration for the promise of other creditors to forbear.

§ 16:7 PRESENT CONSIDERATION VERSUS PAST BENEFITS

Consideration is what the promisor states must be received in return for the promise. Therefore, consideration must be given when or after the promisor states what is demanded.

(a) PAST CONSIDERATION. Past benefits already received by the promisor cannot be consideration for the later promise.

(b) COMPLEX TRANSACTIONS. In applying the rule that past benefits cannot be consideration, care must be taken to distinguish between the situation in which the consideration is in fact past and the situation in which the earlier consideration and subsequent promises were all part of one complex transaction. In such cases, the earlier consideration is not regarded as past and supports the later promises.[11]

In the *Medley* case, a father guaranteed payment of his son's debts but later claimed that the guaranty was not binding because no consideration had been received by him.

---

[10] Upper Avenue National Bank v First Arlington National Bank, 81 Ill App 3d 208, 36 Ill Dec 325, 400 NE2d 1105 (1980); Uniform Commercial Code § 3-408. Official Comment, point 2.

[11] Such a complex transaction is called "contemporaneous" in some states. Soukop v Snyder (Hawaii App) 709 P2d 109 (1985).

MEDLEY V SOUTHTRUST BANK OF QUAD CITIES
(Ala) 500 So 2d 1075 (1986)

Roy Medley borrowed money from the bank. His father, Oscar, gave the bank a guaranty that he would pay his son's existing and future bank loans if his son did not repay them. Roy Medley did not repay the loans, and the bank sued Oscar Medley on the guaranty. Oscar Medley raised the defense that the guaranty was not binding because he had not received any consideration for it. This defense was overruled and judgment was entered against Medley. He appealed.

JONES, J. . . . Medley contends that there is no consideration because the guaranty sued upon 1) included pre-existing debts, 2) was not made contemporaneously with any loan, and 3) contained no expression of new valuable consideration. SouthTrust, on the other hand, argues that its promise of future advances constitutes sufficient consideration.

That portion of the guaranty agreement here contested contains the following language:

> "WHEREAS, the undersigned (if more than one, the undersigned jointly and severally) have requested . . . the Bank to extend credit from time to time to
>
> Roy D. Medley . . . (hereinafter referred to as the debtor), and have agreed to guarantee the payment when due of all such credits, and also of all other indebtedness of every kind and character now or at any time hereafter (before revocation hereof) owing by the debtor to the Bank; and
>
> "WHEREAS, the Bank is willing to extend such credit to the debtor from time to time as, in the Bank's discretion, is prudent and wise, provided this instrument of guaranty is executed to the Bank.
>
> "NOW, THEREFORE, in consideration of the premises, and in order to induce the Bank to extend to the debtor from time to time in the future as requested by the debtor, such loans, extensions of loans and forbearances as to the Bank may seem prudent and wise, the undersigned (if more than one, the undersigned jointly and severally) guarantee(s) the prompt payment on demand of the principal of and interest on any indebtedness of the debtor now, or at any time hereafter, outstanding, and any and all renewals thereof, together with all costs of collection, including a reasonable attorney's fee, as may be provided for in the face of any and all notes heretofore taken, or hereafter executed by the debtor, evidencing any such indebtedness, or any part thereof."

It is true that when someone not a party to the original transaction signs an instrument as guarantor after the original contract has been duly executed and delivered, without agreement at the time of the execution of the original contract that additional security would be furnished, he is entering a new and independent contract; and, to be binding, this agreement must be supported by consideration, independent of the original contract.

When dealing with a guarantee of a pre-existing debt, consideration is essential to sustain the obligation. In the instant case, however, the guaranty agreement is not limited solely to pre-existing debts. Rather, it covers the "indebtedness of debtor now, or at any time hereafter, . . . and any and all renewals thereof. . . ." In other words, Medley agreed to guarantee all of his son's past and future indebtedness to SouthTrust.

This Court has repeatedly held that the promise of extension of credit in the future to the principal debtor is good consideration in a guaranty contract.

It is well established that when the terms of a contract are unambiguous, the contract's construction and legal effect become a question of law for the court, and, when appropriate, may be decided by summary judgment. The contract at issue here is not ambiguous insofar as the issue of consideration is concerned, nor has any such allegation been made. The contention that there was no consideration has been disproved by the undisputed fact that South-Trust subsequently made loans to Medley & Company (from May 1979 through the end of 1979), as contemplated by the guaranty agreement. . . .

[Judgment affirmed]

QUESTIONS

1. What was the consideration for the father's guaranty?
2. What is your opinion of the reasoning of the court?
3. Was any other analysis available to the court?

§ 16:8   FORBEARANCE AS CONSIDERATION

In most cases, consideration consists of the performance of an act or the making of a promise to act. Consideration may also consist of forbearance, which is refraining from doing an act, or a promise of forbearance. In other words, the promisor may desire to buy the inaction or a promise of inaction of the other party.

The waiving or giving up of any right can be consideration for the promise of another. Thus, the relinquishment of a right in property or of a right to sue for damages will support a promise given in return for it.

The promise of a creditor to forbear collecting the debt is consideration for a promise by the debtor to modify the terms of the transaction.[12]

When the creditor agrees to extend the time for paying the debt in return for the debtor's promise of a higher return of interest, the agreement to extend is consideration for the promise to pay the higher rate of interest.

When a supplier has the right to terminate the contract with the dealer selling its products, the promise of the supplier to refrain from revoking the contract with the dealer is consideration for the dealer's agreement to reduce the commissions deducted on the resale of the supplier's product.

The right that is surrendered in return for a promise may be a right against a third person, as well as against the promisor.

As under the rule governing compromises, forbearance to assert a claim is consideration when the claim has been asserted in good faith, even though it is without merit.[13] In the absence of a good faith belief, forbearance with respect to a worthless claim is not consideration.

(a) WHAT CONSTITUTES CONSIDERATION. The consideration for forbearance is anything that constitutes consideration under the general rules discussed in this chapter. Typically it is a payment of money to the promisor or a third person to guarantee the debt of another.

(b) CONSIDERATION IN EMPLOYMENT CONTRACTS. In employment contracts, an employee may promise not to compete with the employer upon leaving the employment. What is the consideration for this promise? When the promise is made at the time of the making of the contract of employment, the promise of the employer to employ and to pay compensation is consideration for the employee's promise to refrain from competing upon leaving the employment. If the employee's promise is made after the contract of employment has

---

[12] Missouri Farmers Ass'n., Inc. v Barry (Mo App) 710 SW2d 923 (1986).

[13] Reed v Hess, 239 Kan 46, 716 P2d 555 (1986).

been made, it is necessary to see whether the contract (a) is for an indefinite duration with no job security provision, or (b) is for a definite period of time, such as five years, or contains job security provisions that prevent the employer from discharging the employee at will. If the employment contract is for a definite period or is covered by job security provisions, the employee's promise not to compete when made after the contract of employment has been made is not binding on the employee unless the employer gives some consideration for the promise not to compete. In the case of the indefinite duration contract that has no job security provision, the employer can ordinarily terminate the contract at will. Therefore, according to some courts, the employer's continuing to employ the employee after the employee's making of the promise not to compete is consideration for that promise, even though the parties did not express these thoughts in words.[14] Other courts, however, do not make a distinction based on the type of employment contract. These courts follow the common-law rule that a restrictive covenant agreed to by an employee already under contract of employment is not binding because it is not supported by consideration.

§ 16:9   ADEQUACY OF CONSIDERATION

Ordinarily courts do not consider the adequacy of the consideration given for a

---

[14] Computer Sales International, Inc. v Collins (Mo App) 723 SW2d 450 (1986).

promise. The fact that the consideration supplied by one party is slight when compared with the burden undertaken by the other party is immaterial. It is a matter for the parties to decide when they make their contract whether each is getting a fair return. In the absence of fraud or other misconduct, the court usually will not interfere to make sure that each side is getting a fair return.

C.   EXCEPTIONS TO THE LAW OF CONSIDERATION

The ever-changing character of law clearly appears in the area of consideration as the rules stated earlier in this chapter are seen slowly eroding.

§ 16:10   EXCEPTIONS TO ADEQUACY OF CONSIDERATION RULE

The insufficiency or inadequacy of the consideration may lead a court to the conclusion that a contract is not binding because it is unconscionable. Inadequate consideration may also indicate that fraud was practiced on the promisor.

The inadequacy of the consideration may be evidence of the exercise of undue influence or the taking advantage of the condition of the other contracting party. Several factors may combine to challenge the validity of the contract. This happened in the *Williamson* case.

WILLIAMSON V MATTHEWS
(Ala) 379 So 2d 1245 (1980)

Williamson owned a house on which there was a mortgage. She was about to lose the house because she could not pay the mortgage. She agreed to sell the house to the Matthews for a price that would pay off the mortgage and leave enough for her to buy a mobile home. Subtracting the amount of the mortgage from the appraised value of the house, it was agreed that Williamson should receive $1,700. After making this sales contract, Williamson consulted an attorney and two days later began a lawsuit to stop the sale on the ground that her mental capacity had been impaired by drinking, she had been drinking on the day the sale was negotiated, and she had been pressured into making the sale because of the fear of losing her house. She also claimed that the actual value was much greater than the appraisal that had been used in calculating the sales price and that the actual amount that should have been paid to her was somewhere between $8,300 and $15,300 more than she actually received, depending on which appraisal was used. The court refused to cancel the sale, and Williamson appealed.

PER CURIAM . . . Williamson's contention of inadequacy of consideration is based upon evidence which she introduced at trial showing a property appraisal of $16,500. Using this figure and deducting the existing mortgage of approximately $6,500, Williamson's equity would amount to $10,000, $8,300 more than the $1,700 she was paid. Williamson contends that she was due $17,000 for her equity, which would result in the property being valued at $23,500 (adding the mortgage of $6,500). In other words, accepting Williamson's first contention, the Matthews should have paid her *$8,300 more;* accepting the second contention, Williamson should receive *$15,300 more.* There was also evidence that the credit union appraised the property for $19,500. This would reflect an equity of $13,000. Accepting this figure, she should have been paid *$11,300 more.* Thus, the claim of inadequacy of consideration (and it would seem to be well established) varied from *$8,300 to $15,300.*

Although it is a fundamental principle of law that inadequacy of consideration is not, by itself, a sufficient ground to set aside a contract for the sale of land, in *Judge v Wilkins,* 19 Ala 765 (1851), over 128 years ago, this Court stated that:

> . . . Inadequacy of price *within itself,* and disconnected from all other facts, cannot be a ground for setting aside a contract, or affording relief against it. There must be something else besides the mere inadequacy of consideration or inequality in the bargain, to justify a court in granting relief by setting aside the contract. *What this something else besides the inadequacy* should be, perhaps no court ought to say, lest the wary and cunning, by employing other means than those named, should escape with their fraudulent gains. I, however, will venture to say, that it ought, in connection with the inadequacy of consideration, to superinduce the belief that there had been either a suppression of the truth, the suggestion of falsehood, abuse of confidence, a violation of duty arising out of some fiduciary relation between the parties, the exercise of undue influence, or the taking of an unjust and inequitable advantage of one whose peculiar situation at the time would be calculated to render him an easy prey to the cunning and the artful. But if no one of these appears, or if no fact is proved that will lead the mind to the conclusion, that the party against whom relief is sought has suppressed some fact that he ought to have disclosed, or that he has suggested some falsehood, or abused in some manner the confidence reposed in him, or that some fiduciary relation existed between the parties, or that the party complaining was under his influence, or at the time of the trade was in a condition, *from any cause,* that would render him an easy victim to the unconscientious, then relief cannot be afforded; for inadequacy of consideration, *standing alone and unsup-*

ported by any thing else, can authorize no court, governed by the rules of the English law, to set aside a contract. . . .

Williamson contends that the "something else" in the case at bar is mental weakness, either due to some form of permanent mental incapacity or due to intoxication. Of course, the contracts of an insane person are absolutely void. *Walker v Winn*, 142 Ala 560, 39 So 12 (1904). Williamson, however, is not contending that she was insane at the time of the contract, but rather is contending that she had a mental incapacity, which coupled with inadequacy of consideration requires the setting aside of the transaction.

Our rule in such a case is that a party cannot avoid, free from fraud or undue influence, a contract on the ground of mental incapacity, unless it be shown that the incapacity was of such a character that, at the time of execution, the person had no reasonable perception or understanding of the nature and terms of the contract. *Weaver v Carothers*, 228 Ala 157, 153 So 201 (1934).

Our rule regarding incapacity due to intoxication is much the same. The drunkenness of a party at the time of making a contract may render the contract voidable, but it does not render it void; and to render the contract voidable, it must be made to appear that the party was intoxicated to such a degree that he was, at the time of the contracting, incapable of exercising judgment, understanding the proposed engagement, and of knowing what he was about when he entered into the contract sought to be avoided. *Snead v Scott*, 182 Ala 97, 62 So 36 (1913). Proof merely that the party was drunk on the day the sale was executed does not per se show that he was without contractual capacity; there must be some evidence of a resultant condition indicative of that extreme impairment of the faculties which amounts to contractual incapacity.

The burden was therefore cast on Williamson to show, by clear and convincing evidence, that she was incapable, at the time of execution, of executing the contract for sale and of executing the deed.

We hold that Williamson met this burden. The testimony elicited at trial by Williamson's attorney charted a history of aberrative behavior. A Mrs. Logan, Williamson's mother, provided lengthy testimony about her daughter's past aberrations. Additionally, Dr. Fredric Feist provided expert testimony regarding Williamson. . . . He stated that she showed signs of an early organic brain syndrome due to her excessive drinking, that she had emotional problems, that he thought that some of her brain cells were destroyed, and that her ability to transact business had been impaired.

. . . We do not hold that Williamson was so intoxicated as to render her incapable of contracting. However, numerous factors combine to warrant the conclusion that she was operating under diminished capacity. Testimony showed that Williamson's capacity to transact business was impaired, that she had a history of drinking, that she had been drinking the day she conducted negotiations, and that she had an apparent weakened will because she was pressured by the possibility of an impending foreclosure. Moreover, Williamson made complaint to an attorney only hours after the transaction. These factors are combined with a gross inadequacy of consideration.

[Judgment reversed and action remanded]

QUESTIONS

1. Did the court hold that Williamson lacked capacity to make the contract of sale?
2. Was the consideration for the sale of Williamson's house adequate?
3. Does the court avoid the contract because of inadequacy of consideration?

§ 16:11   EXCEPTIONS TO REQUIREMENT OF CONSIDERATION

By statute or decision, consideration is no longer required in a number of situations.

(a) CHARITABLE SUBSCRIPTIONS. charitable enterprises are financed by voluntary subscriptions of a number of persons, the promise of each is generally enforceable. For example, when a number of people make pledges or subscriptions for the construction of a church, for a charitable institution, or for a college, the subscriptions are binding.

The theories for sustaining such promises vary. Consideration is lacking according to the technical standards applied in ordinary contract cases. Nevertheless, the courts enforce such promises as a matter of public policy.

(b) UNIFORM COMMERCIAL CODE. In a number of situations, the Uniform Commercial Code abolishes the requirement of consideration. For example, under the Code, consideration is not required for (1) a merchant's written, firm offer as to goods, stated to be irrevocable; (2) a written discharge of a claim for an alleged breach of a commercial contract; or (3) an agreement to modify a contract for the sale of goods.[15]

(c) SEALED AND WRITTEN INSTRUMENTS. At common law, consideration was not necessary to support a promise under seal. In a state that gives the seal its original common-law effect, the gratuitous promise or a promise to make a gift is enforceable when it is set forth in a sealed instrument.

In some states, a promise under seal must be supported by consideration, just as though it did not have a seal. Other states take a middle position and hold that the presence of a seal is prima facie proof that there is consideration to support the promise. This means that if nothing more than the existence of the sealed promise is shown, it is deemed supported by consideration. The party making the promise, however, may prove that there was no consideration. In that case, the promise is not binding.

In some states a rebuttable presumption arises whenever a contract is in writing that the promises of the parties are supported by consideration.[16]

§ 16:12   PROMISSORY ESTOPPEL

Most courts enforce some promises that are not supported by consideration by applying the doctrine of **promissory estoppel**. A person may make a promise to another under such circumstances that the promisor should reasonably foresee that the promisee will be induced to rely thereon and that the promisee will then sustain substantial loss if the promise is not kept. Under the doctrine of promissory estoppel, such a promise is binding, even though there is no consideration for it. In applying the doctrine of promissory estoppel, courts are ignoring the requirement of

---

[15]   UCC § 2-209(1).

[16]   Nordwick v Berg, __ Mont __, 725 P2d 1195 (1986).

consideration in order to attain a just result.

Legal difficulties often arise because parties take certain things for granted. Frequently they will be sure that they have agreed to everything and that they have a valid contract. Sometimes they do not. The courts are then faced with the problem of leaving them with their broken dreams or coming to their rescue, as in the *Hoffman* case.

HOFFMAN v RED OWL STORES, INC.

26 Wis 2d 683, 133 NW2d 267 (1965)

Joseph H. Hoffman wanted to acquire a franchise for a Red Owl Grocery Store. (Red Owl was a corporation that maintained a system of chain stores.) The agent of Red Owl informed Hoffman and his wife that if they would sell their bakery in Wautoma, acquire a certain tract of land in Chilton, another city, and put up a specified amount of money, they would be given a franchise as desired. Hoffman sold his business and acquired the land in Chilton, but was never granted a franchise. He and his wife sued Red Owl, which raised the defense that there had only been an assurance that Hoffman would receive a franchise, but no promise supported by consideration. Thus, there was no binding contract to give him a franchise. From a judgment in the Hoffman's favor, Red Owl appealed.

CURRIE, C. J. . . .The development of the law of promissory estoppel "is an attempt by the court to keep remedies abreast of increased moral consciousness of honesty and fair representations in all business dealings." *Peoples National Bank of Little Rock v Lineberger Constr. Co.*, 219 Ark. 11, 240 SW2d 12, (1951). . . .

The Restatement avoids use of the term "promissory estoppel," and there has been criticism of it as an inaccurate term . . . Use of the word "estoppel" to describe a doctrine upon which a party to a lawsuit may obtain affirmative relief offends the traditional concept that estoppel merely serves as a shield and cannot serve as a sword to create a cause of action. . . .

Because we deem the doctrine of promissory estoppel, as stated in Sec 90 of Restatement, 1 Contracts, as one which supplies a needed weapon which courts may employ in a proper cause to prevent injustice, we endorse and adopt it.

The record here discloses a number of promises and assurances given to Hoffman by Lukowitz in behalf of Red Owl upon which plaintiffs relied and acted upon to their detriment. . . .

Originally the doctrine of promissory estoppel was invoked as a substitute for consideration rendering a gratuitous promise enforceable as a contract. . . . In other words, the acts of reliance by the promisee to his detriment provided a substitute for consideration. . . . [Under] Sec 90 of Restatement, 1 Contracts, . . . the conditions imposed are:

(1) Was the promise one which the promisor should reasonably expect to in-

duce action or forbearance of a definite and substantial character on the part of the promisee?

(2) Did the promise induce such action or forbearance?

(3) Can injustice be avoided only by enforcement of the promise? . . .

We conclude that injustice would result here if plaintiffs were not granted some relief because of the failure of defendants to keep their promises which induced plaintiffs to act to their detriment. . . .

[Judgment affirmed on this phase of the case]

QUESTIONS

1. Could the court in the *Hoffman* case have reached the same conclusion by applying the common-law rule as to consideration?
2. Compare the concept of firm offer with promissory estoppel.
3. How could Hoffman have avoided the problem that arose in his case?

(a) PROMISSORY ESTOPPEL DISTINGUISHED FROM CONSIDERATION. Promissory estoppel differs from consideration in that the reliance of the promisee is not the bargained-for price or response sought by the promisor. Under promissory estoppel, it is sufficient that the promisor foresees that there will be such reliance. The doctrine of promissory estoppel applies only when (1) the promisor has reason to foresee the detrimental reliance by the promisee, and (2) the promisee in fact would sustain a substantial loss because of such reliance if the promise were not performed.

(b) DETRIMENTAL RELIANCE ESSENTIAL. Promissory estoppel cannot be applied merely because the promisor has not performed the promise.[17] In the absence of detrimental reliance on the promise, the doctrine of promissory estoppel is not applicable. Thus, a promise made to the debtor by the creditor that the creditor would collect only $20 a month on the debt of approximately $12,000 was not binding because there was no proof that the debtor relied in any manner upon such promise.[18]

[17] Tutak v Tutak, 123 App Div 2d 758, 507 NYS2d 232 (1986).

[18] Lawrence v Board of Education, 152 Ill App 3d 187, 105 Ill Dec 195, 503 NE2d 1201 (1987). Some courts hold the promisor liable for tort damages when the promisee has sustained harm because the promisee relied on the promise, but the promise was never kept. ITT Terryphone Corp. v Tri-State Steel Drum, Inc. 178 Ga App 694, 344 SE2d 686 (1986). The explanation for these differing views is that those courts do not believe it is just for the promisor to break a promise on which the promisee had detrimentally relied, but at the same time they do not feel that they can come out flatly and state that consideration is not required to make the broken promise binding on the defendant.

SUMMARY

A promise is not binding if there is no consideration for the promise. Consideration is the price required by the promisor as the price for the promise. That price may be the doing of an act, the refraining from the doing of an act, or merely a promise to do or to refrain. In a bilateral contract, it is necessary to find that the promise of each party is supported by consideration. If either promise is not so supported, it is not binding, and the agreement of the parties is not a contract. Consequently, the agreement cannot be enforced. When a promise is the consideration, it must be a binding promise. The binding character of a promise is not affected by the circumstance that there is a condition precedent to the performance promised. Likewise, the binding character of the promise and of the contract is not affected by a provision in the contract for its cancellation by either one or both of the parties. A promise to do what one is already obligated to do is not consideration, although some exceptions are made when the rendering of a partial performance or a modified performance is accepted as a good faith adjustment to a changed situation, a compromise and release of claims, a part payment check, or a compromise of creditors. As consideration is the price that is given to obtain the promise, past benefits conferred upon the promisor cannot be consideration. In the case of a complex transaction, however, the past benefit and the subsequent transaction relating to the promise may in fact have been intended by the parties as one transaction. In such a case, the earlier benefit is not past consideration but is the consideration contemplated by the promisor as the price for the promise subsequently made.

A promise to refrain from doing an act can be consideration. A promise to refrain from suing or asserting a particular claim can be consideration. Generally the promise to forbear must be for a specified time, as distinguished from agreeing to forbear at will. When consideration is forbearance to assert a claim, it is immaterial whether the claim is valid, as long as the claim has been asserted in good faith in the belief that it was valid.

When the promisor obtains the consideration specified for the promise, the law is not ordinarily concerned with the value or adequacy of that consideration. Exceptions are sometimes made in the case of fraud or unconscionability and under consumer protection statutes.

There is a trend to abandon the requirement of consideration. Exceptions to the requirement of consideration are made in the case of charitable subscriptions and contracts governed by certain statutory provisions, such as a contract for the modification of a sale of goods under the Uniform Commercial Code. In some states, the common-law effect of the seal continues and makes a promise binding, although there is no consideration to support it. Promissory estoppel is the most extensive repudiation of the requirement of consideration. Under this doctrine, a promise not supported by consideration is binding when the promisor should have realized that the promise would be relied on by the promisee, and when the promisee would sustain substantial loss as a result of this reliance if the promisor did not keep the promise.

All transactions must be lawful; therefore, consideration for a promise must be legal. If it is not, there is no consideration, and the promise is not binding.

When the promisor does not actually receive the price promised for the promise, it is said that there is a failure of consideration. This is merely a default in performance, and the binding character of the agreement is not affected by the subsequent failure of consideration. Such failure constitutes a breach of the contract.

Although consideration is required to make a promise binding, the promise that is not supported by consideration is not unlawful or illegal. If the promisor voluntarily performs the promise, the promisor cannot undo the performance and restore matters to their position prior to the making of the agreement. The parties are free to perform their agreement, but the courts will not help either of them because there is no contract.

QUESTIONS AND CASE PROBLEMS

1. What is the objective of each of the following rules of law?
   (a) An executed gift or a performance that has been rendered without consideration cannot be rescinded for lack of consideration.
   (b) In the absence of fraud, the adequacy of consideration is usually immaterial.
2. What is consideration?
3. Sarah's house caught on fire. Through the prompt assistance of her neighbor, Odessa, the fire was quickly extinguished. In gratitude, Sarah promised to pay Odessa $1,000. Can Odessa enforce this promise if Sarah does not pay the money?
4. Clifton agreed to work for Acrylics Incorporated for $400 a month. Clifton later claimed that there was no contract because the consideration for the services to be rendered was inadequate. Is there a binding contract?
5. Frank promised to paint Cynthia's house. There was nothing given in return for the promise. Frank did not paint the house. Cynthia sued Frank for damages on the theory that the promise was binding because of promissory estoppel, as she had waited for him to paint the house. Is Frank liable?
6. Compare (a) adequate consideration, (b) moral obligation, and (c) past consideration.
7. Galloway induced Marian to sell Marian's house to Galloway by false statements that a factory was going to be built on the vacant lot adjoining Marian's house. No factory was ever built, and Marian then sued Galloway for damages for fraud. Marian offered to prove that Galloway had paid Marian only a fraction of the true value of Marian's house. Galloway claimed that this evidence as to value could not be admitted because it was immaterial whether the consideration paid Marian was adequate. Is Galloway correct?
8. Koedding hired the West Roofers to put a roof on her house. She later claimed that the roofing job was defective and threatened to sue West. Both parties discussed the matter in good faith and finally West guaranteed that the roof would be free from leaks for twenty years in return for which guarantee Koedding agreed not to sue West for dam-

ages. The roof leaked the next year. Koedding sued West on the guarantee. West claimed that the guarantee was not binding because there was no consideration for it. According to West, Koedding's promise not to sue had no value, because Koedding in fact did not have any valid claim against West; therefore she was not entitled to sue. Was this defense valid?
9. Fedun rented a building to Gomer, who did business under the name of Mike's Cafe. Later, Gomer was about to sell out the business to Brown and requested Fedun to release him from his liability under the lease. Fedun agreed to do so. Brown sold out shortly thereafter. The balance of the rent due by Gomer under the original lease agreement was not paid, and Fedun sued Gomer on the rent claim. Could he collect after having released Gomer? [Fedun v Mike's Cafe, 204 Pa Super 356, 204 A2d 776]
10. Alexander Proudfoot Company was in the business of devising efficiency systems for industry. It told the Sanitary Linen Service Company that it could provide an improved system for Sanitary Linen that would save it money. It made a contract with Sanitary Linen to provide a money-saving system. The system was put into operation, and Proudfoot was paid the amount due under the contract. The system failed to work and did not save money. Sanitary Linen sued to get the money back. Was it entitled to do so? [Sanitary Linen Service Co. v Alexander Proudfoot Co. (CA5 Fla) 435 F2d 292]
11. Allen owned land that was being developed. Allen's brother, Norburn, wrote to the vice-president of Investment Properties of Asheville, Inc., stating that "this is to certify that I will stand personally liable" for the land preparation expenses. When Investment Properties sued Norburn on this guaranty, he raised the defense that he did not receive any consideration for his promise and therefore it was not binding. Was this a valid defense? [Investment Properties of Asheville, Inc. v Norburn, 281 NC 300, 188 SE2d 342]
12. Sears, Roebuck & Co. promised to give For-

rer "permanent employment." Forrer sold his farm at a loss in order to take the job. Shortly after commencing work, he was discharged by Sears, which claimed that the contract could be terminated at will. Forrer claimed that promissory estoppel prevented Sears from terminating the contract. Was he correct? [Forrer v Sears, Roebuck & Co., 36 Wis 2d 388, 153 NW2d 587]

13. Elena O'Brien was an interior decorator. The owner of two condominium buildings agreed to hire her to decorate the building interiors if she promised to split her commission with Victor Hovas, the son-in-law of the owner. She promised to do so and was given the job. Elena and Hovas then signed a separate contract in which she agreed to split the commission. Elena did not split the commission, and Hovas sued her on their contract. She raised the defense that there was no consideration for her promise. Was she correct? [Hovas v O'Brien (Tex App) 654 SW2d 801]

14. Bogart owed several debts to the Security Bank & Trust Company. He applied to the bank for a loan to pay the various debts. The bank's employee stated that he would take the application for the loan "to the loan committee and within two or three days, we ought to have something here, ready for you to go with." The loan was not made. The bank sued Bogart for his debts. He filed a counterclaim on the theory that the bank had broken its contract to make a loan to him, and that promissory estoppel prevented the bank from going back on what the employee had said. Was this counterclaim valid? [Security Bank & Trust Co. v Bogart (Ind App) 494 NE2d 965]

15. Hubbard made an oral agreement renting a farm combine from Farm Machinery, Inc. While in use, the combine was destroyed by fire. Following the fire, Farm Machinery and Hubbard signed a written contract. The contract stated that Hubbard was responsible for any damage to the combine. Nothing had been said on this point in the original oral agreement. Farm Machinery was paid by its insurer, Liberty Mutual Fire Insurance Company. Liberty Mutual then sued Hubbard on the provision of the written contract stating that he was liable for the loss. Was he liable? [Liberty Mutual Fire Ins. Co. v Hubbard, 275 Or 567, 551 P2d 1288]

17

LEGALITY AND PUBLIC POLICY

If society were totally committed to free enterprise and freedom of contract, anyone could make a contract on any subject. But as you might suspect, society does not wish to go that far. In Chapters 9 and 10 you saw that certain conduct is prohibited as crimes and torts. Logically it follows that society will not allow the making of a contract that calls for conduct that would be a crime or a tort.

In its most obvious form, the rule has developed that a contract calling for the commission of a crime is void. However, the criminal law generally lags behind the societal judgment of what is right and what is wrong. What happens when a court is faced with a contract that it believes is wrong, but there is no statute making the transaction illegal? In such case, the court will declare that the contract is void as contrary to public policy. In recent years the judges have ventured even further in order to declare a contract or a contract provision invalid because unconscionable. All three limitations: (1) illegality, (2) contravention of public policy, and (3) unconscionability, represent society, speaking through the lawmaker or the judge for the purpose of striking a balance between freedom of contract and protection of the public.

A.   GENERAL PRINCIPLES

An agreement is illegal when either its formation or performance is a crime or a tort, or it is contrary to public policy. Ordinarily an illegal agreement is void.

§ 17:1   EFFECT OF ILLEGALITY

When an agreement is illegal, the parties are usually not entitled to the aid of the courts. If the illegal agreement has not been performed, neither party can sue the other to obtain performance or damages.[1] If the agreement has been performed, neither party can sue the other for damages or to set it aside. In the *Jackson Purchase* case, the validity of a contract provision was challenged on the ground that it called for a practice that was unlawful.

[1]   Kaszuba v Zientara (Ind App) 495 NE2d 761 (1986).

JACKSON PURCHASE ELECTRIC COOPERATIVE V LOCAL UNION 816

(CA6 Ky) 646 F2d 264 (1981)

When employees of an employer belong to a union, it is common for the union and the employer to agree that the employer shall deduct the union dues of the employees from their wages and pay such amounts directly to the union. This is called a checkoff of union dues. Under federal law, this is unlawful if done without written authorization from the employees affected. Moreover, if a checkoff of union dues is willfully made without such written authorization, the employer is guilty of a crime. The employees of Jackson Purchase Rural Electric Cooperative Association belonged to Local Union 816 of the electrical workers union. For sixteen years, the employer made a checkoff of union dues without any written authorization. The practice was unilaterally terminated by the employer in 1978. The union protested, and the matter was referred to an arbitrator. The arbitrator ordered the employer to reinstate dues checkoff, but also provided that such checkoff should only be made upon the submission of a written authorization of the employees affected. The union appealed to the district court on other grounds. The district court held that the checkoff practice that had been followed in the prior years was illegal and therefore could not be reinstated. A further appeal was taken by the union.

KENNEDY, J. . . . Section 302(a)(1) of the Labor Management Relations Act, 29 U.S.C. § 186(a)(1), states that

> it shall be unlawful for any employer . . . to pay, lend, or deliver, or agree to pay, lend, or deliver, any money or any other thing of value to any representative of any of his employees who are employed in an industry affecting commerce.

Subsection (c)(4) creates an exception

> with respect to money deducted from the wages of employees in payment of membership dues in a labor organization: *Provided*, That the employer has received from each employee, on whose account such deductions are made, a written assignment which shall not be irrevocable for a period of more than one year, or beyond the termination date of the applicable collective bargaining agreement, whichever occurs sooner. . . .

Subsection (d) makes it a misdemeanor willfully to violate the above provisions.

Local 816 first argues that because subsection (d) makes it a crime willfully to violate § 302, a willful violation is the only violation that Congress contemplated. Because the District Court found that Jackson Purchase and Local 816 did not *intend* to violate § 302, Local 816 claims that [the District Court] erred in finding that the Local *did* violate that section. This argument is devoid of merit. The fact that willful violations of § 302 are to be met with a criminal sanction does not render an unwitting violation lawful. Congress need not prescribe a criminal penalty, or any penalty for that matter, to make an action illegal. As noted above, subsection (a) expresses Congress' intent that an agreement to check off union dues without written employee authorization "shall be unlawful." . . .

Local 816 next observes that the long-continued practice of checking off union dues necessarily implies an underlying agreement to check off union dues. It argues that although the implementation of the agreement in this case was unlawful, the agreement itself is not, because the agreement does not specify that unlawful means shall be used to accomplish its ends. Thus, Local 816 contends that we should sever the agreement to check off from the manner in which the checking off was accomplished, and enforce only the agreement to check off through the past practice doctrine. The distinction that the Union is making may have merit in the appropriate case, where there is evidence of a lawful agreement which is independent of the illegal act. However, that is not the case here. The only implied agreement that could be said to have become, by long-continued practice, a part of the contract is the agreement to check off without written authorizations from the employees. Such agreement to check off without written authorizations, although not willful and therefore not criminal, is clearly unlawful under the terms of the applicable statute.

The next question is what effect, if any, should be given the illegal past practice and past agreement. The *Restatement (Second) of Contracts* § 302(1) (Tent. Draft No. 12, 1977) states the rule that a promise is unenforceable if legislation so provides, or if the interest in enforcement is clearly outweighed by the public policy against enforcement. Generally, one who has himself participated in an illegal act cannot be permitted to assert in a court of justice any right founded upon or growing out of the illegal transaction. . . .

However, it is not the case that all unlawful agreements are *ipso facto* void. If the denial of relief is disproportionately inequitable the right to recover will not be denied. 14 *Williston on Contracts* § 1630A (3d ed. 1972). Factors a court should consider in performing this balancing include: the justified expectations of the parties; the forfeiture that would result from nonenforcement of the agreement; any special public interest in enforcement; the strength of the public policy that the agreement violates, as shown by legislation or court decision; the likelihood that refusal to enforce will further that policy; and the seriousness of the misconduct. *Restatement (Second) of Contracts* § 320(1) (Tent. Draft No. 12, 1977).

As the authorities cited above make clear, there is a strong presumption that agreements in violation of a statute will not be sanctioned by the courts. That presumption is stronger than usual in this case, as Congress not only made the act of unauthorized checking off of union dues illegal, it also made the agreement to do that act illegal. This is not a case where a party is trying to have an entire contract declared illegal on the basis that a minor provision violates the law. . . . Local 816 is trying to enforce the illegal agreement itself. There is no specific public interest in enforcing this agreement. Rather, the public's interest is promoted by non-enforcement. The public policy advanced by § 302 is to protect employees in dealings between the union and employer. The relief ordered by the arbitrator is prospective and there is no contention that any employee was actually injured by this past practice. However, enforcement of an illegal agreement on the ground that the evil concerned did not follow would destroy the safeguards of law and lessen the prevention of abuses. Local 816 had no justified expectation that its agreement with Jackson Purchase was lawful, nor was it misled in any way by Jackson Purchase. No forfeiture or unjust enrichment will result to any party if this past practice or agreement is not made a part of future collective bargaining agreements. Although the misconduct in this case was not serious, that factor by itself is entitled to little weight. In short, Local 816 has given us no reason to disregard the presumption that courts will not give legal effect to illegal acts.

[Judgment affirmed]

QUESTIONS

1. What is the difference in stating that checking off union dues without written authorization is unlawful and saying that when done willfully it is criminal?
2. Did the arbitrator authorize a continuation of the past practice of checking off union dues?

§ 17:2 EXCEPTIONS TO EFFECT OF ILLEGALITY

In some situations, the rules stated in § 17:1 produce a result that society deems too harsh and unjust. Thus, the following exceptions are made.

(a) PROTECTION OF ONE PARTY. When the law that the agreement violates is intended for the protection of one of the parties, that party may seek relief. For example, when, in order to protect the public, the law forbids the issuance of securities or notes by certain classes of corporations, a person who has purchased them may recover the money paid.

(b) UNEQUAL GUILT. When the parties are not *in pari delicto*, or are not equally guilty, the one less guilty is granted relief when public interest is advanced by so doing. For example, when a statute is adopted to protect one of the parties to a transaction, such as a usury law adopted to protect borrowers, the person to be protected will not be deemed to be *in pari delicto* with the wrongdoer when entering into a transaction that is prohibited by the statute.

(c) KNOWLEDGE OF ILLEGAL PURPOSE OF OTHER CONTRACTING PARTY. A contract that is in itself lawful is not made unlawful by the fact that one of the parties intends to make an unlawful use of the subject matter of the contract, and this intention is known to the other contracting party. In the *Potomac Leasing Company* case, the defendant claimed that the plaintiff could not recover because the plaintiff knew that the defendant intended to make an illegal use of the goods involved.

POTOMAC LEASING CO. V VITALITY CENTERS, INC.
290 Ark 265, 718 SW2d 928 (1986)

> The Potomac Leasing Company leased an automatic telephone system to Vitality Centers. Claudene Cato signed the lease as guarantor of payments. When the rentals were not paid, Potomac Leasing brought suit against Vitality and Cato. They raised the defense that the rented equipment was to be used for an illegal purpose, that this purpose was known to Potomac Leasing, and that therefore Potomac Leasing could not enforce the lease. The lower court sustained this defense, and Potomac Leasing appealed.

HOLT, C. J. . . . Vitality Centers, Inc., appellee, entered into a lease agreement, which was guaranteed by Claudene Cato, co-appellee, to lease an automated telephone system from Potomac Leasing, Co., appellant. Leads Unlimited, Inc., not a party, manufactured the telephone system and it was apparently a Leads Unlimited salesman whom Cato dealt with in deciding to acquire the equipment while at a convention in Cincinnati. Potomac's manager testified that the salesman never worked for Potomac and that Potomac only becomes involved after the vendor and customer have reached an agreement. Potomac simply buys equipment from the vendor and enters a lease agreement with the customer after the vendor and customer have agreed on the product and its financing.

The lease stated that the "lessee acknowledges that Potomac Leasing Company is neither the manufacturer, distributor or seller of the equipment and has no control, knowledge or familiarity with the condition, capacity, functioning or other characteristics of the equipment." Potomac's manager testified that he did not know if Leads Unlimited was one of the more than 3,000 vendors that Potomac had dealt with before and that Potomac merely distributes literature on its leasing arrangements to salesmen for many such vendors.

After appellees made a few payments on the noncancellable, 48-month lease, the equipment was sent back to Potomac. When Potomac sued to enforce the lease, appellees answered, claiming that the subject matter of the lease was illegal. Appellees had intended to use the equipment to randomly dial phone numbers, give a message advertising certain products, and record the responses of the person answering the call. Arkansas Stat.Ann. § 41-4162 (Supp.1985) prohibits this use:

> It shall be unlawful for any person to use a telephone for the purpose of offering any goods or services for sale, or for conveying information regarding any goods or services for the purpose of soliciting the sale or purchase thereof, or for soliciting information, gathering data, or for any other purpose in connection with a political campaign when such use involves an automated system for the selection and dialing of telephone numbers and the playing of recorded messages when a message is completed to the called number. Provided, however, that nothing in this Act [§ § 41-4162-41-4164]shall prohibit the use of a telephone involving an automated system for the selection and dialing of telephone numbers, and the play of recorded messages to inform the purchaser of such goods or services concerning receipt and availability of such goods or services for delivery to the purchaser, or to convey information concerning any delay or pertinent information about the current status of any purchase order previously made.
>
> Nothing herein shall prohibit the use of automated telephone systems with recorded messages when the calls are made or messages given solely in response to calls initiated by the person to which the automatic call or recorded message is directed. [Acts 1981, No. 947, § 1, p. 2271.] . . .

The trial court, in its letter opinion, stated: "The equipment involved here, the subject matter of the lease, is specifically the type of equipment prohibited by statute. With the subject matter of the lease being illegal, the contract is void." We disagree. That the subject matter of a contract is to be used for an illegal purpose, does not in itself make a contract for the sale of the product void. In *Dillard v Kelley*, 205 Ark. 848, 171 S.W.2d 53 (1943), we said, "While a transaction contrary to public policy is void, however, one who is not in *pari delicto*, or who is not a participant in the wrong at all, is not, on account of the character of the transaction, barred from asserting rights under it."

This is so even when the seller has knowledge of the illegal purpose as long as he has not participated in that use:

> The rule supported by the weight of authority and approved by this court is that, though the contract is entered into by one of the parties for the furtherance of an illegal purpose, the contract will not be rendered illegal as to the other party, though he had knowledge of such illegal purpose, provided he does nothing in furtherance thereof.

Ashford v. Mace, 103 Ark. 114, 143 S.W. 1081 (1912), quoting *Hollenberg Music Co. v. Berry*, 85 Ark. 9, 106 S.W. 1172 (1907).

An exception is when the seller knows the product will be used in "flagrant violation of the fundamental rights of man or society." *Ashford, supra*.

6A *Corbin on Contracts*, § 1519 (1962) states essentially the same rule as the Arkansas cases:

> If the terms of a contract and its actual performance are all in themselves lawful, it is not made unlawful by the fact that the subject matter is capable of being put to illegal uses. Fire arms, a house, a motor car, liquors, a fountain pen can all be used for tortious or criminal purposes; but a contract for their sale is not for that reason invalid. Such a bargain is not enforceable by the buyer, however, if he buys with the purpose of making an illegal use of the subject matter. A seller who, with knowledge of the buyer's illegal purpose, makes the sale and delivers the subject matter, thereby increases the probability that the illegal purpose will

be carried out, even though he does not participate in the purpose, urges its abandonment, and hopes for the best. This fact makes the bargain unenforceable by
the seller also, if the illegal purpose of which he has knowledge involves the commission of a serious crime or an act of great moral turpitude. In cases other than
these, the seller's knowledge of the purpose does not prevent his enforcement of
the bargain, if he in no way participates in the purpose and does not act in furtherance of it aside from making the sale.

Accord, Restatement of Contracts 2d, §182 (1981).

The evidence did not establish that Potomac knew of or did anything in
furtherance of the appellees' illegal purpose. Likewise, the illegality involved
is clearly not a "flagrant violation of the fundamental rights of man or society." Section 41-4162 allows certain legal uses of automated telephones and
Cato testified that the equipment she bought could perform legal functions.
The only testimony offered to show Potomac even knew of the appellees' intended use was Cato's testimony that she thought Leads Unlimited's salesman was a Potomac employee. This is not sufficient to establish that Potomac,
aside from simply leasing the equipment to the appellees, acted in furtherance
of the appellees' intended illegal use so as to void the contract. . . .

[Judgment reversed and action remanded]

QUESTIONS

1. What was the basis for the claim of illegality?
2. Are there any exceptions to the rule stated by the court?
3. What is the justification of the rule applied in the *Potomac Leasing* case?

§ 17:3   PARTIAL ILLEGALITY

An agreement may involve the performance of several promises, some of which
are illegal and some legal. The legal parts
of the agreement may be enforced, provided that they can be separated from the
parts which are illegal. The same rule applies when the consideration is illegal in
part. The rule is not applied, however, to
situations in which the illegal act or consideration is said to taint and strike down the
entire agreement. Thus, an employee
could not recover for services when the
employee had performed some lawful
work but had also taken part in a fraudulent scheme of the employer.[2]

If a contract is susceptible to two interpretations, one legal and the other illegal,
the court will assume that the legal meaning was intended unless the contrary is
clearly indicated.

§ 17:4   CRIMES AND CIVIL WRONGS

An agreement is illegal, and therefore
void, when it calls for the commission of
any act that constitutes a crime. To illustrate, one cannot enforce an agreement by
which the other party is to commit an assault, to steal property, to burn a house, or
to kill a person.

An agreement that calls for the commission of a civil wrong is also illegal and void.
Examples are agreements to slander a third
person; to defraud another; to infringe another's patent, trademark, or copyright; or
to fix prices.

[2] Sacks v Dallas Gold & Silver Exchange, Inc. (Tex
App) 720 SW2d 177 (1986).

§ 17:5   GOOD FAITH AND FAIRNESS

The law is evolving toward requiring that contracts be fair and be made in good faith. The law is becoming increasingly concerned with whether *A* has utilized a superior bargaining power or superior knowledge to obtain better terms from *B* than *A* would otherwise have obtained.

In the case of goods, the seller must act in good faith, which is defined as to merchant sellers as "honesty in fact and the observance of reasonable commercial standards of fair dealing in the trade."[3]

§ 17:6   UNCONSCIONABLE AND OPPRESSIVE CONTRACTS

Ordinarily a court will not consider whether a contract is fair or unfair, wise or foolish, or operates unequally between the parties. However, in a number of instances the law holds that contracts or contract clauses will not be enforced because they are too harsh or oppressive to one of the two parties. This principle is most commonly applied to invalidate a clause providing for the payment by one party of a large penalty upon breaking the contract or a provision declaring that a party shall not be liable for the consequences of negligence. This principle is extended in connection with the sale of goods to provide that "if the court . . . finds the contract or any clause of the contract to have been unconscionable at the time it was made, the court may refuse to enforce the contract, or it may en-

force the remainder of the contract without the unconscionable clause, or it may so limit the application of any unconscionable clause as to avoid any unconscionable result."[4]

A provision that gives what the court believes is too much of an advantage over a buyer is likely to be held void as **unconscionable**.

In order to bring the unconscionability provision into operation, it is not necessary to prove that fraud was practiced. When there is a grossly disproportionate bargaining power between the parties so that the weaker or inexperienced party cannot afford to risk confrontation with the stronger party but just signs on the dotted line, courts will hold that grossly unfair terms obtained by the stronger party are void as contrary to public policy.

Under the UCCC a particular clause or an entire agreement relating to a consumer credit sale, a consumer lease, or a consumer loan is void when such provision or agreement is unconscionable.[5]

However, the fact that a contract is a bad bargain does not make it unconscionable. Moreover, unconscionability is to be determined in the light of the circumstances existing at the time when the contract was made. The fact that later events make the contract unwise or undesirable does not make the contract unconscionable. Hence, the fact that there is a sharp rise in the market price of goods after the contract has been made does not make the contract unconscionable. The decision that a provision or a contract is unconscionable can only be made by a court after holding a hearing in order to determine the real effect of the contract when viewed in its commercial setting. In a particular state, the concept of unconscionability may be based on the Uniform Commercial Code, the Uniform Consumer Credit Code, local nonuniform code statutes, or general principles of equity ab-

---

[3] Uniform Commercial Code § 2-103 (1) (b). Higher standards are also imposed on merchant sellers by other provisions of UCC. See § 2-314, as to warranties; § 2-603, as to duties with respect to rightfully rejected goods; and § 2-509(3), as to the transfer of risk of loss. While the provisions of the Code above noted do not apply to contracts generally, there is a growing trend of courts to extend Article 2 of the Code, which relates only to the sale of goods, to contract situations generally, on the theory that it represents the latest restatement of the law of contracts made by expert scholars and the legislators of the land.

[4] UCC § 2-302(1).
[5] Uniform Consumer Credit Code § 5.108.

sorbed by the common law. The concept of unconscionability is given the same interpretation by the courts regardless of the source of the concept.

The concept of unconscionability is frequently used by the court to protect consumers. This is seen in the *Williams* case.

WILLIAMS V WALKER-THOMAS FURNITURE CO.
(CA Dist Col) 350 F2d 445 (1965)

The Walker-Thomas Furniture Co. sold furniture on credit under contracts that contained a provision that a customer did not own the purchase as long as any balance on any purchase remained due. It sold goods to Ora Lee Williams. At the time when the balance of her account was $164, Walker-Thomas Furniture Co. sold her a $514 stereo set with knowledge that she was supporting herself and seven children on a government relief check of $218 a month. From 1957 to 1962, Williams had purchased $1,800 worth of goods and made payments of $1,400. When she stopped making payments in 1962, Walker-Thomas sought to take back everything she had purchased since 1957. From a judgment in favor of Walker-Thomas, Williams appealed.

WRIGHT, J. . . . The notion that an unconscionable bargain should not be given full enforcement is by no means novel. In Scott v United States, 79 U.S. (12 Wall) 443, 445 (1870), the Supreme Court stated: "If a contract be unreasonable and unconscionable, but not void for fraud, a court of law will give to the party who sues for its breach damages, not according to its letter, but only such as he is equitably entitled to." . . .

Congress has recently enacted the Uniform Commercial Code, which specifically provides that the court may refuse to enforce a contract which it finds to be unconscionable at the time it was made. 28 DC Code § 2-302 (Supp IV 1965). The enactment of this section, which occurred subsequent to the contracts here in suit, does not mean that the common law of the District of Columbia was otherwise at the time of enactment, nor does it preclude the court from adopting a similar rule in the exercise of its powers to develop the common law for the District of Columbia. In fact, in view of the absence of prior authority on the point, we consider the congressional adoption of § 2-302 persuasive authority for following the rationale of the cases from which the section is explicitly derived. Accordingly, we hold that where the element of unconscionability is present at the time a contract is made, the contract should not be enforced.

Unconscionability has generally been recognized to include an absence of meaningful choice on the part of one of the parties together with contract terms which are unreasonably favorable to the other party. Whether a meaningful choice is present in a particular case can only be determined by consideration of all the circumstances surrounding the transaction. In many cases the meaningfulness of the choice is negated by a gross inequality of bargaining power. *Henningsen v Bloomfield Motors, Inc.* [32NJ 358 (1960)] The manner in which the contract was entered is also relevant to this consideration. Did each party to the contract, considering his obvious education or lack of it, have a reasonable opportunity to understand the terms of the contract, or were the important terms hidden in a maze of fine print and minimized by deceptive sales practices? Ordinarily, one who signs an agreement without full knowledge of its terms might be held to assume the risk that he has entered a one-sided bargain. But when a party of little bargaining power, and hence little real choice, signs a commercially unreasonable contract with little or no knowledge of its terms, it is hardly likely that his consent, or even an objective manifestation of his consent, was ever given to all the terms. In such a case the usual rule that the terms of the agreement are not to be questioned should be abandoned and the court should consider whether the terms of the contract are so unfair that enforcement should be withheld. . . .

Because the trial court and the appellate court did not feel that enforcement could be refused, no findings were made on the possible unconscionability of the contracts in [this case]. Since the record is not sufficient for our deciding the issue as a matter of law, the [case is] remanded to the trial court for further proceedings.

So ordered.

QUESTIONS

1. Did the court hold that the contract in the *Williams* case was illegal?
2. What is the difference between holding that a contract is unconscionable and holding that the contract is illegal?
3. Why did the court not say that the contract was or was not unconscionable?

§ 17:7   SOCIAL CONSEQUENCES OF CONTRACTS

The social consequences of a contract are an important element today in determining its validity and the power of government to regulate it. The social consequences of a contract are related to the concept of unconscionability. This is true although unconscionability would seem to be concerned with the effect of the contract as between the parties, whereas social consequences have a broader concern for the effect of the particular contract and other similar contracts upon society in general.

(a) THE PRIVATE CONTRACT IN SOCIETY. The law of contracts, originally oriented to private relations between private individuals, is moving from the field of bilateral private law to multi-party societal considerations. The Supreme Court has held that private contracts lose their private, do-not-touch characteristic when they become such a common part of our way of life that society deems it necessary to regulate them.

The significance of the socioeconomic setting of the contract is seen in the minimum wage law decisions. The Supreme Court at first held such laws unconstitutional as an improper interference with the rights of two adult contracting parties. Thereafter it changed its point of view to sustain such laws because of the consequences of substandard wages upon the welfare of the individual, society, and the nation.

This reevaluation of old standards is part of the general move to make modern law more "just."

(b) THE N FACTOR. With the expansion of the concepts of "against public policy" and unconscionability on the one hand, and government regulation of business on the other, the importance of a given contract to society becomes increasingly significant in determining the validity of the contract as between the parties. Less and less are courts considering a contract as only a legal relationship between *A* and *B*. More and more, the modern court is influenced in its decision by the recognition of the fact that the contract before the court is not one in a million but is one of a million.

For example, *J* Company makes an insurance contract with *K* that is of the same nature as one that *J* makes with *M*. Also, these contracts are the same as the one that Company *R* makes with *S*, and so on. A like industry-wide pattern is seen in the case of the bank loan made by bank *O* to borrower *P*, by bank *Q* to borrower *T*, and so on.

The appreciation that a particular contract is merely one of many has not only influenced the courts in the interpretation of such contracts but has also been held to justify regulation of the contract by government. The view has been adopted that "when a widely diffused public interest has become enmeshed in a network of multitudinous private arrangements, the authority of the state 'to safeguard the vital interests of its people' . . . is not to be gainsaid by abstracting one such agreement from its public context and treating it as though it were an isolated private contract constitutionally immune from impairment."[6]

AGREEMENTS CONTRARY TO PUBLIC POLICY
AGREEMENTS EVADING STATUTES
AGREEMENTS INJURING PUBLIC SERVICE
AGREEMENTS INVOLVING CONFLICTS
  OF INTEREST
AGREEMENTS OBSTRUCTING LEGAL PROCESS
AGREEMENTS INVOLVING ILLEGAL
  DISCRIMINATION
WAGERS AND PRIVATE LOTTERIES

FIGURE 17-1
ILLEGAL AGREEMENTS AFFECTING PUBLIC
WELFARE

---

[6]   East New York Savings Bank v Hahn, 326 US 230, 232 (1945).

B.   AGREEMENTS AFFECTING PUBLIC WELFARE

Agreements that may harm the public welfare are condemned as contrary to public policy and are not binding. Agreements that interfere with public service or the duties of public officials, obstruct legal process, or discriminate against members of minority groups are considered detrimental to public welfare and, as such, are not enforceable.

§ 17:8   AGREEMENTS CONTRARY TO PUBLIC POLICY

A given agreement may not violate any statute but may still be so offensive to society that the courts feel that to enforce the contract would be contrary to public policy.

(a) THE CONCEPT OF PUBLIC POLICY. **Public policy** cannot be defined precisely, but is loosely described as "protecting from that which tends to be injurious to the public or contrary to the public good, or which violates any established interest of society." Contracts condemned as contrary to public policy frequently relate to the protection of the public welfare, health, or safety; to the protection of the person; and to the protection of recognized social institutions. For example, a contract that prohibits marriage under all circumstances or that encourages divorce is generally held invalid as contrary to public policy. Courts are slow and cautious in invalidating a contract on the ground that it is contrary to public policy. This is so because the courts recognize that, on the one hand, they are applying a very vague standard, and, on the other hand, they are restricting the freedom of the contracting parties to contract freely as they choose.

(b) AGREEMENTS EVADING STATUTORY PROTECTION. Statutes frequently confer benefits or provide protection. If an agreement is made that deprives a person of such a statutory benefit, it is generally held that the agreement is invalid because it is contrary to the public policy declared by the statute. For example, where a state law provided that automobile insurance policies should cover certain persons, a policy provision that excluded certain persons who would be covered by the statutory provision is not valid because it is contrary to the public policy declared in the statute.

§ 17:9   AGREEMENTS INJURING PUBLIC SERVICE

An agreement that tends to interfere with the proper performance of the duties of a public officer — whether legislative, administrative, or judicial — is contrary to public policy and void. Thus, an agreement to procure the award of a public contract by corrupt means is not enforceable. Other examples are agreements to sell public offices, to procure pardons by corrupt means, or to pay a public officer more or less than legal fees or salary.

One of the most common agreements within the class is the **illegal lobbying agreement.** This term is used to describe an agreement to use unlawful means to procure or prevent the adoption of legislation by a lawmaking body, such as Congress or a state legislature. Such agreements are clearly contrary to the public interest since they interfere with the workings of the democratic process. They are accordingly illegal and void.

Some courts hold illegal all agreements to influence legislation, regardless of the means contemplated or employed. Other courts adopt the rule that such agreements are valid in the absence of the use of improper influence or the contemplation of using such influence.

§ 17:10   AGREEMENTS INVOLVING CONFLICTS OF INTERESTS

Various statutes prohibit government officials from being personally interested, directly or indirectly, in any transaction entered into by such officials on behalf of the government. When there is a prohibited conflict of interests, a contract is invalid without regard to whether its terms are fair or advantageous to the public.

§ 17:11   AGREEMENTS OBSTRUCTING LEGAL PROCESSES

Any agreement intended to obstruct or pervert legal processes is contrary to public interest and therefore void. Agreements that promise to pay money in return for the abandonment of the prosecution of a criminal case, for the suppression of evidence in any legal proceeding, for initiating litigation, or for the perpetration of any fraud upon the court are therefore void.

An agreement to pay an ordinary witness more than the regular witness fee allowed by law or a promise to pay a greater amount if the promisor wins the lawsuit is void. The danger here is that the witness will lie in order to help win the case.

§ 17:12   ILLEGAL DISCRIMINATION CONTRACTS

A contract that a property owner will not sell to a member of a particular race cannot be enforced because it violates the Fourteenth Amendment of the Constitution.[7] Hotels and restaurants may not deal with their customers on terms that discriminate because of race, religion, color, or national origin.[8]

§ 17:13   WAGERS AND LOTTERIES

Largely as a result of the adoption of antigambling statutes, wagers or bets are generally illegal. Private lotteries involving the three elements of prize, chance, and consideration, or similar affairs of chance, also are generally held illegal, though in many states public lotteries (lotteries run by a state government) have been legalized

---

[7]   Shelley v Kraemer, 334 USI (1948).
[8]   Federal Civil Rights Act of 1964, 42 United States Code § 2000a et seq.

by statute. Raffles are usually regarded as lotteries. Sales promotion schemes calling for the distribution of property according to chance among the purchasers of goods are held illegal as lotteries, without regard to whether the scheme is called a guessing contest, raffle, or gift.

Giveaway plans and games are lawful as long as it is not necessary to buy anything or to give anything of value in order to participate. If participation is free, the element of consideration is lacking, and there is no lottery.

An activity is not gambling when the result is solely a matter of skill. In contrast, it is gambling when the result is solely a matter of luck. Rarely is any activity one hundred percent skill or one hundred percent luck. In the *Seattle Times* case, the court was faced with the problem of how to classify a contest that involved both skill and chance.

SEATTLE TIMES COMPANY v TIELSCH
80 Wash App 2d 502, 495 P2d 1366 (1972)

The *Seattle Times* ran a football game forecasting contest, called "Guest-Guesser." George Tielsch, the Seattle Chief of Police, claimed that this was illegal as a lottery. The *Times* brought a declaratory judgment action to determine the legality of the contest. The court held the contest was a lottery and the *Seattle Times* appealed.

ROSELLINI, J. . . . The result of a football game may depend upon weather, the physical condition of the players and the psychological attitude of the players. It may also be affected by sociological problems between and among the members of a football team. The element of chance is an integral part of the game of football as well as the skill of the players.

The lure of the "Guest-Guesser" contest is partially the participant's love of football, partially the challenge of competition and partially the hope enticingly held out, which is often false or disappointing, that the participant will get something for nothing or a great deal for a very little outlay. . . .

The elements of a lottery are prize, consideration and chance.

The appellant maintains that chance is not a dominant element in football forecasting contests. . . . The trial court found to the contrary upon that evidence, and we think the finding is justified. The appellant's expert statistician who testified at the trial did not state that chance plays no part in the outcome of such a contest or even that it does not play a dominant role. He merely testified that such a contest is not one of "pure chance." Pure chance he defined as a 50-50 chance. He acknowledged that a contestant who consistently predicted the outcome of 14 out of 20 games correctly would be a "highly skilled" contestant. . . .

. . . Where a contest is multiple or serial, and requires the solution of a number of problems to win the prize, the fact that skill alone will bring contestants to a correct solution of a greater part of the problems does not make the contest any the less a lottery if chance enters into the solution of another lesser part of the problems and thereby proximately influences the final result. . . .

Our research has revealed only one case involving a football forecasting game and the game there was a "pool," that is, a gambling game wherein wagers were placed. The Superior Court of Pennsylvania held that it was a lottery. What is most relevant in the case for our consideration here is the court's discussion of the element of chance in forecasting the result of football games. That court said: It is true that for an avid student of the sport of football the chance taken is not so great as for those who have little interest in the game. However, it is common knowledge that the predictions even among these so-called "experts" are far from infallible. Any attempt to forecast the result of a single athletic contest, be it football, baseball, or whatever, is fraught with chance. This hazard is multiplied directly by the number of predictions made. The operators of the scheme involved in this case were all cognizant of this fact for the odds against a correct number of selections were increased from 5 to 1 for three teams picked up to 900 to 1 for fifteen teams. *Commonwealth v Laniewski*, 173 Pa Super 245, 98 A2d 215 (1953).

The trial court in the instant case recognized the same basic realities attendant upon the enterprise of football game-result forecasting. We are convinced that it correctly held that chance, rather than skill, is the dominant factor in the Times' "Guest-Guesser" contest. The very name of the contest conveys quite accurately the promoter's as well as the participants' true concept of the nature of the contest.

We conclude that the contest, however harmless it may be in the opinion of the participants and the promoters, is a lottery. . . .

[Judgment against Seattle Times]

QUESTIONS

1. What kind of contracts were involved in the *Seattle Times* case?
2. Does the court classify the mixed skill-luck transaction according to which element predominates?
3. In order to be condemned as a lottery, a plan must be shown to have harmful effects upon some members of society. Appraise this statement.

CONTRACTS WITH UNLICENSED PERSONS IN LICENSED CALLINGS OR DEALINGS
FRAUDULENT SALES
AGREEMENTS RESTRAINING TRADE
AGREEMENTS NOT TO COMPETE
USURIOUS AGREEMENTS

FIGURE 17-2
ILLEGAL AGREEMENTS AFFECTING BUSINESS

C.   REGULATION OF BUSINESS

Local, state, and national laws regulate a wide variety of business activities and practices. A person violating such regulations may under some statutes be subject to a fine or criminal prosecution or under others to an order to cease and desist by an administrative agency or commission.

Whether an agreement made in connection with business conducted in violation of the law is binding or void depends upon how strongly opposed the public policy is to the prohibited act. Some courts take the view that the agreement is not void unless the statute expressly so specifies. In some instances, the statute expressly preserves the validity of the contract. For example, if someone fails to register a fictitious name under which the business is done, the violator, after registering the name as required by the statute, is permitted to sue on a contract made while illegally conducting business.

§ 17:14 STATUTORY REGULATION OF CONTRACTS

In order to establish uniformity or to protect one of the parties to a contract, statutes frequently provide that contracts of a given class must follow a statutory model or must contain specified provisions. For example, statutes commonly specify that particular clauses must be included in insurance policies in order to protect the persons insured and their beneficiaries. Others require that contracts executed in connection with credit buying and loans contain particular provisions designed to protect the debtor.

Consumer protection legislation gives the consumer the right to rescind the contract in certain situations. Laws relating to truth in lending, installment sales, and home improvement contracts commonly require that an installment-sale contract specify the cash price, the down payment, the trade-in value, if any, the cash balance, the insurance costs, the interest and finance charges.

When the statute imposes a fine or imprisonment for violation, the court should not hold that the contract is void since that would increase the penalty that the legislature had imposed. If a statute prohibits the making of certain kinds of contracts or imposes limitations on contracts that can be made, the attorney general or other government official may generally be able to obtain an **injunction,** or court order, to stop the parties from entering into a prohibited kind of contract.

§ 17:15 LICENSED CALLINGS OR DEALINGS

Statutes frequently require that a person obtain a license, certificate, or diploma before practicing certain professions, such as law or medicine, or before carrying on a particular business or trade, such as that of a real estate broker, peddler, stockbroker, hotelkeeper, or pawnbroker. If a license is required to protect the public from unqualified persons, a contract made by an unlicensed person is void.[9]

Thus, an agreement with an unlicensed physician for services cannot be enforced by the physician. The patient of the unlicensed physician, however, may sue for damages if the contract is not properly performed.

The illegality of contracts often comes into the picture when parties seek to set up some arrangement to evade government regulations or prohibitions of the criminal law or to avoid paying taxes.

In contrast with the protective license, a license may be required solely as a revenue measure by requiring the payment of a fee for the license. In that event, an agreement made in violation of the statute by one not licensed is generally held valid. The contract may also sometimes be held valid when it is shown that no harm has resulted from the failure to obtain a permit to do the work contemplated by the particular contract.

§ 17:16 FRAUDULENT SALES

Statutes commonly regulate the sale of certain commodities. Scales and measures of grocers and other vendors must be checked periodically, and they must be approved and sealed by the proper official. Certain articles must be inspected before they are sold. Others must be labeled in a particular way to show their contents and to warn the public of the presence of any

---

[9]   Hoffman v Dunn (Ind App) 496 NE2d 818 (1986).

dangerous or poisonous substance. Since these laws are generally designed for the protection of the public, transactions in violation of such laws are void.

§ 17:17 ADMINISTRATIVE AGENCY REGULATION

Large segments of the American economy are governed by federal administrative agencies created to carry out the general policies specified by Congress. A contract must be in harmony with public policy not only as declared by Congress and the courts but also as applied by the appropriate administrative agency. For example, a particular contract to market goods might not be prohibited by any statute or court decision but may still be condemned by the Federal Trade Commission as an unfair method of competition. When the proper commission has made its determination, a contract not in harmony therewith, such as a contract of a railroad charging a higher or a lower rate than that approved by the Interstate Commerce Commission, is illegal.

§ 17:18   CONTRACTS IN RESTRAINT OF TRADE

An agreement that unreasonably restrains trade is illegal and void on the ground that it is contrary to public policy. Such agreements take many forms, such as a combination to create a monopoly or to obtain a corner on the market, or an association of merchants to increase prices. In addition to the illegality of the agreement based on general principles of law, statutes frequently declare monopolies illegal and subject the parties to various civil and criminal penalties.[10]

§ 17:19   AGREEMENTS NOT TO COMPETE

When a going business is sold, it is commonly stated in the contract that the seller shall not go into the same or a similar business again within a certain geographical area, or for a certain period of time, or both. In early times, such agreements were held void since they deprived the public of the service of the person who agreed not to compete, impaired the latter's means of earning a livelihood, reduced competition, and exposed the public to monopoly. To the modern courts, the question is whether, under the circumstances, the restriction imposed upon one party is reasonably necessary to protect the other party. If the restriction is reasonable, it is valid.

Restrictions to prevent competition by an employee are held valid when reasonable and necessary to protect the interest of the employer. For example, a provision that a doctor employed by a medical clinic would not practice medicine for one year within a 50-mile radius of the city in which the clinic was located is reasonable and will be enforced. Likewise, a provision is valid that prohibited an employee for two years from calling upon any customer of the employer called upon by the employee during the last six months of employment.[11]

The more unusual the business, the greater will be the geographic area that will be allowed.[12] This is so because the more unusual the business is, the more likely it is to draw customers from a greater distance than an ordinary business.

If there is no sale of a business or the making of an employment contract, an agreement not to compete is illegal as a restraint of trade and a violation of the antitrust law. The agreement is therefore void. A restrictive convenant is not binding when it places a restriction on the employee that is broader than reasonably necessary to protect the employer.

---

[10]   Sherman Antitrust Act. 15 USC §§ 1-7; Clayton Act, 15 USC §§ 12-27; Federal Trade Commision Act, 15 USC §§ 41 to 58.

[11]   Nunn v Orkin Exterminating Co. Inc. 256 Ga 558, 350 SE2d 425 (1986).
[12]   National Settlement Associates of Georgia, Inc. v Creel, 256 Ga 329, 349 SE2d 177 (1986).

The employer cannot prohibit competition by a former employee for all time or for the entire world merely because some customer might follow the former employee.[13]

When a restriction of competition agreed to by the parties is invalid because its scope as to time or geographical area is too great, how does this affect the contract? Some courts trim the restrictive covenant down to a scope that the court deems reasonable and require the parties to abide by that revision. This rule is nicknamed the "blue pencil" rule. Other courts refuse to apply the blue pencil rule and hold that the restrictive convenant is void or that the entire contract is void.[14]

§ 17:20 USURIOUS AGREEMENTS

Usury is committed when money is loaned at a greater rate of interest than is allowed by law. Most states prohibit by statute the taking of more than a stated amount of interest. These statutes provide a *maximum contract rate* of interest that is the highest annual rate that can be exacted or demanded under the law of a given state. This maximum is often stated as a flat percentage rate though there is a trend to tie the usury ceilings to current market rates. Intentionally charging greater interest on a loan than allowed by law constitutes usury. It is not necessary to prove that the defendant knew that there was a violation of the usury law.

When a lender incurs expenses in the making of a loan, such as the cost of appraising property or making a credit investigation of the borrower, the lender will require the borrower to pay the amount of such expenses. Lenders may attempt to obtain more than the expenses from the borrowers. Any fee charged by a lender that goes beyond the reasonable expense of

making the loan constitutes "interest" for the purpose of determining whether the transaction is usurious.[15]

§ 17:21 CREDIT SALE CONTRACTS

Sales of goods and services on credit are not technically within the scope of the usury laws as the seller does not make an express "loan" to the buyer. When the sale is made on credit, the price that the seller charges is ordinarily not controlled by the usury law.

(a) CREDIT SALE PRICE. A seller may charge one price for cash sales and a higher price for credit or installment sales. The difference between these two prices is called the **time-price differential**. As the usury law is not applicable, the time price differential may be greater than the maximum amount of interest that could be charged on a loan equal to the cash price.

A few states, however, hold that the time-price differential is subject to the usury law or have amended their usury laws or have adopted statutes to regulate the differential between cash and time prices charged by the seller. Such statutes, however, are sometimes limited to sales by retailers to consumers or apply only to sales under a stated dollar maximum.

Many states have adopted retail and installment sale laws that apply whenever the sale price is to be paid in installments and the seller retains a security interest in the goods. These laws frequently fix a maximum for the time-price differential, thereby remedying the situation created by the fact that the price differential is not subject to the usury laws.

In the *Midland Guardian Company* case, the buyer defended an action brought by the finance company on the ground that any liability to the plaintiff could not be enforced because it was usurious. The buyer asserted that she was entitled to statutory damages.

---

[13] Hill v Mobile Auto Trim, Inc. (Tex) 725 SW2d 168 (1987).

[14] Jarrett v Hamilton, 179 Ga App 422, 346 SE2d 875 (1986).

[15] First American Bank & Trust v Windjammer Time Sharing Resort, Inc. (Fla App) 483 So 2d 732 (1986).

MIDLAND GUARDIAN CO. V THACKER

280 SC App 584, 314 SE2d 26 (1984)

Sarah Thacker purchased a mobile home from a dealer, Colonial. Thacker paid for it with the money borrowed from a finance company, Midland Guardian Co. When she stopped making payments on the loan, Midland sued to get the home. Thacker asserted that the transaction was usurious and counterclaimed against Midland to recover the statutory damages authorized in cases of usury. From a decision in favor of Midland, Thacker appealed.

GOOLSBY, J. . . . [The counterclaim for usury damages raises the question] whether a transaction involving the sale of a mobile home on deferred payments constitutes a sale at a time price or a loan and cloak for usury. . . .

We recognize . . . that a bona fide sale of property on credit at a price which exceeds the cash price by more than the legal rate of interest does not constitute usury. But the sale will be considered usurious when the sale is in fact at an agreed cash price and the form of a sale on credit is employed for the purpose of evading the usury statute. Our task, then, is to examine the real nature of the transaction questioned here. As the court asked in *Daniel v. First National Bank of Birmingham*, 227 F2d 353 (5th Cir. 1955), "Was the sale at a bona fide time price or at a cash price combined with a loan or extension of credit?"

A close relationship between the seller of personal property and the financing institution can trigger an application of the usury statute despite language in the contract appearing to invoke the time price exception. Indeed, the time price exception has no application to a lending company that purchases the loan instrument from the merchant for the actual cash price when it is privy to the terms of the original transaction.

Here, the evidence shows that Colonial, the seller, and Midland Guardian, the finance company, were so closely allied that the original transaction was, in substance, a direct loan from Midland Guardian to the Thackers. As the record discloses, the finance company furnished the seller with security agreement forms and rate charts. And while the seller undertook to obtain credit information from the buyer, the seller did nothing with the data except transmit it to the finance company. Further, the finance company conducted the credit check and indicated approval of the credit application before any contract was made. Also, the security agreement was assigned to the finance company on the same day of its execution. . . .

Moreover, there are other indicia that the purported time price sale involved a usurious loan. The time price, here referred to as the "deferred payment price," was determined by adding amounts for insurance and a "finance charge" to the "cash price." Additionally, Colonial received from Midland Guardian in exchange for the security agreement its cash price and nothing else. Finally, and in many ways the most revealing, Colonial never contemplated that it would extend credit to the Thackers. This fact is made clear by the following exchange between the buyers' attorney and the mobile home salesman:

Q. . . . You stated that if the finance company turned you down on a customer's application for credit, you would go to another finance company?
A. Yes, M'am.
Q. . . . If all the finance companies that you normally dealt with turned you down, would you indeed make a credit sale to that customer?
A. No, m'am.

Thus, the correct conclusion to be drawn from the undisputed facts is "that the real transaction was a sale at a cash price accompanied by a loan or extension of credit to which the [finance company] was privy throughout." When so viewed, the finance charge of Six Thousand One Hundred Sixty-six Dollars ($6,166) on a mobile home costing, exclusive of insurance, Six Thousand Four Hundred Forty-two and 80/100 Dollars ($6,442.80) clearly emerges as usurious interest on a loan and not as an additional price paid for credit. The trial judge, therefore, erred as a matter of law in not holding that the time price rule was inapplicable. The usury law was violated when the undisputed evidence showed Midland Guardian was privy to the terms of the original transaction and purchased the security agreement from Colonial for the cash price of the mobile home. In our judgment, no other reasonable conclusion can be drawn from the undisputed facts.

Midland Guardian argues, however, that *Carolina Industrial Bank v. Merrimon*, 260 N.C. 335, 132 SE2d 692 (1963), the principal case on which the trial court relied, supports its contention that the transaction in this case constituted a credit sale and not a loan. We do not agree. There is nothing in *Merrimon* to indicate that the sale in that case was dependent on the acceptance of the assignment of the contract by a finance company, as was the case here. Also, the purchase of the note and mortgage by the bank in *Merrimon* took place three (3) days after their execution whereas the assignment of the security agreement in this case occurred on the same day as its execution, in fact, on the same form.

Because we have concluded that the transaction involved here did not constitute, under the particular facts shown, a valid time price sale, the judgment appealed from is reversed and the case is remanded to the Court of Common Pleas for a determination of the amount to which the appellant is entitled on her counterclaim as statutory damages.

[Judgment reversed and action remanded]

QUESTIONS

1. What was the basis for Thacker's claim that the transaction was usurious?
2. Would it affect the decision of the court if Colonial had sold the mobile home to Thacker on credit?
3. The parties agreed to a transaction in the form of a sale. Why doesn't the court accept the agreement and treat the transaction as a sale?

(b) REVOLVING CHARGE ACCOUNTS. When a merchant sells on credit and puts the bill on a charge account and then adds a charge to the unpaid balance due by the customer, most courts hold that the amount of such charge is not controlled by the usury law.

SUMMARY

When an agreement is illegal, it is ordinarily void, and no contract arises therefrom. Courts will not allow one party to an illegal agreement to bring suit against the other party. There are some exceptions to this, as when the parties are not equally guilty or when the law's purpose in making the agreement illegal is to protect the person who is bringing suit. When possible, an agreement will be interpreted as being lawful. Even when a particular provision is held unlawful, the balance of the agreement will generally be saved, so that the net result is that there is a contract minus the clause that was held illegal.

The term *illegality* embraces situations in which a statute declares that certain conduct is unlawful or a crime, contracts requiring the commission of a tort, contracts that are contrary to public policy, contracts that are unconscionable, and, to some extent, to contracts that are oppressive, unfair, or made in bad faith. The question of the legality of an agreement is not considered in the abstract but the effect of the decision upon the rest of society is considered. Increasingly, a given contract is not in a class by itself but is the same as thousands and even millions of other contracts.

Whether a contract is contrary to public policy may be difficult to determine because public policy is not precisely defined. That which is harmful to the public welfare or general good is contrary to public policy. Contracts condemned as contrary to public policy include those designed to deprive the weaker of a benefit that the lawmaker desired to provide; agreements injuring public service, such as an agreement to buy a government job for an applicant; agreements involving conflicts of interests, as when the purchasing officer of a government buys from a company that the officer privately owns; agreements obstructing legal process, such as an agreement with a witness to disappear; illegal discrimination contracts; and wagers and private lotteries. Statutes commonly make the wager illegal as gambling. The lottery is any plan under which, for a consideration, a person has a chance to win a prize.

Illegality may consist of the violation of a statute or administrative regulation adopted to regulate business. Statutes may make it illegal to do business unless a particular form of contract is used or unless the party promoting the transaction is licensed. The protection of buyers from fraud of sellers may make it unlawful to sell under certain circumstances or without making certain disclosures. Contracts in restraint of trade are generally illegal as violating federal or state antitrust laws. An agreement not to compete is illegal as a restraint of trade except when reasonable in its terms and when it is incidental to the sale of a business or to a contract of employment.

The charging by a lender of a higher rate of interest than allowed by law is usurious. Courts must examine transactions carefully to see if there is a usurious loan disguised as a legitimate transaction. When sellers of goods offer their buyers one price for a cash sale and another higher price for a credit sale, the higher price is lawful and is not usurious, even though the difference between the cash price and the credit price is greater than the amount that could be charged as interest on a loan equal to the cash price. This concept is called the time-price differential. A minority of states reject or abolish it or limit the increase of the credit price over the cash price to a specified percentage or to the maximum amount that could be charged on a loan equal to the cash price. Most states do not apply the usury law to a revolving charge account, but a minority do so, with the result that

the charges imposed on the account must not exceed the amount that could be charged as interest on a loan of the amount due in the account.

QUESTIONS AND CASE PROBLEMS

1. What social forces are affected by the rule that a credit sale price is not usurious, although the difference between the credit price and the cash price is greater than the interest that could be charged on a loan in the amount of the cash price?

2. When are the parties to an illegal agreement *in pari delicto*?

3. Alman made a contract to purchase an automobile from Crockett Motors on credit. Alman failed to make payments on time. When Crockett sued to enforce the contract, Alman raised the defense that the price of the car had been increased because she was buying on credit and that this increase was unconscionable. Crockett proved that the automobile was exactly what it was represented to be and that no fraud had been committed in selling the car to Alman. Does Crockett's evidence constitute a defense to Alman's claim of unconscionability?

4. The Civic Association of Plaineville raffled an automobile in order to raise funds to build a hospital. Lyons won the automobile, but the Association refused to deliver it to her. She sued the Association for the automobile. Can Lyons enforce the contract?

5. Oakes made a contract with the Guarantee Insurance Co. to act as its agent. He should then have obtained a certificate from the State Board of Insurance showing his authority to act as agent for the company. A statute imposed a penalty on agents failing to obtain the required certificate. No penalty was imposed upon insurance companies employing agents who did not obtain the necessary certificate. Oakes did not obtain the certificate required by statute but just went ahead and acted as agent. He collected over six thousand dollars of premiums that he should have paid over to the Guarantee Insurance Co. He did not make such payment, and Guarantee sued him. He raised the defense that Guarantee could not recover because the obligation to pay the premiums was based

on the contract of agency with the company and that contract was illegal because the certificate of authority had not been obtained. Was this a valid defense?

6. The Creswell Department Store sold for cash and for credit. A customer purchasing on credit paid in twelve monthly installments and paid a purchase price that was 20 percent higher than a person buying for cash. Rose purchased a refrigerator from Creswell on the credit plan. After paying for it in full, she sued Creswell for the penalties prescribed by the state usury law. She claimed that the price increase of 20 percent for the credit sale violated the state usury law that allowed a maximum of only 6 percent interest on loans. Was she entitled to recover the penalties?

7. Compare the legality of a prize drawing with winners selected by a random drawing from (a) names in the telephone book, (b) names of persons attending a television show, and (c) names of persons written on entry blanks obtained on purchasing goods from the sponsoring store.

8. Burgess, a salesperson for Bowyer, failed to turn over to Bowyer an indefinite amount of money collected by him. In order to avoid a criminal prosecution of Burgess by Bowyer, Burgess and his brother-in-law entered into a contract with the employer by which they agreed to pay Bowyer $5,000 if full restitution was not made. No restitution was made, and Bowyer sued Burgess and his brother-in-law on the contract for $5,000. Was he entitled to recover?

9. Compare the legality of (a) a door prize given to the lucky customer of a supermarket on its opening day and (b) a door prize given to the lucky person coming to the opening of the supermarket.

10. A entered a retirement home operated by B. The contract between A and B required A to make a specified monthly payment that could be increased by B as the cost of opera-

tions of the home increased. The contract and the payment plan were thoroughly explained to *A*. As the cost of operations rose, the monthly payments were continually raised by *B*. *A* objected to the increases on the ground that the increases were far more than had been anticipated and the contract was therefore unconscionable. Was his objection valid? [Onderdonk v Presbyterian Homes, 171 NJ Super 529, 410 A2d 252]

11. Smith was employed as a salesman for Borden, Inc., which sold food products in 63 counties in Arkansas, 2 counties in Missouri, 2 counties in Oklahoma, and 1 county in Texas. The contract with Smith prohibited him from competing with Borden after leaving its employ. Smith left Borden and went to work for a competitor, Lady Baltimore Foods. Working for this second employer, Smith sold in three counties of Arkansas. He had sold in two of these counties while he worked for Borden. Borden brought an injunction action against Smith and Lady Baltimore to enforce the anticompetitive covenant in Smith's former contract. Was Borden entitled to the injunction? [Borden, Inc. v Smith, 252 Ark 295, 478 SW2d 744]

12. Doherty ran a lounge and bar, known as the Orchid Room, in California, where betting is illegal. Bradley, a patron in the Orchid Room, made bets with Doherty on the scores he could attain on the pinball machine. Bradley lost $70,000 on such bets. He later sued Doherty to recover the money. Doherty raised the defense that Bradley was *in pari delicto* and therefore could not recover. Bradley claimed that this defense did not apply because the pinball machines were fixed by electronic devices, and also because he, Bradley, was a compulsive gambler. Was Bradley correct? [Bradley v Doherty, 30 Cal App 3d 991, 106 Cal Rptr 725]

13. Credit Alliance Corporation loaned money to Westland Machine Company, Inc. Both companies had business experience, and the contract was signed on behalf of Westland by its president, who was also an attorney. He apparently did not read the contract and did not see that, buried in standard clauses, there was a provision waiving trial by jury. Credit Alliance later sued Westland on the debt. Westland demanded a jury trial and claimed that the waiver was invalid because it was unconscionable and contrary to public policy. Should a jury trial be granted? [Credit Alliance Corp. v Westland Machines Co. Inc. (Fla App) 439 So 2d 332]

14. Vodra was employed as a salesperson and contract person for American Security Services. As part of his contract of employment, Vodra signed an agreement that for 3 years after leaving this employment, he would not solicit any customer of American. Vodra had no experience in the security field when he went to work for American. To the extent that he became known to American's customers, it was by virtue of being the representative of American rather than because of his own reputation in the security field. After some years, Vodra left American and organized a competing company that solicited American's customers. American sued him to enforce the restrictive convenant. Vodra claimed that the restrictive convenant was illegal and not binding. Was he correct? [American Securities Services, Inc. v Vodra, 222 Neb 480, 385 NW2d 73]

15. John and Georgeann Dodge were married. They were later divorced and then made an agreement that John would pay real estate taxes on Georgeann's home until she remarried. She remarried, and John stopped paying the real estate taxes. Georgeann sued John for the taxes. He raised the defense that his duty to pay taxes stopped when she remarried. She replied that this provision was invalid because it imposed a restraint on remarriage and was therefore against public policy. Was she correct? [Re Dodge Marriage, 150 Ill App 3d 486, 103 Ill Dec 816, 501 NE2d 1354]

18

FORM OF CONTRACT

There was a time, in the history of the common law, when there was no requirement that a promise be in writing in order to be enforceable — a promise was a promise irrespective of its form (oral or written). Experience proved that this degree of freedom created too great an opportunity for abuse, and perjury became commonplace. In order to prevent this type of fraud, the law was changed to require that certain kinds of contracts be evidenced by a writing. In practice, this flat requirement was found also to open the door to fraud when in fact there was an oral contract, but the existence of the contract was falsely denied. So the law shifted once again and

now recognizes certain exceptions to the writing requirement. As an example, the requirement may be satisfied by a sufficient part performance. Some courts have gone further to ignore the writing requirement in certain cases of detrimental reliance upon an oral contract.

Assuming that a contract had been evidenced by a writing, whether or not the writing was required by statute, society was next faced with the policy of what effect was to be given the writing. Specifically, was the writing the final word or could it be modified or contradicted by the testimony of witnesses? Society has made a compromise between two extremes, hold-

WRITING REQUIRED:

STATUTE OF FRAUDS

MORE THAN ONE YEAR TO PERFORM
SALE OF LAND
ANSWER FOR ANOTHER'S DEBT OR DEFAULT
PERSONAL REPRESENTATIVE TO PAY DEBT
    OF DECEDENT
PROMISE IN CONSIDERATION OF MARRIAGE
SALE OF GOODS FOR $500 OR MORE
MISCELLANEOUS

EXCEPTIONS

PART PERFORMANCE
PROMISOR BENEFIT
DETRIMENTAL RELIANCE

PAROL EVIDENCE RULE

EVERY COMPLETE, FINAL WRITTEN
    CONTRACT

EXCEPTIONS

INCOMPLETE CONTRACT
AMBIGUOUS TERMS
FRAUD, ACCIDENT, OR MISTAKE
TO PROVE EXISTENCE OR NONBINDING
    CHARACTER OF CONTRACT
MODIFICATION OF CONTRACT
ILLEGALITY

FIGURE 18-1
HURDLES IN THE PATH OF A CONTRACT

ing by what is called the parol evidence rule that ordinarily the writing is the final word, but that in certain circumstances it is not.

A.   STATUTE OF FRAUDS

In Chapter 12 it was stated that a contract is a binding agreement. Must the agreement be evidenced by a writing?

§ 18:1   ORAL CONTRACTS VALID

Generally a contract is valid whether it is written or oral. By statute, however, some contracts must be evidenced by a writing. Such statutes are designed to prevent the use of the courts for the purpose of enforcing certain oral agreements or alleged oral agreements. The statutes do not apply when an oral agreement has been voluntarily performed by both parties.

The failure to sign and return a written contract does not establish that there is no contract as there may have been an earlier oral contract. Whether such a prior oral contract exists is to be determined from all the circumstances, the test being what intent was manifested by the parties.[1] If one of the parties, with the knowledge or approval of the other contracting party, undertakes performance of the contract before it is reduced to writing, it is generally held that the parties intended to be bound from the moment the oral contract was made.

Although ordinarily oral agreements are binding and are therefore contracts, an exception will arise when it is the intent of

---

[1]   Mal Spinrad of St. Louis, Inc. v Karman, Inc. (Mo App) 690 SW2d 460 (1985).

the parties that there is no binding agreement until a written contract is prepared and signed. If, in fact, the parties intend not to be bound until a written contract is executed, their preliminary oral agreement does not constitute a contract and cannot be enforced when no writing is thereafter executed.[2]

§ 18:2 CONTRACTS THAT MUST BE EVIDENCED BY A WRITING

Ordinarily a contract, whether oral or not, is binding if the existence and terms of the contract can be established to the satisfaction of the trier of fact, ordinarily the jury. In some instances a statute, commonly called a **statute of frauds**,[3] requires that certain kinds of contracts be evidenced by a writing or they cannot be enforced. This means that either (a) the contract itself must be in writing and signed by both parties, or (b) there be a sufficient written memorandum of the oral contract signed by the person being sued for breach of contract.

(a) AGREEMENT THAT CANNOT BE PERFORMED WITHIN ONE YEAR AFTER THE CONTRACT IS MADE. A writing is required when the contract by its terms or subject matter cannot be performed within one year after the date of the agreement. Thus, a joint venture agreement to construct a condominium complex was subject to the one-year provision of the statute of frauds where the contract could not reasonably have been performed within one year. This was due to the complex nature of the project and the fact that the plans of the parties projected a development over the course of three years. The year runs from the time of the making of the oral contract rather than from the date when performance is to begin. In computing the year, the day on which the contract was made is excluded. The year begins with the following day and ends at the close of the first anniversary of the day on which the agreement was made.

The statute of frauds does not apply if it is possible under the terms of the agreement to perform the contract within one year. Thus, a writing is not required when no time for performance is specified, and the performance will not necessarily take more than a year.[4] In this case the statute is inapplicable without regard to the time when performance is actually begun or completed.

Since a contract of indefinite duration is terminable by either party at will, the statute of frauds is not applicable since the contract may be terminated within a year.[5] In the *Boening* case, it was claimed that there was no binding contract when there was only an oral agreement to continue the plaintiff's franchise for so long as performance thereunder was satisfactory.

---

[2] Lal v Naffah, 149 Ill App 3d 245, 102 Ill Dec 803, 500 NE2d 699 (1986).

[3] The name is derived from the original English Statute of Frauds and Perjuries, which was adopted in 1677 and became the pattern for similar legislation in America. The seventeenth section of that statute governed the sale of goods, and its modern counterpart is § 2-201 of the Uniform Commercial Code, discussed in Chapter 27. The fourth section of the English statute provided the pattern for American legislation with respect to contracts other than for the sale of goods described in this section of the chapter. The English statute was repealed in 1954, except as to land sale and guaranty contracts. The American statutes remain in force, but the liberalization by Uniform Commercial Code § 2-201 of the pre-Code requirements with respect to contracts for the sale of goods may be regarded as a step in the direction of the abandonment of the statute of frauds concept.

When the English Statute of Frauds was adopted, the parties to a lawsuit were not permitted to testify on their own behalf, with the result that a litigant had difficulty in disproving perjured testimony of third persons offered as evidence on behalf of the adverse party. The Statute of Frauds was repealed in England partly because it was felt that it permitted the assertion of a "technical" defense as a means of avoiding just obligations and partly on the ground that with parties in interest now having the right to testify there is no longer the need for a writing to protect the parties from perjured testimony of third persons. Azevedo v Minister, 86 Nev 576, 471 P2d 661 (1970).

[4] Vitner v Funk, 182 Ga App 39, 354 SE2d 666 (1987).

[5] Fisher v Ken Carter Industries, Inc. 127 App Div 2d 817, 512 NYS2d 408 (1987).

D & N Boening, Inc. v Kirsch Beverages, Inc.
63 NY2d 449, 483 NYS2d 164, 472 NE2d 992 (1984)

D & N Boening, Inc. was franchised by the American Beverage Corporation to sell the "Yoo-Hoo" beverage in a certain portion of New York state. The franchise was to continue as long as the franchisee rendered satisfactory performance. This agreement was oral, and several requests to put it in writing were refused. Thereafter Kirsch Beverages bought out American Beverage Corporation and notified Boening that its franchise was terminated. No cause for termination was given, and Boening then sued Kirsch and American for breach of the franchise. From a judgment for the defendants, the plaintiff appealed.

JASEN, J. . . . The ancient Statute of Frauds . . . was intended to prevent fraud in the proving of certain legal transactions particularly susceptible to deception, mistake and perjury and, with regard specifically to the requirement for a signed writing for a contract not to be performed within one year, "the design of the statute was, not to trust to the memory of witnesses for a longer time than one year".

Unfortunately, the Statute does not in many cases provide an effective means of serving that purpose. There is no necessary relationship between the time of the making of a contract, the time within which its performance is required, and the time when it might come to court to be proven. Accordingly, the courts have generally been reluctant to give too broad an interpretation to this provision of the Statute and instead have limited it to those contracts only which by their very terms have absolutely no possibility in fact and law of full performance within one year.

In a leading case on this provision of the Statute of Frauds, the United States Supreme Court in 1896 reviewed the case law of both Great Britain and the several States throughout this country and concluded, with regard to the oral agreement before it, that "the parties may well have expected that the contract would continue in force for more than one year; it may well have been very improbable that it would not do so; and it did in fact continue in force for a much longer time. But they made no stipulation which in terms, or by reasonable inference, required that result. The question is not what the probable, or expected, or actual performance of the contract was; but whether the contract, according to the reasonable interpretation of its terms, required that it should not be performed within the year." (*Warner v. Texas & Pacific Ry.*, 164 U.S. 418.) Likewise, this court almost 40 years previous gave a similar construction of this State's Statute of Frauds. At that time, we explained that "[i]t is not the meaning of the statute that the contract must be performed within a year. If it can be so performed consistently with the language in which the parties have expressed themselves; in other words, if the obligation of the contract is not, by its very terms, or necessary construction, to endure for a longer period than one year, it is a valid agreement, although it may be capable of an indefinite continuance."

. . . Moreover, consistent with that narrow interpretation, this court has continued to analyze oral agreements to determine if, according to the parties' terms, there might be any possible means of performance within one year. Wherever an agreement has been found to be susceptible of fulfillment within that time, in whatever manner and however impractical, this court has held the one-year provision of the Statute to be inapplicable, a writing unnecessary, and the agreement not barred. . . .

On the other hand, while the foregoing oral agreements and similar ones which are performable within one year are saved from the writing requirement of the Statute of Frauds, clearly there are others which simply are impossible of completion within that time by their own terms and are, therefore, void if unwritten. Prominent among these latter agreements falling within the Statute are those which are terminable within one year only upon a breach by one of the parties. A breach can in no way be equated with an option to discontinue or cancel, the exercise of which would constitute an alternative performance of the agreement. . . .

As this court early explained, "termination is not performance, but rather the destruction of the contract . . . where there is no provision authorizing either of the parties to terminate as a matter of right." And, more recently, in deciding that the contract then under review fell within the Statute because not truly performable within one year, this court held that "[t]he contract was not, then, one which might be *performed* within a year, but rather one which could only be *terminated* within that period by a breach of one or the other party to it [emphasis in original]. *The possibility of such wrongful termination is not, of course, the same as the possibility of performance* within the statutory period."

Here, as the Appellate Division correctly held, the oral agreement between the parties called for performance of an indefinite duration and could only be terminated within one year by its breach during that period. . . .

According to its terms, the agreement required defendants to continue plaintiff's subdistributorship indefinitely. It provided for no expiration and there was no contemplation of any completion or final discharge. The sole limitation on the agreement's duration was its explicit requirement — especially crucial to an exclusive agency — that plaintiff conduct its subdistributorship satisfactorily, exerting its best efforts and acting in good faith. Only upon plaintiff's failure to do so within the first year could the agreement have been terminated during that period.

Such a failure would not have constituted a permitted manner of performance or exercise of an option, but rather, a breach of the agreement. And other than such a breach, there was no provision under the terms of the agreement for it to come to an end. Neither party had an option to cancel, and there was no specified time or event which automatically would cause the agreement to terminate. Instead, under a reasonable interpretation of its own terms, the agreement would extend beyond the first year and, indeed, would continue in perpetuity unless plaintiff failed to perform its part of the bargain.

Being terminable only by plaintiff's breach, the agreement alleged in the complaint was not one which by its terms could be *performed* within one year. As such, it came within the ambit of the Statute of Frauds and is void for being unwritten. . . .

[Judgment affirmed]

QUESTIONS

1. What was the evil against which the statute of frauds was intended to guard in connection with the provision involved in the *Boening* case?

2. What has been the attitude of the courts to the one-year provision of the statute of frauds?
3. Why didn't the court sustain the oral contract in view of the fact that it could have ended in less than a year if Boening's performance was not satisfactory to Kirsch?

The fact that an oral contract for a specified number of years would be terminated by the death of a party thereto does not take the oral contract out of the statute of frauds. Thus, an oral contract of employment not to compete with the employer for five years is not binding, even though the contract would be discharged by the death of the employee, which could occur within one year.[6]

(b) AGREEMENT TO SELL OR A SALE OF ANY INTEREST IN REAL PROPERTY. All contracts to sell as well as sales of land, buildings, or interests in land, such as mortgages, must be evidenced by a writing.

The statute applies only to the agreement between the owner and purchaser, or between their agents. It does not apply to collateral agreements, such as those that the purchaser may make in order to raise the money to pay for the property or to agreements to pay for an examination or search of the title of the property. Similarly, a partnership agreement to deal in real estate is generally not required by this provision of the statute of frauds to be in writing. The statute ordinarily does not apply to a contract between a real estate agent and one of the parties to the sales contract employing the agent.

An agreement to cancel or set aside a contract for the sale of land must satisfy the statute of frauds.[7]

(c) PROMISE TO ANSWER FOR THE DEBT OR DEFAULT OF ANOTHER. When A promises C to pay B's debt to C if B does not do so, A is promising to answer for the debt of another. Such a promise must usually be evidenced by a writing to be enforceable.[8] Thus, the oral promise of the president of a corporation to pay the debts owed by the corporation to its creditors if they will not sue the corporation does not bind the president. A promise to pay an attorney the fee owed by a third person cannot be enforced when there was no writing to satisfy the statute of frauds.[9]

If the promise is made directly to the debtor that the promisor will pay the creditor of the debtor what is owed, the statute of frauds is not applicable. In contrast, if the promisor makes the promise to the creditor, it comes within the category of a promise made for the benefit of another and must therefore be evidenced by a writing that satisfies the statute of frauds.

(d) PROMISE BY THE EXECUTOR OR ADMINISTRATOR OF A DECEDENT'S ESTATE TO PAY A CLAIM AGAINST THE ESTATE FROM PERSONAL FUNDS. The personal representative (executor or administrator) has the duty of winding up the affairs of a deceased person, paying the debts from the proceeds of the estate, and distributing any balance remaining. The executor or administrator is not personally liable for the claims against the estate of the decedent. If the personal representative promises to pay the decedent's debts with the representative's own money, the promise cannot be enforced unless it is evidenced by a writing that complies with the terms of the statute of frauds.

If the personal representative makes a

---

[6] Frantz v Parke (Idaho App) 729 P2d 1068 (1986).
[7] Saikowski v Manning (Tex App) 720 SW2d 275 (1986).

[8] Lichtman v Grossbard, 129 App Div 2d 437, 514 NYS2d 9 (1987).
[9] Cook & Franke v Mailman (App) 136 Wis 2d 434, 402 NW2d 361 (1987).

contract on behalf of the estate in the course of administering the estate, a writing is not required since the representative is then contracting on behalf of the estate. Thus, if the personal representative employs an attorney to settle the estate or makes a burial contract with an undertaker, no writing is required.

(e) PROMISE MADE IN CONSIDERATION OF MARRIAGE. If a person makes a promise to pay a sum of money or to give property to another in consideration of marriage or a promise to marry, the agreement must be evidenced by a writing. This provision of the statute of frauds is not applicable to ordinary mutual promises to marry, and it is not affected by the statutes in some states that prohibit the bringing of any action for breach of promise of marriage.

(f) SALE OF GOODS. When the contract price for goods is $500 or more, the contract must ordinarily be evidenced by a writing.

(g) MISCELLANEOUS STATUTES OF FRAUDS. In a number of states, special statutes require other agreements to be in writing or evidenced by a writing. Thus, a statute may provide that an agreement to name a person as beneficiary in an insurance policy must be evidenced by a writing.

The Uniform Commercial Code contains three statutes of frauds relating to sales of personal property: (1) goods, (2) securities, such as stocks and bonds; (3) personal property other than goods and securities.

In some states contracts with brokers relating to the sale of land are also subject to the statute of frauds.

§ 18:3 NOTE OR MEMORANDUM

The statute of frauds requires a writing to evidence those contracts that come within its scope. This writing may be a note or memorandum, as distinguished from a contract. It may be in any form because its only purpose is to serve as evidence of the contract. The statutory requirement is, of course, satisfied if there is a complete written contract signed by both parties.

(a) SIGNING. The note or memorandum must be signed by the party sought to be charged or that person's agent. A letter from an employer setting forth the details of an oral contract of employment satisfies the statute of frauds in a suit brought by the employee against the employer, as the writing was signed by the party "sought to be charged." If the employer had sued the employee in such case, the employer's letter would not satisfy the statute of frauds as it would not be signed by the employee.

Some states require that the authorization of an agent to execute a contract coming within the statute of frauds must also be in writing. In the case of an auction, it is the usual practice for the auctioneer to be the agent of both parties for the purpose of signing the memorandum.

Ordinarily the signature may be made at any place on the writing, although in some states it is expressly required that the signature appear at the end of the writing. The signature may be an ordinary one or any symbol that is adopted by the party as a signature. It may consist of initials, figures, or a mark. When a signature consists of a mark made by a person who is illiterate or physically incapacitated, it is commonly required that the name of the person be placed upon the writing by someone else, who may be required to sign the instrument as a witness. A person signing a trade or assumed name is liable to the same extent as though the contract had been signed with the signer's name. In the absence of a local statute that provides otherwise, a signature may be made by pencil, pen, typewriter, print, or stamp.

(b) CONTENT. Except in the case of a sale of goods, the note or memorandum must contain all the material terms of the contract so that the court can determine just what was agreed.[10] A writing that does not describe the land or identify the buyer does not satisfy the statute of frauds.[11] Likewise,

---

[10] Elghanayan v Forest Hills Co 2 Company, 123 App Div 2d 417, 506 NYS2d 720 (1986).
[11] Rodman v Aivagedis, 123 App Div 2d 428, 506 NYS2d 733 (1986).

a writing is insufficient if the contract is partly oral and partly written. The subject matter must be identified either within the writing itself or in other writings to which it refers. A writing is not sufficient that does not identify the subject of the contract. A deposit check given by the buyer to the seller does not take the oral land sales contract out of the statute of frauds. This is because the check does not set forth the terms of the sale.

The note or memorandum may consist of one writing or of separate papers, such as letters or telegrams, or of a combination of such papers. The writing that satisfies the statute of frauds may be a letter written by a party's attorney.[12]

Separate writings cannot be considered

together unless they are linked, either by express reference in each writing to the other or by the fact that each writing clearly deals with the same subject matter.

It is not necessary that the writing be addressed to the other contracting party or to any other person, nor is it necessary that the writing be made with the intent to create a writing to satisfy the statute of frauds. When a corporation made an oral contract of employment with an employee, the minutes of the corporation reciting the adoption of the resolution to employ the employee (which minutes were signed by the president of the corporation) together with the salary check paid the employee constituted a sufficient writing to satisfy the statute of frauds. In the *Socarras* case, the question was whether a writing satisfied the statute of frauds.

[12] Smith v McClam (SC) 346 SE2d 720 (1986).

SOCARRAS V CLAUGHTON HOTELS, INC.

(Fla App) 374 So 2d 1057 (1979)

Edward Claughton was president and principal stockholder of Claughton Hotels, Inc. William Socarras wanted to purchase the Silver Sands Oceanfront Motel from the corporation. He filled out and submitted a printed form, referred to as the RAMCO form, which stated the terms of his offer. After some days of discussion, the parties were near agreement but held back until the tax consequences of the sale could be studied. To protect the transaction during this interval, Socarras asked Claughton for something in writing to show his financial backers so that they would know that the deal was proceeding favorably. Claughton then wrote by hand the note that is set forth in the beginning of the opinion of the court. The deal fell through, and Socarras then sued Claughton Hotels to enforce the sales contract that Socarras claimed arose from combining the RAMCO form and the handwritten note. Claughton Hotels claimed that these two writings did not establish the existence of a contract and did not satisfy the statute of frauds. The court agreed with Claughton Hotels and entered summary judgment against Socarras. He appealed.

EZELL, A. J. . . . Socarras delivered to Claughton a RAMCO deposit receipt form appropriately completed and signed by Socarras. This completed form comprised the basic terms of his proposal to buy the motel. . . .

A short time later the parties again met to discuss the contemplated sale. Claughton returned the RAMCO form on which he had made a number of

handwritten notations materially varying the original offer submitted by Socarras. . . .

At their next meeting, Socarras handed Claughton a retyped version of the
RAMCO form containing essentially his original offer, . . . After consulting
with his tax advisor, Claughton again informed Socarras that he would not
sign any contract until it could be thoroughly reviewed regarding its possible
tax consequences. When Socarras responded that he needed something to
show his financial backers that an agreement was imminent, Claughton
obliged by drafting a handwritten note which read as follows:

> Mr. Bill Socarras,
> Dear Bill,
>   I would like to sell the Silver Sands Oceanfront Motel with an area of approxi-
> mately 4.3 acres on Key Biscayne under the following terms and conditions:
>   Price — $3,000,000.00
>   Terms: — $150,000 at closing about 90 days after contract with a $50,000.00 de-
> posit with your attorneys; of which shall be a part of the sum at closing.
> $720,000.00 payable on or about August 1, 1978; and the balance in a purchase
>   money mortgage payable over three years at 8 1/2 % interest while 1st mtg. status
>   and 10% interest while subordinated; payable in full or in part at any time after
>   the first year without penalty; and may be subordinated to an institutional first
>   mortgage
>   Sale includes personal property owned by the seller except for certain personal
> items such as paintings, wall coverings, boats and the like, except for the 2
> duplexes.
>   This is an exclusive offer to sell net at this price for a period of time not to exceed
> Aug. 15, 1977.
>   Many thanks for your understanding.
> Sincerely,
> Claughton Hotels, Inc.
> by: E. N. Claughton, Jr.
> attest: Suzanne C. Matthews

Claughton signed and delivered the handwritten note to Socarras and returned the retyped RAMCO form unsigned.

Three weeks later, after further extensive negotiations, the transaction fell
through when Claughton learned that the sale would have very adverse tax
consequences to his corporation. Although Socarras was given another opportunity to work out acceptable terms, when he returned with another RAMCO
form containing essentially the same terms as originally proposed, Claughton
refused to sign. After several subsequent fruitless meetings failed to produce
any written agreement, the negotiations concluded without a sale.

Socarras then filed a complaint in the circuit court. . . . He contended that
the parties entered into an enforceable contract. . . . He maintained that the
RAMCO form and the handwritten note were sufficient, when taken together,
to satisfy the statute of frauds. . . .

To be an enforceable land sales contract, the statute of frauds requires the
contract to satisfy two threshold conditions. First, the contract must be embodied in a written memorandum signed by the party against whom enforcement is sought. Second, the written memorandum must disclose all of the
essential terms of the sale and these terms may not be explained by resort to
parol evidence. . . . Neither of these two essential prerequisites were met.

. . . The appellant concedes that the RAMCO form was never signed by the appellee. Appellant's ingenuous effort to persuade the court that an enforceable agreement was created by the physical attachment of the unsigned RAMCO form to the signed handwritten note must fail. It is established law that in order for an unsigned writing to be used to supply the essential elements of an enforceable contract, there must be some reference to that unsigned writing in the signed writing. Nowhere in Claughton's handwritten note is there the slightest reference to the RAMCO form or any other document. . . . The handwritten note and the RAMCO form were separately discussed and treated by the parties. Even if the two documents were attached and discussed together, this would not be sufficient to constitute an enforceable contract where the writings were not connected by internal reference.

Further, the handwritten note is not enforceable by itself since it contains numerous unclear terms that could not be known or understood without recourse to inadmissible parol evidence. There is no definitive list of essential terms that must be present and certain to satisfy the statute of frauds. Rather, the essential terms will vary widely according to the nature and complexity of each transaction and will be evaluated on a case by case basis:

> Where it is sought to enforce in equity a contract for the sale of land, it is essential that the terms of the contract shall be expressed with reasonable certainty, and what is reasonable in any case must depend upon the subject-matter of the agreement, the purpose for which it was entered into, the situation and relation of the parties, and the circumstances under which it was made.

In a situation such as the present case, where the alleged agreement involves a large and very complex real estate transaction, it is readily apparent that all of the essential terms of that transaction were not included in Claughton's handwritten note. An examination of the note reveals some of the more conspicuous omissions. For instance, it contains only the suggestion that the appellee "would like to sell" the Silver Sands Motel. The identity of the ultimate purchasers is not given and it is not clear as to how the deferred payment financing arrangement would work, or when the purchase money mortgage payments would begin. The note makes reference to personal property to be excepted from the contemplated sale, but there is no clear identification of the items that Claughton Hotels would retain. The note also makes mention of a possible future subordination of the purchase money mortgage to a new first mortgage, but none of the terms of this contemplated subordination were delineated.

In short, the handwritten note evidences only Claughton's willingness to negotiate a contract with potential purchasers who might be interested in the general terms that he outlined. The note did not incorporate all of the essential terms necessary to make an enforceable contract for the sale of the land. It reflected only the state of negotiations at that point, preliminary negotiations which never ripened into a formal agreement. Under these circumstances, the trial court was eminently correct in entering summary judgment for the appellee.

[Judgment affirmed]

QUESTIONS

1. Was the unsigned printed form sufficient to satisfy the statute of frauds?

2. What test must be satisfied before two separate papers may be considered together for the purpose of meeting the requirements of the statute of frauds?
3. Did the handwritten note satisfy the statute of frauds?

(c) TIME OF WRITING. The memorandum may be made at the time of the original transaction or at a later date. It must, however, ordinarily exist at the time a court action is brought upon the agreement.

§ 18:4   EFFECT OF NONCOMPLIANCE

The majority of states hold that a contract which does not comply with the statute of frauds is voidable.[13] A small minority of states hold that such an agreement is void. Under either view, if an action is brought to enforce the contract, the defendant can raise the objection that it is not evidenced by a writing. However, when it is held that the oral contract is not void but merely voidable, it can be enforced if the defendant does not raise the statute of frauds. That is, the court will not refuse to enforce the contract when it notices that it is oral unless the opposing party objects thereto.[14] No one other than the defendant, however, can make the objection. Thus, an insurance company cannot refuse to pay on its policy on the theory that the insured did not have any insurable interest in the insured property because there was no writing relating to the property that satisfied the statute of frauds.

(a) RECOVERY OF VALUE CONFERRED. In most instances, a person who is prevented from enforcing a contract because of the statute of frauds is nevertheless entitled to recover from the other party the value of any services or property furnished or money given under the oral contract. Recovery is not based upon the terms of the contract but upon the quasi-contractual obligation of the other party to restore to the plaintiff what was received in order to prevent unjust enrichment at the plaintiff's expense. For example, when an oral contract for services cannot be enforced because of the statute of frauds, the person performing the work may recover the reasonable value of the services rendered.

(b) PROOF OF FRAUD. The statute of frauds does not bar proof that the promisor had no intention to pay the debt of the third person but had made such promise fraudulently to induce the promisee to supply goods.

§ 18:5   JUDICIAL RELIEF FROM STATUTE OF FRAUDS

The requirements of the statute of frauds are easily met. Often, however, because people are in a hurry or do not know the law, transactions consist only of spoken words. No writing is made that satisfies the statute of frauds. If one of the parties double-crosses the other by claiming that the transaction is not binding because of the statute of frauds, a real injustice can be inflicted. To prevent this hardship, the courts have created certain exceptions to the statute of frauds.

(a) PART PERFORMANCE OF LAND CONTRACT. In spite of the statute of frauds, an oral contract for the sale of an interest in land will be enforced if the buyer has gone into possession of the land and has made

---

[13] The Uniform Commercial Code creates several statutes of frauds of limited applicability in which it uses the term *not enforceable*. § 1-206 (sale of intangible personal property); § 2-201 (sale of goods); and § 8-319 (sale of securities). The Official Code Comment, point 4, to § 2-201 describes *not enforceable* as meaning what would ordinarily be called *voidable*.

[14] Joiner v Elrod (Tex App) 716 SW2d 606 (1986).

substantial valuable improvements to the land, and the value of such improvements cannot be easily measured in dollars.[15]

(b) PROMISOR BENEFITED BY PROMISE TO PAY DEBT OF ANOTHER. If a person orally promises a creditor to pay the debt owed to that creditor by a debtor, the promise is ordinarily not binding because of the statute of frauds. If the promise is not made by the promisor to help the debtor but is made primarily to benefit the promisor, the courts refuse to apply the statute of frauds. In such case, the promise to pay the debt of the third person is binding, even though it is oral and benefits the debtor by discharging the debt that was due.

For example, when a contractor promises to pay the debt owed by a subcontractor to the supplier of materials needed by the subcontractor for the construction work, it can be found that the primary purpose of the contractor's making such promise was to assure the uninterrupted work on the construction and thus protect the contractor from liability for delay that would result from an interruption. If so found, the contractor is liable on the promise, although there is no writing as would be required by the statute of frauds for a promise to pay the debt of another. When the purpose of a majority stockholder's promise to pay the debt of the corporation is to benefit the stockholder, the statute of frauds is not applicable to that promise.[16]

(c) DETRIMENTAL RELIANCE ON ORAL CONTRACT. The extent to which judicial relief from the statute of frauds will be granted in cases other than land sales and debt guaranties is not clear. The same forces that gave rise to the doctrine of promissory estoppel in connection with the law of consideration are to some extent causing courts to recognize detrimental reliance as excusing noncompliance with the statute of frauds. In the *Kiely* case, it was claimed that an oral contract could be enforced in spite of the statute of frauds because of the plaintiff's reliance on the contract.

---

[15]   Penwell v Barrett (Tex App) 724 SW2d 902 (1987).

[16]   Baron v Lerman (Mo App) 719 SW2d 72 (1986).

KIELY V ST. GERMAIN
(Colo) 670 P2d 764 (1983)

Joel St. Germain was employed by the Public Service Company. William Boshouwers owned 100 percent of the stock of Boshouwers Color Laboratory, Inc. St. Germain and Boshouwers, in the office of St. Germain's attorney, reached an agreement that they would begin a new business venture, that St. Germain would come to work for Boshouwers Color Laboratory and that William Boshouwers would sell 49 percent of the stock of the laboratory to St. Germain for $25,000. At the end of the meeting, Boshouwers stated to St. Germain "We have a deal and you can tell your employer that you are leaving." St. Germain then quit his job and obtained a second mortgage on his home to raise the money to purchase the stock of the laboratory. A document was prepared setting forth the terms of the oral agreement, but Boshouwers then refused to sign it and denied that there was ever such an agreement. St. Germain brought suit on the oral contract. With respect to the shares of the laboratory stock, he claimed the profit that he would have made if Boshouwers had sold the stock as orally agreed. Boshouwers raised the defense that the statute of frauds, Uniform Commercial Code, § 8-319, required that the contract be evidenced in writing and that in the absence of a writing, there was no contract. St. Germain claimed that because of his reliance on the oral contract the doctrine of promissory estoppel barred Boshouwers from raising the defense of the statute of frauds. The trial court held that the statute of frauds barred proof of the oral contract for the sale of stock, but awarded other damages for lost wages and legal costs. By this time, Boshouwers and the laboratory had become bankrupt, and Kiely, as the trustee in bankruptcy, then appealed.

KIRSHBAUM, J. . . . Although the doctrine of promissory estoppel is based in part upon the premise that statute of frauds provisions need not defeat meritorious claims for enforcement of oral promises, the results are far from uniform in cases wherein a claim based on promissory estoppel is challenged by a defense based squarely on the provisions of a particular statute of frauds. Some jurisdictions suggest that in such circumstances the absence of compliance with statute of frauds requirements invariably will result in the defeat of the promissory estoppel claim. . . . Other jurisdictions have permitted recovery on the promissory estoppel claim when the evidence establishes that the defendant relying on the statute of frauds defense orally agreed to reduce the operative promise to writing.

The majority of jurisdictions faced with resolving a confrontation between promissory estoppel claims and statute of frauds defenses have adopted a more flexible, albeit a more complex, approach. The courts in those jurisdictions are required to examine the policies furthered by the doctrine of promissory estoppel and by the particular statute of frauds in the total context of the case and to render a decision which is basically fair to all the parties. . . . The effort to compare the strengths of the doctrine and of the statute in particular cases gives maximum recognition to the central policy furthered by each — preventing unjust results when parties deal with each other by means of oral rather than written communication.

In response to judicial development of the doctrine of promissory estoppel, the American Law Institute in 1979 adopted a new section articulating principles directly applicable to the promissory estoppel claim/statute of frauds defense quagmire. . . . In essence, section 139 provides the equitable balancing test utilized by the majority of jurisdictions. This court has previously recognized that a plaintiff's full or partial performance of an oral agreement, when done in reasonably justifiable reliance thereon, is sufficient to overcome a statute of frauds defense. . . . Thus, the principle embodied in section 139 of the *Restatement (Second) of Contracts* that detrimental action performed in justifiable reliance upon oral promises may be sufficient to compel full or partial performance of the promise in spite of the applicability of a statute of frauds defense is but a slight extension of the principles well settled in Colorado. Thus, we conclude that the Court of Appeals correctly concluded that section 139 of the *Restatement (Second) of Contracts* is applicable to this case.

The statute of frauds relied on by defendants, [UCC § 8-319] states in pertinent part as follows:

A contract for the sale of securities is not enforceable . . . unless: (a) There is some writing signed by the party against whom enforcement is sought or by his authorized agent or broker sufficient to indicate that a contract has been made for sale of a stated quantity of described securities at a defined or stated price. . . .

The statute, a part of the Uniform Commercial Code (the Code), is designed to ensure certainty in the sale and purchase of securities. It prohibits the sale of or purchase of this type of asset in the absence of a complete written agreement concerning the essential terms of such transaction. However, [UCC § 1-103] contains the following provision concerning construction of other provisions of the Code:

> Unless displaced by the particular provisions of this title, the principles of law and equity, including . . . the law relative to . . . estoppel . . . shall supplement its provisions.

This recognition that general principles of estoppel should be considered in applying the provisions of the Code indicates a strong legislative concern that the statute not be utilized to perpetrate a fraud or to achieve inequitable results in particular cases. Section 8-319 contains no indication that transactions involving the sale of securities are exempt from the general caveat of section 1-103. Thus, this particular statute of frauds may be "supplemented" by the doctrine of promissory estoppel — a virtual requirement that courts utilize a balancing test to prevent use of the statute to effect inequitable results.

The trial court has not had an opportunity to analyze the merits of St. Germain's claim for "lost profits" under the principles enunciated in section 139 of the *Restatement (Second) of Contracts*. It must be permitted to do so in light of the evidence adduced at trial or in light of any additional evidence it might in its discretion permit to be presented on the matter.

[Judgment reversed and action remanded]

QUESTIONS

1. List and explain the different views as to the relationship of promissory estoppel to the statute of frauds.
2. Compare promissory estoppel and part performance.
3. State whether (a) St. Germain's claim was based on promissory estoppel or whether (b) St. Germain relied on promissory estoppel as a defense against Boshouwers' claim that the statute of frauds barred enforcement of an oral contract.

There is a conflict of authority on whether detrimental reliance excuses non-compliance with the statute of frauds. Some courts refuse to apply the doctrine of detrimental reliance to avoid the defense of the statute of frauds because that would defeat the policy of the statute.[17]

The mere fact that the promisee relies on the oral promise is generally not sufficient to entitle the promisee to enforce the oral

[17]   Meinhold v Huang (Mo App) 687 SW2d 596 (1985). Courts commonly refer to this doctrine as "promissory estoppel." The term *detrimental reliance* is used in the text because the promissory estoppel applied in connection with the question of consideration requires greater detriment than is required by those courts recognizing reliance as avoiding the statute of frauds. See § 16:10 as to consideration and promissory estoppel.

promise. The promisee must show that (1) because of the reliance on the promise substantial or unconscionable injury would be sustained by the promisee, or (2) the promisor would be unjustly enriched if the oral promise was not enforced.

B.   PAROL EVIDENCE RULE

When the contract is evidenced by a writing, may the contract terms be changed by the testimony of witnesses? The answer depends upon the circumstances surrounding the execution of the writing and the nature of the writing.

§ 18:6   EXCLUSION OF PAROL EVIDENCE

The general rule is that spoken words, that is, **parol evidence,** will not be allowed to modify or contradict the terms of a written contract that is complete on its face unless there is clear proof that because of fraud, accident, or a mistake, the writing is not in fact the contract or the complete or true contract. This is called the **parol evidence rule.** It excludes words spoken before or at the time the contract was made.

The parol evidence rule prevents a party from avoiding liability on a written contract by evidence that the writing does not mean what it says. Thus, the parol evidence rule bars proof that the obligee stated that the guaranty contract signed by the defendant was a "mere technicality" and that the defendant would not be required to make payment.[18]

In the *Gerlund* case, evidence was offered that contradicted the express provision of an employment contract.

---

[18] Simpson v MBank Dallas (Tex App) 724 SW2d 102 (1987).

GERLUND V ELECTRONIC DISPENSERS INTERNATIONAL
190 Cal App 3d 263, 235 Cal Rptr 279 (1987)

Leroy and Susan Gerlund were sales representatives of Electronic Dispensers International (EDI). They worked under a contract that specified that the employment could be terminated for any reason. The Gerlunds were the best sales representatives of EDI. After some years, EDI wanted to change the rate of commissions paid to sales representatives. When the Gerlunds did not agree to the changes, EDI discharged them. They sued EDI and offered evidence that EDI had stated they would be employed as long as they did a good job. From a judgment in the Gerlunds' favor, EDI appealed.

BRAUER, J. . . . We quote here the pertinent portions of the agreement:

11. EFFECTIVE PERIOD: TERMINATION
    This agreement shall be effective until thirty (30) days after notice of termination given by either party. Notice of termination may be given at any time and for any reason, and the date of any such notice shall be the postmark date if mailed, or the transmission date if wired. . . .
13. THE AGREEMENT COMPLETE.
    This agreement contains the entire agreement between the Company and the Representative. There are no oral or collateral agreements of any kind. . . .

. . . The parol evidence rule generally prohibits the introduction of any extrinsic evidence to vary or contradict the terms of an integrated written instrument. It is based upon the premise that the written instrument *is* the agreement of the parties. Its application involves a two part analysis: 1) was the writing intended to be an integration, i.e. a complete and final expression of the parties' agreement, precluding any evidence of collateral agreements, and 2) is the agreement susceptible of the meaning contended for by the party offering the evidence? . . .

In regard to the question of integration, the written agreement of the parties contained an expression of their intent that it supersede any and all other agreements between them and that it constitute their entire agreement. It specifically recited that "there are no oral or collateral agreements of any kind." Our Supreme Court held in *Masterson v Sine,* 68 Cal.2d 222, 65 Cal.Rptr. 545, 436 P.2d 561 that such a clause, while it certainly helps to resolve the issue, does not of itself establish an integration; the collateral agreement itself must be examined in order to determine whether the parties intended it to be a part of their bargain. *Masterson,* however, does not go so far as to permit proof of a collateral agreement which contradicts an express provision of the written agreement. The reason for this clear: it cannot reasonably be presumed that the parties intended to integrate two directly contradictory terms in the same agreement. Under *Masterson* then, parol evidence can be admitted only "'to prove the existence of a separate oral agreement as to any matter on which the document is silent and which is not inconsistent with it terms. . . '" (*Id.* p. 226, 65 Cal.Rptr. 545, 436 P.2d 561.)

. . . The contract provides that either party can give written notice of termination *for any reason.* Thus there is no room for a separate collateral agreement regarding reasons for termination; the precise subject is already covered in the writing. Any additional agreement would "certainly" have been included in paragraph 11. (Com. Code § 2202.)

. . . We find that the alleged oral agreement is completely inconsistent with the language of the written contract. Thus the proffered parol understanding as to grounds for termination would be inadmissible to vary the contractual terms even if the contract were *not* an integration.

We now move on to the second part of our analysis: whether the offered evidence is nonetheless admissible to explain the meaning of the contractual language.

We do not find that the language of the contract lends itself to the proposed meaning. The term "any reason" is plainly all-inclusive, encompassing all reasons "*of whatever kind,*" good, bad, or indifferent. (quoting Webster's Dictionary definition of "any"). Adding the modifier "good" has a delimiting effect which changes the meaning entirely. As written the contract is one which is terminable at will; the interpretation sought by the Gerlunds is that the contract is terminable only for good cause. The two are totally inconsistent. The trial court admitted the evidence on the ground that "both parties have testified as to what they interpreted the contract to mean." Testimony of intention which is contrary to a contract's express terms, however, does not give meaning to the contract: rather it seeks to substitute a different meaning. It follows . . . that such evidence must be excluded.

[Judgment reversed]

1. What does the court mean when it speaks of the contract as being an "integration"?
2. How would the *Gerlund* case have been decided if Paragraph 13, stating that it was the complete contract, had not been included?
3. Could the parol evidence in the *Gerlund* case have been admitted to explain the meaning of the terms used in the written contract?

(a) REASON FOR THE PAROL EVIDENCE RULE. The parol evidence rule is based on the theory that either (1) there never was an oral agreement or (2) if there was, the parties purposely abandoned it when they executed their written contract. The social objective of the parol evidence rule is to give stability to contracts and to prevent the fraudulent assertion of oral terms that never actually existed. Some courts apply the parol evidence rule strictly.

To illustrate the parol evidence rule, assume that L, the landlord who is the owner of several new stores in the same vicinity, discusses leasing one of them to T (tenant). L agrees to give to T the exclusive right to sell soft drinks and agrees to stipulate in the leases with the tenants of other stores that they cannot do so. L and T then execute a detailed written lease for the store. The lease with T makes no provision with respect to an exclusive right of T to sell soft drinks.Thereafter L leases the other stores to A, B, and C, without restricting them as to the sale of soft drinks, which they then begin to sell, causing T to lose money. T sues L, claiming that the latter has broken the contract by which T was to have the exclusive right to sell soft drinks. L defends on the ground that there was no prior oral agreement to that effect. Will the court permit T to prove that there was such an oral agreement?

On the facts as stated, if nothing more is shown, the court will not permit such parol evidence to be presented. The operation of this principle can be understood more easily if the actual courtroom procedure is fol-lowed. When T sues L, the first step will be to prove that there is a lease between them. Accordingly, T will offer in evidence the written lease between T and L. T will then take the witness stand and begin to testify about an oral agreement giving an exclu-sive right. At this point, L's attorney will object to the admission of the oral testimo-ny by T because it would modify the terms of the written lease. The court will then ex-amine the lease to see if it appears to be complete. If the court decides that it is, the court will refuse to allow T to offer evi-dence of an oral agreement. The only evi-dence before the court then will be the written lease. T will lose because nothing is in the written lease about an exclusive right to sell soft drinks.

If a written contract appears to be com-plete, the parol evidence rule prohibits its alteration not only by oral testimony but also by proof of other writings or memo-randums made before or at the time the written contract was executed. An excep-tion is made when the written contract re-fers to and identifies other writings or memorandums and states that they are to be regarded as part of the written con-tract. In such a case, it is said that the other writings are integrated or incorpo-rated by reference.

(b) CONFLICT BETWEEN ORAL AND WRITTEN CONTRACTS. Initially, when there is a conflict between the prior oral contract and the later written contract, the variation is to be regarded as (1) a mistake, which can be corrected by reformation, or (2) an additional term in the written contract, which is not binding because it was not part of the agreement.

Conflicts between written contracts and spoken words frequently arise when an agent or employee gives an explanation that is not what the written contract says.

§ 18:7 LIBERALIZATION OF PAROL EVIDENCE RULE

The strictness of the parol evidence rule has been relaxed in a number of jurisdictions. A trend is beginning to appear that permits parol evidence as to the intention of the parties when the claimed intention is plausible from the face of the contract, even though there is no ambiguity. There is likewise authority that parol evidence is admissible as to matters occurring before the execution of the contract in order to give a better understanding of what the parties meant by their written contract.[19]

The liberalization approach is not followed by all courts, and some apply the **four corners rule** under which the court must look for the contract within the four corners of the writing and may not look beyond the paper in the absence of an exception to the parol evidence rule.

§ 18:8   WHEN THE PAROL EVIDENCE RULE DOES NOT APPLY

The parol evidence rule may not apply in certain cases. The most common of these are discussed in the following paragraphs.

(a) INCOMPLETE CONTRACT. The parol evidence rule necessarily requires that the written contract sum up or integrate the entire contract. If the written contract is on its face, or is admittedly, not a complete summation, the parties naturally did not intend to abandon the points upon which they agreed but which were not noted in the contract; and parol evidence is admissible to show the actual agreement of the parties.[20]

A contract may appear on its face to be complete and yet not include everything the parties agreed upon. It must be remembered that there is no official standard by which to determine when a contract is complete. All that the court can do is to consider whether all essential terms of the contract are present, that is, whether the contract is sufficiently definite to be enforceable, and whether it contains all provisions that would ordinarily be included in a contract of that nature.

The fact that a contract is silent as to particular matter does not mean that it is incomplete, for the law may attach a particular legal result (called *implying a term*) when the contract is silent. In such a case, parol evidence that is inconsistent with the term that would be implied cannot be shown. For example, when the contract is silent as to the time of payment, the obligation of making payment concurrently with performance by the other part is implied, and parol evidence is not admissible to show that there was an oral agreement to make a payment at a different time.

(b) AMBIGUITY. Parol evidence is admissible to explain ambiguous terms of a contract in order to ascertain the real intent of the parties.

If a written contract may have two different meanings, parol evidence may generally be admitted to clarify the meaning. This is particularly true when the contract contains contradictory measurements or descriptions, or when it employs symbols or abbreviations that have no general meaning known to the court.

---

[19]   This is also the view followed by UCC § 2-202(a) which permits terms in a contract for the sale of goods to be "explained or supplemented by a course of dealing or usage of trade . . . or by course of performance." Such evidence is admissible not because there is an ambiguity but "in order that the true understanding of the parties as to the agreement may be reached." Official Code Comment to § 2-202.

It has also been held that UCC § 1-205 permits proof of trade usage and course of performance with respect to non-Code contracts even though there is no ambiguity. Chase Manhattan Bank v First Marion Bank (CA5 Fla) 437 F2d 1040 (1971).

[20]   Marani v Jackson, 183 Cal App 3d 695, 228 Cal Rptr 518 (1986).

Parol evidence may also be admitted to show that a word used in a contract has a special trade meaning or a meaning in the particular locality that differs from the common meaning of that word.

The fact that the parties disagree as to the meaning of the contract does not mean that it is ambiguous.

(c) FRAUD, ACCIDENT, OR MISTAKE. A contract apparently complete on its face may have omitted a provision that should have been included. Parol evidence may be admitted to show that a provision was omitted as the result of fraud, accident, or mistake, and to further show what that provision stated.

When one party claims to have been fraudulently induced by the other to enter into the contract, the parol evidence rule does not bar proof that there was fraud.[21]

(d) EXISTENCE OF CONTRACT. Parol evidence is admissible to identify the writing of the parties. When several documents are executed as part of one transaction, parol evidence is admissible to show the relationship of the documents as forming one transaction.

When it is claimed that there is in fact no contract because of a mutual mistake, parol evidence is admissible to show the existence of such a mistake.

The parol evidence rule does not bar poof that the written contract is in fact not a binding agreement. Thus, it can be shown that there was no consideration for the contract, that the contract was void because it was illegal, or that the contract was voidable because of the incapacity of a party or because of fraud. Likewise, parol evidence may be used to show in a lawsuit between the original parties that a promissory note signed by the defendant was never to be enforced, and that it was merely a dummy note intended to create a paper loss for tax purposes.[22]

(e) MODIFICATION OF CONTRACT. The parol evidence rule prohibits only the contradiction of a complete written contract. It does not prohibit proof that the contract was thereafter modified or terminated.

Written contracts commonly declare that they can only be modified by a writing. In the case of construction contracts, there is ordinarily a statement that no payment will be made for extra work unless there is a written order from the owner or architect calling for such extra work. If the parties proceed in disregard of such a clause requiring a writing, it may be shown by parol evidence that they have done so, and the contract will be modified accordingly.

(f) ILLEGALITY. The parol evidence rule does not bar proof of conduct that violates the law. In the *Honeywell* case, evidence of pre-contracting statements was offered to show that the defendant had violated the state Deceptive Trade Practices Act.

---

[21] Teague Motor Co. v Rowton, 84 Or App 72, 733 P2d 93 (1987).

[22] Bill Shannon, Inc. v San Clemente (Tex App) 724 SW2d 941 (1987).

HONEYWELL, INC. V IMPERIAL CONDOMINIUM ASS'N.

(Tex App) 716 SW2d 75 (1986)

Honeywell made a contract with the Imperial Condominium Association to install and service a heating and cooling system. The system did not function properly, and Imperial Condominium sued Honeywell for treble damages under the Texas Deceptive Trade Practices Act (DTPA). Imperial offered in evidence the promotional literature of Honeywell to show that false statements had been made to induce the making of the contract and that this constituted deceptive trade practices. The trial court admitted this evidence, and the jury returned a verdict in favor of Imperial. From the judgment against it, Honeywell appealed.

HOWELL, J. . . .

I. *Extrinsic Evidence of Misrepresentation*

Honeywell first complains that the trial court violated the parol evidence rule by admitting extrinsic evidence of Honeywell's pre-contractual representations. Over Honeywell's objection, the court allowed the consumer to introduce Honeywell's promotional literature for the limited purpose of proving that Honeywell's representations concerning the quality and benefits of its services did not accurately depict those actually received. We find no merit in Honeywell's complaint.

Agreeing with the decisions of the courts of appeals in *Oakes v Guerra*, 603 S.W.2d 371, 374 (Tex.Civ.App. — Amarillo 1980, no writ), and *United Postage Corp. v. Kammeyer*, 581 S.W.2d 716, 720-21 (Tex.Civ.App. — Dallas 1979, no writ), the supreme court recently decided that the parol evidence rule does not prevent a consumer from introducing statements made before the formation of a contract to show that the provider of goods or services engaged in a deceptive trade practice. *Weitzel v. Barnes*, 691 S.W.2d 598, 600 (Tex.1985). This holding was based upon the differences between the nature of an action for a breach of contract and that of an action for a deceptive trade practice.

The Supreme Court reasoned that the justifications for the parol evidence rule do not apply in deceptive trade practices cases where the consumer sues on the basis of pre-contractual representations because the consumer's recovery is not dependent upon the alteration or contradiction of a contract but rather upon conduct which was itself actionable under the DTPA without regard to the obligations imposed on the parties by the contract.

In other words, the supreme court recognized that contractual liability and liability under the DTPA derive from two different sources. Contractual liability turns solely on the agreement of the parties whereas liability under the DTPA springs from the statute. As a general proposition, liability under the DTPA is neither increased nor diminished by the presence of a formal written contract covering the identical subject matter.

Unlike contractual liability, resulting from the voluntary agreement of the parties, liability for false, misleading and deceptive acts is provided by the legislature for the breach of a duty imposed by it. These duties cannot be altered by the agreement of the parties. To apply the parol evidence rule in DTPA cases would frustrate the legislature's purpose in passing the statute without furthering the objectives of the parol evidence rule. As the supreme court succinctly announced in *Weitzel*, "traditional contractual notions do not apply" when the consumer seeks recovery for the breach of duty imposed by the DTPA. 691 S.W.2d at 600. Although the *Weitzel* decision addressed the admissibility of oral representations, its rationale compels the same result in this case where the representations were written. Consequently, we hold that trial court did not err when it allowed the consumer to introduce Honeywell's promotional literature for the purpose of proving that Honeywell violated the DTPA.

II. *Misrepresentation Under the DTPA*

Honeywell next contends that as a matter of law the consumer could not recover under the DTPA because a mere breach of contract, without more, is not a false, misleading or deceptive act. Honeywell argues that this case involves a mere breach of contract because all of the representations in its promotional literature were incorporated into the terms of the contract and, therefore, the consumer can show no failure to comply with a pre-contractual representation that was not also a breach of contract. This proposition is untenable in light of the supreme court's decision in *Smith v Baldwin*, 611 S.W.2d at 615-16.

The consumer there counterclaimed against his builder alleging that the builder failed to build a home which, as promised both in the contract and in discussions with the consumer, would qualify for financing by the Veteran's Administration. The consumer sought to recover on the grounds that the builder both breached the construction contract and misrepresented his services in violation of section 17.46 (b)(7) of the DTPA. A trial before the court resulted in a DTPA judgment for the consumer. The court of appeals disallowed a DTPA recovery and limited the consumer's relief to an award of the cost of remedying construction defects; the builder having substantially performed. The supreme court reversed and held that the consumer was entitled to his DTPA remedies. The court ruled that "representing that goods or services are of a particular standard, quality or grade . . . if they are of another" applies to goods and services to be provided in the future, and concluded that the builder committed a deceptive act by representing that the house when built would qualify for V.A. financing.

The case at bar is indistinguishable from *Smith v. Baldwin*. Honeywell by its literature and by the formal contract represented that it would provide proper water treatment to extend equipment life. These representations later proved to be false. Nothing further is required in order to meet the *Baldwin* test. We reject Honeywell's argument that intentional, reckless or negligent conduct must be proved in order to invoke the act.

Because both the pre-contractual and the contractual representations proved to be false in the instant case, we need not decide whether the supreme court's holding in *Smith v. Baldwin* was based exclusively upon the pre-contractual representations. Nor is it necessary for us to explore whether Honeywell could have been held liable for the damages found by the jury under the alternative theories of unconscionability or breach of an express warranty. The misrepresentation is enough to establish that Honeywell breached its statutory duty. Honeywell's points of error complaining that the DTPA is inapplicable are overruled.

[Judgment affirmed]

QUESTIONS

1. Does the parol evidence rule bar proof of statements that constitute a violation of a consumer protection statute? Explain.
2. Were the precontract statements oral or written?
3. What significance is there to the fact that precontract statements are or are not included in the written contract?

Summary

An oral agreement can be a contract unless it is the intention of the parties that they should not be bound by the agreement unless a writing is executed by them. If the parties intend to be bound by the oral agreement it is a contract, even though it is oral. As an exception to this statement, certain contracts must be evidenced by a writing or they cannot be enforced. The statutes that declare this exception are called statutes of frauds and commonly require that a contract be evidenced by writing in the case of (a) an agreement that cannot be performed within one year after the agreement is made, (b) an agreement to sell or a sale of any interest in real property, (c) a promise to answer for the debt or default of another, (d) a promise by the executor or administrator of a decedent's estate to pay a claim against the estate from personal funds, (e) a promise made in consideration of marriage, and (f) a contract for the sale of goods for a purchase price of $500 or more. Local statutes may expand the above list to include other types of contracts, such as a contract between a landowner and a real estate agent employed to sell the land.

In order to evidence a contract so as to satisfy a statute of frauds, there must be some permanent record, a writing, of all material terms, and this must be signed by the defendant against whom enforcement of the contract or damages for its breach is sought. The signing may be made by printing, stamping, or typewriting or any other means that is intended to identify the particular party. Two or more writings can be combined to form a writing sufficient to satisfy the statute of frauds, provided there is an express internal reference in the writings that ties them together.

If the applicable statute of frauds is not satisfied, the oral contract cannot be enforced. In order to avoid unjust enrichment, a plaintiff barred from enforcing an oral contract may recover from the other contracting party the reasonable value of the benefits conferred by the plaintiff upon the defendant. In order to prevent the statute of frauds from being used to defraud a party to an oral contract, the courts by decision have made certain exceptions to the statute of frauds. Under the partial performance exception, an oral contract for the sale of land is binding when the buyer has gone into possession and made substantial improvements to the land of such a nature that they cannot be compensated for by the payment of money damages. Under the primary or main purpose exception, an oral promise to pay the debt of another can be enforced when the main purpose of the promisor in making such promise is to benefit the promisor rather than to benefit the debtor. Under the detrimental reliance exception, many courts will enforce an oral contract in spite of the statute of frauds when the party seeking performance has relied on the oral contract to such an extent that it would be an unconscionable hardship if the contract were not enforced and this reliance on the oral contract was reasonably foreseeable to the other contracting party.

When there is a written contract, the question arises as to whether that writing is the exclusive statement of the agreement of the parties. If the writing is the complete and final statement of the contract, parol evidence as to matters agreed to before or at the time the writing was signed is not admissible to contradict the writing. This is called the parol evidence rule. Some courts have liberalized the rule so that parol evidence is admitted when it will aid in interpreting what the writing says. In any case, the parol evidence rule does not bar parol evidence when (a) the writing is incomplete; (b) the writing is ambiguous; (c) the writing is not a true statement of the agreement of the parties because of fraud, accident, or mistake; or (d) the existence, (e) modification, or (f) illegality of a contract is in controversy. The fact that the parties disagree as to the meaning of a contract or that a court decision is required to settle the point does not make the writing ambiguous. The exception as to mistake permits proof that there is in fact no contract because there is a mutual mistake or that the writing that has been executed does not correctly set forth the terms of the contract.

QUESTIONS AND CASE PROBLEMS

1. What social forces are affected by the following rule of law? "Parol evidence is not admissible for the purpose of modifying a written contract when that evidence relates to an agreement made before or at the time that the written contract was executed."

2. What is the primary purpose exception to the statute of frauds?

3. In a telephone conversation, Roderick agrees to buy Dexter's house. All the details of the transaction were agreed to in the conversation. The next day Dexter wrote Roderick a letter stating, "This confirms the agreement we made last night that I should sell you my home." Later, Dexter refused to go through with the transaction. Roderick sued Dexter. Will Roderick recover?

4. Potack made a contract to build a house for Nathan by July 1. After construction was commenced, heavy rains began and continued. Because it was impossible to continue building in the rain, Potack and Nathan orally agreed that Potack could have one extra day in which to complete the work for every day lost because of bad weather and that in return Potack would reduce the contract price by $100 for every day's delay. The work was not completed until August 1. When Nathan sues Potack for damages for delay, can Potack prove that there were thirty bad weather days and that the oral agreement therefore entitled him to an extension of thirty days?

5. Martin made an oral contract with Cresheim Garage to work as its manager for two years. Cresheim wrote Martin a letter stating that the oral contract had been made and setting forth all its terms. Cresheim later refused to recognize the contract. Martin sued Cresheim for breach of the contract and offered Cresheim's letter in evidence as proof of the contract. Cresheim claimed that the oral contract was not binding because the contract was not in writing and its letter referring to the contract was not a contract but only a letter. Was the contract binding?

6. Lawrence loaned money to Moore. Moore died without repaying the loan. Lawrence claimed that when he mentioned the matter to Moore's widow, she promised to pay the debt. She did not do so, and Lawrence sued her on her promise. Does she have any defense? [Moore v Lawrence, 252 Ark 759, 480 SW2d 941]

7. Investors Premium Corporation purchased computer equipment from Burroughs Corporation. It made the purchase because of various statements made by the Burroughs sales representative. A written contract was executed for the purchase of the system. The contract stated that there were no warranties that were not stated in the contract and that the written contract was the complete statement of the obligation of Burroughs. The system did not work properly, and Investors claimed that Burroughs was liable because the system did not perform as the salesman had warranted. Is Burroughs liable for breach of the agent's warranty? [Investors Premium Corp. v Burroughs Corp. (DC SC) 389 F Supp 39]

8. Evans made a written contract to buy property from Borkowski. Under the sales contract the buyer was to make payment in certain installments prior to the delivery of the deed. When the buyer could not make payments on time, the parties entered into a new written agreement, the buyer persuading the seller to do so by orally promising him that he would pay interest on late payments. He was late in making the payments and paid the interest under protest. The buyer later

sued the seller to recover the interest payments. Was the buyer entitled to recover the interest? [Evans v Borkowski (Fla) 139 So 2d 472]

9. An accounting firm sold out its business to a new firm. The sales contract stated that it was the intention of the parties that the new firm should provide service for clients of the old firm. The new firm agreed to pay the old firm 15 percent of the gross billings for assignments performed by the new firm for a period of 84 months. Later a dispute arose as to whether the 15 percent of gross billings was limited to the billings of those who were originally clients of the old firm or whether it also included billings of new clients of the new firm. In a lawsuit over this point, parol evidence was offered to show what the contract covered. Was this evidence admissible? [Rullman v LaFrance, Walker, Jackley & Saville, 206 Neb 180, 292 NW2d 19]

10. When will improvements made by a buyer bar the seller from claiming that the purchase contract was not binding because it was oral?

11. Roth made a contract to sell her house to Eric. They signed a written contract but left the purchase price blank because they had agreed that the selling price was to be reduced by the cost of certain necessary repairs that the buyer would be required to make. They later agreed on this amount, but the amount was never filled in on the written contract. Is the contract binding?

12. With respect to the applicability of the statute of frauds, compare
(a) a promise made by an aunt to her niece to pay the niece's bill owed to the department store;
(b) a promise made by the aunt to the department store to pay the amount the aunt owes the store for a television set the aunt purchased as a present for her niece; and
(c) a promise made by the aunt to the department store that she would pay her niece's bill if the niece did not do so.

13. Louise Pulsifer owned a farm. She desired to sell the farm and ran an ad in the local newspaper. Russell Gillespie agreed to purchase the farm. Louise then wrote him a letter stating that she would not sell the farm. He sued her in order to enforce the contract. Louise raised the defense of the statute of frauds. The letter signed by her did not contain any of the terms of the sale. Gillespie, however, claimed that the newspaper ad could be combined with her letter in order to satisfy the statute of frauds. Was he correct? [Gillespie v Pulsifer (Mo App) 655 SW2d 123]

14. McLarty claimed that he and Wright made an oral contract to start a business under the name of DeKalb Textile Mill, Inc., to incorporate the business, and to divide the stock equally. The alleged contract was not performed. McLarty sued Wright for breach of contract. Wright raised the defense of the statute of frauds, asserting that it was not specified that the contract should be performed within one year of making. Was this defense valid? [McLarty v Wright (Ala Civ App) 321 So 2d 687]

15. Callicutt Enterprises purchased tires from Brad Ragan. The tires were mounted on trucks that were then sold to Bobbie Ray Lewis. As part of the sales contract, Lewis orally promised Callicutt that Lewis would pay the debt that Callicutt owed to Ragan for the tires. Later Ragan sued Callicutt and Lewis. Ragan claimed that it was the third party beneficiary of the promise made by Lewis to pay the debt of Callicutt. Lewis raised the defense that the statute of frauds prohibited proof of an oral promise to pay the debt of another. Was he correct? [Brad Ragan, Inc. v Callicutt Enterpise, Inc. 73 NC App 134, 326 SE2d 62]

19

INTERPRETATION OF CONTRACTS

When it has been decided that there is a contract between the parties, the next step is to determine the terms of that contract. Should a contract be interpreted to mean what one of the parties intended it to mean, or should it mean what a reasonable person would believe was intended? Should the contract be held to mean only what it expressly says, or can additional terms be implied or read into the contract? What if additional terms are needed to protect one of the parties to the contract from hardship or oppression?

If the parties disagree as to the terms, society has the task of determining just what the contract means and of deciding if society wants to enforce the contract according to its terms. The rules of law that have evolved in finding answers to these questions are the rules governing the interpretation of contracts.

A. RULES OF CONSTRUCTION AND INTERPRETATION

An understanding of the rules discussed in the following paragraphs will help contracting parties avoid many of the difficulties that may arise when a contract is not drafted carefully.

§ 19:1 INTENTION OF THE PARTIES

A contract is to be enforced according to its terms. A court cannot remake or rewrite the contract of the parties under the pretense of interpreting it.[1] If there is a dispute as to the meaning of a contract, the court examines the contract to determine what the parties intended. It will then give effect to what the parties intended, as long as it is lawful.

No particular form of words is required, and any words manifesting the intent of the parties are sufficient. In the absence of proof that a word has a peculiar meaning or that it was employed by the parties with a particular meaning, a common word is given its ordinary meaning.

A word will not be given its literal meaning when it is clear that the parties did not intend such a meaning. For example, *and*

may be substituted for *or*, *may* for *shall*, and *void* for *voidable*, and vice versa, when it is clear that the parties so intended.

(a) OBJECTIVE INTENT. When it is stated that the law seeks to enforce the intent of the parties, this means the intent that is outwardly manifested. That is, what would a reasonable third person believe the parties intended? It is this **objective intent** that will be enforced. A party cannot claim that secretly something else was intended. Such secret or **subjective intent** cannot be proven.[2]

The use of the objective intent standard means that an unambiguous contract must be interpreted as written. It cannot be given a different meaning that one party thinks it has. In the *Sterling Merchandise* case the court was faced with the question of whether an insurance policy meant just what it said.

---

[1]   Borders v KRLB, Inc. (Tex App) 727 SW2d 357 (1987).

[2]   Cherry v Anthony, Gibbs, Sage (Miss) 501 So 2d 416 (1987).

STERLING MERCHANDISE CO. V HARTFORD INS. CO.
30 Ohio App 3d 131, 506 NE2d 1192 (1986)

Sterling Merchandise Company obtained policies of insurance from the Hartford Insurance Company and from Underwriters at Lloyd's of London to protect the contents of the safe in its jewelry store from burglary. The policy stated that there was coverage of theft from the safe provided that there were visible marks on the safe of a forcible entry. The Sterling safe was robbed. The robber set off the electronic alarm system, but there were no visible marks of forcible entry. The insurer refused to pay for the loss. Sterling claimed that it reasonably expected that the contents of the safe would be covered whenever there was an opening of the safe by a robber. Sterling sued the insurers. From a decision in favor of Sterling, the insurers appealed.

GEORGE, P.J. . . . The insurance contracts issued to Sterling by Underwriters define a ''safe burglary'' as follows:

'SAFE BURGLARY' means the felonious abstraction of the insured property from within a safe or vault in the premises (or after removal therefrom by burglars) by any person or persons making felonious entry into such safe and also into the vault, if any, containing such safe, when all doors of such safe and vault are duly closed and locked by at least one combination, key or timelock thereof; provided that such entry shall be made by actual force or violence of which there shall be visible marks made by tools, explosives, electricity, gas or chemicals, upon the exterior of (1) all of said doors of such safe and vault, if any, containing such safe if entry is made through such doors, or (2) the top, bottom, or walls of such safe and of the vault through which entry is made, if not made through such doors.

. . . The trial court's decision is based entirely on the doctrine of reasonable expectations. . . .

The doctrine of reasonable expectations is a theory of recovery employed in contract actions. It has been articulated in the following passage contained in the Restatement of the Law 2d, Contracts (Tent. Drafts Nos. 1-7 Rev. 1973), Section 237 ("Standardized Agreements"), Comment f, at 540-541:

> *Terms excluded.* . . . Although customers typically adhere to standardized agreements and are bound by them without even appearing to know the standard terms in detail, they are not bound to unknown terms which are beyond the range of reasonable expectation. A debtor who delivers a check to his creditor with the amount blank does not authorize the insertion of an infinite figure. Similarly, a party who adheres to the other party's standard terms does not assent to a term if the other party has reason to believe that the adhering party would not have accepted the agreement if he had known that the agreement contained the particular term. Such a belief or assumption may be shown by the prior negotiations or inferred from the circumstances. Reason to believe may be inferred from the fact that the term is bizarre or oppressive, from the fact that it eviscerates the nonstandard terms explicitly agreed to, or from the fact that it eliminates the dominant purpose of the transaction. The inference is reinforced if the adhering party never had an opportunity to read the term, or if it is illegible or otherwise hidden from view. This rule is closely related to the policy against unconscionable terms and the rule of interpretation against the draftsman. . . .

This doctrine is grounded on several beliefs. First, that most people never read the insurance contracts they sign, but merely adhere to them. Second, that insurers write the terms of the contracts and usually offer the consumer only a standard preprinted form which the latter is ill-equipped to understand. Third, that the insured lacks any real bargaining power in such a situation because the insurer assumes a take-it-or-leave-it attitude. Fourth, that to enforce the terms of the contract in favor of the insurer is somehow unconscionable. . . .

Although Ohio has adopted rules of construction of insurance contracts which favor the insured, it has not implicitly adopted the theory of recovery known as the reasonable expectations doctrine. That doctrine is based on principles which go far beyond the liberal rules of construction employed by Ohio courts. . . .

The reasonable expectation doctrine requires a court to rewrite an insurance contract which does not meet popular expectations. Such rewriting is done regardless of the bargain entered into by the parties to the contract. Such judicial activism has not been adopted in Ohio by its courts and the courts' use of liberal rules of construction. Further, this court declines to do so. . . .

The facts of this case, as evidenced by the stipulations of the parties, do not indicate any misrepresentation, overreaching, or other conduct on behalf of the insurer which would justify abrogating the parties' agreement. Nor was there any evidence that Sterling was beguiled into believing it had more protection than it actually did.

Sterling tacitly refused to read its policies. The provision defining "safe bur-glary" was written in the same style and size type as the rest of the policy provisions. The definition was not hidden away in fine print in an obscure place, but was plainly set out. The definition was not so complex or esoteric that a competent businessman could not understand it. . . .

The record in the instant case also reveals that there was comprehensive crime coverage available to Sterling, but at an additional cost. This additional coverage was noted in part seven of Sterling's policy. . . .

The trial court did not find the "safe burglary" definition to be ambiguous. Neither does this court. Provisions requiring visible marks of entry by actual force or violence before coverage is allowed are not ambiguous. Because the definition is not ambiguous, it must be given its plain and ordinary meaning. . . .

[Judgment reversed]

QUESTIONS

1. Was the safe burglary paragraph of the policy ambiguous?
2. Why does the court mention the fact that Sterling could have obtained comprehensive crime coverage by paying an additional amount?
3. What effect would the adoption of the Restatement rule have on the business world?

Society balances the risks involved in enforcing a contract that does not accurately state the intent of the parties with the danger of giving effect to a subjective intent that is falsely asserted. The enforcing of the objectively determined intent appears to society to hold the smaller risk of harm and injury. Giving effect to a subjective intent would open the door to fraudulent claims that a contract was secretly intended to mean something else.

Thus, the objectively shown intent controls, and the secret or subjective intent is ignored.

(b) MEANING OF WORDS. Ordinary words are to be interpreted according to their ordinary meaning.

In the *Bartlett* case, property owners claimed to be covered by insurance when a breaking dam caused damage to the property. The insurance claimed there was no liability for "flood damage."

BARTLETT V CONTINENTAL DIVIDE INS. CO.
(Colo App) 697 P2d 412 (1984)

Perry Bartlett and his wife owned and operated a resort. They obtained a policy of insurance from the Continental Divide Insurance Company protecting the resort from damage. A nearby dam broke, and water from the dam and the debris carried by the water damaged the resort. The Bartletts claimed the insurance company was liable for the loss. It denied liability on the ground that the policy expressly excluded flood damage. The Bartletts claimed that what had happened was not a flood and brought suit against the insurance company. The court decided in favor of the insurance company, and the Bartletts appealed.

STERNBERG, J. . . . The plaintiffs' property was damaged by released water and debris as a result of the failure of Lawn Lake Dam. They filed a claim under their Special Businessowners Policy issued by Continental Insurance Co. Continental denied coverage because the policy contained an exclusion for losses "caused by, resulting from, contributed to, or aggravated by . . . flood, surface water [or]. . . overflow of streams or other bodies of water. . . ."

The plaintiffs filed this action for declaratory relief and damages. After both parties filed motions for partial summary judgment, the trial court ruled in Continental's favor. The court found that the insurance policy expressly excluded damage due to flood, the term "flood" was not vague or ambiguous in this case, and the failure of Lawn Lake Dam did in fact cause a flood resulting in damage to plaintiff's property. Contending that the language of the exclusion was ambiguous, the plaintiffs appeal. We affirm.

The term "flood" is not defined within the policy, and it therefore retains its ordinary, customary meaning. . . . Ordinarily, "flood" means "a body of water (including moving water) . . . overflowing or inundating land not usually covered," . . . and no distinction is made between natural and artificial causes. . . .

Notwithstanding the ordinary meaning of "flood," plaintiffs urge us to distinguish between natural and artificial causes when reading the terms of the insurance policy. However, there is no such distinction in the contract, and the event in question falls well within the ordinary use of the term; therefore, to make such distinction would be to rewrite terms of the policy, and that is beyond our power. Although the use of the term may in some cases result in ambiguity, we agree with the trial court's conclusion that there was no ambiguity here.

Similarly, the trial court properly refused to address the question of the "efficient moving cause" of the loss. The insurance policy excludes coverage for "all direct loss by flood or overflow," and contains no provision for coverage of flood losses that result from the negligence of a third party. Thus, the trial court properly limited the inquiry to the immediate cause of the loss.

. . . The only event alleged as the cause of the loss was the flood caused by the failure of the dam; and loss by flood was specifically excluded from coverage.

[Judgment affirmed]

QUESTIONS

1. Why wasn't the word *flood* defined in the insurance policy?
2. What effect does the decision have on the social force of protecting from hardship?
3. How would it have affected the decision of the court if the dam had failed because of sabotage by discontented workers?

If technical or trade terms are used in a contract, they are to be interpreted according to the area of technical knowledge or trade from which the terms are taken. If there is a common meaning to a term, that meaning will be followed, even though the dictionary may give a different meaning.

The prior relationships of the parties may give meaning to the words used by the parties.[3]

(c) INCORPORATION BY REFERENCE. The contract may not cover all the terms agreed upon. The missing terms may be found in another document. Frequently the parties executing the contract will state that it embraces or incorporates the other document. Thus, a contract for storage will simply state that a storage contract is entered into and that the contract applies to the goods that are listed in the schedule that is attached to the contract and made part of the contract. Likewise, a contract for the construction of a building will simply state that the building is to be constructed according to the plans and specifications "which are incorporated herein and made part of this contract." When there is such an **incorporation by reference,** the contract consists of both the original or skeleton document and the detailed statement that is incorporated therein.

§ 19:2   WHOLE CONTRACT

The provisions of a contract must be construed as a whole.[4] This rule is followed even when the contract is partly written and partly oral. Every word of a contract is to be given effect if reasonably possible.

(a) DIVISIBLE CONTRACT. A contract may contain a number of provisions or performances to be rendered. If so, the question arises as to whether the parties intended merely a group of separate contracts (a *divisible contract)* or whether they intended a package deal so that complete performance

of every provision of the contract was essential.[5]

(b) WHAT CONSTITUTES THE WHOLE CONTRACT. The question may arise whether separate papers or particular parts of a paper constitute part of the whole contract.

Terms in a printed letterhead or billhead or on the reverse side of the printed contract form are not part of a contract written thereon unless a reasonable person would regard such terms as part of the contract. An employer's manual that is shown to the job applicant after the signing of an employment contract is not part of that contract. Similarly, provisions in a manufacturer's instruction manual, or in invoices, or on labels that are not seen or called to the attention of a buyer until after a contract of sale has been made are not part of the contract and do not bind the buyer.

§ 19:3   CONDITIONS

When the occurrence or nonoccurrence of an event affects the existence of a contract or the obligation of a party to a contract, the event is called a **condition**.

Courts do not favor conditions because they cause a loss of rights, and therefore courts will interpret a contract provision as not creating a condition when that interpretation is reasonably possible.[6]

(a) CONDITION PRECEDENT. A condition or obligation-triggering event may be described as a **condition precedent** because it precedes the existence of the obligation.

In a fire insurance policy, there is no obligation on the insurer to make any payment until there is a fire loss. The occurrence of such a loss is thus a condition precedent to the duty of the insurer to make payment under the policy. Likewise, when an employee is required to give notice to

---

[3]   See § 19:6 of this book.
[4]   Buhl v Bak (SD) 400 NW2d 903 (1987).

[5]   Stika v Albion (App) 150 Ariz 521, 724 P2d 607 (1986).
[6]   Vergote v K Mart Corp. 158 Mich App 96, 404 NW2d 711 (1987).

the employer in order to obtain a particular benefit, the giving of notice is a condition precedent to the duty of the employer to provide the benefit.

(b) CONDITION SUBSEQUENT. The parties may specify that the contract shall terminate when a particular event occurs or does not occur. Such a provision is a **condition subsequent.** If government approval is required, the parties may specify that the contract shall not bind them if the government approval cannot be obtained.

A contract for the purchase of land may contain a condition subsequent that cancels the contract if the buyer is not able to obtain a zoning permit to use a building for a particular purpose.

In the *K & K Pharmacy*, case the presence of a condition affected the existence of the contract.

K & K PHARMACY, INC. V BARTA
222 Neb 215, 382 NW2d 363 (1986)

K & K ran a pharmacy in space rented from the Millard Shopping Center. K & K made a contract with Barta to sell the pharmacy to him. Barta did not go through with the purchase. K & K sued him for breach of contract. He raised the defense that there was no contract because a condition in the agreement of the parties had not been satisfied. The lower court entered judgment for Barta, and K & K appealed.

BOSLAUGH, J. . . . On June 8, 1983, the plaintiff, K & K Pharmacy, Inc., entered into a written contract with the defendant, James R. Barta, for the sale of the pharmacy to the defendant. The contract contained the following provision regarding a new lease of the premises to be obtained by the defendant:

13. *New Lease.* This Agreement shall be contingent upon Buyer's ability to obtain a new lease from Larsen Enterprises, Inc., for the premises presently occupied by Seller. In the event Buyer is unable to obtain a new lease satisfactory to Buyer, this Agreement shall be null and void.

The defendant owned a number of full-line pharmacies and employed a specific marketing strategy which he intended to use in the operation of the pharmacy to be purchased from the plaintiff. The defendant carried high-traffic grocery items, such as bread, milk, and coffee, and sold those items at a low price in order to generate volume traffic into the drugstore.

Early in the negotiations for the sale of the pharmacy, the defendant advised the agent of the seller that the defendant would require the right or privilege to sell foodstuffs in the pharmacy. However, prior to signing the contract, the defendant did not know that Millard Food Mart, a grocery store located in the same shopping center as plaintiff's pharmacy, had a lease giving it the exclusive right to sell grocery items in the shopping center.

The record also shows that after signing the purchase agreement, the defendant entered into negotiations with the owner of the shopping center and other interested parties for the purpose of agreeing upon a satisfactory lease. At the first meeting of the parties, the grocer, who had the exclusive right to sell grocery items, indicated that he also used high-traffic items such as milk and bread as loss leaders to attract traffic into his store, that the exclusive right to sell groceries was important to him, and that he was not willing to give up any of his rights under his lease. Although lease negotiations continued, the grocer never agreed to allow Barta to carry any food items.

The original agreement provided for the closing of the sale on or about June 24, 1983. On the 24th of June the parties added an addendum to the agreement providing that the defendant would take possession of the pharmacy beginning June 25 and operate the pharmacy until the anticipated closing on Monday, June 27. The defendant did go into possession on the 25th and operated the business until June 30, at which time he ceased operations in the drugstore because he had not been able to obtain a satisfactory lease.

This action was commenced on January 26, 1984, to recover damages resulting from the defendant's alleged breach of the contract. On November 19, 1984, the trial court sustained the defendant's motion for summary judgment and dismissed the action. The plaintiff has appealed.

The case turns on the meaning and effect of the "New Lease" provision in the contract. Generally, in negotiating a contract the parties may impose any condition precedent, a performance of which is essential before the parties become bound by the agreement. . . .The provision entitled "13. *New Lease*" was clearly a condition precedent to the existence of binding contractual obligations between the parties. The contract was *contingent* upon the defendant obtaining a new lease *satisfactory* to him. This court has held that "where a contract is executed but its effectiveness is dependent upon the fulfillment of an agreed condition before it can become a binding contract, such contract cannot be enforced unless the condition is performed." . . .

The party seeking to enforce a contract containing a condition precedent bears the burden of proof as to the occurrence of the condition, and if there is no evidence of the occurrence of the condition, the contract is not binding and cannot be enforced. In the present case the plaintiff had the burden to prove that the condition precedent contained in the contract had been met before the contract was enforceable. . . .

[Judgment affirmed]

QUESTIONS

1. Did the defendant break his contract?
2. What effect was the condition in this case intended to have?
3. Do you agree with the court's classification of that condition?

(c) CONCURRENT CONDITIONS. In most bilateral contracts, the performances by the parties are **concurrent conditions,** that is, the duty of each party to perform is dependent upon the other party's performing. Thus, neither is required to perform until the other performs or tenders performance. Frequently the contract will specify or indicate that one person must perform first. In such case, that performance is a condition precedent and the conditions are not concurrent. For example, in a contract to pay a painter $1,000 for painting a house, the painter must perform the painting work before the owner is required to perform the promise of paying for the work. Performance by the painter is thus a condition precedent to the owner's obligation to pay.

§ 19:4   CONTRADICTORY AND AMBIGUOUS TERMS

One term in a contract may conflict with another term, or one term may have two different meanings. It is then necessary for the court to determine whether there is a contract, and, if so, what the contract really means. When the terms of a contract are contradictory or conflict as to a significant matter, the existence of such conflict prevents there being any contract.

In some instances, the conflict between the terms of a contract is eliminated by the introduction of parol evidence or by applying an appropriate rule of construction.

(a) NATURE OF WRITING. When a contract is partly printed or typewritten and partly written and the written part conflicts with the printed or typewritten part, the written part prevails. When there is a conflict between a printed part and a typewritten part, the latter prevails. Consequently, when a clause typewritten on a printed form conflicts with what is stated by the print, the conflicting print is ignored and the typewritten clause controls.[7] When there is a conflict between an amount or quantity expressed both in words and figures, as on a check, the amount or quantity expressed in words prevails.

(b) AMBIGUITY. A contract is **ambiguous** when it is uncertain what was the intent of the parties, and the contract is capable of more than one reasonable interpretation.[8]

Disagreement as to the legal effect of the terms used by the parties does not make the contract ambiguous. This is so because the court, by applying the law to their terms can reach a conclusion as to the intent manifested by the contract. In contrast, if the intent would still be uncertain even after rules of law were applied, the contract is ambiguous.

The fact that a particular situation is not provided for by the contract does not make it ambiguous. For example, a summer camp contract is not ambiguous because it does not contain any provision relating to refunds upon cancellation.

(c) STRICT CONSTRUCTION AGAINST DRAFTING PARTY. An ambiguous contract is interpreted strictly against the party who drafted it.[9] Thus, printed forms of a contract, such as insurance policies, which are supplied by the insurer, are interpreted against the insurer and in favor of the insured when two interpretations are reasonably possible. If the contract is clear and unambiguous, it will be enforced according to its terms, even though this benefits the party who drafted the contract.

Whether a contract is ambiguous cannot always be determined merely by looking at the contract. In some cases, the written contract will look perfectly clear, and the ambiguity does not become apparent until the contract is applied to the facts or the property concerned. Such an application ambiguity was present in the *Grove* case.

---

[7]   Rubin v Centerbanc Federal S & L Ass'n (Fla App) 487 So 2d 1193 (1986).
[8]   Horizon Aviation, Inc. v Pirfil Cam, 80 Or App 577, 722 P2d 1291 (1986).

[9]   Investors Associates Ltd. v B.F. Trappey's Sons Inc. (La App) 500 So 2d 909 (1987).

GROVE V CHARBONNEAU BUICK-PONTIAC, INC.
(ND) 240 NW2d 853 (1976)

The Dickinson Elks Club conducted an annual Labor Day golf tournament. Charbonneau Buick-Pontiac offered to give a new car as a prize to any one making a hole in one on hole No. 8. The golf course of the club was only nine holes so that in order to play eighteen holes, the players

would go around the course twice, although they would play from different tees or locations for the second nine holes. On the second time
around, what was originally the eighth hole became the seventeenth
hole. Lloyd Grove was a contestant in the tournament. On the first day
he scored three on the No. 8 hole, but on approaching it for the second
time as the seventeenth hole, he made a hole in one. He claimed the
prize car from Charbonneau. The latter claimed that Grove had not won
the prize because he did not make the hole in one on the eighth hole.
Grove sued Charbonneau for the value of the prize car. From a judgment
in favor of Grove, Charbonneau appealed.

SAND, J. . . . The general rule of the law of contracts which provides that where
an offer or promise for an act is made, the only acceptance of the offer that is
necessary is the performance of the act, applies to prizewinning contests.
When a word is used in an agreement between two parties, . . . such word is
to be given its ordinary, popular meaning. The words are given the common
prevailing meaning as generally understood among people.

Grove contends that the words of the offer, when used in their ordinary
sense, mean that any time in the process of an official play in the tournament a
ball is hit into the eighth hole in one stroke, from either tee No. 8 or tee No. 17,
the conditions of the offer are satisfied. Charbonneau, however, contends that
the language of the offer has a technical meaning under the rules of golf and
that there cannot be a hole-in-one on hole No. 8 unless the ball, with a single
stroke, is hit from tee area No. 8 and lands in hole No. 8.

. . . Where a contract contains ambiguous terms which are in dispute it is
the duty of the court to construe them. . . . The ambiguous terms of a contract
will be interpreted most strongly against the party who caused the ambiguity.
. . .

The rule on ambiguous contracts applies to this case, and therefore any
language of this contract which is not clear and definite or in which an uncertainty exists as to its meaning must be interpreted most strongly against
Charbonneau.

The crucial or pivotal point in this case rests upon the meaning of the language "a hole-in-one on Hole No. 8," where the 9-hole golf course was converted to or used as an 18-hole course without adding any additional holes.
Does this language, "on Hole No. 8," refer to the actual, physical designation
of the hole, which is generally identified with the number on the flagstick, or
does it refer to the hypothetical number given to the hole because of the sequence in which it is "played"? . . .

The offer does not contain any qualifications, restrictions, or limitations as
to what is meant by the phrase "on hole No. 8." Neither does the award or
offer make any statement restricting or qualifying that the hole-in-one on hole
No. 8 may be accomplished only from tee No. 8. If Charbonneau had in mind
to impose limitations, restrictions, or qualifications he could have made this in
the offer so that a person with ordinary intelligence would have been fully
apprised of the offer in every respect.

The distance from tee No. 17 to hole No. 8 was greater than the distance
from tee No. 8 to hole No. 8. Thus an argument cannot be made that a player
had an advantage playing from tee No. 17 to hole No. 8, as compared to playing from tee No. 8 to hole No. 8. Actually, it would be a disadvantage.

When good arguments can be made for either of two contrary positions as to the meaning of a term in a document an ambiguity exists. . . . The contending parties have made good arguments, if not convincing arguments, for their positions. . . .

We have no reason to suspect that anyone other than Charbonneau deliberately chose the ambiguous language. We are not suggesting that Charbonneau intended to trifle with the public, but if we do not apply the rule of law on ambiguous contracts, as set out earlier herein, to this situation we would permit promoters to trifle with the public, which we do not believe the law should permit, and in fact, does not permit.

If this rule of law were not applied it would permit the promoter who is so inclined, where there has been a performance, to keep adding requirements or conditions which were not stated in the offer. As an example, such as, "must use a certain club; the ball must be of a certain brand; the play must be accomplished by a person left-handed," to name only a few.

Both of the constructions and interpretations of the language in the offer as contended by the parties are reasonable and each has some strong convincing points, but that does not constitute legal grounds for not applying the rule of law as to how ambiguities in a contract are to be resolved in a situation or setting we have here.

By interpreting and construing the ambiguous provisions of the offer most strongly against the party who caused them . . . we construe it to mean that an entrant in the golf tournament who had paid the fee and who during regular tournament play drives the ball in one stroke into hole No. 8 from either the 8th or 17th tee has made a hole-in-one on hole No. 8, and has met the conditions of the offer and is entitled to the award or the equivalent in money damages. . . .

[Judgment affirmed]

QUESTIONS

1. Was there an ambiguity in the prize offer itself?
2. Why does the court decide the case as it did?
3. How could the lawsuit have been avoided?

---

§ 19:5   IMPLIED TERMS

In some cases the court will imply a term to cover a situation for which the parties failed to provide or when needed to give the contract a construction or meaning that is reasonable.

A term will not be implied in a contract when the court concludes that the silence of the contract on the particular point was intentional.

(a) DURATION OF CONTRACT. When a contract does not state any time for its duration, three alternatives are possible. It could be held that there is no contract at all because an essential term is missing and without the term the agreement is too vague to enforce. It could also be held that as no termination is stated, the contract runs on forever. Neither of these views is adopted by the law.

Instead, when no duration is specified in the contract, courts will imply that the contract is to be performed or will continue for a reasonable time. But either party may terminate the contract by giving notice to the other party. Thus, an employment contract that only specifies the rate of pay but not the duration of employment may be terminated by the employer or the employee at any time.[10]

Note that in effect the court is trying to salvage the transaction and give some effect to the intent of the parties to have a contract. But one should not jump to the conclusion that whenever a term is missing from a contract the word *reasonable* is to be implied. For example, an agreement to sell your house is not a contract when no price is stated and the omission of the price will not be cured by implying that a reasonable price is to be paid.

(b) DETAILS OF PERFORMANCE. Details of performance of a contract not expressly stated in the contract will often be implied by the court. Thus, an obligation to pay a specified sum of money is implied to mean payment in legal tender. In a contract to perform work there is an implied promise to use such skill as is necessary for the proper performance of the work. In a "cost plus" contract an undertaking is implied that the costs will be reasonable and proper. When payment is made "as a deposit on account," there is an implied term that if the payment is not used for the purpose stated, the payment will be returned to the person who made the deposit. When a contract does not specify where money is to be paid, it will be implied that the payment is to be made to the creditor at the creditor's office or place of business.[11]

A local custom or trade practice, such as that of allowing thirty days' credit to buyers, may form part of the contract when it is clear that the parties intended to be governed by this custom or trade practice or when a reasonable person would believe that they had so intended.

When a written contract does not specify the time for performance, a reasonable time is implied.

(c) GOOD FAITH. In every contract there is an implied obligation that neither party shall do anything that will have the effect of destroying or injuring the right of the other party to receive the fruits of the contract. This means that in every contract there exists an implied covenant of good faith and fair dealing.

When the satisfaction of a condition involves action by a party to the contract, the implied duty to act in good faith requires that such party make an honest, good-faith effort to bring about the satisfaction of the condition. For example, when a contract is made subject to the condition that one of the parties obtain financing, that party must make reasonable, good-faith efforts to obtain financing.[12] The party is not permitted to do nothing and then claim that the contract is not binding because the condition has not been satisfied.

The obligation to act in good faith does not require a party to agree to a modification of the contract or to surrender any right. Likewise, a franchisor having a right to terminate the franchise without cause is not barred from so doing because of the duty of good faith. When a franchisee has been granted a nonexclusive franchise, good faith does not prevent the franchisor from granting another franchise that competes with the original franchise.[13]

(d) GOVERNMENTAL APPROVAL. In some situations, the ability to perform a contract will depend upon obtaining a governmental permit or approval. When this is so, the failure to obtain such approval or permit may be made an express condition subsequent so that the contract is discharged by such failure. An implied term generally

[10] Khalifa v Henry Ford Hospital, 156 Mich App 485, 401 NW2d 884 (1987). Note that there is a modern trend to prevent the employer from firing an employee without cause when the employer is retaliating against the employee. See § 45:3.
[11] Valiant Air Command, Inc. v Frank K. Collins & Associates (Fla App) 500 So 2d 577 (1986).

[12] EKE Builders, Inc. v Quail Bluff Associates (Okla App) 714 P2d 604 (1985).
[13] Patel v Dunkin' Donuts of America, Inc. 146 Ill App 3d 233, 100 Ill Dec 94, 496 NE2d 1159 (1986).

arises that one party to the contract will co-operate with the other in obtaining any necessary governmental permit or approval.

(e) STATUTORY TERMS. Statutes commonly require that certain kinds of contracts contain particular clauses. For example, automobile insurance contracts are often required by statute to contain clauses with respect to no-fault liability and uninsured motorists. When a contract is written that does not contain the required statutory terms, the courts will ordinarily imply the statutory terms and interpret the contract as though it complied with the statute. Similarly, a provision in a contract that would be contrary to a required statutory provision will be ignored.[14]

§ 19:6 CONDUCT AND CUSTOM

The conduct of the parties and the customs and usages of a particular trade may give meaning to the words of the parties and thus aid in the interpretation of their contract.

(a) CONDUCT OF THE PARTIES. The conduct of the parties in carrying out the terms of a contract may be considered in determining just what they meant by the contract. When performance has been repeatedly tendered and accepted without protest, neither party will be permitted to claim that the contract was too indefinite to be binding. For example, when a travel agent made a contract with a hotel to arrange for junkets to the hotel, any claim that it was not certain just what was intended must be ignored when some eighty junkets had already been arranged and paid for by the hotel at the contract price without any dispute as to whether the contract obligation was satisfied.[15] Moreover, when the conduct of the parties is inconsis-

tent with the original written contract, proof of such conduct may justify concluding that the parties had orally modified the original agreement.

(b) CUSTOM AND USAGE OF TRADE. The customs and usages of the trade or commercial activity to which the contract relates may give to the terms of a contract a meaning that the terms would not have in ordinary speech or a meaning where the words of the contract would otherwise appear to have no meaning. For example, when a contract for the construction of a house calls for a "turn-key construction," industry usage is admissible to show that this means a construction in which all the owner need do is "turn the key" in the lock to open the building for use and that all risks are assumed by the contractor.[16]

Custom and usage, however, cannot override express provisions of a contract that are inconsistent with such customs and usage.

§ 19:7 AVOIDANCE OF HARDSHIP

As a general rule, a party is bound by a contract, even though it proves to be a bad bargain. If possible, a court will interpret a contract to avoid hardship, particularly when the hardship will hurt the weaker of the two parties to the contract.

When there is ambiguity as to the meaning of a contract, a court will avoid the interpretation that gives one contracting party an unreasonable advantage over the other or that causes a forfeiture of a party's interest. When there is an inequality of bargaining power between the contracting parties, courts will sometimes classify the contract as a contract of adhesion in that it was offered on a take-it-or-leave-it basis by the stronger party. The court will then interpret the contract as providing what appeared reasonable from the standpoint of the weaker bargaining party.

In some instances, if hardship cannot be

---

[14] Florida Beverage Corp. v Division of Alcoholic Beverages (Fla App) 503 So 2d 396 (1987).

[15] See Uniform Commercial Code § 2–208(1) as to course of performance in the interpretation of contracts for the sale of goods and UCC § 1–205 as to both Code and non-Code transactions.

[16] Blue v R. L. Glossen Contracting, Inc. 173 Ga App 622, 327 SE2d 582 (1985).

avoided in this manner, the court may hold that the contract or a particular provision is not binding because it is unconscionable or contrary to public policy. The extent to which this protection is available is uncertain.

When the hardship arises because the contract makes no provision for the situation that has occurred, the court will sometimes imply a term in order to avoid the hardship. In the *Perkins* case, the weaker party claimed that the court should imply or read into the contract a protective term that was not there.

PERKINS V STANDARD OIL CO.
235 Or 7, 383 P2d 107 (1963)

Standard Oil made a jobbing or wholesale dealership contract with Clyde Perkins that limited him to selling Standard's products and required Perkins to maintain certain minimum prices. Standard Oil had the right to approve or disapprove of Perkins' customers. In order to be able to perform under this contract, Perkins had to make a substantial monetary investment, and his only income was from the commissions on the sales of Standard's products. Standard Oil made some sales directly to Perkins' customers. When Perkins protested, Standard Oil pointed out that the contract did not contain any provision making his rights exclusive. Perkins sued Standard Oil to compel it to stop dealing with his customers. From a decision in Standard's favor, Perkins appealed.

ROSSMAN, J. . . . The contract authorized the plaintiff [Perkins] to sell without Standard's written consent "on a nonexclusive basis" the products which Standard consigned to him but only to service stations or consuming accounts. Standard's written consent was required before the plaintiff could sell to any other account. The plaintiff promised in the contract to use his "best efforts to promote the sale of products consigned hereunder" and to sell a specified minimum amount during each year. . . . The plaintiff was required to deliver to Standard a complete list of the names and addresses of all his distributors and submit to it the names of any new potential distributors. . . .

The plaintiff claims that the contract by its very nature contains an implied condition that Standard would not solicit business directly from his (plaintiff's) customers. Standard protests that such an implied condition would be contrary to the express terms of the contract since the latter (1) provides that the plaintiff was authorized to sell Standard's products only "on a nonexclusive basis" and (2) reserved to Standard the "right to select its own customers." Plaintiff proposes a more restricted interpretation. . . . He concedes that the contract reserved to Standard the right to sell to any new accounts which it found, and to accept or reject any new accounts which he (the plaintiff) might obtain, but he insists that it does not permit Standard to solicit accounts which it had approved as his customers. . . .

In order to be successful in his business and to comply with the terms of his contract, the plaintiff was obliged to make substantial investments in storage facilities, delivery trucks, and other equipment. He was also obliged to hire employees. He was required to use his "best efforts" to promote the sale of Standard's products. Only if he sold Standard's products exclusively could it be said that he was using his best efforts to promote their sale. It is clear, then, that the contract limited his dealership to Standard products. Plaintiff was also required to sell a minimum quantity of other designated Standard petroleum products. If he at any time failed to sell the minimum quantity, Standard was at liberty to terminate its contract with him. Plaintiff's compensation was based exclusively on the sales he made to customers, which he secured through his own efforts. No compensation was available for the plaintiff if he obtained customers for Standard who bought directly from it. Nor does the contract obligate Standard to compensate him for sales made directly by Standard to plaintiff's customers. . . .

. . . . A condition must be implied that Standard would not solicit customers which had been obtained through plaintiff's efforts. The interpretation of the contract for which Standard contends would leave plaintiff and others in a position similar to his completely at the mercy of Standard. . . .

"We cannot accept [Standard's] construction of its meaning. An intention to make so one-sided an agreement is not readily to be inferred. . . .

"In every contract there is an implied covenant that neither party shall do anything that will have the effect of destroying or injuring the right of the other party to receive the fruits of the contract, which means that in every contract there exists a covenant of good faith and fair dealing." . . . 3 *Corbin* [*on Contracts 278*] 349-352 . . .

The implication of a condition finds support in many circumstances. . . . Plaintiff's only source of return on his substantial investments in the business was the sales he made to his customers. If Standard was at liberty to solicit his direct customers, as it contends, . . . plaintiff was in a state of economic servility; we do not believe that the parties intended such a result at the time the contract was signed. . . .

The contract before us is obviously a form contract prepared by Standard. It is a contract of "adhesion" in the sense that it is a take-it-or-leave-it whole. Such contracts are regarded by some authorities as anachronistic or inconsistent with real freedom of contract. At least they should be construed with an awareness of the inequality of the bargainers. . . .

[Judgment reversed]

QUESTIONS

1. What created the problem in the *Perkins* case?
2. Could the problem in the *Perkins* case have been avoided?

---

§ 19:8   **JOINT, SEVERAL, AND JOINT AND SEVERAL CONTRACTS**

The obligation of defendants bound by a contract may be several (separate), joint, or joint and several.[17] Printed forms will commonly specify that liability is joint and several.

[17]   Chun v Chun, 190 Cal App 589, 235 Cal Rptr 553 (1987).

B. CONFLICT OF LAWS

When a lawsuit is brought on a contract, the court will seek to apply the law under which the contract was made. That is, a California court in many cases will not apply California law to a foreign (out-of-state) contract. The principles that determine when a court applies the law of its own state — the **law of the forum** — or some foreign law are called **conflict of laws.**

Because there are fifty state court systems and a federal court system, and a high degree of interstate activity, these conflict of laws questions arise frequently.

§ 19:9 STATE COURTS

It is important to distinguish between the state in which the parties are **domiciled** or have their permanent home, the state in which the contract is made, and the state in which the contract is to be performed. The law of the state where the contract is made determines whether it is valid in substance and satisfies requirements as to form. Matters relating to the performance of the contract, excuse or liability for nonperformance, and the measure of damages for nonperformance are generally governed by the law of the state where the contract is to be performed.

When a lawsuit is brought on a contract, the law of the forum determines the procedure and the rules of evidence.

(a) PLACE OF CONTRACTING. The state in which the contract is made is determined by finding the state in which the last act essential to the formation of the contract was performed. Thus, when an acceptance is mailed in one state to an offeror in another state, the state of formation of the contract is the state in which the acceptance is mailed if the acceptance becomes effective at that time.

If acceptance by telephone is otherwise proper, the acceptance takes effect at the place where the acceptance is spoken into the phone. Thus, an employment contract is made in the state in which the job applicant telephones an acceptance, and consequently, the law of that state governs a claim to workers' compensation, even though the injuries were sustained in another state.

If an action on a contract made in one state is brought in a court of another state, an initial question is whether that court will lend its aid to the enforcement of a foreign contract. Ordinarily suit may be brought on a foreign contract. If there is a strong contrary local policy, however, recovery may be denied, even though the contract was valid in the state where it was made.

The capacity of a natural person to make a contract is governed by the place of contracting. A corporation's capacity to make a contract is determined by the law of the state of incorporation.

(b) CENTER OF GRAVITY. It is common for contracts with interstate aspects to specify that they shall be governed by the law of a particular state. In the absence of a law-selecting provision in the contract, there is a growing acceptance of the rule that a contract should be governed by the law of the state that has the most significant contacts with the transaction. This is the state to which the contract may be said to gravitate.

For example, when the buyer's place of business and the seller's factory are located in state A, and the buyer is purchasing to resell to customers in state A, many courts will hold that this is a contract governed by the law of state A in all respects, even though it may happen to be a state B contract by virtue of the chance circumstance that the seller's offer was accepted by the buyer in state B. In determining which state has the most significant contacts, the court is to consider the place of contracting, negotiating, and performing; the location of the subject matter of the contract; and the domicile, residence, and states of incorporation and principal place of business of the parties.

When all states have the same rule of law, it is not important which state's law is followed. If, however, the law of the states involved is not the same, the choice of the state whose law is to govern will determine how the lawsuit will end. This is seen in the *Wood* case in which the plaintiff would win if the law of the state of contracting was followed but would lose if the law of the state of performance was followed.

WOOD BROS. HOMES V WALKER ADJUSTMENT BUREAU

198 Colo 444, 601 P2d 1369 (1979)

Fred Gagnon was a California contractor. He signed a contract with Wood Bros. Homes of Colorado to do some construction work for it on an apartment complex in New Mexico. Negotiations leading up to the contract took place in California, Colorado, and New Mexico. The contract was signed in Colorado. Gagnon did not have a New Mexico contractor's license, and the New Mexico officials ordered him to stop work when the contract was partly finished. He wanted to be paid for what he had done and sold his claim against Wood Brothers to a collection agency, the Walker Adjustment Bureau. Walker, an assignee of Gagnon, sued Wood Bros. in Colorado. By the law of New Mexico, Gagnon could not have sued because he did not have a license. By the law of Colorado, the absence of a license did not bar suit. The trial court held that the New Mexico law applied. This was reversed by the court of appeals. An appeal was then taken to the state supreme court.

HODGES, C. J. . . . Under the traditional conflict of laws rule for contract actions, the law of the place of execution governs questions regarding the formation of the contract, while the law of the place of performance governs issues relating to the performance of the contract. This rule, however, has frequently proven unduly inflexible, leading to harsh and unjust results. Courts have often been forced to employ a multitude of escape devices to reach an equitable result. Therefore the traditional choice of law rules no longer provide the predictability and uniformity which were considered their primary virtues.

In adopting the *Restatement (Second)* approach for tort actions, this court recognized the shortcomings of the traditional conflict of laws rule and the benefits of the most significant relationship approach of the *Restatement (Second)*. . . . We now adopt the *Restatement (Second)* approach for contract actions.

Where a conflict of laws question is raised, the objective of the *Restatement (Second)* is to locate the state having the "most significant relationship" to the particular issue. . . . Once the state having the most significant relationship is identified, the law of that state is then applied to resolve the particular issue. . . .

The court of appeals held that under the *Restatement (Second)* Colorado would be the state having the most significant relationship. . . . We disagree.

Colorado's interest in the validation of agreements and protection of the parties' expectations is a central policy underlying the law of contracts. . . . While this interest is strong, it does not necessarily supersede all others.

The New Mexico Construction Industries Licensing Act provides a comprehensive and mandatory system of licensing for persons engaged in construction work in New Mexico. The act is designed to protect New Mexico citizens against "substandard or hazardous construction . . . and by providing protection against the fiscal irresponsibility of persons engaged in construction occupations or trades. . . ." Potential contractors must present evidence of financial responsibility, demonstrate a familiarity with building regulations, submit proof of registration with the tax office, pass an examination, and must not have engaged illegally in the contracting business in New Mexico within the past year. Those who build without a license are subject to a criminal sanction and are expressly barred from obtaining judicial enforcement of their contract or from recovery for the value of services performed.

In this situation, the value of protecting the parties' contractual expectations is outweighed by New Mexico's interest in applying its invalidating rule. *A fortiori,* the presumption of section 196 that New Mexico law applies has not been rebutted. The law of New Mexico applies to resolve this issue, and as discussed above, the action is consequently barred. This conclusion is in accord with *Restatement (Second)* section 202(2) (1971) which provides: "When performance is illegal in the place of performance, the contract will usually be denied enforcement."

[Judgment Reversed]

QUESTIONS

1. Why did the plaintiff sue in Colorado?
2. Did the court follow the traditional rule of conflicts of laws?
3. What was the reason for the decision that the court made?

§ 19:10   FEDERAL COURTS

When the parties to a contract reside in different states and an action is brought on the contract in a federal court because of their different citizenship, the federal court must apply the same rules of conflict of laws that would be applied by the courts of the state in which the federal court is sitting. Thus, a federal court in Chicago deciding a case involving parties from different states must apply the same rule of conflict of laws as would be applied by the state courts in Illinois. The state law must be followed by the federal court in such a case whether or not the federal court agrees with the state law.

SUMMARY

As a contract is based on the agreement of the parties, courts must give effect to the intent of the parties manifested thereby. The intent that is to be enforced is the intent as it reasonably appears to a third person. This objective intent is followed, and the subjective or secret intent is ignored because the recognition of secret intention would undermine the stability of contracts and open the door to fraud.

In interpreting a contract, words are to be given their ordinary meaning unless there is some reason, as in the case of trade or technical terms, to conclude that the parties gave the words a special meaning. The court must consider the whole contract and not read a particular part out of context. When different writings are executed as part of the same transaction or one writing refers to or incorporates another, all the writings are to be read together as constituting the contract of the parties. In some cases, the reverse is done, and a contract is held divisible because it is proper to conclude that the parties were in fact making two or more separate contracts and intended that each contract should stand by itself.

When provisions of a contract are contradictory, the court will try to reconcile or eliminate the conflict. If this cannot be done, the conclusion may be reached that there is no contract because the conflict makes the agreement indefinite as to a material matter. In some cases, conflict is solved by considering the form of the conflicting terms. Handwriting prevails over typing and printing, and typing prevails over printing. Ambiguity will be eliminated in some cases by the admission of parol evidence as discussed in Chapter 18 or by interpreting the provision strictly against the party preparing the contract, particularly when the party has significantly greater bargaining power or the contract can be described as an adhesion contract.

In most cases, the parties are held to their contract exactly as it has been written. In other cases, the courts will imply certain terms to preserve the contract against the objection that essential terms are missing or to prevent hardship. The law will imply that performance be made within a reasonable time and that details of performance be reasonable when the contract fails to be specific on these points. Also, the law will imply an obligation to act in good faith and a limitation to prevent a franchisor from competing with its franchisee.

When a contract has interstate aspects, it is necessary to determine which state's law governs the contract. The rules that govern that decision are called the law of conflict of laws. The parties may specify the jurisdiction whose law is to govern. If that jurisdiction bears a reasonable relationship to the contract, it will be given effect by the court. In the absence of such a provision, the older courts will apply the law of the state where the contract was made with respect to most matters and the law of the state where performance is to be made as to matters relating to performance. The modern, or center of gravity view, is to choose that jurisdiction that has the most significant relationship to the parties, the contract, and its performance. When an action is brought in a federal court because it involves citizens of different states (diversity of citizenship), the federal court must apply the conflict of laws principles that would be applied by the courts of the state in which the federal court is sitting.

QUESTIONS AND CASE PROBLEMS

1. What social forces are affected by the rule that a secret intention that is not expressed has no effect?
2. What is a condition precedent?
3. Harrison Builders made a contract to build a house for Kendall on a cost plus 10 percent profit basis. The cost of the finished house was approximately $100,000. Kendall had expected that it would have been $60,000 and

claimed that Harrison was careless and extravagant in piling up costs of $100,000. Harrison asserted that as Kendall did not deny that the costs were $100,000, he could not dispute that they were proper. Is Harrison correct?
4. In letters between the two, Rita contracted to sell "my car" to Viola for $2,000. It is later shown that Rita owned two cars. Rita re-

fused to deliver either car to Viola. Viola sues Rita for breach of contract. Rita raised the defense that the contract is too indefinite to be enforced because it cannot be determined from the writing which car is the subject matter of the contract. Is the contract too indefinite to be enforced?

5. Quinn of Ohio sues Norman of California in the federal district court for the southern district of New York. Quinn claims that the court should apply the conflicts of laws rules of Ohio because he is from Ohio and the plaintiff should have the choice of law. Norman claims that the federal court should apply federal law and not the law of any particular state. Who is correct?

6. The Wendell Saw Company contracted to sell to the Harris Industrial Equipment Company a new power saw if it could be developed and made operational by the Wendell Company. Wendell was not able to make the new saw operate consistently and never delivered it to Harris. Harris sued Wendell for breach of contract. Was Wendell liable?

7. Compare (a) the rule that a contract will be construed strictly against the person preparing it, and (b) the rule that a typewritten provision prevails over a printed provision.

8. McGill and his grandson, Malo, made an agreement by which the former would live with the latter and receive support and maintenance in return for deeding to the grandson the house of the former. After a number of years, the grandfather left the house because of the threats and physical violence of the grandson. There was no complaint of lack of support and maintenance. Had the grandson broken the contract? [McGill v Malo, 23 Conn Supp 447, 184 A2d 517]

9. A contract was made for the sale of a farm. The contract stated that the buyer's deposit would be returned "if for any reason the farm cannot be sold." Thereafter the seller stated that she had changed her mind, and would not sell, and offered to return the deposit. The buyer refused to take the deposit back and brought suit to enforce the contract. The seller defended on the ground that the "any reason" provision extended to anything, including the seller's changing her mind. Was the buyer entitled to recover? [Phillips v Rogers, 157 W Va 194, 200 SE2d 676]

10. Gerson Realty Co. rented an apartment to Casaly. The lease stated that it could be renewed on giving notice but declared that "such notice . . . shall be given or served and shall not be deemed to have been duly given or served unless in writing and forwarded by registered mail." Casaly sent a renewal notice by certified mail. Two years after receiving the notice, Gerson claimed that it was not effective because it had not been sent by registered mail. Was this notice effective? [Gerson Realty Inc. v Casaly, 2 Mass App 875, 316 NE2d 767]

11. Harwood rented an apartment in an apartment house complex from Lincoln Square Apartments. Air conditioning was among the services to be provided by the landlord. The lease stated that the landlord was not liable for "any interruption or curtailment of any service." The central air conditioning system in the apartment house broke down and would not function for six weeks in the summer. Harwood rented an air conditioning unit that he placed in his apartment and then sued the landlord for the cost thereof. The landlord denied liability because of the disclaimer clause. Was the landlord right? [Harwood v Lincoln Square Apartments Section 5, Inc. 359 NYS2d 387]

12. Physicians Mutual Insurance Company issued a policy covering the life of Brown. The policy declared that it did not cover any deaths resulting from "mental disorder, alcoholism, or drug addiction." Brown was killed when she fell while intoxicated. The insurance company refused to pay because of the quoted provision. Her executor, Savage, sued the insurance company. Did the insurance company have a defense? [Physicians Mut. Ins. Co. v Savage, 156 Ind App 283, 296 NE2d 165]

13. Buice was employed by the Gulf Oil Corporation as a driver. His contract of employment did not state that it was to continue for any specified time. Buice was fired because of excessive drinking. He was treated for alcoholism and was cured. He then applied to Gulf for reinstatement. Gulf refused to reinstate him. Buice then sued Gulf claiming that Gulf had followed the practice of reinstating addiction patients who were cured of their addictions, and it was his understanding that this was an implied term of his employment contract. Was Buice enti-

tled to reinstatement? [Buice v Gulf Oil Corp. 172 Ga App 93, 322 SE2d 103]

14. The McBride & Dehmer Construction Company was doing construction work in Oklahoma. Smith lived in Kansas and was notified by McBride's foreman that if he wanted to go to work he should show up at the job site in Oklahoma. He did so and was put to work. He was injured and then claimed workers' compensation under the Kansas statute, on the theory that the contract for employment had been made in Kansas. Was he correct? [Smith v McBride & Dehmer Constr. Co. 216 Kan 76, 530 P2d 1222]

15. Carol and John were married. They separated and signed an agreement by which John promised to pay Carol $100 a month. A year later, they were divorced, and John stopped making payments. Carol sued him for breach of the contract. John offered to testify that it was his intention that the payments would stop when the parties were divorced. Is this testimony admissible? [Grady v Grady, 29 NC App 402, 224 SE2d 282]

20

THIRD PERSONS AND CONTRACTS

When the economy was agrarian and the modern era of mass selling on credit had not begun, it was logical to regard a contract as a matter that concerned only the contracting parties. It was their private affair, and the relationship between them was described as privity of contract. Persons not in privity of contract had no rights with respect to contracts made by other persons. As time went by, society became aware that there were needs that could not be met by this concept of privity of contract. Life insurance would not be possible because the beneficiary, not being in privity of contract, would not have an enforcea-

ble claim against the insurance company. Faced with such situations, society modified the rule of law so that third party beneficiaries could sue for breach of a contract to which they were strangers. This decision, however, led to another problem: that of defining third party beneficiaries so as to limit contract rights to those third parties that the original contracting parties sought to benefit. Society chose the policy of drawing a line so that those who are merely incidentally benefited cannot sue on a contract to which they are strangers.

The social decision of allowing strangers to get involved in a contract made by others also arose in connection with determining whether a party to a contract could transfer a right to receive money or to receive a performance or to delegate the duties imposed by the contract to another person. Subject to certain practical limitations, society gradually chose to allow the free transfer of rights and the free delegation of duties. Society has done this to provide the economy with greater flexibility in making financial and working arrangements. This has given rise to the body of law governing assignment of rights and delegation of duties.

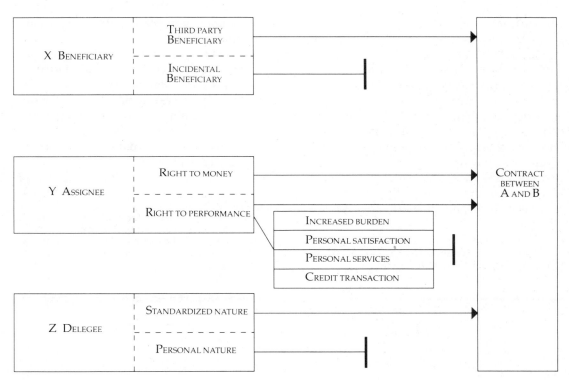

FIGURE 20-1
CAN A THIRD PERSON SUE ON A CONTRACT?

A. THIRD PARTY BENEFICIARY CONTRACTS

In some cases a third person who is not a party to the contract may sue on the contract.

§ 20:1 DEFINITION

When a contract is intended to benefit a third person, such person is a third party beneficiary and may bring suit on and enforce the contract. In some states, the right of the third party beneficiary to sue on the contract is declared by statute.[1]

Ordinarily A and B will make a contract that concerns only them. However, they may make a contract by which B promises A that B will make a payment of money to C. That is, the contracting parties intend to benefit C. Because of this intent, if B fails to peform that promise, C, who is not the original promisee, may enforce the con-

[1] Outdoor Services, Inc. v Pabagold, Inc. 185 Cal App 3d 676, 230 Cal Rptr 73 (1986).

tract against *B*, the promisor. Such an agreement is a **third party beneficiary contract.** A life insurance contract is a third party beneficiary contract, as the insurance company promises the insured to make payment to the beneficiary. Such a contract entitles the beneficiary to sue the insurance company upon the insured's death, even though the insurance company never made any agreement directly with the beneficiary.

It is not necessary that the third party beneficiary be identified by name. It is sufficient to identify such beneficiary by class with the result that any member of that class is a third party beneficiary.[2] For example, when a contract between the promoter of an automobile stock car race and the owner of the race track contains a promise to pay specified sums of money to each driver racing a car in certain races, a person driving in one of the designated races is a third party beneficiary and can

sue on the contract for the promised compensation.

At times it is difficult to decide whether a stranger to a contract should be called a third party beneficiary, and therefore be entitled to sue on the contract. At other times, the question is easily answered because one purpose dominates the entire transaction. In any case, it is a question of intention whether the third person is an intended beneficiary.[3] If a contract expressly states that no third person may sue for its breach and that only the other contracting party may do so, it is obvious that there can be no third party beneficiary.[4]

In the *Dagen* case a third person who was injured claimed that the dangerous condition that caused his injury was a breach of contract and that he could sue as a third party beneficiary.

[2] J.F. Inc. v S.M. Wilson & Co. 152 Ill App 3d 893, 105 Ill Dec 748, 504 NE2d 1266 (1987).

[3] Valdex v Cillessen & Son, Inc. 105 NM 575, 734 P2d 1258 (1987).
[4] Moore Construction Co., Inc. v Clarksville Department of Electricity (Tenn App) 707 SW2d 1 (1986). An exception would be made in the case in which a statute or a court would declare such a limitation invalid.

DAGEN V VILLAGE OF BALDWIN
159 Mich App 620, 406 NW2d 889 (1987)

Richard Dagen was on state welfare. He was assigned by the county Department of Social Services (DSS) to work in repairing a building owned by the Village of Baldwin. While so working, he fell and was injured. He, claiming to be a third party beneficiary, sued the village. The lower court entered summary judgment in favor of the village, and Dagen appealed.

HOLBROOK, J. . . .On August 24, 1982, plaintiff suffered a permanent knee injury when he fell from the roof of a building owned and maintained by the village. At the time of his injury, plaintiff was a welfare recipient who was required to participate in the Community Work Experience Program (CWEP) sponsored by the Department of Social Services. Under the program plaintiff was sent by the DSS to work for the village. Plaintiff was shingling the roof of a village maintenance building when he fell. . . .

Although plaintiff was not a party to the CWEP contract between the Department of Social Services and defendant, we find that plaintiff has sufficiently pled that he was a third-party beneficiary to the contract. By statute, any person, for whose benefit a promise is made by way of contract, has the same right to enforce the promise that he would have had if the promise had been made directly to him as the promisee. . . . A promise is construed to have been made for the benefit of a person whenever the promisor has undertaken to give or to do or to refrain from doing something directly to or for said person. . . .

The contract in the case at hand provides that CWEP participants shall not be assigned to work involving a significant degree of risk to life or health, and shall be provided training and instruction on safety:

> 3. Working Conditions
> A. Work assignments may be made for any work typical of that performed by the agency. However, CWEP participants shall not be assigned to perform work that entails a significant degree of risk to life or health. . . .
> CWEP AGENCY . . .
> 2. Training
> The CWEP agency must provide orientation and training to include teaching the skills which are required of the job to be performed as well as instruction about safety and proper work attitudes and habits.

We find that the contract at issue may be construed to benefit plaintiff, since the promises made by defendant village upon entering into the agreement clearly and directly benefitted plaintiff's health and safety. Consequently, we conclude that plaintiff is a third-party beneficiary to the contract between the DSS and defendant village. Plaintiff sufficiently alleged a third-party beneficiary theory in his amended complaint:

> COUNT III: BREACH OF CONTRACT . . .
> 13. In return for the free labor provided by the Lake County Department of Social Services under the CWEP, Defendant Village of Baldwin promised
> (a) not to assign CWEP workers to work entailing a significant degree of risk to life or health;
> (b) to adequately supervise CWEP workers;
> (c) to adequately train CWEP workers so as to do their job properly and safely;
> (d) to provide reasonable work conditions; and
> (e) to assume liability for personal injuries incurred by CWEP workers while performing their assigned duties.
> 14. *Said promises were made in contemplation of and for the benefit and protection of, third persons such as plaintiff Richard R. Dagen.*

Hence we find that plaintiff's amended complaint states a claim upon which relief can be granted and the trial court erred in granting defendant summary judgment on this claim. . . .

[Judgment reversed as to right of plaintiff to sue]

QUESTIONS

1. Why was Dagen allowed to sue on the contract between the county board and the village?
2. Upon what did the court base its decision as stated in your answer to Question 1?
3. Did the contract sued upon name the plaintiff as a beneficiary?

§ 20:2   Modification or Termination of Third Party Beneficiary Contract

Can the parties to the contract modify or terminate it so as to destroy the right of the third party beneficiary? If the contract contains an express provision to change beneficiaries or to cancel the contract without the consent of the third party beneficiary, the parties to the contract may destroy the rights of the third party beneficiary by acting in accordance with such contract provision.[5]

In addition, the rights of a third party beneficiary are destroyed if the contract is discharged or ended by operation of law, as discussed in Chapter 21.

In the absence of a proper change or termination under a term of the contract or a discharge of the contract by operation of law, the parties to the contract cannot affect the rights of the third party beneficiary. However, if the third party beneficiary consents to the change or termination or acts in such a way as to mislead others, the beneficiary is barred or estopped from complaining.

§ 20:3   Limitations on Third Party Beneficiary

While the third party beneficiary rule gives the third person the right to enforce the contract, it obviously gives no greater rights than the contract provides. Otherwise stated, the third party beneficiary must take the contract as it is. If there is a time limitation or any other restriction in the contract, the third party beneficiary cannot ignore it but is bound thereby. Likewise, a third party beneficiary is required to arbitrate a dispute arising under the contract when the original parties to the contract were bound to arbitrate.

§ 20:4   Incidental Beneficiaries

Not everyone who benefits from the performance of a contract between other persons is entitled to sue as a third party beneficiary.[6] If the benefit was intended, the third person is a third party beneficiary with the rights described in the preceding sections. If the benefit was not intended, the third person is an incidental beneficiary.

(a) Direct Incidental Beneficiary. When the performance of the contract will confer a direct, although not intended, benefit on the third person, that person is a **direct incidental beneficiary.** For example, when a private employer makes a contract with the U. S. government to employ and train disadvantaged unemployed persons, such persons are merely incidental beneficiaries of the contract and therefore cannot sue for damages when the contract with the government is broken by the employer. Such persons are direct incidental beneficiaries as the performance of the contract would have directly benefited them.

The fact that a contract requires one of the parties to take steps that will protect or benefit a third person does not make such person a third party beneficiary. For example, when the city hired a contractor to do excavation work, and the contract specified that the contractor should be careful of underground facilities, such care benefited the electric power company that had underground facilities. However, that direct benefit did not make the power company a third party beneficiary to the contract. The power company was merely a direct incidental beneficiary.[7]

---

[5]   A common form of reservation is the life insurance policy provision by which the insured reserves the right to change the beneficiary. § 142 of the Restatement of Contracts 2d provides that the promisor and promisee may modify their contract and affect the right of the third party beneficiary thereby unless the agreement expressly prohibits this or the third party beneficiary has changed position in reliance on the promise or has manifested assent to it.

[6]   Davidson v Marshall-DeKalb Electric Cooperative (Ala) 495 So 2d 1058 (1986).
[7]   New York v Consolidated Edison Co. 114 App Div 2d 217, 498 NYS2d 369 (1986).

Likewise, a contractor was merely a direct incidental beneficiary of the contract between the city and the supervising engineer by which the engineer agreed that proper payment would be made to contractors.[8]

(b) CONTINGENT INCIDENTAL BENEFICIARY. In contrast with the incidental beneficiary who is directly benefited by the performance of the contract, the situation may be such that the third party will benefit only if the obligee of the original contract takes some further action that will benefit the third person. For example, a landlord is not a third party beneficiary of the contract by which a bank agreed to lend money to the tenant, even though the tenant intended to use the money to make improvements to the rented premises.[9] In effect, the landlord was an incidental beneficiary once removed. The landlord would benefit only (a) if the bank loaned the money to the tenant, and (b) if the tenant used the money to make the improvements. Thus, the bank could perform its duty by making the loan, but if the tenant never used the money to make the improvements, the landlord would never receive any benefit from that loan. The benefit to the landlord was therefore contingent upon the tenant's using proceeds of the loan for making improvements.

(c) CONSEQUENCE OF INCIDENTAL BENEFICIARY STATUS. An incidental beneficiary cannot sue the parties to the contract that gave rise to the benefit or the possible benefit.

The importance in making the distinction between the direct and the contingent incidental beneficiary lies in the value of the distinction as proof of lack of intent to benefit the third person. For example, when the performance of a contract directly benefits the third person, it is necessary to go further and determine whether the parties to the contract had intended to confer that benefit on the third person. In contrast, in the contingent incidental beneficiary case it is obvious that the parties to the original contract did not intend to confer a benefit on that person who would only benefit if the obligee in turn would *choose* to confer a benefit. Consequently, once it is established that the third party is, at best, a contingent incidental beneficiary, the lawsuit is ended, and there is no need to make further inquiry as to the intent of the original parties.

B.   ASSIGNMENTS

The parties to a contract have both rights and duties. Can rights be transferred or sold to another person? Can duties be transferred to another person?

§ 20:5   DEFINITIONS

An **assignment** is a transfer of rights. The party making the assignment is the **assignor,** and the person to whom the assignment is made is the **assignee.** An assignee of a contract may generally sue directly on the contract, rather than suing in the name of the assignor.

§ 20:6   FORM OF ASSIGNMENT

Generally an assignment may be in any form. Any words, whether written or spoken, that show an intention to transfer or assign will be given the effect of an assignment. Statutes, however, may require that certain kinds of assignments be in writing or be executed in particular form. This requirement is common in respect to statutes limiting the assignment of claims to wages. It is not necessary to use the words *assign* or *transfer*. A statement that "you will be entitled to" a specific sum of money owed by a named person is sufficient to assign the right to that money.

As no particular words are necessary to create an assignment, an authorization to

---

[8]   Santucci Construction Co. v Baxter & Woodman, Inc. 151 Ill App 3d 547, 104 Ill Dec 474, 502 NE2d 1134 (1987).
[9]   Popp v Dyslin, 149 Ill App 3d 956, 102 Ill Dec 938, 500 NE2d 1039 (1986).

the obligor (the other party to the original contract) to pay a third person is an assignment to such third person. For example, the printed forms supplied by the health insurer that read "I hereby authorize payment directly to the below named dentist of the group insurance benefits otherwise payable to me" constitute an assignment to the dentist of such benefits.

Whether there is consideration or not for the assignment does not affect the validity of the assignment, and an assignment cannot be challenged by the obligor on the ground that there was no consideration. This is so because an assignment is not a contract. It is a transfer of a property right. An assignment may therefore be made as a gift, although it is usually part of a business transaction.

§ 20:7   ASSIGNMENT OF RIGHT TO MONEY

A person entitled to receive money, such as payment for the price of goods or for work done under a contract, may generally assign that right to another person. A claim or cause of action against another person may be assigned. A contractor entitled to receive payment from the owner can assign that right to the bank as security for a loan or can assign it to anyone else.

A partial assignment is valid but may be ignored by the debtor unless the owners of all parts of the claim in question demand payment or bring one lawsuit against the debtor.[10]

(a) FUTURE RIGHTS. By the modern rule, future and expected rights may be assigned. Thus, the contractor may assign the money that is not yet due under the contract because the building has not yet been constructed. Likewise, an author may assign royalties that are expected to be received from contracts that the author expects to enter into in the future. The fact that there is nothing in existence now does not prohibit the assignment of what is expected to be existing in the future.

(b) CONSENT TO ASSIGNMENT OF RIGHTS. The party who is subject to the right of the other party that is, the obligor, may expressly consent to the assignment of the right. A provision that the contract should bind the successors to the parties constitutes consent to future assignments thereof.

(c) PROHIBITION OF ASSIGNMENT OF RIGHTS. A contract may prohibit the assignment of any rights arising thereunder. Some courts hold that such a prohibition is binding. This means that an assignment made in violation of the prohibition has no effect. By the modern view, a prohibition against assignment has no effect. Thus, an assignment is valid even though prohibited by the contract. By this view, a provision in a construction contract that the contractor may not assign money to become due under the contract without the consent of the other contracting party is not binding, and the assignee may recover the amounts due from the obligor. Under the Uniform Commercial Code, the assignment of accounts receivable cannot be prohibited by the parties.[11]

§ 20:8   ASSIGNMENT OF RIGHT TO A PERFORMANCE

When the contractual right of the obligee is that of receiving a performance by the other party, the obligee may assign that right, provided the performance required of the other party will not be materially altered or varied by such assignment. If a transfer of a right to a performance would materially affect or alter a duty or the rights of the obligor, an assignment of the rights to the performance is not permitted. When an obligee is entitled to assign a right, it may be done by unilateral act.

---

[10] Space Coast Credit Union v Walt Disney World Co. (Fla App) 483 So 2d 35 (1986).

[11] UCC § 9-318(4). Although some cases still follow the contrary pre-Code law. See, for example, Cordis Corp. v Sonies International, Inc. (Fla App) 427 So 2d 782 (1983).

There is no requirement that the obligor consent or agree. Likewise, the act of assigning does not constitute a breach of the contract, unless the contract specifically declares so.

Thus, when repairs or improvements are made to a building by one who guarantees the work to the owner, the owner, on selling the building, may assign the guarantee to the buyer.[12]

(a) ASSIGNMENT INCREASING BURDEN OF PERFORMANCE. When the assigning of a right would increase the burden of the obligor in performing, an assignment is ordinarily not permitted. To illustrate, if the assignor has the right to buy a certain quantity of a stated article and to take such property from the seller's warehouse, this right can be assigned. If, however, the sales contract stipulated that the seller should deliver to the buyer's premises, and the assignee lived or had a place of business a substantial distance from the assignor's place of business, the assignment would not be given effect. In this case, the seller would be required to give a different performance by providing greater transportation if the assignment were permitted.

(b) PERSONAL SATISFACTION. A similar problem arises when the goods to be furnished must be satisfactory to the personal judgment of the buyer. Since the seller only contracted that the performance would stand or fall according to the buyer's judgment, the buyer may not substitute the personal judgment of an assignee.

(c) PERSONAL SERVICES. An employer cannot assign to another the employer's right to have an employee work. The relationship of employer and employee is so personal that the right cannot be assigned. The performance contracted by the employee was to work for a particular employer at a particular place and at a particular job. To permit an assignee to claim the employee's services would be to change that contract.

(d) CREDIT TRANSACTION. When a transaction is based on extending credit, the person to whom credit is extended cannot assign any rights under the contract to another. For example, when land is sold on credit, the buyer cannot assign the contract unless the seller consents thereto. The making of an assignment is here prohibited because the assignee is a different credit risk. Whether the assignee is a better or worse credit risk is not considered.

§ 20:9   RIGHTS OF ASSIGNEE

An assignee stands exactly in the position of the assignor.[13] The assignee's rights are no greater nor less than those of the assignor. If the assigned right to payment is subject to a condition precedent, that same condition exists for the assignee. For example, when a contractor is not entitled to receive the balance of money due under the contract until all bills of suppliers of materials have been paid, the assignee to whom the contractor assigns the balance due under the contract is subject to the same condition and cannot obtain the money until that condition is satisfied.

§ 20:10   DELEGATION OF DUTIES

A **delegation of duties** is a transfer of duties by a contracting party to another person who is to perform them. Under certain circumstances, a contracting party may obtain someone else to do the work. When the performance is standardized and nonpersonal, so that it is not material who performs, the law will permit the delegation of the performance of the contract. In such cases, however, the contracting party remains liable for the default of the person doing the work just as though no assignment had been made.

(a) INTENTION TO DELEGATE DUTIES. In the absence of clear language in the assignment stating that duties are or are not dele-

---

[12] Decatur North Associates, Ltd. v Builders Glass, Inc. 180 Ga App 862, 350 SE2d 795 (1986).

[13] H. Freeman & Son v Henry's, Inc. 239 Kan 161, 717 P2d 1049 (1986).

gated, all circumstances must be examined to determine whether there is a delegation. When the total picture is viewed, it may become clear what was intended.

A question of interpretation arises as to whether an assignment of "the contract" is only an assignment of the rights of the as-signor or is both an assignment of those rights and a delegation of duties. The trend of authority is to regard such a general assignment as both a transfer of rights and a delegation of duties. The *Radley* case involved the effect of a blanket assignment of "the contract."

RADLEY V SMITH
6 Utah 2d 314, 313 P2d 465 (1957)

Smith, who owned the Avalon Apartments, a condominium, sold individual apartments under contracts that required each purchaser to pay $15 a month extra for hot and cold water, heat, refrigeration, taxes, and fire insurance. Smith assigned his interest in the apartment house under the various contracts to Roberts. She failed to pay the taxes on the building. Radley and other purchasers sued Smith and Roberts to compel them to pay the taxes. The action was dropped as to Smith. From a judgment against Roberts, she appealed.

CROCKETT, J. . . . The first of defendant's contentions is that the trial court erred in finding she had assumed any of the duties and obligations arising under the contracts between Smith and the plaintiffs. She maintains that in purchasing Smith's interest she was acquiring only the right to collect payments from the plaintiffs and that she had no intention of assuming the burdens of the contracts. While it is no doubt possible for a party to become the assignee of the rights under a contract without becoming responsible for the duties, the question whether a purported assignment of an entire contract includes such assumption depends upon its terms and the intent of the parties. Whenever uncertainty or ambiguity exists with respect thereto, it is proper for the court to consider all the facts and circumstances, including the words and actions of the parties forming the background of the transaction. . . .

It appears that the defendant had available Smith's contracts which set forth the corresponding rights and duties of the parties, and expressly stated that the provisions would bind the "successors and assigns." She, therefore, knew of the services required of the seller and in fact initially accepted and performed those responsibilities, and further, accepted the $15 per month which the contract recited was to pay for them, and for the payments of taxes. Applicable to this situation is the rule of construction stated in §164 (1) of the Restatement of Contracts:

> Where a party to a bilateral contract, which is at the time wholly or partially executory on both sides, purports to assign the whole contract, his action is interpreted, in the absence of circumstances showing a contrary intention, as an assignment of the assignor's rights under the contract and a delegation of the performance of assignor's duties.

There is nothing in this case to affirmatively indicate anything other than that defendant was to assume the responsiblities of the seller under the contracts and the trial court's finding with respect to that issue must therefore be affirmed. . . .

[Judgment affirmed]

QUESTIONS

1. Was the intention of Roberts important in determining whether duties had been delegated to her?
2. Was it reasonable to believe the statement of Roberts that she did not intend to take over the performance of the duties?
3. What is the view of the Restatement of Contracts with respect to the assignment of a "contract"?

(b) DELEGATION OF DUTIES UNDER THE UCC. With respect to contracts for the sale of goods, "an assignment of 'the contract' or of 'all my rights under the contract' or an assignment in similar general terms is an assignment of rights and unless the language or the circumstances (as in an assignment for security) indicate the contrary, it is a delegation of performance of the duties of the assignor and its acceptance by the assignee constitutes a promise . . . to perform those duties. This promise is enforceable by either the assignor or the other party to the original contract."[14]

§ 20:11   CONTINUING LIABILITY OF ASSIGNOR

The making of an assignment does not relieve the assignor of any obligation of the contract. In the absence of a contrary agreement, an assignor continues to be

---

[14]   UCC § 2-210(4).

---

bound by the obligations of the original contract. Thus, the fact that a buyer assigns the right to goods under a contract does not terminate the buyer's liability to make payment to the seller. Likewise, when an independent contractor is hired to perform a party's obligations under a contract, that party is liable if the independent contractor does not properly perform the contract.

§ 20:12   LIABILITY OF ASSIGNEE

It is necessary to distinguish between the question of whether the obligor can assert a particular defense against the assignee and the question of whether any person can sue the assignee for failing to perform the contract.

Ordinarily the assignee is not subject to suit by virtue of the fact that the assignment has been made. In the *Cuchine* case the buyer of a truck claimed that the dealer's assignee was liable for defects in the truck.

CUCHINE v H. O. BELL, INC.
—— Mont ——, 682 P2d 723 (1984)

Cuchine purchased a pickup truck from H. O. Bell, Inc. The sale was made as a credit installment sale. Bell assigned the contract to the Ford Motor Credit Co. Cuchine brought the truck back to Bell for repairs. When it became apparent that the truck could not be repaired, Cuchine sued Bell and Ford. As to Ford, he claimed that by taking the assignment, Ford guaranteed that the truck would perform properly. Ford asserted that it was not liable for the truck because it was merely an assignee of the right to collect the money from Cuchine and was not a guarantor of the truck. Judgment was entered in favor of Ford, and Cuchine appealed.

SHEEHY, J. . . . Cuchine contends that the credit company assumed full contract liability when the assignment was accepted. Cuchine further contends that the credit company could not avoid this liability during the pendency of the action by reassigning the contract to H. O. Bell. Cuchine predicates the credit company's liability under the contract upon the following language which appears in the contract in bold, capital letters:

> NOTICE — ANY HOLDER OF THIS CONSUMER CREDIT CONTRACT IS SUBJECT TO ALL CLAIMS AND DEFENSES WHICH THE DEBTOR COULD ASSERT AGAINST THE SELLER OF GOODS OR SERVICES OBTAINED PURSUANT HERETO OR WITH THE PROCEEDS HEREOF. RECOVERY HEREUNDER BY THE DEBTOR SHALL NOT EXCEED AMOUNTS PAID BY THE DEBTOR HEREUNDER.

This language is consistent with section 9-318 of the Uniform Commercial Code, adopted in Montana as section 30-9-318. MCA. That section reads in pertinent part.

> Unless an account debtor has made an enforceable agreement not to assert defenses or claims arising out of a sale as provided in 30-9-206, the rights of an assignee are subject to:
> (a) all the terms of the contract between the account debtor and assignor and any defense or claim arising therefrom; . . .

At common law, it is a well established rule that a party to a contract cannot relieve himself of the obligations which the contract imposed upon him merely by assigning the contract to a third person. Therefore, we must determine whether, under the Uniform Commercial Code, the assignment of the contract to the credit company imposed full contract liability on the credit company as assignee.

The case law as to the effect of section 9-318 of the UCC on the liabilities of an assignee of contract rights is scant, but conclusive. In *Michelin Tires v. First National Bank of Boston* (1st Cir. 1981), 666 F.2d 673, the court examined section 9-318 and determined that:

> The key statutory language is ambiguous. That 'the rights of an assignee are *subject to* . . . (a) all the terms of the contract' connotes only that the assignee's rights to recover are limited by the obligor's rights to assert contractual defenses as a set-off, implying that affirmative recovery against the assignee is not intended.

The court also noted that:

> The words 'subject to,' used in their ordinary sense, mean 'subordinate to,' 'subservient to,' or 'limited by.' There is nothing in the use of the words 'subject to,' in their ordinary use, which would even hint at the creation of affirmative rights.

Such a conclusion is buttressed by the official comment to section 9-318. Official Comment 1 provides in pertinent part:

Subsection (1) makes no substantial change in prior law. An assignee has traditionally been subject to defenses or set-offs existing before an account debtor is notified of the assignment.

Under prior law, the assignee of a contract was generally not held liable for the assignor's breach of contract. . . . This rule has been carried into current law as well; where it is not clearly shown that the assignee under a contract expressly or impliedly assumed the assignor's liability under the contract the assignee is not subject to the contract liability imposed by the contract on the assignor.

We believe that the intent of section 9-318 of the Uniform Commercial Code and section 30-9-318, MCA, was to allow an account debtor to assert contractual defenses as a set-off; the provisions were not intended, generally, to place the assignee of a contract in the position of being held a guarantor of a product in place of the assignor. . . .

[Judgment affirmed]

QUESTIONS

1. What is the effect of the notice set forth in the first paragraph of the opinion?
2. Why is the assignee of a right not subject to the duties of the assignor?
3. Does the court recognize any exception to the rule of nonliability of the assignee?

(a) CONSUMER PROTECTION LIABILITY OF ASSIGNEE. The assignee of a right to money typically has no relationship to the original debtor except with respect to receiving payments or collecting. Consumer protection laws, however, may subject the assignee to liability for the misconduct of the assignor. When the circumstances are such that the debtor could recover the money paid to the assignor, the debtor may recover that amount from the assignee by virtue of the Federal Trade Commission Regulation preserving consumer defenses.[15]

Some state statutes go beyond this and declare that the assignee must pay the debtor the same penalties that the seller-assignor would have been required to pay under a consumer protection law.[16]

(b) DEFENSES AND SETOFFS. The assignee's rights are no greater than those of the assignor. If the obligor could successfully defend against a suit brought by the assignor, the obligor will also prevail against the assignee. The fact that the assignee has given value for the assignment does not give the assignee any immunity from defenses that the other party, the obligor, could have asserted against the assignor. The rights acquired by the assignee remain subject to any limitations imposed by the contract.

Modern contract forms commonly provide that the debtor waives or will not assert against an assignee of the contract exemptions and defenses that could have been raised against the assignor. Such waivers are generally valid, although consumer protection statutes often prohibit them. Some statutes take a modified position and permit barring a buyer if, when notified of the assignment, the buyer fails to inform the assignee of the defense against the seller.

[15] See § 8:13.
[16] Home Savings Ass'n. v Guerra (Tex App) 720 SW2d 636 (1986).

Assignments of contracts are generally made to raise money. For example, an automobile dealer assigns a customer's credit contract to a finance company and receives cash for it. Sometimes assignments are made when an enterprise closes down and transfers its business to a new owner. The availability of defenses and setoffs is the same for both cases.

§ 20:13 NOTICE OF ASSIGNMENT

An assignment, if otherwise valid, takes effect the moment it is made. It is not necessary that the assignee or the assignor give notice to the other party to the contract that the assignment has been made.

It is highly desirable, however, that the other party be notified as soon as possible after the making of the assignment. The notice must identify the particular claim against the defendant.

(a) PRIORITY. If a person assigns the same right to two different assignees, the question arises as to which assignee has obtained the right. By the American rule, the assignee taking the first assignment prevails over the subsequent assignees.

(b) EFFECT ON DEFENSES AND SETOFFS. Notice of an assignment prevents the obligor from asserting against the assignee any matter not related to the assigned claim that arose after such notice.

(c) DISCHARGE. If the obligor is notified that there has been an assignment and that any money due must be paid to the assignee, the obligor's obligation can only be discharged by making payment to the assignee. Before the obligor knows of an assignment and before being notified that payment must be made to the assignee, any payment made by the obligor to the assignor reduces or cancels the debt, even though as between the assignor and the assignee it is the assignee who is entitled to the money. The only remedy of the assignee is to sue the assignor to recover the payments that were made by the obligor.

If the obligor both knows of the assignment and has been notified to make future payments to the assignee, any payment made by the obligor to the assignor has no effect and does not reduce or discharge the debt of the obligor.

In the *First Trust and Savings* case, the obligor on the assigned claim continued to make payments to the assignor after learning of the assignment. The assignee claimed that such payments did not discharge the obligor's liability.

FIRST TRUST AND SAVINGS BANK V SKOKIE SAVINGS AND LOAN ASS'N

126 Ill App 3d 432, 81 Ill Dec 246, 466 NE2d 1048 (1984)

Skokie Federal Savings and Loan Association made an agreement to lend money in installments to Spanish Court II for construction of a condominium. Spanish Court borrowed additional money from First Trust and Savings Bank and assigned to it the right to receive payments from Skokie. The assignment also authorized Skokie to make payments directly to First Trust. Skokie was given a copy of the assignment and authorization but continued to make payments directly to Spanish Court. Two and one-half years later, by which time all the money had been paid by Skokie to Spanish Court, First Trust sued Skokie claiming that it was liable for payments made to Spanish Court after Skokie had notice of the assignment made to First Trust. From a judgment for Skokie, First Trust appealed.

McGLOON, J. . . . In October, 1978, Skokie Federal loaned Spanish Court II, Ltd. (Spanish Court) $2,400,000 to finance the construction of a 32-unit condominium in Highland Park, Illinois. Under the terms of the construction loan agreement, proceeds for the payment of "profit and overhead expenses" were to be disbursed to Spanish Court as various phases of the project were completed. An additional $100,000, needed to purchase labor and materials to commence construction, was obtained from First Trust. This loan was secured by the collateral assignment of the construction loan proceeds that Spanish Court was to receive from Skokie Federal. The language contained in the agreement read as follows:

> For value received, I hereby sell, assign, transfer and set unto The First Trust and Savings Bank, Glenview and Robert L. Munzer, their successors and assigns all rights to profit and overhead from a certain construction loan granted to Spanish Court II, Ltd. by Skokie Federal Savings and Loan Association per their Loan Commitment and Construction Loan Agreement dated October 16, 1978 attached hereto as Exhibit "A" and made a part hereof and General Contractor's sworn statement attached hereto as Exhibit "B" and made a part hereof.
>
> Said Assignment is made to secure a loan in the amount of $100,000.00 to Spanish Court II, Ltd., which will be used for the start-up costs (labor and materials) prior to the opening of Skokie Federal Savings and Loan Association's Construction Loan.
>
> I hereby authorize Skokie Federal Savings and Loan Association to direct Pioneer National Title Insurance Company as Construction Payout Agent to make all payouts for profit and overhead payable to The First Trust and Savings Bank and Robert L. Munzer.

The assignment was accepted by First Trust and acknowledged by Skokie Federal on October 23, 1978. Between October, 1978 and May, 1981, First Trust did not receive any payments of profit and overhead. Although the owner of Spanish Court, Louis Frappier, occasionally discussed the $100,000 loan with a loan officer at First Trust, Stephen Miles, he never disclosed that Spanish Court was receiving disbursements of construction loan proceeds from Skokie Federal. On May 15, 1981, the final installment of the construction loan proceeds was made to Spanish Court. Thereafter, First Trust made a demand upon Skokie Federal for payment of the construction loan proceeds due under the assignment. Skokie Federal rejected the demand.

First Trust filed an action for declaratory judgment urging the court to determine that Skokie Federal had wrongfully paid funds directly to Spanish Court in derogation of First Trust's rights under the assignment. Thereafter, a motion for summary judgment was filed by Skokie Federal. After a hearing, the trial court granted summary judgment in favor of Skokie Federal based upon its finding that Skokie Federal did not receive an explicit direction to pay First Trust the assigned proceeds.

The sole issue presented for our determination is whether Skokie Federal, as the debtor of an account that had been assigned to First Trust, received sufficient notification that future payments should be made to the assignee to render it liable for continuing to disburse construction loan proceeds directly to Spanish Court.

Section 9-318(3) of the Uniform Commercial Code governs the situation in which a creditor has assigned its right to receive payments to another party. . . . That section provides:

The account debtor is authorized to pay the assignor until the account debtor receives notification that the amount due or to become due has been assigned and that payment is to be made to the assignee. A notification which does not reasonably identify the rights assigned is ineffective. If requested by the account debtor, the assignee must seasonably furnish reasonable proof that the assignment has been made and unless he does so the account debtor may pay the assignor.

Section 9-318(3) has been interpreted as an express authorization for an account debtor to make payments to an assignor until the account debtor receives notification that the right to receive payments has been assigned and that the future payments are to be made to the assignee. Uniform Commercial Code Comment to section 9-318 further indicates that an account debtor may continue to pay the assignor even though the account debtor has knowledge of the assignment. The Illinois cases which rely on section 9-318(3) of the Code hold that enforcement of an assignee's rights under the assignment requires *both* notification of the assignment and a demand that future payments be made to the assignee. This holding is in accord with the plain language of the statute as clarified by Uniform Commercial Code Comment to section 9-318(3).

In the instant case, the assignment does not contain an explicit demand for Skokie Federal to make future disbursements of its construction loan proceeds to First Trust. The relevant language, which we have quoted above, merely "authorizes" Skokie Federal to direct the payout agent to make the disbursements to First Trust. Our review of the record supports the trial court's conclusion that, although Skokie Federal received notice of the existence of the assignment, it did not receive a demand that payments were to be made to First Trust. The uncontradicted affidavit of Steven Munson, an officer of Skokie Federal, states that Skokie Federal received no notification to pay any amount due under the assignment until after Skokie Federal made its final payment to Spanish Court.

Here . . . the trial court's conclusion that the assignment itself was not intended as a demand for payment directly to First Trust is fortified by the fact that First Trust acquiesced for so long in the payments to the assignor. . . . First Trust's failure in the present case to investigate whether and to whom payments were being made for over a 2 1/2 year period constituted a lack of common prudence. . . . Accordingly, we hold that First Trust, by its failure to demand direct payments, waived its rights to impose liability upon Skokie Federal.

[Judgment affirmed]

QUESTIONS

1. Was it not wrong for Skokie to pay Spanish Court when it knew that the money had been assigned to First Trust?
2. What remedy was available to First Trust?
3. Why was it important for the assignment agreement to authorize Skokie to pay First Trust?
4. What was the basis for the court's decision?

The Uniform Consumer Credit Code restates the protection of the consumer-debtor making payment to the assignor without knowledge of the assignment and imposes a penalty for using a contract term that would destroy this protection of the consumer.

§ 20:14   WARRANTIES OF ASSIGNOR

When the assignment is made for a consideration, the assignor is regarded as impliedly warranting that the right assigned is valid, that the assignor is the owner of the claim or right assigned, and that the assignor will not interfere with the assignee's enforcement of the obligation. The assignor does not warrant that the other party will pay or perform as required by the contract.

SUMMARY

Ordinarily only the parties to contracts have rights and duties with respect to such contracts. Exceptions are made in the case of third party beneficiary contracts and assignments.

When a contract shows a clear intent to benefit a third person or class of persons, those persons are called third party beneficiaries, and they may sue for breach of the contract. A third party beneficiary is subject to any limitation or restriction found in the contract and loses all rights when the original contract is terminated by operation of law or the contract reserves the right to change beneficiaries and such a change is made. In contrast with a third party beneficiary, is the incidental beneficiary who benefits from the performance of the contract but the conferring of this benefit was not intended by the contracting parties. An incidental beneficiary cannot sue on the contract.

An assignment is a transfer of a right by which the assignor transfers a right to the assignee. In the absence of local statute, there are no formal requirements for an assignment. Any words manifesting the intent to transfer are sufficient to constitute an assignment. No consideration is required. Any right to money may be assigned, whether the assignor is entitled to the money at the time of the assignment or will be entitled or expects to be entitled at some time in the future. A contract term prohibiting the assignment of a right to money is invalid and does not prevent the making of an assignment. The right to make an assignment of money may be prohibited by statute, as in the case of contracts involving the construction of public works.

A right to a performance may also be assigned except when it would increase the burden of performance, when performance under the contract is to be measured by the personal satisfaction of the obligee, or when it involves the performance of personal services or the credit of the person entitled to the performance.

When a valid assignment is made, the assignee has the same rights — and only the same rights — as the assignor and is subject to the same defenses and setoffs as the assignor had been.

The performance of duties under a contract may be delegated to another person, except when a personal element of skill or judgment of the original contracting party is involved. The intent to delegate duties may be expressly stated. The intent may also be found in an "assignment" of "the contract," unless the circumstances make it clear that only the right to money was intended to be transferred, as when an automobile dealer assigns "the contract" of the buyer to a finance company. The fact that there has been a delegation of duties does not release the assignor from responsibility for performance, and the assignor is liable for breach of the contract if the assignee does not properly perform the delegated duties. In the absence of an effective delegation or the formation of a third party beneficiary contract, an assignee of rights is not liable to the obligee of the contract for its performance by the assignor. Notice is not required to effect an assignment, but it has importance in determining the priority between competing assignees of the same rights, and in terminating the ability of the obligor to assert defenses and setoffs not related to the assigned right. When notice of the assign-

ment is given to the assignee together with a demand that future payments be made to the assignee, the obligor cannot discharge liability by payment to the assignor.

When an assignment is made for a consideration, the assignor makes implied warranties that the right assigned is valid, and that the assignor owns that right and will not interfere with its enforcement by the obligee. The assignor does not warrant that the obligor on the assigned right will perform the obligation of the contract.

QUESTIONS AND CASE PROBLEMS

1. What social forces are affected by allowing an obligee to assign the right to obtain payment?
2. Give an example of a third party beneficiary contract.
3. Gilbert Chapman owes Jeanette Sandburg $100. Jeanette gets a job in another city and cannot wait to collect the money from Gilbert. Jeanette gives Barton Wilkins a letter stating: "To Barton Wilkins: I hereby give you the right to the $100 owed to me by Gilbert Chapman. (signed) Jeanette Sandburg." Barton shows this letter to Gilbert and requests that Gilbert make payment of the money. Gilbert refuses to do so on the ground that a letter cannot operate as an assignment because it is not sealed and is not sworn to before a notary public. Are these objections valid?
4. Lee contracts to paint Sally's two-story house for $1,000. Sally realizes that she will not have sufficient money so she transfers her rights under this agreement to her neighbor Karen who has a three-story house. Karen notifies Lee that Sally's contract has been assigned to her and demands that Lee paint Karen's house for $1,000. Is Lee required to do so?
5. Assume that Lee agrees to the assignment of the house-painting contract to Karen as stated in Question 4. Thereafter Lee fails to perform the contract to paint Karen's house. Karen sues Sally for damages. Is Sally liable?
6. Jessie borrows $1,000 from Thomas and agrees to repay the money in thirty days. Thomas assigns the right to the $1,000 to the Douglas Finance Company. Douglas sues

Jessie. Jessie raises the defense that she had only agreed to pay the money to Thomas and that when she and Thomas had entered into the transaction there was no intention to benefit the Douglas Finance Company. Are these objections valid?
7. Classify the following as beneficiaries of an accident insurance policy obtained by an employer to cover accidents of the employees:
(a) the employer,
(b) the employee,
(c) a hospital providing medical care for an injured employee, and (d) a doctor treating an injured employee for the injury after the employee is discharged from the hospital.
8. When a seller defrauds the buyer and then assigns the seller's claim for the balance due to a bank, what difference does it make if the bank in taking the assignment
(a) knew of the fraud,
(b) did not know of the fraud, or
(c) acted in good faith and paid full value for the assigned claim?
9. Lone Star Life Insurance Company agreed to make a long-term loan to Five Forty Three Land, Inc. whenever requested to do so by that corporation. Five Forty Three wanted this loan in order to pay off its short-term debts. The loan was never made as it was never requested by Five Forty Three. That corporation owed the Exchange Bank & Trust Company on a short-term debt. Exchange Bank then sued Lone Star for breach of its promise on the theory that the Exchange Bank was a third party beneficiary of the contract to make the loan. Was the Exchange Bank correct? [Exchange Bank &

Trust Co. v Loan Star Life Ins. Co. (Tex Civ App) 546 SW2d 948]

10. The New Rochelle Humane Society made a contract with the city of New Rochelle to capture and impound all dogs running at large. Spiegler, a minor, was bitten by some dogs while in the school yard. She sued the school district of New Rochelle and the Humane Society. With respect to the Humane Society, she claimed that she was a third party beneficiary of the contract that the Society had made with the City and could therefore sue it for its failure to capture the dogs by which she had been bitten. Was she entitled to recover? [Spiegler v School District, 39 Misc 2d 946, 242 NYS2d 430]

11. Helen owned a store and a home. She made separate contracts with Donna to put a new roof on each building. Payment was to be made by Helen in installments over a three-month period. When Donna finished the work she immediately assigned the store contract to the First National Bank. She did not assign the house contract because the amount involved was not large. First National promptly notified Helen of the assignment. A week later Helen notified First National that she would not pay on the assignment because both the store roof and the house roof were leaking. Can Helen assert counterclaims for the leaking of each roof?

12. An electric power company made a contract for the construction of a dam to supply water power for the generation of electricity. The dam collapsed. Customers of the power company brought suit against the contractors who had constructed the dam and various persons who had inspected it, claiming that those persons had improperly performed their duties under their contracts and that the customers of the power company were third party beneficiaries of those contracts. Were the customers of the power company entitled to bring suit on the contract made by the power company with such inspectors and contractors? [Ziegler v Blount Bros. Constr. Co. (Ala) 364 So2d 1163]

13. The Byron Chamber of Commerce hired Long, an attorney, to petition the local court to put on the next election ballot the question whether the voters wanted to set up a park district. The petition was rejected by the court because the description of the park area was not adequate. Residents and taxpayers who lived in what would be the park area brought a lawsuit against Long on the theory that he had broken a contract of which they were third party beneficiaries. They claimed that they would have received the benefit of the creation of a park district. Were they entitled to recover damages from Long? [Byron Chamber of Commerce, Inc. v Long, 92 Ill App 3d 364, 48 Ill Dec 77, 415 NE2d 1361]

14. Brooks made a contract with Hayes by which he agreed to construct a house for Brooks. Hayes made a contract with Marr to do the masonry work. The masonry work was defective. Brooks sued Hayes for the damages. Hayes raised the defense that the work had been delegated to Marr and therefore was not Hayes' fault. Is this a valid defense? [Brooks v Hayes, 133 Wis 2d 228, 395 NW2d 167]

15. Ralph Gilmore was an employee of Stevens Air Systems. Stevens contracted with Health Care Services (HCS) to provide health care for its employees. In order to enable it to make payments for major catastrophic expenses, HCS contracted with Omaha Indemnity to reimburse it for major medical expenses paid by HCS to employees of Stevens. While employed at Stevens, Gilmore had a heart attack and underwent open heart surgery. Stevens claimed that Omaha was required to pay a share of his medical bills. Omaha refused to make payment on the ground that its only obligation was to HCS. Gilmore sued Omaha. Was he entitled to recover? [Gilmore v Omaha Indemnity, 96 Cal App 3d 750, 158 Cal Rptr 229]

21

DISCHARGE OF CONTRACTS

In the preceding chapters you have studied how a contract is formed, what it means, and who has rights under a contract. In this chapter, attention is turned to how a contract is ended or discharged.

A. DISCHARGE BY PERFORMANCE

When it is claimed that a contract is discharged by performance, questions arise as to the nature, time, and sufficiency of the performance.

§ 21:1 THE NORMAL DISCHARGE OF CONTRACTS

A contract is usually discharged by the performance of the terms of the agreement. In most cases, the parties perform their promises and the contract ceases to exist or is thereby discharged.

§ 21:2 NATURE OF PERFORMANCE

Performance may be the doing of an act or the making of payment.

(a) TENDER. An offer to perform is known as a **tender**. If performance of the

440

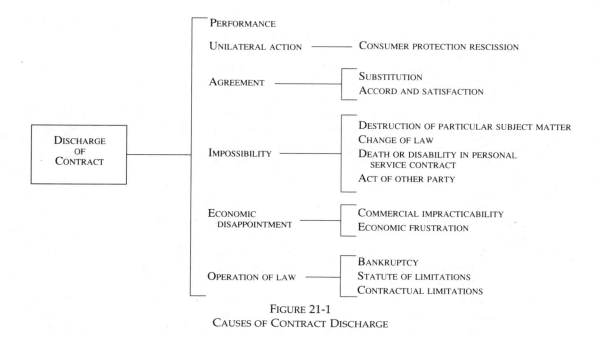

FIGURE 21-1
CAUSES OF CONTRACT DISCHARGE

contract requires the doing of an act, a tender that is refused will discharge the party offering to perform. If performance requires the payment of a debt, however, a tender that is refused does not discharge the debt. It does stop the running of interest and does prevent the collection of court costs if the party is sued, providing the tender is kept open and the money is produced in court.

A valid **tender of payment** consists of an unconditional offer of the exact amount due on the date when due or an amount from which the creditor may take what is due without the necessity of making change. The debtor must offer **legal tender** or, in other words, such form of money as the law recognizes as lawful money and declares to be legal tender for the payment of debts. The offer of a check is not a valid tender of payment, as a check is not legal tender even when it is certified. A tender of part of the debt is not a valid tender. In addition to the amount owed, the debtor must tender all accrued interest and any costs to which the creditor is entitled. If the debtor tenders less than the amount due, the creditor may refuse the offer without

affecting the right to collect the amount that is due. If the creditor accepts the smaller amount, the question arises whether it has been accepted as payment on account or as full payment of the balance that was due.

(b) PAYMENT. When payment is required by the contract, performance consists of the payment of money or, if accepted by the other party, the delivery of property or the rendering of services.

(1) Application of Payments. If a debtor owes more than one debt to the creditor and pays money, a question may arise as to which debt has been paid. If the debtor specifies the debt to which the payment is to be applied and the creditor accepts the money, the creditor is bound to apply the money as specified. Thus, if the debtor specifies that a payment is to be made for a current purchase, the creditor may not apply the payment to an older balance.

If the debtor does not specify the application to be made, the creditor has the choice of deciding to which debt the payment should be applied. As between secured and unsecured claims, the creditor is free to apply the payment to the unsecured claim. The creditor, however, must apply the payment to a debt that is due as contrasted with one that is not yet due. The creditor cannot apply a payment to a claim that is illegal or invalid, but may apply the payment to a claim that cannot be enforced because it is barred by the statute of limitations. According to some authorities, the creditor may also apply the payment to a claim that cannot be enforced for lack of a writing required by the statute of frauds.

(2) No Application Specified. If neither the debtor nor the creditor has specified any application of the payment, application will be made by the court. There is a division of authority, however, whether the court is to make such application as will be more favorable to the creditor or the debtor.[1] Consumer protection statutes commonly require application to the oldest debt.

(3) Payment by Check. Payment by commercial paper, such as a check, is ordinarily a conditional payment. A check merely suspends the debt until the check is presented for payment.[2] If payment is then made, the debt is discharged; if not paid, the suspension terminates and suit may be brought on either the debt or the check. Frequently payment must be made by a specified date. It is generally held that the payment is made on time if it is mailed on or before the final date for payment.

§ 21:3   TIME OF PERFORMANCE

When the date or period of time for performance is specified in the contract, performance should be made on that date or within that time period.

(a) No TIME SPECIFIED. When the time for performance is not specified in the contract, an obligation to perform within a reasonable time will be implied. The fact that no time is stated does not impair the contract on the ground that it is indefinite, nor

does it allow an endless time in which to perform.

(b) WHEN TIME IS ESSENTIAL. If performance of the contract on or within the exact time specified is vital, it is said that "time is of the essence." Time is of the essence when the contract relates to property that is perishable or that is fluctuating rapidly in value.

An express statement in the contract that time is of the essence may not be controlling. When it is obvious that time is not important, such a statement will be ignored by the courts. It is the nature of the subject matter of the contract and the surrounding circumstances, rather than the declaration of the parties, that control.

(c) WHEN TIME IS NOT ESSENTIAL. Ordinarily, time is not of the essence, and performance within a reasonable time is sufficient. In the case of the sale of property, time will not be regarded as of the essence when there has not been any appreciable change in the market value or condition of the property and when the person who delayed does not appear to have done so for the purpose of speculating on a change in market price.

§ 21:4   ADEQUACY OF PERFORMANCE

When a party renders exactly the performance called for by the contract, no question arises as to whether the contract has been performed. In other cases, there may not have been a perfect performance or a question arises as to whether the performance made satisfies the standard set by the contract.

(a) SUBSTANTIAL PERFORMANCE. Perfect performance of a contract is not required. A party who in good faith has substantially performed the contract may sue to recover the payment specified in the contract. However, because the performance was not perfect, the performing party is subject to a counterclaim for the damages caused the other party. When a building contrac-

---

[1]   Carter's Insurance Agency, Inc. v Franklin (La App) 428 So 2d 808 (1983) (favoring debtor).
[2]   Uniform Commercial Code § 3–802(1)(b).

tor has substantially performed the contract to construct a building, the measure of damages is the cost of repairing or correcting the defects if that can be done at a reasonable cost.[3] If, however, the cost would be unreasonably disproportionate to the importance of the defect, as when a virtual rebuilding of the finished building would be required to make a minor correction, the measure of damages is the difference between the value of the building as completed and the value that the building would have had if the contract had been performed perfectly.

This rule of **substantial performance** applies only when departures from the contract or the defects were not made willfully. A contractor who willfully makes a substantial departure from the contract is in default and cannot recover any payment from the other party to the contract. In large construction contracts when the total value of the partial performance is large compared to the damages sustained through incomplete or imperfect performance, the courts tend to ignore whether or not the breach was intentional on the part of the contractor.

A performance cannot be regarded as substantial if what has been done is of no use to the defendant. Thus, when a contractor failed to follow specifications for the construction of a swimming pool and the result was a pool that was so cracked that it would not hold water, the work of the contractor was not of any use to the other party. Therefore the contractor could not recover on the ground of substantial performance.[4]

The doctrine of substantial performance does not apply to a condition precedent. Consequently, a lender, obligated to lend a specified amount for the purchase and renovation of an office building, was excused from making such loan when the duty to lend was subject to a condition precedent that a specific number of office space leases had to be signed, but the required number was not obtained. The claim of the borrower that the substantial performance rule should be applied to hold that there was a sufficient compliance with the rental condition was defeated.

(b) SATISFACTION OF PROMISEE OR THIRD PERSON. When the agreement requires that the promisor perform an act to the satisfaction, taste, or judgment of the other party on the contract, the courts are divided as to whether the promisor must so perform the contract as to satisfy the promisee or whether it is sufficient that the performance be such as would satisfy a reasonable person under the circumstances. When personal taste is an important element, the courts generally hold that the performance is not sufficient unless the promisee is actually satisfied, although in some instances it is insisted that the dissatisfaction be shown to be in good faith and not merely to avoid paying for the work that has been done. The personal satisfaction of the promisee is generally required under this rule when one promises to make clothes or to paint a portrait to the satisfaction of the other party.

There is a similar division of authority when the subject matter involves the fitness or mechanical utility of property. With respect to things mechanical and to routine performances, however, the courts are more likely to hold that the promisor has satisfactorily performed if a reasonable person should be satisfied with what was done.

When a building contract requires the contractor to perform the contract to the "satisfaction" of the owner, the owner generally is required to pay if a reasonable person would be satisfied with the work of the contractor.

When performance is to be approved by a third person, the tendency is to apply the reasonable-person test of satisfaction, es-

[3] Shaddock v Storm King Window Co. (Tex App) 696 SW2d 271 (1985).
[4] Levan v Richter, 152 I11 App 3d 1082, 105 I11 Dec 855, 504 NE2d 1373 (1987).

pecially when the third person has wrongfully withheld approval or has become incapacitated.

When work is to be done subject to the approval of an architect, engineer, or other expert, the determination of that expert is ordinarily final and binding upon the parties in the absence of fraud.

The *Forman* case raised the question whether a seller should have been satisfied with the report as to the buyer's credit.

FORMAN V BENSON
112 Ill App 3d 1070, 68 Ill Dec 629, 446 NE2d 535 (1983)

Art Benson owned a tract of land. Eric Forman wanted to buy the land and to pay for it in ten annual installments. Benson was at first unwilling to extend such long credit but agreed to do so if the buyer agreed to include in the contract a provision "subject to the seller's approving buyer's credit report." The buyer agreed to this, and the provision was included in the contract. When the credit report was given to Benson, he stated that it "looked real good" and that he would give it to his attorney to examine. Thereafter Benson tried to get Forman to pay more for the land than stated in the contract. Forman refused to agree to the higher price. Benson then stated that he did not approve the credit report because Forman's liabilities were slightly more than four times his liquid assets. Forman sued to enforce the contract. From a decision in Forman's favor, Benson appealed.

HOPF, J. . . . We have discovered no case dealing with the interpretation of the specific clause in question. However, there is some Illinois case law regarding the interpretation of "satisfaction" clauses in general. In *Reeves & Co. v. Chandler* (1903), 113 Ill. App. 167, 170, the court found that satisfaction clauses generally fall into one of two classes. In one class, the decision as to whether a party is satisfied is completely reserved to the party for whose benefit the clause is inserted, and the reasons for his decision may not be inquired into and overhauled by either the other party or the courts. Cases falling into this class generally involve matters which are dependent upon the feelings, taste, or judgment of the party making the decision. The second class of cases are those in which the party to be satisfied is to base his determination on grounds which are just and reasonable. These cases generally involve matters which are capable of objective evaluation, or which involve considerations of operative fitness or mechanical utility. Matters of financial concern generally fall into this second category of cases. The adequacy of the grounds of a determination in this class are open to judicial scrutiny and are judged by a reasonable man standard.

However, the *Reeves* case also made it clear that the parties may agree to a reservation in one party of the absolute and unqualified freedom of choice on a matter not involving fancy, taste, or whim.

It sometimes happens that the right is fully reserved where it is the chief ground, if not the only one, that the party is determined to reserve an unqualified option, and is not willing to leave his freedom of choice exposed to any contention or subject to any contingency. He will not enter into any bargain except upon the condition of reserving the power to do what others might regard as unreasonable.

Applying this reasoning, the court in *Reeves* found that a satisfaction clause regarding certain machinery — a matter which would normally be capable of objective evaluation — was intended to allow the purchaser of the machinery to exercise his judgment in accepting or rejecting the machinery:

> It is apparent from the grammatical construction and arrangement of the clause in question that the words 'and satisfactory' were added thereto after the preceding portion was written and as a concession to defendant in error. It may be reasonably inferred that he was determined that no opportunity should be given plaintiff in error to force the outfit upon him if he finally concluded not to take it. The words referred to were undoubtedly added to the clause at his request or suggestion and for the purpose of inducing him to sign the order.

Thus, it is apparent that under *Reeves* the fact that the clause was added as a concession or inducement to one of the parties is significant in determining whether the reasonableness standard should be applied. . . .

It seems clear from the foregoing cases that a reasonableness standard is favored by the law when the contract concerns matters capable of objective evaluation. However, where the circumstances are such that it is clear the provision was added as a personal concession to one of the contracting parties, the subjective, rather than the objective standard, should be applied.

In the present case, it is uncontroverted that the clause in question was inserted as a concession to the defendant and as an inducement to him to sign the contract, which he subsequently did. Ken Burnell testified that the addition of the provision indeed eased defendant's mind about the plaintiff's credit worthiness. In light of the fact that the relationship between the parties was to endure over a ten-year period of time, we think it is a reasonable construction of the provision that it was intended to allow defendant the freedom of making a personal and subjective evaluation of plaintiff's credit worthiness. We, therefore, conclude that the trial court erred in applying a reasonableness standard to the instant case.

The personal judgment standard, however, does not allow the defendant to exercise unbridled discretion in rejecting plaintiff's credit, but rather is subject to the requirement of good faith. . . . In the instant case the trial court made no specific finding whether defendant Benson rejected plaintiff's credit in good faith. However, the trial court did find that between the time the contract was executed and the time the offer was rejected, defendant attempted to renegotiate the purchase price of the building as well as the interest rate. Defendant has challenged this finding on appeal, claiming it was against the manifest weight of the evidence. We disagree. Both plaintiff and defendant testified that an increased purchase price was discussed. Thus, the trial court's finding in this regard was supported by the record and was not against the manifest weight of the evidence. Further, we hold that while defendant may have had a basis in his personal judgment for rejecting plaintiff's credit (*i.e.*, outstanding debts and a $2,000 loss reflected in an income tax return), his attempted renegotiation demonstrates that his rejection was based on reasons other than plaintiff's credit rating and was, therefore, in bad faith. . . .

[Judgment affirmed]

QUESTIONS

1. Did the contract specify that the credit report had to be satisfactory to the seller?
2. A satisfaction clause is governed by the objective standard. Comment on this statement and explain your answer.
3. What was the significance of the seller's seeking a higher price?

§ 21:5   GUARANTEE OF PERFORMANCE

It is common for an obligor to guarantee the performance. Thus, a builder may guarantee for one year that the work will be satisfactory.

The guarantee may be made by a third person. Thus, a surety company may guarantee to the owner that a contractor will perform the contract. In such case, it is clear that the obligation of the surety is in addition to the liability of the contractor and does not take the place of such liability.

B.   DISCHARGE BY ACTION OF PARTIES

Contracts may be discharged by the joint action of both contracting parties and, in some cases, by the action of one party alone.

§ 21:6   DISCHARGE BY UNILATERAL ACTION

Ordinarily, a contract cannot be discharged by the action of either party alone. In some cases, the contract will give one or either party the right to cancel the contract by unilateral action, such as by notice to the other party. If the contract does not specify any duration, or it states a duration in such vague terms as "for life," the contract may be terminated by either party at will.

(a) CONSUMER PROTECTION RESCISSION. Contrary to the basic principle of contract law that a contract between competent persons is a binding obligation, consumer protection legislation is introducing into the law a concept of giving the consumer a chance to think things over and to rescind the contract. Thus, the federal Consumer Credit Protection Act (CCPA) gives the debtor the right to rescind a credit transaction within three days when the transaction would impose a lien upon the debtor's home. A homeowner who mortgages the home to obtain a loan may cancel the transaction for any reason by notifying the lender before midnight of the third full business day after the loan is made.[5]

A Federal Trade Commission regulation gives the buyer three days in which to avoid a home-solicited sale of goods or services costing more than $25.[6]

§ 21:7 DISCHARGE BY AGREEMENT

A contract may be discharged by the operation of one of its provisions or by a subsequent agreement. Thus, there may be a discharge by (a) terms of the original contract, as a provision that the contract should end on a specified date; (b) a mutual cancellation, in which the parties agree to end their contract; (c) a mutual **rescission** in which the parties agree to undo the contract and return both parties to their original positions before the contract had

---

[5]   If the owner is not informed of this right to cancel, the three-day period does not begin until that information is given. In any case, however, the right to cancel is lost if the owner sells the house or three years elapse after the loan transaction. Consumer Credit Protection Act (CCPA) § 125, 15 USC § 1635 (a), (e), (f).

[6]   16 CFR § 429.1. This displaces state laws making similar provision for rescission, such as UCCC § 2.502.

been made; (d) substitution of a new contract between the same parties; (e) a **novation** or substitution of a new contract involving a new party;[7] (f) an accord and satisfaction; (g) a release; or (h) a waiver. Of these, the discharge by substitution and by accord and satisfaction are the more common.

(a) SUBSTITUTION. The parties may decide that their contract is not the one they want. They may then replace it with another contract. If they do so, the original contract is discharged by substitution.

It is not necessary for the parties to expressly state that they are making a substitution. Whenever they make a new contract that is clearly inconsistent with a former contract, the court will conclude that the earlier contract has been superseded by the later of the two. Since the new contract must in itself be a binding agreement, it must be supported by consideration. Any suit thereafter brought must show a breach of the second or subsequent contract.[8]

The fact that a second contract is entered into does not establish that the original contract is canceled. The later contract may merely add to or supplement the original contract or it may merely modify part of the original contract. In order for the later contract to displace the first, the later contract must show the intent of the parties to substitute the later contract for the earlier contract. This intent may be shown by an express statement in the later contract that the parties thereby cancel or set aside the earlier contract, or the later contract may be so complete and so inconsistent with the earlier writing that the intent is clear that the later writing was a substitute for the earlier one.[9]

The agreement modifying the original contract may be expressed in words or by conduct, but in any event, it is essential that an agreement to modify be found.

A written contract may be modified by a subsequent oral agreement, even though the contract itself prohibits oral modification.[10] However, the modification contract must be evidenced by a writing when the modified contract comes within the statute of frauds.

(b) ACCORD AND SATISFACTION. In lieu of the performance of an obligation specified by a contract, the parties may agree to a different performance. Such an agreement is called an **accord**. When the accord is performed or executed, there is an **accord and satisfaction,** which discharges the original obligation.[11]

The accord that is the basis for the accord and satisfaction must be a binding agreement, that is, a contract. It must therefore meet the basic requirements of a simple contract.[12] If it is not a contract, as for example, if it is not supported by consideration, there is no binding accord, and the prior contract is not discharged. The making of an accord does not by itself discharge the prior contract. It is not until the terms of the accord are carried out that there is a discharge of the earlier contract.

C.   DISCHARGE BY EXTERNAL CAUSES

Circumstances beyond the control of the contracting parties may discharge the contract.

§ 21:8   DISCHARGE BY IMPOSSIBILITY

Impossibility of performance refers to external or extrinsic conditions as contrasted with the obligor's personal inability to perform. Thus, the fact that a debtor does not

---

[7] In a few jurisdictions , the term novation is used generally to embrace the substitution of any new contract whether between the original parties or not.

[8] George Vining & Sons, Inc. v Jones (Fla App) 498 So 2d 695 (1986).

[9] Costello v Watson (App) 111 Idaho 68, 720 P2d 1033 (1986).

[10] Kern's Estate, 142 Ill App 3d 506, 96 Ill Dec 815, 491 NE2d 1275 (1986).

[11] Polin v Major, 150 Ill App 3d 988, 104 Ill Dec 122, 502 NE2d 355 (1986).

[12] Schroeder v Dy-Tronix, Inc. (Mo App) 723 SW2d 934 (1987).

have the money to pay and cannot pay a debt does not present a case of impossibility.

Riots, shortages of materials, and similar factors, even though external, usually do not excuse the promisor from performing a contract. The fact that a seller cannot obtain from any supplier the goods that the seller has already contracted to sell to the buyer does not excuse the seller from liability to the buyer, unless the inability to procure the goods was made a condition subsequent to the sales contract. Thus, the fact that the road contractor's contemplated gravel source cannot be used, and it is necessary to transport gravel from a more distant source making performance more costly, does not discharge the contractor from the obligation to construct a road. If there is nothing in the contract requiring that the gravel be obtained from the unavailable source, no question of impossibility of performance exists.

The fact that it will prove more costly to perform the contract than originally contemplated, or that the obligor has voluntarily gone out of business, does not constitute impossibility that excuses performance. No distinction is made in this connection between the acts of nature, people, or governments.

(a) DESTRUCTION OF PARTICULAR SUBJECT MATTER. When the parties contract expressly for or with reference to a particular subject matter, the contract is discharged if the subject matter is destroyed through no fault of either party. When a contract calls for the sale of a wheat crop growing on a specific parcel of land, the contract is discharged if that crop is destroyed by blight.

On the other hand, if there is merely a contract to sell a given quantity of a specified grade of wheat, the seller is not discharged when the seller's crop is destroyed by blight. The seller had made an unqualified undertaking to deliver wheat of a specified grade. No restrictions or qualifications were imposed as to the source from which the wheat would be obtained. If the seller does not deliver the goods called for by the contract, the contract is broken and the seller is liable for damages.

The parties may by their contract allocate the risk of loss. Thus, a contract for the sale of a building and land may specify that any loss from damage to the building should be borne by the seller.[13]

(b) CHANGE OF LAW. A contract is discharged when its performance is made illegal by a subsequent change in the law of the state or country in which the contract is to be performed. Thus, a contract to construct a nonfireproof building at a particular place is discharged by the adoption of a zoning law prohibiting such a building within that area. Mere inconvenience or temporary delay caused by the new law, however, does not excuse performance. Likewise, a change of law that merely increases the cost of the promisor is not a "change of law" that discharges the contract.

A change in government controls is distinguished from a change in law. In the N.C. Coastal Motor Line case a buyer refused to make payments because of the effect of government deregulation of the trucking business.

---

[13] Bryant v Willison Real Estate Co. (WVa App) 350 SE2d 748 (1986).

N.C. COASTAL MOTOR LINE, INC. V EVERETTE TRUCK LINE, INC.

77 NC App 149, 334 SE2d 499 (1985)

N.C. Coastal Motor Line was authorized by the Interstate Commerce Commission to engage in interstate trucking operations. It made a contract to sell this authority to Everette Truck Line. Payment was to be made in eight annual installments. At the time of making the contract, it was unlawful to engage in interstate trucking without such an authority. Everette made four annual payments. The trucking industry was then deregulated by the government, and the authority of the Interstate Commerce Commission was no longer required to engage in interstate trucking. Everette refused to make any more payments on the ground that what it was paying for was worthless. N.C. Coastal sued Everette. Judgment was entered for Everette, and Coastal appealed.

JOHNSON, J. . . . Everette admits the signing of the contract, validity of the contract, and the sale price, which are the essential terms of any instrument. . . . Under section nine (9) entitled, SELLER'S WARRANTIES, it states in subsection (a) "There are *no proceedings pending* which adversely affect the operating rights proposed to be transferred." (emphasis added). Everette now argues that government deregulations in 1980, three years after the contract was entered into, rendered plaintiff's operating rights worthless, and thus breaches an "express but implied warranty" of permanent economic value. We find nothing . . . which gives rise to such an implied warranty. . . . Everette's attorney drafted the terms of the agreement whereby Coastal's warranty was expressly limited to no *pending* actions or proceedings which would affect the operating rights purchased by Everette. . . . Everette contends governmental deregulation was not foreseeable and that there were representations by Coastal to the effect that the operating authority would retain permanent value. Everette's pleadings and affidavits regarding the existence of an oral warranty through representations by Coastal do not establish a material issue of fact. "The obligation arising upon a warranty is that of an undertaking or promise that the goods shall be as represented or, more specifically, a *contract of indemnity* against loss by reason of defects therein." *Prod. & Dev. Sales Co.*, at 669, 136 S.E.2d at 63. In the agreement we find a written expression of Coastal's warranty which defendant in essence is seeking to expand. "The general rule is that when a written instrument is introduced into evidence, its terms may not be contradicted by parol or extrinsic evidence, and it is presumed that all prior negotiations are merged into the written instrument." *Root v. Allstate Ins. Co.*, 272 N.C. 580, 587, 158 S.E.2d 829, 835 (1968). In the absence of allegations of fraud, mistake, duress or ambiguous terms, which Everette did not allege, any allegations of additional warranties or variation of the written agreement would not raise any issue of material fact and would be properly excludable.

Everette also raised lack of consideration as an affirmative defense. . . . At the time of purchase Coastal's operating rights were as represented, a valuable set of rights which Everette could not have otherwise acquired. Everette is without a legal defense to Coastal's claim.

[Judgment reversed and action remanded]

QUESTIONS

1. When the trucking industry was deregulated there was a change of law. What effect did that have on the contract of the parties? Explain.
2. What defenses were raised by the defendant?
3. How did the court dispose of the defenses of the defendant?

(c) DEATH OR DISABILITY. When the contract obligates a party to perform an act that requires personal skill or that contemplates a personal relationship with the obligee or some other person, the death or disability of the obligor, obligee, or other person (as the case may be) discharges the contract, as when a newspaper cartoonist dies before the expiration of the contract. If the act called for by the contract can be performed by others or by the promisor's personal representative, however, this rule does not apply.

The death of a person to whom personal services are to be rendered also terminates the contract when the death of that person makes impossible the rendition of the services contemplated. Thus, a contract to employ a person as the musical director for a singer terminates when the singer dies.

When the contract calls for the payment of money, the death of either party does not affect the obligation. If the obligor dies, the obligation is a liability of the obligor's estate. If the obligee dies, the right to collect the debt is an asset of the obligee's estate. The parties to a contract may agree, however, that the death of either the obligee or the obligor shall terminate the debt. In any case, the creditor can obtain insurance on the life of the debtor. In the *Shutt* case, it was claimed by the ex-husband that the agreement with his ex-wife to sell their home was discharged by her death.

SHUTT V BUTNER
62 NC App 701, 303 SE2d 399 (1983)

When Jean and Jerry Butner were divorced, their property settlement and divorce decree specified that when their son no longer needed their home, the home would be sold and the proceeds divided equally between Jean and Jerry. Jean died and Marie Shutt, her mother, was appointed her executrix. In a lawsuit between Shutt and Jerry, the court refused to order the sale of the home. Shutt appealed.

PHILLIPS, J. . . . The trial court erred in denying the plaintiff's motion for the sale of the marital homeplace. Though the defendant did become the *record* fee simple owner of the entirety held realty by operation of law upon the death of his wife, as the court concluded, he became so subject to his promise and agreement as follows:

(8) It is agreed that the wife shall have complete possession of the homeplace of the parties until the minor child TIMOTHY EUGENE BUTNER attains the age of 18 years or until the child respectively dies, marries, or is otherwise emancipated, at which time the homeplace of the parties will be sold and the proceeds will be divided equally among the parties. It is further agreed that the wife shall make monthly payments on the homeplace . . . and that the husband shall reimburse to the wife the amount by which her monthly mortgage payments have reduced the principal on the mortgage.

This agreement to sell their property and divide the proceeds between them, solemnly and deliberately made twice, was therefore doubly binding — first as an ordinary separation and settlement agreement, *Lane v. Scarborough*, 284 N.C. 407, 200 S.E.2d 622 (1973), and second as a consent judgment in compromise and settlement of matters that were then being disputed in this litigation. *Price v. Horn*, 30 N.C. App. 10, 226 S.E.2d 165 (1976).

Unlike the agreements involved in those cases, however, the agreement here requires little or no construction, only enforcement. The parties' obligation to sell the property and divide the proceeds was explicit and without ambiguity; nor was it contingent upon either party being alive when the time to sell came or anything else. The agreement to sell and divide was absolute and unequivocal; only the time was uncertain and that was clearly ascertainable from the terms used — no later than the boy's eighteenth birthday, then less than two years away, and sooner than that if the boy married, was otherwise emancipated, died, or stopped living there. Though the latter eventuality was not expressly provided for in the agreement as the others were, it is impliable from the obvious fact that the parties delayed the sale as they did only so that the boy could dwell there rent-free until his legally dependent status ended. Therefore, upon him ceasing to live there after his mother died, the reason for delaying the sale vanished, and the parties were obligated to go ahead with the sale if either so requested. That this is so, however, need not be demonstrated or even relied upon, since the son's eighteenth birthday has passed, and the property must be sold now in any event.

Nor were the defendant's obligations under the contract terminated by the death of the other contracting party. Few contracts are terminated by death in the absence of explicit provisions therein to the contrary. This is because all know that unexpected and untimely death is a constant possibility and are deemed to make their contracts in light thereof, and also because most contracts can be satisfactorily performed by personal representatives. The general rule is that "contracts bind the executor or administrator, though not named therein, and that death does not absolve a man from his engagements." *Burch v. Bush,* 181 N.C. 125, 106 S.E. 489 (1921). But in this instance it is unnecessary to resort to the general rule, because the parties themselves, leaving nothing to chance or the law's operation, had their agreement to provide that:

> . . . this Judgment shall be enforceable against the parties, their personal representatives, heirs and assigns.

Having so contracted, the defendant is bound thereby.

It is true, of course, for obvious reasons, that contracts of a personal nature or that require special talent — to marry, to draw a picture, write a book, perform on the stage, be one's companion, etc. — do come to an end upon the death of a party, unless the parties agree otherwise. *Burch v. Bush, supra.* But selling a house and lot and dividing the proceeds does not depend upon talent or personality and the defendant's obligation with respect thereto still abides. . . .

[Judgment reversed]

QUESTIONS

1. How did the court classify the contract to sell the house?
2. Suppose that a contract is made between a real estate agent and the owner of an apartment house complex for the agent to sell the property. The agent

dies before the sale is made. What effect does the death have on the contract?

3. As the ex-wife is no longer alive to receive one half of the proceeds from the sale of the property, the agreement to sell and divide the proceeds had failed; therefore, there was no reason to go through with the transaction. Appraise this statement and argument.

(d) ACT OF OTHER PARTY. There is in every contract "an implied covenant of good faith and fair dealing" in consequence of which a promisee is under an obligation to do nothing that would interfere with performance by the promisor. When the promisee prevents performance or otherwise makes performance impossible, the promisor is discharged from the contract. Thus, a subcontractor is discharged from any obligation when unable to do the work because the principal contractor refuses to deliver the material, equipment, or money required by the subcontract. When the default of the other party consists of failing to supply goods or services, the duty may rest upon the party claiming a discharge of the contract to show that substitute goods or services could not be obtained elsewhere, either because they were not reasonably available or were not acceptable under the terms of the contract.

When the conduct of the other contracting party does not make performance impossible but merely causes delay or renders performance more expensive or difficult, the contract is not discharged; but the injured party is entitled to damages for the loss incurred.

A promisor is not excused from performing under the contract when it is the act of the promisor that has made performance impossible. Consequently, when a data service contracted with a bank to keypunch all its daily operations and to process the cards, the bank was not excused from its obligation under the contract by the fact that it converted to magnetic tapes and installed its own computers. The bank could not ignore its contract. It could only terminate the contract with the data service by giving the notice required by the contract.

When one party is to make installment payments as work is done by the other party, the making of the payments as specified is of course the legal obligation of the person required to pay. In many instances, payment is essential to provide the other party with the funds necessary for the continuation of the work.

§ 21:9   ECONOMIC
           DISAPPOINTMENT

Some courts hold that a contract is discharged when, because of a change of circumstances, the performance of the contract has become such an economic disappointment that it would be unjust and oppressive to insist on the performance of the contract.

(a) COMMERCIAL IMPRACTICABILITY. When the cost of performance has risen suddenly and so greatly that performance of the contract will result in a substantial loss, some courts hold that the contract is discharged because it is **commercially impracticable** to perform. Although it is possible to perform, it has become such a bad bargain that the courts will not enforce it.

When future developments prove to be different than was assumed by the parties, there is a growing trend in finding that there is an impossibility that discharges the contract.[14] This doctrine is described as the doctrine of supervening impracticability:

---

[14] Landis v Hodgson (App) 109 Idaho 252, 706 P2d 1363 (1985).

Where after a contract is made, a party's performance is made impracticable without his fault by the occurrence of an event the non-occurrence of which was the basic assumption on which the contract was made, his duty to render that performance is discharged, unless the language or the circumstances indicates the contrary.[15]

(b) ECONOMIC FRUSTRATION. Because of a change of circumstance the performance of the contract may have no value to the party entitled to receive performance. For example, the holder of a franchise may make a contract for the construction of a building that will be used for the purpose of the franchise. If the franchise is terminated before the construction of the building begins, the former franchisee no longer has any use for the building and will want to get out of the contract. Some courts sympathize with the franchisee and hold that the contract with the contractor has been discharged by **economic frustration.**

(c) THE MAJORITY RULE COMPARED. The majority or traditional common-law rule refuses to recognize commercial impracticability or economic frustration. By the common law-rule, the losses and disappointments against which commercial impracticability and economic frustration give protection are merely the risks that one takes in entering into a contract. Moreover, the situations could have been guarded against by including an appropriate condition subsequent in the contract declaring that the contract should be void if a specified event occurred. Or the contract could have provided for a readjustment of compensation when there was a basic change of circumstances. The common-law approach also rejects these two new concepts because they weaken the stability of a contract. The net result of these new concepts is that a contract ceases to be binding when there is a significant change in circumstances. That is, when a contract is most needed to give stability, the courts by these new concepts hold that there is no contract.

The common-law rule is also opposed because the new concepts raise questions of measurement of matters that cannot be measured. How much change is needed in order to make a change "significant"?

In spite of the logical and practical objections to the new doctrines, it is likely that they will be given greater recognition by the courts in the future. The expanded recognition of the doctrine of unconscionability is developing a pattern of the judicial monitoring of contracts to prevent injustice. Further indication of a wider recognition of the concept that "extreme" change of circumstances can discharge a contract is found in the fact that the Uniform Commercial Code provides for the discharge of a contract for the sale of goods when a condition that the parties assumed existed or would continue ceases to exist.[16]

It must be remembered that if a contract clearly places upon one of the parties a particular risk, the contract is not discharged when that risk is realized and loss is sustained. Neither the concept of commercial impracticability nor economic frustration will be applied to cancel out provisions of a contract that allocate the risk of loss.

In the *Agosta* case it was claimed that economic frustration discharged a contract for the sale of stock of a corporation when the corporation went out of business.

---

[15] Restatement (2d) of Contracts, § 261.

[16] UCC § 2-615.

RE AGOSTA
122 Misc 2d 1091, 472 NYS2d 538 (1983)

John Agosta and his brother Salvatore each owned one half of the stock of Fontana D'Oro, Inc. The corporate business was the storing and saling of food materials used in the pizza trade. Its major asset was the warehouse where it stored the food materials. Because of disputes, an action was brought to end the business. The action was settled by Salvatore's agreeing to sell his stock to John for $505,000. Shortly thereafter, a fire destroyed the warehouse, and the business had to shut down. John refused to go through with the settlement, and Salvatore brought an action for specific performance to compel him to perform his contract.

GOLDBERG, J. This decision presents a novel question in this jurisdiction; whether an agreement for the sale of stock in a business corporation may be set aside when the underlying purpose of the sale is frustrated by unforeseeable circumstances. . . .

Concededly, the value of the stock has declined as a result of the fire. However, John could not be heard to complain on this account because of the well-known commercial policy which prevents one who has contracted to purchase securities from avoiding his obligation by reason of a decline, even a severe one, in the value of what he has agreed to buy. Additionally, the doctrine of impossibility of performance is inapplicable to the case at bar. In general, impossibility of performance may be equated with an inability to perform as promised due to intervening events, such as an act of state or destruction of the subject matter of the contract. When performance depends on the continued existence of a thing, and such continued existence was assumed as the basis of the agreement, the destruction of the thing puts an end to the obligation. Here, the subject matter, the shares of stock in the corporation, were not destroyed. The shares of stock are presently capable of being transferred. . . .

However, to consider the [settlement agreement] as merely a contract for the transfer of corporate stock as it might appear on its face would be to focus on one aspect of the agreement and to ignore the real intent of the parties. It would ignore the very context in which the agreement was entered into. It was contemplated that Fontana D'Oro Foods, Inc. would continue as a going business enterprise, changing merely from a company jointly owned and operated by John and Salvatore to one owned and operated by John alone. Transfer of the securities was a coincidental formality.

Analysis of the [settlement agreement] as a whole clearly demonstrates the accuracy of the foregoing conclusion. . . . It is clear that both parties were treating the underlying corporate assets and liabilities and, indeed, the operation of the corporation itself, as their own personal property and obligations and that the terminology of the [agreement] classifying the transaction as one for the sale of stock was an unfortunate misnomer not representing the true intent of the parties. While transfer of the corporate securities was most certainly contemplated it was but a minor ministerial act when viewed in the overall context of the transaction. . . .

To view this agreement as simply one for the sale of stock and not as one for the sale of a going business would be to exalt form over substance.

The Court now turns to the question of whether a supervening event has occurred of the type necessary to excuse non-performance.

Frustration of purpose is a corollary of the defense of impossibility of performance. The doctrine has its origin in what are known as the coronation cases. In *Krell v. Henry*, 2 K.B. 740 (1903), the defendant was excused from his duty of payment for use of the plaintiff's apartment along the route of the coronation procession, when the procession was cancelled because the King became ill.

In modern legal parlance, frustration of purpose refers to a situation where an unforeseen event has occurred, which, in the context of the entire transaction, destroys the underlying reasons for performing the contract, even though performance is possible, thus operating to discharge a party's duties of performance. . . .

We are faced with just such a set of circumstances in the instant case. As a result of the fire, performance by Salvatore Agosta would no longer give John Agosta a going business, which is what induced John Agosta to enter into the contract. Although some parts of the business still exist, for all practical purposes that business has been destroyed by the fire. As a result of that fire, the purpose of the contract has been frustrated since there is no longer a functioning business to purchase.

In order to succeed under the doctrine of frustration of purpose, the supervening event must be one which was not foreseeable by the parties. That the parties anticipated the possibility that a fire could destroy their warehouse and inventory is not in doubt. Both must have known, through their involvement in the company's affairs, of insurance coverage on these assets, as well as the existence of a policy covering business interruption. What could not have been foreseen, was the possibility (which has matured into a fact) that the insurance carrier would withhold payment of the corporation's claim based upon its arson investigation. Counsel has advised the Court that the present status of that investigation is not known, but it is not likely that the company will receive compensation for its losses in the foreseeable future, if at all. It is conceivable that the company will recover nothing, and also possible that due to the extended interruption in the company's operations, it may be difficult or impossible for the company ever to resume business, even if the insurance claim is paid in full.

When viewing the stipulation as one for the conveyance of an interest in an operating business it becomes apparent that this purpose has been frustrated by subsequent events that neither side could have reasonably anticipated.

The commercial policy which prevents a contract vendee of corporate stock from escaping his obligation to complete the purchase despite a diminution in value between the time of contract and the time of closing clearly applies when dealing with publicly traded securities or stock purchased primarily for investment purposes. Where, as here, the purpose of the contract to buy or sell corporate stock is to convey control of a functioning business, the Court has the equitable power to set aside the purchase agreement when the purpose has been frustrated by unforeseeable circumstances.

[The motion for specific performance is denied.]

[The above Agosta case was appealed several times and was reversed. Re Fontana D'Oro, 65 NY2d 886, 493 NY2d 300, 428 NE2d 1216 (1985). The following memorandum opinion was filed by the court of last resort:]

While the Appellate Division properly directed specific performance, both lower courts erroneously disregarded the form of the transaction — which was a stock transfer — and treated the transaction instead as a sale of a business or tangible assets. The well-settled rule is that "ownership of capital stock is by no means identical with or equivalent to ownership of corporate property." We recently reaffirmed this rule in *5303 Realty Corp. v. O & Y Equity*

Corp., 64 N.Y.2d 313, 486 N.Y.S.2d 877, 476 N.E.2d 276, in which we held that a notice of pendency was unavailable to a plaintiff in an action for specific performance of a contract to sell 100% of the stock in a corporation whose sole asset was an office building. Here, too, we cannot disregard the fact that the parties chose to structure their transaction as one involving stock, or that John agreed to pay $505,000 for Salvatore's stock. Given the form of their transaction, whether the parties might really have intended to transfer control of an ongoing business enterprise, rather than stock, can have no bearing on this conclusion. . . .

Since an agreement to convey stock in a close corporation may be enforced by specific performance, it was within the power of the Appellate Division to award such relief to Salvatore by directing Supreme Court to execute as nominee for John the various documents contemplated by the parties' stipulation.

[Specific performance ordered]

QUESTIONS

1. What social forces are advanced and what defeated by each of the two opinions in the *Agosta* case?
2. Does the appellate court opinion answer the basic question involved?

§ 21:10 TEMPORARY IMPOSSIBILITY

Ordinarily a temporary impossibility has either no effect on the obligation to perform of the party who is affected thereby, or at most suspends the duty to perform so that the obligation to perform is revived upon the termination of the impossibility. If, however, performance at that later date would impose a substantially greater burden upon the obligor, some courts discharge the obligor from the contract.

(a) WEATHER. Acts of God, such as tornadoes, lightning, and sudden floods, usually do not terminate a contract, even though they make performance difficult or impossible. Thus, weather conditions constitute a risk that is assumed by a contracting party in the absence of a contrary agreement. Consequently, extra expense sustained by a contractor because of weather conditions is a risk that the contractor assumes in the absence of an express provision for additional compensation in such case.

(b) WEATHER CLAUSES. Modern contracts commonly contain a "weather" clause, which either expressly grants an extension for delays caused by weather conditions or expressly denies the right to any extension of time or additional compensation because of weather condition difficulties. Some courts hold that abnormal weather conditions excuse what would otherwise be a breach of contract. Thus, nondelivery of equipment has been excused when the early melting of a frozen river made it impossible to deliver.

§ 21:11   DISCHARGE BY OPERATION OF LAW

A contract is discharged by operation of law by (a) alteration or a material change made by a party; (b) destruction of the written contract with intent to discharge it; (c) merger when a judgment is obtained on the contract; (d) bankruptcy; (e) the operation of a statute of limitations; or (f) a contractual limitation. The last three have the most practical importance.

(a) BANKRUPTCY. Most insolvent debtors

may voluntarily enter into a federal court of bankruptcy or be compelled to do so by creditors. The trustee in bankruptcy then takes possession of the debtor's property and distributes it as far as it will go among the creditors. After this is done, the court grants the debtor a discharge in bankruptcy if it concludes that the debtor has acted honestly and has not attempted to defraud creditors.

Even though all creditors have not been paid in full, the discharge in bankruptcy discharges ordinary contract claims against the debtor.

(b) STATUTES OF LIMITATIONS. Statutes provide that after a certain number of years have passed a contract claim is barred. The time limitation provided by state statutes of limitations vary widely. The period usually differs with the type of contract — ranging from a relatively short time for open accounts (ordinary custom-ers' charge accounts) and other sales of goods (4 years);[17] to a somewhat longer period for written contracts (usually 5 to 10 years); to a maximum period for judgments of record (usually 10 to 20 years).

(c) CONTRACTUAL LIMITATIONS. Some contracts, particularly insurance contracts, contain a time limitation within which suit may be brought. This is, in effect, a private statute of limitations created by the agreement of the parties.

A contract may also require that notice of any claim be given within a specified time. A party who fails to give notice within the time specified by the contract is barred from suing thereon. What if the notice is not given because a party wrongly believes that there was no claim about which to give notice? This was the problem in the *State Bank* case.

---

[17]   UCC § 2-725(1).

STATE BANK OF VIROQUA V CAPITOL INDEMNITY CORP.

61 Wis 2d 699, 214 NW2d 42 (1974)

The State Bank of Viroqua obtained a bankers blanket bond from the Capitol Indemnity Corporation to protect it from loss by forgery. The bond required that the bank give the insurer notice of any loss at "the earliest practicable moment." James DeLap borrowed money from the bank by means of paper on which he forged the name of Leon Mellem. This was learned in October 1969. In October 1970 an agent of Capitol was discussing the bond with the bank. The bank then realized for the first time that the bond covered the DeLap forgery loss. Fifteen days later the bank notified Capitol of that claim. Capitol denied liability because of the delay. The bank sued Capitol. From a judgment in favor of Capitol, the bank appealed.

HALLOWS, C. J. . . . The trial court held the giving of notice . . . was too late as a matter of law and constituted noncompliance with the contract unless excusable. . . .

The bank claims error on the theory that the language in the bond requiring notice to be given at "the earliest practicable moment" means within a reasonable time under all the circumstances and such circumstances in this case consist of the uncertainty of coverage, the lack of a forfeiture clause and the lack of prejudice to Capitol Indemnity because of the delay.

. . . Most courts have regarded the notice of loss provision as a condition precedent even though the contract does not expressly say so or contain a forfeiture clause and have held that noncompliance will defeat recovery on the bond. The rationale behind the majority rule is to give the earliest opportunity to the surety to investigate, minimize and recoup losses while the time is ripe for such purpose, and to give the surety a reasonable opportunity to protect its rights. Under this view, the failure to comply with the condition precedent to liability vitiates the insured's claim regardless of whether or not prejudice to the surety resulted from the delay or the relative carelessness of the insured in giving notice or the insured's ignorance of coverage under the bond.

. . . We hold that where the giving of timely notice is required by the Bankers Blanket Bond prior to the maturity of the liability of the insurer, such requirement is a condition precedent in fact to liability whether or not expressly so stated and is to be enforced as written whether or not its importance is emphasized by further language that noncompliance works a forfeiture or voids the policy.

Ignorance of policy provisions or a belief that coverage is questionable is no excuse for failure to give notice of loss under the Bankers Blanket Bond. In case of questionable coverage, notice of loss to the insurance company would start the investigative process in motion and resolve the uncertainty of coverage. As for ignorance of coverage, a bank should know its business and the ordinary terms of standard insurance contracts applying to banking business. The existence of such ignorance on the part of a bank would seem to be inexcusable and unreasonable.

The fact that Capitol Indemnity was not prejudiced is irrelevant. The contract language requiring timely notice of loss is designed to prevent prejudice or harm to the insurer. It is a fact of life in the insurance field that a timely notice of loss is important. It is a notice of loss that starts the investigation by the insurance company while the evidence is fresh and gatherable. Insurers are entitled to contract for this protection.

[Judgment affirmed]

Questions

1. Is there a statutory basis for the time limitation imposed in the *State Bank* case?
2. How could the bank have protected itself?
3. How could the bank have protected itself under the policy as actually written?

Summary

Most contracts are discharged by performance. An offer to perform is called a tender of performance. If a tender of performance is wrongfully refused, the duty of the tenderer to perform is terminated. If the performance required was the payment of money, the refusal of a proper tender does not discharge the debt but prevents the creditor from recovering interest or costs if suit is thereafter brought against the tenderer to recover the amount owed. When the performance called for by the contract is the payment of money, it must be legal tender that is tendered. In actual practice, it is common to pay and to accept payment by checks or other commercial paper. When the debtor owes the creditor on several accounts and makes a payment, the debtor may specify which account is to be credited with the payment. If the debtor fails to do so, the creditor may make the application. If neither the creditor nor the debtor makes an application of the payment, the court may do so. There is a conflict of authority as to whether a court's application of the payment should be made so as to favor the creditor or the debtor.

When a contract does not state when it is to be performed, it must be performed within a reasonable time. If time for performance is stated in the contract, the contract must be performed at the time specified if such time is essential (is of the essence). Performance within a reasonable time is sufficient if the specified time is not essential.

Ordinarily a contract must be performed exactly in the manner specified by the contract. A less than perfect performance is allowed if it is a substantial performance and if damages are allowed the other party sufficient to compensate for the loss sustained because the performance was not perfect. The other contracting party or a third person may guarantee a perfect performance and such a guarantor is then liable if the performance is less than perfect.

A contract cannot be discharged by unilateral action unless authorized by the contract itself or by statute, as in the case of consumer protection rescission.

As a contract arises from an agreement,

it may also be terminated by an agreement. This may be a provision in the original contract or a subsequent agreement to rescind the contract. A contract may also be discharged by substitution of a new contract for the original contract; by a novation by making a new contract with a new party; by accord and satisfaction; by release; or by waiver.

A contract is discharged when it is impossible to perform as in the case of the destruction of the subject matter of the contract, the adoption of a new law that prohibits performance, the death or disability of a party whose personal action was required for performance of the contract, or the act of the other contracting party to the contract. Some courts will also hold that a contract is discharged when its performance is commercially impracticable or there is economic frustration of one of the parties. Although increased cost of performance ordinarily has no effect on a contract, if that increase is grossly disproportionate to the original performance cost, some courts will classify the situation as one of commercial impracticability and hold that the contract is discharged. In the case of economic frustration, the contract can be performed, but the performance has ceased to have any significant value to the party who originally contracted to obtain that performance. Temporary impossibility, such as a labor strike or bad weather, has no effect upon a contract, although it is common to include protective clauses that excuse delay caused by temporary impossibility. A contract may be discharged by operation of law. This occurs when (1) the liability arising from the contract is discharged by bankruptcy, (2) suit on the contract is barred by the applicable statute of limitations, or (3) a time limitation is stated in the contract.

QUESTIONS AND CASE PROBLEMS

1. What social forces are affected by the doctrine of economic frustration?

2. Parties to a contract must perform their obligations entirely on the dates specified by the

contract and will forfeit all rights if performance is not so made. Appraise this statement.

3. McMullen Contractors made a contract with Richardson to build an apartment house for a specific price. A number of serious apartment house fires broke out in the city, and an ordinance was adopted by the city council increasing the fire precautions that had to be taken in the construction of a new building. Compliance with these new requirements would make the construction of the apartment house for Richardson more expensive than McMullen had originally contemplated. Is McMullen discharged from the contract to build the apartment house?

4. Grattan contracted to build a house and garage for Boris for $50,000. The job was completed according to the specifications in all respects except that Grattan forgot to put a tool shed next to the garage as was required by the contract specifications. Boris refused to pay Grattan. Grattan sued Boris. Boris raised the defense that Grattan was not entitled to any money until the contract was completely performed and that the performance was incomplete because the tool shed had not been constructed. Was Boris correct?

5. Johnson made a contract with Hanes to paint her house for $1,000. Thereafter, Johnson, Hanes, and Plaskey agreed that Plaskey would do the painting and that Johnson would have no further obligation with respect to the painting. Plaskey failed to paint the house, and Hanes sued Johnson for damages. Is Johnson liable?

6. Compare (a) the principle that time is generally not of the essence, with (b) the right of a construction contractor to recover for a substantial performance of the contract.

7. Metalcrafters made a contract to design a new earth-moving vehicle for Lamar Highway Construction Company. Metalcrafters was depending upon the genius of Samet, the head of its research department, to design a new product. Shortly after the contract was made between Metalcrafters and Lamar, Samet was killed in an automobile accident. Metalcrafters was not able to design the product without Samet. Lamar sued Metalcrafters for damages for breach of the contract. Metalcrafters claimed that the contract was discharged by Samet's death. Is it correct?

8. The Tinchers signed a contract to sell land to Creasy. The contract specified that the sales transaction was to be completed in 90 days. At the end of the 90 days, Creasy requested an extension of time. The Tinchers refused to grant an extension and stated that the contract was terminated. Creasy claimed that the 90-day clause was not binding because the contract did not state that time was of the essence. Was the contract terminated? [Creasy v Tincher, 154 W Va 18, 173 SE2d 332]

9. The Powers entered into a home improvement contract with Sims and Levin. The contract declared that the amount due was a lien on the home of the Powers and that they had two days in which to cancel the contract if they changed their minds. Was this cancellation provision valid?

10. Dickson contracted to build a house for Moran. When it was approximately 25-40 percent completed, Moran would not let Dickson work any further because he was not following the building plans and specifications, and there were many defects. Moran hired another contractor to correct the defects and finish the building. Dickson sued Moran for breach of contract, claiming that he had substantially performed the contract up to the point where he had been discharged. Was Dickson correct? [Dickson v Moran (La App) 344 So 2d 102]

11. Compare a novation and a delegation of duties.

12. A leased a trailer park to B. At the time, sewage was disposed of by a septic tank system that was not connected with the public sewage system. B knew this, and the lease declared that B had examined the premises and that A made no representation or guarantee as to the condition of the premises. Some time thereafter, the septic tank system stopped working properly, and the county health department notified B that he was required to connect the sewage system with the public sewage system or else close the trailer park. B did not want to pay the additional cost involved in connecting with the public system. B claimed that he was released from the lease and was entitled to a refund of the deposit that he had made. Was he correct? [Glen R. Sewell

Sheet Metal v Loverde, 70 Cal 2d 666, 75 Cal Rptr 889, 451 P2d 721]

13. A farmer made a contract to sell and deliver 10,000 bushels of soybeans. A flood destroyed his entire crop. He claimed that he was discharged from his obligation under the contract. Was he correct?

14. Northwest Construction, Inc. made a contract with the state of Washington for highway construction. Part of the work was turned over under a subcontract to the Yakima Asphalt Paving Company. The contract required that any claim be asserted within 180 days. Yakima brought an action for damages after the expiration of 180 days. The defense was raised that the claim was too late. Yakima replied that the action was brought within the time allowed by the statute of limitations and that the contractual limitation of 180 days was therefore not binding. Was Yakima correct? [Yakima Asphalt Paving Co. v Washington State Department of Transportation, 45 Wash App 663, 726 P2d 1021]

15. The Metropolitan Park District of Tacoma gave Griffith a concession to run its park. The agreement gave the right to occupy the parks and use any improvements found therein. The District later wished to set this agreement aside because it was not making sufficient money from the transaction. While it was seeking to do so, a boathouse and giftshop in one of the parks was destroyed by fire. The District then claimed that the concession contract with Griffith was discharged by impossibility of performance. Was it correct? [Metropolitan Park District of Tacoma v Griffith, 106 Wash 2d 5, 723 P2d 1093]

22

BREACH OF CONTRACT AND REMEDIES

When a party breaks a contract, society gives the other party — the injured party — a remedy against the defaulter. As seen in Chapter 20, sometimes the right to obtain a remedy for breach has been extended beyond the contracting parties to include third party beneficiaries and assignees.

Assume that the fact situation that constitutes a breach of contract is also a tort, as described in Chapter 10. Can an aggrieved party sue the defaulter for the tort? Society could have taken the position that, as the parties had made a contract, their respec-

tive rights must stand or fall as contract rights and that any other kind of liability was excluded. In the interest of putting the aggrieved person in as nearly as possible the same position that such person would have held had the contract been performed, the aggrieved person is given the choice of seeking a remedy for breach of contract or for tort.

Once society decided to make a tort remedy available, it was necessary to decide who could seek such tort remedy. Could third person victims of the default be allowed to sue for the tort involved in the breach of the contract? Unlike the third party beneficiary, there is often nothing in the contract that shows any intent to benefit such victims. Unlike the assignee, there is no relationship between the third person tort victim and a party to the original contract. Society was thus faced with the necessity of deciding whether only a contracting party could sue the other contracting party for a tort or whether anyone who could show injury could sue for such tort. The first choice seemed too narrow, and the second seemed too broad. Somewhere between the two extremes society has been struggling to develop a dividing line that will allow some third person victims to sue for tortious breach of contract but that will not allow too many to sue.

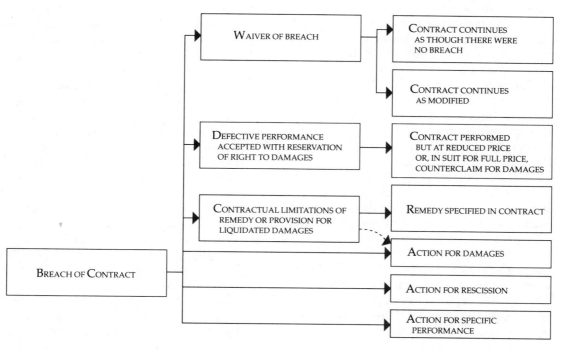

FIGURE 22-1
What Follows the Breach?

A. What Constitutes a Breach of Contract

The question of remedies does not become important until it is first determined that there has been a breach of the contract.

§ 22:1 Definition of Breach

A breach is the failure to act or perform in the manner called for by the contract. When the contract calls for performance, such as the painting of the owner's house, the failure to paint or to paint properly is a breach of contract. If the contract calls for forbearance, the action of the creditor in bringing a lawsuit is a breach of the contract.

§ 22:2 Anticipatory Breach

When the contract calls for performance, the question of whether there has been a breach is determined by whether performance was made at the proper time. A party may make it clear before that time arrives that the contract will not be performed.

(a) ANTICIPATORY REPUDIATION. When a party expressly declares that performance will not be made when required, such declaration is called an **anticipatory repudiation** of the contract. To constitute such a repudiation there must be a clear, absolute, unequivocal refusal to perform the contract according to its terms.

When a party insists that the contract has a meaning that it could not possibly have, such insistence is regarded as an anticipatory repudiation because it clearly manifests that the declarant will not perform the contract according to its reasonable terms.[1]

A party making an anticipatory repudiation may retract or take back the repudiation providing the other party has not changed position in reliance on the repudiation. For example, if the buyer makes another purchase when the seller declares that the seller will not perform the contract, the buyer has acted in reliance on the seller's repudiation. The seller will therefore not be allowed to retract the repudiation.

(b) ANTICIPATORY REPUDIATION BY CONDUCT. The anticipatory repudiation may be expressed by conduct that makes it impossible for the repudiating party to perform thereafter. To illustrate, there is a repudiation by conduct if a farmer who made a contract to sell an identified mass of potatoes, sells and delivers them to another buyer before the date specified for the delivery of the potatoes to the first buyer.

B.   WAIVER OF BREACH

The breach of a contract may have no importance because the other party to the contract waives the breach.

§ 22:3   CURE OF BREACH BY WAIVER

The fact that one party has broken a contract does not necessarily mean that there will be a lawsuit or a forfeiture of the contract. For practical business reasons, one party may be willing to ignore or **waive** the breach. When it is established that there has been a waiver of a breach, the party waiving the breach cannot take any action on the theory that the contract was broken. The waiver, in effect, erases the past breach, and the contract continues as though the breach had not existed.

Many times a tender of performance will be defective in some respect. There may be delays or the product tendered may not be exactly what was ordered. Because the obligee is not really troubled by the defect or because the obligee is in such a position that the defective performance must be accepted as better than none, the obligee will frequently accept the performance, although defective, without making any complaint as to the defect.

The waiver may be express or it may be implied from the continued recognition of the existence of the contract by the aggrieved party.[2] In the *Seismic* case, the question arose as to whether a buyer had waived defects in the performance of the seller.

[1]   United California Bank v Prudential Ins. Co. (App) 140 Ariz 238, 681 P2d 390 (1983).

[2]   Creative Communications Consultants, Inc. v Gaylord (Minn App) 403 NW2d 654 (1987).

SEISMIC & DIGITAL CONCEPTS INC. V DIGITAL RESOURCES CORP.
(Tex Civ App) 590 SW2d 718 (1979)

Computers and physical equipment used in connection with computers are called hardware. The programs or instructions on how to use the hardware to produce certain desired results are called software. Without the proper software, the hardware is useless. Digital Resources made a contract to supply Seismic and Digital Concepts Inc. with software that it needed to produce the desired results with its hardware. When Digital Resources was not paid, it sued Seismic. Seismic asserted a counterclaim for damages because of late delivery of the software. The evidence showed that the software was not delivered by Digital on the date of October 21, as specified in the contract, but was delivered ten to twenty-five days late. Seismic accepted the software, made use of it for many months and requested Digital to do additional work to speed up the programs. On the basis of this evidence, judgment was entered against Seismic on the counterclaim. Seismic appealed.

PEDEN, J. . . . Seismic argues that Digital breached whatever contractual arrangement the parties may have had by failure to deliver the software program to appellant within the contract time, and that Digital is itself in default on the contract and cannot now maintain a suit for its breach.

It is clear . . . that Digital did not deliver the software programs by October 21, 1974, the date agreed upon in the contract, but it does not follow that such late delivery necessarily precludes Digital's recovery of the contract price.

When, as here, there is no indication that time was of the essence, failure to preform a contract on the exact date specified is not such a breach as justifies nonperformance by the other party. . . . In our case, Digital's delivery of the software programs from ten to twenty-five days after the date agreed upon was followed by some five months of additional work performed either at Seismic's request or because of its errors. During those five months Seismic never rejected the programs. On the contrary, the trial judge explicitly found that Seismic accepted them and approved them "as to speed and performance" sometime after April, 1975. Under these circumstances, Digital's failure to comply exactly with the delivery schedule did not justify Seismic's refusal to perform its own obligations.

Even if Digital's initial delay in delivering the software programs had constituted a breach of the agreement, we agree with the trial court's conclusion that as a matter of law Seismic effectively waived strict compliance with the delivery schedule.

Waiver of strict performance may be inferred from the circumstances or course of dealings between the parties. A waiver may result from one party's express or implied assent to the continued performance of the other party without objection to the delay, as in . . . *Ryan v Thurmond*, 481 SW2d 199 (TexCivApp 1972). In addition, express representations by one party that strict compliance with a deadline will not be required, or other actions that reasonably lead the other party to believe such, will also cause an effective waiver of a time provision in a contract. . . . Finally, a party may effectively waive a breach of agreement by the other party by continuing to insist on performance by the other party even after the breach. In our case, Seismic waived the contract provision as to time of performance through its failure to object to the delay, its failure to reject the software programs when delivered, and its subsequent conduct in both assenting to the delay and requesting additional work from Digital on the completed programs.

[Judgment affirmed]

QUESTIONS

1. Why did the court decide against Seismic on its counterclaim?
2. What was the basis of the court's decision?
3. How could the parties have protected themselves from this lawsuit?

§ 22:4 EXISTENCE AND SCOPE OF WAIVER

It is a question of fact whether there has been a waiver.

(a) EXISTENCE OF WAIVER. A party may express or declare that the breach of the contract is waived. A waiver of breach is more often the result of silence or failure to object in timely fashion than it is the result of an express forgiving of a breach. Thus, a party allowing the other party to continue performance without objecting that that performance is not satisfactory, waives the right to raise that objection when sued for payment by the performing party.[3]

(b) SCOPE OF WAIVER. The waiver of a breach of contract only extends to the matter waived. It does not show any intent to ignore other provisions of the contract. For example, a contractor may be late in completing the construction of a building. The owner could waive objection to the lateness and permit the contractor to finish the construction. Such waiver as to time does not waive the obligation of the contractor to complete the building according to the plans and specifications. Only the time of performance requirement is waived.

§ 22:5 WAIVER OF BREACH AS MODIFICATION OF CONTRACT

When the contract calls for a continuing performance, such as making delivery of

goods or paying an installment on the first of each month, the acceptance of a late delivery or a late payment may have more significance than merely waiving a claim for damages because of the lateness.

(a) REPEATED BREACHES AND WAIVERS. Repeated breaches and repeated waivers may show that the parties had modified their original contract. For example, the contract calling for performance on the first of the month may have been modified to permit performance in the first week of the month. When there is a modification of the contract, neither party can go back to the original contract without the consent of the other.

(b) ANTI-MODIFICATION CLAUSE. Modern contracts commonly specify that the terms of a contract shall not be deemed modified by waiver as to any breaches. This means that the original contract remains as agreed to, and either party may therefore return to and insist upon compliance with the original contract.

§ 22:6 RESERVATION OF RIGHT

It may be that a party is willing to accept a defective performance but does not wish to surrender any claim for damages for the breach. For example, the buyer of coal may need a shipment of coal so badly as to be forced to accept it although it is defective; yet at the same time, the buyer does not wish to be required to pay the full purchase price for the defective shipment. The buyer wants to claim a deduction for damages because the shipment

[3] Old Mill Printers v Kruse (Minn App) 392 NW2d 621 (1986).

was defective. In such a case, the buyer should accept the tendered performance with a **reservation of right.** In the above illustration, the buyer would state that the defective coal was accepted but that the right to damages for nonconformity to the contract was reserved.[4] Frequently the buyer will express the same thought by stating that the coal is accepted without prejudice to a claim for damages for nonconformity or that the shipment is accepted under protest.

The acceptance under reservation described above may be oral. It is preferable for practical reasons that it be in writing. In many cases the practical procedure is to make the declaration orally as soon as possible and then send a confirming letter. When the matter is sufficiently important, it is also desirable to have the wrongdoer countersign or make a written acknowledgment of the reservation letter.

C. REMEDIES FOR BREACH OF CONTRACT

When a party has broken a contract there are several remedies, one or more of which may be available to the injured party. The injured party may bring an action for damages, rescind the contract, bring a suit in equity to obtain specific performance, or commence a proceeding to obtain relief from an administrative agency of the government. There is also the possibility that arbitration or a streamlined procedure discussed in Chapter 1 is available for the determination of the rights of the parties.

§ 22:7 REMEDIES UPON ANTICIPATORY REPUDIATION

When there has been an anticipatory repudiation of a contract, the aggrieved person has the option of (a) doing nothing beyond stating that the performance at the proper time will be required, (b) regarding the contract as having been definitively broken and bringing a lawsuit against the repudiating party, without waiting to see if there will be a proper performance when the performance date arrives, or (c) regarding the repudiation as an offer to cancel the contract, which offer can be accepted or rejected. If accepted, there is a discharge of the original contract by the subsequent cancellation agreement of the parties.

§ 22:8 ACTION FOR DAMAGES

When a breach of contract occurs, the injured party is entitled to bring an action for damages to recover such sum of money as will place the injured party in the same position that would have been attained if the contract had been performed.[5]

If the defendant has been negligent in performing the contract, the plaintiff may sue for the damages caused by the negligence. Thus, a person contracting to drill a well for drinking water can be sued for the damage caused by negligently drilling the well so as to cause the water to become contaminated. However, damages representing annoyance ordinarily may not be recovered for breach of contract. Likewise, the mere fact that the breaking of the contract causes the injured party to be emotionally upset does not ordinarily entitle that person to recover damages for such emotional distress.[6]

(a) MEASURE OF DAMAGES. A plaintiff who has sustained actual loss is entitled to a sum of money that will, so far as possible, compensate for that loss; such damages are called **compensatory damages.** An injured party who does not sustain an actual loss from the breach of a contract is entitled to a

---

[4] UCC § 1-207.

[5] Turner v Alberts 224 Neb 632, 399 NW2d 817 (1987).
[6] Brown v Fritz (Idaho) 699 P2d 1371 (1985).

judgment of a small sum, such as $1, known as **nominal damages.**

The fact that damages cannot be established with mathematical certainty is not a bar to their recovery. All that is required is reasonable certainty.[7] The trier of fact is given a large degree of discretion in determining the damages.

(b) PUNITIVE DAMAGES. Damages in excess of actual loss, imposed for the purpose of punishing or making an example of the defendant, are known as **punitive damages** or **exemplary damages.** In contract actions, punitive damages are not ordinarily awarded. In some consumer situations, the recovery of punitive damages is allowed in order to discourage the defendant from breaking the law with others. For example, in cases in which the plaintiff is a consumer and the seller has acted wrongfully and stubbornly, there is an increasing trend to award punitive damages in order to prevent a repetition of such conduct.

The fact that the breaching party made prompt efforts to correct the situation when notified of the breach is strong evidence of the lack of the mental state justifying the imposition of punitive damages.[8]

In the *Morrow* case the plaintiff claimed the right to recover punitive damages because the defendant's breach of contract had been "wilful and wanton."

[7]   Crystal Springs Trout Co. v First State Bank, ___ Mont ___, 732 P2d 819 (1987).

[8]   McDaniel v Bass-Smith Funeral Home, Inc. 80 NC App 629, 343 SE2d 228 (1986).

MORROW V L. A. GOLDSCHMIDT ASSOCIATES, INC.

112 Ill 2d 87, 96 Ill Dec 939, 492 NE2d 181 (1986)

L. A. Goldschmidt Associates constructed townhouses that were purchased by Morrow and others. The construction contracts were not properly performed, and Morrow and the other purchasers sued Goldschmidt for breach of the contract. In their complaint, they stated that the breach of the contract had been "wilful and wanton" and claimed punitive damages. Punitive damages were awarded the plaintiffs, and the defendant appealed.

MORAN, J. . . . As a general rule, punitive damages are not recoverable for breach of contract. . . . The sole purpose of contract damages is to compensate the nonbreaching party, and punitive damages are not available even for a "wilful" breach of contract. . . .

The rule against awarding punitive damages for breach of contract has been applied to situations, like the present case, where homeowners have sued builders or contractors for construction defects. Courts traditionally have refused to award punitive damages in such cases where the allegations against the builder or contractor amounted to nothing more than a breach of contract. . . .

An exception to the general rule that punitive damages are not recoverable for breach of contract is when the conduct causing the breach is also a tort for which punitive damages are recoverable. . . . That is, punitive damages are recoverable "where the breach amounts to an independent tort and there are proper allegations of malice, wantonness or oppression."

. . . Defendants, however, argue that plaintiffs have not alleged a separate tort for which punitive damages are available. They note that the complaint does not allege that the defects in workmanship and construction caused personal injury or damage to property other than to the townhouse units themselves. As such, they argue that plaintiffs have incurred only "economic losses" for which there is no tort recovery.

The line of demarcation between tort and contract is sometimes difficult to make, and occasionally, the conduct complained of can constitute both a breach of contract and a tort. . . . Nevertheless, this court held in *Moorman Manufacturing Co. v. National Tank Co.* (1982), 91 Ill.2d 69, 61 Ill.Dec. 746, 435 N.E.2d 443, that recovery for solely economic losses is more appropriately governed by contract, rather than tort, law principles. . . .

Subsequently, in *Redarowicz v. Ohlendorf* (1982), 92 Ill.2d 171, 65 Ill.Dec. 411, 441 N.E.2d 324, this court held that . . . when a purchaser of a defectively constructed residence sues the builder and alleges solely economic losses, the purchaser cannot recover under a negligence theory in tort. The court explained:

> This is not a case where defective construction created a hazard that resulted in a member of the plaintiff's family being struck by a falling brick from the chimney. The adjoining wall has not collapsed on and destroyed the plaintiff's living room furniture. The plaintiff is seeking damages for the costs of replacement and repair of the defective chimney, adjoining wall and patio. While the commercial expectations of this buyer have not been met by the builder, the only danger to the plaintiff is that he would be forced to incur additional expenses for living conditions that were less than what was bargained for. (92 Ill.2d 171, 178, 65 Ill.Dec. 411, 441 N.E.2d 324)

Similarly, in the present case, plaintiffs seek to recover only the costs of repairs to their homes caused by defendants' alleged faulty workmanship. Like the plaintiff in *Redarowicz,* the plaintiffs here have not alleged a harm "above and beyond disappointed expectations." (*Redarowicz v. Ohlendorf* (1982), 92 Ill.2d 171, 177, 65 Ill.Dec. 411, 441 N.E.2d 324.) They do not complain that the defects caused an accident which resulted in physical injury or damage to other property. Indeed, contrary to the findings of the appellate court, nowhere in plaintiffs' complaint is it alleged that the defects were a threat to health or safety. As such, the plaintiffs essentially are complaining that they did not receive the benefit of their bargain — a harm which is appropriately remedied by bringing an action for breach of contract.

Plaintiffs argue that the present case is distinguishable from *Moorman* and *Redarowicz* because the defendants' conduct in those cases was merely negligent whereas the defendants' conduct here was allegedly "wilful and wanton." We disagree. Simply characterizing a breach of contract as "wilful and wanton" does not change the fact that plaintiffs are only seeking recovery for harm to a contract-like interest. We cannot agree that a breach of contract becomes a tort just because the breach was wilful and wanton. . . . Where the construction defects do not cause physical injuries or damage to other property, we are unwilling to impose tort liability on a builder for breach of his contract with the purchaser, even if the breach was willful and wanton.

Moreover, we decline to adopt plaintiffs' alternative argument that punitive damages should be awarded for certain wilful and wanton breaches of contract, even though the breach is not accompanied by an independent tort. Although punitive damages appear to be recoverable in a few other jurisdictions for certain wilful breaches of contract . . ., we continue to adhere to the view that tort and contract law are founded on different policies which justify separate rules with respect to recovery of punitive damages. (See Corbin, Contracts sec. 1077, at 437-38 (1964).) We hold that counts VIII through XI of plaintiffs' complaint do not state a cause of action for the tort of wilful and wanton misconduct and punitive damages.

[Judgment allowing punitive damages reversed]

QUESTIONS

1. What did the court decide?
2. Did the court recognize any exception to the rule stated in its decision? Explain.
3. Under what circumstances could the plaintiffs in the *Morrow* case have recovered punitive damages in the action for breach of contract?

(c) DIRECT AND CONSEQUENTIAL DAMAGES. The breach of a contract may cause the other party *direct* and *consequential loss*. A **direct loss** is one that necessarily is caused by the breach of contract. A **consequential loss** is one that does not necessarily follow the breach of the contract, but happens to do so in a particular case because of the circumstances of the injured party. For example, if the seller breaks the contract to deliver a truck that operates properly, the buyer sustains the damages of receiving a truck that cannot be used. This is the direct loss. If the buyer of the truck needed the truck to take a harvest of ripe tomatoes to the cannery but was unable to do so because the truck would not operate, the loss of the crop that could not be transported would be the consequential loss sustained by the farmer-buyer.

Consequential damages may be recovered if they were within the contemplation of the parties at the time they entered into

their contract.[9] This does not mean that the parties must have actually thought of the consequential damage that would follow from a breach of the contract. It is sufficient that a reasonable person in their position would have foreseen the probability of such damage.

In order to recover damages for a particular consequential loss, the plaintiff must show that it was within the defendant's contemplation, that is, it was foreseeable that the kind of loss in question could be sustained by the plaintiff if the contract was broken.

(d) MITIGATION OF DAMAGES. The injured party is under the duty to **mitigate the damages** if reasonably possible. That is, damages must not be permitted to increase if this can be prevented by reasonable efforts. This means that the injured party must generally stop any perfor-

---

[9]   Fairfax County Redevelopment and Housing Authority v Hurst and Associates Consulting Engineers, Inc. 231 Va 164, 343 SE2d 294 (1986).

mance under the contract in order to avoid running up a larger bill. It may require the injured party to buy or rent elsewhere the goods that the wrongdoer was obligated to deliver under the contract. In the case of the breach of an employment contract by the employer, the employee is required to seek other similar employment, and the wages earned or that could have been earned from similar employment must be deducted from the damages claimed.

(1) Effect of failure to mitigate damages. The effect of the requirement of mitigating damages is to limit the recovery by the injured party to the damages that would have been sustained had the injured party mitigated the damages. That is, recovery is limited to the direct loss, and damages for consequential loss are excluded. For example, assume that a commercial hauler makes a contract to buy a truck. Because the seller fails to deliver the truck, the buyer loses a hauling job on which a profit of $500 would have been made. Assume that the hauler could have rented a truck for $150 in time to do the hauling job. The hauler would then be under a duty to rent the truck so that the $500 profit would not be lost. By failing to do this, the hauler permitted the damages to grow from a rental cost of $150 to a loss of profit of $500. When the hauler sues the seller for breach of the sales contract, the rule of mitigation of damages will limit the hauler to recovering only $150 because the additional $350 loss was unnecessarily sustained. If in fact the hauler had rented a truck, the rental of $150 would be recoverable as damages from the seller. Thus, the hauler will only receive $150 damages whether or not a truck is rented in order to mitigate the damages.

(2) Excuse for failure to mitigate damages. If there is nothing that the injured party can reasonably do to reduce damages, there is, by definition, no duty to mitigate damages. For example, a leasing company broke its contract to supply a speci-fied computer and auxiliary equipment by delivering a less desirable computer. The specified computer and equipment could not be obtained elsewhere by the customer. Therefore, the customer was entitled to recover full damages.

When the cost of mitigating, as by purchasing elsewhere the goods that the seller failed to deliver, is unreasonably great, there is no duty to mitigate damages.

§ 22:9 RESCISSION

When there has been a material breach of the contract, the aggrieved party may rescind the contract. If this is objected to by the wrongdoing party, the aggrieved party may bring an action for rescission.

(a) RIGHT TO RESCIND. When one party commits a material breach of the contract, the other party may rescind the contract because of such breach. In some situations, the right to rescind may be governed or controlled by civil service statutes or similar regulations or by an obligation to submit the matter to arbitration or to a grievance procedure.

An injured party who rescinds after having performed or paid money under the contract may recover the reasonable value of the performance rendered or the money paid. This recovery is not based on the contract that has been rescinded but on a quasi contract that the law implies to prevent the defaulter from keeping the benefit received and thus being unjustly enriched.

The rescinding party must restore the other party to that party's original position. If the rescinding party's own acts make this impossible, the contract cannot be rescinded. Thus, a buyer who has placed a mortgage on property purchased cannot rescind the sales contract because the property cannot be returned to the seller in its original, unmortgaged condition.

Care must be exercised in deciding to rescind a contract. If proper ground for rescission does not exist, the party who rescinds is guilty of repudiating the contract and is liable for damages for its breach.[10] Rescission and recovery of monetary damages are alternative remedies except in a contract for the sale of goods, in which case both remedies are available.

(b) JUDICIAL RESCISSION. If the party breaking the contract does not recognize the right of the aggrieved party to rescind the contract, the aggrieved party may bring an action in which the court will declare that the contract has been rescinded. In that action, the court will also specify what payments or exchanges of property are to be made by the parties in order to return matters to the conditions existing before the contract was made.

§ 22:10 ACTION FOR SPECIFIC PERFORMANCE

Under special circumstances, the injured party may obtain the equitable remedy of specific performance that compels the other party to carry out the terms of a contract. Specific performance is ordinarily granted only if the subject matter of the contract is unique, thereby making a monetary award of damages an inadequate remedy. Monetary damages may be inadequate either because it is not possible to make a reasonable determination of the damages the plaintiff will sustain by the breach of the contract or because a replacement or substitute performance cannot be obtained in the market-place. Contracts for the purchase of land will be specifically enforced, as will contracts for the sale of a business and the franchise held by the business.

Specific performance of a contract to sell personal property can generally be obtained only if the article is of unusual age, beauty, unique history, or other distinction, as in the case of heirlooms, original paintings, old editions of books, or relics. In these cases identical articles could not be obtained in the market. Specific performance is also allowed a buyer in the case of a contract to buy shares of stock essential for control of a close corporation when those shares have no fixed or market value and are not quoted in the commercial reports or sold on a stock exchange.[11]

The granting of specific performance is discretionary with the court. This relief will be refused (a) when the contract is not definite; (b) when there is an adequate legal remedy (usually a monetary award); (c) when it works an undue hardship or an injustice on the defaulting party or the consideration is inadequate; (d) when the agreement is illegal, fraudulent, or unconscionable; (e) when the court is unable to supervise the performance of such acts, as when services of a technical nature are to be rendered; or (f) when there has been unreasonable delay in bringing suit.

If the subject matter of the contract lacks uniqueness, specific performance cannot be obtained when the contract is broken. The *Van Wagner Advertising* case turned on what constituted being "unique."

---

[10] Joshua v McBride 19 Ark App 31, 716 SW2d 215 (1986).

[11] Brown v Knox, 219 Neb 189, 361 NW2d 540 (1985).

VAN WAGNER ADVERTISING CORP. V S & M ENTERPRISES

67 NY2d 177, 501 NYS2d 628, 492 NE2d 756 (1986)

Michaels owned a building. She made a lease with Van Wagner Advertising Corporation giving it the right to erect a sign on one of the walls of the building facing automobile traffic entering Manhattan through the

Midtown Tunnel. The lease ran for three years with options to renew up to ten years. Van Wagner erected an illuminated billboard and then leased it to Asch Advertising. Michaels later sold the building to S & M Enterprises. S & M was buying up the property on the block in order to construct a residential-commercial complex. S & M notified Van Wagner that it was terminating the lease. Van Wagner sued S & M for specific performance to make it adhere to the terms of the lease. The court held that the lease was improperly broken but refused to grant specific performance to compel obedience to the lease terms. Van Wagner appealed.

KAYE, J. . . . Whether or not to award specific performance is a decision that rests in the sound discretion of the trial court, and here that discretion was not abused. Considering first the nature of the transaction, specific performance has been imposed as the remedy for breach of contracts for the sale of real property . . . , but the contract here is to lease rather than sell an interest in real property. While specific performance is available, in appropriate circumstances, for breach of a commercial or residential lease, specific performance of real property leases is not in this State awarded as a matter of course. . . .

Van Wagner argues that specific performance must be granted in light of the trial court's finding that the "demised space is unique as to location for the particular advertising purpose intended". The word "uniqueness" is not, however, a magic door to specific performance. . . . Putting aside contracts for the sale of real property, where specific performance has traditionally been the remedy for breach, uniqueness in the sense of physical difference does not itself dictate the propriety of equitable relief. . . .

The point at which breach of a contract will be redressable by specific performance . . . must lie . . . in the uncertainty of valuing it: "What matters, in measuring money damages, is the volume, refinement, and reliability of the available information about substitutes for the subject matter of the breached contract. When the relevant information is thin and unreliable, there is a substantial risk that an award of money damages will either exceed or fall short of the promisee's actual loss. Of course this risk can always be reduced — but only at great cost when reliable information is difficult to obtain. Conversely, when there is a great deal of consumer behavior generating abundant and highly dependable information about substitutes, the risk of error in measuring the promisee's loss may be reduced at much smaller cost. In asserting that the subject matter of a particular contract is unique and has no established market value, a court is really saying that it cannot obtain, at reasonable cost, enough information about substitutes to permit it to calculate an award of money damages without imposing an unacceptably high risk of undercompensation on the injured promisee. Conceived in this way, the uniqueness test seems economically sound." (45 U Chi L Rev, at 362.) This principle is reflected in the case law . . . , and is essentially the position of the Restatement (Second) of Contracts, which lists "the difficulty of proving damages with reasonable certainty" as the first factor affecting adequacy of damages (Restatement [Second] of Contracts § 360[a]).

Thus, the fact that the subject of the contract may be "unique as to location for the particular advertising purpose intended" by the parties does not entitle a plaintiff to the remedy of specific performance.

Here, the trial court correctly concluded that the value of the "unique qualities" of the demised space could be fixed with reasonable certainty and without imposing an unacceptably high risk of undercompensating the injured tenant. Both parties complain: Van Wagner asserts that while lost revenues on the Asch contract may be adequate compensation, that contract expired February 28, 1985, its lease with S & M continues until 1992, and the value of the demised space cannot reasonably be fixed for the balance of the term. S & M urges that future rents and continuing damages are necessarily conjectural, both during and after the Asch contract, and that Van Wagner's damages must be limited to 60 days — the period during which Van Wagner could cancel Asch's contract without consequence in the event Van Wagner lost the demised space. S & M points out that Van Wagner's lease could remain in effect for the full 10-year term, or it could legitimately be extinguished immediately, either in conjunction with a bona fide sale of the property by S & M, or by a reletting of the building if the new tenant required use of the billboard space for its own purposes. Both parties' contentions were properly rejected.

First, it is hardly novel in the law for damages to be projected into the future. Particularly where the value of commercial billboard space can be readily determined by comparisons with similar uses — Van Wagner itself has more than 400 leases — the value of this property between 1985 and 1992 cannot be regarded as speculative. Second, S & M having successfully resisted specific performance on the ground that there is an adequate remedy at law, cannot at the same time be heard to contend that damages beyond 60 days must be denied because they are conjectural. If damages for breach of this lease are indeed conjectural, and cannot be calculated with reasonable certainty, then S & M should be compelled to perform its contractual obligation by restoring Van Wagner to the premises. Moreover, the contingencies to which S & M points do not, as a practical matter, render the calculation of damages speculative. While S & M could terminate the Van Wagner lease in the event of a sale of the building, this building has been sold only once in 40 years; S & M paid several million dollars, and purchased the building in connection with its plan for major development of the block. The theoretical termination right of a future tenant of the existing building also must be viewed in light of these circumstances. If any uncertainty is generated by the two contingencies, then the benefit of that doubt must go to Van Wagner and not the contract violator. Neither contingency allegedly affecting Van Wagner's continued contractual right to the space for the balance of the lease term is within its own control; on the contrary, both are in the interest of S & M. Thus, neither the need to project into the future nor the contingencies allegedly affecting the length of Van Wagner's term render inadequate the remedy of damages for S & M's breach of its lease with Van Wagner.

The trial court, additionally, correctly concluded that specific performance should be denied on the ground that such relief "would be inequitable in that its effect would be disproportionate in its harm to defendant and its assistance to plaintiff." It is well settled that the imposition of an equitable remedy must not itself work an inequity, and that specific performance should not be an undue hardship. . . .

[Judgment affirmed as to denial of specific performance]

QUESTIONS

1. What did the court hold and why?
2. How would the case have been decided if the action for specific performance had been brought by Asch Advertising?
3. Could the damages in the *Van Wagner* case be proven with mathematical certainty?

Ordinarily contracts for the performance of personal services will not be specifically ordered, both because of the difficulty of supervision by the court and because of the restriction of the Thirteenth Amendment of the federal Constitution prohibiting involuntary servitude except as criminal punishment. In some instances, a court will issue a negative injunction that prohibits the defendant from rendering a similar service for anyone else. This may indirectly have the effect of compelling the defendant to work for the plaintiff.

In order to do complete justice, the court in awarding specific performance, can also award damages to compensate for the direct and consequential loss caused by the defendant's refusal to perform the contract.

D. CONTRACT PROVISIONS AFFECTING REMEDIES AND DAMAGES

The contract of the parties may contain provisions that affect the remedies available or the recovery of damages.

§ 22:11 LIMITATION OF REMEDIES

The contract of the parties may limit the remedies of the aggrieved parties. For example, the contract may give one party the right to repair or replace a defective item sold or to refund the contract price. The contract may require both parties to submit any dispute to arbitration or other streamlined procedure.

§ 22:12 LIQUIDATED DAMAGES

The parties may stipulate in their contract that a certain amount should be paid in case of a breach. This amount is known as **liquidated damages.** Liquidated damages may be variously measured by the parties. When delay is in mind, liquidated damages may be a fixed sum, as $100 for each day of delay. When there is a total default, damages may be a percentage of the contract price or may be the amount of the down payment.

(a) EFFECT. When a liquidated damage clause is held valid, the injured party cannot collect more than the amount specified by the clause, and the defaulting party is bound to pay such damages once the fact is established that there has been a default. The injured party is not required to make any proof as to damages sustained, and the defendant is not permitted to show that the damages were not as great as the liquidated sum.

(b) VALIDITY. In order to be valid, a liquidated damage clause must satisfy two requirements: (1) the situation must be one in which it is difficult or impossible to determine the actual damages, and (2) the amount specified must not be excessive when compared with the probable damages that would be sustained.

If the liquidated damages clause calls for the payment of a sum that is clearly unreasonably large and unrelated to the possible actual damages that might be sustained, the clause will be held to be void as a **penalty**.

In the *Walter Implement* case the validity of a liquidated damage clause was challenged.

WALTER IMPLEMENT, INC. V FOCHT
107 Wash 2d 533, 730 P2d 1340 (1987)

Walter Implement, Inc. was a dealer for farm equipment. It leased five pieces of farm equipment to Focht and his wife for five years. The lease provided that if annual rental payments were not made, Walter could take back the equipment, resell it, and then sue Focht for any unpaid balance. The lease also required Focht to pay Walter liquidated damages in such case. These damages were to be "20 percent of the aggregate minimum rental charges for the unexpired portion of the term [of the lease], not as a penalty, but as and for liquidated damages." Focht could not make the second annual payment and returned the equipment to Walter. It sold the equipment and then sued Focht for the liquidated damages. The court entered judgment for Walter for the liquidated damages, computing them by the formula contained in the lease. Focht appealed. The court of appeals held the liquidated damage clause void. Walter then appealed to the state supreme court.

GOODLOE, J. . . . The . . . issue we must decide is whether the liquidated damages clause in the resell remedy provision is enforceable. The clause provides for "an amount equal to twenty (20) percent of the aggregate minimum rental charges for the unexpired portion of the term of this agreement, not as a penalty, but as and for liquidated damages". Exhibit 1. The trial court enforced this clause. The court calculated that Focht, having made only one of the five annual payments, had an unexpired portion of $43,255.28 (four payments at $10,806.32) which was multiplied by 20 percent to get the liquidated damages figure of $8,645.06. The Court of Appeals reversed. It held the clause was unenforceable because it was not a product of the parties' negotiations, was inherently unfair, and bore no relation to the anticipated actual damages.

True liquidated damages clauses, those that are not penalties, are favored and will be upheld. This court follows the United States Supreme Court view that liquidated damages agreements fairly and understandingly entered into by experienced, equal parties with a view to just compensation for the anticipated loss should be enforced. The fact that the contracting parties designate a sum as liquidated damages is a circumstance given serious consideration, but it is not necessarily controlling or conclusive. The designation in this contract that the additional amount is not a penalty but is liquidated damages, therefore, does not decide the issue. Courts will look to the intention of the parties to make an accurate assessment of the clause's purpose. "A provision in a contract which bears no reasonable relation to actual damages will be construed as a penalty." *Enders,* 74 Wash.2d at 594, 446 P.2d 200.

This court has adopted and applied a 2-part test to determine whether a liquidated damages clause is enforceable. First, the amount fixed must be a reasonable forecast of just compensation for the harm that is caused by the breach. Second, the harm must be such that it is incapable or very difficult of ascertainment. Reasonableness of the forecast will be judged as of the time the contract was entered. Determination of whether the test is met depends upon the facts and circumstances of each case.

. . . Most of the cases addressing liquidated damages clauses have involved contracts not to compete in business. With contracts not to compete in business it has been conceded and held that the harm caused by the breach is very difficult to ascertain. . . .

First, we look at the amount fixed to see if it is a reasonable forecast of just compensation for the harm caused by the breach. The involved liquidated damages clause which does not require a fixed amount but instead requires 20 percent of the outstanding rental payments does not appear to have any relation, reasonable or not, to an estimation of damages. A fixed amount of 20 percent of the full lease figure may be a reasonable forecast. In fact, the parties orally agreed that if Focht wished to buy the equipment at the end of the lease term, the cost would be 20 percent of the entire lease figure. This liquidated damages clause by containing a variable makes the amount of liquidated damages depend upon when the default occurs. Even this could be acceptable if . . . the variable was reasonably related to the damages. Here, the liquidated damages could vary from $2161.26 (default in the 4th year) to $8645.06 (default in the first year). No reasoning has been offered explaining how the variation reflects a reasonable forecast of the harm that is caused by the breach. For example, using this formula, the earlier the default the greater the penalty although the equipment is returned sooner resulting in less depreciation of the equipment.

Besides the formula not appearing to have any relation to the anticipated actual damages, such damages are not difficult to ascertain. *American Fin. Leasing & Servs. Co. v. Miller*, 41 Ohio App.2d 69, 322 N.E.2d 149 (1974), which uses the same 2-part test to evaluate liquidated damages clauses, involved a similar equipment lease provision. The *Miller* lease contained several optional remedies, one of which included a recovery of 10 percent of the actual cost to lessor of equipment sold in the event of a default. The court held that actual damages could be easily ascertained. Because of recoupment of the actual damages, the court determined the 10 percent figure

> neither bears a reasonable relationship to such damage, nor is in a reasonable proportion thereto.
>
> Such amount is patently in excess of the actual damage which could be suffered by the lessor, and therefore must be considered as a 'penalty' rather than a stipulated 'liquidated damage.'

Miller, at 75, 322 N.E.2d 149. Using the same reasoning, the liquidated damages clause in this case fails. . . .

The consequence of the preceding analysis is that Walter Implement is entitled to a deficiency judgment. The deficiency judgment is based on actual damages. . . . In a true lease situation, the lessor has a right not only to the contract price but also to the return of the leased goods. The lessor is thus entitled at breach to the value the goods would have had at the expiration of the lease term in addition to the unpaid portion of the contract price. . . .

Evidence presented at trial suggested that the equipment was expected to be worth about 20 percent of the total lease price at the end of the lease, or about $10,000. If that forecast was reasonable, then Walter Implement's damages are the unpaid rents ($43,225.28) plus about $10,000, both reduced to present value, minus the value of the recovered equipment (about $35,000). We affirm the Court of Appeals and find the liquidated damages clause is a penalty and unenforceable. We remand to the trial court to determine how much the equipment reasonably could have been expected to be worth at the end of the lease term. That value should be included in the Fochts' debt and the deficiency adjusted accordingly.

[Judgment affirmed and action remanded]

QUESTIONS

1. Did the court hold that the lease arrangement for damages was illegal?
2. In view of the fact that the Washington supreme court affirmed the judgment of the court of appeals, why did it remand the action?
3. What was the basis for the court's decision?

§ 22:13 LIMITATION OF LIABILITY CLAUSES

A contract may contain a provision stating that one of the parties shall not be liable for damages in case of breach. Such a provision is called an **exculpatory clause** or a limitation of liability clause. As an example of such a provision, a construction contract may state that the contractor shall not be liable for damages from delay caused by third persons.

(a) CONTENT AND CONSTRUCTION. An exculpatory clause must be clear and unambiguous. Moreover, such a clause is strictly construed. For example, a limitation of liability for negligence does not bar liability for violation of a consumer protection statute.[12]

(b) VALIDITY. Exculpatory clauses are generally valid, particularly between experienced business persons. Thus, a telephone company may limit its liability to a nominal amount for the omission of a customer's name and number from the yellow page directory where the limitation is conspicuous, the customer is experienced in business, and the omission was merely the result of simple negligence.[13]

There is a growing trend, however, to limit such exculpatory provisions or to hold them invalid when it is felt that, because of the unequal bargaining power of the contracting parties, the surrender of a right to damages for breach by the other is oppressive or unconscionable. For example, when the subject of a contract is affected with a public interest, and the party exculpating itself has a legal economic monopoly, some courts hold that the exculpatory clause is invalid as contrary to public policy or unconscionable. When the provision is expanded so as to free the contracting party from liability for that party's own negligence, the provision is sometimes held void as contrary to public policy. This is particularly likely to be the result when the party in question is a public utility, which is under the duty to render the performance or to provide the service in question in a nonnegligent way.

[12] Corral v Rollins Protective Services Co. 240 Kan 678, 732 P2d 1260 (1987).

[13] Electronic Security Systems Corp. v Southern Bell Tel. and Tel. Co. (Fla App) 482 So 2d 518 (1986).

In recent years, the concept has developed that a limitation of liability is invalid when persons in an inferior bargaining position are involved. In any case, a limitation of liability is not binding if obtained by misconduct or deception. Also, some courts refuse to recognize provisions releasing a party from liability for negligence when the provisions are so inconspicuous as to raise a question of whether they were knowingly agreed to.[14]

In the *Schutkowski* case the plaintiff claimed that the release she signed did not release the defendant from liability for negligence.

[14] Conradt v Four Star Promotions, Inc. 45 Wash App 847, 728 P2d 617 (1986).

SCHUTKOWSKI V CAREY

(Wyo) 725 P2d 1057 (1986)

Schutkowski went to the Cheyenne Parachute Club to learn skydiving. Before taking her first lesson, she signed a "release and indemnity" form. On her first parachute jump, she was injured. She sued the instructors, Carey and Rodekohr, claiming that they were negligent. They raised the defense that they were protected by the release that she had signed. The court agreed with them, and she appealed.

BROWN, J. . . . [The release stated]

. . . I Barbara Schutkowski of Cheyenne, Wy for myself, my heirs . . . do hereby *fully and forever release* and discharge the said Cheyenne Parachute Club and Bob Rodekohr, Cheyenne, Wyo, and their divisions, and their employees . . . and *all persons whomsoever directly or indirectly liable, from any and all other claims and demands,* actions, and causes of action, damages, costs, loss of services, expenses, and any and all other claims of damages whatsoever both in law and in equity, on account of, or *in any way resulting from, personal injuries,* conscious suffering, death, or property damages sustained by me, arising out of aircraft flights, parachute jumps, or any other means of lift, ascent, or descent from an aircraft . . . on the ground or in flight, and meaning and intending to include herein all such personal injuries, conscious suffering, death or property damage resulting from or in any way connected with or arising out of instructions, training, and ground or air operations incidental thereto, and in consideration of the foregoing premises I . . . hereby expressly stipulate, covenant and agree to indemnify and hold forever harmless the said Cheyenne Parachute Club . . . from any and all actions . . . and any and all other claims for damages whatsoever which may hereafter arise . . . from my negligent, willful or wanton, or intentional act or actions. (Emphasis added.)

The terms of this release and indemnification agreement are contractual and not a mere recital and contain the entire agreement between the parties hereto.

Wyoming courts enforce exculpatory clauses releasing parties from liability for injury or damages resulting from negligence if the clause is not contrary to public policy. Generally, specific agreements absolving participants and proprietors from negligence liability during hazardous recreational activities are enforceable, subject to willful misconduct limitations. *Cain v. Cleveland Para-*

chute Training Center, 9 O.R.B. 28, 9 Ohio App.3d 27, 457 N.E.2d 1185 (1983).
The Ohio court observed in Cain:

> A participant in recreational activity is free to contract with the proprietor of such
> activity so as to relieve the proprietor of responsibility for damages or injuries to the
> participant caused by the negligence of the proprietor, except when caused by will-
> ful or wanton misconduct. [Citations omitted.]

Id., 457 N.E.2d at 1187.
. . . In reaching its determination a court considers (1) whether a duty to the
public exists; (2) the nature of the service performed; (3) whether the contract
was fairly entered into; and (4) whether the intention of the parties is expressed in clear and unambiguous language. Only exculpatory agreements
meeting these requirements are enforceable.

Private recreational businesses generally do not qualify as services demanding a special duty to the public, nor are their services of a special, highly necessary nature. The California Supreme Court, in *Tunkl v. Regents of University of
California*, 60 Cal.2d 92, 32 Cal.Rpt. 33, 36, 383 P.2d 441, 445-446, 6 A.L.R.3d
693 (1963), described the elements of an agreement affecting the public
interest:

> [The agreement] concerns a business of a type generally thought suitable for public
> regulation. The party seeking exculpation is engaged in performing a service of
> great importance to the public, which is often a matter of practical necessity for
> some members of the public. The party holds himself out as willing to perform this
> service for any member of the public who seeks it. . . . As a result of the essential
> nature of the service, in the economic setting of the transaction, the party invoking
> exculpation possesses a decisive advantage of bargaining strength against any
> member of the public who seeks his services. . . .

The service provided by appellees was not a matter of practical necessity for
any member of the public. It was not an essential service, so no decisive bargaining advantage existed. Further, no evidence suggests that appellant was
unfairly pressured into signing the agreement or that she was deprived of an
opportunity to understand its implications. The agreement meets the first
three criteria for determining if the exculpatory clause is valid.

Finally, we must determine if the release clearly shows the intent to eliminate appellee's liability for negligent acts. Public policy disfavors clauses exculpating liability for negligence, and a court must closely scrutinize such
clauses. The exculpatory clause must clearly and unequivocally demonstrate
the parties' intent to eliminate liability for negligence. The question here is
whether "negligence" or other specific words are required to clearly show
intent.

Courts disagree on the specific language needed to show such intent. In
some jurisdictions the word "negligence" or equally precise language is required in order to bar liability for negligent acts. . . .

Conversely, the absence of the word "negligence" is not fatal to an exculpatory clause in many courts if the terms of the contract clearly show intent to
extinguish liability. . . .

Considering all of the language of the agreement in context, it is clear that
the parties' intent was to release appellees from liability for negligence. The
contract wording focuses particular attention on the unconditional nature of

the exculpatory agreement. It specifically and repeatedly exempts appellants from any responsibility for potential consequences. By signing the release, Barbara Schutkowski voluntarily waived her potential claims against

> all persons whomsoever directly or indirectly liable, from *any and all* . . . claims and demands, actions and causes of action . . . and *any and all other claims* of damages *whatsoever both in law and in equity,* and *in any way* resulting from, personal injuries. . . . (Emphasis added.)

Common sense is one of the leading characteristics of contract interpretation and construction. In construing this contract the nature of the service and the purpose of the release must be considered. . . .

In this case it is difficult to envision any claim other than one based on negligence that appellant might have had against appellees. If it was not the intent of the parties to release appellees from liability for negligent acts, we see little purpose in the Release and Indemnity Agreement.

Adult private parties should not enter into a contract for hazardous recreational service lightly. The agreement language is unambiguous; it clearly shows that appellant intended to relinquish all liability claims she might accrue against appellees. We will enforce the exculpatory clause. . . .

[Judgment affirmed]

QUESTIONS

1. What is the public policy toward clauses excluding liability for negligence?
2. Are there any exceptions to the rule stated in your answer to Question 1?
3. What is the basic question involved in the *Schutkowski* case?

---

§ 22:14   ## INVALIDITY OF CONTRACT PROVISION RELATING TO REMEDIES OR DAMAGES

When a contract contains a valid provision governing remedies or damages, the parties are bound thereby. That means that they must follow the procedures specified or the aggrieved person is bound by the provision as to damages. What happens if the provision in question is invalid? The provision is merely ignored. The balance of the contract remains valid. This means that if the limitation of remedies is not valid, an aggrieved person may follow any remedy that would otherwise be available. If a liquidated damages or a limitation of damages clause is invalid, the aggrieved person may sue for the damages sustained, but must actually prove what those damages were.

SUMMARY

When a party fails to perform a contract or performs improperly, the other contracting party may sue for damages caused by the breach. What may be recovered by the aggrieved person is stated in terms of being direct or consequential damages. Direct damages are those that ordinarily will result from the breach. Consequential damages are those that are in fact caused by the breach but do not ordinarily or necessarily result from every breach of the particular kind of contract. Direct damages may be recovered on proof of causation and amount. Consequential damages can only be recovered if, in addition to causation and amount, it is shown that they were reasonably within the contemplation of the contracting parties as a probable result of a breach of the contract. The right to recover consequential damages is lost if the aggrieved party could reasonably have taken steps to avoid such damages. That is, the aggrieved person has a duty to mitigate or reduce damages by reasonable means.

In any case, the damages recoverable for breach of contract may be limited to a specific amount by a liquidated damage clause or may be canceled out completely by a limitation of liability clause. A liquidated damage clause is valid when the circumstances are such that the actual damages cannot be reasonably determined, and the amount specified is not unreasonably disproportionate to the damages that could be caused by a breach of the contract. If both of these conditions are satisfied, the liquidated damage clause is valid, and the injured party recovers the specified amount and cannot recover any greater amount. If both conditions are not satisfied, the liquidated damage clause is held invalid as imposing a penalty, and damages are recovered as though the clause never existed. A clause limiting (excluding) liability for harm caused by the conduct of third persons is valid. When the cause of the harm has been the negligence or the willful misconduct of the person protected by the clause, the limitation is frequently held invalid. Limitations of liability are often held invalid when the effect is to allow a contracting party to evade a duty imposed by law or when there is such a bargaining inequality between the parties as to make the limitation appear unconscionable.

In a limited number of situations, the aggrieved party may bring an action for specific performance to compel the other contracting party to perform the acts called for by the contract. Specific performance is always obtainable of a contract to sell land or real estate on the theory that such property has a unique value. With respect to other contracts, specific performance will not be ordered unless it is shown that there was some unique element present so that the aggrieved person would suffer a damage that could not be compensated for by the payment of money damages.

The aggrieved person also has the option of rescinding the contract if (1) the breach has been as to a material term and (2) the aggrieved party returns everything to the way that it was before the contract was made. Rescission and recovery of monetary damages are alternative remedies except when the contract relates to the sale of goods. In the latter case, the aggrieved party may both rescind and obtain money damages.

Although there has been a breach of the contract, the effect of this breach is nullified if the aggrieved person by word or conduct waives the right to object to the breach. Conversely, an aggrieved party may accept a defective performance without thereby waiving a claim for breach if the party makes a reservation of rights as by stating that the defective performance is accepted without prejudice, under protest, or with reservation of rights.

The continued waiver of a breach of a particular clause may indicate that the parties have modified their contract by abandoning the clause to which the waiver relates. To guard against the unintended modification of a contract by waiver, the contract may contain a clause stating that nothing shall constitute a modification of the contract unless stated in writing. Such a clause, however, may itself be waived.

QUESTIONS AND CASE PROBLEMS

1. What social forces are affected by the rule governing the mitigation of damages?

2. When must a party to a contract mitigate damages caused by the breach of the contract by the other party?

3. Anthony makes a contract to sell a rare painting to Laura for $100,000. The written contract specifies that if Anthony should fail to perform the contract he will pay to Laura $50,000 as liquidated damages. Anthony fails to deliver the painting and is sued by Laura for $50,000. Can she recover this amount?

4. Hogarth owned a factory that used coal for heat and power. He purchased grade A coal from Kay who owned a coal mine. When one of the truckloads of coal was delivered to Hogarth, it was apparent that there was a large quantity of wood and slate mixed in with the coal. Hogarth would have been within his rights if he had rejected the coal as not conforming to the contract, but he needed the coal desperately to keep the furnaces in his factory from going out. He therefore accepted the coal in spite of its defect but expressly stated that he accepted it with a reservation of rights. Kay billed Hogarth for the full price of grade A coal. Hogarth claimed that Kay should reduce the price because of the inferior quality. Kay claimed that Hogarth was not entitled to any reduction. Kay further claimed that Hogarth had the choice only of rejecting the coal because it was poor or of accepting the coal and paying for it at the contract price. Was Kay correct?

5. A, who had contracted to build a house for B, departed from the specifications at a number of points. It would cost approximately $1,000 to put the house in the condition called for by the contract. B sued A for $5,000 for breach of contract and emotional disturbance caused by the breach. Decide.

6. Protein Blenders, Inc., made a contract with Gingerich to buy from him the shares of stock of a small corporation. When the buyer refused to take and pay for the stock, Gingerich sued for specific performance on the contract on the ground that the value of the stock was unknown and could not be readily ascertained because it was not sold on the general market. Was he entitled to specific performance? [Gingerich v Protein Blenders, Inc. 250 Iowa 646, 95 NW2d 522]

7. The buyer of real estate made a down payment. In the contract it was stated that the buyer would be liable for damages in an amount equal to the down payment if the buyer broke the contract. The buyer refused to go through with the contract and demanded his down payment back. The seller refused to return it and claimed that he was entitled to additional damages from the buyer because the damages that he had suffered were greater than the amount of the down payment. Decide. [Waters v Key Colony East, Inc. (Fla App) 345 So 2d 367]

8. Kuznicki made a contract for the installation of a fire detection system by Security Safety Corp. for $498. The contract was made one night and canceled at 9:00 a.m. the next morning. Security then claimed one-third of the purchase price from Kuznicki by virtue of a provision in the contract that "in the event of cancellation of this agreement . . . the owner agrees to pay 33-1/3 percent of the contract price, as liquidated damages." Was Security Safety entitled to recover the amount claimed? [Security Safety Corp. v Kuznicki, 350 Mass 157, 213 NE2d 866]

9. Stabler was under contract to play professional football for Alabama Football, Inc. The corporation was not able to pay Stabler the amount due him under the contract. He sued for rescission. The club defended on the theory that nonpayment was not a sufficiently substantial breach of the contract to justify rescission. Was the club correct? [Alabama Football, Inc. v Stabler, 294 Ala 551, 319 So 2d 678]

10. Melodee Lane Lingerie Co. was a tenant in a building that was protected against fire by a sprinkler and alarm system maintained by the American District Telegraph Co. Because of the latter's fault, the controls on the system were defective and allowed the discharge of water into the building, which damaged Melodee's prop-

erty. When Melodee sued A.D.T., it raised the defense that its service contract limited its liability to 10 percent of the annual service charge made to the customer. Was this limitation valid? [Melodee Lane Lingerie Co. v American District Telegraph Co. 18 NY2d 57, 271 NYS2d 937, 218 NE2d 661]

11. A owned a house. In May he made a contract with B, a roofer, to repair the roof on the house by July 1. B never came to repair the roof and heavy rains in the fall damaged the interior of A's house. A sues B for breach of contract and claims damages for the harm done to the interior of the house. Is A entitled to recover such damages?

12. Compare the purpose, effect, and validity of a liquidated damage clause and a limitation of liability clause.

13. Lowell Prentice wanted to sell his farm, house, and land. After negotiation with Charles Classen, who wanted the property to operate a dairy, the price was agreed to as $45,000. Classen signed a contract for the purchase of the land. Under the contract, Classen made an initial deposit of 10 percent of the purchase price, and he was required to pay the balance in specified installments with 8 percent interest. The contract stated that if the buyer broke the contract, the seller could retain the initial payment of 10 percent and all improvements that had been made to the property by the buyer. Classen moved into the farmhouse with his family and lived there for the next year, during which time he improved the property by adding dairy equipment, a bulk tank, and cement floors in the dairy building. After a year, Classen failed to make necessary payments, and Prentice declared him in default. Classen claimed he was entitled to a refund of the initial 10 percent payment. He claimed that the contract provision allowing Prentice to retain this amount was unconscionable and void. Was he correct? [Prentice v Classen (SD) 355 NW2d 352]

14. Dr. Guinan, acting on behalf of the Cook County Hospital, made a contract to hire Dr. Feldstein as a resident physician for one year. The contract prohibited Feldstein from rendering any medical service outside of the hospital. Guinan then notified Feldstein that the hospital was not going to live up to its contract and that another doctor had been selected as the resident physician. Feldstein then went into private practice and later sued Guinan and the hospital for the salary that he would have received for the year that he would have been a resident physician. The defendants claimed that the amount of Feldstein's claim should be reduced by the fees that he had received from private practice during the year that he would have been a resident physician. Were they correct? [Feldstein v Guinan, 148 Ill App 3d 610, 101 Ill Dec 947, 499 NE2d 535]

15. Wassenaar worked for Panos under a three-year contract which stated that if the contract was terminated wrongfully by Panos before the end of the three years, he would pay as damages the salary for the remaining time that the contract had to run. After three months, Panos terminated the contract and Wassenaar sued him for twenty-one months' pay. Panos claimed that this amount could not be recovered because the contract provision for the payment of such amount was a void penalty. Was this provision valid? [Wassenaar v Panos, 111 Wis 2d 518, 331 NW2d 357]

23

ACCOUNTANTS' LIABILITY AND MALPRACTICE

When is a professional, such as an accountant, an attorney, or a physician, liable for harm caused by improper performance? Under what circumstances can third persons sue for harm?

A. GENERAL PRINCIPLES

The liability of a contracting party for malpractice raises questions of what constitutes malpractice, what remedies are available to enforce liability for malpractice, and the effect of conduct of the plaintiff and of limitations of liability.

§ 23:1 WHAT CONSTITUTES MALPRACTICE

When an accountant, a physician, or an attorney makes a contract to perform services, there is a duty to exercise such skill and care as is common within the community for persons performing similar services. If the services are not properly rendered in accordance with those standards, there is an improper practicing of the particular profession or, as it is commonly called, **malpractice**.

§ 23:2   CHOICE OF REMEDY

Because performance falls below the proper standard in cases of malpractice, malpractice is classified as negligence and constitutes a tort. In addition, because the services called for by the contract have not been rendered, malpractice is also a breach of the contract.

(a) BREACH OF CONTRACT OR TORT ACTION. As malpractice is both a breach of the contract and an independent tort, the client or patient who is harmed has the choice of suing for breach of contract or for the particular tort that is involved. Generally the client or patient will bring a tort action when justified by the facts. This is so because the tort claimant may recover greater damages than the breach-of-contract plaintiff. Moreover, the tort claimant may have a longer period of time in which to sue. The statute of limitations runs on the tort claim from the date when the harm was discovered. In a contract action the statute of limitations runs from the date when the contract was broken. This may be very important, because in some cases the plaintiff does not realize that any harm has been sustained until a substantially long period of time after there was a breach of the contract.

The plaintiff does not have a choice of action when the only misconduct of the defendant is a breach of contract. In order to sue for a tort, the plaintiff must show that the defendant's breach was negligent or willful so that it was tortious as well as being a breach of contract.[1]

(b) ACTION BY THIRD PERSON. When the malpractice claim is brought by a third person rather than a client or patient of the defendant, the malpractice action will be brought on the tort theory. Suit cannot be brought by the third person on the original contract, as the third person is not a party to that contract and ordinarily cannot be classified as a third party beneficiary of that contract.

§ 23:3   THE ENVIRONMENT OF ACCOUNTANTS' MALPRACTICE LIABILITY

In the course of this century, several changes have taken place that have influenced the law of malpractice liability as it relates to accountants.

First, the accountant has in many cases moved from being merely a clerical employee to being an essential participant in the planning of business strategies. In addition, the accountant in many instances has moved from being an employee of one employer to being an independent contractor performing accounting services for many clients. Also, the accountant is now employed in many cases for the purpose of producing data on which third persons will rely. For example, the accountant will prepare statements that will be submitted to banks to induce them to lend to the accountant's client. Likewise, such information may be supplied to prospective purchasers of stock of the client corporation.

As the above changes took place, it became natural for courts to allow third persons relying upon the work product of the accountant to sue the accountant when malpractice caused loss to the third person.

At the same time that the changes noted above were taking place in the economy and in the legal status of the accountant, changes were taking place in other areas of the law. As will be seen in Chapter 30, manufacturers and remote sellers became liable to the ultimate users for damages caused by defective products. Technicians became liable to third persons harmed by their negligence. Thus, this century brings a rising tide of liability to third persons. This background of liability to third per-

---

[1]   Computerized Design and Manufacturing, Inc. v Genrad, Inc. 84 Or App 189, 733 P2d 485 (1987).

sons in other areas naturally influenced the law with respect to accountants.[2]

A word of caution is necessary. Just as the ocean moving up the shore does not move in a straight line but runs higher up the coast at some points, so the law did not change in all states at the same time. For example, some states limit recovery by third persons to cases where personal injuries are sustained. Other courts impose liability if third persons have suffered economic loss. It is this latter wave that is important to accountants, because negligence or false accounting will inflict economic loss. States that recognize the right of third persons to sue for economic loss will naturally tend to permit third persons to sue accountants for malpractice. This will be considered in greater detail in Part C of this chapter.

§ 23:4   ASSIGNMENT OF CLAIM

Much of this chapter is concerned with the right of third persons to recover damages from accountants for malpractice. Distinct from the right of the third person to sue as a "third person" is the right of such person to sue as assignee of the client. The client with a malpractice claim against the accountant may assign this claim to a third person who can then sue the accountant for malpractice.

The same is true of malpractice claims against a technician. For example, an owner of land hired a surveyor to survey the land. Then the owner sold it to a buyer who resold it to another buyer. The court held that a subsequent buyer could not sue the surveyor for negligence in preparing a defective survey, but then held that the owner who hired the surveyor could assign to the subsequent buyer the owner's right under the survey contract. As a consequence, the subsequent buyer could sue the surveyor as assignee of the owner.[3] The net result was the same as though the subsequent buyer had been allowed to sue the surveyor as a third person injured by the surveyor's negligence.

The rule that a client may assign a claim to a third person who can then sue is subject to certain restrictions. In some states, such an assignment will not be recognized because the claim is an unliquidated tort claim. Assuming that the claim can be assigned, it is merely the claim of the client and does not extend to damages sustained by the third person. Because of these limitations, third persons will seek to recover in their own right, rather than as assignees of clients.

§ 23:5   LIMITATION OF LIABILITY

Can accountants protect themselves from liability for malpractice with respect to their clients and third persons? As the law generally permits any contracting party to limit or disclaim liability for negligence, an accountant may exclude liability for malpractice based on the theory of negligence. Influenced by the consumer protection movement and by the law as to product liability, courts will require such disclaimers to be (1) clear and unambiguous and (2) conspicuous. If these requirements are not met, the disclaimers will not be held effective.

(a) SCOPE OF LIMITATION. Disclaimers are valid when the circumstances are such that it is not reasonable to expect the accountant to stand behind particular data. For example, when the client owns land in a foreign country, it is reasonable for the accountant to accept the valuation placed on

---

[2]   The interplay between the various areas of malpractice liability and that of accountants is further seen in the fact that the Restatement of Torts, 2d, does not contain a separate provision applicable only to accountants, but deals with the subject of malpractice liability of accountants to third persons in a general section, § 552. Section 552 declares that "one who in the course of his business, profession or employment, or in any other transaction in which he has a pecuniary interest, supplies false information for the guidance of others in their business transactions, is subject to liability for pecuniary loss caused to them by their justifiable reliance on the information, if he fails to exercise reasonable care or competence in obtaining or communicating the information." The section then continues to define what persons can enforce this liability.

[3]   Essex v Ryan (Ind App) 446 NE2d 368 (1983).

the land by someone in that foreign country. If the accountant includes in the financial statement prepared for the client a statement that the valuation of that land was obtained from an identified person in the foreign country and that the accountant assumes no responsibility for the accuracy of that valuation, the accountant is protected from the falsity of that information. Likewise, if the accountant's examination has been restricted, the accountant is protected from claims of third persons when the accountant makes a certification or statement that certain assets were not examined and that the figures relating thereto had not been verified. For example, when the accountant was restricted from examining accounts receivable and the certificate stated that no opinion was expressed as to accounts receivable, the accountant could not be held liable because the information relating to accounts receivable was not accurate.[4]

(b) LIMITATIONS ON EXCULPATORY PROVISIONS. A disclaimer based on lack of knowledge does not protect the accountant from liability if the accountant had knowledge or reason to know that the statements so made were in fact false. In such a case, a court would hold that the disclaimer was not binding, on the theory that when the accountant stated that personal knowledge was lacking, the accountant impliedly represented that the accountant did not have any knowledge or reason to know that the statements were not correct.

In some states, a limitation of liability or exculpatory clause will only protect the accountant from a malpractice suit brought by the client and not from a suit brought by a third person. In such cases the court applies the general rule of contract law that only a party to a contract is bound by an exculpatory or limitation of liability clause of the contract.[5]

When the malpractice liability of the accountant is based upon an intentional falsification of data, a limitation of liability will not be binding. This follows from the general rule of law that it is against public policy to permit a limitation of liability to immunize an intentional tort.

§ 23:6   CONTRIBUTORY NEGLIGENCE OF PLAINTIFF

When suit is brought by a third person for malpractice, the defendant accountant may raise the defense of the contributory negligence of the plaintiff. If the circumstances are such that the plaintiff acted negligently in relying on a financial statement, the plaintiff cannot sue the accountant because of the latter's negligence in preparing the statement.

For example, when the statement recites that it is merely a working examination and is not certified by the accountant, the third person is negligent if reliance is placed on the statement. In harmony with general principles of negligence law, the plaintiff is then barred by such contributory negligence.

In some cases it may be apparent from the face of the financial statement that the business represented therein is in poor financial condition. When a prudent person would see danger in the financial statement, the plaintiff not perceiving such danger cannot sue the accountant on the ground that the statement was negligently prepared.[6]

B.   MALPRACTICE LIABILITY OF NON-ACCOUNTANTS

The law governing the accountant's liability for malpractice has developed against the background of general principles governing the liability for improper perfor-

---

[4]   Stephans Industries Inc. v Haskins & Sells (CA10 Colo) 438 F2d 357 (1971).
[5]   American Centennial Ins. Co. v Wells Fargo Alarm Service, 152 Ill App 3d 503, 105 Ill Dec 457, 504 NE2d 742 (1986).

[6]   Hasbro Bradley, Inc. v Coopers & Lybrand, 128 App Div 2d 218, 515 NYS2d 461 (1987).

mance of contract by technicians, surveyors, inspectors, and by professionals other than accountants.

§ 23:7   STANDARD OF CARE

When is a contracting party guilty of such poor performance that the conduct may be called "malpractice"? Historically, the term *malpractice* was applied only to persons engaged in the practice of medicine or of law. In the last half century, the concepts of liability for poor performance of a professional have been extended to technicians, surveyors, and safety inspectors. All of these, as well as the lawyer and the doctor, must exercise that degree of care and skill commonly exercised by others following the same calling within the same community.

The standard just described is a variable standard affected by time and place. As new knowledge develops and is accepted within the community, it is malpractice to fail to keep in step with the changing times. With respect to place, the community standards of one geographic area may differ from those of another. With modern methods of transportation and communication, the geographic differential becomes less significant as there is a greater degree of exchange of knowledge and skills between different parts of the country.

§ 23:8   PERSONS ENTITLED TO DAMAGES

Once it is shown that a contracting party is guilty of malpractice, the next step is to determine who may recover damages for such improper conduct.

(a) OTHER CONTRACTING PARTY. When a party is guilty of malpractice, there is a breach of contract and the other contracting party can sue for the damages caused by such breach of contract. Before this century, liability for malpractice in the performance of a contract stopped with the other contracting party.

(b) THIRD PERSONS. Prior to this century, there was no malpractice liability to third persons. In this century, liability to third persons is recognized to some extent.

(1) Privity of contract rule. The rule of law that bars a third person from suing for malpractice is called the **privity of contract rule.** It is explained in terms that there could not be a suit for breach of a contract because there was no privity of contract between the third person and the defendant. This is the same concept that for several centuries barred a third person from claiming the right to sue on a contract as a third party beneficiary. The privity of contract rule also barred the stranger to the contract from suing one of the contracting parties for malpractice. Many courts continue to follow this rule today for fear that by abandoning the requirement of privity, they may be subjecting the defendant to an endless number of lawsuits that in effect would cause the economic death of the defendant.

(2) Abandonment of privity of contract rule. In this century, a number of courts have abandoned the privity of contract rule and allowed third persons to sue for malpractice by a contracting party. In some cases, the court felt that no evil would follow the abandonment of the privity of contract rule. The number of persons who might be affected would be small, and therefore there was no danger of a flood of litigation. The defendant would not be economically destroyed because insurance was available or the burden of liability could be passed on to other customers and clients by the defendant's raising fees and charges.

Rejecting the privity of contract rule, one court held that when an insurance company was negligent in making a safety examination of the boiler in the insured building and because of that negligence an employee was scalded from a bursting boiler, suit could be brought against the insurance company by the widow of the employee who died from the burn.[7] Likewise,

---

[7]   Seay v Travelers Indemnity Co. (Tex App) 730 SW2d 774 (1987).

the repairer of an automobile who negligently repairs the brakes is liable to a pedestrian injured when the brakes fail. A surveyor making a negligent survey for a real estate developer is liable to a subsequent purchaser of the land for loss caused by a mistake in the survey.[8] An architect negligently preparing an inspection report on the condition of the building for a building owner is liable to the buyer who sustains loss by purchasing the building on the basis that its condition was good, as stated in the erroneous report. When a lawyer is retained to draw a will to leave property to particular persons, those persons can sue the lawyer for negligence when the lawyer improperly prepares the will with the result that the third persons do not receive the property intended for them.

In the *A. E. Investment Corporation* case, the third person sued the architect for economic loss.

[8]   Cook Consultants, Inc. v Larson (Tex App) 700 SW2d 231 (1985).

A. E. INVESTMENT CORP. V LINK BUILDERS, INC.
62 Wis 2d 479, 214 NW2d 764 (1974)

The More-Way Development Company contracted with Link to construct a building. DeQuardo, Robinson, Crouch & Associates, Inc., were the architects who designed the building. After the building was constructed, A. E. Investment Corporation rented a part of the building. Because of the negligence of the architects, the building settled. A. E. Investment Corporation was forced to leave the building because of this condition. It then sued the architects for the economic loss sustained thereby. The architects filed a demurrer to the complaint. The lower court overruled the demurrer. The defendant architects appealed.

HEFFERNAN, J. . . . It was alleged that the architect was negligent in its failure to adequately supervise the construction, in that it failed to determine the nature and condition of the subsoil prior to and during construction. It was also alleged that, in view of the subsoil conditions, the plans were negligently drawn because they did not provide for the construction of a floor that was necessary to accommodate the plaintiff's business enterprise.

It was alleged that the defendant knew that the building would be used as a commercial store and the plaintiff would therein operate a supermarket. It was alleged that, as the direct and proximate result of the negligence, the floor space leased to the plaintiff began to settle, damage was caused to the walls, the floor became uneven, and eventually the premises became untenantable. . . .

. . . The defendant defines the question . . . as being whether the defendant had a "duty to protect the subtenant plaintiff's future economic interests from loss allegedly resulting from a condition of the building." It responds to that question only by attempting to show that an architect owes no duty to a person with whom he is not in privity of contract. As a consequence, the defendant relies on the narrow argument that it has no responsibility for any economic loss to the plaintiff because it has no duty to the plaintiff at all and no responsibility to be answerable for any damages, irrespective of the nature of the loss. . . .

We believe that the narrow concept of duty relied on by the defendant architect has long been discarded in Wisconsin law. The duty of any person is the obligation of due care to refrain from any act which will cause foreseeable harm to others even though the nature of that harm and the identity of the harmed person or harmed interest is unknown at the time of the act. . . . ". . . Once an act has been found to be negligent, we no longer look to see if there was a duty to the one who was in fact injured." . . .

In the instant case . . . the defendant's alleged failure to properly take into account the condition of the subsoil when designing and supervising the construction of the building was an act or omission that would foreseeably cause some harm to someone. The duty was to refrain from such act or omission. Where, as here, it is alleged that the architect knew the purpose for which the building was being constructed, it was clearly foreseeable that a future tenant of the building was within the ambit of the harm. Hence, the harm to the particular plaintiff was foreseeable, although under the methodology of this court, it is not necessary that either the person harmed or the type of harm that would result be foreseeable. The act or omission in the face of foreseeable harm was negligence. . . .

Under Wisconsin negligence law, architects may be liable to third parties with whom they are not in privity of contract. The lack of privity does not constitute a policy reason for not imposing liability where negligence is shown to be a substantial factor in occasioning the harm.

The defendant also argues that, since an architect is a professional, his paramount duty is to his client, and that, if no duty is breached in connection with the architect-client relationship, there is no responsibility to third parties. We disagree with the argument that a professional can exonerate himself from liability for a negligent act which will foreseeably cause harm to third parties, merely because his client does not object. The very essence of a profession is that the services are rendered with the understanding that the duties of the profession cannot be undertaken on behalf of a client without an awareness and a responsibility to the public welfare. The entire ambit of state regulations as they apply to the profession of architecture is intended, not solely for the protection of the person with whom the architect deals, but for the protection of the world at large. Professionalism is the very antithesis to irresponsibility to all interests other than those of an immediate employer.

In the instant case, however, if, as it is alleged, the defendant architect negligently designed or permitted the erection of an unsuitable or unstable structure, it was hardly acting in the interests of its client, whether that client has seen fit to complain or not. . . .

[Judgment affirmed]

QUESTIONS

1. Was there a contract between the architect and the tenants of the building?
2. Were the tenants third party beneficiaries of the contract between the building owner and the architect?
3. Only a party to a contract or a third party beneficiary of a contract can sue for harm caused by the improper performance of a contract. Appraise this statement.

(3) Relaxation of Privity of Contract Rule. Some courts have been unwilling to follow the privity rule and yet have been faced with a case in which they were reluctant to abandon that rule. At times, such a court has escaped from this dilemma by reaching the conclusion that the facts presented a situation that could be described as presenting the equivalent of privity or substantially the same as privity of contract.

Such a court will allow the recovery of malpractice damages by the stranger to the contract when there is a sufficiently close connection of the stranger to the transaction or sufficient contact with the defendant that it appears proper to allow suit by the stranger.

C.   ACCOUNTANTS' MALPRACTICE LIABILITY

There is not much litigation on the subject of what standards of conduct accountants should observe. Most of the litigation involves the question whether third persons may sue an accountant for malpractice.

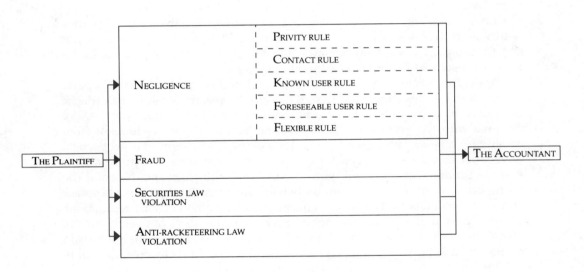

FIGURE 23-1
SUING THE ACCOUNTANT

§ 23:9   STANDARDS OF CONDUCT FOR ACCOUNTANTS

Accountants are liable to their clients when loss is caused the clients because the accountants failed to observe the standards of sound accounting practices, and the clients sustain loss or fail to prevent loss because of such malpractice. Basically the concept is the same as is applied to doctors and attorneys.

An accountant is liable to the client when the accountant negligently fails to detect or fraudulently conceals signs that an employee of the client is embezzling from the client or that the internal audit controls of the client's business are not being observed. An accountant who prepares tax returns and acts as tax manager for the client will be liable when negligently given advice results in additional taxes or penalties being assessed against the client.

§ 23:10 NONLIABILITY TO THE INTERLOPER

No court imposes liability on the accountant to a total stranger who gets possession of the accountant's work and then sustains a loss because of a false statement in the work, whether such statement was negligent or intentional. For example, assume that a negligently prepared financial statement of a corporation is thrown in the wastepaper basket and is then retrieved by a security guard. If the guard thinks that the statement is a "hot tip" and invests in the stock of the corporation on the basis of the statement, the guard cannot sue the accountant for negligence in preparing the statement. The problem considered in the sections that follow represents the struggle of the courts to form a rule that will exclude what the court regards as interlopers but permit suits by those the courts regard as proper plaintiffs.

§ 23:11 NONLIABILITY TO PERSON AFFECTED BY THE DECISION OF ACCOUNTANT'S CLIENT

On the basis of information furnished by the accountant to the client, the client may make a decision that affects a third person. For example, the report of the independent auditor may indicate that the business manager or fiscal officer of the client has not handled funds properly or that it is economically unsound to enter into a contract with a third person. Assume that the client relies on the accountant's report and fires the employee or refuses to make a contract with the third person. If, in fact, the report of the accountant was negligently made, and the true facts would not have justified the action taken by the client, the question arises whether the third person or the discharged employee may sue the negligent accountant. It has been held that such a suit may not be brought.[9]

---

[9] Harper v Inkster Public Schools and Arthur Andersen & Co. 158 Mich App 456, 404 NW2d 776 (1987).

§ 23:12 ACCOUNTANTS' NEGLIGENCE MALPRACTICE LIABILITY TO THIRD PERSONS

In the last century, the negligence of the accountant would impose liability only to the client of the accountant. Today, many states permit third persons to recover damages from the accountant.

(a) STATUS OF ACCOUNTANT. The accountant sued by the third person for malpractice may be an in-house accountant working full-time for the particular employer; an independent contractor who regularly does accounting-related work, such as preparing financial statements and tax returns for different clients; or an independent auditor.

What constitutes negligence is the same for all three types of accountants. As a practical matter, a third person would not ordinarily sue the employee-accountant because the claim would probably be much more than the employee could pay.

It is the independent contractor accountant and the independent auditor accountant who are more likely to be sued by third persons for negligent malpractice. The very fact that the accountant is an independent auditor indicates an intention and an awareness that the accountant prepares something on which third persons would rely.

(b) CONFLICTING THEORIES. A number of theories have been developed in this century to determine whether a third person sustaining a loss because of the accountant's negligence can sue the accountant for loss or whether he/she is an interloper who cannot sue. These views may be identified as (1) the privity rule, (2) the contact rule, (3) the known-user rule, and (4) the foreseeable-user rule. In addition, some courts follow a flexible rule, deciding each case as it arises.

Each of these views represents an attempt to draw a boundary line between the interloper and the "proper" plaintiff. Each view is supported by honest judges seeking to do justice. They have the same goal and are all guided by ethics, but the resultant rule of law is different.

(1) THE PRIVITY RULE. The privity rule excludes a negligence malpractice suit by a third person. This rule holds that only the person in privity with the accountant, that is, the client of the accountant, may sue the accountant.

This rule was originally known as the New York rule,[10] although it has been replaced in New York by the contact rule. The privity rule is still the law in many jurisdictions, although many have departed from it.

(2) THE CONTACT RULE. As a relaxation of the privity requirement, New York now holds that a third person may sue a negligent accountant when there was some contact between the third persons and the accountant. For example, when the accountant goes to the bank to see what information the bank requires in order for the accountant's client to obtain a loan, there is a sufficient "link" or "contact" between the bank and the accountant to allow the bank to sue the accountant if it sustains loss because of the accountant's negligence.[11]

(3) THE KNOWN-USER RULE. By this rule, the accountant is liable for a third person's negligently caused loss when the accountant knew the third person would be using the accountant's work product. For example, when the accountant prepares a financial statement for the client with the knowledge that it will be taken by the client to the First National Bank in order to obtain a loan, the First National Bank may sue the accountant for negligent loss, even though the bank never had any direct contact or dealings with the accountant and was not in privity with the accountant. However, no one other than the known user may sue the accountant for negligence. The fact that the plaintiff was a foreseeable user does not give the right to sue in a known-user state. Accordingly, when the accountant prepared a financial statement for the client and nothing was said as to what further use of the statement would be made, creditors of the client could not sue the accountant for negligence in the preparation of the statement, because it was the client who was the known user.[12]

If the court follows the privity rule or the contact rule described in the two preceding sections, the known user cannot sue the accountant for negligent malpractice. Moreover, some courts that follow the known-user rule apply it so strictly that a substitute foreseeable user is not allowed to sue. To illustrate, assume that in the case just stated the client was refused the loan by the First National Bank. The client might then make an application for a loan to the Second National Bank. It has been held that the Second National Bank could not sue the accountant because the Second National Bank was not a known user. The Second National Bank, however, would be allowed to sue, under the views discussed in the sections that follow.

(4) THE FORESEEABLE-USER RULE. The accountant may foresee that a particular class of unknown persons will rely on the accountant's work. For example, when the accountant prepares a financial statement knowing that the client is going to use it to borrow money from some bank or finance company, the accountant foresees that there is a class of lenders, even though the accountant does not have any particular lender in mind. Likewise, the accountant may know that the financial statement will be used to sell the stock of the client corpo-

[10] Ultramares Corp. v Touche, 255 NY 170, 174 NE 441 (1931).
[11] Credit Alliance Corp. v Arthur Andersen & Co. 65 NY2d 536, 483 NE2d 110 (1985). Some courts are reluctant to turn their backs on the requirement of privity and describe the contact rule not as a different rule but as requiring "a relationship sufficiently intimate to be equated with privity." Empire of America v Arthur Andersen & Co. ___ App Div 2d ___, 514 NYS2d 578 (1987).

[12] Badische Corp. v Caylor, 257 Ga 131, 356 SE2d 198 (1987).

ration. Here again there is a class consisting of unknown persons.

When it is reasonable to foresee that there will be persons who will rely on the statement of the accountant, the foreseeable-user rule imposes liability on the accountant for negligent malpractice and allows such third persons to sue for their loss without regard to the lack of privity of contract between the third persons and the ac-

countants.[13] In the *Spherex* case, the lawsuit turned on whether the plaintiff could recover from the accountant hired by the plaintiff's customer.

[13] H. Rosenblum, Inc. v Adler, 93 NJ 324, 461 A2d 138 (1983). This rule is now regarded by some courts as representing the majority view. The foreseeable-user rule brings the law as to accountants in harmony with the tort law relating to other persons and activities.

SPHEREX, INC. V ALEXANDER GRANT & CO.
122 NH 898, 451 A2d 1308 (1982)

General Home Products (GHP) hired the accounting firm of Alexander Grant & Company to prepare a financial statement of GHP. GHP submitted this financial statement to Spherex so that it could buy on credit. The financial statement had been negligently prepared, and Spherex lost money by selling to GHP on credit. Spherex then sued Alexander Grant on the ground that it knew that the financial statement prepared by it would be submitted to Spherex to obtain credit, but Grant was negligent in preparing it. Suit was brought in the federal district court for the District of New Hampshire, and that court certified to the state supreme court the question of liability of an accountant to a non-privity plaintiff.

DOUGLAS, J. . . . The facts certified by the district court are that the defendant, Alexander Grant and Company (Alexander Grant), a partnership with its principal place of business in Philadelphia, contracted to perform accounting services for General Home Products Corporation (GHP) of Pennsauken, New Jersey. GHP engaged Alexander Grant to prepare an unaudited financial statement for the twelve-month period ending December 31, 1977, based on financial information provided by GHP. GHP submitted copies of this statement to the plaintiff, Spherex, Inc. (Spherex), a New Hampshire-based manufacturer of spoked wheels for baby carriages and shopping carts, for the purpose of obtaining credit. Spherex subsequently sustained a financial loss in its dealings with GHP and filed suit in United States district court alleging: that Alexander Grant either knew that the unaudited financial statement was inaccurate or was negligent in preparing the statement; that Alexander Grant knew GHP would show the statement to Spherex; and, that Spherex detrimentally relied on the statement in extending credit to GHP. Alexander Grant, in defense, contended its potential liability did not extend to a third-party creditor of GHP with whom Alexander Grant was not in privity. Alexander Grant further asserted it is unreasonable, as a matter of law, for a third party to rely upon an unaudited financial statement.

. . .

It should be noted at the outset that the question before this court is not Alexander Grant's liability to Spherex for intentional misrepresentation, or fraud. *Ultramares Corp. v. Touche*, 255 N.Y. 170, 174 N.E. 441 (1931), the semi-nal case on an accountant's liability to third parties, from which Alexander Grant's privity defense stems, distinguished intentional from negligent mis-representation, and held that an accountant could be liable to a non-client whom he intentionally deceived. Justice Cardozo, writing for the New York Court of Appeals, took note of the defendant accountant's liability in that case to a plaintiff who detrimentally relied on *intentional* material misstatements:

> The defendants owed to their employer a duty imposed by law to make their certificate without fraud, and a duty growing out of contract to make it with the care and caution proper to their calling. Fraud includes the pretense of knowledge when knowledge there is none. To creditors and investors to whom the employer exhibit-ed the certificate, the defendants owed a like duty to make it without fraud, since there was notice in the circumstances of its making that the employer did not intend to keep it to himself.

In other words, where an accountant or other supplier of information knows that a materially false statement is to be conveyed to some party other than to whom it is made, public policy is served by holding the intentional wrongdoer accountable to the one who relies to his detriment on the misstatement of fact.

The considerations are different when the misrepresentation is *negligently* made. "If liability for negligence exists, a thoughtless slip or blunder, the fail-ure to detect a theft or forgery beneath the cover of deceptive entries, may expose accountants to a liability in an indeterminate amount for an indetermi-nate time to an indeterminate class." Courts have read this language in *Ul-tramares* as requiring privity between a defendant-accountant and a plaintiff before liability for negligent misrepresentation can attach. . . .

Counsel for both parties agree, and our research has revealed no cases to the contrary, that this question is unsettled in New Hampshire. Yet, we have expressed our disfavor for the privity doctrine in personal injury cases. Our reluctance to apply the privity rule has extended to allowing a proper plaintiff to recover for mere financial loss resulting from the negligent per-formance of services. The duty that Spherex alleges it was owed by Alex-ander Grant is not entirely dissimilar to the duty we have held a promisor owes to an intended third-party beneficiary. In *Tamposi Associates v. Star Mkt. Co.*, 119 N.H. 630, 406 A.2d 132 (1979), we said "[a] third-party benefi-ciary relationship exists if . . . the contract is so expressed as to give the promisor reason to know that a benefit to a third party is contemplated by the promisee as one of the motivating causes of his making the contract." In the instant case, Spherex claims Alexander Grant's duty to produce an unaudited financial statement in a non-negligent manner grew out of Alex-ander Grant's engagement contract with GHP. Spherex's status as a third-party user of the financial statement prepared by Alexander Grant, if proved at trial, would be akin to an intended third-party beneficiary to whom Alex-ander Grant owed a duty of due care.

The *Ultramares* holding, and its apparent privity requirement, has been dis-tinguished primarily on two bases. First, courts have sought to link the privity doctrine with Justice Cardozo's "social utility" rationale of protecting profes-sionals from the specter of unlimited liability to a virtually limitless class of plaintiffs. Thus, judges have not hesitated to permit recovery where the plain-tiff's identity was specifically known to the negligent defendant. . . . Beyond that, courts have been less willing to expand the frontier of liability. The question is "whether the defendant has some special reason to anticipate the reliance of the plaintiff."

Second, *Ultramares* has been distinguished as a relic of a bygone economic era. Both the sophistication of modern accounting procedures and the accountant's central role in the financing and investment industry are a far cry from the fledgling profession in need of judicial protection that existed at the time of *Ultramares*. One commentator has stated:

> The accountant today has a role of central responsibility in the business community. . . . This new circumstance, not present when *Ultramares* was decided, makes it clear that 'between the innocent reliant party and the negligent public accountant, the accountant should bear the burden of his negligence.' The accountant then must accept the burdens of legal responsibility that go along with the benefits derived from his important role in the modern business community.

The Restatement (Second) of Torts § 552 has sought to harmonize the accountant's contemporary role and his potential liability by holding him accountable to a "person or one of a limited group of persons for whose benefit and guidance he intends to supply the information or knows that the recipient intends to supply it. . . . " In effect, an accountant who negligently misrepresents information is held liable not only to known third parties but to an actually foreseeable class of third persons. As comment *a* to section 552 explains, extending an accountant's liability to an intended recipient of information "promotes the important social policy of encouraging the flow of commercial information upon which the operation of the economy rests." Furthermore, an accountant, like the manufacturer under products liability law, is in the best position to regulate the effects of his conduct by controlling the degree of care exercised during the performance of his professional duties. The accountant, through the fee structure, can pass along to his clients the cost of insuring against financial loss sustained by them through reliance upon his negligent misstatement of fact.

We believe section 552 of the Restatement represents a reasoned approach to the issue of professional liability for negligent misrepresentation. . . .

Nevertheless, we acknowledge that an accountant's potential liability is not boundless. "It is not enough that the maker merely knows of the ever-present possibility of repetition [of information supplied by him] to anyone, and the possibility of action in reliance upon it, on the part of anyone to whom it may be repeated." Restatement (Second) of Torts § 552 comment *h*, at 133. The plaintiff's relationship to the accountant becomes crucial because

> the risk of liability to which the supplier subjects himself by undertaking to give the information, while it may not be affected by the identity of the person for whose guidance the information is given, is vitally affected by the number and character of the persons, and particularly the nature and extent of the proposed transaction.

Therefore, while an accountant is to employ a sufficient degree of care in the performance of professional activities in order to protect himself from liability, the law must not arbitrarily extend that liability beyond his reasonable expectations as to whom the information will reach. "The risk reasonably to be perceived defines the duty to be obeyed. . . . " *Palsgraf v. Long Island R. Co.*, 248 N.Y. 339, 162 N.E. 99 (1928). We believe section 552 of the Restatement preserves such reasonable boundaries of liability.

We are unable, as a matter of law, to consider it unreasonable for a third party to rely upon information presented in an unaudited financial statement prepared by the defendant accountant, or to rely upon an accountant to verify the substantive accuracy of the information presented in an unaudited financial statement. It is for Spherex at trial to adduce evidence as to any duty undertaken by the accounting firm in its engagement contract with the client, irrespective of the unaudited nature of the financial statement it prepared.

[Action remanded]

QUESTIONS

1. Why does the court begin the discussion of the case with the statement that the case did not involve liability for intentional misrepresentation or fraud?
2. Was the court influenced by a change in the role of accountants? Explain your answer.
3. What standard is adopted by the Restatement of Torts for determining the negligence liability of accountants to third persons?

(5) THE FLEXIBLE RULE. Some courts have rejected the requirement of privity in malpractice suits against accountants but have not adopted any one of the rules discussed in the preceeding sections. These courts prefer to keep the question open and to decide each case as it arises. In the *Raritan River* case, the plaintiffs claimed that the court should adopt the flexible view.

RARITAN RIVER STEEL COMPANY V CHERRY, BEKAERT & HOLLAND

79 NC App 81, 339 SE2d 62 (1986)

Intercontinental Metals Corporation (IMC) hired Cherry, Bekaert & Holland (Cherry) to prepare financial statements of its business. Cherry prepared the statements and gave IMC seventy copies. Relying on the financial statement, the Raritan River Steel Company and Sidbec-Dosco, Inc. extended credit to IMC. It was later shown that the financial statements negligently reported IMC as having much greater assets than it in fact had. IMC went into bankruptcy. Raritan and Sidbec then sued Cherry for the amounts that IMC had not paid them. From a decision in favor of Cherry, the creditors appealed.

WHICHARD, J. . . . The issue is whether a third person not in privity with a certified public accountant may bring a claim against that accountant for negligent misrepresentation concerning the preparation of an audit opinion which the third person allegedly relied on to his or her detriment.

. . . The judicial trend is toward an abrogation of the privity requirement in favor of a more flexible and equitable standard. Justice Cardozo's decision in

Ultramares Corp. v. Touche, 255 N.Y. 170, 174 N.E. 441 (1931) first established the privity requirement. It warned:

> If liability for negligence exists, a thoughtless slip or blunder, the failure to detect a theft or forgery beneath the cover of deceptive entries, may expose accountants to a liability in an indeterminate amount for an indeterminate time to an indeterminate class. The hazards of a business conducted on these terms are so extreme as to enkindle doubt whether a flaw may not exist in the implication of a duty that exposes to these consequences.

Id. at 179-80, 174 N.E. at 444.

This Court, however, has stated that "the rationale of *Ultramares* is not . . . controlling where the damages to an identified third party are reasonably foreseeable by the defendant." *Howell*, 49 N.C.App. at 495, 272 S.E.2d at 24. Following that reasoning, it held that plaintiff shareholders had a claim against defendant engineers for negligent misrepresentation concerning a soil report prepared by defendants for plaintiff shareholders' corporation, despite the absence of privity between plaintiffs and defendants.

"It is well settled in North Carolina that privity of contract is not required in order to recover against a person who negligently performs service for another and thus injures a third party." *Ingle v. Allen*, 71 N.C.App 20, 26, 321 S.E.2d 588, 594 (1984). In particular, under certain circumstances a third person not in privity of contract with an attorney may recover for negligence in the performance of the attorney's employment contract with his or her client. *See, e.g., Leasing Corp.*, 45 N.C.App at 406-07, 263 S.E.2d at 317-18. In *Leasing Corp.* the Court held that plaintiff, a lessor of equipment to defendant attorneys' client, adequately stated a claim against defendants for negligence concerning a title opinion letter issued by defendants to their client and relied on by plaintiff.

We find no compelling basis for distinguishing accountants from other professionals in this regard. Following *Leasing Corp.* and *Howell*, we thus hold that lack of privity of contract is not a bar to actions by third parties against certified public accountants for negligent misrepresentation.

Jurisdictions which have abandoned the privity requirement have adopted several standards for determining accountants' liability in tort. The most commonly applied alternative to the privity rule is that in the Restatement (Second) of Torts Sec. 552 (1977). It provides that:

> (1) One who, in the course of his business, profession or employment, or in any other transaction in which he has a pecuniary interest, supplies false information for the guidance of others in their business transactions, is subject to liability for pecuniary loss caused to them by their justifiable reliance upon the information, if he fails to exercise reasonable care or competence in obtaining or communicating the information. (2) Except as stated in Subsection (3), the liability stated in Subsection (1) is limited to loss suffered
>
> (a) by the person or one of a limited group of persons for whose benefit and guidance he intends to supply the information or know that the recipient intends to supply it; and
>
> (b) Through reliance upon it in a transaction that he intends the information to influence or knows that the recipient so intends or in a substantially similar transaction.

Restatement (Second) of Torts Sec. 552 (1977).

This Court has followed the Restatement approach to negligent misrepresentation actions by third parties not in privity in suits against engineers and real estate appraisers. As construed in *Howell*, the Restatement restricts actions to a plaintiff or limited group of plaintiffs "to whom defendant intended the information to be supplied, who have suffered a loss in reliance upon the information in a transaction which defendant intended the information to influence." *Howell*, 49 N.C.App. at 497, 272 S.E.2d at 25. Accordingly, in *Howell* plaintiffs established a claim for relief under this test by alleging "that defendants prepared the soil test reports with express knowledge that they would be used to induce plaintiffs to invest in the corporation and defendants' agent so advised plaintiffs upon the reliability of the soil reports." *Id.*

Another standard is a balancing test containing several factors. This standard originates with *Biakanja v. Irving*, 49 Cal.2d 647, 320 P.2d 16 (1958). In *Biakanja* a will was denied probate because the notary public who prepared it negligently failed to have it attested. Plaintiff, a beneficiary under the will, sought damages from the notary public. The Court held that third-party liability was a policy matter and applied the following six-factor balancing test:

> The extent to which the transaction was intended to affect the plaintiff; the foreseeability of harm to [plaintiff], the degree of certainty that the plaintiff suffered injury, the [proximity] between the defendant's conduct and the injury suffered, the moral blame attached to the defendant's conduct, and the policy of preventing future harm.

In *Aluma Kraft Manufacturing Co. v. Elmer Fox & Co.*, 493 S.W.2d 378 (Mo.App 1973), the court applied the *Biakanja* test to accountants. Plaintiff there, a buyer of stock of defendant accounting firms' client, sought damages for negligence in the performance of an audit it detrimentally relied on in the stock purchase. Applying the *Biakanja* test, the Court held that plaintiff had stated a claim sufficient to withstand defendants' motion to dismiss.

This Court has acknowledged or applied the *Biakanja* test to find a third-party claim against architects. It has also applied this test to find a third-party claim against attorneys.

Two jurisdictions have adopted a standard negligence theory of recovery known as the reasonably foreseeable test. Under this theory, accountants owe a duty of care to all parties who are reasonably foreseeable recipients of financial statements for business purposes, provided the recipients rely on the statements pursuant to those business purposes. *Rosenblum v. Adler*, 93 N.J. 324, 352, 461 A.2d 138, 153 (1983); *see also Citizens State Bank v. Timm, Schmidt & Co.*, 113 Wis.2d 376, 386, 335 N.W.2d 361, 366 (1983). In *Rosenblum* a corporate plaintiff acquired the stock of defendant accounting firm's client. When the stock later proved worthless, plaintiff sued defendants alleging negligence and detrimental reliance. Applying the reasonably foreseeable test, the Court found defendants liable for negligent misrepresentation.

The courts of this jurisdiction have not applied the reasonably foreseeable test to find liability to third parties in any negligent misrepresentation action. We also decline here to apply it to accountants. Especially in the field of accounting, "it [is] necessary to adopt a more restricted rule of liability [for pecuniary loss], because of the extent to which misinformation may be, and may be expected to be, circulated, and the magnitude of the losses which may follow from reliance upon it." Restatement (Second) of Torts 2d Sec. 552, comment a (1977).

We also do not adopt the Restatement test. The Restatement approach "is similar to the privity rule in that it draws an arbitrary limit on the class of potential plaintiffs." *Negligent Misrepresentation*, 18 Suffolk L.Rev. at 445. "While the *Restatement* position is easily applied, its arbitrary limitations create an undesirable inflexibility which denies injured third parties recovery simply because they do not fall within a specific class of persons." *Id.* at 445-46; *see also* Restatement (Second) of Torts Sec. 552, comment h, illustrations 5-7 (1977). In essence, liability hinges on the purpose of a particular audit. While the purpose of a particular audit may be relevant to foreseeability, it should not be exclusively determinative.

The *Biakanja* test, by contrast, avoids the necessity of an arbitrary, purpose-based determination of liability by allowing a court to weigh the purpose of the audit as one of several determinative factors. As noted, this Court has applied this test to find third-party liability for professionals in law and architecture. We now adopt it for determining professional accountants' liability to third parties as well.

[Judgment affirmed as to right of plaintiffs to sue]

QUESTIONS

1. What defense was raised by Cherry?
2. On what does the court base its decision?
3. What is the significance of the fact that the accountant furnished the client with seventy copies of the financial statement?

§ 23:13   ACCOUNTANTS' FRAUD MALPRACTICE LIABILITY TO THIRD PERSONS

Society in general condemns fraud more strongly than it does negligence. This is seen in the greater liability of accountants for fraudulent malpractice.

(a) WHAT CONSTITUTES FRAUD WITH RESPECT TO ACCOUNTANTS. In Chapter 15, fraud was defined as a false statement made with knowledge that it was false, or with reckless indifference as to whether it was true or not. This statement was made with the intent that the listener rely thereon, and the listener did so rely and sustained loss. In the field of accounting, the false statement will typically be one of accounting in such manner as to make the client appear to be in a better financial position than is actually the case. For example, the client may own assets that are worthless, but the accountant retains them on the financial statement at cost or some other unreasonable value.

At times, the falsification of the financial statement may be designed to downgrade the financial condition of the corporation. This has been done when the object was to induce shareholders to sell their stock to a dominant group of shareholders. The false financial statement purposely undervalued the assets of the corporation to make the stockholders believe that their stock had little value and that, therefore, they should sell at the low price offered by the dominant group.

(b) FRAUD LIABILITY OF ACCOUNTANTS TO INTENDED VICTIMS. When an accountant commits fraud, it is typically aimed to mislead a third person whose identity is known to the accountant or to a class of persons whose identity is known to the accountant. Any such victim, whether an identified person or the member of a contemplated class of potential victims, may sue the accountant for loss caused by fraud. The problem of privity (relating to liability for negligence) is ignored when the basis of the malpractice suit is fraud. The social force of preventing fraud overrides the concern for creating a hardship upon the accountant by allowing third persons to bring suit.

When accountants make a false financial statement for a corporate client with knowledge that it will be used in selling securities of the corporation to third persons, such third persons may sue the accountant for the damages sustained. Thus, the accountant has been held liable for disguising the true character of a hoped-for profit from the sale and resale of real estate by describing it as "deferred income," although there was little reason to believe that the transaction could ever be completed. In this case, the buyer, who was obligated to pay $5 million for the property, had assets of only $100,000. The financial statement would have shown a loss instead of a substantial profit if the true character of the transaction had been disclosed.

§ 23:14   ACCOUNTANTS'
          MALPRACTICE LIABILITY
             UNDER STATUTES

Statutes, particularly those relating to the sale of securities, may impose liability upon accountants to third persons not in privity.

(a) FEDERAL SECURITIES STATUTES. Federal statutes regulate the sale of stocks and bonds. This is described in detail in Chapter 51, Sections 51:11 through 51:14. Accountants involved in the issuance and sale of securities may be liable to investors under a number of provisions of the Securities Act of 1933 and the Securities Exchange Act of 1934.

The Securities Act of 1933 deals with the original distribution of securities and requires disclosure of specific financial information in a **registration statement** filed with the Securities and Exchange Com-

mission. Under Section 11 of the 1933 act, accountants, lawyers, engineers, and appraisers who consent to being named in the registration statement as preparing any part of that statement are liable to purchasers of the securities for any untrue statement or omission of material fact made in the registration statement. "Due diligence" is a defense for these professionals.

Section 12 of the 1933 act applies to those who "offer or sell" securities and employ any device or scheme to defraud and obtain money by means of any untrue statement of material fact. Liability may be imposed on accountants whose conduct is a substantial factor in bringing about the fraudulent sale of a security. The more extensive the involvement or control of an accountant over a sale, the more likely the accountant is to be considered a seller under Section 12. Accountants who, in conjunction with clients, prepare fraudulent registration statements may be subject to civil liability as "aiders and abettors" under Section 12(2) of the 1933 act. They may also be subject to criminal liability under Section 17 (a) of the 1933 act.

The Securities Exchange Act of 1934 regulates the secondary distribution of securities. Section 10(b) of the 1934 act and SEC Rule 10b-5 impose liability on any person who employs any device, scheme, or artifice to defraud in connection with the purchase or sale of any security. Section 10(b) and Rule 10b-5 are the most effective federal security law provisions against accountants who participate in a fraudulent securities transaction. Under Section 10(b) and Rule 10b-5 a civil action for damages may be brought by any injured party who purchased or sold securities because of false, misleading, or undisclosed information. However, *scienter* or proof that the accountant acted with guilty knowledge or intent to deceive is required. Liability cannot be based on negligence. Because fraudulent intent is required, an accountant is not liable to the purchaser of corporate securities when the accountant was negligent in failing to use appropriate auditing procedures and thereby failed to discover internal accounting practices of the corporate client that prevented the making of an effective audit.[14] However, a showing of shady accounting practices amounting to a "pretended audit" or of grounds supporting a representation so flimsy as to lead to the conclusion that there was no genuine belief behind it have supported findings of liability.[15]

(b) LIABILITY OF ACCOUNTANTS UNDER ANTI-RACKETEERING STATUTES. The federal Racketeer Influenced and Corrupt Organizations Act (RICO) authorizes the victim of a pattern of racketeering practices to sue for treble damages. Many states have similar laws.[16] When an accountant's conduct that constitutes malpractice aids or furthers a pattern of racketeering practices, the person injured may bring suit under RICO.[17]

---

[14] Ernst & Ernst v Hochfelder, 425 US 185(1976).
[15] McLean v Alexander (CA3) 599 F2d 1190, 1198 (1979).

[16] See §§ 9:7, 8(c).
[17] Bank of America v Touche Ross & Co. (CA11 Ga) 782 F2d 966 (1986); Equitable Life Assur. Soc. v Alexander Grant & Co. (DC NY) 627 F Supp 1023 (1985); First Fed. S. & L. Ass'n v Oppenheim, Appel, Dixon & Co. (SC NY) 629 F Supp 427 (1986). Criminal liability is also imposed by the anti-racketeering statutes. If the accountant has the intent to defraud, there may be federal criminal liability for using the mail, a wire, radio or television with intent to defraud, or for defrauding a bank, 18 USC §§ 1341 et seq. Most states have similar antifraud laws.

SUMMARY

When a contract requires a party to perform services, the party must perform with the care exercised by persons performing similar services within the same community. If the party negligently fails to observe those standards, there is both a breach of contract and a tort. This tort of negligent breach of contract constitutes malpractice, and the other party to the contract can sue the wrongdoer for either breach of contract or for the tort involved.

By the modern view, third persons may also sue the wrongdoer for malpractice. In states that follow the older law, the third person is barred from suing because of lack of privity. The rules governing the right of the third person to sue are applied in suits against technicians, architects, attorneys, and physicians.

When the malpractice suit is brought against an accountant for negligence, courts differ as to when a third person may sue. Some courts refuse to let the third person sue by requiring privity of contract between the parties. Most courts allow suit by the third person against the wrongdoer but differ as to what the plaintiff must show in order to bring such a suit. In New York, the plaintiff must show as a minimum that there was a "contact" with the accountant. In some states, it is sufficient that the third person was a known user of the accountant's information. Other courts go further and allow the third person to sue if it was reasonable to foresee that that third person would make use of the accountant's information.

When the accountant is guilty of fraud, the intended victim of the fraud may sue the accountant, even though privity of contract is lacking.

In a suit brought under federal securities statutes, lack of privity is not a defense for an accountant.

To a limited degree, an accountant is protected from malpractice liability by a disclaimer of liability or by the contributory negligence of the plaintiff.

When the malpractice of the accountant involves or promotes racketeering activity or fraud, the accountant is subject to civil and criminal liability under RICO and similar state laws.

QUESTIONS AND CASE PROBLEMS

1. What social forces are affected by allowing a stranger to a contract to sue for the harm caused by the negligent performance of the contract?

2. The president of Jones Corporation was concerned as to whether it would be necessary to borrow money to pay taxes. The corporation employed Roanne to prepare a financial statement of the corporation. When the president saw this statement, he decided that money should be borrowed. The lending bank required that the corporation submit a financial statement. The statement prepared by Roanne was submitted. It contained a number of negligent mistakes that misled the bank into lending the money to Jones. Jones went into bankruptcy shortly thereafter, and the bank recovered only a small percentage of the loan. The bank sued Roanne for the amount it could not collect. Was she liable in a state that followed the known-user rule?

3. Thomas & Sons, certified public accountants, prepared a financial statement of the Continental Land Development Company. Much of the assets of the company consisted of land in foreign countries. Some of the land had been confiscated by the local governments. The financial statement prepared by Thomas stated that, based on the best information available, the land described therein was owned by Continental and had not been confiscated. The financial statement further recited that Thomas was entirely dependent upon foreign sources for the information relating to the foreign land and had no knowledge of its accuracy. On the strength of this financial statement, the Fifth National Bank loaned money to Continental. The recitals as to the land owned by Continental and its value proved false, and the bank could not get back its loan. The bank sued Thomas. Was Thomas liable?

4. Compare the right of a third party beneficiary and the right of a third person to sue for a negligent breach of a contract.

5. Matthew is a certified public accountant. He prepared a balance sheet statement for the Stanley Corporation that he knew would be used by Stanley to obtain a loan from the Third National Bank. In order to satisfy Stanley, Matthew prepared the statement in such a way that the false impression was created that Stanley was a thriving, prosperous corporation. If the statement had been prepared in accordance with standard accounting procedures, it would have shown that Stanley was just about to become insolvent. The Third National Bank, relying on this financial statement, loaned money to Stanley. Shortly thereafter, Stanley went into bankruptcy, and the Third National Bank lost virtually the full amount of the loan. The bank sued Matthew for the loss. Matthew asserted that he could not be sued by a third person as his only duty was to his client, the Stanley Corporation. Is this a valid defense?

6. Samari Brothers built an office building for the Pierce Corporation. Pierce rented one of the first floor stores of the building to Byron. Because of defective construction work, there were water leaks into Byron's store. Byron sued Samari for the damage caused to his inventory by such leaks. Samari denied liability on the ground that the building had been approved by the architect and accepted by the Pierce Corporation, and therefore a third person, such as Byron, could not bring suit against Samari. Samari claimed Byron was merely an incidental beneficiary of the contract between Samari and Pierce. Is this a valid defense?

7. Compare the malpractice liability of accountants and doctors.

8. Air-Speed, Inc. retained Hansman to obtain insurance to cover workers' compensation payments for its employees. Hansman notified Air-Speed that the insurance had been obtained. In fact it had not been because Hansman negligently did not forward the premiums to the insurance company to pay for the insurance. Thomas Rae was an employee of Air-Speed. He was killed in the course of his employment. His wife Christine was appointed as administratrix of his estate. She sued Air-Speed and Hansman for the payments that would have been received under a workers' compensation insurance policy if one had been obtained. Hansman denied liability on the ground that he had not made any contract with Christine to ob-

tain insurance. Was this defense valid? [Rae v Air-Speed, Inc. 386 Mass 167, 435 NE2d 628]

9. Johnson was a notary public. Albin, pretending to be Werner, showed him a deed signed with the name of Werner. Johnson did not do anything to determine the true identity of Albin as required by law. Instead he assumed that the signature was genuine and filled in the acknowledgment form on the deed, falsely reciting that Werner had appeared before him and that Werner had acknowledged the deed as being his deed. Actually the deed was a forgery. Suit was brought by a member of the Werner family who had relied on the forged deed and thereby sustained damage when the true owner reclaimed the land. Decide. [Werner v Werner, 84 Wash 2d 360, 526 P2d 370]

10. A certified public accounting partnership of James, Guinn and Head prepared a certified audit report of four corporations, known as the Paschal Enterprises, with knowledge that their report would be used to induce Shatterproof Glass Corporation to lend money to those corporations. The report showed the corporations to be solvent when in fact they were insolvent. Shatterproof relied upon the audit report and loaned approximately one half million dollars to the four corporations and lost almost all of it because the liabilities of the companies were in excess of their assets. Shatterproof claimed that James and other accountants had been negligent in preparing the report and sued them to recover the loss on the loan. The accountants raised the defense that they had not been retained by the plaintiff and had instead been retained by Paschal. Was this defense valid? [Shatterproof Glass Corporation v James (Tex Civ App) 466 SW2d 873]

11. Melvin Jacobs was a patient at the Horton Memorial Hospital. The doctors negligently made a wrong diagnosis of his case and told his wife that Melvin had only six months to live. When it was later discovered that the diagnosis was wrong, the wife sued the hospital for the emotional distress that she had suffered. Was it liable to the wife? [Jacobs v Horton Memorial Hospital, 130 App Div 2d 546, 515 NYS2d 281]

12. Murphy Bros. wished to obtain a loan from the First National Bank. It employed Kaman to prepare a certified financial statement of its business. In order to make Murphy Bros. appear to be a good credit risk, Kaman described a million dollars worth of accounts receivable as being "deferred income" and failed to indicate that most of these accounts were uncollectible. The financial statement as prepared by Kaman made Murphy appear to be solvent. If Kaman had prepared the financial statement properly, it would have been seen that Murphy was near financial collapse. First National Bank made the loan requested, but several months later Murphy was forced into bankruptcy. First National did not recover the full amount of its loan, and sued Kaman for her malpractice. She raised the defense that she could not be sued by First National as there was no privity of contract between them. Was this a valid defense?

13. Suits Galore, Inc. was a clothing manufacturer. Landau made an audit and a financial report of Suits Galore. The statement prepared by Landau was not certified, stated that it was a review report only, and that no opinion was expressly stated by the accountant. On the basis of this report, William Iselin & Co., Inc. extended credit to Suits Galore. Shortly thereafter Suits Galore went into bankruptcy. Iselin was not repaid the money it had loaned. Iselin sued Landau on the ground that the financial report had been negligently prepared and that Iselin could sue Landau for the loss sustained. Was it correct? [William Iselin & Co., Inc. v Landau, 128 App Div 2d 453, 513 NYS2d 3]

14. Alton Packaging owned an airplane that it had serviced by Garrett. Garrett found corrosion in the fuel tanks and replaced some of the tanks. Garrett did not enter into the logbook of the plane the making of the repairs or the existence of the corrosion problem. Alton sold the plane to B.L. Jet Sales, Inc. Difficulties developed because of the corrosion problem. B.L. sued Alton and Garrett. The claim against Garrett was the negligent failure to make the proper repair entry in the logbook of the plane so that subsequent purchasers would be aware of the problem. Garrett raised the defense that there was no privity of contract between him and the plaintiff and that the plaintiff was seeking to recover only for economic loss. Was this defense valid? [B.L. Jet Sales,

Inc. v Alton Packaging Corp. (Mo App) 724 SW2d 669]

15. The U. S. F. & G. Co. issued policies of fire and public liability insurance to the Roosevelt Hotel and agreed to make periodic inspections of the premises for fire hazards and conditions dangerous to guests. Marie Hill and her husband were guests at the hotel. The insurer negligently failed to find a hazard that resulted in a fire that injured Marie Hill and killed her husband. She sued the insurer for damages for her injuries and for the wrongful death of her husband. The insurer denied liability because there was no privity of contract between the plaintiff and the insurer. Was this defense valid? [Hill v U.S.F. & G. Co. (CA5 Fla) 428 F2d 112]

PART 3

PERSONAL PROPERTY AND BAILMENTS

24

PERSONAL PROPERTY

Property includes the rights of any person to possess, use, enjoy, and dispose of a thing or object of value. Property is classified as real property and personal property. **Real property** means land and things permanently affixed to land, such as trees or buildings. **Personal property** includes all other property. This chapter develops the law of personal property, setting forth (1) the basic legal principles of personal property, (2) how title to personal property is acquired, and (3) the law concerning multiple owners of specific personal property.

A. GENERAL PRINCIPLES

In common usage, the term *property* refers to a piece of land or a thing or an object. As a legal concept, however, *property* refers to the rights that an individual may possess in that piece of land or that thing or that object.[1] A right in a thing is property, without regard to whether such right is absolute or conditional, perfect or imperfect, legal or equitable.

§ 24:1 PERSONAL PROPERTY

Personal property consists of: (a) whole or fractional rights in things that are tangible and movable, such as furniture and books; (b) claims and debts, which are called **choses in action;** and (c) intangible proprietary rights, such as trademarks, copyrights, and patents.

The concept of personal property is expanding. For example, courts now generally include gas and water within the definition of *property*. Thus, persons who tap water mains and gas pipes and so obtain water and gas without paying are guilty of taking property.

The modern techniques of sound and image recording have led to the necessity of giving protection against copying. Federal and state statutes provide for the copyright protection of compositions and create crimes of record and tape piracy.[2]

The theft of personal property that relates to computers is covered in Chapter 11.

§ 24:2 LIMITATIONS ON OWNERSHIP

A person who has all possible rights in and over a thing is said to have **absolute ownership** of it. The term *absolute*, however, is somewhat misleading, for one's rights in respect to the use, enjoyment, and disposal of things are subject to certain restrictions. An owner's property is subject to the government's powers to tax, to regulate under the police power, and to take by eminent domain. It is subject to the creditors of the owner. Above all, the owner may not use property in a way that will unreasonably injure others.

B. ACQUISITION OF TITLE TO PERSONAL PROPERTY

Title to personal property may be acquired in different ways. For example, property is commonly purchased. The purchase and sale of goods is governed by the law of sales, covered in Part 4 of this book. In this chapter the following methods of acquiring personal property will be discussed: gift, the finding of lost property, transfer by a nonowner, occupation, and escheat.

§ 24:3 GIFTS

Title to personal property may be transferred by the voluntary act of the owner without receiving anything in exchange, that is by *gift*. The person making the gift, the **donor**, may do so because of things that the recipient of the gift, the **donee**, has done in the past or is expected to do in the future. However, such matters of inducement are not deemed consideration so as to alter the "free" character of the gift.

(a) INTER VIVOS GIFTS. The ordinary gift that is made between two living persons is an **inter vivos gift.** For practical purposes, such a gift takes effect upon the donor's expressing an intent to transfer title and making delivery, subject to the right of the donee to disclaim the gift within a reasonable time after learning that it has been made.[3] As there is no consideration for a gift, there is no enforceable contract, and an intended donee cannot sue for breach of contract if the donor fails to complete the gift.

(1) Intent. The intent to make a gift re-

---

[1] Virginia Marine Resources Commission v Forbes, 214 Va 109, 197 SE2d 195 (1973).
[2] PL 92-140, 85 Stat 391, 17 United States Code §§ 1, 5, 20, 101; Pennsylvania Act of January 10, 1972, PL 872, 18 PS § 1878.1.

[3] Owen v Owen (SD) 351 NW2d 139 (1984).

quires an intent to transfer title at that time. In contrast, an intent to confer a benefit at a future date is not a sufficient intent to create any right in the intended donee. A delivery of property without the intent to make a gift does not transfer title.[4]

(2) Delivery. Ordinarily the delivery required to make a gift will be an actual handing over to the donee of the thing that is given.

The delivery of a gift may also be made by a **symbolic delivery,** as by the delivery of means of control of property. Such means of control might be keys to a lock or keys to an automobile, or papers that are essential to or closely associated with the ownership of the property, such as documents of title or a ship's papers. The deliv-

[4] Re Jacobs' Marriage, 128 Cal App 3d 273, 180 Cal Rptr 234 (1982).

ery of a symbol is effective as a gift if the intent to make a gift is established. This is in contrast to merely giving the recipient of the token temporary access to the property, as for example, until the deliveror comes back from the hospital.

A gift may be made by depositing money in the bank account of an intended donee. If the account is a joint account in the names of two persons, a deposit of money in the account by one person may or may not be a gift to the other. Parol evidence is generally admissible to show whether there was an intention to make a gift.

When a savings account passbook is essential to the withdrawal of money from a savings account, parents do not make a gift to a minor child when they open a savings account in the child's name but keep possession of the passbook.

Inter Vivos Gift

		1. INTENT	UNLESS THE GIFT IS DISCLAIMED, TITLE PASSES TO
LAW:	DONOR	AND	
		2. DELIVERY	DONEE
APPLICATION:	SMITH OWNS THE VAN GOGH PAINTING "THE IRISES"	1. HE STATES, "THIS IS FOR YOU MICHAEL," AND 2. PERSONALLY PRESENTS THE PAINTING TO HIS SON MICHAEL	MICHAEL BECOMES THE OWNER

FIGURE 24-1
INTER VIVOS GIFT

(3) Donor's Death. If the donor dies before doing what is needed to make an effective gift, the gift fails. An agent or the executor or administrator of the donor cannot thereafter perform the missing step on behalf of the donor. For example, in a state where a transfer of title to a motor vehicle could not be made without a transfer of the title certificate, that transfer must be made

while the donor is living and cannot be made after the donor's death by the executor of the donor.

(b) GIFTS CAUSA MORTIS. A **gift causa mortis** is made when the donor, contemplating imminent and impending death, delivers personal property to the donee with the intent that the donee shall own it if the donor dies. This is a conditional gift, and the donor is entitled to take the property back if (1) the donor does not die; (2) the donor revokes the gift before dying; or (3) the donee dies before the donor.

(c) UNIFORM GIFTS TO MINORS ACT. The Uniform Gifts to Minors Act (UGMA), provides an additional method for making gifts of money and of registered and unregistered securities to minors.[5] Under the act, a gift of money may be made by an adult to a minor by depositing it with a broker or a bank in an account in the name of the donor or another adult or a bank with trust powers "as a custodian for [*name of minor*] under the [*name of state*] Uniform Gifts to Minors Act." If the gift is a registered security, the donor registers the security in a similar manner. If the security is unregistered, it must be delivered by the donor to another adult or a trust company accompanied by a written statement

signed by the donor and the custodian acknowledging receipt of the security.[6]

Under the act, the custodian is in effect a guardian of the property for the minor, but the custodian may use the property more freely and is not subject to many restrictions applicable to true guardians. When property is held by a custodian for the benefit of a minor under UGMA, the custodian has discretionary power to use the property for the "support, maintenance, education, and benefit" of the minor, but the custodian may not use the custodial property for the custodian's own personal benefit. The gift is final and irrevocable for tax and all other purposes upon complying with the procedure of the act.

The *Heath* case involved a dispute over the ownership of two bank accounts established under UGMA. The court was faced with deciding whether the donative intent and delivery, the two basic elements of every *inter vivos* gift of personal property, were present.

---

[5]   The Uniform Gifts to Minors Act (UGMA) was originally proposed in 1956. It was revised in 1965 and again in 1966. One of these versions, often with minor variations, has been adopted in every state. It has been adopted for the Virgin Islands and the District of Columbia.

[6]   UGMA § 2.

HEATH V HEATH

143 Ill App 3d 390, 97 Ill Dec 615, 493 NE2d 97 (1986)

In 1980 Larry Heath received $10,000 from his father. These funds grew to $13,381 by 1983, and in March he used this money to establish two custodian bank accounts for his minor children under the Uniform Gifts to Minors Act. Larry was listed as custodian on each account. In August of 1984 Larry closed both accounts and returned the proceeds to his mother, because his father was in Europe. The childrens' mother, Pamela, brought suit to recover the funds, contending that the deposits were irrevocable gifts. Larry Heath contends that the money was his father's and it was never intended as a gift. From a judgment for the children, Larry Heath appealed.

HOPF, J. . . . In the instant case, sections 2 and 3 of the Illinois Uniform Gifts to Minors Act (the Act) are particularly relevant to a determination whether an irrevocable gift was created. These sections provide in part:

> An adult may, during his lifetime make or provide for a gift of custodial property to a person who is a minor on the date of the gift or distribution: . . .
> (2) if the subject of the gift is money, by paying or delivering it to a broker or domestic financial institution for credit to an account in the name of the donor, another adult or a trust company, followed, in substance, by the words: "as custodian for . . . (name of minor) under the Illinois Uniform Gifts to Minors Act." . . .
> A gift made in a manner prescribed in this Act is irrevocable and conveys to the minor indefeasibly vested legal title to the custodial property given, but no guardian of the minor has any right, power, duty or authority with respect to the custodial property except as provided in this Act. Ill. Rev. Stat. 1983, ch. 110 1/2, pars. 202(a)(2), 203(a).

The Act is designed to make an *inter vivos* gift to a minor in a relatively simplified manner. By conveying the gift in the manner presented by the Act, the minor obtains indefeasibly vested legal title to the property which is gifted, and once the gift is made, it is irrevocable. A valid *inter vivos* gift requires proof of donative intent and delivery of the subject matter. As noted in section 2 above, the Act expressly addresses the element of delivery by providing that such element shall be satisfied by following the procedures set forth in the statute. However, the Act contains no provision regarding the element of donative intent and that element is the one at issue in the case at bar.

. . . Defendant has presented this court with three cases from other jurisdictions which have dealt with this issue and we find the holdings reached therein both persuasive and applicable to the instant case.

All three cases, *Gordon v. Gordon* (1979), 419 N.Y.S.2d 684; *In re Marriage of Jacobs* (1982), 128 Cal.App.3d 273 and *Golden v. Golden* (Fla. Dist.Ct.App.1983), 434 So.2d 978, held that, although establishing a bank account in a minor's name in compliance with the provisions of the Uniform Gifts to Minors Act is highly probative on the issue of donative intent, it did not create an irrebutable presumption of intent. Thus, documentary compliance with the statutory mechanisms of the Act constitutes *prima facie* evidence that a gift was made and intended. (*Gordon v. Gordon.*) But, in appropriate circumstances, extrinsic evidence may be introduced to rebut the *prima facie* showing provided by the prescribed documentation of the Act.

In the instant case the documentary evidence, in particular, the account signature cards signed by the defendant, clearly constituted a *prima facie* showing that the bank accounts established at the Home Savings & Loan Association were intended to be irrevocable gifts to the named minors under the Act. At the citation proceeding, defendant admitted opening the accounts in the names of his children and signing the signature cards. However, defendant argues in this court that his testimony was sufficient to rebut this documentary showing of donative intent. . . .

Defendant maintains that his testimony at the hearing shows he was unaware of the legal effect the account signature cards acquired upon his signing of them. Defendant attempts to pass himself off as a mere "factory worker" with apparently little knowledge of such matters. However, it is a matter of common knowledge that one should always read any document before signing it. Moreover, even a casual glance at the signature cards would have warned defendant that he was making a gift to a minor. At the top of the signature cards it clearly stated in capital letters "GIFT TRANSFERRED TO MINOR." On both sides of the signature cards it indicates that defendant is opening savings accounts for the children "as Custodian for" them under the Illinois Uniform Gifts to Minors Act. Additionally, directly above defendant's signature it states:

> This gift of money to the minor named, which gift shall be deemed to include all earnings thereon and any future earnings thereto, is irrevocable and is made in accordance with and to include all the provisions of the said Statute of this state as it is now or hereafter may be amended.

Underneath defendant's signature appear the words "Signature of Donor." This court finds defendant's claim of ignorance, regarding the legal effect of what he was signing, unworthy of belief.

Consequently, in our view, defendant's testimony regarding his alleged ignorance regarding the opening of the bank accounts in the names of his minor children was insufficient to rebut plaintiff's strong documentary showing that defendant had created irrevocable gifts. Additionally, although defendant testified the monies used for the accounts in question constituted a loan from his father which had to be repaid, defendant offered no other evidence to substantiate this contention.

. . . In our opinion, the trial court was correct in concluding that irrevocable gifts were created at the time defendant opened the bank accounts in the names of the minors under the Illinois Uniform Gifts to Minors Act.

[Judgment affirmed]

QUESTIONS

1. What are the two basic elements of every *inter vivos* gift of personal property?
2. Was the court influenced by the documentary compliance with the UGMA in reaching the determination on whether or not there was a "gift"?
3. After Larry Heath had opened the UGMA accounts, could he change his mind and revoke the transfer?

(d) CONDITIONAL GIFTS. A gift may be made on condition, such as "This car is yours when you graduate" or "This car is yours unless you drop out of school." The former gift is subject to a condition precedent, and the latter to a condition subsequent. The condition to the first gift must be satisfied before any gift or transfer takes place. The satisfaction of the second condition operates to destroy or divest a title that had already been transferred. Ordinarily no condition is recognized unless it is expressly stated. However, most courts regard an engagement ring as a conditional gift subject to the condition subsequent of a failure to marry. The inherent symbolism of the gift itself is deemed to foreclose the need to establish an express condition that the marriage will ensue. Most jurisdictions allow recovery of conditional engagement gifts only if the party seeking recovery has not unjustifiably broken off the engagement. The *Harris* case illustrates the application of this rule. However, a few states reject considerations of "fault" as to the breaking of an engagement and always require the return of the ring to the donor where there is a broken engagement on the theory that in most cases there is no real fault as such, but rather a change of mind.[7]

[7]   Brown v Thomas __ Wis App __, 379 NW2d 868 (1985); Gaden v Gaden 29 NY2d 471 (1971).

HARRIS V DAVIS

139 Ill App 3d 1046, 94 Ill Dec 326, 487 NE2d 1204 (1986)

Chip Harris gave Rebecca Davis a diamond ring upon their engagement to be married. Some time later Davis informed Harris that she no longer wanted to see him and that she had thrown the ring into a drainage ditch near her mother's home. Harris rented a metal detector and searched the area to no avail. He sued Davis for the value of the ring. From a judgment for Davis, Harris appealed.

JONES, J. . . . On appeal, the plaintiff argues that under Illinois law, the party failing to comply with an engagement or a contract to be married has no right to property acquired in contemplation of the marriage. (*Urbanus v. Burns* (1939), 300 Ill.App. 207, 20 N.E.2d 869; *Rockafellow v. Newcomb* (1870), 57 Ill. 186.) Plaintiff further argues that where an engagement is terminated because of the fault of the woman, the man is ordinarily entitled to the return of gifts made in contemplation of the marriage. (20 Ill.L. & Prac. § 22 (1968).) We agree.

The law in Illinois appears established that a gift given in contemplation of marriage is deemed to be conditional on the subsequent marriage of the parties, and the party who fails to perform on the condition of the gift has no right to property acquired under such pretenses.

A Pennsylvania court said: "A gift given by a man to a woman on condition that she embark on the sea of matrimony with him is no different from a gift based on the condition that the donee sail on any other sea", and "if, after receiving the provisional gift, the donee refuses to leave the harbor, — if the anchor of contractual performance sticks in the sands of irresolution and procrastination — the gift must be restored to the donor". *Pavlicic v. Vogtsberger* (1957), 390 Pa. 502, 507-09, 136 A.2d 127, 130.

There can be no question that the ring in the instant case was given by the plaintiff to the defendant in contemplation of marriage. Neither party disputes that fact. Neither is there any question that it was the defendant fiancee who broke the engagement. There is no allegation that plaintiff's acts caused the defendant to break the engagement. The record does not reveal the cause of the break-up. At any rate, the defendant failed to perform on the condition of the gift and, therefore, had no right either to retain the ring or to dispose of it. We, therefore, reverse the judgment of the trial court and hold that the defendant is liable to the plaintiff for the $1,390 value of the engagement ring.

[Judgment reversed]

QUESTIONS

1. State the rule of law set forth in this decision.
2. If Chip Harris had broken off the engagement, would he have been entitled to the return of the ring?

(e) ANATOMICAL GIFTS. The Uniform Anatomical Gift Act[8] permits persons eighteen years or older to make a gift of their body or any part or an organ to take effect upon their death. The gift may be made to a school, a hospital, or organ bank, or to a named patient. Such a gift may also be made, subject to certain restrictions, by the spouse, adult child, parent, adult brother or sister, or guardian of a deceased person.[9] Independently of the act, a living person may make a gift, while living, of part of the person's body, as in the case of a blood transfusion or a kidney transplant.

§ 24:4   LOST PROPERTY

Personal property is *lost* when the owner does not know where it is located but intends to retain title or ownership to it. The person finding lost property does not acquire title but only possession. Ordinarily the finder of lost property is required to surrender the property to the true owner when the latter establishes ownership. Meanwhile the finder is entitled to retain possession as against everyone else.

Without a contract with the owner or a statute so providing, the finder of lost property is not entitled to a reward or to compensation for finding or caring for the property.

(a) FINDING IN PUBLIC PLACE. If the lost property is found in a public place, such as a hotel, under such circumstances that to a reasonable person it would appear that the property had been intentionally placed there by the owner and that the owner would be likely to recall where the property had been left and to return for it, the finder is not entitled to possession of the property. The finder must give it to the proprietor or manager of the public place to keep it for the owner. This exception does not apply if it appears that the property was not intentionally placed where it was found, because in that case, it is not likely that the owner will recall having left it there.

(b) STATUTORY CHANGE. In some states, statutes have been adopted permitting the finder to sell the property or keep it if the owner does not appear within a stated period of time. In such a case, the finder is required to give notice, as by newspaper publication, in order to attempt to reach the owner.

§ 24:5   TRANSFER BY NONOWNER

Ordinarily a sale or other transfer by one who does not own the property will pass no title. No title is acquired by theft. The thief acquires possession only; and if the thief makes a sale or gift of the property to another, the latter only acquires possession of the property. The true owner may reclaim the property from the thief or from the thief's transferee.[10]

(a) AUTOMOBILES. In some states the general rule stated above is fortified by statutes that declare that the title to an automobile cannot be transferred, even by the true owner, without a delivery of a properly endorsed title certificate. The states that follow the common law do not make the holding of a title certificate essential to the ownership of an automobile, although as a matter of police regulation, the owner must obtain such a certificate.

(b) EXCEPTIONS. As an exception to the rule that a nonowner cannot transfer title, an agent, who does not own the property but who is authorized to sell it, may tranfer the title of the agent's principal. Likewise, certain relationships, such as a pledge or an entrustment, create a power to sell and to transfer title. Likewise, an owner of property may be barred or estopped from claiming ownership when the owner has acted to deceive an innocent buyer into be-

---

[8]   This Act has been adopted in every state.
[9]   Uniform Anatomical Gift Act (UAGA) § § 2, 3.

[10]   As to the right of the owner to sue for monetary damages see § 24:15 of this book.

lieving that someone else was the owner or had authority to sell.

§ 24:6 OCCUPATION OF PERSONAL PROPERTY

In some cases, title to personal property may be acquired by occupation, that is, by taking and retaining possession of the property.

(a) WILD ANIMALS. Wild animals, living in a state of nature, are not owned by any individual. In the absence of restrictions imposed by game laws, the person who acquires dominion or control over a wild animal becomes its owner. What constitutes sufficient dominion or control varies with the nature of the animal and all the surrounding circumstances. If the animal is killed, tied, imprisioned, or otherwise prevented from going at its will, the hunter exercises sufficient dominion or control over the animal and becomes its owner. If the wild animal, subsequent to its capture, should escape and return to its natural state, it resumes the status of a wild animal.[11]

As a qualification to the ordinary rule, the following exception developed. If an animal is killed or captured on the land of another while the hunter is upon the land without permission of the landowner, the animal, when killed or captured, does not belong to the hunter but to the landowner.

(b) ABANDONED PERSONAL PROPERTY. Personal property is deemed abandoned when the owner relinquishes possession of it with the intention to disclaim title to it. Yesterday's newspaper that is thrown out in the trash is abandoned personal property. Title to abandoned property may be acquired by the first person who obtains possession and control of it. A person becomes the owner at the moment of taking possession of the abandoned personal property.

When the owner of property flees in the face of an approaching peril, property left behind is not abandoned. An abandonment occurs only when the leaving of the property is the voluntary act of the owner.

§ 24:7 ESCHEAT

Who owns unclaimed property? In the case of personal property, the practical answer is that the property will probably "disappear" after a period of time, or, if in the possession of a carrier, hotel, or warehouse, it may be sold for unpaid charges. A growing problem arises with respect to unclaimed corporate dividends, bank deposits, insurance payments, and refunds. Most states have a statute providing for the transfer of title of such unclaimed property to the state government. This transfer of ownership to the government is often called by its feudal name of **escheat.** To provide for unclaimed property, many states have adopted the Uniform Disposition of Unclaimed Property Act.[12]

C. PROTECTION OF PERSONAL PROPERTY

Property rights in trademarks, copyrights, and patents are acquired as provided by federal statutes, and the nature and extent of their legal protection will be covered in this chapter.

§ 24:8 TRADEMARKS AND SERVICE MARKS

A *mark* is any word, name, symbol, or design, or a combination of these used to

---

[11] Wiley v Baker (Tex Civ App) 597 SW2d 3 (1980).

[12] The 1954 version of the Act has been adopted in Arkansas, Florida, Maryland, New Hampshire, Vermont. A 1966 version of the Act has been adopted in Alabama, Georgia, Hawaii, Illinois, Indiana, Louisiana, Maine, Minnesota, Mississippi, Missouri, Nebraska, New Mexico, Oklahoma, Rhode Island, South Carolina, South Dakota, Tennessee, and the District of Columbia. A 1981 version of the Act has been adopted in Arizona, Idaho, Montana, Nevada, North Dakota, Oregon, Utah, Virginia, Washington and West Virginia.

identify a product or service.[13] If the mark identifies a product, such as an automobile or soap, it is called a **trademark**. If it identifies a service, such as a restaurant or clothes cleaner, it is called a **service mark**.

The owner of a mark may obtain protection from its use by others by registering the mark in accordance with federal law.[14] In order to be registered, a mark must distinguish the goods or service of the applicant from those of others. Under the federal statute, a register, called the Principal Register, is maintained for the recording of such marks. Registration on the Principal Register grants the registrant the exclusive right to use the mark. Challenges may be made to the registrant's rights within five years of registration; but after five years, the rights of the registrant are incontestable.

(a) REGISTRABLE MARKS. Marks that are coined, completely fanciful, or arbitrary are capable of registration on the Principal Register. The mark *Exxon,* for example, was coined by the owners. The name *Kodak* is also a creation of the owners of this trademark, has no other meaning in our language, and obviously serves to distinguish the goods of its owners from all others.

A suggestive term may also be registered. Such a term suggests rather than describes some characteristics of the goods to which it applies and requires the consumer to exercise some imagination to reach a conclusion as to the nature of the goods. For example, as a trademark for refrigerators, the term *Penguin* would be suggestive. As a trademark for paperback books, the term *Penguin* is arbitrary and fanciful.

Ordinarily, descriptive terms, sur-names, and geographical terms are not registrable on the Principal Register.[15] A descriptive term identifies a characteristic or quality of an article or service, such as color, odor, function, or use.[16] Thus, *Cough Calmers* was held not to be registrable on the Principal Register because it was merely descriptive of the goods normally called cough drops. However, an exception is made where a descriptive or geographic term or a surname has acquired a **secondary meaning;** and such a mark is registrable. A term or terms that have a primary meaning of their own acquire a secondary meaning when, through long use in connection with a particular product, they have come to be known by the public at large as identifying the particular product and its origin.[17] For example, the geographic term, *Philadelphia* has acquired a secondary meaning as applied to cream cheese, and is widely accepted by the public as denoting a particular brand, rather than any cream cheese made in Philadelphia. Factors considered by a court in determining whether a trade mark has acquired secondary meaning are the amount and manner of advertising, volume of sales, and length and manner of use, direct consumer testimony, and consumer surveys.

Generic terms that designate a kind or class of goods, such as *cola* or *rosé wine,* are never registrable.

(b) INJUNCTION AGAINST IMPROPER USE OF MARK. A person who has the right to use a mark may enjoin a competitor from imitating or duplicating the mark. The basic question in such litigation is whether the general public is likely to be confused by the mark

---

[13] 15 USC § 1127; Safeway Stores, Inc. v Safeway Discount Drugs, Inc. (CA11 Fla) 675 F2d 1160 (1982). See also Trademark Clarification Act of 1984, PL 98-620, 98 Stat 333.

[14] Lanham Act, 15 USC § § 1050-1127.

[15] A Supplemental Register exists for recording such marks. This recording does not give the registrant any protection but it provides a source to which other persons designing a mark can go to make sure they are not duplicating an existing mark.

[16] Soweco Inc. v Shell Oil Co. (CA5 Tex) 617 F2d 1178 (1980).

[17] Volkswagen v Richard (CA5 Tex) 492 F2d 474 (1974).

of the defendant and to wrongly believe that it identifies the plaintiff. If there is this danger of confusion, the court will enjoin the defendant from using the particular mark.

In some cases, the fact that the products of the plaintiff and the defendant did not compete in the same market was held to entitle the defendant to use a mark that would have been prohibited as confusingly similar if the defendant manufactured the same product as the plaintiff. For example, it has been held that *Cadillac* as applied to boats is not confusingly similar to

Cadillac as applied to automobiles, and therefore its use cannot be enjoined.[18]

In the *University of Georgia Athletic Association* case, the court was faced with the question of whether there was likelihood of confusion between the UGAA's service mark and athletic symbol *Bulldogs* and the trademark *Battlin' Bulldog Beer*.

[18] General Motors Corporation v Cadillac Marine and Boat Co. 140 USPQ 447 (1964). See also Amstar Corp. v Domino's Pizza Inc. (CA5 Ga) 615 F2d 252 (1980), where the mark *Domino* as applied to pizza held not to be confusingly similar to *Domino* as applied to sugar.

UNIVERSITY OF GEORGIA ATHLETIC ASS'N V LAITE
(CA11 Ga) 756 F2d 1535 (1985)

The University of Georgia Athletic Association (UGAA) brought suit against beer wholesaler, Bill Laite, for marketing *Battlin' Bulldog Beer*. The UGAA claimed that the cans infringed on its symbol for its athletic teams, which it had registered as a service mark and which depicted an English Bulldog wearing a sweater with a *G* and the word *BULLDOGS* on it. Soon after the beer appeared on the market, the University received telephone calls from friends of the University, who were concerned that Battlin' Bulldog Beer was not the sort of product that should in any way be related to the University of Georgia. The University's suit was based on the theory of false designation of origin in violation of the Lanham Act. Laite contended that the University of Georgia Bulldog was not a valid service mark; that his bulldog was different than the University's; and that his cans contained the disclaimer "Not associated with the University of Georgia." The district court permanently enjoined Laite from marketing the beer under the challenged label design. Laite appealed.

KRAVITCH, C. J. . . . Laite's first argument on appeal is that the "University of Georgia Bulldog" is not a valid trade or service mark worthy of protection. Laite cites *Universal City Studios, Inc. v. Nintendo Co.*, 578 F. Supp. 911 (S.D.N.Y. 1983), for the proposition that "[t]o make a successful claim of false designation of origin in violation of § 43(a) of the Lanham Act, 15 U.S.C. § 1125(a), [plaintiff] must demonstrate that its trademark possesses 'secondary meaning' — '[t]he power of a name or other configuration to symbolize a particular business, product or company. . . . '" Laite contends that the record does not contain sufficient proof of secondary meaning, and that the vagueness of UGAA's mark, coupled with extensive third-party uses of the same or similar marks, demonstrates the absence of secondary meaning. . . . The general rule in this circuit is that proof of secondary meaning is required *only* when protection is sought for descriptive marks, as opposed to arbitrary or suggestive marks. We have long recognized that:

> Service marks fall into four categories. A strong mark is usually fictitious, arbitrary or fanciful and is generally inherently distinctive. It is afforded the widest ambit of protection. . . . A descriptive mark tells something about the product; it is protected only when secondary meaning is shown. . . . In contrast to the above is the suggestive mark, which subtly connotes something about the service or product. Although less distinctive than a fictitious, arbitrary or fanciful mark . . . a suggestive mark will be protected without proof of secondary meaning. . . . Lastly, there are generic terms, which communicate 'information about the nature or class of an article or service,' and therefore can never become a service or trademark.

Thus, secondary meaning is best characterized not as a general prerequisite for trade or service mark protection, but as a means by which otherwise unprotectible descriptive marks may obtain protection. As one commentator has explained:

> Secondary meaning converts a word originally incapable of serving as a mark into a full fledged trademark. . . . An arbitrary, fanciful, or otherwise distinctive word qualifies as a trademark immediately, because in the particular industry it has no primary meaning to overcome. Therefore it is initially registrable, and also protectible at common law. In the case of words with primary meaning, the reverse is true. Such words, be they descriptive or geographical, are initially nonregistrable and unprotectible unless and until they have attained secondary meaning as trademarks.

We therefore hold that, . . . proof of secondary meaning is required in an action under section 43(a) *only* when protection is sought for a descriptive mark, as opposed to an arbitrary or suggestive mark. Turning to the mark at issue in the instant case, we are convinced beyond a shadow of a doubt that the "University of Georgia Bulldog" is not a descriptive mark. In our view, the portrayal of an English bulldog chosen by the university as a symbol for its athletic teams is, at best, "suggestive," if not downright "arbitrary." Thus, contrary to Laite's assertion, UGAA was not required to prove secondary meaning in order to prevail on its Lanham Act claim, and the district court did not err in granting injunctive relief to UGAA under section 43(a) despite the absence of proof of secondary meaning.

Laite's next argument is that the district court used the wrong factors in comparing the "Battlin' Bulldog" with the "University of Georgia Bulldog." Laite correctly points out that this circuit has recognized seven factors as relevant to the determination of a "likelihood of confusion" between two trade or service marks: (1) the type of mark at issue, (2) the similarity of design between the two marks, (3) the similarity of product, (4) the identity of retail outlets and purchasers, (5) the identity of advertising media utilized, (6) the defendant's intent, and (7) actual confusion between the two marks. According to Laite, the court below erred by failing to consider all seven of the relevant factors before deciding that the sale of "Battlin' Bulldog Beer" created a "likelihood of confusion."

. . . [W]e are not convinced, after examining the record and the orders entered by the district court, that the court failed to consider all seven of the relevant factors. At the preliminary injunction hearing, counsel for Laite discussed at length the seven factors, as set out in the *Amstar Corp.* case. Moreover, in the order granting the preliminary injunction, the district court cited *Amstar Corp.* and specifically mentioned two of the seven factors, namely, the similarity of design and the defendant's intent. The fact that the court did not discuss the other five factors may indicate only that the court found those factors insignificant under the circumstances. . . .

Laite's final argument is that the district court's conclusion that the sale of "Battlin' Bulldog Beer" created a "likelihood of confusion" is clearly erroneous. . . .

After reviewing the record, we cannot say that we are "left with the definite and firm conviction that a mistake has been committed." On the contrary, we agree with the district court that the sale of "Battlin' Bulldog Beer" created a "likelihood of confusion." We find most significant the same two factors that were identified by the district court, the similarity of design between the two marks and the defendant's intent. In our view, these two factors alone are sufficient to support the conclusion reached by the court below.

The most cursory visual examination of the two bulldogs in this case reveals their similarity.

As the district court pointed out, it is the combination of similar design elements, rather than any individual element, that compels the conclusion that the two bulldogs are similar. Had the cans of "Battlin' Bulldog Beer" been printed in different colors, or had the "Battlin' Bulldog" worn a different monogram on its sweater, we might have a different case. Instead, the cans are red and black, the colors of the University of Georgia, and the "Battlin' Bulldog" wears the letter "G." To be sure, the "Battlin' Bulldog" is not an exact reproduction of the "University of Georgia Bulldog." Nevertheless, we find the differences between the two so minor as to be legally, if not factually, nonexistent.

The defendant's intent likewise is apparent from the record. The record establishes that the Royal Brewing Company of New Orleans, Louisiana, the brewer of "Battlin' Bulldog Beer," wrote to several southeastern colleges, including the University of Georgia, seeking permission to use the colleges' symbols on cans of beer. Furthermore, Laite candidly admitted in the court below, and at oral argument in this court, that "Battlin' Bulldog Beer" was intended to capitalize on the popularity of the University of Georgia football program. In short, there can be no doubt that Laite hoped to sell "Battlin' Bulldog Beer" not because the beer tastes great, but because the cans would catch the attention of University of Georgia football fans.

Although we find the defendant's intent and the similarity of design between the two marks sufficient to support the district court's finding of a "likelihood of confusion," we also note that the remaining five factors either support the same conclusion or, at least, do not undermine it. For example, as we previously noted, the type of mark at issue in this case is at best "suggestive," if not downright "arbitrary." Such marks traditionally have been characterized as "strong." The fact that many other colleges, junior colleges, and high schools use an English bulldog as a symbol does not significantly diminish the strength of UGAA's mark, since almost all of the other schools (1) are geographically remote, (2) use a different color scheme, or (3) have names that begin with a letter other than "G." . . .

Laite also argues that no confusion could result from the sale of "Battlin' Bulldog Beer" because the cans contain the disclaimer, "Not associated with the University of Georgia." We reject this argument for two reasons. First, the disclaimer is relatively inconspicuous on the individual cans, and practically invisible when the cans are grouped together into six-packs. Second, in the *Boston Pro. Hockey* case we dismissed a similar argument, stating:

> The exact duplication of the symbol and the sale as the team's emblem satisfying the confusion requirement of the law, words which indicate it was not authorized by the trademark owner are insufficient to remedy the illegal confusion. Only a prohibition of the unauthorized use will sufficiently remedy the wrong.

The "Battlin' Bulldog's" football career thus comes to an abrupt end. Laite devised a clever entrepreneurial "game plan," but failed to take into account the strength of UGAA's mark and the tenacity with which UGAA was willing to defend that mark. Like the University of Georgia's famed "Junkyard Dog" defense, UGAA was able to hold its opponent to little or no gain. . . . [W]e find that the district court did not err, in fact or in law, when it granted permanent injunctive relief to UGAA. . . .

[Judgment affirmed]

QUESTIONS

1. When is proof of secondary meaning required in a trademark or service mark infringement lawsuit?
2. In what category of service mark is the University of Georgia Bulldog?
3. What are the seven factors considered by this circuit court in determining whether "likelihood of confusion" exists between two marks?

(c) ABANDONMENT OF EXCLUSIVE RIGHTS TO MARK. An owner who has an exclusive right to use a mark may lose that right. If other persons are permitted to use the mark, it loses its exclusive character and is said to pass into the English language and become generic. Examples of formerly enforceable marks that have made this transition into the general language are *aspirin, thermos, cellophane,* and *shredded wheat.*

§ 24:9   COPYRIGHTS

A **copyright** is the exclusive right given by federal statute to the creator of a literary or artistic work to use, reproduce, or display the work. By international treaties, copyrights given under the laws of one nation are generally recognized in another. Works produced in this country for export to foreign countries that have ratified the Universal Copyright Convention may use the internationally accepted copyright symbol © in place of or in addition to the word "copyright" or its abbreviation.

A copyright does not prevent the copying of an idea but only the copying of the way the idea is expressed.[19] That is, the copyright is violated when there is a duplicating of the words or the pictures of the creator but not when there is merely a copying of the idea which those words or pictures express.

(a) WHAT IS COPYRIGHTABLE. Copyrights protect literary, musical, dramatic, and artistic work. Protected are books and periodicals; musical and dramatic composi-

[19] Atari, Inc. v North American Philips Consumer Electronics Corp., (CA7 Ill) 672 F2d 607 (1982).

tions; choreographic works; maps; works of art, such as paintings, sculptures, and photographs; motion pictures and other audiovisual works; sound recordings; and computer programs, discussed in § 24:12.

(b) UNPUBLISHED WORK. As long as a work is not made public, it has the same protection as though it had been copyrighted. Once it is made public, however, anyone can use or copy it if it has not been copyrighted.

(c) DURATION OF COPYRIGHT. For works created after January 1, 1978, a copyright lasts for the creator's lifetime plus fifty years.[20] After a copyright has expired, the work is in the public domain and may be used by anyone without cost.

(d) LIMITATIONS ON EXCLUSIVE CHARACTER OF COPYRIGHT. A limitation on the exclusive rights of copyright owners exists under the principle of "fair use," which allows for the limited usage of copyrighted material in connection with criticism, news reporting, teaching, and research. Two important factors in judging if the usage is a fair use are: (1) the amount of text used in relation to the copyrighted work as a whole and (2) the effect of the use on the value of the work.[21]

§ 24:10   PATENTS

A **patent** is the exclusive right that the inventor of a device can obtain under federal law. The patent gives the inventor an exclusive seventeen-year right to make, use, and sell the thing invented. At the end of seventeen years the patent expires and cannot be renewed. Patents cannot be defeated by the improper combination of components outside the United States for sale in global markets. U. S. suppliers of components of a patented invention who actively induce the combination of components outside the United States in a manner that would infringe the patent if the activity occurred in the United States are lia-

ble as infringers under the Patent Law Amendments Act of 1984.[22]

If a patent is not obtained or if the patent has expired, anyone may make, use, or sell the invention without permission of the inventor and without making any payment therefor.

(a) WHAT IS PATENTABLE. In order to be patentable, the invention must be something that is new and useful and must be something that would not have been obvious to a person of ordinary skill or knowledge in the art or technology to which the invention is related.[23]

It is the thing that is patented: whether it be a machine, a process, or a particular chemical composition of matter. The idea or inspiration, ways of doing business, and scientific principles cannot be patented unless there is some physical thing that is based upon them. Patent law has been interpreted to permit the patenting of human-made life forms.

(b) CONTRACTUAL PROTECTION OF INVENTIONS. Frequently an employee will invent a patentable device during working hours or use the employer's equipment and materials. To protect the employer in such situations, employment contracts commonly provide that any invention relating to the employer's business that is discovered by the employee while still an employee or during the first one or two years after leaving the employment shall be assigned to the employer. Such provisions are generally held valid, although a provision requiring the assignment of all inventions, whether or not related to the employer's business, has been held contrary to public policy and therefore invalid.

§ 24:11   SECRET BUSINESS
       INFORMATION

A business may have developed information that is not generally known but that

---

[20] Copyright Act of 1976, § 302(a), 17 USC § 302(a).
[21] Copyright Act of 1976, § 107, 17 USC § 107.

[22] PL 98-622, 98 Stat 3383, 35 USC 361.
[23] 35 USC § § 101, 102, 103, Park-Ohio Industries, Inc. v Letica Corp.(CA6 Mich) 617 F2d 450 (1980).

cannot be properly protected under federal law. As long as such information is kept secret, it will be protected under state law relating to trade secrets.[24] The protection of trade secrets is necessary to encourage and protect invention and commercial enterprise, and to maintain standards of commercial ethics in the marketplace.

(a) TRADE SECRETS. A trade secret may consist of any formula, device, or compilation of information that is used in one's business that is of such a nature that it gives an advantage over competitors who do not have such information. It may be a formula for a chemical compound; a process of manufacturing, treating, or preserving materials; and, to a limited extent, certain confidential customer lists.[25] The courts in some states will not protect customer lists where customer identities are readily ascertainable from industry or public sources or where products or services are sold to a wide group of purchasers based on their individual needs.[26]

(b) LOSS OF PROTECTION BY PUBLICATION. When secret business information is made public, it loses the protection it had while secret. Such loss of protection by publication occurs when the information is made known without any restrictions. In contrast, there is no loss of protection when secret information is shared or communicated for a special purpose and the person receiving the information knows that it is not to be made public.

(c) DEFENSIVE MEASURES. Employers have adopted measures to avoid the expense of trade secret litigation by limiting disclosure of trade secrets to only those employees with a "need to know," having employees sign nondisclosure agreements, and conducting exit interviews when an employee with confidential information terminates employment with the business, reminding the employee of the intent to enforce the nondisclosure agreement.

Employers also have adopted industrial security plans to protect their unique knowledge and competitive advantages from "outsiders," who may engage in theft, trespass, wiretapping, or other forms of commercial espionage.

§ 24:12   PROTECTION OF COMPUTER PROGRAMS

Computer programs may be protected by copyright law, patent law, trade secrecy law, and contract law. Difficulties exist, however, in the application of these traditional legal theories to the new technology of computer programming.

(a) COPYRIGHTS. Under the Computer Software Copyright Act of 1980[27] computer programs, including program instructions in machine or symbolic languages, now receive the same protection as the other works of authorship covered by the Copyright Act of 1976. Thus, if the owner utilizes the proper copyright notice, the copyright will protect the program's literal code. It should be remembered that a copyright does not prevent the copying of the basic "ideas" found in a copyrighted work, but only the way the ideas are "expressed." Court decisions have added significant substance to the protection provided computer program developers under the Computer Software Copyright Act by considering a program's structure, sequence and organization a part of the "expression" of the program, rather than considering such "ideas," which would not be protected. Moreover, the courts in their in-

---

[24] The Uniform Trade Secrets Act has been adopted by Arkansas, California, Connecticut, Delaware, Idaho, Indiana, Kansas, Louisiana, Minnesota, Montana, North Dakota, Oklahoma, Washington, and West Virginia. Trade secrets are protected in all states either under the Uniform Act or the common law, and under both criminal and civil statutes.

[25] Restatement of Torts § 757, comment b.

[26] American Paper & Packaging Products v Kirgan, 183 Cal App 3d 1318, 228 Cal Rptr 713 (1986); Steenhoven v College Life Insurance Co. (Ind App) 48 NE2d 661 (1984).

[27] PL 96-517, 17 USC § § 101 and 117.

fringement analysis look to see if the most significant steps of the program are similar, rather than whether most of the program's steps are similar. To illustrate a copyright violation, substantial similarity in structures of two computer programs for dental laboratory record keeping was found, even though the programs were dissimilar in a number of respects, where five particularly important subroutines within both programs performed almost identically.[28] Copyright protection then extends beyond literal copying to the manner in which the program operates — its structure, sequence, and organization. However, because the law is still developing and uncertainties exist, many computer program developers seek additional or alternative protection for their programs through other legal means.

(b) PATENTS. The extent to which computer programs can be patented is not settled. Many programs are not patentable because they contain mathematical formulas, and the courts are reluctant to grant a monopoly on a method of solving a mathematical problem since such are the basic tools of scientific work.[29] Patents have been granted for computer programs, however. For example, a method of using a computer to carry out translations from one language to another was held to be patentable. Developers of computer programs often will not attempt to obtain a patent because, once a patent is obtained, the program is available for public inspection at the U.S. Patent Office. Should the program be improperly used by the public, detection of the infringement may be difficult.

(c) TRADE SECRETS. Trade secrecy is widely used in the computer industry to protect computer programs. There are no time limitations on the protection of trade secrets, as exist with patents and copyrights. Also, there is no necessity for filing and disclosure as is required by the patent and copyright laws.

The *Aries* case illustrates the application of trade secrecy laws in the protection of computer software.

[28] Whelan Associates v Jaslow Dental Laboratory (CA3 Pa) 797 F2d 1222 (1986).

[29] Gottschalk v Benson, 409 US 63 (1972); Parker v Flook, 437 US 584 (1978). But see Diamond v Diehr, 450 US 175 (1981), where a computerized process for curing rubber was held to be patentable, even though the process was based on a mathematical formula, since the inventor did not seek to prevent all others from using the formula, but only to prevent the use of the formula in conjunction with the other steps in his rubber curing process.

ARIES INFORMATION SYSTEMS, INC. V PACIFIC MANAGEMENT SYSTEMS CORP.

(Minn App) 366 NW2d 366 (1985)

Aries Information Systems, Inc. (Aries), develops and markets computer software specially designed to meet the financial accounting and reporting requirements of public bodies such as school districts and county governments. One of Aries principal products is the POBAS III accounting program. Pacific Management Systems Corporation (Pacific) was organized in March 1980 by Scott Dahmer, John Laugan, and Roman Rowan for the purpose of marketing a financial accounting and budgeting system known as FAMIS. Dahmer, Laugan, and Rowan were Aries employees before, during, and shortly after they organized Pacific. As employees, they each gained access to Aries' software materials (including the POBAS III system) and had information about Aries' existing and prospective clients. Proprietary notices appeared on every client contract, source code list, and magnetic tape. The software user manuals of Aries were copyrighted. Dahmer, Laugan, and Rowan signed an "Employee Confidential Information Agreement" after beginning employment with Aries. They did not receive any consideration for signing the agreements. The agreements also restricted these individuals from competing with Aries during or for a three-year period after their employment with Aries. Dahmer, Laugan, and Rowan — while still employees of Aries — submitted a bid on behalf of Pacific to Rock County and were awarded the contract. Pacific's FAMIS software system is substantially identical to Aries' proprietary POBAS III system. The differences that do exist are superficial and do not make the FAMIS system different in form or capacity from POBAS III. Pacific failed to present any evidence or documentation at trial that showed either how they developed or acquired the FAMIS system. The POBAS III system is not available from any source but Aries. Aries sued Pacific to recover damages for misappropriation of its trade secrets. Pacific defended that Dahmer, Laugan, and Rowan were not bound by the "Employee Confidential Information Agreement" because of lack of consideration. From a judgment for Aries, Pacific appealed.

POPOVICH, C. J. . . . The definition of a trade secret is set forth in the Minnesota Trade Secrets Act:

> "Trade secret" means information, including a formula, pattern, compilation, program, device, method, technique, or process, that:
>   (i) derives independent economic value, actual or potential, from not being generally known to, and not being readily ascertainable by proper means by, other persons who can obtain economic value from its disclosure or use, and
>   (ii) is the subject of efforts that are reasonable under the circumstances to maintain its secrecy.

Minn. Stat. § 325C.01, subd. 5 (1984).

Aries' POBAS III system is a trade secret. The system derived independent economic value from being generally unknown and available solely from Aries. The economic value is evidenced by the $2 million generated by Aries from the sale of POBAS III between 1979 and 1983.

Aries can assert POBAS III was a trade secret only if they made reasonable efforts to maintain the secrecy of POBAS III. The law requires more than mere intent to keep it secret yet does not require absolute secrecy if the circumstances do not demand it. The possessor of a trade secret is not required to guard against unanticipated, undetectable or unpreventable methods of discovery.

Aries took reasonable efforts to maintain the secrecy of POBAS III. The efforts constituted more than mere intent: (a) all of the source code listings and magnetic tapes incorporating the POBAS system bore proprietary notices; (b) the Aries user manuals were copyrighted and stated that all system information was proprietary; and (c) every client contract stated that POBAS was the exclusive proprietary property of Aries. Although absolute security was not achieved, Aries took reasonable efforts to protect the secrecy of POBAS III from third parties.

Aries' greatest exposure arose from its own employees. It is difficult, if not impossible, to prevent an employee from discovering his employer's trade secrets. Aries took reasonable steps to maintain the secrecy of POBAS III by having Dahmer, Laugan and Rowan sign confidentiality agreements. . . .

> "Misappropriation" means: . . . disclosure or use of a trade secret of another without express or implied consent of a person who . . . at the time of disclosure or use, knew or had reason to know that his knowledge of the trade secret was . . . acquired under circumstances giving rise to a duty to maintain its secrecy or limit its use. . . .

Minn. Stat. § 325C.01, subd. 3(B)(II) (1984).

Appellants made use of the POBAS III trade secret without any express or implied consent from Aries. At the time appellants made use of the trade secret, they were still employed by Aries. By reading and signing the confidentiality agreements, appellants knew they were under a duty to maintain the secrecy and limit the use of all Aries' information. A duty of employer/employee confidentiality can arise at common law if the employee is given notice of what material is to be kept confidential. The duty existed because the confidentiality agreements, whether supported by consideration or not, put appellants on notice that all Aries' information was confidential.

Appellants' misappropriation is further demonstrated by (a) there were no material differences between Pacific's FAMIS system and Aries' POBAS III system; (b) Pacific failed to show how they developed or acquired the FAMIS system; and (c) the POBAS III system was not available from any source but Aries.

A complainant may recover the actual loss caused by the misappropriation in addition to the unjust enrichment enjoyed by the wrongdoer. The trial court based the compensatory damages on the revenues gained by Pacific during the period of misappropriation and on the revenues which Aries lost because its clients were diverted to Pacific. A 33 percent industry standard royalty fee was also assessed to Pacific because the royalties would have gone to Aries but for the misappropriation. The trial court found that appellants' conduct was willful and malicious and properly awarded punitive damages and attorney's fees.

[Judgment affirmed]

QUESTIONS

1. Did Aries make reasonable efforts to maintain the secrecy of POBAS III?
2. What factors supported the conclusion that Pacific had misappropriated Aries' trade secrets?
3. Why didn't Aries sue its three former employees on a breach of contract theory for violating the "Employee Confidential Information Agreement" that also included a three-year noncompetition agreement?

(d) CONTRACTS. Where the owner of a computer program desires to sell or lease the program to others, such use is usually controlled by a contract between the owner and customer. Owners also may choose to copyright their programs in order to give notice to third parties who may have innocently received the program.

Owners and developers of computer software commonly utilize noncompetition agreements and nondisclosure agreements as parts of their initial or renewal employment contracts with employees working on research and development. (See § 17:19 on agreements not to compete.) These agreements are used to protect the owner's computer software from unauthorized disclosures by ex-employees to competitors. A **noncompetition agreement,** reasonable in geographic scope and duration, is an effective deterrent to unauthorized disclosures to competitors because it forecloses employees' freedom to accept employment with competitors. A **nondisclosure agreement** identifies what information the parties consider to be confidential, as opposed to the general skills and knowledge of the business. Even if the confidential information does not meet the requirements for classification as a trade secret, nevertheless it will be protected as a matter of contract.

§ 24:13   SEMICONDUCTOR CHIP PROTECTION

The Semiconductor Chip Protection Act of 1984[30] (SCPA) created a new form of industrial intellectual property, protecting "mask works" and the semiconductor chip products in which they are embodied from chip piracy. **Mask works** refer to the specific form of expression embodied in chip design, including the stencils used in manufacturing semiconductor chip products. A **semiconductor chip product** is a product placed on a piece of semiconductor material in accordance with a predetermined pattern, and intended to perform electronic circuitry functions. This definition includes products such as analog chips, logic function chips such as microprocessors, and memory chips such as RAMs and ROMs.

(a) DURATION AND QUALIFICATIONS FOR PROTECTION. The SCPA provides the own-

ers of a mask work fixed in a semiconductor chip product the exclusive right for ten years to reproduce and distribute their products in the United States and to import them into the United States. These rights fully apply to works first commercially exploited after November 8, 1984, the date of the enactment of the law. However, the protection of the act only applies to those works that, when considered as a whole, are not commonplace, staple, or familiar in the semiconductor industry.

(b) APPLICATION PROCEDURE. The owner of a mask work subject to protection under the SCPA must file an application for a certificate of registration with the Register of Copyrights within two years of the date of the work's first commercial exploitation. Failure to do so within this period will result in forfeiture of all rights under the act. Questions concerning the validity of the works are to be resolved through litigation or arbitration.

(c) LIMITATIONS ON EXCLUSIVE RIGHTS. Under the SCPA's reverse engineering exemption, competitors may not only study mask works, but may use the results of that study to design their own semiconductor chip products embodying their own original masks, even if the masks are substantially similar (but not substantially identical), so long as their products are the result of substantial study and analysis and not the mere result of plagerism.[31]

Innocent infringers are not liable for infringements occurring before notice of protection is given them and are liable for reasonable royalties on each unit distributed after notice has been given them. However, the continued purchasing of infringing semiconductors after notice has been given can result in penalties up to $250,000.

(d) REMEDIES. The SCPA provides that the infringer will be liable for actual damages, and will forfeit its profits to the owner. As an alternative the owner may elect to

---

[30]   PL 98-620, 98 Stat 3347, 17 USC 901.

[31]   17 USC § 906.

receive statutory damages of up to $250,000 as determined by the court.[32] The court may also order destruction or other disposition of the products and the equipment used to make the products.

§ 24:14 REMEDIES FOR VIOLATION OF PROPERTY RIGHTS

The remedy most commonly used by the owner of personal propety for violations of property rights is an action for monetary damages when the property is negligently or willfully harmed, taken, or destroyed by the act of another. When the owner's property is taken under circumstances that would constitute larceny, the owner may sue for the wrong, called conversion, and will recover the monetary value of the property at the time of the unlawful taking, or may recover the property itself by an action at law.

The owner's right to recover damages for conversion may also be asserted against an innocent wrongdoer; that is a person who in good faith has exercised dominion over the property of the plaintiff. For example, although the buyer of a stolen television set gave value and acted in good faith in the belief that the seller was the owner of the set, the conduct of the innocent buyer in taking possession of the set and exercising control over it is a conversion for which the innocent buyer is liable to the true owner.

If the defendant has infringed copyrights, patents, or marks of the plaintiff, the plaintiff may obtain an injunction ordering the defendant to stop such practices. If the infringement was intentional, the plaintiff may also recover from the defendant any profits obtained by the defendant from such infringement. If the infringement conduct is such as to constitute an unfair trade practice, the plaintiff may obtain a cease and desist order against the defendant from the Federal Trade Commission.

---

[32] 17 USC § 911(c).

D. MULTIPLE OWNERSHIP OF PERSONAL PROPERTY

When all rights in a particular object of property are held by one person, that property is held in **severalty.** However, two or more persons may hold concurrent rights and interests in the same property. In that case, the property is said to be held in **cotenancy.** The various forms of cotenancy include (1) tenancy in common, (2) joint tenancy, (3) tenancy by entirety, and (4) community property.

§ 24:15 TENANCY IN COMMON

A tenancy in common is a form of ownership by two or more persons. The interest of a tenant in common may be transferred or inherited, in which case the taker becomes a tenant in common with the others. This tenancy is terminated only when there is a partition or division, giving each a specific portion, or when one person acquires all of the interests of the co-owners.

§ 24:16 JOINT TENANCY

A joint teneancy is another form of ownership by two or more persons. A joint tenant's interest may be transferred to a third person, but this destroys the joint tenancy. In such a case, the remaining joint tenant becomes a tenant in common with the third person.

Upon the death of a joint tenant, the remaining tenants take the share of the deceased tenant. The last surviving joint tenant takes the property as a holder in severalty.

(a) STATUTORY CHANGE. Statutes in many states have modified the common law by adding a formal requirement to the creation of a joint tenancy with survivorship. At common law, such an estate would be created by a transfer of property to "A and B as joint tenants." Under these statutes, it is necessary to add the words *with right of survivorship*, or other similar words, if it is desired to create a right of survivorship. If no words of survivorship are used, the transfer of property to two or more persons will be construed as creating a tenancy in common. Under such a statute, a certificate of deposit issued only in the name of "A or B" does not create a joint tenancy because it does not add words of survivorship.

(b) BANK ACCOUNTS. The deposit of money in a joint account constitutes a gift of a joint ownership interest in the money when that is the intent of the depositor. The mere fact that money is deposited in a joint account does not in itself establish that there was such a gift, particularly when it can be shown by clear and convincing evidence that the deposits were made in the joint account "solely for the convenience of enabling either of the parties to draw therefrom for family purposes." When the joint account is merely an agency device, the account agent is not entitled to use any part of the account for personal purposes.

The effect of creating a joint bank account with the right of survivorship can be seen in the *Coddington* case, where the deceased depositor's bank account was claimed by both his mother and his widow.

CODDINGTON V CODDINGTON

56 App Div 2d 697, 391 NYS2d 760 (1977)

The New York Banking Law provides that a presumption arises that a joint tenancy has been created when a bank account is opened in the names of two persons "payable to either or the survivor." While he was still single, Richard Coddington opened a savings account with his mother Amelia. The signature card they signed stated that the account was owned by them as joint tenants with the right of survivorship. No statement as to survivorship was made on the passbook. Richard later married Margaret. On his death, Margaret claimed a share of the account on the ground that it was not a joint tenancy because the passbook did not contain words of survivorship and because the statutory presumption of a joint tenancy was overcome by the fact that Richard had withdrawn substantial sums from the account during his life. The court awarded the entire account to the mother, and Margaret appealed.

PER CURIAM. . . . Appellant urges that the absence of the words "payable to either or the survivor" on the passbook and some of the ledger cards prevents the operation of the presumption because no joint tenancy was created. While appellant is correct in maintaining that a joint tenancy cannot be created without words of survivorship . . . what is controlling is the form in which the initial deposit was made (*Matter of Fenelon*, 262 NY 308, 186 NE 794). In the case at bar, the signature card contained the agreement of the bank and the depositor and provided as follows:

Joint Account Payable to Either or Survivor. We agree and declare that all funds now, or hereafter, deposited in this account are, and shall be, our joint property and owned by us as joint tenants with right of survivorship, and not as tenants in common; and upon the death of either of us any balance in said account shall become the absolute property of the survivor.

The deposit was clearly in the statutory form and prima facie presumption of subdivision (b) of . . . the Banking Law applies.

Addressing our attention to the . . . assertion of the appellant . . . that the facts adduced at trial were sufficient to overcome the presumption, we must again disagree. The heavy burden of rebutting the presumption rests upon the challenger . . . and for the appellant to prevail there must be direct proof or substantial circumstantial proof, clear and convincing and sufficient to support an inference that the joint account had been opened in that form as a matter of convenience only (*Matter of Murphy*, 23 AD2d 866, 259 NYS2d 228 . . .). We find no such proof here. It is true that the appellant was able to demonstrate that Richard Coddington had, in fact at one time withdrawn most of the money in the account. It is true, too, that withdrawal by one depositor of the whole fund or more than his share is some evidence that no true joint tenancy was intended. . . . However, such action, standing alone, is insufficient to overcome the presumption.

[Judgment affirmed]

QUESTIONS

1. What did the widow, Margaret Coddington, claim?
2. Did the court agree with Margaret Coddington?
3. Did the court find the signature card signed by the depositors when the account was opened to be important?

§ 24:17   TENANCY BY ENTIRETY

At common law a **tenancy by entirety** or **tenancy by the entireties** was created when property was transferred to both husband and wife. It differs from joint tenancy in that it requires a transfer to husband and wife and also in that the right of survivorship cannot be extinguished and one spouse's interest cannot be transferred to a third person, although in some jurisdictions a spouse's right to share the possession and the profits may be transferred. This form of property holding is popular in common-law jurisdictions because creditors of one of the spouses cannot reach the property while both are living. Only a creditor of both the husband and wife under the same obligation can obtain execution against the property. Moreover, the tenancy by en-tirety is in effect a substitute for a will since the surviving spouse acquires the complete property interest upon the death of the other. There are usually other reasons, however, why each spouse should make a will.

In many states the granting of an absolute divorce converts a tenancy by the entireties into a tenancy in common.

§ 24:18   COMMUNITY PROPERTY

In some states property acquired during the period of marriage is the community property of the husband and wife. Some statutes provide for the right of survivorship; others provide that half of the property of the deceased husband or wife shall go to the heirs, or permit such half to be disposed of by will. It is commonly provided that property acquired by either spouse during the marriage is prima facie community property, even though title is taken in the spouse's individual name,

unless it can be shown that it was obtained with property possessed by the spouse prior to the marriage.

SUMMARY

Personal property consists of whole or fractional ownership rights in things that are tangible and movable as well as rights in things that are intangible.

Personal property may be acquired by purchase. Personal property may also be acquired by gift where the donor has present intent to make a gift and delivers possession to the donee. Personal property may also be acquired by finding lost property and by occupation.

Property rights in trademarks, copyrights, and patents are acquired as provided in federal statutes. A trademark or service mark is any word, symbol, or design, or combination of these used to identify a product in the case of a trademark, and a service in the case of service mark. Terms for which protection is claimed will fall into one of four categories: (1) generic, (2) descriptive, (3) suggestive, or (4) arbitrary of fanciful. Generic terms are never registrable. Ordinarily descriptive terms are not registrable; however, if a descriptive term has acquired a "secondary meaning" it is registrable. Suggestive and arbitrary marks are registrable. If there is likelihood of confusion, a court will enjoin the second user from using a particular mark.

A copyright is the exclusive right given by federal statute to the creator of a literary or artistic work to use, reproduce, or display the work for the life of the creator and fifty years after the creator's death. A patent gives the inventor an exclusive right for seventeen years to make, use and sell an invention that is new and useful and not obvious to those in the business to which the invention is related. Trade secrets that give an owner an advantage over competitors are protected under state law for an ulimited period so long as they are not made public. Computer programs may be protected under the Computer Software Copyright Act, patent law, trade secrecy law, and contract law. Qualifying mask works and the semiconductor chip products in which they are embodied are protected from piracy by the Semiconductor Chip Protection Act for a period of ten years.

All rights in a particular object of property can be held by one individual, in which case it is said to be held in severalty. Ownership rights may be held concurrently by two or more individuals, in which case it is said to be held in cotenancy. The major forms of cotenancy include (1) tenancy in common, (2) joint tenancy, (3) tenancy by the entireties, and (4) community property.

QUESTIONS AND CASE PROBLEMS

1. What social forces give rise to the rule of law requiring that there be an actual or symbolic delivery in order to make a gift?
2. What qualities must an invention possess in order to be patentable?
3. Compare the protection afforded by a patent and the protection afforded by a trademark registration.
4. How does (a) capturing a wild game animal during the hunting season compare with (b) finding lost property?
5. The Mackey Corporation manufactures fur-

niture polishes. Mackey develops a new polish that it markets under the name of "Super-polish." Mackey wants to register this name as a trademark and prevent anyone else from using it. Can Mackey do so?

6. General Computers Corporation developed a new generation computer at its research and development facility in Bedford, California. Prior to marketing the computer, a competitor, World Data Systems Inc., of Piscataway, New Jersey hired away General's chief research engineer, Tyler Moore. General is worried that World will obtain secret information about the new computer from Moore and consults you. Your investigation reveals that General did not have a corporate policy of utilizing contracts of employment to protect against disclosure of secret business information and to reasonably restrict employees from working for direct competitors. General did not patent its new computer because of the disclosure requirements necessary to obtain a patent. Is there any legal theory by which General can prohibit Moore from disclosing secret information about the new computer to World?

7. Sony Corporation manufactures video cassette recorders (VCR's) to tape television shows for later home viewing (time-shifting). Sony sells them under the trade name Betamax through retail establishments throughout the country. Universal City Studios and Walt Disney Productions own the copyrights on some of the television programs that are broadcast on public airwaves. Universal and Disney bring an action against Sony and certain large retailers contending that VCR consumers have recorded some of their copyrighted works that had been shown on commercially sponsored television and thereby infringed on these copyrights. These plaintiffs seek damages and an injunction against the manufacture and marketing of VCR's. Sony contends that the non-commercial, home-use recording of material broadcast over public airwaves for later viewing is a "fair use" of copyrighted works. Decide. [Sony Corp v Universal Studios, 464 US 417.]

8. Ruth and Stella were sisters. They owned a house as joint tenants with right of survivorship. Ruth sold her half interest to Roy. Thereafter, Stella died and Roy claimed the entire property by survivorship. Was he entitled thereto?

9. Mona finds a wallet on the floor of an elevator in the office building in which she works. She posts several notices in the building informing of the finding of the wallet, but no one appears to claim it. She waits for six months and then spends the money in the wallet in the belief that she owns it. Thereafter Jason, the person who lost the wallet, brings suit to recover the money. Mona defends that the money was hers, since Jason did not claim it within a reasonable time after she posted the notice. Is she correct?

10. In 1971 Harry Gordon turned over $40,000 to his son, Murray Gordon. Murray opened two $20,000 custodian bank accounts under the Uniform Gifts to Minors Acts for his minor children, Eden and Alexander. Murray was listed as the custodian of both accounts. On January 9, 1976, both accounts were closed, and a single bank check representing the principal of the accounts, was drawn to the order of Harry Gordon. In April of 1976, Murray and his wife, Joan, entered into a separation agreement and were later divorced. Thereafter, Joan, on behalf of her children, Eden and Alexander, brought suit against Murray to recover the funds withdrawn in January of 1976, contending that the deposits in both accounts were irrevocable gifts. Murray contended that the money was his father's and it was never intended as a gift, but was merely a means of avoiding tax liability. [Gordon v Gordon, 419 NYS2d 684, 70 App Div 2d 86 (1979)]

11. Carol and Robert, both over twenty-one, became engaged. Robert gave Carol an engagement ring. He was killed in an automobile crash before they were married. His estate demanded that Carol return the ring. Was she entitled to keep it? [Cohen v Bayside Federal Savings and Loan Ass'n, 62 Misc 2d 738, 309 NYS2d 980]

12. The plaintiff, Herbert Rosenthal Jewelry Coporation, and the defendant, Kalpakian, manufactured jewelry. The plaintiff obtained a copyright registration of a jeweled pin in the shape of a bee. Kalpakian made a similar pin. Rosenthal sued Kalpakian for infringement of copyright registration. Kalpakian raised the defense that he was

only copying the idea and not the way the idea was expressed. Was he liable for infringement of the plaintiff's copyright? [Herbert Rosenthal Jewelry Corp. v Kalpakian (CA9 Cal) 446 F2d 738]

13. Brogden acquired a biblical manuscript in 1945. In 1952 he told his sister Lucy that he wanted Texas A & M University to have this manuscript. He dictated a note so stating and placed it with the manuscript. He made some effort to have an officer of the college come for the manuscript. In 1956 he delivered the manuscript to his sister, stating that he was afraid someone would steal it. Later in the year he told a third person that he was going to give the manuscript to the university. In 1957 he was declared incompetent. In 1959 the sister delivered the manuscript to the university. In April, 1960, Brogden died, and his heirs, Bailey and others, sued Harrington and other officers of the university to have the title to the manuscript determined. Decide. [Harrington v Bailey (Tex Civ App) 351 SW2d 946]

14. From October, 1965, through July, 1967, Union Carbide Corporation sold certain bulbs for high-intensity reading lamps under its EVEREADY trademark. Carbide's sales of electrical products under the EVEREADY mark exceeded $100 million for every year after 1963; from 1963-67 Carbide spent $50 million in advertising these products. In 1969 the defendant, Ever-Ready, Inc., imported miniature lamp bulbs for high-intensity lamps with "Ever-Ready" stamped on their bases. In two surveys conducted by Carbide, 50 percent of those interviewed associated Carbide products with the marks used by Ever-Ready Inc. Carbide sought an injunction against Ever-Ready's use of the name Ever-Ready on or in connection with the sale of electrical products. No monetary damages were sought. Ever-Ready Inc. defended that Carbide's trademark EVEREADY was descriptive, and therefore the registration of the mark was improper and invalid. Carbide responded that its mark had acquired secondary meaning. Decide. [Union Carbide Corp. v Ever-Ready Inc. (CA7 Ill) 531 F2d 366.]

15. Anheuser-Busch had been interested in producing a low-alcohol beer, both because of its need to develop new markets for growth and because of growing public concern over the health aspects of beer consumption and the problem of drunken driving. Other breweries had similar interests and, in fact, two smaller companies, Hudepohl Brewery and Christian Schmidt Brewing Company, had marketed reduced alcohol beers under the brand names of Pace and Break. Anheuser-Busch made an application for registration of the trademark LA and soon thereafter began marketing its low alcohol product under the LA label. Following Anheuser-Busch's introduction of its product, the Stroh Brewery Company introduced "Schaefer LA," also a low alcohol beer. An action to enjoin Stroh's use of LA followed. Anheuser-Busch contends that the term LA was suggestive in that it required some imagination to connect it with the product and, accordingly, was a protectible trademark. Stroh argues that LA is generic or descriptive in nature, since the term is comprised of the initials of the phrase low alcohol. Decide. [Anheuser-Busch Inc. v The Stroh Brewery Company (CA8 Mo) 750 F2d 631.]

25

BAILMENTS

Many instances arise in which the owner of personal property entrusts it to another. A person checks a coat at a restaurant, delivers a watch to a jeweler for repairs, or loans hedge clippers to a neighbor; or a company rents a car to a tourist for a weekend. The delivery of property to another under such circumstances is a bailment.

A. GENERAL PRINCIPLES

A **bailment** is the legal relationship that arises whenever one person delivers possession of personal property to another under an agreement, express or implied, by which the latter is under a duty to re-turn the identical property to the former or to deliver it or dispose of it as agreed. The person who turns over the possession of the property is the **bailor**. The person who accepts possession is the **bailee**.

§ 25:1 ELEMENTS OF BAILMENT

A bailment is created when the following elements are present:

(a) AGREEMENT. The bailment is based upon an agreement. Generally this agreement will contain all the elements of a contract so that the bailment transaction in fact consists of (1) a contract to bail and (2) the actual bailing of the property. Ordinarily there is no requirement that the contract of bailment be in writing. The subject of a bailment may be any personal property of which possession may be given. Real property cannot be bailed.

(b) DELIVERY AND ACCEPTANCE. The bailment arises when, pursuant to the agreement of the parties, the property is delivered to the bailee and accepted by the bailee as subject to the bailment agreement.[1]

Delivery may be **actual,** as when the bailor physically hands a book to the bailee, or it may be **constructive,** as when the bailor points out a package to the bailee who then takes possession of it. In the absence of a prior agreement to the contrary, a valid delivery and acceptance gener-

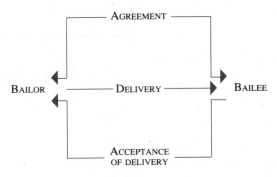

FIGURE 25-1
BAILMENT OF PERSONAL PROPERTY

ally requires that the bailee be aware that goods have been placed within the bailee's control. The *Berglund* case illustrates a situation where this element was not present.

---

[1]   Merrit v Nationwide Warehouse Co., Ltd. (Tenn App) 605 SW2d 250 (1980).

BERGLUND V ROOSEVELT UNIVERSITY
18 Ill App 3d 842, 310 NE2d 773 (1974)

Richard Berglund, the plaintiff, was a full-time student at Roosevelt University. He was also the editor and photographer of the student newspaper. The University was unaware that Richard kept his own photographic equipment in the rooms it had assigned to the newspaper. One night this equipment was stolen from the newspaper office. Richard sued the University on the theory that it had breached its duty as a bailee. He showed that former editors had also left their equipment in the University rooms. The University denied that it was a bailee. The trial court awarded $1,789.15 to Richard on the theory of an implied bailment, and the University appealed.

McNAMARA, J. . . . The characteristics common to every bailment are the intent to create a bailment, delivery of possession of the bailed items, and the acceptance of the items by the bailee. . . . A bailment can be established by express contract or by implication. (*Chesterfield Sewer & Water v Citizens Ins. Co.* (1965) 57 Ill App 2d 90, 207 NE2d 84). . . . In determining the existence of an implied-in-fact bailment, one must analyze the facts surrounding the transaction, such as the benefits to be received by the parties, their intentions, the kind of property involved, and the opportunity of each to exercise control over the property. . . .

In the present case, plaintiff attempted to show that an implied-in-fact bailment had arisen between the parties. It is clear, however, that the failure of the plaintiff to prove any knowledge on the part of the defendant of the storage of the items doomed this attempt.

Knowledge on the part of the bailee is essential to prove proper delivery and acceptance. Physical control over the property allegedly bailed and an intention to exercise that control are needed to show that one is in possession of the bailed item. . . . And before acceptance can be inferred on the part of the alleged bailee of the goods purportedly bailed, there must be evidence to show notice or knowledge on the part of the bailee that the goods are in fact in his possession. . . . Yet in the present case defendant's consistent denial of having any knowledge that plaintiff had stored his camera equipment on the premises is supported by plaintiff's own testimony. Although normal procedure required plaintiff to seek permission of certain agents of defendant to store his property on the premises, plaintiff never bothered to do so. . . . Nor does the fact that prior student paper photographers may have similarly stored their equipment in the darkroom, without more, prove knowledge on the part of defendant. The record also reveals that defendant's security officers never exercised any degree of intentional control over plaintiff's goods. We conclude that plaintiff's failure to prove knowledge on the part of defendant of the goods stored resulted in his inability to prove a valid delivery of the camera equipment and a true acceptance of the goods by defendant. . . . Our holding on this issue obviates the necessity of considering whether defendant was negligent in its capacity as bailee.

[Judgment reversed]

QUESTIONS

1. What did the plaintiff claim?
2. Was it essential for the plaintiff to prove the defendant had knowledge of the storage of the items in order to prove proper delivery and acceptance in this case?
3. Did the court find that there was a bailment?

§ 25:2 NATURE OF THE PARTIES' INTERESTS

The bailor and bailee have different legal interests in the bailed property.

(a) BAILOR'S INTEREST. The bailor is usually the owner, but ownership by the bailor is not required. It is sufficient that the bailor have physical possession. Thus, an employee may be a bailor in leaving the employer's truck at a garage.

(b) BAILEE'S INTEREST. The bailee has only possession of the property. Title to the property does not pass to the bailee, and the bailee cannot sell the property to a third person unless the bailee is also an agent authorized to make such a sale. If the bailee attempts to sell the property, such sale only transfers possession, and the owner may recover the property from the buyer.

The bailor may cause third persons to believe that the bailee is the owner of the bailed property. If the bailor does so, the bailor is estopped from denying that the bailee is the owner as against persons who have relied on the bailor's representations. As a further exception, if the bailee is a dealer in goods of the kinds entrusted to the bailee by the bailor, a sale by the bailee to a buyer in the ordinary course of business will pass the bailor's title to the buyer.

§ 25:3   CLASSIFICATION OF BAILMENTS

Bailments are classified as ordinary and extraordinary (or special). **Extraordinary bailments** are those in which the bailee is under unusual duties and liabilities by law, as in the case of bailments in which a motel or a common carrier is involved. **Ordinary bailments** include all other bailments.

Bailments may or may not provide for compensation to the bailee. Upon that basis they may be classified as **contract bailments** and **gratuitous bailments.** The fact that no charge is made by the bailor does not necessarily make the transaction a gratuitous bailment. If the bailment is made to further a business interest of the bailor, as when something is loaned free to a customer, the bailment is not gratuitous.

Bailments may also be classified in terms of benefit. A bailment may be for the sole benefit of the bailor, as when a farmer gratuitously transports another's produce to the city. A bailment may be for the sole benefit of the bailee, as when a person borrows a friend's automobile. A bailment may be for the benefit of both parties (mutual-benefit bailment), as when one rents a power tool. A mutual-benefit bailment also arises when a prospective buyer of an automobile leaves the automobile that is to be traded in with the dealer so that the latter may test it and appraise it.

§ 25:4   CONSTRUCTIVE BAILMENTS

When one person comes into possession of personal property of another without the owner's consent, the law treats the possessor as a bailee and calls the relationship a **constructive bailment.**[2] It is thus held that the finder of lost property is a bailee of that property.

When a city impounds an automobile, a bailment arises as to the vehicle and its contents. A seller who has not yet delivered the goods to the buyer is treated as bailee of the goods if title has passed to the buyer. Similarly, a buyer who is in possession of goods, the title to which has not yet passed from the seller, is a bailee.

§ 25:5   RENTING OF SPACE DISTINGUISHED

When a person rents space in a locker or building under an agreement that gives the renter the exclusive right to use that space, the placing of goods by the renter in that space does not create a bailment.[3] In such a case, putting property into the space does not constitute a delivery of goods into the possession of the owner of the space. On this basis, there is no bailment in a self-service parking lot when the owner of a car parks it, retains the key, and the owner's only contact with any parking lot employee is upon making a payment when leaving the lot. In such situations, the car owner merely rents the space for parking.

The practical consequence of this conclusion is that if the car is damaged or stolen, the car owner cannot recover damages from the parking lot management unless the owner can show some fault on the part of the parking lot. If the transaction were a bailment, the owner of the car would establish a prima facie right to recover by proving the fact of the bailment and that there was a loss.

If the parking lot is a locked enclosure with a guard to whom the patron must surrender a parking ticket received on entering the lot in order to regain possession of the car, a modern trend regards the transaction as a bailment. The theoretical objection to this view is that the lot does not have full dominion and control over the car since it cannot move the car because the patron has retained possession of the keys. At the same time, as the lot has the power to exclude others from the car, courts have

---

[2]   Hertz Corp. v Paloni, (App) 95 NM 212, 619 P2d 1256 (1980).

[3]   Magliocco v American Locker Co. 239 Cal Rptr 497 (1987).

found it "realistic" to treat the parking lot as a bailee and hold it to a bailee's standard of care.

§ 25:6 BAILMENT OF CONTENTS OF CONTAINER

It is a question of the intention of the parties, as that appears to a reasonable person, whether a bailment of a container also constitutes a bailment of articles contained in it; for example, whether a bailment of a coat is a bailment of articles in the coat. When the contained articles are of a class that is reasonably or normally to be found in the container, they may be regarded as bailed in the absence of an express disclaimer. If the articles are not of such a nature and their presence in the container is unknown to the bailee, there is no bailment of such articles. Consequently, although the circumstances are such that the parking of a car constitutes a bailment, there is no bailment of valuable drawings and sporting equipment that are on the back seat but that are not visible from the outside of the car. However, there is ordinarily a bailment of whatever is locked in the trunk.

B. RIGHTS AND DUTIES OF THE PARTIES

A bailment creates certain rights and imposes certain duties upon each party. These may be increased or modified by statute, by custom, or by the express agreement of the parties.

§ 25:7 DUTIES OF THE BAILEE

The bailee has certain duties concerning performance, care, maintenance, and return of the bailed property. A bailee's lien allows for the retention of goods until charges are paid. Unauthorized use is forbidden.

(a) PERFORMANCE. If the bailment is based upon a contract, the bailee must per-form the bailee's part of the contract and is liable to the bailor for ordinary contract damages arising out of the failure to perform the contract.[4] Thus, if the bailment is for repair, the bailee is under the duty to make the repairs properly. The fact that the bailee used due care in attempting to perform the contract does not excuse the bailee from liability for failing to perform the contract.

(b) CARE OF PROPERTY. The bailee is under a duty to care for the bailed property. If the property is damaged or destroyed, the bailee is liable for the loss (1) if the harm was caused in whole or in part by the bailee's failure to use reasonable care under the circumstances, or (2) if the harm was sustained during the unauthorized use of the property by the bailee. Otherwise the bailor bears the loss. Thus, if the bailee was exercising due care and was making an authorized use of the property, the bailor must bear the loss of or damage to the property caused by an act of a third person, whether willful or negligent; by an accident or occurrence for which no one was at fault; or by an act of God.[5] In this connection, the term, *act of God*, means a natural phenomenon that is not reasonably foreseeable, such as a sudden flood or lightning.

(1) Standard of Care. The standard for ordinary bailments is reasonable care under the circumstances, that is, the degree of care that a reasonable person would exercise in the situation in order to prevent the realization of reasonably foreseeable harm. The significant factors in determining what constitutes reasonable care in a bailment are the time and place of making the bailment, the facilities for taking care of the bailed property, the nature of the bailed property, the bailee's knowledge of its nature, and the extent of the bailee's skills and experience in taking care of goods of that kind.

---

[4] Computer Systems v Western Reserve Life, 19 Mass App 430, 475 NE2d 745 (1985).

[5] Andrews v Allen (Tex Civ App) 724 SW2d 893 (1987).

Some courts state the standard of care in terms of the benefit characteristic of the bailment. Thus, when the bailment is for the sole benefit of the bailee, the bailee is held liable for the slightest negligence. When the bailment is for the mutual benefit of the parties, the bailee is held liable for ordinary negligence. In contrast, if the benefit is for the sole benefit of the bailor, the bailee is only required to exercise slight care and will only be liable for gross negligence.

The *Mahallati* case illustrates the degree of care owed in mutual-benefit bailments and the problems that can result from a business's imprecise administrative practices.

MAHALLATI V WILLIAMS

(Dist Col App) 479 A2d 300 (1984)

On May 14, 1980, Clarence Williams brought his wife's fur coat to Debonair Cleaners for cleaning and storage. Williams testified that the cleaners' co-owner, Massoud Mahallati, told him that Debonair was experienced in such matters and that the charge would be 3 percent of the stated value of the coat. Williams stated that the coat was worth $13,000, and Mahallati wrote a figure on the claim check that Williams believed at that time to be "$13,000." He also testified that the clerk informed him that the total fee for storage would be $390 (3 percent of $13,000) to be paid when the coat was returned. Mahallati testified that he received the coat from Williams, who told him the coat was worth only $130. Mahallati said that he wrote $130, not $13,000, on the claim ticket. Approximately eight months later, Arnicia Williams went to Debonair Cleaners to retrieve her coat. She presented the claim check to the clerk who, after searching the premises for the coat, told her that it could not be located. She was informed that the coat had probably been stolen during a break-in. Arnicia Williams described the missing coat as a full length, very dark Blackglama mink coat purchased from the Henri Bendel department store in New York City. The Williamses brought an action against the bailees for the value of the missing coat. From a judgment for the Williamses for $13,000, the bailees appealed.

PAIR, A. J. . . . Appellants [bailees] now maintain that the trial court erred in denying their motion for a directed verdict because there was insufficient evidence to permit the jury to find that they were negligent. We disagree. . . .

In support of their claim of negligence, appellees [the Williamses] presented evidence that in December 1980 there had been two burglaries at Debonair Cleaners. Nothing appeared to have been missing as a result of the first break-in which occurred through a window at the rear of the store. Just five days later, however, a second break-in through a back door resulted in the loss of several items. Presumably, the Williams' coat was stolen in the second burglary. At trial, Nasser Mahallati testified that after the first break-in, steel bars with anchor bolts were installed inside the rear window. He admitted, however, that no major steps were taken to generally upgrade the physical security of the premises. He explained that his family was in the process of negotiating the sale of the business and did not wish to make any substantial investment to improve the premises.

Appellants argue that this evidence was not sufficient to prove the absence of ordinary care usually required in a mutual benefit bailment contract.* The weakness in appellants' argument is that it assumes that appellees-bailors were required to prove negligence to an absolute certainty. This is simply incorrect. Where a bailor's right to recover is dependent upon a finding of the bailee's negligence, he need only introduce evidence with sufficient probative force to demonstrate a reasonable probability that the loss was caused by the defendant's negligence. Our review of the evidence indicates that, contrary to appellants' assertions, it is not clear, as a matter of law, that they were not negligent. Therefore, we conclude that the trial court did not err in refusing to direct a verdict for appellants. . . .

Appellants . . . assert that the trial court committed error by failing to instruct the jury to limit their potential liability to $130, the amount appearing on the face of the claim check. Appellants argued at trial and now on appeal that the placement of the numbers of the claim ticket unambiguously represented the value of the coat to be $130 and that parol evidence was improperly admitted to alter the meaning of these figures.

The claim check in the instant case is an ordinary dry cleaning receipt form filled with handwritten notations. At the right side of the claim check is a column with the caption "amount." This column is divided by a vertical line. To the left of the vertical line, the digits "130" appear; to the right of the line is written "00." On the bottom of the ticket, the handwritten words "Storage" and "3% for insurance only" are conspicuously written. In our opinion, not only is the meaning of the figures "130/00" ambiguous, but it is also unclear whether these numbers represent the cost for cleaning and storage of the coat, the cost of insurance, or the value of the coat itself.

When words whose meaning might ordinarily be clear and unambiguous are susceptible to a variety of interpretations, it is entirely appropriate for the trial judge to admit extrinsic evidence to aid in their construction. Therefore, in the instant case parol evidence was properly admitted and the construction of the claim ticket necessarily became a question of fact for the jury to resolve. Therefore, in light of the ambiguity surrounding the construction of the meaning of the claim ticket, we hold that the trial court acted properly in refusing to instruct the jury to limit appellant's liability to $130.

Still another issue exists with respect to the award of damages — whether the award of $13,000 was excessive and against the weight of evidence. . . .

. . .The sole proof of the value offered by appellees was Mrs. William's observations and comparison shopping. On this basis alone, appellees claimed coat was worth $13,000. We do not here dispute whether Mrs. Williams, as owner was competent to testify as to her personal opinion of value, for that question has long been settled in this jurisdiction. We do, however, question on the facts of this case, whether an owner's opinion of value standing alone is sufficient proof of the value of the lost fur.

---

*   A "mutual benefit" bailment arises when the bailor receives a particular storage service and in return the bailee is to be paid for that service. By depositing her fur coat for cleaning and storage with Debonair Cleaners, Arnicia Williams established a mutual benefit bailment with appellants.

During cross-examination, Arnicia Williams conceded that she had no bill of sale, no insurance policies and no photographs of the coat. Arguably then, her testimony was the best available evidence of the coat's value. We, however, are compelled to disagree. From the very nature of the situation, we recognize that the amount of appellees' loss in the instant case cannot be proven with exactitude. While this should not preclude a bailor from recovering damages, nevertheless, he must present some evidence, with such certainty as the nature of the particular case may permit, to lay a foundation which will enable the trier of fact to make a reasonable estimate of damages.

In short, we conclude that the jury did not have sufficient evidence before it to make a reasonable determination on the issue of the amount of damages to be awarded. Accordingly, we must remand for a new trial. But because the lower court fairly determined the question of liability and because the issues of liability and damages are separate, our remand for a new trial is limited solely to the issue of damages.

The case is therefore remanded for proceedings consistent with this opinion.

[Affirmed in part; reversed in part]

QUESTIONS

1. Why did the court consider the bailment to be a mutual-benefit bailment?
2. What duty of care was owed to the bailor in this case?
3. If the bailment receipt had stated on its face the customer's declared value as "$130" and stated that "our liability in case of loss is limited to the valuation shown on the receipt," would the bailee's liability have been limited to that amount if in fact it could be shown that the coat was actually worth $13,000?

(2) Contract Modification of Liability. A bailee's liability may be expanded by contract. A provision that the bailee assumes absolute liability for the property is binding, but there is a difference of opinion as to whether a stipulation to return the property "in good condition" or "in as good condition as received" has the effect of imposing such absolute liability.

An ordinary bailee may limit liability, except for willful misconduct, by agreement or contract.[6] However in some states, statutes prohibit certain kinds of paid bailees, such as automobile parking garages, from limiting their liability for negligence.

Also, statutes in some states declare that a party cannot bar liability for negligent violations of common law standards of care where a public interest is involved. In the *Gardner* case the court was faced with the problem of whether an automobile repair business could exempt itself from liability for ordinary negligence by a clause in its service order contract where the service it performed implicates public interest.

---

[6] Blume v Evans Fur Co. 126 Ill App 3d 52, 81 Ill Dec 335, 466 NE2d 1366 (1984).

GARDNER V DOWNTOWN PORSCHE AUDI

180 Cal App 3d 713, 225 Cal Rptr 757 (1986)

In June 1978, Bruce Gardner took his 1976 Porsche 911 automobile to be repaired at Downtown Porsche Audi (Downtown). Gardner signed a repair order bearing the disclaimer "not responsible for loss (of) cars . . . in case of . . . theft." While it was parked in the repair garage the car was stolen because of Downtown's negligence. Gardner sued Downtown for failing to redeliver his car. Downtown defended that the disclaimer absolved it of liability for its negligence. From a judgment in favor of Gardner for $16,000, Downtown appealed.

JOHNSON, A. J. . . . Downtown concedes negligence but argues the disclaimer absolves it of liability for this failure to exercise due care. Assuming the truth of Downtown's contention Gardner signed a repair slip containing this exculpatory language, and even assuming he read and understood it, we find the attempted exemption from liability to be against public policy and thus ineffective to excuse Downtown's negligence.

In the absence of a disclaimer the duties and liabilities of a bailee for hire — such as Downtown — are clear. Unless it can redeliver the subject of the bailment — in this instance, the 1976 Porsche — the bailee must prove it exercised due care in its care and custody of this property. If it fails to establish the absence of negligence the bailee is liable to the bailor for any damages suffered due to the failure to redeliver the bailed property. . . .

Traditionally the law has looked carefully and with some skepticism at those who attempt to contract away their legal liabilities for the commission of torts. (Prosser and Keeton, *Torts, Fifth Edition* (1984) pp. 482-483.) This general policy of the common law found legislative expression early in California's history with the enactment of Civil Code section 1668. This 1872 statute reads:

CERTAIN CONTRACTS UNLAWFUL. All contracts which have for their object, directly or indirectly, to exempt any one from responsibility for his own fraud, or willful injury to the person or property of another, or violation of law, *whether willful or negligent*, are against the policy of the law.

(Civ. Code § 1668, italics added.)

This section made it clear a party could not contract away liability for his fraudulent or intentional acts or for his negligent violations of *statutory* law. Less clear was the status of negligent violations of *common law* standards of care. While acknowledging some conflict in the cases, Witkin concludes California now follows the modern view of the Restatement of Contracts — "a contract exempting from liability for *ordinary* negligence is valid where *no public interest* is involved . . . and no statute expressly prohibits it. . . ."

The converse is also true, however. Under Civil Code section 1668 an automobile repair garage cannot exempt itself from liability even for ordinary negligence if the service it provides implicates the public interest. In a leading case striking down exculpatory clauses in hospital admission forms, *Tunkl v. Re-*

gents of University of California (1963) 60 Cal.2d 92, the Supreme Court set forth six characteristics typical of contracts affecting the public interest.

(1) It concerns a business of a type generally thought suitable for public regulation. (2) The party seeking exculpation is engaged in performing a service of great importance to the public, which is often a matter of practical necessity for some members of the public. (3) The party holds himself out as willing to perform this service for any member of the public who seeks it, or at least any member coming within certain established standards. (4) As a result of the essential nature of the service, in the economic setting of the transaction, the party invoking exculpation possesses a decisive advantage of bargaining strength against any member of the public who seeks his services. (5) In exercising a superior bargaining power the party confronts the public with a standardized adhesion contract of exculpation, and makes no provision whereby a purchaser may pay additional fees and obtain protection against negligence. (6) Finally, as a result of the transaction, the person or property of the purchaser is placed under the control of the seller, subject to the risk of carelessness by the seller or his agents. . . .

To begin with, automobile repair shops are in a "business of a type . . . thought suitable for public regulation" in the state of California. They are licensed by the state and their performance is regulated by the Bureau of Automotive Repair of the State Department of Consumer Affairs.

Secondly, these repair shops are most definitely engaged in "performing a service of great importance to the public, . . ." and, moreover, one which is a "matter of practical *necessity*" for nearly *all* not just "*some* members of the public." . . .

The modern citizen lives — and all too frequently dies — by the automobile. Members of the general public need cars not merely for discretionary recreational purposes but to get to and from their places of employment, to reach the stores where they can purchase the necessities — as well as the frivolities — of life, and the like. An out of repair automobile is an unreliable means of transportation. Moreover, it is a dangerous one as well — to pedestrians and other drivers not just the owner. What is true of modern society in general is doubly true in Southern California, the capital of the motor vehicle. Indeed it is virtually impossible to exist in the Los Angeles area without a fully operational automobile. Thus, except for the few who can afford to buy a new car every time the ash trays fill up, people in this area find the automobile repair business a "service of great importance" and a "practical necessity."

Thirdly, Downtown held itself "out as willing to perform" this important service "for any member of the public" or at least for any member of the public who fell within the "established standard" of owning an automobile of the type it was equipped to repair, in this case a Porsche.

Fourthly, Downtown indisputably "possesses a decisive advantage of bargaining strength against" Gardner or almost "any member of the public who seeks [its] services." Like the hospital in *Tunkl* it is one of a relatively small number of entities dispensing a service which is a "practical necessity" to a large number of consumers.

Fifthly, it is apparent Downtown "confronts the public with a standardized adhesion contract of exculpation." The exculpatory language is incorporated in the printed form "repair order" all customers are expected to sign before Downtown will begin work on the car.

Finally, Gardner's Porsche was "placed under the control of" Downtown, "subject to the risk of carelessness by" Downtown and its employees. In order to make the repairs on Gardner's vehicle, Downtown took possession of the car and keys to the car. During this period, the security of the automobile was entirely in Downtown's hands. If this dealer were careless in storing the vehicle or the keys, the Porsche would become an easy target for theft and there would be little the owner could do about it.

Based on application of the *Tunkl* criteria, we therefore conclude automobile repair contracts "affect the public interest." It follows that clauses which exculpate repair firms for ordinary negligence in handling and securing vehicles under repair run afoul of Civil Code section 1668 and are "invalid as contrary to public policy."

Downtown concedes it was negligent. We hold its attempt to avoid legal responsibility for this negligence is unavailing. It follows Downtown is liable for non-delivery of the subject of the bailment, Gardner's Porsche.
[Judgment affirmed]

QUESTIONS

1. Was Gardner bound by the clear language of the repair order that he signed that said that Downtown was "not responsible for loss (of) cars . . . in case of . . . theft?
2. Did Downtown admit it was negligent in taking care of the automobile during the bailment?
3. What characteristics are typical of contracts affecting the public interest?

By definition, a limitation of liability must be a term of the bailment contract before any question arises as to whether it is binding. Thus, a limitation contained in a receipt mailed by a bailee after receiving a coat for storage is not effective to alter the terms of the bailment as originally made. Likewise, a bailor is not bound by a limitation of liability that was not known at the time the bailment was made. In the *Allright* case, the court was called upon to decide whether a parking lot had given notice to a customer concerning its intention to limit liability.

ALLRIGHT, INC. V SCHROEDER
(Tex Civ App) 551 SW2d 745 (1977)

Schroeder parked his car on a parking lot operated by Allright, Inc. It was stolen from the lot. The lot denied liability to Schroeder on the ground that the parking ticket given stated there was no liability for theft and that the parking lot closed at 6 p.m. and that a sign stated that after 6 p.m. patrons of the lot could obtain the keys of their cars at another location. From a judgment for Schroeder, Allright appealed.

COLEMAN, C. J. . . . On September 8, 1969, at approximately 1:30 p.m. plaintiff drove his automobile into defendant's parking lot in downtown Houston. He turned possession of the automobile over to one of the defendant's employees, who proceeded to park the automobile, and received a claim ticket from another employee. The words "We close at 6 o'clock p.m." were printed on the ticket in heavy type. A copy of the ticket is attached as an appendix. It can be seen that the provision limiting liability would not be so readily noticed.

Signs were located throughout the parking lot which stated that the lot closed at 6 o'clock p.m. and that anyone returning after that time could pick up their keys at another parking lot operated by defendant at a specified location. Plaintiff had parked his automobile at this lot previously. He was aware at the time he left the car at the station on the occasion in question that the signs and the claim ticket said the lot closed at 6 o'clock.

When the plaintiff returned to the lot around midnight his car was missing. He inquired at defendant's parking lot at 503 Fannin as to the whereabouts of his car. The attendant did not have his keys and knew nothing about the car. Plaintiff filed an offense report with the Houston police reporting the theft of his automobile, and the car was recovered on September 10 by the Harris County Sheriff's Department. It had been partially "stripped" and suffered other damage. . . .

The defendant contends that the fact issues submitted were designed to establish that the plaintiff knew the lot closed at 6 o'clock p.m. and that the plaintiff had impliedly agreed to the limitation of liability provision printed on the stub of the parking ticket. The defendant further asserts that once it is established that the defendant knew of the closing time a finding that the automobile was stolen after that time would establish a defense to suit in that the operator of a parking lot would have no duty to protect the patron's automobile after the time of closing. The defendant also contends that where a patron of a public parking lot is aware of a statement limiting liability which appears on the parking stub given him at the time he leaves his automobile in the lot, he impliedly agrees to this limitation as a provision of the contract of bailment.

Where parking lot owners attempt to limit liability by posting notices on the wall or by printing such a limitation on the claim check, the limitation must be called to the attention of the bailor before it may become part of the bailment contract. Allright, Inc. v Elledge, 515 SW2d 266 (Tex 1974). These provisions are strictly construed against the bailee. . . . In *Elledge* the Supreme Court of Texas held that a provision limiting liability of the parking lot owner to a maximum of $100.00 for loss of the bailor's automobile due to theft occasioned by the ordinary negligence of the parking lot owner was enforceable where this provision was inserted in a written contract signed by the bailor.

In this case the limitation provision printed on the claim check was not specifically called to the attention of the bailor at the time he left his automobile at the parking lot. Plaintiff testified that at the time he left his automobile with the defendant he knew that the claim check stated that the lot closed at 6 o'clock. The defendant asserts that this evidence also raises an issue of fact as to whether or not the plaintiff had read the provision limiting liability printed on the check.

There is no evidence that the plaintiff read the material appearing on the claim check which was given him on September 8. . . .

Notice that a lot will "close at 6 o'clock p.m." does not give notice that cars left after such time will be at the owner's risk. Such a sign might be construed to mean that no automobile would be accepted after 6 o'clock p.m. The fact that the closing time of the lot was posted on signs and was printed on the claim ticket does not exempt the operator of the lot from the exercise of ordinary care with respect to the safety of the property. . . .

The evidence does not establish whether the automobile was stolen before or after the lot had closed for the day on September 8, 1969. There was testimony that on special occasions the lot stayed open to a later hour. The plaintiff testified that he knew that the lot had been open after 6 o'clock closing time on previous occasions and that he inquired of the attendant whether or not the lot would be open later on this night. He testified that he was told that it would be open later. There was testimony that it closed at 6:00 p.m. on September 8, 1969. When his car was recovered the trunk was open, his spare tire was missing, and the keys were found in the trunk. The defendant represented that the keys to the car would be in its custody until returned to the owner.

The requested issue related to an immaterial fact. The operator had a duty to remove the keys from the car at closing time and to transport them to the place mentioned in their sign. The trial court submitted a general negligence issue and the jury found that the defendant's negligence proximately caused plaintiff's automobile to be stolen. . . .

Here the sign clearly represented to the patrons that some degree of care would be exercised for the safety of their automobiles after the closing time by reason of the notice that the car keys could be picked up after closing time at another location. No agreement that the bailment would expire at 6 o'clock p.m. will be implied from the fact that the plaintiff knew the signs stated that the lot would close at 6 o'clock p.m. under these circumstances.

ALLRIGHT, INC.

320 TRAVIS
WE CLOSE AT 6:00 P.M.
IMPORTANT — READ CAREFULLY

In consideration of low rates charged for parking, customer agrees that parking operator won't be responsible for loss by fire, misdelivery or theft, except such loss be occasioned by negligence of operator, and then only up to a maximum value of $100. Proportionately greater rates must be paid in advance if customer sets larger limits of liability.

**Articles
Left In
Car At
Own Risk**

ALLRIGHT
AUTO PARKS

191

[Judgment affirmed]

QUESTIONS

1. What did Allright contend?
2. What rule of construction is generally applied in interpreting limitation of liability provisions posted on walls or contained in claim checks?
3. How did court decide the case?

(3) Insurance. In the absence of a statute or contract provision, a bailee is not under any duty to insure for the benefit of the bailor the property entrusted to the bailee.

(c) MAINTENANCE OF PROPERTY. In the situation of a bailment for hire, such as when a business rents an office copier from a leasing firm, the bailee must bear the expense of repairs that are ordinary and incidental to the use of the machine, in the absence of a contrary contract provision. If, however, the repairs required are of an unusual nature or if the bailment is for a short period of time, the bailor is required to make the repairs unless the need for the repairs arose from the fault of the bailee.

(d) UNAUTHORIZED USE. The bailee is liable for conversion, just as though the bailee stole the property, if the bailee uses the property without authority or uses it in any manner to which the bailor had not agreed. Ordinarily the bailee will be required to pay compensatory damages, although punitive damages may be imposed when the improper use was deliberate and when the bailee was recklessly indifferent to the effect of the use upon the property.

(e) RETURN OF PROPERTY. The bailee is under a duty to return the identical property that is the subject of the bailment or to deliver it as directed by the bailment agreement. An exception exists for **fungible goods,** which are those goods of a homogeneous nature of which any unit is the equivalent of any other like unit. Examples of fungible goods are grain, potatoes (within the same grade), and petroleum (within the same grade). In the case of fungible goods, if the bailee contracts to return an equal amount of the same kind and quality, the transaction is a bailment. If the bailee has the option of paying an amount of money or returning property other than that which was delivered by the bailor, there is generally no bailment, but rather a "sale." Thus, when a farmer delivers wheat to a grain elevator that gives the farmer a receipt that promises to return either a similar amount of wheat or a certain sum of money upon presentment of the receipt, the relationship is generally not a bailment.[7]

The redelivery to the bailor or delivery to a third person must be made in accordance with the terms of the bailment contract as to time, place, and manner. When the agreement between the parties does not control these matters, the customs of the community govern.

(1) Bailee's Lien. By common law or statute, a bailee is given a **lien** or the right to retain possession of the bailed property until the bailee has been paid for any charges for storage or repairs.[8] If the bailee has a lien on the property, the bailee is entitled to keep possession of the property until payment has been made for the claim on which the lien is based. The lien is lost if the property is voluntarily returned to the bailor. If the bailor is guilty of any miscon-

---

[7]   In some states statutes declare that the relationship between farmer and the grain elevator is a bailment and not a sale. United States v Haddix & Sons, Inc. (CA6 Mich) 415 F2d 584 (1969).

[8]   Burns v Miller, 107 Wash 2d 778, 733 P2d 522 (1987).

duct in regaining possession of the property, there is no loss of lien, and the bailee may retain possession if possession can be reacquired.[9]

A bailee who is authorized by statute to sell the bailed property to enforce a charge or claim against the bailor must give such notice as is required by the statute. A bailee who sells without giving the required notice is liable for conversion of the property.

In some states a bailee's lien may be extinguished where the bailee intentionally claims an amount greater than that to which the bailee is entitled. Thus, a car stereo seller's lien was extinguished when he knowingly demanded in his lien statement an additional charge of $50 per day for storage of the bailor's truck.[10] This charge was clearly excessive and an intentional demand for an amount in excess of that due the bailee.

(2) Constitutionality of Bailee's Lien. Historically, the bailee's lien was merely a right to retain the goods until paid, and a statute that goes no further than to authorize such retention is constitutional. There is authority, however, that when the statute goes beyond this common-law pattern and authorizes a sale of the goods, the statute is unconstitutional if it permits the sale of the property without prior notice and hearing as to the existence of the amount alleged to be due.[11]

§ 25:8   BURDEN OF PROOF

When the bailor sues the bailee for damages to the bailed property, the bailor has the burden of proving that the bailee was at fault and that such fault was the proximate cause of the loss. A prima facie right of the bailor to recover is established, however, by proof that the property was delivered by the bailor to the bailee and thereafter could not be returned or was returned in a damaged condition. When this is done, the bailee has the burden of proving that the loss or damage was not caused by the bailee's failure to exercise the care required by law or by an unauthorized use of the property.[12]

§ 25:9   RIGHTS OF THE BAILOR

The typical commercial bailment is a mutual-benefit bailment. Under such a bailment, the bailor has the right to compensation, commonly called rent, for the use of the bailed property. If the bailor is obligated to render a service to the bailee, such as maintenance of the rented property, the bailor's failure to do so will ordinarily bar the bailor from recovering compensation from the bailee.

(a) RIGHTS AGAINST THE BAILEE. The bailor may sue the bailee for breach of contract if the goods are not redelivered to the bailor or delivered to a third person as specified by the bailment agreement. The bailor may also maintain an action against a bailee for negligence, willful destruction, and unlawful retention or conversion of the goods.

(b) RIGHTS AGAINST THIRD PERSONS. The bailor may sue third persons damaging or taking the bailed property from the bailee's possession, even though the bailment is for a fixed period that has not yet expired. In such a case, the bailor is said to recover damages for injury to the bailor's **reversionary interest,** that is, the right that the bailor has to regain the property upon the expiration of the period of the bailment.

§ 25:10   DUTIES OF THE BAILOR

The bailor has certain duties concerning the condition of the property bailed. Some-

---

[9]   Smith v Cooper Chevrolet, Inc. (Ala) 404 So 2d 49 (1981).
[10]   First Bank Southdale v Kinney (Minn App) 392 NW2d 740 (1986).
[11]   Hernandez v European Auto Collision, Inc. (CA2 NY) 487 F2d 378 (1973); Whitmore v New Jersey Division of Motor Vehicles, 137 NJ Super 492, 349 A2d 560 (1975).

[12]   Subler Trucking Co., Inc. v Splittorf, (Ind App) 482 NE2d 295 (1985); Howard's Cleaners v Munsey (Ark) 708 SW2d 629 (1986).

times the duty concerning goods furnished by the bailor is described as an implied warranty.

(a) CONDITION OF THE PROPERTY. In a mutual-benefit bailment, as a bailment for hire, the bailor is under a duty to furnish goods reasonably fit for the purpose contemplated by the parties. If the bailee is injured or the bailee's property is damaged because of the defective condition of the bailed property, the bailor may be held liable.[13] If the bailment is for the sole benefit of the bailee, the bailor is under a duty to inform the bailee of known defects. If the bailee is harmed by a defect that was known by the bailor, the bailor is liable for damages.[14] If the bailor receives a benefit from the bailment, the bailor must not only inform the bailee of known defects, but must also make a reasonable investigation to discover defects. The bailor is liable for the harm resulting from those defects that would have been disclosed had the bailor made such an examination, in addition to those defects that were known to the bailor.

If the defect would not have been revealed by a reasonable examination, the bailor, regardless of classification of the bailment, is not liable for the harm that results.

In any case, a bailee who is aware of a defective condition of the bailed property but makes use of the property and sustains injury because of its condition is barred by contributory negligence or assumption of risk from collecting damages from the bailor.

(b) BAILOR'S IMPLIED WARRANTY. In many cases, the duty of the bailor is described as an implied warranty that the goods will be reasonably fit for their intended use. Apart from an implied warranty, the bailor may expressly warrant the condition of the property. In this event the bailor will be liable for breach of the warranty to the same extent as though the bailor had made a sale rather than a bailment of the property.

With the increase in car and equipment leasing, a new trend in the cases is beginning to appear. This trend extends to the bailee and third persons the benefit of an implied warranty by the bailor that the article is fit for its intended use and will remain so. This is distinguished from the warranty that the article was merely reasonably fit, or that it was fit at the beginning of the bailment, or that the property was free from defects known to the bailor or which a reasonable investigation would disclose. The significance of an analysis on the basis of warranty lies in the fact that warranty liability may exist even though the bailor was not negligent.[15]

The court in the *Cintrone* case considered the question of whether a commercial truck rental company was subject to an implied warranty that the truck was fit for its intended use for the rental period.

---

[13] Hall v Skate Escape, Ltd. 171 Ga App 178, 319 SE2d 67 (1984).
[14] Burke Enterprises Inc. v Mitchell (Ky) 700 SW2d 789 (1987).

[15] Jones v Keetch, 388 Mich 164, 200 NW2d 227 (1972), sustaining right of plaintiff to a new trial on the warranty theory, although the first trial on the theory of negligence had ended with a verdict in favor of the defendant. The commercial lessor may also be liable on the strict tort theory.

CINTRONE V HERTZ TRUCK LEASING & RENTAL SERVICE

45 NJ 434, 212 A2d 769 (1965)

Contract Packers rented a truck from Hertz Truck Leasing. Packers' employee, Cintrone, was injured while riding in the truck being driven by his helper. The brakes of the truck did not function properly, and the truck crashed. Cintrone sued Hertz. From a judgment in favor of Hertz, Cintrone appealed.

FRANCIS, J. . . . Under the lease the trucks were kept at Contract Packers' premises but Hertz agreed to service, repair, and maintain them. . . .

The failure of the brakes at the time of the accident was not chargeable to negligence on defendant's part. Plaintiff seeks a reversal of the adverse judgment, however, on the ground that the contractual relationship between Hertz and his employer gave rise to an implied continuing promissory warranty by Hertz that the truck in question was fit for the purposes for which plaintiff's employer rented it, *i.e.*, operation and transportation of goods on the public highways. . . .

If the relationship in the present case between Contract Packers and Hertz were manufacturer or dealer and purchaser, an implied warranty of fitness for operation on the public highway would have come into existence at the time of the sale. . . .

There is no good reason for restricting such warranties to sales. Warranties of fitness are regarded by law as an incident of a transaction because one party to the relationship is in a better position than the other to know and control the condition of the chattel transferred and to distribute the losses which may occur because of a dangerous condition the chattel possesses. These factors make it likely that the party acquiring possession of the article will assume it is in a safe condition for use and therefore refrain from taking precautionary measures himself. . . .

In this connection it may be observed also that the comment to the warranty section of the Uniform Commercial Code speaks out against confining warranties to sales transactions. The comment says: "Although this section is limited in its scope and direct purpose to warranties made by the seller to the buyer as part of a contract of sale, the warranty sections of this Article are not designed in any way to disturb those lines of case law growth which have recognized that warranties need not be confined either to sales contracts or to the direct parties to such a contract. They may arise in other appropriate circumstances such as in the case of bailments for hire, whether such bailment is itself the main contract or is merely a supplying of containers under a contract for the sale of their contents. . . ." See Comment. [UCC §] 2-313. . . . See also . . . "Implied Warranties of Quality in Non-Sales Cases" 57 Colum. L. Rev. 653, 673-674 (1957):

> The expansion of enterprises engaged solely in bailment for hire seems to justify increasing imposition of absolute warranties, at least to the extent that they would be imposed upon a seller of similarly used goods. In addition, reliance is greater than in the typical sale, for it is generally true that the bailee for hire spends less time shopping for the article than he would in selecting like goods to be purchased, and since the item is not one he expects to own, he will usually be less competent in judging its quality.

A sale transfers ownership and possession of the article in exchange for the price; a bailment for hire transfers possession in exchange for the rental and contemplates eventual return of the article to the owner. By means of a bailment parties can often reach the same business ends that can be achieved by selling and buying. The goods come to the user for the time being, and he benefits by their use and enjoyment without the burdens of becoming and remaining the owner. The owner-lessor benefits by receiving the rent for the temporary use. . . . We may take judicial notice of the growth of the business of renting motor vehicles, trucks and pleasure cars. . . . The offering to the public of trucks and pleasure vehicles for hire necessarily carries with it a representation that they are fit for operation. This representation is of major significance because both new and used cars and trucks are rented. In fact, . . . the rental rates are the same whether a new or used vehicle is supplied. In other words, the lessor in effect says to the customer that the representation of fitness for use is the same whether the vehicle supplied is new or old. From the standpoint of service to the customer, therefore, the law cannot justly accept any distinction between the obligation assumed by a U-drive-it company whether the vehicle is new or old when rented. The nature of the business is such that the customer is expected to, and in fact must, rely ordinarily on the express or implied representation of fitness for immediate use. . . . To illustrate, if a traveler comes into an airport and needs a car for a short period and rents one from a U-drive-it agency, when he is "put in the driver's seat," his reliance on the fitness of the car assigned to him for the rental period whether new or used usually is absolute. In such circumstances the relationship between the parties fairly calls for an implied warranty of fitness for use, at least equal to that assumed by a new car manufacturer. The content of such warranty must be that the car will not fail mechanically during the rental period.

In the case before us, it is just as obvious that when a company like Contract Packers rents trucks for limited or extended periods for use in its occupation of transportation of goods, it too relies on the express or implied representation of the person in the business of supplying vehicles for hire, that they are fit for such use. . . .

When the implied warranty or representation of fitness arises, . . . it continues for the agreed rental period. The public interests involved are justly served only by treating an obligation of that nature as an incident of the business enterprise. The operator of the rental business must be regarded as possessing expertise with respect to the service life and fitness of his vehicles for use. That expertise ought to put him in a better position than the bailee to detect or to anticipate flaws or defects or fatigue in his vehicles. Moreover, as between bailor for hire and bailee, the liability for flaws or defects not discoverable by ordinary care in inspecting or testing ought to rest with the bailor just as it rests with a manufacturer who buys components containing latent defects from another maker, and installs them in the completed product, or just as it rests with a retailer at the point of sale to the consumer. . . .

The warranty or representation of fitness is not dependent upon existence of Hertz' additional undertaking to service and maintain the trucks while they were leased. That undertaking serves particularly to instill reliance in Contract Packers upon mechanical operability of the trucks throughout the rental period. But the warranty or representation that the vehicles will not fail for that period sprang into existence on the making of the agreement to rent the trucks, and was an incident thereof, irrespective of the service and maintenance undertaking. . . .

In this developing area of the law, we perceive no sound reason why a distinction in principle should be made between the sale of a truck to plaintiff's employer by a manufacturer, and a lease for hire of the character established by the evidence. . . .

[Judgment reversed and new trial ordered]

Authors' Note. California and a growing number of states have imposed strict tort liability (see § 30:1) on the commercial lessors of motor vehicles, thereby achieving independently of the warranty concept a result similar to that reached in the *Cintrone* case on the basis of a warranty concept. [*Price v Shell Oil Co.*, 2 Cal 3d 245, 85 Cal Rptr 178, 466 P2d 722]

QUESTIONS

1. What did the court hold?
2. What is the basis for the court's decision?
3. What effect does the decision have on the cost of renting a car or truck?

§ 25:11 LIABILITY TO THIRD PERSONS

When injuries are sustained by third persons resulting from the use of bailed property, liability may, under certain circumstances, be imposed on the bailee or the bailor.

(a) LIABILITY OF BAILEE. When the bailee injures a third person with the bailed property, as when the bailee runs into a third person while driving a rented automobile, the bailee is liable to the third person to the same extent as though the bailee were the owner of the property. When the bailee repairs bailed property, the bailee is liable to a third person who is injured as a result of the negligent way in which the repairs were made.

(b) LIABILITY OF BAILOR. The bailor is ordinarily not liable to a third person injured by the bailee while using the bailed property. In states that follow the common law, a person lending an automobile to another is not liable to the third person injured by the bailee when the lender did not know or have reason to know that the bailee was not a fit driver.

The bailor is liable, however, to the injured third person: (a) if the bailor has entrusted a dangerous instrumentality to one known to the bailor to be ignorant of its dangerous character; (b) if the bailor has entrusted an instrumentality, such as an automobile, to one known to the bailor to be so incompetent or reckless that injury of third persons is a foreseeable consequence; (c) if the bailor has entrusted property with a defect that causes harm to the third person when the circumstances are such that the bailor would be liable to the bailee if the bailee were injured by the defect; or (d) if the bailee is using the bailed article, such as driving an automobile, as the bailor's employee in the course of employment.

(c) STATUTORY CHANGE. A number of states have enacted statutes by which an automobile owner granting permission to another to use the automobile automatically becomes liable for any negligent harm caused by the person to whom the automobile has been entrusted. That is, permissive use imposes liability on the owner or provider for the permittee's negligence. In some states, the statute is limited to cases where the permittee is under a specified age, such as sixteen years. Under some statutes, the owner is only liable with respect to harm sustained while the permittee is using the automobile for the specific purpose for which permission was granted.

(d) FAMILY PURPOSE DOCTRINE. Under what is called the **family purpose doctrine,** some courts hold that when the bailor supplies a car for the use of members of the bailor's family, the bailor is liable for harm caused by a member of the family while negligently driving the car. Other jurisdictions reject this doctrine and refuse to impose liability on the bailor of the automobile unless there is an agency relationship between the bailor and the driver.

SUMMARY

A bailment is the legal relationship that exists when personal property is delivered by the bailor into the possession of the bailee, under an agreement, express or implied, that the identical property will be returned or will be delivered in accordance with the agreement. In a bailment, the title remains with the bailor (or the principal or employer of the bailor) while the bailee has the right of possession. When a person comes into the possession of the personal property of another without the owner's consent, the law refers to the relationship as a constructive bailment.

Bailments may be classified in terms of benefit as for the (a) sole benefit of the bailor, (b) sole benefit of the bailee, or (c) benefit of both parties (mutual-benefit bailment). Some courts state the standard of care required of a bailee in terms of the class of bailment. Thus, if the bailment is for the sole benefit of the bailor, the bailee is only required to exercise slight care and is only liable for gross negligence; when the bailment is for the sole benefit of the bailee, the bailee is liable for the slightest negligence; and when the bailment is for the mutual benefit of the parties, which is the typical commer-

cial bailment, the bailee is liable for ordinary negligence. In other states the courts do not make the above distinctions based on the class of bailment but apply a "reasonable care under the circumstances" standard of care. An ordinary bailee may limit liability, except for willful misconduct or where prohibited by statute, by a provision in the bailment contract. A bailee (1) must perform the bailee's part of the contract; (2) unless otherwise agreed, must bear the repair expenses incidental to the use of a machine in a bailment for hire situation; (3) must return the identical property; and (4) must otherwise fulfill the bailment agreement. The bailee has a lien on the bailed property until paid for storage or repair charges.

In a bailment for hire situation, such as the renting of a motor vehicle or a tool, the bailor is under a duty to furnish goods reasonably fit for the purposes contemplated by the parties. The bailor may be held liable for damages or injury caused by the defective condition of the bailed property. Should a bailee injure a third person while driving a rental motor vehicle, the bailee is liable to the third person as though the bailee were the owner of the vehicle.

QUESTIONS AND CASE PROBLEMS

1. What social forces are affected by the recognition of a bailment relationship?
2. Mercedes is employed by Park Lane Supply Company to sell its merchandise. In the course of the day she stops and leaves the company car she is driving on a parking lot operated by Simms Garage. The car is stolen from the lot. In a lawsuit brought against Simms on the theory that Simms was a negligent bailee, Simms raises the defense that there was no bailment because Mercedes did not own the car that was left with Simms. Is Simms correct?
3. What is a bailee's lien?
4. Compare a gift with a bailment.
5. Lillian loaned her automobile to Harry.

Harry carelessly drove the automobile and hit Mark. Mark sued Lillian for damages. Is Lillian liable?

6. Compare a bailment with a constructive bailment.

7. John Hayes and Lynn Magosian, auditors for Lloyd, Little & Co., a public accounting firm, went to lunch at the Bay View Restaurant in San Francisco. John left his raincoat with a coatroom attendant, while Lynn chose to bring her new raincoat with her to the dining room, where she hung it on a coat hook near her booth. When leaving the restaurant, Lynn discovered that an individual had taken her new, expensive raincoat and left behind a coat of little value. When John sought to claim his raincoat at the coatroom, it could not be found; and the attendant advised that it might have been taken while he was on his break. John and Lynn sue the restaurant claiming that the restaurant was a bailee of the raincoats and had a duty to return them. Are both John and Lynn correct?

8. When Todd departed for college in late August, he left his Boston Whaler motor boat at Terry's Low Tide Marina for land storage during the fall and winter months. Terry rented the boat to his customers on a daily basis for the entire month of September. When Todd discovered this, he sued Terry for conversion. Terry contends that he has the legal status of bailee, had proper possession of the boat, and that he cannot be held liable for conversion. Decide.

9. Rhodes parked his car on the self-service, park-and-lock lot of Pioneer Parking Lot, Inc. The ticket that he received from the ticket meter stated the following, "NOTICE. THIS CONTRACT LIMITS OUR LIABILITY — READ IT. WE RENT SPACE ONLY. NO BAILMENT IS CREATED. . . ." Rhodes parked the car himself and kept the keys. There was no attendant at the lot. The car was stolen from the lot. Rhodes sued the parking lot on the theory it had breached its duty as a bailee. Was there a bailment? [Rhodes v Pioneer Parking Lot, Inc. (Tenn) 501 SW2d 569]

10. Lewis put a paper bag containing $3,000 in cash in a railroad station coin-operated locker. After the period of the coin rental expired, a locker company employee opened the locker, removed the money, and be-

cause of the amount, surrendered it to the police authorities, as was required by the local law. When Lewis demanded the return of the money from Aderholdt, the police property clerk, the latter required Lewis to prove his ownership to the funds because there were circumstances leading to the belief that the money had been stolen by Lewis. He sued the police property clerk and the locker company. Was the locker company liable for breach of duty as a bailee? [Lewis v Aderholdt (Dist Col App) 203 A2d 919]

11. Joan took driving lessons at the A-North Shore Driving School. Later the school loaned her an automobile and took her for her state driving test. Crowley was the state examiner. Joan drove into a signal box on the side of the road. Crowley was seriously injured. He sued the driving school. Was it liable? [Crowley v A-North Shore Driving School, 19 Ill App 3d 1035, 313 NE2d 200]

12. Gilchrist took an automobile to a dealer, Winmar J. Ford, Inc., to have the tires rotated. Gilchrist was a refrigerator mechanic and had a special set of tools in the trunk of the car. He did not inform Ford that the tools were in the car. The car was stolen. Ford was sued for the value of the tools. Ford defended on the ground that it was not liable for the value of the tools and that it had never been informed of their value and therefore was not alerted to take special precautions. Was this a valid defense? [Gilchrist v Winmar J. Ford, Inc. 355 NYS2d 261]

13. Morse, who owned a diamond ring valued at $2,000, took the ring to Homer's, Inc., to sell for him. Homer placed the ring in the window display of his store. There was no guard or grating across the opening of the window inside his store. There was a partitioned door that was left unlocked. On two former occasions Homer's store had been robbed. Several weeks after Morse left his ring, armed men robbed the store and took several rings from the store window, including Morse's ring. Morse sued Homer, who defended on the ground that he was not liable for the criminal acts of others. Decide. [Morse v Homer's, Inc. 295 Mass 606, 4 NE2d 625]

14. June Southard was employed at K-Mart in its Sporting Goods Department when she

was struck by a mounted fish that fell from the wall. The fish was owned by taxidermist Marty Hansen, and it had been delivered to K-Mart as a sample of Hansen's work should the public wish to contact him directly. Southard sued Hansen for her injuries on the basis that Hansen was vicariously liable for the negligence of his agent, K-Mart, in improperly handling the fish. Hansen contended that his legal relationship with K-Mart was that of bailor and bailee respectively, and that as the bailor he was not liable to Southard. Decide. [Southard v Hansen (SD) 376 NW2d 56]

15. Welge owned a sofa and chair that Baena Brothers agreed to reupholster and to reduce the size of the arms. The work was not done according to the contract, and the furniture when finished had no value to Welge and was not accepted by him. Baena sued him for the contract price. Welge counterclaimed for the value of the furniture. Decide. [Baena Brothers v Welge, 3 Conn Cir 67, 207 A2d 749]

26

SPECIAL BAILMENTS AND DOCUMENTS OF TITLE

Because of the nature of the property involved or because of the circumstances under which possession of that property is transferred, some bailments have a particularly strong effect on the public interest. These bailments are called **special bailments** and include the storage of goods in a warehouse as well as the transportation of goods by a carrier. The warehouses may be general warehouses, refrigerated or cold-storage warehouses, farm-products warehouses, or special-purpose warehouses. The carriers may be motor, rail, or air carriers; they may be water carriers utilizing boats or barges on the coastal waters, the Great Lakes, or the inland waterways; they may even be pipeline companies transporting oil and gas.

The storage and transportation of goods as well as the documents used to evidence their ownership are vital to American com-

557

merce. For this reason, the law has imposed upon the special bailee a liability more stringent than that imposed upon ordinary bailees.

Because of the public interest in protecting the property of travelers, hotelkeepers were absolutely liable for loss or damage to their guests' property at common law. Most states, however, have reduced this liability by statute for the benefit of hotelkeepers, allowing for the limitation of liability where notices inform guests of the existence of a safe where valuables may be deposited.

A.   WAREHOUSERS

The storage of goods by a warehouser is a special bailment. The rights and duties of warehousers are defined by the common law and Article 7 of the UCC.

§ 26:1   DEFINITIONS

A **warehouser** is a person engaged in the business of storing the goods of others for compensation. **Public warehousers** hold themselves out to serve the public generally without discrimination.

A building is not essential to warehousing. Thus, an enterprise that stores boats outdoors on land is engaged in warehousing, since it is engaged in the business of storing goods for hire.

§ 26:2   RIGHTS AND DUTIES OF WAREHOUSERS

The rights and duties of a warehouser are for the most part the same as those of a bailee under a mutual-benefit bailment.[1] The standard of care required of a warehouser is set forth in the *Singer* case where the court applied that standard to a warehouser who was unable to return the bailor's goods because they had been destroyed.

[1] Uniform Commercial Code § 7-204; F-M Potatoes, Inc. v Suda (ND) 259 NW2d 487 (1977).

SINGER CO. V STODA
79 App Div 2d 227, 436 NYS2d 508 (1981)

The Singer Corporation had been storing air conditioners in Stoda warehouses for several years. In May of 1974, Singer's transportation manager, Guy Bataglia, went to Stoda's "Hoffman Plant" warehouse accompanied by the president of Stoda, Larry Ellis. While looking over the building, Bataglia noticed the sprinkler system and inquired about it. Ellis, who knew the system had been turned off, said the system was active. Singer stored 133 cartons of air conditioning units at the Hoffman Plant as of that day. On July 7, 1974, a fire broke out in the Hoffman Plant, totally destroying Singer's goods. Singer's action to recover damages for the destroyed property was dismissed by the trial court judge at the close of the evidence for failure to prove a prima facie case, and Singer appealed.

MOULE, J. . . . At trial, plaintiff presented evidence tending to show inadequate fire precautions by defendant. The sprinkler system had been shut down for repairs and was not working. . . . An experienced fire protection engineer testified not only that sprinkler systems are effective in controlling a fire and preventing extensive damage but also that the leaks in the system could have been repaired without shutting down every sprinkler system in the building. While the building was equipped with an operable fire alarm box, it had to be manually operated and would not come on automatically in the event of fire. Even though the fire alarm was manually operated, and Stoda was aware the sprinkler system was shut down, there were no watchmen at the plant. The evidence showed that fire trucks arrived about one and one-half minutes after an alarm went off, but that the fire had been burning for about 20 to 45 minutes prior to the alarm. . . . . If plaintiff is to recover for bailee negligence, he must establish that a bailment relationship existed with respect to the destroyed goods, and that the bailee failed to exercise the required standard of care in storing the goods (*Proctor & Gamble Distr. Co. v. Lawrence Amer. Field Warehousing Corp.*, 16 NY2d 344, 266 NYS 785, 213 NE2d 873; *Claflin et al v Meyer*, 75 NY 260). The statutorily defined standard of care provides:

> (1) A warehouseman is liable for damages for loss of or injury to the goods caused by his failure to exercise such care in regard to them as a reasonably careful man would exercise under like circumstances but, unless otherwise agreed, he is not liable for damages which could not have been avoided by the exercise of such care.

(Uniform Commercial Code, § 7-204). This statute does not alter the common law, but codifies it (*Proctor & Gamble Distr. Co. v. Lawrence Amer. Field Warehousing Corp.*, supra.) . . .

Once plaintiff establishes delivery of the goods and the failure of the bailee to return them on demand, a prima facie case of negligence is made and the burden of coming forward with evidence tending to show due care shifts to the bailee. . . . However, the burden of persuasion never shifts from the plaintiff to the bailee, and the bailee can rebut the prima facie case if it shows either how the loss occurred and that this was in no way attributable to its negligence, or that the requisite care was exercised in all respects to the bailed goods so that, regardless of how the accident transpired, it could not have been caused by any negligence on the bailee's part (*R. L. Pritchard & Co., Inc. v. Steamship Hellenic Laurel*, 342 F.Supp. 388). If the goods have been destroyed by fire, the plaintiff has the burden to show that the loss resulted from the bailee's negligence (*Claflin et al. v. Meyer*, supra, 263). . . .

The evidence presented at trial established a bailment relationship between plaintiff and Stoda, delivery of the goods to Stoda and its failure to return them upon demand. This proof established plaintiff's prima facie case of negligence and shifted the burden to the bailee of coming forward with evidence tending to show due care. Plaintiff also went forward with proof of negligence on the part of Stoda, the evidence showing that the sprinkler system was inoperable; that Stoda was aware of this condition; that no watchmen were present; and that the fire alarm system could not be automatically activated. Expert testimony established that a properly operating sprinkler system could control the spread of the fire, and that an automatic alarm system would have been helpful given the close proximity of the fire department.

Under these circumstances, the issue of bailee negligence should have been submitted to the jury. Stoda did not successfully rebut plaintiff's prima facie case of negligence by merely showing the fact that the goods were destroyed by fire, especially where plaintiffs went forward with proof of negligence. Plaintiff produced sufficient evidence to establish a rational basis by which the jury could have found in their favor. Whether due caution requires a bailee to furnish the means for extinguishing fire, or provide an all-night watchman, has been held to be a question for the jury. . . . Consequently, this cause of action by Singer. . . . against Stoda should not have been dismissed. . . .

[Judgment reversed and new trial ordered]

QUESTIONS

1. What must a warehouse customer prove in order to recover for damage to stored property?
2. Did Stoda successfully rebut the plaintiff's prima facie case of negligence by merely showing that the goods were destroyed by fire?
3. How does the statutory standard, set forth in the second paragraph of the opinion, compare with the standard of care required of an ordinary bailee as set forth in § 25:7(b)(1) of the previous chapter?

(a) STATUTORY REGULATION. Most states have passed warehouse acts defining the rights and duties of warehousers and imposing regulations. Regulations affect charges and liens, bonds for the protection of patrons, maintenance of storage facilities in a suitable and safe condition, inspections, and general methods of transacting business.

(b) LIEN OF WAREHOUSER. The public warehouser has a lien against the goods for reasonable storage charges.[2] It is a **specific lien** in that it attaches only to the property with respect to which the charges arose and cannot be asserted against any other property of the same owner in the possession of the warehouser. The warehouser, however, may make a lien carry over to the other goods by noting on the receipt for one lot of goods that a lien is also claimed thereon for charges as to the other goods. The warehouser's

lien for storage charges may be enforced by sale after due notice has been given to all persons who claim any interest in the property stored.[3]

§ 26:3   WAREHOUSE RECEIPTS

A **warehouse receipt** is a written acknowledgment by a warehouser (bailee) that certain property has been received for storage from a named person called a **depositor** (bailor). The warehouse receipt is a memorandum of a contract between the **issuer**, the warehouse that prepares the receipt, and the depositor. It sets forth the terms of the contract for storage. While no particular form is required, the failure to

---

[2]   UCC § 7-209(1). The warehouser's lien provision of the UCC is constitutional as a continuation of the common-law lien.

[3]   UCC § 7-210. In Svendsen v Smith's Moving and Trucking Co., 76 App Div 2d 504, 431 NYS2d 94 (1980) it was held that this provision of the New York UCC authorizing a warehouse to sell stored property without first affording the customer an opportunity for a hearing violated the constitution of the state of New York. However, the same provision of the New York UCC had previously survived a challenge based on the federal Constitution. Flagg Bros. v Brooks, 436 US 149 (1978).

include certain terms within the written or printed provisions of the warehouse receipt may lead to the issuer's being held liable for damages to a person injured by the omission. Some of the essential terms are: (a) the location of the warehouse where the goods are stored, (b) date of issuance of the receipt, (c) the number of the receipt, (d) information on negotiability or nonnegotiability of the receipt, (e) the rate of storage and handling charges, (f) a description of the goods or the packages containing them, and (g) a statement of any liabilities incurred for which the warehouser claims a lien or security interest.[4]

The warehouse receipt is also a **document of title;** that is, a document that in the regular course of business or financing is treated as adequately evidencing that the person in possession of it is entitled to receive, hold, and dispose of the document and the goods it covers.[5] The person lawfully holding this receipt then is entitled to the goods represented by the receipt. A warehouse receipt as a document of title is a symbol representing the goods. This receipt can be bought or sold, and can be used as security to obtain credit from a financial institution.

§ 26:4 RIGHTS OF HOLDERS OF WAREHOUSE RECEIPTS

The rights of the holders of warehouse receipts differ depending on whether the receipts are nonnegotiable or negotiable.

(a) NONNEGOTIABLE WAREHOUSE RECEIPTS. A warehouse receipt in which it is stated that the goods received will be delivered to a specified person is a **nonnegotiable warehouse receipt.** A transferee of a nonnegotiable receipt acquires only the title and rights that the transferor had actual authority to transfer.[6] As such, the transferee's rights may be defeated by a good faith purchaser of the goods from the transferor of the receipt.[7]

(b) NEGOTIABLE WAREHOUSE RECEIPTS. A warehouse receipt stating that the goods will be delivered to the "bearer," or "to the order of" any named person is a negotiable warehouse receipt. If such a receipt is duly negotiated, the person to whom it is negotiated may acquire rights superior to those of the transferor.

(1) Negotiation. If the receipt provides for the delivery of the goods "to the bearer," the receipt may be negotiated by delivery of the document. If the receipt provides for delivery of the goods "to the order of" a named individual, the document must be indorsed by that person and delivered.

(2) Due Negotiation. A warehouse receipt is "duly negotiated" when the holder purchases the document in good faith, without notice of any defense to it, for value in the regular course of business or financing.[8] The holder of such a duly negotiated document acquires title to the document and title to the goods.[9] The holder also acquires the direct obligation of the issuer to hold or deliver the goods according to the terms of the warehouse receipt.

The holder's rights cannot be defeated by the surrender of the goods by the warehouser to the depositor. Indeed, it is the duty of the warehouser to deliver the goods only to the holder of the negotiable receipt and to cancel such receipt upon surrendering the goods.[10]

The rights of a purchaser of a warehouse receipt by due negotiation are not cut off, for example, by the claim that: (a) an original owner was deprived of the receipt in "bearer" form by misrepresentation, fraud, mistake, loss, theft, or conversion; or (b) that a bona fide purchaser bought the goods from the warehouser.

---

[4] UCC § 7-202(2).
[5] UCC § 1-201(15); § 7-102(1)(e).
[6] UCC § 7-504(1).

[7] UCC § 7-504(2)(b).
[8] UCC § 7-501(4).
[9] UCC § 7-502(1).
[10] UCC § 7-403(3).

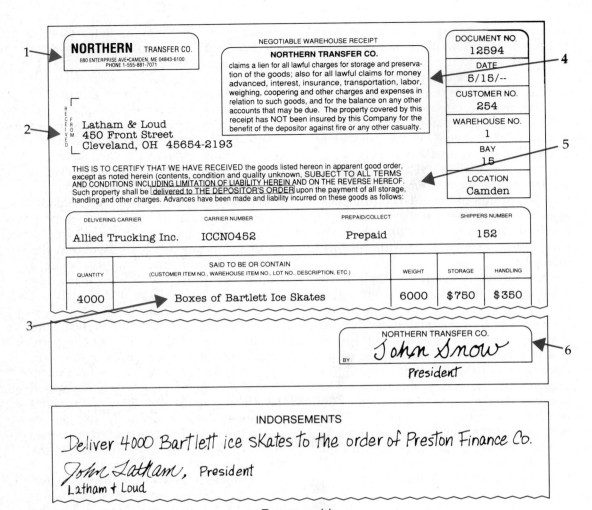

FIGURE 26-1   NEGOTIABLE WAREHOUSE RECEIPT
(1) warehouser, (2) depositor, (3) goods, (4) warehouser's lien, (5)
negotiable delivery terms, (6) warehouser's authorized agent. A
negotiable warehouse receipt contains a promise to deliver to bearer or
to depositor's *order*, unlike a nonnegotiable warehouse receipt that
promises only to deliver to depositor. Case Question 6 presents a
problem related to the above document.

A purchaser of a warehouse receipt who takes by due negotiation does not cut off all prior claims, however. If the person who deposited the goods with the warehouser did not own the goods or did not have power to transfer title to them, the purchaser of the receipt is subject to the title of the true owner.[11] Accordingly, when goods are stolen and delivered to a warehouse and a warehouse receipt is issued for them, the owner prevails over the purchaser by due negotiation.

(c) WARRANTIES. The transferor of a negotiable or nonnegotiable warehouse receipt makes certain implied warranties for the protection of the transferee. These warranties are that the receipt is genuine, that its transfer is rightful and effective, and

[11]   UCC § 7-503(1).

that the transferor has no knowledge of any facts that impair the validity or worth of the receipt.[12]

§ 26:5 FIELD WAREHOUSING

Ordinarily, stored goods are placed in a warehouse belonging to the warehouser. The owner of goods, such as a manufacturer, may keep the goods in the owner's own storage room or building. The warehouser may then take exclusive control over the room or the area in which the goods are stored and issue a receipt for the goods just as though they were in the warehouse. Such a transaction has the same legal effect with respect to other persons and purchasers of the warehouse receipts as though the property were in fact in the warehouse of the warehouser. This practice is called **field warehousing** since the goods are not taken to the warehouse but remain "in the field."

The purpose of field warehousing is to create warehouse receipts that the owner

of the goods is able to pledge as security for loans. The owner could, of course, have done this by actually placing the goods in a warehouse, but this would have involved the expense of transportation and storage.

§ 26:6 LIMITATION OF LIABILITY OF WAREHOUSER

A warehouser may limit liability by a provision in the warehouse receipt specifying the maximum amount for which the warehouser can be held liable. This privilege is subject to two qualifications: (a) the customer must be given the choice of storing the goods without such limitation if the customer pays a higher storage rate, and (b) the limitation must be stated as to each item or as to each unit of weight. A limitation is proper when it states that the maximum liability for a piano is $1,000 or that the maximum liability per bushel of wheat is a stated amount. Conversely, there cannot be a blanket limitation of liability, such as "maximum liability $50," when the receipt covers more than one item. The *Allstate* case illustrates that a warehouser cannot contract for a total exemption from all liability for losses, including losses due to its own negligence.

---

[12] UCC § 7-507. These warranties are in addition to any that may arise between the parties by virtue of the fact that the transferor is selling the goods represented by the receipt to the transferee. See Chapter 30 as to sellers' warranties.

ALLSTATE V WINNEBAGO COUNTY FAIR ASSOCIATION, INC.

(Ill App) 475 NE2d 230 (1985)

Richard Schewe, Charles Lane, Richard Fisher, and others had placed personal property in a building occupied by the Winnebago County Fair Association, Inc. The property was destroyed by fire. These individuals admitted that prior to placing their property in storage they signed a "Storage Rental Agreement" prepared by the County Fair Association, which stated in part that: "No liability exists for damage or loss to the stored equipment from the perils of fire. . . ." The individuals brought suit against the County Fair Association to recover damages for the losses on the theory of negligence of a warehouser. Allstate Insurance Company, having paid the claims of certain individuals based on losses suffered in the fire, joined in the suit. The County Fair Association defended that the language in the storage agreement relieved it of all liability. The court agreed with the Fair Association and dismissed the plaintiffs' complaints with prejudice. The plaintiffs appealed.

UNVERZAG, J. . . . The . . . issue presented is whether the defendant could validly contract away its liability for fire damage. . . . Illinois law recognizes as part of one's freedom to contract, the validity of exculpatory clauses in many cases as relieving a party of liability for negligence. However, the provisions of the Uniform Commercial Code have full force and effect with respect to warehouses, warehousemen, personal property, persons, depositions and receipts and are determinative of what can be varied by agreement. Section 1–102(3) of the Uniform Commercial Code states:

> The effect of provisions of this Act may be varied by agreement, except as otherwise provided in this Act and except that the obligations of good faith, diligence, reasonableness and care prescribed by this Act may not be disclaimed by agreement but the parties may by agreement determine the standards by which the performance of such obligations is to be measured if such standards are not manifestly unreasonable.

Although freedom of contract is emphasized in the Code, the principle is subject to certain stipulated exceptions. . . . A warehouseman may limit his liability generally on the condition that the depositor be afforded an opportunity to declare a higher value for which the warehousemen may charge an increased rate. Thus a warehouse receipt may legally contain a provision exempting the warehouseman from total liability for loss or damage to the goods in storage. In the present case, the agreement provided that "no liability exists for damage or loss to the stored equipment from the perils of fire. . . ." At issue in the present case, however, is exemption from all liability for fire damage including loss attributed to negligence which is not expressly stated in the disclaimer. . . . Our research has revealed no Illinois cases which have allowed total exemption from such liability. Decisions in other jurisdictions indicate that even when such agreements have sought explicitly to relieve warehousemen from the consequences of their negligence, they have often been regarded as invalid or ineffective . . . and warehousemen are not relieved from the duty of exercising ordinary care. . . .

Based on the above, it is our opinion that defendant . . . was bound by the provisions of the Uniform Commercial Code and could not validly contract away all liability for negligently caused fire damage.

The judgment of the circuit court of Winnebago County dismissing the complaints is reversed and the cause is remanded for further proceedings consistent with this opinion.

[Reversed and remanded]

QUESTIONS

1. Did the agreement language, "no liability exists for damage . . . from the perils of fire," relieve the defendant of all liability for fire damage to the stored property?
2. What should the defendant have done to limit its liability in this case?

General contract law determines whether a limitation clause is a part of the contract between the warehouser and the customer. A limitation in a warehouse receipt is not part of the contract when the receipt is delivered to the customer a substantial period of time after the goods have been left for storage.

B.   COMMON CARRIERS

The purpose of a bailment may be transportation and not storage. In such case, the bailee may be a common carrier.

§ 26:7   DEFINITIONS

A **carrier** of goods is an individual or organization undertaking the transportation of goods, regardless of the method of transportation or the distance covered. The **consignor** or shipper is the person who delivers goods to the carrier for shipment. The **consignee** is the person to whom the goods are shipped and to whom the carrier should deliver the goods.

A carrier may be classified as (a) a **common carrier,** which holds itself out as willing to furnish transportation for compensation without discrimination to all members of the public who apply, assuming that the goods to be carried are proper and the facilities of the carrier are available;[13] (b) a **contract carrier,** which transports goods under individual contracts; or (c) a **private carrier,** which is owned and operated by the firm transporting goods by it, such as a truck fleet owned and operated by an industrial firm. The common carrier law applies to the first class, the bailment law to the second, and the law of employment to the third.

§ 26:8   BILLS OF LADING

When the carrier accepts goods for shipment or forwarding, the carrier ordinarily issues to the shipper a **bill of lading** in the case of land or water transportation or an **airbill** for air transportation.[14] This instrument is a document of title and provides rights similar to those provided by a warehouse receipt. A bill of lading is both a receipt for the goods and a memorandum of a contract stating the terms of carriage. Title to the goods may be transferred by transfer of the bill of lading made with that intention.

With respect to intrastate shipments, bills of lading are governed by the Uniform Commercial Code.[15] As to interstate shipments, bills of lading are regulated by the Federal Bills of Lading Act.[16]

(a) CONTENTS OF BILL OF LADING. The form of the bill of lading is regulated in varying degrees by administrative agencies.[17] For example, the Interstate Commerce Commission requires that negotiable bills of lading must be printed on yellow paper, and nonnegotiable or straight bills of lading must be printed on white paper.[18]

As against the bona fide transferee of the bill of lading, a carrier is bound by the recitals in the bill as to the contents, quantity, or weight of goods.[19] This means that the carrier must produce the goods that are described or pay damages for failing to do so. This rule is not applied if facts appear on the face of the bill that should keep the transferee from relying on the recital.

(b) NEGOTIATION. A bill of lading is a **negotiable bill of lading** when by its terms the goods are to be delivered ''to bearer'' or ''to the order of'' a named person.[20] Any other bill of lading, such as one that consigns the goods to a named person is a **nonnegotiable** or **straight bill of lading.** Like transferees of warehouse receipts who take by due negotiation, holders of

---

[13]   Market Transport Ltd. v Maudlin, 301 Or 727, 725 P2d 914 (1986).

[14]   Imtiaz v Emery Airfreight, Inc. (Tex Civ App) 728 SW2d 897 (1987).
[15]   UCC, Article 7.
[16]   Title 49, United States Code § 81, et seq.
[17]   The UCC contains no provision for regulating the form of the bill of lading.
[18]   Bill of Lading 55 ICC 671.
[19]   UCC § 7-301(1).
[20]   UCC § 7-104(1)(a).

bills of lading who take by due negotiation ordinarily also acquire the title to the bills and title to the goods represented by them. These rights are not affected by the fact that (1) the original owner has been somehow deprived of the bill in bearer form, (2) the goods had already been surrendered by the carrier, or (3) the goods had been stopped in transit.[21] The rights are defeated by the true owner, however, when a thief delivers the goods to the carrier and then negotiates the bill of lading.[22]

(c) WARRANTIES. By transferring for value a bill of lading, whether negotiable or nonnegotiable, the transferor makes certain implied warranties to the transferee. The transferor impliedly warrants that (1) the bill of lading is genuine, (2) its transfer is rightful and is effective to transfer the goods represented thereby, and (3) the transferor has no knowledge of facts that would impair the validity or worth of the bill of lading.[23]

§ 26:9   RIGHTS OF COMMON CARRIER

A common carrier of goods has the right to make reasonable and necessary rules for the conduct of its business. It has the right to charge such rates for its services as yield it a fair return on the property devoted to the business of transportation, but the exact rates charged are regulated by the Interstate Commerce Commission in the case of interstate carriers and by state commissions in the case of intrastate carriers.[24] As an incident of the right to charge for its services, a carrier may charge **demurrage** — a charge for the detention of its cars or equipment for

an unreasonable length of time by either the consignor or consignee.[25]

As security for unpaid transportation and service charges, a common carrier has a lien on goods that it transports. The carrier's lien also secures demurrage charges, the costs of preservation of the goods, and the costs of sale to enforce the lien.[26] The lien of a carrier is a specific lien. It attaches only to goods shipped under the particular contract, but includes all of the shipment even though it is sent in installments. Thus, when part of the shipment is delivered to the consignee, the lien attaches to the portion remaining in possession of the carrier.

§ 26:10   DUTIES OF COMMON CARRIER

A common carrier is generally required (a) to receive and carry proper and lawful goods of all persons who offer them for shipment so long as the carrier has room; (b) to furnish facilities that are adequate for the transportation of freight in the usual course of business, and to furnish proper storage facilities for goods awaiting shipment or awaiting delivery after shipment;[27] (c) to follow the directions given by the shipper; (d) to load and unload goods delivered to it for shipment (in less-than-carload lots in the case of railroads), but the shipper or consignee may assume this duty by contract or custom; (e) to deliver the goods in accordance with the shipment contract.

Goods must be delivered at the usual place of delivery at the specified destination. When goods are shipped under a negotiable bill of lading, the carrier must not deliver the goods without obtaining possession of the bill properly indorsed. When goods are shipped under a straight bill of lading, the carrier is justified in delivering the goods to the consignee or the consignee's agent without receiving the bill of

---

[21] UCC § 7-502(2).
[22] UCC § 7-503(1).
[23] UCC § 7-507; Federal Bills of Lading Act (FBLA), 49 USC § 114, 116. When the transfer of the bill of lading is part of a transaction by which the transferor sells the goods represented thereby to the transferee, there will also arise the warranties that are found in other sales of goods.
[24] GMW, Inc. v Certified Parts Corporation, 135 Wis 2d 503, 400 NW2d 512 (1986).

[25] Betsy Ross Foods v A, C & Y Ry. Co. 17 Ohio App 3d 145, 468 NE2d 338 (1983).
[26] UCC § 7-307(1); FBLA, 49 USC § 105.
[27] Exquisite Form Industries v Transporters Ragat (DC Tex) 585 F Supp 473 (1984).

lading, unless notified by the shipper to deliver the goods to someone else. If the carrier delivers the goods to the wrong person, the carrier is liable for breach of contract and for the tort of conversion.

§ 26:11 LIABILITIES OF COMMON CARRIER

When goods are delivered to a common carrier for immediate shipment and while they are in transit, the carrier is absolutely liable for any loss or damage to the goods unless it can prove that it was due solely to one or more of the following excepted causes: (a) act of God, meaning a natural phenomenon that is not reasonably foreseeable; (b) act of public enemy, such as the military forces of an opposing government, as distinguished from ordinary robbers; (c) act of public authority, such as a health officer removing goods from a truck; (d) act of the shipper, such as fraudulent labeling or defective packing; or (e) inherent nature of the goods, such as those naturally tending to spoil or deteriorate.

The *Smith* case illustrates the extent of a common carrier's liability for damages to goods in transit.

SMITH V WATSON

(ND) 406 NW2d 685 (1987)

Glen Smith contracted with Dave Watson, a common carrier, to transport 720 hives of live bees along with associated equipment from Idabel, Oklahoma to Mandan, North Dakota. At 9:00 a.m. on May 24, 1984, while en route, Watson's truck skidded off the road and tipped over, severly damaging the cargo. Watson notified Smith of what had happened, and Smith immediately set out for the scene of the accident. He arrived at 6:00 p.m. with two bee experts and a Bobcat loader. They were hindered by the turned-over truck on top of the cargo, and they determined that they could not safely salvage the cargo that evening. The next day an insurance adjuster determined that the cargo was a total loss. The adjuster directed a bee expert, Dr. Moffat, to conduct the cleanup. Smith sued Watson for damages. The trial court found in favor of Smith but reduced his damages by $12,326.98 for failure to mitigate damages. Both Smith and Watson appealed.

VANDE WALLE, J. . . . A plaintiff seeking to recover damages has a duty to minimize or mitigate his damages and may not recover for damages which could have been avoided by reasonable efforts under the existing circumstances. However, the duty of a plaintiff to mitigate damages is not applicable where the defendant, who by breach of contract has caused injury to the plaintiff, has equal knowledge and opportunity to minimize the damages by performing the contract as he has obligated himself to do. . . .

Pursuant to Section 8-09-01, N.D.C.C., a common carrier is liable for loss or injury to property for any cause whatever, except for specified causes not relevant to this case, from the time the carrier accepts the property until proper delivery. Even when goods being transported by common carrier are initially damaged by an act of God or other cause for which the carrier is exempt from liability, the common carrier has a duty to minimize or mitigate damages to the property and is liable for failure to do so.

In this case the damage to Smith's bees, hives, and equipment resulted from a highway accident involving Watson's driver for which, the trial court determined, Smith was not responsible. It is undisputed that the cleanup and salvage operation for the accident was conducted through the efforts of Watson's insurance company. It is also undisputed that whatever cargo was salvageable was used as payment for the cleanup operation. Although Smith happened to be in the vicinity of the accident [after] it occurred, Watson had the primary responsibility to retain the necessary personnel and machinery to effectuate a cleanup and salvage operation to minimize loss of or damage to the cargo. Watson, as the carrier responsible for the accident, was liable for the cost of the cleanup operation. Therefore, Watson was the beneficiary of the salvaged cargo which was used as payment for those cleanup costs. We hold that, under these circumstances, Watson had a duty to mitigate the damages to Smith's property as a result of the accident occurring during Watson's transport of the property and that Watson cannot assert a failure by Smith to minimize damages where Watson had the primary responsibility as well as equal opportunity and knowledge to mitigate damages. . . .

[The district court judgment is increased by $12,096 and, as so modified, is affirmed.]

QUESTIONS

1. State the rule that governs the liability of a common carrier for loss or damage to goods occurring after the carrier has accepted the goods and before proper delivery of the goods has been made.
2. Does the shipper have an obligation to mitigate damages when goods being transported by a common carrier are initially damaged by an "act of God"?
3. Which party, the shipper or carrier, was responsible for the cost of the cleanup operation required after Watson's accident?

(a) CARRIER'S LIABILITY FOR DELAY. A carrier is liable for losses caused by its failure to deliver goods within a reasonable time. Thus, the carrier is liable for losses arising from a fall in price or a deterioration of the goods caused by its unreasonable delay. The carrier, however, is not liable for every delay. The risk of ordinary delays incidental to transporting goods is assumed by the shipper.

(b) LIABILITY OF INITIAL AND CONNECTING CARRIERS. When goods are carried over the lines of several carriers, the initial and the final carrier, as well as the carrier on whose lines the loss is sustained, may be liable to the shipper or the owner of the goods. Only one payment, however, may be obtained by the shippper.

(c) LIMITATION OF LIABILITY OF CARRIER. In the absence of a constitutional or statutory prohibition, a carrier generally has the right to limit its liability by contract.[28] A clause limiting the liability of the carrier is not enforceable unless (1) consideration is given for it, usually in the form of a reduced rate, and (2) the shipper is allowed to ship without limitation of liability if the shipper chooses to pay the higher or ordinary rate.

[28] Star-kist Foods v Chicago, Rock Island & Pacific R.R. (DC Ill) 586 F Supp 252 (1984).

A carrier may by contract exempt itself from liability for losses not arising from its own negligence, but may not exempt itself from liability for loss due to its own negligence. Thus, a provision that purports to exempt an air carrier from liability for its own negligence in the carriage of live animals as baggage has been held invalid.

(d) NOTICE OF CLAIM. The bill of lading and applicable government regulations may require that a carrier be given notice of any claim for damages or loss of goods within a specified time, generally within nine months.

(e) C.O.D. SHIPMENT. A common carrier transporting goods under a C.O.D. (cash on delivery) shipment may not make delivery of the goods without first receiving payment. If it does so, it is liable to the shipper for any loss resulting therefrom. If the carrier accepts a check from the consignee and the check is not honored by the bank on which it is drawn, the carrier is liable to the shipper for the amount thereof.[29]

C.   FACTORS

Some selling agents are called factors. A **factor** is a special type of bailee who sells goods consigned to the factor as though the factor were the owner of the goods.

§ 26:12   DEFINITIONS

Entrusting a person with the possession of property for the purpose of sale is commonly called **selling on consignment**.[30] The owner who consigns the goods for sale is the **consignor**. The person or agent to whom they are consigned is the **consignee**; the consignee may also be known as a commission merchant. A consignee's compensation is known as a **commission** or **factorage**. In a sale on consignment, the property remains the property of the owner or consignor, and

the consignee acts as the agent of the owner to pass the owner's title to the buyer.

§ 26:13   EFFECT OF FACTOR TRANSACTION

As a factor is by definition authorized by the consignor to sell the goods entrusted to the factor, such a sale will pass the title of the consignor to the purchaser. Before the factor makes the sale, the goods belong to the consignor, but in some instances, creditors of the factor may ignore the consignor and treat the goods as though they belonged to the consignee.[31] If the consignor is not the owner, as when a thief delivers stolen goods to the factor, a sale by the factor is an unlawful conversion.[32] It is constitutional, however, to provide by statute that the factor who sells in good faith in ignorance of the rights of other persons in the goods is protected from liability and cannot be treated as a converter of the goods, as would be the case in the absence of such statutory immunity.

D.   HOTELKEEPERS

A hotelkeeper has a bailee's liability with respect to property specifically entrusted to the hotelkeeper's care. In addition, the hotelkeeper has special duties with respect to a guest's property brought into the hotel.

§ 26:14   DEFINITIONS

The rules governing the special relationship between a hotelkeeper and guest arose in part because of the special needs of travelers. The legal definitions of *hotelkeeper* and *guest* are meant to exclude lodging of a more permanent character, such as that provided by boardinghouse keepers to boarders.

(a) HOTELKEEPER. The term *hotelkeeper* is used by law to refer to an operator of a hotel, motel, tourist home, or to anyone who is regularly engaged in the business of

---

[29]   Mountain States Waterbed v O.N.C. Freight System, 44 Colo App 433, 614 P2d 906 (1980).
[30]   Matter of Freidman, 54 App Div 2d 70, 407 NYS2d 999 (1978).

[31]   UCC § 2-326.
[32]   De Vore v McClure Livestock Commission Co. 207 Kan 499, 485 P2d 1013 (1971).

offering living accommodations to all transient persons.[33] In the early law, the hotelkeeper was called an innkeeper or a tavernkeeper.

(b) GUEST. The essential element in the definition of a **guest** is that the guest is a transient. The guest need not be a traveler nor come from a distance. A person living within a short distance of a hotel who engages a room at the hotel and remains there overnight is a guest.

A person who enters a hotel at the invitation of a guest or attends a dance or a banquet given at the hotel is not a guest. Similarly, the guest of a registered occupant of a motel room who shares the room with the occupant without the knowledge or consent of the management is not a guest of the motel, since there is no relationship between that person and the motel.

§ 26:15   DURATION OF GUEST RELATIONSHIP

The relationship of guest and hotelkeeper does not begin until a person is received as a guest by the hotelkeeper. The relationship terminates when the guest leaves or when the guest ceases to be a transient, as when the guest arranges for a more or less permanent residence at the hotel. The transition from the status of guest to the status of boarder or lodger must be clearly indicated. It is not established by the mere fact that one remains at the hotel for a long period, even though it runs into months.

§ 26:16   HOTELKEEPER'S LIABILITY FOR GUEST'S PROPERTY

As to property expressly entrusted to the hotelkeeper's care, the hotelkeeper has a bailee's liability. At common law, the hotelkeeper was an insurer of any other property of a guest.[34] As exceptions to this absolute liability at common law, the hotelkeeper is not liable for loss caused by an act of God, public enemy, act of public authority, the inherent nature of the property, or the fault of the guest.

In most states, statutes limit or provide a method of limiting the common-law liability of a hotelkeeper. The statutes may limit the extent of liability, reduce the liability of a hotelkeeper to that of an ordinary bailee, or permit the hotelkeeper to limit liability by contract or by posting a notice of the limitation. Some statutes relieve the hotelkeeper from liability when directions for depositing valuables with the hotelkeeper are posted on the doors of the rooms occupied, and the guest fails to comply with the directions. When a statute permits a hotel receiving valuables for deposit in its safe-deposit box to limit its liability to the amount specified in the agreement signed by the guest, such limitation binds the guest even though the loss was caused by negligence on the part of the hotel. A hotelkeeper must substantially comply with such a statute in order to obtain its protection.[35]

In the *Hicks* case the court considered the question of whether a statute limiting a hotelkeeper's liability for the loss of a guest's property applies to a situation in which the hotel's negligence caused the loss.

---

[33] A person furnishing the services of a hotelkeeper has the status of such even though the word *hotel* is not used in the business name. Lackman v Department of Labor and Industries, 78 Wash 2d 212, 471 P2d 82 (1970).

[34] Hanover Ins. Co. v Alamo Hotel (Iowa) 264 NW2d 774 (1978).

[35] Zacharia v Harbor Island Spa, Inc. (CA2 NY) 684 F2d 199 (1982).

HICKS V DAYS INNS OF AMERICA INC.
183 GA App 4, 357 SE2d 847 (1987)

The Hicks family, thinking that their room at the Days Inn was secure against theft, left several hundred dollars and a valuable antique pistol there for a short period of time. When they returned to their room they discovered that the money and pistol had been stolen. They sued the hotelkeeper, contending that it was responsible for the loss of the money and the valuable pistol due to its negligence in not providing better security for the room. They further asserted that the limitation of liability under state law does not apply to limit a hotelkeeper's liability for its own negligent acts. Days Inn disagreed. The court held that under state law the hotelkeeper's liability for negligence in the loss of a guest's property was limited to $100. The Hick's family appealed.

CARLEY, J. The evidence of record is undisputed that appellee had posted, on the inside of the door to appellants' motel room, a notice which required guests to store their valuables in the motel's safe and which otherwise limited appellee's liability for the loss of a guest's property to $100 unless the guest had made prior written notification that the value of his property exceeded that amount. See OCGA § 43-21-10; former OCGA § 43-21-12. This was a sufficient disclosure of the security measures that were made available by appellee for its guests' property and of the limitation on its liability as provided by the applicable statutes. . . .

In support of its motion for summary judgment as to appellants' negligence claim, appellee did not rely upon its publication of the notice authorized by OCGA § 43-21-10, pursuant to which it would "be relieved from responsibility" for appellants' "valuable articles" which were not placed in appellee's safe. Instead, appellee relied only upon its publication of the notice that is authorized by OCGA § 43-21-12 and which applies to the loss of property "other than valuable articles." The evidence is undisputed that appellee had posted, on the inside of the door to appellants' room, the notice authorized by OCGA § 43-21-12. Appellants assert only that they did not read the entire notice. They did not notify appellee in writing that their property's value was in excess of $100. Under these circumstances and OCGA § 43-21-12 as it existed at the time of appellants' loss, appellee's liability for their property damage was limited to $100. Accordingly, the trial court was correct in granting summary judgment limiting appellee's liability for its alleged negligence to a recovery of this amount. "The General Assembly by [enacting OCGA § 43-21-12] authorizing a limitation of liability has pre-empted the field on that subject." *Ellerman v. Atlanta American Hotel Corp.*, 126 Ga. App. 194, 196 (2), 191 S.E.2d 295 (1972).

[Judgment affirmed]

QUESTIONS

1. Did Days Inns comply with the state law limiting the common-law liability of hotelkeepers?
2. Does the statutory limitation of liability for loss of a guest's property to $100 apply to situations where it is proven that the hotel's negligence caused the loss?

§ 26:17 HOTELKEEPER'S LIEN

The hotelkeeper has a lien on the baggage of guests for the agreed charges, or if no express agreement was made, for the reasonable value of the accommodations furnished. Statutes permit the hotelkeeper to enforce this lien by selling the goods of the guests at a public sale.[36] The lien of the hotelkeeper is terminated by (a) the guest's payment of the hotel charges, (b) any conversion of the guest's goods by the hotelkeeper, and (c) surrender of the goods to the guest. In the last situation, an exception is made

[36] There is authority that the hotelkeeper's lien may not be exercised unless the guest is given an impartial hearing and that it is unconstitutional as a denial of due process to permit the hotelkeeper to hold or sell the guest's property without such a hearing. Klim v Jones (DC Cal) 315 F Supp 109 (1970). A hotel cannot seize the goods of a guest under a statutory lien law without first affording the guest a hearing as to liability, and the failure to do so deprives the guest of the due process guaranteed by the federal Constitution. New York v Skinner, 33 NYS2d 23, 300 NE2d 716 (1973).

when the goods are given to the guest for temporary use.

§ 26:18   BOARDERS OR LODGERS

To those persons who are permanent boarders or lodgers, rather than transient guests, the hotelkeeper owes only the duty of an ordinary bailee of personal property under a mutual-benefit bailment.

A hotelkeeper has no common-law right of lien on property of boarders or lodgers, as distinguished from guests, in the absence of an express agreement creating such a lien. In a number of states, however, legislation giving a lien to a boarding house or a lodging housekeeper has been adopted.

SUMMARY

A warehouser stores the goods of others for compensation, and for the most part has the rights and duties of a bailee in an ordinary mutual-benefit bailment. A warehouser issues a warehouse receipt to the depositor of the goods, and this receipt is a document of title that entitles the person in possession of the receipt to receive the goods. The warehouse receipt can be bought or sold, or used as security to obtain financing from banks. A nonnegotiable warehouse receipt states that the goods received will be delivered to a specified person. A negotiable warehouse receipt states that the goods will be delivered to the "bearer," or "to the order of" a named person, and if such a receipt is duly negotiated, the transferee may acquire rights superior to the transferor. A warehouser may limit its liability for loss or damage to goods due to its own negligence to an agreed valuation of the property stated in the warehouse receipt, provided the depositor is given the right to store the goods without the limitation at a higher storage rate.

A common carrier is in the business of accepting goods from the public for transportation to a designated destination for compensation. It issues to the shipper a bill of lading or an air bill, both of which are documents of title and provide rights similar to those provided by a warehouse receipt. A common carrier is absolutely liable for any loss or damage to the goods unless the carrier can show that the loss was caused by an act of God, an act of a public enemy, an act of a public authority, an act of the shipper, or the inherent nature of the goods. The carrier may limit its liability by contract.

A factor is a special type of bailee, who has possession of the owner's property for the purpose of sale. The factor or consignee receives a commission on the sale.

A hotelkeeper is in the business of providing living accommodations to transient persons. These persons are called guests. Subject to exceptions, hotelkeepers were absolutely liable for loss or damage to their guests' property at common law. Most states, however, provide a method of limiting the common-law liability of a hotelkeeper. A hotelkeeper has a lien on the property of the guest for the agreed charges.

QUESTIONS AND CASE PROBLEMS

1. What social forces are involved in the rule of law governing the liability of a common carrier for loss of freight?

2. Gowan sent goods by the Southern Mississippi Railroad to Robert in New Orleans. Fulton appeared in the New Orleans freight office of the railroad and stated that he was Robert's employee, sent to pick up the shipment. The shipment was given to Fulton without any proof of his authority from Robert. Robert later demanded the goods, and it was then learned that Fulton did not have any authority from Robert and had disappeared with the shipment. Is the railroad liable to Robert?

3. Compare the liens of carriers, warehousers, and hotels in terms of being specific.

4. Compare the limitation of the liability of a warehouser and of a hotel.

5. Compare warehouse receipts and bills of lading as to negotiability.

6. Latham and Loud, sporting goods manufacturers' representatives in Cleveland, Ohio, hijacked a truckload of ice skates from the Bartlett Shoe and Skate Company of Bangor, Maine. Latham and Loud warehoused the skates at the Northern Transfer Company's warehouse and received a negotiable warehouse receipt. Preston, a lender who had had business dealings with Latham and Loud in the past and believed them to be honest individuals, made a bona fide purchase of the receipt. Bartlett discovered that the skates were at Northern's Warehouse and informed Northern of the hijacking. Northern delivered the skates to Bartlett. Latham and Loud fled the state. Preston, claiming that he was entitled to delivery of the skates, brought an action against Northern since he acquired the negotiable receipt by due negotiation. Was Preston entitled to the skates?

7. Welch Brothers Trucking, Inc., a common carrier, made an agreement with B & L Export and Import Co. of San Francisco to transport a shipment of freshly harvested bluefin tuna from Calais, Maine to the Japan Air Lines freight terminal at New York's Kennedy Airport. The bluefin had been packed in ice and were to be shipped by Japan Air to Tokyo. Fresh bluefin at the peak of their autumnal fattening are used in the traditional Japanese raw fish dish *sashimi* and command very high prices. When transportation charges were not paid by B & L's representative in New York, Welch Brothers refused to release the shipment to Japan Air Lines. B & L's representative in New York explained that he had no check-writing authority, but assured Welch that it would be paid and pleaded for the release of the cargo because of its perishable nature. Transportation charges were not paid in the next twelve-hour period because the principals of B & L were on a business trip to the Far East and could not be contacted. After waiting the twelve-hour period, Welch sent a telegram to B & L's offices in San Francisco stating the amount due and that it intended to auction the cargo in twenty-four hours if transportation charges were not paid. Welch also sent telegrams to all fish wholesalers listed in the New York City Yellow Pages seeking bidders after advising that the cargo would be sold at auction in twenty-four hours if the charges were not paid. Welch sold the shipment to the highest bidder at the appointed time for an amount just in excess of the transportation charges plus a demurrage charge for the thirty-six hour waiting period. When the principals of B & L were later informed of what happened, they were outraged and initiated suit against Welch for the profits they would have earned had the cargo been shipped and sold in Japan. Decide.

8. Evers owned and operated a warehouse. DeCecchis phoned and inquired as to the rates and then brought furniture in for storage. Nothing was said at any time about any limitation of the liability of Evers as a warehouser. A warehouse receipt was mailed to DeCecchis several days later. The receipt contained a clause that limited liability to $50 per package stored. Was the limitation of liability binding on DeCecchis? [DeCecchis v Evers, 54 Del 99, 174 A2d 463]

9. Vanguard Transfer Co. ran a moving and storage business. It obtained an insurance policy from the St. Paul Fire & Marine Insurance Co. covering goods that it had "accepted at the warehouse for storage." Dahl rented a room in Vanguard's building. Both Dahl and Vanguard had keys to the room. Dahl was charged a flat monthly rental for the room and could keep any property there that he desired.

Vanguard did not make any record of the goods that Dahl brought to the warehouse. There was a fire in the warehouse and, Dahl's property was destroyed. He sued the insurance company. Was it liable? [Dahl v St. Paul Fire & Marine Insurance Co. 36 Wis 2d 420, 153 NW2d 624]

10. Dovax Fabrics, Inc. had been shipping goods by a common carrier, G & A Delivery Corp., for over a year, during which all of G & A's bills to Dovax bore the notation, "Liability limited to $50 unless value is declared and paid for. . . ." Dovax gave G & A three lots of goods, having a total value of $1,799.95. A truck containing all three was stolen that night, without negligence on the part of G & A. Should Dovax recover from G & A (a) $1,799.95, (b) $150 for three shipments, or (c) nothing? [Dovax Fabrics, Inc. v G & A Delivery Corp. (NY Civ Ct) 4 UCCRS 492]

11. The guest in a motel opened the bedroom window at night and went to sleep. During the night a prowler pried open the screen, entered the room and stole property of the guest. The guest sued the motel. The motel asserted that it was not responsible for property in the possession of the guest and that the guest had been contributorily negligent in opening the window. Could the guest recover damages? [Buck v Hankin, 217 Pa Super 262, 269 A2d 344]

12. On March 30, Emery Air Freight Corp. picked up a shipment of furs from Hopper Furs, Inc. Hopper's chief of security filled in certain items in the air bill. In the box entitled zip code, he placed the figure "61,045." The zip code box is immediately above the "declared value" box. The air bill contained a clause limiting liability to $10 per pound of cargo lost or damaged, unless the shipper makes a declaration of value in excess of the amount and pays a higher fee. A higher fee was not charged in this case, and Gerald Doane signed the air bill for the carrier and took possession of the furs. The furs were lost by Emery in transit, and Hopper sued for the value of the furs, $61,045. Emery's offer to pay $2,150, the $10 per pound rate set forth in the air bill, was rejected. Hopper claims that the amount $61,045, which was mistakenly placed in the zip code box, was in fact part of the contract set forth in the air bill and that Emery, upon reviewing the contract, must have realized a mistake was made. Decide. [Hopper Furs, Inc. v. Emery Air Freight Corporation (CA8 Mo) 749 F2d 1261]

13. Jose Maria Berga de Lema, a Brazilian resident, arrived in New York City. His luggage consisted of three suitcases, an attache case, and a cylindrical bag. The attache case and the cylindrical bag contained jewels, valued at $300,000. Mr. de Lema went from JFK Airport to the Waldorf Astoria Hotel where he gave the three suitcases to hotel staff in the garage, and then he went to the lobby to register. The assistant manager, Mr. Baez, summoned room clerk Mr. Tamburino to assist him. Mr. de Lema stated, "The room clerk asked me if I had a reservation. I said, 'Yes. The name is Jose Berga de Lema.' And I said, 'I want a safety deposit box.' He said, 'Please fill out your registration.'" While de Lema was filling out the reservation form, paying $300 in cash as an advance, and Tamburino was filling out a receipt for that amount, de Lema had placed the attache case and the cylindrical bag on the floor. A blond woman jostled de Lema, apparently creating a diversion, and when he next looked down, he discovered that the attache case was gone. Mr. de Lema brought suit against the hotel for the value of the jewels stolen in the hotel's lobby. The hotel maintained a safe for valuables and posted notices in the lobby, garage, and rooms, as required by the New York law that modifies a hotelkeeper's common-law liability. The notices stated in part that the hotel is not liable for the loss of valuables that a guest neglects to deliver to the hotel for safekeeping. The hotel defends that de Lema neglected to inform it of the presence of the jewels and to deliver the jewels to the hotel. It states that it is not liable. Decide. [De Lema v Waldorf Astoria Hotel, Inc. (SDNY) 588 F Supp 19]

14. Frosty Land Foods shipped a load of beef from its plant in Montgomery, Alabama, to Scott Meat Company in Los Angeles via the Refrigerated Transport Co. (RTC), a common carrier. Early Wednesday morning, December 7, at 12:55 a.m., two of RTC's drivers departed from the Frosty Land facility with the load of beef. The bill of lading called for delivery at Scott Meat Company on Friday, December 9, at 6:00 a.m. The RTC drivers arrived in Los Angeles at approximately 3:30 p.m. on Friday, December

9; Scott notified the drivers that it could not process the meat at that time. The drivers checked into a motel for the weekend and the load was delivered to Scott on Monday, December 12, 1977. After inspecting 65 of the 308 carcasses, Scott determined that the meat was in "off condition" and refused the shipment. On Tuesday, December 13, 1977, Frosty Land sold the meat, after extensive trimming, at a loss of $13,529. Frosty Land brought suit against RTC for its loss. Decide. [Frosty Land Foods v Refrigerated Transport Co. (CA5) 613 F2d 1344]

15. An employee of General Foods Corporation was a paying guest of the Skyways Motor Lodge. Certain airplane parts, the property of General Foods, were stolen from the employee's room. The employee did not see the motel's limitation-of-liability notice that appeared at the bottom of the room-rate sign on the back of the motel door. The notice stated that all valuables should be left at the office. A state statute that limited hotel-keepers' common-law liability required that notices be placed in every room stating the fact that "such safe or vault is provided" for the valuables. General Foods sued Skyways on the theory that the motel had breached its common-law duty as an innkeeper to safeguard a guest's property since Skyways had not fully complied with the notice requirements of the state statute. Skyways contends it substantially fulfilled the statutory requirement by posting the notice to leave "all valuables at the office." Decide. [Skyways Motor Lodge v General Foods Corp. (Del) 403 A2d 722]

PART 4

SALES

27

---◆---

NATURE AND FORM OF SALES

The most common business transaction is the sale of goods, such as food, clothing, or books. The law of sales is a combination of the law merchant, the common law of England, and former statutes as modified and codified by Article 2 of the Uniform Commercial Code.

A. NATURE AND LEGALITY

A **sale of goods** is a present transfer of title to movable property for a price. This price may be a payment of money, an ex-change of other property, or the performance of services.[1] When a free item is given with the purchase of other goods, it is the purchasing of the other goods that is the price for the "free" goods; hence, the transaction as to the free goods is a sale.

The parties to a sale are the person who owns the goods and the person to whom the title is transferred. The transferor is the

---

[1]   Uniform Commercial Code § 2-304(1). O'Keefe Elevator Co. v Second Ave. Properties, Ltd. 216 Neb 170, 343 NW2d 54 (1984).

seller or vendor, and the transferee is the buyer or vendee.

§ 27:1 Subject Matter of Sales

Goods, the subject matter of a sale under Article 2 of the Uniform Commercial Code, includes any thing movable at the time it is identified as the subject of the transaction.[2] The subject matter may not be (a) investment securities, such as stocks and bonds, the sale of which is regulated by Article 8 of the UCC; (b) choses in action, such as insurance policies and promissory notes since they are assigned or negotiated rather than sold, or which, because of their personal nature, are not transferable in any case; or (c) real estate, such as a house, factory, or farm.

(a) Nature of Goods. Most goods are tangible and solid, such as an automobile or a chair. But goods may also be fluid, as oil or gasoline. Goods may also be intangible, as natural gas and electricity. The UCC is applicable to both new and to used goods.[3]

(b) Existing and Future Goods. Goods physically existing and owned by the seller at the time of the transaction are called **existing goods.** All other goods are called **future goods.** Future goods include both goods that are physically existing but not owned by the seller and goods that have not yet been manufactured.

A person can make a contract to sell goods at a future date. No sale can be made of future goods. As the "seller" does not have any title to future goods, there can be no transfer of that title now, and hence no sale. For example, an agreement made today that all fish caught on a fishing trip tomorrow shall belong to a particular person does not make that person the owner of any fish today.

When the parties attempt to effect a present sale of future goods, the agreement operates only as a contract to sell the goods. Thus, a farmer purporting to transfer the title today to a future crop would be held subject to a duty to transfer the crop when it came into existence. The contract itself does not pass the title to the crop.

§ 27:2 Sale Distinguished

A sale is an actual present transfer of title. If there is a transfer of a lesser interest than title, the transaction is not a sale.

(a) Bailment. A bailment is not a sale because only possession is transferred to the bailee. Title to the property is not transferred. A lease of goods, such as an automobile, is a bailment.[4]

Although a bailment is not a sale, there is a trend in the law to hold the commercial bailor to the same responsibilities as a seller.

(b) Gift. There can be no sale without a price. A **gift** is a gratuitous or free transfer of the title to property.

(c) Contract to Sell. When the parties intend that title to goods will pass at a future time and they make a contract so providing, a **contract to sell** is created.

(d) Option to Purchase. A sale, a present transfer of title, differs from an **option to purchase.** The latter is neither a transfer of title nor a contract to transfer title, but a power to make a contract to sell.

(e) Conditional Sale. A **conditional sale** customarily refers to a "condition precedent" transaction by which title does not vest in the purchaser until payment in full has been made for the property purchased.

---

[2] It may also include things that are attached to the land, such as (a) minerals or buildings or materials forming part of buildings if they are to be removed or severed by the seller, (b) other things attached to the land to be removed by either party. UCC § 2-107.

[3] Rose v Epley Motor Sales, 288 NC 53, 215 SE2d 573 (1975).

[4] Under a proposed amendment to Article 2 of the UCC, there has been a codification of the law of leases. This Article 2A will apply to any transaction, regardless of form, that creates a lease. Many of the provisions of the law of sales were carried over and changed to reflect differences in style, leasing terminology, or leasing practices. These include among others, statute of frauds provisions, rules relating to offer and acceptance, and warranties.

This was formerly a common type of sale used when the purchase was made on credit and payment was to be made in installments. The conditional sale has been replaced by a secured transaction under Article 9 of the UCC.

TRANSACTION	TYPE OF PROPERTY	ESSENTIAL CHARACTERISTIC
SALE	PERSONAL OR REAL	PRESENT TRANSFER OF TITLE FOR A PRICE
BAILMENT	GOODS	TRANSFER OF POSSESSION WHILE RETAINING TITLE
GIFT	PERSONAL OR REAL	GRATUITOUS TRANSFER OF TITLE
CONTRACT TO SELL	PERSONAL OR REAL	TRANSFER OF TITLE AT A FUTURE DATE
OPTION TO PURCHASE	PERSONAL OR REAL	POWER TO MAKE A CONTRACT TO SELL
CONDITIONAL SALE	PERSONAL OR REAL	TITLE PASSES TO PURCHASER WHEN CONDITION IS SATISFIED

FIGURE 27-1
COMPARISON OF SALES WITH OTHER
TRANSACTIONS

(f) CONTRACT FOR SERVICES. A contract for services is an ordinary contract and is not governed by the UCC.[5]

(g) CONTRACT FOR GOODS AND SERVICES. If a contract calls for both the rendering of services and the supplying of materials to be used in performing the services, the contract is classified according to its dominant element. If the sale of goods is dominant, it is a sales contract. If the service element is dominant, it is a service contract.

[5] Professional Recruiters, Inc. v Oliver (Neb) 409 NW2d 304 (1987).

For example, the contract of a repairer is a contract for services, even though in making the repairs, parts are supplied to perform the task. The supplying of such parts is not regarded as a sale but is merely incidental to the primary contract of making repairs. In contrast, the purchase of a television set, with incidental service of installation, is a sale of goods because the purchase of the set is the dominant element.

In the *Meyers* case, the court was faced with whether a person assembling and installing prefabricated items was making a sale of goods or was rendering a service.

MEYERS V HENDERSON CONSTRUCTION CO.
147 NJ Super 77, 370 A2d 547 (1977)

The Henderson Construction Co. was building a factory. Cyril Meyers contracted to install overhead doors in the factory. Meyers obtained the prefabricated but disassembled doors from the manufacturer. His contract with Henderson required Meyers to "furnish all labor, materials, tools and equipment to satisfactorily complete the installation of all overhead doors." Five years later, when Meyers sued Henderson for breach of contract, Henderson raised the defense that the contract was for the sale of goods, in which case it would be barred by the UCC's four-year statute of limitations. Meyers claimed that it was a contract for services, for which the UCC's statute of limitation was not applicable, and suit could be brought within six years.

WEISS, J. D. C. . . . Which statute properly applies depends upon how the contract may be most accurately characterized — as one for the sale of goods (as defined in [UCC §] 2-105(1)) plus incidental services, or as one for construction services with the subcontractor furnishing materials as well as labor. . . .

[UCC §] 2-105 requires that, in order to be classified as goods, the subject matter of a contract must be "movable at the time of identification to the contract." This definitional section continues, excluding some "things" from UCC coverage. But there is no exception for goods which require servicing before they can be used. . . . Some courts have characterized contracts as involving primarily services, with the transfer of materials being so incidental to the services as to exclude coverage by the UCC, . . . [when those contracts involved] the sale and installation of blacktop, construction of a house with a builder furnishing all materials and labor, construction of electrical equipment, construction and sale of a house, and finally sale and erection of structural steel in the construction of a bridge.

It is apparent that at some point the service element may so dominate the subject matter of a contract as to bring it outside UCC coverage. An agreement to paint a house is a classic example of this situation. In *Bonebrake v Cox*, [(CA8 Iowa) 499 F2d 951] the Eighth Circuit was faced with the task of enunciating a test to cover borderline cases. There the issue was whether the four-year UCC limitation period barred an action of allegedly defective used bowling equipment which had been supplied and installed by defendant. . . .

As is the case here, *Bonebrake* involved the purchase of manufactured goods which were useless without a substantial amount of labor. One lump sum was charged for the equipment and its installation. . . .

The cases presenting mixed contracts of this type are legion. The test for inclusion or exclusion is not whether they are mixed, but, granting that they are mixed, whether their predominant factor, their thrust, their purpose, reasonably stated, is the rendition of service, with goods incidentally involved (e.g., contract with artist for painting) or is a transaction of sale, with labor incidentally involved (e.g., installation of a water heater in a bathroom). . . . See also *Cleveland Lumber Co. v Proctor and Schwartz, Inc.* 397 F Supp 1088 (ND Ga 1975).

It cannot be denied that the overhead doors were useless without the performance of installation services. . . .

When presented with two elements of a contract, each absolutely necessary if the subject matter is to be of any significant value to the purchaser, it is a futile task to attempt to determine which component is "more necessary." Thus the *Bonebrake* test looks to the predominant purpose, the thrust of the contract as it would exist in the minds of reasonable parties. There is no surer way to provide for predictable results in the face of a highly artificial classification system.

Applying the test here, we find the predominant reason for the agreement to have been the procurement of overhead doors, with the installation services being incidental. The contract is, therefore, governed by the UCC, and the four-year limitation period of [UCC §] 2-725 is properly applicable. . . .

[Judgment for defendant]

QUESTIONS

1. What was the importance of determining whether Meyers was selling services or goods?
2. What provision does the UCC make with respect to goods that require servicing by the supplier before they can be used by the customer?
3. Would it have affected the decision if Meyers had constructed the doors from building materials rather than having assembled and installed prefabricated doors?

§ 27:3   LAW OF CONTRACTS APPLICABLE

A sale is a voluntary transaction between two persons. Accordingly, most of the principles that apply to contractual agreements in general are equally applicable to a sale of goods.

Modern marketing practices have modified the strict principles of contract law, and this approach is carried into the UCC. Thus, not only can a sale be made in any manner; but it is sufficient that the parties by their conduct recognize the existence of a contract, even though it cannot be determined when the contract was made, and generally, even though one or more terms are left open.[6]

In most instances, the UCC treats all buyers and sellers alike. In some, it treats merchants differently than it does the occasional or casual buyer or seller. In this way, the UCC recognizes that the merchant is experienced and has a special knowledge of the relevant commercial practices.

(a) OFFER. Contract law as to offers is applicable to a sales contract with the following exception. A **firm offer** by a merchant cannot be revoked if (1) the offer expresses an intention that it will not be revoked, and is (2) in a writing, (3) signed by the merchant. An express period of irrevocability in the offer cannot exceed three months. If nothing is said as to the duration of the offer, irrevocability continues only for a reasonable time. This firm offer exception applies without regard to whether the merchant received any consideration to keep the offer open.

(b) ACCEPTANCE. An offer to buy or sell goods may be accepted in any manner and by any medium that is reasonable under the circumstances.[7] However, if a specific manner or medium is clearly indicated by the terms of the offer or the circumstances of the case, the offer can only be accepted in that manner.

Unless it is expressly specified that an offer to buy or sell goods must be accepted just as made, the offeree may accept an offer and at the same time propose an additional term. Contrary to the general contract-law rule, the new term does not reject the original offer. A contract arises on the terms of the original offer, and the new term is a counteroffer. If, however, the offer states that it must be accepted exactly as made, the ordinary contract-law rules apply. If the additional term is treated as a counteroffer, that term does not become binding until accepted by the original offeror.

In a transaction between merchants, the additional term becomes part of the con-

---

[6]   UCC § 2-204. This provision is limited by requiring that there be "a reasonably certain basis for giving an appropriate remedy."

[7]   UCC § 2-206(1). An order or other offer to buy goods that are to be sent promptly or currently can be accepted by the seller by actually shipping the goods.

tract if that term does not materially alter the offer and no objection is made to it. If such an additional term in the seller's form of acknowledgment operates solely to the seller's advantage, however, it is a material term and must be accepted to be effective.

The acceptance by the buyer of a term added by the seller to the acceptance of the buyer's offer may be found in an express statement or in conduct. The buyer may state orally or in writing agreement to the additional term. There is an acceptance by conduct if the buyer accepts the goods with knowledge that the term has been added by the seller.

When a term of an acceptance conflicts with a term of an offer, but it is clear that the parties intended to be bound by a contract, the UCC recognizes the formation of a contract. The terms that are conflicting cancel out and are ignored. The contract then consists of the terms of the offer and acceptance that agree, together with those terms that the UCC or contract law implies into a contract.

(c) DETERMINATION OF PRICE. The price for goods may be expressly fixed by the contract. If not fixed by the contract, the price may be an open term whereby the parties merely indicate how the price should be determined at a later time or make no provision whatever as to the price.

When persons experienced in a particular industry make a contract without specifying the price to be paid, the price will be determined by the manner that is customary in the industry. Ordinarily if nothing is said as to price, the buyer is required to pay the reasonable value of the goods, which is generally the market price.

In recent years there has been an increase in use of the "cost plus" formula for determining price. Under this form of agreement, the buyer pays the seller a sum equal to the cost to the seller of obtaining the goods plus a specified percentage of that cost representing the seller's profit.

The contract may expressly provide that one of the parties may determine the price,

in which case that party must act in good faith in so doing.[8] Likewise, the contract may specify that the price shall be determined by some standard or by a third person.

(d) OUTPUT AND REQUIREMENTS CONTRACTS. Somewhat related to the open term concept concerning price is the concept involved in the output and requirements contracts that the quantity to be sold or purchased is not a specific quantity. Instead it is such amount as the seller should produce or the buyer should require. Although this introduces an element of uncertainty, such sales contracts are valid. To prevent oppression, they are subject to two limitations: (1) the parties must act in good faith, and (2) the quantity offered or demanded must not be unreasonably disproportionate to prior output or requirements or to a stated estimate.

When the sales contract is a continuing contract, as one calling for periodic delivery of fuel, but no time is set for the life of the contract, the contract runs for a reasonable time. It may be terminated on notice by either party.

(e) SEALS. A seal on a sales contract or on an offer of sale has no effect. Thus, in determining whether there is consideration or if the statute of limitations is applicable, the fact that there is a seal on the sales contract is ignored.

(f) IMPLIED CONDITIONS. The field of implied conditions under contract law is broadened by the UCC to permit the release of a party from any obligation under a sales contract when performance has been made commercially impracticable, as distinguished from impossible: (1) by the occurrence of a contingency, the nonoccurrence of which was a basic assumption on which the contract was made; or (2) by compliance in good faith with any applicable governmental regulation or order. "A

[8] Good faith requires that the party act honestly and, in the case of a merchant, also requires the party to follow reasonable commercial standards of fair dealing that are recognized in the trade. UCC § § 1-201(19), 2-103(1)(b).

severe shortage of raw materials or of supplies due to a contingency such as war, embargo, local crop failure, unforeseen shutdown of major sources of supply or the like, which either causes a marked increase in cost or altogether prevents the seller from securing supplies necessary to his performance, is within the contemplation" of this provision of the Code.[9]

(g) MODIFICATION OF CONTRACT. An agreement to modify a contract for the sale of goods is binding even though the modification is not supported by consideration.[10]

(h) PAROL EVIDENCE RULE. The parol evidence rule applies to the sale of goods with the slight modification that a writing is not presumed or assumed to represent the entire contract of the parties unless the court specifically decides that it does. If the court so decides, parol evidence is admissible to show what the parties meant by their words, but additional terms cannot be added to the writing by parol evidence.

If the court decides that the writing was not intended to represent the entire contract, the writing may be supplemented by parol proof of additional terms as long as such terms are not inconsistent with the original written terms.

(i) USAGE OF TRADE AND COURSE OF DEALING. Established usages or customs of trade and prior course of conduct or dealings between the parties are to be considered in connection with any sales transaction. If there is no express term excluding or "overruling" the prior pattern of dealings between the parties and the usages of the trade, it is concluded that the parties contracted on the basis of those patterns of doing business. More specifically, the patterns of doing business as shown by the prior dealings of the parties and the usages of the trade enter into and form part of their contract. These patterns may be looked to in order to find what was intend-

ed by the express provisions and to supply otherwise missing terms.

(j) FRAUD AND OTHER DEFENSES. The defenses that may be raised in a suit on a sales contract are in general the same as those that may be raised in a suit on any other contract. A defrauded party may cancel the transaction and recover what was paid or the goods that were delivered, together with damages for any loss sustained. If title was obtained by the buyer by means of fraud, the title is voidable by an innocent seller.

If the sales contract or any clause in it was unconscionable when made, a court may refuse to enforce it.

§ 27:4   ILLEGAL SALES

At common law, a sale was illegal if the subject matter itself was illegal. A transaction may also be illegal even though the subject matter of the sale is unobjectionable, if the agreement provides that the goods sold shall be employed for some unlawful purpose or if the seller assists the buyer in an unlawful act. To illustrate, when the seller falsely labels domestic goods, representing them to be imported, to assist the buyer in perpetrating a fraud upon the buyer's customers, the sale is illegal. The mere fact, however, that the seller has knowledge of the buyer's unlawful purpose does not, under the general rule, make the sale illegal unless the purpose is the commission of a serious crime.

(a) ILLEGALITY UNDER STATUTES. Every state has legislation prohibiting certain sales when they are not conducted according to the requirements of the statutes. Statutes commonly regulate sales by establishing standards as to grading, size, weight, and measure, and by prohibiting adulteration.

Statutes may regulate the sale of "secondhand" goods. Such a statute does not apply to a casual seller, but only applies to one whose regular business consists of selling goods of the kind covered by the statute.

---

[9]   UCC § 2-615, Official Comment, point 4.
[10]   UCC § 2-209(1).

States may prohibit the making of sales on Sunday. This may apply either to sales generally or to particular classes of commodities or stores.

The federal Food, Drug, and Cosmetic Act prohibits the interstate shipment of misbranded or adulterated foods, drugs, cosmetics, and therapeutic devices. A product that does not carry adequate use instructions and warnings is deemed "misbranded."

(b) EFFECT OF ILLEGAL SALE. An illegal sale or contract to sell cannot be enforced. As a general rule, courts will not aid either party in recovering money or property transferred pursuant to an illegal agreement. Here, the ordinary contract-law rule as to illegality is applied. However, if a sale is made illegal by statute, a seller who violates the law may be held liable for the damage caused.

§ 27:5 BULK TRANSFERS

Whenever a merchant is about to transfer a major part of the merchant's materials, supplies, merchandise, or other inventory, not in the ordinary course of business, advance notice of the transfer should be given to creditors by the transferee in accordance with Article 6 of the Uniform Commercial Code. The essential characteristic of businesses subject to Article 6 is that they sell from inventory or a stock of goods, as contrasted with businesses that render services.[11] Thus, a beauty salon is ordinarily a service enterprise and is not subject to the bulk transfer article, as contrasted with a store selling cosmetics, which is so subject.

(a) EFFECT OF NONCOMPLIANCE WITH ARTICLE 6. If the notice required by Article 6 is not given, the creditors of the seller may reach the sold property in the hands of the buyer. Creditors may also reach the property in the hands of any subsequent transferee who knew that there had not been compliance with the UCC or who did not pay value. This provision is designed to protect the creditors of a merchant from the merchant's selling all the inventory, pocketing the money, and then disappearing, leaving the creditors unpaid. The protection given to creditors by the bulk transfer legislation is in addition to the protection that they have against their debtor for fraudulent transfers or conveyances, and the remedies that can be employed in bankruptcy proceedings.

In the *Republic Steel* case, a creditor claimed that a transfer of equipment was a bulk transfer requiring notice to creditors, since it was made in connection with a bulk transfer of inventory.

---

[11] J.I. Hass Co. Inc. v Frank A. Kristal Associates, Inc. (NY) 512 NYS2d 104 (1987).

REPUBLIC STEEL CORPORATION V CANYON CULVERT COMPANY INC.
__ NM __, 722 P2d 647 (1986)

Canyon Culvert sold most of its equipment to Armco. A short time thereafter, Canyon Culvert transferred its remaining equipment, its office furniture, and its inventory to Canyon Steel, a new corporation formed by the former owner of Canyon Culvert. Having received written assurance from Canyon Culvert's lawyer that Canyon Culvert had complied with any pertinent provisions of the bulk transfer sections of the UCC, Armco did not provide Canyon Culvert's creditors with formal notice of sale. Republic Steel, a creditor of Canyon Culvert, subsequently brought suit against Canyon Culvert and against Armco, seeking a declaration that the transfer to Armco was ineffective against Republic. From a judgment in favor of Armco, Republic appealed.

WALTERS, J. . . . Article VI of New Mexico's UCC provides in part:

> (1) A "bulk transfer" is any transfer in bulk and not in the ordinary course of the transferor's business of a major part of the . . . inventory . . . of an enterprise subject to this article. (2) A transfer of a substantial part of the equipment . . . of such an enterprise is a bulk transfer if it is made *in connection with* a bulk transfer of inventory, but not otherwise. (3) The enterprises subject to this article are all those whose principal business is the sale of merchandise from stock, including those who manufacture what they sell.

NMSA 1978, § 55-6-102 (emphasis added). Where a sale embodies the statutory elements of a bulk transfer, the transferee is required to obtain a list of the seller's creditors and notify them of the impending sale no later than ten days before the transferee pays for or takes possession of the goods. *See* §§ 55-6-104, -105.

Republic argues that, because the purpose of Article VI is to protect creditors from debtors who might otherwise liquidate assets and abscond with the proceeds (*see* § 55-6-101, comments 3 and 4), the words "in connection with" as used in Section 55-6-102(2) must necessarily mean closely related in time to or part of the overall process of going out of business. Thus, claims Republic, the sale of equipment to Armco, made shortly before the sale of inventory to Canyon Steel, was a transfer of equipment "made in connection with a bulk transfer of inventory," *i.e.*, a bulk transfer subject to the notice requirements of Article VI.

The case law dealing with this issue is sparse. . . . Nonetheless, the majority of jurisdictions have held in the past that their pre-code Bulk Sales Acts were to be strictly construed because they were in derogation of the common-law rules which secure the right to alienate one's property without restriction. For example, where a bulk sales statute applied only to a bulk transfer of "merchandise or merchandise and fixtures," the statute was held not applicable to a transfer of fixtures only, or to a transfer of merchandise to one purchaser accompanied by a transfer of fixtures to a different purchaser on the same day.

When the various bulk sales laws were codified into UCC, Article VI, the word "equipment" was substituted for "fixtures," and those courts that have dealt with UCC Section 6-102(2) have construed that subsection narrowly. In *H.L.C. Imports Corp. v M & L Siegel, Inc.*, 94 Misc.2d 179, 413 N.Y.S.2d 605 (N.Y.Civ.Ct. 1979), the sale of all office supplies, equipment, and furniture by a jeweler who subsequently "disappeared" was held not to be a bulk transfer because there had been no sale of inventory. Similarly, a Pennsylvania trial court found that where a private club sold all its personal property, equipment, and fixtures, excluding its liquor and other inventory, there was no bulk transfer subject to Article VI. *Brooks v Lambert*, 44 Del.Co. 153, 10 Pa.D.&C.2d 237 (1957). The *Brooks* court did not specify when or to whom the defunct club had sold its inventory. It did, however, observe that under state law the bulk sale of the liquor was governed exclusively by liquor board regulations and could not therefore be subject to Article VI, and that the remaining inventory of that particular business would logically consist of goods unsaleable in bulk.

Other courts, while holding that the defendant transferor was not the sort of *enterprise* subject to Article VI, have stated in dicta that even if the transferor had satisfied the elements of Section 6-102(3), its sale of equipment only was not a bulk transfer within the meaning of Section 102(2).

We agree with the cases that have construed Section 6-102(2) narrowly. Because Article VI restricts the free alienation of property (*see* § 55-6-101, comment 5) and imposes an unusual obligation on the *buyer* (§ 55-6-110, comment 1), the determination whether equipment is transferred "in connection with" a bulk transfer of inventory should logically be made from the *buyer's* point of view as of the date that negotiations are completed. If, at that time, the buyer has not purchased or agreed to purchase a major part of the seller's inventory (*see* § 55-6-102(1)), and has not been alerted to the likelihood of such a concurrent sale, the buyer has no reason to know or to believe that the transfer of the seller's equipment is being made "in connection with" a bulk transfer of inventory as described in Section 55-6-102(2).

In the instant case, Armco bargained for and negotiated a purchase of equipment only. That transaction, in and of itself, was not a bulk transfer within the literal meaning of Section 55-6-102(2). As an added precaution, however, Armco drafted a purchase agreement in which Canyon Culvert promised that its attorney would provide a letter verifying that Canyon Culvert had complied with any applicable provisions of Article VI. Armco was justified in believing that the transaction was not a bulk transfer within the meaning of Section 55-6-102(2). Indeed, as of the date of the sale, Article VI could not have applied because there had been no transfer of Canyon Culvert's inventory to anyone. It would be illogical and unfair to hold that Canyon Culvert's subsequent sale of inventory to Canyon Steel operated retroactively to impose on Armco the requirements of Article VI simply because of Armco's status as a buyer, and regardless of its lack of knowledge of Canyon's plans or later conduct.

We therefore hold that, under Section 55-6-102(2), the sale of equipment occurs in connection with a bulk transfer of inventory and notice to creditors is required if and only if the purchaser of the equipment has reason to know that a substantial part of the seller's inventory has been or will be sold in a reasonably contemporaneous transaction.

[Judgment affirmed]

QUESTIONS

1. What was the argument of Republic?
2. How does failure to comply with the bulk transfer article affect the buyer?
3. What was the basis for the court's decision?

The fact that there has been noncompliance with Article 6 of the UCC regulating bulk transfers, however, does not affect the validity of a bulk sale of goods as between the immediate parties to the transfer. Article 6 governs only the rights of creditors of the transferor.

(b) LIABILITY OF BULK PURCHASER. Ordinarily the bulk purchaser who receives the goods does not become liable for the debts of the bulk seller merely because the requirements of Article 6 have not been satisfied. In contrast, if the buyer mixes the transferred goods with other goods so that it is not possible for the creditor to identify the transferred goods that are subject to the creditor's claim, the bulk buyer is personally liable for the debts of the bulk seller. The liability of the bulk buyer will not exceed the value of the goods transferred, however.

B. FORM OF SALES CONTRACT

A contract for the sale of goods may be oral or written. In some cases, it must be evidenced by a writing or it cannot be enforced in court.

§ 27:6 AMOUNT

Whenever the sales price of goods is $500 or more, the sales contract must be evidenced by a writing to be enforceable.[12] The section of the UCC setting forth this requirement is known as the statute of frauds.

§ 27:7 NATURE OF THE WRITING REQUIRED

The writing evidencing the sales contract may be either (1) a complete written contract signed by both parties or (2) a memorandum signed by the defendant. In any case, it must meet the following requirements:

(a) TERMS. The writing must indicate that there has been a completed transaction as to certain goods. Specifically, it need only (1) indicate that a sale or contract to sell has been made[13] and (2) state the quantity of goods involved. Any other missing terms may be shown by parol evidence.

(b) SIGNATURE. The writing must be signed by the person who is being sued or by the authorized agent of that person. The signature must be placed on the paper with the intention of authenticating the writing. It may consist of initials or be printed, stamped, or typewritten, as long as made with the necessary intent.

When the transaction is between merchants, an exception is made to the requirement of signing. The failure of a merchant to repudiate a confirming letter sent by another merchant within ten days of receiving such a letter binds the nonsigner just as if the receiving merchant had signed the letter. This makes it necessary for a merchant seller to watch the mail and to act within ten days of receiving a mailed confirmation. This was the problem that arose in the *Thompson Printing* case.

---

[12] UCC §2-201.

[13] Martco, Inc. v Doran Chevrolet, Inc. (Tex Civ App) 632 SW2d 927 (1982).

THOMPSON PRINTING MACHINERY CO. V B. F. GOODRICH CO.
(CA7 Ill) 714 F2d 744 (1983)

Thompson Printing buys and sells used printing machinery. Thompson brought suit on an oral contract for the purchase from B. F. Goodrich Company of printing machinery. Goodrich defended on the basis that the Statute of Frauds required a writing. Thompson argued that the Statute had been satisfied when Goodrich failed to object to a memorandum of the sale that had been sent within four days after the oral agreement had been made. Goodrich alleged that Thompson had not sufficiently addressed the envelope containing the contents of the memorandum, and that consequently, it had never been received by anyone who had reason to know what it concerned. The court sustained these objections and held that the "between merchants" provision had not been satisfied and that accordingly any oral contract between the parties could not be enforced. From a judgment in favor of the defendant, Thompson appealed.

CUDAHY, C. J. . . . A modern exception to the usual writing requirement is the "merchants" exception of the Uniform Commercial Code, § 2-201(2), which provides:

> Between merchants if within a reasonable time a writing in confirmation of the contract and sufficient against the sender is received and the party receiving it has reason to know its contents, it satisfies the [writing requirement] against such party unless written notice of objection to its contents is given within 10 days after it is received.

We must emphasize that the only effect of this exception is to take away from a merchant who receives a writing in confirmation of a contract the Statute of Frauds defense if the merchant does not object. The sender must still persuade the trier of fact that a contract was in fact made orally, to which the written confirmation applies.

In the instant case, James Thomson sent a "writing in confirmation" to Goodrich four days after his meeting with Ingram Meyers, a Goodrich employee and agent. The purchase order contained Thomson Printing's name, address, telephone number and certain information about the machinery purchase. The check James Thomson sent to Goodrich with the purchase order also had on it Thomson Printing's name and address, and the check carried notations that connected the check with the purchase order.

Goodrich argues, however, that Thomson's writing in confirmation cannot qualify for the 2-201(2) exception because it was not received by anyone at Goodrich who had reason to know its contents. Goodrich claims that Thomson erred in not specifically designating on the envelope, check or purchase order that the items were intended for Ingram Meyers or the surplus equipment department. Consequently, Goodrich contends, it was unable to "find a home" for the check and purchase order despite attempts to do so, in accordance with its regular procedures, by sending copies of the documents to several of its various divisions. Ingram Meyers testified that he never learned of the purchase order until weeks later when James Thomson called to arrange for removal of the machines. By then, however, the machines had long been sold to someone else.

We think Goodrich misreads the requirements of 2-201(2). First, the literal requirements of 2-201(2), as they apply here, are that a writing "is received" and that Goodrich "has reason to know its contents." There is no dispute that the purchase order and check were received by Goodrich, and there is at least no specific or express requirement that the "receipt" referred to in 2-201(2) be by any Goodrich agent in particular.

These issues are not resolved by [2-201(2)], but it is probably a reasonable projection that a delivery at either the recipient's principal place of business, a place of business from which negotiations were conducted, or to which the sender may have transmitted previous communications, will be an adequate receipt.

As for the "reason to know its contents" requirement, this element "is best understood to mean that the confirmation was an instrument which should have been anticipated and therefore should have received the attention of appropriate parties. The receipt of a spurious document would not burden the recipient with a risk of losing the [Statute of Frauds] defense. . . . " In the case before us there is no doubt that the confirmatory writings were based on actual negotiations (although the legal effect of the negotiations was disputed), and therefore the documents were not "spurious" but could have been anticipated and appropriately handled.

Even if we go beyond the literal requirements of 2-201(2) and read into the "receipt" requirement the "receipt of notice" rule of 1-201(27), we still think Thomson Printing satisfied the "merchants" exception. Section 1-201, the definitional section of the U.C.C., provides that notice received by an organization

> is effective for a particular transaction . . . from the time when it would have been brought to [the attention of the individual conducting that transaction] if the organization had executed *due diligence*.

The Official Comment states:

> reason to know, knowledge, or a notification, although "received" for instance by a clerk in Department A of an organization, is effective for a transaction conducted in Department B only from the time when it was *or should have been* communicated to the individual conducting that transaction.

Thus, the question comes down to whether Goodrich's mailroom, given the information it had, should have notified the surplus equipment manager, Ingram Meyers, of Thomson's confirmatory writing. At whatever point Meyers should have been so notified, then at that point Thomson's writing was effective even though Meyers did not see it.

The definitional section of the U.C.C. also sets the general standard for what mailrooms "should do":

> An organization exercises due diligence if it maintains reasonable routines for communicating significant information to the person conducting the transaction and there is reasonable compliance with the routines.

One cannot say that Goodrich's mailroom procedures were reasonable as a matter of law: if Goodrich had exercised due diligence in handling Thomson Printing's purchase order and check, these items would have reasonably promptly come to Ingram Meyers' attention. First, the purchase order on its face should have alerted the mailroom that the documents referred to a purchase of used printing equipment. Since Goodrich had only one surplus machinery department, the documents' "home" should not have been difficult to find. Second, even if the mailroom would have had difficulty in immediately identifying the kind of transaction involved, the purchase order had Thomson Printing's phone number printed on it and we think a "reasonable routine" in these particular circumstances would have involved at some point in the process a simple phone call to Thomson Printing. Thus, we think Goodrich's mailroom mishandled the confirmatory writings. This failure should not permit Goodrich to escape liability by pleading nonreceipt.

We note that the jury verdict for Thomson Printing indicates that the jury found as a fact that the contract had in fact been made and that the Statute of Frauds had been satisfied. Also, Goodrich acknowledges those facts about the handling of the purchase order which we regard as determinative of the "merchants" exception question. We think that there is ample evidence to support the jury findings both of the existence of the contract and of the satisfaction of the Statute.

The district court, in holding as a matter of law that the circumstances failed to satisfy the Statute of Frauds, was impressed by James Thomson's dereliction in failing to specifically direct the purchase order and check to the attention of Ingram Meyers or the surplus equipment department. We agree that Thomson erred in this respect, but, for the reasons we have suggested, Goodrich was at least equally derelict in failing to find a "home" for the well-identified documents. Goodrich argues that in the "vast majority" of cases it can identify checks within a week without contacting an outside party; in the instant case, therefore, if Goodrich correctly states its experience under its procedures, it should presumably have checked with Thomson Printing promptly after the time it normally identified checks by other means — in this case, by its own calculation, a week at most. Under the particular circumstances of this case, we therefore think it inappropriate to set aside a jury verdict on Statute of Frauds grounds.

The district court's order granting judgment for Goodrich is reversed and the cause is remanded for further proceedings consistent with this opinion.

[Reversed and remanded]

QUESTIONS

1. What does the UCC provide when a merchant sends to another merchant a signed, written confirmation of their oral contract?
2. Does a signed confirmation have to be actually received at the seller's principal place of business?
3. How did the court decide the contention of Goodrich that the confirmation was not received by anyone who had reason to know its contents?

(c) PURPOSE OF EXECUTION. A writing can satisfy a statute of frauds, although it was not made for that purpose. Accordingly, when the buyer writes a reply to the seller, after a 45-day delay, and merely criticizes the quality of the goods, the letter of the buyer satisfies the statute as it indicates that there was a sale of those goods.

(d) PARTICULAR WRITINGS. Formal contracts, bills of sale, letters, and telegrams are common forms of writings that satisfy the requirement. Purchase orders, cash register receipts, sales tickets, invoices, and similar papers generally do not satisfy the requirement as to a signature, and sometimes they do not specify any quantity or commodity.

Two or more writings may constitute the "writing" that satisfies the statute of frauds.[14]

[14] West Cent. Packing, Inc. v A. F. Murch Co. 109 Mich App 493, 311 NW2d 404 (1981).

§ 27:8 EFFECT OF NONCOMPLIANCE

A sales agreement that does not satisfy the statute of frauds cannot be enforced. However, the oral contract itself is not unlawful and may be voluntarily performed by the parties.[15]

§ 27:9 WHEN PROOF OF ORAL CONTRACT IS PERMITTED

The absence of a writing does not always bar proof of a sales contract.

(a) NONRESELLABLE GOODS. No writing is required when the goods are specially made for the buyer and are of such an unusual nature that they are not suitable for sale in the ordinary course of the seller's business. For example, when fourteen steel doors were tailor-made by the seller for the buyer's building, and were not suitable for sale to anyone else in the ordinary course of the seller's business, and could only be sold as scrap, the oral contract of sale could be enforced.

In order for the nonresellable goods exception to apply, the seller must have made a substantial beginning in manufacturing the goods, or, if a distributor, in procuring them, before notice of repudiation by the buyer is received.

(b) RECEIPT AND ACCEPTANCE. An oral sales contract may be enforced if it can be shown that the goods were delivered by the seller and were received and accepted by the buyer. Thus, if the buyer receives and accepts goods on credit, the seller may sue for the purchase price even though it is over five hundred dollars and there is no writing. The receipt and acceptance of the goods by the buyer took the contract out of the statute of frauds. Both a receipt and an acceptance by the buyer must be shown. If only part of the goods had been received and accepted, the contract may be enforced only insofar as it relates to those goods received and accepted.[16]

(c) PAYMENT. An oral contract may be enforced if the buyer has made full payment. In the case of part payment for divisible units of goods, a contract may be enforced only with respect to the goods for which payment has been made and accepted. If part payment is made for indivisible goods, such as an automobile, a part payment avoids the statute of frauds and permits proof of the entire oral contract.

(d) ADMISSION. An oral contract may be enforced if the party against whom enforcement is sought admits in pleadings, testimony, or otherwise in court that a contract for sale was made. The contract, however, is not enforceable beyond the quantity of goods admitted.[17]

§ 27:10 NON-CODE REQUIREMENTS

In addition to the UCC requirement as to a writing, other statutes may impose requirements. For example, state consumer protection legislation commonly requires the execution of a detailed contract and the giving of a copy thereof to the consumer. The result is that even though the UCC requirements have been satisfied, the buyer may still be able to avoid the transaction for noncompliance with the requirements of other statutes.

§ 27:11 BILL OF SALE

Regardless of the requirement of the statute of frauds, the parties may wish to execute a writing as evidence or proof of the sale. Through custom this writing has become known as a **bill of sale,** but it is neither a bill nor a contract. It is merely a receipt or writing signed by the seller reciting the transfer to the buyer of the title to the described property. The only effect of the bill of sale is to bar the seller from later

---

[15] Duffee v Judson, 251 Pa Super 406, 380 A2d 843 (1977).

[16] Trimble v Todd (Ala) 510 So2d 810 (1987).
[17] Jackson v Meadows, 153 Ga App 1, 264 SE2d 503 (1980).

denying the making of the sale. If the seller did not have title to the goods, the bill of sale does not give the buyer any title.

In some states, provision is made for the public recording of bills of sale when goods are left in the seller's possession. Some states require the production of the bill of sale before the title to any automobile will be registered in the name of the purchaser.

Although the bill of sale states that the full purchase price has been paid, the seller may show that in fact it has not been so paid.

C. UNIFORM LAW FOR INTERNATIONAL SALES

The United Nations Convention on Contracts for the International Sale of Goods (CISG) applies to contracts made after January 1, 1988, between the parties in the United States and parties in the other nations that have ratified the convention.[18] The provisions of this convention or international agreement have been strongly influenced by Article 2 of the Uniform Commercial Code. The international rules of the convention automatically apply to contracts for the sale of goods if the buyer and seller have places of business in different

---

[18] 52 Fed. Reg. 6262 (1987) Argentina, Austria, China, Egypt, Finland, France, Hungary, Italy, Lesotho, Mexico, Sweden, Syria, the United States, Yugoslavia, and Zambia have ratified thus far. Ratification proceedings are under way in other countries.

countries that have ratified the convention. The sales contract, however, may exclude the convention provisions.

§ 27:12   SCOPE OF THE CISG

The CISG does not govern all contracts between parties in the countries that ratified it. The CISG does not apply to goods bought for personal, family, or household use, nor does it apply to contracts in which the preponderant part of the obligations of the party who furnishes the goods consists of the supply of labor or other services. In addition, it does not apply to the liability of the seller to any person for death or personal injury caused by the goods.

The CISG governs the formation of the contract of sale and the rights and obligations of the seller and the buyer arising from such a contract. The CISG provides a basis for answering questions and settling issues the parties failed to deal with in their contracts.

§ 27:13   STATUTE OF FRAUDS

Under the CISG a contract for the sale of goods need not be in any particular form and can be proved by any means. The convention, by this provision, has abolished the statute of frauds requirement of a writing. Countries may, however, retain the UCC requirements of the statute of frauds by requiring certain contracts to be evidenced by a writing.

SUMMARY

A sale of goods, governed by Article 2 of the UCC, is a present transfer of title to movable property for a price. Goods, the subject matter of a sale, include anything movable at the time they are identified as the subject of the transaction. Goods physically existing and owned by the seller at

the time of the transaction are existing goods. Goods that are not existing goods are known as future goods. There can be no present sale of future goods, and any agreement to sell such goods operates as a contract to sell.

A bailment is not a sale because no title

is transferred. A gift is not a sale since there is no price paid for the gift. A contract for services is an ordinary contract and is not governed by the UCC. If a contract calls for both the rendering of services and the supplying of goods, the contract is classified according to its dominant element.

The law of contracts is applicable to a sale of goods. Contract law as to offers is applicable to a sale of goods except for rules concerning an acceptance with new terms. In sales contracts, a contract arises on the terms of the original offer and the new terms are considered counteroffers. If the transaction is between merchants, the additional terms become part of the contract if those terms do not materially alter the offer and no objection is made to them.

The price term may be expressly fixed by the parties or the parties may make no provision as to price or may indicate how the price should be determined later. In output or requirements contracts, the quantity that is to be sold or purchased is not specified, but such contracts are nevertheless valid. Output and requirements contracts are contracts to sell, and the specific quantities are identified at the time of the sale. A seal has no effect on a contract. A contract relating to a sale of goods may be modified even though the modification is not supported by consideration. The parol evidence rule applies to a sale of goods in much the same manner as to ordinary contracts not for sale of goods. There is the slight modification that a writing is not presumed to represent the entire contract of the parties unless the court specifically decides that it does. Most contract defenses may be raised in a suit on a sales contract. An illegal sale or a contract to sell cannot be enforced.

Any merchant who transfers a major part of the merchant's merchandise or inventory not in the ordinary course of business must comply with the bulk transfer provisions of the UCC.

A sales contract for $500 or more must be evidenced by a writing unless the goods are specially made for the buyer and are nonresellable, or the buyer received and accepted the goods, or the buyer has made either full or part payment, or the party against whom enforcement is sought admits in court pleadings or testimony that a contract for sale was made.

Uniform rules for international sales are applicable to contracts made after January 1, 1988, for sales among parties in the contracting states. Under the CISG, a contract for the sale of goods need not be in any particular form and can be proved by any means.

QUESTIONS AND CASE PROBLEMS

1. What social forces are affected by the rule that consideration is not required for a modification of a contract for the sale of goods?
2. On Monday, Nancy sells her sewing machine to Irma. It is agreed that Irma will pay for the sewing machine on the next Friday, payday, and that Nancy will retain title and possession until such payment is made. Is there a sale of the sewing machine on Monday?
3. Ethel wrote to Lasco Dealers inquiring as to the price of a certain freezer. Lasco wrote her a letter signed by its credit manager stating that Ethel could purchase the freezer in question during the next 30 days at the price of $400. Ethel wrote back the next day ordering a freezer at that price. Ethel's letter was received by Lasco the following day, but Lasco wrote an answering letter stating that it had changed the price to $450. Ethel claims that Lasco could not change its price. Is Ethel correct?
4. Emily purchases a refrigerator-freezer from the Elton Appliance Shop for $600. The purchase is made over the phone. Thereafter Elton sends Emily a letter thanking her for the purchase of the refrigerator-freezer. Before the refrigerator-freezer is delivered to Emily, she telephones Elton and cancels the purchase. Elton then sues her for damages. She raises the defense of the statute of frauds. Elton produces a copy of the letter that it sent

to Emily. Does this letter avoid the defense of the statute of frauds?

5. Danfie Company of New York owns leather hides stored in a warehouse in the south of France. Danfie sells some of these hides to the Haldane Company of Chicago. Danfie and Haldane agree that the price shall be determined by Rumfort who lives in the south of France and is recognized in the trade as an expert in leather. Haldane becomes dissatisfied with the contract and claims that it is not binding because it is too indefinite because it does not state the price to be paid for the leather. Is Haldane correct?

6. Raymond International, Inc., was a highway contractor. Blue Rock Industries sold Raymond large quantities of sand for use in the construction of highways. Raymond did not pay for the sand. Was the liability of Raymond governed by the Uniform Commercial Code? [Blue Rock Industries v Raymond International, Inc. (Me) 325 A2d 66]

7. The Tober Foreign Motors, Inc., sold an airplane to Skinner on installments. Later it was agreed that the amount of the monthly installments should be reduced by one half. Thereafter Tober claimed that the reduction agreement was not binding because it was not supported by consideration. Was this claim correct? [Skinner v Tober Foreign Motors, Inc. 345 Mass 429, 187 NE2d 669]

8. The LTV Aerospace Corporation manufactured all-terrain vehicles for use in Southeast Asia. LTV made an oral contract with Bateman under which he would supply the packing cases needed for their overseas shipment. Bateman made substantial beginnings in the production of packing cases following LTV's specifications. LTV thereafter stopped production of its vehicles and refused to take delivery of any cases. When sued by Bateman for breach of contract, LTV raised the defense that the contract could not be enforced because there was no writing that satisfied the statute of frauds. Was this a valid defense? [LTV Aerospace Corp. v Bateman (Tex Civ App) 492 SW2d 703]

9. Suburban Gas Heat of Kennewick sold propane gas for domestic consumption. As the result of its negligence in supplying propane gas mixed with water, there was an explosion that caused damage to Kasey. When Kasey sued to enforce the liability of Suburban Gas Heat as a seller, Suburban raised the defense that it was engaged in furnishing a public service and not in the sale of goods. Was Suburban correct? [Kasey v Suburban Gas Heat of Kennewick, Inc. 60 Wash 2d 468, 374 P2d 549]

10. Members of the Colonial Club purchased beer from outside the state and ordered it sent to the Colonial Club. The club then kept it in the club refrigerator and served the beer to its respective owners upon demand. The club received no compensation or profit from the transaction. The club was indicted for selling liquor. Was it guilty? [North Carolina v Colonial Club, 154 NC 177, 69 SE 771]

11. A merchant made an oral contract to sell $1,000 worth of goods to another merchant. The buyer broke the contract, and the seller sued for breach of contract. The buyer raised the defense that suit could not be brought on the oral contract because there was no writing satisfying UCC § 2-201. The seller offered evidence showing that it was customary for merchants in the trade to deal on the basis of oral contracts. Was the seller entitled to recover on the oral contract?

12. A college senior furnished a carpenter a unique design for a bookshelf to be built in her dorm. The carpenter orally agreed to follow the design and build the bookshelf for a total price of $1,000. When the carpenter started the work, the senior informed him that she no longer wished the bookshelf. What are the rights of the carpenter, if any, against the college senior?

13. Lukas ordered goods from the Farbar Tool and Die Corp. The goods were received and accepted by Lukas, but at no time was anything agreed as to the price for the goods. Was there a binding sales contract?

14. Lawrence Fashions, a retail dress merchant, placed a telephone order with Bentley Company for twenty dozen dresses for $5,000. The next week Lawrence Fashions received, inspected, and accepted ten dozen dresses. Lawrence Fashions refused to accept the balance when tendered and sought to return the other ten dozen dresses claiming it was not obligated. Decide.

15. Compare a sale, bailment, and a gift.

28

RISK AND PROPERTY RIGHTS

In most sales, the buyer receives the proper goods, makes payment, and the transaction is thus completed. However, problems may arise. If the parties can foresee potential problems, they can state in their contract what results they desire if such problems do, in fact, occur. If the parties do not provide in their contract for potential problems, the rules in this chapter apply.

A. TYPES OF TRANSACTIONS AND POTENTIAL PROBLEMS

The solutions to problems of risk and property rights vary with the kind and terms of the transaction between the seller and the buyer.

§ 28:1 TYPES OF PROBLEMS

Problems involving risk and property rights in sales transactions will often relate to damage to the goods, the claims of creditors of the parties to the sales contract, or the obtaining of insurance by those parties.

(a) DAMAGE TO GOODS. If the goods are damaged or totally destroyed without any fault of either the buyer or the seller, must the seller bear the loss and supply new goods to the buyer? Or is it the buyer's loss, so that the buyer must pay the seller the purchase price even though the goods are damaged or destroyed?[1] The fact that there may be insurance does not avoid this question, for the answer to it determines whose insurer is liable and the extent of that insurer's liability.

(b) CREDITORS' CLAIMS. Creditors of a delinquent seller may seize the goods as belonging to the seller. The buyer's creditors may seize them on the theory that they belong to the buyer. In such cases the question arises whether the creditors are correct as to who owns the goods. The question of ownership is also important in connection with the consequence of a resale by the buyer, or the liability for or the computation of certain kinds of taxes, and the liability under certain registration and criminal law statutes.[2]

(c) INSURANCE. Until the buyer has received the goods and the seller has been paid, both the seller and buyer have an economic interest in the sales transaction.[3] The question arises as to whether either or both have enough interest to entitle them to insure the property involved; that is, whether they have an insurable interest.[4]

§ 28:2   NATURE OF THE
            TRANSACTION

The answer to be given to each of the questions noted in the preceding section depends upon the nature of the transaction between the seller and the buyer. Sales transactions may be classified according to the nature of the goods and the terms of the transaction.

(a) EXISTING AND IDENTIFIED GOODS. Existing goods are (1) physically in existence and (2) owned by the seller. When particular goods have been selected by either the buyer or the seller, or both of them, as being the goods called for by the sales contract, the goods are called identified goods. Thus, when you go into a store, point at a particular item, and tell the clerk, "I'll take that one," the sales transaction relates to existing and identified goods.

(b) FUTURE AND UNIDENTIFIED GOODS. Goods are future goods when they are not yet owned by the seller, or when they are not yet in existence. Before goods have been identified to the contract, they are unidentified. Consequently, when you tell the clerk in the store you want one of the items advertised in the paper, the transaction relates to unidentified goods. Your reference to the newspaper ad described the thing you wanted, but it did not identify any particular item as the one the seller was to deliver. Future goods are involved if a store tells you that they are out of the advertised item but can order it from the factory or that the factory is going to make a new run of the item that will arrive next month.

(c) TERMS OF THE TRANSACTION. Ordinarily, the seller is only required to make the goods available to the buyer. If transportation is provided, the seller is normally only required to make shipment, and the seller's part of the contract is performed by handing the goods over to a carrier for shipment to the buyer. The terms of the contract, however, may obligate the seller to deliver the goods at a particular place, for example, to make delivery at the buyer's warehouse. The seller's part of the contract is then not completed until the goods are brought to the destination point and there tendered to the buyer. If the transaction calls for sending the goods to the buyer, it is ordinarily required that the seller deliver the goods to a carrier under a proper contract for shipment to the buyer. Actual physical delivery at destination is only required when the contract expressly so states.

Instead of calling for the actual delivery of goods, the sales transaction may relate to a transfer of the document of title representing the goods. For example, the goods

---

[1]   The subject is regulated by UCC § 2-509.
[2]   UCC § 2-401.
[3]   See UCC § 2-501(1)(a).
[4]   In order to insure property, a person must have such a right or interest in the property that its damage or destruction would cause financial loss. This is called an insurable interest in the property. The ownership of goods that are the subject of a sales transaction is determined by the UCC for the purpose of insurance.

may be stored in a warehouse, and the seller and the buyer have no intention of moving the goods, but intend that there shall be a sale and a delivery of the warehouse receipt that stands for the goods. Here the obligation of the seller is to produce the proper paper as distinguished from the goods themselves. The same is true when the goods are represented by any other document of title, such as a bill of lading issued by a carrier.

§ 28:3   EXISTING GOODS IDENTIFIED AT TIME OF CONTRACTING

In a transaction relating to existing and identified goods, where there is no document of title, such as a warehouse receipt or a bill of lading, the title to the goods passes to the buyer at the time the parties agree to the transaction. They may, however, state in the contract that the title shall not pass to the buyer until the full purchase price has been paid.

When the buyer becomes the owner of the goods in the situation here considered, the buyer has an insurable interest in them. The seller has an insurable interest in the goods before title passes to the buyer. The insurable interest of the seller terminates when title passes to the buyer unless the seller has reserved a security interest to protect any balance due.

As to risk of loss, a distinction must be made between a merchant seller and a nonmerchant seller. If the seller is a merchant, the risk of loss passes to the buyer on receiving the goods from the merchant. If the seller is a nonmerchant, the risk of loss passes when the seller makes the goods available to the buyer. The risk thus remains longer on the merchant seller. Receiving the goods from a merchant means that the buyer takes actual physical possession of the goods.[5]

When the buyer leaves the purchased goods with the seller, who bears the risk of loss if the goods are destroyed? In the *Schock* case, the buyer claimed that the seller bore the risk of loss.

---

[5]   Spikes v Baier, 6 Kan App 2d 45, 626 P2d 816 (1981).

SCHOCK V RONDEROS

(ND) 394 NW2d 697 (1986)

Schock negotiated to purchase a mobile home that was owned by and located on the sellers' property. On April 15, buyer appeared at sellers' home and paid to them the agreed-upon purchase price of $3,900. Schock received a bill of sale and an assurance from sellers that title to the mobile home would be delivered soon. On that date, with the permission of sellers, Schock prepared the mobile home for removal. His preparations included the removal of skirting around the mobile home's foundation, removal of the tie-downs and removal of the foundation blocks causing the mobile home to rest on the wheels of its chassis. Schock intended to remove the mobile home from the sellers' property a week later, and sellers had no objection to having the mobile home remain on their premises until that time. Sellers also promised to have the electricity and natural gas disconnected by that time. Two days later, the mobile home was destroyed by high winds as it sat on sellers' property. Schock received in the mail a clear certificate of title to the mobile home. Thereafter, Schock sued the sellers for return of his money on the ground that when the mobile home was destroyed, the risk of loss was on the sellers. From a judgment in favor of the sellers, buyer appealed.

ERICKSTAD, J. . . . The issue of which party in this case must bear the loss of the mobile home is determined by the risk of loss provisions under Section 41-02-57, N.D.C.C., which provide in relevant part:

> 3. In any case not within subsection 1 or 2, the risk of loss passes to the buyer on his receipt of the goods if the seller is a merchant; otherwise the risk passes to the buyer on tender of delivery.

It is undisputed that the Sellers are not merchants; therefore, the risk of loss was on them until they made a "tender of delivery" of the mobile home at which time the risk of loss passed to Buyer. The location or status of the title is not a relevant consideration in determining which party must bear the loss of the mobile home. *Martin v Melland's Inc.*, 283 N.W.2d 76 (N.D.1979).

Pursuant to Section 41-02-51, N.D.C.C., tender of delivery requires that the seller "put and hold conforming goods at the buyer's disposition. . . ." The trial court determined that there had been payment for and acceptance of the mobile home by Buyer. Within that conclusion is an implicit determination that there was a completed tender of delivery by Sellers.

The Sellers disconnected the electricity and natural gas to the mobile home prior to its destruction, and nothing remained for them to do as a prerequisite to Buyer's taking possession of the home. . . . The Sellers testified that following Buyer's payment for the home on April 15, 1985, Buyer could have removed the home from their premises at any time. . . . The Sellers, consistent with a completed tender of delivery, acquiesced in Buyer's decision to prepare, on April 15, 1985, the mobile home for removal. As part of those preparations Buyer removed the skirting, the tie downs, and the blocks. He also removed and took with him a set of steps to the mobile home. We believe those actions by Buyer constituted an exercise of possession which is consistent with our conclusion that Sellers had tendered delivery of the mobile home to him on that date. Thus, we hold that on April 15, 1985, the Sellers tendered delivery of the mobile home and the risk of loss passed to Buyer. Accordingly, we further hold that the trial court did not err in denying Buyer's claim for return of the $3,900 purchase money. . . .

[Judgment affirmed]

QUESTIONS

1. Did the title certificate have any bearing on who had risk of loss?
2. Was there a tender of delivery of the mobile home?
3. Would the result have been different if the sellers were merchants?

§ 28:4 GOODS REPRESENTED BY NEGOTIABLE DOCUMENT OF TITLE

Merchants dealing in large quantities of goods will often prefer to deal with negotiable documents of title to the goods instead of making a physical delivery of the goods. In such a transaction, the buyer acquires an insurable interest in the goods at the time and place of contracting but, unless otherwise provided in the contract, does not become subject to the risk of loss nor acquire the title until delivery of the document is made.[6]

§ 28:5 FUTURE AND UNIDENTIFIED GOODS

If the goods are either future goods or have not been identified by the time the transaction is agreed to, the rules stated in § 28:3 and § 28:4 do not apply. Instead, the following rules govern the transaction if the parties do not state otherwise.

(a) MARKING FOR BUYER. If the buyer sends an order for goods to be manufactured by the seller or to be filled from inventory or by purchases from third persons, one step in the process of filling the order is the seller's act of marking, tagging, labeling, or in some way doing an act for the benefit of the shipping department to indicate that certain goods are the ones to be sent or delivered to the buyer under the order. This act of unilateral identification of the goods is enough to give the buyer a property interest in the goods, which entitles the buyer to insure them. Neither risk of loss nor title passes to the buyer at that time, however. Risk of loss and title remain with the seller, who, as the continuing owner, also has an insurable interest in the goods. Thus, neither title nor risk of loss passes to the buyer until some later event, such as a shipment or delivery, occurs.

(b) CONTRACT FOR SHIPMENT TO BUYER. In a contract for shipment to a buyer, the buyer has placed an order for future goods, and the contract is performed by the seller by delivering the goods to a carrier for shipment to the buyer. Under such a contract, the risk of loss and the title pass to the buyer when the goods are delivered to the carrier, that is, at the time and place of shipment. After the goods are delivered to the carrier, the seller has no insurable interest unless the seller has reserved a security interest in the goods.

The fact that a shipment of goods is represented by a bill of lading or an airbill issued by the carrier, and that in order to complete the transaction it will be necessary to transfer that bill to the buyer, does not affect these rules or bring the transaction within § 28:4.

(c) CONTRACT FOR DELIVERY AT DESTINATION. When the contract requires the seller to make delivery of future goods at a particular destination point, the buyer acquires a property right and an insurable interest in the goods at the time and place they are marked or shipped. However, the risk of loss and the title do not pass until the carrier tenders or makes the goods available at the destination point. The seller retains an insurable interest until that time.

A provision in the contract directing the seller to "ship to" the buyer does not convert the contract into a contract calling for delivery at destination.

§ 28:6 DAMAGE TO OR DESTRUCTION OF GOODS

In the absence of a contrary agreement, damage to or destruction of the goods affects the transaction as follows:

(a) DAMAGE TO IDENTIFIED GOODS BEFORE RISK OF LOSS PASSES. When goods that were identified at the time the contract was made are damaged or destroyed without the fault of either party before the risk of loss has passed, the contract is avoided if the loss is total. If the loss is partial or if the goods have so deteriorated that they do not conform to the contract, the buyer has the option, after inspection of the goods, to (1) avoid the contract or (2) accept the goods subject to an allowance or deduction from the contract price. In either case, the buyer cannot assert any claim against the seller for breach of contract.[7]

(b) DAMAGE TO IDENTIFIED GOODS AFTER RISK OF LOSS PASSES. If partial damage or total destruction occurs after the risk of loss has passed to the buyer, it is the buyer's

---

[6] Express provision is made for the case of a nonnegotiable document and other factual variations. UCC § 2-509(2)(c), § 2-503(4).

[7] UCC § 2-613. Carlson v Nelson, 204 Neb 765, 285 NW2d 505 (1979).

NATURE OF GOODS	TERMS OF TRANSACTION	TRANSFER OF RISK OF LOSS TO BUYER	TRANSFER OF TITLE TO BUYER	ACQUISITION OF INSURABLE INTEREST BY BUYER *
EXISTING GOODS IDENTIFIED AT TIME OF CONTRACTING	1. WITHOUT DOCUMENT OF TITLE	BUYER'S RECEIPT OF GOODS FROM MERCHANT SELLER, TENDER OF DELIVERY BY NONMERCHANT SELLER § 2-509(3)	TIME AND PLACE OF CONTRACTING § 2-401(3)(b)	TIME AND PLACE OF CONTRACTING § 2-501(1)(a)
	2. DELIVERY OF DOCUMENT OF TITLE ONLY	BUYER'S RECEIPT OF NEGOTIABLE DOCUMENT OF TITLE § 2-509(2)(a)	TIME AND PLACE OF DELIVERY OF DOCUMENTS BY SELLER § 2-401(3)(a)	TIME AND PLACE OF CONTRACTING § 2-501(1)(a)
FUTURE GOODS	3. MARKING FOR BUYER	NO TRANSFER UNTIL A LATER EVENT	NO TRANSFER UNTIL A LATER EVENT	AT TIME OF MARKING § 2-501(1)(b)
	4. CONTRACT FOR SHIPMENT TO BUYER	DELIVERY OF GOODS TO CARRIER § 2-509(1)(a)	DELIVERY OF GOODS TO CARRIER § 2-401(2)(a)	DELIVERY TO CARRIER OR MARKING FOR BUYER § 2-501(1)(b)
	5. CONTRACT FOR DELIVERY AT DESTINATION	TENDER OF GOODS AT DESTINATION § 2-509(1)(b)	TENDER OF GOODS AT DESTINATION § 2-401(2)(b)	DELIVERY TO CARRIER OR MARKING FOR BUYER § 2-501(1)(b)

* THE SELLER RETAINS AN INSURABLE INTEREST IN THE GOODS AS LONG AS THE SELLER HAS A SECURITY INTEREST IN THEM. WHEN THE BUYER ACQUIRES AN INSURABLE INTEREST, THE BUYER ALSO ACQUIRES A SPECIAL PROPERTY IN THE GOODS, LESS THAN TITLE, WHICH ENTITLES THE BUYER TO ASSERT CERTAIN REMEDIES AGAINST THE SELLER.

FIGURE 28-1
RISK AND PROPERTY RIGHTS IN SALES CONTRACTS

loss. The buyer may be able to recover the amount of the damages from the person in possession of the goods or from a third person causing the loss.

(c) DAMAGE TO UNIDENTIFIED GOODS As long as the goods are unidentified, no risk of loss passes to the buyer. If any goods are damaged or destroyed during this period, the loss is the seller's. The buyer is still entitled to receive the goods described by the contract. The seller is therefore liable for breach of contract if the proper goods are not delivered.

The only exception arises when the parties have expressly provided in the contract that the destruction of the seller's supply shall release the seller from liability or when it is clear that the parties contracted for the purchase and sale of part of the seller's supply to the exclusion of any other possible source of such goods. In such case, the destruction of or damage to the seller's supply is a condition subsequent that discharges the contract.

(d) RESERVATION OF TITLE OR POSSESSION. When the seller reserves title or possession solely as security to make certain that the buyer will pay the purchase price, the risk of loss is borne by the buyer if the circumstances are such that the loss would be on the buyer in the absence of such a reservation.

§ 28:7   EFFECT OF SELLER'S BREACH

When the seller breaches the contract by sending the buyer goods that do not conform to the contract and the buyer rejects the goods, the risk of loss does not pass to the buyer.[8] This means that the risk of loss remains on the seller even though the risk would ordinarily have passed to the buyer. If, because of the nature of the transaction, the risk of loss had already passed to the buyer before there was the opportunity to inspect the goods, the buyer's rejection of the goods returns the risk of loss to the seller.

In the *Graybar* case, the seller claimed that the buyer should bear the loss of rejected goods when the loss occurred before the seller took the goods back.

[8]   United Air Lines, Inc. v Conductron, Corp. 69 Ill App 3d 847, 26 Ill Dec 344, 387 NE2d 1272 (1979).

GRAYBAR ELECTRIC CO. V SHOOK

283 NC 213, 195 SE2d 514 (1973)

> Harold Shook ordered three reels of burial cable from Graybar Company for use in construction work. By mistake, two of the three reels that were sent were aerial cable, although each carton was marked "burial cable." Shook accepted the one reel of proper cable and rejected the two nonconforming reels. Because of their size they were left on the ground at the construction site and Graybar was notified of the rejection. Graybar did not collect the cable. Shook attempted to return the cable but could not do so because there was a strike of truck drivers. About four months later the two reels of cable were stolen by unidentified persons. Graybar sued Shook for the purchase price. Graybar claimed that after the rejection was made by Shook, it had been agreed that Shook would return the nonconforming reels to Graybar. From a judgment for Shook, Graybar appealed.

HIGGINS, J. . . . The parties admitted the following: (1) The defendant placed an order with the plaintiff for three reels of burial (underground) cable to be delivered at Six Run Grocery Store, a rural community sixteen miles south of Clinton. (2) On April 6 the plaintiff delivered one reel of burial cable and, by mistake, delivered two reels of aerial cable. The aerial cable was totally unsuited to the defendant's use. Defendant notified the plaintiff of the mistake and received a request that the nonconforming reels be returned. Here the parties disagree. The plaintiff contends the defendant contracted to make the return. The defendant contends he agreed to contact a trucking company and request that it pick up and return the nonconforming reels. The defendant's request was turned down by three different trucking concerns on account of a strike in the trucking industry.

As the defendant's underground cable work progressed beyond the Six Run Grocery Store, the defendant left the nonconforming cable at the store and so notified the plaintiff. The evidence discloses that the cable was stored directly beside the grocery store building near the owner's dwelling in a space which the defendant rented for storage purposes. "The area where the cable was stored was well lighted at all times."

On July 20, 1970, the defendant discovered that one of the reels had been stolen and the following day notified the plaintiff. On that day, also, the defendant contacted a garage operator who promised to pick up the remaining reel and store it in his garage some distance from Six Run. However, before the transfer, the second reel was stolen. The defendant so notified the plaintiff.

The court, upon the disputed facts, found the defendant had not entered into a contract to return the nonconforming cable. A finding supported by evidence "must be accepted as final truth upon the appeal to the Supreme Court." . . . When findings of fact sufficient to determine the entire controversy are made by the court, failure to find other facts is not error. . . . The plaintiff's claim, therefore, that it was prejudiced by the court's failure to make requested findings is not error. The court's actual finding determined the entire controversy.

The plaintiff, having made the error of delivering the nonconforming goods on a moving job in the country, was entitled to notice of the nonconformity sufficient to enable it to repossess the nonconforming goods. The plaintiff was given prompt notice but delayed action for more than three months. The cable was stolen from the defendant's regular storage space where the plaintiff had delivered it. Evidence is lacking that a safer storage space was available. The defendant's workmen moved on, leaving the cable and the responsibility for its safety on the owner.

The plaintiff, failing in its efforts to establish a contract on the part of the defendant to return the shipment, however, contends in the alternative that [UCC §] 2-602(2)(b) . . . required the defendant to exercise reasonable care in holding the rejected goods pending the plaintiff's repossession and removal and that the defendant failed to exercise the required care in storage.

Actually, the plaintiff made an on the spot delivery at a store and dwelling in the country. The defendant's work force was stringing underground cable along the highway and the crew was in continual movement. Obviously the crew could not be expected to carry with it two thousand pounds of useless cable and was within its rights placing the cable in its regular storage space and notifying the plaintiff of the place of storage. Both parties realized that cable weighing almost a ton would require men and a truck to remove it. Also both parties assumed that the danger of theft from a well lighted store area was a minimal risk. The property itself was a poor candidate for larceny. The cable was permitted to remain where the plaintiff knew it was located for more than three months. The plaintiff, therefore, had ample opportunity to repossess its property.

The Uniform Commercial Code emphasizes promptness and good faith. The prospective purchaser may exercise a valid right to reject and even if he takes possession, responsibility expires after a reasonable time in which the owner has opportunity to repossess. "Where a tender or delivery of goods so fails to conform to the contract as to give a right of rejection the risk of their loss remains on the seller until cure or acceptance." [UCC §] 2-510(1). The defendant did not accept the aerial cable. According to the evidence and the court's findings, the defendant acted in accordance with the request of the owner in attempting to facilitate the return of that which the defendant rejected. The plaintiff with full notice of the place of storage which was at the place of delivery did nothing but sleep on its rights for more than three months.

The superior court was fully justified in the findings of fact, conclusions of law, and in the judgment dismissing the action. The judgment of the Court of Appeals affirming the superior court was correct. . . .

[Judgment affirmed]

QUESTIONS

1. What was the theory of the plaintiff seller?
2. Did the court agree with the seller's theory? Explain.
3. What decision would the court have made if the cable had been stolen within twenty-four hours after the seller was notified of the buyer's rejection?

§ 28:8   RETURNABLE GOODS TRANSACTIONS

The parties may agree for the return of conforming goods to the seller. This may be (a) a sale on approval, (b) a sale or return, or (c) a consignment sale. In the first two types of transactions, the buyer is allowed to return the goods as an added inducement to purchase. The consignment sale is used when the buyer is actually the seller's agent.

Classifying the transaction is the first step in determining the relevant rights of the parties when the buyer may return the goods to the seller. A consignment sale is easily recognized because of its agency characteristics. The agreement of the parties may expressly state that the transaction is a sale on approval or a sale or return. If the agreement of the parties is not clear on this point, and the transaction is not an agency or consignment, classification of the transaction is controlled by the use the buyer will make of the goods. It is a **sale on approval** if the goods are purchased for use, that is, by a consumer. It is a **sale or return** if purchased for resale, that is, by a merchant.[9]

If the transaction does not give the buyer the right to return the goods, the buyer cannot return goods that conform to the contract if the seller refuses to take them back.

(a) SALE ON APPROVAL. In a sale on approval, no sale takes place, meaning there is no transfer of title, until the buyer approves. Title and risk of loss remain with the seller until there is an approval. As the buyer is not the "owner" of the goods before approval, the buyer's creditors cannot reach the goods.

Approval of the buyer may be shown by (1) express words, (2) conduct, or (3) the lapse of time. Use of the goods that is merely a trying out or testing does not constitute approval. Any use that goes beyond trying out or testing, such as repairing or giving away as a present, is inconsistent with the continued ownership of the seller and therefore shows approval by the buyer. The contract may give the buyer a fixed number of days for approval. The expiration of that period of time without any action by the buyer constitutes an approval. If no time is stated in the contract, the lapse of a reasonable time without action by the buyer constitutes an approval. If the buyer gives the seller notice of disapproval, the lapse of time thereafter has no effect.

If the goods are returned by the buyer, the seller bears the risk and expense of the return.[10]

(b) SALE OR RETURN. A sale or return is a completed sale with an option for the buyer to return the goods and thereby sell or transfer back to the seller the title that had already passed to the buyer. As to the original sale, title and risk of loss pass to the buyer as in the case of the ordinary or absolute sale. Until the actual return of the goods is made, the title and risk of loss remain with the buyer. The expense and risk of return is on the buyer.

As long as the goods remain in the buyer's possession, the buyer's creditors may treat the goods as belonging to the buyer. The buyer under a sale or return may return all of the goods or any commercial unit thereof. A **commercial unit** is any article, group of articles, or quantity that commercially is regarded as a separate unit or item, such as a particular machine, a suite of furniture, or a carload lot. In order to exercise the right to return the goods, they must be substantially in their original condition, and the option to return must be exercised within the time specified by the contract or within a reasonable time if none is specified.

(c) CONSIGNMENT SALE. By a consignment or sale on consignment, the owner of goods sends them to a dealer to sell. As

---

[9]   UCC § 2-326(1). An "or return" provision is treated as a sales contract for the purpose of applying the statute of frauds, and cannot be established by parol evidence when it would contradict a sales contract indicating an absolute sale. § 2-326(4).

[10]   UCC § 2-327(1).

between the owner and the dealer, there is no transfer of title. The relationship is merely an agency relationship. A consignee is of course required to return any goods not sold, but this does not make it either a sale on approval or a sale or return. When a sale is made by the consignee to a third person, the title of the consignor passes from the consignor directly to the third person.

At no time is the consignee the owner of the goods. In some instances, however, the creditors of the consignee may treat the goods held by the consignee on consignment as though they belonged to the consignee, thereby ignoring and destroying the consignor's ownership.[11]

§ 28:9   RESERVATION OF A SECURITY INTEREST

The seller may fear that the buyer will not pay for the goods. The seller could protect against this danger by insisting that the buyer pay cash immediately. This may not be practical for geographic or business reasons. The seller may then give credit to the buyer but can obtain protection by retaining a security interest in the goods. When goods are shipped to the buyer, the creditor may create a temporary security interest so that the buyer must make payment before obtaining the goods from the carrier. Between merchants this will be done by various ways of handling the bill of lading issued by the carrier. In the case of a consumer buyer, it is customary for the seller to make the shipment C.O.D. In a C.O.D. shipment, the consumer must pay for the goods before taking possession from the carrier. Under the bill of lading or the C.O.D. shipment, the security interest of the seller ends when the goods are delivered to the buyer. If a seller desires a security interest that will continue as long as the purchase price remains unpaid, a secured

transaction under Article 9 of the Uniform Commercial Code will be created.

The fact that a seller has a security interest in the goods, by virtue of a C.O.D. provision or any other device, has no effect on the question of whether title or risk of loss has passed to the buyer. These questions are answered just as though there were no security interest. For example, under a shipment contract of future goods from a distant seller, the risk of loss and the title pass to the buyer on delivery to the carrier. The result is the same even though such shipment is made C.O.D.

§ 28:10   EFFECT OF SALE ON TITLE

As a general rule, a seller can only sell what the seller owns. If a person in possession of goods is not the owner, as in the case of a finder, thief, or a bailee, a sale by such possessor passes only possession. It is immaterial that the buyer from the possessor had purchased in good faith and had given value. The attempted sale does not pass any title. Consequently, the buyer of stolen goods must surrender them to the true owner and can be sued by the true owner for damages for conversion of the goods. The fact that the negligence of the owner made the theft possible or contributed to the losing of the goods does not bar the owner from recovering the goods or money damages from the thief, the finder, or the purchaser from either of them.[12]

There are instances, however, when either because of the conduct of the owner or the desire of society to protect the bona fide purchaser for value, the law permits a greater title to be transferred than the seller possessed.

(a) CONSIGNMENT SALE. A manufacturer or distributor may send goods to a dealer for sale to the public with the understanding that the manufacturer or distributor is to remain the owner, and the dealer in effect is to act as selling agent. When the

[11]   Escrow Connection v Haas __ Cal App 3d __, 235 Cal Rptr 200 (1987).

[12]   Pate v Elliott, 61 Ohio App 2d 144, 400 NE2d 910 (1978) (theft).

dealer maintains a place of business at which the dealer sells goods of the kind in question under a name other than that of the consigning manufacturer or distributor, the creditors of the dealer may reach the goods as though they were owned by the dealer. Such goods are deemed to be on sale or return with title and risk of loss passing to the dealer as in the case of an ordinary sale or return. The consignor can avoid this result by complying with an applicable law providing for the consignor's interest to be evidenced by a sign, or showing that the person conducting the business is generally known by the creditors to be substantially engaged in selling goods of others, or complying with the filing provisions of Article 9.[13]

(b) ESTOPPEL. The owner of property may be estopped from asserting ownership and thus be barred from denying the right of another person to sell the property. A person may purchase something and have the bill of sale made out in the name of a friend to whom possession of the property and the bill of sale are given. This might be done in order to deceive creditors of the true owner or to keep other persons from knowing that the purchase was made. If the friend should sell the property to a bona fide purchaser who relied on the bill of sale as showing that the friend was the owner, the true owner is estopped or barred from denying the friend's apparent ownership and right to sell.

(c) POWERS. In certain circumstances, persons in possession of someone else's property may sell the property. This is true in the case of pledgees, lienholders, and some finders who, by statute, may have authority to sell the property to enforce their claim or when the owner cannot be found.

(d) NEGOTIABLE DOCUMENTS OF TITLE. By statute, certain documents of title, such as bills of lading and warehouse receipts, have been clothed with a degree of negotiability when executed in proper form. By

virtue of such provisions, the holder of a negotiable document of title may transfer to a good faith purchaser for value such title as was possessed by the person leaving the property with the issuer of the document. In such cases, it is immaterial that the holder had not acquired the document in a lawful manner.

(e) VOIDABLE TITLE. If the buyer has a voidable title, as when the goods were obtained by fraud, the seller can rescind the sale while the buyer is still the owner. If, however, the buyer resells the property to a bona fide purchaser before the seller has rescinded the transaction, the subsequent purchaser acquires valid title. It is immaterial whether the buyer having the voidable title had obtained title by fraud as to identity or by larceny by trick, or had paid for the goods with a bad check, or that the transaction was a cash sale and the purchase price had not been paid.[14]

If the transferee from the holder of the voidable title is not a good faith purchaser, the title remains voidable, and the true owner may reclaim the goods.[15]

(f) SALE BY ENTRUSTEE. If the owner entrusts goods to a merchant who deals in goods of that kind, the latter has the power to transfer the entruster's title to anyone who buys from the entrustee in the ordinary course of business.

It is immaterial why the goods were entrusted to the merchant. Hence the leaving of a watch for repair with a jeweler who sells new and secondhand watches gives the jeweler the power to pass the title of the repair customer to a buyer in the ordinary course of business. Goods in inventory thus have a degree of "negotiability" so that the ordinary buyer, whether a consumer or another merchant, buys the goods free of the ownership interest of the person entrusting the goods to the seller.[16]

---

[13]   UCC § 2-326(3).

[14]   Ledbetter v Darwin Dobbs Co., Inc. (Ala) 473 SW2d 197 (1985).
[15]   Kimberly & European Diamonds, Inc. (CA6 Ky) 684 F2d 363 (1982).
[16]   UCC § 2-403(1). Executive Financial Services, Inc. v Pagel, ___ Kan ___, 715 P2d 381 (1986).

The entrustee is, of course, liable to the owner for damages caused by the entrustee's sale of the goods and is guilty of some form of statutory offense of embezzlement.

If the entrustee is not a merchant, such as a prospective customer trying out an automobile, there is no transfer of title to the buyer from the entrustee. Likewise, there is no transfer of title when a mere bailee, such as a repairer, who is not a seller of goods of that kind, sells the property of a customer.

If a third person has a claim to the goods that is superior to the entruster, a sale by the entrustee does not destroy that claim but passes the title of the entruster subject to such claim.[17]

The *Porter* case involved a sale by an entrustee and the defense of equitable estoppel.

[17] Commercial Credit Equipment Corp. v Bates, 154 Ga App 71, 267 SE2d 469 (1980).

PORTER V WERTZ
53 NYS2d 696, 421 NE2d 500 (1981)

Samuel Porter, an art collector, owned a valuable Utrillo painting. Porter entrusted the painting to Von Maker, an art merchant. Von Maker, in turn, delivered the painting to Wertz (a delicatessen employee with whom Von Maker was acquainted) and asked Wertz to try to find a buyer for the painting. Wertz approached the Feigen Gallery, which purchased the Utrillo painting. Porter brought actions for conversion against Wertz, Von Maker, and Feigen. Feigen raised two defenses: (1) entrustment under UCC § 2-403 and (2) equitable estoppel. From a judgment in favor of Porter, defendants appealed.

PER CURIAM . . . While the Utrillo painting was entrusted to Harold Von Maker, an art merchant, the Feigen Gallery purchased the painting not from Von Maker, but from one Peter Wertz, who turns out to have been a delicatessen employee acquainted with Von Maker. It seems that Von Maker frequented the delicatessen where Peter Wertz was employed and that at some point Von Maker began to identify himself as Peter Wertz in certain art transactions. Indeed, Von Maker identified himself as Peter Wertz in his dealings with Porter.

Defendants argued that Feigen reasonably assumed that the Peter Wertz who offered the Utrillo to him was an art merchant because Feigen had been informed by Henry Sloan that an art dealer named Peter Wertz desired to sell a Utrillo painting. Feigen therefore argues that for purposes of subdivision (2) of section 2-403 of the Uniform Commercial Code it is as though he purchased from a merchant in the ordinary course of business. Alternatively, he claims that he actually purchased the Utrillo from Von Maker, the art dealer to whom it had been entrusted, because Peter Wertz sold the painting on Von Maker's behalf. Neither argument has merit.

Even if Peter Wertz were acting on Von Maker's behalf, unless he disclosed this fact to Feigen, it could hardly be said that Feigen relied upon Von Maker's status as an art merchant. It does not appear that the actual Peter Wertz ever represented that he was acting on behalf of Von Maker in selling the painting.

As to the argument that Feigen reasonably assumed that Peter Wertz was an art merchant, it is apparent from the opinion of the Appellate Division that the court rejected the fact finding essential to this argument, namely, that Peter Wertz had been introduced to Feigen by Henry Sloan as an art merchant. The court noted that in his examination before trial Richard Feigen had testified that he could not recall whether Henry Sloan had described Peter Wertz as an art dealer and concluded that this substantially weakened the probative force of Feigen's trial testimony on this point. Indeed, Peter Wertz testified that Von Maker had not directed him to the Feigen Gallery but had simply delivered the painting to Wertz and asked him to try to find a buyer for the Utrillo. Wertz had been to several art galleries before he approached the Feigen Gallery. Thus, the Appellate Division's finding has support in the record.

Because Peter Wertz was not an art dealer and the Appellate Division has found that Feigen was not duped by Von Maker into believing that Peter Wertz was such a dealer, subdivision (2) of section 2-403 of the Uniform Commercial Code is inapplicable for three distinct reasons: (1) even if Peter Wertz were an art merchant rather than a delicatessen employee, he is not the same merchant to whom Porter entrusted the Utrillo painting; (2) Wertz was not an art merchant; and (3) the sale was not in the ordinary course of Wertz' business because he did not deal in goods of that kind.

Nor can the defendants-appellants rely on the doctrine of equitable estoppel. It has been observed that subdivision (1) of section 2-403 of the Uniform Commercial Code incorporates the doctrines of estoppel, agency and apparent agency because it states that a purchaser acquires not only all title that his transferor had, but also all title that he had power to transfer.

An estoppel might arise if Porter had clothed Peter Wertz with ownership of or authority to sell the Utrillo painting and the Feigen Gallery had relied upon Wertz' apparent ownership or right to transfer it. But Porter never even delivered the painting to Peter Wertz, much less create apparent ownership in him; he delivered the painting to Von Maker for his own personal use. It is true, as previously noted, that Von Maker used the name Peter Wertz in his dealings with Porter, but the Appellate Division found that the Feigen Gallery purchased from the actual Peter Wertz and that there was insufficient evidence to establish the claim that Peter Wertz had been described as an art dealer by Henry Sloan. Nothing Porter did influenced the Feigen Gallery's decision to purchase from Peter Wertz, a delicatessen employee. Accordingly, the Feigen Gallery cannot protect its defective title by a defense of estoppel.

The Appellate Division opined that even if Von Maker had duped Feigen into believing that Peter Wertz was an art dealer, subdivision (2) of section 2-403 of the Uniform Commercial Code would still not protect his defective title because as a merchant, Feigen failed to purchase in good faith. Among merchants good faith requires not only honesty in fact but observance of reasonable commercial standards. The Appellate Division concluded that it was a departure from reasonable commercial standards for the Feigen Gallery to fail to inquire concerning the title to the Utrillo and to fail to question Peter Wertz' credentials as an art dealer.

[Judgment affirmed]

QUESTIONS

1. Was there an entrustment of the painting that would allow a buyer to obtain title?

2. State how the sale was classified by the court. Explain.

3. Under what conditions would the court have found an equitable estoppel?

B.   SPECIAL SITUATIONS

Risk and property rights in the case of goods in self-service stores, automobiles, and goods sold at auction will be discussed in the following sections.

§ 28:11   SELF-SERVICE STORES

In the case of goods in a self-service store, the reasonable interpretation of the circumstances is that the store, by its act of putting the goods on display on the shelves, makes an offer to sell such goods for cash and confers upon a prospective customer a license to carry the goods to the cashier in order to make payment. Most courts hold that there is no transfer of title until the buyer makes payment to the cashier.

A contrary rule adopts the view that "a contract to sell" is formed when the customer "accepts" the seller's offer by taking the item from the shelf.

By another contrary view, a sale actually occurs when the buyer takes the item from the shelf. That is, title passes at that moment to the buyer even though the goods have not yet been paid for. Under this view, if the buyer places the item back on the shelf this is merely a "return" by the buyer. By this return the buyer transfers back to the seller the title that had already passed to the buyer when the item was removed from the shelf.

In the *Fender* case, a customer in a self-service store was injured by an item that she was about to pay for. This raised the question of whether she had the status of a buyer under a sales contract.

FENDER V COLONIAL STORES, INC.
138 Ga App 138, 225 SE2d 691 (1976)

Fender was a customer in the Big Star self-service store owned by Colonial Stores, Inc. She placed her selections on the cashier's counter. While lifting a six-pack of Coca Cola from her cart to the counter, one of the bottles exploded, and she was injured by the flying glass. She sued Colonial Stores. She claimed that the defendant was liable for breach of warranty. The defendant denied this liability on the ground that there could be no warranty liability until there was a sale and that the Coca Cola had not been sold to Fender because she had not yet paid for it. From a judgment for Colonial, Fender appealed.

DEEN, P. J. . . . An action based on breach of warranty necessitates a showing of the existence of the warranty, the fact that the warranty was broken and that the breach of the warranty was the proximate cause of the loss sustained. . . . The defendant-retailer contends that the plaintiff's evidence failed to establish the existence of a warranty. [UCC §] 2-314(1) provides . . . a warranty that the goods shall be merchantable is implied in a *contract for their sale* if the seller is a merchant with respect to goods of that kind . . . " (Emphasis supplied.) The retailer urges there was no warranty because at the moment of explosion the plaintiff had as yet not paid for the bottle.

The retailer argues that no title had passed on the goods; this ignores, however, the clear language of [UCC §] 2-314 that a warranty is implied upon a contract for sale and not solely upon the execution of the sale itself. [UCC §] 2-106(1) defined "contract for sale" as "both a present sale of goods and a contract to sell goods at a future time . . . " We therefore see this issue as not one of title passing from the retailer to the consumer but one of the existence of a contract between the parties to sell goods at a future time. A contract is of course "an agreement between two or more parties for the doing or not doing of some specified thing" and requires "parties able to contract, a consideration moving to the contract, the assent of the parties to the terms of the contract, and a subject-matter upon which it can operate." . . . The plaintiff has the burden of showing the existence of the warranty by establishing that at the time the bottle exploded there was a contract for its sale existing between herself and the retailer.

The plaintiff's evidence in this case showed that the retailer's store was of the usual "self-service" type, in which customers were supplied with carts and allowed to roam the aisles at will, selecting items from the shelves and cases and then negotiating the check-out line where the purchases are rung up on the register and the total price is paid. The plaintiff testified that she had finished her shopping and was in the physical act of placing the bottles on the counter for payment when the explosion occurred; she further testified that she was at the check-out counter to pay for her purchases.

We think this evidence sufficient to show that the retailer's act of placing the bottles on the shelf with the price stamped upon them manifested an intent to offer them for sale, the terms of the offer being that it would pass title to the customer when they were presented at the check-out counter and paid for. Likewise we think that the evidence shows that the plaintiff's act of taking physical possession of the goods with the intent to purchase them manifested an intent to accept the offer and a promise to take them to the check-out counter and to there pay for them. . . . Placing the goods on the shelf for customer inspection and selection was clearly an offer to sell them at the stated price; the retailer did not indicate by language or circumstances that acceptance of this offer could not be accomplished by taking possession of the goods with an implied *promise* to pay for them upon check-out rather than by the actual act of exchanging money. It is equally reasonable under the terms of the offer that acceptance could occur in any one of three ways: (1) by delivering the goods to the check-out counter and paying for them; (2) by the promise to pay for the goods as evidenced by their physical delivery to the check-out counter; and (3) by the promise to deliver the goods to the check-out counter and to pay for them there as evidenced by taking physical possession of the goods by their removal from the shelf. Under the circumstances surrounding this transaction we believe reasonable men could conclude that the plaintiff's act of taking physical possession of the goods with the intent to pay for them constituted a reasonable mode of acceptance; that by taking physical possession and delivering to the check-out counter the plaintiff promised to pay for them at the stated price and that this promise is sufficient consideration to support a contract . . . ; that a contract for the sale of the goods came into being when the plaintiff accepted the offer by taking physical possession thereof with the intent to pay for them; and that from that moment forward the implied warranties of [UCC §] 2-314 were applicable. See *Seigel v Giant Food, Inc.* 20 Md App 611, 318 A2d 874. "A contract for sale of goods may be made in any manner sufficient to show agreement, including conduct by both parties which recognizes the existence of such a contract. An agreement sufficient to constitute a contract for sale may be found even though the moment of its making is undetermined." . . .

Nor do we believe that the fact that the customer in a "self-service" store has the right to return merchandise to the shelves at any time before payment is made militates against a finding that a contract for the sale of goods has come into being before such payment. " 'Termination' occurs when either party pursuant to a power created by agreement or law puts an end to the contract otherwise than for its breach . . . " [UCC §] 2-106(3). We believe that the fact that the retailer permits the customer to "change his mind" indicates only an agreement between the parties to allow the customer to end his contract with the retailer irrespective of a breach of the agreement by the retailer. . . .

In reaching this decision that in the context of a self-service store a contract for sale of goods may arise before payment is actually made for the goods, we are not unaware of decisions in other jurisdictions to the contrary. *Loch v Confair*, 361 Pa 158, 63 A2d 24; *Lasky v Economy Grocery Stores*, 319 Mass 224, 65 NE2d 305; *Day v Grand Union Co.*, 280 AppDiv 253, 113 NYS2d 436. These cases were all decided prior to the adoption in their jurisdictions of the Uniform Commercial Code with its liberalized concept of contract formation and at a time when passage of "title" was the relevant legal prerequisite to a warranty action. It is true that the Court of Appeals of our sister state of North Carolina by discussion of the "passage of title" in a recent decision reached a similar result to that we have reached here. *Gillispie v The Great Atlantic and Pacific Tea Co.*, 14 NCApp 1, 187 SE2d 441. While we agree with the result reached in the *Gillispie* decision we do not agree that the question of whether a contract for sale exists is dependent upon the passage of title. We embrace rather the well-reasoned opinions of *Seigel v Giant Foods, Inc.*, [20 MdApp 611, 318, A2d 874] and *Giant Food, Inc. v Washington Coca-Cola Bottling Co., Inc.*, 273 Md 592, 332 A2d 1, 16 UCC 340 (1975) to the effect that a contract of sale of goods in the self-service supermarket context may arise before payment is actually made for the goods and title passes.

The retailer urges that even if we find a warranty has arisen in this case, as we have in fact so found, that the plaintiff's evidence fails to show a breach thereof. The testimony was that the goods selected were normal in appearance, that the bottles had not struck or touched the carton or any of the bottles against any object at any time after they were removed from the shelf, but that the bottle exploded as it was being placed on the counter for check-out and that the plaintiff was injured by flying glass. "It is obvious that Coca Cola bottles which would break under normal handling are not fit for the ordinary use for which they were intended and that the relinquishment of physical control of such a defective bottle to a consumer constitutes a breach of warranty. Thus the evidence was sufficient to show that when the bottles left the retailer's control they did not conform to the representations of the warranty of merchantability, and that this breach of the warranty was the cause of the loss sustained. Having made this *prima facie* showing appellant was entitled to have the jury pass upon the questions of whether the warranty was breached, and if so, whether the breach caused his injury." . . .

[Judgment reversed]

QUESTIONS

1. Did the customer own the six-pack at the time one of the bottles exploded?
2. Was the case affected by your answer to Question 1?
3. The fact that the customer in a self-service store may return a selected item to the shelf means that the customer does not have any contract of purchase with the store. Appraise this statement.

§ 28:12 AUTOMOBILES

Most states provide for the registration of the title to automobiles. These states ordinarily provide for the transfer of the title certificate upon the making of a sale of a registered automobile. As between the seller and a buyer, however, the transfer of such a title certificate is not essential. That is, title passes from the seller to the buyer in accordance with the provisions of the Uniform Commercial Code.[18] After it has so passed, the new owner is entitled to obtain a title certificate showing such ownership.

In states that follow the view just stated, the automobile title certificate is merely evidence of the ownership of the automobile. It is not a document of title. Possession or ownership of the title certificate has no importance in determining who is the owner of the automobile.

In contrast to the view that the transfer of title to an automobile is governed by the UCC, some states by statute have declared that the title to an automobile cannot be transferred without an indorsement and delivery of the certificate of title. In those states, the parties must satisfy the requirement of such a statute, and it is immaterial that title would otherwise pass under the Uniform Commercial Code.

§ 28:13 AUCTION SALES

When goods are sold at an auction in separate lots, each lot is a separate transaction, and title to each passes independently of the other lots. Title to each lot passes when the auctioneer announces by the fall of the hammer or in any other customary manner that the auction is completed as to that lot,[19] that is, the lot in question has been sold to the bidder.

[18] Bacheller v Employers Mutual Liability Ins. Co. 290 Wis 2d 564, 290 NW2d 872 (1980).

[19] UCC § 2-328.

SUMMARY

Problems relating to risk and property rights in sales transactions will often involve damage to the goods, the claims of creditors, and insurance. The solution to these problems often depends upon the

nature of the transaction between the seller and the buyer. Sales transactions may be classified according to the nature of the goods and the terms of the transactions.

Existing goods are physically in existence

and owned by the seller. Future goods are not yet owned by the seller or are not yet in existence. The title to existing goods identified at the time of the contract passes to the buyer at the time the parties agree to the transaction. Once the goods are identified, both the buyer and the seller have an insurable interest in the goods. If the goods are damaged after the sales agreement has been made, a merchant seller bears the loss occurring until the time the buyer receives the goods. If the seller is not a merchant, the risk of loss passes to the buyer when the goods are tendered or made available to the buyer. In a shipment contract, title and risk of loss pass at the time and place of shipment; in a destination contract, title and risk pass when the goods are made available at the destination. As long as the goods are unidentified, neither title nor risk of loss passes to the buyer.

In cases where the risk of loss would ordinarily pass to the buyer, the risk nevertheless remains with the seller if the goods do not conform to the contract. Even when the goods do conform to the contract, the buyer and seller could have agreed in their contract that the goods may be returned. The nature of their agreement, as a sale on approval, sale or return, or consignment sale, determines who has title and who bears the risk of loss.

The reservation of a security interest in goods does not affect the question of whether title or risk of loss has passed to the buyer.

Ordinarily, sellers cannot pass any better title than they possess. In some cases, however, the law permits a greater title to be transferred.

In an auction sale, title passes when the auctioneer accepts the bidder's offer.

QUESTIONS AND CASE PROBLEMS

1. What social forces are affected by the rule that the buyer has an insurable interest when future goods are marked for shipment to the buyer?

2. By letter, Felicia in Oklahoma, orders a sewing machine from the Jakoby Sewing Machine Company in Chicago. The order of Felicia is accepted but nothing is said as to whether the sale is for cash or on credit. How can Jakoby be sure that payment is made before Felicia gets possession of the sewing machine?

3. Kirk buys a television set from the Janess Television Store. At the time of the sale, Kirk gives Janess a check for the purchase price and obtains a receipt marked "paid in full." The check is a bad check as it is drawn on an account in which the balance is not sufficient to cover the amount of the check. Kirk knows this but hopes to leave town with the television set before Janess learns that the check is bad. Is Kirk the owner of the television set?

4. Compare the legal classification of (a) goods physically existing and owned by the seller at the time of contracting, (b) goods physically existing but not owned by the seller at the time of contracting, and (c) goods not physically existing at the time of contracting.

5. Jamison wants to buy a new truck. Kenton, a dealer, tries to sell him a particular truck. Jamison is not certain that this is the truck he wants. To encourage him to buy, Kenton sells the truck to him on "thirty-day approval." Jamison owes the First National Bank on an overdue debt and twenty-five days later the bank has the sheriff seize the truck in order to sell it to pay off the debt owed by Jamison. Both Kenton and Jamison object that the bank cannot do this. Are they correct?

6. O owned a television set. T stole the set and sold it to A who purchased for value and in good faith. A resold the set to B who also purchased in good faith and for value. O sued B for the set. B raised the defense that he had purchased it in good faith from a seller who had sold in good faith. Was this defense valid? [Johnny Dell, Inc. v New York State Police, 84 Misc 2d 360, 375 NYS2d 545]

7. B purchased a used automobile from A with a bad check. B then took the automobile to an auction in which the automobile was sold to C, who had no knowledge of the prior history of the automobile. When B's check was

dishonored, *A* brought suit against *C* to reclaim the automobile. Was he entitled to do so? [Greater Louisville Auto Auction, Inc. v Ogle Buick, Inc. (Ky) 387 SW2d 17]

8. Coppola collected coins. He joined a coin club, First Coinvestors, Inc. The club would send coins to its members who were to pay for them or return them within ten days. What was the nature of the transaction? [First Coinvestors, Inc. v Coppola, 88 Misc 2d 495, 388 NYS2d 833]

9. Eastern Supply Co. purchased lawn mowers from the Turf Man Sales Corp. The purchase order stated on its face "Ship direct to 30th & Harcum Way, Pitts., Pa." Turf Man delivered the goods to Helm's Express, Inc. for shipment and delivery to Eastern at the address in question. Did title pass on delivery of the goods to Helm or on their arrival at the specified address? [In re Eastern Supply Co. 21 (Pa) D&C 2d 128, 107 Pitts Leg J 451]

10. A manufacturer of knitwear loaded a trailer with goods ordered by the buyer. The loaded trailer was to be hauled away by a carrier. After the trailer was loaded but before it was taken away, it was damaged by fire. The manufacturer claimed that the buyer must bear the risk of loss because the goods were future goods covered by a shipment contract. Was the manufacturer correct? [A. M. Knitwear Corp. v All America Export-Import Corp. 50 App Div 2d 558, 375 NYS2d 23]

11. Compare the effect upon title of an unauthorized sale made by a repair shop of a customer's television set when (a) the repair shop only makes repairs, and (b) the repair shop also sells new and used television sets.

12. The Leton Wholesale Company sold and delivered ten executive desks on consignment to Lois, the owner and manager of the Handy Office Supply Company. Lois had severe financial problems, and her creditors petitioned the court to allow attachment of her inventory. A marshall seized the entire inventory of the Handy Office Supply Company including the ten executive desks. Explain how the Leton Wholesale Company could have prevented the desks from becoming subject to the claim of the creditors of Lois.

13. Smith operated a marina and sold and repaired boats. Gallagher rented a stall at the marina where he kept his vessel, the River Queen. Without any authorization, Smith sold the vessel to Courtesy Ford. Gallagher sued Courtesy Ford for the vessel. What was the result? [Gallagher v Unenrolled Motor Vessel River Queen (CA5 Tex) 475 F2d 117]

14. Grissom, without permission, entered onto land owned by another. He then proceeded to cut and sell the timber from the land. Upon learning that the timber had been sold, the owner of the land brought an action to recover the timber from the purchaser. The purchaser argued that he was a good faith purchaser who had paid value and therefore was entitled to keep the timber. Decide. [Baysprings Forest Products, Inc. v Wade, (Miss) 435 So 2d 690]

15. Compare or contrast a sale on approval with a sale or return with respect to risk of loss and title.

29

OBLIGATIONS AND PERFORMANCE

Each party to a sales contract must perform according to its terms. Each is likewise under the duty to act with good faith in its performance and to do nothing to impair the other party's expectation that the contract will be performed.

A.   GENERAL PRINCIPLES

Contracts for the sale of goods impose certain obligations on the parties to the contracts.

§ 29:1   OBLIGATION OF GOOD FAITH

"Every contract or duty within [the UCC] imposes an obligation of good faith in its performance or enforcement."[1] The UCC defines good faith as meaning "honesty in fact in the conduct or transaction concerned."[2] In the case of a merchant seller or buyer of goods, the UCC carries the concept of good faith further and imposes the additional requirement that the merchant seller or buyer observe "reasonable commercial standards of fair dealing in the trade."[3]

In the *Umlas* case, the owner of a car wanted to trade it in on the purchase of a new car. He claimed that the dealer did not observe good faith in making a reappraisal of the used car.

[1]   Uniform Commercial Code § 1-203. Servbest Foods, Inc. v Emessee Industries, Inc. 82 Ill App 3d 662, 37 Ill Dec 945, 403 NE2d 1 (1980).
[2]   UCC § 1-201(19); Chemical Bank of Rochester v Haskell, 51 NY2d 85, 432 NYS2d 478, 411 NE2d 1339 (1980).
[3]   UCC § 2-103(1)(b).

UMLAS V ACEY OLDSMOBILE, INC.

(NY Civil Court) 62 Misc 2d 819, 310 NYS2d 147 (1970)

Harry Umlas made a contract to buy a new automobile from Acey Olds-mobile. He was allowed to keep his old car until the new car was deliv-ered. The sales contract gave him a trade-in value on the old car of $650, but specified that it would be reappraised when it was actually brought in to the dealer. When Umlas brought the trade-in to the dealer, an em-ployee of Acey took it for a test drive and told Acey that it was worth from $300 to $400. Acey stated to Umlas that the trade-in would be ap-praised at $50. Umlas refused to buy from Acey and purchased from an-other dealer who appraised the trade-in at $400. Umlas sued Acey for breach of contract. Acey defended on the ground that its conduct was authorized by the reappraisal clause.

SANDLER, J. . . . Underlying plaintiff's lawsuit is the charge . . . that the reap-praisal was not done in good faith.

The defendant interposed a counterclaim for an amount just in excess of $300.00 that is totally without any semblance of merit, and that was obviously designed to harass the plaintiff by removing the case from the Small Claims Part of this Court.

I find as a fact that defendant's employee did state to plaintiff that he had reappraised plaintiff's car in the amount of $50.00 . . . and that this valuation was not made in good faith.

The critical legal question thus becomes whether the provision of the form order, under which defendant reserved the right to reappraise the used car allowance at the time of delivery where delivery is deferred, implies that the right of reappraisal is to be exercised in good faith. I conclude as a matter of law that good faith is an essential implied condition for the exercise of the right of reappraisal. See Uniform Commercial Code, 1-201, 2-103; c.f. 2-305.

To hold otherwise would mean that the order agreement, and the promises exchanged therein, was intended to be wholly illusory until delivery had been completed. Such a construction would make a travesty of an agreement that evoked from the plaintiff, as it was intended to, the following substantial reli-ance: a down payment, suspension for a period of his right to acquire a car elsewhere, and the securing of a bank loan. . . .

In reaching the above conclusion, I do not wish to be understood as doubt-ing the legitimate considerations prompting the provision in question when the delivery of the car is to be deferred. Obviously, the buyer's car may suffer some deterioration during the intervening period. . . .

But the fact that the clause represents a reasonable response to a practical problem does not obscure the reality that it is open to, and indeed lends itself to, serious and recurrent abuse. In the presence of a potential buyer, searching for the optimum price for his used car, a dealer may well be disposed to place a generous value on the used car, realizing that he could later renegotiate the figure when his bargaining position was immensely strengthened.

For it is surely clear that when a buyer has signed an order for a particular car of a certain color and with special accessories, has made a cash down pay-ment, has secured a bank loan, and has arrived in his somewhat worn old car ready to receive a resplendent new vehicle, his ability to resist a new less-favorable deal is at a very low ebb indeed.

Surely, it is no surprise that defendant's witness acknowledged that used car allowances are often lowered at the delivery date. And although no testimony was presented directly, it is surely a fair surmise that instances in which used cars are found to have a higher value at the delivery date would represent extraordinary phenomena in the annals of any car dealer.

In evaluating the appropriate remedy for the kind of breach presented, I have considered that the arrangement of circumstances in this very common situation presents car dealers with a powerful inducement to place high values on used cars when attempting to land the order and low values when the physical presence of the new car after an intervening period has substantially reduced the purchasers' resistance. Car dealers should be encouraged to withstand this temptation. *Corbin on Contracts*, Vol 5, Sections 997, 1002 (1960 Edition).

The plaintiff, like any purchaser under the circumstances, was entitled to a good faith valuation of his car on the delivery date.

In the absence of any good faith reappraisal by the defendant, the only valuation by the defendant is that fixed at the time of the original order, and I find that to be controlling.

Accordingly, I find for the plaintiff . . .

QUESTIONS

1. What part of the contract between Umlas and Acey was violated?
2. What could Umlas have done for his protection?
3. Compare the *Umlas* decision and the common-law concept of "let the buyer beware."

§ 29:2   TIME REQUIREMENTS OF OBLIGATIONS

In the case of a cash sale not requiring the physical moving of the goods, the duties of the seller and buyer are concurrent. Each one has the right to demand that the other perform at the same time. That is, as the seller hands over the goods, the buyer theoretically must hand over the purchase money. If either party refuses to act, the other party has the right to withhold performance. In the case of a shipment contract, there is a time interval between the performance of the parties; the seller will have performed by delivering the goods to the carrier, but the buyer's obligation will not arise until the goods have been received and accepted by the buyer.

§ 29:3   REPUDIATION OF THE CONTRACT

The seller or the buyer may refuse to perform the contract when the time for performance arises. This is a **repudiation** of the contract.[4] Likewise, before that time arrives, one party may inform the other that the contract will never be performed. This repudiation made in advance of the time for performance is called an **anticipatory repudiation**.

(a) ACTION OF AGGRIEVED PARTY. If there is a clear repudiation of the contract and the loss of the repudiated performance substantially impairs the value of the con-

---

[4]   Unique Systems, Inc. v Zotos International, Inc. (CA8 Minn) 622 F2d 373 (1980).

tract to the other party, the aggrieved party may request the repudiating party to retract or take back the repudiation. While waiting to see what happens, the aggrieved party may hold up rendering any further performance under the contract. In any case, the aggrieved party may assert that the contract has been broken and utilize any of the remedies available for breach.[5]

If the aggrieved party has acted without sufficient justification, that is, if in fact there was no anticipatory repudiation, the aggrieved party who withholds performance will be the one who is breaking the contract and will be liable for damages for breach.

(b) RETRACTION OF ANTICIPATORY REPUDIATION. Prior to the time when performance is due, the party who made the anticipatory repudiation may retract it or take it back. This cannot be done if the other party has (a) canceled the contract because of the repudiation, (b) has materially changed position, as by making other sales or purchases, or (c) has expressly accepted the repudiation as final.

§ 29:4   ADEQUATE ASSURANCE OF PERFORMANCE

A party to a sales contract may think that the other party will not perform the contract. For example, the seller's warehouse is destroyed by fire. The buyer could fear that the seller would not be able to make a delivery scheduled for the following month. Whenever a party to a sales contract has reasonable grounds for being concerned about the future performance of the other party, a written demand may be made upon such other party for assurance that the contract will be performed.

(a) FORM OF ASSURANCE. The person upon whom demand for assurance is made must give "such assurance of due performance as is adequate under the circum-

stances of the particular case." The exact form of assurance is not specified by the UCC. If the party on whom demand is made has an established reputation, a reaffirmation of the contract obligation and a statement that it will be performed may be sufficient to assure a reasonable person that it will be performed. In contrast, the person's reputation or economic position at the time may be such that mere words and promises would not give any real assurance. In such case, it may be necessary to have a third person (or an insurance company) guarantee performance or to put up property as security for performance.

(b) FAILURE TO GIVE ASSURANCE. If adequate assurance is not given, the demanding party may treat the contract as repudiated.[6] The demanding party is then free to make a substitute contract with a third person to replace the repudiated contract.

B.   DUTIES OF THE PARTIES

The obligations of the parties to a sales contract include: (1) the seller's duty to deliver the goods, (2) the buyer's duty to accept the goods, (3) the buyer's duty to pay for the goods, and (4) duties of the parties under particular contract terms.

§ 29:5 SELLER'S DUTY TO DELIVER

The seller has the duty to deliver the goods in accordance with the terms of the contract. This duty to make "delivery" does not require physical transportation but merely means that the seller must permit the transfer of possession of the goods to the buyer. That is, the seller makes the goods available to the buyer. The delivery is sufficient if it is made in accordance with the terms of the sale or contract to sell.

(a) PLACE, TIME, AND MANNER OF DELIVERY. The terms of the contract determine whether the seller is to send the goods or

---

[5]   UCC § 2-610; Crowder v Aurora Co-op Elevator Co. ___ Neb ___, 393 NW2d 250 (1986).

[6]   UCC § 2-609(4). This assurance must ordinarily be given within thirty days.

the buyer is to call for them, or whether the goods must be transported by the seller to the buyer, or whether the transaction is to be completed by the delivery of documents without the movement of the goods. In the absence of a provision in the contract or a contrary course of performance or usage of trade, the place of delivery is the seller's place of business, if the seller has one; otherwise it is the seller's residence. If, however, the subject matter of the contract consists of identified goods that are known by the parties to be in some other place, that place is the place of delivery. Documents of title may be delivered through customary banking channels.[7]

When a method of transportation called for by the contract becomes unavailable or commercially unreasonable, the seller must make delivery by means of a commercially reasonable substitute if available, and the buyer must accept such substitute.[8] This provision is applicable when a shipping strike makes impossible the use of the method of transportation specified in the contract of sale.

(b) QUANTITY DELIVERED. The buyer has the right to insist that all the goods be delivered at one time. If the seller delivers a smaller or larger quantity than that stipu-lated in the contract, the buyer may refuse to accept the goods.

(c) CURE OF DEFECTIVE TENDER OR DELIVERY. If the seller tenders or delivers non-conforming goods, the buyer may reject them. This does not end the transaction because the seller is given a second chance to make a proper or curative tender of conforming goods.[9]

This right is restricted in terms of whether the second tender can be made within the time called for by the contract. If the time for making delivery under the contract has not expired, the seller need only give the buyer seasonable (timely) notice of the intention to make a proper delivery within the time allowed by the contract, and the seller may then do so. If the time for making the delivery has expired, the seller is given an additional reasonable time in which to make a substitute conforming tender if (1) the seller so notifies the buyer, and (2) the seller had acted reasonably in making the original tender, believing that it would be acceptable to the buyer.

The *T.W. Oil* case deals with the right of the seller to cure a delivery of goods that did not conform to the contract specifications.

---

[7] UCC § 2-308.
[8] UCC § 2-614(1).

[9] UCC § 2-508. Stephenson v Frazier, (Ind App), 399 NE2d 794 (1980).

T. W. OIL V CONSOLIDATED EDISON

57 NY2d 574, 443 NE2d 932 (1982)

Con Ed purchased a cargo of fuel oil from plaintiffs. The plaintiffs were aware that Con Ed was authorized to buy and burn oil with a sulfur content of up to 1 percent. The oil that plaintiffs supplied was originally represented to have a sulfur content of no greater than 1 percent. Later, in the written purchase contract, the oil was described as .5 percent sulfur content. When the oil was delivered and tested, its sulfur content was found to be .92 percent. Con Ed rejected the fuel oil. Negotiations to adjust the price failed, and plaintiffs then offered to cure the defect with a substitute shipment of oil. After Con Ed rejected the plaintiff's proposal, plaintiffs brought suit for breach of contract. The trial court ruled for the plaintiffs, and Con Ed appealed.

FUCHSBERG, J. . . . In January, 1974, midst the fuel shortage produced by the oil embargo, the plaintiff (then known as Joc Oil USA, Inc.) purchased a cargo of fuel oil whose sulfur content was represented to it as no greater than 1%. While the oil was still at sea en route to the United States in the tanker *M T Khamsin*, plaintiff received a certificate from the foreign refinery at which it had been processed informing it that the sulfur content in fact was .52%. Thereafter, on January 24, the plaintiff entered into a written contract with the defendant (Con Ed) for the sale of this oil. The agreement was for delivery to take place between January 24 and January 30, payment being subject to a named independent testing agency's confirmation of quality and quantity. The contract, following a trade custom to round off specifications of sulfur content at, for instance, 1%, .5% or .3%, described that of the *Khamsin* oil as .5%. In the course of the negotiations, the plaintiff learned that Con Ed was then authorized to buy and burn oil with a sulfur content of up to 1% and would even mix oils containing more and less to maintain that figure.

When the vessel arrived, on January 25, its cargo was discharged into Con Ed storage tanks in Bayonne, New Jersey. In due course, the independent testing people reported a sulfur content of .92%. On this basis, acting within a time frame whose reasonableness is not in question, on February 14 Con Ed rejected the shipment. Prompt negotiations to adjust the price failed; by February 20, plaintiff had offered a price reduction roughly responsive to the difference in sulfur reading, but Con Ed, though it could use the oil, rejected this proposition out of hand. It was insistent on paying no more than the latest prevailing price, which, in the volatile market that then existed, was some 25% below the level which prevailed when it agreed to buy the oil.

The very next day, February 21, plaintiff offered to cure the defect with a substitute shipment of conforming oil scheduled to arrive on the *S. S. Appollonian Victory* on February 28. Nevertheless, on February 22, the very day after the cure was proffered, Con Ed, adamant in its intention to avail itself of the intervening drop in prices, summarily rejected this proposal too. The two cargos were subsequently sold to third parties at the best price obtainable, first that of the *Appollonian* and, sometime later, after extraction from the tanks had been accomplished, that of the *Khamsin*.

. . . We turn then to the central issue on this appeal: Fairly interpreted, did subdivision (2) of section 2-508 of the Uniform Commercial Code require Con Ed to accept the substitute shipment plaintiff tendered? In approaching this question, we, of course, must remember that a seller's right to cure a defective tender, as allowed by both subdivisions of section 2-508, was intended to act as a meaningful limitation on the absolutism of the old perfect tender rule, under which, no leeway [was] allowed for any imperfections. . . .

Section 2-508 may be conveniently divided between provisions for cure offered when "the time for performance has not yet expired", and ones which, by newly introducing the possibility of a seller obtaining "a further reasonable time to substitute a conforming tender", also permit cure beyond the date set for performance. In its entirety the section reads as follows:

(1) Where any tender or delivery by the seller is rejected because non-conforming

and the time for performance has not yet expired, the seller may seasonably notify the buyer of his intention to cure and may then within the contract time make a conforming delivery.

(2) Where the buyer rejects a non-conforming tender which the seller had reasonable grounds to believe would be acceptable with or without money allowance, the seller may if he seasonably notifies the buyer have a further reasonable time to substitute a conforming tender.

Since we here confront circumstances in which the conforming tender came after the time of performance, we focus on subdivision (2). On its face, taking its conditions in the order in which they appear, for the statute to apply (1) a buyer must have rejected a nonconforming tender, (2) the seller must have had reasonable grounds to believe this tender would be acceptable (with or without money allowance), and (3) the seller must have "seasonably" notified the buyer of the intention to substitute a conforming tender within a reasonable time.

In the present case, none of these presented a problem. The first one was easily met for it is unquestioned that, at .92%, the sulfur content of the *Khamsin* oil did not conform to the .5% specified in the contract and that it was rejected by Con Ed. The second, the reasonableness of the seller's belief that the original tender would be acceptable, was supported not only by unimpeached proof that the contract's .5% and the refinery certificate's .52% were trade equivalents, but by testimony that, by the time the contract was made, the plaintiff knew Con Ed burned fuel with a content of up to 1%, so that, with appropriate price adjustment, the *Khamsin* oil would have suited its needs even if, at delivery, it was, to the plaintiff's surprise, to test out at .92%. Further, the matter seems to have been put beyond dispute by the defendant's readiness to take the oil at the reduced market price on February 20.

As to the third, the conforming state of the *Appollonian* oil is undisputed, the offer to tender it took place on February 21, only a day after Con Ed finally had rejected the *Khamsin* delivery and the *Appollonian* substitute then already was en route to the United States, where it was expected in a week and did arrive on March 4, only four days later than expected. . . . it is almost impossible, given the flexibility of the Uniform Commercial Code definitions of "seasonable" and "reasonable", to quarrel with the finding that the remaining requirements of the statute also had been met.

In dealing with the application of subdivision (2) of section 2–508, courts have been concerned with the reasonableness of the seller's belief that the goods would be acceptable rather than with the seller's pretended knowledge or lack of knowledge of the defect.

. . . A seller should have recourse to section 2–508 of the Uniform Commercial Code as long as it can establish that it had reasonable grounds, tested objectively, for its belief that the goods would be accepted. It goes without saying that the test of reasonableness, in this context, must encompass the concepts of "good faith" and "commercial standards of fair dealing" which permeate the code.

[Judgment affirmed]

QUESTIONS

1. Is a buyer's rejection of a seller's tender conditioned by a requirement that it be reasonable?

2. What are the requirements for a seller's right to cure?
3. Did the seller act properly in exercising the right to cure?

§ 29:6   BUYER'S DUTY TO
          ACCEPT GOODS

The buyer must accept goods that conform to the contract. Refusal to do so is a breach of the contract.

(a) RIGHT TO EXAMINE GOODS. In order to see if the goods in fact conform to the contract, the buyer has the right to examine the goods when tendered by the seller. As an exception to this rule, the buyer must pay for goods sent C.O.D. and has no right to examine the goods until payment is made.

(b) WHAT CONSTITUTES ACCEPTANCE OF GOODS. Acceptance of goods means that the buyer shows in some way that the goods conform to the contract. This may be shown by (a) an express statement of approval, (b) conduct inconsistent with rejection, as illustrated in the *Fram* case, or (c) lapse of time.[10]

[10]   UCC § 2-602(1) and § 2-606(1). Danjee, Inc. v Addressograph Multigraph Corp. 44 NC App 626, 262 SE2d 665 (1980).

UNITED STATES FOR THE USE OF FRAM CORP. V CRAWFORD

(CA5 Ga) 443 F2d 611 1971)

Floyd Crawford, who was constructing a building for the United States Navy, purchased fuel equipment from Fram Corp. and installed the equipment in the building. Fram sued for the purchase price. Crawford claimed that he had not accepted the equipment because it was defective. From a judgment for Crawford, Fram appealed.

AINSWORTH, C. J. . . . The contract price for the fuel filter/separator units was $55,564.20. Floyd Crawford admitted at the trial that of that sum, $6,298.50 had not been paid. There was no testimony to the contrary. The appellees maintain that they are excused from further payment by the deficiencies in Fram's performance on the contract. Fram contends, to the contrary, that the Trial Judge should have directed a verdict in its favor on its claim for the $6,298.50. We sustain Fram's contention.

It is undisputed that Fram furnished the eighteen fuel filter/separator units called for by the contract, and that Crawford received and installed all eighteen units. Section 2-607 of the Uniform Commercial Code . . . provides . . . "The buyer must pay at the contract rate for any goods accepted." Acceptance of goods occurs when the buyer "does any act inconsistent with the seller's ownership." Georgia UCC § 2-606(1)(c). No case is reported in which the Georgia courts have had occasion to interpret section 2-606(1)(c). Courts in other jurisdictions, interpreting the same section of the Uniform Commercial Code, have held that installation by the buyer of heavy equipment supplied by the seller is an act inconsistent with the seller's ownership. See *Marbelite Company v City of Philadelphia*, 208 Pa Super 256, 222 A2d 443 (1966) (traffic signal equipment); *Park County Implement Co. v Craig* (Wyo) 397 P2d 800 (1964) (hoist and dump bed on vehicle). We believe that the Georgia courts, confronted with the same issue in the instant case, would give section 2–606(1)(c) the same construction. A buyer who has accepted goods may under certain conditions revoke his acceptance. Georgia UCC § 2–608. However, once Crawford had accepted and installed the units supplied in place on the Albany site, any subsequent attempt at revocation was ineffective. . . .

[Judgment reversed and action remanded]

QUESTIONS

1. Who was the plaintiff?
2. Was it important whether the buyer had accepted the equipment? Explain.
3. Did Crawford ever inform Fram Corporation that the equipment was accepted?

A buyer accepts the goods by making continued use of them and by not attempting to return the goods. A buyer, of course, accepts the goods by modifying them because such action is inconsistent with a rejection or with the continued ownership of the goods by the seller. Consequently, when the purchaser of a truck installs a hoist and a dump bed on it, such action constitutes an acceptance by conduct. The buyer therefore becomes liable for the contract price of the truck.

§ 29:7   BUYER'S DUTY TO PAY

The buyer must pay for goods accepted and must pay the amount stated in the sales contract.

(a) TIME OF PAYMENT. The sales contract may require payment in advance or may give the buyer credit by postponing the time for payment.[11]

(b) FORM OF PAYMENT. Unless otherwise agreed, payment by the buyer requires payment in cash.

The seller may accept a check or a promissory note from the buyer. If the check is not paid by the bank, the purchase price remains unpaid. A promissory note payable at a future date gives the buyer credit by postponing the time for payment.

The seller may refuse to accept a check or promissory note. When the seller does so, the seller must give the buyer reasonable time in which to obtain legal tender with which to make payment.

§ 29:8   DUTIES UNDER PARTICULAR TERMS

A sale may be as simple as a face-to-face exchange of money and goods, but it frequently involves a more complicated pattern, with some element of transportation, generally by a common carrier. This, in turn, generally results in the addition of certain special terms to the sales transaction.

(a) C.I.F., C. & F. Under a C.I.F. contract, the buyer pays the seller a lump sum covering the cost (selling price) of the goods, insurance on the goods, and freight to the specified destination. C. & F. contracts are similar except that under such contracts the seller is not obligated to insure the goods for the buyer's benefit. Under both these terms, the risk of loss

---

[11] UCC § 2-310(a). If delivery under the contract is to be made by delivery of a document of title, payment is due at the time and place at which the buyer is to receive the document regardless of where the goods are to be received. § 2-310(c).

and title to the goods pass to the buyer after the goods have been delivered to the carrier.

(b) F.O.B. The term *F.O.B.* or "free on board" is a condensed way of saying that the seller has the obligation of (a) putting the goods on board a named vessel, truck, or other carrier, or of (b) making tender at a named geographical point. When used to specify a geographical point, it may be F.O.B. the seller's city, the buyer's city, or an intermediate point, such as the Port of New York for goods that are to be sent by land to New York and by water to a foreign country. Under the F.O.B. term (1) risk of loss and (2) title pass to the buyer at the F.O.B. point. This is so even though such transfer would have occurred at a different point if the shipment had not been F.O.B.

The seller pays the cost of transporting the goods to the F.O.B. point.[12] The buyer pays transportation costs from that point on.

(c) F.A.S., Ex-Ship. The term *F.A.S.* means free alongside the named vessel. The seller, at the seller's own expense and risk, must deliver the goods alongside a named vessel. Risk of loss and title pass to the buyer at the shipping point.

The term *ex-ship* obligates the seller to deliver or unload the goods from a ship that has reached a place at the named port of destination where goods of the kind are usually discharged. Risk of loss and title pass to the buyer when the goods leave the ship's tackle or are otherwise properly unloaded.

---

[12] Buenger v Pruden (Wyo) 713 P2d 771 (1986).

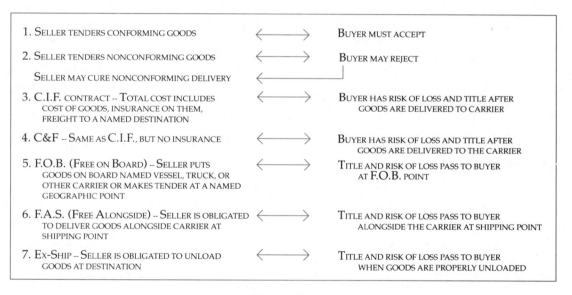

1. Seller tenders conforming goods ⟵⟶ Buyer must accept

2. Seller tenders nonconforming goods ⟵⟶ Buyer may reject

   Seller may cure nonconforming delivery ⟵

3. C.I.F. contract -- Total cost includes cost of goods, insurance on them, freight to a named destination ⟵⟶ Buyer has risk of loss and title after goods are delivered to carrier

4. C&F -- Same as C.I.F., but no insurance ⟵⟶ Buyer has risk of loss and title after goods are delivered to the carrier

5. F.O.B. (Free on Board) -- Seller puts goods on board named vessel, truck, or other carrier or makes tender at a named geographic point ⟵⟶ Title and risk of loss pass to buyer at F.O.B. point

6. F.A.S. (Free Alongside) -- Seller is obligated to deliver goods alongside carrier at shipping point ⟵⟶ Title and risk of loss pass to buyer alongside the carrier at shipping point

7. Ex-Ship -- Seller is obligated to unload goods at destination ⟵⟶ Title and risk of loss pass to buyer when goods are properly unloaded

FIGURE 29-1
OBLIGATIONS AND PERFORMANCE

SUMMARY

Every sales contract imposes an obligation of good faith in its performance or enforcement. Good faith means honesty in fact in the conduct or transaction concerned. For merchants, the UCC imposes the additional requirement of observing "reasonable commercial standards of fair dealing in the trade.''

In the case of a cash sale where no transportation of the goods is required, both the buyer and the seller may demand concurrent performance.

If a buyer or seller refuses to perform a contract, it is called a repudiation. A repudiation made in advance of the time for performance is called an anticipatory repudiation. If either party to a contract feels insecure about the performance of the other, that party may demand adequate assurance of performance and, if not given, the demanding party may treat the contract as repudiated.

The seller has the duty to deliver the goods in accordance with the terms of the contract. This duty does not require physical transportation; it requires that the seller permit the transfer of possession of the goods to the buyer. If the seller tenders nonconforming goods, the buyer may reject them. Subject to certain limitations, the seller may then make a curative tender. The buyer has a duty to accept goods that conform to the contract. Refusal to do so is a breach of contract. The buyer is deemed to have accepted the goods when the buyer expresses acceptance, does something inconsistent with rejection, or fails to reject the goods after having a reasonable opportunity to inspect them, or if a reasonable time has elapsed after the buyer inspected the goods or had the opportunity to inspect them. The buyer must pay for the goods accepted in accordance with the terms of the contract.

The parties to a sales contract assume certain duties where goods are shipped under particular shipping terms. In a C.I.F. contract the buyer pays the seller the cost of the goods, insurance, and freight to the specified destination. In a C. & F. contract, the seller is not obligated to insure the goods for the buyer's benefit. Under both these terms, the risk of loss and title to the goods pass to the buyer after the goods have been delivered to the carrier.

In an F.O.B., or free on board, contract the seller has the obligation of putting the goods on board a named carrier or making delivery at a particular destination. The risk of loss and title to the goods pass to the buyer at the F.O.B. point.

In an F.A.S. contract, the seller at the seller's own expense and risk must deliver the goods alongside a named vessel. Risk of loss and title pass to the buyer at the shipping point. The term *ex-ship* obligates the seller to unload the goods at the named port of destination. Risk of loss and title pass to the buyer when the goods are properly unloaded.

QUESTIONS AND CASE PROBLEMS

1. What social forces are involved in the rule of law governing the substitution of a different method of transportation to replace the method specified in the contract of sale?

2. Elkins Appliance Store makes a contract to purchase 100 electric toasters from the Greystone Electric Company, delivery to be made on November 1. A week later Greystone informs Elkins that its factory has been severely damaged by fire and that Greystone is uncertain as to whether it will be able to deliver the toasters by November 1 or at any time. Elkins claims that this statement is an anticipatory repudiation of the contract. Is Elkins correct?

3. The Wolfson Paint Store wants to build up its inventory. It makes a contract to purchase 1,000 cans of paint from the Gordon Paint Factory. A truck from the Gordon Paint Factory delivers 400 cans of paint, and the driver tells Wolfson that the balance will come later. Wolfson rejects the 400 cans. Has he broken the contract by so doing?

4. Louise in St. Louis orders a set of kitchen knives by mail from Grant Company in Seattle. They are sent C.O.D. to Louise. In order to be sure that there has been no mistake, Louise wants to examine the knives before she pays the carrier. Can she do so?

5. The Melvin Electric Motor Corporation makes a contract with the Raskob Gear Company for the latter to supply 10,000 sets of reduction gears according to specifications

supplied by Melvin. The president of Melvin reads in the newspaper that there is a strike in the Raskob plant. The president of Melvin telephones the president of Raskob to express concern over whether Raskob will be able to perform the contract. The conversation does not lessen the fears of the president of Melvin, and the conversation concludes with Melvin's president demanding assurance from Raskob that performance will be made. The president of Melvin does not hear anything further from Raskob during the next thirty days. Can Melvin treat the contract as repudiated by Raskob?

6. International Minerals and Metals Corporation contracted to sell Weinstein scrap metal to be delivered within thirty days. Later the seller informed the buyer that it could not make delivery within that time. The buyer agreed to an extension of time, but no limiting date was set. Within what time must the seller perform? [International Minerals and Metals Corp. v Weinstein, 236 NC 558, 73 SE2d 472]

7. Carlson ordered equipment from the Ventresca Foundry in St. Louis, Missouri, to be sent "F.O.B. Chicago, Illinois." The equipment was placed on a motor freight truck under a proper shipment contract. The truck was wrecked before it reached Chicago. Ventresca demanded payment of the purchase price from Carlson on the theory that the contract was a shipment contract and that the risk of loss passed to Carlson when the equipment was delivered to the carrier in St. Louis. Was Ventresca correct?

8. The Spaulding & Kimball Co. ordered from the Aetna Chemical Co. seventy-five cartons of window washers. The buyer received them and sold about a third to its customers. The buyer later refused to pay for them, claiming that the quality was poor. The seller sued for the price. Decide. [Aetna Chemical Co. v Spaulding & Kimball Co. 98 Vt 51, 126 A 582]

9. A computer manufacturer promoted the sale of a digital computer as a "revolutionary breakthrough." It made a contract to deliver one of these computers to a buyer. It failed to deliver the computer and explained that its failure was caused by unanticipated technological difficulties. Was this an excuse for nonperformance by the seller? [United States v Wegematic Corp. (CA2 NY) 360 F2d 674]

10. A buyer made a contract for equipment that was to be installed in a new building that was being constructed. When the equipment was delivered to the buyer, the buyer refused to accept it on the ground that the architect had made a mistake and the tendered goods could not be used in the new building. The seller sued the buyer for breach of contract. Was the buyer entitled to reject the goods? [R. R. Waites Co. v E. H. Thrift Air Conditioning, Inc. (Mo App) 510 SW2d 759]

11. Teeman made a contract to purchase lumber from the Oakhill Mill. The contract called for payment to be made upon delivery to Teeman. When the truck from the Mill arrived to deliver the lumber, Teeman gave the driver a check for the purchase price. The driver refused to take the check, returned to the Mill, and the Mill then notified Teeman that the contract was canceled. Was the Mill entitled to cancel the contract?

12. Lury has a contract to sell with Burns, with whom he has not previously dealt, to make four quarterly deliveries of Product Z on thirty days' credit. Two months after the first delivery under the contract, Burns has not yet paid. May Lurie demand adequate assurance of performance?

13. Francine Moss was in the process of furnishing her apartment. She purchased a leather sofa and three leather chairs from Davenport Furniture, Inc. to be delivered in twenty days. She paid part of the purchase price upon executing the order and agreed to pay the balance on delivery. Davenport delivered the sofa and the chairs a week later, but the leather chairs did not match the sofa. Francine thereupon rejected the sofa and the chairs. She also demanded the return of her money. What rights, if any, does Davenport have?

14. The Singer Appliance Co. purchased refrigerators from the Specialty Refrigerator Co. It used them as demonstrators for eight and a half months and then notified Specialty Refrigerator Co. that the refrigerators did not work. Singer Appliance offered to return the refrigerators. Was Specialty Refrigerator required to take back the goods?

15. Compare or contrast an F.O.B. shipping term with a C.I.F. contract provision with respect to when the risk of loss passes to the buyer.

30

WARRANTIES AND OTHER PRODUCT LIABILITY THEORIES

When goods are defective and cause injury or loss, the person harmed has a claim for product liability.

A. GENERAL PRINCIPLES

The remedy of the harmed person may be governed by the common law, by the UCC, or by the newly emerging case law.

§ 30:1 THEORIES OF LIABILITY

Two centuries ago, a buyer was limited to suing a seller for breach of an express guarantee or for negligence or fraud. After the onset of mass production and distribution, however, these remedies had little value. A guarantee was good, but in the ordinary sales transaction no one stopped to get a guarantee. One never asked the manager of the supermarket to give a guarantee that the loaf of bread purchased was fit to eat. Further, negligence and fraud have become generally impossible to prove in a mass production world. How can one prove how a can of soup was prepared months ago? The making of fraudulent statements by the seller is rather rare.

In order to give protection from harm-causing products, the law developed the concept of warranty liability. Warranties are either express or implied and are governed by the UCC. Within the last few decades, many courts have decided that still broader protection was required and created an additional concept of strict tort liability.

There are accordingly six theories in the law to protect from harm caused by defective products: guarantee, negligence, fraud, express warranty, implied warranty, and strict tort liability. If the plaintiff is a consumer or an employee, there might also be consumer protection liability and employee protection liability. In every case, the plaintiff does not have a choice of all theories. The facts of the case will ordinarily exclude some theories. In other situations, the plaintiff will have the choice of two or more theories.

§ 30:2   NATURE OF HARM

When a product is defective, harm may be caused to (a) person, (b) property, or (c) economic or commercial interests. Under (a), the buyer of a truck may be injured when it goes out of control and plunges down the side of a hill. Third persons may also be injured, such as passengers in the truck, bystanders, or the driver of a car hit by the truck. The defective truck may also cause injury to a total stranger who seeks to rescue one of the victims. Property damage under (b) is sustained when the buyer's

truck is damaged when it plunges down the slope. The car of the other driver may be damaged or a building into which the runaway truck careens may be damaged. Under (c), commercial and economic interests of the buyer are affected by the fact that the truck is defective. Even if no physical harm is sustained, the fact remains that the truck is not as valuable as it would have been. The buyer who has paid for the truck on the basis of the value it should have had has sustained an economic loss. If the buyer is required to rent a truck from someone else or loses an opportunity to haul freight for compensation, the fact that the truck was defective also causes economic or commercial loss.

§ 30:3   WHO MAY SUE AND BE SUED

Until the early part of this century, only the parties to the sales contract could sue each other. Thus, a seller could be sued by the buyer, but other persons could not sue because they were not in privity of contract.

This requirement of privity of contract has been widely rejected, and the law is moving toward the conclusion that persons harmed because of an "improper" product may sue anyone who is in any way responsible.

(a) THE PLAINTIFF. By the modern view, not only the buyer, but also customers and employees of the buyer and even third persons or bystanders may sue because of harm caused by an improper product. The UCC expressly abolishes the requirement of privity when the plaintiff is a member of the buyer's family or household or a guest of the buyer and has sustained personal injury because of the product.[1]

Some states require privity of contract, particularly when the plaintiff does not sustain personal injury or property damage and seeks to recover only economic loss. However, a manufacturer making an express warranty as to a consumer product

---

[1]   Uniform Commercial Code § 2-318.

costing over $15 that was manufactured after July 4, 1975, may be sued for the economic loss sustained by the buyer.

(b) THE DEFENDANT. The plaintiff who is entitled to sue may sue the seller, a remote seller, a manufacturer, and generally even the manufacturer of the component part of the product that caused the harm.[2] For example, when a person is struck by an automobile because of its defective brakes, the victim may sue the seller and the manufacturer of the car and the maker of the brake assembly or system that the car manufacturer installed in the car.

(c) DIRECT SALES CONTACT. In many instances recovery is allowed by a buyer against a remote manufacturer because there have been direct dealings between them that justify regarding the buyer and the manufacturer as being in privity, as against the contention that the buyer was only in privity with the local dealer from whom the product was bought.[3] When the manufacturer enters into direct negotiations with the ultimate buyer with respect to any phase of the manufacturing or financing of the transaction, the sale will probably be treated as though it were made directly by the manufacturer to the ultimate purchaser even though, for the purpose of record keeping, the transaction is treated as a sale by the manufacturer to the dealer and by that dealer to the ultimate purchaser. Likewise, recovery may be allowed when the consumer mails to the manufacturer a warranty registration card that the manufacturer packed with the manufactured article.

In the *Nobility Homes* case, the purchaser of a mobile home sued the manufacturer for breach of warranty. The manufacturer claimed that the purchaser could only sue the dealer from whom the home had been purchased.

---

[2]   Mendelson v General Motors Corp. 432 NYS2d 132 (1980).

[3]   Richards v Goerg Boat & Motors, Inc. (Ind App) 384 NE2d 1084 (1979).

NOBILITY HOMES OF TEXAS V SHIVERS

(Tex Civ App) 539 SW2d 190 (1976)

John Shivers and his wife purchased a mobile home from Marvin Hurley. Because of many defects, the home had a market value of approximately $9,000 less than the contract price. The buyers sued the manufacturer, Nobility Homes of Texas, for this amount. From a judgment in favor of the plaintiffs, Nobility Homes appealed.

DIES, C. J. . . . Hurley had previously purchased this unit from the defendant, the manufacturer thereof. Hurley was not an agent for the defendant. . . .

Defendant . . . asserts that it could not be liable for any damages to plaintiffs because there was no privity of contract between them, and plaintiffs are only seeking economic loss. . . . The generally recognized landmark case for support of the principle that privity is not required in pure economic loss cases is *Santor v A & M Karagheusian, Inc.* 44 NJ 52, 207 A2d 305 (1965). There, Santor brought suit against the manufacturer of a carpet which he had purchased from one of its distributors. The only contract was between Santor and the distributor, which had subsequently gone out of business. Santor sought recovery only for the loss of value of the carpeting.

After a thorough discussion of the positions of the various states and the concomitant rationale of the divergent views, the New Jersey Supreme Court held that privity was not necessary to maintain an action by a consumer against the manufacturer for redress of an economic loss. The Court restated the holdings which do not require privity for recovery in instances of personal injury and said:

> But we see no just cause for recognition of the existence of an implied warranty of merchantability and a right to recovery for breach thereof regardless of lack of privity of the claimant in the one case [as in personal injury] and the exclusion of recovery in the other simply because loss of value of the article sold is the only damage resulting from the breach. . . .
>
> From the standpoint of principle, we perceive no sound reason why the implication of reasonable fitness should be attached to the transaction and be actionable against the manufacturer where the defectively made product has caused personal injury, and not actionable when inadequate manufacture has put a worthless article in the hands of an innocent purchaser who has paid the required price for it. In such situations considerations of justice require a court to interest itself in originating causes and to apply the principle of implied warranty on that basis, rather than to test its application by whether personal injury or simply loss of bargain resulted from the breach of the warranty. True, the rule of implied warranty had its gestative stirrings because of the greater appeal of personal injury claim. But, once in existence, the field of operation of the remedy should not be fenced in by such a factor.

The court accepted these logical principles of equity and incorporated with them the substantive law of strict liability in tort. It again refused to accept the personal injury/economic loss dichotomy and held that only through tort liability would the burden of the injury be placed where it should be — on the maker of the product. This is because, though the breach arose initially from the sales contract, it was a " 'tortious wrong suable by a noncontracting party . . .' "

It is our opinion that the interests of equity and justice will best be served by accepting the view that privity in cases now under consideration should not be required. Matters of public policy dictate that no different treatment should be accorded in instances where a consumer suffers personal injury or damage to other property, and situations where the harm is the diminution of value of the product itself and the resulting economic loss. In both circumstances there is an "injury" to the public sector, whose only action in the commercial transaction is to purchase goods placed in the stream of commerce by the manufacturer. To insulate the maker of the goods under these conditions can result only by resort to reasoning which is no longer viable in our current economic practices and present sense of justice. . . .

A practical consideration also supports the position advanced by this Court today; the problem of wasteful litigation. In quoting from *Randy Knitwear, Inc. v American Cyanamid Company* (226 NYS2d 363, 181 NE2d 399) the Court in Santor restated:

> It is true that in many cases the manufacturer will ultimately be held accountable for the falsity of his representations, but only after an unduly wasteful process of litigation. Thus, if the consumer or ultimate business user sues and recovers, for breach of warranty, from his immediate seller and if the latter, in turn, sues and recovers against his supplier in recoupment of his damages and costs, eventually, after several separate actions by those in the chain of distribution, the manufacturer may finally be obliged to shoulder the responsibility which should have been his in the first instance.

. . . The pursuit of such wasteful litigation which is often inadequate should not be required in this State.

This jurisdiction should refrain from the "narrow legalistic view" that privity is necessary before the public may recover for damages suffered when the product diminishes in value and/or becomes worthless because of the defective workmanship of the manufacturer. . . .

[Judgment affirmed]

QUESTIONS

1. What was the theory on which the plaintiff sued the defendant?
2. What kind of loss was sustained by the plaintiff?
3. Was the court in the *Nobility Homes* case influenced by the nature of the plaintiff's loss?

B.   EXPRESS WARRANTIES

A warranty may be express or implied. Both have the same effect and operate as though the defendant had made an express guarantee. An express guarantee is governed by the common law of contracts. Warranties are governed primarily by the UCC.

§ 30:4   DEFINITION OF EXPRESS WARRANTY

An **express warranty** is a statement by the defendant relating to the goods, which statement is part of the basis of the bargain. That is, the statement is part of the basis of the sale. This means that the buyer has purchased the goods on the reasonable assumption that they were as stated by the seller. Thus, a statement by the seller with respect to the quality, capacity, or other characteristic of the goods is an express warranty. To illustrate, the seller may say: "This cloth is all wool," "This paint is for household woodwork," or "This engine can produce 50 horsepower."

A representation that an airplane is a 1983 model is an express warranty. A statement that a product was particularly developed for a special purpose is an express warranty that it will achieve that purpose.[4]

There is no requirement of reliance upon an express warranty. The question is merely whether the statement of the seller became part of the bargain of the parties.

§ 30:5   FORM OF EXPRESS WARRANTY

No particular form of words is necessary to constitute an express warranty. A seller need not state that a warranty is being made nor that one is intended. It is sufficient that the seller assert a fact that becomes a part or term of the bargain or transaction between the parties.

It is not necessary that the seller make an express statement, for the express warranty may be found in conduct. Accordingly, if the buyer asks for a can of outside house paint and the seller hands over a can of paint, the seller's conduct expresses a warranty that the can contains outside house paint.

The seller's statement may be written or printed, as well as oral. The words on the label of a can and in a newspaper ad for "boned chicken" constitute an express warranty that the can contains chicken that is free of bones.

The illustrations in a seller's catalog are

---

4   Swenson v Chevron Chemical Co. (SD) 234 NW2d 38 (1975).

descriptions of the goods. Therefore an express warranty arises that the goods will conform to a catalog illustration.

§ 30:6   TIME OF MAKING EXPRESS WARRANTY

It is immaterial whether the express warranty is made at the time of or after the sale. No separate consideration is required for the warranty when it is a part of a sale. If a warranty is made after the sale, no consideration is required as it is regarded as a modification of the sales contract.

In the *Werner* case, the buyer claimed that oral statements made by the seller before the sale were express warranties as to the future performance of the goods.

WERNER V MONTANA

117 NH 721, 378 A2d 1130 (1977)

Peter Werner purchased the *White Eagle*, a wooden sailing sloop, from Robert Montana. The sloop leaked, and Werner brought an action to cancel the sale on the ground that there had been an express oral warranty that it would not leak. Montana contended that no warranty was stated in any of the writings involved in the transaction and that the parol evidence rule prevented proof of statements made in the course of negotiations and that accordingly there was no express warranty. The case was heard by a master who recommended that judgment be entered for Werner. Montana appealed.

LAMPRON, J. . . . Plaintiff put the White Eagle into the water. After allowing ordinarily sufficient time for the planking to swell, or "make up," to form a watertight hull, plaintiff found that the White Eagle still leaked and could not be sailed. Plaintiff then discovered that there was extensive dry rot in the hull and that the cost of repairs would be substantial. After some discussions with defendant in the course of the summer concerning the problem, on September 8, 1972, plaintiff wrote defendant a letter complaining about the dry rot and unseaworthiness of the White Eagle and demanding that defendant take back the White Eagle and refund the purchase price. Defendant refused and plaintiff brought this action.

The basis for plaintiff's action is that there was a breach of an express warranty. [UCC §] 2-313. Plaintiff alleged that defendant, in the course of negotiations prior to sale, made certain statements to the effect that the White Eagle would "make up" when placed in the water and become watertight and that such statements amounted to an express warranty as to the sloop's condition. Defendant argues that any statements made by the defendant prior to sale could not be admitted or considered as constituting an express warranty by virtue of [UCC §] 2-202 (Parol or extrinsic Evidence Rule). . . .

Under the Uniform Commercial Code an express warranty may be created by a seller who makes "any affirmation of fact or promise . . . to the buyer which relates to the goods and becomes part of the basis of the bargain." [UCC §] 2-313(1)(a). In addition, "any description of the goods which is made part of the basis of the bargain creates an express warranty that the goods shall conform to the description." [UCC §] 2-313(1)(b).

In general, affirmations of fact made by a seller about the goods being sold are considered a part of the description of the goods and are regarded as forming a part of the sales agreement. Uniform Laws Comment 3 to [UCC §] 2-313; 1 R. Anderson, Uniform Commercial Code § 2-313:45 (2d ed 1970). There was evidence that during the course of negotiations the parties had discussed the ship's watertightness and that defendant had told plaintiff that the White Eagle would become watertight once placed in water and allowed sufficient time to "make up." Considering the negotiations of the parties as a whole, particularly plaintiff's concern with whether the White Eagle was watertight, and considering the importance of watertightness for a ship, these assurances by defendant regarding the condition of the White Eagle could properly be considered as making part of the basis of the bargain. *See* 1 R. Anderson, *supra* § 2-313:7. Therefore, . . . the master did not err in ruling that these affirmations or descriptions of the White Eagle by the defendant created an express warranty under both [UCC §] 2-313(1)(a) and (b).

[UCC §] 2-202 excludes evidence of any additional oral agreement or terms when a written agreement is intended by the parties to be a final expression of their agreement. However, unless the writing was intended as a complete and exclusive statement of the terms of the agreement, evidence of consistent additional terms are admissible. [UCC §]2-202(b). There was no evidence that the writings in this case, the notice of intent to purchase, the bill of sale, and the advertisement incorporated therein by reference, were intended by the parties as constituting a complete and exclusive statement of the terms of their agreement. The master therefore could properly find defendant's statements regarding the White Eagle's watertightness as being an express warranty which was a consistent additional term of the agreement . . . 1 R. Anderson, Uniform Commercial Code § 2-313:22; R. Nordstrom, Sales § 53 (1970). . . .

Defendant argues that plaintiff failed to prove a breach of warranty because the evidence did not establish that the leaking of the White Eagle was caused by the dry rot, or by any other cause, and therefore did not establish that the leaking constituted a breach of the alleged warranty. It is true that the master found there was no evidence to connect the leaking with the dry rot in the hull. However, the master did not find that defendant had made any warranty that the White Eagle was free from dry rot. Rather, the master found that defendant had told plaintiff that the White Eagle was suitable for sailing, and that defendant's statements which created the warranty were to the effect that the White Eagle had not leaked and would not leak after a sufficient swelling period was allowed. The master found that the White Eagle's "inability to 'make up' " created a breach of this warranty. While it is true that there was no evidence to establish the cause of the leaking, such evidence was not necessary. The plaintiff was required only to establish the existence of an express warranty and to establish that the White Eagle was defective in that its condition did not comply with the condition warranted by defendant. . . . The evidence was undisputed that the White Eagle continued to leak and was not seaworthy despite being allowed to soak for over six weeks. Plaintiff therefore met his burden establishing the boat's defective condition.

Defendant also argues that any warranty made related only to the condition of the White Eagle at the time of sale and that plaintiff failed to prove that the

White Eagle was not as warranted at that time. While an express warranty generally relates only to the condition of the goods at the time of sale, a warranty may relate to another point in time if so specified. 1 R. Anderson, supra § 2–313:12. The warranty found by the master to have been made by defendant was that the White Eagle would not leak; that it would be tight after a two-week swelling period. The discussions between the parties prior to sale occurred after September 1, 1971, and the bill of sale was dated January 1, 1972. It would not be until the following spring or summer that plaintiff would have the first occasion to put the White Eagle in the water and allow for the swelling defendant indicated would occur. The warranty as to tightness therefore did not relate simply to the condition of the White Eagle as of the date of sale, but necessarily related to the time when the boat would be put in the water and prepared for sailing. Under these circumstances defendant's statement amounted to an express warranty.

Although reliance on the part of the buyer is not necessary for the creation of an express warranty, the master properly found that plaintiff did in fact rely on defendant's affirmation that the boat would not leak and it became part of the bargain. . . .

[Judgment affirmed]

QUESTIONS

1. Why did the plaintiff sue the defendant?
2. Did the seller guarantee that the sloop would not leak?
3. Did the seller say that he warranted that the sloop would not leak after being placed in the water?

---

§ 30:7   SELLER'S OPINION OR STATEMENT OF VALUE

"An affirmation merely of the value of goods or a statement purporting to be merely the seller's opinion or commendation of the goods does not create a warranty."[5] A purchaser, as a reasonable person, should not believe such statements implicitly, and therefore cannot hold the seller to them should they prove false. Thus, "sales talk" by a seller that "this is the best piece of cloth in the market" or that glassware "is as good as anyone else's" is merely an opinion that the buyer cannot ordinarily treat as a warranty.

Statements made by the seller of cosmetics that its products were "the future of beauty" and that they were "just the product for you [the plaintiff]" were "sales talk" arising "in the ordinary course of merchandising" and did not constitute warranties.

It is probable, however, that the UCC will permit an exception to be made, as under the prior law, when the circumstances are such that a reasonable person would rely on such a statement. If the buyer has reason to believe that the seller has expert knowledge of the conditions of the market and the buyer requests the seller's opinion as an expert, the buyer would be entitled to accept as a fact the seller's statement as to whether a given article was the best obtainable. The statement could be reasonably regarded as forming part of the basis of the bargain. Thus, a statement by a florist that bulbs are of first-grade quality may be a warranty.

[5]   UCC § 2-313(2).

§ 30:8   WARRANTY OF CONFORMITY TO DESCRIPTION, SAMPLE, OR MODEL

When the contract is based in part on the understanding that the seller will supply goods according to a particular description or that the goods will be the same as the sample or a model, the seller is bound by an express warranty that the goods shall conform to the description, sample, or model.[6] Ordinarily a **sample** is a portion of the whole mass that is the subject of the transaction, while a **model** is a replica of the article in question.

§ 30:9   FEDERAL REGULATION OF EXPRESS WARRANTIES

A seller who makes an express warranty as to a consumer product costing more than $15 must conform to certain standards imposed by federal statute[7] and by regulations of the Federal Trade Commission.[8] Initially, the seller is not required to make any express warranty but if one is made, it must be stated in ordinary understandable language and must be made available for inspection before purchasing so that the consumer may comparison shop.

(a) FULL WARRANTIES. If the seller or the label states that a **full warranty** is made, the seller is obligated to fix or replace a defective product within a reasonable time, without cost to the buyer. If the product cannot be fixed or if a reasonable number of repair attempts are unsuccessful, the buyer has the choice of a cash refund or a free replacement. No unreasonable burden may be placed on a buyer seeking to obtain warranty service. A full warranty runs for its specified life without regard to the ownership of the product.

(b) LIMITED WARRANTIES. Any warranty that does not provide the complete protection of a full warranty is a **limited warranty** and must be conspicuously described as

---

[6]   UCC § 2-313(1)(b), (c).
[7]   PL 93-637, 15 USC § 2301 et seq.
[8]   16 CFR § 700.1 et seq.

such by the seller. For example, a warranty is limited if the buyer must pay any cost for repair or replacement of a defective product, or if only the first buyer is covered by the warranty, or if the warranty only covers part of the product. A warrantor making a full warranty cannot require that the buyer pay the cost of sending the product to or from a warranty service point. A warrantor making a full warranty cannot require the buyer to return the product to such a point if it weighs over 35 pounds, or to return a part for service unless it can be easily removed, or to fill and return a warranty registration card shortly after purchase in order to make the warranty effective. If the warrantor imposes any of these burdens the warranty must be called a limited warranty.

§ 30:10   EFFECT OF BREACH OF EXPRESS WARRANTY

If the express warranty is false, there is a breach of the warranty. The warrantor is then liable just as though the truth of the warranty had been guaranteed. It is no defense that the defendant honestly believed that the warranty was true, or had exercised due care in manufacturing or handling the product, or had no reason to believe that the warranty was false.

C.   IMPLIED WARRANTIES

Whenever a sale of goods is made, certain warranties are implied unless they are expressly excluded. The scope of these warranties may differ in terms of whether the seller is a merchant or a casual seller.

§ 30:11   DEFINITION OF IMPLIED WARRANTY

An **implied warranty** is one that was not made by the seller but which is implied by the law. In certain instances, the law implies or reads a warranty into a sale although the seller did not make it. That is, the implied warranty arises automatically from the fact that a sale has been made; express warranties arise because they form part of the basis on which the sale has been made.

The fact that express warranties are made does not exclude implied warranties. When both express and implied warranties exist, they should be construed as being consistent with each other and as cumulative if such construction is reasonable. In case it is unreasonable to construe them as consistent and cumulative, an express warranty prevails over an implied warranty as to the subject matter, except in the case of an implied warranty of fitness for a particular purpose. When there is an express warranty as to a particular matter, it is unnecessary to find an implied warranty relating thereto.

§ 30:12 IMPLIED WARRANTIES OF ALL SELLERS

A distinction is made between a merchant seller and the casual seller. There is a greater range of warranties in the case of the merchant seller.

(a) WARRANTY OF TITLE. Every seller, by the mere act of selling, makes a warranty that the seller's title is good and that the transfer is rightful.

A warranty of title may be specifically excluded, or the circumstances may be such as to prevent the warranty from arising. The latter situation is found when the buyer has reason to know that the seller does not claim to hold the title or that the seller is purporting to sell only such right or title as the seller or a third person may have. For example, no warranty of title arises when the seller makes the sale in a representative capacity, such as a sheriff, an auctioneer, or an administrator of a decedent's estate. Likewise, no warranty arises when the seller makes the sale as a pledgee or mortgagee.

(b) WARRANTY AGAINST ENCUMBRANCES. Every seller by the mere act of selling makes a warranty that the goods shall be delivered free from any security interest or any other lien or encumbrance of which the buyer at the time of the sales transaction had no knowledge. Thus, there is a breach of warranty if the automobile sold to the buyer is delivered subject to an outstanding encumbrance that had been placed on it by the original owner and that was unknown to the buyer at the time of the sale.

This warranty refers to the goods only at the time they are delivered to the buyer and is not concerned with an encumbrance that existed before or at the time the sale was made. For example, a seller may not have paid in full for the goods, and the original supplier may have a lien on them. The seller may resell the goods while that lien is still on them, and the seller's only duty is to pay off the lien before delivering the goods to the buyer.

(c) WARRANTY OF FITNESS FOR A PARTICULAR PURPOSE. If the buyer intends to use the goods for a particular or unusual purpose, as contrasted with the ordinary use for which they are customarily sold, the seller makes an implied warranty that the goods will be fit for the purpose when the buyer relies on the seller's skill or judgment to select or furnish suitable goods, and when the seller at the time of contracting knows or has reason to know the buyer's particular purpose and the buyer's reliance on the seller's judgment.[9] When the seller knows that the buyer is purchasing an accounting machine in order to produce a payroll on time and with reduced work hours, an implied warranty arises that the machine will perform as desired by the buyer.

When the buyer makes the purchase without relying on the seller's skill and judgment, no warranty of fitness for a particular purpose arises.[10]

In the *Lewis and Sims* case, the buyer ordered goods and then sued the seller when the goods did not do what the buyer wanted.

[9] UCC § 2-315. This warranty applies to every seller, but as a matter of fact it will probably always be a merchant seller who has such skill and judgment so that the UCC provision would be applicable.
[10] B. W. Feed Co., Inc. v General Equipment Co. 44 Or App 467, 605 P2d 1205 (1980).

LEWIS AND SIMS, INC. V KEY INDUSTRIES, INC.

16 Wash App 619, 557 P2d 1318 (1976)

> Lewis and Sims, a contracting corporation, was installing a water and sewer system in the town of North Pole, Alaska. It ordered pipe stating only the size and quantity of the pipe and that the pipe be "coal tar enamel lined." The pipe could not withstand the intense cold and before the pipe lines could be constructed, the enamel lining had pulled away from the pipe. Because of this it was rejected, and Lewis and Sims were required to purchase other pipe. It then sued the suppliers of the original pipe for damages for breach of a warranty of fitness for a particular purpose. From a judgment in favor of Lewis and Sims, the defendants appealed.

SWANSON, J. . . . In order to invoke the provisions of the Section 2-315 warranty, the evidence must be sufficient to show that (1) the seller at the time of contracting had reason to know the particular purpose for which the goods were required, and (2) that the buyer relied upon the seller's skills or judgment in selecting or furnishing suitable goods. In marked contrast to other commercial code warranties, it is imperative to the existence of a warranty of fitness for a particular purpose that the buyer relied upon the seller's skill or judgment in selecting the appropriate goods. In so relying, the buyer generally is ignorant of the fitness of the article offered by the seller and thus relies on the superior skill, information or judgment the seller possesses and not on his own judgment.

In *Frisken v Art Strand Floor Coverings, Inc.*, 47 Wash 2d 587, 288 P2d 1087 (1955),* the owner of a commercial building entered into an agreement with a corporation engaged in the business of selling and laying floor coverings whereby the latter contracted [to] furnish and install asphalt tile on the floor of the premises. The building's floor was concrete covered with magnesite. The corporation's agent, after viewing the premises, recommended a certain tile suitable for the building owner's needs. The tile, as it turned out, was incompatible with the magnesite underflooring such that the tile floor became uneven and buckled. Our Supreme Court held that the seller impliedly warranted that the floor would be fit for the intended use regardless of the structure of the underflooring. In so holding, the court found that the buyer was ignorant of the risk involved in the covering magnesite with tile and that she relied on the seller's knowledge and judgment in the matter. . . . In similar fashion, the Catania case [4 Conn Cir 344, 231 A2d 668 (1967)] involved a fairly typical situation where application of the implied warranty of fitness for a particular purpose is deemed appropriate. In Catania, the buyer asked the seller, who was engaged in the retail paint business, to recommend a paint to cover the exterior stucco walls of the buyer's house. The seller was told that the stucco was in a chalky or powdery condition. Based on this information, the seller recommended a particular brand name product and also provided instructions on its

---

*   This case arose before enactment of the present-day UCC; however, the same principles are still applicable.

use. Subsequent to its application, the paint began to flake and blister. The Connecticut Supreme Court found that the implied warranty liability existed since the buyer justifiably relied on the superior information, skill, and judgment of the seller.

If, as has been shown, liability for the implied warranty for fitness for a particular purpose flows from the existence of: (1) reliance by the buyer on the judgment of the seller and (2) the fact that the seller had reason to know the buyer's particular purpose, . . . then it conversely follows that no warranty of fitness for a particular purpose arises when it is clear that the buyer orders goods according to his own specifications. As stated in 1 R. Anderson, *Uniform Commercial Code,* § 2-315:21 at 666 (1970), a buyer does not rely upon the seller's judgment, skill, or experience where an article, although intended for a disclosed purpose, is to be made or manufactured or furnished by the seller in accordance with plans and specifications furnished by the purchaser; there is in such case no implied warranty that the article, if in accordance with the specifications, will answer the intended purpose, or in other words, no warranty against unfitness arising out of defects in the plans and specifications. . . .

We turn now from the abstract legal aspects of the warranty of fitness for purpose to a discussion of that warranty as it applies to the facts before us. In order to prevail in the instant action, the respondent-buyer was under an obligation to show that he relied on the seller's judgment in choosing a pipe that best suited the needs of an underground water-sewer system in North Pole, Alaska. While the trial court apparently believed such reliance existed, we are at a loss to find substantial evidence within the record to sustain the trial court. On the contrary, after carefully reviewing the record, we find ample evidence to conclude that Lewis and Sims ordered a specific size and type of pipe and that any deviation from the coal tar enamel lined pipe that was manufactured would not have been accepted by Lewis and Sims. In short, neither supplier was asked for its recommendations, nor did either select the pipe or lining to be used. The warranty for fitness for a particular purpose was not meant to be applied in a situation such as we face today. The central tenet — reliance upon the skill, judgment, or experience of the seller — is not manifested. What is apparent is the fact that both parties to this action knew what was desired, and that desire was fulfilled. It is also important to note that the pipe itself was not negligently manufactured; rather, the lining was susceptible to cracking upon exposure to exteme cold. . . .

In summary then, we find no breach of an implied warranty of fitness for purpose owed to Lewis and Sims. . . .

[Judgment reversed]

QUESTIONS

1. What was the basis or theory of the plaintiff's suit?
2. Why was the purpose of the buyer a "particular purpose"?
3. How would the case have been decided if the pipes were cracked and leaked under all temperature conditions?

§ 30:13 ADDITIONAL IMPLIED WARRANTIES OF MERCHANT SELLER

A seller who deals in goods of the kind in question is classified as a **merchant** by the UCC and is held to a higher degree of responsibility for the product than one who is merely making a casual sale.

(a) WARRANTY AGAINST INFRINGEMENT. Unless otherwise agreed, every merchant seller warrants that the goods will be delivered free of the rightful claim of any third person by way of patent or trademark infringement or the like.

(b) WARRANTY OF MERCHANTABILITY OR FITNESS FOR NORMAL USE. A merchant seller makes an implied warranty of the merchantability of the goods sold.[11] This warranty is in fact a group of warranties, the most important of which is that the goods are fit for the ordinary purposes for which they are sold.

A merchant is not protected from warranty liability by the fact that every possible step was taken to make the product safe. Similarly, it is no defense that the defendant could not have known of or discovered the defective character of the product, for warranty liability is not merely an assurance that the defendant has exercised due care but is an undertaking or guarantee that the product is fit for use.

In the *Shell* case, the plaintiff alleged a breach of warranty of merchantability and a breach of the warranty of fitness for a particular purpose.

[11] Maybank v S. S. Kresge Co. 46 NC App 687, 266 SE2d 409 (1980).

SHELL V UNION OIL CO.
(Ala) 489 So 2d 569 (1986)

John Shell, an employee of the Goodyear Tire and Rubber Company, came into contact with a naphtha product supplied by Union Oil. The product contained benzene, a carcinogen known to cause leukemia. The product complied with specifications established by Goodyear that limited the amount of benzene any shipment could contain. In addition, Union supplied Goodyear with safety data sheets setting forth precautions that should be taken to prevent exposure when using benzene. Shell brought an action against the suppliers of the chemical compound alleging breach of warranties. From a judgment in favor of the suppliers, Shell appealed.

JONES, J. . . . In its simplest terms, the questions presented are:

1. Was there a duty owed, i.e., was there an implied promise?
2. If so, was that duty breached, i.e., was the promise unperformed? and
3. Did that duty extend to this Plaintiff, i.e., was the obligation of performance intended for Shell's protection? Shell can prevail, of course, only if the answer to *all* three questions is "yes."

If we assume a "yes" answer to each of the first two questions, then the third question must be answered in the affirmative, in light of Code 1975, § 7-2-318:

Third-party beneficiaries of warranties express or implied.
    A seller's warranty, whether express or implied, extends to any natural person if

it is reasonable to expect that such person may use, consume or be affected by the goods and who is injured in person by breach of the warranty. A seller may not exclude or limit the operation of this section.

Therefore, we will concentrate on the first two questions.

I

Plaintiff's first theory is based upon breach of warranty of merchantability, and he relies on § 7-2-314, which reads in part:

Implied warranty: Merchantability.
    (1) Unless excluded or modified (section 7-2-316), a warranty that the goods shall be merchantable is implied in a contract for their sale if the seller is a merchant with respect to goods of that kind. Under this section the serving for value of food or drink to be consumed either on the premises or elsewhere is a sale.
    (2) Goods to be merchantable must be at least such as:
        (a) Pass without objection in the trade under the contract description; and
        (b) In the case of fungible goods, are of fair average quality within the description; and
        (c) Are fit for the ordinary purposes for which such goods are used; and
        (d) Run, within the variations permitted by the agreement, of even kind, quality and quantity within each unit and among all units involved; and
        (e) Are adequately contained, packaged, and labeled as the agreement may require; and
        (f) Conform to the promises or affirmations of fact made on the container or label if any.

Plaintiff's implied warranty of merchantability theory, as we understand it, is to the effect that, because the substance supplied by Defendants caused cancer, it could not be "fit for ordinary purposes for which such goods are used"; that is, because this is a cancer-causing substance, it is unreasonably dangerous, and, therefore, cannot be merchantable. Such an argument ignores the clear distinction between causes of action arising under tort law and those arising under the U.C.C. as adopted in Alabama. A Texas court recognized that distinction in *Mid Continent Aircraft Corp. v. Curry County Spraying Service, Inc.*, 553 S.W.2d 935 (Tex.Civ.App. 1977):

[U.C.C.] law, whose statutory language makes no reference to tort law in connection with products liability, concerns itself with the quality of the product by establishing standards of merchantability for a particular purpose . . . [while the tort law] concerns itself with safety standards by imposing strict liability upon one who sells an unreasonably dangerous product which causes physical harm. The considerations supporting either of the principles are not affected by the considerations underlying the other, and the standards of quality of a product, with the attendant risk of the bargain, are entirely distinct from its standards of safety, with a possible unreasonable risk of harm. It follows that a violation of the standards of safety which results in physical harm to the unreasonably dangerous product itself subjects the seller to the tort rule of strict liability.

553 S.W.2d at 940.

Whether this product was unreasonably dangerous, therefore, is not a question properly addressed in an action brought under the provisions of the U.C.C.

To cover the initial bare bones question (Was there a duty owed?) with flesh, we should reask the question: Did the sale of the subject product give rise to an implied warranty of merchantability in the sense that these two manufacturers promised the employee that he would not be injured by his use of or contact with their product? The answer must be made in the context of § 7-2-314: "[Whether this product was] fit for the ordinary purposes for which such goods are used." In this instance, the product — made to Goodyear's specifications — performed the job it was intended to do; and the manufacturers' warnings and precautions, accompanying the products, were in keeping with their knowledge of its inherent dangers. Thus, any duty arising under this section of the Code was not breached. Indeed, more precisely, these undisputed facts do not give rise to a warranty of merchantability, as contended by Shell.

The implied warranty mandated by this section of the U.C.C. is one of *commercial* fitness and suitability, and a private right of action is afforded only where the user or consumer is injured by the breach of *that* warranty. That is to say, the U.C.C. does not impose upon the seller the broader obligation to warrant against health hazards inherent in the use of the product when the warranty of commercial fitness has been complied with. Those injured by the use of or contact with such a product, under these circumstances, must find their remedy outside the warranty remedies afforded by the U.C.C. . . . The Defendants were entitled to judgment as a matter of law.

II

The second action was brought under the theory of breach of the warranty of fitness for a particular purpose provided for in the Code as follows:

§ 7-2-315. Implied warranty: Fitness for particular purpose.

Where the seller at the time of contracting has reason to know any particular purpose for which the goods are required and that the buyer is relying on the seller's skill or judgment to select or furnish suitable goods, there is unless excluded or modified under section 7-2-316 an implied warranty that the goods shall be fit for such purpose.

While privity is not a requirement, the injured third party beneficiary can have no more interest than the principal parties. Because Goodyear set the specifications for this product, it did not rely on "the seller's skill or judgment to select or furnish suitable goods." Goodyear was well aware of the connection between benzene and leukemia at the time it set the standards which these Defendants were required to meet. Because Goodyear, the buyer, did not rely on the seller's skill or expertise, as required by § 7-2-315, no duty on the part of Defendants arose under this section of the Code.

[Judgment affirmed]

QUESTIONS

1. Why did Shell allege a breach of warranty of merchantability?
2. Was there a breach of warranty of fitness for a particular purpose?
3. What disposition did the court make of the claim that there was a breach of warranty of merchantability?

§ 30:14   WARRANTIES IN PARTICULAR SALES

Particular types of sales may involve special considerations.

(a) SALE ON BUYER'S SPECIFICATIONS. When the buyer furnishes the seller with exact specifications for the preparation or manufacture of such goods, the same warranties arise as in the case of any other sale of such goods by the particular seller. No warranty of fitness for a particular purpose can arise, however, since it is clear that the buyer is purchasing on the basis of the buyer's own decision and is not relying on the seller's skill and judgment. Likewise, the manufacturer is not liable for loss caused by a design defect.[12]

(b) SALE OF SECONDHAND OR USED GOODS. As far as the UCC is concerned, there is no difference between the warranties arising in the sale of used or secondhand goods and those arising in the sale of new goods.[13] As to ordinary goods, what is "fit for normal use" will be a lower standard for used than for new goods. Some courts still follow their pre-Code law under which no warranties of fitness arose in the sale of used goods.

(c) SALE OF FOOD OR DRINK. The sale of food or drink, whether to be consumed on or off the seller's premises, is a sale. When made by a merchant, a sale of food or drink carries the implied warranty that the food is fit for its ordinary purpose, that is, human consumption.[14]

Thus, the seller of canned crabmeat has broken this warranty when the can contains a nail. Does it make any difference if the thing which harms the buyer is a crabshell? Some courts refuse to impose warranty liability if the thing in the food which causes the harm was naturally pre-

sent, as the crabshell in crabmeat, prune stones in stewed prunes, or bones in canned fish. Other courts reject this natural substance exception. They hold that there is liability if the seller does not deliver to the buyer goods of the character that the buyer reasonably expected. Thus, there is a breach of the implied warranty of fitness for normal use if the buyer reasonably expected the food to be free of harm-causing natural things, such as shells and bones.

§ 30:15   NECESSITY OF DEFECT

In order to impose liability for breach of an implied warranty, it is ordinarily necessary to show that there was a defect in the product and that this defect was the cause of the plaintiff's harm. A product may be defective because there is (a) a manufacturing defect, (b) a design defect, (c) inadequate instruction on how to use the product, or (d) inadequate warning against dangers involved in using the product.

If the manufacturer's blueprint shows that there should be two bolts at a particular place and the factory puts in only one bolt, there is a manufacturing defect. If the two bolts are put in but the product breaks because four bolts are required to provide sufficient strength, there is no manufacturing defect, but there is a design defect. A product that is properly designed and properly manufactured may be dangerous because the user is not given sufficient instructions on how to use the product. Also a product is defective if there is a danger that is not obvious, and there is no warning at all or a warning that does not describe the full danger. For example, a can of adhesive used to cement tiles to a floor is defective when the can merely says that the cement should not be used near an open flame, but does not state that a newly cemented floor would throw off vapor that would stay in the room for several hours and

---

[12] Wisconsin Electric Power Co. v Zallea Brothers, Inc. (CA7 Wis) 606 F2d 697 (1979).

[13] Hargett v Midas Intern. Corp. (Miss) 508 So 2d 663 (1987).

[14] Fernandes v Union Bookbinding Co. Inc. ___ Mass ___, 507 NE2d 728 (1987).

would explode if any spark or flame were present.

Many courts are relaxing the requirement of proving the existence of a specific defect. These courts impose liability when the goods are in fact not fit for their normal purpose. These courts allow the buyer to prove goods are not fit for their normal purpose by evidence that the goods do not function properly, even though the buyer does not establish the specific defect that made the goods malfunction.

In contrast with the suit for breach of an implied warranty, when the plaintiff sues for breach of an express warranty or a guarantee, it is not necessary to show that there was a defect that caused the breach. It is sufficient to show that the goods did not conform to the guarantee or to the express warranty. Why they did not is not material.

§ 30:16   WARRANTIES IN THE INTERNATIONAL SALE OF GOODS

Both the warranties of merchantability and fitness for a particular purpose exist under the Convention on Contracts for the International Sale of Goods. (See Part C, Chapter 27.) In most cases the provisions are identical to the UCC. Sellers, however, can expressly disclaim the convention's warranties, without mentioning merchantability or making the disclaimer conspicuous.

D.   DISCLAIMER OF WARRANTIES

The seller and the buyer may agree that there shall be no warranties. In some states this is limited in terms of public policy or consumer protection.

§ 30:17   VALIDITY OF DISCLAIMER

Warranties may be disclaimed by agreement of the parties, subject to the limita-

tion that such a provision must not be unconscionable.[15]

If a warranty of fitness[16] is excluded or if it is modified in writing, it must be conspicuous in order to make certain that the buyer will be aware of its presence. If the implied warranty of merchantability is excluded, the exclusion clause must expressly mention the word *merchantability*, and the exclusion must be conspicuous.

(a) CONSPICUOUSNESS. A disclaimer provision is made conspicuous by printing it under a conspicuous heading, but in such case the heading must indicate that there is an exclusion or modification of warranties. Conversely, a heading cannot be relied upon to make such a provision "conspicuous" when the heading is misleading and wrongfully gives the impression that there is a warranty. For example, the heading "Vehicle Warranty" is misleading if the provision that follows contains a limitation of warranties. A disclaimer that is hidden in a mass of printed material handed to the buyer is not conspicuous and is not effective to exclude warranties. Similarly, an inconspicuous disclaimer of warranties under a heading of "Notice to retail buyers" has no effect.

When a waiver of warranties fails to be effective because it is not conspicuous, the implied warranties that would arise in the absence of any waiver are operative.

(b) UNCONSCIONABILITY AND PUBLIC POLICY. An exclusion of warranties made in the manner specified by the UCC is not unconscionable. There is also authority that when the breach of warranty is the result of negligence of the seller, the disclaimer of warranty liability and a limitation of remedies to re-

---

[15]   UCC § § 2-316(1), 2-302(1). A distinction must be made between holding that the circumstances do not give rise to a warranty, thus precluding warranty liability, and holding that the warranty that would otherwise arise was excluded or surrendered by the contract of the parties. Dubbe v A.O. Smith Harvestore Products (Minn App) 399 NW2d 644 (1987).

[16]   By the letter of the Code, the text statement is applicable to any warranty of fitness, see UCC § 2-316(2), although by the Official Comment to § 2-316, point 4, it would appear to be only the warranty of fitness for a particular purpose.

funding the purchase price is not binding. Such a limitation is unreasonable, unconscionable, and against sound public policy. In some states, warranty disclaimers are invalid as contrary to public policy or because they are prohibited by consumer protection laws.

If a seller makes any written warranty of a consumer product costing more than $15, the seller is barred from excluding any implied warranty that would be implied under the law of sales.

§ 30:18   PARTICULAR PROVISIONS

A statement such as "There are no warranties that extend beyond the description on the face hereof" excludes all implied warranties of fitness. Implied warranties are excluded by the statement of "as is," "with all faults," or other language that in normal, common speech calls attention to the warranty exclusion and makes it clear that there is no implied warranty.

In order for a disclaimer of warranties to be a binding part of an oral sales contract, the disclaimer must be called to the attention of the buyer.

Provisions in a sales contract excluding warranties have only that effect. They do not bar the buyer from recovering damages for fraud, negligence, or strict tort liability.

§ 30:19   EXCLUSION OF WARRANTIES BY EXAMINATION OF GOODS

There is no implied warranty with respect to defects in goods that an examination should have revealed when the buyer, before making the final contract, has examined the goods, or model or sample, or has refused to make such examination.

The examination of the goods by the buyer does not exclude the existence of an express warranty unless it can be concluded that the buyer thereby learned of the falsity of the statement claimed to be a warranty, with the consequence that such

statement did not in fact form part of the basis of the bargain.

§ 30:20   POST-SALE DISCLAIMER

Frequently the statement excluding or modifying warranties appears for the first time in a written contract sent to confirm or memorialize the oral contract made earlier; or it appears in an invoice,[17] a bill, or an instruction manual delivered to the buyer at or after the time the goods are received. Such post-sale disclaimers have no effect on warranties that arose at the time of the sale.

An exclusion of warranties in a manufacturer's manual given to the buyer after the sale is not binding on a buyer because it is not a term of the sales contract.

If the buyer assents to the post-sale disclaimer, however, it is effective as a modification of the sales contract.

---

[17]   Old Albany Estates, Ltd v Highland Carpet Mills, Inc. (Okla) 604 F2d 849 (1979).

WARRANTIES

1. EXPRESS
   A. MAY BE ORAL OR WRITTEN
   B. FORM PART OF BASIS OF BARGAIN
   C. STATEMENT OF FACT
2. IMPLIED
   A. GOOD TITLE
   B. NO ENCUMBRANCES
   C. FITNESS FOR PARTICULAR PURPOSE
   D. NO INFRINGEMENT OF PATENT OR TRADEMARK
   E. MERCHANTABILITY
3. DISCLAIMERS
   A. MUST NOT BE UNCONSCIONABLE
   B. IF WRITTEN, MUST BE CONSPICUOUS
   C. IF DISCLAIM WARRANTY OF MERCHANTABILITY, MUST EXPRESSLY MENTION *MERCHANTABILITY*
   D. NO IMPLIED WARRANTIES WHERE GOODS SOLD "AS IS" OR "WITH ALL FAULTS"

FIGURE 30-1
WARRANTIES

E.   OTHER THEORIES OF PRODUCT LIABILITY

In addition to suit for breach of an express guarantee, an express warranty, or an implied warranty, a plaintiff in a given product liability case may be able to sue for negligence, fraud, or strict tort liability.

§ 30:21   NEGLIGENCE

A person injured because of the defective condition of a product may be entitled to sue the seller or manufacturer for the damages. The injured person must be able to show that the defendant was negligent in the preparation or manufacture of the article or failed to provide proper instructions and warnings as to dangers. An action for negligence rests upon common law tort principles and does not require privity of contract.

§ 30:22   FRAUD

The UCC expressly preserves the pre-Code law as to fraud. Thus, a person defrauded by false statements as to a product obtained from a distributor or manufacturer will generally be able to recover damages for the harm sustained because of such misrepresentations when the statements were made with knowledge that they were false or with reckless indifference as to whether they were true.

§ 30:23   STRICT TORT LIABILITY

Independently of the UCC, a manufacturer or distributor of a defective product is liable to a person who is injured by the product without regard to whether the person injured is a purchaser, a consumer, or a third person such as a bystander.[18] It is no defense that privity of contract does not exist between the injured party and the seller nor that the defect was found in a component part purchased from another manufacturer.[19] This concept is not one of absolute liability; that is, it must first be shown that there was a defect in the product at the time it left the control of the seller.[20] The seller is liable because the product is defective and unreasonably dangerous and has caused harm. It is immaterial whether or not the seller was negligent or whether the user was guilty of contributory negligence. Assumption of risk by the injured party, on the other hand, is a defense available to the seller.[21]

§ 30:24   CUMULATIVE THEORIES OF LIABILITY

The theories of product liability are not mutually exclusive. Thus, a given set of facts may give rise to two or more theories of liability as in the *Shaw* case.

---

[18]   Walker v Clark Equipment Co. (Iowa) 320 NW2d 561 (1982).
[19]   The concept of strict tort liability was judicially declared in Greenman v Yuba Power Products, 59 Cal 2d 57, 27 Cal Rptr 697, 377 P2d 897 (1963). This concept has been incorporated in the Restatement of Torts 2d as § 402A.
[20]   Shultz v Linden-Alimak, Inc. (Colo App) 734 P2d 146 (1986).
[21]   Central Telephone Co. v Fixtures Mfg. __ Nev __, 738 P2d 510 (1987).

SHAW V GENERAL MOTORS
(Colo App) 727 P2d 387 (1986)

General Motors (GM) manufactured the cab and chassis of a truck that was sold unchanged by Daniels Motors (DM) to the city of Colorado Springs. Fontaine Truck Equipment Co. (FTE) manufactured a dump bed and hoist that was sold by another equipment company to the City of Colorado Springs. Fontaine installed the dump bed and hoist on the General Motors truck and made further modifications as specified by the City so that the truck would be usable as a pothole repair truck by the city. Shaw, while in the city's employ, was injured when his co-worker backed the pothole repair truck over him. Shaw brought suit against GM, DM, and FTE. Shaw argued that the truck was defective and unreasonably dangerous to its user because of defendants' failure to warn of the necessity of installing a back-up alarm, and because of defendants' alleged failure to fulfill their duty in installing such a back-up alarm. He claimed liability because of (1) strict liability, (2) negligence, (3) breach of implied warranties of fitness and merchantability, and (4) breach of express warranties. From a judgment in favor of defendants, Shaw appealed.

PIERCE, J. . . .

I. Strict Liability
A. General Motors

A manufacturer of component parts, such as GM here, may be held strictly liable for injuries as a result of design defects in the component when it is expected to and does reach the consumer without substantial change in condition. While it may be arguable whether GM's cab and chassis underwent "substantial change in condition" because of the modifications made by the City, other issues regarding strict liability must be considered as to GM.

The critical questions as concerns GM are whether the condition of the truck at the time of its delivery to DM was defective and unreasonably dangerous without a back-up alarm or unreasonably dangerous as a result of a failure to warn. Based on the pleadings and other materials submitted, the truck was not in such a defective condition so as to impose strict liability upon GM.

The record here shows that the GM cab and chassis could be equipped for numerous different uses; that, at the time of assembly by GM, there was no restriction of rear vision; and that it was assembled by GM with two rear-view mirrors for visibility around most body installations. In rebuttal, plaintiff points to deposition testimony by a GM engineer who admitted that a back-up alarm system would be "desirable" given the City's use of the truck as a pothole repair truck. This testimony, however, does not show that a defective condition existed at the time of the truck's delivery to DM.

As a result, at the time that the truck left GM's control, it had no "inherent dangers" such as would expose GM to liability for failure to warn of an unreasonably dangerous condition. Based on the record, the likelihood of an accident resulting from the GM truck in the condition in which it was delivered was not such as to require warnings.

Plaintiff argues that GM should have foreseen that its truck would be transformed into a pothole filling truck which had visual impairment. Under the circumstances of this case, to require such foreseeability would be tantamount to making GM an insurer against all accidents. The principle of strict liability does not impose such absolute liability.

Thus, plaintiff could not have prevailed against GM on a theory of strict liability. Accordingly, judgment was proper.

B. Daniels Motors

The pleadings and affidavits . . . show that DM is not a "manufacturer" and, therefore, cannot be strictly liable. . . .

C. Fontaine

The critical questions as to FTE are whether the dump bed and hoist were in such a condition at the time of their delivery to the equipment company as to be defective and unreasonably dangerous without a back-up alarm or unreasonably dangerous as a result of a failure to warn. . . .

The fundamental bases for plaintiff's allegations that the dump bed and hoist are defective are that: (1) it lacked a back-up alarm and (2) FTE failed to warn that lack of a back-up alarm constituted an inherent danger. The lack of a back-up alarm cannot be considered an unreasonably dangerous or defective condition until final assembly of all components, because, until assembled, there can be no need for the back-up device.

Similarly, with respect to plaintiff's allegation that FTE failed to warn, considering the unlikelihood of the dump bed and hoist backing up by themselves, we conclude there is no reasonable likelihood of an accident as a result of FTE's failure to warn. The condition of FTE's product was not, therefore, defective and unreasonably dangerous without a warning. Thus, liability could not attach to FTE. Strict liability does not equate to absolute liability.

Therefore, plaintiff's allegations did not provide a valid basis for relief, and judgment was proper in favor of FTE.

II. Negligence

Before liability can be found in a negligence action, the existence of a duty of care must be determined. This is a question of law. Whether the law should impose a duty requires consideration of the risk involved, the foreseeability and likelihood of injury as weighed against the social utility of the actor's conduct, the magnitude of the burden of guarding against injury or harm, and the consequences of placing the burden upon the actor.

Based on these considerations, there may be a duty to install an alarm system, but it does not lie with the defendants here.

We rule that defendants here owed no duty to the class to which plaintiff belongs. GM, DM, and FTE, as manufacturers and sellers of component parts that were assembled by the City, could not properly evaluate, or likely foresee, the risks arising from not installing a specific safety feature such as a back-up alarm. The burden of guarding against the injury suffered here should appropriately be placed upon the entity that designed the final product, arranged for acquisition of all the component parts, and directed their assembly. We find little social utility in placing this burden upon the manufacturers and sellers of the component parts, who did not partake in the designing or assembling of the final product.

Thus, absent a duty of care, plaintiff's claims of negligence were properly dismissed against GM, DM, and FTE.

III. Implied Warranties

Implied warranty liability can extend to the manufacturer of component parts. Such liability can also extend to sellers of component parts. However, the lack of fitness for ordinary purposes as well as for particular purposes must be found in the component parts before they leave the component parts manufacturers or sellers.

Plaintiff claims that the GM cab and chassis were not safe and fit for this use and application. However, as was discussed in Part I herein, the record does not show that a defective condition existed at the time that the truck left GM and DM. The documentation presented here unrebuttably shows that the GM truck was safe and fit for ordinary use and for its particular purpose, as that particular purpose was identifiable prior to assembly by the City. Therefore, based on the record, plaintiff could not prevail on his claims of breach of implied warranties against GM and DM.

Moreover, the record shows that DM sold to the City a truck which met the specifications set forth in the City's bidding form. DM, having substantially complied with the specifications will not be held to have extended a warranty of fitness.

The record also supports FTE's substantial compliance with the City's specifications. Therefore, it too cannot be held liable on implied warranties of fitness for particular or ordinary purposes.

IV. Express Warranties

In their pleadings, plaintiff alleges that GM, DM, and FTE breached express warranties of safety and fitness, and other express warranties set forth in their publications. On appeal, plaintiff specifically argues that deposition testimony stating that "Chevy's business is providing the right truck for your business" represents an express warranty to which the GM truck did not conform. This language does not constitute an affirmation of fact or a promise; it is "merely the sellers' opinion or commendation of the goods." See § 4-2-313(2), C.R.S. Thus, no warranty was created. . . .

[Judgments affirmed]

QUESTIONS

1. How did the court decide the question of strict liability against the defendants?
2. How did the court decide the issue of negligence?
3. Was there a breach of either express or implied warranties?

SUMMARY

There are six theories in the law to protect from harm caused by defective products. They are: (a) guarantee, (b) negligence, (c) fraud, (d) express warranty, (e) implied warranty, and (f) strict tort liability.

Theories of product liability are not mutually exclusive, and a given set of facts may give rise to two or more theories of product liability.

The requirement of privity of contract, that is, that only the parties to the sales contract could sue each other, has been widely rejected. The law is moving toward the conclusion that persons harmed because of an improper product may sue anyone who is in any way responsible. The requirement of privity has been abolished by the UCC in cases where the plaintiff is a member of the buyer's family or household or a guest of the buyer and has sustained personal injury because of the product.

Warranties may be express or implied. Both have the same effect and operate as though the defendant had made an express guarantee.

A warranty made after a sale does not require consideration as it is regarded as a modification of the sales contract.

Express warranties are regulated by federal statute and the FTC. These warranties are labeled as full or limited warranties and must conform to certain standards.

A distinction is made between a merchant seller and the casual seller. There is a greater range of warranties in the case of the merchant seller.

A seller makes a warranty of good title unless such warranty is excluded. Warranties that the goods shall conform to the description sample or model are express warranties, while warranties of fitness for a particular purpose and merchantability are implied warranties.

Warranties may be disclaimed by agreement of the parties, provided the disclaimer is not unconscionable. Disclaimer provisions to exclude warranties must be conspicuous. Post-sale disclaimers have no effect on warranties that arose at the time of the sale.

The warranties of merchantability and fitness exist under the CISG, but disclaimers need not mention merchantibility nor must the disclaimer be conspicuous.

The strict tort liability plaintiff must show that there was a defect in the product at the time it left the control of the seller. No negligence need be established on the part of the manufacturer, nor is contributory negligence of the plaintiff a defense. The seller may show that the injured party assumed the risk.

Questions and Case Problems

1. What social forces are affected by the abolition of the requirement of privity in product liability suits?

2. Norma purchases a dress from the Borolsky Dress Shop. After she gets the dress home, she is doubtful as to the quality of the cloth. When she complains to Borolsky, they assure her that the cloth is 100 percent wool. Later, Norma proves that the dress is only 60 percent wool. Can she hold Borolsky liable on the statement that it was 100 percent wool?

3. The Erie Railroad holds a public auction sale of unclaimed baggage. Mayo purchases a trunk at the sale. Later the police take the trunk from Mayo on the ground that it had been stolen from its true owner. Mayo sues the Erie Railroad on the ground that by selling the trunk it had made an implied warranty that it had the title or the right to sell. Since it did not have title, Mayo claims Erie must pay Mayo for the loss sustained because of the taking of the trunk by the police. Is Mayo correct?

4. Steve purchases an electric kitchen range from the Shermack Electric Appliance Company. In the instruction manual that is enclosed in the crate in which the range is delivered to Steve's home, there is a statement that Shermack makes no warranty, express or implied, with respect to the range. The range works properly for two weeks and then ceases to function. When Steve demands his money back from Shermack, it raises the defense that all warranties, including that of fitness for normal use, were excluded by the statement in the manual. Is Shermack correct?

5. Edgmore has a class reunion at his house. There is a substantial amount of food that is left over. He sells the surplus food to his neighbor Hartranft for a fraction of its price. In eating this food, Hartranft is injured from a piece of glass that was contained in a can of salmon. Hartranft sued Edgmore for the injuries sustained. Is Edgmore liable?

6. A buyer purchased a new car wash from a dealer. It washed the cars effectively, but it would knock off external accessories such as mirrors and radio antennas. When the buyer complained, the seller stated that the contract made no provision with respect to such matters. Was this a valid defense?

7. A purchased a refrigerator from the B store. The written contract stated that the refrigerator was sold "as is" and that the warranty of merchantability and all warranties of fitness were excluded. This was stated in large cap-

ital letters printed just above the line on which *A* signed her name. The refrigerator worked properly for a few weeks and then stopped. *B* refused to do anything about it because of the exclusion of the warranties made by the contract. *A* claimed that this exclusion was not binding because it was unconscionable. Was *A* correct? [Avery v Aladdin Products Div., Nat. Service Industries, Inc. 128 Ga App 266, 196 SE2d 357]

8. A manufacturer advertised its product in national magazines. The advertisement induced a buyer to purchase the product. The product did not live up to the statements in the advertisement. The buyer claimed that there was a breach of warranty. The manufacturer contended that the statements in the advertisement were obviously sales talk and therefore could not constitute a warranty. Was this a valid defense? [Westrie Battery Co. v Standard Electric Co. (CA10 Colo) 482 F2d 1307]

9. Joyce worked in a business office. She sold her motorcycle to James. The motorcycle did not run properly. James demanded the return of his money because there had been a breach of the implied warranty that the motorcycle would be fit for normal use. Was James entitled to recover the purchase price on this ground?

10. The defendant, Zogarts, manufactured and sold a practice device for beginning golfers. The statements on the package stated that the device was completely safe and that a player could never be struck by the golf ball of the device. Hauter was hit by the ball when practicing with the device. He sued Zogarts. Zogarts denied liability on the ground that the statements were merely matters of opinion, and therefore liability could not be based on them. Was this a valid defense? [Hauter v Zogarts, 14 Cal 104, 120 Cal Rptr 681, 534 P2d 377]

11. The buyer purchased an engine to operate an irrigation pump. The buyer selected the engine from a large number that were standing on the floor of the seller's stockroom. A label on the engine stated that it would produce 100 horsepower. The buyer needed an engine which would generate at least 80 horsepower. In actual use in the buyer's irrigation system, the engine only generated 60 horsepower. The buyer sued the seller for damages. The seller raised the defense that no warranty of fitness for the buyer's particular purpose of operating an irrigation pump had arisen because the seller did not know of the use to which the buyer intended to put the engine, and the buyer had not relied on the seller's skill and judgment in selecting the particular engine. Was the seller liable? [Potter v Ryndall, 22 NC App 129, 205 SE2d 808, cert den 285 NC 661, 207 SE2d 762]

12. Roberts, a certified public accountant, explained to Haynes, a sales agent for a manufacturer of calculating machines, a certain kind of accounting work for which he needed a machine. He asked Haynes to select a machine from his principal's stock and deliver it. Haynes had his firm to deliver a machine to Roberts, for which Roberts paid cash. Later, Roberts discovered that the machine would not do the required work. What warranty, if any, has been breached?

13. A new Dodge automobile was purchased from a Dodge dealer. Numerous problems existed with the transmission, and it had to be replaced a few times. Soon the purchaser was having other problems with the car. The purchaser sued the Dodge dealer for breach of the implied warranty of merchantability. The dealer argued that he was not liable as he had disclaimed all warranties, and furthermore, the purchase order signed by the buyer contained a clause on its front stating that the automobile was sold "AS IS." In addition, a disclaimer of the warranties of merchantability and fitness was printed in contrasting red type. Decide. [Koperski v Husker Dodge, Inc., 208 Neb 29, 302 NW2d 655]

14. A strict tort liability defendant may raise the defense that there was no negligence involved and that even if there was negligence, the plaintiff cannot recover because the plaintiff was guilty of contributory negligence. Appraise this statement.

15. Mark went to the Happy Hour Cafe to eat breakfast. He ordered grapefruit juice, french toast, and milk. While drinking the milk, his throat was cut because the milk contained a piece of glass. Mark thereupon brought an action against Happy Hour to recover damages for personal injuries resulting from an implied breach of warranty. Will he be successful?

31

REMEDIES FOR BREACH OF SALES CONTRACTS

If one of the parties to a sale fails to perform the contract duties, the law makes several remedies available to the other party. In addition, the parties may have included provisions pertaining to remedies in their contract.

A. STATUTE OF LIMITATIONS

Judicial remedies are ordinarily subject to a time limitation that bars resort to the courts after the expiration of a particular period of time. The UCC supplies the statute of limitations for sales of goods except when suit is brought on a theory of tort, such as negligence, fraud, or strict tort.

§ 31:1   CODE CLAIM

An action for a breach of a sales contract must be commenced within four years after the cause of action arises, regardless of when the aggrieved party learned that there was a cause of action. In the case of a warranty, the breach occurs when tender of delivery is made to the buyer even though no defect then appears and no harm is sustained until a later date.[1]

(a) FUTURE PERFORMANCE WARRANTY. When an express warranty is made as to future performance, the statute of limitations does not run from the time of the tender but from the date when the future performance begins.[2]

(b) NOTICE OF DEFECT. In addition to bringing suit within four years under the UCC statute of limitations, the buyer who sues the seller for damages claimed because of a breach of the sales contract must give the seller notice of such breach within a reasonable time after the buyer discovers or should have discovered the defect.[3]

§ 31:2   NON-CODE CLAIM

When the plaintiff sues on a non-Code theory, even though it relates to goods, the UCC statute of limitations does not apply. Thus, when the plaintiff sues on the basis of strict tort, fraud, or negligence, the action is subject to the tort statutes of limitations. When the plaintiff sues on the basis of an express guarantee, the action is governed by the contract statute of limitations.

B.   REMEDIES OF THE SELLER

When a sales contract is broken by the buyer, the seller has a number of remedies available. The more common ones are discussed in the following sections.[4]

§ 31:3   SELLER'S LIEN

In the absence of an agreement for the extension of credit to the purchaser, the seller has a lien on the goods, that is, the right to retain possession of the goods until the seller is paid for them. Even when the goods are sold on credit, the seller has a lien on the goods if the buyer becomes insolvent or if the credit period expires while the goods are in the seller's possession.

The seller's lien may be lost by (a) waiver, as by a later extension of credit, (b) delivery of the goods to a carrier or other bailee, without a reservation of title or possession, for the purpose of delivery to the buyer, (c) acquisition of the property by the buyer or an agent by lawful means, or (d) payment or tender of the price by the buyer.

§ 31:4   RESALE BY SELLER

When the buyer has broken the contract by wrongfully rejecting the goods, wrongfully revoking acceptance, failing to pay, or repudiating the contract, the seller may resell the goods or the balance of them in the seller's possession. After the resale, the seller is not liable to the original buyer upon the contract or for any profit obtained on the

---

[1]   Nelson v International Harvester Corp. (Minn App) 394 NW2d 578 (1986).

[2]   Jones & Laughlin Steel Corp. v Johns-Manville Sales Corp. (CA3 Pa) 626 F2d 280 (1980).

[3]   UCC § 2-607(3)(a).

[4]   When the goods purchased by the buyer are being shipped to the buyer or are held in a warehouse, an unpaid seller has a limited right to prevent delivery of the goods to the buyer. UCC § 2-705. If the buyer repudiates the contract while the goods are being manufactured, the seller-manufacturer may stop further production or may continue to complete the manufacturing of the goods. UCC § 2-704(2). An unpaid seller who sold on credit has a limited right to take the goods back if the buyer was insolvent. UCC § 2-702.

resale. On the other hand, if the proceeds are less than the contract price, the seller may recover the loss from the original buyer.[5]

Reasonable notice must be given to the original buyer of the intention to make a private sale. Such notice must also be given of a public sale unless the goods are perishable in nature or threaten to decline rapidly in value. Notice of a public sale must also be given to the general public in such manner as is commercially reasonable under the circumstances.

§ 31:5 CANCELLATION BY SELLER

When the buyer wrongfully rejects the goods, wrongfully revokes an acceptance of the goods, repudiates the contract, or fails to make a payment due on or before delivery, the seller may cancel the contract. Such action puts an end to the contract, discharging all obligations on both sides that are still unperformed, but the seller retains any remedy with respect to the breach by the buyer. Cancellation revests the seller with title to the goods.

A seller may only cancel the contract if the buyer's breach substantially impairs the value of the contract to the seller.

§ 31:6 SELLER'S ACTION FOR DAMAGES

If the buyer wrongfully refuses to accept the goods or repudiates the contract, the seller may sue for the damages that the seller sustains. In the ordinary case, the amount of damages is to be measured by the difference between the market price at the time and place of the tender of the goods and the contract price.

If this measure of damages does not place the seller in the position in which the seller would have been placed by the buyer's performance, recovery may be permitted of lost profits, together with an allowance for overhead. The seller may in any

case recover, as incidental damages, any commercially reasonable charges, expenses, or commissions incurred in enforcing that remedy, such as those sustained in the transportation, care, and custody of the goods after the buyer's breach; and in the return or resale of the goods. Such additional damages are recovered in addition to any other damages that may be recovered by the seller.

The seller is not entitled to recover the contract or purchase price except as stated in § 31:7.

§ 31:7 SELLER'S ACTION FOR THE PURCHASE PRICE

The seller may bring an action to recover the purchase price, together with incidental damages as described in connection with the action for damages, if (a) the goods have been accepted, and there has not been any rightful revocation of acceptance; (b) conforming goods were damaged or destroyed after the risk of loss passed to the buyer; or (c) the seller has identified proper goods to the contract but, after the buyer's breach, has been or will be unable to resell them at a reasonable price. In consequence of these limitations, the right to sue for the contract price, as distinguished from a suit for damages for breach of contract, is a remedy that is not ordinarily available to the seller.

C. REMEDIES OF THE BUYER

When a sales contract is broken by the seller, the buyer has a number of remedies provided by Article 2 of the UCC.

§ 31:8 REJECTION OF IMPROPER TENDER OR DELIVERY

If the goods or the tender made by the seller do not conform to the contract in any respect, the buyer may reject the goods. For example, the buyer may reject a mobile

---

[5]   UCC § 2-706(1),(6).

home when it does not contain an air conditioner with the capacity specified by the contract.

The buyer may reject a tender that is not perfect, as against the contention that a substantial performance is sufficient.

When the goods tendered consist of different units some of which conform to the contract, the buyer has the choice of (a) rejecting the entire quantity tendered, (b) accepting the entire tender, or (c) accepting any one or more commercial units and rejecting the rest.[6]

The rejection must be made within a reasonable time after the delivery or tender, and the buyer must notify the seller of the choice made.[7]

After rejecting the goods, the buyer may not exercise any right of ownership as to the goods but must hold them awaiting instructions from the seller.

§ 31:9 REVOCATION OF ACCEPTANCE

The buyer may revoke acceptance of the goods when they do not conform to the contract to such an extent that the defect substantially impairs the value of the contract to the buyer. For example, a buyer purchased an emergency electric power plant. The plant only produced about 65 percent of the power called for by the contract, and this was not sufficient to operate the buyer's equipment. Repeated attempts to improve the system failed. There was such a nonconformity as substantially impaired the value of the contract to the buyer, and the buyer was entitled to revoke acceptance.

Proof of substantial impairment is required to justify revocation of acceptance. The mere fact that the goods do not conform to the contract does not entitle the buyer to revoke acceptance. On the other hand, it is not necessary that the buyer show that the goods are worthless.

The revocation of acceptance does no more than revoke the acceptance. In itself, it does not cancel the contract with the seller. After revoking acceptance, the buyer has the choice of canceling that contract or insisting that the seller deliver conforming goods in place of the goods originally delivered.

In the *Asciolla* case, the court faced the question of whether the seller could prevent the buyer from revoking acceptance by offering to repair the defects.

---

[6] McClure Oil v Murray Equipment, Inc. (Ind App) 515 NE2d 546 (1987).

[7] UCC § 2-602(1).

ASCIOLLA V MANTER OLDSMOBILE-PONTIAC, INC.
8 NH 91, 370 A2d 270 (1977)

Angello Asciolla purchased a new automobile in December. The car was waterproofed and then delivered to the buyer. He drove it to Wisconsin the following January. The car stood outside overnight. The next day the car would not run because the transmission was inoperable. There was ice in the transmission and substantial rust. These facts seemed to confirm the statement that was later made to the buyer that the car had been flooded before it had been sold to him. The dealer offered to repair the car. The buyer refused to accept repairs and insisted that he could revoke his acceptance and demanded a new car. He sued the dealer and the manufacturer. The case was referred to a master who recommended that damages be awarded to the buyer. However, the master decided that the buyer should not be allowed to revoke the acceptance because a reasonable person would have been satisfied with the repairs that were offered by the seller. From this judgment, the plaintiff appealed.

DOUGLAS, J. . . . The question . . . is whether the inoperable transmission of the plaintiff's car was a defect that substantially impaired the value of the product to him. [UCC §] 2–608, Comment 2 states that the test of "substantial impairment" is "whether the non-conformity is such as will *in fact* cause a substantial impairment of value *to the buyer* . . ." (Emphasis added). This section, therefore, creates a subjective test in the sense that the needs and circumstances of the particular buyer must be examined. . . . The trier of fact must make an objective determination that the value of the goods to the buyer has in fact been substantially impaired. . . . *Tiger Motor Co. v McMurtry*, 284 Ala 283, 224 So 2d 638 (1969). . . .

We find . . . that the value of the subject automobile to [the buyer] was substantially impaired. In purchasing a new car the plaintiff was making a major investment. Few items which are considered necessities occupy such a significant portion of an individual consumer's income as does a new automobile. Few purchases are made with more care and deliberation. The record indicates that the plaintiff was a particularly prudent and painstaking car buyer and that he had indeed once before refused to accept an automobile from the defendants which merely had a dented fender which had been repaired. Within three weeks of the purchase of the car at issue in this case he found it to be totally inoperable. He was informed by franchised representatives of the manufacturer that the car had been flooded or submerged. While the master found that the evidence presented at the hearing did not support such a conclusion, no satisfactory reason was ever presented to the plaintiff to otherwise explain the presence of ice in his transmission. Nor was [the buyer] offered any guarantees concerning other deficiencies, caused by the same mysterious condition, which he very reasonably apprehended might arise in the future.

Under these facts, we think it clear that the plaintiff's confidence in the reliability and integrity of his new automobile was severely undermined. He had bargained for a new car, expecting to receive a vehicle upon whose dependability and safety he could comfortably rely. Instead he received a product which he understandably feared was what is known in popular parlance as "a lemon." The plaintiff is correct in his assertion that a new automobile is more than the sum of its various components. It is the integrity of the vehicle as a whole which is the essence of the consumer's bargain. As the Superior Court of New Jersey said in a markedly similar case concerning a new car with a defective transmission "[the buyer] assumed what every new car buyer has a right to assume and, indeed, has been led to assume by the high powered advertising techniques of the auto industry — that his new car, with the exception of very minor adjustments, would be mechanically new and factory-furnished, operate perfectly, and be free of substantial defects." *Zabriskie Chevrolet, Inc. v Smith*, 99 NJ Super 441, 240 A2d 195 (1968). The plaintiff's situation cannot be accurately compared to cases . . . in which the cars presented defects which were trivial and readily repaired. The new car in the instant case was rendered wholly inoperable by a defective condition which permeated one of its most essential systems. Under such circumstances, his revocation of acceptance is justified. . . .

The defendants contend that they are entitled to cure the nonconformity in the tendered goods. Although a seller is given the right to cure under [UCC §] 2–508 in the context of rejection of goods, no such right is granted by [UCC §] 2–608(1)(b) when acceptance is being revoked. Whether a seller's right to cure may be implied under this section has been the subject of considerable dispute. . . . We need not decide the question in this case, however. For the reasons set forth above, any cure other than replacement of the automobile with a new one would, under the facts of this case, be insufficient to accomplish a conforming tender. See *Zabriskie Chevrolet, Inc. v Smith, supra;* 2 R. Anderson, Uniform Commercial Code § 2–608:10 (2d ed. 1971). . . .

[Judgment reversed and action remanded]

QUESTIONS

1. What remedy did the buyer exercise?
2. Was he entitled to do so?
3. Was it important that the seller offered to repair the defects?

§ 31:10 PROCEDURE FOR REVOKING ACCEPTANCE

In order to revoke acceptance of the goods, the buyer must take certain steps.

(a) NOTICE OF REVOCATION. The acceptance of goods cannot be revoked unless the buyer gives the seller a notice of revocation. The revocation of acceptance is effective when the buyer notifies the seller. It is not necessary that the buyer make an actual return of the goods in order to make the revocation effective.

(b) TIME FOR REVOCATION. The notice of revocation must be given within a reasonable time after the buyer discovers that the goods do not conform or after the buyer should have discovered such nonconformity. A buyer is not required to notify the seller of the revocation of acceptance until the buyer is reasonably certain that the nonconformity of the goods substantially impairs the value of the contract. Thus, the mere fact that the buyer suspects that the goods do not conform and that such nonconformity may substantially impair the value of the contract does not itself require that the buyer immediately give notice to the seller.

In the *Central Florida* case, the buyer of a satellite television system used the goods for one and a half years before revoking his acceptance.

CENTRAL FLORIDA ANTENNA SERVICE V CRABTREE
(Fla App) 503 So 2d 1351 (1987)

Crabtree purchased from Central a satellite system capable of producing stereo sound. Relying upon representations of employees of Central, Crabtree purchased a system for his home in 1983. Crabtree made numerous complaints about the quality of the stereo sound and clarity of the picture. In December of 1984, one year after purchase, Central adjusted and connected the equipment to Crabtree's satisfaction, and Crabtree paid the balance on the purchase price. In April of 1985, Crabtree again complained that the equipment was not working properly. Crabtree then brought an action seeking revocation of his acceptance and refund of the purchase price. He did not seek damages or other relief although there was an existing eighteen-month warranty on defective parts. From a judgment in favor of Crabtree, the seller appealed.

SHAYS, J. . . . Section 672.608, Florida Statutes (1985) [UCC § 2-608] entitled "Revocation of Acceptance," is controlling. Article Two of the Code impacts on this case. . . .

> 672.608 Revocation of acceptance in whole or in part.
>   (1) The buyer may revoke his acceptance of a lot or commercial unit whose nonconformity substantially impairs its value to him if he has accepted it:
>   (a) On the reasonable assumption that its nonconformity would be cured and it has not been seasonably cured; or
>   (b) Without discovery of such nonconformity if his acceptance was reasonably induced either by the difficulty of discovery before acceptance or by the seller's assurances.
>   (2) *Revocation of acceptance must occur within a reasonable time after the buyer discovers or should have discovered the ground for it and before any substantial change in condition of the goods which is not caused by their own defects. It is not effective until the buyer notifies the seller of it.*
>   (3) A buyer who so revokes has the same rights and duties with regard to the goods involved as if he had rejected them. (Emphasis added).

In this case, based on the stipulated record, Crabtree accepted the system by keeping it for in excess of a year, and paying for it in full after it was made to function to his satisfaction. Thereafter, section 672.608 limited and controlled his ability to revoke his acceptance. By waiting until May of 1985 to seek rescission, having had possession and use of the system for one and a half years, Crabtree clearly did not act "within a reasonable time" after discovering the system's defects. In most cases the reasonableness of the delay is a fact question. However here, Crabtree's one and a half year delay after knowledge of the system's problems forecloses his remedy of revocation as a matter of law.

While a failure to properly reject goods may affect the amount of damages a buyer can recover, it does not preclude him from making a claim for breach of warranty. *United States Fidelity & Guaranty v. North American Steel Corp.*, 335 So 2d 18 (Fla.2d DCA 1976).

Accordingly, we reverse the judgment because there was no basis upon which to find a "revocation of acceptance" under section 672.608. However, this does not preclude the trial court from awarding damages under a claim of breach of warranty, if appropriate, and we remand this cause for further proceedings not inconsistent with this decision.
[Judgment reversed]

QUESTIONS

1. When must revocation of acceptance occur?
2. What did the court decide as to the issue of timely revocation?
3. Could Crabtree have sued for breach of warranty?

A buyer is not barred from revoking acceptance of the goods because the buyer has delayed until attempts of the seller to correct the defects proved unsuccessful. For example, the lapse of even a year does not bar revocation of acceptance where the goods are of a complex nature, such as a computer, and the seller was continuously experimenting and assuring the buyer that the goods would be made to work.

(c) DISPOSITION OF GOODS AFTER REVOCATION. After making a revocation of acceptance, the buyer must hold the goods awaiting instructions from the seller. If the buyer has paid the seller in advance, the buyer may retain possession of the goods after revoking acceptance as security for the refund of the money that has been paid. Postrevocation use of the goods does not nullify the prior revocation of acceptance when such use is reasonable under the circumstances.[8]

§ 31:11 BUYER'S ACTION FOR DAMAGES FOR NONDELIVERY

If the seller fails to deliver as required by the contract or repudiates the contract, or if the buyer properly rejects tendered goods or revokes acceptance of nonconforming goods, the buyer is entitled to sue the seller for damages for breach of contract. The buyer is entitled to recover the difference between the market price at the time the buyer learned of the breach and the contract price.

Within a reasonable time after the seller's breach, the buyer may **cover,** that is, procure the same or similar goods elsewhere.[9] If the buyer acts in good faith, the measure of damages for the seller's nondelivery or repudiation is then the difference between the cost of cover and the contract price.

§ 31:12 ACTION FOR BREACH OF WARRANTY

One remedy that may be available to a buyer is an action for breach of warranty.

(a) NOTICE OF BREACH. If the buyer has accepted goods that do not conform to the contract or as to which there is a breach of warranty, the buyer must notify the seller of the breach within a reasonable time after the breach is discovered or should have been discovered. Otherwise the buyer is not entitled to complain.[10]

(b) MEASURE OF DAMAGES. If the buyer has given the necessary notice of breach, the buyer may recover damages measured by the loss resulting in the normal course of events from the breach. If suit is brought for breach of warranty, the measure of damages is the difference between the value of the goods as they were when accepted and the value that they would have had if they had been as warranted.

In other cases, the buyer may recover the difference between the contract price and the actual value of the goods.

The buyer may also recover as damages the loss directly and naturally resulting from that breach. In other words, the buyer may recover for the loss proximately resulting from the failure to deliver the goods as warranted. Thus, a buyer may recover the cost of renting other equipment when the equipment sold by the defendant did not work because of its defective condition. When the buyer resells the goods and then, because of their defective condition, is required to indemnify customers of the buyer, the original buyer may recover such loss from the original seller as consequential damages.

Where the condition that breaches the warranty induces fright that causes illness, the warranty liability includes damages for such illness.

A buyer who is entitled to recover damages from the seller may deduct the

---

[8] Johannsen v Minnesota Valley Ford Tractor Co. (Minn) 304 NW2d 654 (1981).
[9] Banner Iron Works, Inc. v Amax Zinc Co. (CA8 Mo) 621 F2d 883 (1980).

[10] Armco Steel Corp. v Isaacson Structural Steel Co. (Alaska) 611 P2d 507 (1980).

amount of such damages from any balance remaining due on the purchase price, provided the seller is notified of the buyer's intention to do so.[11]

(c) Notice of Third Party Action Against Buyer. The buyer may be sued in consequence of the seller's breach of warranty, as when the buyer's customers sue because of the condition of the goods that the buyer has resold to them. In such a case, it is optional with the buyer whether or not to give the seller notice of the action and to request the seller to defend that action.

The buyer may also be sued by a third person because of patent infringement. In this case, however, the buyer must give notice of the action to the seller. Moreover, the seller can demand control over the defense of that action.[12]

§ 31:13 Cancellation by Buyer

The buyer may cancel or rescind the contract if the seller fails to deliver the goods or repudiates the contract or if the buyer has rightfully rejected tender of the goods or rightfully revoked acceptance of them. A buyer who cancels the contract is entitled to recover as much of the purchase price as has been paid, including the value of any property given as a trade-in as part of the purchase price. The fact that the buyer cancels the contract does not destroy the buyer's cause of action against the seller for breach of that contract. The buyer may therefore recover from the seller not only any payment made on the purchase price, but, in addition, damages for the breach of the contract. The damages represent the difference between the contract price and the cost of cover.[13]

The right of the buyer to cancel or rescind the sales contract may be lost by a delay in exercising the right. A buyer who

with full knowledge of the defects in the goods makes partial payments or performs acts of dominion inconsistent with any intent to cancel cannot thereafter cancel the contract.

§ 31:14 Buyer's Resale of Goods

When the buyer has possession of the goods after rightfully rejecting them or after rightfully revoking acceptance, the buyer is treated the same as a seller in possession of goods after the default of a buyer. That is, the aggrieved buyer has a security interest in the goods to protect the claim against the seller and may resell the goods as though the aggrieved buyer were a seller. From the proceeds of the sale, the aggrieved buyer is entitled to deduct any payments made on the price and any expenses reasonably incurred in the inspection, receipt, transportation, care and custody, and resale of the goods.[14]

§ 31:15 Action for Conversion or Recovery of Goods

When, as a result of the sales agreement, ownership passes to the buyer and the seller wrongfully refuses or neglects to deliver the goods, the buyer may maintain any action allowed by law to the owner of goods wrongfully converted or withheld. The obligation of the seller to deliver proper goods may be enforced by an order for specific performance when the goods are "unique or in other proper circumstances."[15] Distributors have been granted specific performance against suppliers to deliver the goods covered by supply contracts. Specific performance will not be granted, however, merely because the price of the goods purchased from the seller has gone up. In such a case, the buyer can still purchase the goods in the open

---

[11] UCC § 2-717.
[12] UCC § 2-607.
[13] UCC § 2-712(1), (2).

[14] UCC § 2-715(1).
[15] UCC § 2-716(1).

market, and the fact that it will cost more to cover can be compensated for by allowing the buyer to recover greater damages from the seller.

§ 31:16 REMEDIES FOR FRAUD OF SELLER

Independently of the preceding remedies, the buyer has the right to sue the seller for damages for the latter's fraud and to cancel the transaction on that ground.[16]

As these remedies for fraud exist independently of the provisions of the UCC, the buyer may assert such remedies even though barred by the UCC from exercising any remedy for a breach of warranty. Likewise a limitation on remedies or exclusion of warranty liability has no effect on the buyer's claim for damages for fraud.

REMEDIES OF SELLER	REMEDIES OF BUYER
LIEN RESALE CANCELLATION ACTION FOR DAMAGES ACTION FOR PRICE	REJECTION OF IMPROPER TENDER OR DELIVERY REVOCATION OF ACCEPTANCE ACTION FOR DAMAGES FOR NONDELIVERY ACTION FOR DAMAGES FOR BREACH OF WARRANTY CANCELLATION RESALE ACTION FOR CONVERSION OR RECOVERY ACTION FOR FRAUD

FIGURE 31-1
REMEDIES FOR BREACH OF SALES CONTRACT

D. CONTRACT PROVISIONS ON REMEDIES

The UCC permits the parties to modify or limit by their contract the remedies that they otherwise possess.

§ 31:17 LIMITATION OF DAMAGES

The parties to the sales contract may seek to limit or exclude the recovery of damages in case of breach.

(a) LIQUIDATION OF DAMAGES. The parties may specify the exact amount of damages that may be recovered in case of breach. Such a **liquidation of damages** is valid if the amount so specified is reasonable in the light of the actual harm that would be caused by the breach, the difficulty of proving the amount of such loss, and the inconvenience and impracticality of suing for damages or enforcing other remedies for breach.

(b) EXCLUSION OF DAMAGES. The sales contract may provide that in case of breach no damages may be recovered or that no consequential damages may be recovered. Such total exclusions are prima facie unconscionable, and therefore prima facie not binding, when goods are sold for consum-

---

[16] Stephenson v Frazier, ___ Ind App ___, 399 NE2d (1980).

er use and personal injuries are sustained. Thus, a defendant, in such a case, cannot rely on the contract limitation unless the defendant is able to prove that the limitation of liability was commercially reasonable and fair, rather than oppressive and surprising. Moreover, when the seller would be liable to the buyer for damages, the seller cannot exclude liability for personal injuries to members of the buyer's family or household, or to guests of the buyer.

In cases not involving consumer goods and personal injuries, the plaintiff has the burden of proving that a limitation on damages is not binding because unconscionable. When the seller knows that the failure of the product, such as a harvester, to perform will cause serious economic loss, a limitation of damages for breach to the return of the purchase price is void as unconscionable.

A limitation of damages that is hidden in a paragraph headed *guarantee* is misleading and unconscionable.[17]

§ 31:18   DOWN PAYMENTS AND DEPOSITS

The buyer may have made a deposit with the seller or an initial or down payment at the time of making the contract. If the contract contains a valid liquidation-of-damages provision and the buyer defaults, the seller must return any part of the down payment or deposit in excess of the amount specified by the liquidated damages clause. In the absence of such a clause, and in the absence of proof of greater damages sustained, the seller's damages are computed as 20 percent of the purchase price or $500, whichever is the smaller. The extent to which the down payment exceeds such amount must be returned to the buyer.

In the *Stanturf* case, the buyer defaulted, and the seller refused to return the money and the trade-in received by the seller.

[17] Jutta's Incorporated v Fireco Equipment Co. 150 NJ Super 301, 375 A2d 687 (1977).

STANTURF V QUALITY DODGE, INC.

3 Kan App 2d 485, 596 P2d 1247 (1979)

Keith Stanturf wanted a van. He went to Quality Dodge, Inc. and selected a particular van, left his car as a trade-in valued at $1,000 and made a cash payment of $500. He later refused to go through with the sale because he believed that the seller had substituted another van in place of the one he had selected. He demanded the return of his money, damages, and the trade-in. Quality Dodge refused to make such return. Stanturf then sued Quality Dodge. From a judgment refusing to require the return of the deposit and the trade-in, Stanturf appealed.

ABBOTT, J. . . . The common law rule regarding restitution of property advanced by a breaching buyer was stated in *Gibbons v Hayden*, 3 Kan App 38, 40-41, 44 P 445, 445 (1896).

. . . The party who has advanced money in part performance of such an agreement — the other party being ready and willing to perform on his part — cannot, without just cause or excuse, refuse to proceed with the contract, and recover back what he has advanced. . . .

The early common law rule in this instance, however, has been replaced by statute. [UCC §] 2–718(2) provides:

> (2) Where the seller justifiably withholds delivery of goods because of the buyer's breach, the buyer is entitled to restitution of any amount by which the sum of his payments exceeds
>
> (a) the amount to which the seller is entitled by virtue of terms liquidating the seller's damages in accordance with subsection (1), or
>
> (b) in the absence of such terms, twenty percent of the value of the total performance for which the buyer is obligated under the contract or $500, whichever is smaller.

The above provision is discussed in Anderson, Uniform Commercial Code, § 2–718:7 (2d ed 1971).

> The general objective of Code § 2–718 is to prevent the oppression of the buyer who has breached the contract, by requiring that the seller return to the buyer so much of any deposit or down payment as exceeds the damages which the seller in fact sustains.
>
> This principle is applicable to anything paid or delivered by the buyer to the seller, whether as a part or down payment on the purchase price or as security for performance, and without regard to whether the buyer's payment was in money or goods.
>
> The applicability of the refund clause of the Code is not affected by the fact that the breach by the buyer was willful or without justification. . . .

As there is no liquidated damages provision involved, application of [UCC §] 2–718(2) to the present case may limit defendant's retention of plaintiff's property to $500. If Quality Dodge, Inc., can prove special damages, authority exists which recognizes a seller's right to prove and recover additional damages. . . . If special damages are not applicable, the trial court should order restitution of all but $500 to plaintiff.

. . . We remand to the trial court to fix damages.

[Action remanded]

Questions

1. Did the buyer act in good faith in refusing to go through with the contract?
2. What social force is furthered by the rule adopted and created by the Code as applied in the *Stanturf* case?
3. How is the rule of the Code that is applied in the *Stanturf* case related to the rule as to the mitigation of damages?

---

§ 31:19 Limitation of Remedies

The parties may validly limit the remedies that are provided by the Code in the case of breach of contract. Thus, a seller may specify that the only remedy of the buyer for breach of warranty shall be the repair or replacement of the goods or that the buyer shall be limited to returning the goods and obtaining a refund of the purchase price. A limitation of remedies need not be conspicuous.

(a) Construction Favoring Cumulative Remedies. When the sales contract specifies a remedy to which a party will be entitled, a question arises whether the parties intended that that should be the sole or exclusive remedy. It must be clearly stated that the remedy was to be the exclusive remedy. If it is not clearly stated, the remedy stated will be regarded as being in addition or cumulative to the remedies already existing under the Code.[18]

(b) FAILURE OF LIMITED REMEDY. A provision limiting the seller's obligation to the repair of the goods or the replacement of defective parts fails of its essential purpose and is not binding when the seller is

[18] Zappala & Co. v Pyramid Co. 81 App Div 2d 983, 439 NYS2d 765 (1981).

unable or refuses to make the goods function properly within a reasonable time. The buyer is entitled to goods that will be fit to the extent required by the particular express or implied warranties. When there is such a failure to correct the defect, the buyer may use any remedy authorized by the Code, just as though the contract had not contained any limitation on remedies.

In the *Osburn* case, the dealer and the manufacturer of a mobile home claimed that their only obligation was to make repairs and that it did not matter if the repairs were unsuccessful.

OSBURN V BENDIX HOME SYSTEMS, INC.
(Okla) 613 P2d 445 (1980)

Vernon and Phyllis Osburn purchased a mobile home from Bendix Home Systems, Inc. The "warranty" of the dealer and of the manufacturer stated that the liability for breach of warranty was limited to repairing any defects. The Osburns' home had numerous defects. After repeated repairs, the home was still defective. The Osburns sued the dealer and the manufacturer for breach of warranty. The defendants asserted that their only obligation was to make repairs. From a judgment for the Osburns, the defendants appealed.

OPALA, J. . . . Was the evidence with respect to the existence of defects sufficient to sustain a legal claim for breach of warranty? Did the limitation-of-remedy clause in [the] manufacturer's warranty "fail of its essential purpose" so as to make expanded UCC remedies available to the buyer under [UCC §] 2–719(2)? . . .

The proof here amply shows that, in addition to the substantial water leakage, numerous other defects and deficiencies existed. These consisted of (a) leaking water faucets, (b) buckled wall paneling, (c) missing interior trim, (d) insecurely fastened kitchen cabinets, (e) torn carpet and (f) a roof that made rumbling noises. All of these defects came to be discovered by the buyer shortly after he had moved into the home and all were promptly reported to the dealer pursuant to the warranty requirements. . . .

The warranty here in suit restricts the buyer's right of recovery for its breach to "repair or replacement of defective parts." The limitation so imposed is not, on its face, unconscionable. In fact, § 2–719(1)(a) expressly sanctions its employment. Limiting the buyer to the remedy of repair or replacement does not appear unfair because the warranty clause amply assures him of receiving the goods which either do or will conform to the contract. The purpose of the clause, as applied to this case, was hence to provide the buyer with a mobile home substantially free of defects. Implicit in the warranty-imposed obligation to repair or replace is the duty of providing conformable goods within a reasonable time after a defect in the original delivery is discovered.* Where the seller is afforded a reasonable opportunity to correct the defect and fails timely to respond or is repeatedly unsuccessful in the efforts to meet the warranty-imposed obligation, the limitation of remedy is deemed to have failed of its essential purpose *eo instante* and without the necessity of a prior judicial declaration.** The buyer is then free to invoke any of the broader remedies available under the Code.

Neither the seller nor the manufacturer was successful in the effort of rectifying the faulty conditions before the home was severely damaged by water leakage. When the home was not made to conform to the warranty within a reasonable time, the buyer — then left without the substantial value of his bargain — was relieved by the Code of the warranty-imposed limitation and hence able to seek broader recovery.

Manufacturer next complains that the trial court gave improper instructions upon the measure of damages for the breach in suit. The charge given called upon the jury to apply the difference — at the time and place of acceptance — between the actual value of the goods accepted and the value they would have had if they had been as warranted. This measure is, of course, proper when the evidence shows, as it did here, that the warranty-imposed limited-recovery clause "failed of its essential purpose."

[Judgment affirmed]

---

* What is a "reasonable time" for taking any action under the UCC depends on the nature, purpose, and circumstance of such action. . . . The terms of § 2-719(1) permit parties to tailor the outer limit of allowable recovery to their particular requirements, giving effect to reasonable agreements limiting or modifying existing remedies. They are designed to facilitate a fair recompense for breach of the contractual obligations. UCC § 2-719, Official Comment No. 1. *Conte v Dwan Lincoln-Mercury*, 172 Conn 112, 374 A2d 144 [1976]; . . . "The purpose of an exclusive remedy of replacement or repair of defective parts, whose presence constitute a breach of an express warranty, is to give the seller an opportunity to make the goods conforming while limiting the risks to which he is subject by excluding direct and consequential damages that might otherwise arise." *Beal v General Motors Corp.* 354 F Supp 423, 426 [D Del 1973].

** When a manufacturer limits its obligation to repair and replacement of defective parts, and repeatedly fails to correct the defect as promised within a reasonable time, it is liable for the breach of that promise as a breach of warranty. *Matthews v Ford Motor Co.*, 479 F.2d 399 [4th Cir. 1973]. . . . The fact that a manufacturer in good faith attempts to repair the defect whenever requested to do so is not a fulfillment of the warranty; he must demonstrate that the defect is permanently remedied as promised in the express warranty. . . . He can be liable for failure to fulfill the warranty obligation even if his failure to repair is neither wilful nor negligent. *Soo Line R. Co. v Fruehauf Corp.*, 547 F.2d 1365 [8th Cir. 1977].

QUESTIONS

1. What defense did the defendants raise?
2. How did the plaintiffs meet this argument?
3. Is there any relationship between the implied warranty provisions of the Code and the Code's provision as to the failure of a limited remedy?

---

§ 31:20   WAIVER OF DEFENSES

A buyer may be barred from objecting to a breach of the contract by the seller because the buyer has waived the right to do so.

(a) EXPRESS WAIVER. When sales are made on credit, the seller will ordinarily plan to assign the sales contract to a bank or other financer and thereby convert into immediate cash the customer's obligation to pay in the future. To make the transaction more attractive to banks and financers, the credit seller will generally include in the sales contract with each buyer a **waiver of defense** clause. By this clause, the buyer agrees not to assert against the seller's assignee any defense held against the seller. For example, if the television set does not work properly, the buyer agrees to complain only to the seller. The buyer agrees not to complain to the seller's assignee but will continue to pay the assignee just as though everything were satisfactory.

(b) IMPLIED WAIVER. When the buyer executes a promissory note as part of the credit transaction described above, the buyer automatically waives with respect to the seller's assignee any defense that could not be raised against a holder in due course of the note. This will be considered in greater detail in Chapter 35. What it means in the ordinary situation is that when the buyer signs a promissory note for the balance due, the buyer cannot assert against the finance company or the bank the defense that the buyer never got the goods called for by the contract, that the goods were defective and did not work, or that the contract had been entered into because of the fraudulent misstatements of the seller.

§ 31:21   PRESERVATION OF DEFENSES

Consumer protection laws and regulations seek to protect consumers by preserving defenses. In such cases, there is no waiver of defenses as described in § 31:20. If the basis for the defense to a home-solicited sale becomes apparent within time to cancel the sale, it is possible that the consumer may assert the defense by exercising the right of cancellation as described in § 21:6(a).

(a) PRESERVATION NOTICE. Consumer defenses will be preserved by the Federal Trade Commission regulation requiring that the papers signed by a consumer contain a provision which expressly states that the consumer is reserving any defense arising from the transaction.[19] A third person acquiring such paper is necessarily charged with knowledge of such provision and a defense of the consumer arising from the original transaction may therefore be asserted against such third person.

(b) PROHIBITION OF WAIVER. When the Federal Trade Commission preservation notice is included in the paper that is received by the third person, it is unnecessary to consider whether a waiver of defenses could be validly made. If the preservation notice is not included, the seller has committed an unfair trade practice. The question then arises of whether the buyer may assert against an assignee a defense that could have been asserted against the seller. The answer to this question depends upon state law. In many states, consumer protection statutes nullify a waiver of defenses by expressly providing that the buyer may assert against the seller's transferee any defense that might have been raised against the seller. Under some statutes, the buyer must give notice of any defense within a specified number of days after being notified of the assignment. Some courts extend consumer protection beyond the scope of the statute by ignoring a time limitation on the giving of notice of defenses and allow consumers to give late notice of defenses.

E.   REMEDIES IN THE INTERNATIONAL SALE OF GOODS

The United Nations Convention on Contracts for the International Sale of Goods (CISG) provides remedies for breach of a sales contract between parties from nations that have approved the CISG.

---

[19]   16 CFR § 433.1. It is an unfair or deceptive trade practice to take or receive a consumer credit contract that fails to contain such a preservation notice. See § 34:7 of this text.

§ 31:22 Remedies of the Seller

Under the CISG, if the buyer fails to perform any obligations under the contract, the seller is given various remedies. The seller may require the buyer to pay the price, take delivery, and perform other obligations under the contract. The seller may also declare the contract avoided if the failure of the buyer to perform obligations under the contract amounts to a fundamental breach of contract.

§ 31:23 Remedies of the Buyer

Under the CISG, a buyer may reject goods only if the tender is a fundamental breach of the contract. This is in contrast to the UCC requirement of perfect tender. Under the CISG, a buyer may also reduce the price when nonconforming goods are delivered even though no notice of nonconformity is given. The buyer in this case must have a reasonable excuse for failure to give notice.

Summary

The law provides a number of remedies for the breach of a sales contract. Remedies based on UCC theories are subject to a four-year statute of limitations. If the remedy sought is based on a non-UCC theory, the four-year limitation does not apply. A tort or contract statute of limitations will apply.

Remedies of the seller may include (1) a lien on the goods until the seller is paid, (2) the right to resell goods, (3) the right to cancel the sales contract, and (4) the right to bring an action for damages or, in some cases, for the purchase price.

Remedies of the buyer may include (1) rejection of nonconforming goods, (2) revocation of acceptance, (3) an action for damages for nondelivery of conforming goods, (4) an action for breach of warranty, (5) cancellation of the sales contract, (6) the right to resell the goods, (7) the right to bring an action for conversion, recovery of goods, or specific performance, and (8) the right to sue for damages and cancel the transaction because of the seller's fraud.

The parties may modify their remedies by contractual provision for liquidated damages, limitations on statutory remedies, or waiver of defenses. Legislative and administrative regulations restrict this freedom of contract to some extent for the benefit of consumers.

Under the CISG, the seller may require the buyer to pay the price, take delivery, and perform obligations under the contract, or may declare the contract avoided if there is a fundamental breach of contract.

Under the CISG, a buyer may reject goods only if there is a fundamental breach of contract. The buyer may also reduce the price of goods if nonconforming even without notice to the seller of nonconformity. The buyer must, however, have a reasonable excuse for failure to give notice.

Questions and Case Problems

1. What social forces are involved in the rule of law allowing the buyer to cover upon the seller's breach?
2. Donna purchased a snowmobile from the Park Manufacturing Company. Three years later it rolled over and injured her. She sued Park two years after her accident, alleging that Park had breached its implied warranty of merchantability on the theory that the snowmobile had rolled over because of a design defect and that this defect showed that the snowmobile was not fit for its normal

use. Is Park liable for the injuries sustained by Donna?

3. Gwendolyn purchased a washing machine from the Melvin Appliance Center. She did not notice that on the back of the contract that she signed there was a statement in fine print that in the event of any defects, Melvin's liability was limited to repairing or replacing the defective parts. There was a defective switch in the washing machine. The switch caused the machine to overheat and set fire to the laundry room of Gwendolyn's house. She demanded that Melvin pay her for the damage caused to the laundry room. Melvin offered to repair the washing machine free of charge and insisted that it had no greater liability because of the limitation of liability in the contract. Gwendolyn claimed that the limitation clause was not binding because it was not conspicuous. Is she correct?

4. Ward ordered a $500 television set from Greyline Markets Inc. Greyline wrote Ward an acceptance of his order. The next day Ward found a store selling the same set for $400. He notified Greyline that he was canceling his order of the day before. Greyline insisted that he could not do this and that he must pay $500 for the set. Was Greyline correct?

5. Compare a buyer's rejection of nonconforming goods with the buyer's revocation of acceptance of goods.

6. The goods purchased by the buyer were defective. The seller made repeated attempts to correct the defect. It became apparent that it was impossible to correct the defect. The buyer notified the seller that the buyer was revoking acceptance of the goods. The seller offered to try again to repair the goods. The buyer rejected this offer and repeated that acceptance of the goods was being revoked. The seller claimed that the buyer could not revoke acceptance as long as the seller offered to repair the goods. Was the seller correct? [See Fenton v Contemporary Development Co. 12 Wash App 345, 529 P2d 883]

7. After a sales contract was made, the seller's factory was destroyed by fire. The seller and the buyer then agreed to cancel the contract. Thereafter the seller's factory was rebuilt, and the buyer demanded that the seller perform the contract. Was the seller required to do so? [Goddard v Ishikawajima-Harima Heavy Industries Co. 29 App Div 2d 754, 287 NYS2d 901]

8. Sam wants to buy a car on credit from Henry Motors. He is afraid, however, that Henry will assign his contract to a finance company and that the finance company will be able to collect the balance due on the car even if the car does not run properly. Sam wants to be able to defend against the finance company by showing that there are defects in the car. Is this possible?

9. Wolosin purchased a vegetable and dairy refrigerator case from the Evans Manufacturing Corp. Evans sued Wolosin for the purchase price. Wolosin raised as a defense a claim for damages for breach of warranty. The sales contract provided that Evans would replace defective parts free of charge for one year and that "This warranty is in lieu of any and all other warranties stated or inferred, and of all other obligations on the part of the manufacturer, which neither assumes nor authorizes anyone to assume for it any other obligations or liability in connection with the sale of its products." Evans claimed that it was only liable for replacement of parts. Wolosin claimed that the quoted clause was not sufficiently specific to satisfy the limitation of remedies requirement of UCC § 2-719. Decide. [Evans Mfg. Corp. v Wolosin (Pa) 47 Luzerne County Leg Reg 238]

10. McInnis purchased a tractor and scraper as new equipment of current model from the Western Tractor & Equipment Co. The written contract stated that the seller disclaimed all warranties and that no warranties existed except as were stated in the contract. Actually, the equipment was not the current model but that of the prior year. Likewise, the equipment was not new but had been used for 68 hours as a demonstrator model and then the hour meter had been reset to zero. The buyer sued the seller for damages. The latter defended on the ground that all liability for warranties had been disclaimed. Was this defense valid? [McInnis v Western Tractor & Equipment Co. 63 Wash 2d 652, 388 P2d 562]

11. Compare the right of a buyer to a refund of a deposit when (a) the seller has repudiated the contract, and (b) the buyer has repudiated the contract.

12. Keenan rejected nonconforming goods delivered to him by Ross. After such rejection, but before Ross had been allowed a reasonable time to give instructions for the goods' disposition, Keenan arranged a sale of the goods at a substantially reduced price. Ross in the meantime had sold the goods to another of his customers. What rights, if any, does Ross have against Keenan?

13. Peters, the buyer, received merchandise from Hadley, the seller. Upon looking over the goods, Peters noticed that certain of the goods did not conform to the contract. He therefore called Hadley, who stated, "We always take care of our customers." Peters then accepted the goods. The nonconformity not being remedied within a reasonable time, Peters informed Hadley that he revoked his acceptance. Hadley refused to take back the goods. Who will prevail?

14. A buyer purchased goods from a seller. He telephoned the seller that he revoked his acceptance of the goods. The seller claimed that the revocation of acceptance was not effective because it was not accompanied by a return or offer to return the goods. Was the seller correct?

15. Duran Corporation purchased 25 dozen all-linen suits from Rober Company after examining a sample all-linen suit that Rober Company submitted. The written confirmation received by Duran Corporation contained the words "as per sample submitted to the company." Upon delivery, inspection, and testing, the Duran Company determined that the suits were 65 percent linen and 35 percent cotton. Duran immediately informed Rober that it wanted to return the suits for full credit. Rober insisted that Duran take the suits less a 25 percent discount, but Duran refused to do so. What will the result be?

PART 5

COMMERCIAL PAPER

32

KINDS OF PAPER, PARTIES, AND NEGOTIABILITY

Under the law of contracts a promise, when supported by consideration, creates certain legal rights that may be assigned to another person. Even before these common-law rules relating to contracts were developing, another body of law, the law merchant, was creating principles relating to a different type of obligation and the transfer of rights arising therefrom. In the course of time this obligation became the bill of exchange, which today we also know as a draft, a trade acceptance, or, with certain modification, a check. In time, another type of instrument, the promissory note, appeared. Both drafts and promissory notes may have the quality of negotiability. This is a quality that distinguishes them from contracts because the rights they represent can be transferred in such a way that the transferee may be immune from certain contract defenses. As a group, these instruments are known as commercial paper or negotiable instruments.

A. KINDS OF COMMERCIAL PAPER AND PARTIES

Commercial paper, such as checks and promissory notes, provide a substitute for money and can be used as a means of providing credit.

§ 32:1 DEFINITION

Commercial paper includes written promises (such as promissory notes) or orders (such as checks or drafts) to pay money, and it may be transferred by the process of negotiation. Much of the importance of commercial paper lies in the fact that it is more readily transferred than ordinary contract rights and that the transferee of commercial paper may acquire greater rights than would an assignee of a contract. A person who acquires a commercial paper may therefore be subject to less risk.

§ 32:2 KINDS OF COMMERCIAL PAPER

Commercial paper falls into four categories: (a) promissory notes, (b) drafts or bills of exchange, (c) checks, and (d) certificates of deposit.

(a) PROMISSORY NOTES. A **negotiable promissory note** is an unconditional promise in writing made by one person to another, signed by the maker, engaging to pay on demand or at a definite time a sum certain in money to order or to bearer.[1] (See Figure 32-1.)

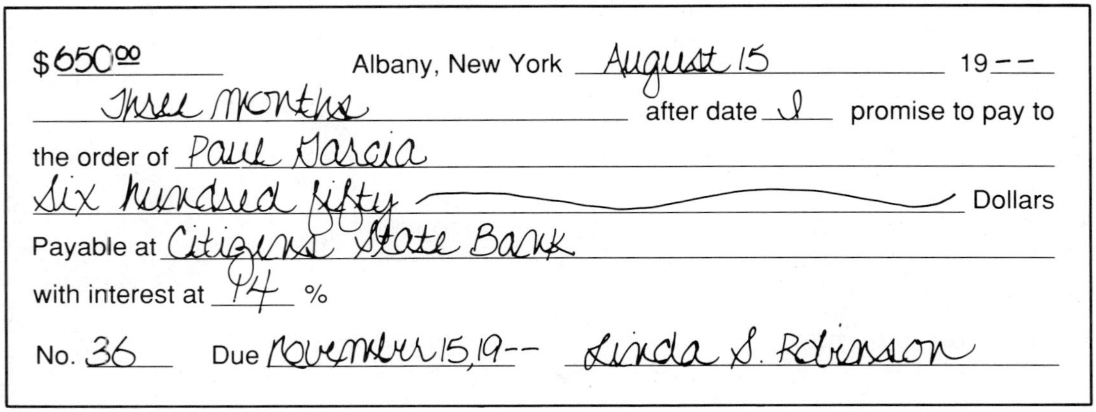

FIGURE 32-1
PROMISSORY NOTE
Parties: maker (buyer, borrower, or debtor) — Linda Robinson; payee
(seller, lender, or creditor) — Paul Garcia.

(b) DRAFTS. A **negotiable draft** or **bill of exchange** is an unconditional order in writing addressed by one person to another, signed by the person giving it, requiring the person to whom it is addressed to pay on demand, or at a definite time, a sum certain in money to order or to bearer.[2] (See Figure 32-2.) In effect, it is an order by one person upon a second person to pay a sum of money. The person who gives the order is called the **drawer** and is said to draw the bill. The person on whom the order to pay is drawn is the **drawee**. The person to whom payment is to be made is the **payee**. The drawer may also be named as the payee.

The drawee who is ordered to pay the paper is not bound to do so. The drawee, however, may agree to pay the paper, in which case the drawee is called an **acceptor**.

---

[1] Uniform Commercial Code § 3-104(1).

[2] UCC § 3-104(1).

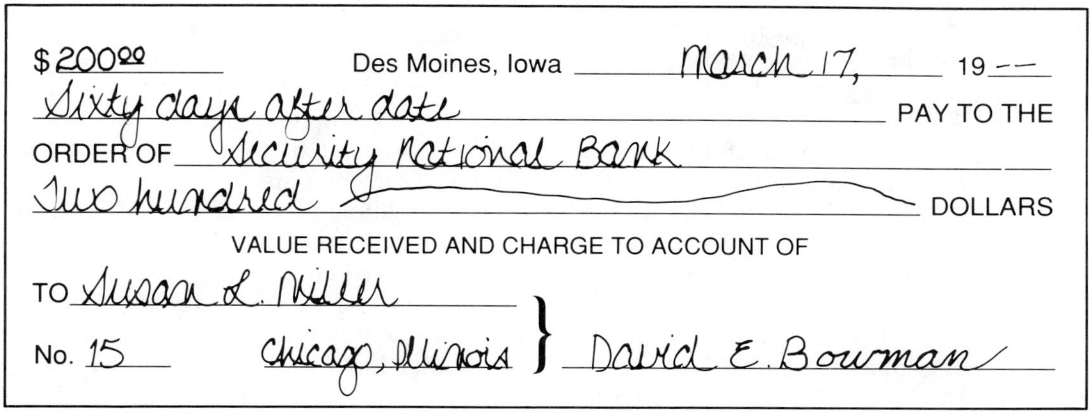

$200.00 _____ Des Moines, Iowa _____ March 17, _____ 19 - -

Sixty days after date _____ PAY TO THE

ORDER OF *Security National Bank* _____

Two hundred _____ DOLLARS

VALUE RECEIVED AND CHARGE TO ACCOUNT OF

TO *Susan L. Miller* _____ }

No. 15 _____ Chicago, Illinois } *David E. Bowman*

FIGURE 32-2
DRAFT (BILL OF EXCHANGE)
Parties: drawer (seller or creditor) — David Bowman; drawee (buyer or
debtor) — Susan Miller; payee (seller's or creditor's bank) — Security
National Bank.

(c) CHECKS. A **check** is a draft drawn on a bank and is payable on demand.[3] It is an order by a depositor (the drawer) upon a bank (the drawee) to pay a sum of money to the order of another person (the payee). A check is always drawn upon a bank as drawee and is always payable upon demand.

(d) CERTIFICATES OF DEPOSIT. A **certificate of deposit** is an instrument issued by a bank that acknowledges the deposit of a specific sum of money and promises to pay the holder of the certificate that amount, usually with interest, when the certificate is surrendered.[4]

§ 32:3 PARTIES TO COMMERCIAL PAPER

A note has two original parties — the maker and the payee; and a draft or a check has three original parties — the drawer, the drawee, and the payee. In addition to these original parties, a commercial paper may have one or more of the parties described under (e) through (k) of this section.

(a) MAKER. The **maker** is the person who writes out and creates a promissory note. If the paper is not a promissory note, this person has a different name, as the drawer of a check.

(b) DRAWER. The **drawer** is the person who writes out and creates a draft. This includes bills of exchange, trade acceptances, and checks. It is essential to bear in mind the distinction between a maker and a drawer because the liability of the maker is primary while that of a drawer is secondary.

(c) DRAWEE. The **drawee** is the person to whom the draft is addressed and who is ordered to pay the amount of money specified in the draft.

(d) PAYEE. The **payee** is the person named on the face of the paper to receive payment. In a check stating "pay to the order of John Jones," the named person, John Jones, is the payee.

A payee has no rights in the paper until it has been delivered by the drawer or the maker. Likewise, the payee is not liable on the paper in any way until the payee transfers the paper to someone else or receives payment of it.

(e) ACCEPTOR. When the drawee has sig-

---

[3]   UCC § 104(2)(b).
[4]   A certificate of deposit "is an acknowledgment by a bank of receipt of money with an engagement to repay it," as distinguished from a note, which "is a promise other than a certificate of deposit." UCC § 3-104(2)(c), (d).

nified in writing on the draft the willingness to make the specified payment, the drawee is called the **acceptor**.

(f) INDORSER.[5] The owner of commercial paper who signs on the back of the paper is an **indorser**. Thus, if a check is made payable to the order of *P*, *P* may indorse it to *E* to pay a debt that *P* owes *E*. In such a case, *P*, who is the payee of the check, is now also an indorser.

(g) INDORSEE. The person to whom an indorsement is made payable is called an **indorsee**. The indorsee may in turn indorse the instrument and then is also an indorser.

(h) BEARER. The person in physical possession of a commercial paper that is payable to bearer is called a **bearer**.

(i) HOLDER. A **holder** is a person in possession of commercial paper that is payable at that time either to such person, as payee or indorsee, or to bearer. For example, if *H* has possession of a check made payable to the order of *H*, *H* is a holder.

A person who takes the paper for value, in good faith, and without notice that it is overdue or has been dishonored or that there are defenses against or claims to it is called a **holder in due course**. The law gives a holder in due course preferred status. A holder in due course is immune from certain defenses when such favored holder brings suit on the paper. (See Chapter 34 for rights and defenses of holders.) A person becoming the holder of an instrument at any time after it was once held by a holder in due course is described as a **holder through a holder in due course**. Ordinarily, a holder through a holder in due course is given the same special rights as a holder in due course.

(j) ACCOMMODATION PARTY. A person who becomes a party to a commercial paper in order to add strength to the paper for the benefit of another party to the paper is called an **accommodation party.**

(k) GUARANTOR. A **guarantor** is a person who signs a commercial paper and adds a promise to pay the instrument under certain circumstances. Ordinarily this is done by merely adding *payment guaranteed* or *collection guaranteed* to the signature of the guarantor on the paper.

The addition of *payment guaranteed* or similar words mean that the guarantor will pay the instrument when due. *Collection guaranteed* or similar words mean that the guarantor will not pay the paper until after the holder has sought to collect payment from the maker or acceptor and has been unable to do so.

If the meaning of the guaranty is not clear, it is construed as a guaranty of payment. For example, when an indorser adds a statement that the paper is *guaranteed* or adds the word *guarantor* to the indorsement without specifying whether it is payment or collection that is guaranteed, the indorser is deemed to be a guarantor of payment. As a consequence, the holder of the paper may proceed directly against such guarantor without first proceeding against any other party on the paper.

The liability of a guarantor of payment is as extensive as that of the original debtor.

§ 32:4   LIABILITY OF PARTIES

A person who by the terms of the instrument is absolutely required to pay is primarily liable. For a note, the maker is primarily liable; for a draft, the acceptor (the drawee who has accepted) is primarily liable. A guarantor of payment is primarily liable in any case. Other parties are either secondarily or conditionally liable, as in the case of an indorser, or they are not liable in any capacity. A person who transfers the paper but does not sign it is not liable for its payment.[6]

(a) ACCOMMODATION PARTIES. An accommodation party is liable on the paper regardless of whether the paper is signed merely as a matter of friendship or in re-

---

[5] The spelling *endorse* is commonly used in business. The spelling *indorse* is used in the UCC.

[6] Pike Burden Printing, Inc. v Pike Burden, Inc. (La App) 396 So2d 361 (1981).

turn for payment. When suit is brought against an accommodation party by a plaintiff who gave value for it, the accommodation party cannot avoid liability on the ground that the plaintiff knew of the accommodation character.

The accommodation party is not liable to the party accommodated.[7] If the accommodation party is required to pay the paper, that party has a right to recover the payment from the person accommodated. Parol evidence may be admitted to show that a party to the paper had signed to accommodate another party.[8]

(b) GUARANTORS. A **guarantor of payment** has primary liability. The guarantor of payment is liable for payment of the paper even though the holder has not sought to obtain payment from any other party. It is immaterial that payment was not demanded from the primary party or that the primary party had sufficient assets to pay the paper.

The **guarantor of collection** is not required to pay the paper until collection has been attempted and has failed, or an attempt to collect would obviously be useless.

B.   NEGOTIABILITY

As noted early in this chapter, one of the important qualities of commercial paper is its negotiability. It is this quality of negotiability that makes commercial paper acceptable as a circulating medium of exchange, that is, a substitute for money or credit, in commercial transactions.

§ 32:5   REQUIREMENTS OF NEGOTIABILITY

In order to be negotiable, an instrument must be (a) in writing and (b) signed by the maker or drawer; it must contain (c) a promise or order (d) of an unconditional character (e) to pay in money (f) a sum certain; (g) it must be payable on demand or at a definite time; (h) it must be payable to order or bearer;[9] and (i) a party who is a drawee must be identified with reasonable certainty.

In addition to these formal requirements, the instrument must be delivered or issued by the maker or drawer to the payee or the latter's agent with the intent that it be effective and create a legal obligation.

If an instrument is not negotiable, the rights of the parties are governed by the general body of contract law.[10] If there is any uncertainty as to whether a paper is negotiable, it is deemed nonnegotiable.

Sometimes, as in the *Frank* case, what appears to be a negotiable instrument may contain a provision that impairs its negotiability and converts it to a simple contract.

---

[7]   UCC § 3-415(5).
[8]   Citizens Sav. Bank and Trust Co. v Hardaway (Tenn App) 724 SW2d 352 (1986).

[9]   Smith v Rushing Const. Co. 84 NC App 692, 353 SE2d 692 (1987).
[10]   First Investment Co. v Andersen (Utah) 621 P2d 683 (1980). Note, however, that if the nonnegotiability results from the fact that the instrument is not payable to order or bearer, it is governed by Article 3 of the Code with the limitation that there cannot be a holder in due course of such paper. UCC § 3-805.

FRANK V HERSHEY NATIONAL BANK

269 Md App 138, 306 A2d 207 (1973)

East Penn Broadcasting Company borrowed money from the Hershey National Bank. The promissory note representing the loan was made payable "to the Hershey National Bank." It also contained a provision authorizing confession of judgment against the borrower at any time. This provision allowed a judgment to be entered against East Penn without the formality involved in an ordinary action or proceeding. The note was signed with the typewritten name of the borrowing corporation and the handwritten signature of three individuals including the plaintiff, Frank. The loan was not paid. Frank and the others were sued on the note by the bank. Frank and the other individuals raised defenses under the UCC. The bank claimed that the UCC was not applicable. From a judgment in favor of the bank, Frank and the others appealed.

DIGGES, J. . . . The parties have proceeded . . . on the assumption that these notes were negotiable and therefore governed by the provisions of the UCC. We find the notes to be nonnegotiable and the UCC to be inapplicable. Therefore, the liability of the parties is determined as a matter of simple contract law. . . .

. . . To be negotiable, an instrument must, among other requirements, "be payable to order or to bearer." (§ 3–104(1)(d)) The absence of these magic words renders a note nonnegotiable. Here, the notes in question contain just a "promise to pay to the Hershey National Bank" the amount due. However, § 3–805 entitled "instruments not payable to order or to bearer" specifies that: "This subtitle *applies* to any instrument whose terms do not preclude transfer and *which is otherwise negotiable within this subtitle* but which is not payable to order or to bearer, except that there can be no holder in due course of such an instrument." . . . The official comments to this section indicate that: "This section covers the 'nonnegotiable instrument.' As it has been used by most courts, this term has been a technical one of art. It does not refer to a writing, such as a note containing an express condition, which is not negotiable and is entirely outside of the scope of this Subtitle and to be treated as a simple contract. It refers to a particular type of instrument which meets all requirements as to form of a negotiable instrument except that it is not payable to order or to bearer."

Thus, while these notes could still be governed by the Code even though they lack words of negotiability, they must meet all other "requirements as to form of a negotiable instrument" except for that. The notes here do not conform to this standard. The UCC § 3–112(1)(d) provides that the negotiability of an instrument is not affected by "a term authorizing confession of judgment on the instrument if it is not paid when due." We held in *Stankovich v Lehman*, 230 Md 426, 187 A2d 309 (1963), a case decided under the Negotiable Instruments Act, that the authorization to confess judgment "as of any term" permitted entry of judgment at any time prior to the maturity of the note and therefore destroyed negotiability. . . . "It would seem logical that if the statute, as it does, preserves negotiability only if the confession of judgment is at or after maturity, the warrant to confess must expressly, or by necessary implication, restrict its exercise to that time if the note is to be negotiable, and that if the warrant is silent as to the time when it can be exercised, the reasonable implication must be that it can be done at any time. Most of the cases involving this general area of the law have arisen in Pennsylvania, and the Courts of that State have held that notes containing stipulations for confession of judgment without specification or limitation as to time are, like those expressly authorizing judgment prior to maturity, nonnegotiable." . . .

Since these nonnegotiable notes are not governed by the UCC, their effect is, as already noted, determined under principles of simple contract law.

[Judgment affirmed]

QUESTIONS

1. What made the instrument nonnegotiable? Explain.
2. Why was the issue of negotiability important?

(a) WRITING. A commercial paper must be in writing. "Writing" includes handwriting, typing, printing, and any other method of setting words down in a permanent form. The use of a pencil is not wise because such writing is not as durable as ink, and the instrument may be more easily altered. A commercial paper may be partly printed and partly typewritten.

As the commercial paper is a writing, the parol evidence rule applies. This rule prohibits modifying the instrument by proving the existence of a conflicting oral agreement alleged to have been made before or at the time of the execution of the commercial paper.

(b) SIGNATURE. The instrument must be signed by the maker or drawer. The signature usually appears at the lower right-hand corner of the face of the instrument, but it is immaterial whether the signature is so placed. However, if the signature is placed on the instrument in such a manner that it does not in itself clearly indicate that the signer was the maker, drawer, or acceptor, the signer is held to be only an indorser.

The signature itself may consist of the full name or of any symbol adopted for that purpose. It may consist of initials, figures, or a mark. A person signing a trade or an assumed name is liable to the same extent as though the signer's own name had been used.

(1) Agent. A signature may be made by the drawer or maker or by an authorized agent.[11] No particular form of authorization to an agent to execute or sign a commercial paper is required.

An agent signing commercial paper should disclose on the paper (a) the identity of the principal, and (b) the fact that the signing is made in a representative capacity. When both are done, an authorized agent is not liable on the paper. The representative capacity of an officer of an organization is sufficiently shown by the signature of the officer preceded or followed by the title of the office and the organization name.

(2) Nondisclosure of Agency or Principal. If a person who signs a commercial paper in a representative capacity, such as an agent or an officer of a corporation, executes the paper without disclosing both the identity of the principal and the existence of the representative capacity, the agent appears to be signing the paper as a personal obligation. Under these circumstances, the agent is personally bound by the paper with respect to subsequent holders, regardless of whether the agent had intended to be personally bound or to act in a representative capacity.

In the *First National Bank* case, the question was whether corporate officers were personally liable on the notes of the corporation where there was no indication of signing in a representative capacity.

[11] UCC § 3-403(1).

FIRST NATIONAL BANK V BLACKHURST

(W Va) 345 SE2d 567 (1986)

Long, Blackhurst, and Sheets formed a corporation to own and operate a ski apparel shop. They served as president, vice president, and secretary-treasurer respectively of the corporation, Josh, Inc. Before opening the store, the three officers established a line of credit with the First National Bank. This line of credit was to be used to finance the purchase of inventory. On different dates they executed eight notes of varying amounts totaling $94,190. The shop failed and filed for bankruptcy and was unable to pay its debt to the bank. The bank instituted an action against the officers claiming that the notes were personal obligations of the defendants and not exclusively the corporate obligations of Josh, Inc. The defendants argued that at all times they were acting in a representative capacity as officers of Josh, Inc., that the loans were made to the corporation, and that they were not personally liable. From a judgment in favor of the bank, the officers appealed.

NEELY, J. . . . In this case we decide whether the defendants, Jo Debra Long, A. A. Blackhurst, and Robert A. Sheets, are personally liable on notes they executed in favor of the plaintiff, First National Bank in Marlinton. . . .

Commercial paper's value lies largely in its negotiability. Accordingly, Article Three of the *Uniform Commercial Code*, which governs commercial paper, was designed to avoid situations where it would be unclear whether a representative signing a negotiable instrument obligated his principal or himself. *W.Va. Code*, 46-3-403 [1963] establishes rules to enable subsequent holders to determine, by reference solely to the instrument itself, which party is liable on the instrument. In general, representative capacity must be shown on the face of the instrument if a representative signs his own name to an instrument but wishes to avoid personal liability. On each of the notes in this case the three defendants' signatures are affixed in the bottom right hand corner under a typewritten legend stating "Josh, Inc." The defendants argue that the legend indicates that they were signing in their corporate capacity rather than as individuals. The legend alone is not enough to free the defendants of personal liability. . . .

[Judgment affirmed]

QUESTIONS

1. Did the notes show the name of the principal?
2. How should officers of a corporation sign notes of the corporation to avoid personal liability?
3. What was the basis for the court's decision?

(c) PROMISE OR ORDER TO PAY. A promissory note must contain a promise to pay money. No particular form of promise is required; the intention as gathered from the face of the instrument controls.[12] If the maker uses such a phrase as, "I certify to pay," a promise is implied. A mere acknowledgment of a debt, such as a writing stating "I.O.U.," is not a commercial paper.

A draft or check must contain an order or command to pay money.[13] As in the case of a promise in a note, no particular form of order is required.

(d) UNCONDITIONAL PROMISE OR ORDER. For an instrument to be negotiable, the promise or order to pay must be unconditional. For example, when an instrument makes the duty to pay dependent upon the completion of the construction of a building, the promise is conditional, and the instrument is nonnegotiable. Also, the promise or order is conditional, and the instrument is nonnegotiable if the instrument states that it is subject to another agreement. In such a case, the paper is not negotiable because the obligation of the paper is dependent upon the performance of the other agreement.

An order for the payment of money out of a particular fund, such as ten dollars from next week's salary, is conditional.[14] If, however, the instrument is based upon the general credit of the drawer and the reference to a particular fund is merely to indicate a source of reimbursement for the drawee, such as "charge my expense account," the order is considered unconditional.[15] The effect of a reference to a source of payment was involved in the *Bank of Viola* case.

---

[12] Fejta v Werner Enterprises (La App) 412 So 2d 155 (1982).
[13] UCC § 3–104(1)(b).

[14] UCC § 3–105(2)(b).
[15] Rogers v Willard (Fla App) 453 So 2d 1175 (1984).

BANK OF VIOLA V NESTRICK

72 Ill App 3d 276, 390 NE2d 636 (1979)

The *Liberty Advertiser* was a weekly advertising paper published in Aledo, Illinois. Donald Nestrick, the defendant, executed a promissory note on May 7, 1975, purportedly to secure a line of credit on behalf of the *Liberty Advertiser*. The note was made payable to the Bank of Viola, and provided in part:

"For value received, the undersigned promises to pay to the Order of Bank of Viola, Viola, Illinois, the principal sum of $15,884.54 payable in installments Or as follows: Or *payable $80.00 per week from Jack & Jill contract* with interest at the rate of *8.00* per cent per annum from date until paid." (Italicized words were handwritten in original.)

The Jack & Jill contract referred to in the instrument was a contract entered into by the Aledo Jack & Jill store for advertising space in the *Liberty Advertiser*. When the Bank of Viola sued Nestrick to recover on the note, he claimed that the provision for payment from the proceeds of the Jack & Jill contract made the note conditional and therefore nonnegotiable and that, consequently, the Bank of Viola could not look either to him or to the general assets of the *Liberty Advertiser* for payments of the note as long as all proceeds from the Jack & Jill contract were being used to make the payments required by the note. The circuit court agreed with Nestrick, and the Bank of Viola appealed from that decision.

SCOTT, P. J. . . . A promissory note is conditional if it is to be paid only from a particular fund. In the instant case, if the note in question was a conditional note, it was fully paid if the payments made by the Jack & Jill store were properly credited to the note. In short, if the note is conditional, the plaintiff bank has no recourse against the defendant Nestrick on his personal liability.

There is considerable discussion in the case law as to whether a note or draft is conditional. Most of the case law hinges on the question of negotiability. . . . The statutory standard for determining whether a note is conditional is set forth in [UCC§] 3–105(2)(b). Therein it states:

> (2) A promise or order is not unconditional if the instrument . . .
> (b) states that it is to be paid only out of a particular fund or source . . .

. . . A promise will be held unconditional whenever it is possible to do so without doing violence to the ordinary meaning of the language used.

The current statute provides that a promise is not unconditional if the instrument states that it is to be paid *only* out of a particular fund or source. (Emphasis added.) This is in accord with prior law. In the Washington case of *First National Bank v Sullivan* (1911), 66 Wash 375, 119 P 820, the court held that an instrument to be negotiable must contain an unconditional promise to pay; but an unqualified order to pay was unconditional even though coupled with an indication of a particular fund out of which reimbursement was to be made. The same court held that a promise to pay *only* out of a particular fund was not unconditional. Similarly, the Florida court in *Wright v Board of Public Instruction* (1955), 77 So2d 435, held that ''a provision for payment from a certain source, in the absence of language limiting payment to the source alone, 'does not constitute a mandatory restriction on the source of payment and does not render the [instruments] non-negotiable if they are issued as general obligations of the maker'.'' The court went on to determine that if the instrument reads ''shall be payable out of a certain fund'', the restriction is merely advisory. . . .

Negotiability is favored in the law. It follows that construing an instrument as unconditional is favored in the law. An instrument may be unconditional which indicates a particular account or fund or source from which reimbursement is expected. ([UCC] § 3–105(1)(f).) A line of judicial precedents unbroken through this century requires words of explicit limitation before an instrument is said to be payable only out of a particular account, fund or source. Those words of explicit limitation are absent here. It does no violence to the statute or to the ordinary language of the instrument to conclude that this note is unconditional.

As set forth earlier, the mere wording of an instrument is not determinative of the issue. Rather, the intention of the parties as disclosed by the surrounding circumstances must be considered, and the language of the instrument is but one of many probative elements considered in determining the intention which requires the conclusion that this instrument was not conditional, but an unconditional promise to pay backed by the general credit of the maker. The face amount of the note was $15,884.54, and the handwritten portion provides that it is payable $80.00 per week from the Jack & Jill contract. Further, the note recites a due date of May 7, 1976. The court takes judicial notice of the fact that the year from the date of execution, May 7, 1975, until the due date, May 7, 1976, was but 52 weeks in length. Thus the maximum payment that could be paid before the due date would be $4,160.00. This amount is less than half the face amount of the note, to say nothing of interest which might accrue. Absent an extraordinary philanthropic motive on the part of the plaintiff bank, this arithmetic mandates the conclusion that the parties intended that the general credit of the defendant-maker would provide the means of payment when the balance of the note became due on May 7, 1976.

Because we agree with plaintiff, for the reasons set forth above, that the decision of the trial court holding the note conditional is not supported by the evidence, it is necessary to reverse that decision.

[Judgment reversed]

QUESTIONS

1. What changes in the terms of the note would have made it conditional? Explain.
2. Why did Nestrick claim that the note was conditional?

(e) PAYMENT IN MONEY. A commercial paper must call for payment in *money*, that is, any circulating medium of exchange that is legal tender at the place of payment. If the order or promise is not for money, the instrument is not negotiable. For example, an instrument that requires the holder to take stock or goods in place of money is nonnegotiable.

(f) SUM CERTAIN. This means an exact amount. Unless the instrument is definite on its face as to how much is to be paid, there is no way of determining how much the instrument is worth.

Minor variations from the above rule are allowed in certain cases. Thus, commercial paper is not made nonnegotiable because the interest rate changes at maturity or because certain costs and attorney's fees may be recovered by the holder.[16]

(g) TIME OF PAYMENT. A commercial paper must be payable on demand or at a definite time. If it is payable "when convenient" the instrument is nonnegotiable because the day of payment may never arrive. An instrument payable only upon the happening of a particular event that may never happen is not negotiable. For example, a provision to pay when a person marries is not payable at a definite time since that particular event may never occur. It is immaterial whether the contingency in fact has happened, because from an examination of the instrument alone it still appears to be subject to a condition that may never happen.

(1) Demand. An instrument is payable on **demand** when it is expressly specified to be payable "on demand," or at sight or upon presentation, that is, whenever the holder presents the instrument to the party required to pay and demands payment. Commercial paper is also payable on demand when no time for payment is stated in the instrument.[17]

(2) Definite Time. The time of payment is **definite** if the instrument is payable (a) on or before a stated date, (b) at a fixed period after a stated date, (c) at a fixed period after sight, (d) at a definite time subject to any acceleration, (e) at a definite time subject to extension at the option of the hold-

---

[16]   Means v Clardy (Mo App) 735 SW2d 6 (1987).

[17]   UCC § 3-108.

er, (f) at a definite time subject to extension to a further definite date at the option of the maker or acceptor, or (g) at a definite time subject to an extension to a further definite date automatically upon or after the occurrence of a specified act or event.[18]

(3) Missing or Incorrect Date. Paper that is not dated is deemed dated on the day it is issued to the payee. Any holder may add the correct date to the paper.

When a commercial paper is dated, the date is deemed prima facie to be the true date, whether the date was originally inserted or was thereafter added.[19] A commercial paper may be antedated or postdated, provided that it is not done to defraud anyone. The holder acquires title as of the date of delivery without regard to whether this is the date stated in the instrument.

(h) ORDER OR BEARER. A commercial paper must be payable to order or bearer.[20] This requirement is met by such expressions as "Pay to the order of John Jones," "Pay to John Jones or order," "Pay to bearer," and "Pay to John Jones or bearer." The use of the phrase "to the order of John Jones" or to "John Jones or order" is important in showing that the person executing the instrument is indicating that there is no intention to restrict payment of the instrument to John Jones only and that there is no objection to paying anyone to whom John Jones orders the paper to be paid. Similarly, if the person executing the instrument originally states that it will be paid to "bearer" or "to John Jones or bearer," there is no restricting of payment of the paper to the original payee. If the instrument is payable on its face "to John Jones," however, the instrument is not negotiable.

(1) Order Paper. An instrument is payable to **order** when by its terms it is payable to the order of any person specified therein with reasonable certainty (pay to the order of K. Read), or to a person so described or order (pay to K. Read or order).

(2) Bearer Paper. An instrument is **payable to bearer** when by its terms it is payable (a) to bearer or the order of bearer, (b) to a specified person or bearer, or (c) to "cash," or "the order of cash," or any other designation that does not purport to identify a person, or (d) if the last or only indorsement is a blank indorsement (an indorsement that does not name the person to whom the paper is negotiated), the paper is bearer paper.

§ 32:6   EFFECT OF PROVISIONS FOR ADDITIONAL POWERS OR BENEFITS

Certain provisions in an instrument that give the holder certain additional powers and benefits may or may not affect negotiability.

(a) COLLATERAL. The inclusion of a power to sell collateral security, such as corporate stocks and bonds, upon default does not impair negotiability. An instrument secured by collateral contains as absolute a promise or order as an unsecured instrument. Negotiability is not affected by a promise or power to maintain or protect collateral or to give additional collateral or to make the entire debt due if the additional collateral is not supplied according to the terms of the promise.

(b) ACCELERATION. A power to accelerate the due date of an instrument upon a default in the payment of interest or of any installment of the principal, or upon the failure to maintain or provide collateral does not affect the negotiability of an instrument. However, a holder's power to accelerate the due date "at will" or when a person "deems himself insecure" must be exercised in good faith.[21]

---

[18] UCC § 3-109(1).
[19] UCC § 3-114(3). If the wrong date is inserted, the true date can be proved unless the holder is a holder in due course or a holder through a holder in due course, in which case the date, even though wrong, cannot be contradicted.
[20] Beyer v First National Bank (Mont) 612 P2d 1285 (1980).

[21] UCC § 1-208.

```
$10,000.00                              September 1, 19--


Six months after date I promise to pay to the order of

Sally Kase Ten Thousand and no/100 Dollars with interest

at 5 percent.
                                    Donald C. Rich
```

FIGURE 32-3
REQUIREMENTS OF NEGOTIABILITY
In writing and signed by maker — Donald Rich; containing an
unconditional promise or order to pay — "I promise to pay"; sum
certain in money — ten thousand and no/100 dollars; payable on
demand or at a definite time — six months after date; payable to order
or to bearer — "pay to the order of Sally Kase."

(c) REQUIREMENT OF ANOTHER ACT. A provision authorizing the holder to require an act other than the payment of money, such as the delivery of goods, makes the instrument nonnegotiable.[22]

§ 32:7 ADDITIONAL DOCUMENTS

The fact that a separate document is executed that gives the holder additional protection, as a mortgage on real estate, or the right to repossess goods sold to the maker of the instrument, does not impair the negotiability of the commercial paper.

As between the parties to the original paper, the liability on the paper will be controlled by the terms of any other documents as well as the commercial paper. In contrast, subsequent holders of the commercial paper can rely on the face of the paper and are not affected by the terms of any additional separate document.

[22] UCC § 3-104(1)(b).

SUMMARY

Commercial paper includes written promises or orders to pay money and may be transferred by negotiation. A transferee of commercial paper may be immune from certain contract defenses. Because of this, commercial paper is more acceptable to transferees.

There are four categories of commercial paper: (1) promissory notes, (2) drafts or bills of exchange, (3) checks, and (4) certificates of deposit.

A negotiable promissory note is an unconditional promise in writing, made by one person to another, signed by the maker, promising to pay on demand or at a definite time, a sum certain in money, to order or to bearer. A negotiable draft or bill of exchange is an unconditional order in writing, addressed by one person to another, signed by the one giving it, requiring the person to whom it is addressed to pay on demand or at a definite time, a sum certain in money, to order or to bearer. A check is a draft drawn on a bank and payable on demand. A certificate of deposit is an instrument issued by a bank that acknowledges the deposit of a specified sum of money and promises to pay the holder of the certificate that amount, usually with interest, upon surrender of the certificate.

The original parties to a note are the maker and payee. The original parties to a draft are the drawer, the drawee, and the payee. The owner of commercial paper who signs on the back of the paper is called an indorser. The person to whom an indorsement is made payable is called an indorsee. A person in physical possession of a commercial paper that is payable to bearer is called a bearer and a holder.

A holder in due course is a favored holder of commercial paper. A person taking commercial paper through a holder in due course is a holder through a holder in due course and is immune from certain defenses.

The requirements of negotiability are: (1) the instrument must be in writing, (2) signed by the maker or drawer, (3) contain an unconditional promise or order, (4) to pay a sum certain in money, (5) on demand or at a definite time, (6) to order or to bearer. If an instrument is not negotiable, it is governed by the rules of contract law.

QUESTIONS AND CASE PROBLEMS

1. What social forces are affected by the rule of law governing the nature of a signature on commercial paper?
2. Name the four kinds of commercial paper.
3. Dorothy purchased a power mower from Reilly Brothers on credit. She gave Reilly a promissory note for the balance due. To induce Reilly to accept this note, Jeanette wrote on the back *guaranteed* and then signed her name. Dorothy promised Jeanette that Jeanette would never be required to pay this note. Dorothy did not pay the note to Reilly, and Reilly sued Jeanette. Jeanette claimed that Reilly could not sue her because of Dorothy's promise and that, in any case, Reilly could not sue Jeanette until Reilly had attempted to collect the money from Dorothy. On the facts stated, is Jeanette liable?
4. Hampton purchased cloth from Regal Fibres, Inc., on behalf of Twentieth Century Clothing Company, by whom Hampton was employed. Hampton informed Regal that she was acting for Twentieth Century and signed a promissory note for the purchase price of the cloth. The note stated, "I promise to pay . . ." and was signed "Gertrude Hampton." Regal sold the note to the Commercial Finance Company. Commercial sued Hampton on the note. She claimed that she was not liable because she had acted as agent for Twentieth Century and had so informed Regal Fibres. Is this a valid defense?
5. Adolph gave Benjamin a note that promised to pay $10,000 to the order of Benjamin when Adolph sold his house. Adolph thereafter sold his house and made a net profit of $40,000. Benjamin sued Adolph on the note. Is the note negotiable?
6. Compare the obligation of a party to a contract and the obligation of a party to commercial paper.
7. Nelson gave Buchert the following instrument, dated July 6, 1988:
   One year after date I promise to pay to the order of Dale Buchert one thousand dollars in United States Savings Bonds payable at Last Mortgage Bank. (signed) Ronald K. Nelson
   Does this instrument qualify as a negotiable instrument?
8. Compare the liability of the acceptor of a draft with the liability of the maker of a note.
9. Money was borrowed from a bank by a corporation. The president of the corporation negotiated the loan and signed the promissory note. On the first line he wrote the name of the corporation. On the second line he signed his own name. The note was negotiated by the lending bank to the Federal Reserve Bank. The note was not paid when due, and the Federal Reserve Bank sued the

corporation and the president. The president raised the defense that he was not bound on the note because he did not intend to bind himself and because the money obtained by the loan was used by the corporation. Is the president liable on the note? [See Talley v Blake (La App) 322 So 2d 877 (non-Code); Geer v Farquhar, 270 Or 642, 528 P2d 1335]

10. Rinehart issues a check that satisfies all the requirements of negotiability. It is payable to the order of cash. Is the instrument payable to order or to bearer?

11. Is the following instrument negotiable?

I, Richard Bell, hereby promise to pay to the order of Lorry Motors Ten Thousand Dollars ($10,000) upon the receipt of the final distribution from the estate of my deceased aunt, Rita Dorn. This negotiable instrument is given by me as the down payment on my purchase of a 1986 Buick to be delivered in three weeks.

Richard Bell (signature)

12. Smith has in his possession the following instrument.

September 1, 1986

I, Selma Ray, hereby promise to pay Helen Savit One Thousand Dollars ($1,000) one year after date. This instrument was given for the purchase of Two Hundred (200) shares of Redding Mining Corporation, Interest 6%.

Selma Ray (signature)

Smith purchased the instrument from Helen Savit at a substantial discount. Savit specializes in the sale of counterfeit stock. Selma Ray was one of her innocent victims. Smith is seeking to collect on the instrument. What are the rights of Smith against Ray on the instrument?

13. Master Homecraft Company received a promissory note with a stated face value from Mr. and Mrs. Zimmerman. The note was payment for remodeling of their home. The note contained unused blanks for installment payments. There was no maturity date. Master Homecraft sued the Zimmermans on the note. They argue that they should not be liable on the note because it is impossible to determine from its face the amount due or the date of maturity. Decide. [Master Homecraft Co. v Zimmerman, 208 Pa 401, 22 A2d 440]

14. On July 1, 1989, Ralph Golde signed a promissory note that was made payable to the order of Williams, Inc. for $20,000 plus 6 percent interest, payable 90 days from date. On the front of the note above his signature Golde wrote: "Subject to satisfactory delivery of goods purchased this date. Delivery to be made not later than July 31, 1989." Is the note negotiable commercial paper? Explain.

15. Nation-Wide Check Corp. sold money orders through agents. A customer would purchase a money order by paying an agent the amount of the desired money order plus a fee. The customer would then sign the money order as the remitter or sender and would fill in the name of the person who was to receive the money following the printed words "Payable to." In a lawsuit between Nation-Wide and Banks, a payee on some of these orders, the question was raised whether these money orders were negotiable. Decide. [Nation-Wide Check Corp. v Banks (Dist Col App) 260 A2d 367]

33

TRANSFER OF COMMERCIAL PAPER

Commercial paper may be transferred by negotiation or assignment. If the transfer is made in the manner required by the UCC, the transfer is called a negotiation and the transferee becomes a holder. If there is no negotiation, the transferee is merely an assignee. When the transfer is made by negotiation, the rights of the transferee may rise higher than those of the transferor, depending upon the circumstances attending the negotiation. When the transfer is made by assignment, the assignee has only those rights which the assignor possessed.

The transfer of ownership of commercial paper may be made as a gift. In most cases it will be made for value.[1]

A. NEGOTIATION OF COMMERCIAL PAPER

Negotiation is the transferring of commercial paper in such a way as to make the transferee the holder of the paper. This, in

---

[1] Brown v Bell (Ark) 722 SW2d 592 (1987).

turn, is controlled by whether the paper is order paper or bearer paper.

§ 33:1 TIME FOR DETERMINING ORDER OR BEARER CHARACTER OF PAPER

The order or bearer character of the paper is determined as of the time when the negotiation is about to take place, without regard to the character of the paper originally or at any intermediate time. Accordingly, when the last indorsement specifies the person to whom the indorser makes the instrument payable, the paper is order paper without regard to whether it was bearer paper originally or at any intermediate time. The holder cannot treat the paper as bearer paper merely because it had once been bearer paper.

§ 33:2 NEGOTIATION OF ORDER PAPER

An instrument payable to order may be negotiated only by indorsement by the person to whom it is payable at that time and the delivery of the paper by such person. Indorsement and delivery may also be made by an authorized agent of the person to whom the paper is then payable.

(a) MULTIPLE PAYEES AND INDORSEES. Ordinarily one person is named as the payee in the instrument, but two or more payees may be named. In that case, the instrument may specify that it is payable to any one or more of them or that it is payable to all jointly. If nothing is specified, the instrument is payable to all of the payees and they are **joint payees.** For example, if the instrument is made payable "to the order of A and B," the two persons named are joint payees. The indorsements of both A and B are required to negotiate the instrument.

If the instrument is payable to **alternate payees** or if it has been negotiated to alternate indorsees, as A or B, it may be indorsed and delivered by either of them.

(b) AGENT OR OFFICER AS PAYEE. The in-

strument may be made payable to the order of an officeholder. For example, a check may read "Pay to the order of Receiver of Taxes." Such a check may be received and negotiated by the person who at the time is the Receiver of Taxes. This is a matter of convenience since the person writing the check is not required to find out the actual name of the Receiver of Taxes at that time.

If the instrument is drawn in favor of a person as "Cashier" or some other fiscal officer of a bank or corporation, it is prima facie payable to the bank or corporation of which such person is an officer; it may be negotiated by the indorsement of either the bank or the corporation, or of the specified officer. If drawn in favor of an agent, it may similarly be negotiated by the agent or the agent's principal.[2]

(c) MISSING INDORSEMENT. Although order paper cannot be negotiated without indorsement, it can be assigned to another without indorsement. In such a case, the transferee has the same rights as the transferor; and if the transferee gave value for the paper, the transferee also has the right to require that the transferor indorse the instrument unqualifiedly and thereby effect a negotiation of the instrument.

When the transferor fails to indorse, the transferee may bring suit as an assignee. It is no defense to the obligor that there was no indorsement.

§ 33:3 NEGOTIATION OF BEARER PAPER

Any commercial paper payable to bearer may be negotiated by a mere transfer of possession. Thus, bearer paper is negotiated to a person taking possession of it, without regard to whether such taking of possession was done with the consent of the owner of the paper.

The paper may be negotiated by a mere transfer of possession not only when the instrument expressly states that it is pay-

---

[2] UCC § 3-117.

able to bearer, but also when the law interprets it as being payable to bearer, as in the case of a check payable to the order of "Cash."

Although bearer paper may be negotiated by such transfer, the one to whom it is delivered may insist that the bearer indorse the paper so as to impose the liability of an indorser. This situation most commonly arises when a check payable to "Cash" is presented to a bank for payment.

§ 33:4   FORGED AND UNAUTHORIZED INDORSEMENTS

A forged or unauthorized indorsement is by definition no indorsement of the person by whom it appears to have been made. Accordingly, the possessor of the paper is not the holder when the indorsement of the person whose signature was forged

was necessary for effective negotiation of the paper to the possessor.

If payment of commercial paper is made to one claiming under or through a forged indorsement, the payor is ordinarily liable to the person who is the rightful owner of the paper, unless such person is estopped or barred by negligence or other conduct from asserting any claim against the payor.

A forged or unauthorized indorsement may be ratified.[3] In that case, it is effective as though it had been genuine and authorized.

The *Mott* case deals with the question of whether a bank should be held liable for allowing the manager of a corporation to deposit in his own account checks which were payable to the corporation.

[3]   American Travel Corp. v Central Carolina Bank & Trust Co., 57 NC App 437, 291 SE2d 892 (1982).

MOTT GRAIN CO. V FIRST NATIONAL BANK & TRUST CO.
(ND) 259 NW2d 667 (1977)

Baszler was a manager of the grain elevator of the Mott Company and an officer of the company. He had expensive tastes and always needed money for his life-style. A corporate resolution executed by the Mott Company with the bank authorized officers to indorse or deposit in the corporate account checks payable to the corporation. Baszler took seventeen checks payable to the company and, instead of depositing them in the company account, indorsed and deposited them in his own account with the bank. The Mott Company claimed that the bank was liable for the amount of these checks that were improperly deposited. From a judgment in favor of the Mott Company, the bank appealed.

VOGEL, J. . . . This case is governed by the Uniform Commercial Code.

Leaving aside for the moment questions raised by the "Corporate Authorization Resolution" . . ., there can be little doubt that the bank is liable to the payee of checks which are negotiated upon indorsements which are forged or unauthorized.

Under UCC § 3-404, a payee of a check may recover from a bank which cashes a check on which the payee's signature is unauthorized.

An unauthorized signature is one which is either forged or made without actual, apparent, or implied authority. [UCC § 1-201 (43)].

Forged indorsements are inoperative as signatures of the payee, whether they are indorsements for deposit UCC § 3-205 or in blank UCC § 3-204, unless ratified or unless the owner is precluded from denying authority. [UCC § 3-404].

A bank which negotiates checks bearing forged or unauthorized indorsements is therefore liable in conversion to the true owner of the checks.

The bank asserts that the general law stated above does not apply because of the terms of the "Corporate Authorization Resolution." It points in particular to the language [of the resolution] authorizing any of the three owner-officers of the grain company to sign "checks, drafts and other withdrawal orders and any and all other directions and instructions of any character with respect to funds of this corporation now or hereafter with said Bank" and that the bank is authorized to "pay and charge to such account or accounts any checks, drafts and other withdrawal orders so signed, and to honor any directions or instructions so signed, whether or not payable to the individual order of or deposited to the individual account of or inuring to the individual benefit of any of the foregoing officers or persons."

Since the meaning of this terminology is unclear, we could simply hold that it is ambiguous and construe it against the party which drew it and submitted it to the grain company.

However, we believe that accepted methods of construing contractual language require us to hold that the language in question does not authorize the bank to negotiate checks payable to the grain company but indorsed by one of the officers and either cashed or deposited to his own account. The quoted language authorizes the bank to honor checks, drafts, and other withdrawal orders and directions and instructions of any character "with respect to funds of this corporation now or hereafter *with* said Bank . . ." While the use of the word "with" is unfortunate and less than clear, we understand the language to mean that money of the corporation on deposit with the bank is subject to being withdrawn by checks, drafts, or other withdrawal orders, or transferred as directed or instructed by any one of the officers. However, the language does not cover money which is not deposited with the bank or in its hands. When the improperly indorsed checks involved in this appeal were presented to the bank, they were not presented as funds of the corporation, but as funds of the individual officer indorsing them. The bank did not treat them as funds of the corporation, but treated them as funds of the individual. The checks therefore were not "funds of this corporation now or hereafter with said Bank" and were not within the description of the language quoted above in the "Corporate Authorization Resolution."

[Judgment affirmed]

QUESTIONS

1. What is the liability of a bank that negotiates a check bearing a forged or unauthorized indorsement?
2. What was the argument of the bank?
3. Was the bank correct?

§ 33:5   IMPOSTOR RULE

Ordinarily when the name of the payee is indorsed on commercial paper by a person who is not the payee or the agent of the payee, such indorsement is not effective to negotiate the paper. This signature is ineffective to negotiate the paper because the paper has not been indorsed and delivered by the person to whom it was then payable, namely the payee, or by his authorized agent.

The UCC makes exceptions to this general rule in three situations. In these situations, the unauthorized or forged character of the payee's signature is ignored as far as negotiation is concerned, and the signature is given the same effect as though it had been authorized by the named payee: (a) an impostor has induced the maker or drawer to issue the instrument to the person whose identity has been assumed by the impostor, or to a confederate, in the name of that payee; (b) the person signing as, or on behalf of, the drawer or maker intends the named payee to have no interest in the paper, or (c) an agent or employee of the maker or drawer has supplied the name used for the payee, intending that the payee should not have any interest in the paper. These three exceptions are known as the **impostor rule**.[4]

The first situation is present when a person impersonates the holder of a savings account and, by presenting a forged withdrawal slip to the savings bank, gets the bank to issue a check payable to the bank's customer that it hands to the impersonator in the belief that the impersonator is the customer. The second situation arises when the owner of a checking account, who wishes to conceal the true purpose of taking money from the bank, makes out a check purportedly in payment of a debt that in fact does not exist.

The last situation is illustrated by the case of the employee who fraudulently causes the employer to sign a check made to a customer or another person, whether existing or not. The employee does not intend to send it to that person but rather intends to forge the latter's indorsement, to cash the check, and to keep the money.

The impostor rule does not apply when there is a valid check to an actual creditor for a correct amount owed by the drawer and someone thereafter forges the payee's name, even though the forger is an employee of the drawer.

Even when the unauthorized indorsement of the payee's name is effective by virtue of the impostor rule, a person forging the payee's name is subject to civil and criminal liability for making such indorsement.

The impostor rule applies without regard to whether or not the drawee acted with reasonable care. The *Northbrook Property* case deals with the question of negligence of a drawee bank in accepting forged checks.

---

[4]   UCC § 3-405.

NORTHBROOK PROP. V CITIZENS & SOUTHERN

__ Ga App __ 361 SE2d 531 (1987)

Northbrook Property and Casualty Insurance Company, as subrogee of Devin Management Company, Inc., brought suit against the Citizens and Southern National Bank seeking damages in the amount of $75,805.89. Northbrook alleges, as insurer of Devin, that Devin's employee, Patricia Ferguson, cashed numerous unauthorized checks drawn by her on Devin's account and payable to fictitious individuals. She then indorsed these checks and presented them to C & S. Northbrook further alleges that C & S negligently accepted the checks and without further inquiry or authorization paid the funds to Patricia Ferguson in contravention of accepted banking practices and in violation of its contractual obligation to its depositors. From a judgment in favor of Citizens & Southern bank, Northbrook Property appealed.

BEASLEY, J. . . . Patricia Ferguson, Devin's office manager and bookkeeper, was authorized to sign the checks on behalf of the maker, Devin, and all checks for which recovery is sought were signed on Devin's behalf by her. . . . The controversy centers on checks . . . which were made payable to fictitious persons or to actual persons who were not intended by Patricia Ferguson to have any interest in the items. During the time in question 369 checks were presented to branches of C & S for cashing, only 11 of which bore Patricia Ferguson's indorsement (the others were indorsed in the payee's name). C & S was informed of Devin's claim in February 1983.

The trial court granted C & S's partial motion for summary judgment finding OCGA § 11-3-405 to be controlling. Northbrook appeals to this court and contends that although OCGA § 11-3-405 is applicable, the fictitious payee/padded payroll defense contained therein is not absolute but should further involve the issue of whether the drawee bank was negligent in accepting forged items from an employee of the drawer.

As stated in the briefs, this is a question of first impression in Georgia. OCGA § 11-3-405(1)(b) and (c) [adopted from the Uniform Commercial Code] states: "An indorsement by any person in the name of a named payee is effective if: . . . A person signing as or on behalf of a maker or drawer intends the payee to have no interest in the instrument; . . . or An agent or employee of the maker or drawer has supplied him with the name of the payee intending the latter to have no such interest."

Anderson, Uniform Commercial Code, p. 163 § 3-405.3 points out that Code § 3-405 "permits anyone to indorse paper made payable to a fictitious person or to one who was not intended to acquire any interest in the paper. The purpose of § 3-405 is to promote negotiability and foster the commercial reliability of paper. The rationale of UCC § 3-405 is that the employer-drawer should bear the loss caused by his dishonest employee rather than thrusting it upon the drawee bank."

The Official Code Comment to U.C.C. § 3-405 explains that the test of subsection (1)(b) "is not whether the named payee is 'fictitious,' but whether the signer intends that he shall have no interest in the instrument. The following situations illustrate the application of the subsection. (a) The drawer of a check, for his own reasons, makes it payable to P knowing that P does not exist. . . . (c) The drawer makes the check payable to, an existing person whom he knows, intending to receive the money himself and that P shall have no interest in the check. (d) The treasurer of a corporation draws its check payable to P, who to the knowledge of the treasurer does not exist. (e) The treasurer of a corporation draws its check payable to P. P exists but the treasurer has fraudulently added his name to the payroll intending that he shall not receive the check."

Thus, a loss from the activities of a faithless employee must be borne by the employer rather than the drawee bank. This is accomplished by making the indorsement effective even though it is unauthorized. ''The principle followed is that the loss should fall upon the employer as a risk of his business enterprise rather than upon the subsequent holder or drawee. The reasons are that the employer is normally in a better position to prevent such forgeries by reasonable care in the selection or supervision of his employees, or, if he is not, is at least in a better position to cover the loss by fidelity insurance, and that the cost of such insurance is properly an expense of his business rather than of the business of the holder or drawee.'' Official Code Comment, U.C.C. § 3-405.

An overwhelming majority of the jurisdictions confronted with this issue have recognized the import of the code section to be that any loss arising from situations provided for therein should fall upon the employer and negligence on the part of the bank is irrelevant. Only bad faith by a bank prevents invoking the code section to defeat a claim.

Northbrook asks that we choose the minority position which is now viable in only one jurisdiction, California. Some strong policy arguments have been proffered in support of this position. . . . But these policy considerations are for the legislature. We are charged solely with construing the statutory language. We come to the . . . result . . . that the code section makes no provision for negligence by the bank. Fortification for this plain meaning construction is implicit from the tenor of the U.C.C. In those situations where negligence is a factor, it invariably expressly appears in the section involved.

We therefore adopt the construction called for by the official comment and recognized by the near unanimous majority of other states which have considered the issue. Northbrook cannot recover because of mere negligence on the part of C & S.

[Judgment affirmed]

QUESTIONS

1. What was the argument of Northbrook Property?
2. How did the court decide the issue?

---

§ 33:6   EFFECT OF INCAPACITY
         OR MISCONDUCT ON
         NEGOTIATION

A negotiation is effective even though (a) it is made by a minor or any other person lacking capacity; (b) it is an act beyond the powers of a corporation; (c) it is obtained by fraud, duress, or mistake of any kind; (d) or the negotiation is part of an illegal transaction or was made in breach of duty. Under general principles of law apart from the UCC, the transferor in such cases may be able to set aside the negotiation or to obtain some other form of legal relief. If, however, the instrument has in the meantime been acquired by a holder in due course, the negotiation can no longer be set aside.

§ 33:7   LOST PAPER

The effect of losing commercial paper depends upon who is suing or demanding payment from whom and whether the paper was order paper or bearer paper when it was lost. If the paper is order paper, the finder does not become the holder because the paper, by definition, is not indorsed and delivered by the person to whom it was then payable. The former holder who lost it is still the rightful owner of the paper, although technically not the holder because not in possession of the paper.

When a commercial paper is lost, it may be possible to have a new paper issued in its place. Thus, an employer may issue a new paycheck to replace the check lost by the employee. If the lost paper is a promissory note, it is less likely that the maker will oblige by executing a new promissory note. The *Kraft* case deals with whether the owner of the lost paper may bring suit on it against any party liable thereon.

KRAFT V SOMMER

54 App Div 2d 598, 387 NYS2d 318 (1976)

> Sommer delivered a check to Kraft. Kraft deposited the check but the bank refused to pay it. Sommer refused to pay the check to Kraft since the original had been lost and all that Kraft had was a copy. The lower court agreed with Sommer and Kraft appealed.

MEMORANDUM* . . . Plaintiff alleges . . . that she "is the owner and holder of a check, no part of which has been paid" and she seeks payment of the check. It is undisputed that the check was delivered to her by the [drawer] and that the bank in which she deposited the check refused to honor it because payment had been stopped by defendant Sommer, one of the executors of the deceased [drawer]. [The] plaintiff claims [the original check] was not returned to her by the bank to which she had presented it. The bank's affidavit states that it was its standard practice to photograph such a check, to mark it "payment stopped" and to return it by regular mail to the depositor. . . . Plaintiff's inability to produce the original check [does not] require the dismissal of the causes of action relating to the check.

Section 3-804 of the Uniform Commercial Code makes manifest that a suit may be brought by the "owner" of a lost instrument. Although requirements of "proof" as to the ownership of the check, circumstances of the loss and its terms are required, these matters go to the evidence necessary at trial and not to the sufficiency of the pleadings. "The fact that a negotiable instrument is lost, stolen or destroyed does not defeat the right of the holder or discharge his interest. The holder may bring suit upon the instrument in his own name just as if the instrument were available for production in court. It is, of course, necessary for him to prove the terms of the missing instrument, and this requires that there be sufficient evidence produced of his ownership of the instrument and of the facts which prevent its production in court." (1 Anderson, Uniform Commercial Code, § 3-804:3).

. . . The parties should proceed to trial. . . .

[Judgment reversed and action remanded]

---

*   [Authors' note] Ordinarily an opinion of the court is filed under the name of the judge who wrote the opinion. When a case is perfectly clear and obvious, the opinion will frequently be filed without naming the writing judge and will then have a heading of "memorandum" or "per curiam" (by the court).

QUESTIONS

1. Why did the bank refuse to honor the check?
2. Was Kraft correct in claiming that she was a holder of the check?
3. Does the owner of a check that is lost have a right to enforce payment of the check?

There is, of course, the practical difficulty of proving just what the lost paper provided and explaining the loss of the paper. The court may also require that the plaintiff suing on the lost instrument furnish the defendant with security to indemnify the defendant against loss by reason of any claim that might thereafter be made on the lost instrument.[5]

If the paper is in bearer form when it is lost, the finder, as the possessor of bearer paper, is the holder, and is entitled to enforce payment.

B.   KINDS OF INDORSEMENTS

Some commercial paper may be transferred without an indorsement. An indorsement is required in other cases.

The person to whom an instrument is payable, either on its face or by indorsement, or the person in possession of bearer paper may indorse it for the purpose of negotiating it by merely signing it. The person may add certain words or statements as part of the indorsement. By definition, an indorsement is written on the back of an instrument.

§ 33:8   BLANK INDORSEMENT

When the indorser merely signs the paper, the indorsement is called a **blank indorsement.** (See Figure 33-1.) A blank indorsement does not indicate the person to whom the instrument is to be paid, that is

the transferee. A person who is in possession of paper on which the last indorsement is blank is the holder.

FIGURE 33-1
BLANK INDORSEMENT

(a) CONVERTING THE BLANK INDORSEMENT. The holder of an instrument on which the last indorsement is blank may write above the blank indorsement a statement that the instrument is payable to that particular holder.[6] This is called "completing" the indorsement or "converting" the blank indorsement to a special indorsement by specifying the identity of the indorsee. It protects the holder because the paper cannot be negotiated thereafter without the indorsement and delivery of such holder.

(b) EFFECT OF BLANK INDORSEMENT. Negotiation by a blank indorsement does four

---

[5]   UCC § 3-804.

[6]   UCC § 3-204(3).

things: (1) it passes the ownership of the instrument; (2) it gives rise to certain implied warranties; (3) it imposes upon the indorser secondary liability for payment of the paper; and (4) it changes the paper to bearer paper, which may be negotiated by transfer of possession alone.

§ 33:9 SPECIAL INDORSEMENT

A **special indorsement** consists of the signature of the indorser and words specifying the person to whom the indorser makes the instrument payable, that is, the indorsee. (See Figure 33-2.) Common forms of this kind of indorsement are "Pay to the order of Roberta Hicks, E. S. Flynn" and "Pay to Roberta Hicks or order, E. S. Flynn." It is not necessary that the indorsement contain the words "order" or "bearer." Thus, a commercial paper indorsed in the form "Pay to Roberta Hicks, E. S. Flynn" continues to be negotiable and may be negotiated further. In contrast, an instrument that on its face reads "Pay to E. S. Flynn" is not negotiable.

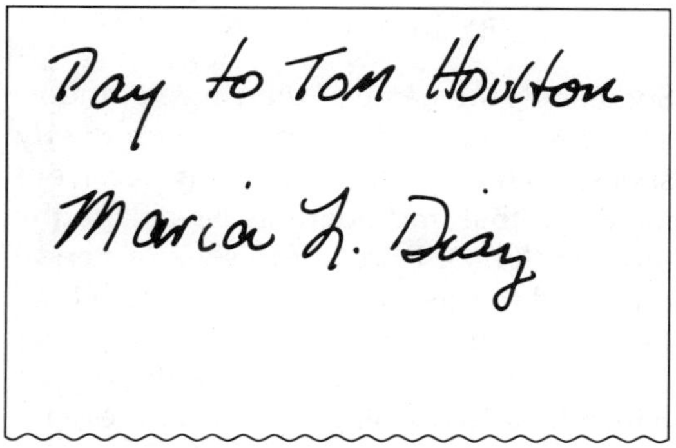

FIGURE 33-2
SPECIAL INDORSEMENT

As in the case of the blank indorsement, a special indorsement transfers title to the instrument. It also results in the indorser making certain warranties about the in-

strument and imposes upon the indorser a secondary liability to pay the amount of the instrument when certain requirements are satisfied. When a special indorsement is made, the paper becomes order paper and may only be negotiated by an indorsement and delivery.

§ 33:10 QUALIFIED INDORSEMENT

A **qualified indorsement** is one that qualifies the effect of a blank or a special indorsement by disclaiming or destroying the liability of the indorser to answer for dishonor by the maker or drawee. This may be done by including the words "without recourse" in the body of the indorsement or by using any other words that indicate an intention to destroy the indorser's secondary liability for dishonor by the maker or drawee.[7] (See Figure 33-3.)

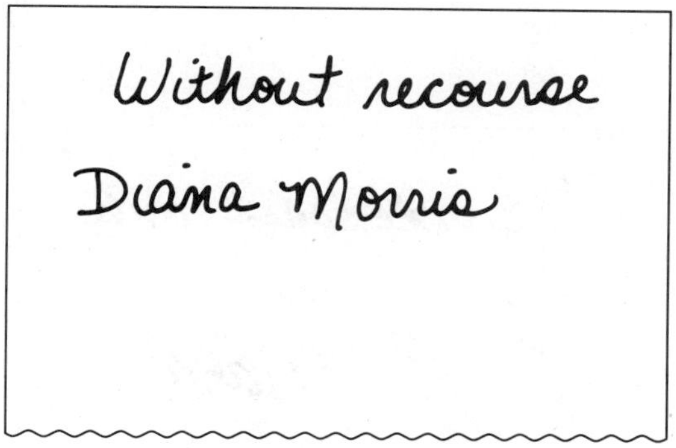

FIGURE 33-3
QUALIFIED INDORSEMENT

The qualification of an indorsement does not affect the passage of title or the negotiable character of the paper. It merely disclaims the indorser's secondary liability for payment of the paper.

---

[7] Florida Coast Bank v Monarch Dodge (Fla App) 430 So 2d 607 (1983).

This form of indorsement is most commonly used when the qualified indorser is known to be a person who has no personal interest in the transaction. For example, an agent or an attorney who is merely indorsing to a principal or client a check of a third person made payable to the agent or attorney might make a qualified indorsement. Here the transferee recognizes that the transferor is not a party to the transaction and therefore should not be asked to vouch for the payment of the paper.

§ 33:11   RESTRICTIVE
              INDORSEMENTS

A restrictive indorsement specifies the purpose of the indorsement or the use to be made of the paper. (See Figure 33-4.) An indorsement is restrictive when it includes words showing that the paper is to be deposited (as "for deposit") or is negotiated for collection, or to an agent or trustee, or the negotiation is conditional.[8]

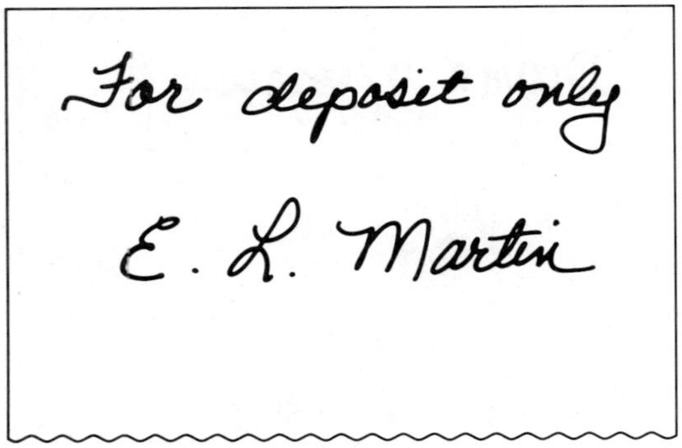

FIGURE 33-4
RESTRICTIVE INDORSEMENT

A restrictive indorsement does not prevent transfer or negotiation of the paper even when it expressly states that transfer or negotiation is prohibited.

If the restriction is in the form of a conditional indorsement, the holder may be a holder in due course — subject only to the requirement that the maker must pay only if the condition is fulfilled. For example, an instrument payable to the order of P is indorsed by P, "Pay Allen Weber if X ship arrives at port before October 1." Weber indorsed the instrument to Byrd. Byrd cannot collect from the maker unless the X ship arrives at port before October 1. If the maker pays Byrd, the maker may have to pay again to P, who indorsed restrictively.

A bank may ignore and is not affected by the restrictive indorsement of any person except the holder transferring the instrument to the bank or the person presenting it to the bank for payment. However, a **depositary bank,** that is, the one in which the customer deposits the item, and persons not in the bank collection process must recognize the restrictive indorsement to the extent of applying any value given in a manner consistent with the indorsement.[9]

§ 33:12   CORRECTION OF NAME
              BY INDORSEMENT

Sometimes the name of the payee or indorsee of a commercial paper is improperly spelled. Thus, H. A. Price may receive a paycheck that improperly is payable to the order of "H. O. Price." If this was a clerical error and the check was intended for H. A. Price, the employee may ask the employer to write a new check payable in the proper name. Instead of doing this, the payee or indorsee whose name is misspelled may indorse the wrong name, the correct name, or both. A person giving or paying value for the instrument may require both.[10]

This correction of name by indorsement may only be used when it was intended that the indorsement should be payable to

8   UCC § 3-205. Walcott v Manufacturers Hanover Trust, 133 Misc 2d, 725 507 NYS2d 961 (1986).

9   Marine Midland Bank, N.A. v Prince, 157 NYS2d 220, 443 NE2d 932 (1982).
10   UCC § 3-203.

the person making the corrective indorsement. If there were in fact two employees, one named H. A. Price and the other H. O. Price, it would be illegal as a forgery for one to take the check intended for the other and by indorsing it obtain the benefit of the proceeds of the check.

§ 33:13 BANK INDORSEMENTS

In order to simplify the transfer of commercial paper from one bank to another in the process of collecting items, "any agreed method which identifies the transferor bank is sufficient for the item's further transfer to another bank."[11] Thus, a bank may indorse with its Federal Reserve System number instead of using its name.

Likewise, when a customer has deposited an instrument with a bank but has failed to indorse it, the bank may make an indorsement for the customer unless the instrument expressly requires the payee's personal indorsement. Furthermore, the mere stamping or marking on the item of any notation showing that it was deposited by the customer or credited to the customer's account is declared to be as effective as an indorsement by the customer would have been.[12]

C. WARRANTIES OF TRANSFEROR BY NEGOTIATION

When commercial paper is transferred, certain implied warranties are imposed by law upon the transferor. When an instrument is transferred in exchange for value, the transaction is similar in some respects to a sale of merchandise. In the case of a sale of merchandise, certain warranties as to title, description, and quality arise, which, if breached, give the buyer a cause of action against the seller. The transferor of commercial paper, by the act of making the transfer, warrants the existence of certain facts. These warranties vary according to whether the instrument is transferred with or without an indorsement and according to the nature of the indorsement.

§ 33:14 WARRANTIES OF UNQUALIFIED INDORSER

When the holder of a commercial paper negotiates it by an unqualified indorsement, and receives consideration, the transferor warrants:

(a) Ownership of good title, which includes the genuineness of all indorsements necessary to title to the instrument, or authorization to act for one who has such good title. For example, Rita makes a note payable to the order of Jorge. The note is stolen and the thief forges Jorge's signature on the back of the note, making it payable to the order of Lawten. Lawten, without knowledge of the forged indorsement, transfers and indorses the note to Selma for value. Selma could not recover from the maker since she did not have good title. Selma, however, can sue Lawten for breach of warranty of good title because a necessary signature (Jorge's) was not genuine.

(b) The act of transferring the instrument is rightful, independent of the question of title or authority to act. For example, if a payee of a note breaches a contract with the maker to hold the note until certain goods are shipped by transferring the note before the goods are shipped, the transfer is not rightful. This payee becomes liable to the transferee for any loss occasioned by the early transfer of the note.

(c) The signatures on the instrument are genuine or executed by authorized agents.

11 UCC § 4-206.
12 UCC § 4-205(1).

(d) The instrument has not been materially altered.

(e) The indorser has no knowledge of the existence or commencement of any insolvency proceeding against the maker or acceptor of the instrument, or against the drawer of an unaccepted draft or bill of exchange.

(f) No defense of any party is good against the indorser.

These warranties made by the unqualified indorser pass to the transferee and to any subsequent holder who acquires the instrument in good faith.[13]

The holder's indorsement of the check does not give rise to any warranty that the account of the drawer in the drawee bank contains funds sufficient to cover the check.

§ 33:15 WARRANTIES OF OTHER PARTIES

Warranties are also made by the indorser who indorses "without recourse" and by one who transfers by delivery only.

(a) QUALIFIED INDORSER. The warranty liability of the indorser who indorses "without recourse" is the same as that of the unqualified indorser with one difference. The warranty as to "no defenses" (f) is limited to a warranty that the indorser does not have knowledge of any defense rather than that no defense exists.[14] The

warranties of a qualified indorser run to the same persons as those of an unqualified indorser.

(b) TRANSFEROR BY DELIVERY. The warranties made by one who transfers a commercial paper by delivery are the same as those made by an unqualified indorser except that they run only to the immediate transferee and then only if consideration has been given for the transfer.[15] Subsequent holders cannot enforce such warranties against this prior transferor by delivery regardless of the character of such holders.

D.   ASSIGNMENT OF COMMERCIAL PAPER

Although commercial paper may be negotiated, it may also be assigned. The assignment may result from the act of the parties or by operation of law.

§ 33:16 ASSIGNMENT BY ACT OF THE PARTIES

Commercial paper may be assigned in the same manner as any other contract right by the express act of the holder. A commercial paper is also regarded as assigned when a person whose indorsement is required to negotiate the instrument transfers it without indorsing it. In *Duxbury* the court dealt with a promissory note that was transferred without indorsement.

---

[13] UCC § 3-417(2).
[14] UCC § 3-417(3). The qualified indorsement does not exclude other warranties unless it is specified to be "without warranties."

[15] UCC § 3-417(2).

DUXBURY V ROBERTS
338 Mass 385, 446 NE2d 401 (1983)

Roberts issued a promissory note payable to the order of Baines. Baines handed this note over to Duxbury without indorsing it. Baines also gave him a separate paper in which Baines stated that the note was being transferred to Duxbury. When Duxbury sued Roberts on the note, Roberts contended that he was not liable because Duxbury was not a holder in due course of the paper. From a judgment in favor of Duxbury, Roberts appealed.

HENNESSEY, C. J. . . . The defendants argue that the trial judge improperly determined that Duxbury was a holder in due course. The Appellate Division found the trial judge to be in error on this issue because the note was not negotiated properly to Duxbury. We agree with the Appellate Division. One does not become a holder of a negotiable instrument unless there is a negotiation of that instrument as required under the Uniform Commercial Code, § 3-202(1). To have a negotiation of an instrument payable to order, the instrument must be delivered with any necessary indorsement. "An indorsement must be written by or on behalf of the holder and on the instrument or on a paper so firmly affixed thereto as to become a part thereof." In this case Baines did not sign the note when he transferred it to Duxbury. Rather, he signed only the document entitled, "Partial Assignment of Note and Mortgage." His signing of this document does not constitute an indorsement of the note because it was not "so firmly affixed thereto as to become a part thereof." Therefore, Duxbury did not become a holder or a holder in due course. We agree, however, with the Appellate Division which determined further that notwithstanding the trial judge's improper resolution of the holder in due course issue, the plaintiff was properly entitled to judgment on the merits.

We, thus, reject the defendants' final contention that the assignment to Duxbury was not valid. Under [UCC] § 3-201(1), even though the instrument was not negotiated, Duxbury acquired the rights of his transferor, Baines, subject to all defenses available against Baines. . . .

[Judgment affirmed]

QUESTIONS

1. How is order paper negotiated?
2. Was there a negotiation by Baines to Duxbury?
3. What rights did Duxbury have on the note?

When a necessary indorsement is missing, the transferee has only the rights of an assignee. If the transferee acquires the paper for value, the transferee is entitled, however, to require that the transferor indorse the instrument.[16] If the indorsement is obtained, then the transferee is deemed a holder but only as of the time when the indorsement is made.

§ 33:17   ASSIGNMENT BY OPERATION OF LAW

An assignment by operation of law occurs when by virtue of the law the title of one person to commercial paper is vested in another. For example, if the holder of a

---

[16]   UCC § 3-201(3).

commercial paper becomes a debtor under the Bankruptcy Code or dies, the title to the instrument vests automatically in the trustee in bankruptcy or in the personal representative of the decedent's estate, respectively.

SUMMARY

Commercial paper may be transferred by negotiation or assignment. If an instrument is negotiated, the rights of the transferee may rise higher than those of the transferor. If an instrument is assigned, the assignee has only those rights that the assignor had.

Negotiation is the transfer of commercial paper in such a way as to make the transferee the holder of the paper. Order paper is negotiated by an indorsement and a delivery by the person to whom it is then payable. Bearer paper is negotiated by a transfer of possession. The order or bearer character of paper is determined by the face of the paper as long as the paper is not indorsed. If the paper has been indorsed, the character is determined by the last genuine indorsement.

A forged or unauthorized indorsement is no indorsement, and the possessor of the paper cannot be a holder. The UCC makes exceptions to this general rule in three situations and the indorsement is given the same effect as though it had been authorized by the named payee: (1) an impostor has induced the maker or drawer to issue the instrument to the person whose identity has been assumed by the impostor, (2) the person signing as or on behalf of the drawer intends that the named payee shall have no interest in the paper, or (3) an agent or employee of the drawer has given the drawer the name used as the payee, intending that the payee should not have any interest in the paper.

A negotiation is effective even though: (1) it is made by a minor, (2) it is an act beyond the powers of a corporation, (3) it is obtained by fraud, or (4) the negotiation is part of an illegal transaction. The transferor may be able to set aside the negotiation.

There are a number of different kinds of indorsements that can be made on commercial paper. When an indorser merely signs the paper, the indorsement is called a blank indorsement. If the last indorsement is a blank indorsement, the paper is bearer paper, which may be negotiated by transfer of possession alone. A special indorsement consists of the signature of the indorser and words specifying the person to whom the indorser makes the instrument payable. If the last indorsement is a special indorsement, the paper is order paper and may only be negotiated by an indorsement and delivery. A qualified indorsement destroys the liability of the indorser to answer for dishonor by the maker or drawee. A restrictive indorsement specifies the purpose of the indorsement or the use to be made of the paper.

An indorser who negotiates by an unqualified indorsement and receives consideration makes the following warranties: (1) title is good, (2) all the signatures are genuine, (3) the instrument has not been materially altered, (4) the indorser has no knowledge of any insolvency proceeding against the maker or drawer, and (5) no defense of any party is good against the indorser. A transferor indorsing with a qualified indorsement warrants only that the transferor has no knowledge of any defense rather than that no defense exists. A transferor who does not indorse the instrument makes these warranties only to the immediate transferee.

QUESTIONS AND CASE PROBLEMS

1. What social forces are affected by the law as to qualified indorsements?

2. As soon as Bertha gets her weekly paycheck, she carefully writes her name on the back so that everyone will know that it is her check. Is Bertha protected by doing this?

3. Allan pays Bestor the $100 which Allan owes Bestor with a check stating "pay to the order of Dale Bestor $100." How can Bestor transfer this check to Wickard in such a way as to make Wickard the holder of the check?

4. Higgins owes the Packard Appliance store $100. He mails a check to Packard. The check is drawn on the First National Bank and states "pay to the order of cash $100." This check is stapled to a letter stating that the $100 is in payment of the debt owed by Higgins. Edwards is employed by Packard in the mailroom. Edwards removes the letter from its envelope, detaches the check, and disappears. No one knows what becomes of the check until it is presented at the First National Bank by a person identifying himself as Gene Howard. The bank pays this person $100 and debits that amount against the account of Higgins. Higgins protests that this cannot be done because the check was lost and never belonged to Howard. Is Higgins correct?

5. When the holder presents a check to the drawee bank for payment, does an indorsement of the check give rise to any warranty that the account of the drawer in the drawee bank is sufficient to cover the check?

6. Huff, the assistant to the controller of a general partnership, told the controller that the firm owed Janet Richards $250. Richards was a fictitious person, but relying upon Huff's statement, the controller signed the partnership's name to a check. Huff indorsed the check on its back, signing the name "Janet Richards," and cashed it at a liquor store. Hudson Bank charged the partnership's account for the $250 and returned it with the rest of the checks for the month. Subsequently, the fraudulent conduct of Huff was discovered by the partnership's auditors. Must the Hudson Bank recredit the partnership's account with $250?

7. Gellert paid her rent by indorsing to Parker, her landlord, a check payable to the order of Gellert. The check appeared to have been drawn by McCoy. Actually the signature of McCoy was a forgery. The check is indorsed by Parker with only his name and delivered by him to Tipton, a roofer who had repaired the roof. Tipton delivers the check without any indorsement to the Ruane Supply Company, the supply house from which he purchased the roofing materials. Ruane transfers the check without indorsement to the Metropolitan Manufacturing Company which manufactured the supplies sold to the supply house. Metropolitan presents the check to the bank. The bank refuses to pay the check. Metropolitan demands payment from McCoy. McCoy refuses to pay because the check is a forgery. Metropolitan then sues Tipton for breach of warranty. Is Tipton liable?

8. Benton, as agent for Savidge, received an insurance settlement check from the Metropolitan Life Insurance Co. He indorsed it "For deposit" and deposited it in the Bryn Mawr Trust Company in the account of Savidge. What was the nature and effect of this indorsement? [Savidge v Metropolitan Life Insurance Co. 380 Pa 205, 110 A2d 730]

9. Humphrey drew a check for $100. It was stolen and the payee's name forged as an indorser. The check was then negotiated to Miller who had no knowledge of these facts. Miller indorsed the check to the Citizens Bank. Payment of the check was voided on the ground of the forgery. The Citizens Bank then sued Miller as indorser. Decide. [Citizens Bank of Hattiesburg v Miller, 194 Miss 557, 11 So 2d 457]

10. When claims filed with the insurance company were approved for payment, they were given to the claims clerk who would prepare checks to pay those claims and then give the checks to the treasurer to sign. The claims clerk of the insurance company made a number of checks payable to persons who did not have any claims, gave them to the treasurer together with the checks for valid claims, and the treasurer signed all the checks. The claims clerk then

removed the false checks, indorsed them with the names of their respective payees, and cashed them at the bank where the insurance company had its account. The bank debited the account of the insurance company with the amount of these checks. The insurance company claimed that the bank could not do this because the indorsements on the checks were forgeries. Is the insurance company correct? [General Acci. Fire & Life Assur. Corp. v Citizens Fidelity Bank & Trust Co. (Ky) 519 SW2d 817]

11. Vance issued a negotiable promissory note payable to the order of Adams. Adams transferred by delivery this note for value and before maturity to Reisman. Was this a proper negotiation by Adams to Reisman?

12. Jerry Waters and his wife Patsy were not getting along well. Patsy commenced a divorce proceeding against Jerry. As a result of the proceeding, Patsy received a property settlement. Under the terms of the settlement, it was agreed that a demand note signed by Jerry and payable to the order of Patsy's father should be transferred to Patsy in the future. Her father delivered the note to her but did not indorse the paper or write anything on the note. Upon the death of her father, Patsy sued her former husband on the note. Jerry refused to pay, alleging that she could not sue as she was not the owner of the note. Decide. [Waters v Waters (Tex Civ App) 498 SW2d 236]

13. Fisher wanted to have his house painted. His father wrote out a check to the order of Fisher for $200 as a down payment for the painting. Fisher then made a contract with Denny to paint the house. For the down payment on this contract he took his father's check and indorsed on it "Pay to Denny upon condition of the proper painting of my home at 510 N. Maine St., Jonesville." He then delivered the check to Denny. Could Denny cash the check before he completed the painting work?

14. A note was indorsed "without recourse" to the Hudson Bank by Starlit Equipment. When the bank tried to collect on the note, the maker of the note alleged that his signature was forged. The bank then sued Starlit. Starlit defended the action on the basis that the instrument was signed "without recourse." Decide.

15. Two employees of the state of New Mexico fraudulently procured and indorsed a warrant (that is, a draft drawn against funds of the state) made out to the Greater Mesilla Valley Sanitation District. There was no such sanitation district. The employees obtained payment from the Citizens Bank. Western Casualty, the state's insurer, reimbursed the state for its loss and then brought suit against the bank for negligently paying the warrant. Decide. [Western Casualty & Surety Co. v Citizens Bank of Las Cruces (CA10 NM) 676 F2d 1344]

34

RIGHTS OF HOLDERS AND DEFENSES

Commercial paper litigation may arise between the original parties to the instrument or, where commercial paper has been negotiated, may arise between the maker or drawer and a holder or between subsequent holders. When the original parties are involved, ordinary contract defenses, such as failure of consideration, may be asserted. When the instrument has left the hands of the payee and has been negotiated to a holder in due course, such holder will take the instrument free from many kinds of claims that might be asserted by a party to the instrument.

A. KINDS OF HOLDERS

When a commercial paper is negotiated to a person, that person is the holder: either an ordinary holder or a favored holder.

§ 34:1 ORDINARY HOLDERS AND ASSIGNEES

Any holder has all the rights relating to the paper. The holder, although an ordinary holder, is the only person who may demand payment, bring suit for the collection of the paper, give a discharge or release from liability on the paper, or cancel the liability of another party to the paper.

When the holder sues on the paper, the holder is only required to produce the paper in court and show that the signature of the defendant is genuine. If that is done and there is no evidence of a defense, the holder is entitled to a judgment for the full face amount of the paper.

The holder may generally sue any one or more prior parties on the paper without regard to the order in which such persons signed the paper or the order in which such persons may be liable to each other.

The fact that the holder is merely an ordinary holder has no significance if the defendant does not have any defense.

The assignee of a commercial paper is in the same position and has the same rights as an ordinary holder. It is immaterial whether the person is an assignee by express assignment, by operation of law, or in consequence of the omission of an essential indorsement.

§ 34:2   FAVORED HOLDERS

The law gives certain holders of commercial paper a preferred standing by protecting them from certain defenses when they sue to collect payment. This protection is given in order to make commercial paper more attractive by giving the favored holder an immunity not possessed by an ordinary holder or an assignee. The favored holders are known as the holder in due course and the holder through a holder in due course.

(a) HOLDER IN DUE COURSE. In order to have the preferred status of a holder in due course, a person must first be a holder. This means that the possessor of the paper must have acquired it by proper negotiation. That is, the person in question must be the possessor of bearer paper or must be the possessor of order paper payable to that person as payee or in-

dorsee.[1] The concept of due course may be understood better if modern terminology is substituted and "due course" is thought of as an ordinary transaction.

In addition to being a holder, the holder in due course must meet certain conditions that pertain to (1) value, (2) good faith, (3) ignorance of paper's being overdue or dishonored, and (4) ignorance of defenses and adverse claims.[2]

(1) Value. Since the law of commercial paper is fundamentally a merchant's or business person's law, it favors only the holders who have given value for the paper. For example, since a legatee under a will does not give value, a person receiving bonds as a legacy is not a holder in due course.

A person takes an instrument for value (a) by performing the act for which the instrument was given, such as delivering the goods for which the check was sent in payment; (b) by acquiring a security interest in the paper, as when it has been pledged as security for another obligation; or (c) by taking the instrument in payment of, or as security for a debt.[3] When value is given, the courts do not measure or appraise the value given.

A promise not yet performed, although sufficient as consideration for a contract, does not constitute value to satisfy this requirement for a holder in due course.[4]

---

[1] Although it is an uncommon occurrence, the original payee may also be a holder in due course provided the necessary elements are satisfied. UCC § 3-302(2). Hartford Acc. & Indem. v American Express (NY) 518 NYS2d 93 (1987).

[2] In a few special cases, a purchaser of commercial paper will not be considered a holder in due course even though all these elements have been satisfied. This is true when the sales are not of an ordinary commercial nature, such as when paper is acquired by judicial sale, sale of the assets of an estate, or a bulk sale not in the regular course of business of the transferor. UCC § 3-302(3).

[3] UCC § 3-303. It is also provided that there is a taking for value when another commercial paper is given in exchange or when the taker makes an irrevocable commitment to a third person as by providing a letter of credit, UCC § 3-303(c).

[4] Sea Air Support, Inc. v Herrmann (Nev) 613 P2d 413 (1980).

A bank does not give value for a deposited check when it credits the depositor's account with the amount of the deposit. The bank gives value to the extent that the depositor withdraws money against that credit.

(2) Good Faith. The element of good faith requires that the taker of commercial paper act honestly in the acquisition of the instrument. Bad faith may sometimes be indicated by the small value given. This does not mean that the transferee must give full value, but it does mean that a gross inadequacy of value may be evidence of bad faith. Bad faith is established by proof that the transferee had knowledge of such facts as rendered it improper to acquire the instrument under the circumstances.

The fact that a transferee acted carelessly does not establish that it acted in bad faith.[5] If the transferee takes the instrument in good faith, it is immaterial whether the transferor acted in good faith.

(3) Ignorance of Paper's Being Overdue or Dishonored. Commercial paper may be negotiated even though (a) it has been dishonored, whether by nonacceptance or nonpayment; or (b) the paper is overdue, whether because of lapse of time or the acceleration of the due date; or (c) it is demand paper that has been outstanding more than a reasonable time. In other words, ownership may still be transferred. Nevertheless, the fact that the paper is circulating at a late date or after it has been dishonored is a suspicious circumstance that is deemed to put the person acquiring the paper on notice that there is some adverse claim or defense. A person who acquires title to the paper under such circumstances, therefore, cannot be a holder in due course.

(4) Ignorance of Defenses and Adverse Claims. Prior parties on the paper may have defenses that they could raise if sued by the person with whom they dealt. For example, the drawer of a check, if sued by the payee, might have the defense that the merchandise delivered by the payee was defective. In addition, third persons, whether prior parties or not, may be able to assert that the instrument belongs to them and not to the possessor. A person who acquires the commercial paper with notice or knowledge that any party might have a defense or that there is any adverse claim to the ownership of the instrument cannot be a holder in due course. Thus, the holder of commercial paper cannot be a holder in due course when the holder acquired the paper with knowledge that there had been a failure of consideration with respect to the contract for which the paper had been given.

Knowledge acquired by the taker after acquiring the paper does not prevent the taker from being a holder in due course. Consequently, the fact that the payee, after acquiring the paper, learns of a defense does not operate retroactively to destroy the payee's character as a holder in due course.

Knowledge of certain facts constitutes notice to the person acquiring a commercial paper that there is a defense or an adverse claim. The holder or purchaser of the paper is deemed to have notice of a claim or defense (a) if the instrument is so incomplete, bears such visible evidence of forgery or alteration, or is otherwise so irregular as to call into question its validity, terms, or ownership, or to create an ambiguity as to the party who is required to pay; or (b) if the purchaser has notice that the obligation of any party is voidable in whole or in part, or that all parties to the paper have been discharged.[6] For example, if the subsequent holder knows that a note given for home improvement work in fact covers both the improvements and a loan and that the transaction is usurious because excessive costs were charged for the work to conceal the usurious interest, the subsequent holder is not a holder in due course.

[5] Funding Consultants, Inc. v Aetna Casualty and Surety Co. 187 Conn 637, 447 A2d 1163 (1982).

[6] UCC § 3-304(1).

In general, a holder who has knowledge of such facts as would put a reasonable person upon inquiry is deemed to have knowledge of the facts that would be learned if such inquiry were made.

The purchaser of commercial paper does not have notice of a defense that bars such purchaser from being a holder in due course merely because the purchaser knows that the instrument is antedated or postdated; that any person has signed for accommodation; that an incomplete instrument has been completed, unless the purchaser has notice of any improper completion; that there was a negotiation by a fiduciary unless the purchaser has knowledge that the fiduciary is breaching a duty; or that there is a default in payment of interest on the instrument.[7]

In the *Money Mart* case, the drawer of a payroll check argued that the purchaser of that check should have inquired as to whether the check would be honored before cashing it.

[7]   UCC § 3-304.

MONEY MART CHECK CASHING CENTER INC.
v EPICYCLE CORPORATION
(Colo) 667 P2d 1372 (1983)

An employee of Epicycle cashed his final payroll check at Money Mart Check Cashing Center. Epicycle had issued a stop payment order on the check. Money Mart deposited the check through normal banking channels. The check was returned to Money Mart marked "Payment Stopped." Money Mart brought an action against Epicycle claiming that, as a holder in due course, it was entitled to recover against Epicycle. Epicycle argued that Money Mart could not be a holder in due course because it failed to verify the check as good prior to cashing it. From a judgment in favor of Epicycle, Money Mart appealed.

ROVIRA, J. . . . The question before us is whether Money Mart is a holder in due course. If it is, it takes the check free of any of Epicycle's claims to the check or defenses against [its employee. UCC § 3-302(1)] provides:

(1) A holder in due course is a holder who takes the instrument:
    (a) For value; and
    (b) In good faith; and
    (c) Without notice that it is overdue or has been dishonored or of any defense against or claim to it on the part of any person.

That Money Mart took the check for value is undisputed, leaving the questions of "good faith" and "notice."

"Good faith" is defined as "honesty in fact in the conduct or transaction concerned." The drafters of the Uniform Commercial Code intended that this standard be a subjective one. Thus, the question is: "[W]as this alleged holder in due course acting in good faith, however stupid and negligent his behavior might have been?"

The only testimony on the question of good faith is that Money Mart cashed the check without knowing that a stop payment order had been issued on it. The Superior Court concluded that Money Mart was not a holder in due course because it "did not inquire as to the check itself and had no knowledge as to whether the check was stolen, incomplete, or secured by fraud." Under a subjective standard, an absence of knowledge is not equivalent to a lack of good faith.

We now consider whether Money Mart had "notice" of the fact that payment had been stopped on the check or that Cronin had obtained the check improperly. A person has "notice" of a fact when:

(a) He has actual knowledge of it; or
(b) He has received a notice or notification of it; or
(c) From all the facts and circumstances known to him at the time in question he has reason to know that it exists.

As can be seen, tests other than "actual knowledge" may be used in determining whether a person is a holder in due course. There is no allegation that Money Mart had received notification of the defenses, so we must now determine whether Money Mart had "reason to know" of them. . . .

The Superior Court held that Money Mart's failure to inquire about the validity of the check constituted negligence. However, there is nothing in the Uniform Commercial Code and nothing in the record to support such a conclusion.

A determination of whether a holder has "reason to know" is based upon "all the facts and circumstances known to him." A person "knows" of a fact when he has "actual knowledge" of it. The question therefore is whether Money Mart had actual knowledge of facts giving it reason to know that a defense existed. There is nothing to distinguish the facts of this case from any other of the thousands of checks that Money Mart and others cash each year: A man came to Money Mart to cash his paycheck; Money Mart is in the business of cashing paychecks; the face of the check disclosed nothing to raise even a suspicion that there was something wrong with it.

It has often been held that where an instrument is regular on its face there is no duty to inquire as to possible defenses unless the circumstances of which the holder has knowledge are of such a nature that failure to inquire reveals a deliberate desire to evade knowledge because of a fear that investigation would disclose the existence of a defense. There is nothing in using a check-cashing service instead of a bank that would lead to a rule imposing different standards on the two kinds of institutions.

Accordingly, we hold that Money Mart is a holder in due course and, as such, is not subject to the defenses Epicycle may have against Cronin.

[Judgment reversed]

QUESTIONS

1. Did Money Mart take the check for value?
2. Did Money Mart take the check in good faith and without notice?
3. What was the basis for the court's decision?

(b) HOLDER THROUGH A HOLDER IN DUE COURSE. Those persons who become holders of the instrument after a holder in due course are given the same protection as the holder in due course provided they are not parties to fraud or illegality that affects the instrument.

This means that if an instrument is negotiated from *A* to *B* to *C* to *D* and *B* is a holder in due course, both *C* and *D* will enjoy the same rights as *B*. If *C* received the instrument as a gift or with knowledge of failure of consideration or other defense, or if *D* took the instrument after maturity, they could not themselves be holders in due course. Nevertheless, they are given the same protection as a holder in due course because they took the instrument through such a holder, namely, *B*. It is not only *C*, the person taking directly from *B*, but also *D*, who is given this extra protection.

B.   DEFENSES

The importance of being a holder in due course or a holder through a holder in due course is that those holders are not subject to certain defenses when they demand payment or bring suit upon a commercial paper. These defenses may be described as **limited defenses.** Another class of defenses, **universal defenses,** may be asserted against any plaintiff, whether the party is an assignee, an ordinary holder, a holder in due course, or a holder through holder in due course.

§ 34:3   DEFENSES AGAINST AN ORDINARY HOLDER OR ASSIGNEE

A holder who is neither a holder in due course nor a holder through a holder in due course is subject to every defense just as though the instrument were not negotiable. Thus, an ordinary holder suing on the promissory note of the buyer is subject to the latter's defense of breach of warranty.[8]

§ 34:4   LIMITED DEFENSES NOT AVAILABLE AGAINST A HOLDER IN DUE COURSE

Neither a holder in due course nor one having the rights of such a holder is subject

to any of the following defenses.[9] They are limited defenses. These defenses are also barred with respect to any instrument that is executed to renew or extend the original instrument.

(a) ORDINARY CONTRACT DEFENSES. In general terms, the defenses that could be raised against a suit on an ordinary contract cannot be raised against a holder in due course. Accordingly, the defendant cannot assert against the holder in due course the defense of lack, failure, or illegality of consideration with respect to the transaction between the defendant and the person with whom the defendant dealt.

(b) INCAPACITY OF DEFENDANT. The incapacity of the defendant may not be raised against a holder in due course unless by general principles of law that incapacity, such as insanity of a person for whom a guardian has been appointed by a court, makes the instrument a nullity.[10]

(c) FRAUD IN THE INDUCEMENT. When a person knowingly executes commercial paper and knows its essential terms but is persuaded or is induced to execute it because of fraudulent statements, such fraud cannot be raised against a holder in due course nor a holder through a holder in due course. As an illustration, *M* is persuaded to purchase an automobile because of *P*'s statements concerning its condition. *M* gives *P* a note, which is negotiated until it reaches *H*, who is a holder in due course. *M* meanwhile learns that the car is not as represented and that *P*'s statements were fraudulent. When *H* demands payment of the note, *M* cannot refuse to pay on the ground of *P*'s fraud. *M* must pay the note. *M* may then sue *P* for damages for fraud.

(d) PRIOR PAYMENT OR CANCELLATION. When a commercial paper is paid, the person making the payment should demand the surrender of the instrument. If this is not done, it is possible for the holder to continue to negotiate it. Another person may thus become the holder of the instru-

---

8   Pascal v Tardera (NY) 507 NYS2d 225 (1986).

9   UCC § 3-305.
10   UCC § 3-305(2)(b).

ment. When the new holder demands payment of the instrument, the defense cannot be raised that payment had been made to a former holder if the new holder is a holder in due course. The fact that the person making the payment obtained a receipt from the former holder does not affect the application of this principle.

When the holder and the party primarily liable have agreed to cancel the instrument but the face of the instrument does not show any sign of cancellation, the defense of cancellation cannot be asserted against a holder in due course. Similarly, an order to stop payment of a check cannot be raised as a defense by the drawer of a check against a holder in due course.

(e) NONDELIVERY OF AN INSTRUMENT. A person may write out a commercial paper or indorse an existing paper and leave it on a desk for future delivery. At that moment, the instrument or the indorsement is not effective because there has been no delivery.

Assume that through the negligence of an employee or through the theft of the instrument, it comes into the hands of another person. If the instrument is in such form that it can be negotiated, as when it is payable to bearer, a subsequent receiver of the instrument may be a holder in due course or a holder through a holder in due course. As against that holder, the person who wrote the instrument or indorsed it cannot defend on the ground that there had been no delivery.

(f) CONDITIONAL OR SPECIFIED PURPOSE DELIVERY. As against a favored holder, a person who would be liable on the instrument cannot show that the instrument, unconditional on its face, was in fact delivered subject to a condition that had not been satisfied or that it was delivered for a particular purpose but was not so used. Assume A makes out a check to the order of B and hands it to C with the understanding that C shall not deliver the check to B until B delivers certain merchandise. If C should deliver the check to B before the condition is satisfied and B then negotiates

the check, a holder in due course or a holder through a holder in due course may enforce the instrument.

(g) DURESS CONSISTING OF THREATS. The defense that a person signed or executed a commercial paper under threats of harm or violence may not be raised as a defense against a holder in due course when the effect of such duress is merely to make the contract voidable at the election of the victim of the duress.

(h) UNAUTHORIZED COMPLETION. If a maker or drawer signs a commercial paper and leaves blank the name of the payee, the amount, or any other term, and then hands the instrument to another to be completed, the defense of an improper completion cannot be raised when payment is demanded or suit brought by a subsequent holder in due course or a holder through a holder in due course. For example, Fulton gave Perry a note duly executed except for the amount. Fulton gave Perry authority to fill in an amount not to exceed $300. Perry filled in the note for $500. If Perry had negotiated the instrument to a holder in due course, the instrument could have been enforced as completed.[11]

(i) THEFT. As a matter of definition, a holder in due course will not have acquired the paper through theft and any defense of theft therefore must relate to the conduct of a prior party. Assuming that the theft of the paper does not result in a defect in the chain of necessary indorsements, the defense that the instrument has been stolen cannot be raised against a holder in due course or a holder through a holder in due course.[12]

§ 34:5 UNIVERSAL DEFENSES AVAILABLE AGAINST ALL HOLDERS

Certain defenses are regarded as so basic that the social interest in preserving them

---

[11] UCC § 3-407(3). Virginia Capital Bank v Aetna Cas. & Sun. (Va) 343 SE2d 81 (1986).
[12] UCC § 3-305(1).

outweighs the social interest of giving commercial paper the free-passing qualities of money. Accordingly, such defenses are given universal effect and may be raised against all holders, whether ordinary holders, holders in due course, or holders through a holder in due course. Such defenses are therefore appropriately called **universal defenses.**

(a) FRAUD AS TO THE NATURE OR ESSENTIAL TERMS OF THE PAPER. The fact that a person signs a commercial paper because fraudulently deceived as to its nature or essential terms is a defense available against all holders. This is the situation when an experienced business person induces an illiterate person to sign a note by falsely representing that it is a contract for repairs or, as in the *Schaeffer* case, by representing that it is a character reference. This defense, however, cannot be raised when it is the negligence of the defending party that prevented learning the true nature and terms of the instrument.

SCHAEFFER V UNITED BANK AND TRUST COMPANY
32 Md App 339, 360 A2d 461 (1976)

Estepp and Schaeffer both worked at the same country club. Estepp was Schaeffer's supervisor. Estepp borrowed money from the United States Bank and Trust Company. Estepp asked his good friend Schaeffer to give him a character reference for the bank. Schaeffer could not read and did not realize he was signing a note to the bank as an accommodation maker on behalf of Estepp so that the bank would make the loan. Estepp did not pay the note. The bank sued Schaeffer who raised the defense of fraud. From a judgment in favor of the bank, Schaeffer appealed.

MOORE, J. . . . [The lower court stated] *I do not think that the United Bank did anything wrong in this case in its dealings and I have not seen any evidence here today that it committed any kind of fraud on this particular defendant.* . . .

It is manifest that the court overlooked evidence of fraud on the part of the maker, James Estepp, and herein resides reversible error. . . .

The evidence. . . . would establish (1) that [Schaeffer] was almost illiterate, (2) that the nature of the transaction was not explained to him by the bank, (3) that he did not understand that he was assuming any financial responsibility when he signed the note and (4) that Mr. Estepp falsely and fraudulently misrepresented the document. This evidence mounts up to fraud in the *factum*.

Fraud in the *factum*, unaccompanied by negligence, is one of the most potent defenses in the realm of commercial law. When it is successfully interposed it bars recovery not only by the promisee on a simple contract . . . , but also by a holder in due course. . . .

In discussing the elements of fraud in the *factum*, [UCC § 3-305, Official Comment 7] is instructive:

The test of the defense here stated is that of excusable ignorance of the contents of the writing signed. The party must not only have been in ignorance, but must also have had no reasonable opportunity to obtain knowledge. In determining what is a reasonable opportunity all relevant factors are to be taken into account, including the age and sex of the party, his intelligence, education and business experience; his ability to read or to understand English, the representations made to him and his reason to rely on them or to have confidence in the person making them; the presence or absence of any third person who might read or explain the instrument to him, or any other possibility of obtaining independent information; and the apparent necessity, or lack of it, for acting without delay.

Here appellant was a man of limited intelligence, little education, and virtually no ability to read English. His supervisor at work, who had assisted him in the funeral of his wife, and in whom he "had complete confidence in what he said" at the time the note was signed, misrepresented the very essence of the transaction.

In a strikingly similar case, a New Jersey court observed:

> The evidence supports the trial court's finding that De Paul signed the note in issue in reliance upon the false representation made to him by the maker Ronald Perkowsky, that he was signing only a "character reference" which Perkowsky needed in connection with the purchase of merchandise from Bushberg Brothers of Union City, the payee of the instrument. Because of his subnormal mentality, his only schooling having been in a "special class" of the public school, De Paul was not able to read, except small words, and then he needed reading glasses for this purpose. When he signed this note, he did not read it; he had no reading glasses with him, and the note was not read to him by Perkowsky or the representative of Bushberg Brothers who witnessed his signature. It seems clear, therefore, that the district court was correct in finding that De Paul's signature was obtained as the result of fraud in the *factum*, without any negligence on his part. . . .
>
> The rationale of the defense is the fundamental of contract law that one cannot be bound on an obligation he does not know he is entering into.

Here, . . . the same considerations lead us to the conclusion that appellant was a victim of fraud in the *factum*.

In *Amsterdam* the plaintiff holder in due course argued that since the fraud was perpetrated by a maker upon a co-maker rather than by the payee, "the defense was not available as against the payee or its transferee, the plaintiff." In the instant case the bank correctly argues that "there was no testimony or evidence of fraud perpetrated by the appellee [Bank] on the appellant" [Schaeffer]. This argument is, however, irrelevant. When the individual charged on a note successfully interposes the defense of fraud in the *factum* it is immaterial *who* perpetrated the fraud. . . .

[Judgment reversed]

Questions

1. What kind of fraud was committed by Estepp?
2. Did Schaeffer take reasonable steps to determine that he was signing a character reference?
3. When suit is brought on commercial paper and a defense is raised by the defendant, can the plaintiff avoid the defense by showing that he or she personally was innocent of any wrong?

(b) FORGERY OR LACK OF AUTHORITY. The defense that a signature was forged or signed without authority may be raised against any holder unless the person whose name was signed has ratified it or is estopped by conduct or negligence from denying it.[13]

The fact that the negligence of the drawer helped the wrongdoer does not bar the drawer from raising the defense of forgery.

(c) DURESS DEPRIVING CONTROL. When a person executes or indorses a commercial paper in response to a force of such a nature that, under general principles of law, there is duress that makes the transaction a nullity rather than merely voidable, such duress may be raised as a defense against any holder.

(d) INCAPACITY. The fact that the defendant is a minor, who under general principles of contract law may avoid the obligation, is a matter that may be raised against any kind of holder. Other kinds of incapacity may only be raised as a defense if the effect of the incapacity is to make the instrument a nullity.

(e) ILLEGALITY. If the law declares that an instrument is void when executed in connection with certain conduct, such as gambling or usury, that defense may be raised against any holder. Similarly, when contracts of a corporate seller are a nullity because its charter has been forfeited for nonpayment of taxes, a promissory note given to it by a buyer is void and that defense may be raised as against a holder in due course. If the law merely makes the transaction illegal but does not make the instrument void, the defense cannot be asserted against a holder in due course or a holder through a holder in due course.

(f) ALTERATION. An alteration is a change to an instrument that is both material and fraudulently made. An alteration is material when it changes the contract of any party, as by changing the date, place of payment, rate of interest, or any other term. Material alterations also include any modification that changes the number or the relationship of the parties to the paper, by adding new terms or by cutting off a part of the paper itself.

An alteration must be made to the instrument itself. An oral or a collateral written agreement between the holder and one of the parties that modifies the obligation of the party is not an "alteration" within the sense just discussed, even though the obligation of a party is changed or altered thereby.

(1) Person Making Alteration. By definition, an **alteration** is a change made by a party to the instrument. A change of the instrument made by a nonparty has no effect, and recovery may be had on the instrument as though the change had not been made, provided it can be proved what the instrument had been in its original form.

(2) Effect of Alteration. The fact that an instrument has been altered may be raised against any holder. Unlike other defenses, however, it is only a partial defense as against a favored holder. That is, a holder in due course or a holder through a holder in due course may enforce the instrument according to its original terms prior to its alteration.[14]

For example, Ryan signed a negotiable demand note for $500, made payable to Long. A subsequent holder changed the amount from $500 to $700. A later holder in due course presented the note to Ryan for payment. Ryan would still be liable for the original amount, $500. However, if the person sued by the holder in due course has by negligence substantially contributed to making the alteration possible, that defendant is precluded or barred from asserting the defense of alteration.

---

[13] UCC § 3-404(1); Eutsler v First Nat. Bank (Okla) 639 P2d 1245 (1982).

[14] UCC § 3-407(3).

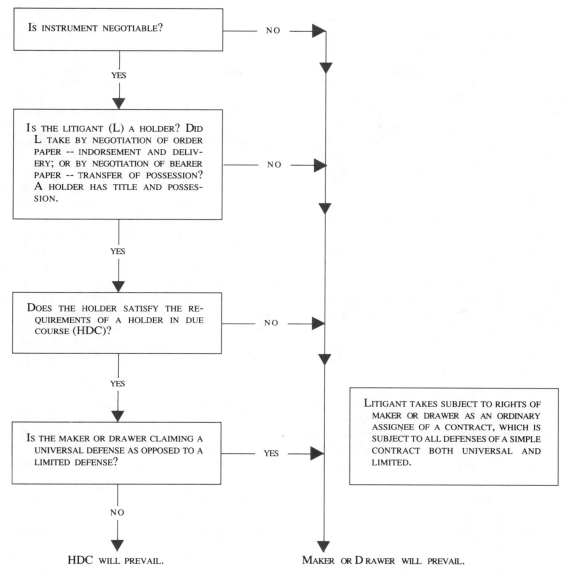

FIGURE 34-1
COMMERCIAL PAPER LITIGATION

§ 34:6 ADVERSE CLAIMS TO THE PAPER

Distinct from a defense that a defendant may raise against the plaintiff as a reason against paying the instrument is a claim of a third person to be the owner of the paper. Assume that a check was made payable to the order of *B*; that thereafter blank indorse-ments are made by *B*, *C*, and *D*; and that *E* in possession of the check appears to be the holder. *B* might then claim and show, if such be the case, that *C* had fraudulently deceived *B* into indorsing the check; and that *B* therefore avoids the indorsement because of such fraud; and that accordingly the check still belongs to *B*. *B* in such case is making an adverse claim to the instrument.

(a) EFFECT OF ADVERSE CLAIM. A holder in due course holds commercial paper free and clear from all adverse claims of any other person to the paper, including both equitable and legal interests of third persons, and the right of a former holder to rescind negotiation.[15]

In contrast, such adverse claims may be asserted against a holder who is not a holder in due course. This means that the adverse claimant may bring an action against the holder to obtain the paper as the law generally provides for the recovery of property by the owner from anyone else.

(b) DEFENDANT'S ASSERTION OF ADVERSE CLAIM. Ordinarily a defendant when sued by a holder cannot raise against the holder the defense that the holder's ownership is subject to an adverse claim. This may be done only when the adverse claimant has also become a party to the action or is defending the action on behalf of the defendant.

This limitation is imposed to protect the adverse claimant from a decision in an action to which the adverse claimant was not a party and to prevent opening the door to perjury by giving any defendant the opportunity of beclouding the issues by raising a false claim that a third person has an adverse interest.

§ 34:7 AVOIDANCE OF HOLDER IN DUE COURSE PROTECTION

In certain situations, the taker of a commercial paper is denied the status of a holder in due course or is denied the protection of a holder in due course.

(a) PARTICIPATING TRANSFEREE. The seller of goods on credit frequently assigns the sales contract and buyer's promissory note to the manufacturer who made the goods, to a finance company, or to a bank. In such a case, the assignee of the seller will be a holder in due course of the buyer's commercial paper if the paper is properly negotiated and the transferee satisfies all the elements of being a holder in due course. The transferee, however, may take such an active part in the sale to the seller's customer or may be so related to the seller that it is proper to conclude that the transferee was in fact a party to the original transaction and had notice or knowledge of any defense of the buyer against the seller, which conclusion automatically bars holding that the transferee is a holder in due course.

In the *Cessna Finance* case, a transferee of a promissory note and installment contract claimed holder in due course status.

[15] UCC § 3-305(1), 3-207(2).

CESSNA FINANCE CORP. V WARMUS

—— Mich App ——, 407 NW2d 66 (1987)

Warmus purchased an airplane from Cessna Aircraft. He executed an installment sales contract and promissory note. The sales contract named Cessna Finance as assignee.* After allegedly encountering mechanical difficulties with the plane, Warmus ceased payments on the installment contract. Assignee Cessna Finance sued Warmus claiming holder in due course status. Warmus defended on the ground that the sole consideration for the execution of the installment contract failed and that assignee financing company is so closely connected with the sales

* Authors' Note: In the trade, "assignment of the note and contract" is used to mean negotiation of the note and assignment of the contract.

transaction, that it cannot be a holder in due course. From a judgment in favor of Cessna Finance Corporation, Warmus appealed.

CARNOVALE, J. . . . Warmus requested a ruling that Cessna Finance was not a holder in due course of the promissory note and installment sales contract it took by assignment from Cessna Aircraft. To support his motion, Warmus submitted: (1) Cessna Finance's admissions that it drafted the installment sales contract form used by Cessna Aircraft in defendant's purchase transaction and that its own name was preprinted thereon under "assignments"; (2) Cessna Finance's admission that it drafted the promissory note form that was used by Cessna Aircraft; (3) Cessna Finance's admission that it performed a credit check on defendant before he purchased the airplane from Cessna Aircraft; (4) the deposition testimony of Cessna Finance's administrative manager, David Carl Peaden, that more than fifty percent of Cessna Finance's income derives from the sale of aircraft manufactured by Cessna Aircraft; (5) interrogatory answers that five persons from Cessna Finance's seven-member board were on Cessna Aircraft's board at the time Warmus executed the contract, three of whom were corporate officers of Cessna Aircraft.

Cessna Finance replied with its own motion . . . predicated upon a waiver of defenses clause which provided for assignment of the contract and stated "when so assigned the contract shall be free from any claims whatsoever which buyer might have against seller."

. . . Warmus contends he may assert the defense of failure of consideration against Cessna Finance because Warmus is a party with whom the holder, Cessna Finance, has dealt. To avoid Cessna Finance's argument that only Cessna Aircraft owed a duty to Warmus under the installment sales contract, Warmus urges this Court to adopt the "close-connections" or "close-connectedness" doctrine. Under that doctrine, if the assignee financing company is closely connected with the sales transaction, it cannot claim that it is a holder in due course.

The trial court rejected Warmus' reliance on the close-connections doctrine, reasoning that the majority of states which have adopted the doctrine apply it only to consumer transactions. The court further relied on M.C.L. § 445.865(d); M.S.A. § 19.416(115)(d), which provides that holders of retail installment contracts are subject to all claims and defenses of a buyer of *consumer goods* arising out of the retail transaction, notwithstanding any other provision of law. By negative implication, the court reasoned that the Legislature intended no similar protection for persons such as Warmus, who enter into business transactions.

We believe that the trial judge has erred . . . because a question of fact existed as to whether Cessna Finance was a holder in due course.

M.C.L. § 440.9206; M.S.A. § 19.9206 provides:

> Subject to any statute or decision which establishes a different rule for buyers or lessees of consumer goods, an agreement by a buyer or a lessee that he will not assert against an assignee any claim or defense which he may have against the seller or lessor is enforceable by an assignee who takes his assignment for value, in good faith and without notice of a claim or defense, except as to defenses of a type which may be asserted against a holder in due course of a negotiable instrument under the article on commercial paper (article 3). A buyer who as part of one transaction signs both a negotiable instrument and a security agreement makes such an agreement.

Pursuant to the above statute, an assignee may rely on an agreement precluding an assertion of certain defenses against an assignee only if the assignee is a holder in due course.

A holder in due course of an instrument is one who takes the instrument (1) for value, (2) in good faith, and (3) without notice that it is overdue or has been dishonored, or of any defenses or claims to it. M.C.L. § 440.3302; M.S.A. § 19.3302. Holder-in-due-course status operates to insulate the holder from certain defenses to the instrument of any party with whom the holder has not dealt. However, a holder is subject to all defenses of a party with whom the holder has dealt. M.C.L. § 440.3305; M.S.A. § 19.3305. . . .

We believe issues of material fact remain in the instant case, and thus that the question of good faith and notice should properly be submitted to the trier of fact. Evidence exists that Cessna Finance's name, as assignee, was on the preprinted form at the time of the execution of the lease agreement. Evidence exists that Cessna Finance made an independent check of Warmus' credit. Evidence exists that management of Cessna Finance and Cessna Aircraft was related by common members of their boards of directors and corporate officers. . . .

Under our disposition, it is unnecessary to adopt the close-connectedness doctrine. We believe that the doctrine is only a substitute for a proper analysis under existing law. Stated otherwise, it is unnecessary to adopt the doctrine when the issue can be properly addressed under existing law. To the extent that the factors relied on by other courts as indicative of close-connectedness are within the totality of the circumstances of a particular case, the parties may rely on them to establish that an assignee is not a holder in due course.

[Judgment reversed]

QUESTIONS

1. What is meant by the close-connections doctrine?
2. Did court adopt the doctrine?
3. What was the basis for the court's decision?

(b) THE FEDERAL TRADE COMMISSION RULE. In 1976, the FTC adopted a rule that to some extent limits the rights of a holder in due course in a **consumer credit transaction.** The rule protects consumers who purchase goods or services for personal, family, or household use.[16] When the buyer is sued by a finance company on the note given to the seller, the buyer may raise any defense that could have been raised against the seller if the consumer's contract contains the notice required by the FTC regulation. The Commission regulation requires that the following notice be included in boldface type at least ten points in size:

NOTICE

ANY HOLDER OF THIS CONSUMER CREDIT CONTRACT IS SUBJECT TO ALL CLAIMS AND DEFENSES WHICH THE   DEBTOR   COULD   ASSERT

---

[16] The regulation does not cover purchases of real estate, securities, or consumer goods or services of which the purchase price is more than $25,000. Roosevelt Federal Sav. & Loan Assn. v Crider, (Mo App) 722 SW2d 325 (1986).

AGAINST THE SELLER OF GOODS OR SERVICES OBTAINED WITH THE PROCEEDS HEREOF. RECOVERY HEREUNDER BY THE DEBTOR SHALL NOT EXCEED AMOUNTS PAID BY THE DEBTOR HEREUNDER.

SUMMARY

A holder of commercial paper can be either an ordinary holder or a favored holder. The ordinary holder has the same rights that an assignee would have. Favored holders are protected from certain defenses. Favored holders are (1) holders in due course, and (2) holders through holders in due course. To be a holder in due course, a person must first be a holder, that is, the paper must have been acquired by a proper negotiation. The holder must meet certain requirements to be a holder in due course. The holder must take for value, in good faith, without notice of paper overdue or dishonored, and without notice of defenses and adverse claims. Those persons who become holders of the instrument after a holder in due course are given the same protection as the holder in due course provided they are not parties to any fraud or illegality affecting the instrument.

The importance of being a holder in due course or a holder through a holder in due course is that those holders are not subject to certain defenses when they demand payment or bring suit on commercial paper. These defenses are limited defenses and include ordinary contract defenses, incapacity unless it makes the instrument a nullity, fraud in the inducement, prior payment or cancellation, nondelivery of an instrument, duress consisting of threats, unauthorized completion, and theft of the paper that does not result in a defect in the chain of necessary indorsements. Universal defenses may be asserted against any plaintiff, whether that party is an assignee, an ordinary holder, a holder in due course, or a holder through a holder in due course. Universal defenses include fraud as to the nature or essential terms of the paper, forgery or lack of authority, duress depriving control, infancy, illegality, and alteration. With regard to alteration, it is only a partial defense, as the favored holder may enforce the instrument according to its original terms.

The Federal Trade Commission provides for limiting the immunity of a holder in due course from defenses of consumer buyers against their sellers. Immunity is limited in consumer credit transactions if the notice specified by the FTC regulation is included in a sales contract.

QUESTIONS AND CASE PROBLEMS

1. What social forces are affected by the holder in due course rule?
2. Holton owes Zeigler $100. Holton draws a check on her bank payable to the order of Zeigler for $100, and delivers the check to Zeigler. The question arises whether Zeigler has taken the check for value. The argument is made that Zeigler did not give anything in return for the check and, therefore, has not given value. Is this argument correct?
3. Bushnell purchased an automobile from Gable because of the latter's fraudulent statements as to the condition of the car. Bushnell gave Gable a check drawn on the Exchange Bank for the purchase price. Gable cashed the check at the Industrial Bank. When Bushnell learned that he had been defrauded, he stopped payment on the check. Bushnell also informed the Exchange Bank and the Industrial Bank of Gable's misconduct. Indus-

trial Bank claimed that Bushnell was liable to it on the dishonored check. Bushnell claimed that the Industrial Bank was subject to the defense of fraud in the inducement. Industrial Bank denied this on the ground that it was a holder in due course. Bushnell claimed that Industrial Bank was not a holder in due course because it knew of Gable's fraud. Was Bushnell correct?

4. Dawn gave Cleo a promissory note promising to pay $1,000 to the order of Cleo in thirty days. Cleo transferred this note to Carlos thirty-five days later. When Carlos demanded payment from Dawn, Dawn raised the defense that Cleo did not perform the work for which the note was given as payment in advance. Carlos replied that the defense of Dawn was a matter between Dawn and Cleo only and that he was not concerned with it. Is Carlos correct?

5. What is the underlying reasoning behind making universal defenses available against all holders?

6. Compare (a) an assignee, (b) a holder, (c) a holder in due course, and (d) a holder through a holder in due course, with respect to the defense that the defendant is seventeen years of age.

7. How does fraud as a limited defense differ from fraud as a universal defense?

8. Jones, wishing to retire from a business enterprise which he had been conducting for a number of years, sold all the assets of the business to Jackson Corporation. Included among such assets were a number of promissory notes that he had taken from his customers payable to the order of Jones. On maturity of one such note, the maker would not pay, alleging failure of consideration (which was a fact). Jackson Corporation sues the maker of the note. Who should succeed?

9. D drew a check to the order of P. It was later claimed that P was not a holder in due course because the check was postdated and because P knew that D was having financial difficulties and that the particular checking account on which this check was drawn had been frequently overdrawn. Do these circumstances prevent P from being a holder in due course? [Citizens Bank, Booneville v National Bank of Commerce (CA10 Okla) 334 F2d 257; Franklin National Bank v Sidney Gotowner (NY Sup Ct) 4 UC-CRS 953]

10. H acquired a check by indorsement. At the time that H acquired the check he knew of all the circumstances surrounding the original issue of the check. If H knew the legal significance of those circumstances, he would have realized that the drawer of the check had a valid defense. Because H did not know the law, he did not realize that the drawer had a defense and took the check in good faith believing that everything was proper. In a subsequent lawsuit on the check, the question arose whether H was a holder in due course. The defendant claimed that H was not because H knew of the defense based on the surrounding circumstances and H's ignorance of the law did not excuse him from the consequence of that knowledge, because ignorance of the law is no excuse. Is H a holder in due course? [Hartford Life Ins. Co. v Title Guarantee Co. 172 App DC 156, 520 F2d 1170]

11. A customer of a bank purchased a bank money order and paid for it with a forged check. The money order was negotiable and was acquired by N who was a holder in due course. When N sued the bank on the money order, it raised the defense that its customer had paid with a bad check. Could this defense be raised against N? [Bank of Niles v American State Bank, 14 Ill App 3d 729, 303 NE2d 186]

12. Statham drew a check. The payee indorsed it to the Kemp Motor Sales Co. Statham then stopped payment on the check on the ground that there was a failure of consideration for the check. Kemp sued Statham on the check. When Statham raised the defense of failure of consideration, Kemp replied that it was a holder in due course. Statham claimed that Kemp could not recover because it learned of his defense before it deposited the check in its bank account. Decide. [Kemp Motor Sales v Statham, 120 Ga App 515, 171 SE2d 389]

13. Layton wished to make a gift to his niece of $2,000, but he did not have the cash. Layton therefore executed a demand negotiable promissory note for $2,000 payable to the order of his niece, delivered the note to his niece, and stated: "You can present this note as a claim against my estate if the note is not paid before my death." The niece immediately sold the note to Richards, a hold-

er in due course. Richards presented the note to Layton for payment, and Layton refused payment. What defense is available to Layton?

14. Abbott gives his note to Brown, no interest being specified. Brown adds thereto a provision for interest and conveys the note for value before maturity to Jones, who takes it without notice. Can Jones enforce the note against Abbott for principal and interest? Why or why not?

15. Dorsey was negligent in not determining that the paper he was signing was actually a promissory note. The note was negotiated by proper indorsement and delivery to the New Jersey Mortgage and Investment Co. The evidence established that New Jersey Mortgage and Investment was a holder in due course. Dorsey refuses to pay, alleging fraud as to the nature of essential terms. Decide. [New Jersey Mortgage and Investment Co. v Dorsey, 33 NJ 448, 165 A2d 297]

35

LIABILITIES OF THE PARTIES AND DISCHARGE FROM LIABILITY

The law of commercial paper relating to presentment, dishonor, and discharge is regulated by Part 5 of Article 3 of the UCC. Much of this law, however, does not have practical importance because it relates to situations that rarely occur in the world of business. The following discussion is, therefore, a simplified presentation of the subject aimed at basic requirements and the points that have given rise to litigation.

A.   PARTIES TO AN INSTRUMENT

Parties to an instrument may be classified as primary or secondary.

§ 35:1   PRIMARY PARTIES

Primary parties are the parties required to pay the instruments when they are due. The maker in the case of a promissory note and the drawee-acceptor in the case of a draft are primary parties. A drawee is not liable for payment of a draft before acceptance. An **acceptance** is the drawee's written and signed assent to the order of the drawer. The act of refusing to accept the draft does not give the holder any right to sue the drawee on the paper. The draft does not operate as an assignment of money, even though the drawee has possession of funds of the drawer.[1]

---

[1] Holsombach v Akins, 134 Ga App 513, 215 SE2d 306 (1975).

722

The liability of a primary party on an instrument continues for the period of the statute of limitations. The holder need not give the primary party any advance notice of demand.

§ 35:2   SECONDARY PARTIES

Secondary parties have conditional liability that may be enforced when the primary parties fail to pay. Secondary parties include the drawer of a draft and the unqualified indorser of a draft or a note.

B.   PRESENTMENT AND DISHONOR

The conditional liability of secondary parties does not arise until three conditions precedent are met — presentment of the instrument for payment or acceptance, dishonor, and notice of dishonor.[2]

§ 35:3   PRESENTMENT

Presentment is a demand for acceptance upon a drawee or a demand for payment upon a maker, acceptor, or indorser.[3] Commercial paper should be presented to any primary party for payment at the time of maturity. However, a failure to make a presentment for payment will not discharge primary parties from their obligation. Liability continues until barred by the statute of limitations. Failure to make presentment when the paper is due will discharge all secondary parties.

(a) HOW PRESENTMENT IS MADE. Presentment must be made by or on behalf of the holder to the party primarily liable at the place specified in the instrument. The presentment must be made at a reasonable time, and if made at a bank, must be made during its banking day. It is not necessary that there be actual physical presentation of the paper, although the person to whom presentment is made usually will ask that the instrument be shown. Once the paper is paid, the holder must offer to surrender the instrument.[4]

(b) WHEN PRESENTMENT IS EXCUSED OR UNNECESSARY. Presentment for payment may not be made for various reasons. It will be excused or unnecessary (1) if presentment has been waived by the secondary party in question; (2) if presentment cannot be made in spite of due diligence; (3) if the primary party has died; or (4) if the secondary party has no reason to believe that the instrument will be paid.[5]

§ 35:4   DISHONOR

Dishonor occurs when an instrument has been duly presented for acceptance or payment and acceptance or payment cannot be obtained or is refused. If proper notice has been given to the secondary parties — the drawer and the indorsers — the holder has an immediate right of recourse against them.[6]

§ 35:5   NOTICE OF DISHONOR

If commercial paper is dishonored, any secondary party who is not given proper notice thereof is released from liability, unless the giving of notice is excused. It was a failure to give proper notice of dishonor that caused problems for the holder in the *Hane* case.

---

[2]   Binford v Lichtenberger Estate (Or App) 660 P2d 1077 (1983).
[3]   UCC § 3-504(1)

[4]   UCC §§ 3-503, 3-504, 3-505.
[5]   UCC § 3-511.
[6]   UCC § 3-507.

HANE V EXTEN
255 Md 668, 259 A2d 290 (1969)

Theta Electronic Laboratories executed a promissory note payable to Thomson and his wife. The note was indorsed by Exten, O'Neil, and

James Hane, and their wives. The Thomsons assigned the note to John Hane. The note was not paid when due. John Hane took judgment by confession against the maker and the Extens. Upon learning of the judgment, the Extens moved that the judgment be vacated as to them and their motion was granted. John Hane appealed.

SINGLEY, J. . . . John B. Hane is the assignee of the note of Theta Electronic Laboratories, Inc. (Theta) in the stated amount of $15,377.07. . . . [The note provided] that "In the event of the failure to pay the interest or principal, as the same becomes due on this Note, the entire debt represented hereby shall at the end of thirty (30) days become due and demandable. . . ." The note was assigned without recourse to Hane by George B. and Marguerite F. Thomson, the original payees, on 26 November 1965. A default having occurred in the making of the monthly payments, Hane took judgments by confession in the Circuit Court for Montgomery County on 7 June 1967 against Theta and three individuals, Gerald M. Exten, Emil L. O'Neil, and James W. Hane, and their wives, who had indorsed Theta's note. On motion of the Extens, the judgment was vacated as to them. . . . From a judgment for the Extens, Hane has appealed.

This case raises the familiar question: Must Hane show that the Extens were given notice of presentment and dishonor before he can hold them on their indorsement?

The court below, in finding for the Extens, relied on the provisions of Uniform Commercial Code. . . . Section 3-414(1) provides:

Unless the indorsement otherwise specifies (as by such words as "without recourse") every indorser engages that upon dishonor and any necessary notice of dishonor and protest he will pay the instrument according to its tenor at the time of his indorsement to the holder or to any subsequent indorser who takes it up, even though the indorser who takes it up was not obligated to do so.

§ 3-501(1)(b) provides that "Presentment for payment is necessary to charge any indorser" and § 3-501(2)(a) that "Notice of any dishonor is necessary to charge any indorser," in each case subject, however, to the provisions of § 3-511 which recite the circumstances under which notice of dishonor may be waived or excused, none of which is here present. § 3-502(1)(a) makes it clear that unless presentment or notice of dishonor is waived or excused, unreasonable delay will discharge an indorser.

There was testimony from which the trier of facts could find as he did that presentment and notice of dishonor were unduly delayed.

It is clear that Hane held the note from November 1965, until some time in April, 1967, before he made demand for payment. UCC § 3-503(1)(d) provides that "Where an instrument is accelerated, presentment for payment is due within a reasonable time after the acceleration." "Reasonable time" is not defined in § 3-503, except that § 3-503(2) provides, "A reasonable time for presentment is determined by the nature of the instrument, any usage of banking or trade, and the facts of the particular case." But § 1-204(2) characterizes it: "What is a reasonable time for taking any action depends on the nature, purpose, and circumstances of such action."

Reasonableness is primarily a question for the fact finder. *Vanderberg & Sons, N. V. v Siter*, 204 PaSuper 392, 204 A2d 494 (1964); . . . 1 Anderson's Uniform Commercial Code, Commentary, § 1-204:3. . . . We see no reason to disturb the lower court's finding that Hane's delay of almost 18 months in presenting the note "was unreasonable from any viewpoint." . . .

As regards notice of dishonor, § 3-508(2) requires that notice be given by persons other than banks "before midnight of the third business day after dishonor or receipt of notice of dishonor." Exten, called as an adverse witness by Hane, testified that his first notice that the note had not been paid was the entry of the confessed judgment on 7 June 1967. Hane's brother testified that demand had been made about 15 April 1967. He was uncertain as to when he had given Exten notice of dishonor, but finally conceded that it was "within a week." The lower court found that the ambiguity of this testimony, coupled with Exten's denial that he had received *any* notice before 7 June fell short of meeting the three-day notice requirement of the UCC. The date of giving notice of dishonor is a question of fact, solely for determination by the trier of facts. . . . We cannot say that the court erred in its finding.

In the absence of evidence that presentment and notice of dishonor were waived or excused, Hane's unreasonable delay discharged the Extens, § 3-502(1)(a). . . .

[Judgment affirmed]

QUESTIONS

1. Within what time must notice of dishonor be given?
2. Within what time must a holder in due course give notice of dishonor?

(a) HOW NOTICE IS GIVEN. Notice is ordinarily given by the holder who has been refused payment. It may be given in any reasonable manner, oral or written. It may have any terms as long as it identifies the instrument and states that it has been dishonored. Any necessary notice must be given by a bank before midnight of the next banking day following the business day on which the bank receives the instrument or notice. By a nonbank, notice must be given before midnight of the third full business day following the dishonor or receipt of notice of dishonor. Written notice is effective when sent, although it is not received.

In the *Greer* case, a bank claimed that it had acted promptly in giving notice.

GREER v WHITE OAK STATE BANK
(Tex App) 673 SW2d 326 (1984)

Jack Greer and Donald Biesel owned a bowling alley. George Ford and Bowling and Billiard Supply of Dallas (B & B) had outstanding liens on the alley. Greer, Biesel, Ford, and B & B were named as beneficiaries of an insurance policy on the bowling alley. The bowling complex burned and a check from the insurance company was issued to Greer, Biesel, Ford, and B & B. All the parties indorsed the check. The insurance check was deposited in Greer's account at the White Oak State Bank. Greer then issued checks drawn on that account to Ford and B & B in payment of their claims. The insurance company was insolvent; therefore, the drawee bank dishonored the insurance check on August 3, 1981, and notified the White Oak Bank that same day by telephone. The oral notification was followed by written notice of dishonor which was received by the White Oak Bank ten days later, on August 13, 1981. White Oak then notified the indorsers of the dishonor on August 14, 1981. White Oak brought suit against the indorsers on the dishonored check. They denied liability because of White Oak's failure to promptly notify them of the dishonor. From a judgment in favor of White Oak, the indorsers appealed.

CORNELIUS, C. J. . . . [UCC §§ 3-501, 3-503, and 3-502], respectively, provide that unless excused, notice of dishonor is necessary to charge any indorser of an item; notice must be given by a bank before its midnight deadline (the next banking day after the banking day it received the item); and that any unexcused delay in giving notice of dishonor discharges any indorser. The bank argues that these code provisions do not apply to Greer, Ford and B & B because (1) oral notice of dishonor is not effective and the indorsers were promptly notified after the bank received written notice of the check's dishonor on August 14, 1981, and (2) the telephone notice from the bank in Dallas did not specify that Ford and B & B were indorsers, so in any event it did not receive notice of dishonor *as to them* until August 13, 1981. We cannot agree with either of these propositions.

Section 3-508 expressly provides that notice of dishonor may be oral. The bank contends that Section 4-202(1)(b) supersedes Section 3-508 with respect to notice from a collecting bank, and because that section refers to "sending" notice of dishonor, only a written notice is contemplated. We disagree. The adequacy of oral notice is confirmed by Section 4-104(3) which specifically makes the notice of dishonor provisions of Section 3-508 applicable to transactions under Article 4. Moreover, the jury found upon sufficient evidence that White Oak State Bank and the First National Bank in Dallas had agreed prior to August 3, 1981, that notice of returned items could be sent by telephone. The requirements of Article 4 may be modified by agreement.

The failure of the telephone notice to name Ford and B & B as indorsers did not render the notice ineffective as to them. Section 3-502(1)(a) provides that if notice of dishonor is not given when due, *any* indorser is discharged. Delay in giving notice may be excused when a party does not know it is due or when the delay is caused by circumstances beyond his control. But there was no jury finding here that any circumstance existed which would excuse the Bank from notifying Ford and B & B. In fact, the employee who received the telephone notice testified that the information she received was sufficient to enable her to identify the check and all parties to it.

As indicated, Greer, Ford and B & B were all discharged, *as indorsers*, from any obligation on the check. . . .

[Judgment reversed]

QUESTIONS

1. What was the argument of White Oak Bank?
2. Why was it important that the indorsers receive timely notice of dishonor?
3. State the decision of the court and the basis for the decision.

(b) EXCUSE FOR DELAY OR ABSENCE OF NOTICE OF DISHONOR. Delay in giving notice of dishonor is excused under the same circumstances as delay in making presentment for payment. It is excused for any of the following: (1) waiver; (2) inability to give notice in spite of due diligence; and (3) the fact that the party notified did not have any reason to believe that the instrument would be paid.[7]

PARTY	PRIMARY LIABILITY	SECONDARY LIABILITY
ACCEPTOR	X	
DRAWEE		
DRAWER		X
GUARANTOR OF PAYMENT	X	
MAKER OF NOTE	X	
UNQUALIFIED INDORSER		X

FIGURE 35-1
LIABILITIES OF PARTIES FOR PAYMENT

C.   DISCHARGE FROM LIABILITY

A party may be discharged individually or by some act that discharges all parties to the paper at one time.

§ 35:6   DISCHARGE OF INDIVIDUAL PARTIES

A party to a commercial paper, just as a party to an ordinary contract, is usually discharged from liability when payment is made to the proper person; but the discharge from liability may be effected in a number of other ways.

(a) THE LAW OF CONTRACTS. Commercial paper may be discharged in the same manner as an ordinary contract for the payment of money. Accordingly, there may be a discharge by accord and satisfaction, by a novation, or by operation of law, such as a discharge in bankruptcy and the operation of the statute of limitations.[8]

(b) PAYMENT. The obligation of a particular party on commercial paper is discharged by payment of the amount of the instrument to the holder or to the holder's authorized agent.[9] Payment to anyone else is not effective to discharge the liability of the payor.

(c) CANCELLATION AND RENUNCIATION. The holder of an instrument may discharge the liability of a party by placing something indicative of discharge on the paper, such as intentionally marking the instrument canceled, or by destroying or mutilating the instrument or a party's signature. There is no cancellation when the paper is destroyed by accident or mistake.

A holder can also discharge a party's liability by renouncing the holder's rights against the party in a written paper to that

[7]   UCC § 3-511.
[8]   Duke v Young (Ala) 496 So 2d 37 (1986).
[9]   UCC § 3-603(1).

effect delivered with the instrument or by surrendering the instrument to the party to be discharged.[10]

No consideration is needed for a discharge by cancellation or renunciation.

(d) IMPAIRMENT OF RIGHT OF RECOURSE OR OF COLLATERAL. If the holder extends the time of payment or releases the principal debtor or impairs collateral security furnished as security for the payment of the instrument, such action will discharge any party whose rights are affected by such impairment.[11]

(e) ALTERATION. When an instrument is materially and fraudulently altered by the holder, any party whose obligation is changed thereby is discharged, unless such party has assented to the alteration or is barred by conduct from asserting a discharge. The effect of the discharge is limited, however, for a holder in due course may enforce the paper according to its original terms.[12]

In the *Citizen's National Bank* case, a maker of a promissory note to the bank claimed a discharge by alteration.

---

[10] UCC § 3-605.
[11] Valley Bank & Trust v Rite Way Concrete (Utah App) 742 P2d 105 (1987).

[12] UCC § 3-407.

CITIZEN'S NATIONAL BANK OF WILMAR V TAYLOR
(Minn) 368 NW2d 913 (1985)

Douglas Taylor executed three promissory notes to the Citizen's National Bank in the amount of $48,991.96 together with 15 percent interest. After the notes became past due, the bank sent Taylor a letter informing him that since the maturity date had passed, the bank was increasing the interest on those notes to 22½ percent. The three notes had been altered by crossing out the interest figure of 15 percent in pencil and writing in its place the new rate of 22½ percent. When the bank sued Taylor to recover on the three notes, Taylor claimed that he had been discharged because the bank had fraudulently altered the interest rate on the notes. From a judgment in favor of the bank, Taylor appealed.

AMDAHL, C. J. . . . [A] letter was sent to Taylor regarding his indebtedness on June 2, 1981. In that letter, the bank noted that Taylor had not responded to previous letters concerning the notes, and asked Taylor to "stop in right away and take care of these past due items." Taylor testified that he did not receive any of these notices or letters. The bank officer to whom returned mail is brought testified that these notices were not returned undelivered. The bank received no response from Taylor.

On May 26, 1981, the bank sent Taylor the following letter:

Your three notes came due May 1, 1981, in excess of $40,000.00. The interest on those notes effective today is 22½%.

It is necessary that you stop in the bank and pay the interest to bring the notes current and take them off a past due status. You should do that this week.

The three notes were altered by crossing out the 15% interest figure in pencil and writing in its place on the face of each note "22½ eff. 5/26/81." Paul Peterson, the loan officer who dealt with Taylor, said the notes would have been changed on the date indicated, May 26. The alteration was not made by Peterson, but by a bank employee in accordance with what Peterson described as "normal banking procedures" when a demand note is overdue. Peterson testified that in May of 1981, interest rates were changing and the bank renewed demand notes as they came due at the current rate. The bank would notify the customer and change the note. Peterson testified that the bank always notified the customer when it changed the interest rate on any note, and that interest rates have been lowered, as well as raised, in this manner in the past.

Taylor admitted that he received the bank's May 26 letter. Taylor apparently did not go to the bank before June 8 because the bank sent him a letter on that date advising him that no more credit would be extended and that the bank expected full payment on the notes "around the first of July." Taylor eventually went to the bank and discussed his situation with loan officer Peterson. As a result of this visit, the bank agreed to extend the notes to August 1, 1981. A statement that the notes were extended was stamped on the back of each note, Peterson initialed the back of each note, and Taylor signed on the back of each note.

After the bank sued Taylor to recover on the three demand notes, Taylor counterclaimed for . . . punitive damages, alleging that the bank had fraudulently altered the notes with willful indifference to Taylor's rights. . . .

The trial court . . . issued findings of fact and conclusions of law, finding Taylor liable on the notes according to their original tenor. In reaching its conclusion, the trial court found that the bank altered the notes in the good faith, but mistaken, impression that it could change the interest rate after a default on a demand note. The court concluded that the alteration was not fraudulent. The court also found that Taylor consented to the alteration. . . . [UCC §] 3-407(2)(a) (1984) provides that:

> (2) As against any person other than a subsequent holder in due course
>   (a) alteration by the holder which is both fraudulent and material discharges any party whose contract is thereby changed unless that party assents or is precluded from asserting the defense . . . .

Taylor claimed that he was discharged from his obligation under all three notes because the bank fraudulently altered the interest rate on the notes. In order to prevail, Taylor had to show that the alteration was (1) made by the holder of the note, (2) was material, and (3) was made for a fraudulent purpose. The bank was clearly the holder of the notes, and the change in interest rate from 15% to 22½% was clearly material. The trial court found, however, that the bank did not fraudulently alter the note.

Fraud, under the Uniform Commercial Code, "requires a dishonest and deceitful purpose to acquire more than one was entitled to under the note as signed by the maker rather than only a misguided purpose." . . . The general rule is that a party seeking discharge on an instrument under 3-407 must show that the holder altered the instrument with a deceitful purpose.

The evidence at trial supports the directed verdict finding that the bank did not alter Taylor's notes with fraudulent intent. The evidence showed that the bank notified Taylor several times that his notes were due. The bank notified Taylor of the change in interest rate on the day the alterations were made, and Taylor admitted receiving this notice. Bank officers testified that they thought they were entitled to renew overdue demand notes at the current rate if the customer was given notice, and said that as notes came due in May of 1981, they were changing notes in this way. They also said that they had lowered interest rates on notes in this manner in the past if the market rates were lower than the interest rate on the note. This was described as a "normal banking procedure." There was no evidence tending to show deceit on the part of the bank in their dealings with Taylor on the notes. . . .

. . . Fraudulent alteration of an instrument does not discharge a party if that party consents to the alteration. The trial court, after finding that the bank did not fraudulently alter the instrument, also found that Taylor consented to the alteration. The evidence supports the trial court's . . . finding of consent. Taylor was notified of the change in interest rate and later signed an extension of the notes after the alteration had taken place. Peterson testified that he and Taylor specifically discussed the interest rate and that Taylor said the rate was "awfully high." Taylor said the May 26 letter made him aware that the bank wanted to charge 22½% interest. We affirm the trial court's direction of the verdict on the issue of consent.

[Judgment affirmed as to alteration]

QUESTIONS

1. Was the Citizen's Bank a holder?
2. Was the alteration material and made for a fraudulent purpose?
3. Was Taylor liable on the notes? Explain.

§ 35:7 DISCHARGE OF ALL PARTIES

The primary party on an instrument, that is, the maker of a note or the acceptor of a draft, has no right of recourse against any party to the paper. Conversely, every other party who may be liable on the paper has a right of recourse against the party primarily liable. If the holder discharges in any way a party who is primarily liable, all parties to the instrument are discharged, as the discharge of the primary party discharges the person who had a right of recourse against the primary party.[13]

In much the same manner, when a party primarily liable on the paper reacquires it as owner at any time, the instrument is then held by the one who has no right to sue any other party on the instrument. Such reacquisition therefore discharges the liability of all intervening parties to the instrument.

No discharge is effective against a holder in due course unless such holder has notice of the discharge when taking the instrument.[14]

[13]   UCC § 3-601(3).

[14]   UCC § 3-602. As an exception to this rule, a holder in due course is subject to a discharge in insolvency proceedings of any party, even though the paper was taken without notice or knowledge of such discharge. UCC § 3-305(2)(e).

SUMMARY

The maker of a promissory note and the acceptor of a draft are primarily liable for its payment. Payment may be demanded from them as soon as the paper is due.

Secondary parties are required to pay the paper if the primary party failed to do so upon proper presentment and proper notice of default was given to the secondary party.

Presentment and notice of dishonor may be excused under certain circumstances.

Dishonor occurs when an instrument has been duly presented for acceptance or payment and such acceptance or payment cannot be obtained or is refused. Upon proper notice to the secondary parties of such refusal or inability to obtain acceptance or payment, the holder has an immediate right of recourse against them. Any secondary party not given proper notice will be discharged from liability on the instrument. Notice of dishonor is excused under the same circumstances as delay in making presentment for payment. Notice may be given in any reasonable manner; it may be oral or written; and it must be given (if the holder is not a bank) before midnight of the third full business day after dishonor.

A party may be discharged individually or by some act that has discharged all parties to the paper at one time. There may be a discharge by accord and satisfaction, novation, or operation of law. There may be a discharge by payment of the instrument to the holder or the holder's authorized agent, by cancellation, renunciation, impairment of right of recourse or of collateral, or by an alteration.

A discharge of the party primarily liable discharges all persons who had a right of recourse against the primary party. No discharge is effective against a holder in due course, unless such holder has notice of the discharge when taking the instrument.

QUESTIONS AND CASE PROBLEMS

1. What social forces are affected by the rule that giving notice of dishonor to a secondary party before midnight of the third business day following dishonor is sufficient?
2. Ragno borrows money from the Main Street Bank and gives a promissory note for the amount of the loan. The note is due in sixty days. Main Street indorses and delivers the note to the Third National Bank. Ragno fails to pay the note when it is due. A month after it is due, the Third National Bank sues the Main Street Bank for the amount of the note. Is it liable?
3. Henri draws a draft on Marchamp directing Marchamp to pay $1,000 on demand to the order of Clara. Marchamp is indebted to Henri for $10,000. When Clara presents the draft of Henri, Marchamp refuses to make any payments to Clara. Clara sues Marchamp. Can she recover?
4. Compare a note and draft both payable at a definite time with regard to the need of presentment for payment with respect to
   (a) the maker,
   (b) an acceptor, and
   (c) an unqualified indorser.
5. State how notice of dishonor may be given.
6. Four promissory notes were executed by Continental Diamond Mines, Inc. payable to the order of M. Kopp. The notes were thereafter indorsed to M. Kopp, Inc. and then to Rafkin. Rafkin was the holder on the due date. Was it necessary for him to make a presentment of the notes to Continental Diamond Mines in order to hold it liable on the notes? [Rafkin v Continental Diamond Mines, Inc. 33 Misc 2d 156, 228 NYS2d 317]
7. A indorsed a promissory note on the back. At the top of the back, above all indorsements, there were printed the words "Notice of protest waived." The note was not paid when due. The holder sent A notice that the note was not paid, but A did not receive the notice because it was sent to a former address at which he no longer lived. A denied liability because he had not been properly notified. Decide. [Lizza Asphalt Construction Co. v Greenvale Construction Co. (NY Sup Ct) 4 UCCRS 954]
8. Mellen-Wright Lumber Co., the holder of a note, sued McNett, as maker, and Kendall, as indorser. The latter claimed that he had not received notice of the dishonor of the note by the maker. The holder proved that he had sent the following letter, dated June 10, to Kendall:
   Dear Sir: We hold note for $2,000 with interest at 7 percent signed by Earl P. McNett and Anna J. McNett, his wife, on which you indorsed guaranteeing payment.
   This note will be due June 12 and we are going to ask that you arrange to pay same

promptly. We would appreciate this being paid by not later than Friday, June 18.
Kindly advise if you wish to make payment at our office or at one of our local banks.
We are enclosing stamped envelope for reply.
Was Kendall liable? [Mellen-Wright Lumber Co. v McNett, 242 Mich 369, 218 NW 709]

9. Donavan owed the A & B Body Works for repairs to her auto. She gave the Body Works a promissory note payable to its order for the amount that was due. When she found that she could not pay the note when due, she so informed Ray, the son of one of the owners of Body Works. He told her to forget the debt. Later Body Works sued Donavan on the note. She claimed that the note had been discharged by cancellation. Was she correct?

10. Harrison gave the Construction Transport Company a promissory note representing a freight bill owed it. The note was payable in sixty days. The transport company wanted the money sooner and changed the note to make the amount due in thirty days. Harrison refused to pay the note and was sued on the sixty-first day. Is Harrison liable?

11. On August 15, Janet borrowed $3,000 from Richard, giving Richard in return a negotiable promissory note for $3,000 payable to the order of Richard. The note was due in thirty days. On September 10th, Richard indorsed the note to the Alden Car Co. On September 12th, Alden Car Co. learned that Janet was seriously ill. Alden Car Co. wrote Janet that they were discharging her from liability on the instrument. On the due date, Alden Car Co. asked Richard to pay the note as an indorser, explaining why they did not collect from Janet. Is Richard obligated to pay?

12. As part of a business plan, Schwald executed and delivered a note to Montgomery. The parties then made a new business arrangement, and Montgomery intentionally tore up the note and threw it into the wastebasket. It was subsequently contended that this note had been canceled. Do you agree? [Montgomery v Schwald, 117 Mo App 75, 166 SW 831]

13. Gorman executed and delivered to the First National Bank a negotiable promissory note payable to its order. The note was stolen from the bank. Some time later, Richardson, a former employee of the bank, delivered the note to Gorman in return for Gorman's payment of the balance then due. The note was returned to Gorman marked "paid." First National Bank sued Gorman for the balance of the loan. He raised the defense that the note had been discharged by payment. Decide. [First National Bank v Gorman, 45 Wyo 519, 21 P2d 549]

14. Rochelle executed a promissory note. Nevis was the holder of the note. Nevis renounced his claim against Rochelle on the note. Thereafter, he asserted that his renunciation was not binding because he had not received any consideration for it. Is Rochelle liable on the note?

15. The Citizens State Bank issued a cashier's check payable to the order of Donovan. He indorsed it to Denny, who did business as the Houston Aircraft Co., and included in the indorsement a recital that it was "in full satisfaction of any and all claims of any character whatever." Denny crossed out this quoted phrase and wrote Donovan and the bank that he had done so. The Houston Aircraft Co. sued the Citizens National Bank on the check. Was the bank liable? [Houston Aircraft v Citizens State Bank (Tex Civ App) 184 SW2d 335]

16. In the following circumstances, state the respective rights and obligations of (a) the maker, (b) the payee, and (c) the holder. Ann Lane gave her promissory note for $1,000, due Feb. 15, payable at the First Bank, to Sally Parks, who for value, indorsed and delivered it to Robert Davis. Through an oversight, the note was not presented for payment until February 25. As of February 15 and thereafter, Lane had more than $1,000 on deposit in the First Bank.

17. First Properties, Inc. issued a promissory note to the order of Fletcher. Fletcher indorsed the note to Dannon, who in turn took the note to his bank for collection. The teller at the bank mistakenly stamped the note "paid" although payment had not yet been received. Dannon had no knowledge that the note was so stamped. A question arose by the creditors of First Properties, Inc. to determine whether the note had been canceled. Decide.

36

CHECKS AND CUSTOMER-BANK RELATIONSHIP

A deposit of money in a bank to the depositor's credit creates the relationship of debtor and creditor between the bank and depositor. This deposit creates a liability upon the bank to repay upon demand, on the written order of the depositor, the credit established. This written order is known as a check.

A. CHECKS

In business the majority of money obligations are settled by means of checks. By using checks it is possible to make payment safely and conveniently without the need for safeguarding a shipment of money. The checkbook stub and the canceled check make a written record which may be used at a later date to show that payment was made.

§ 36:1   NATURE OF A CHECK

A **check** is a particular kind of draft. The first three of the following features of a check distinguish it from other drafts or bills of exchange.[1]

(a) DRAWEE. The drawee of a check is always a bank.

(b) SUFFICIENT FUNDS ON DEPOSIT. As a practical matter, the check is drawn on the assumption that the bank has on deposit in the drawer's account an amount sufficient to pay the check. In the case of a draft, there is no assumption that the drawee has any of the drawer's money with which to pay the instrument. Actually, the rights of the parties are not affected by the fact that the depositor does not have funds on deposit with the bank sufficient to pay the check.

If a draft is dishonored, the drawer is civilly liable; but if a check is drawn with intent to defraud the person to whom it is delivered, the drawer is also subject to criminal prosecution in most states under what are known as *bad check laws*. Most states provide that if the check is not made good within a stated period, such as 10 days, it will be presumed that the check was originally issued with the intent to defraud.

(c) DEMAND PAPER. A check is demand paper. A draft may be payable either on demand or at a future date. The standard form of check does not specify when it is payable, and it is therefore automatically payable on demand. This eliminates the need for an acceptance since the holder of the check will merely present it for payment.

One exception arises when a check is postdated, that is, when the check shows a date later than the actual date of execution. Here the check is not payable until the date arrives.[2] This, in effect, changes the check from demand paper to time paper without expressly stating so.

While it is customary for banks to supply depositors with printed forms of checks, a check may be any writing.[3] A card, given to a computer terminal located away from a bank for the purpose of withdrawing money from the bank or making a repayment on a loan, is also a check.[4]

(d) DELIVERY NOT ASSIGNMENT. The delivery of a check is not an assignment of the money on deposit. Therefore, it does not automatically transfer the rights of the depositor against the bank to the holder of the check, and there is no duty on the part of the drawee bank to the holder to pay the holder the amount of the check.[5]

§ 36:2   CERTIFIED CHECKS

The drawee bank may certify or accept a check drawn on it. The certification must be written on the check and signed by an authorized representative of the bank.

The effect of the certification is to set aside in a special account maintained by the bank as much of the depositor's account as is needed to pay the certified check. With respect to the holder of the check, the certification is an undertaking by the bank that when the check is presented for payment, it will make payment according to the terms of the check without regard to the standing of the depositor's account at that time.

A check may be certified by a bank upon the request of the drawer or the holder. In the latter case all prior indorsers and the

---

[1]   Checks are governed by both Article 3 of the UCC relating to commercial paper and Article 4 governing bank deposits and collections.

[2]   Howells, Inc. v Nelson (Utah) 565 P2d 1147 (1977).
[3]   The printed bank check is preferable because it generally carries magnetic ink figures that facilitate sorting and posting.
[4]   Illinois v Continental Illinois National Bank (CA7 Ill) 536 F2d 176 (1976).
[5]   UCC § 3-409(1). Galaxy Boat Mfg. Co. v East End State Bank (Tex App) 641 SW2d 594 (1982).

CHECK	DRAFT
1. DRAWEE IS ALWAYS A BANK 2. CHECK IS DRAWN ON ASSUMPTION MONEY IN BANK TO COVER CHECK 3. CHECK IS PAYABLE ON DEMAND (UNLESS POSTDATED)	1. DRAWEE IS NOT NECESSARILY A BANK 2. NO ASSUMPTION DRAWEE HAS ANY OF DRAWER'S MONEY TO PAY INSTRUMENT 3. DRAFT MAY BE PAYABLE ON DEMAND OR AT FUTURE DATE

FIGURE 36-1
DIFFERENCES BETWEEN A CHECK AND A DRAFT

drawer are released from liability.[6] Since the holder could have received payment, as the bank was willing to certify the check, and since the holder did not take the payment but chose to take the certification, the prior secondary parties are released from liability. When the certification is obtained by the drawer, there is no release of the secondary parties.

§ 36:3   LIABILITY OF DRAWER

If the check is presented for payment and paid, no liability of the drawer arises. If the bank refuses to make payment, the drawer is then subject to the same liability as in the case of the nonpayment of an ordinary draft. If proper notice of dishonor is not given the drawer of the check,[7] the drawer will be discharged from liability to the same extent as the drawer of an ordinary draft.

§ 36:4   THE DEPOSITOR-BANK RELATIONSHIP

The depositor-bank relationship imposes duties upon the bank.

(a) PRIVACY. The bank owes the depositor the duty of maintaining secrecy concerning information that the bank acquires in connection with the depositor-bank relationship. Law enforcement officers and administrative agencies cannot require the disclosure of information relating to a depositor's account without obtaining the depositor's consent, a search warrant, or following the statutory procedures designed to protect depositors from unreasonable invasions of privacy.[8]

(b) PAYMENT. A bank is under a general contractual duty to its depositor to pay on demand all checks to the extent of the funds in the depositor's account. When the bank breaches this contract, the bank is liable to the drawer for damages. As in the case of an unaccepted draft, in the absence of an independent contractual duty, the bank owes no duty to the holder to accept or pay a check.

(1) Stale Checks. A bank acting in good faith may pay a check presented more than six months after its date (commonly known as a **stale check**); but, unless the check is certified, the bank is not required to do so. The fact that a bank may refuse to pay a check that is more than six months old does not mean that it must pay a check that is less than six months old or that it is not required to exercise reasonable care in making payment of any check.

(2) Payment After Depositor's Death. Subject to certain exceptions, the authority of a bank to act with respect to its depositor's check terminates with the death of the depositor. As exceptions to this general rule, the drawee bank's power continues

---

[6]   UCC § 3-411(1). Sherwin-Williams Co. v Sarrett (Miss) 405 So 2d 842 (1981).

[7]   Under Federal Reserve regulations notice of dishonor may be given by telephone. Security Bank and Trust Co. v Federal National Bank (Okla App) 554 P2d 119 (1976).

[8]   Right to Financial Privacy Act of 1978, PL 95-630, 92 Stat 3697, 12 USC § 3401 et seq.

for some time after the death of the depositor. For the first ten days after the depositor's death, the bank may continue to pay or certify checks of the depositor even though it knows of the depositor's death, unless ordered to stop payment by a person claiming an interest in the account.[9] If the bank does not know of the death of the drawer, its power to pay and certify checks of the depositor continues until it learns of the death.

§ 36:5   STOPPING PAYMENT OF CHECK

The drawer may **stop payment** of a check by notifying the drawee bank not to pay it

[9]   UCC § 4-405.

when it is presented for payment. This procedure is useful when a check is lost or mislaid. A duplicate check can be written, and, to make sure that the payee does not receive payment twice or that an improper person does not receive payment on the first check, payment on the first check can be stopped. Likewise, if payment is made by check and then the payee defaults on the contract so that the drawer would have a claim for breach of contract, payment on the check can be stopped, provided the check has not been paid.

The drawer cannot stop payment of a certified check. A bank customer cannot stop payment of a cashier's check.

The *First Financial* case, involved the question of whether payment could be stopped on a cashier's check.

FIRST FINANCIAL V FIRST AMERICAN BANK
(La App) 489 So 2d 388 (1986)

First Financial filed suit against First American Bank, seeking payment of a cashier's check issued by First American to First Financial in the amount of eighteen-hundred dollars ($1,800). First American had issued its cashier's check in exchange for a personal check on which a stop payment order had been issued. From a judgment in favor of First Financial, First American appealed.

WICKER, J. . . . On Friday, May 3, 1985, Mrs. Tommy Marzoni, a customer of First American deposited a personal check in the amount of Eighteen Hundred Dollars ($1,800.00) into First Financial. The check was drawn on her account at First American. On that same date, she spoke to Cindy Pilgram, an employee at First American, and informed her that she wished to stop payment on her personal check. She was informed, however, that she would have to place her request in writing. Consequently, she appeared at First American on Monday, May 6, 1985 at 9:00 a.m. to institute the stop payment order. On that same date, subsequent to her written request, but prior to the time at which all window tellers could be informed of the order, one of First Financial's employees appeared at First American and presented the personal check to Gloria Detillier, a cashier at First American, and requested a cashier's check in exchange. Such a check in the amount of Eighteen Hundred Dollars ($1,800.00) was issued by First American in exchange for Mrs. Marzoni's personal check.

Shortly thereafter, the employees of First American learned of the stop payment order on the personal check and immediately notified First Financial that the bank would not honor the cashier's check. On Tuesday, May 7, 1985, First

American issued a stop payment order on its cashier's check. Prior to that order reaching First Financial, it credited the amount to pay off a loan in the name of Mr. Tommy Marzoni and to credit the account of Mrs. Marzoni with the remaining funds. The amount so credited to the account was subsequently withdrawn prior to the stop payment order on the cashier's check reaching First Financial . . . .

This appeal presents questions of first impression in this jurisdiction, namely, whether a bank can stop payment on its cashier's check and whether it can assert a defense of failure of consideration in that payment on the personal check accepted in exchange for the cashier's check had been stopped.
. . .

Louisiana's version of Articles 1, 3, 4 and 5 of the Uniform Commercial Code (U.C.C.) and Articles 7 and 8 is contained in L.S.A.- R.S. 10:1-101 et seq. Our version is similar to that of the U.C.C. in that it also has only one reference to cashier's checks. L.S.A.-R.S. 10:4-211 provides in pertinent part that:

> 1) A collecting bank may take in settlement of an item. . . .
>   (b) a *cashier's check* or similar primary obligation of a remitting bank which is a member of or clears through a member of the same clearing house or group as the collecting bank . . .

[Emphasis supplied]

A review of our Louisiana jurisprudence reveals that no court has specifically addressed the issue of whether a bank can stop payment on its own cashier's check. . . .

Since Louisiana law does not address the issue of whether a bank can stop payment on its cashier's check or whether it can assert the defense of failure of consideration, we now turn to a view of other jurisdictions to determine their treatment of such a check.

The majority of jurisdictions define a cashier's check as a substitute for cash.

Most of the courts which follow the majority view disallow defenses on the part of the issuing bank.

New York courts in particular have favored a rule which opposes the stopping of payment of a cashier's check. In *Kaufman,[v Chase Manhattan Bank*, 370 F Supp 276 (SDNY 1973)] the court summarized New York law as having accorded a special status to a cashier's check as follows:

> An ordinary check is an order by one party (drawer) directing a second party (drawee) to pay, on demand, a fixed sum of money to a third party (payee). The drawer is primarily liable to the payee for the amount of the check until that check has been accepted by the drawee. Payment on the check may be stopped by the drawer only if the drawee receives notice prior to acceptance. . .
>
> *A cashier's check, however, is a check drawn by the bank upon itself, payable to another person, and issued by an authorized officer of the bank. The bank, therefore, becomes both the drawer and drawee; and the check becomes a promise by the bank to draw the amount of the check from its own resources and to pay the check upon demand. Thus, the issuance of the cashier's check constitutes an acceptance by the issuing bank; and the cashier's check becomes the primary obligation of the bank. . . .*

In *Kaufman, supra,* a cashier's check was presumed to have been issued for value and this presumption could not be overcome by evidence that the bank did not receive consideration. The court found that the bank was both the drawer and the drawee of the check and that upon issuance the bank promised to pay the check upon demand from its own resources. The *Kaufman* court looked to the public policy regarding the nature and usage of cashier's checks in the commercial world and the fact that such a policy would favor a rule which prohibits the stop payment of a cashier's check.

The rationale behind an approach which treats cashier's checks as cash equivalents is explained in the leading case of *National Newark & Essex Bank [v Giordano*, III NJ Super 347, 268 A2d 327 (1970)] as follows:

> a cashier's check circulates in the commercial world as the equivalent of cash. . . People accept a cashier's check as a substitute for cash because the bank stands behind it, rather than an individual. In effect the bank becomes a guarantor of the value of the check and pledges its resources to the payment of the amount represented upon presentation. To allow the bank to stop payment on such an instrument would be inconsistent with the representation it makes in issuing the check. Such a rule would undermine the public confidence in the bank and its checks and thereby deprive the cashier's check of the essential incident which makes it useful. People would no longer be willing to accept it as a substitute for cash if they could not be sure that there would be no difficulty in converting it into cash. . . .

In contrast, a minority of the jurisdictions look to the status of the instrument and view the cashier's check as a negotiable instrument. Of this minority, most of these courts view it as a bank draft, the others view it as a negotiable promissory note.

These courts, however, do recognize the validity of certain defenses to payment. In the instant case, appellant raises the defense of lack of consideration. It contends that since it issued a cashier's check for a personal check which it subsequently learned had a stop payment order, it received no consideration and thus can assert this defense. It relies on the legal analysis which treats the cashier's check as a negotiable instrument subject to the defenses relative to a holder or a holder in due course.

We adhere to the majority view that a cashier's check is a substitute for cash or a cash equivalent. Moreover, we adopt the analysis used by several courts of applying U.C.C. Section 4-303(1)(a) to prohibit a bank from asserting a defense to payment of a cashier's check.

In *Kaufman, supra*, the court held that:

> Since a cashier's check is a bank's primary obligation, a cashier's check is presumed to have been issued for value. This presumption cannot be overcome by evidence that the bank did not receive consideration for the cashier's check from the payee. Such proof is irrelevant and provides no defense.

By its act of issuing the cashier's check, the bank undertakes a primary obligation to pay the amount when presented. In particular, it undertakes the obligation to pay the amount from its own resources.

The applicable section in our statute is L.S.A.-R.S. 10:4-303(1)(a) which provides that:

> (1) Any knowledge, notice or stop-order received by, legal process served upon or setoff exercised by a payor bank, whether or not effective under other rules of law to terminate, suspend or modify the bank's right or duty to pay an item or to charge its customer's account for the item, comes too late to so terminate, sus-

pend or modify such right or duty if the knowledge, notice, stop-order or legal process is received or served and a reasonable time for the bank to act thereon expires or the setoff is exercised after the bank has done any of the following:
(a) accepted or certified the item . . .

Accordingly, since L.S.A.-R.S. 10:4-303(1)(a) disallows stop payment orders on accepted items, the bank cannot issue a stop payment order on its cashier's check. Thus, any defenses allowed in L.S.A.-R.S. 10:3-305 and 306 relative to the status of holder or holder in due course do not apply. Moreover, the court in *Kaufman, supra*, felt that the bank could have protected itself by ensuring that it had received payment before issuing.

Considering the law and the views expressed, we hold that a cashier's check is a cash equivalent and therefore a bank is prohibited from issuing a stop payment order on its own cashier's check for failure of consideration.

[Judgment affirmed]

QUESTIONS

1. What is meant by a cashier's check?
2. What was the argument of the appellant, First American?
3. What reason did the court give for rejecting the argument of the appellant?

(a) FORM OF STOP PAYMENT ORDER. The stop payment order may be either oral or written. If oral, however, it is only binding on the bank for 14 calender days unless confirmed in writing within that time. A written stop payment order or confirmation is effective for six months.

(b) LIABILITY TO HOLDER FOR STOPPING PAYMENT. The act of stopping payment may in some cases make the depositor liable to the holder of the check. If the depositor has no proper ground for stopping payment, the depositor is liable to the holder of the check. In any case, the depositor is liable for stopping payment with respect to any holder in due course or other party having the rights of a holder in due course, unless payment was stopped for a reason that may be asserted against such a holder as a defense. The fact that payment of a check has been stopped does not affect its negotiable character.[10]

§ 36:6   TIME OF PRESENTMENT OF CHECK FOR PAYMENT

In order to charge a secondary party to demand paper, presentment for payment must generally be made upon the primary party to the instrument within a reasonable time after that secondary party has signed it. Reasonable time is determined by the nature of the instrument, by commercial usage, and by the facts of the particular case.[11]

Failure to make timely presentment discharges all prior indorsers of the instrument. It also discharges the drawer, if the draft was payable at a bank, to the extent that the drawer has lost, through the bank's failure, money which was on deposit at the bank to meet the payment of the instrument.[12]

The UCC establishes two presumptions as to what is a reasonable time in which to

---

[10]   Bigbee v Indiana, __ Ind App __, 364 NE2d 149 (1977).

[11]   UCC § 3-503(1)(e),(2).
[12]   UCC § 3-502(1).

present a check for payment.[13] If the check is not certified and is both drawn and payable within the United States, it is presumed as to the drawer that thirty days after the date of the check or the date of its issuance, whichever is later, is the reasonable period in which to make presentment for payment. With respect to the liability of an indorser, seven days after indorsing is presumed to be a reasonable time.[14]

§ 36:7   DISHONOR OF CHECK

When a check is dishonored by nonpayment, the holder must follow the same procedure of notice to the secondary parties as in the case of a draft or bill of exchange in order to hold them liable for payment. As in the case of any drawer of a draft or bill of exchange who countermands payment, notice of dishonor need not be given to the drawer who has stopped payment on a check. Notice is also excused under any circumstances that would excuse notice in the case of a promissory note. For example, no notice need be given a drawer or an indorser who knows that sufficient funds to cover the check are not on deposit, since such party has no reason to expect that the check will be paid by the bank.[15]

When a check is sent in the course of the collection process to the bank on which it is drawn, that bank must either pay or promptly return the check as unpaid, or send notice of its dishonor, as by returning the check unpaid for "insufficient funds." If the drawee bank does not act before its midnight deadline, it automatically becomes liable for the face of the instrument.[16] Oral notice of dishonor is sufficient.

(a) BANK'S LIABILITY TO DRAWER OF CHECK. The contract between the depositor (drawer) and the bank (drawee) obligates the latter to pay in accordance with the orders of its depositor as long as there is sufficient money on deposit to make such payment. If the bank improperly refuses to make payments, it is liable to the drawer for damages sustained by the drawer in consequence of such dishonor.

(b) BANK'S LIABILITY TO HOLDER. If the check has not been certified, the holder has no claim against the bank for the dishonor of the check, regardless of the fact that the bank had acted in breach of its contract with its depositor. If the bank had certified the check, it is liable to the holder when it dishonors the check, as the certification imposes upon the bank a primary liability to pay the face amount of the check.

The liability of secondary parties on the check is not affected by whether the holder has any right against the drawee bank.

§ 36:8   AGENCY STATUS OF COLLECTING BANK

When a person deposits a commercial paper in a bank, the bank is ordinarily thereby made an agent to collect or obtain the payment of the paper. Unless the contrary intent clearly appears, a bank receiving an item is deemed to take it as agent for the depositor rather than as becoming the purchaser of the paper. This presumption is not affected by the form of the indorsement nor by the absence of any indorsement. The bank is also regarded as being merely an agent even though the depositor has the right to make immediate withdrawals against the deposited item.[17] In consequence of the agency status, the depositor remains the owner of the item and is, therefore, subject to the risks of ownership involved in its collection, in the absence of fault on the part of any collecting bank.[18]

When a bank cashes a check deposited by its customer or cashes a check drawn by

---

[13] A presumption means that the trier of fact must find the existence of the fact presumed in the absence of evidence that supports a contrary conclusion. UCC § 1-201(31).

[14] UCC § 3-503(2).

[15] UCC § 3-511(2)(b).

[16] UCC § 4-302, 4-104(1)(h). Southwest Nat. Bank v ATG Const. ___ Kan ___, 736 P2d 894 (1987).

[17] UCC § 4-201(1).

[18] UCC § 4-202.

its customer on the strength of a deposited check, it is a holder of the check deposited by its customer. The bank may sue the parties thereon, even though as between the customer and the bank the latter is an agent for collection and has the right to charge back the amount of the deposited check if it cannot be collected. When the bank receives final settlement for an item taken for collection, the agency status ends and the bank is merely a debtor of its customer just as though the customer had made an ordinary cash deposit in the bank.[19]

B. LIABILITY OF BANK FOR IMPROPER PAYMENT AND COLLECTION

The drawee bank may be liable for paying a check contrary to a stop payment order or when there has been a forgery or alteration.

§ 36:9   PAYMENT OVER A STOP PAYMENT ORDER

A bank must be given a reasonable time to put a stop payment order into effect. However, if the bank makes payment of a check after it has been properly notified to stop payment, it is liable to the depositor for the loss the depositor sustains, in the absence of a valid limitation of the bank's liability.[20] The burden of establishing the loss resulting in such case rests upon the depositor. In the *Tusso* case, the court found that one and one-half hours was a reasonable time to put the stop payment order into effect.

---

[19]   Cooper v Union Bank, 9 Cal 3d 123, 107 Cal Rptr 1, 507 P2d 609 (1973).

[20]   A bank cannot contractually limit its liability for paying over a valid stop payment order when the bank has failed to exercise ordinary care. UCC § 4-403, Comment 8.

TUSSO V SECURITY NATIONAL BANK
349 NYS2d 914 (1973)

Tusso sent a check for $600 drawn on the Security National Bank to the Adamson Company. He then realized that he had already paid Adamson. Tusso was at the bank the next morning at 9:00 a.m. when it opened. He notified the bank to stop payment on the $600 check he had written the day before. At 10:40 a.m., about an hour and a half later, the payee arrived at the bank with the check. The bank certified the check and charged it to Tusso's account. Tusso sued the bank to recover the amount so charged. The bank claimed that he was required to prove that the bank was negligent.

COLANERI, J. . . . The bank's . . . defense is incorrect. [UCC §] 4-403(1) entitles a bank customer to stop payment on his check by giving notice to that effect "at such time and in such manner as to afford the bank a reasonable opportunity to act on it prior to any action by the bank with respect to the item . . ." The statute does not place any other affirmative burden of proof upon the plaintiff with respect to the stop payment order other than the "burden of establishing the fact and amount of loss resulting from the payment of an item contrary to a binding stop payment order . . ." (UCC § 4-403(3)). . . .

To read into this statute the additional requirement that the drawer prove the commission of a negligent act by the bank in order to recover would, in effect, alter the statute in a manner not intended by the legislature. . . . A valid stop payment order received by the bank prior to payment or certification renders subsequent payment wrongful, whether or not the bank was shown to be negligent in making such payment. . . .

The plaintiff in this case has the burden of proving that the stop payment order was received by the bank at such time as to afford it a reasonable opportunity to act on such order. . . . The facts as presented support this contention and therefore the court finds in favor of the plaintiff and against the defendant bank.

It has been held that a bank which improperly paid a check on which payment had been stopped may recover from the one who received payment, if such payee was not a holder for value. . . . The facts developed in this case indicate that the defendant construction corporation was already fully paid for its services. Therefore the construction corporation has no right to retain the additional funds improperly paid by the bank, and the court finds that the bank is entitled to judgment against the third party defendant for the amount of the improperly certified check.

Accordingly, judgment for the plaintiff against the defendant (Security National Bank) in the sum of $600.00 with interest thereon from July 25, 1972, together with the costs and disbursements of this action, and, further, the defendant and third-party plaintiff (Security National Bank) may have judgment over and against the third party defendant (Adamson Construction Corporation) in the sum of $600.00 with interest thereon from July 25, 1972, together with the costs and disbursements of this action.

QUESTIONS

1. What would the result have been if the check issued by Tusso had been certified when it was sent to the Adamson Company?
2. When a bank makes payment of check in violation of a proper stop payment order, is the bank protected from liability if it exercised reasonable care?
3. Was the drawer required to prove that the bank was negligent in paying the check over the stop payment order?

---

§ 36:10 PAYMENT ON FORGED SIGNATURE OF DRAWER

A **forgery** of the signature occurs when the name of the depositor has been signed by another person without authority to do so and with the intent to defraud by making it appear that the check was signed by the depositor. The bank is liable to the depositor (drawer) if it pays a check upon which the drawer's signature has been forged since a forgery ordinarily has no effect as a signature. The risk of loss caused by the forged signature of the drawer is thus placed upon the bank without regard to whether the bank could have detected the forgery.[21]

Although the bank has no right to pay a check upon which the drawer's signature is forged, the drawer may be barred from objecting that the signature was a forgery.

[21] Perini Corp. v First National Bank (CA5 Ga) 553 F2d 398 (1977).

If the drawer's negligence contributed substantially to the forging of the signature, the drawer cannot assert that it was forged when the drawee bank makes payment of the check while acting in good faith and conforming to reasonable commercial standards. For example, if the drawer signs checks with a mechanical writer, reasonable care must be exercised to prevent unauthorized persons from making use of it to forge or "sign" the drawer's name with such device. If the depositor's negligence enables a third person to make such improper use of it, the depositor is barred from objecting to the payment of the check by the bank.

When a check is presented to the drawee bank for payment, the drawee alone is responsible for determining whether the signature of the drawer, its customer, is a forgery. Prior indorsers do not warrant that the signature of the drawer is genuine; and, if the bank pays money or gives a cashier's check in payment of the depositor's check, the drawee cannot thereafter recover the money paid or defend against payment on the cashier's check on the ground that the drawer's signature had been forged.

§ 36:11 PAYMENT ON FORGED OR MISSING INDORSEMENT

A drawee bank that honors a depositor's check bearing a forged indorsement must recredit the drawer's account upon the drawer's discovery of the forgery and notification to the bank. Since the bank paid out the money to a person who was not the holder of the instrument, the drawer could bring an action against the bank in conversion should the bank fail to recredit the drawer's account.[22]

A drawee bank is liable for the loss when it pays a check that lacks an essential indorsement. In such a case, the instrument is not properly payable; and by defi-nition the person presenting the check for payment is not the holder of the instrument and is not entitled to demand or receive payment.

When a person deposits a check but does not indorse it, the depositor's bank may make an indorsement on behalf of the depositor unless the check expressly requires the customer's indorsement. A bank cannot add the missing indorsement of a person who is not its customer depositing the item in the customer's account in the bank.[23]

§ 36:12 ALTERATION OF CHECK

If the face of the check has been altered so that the amount to be paid has been increased, the bank is liable to the drawer for the amount of the increase when it makes payment for the greater amount.

The drawer may be barred from claiming that there was an alteration by conduct with respect to writing the check or conduct after receiving the canceled check from the bank. As to the former, the drawer is barred if the check was carelessly written and the negligence substantially contributed to the making of the material alteration and the bank honored the check in good faith and observed reasonable commercial standards in so doing.[24] For example, the drawer is barred when the check was written with blank spaces so that it was readily possible to change "four" to "four-hundred," and the drawee bank paid out the latter sum without any cause to know that there was an alteration. Therefore, a careful person will write figures and words close together and run a line through or cross out any blank spaces.

In the *Ray* case the drawer of a check brought an action against the drawee bank for a loss suffered from a check that a third party altered.

---

[22] UCC § 3-419(1)(c).

[23] Krump Construction Co., Inc. v First National Bank, ___ Nev ___, 655 P2d 524 (1982).
[24] UCC § 3-406.

RAY V FARMERS STATE BANK OF HART

(Tex) 576 SW2d 607 (1979)

Robert Freeman, posing as an electrical utility repairman, gained entrance to the home of Nora Ray, an eighty-year-old widow. Freeman told the woman that he needed a check for $1.50 to cover the "service charge." To accommodate Nora, Freeman volunteered to fill out the check for her. He then filled in a check on one of the widow's blank check forms, writing the number "1.50" far to the right of the dollar mark, and filling in the words for the amount far to the right also. Nora signed the check, and Freeman left. Freeman added "185" between the dollar sign and the $1.50 number and filled in the amount in words. Freeman cashed the check, which now read "Eighteen Hundred Fifty-One and 50/100," at the payor bank after furnishing identification. Ray sought recovery against the bank for the raised amount. The bank alleged that her negligence substantially contributed to the alteration.

POPE, J. . . . The question presented is whether Mrs. Nora Ray, the drawer, or Farmers' State Bank of Hart, Texas, the drawee, is liable for the loss occasioned by a check that a third party altered. In a case tried before the court without a jury, Mrs. Ray recovered judgment for $1,850.00, which was the amount of the alteration. The court of civil appeals reversed the judgment and rendered judgment that Mrs. Ray take nothing. 565 S.W.2d 103. We reverse the judgment of the court of civil appeals and affirm that of the trial court.

The controlling issue in the case is whether Mrs. Ray was negligent as a matter of law. On May 7, 1975, Mrs. Ray, an eighty-year-old lady, was awakened from a nap by a man who was shaking the screen to her front door. He gave his name as Robert Freeman, said he worked for the utility company, and that he needed to check the electrical system of her home because the power was off along the block. Mrs. Ray testified that when she unlatched the screen to look down the street for a utility vehicle, Freeman pushed his way inside the house. He went around the house placing a device in the electrical outlets and then went outside to check in the garage. While he was outside, as she later discovered, he cut the telephone wire to her house. Upon returning, he told Mrs. Ray that he was not through, but that he was awaiting the arrival of someone else from the utility company. He said that he was going to get a hamburger and would return after lunch, but that she should give him $1.50 for the service charge. Mrs. Ray testified that she could not see what he had done to earn $1.50 but was willing to give him the money to get him out of the house. She reached for her purse, but Freeman picked up her checkbook that was lying on the table telling her that his company required payment by check. He proceeded to fill it in, then shoved it over to her to be signed. She noted to herself that the check was for $1.50 and was in ink so it couldn't be changed. She signed the check and Freeman left.

After waiting a considerable period of time, Mrs. Ray concluded that Freeman was not going to return. She decided to phone the bank to stop payment on the check because he had not earned the money. She then discovered the phone was dead. Mrs. Ray walked down the street to use a neighbor's phone but could find nobody at home. About two hours later, when she finally talked to a lady at the bank, she learned that Freeman had cashed the check and that it was for $1,851.50 instead of $1.50.

When Freeman filled out the check at Mrs. Ray's home, he wrote the figures "1.50" far to the right of the dollar mark, leaving space in which he later added the figures "185." That made the amount appear as $1,851.50. There is some evidence that he also left space on the next line where he wrote the words "one and 50/100." He later placed in front of those words, "Eighteen Hundred & Fifty."

When Freeman presented the check at the bank, the teller required him to produce identification which he did by showing his driver's license and another identification card that showed his picture. Freeman had endorsed the check and beneath his signature he had stamped the words, "Allied Construction and Commercial-Residential."

The trial court made a number of findings of fact and also filed conclusions of law. The findings relevant to this appeal are:

1a. The Defendant Bank paid the check in question in good faith and in accordance with the reasonable commercial standards of the Bank's business.
2a. The Defendant Bank paid the check in due course of its banking business.

The relevant "conclusion of law" was that the conditions and circumstances under which Nora Ray signed and delivered the check did not amount to negligence substantially contributing to the material alteration of the instrument as required by Section 3:406 of the Uniform Commercial Code to constitute a defense.

We must begin with article 4:401 of the Code since it sets forth the general rule when a bank may charge an item against a customer's account. It states that a bank may charge against a customer's account any item properly payable from that account. Further, the bank may charge the account if it pays in good faith, even though the item has been altered, but only according to the original tenor of the altered item. We are here dealing with an alteration as explained by article 3:407(a)(3) since there were additions to Mrs. Ray's check. If we look only to these two statutes, the bank had the right to charge Mrs. Ray's account according to the original tenor of the item — $1.50 — because, according to the findings, the bank acted in good faith.

We still need, however, to fit article 3:406 into the scheme of the statutes. That article cuts off rights that a person might have against a holder in due course or against a drawee or other payor who pays an instrument in good faith and in accordance with reasonable commercial standards of the drawee's or payor's business. This means that Mrs. Ray would be precluded from asserting the alteration against Farmers' State Bank if her negligence substantially contributed to the alteration of the check.

In determining whether the bank may charge Mrs. Ray's account, there are steps that must be taken sequentially. First, the instrument must have been paid in good faith and in accordance with the reasonable commercial standards of the drawee's business. Second, the person seeking to assert the alteration must be found negligent. Third, the negligence must have substantially contributed to the alteration of the instrument.

It can be concluded that the bank did pay the check in good faith and in accordance with reasonable commercial standards. There was a finding of fact to this effect by the trial court, and there was no dispute concerning this issue before the court of civil appeals. The trial court and the court of civil appeals, however, differ on the question of negligence. The trial court found that Mrs. Ray was not negligent under the circumstances, but the court of civil appeals found negligence as a matter of law.

Official Comment 3 to this section of the Uniform Commercial Code includes this explanation of how negligence is to be determined.

> 3. No attempt was made to define negligence which will contribute to an alteration. The question is left to the court or the jury upon the circumstances of the particular cases. Negligence usually has been found where spaces are left in the body of the instrument in which words or figures may be inserted.

As a general rule, the determination of negligence is the province of the trier of fact. . . . In determining whether there was any evidence of probative force to sustain the trial judge's finding, the court of civil appeals was required to consider only that evidence favorable to the finding and the judgment rendered thereon and to disregard all evidence to the contrary. The judgment of a trial court will not be set aside if there is any evidence of a probative nature to support it, and a court of civil appeals cannot substitute its findings of fact for those of the trial court if there is any evidence in the record to sustain the trial court's findings.

When viewed in the light most favorable to the trial court's judgment, we think there is at least some evidence of probative force to support the trial court's finding. At most, the evidence is conflicting. Under such circumstances, the trial court's finding is binding on the court of civil appeals. It is our opinion that the nature of the evidence introduced at trial was such that reasonable minds might differ as to whether Nora Ray was negligent under the circumstances. The court of civil appeals, therefore, erred in reversing the judgment of the trial court and rendering judgment that Nora Ray was negligent as a matter of law. Because of this determination, we do not reach the causation issue.

[The judgment of the court of civil appeals is reversed and that of the trial court is affirmed.]

QUESTIONS

1. Did the bank pay the check in good faith and in accordance with reasonable commercial standards?
2. Does the UCC define negligence that will contribute to an alteration?
3. Was Nora Ray ultimately found guilty of negligence?

---

§ 36:13   UNAUTHORIZED
            COLLECTION OF CHECK

Although a bank acts as agent for its customer in obtaining payment of a check deposited with it by its customer, it may be liable to a third person when the act of its customer is unauthorized or unlawful with respect to the third person. That is, if the customer has no authority to deposit the check, the bank, in obtaining payment from the drawee of the check and thereafter depositing the proceeds of the check in the account of its customer, may be liable for conversion of the check to the person lawfully entitled to the check and its proceeds.

§ 36:14   INDEMNITY RIGHT OF BANK

When a bank is held liable to a drawer or a depositor for a payment or collection that is improper because a signature on the check is a forgery, the bank will in many instances be able to recover its loss from a prior party to the paper who has made either an express or implied warranty that signatures are genuine.

§ 36:15   TIME LIMITATIONS

The liability of the bank to its depositor is subject to certain time limitations.

(a) NON-CODE STATUTE OF LIMITATIONS. A local non-Code statute of limitations will fix the maximum time for asserting a claim against a bank for the breach of the customer-bank deposit contract, an action against any bank for conversion of an item of commercial paper, or an action by one bank against another bank or party to paper to obtain indemnity or contribution.

(b) FORGERY AND ALTERATION REPORTING TIME. A depositor must examine with reasonable care and promptness a bank statement and relevant checks that are paid in good faith and sent to the depositor by the bank, and to discover any unauthorized signature or alteration on the checks. The depositor must notify the bank promptly after discovering either of the foregoing. If the bank exercises ordinary care in paying a forged or altered check and suffers a loss because the depositor fails to discover and notify the bank of the forgery or alteration, the depositor cannot assert the unauthorized signature or the alteration against the bank.[25]

Regardless of the care or lack of care of either the depositor or the bank, the depositor is precluded from asserting the depositor's unauthorized signature or any alteration if the depositor does not report it within one year from the time the bank state-ment is received. A forged indorsement must be reported within three years.[26]

(c) UNAUTHORIZED SIGNATURE OR ALTERATION BY SAME WRONGDOER. Often the same wrongdoer perpetrates a series of forgeries or alterations. The depositor must warn the bank as soon as possible of the first forgery or altered item so that the bank can protect itself from a repetition of the misconduct. A failure by the depositor to notify the bank within fourteen days after a statement of account with the paid items is sent bars the depositor from holding the bank liable for the loss on additional checks forged or altered by the same wrongdoer thereafter paid in good faith by the bank.[27]

C.   ELECTRONIC FUND TRANSFERS ACT

The primary objective of the **Electronic Fund Transfers Act (EFTA)** is to provide for individual consumer rights when participating in electronic fund transfer systems.[28] The term **electronic fund transfer** means any transfer of funds (other than a transaction originated by check, draft, or similar paper instrument) that is initiated through an electronic terminal, telephone, computer, or magnetic tape so as to authorize a financial institution to debit or credit an account. The service available from an automated teller machine is a common form of EFT.

§ 36:16   KINDS OF ELECTRONIC FUND TRANSFER SYSTEMS

There are currently four common kinds of EFT systems in use. In some of these systems, the consumer has a card giving him or her access to the machine. The consumer usually has a private code which prevents others from using the card if they obtain possession of it.

---

[25] Vending Chattanooga v. Am. Nat. Bank and Trust (Tenn) 730 SW2d 624(1987).

[26] UCC § 4-406(4).
[27] UCC § 4-406(2)(b)
[28] 15 USC §§ 1693 et seq.

(a) AUTOMATED TELLER MACHINE. The automated teller machine (ATM) performs many of the tasks of human bank tellers. Once an individual activates the ATM, it allows the user to deposit and withdraw funds from his or her account, to transfer funds between accounts, to make payments on loan accounts, and to obtain cash advances from bank credit cards.

(b) PAY-BY-PHONE SYSTEM. This system facilitates the paying of telephone and utility bills without writing checks. The consumer calls the bank and directs the transfer of funds to a designated third party.

(c) DIRECT DEPOSIT AND WITHDRAWAL. An employee may authorize an employer to deposit the former's wages directly to the employee's account. A consumer who has just purchased an automobile on credit may elect to have monthly payments withdrawn from the consumer's bank account and paid directly to the seller.

(d) POINT-OF-SALE-TERMINAL. This device allows the business with a terminal to transfer funds from the consumer's account to the store account.

§ 36:17   RESPONSIBILITY AND LIABILITY OF FINANCIAL INSTITUTION

The consumer must be furnished with the prescribed terms and conditions of all EFT services in advance, and must be given periodic statements covering account activity. Any automatic EFT from an individual's account must be authorized in writing in advance.

The financial institution is liable to a consumer for all damages proximately caused by its failure to make an EFT in accordance with the terms and conditions of an account, unless the consumer's account has insufficient funds, the funds are subject to legal process, the transfer would exceed an established credit limit, or insufficient cash is available in an ATM.

§ 36:18   CONSUMER LIABILITY

A consumer who notifies the issuer of the EFT card within two days after learning of a loss or theft of the card is limited to a maximum liability of $50 for unauthorized use of the card. Failure to notify within this time will increase the consumer's liability for losses to a maximum of $500.

The consumer has a responsibility to examine periodic statements provided by the financial institution. If it is established that a loss would not have occurred but for the failure of the consumer to report within sixty days of the transmittal of the statement any unauthorized transfer, then the loss is borne by the consumer.

SUMMARY

A check is a particular kind of draft; it is drawn on a bank and payable on demand. A delivery of a check is not an assignment of money on deposit with the bank on which it is drawn. Therefore, it does not automatically transfer the rights of the depositor against the bank to the holder of the check, and there is no duty on the part of the drawee bank to the holder to pay the holder the amount of the check.

Certification of a check by the bank is the acceptance of the draft — the bank becomes the primary party. Certification may be at the request of the drawee or the holder. Upon certification by the holder, all prior indorsers and the drawer are released from liability. Notice of nonpayment of a check must be given to the drawer of a check. If no notice is given, the drawer will be discharged from liability to the same extent as the drawer of an ordinary draft. The drawee bank owes the depositor certain duties, such as not disclosing information relating to the depositor's account and paying on demand all checks issued by the depositor.

A depositor may stop payment on a check. However, the depositor may become liable to a holder in due course unless such stopping of payment was for a reason that may be raised against a holder in due course. The stop payment order may be oral (binding for 14 calendar days) or written (effective for six months).

Liability of a secondary party cannot be enforced unless that party was given proper notice of the dishonor.

The depositary bank is the agent of the depositor for the purpose of collecting the deposited item. The bank may become liable for paying a check contrary to a stop payment order or when there has been a forgery or alteration. The bank will not be liable, however, if the drawer's negligence has substantially contributed to the forgery. A bank that pays on a forged indorsement must recredit the drawer's account. A depositor is subject to certain time limitations in order to enforce liability upon the bank.

An electronic fund transfer is a transfer of funds (other than a transaction originated by check, draft, or other commercial paper) that is initiated through an electronic terminal, telephone, computer, or magnetic tape so as to authorize a financial institution to debit or credit an account. The Electronic Fund Transfers Act requires that a financial institution furnish consumers with specific information containing all the terms and conditions of all EFT services. Under certain conditions, the financial institution will bear the loss for unauthorized transfers. Under other circumstances, the loss will be borne by the consumer.

QUESTIONS AND CASE PROBLEMS

1. What social forces are involved in the common statutory provision that it will be presumed that a check was issued with intent to defraud if the drawer does not pay the amount of the check within ten days after its dishonor?

2. When a bank certifies a check, what does it undertake to do with respect to the holder of the check?

3. Shirley drew a check on her account in the First Central Bank. She later telephoned the bank to stop payment on the check. The bank agreed to do so. Sixteen days thereafter the check was presented to the bank for payment and was paid by the bank. Shirley sued the bank for violating the stop payment order. The bank claimed it was not liable. Is Shirley entitled to recover?

4. Tom had a checking account with the Farmers National Bank. A check was written by an unknown person who forged the signature of Tom as a drawer of the check and then presented the check to the Farmers National Bank for payment. The bank paid the check and debited Tom's account for the amount of the check. When Tom received the monthly statement from the bank, he demanded that the bank restore the amount of this debit. Was he correct?

5. A check on the Central Exchange Bank was drawn by Seward payable to the order of Kolp. The check was indorsed by Carlson by writing on the back "pay to Maria Hehn (signed) Kevin Carlson." Hehn cashed the check at the Central Bank. Kolp then sued Central. Is it liable?

6. Gloria maintains a checking account at the First Bank. On the third day of January, the bank sent to Gloria a statement of her account for December, accompanied by the checks that the bank had paid. One of the checks had her forged signature, which Gloria discovered on the 25th of the month when she prepared a bank reconciliation. Upon this discovery, Gloria immediately notified the bank. On January 21 the bank paid another check forged by the same party who had forged the December item. Who must bear the loss on the forged January check?

7. Dean bought a car from Cannon. In payment, Dean gave him a check drawn on the South Dorchester Bank of the Eastern Shore Trust Company. The payee, Cannon, cashed the check at the Cambridge Bank of the Eastern Shore Trust Company. The drawee bank refused payment when the check was presented on the ground that Dean had stopped payment because of certain misrepresenta-

tions made by Cannon. Will the Eastern Shore Trust Company succeed in an action against Dean for payment? [Dean v Eastern Shore Trust Co. 159 Md 213, 150 A 797]

8. A depositor drew a check and delivered it to the payee. Fourteen months later the check was presented to the drawee bank for payment. The bank did not have any knowledge that anything was wrong and paid the check. The depositor then sued the person receiving the money and the bank. The depositor claimed that the bank could not pay a stale check without asking the depositor whether payment should be made. Was the depositor correct? [Advanced Alloys, Inc. v Sergeant Steel Corp. 340 NYS2d 266]

9. Siniscalchi drew a check on his account in the Valley Bank of New York. About a week later, the holder cashed the check at the bank on a Saturday morning. The following Monday morning, Siniscalchi gave the bank a stop payment order on the check. The Saturday morning transactions had not yet been recorded and neither the bank nor Siniscalchi knew that the check had been cashed. When that fact was learned, the bank debited Siniscalchi's account for the amount of the check. He claimed the bank was liable because the stop payment order had been violated. Was the bank liable? [Siniscalchi v Valley Bank of New York, 359 NYS2d 173]

10. Bogash drew a check on the National Safety Bank and Trust Co. payable to the order of the Fiss Corp. At the request of the Fiss Corp., the bank certified the check. The bank later refused to make payment on the check because there was a dispute between Bogash and the corporation as to the amount due to the corporation. The corporation sued the bank on the check. Decide. [Fiss Corp. v National Safety Bank and Trust Co. 191 Misc 397, 77 NYS2d 293]

11. Gracious Homes maintained a checking account with the Crandall Bank. Dawson, owner of Gracious Homes, and his daughter Linda were the only persons authorized to sign checks on behalf of the store. Lawrence, who was the bookkeeper for the store, had forged checks drawn on the Gracious Homes account for almost two years. Lawrence had escaped detection of the forgeries because he had done the bank reconciliation each month. An examination by Linda of the books and records disclosed the forgeries. Gracious Homes brought an action against the Crandall Bank to recover the amount paid out on the forged checks. Will Gracious Homes be successful?

12. Steinbaum executed and delivered a check to the order of the White Way Motors, the name under which DiFranco was doing business. Before the check was paid, Steinbaum stopped payment on the check. DiFranco sued Steinbaum on the check. Decide. [DiFranco v Steinbaum (Mo App) 177 SW2d 697]

13. Sandra died on April 5. Three days prior to her death, Sandra had issued a check to Galt in payment of a debt. The bank on which the check was drawn made payment to Galt on April 13. The bank had no knowledge of the death of Sandra. Was payment of the check proper?

14. Shortly before the close of banking hours on Friday, a creditor receives from his debtor two checks, one of which has been certified before its delivery to the creditor. Certification of the other check is secured by the creditor, but too late for the deposit of either check in the creditor's bank until Monday. On Monday, the bank on which both checks were drawn does not open for business; it has been taken over by the State Banking Department. What is the position of the creditor with respect to each check. Give reasons.

15. Stanley Salton delivered a $50 check to Doris Dean. Dean wrongfully raised the amount to $250 using spaces that Salton negligently had left blank. Dean then indorsed and delivered the check to Watkins who took it for value, in good faith, and without notice of the alteration. In due course the check was presented for payment to Salton's bank which paid it in good faith and in accordance with reasonable commercial standards. Salton protested when the bank charged his account for $250. What is the argument of the bank?

PART 6

SECURED TRANSACTIONS, CREDITORS' RIGHTS, AND INSURANCE

37

SECURED TRANSACTIONS UNDER ARTICLE 9

A person selling goods on credit or lending money has a right, grounded in contract, to receive from the debtor the amount due under the terms of the agreement. If the debtor defaults, the creditor has the right to sue for damages. However, the creditor may want more protection than that afforded by this right to sue on the debt.

Prior to the adoption of the UCC there were a number of devices designed to give the lender/seller an interest in specific

property of the borrower/buyer. This interest could be used to satisfy any claims of the creditor resulting from the debtor's breach. These devices included: (1) conditional sales, wherein the seller retained title until the condition of payment in full had been satisfied; (2) bailment leases, by which the buyer rented the property and could only acquire title after the payment of sufficient rentals to equal the purchase price; (3) chattel mortgages, by which the buyer, upon taking title from the seller, gave the seller a mortgage on the property for the amount of the purchase price; and (4) trust receipts, by which the borrower/buyer agreed to hold the goods in trust for the lender.

A.   General Principles

Article 9 of the UCC consolidates this fragmented field of security devices into one device called a **secured transaction.**[1] A creditor who complies with the requirements of Article 9 may create a security interest that protects the creditor against the debtor's default by allowing the creditor to recover the goods in the debtor's possession. Any transaction intended to create such an interest (regardless of its form) is subject to the requirements of Article 9.

§ 37:1   Creation of a Security Interest

A **security interest** is an interest in personal property or fixtures that secures payment or performance of an obligation.[2] The property in which the interest is held is called the **collateral**. The party holding the interest is termed the **secured party.**[3] The interest may be possessory, wherein the collateral is in the possession of the secured party; or it may be nonpossessory, wherein the debtor is in possession of the collateral.

A security interest is said to **attach** at the time it becomes enforceable. There are three prerequisites to the attachment of a security interest: (a) there must be a security agreement; (b) value must be given; and (c) the debtor must have rights in the collateral.[4]

(a) Security Agreement. The agreement of the creditor and the debtor that the creditor shall have a security interest in the goods must be evidenced by a written **security agreement** unless the creditor retains a possessory security interest by taking possession of the collateral. The agreement must be signed by the debtor and reasonably describe the collateral.

(b) Value. To be effective for the attaching of a security interest, value is given when the secured party lends money to the debtor or agrees to lend money to the debtor. In most cases value is any consideration that supports a simple contract.

(c) Debtor has Rights in the Collateral. The debtor must have rights in the collateral. That is, the debtor must either own or have the right to possession of the collateral.

(d) Future Transactions. The security agreement may contemplate future action by extending to future advances if money is lent or to **after-acquired goods**, that is, goods to be acquired and delivered to the buyer at a future date. In general, the security interest does not attach to future goods until the buyer has rights in such goods.[5]

In order to protect consumers, a limit is placed upon the extent to which after-acquired property may be bound by a security interest. In order to be collateral for a consumer obligation, the consumer must acquire the later property within ten days after the creditor gave value to the consumer. That is, the creditor cannot bind all property acquired at any time in the future but only that which is acquired within ten days after the creditor sells the goods or lends the money to the consumer.

(e) Perfection. When a security interest in property is superior to other interests and claims to the property, it is said to be **perfected**. Perfection may generally be obtained by filing a financing statement in the proper governmental office. If the collateral is tangible personal property, the credi-

---

[1]   This chapter is based on the UCC, including the 1972 amendments, which is set forth in the Appendix. The changes made by the 1972 amendments are confined mainly to Article 9 on secured transactions.

[2]   UCC § 1-201(37).

[3]   UCC § 9-105(1).

[4]   UCC § 9-203(1),(2). Louis & Diederich v Cambridge European Imp., __ Cal App 3d __, 234 Cal Rptr 889 (1987).

[5]   UCC § 9-204.

tor has the alternative of perfecting the security interest by taking possession of the collateral. If the collateral is consumer goods neither filing nor taking possession is required to perfect a purchase money security interest in the goods, because such an interest is perfected as soon as it attaches. A creditor who has a security agreement and either sells goods to a consumer on credit or lends money to enable the debtor to purchase goods, has a **purchase money security interest**.[6] Perfection of a purchase money security interest is more readily lost than perfection based upon filing or possession.

§ 37:2   CLASSIFICATION OF COLLATERAL

The Code divides tangible personal property or goods into four different classes: consumer goods, equipment, inventory, and farm products.[7] These goods are classified by the debtor's intended use, not their physical characteristics. For example, a television set in the hands of a manufacturer or retailer would be inventory. However, in the buyer/borrower's hands, it is a consumer good.

(a) CONSUMER GOODS. Goods are **consumer goods** if they are used or bought primarily for personal, family, or household use (for example, a television set).

(b) EQUIPMENT. Goods are classified as **equipment** if they are used or bought primarily for use in a business (for example, a musical instrument used by a night club entertainer).

(c) INVENTORY. Goods are classified as **inventory** if they are held by the debtor primarily for sale or lease to others (for example, a refrigerator bought by a dealer) or if they are raw materials, work in process, or materials consumed in a business.

(d) FARM PRODUCTS. Goods are **farm products** if they are crops or livestock or supplies used or produced in farming operations.

B.   SECURED CREDIT SALES OF CONSUMER GOODS

Consumer credit sales are treated differently than secured credit sales of inventory. Perfection by filing in a public office is not required for consumer goods. For most consumer transactions, the amount involved would not warrant the filing expense.

§ 37:3   RIGHTS OF THE SELLER OF CONSUMER GOODS INDEPENDENT OF DEFAULT

The seller stands in a dual position of being both a seller, having rights under Article 2 of the UCC governing sales, and a secured creditor, having rights under Article 9 of the UCC regulating secured transactions.[8]

The secured credit seller of consumer goods has rights that are effective not only against the buyer, but also against purchasers of the property from the buyer as soon as the security agreement is executed with respect to goods in which the buyer has acquired an interest. From that moment on, the seller's interest is generally effective against third persons[9] and is described as a **perfected security interest.**

(a) FILING NOT REQUIRED. In an ordinary, intrastate sale of consumer goods under a secured transaction, no filing in any state or government office is required in order to perfect the secured seller's interest. The security agreement will protect the seller against creditors of the buyer and most third parties who thereafter buy the property from the buyer.[10]

(b) INTERSTATE SECURITY INTERESTS. The UCC regulates not only transactions within the state, but also the effect to be given

---

[6]   DeKalb Bank v Klotz, ___ Ill App 3d ___, ___ Ill Dec ___, 502 NE2d 1256 (1986).
[7]   UCC § 9-109.

[8]   UCC § 9-113.
[9]   UCC § 9-201.
[10]   UCC § 9-302(1)(d).

security interests in property brought into the state from another state. If the interest of the secured party was perfected in the other state, that interest will be regarded as perfected by the state into which the property is brought. Within the second state, however, it is necessary to file within four months in order to keep the security interest continuously perfected.

If title to the property, such as an automobile, is represented by a title certificate, the law of the state that issued the certificate determines whether an interest is perfected. Accordingly, if the law of the certificate-issuing state requires that a security interest be noted on the title certificate in order to be perfected, that requirement is the exclusive means of perfecting the interest of the secured creditor.[11]

(c) REPAIR AND STORAGE LIEN. In most states, persons making repairs to or storing property have a right to assert a lien against the property for the amount of their charges. A question of priority arises when there is an outstanding security interest in the goods that the customer brings for repair or storage. In such a case, the lien for repairs or storage charges has priority over the outstanding security interest.[12]

In the *National Bank* case a car dealer who had repaired an automobile claimed priority to the car over a bank that had financed the debtor's purchase.

---

[11] UCC § 9-103(2).
[12] UCC § 9-310.

NATIONAL BANK V BERGERON CADILLAC, INC.
66 Ill 2d 140, 361 NE2d 1116 (1977)

In order to finance the purchase of a new automobile, Gladys Schmidt obtained a loan from the National Bank and gave the bank a security interest in the new automobile to protect its loan. The bank perfected the security interest in accordance with the UCC. Gladys later took the automobile to Bergeron Cadillac for repairs. Thereafter, she stopped paying installments to the bank and the bank sought to repossess the automobile from Bergeron Cadillac. The latter refused to surrender the automobile until paid for the repairs. The bank claimed that it was entitled to the automobile because it had perfected its security interest. The bank brought an action of replevin against Bergeron to recover the automobile. From a decision in favor of Bergeron, National Bank appealed.

WARD, C. J. . . . The trial court entered judgment for the defendant, holding that its common law possessory lien based on repairs it had made on the auto had priority over the plaintiff's prior security interest under section 9-310 of the Uniform Commercial Code. . . .

In February of 1973 the plaintiff loaned Gladys Schmidt $4,120 to enable her to purchase the automobile, taking a security interest in the automobile to secure the loan. This security interest was perfected by filing in the office of the Secretary of State. . . . In August of 1973 Schmidt brought the auto to the defendant's shop for repairs. The cost of the materials and service was approximately $2,000, and, when Schmidt failed to pay, the defendant, through an inquiry to the Secretary of State, learned of the plaintiff's security interest. The defendant exercised its right of lien for the unpaid charges and retained possession of the auto. In September, Schmidt defaulted on her loan payments, and in October the plaintiff ascertained that the Cadillac was in the defendant's possession. The plaintiff's demand on the defendant for the Cadillac under its security interest was refused, and the plaintiff filed the action in replevin.

The plaintiff contends that the right to a common law possessory lien has been superseded in Illinois by two statutes which provide for repairmen's liens. Ill Rev Stat 1973, ch. 82, pars. 40 through 47 and 47a through 47f.

Section 9-310 of the Uniform Commercial Code . . . provides:

> When a person in the ordinary course of his business furnishes services or materials with respect to goods subject to a security interest, a lien upon goods in the possession of such person given by statute or rule of law for such materials or services takes priority over a perfected security interest unless the lien is statutory and the statute expressly provided otherwise. . . .

The plain language of section 9-310 gives the lien of persons furnishing services or materials upon goods in their possession priority over a perfected security interest unless the lien is created by statute and the statute expressly provides otherwise.

The comment of Anderson (Anderson, Uniform Commercial Code) is:

> Code section 9-310 declares the priority of the lien of persons furnishing services or materials with respect to goods in their possession. Such a lien is, basically, the artisan's lien of the common law. Whether such a lien is based upon decision or statute law, Code section 9-310 gives it priority, with one exception, over a preexisting security interest in the goods. . . .
>
> The single exception relates to a lien created by statute; such a lien does not have such priority if the statute expressly provides otherwise. Accordingly, the lien has priority when it is based upon the common law or decision, or when it is based upon a statute which is silent as to priorities or which gives the lien priority. The lien is subordinated to the security interest only when the lien statute expressly so declares. 4 Anderson, Uniform Commercial Code sec. 9-310, at 341-42(2 ed. 1971). . . .

The artisan's possessory lien of the common law is recognized in Illinois. . . .

We cannot accept the plaintiff's contention that the General Assembly's enactment of the two statutes creating liens in favor of repairmen with respect to personal property . . . evidenced an intent to supersede the artisan's common law lien. Both of the statutes expressly provide that the liens created shall be in addition to, and shall not exclude, any lien existing by virtue of the common law. . . .

As the defendant had a common law possessory lien for services and materials in connection with the repairs it made, its lien takes priority over the plaintiff's earlier perfected security interest under the provisions of section 9-310 of the Uniform Commercial Code. . . .

[Judgment affirmed]

QUESTIONS

1. Did the repairer have a common-law lien?
2. Would the decision have been changed if the lien of the repairer had been created by statute?

§ 37:4   RIGHTS OF THE BUYER OF CONSUMER GOODS INDEPENDENT OF DEFAULT

In a secured transaction the buyer, like the seller, has a double status under the UCC. By virtue of Article 2, the buyer has certain rights as a buyer, and by virtue of Article 9, the buyer has certain rights as a debtor in a secured transaction.

(a) RIGHTS AS A BUYER. The buyer has certain rights of ownership in the collateral. It is not material whether technically the buyer is the owner of the title. The buyer may voluntarily transfer whatever interest is owned by the buyer, and the creditors of the buyer may reach that interest by the process of law as fully as though there were no security agreement. Such third persons generally cannot acquire any greater rights than the buyer, and therefore they hold the property subject to the security interest of the seller.

(b) RIGHTS AS A DEBTOR. The secured transaction buyer is a debtor to the extent that there is a balance due on the purchase price. In order for the buyer to know just how much is owed and to check what the seller claims is due, the buyer has the right to compel the seller to state what balance is owed and also to specify in which collateral the seller claims a security interest. This is done by the buyer's sending the seller a statement of the amount believed to be due, or a statement of the collateral believed to be subject to the security agreement, with the request that the seller approve or correct the statement. The seller must so indicate; and if there has been an assignment of the contract and the security interest to a third person, the seller must furnish the buyer with the name and address of such successor in interest.

§ 37:5   PROTECTION OF SUBPURCHASER

When the seller of consumer goods sells on credit, filing of a financing statement is not necessary to protect the seller's security interest in the goods against other creditors of the buyer. A security interest in the goods is perfected or arises by attachment alone, even though the seller gives the buyer possession of the goods. This rule relieves retail merchants who sell many articles on installment plans of the burdens of filing and of paying filing fees.

When no financing statement is filed, however, a resale by the consumer to another consumer will destroy the seller's security interest if the second purchaser does not have knowledge of the security interest of the original party and buys for personal, family, or household use.[13] For example, a consumer buys a refrigerator under an installment contract whereby the appliance store retains a security interest in the refrigerator. The appliance store does not file a financing statement, though its interest is perfected by attachment. Some time later, the consumer sells the refrigerator to a neighbor who is unaware of the prior security interest. The neighbor will take free of the security interest.

The *Balon* case illustrates the rights of subpurchasers of consumer goods who purchased the goods from a consumer/purchaser.

---

[13]   UCC § 9-307(2).

BALON V CADILLAC AUTOMOBILE CO.
113 NH 108, 303 A2d 194 (1973)

Balon and Gibert each purchased a Cadillac for personal use from Russell Saia, a private owner. They did not know that each car was subject to an unfiled security interest in favor of the original seller, the Cadillac Automobile Company of Boston. Balon and Gibert claimed that they owned their cars free of the security interest of Cadillac. Cadillac contended that Balon and Gibert did not believe that they were purchasing a clear title and were subject to its unfiled security interests. Cadillac repossessed the cars. Balon and Gibert sued Cadillac. From judgment in favor of Balon and Gibert, Cadillac appealed.

LAMPRON, J. . . . The issue to be decided is whether the trial court properly found and ruled that Balon and Gibert each had clear title to his automobile by virtue of § 9-307 of the [UCC]. . . .

On September 28, 1965, Charles Pernokas was a salesman for Cadillac Automobile in Boston, Massachusetts. He had previously worked for another employer as a car salesman with Russell Saia. On that day Saia came to Cadillac Automobile looking for a convertible for a customer. Pernokas showed him two cars and Saia said he would hear from him shortly. He telephoned soon thereafter saying that his customer, Peter J. Russell, would take one of the Cadillac convertibles and gave the required credit information and references. On the next day, Saia telephoned Pernokas again and told him another customer, Joseph P. DeLuca, would take the other convertible and gave credit information on him.

Pernokas testified that in each instance he delivered the car to Saia's place and that Saia and another person, supposedly Russell in one instance and DeLuca in the other, identified himself and signed the security agreements. The selling price, $5300 for each car, was paid by a $1000 cash down payment on each and the balance financed on a conditional sale agreement.

At about that time, an individual named Arthur Freije told Balon in Manchester that "somebody" had "a friend" who could get a good deal on Cadillacs. "Somebody" was Fred Sarno who had accompanied Saia on his visit to the Cadillac garage after which the two cars in question were bought. The "friend" was Russell Saia. Balon passed the information along to his stepfather, Gibert, and eventually both Balon and Gibert purchased a Cadillac convertible through Freije for $4300 each.

The October and November payments on these Cadillacs were not made to Cadillac Automobile. As a result of these defaults, Simons, its credit manager, made an investigation and concluded that Peter J. Russell and Joseph P. DeLuca, the apparent purchasers, did not exist and decided that "both of these were two straw deals." The trial court properly found on the evidence that the two Cadillac automobiles in question were purchased by Russell Saia and that he was the principal in their sale to Balon and Gibert.

[UCC §] 9-307 . . . reads as follows:

(1) A buyer in the ordinary course of business . . . takes free of a security interest created by his seller even though the security interest is perfected and even though the buyer knows of its existence.

(2) In the case of consumer goods . . . a buyer takes free of a security interest even though perfected if he buys without knowledge of the security interest, for value and for his own personal, family or household purposes . . . unless prior to the purchase the secured party has filed a financing statement covering such goods.

The secured interest of Cadillac Automobile was perfected when the agreement of the parties was executed. . . . However the security agreements covering these two automobiles were never filed. . . .

The buyer protected by § 9-307(1) is one who purchases in the ordinary course of business from a person in the business of selling goods of the kind involved. § 1-201(9). Hence § 9-307(1) applies primarily to purchases from the inventory of a dealer in the type of goods sold. 4 Anderson, Uniform Commercial Code 323:24 (2d ed. 1971); *see National Shawmut Bank v Jones*, 108 NH 386, 236 A2d 484 (1967). The buyer protected under § 9-307(2) is one who purchases goods for consumer use, that is, for personal, family or household purposes, from a consumer seller. In order to fall within the protection of this section the goods must be consumer goods in the hands of both the buyer and the seller. . . .

The categorization of these automobiles at the time of the execution of the security agreement with Cadillac Automobile is an important factor in determining whether they were inventory or consumer goods in the hands of Saia when he sold them. . . . This classification of the goods remains unchanged in the controversy between Balon, Gibert, and Cadillac Automobile when it seeks to enforce its security agreement. Simon, Cadillac's credit manager, testified that it is company policy to record security agreements except when the buyer is an individual consumer as determined by the contract. Their security agreement provides that if the car is purchased for business purposes the address of the buyer's place of business must appear as the address on the front of the contract. There was evidence that the address on the front of the Peter Russell contract was listed in the Boston directory as the residence of Mrs. Jean Saia. Simon also testified that as far as the seller was concerned these sales were made to two private consumers for their personal, family and household use. Accordingly, following its policy with respect to consumer purchasers, the security agreements were not filed.

We hold that the trial court properly found and ruled that Russell Saia was a dishonest consumer purchaser of these automobiles. We further hold that these cars remained consumer goods in his hands at the time of the sales to Balon and Gibert who are protected by [UCC §] 9-307(2) if they were good faith consumer buyers for value without knowledge of Cadillac's security interest.

The company maintains, however, that the only conclusion which can be reached on the evidence is that Balon and Gibert "could not have conceivably held honest convictions that these transactions were legitimate." In support it cites § 1-201(19) which provides: " 'Good faith' means honesty in fact in the conduct or transaction concerned." By its terms this is a subjective standard of good faith, that is, whether the particular purchaser believed he was in good faith, not whether anyone else would have held the same belief. The test is what the particular person did or thought in the given situation and whether or not he was honest in what he did. . . .

There was evidence that Gibert had known Freije, who made the approaches which culminated in these sales, in a social way for about fifteen years. His wife had known him all her life. Balon knew him also and had purchased a 1963 Cadillac from him without any untoward incidents. Balon and Gibert learned from inquiries made to dealers known to them that the asking price of $4300 was consistent with prices at which such cars could be bought. The explanation advanced that these convertibles sold in September, when the new models were due, could be found by them plausible reasons for the price quoted. Simon testified that when Balon and Gibert came to Boston after their cars were taken they seemed genuinely concerned [in] trying to figure out what happened. There was no evidence that they had actual knowledge of the status of the title to these cars. The fact that others might have acted differently, made more inquiries, or been more suspicious does not require a conclusion that they lacked good faith when they purchased these cars. . . . The evidence is clear that they paid value and bought for personal, family, or household purposes.

We hold that the trial court properly found and ruled that Balon and Gibert were good faith consumer buyers for value from a consumer seller without knowledge of Cadillac Automobile's security interest which had not been filed. . . . Consequently they were entitled to the protection of [UCC §] 9-307(2). . . .

[Judgment affirmed]

QUESTIONS

1. Classify the collateral in the hands of Russell Saia.
2. Why did Cadillac Automobile not file a financing statement?
3. Did Balon and Gibert acquire title clear of any prior security interest?

C. SECURED CREDIT SALES OF INVENTORY

In contrast with one who buys goods for personal use, the buyer may be a merchant or dealer who intends to resell the goods. The goods that such a merchant or dealer buys are classified as inventory. The financing of the purchase of inventory may involve a third person, rather than the seller, as creditor. For example, a third person, such as a bank or finance company, may lend the dealer the money with which to make the purchase and to pay the seller in full. In such a case the security interest in the goods may be given by the buyer to the third person and not to the seller. Accordingly, the terms *creditor* and *secured party* may refer to a seller who sells on credit or to a third person who finances the purchase of goods.

In general, the provisions regulating a secured transaction in inventory follow the same pattern as is applicable to the secured credit sale of consumer goods. Variations recognize the differences in the commercial settings of the two transactions.

Initially there must be possession of the goods or there must be a security agreement to give rise to the security interest. If perfection of the interest is desired, there must also be a filing of a financing statement or the creditor must hold possession of the collateral.

§ 37:6 USE OF PROPERTY AND EXTENT OF SECURITY INTEREST

A secured transaction relating to inventory will generally give the buyer full freedom to deal with the collateral goods as though the goods were not subject to a security interest. Thus, the parties may agree that the buyer/dealer may mingle the goods with existing inventory, resell the goods, take goods back and make exchanges, and so on, without being required to keep any records of just what became of the goods covered by the security agreement, or to replace the goods sold with other goods, or to account for the proceeds from the sale of the original goods.

(a) AFTER-ACQUIRED PROPERTY. The security agreement may expressly provide that the security interest of the creditor shall bind after-acquired property, that is, other goods thereafter acquired by the buyer. The combination of the buyer's freedom to use and dispose of the collateral and the subjecting of after-acquired goods to the interest of the secured creditor permits the latter to have a **floating lien** on a changing or shifting stock of goods of the buyer. Conversely stated, the UCC rejects the common-law concept that the security interest was lost if the collateral was not maintained and accounted for separately and that a floating lien upon the buyer's property was void as a fraud against the latter's creditors.

The security interest in inventory covered as after-acquired property has priority over claims of subsequent creditors and third persons, except buyers in the ordinary course of business and sellers to the debtor holding perfected purchase money security interests in the goods sold to the debtor.

(b) PROCEEDS OF COLLATERAL. The secured transaction covers proceeds from the collateral unless such interest is expressly excluded. **Proceeds** includes cash, checks, and accounts receivable arising on a sale of the collateral and also indemnification from an insurer for damage to the collateral.[14]

§ 37:7   FILING OF FINANCING STATEMENT

Filing is usually required to perfect the creditor's interest in inventory or the proceeds therefrom. An exception is made when a statute requires the security inter-

est to be noted on the title certificate issued for the property. A security interest in a motor vehicle that is inventory is perfected by filing under the Code; but a privately owned vehicle is perfected by a notation on the title registration certificate.

An unperfected security interest is valid as against anyone standing in the position of the debtor.

(a) FINANCING STATEMENT. The paper that is filed is a financing statement (See Figure 37-1) and is distinct from the security agreement that was executed by the parties to give rise to the secured transaction.[15] The **financing statement** must be signed by the debtor; it must give an address of the secured party from which information concerning the security interest may be obtained; it must give a mailing address of the debtor; and it must contain a statement indicating the kinds, or describing the items, of collateral.

The financing statement does not set forth the terms of the agreement between the parties. This is done in the security agreement. All that the financing statement does is give notice to the world that the secured creditor who has filed may have a security interest in the collateral described in the statement.

Can a financing statement signed by a debtor extend the security interest of the creditor to collateral not described in an underlying security agreement? This was the issue in the *Whitmore* case.

---

[14] UCC § 9-306(1), C. O. Funk & Son Inc. v Sullivan Equipment, Inc. 89 Ill 2d 27, 431 NE2d 370 (1982).

[15] UCC § 9-402. However, the security agreement may be filed as a financing statement if it contains the required information.

WHITMORE & ARNOLD INC. V LUCQUET
___ Va ___, 353 SE2d 764 (1987)

The Lucquets, the debtors, purchased fertilizer and other goods from Whitmore. The purchases were financed by two loans from Farmers & Merchants National Bank, aggregating $27,460 and evidenced by two promissory notes. Each note contained a security agreement. The Luc-

Uniform Commercial Code — FINANCING STATEMENT

This FINANCING STATEMENT is presented to a Filing Officer for filing pursuant to the Uniform Commercial Code.	No. of Additional Sheets Presented:	3. ☐ The Debtor is a transmitting utility.
1. Debtor(s) (Last Name First) and Address(es):	2. Secured Party(ies) Name(s) and Address(es)	4. For Filing Officer: Date, Time, No. Filing Office

5. This Financing Statement covers the following types (or items) of property:	6. Assignee(s) of Secured Party and Address(es)

☐ Products of the Collateral are also covered.

7. ☐ The described crops are a growing or to be grown on:*
☐ The described goods are or are to be affixed to:*
☐ The lumber to be cut or minerals or the like (including oil and gas) is on:*
*(Describe Real Estate Below)

8. Describe Real Estate Here: ☐ This statement is to be indexed in the Real Estate Records: 9. Name of a Record Owner

No. & Street	Town or City	County	Section	Block	Lot

10. This statement is filed without the debtor's signature to perfect a security interest in collateral (check appropriate box)
☐ under a security agreement signed by debtor authorizing secured party to file this statement, or
☐ which is proceeds of the original collateral described above in which a security interest was perfected, or
☐ acquired after a change of name, identity or corporate structure of the debtor, or ☐ as to which the filing has lapsed, or already subject to a security interest in another jurisdiction:
☐ when the collateral was brought into the state, or ☐ when the debtor's location was changed to this state.

By _____   By _____
       Signature(s) of Debtor(s)   Signature(s) of Secured Party(ies)

(1) Filing Officer Copy-Numerical

FIGURE 37-1
FINANCING STATEMENT

quets were the makers, and Whitmore was the indorser on the notes. One note gave the bank a security interest in a soybean crop; the other created a security interest in a corn crop. The security agreement contained the following: "the collateral subject to this agreement is more particularly described on the front of this note, but may also be described and supplemented by other security agreements or financing statements executed by the Makers and/or Endorsers of this note. Proceeds and after-acquired property are also covered by this Agreement." Whitmore filed a financing statement that was signed by the debtors. It covered specific farm equipment and a "1983 wheat crop." The financing statement named the Lucquets as "debtors" and Whitmore as both "secured party" and "assignee of secured party." The Lucquets defaulted on the notes and Whitmore, as indorser, paid the balance on the debt to the bank. The bank then assigned the notes and security agreements to Whitmore. Whitmore then brought this action for seizure of the farm equipment and wheat crop to satisfy the debt. The trial court ruled in favor of the Lucquets. The court found that the financing statement did not add collateral to the underlying security agreement because it failed to comply with the requirements of the Code. It omitted the names and address of the bank as the secured party and the name of the record owner of the real estate upon which the wheat crop was grown. Whitmore appealed.

STEPHENSON, J. . . . Generally, two documents are required to create a perfected security interest in a debtor's collateral. First, a *security agreement* must give a creditor an interest in the collateral. Code § 8.9-203(1)(a) requires that a security agreement be embodied in a writing that contains the debtor's signature and a description of the collateral. The requisites of Code § 8.9-203(1)(a) serve an evidentiary function by requiring a signed agreement and obviate any Statute of Frauds problems between the debtor and creditor by requiring a writing.

The second document required to create a perfected security interest is a *financing statement*, a writing filed for public record. It serves the purpose of giving notice to third parties that a security interest is claimed in the debtor's collateral. The requisites of a financing statement are set forth in Code § 8.9-402(1).*

The trial court rejected Whitmore's claim of a security interest in the collateral described in the financing statement, concluding that the financing statement did not comply with the requirements of Code § 8.9-402(1). The present case, however, involves only a debtor-creditor relationship and the *creation* of a security interest, not third-party claims or the *perfection* of a security interest. Thus, we conclude that the deficiencies in the financing statement noted by the trial court are immaterial to the question presented in this appeal.

The dispositive question is whether, as between the parties, the financing statement can supplement the underlying security agreements by adding other collateral. To answer this question, we need not look beyond the security agreements themselves. They provide that "[t]he collateral subject to this agreement . . . may also be . . . supplemented by . . . financing statements executed by the Makers . . . of this note."

Ordinarily, persons are free to contract as they wish with respect to their property rights, and a court will not annul their agreement unless it is contrary to law. We find nothing in the U.C.C. that prohibits parties from contracting to supplement a security agreement with a separate document adding other collateral.

Here, the parties executed security agreements providing that the collateral

---

* Code § 8.9-402, in pertinent part, provides:

(1) A financing statement is sufficient if it gives the names of the debtor and the secured party, is signed by the debtor, gives an address of the secured party from which information concerning the security interest may be obtained, gives a mailing address of the debtor and contains a statement indicating the types, or describing the items, of collateral. A financing statement may be filed before a security agreement is made or a security interest otherwise attaches. When the financing statement covers. . .crops growing or to be grown or goods which are or are to become fixtures, the statement must also contain a description of the real estate concerned and the name of the record owner. . . .A copy of the security agreement is sufficient as a financing statement if it contains the above information and is signed by the debtor.

described therein could be supplemented, i.e., added to, by financing statements signed by the debtors. The Lucquets signed the financing statement that added the subject collateral. We conclude, therefore, that the financing statement, coupled with the security agreements, furnishes a sufficient description of the collateral, *see* Code § 8.9-110, and meets the requirements of Code § 8.9-203(1)(a).

Thus, we hold that Whitmore had a security interest in the farm equipment and the wheat crop. Additionally, under the terms of the security agreement and Code § 8.9-203(3), Whitmore's security interest in the wheat crop extends to the proceeds from the crop's sale.

Accordingly, we will reverse the judgment and remand the case to the trial court. On remand, the trial court shall order the seizure of the farm equipment and direct the debtors to pay the proceeds of the sale of the 1983 wheat crop.

[Judgment reversed]

QUESTIONS

1. What two documents are required to create a perfected security interest in collateral in the possession of the debtor?
2. What was the relationship between the parties?
3. What was the reason for the court's decision?

(b) ERRORS IN THE FINANCING STATEMENT. Errors in the financing statement have no effect unless they are seriously misleading. If they are seriously misleading, the filing has no effect and does not perfect the security interest. For example, a description of the collateral in the financing statement as "all personal property" is not sufficient, and therefore, the filing of the statement does not perfect the security interest.

(c) PLACE OF FILING. The Code gives each state the option to provide for the filing of the financing statement under (1) **local filing,** as in the county of residence or place of business of the debtor, (2) **central filing,** as in a particular office in the state capitol, or (3) **dual filing,** a combination of both local and central filing.

(d) DEFECTIVE FILING. When the filing of the statement is defective either because the statement is so erroneous as to be seriously misleading or the filing is made in a wrong county or office, the filing fails to perfect the security interest. This means that other creditors who have liens on the collateral and the trustee in bankruptcy of the debtor have a right to the collateral superior to that of the original secured creditor.

§ 37:8 DURATION AND CONTINUATION OF FILING

The filing of the financing statement is effective for 5 years. At the expiration thereof, the perfection of the security interest terminates unless a continuation statement has been filed prior thereto. The **continuation statement** is merely a written declaration by the secured party that identifies the original filing statement by its file number and declares that it is still effective. The filing of the continuation statement continues perfection of the security for a period of 5 years after the last date upon which the original filing was effective. The filing of successive continuation statements will continue the perfection indefinitely.[16]

§ 37:9   TERMINATION OF THE BUYER'S OBLIGATION

A buyer who has paid the debt in full may make a written demand on the secured party, or the latter's assignee if the security interest has been assigned, to send the buyer a *termination statement* that a security interest is no longer claimed under the specified financing statement. The buyer then may present this statement to the filing officer who marks the record "terminated" and returns to the secured party the various papers that had been filed. Public notice is thereby given that the secured obligation is discharged and the financing transaction terminated.[17]

§ 37:10   PROTECTION OF CUSTOMERS OF THE BUYER

The customer of the dealer selling from inventory takes the goods free from the security interest of the dealer's supplier. That is, one who buys in the ordinary course of business items of property taken from the original buyer's inventory is free of the secured party's interest, even though the interest was perfected by filing and even though such ultimate customer knew of the secured party's interest.[18] For example, a finance company lends money to a retailer to finance the retailer's inventory of new refrigerators. It takes a security interest in the inventory and files a financing statement. The retailer then sells a refrigerator to a customer. The customer will take the refrigerator free of the finance company's security interest even though the dealer may be in default on its loan to the finance compa-

ny. If this were not so, buyers would be reluctant to buy goods. The sale to the consumer was obviously contemplated by the parties. The finance company really expected to be paid from the proceeds of the sale of the collateral.

D.   SECURED CREDIT SALES OF EQUIPMENT

In general, secured credit sales of equipment are treated the same as secured transactions with regard to inventory. However, the various provisions relating to resale by the buyer and the creditor's rights in proceeds have no practical application because the buyer does not resell the property but makes the purchase with the intention of keeping and using or operating it.

§ 37:11   USE OF COLLATERAL

For the purpose of secured transactions, a distinction is made as to the purpose for which the buyer procures the goods. If an ultimate consumer purchases primarily for personal, family, or household use, the goods are described as consumer goods. The consumer's purchase, however, is described as equipment if used or purchased for use primarily in a business, in farming, or in a profession.

§ 37:12   FILING

In the ordinary sale of consumer goods, filing of a financing statement is not required. In contrast, filing is required to perfect a security interest in equipment.

E.   RIGHTS OF PARTIES AFTER DEFAULT

When a debtor defaults on an obligation in a secured transaction, the secured party

---

[16] UCC § 9-403(3).

[17] UCC § 9-404.

[18] UCC § 9-307(1), Central Finance Loan v Bank of Illinois, __ Ill App 3d __, __ Ill Dec __, 500 NE2d 1066 (1986).

has certain rights with respect to the enforcement of the claim against the collateral.[19] These rights can be spelled out by the security agreement itself. The UCC also provides for procedures that the secured party can follow in the event the security agreement does not itself make provisions for them.

§ 37:13   SECURED SELLER'S REPOSSESSION AND RESALE OF COLLATERAL

Upon the buyer's default, the secured party is entitled to take the collateral or purchased property from the buyer. Self-help repossession is allowed if this can be done without causing a breach of the peace. If a breach of the peace might occur, the seller must use court action to regain the collateral.

If the debtor defaults, the secured creditor may sell the collateral at a private or public sale at any time and place and on any terms, provided such sale is done in a manner that is commercially reasonable.[20] The seller must give the debtor reasonable advance notice of a resale unless the goods are perishable, or unless they threaten to decline speedily in value, or unless they are of a kind customarily sold on a recognized market. The seller's resale destroys all interest of the debtor in the goods.

(a) COMPULSORY RESALE. If the buyer has paid 60 percent or more of the cash price of the consumer goods, the seller must resell them within 90 days after repossession, unless the buyer, after default, has signed a written statement surrendering the right to require the resale. If the seller does not resell within the time specified, the buyer may sue for conversion of

the collateral or proceed under the UCC provision applicable to failure to comply with the UCC.[21]

(b) NOTICE. Ordinarily notice must be given of the sale of collateral. The UCC does not specify the form of notice, and any form of notice that is reasonable is sufficient. A letter to the debtor can satisfy this requirement. If a public sale is made, the notice must give the time and place of the sale. If a private sale is made, it is sufficient to give reasonable notice of the time after which the private sale will be made. No notice is required when the collateral is perishable or is threatening to decline rapidly in value or is sold on a recognized market or exchange.

§ 37:14   DEBTOR'S RIGHT OF REDEMPTION

The debtor may exercise the right to redeem the collateral at any time prior to the time the secured party has disposed of the collateral or entered into a binding contract for resale. To redeem, the debtor must tender the entire obligation that is owed plus any legal costs and expenses incurred by the secured party.[22]

§ 37:15   DISPOSITION OF COLLATERAL BY SALE

Upon the debtor's default, the creditor may sell the collateral at public or private sale or may lease it to a third party as long as the creditor acts in a commercially reasonable manner. The proceeds of the sale are applied in the following order: (a) to pay the expenses of the secured party in connection with the default; (b) to pay the debt owed the secured party; and (c) to pay the indebtedness owed other secured parties in the collateral.

---

[19] The term *default* is not defined in Article 9. The parties to a secured transaction may specify in their agreement what constitutes a default. If they say nothing, default means the failure to perform the obligation underlying the transaction.
[20] UCC § 9-504, John Deere Leasing Co. v Fraken (Iowa) 395 NW2d 885 (1986).

[21] UCC § 9-507.
[22] UCC § 9-506.

SUMMARY

A security interest is an interest in personal property or fixtures that secures payment or performance of an obligation. The property that is subject to the interest is called the collateral, and the party holding the interest is called the secured party. Attachment is the creation of a security interest. To secure protection against third parties' claims to the collateral, the secured party must perfect the security interest.

Tangible collateral is divided into four classes: consumer goods, equipment, inventory, and farm products. These goods classifications are based upon the debtor's intended use and not upon the physical characteristics of the goods.

In the ordinary credit sale of consumer goods, no filing in any state or government office is required in order to perfect the secured party's interest. The secured party who does not file will still have priority over other creditors of the buyer, but will not have priority over a subpurchaser of the debtor who buys for personal, family, or household use without knowledge of the security interest. If the secured party wants to be protected against the subpurchaser, a financing statement must be filed.

In the case of goods classified as inventory, unless the secured party holds possession of the collateral, the secured party must file a financing statement. A financing statement must be signed by the debtor, must have the names and addresses of the parties, and must describe the collateral. Inventory financing covers proceeds from the sale of the collateral unless such interest is expressly excluded. Any customer of the dealer selling from inventory will take the goods free from the security interest of the dealer's supplier even though the customer knows that the goods are subject to a perfected security interest. The filing, however, will protect the secured creditor from certain other creditors.

A secured credit sale of equipment is treated the same as a secured credit sale of inventory except that the provisions relating to resale by the buyer have no practical application.

Upon default, a secured party may repossess the collateral from the buyer if this can be done without a breach of the peace. If a breach of the peace might occur, the secured party must use court action to regain the collateral. If the buyer has paid 60 percent or more of the cash price of the consumer goods, the seller must resell them within 90 days after repossession unless the buyer after default has waived this right in writing. Notice to the debtor of the sale of the collateral is usually required. A debtor may redeem the collateral prior to the time the secured party disposes of it or contracts to resell it.

QUESTIONS AND CASE PROBLEMS

1. What social forces are affected by the destruction of a security interest in consumer goods when a consumer-debtor resells the goods to another consumer who does not know of the security interest?
2. List three ways for a secured party to perfect a security interest.
3. Natasha purchases on credit a $1,000 freezer from the Silas Household Appliance Store. Af-

ter she had paid approximately $700, Natasha missed the next monthly installment payment. Silas repossessed the freezer and billed Natasha for the balance of the purchase price of $300. Natasha claimed that the freezer, now in the possession of Silas, was worth much more than the balance due and requested Silas to sell the freezer in order to wipe out the balance of the debt and to leave something for

Natasha. Silas claimed that as Natasha had broken her contract to pay the purchase price, she had no right to say what should be done with the freezer. Was Silas correct?

4. Thompson Home Appliance Store purchased refrigerator-freezers from the Henson Manufacturing Company and financed the purchase by obtaining a loan from the First National Bank. Thompson signed an agreement giving the bank a security interest in its inventory of refrigerator-freezers. Erhart purchased a refrigerator-freezer from Thompson on credit. The bank claimed that its security interest extended to the down payment that Erhart had made and to the unpaid balance which she owed Thompson. Was the bank correct?

5. The Start Television Co. sold a portable TV set to an accountant to be used in her home. Classify the TV as collateral with respect to
   (a) the Television Co., and
   (b) the accountant.

6. Compare or contrast attachment of a security interest with perfection of a security interest.

7. Rawlings purchased a typewriter from the Kroll Typewriter Co. for $600. At the time of the purchase, he made an initial payment of $75 and agreed to pay the balance in monthly installments. A security agreement was prepared which complied with the UCC. The agreement, however, was never filed. Rawlings, at a time when he still owed a balance on the typewriter and without the consent of Kroll, sold the typewriter to a neighbor. The neighbor, who had no knowledge of the security interest, used the typewriter in her home. Will Kroll be able to repossess the typewriter from the neighbor?

8. Compare or contrast a financing statement, a continuation statement, and a termination statement.

9. Benson purchased a new Ford Thunderbird automobile. She traded in her old car and used the Magnavox Employees Credit Union to finance the balance. The Credit Union took a security interest in the Ford. Subsequently, the Ford was involved in a number of accidents. It was taken to a dealer for repairs. Benson was unable to pay for the work done. The dealer claimed a lien on the car for services and materials furnished. The Magnavox Employees Credit Union also claimed priority. Which claim has priority? [Magnavox Employees Credit Union v Benson, 165 Ind App 155, 331 NE2d 46]

10. A owned a store. He borrowed from the B Bank and gave the bank a security interest in the "inventory" of the store. The security agreement described the collateral as inventory but did not contain any provision as to after-acquired property. A later became subject to bankruptcy proceedings, and his trustee in bankruptcy claimed the secured transaction did not bind after-acquired property because the security agreement did not expressly state that it did. Was the trustee correct? [Re Fibre Glass Boat Corp. (DC Fla) 324 F Supp 1054, aff'd (CA5 Fla) 448 F2d 781]

11. Hull-Dobbs sold an automobile to Mallicoat and then assigned the sales contract to the Volunteer Finance & Loan Corp. Later Volunteer repossessed the automobile and sold it. When Volunteer sued Mallicoat for the deficiency between the contract price and the proceeds on resale, Mallicoat raised the defense that he had not been properly notified of the resale. The loan manager of the finance company testified that Mallicoat had been sent a registered letter stating that the car would be sold. He did not state whether the letter merely declared in general terms that the car would be sold or specified a date for its resale. He admitted that the letter never was delivered to Mallicoat and was returned to the finance company "unclaimed." The loan manager also testified that the sale was advertised by posters, but on cross examination he admitted that he was not able to state when or where it was thus advertised. It was shown that Volunteer knew where Mallicoat and his father lived and where Mallicoat was employed. Mallicoat claimed that he had not been properly notified. Volunteer asserted that sufficient notice had been given. Was the notice of the resale sufficient? [Mallicoat v Volunteer Finance & Loan Corp. 57 Tenn App 106, 415 SW2d 347]

12. A borrowed money from B. He orally agreed that B should have a security interest in certain equipment that was standing in A's yard. There was nothing in writing, and no filing of any kind was made. Nine days later, B took possession of the equipment. What kind of interest did B have in the equipment? [Transport Equipment Co. v Guaranty State Bank (CA10 Kan) 518]

13. Cook sold to Martin a new tractor truck for

approximately $13,000 with a down payment of approximately $3,000 and the balance to be paid in 30 monthly installments. The sales agreement provided that upon default in any payment Cook could take "immediate possession of the property . . . without notice or demand. For this purpose vendor may enter upon any premises the property may be." Martin failed to pay the installments when due, and Cook notified him that the truck would be repossessed. Martin had the tractor truck, attached to a loaded trailer, locked on the premises of a company in Memphis. Martin intended to drive to the West Coast as soon as the trailer was loaded. When Cook located the tractor truck, no one was around. In order to disconnect the trailer from the truck, as Cook had no right to the trailer, Cook removed the wire screen over a ventilator hole by unscrewing it from the outside with his penknife. He next reached through the ventilator hole with a stick and unlocked the door of the tractor truck. He then disconnected the trailer and had the truck towed away. Martin sued Cook for unlawfully repossessing the truck by committing a breach of the peace. Decide. [Martin v Cook, 237 Miss 267, 114 So 2d 669]

14. Scott, an automobile dealer, sold Colbert a used truck on an installment sales contract. Colbert defaulted in his installment payments, and Scott brought an action requesting the court to issue an order for a sheriff to seize the truck and offer it for sale at a public auction. The truck was seized by the sheriff of the county and advertised to be sold at public auction. It was sold to Roberts for $2,500. Used trucks of a similar kind were selling on the open market for $3,000. Does Colbert have any rights against Scott? Explain.

15. O'Donnell sells a refrigerator to Garnet on credit and obtains a proper security agreement so that the refrigerator may serve as collateral for the payment of the amount due. Does O'Donnell have a purchase money security interest? Why or why not?

38

OTHER SECURITY DEVICES

Subject to certain exceptions, Article 9 of the UCC regulates all secured transactions dealing with personal property. The secured credit sales of consumer goods, inventory, and equipment were discussed in Chapter 37. This chapter considers other common forms of security devices.

A. SURETYSHIP AND GUARANTY

Parties may make a contract by which one party agrees to pay if another party does not pay or defaults in the performance of an obligation. The relationship by which one person becomes responsible for the debt or undertaking of another person is used most commonly to insure that a debt will be paid or that a contractor will perform the work called for by the contract. A distinction may be made between the two kinds of such agreements.

§ 38:1 DEFINITIONS

One kind of agreement to answer for the debt or default of another is called a contract or undertaking of **suretyship**, and the third person is called a **surety**. The other kind of agreement is called a contract or undertaking of **guaranty**, and the third person is called a **guarantor**. In both cases the person who owes the money or is under the original obligation to pay or perform is called the **principal**, the principal debtor, or debtor. The person to whom the debt or obligation is owed is known as the **creditor**.[1]

Suretyship and guaranty undertakings have the common feature of a promise to answer for the debt or default of another, but they have a basic difference. The surety is primarily liable for the debt or obligation

[1] Unless otherwise stated, *surety* as used in the text includes guarantor as well as surety, and *guaranty* is limited to a conditional guaranty. The word *principal* is also used by the law to identify the person who employs an agent. The *principal* in suretyship must be distinguished from the agent's *principal*.

of the principal; ordinarily the guarantor is only secondarily liable. This means that the moment the principal is in default, the creditor may demand performance or payment of the surety. The creditor generally cannot do so in the case of the guarantor and must first attempt to collect from the principal. An exception is an **absolute guaranty**, which creates the same obligation as a suretyship. A guaranty of payment creates an absolute guaranty.

The *General Motors Acceptance Corporation* case illustrates the difference between a surety and a guarantor.

GENERAL MOTORS ACCEPTANCE CORPORATION v DANIELS
—— Md ——, 492 A2d 1306 (1985)

In June, 1981, John Daniels agreed to purchase a used automobile from Lindsay Cadillac Company. Because John had a poor credit rating, his brother Seymoure agreed to cosign the installment sales contract. On June 23, 1981, Seymoure accompanied John to Lindsay Cadillac and signed the contract on the line designated *Buyer*. John signed the contract on the line designated *Co-Buyer*. Lindsay Cadillac then assigned the contract to General Motors Acceptance Corporation (GMAC), a company engaged in the business of financing automobiles. Installment payments were not made, and GMAC then sued Seymoure to collect the amount due. No suit was brought against John because he could not be served with process. Seymoure claimed that he was simply a guarantor not a surety and, therefore, he could not be sued until GMAC had brought suit against John. From a judgment in favor of Seymoure, GMAC appealed.

COLE, J. . . . GMAC marshals several alternative arguments in support of its position that the District Court was clearly erroneous in finding that Seymoure was a guarantor of the contract between John and itself. In particular, GMAC argues that Seymoure was a surety for his brother in this transaction. We agree.

Maryland law has consistently maintained a distinction between a contract of suretyship and a contract of guaranty. A review of the distinguishing characteristics of each of these contracts, together with a summary of the relevant principles governing the interpretation and construction of contracts, provides a useful, if not necessary, predicate to the resolution of the issue presented in this case.

A contract of suretyship is a tripartite agreement among a principal obligor, his obligee, and a surety. This contract is a direct and original undertaking under which the surety is primarily or jointly liable with the principal obligor, and therefore is responsible at once if the principal obligor fails to perform. A surety is usually bound with his principal by the same instrument, executed at the same time, and on the same consideration. As Judge Rodowsky explained in *Rosenbloom v. Feiler*, 290 Md. 598, 604, 431 A.2d 102, 106 (1981) (quoting L. Simpson, *Handbook on the Law of Suretyship* § 17, at 28 (1950)), "[i]n suretyship the [obligee] has or is about to extend credit to [the principal obligor], and the promise is made to protect the [obligee] in case the principal fails to perform."

Ultimate liability rests upon the principal obligor rather than the surety, but the obligee has remedy against both. The surety, however, becomes subrogated to the rights of the obligee when the surety pays the debt for the principal obligor. With respect to notice of default, the surety is ordinarily held to know every default of his principal because he is under a duty to make inquiry and ascertain whether the principal obligor is discharging the obligation resting on him. *See* L. Simpson, *supra*, § 41 ("[I]t is generally not necessary for the creditor to notify the surety of the fact that the principal debtor is in default on his promise. It is the duty of the surety to the creditor to see that the debt is paid."). Consequently, the surety is ordinarily liable without notice.

A contract of guaranty, similar to a contract of suretyship, is an accessory contract. Despite this similarity, a contract of guaranty has several distinguishing characteristics. First, this particular contract is collateral to and independent of the principal contract that is guaranteed and, as a result, the guarantor is not a party to the principal obligation. A guarantor is therefore secondarily liable to the creditor on his contract and his promise to answer for the debt, default, or miscarriage of another becomes absolute upon default of the principal debtor and the satisfaction of the conditions precedent to liability. Second, the original contract of the principal is not the guarantor's contract, and the guarantor is not bound to take notice of its nonperformance. Rather, the guarantor agrees that the principal is able to and will perform a contract that he has made or is about to make, and that if he defaults the guarantor will pay the resulting damages provided the guarantor is notified of the principal's default. As such, the guarantor insures the ability or solvency of the principal. Third, the contract of guaranty is often founded upon a separate consideration from that supporting the contract of the principal and, consequently, the consideration for the guarantor's promise moves wholly or in part to him. Fourth, and in sum, the guarantor promises to perform if the principal does not. By contrast, a surety promises to do the same thing that the principal undertakes. . . .

Our review of the evidence in this case convinces us that the District Court erred in finding that Seymoure was a guarantor rather than a surety with respect to the installment sales contract. In our judgment the indicia for determining whether a contract is one for suretyship or one for guaranty all point to the existence of a suretyship agreement.

Initially, we note that because the contractual language is clear and unambiguous on its face, we confine our review to the contract itself. Seymoure agreed to purchase the subject automobile by affixing his signature to the installment sales contract on the line designated "Buyer."

The contract clearly stated that all buyers agreed to be jointly and severally liable for the purchase of that vehicle. Therefore, under the objective law of contracts, a reasonable person knew or should have known that he was subjecting himself to primary liability for the purchase of the automobile. In short, although uncompensated sureties are favorites of the law, Seymoure's careless indifference does not insulate him from primary liability on that agreement.

Seymoure executed the same contract as his brother, thereby making himself a party to the original contract. There is no evidence that Seymoure executed an agreement collateral to and independent of this contract. This fact, standing alone, ordinarily negates the existence of a guaranty. As one court observed, "[i]t is certain that in most cases 'the joint execution of a contract by the principal and another operates to exclude the idea of a guaranty and that in all cases such fact is an index pointing to suretyship.' " *Phoenix Insurance Co. v. Lester Bros.*, 203 Va. 802, 807, 127 S.E.2d 432, 436 (1962).

Both Seymoure and John signed the contract at the same time. Although not dispositive, this fact tends to establish the existence of a contract of suretyship rather than a contract of guaranty. Furthermore, there are no competent facts indicating that Seymoure expressly agreed to pay for the automobile only upon the default of John. Seymoure also did not qualify his signature in any manner. Thus, by the terms of the contract Seymoure agreed to be primarily and jointly liable with John for the purchase of the automobile. GMAC was therefore not required to proceed against John in the first instance, and the failure of GMAC promptly to notify Seymoure of the default in payments and of the lapse in physical damage insurance coverage does not constitute a discharge.

Finally, on the facts of this case it is immaterial that the contract did not expressly designate Seymoure as a "surety." Whether a party has entered into a contract of suretyship or guaranty is to be determined by the substance of the agreement and not by its nomenclature.

[Judgment reversed]

QUESTIONS

1. What is the principal difference between a surety and a guarantor?
2. Was Seymoure a surety or a guarantor?
3. What was the basis for the court's decision?

§ 38:2 INDEMNITY CONTRACT DISTINGUISHED

Both suretyship and guaranty differ from an **indemnity contract,** which is an undertaking by one person, for a consideration, to pay another person a sum of money in the event that the other person sustains a specified loss. A fire insurance policy is an example of an indemnity contract.

§ 38:3 CREATION OF THE RELATION

The suretyship and guaranty relationships are based upon contract. The principles relating to capacity, formation, validity, and interpretation of contracts are applicable. Generally, the ordinary rules of offer and acceptance apply. Notice of acceptance must usually be given by the creditor to the guarantor.

In most states, the statute of frauds requires that contracts of guaranty be in writing in order to be enforceable, subject to the exception that no writing is required when the promise is made primarily for the promisor's benefit.

In the absence of a special statute, no writing is required for contracts of suretyship or indemnity, because they impose primary liability, and not a secondary liability to answer for the debt or default of another. Special statutes or sound business practice, however, commonly require the use of written contracts for both suretyship and indemnity.

When the contract of guaranty is made at the same time as the original transaction, the consideration for the original promise that is covered by the guaranty is also consideration for the performance of the guarantor. When the guaranty contract is entered into subsequent to the original transaction, there must be new consideration for the promise of the guarantor.

§ 38:4   RIGHTS OF SURETY

Sureties have a number of rights to protect them from sustaining loss, to obtain their discharge because of the conduct of others that would be harmful to them, or to recover money that they were required to pay because of the debtor's breach.

(a) EXONERATION. If the position of the surety becomes endangered, as when the debtor is about to leave the state, the surety may call upon the creditor to take action against the debtor. If at that time, the creditor could proceed against the debtor and fails to do so, the surety is released or exonerated from liability to the extent that the surety has been harmed by such failure.

(b) SUBROGATION. When a surety pays a debt that it is obligated to pay, it automatically acquires the claim and the rights of the creditor. This is known as **subrogation.** That is, once the creditor is paid in full, the surety stands in the same position as the creditor and may sue the debtor or enforce any security that was available to the creditor in order to recover the amount it has paid. The effect is the same as if the creditor, upon being paid, made an express assignment of all rights to the surety.

(c) INDEMNITY. A surety that has made payment of a claim for which it was liable as surety is entitled to indemnity from the principal; that is, it is entitled to demand from the principal reimbursement of the amount that it has paid.

(d) CONTRIBUTION. If there are two or more sureties, each is liable to the creditor for the full amount of the debt, until the creditor has been paid in full. As between themselves, however, each is only liable for a proportionate share of the debt. Accordingly, if the surety has paid more than its share of the debt, it is entitled to demand that its co-sureties contribute to it in order to share the burden, which in the absence of a contrary agreement, must be borne equally.

In the *Collins* case, a person paying a debt claimed that he was entitled to contribution.

COLLINS V THROCKMORTON

(Del App) 425 A2d 146 (1981)

Throckmorton and Collins were the sole stockholders as well as officers and directors in Central Ceilings Inc. Central borrowed money from the Wilmington Trust Co. A demand note was executed by the corporate officers. Throckmorton, and his wife, and Collins, and his wife, signed as unconditional guarantors of the note on behalf of Central. Central eventually went out of business. Throckmorton and his wife took out a bank loan to satisfy the demand note. The bank then assigned the original demand note with all its rights to Throckmorton. He claimed contribution from the Collinses for half of the amounts paid by him. From a judgment in favor of the plaintiff, the defendants appealed.

MCNEILLY, J. . . . The right of a surety or guarantor, upon being compelled to pay more than his just proportion of the principal's debt, to be reimbursed by his fellow guarantors for the excess is grounded on equitable principles. . . .

The Restatement of the Law of Security, provides in pertinent part:

(1) A surety who has discharged more than his proportionate share of the principal's duty is entitled to contribution from a co-surety.
   (a) who has consented to the surety's becoming bound, in the proportionate amount of the net outlay property expended. . . .

The undisputed facts show that the 1973 note was guaranteed by four persons. Consequently, each was potentially liable for one-quarter of Central's default on the note. Although the complaint alleged the plaintiff [Throckmorton] personally satisfied Central's default by paying the entirety of the principal and interest owed on the note in May, 1975, the defendants argue that the trial proofs show that the plaintiff's wife, the fourth co-guarantor, contributed equally with the plaintiff to this satisfaction. Thus, of the $9,668.73 paid to satisfy the 1973 note, the defendants claim the plaintiff contributed only half ($4,834.36). Of that amount the plaintiff was personally liable for half, which constituted one-quarter of Central's total default ($2,417.18). Thus argue the defendants, the maximum amount of contribution which the plaintiff could recover from the two defendants was $2,417.18, *i.e.*, the amount in excess of his share of Central's default which the plaintiff personally paid to satisfy the 1973 note. Therefore, the defendants argue that the Trial Court's decision, which was premised on the assumption that the plaintiff satisfied the entire default by Central (or at least three-quarters thereof), erroneously awarded judgment against each defendant in the amount of $2,417.18, double the excess amount which the plaintiff allegedly paid in satisfaction of the note and, thus, double the total amount of contribution which he was entitled to recover from the defendants collectively. . . .

Although there was no direct testimony concerning the respective amounts which the plaintiff and his wife contributed to satisfaction of the 1973 note, the bank's assignment of the note to the plaintiff, individually, gives rise to a reasonable inference that, as between the plaintiff and his wife, the plaintiff alone was entitled to seek contribution from the defendants. While it would obviously be desired to have a more detailed and explicit factual record on this point, the failure to so develop the record must be laid at the defendants' doorstep. Therefore, we will not disturb that portion of the Trial Court's judgment which requires each defendant to pay the plaintiff $2,417.18 for their contributive shares on the demand note as satisfied. . . .

[Judgment affirmed]

QUESTIONS

1. What was the basis for the court's decision?
2. When there is more than one surety, can the creditor hold one surety liable for the full amount of the debt?

§ 38:5 Defenses of the Surety

The surety's defenses include not only those that may be raised by a party to any contract but also the special defenses that are peculiar to the suretyship relation.

(a) Ordinary Contract Defenses. Since the relationship of suretyship is based upon a contract, the surety may raise any defense that a party to an ordinary contract may raise, such as lack of capacity of parties, absence of consideration, fraud, or mistake.

Fraud and concealment are common defenses. Since the risk of the principal's default is thrown upon the surety, it is unfair for the creditor to conceal from the surety facts that are material to the surety's risk.

Fraud on the part of the principal that is unknown to the creditor and in which the creditor has not taken part does not ordinarily release the surety.

By common law the creditor was not required to volunteer information to the surety and was not required to disclose that the principal was insolvent. There is a growing modern view that the creditor should be required to inform the surety of matters material to the risk when the creditor has reason to believe that the surety does not possess such information.

(b) Suretyship Defenses. In addition to the ordinary defenses that can be raised against any contract, the following defenses are peculiar to the suretyship relation:

(1) The original obligation was invalid.
(2) The principal was discharged by payment or some other means.
(3) The original contract was modified without the surety's consent.

In the *Gilbert* case, a guarantor argued that he was discharged on his son's note by a renewal that added $600 to the original obligation.

L. A. Gilbert v Cobb Exchange Bank

140 Ga App 514, 231 SE2d 508 (1976)

Gilbert signed a guaranty for the benefit of his son with the Cobb Exchange Bank. The guaranty included all extensions and renewals of the obligation. Subsequently, a renewal of the note added $600 to the original obligation. Upon the son's default, the Cobb Bank brought suit on the guaranty. From a judgment in favor of the Cobb Bank, Gilbert appealed.

Bell, C. J. . . .The defendant argued at trial and here that the addition of the $600 constituted a [modification of contract] and was accomplished without his consent which operated to discharge him. A [modification of contract] without the consent of the surety will discharge the surety. . . . Plaintiff contends that since the guaranty covered all renewals of the note, there was no discharge. While the guaranty did cover extensions or renewals, it could only apply to a renewal of the same obligation and not a new one. The guaranty very clearly guaranteed payment of "that certain note dated July 31, 1970 in the amount of $3,100.00. . . and all extensions or renewals thereof,. . ." and nothing else. The addition of the $600 to principal constituted a material change in the terms of the note. A [modification of contract] resulted which discharged defendant.

[Judgment reversed]

Questions

1. Was the Bank required to attempt to recover payment from the son before bringing suit against the plaintiff?
2. What effect does a material change in the terms of the original contract have on a contract of guaranty?
3. Was the guarantor discharged?

B.   Letters of Credit

A letter of credit is a form of agreement that the issuer of the letter will pay drafts drawn by the creditor. It is thus a form of advance arrangement for financing in that it is known in advance how much money may be obtained from the issuer of the letter. It is likewise a security device because the creditor knows that the drafts that the creditor draws will be accepted or paid by the issuer of the letter.

The use of letters of credit arose in international trade. While this continues to be the primary area of use, there is a growing use of letters in domestic sales and in transactions in which the letter of credit takes the place of a surety bond. Thus, a letter of credit has been used to assure that a borrower would repay a loan, that a tenant would pay the rent due under a lease, and that a contractor would properly perform a construction contract.[2]

[2] Barclays Bank D.C.O. v The Mercantile National Bank (CA5 Ga) 481 F2d 1224 (1973).

§ 38:6   Definition

A **letter of credit** is an engagement by its issuer that it will pay or accept drafts when the conditions specified in the letter are satisfied. The issuer is usually a bank.

Three contracts are involved in letter-of-credit transactions: (a) the contract between the issuer and the customer of the issuer; (b) the letter of credit itself; and (c) the underlying agreement, often a contract of sale, between the beneficiary and the customer of the issuer of the letter of credit. The letter of credit is completely independent from the other two contracts.

The issuer of the letter of credit is not a surety that is underwriting payment by its customer. The issuer of the letter is in effect the obligor on a third party beneficiary contract made for the benefit of the beneficiary of the letter.

The *Traveler's* case is an illustration of the use of a letter of credit and how it differs from a contract of suretyship. The case also illustrates the contractual commitment of a bank to make payment under specified conditions.

Travelers Indemnity Company v Flushing National Bank

90 Misc 2d 964, 396 NYS2d 754 (1977)

Berley was a party to a lawsuit. The court required him to file a $40,000 bond. The Travelers Indemnity Company issued the bond but required him to give it a certified check for $40,000 as security. Subsequently Berley obtained a letter of credit for $40,000 from the Flushing National Bank by which the bank agreed to honor drafts drawn upon it by the indemnity company when it incurred liability on the Berley bond. Berley gave this letter of credit to the indemnity company and took back his certified check. Thereafter, a claim was made on the Berley bond. The indemnity company then drew a draft upon the bank pursuant to the letter of credit. The bank refused to pay the draft on the ground that the indemnity company had not given any consideration for the letter of credit and that the bank was released from liability because the indemnity company's release of the certified check constituted an impairment of collateral which released the bank as a surety.

FINZ, J. . . . The defendant bank now claims that it should be released from the terms of the letter of credit. . . .

It claims, first of all, that there was no consideration for the issuance of the letter of credit. . . . In addition, it asserts that the credit is unenforceable by reason of the fact that the plaintiff, having in its hands a certified check in the sum of $40,000, released the check and thereby released the defendant since the defendant was, in effect, a guarantor or a surety to the plaintiff. Lastly, the defendant bank alleges that it was the plaintiff's fraud and concealment of facts which have rendered the letter of credit unenforceable.

Before proceeding in any direction it is necessary to make clear the nature of a letter of credit.

"Credit" or "letter of credit" means an engagement by a bank or other person made at the request of a customer and of a kind within the scope of this Article (Section 5-102) that the issuer will honor drafts or other demands for payment upon compliance with the conditions specified in the credit. . . .

A letter of credit is a contract. It is distinguished by the fact that it is inevitably linked to another understanding, usually also a contract, but is independent of that other understanding or contract. Appreciation of these two simple concepts: that a letter of credit is a contract, and that the letter of credit contract stands alone to be construed within its own four corners, is sufficient to provide understanding, it is indispensable to avoid confusion.

Confining ourselves, as noted above, to bank letters of credit, the first fundamental is that the bank engage itself as a principal in the letter of credit transaction but is neither engaged in nor . . . in any way concerned with the understanding, contract, or transaction which may have made the letter of credit necessary or convenient.

The purpose of the letter of credit is to provide a method of payment, through banking channels, which defines the terms and conditions upon which *and only upon which the payment will be made*, and which, within the strict limits of those terms and conditions, engages the full *primary* responsibility of the bank to make the payment, in addition to whatever obligation may lie upon the party for whose account the bank has issued or confirmed the letter of credit. This is the only role which the bank undertakes, and its only engagement, legal, commercial, or moral. This is, in short, the limitation of the letter of credit. If the limitation is recognized at all times by all interested parties, there is room neither for dispute nor for disappointment. Disappointment, disputes, and litigation arise only when one or another of the parties overlooks the functional limitation and takes the bank's letter of credit to be a guaranty of performance of some related but separate mercantile contract. (McKinney's Consolidated Laws Uniform Commercial Code, Practice Commentary p. 642.)

The letter of credit, probably because of its simple structure and its unqualified agreement to pay, notwithstanding any condition outside of its own terms, has become a principal instrument of international trade and, increasingly, of domestic transactions. It is in this framework that the defenses raised by the defendant should be considered.

The fact that plaintiff did not rely on the letter of credit when it issued its bond is not relevant to the question of consideration for the issuance of the letter of credit. If this were an issue at all, the question of consideration only arises as between the issuers of the credit and its customer. The beneficiary . . . would not in any event give consideration to the issuer.

The problem of consideration does not arise, however, in view of UCC § 5-105, which states: "No consideration is necessary to establish a credit or to enlarge or otherwise modify its terms. . . ."

A letter of credit, insofar as it is a contract, partakes of the rules of construction generally applicable to contracts. . . . Since there were no special rules adopted with regard to interpretation of the terms of a letter of credit, the ordinary rules of law apply (UCC § 1-103). "The same general principles which apply to other contracts in writing govern letters of credit. . . . Moreover, as between the beneficiary of a letter of credit and the issuer. . .if ambiguity exists, the words are taken as strongly against the issuer as a reasonable reading will justify. . . ."

In addition, the beneficiary, when it presents a demand for payment or a draft, warrants that there has been compliance with the necessary conditions of the letter of credit (UCC § 5-111[1]).

The claim that the release of the collateral without knowledge or consent of the defendant, discharged the defendant's obligation as a surety, depends upon the relationship of the defendant and plaintiff.

> The issuer of a letter of credit does not have the status of a surety or guarantor. A surety is generally not liable on his undertaking unless his principal is liable and in default on the underlying liability. The defenses of the principal are available to the surety and, if the underlying debt is canceled, the surety's obligation ceases. (*Association de Axucareros de Guatemala v United States Nat. Bank* (CA9 Or) 423 F2d 638).
>
> The letter of credit, unlike the classic surety undertaking, is a primary obligation between the issuer and the beneficiary. (See UCC § 5-114:1, pt 1,) [(Anderson Uniform Commercial Code, Second Edition, § 5-114:7.)]

Undoubtedly, a guarantor or a surety has the right to expect that the terms upon which the guarantee was made would remain unchanged, absent the knowledge and consent to such change by the guarantor. A release of collateral or a change in the terms would certainly operate to release the surety or guarantor. . . .

In this case, the letter was not issued on the strength of any collateral held by the plaintiff. It is admitted in the affidavit in opposition that defendant had no knowledge that the bond was issued or how it was collateralized. It offered no guarantee to the plaintiff. It dealt entirely with its own customer. It had dealt with him on previous occasions and it knew that he had obligations which "were very substantial" and "the Bank was becoming concerned about Berley's ability to pay the loans. . . . Berley owed the Bank nearly $300,000 when the letter of credit was issued." They had nearly five weeks, after being informed of all the circumstances, to inquire of the defendant as to the status of the bond. They questioned Berley as to the wording of the letter of credit and then, finally, accepted it, issuing the letter in the form suggested.

[Judgment for Travelers Indemnity Company]

QUESTIONS

1. Must the customer or the beneficiary give consideration for a letter of credit?
2. Why was the issuer of the letter not discharged when the certified check was given back to the customer?

§ 38:7   PARTIES

The parties to a letter of credit are (a) the issuer, (b) the customer who makes the arrangements with the issuer, and (c) the beneficiary who will be the drawer of the drafts which will be drawn under the letter of credit. There may also be (d) an advising bank[3] if the local issuer of the letter of credit requests its correspondent bank where the beneficiary is located to notify or advise the beneficiary that the letter has been issued.

As an illustration of the above definitions, an American merchant may buy goods from a Spanish merchant. There may be a prior course of dealings between the parties so that the seller is willing to accept the buyer's commercial paper as payment or to accept trade acceptances drawn on the buyer. If the foreign seller is not willing to do this, the American buyer, as customer, may go to a bank, the issuer, and obtain a letter of credit naming the Spanish seller as beneficiary. The American bank's correspondent or advising bank in Spain notifies the Spanish seller that this has been done. The Spanish seller will then draw drafts on the American buyer. By the letter of credit, the issuer is required to accept or pay these drafts.

§ 38:8   DURATION

A letter of credit continues for any time specified therein. Generally, a maximum money amount is stated in the letter so that the letter is exhausted or used up when drafts aggregating that maximum have been accepted or paid by the issuer. A letter of credit may be used in installments as the beneficiary chooses. A letter of credit cannot be revoked or modified by the issuer or the customer without the consent of the beneficiary unless that right is expressly reserved in the letter.

§ 38:9   FORM

A letter of credit must be in writing and signed by the issuer. If the credit is issued by a bank and requires a documentary draft or a documentary demand for payment[4] or if the credit is issued by a nonbank and requires that the draft or demand for payment be accompanied by a document of title, the instrument will be presumed to be a letter of credit (rather than a contract of guaranty). Otherwise, the instrument must conspicuously state that it is a letter of credit.[5] Consideration is not required to establish or modify a letter of credit.

§ 38:10   DUTY OF ISSUER

The issuer is obligated to honor drafts drawn under the letter of credit if the conditions specified in the letter have been satisfied. Generally, this means that the bank must assure itself that all specified papers have been submitted. The issuer has no

---

[3]   UCC § 5-103(1)(e).

[4]   A documentary draft or a documentary demand for payment is one the honor of which is conditioned upon the presentation of a document(s). A document could be a document of title, security, invoice, certificate, notice of default, or other similar paper. UCC § 5-103(1)(b).

[5]   Western Petroleum Co. v First Bank Aberdeen (SD) 367 NW2d 773 (1985).

THE NATIONAL BANK OF COMMERCE
St. Louis, MO

To: _____

DATE _____

BRANCH _____

LADIES and GENTLEMEN,

We open an IRREVOCABLE DOCUMENTARY CREDIT NO

in favor of _____

_____

For account of _____

_____

For an amount not exceeding _____

Valid until _____ Available by beneficiary's draft in duplicate on accountees at _____

_____ drawn to the order of negotiating Bank (without recourse) for 100% of net invoice value bearing date, credit number and accompanied by documents (marked X below) at least in duplicate, unless otherwise specified.

☐   Full set of CLEAN ON BOARD OCEAN BILLS OF LADING to order endorsed in blank, marked "freight paid/ payable at destination" and notify accreditors.

☐   INSURANCE POLICY OR UNDERWRITERS' CERTIFICATE in duplicate, blank endorsed in currency of credit for at least _____ % of invoice value against Marine, War and Strike risks.

☐   PACKING SPECIFICATION in quadruplicate.

☐   INVOICE in sextuplicate in English duly signed by beneficiaries certifying that the goods shipped are in accordance with order / indent/pro-forma Invoice No. _____ dated _____ showing Import Licence No. _____

Documents to cover shipment of:

From:	To:	Shipment not later than	Partshipment	Transhipment

All bank charges, including postage s for beneficiaries account.

Original draft and one set of documents to be sent to us by registered airmail and the duplicate draft with the remaining documents by subsequent registered air-mail.

REIMBURSEMENT INSTRUCTIONS.

Yours faithfully,

THE NATIONAL BANK OF COMMERCE,

_____   _____

ACCOUNTANT   MANAGER

No. 4355610

FIGURE 38-1
LETTER OF CREDIT
While there are few formal requirements for creating a letter of credit, banks often use a standard form (similar to the one pictured here) for convenience.

duty to verify that the papers are properly supported by facts or that the underlying transaction has been performed. It is thus immaterial that the goods sold by the seller in fact do not conform to the contract as long as the seller tenders the documents specified by the letter of credit.[6] If the issuer dishonors a draft without justification, it is liable to its customer for breach of contract.

[6]   Intraworld Industries, Inc. v Girard Trust Bank, 461 Pa 343, 336 A2d 316 (1975).

SUMMARY

Suretyship and guaranty undertakings have the common feature of a promise to answer for the debt or default of another. A surety is primarily liable for the debt or obligation of the principal debtor. The guarantor is ordinarily only secondarily liable unless the guarantor has made an absolute guaranty, in which case the guarantor becomes primarily liable. The surety and guaranty relationships are based upon contract. Sureties have a number of rights to protect them. They are exoneration, subrogation, indemnity, and contribution. In addition to those rights, sureties also have certain defenses. They include ordinary contract defenses as well as some defenses peculiar to the suretyship relationship, such as, that the original contract was invalid, that the principal obligation was discharged, or that the original contract was modified without the surety's consent.

A letter of credit is an agreement that the issuer of the letter will pay drafts drawn on the issuer by the beneficiary of the letter. The issuer of the letter of credit is usually a bank. There are three contracts involved in letter-of-credit transactions: (1) the contract between the issuer and the customer of the issuer, (2) the letter of credit itself, and (3) the underlying agreement between the beneficiary and the customer of the issuer of the letter of credit. The parties to a letter of credit are the issuer, the customer who makes the arrangement with the issuer, and the beneficiary who will be the drawer of the drafts to be drawn under the letter of credit. The letter of credit continues for any time specified therein. The letter of credit must be in writing and signed by the issuer. Consideration is not required to establish or modify a letter of credit. If the conditions in the letter of credit have been complied with, the issuer is then obligated to honor drafts drawn under the letter of credit.

QUESTIONS AND CASE PROBLEMS

1. What social forces are affected by the use of a letter of credit?
2. Kiernan Construction Company makes a contract with Jackson to build a house for her. The Century Surety Company executes a bond to protect Jackson from loss should Kiernan fail to construct the house or pay labor and material bills. Kiernan fails to build the house. Jackson sues the Century Surety Company. It raises the defense that Jackson must first sue Kiernan. Is it correct?
3. Identify the parties to a letter of credit.
4. What is the duration of a letter of credit?
5. The surety's right of subrogation arises as soon as the surety pays any part of the debt that the surety is obligated to pay. Appraise this statement.
6. Eberstadt owed Terence $500. He gave his note for that amount to Terence. At the same time, an agreement signed by Reid and given to Terence was as follows:
I agree to be surety for the payment of Eber-

stadt's note for $500.

On maturity of the note, Eberstadt paid $200 on account and gave a new note for $300 due in three months. Reid was not informed of this transaction. The new note was not paid at maturity. Terence sues Reid. Does Reid have any defense?

7. Vort owed Yarrow the sum of $500. When it appeared that Vort would probably not be able to pay when his obligation came due, Grant orally advised Yarrow, "Don't worry, if you cannot collect from Vort, I will pay you." Vort did not pay the $500 when it became due, and Yarrow sued Grant. State any defenses available to Grant.

8. A made a contract to purchase goods from B. In order to assure B that he would be paid, A obtained a letter of credit from the C bank. The letter was irrevocable and provided that C would honor drafts for the purchase price of goods shipped to A upon presentment to the bank of the drafts, the bill of lading showing shipment to A, and the invoice showing the nature and price of the goods shipped. Because of financial difficulties, A did not want to receive the goods under the contract and made an agreement with C that no drafts would be honored pursuant to the letter of credit. B shipped goods to A under the contract and presented drafts, and the proper bills of lading, and invoices to C. C refused to honor the drafts. B sued C. It claimed that it was not liable because the letter of credit that had obligated it to accept the drafts had been terminated by the agreement of its customer. Was this a valid defense?

9. The Kitsap County Credit Bureau held against Alderman a claim, the payment of which had been guaranteed by Richards. When Richards was sued on his guaranty, he proved that the claim against Alderman had been settled by compromise upon Alderman's paying $100 to the creditor. What result? [Kitsap County Credit Bureau v Richards, 52 Wash 381, 325 P2d 292]

10. Hugill agreed to deliver shingles to the W. I. Carpenter Lumber Co. He furnished a surety bond to secure the faithful performance of the contract on his part. After a breach of the contract by Hugill, the lumber company brought an action to recover its loss from the surety, the Fidelity & Deposit Co. of Maryland. The surety denied liability on the ground that there was concealment of (a) the price to be paid for the shingles, and (b) the fact that a material advance had been made to the contractor equal to the amount of the profit that he would make by performing the contract. Decide. [W. I. Carpenter Lumber Co. v Hugill, 149 Wash 45, 270 P 94]

11. Donaldson sold plumbing supplies. The St. Paul-Mercury Indemnity Co., as surety for him, executed and delivered a bond to the State of California for the payment of all sales taxes. Donaldson failed to pay, and the company paid the taxes that he owed. The company then sued him for the taxes. What result? [St. Paul-Mercury Indemnity Co. v Donaldson, 225 SC 476, 83 SE2d 159]

12. Stewart, Brown, and James were sureties on a $9,000 promissory note signed by Hunter, as maker, in favor of the Fanton Finance Company. When the note became due, Stewart paid the $9,000 to the Fanton Finance Company. Stewart then brought an action against Brown and James to recover $6,000. Brown and James contend that Stewart must first proceed against Hunter. Decide.

13. First National Bank hired Longdon as a secretary and obtained a surety bond from Belton covering the Bank against losses up to $100,000 resulting from Longdon's improper conduct in the performance of his duties. Both Longdon and the Bank signed the application for the bond. After one year of service Longdon was promoted to the position of teller in the Bank and the original bond remained in effect. Shortly after Longdon's promotion a surprise examination revealed that Longdon had taken advantage of his new position and had stolen $50,000 from the Bank. He was arrested and charged with embezzlement. Longdon had only $5,000 in assets at the time of his arrest.

    (a) If the Bank demands a payment of $50,000 from Belton, what defense, if any, might Belton raise to deny any obligation to the Bank?

    (b) If Belton fully reimburses the Bank for its loss, under what theory or theories, if any, may Belton attempt to recover from Longdon?

14. Glen is surety for Brady for $10,000. Brady defaults, and Glen is sued by the creditor. He settles for $8,000 and then sues Brady

for the full amount of $10,000. Can Glen recover the full $10,000? Explain?

15. Partridge lends $1,000 to Fazio, who agrees to repay the amount in three months. A month after the loan, Partridge requests security, and Shank without asking or receiving payment for so doing, gives Partridge a written promise to answer in the event of default by Fazio. Fazio defaults. Partridge sues Fazio, obtains judgment, execution is issued and returned unsatisfied. Partridge then sues Shank, who claims there is no consideration for her promise. Is this defense valid? Explain.

39

BANKRUPTCY

Our society has provided a system by which the honest but financially overburdened debtor can pay into court whatever property the debtor possesses, be relieved of most obligations, and begin economic life anew. This system is called **bankruptcy**.

Historically the bankruptcy law was not concerned with benefiting the debtor as much as it was with benefiting the debtor's creditors. In its origin, the law was designed to compel fraudulent debtors to bring their property into court and to pay it to their creditors, thus preventing them from concealing their property or from paying it to only some of their creditors. Today, a bankruptcy proceeding is concerned with benefiting both debtor and creditors, as can be seen from the fact that a

786

case in bankruptcy may be initiated by the debtor (a voluntary case) or by creditors (an involuntary case).

A.   BANKRUPTCY LAW

Congress, under the power granted to it by the Constitution, enacted the Bankruptcy Act in 1898. This legislation was subsequently amended by the Chandler Act of 1938. However, the Bankruptcy Reform Act of 1978 (the Bankruptcy Code) was the first comprehensive revision to modernize the bankruptcy laws by making both substantive and procedural changes. The Bankruptcy Amendments Act of 1984 and Supreme Court Bankruptcy Rules supplement the 1978 Act.

§ 39:1   BANKRUPTCY COURTS

The 1978 Act established a United States Bankruptcy Court as an adjunct to the federal district court in each judicial district. This measure greatly expanded the jurisdiction of the bankruptcy courts. Under the 1978 Act, the bankruptcy courts could not only hear and decide all bankruptcy cases but were also granted nonexclusive jurisdiction to hear and decide all civil proceedings arising under the bankruptcy law or related to cases under the bankruptcy law. However, this expansion of bankruptcy court jurisdiction was held by the United States Supreme Court to violate Article III of the U.S. Constitution.[1] The 1978 Act had given bankruptcy judges most of the authority of federal district court judges, but none of their tenure or salary protection.

The Bankruptcy Amendments Act of 1984 restructured the bankruptcy court system, limiting the powers of bankruptcy judges. The amendments removed the authority of bankruptcy judges over non-bankruptcy issues. In effect, the amend-

ments vested all jurisdiction over bankruptcy cases in the United States District Courts, which may refer all cases and related proceedings to adjunct bankruptcy courts.

§ 39:2   KINDS OF BANKRUPTCY PROCEEDINGS

Under the 1978 Act, three kinds of bankruptcy proceedings are available to individuals and businesses:

(a) liquidation, sometimes called a "Chapter 7" bankruptcy;
(b) reorganization, sometimes called a "Chapter 11" bankruptcy; and
(c) extended time payment, sometimes called a "Chapter 13" bankruptcy.

B.   LIQUIDATION UNDER CHAPTER 7

In liquidation proceedings, the debtor's nonexempt assets are collected by the trustee representing the creditors. The trustee liquidates the assets and distributes the proceeds to the creditors. The debtor is then discharged from most debts. A liquidation can be voluntary or involuntary.

§ 39:3   COMMENCEMENT OF THE CASE

A bankruptcy case refers to the proceeding in the bankruptcy court. The principal difference between a voluntary case and an involuntary case lies in the manner in which the proceedings are initiated.

(a) VOLUNTARY. A **voluntary case** is commenced by the debtor's filing a petition with the bankruptcy court. A joint petition may be filed by a husband and wife. The commencement of a voluntary case constitutes an order for relief, no formal adjudication is needed.[2] Unless the court orders otherwise, a debtor must also file a sched-

---

[1]   Northern Pipeline Constr. Co. v Marathon Pipe Line Co. 458 US 50 (1982).

[2]   11 USC § 301.

ule of current income and current expenditures.

Individuals, partnerships, and corporations, except railroads, banks, insurance companies, savings and loan associations, and credit unions, may file a voluntary petition.[3]

(b) INVOLUNTARY. An **involuntary case** is commenced by the creditors by filing a petition with the bankruptcy court.

An involuntary case may be commenced against any individual, partnership or corporation, except those excluded from filing voluntary petitions, as well as farmers and nonprofit corporations.[4]

§ 39:4 NUMBER AND CLAIMS OF PETITIONING CREDITORS

If there are twelve or more creditors, at least three, whose unsecured claims total $5,000 or more, must sign the involuntary petition. If there are fewer than twelve creditors, excluding employees or insiders, any creditor whose unsecured claim is at least $5,000 may sign the petition.

---

[3] 11 USC § 109(b).
[4] 11 USC § 303(a).

If the creditor holds security for the claim, only the amount of the claim in excess of the value of the security is counted. The holder of a claim that is the subject of a bona fide dispute may not be counted as a petitioning creditor.[5]

§ 39:5 GROUNDS FOR RELIEF FOR INVOLUNTARY CASE

The mere filing of an involuntary case petition does not constitute an order for relief. The debtor may contest the bankruptcy petition. If the debtor does not contest the petition, the court will enter an order for relief if at least one of the following grounds exists: (a) the debtor is generally not paying debts as they become due, or (b) within 120 days before the filing of the petition, a custodian has been appointed for the debtor's property. No act of misconduct on the part of the debtor need be shown.[6]

In the *Arker* case, the court was faced with the problem of whether a failure to pay a debt to a single creditor should be grounds for relief in an involuntary case.

---

[5] 11 USC § 303(b)(1).
[6] 11 USC § 303(h)(1) and (2).

IN RE SOL ARKER
6 BR 632 (ED NY 1980)

Bank Leumi Trust Company commenced an involuntary case in bankruptcy against Sol Arker. The bank claimed that Arker was generally not paying his debts since the bank had been unable to collect on a $190,000 judgment that it held against Arker. Arker denied that he was generally not paying his debts and asserted further that he had no assets that could be used to satisfy the bank's claim.

PARENTE, B. J. . . . The alleged debtor denies that he is generally not paying his debts as they become due.

Whether the Court should grant an order for relief against the alleged debtor rests on the resolution of the following:

Should the Court grant an order for relief where the petitioning creditor contends that the alleged debtor has failed to pay one creditor and where the alleged debtor has no assets for the Bankruptcy Court to administer.

As set forth in 11 U.S.C. § 303 and as is relevant to the case now before the Court, an involuntary case may be commenced under Chapter 7 or Chapter 11 of the Bankruptcy Code against any person that may be a debtor under those chapters. In cases such as the case at bar, where the debtor has fewer than twelve creditors, § 303(b)(2) provides that a petition may be brought by a single entity which is a holder of a claim against the alleged debtor that is not contingent as to liability. . . .

Subsection (h) of § 303 enunciates the standard for an order for relief on an involuntary petition.

Section 303(h) provides in relevant part:

> (h) If the petition is not timely controverted, the court shall order relief against the debtor in an involuntary case under the chapter under which the petition was filed. Otherwise, after trial, the court shall order relief against the debtor in an involuntary case under the chapter which the petition was filed, only if
> (1) The debtor is generally not paying such debtor's debts as such debts become due: or . . .

The phrase "the debtor is generally not paying such debtor's debts as such debts become due" is not defined in the Bankruptcy Code.

However, when faced with this issue, the bankruptcy courts have consistently held that in order to determine whether the alleged debtor is generally paying his debts as they become due, the amount of the debts not being paid and the number of creditors not being paid are significant factors. . . .

Specifically, in the *Matter of 7H Land & Cattle Co.*, 2 CBC 2d 554 (D Nev. 1980), the bankruptcy court was faced with the following issue:

Does an allegation that the alleged debtors have failed to pay one creditor constitute 'generally not paying such debtors' debts as they become due."

The Court stated that as a general rule:

> It may be assumed that in the ordinary case there can be no order for relief with no more proof than mere failure to meet liability to a single creditor.

However, the Court further states that there should be two exceptions to this general rule:

> First: An order for relief should be granted in the exceptional case of an alleged debtor with a sole creditor who would otherwise be without an adequate remedy under non-bankruptcy law.
>   Second: If the petitioning creditor makes a showing of special circumstances amounting to fraud, trick, artifice, or scam, then an order for relief should be granted.

This Court agrees with the principle of law enunciated in the *Matter of 7H Land and Cattle Co.* Thus, given the facts of the case at bar, unless one of the exceptions to the general rule stated in said case applies, the petitioning creditor's request for an order for relief should be denied.

The petitioning creditor did not put before this Court a claim that there were circumstances surrounding the petitioning creditor which bear closely upon trick, artifice, scam or fraud by the alleged debtor. Therefore, the second exception to the general rule does not apply to the case at bar.

With respect to the first exception, i.e., an alleged debtor with a sole creditor who would otherwise be without an adequate remedy under non-bankruptcy law, although there is ample evidence in the record to support the Court's finding that the petitioning creditor has exhausted all possible non-bankruptcy remedies, there is an additional factor in this case which was not present in the *Matter of 7H Land and Cattle Co.*

The Court in the case at bar is faced with the following situation: an involuntary petition has been filed against an alleged debtor who has no free assets which could be liquidated for the benefit of his creditors and who has only one creditor which has yet to be paid. It is manifest that the alleged debtor has no free assets to be liquidated which is decisive to this Court's conclusion that an order for relief should not be granted in the case at bar. This conclusion is predicated on the purpose of an involuntary proceeding which is to secure an equitable distribution of the assets of the alleged debtor among all his creditors. . . . To grant an order for relief in a case where there are no assets to be liquidated for the benefit of creditors would not be in comport with this long standing policy underlying involuntary proceedings.

Further support for this precept is found in the *Matter of Oak Winds,* 2 CBC 2d 417 (MD Fla 1980). In that case, an involuntary petition under Chapter 11 of the Bankruptcy Code was filed against the alleged debtor. The petitioning creditor entered into a stipulation with the alleged debtor wherein, among other things, the alleged debtor consented to the granting of an order for relief. An order for relief was never entered by the court due to the filing of a joint application to dismiss the involuntary petition by the alleged debtor and the petitioning creditor. An objection to said application was filed by a creditor of the alleged debtor. In overruling the objection, the court stated in relevant part:

> In sum, it is evident and this Court is satisfied that there would not be any useful purpose to retain jurisdiction of this case either as a reorganization case under Chapter 11 of the Code since there is obviously no desire by the debtor to effectuate any involuntary reorganization *nor would it serve any useful purpose to consider a conversion of this case into a liquidating case under Chapter 7 simply because there are no free assets which could be liquidated for the benefit of the general unsecured creditors or, the only one in this instance.* (emphasis added)

Just as the court in the *Matter of Oak Winds* refused to convert the involuntary Chapter 11 case to a Chapter 7 case on the ground that there were no free assets to liquidate, this Court is constrained to deny the granting of an order for relief in the case at bar. To grant an order for relief in the case at bar would serve no purpose since there are not assets for this Court to administer.

[Petition denied]

QUESTIONS

1. What are the requirements for the commencement of an involuntary case?
2. How many creditors signed the petition?
3. Did the court grant the relief requested?

---

§ 39:6   AUTOMATIC STAY

After the filing of the bankruptcy petition, the debtor needs protection from the collection efforts of creditors. The filing of either a voluntary or involuntary petition operates as an **automatic stay**, which prevents creditors from taking action against the debtor.[7] This automatic stay ends when the bankruptcy case is closed or dismissed or the debtor is granted a discharge.

§ 39:7 RIGHTS OF DEBTOR IN INVOLUNTARY CASE

If an involuntary petition is dismissed other than by consent of all petitioning creditors and the debtor, the court may award costs, reasonable attorney fees, or damages to the debtor. The damages are those that may be caused by the taking of possession of the debtor's property. The debtor may also recover damages against any creditor who filed the petition in bad faith.[8]

§ 39:8 TRUSTEE IN BANKRUPTCY

The trustee in bankruptcy is elected by the creditors. An interim trustee will be appointed by the court or the United States Trustee if a trustee is not elected by the creditors.

(a) STATUS OF THE TRUSTEE. The trustee is deemed to be the successor to and stand in the shoes of the debtor. The trustee automatically becomes by operation of law the owner of all the property of the debtor in excess of the property to which the debtor is entitled under exemption laws. Property inherited by the debtor within six months after the filing of the petition also passes to the trustee.

(b) RIGHTS OF THE TRUSTEE. The bankruptcy trustee possesses the rights and the powers of the most favored creditor of the debtor. This means that the trustee can avoid (1) transfers by the debtor that a creditor holding a valid claim under state law could have avoided at the commencement of the bankruptcy case, (2) preferences, that is, a transfer of property by the debtor to a creditor, the effect of which enables the creditor to obtain a greater percentage of the creditor's claim than the creditor would have received had the debt-

or's assets been liquidated in bankruptcy, and (3) statutory liens that became effective against the debtor at the commencement of the bankruptcy.

§ 39:9 VOIDABLE TRANSFERS

A debtor may not transfer property to prevent creditors from satisfying their legal claims. The trustee may avoid any such transfer made or obligation incurred by the debtor within one year of bankruptcy when the debtor's actual intent was to hinder, delay, or defraud creditors by so doing.

The trustee may also avoid certain transfers of property made by a debtor merely because their effect is to make the debtor insolvent or to reduce the debtor's assets to an unreasonably low amount.[9]

(a) THE INSOLVENT DEBTOR. A debtor is insolvent when the total fair value of all the debtor's assets does not exceed the debts owed by the debtor. This is commonly called the **balance sheet test** because it is merely a comparison of assets to liabilities without considering whether the debtor will be able to meet future obligations as they become due.

(b) PREFERENTIAL TRANSFERS. A transfer of property by the debtor to a creditor may be set aside and the property recovered by the debtor's trustee in bankruptcy if (1) the transfer was to pay a debt incurred at some earlier time, (2) the transfer was made when the debtor was insolvent and within 90 days before the filing of the bankruptcy petition, and (3) by the transfer the creditor received more than such creditor would have received in a liquidation of the debtor's estate. A debtor is presumed to be insolvent on and during the 90 days immediately preceding the date of the filing of the bankruptcy petition.[10]

Transfers made to **insiders,** that is, the debtor's relatives, partners, directors, and controlling persons, within the 12 months

---

[7] 11 USC § 362.
[8] 11 USC § 303(i).

[9]   11 USC § 548.
[10] 11 USC § 547(f).

prior to the filing of the petition may be set aside.[11]

Certain transfers by a debtor may not be attacked by the trustee as preferences. A transaction for a present consideration, such as a cash sale, is not subject to attack. A payment by a debtor in the ordinary course of business, such as the payment of a utility bill, is not subject to attack. A payment by an individual debtor whose debts are primarily consumer debts is not subject to attack if the aggregate value of the transfer is less than $600.[12]

In the *Jaggers* case, a trustee objected to a debtor's payments on a promissory note on the grounds that these payments were preferences.

[11]   11 USC § 547(b)(4)(B).

[12]   11 USC § 547(c)(7).

IN RE JAGGERS
48 BR 33 (WD Tex 1985)

On May 7, 1981, Joseph Jaggers filed a petition under Chapter 7 of the Bankruptcy Code. At the time the petition was filed, he was indebted to the Cove State Bank on a promissory note. The principal amount of the note had originally been in excess of $68,000. Two payments had been made on the note: one on February 23, 1981, in the form of a check drawn on the account of T-Vest Corporation and signed by Dorothea M. Kerr, an authorized signatory on the T-Vest account; another on March 23, 1981, in the form of a check drawn on the account of J. & D. Finance and signed by Jaggers, an authorized signatory on the J. & D. account. The trustee in bankruptcy claimed that these payments were preferential transfers.

THOMPSON, C. J. . . . The T-Vest Corporation is a Texas Corporation. The Debtor and his wife were directors of the corporation. The Debtor was the Chairman of the Board of Directors and his wife was the secretary of the corporation. One Hundred percent of the stock of T-Vest Corporation was owned by the Debtor and his wife. The Debtor controlled and directed the disbursement of the funds from the T-Vest Corporation account. At the direction of the Debtor, payments of both personal and business expenses were made as well as payments to the Debtor and his associates for consulting fees.

[The account] maintained by the T-Vest Corporation and controlled by the Debtor was a "conduit" or depository account for funds received by the T-Vest Corporation from Astroglass Boat Company, Star Custom Trailers, and other entities with which the Debtor was associated. Funds belonging to the various entities and funds belonging to the Debtor were commingled in the T-Vest account. At the time of the payments in question the Debtor exercised effective control over Astroglass Boat Company and Star Custom Trailers. The T-Vest account was also used for the receipt of consulting fees earned by the Debtor, Monty Tounsend, and other associates of the Debtor. . . .

J. & D. Finance Co. was not a corporation. The account in the name of J. & D. Finance was used for both personal and business purposes of the Debtor. All disbursements from this account were controlled by the Debtor. Funds from Astroglass Boat Company and Maiden-Craft, a Tennessee Corporation wholly owned and controlled by the Debtor and his wife, were funneled through the J. & D. Finance Co. account for payment of various operating and business expenses. The J. & D. Finance Co. account was used as a depository account for funds from Astroglass Boat Co., Maiden-Craft and the T-Vest Corporation. Funds belonging to these entities and the Debtor were commingled in the account. . . .

The payments to Cove State Bank from the T-Vest and J. & D. Finance Co. accounts directly benefited the Debtor because Joseph N. Jaggers was personally liable on the debt to Cove State Bank. The disbursements from these funds were credited on the general ledgers of Joseph Jaggers as salary fulfillments.

The threshold question before the Court is whether the payments . . . by the Debtor to Cove State Bank constituted a preferential transfer in violation of 11 U.S.C. Section 547(b).

In order to avoid a transfer, the trustee must establish by a fair preponderance of the evidence each controverted element of a voidable preference. The six elements which must be present for this Court to find that a preference exists under 11 U.S.C. Section 547(b) are:

(1) The property transferred was the property of the Debtor;
(2) The transfer was "to or for the benefit of a creditor;"
(3) The payment was made "for or on account of an antecedent debt owed by the debtor before such transfer was made;"
(4) The transfer was made while the Debtor was insolvent;
(5) The transfer was made on or within 90 days before the date of the filing of the petitions; and
(6) The transfer enabled the creditor to receive more than such creditor would have received if the transfer had not been made, and the creditor received payment of the debt to the extent provided under the bankruptcy code.

The parties have stipulated that the payments . . . were for the benefit of Cove State Bank, that they were made on or before 90 days before the date of the filing of the Debtor's petition, that the payments were made while the debtor was insolvent, and that these payments enabled Cove State Bank to receive more than it would otherwise have received in the Debtor's Chapter 7 case. The only issue then before the Court is whether the funds transferred constituted "property of the estate" within the meaning of 11 U.S.C. Section 547(b).

In order to ascertain whether certain monies constitute property of the debtor the Court must determine whether the debtor had an interest in the funds such that a transfer thereof would result in a diminution of the estate.

In the case at bar, though the Debtor did have ownership rights in the accounts from which the payments to Cove State Bank were made, it is apparent that he did not own the funds in their entirety. The Debtor shared ownership interests in the accounts in question with Astroglass Boat Co., Star Custom Trailers and Mr. Monty Tounsend. It is clear, therefore, that the funds which the debtor used to pay Cove State Bank were, in part, the property of a third party.

When a debtor uses the funds of a third party to pay an obligation of the debtor the Court must look to the source of the control over the disposition of the funds in order to determine whether a preference exists. If the debtor controls the disposition of the funds and designates the creditor to whom the monies will be paid independent of the third party whose funds are being used in partial payment of the debt, then the payments made by the debtor to the creditor constitute a preferential transfer. Hence, if the funds are available for payment to the creditors of the debtor generally the funds are an asset of the estate and payment thereof constitutes a diminution of the estate.

The question the Court must ask is whether the funds of the third party were available for use by the debtor generally or were the funds solely available for the purpose of discharging a particular debt to a particular creditor. . . .

In the case at bar, the Debtor made two payments to Cove State Bank in check form in the amounts of $7,900.43 and $5,000.000 respectively. The $5,000.00 check on the account of J. & D. Finance Company was signed by the Debtor and the Debtor directed that payment be made to Cove State Bank. This transfer, on its face, was directed solely by the Debtor. By virtue of the Debtor's exclusive control over the disposition of the funds in payment of a personal obligation of the Debtor, the funds were available for payment to creditors of the Debtor generally and constituted an asset of the estate. The $7,900.43 check on the T-Vest Corporation account was tendered to Cove State Bank for the purpose of reducing the balance on the promissory note owed by the Debtor to Cove State Bank. Though the check was not signed by the Debtor, there is no evidence that the use of the funds in the T-Vest account by the Debtor was conditioned upon payment of those funds to Cove State Bank. It is apparent that the Debtor controlled the distribution of funds from the T-Vest Corporation account. As a result of that control, the funds used by the Debtor for the payment of Cove State Bank were available to the creditors of the Debtor generally and constituted assets of the estate. The payments to Cove State Bank, therefore, were made with property of the estate. The payments resulted in a diminution of the estate and thereby constituted a preferential transfer of the property of the estate. . . .

[Judgment for the trustee]

QUESTIONS

1. When does payment to a creditor constitute a voidable preference?
2. Did Jaggers intend to prefer Cove State Bank over other creditors?
3. Did the court agree with the trustee?

C.   ADMINISTRATION OF DEBTOR'S ESTATE

Bankruptcy law regulates the manner in which creditors present their claims and how the assets of the debtor are to be distributed in payment of such claims.

§ 39:10   PROOF OF CLAIM

In a bankruptcy case, the debtor will file a list of creditors. The court will then send a notice of the case to listed creditors. The creditors that wish to participate in distribution of the proceeds of the liquidation of the debtor's estate must file a proof of claim. A **proof of claim** is a written statement signed by the creditor or an authorized representative setting forth any claim made against the debtor and the basis thereof. It must ordinarily be filed within 90 days after the first meeting of creditors.[13] A creditor is not excused from filing within that time even though the trustee in bankruptcy in fact knew of the existence of the creditor's claim. A **claim** is a right to payment whether liquidated (certain and not disputed), unliquidated, contingent, unmatured, disputed, legal, or equitable.

§ 39:11   PRIORITY OF CLAIMS

Creditors who hold security for payment, such as a lien or a mortgage on the debtor's property, are not affected by the debtor's bankruptcy. Secured creditors may enforce their security in order to obtain payment of their claims. The unsecured creditors share in the remaining assets of the debtor. Some have priority over others. Any balance remaining after all creditors have been paid is turned over to the debtor.

The unsecured debts that have priority and the order of priority are:[14]

(a) Costs and expenses of administration of the bankruptcy case, including fees to trustees, attorneys, and accountants, and the reasonable expenses of creditors in recovering property transferred or concealed by the debtor.

(b) Claims arising in the ordinary course of a debtor's business or financial affairs after the commencement of the case and before the appointment of a trustee.

(c) Claims for wages, salaries, or commissions, including vacation, severance, or sick leave pay earned within 90 days before the filing of the petition or the date of cessation of the debtor's business, whichever occurred first. The amount of such claims is limited, however, to $2,000 for each person.

(d) Claims arising for contributions to employee benefit plans. The amount is limited by the Code, and services must have been rendered within 180 days before the filing of the petition or when the debtor ceased doing business, whichever occurred first.

(e) Claims by consumer creditors, not to exceed $900 for each claimant, arising from the purchase of consumer goods or services, where such property or services were not delivered or provided.

(f) Federal and state income taxes due within three years of the filing of the petition.

D.   DEBTOR'S DUTIES AND EXEMPTIONS

The Bankruptcy Code imposes certain duties upon the debtor and provides for specific exemptions of some of the debtor's estate from the claims of creditors.

§ 39:12   DEBTOR'S DUTIES

The debtor must file with the court a list of creditors, a schedule of assets and liabilities, and a statement of the debtor's financial affairs. The debtor must also appear for examination under oath at the first meeting of creditors.

§ 39:13   DEBTOR'S EXEMPTIONS

The debtor is permitted to claim certain property of the estate in the trustee's possession and keep it free from claims of creditors. Unless state law forbids the choice, the debtor may elect either the exemptions permitted by the laws of his or her state of domicile or those set forth in the Bankruptcy Code. If a husband and wife file a joint petition, they must elect together to use either the state or federal exemptions. If they cannot agree upon which to elect, they will be

---

[13] Bankruptcy Rule 3002(c).
[14] 11 USC § 507(1) to (6).

deemed to have chosen the federal exemptions. The Bankruptcy Code provides for the following exemptions, among others: the debtor's interest in real or personal property used as a residence to the extent of $7,500; the debtor's interest in a motor vehicle to the extent of $1,200; household furnishings of the debtor or the debtor's dependents, not to exceed $200 per item, or $4,000 in aggregate value; payments under a life insurance contract; alimony and child support payments; and awards from personal injury causes of action.[15]

E.   DISCHARGE IN BANKRUPTCY

The main objectives of a bankruptcy proceeding are the collection and distribution of the debtor's assets and the discharge of the debtor from obligations. The decree terminating the bankruptcy proceeding is generally a **discharge** which releases the debtor from debts.

§ 39:14   DENIAL OF DISCHARGE

The court will refuse to grant a discharge if the debtor has: (a) within one year of the filing of the petition, fraudulently transferred or concealed property with intent to hinder, delay, or defraud creditors; (b) failed to keep proper financial records; (c) made a false oath or account; (d) failed to explain satisfactorily any loss of assets; (e) refused to obey any lawful order of the court, or refused to testify after having been granted immunity; (f) obtained a discharge within the last six years; or (g) filed a written waiver of discharge that is approved by the court.[16]

---

[15]   11 USC § 522.

[16]   11 USC § 727.

NONDISCHARGEABLE DEBTS
A.   TAX PENALTY
B.   STUDENT LOANS RECEIVED WITHIN FIVE YEARS OF BANKRUPTCY
C.   LOANS OBTAINED BY USE OF FALSE FINANCIAL STATEMENT
D.   UNSCHEDULED DEBTS
E.   ALIMONY AND CHILD SUPPORT
F.   LIABILITY FOR WILLFUL AND MALICIOUS INJURY TO PROPERTY
G.   JUDGMENTS BASED UPON DRIVING WHILE INTOXICATED
H.   CONSUMER DEBTS FOR LUXURY GOODS
I.   CASH ADVANCES

FIGURE 39-1
DEBTS FROM WHICH A DEBTOR IS NOT RELEASED

§ 39:15 EFFECT OF DISCHARGE

A discharge releases the debtor from the unpaid balance of most debts. However, a discharge does not release a person from: (a) a tax, customs duty, or tax penalty; (b) student loans unless the loan first became due more than five years before bankruptcy or unless excepting the loan from discharge would impose undue hardship upon the debtor; (c) loans obtained by use of a false financial statement, made with intent to deceive, and upon which the creditor reasonably relied; (d) debts not duly scheduled in time for allowance; (e) liability for fraud while acting in a fiduciary capacity or by reason of embezzlement or larceny; (f) liability for alimony and child support; (g) liability for willful and malicious injury to property; (h) judgments against the debtor for liability for driving while intoxicated; (i) a consumer debt to a single creditor aggregating more than $500 for luxury goods or services; and (j) cash advances based upon consumer credit exceeding $1,000.[17]

The debt for luxury goods must be incurred within 40 days of the order for relief; the cash advances must be incurred within 20 days of the order for relief.

In the *Cunningham* case, a passenger injured as a result of the debtor's driving while intoxicated sought to have his judgment declared nondischargeable.

[17] 11 USC § 523.

IN RE CUNNINGHAM

48 BR 641 (WD Tenn 1985)

Cunningham pleaded guilty to driving while intoxicated after having an accident. Brunswick, a passenger in the car brought a civil action against the debtor and recovered a judgment of $800,000. Cunningham had $10,000 worth of insurance. This amount was paid to Brunswick, leaving Cunningham liable for the remaining portion of the judgment. In the subsequent bankruptcy proceeding, Brunswick sought to have his judgment declared nondischargeable pursuant to the bankruptcy law.

LEFFLER, W.B. . . . On Sunday, October 3, 1982 the Debtor and a friend purchased three six-packs of beer and proceeded to drive around Obion County and drink. The friend drove and the Debtor was a passenger. Between the hours of two o'clock P.M. and ten o'clock P.M. the Debtor and his drinking partner consumed all eighteen beers, sharing the beer equally. After the young men finished the beer they continued to drive around town and talk. At about eleven-thirty P.M. the Debtor and his friend parked the friend's car and got into the Debtor's new Trans-Am automobile. Shortly thereafter the Debtor and his friend encountered the Plaintiff and his fiancée. The Plaintiff and his fiancée got in the back seat of Debtor's automobile and the Debtor drove; they traveled out a rural road in Obion County, Tennessee. Sometime near midnight Debtor turned south on Pleasant Hill Road and traveled for about one mile at which point he turned around and proceeded to travel in a northern direction from whence he just came. For some unknown reason the Debtor increased the speed of his automobile to about sixty miles per hour, an unsafe speed considering that it was a foggy night and they were traveling on a dark rural road. Debtor did not stop at the intersection, nor did he reduce the speed of his automobile as he approached the intersection. Debtor drove his automobile through the intersection, across the road, and into a dirt embankment. The accident caused serious and permanent injuries to the Plaintiff and less serious injuries to the other passengers. By virtue of the accident, the Plaintiff is permanently paralyzed from the waist down and he is confined to a wheelchair.

After the Debtor drove through the intersection and crashed into the dirt embankment the investigating police officers charged the Debtor with the criminal offense of driving while intoxicated ("DWI") and indicated in the Arrest Report that the Debtor had a strong odor of alcohol on his breath. As a result of that charge the Debtor pled guilty to DWI in the General Sessions Court of Obion County, Tennessee, on December 1, 1982. The Debtor was fined Two Hundred Fifty Dollars ($250.00), plus costs, and sentenced to serve forty-eight (48) hours in the county jail. Additionally, as a result of that guilty plea, the Court suspended the Debtor's driving privileges for a period of one (1) Year.

On August 24, 1983 the Plaintiff instituted the civil action against the Debtor. The Complaint in the state court action alleged that the Debtor operated his motor vehicle in violation of Tenn.Code Ann. § 55-10-401, which makes it unlawful for any person to drive an automobile while under the influence of an intoxicant. The Complaint additionally set forth that the accident was a direct result of the Debtor's operation of his automobile recklessly and negligently and that he intentionally drove his automobile while under the influence of alcohol.

In the civil proceeding in state court the Debtor never denied that he was intoxicated at the time of the accident. His defense was based upon contributory negligence and assumption of the risk on the part of the Plaintiff. The essence of the defense was that the Plaintiff knew that the Debtor was drunk when he got in the car with him.

On November 7, 1984 the Debtor filed a Chapter 7 Petition in Bankruptcy. The Plaintiff has been listed as an unsecured creditor in the amount of $790,000.

In the instant proceeding the Debtor takes the position that he was not intoxicated at the time of the accident and that the accident was merely a result of Debtor's negligence, therefore, neither section 523(a)(9), nor section 523(a)(6) is applicable and a debt based on mere negligence is dischargeable pursuant to 11 U.S.C. § 727.

The Debtor put into evidence a copy of the hospital report showing that debtor's blood alcohol level was .05 when Debtor was treated at the hospital after the accident. In rebuttal, the Plaintiff pointed out that the accident occurred after midnight on a Sunday on an isolated rural road and that it is not noted on the hospital record what time the blood test was performed.

The Debtor also challenges the voluntariness of his guilty plea in state court to DWI. This claim is without merit. Debtor's attempt to overturn the guilty plea must be pursued in state court. . . .

Conclusions of Law

Section 523(a)(6) states as follows:

(a) A discharge under section 727, 1141, or 1328(b) of this title does not discharge an individual debtor from any debt —
  (6) for willful and malicious injury by the debtor to another entity or to the property of another entity.

A split of authority exists on the question of the dischargeability of an indebtedness arising from an automobile accident caused by a debtor while intoxicated.

The division of authority seems to have been resolved by the recently enacted Bankruptcy Amendments of 1984.

Section 523 was amended by adding paragraph (a)(9), that states as follows:

> (a) A discharge under section 727, 1141, or 1328(b) of this title does not discharge an individual debtor from any debt —
>
> > (9) to any entity, to the extent that such debt arises from a judgment or consent decree entered in a court of record against the debtor wherein liability was incurred by such debtor as a result of the debtor's operation of a motor vehicle while legally intoxicated under the laws or regulations of any jurisdiction within the United States or its territories wherein such motor vehicle was operated and within which such liability was incurred; . . .

When dealing with the question of dischargeability of an indebtedness arising from an automobile accident caused by a debtor while intoxicated under section 523(a)(6) the Court had to determine whether the actions by a debtor were "willful" and "malicious", since these terms are not defined by the Bankruptcy Act. This problem does not exist under Section 523(a)(9). Section (a)(9) allows the court to rely on state laws or regulations in determining whether a debtor was legally intoxicated at the time of the accident.

It seems obvious from the plain language of the statute that Section 523 (a)(9) was meant to apply to situations exactly like the one that is now before this Court. Although the legislative history regarding Section 523 (a)(9) is sparse, there are references to the effect that the amended paragraph was added in order to clear up the above mentioned problems relating to 523 (a)(6):

> Judgments against drunk drivers for personal injuries . . . could be discharged in bankruptcy like any other judgment; now that is prohibited. Just a number of distinct improvements. 130 Cong. Rec. H7492 (daily ed. June 29, 1984) (statement by Rep. Sawyer).
>
> . . . this bill provides important new protections . . . reforms in the law of bankruptcy as it treats claims against drunk drivers, to ensure that victims of the drunk driver do not have their judgments against the drunk driver discharged in bankruptcy. . . 130 Cong. Rec. § 8890 (daily ed. June 29, 1984) (statement by Sen. Dole).

In the case at bar, all the requirements to except a debt from discharge under Section 523(a)(9) are present. The Plaintiff has a valid judgment against the Debtor, the liability was incurred by the Debtor as a result of the Debtor driving his automobile while legally intoxicated under Tennessee law, as evidenced by the guilty plea entered by the Debtor in the state court. Therefore, this Court holds that the $790,000.00 debt in question is nondischargeable pursuant to 11 U.S.C. § 523(a)(9).

[Judgment for plaintiff]

QUESTIONS

1. What was the argument of the debtor in the bankruptcy court?
2. Did the bankruptcy court agree with the debtor?
3. Was the judgment nondischargeable?

F. Reorganizations and Payment Plans Under Chapters 11 and 13

In addition to liquidation as above described, the Bankruptcy Code permits the parties to restructure the organization and finances of a business so that it may continue to operate. The Code also provides for the adoption of extended time payment plans for individual debtors who owe unsecured debts of less than $100,000 and secured debts of less than $350,000.

In these so-called rehabilitation plans, the debtor keeps all the assets (exempt and nonexempt), remains in business, and makes a settlement that is acceptable to the majority of the creditors, whose decision is binding upon the minority.

§ 39:16   Business Reorganizations Under Chapter 11

Individuals, partnerships, and corporations in business may be reorganized under the Bankruptcy Code. The first step is to file a plan for the reorganization of the debtor. This plan may be filed by the debtor or by any party in interest or committee of creditors.

(a) Contents of Plan. The plan divides ownership interests and debts into those that will be affected by the adoption of the plan and those that will not. It then specifies what will be done to those interests and claims that are affected. For example, where mortgage payments are too high for the income of the enterprise, a possible plan would be to reduce the mortgage payments and give the mortgage holder preferred stock to compensate for the loss sustained.

Persons within a particular class must all be treated the same way. For example, the holders of first mortgage bonds must all be treated the same way.

A plan may also provide for the assumption, rejection, or assignment of executory contracts. Thus, the trustee or debtor may under certain circumstances suspend performance of a contract not yet fully performed. Collective bargaining agreements may be rejected in this manner with the approval of the bankruptcy court.[18]

(b) Confirmation of Plan. When the plan is prepared, it must be approved or **confirmed** by the court. This confirmation will be realized if the plan has been submitted in good faith and if its provisions are reasonable.[19]

After the plan is confirmed, the owners and creditors of the enterprise have only such rights as are specified in the plan and cannot go back to their original positions.

§ 39:17   Extended Time Payment Plans Under Chapter 13

An individual debtor who has a regular income may submit a plan for the installment payment of outstanding debts. If approved by the court, the debtor may then pay the debts in the installments specified by the plan even though the creditors had not originally agreed to such installment payments.

(a) Contents of Plan. The individual debtor plan is, in effect, a budget of the debtor's future income with respect to outstanding debts. The plan must provide for the eventual payment in full of all claims entitled to priority under the Bankruptcy Code. Creditors holding the same kind or class of claim must all be treated the same way.

(b) Confirmation of Plan. The plan has no effect until it is approved or confirmed by the court. This confirmation will be realized if the plan was submitted in good faith and is in the best interests of the creditors.[20]

When the plan is confirmed, debts are

---

[18]   11 USC § 1113, modifying the holding of the U.S. Supreme Court in *NLRB v Bildisco*, 104 US 1188 (1984).
[19]   11 USC § 1129.
[20]   11 USC § 1325.

payable in the manner specified in the plan.

(c) DISCHARGE OF DEBTOR. After all the payments called for by the plan have been made, the debtor is given a discharge which releases him from liability for all debts except those that would not be discharged by an ordinary bankruptcy discharge.[21]

§ 39:18 PROTECTION AGAINST DISCRIMINATION

Federal, state, or local law may not discriminate against anyone on the basis of a discharge in bankruptcy.[22] This principle is illustrated in the *Young* case.

---

[21] 11 USC § 1328. See § 38:12 of this book.

[22] 11 USC § 525.

IN RE YOUNG, DEBTOR
10 BR 17 (SD Cal 1980)

Marion Young, the debtor, filed her extended time payment plan with the court. Subsequent to the filing of the petition, she was issued a citation for a traffic violation. In her confirmed plan, she proposed to pay 100 percent of her debts. Her application for renewal of her driver's license was denied because of her failure to pay the traffic tickets. She then moved to have the bankruptcy court order the state to renew her license.

KATZ, B. J. . . . . After hearing arguments presented by counsel, the court hereby makes the following findings of fact and conclusions of law:

Findings of Fact

1. Plaintiff filed her voluntary petition on May 19, 1980 under the provisions of Chapter 13 of Title 11 of the United States Code. The debtor's plan filed in the case provides for payment of 100% of creditor's claims as allowed, and was confirmed on July 8, 1980.
2. Plaintiff was issued a citation on May 31, 1979 for a traffic violation and executed a written promise to appear or post bail with the Municipal Court, West Orange County Judicial District. This obligation was listed in plaintiff's bankruptcy schedules for payment under her Chapter 13 plan. Plaintiff has not appeared in court on the offense nor posted bail in lieu of her appearance, and a bench warrant has been issued for her arrest.
3. Plaintiff's application for renewal of her California driver's license has been denied by defendant Department of Motor Vehicles under the authority of sections 12807(c) and 40508(a) of the California Vehicle Code, stating as grounds therefore plaintiff's failure to appear on the traffic violation.

Conclusions of Law

1. Section 525 of the Code provides in pertinent part that "A governmental unit may not deny, revoke, suspend, or refuse to renew a license . . . solely because the bankrupt or debtor . . . has not paid a debt that is dischargeable in the case under this Title or that was discharged under the Bankruptcy Act." *11 USC § 525.*
2. Plaintiff's obligation on account of the traffic citation is a criminal fine that is

not dischargeable under section 523(a)(7) of the Code. *11 USC § 523(a)(7).* . . . .

4. Section 1328(a) provides that after completion by the debtor of all payments under the plan, the court shall grant the debtor a discharge of all debts provided for by the plan or disallowed under section 502 except for certain debts and obligations on account of support excepted from discharge. Other obligations, including fines excepted from discharge under section 523(a)(7) of the Code, are dischargeable in a Chapter 13 case. *11 USC § 1328(a).*

5. A criminal fine dischargeable in a Chapter 13 case is a dischargeable debt within the provisions of section 525 of the Code, and defendant Department of Motor Vehicles is a governmental unit subject to the provisions of that section. *11 USC §§ 1328(a)(2), 525.*

6. Defendant's action in denying plaintiff's application for a renewal license is in violation of the anti-discrimination provisions of the Bankruptcy Code. *11 USC § 525.*

7. Plaintiff is entitled to a renewal license during the pendency of her Chapter 13 case, and discharge of her obligations upon completion of the payments provided for in her Chapter 13 plan. Should plaintiff convert to a liquidation case . . . the obligation for the traffic fine would not be dischargeable, and the Department of Motor Vehicles would be justified in revoking plaintiff's license. Likewise if plaintiff receives a hardship discharge under the provisions of section 1328(b), the Department could revoke plaintiff's license.

For the reasons stated above, plaintiff's motion for partial summary judgment shall be *Granted,* and defendant's crossmotion for summary judgment *Denied.* On stipulation of the parties, plaintiff's complaint in this action shall be dismissed as to all defendants without prejudice. Counsel for plaintiff shall prepare an order directing the Department of Motor Vehicles to issue plaintiff a renewal California driver's license.

QUESTIONS

1. What are the requirements for an extended time payment plan?
2. Was the Department of Motor Vehicles required to issue a license to Young? Why or why not?

SUMMARY

Jurisdiction over bankruptcy cases is in the United States District Courts, which may refer all cases and related proceedings to adjunct bankruptcy courts.

Three bankruptcy proceedings are available to individuals and businesses: (a) liquidation, (b) reorganization, and (c) extended time payment.

A liquidation proceeding under Chapter 7 may be either voluntary or involuntary. The voluntary case is commenced by the debtor by filing a petition with the bankruptcy court. An involuntary case is commenced by the creditors by filing a petition with the bankruptcy court. If there are twelve or more creditors, at least three, whose unsecured claims total at least $5,000 or more must sign the involuntary petition. If there are fewer than twelve such creditors, any creditor whose unsecured claim is at least $5,000 may sign the petition. If the debtor contests the bankruptcy petition, it must be shown that the debtor is not paying debts as they become due, or that within 120 days before the date of the filing of the petition a custodian had been appointed for the debtor's property.

An automatic stay prevents creditors from taking action against the debtor after a bankruptcy petition is filed.

The trustee in bankruptcy is elected by the creditors and is the successor to and stands in the place of the debtor. The trustee can avoid transfers of property to prevent creditors from satisfying their legal claims. Preferential transfers to creditors and to insiders may be set aside. A transaction for a present consideration such as a cash sale is not a preference.

Bankruptcy law regulates the manner in which creditors present their claims and how the assets of the debtor are to be distributed in payment of the claims.

Claims are paid in the following order of priority: (a) secured creditors, (b) adminis-trative expenses, (c) claims arising in the ordinary course of the debtor's business, (d) wage claims limited to $2,000 for each claimant earned within 90 days before the filing of the petition, (e) claims for contributions to employee benefit plans, (f) claims by consumer creditors, (g) taxes, and (h) general creditors. Certain property of the debtor is exempt from the claims of creditors.

The decree terminating the bankruptcy proceedings is generally a discharge which releases the debtor from most debts. If the debtor is a dishonest debtor, no discharge will be given. Dishonesty exists when the debtor has fraudulently transferred property, failed to keep proper records, or failed to obey a court order, among others. Certain debts, such as taxes, student loans, loans obtained by use of a false financial statement, alimony, and debts not duly scheduled, are not dischargeable.

Individuals, partnerships, and corporations in business may be reorganized so that a business may continue to operate. A plan for reorganization must be approved by the court. Individual debtors may adopt extended time payment plans for the payment of debts. A plan for extended time payment must also be confirmed by the court.

Federal, state, or local law may not discriminate against anyone on the basis of a discharge in bankruptcy.

QUESTIONS AND CASE PROBLEMS

1. What social forces are affected by permitting a debtor to avoid paying debts by going into bankruptcy?
2. Compare a release of claims given by a creditor with a discharge in bankruptcy.
3. Barron sold goods on credit to Charles by relying upon a false financial statement issued by Charles. Charles later filed for voluntary bankruptcy still owing this debt to Barron. Barron claimed that Charles was not entitled to a discharge from this particular debt because of the fraud. Was Barron correct?

4. Ruth commenced a voluntary case with the bankruptcy court. After her assets subject to the claims of creditors were liquidated, her trustee had possession of $2,000 in cash. Various creditors had filed claims for $20,000. Ruth's trustee claimed that the $2,000 should be used to pay the fee of the trustee, the fee of Ruth's accountant, and other administrative expenses of the bankruptcy case. The other creditors claimed that they were entitled to a portion of the $2,000. Were the other creditors correct?
5. Anita knows Jean to be insolvent. She sells

Jean her auto for $500 and receives cash in payment for the car. An involuntary bankruptcy case is commenced by the creditors sometime later against Jean. The trustee in bankruptcy attempts to recover the $500 on the ground that it was a preferential transfer. Will the trustee be successful?

6. Smith has twenty creditors. Three creditors with unsecured claims that total $10,000 signed an involuntary bankruptcy petition against Smith. Smith has been unable to pay debts as they become due. Smith objects to the petition being filed since the creditors have failed to allege that Smith has engaged in any misconduct. Will the creditors be successful?

7. Which of the following, if any, survive Rogers' discharge in bankruptcy.
   a. Wages amounting to $400 to three employees earned within 60 days of the bankruptcy.
   b. A judgment against Rogers for injuries received because of Rogers' negligent operation of an automobile.
   c. A judgment against Rogers by Landers for breach of contract.
   d. Rogers' obligation for alimony and child support.

8. Between March 26, 1979, and May 25, 1979, the debtor, Gulf States Marine, Inc. incurred certain obligations to the creditor, Lake Charles Diesel, Inc. on an open account. On September 29, 1979, the debtor paid the creditor the sum of $879.75 in full satisfaction of the obligation. The debtor filed its petition for relief in early October. The trustee seeks to recover the sum of $879.75 from the creditor alleging that the payment to the creditor was a voidable preference. The creditor denies that the debtor was insolvent but offers no proof to the contrary. Decide. [In re Gulf States Marine, Inc. Debtor, 6 BCD 79 (WD La)]

9. Essex is in serious financial difficulty and is unable to meet current unsecured obligations of $40,000 to some 20 creditors who are demanding immediate payment. Essex owes Stevens $5,000, and Stevens has decided to file an involuntary petition against Essex. Can Stevens file the petition?

10. Sonia, a retailer, has the following assets: a factory worth $100,000; accounts receivable amounting to $75,000, which fall due in from four to six months; and $2,000 cash in the bank. Sonia's sole liability is a $20,000 note falling due today, which Sonia is unable to pay. May Sonia be forced into involuntary bankruptcy under the Bankruptcy Code?

11. Samson Industries, Inc. ceased doing business and is in bankruptcy proceedings. Among the claimants are five employees seeking unpaid wages. Three of the employees are owed $3,500, and two are owed $1,500. These amounts became due within ninety days preceding the filing of the petition. How much, if anything, will the employees receive?

12. What is the importance of an automatic stay?

13. Carol Cott, doing business as Carol Cott Fashions, is worried about an involuntary bankruptcy proceeding being filed by her creditors. Her net worth using a balance-sheet approach is $8,000 ($108,000 assets - $100,000 liabilities.) However, her cash flow is negative, and she has been hard pressed to meet current obligations as they mature. She is, in fact, some $12,500 in arrears in payments to her creditors on bills submitted during the past two months. Will the fact that Carol is solvent in the bankruptcy sense result in the court's dismissing the creditor's petition if Carol contests the propriety of the filing of the petition? Explain.

14. A trustee, the United States government, and wage earners all claim first priority in bankruptcy for their claims. Who will be paid first. Explain.

15. On July 1, Roger Walsh, a sole proprietor operating a grocery, was involuntarily petitioned into bankruptcy by his creditors. At that time, and for at least 90 days prior thereto, Walsh was unable to pay current obligations. On June 16, Walsh paid the May electric bill that was incurred in his business. The trustee in bankruptcy claims this payment was a voidable preference. Is the trustee correct? Explain.

40

INSURANCE

Insurance is a multimillion-dollar industry in the United States. The function of insurance is to distribute the risk of substantial, individual loss over a large group of individuals who are exposed to similar risks. Insurance companies, through actuarial and other data-collecting devices, measure the risks of loss from the perils covered and set a premium or price for the insurance protection provided.

Insurance companies perform a wide range of services such as training businesses in loss prevention, investigating and appraising losses, and managing the vast sums of money they collect as premiums.

However, the cornerstone upon which the insurance industry is built is the contract.

A. INTRODUCTION TO THE INSURANCE CONTRACT

Insurance is a contract by which one party for a stipulated consideration promises to pay another party a sum of money upon the destruction of, loss of, or injury to something in which the other party has an interest.

§ 40:1   THE PARTIES

The promisor in an insurance contract is called the **insurer** or **underwriter**. The person to whom the promise is made is the **insured**, the assured, or the policyholder. The promise of the insurer is generally set forth in a written contract called a **policy**.

As a result of statutory regulation, virtually all insurance policies today are written by corporations, fraternal or benefit societies, and national or state governments.

The insured must have the capacity to make a contract. At common law, a minor's insurance contract could be avoided. Statutes increasingly change this and make the minor's contract of insurance as binding as though the minor were an adult.

Insurance contracts are ordinarily made through an agent or broker. The **insurance agent** is an agent of the insurance company, generally working exclusively for one company. For the most part, the ordinary rules of agency law govern the dealings between this agent and the applicant for insurance.[1]

The **insurance broker** is generally an independent contractor who is not employed by any one insurance company. When a broker obtains a policy for a customer, the former is the agent of the latter for the purpose of that transaction. Under some statutes, the broker is made an agent of the insurer with respect to transmitting the applicant's payments to the insurer.

§ 40:2   INSURABLE INTEREST

A person obtaining insurance must have an insurable interest in the subject matter insured. If not, the insurance contract cannot be enforced.

(a) INSURABLE INTEREST IN PROPERTY. A person has an insurable interest in property whenever the destruction of the property will cause a direct pecuniary loss to that person.[2]

It is immaterial whether the insured is the owner of the legal or equitable title, a lien holder, or merely a person in possession of the property. Thus, a person who is merely a possessor, such as the innocent purchaser of a stolen automobile, has an insurable interest therein.[3] Likewise, a contractor remodeling a building has an insurable interest in the building to the extent of the money that will be paid under the contract because the contractor would not be able to receive that money if the building were destroyed by fire.

In the case of property insurance, the insurable interest must exist at the time the loss occurs. Except when expressly required by statute, it is not necessary that the interest exist at the time when the policy or contract of insurance is made.

(b) INSURABLE INTEREST IN LIFE. A person who obtains life insurance can generally name anyone as beneficiary regardless of whether that beneficiary has an insurable interest in the life of the insured. If the beneficiary obtains the policy, however, he or she must have an insurable interest in the life of the insured. Such an interest exists if the beneficiary can reasonably expect to receive pecuniary gain from the continued life of the other person and, conversely, would suffer financial loss from the latter's death.[4] Thus, a creditor has an insurable interest in the life of the debtor since the death of the debtor may mean that the creditor will not be paid the amount owed.

A partner or partnership has an insurable interest in the life of each of the partners because the death of any one of them will dissolve the firm and cause some degree of loss to the partnership. A business enterprise has an insurable interest in the life of an executive or a key employee be-

---

[1]   Tidelands Life Insurance Co. v France (Tex Civ App) 711 So 2d 728 (1986).

[2]   DeWitt v American Family Mutual Ins. Co. (Mo) 667 SW2d 700 (1984).

[3]   Castle Cars, Inc. v United States Fire Ins. Co. 221 Va 773, 273 SE2d 793 (1981).

[4]   New York Life Ins. Co. v Port City Construction Co. 128 Cal App 3d 482, 180 Cal Rptr 359 (1982).

cause that person's death would inflict a financial loss upon the business to the extent that a replacement might not be readily available or could not be found.

In the case of life insurance, the insurable interest must exist at the time the policy is obtained. It is immaterial that the interest no longer exists when the loss is actually sustained. Thus, the fact that the insured husband and wife beneficiary are divorced after the life insurance policy was procured does not affect the validity of the policy.

In the *Graves* case the court was faced with two questions: (1) does a partner have an insurable interest in the life of another partner, and (2) was the surviving partner required to remit the proceeds to the estate of the deceased partner as a payment for the deceased partner's interest?

GRAVES V NORRED
(Ala) 510 So 2d 816 (1987)

Jewell Norred's husband, James Norred, was the business partner of Clyde Graves for some ten years. On May 7, 1979, Graves and Norred took out $25,000-level term life insurance policies, with Graves being the beneficiary of Norred's policy and Norred being the beneficiary of Graves' policy. Premiums were paid out of partnership funds. On February 28, 1983, Graves and Norred divided the partnership assets, but did not perform the customary steps of dissolving the partnership. Graves became the sole owner of the business and continued to pay the premiums on both insurance policies until James Norred died on December 5, 1983. Jewell Norred sued Graves seeking the proceeds of the insurance policy for herself, alleging that Graves had no insurable interest in the life of James Norred at the time of his death. She also contended that the proceeds should go to the estate as a payment for Norred's interest in the partnership. From a judgment on behalf of the estate, Graves appealed.

ADAMS, J. . . . Jewell Norred argues that she should receive the benefits of the insurance policy because she alone had an insurable interest in the insurance contract. . . . The prevailing rule among the states is that a partner or partnership has an insurable interest in the life of one of the partners. 43 Am.Jur.2d *Insurance* § 989 (1982). It is not the mere existence of the partnership which provides the basis for the insurable interest. It is the insuring partner's "reasonable expectation of pecuniary benefit from the continuance of the insured's life." *Id.*, at 1000. This interest continues even if the partnership is discontinued prior to the death of one of the partners. *Id.* . . .

In the instant case, each partner took out a life insurance policy on the other. Both sides testified that the purpose was to provide for one partner at the other partner's death. The manner of providing for the surviving partner is in dispute between the parties. However, there is not legal uncertainty that both partners had an insurable interest in the life of the other partner.

We next turn our analysis to the designation of the beneficiary in order to determine who should be entitled to the proceeds of the life insurance policy. In the case of *Williams v Williams*, 438 So.2d 735 (Ala.1983), a partner designated the other partners (his brothers), as the beneficiaries of his life insurance policy. Pursuant to the partnership's dissolution agreement, the surviving partners were to receive the insurance proceeds and then use those proceeds to purchase the deceased partner's interest. Although it was written in an awkward manner, the dissolution agreement was held to be valid and enforceable. 438 So.2d at 735. Unlike the present case, in *Williams* a written partnership agreement and a dissolution agreement existed. However, both agreements involved the designation of the partners as beneficiaries instead of the spouse or estate. As stated by Chief Justice Torbert, "The fact that the decedent selected his partners, as opposed to his spouse or estate, as beneficiaries of the life insurance . . . is unquestionably permissible. Partners continue to be free to select whomever they wish to benefit from insurance on their lives." *Williams*, 438 So.2d at 739. In this case, the plaintiff's evidence that the decedent intended for the proceeds to go to his estate consisted solely of oral testimony from the plaintiff's brother (the insurance agent), and an ambiguous statement from a mutual friend of both partners. No ambiguity existed in the designation of the beneficiary. There was no written agreement like the dissolution agreement in *Williams, supra*, which provided that the surviving partners were to use the proceeds to purchase the deceased partner's interest. We require more than oral testimony, like the testimony presented here, in order to show that it was not the intention of the decedent that the designated beneficiary retain the proceeds. Therefore, we reverse the trial court's judgment designating Norred's estate as the rightful recipient of the proceeds instead of the designated beneficiary.

[Reversed and remanded]

QUESTIONS

1. Did Graves have an insurable interest in the life of Norred following the discontinuance of the partnership?
2. Was Graves required to remit the proceeds of the insurance to Norred's estate as payment for Mr. Norred's partnership interest, subject to set-offs due Graves?
3. Can a partner select his or her partner, as opposed to his or her spouse or estate, as beneficiary under a life insurance policy?

§ 40:3　THE INSURANCE CONTRACT

The formation of the contract of insurance is governed by the general principles applicable to contracts.[5] Frequently, a question arises as to whether advertising material, estimates, and statistical projections constitute a part of the contract.

By statute it is now commonly provided that an insurance policy must be written. In order to avoid deception, many statutes also specify the content of certain policies, in whole or in part, and some specify the size and style of type to be used in printing them. Provisions in a policy that conflict with statutory requirements are generally void.

(a) THE APPLICATION AS PART OF THE CONTRACT. The application for insurance is generally attached to the policy when issued and is made part of the contract of insurance by express stipulation of the policy.

The insured should examine the policy and an attached application. Any false

[5]　Employers Mutual Casualty Co. v Pigeon Creek Corp. 1 Ark App 179, 614 SW2d 516 (1981).

statement in the application binds the insured, if the policy and the attached application are retained without objection to such statement.

(b) STATUTORY PROVISIONS AS PART OF THE CONTRACT. When a statute requires that insurance contracts contain certain provisions or cover certain specified losses, a contract of insurance that does not comply with the statute will be interpreted as though it contained all the provisions required by the statute.[6] When a statute requires that the insurance contract include any exceptions, limitations, or restrictions, then the insurer may not rely upon an exception, limitation, or restriction not stated in the contract to defeat an insured's claim, as illustrated in the *Domke* case.

[6] Samson v Transamerica Ins. Co. 30 Cal 3d 220, 178 Cal Rptr 343, 636 P2d 32 (1981).

DOMKE V F&M SAVINGS BANK & N.C. LIFE INS. CO.
(Minn App) 363 NW2d 898 (1985)

On April 16, 1975, Edwin Domke submitted an application for disability insurance, under a group insurance plan, to cover the mortgage on his house. He filled out the application listing a hearing impairment as "slight" and setting forth a medical history. Domke was issued a four-page Certificate of Insurance and was not given a copy of the group master policy that excluded from coverage preexisting conditions. In January 1977, Domke resigned his employment because of his hearing loss, related vertigo problems, and arthritis, and applied for benefits under the mortgage disability policy. The insurance company denied benefits because of alleged false statements in his application and the fact that the master policy excluded coverage for preexisting conditions. From a judgment for Domke, the insurance company appealed.

RANDALL, J. . . . [A Minnesota statute regulating insurance] provides that:

The falsity of any statement in the application for any policy . . . may not bar the right to recovery thereunder unless such false statement materially affected either the acceptance of the risk or the hazard assumed by the insurer.

Appellant contends that respondent materially misrepresented his hearing condition on the application by failing to list the physicians who treated him at Mayo and by describing his hearing loss as "slight." The trial court, however, found as a fact that there was no material misrepresentation by respondent, since respondent's description of his hearing loss as "slight" was the one used by doctors at Mayo in the mid-60's, and since his failure to list the name of his doctor at Mayo was due simply to his inability to remember. Findings of fact of the trial court may not be disturbed unless they are clearly erroneous. There is evidence in the record to support the court's finding; therefore, we do not disturb it.

Further, even if respondent's statements in his application could be construed as false, support for the position that they did not affect either the acceptance of the risk or the hazard assumed comes from the insurer's failure to inquire or investigate further before issuing coverage. While the insurer did not have the name of the physician who treated respondent for hearing loss, it did have the name of respondent's family physician and the name of a physician who had given respondent an annual physical. It did not ask either of those physicians any questions about respondent's hearing loss, nor did it ask respondent to supply the name of the treating physician before it took action on the application. An insurer's failure to inquire when a basis for inquiry is set out on the application may constitute a waiver of the right to use the nondisclosure as a basis for denying coverage. Respondent's application clearly set out a basis for inquiry.

The trial court found that the language in the Certificate of Insurance issued to respondent should constitute the contract between the parties. The certificate did not include any reference to pre-existing conditions; the master policy did. Appellant argues that the certificate stated it was subject to the terms of the master policy and that respondent was familiar enough with insurance contracts to know that. The language of the master contract should, therefore, be controlling, appellant argues.

Respondent himself testified that he knew the *brochure* sent him by F & M was only advertising. He thought, however, that all the essential aspects of the policy's coverage were described in the *certificate* and that he could rely on it. The certificate itself stated that it summarized the "principal provisions" of the master policy.

Minn.Stat. § 62B.06, subd. 2 (1982) provides that[:]

Each individual . . . group certificate of . . . credit, accident and health insurance shall . . . set forth . . . a description of the amount, term and coverage *including any exceptions, limitations and restrictions*. . . . [Emphasis supplied.]

The exclusion of pre-existing conditions from coverage is clearly an exception, limitation, or restriction. Since it was not set forth in the certificate issued to respondent, appellant may not rely upon it to defeat respondent's claim. . . .

Trial court did not err in finding that respondent made no misrepresentations or false statements in his application. The insurer could not rely upon the master policy to deny coverage because respondent's disability resulted from a pre-existing condition. The Certificate of Insurance supplied to insured contained no such exclusion or exemption. . . .

[Judgment affirmed]

QUESTIONS

1. May an insurer waive its right to use an applicant's nondisclosure as a basis for denying liability?
2. What was the contract between the parties?
3. Could the insurer rely upon the exclusion of preexisting conditions set forth in the master policy as a basis for denying coverage?

(c) **DUTIES OF PARTIES TO INSURANCE CONTRACT.** The insured and the insurer owe each other the obligations imposed by the insurance contract. The duty to act in good faith requires that an applicant for insurance tell the insurer any fact material to the risk.[7] The insurer is under the obligation to make any investigation that is required to determine the facts of the case, to make reasonable efforts to settle any claim asserted against the insured when the insurance provides protection from claims of third persons, and to defend the insured if such claims cannot be settled.[8]

§ 40:4   WHEN THE INSURANCE CONTRACT IS EFFECTIVE

An applicant for insurance may or may not be protected by insurance before the written policy is issued. Four situations may arise:

(1) When the applicant tells a broker to obtain property or liability insurance, the applicant is merely employing the broker as an agent. If the broker procures a policy, the customer is insured. If the broker fails to do so, the customer does not have any insurance, but the broker may be personally liable to the customer for the loss.

(2) The person seeking insurance and the insurer or its agent may agree that the applicant will be protected by insurance during the interval between the time the application is received and the time when the insurer either rejects the application, or accepts it and issues a policy. This agreement to protect the applicant by insurance during such an interval is binding even though it is oral. Generally, however, when such a preliminary contract is made, the agent will sign a memorandum stating the essential terms of the policy to be executed. This oral contract and the written memorandum are called **binders.**

An **oral binder** of insurance is a temporary contract that terminates when the written policy contemplated by it is issued.[9] In some states, a maximum duration for an oral contract of insurance is set by statute.

(3) The parties may agree that at a later time a policy will be issued and delivered. In that case the insurance contract is not in effect until the policy is delivered or sent to the applicant. Accordingly, loss sustained after the transaction between the applicant and the insurance agent but before the delivery of the policy is not covered by the policy thereafter delivered.

(4) The parties may agree that a policy of life insurance shall be binding upon the payment of the first premium, even though the applicant has not been examined, provided the applicant thereafter passes an examination.

(a) *Delivery of Policy.* Ordinarily, delivery of the policy is not essential to the existence of a contract of insurance. As an exception, delivery of the policy may be made an express condition to coverage.

(b) *Prepayment of Premiums.* Ordinarily, a contract of property insurance exists even though the premium due has not been paid. Thus, it is possible to effect property and liability insurance in most cases by an oral binder or agreement, as by a telephone call. In the case of life insurance policies, it is common to require both (1) delivery of the policy to the insured while the insured is in a condition of good health and (2) the prepayment of the first premium on the policy.

(c) *When Coverage Is Effective.* Distinct from the question of when is there a contract of insurance is the question of when does the coverage of the risk commence under a contract of insurance. Some policies of insurance do not cover the specified risk

---

[7]   Topps v Universal Life Ins. Co. (La App) 396 So 2d 394 (1981).
[8]   Hartford Insurance Group v District Court (Colo) 625 P2d 1013 (1981).

[9]   Terry v Mongin Insurance Agency, 102 Wis 2d 239, 306 NW2d 270 (1981).

until after a certain period of time has elapsed. That is, there is a waiting period before the contract of insurance provides protection. In most kinds of insurance, the coverage is immediately effective so that there is no waiting period once the insurer has accepted the application and has thereby created a contract of insurance between the parties.

(d) *Machine-Vended Insurance*. When insurance is sold by a vending machine, as in the case of air flight insurance, it becomes effective when the applicant places the application and the premium in the machine and receives a receipt.

§ 40:5   MODIFICATION OF CONTRACT

As is the case with most contracts, a contract of insurance can be modified if both insurer and insured agree to the change. The insurer cannot modify the contract without the consent of the insured when the right to do so is not reserved in the insurance contract.[10]

In order to make changes or corrections to the policy, it is not necessary to issue a new policy. An indorsement on the policy or the execution of a separate **rider** is effective for the purpose of changing the policy.

---

[10]   Krebs v Strange (Miss) 419 So 2d 178 (1982).

When a provision of an indorsement conflicts with a provision of the policy, the indorsement controls because it is the later document.

§ 40:6   INTERPRETATION OF CONTRACT

The contract of insurance is interpreted by the same rules that govern the interpretation of ordinary contracts. Words are to be given their ordinary meaning and interpreted in light of the nature of the coverage intended. Thus, an employee who had been killed was not regarded as disabled within the meaning of a group policy covering employees.

The courts are increasingly recognizing the fact that most persons obtaining insurance are not specially trained, and therefore, the contract of insurance is to be read as it would be understood by the average person or by the average person in business, rather than by one with technical knowledge of the law or of insurance.[11]

If there is an ambiguity in the policy, the provision is interpreted against the insurer. In some instances courts will give a liberal interpretation to the policy terms in order to favor the insured or the beneficiary on the basis that the insured did not in fact have a free choice. As the *Baurer* case illustrates, exclusionary clauses are commonly subject to interpretation that favors the insured.

---

[11]   Coconio County v Fund Administrators Assn. Inc. 49 Ariz 42, 719 P2d 693 (1986).

BAURER V MOUNTAIN WEST FARM BUREAU INS.
__ Mont __, 695 P2d 1307 (1985)

R. F. Baurer purchased a White freightliner tractor for $56,000 in August of 1980 under an agreement with his son-in-law Craig Britton. Under the agreement, Britton would care for the vehicle and use it in the trucking business. In return, Britton would haul Baurer's hay and cattle at no charge. Baurer had been paying approximately $30,000 for such service.

Baurer at all times had the right to control the vehicle. Baurer insured the vehicle with Mountain West Farm Bureau Insurance Co. On December 8, 1982, the vehicle was destroyed while pulling a trailer load of cattle belonging to Britton. Mountain West refused to pay on the policy contending that the arrangement between Baurer and Britton was a lease of the tractor which was excluded under the policy. Baurer brought suit contending that it was a "share expense basis" allowed under the policy. From a judgment for Baurer, Mountain West appealed.

SHEEHY, J. . . . In truth, there is little dispute between the parties as to the facts of this case. What is in dispute is the legal effect of the arrangement between Baurer and Britton, that is whether the arrangement constituted a lease as a matter of law, or an arrangement for shared expenses, as determined by the District Court.

An ambiguous provision in an insurance policy is construed against the insurance company. A clause in an insurance policy is ambiguous when different persons looking at it in the light of its purpose cannot agree upon its meaning. If the language is unambiguous, and subject to only one meaning, there is no basis for the interpretation of policy coverage under the guise of ambiguity. In interpreting and applying insurance contracts, the common rather than technical usage and meaning of definitional terms and policies should be used. Regardless of ambiguity, however, exclusions and words of limitation in a policy must be strictly construed against the insurer. . . . If the policy language is ambiguous as applied to the facts of a case, the construction most favorable to the insured should be adopted. Such construction applies particularly to exclusionary clauses.

With the foregoing background of applicable law on the construction of insurance contracts, we look at the exclusionary clause relied on by Mountain West:

> We don't insure your [truck] while it is rented or leased to others or used to carry persons for a charge. This does not apply to the use of your [truck] on a share expense basis.

Under the facts of this case, the truck was not being used to carry persons for a charge, and that exclusion does not apply. Without quibble we can say the exclusion does not apply to the use of the truck on a "share expense basis." The exclusion does apply if the truck is rented or leased to others, but it is arguable under the language used that the exclusion would not apply if it were rented or leased on a share expense basis.

We are unable to say that the arrangement between Baurer and Britton here was a lease or rental as a matter of law. Although it was a contract by which Baurer gave to Britton the temporary use of his property for a reward, and it was to be returned to him at a future time, and Britton had the duty of keeping the tractor in repair; yet the agreement did not contemplate that Baurer would have to put the tractor in the condition fit for the purpose for which it was delivered to Britton or to repair all deteriorations thereof not occasioned by the fault of Britton. In an ordinary rental of personal property, the hirer must bear all the expenses concerning it as might naturally be foreseen to attend it during its use by him. It would seem that the cost of insurance against physical damage is an expense that might naturally be foreseen, and an expense that must be borne by Britton, if the arrangement were a lease. . . .

We are convinced in this case that the arrangement between Baurer and Britton was one for sharing of expenses. Baurer as owner bore the expense of the purchase of the truck and providing its insurance. In return for its use, Britton hauled Baurer's cattle and hay for no charge whenever it was demanded of him. Thus Britton bore the expense that would ordinarily be borne by Baurer for that item. It is clear therefore that the arrangement between Baurer and Britton, whatever else it was, was one for the sharing of expenses that were incidental to the operation of the use of the tractor. In that circumstance, the use was not within the exclusion to the policy coverage relating to leased and rented vehicles. . . .

[Judgment affirmed]

Questions

1. Identify the contractual language at the heart of the dispute.
2. What standards of contract interpretation were applied in construing the exclusionary clause?
3. Did the court find that the truck in question was "rented or leased to others"?

---

§ 40:7   Premiums

Premiums may be paid by check. If the check is not paid by the bank, however, the instrument loses its character as payment.

If the premiums are not paid, the policy will ordinarily lapse because of nonpayment, subject to anti-lapse statutes or provisions.

(a) Return of Unearned Premiums. When an insurance policy is canceled before the expiration of the term for which premiums have been paid, the insurer is required to return any unearned premiums.

(b) Nonforfeiture and Anti-lapse Provisions. As to the payment of premiums due on life insurance policies subsequent to the first premium, the policies now in general use provide, or a statute may specify, that the policy shall not automatically lapse upon the date the premium is due if payment is not then made. By policy provision or statute, the insured is also allowed a **grace period** of 30 to 31 days in which to make payment of the premium due.[12] When there is a default in the payment of a premium by the insured, the insurer may be required by statute (1) to issue a paid-up policy in a smaller amount, (2) to provide extended insurance for a period of time, or (3) to pay the cash surrender value of the policy.

§ 40:8   Extent of Insurer's Liability

In the case of life and disability insurance, the insurer is required to pay the amount called for by the contract of insurance. When the policy is one to indemnify against loss, the liability of the insurer is to pay only to the extent that the insured sustains loss, subject to a maximum amount stated in the contract. Thus, a fire insurer is liable for only $1,000, even though it has written a $20,000 policy, when the fire loss sustained by the insured is in fact only

---

[12]   Flowers v Provident Life and Acc. Ins. Co. (Tenn) 713 SW2d 6 (1986).

$1,000. If the loss were $22,000, the liability of the insurer would be limited by the face amount of the policy to only $20,000.

§ 40:9   CANCELLATION

The contract of insurance may expressly declare that it may or may not be canceled by the insurer's unilateral act. By statute or policy provision, the insurer is commonly required to give a specific number of days' written notice of cancellation.

Property and liability policies generally reserve to the insurer the right to cancel the policy upon giving a specified number of days' notice. In some states, antidiscrimination statutes restrict the right of insurers to cancel. An insurance company may not exercise its right to cancel the policy when it does so to punish the insured for having appeared as a witness in a case against it.

Only the insured is entitled to notice of cancellation unless the policy or an indorsement expressly declares otherwise. The mere fact that a creditor is entitled to the proceeds of the insurance policy in the case of loss does not in itself entitle the creditor to notice of cancellation of the policy.

§ 40:10   COVERAGE OF POLICY

When an insurance claim is disputed by the insurer, the person bringing suit has the burden of proving that there was a loss, that it occurred while the policy was in force, and that the loss was a kind that was within the coverage or scope of the policy.

A policy will contain exceptions to the coverage. This means that the policy is not applicable when an exception applies to the situation.[13] Exceptions to coverage are generally strictly interpreted against the insurer. The insurer has the burden of proving that the facts were such that there was

no coverage because an exception applied. There is also a modern trend that holds that although an exception is literally applicable to the situation it will be ignored and coverage sustained when there is no cause and effect relationship between the loss and the conduct that was the violation of the exception.

B.   OTHER
         CONSIDERATIONS

Insurer defenses, bad faith on the part of the insurer, time limitations on the insured, and the insurer's subrogation rights are now considered.

§ 40:11 DEFENSES OF THE INSURER

The insurer may raise any defense that would be valid in an action upon a contract. Some defenses that do not apply to an action on an ordinary contract may also be raised. In a given case, the insurer may be barred from raising a particular defense because it has waived that defense or is estopped from asserting it.

§ 40:12   INSURER BAD FAITH

When it is the insurer's duty to defend the insured and the insurer wrongfully refuses to do so, the insurer is guilty of breach of contract and is liable for all consequential damages resulting from the breach. In some jurisdictions an insured can recover for an excess judgment rendered against the insured when it is proven that the insurer was guilty of negligence or bad faith in failing to defend the action and settle the matter within policy limits.[14]

In some states laws have been enacted making an insurer liable for a statutory penalty and attorneys' fees in case of a failure or delay, in bad faith, to pay a valid claim within a specified period of time. A

[13] Fireman's Fund Ins. v Fibreboard Corp. 182 Cal App 3d 462, 227 Cal Rptr 203 (1986).

[14] Hodges v State Farm (DC SC) 488 F Supp 1057 (1980).

bad faith refusal is generally considered to be any frivolous or unfounded refusal to comply with the demand of a policyholder to pay according to the policy.[15] Penalties are improper when the insurer has any reasonable ground to contest the claim or when there is a bona fide dispute as to a material fact relevant to whether the insurer is liable.

In the *Filasky* case the court was faced with the questions of whether, in addition to the benefits due the insured under her policies, she was entitled to compensatory and punitive damages for bad faith failure to investigate and pay her claims.

[15]   White v Unigard Mutual Ins. Co. 112 Idaho 94, 730 P2d 1014 (1986).

FILASKY V PREFERRED RISK MUTUAL INS. CO.
___ Ariz ___, 734 P2d 76 (1987)

Linda Filasky was insured by Preferred Risk Mutual Insurance Company under automobile and homeowner's insurance policies. On June 17, 1982, while working, she was injured in an automobile accident and was hospitalized for two weeks. While in the hospital, her home was burglarized and many valuable items were stolen. On July 7, 1982, a rain storm damaged her roof and family room. She filed a claim for lost income benefits under her automobile policy and filed claims for theft loss and water damage under her homeowner's policy. Filasky sued Preferred Risk for the bad faith delay in settling claims under her two policies, contending that it took groundless positions and failed to adequately investigate her claims. Ultimately, all benefits due Filasky were paid by January 25, 1984. From a judgment for Filasky for $100,000 compensatory damages and $1,000,000 in punitive damages, Preferred Risk appealed.

GORDON, C.J. . . . In 1981 we recognized that an insurer has a legal duty to act in good faith when settling its policyholders' claims; violation of that duty constitutes a tort. An insurer can challenge claims that are "fairly debatable"; however, it breaches its legal duty when it "intentionally denies or fails to process or pay a claim without a reasonable basis for such action." *Linthicum v. Nationwide Life Insurance Company*, 150 Ariz. 354, 362 (App. 1985); *aff'd*, 150 Ariz. 36 (1986). We recently wrote:

> To be liable for tort damages, it [the insurer] need only to have intended its act or omission [of denying or failing to provide the insured with the security and protection from calamity which is the object of the relationship], lacking a founded belief that such conduct was permitted by the policy.
>
> The founded belief is absent when the insurer either knows that its position is groundless or when it fails to undertake an investigation adequate to determine whether its position is tenable. In either event, its position is without reasonable basis and subjects it to payment of damages in addition to those traditionally recoverable in a breach of contract action.

Rawlings v. Apodaca, 151 Ariz. 149, 160, 726 P.2d 565, 576 (1986).

. . . All of the evidence clearly suggests that reasons given by Preferred Risk for delaying settlement of Filasky's three claims were groundless or inadequately investigated and supports the jury's conclusion that Preferred Risk breached its duty to deal with Filasky in good faith.

Compensatory Damages

The jury awarded compensatory damages of $100,000 to Filasky for her emotional distress and attorneys' fees. To recover damages for emotional distress caused by the insurer's bad faith, the insured must demonstrate that the insurer's bad faith resulted in an invasion of property rights. . . . Damages for pain, humiliation, or inconvenience, as well as pecuniary losses for expenses such as attorney's fees, trigger an invasion of protected property rights.

Evidence supports the jury's $100,000 compensatory damage award. Not only did Filasky incur economic losses of approximately $4000 in attorney's fees and the lost time value of her insurance proceeds, she also endured months of overwhelming inconvenience and frustration caused by Preferred Risk's callous disregard for her plight. The record indicates that Filasky may have been able to maintain her house payments if Preferred Risk had paid her lost wages claim on a timely basis. The record also indicates that Preferred Risk frustrated Filasky's attempts at resolving her claims by engaging in such dilatory tactics as not returning her telephone calls, ignoring her pleas for personal assistance in completing forms, repeating requests with which Filasky had already complied, and rejecting her claims but providing no reasons for doing so.

We do not believe the jury's compensatory damage award of $100,000 was motivated by passion or prejudice; nor do we believe the amount is excessive or grossly disproportionate to the damage incurred. The evidence reveals that Filasky suffered pecuniary losses and damages for frustration, inconvenience, and humiliation. In our opinion, the record fully justifies the jury's award of $100,000 in compensatory damages for emotional distress and attorneys' fees.

Punitive Damages

Punitive damages may be awarded in a bad faith insurance case. However, punitive damages may not be awarded in a bad faith insurance case absent evidence reflecting "something more" than conduct necessary to establish the tort. We recently articulated a standard for determining whether the requisite "something more" exists:

> To obtain punitive damages, plaintiff must also show that the evil hand that unjustifiably damaged the objectives sought to be reached by the insurance contract was guided by an evil mind which either consciously sought to damage the insured or acted intentionally, knowing that its conduct was likely to cause unjustified, significant damage to the insured. When defendant's motives are shown to be so improper, *or* its conduct so oppressive, outrageous or intolerable that such an "evil mind" may be inferred, punitive damages may be awarded.

Rawlings, 151 Ariz. at 162-63, 726 P.2d at 578-79. . . .

. . . Preferred Risk's reasons for its dilatory settlement of Filasky's three claims were either groundless or inadequately investigated. This conduct supported the jury's conclusion that Preferred Risk acted in bad faith. However, evidence of "something more" than indifference to facts and failure to properly and timely investigate an insurance claim must exist before the trial court can instruct the jury on punitive damages. We have read the record and conclude that evidence that Preferred Risk acted toward Filasky in an aggravated, outrageous, malicious, or fraudulent manner, that Preferred Risk was guided by an evil mind which either consciously sought to injure Filasky or acted intentionally, knowing that its conduct was likely to cause unjustified, significant damage to Filasky, is slight and inconclusive at best. Therefore, the trial judge erred in submitting the issue of punitive damages to the jury.

Conclusion

We affirm the jury's finding of bad faith and its compensatory damage award of $100,000. We reverse its punitive damage award of $1,000,000 and remand this case to the trial court for entry of judgment consistent with this opinion.

[Affirmed in part; reversed in part]

QUESTIONS

1. Does an insurer's failure to settle the insured's claims in good faith constitute a tort?
2. Did the appeals court allow a compensatory award for pecuniary losses and damages for frustration, inconvenience, and humiliation in addition to the insurance benefits due the insured under the two policies?
3. What must an insured prove to be entitled to recover punitive damages in an action claiming that the insurer had failed to act in good faith?

---

§ 40:13   TIME LIMITATIONS ON INSURED

The insured is subject to a number of time limitations in making a claim against the insurer. If the insured does not satisfy all time limitations, the insurer is not liable.

(a) NOTIFICATION OF CLAIM. The insured is generally required to give the insurer prompt or immediate notice of any claim that arises under the policy. Notice that is given within a reasonable time is ordinarily sufficient, even though the policy requires "immediate" notice or notice "as soon as practicable."[16]

(b) PROOF OF LOSS. Within a stated number of days after an occurrence within the coverage of the policy, the insured must file a formal written statement of the claim that is made against the insurer. This written claim is called a **proof of loss**.

(c) CONTRACT LIMITATION ON TIME FOR SUIT. The policy or contract of insurance will ordinarily state that suit must be brought on the policy within a specified period of time.[17]

(d) STATUTE OF LIMITATIONS. Without regard to any time limitation in the contract between the parties, the general statute of limitations applicable to contract actions will set a time limit after the expiration of which no suit may be brought on the policy.[18]

Typically, the period allowed by the statute of limitations is longer than the period specified in the contract or policy of insurance.

§ 40:14   SUBROGATION OF INSURER

In some instances, the insured has a claim against a third person for the harm covered by the insurance policy. For example, the insured (who has an automobile collision insurance policy) who is in a collision may have a claim against the other driver. If the insurer pays the insured the full amount of the insured's claim, the insurer is then subrogated to the insured's claim against the third person who caused the harm.[19] This means that the insurer acquires the claim

---

[16]   Allstate Ins. Co. v Moon, 89 App Div 2d 804, 453 NYS2d 467 (1982).
[17]   Herring v Middle Georgia Mutual Ins. Co. 149 Ga App 585, 254 SE2d 904 (1979).

[18]   Hearn v Rickenbacker, 140 Mich App 525, 364 NW2d 371 (1985).
[19]   Johnson v State Farm Fire and Casualty Co. 151 Ill App 3d 879, 104 Ill Dec 890, 503 NE2d 602 (1987).

of the insured against the third person just as though the insured had assigned the claim to the insurer. When the insurer is subrogated to the insured's claim, the insurer may enforce that claim against the third person.[20] The insurer is entitled to keep from the money recovered from the third person an amount equal to the payment made by the insurer to the insured, together with interest and costs.

[20]   Bowen v Waters, 170 Ga App 65, 316 SE2d 497 (1984).

1.

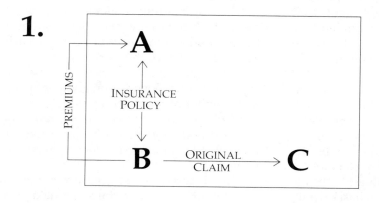

A = INSURER

B = INSURED

2.

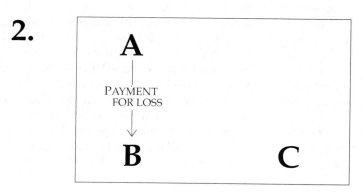

C = THIRD PARTY
WHO CAUSED
B TO
SUSTAIN
LOSS

3.

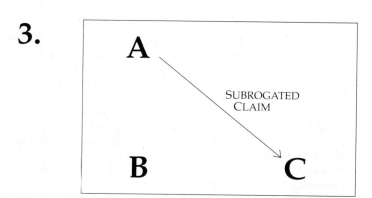

FIGURE 40-1
SUBROGATION

Summary

Insurance is a contract, called a policy, by which a provision is made by the insurer, in consideration of premium payments made by the insured, to pay the insured or beneficiary a sum of money if the insured sustains a specified loss. These contracts are made through an insurance agent, who is an agent for the insurance company, or through an insurance broker, who is the agent of the insured when obtaining a policy for the latter.

The person purchasing an insurance contract must have an insurable interest in the subject matter insured, be it life or property. An insurable interest in property exists when the damage or destruction of the property will cause a direct monetary loss to the insured. An insurable interest in the life of the insured exists if the purchaser would suffer a financial loss from the insured's death, as of the time the policy is obtained.

The insurer may agree to protect the applicant by an oral binder during the interval while the insurance application is being processed. A binder is a temporary contract that terminates when the written policy contemplated is issued.

Changes to an insurance policy may be made by executing a rider or adding an indorsement to the policy.

If premiums are not paid, the policy will ordinarily lapse, subject to anti-lapse statutes that may provide for a thirty-day grace period in which to make the payment. In the case of some forms of life insurance, the insurer may be required by statute (1) to issue a paid-up policy in a smaller amount, (2) to provide extended insurance for a period of time, or (3) to pay the cash surrender value of the policy.

The insurer may expressly reserve the right to cancel a policy upon giving a specified number of days written notice.

Insurance policies commonly contain exceptions to coverage, which exceptions are generally strictly construed against the insurer.

The insured must comply with a number of time limitations in making a claim; such as, promptly notifying the insurer of any claim that may arise, submitting a proof of loss statement within the time set forth in the policy, and bringing any court actions based upon the policy within a specified time period.

When the insurer pays a claim under a policy, it is then subrogated to the insured's claim against the third party and may enforce the insured's claim against the third party.

Questions and Case Problems

1. What social forces are affected by imposing the requirement of insurable interest?
2. Vazquez told Litchfield to obtain a policy of insurance on the former's house. Litchfield was in the business of obtaining policies of insurance for members of the general public. He obtained a policy of insurance for Vazquez from the Century Indemnity Company. She paid Litchfield the money due for the premium on the policy but he never sent the money to Century which then canceled Vazquez' policy. She claimed that it could not do this because she had paid Litchfield. Was she correct?
3. How may a contract of insurance be modified?
4. Schellinger obtained a policy of insurance on his life from the Simpson Insurance Company. In order to obtain the policy he made false statements as to his prior medical history. The company learned of the misrepresentation and brought a suit a few months later to cancel the policy for fraud. Schellinger claimed that the policy, once issued, could not be set aside even if he were guilty of fraud because the policy exceptions did not include fraud as one of the situations in which the insurer would not be liable. Was he correct?

5. Compare (a) a contract of insurance, and (b) an ordinary contract.

6. What time limits may bar an insured from recovering on the policy questioned?

7. Lisle applied for life insurance with the Federal Life & Casualty Co. Both Lisle and his wife made false, fraudulent statements to the insurer in connection with the application. The insurer's physician examined Lisle twice but did not ascertain anything that revealed the falsity of those statements. After the insured's death about a year later, the insurer denied liability on the ground of fraud. Lisle's widow claimed that the insurer could not raise the question of fraud since it had examined the insured before accepting his application. Was the insurer liable? [Federal Life & Casualty Co. v Lisle, 140 Ohio 2d 269, 172 NE2d 919]

8. James Butler purchased a stolen automobile without knowing that it had been stolen. He insured it with Farmers Insurance Company. The policy covered loss by accidental means. The automobile was seized by the local police and returned to its true owner. Butler then sued on his insurance policy, claiming that there had been a loss by accidental means. The insurer raised the defense that Butler did not have an insurable interest in the automobile because it was a stolen car. Was this defense valid? [Butler v Farmers Insurance Co. 126 Ariz 377, 616 P2d 46]

9. On October 29, Griffin sent an application for life insurance and the first premium to the Insurance Company of North America. In the application, her son, Carlisle Moore, was named as beneficiary. On November 25 of the same year, Griffin died. On November 26, the company rejected the application and notified the broker who took the application, who in turn notified Moore by letter dated November 30. Moore sued the company for breach of contract. Decide. [Moore v Insurance Co. of North America, 49 Ill App 2d 287, 200 NE2d 1]

10. From the United Insurance Co., Rebecca Foster obtained a policy insuring the life of Lucille McClurkin and naming herself as beneficiary. Lucille did not live with Rebecca, and Rebecca did not inform Lucille of the existence of the policy. Rebecca paid the premiums on the policy and, upon the death of Lucille, sued the United Insurance Co. for the amount of the insurance. At the trial, Rebecca testified vaguely that her father had told her that Lucille was her second cousin on his side of the family. Was Rebecca entitled to recover on the policy? [Foster v United Insurance Co. 250 SC 423, 158 SE2d 201]

11. Moore's wife applied for accident insurance on her husband. She paid the premium due. Unknown to her, the application was rejected. However, when she inquired of the agent as to the status of the application, the agent said that he had had no word. When she inquired some time later, the agent said he thought that the policy had come in and, if it had not, she would be notified in a few days. She heard nothing. Two weeks later her husband was killed accidentally. After his death the insurance company informed her that the application had been rejected. She sued the insurance company. Decide. [Moore v Palmetto State Life Insurance Co. 222 SC 492, 73 SE2d 688]

12. Mike Edwards insured his car against theft with the State Farm Mutual Automobile Insurance Company. He later sold the car to Steven Davis who paid for the car with a bad check that the bank refused to honor because of insufficient funds. Neither Steven nor the car were ever seen again. Mike claimed that his insurance company was liable for the loss on the ground that the policy covered theft, and there had been a theft of his car. The insurance company answered that Edwards had been defrauded by the use of the bad check but that this was not a theft of the car. [Edwards v State Farm Automobile Ins. Co. (Iowa) 296 NW2d 804]

13. Assistant manager trainee R. G. Smith suspected Bowen of shoplifting at Broad & Marshall Department Store. After getting permission from the store manager to follow her, he observed Bowen driving out of the store's parking lot. Smith followed her in his car and forced her into a ditch, where her car overturned and was destroyed. Bowen received the fair market value for her car from her insurance company, General National Mutual (GNM), and executed a subrogation agreement in connection with this payment. Bowen is planning on bringing suit against Smith and the store for actual and punitive damages for the injury and

indignity suffered. GNM brought suit against Smith and the store for damage to the car. They defend that GNM is not the proper party plaintiff. Decide.

14. Stefan Etterle and his wife, Justyna, insured their house with Excelsior Insurance Co. The policy protected them from damage to the dwelling by fire. Some time later, they transferred the title of the house to their son Stephen as a matter of convenience because of their ill health. Two months later, the house was damaged by fire. The parents and the son demanded payment on the policy for the loss sustained. Excelsior refused to make payment on the ground that the parents did not have any insurable interest in the property and that the son was not named on the policy. Decide. [Etterle v Excelsior Ins. Co., 74 App Div 2d 436, 428 NYS2d 95]

15. Collins owned a Piper Colt airplane. He obtained from the South Carolina Insurance Company a liability policy covering the plane. The policy provided that it did not cover loss sustained while the plane was being piloted by a person who did not have a valid pilot's certificate and a valid medical examination certificate. Collins held a valid pilot's certificate but his medical examination certificate had expired three months before. Collins was piloting the plane when it crashed, and he was killed. The insurer denied liability because Collins did not have a valid medical certificate. It was stipulated by both parties that the crash was in no way caused by the absence of the medical certificate. [South Carolina Insurance Company v Collins (SC) 237 SE2d 358]

41

KINDS OF INSURANCE

Both businesses and individuals are exposed to the risk of loss of property due to damage, destruction, or theft as well as the risk of economic losses due to legal liability for individual actions and the actions of employees. Employers and employees seek protection against the risk of economic losses due to employees' sicknesses or accidents, and employers seek protection against the risks involved in the unforeseeable events that may cause the interruption of their businesses. Individuals seek to protect their families' financial security in case of their own untimely deaths, while businesses seek to protect against economic harm resulting from the death of key employees. The insurance industry offers a wide range of insurance plans to provide protection suited to the wide range of needs faced by businesses and individuals.

Businesses today have specialized risk managers who identify the risks to which individual businesses are exposed, measure those risks, and purchase insurance to cover those risks (or decide to self-insure in whole or in part).

Businesses may purchase comprehensive "all risk" business liability and indemnity policies. Businesses may also purchase policies providing liability insurance for their directors and officers. (As will be seen in Chapter 52, because of recent adverse court decisions against corporate directors and officers, premiums and deductibles for this kind of insurance have increased, and availability has decreased.) Businesses may purchase specialized insurance to meet their individual needs. For example, computer hardware and software companies purchase insurance policies to protect against the losses caused by computer products.

Professionals such as doctors, lawyers, accountants, architects, and engineers commonly purchase malpractice insurance. This insurance provides comprehensive coverage for liability due to mistakes made while practicing their professions.

Insurance policies can be grouped into a few categories in terms of the nature of the interest protected. Fire, homeowner's, automobile, and life insurance will be considered in this chapter.

A.   Fire Insurance

A **fire insurance policy** is a contract to indemnify the insured for destruction of or damage to property caused by fire. In almost every state, the New York standard fire insurance form is the standard policy.

§ 41:1   Nature of Contract

In order for fire loss to be covered by fire insurance, there must be an actual, hostile fire that is the immediate or proximate cause of the loss.

(a) Actual, Hostile Fire. The hostile character is easily determined when the fire is caused by accident, such as a short circuit in electric wiring; but it is often difficult to determine if the fire is intentional when, for example, it is being used for heating or cooking. A **hostile fire** in the latter case is one which to some extent becomes uncontrollable, burns with excessive heat, or escapes from the place where it is intended to be.[1] To illustrate, when soot is ignited and causes a fire in the chimney, the fire is hostile. On the other hand, a loss caused by the smoke or heat of a fire in its ordinary container, which has not broken out or become uncontrollable, results from a **friendly fire**, and is not covered by the policy.

By policy endorsement, the coverage may be, and frequently is, extended to include loss by a friendly fire.

(b) Immediate or Proximate Cause. In addition to direct destruction or damage by fire, a fire may set in motion a chain of events that damages property. When there is a reasonable connection between a fire and the ultimate loss sustained, the insurer under a fire insurance policy is liable for the loss.

The New York standard form of fire insurance policy excludes loss or damage caused directly or indirectly by enemy attack by armed forces, invasion, insurrection, rebellion, revolution, civil war, or usurped power, or by order of any civil authority; or by neglect of the insured to use all reasonable means to save and preserve the property at and after a fire or when the property is endangered by fire in neighboring premises; or by theft.

§ 41:2   Determination of Insurer's Liability

Basically, the insurer is liable for the actual amount of the loss sustained. This liability

---

[1] Schulze and Burch Biscuit Co. v American Protection Ins. Co. 96 Ill App 3d 350, 421 NE2d 331 (1981).

is limited, however, by the maximum amount stated in the policy or the amount of damages sustained by total destruction of the property, whichever is less.

(a) AMOUNT OF LOSS. The amount of a total loss, in the absence of statute or agreement to the contrary, is the actual cash value of the property at the time of the loss. If the insurer and the insured cannot agree, policies commonly provide for the determination of the amount of loss by appraisers or arbitrators.

(b) TOTAL LOSS. A **total loss** does not necessarily mean that the property has been completely destroyed. The loss is regarded as being total if the unconsumed portion is of no value for the purposes for which the property was utilized at the time of the insurance. Consequently, the mere fact that some of the walls and the roof remain after the fire does not prove that the loss of a house was not total.

(c) REPLACEMENT BY INSURER. Frequently, the insurer will stipulate in the policy that it has the right to replace or restore the property to its former condition in lieu of paying the insured the cash value of the loss.[2]

(d) COINSURANCE. A **coinsurance clause** requires the insured to maintain insurance on the covered property up to a certain amount or a certain percent of the value, generally 80 percent. Under such a provision, if the policyholder insures the property for less than the required amount, the insurer is liable only for the proportionate share of the amount of insurance required to be carried. To illustrate, suppose the owner of a building with a value of $200,000 insures it against loss to the extent of $120,000, and the policy contains a coinsurance clause requiring that insurance of 80 percent of the value of the property be carried. Assume that an $80,000 loss is then sustained. The insured would not receive $80,000 from the insurer but only three-fourths of that amount, which is $60,000, because the amount of the insurance carried ($120,000) is only three-fourths of the amount required ($160,000, that is, 80 percent of $200,000).

The use of a coinsurance clause is not permitted in all states. In some states, it is prohibited or is permitted only with the consent of the insured.

§ 41:3   ASSIGNMENT OF FIRE
          INSURANCE POLICY

Fire insurance is a personal contract, and in the absence of statute or contractual authorization it cannot be assigned before a loss is sustained without the consent of the insurer. In addition, it is commonly provided that the policy shall be void if an assignment to give a purchaser of the property the protection of the policy is attempted. Such a forfeiture clause applies only when the insured attempts to transfer total ownership of the policy. It does not apply to an assignment as security for a loan to the insured.

§ 41:4   MORTGAGE CLAUSE

If the insured property is subject to a mortgage, either or both the mortgagor and mortgagee may take out policies of fire insurance to protect their respective interests in the property. Each has an insurable interest therein. In the absence of a contrary stipulation, the policy taken out by either covers only that insured's own interest. That is, the mortgagor's policy protects only the value of the mortgagor's right to redemption or the value of the property in excess of the mortgage, while the policy of the mortgagee covers only the debt. Neither can claim the benefit of insurance money paid to the other.

It is common, however, for the mortgagee to insist as a condition of making the loan that the mortgagor obtain and pay the premiums on a policy covering the full value of the property and providing that in case of loss the insurance money shall be paid to the mortgagor and the mortga-

---

[2] Allstate Ins. Co. v Kleveno, 81 App Div 2d 648, 438 NYS2d 384 (1981).

gee as their respective interests may appear. As the amount of the mortgage debt is reduced, the interest of the mortgagee in the property becomes less and the share of insurance proceeds that the mortgagee would receive accordingly becomes less. Such a mortgage clause has the advantage of protecting both the mortgagor and mortgagee by one policy and of providing a flexible method of insuring each of them.[3]

§ 41:5   Extended Coverage

The term **extended coverage** generally refers to protection of property against loss from windstorm, hail, riot, civil commotion, aircraft damage, vehicle damage, smoke damage, and most explosions.

A special form of extended coverage may be obtained to protect property from vandalism. **Vandalism** is the intentional senseless or malicious destruction or damaging of property.

If vandals burn a building, fire insurance would provide protection. If the harm occurred as part of a riot, the standard extended coverage would afford protection.

§ 41:6   Other Provisions

Fire insurance policies commonly prohibit the insured from performing certain acts that may increase the risk involved and provide that the policy is void if the insured commits the prohibited acts.

It is commonly provided that false statements made by the insured when they are known to be false shall avoid the policy.[4] Under such a provision a fraudulent misstatement of the value of the property avoids the policy.

The insured may take out more than one policy on the same property, in the absence of a provision in any of the policies to the contrary; but in the event of loss, recovery cannot be greater than the total loss sustained. Such a loss is prorated among the insurers.

An insurer is not liable when the damage or destruction of the property was intentionally caused by the insured.[5] However, the fact that the insured negligently caused a fire is not a defense to the insurer, even when there is a stipulation that the insured shall not change or increase the hazard insured against.

Provisions in a policy of fire insurance relating to the use and occupancy of the property are generally strictly construed because they relate to the hazards involved. In the *Miller* case the court was faced with determining the effect upon the policy of a violation of such provisions.

---

[3]   495 Corp. v New Jersey Insurance Underwriting Association, 86 NJ 159, 430 A2d 203 (1981).

[4]   Morgan v Cincinnati Ins. Co. 411 Mich 267, 307 NW2d 53 (1981).
[5]   Neises v Solomon State Bank, 236 Kan 767, 696 P2d 372 (1985).

Miller v Underwriters at Lloyd's, London
(La App) 398 So 2d (1981)

Miller owned a house. He insured it against fire with Lloyd's of London. In the policy, the house was described as "owner occupied." In fact it was not occupied by Miller but by various tenants to whom Miller successively rented the house, the last tenant being Gus Tynes. The policy also stated that if the house became vacant or was unoccupied for more than 60 days the insurer would be notified. Tynes moved away and the house remained vacant. Miller made repairs to the empty house from time to time, but the house remained unoccupied for more than 60 days. A fire oc-curred. Miller claimed that Lloyd's was liable for the loss. It denied liability because of the falsity of the statement of being "owner occupied" and be-cause there had been a vacancy in excess of 60 days. Miller sued Lloyd's. The court entered judgment in his favor and Lloyd's appealed.

WATKINS, J. . . . The property that was destroyed by fire on November 13, 1978, was located at 1505 Dan Street, Bogalusa, Louisiana. Plaintiff and his wife lived at the Pooles Bluff Community, some four miles away. Plaintiff's agent, James Stevenson, president of the GAR Real Estate & Insurance Agency, Inc., Bogalusa, Louisiana had secured fire coverage on the tenant dwelling since 1969. He was fully aware of the fact it was not occupied by Miller. The last policy issued was . . .obtained by GAR through Dupuy Busch-ing General Agency, Inc., Jackson, Mississippi, an insurance broker. The poli-cy was delivered to First Financial Services, Bogalusa, mortgagee of the tenant property, and a certificate of insurance was delivered to Miller. Both the policy and certificate indicated the property was "owner occupied". In addition, a "permission granted clause" was contained in an endorsement attached to the policy, which clause read as follows:

> PERMISSION GRANTED CLAUSE (OCCUPANCY CLAUSE): In the event the prop-erty insured under this policy becomes vacant or unoccupied or if there is a change of occupancy from that indicated in the policy for more than 60 days, then the insured must notify the Company in writing and the insured's failure to so notify the Compa-ny in writing will render the coverage on that item null and void and the insured shall be entitled to a pro rata return premium as of that date, except, if this policy shall cover more than four dwellings of four families or less, the vacancy or unoccupancy period is extended to 90 days. Vacancy or unoccupancy of part of the units of a multi-ple family dwelling shall not be deemed as vacancy or unoccupancy.

The last tenant to reside on the premises was Gus Tynes, who moved out about June 27, 1978. All utilities were cut off, and all furnishings removed. Miller went to the V.A. Hospital intermittently for about a month after Tynes vacated the premises. He then commenced a rather protracted period of re-pairs to the premises, the repairs still having been in progress, although pro-ceeding extremely slowly, at the time of the fire. Miller testified that he slept on the premises in a sleeping bag on several occasions.

We find that the premises were not owner occupied in compliance with the terms of the policy. Clearly the premises were occupied by a tenant, not the owner at the time when the policy was issued and the certificate of insurance was delivered to Miller. Miller appears not to have called GAR's, Dupuy Busching's, or Underwriters' attention to the incorrectness of the description "owner occupied". We would find lack of owner occupancy alone sufficient reason to hold there was no coverage, but in addition, we see, Miller failed to notify Underwriters of the fact that the property had been "vacant or unoccu-pied" for more than 60 days, thereby violating the permission granted clause of the policy. . . .

We note that in the present case the insurance agent, GAR, was largely responsible for the mistake found in the policy and certificate in their indicat-ing that the premises were "owner occupied", as that description was appar-ently taken from the application prepared by GAR. . . . We are thus faced with the question of whether or not GAR's negligence was imputable to Underwriters.

. . . [T]here is nothing in the present case that would indicate that any form of agency, either under the statutory laws regulating insurance or under the Codal laws regulating mandate, existed between GAR and the insurer, Underwriters. Thus, GAR's negligence was in no way imputable to Underwriters. . . .

[Judgment reversed]

QUESTIONS

1. Did the court hold the insurer liable on its policy?
2. Did Miller intentionally lie to the insurer in stating that the property was owner occupied?
3. What difference does it make to the insurer whether the property was owner occupied or tenant occupied, or whether it was occupied or vacant?

§ 41:7   CANCELLATION

It is common to provide by statute or by the terms of the policy that under certain circumstances the policy may be terminated or canceled by the act of one party alone. When this is done, the provisions of the statute and the policy must be strictly followed in order to make the cancellation effective.

B.   HOMEOWNER'S INSURANCE

A homeowner's insurance policy provides coverage for multiple perils that relate to home or condominium ownership or to the rental of an apartment. It is a combination of the standard fire insurance policy and comprehensive personal liability insurance. It thus provides fire, theft, and certain liability protection in a single insurance contract.

§ 41:8   COVERAGE AND EXCLUSIONS

In addition to providing protection against losses due to fire, the homeowner's policy provides liability coverage for accidents or injuries that occur on the premises of the insured. Moreover, the liability provisions provide coverage for unintentional injuries to others away from home for which the insured or any member of the resident family is held responsible, such as injuries caused others by golfing, hunting, or fishing accidents. Generally, motor vehicles including mopeds and recreation vehicles are excluded from such personal liability coverage.[6]

A homeowner's policy also provides protection from losses due to theft.

(a) PERSONS COVERED. A homeowner's policy provides protection for all permanent residents of the household, which includes all family members living with the insured. Thus, a son of the insured who lives at home has the right to bring suit against the insurer, under the homeowner's policy, for the value of personal property lost when the home is destroyed by fire.[7]

Injuries to household members are not covered by a homeowner's policy. However, visitors, including relatives tempora-

---

[6] Western v Home Owners Insurance Co. 157 Mich App 261, 403 NW2d 115 (1987).
[7] Gulf Insurance Co. v Mathis, 183 Ga App 323, 358 SE2d 307 (1987).

rily living with the insured, are covered under such a policy.[8]

(b) COMMON EXCLUSIONS. A homeowner's policy commonly excludes liability for intentional injuries. Also, personal injuries relating to boats or motor vehicles are ordinarily excluded from homeowner's policies.[9]

§ 41:9 ENDORSEMENTS FOR SCHEDULED PERSONAL PROPERTY

Personal property floaters may be added to a homeowner's policy to protect against the loss or theft of items of special value, such as jewelry, paintings, and fur coats. A schedule or listing of the items is made part of the policy, with the additional premiums charged being less than that which would be paid if the items were insured under separate policies.

C. AUTOMOBILE INSURANCE

Associations of insurers, such as the National Bureau of Casualty Underwriters and the National Automobile Underwriters Association, have proposed standard forms of automobile insurance policies that have been approved by their members in virtually all states.

§ 41:10 NATURE OF CONTRACT

In the case of insurance to compensate the insured driver or car owner for damages to the insured's own car, it is immaterial whether the insured's negligence caused or contributed to the harm sustained. In the case of insurance that protects the insured driver or owner from claims of others (**liability insurance**), no liability of

the insurer for a claim arises unless the insured was negligent in the operation of the automobile. To some extent this has been altered by no fault insurance as discussed in § 41:15.

§ 41:11 FINANCIAL RESPONSIBILITY LAWS

In a few states and under some no fault insurance statutes, liability insurance must be obtained before a driver's license will be issued. In most states **financial responsibility laws** require that if a driver is involved in an accident, proof of financial responsibility must be furnished. Under some laws this means that the driver must deposit security sufficient to pay any judgment that may be entered with respect to that accident. Under other statutes, it is sufficient that the driver produce a liability policy in a specified amount as to future accidents.

The security form of statute may not protect the victim of the first accident. If the driver is unwilling or unable to deposit the required security, the driver's license is forfeited; but this does not provide any payment to the victim of the first accident. By definition, the second kind of law does not protect the victim of the first accident. Moreover, the efficiency of financial responsibility laws has been reduced by the decision that the United States Constitution requires that there be a hearing to establish the probable liability of a driver to the victim before the driver's license can be suspended or revoked. The requirement of such a hearing has the effect of delaying and making cumbersome what was formerly a relatively simple and swift administrative remedy.

§ 41:12 LIABILITY INSURANCE

The owner or operator of a motor vehicle may obtain **liability insurance** for protection from claims made by third persons for damage to their property (property damage liability) or person (bodily injury liabili-

---

[8] Farmers Ins. Co. v Oliver, 154 Ariz 174, 741 P2d 307 (1987).

[9] Behrens v Aetna Life and Casualty, 153 Ariz 301, 736 P2d 385 (1987); State Farm Fire and Casualty Co. v Pahl, 191 Cal App 3d 74, 236 Cal Rptr 216 (1987).

ty) arising from the use or operation of an automobile. When the insurer pays under such a policy, it is liable to pay for the same items as the insured would be required to pay, but for not more than the maximum amount stated in the policy.

If the insurer is liable for the damage caused a third person or such person's property, it is likewise liable for cost of repairs, loss by destruction of property, loss of services, and other damages for which the insured would be liable, subject to the policy maximum.

(a) OWNERSHIP OF AUTOMOBILE. Basically, liability insurance protects the insured with respect to an *owned* automobile. Whether a given automobile is owned by the insured is determined by

Article 2 of the UCC, and it is immaterial whether the steps required by a motor vehicle statute have been taken to transfer the title.

(b) USE AND OPERATION. The terms *use* and *operation* as found in a liability policy are liberally interpreted to include events in which there is some involvement of the automobile even though not for the purpose of transportation.[10] For example, the insured *uses* the automobile when packages are being loaded into it.

In the *McNeill* case, the court was faced with how broadly *use* of an automobile should be interpreted.

[10]   State Farm Ins. v Whithead (Mo App) 711 SW2d 198 (1986).

McNeill v Maryland Insurance Guaranty Association

48 Md App 411, 427 A2d 1056 (1981)

Evelyn Watkins obtained insurance to protect her from liability arising out of the "ownership, maintenance and use" of her automobile. Her friend, Charlie McNeill, could not start his car. He phoned Evelyn who had Edward Hill take her car to the place where McNeill was stalled. The battery of the Watkins car was then connected to the battery of the McNeill car in order to give the battery a quick charge. McNeill took some of the caps off his battery. Hill was standing nearby and lit a match, which caused the battery of the McNeill car to explode. McNeill was seriously injured by the explosion. He claimed that he was entitled to recover damages under the Watkins policy. The insurer denied liability on the ground that McNeill had not been injured as the result of the "ownership, maintenance or use" of the Watkins car. A declaratory judgment action was brought to determine the question. From a judgment against McNeill, he appealed.

LISS, J. . . . "Ownership, maintenance or use clauses" do not limit recovery solely to injuries that are caused by direct physical contact with the injured vehicle; nor is it necessary that the damages be directly sustained or inflicted by the operation of the motor vehicle. . . .

The Court of Appeals, in *Frazier v Unsatisfied Claim and Judgment Board,* 262 Md 115, 277 A2d 57 (1971) had before it a factual situation in which a child of five years was a passenger in the rear seat of an open convertible vehicle which was being operated by the child's mother. An unidentified vehicle proceeding in the opposite direction passed the convertible and a lighted firecracker was thrown from the unidentified vehicle into the rear seat of the convertible. Distracted by the occurrence, the mother lost control of her car and struck a tree, severely injuring her child. The trial court concluded as a matter of law that the injuries did not arise out of the ownership, maintenance and use of the unidentified automobile. In reversing the trial court, the Court of Appeals held:

> [there seemed to be support for] the proposition that whether an injury is or is not within the coverage provided by an automobile insurance policy may well turn on the question whether the use of an automobile is directly or merely incidentally causally connected with the injury, even though the automobile itself may not have proximately caused the injury. Compare, for example, *National Indemnity Co. v Ewing*, 235 Md 145, 200 A2d 680 (1964) (recovery allowed plaintiff, who fell from insured's car, and was injured while being escorted back to car on foot) and *Mullen v Hartford Accident & Indemnity Co.* 287 Mass 262, 191 NE 394 (1934) (injury sustained from slipping on oil leaking from car held to be within provisions of policy) with *Commercial Union Ins. Co. of New York v Hall*, 246 FSupp 64 (EDSC 1965) (no liability to plaintiff, whose way was blocked by insured's car and was then assaulted by insured) and Kraus v Allstate Ins. Co. 258 FSupp 407 (WD Pa 1966) *aff'd* 379 F2d 443 (3d Cir 1967) (insurer not liable to pedestrians when insured detonated dynamite in his car). [262 Md at 118, 277 A2d 57.]

The proposition had previously been established in *National Indemnity Co. v Ewing, supra*, where recovery was permitted by a plaintiff who had been thrown uninjured from the insured car but had subsequently sustained injury when the insured driver negligently escorted the plaintiff back to the car on foot by leading plaintiff down the center of the road. The Court permitted recovery under the insurance policy which provided for compensation of injuries arising out of the "ownership, maintenance or use" of the automobile, where it held:

> Language in automobile liability policies, identical to that in the case before us, has been construed by the courts of other states, and it has generally been held that, while the words import and require a showing of causal relationship, recovery is not limited to the strict rules developed in relation to direct and proximate cause. . . . The same rule was applied in *Merchants Co. v Hartford Accident & Indemnity Co.* [187 Miss 301], 188 So 571, 572, where the injury was caused by poles negligently left in the road after the covered vehicle had been extricated from a ditch and had departed. The court said:
> "Our conclusion, under a policy such as is here before us, is that where a dangerous situation causing injury is one which arose out of or had its source in, the use or operation of the automobile, the chain of responsibility must be deemed to possess the requisite articulation with the use or operation until broken by the intervention of some event which has no direct or substantial relation to the use or operation, — which is to say, that the event which breaks the chain, and which, therefore, would exclude liability under the automobile policy, must be an event which bears no direct or substantial relation to the use or operation; and until an event of the latter nature transpires the liability under the policy exists." . . .

The use of the Watkins vehicle was clearly a use which was or should have been contemplated and anticipated by the insurance carrier and the owner of the vehicle. It is not unusual that an insured might on occasion be required to use his vehicle to charge the battery of another vehicle. At the time the explosion took place, the Watkins vehicle was still being used in an activity permitted by her policy. . . . The Watkins vehicle was still attached by the jumper cables to McNeill's vehicle at the time Watkins' driver negligently threw the match. McNeill's activity in unscrewing the battery caps was entirely consistent with an effort to determine whether the battery had sufficient fluid and charge to permit McNeill's car to operate without being attached to the jumper cables. The lighting of the cigarette by Watkins' driver was not an intervening or independent cause, . . . There was a causal relationship between the use of the Watkins vehicle to start McNeill's automobile and that the explosion was caused by the careless throwing of the match by Watkins' driver which ignited the fumes released when the battery caps were unscrewed. We find that at the time this occurred the Watkins vehicle was being "used" as contemplated by the Watkins liability insurance policy.

[Judgment reversed]

QUESTIONS

1. In order to recover on an automobile liability policy it is necessary to show that the use of the automobile was the cause of the harm sustained by the plaintiff. Appraise this statement.
2. Did foreseeability have any significance in the *McNeill* decision?
3. Public liability insurance covers only harm arising from collision with the insured automobile. Appraise this statement.

(c) PERSON OPERATING. Liability policies ordinarily protect the owner of the auto from liability when it is operated by another person with the permission of the insured, as in the case of an employee or agent of the owner.

Liability insurance may also protect an insured individual or the insured's spouse against liability incurred while operating another person's automobile. This protection is referred to as **D.O.C.** (drive-other-car) **coverage**, or **temporary replacement coverage.**

(1) Members of Household of Insured. Automobile liability policies variously extend coverage to members of the insured's household or residence. Such terms are generally liberally construed to reach the conclusion that a given relative is a member of the insured's household or residence.

(2) Other Driver. The automobile liability policy protects the insured when driving. If someone else is driving with the insured's permission, the policy protects

both the original insured and such other driver.[11] This **omnibus** or **other driver clause** is generally liberally interpreted so that permission is often found in acquiescence in the other driver's use or in the insured's failing to object or to prevent such use. In the absence of an express prohibition by the insured against the permittee's lending the car to another, a permission by A given to B to use the car generally includes an implied permission to B to permit C to drive, in which case the liability of the insurer is the same as though A or B were driving.[12]

The buyer of an automobile does not come within the scope of an omnibus clause because the buyer's operation of the automobile is not based upon the permis-

---

[11] DeWitt v Young (Kan) 625 P2d 478 (1981).
[12] Some courts interpret the omnibus clause more strictly and refuse to recognize a second permittee when the original insured did not expressly authorize such relending or when the use made by the second permittee was not the same use that the insured contemplated would be made by the first permittee.

sion of the seller but upon the buyer's ownership of the automobile. To avoid litigation, policies commonly expressly exclude buyers from the scope of the omnibus clause.

(d) EXCLUSIONS. A liability policy does not cover every harm sustained. Such policies may exclude claims of employees of the owner or claims under the workers' compensation laws, liability for harm intentionally caused by the insured,[13] or liability for claims when the insured admits to the injured third person that the insured is liable and agrees to pay the claim.

In the case of commercial vehicles the insurer may stipulate that it shall only be bound by the policy "provided: (a) the regular and frequent use of the automobile is confined to the area within a fifty-mile radius of the limits of the city or town where the automobile is principally garaged . . . , (b) no regular or frequent trips are made by the automobile to any locations beyond such radius."

(e) CANCELLATION. Automobile liability policies generally contain a provision authorizing the insurer to cancel the policy before a loss is sustained upon giving the insured a stated number of days' notice.[14]

(f) NOTICE AND COOPERATION. A liability policy generally provides that the insurer is not liable unless the insured (1) gives the insurer prompt notice of any serious accident or claim or lawsuit brought against the insured, (2) furnishes the insurance company with all details of the occurrence, and (3) cooperates with the insurer in the preparation of the defense against a lawsuit brought on the policy and participates at the trial. Notice and cooperation under such a policy are conditions precedent to the liability of the insurer.

These requirements are subject to modification in terms of reasonableness. Thus, the insured is not required to report a trivi-

al accident when there was no reason to believe that the injured person was going to proceed further with the matter. The notice to the insurer need only be given within a reasonable time after the occurrence, and "reasonable" is determined in the light of all the surrounding circumstances.

(g) DUTY TO DEFEND. A liability insurer has the duty to defend any suit brought against its insured on a claim that, if valid, would come within the policy coverage. The liability insurer cannot refuse to defend the insured on the ground that it does not believe the claim of the third person. Consequently, when the third person's complaint against the insured states a claim within the coverage of the policy, a liability insurer cannot refuse to defend on the ground that its investigation shows that the claim is without merit.

If the insurer wrongly refuses to defend and the third person recovers a judgment against the insured even though it exceeds the policy maximum, the insurer is liable to the insured for the full amount of the judgment. Under statutes in some states, the insurer may also be required to pay the insured the litigation costs and attorney's fees when the insurer refuses in bad faith to settle or defend the action.

§ 41:13 COLLISION AND UPSET INSURANCE

Liability insurance does not indemnify the insured for damage to his or her own property. In order to obtain this protection for an auto, its owner must obtain property insurance. One such kind of insurance covers damage from collision and upset.

The term *collision* is generally liberally interpreted so that there is insurance coverage whenever there is an unintended striking of another object even though the object is not an automobile or is not moving. For example, there is a collision when a wheel comes off of the automobile and the automobile falls to the ground.

The phrase *struck by automobile* is likewise liberally interpreted so that there is

[13] Globe American Cas. Co. v Lyons, 131 Ariz App 337, 641 P2d 251 (1982).
[14] Ophus v Tri-State Ins. Co. __ Minn __, 392 NW2d 653 (1986).

coverage when the insured ran a motor scooter into an automobile, as against the contention that *struck by automobile* required that the automobile run into the insured.

(a) EXCLUSIONS. The insurer against collision is not required to pay in every case. It is commonly provided that the insurer is not liable when the automobile is used by a person who is violating the law. It may also be stipulated that liability is avoided if the auto is subject to a lien or encumbrance that has not been disclosed. It is common to exclude damages resulting from collision for the loss of the use of the auto, for depreciation, or for loss of personal property in the auto.

(b) NOTICE AND COOPERATION. As in the case of public liability insurance, the auto owner is under a duty to give notice, to inform, and to cooperate with the insurer. The owner must also give the insurer an opportunity to examine the automobile to determine the extent of damage before making repairs.

§ 41:14   UNINSURED MOTORIST

Statutes and liability policies commonly provide for special coverage when the insured sustains loss because of an uninsured motorist.[15] Since the **uninsured motorist coverage** is a liability coverage, there is no liability of the insurer in the absence of establishing that the uninsured motorist was negligent and would be held liable if sued by the insured. Consequently, collision and accident insurance provide greater protection in that under such coverage the insurer is bound by its contract without regard to whether anyone could be held liable to the insured.

Uninsured motorist coverage generally includes the hit-and-run driver who leaves the scene of the collision before being identified. Policies commonly require that the collision be reported to the police or other

appropriate authorities within 24 hours and that diligent effort be made to locate the hit-and-run driver. These restrictions are imposed in order to guard against the fraud of reporting the other car as "unknown" when its driver was in fact known, or against the fraud of having a one-car accident and then falsely claiming that the damage was the result of a collision with a hit-and-run driver.

This coverage differs from other insurance that the insured could obtain in that only personal injury claims are covered and generally only up to $10,000. Contact with the uninsured or unidentified vehicle is required, so that there is no uninsured motorist coverage when the insured runs off the road to avoid a collision and sustains injury thereby, or when the insured is injured upon striking oil or an object dropped from the uninsured vehicle.

§ 41:15   NO FAULT INSURANCE

A state statute may require that every automobile liability policy provide for **no fault coverage.**

(a) HARM TO THE INSURED. No fault coverage means that when the insured is injured while using the insured automobile, the insurer will make a payment without regard to whose fault caused the harm.[16] In effect, this is insurance for medical expense and loss of wages that runs in favor of the holder of the liability policy and is in addition to or in lieu of the coverage that the policy provides with respect to liability to other persons.

The no fault insurance statutes generally do not provide for payment for pain and suffering. Under some statutes recovery is allowed for pain and suffering if the medical expenses exceed $500 or if certain specified injuries have been sustained by the insured.

(b) OTHER PARTY INJURY. If another person is harmed, such as a pedestrian or an-

---

[15]   Guess v Gulf Ins. Co. 96 N Mex 27, 627 P2d 869 (1981).

[16]   Brehm v Illinois Farmers Insurance, ___ Minn ___, 390 NW2d 475 (1986).

other driver, no fault insurance statutes generally provide for a similar kind of payment to such third person by that person's auto insurer or by the insurer of the car inflicting the injury.

(c) SUIT AGAINST PARTY AT FAULT. No fault insurance laws bar the claimant from suing the party at fault for ordinary claims. If the automobile collision results in a permanent serious disablement or disfigurement, or death, or if the medical bills and lost wages of the plaintiff exceed a specified amount, suit may be brought against the party who was at fault. A person who is entitled to sue the at-fault party may collect the maximum amount of no fault insurance and then sue the at-fault party for the total damages, just as though no payment had been received from the insurer. However, if the injured party recovers the total amount from the at-fault party, the injured party must ordinarily repay the insurance company the amount that had been received from it under the no fault coverage.

(d) ARBITRATION. Disputes under no fault insurance are sometimes determined by arbitration. In addition, some states require the arbitration of small claims of any nature.

(e) CONSTITUTIONALITY. No fault insurance is generally held constitutional, as against the contention that it violates the guarantees of equal protection and due process. It has been sustained as a carefully studied plan to provide a new remedy to meet the problems caused by the automobile: rising cost of insurance, overloading of courts, and delay in making payment to the injured person.

§ 41:16 THEFT INSURANCE

The owner of an automobile can secure theft insurance that will protect from loss through theft and from damage to the auto caused by a theft.

An automobile theft policy does not ordinarily protect against loss of contents. It is common to exclude liability for equipment or personal property taken from the auto, but additional insurance protecting from such theft can be secured. It is common also to exclude liability for loss sustained while a passenger auto is used for commercial transportation or is rented to another.

§ 41:17 FIRE, LIGHTNING, AND TRANSPORTATION INSURANCE

In this kind of insurance the insurer agrees to pay for any loss arising out of damage to or the destruction of a motor vehicle or its equipment caused by fire originating in any manner, by lightning, or by the stranding, sinking, burning, collision, or derailment of any conveyance in or upon which the automobile or the truck is being transported. This kind of policy is commonly combined with a policy against theft and pilferage and is usually subject to the same exclusions.

§ 41:18 COMPREHENSIVE INSURANCE

In many automobile insurance policies, comprehensive material damage coverage, which protects the policyholder against virtually all such risks except collision or upset, replaces fire and theft insurance. The exclusions for this kind of insurance include wear and tear, freezing, mechanical breakdown, and loss of personal effects.

D. LIFE INSURANCE

A contract of **life insurance** requires the insurer to pay a stipulated sum of money upon the death of the insured. It is not a contract of indemnity since the insurer does not undertake to indemnify the beneficiary for the financial loss sustained as the result of the death of the insured.

§ 41:19   KINDS OF LIFE INSURANCE POLICIES

Life insurance policies may be classified in terms of their duration and extent of coverage and of the pattern of payment of premiums.

(a) ORDINARY LIFE INSURANCE. Ordinary life insurance may be subclassified as (1) **straight life insurance,** which requires payment of premiums throughout the life of the insured; (2) **limited payment insurance,** requiring the payment of premiums during a limited period, such as ten, twenty, or thirty years, or until the death of the insured if that should occur before the end of the specified period; (3) **endowment insurance,** under which the insurer agrees to pay a stipulated sum when the insured reaches a specified age, or upon death if that occurs sooner; and (4) **term insurance,** under which the insurer agrees to pay a stipulated sum only in the event of the death of the insured during a specified period, such as one, two, five, or ten years.

Somewhat similar to policies of endowment insurance are **annuity policies** and **retirement income insurance** under which the insured either pays a lump sum to the insurer and thereafter receives fixed annual payments, or pays periodic premiums to the insurer until a certain date and then receives fixed annual payments.

(b) GROUP INSURANCE. **Group life insurance** is insurance of the lives of members of a group, such as employees of a particular employer or persons engaged in a particular business or profession. Such policies are usually either term policies or straight life insurance.

(c) DOUBLE INDEMNITY. Many life insurance companies undertake to pay double the amount of the policy, called **double indemnity,** if death is caused by an accident and death occurs within ninety days after the accident.[17] A comparatively small, additional premium is charged for this special protection.

(d) DISABILITY INSURANCE. In consideration of the payment of an additional premium, many life insurance companies also provide insurance against total permanent disability of the insured. **Disability** is usually defined in a life insurance policy as any "incapacity resulting from bodily injury or disease to engage in any occupation for remuneration or profit." The policy generally provides that a disability that has continued for a stated minimum period, such as four to six months, will be regarded as a **total permanent disability.**

(e) EXCLUSIONS. Life insurance policies frequently provide that death shall not be within the protection of the policy or that a double indemnity provision shall not be applicable when death is caused by (1) suicide,[18] (2) narcotics, (3) the intentional act of another, (4) execution for a crime, (5) war activities, or (6) operation of aircraft.

The *Evans* case illustrates the judicial applications of a plainly expressed exclusion from double indemnity coverage.

[17] Valley National Bank v J. C. Penney Ins. Co. 129 Ariz App 108, 628 P2d 991 (1981).
[18] Southern Farm Bureau Life Ins. Co. v Dettle (Tex Civ App) 707 SW2d 271 (1986).

EVANS V NATIONAL LIFE ACCIDENT INSURANCE CO.

(Ind App) 467 NE2d 1216 (1984)

In 1970, Jerome Evans (the Insured) purchased a life insurance policy from National Life Accident Insurance Co. (National) with a death benefit amount of $10,000. At the same time, he purchased an Additional Indemnity Agreement (Agreement) that provided an additional $10,000 in benefits if death resulted from "accidental means." The Insured died on the evening of February 23, 1979, as a result of a shotgun wound to the heart. The fatal shot was fired by Thomas Cox sometime after Cox and the Insured argued at a tavern in Marion, Indiana. National paid the Evanses, the named beneficiaries, the face amount of the life insurance policy, $10,000, but refused to pay the additional $10,000 in benefits under the Agreement. The Additional Indemnity Agreement provided benefits only for death resulting from "external, violent and accidental means" and enumerated seven specific exclusions from coverage, including death resulting from suicide, poisoning, disease, war, the intentional act of another, commission of an assault or felony, or operation of an aircraft.

The Evanses sued National for the additional $10,000 in benefits. From a judgment for National, the Evanses appealed.

SHIELDS, J. . . . The Evanses correctly define the "intentional act" exclusion as an affirmative defense. Consequently, National had the burden of proving facts sufficient to demonstrate the Insured's death was the result of Cox's intentional conduct.

Based on this burden of proof, the Evanses first challenge the sufficiency of the evidence to support the trial court's finding that the Insured's death resulted "directly or indirectly and wholly or partially as a result of the intentional act of another person." The Evanses highlight Cox's testimony that he did not intend to fire the shotgun or to shoot the Insured. However, on appeal we only consider the evidence and reasonable inferences which support the trial court's judgment; we neither weigh conflicting evidence nor judge the credibility of witnesses. The trial court's findings and conclusions will not be set aside unless clearly erroneous. . . .

The evidence amply supports the court's conclusion the Insured's death was the result of Cox's intentional conduct. Contrary to the Evanses assertion, the evidence clearly supports the conclusions that Cox intended to fire the shotgun and to shoot the Insured. Upon the Insured's return to the tavern, Cox left the tavern but, rather than staying away, returned armed with a shotgun, raised the shotgun, specifically called the Insured's name, shot the Insured in the back from a few feet away, and then kicked the dying man in the head. It was within the evidence for the trial court, as the trier of fact, to conclude Cox "intentionally" and "deliberately" "murdered" the Insured.

Even assuming the sufficiency of the evidence, the Evanses contend the policy exclusion for intentional conduct was ambiguous and unconscionable. The Agreement, however, expressly excluded coverage "if the death of the Insured resulted either directly or indirectly, or wholly or partially from . . . the intentional act of another person. . . ." Regardless, the Evanses contend the court must give effect only to the average insured's reasonable expectations of coverage. They argue "[i]t is reasonable to assume Jerome Evans intended to purchase coverage of 'accidents' being any unexpected death not due to medical or health causes as he was familiar with the term." In effect, the Evanses would have this Court hold all clearly expressed exceptions to coverage, unconscionable and void as against public policy; the insured's expectations would substitute for clear contractual provisions.

We are unaware of any cases or reasoning supporting the intentional act exclusion as unconscionable. Furthermore, the Evanses' arguments confuse unconscionability and ambiguity. The insured's expectations of coverage are significant in construing ambiguities. An insurance policy is a contract and is consequently governed by the law of contracts. The objective of the court is to enforce the intent of the parties as manifested by the contract. Since insurance contracts are typically contracts of adhesion, any ambiguities must be construed in favor of the insured. . . .

Exclusionary provisions in insurance contracts are equally susceptible to construction against the insurance company if the exclusionary language is ambiguous. An exclusion will be given only if it unmistakably brings the act or omission within its scope. Nonetheless, the parties are still entitled to make their contract; an exclusion plainly stated in the policy is enforceable. . . .

In the instant case, there is no ambiguity. . . .

Once the trial court resolved the conflicting testimony regarding Cox's intent, application of the exclusion was clear.

"An insurance company is free to determine by its contract what risks it is undertaking to insure, provided policy provisions do not violate statutory mandates or are not against public policy." Insurance companies, like individuals, are free to limit their liability in a manner not inconsistent with public policy. Consequently, plainly expressed exceptions, exclusions and limitations are entitled to construction and enforcement as expressed. We cannot rewrite the insurance contract for the parties.

[Judgment affirmed]

QUESTIONS

1. Did the insurer have the burden of proving facts sufficient to demonstrate that the insured's death was the result of intentional conduct?
2. Did the evidence support the conclusion that the insured's death was the result of intentional conduct?
3. Is a plainly expressed "intentional act" exclusion in a life insurance policy enforceable?

§ 41:20   The Beneficiary

The recipient of proceeds of a life insurance policy that are payable upon the death of the insured is called the **beneficiary.** The beneficiary may be a third person or the estate of the insured. There may be more than one beneficiary.

The beneficiary named in the policy may be barred from claiming the proceeds of the policy. There may be a prior settlement agreement by which it was agreed that the beneficiary would not claim the insurance. Likewise, it is generally provided by stat-ute or stated by court decision that a beneficiary who has feloniously killed the insured is not entitled to receive the proceeds of the policy.[19]

(a) Primary and Contingent Beneficiaries. It is desirable to name a primary and a contingent beneficiary. Thus, A may make insurance payable to B, but provide that if B dies before A, the insurance shall be payable to C. In such case, B is the **primary beneficiary,** and C is the **contingent**

[19] State Farm Life Ins. Co. v Smith, 66 Ill 2d 591, 363 NE2d 785 (1977).

beneficiary because *C* takes the proceeds as beneficiary only upon the contingency that *B* dies before *A*.

(b) CHANGE OF BENEFICIARY. The customary policy provides that the insured reserves the right to change the beneficiary without the latter's consent. When the policy contains such a provision, the beneficiary cannot object to a change that destroys all of that beneficiary's rights under the policy and that names another person as beneficiary.

The insurance policy will ordinarily state that in order to change the beneficiary, the insurer must be so instructed in writing by the insured and the policy must then be endorsed by the company with the change of the beneficiary. These provisions are generally liberally construed. If the insured has notified the insurer but dies before the endorsement of the change by the company, the change of beneficiary is effective. If, however, the insured has not taken any steps to comply with the policy requirements, a change of beneficiary is not effective, even though a change was intended.

The *Puricelli* case illustrates the liberal construction of policy requirements so that the intentions of the insured may be carried out.

WOODMAN ACCIDENT AND LIFE CO.V PURICELLI
(Mo App) 669 SW2d 64 (1984)

Lesley Puricelli was the estranged wife of the insured, Michael J. Puricelli, and was originally named as beneficiary in his two life insurance policies. Mr. Michael M. Puricelli and Mrs. Rose H. Puricelli were the insured's parents and were named the new beneficiaries in changes of beneficiary forms executed a few days before the insured's death but not delivered to the two insurance companies in question until two days after the insured's death. Lesley and Mr. and Mrs. Puricelli all claim entitlement to the proceeds of the life insurance policies. From a judgment for Mr. and Mrs. Puricelli, Lesley appealed.

CLEMENS, S. J. . . . According to insurance agent Thomas H. Lake the insured brought him the policies and requested the changes in beneficiaries. Mr. Lake prepared the requested change of beneficiary forms; the insured executed the forms and left them and the policies with Mr. Lake for delivery to the two insurers. However — and here is the gist of this case — due to press of other business Mr. Lake did not send the policies and the new beneficiary forms to the insurers until two days after the insured's death.

The trial court found the facts as stated above. By a formal memorandum it ruled that when the insured left Mr. Lake's office all that remained to be done was the simple ministerial act of Mr. Lake mailing the policies and new beneficiary forms to the insurers, and the insured believed this was being done.

The trial court concluded a court of equity regards that as done which ought to have been done. So the court ordered the insurers to pay the policy proceeds to the new beneficiaries, the defendant parents.

Defendant widow has appealed. She contends the insured's death revoked Mr. Lake's authority to thereafter send the change of beneficiary forms to the insurers. We disagree.

A leading case concerning the change of a beneficiary is *Persons v. Prudential*

Ins. Co. of America, 233 SW2d 729 (Mo. 1950). There as here the insured executed a change of beneficiary form two days before his death, but prior to the
insurer receiving notice thereof. In upholding the change in beneficiary the
court ruled:

> So where, as in this state, the substantial compliance rule prevails, and the insured
> has done all within his power to exercise his right to change the beneficiary, the
> *change* itself is effective before his death.

In this, the court followed the earlier case of *Mutual Life Ins. Co. of Baltimore
v. Burger*, 50 SW2d 765 (Mo App 1932) where Judge Bennick wrote:

> One of the familiar maxims of equitable jurisprudence is that equity regards that as
> done which ought to be done; and, inasmuch as equity does not demand impossible
> things, but is free to view the case in the light of the above principle, a court of
> equity will hold that the insured has done all that equity demands of him when it
> appears that he has complied with all the requirements of the policy within his pow-
> er for the purpose of making a change of beneficiary.

We therefore hold the trial court properly held the changes of beneficiary
were effective, in favor of the new beneficiary, the insured's parents.
[Judgment affirmed]

QUESTIONS

1. Summarize the facts of this case.
2. What did Lesley contend?
3. What maxim of equitable jurisprudence was applied in this case?

---

§ 41:21 INCONTESTABILITY CLAUSE

Statutes commonly require the inclusion of
an incontestability clause in life insurance
policies. Ordinarily this clause states that
after the lapse of two years the policy cannot be contested by the insurance company. The insurer is free to contest the validity of the policy at any time during the con-
testable period; but once the period has expired, it must pay the stipulated sum upon
the death of the insured and cannot claim
that in obtaining the policy the insured had
been guilty of misrepresentation, fraud, or
any other conduct that would entitle it to
avoid the contract of insurance.[20]

[20] Chavis v Southern Life Ins. Co. 318 NC 259, 347
SE2d 425 (1986).

§ 41:22 SURRENDER OF POLICY AND ALTERNATIVES

The insured may give up or **surrender** the
policy of insurance or may use it to raise
money in several ways.

(a) CASH SURRENDER VALUE. By modern
statute or policy provision, it is commonly
provided that if the life insurance policy
has been in force a stated number of years,
usually two or three, the insured may surrender the policy and the insurer will then
make a payment of the cash value of the
policy to the insured. Term policies do not
have a cash surrender value.

Each year a certain percentage of the
premiums is set aside by the insurer to
hold as a reserve against the date when
payment must be made under the policy. If
the policy is surrendered or canceled, the
potential liability of the reserve fund is re-

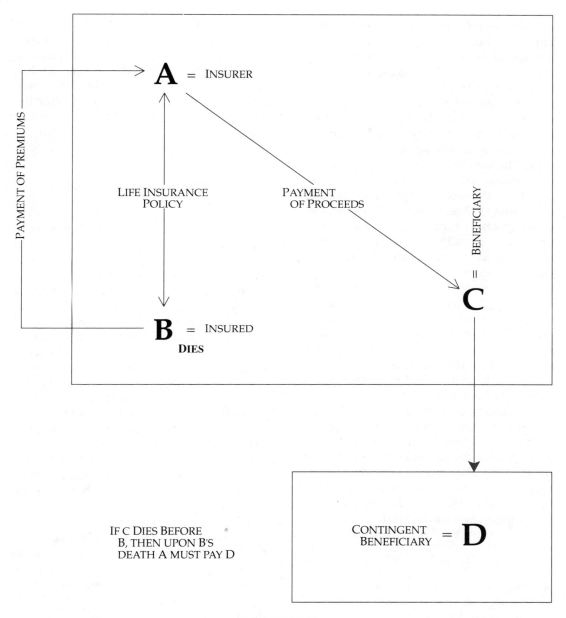

FIGURE 41-1
LIFE INSURANCE

moved and part of the fund can then be released as a payment to the insured. The longer the policy has been in existence, the larger the cash surrender value.

(b) LOAN ON POLICY. The insured can generally obtain funds by borrowing from the insurer. The modern policy contains a definite scale of maximum amounts that can be borrowed depending upon the age of the policy. The insurer is able to make such loans because it has the security of the cash surrender value if the loan is not repaid; or if the insured dies without making repayment, it may deduct the debt from the proceeds payable to the beneficiary.

The loan value of a policy is usually the

same amount as the cash surrender value. The policy holder, as a borrower, must pay interest to the insurance company on the loan.

(c) PAID-UP POLICY. Under modern statutes or common forms of policies, an insured who can no longer afford the expense of insurance, may request the insurer to issue a new policy of paid-up insurance. The insured in effect takes out a new but smaller paid-up policy through the transfer of the reserve value of the old policy. In some states, when a policy lapses for nonpayment of premiums, the insurer must automatically issue a paid-up policy on the basis of the reserve value of the lapsed policy.

(d) EXTENDED INSURANCE. Instead of a paid-up policy for a smaller amount, it is generally possible under modern statutes and policies for the insured to obtain term insurance that provides the original amount of protection. This remains effective until the reserve value of the original policy has been consumed.

(e) REINSTATEMENT OF LAPSED POLICY. When a premium on a policy is not paid within the required period or within the grace period, the insured generally may reinstate the policy within a reasonable time thereafter as long as the insured is still an insurable risk and provided all premiums that were in arrears are paid.

§ 41:23   SETTLEMENT OPTIONS

Although an ordinary life insurance policy will provide for the payment of a specified amount upon the death of the insured, the insured generally may designate one or several plans of distribution of this fund. These plans of distribution are called **settlement options.** When the insured has designated a particular option, the beneficiary generally cannot change it after the insured's death. Sometimes the policy reserves to the beneficiary the right to change the settlement option.

§ 41:24   RIGHTS OF CREDITORS

Can creditors complain when a debtor obtains a policy of life insurance? To the extent that the debtor is paying premiums to the insurance company, there is less money with which to pay the creditors. Can the creditors reach the cash surrender value of the policy during the insured's life or the proceeds of the policy upon the insured's death?

If the insured makes the policy payable to the estate of the insured, the proceeds become part of the general assets of the insured's estate upon death, and, in the absence of statute, are subject to claims of the insured's creditors. If the insured is solvent at all times when premiums are paid, the creditors cannot reach the policy in payment of their claims, and if the insured makes the policy payable to a named beneficiary, the beneficiary is entitled to the entire proceeds of the policy.

Between these two extremes are a variety of situations. The insured may have been insolvent during part or all of the life of the policy; or the obtaining of the insurance policy or the assignment of it or the changing of the beneficiary may have been done to defraud the creditors.

SUMMARY

In order for a fire loss to be covered by fire insurance there must be an actual, hostile fire and that fire must be the immediate cause of the loss. The insurer is liable for the actual amount of the loss sustained up to the maximum amount stated in the policy. An exception exists when the policy contains a coinsurance clause requiring the insured to maintain insurance up to a certain percentage of the value of the property. To the extent this is not done, the insured is deemed a coinsurer with the insurer, and the insurer is liable for only its proportional share of the amount of insurance required to be carried. A fire insurance policy usually cannot be assigned without the consent of the insurer. It is common for lenders to insist as a condition of making a mortgage loan on real estate that the mortgagor obtain and pay the premiums on a fire insurance policy on the full value of the property, and in case of loss that the insurance money be paid to the mortgagor and mortgagee as their respective interests may appear. Extended coverage generally refers to protection against losses due to wind, hail, riot, aircraft, vehicular damage, and smoke damage. When the insurer cancels a policy, the provisions of the policy or applicable statute must be strictly followed in order for the cancellation to be effective.

A homeowner's insurance policy provides fire, theft, and liability protection in a single contract. A homeowner's policy covers all permanent residents of the insured's household. Liability protection covers accidents or injuries that occur on the premises of the insured and unintentional injuries to others away from home but for which the insured or any member of the resident family is held responsible. Injuries to household members are not covered by a homeowner's policy. Personal property floaters may be added to a homeowner's policy to cover loss or theft of items of special value.

The owner or operator of a motor vehicle may purchase liability insurance for protection from claims made by third persons for their bodily injuries or the damage to their property caused by the operation or use of the motor vehicle. The owner may also purchase insurance to cover the damage to the owner's property, regardless of whether the owner was at fault. This kind of insurance is called collision insurance. Special limited coverage insurance is required by law in most states to cover personal injuries caused by uninsured motorists. A state statute may require no fault coverage, which means that when the insured is injured while using the insured automobile the insurer will make payment without regard to whose fault caused the harm. No fault laws bar suits against the party at fault for ordinary claims. However in serious matters, as defined by law, suits may be brought against the party at fault. The insured may purchase theft and fire insurance, or comprehensive coverage, which protects against all risks including fire and theft, except collision or certain other exclusions.

A life insurance policy requires the insurer to pay a stipulated sum of money to a named beneficiary upon the death of the insured. It may be a straight life policy, a limited payment policy, an endowment policy, or (as is most common today) a term insurance policy. State law commonly requires the inclusion of an incontestability clause, whereupon at the conclusion of a two-year period, the insurer cannot contest the validity of the policy based on misstatements or misrepresentations of the insured in the application for insurance and must pay the claim. Various settlement options exist.

QUESTIONS AND CASE PROBLEMS

1. What social forces are affected by the concept of no fault insurance?
2. Hernandez owned and operated a grocery store. He obtained a policy of fire insurance on the store and contents from the Casandra Casualty Company. The oil furnace that heated the store became clogged, and heavy smoke poured into the store. Much of the food in the store absorbed the smoke, and the contaminated food had to be thrown away. Hernandez sued Casandra for the loss. Is he entitled to recover?

3. Explain the terms *use* and *operation* as found in automobile liability policies.

4. Compare the nature of and extent of coverage of:
   (a) life insurance,
   (b) fire insurance, and
   (c) automobile liability insurance.

5. Caroline drives her car off of the road to avoid a collision with an oncoming truck. In so doing, she hits a tree. The truck and its driver cannot be located or identified. Caroline sues her own insurer claiming that it is liable to her for the damage to the car under its uninsured motorist coverage. Is the insurer liable?

6. Joan owns an automobile. She carries liability insurance. The policy contains an omnibus clause. Joan is discussing selling her car to Carlos. With her consent, he drives the car in the morning to test it out. At noon he tells Joan he will take the car but that he cannot pay for it until the end of the week. Joan tells Carlos that he can drive the car and that she will trust him to come back with the money. Carlos drives away and later that afternoon runs into Oki. Oki sues Joan's insurance company on the theory that Carlos was driving with the insured's permission and, therefore, was covered by the omnibus clause of Joan's insurance policy. Is Oki correct?

7. Turner had a policy of life insurance issued by the Equitable Life Assurance Society. His wife was the beneficiary. When she died, Turner changed the beneficiary to Olsen. Thereafter, he began drinking heavily and was committed two times to institutions for alcoholism. About two years after he was released the second time, he changed the beneficiary of the policy to Hawkins. When Turner died, Olsen sued Hawkins and the insurance company for the proceeds of the policy, claiming that the change of beneficiary was not valid on the theory that Turner lacked capacity to change the beneficiary. In addition to Turner's confinement to institutions for alcoholism, it was shown that on a number of instances he had been arrested for minor offenses committed while intoxicated. There was evidence that he was childish and forgetful. Was Olsen entitled to the proceeds of the policy? [Olsen v Hawkins, 90 Idaho 28, 408 P2d 462]

8. Marshall Produce Co. insured its milk and egg processing plant against fire. Smoke from a fire near its plant was absorbed by its egg powder. Cans of the powder delivered to the United States Government were rejected as contaminated. Marshall Produce sued the insurance company for a total loss. The insurer contended that there had been no fire involving the insured property and no total loss. Decide. [Marshall Produce Co. v St. Paul Fire & Marine Insurance Co. 256 Minn 404, 98 NW2d 280]

9. George Rogers insured his life with the National Producers Life Insurance Company. Ten years later he committed suicide. The insurance company denied liability because the policy stated that death by suicide was excepted. The beneficiary of the policy claimed that the insurer could not raise this defense because the two years specified by the two-year incontestability clause had expired. She sued the insurance company. Was she entitled to recover? [National Producers Life Ins. Co. v Rogers, 8 Ariz App 53, 442 P2d 876]

10. A father told his son that the latter could have the former's car but must not drive it. The son had a friend drive the car. The friend ran into another car. The insurer denied liability on the ground that the father had not given permission to the friend to drive the car and that, therefore, the friend was not an "other driver" within the protection of the omnibus clause. Decide. [Esmond v Liscio, 209 Pa Super 200, 224 A2d 793]

11. Leverette had a policy insuring his pickup truck. The policy covered harm sustained through the operation, maintenance, or use of a motor vehicle. Leverette was driving his truck on the highway. He stopped his truck so that he could pick plums from a tree growing by the side of the road. In order to reach the higher plums, he stood on the side panel of the truck. He fell and was injured. He then sued the insurer, claiming that his injury was sustained through the use of the truck. Was his injury covered by the policy? [Leverette v Aetna Casualty & Surety Co. 157 Ga App 175, 276 SE2d 859]

12. Amador Pena had three insurance policies on his life. He wrote a will in which he specified that the proceeds from the insurance policies should go to his children instead of to Leticia Pena Salinas and other beneficiaries named in the policies. He died the

next day. The insurance companies paid the proceeds of the policies to the named beneficiaries. The executor of Pena's estate sued Salinas and the other beneficiaries for the insurance money. Decide. [Pena v Salinas (Tex Civ App) 536 SW2d 671]

13. Spector owned a small automobile repair garage in rural Kansas valued at $40,000. He purchased fire insurance coverage against loss to the extent of $24,000. The policy contained an 80 percent coinsurance clause. A fire destroyed a portion of his parts room, causing a loss of $16,000. Spector believes he is entitled to be fully compensated for this loss since it is less than the $24,000 of fire protection that he purchased and paid for. Is Spector correct?

14. The Springfield Life Insurance Company issued a group policy on the lives of the employees of Chickasha Transit Mixed Concrete, Inc. Richard Kamm was included in the list of employees, and a certificate of insurance was issued to him. Homer Hulme was named in the certificate as the beneficiary. The master contract between the insurer and the employer stated "this contract shall be incontestable after two years from date of issue, except for nonpayment of premiums." Kamm died four years later. The insurer refused to pay the death benefit on the theory that Kamm was not an employee and, therefore, was not covered by the policy. Hulme claimed that the incontestable clause prevented raising this issue. Decide. [Hulme v Springfield Life Insurance Company, Inc. (Okla) 565 P2d 666]

15. Daniel Corrales, the minor son of Gilbert and Edna Corrales, while waterskiing in the family boat caused serious injury to Andrea Behrens. Claiming that the parents had negligently entrusted the boat to Daniel and had negligently "failed to provide supervision of the operation of the boat," Andrea brought suit against them. The Corraleses requested that Aetna defend this action under their homeowner's policy. They contend that such a policy covers such an injury to another away from home since the lawsuit against them dealt with their negligence in entrustment and supervision and not the operation of the boat. Aetna declined because of a policy exclusion for "bodily injury or property damage arising out of the ownership, maintenance, operation, use, loading or unloading of any water craft" of the kind involved in this case. Andrea was awarded a judgment against the parents for $100,000 and brought a declaratory judgment action against Aetna to establish that the policy provided coverage. Aetna disagrees. Decide. [Behrens v Aetna Life and Casualty, ___ Ariz ___, 736 P2d 385]

PART 7

AGENCY AND EMPLOYMENT

42

AGENCY — CREATION AND TERMINATION

One of the most common legal relationships is that of agency. By virtue of the agency device, one person can make contracts at numerous places with many different parties at the same time. A principal or employer can sometimes be held liable in tort when an agent or employee injures a third person while performing business-related tasks directed by the principal or employer. Thus, disputes based upon contract law and tort law may arise out of transactions or work done for others. The rights and liabilities of the parties to the dispute may turn not only on the point of contract or tort law, but also on whether or not an agency relationship existed.

A. NATURE OF THE AGENCY RELATIONSHIP

Agency is based upon the consent of the parties, and, for that reason, is called a consensual relation. If consideration is present, the relationship is also contractual. The law sometimes imposes an agency relationship.

849

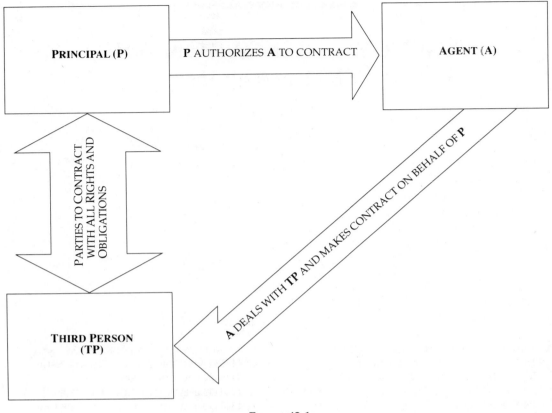

FIGURE 42-1
AGENCY RELATIONSHIP

§ 42:1   DEFINITIONS AND
             DISTINCTIONS

Agency is a relationship based upon an express or implied agreement by which one person, the **agent,** is authorized to act under the control of and for another, the **principal,** in negotiating and making contracts with third persons.[1] The acts of the agent obligate the principal to third persons and give the principal rights against third persons.

The term *agency* is frequently used with other meanings. It is sometimes used to denote the fact that one has the right to sell certain products, such as when a dealer is said to possess an automobile agency. In other instances, the term is used to mean an exclusive right to sell certain articles within a given territory. In these cases, however, the dealer is not an agent in the sense of representing the manufacturer.[2]

In the *Hutton* case the court was called upon to determine if an agency relationship existed although the term *agent* had not been used.

---

[1]   Restatement, Agency, 2d § 1; Botticello v Stefanovicz, 177 Conn 22, 411 A2d 16 (1979). When the question is the tax liability of an enterprise (see Boise Cascade Corp. v Washington, 3 Wash App 78, 473 P2d 429 (1970)), the definition of agency may be different than when the question is contract or tort liability, which are the areas of law considered in this part.

[2]   Professional Lens Plan, Inc. v Polaris Leasing Corp, 238 Kan 384, 710 P2d 1297 (1985).

HUTTON V ANITA BECK CARDS & SUCH INC.

(Minn App) 366 NW2d 358 (1985)

Anita Beck Bosiger, president of Anita Beck Cards & Such Inc. (Beck), and Shirley Hutton, a national sales director for Mary Kay Cosmetics, agreed that Beck would manufacture calendars and stationery to be sold at Mary Kay conventions. To finance the project Hutton gave $20,000 to Beck. The sales undertaking proved to be a substantial failure. In the lawsuit that followed, Hutton claimed that she was Beck's agent and the $20,000 had been a loan. Beck claimed that the money was the down payment on the actual purchase of the goods by Hutton. From a judgment for Hutton, Beck appealed.

HUSPENI, J. . . . Bosiger and Hutton agreed that Beck would manufacture 5,000 sets of a product that included a calendar, notebook, notes, box, decorative bee and ribbon. Bosiger contended at trial that Hutton purchased the sets herself, at a 15% discount, for resale to Mary Kay personnel. Hutton contended that she was an agent for Beck and was to receive a 15% commission on her sales. A document encaptioned "order" lists some terms of their agreement, but does not address whether Hutton was to be an agent or a purchaser. . . .

Beck delivered 300 sets of merchandise for Hutton to test market at an Iowa Mary Kay convention in November 1980. Sales were weak. Thereafter, Hutton and Bosiger decided to break down the sets into individual components and market them separately. They intended to target a Dallas Mary Kay convention scheduled in June 1981.

In preparation for the convention, Bosiger shipped goods at her own expense to Dallas. She forwarded to Dallas price sheets and mail order forms, flowers, posters and a tablecloth to decorate the Dallas sales room. The room in Dallas was rented in Bosiger's name. This was done, she argued, so that Hutton could avoid any appearance of conflict of interest with her Mary Kay duties. Hutton paid for the room. She also paid two sales persons hired for the Dallas convention. She stated that this was her responsibility as agent.

A document was prepared to reflect the dates, numbers and prices of the goods shipped to Iowa and Dallas. Both parties signed it. The document did not reflect whether Hutton's role was that of purchaser or agent. It did, however, contain the remark "commission is 15% on all but calendars."

Unfortunately, only $207.09 of the merchandise was sold. Checks were made out directly to Beck and all proceeds of the sale were turned over to Bosiger. Bosiger shipped 67 cartons of unsold merchandise back to her warehouse at her own expense. She stated that this was to accommodate Hutton, who had no storage facility. Bosiger never requested that Hutton pay for the shipping and never demanded that she pick up the merchandise. Attempts to mitigate the losses were futile. The enterprise was a substantial failure.

There was evidence from Beck's accountant that the $20,000 was not included in income but was treated as a liability for "prepaid sales." Further, the parties' transaction was not recorded on an accounts receivable ledger. In a sales transaction, such recording would have been an ordinary practice for Beck. Standard shipping and billing forms were not used. No invoices were sent to Hutton. No changes were made in inventory when the 67 cartons were shipped or returned. . . .

Following trial, the court determined that the $20,000 was a loan which Bosiger and Beck were required to repay. The trial court's award to Hutton represented this $20,000, plus 15% commission on sales of $207.09. . . .

Bosiger and Beck . . . allege that there is no support in the record for the trial court's determination that the parties' transaction was a loan, not a sale. . . .

Beck's accounting books were at best, inconclusive on the issue of whether the transaction was a loan or a sale. Certainly, Beck did not treat Hutton as it did its other sales customers. The trial court recognized that the documents were not skillfully drafted and did not reflect the nature of the transaction.

Hutton testified that she did not buy the merchandise at issue. This position is consistent with the parties' stated overall intent to treat Mary Kay personnel as the ultimate purchasers. It is also consistent with the notation "commission is 15% on all but calendars" on the transaction document. The trial court was required to make its factual determinations on the basis of conflicting testimony. We cannot conclude that it committed error in determining that the $20,000 was a loan, not a sale.

Finally, Bosiger and Beck claim that there is no evidence to support the trial court's determination that Hutton was their agent. We cannot agree. The events occurring at Dallas support Hutton's argument that she was acting as an agent. Beck's role appeared to be a proprietary one. Order forms, room decorations, and the document indicating that Hutton was to receive a commission on all goods sold except calendars support an agency determination. Further, checks were made directly to Beck, goods were shipped back to Minnesota at Beck's expense, and Beck did not account for this transaction in the same manner as it did other sales to customers. We find no error by the trial court. . . .

[Judgment affirmed]

QUESTIONS

1. State the contentions of the parties.
2. What evidence supported the decision that Hutton was Beck's agent?
3. Give your opinion as to whether or not a conflict of interest existed in Hutton's acting as agent for Beck while serving as a national sales director for Mary Kay Cosmetics.

Because the agency relationship creates certain rights and liabilities not present in other associations, it is important to be able to distinguish agencies from other similar relationships.

(a) EMPLOYEES AND INDEPENDENT CONTRACTORS. Control and authority are characteristics that distinguish ordinary employees and independent contractors from agents.

(1) Employees. An agent is distinguished from an ordinary employee, who is not hired to represent the employer in dealings with third persons. It is possible, however, for the same person to be both an agent and an employee. For example, the driver of a milk delivery truck is an agent, as well as an employee, in making contracts between the milk company and its customers, but is only an employee

with respect to the work of delivering milk.

(2) Independent Contractors. An agent or employee differs from an **independent contractor** in that the principal or employer has control over and can direct the agent or an employee but does not have control over the performance of work by an independent contractor.[3]

A person who appears to be an independent contractor may in fact be so controlled by the other party that the contractor is regarded as an agent of, or employee of, the controlling person.

The separate identity of an independent contractor may be concealed so that the public believes that it is dealing with the principal. When this situation occurs, the principal is liable for the negligence of the independent contractor.

A person may be an independent contractor generally but an agent with respect to a particular transaction. Thus, an "agency" or a "broker" rendering personal services to customers is ordinarily an independent contractor but will be the agent of a customer when the rendering of a service involves making a contract on behalf of the customer with a third person.

(b) REAL ESTATE BROKERS. A real estate broker is generally not an agent with authority to make a contract with a third person that will bind the broker's client. Typically, the broker's authority is limited to locating a seller or buyer and bringing the parties together. Even when the third person and the broker sign a "contract," it is generally only an offer by the third person, and it does not become a binding contract until accepted by the client of the broker.

(c) BAILEES. When personal property is delivered to another under an agreement that the property will be returned to the deliverer or transferred to a third person, a bailment arises. The person to whom the property is delivered, the bailee, is not an agent because the bailee has no authority

to act for or make any contract on behalf of the bailor.

Situations commonly arise, however, in which the same person is both an agent and a bailee. A salesperson who is lent a company car is a bailee with respect to the car, but with respect to making sales contracts, is an agent.

(d) REQUIRED ACT. The mere fact that one person requires another person to do an act does not make the latter person the agent of the former. For example, when a bank directs a borrower to obtain the signature of another person in order to secure a bank loan, the borrower is not the agent of the bank in making contact with the other person and procuring the required signature.

§ 42:2 PURPOSE OF AGENCY

An agency may be created to perform almost any act that the principal could lawfully do. The object of the agency must not be criminal, nor may it be contrary to public policy. Some acts must be performed in person and cannot be entrusted or delegated to an agent. Voting, swearing to the truth of documents, testifying in court, and making a will are instances where personal action is required. In the preparation of a document, however, it is proper to employ someone else to prepare the paper that is then signed or sworn to by the employing party. Various forms that are required by statute, such as applications for licenses and tax returns, will in some instances expressly authorize the execution of such forms by an agent as long as the identities of both principal and agent and the latter's representative capacity are clearly shown.

§ 42:3 WHO MAY BE A PRINCIPAL

Any person who is competent to act may act through an agent. The appointment of an agent by a person lacking capacity is generally void or voidable to the same extent that a contract made by such person would be. Thus, a minor acting through an agent will

---

[3] Noonan v Texaco, Inc., (Wyo) 713 P2d 160 (1986).

effect a contract that will be voidable to the same extent as though made by the minor.

Groups of persons may also appoint agents to act for them.

§ 42:4   WHO MAY BE AN AGENT

Since a contract made by an agent is, in law, the contract of the principal, it is immaterial whether the agent has legal capacity to make a contract. Therefore, it is permissible to employ as agents persons who are aliens, minors, and others who are under a natural or legal disability.

While ordinarily an agent is one person acting for another, an agent may be a partnership or a corporation.

§ 42:5   CLASSIFICATION OF AGENTS

A **general agent** is authorized by the principal to transact all affairs in connection with a particular kind of business or trade, or to transact all business at a certain place.[4] To illustrate, a person who is appointed as manager by the owner of a store is a general agent.

A **special agent** is authorized by the principal to handle a definite business transaction or to do a specific act. One who is authorized by another to purchase a particular house is a special agent.

A **universal agent** is authorized by the principal to do all acts that can be delegated lawfully to a representative. This form of agency arises when a person absent by virtue of being in the military service gives another person a blanket power of attorney to do anything that must be done during such absence.

§ 42:6   AGENCY COUPLED WITH AN INTEREST

An agent has an **interest in the authority** when consideration has been given or paid for the right to exercise the authority. To

illustrate, when a lender, in return for making a loan of money, is given, as security, authority to collect rents due to the borrower and to apply those rents to the payment of the debt, the lender becomes the borrower's agent with an interest in the authority given to collect the rents.[5]

An agent has an **interest in the subject matter** when for a consideration the agent is given an interest in the property with which the agent is dealing. Hence, when the agent is authorized to sell property of the principal and is given a lien on such property as security for a debt owed to the agent by the principal, the agent has an interest in the subject matter.

B.   CREATING THE AGENCY

An agency may arise by appointment, conduct, ratification, or operation of law.

§ 42:7   AUTHORIZATION BY APPOINTMENT

The usual method of creating an agency is by express authorization; that is, a person is appointed to act for or on behalf of another.

In most instances the authorization of the agent may be oral. Some appointments, however, must be made in a particular way. A majority of the states, by statute, require the appointment of an agent to be in writing when the agency is created to acquire or dispose of any interest in land. A written authorization of agency is called a **power of attorney** and an agent acting under a power of attorney is referred to as an **attorney in fact.**

Ordinarily, no agency arises from the fact that two people are married to each other or that they are co-owners of property. Consequently, when a check was made payable to the order of husband and wife,

---

[4]   Washington National Ins. Co. v Strictland (Ala) 491 So 2d 872 (1986).

[5]   Halloran-Judge Trust Co. v Heath, 70 Utah 124, 258 P 342 (1927). When personal property or rights to money are involved, the creditor should require the creation of a secured transaction, as Article 9 of the UCC will then give the creditor greater protection.

it was necessary for each to indorse the check because there was no agency by which the husband could indorse the wife's name and deposit the money into the husband's own bank account.

§ 42:8   Authorization by Conduct

Conduct consistent with the existence of an agency relationship may be sufficient to bind the principal.

(a) Principal's Conduct as to Agent. Since agency is created by the consent of the parties, any conduct of the principal, including words, that gives a person reason to believe that the principal consents to that person's acting as agent for the principal is sufficient to create an agency. Likewise, if one person, knowingly and without objection, permits another to act as agent, the law will find in such conduct an expression of authorization to the agent, and the principal will not be permitted to deny that the agent was in fact authorized. Thus, if the owner of a hotel allows another person to assume the duties of hotel clerk, that person may infer from the owner's conduct an authority to act as the hotel clerk.

(b) Principal's Conduct as to Third Persons. The principal may have such dealings with third persons as to cause them to believe that the "agent" has authority. Thus, if the owner of a store places another person in charge, third persons may assume that the person in charge is the agent for the owner in that respect. The "agent" then appears to be authorized and is said to have **apparent authority,** and the principal is estopped from contradicting the appearance that has been created.[6]

The term *apparent authority* is used when there is only the appearance of authority but no actual authority and that appearance of authority was created by the principal.[7] The test for the existence of apparent authority is an objective test determined by the principal's outward manifestations through words or conduct that leads a third person reasonably to believe that the "agent" has authority. A principal's express restriction on authority not made known to a third person is no defense. Apparent authority extends to all acts that a person of ordinary prudence, familiar with business usages, and the particular business, would be justified in believing that the agent has authority to perform.

The mere placing of property in the possession of another does not give that person either actual or apparent authority to sell the property.[8]

It is essential to the concept of apparent authority that the third person reasonably believe that the agent has authority. If the basis for such belief is not reasonable, no apparent authority arises.

In the *Lundberg* case, the court was faced with deciding whether a third party was justified in believing that a breeding farm manager had authority to contract on behalf of the owner of the farm.

[6]   Foote & Davis, Inc. v Arnold Craven, Inc. 72 NC App 591, 324 SE2d 889 (1985).
[7]   Foley v Allard (Minn App) 405 NW2d 503 (1987).
[8]   Krick v First National Bank of Blue Island, 8 Ill App 3d 663, 290 NE2d 661 (1972). Note that under UCC, § 2-403, an entrustee who deals in goods of that kind has the power but not the right to transfer the entruster's title to a person buying in good faith in the ordinary course of business.

Lundberg v Church Farms, Inc.
(Ill App) 502 NE2d 806 (1986)

Gilbert Church owned Church Farms, Inc. in Manteno, Illinois, and he advertised its well-bred stallion Imperial Guard for breeding rights at $50,000, directing all inquiries to "Herb Bagley, Manager." Herb Bagley lived at Church Farms and was the only person available to visitors. Vern

Lundberg responded to the advertisement. After discussions with Bagley wherein Bagley stated that Imperial Guard would remain in Illinois for at least a two-year period, Lundberg and Bagley executed a two-year breeding rights and syndication agreement, which was signed by Lundberg and by Bagley as "Church Farms Inc., H. Bagley, Mgr.". When Gil Church moved Imperial Guard to Oklahoma prior to the second year of the contract, Lundberg brought suit for breach of contract. Church testified that Bagley had no authority to sign contracts for Church Farms or to change or add terms. From a judgment for Lundberg, Church appealed.

UNVERZAGI, J. . . . Defendant. . . [contends] that the jury's verdict and the size of its award were contrary to the manifest weight of the evidence. Specifically, defendant contends that plaintiffs have failed to establish that Bagley had apparent authority to negotiate and sign the Lundberg contract for Church Farm. . . .

The party asserting an agency has the burden of proving its existence, but may do so by inference and circumstantial evidence. Additionally, an agent may bind his principal by acts which the principal has not given him *actual* authority to perform, but which he *appears* authorized to perform. An agent's apparent authority is that authority which "the principal knowingly permits the agent to assume or which he holds his agent out as possessing. It is the authority that a reasonably prudent man, exercising diligence and discretion, in view of the principal's conduct, would naturally suppose the agent to possess." The agent's authority must be derived from some act or statement of the *principal*. Defendant argues that plaintiffs' proof is based on Bagley's own assertions of authority rather than the acts or statements of Church Farm or Gil Church. We disagree.

Plaintiffs produced evidence at trial that Gil Church approved the Imperial Guard advertisement listing Herb Bagley as Church Farm's manager, and directing all inquiries to him. Church also permitted Bagley to live on the farm and to handle its daily operations. Bagley was the only person available to visitors to the farm. Bagley answered Church Farm's phone calls, and there was a preprinted signature line for him on the breeding rights package.

The conclusion is inescapable that Gil Church affirmatively placed Bagley in a managerial position giving him complete control of Church Farm and its dealings with the public. We believe that this is just the sort of "holding out" of an agent by a principal that justifies a third person's reliance on the agent's authority. See *Scholenberger v. Chicago Transit Authority* (1980), 84 Ill.App.3d 1132, 1138 (noting that apparent authority exists when principal allows public to deal exclusively with agent).

We cannot accept defendant's contention that the Lundbergs were affirmatively obligated to seek out Church to ascertain the actual extent of Bagley's authority. Where an agent has apparent authority to act, the principal will be liable in spite of any undisclosed limitations the principal has placed on that authority.

[Judgment affirmed]

QUESTIONS

1. Did the court find that Bagley had authority to bind Church Farms, Inc.? Explain.
2. What could Gil Church have done to prevent the dispute in this case?

(c) ACQUIESCENCE BY PRINCIPAL. The conduct of the principal that gives rise to the agent's authority may be acquiescence in or failing to object to acts done by the purported or apparent agent over a period of time.[9] For example, a person collecting payments on a note and remitting the proper amounts to the holder of the note will be regarded as the latter's agent for collection when this conduct has been followed over a period of years without objection.

§ 42:9 AGENCY BY RATIFICATION

An agent may attempt, on behalf of the principal, to do an act that was not authorized, or a person who is not the agent of another may attempt to act as such an agent. Generally, in such cases, the principal for whom the agent claimed to act has the choice of ignoring the transaction or of ratifying it. Ordinarily any unauthorized act may be ratified.

(a) INTENTION TO RATIFY. Initially, ratification is a question of intention. Just as in the case of authorization, when there is a question of whether or not the principal authorized the agent, so there is a question of whether or not the principal intended to approve or ratify the action of the unauthorized agent.[10]

The intention to ratify may be expressed in words or it may be found in conduct indicating an intention to ratify, such as paying for goods ordered by the agent or performing the contract that the agent had made and accepting payments for such performance.

In the *Melancon* case, the court considered the question of whether the conduct of a service contractor evidenced an intention to ratify the actions of its representative.

---

[9] Vacura v Haar's Equipment Co. (Minn) 364 NW2d 387 (1985).

[10] Miles v Plumbing Services of Houston, Inc. (Tex Civ App) 668 SW2d 509 (1984).

MELANCON V A & M PEST CONTROL SERVICE CO., INC.
(La App) 325 So 2d 391 (1976)

Joseph Melancon made a contract with A & M Pest Control Service, Inc., to protect his house against termites. The contract contained a warranty that stated "this warranty agreement is personal to the customer named above [Melancon] and may not be assigned or transferred by any means whatever by the person to whom it is issued." Melancon sold his house to Alan Ruiz in 1970. In 1972, a representative of A & M told Ruiz that he could keep the contract in force by paying the renewal fee. Ruiz did this, and thereafter, A & M made inspections and repairs to the premises. Ruiz claimed that greater repairs should have been made, whereupon A & M claimed that Ruiz could not enforce the warranty because it was limited to Melancon. Ruiz replied that A & M had ratified the action of its representative and was therefore bound by the renewal contract. Melancon and Ruiz jointly sued A & M. From a judgment in favor of Melancon and Ruiz, A & M appealed.

LEMMON, J. . . . Although the contract and warranty were issued to Melancon, Ruiz testified that A & M's representative with apparent authority to do so told him the contract could be kept in effect by paying the renewal fee. A & M not only did not deny this statement, but also accepted the renewal fee from

Ruiz and contacted him to arrange the annual inspection and treatment pursuant to the contract. We therefore conclude that A & M ratified its agent's agreement to allow Ruiz to take over its contract with Melancon by providing service and accepting payment under the contract, and Ruiz therefore had a right of action to enforce the terms of the contract.

[Judgment affirmed]

QUESTIONS

1. What did the plaintiff claim?
2. What did the court hold?
3. What conduct of the principal did the court consider in reaching its decision?

If the conditions of ratification are satisfied, a principal ratifies an agent's act when, with knowledge of the act, the principal accepts or retains the benefit of the act, or brings an action to enforce legal rights based upon the act, or defends an action by asserting the existence of a right based upon the unauthorized transaction, or fails to repudiate the agent's act within a reasonable time. The receipt, acceptance, and deposit of a check by the principal with knowledge that it arises from an unauthorized transaction is a common illustration of ratification of the unauthorized transaction by conduct.

(b) CONDITIONS FOR RATIFICATION. In addition to the intent to ratify, expressed in some instances with certain formality, the following conditions must be satisfied in order that the intention take effect as a ratification:

1. The agent must have purported to act on behalf of or as agent for the identified principal.[11]
2. The principal must have been capable of authorizing the act both at the time of the act and at the time when it was ratified.
3. The principal must ratify the act before the third person withdraws.

[11] Jones v Nunley, 274 Or 591, 547 P2d 616 (1976).

4. The act to be ratified must generally be legal.
5. The principal must have full knowledge of all material facts. If the agent conceals a material fact, the ratification of the principal that is made in ignorance of such fact is not binding. Of course, there can be no ratification when the principal does not know of the making of the contract by the alleged agent. Consequently, when the owner's agent and a contractor make unauthorized major changes to an installation contract without knowledge of the owner, the fact that the owner had no knowledge of the matter bars any claim of ratification of the agent's act.

It is not always necessary, however, to show that the principal had actual knowledge; for knowledge will be imputed if a principal knows of such other facts as would put a prudent person on inquiry, or if that knowledge can be inferred from the knowledge of other facts or from a course of business. Knowledge is likewise not an essential factor when the principal does not care to know the details and is willing to ratify the contract regardless of such lack of knowledge.

(c) FORM OF RATIFICATION. An agreement that is binding, although oral, may be ratified orally or by conduct. If a contract cannot be enforced unless evidenced by a writing, it is generally held that a ratification of the contract must be in writing.[12]

(d) EFFECT OF RATIFICATION. When an unauthorized act is ratified, the effect is the same as though the act had been originally authorized. Ordinarily this means that the principal and the third party are bound by the contract made by the agent.[13] When the principal ratifies the act of the unauthorized person, such ratification releases that person from the liability that would otherwise be imposed for having acted without authority.

§ 42:10   AGENCY BY OPERATION OF LAW

In certain instances, the courts, influenced by necessity or social desirability, create or find an agency when there is none. For example, a person may purchase necessaries and charge them to the spouse's account when the spouse does not supply them. Here the social policy is the furtherance of the welfare of the neglected dependent spouse. As another example of agency by operation of law, a minor may purchase necessaries upon the parent's credit when the latter fails to supply them.

An emergency power of an agent to act under unusual circumstances not covered by the agent's authority is recognized when the agent is unable to communicate with the principal and when failure to act would cause the principal substantial loss.

§ 42:11   PROVING THE AGENCY RELATIONSHIP

The burden of proving the existence of an agency relationship rests upon the person who seeks to benefit by such proof. The third person who desires to bind the principal because of the act of an alleged agent has the burden of proving that the latter person was in fact the authorized agent of the principal and possessed the authority to do the act in question.[14] For example, when the buyer asserts that there has been a breach of an express warranty made by the seller's agent, the buyer must establish that there was an actual or apparent authority to make the warranty. In the absence of sufficient proof, the jury must find that there is no agency. The authority of the agent may be established by circumstantial evidence.

C.   TERMINATION OF AGENCY

An agency may be terminated by the act of one or both of the parties to the agency agreement, or by operation of law. When the authority of an agent is terminated, the agent loses all right to act for the principal.

§ 42:12   TERMINATION BY ACT OF PARTIES

In most cases, either party to an agency relationship has the power to terminate that relationship at any time. In some cases, however, the terminating party may be liable to the other party for damages.

(a) EXPIRATION OF AGENCY CONTRACT. The ordinary agency may expire by the terms of the contract creating it. Thus, the contract may provide that it shall last for a stated period, such as five years, or until a particular date arrives, or until the happening of a particular event, such as the sale of certain property. In such a case, the agency is automatically terminated when the specified date arrives or the event at which it is to end occurs.

When it is provided that the agency shall last for a stated period of time, it terminates upon the expiration of that period without regard to whether the acts contemplated by the creation of the agency have

---

[12]   Monti v Tangora, 99 Ill App 3d 575, 54 Ill Dec 732, 425 NE2d 597 (1981).
[13]   Taylor v Roy (La App) 499 So 2d 595 (1986).

[14]   Durham v Waddell & Reed, Inc. (Tenn App) 723 SW2d 129 (1986).

been performed. If no period is stated, the agency continues for a reasonable time, but it may be terminated at the will of either party.

(b) AGREEMENT. Since the agency relation is based upon consent, it can be terminated by the consent of the principal and agent.

(c) OPTION OF A PARTY. An agency agreement may provide that upon the giving of notice or the payment of a specified sum of money, one party may terminate the relationship.

(d) REVOCATION BY PRINCIPAL. The rela-

tionship between principal and agent is terminated whenever the principal discharges the agent even though the agency was stated to be "irrevocable." If the agency was not created for a specified time but was to exist only at will, or if the agent has been guilty of misconduct, the principal may discharge the agent without liability. The intent to revoke must be clearly and unequivocally expressed.

In the *Kinmon* case the court was called upon to determine whether the principal had revoked his agent's authority to sell a summer estate at auction.

KINMON V J. P. KING AUCTION CO., INC.
290 Ala 323, 276 So 2d 569 (1973)

Kinmon owned a summer home that he wanted to sell at auction. He employed the J. P. King Auction Company (King) to make the sale. King sold the property to the highest bidder for $35,000. Kinmon had expected twice that much and refused to convey title to the buyer or to pay commissions to King. King sued Kinmon to collect the commissions. Kinmon raised the defense that he had revoked King's authority to sell the property. From a judgment for King, Kinmon appealed.

FAULKNER, J. . . ."Bittersweet" is a home in Perdido Beach, Alabama. . . .

On July 29, 1971, George H. Kinmon, the owner, signed a contract with J. P. King Auction Company (King) to sell the property "for the highest price obtainable." Kinmon testified to having "conveyed" to the representatives of King that he expected to realize $103,500 for the property. The latter told Kinmon that Bittersweet would bring what it was worth the day of the sale. The written contract did not incorporate any guaranteed minimum price, referring merely to "the highest price obtainable."

King prepared and distributed a brochure announcing the "absolute auction" of Bittersweet:

This is the place for your Vacation Home or Company Lodge, plenty of room for sleeping and entertaining on Beautiful Soldier Creek just a few minutes by boat to Alabama Point and on out into the Gulf for some of the best fishing in the world. Enjoy swimming and skiing from your own boathouse or just plain fishing from the pier. There is everything to enjoy at "Bittersweet."
Let Today's Investment Be Tomorrow's Security.
"YOUR PRICE IS OUR PRICE."

Kinmon, concerned about the possibility of not realizing an adequate price for his property, protested against the inclusion of the terms "Your Price is Our Price" and ["]absolute auction." However, preparations for the auction continued. Signs announcing the forthcoming auction and stating "Your Price is Our Price" remained undisturbed by Kinmon.

On August 21, 1971, the day of the auction, Kinmon was "upset." He told King's secretary that he wasn't signing anything. At one point during the bidding, Kinmon went up to King and stated that if Bittersweet did not bring $70,000, "I will take you to Supreme Court." King went ahead with the bidding and sold the property to the highest bidder for $35,000. Kinmon subsequently refused to convey the property or pay King's commission. King sued, and the Circuit Court of Baldwin County held that he was entitled to his commission. Kinmon appealed from this decree.

. . . There is no doubt Kinmon and King could have written a $50,000, $70,000, or $100,000 minimum price for Bittersweet into their auction sale contract. They did not do so. The contract recites that Bittersweet would be sold "for the highest price obtainable." Kinmon may have wished or hoped that the sale would realize $100,000. However, it is elementary that it is the terms of the written contract, not the mental operations of one of the parties, that control its interpretation. . . .

Contracting parties are free to modify their contract by mutual assent. . . . After expressing discontent with the advertised slogan "Your Price is Our Price," Kinmon could have asked King to insert a minimum price guarantee into the contract. He did not do so. Unilateral grumbling cannot modify a bilateral contract.

It is the general rule that the agency to sell at auction, whether such auction be "with reserve" or "absolute," may be withdrawn at any time prior to the opening of bids. . . . This withdrawal of authority must be clear and unequivocal. Nowhere in the record is there evidence that Kinmon clearly and unequivocally stated that he no longer wished King to sell his property, that he was revoking King's authority, that he was withdrawing Bittersweet from sale. Being "upset" is not enough; threatening to take King to court if $70,000 were not realized is not enough.

[Judgment affirmed]

QUESTIONS

1. What did Kinmon contend?
2. Did the court agree with Kinmon's contentions?
3. What could the principal have done to avoid liability?

Any conduct that manifests an intent to revoke the authority is sufficient, as when the principal takes back from the agent the property that had been entrusted to the agent for the purpose of the agency or when the principal retains another agent to do what the original agent had been authorized to do. When the agency is based upon a contract to employ the agent for a specified period of time, the principal is liable for damages if the principal wrongfully discharges the agent. The fact that the principal is liable for damages does not, however, prevent the principal from terminating the agency by discharging the agent. In such a case, it is said that the principal has the *power* to terminate the agency by discharging the agent but does not have the *right* to do so.

(e) Renunciation by Agent. The agency relationship is terminated if the agent refuses to continue to act as agent, as when the agent abandons the object of the agency and acts in self-interest by committing a fraud upon the principal.

If the relationship is an agency at will, the agent has the right, as well as the power, to renounce or abandon the agency at any time. The agent has the right of renunciation of the relationship in any case if the principal is guilty of making wrongful demands or of other misconduct.

If, however, the agency is based upon a contract calling for the continuation of the relationship for a specified or determinable period (that is, until a particular date arrives or a certain event occurs), the agent has no right to abandon or renounce the relationship if the principal is not guilty of wrongdoing.

When the renunciation by the agent is wrongful, the agent is liable to the principal for the damages that the principal sustains.

(f) Rescission. The agency contract may be terminated by rescission to the same extent that any other contract may be so terminated.

§ 42:13   Termination by Operation of Law

The agency relationship is a personal one, and anything that renders one of the parties incapable of performing will result in the termination of the relationship by operation of law.

(a) Death. The death of either the principal or agent ordinarily terminates the authority of an agent automatically, even though the death is unknown to the other. Some state statutes provide that the death of the principal is not a revocation until the agent has notice nor as to third persons who deal with the agent in good faith and are ignorant of the death. Generally, however, these statutes are limited to principals who are members of the armed forces.

In an attorney-client relationship the death of the client does not terminate the agency if the client has expressly agreed that the attorney should conduct the proceeding to its conclusion.[15]

(b) Insanity. The insanity of either the principal or agent ordinarily terminates the agent's authority. If the incapacity of the principal is only temporary, the agent's authority may be merely suspended rather than terminated.

(c) Bankruptcy. Bankruptcy of the principal or agent usually terminates the relationship. It is generally held, however, that the bankruptcy of an agent does not terminate the agent's power to deal with goods of the principal held by the agent.

Insolvency, as distinguished from a formal adjudication of bankruptcy, usually does not terminate the agency. In most states, accordingly, the authority of an agent is not terminated by the appointment of a receiver for the principal.

(d) Impossibility. The authority of an agent is terminated when it is impossible to perform the agency for any reason, such as the destruction of the subject matter of the agency, the death or loss of capacity of the third person with whom the agent is to contract, or a change in law that makes it impossible to perform the agency lawfully.

(e) War. When the country of the principal is at war with that of the agent, the authority of the agent is usually terminated or at least suspended until peace is restored. When the war has the effect of making performance impossible, the agency is, of course, terminated. For example, the authority of an agent who is a nonresident enemy alien to sue is terminated, because such an alien is not permitted to sue.

(f) Unusual Events or Changes of Circumstances. The authority of an agent is also terminated by the occurrence of an unusual event or a change in value or busi-

---

[15] Vincent v Vincent, 16 Wash App 213, 554 P2d 374 (1976).

ness conditions of such a nature that the agent should reasonably infer that the principal would not desire the agent to continue to act under the changed circumstances. For example, an agent employed to sell land at a specified price should regard the authority to sell at that price as terminated when the value of the land increases greatly because of the discovery of oil on the land.

§ 42:14 DISABILITY OF THE PRINCIPAL UNDER THE UDPAA

The Uniform Durable Power of Attorney Act (UDPAA) permits the creation of an agency by a writing which specifies that "this power of attorney shall not be affected by subsequent disability or incapacity of the principal." Or the UDPAA permits the agency to come into existence upon the "disability or incapacity of the principal." To be effective the principal must designate the attorney in fact in writing , and the writing must contain words showing the intent of the principal that the authority conferred shall continue notwithstanding the disability or incapacity of the principal. The UDPAA, which is being rapidly adopted by the states,[16] changes the common law and the general rule that insanity of the principal terminates the agent's authority to act for the principal. Society today recognizes that it may be in the best interest of a princi-

[16] The Uniform Durable Power of Attorney Act has been adopted in Alabama, California, Delaware, District of Columbia, Idaho, Indiana, Kansas, Massachusetts, Missouri, Montana, Nebraska, North Dakota, Pennsylvania, Tennessee, West Virginia, and Wisconsin.

pal and good for the business environment for a principal to designate another as an attorney in fact to act for the principal when the principal becomes incapacitated.

§ 42:15 TERMINATION OF AGENCY COUPLED WITH AN INTEREST

An agency coupled with an interest is an exception to the general rule as to the termination of an agency. Such an agency cannot be revoked by the principal before the expiration of the interest and is not terminated by the death or insanity of either the principal or the agent.

§ 42:16 EFFECT OF TERMINATION OF AUTHORITY

If the agency is revoked by the principal, the authority to act for the principal is not terminated until notice of revocation is received by the agent. As between the principal and the agent, the *right* of the agent to bind the principal to third persons generally ends immediately upon the termination of the agent's authority. Such termination is effective without the giving of notice to third persons.

When the agency is terminated by the act of the principal, notice must be given to third persons. If such notice is not given, the agent may have the *power* to make contracts that will bind the principal and third persons. This rule is predicated on the theory that a known agent will have the appearance of still being the agent unless notice to the contrary is given to third persons. This situation arose in the *Record* case.

RECORD V WAGNER
100 NH 419, 128 A2d 921 (1957)

Donald Record owned a farm that was operated by his agent, David Berry, who lived on the property. The latter hired Fred Wagner to bale the hay in 1953 and told him to bill Record for this work. He did so and was paid by Record. By the summer of 1954, the agency had been terminated by Record, but Berry remained in possession as tenant of the farm and nothing appeared changed. Later in the same year, Berry asked Wagner to bale the hay the same as in the prior year and bill Record for the work. Wagner did so, but Record refused to pay on the ground that Berry was not then his agent. When Wagner sued Record and recovered a judgment against him, Record appealed.

DUNCAN, J. . . . "It is a familiar principle of law that the authority of the agent to bind his principal continues, even after an actual revocation, until notice of the revocation is given." *Claflin v Lenheim*, 66 NY 301.

By paying the 1953 bill, the defendant recognized Berry's authority to hire the plaintiff on the former's credit. Berry then resided on the defendant's farm, and was properly found the defendant's agent at that time. In 1954, Berry continued to reside on the main farm, and to all appearances was operating it in the same manner and in the same capacity. If in fact he had ceased to occupy the farm as agent, but did so as a tenant, the defendant made no effort to notify the plaintiff of the change in Berry's status.

It could be found that in the exercise of reasonable diligence the plaintiff was justified as a result of the defendant's conduct in believing that Berry had authority to pledge the defendant's credit in 1954 for the same services which the defendant recognized as a proper charge against himself in 1953. . . . The important fact is that the defendant permitted the outward appearances of Berry's authority to remain unchanged in 1954 from what they were in 1953, and by not notifying the plaintiff of the termination of the agency permitted the plaintiff to be misled. Having done so, he rather than the plaintiff should bear the loss. . . . We do not consider the circumstance that Berry had previously pledged the defendant's credit upon only one occasion. . . to be of controlling importance. . . .The evidence that no question of the agent's authority was raised on the occasion, coupled with the evidence of the misleading circumstances of his continued occupancy and management of the farms and the cattle in the defendant's continued absence, was sufficient to warrant the verdict.

[Judgment for Wagner]

QUESTIONS

1. Was Berry the agent of Record in 1954 when Berry asked Wagner to bale hay and bill Record for the work?
2. After termination of the agency by Record, did Berry continue to have the power to bind Record?
3. Of what significance was the fact that Berry had pledged Record's credit in only one prior transaction?

When the law requires the giving of notice in order to end the power of the agent to bind the principal, individual notice must be given or mailed to all persons who had prior dealings with the agent or the principal. In addition, notice to the general public can be given by publishing a statement that the agency had been terminated in a newspaper of general circulation in the affected geographical area.

If a notice is actually received, the power of the agent is terminated without regard to whether the method of giving notice was proper. Conversely, if proper notice is given, it is immaterial that it does not actually come to the attention of the party notified. Thus, a member of the general public cannot claim that the principal is bound on the ground that the third person did not see the newspaper notice stating that the agent's authority had been terminated.

Summary

An agency relationship is created by an express or implied agreement whereby one person, the agent, is authorized to act on behalf of and subject to the control of another person, the principal. When an agency relationship exists, the acts of the agent obligate the principal to a third person and give the principal rights against the third person. An agent differs from an independent contractor in that the principal, who controls the acts of an agent, does not have control over the details of performance of work by the independent contractor.

A general agent is authorized by the principal to transact all business affairs of the principal at a certain place. A special agent is authorized by the principal to handle a specific business transaction. A universal agent is authorized to perform all acts that can be lawfully delegated to a representative.

The usual method of creating an agency is by express authorization. However, an agency relationship may be found to exist when the principal causes or permits a third person to reasonably believe that an agency relationship exists. The "agent" appears to be authorized and is said to have apparent authority.

An unauthorized transaction by an agent for a principal may be ratified by the principal, when the principal, with knowledge of all material facts, accepts the benefits of the act.

The duration of the agency relationship is commonly stated in the contract creating the relationship. In most cases, either party has the power to terminate the agency relationship at any time. However, the terminating party may be liable for damages to the other if the termination is in violation of the agency contract. When a principal terminates an agent's authority, it is not effective until the notice is received by the agent. Since a known agent will have the appearance of still being an agent, notice must be given to third persons of the termination, and the agent may have the power to bind the principal and third persons until that notice is given. An agency is terminated by operation of law on (1) the death of the principal or agent; (2) insanity of the principal or agent; (3) bankruptcy of the principal or agent; (4) impossibility of performance, such as the destruction of the subject matter; (5) war; or (6) the occurrence of unusual events or changes of circumstances. An agency coupled with an interest is an exception to the above stated rules on termination and cannot be revoked by the principal prior to the expiration of the interest.

In states that have adopted the Uniform Durable Power of Attorney Act (UDPAA), an agency that is not affected by subsequent disability or incapacity of the principal may be created. In UDPAA states, an agency may also be designated to come into existence upon the "disability or incapacity of the principal." The designation of an attorney in fact under the UDPAA must be in writing.

QUESTIONS AND CASE PROBLEMS

1. What social forces are affected by allowing an agent to make a contract that will bind the agent's principal and a third person?

2. How does an agent differ from an independent contractor?

3. Compare authorization of an agent by (a) appointment and (b) ratification.

4. Elbie came to Suzanne's house and showed her order blanks bearing the name of Elco Corporation. Elbie told Suzanne that he was the agent for the Elco Corporation, solicited an order from Suzanne for merchandise manufactured by Elco, and accepted a deposit from Suzanne. Elbie in fact was not the agent of Elco, and the forms that he showed Suzanne were "counterfeit" ones that he had printed. Suzanne sued Elco on the ground that Elbie appeared to be the agent of Elco and, therefore, had apparent authority to bind Elco to Suzanne. Was this correct?

5. Crawford is the agent for Kolb. Kolb mails Crawford a letter informing her that she is discharged. Crawford makes a contract as agent for Kolb prior to receipt of the letter. Was Crawford Kolb's agent when she made this contract so as to bind Kolb?

6. Compare (a) the termination of an agency with (b) the discharge of a contract.

7. Ken Jones, the number one ranked prizefighter in his weight class, signed a two-year contract with Howard Stayword, with Stayword being obligated to represent and promote Jones in all business and professional matters, including the arrangement of fights. For these services, Jones contracted to pay Stayword 10 percent of gross earnings. After a year, when Stayword proved unsuccessful in arranging a title match with the champion, Jones fired Stayword. During the following year Jones earned $4,000,000. Stayword sued Jones for $400,000. Jones defended himself on the basis that a principal has the absolute power at any time to terminate an agency relationship by discharging the agent, and as such he is not liable to Stayword. Is Jones correct?

8. Paula Strich did business as an optician in Duluth, Minnesota. Paula used only the products of the Plymouth Optical Company, a national manufacturer of optical products and supplies, with numerous retail outlets and some franchise arrangements in areas other than Duluth. In order to increase business, Paula renovated her office and changed the sign on her office to read "Plymouth Optical Co." Paula did business in this manner for more than three years — advertised under that name, paid bills with checks bearing the name of Plymouth Optical Co., and listed herself in the telephone and city directories by that name. Plymouth immediately became aware of what Paula was doing. However, since Paula used only Plymouth products, it saw no advantage at that time in prohibiting Paula from using the name and losing her as a customer, since Plymouth did not have a franchisee in Duluth. Paula contracted with the Duluth Tribune for advertising, making the contract in the name of Plymouth Optical Co. When the advertising bill was not paid, the Duluth Tribune sued Plymouth Optical Company for payment. Plymouth defended that it never authorized Paula to do business under the name, nor had it authorized her to make a contract with the newspaper. Decide.

9. Through his agent, Davis, Fieschko executed a written agreement to sell his real estate to Herlich. The agreement had been negotiated by Dykstra as Herlich's agent. The contract for the purchase of the land was signed by Dykstra as the agent for Herlich. Thereafter, Herlich sent a check for the down payment to Davis. The check did not contain any reference to the sale or the terms of the sale. Herlich did not go through with the sale and, when sued for breach of the contract, he argued that he was not bound by the contract since he had not signed it and Dykstra had not been authorized in writing to sign it. Fieschko claimed that Herlich had ratified the contract when he sent the check for the down payment. Decide. [Fieschko v Herlich, 32 Ill App 2d 280, 177 NE2d 376]

10. Mr. and Mrs. Martin owned farmland, which they listed for sale with Schneider, a real estate broker. Schneider agreed to sell the land to Heinrich. When the Martins lat-

er refused to sell the land, Heinrich sued for specific performance claiming that the Martins were bound by the written contract made by their agent, Schneider, and that based upon the written listing agreement given to Schneider by the Martins, Schneider had authority to sell the land for the Martins. Is Heinrich correct? [Heinrich v Martin (ND) 134 NW2d 786]

11. Walker owned a trailer that he wished to sell. He took it to the business premises of Pacific Mobile Homes. The only person on the premises at that time and several other times when Walker was there was Stewart, who identified himself as a salesman of Pacific and who agreed to take possession of Walker's trailer and to attempt to sell it for him. Stewart made out some forms of Pacific Mobile Homes and thereafter wrote some letters to Walker on the letterhead of Pacific. Walker's trailer was sold, but the salesman disappeared with most of the money. Walker sued Pacific for the proceeds of the sale. It denied liability on the ground that Stewart lacked authority to make any sales agreement and that all salesmen of Pacific were expressly forbidden to take used trailers to sell for their owners. Is this defense valid? [Walker v Pacific Mobile Homes, 68 Wash 2d 347, 413 P2d 3]

12. Hill purchased furniture from Grant Furniture. When she complained that it was damaged, she was told that they would send someone to repair the damage. An independent contractor, Newman, was sent to mend the furniture. He identified himself as the man from Grant's. The lacquer he put on the furniture exploded and caused serious injury to Hill. She sued both Newman and Grant. Grant claimed that Newman was an independent contractor and that it was therefore not liable for his conduct. Was Grant correct? [Hill v Newman, 126 NJ Super 557, 316 A2d 8]

13. Mrs. Bird, a woman of means, was living in deplorable conditions. Because of her bizarre behavior, neighbors got in contact with her cousin Logan Ledbetter, who in turn had Mrs. Bird examined by Dr. Phillips, a psychiatrist. Dr. Phillips determined that Mrs. Bird was suffering from "an organic brain syndrome, chronic, probably secondary to cerebral arteriosclerosis," that "her mental function was very impaired,"

and that in his opinion Mrs. Bird was "mentally incompetent at the time of the examination." Ledbetter planned to deal with the situation by selling off a number of valuable real estate holdings owned by Mrs. Bird and using the proceeds to pay for proper care for Mrs. Bird. Soon thereafter Mrs. Bird executed a power of attorney designating Logan Ledbetter as her attorney-in-fact; and Ledbetter entered into a contract to sell a large parcel of land to Andleman Associates. Mrs. Bird's niece, Barbara, who disliked Ledbetter, filed a petition seeking to have Mrs. Bird declared incompetent and herself named guardian of her estate. The court appointed Barbara as guardian, and she refused to allow the sale of the land to Andleman. In the complicated lawsuit that resulted, Ledbetter and Andleman contended that Ledbetter acted in good faith and had a properly executed power of attorney, and therefore, his signing the sales contract with Andleman was binding on Mrs. Bird (the principal). Atkins (the real estate agent who produced the ready, willing, and able buyer) sought his 10 percent commission under the listing agreement signed by Ledbetter as agent for Mrs. Bird. Barbara contended that the power of attorney was void and that Ledbetter owed the real estate commission since he breached his implied warranty that he had a principal with capacity. Decide.

14. Guy Hunt was a Republican candidate for governor. Jim Hooley, who served as paid campaign manager made a fund-raising proposal to Hunt, which consisted of a mass mailing of literature requesting contributions to be used in the campaign. Hunt expressly told Hooley that the campaign could not afford to finance this particular fund-raising plan, and that loans and the proceeds from the fund-raising would have to cover all expenses connected with the plan. Hooley raised some $15,000 in loans and deposited these funds in a special account. Mailing brochures were designed and proofs shown to Hunt. At the bottom of the brochures, the following appeared: "Pd Pol. Adv. by Guy Hunt Campaign." Hooley then got in contact with Oscar Davis, telling Davis he represented the Guy Hunt Campaign. Davis, who had previously done printing for the campaign, printed and

mailed the materials. The fund-raising plan did not produce enough contributions to pay Davis, and he sued Hunt for the balance due. Hunt refused to pay, contending that Hooley did not have authority to obtain credit in Hunt's name. Decide. [Hunt v Davis (Ala Civ App) 387 So 2d 209]

15. Morris Lew owns a store on Canal Street in New Orleans. He paid a person named Mike and other individuals commissions for customers brought into the store. Lew testified that he knew Mike for less than a week. Sherif Boulos and Paul Durso, partners in a wholesale jewelry business were visiting New Orleans on a business trip when Mike brought them into the store to buy a stereo. While Durso finalized the stereo transaction with the store's manager, Boulos and Mike negotiated to buy two cameras, three videos, and twenty gold Dupont lighters. Unbeknown to the store's manager, Mike was given $8,250 cash and was to deliver the merchandise later that evening to the Marriott Hotel where Boulos and Durso were staying. Mike gave a receipt for the cash, but it showed no sales tax or indication that the goods were to be delivered. Boulos testi-

fied that he believed Mike was the store's owner. Mike never delivered the merchandise, and no one has seen or heard from him since. Boulos and Durso contend Lew is liable for the acts of his agent, Miguel "Mike" Felberg or Feldberg. Lew denied that Mike was his agent, and the testimony showed that Mike had no actual authority to make a sale, to use a cash register, or even to go behind a sales counter. Decide. [Boulos v Morrison (La) 503 So 2d 1]

16. John Cartright executed a written power of attorney designating Tom Lawlor, his friend for many years, as his attorney in fact for the sale of the Cartright business. The writing further stated, "This power of attorney shall become effective upon the disability or incapacity of the principal, John Cartright." Several years after the document was signed, John became totally disabled due to mental illness, and Tom initiated action to sell John's business. John's niece, Mary Concannon, notified Tom that he has no authority to act for John since the insanity of the principal terminated Tom's agency. Is she correct?

43

PRINCIPAL AND AGENT

The principal, the person who permits or directs another to act for the principal's benefit, may, under certain circumstances, be held liable by courts for the dealings of the agent, the active participant in a transaction. Clearly the principal should be liable for the acts of the agent when the principal has given the agent express authority to so act. Should the principal be bound by an agent when the agent acts beyond authority or when the agent misrepresents authority? The principal may be held liable on one of the *authority* theories set forth in this chapter, if justice requires it. The courts are concerned with protecting the property of the principal; however, the courts recognize that third persons have to be able to rely upon the reasonable appearance of authority of agents if our commercial markets are going to function effectively.

The nature of the agency relationship is better understood when the duties and liabilities of the agent and principal to each other are studied. For example, agents owe a duty of loyalty to their principals, and should an agent act contrary to the interest of the principal and make a secret profit, the courts will allow the principal to recover the profit from the agent.

A. AGENT'S AUTHORITY

The fact that one person is the agent of another does not dispose of all questions. It is necessary to determine the scope of the agent's authority.

§ 43:1 SCOPE OF AGENT'S AUTHORITY

The scope of an agent's authority may be determined from the express words of the principal to the agent or may be implied from the principal's words or deeds, or from the customs of the trade or business.

(a) EXPRESS AUTHORITY. If the principal tells the agent to perform a certain act, the agent has **express authority** to do so. Express authority can be indicated orally or in writing.

(b) INCIDENTAL AUTHORITY. An agent has implied **incidental authority** to perform any act reasonably necessary to execute the express authority given to the agent. To illustrate, if the principal authorizes the agent to purchase goods without furnishing funds to the agent to pay for them, the agent has implied incidental authority to purchase the goods on credit.

(c) CUSTOMARY AUTHORITY. An agent has implied **customary authority** to do any act that, according to the custom of the community, usually accompanies the transaction for which the agent is authorized to act. For example, an agent who has express authority to receive payments from third persons has implied authority to issue receipts.

One authorized to act as a general manager has the power to make any contract necessary for the usual and ordinary conduct of business. Likewise, an agent authorized to obtain advertising may contract for television time because the use of television as an advertising medium is customary. Authorization to contract for television time can also be regarded as incidental to a general, unrestricted authorization to advertise.[1]

(d) APPARENT AUTHORITY. A person has apparent authority as an agent when the principal, by words or conduct, leads a third person reasonably to believe that such person has that authority and the third person relies upon that appearance.[2]

The elements of incidental, customary, and apparent authority are discussed in the *Jackson* case. The court considered whether a reasonable person, familiar with business conduct in the community would have been justified in believing that the manager of a hotel was authorized to offer a reward for information leading to the arrest and conviction of the killer of one of the hotel's clerks.

[1] Columbia Broadcasting System v Stokely-Van Camp, Inc. (CA2 NY) 522 F2d 369 (1975).
[2] Draemel v Rufenacht, Dromagen & Hertz, Inc. ___ Neb ___, 392 NW2d 759 (1986).

JACKSON V GOODMAN
69 Mich App 225, 244 NW2d 423 (1976)

A clerk in the St. Regis Hotel was killed during a robbery. Frank Bromber, the general manager of the hotel, offered a $1,000 reward for information leading to the arrest and conviction of the killer. Robert Jackson furnished the information and the killer was convicted. However, when Jackson claimed the reward, Albert Goodman and the other owners of the hotel denied that Bromber had authority to offer a $1,000 reward because he had no authority to spend any amount over $50 without approval from the owners of the hotel. Jackson sued Goodman and the other owners for the $1,000 reward. A jury returned a verdict in favor of

Jackson, but the court entered judgment for the owners as a matter of law. Jackson appealed.

KAUFMAN, J. . . . The trial court improperly granted a judgment notwithstanding the verdict because there was sufficient evidence to present jury questions concerning . . . the presence of either inherent authority or ratification.

. . . Any individual with the authority to make a contract may offer a reward. . . The authority to contract may be inferred from the authority to manage a business. Such authority is limited to making "contracts which are incidental to such business, are usually made in it, or are reasonably necessary in conducting it." . . . One of the factors to be considered in determining the extent of authority is the custom of similar businesses at the same time and place. . . .

Other courts have presumed authority in the president of a bank to offer, on behalf of the bank, a reward for information leading to the arrest of a defaulting teller. . . . Similarly the authority to offer a reward for the arrest of persons maliciously destroying railroad tracks has been held to be within the implied authority of the railroad superintendent. . . .

The conflict resulting from an application of agency principles to the instant case is well illustrated by the divergence between our view and that of the dissent. The basic area of disagreement involves a question of perspective. The dissent views the question of implied authority from the perspective of the business. We view this question from the perspective of the plaintiff, especially that concerning the reasonableness of his reliance on the newspaper article.

Normally, the application of rules concerning usual course of business results in an equitable outcome in line with the parties' expectations, advancement of commercial intercourse and considerations of fundamental fairness. Where the specific business exhibits a general course of behavior relative to the questioned acts, the inquiry generally will give greater focus to the specific concern than the course of conduct in similar businesses. Where, as here, the transaction is one unusual to the specific business affected, the emphasis must differ. In such a case, significant emphasis must be placed on the course of business conduct in the community at large concerning rewards and on whether the recipient party "reasonably believes that the agent is authorized to [act] . . . and has no notice that he is not so authorized." 1 Restatement of the Law, Agency 2d, § 161. A jury, as the repository of "community sense," is in a unique position to decide questions of usual course of conduct and reasonable reliance in such unusual cases.

"When there is a disputed question of agency, if there is any testimony, either direct or inferential, tending to establish it, it becomes a question of fact for the jury to determine." *Miskiewicz v Smolenski*, 249 Mich 23, 227 NW 789 (1929). The jury verdict should not have been disturbed.

. . . We reverse . . . and remand this cause to the trial court for entry of judgment in conformance with the jury verdict. . . .

[Judgment reversed and remanded]

MCGREGOR, J. (dissenting) . . . It was the plaintiff's theory that the reward was offered by Frank C. Bromber, a manager of the hotel, and that the offering of the reward was within Bromber's authority. . . .

The resolution of this issue largely involves the law of agency and the application of its principles to the facts of the present case. A principal is subject to liability for the acts of an agent if it can be said that: (a) the agent was authorized to do the act; (b) the agent was apparently authorized to do the act; (c) the act was within the agent's inherent authority; or (d) the act was ratified by the principal.

In the present case, Bromber cannot be said to have been authorized to offer the reward. At trial, defendant Albert Goodman testified that Bromber could not expend more than $50.00 without Goodman's express approval and that such approval was not given here. This testimony was uncontroverted by the plaintiff and, therefore, it must be assumed that Bromber did not have the actual authority to offer a reward of $1,000.00.

Nor do I find any evidence presented at trial which would justify the jury in concluding that Bromber had either the apparent or inherent authority to offer the reward. . . . Can third persons reasonably assume that a general manager of a hotel has the authority to offer a reward for information leading to the arrest and conviction of the person responsible for the murder of a hotel employee? I would hold that third persons cannot reasonably make such an assumption.

A general manager can only have the apparent or inherent authority to do those things which managers in that business at that time and place customarily do. As such, contracts entered into by general managers are only binding on the principal if they are incidental to a business such as the principal's, are usually made in such a business, or are reasonably necessary in conducting such a business. I do not think that it can reasonably be said that the reward in the present case is either incidental to or reasonably necessary in conducting the hotel business. Nor do I think, in the absence of any evidence to the contrary, that it can be assumed that such rewards are usually made in the hotel business. Rather, it would be more reasonable to assume that the offering of a reward is an unusual or extraordinary event which is not customary in most businesses. Thus, since the plaintiff has failed to show that general managers of hotels, or of defendants' hotel in particular, usually offer rewards under circumstances similar to those in the present case, I conclude that there was no evidence presented which showed that Bromber had the apparent or inherent authority to offer the reward in the instant case.

QUESTIONS

1. Did the general manager, Bromber, have express authority to offer the reward?
2. What is the basic disagreement between the opinion of the majority of the court and the dissenting judge?
3. Does the court hold that the manager had authority to offer the reward?

---

§ 43:2   EFFECT OF PROPER
          EXERCISE OF AUTHORITY

When an agent with authority properly makes a contract with a third person that purports to bind the principal, there is by definition a binding contract between the principal and third person. The agent is not a party to this contract. Consequently, when the owner of goods is the principal, the owner's agent is not liable for breach of warranty with respect to the goods "sold" by the agent because the owner-principal, not the agent, was the "seller" in the sales transaction.[3]

§ 43:3 DUTY TO ASCERTAIN EXTENT OF AGENT'S AUTHORITY

A third person who deals with a person claiming to be an agent cannot rely upon the statements made by the agent concerning the extent of authority. If the agent is not authorized to perform the act

[3] Wright Waterproofing Co. v Allied Polymers (Tex Civ App) 602 SW2d 67 (1980).

or is not even the agent of the principal, the transaction between the alleged agent and the third person will have no legal effect between the principal and the third person.

Third persons who deal with an agent whose authority is limited to a special purpose, are bound at their peril to find out the extent of the agent's authority. An attorney is such an agent; unless the client holds the attorney out as having greater authority than usual, the attorney has no authority to settle a claim without approval from a client. The extent of an attorney's authority to settle a claim was disputed in the *Miotk* case.

MIOTK V RUDY
227 Kan 296, 605 P2d 587 (1980)

Irene Miotk was a passenger in a car when it was struck by another car driven by Vernon Rudy. Miotk retained attorney John D. Logsdon to represent her in a personal injury action against Rudy. Logsdon filed suit on behalf of Miotk, and later entered negotiations with Rudy's attorney to settle the case. As an offer of settlement, Rudy's attorney sent Logsdon a check made out to "Irene Miotk and John D. Logsdon, her attorney" along with a release for Ms. Miotk to sign. Logsdon failed to return the signed release by the day the case was set for trial, but he advised Rudy's attorney that the settlement was agreed to; and the court approved the settlement and dismissed the case. Unknown to all parties and the court, Logsdon had apparently forged Irene Miotk's indorsement to the check, and had retained the proceeds. Miotk hired new counsel, who filed a motion to set aside the dismissal of her action. In an accompanying affidavit, Miotk stated that she at no time authorized the settlement of the case; nor was she ever offered any sum of money by Logsdon. The trial court denied the motion to set aside the dismissal and Miotk appealed.

SWINEHART, J. . . . Plaintiff relies on the rule as to an attorney's authority to settle a case stated in *Reimer v Davis*, 224 Kan at 229, 580 P2d at 85.

We have previously considered the nature and extent of an attorney's authority in handling a client's case. It has been recognized generally that a client is bound by the appearance, admissions, and actions of counsel acting on behalf of his client. The client has control over the subject matter of litigation. An attorney has no authority to compromise or settle his client's claim without his client's approval. . . .

Defendant, while recognizing the rule in Reimer, characterizes it as "idealistic in concept, but extremely difficult . . . to follow." He points out that he clearly relied on the representations of plaintiff's attorney and that the dismissal was entered pursuant to the express representation of plaintiff's attorney to the court and defense counsel that the settlement was authorized. Defendant urges as matter of public policy that the dismissal should not be set aside.

Defendant's argument is essentially that an attorney should be held to have apparent authority to settle an action. This appears to be the rationale of the trial court's denial of the plaintiff's motion. This argument is at first glance appealing. It is clear that the relation of attorney and client is one of agency and the general rules of law that apply to agency apply to that relation . . . . The law recognizes two distinct types of agency, actual and ostensible or apparent. *Brown v Wichita State University*, 217 Kan 279, 540 P2d 66 (1975) . . . . The evidence is uncontradicted that Logsdon lacked actual authority to settle plaintiff's case and there is no issue in that regard. However, the liability of the principal for the acts and contracts of his agent is not limited to such acts and contracts of the agent as are expressly authorized, necessarily implied from express authority, or otherwise actually conferred by implication from the acts and conduct of the principal. . . .

The difficulty in the present case is that there is no evidence of apparent authority on the part of Logsdon to settle plaintiff's case other than his retention as her attorney. . . .

Kansas law is in accord on the general agency principle that those who deal with an agent whose authority is limited to special purposes are bound at their peril to know the extent of his authority. . . . It is clear from *Reimer v Davis*, 224 Kan 225, 580 P2d 81, that an attorney as agent for his client, is limited to control over procedural matters incident to litigation. Under the facts of that case it may be said that an attorney ordinarily has no apparent authority to settle his client's action without the client's consent.

There being no evidence other than Logsdon's employment as plaintiff's attorney of Logsdon's apparent authority to settle plaintiff's action, we hold that the trial court abused its discretion in denying plaintiff's motion pursuant to K.S.A. 60-260(b) to set aside the judgment of dismissal. The case is remanded with directions to grant plaintiff's motion and proceed with trial of the issues on the merits.

[Judgment reversed and action remanded]

QUESTIONS

1. What did the defendant contend?
2. Did the court sustain the defendant's contention?
3. Was Irene Miotk bound by the representation of attorney Logsdon to the court that she had authorized the settlement of the case?

(a) AGENT'S ACTS ADVERSE TO PRINCIPAL. The third person who deals with an agent is required to take notice of any acts that are clearly adverse to the interest of the principal. Thus, if the agent is obviously making use of funds of the principal for the agent's personal benefit, persons dealing with the agent should recognize that the agent may be acting without authority and that they are dealing with the agent at their peril.

The only certain way that third persons can protect themselves is to inquire of the principal whether the agent is in fact the agent of the principal and has the necessary authority. If the principal states that the agent has the authority, the principal cannot later deny this authorization unless the subject matter is such that an authorization must be in writing in order to be binding.

(b) Death of Third Person. The extent of the agent's authority becomes particularly significant when the third person dies after the transaction with the agent but before any action has been taken by the principal. If the agent had authority to contract on behalf of the principal, the agent's agreement with the third person would give rise immediately to a binding contract and the third person's subsequent death would ordinarily not affect that contract. In contrast, if the agent did not have authority to contract but only to transmit an offer from the third person, the death of the third person before the principal had accepted the offer would work a revocation of the offer, and the principal could not create a contract by purporting to accept after the death of the third person.

§ 43:4 Limitations of Agent's Authority

A person who has knowledge of a limitation on the agent's authority cannot disregard that limitation. When the third person knows that the authority of the agent depends upon whether financing has been obtained, the principal is not bound by the act of the agent if the financing in fact was not obtained. If the authority of the agent is based upon a writing and the third person knows that there is such a writing, the third person is charged with knowledge of the limitations contained in it.

(a) Apparent Limitations. In some situations, it will be apparent to third persons that they are dealing with an agent whose authority is limited. When third persons know that they are dealing with an officer of a private corporation or a representative of a governmental agency, they should recognize that such person will ordinarily not have unlimited authority[4] and that a contract made with the officer or representative may not be binding unless ratified by the principal.

(b) Secret Limitations. If the principal has clothed an agent with authority to perform certain acts but the principal gives secret instructions that limit the agent's authority, the third person is allowed to take the authority of the agent at its face value and is not bound by the secret limitations of which the third person has no knowledge.

§ 43:5 Delegation of Authority by Agent

As a general rule, an agent cannot delegate to another the authority obtained from the principal. In other words, unless the principal expressly or in an implied manner consents, an agent cannot appoint *subagents* to carry out the agent's duties. The reason for this rule is that since an agent is usually selected because of some personal qualifications, it would be unfair and possibly injurious to the principal if the authority to act could be shifted by the agent to another — particularly when the agent was originally appointed for the performance of a task requiring discretion or judgment. For example, an agent who is appointed to adjust claims against an insurance company cannot delegate the performance of that duty to another. The *Bucholtz* case sets forth reasons for the general rule that an agent cannot avoid responsibility for the carrying out of the tasks of the agency by delegating the tasks to a subagent.

---

[4] Weil and Associates v Urban Renewal Agency, 206 Kan 405, 479 P2d 875 (1971).

BUCHOLTZ V SIROTKIN TRAVEL LTD.

74 Misc 2d 180, 343 NYS2d 438 (1973)

Helen Bucholtz made reservations through the Sirotkin Travel Agency for a three-day trip to Las Vegas. The reservations were in fact not made by the agency, and Bucholtz sued the agency for damages for breach of its contract. The agency raised the defense that the mistake was the fault of another travel agency or "wholesaler" through which the agency made reservations on behalf of its client.

DONOVAN, J. . . . This small claim proceeding involves a matter of increasing importance to the traveling public, namely, the responsibility of a travel agency in connection with the sale of a tour.

Claimant engaged the defendant travel agency to make reservations for a three day trip for herself and her husband to Las Vegas. The agency advised the claimant that they would stay at the Aladdin Hotel. Changes were made in the arrival and departure time of their flight from that originally stated. At the airport tags on the plaintiff's baggage were switched so that the baggage was not directed to the Aladdin Hotel. On arrival in Las Vegas the claimant learned that no reservations had been made for herself or her husband at the Aladdin Hotel. They were required to take alternative accommodations at a motel. The motel was a half mile out of town. This created additional expense and inconvenience for the claimant and her husband in traveling to the places of interest in the town.

The law presently lacks clarity with respect to the relationship between the travel agency and its clients. Obviously the travel agency is an agent, but the question comes, whose agent? Is it the agent of a hotel or other innkeeper with whom, or for whom the agency transacts business? Or the steamship line or airline with whom it does business? Generally the travel agency is neither an agent nor an employee of the common carriers and innkeepers with whom it may do business.

The travel agent deals directly with the traveler. He must be charged with the duty of exercising reasonable care in securing passage on an appropriate carrier and lodging with an innkeeper. The money was paid over by the traveler to the defendant agency for that specific purpose.

News reports are constantly appearing with stories of travelers — many of them quite young — being stranded far from home or having vacation plans ruined because passage or lodging for which they have paid has not been provided. Who is to bear the responsibility? Is it some remote "wholesaler" who is unknown to the traveler, or the traveler himself, or the travel agency in whom the traveler has reposed his confidence?

Sometimes we must go deep into the past to find ancient principles and mold them to take care of new problems. The policy of the common law from ancient times has been to safeguard the traveler. Speaking of the rule at common law which held the innkeeper liable as an insurer of the property left in his custody by a guest, the court, in *Hulett v Swift*, 33 NY 571 (1865) said:

The considerations of public policy in which the rule had its origin, forbid any relaxation of its rigor. The number of travelers was few, when this custom was established for their protection. The growth of commerce and increased facilities of communication, have so multiplied the class for whose security it was designed, that its abrogation would be the removal of a safeguard against fraud, in which almost every citizen has an immediate interest. The rule is in the highest degree remedial. No public interest would be promoted, by changing the legal effect of the implied contract between the host and the guest, and relieving the former from his common law liability. Innkeepers, like carriers and other insurers, at times find their contracts burdensome; but in the profits they derive from the public, and the privileges accorded to them by the law, they find an ample and liberal compensation. The vocation would be still more profitable if coupled with new immunities; but we are not at liberty to discard the settled rules of the common law, founded on reasons which still operate in all their original force. Open robbery and violence, it is true, are less frequent as civilization advances; but the devices of fraud multiply with the increase of intelligence, and the temptations which spring from opportunity, keep pace with the growth and diffusion of wealth.

As foreseen by the court one hundred years ago, the devices of fraud have indeed multiplied.

In this case nothing was done by the travel agency to verify or confirm either the plane reservations or the hotel reservations. If this duty is the responsibility of the travel agency, then the travel agency is liable in negligence for its failure to exercise reasonable care in making the reservations.

It may be urged that the default in this respect is that of the remote "wholesaler."

Where, as here, the agent is selected because he is supposed to have some special fitness for the performance of the duties to be undertaken, the traveler is entitled to rely on the judgment and discretion of that agent as well as his honesty and financial responsibility. The agent may not evade responsibility by delegating to a subagent the carrying out of the task which has been committed to him. . . . Travel agencies may find it convenient, in the course of transacting their business, to deal with wholesalers. The news reports are so voluminous that we may take judicial notice of the vice inherent in conducting business in so loose a fashion. The wholesaler may fail to pay for accommodations or may even fail to book the accommodations and the traveler is left in a helpless situation. He either has no recourse because of financial insufficiency or he may be required to travel to a distant jurisdiction in order to maintain a suit.

Unless the principal, here the traveler, has expressly or impliedly authorized the travel agency to delegate responsibility to a second agency or "wholesaler," the responsibility must remain on the defendant travel agency. In an area so fraught with danger to the traveler, public policy demands that the travel agency be held responsible to: (a) verify or confirm the reservations and (b) use reasonable diligence in ascertaining the responsibility of any intervening "wholesaler" or tour organizer. . . .

Claimant here did not consent to any delegation of the duty owed to her by the defendant travel agency.

The defendant is liable to the claimant for the breach of its fiduciary responsibility in failing to use reasonable care to confirm the reservations. . . .

[Judgment for plaintiff]

Agents, however, may authorize others to perform their work for them in the following instances:

(a) When the acts to be done involve only mechanical or ministerial duties. Thus, an agent to make application for hail insurance on wheat may delegate to another the clerical act of writing the application. And it may be shown that there is customary authority for a clerk in the office of the insurance agent to sign the agent's name so as to have the effect of a signing by the agent and be binding upon the insurance company, the agent's principal.[5]

(b) When a well-known custom recognizes such appointment. To illustrate, if one is authorized to buy or sell a grain elevator, one may do so through a broker when that is the customary method.

(c) When the appointment is justified by necessity or sudden emergency and it is impractical to communicate with the principal, and the appointment of a subagent is reasonably necessary for the protection of the interests of the principal entrusted to the agent.

(d) When it is contemplated by the parties that subagents would be employed. For example, a bank may now generally use subagents to receive payments of notes that have been left for collection since the parties contemplate that this will be done. Also, the authority to appoint subagents can be inferred where the principal knows or has reason to know that the agent employs subagents. Thus, an agent may grant subagents power to bind a principal fire insurance company, when the agent had a long-standing practice of appointing subagents and this was known to the principal.[6]

B. Duties and Liabilities of Principal and Agent

The creation of the principal-agent relationship gives rise not only to powers but also to duties and liabilities.

§ 43:6 Duties and Liabilities of Agent During Agency

While the agency relationship exists, the agent owes certain duties to the principal.

(a) Loyalty. An agent must be loyal or faithful to the principal. The agent must not obtain any secret profit or benefit from the agency.[7] If the principal is seeking to buy or rent property, the agent cannot secretly obtain the property and then sell or lease it to the principal at a profit.

An agent who owns property cannot sell it to the principal without disclosing that ownership to the principal. If disclosure is not made, the principal may avoid the contract even though the agent's con-

---

[5] United Bonding Insurance Co. v Banco Suizo-Panameno (CA5 Fla) 422 F2d 1142 (1970).

[6] Bloom v Wolfe, 37 Colo App 407, 547 P2d 934 (1976).
[7] Kunz v Warren (Colo App) 725 P2d 794 (1986); Johnson v First Nat'l Bank of Rome, 253 Ga 233, 319 SE2d 440 (1984).

duct did not cause the principal any financial loss. Alternatively, the principal can approve the transaction and sue the agent for any secret profit obtained by the agent.

An agent cannot act as agent for both parties to a transaction unless both know of the dual capacity and agree to it. If the agent does so act without the consent of both parties, the transaction is voidable at the election of any principal who did not know of the agent's double status.

An agent must not accept secret gifts or commissions from third persons in connection with the agency. If the agent does so, the principal may sue the agent for those gifts or commissions. Such practices are condemned because the judgment of the agent may be influenced by the receipt of gifts or commissions.

It is a violation of an agent's duty of loyalty to make and retain secret profits.

An agent is, of course, prohibited from aiding the competitors of a principal or disclosing to them information relating to the business of the principal. It is also a breach of duty for the agent knowingly to deceive a principal.

(b) OBEDIENCE AND PERFORMANCE. An agent is under a duty to obey all lawful instructions.[8] The agent is required to perform the services specified for the period and in the way specified. An agent who does not is liable to the principal for any harm caused. For example, if an agent is instructed to take cash payments only but accepts a check in payment, the agent is liable for the loss caused the principal if the check is dishonored by nonpayment. Likewise, when an insurance broker undertakes to obtain a policy of insurance for a principal that will provide a specified coverage but fails to obtain a policy with the proper coverage, the broker, as agent of the principal, is liable to the principal for the loss thereby caused.

If the agent violates instructions, it is immaterial that the agent acted in good faith or intended to benefit the principal. It is the fact that the agent violated the instructions and thereby caused the principal a loss that imposes a liability upon the agent. In determining whether the agent has obeyed instructions, they must be interpreted in a way that a reasonable person would interpret them.

(c) REASONABLE CARE. It is the duty of an agent to act with the care that a reasonable person would exercise under the circumstances. In addition, if the agent possesses a special skill, as in the case of a broker or an attorney, the agent must exercise that skill.

(d) ACCOUNTING. An agent must account to the principal for all property or money belonging to the principal that comes into the agent's possession. The agent should, within a reasonable time, give notice of collections made and render an accurate account of all receipts and expenditures. The agency agreement may state at what intervals or on what dates such accountings are to be made.

An agent should keep the principal's property and money separate and distinct from that of the agent. If property of the agent is mingled with property of the principal so that the two cannot be identified or separated, the principal may claim all of the commingled mass. Furthermore, when funds of the principal and the agent are mixed, any loss that occurs must be borne by the agent.

(e) INFORMATION. It is the duty of an agent to keep the principal informed of all facts relating to the agency that are relevant to protecting the principal's interests.[9]

The *Allen Industries Inc.* decision illustrates the rule that an agent has a duty to disclose to the principal every material fact, circumstance, and advantage in relation to a sale. Moreover, the case points out that an agent's attempt to receive a higher commission is a violation of the duty of honesty and loyalty to the principal.

---

[8] Stanford v Neiderer, 178 Ga 56, 341 SE2d 892 (1986).

[9] Restatement, Agency 2d § 381; Owen v Shelton, 221 Va 1047, 277 SE2d 189 (1981).

ALLEN INDUSTRIES INC. V SHELDON GOOD CO.

153 Ill App 3d 120, 106 Ill Dec 313, 505 NE2d 1104 (1987)

The facts pleaded in the complaint indicate that Mrs. Joan Kulwin owned Allen Industries Inc. which owned a commercial building in Evanston, Illinois. She granted the Sheldon Co. the exclusive right to sell the building and agreed to pay a commission to Sheldon upon the sale. This commission was to be divided in half between Sheldon and a cooperating broker, should a cooperating broker secure the purchaser. On August 21, 1985 Sheldon Co. presented Kulwin a written offer in final contract form from J.W. Collier. She rejected this offer of $335,000 and made a counteroffer of $350,000. On August 22 Collier accepted the counteroffer. The contract called for the seller to take back a mortgage for $249,000. At the closing Sheldon Co. received an $18,000 commission. Mrs. Kulwin later found out one Maurice Leviton, President of TLC, on his third inspection of the property on August 16, 1985, advised Sheldon Co. that he was preparing an all-cash offer on the property. He made this offer to Sheldon Co. on August 22, 1985, and it was rejected by Sheldon Co. because Mrs. Kulwin had accepted Collier's offer at that point. Mrs. Kulwin sued Sheldon Co. for breach of the fiduciary duty in failing to inform her of all facts material to the sale. She asserted that Sheldon Co. failed to do so to avoid sharing half the commission with the cooperating broker who showed TLC the property. Sheldon Co. denies it had a duty to report conversations of a speculative nature to the seller. From a judgment for Sheldon Co., Kulwin appealed.

STAMOS, J. . . . The relationship between principal and agent for the purchase or sale of property is a fiduciary one, and the agent in the exercise of good faith must make known to his principal all material facts within his knowledge which in any way affect the transaction and the subject matter of his agency. Material facts are those facts which the agent should realize have or are likely to have a bearing upon the desirability of the transaction from the viewpoint of the principal.

If a party employs an agent to make a sale of land he is entitled to all the skill, ability and industry of such agent to make the sale on the best terms that can be had. An agent cannot deal for his own advantage with things to be sold because of his confidential relationship with his principal and because of his duty to disclose to his principal every fact, circumstance or advantage in relation to a sale, which may come to his knowledge. . . .

Plaintiffs . . . allege that defendants never informed plaintiffs of TLC's visits to the subject property or of TLC's statements that they were preparing a cash offer for the property. Defendants do not deny that they failed to inform plaintiffs of TLC's interest in plaintiffs' property; rather, they claim that as real estate brokers that had no duty to "report to a seller each and every speculative conversation which (they) had with a prospective purchaser regarding an offer which the purchaser says that he may make in the indeterminate future."

We conclude that a purchaser's expressions of interest in property to be sold and his statements that he is preparing an offer for said property are material facts which a real estate broker has a duty to convey to his client. It is evident that plaintiffs would have been in an improved position to gain a better price or more favorable terms had they known that there was more than one purchaser interested in their property. Plaintiffs would have benefited from the heightened demand for their property by allowing each prospective purchaser to compete against the other for plaintiffs' property. In fact, TLC's offer included more favorable terms than the contract made with the ultimate purchaser, J.W. Collier. Collier's offer called for a price of $350,000, a cash down payment of $97,500 and monthly payments at an interest rate of 11% on a 30-year amortization schedule with the final payment due 5 years from the closing date. While TLC's offer was also for a sale price of $350,000, it was an all cash deal without any seller participating financing. It is possible that plaintiffs would have found TLC's cash offer to have been more favorable than Collier's. In any event, defendants had a duty to inform the seller of all facts that might influence him in accepting or rejecting the offer. It cannot be said that plaintiffs would not have been influenced by TLC's offer in accepting or rejecting Collier's offer. Therefore, we hold that the dismissed counts sufficiently allege the breach of a fiduciary duty to plaintiffs by failing to disclose material facts to them regarding the sale of their property.

Plaintiffs allege, additionally, that defendants' failure to inform plaintiffs of TLC's offer was an attempt to make personal gain by receiving a higher commission. Such conduct, if proven, is strictly prohibited in this state because it violates an agent's duty of honesty and loyalty toward his principal. This obligation toward a principal prohibits an agent from dealing independently of the interests of his principal to his personal gain in the subject matter of the agency, on the grounds that such activities will necessarily tempt that agent to abandon the interests of his principal in favor of his own interests. In fact, an agent who deals independently of the interests of his principal breaches his fiduciary duty and is therefore barred from any recovery for his services. (When a broker breaches his duties toward his employer he will, in almost every case, lose his commission.) In this instance, defendants allegedly received an $18,000 commission from the sale of plaintiffs' property to J.W. Collier, a client brought in by defendants. Under the listing agreement, defendants would have received only 1/2 of that commission or $9,000 and advertising expenses up to $5,000 if the property was sold to TLC, a prospective purchaser not brought in by defendants.

The circuit court erred in dismissing the stricken allegations and the cause is reversed and remanded with directions to reinstate the same consistent with this order.

[Reversed and remanded with directions]

QUESTIONS

1. Did Sheldon Co. have an obligation to report each conversation of a speculative nature that the agent had with a prospective purchaser concerning offers that may be made in the indeterminate future?
2. Did Sheldon Co. have a right to protect its full commission by preserving the sale for its purchaser as opposed to the purchaser produced by another broker?
3. Is a real estate agent who breaches a duty owed the seller entitled to the full commission when the property is sold?

§ 43:7   Duties and Liabilities
of Agent after
Termination of Agency

When the agency relationship ends, the duties of the agent continue only to the extent necessary to perform prior obligations. For example, the agent must return to the former principal any property that had been entrusted to the agent for the purpose of the agency. With the exception of such "winding up" duties, the agency relationship is terminated, and the former agent can deal with the principal as freely as with a stranger.[10] The *Clinkenbeard* case illustrates the strict application of this rule.

[10]   Corron & Black of Illinois, Inc. v Magner, 145 Ill App 3d 151, 98 Ill Dec 663, 494 NE2d 785 (1986).

CLINKENBEARD V CENTRAL SOUTHWEST OIL CORP.

(CA5 Tex) 526 F2d 649 (1976)

The United States Department of the Interior conducted a monthly lottery of oil leases on United States land. In order to take part in the lottery, it was necessary to select the land on which to bid, file various papers, and take other steps. The Central Southwest Oil Corporation was in the business of doing this work for a monthly fee on behalf of members of the general public. Edrel Clinkenbeard retained the corporation to act for him. After approximately one year, he won a lease that he then sold to the corporation because Tom Allen, the corporation president, told him the lease was not particularly valuable. The president knew that oil had been discovered on neighboring land and that there were producing oil wells in the vicinity. He also knew the prices that had been paid for other neighboring leases. Allen did not tell any of this to Clinkenbeard, and Clinkenbeard sold the oil lease to the corporation for a fraction of its true value. When Clinkenbeard learned the truth, he sued to rescind the sale of the lease. The court rescinded the sale on the theory that the corporation was under a fiduciary duty to Clinkenbeard at the time of the sale and had breached that duty by failing to disclose to him all information relevant to the value of the lease. The corporation appealed.

Thornberry, C. J. . . . Any fiduciary duty owed to Clinkenbeard had terminated at the time of the assignment in question. . . .

It is generally recognized that "an agency which is intended to continue only for the performance of a particular task terminates on the performance or completion of that task." *Renchie v John Hancock Mut. Life Ins. Co.* 174 SW2d 87 (Tex Civ App 1943). . . . After an agency is terminated, the agent is free of any fiduciary duty to the principal arising from that relationship and may then deal with the principal on an arm's length basis. *Smith v Grant*, 483 SW2d 871 (Tex Civ App 1972). . . .

. . . The agency relationship between Central Southwest and Clinkenbeard was for the accomplishment of specific tasks: the selection of federal oil and gas properties on which to bid, the entry of bids on those properties in the Department of Interior lotteries, and notification of the results. The record is devoid of evidence indicating that Central Southwest ever undertook to do anything more than this. Thus, at the moment that Tom Allen notified Clinkenbeard that he had won a lease, the agency relationship terminated as a matter of law; *all that Central agreed to do had been done.*

This conclusion is bolstered by Clinkenbeard's unequivocal testimony at trial. He stated that he recognized that Central Southwest had done everything that he expected it to do at the time they notified him that he had won a lease. And he testified that thereafter he knew that he was dealing with Central Southwest as a potential buyer of his lease and that he was a potential seller. The objective facts of the agency relationship between Central Southwest and Clinkenbeard are those that are controlling, but this testimony clearly indicates that, even subjectively, Clinkenbeard knew that his agency relationship with Central Southwest had ended.

We recognize that this conclusion may seem harsh in light of the fact that Clinkenbeard's subjective trust of Allen may have continued beyond, or even have been augmented by, Allen's notification to him that he had won a lease. But there is a very legitimate need for definiteness in the rules that govern fiduciary relationships. Such relationships impose unusual and stringent duties while they subsist. It is only fair that those subject to such duties be reasonably able to determine their extent and duration. Moreover, we note that the Texas Supreme Court has explicitly stated that subjective trust alone is not enough to transform arms-length dealing into a fiduciary relationship. *Thigpen v Locke*, 363 SW2d 247 (Tex 1962). . . . Businessmen generally do trust one another, and their dealings are frequently characterized by cordiality. . . . If we should permit respondents to set aside their conveyances on such slender evidence, the security of contracts and conveyances in this state would be seriously jeopardized. . . .

Clinkenbeard argues, however, that the fiduciary duties once owed by Central Southwest to him as his agent may have continued to exist after the termination of the formal agency. As a strict matter, this is simply incorrect; the termination of the agency relationship terminates also the fiduciary duties which flow from it. . . .

. . . Because no fiduciary duty was owed by Central Southwest at the time of the assignment, reversal of the judgment in favor of Clinkenbeard is required.

[Judgment reversed]

QUESTIONS

1. What did the plaintiff claim?
2. Did the court agree with the plaintiff's claim?
3. What is the underlying basis for the court's decision?

---

§ 43:8   ENFORCEMENT OF LIABILITY OF AGENT

When the agent's breach of duty causes harm to the principal, the amount of the loss may be deducted from any compensation due the agent or may be recovered in an ordinary lawsuit.

When the agent handles money for the principal, the contract of employment may provide that the amount of any shortages in the agent's account may be deducted from the compensation to which the agent would otherwise be entitled.

If the agent has made a secret profit, the principal may recover that profit from the agent. In addition, the agent may forfeit the right to all compensation, without regard to whether the principal benefited from some of the actions of the agent and without regard to whether the principal had actually been harmed.

§ 43:9   DUTIES AND LIABILITIES OF PRINCIPAL TO AGENT

The principal is under certain duties to the agent. The principal must perform the contract, compensate the agent for services, make reimbursement for proper expenditures, and under certain circumstances must indemnify the agent for loss.

(a) EMPLOYMENT ACCORDING TO TERMS OF CONTRACT. When the contract is for a specified time, the principal is under the obligation to permit the agent to act as such for the term of the contract, in the absence of any just cause or contract provision that permits the principal to terminate the agency sooner. If the principal gives the agent an exclusive right to act as such, the principal cannot give anyone else the authority to act as agent nor may the principal do the act to which the exclusive agent's authority relates. If the principal or another agent does so, the exclusive agent is entitled to full compensation as though the act had been performed by the exclusive agent.

(b) COMPENSATION. The principal must pay the agent the compensation agreed upon. If the parties have not fixed the amount of the compensation by their agreement but intended that the agent should be paid, the agent may recover the customary compensation for such services. If there is no established compensation, the agent may recover the reasonable value of the services rendered.[11]

[11]   Flynn v LaVay (Dist Col App) 431 A2d 543 (1981).

(1) Repeating Transactions. In certain industries third persons make repeated transactions with the principal. In such cases the agent who made the original contract with the third person commonly receives a certain compensation or percentage of commissions on all subsequent renewal or additional contracts. In the insurance business, for example, the insurance agent obtaining the policyholder for the insurer receives a substantial portion of the first year's premium and then receives a smaller percentage of the premiums paid by the policyholder in the following years.

Whether an agent or an agent's estate is entitled to receive compensation on repeating transactions, either after the termination of the agent's employment or after the agent's death, depends upon the terms of the agency contract. Frequently, it is provided that the right to receive compensation on repeating transactions terminates upon the termination of the agent's authority or employment by the principal.

(2) Post-Agency Transactions. An agent is not entitled to compensation in connection with transactions, such as sales or renewals of insurance policies, occurring after the termination of the agency, even though the post-agency transactions are the result of the agent's former activities. Some contracts between a principal and an agent expressly state whether the agent has the right to post-termination compensation, however.

(c) REIMBURSEMENT. The principal is under a duty to reimburse the agent for all disbursements made at the request of the principal and for all expenses necessarily incurred in the lawful discharge of the agency for the benefit of the principal. The agent cannot recover, however, for expenses caused by the agent's own misconduct or negligence. By way of illustration, if the agent transfers title to the wrong person, the agent cannot recover from the principal the expense incurred in correcting the error.

(d) INDEMNITY. It is the duty of the principal to indemnify the agent for any losses or damages suffered on account of the agency that were not caused by the agent's fault.

When the loss sustained is not the result of obedience to the principal's instructions but of the agent's misconduct, or of an obviously illegal act, the principal is not liable for indemnification.

AGENT'S DUTIES TO PRINCIPAL	PRINCIPAL'S DUTIES TO AGENT
LOYALTY OBEDIENCE AND PERFORMANCE ACCORDING TO TERMS OF CONTRACT REASONABLE CARE INFORMATION ACCOUNTING	EMPLOYMENT ACCORDING TO TERMS OF CONTRACT COMPENSATION REIMBURSEMENT INDEMNITY

FIGURE 43-1
DUTIES OF PRINCIPALS AND AGENTS

SUMMARY

The scope of an agent's authority is important, since an agent acting with authority has the power to bind the principal. The scope of an agent's authority may be determined from the express words of the principal to the agent, and such is called express authority. An agent has incidental authority to perform any act reasonably necessary to execute the express authority given the agent. An agent's authority may be implied so as to enable the agent to perform any act in accordance with the general customs or usages in the business or industry. This authority is often referred to as customary authority. An individual is cloaked with apparent authority where the principal, by words or conduct, leads a third person reasonably to believe that the individual has the authority of an agent.

The effect of a proper exercise of authority by an agent is to bind the principal and third person to a contract; the agent, not being a party to the contract, is not liable in any respect under the contract. A third person dealing with a person claiming to be an agent, has a duty to ascertain the extent of the agent's authority and has a duty to take notice of any acts that are clearly adverse to the principal's interests. The third person cannot claim that apparent authority existed when the person has notice that the agent's conduct is adverse to the interests of the principal. A third person who has knowledge of limitations on an agent's authority is bound by those limitations. A third person is not bound by secret limitations.

An agent cannot appoint subagents to do the agent's duties unless (a) the duties are ministerial; (b) to do so is a well-established custom in the industry in question; (c) to do so is justified by emergency conditions; or (d) it was contemplated by the parties that subagents would be employed.

While the agency relationship exists, the agent owes the principal the duties of (a) being loyal; (b) obeying all lawful instructions; (c) exercising reasonable care; (d) accounting for all property or money belonging to the principal; and (e) informing the principal of all facts relating to the agency that are relevant to the principal's interests. The duties of an agent continue after

termination of the agency only to the extent necessary to perform prior obligations, such as return of the former principal's property. After termination of the agency, the agent may deal with the principal as freely as with a stranger.

The principal has certain duties to the agent, including fulfilling all terms of their contract, paying the agreed compensation for services of the agent, reimbursing the agent for proper expenditures, and under certain circumstances, indemnifying the agent for losses suffered on account of the agency through no fault of the agent.

QUESTIONS AND CASE PROBLEMS

1. What social forces are affected by the rule that a third person must ascertain the extent of an agent's authority?

2. Pamela was the authorized agent of Nanette. She so informed Sydney and made a contract with him on behalf of Nanette to purchase Sydney's automobile. Thereafter, Sydney failed to deliver the automobile to Nanette. Pamela sued Sydney for breach of contract. Can Pamela recover?

3. Can a person act as agent for both parties to a transaction?

4. Compare (a) secret limitations on authority of an agent with (b) apparent authority of an agent.

5. After an agency has been terminated, the agent is not entitled to further compensation. Appraise this statement.

6. Martha Christiansen owns women's apparel stores bearing her name in New Seabury, Massachusetts; Lake Placid, New York; Palm Beach, Florida; and Palm Springs, California. At a meeting with her four store managers she discussed styles she thought appropriate for the forthcoming season; advised them as always to use their best judgment in the goods they purchased for each of their respective stores; and cautioned "but no blue jeans." Later Jane Farley, the manager of the Lake Placid store, purchased a line of high-quality blue denim outfits (designer jeans with jacket and vest options) from Women's Wear, Inc. for the summer season. The outfits did not sell. Martha refused to pay for

them, contending that she told all of her managers "no blue jeans," and that if it came to a lawsuit, she would fly in three managers to testify that Jane Farley had absolutely no authority to purchase denim outfits and was, in fact, expressly forbidden to do so. Women's Wear sued Martha, and the three managers testified for Martha. Is the fact that Martha had explicitly forbidden Farley to purchase the outfits in question sufficient to relieve her from liability for the purchases made by Farley?

7. The Taylors were depositors of the Equitable Trust Company of Maryland. Equitable issued them a treasurer's check for $20,000. Mr. Vittetoe, a loan officer of the bank, received a long-distance telephone call from a person who identified himself as Mr. Taylor and who requested that the $20,000 represented by the treasurer's check be transferred to the account of Jody Associates at Irving Trust Company in New York. Mr. Vittetoe did not know Mr. Taylor personally and replied that written instructions from Taylor would be required. Some time later, Frank Terranova appeared at the bank and stated that he was Taylor's agent, surrendered the treasurer's check that had not been indorsed, and requested that the money represented thereby be transferred to the account of Jody Associates in the Irving Trust Company. Terranova also presented a letter that he had signed in his own name, in which was repeated the request to trans-

fer the $20,000. Equitable verified Mr. Terranova's signature by checking his driver's license and a major credit card and thereafter made the transfer as requested. Taylor denied that Terranova had the authority to request such transfer and sued Equitable for damages. The bank contends that it was entitled to rely upon the written instructions submitted to the bank by Terranova. Decide.

8. Regional Broadcasters of Michigan, Inc. owned and operated radio station WTRU. Moreschini supplied advertising material to WTRU under contract made with the station manager. When Moreschini sued Regional Broadcasters, it raised the defense that the manager had been instructed not to make any contracts on behalf of the station. Was Regional bound? [Moreschini v Regional Broadcasters, 373 Mich 496, 129 NW2d 859]

9. Hihn and Eastland, doing business in California, were authorized to sell certain land in Texas. They in turn employed Maney, of Texas, to sell the land. He made the sale and then sued them for the commissions due him on the sale. Did Hihn and Eastland have authority to employ Maney to make the sale? [Eastland v Maney, 36 Tex Civ App 147, 81 SW 574]

10. McKinney requested E. M. Christmas, a real estate broker, to sell McKinney's property. A sale was effected with the contract calling for monthly installment payments by the purchaser, which payments were to be collected by the broker. When the purchaser stopped making the payments, McKinney was not notified of that fact but one of the broker's employees bought out the purchaser's contract. Christmas, the broker, continued making payments to McKinney as though they were being made by the purchaser. Later, Christmas resold the land to another buyer at a substantial profit. McKinney sued Christmas for this profit. Decide. [McKinney v Christmas, 143 Colo 361, 353 P2d 373]

11. An attorney received a check made payable to the order of his client. The attorney indorsed the client's name and cashed the check at the bank upon which it was drawn. The client then sued the bank for the amount that had been paid the attorney. The bank raised the defense that the attorney had authority to sign for the client and to receive payment on the client's behalf. Was this a valid defense? [Aetna Casualty & Surety Co. v Traders Nat. Bank & Trust Co. (Mo App) 514 SW2d 860]

12. Kribbs owned real estate that had been leased through his agent, Jackson, at a monthly rental of $275. When this lease terminated, Jackson and a third person, Solomon, made an agreement that if the latter obtained a new tenant for a rental of $500 a month, Jackson would pay Solomon $100 a month. The latter obtained a new tenant who paid a monthly rental of $550. Jackson continued to send Kribbs $275 a month, less his commissions and janitor and utility costs; paid Solomon $100 a month; and kept the balance of the rental for himself. When Kribbs learned of these facts three years later, he sued Jackson for the money he had kept for himself and that which he had paid Solomon. Jackson defended that Kribbs accepted and was satisfied with the $275 per month, that the additional funds were the sole result of Jackson's own entrepreneurship, and that the funds should accrue solely to Jackson's benefit. Decide. [Kribbs v Jackson, 387 Pa 611, 129 A2d 490]

13. DSG is in the government food service contracting business. Fredrick Anderson was employed by DSG to survey contracts in preparation for bids. Edward Mitura served as manager of DSG's Fort Riley, Kansas, contract. In early November 1982, the food service contract at Fort Campbell, Kentucky, became available for bidding. On November 8, Anderson and Mitura toured the Fort Campbell facility with other prospective bidders, and Mitura informed Anderson of his intention to bid personally on the contract. Anderson hired an accountant Larry Golden concerning the cost per hour to be utilized in a bid, and it was determined to be $7.78. Anderson provided Mitura with this figure and Mitura paid Golden's bill. On November 16, DSG submitted a bid. DSG was not notified by Anderson that Mitura was going to submit a bid. On November 22, Mitura, through his wife, submitted a bid. On November 23, Mitura notified DSG that he had submitted a bid on the Fort Campbell contract and quit his job. On November 24, the bids were opened, and Mitura's bid turned out to be the lowest. On

December 12, Anderson resigned from DSG to work with Mitura; and the Fort Campbell contract was subsequently awarded to Mitura. DSG sued Mitura and Anderson for breach of their fiduciary duty to DSG by competing with it while employed by DSG. Mitura and Anderson contend that they were free to compete with their former employer once their employment relationship was terminated. They point out that their contract at Fort Campbell did not begin until well after both had terminated their work for DSG. Decide. [DSG Corp v Anderson (CA6 Ky) 754 F2d 678]

14. Cristallina S.A., a Panamanian corporation engaged in the purchase and sale of works of art, employed Christie's International to sell eight paintings at a May 19 auction. Based upon the assessment of its experts, Christie's notified the press on May 12 that it expected to receive between $5,000,000 and $9,000,000 for the paintings. On the day before the auction, Christie's president David Bathurst recommended that the "reserves" — the private agreement between the seller and auctioneer on the prices below which an item may not be sold — be set at $9,250,000. The auction was a conceded failure, with just one of the eight paintings being sold. Cristallina sued Christie's contending that as its agent Christie's failed to inform it of the information released to the press on May 12 and the underlying information upon which the press estimates were made; and that the released estimates made it virtually impossible to sell the paintings unless the reserves were lowered.

Christie's contends that as an auctioneer it cannot guarantee the results of a sale. Decide. [Christallina S.A. v Christie, Manson & Woods (N.Y. App Div) 502 NYS2d 165]

15. Bankerd and his wife, Virginia, owned, as tenants by the entirety, a home in Maryland. They lived there until 1966, when Mrs. Bankerd moved out as a result of marital problems. Bankerd continued to live in the house until July 1968, when he "left for the west." Mrs. Bankerd thereupon resumed residency and assumed all expenses for the home. Before Bankerd's departure, he executed a power of attorney to King. The power of attorney was later updated to authorize King to sell the property "on such terms as to him seem best." In 1977 Mrs. Bankerd asked King to exercise the power of attorney and to transfer Bankerd's interest in the property to her so that she could sell the property and retire. King wrote to Bankerd on three occasions at various addresses, but was unsuccessful in reaching him. King believed Bankerd didn't care about the property and that Bankerd had abandoned his interest in it. King therefore conveyed Bankerd's interest in the property to Mrs. Bankerd. Mrs. Bankerd paid no consideration for the transfer, and King received no compensation. Later, Bankerd sued King claiming that King had breached his duty of loyalty in connection with the conveyance of the property. King defended that under the broad language of the power of attorney, he had acted within his authority. Decide. [King v Bankerd, 303 Md 98 492 A2d 608]

44

THIRD PERSONS IN AGENCY

In agency transactions, the third person has certain rights and liabilities with respect to the agent and the principal. Many of these rights and liabilities are contractual in nature. However, the agency transaction can also produce tort and criminal liability for the agent and, under certain circumstances, for the principal as well.

A. LIABILITY OF AGENT TO THIRD PERSON

The liability of the agent to the third person depends upon the existence of authority and the manner of executing the contract.

§ 44:1 ACTION OF AUTHORIZED AGENT OF DISCLOSED PRINCIPAL

If an agent makes a contract with a third person on behalf of a disclosed principal and has proper authority to do so and if the contract is executed properly, the agent has no personal liability on the contract. Whether the principal performs the contract or not, the agent cannot be held liable by the third party. Thus, an insurance agency arranging for the insuring of a customer with a named company is not liable on the policy that the company issues to the insured. If the agent lacks authority, however, or if certain other circumstances exist, the agent may be liable.

In speaking of an agent's action as authorized or unauthorized, it must be remembered that "authorized" includes action that, though originally unauthorized, was subsequently ratified by the principal.[1] Once there is an effective ratification, the original action of the agent is no longer treated as unauthorized.

§ 44:2 UNAUTHORIZED ACTION

If a person makes a contract as agent for another but lacks authority to do so, the contract does not bind the principal. When a person purports to act as agent for a principal, an implied warranty arises that such person has authority to do so.[2] If the agent lacks authority there is a breach of this warranty and if the agent's act causes loss to the third person, that third person may generally hold the agent liable for the loss. It is no defense for the agent in such case that the agent acted in good faith or misunderstood the scope of authority. The purported agent is not liable for conduct in excess of authority when the third person knows that the agent is acting beyond the authority given by the principal.

An agent with a written authorization may avoid liability on the implied warranty of authority by showing the written authorization to the third person and permitting the third person to determine the scope of the agent's authority.

§ 44:3 NO PRINCIPAL WITH CAPACITY

A person purporting to act as agent warrants by implication that there is an existing principal and that the principal has legal capacity. If there is no principal or if the principal lacks capacity, the person acting as an agent is liable for any loss caused the third person.

The agent can avoid liability on the implied warranty of the existence of a principal with capacity by making known to the third person all material or pertinent facts or by obtaining the agreement of the third person that the agent shall not be liable.

§ 44:4 DISCLOSURE OF PRINCIPAL

There are three degrees to which the existence and identity of the principal may be disclosed or not disclosed. An agent's liability as a party to a contract with a third person is affected by the degree of disclosure.

(a) DISCLOSED PRINCIPAL. When the agent makes known the identity of the principal and the fact that the agent is acting on behalf of that principal, the principal is called a **disclosed principal.** The third person dealing with an agent of a disclosed principal ordinarily intends to make a contract with the principal and not with the agent. Consequently, the agent is not a party to and is not bound by the contract that is made.[3]

(b) PARTIALLY DISCLOSED PRINCIPAL. When the agent makes known the existence of an unknown principal but not the principal's identity, the principal is a **partially disclosed principal.** As the third par-

---

[1] Benner v Farm Bureau Mut. Ins. Co. 96 Idaho 311, 528 P2d 193 (1974).
[2] Moore v Lewis, 51 Ill 3d 388, 366 NE2d 594 (1977).

[3] Thilman & Co. v Esposito, 87 Ill App 3d 289, 42 Ill Dec 305, 408 NE2d 1014 (1980).

ty does not know the identity of the principal, the third person is making the contract with the agent, and the agent is therefore a party to the contract.

(c) UNDISCLOSED PRINCIPAL. When the third person is not told or does not know that the agent is acting as an agent for anyone else, the unknown principal is called an **undisclosed principal**.[4] In such case, the third person is making the contract with the agent, and the agent is a party to

that contract. For example, an agent selling the goods of an undisclosed principal is the "seller" in the sales contract and is liable for breach of the implied warranty of title if the principal in fact was not the owner of the goods sold by the agent.

In the *Rothschild* case the court was faced with deciding whether an agent was liable under contracts made on behalf of a principal, wherein the agent did not disclose the name of the principal at the time the contracts were made, but the identity of the principal was later made known to the other contracting party.

---

[4]   Crown Controls Inc. v Smiley, 47 Wash App 832, 737 P2d 709 (1987).

ROTHSCHILD SUNSYSTEMS INC V PAWLUS
514 NYS2d 572 (1987)

Richard Pawlus was an owner of Dutch City Wood Products Inc. which did business as "Dutch City Marketing." Pawlus believed he was acting on behalf of the corporation and purchased merchandise from Rothschild Sunsystems Inc. from April 24, 1985 to June 24, 1985 using the designation "Richard Pawlus Dutch Marketing" on orders and correspondence. In October when a balance of $9,882.34 was owed Rothschild, the seller was notified by Pawlus' attorney that Pawlus was acting on behalf of the corporation when the merchandise was purchased. Rothschild sued Pawlus for payment for the merchandise and received a summary judgment. Pawlus contended that he was an agent of the corporation and is thus not personally liable. Pawlus appealed.

MURPHY, P.J. . . . The inquiry here is whether there exist any triable issues of fact. Plaintiff's complaint alleges that it shipped goods to Pawlus at his request, that Pawlus accepted the goods without objection and that the balance due on the account had not been paid despite reasonable demand having been made. Invoices to establish the allegations were submitted. Plaintiff also alleged that Pawlus never stated that he was acting on behalf of a corporation. Thus, plaintiff made out a cause of action on an account. It was then incumbent on Pawlus to demonstrate in acceptable evidentiary form that issues of fact existed. Pawlus, in his opposing papers, did not deny that he placed the orders or received the merchandise. Nor did he dispute any of the items in the account. He simply alleged that he acted on behalf of the corporation, Dutch City Wood Products, Inc., which was doing business as Dutch City Marketing. Further, he stated that plaintiff was made aware of this fact on October 17, 1985. However, this was well after the orders were placed and filled. The record also includes a letter from Pawlus dated September 12, 1985 which he signed "Richard Pawlus Dutch City Marketing" and which bears a letterhead "Dutch City Marketing." No mention of a corporation is made.

An agent will be liable as a principal if the fact of the agency relationship is not known by the person with whom the agent deals. Such disclosure must be made at the time of the contract. Here, Pawlus has failed to even allege that the existence of an agency was made known to plaintiff. Thus, summary judgment was properly granted to plaintiff.

[Judgment affirmed]

QUESTIONS

1. Was Dutch City Wood Products Inc. a partially disclosed principal?
2. Did the fact that Rothschild was notified that Pawlus was acting as an agent prior to the lawsuit relieve Pawlus from liability as a principal?
3. State the rule of the case.

§ 44:5   WRONGFUL RECEIPT OF MONEY

If an agent obtains a payment of money from a third person by use of illegal methods, the agent is liable to the third person.

If the third person makes an overpayment to the agent or a payment when none is due, the agent is also usually liable to the third person for the amount of such overpayment or payment. If the agent has acted in good faith and does not know that the payment was improperly made, however, the agent is liable to the third person only so long as the agent has possession or control of the overpayment. If the agent has remitted the overpayment to the principal before its return is demanded by the third person, the agent is not liable to the third person. In the latter case, the third person's right of action, if one exists, is only against the principal. But payment to the principal does not relieve the agent of liability when the agent knows that the payment was not proper.

§ 44:6   ASSUMPTION OF LIABILITY

Agents may intentionally make themselves liable upon contracts with third persons.[5] This situation frequently occurs when the

agent is a well-established local brokerage house or other agency and when the principal is located out of town and is not known locally.

In some situations, the agent will make a contract that will be personally binding. If the principal is not disclosed, the agent is necessarily the other contracting party and is bound by the contract. Even when the principal is disclosed, the agent may be personally bound if it were the intention of the parties that the agent assume a personal obligation, even though this was done in order to further the business of the principal.

§ 44:7   EXECUTION OF CONTRACT

A simple contract that would appear to be the contract of the agent can be shown by other evidence, if believed, to have been intended as a contract between the principal and the third party. If the intention is established, it will be permitted to contradict the face of the written contract, and the contract as thus modified will be enforced.

In the *Memorial Hospital* case, where a daughter signed a guarantee of payment form upon bringing her incapacitated mother to a hospital, the court considered the daughter's defense that she had signed the guarantee form only as agent for her mother and thus could not be held personally responsible for unpaid charges.

---

[5]   Forbes Homes Inc. v Trimpi, 70 NC App 614, 320 SE2d 328 (1984).

MEMORIAL HOSPITAL V BAUMANN

475 NYS2d 636 (1984)

During the early morning hours of January 10, 1981, Beverly Baumann accompanied her mother to Memorial Hospital, where her mother was placed in intensive care for symptoms of heart ailment. Ms. Baumann was approached by a nurse and signed various documents, including one that authorized the hospital to release medical information and to receive directly the mother's insurance benefits. This form stated, "I understand I am financially responsible to the hospital for charges not covered by this authorization." Ms. Baumann's mother died during the course of her hospitalization. Thereafter, the hospital commenced suit to recover $19,013.42 in unpaid hospital charges based upon the form, signed by Ms. Baumann, that the hospital called a "guarantee of payment." Baumann contended that she signed the document as an agent for a disclosed principal and was thus not personally liable. From a judgment for Ms. Baumann, the hospital appealed.

MEMORANDUM DECISION. . . . Defendant's affidavit clearly states that she "signed [the] documents understanding that it was on behalf of [her] mother", thereby giving notice of an agency claim in this case. Plaintiff made no attempt to refute this assertion and does not claim on this appeal that it was surprised or prejudiced by defendant's reliance on the agency defense. Accordingly, we conclude that the agency defense was properly considered by Special Term.

On the merits, we recognize as well settled the proposition that an agent assumes no personal liability in executing a contract for a disclosed principal, unless it is clear that the agent intends to be bound personally. Defendant's unrefuted affidavit establishes that she did not intend to be bound personally because she signed the forms on behalf of her incapacitated mother who was clearly, as the patient to whom services were to be rendered in an emergency situation, the principal. Thus, Special Term's conclusions that defendant was acting as an agent for a disclosed principal and could not be personally liable to the hospital were correct. Special Term was also correct in distinguishing *Albany Med. Center Hosp. v Purcell*, 67 A.D.2d 761, 412 N.Y.S.2d 461, relied on by plaintiff, on the ground that the issue of agency was not raised therein.

[Judgment affirmed]

QUESTIONS

1. On what basis did the hospital believe Ms. Baumann was responsible for the unpaid bills?
2. What was Ms. Baumann's defense?
3. What action could Ms. Baumann have taken at the hospital that would have avoided any question as to her responsibility for unpaid charges?

To avoid any question of interpretation an agent should execute an instrument by signing the principal's name and either "by" or "per" and the agent's name. For example, if Jane R. Craig is an agent for B. G. Gray, Craig should execute instruments by signing either "B. G. Gray, by Jane R. Craig" or "B. G. Gray, per Jane R. Craig." Such a signing is in law a signing by *Gray*, and the agent is therefore not a party to the contract.[6] The signing of the principal's name by an authorized agent without indicating the agent's name or identity is likewise in law the signature of the principal.

If the instrument is ambiguous as to whether the agent has signed in a representative or an individual capacity, parol evidence is admissible, as between the original parties to the transaction, to establish the character in which the agent was acting. If the body of the contract states an obligation that clearly refers only to the principal, the agent is not bound by the contract even though it is signed in the agent's individual name without indicating any agency.

If an agent executes a sealed instrument in those states in which a seal retains its common-law force and does so without disclosing the agency or the principal's identity, the agent is bound and cannot show that the parties did not intend this result.[7] Because of the formal character of the writing, the liability of the parties is determined from the face of the instrument alone, and it cannot be modified or contradicted by proof of matters not set forth in the writing.

§ 44:8 FAILURE TO OBTAIN COMMITMENT OF PRINCIPAL

In some situations, the agent is in effect an intermediary, or go-between, who has the duty to the third person to see to it that the principal is bound to the third person. For example, when an agent of an insurance company who has authority to write policies of insurance tells a policyholder whose fire policy has been canceled that the agent will look into the matter and that the insured should forget about it unless notified by the agent, the latter is under an obligation to make reasonable efforts to obtain the reinstatement of the policy or to notify the insured that it is not possible to do so. The agent is liable to the insured for the latter's fire loss if the agent does not obtain the reinstatement of the policy and fails to so inform the insured.

§ 44:9 TORTS AND CRIMES

Agents are liable for harm caused third persons by the agent's fraudulent, intentional, or negligent acts. The fact that they were acting as agents at the time or that they had acted in good faith under the directions of a principal does not relieve them of liability if their conduct would impose liability upon them were they acting for themselves. With respect to liability for torts and crimes, no distinction is made as to whether the person causing harm is an agent or an employee.[8]

If an agent commits a crime, such as stealing from a third person or shooting the third person, the agent is liable for the crime without regard to the fact of acting as an agent, and without regard to whether the agent acted in self-interest or sought to advance the interest of the principal.

B. LIABILITY OF THIRD PERSON TO AGENT

A third party may be liable to an agent because of the manner in which the transac-

---

[6] Barnes v Sadler, 95 NM 334, 622 P2d 239 (1981).

[7] Tooke v Thom (Fla App) 281 So 2d 34 (1973). As to the signing of commercial paper by an agent, see § 32:5(b)(1) of this book.

[8] Mannish v Lacayo (Fla App) 496 So 2d 242 (1986).

tion was conducted or because of acts caus-ing harm to the agent.

§ 44:10   ACTION OF AUTHORIZED AGENT OF DISCLOSED PRINCIPAL

Ordinarily the third person is not liable to the agent for a breach of contract that the agent has made with the third person on behalf of a disclosed principal. In certain instances, however, the third person may be liable to the agent.

§ 44:11   UNDISCLOSED AND PARTIALLY DISCLOSED PRINCIPAL

If the agent executed the contract without the third party's knowing both of the exis-tence of the agency and the identity of the principal, and the third party breaches the contract, the agent may sue the third party for the breach.

In such instances, if the contract is a sim-ple contract, the principal may also sue the third person even though the third person thought the contract was only with the agent. In states in which the seal has lost its common-law significance, this same rule is applied to sealed contracts. In all such cases, the right of the principal to sue the third person is superior to the agent's right to do so.

In contrast with the foregoing, if the contract is a commercial paper or sealed contract in a state that gives the seal its common-law force, the undisclosed princi-pal, not appearing on the instrument as a party, may not bring an action to enforce the contract.

§ 44:12   AGENT INTENDING TO BE BOUND

If the third person knew that the agent was acting as an agent but nevertheless the par-ties intended that the agent should be per-sonally bound by the contract, the agent

may sue the third person for breach of contract.

§ 44:13   EXECUTION OF CONTRACT

The principles that determine when an agent is liable to the third person because of the way in which a written contract was executed apply equally in determining when the third person is liable to the agent because of the way in which the contract is executed. If the agent could be sued by the third person, the third person can be sued by the agent. Thus, if the agent executes a sealed instrument in the agent's own name, only the agent can sue the third per-son on that instrument in a common-law state. The same rule applies if the contract is in the form of a commercial paper.

§ 44:14   AGENT AS TRANSFEREE

The agent may sue the third person for breach of the latter's obligation to the prin-cipal when the principal has assigned or otherwise transferred a claim or right to the agent, whether absolutely for the agent's own benefit or for the purpose of collecting the money and remitting it to the principal.

C.   LIABILITY OF PRINCIPAL TO THIRD PERSON

The principal is liable to the third person for the properly authorized and executed contracts of the agent and, in certain cir-cumstances, for the agent's unauthorized contracts.

§ 44:15   AGENT'S CONTRACTS

The liability of a principal to a third person on a contract made by an agent depends upon the extent of disclosure of the princi-pal and the form of the contract that is executed.

   (a)   SIMPLE   CONTRACT   WHEREIN PRINCIPAL DISCLOSED. When a disclosed principal with contractual capacity authorizes or ratifies an agent's transaction with a third person, and when the agent properly executes a contract with the third person as an agency transaction, a binding contract exists between the principal and the third person. The principal and the third person may each sue the other in the event of a breach of the contract. The agent is not a party to the contract and is not liable for its performance and cannot sue for its breach.[9]

The liability of a disclosed principal to a third person is not discharged by the fact that the principal gives the agent money with which to pay the third person. Consequently, the liability of a buyer for the purchase price of goods is not terminated by the fact that the buyer paid the buyer's agent the purchase price to remit to the seller.

(b) SIMPLE CONTRACT WHEREIN PRINCIPAL UNDISCLOSED. An undisclosed principal is liable for a simple contract made by an authorized agent. Though the third person initially contracted with the agent alone, the third person upon learning of the existence of the undisclosed principal, may sue that principal. However, the right to sue the undisclosed principal on a simple contract is subject to two limitations. The third person cannot sue the principal if in good faith the principal has settled the account with the agent with respect to the contract. Some states refuse to apply this limitation, however, unless the third person has led the principal to reasonably believe that the account between the agent and the third person has been settled. Also, the third person cannot sue the principal when satisfaction of the claim has already been obtained from the agent.

(c) SIMPLE CONTRACT WHEREIN PRINCIPAL PARTIALLY DISCLOSED. A partially disclosed principal is liable for a simple contract made by an authorized agent. The right of the third person is concurrent as against either the agent or the principal.[10]

(d) CONTRACT UNDER SEAL AND COMMERCIAL PAPER. If a contract is under seal in a state that preserves the common-law force of a seal, an undisclosed principal cannot sue or be sued. In a state in which the seal no longer has its common-law force, the fact that the contract made by the agent is under seal does not prohibit the third person from suing the undisclosed principal.[11]

An undisclosed principal whose name or description does not appear on commercial paper is not liable as a party thereto.[12] Thus, an undisclosed principal is not liable on commercial paper executed by an agent in the agent's own name.

§ 44:16   PAYMENT TO AGENT

When the third person makes payment to an authorized agent, such payment is deemed made to the principal. The principal must give the third person full credit for the payment made to the agent, even though in fact the agent never remits or delivers the payment to the principal, as long as the third person made the payment in good faith and had no reason to know that the agent would be guilty of misconduct.[13]

As apparent authority has the same legal consequence as actual authority, a payment made to a person with apparent authority to receive the payment is deemed a payment to the apparent principal. When payment by a debtor is made to a person who is not the actual or apparent agent of the creditor, such payment does not discharge the debt unless that person in fact pays the money over to the creditor.

---

[9] Eppler, Guerin & Turner, Inc. v Kasmir (Tex Civ App) 685 SW2d 737 (1985).

[10] James C. Smith & Associates, Inc. v Everett, 1 Ohio App 3d 118, 439 NE2d 932 (1981).
[11] Nalbandian v Hanson Restaurant & Lounge, Inc. 369 Mass 150, 338 NE2d 335 (1975).
[12] UCC §§ 3-401, 3-403.
[13] This general rule of law is restated in some states by § 2 of the Uniform Fiduciaries Act, which is expressly extended by § 1 thereof to agents, partners, and corporate officers. Similar statutory provisions are found in a number of other states.

In the *Liberty Mutual* case, an agent over a period of years altered many checks sent to his principal and converted the proceeds for his own purposes. The debtor did not inspect its canceled checks for unauthorized alterations or fraudulent indorsements. The court was faced with deciding whether the proceeds of these checks should be considered a discharge of the debt or whether the debtor was still obligated for the payments converted by the creditor's agent.

LIBERTY MUTUAL INS. CO. V ENJAY CHEM. CO.
(Del Super) 316 A2d 219 (1974)

E. I. duPont deNemours & Co. licensed Enjay Chemical Company (now Exxon) and Johnson and Johnson, to use certain chemical processes, in return for which royalty payments were to be made to duPont. Liberty Mutual Insurance Company insured the fidelity of the employees of duPont. DuPont claimed that Enjay and Johnson and Johnson had not made royalty payments. The defendants asserted that they had regularly made the payments by check but that an employee of duPont, identified as C. H. D. had altered some of the checks so that he appeared as payee and then converted them. DuPont claimed that the checks thus converted by C. H. D. had never been paid to duPont and that the amount of those checks was still owed to it by Enjay and Johnson and Johnson. Liberty Mutual and duPont sued Enjay and Johnson and Johnson. The defendants filed a motion to dismiss the action.

PER CURIAM. . . As these checks were received C. H. D. physically altered the face thereof by typing under the payee's name (Account of C. H. D. . .). C. H. D. then indorsed the checks for deposit to his personal account at the Bank of Delaware.

All royalty checks during the nine-year period were sent by defendants to E. I. duPont deNemours Elastomer Chemicals Department, Wilmington, Delaware, 19898, Att: C. H. D., Control Division, in accordance with a written directive to that effect sent to defendants on duPont's letterhead by C. H. D.

. . . DuPont concedes that C. H. D. regularly received and indorsed checks from defendants and would indorse the checks sometimes to his personal account and sometimes to duPont's account. This series of transactions occurred over a period of nine (9) years, and not once is it shown that duPont ever challenged or countermanded C. H. D.'s authority to receive and indorse the checks which were properly paid to duPont's account. Nor did duPont ever advise defendants to deal with anyone in the Company other than C. H. D. DuPont did not repudiate C. H. D.'s authority to receive and indorse those checks where the proceeds were paid to duPont, and, therefore, it cannot be permitted to repudiate the same authority where the proceeds were diverted to C. H. D. . . .

The law in other jurisdictions supports defendants' contention that C. H. D. had authority and that payment to duPont was legally made. One factor considered is the length of time that the agent performed similar acts on behalf of the employer. . . . Here C. H. D. acted for duPont for nine years. . . .

An important factor in determining the existence of apparent authority is whether the debtor, upon sending his payments to the creditor's agent, would have any reason to suspect improper designs or acts by the agent. New Jersey, with citations of other jurisdictions, states that it is the established doctrine that when one indebted to a principal makes a payment to a duly authorized agent, having neither notice nor reason to know of any improper designs on the part of the agent, the indebtedness is discharged when the agent obtains the proceeds. *Gross v Grimaldi*, 64 NJ Super 457, 166 A2d 592 (1960). . . .

. . . It is evident from the record that nothing in the nine years of dealing between duPont's employee and the defendants was designed to put defendants on notice that he behaved improperly. It should be self-evident that the employer-creditor is responsible for the acts of his own employee. It should be equally apparent that the employer-creditor is better able to undertake his own inspection and precautions to avoid mishandling of checks by its employees, than is the debtor who sends the checks to the creditor. In our case years had gone by before duPont detected the fraud. Now duPont says that the debtor defendants should have looked at their canceled checks, after having been returned from the presenting bank, to see if there were any fraudulent indorsements. Obviously, large companies like the defendants' here would receive thousands of checks back from their banks each month. It would be extremely burdensome and expensive for defendants to look at the indorsements on the back of each returned check. It would be even more difficult for them to determine if the indorser was authorized by the creditor to indorse the particular check in question. If there was a burden, it was duPont's not the defendants.

Unquestionably obligated to duPont for royalties, defendants discharged their obligation to duPont by timely delivery of a series of checks to C. H. D., duPont's duly authorized agent, which checks were paid by the payee banks. That the proceeds of those checks were fraudulently converted by duPont's own employee C. H. D. is not a circumstance which requires defendants to pay their obligations twice. . . .

To hold that payment had not been made by defendants is to create the harsh result not only of forcing defendants to pay the same obligation twice, but also of allocating the loss against a party which had not power or control over the person who caused the loss. C. H. D. was duPont's employee, not defendants' and nothing defendants could have done would have insured his trustworthiness.

The draftsmen of the Uniform Commercial Code have taken the position that losses caused by an unfaithful employee should be a cost of the business enterprise in the slightly different factual context of a "padded payroll" case. When the employee supplies the name of a fictitious payee. . . , the draftsmen contend that the business, rather than the bank, should bear the loss: "The principle followed is that the loss should fall upon the employer as a risk of his business enterprise rather than upon the subsequent holder or drawee. The reasons are that the employer is normally in a better position to prevent forgeries by reasonable care in the selection or supervision of his employees, or, if he is not, is at least in a better position to cover the loss by fidelity insurance; and that the cost of such insurance is properly an expense of his business rather than of the business of the holder or drawee." Official comment 4 to § 3-405. The reasoning applies equally to third party checks made payable to du-

Pont which C. H. D. diverted. DuPont should have exercised care in his selection and supervision. Defendants should not be held responsible for the faithlessness of duPont's employee over which [they] had no control, which faithlessness was permitted to continue over a period of nine (9) years. . . .

[Judgment for defendants]

QUESTIONS

1. Did "C. H. D." have actual or apparent authority to cash checks received from the licensees of duPont?
2. Did the court hold that it is preferable to place the loss for an employee's dishonesty upon the customer rather than upon the employer?
3. What, if anything, could duPont have done to have prevented the misconduct of its employee?

§ 44:17   AGENT'S STATEMENTS

A principal is bound by a statement made by an agent while transacting business within the scope of authority. This means that the principal cannot thereafter contradict the statement of the agent and show that it is not true. Statements or declarations of an agent, in order to bind the principal, must be made at the time of performing the act to which they relate or shortly thereafter.

§ 44:18   AGENT'S KNOWLEDGE

The principal is bound by knowledge or notice of any fact that is acquired by an agent while acting within the scope of actual or apparent authority.[14] When a commercial paper is indorsed to the principal and the agent acting for the principal has a knowledge of a matter that would be a defense to the paper, such knowledge of the agent is imputed to the principal and bars the principal from being a holder in due course. When a fact is known to the agent of the seller, the sale is deemed made by the seller with knowledge of that fact. For example, where the agent recommending and selling weed eradicator to the buyer

knew that it would be used in a drainage ditch in the Mississippi River delta, a warranty of fitness for that particular purpose arose because the seller was deemed to know what the agent knew. Likewise, when an employee knows that there has been a pollution of water contrary to law, such knowledge is imputed to the corporate employer, even though no officer or director had in fact any knowledge thereof.[15]

The rule that the agent's knowledge is imputed to the principal is extended in some cases to knowledge gained prior to the creation of the agency relationship. The notice and knowledge in any case must be based upon reliable information. Thus, when the agent hears only rumors, the principal is not charged with notice.

(a) EXCEPTIONS. If the subject matter is outside the scope of the agent's authority, the agent is under no duty to inform the principal of the knowledge and the principal is not bound thereby.

The principal is not charged with knowledge of an agent under the following circumstances: (1) when the agent is under a duty to another person to conceal such knowledge; (2) when the agent is acting adversely to the principal's interest; or (3)

---

[14] Baldinger Baking Co. v Stepan (Minn App) 354 NW2d 569 (1984).

[15] Apex Oil Co. v United States (CA8 Mo) 530 F2d 1291 (1976).

when the third party acts in collusion with the agent for the purpose of cheating the principal. In such cases, it is not likely that the agent would communicate knowledge to the principal. The principal, therefore, is not bound by the knowledge of the agent.

(b) COMMUNICATION TO PRINCIPAL. As a consequence of regarding the principal as possessing the knowledge of the agent, when the law requires that a third person communicate with the principal, that duty may be satisfied by communicating with the agent. Thus, an offeree effectively communicates the acceptance of an offer to the offeror when the offeree makes such communication to the offeror's agent. An offeror effectively communicates the revocation of an offer to the offeree by communicating the revocation to the offeree's agent.

D. LIABILITY OF PRINCIPAL FOR TORTS AND CRIMES OF AGENT

Under certain circumstances the principal may be liable to the third person for the torts or crimes of the agent or employee.

§ 44:19 VICARIOUS LIABILITY FOR TORTS AND CRIMES

Assume that an agent or an employee causes harm to a third person. Is the principal or employer liable for this conduct? If the conduct constitutes a crime, can the principal or employer be criminally prosecuted? The answer is that in many instances the principal or employer is liable civilly and may be prosecuted criminally. That is, the principal or employer is liable although personally free from fault and not guilty of any wrong. This concept of imposing liability for the fault of another is known as **vicarious liability.**

The situation arises both when an employer has an employee and a principal has an agent who commits the wrong. The rules of law governing the vicarious liability of the principal and the employer are the same. In the interest of simplicity, this section will be stated in terms of employees acting in the course of employment. It is to be remembered that these rules are equally applicable to agents acting within the scope of their authority. As a practical matter, some situations will only arise with agents. For example, the vicarious liability of a seller for the misrepresentations made by a salesperson will only arise when the seller appointed an agent to sell. In contrast, both the employee hired to drive a truck and the agent being sent to visit a customer could negligently run over a third person. In many situations, a person employed by another is both an employee and an agent and the tort is committed within the phase of "employee" work.

The rule of law imposing vicarious liability upon an innocent employer for the wrong of an employee is also known as the doctrine of **respondeat superior.** In modern times, this doctrine can be justified on the ground that the business should pay for the harm caused in the doing of the business, that the employer will be more careful in the selection of employees if made responsible for their actions, and that the employer may obtain liability insurance to protect against claims of third persons.

(a) NATURE OF ACT. The wrongful act committed by the employee may be a negligent act, an intentional act, a fraudulent act, or a violation of a governmental regulation. It may give rise only to civil liability of the employer or it may also subject the employer to prosecution for crime.

(1) Negligent Act. Historically, the act for which liability would be imposed under the doctrine of respondeat superior was a negligent act committed within the scope of employment.

(2) Intentional Act. Under the common law, a master was not liable for an intentional tort committed by a servant. The modern law holds that an employer is liable for an intentional tort committed by an employee for the purpose of furthering the

employer's business.[16] Thus an employer is not liable for an intentional, unprovoked assault committed by an employee upon a third person or customer of the employer because of a personal grudge or for no reason, but the employer will be held liable by the modern view when the employee's assault was committed in the belief that the employee was thereby advancing the employer's interest.[17] For example, when an employee is hired to retake property, as in the case of an employee of a finance company hired to repossess automobiles on which installment payments have not been made, the employer is generally liable for the unlawful force used by the employee in retaking the property or in committing an assault upon a debtor.

(3) Fraud. The modern decisions hold the employer liable for fraudulent acts or misrepresentations. The rule is commonly applied to a principal-agent relationship. To illustrate, when an agent makes fraudulent statements in selling stock, the principal is liable for the buyer's loss. In states that follow the common-law rule of no liability for intentional torts, the principal is

not liable for the agent's fraud when the principal did not authorize or know of the fraud of the agent.

(4) Governmental Regulation. The principal may be liable because of the agent's violation of a governmental regulation. Such regulations are most common in the areas of business and of protection of the environment. In such case, the employer may be held liable for a penalty imposed by the government. In some cases, the breach of the regulation will impose liability upon the principal in favor of a third person who is injured in consequence of the violation.

(b) SCOPE OF EMPLOYMENT. The mere fact that a tort or crime is committed by an employee does not necessarily impose vicarious liability upon the employer. It must also be shown that the employee was acting within the scope of the authority if an agent, or in the course of employment if an employee.[18] If the agent or employee was not so acting, there is no vicarious liability.

In the *Golden West Broadcasters* case, an off-duty employee who was on an away-from-home assignment injured the plaintiff in a fight outside a bar. The court was called upon to determine if the employee was acting within the scope of his employment at the time of the fight.

---

[16]   Bourk v Iseman Mobile Homes (SD) 316 NW2d 343 (1982).
[17]   Restatement, 2d Agency § 231; Bremen State Bank v Hartford Accident & Indemnity Co. (CA7 Ill) 427 F2d 425 (1970). Some courts follow the older rule that the employer is never liable for a willful or malicious act by an employee regardless of its purpose.

[18]   Rubin v Yellow Cab Co. 154 Ill App 3d 336, 107 Ill Dec 450, 507 NE2d 114 (1987).

GOLDEN WEST BROADCASTERS V BALL

114 Cal App 3d 947, 171 Cal Rptr 95 (1981)

Sanford Prudden was employed by Golden West Broadcasters, Inc., owners of Los Angeles television station KTLA. On Saturday, March 8, 1974, he was assigned to "remote" work at Palm Springs, California, as Senior Stage Supervisor, and was responsible for setting up the cameras and the supporting equipment for telecast of a California Angels spring training baseball game scheduled for Sunday, March 9, 1974. While at Palm Springs, in addition to his regular hourly wages he was paid a per diem by Golden West. These funds could be spent as the employee saw fit. He worked from 7:00 a.m. to 3:30 p.m. on Saturday. That evening he and some fellow employees drove in a station wagon supplied him by Golden West to the bar at the Gene Autry Hotel. During the several hours at the bar Prudden spent some time with his former wife, Barbara Matson. Dean Ball, a patron of the bar, objected to Prudden's treatment of Barbara. Ball invited Prudden outside, where a fight ensued and Ball was injured. After the fight Prudden was observed driving away in a station wagon with a KTLA inscription painted on its side. Ball sued Golden West for damages on the theory of respondeat superior, claiming that Prudden was acting in the scope of his employment at the time of the fight. The lower court refused to grant Golden West's motion for summary judgment, and Golden West appealed.

MCDANIEL, A. J. . . . Generally, liability of an employer under the doctrine of respondeat superior extends to torts of an employee committed within the scope of his employment. As noted by Justice Tamura in *Rodgers* [*v Kemper Constr Co*, 50 Cal App 3d 608, 124 Cal Rptr 123],

> California has adopted the rationale that the employer's liability should extend beyond his actual or possible control over the employees to include risks *inherent in or created by the enterprise* because he, rather than the innocent injured party, is best able to spread the risk through prices, rates or liability insurance.

Many of the cases arising in this area involve, as here, assaults on the plaintiff by an employee of the defendant. In such instances the imputation of liability follows where the employment in some way involves the risk of force being used against the plaintiff, i.e., where the act is connected with the employment. Such a situation is particularly demonstrated in *Stansell v Safeway Stores, Inc.*, 44 Cal App 2d 822, 113 P2d 264, where the altercation occurred when the manager of the defendant's store quarreled with a customer over an order, and, being called an opprobrious name, ran after the plaintiff customer and struck her. In the course of the Stansell opinion, the court recited the proposition just noted.

Rodgers provides a guide for application of this concept. It states,

> . . . where the question is one of vicarious liability, the inquiry should be whether the risk was one "that may fairly be regarded as typical of or broadly incidental" to the enterprise undertaken by the employer.

Pursuing the analysis of these cases finally brings one to the point where it has been held that if a tort is committed for the employee's own purposes, or as the result of a personal quarrel, the employer need not be liable even though at the time the employee is yet engaged in his employer's service. In the case before us we have reached that point. Conceding as fact all of the items urged by plaintiff as demonstrating that Prudden was acting in the scope of his employment when he beat up the plaintiff in the parking lot at the Gene Autry Hotel, we hold as a matter of law that the beating was not inflicted in the scope of Prudden's employment. . . .

Applying the *Rodgers* test, it is specious in our view to argue that the employment of a television technician whose duties are to set up for and to stage telecasts of events remote from the television station creates an inherent risk of the type here involved. Such employment at no time contemplates contacts with the public. In other words, there is no inherent risk incidental to this kind of employment importing forseeability of the type described in *Rodgers.* To invoke the doctrine of respondeat superior here would be to sanction a rule which would impose the liability of an insurer on all employers for every willful tortious act of their employees committed while off duty. Merely to state such a proposition is enough to discredit it, and we do. . . .

[Motion for summary judgment granted]

Questions

1. What did Ball contend?
2. Was Prudden acting within the scope of his employment when he injured Ball?
3. What is the rationale for holding an employer liable for a tort committed by an employee within the scope of employment?

(c) Employee of the United States. The Federal Tort Claims Act declares that the United States shall be liable vicariously whenever a federal employee driving a motor vehicle in the course of employment causes harm under such circumstances that a private employer would be liable. Contrary to the general rule, the statute exempts the employee driver from liability.

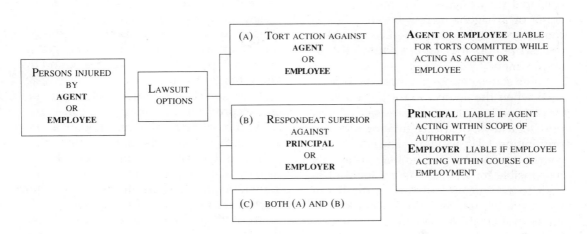

FIGURE 44-1
Liability for Torts of Agent or Employee

§ 44:20 Other Theories of Liability

If an employee is not acting within the course of employment, the employer cannot be held liable on the theory of respondeat superior. This does not mean, however, that the employer will necessarily not be liable. In some cases, the employer will be liable without regard to the nature of the act or whether the employee was acting in the course of employment. For example, the employer may be held liable as a bailor for lending an automobile to a bailee-employee.

An employer is liable for the tortious and criminal consequences of acts expressly authorized. For example, if the employer instructs an employee to hijack a competitor's truck, the employer is both civilly and criminally liable without giving any consideration to the question of whether such activity was within the course of employment of the employee. An employer is also liable upon giving defective equipment to an employee when the defect causes harm or upon giving control of proper equipment to an unfit employee when, because of the latter's lack of qualifications, harm is caused a third person.

§ 44:21   AGENT'S CRIMES

The principal is liable for the crimes of the agent committed at the principal's direction. When not authorized, however, the principal is ordinarily not liable for the crime of an agent merely because it was committed while otherwise acting within the scope of the latter's authority or employment.

Some states impose liability on the principal when the agent has in the course of employment violated liquor sales laws, pure food laws, or laws regulating prices or prohibiting false weights. Thus, by some courts, a principal may be held criminally responsible for the sale by an agent of liquor to a minor in violation of the liquor law, even though the sale was not known to the principal and violated instructions given to the agent.

§ 44:22 OWNER'S LIABILITY FOR ACTS OF AN INDEPENDENT CONTRACTOR

If the work is done by an independent contractor rather than by an employee, the owner is not liable for harm caused by the contractor to third persons or their property nor is the owner bound by the contracts made by the independent contractor.[19] Likewise, the owner is ordinarily not liable for harm caused third persons by the negligence of the employees of the independent contractor.

(a) EXCEPTIONS TO OWNER'S IMMUNITY. There is, however, a trend toward imposing liability upon the owner when the work undertaken by the independent contractor is inherently dangerous. That is, the law is taking the position that if the owner wishes to engage in a particular activity, the owner must be responsible for the harm it causes and cannot be insulated from such liability by the device of hiring an independent contractor to do the work. In such cases, the courts regard the activity as having such a high potential of harm that the owner is not permitted to delegate to another the duty to protect the public from harm.

Regardless of the nature of the activity, the owner may be liable for the torts and contracts of the independent contractor when the owner controls the conduct of the independent contractor. For example, when the franchisor exercises a high degree of control over the franchisee, the relationship will be recognized as an agency relationship and the franchisor is bound by the action of the franchisee.

In certain circumstances such as providing security for a business, bill collecting, and repossessing collateral, there is an increased risk that torts may be committed by the individuals performing such duties. The trend of the law is not to allow the employment of an independent contractor for such work to insulate the employer.[20]

(b) UNDISCLOSED INDEPENDENT CONTRACTOR. In some situations, the owner appears to be doing the act in question because the existence of the independent contractor is not disclosed or apparent. This situation occurs most commonly when a franchisee does business under the

---

[19]   Spivey v Brown, 150 Ill App 3d 139, 103 Ill Dec 876, 502 NE2d 23 (1986).
[20]   General Finance Corp. v Smith (Ala) 505 So 2d 1045 (1987).

name of the franchisor; when a concession-aire, such as a restaurant in a hotel, appears to be the hotel restaurant, although in fact it is operated by an independent concessionaire; or when the buyer of a business continues to run the business in the name of the seller. In such cases of an undisclosed independent contractor, it is generally held that the ostensible owner, that is, the franchisor, the grantor of the concession, or the seller is liable for the torts and contracts of the undisclosed independent contractor.

§ 44:23 ENFORCEMENT OF CLAIM BY THIRD PERSON

A lawsuit by a third person may be brought against the agent or the principal if each is liable. In most states and in the federal courts, the plaintiff may sue either or both in one action when both are liable. If both are sued, the plaintiff may obtain a judgment against both, although the plaintiff will only be allowed to collect the full amount of the judgment once.

E. TRANSACTIONS WITH SALES PERSONNEL

Many transactions with sales personnel do not result in a contract with the third person with whom the salesperson deals.

§ 44:24 SOLICITING AGENT

The giving of an order to a salesperson ordinarily does not give rise to a contract because ordinarily a salesperson is an agent whose authority is limited to soliciting offers from third persons and transmitting them to the principal for acceptance or rejection. Such an agent does not have authority to make a contract that will bind the principal to the third person, and the employer of the salesperson is not bound by a contract until the employer accepts the order.

(a) REASONS FOR LIMITATION ON AUTHORITY OF SALES PERSONNEL. The limitation on the authority of the salesperson is commonly based upon the fact that credit may be involved in the transaction, and the employer of the salesperson does not wish to permit its soliciting agent to make decisions as to the sufficiency of the credit standing of the buyer, but wishes all of these matters to be handled by the credit-management department of the home office.

To avoid difficulties, it is common to limit the authority of a salesperson to that of merely a soliciting agent accepting and transmitting orders to the employer. To make this clear to buyers, order forms signed by the customer, who is given a copy, generally state that the salesperson's authority is limited in this manner and that there is no "contract" with the employer until the order is approved by the home office.

(b) WITHDRAWAL OF CUSTOMER. From the fact that the customer giving a salesperson an order does not ordinarily have a binding contract with the employer of the salesperson until the employer approves the order, it necessarily follows that the customer is not bound by any contract until the employer approves the order. Prior to that time, the "buyer" may withdraw from the transaction. Withdrawal under such circumstances is not a breach of contract, for, by definition, there is no contract to be broken. Likewise, if the "buyer" had given the salesperson any money deposit, down payment, or part payment on the purchase price, the customer on withdrawing from the transaction, is entitled to a refund of the payment that had been made.

§ 44:25 CONTRAST WITH CONTRACTING AGENT

In contrast with the consequences when the salesperson is only a soliciting agent, if the person with whom the buyer deals has authority to make contracts, there is, by definition, a binding contract between the principal and the customer from the moment that the agent agrees with the customer, that is, when the agent accepts the customer's order. Should the customer seek to withdraw from the contract thereafter, the customer must base such action on a ground that justifies the unilateral repudiation or rejection of the contract. If the customer has no such justification, the action of withdrawing is a breach of contract and the customer is liable for the seller's resulting damages. If the buyer has made any down payment, prepayment, or deposit, the seller may deduct damages from the amount thereof before refunding any excess to the buyer. When the transaction relates to the sale of goods, the seller is entitled to retain from such advance payment either $500 or 20 percent of the purchase price, whichever is less, unless the seller can show that greater damages were in fact sustained.[21]

---

[21]   UCC § 2-718(2)(b). See § 21:6(a) of this book as to consumer protection rescission.

SUMMARY

An agent of a disclosed principal who makes a contract within the scope of authority with a third person has no personal liability on the contract. It is the principal and third person who may each sue the other in the event of a breach. A person purporting to act as an agent for a principal warrants by implication that there is an existing principal with legal capacity and that the principal has authorized the agent to act; the person acting as an agent is liable for any loss caused the third person for breach of these warranties. An agent of a partially disclosed or an undisclosed principal is a party to the contract with the third person, may enforce the contract against the third person, and is liable for its breach. To avoid problems of interpretation an agent should execute a contract "Principal, by Agent." Agents are liable for harm caused third persons by their fraudulent, malicious, or negligent acts.

An undisclosed or partially disclosed principal is liable to a third person on a simple contract made by an authorized agent, unless the principal has made a good faith settlement of the account with the agent or where satisfaction of the claim has been obtained from the agent. When a third person makes payment to an authorized agent, it is deemed paid to the principal.

A principal or employer is vicariously liable under the doctrine of respondeat superior for the torts of an agent or employee committed within the course or scope of employment. However, a principal is not liable for the crimes of an agent merely because they were committed while otherwise acting within the scope of employment; rather, it is usually necessary to show that the principal authorized or directed the criminal conduct. An owner is not liable for torts caused by an independent contractor to third persons or their property unless the work undertaken by the independent contractor is inherently hazardous.

A salesperson is ordinarily an agent whose authority is limited to soliciting offers (orders) from third persons and transmitting them to the principal. The principal is not bound until the principal accepts the order, and the customer may withdraw an offer at any time prior to acceptance.

QUESTIONS AND CASE PROBLEMS

1. What social forces are affected by the rule that an agent receiving an overpayment is not liable for the amount thereof when the payment was received in ignorance of the mistake and has been remitted to the principal?

2. Leonard makes a contract with Norma without informing her that he is acting on behalf of Hermes Plastics Company. Leonard has authority to make the contract. Hermes fails to perform the contract. Norma sues Hermes for breach of the contract. Hermes raises the defense that Norma cannot sue on the contract because the only contract she made was with Leonard. Is this a valid defense?

3. Compare a third party beneficiary contract with a contract made by an agent on behalf of an undisclosed principal.

4. What is the justification for the doctrine of respondeat superior?

5. Compare the liability of an agent's undisclosed principal to a third person on (a) a promissory note, (b) a sealed contract, and (c) an oral contract.

6. Mills Electric Company signed a contract with S&S Horticulture Architects, a two-person landscaping partnership operated by Sullivan and Smyth, to maintain the grounds and flowers at the Mills Electric Company plant in Jacksonville, Florida. Mills checked references of S&S and found the company to be highly reputable. The contract set forth that S&S would select the flowers for each season and would determine when to maintain the lawns, so long as the lawns were properly maintained. The contract called for payments to be made to S&S on the first workday of each month, and the contract stipulated that "nothing herein shall make S&S an agent of the company." The contract also required that S&S personnel wear uniforms identifying that they were employed by S&S. S&S had other accounts, but the large Mills Electric plant took up most of their time. While working on a terraced area near the visitors' entrance to the plant, Sullivan lost control of his large commercial mower, and the mower struck Gillespie, a plant visitor, causing serious injury to her. A witness heard Sullivan apologizing to Gillespie, saying "running that mower on the terrace is a two-person job." Gillespie brought suit against Mills Electric Co. contending Mills should be held vicariously liable for the negligence of Sullivan. Will Mills be held liable on this theory?

7. Anthony Perkins was admitted to Children's Hospital by a private pediatric surgeon, Dr. Green. On the evening of July 18, 1984, Dr. Green performed a tracheotomy to correct a congenital condition in the infant's windpipe. Thereafter, Dr. Green examined Anthony in the intensive care unit, where he had been taken after the surgery, and gave instructions as to his treatment. Dr. Green left the hospital at 11:00 p.m., and Anthony came within the exclusive care of the nurses and residents employed by the hospital. At about 3:55 a.m., Anthony stopped breathing, and during the five to seven minutes that elapsed before hospital personnel were able to restore his breathing and heartbeat, he suffered irreversible brain damage. Anthony and his parents brought suit against Children's for negligent post-operative care rendered by the hospital's residents. Expert testimony revealed that the residents who were employed and paid by the hospital had been negligent in failing to employ adequate medical procedures in light of the symptoms that Anthony exhibited for almost two hours before the crisis occurred and in the resuscitation efforts employed after its onset. Children's contends that the residents were under the direction and control of Dr. Green so that he, rather than Children's, was responsible for their negligence. Decide.

8. Weisz purchased a painting at an auction sale in the Parke-Burnett Galleries. It was later shown that the painting was a forgery. When Weisz sued Parke-Burnett for breach of warranty, it raised the defense that it was making the sale for the owner, and therefore, any warranty suit must be brought against the owner. Was it correct? [Weisz v Parke-Burnett Galleries, Inc. 325 NYS2d 576]

9. Video Independent Theaters advertised in newspapers published by the Oklahoma Publishing Company. The Publishing Company would send periodic statements of the amounts due from Video to the advertising agency Ken Guergens and Associates. The latter would then add its fee to the amount due the Publishing Company and would bill Video for the aggregate amount. Upon receiving payment by Video, Guergens was to deduct its fee and then transmit the balance to the Publishing Company. Guergens kept the entire amount paid by Video. The Publishing Company sued Video which claimed that it had paid the bill to Guergens. Was this a defense? [Oklahoma Publishing Company v Video Independent Theaters, Inc. (Okla) 522 P2d 1029]

10. Moritz was a guest at the Pines Hotel. While she was sitting in the lobby, Brown, a hotel employee, dropped a heavy vacuum cleaner on her knee. When she complained, he insulted her and hit her with his fist, knocking her unconscious. She sued the hotel for damages. Was the hotel liable? [Moritz v Pines Hotel, Inc. 53 App Div 2d 1020, 383 NYS2d 704]

11. Phillips was employed as an automobile salesman by an automobile dealer, City Motor Company. He had a driver's license. City Motor lent Phillips a demonstrator car. While Phillips was driving the car from a restaurant to his home, he collided with a third person. The latter sued City Motor in the District Court claiming that City Motor had been negligent in failing to obtain a copy of the driving record of Phillips from the state police before entrusting him with the automobile and claiming that City Motor benefited by having its demonstrator automobile driven on the public streets. Was City Motor liable? [Montana ex rel City Motor Co. v District Court, 166 Mont 52, 530 P2d 486]

12. The Bay State Harness Horse Racing and Breeding Association conducted horse races. Music was supplied for the patrons by an independent contractor hired by the Association. Some of the music played was subject to a copyright held by Famous Music Corporation. The playing of that music was a violation of the copyright unless royalties were paid to Famous Music. None were paid, and Famous Music sued the Association. It raised the defense that the violation had been committed by an independent contractor that was specifically instructed not to play Famous Music copyright material. Decide. [Famous Music Corporation v Bay State Harness Horse Racing and Breeding Association, Inc. (CA1 Mass) 554 F2d 1213]

13. On September 24, 1984, Bernie and Joanne Van Rossem made arrangements for a honeymoon trip to Jamaica with the Penney Travel Service, paying on that date $2,059 to Penney in advance of the scheduled departure date of November 10, 1984. On their wedding day, they received a telephone call from Penney Travel advising them that Lotus Tours, the wholesaler through which Penney had booked their travel reserva-

tions, had gone bankrupt. And, they were further informed that Lotus had paid their airfare prior to bankruptcy, but that their reservation at the Sandles Resort had not been paid by Lotus Tours. The Van Rossems booked new reservations at "Couples" resort where they paid $1,312 for substitute accommodations. The Van Rossems were not told at any time prior to their wedding day of the fact that Penney was acting as agent for the wholesaler Lotus. Penney Travel contends that it is well known by the public that travel agents act as agents for wholesalers in the travel business. Penney can show conclusively that the $2,059 received from the Van Rossems was forwarded to Lotus Travel as of October 4, 1984, and that they had not received any commission because of the bankruptcy. The Van Rossems brought suit against Penney Travel for the cost of the substitute accommodations. Upon what theory or theories could the Van Rossems rely? What defense would Penney Travel raise? Decide. [Van Rossem v Penney Travel Service, 488 NYS 2d 597]

14. Neal Rubin, while driving his car in Chicago, inadvertently obstructed the path of a Yellow Cab Co. taxi driven by Robert Ball, causing the taxi to swerve and come in contact with Rubin's car. Angered by Rubin's driving, Ball got out of his cab and proceeded to hit Rubin over the head and shoulders with a metal pipe. Rubin sued the Yellow Cab Co. for the damages caused by this beating, contending the employer was vicariously liable for the beating under the doctrine of respondeat superior, since the beating occurred in furtherance of the employer's business which is to obtain fares without delay. The company defends that Ball's beating of Rubin was not an act undertaken to further the employer's business. Is the employer liable under respondeat superior? [Rubin v Yellow Cab Co. 154 Ill App 3d 336, 107 Ill Dec 450, 507 NE2d 114]

15. Brazilian & Columbian Co. (B&C), a food broker, ordered 40 barrels of olives from Mawer-Gulden-Annis, Inc. (MGA). MGA's shipping clerk was later communicated with, and advised to make out the bill of lading to B&C's customer, Pantry Queen; the olives were shipped directly to Pantry

Queen. Eight days after the delivery, the president of B&C wrote MGA to give it the name of its principal, Pantry Queen, and advised MGA to bill the principal directly. Pantry Queen was unable to pay for the olives, and MGA sued B&C for payment. B&C defends that it was well known to MGA that B&C was a food broker (agent) and the olives were shipped directly to the principal by MGA. It states that as an agent it was not a party to the contract and is thus not liable. Decide. [Mawer-Gulden-Annis, Inc. v Brazilian & Columbian Coffee Co. 49 Ill App 2d 400, 199 NE2d 222]

45

EMPLOYMENT

The law of employment is structured on the law of contracts. It is the role of the employer and an individual or group of employees to contract on terms for wages, hours, working conditions, and the duration of the employment relationship. The employment relationship is also regulated by statutes known as labor legislation. Labor laws deal with such issues as fair hiring practices, termination of employment for union activities, compensation for injured employees, compensation for the unemployed, the protection of the pension interests of employees, and the protection of the health and safety of employees.

In Chapter 4, "Government Regulation," employment-related law under the National Labor Relations Act and Title VII of the Civil Rights Act was presented. Sections 4:6 through 4:9 of Chapter 4 should be reviewed prior to studying this chapter.

A. THE EMPLOYMENT RELATIONSHIP

The relationship of an employer and an employee exists when, pursuant to an express or implied agreement of the parties, one person, the **employee,** undertakes to perform services or to do work under the direction and control of another, the **employer**, for compensation. In the older cases this relationship was described as the master-servant relationship.[1]

§ 45:1 NATURE OF RELATIONSHIP

An employee without agency authority is hired only to work under the control of the employer, as contrasted with (a) an agent, who is to negotiate or make contracts with third persons on behalf of and under the control of a principal, and with (b) an independent contractor, who is to perform a contract independent of, or free from, control by the other party.[2]

§ 45:2 CREATION OF EMPLOYMENT RELATIONSHIP

The relationship of employer and employee can be created only with the consent of both parties. Generally, the agreement of the parties is a contract, and it is, therefore, subject to all of the principles applicable to contracts. The contract will ordinarily be express but may be implied, as when the employer accepts the rendering of services that a reasonable person would recognize as being rendered with the expectation of receiving compensation.

(a) INDIVIDUAL EMPLOYMENT CONTRACTS. As in contracts generally, both parties must assent to the terms of the employment contract. The parties are free to make a contract on any terms they wish. Historically, wages constituted the sole reward of labor. Today, additional benefits are usually granted employees either by virtue of the contract of employment or by a federal or state statutory provision.

(b) COLLECTIVE BARGAINING CONTRACTS. Collective bargaining contracts govern the rights and obligations of employers and employees in many private and public sector employment relations. Under collective bargaining, representatives of the employees bargain with a single employer or a group of employers for an agreement on wages, hours, and working conditions for the employees. The agreement worked out by the representatives of the employees, usually union officials, is generally subject to a ratification vote by the employees. Terms usually found in collective bargaining contracts are as follows: (1) identification of the work belonging exclusively to designated classes of employees; (2) wage and benefits clauses; (3) promotion and layoff clauses, which are generally tied in part to seniority; (4) a management's rights clause, and (5) a grievance procedure by which persons contending the contract was violated or that they were disciplined or discharged without just cause may ultimately have their cases decided by impartial labor arbitrators.

When there is a collective bargaining contract, the "contract of employment" in effect may consist of two contracts: (1) the collective bargaining contract made by the employees' representative with the employer, and (2) the individual employment contract made by each employee with the employer. Although the individual contracts are distinct, they must conform to the basic plan or terms established by the collective bargaining contract. Examples of

---

[1] The concept of a servant is not identical to that of an employee as the servant was regarded as a chattel or thing owned by the master; whereas, an employee is a free person who works pursuant to a contract of employment. Frank Horton & Co., Inc. v Diggs (Mo App) 544 SW2d 313 (1976).

[2] Bill Rivers Trailers Inc. v Miller (Fla App) 489 So 2d 1139 (1986).

employment situations that may involve two contracts are those involving professional athletes and those involving actors and writers working in the entertainment industries.

§ 45:3   Duration and Termination of Employment Contract

In many instances, the employment contract will not state any time or duration. In such case, it may be terminated at any time by either party. In contrast, the employment contract may expressly state that it shall last for a specified period of time, as a contract to work as general manager for five years. In some instances, a definite duration may be implied by the circumstances.

Ordinarily, a contract of employment may be terminated in the same manner as any other contract. If it is to run for a definite period of time, the employer cannot terminate the contract at an earlier date without justification for so doing. If the employment contract does not have a definite duration, it is terminable at will. Under the employment-at-will doctrine, the employer has historically been allowed to terminate the employment contract at any time for any reason or no reason.[3] Recent decisions, and in some instances statutes, have changed the rule in numerous states by limiting the power of the employer to discharge the employee.

Court decisions in a majority of jurisdictions have carved out exceptions to the employment-at-will doctrine when the discharge violates an established public policy, such as discharging an employee in retaliation for insisting that the employer comply with the state's food and drug act[4] or discharging an employee for filing a workers' compensation claim.[5] The *Phipps* case illustrates an application of the public policy exception to the employment-at-will doctrine.

---

[3]   Elder v Ivey, 171 Ga App 496, 320 SE2d 217 (1984).
[4]   Sheets v Teddy's Frosted Foods, 179 Conn 471, 427 A2d 385 (1980).
[5]   Hunt v Van Der Horst Corp (Tex Civ App) 711 SW2d (1986).

Phipps v Clark Oil & Refining Corp
(Minn App) 396 NW2d 588 (1986)

Mark Phipps was employed as a cashier at a Clark gas station. On November 17, 1984, a customer drove into the station and asked him to pump leaded gasoline into her 1976 Chevrolet — an automobile equipped to receive only unleaded gasoline. The station manager told Phipps to comply with the request, but he refused, believing that his dispensing leaded gasoline into the gas tank was a violation of law. Phipps said that he was willing to pump unleaded gas into the tank; but the manager immediately fired him. Phipps sued Clark for wrongful termination, and the trial court decided the case in favor of Clark, stating Minnesota law allowed Phipps, an employee at will, to be terminated for any reason or for no reason. Phipps appealed.

LANSING, J. . . . Does Minnesota law recognize a cause of action for wrongful discharge if an employee is terminated for refusing to violate a law?

A. Employment-at-Will Doctrine and the Public Policy Exception

The parties concede that there is no formal agreement governing the employment relationship between Phipps and Clark Oil. Thus, Phipps is an at-will employee. The at-will employment doctrine in Minnesota is generally traced to the early case of *Skagerberg v. Blandin Paper Co.*, 197 Minn. 291, 266 N.W. 872 (1936). The *Skagerberg* court interpreted a contract for permanent employment as being merely a contract for employment at will. *Skagerberg* set forth the general rule in Minnesota that employment at will "may be terminated by either party at any time, and no action can be sustained in such case for a wrongful discharge."

The employer's absolute right of discharge has been tempered during the last 50 years. The majority of jurisdictions have adopted, and numerous commentators have advocated, exceptions to the employment-at-will doctrine. Three general exceptions have been judicially created to relieve employees from the strict application of the employment-at-will doctrine:

(1) a contract cause of action based on implied-in-fact promises of employment conditions, generally derived from personnel manuals;
(2) an implied covenant of "good faith and fair dealing" under both contract and tort theories; and
(3) a "public policy" exception, based in tort, which permits recovery upon the finding that the employer's conduct undermines some important public policy.

Although the Minnesota Supreme Court has declined to imply a covenant of good faith and fair dealing into every employment contract, it has followed the modern trend in recognizing exceptions to employment at will.

In *Pine River State Bank v. Mettille*, 333 N.W.2d 622 (Minn. 1983), the supreme court recognized the implied-in-fact contract exception. The *Pine River* court held that an employee manual may constitute an employment contract with enforceable terms preventing termination at will.

Among other states, the most widely adopted exception to the doctrine is the public policy exception. Simply stated, the exception provides that an employer becomes subject to tort liability if its discharge of an employee contravenes some well-established public policy. Although the adoption of this exception has not been addressed in Minnesota, the majority of jurisdictions recognize this exception to the employment-at-will doctrine.

The exception began as a narrow rule permitting employees to sue their employers when a statute expressly prohibited their discharge. The rule later expanded to include any discharge in violation of a statutory expression of public policy. The broadest formulation of the rule permits recovery even in the absence of a specific statutory prohibition.

Courts have reached the public policy exception to accommodate competing interests of society, the employee, and the employer. The Illinois Court of Appeals stated:

> With the rise of large corporations conducting specialized operations and employing relatively immobile workers who often have no other place to market their skills, recognition that the employer and employee do not stand on equal footing is realistic. In addition, unchecked employer power, like unchecked employee power, has been seen to present a distinct threat to the public policy carefully considered and adopted by society as a whole. As a result, it is now recognized that a proper balance must be maintained among the employer's interest in operating a business efficient-

ly and profitably, the employee's interest in earning a livelihood, and society's interest in seeing its public policies carried out.

Palmateer v International Harvester Co., 85 Ill.2d 124, 129, 52 Ill.Dec. 13, 15, 421 N.E.2d 876, 878 (1981).

These courts have also recognized that important societal interests oppose an employer's conditioning employment on required participation in unlawful conduct:

> Although employers generally are free to discharge at-will employees with or without cause at any time, they are not free to require employees, on pain of losing their jobs, to commit unlawful acts or acts in violation of a clear mandate of public policy expressed in the constitution, statutes, and regulations promulgated pursuant to statute. The at-will employment doctrine does not depend upon the employer having such a right. The employer is bound to know the public policies of the state and nation as expressed in their constitutions, statutes, judicial decisions and administrative regulations, particularly, as here, those bearing directly upon the employer's business. . . .
>
> The at-will employment doctrine does not include, contemplate or require a privilege in the employer to subject its employees to the risks of civil and criminal liability that participation in such activities entails.

Boyle v. Vista Eyewear, Inc., 700 S.W.2d 859, 877-78 (Mo.Ct.App.1985).

We find the reasoning of the cases adopting a public policy exception to be persuasive. An employer's authority over its employee does not include the right to demand that the employee commit a criminal act. An employer therefore is liable if an employee is discharged for reasons that contravene a clear mandate of public policy.

Employers may have a legitimate concern that such an exception will allow fraudulent or frivolous suits by disgruntled employees who are discharged for valid reasons. In order to prevent this, the employee should have the burden of proving the dismissal violates a clear mandate of public policy, either legislatively or judicially recognized. Once the employee has demonstrated that the discharge may have been motivated by reasons that contravene a clear mandate of public policy, the burden then shifts to the employer to prove that the dismissal was for reasons other than those alleged by the employee. . . .

Clark Oil argues that the decision to adopt the public policy exception should be left to the legislature, citing *Murphy v. American Home Products Corp.*, 58 N.Y.2d 293. . . .

The at-will doctrine is a creation of common law. Other exceptions to the doctrine have been considered and adopted or rejected by the courts. The judiciary may properly extend or limit a judicially created doctrine. . . .

B. Application of the Public Policy Exception

On appeal from a judgment on the pleadings, this court assumes as true all material facts which are well pleaded. Phipps' complaint alleges that he was terminated for refusing to violate the Federal Clean Air Act, 42 U.S.C. §§ 7401-7642.

Clark Oil argues that this is not the proper case to apply this exception because the penalty for violating this provision is imposed only upon the retailer, not the retailer's employees or agent.

We hold that Phipps has stated a cause of action for wrongful termination under the public policy exception to the at-will employment doctrine. It is not determinative that the employee would not have suffered any monetary loss by violating the law. The law clearly states:

> No retailer or *his employee* . . . shall introduce or allow the introduction of leaded gasoline into any motor vehicle which is labeled "unleaded gasoline only," or which is equipped with a gasoline tank filler inlet which is designed for the introduction of unleaded gasoline. [40 C.F.R. § 80.22(a) (1984) (emphasis added)]. . . .

Complaint which alleges that an at-will employee was terminated for refusing to violate a law states a cause of action in Minnesota for wrongful discharge. . . .

[Reversed and remanded]

QUESTIONS

1. What is the most common exception to the employment-at-will doctrine?
2. How does the court expect to cut down on frivolous lawsuits based upon the public policy exception and instigated by disgruntled former employees?
3. Did the court hold that the public policy exception would apply only to clear mandates of legislative or judicially recognized public policy?

The obligation to act in good faith and deal fairly has been held by some courts to bar the employer's terminating an at-will contract when this is done to benefit the employer financially at the expense of the employee, as by terminating an employee to save the payment of commissions or to save the payment of pension benefits.[6]

Courts may construe employers' statements concerning continued employment as a part of the employment contract, requiring good cause for the discharge of an at-will employee. Also, written personnel policies used as guidelines for the employer's supervisors have been interpreted as being contractual provisions restricting the employer's right to discharge at-will employees without proof of good or just cause.[7] Moreover, employee handbooks that provide for "proper notice and investigation" before termination, may bar employers from terminating employees without providing such notice and an investigation.[8]

Some courts still follow the common-law at-will rule because they believe that a court should not rewrite the contract of the parties to provide a protection for the employee that was never intended. Some courts favor the view limiting the employer from making an at-will discharge but will not adopt such a rule by decision as it is felt that such a significant change should be made, if at all, by the legislature.[9]

If an employment contract provides that an employee can only be fired for "good cause" or "just cause," a lesser standard for discharge will not be allowed by a court.

(a) FEDERAL LAWS. As set forth in Chapter 4, the National Labor Relations Act prohibits dismissal for union activities, and Ti-

---

[6] Siles v Travenol Laboratories, Inc. 13 Mass App 354, 433 NE2d 103 (1982).
[7] Toussaint v Blue Cross and Blue Shield, 408 Mich 579, 292 NW2d 880 (1980).
[8] Duldulao v St. Mary Nazareth Hospital Center 115 Ill 2d 482, 106 Ill Dec 8, 505 NE2d 314 (1987).
[9] Murphy v American Home Products Corp. 58 App Div 2d 286, 461 NY2d 232 (1983).

tle VII of the Civil Rights Act of 1964 as amended prohibits terminating employment for a reason amounting to discrimination because of race, color, sex, religion, or national origin. Sexual harassment is also prohibited by Title VII. The Equal Pay Act provides for equal pay for men and women doing equal work. The Age Discrimination in Employment Act protects certain employees from discrimination and discharge based upon age.[10] The Rehabilitation Act[11] protects certain handicapped persons from termination by federal contractors.

(1) Sexual Harassment. *Quid pro quo* sexual harassment involves supervisors seeking sexual favors from their subordinates in return for job benefits such as continued employment, promotion, a raise, or a favorable job evaluation.[12] In such a case, when a supervisor's actions affect job benefits, Title VII's prohibition against sex discrimination has been violated, and the employer is liable to the employee for lost wages because of the supervisor's misconduct.

A second form of sexual harassment is the so-called hostile working environment harassment — wherein an employee's economic benefits have not been affected by the supervisor's conduct, but the supervisor's sexually harassing conduct nevertheless caused anxiety and has poisoned the work environment. Such conduct may include unwelcome sexual flirtation, propositions or other abuse of a sexual nature, including degrading words or the display of sexually suggestive pictures. While no compensatory or punitive damages are available for so-called pure hostile environment cases, an injunction against such conduct can be obtained and attorney's fees awarded. Moreover, if such conduct drives the employee to quit the job, the employer may be responsible for the economic losses caused the employee.[13]

An employer is liable for the sexual harassment caused its employees by coworkers or its customers only when it fails to take remedial action after being informed of the misconduct. Employers may avoid liability for "hostile environment" sexual harassment by affirmatively raising the subject with all of the employees, expressing strong disapproval of such conduct, advising employees how to inform it of instances of sexual harassment, and taking disciplinary action against wrongdoers.

(2) Equal Pay Act. The Equal Pay Act prohibits employers from paying lower wages to employees of one sex than the rate paid employees of the opposite sex for equal work or substantially equal work in the same establishment on jobs that require substantially equal skill, effort, and responsibility and that are performed under similar working conditions.[14] The Equal Pay Act does not prohibit any variation in wage rates paid men and women, but only those variations based solely upon sex. The act sets forth four exceptions allowing for variances in wages, if paid, pursuant to (1) a seniority system; (2) a merit system; (3) a system that measures earnings by quantity or quality of production; or (4) a differential based upon any factor other than sex.

(3) Age Discrimination. The Age Discrimination in Employment Act (ADEA) forbids discrimination by employers, unions, and employment agencies against men and women over 40 years of age.[15] The ADEA prohibits mandatory retirement for age.[16]

---

[10]   29 USC §§ 621-34.
[11]   29 USC §§ 701-794.
[12]   EEOC *Guidelines* § 1604.11(f) define sexual harassment as follows:
   Unwelcome sexual advances, requests for sexual favors, and other verbal or physical conduct of a sexual nature constitute sexual harassment when (1) submission to such conduct is made either explicitly or implicitly a term or condition of an individual's employment, (2) submission to or rejection of such conduct has the purpose or effect of unreasonably interfering with an individual's work performance or creating an intimidating, hostile, or offensive working environment.

[13]   Meritor Savings Bank v Vinson, 477 US 57 (1986).
[14]   29 USC Section 206(d)(1).
[15]   29 USC Section 623
[16]   PL 99-592 "Age Discrimination in Employment Act of 1986." See the act for exceptions for law enforcement officers, fire fighters, and tenured professors, pending studies to be concluded by 1991.

SEXUAL HARASSMENT

A. DEVELOP AND IMPLEMENT AN EQUAL EMPLOYMENT POLICY THAT SPECIFICALLY INCLUDES
    SEXUAL HARASSMENT AS A PROHIBITED ACTIVITY FOR WHICH DISCIPLINE UP TO AND
    INCLUDING DISCHARGE WILL BE IMPOSED.

B. DESIGNATE A RESPONSIBLE SENIOR OFFICIAL TO WHOM COMPLAINTS OF SEXUAL HARASSMENT
    CAN BE MADE. AVOID ANY PROCEDURE THAT REQUIRES AN EMPLOYEE TO FIRST COMPLAIN
    TO THE EMPLOYEE'S SUPERVISOR, SINCE THAT INDIVIDUAL MAY BE THE OFFENDING PERSON.

C. INVESTIGATE ALL COMPLAINTS THOROUGHLY AND EXPEDITIOUSLY.

D. IF A COMPLAINT HAS MERIT, THE EMPLOYER SHOULD IMPOSE APPROPRIATE AND CONSISTENT
    DISCIPLINE, DEPENDING UPON THE SERIOUSNESS OF THE OFFENSE.

FIGURE 45-1
EMPLOYER POLICY AND PROCEDURE TO AVOID
LIABILITY FOR "HOSTILE ENVIRONMENT" SEXUAL
HARASSMENT

(4) Discrimination Against the Handicapped. The right of handicapped persons to enjoy equal employment opportunities was established on the federal level with the enactment of the Rehabilitation Act of 1973.[17] Although not designed specifically as an employment discrimination measure, but rather as a comprehensive plan to meet many of the needs of the handicapped, the act does contain three sections that provide guarantees against discrimination in employment. Section 501 is applicable to the federal government itself; Section 503 applies to federal contractors; and Section 504 applies to the recipients of federal funds.

Handicapping conditions apply to a wide range of mental and physical disabilities. Some impairments are obvious, such as paraplegia or blindness. Others may not be readily noticeable, such as heart disease, high blood pressure and diabetes. In some cases persons have recovered from their disabilities but have encountered job discrimination because of their past medical records. Cancer and mental or emotional disorders are examples of past medical conditions that may be associated with job discrimination. Sometimes, persons are perceived as having handicaps, when in fact, they do not. One example is a facial disfigurement that causes no disability but which others regard as an impairment.

Under the Rehabilitation Act of 1973, a handicapped person is defined as one who (1) has an impairment that affects a major life activity; (2) has a history of such an impairment; or (3) is considered as having one. The term *major life activity* includes such functions as caring for oneself, seeing, speaking, or walking.

To be entitled to the protection of the act with respect to employment, the individual must meet the requirements set forth in the definition of a handicapped person and must be an "otherwise qualified . . . individual." An otherwise qualified individual is one who can perform "the essential functions" of the job in question. When a handicapped person is not able to perform

[17]   29 USC §§ 701-794.

the essential functions of the job, the court must also consider whether any "reasonable accommodation" by the employer would enable the handicapped person to perform those functions. Reasonable accommodation includes making a facility accessible to the handicapped, as well as job restructuring and modification of work schedules. However, expenses and business necessity are also considered in determining what reasonable accommodation requires.

The Rehabilitation Act does not cover any individual who is an alcoholic or is a drug abuser whose current use of alcohol or drugs prevents such individuals from performing the duties of the job or whose employment constitutes a direct threat to property or the safety of others.

A person afflicted with tuberculosis is a handicapped person under the act, and based upon individualized medical judgment courts will determine if "reasonable accommodation" by the employer can allow the employee to work.[18] AIDS victims are within the protection of the act and must be treated just as anyone else with a disability.

(b) JUSTIFIABLE DISCHARGE. An employer may be justified in discharging an employee because of the employee's (1) nonperformance of duties, (2) misrepresentation or fraud in obtaining the employment, (3) disobedience to proper directions, (4) disloyalty, (5) theft or other dishonesty, (6) possession or use of drugs or intoxicants, (7) misconduct, or (8) incompetency.

Employers generally have the right to lay off employees because of economic conditions including a lack of work. Such actions are sometimes referred to as reductions in force or RIFs. Employers have to be very careful, however, not to make layoffs based on age, for such is a violation of the ADEA.

In some states, a "service letter" statute requires an employer upon request to furnish a discharged employee with a letter stating the reason for the discharge.[19]

(c) REMEDIES. An employee who has been wrongfully discharged may bring against the employer an action to recover (1) wages, (2) damages for breach of contract, or (3) damages representing the value of services already performed. In certain instances, the employee may also bring (4) an action to compel the employer to specifically perform the employment contract, or (5) a proceeding under federal or state labor relations or antidiscrimination statute, seeking reinstatement with back pay and the reinstatement of full seniority rights.

§ 45:4 DUTIES OF THE EMPLOYEE

The duties of an employee are determined primarily by the contract of employment with the employer. The law also implies certain obligations.

(a) SERVICES. Employees are under the duty to perform or hold themselves in readiness to perform such services as may be required by the contract of employment. If employees hold themselves in readiness to comply with their employer's directions, they have discharged this obligation, and they will not forfeit the right to compensation because the employer has withheld directions and has thus kept them idle.

Employees agree by implication to serve their employer honestly and faithfully. They also agree by implication to serve the employer exclusively during the hours of employment. The employee may do other work, however, if the time and nature of such other employment are not inconsistent with the duties owed to the first employer and if the contract of employment with the first employer does not contain any provision against it.

An employee must obey reasonable regulations and requirements adopted by the employer.

---

[18] Nassau County Florida v Arline (US Sup Ct) 43 FEP 81 (1987).

[19] Eimer v Texaco, Inc. (CA8 Mo) 518 F2d 807 (1975).

Employees imply by acceptance of a job that, in performing their duties, they will exercise due care and ordinary diligence in view of the nature of the work. When skill is required, employees need exercise only ordinary skill, unless the employees have held themselves out as possessing special skills.

(b) TRADE SECRETS. An employee may be given confidential trade secrets by the employer. In such case, the employee must not disclose such knowledge to others. An agreement by the employee to refrain from disclosing trade secrets is binding. Even in the absence of such an agreement, an employee is prohibited from disclosing the trade secrets of the employer. If the employee violates this obligation, the employer may enjoin the use of the information by the employee and by any person to whom it is disclosed by the employee.[20]

Former employees who are competing with their former employer may be enjoined from utilizing information as to suppliers and customers that they obtained while employees, when such information is of vital importance to the employer's business. Such relief is denied if the information is not important or not secret.

(c) INVENTIONS. In the absence of an express or implied agreement to the contrary, the inventions of an employee belong to the employee even though the latter used the time and property of the employer in their discovery, provided that the employee had not been employed for the express purpose of inventing the things or processes that were discovered.

If the invention is discovered during working hours and with the employer's materials and equipment the employer has the right, called a **shop right,** to use the invention without charge in the running of the employer's business. If the employee has obtained a patent for the invention, the employee must grant the employer a nonexclusive license to use the invention without the payment of any royalty. The shop right of the employer does not give the right to make and sell machines that embody the employee's invention; it only entitles the employer to use the invention without cost in the operation of the employer's plant.

In contrast, when an employee is employed to secure certain results from experiments to be conducted in the course of employment, the inventions so discovered belong to the employer. The grounds are that there is a trust relationship or that there is an implied agreement by the employee to make an assignment of the inventions to the employer.

§ 45:5 RIGHTS OF THE EMPLOYEE

The rights of an employee are determined primarily by the contract of employment. As in the case of duties, the law also implies certain rights.

(a) COMPENSATION. The rights of an employee with respect to compensation are governed in general by the same principles that apply to the compensation of an agent. In the absence of an agreement to the contrary, when an employee is discharged, whether for cause or not, the employer must pay wages down to the expiration of the last pay period.[21] The express terms of employment, or of collective bargaining contracts, or custom frequently provide for payment of wages for fractional terminal periods, and they may even require a severance pay equal to the compensation for a full period of employment. Provisions relating to deferred compensation under a profit sharing trust for employees are liberally construed in favor of employees.

(b) EMPLOYEE'S LIEN OR PREFERENCE. Most states protect an employee's claim for compensation either by a lien or preference over other claimants of payment out of

[20] Henry Hope X-Ray Products, Inc. v Marron Carrel, Inc. (CA9 Ariz) 674 F2d 1336 (1982).

[21] Alexander v Brown Builders Inc. (La App) 490 So 2d 653 (1986).

proceeds from the sale of the employer's property. These statutes vary widely in their terms. They are usually called **laborers'** or **mechanics' lien laws.** Sometimes the statutes limit their protection to workers of a particular class, such as plasterers or bricklayers. Compensation for the use of materials or machinery is ordinarily not protected by such statutes.

§ 45:6   PENSION PLANS AND FEDERAL REGULATION

Many employers have established pension plans as postretirement benefits to their employees. The Employees Retirement Income Security Act (ERISA)[22] was adopted in 1974 to provide protection for the pension interests of employees.

(a) FIDUCIARY STANDARDS AND REPORTING. Persons administering a pension fund must handle it so as to protect the interest of the employees. The fact that an employer contributed all or part of the money does not entitle the employer to use the fund as though it were still owned by the employer. Persons administering pension plans must make detailed reports to the Secretary of Labor.

(b) VESTING. Vesting refers to the right of an employee to pension benefits paid into a pension plan in the employee's name by the employer. Prior to ERISA many pension plans did not vest accrued benefits until 20 to 25 years of service by an employee. Thus, an employee who was forced to terminate service after 18 years would not receive any pension rights or benefits whatsoever. Under ERISA, employers implementing pension plans must select one of three vesting schedules ranging from 100 percent vesting after 10 years of service to partial or graduated vesting beginning at an earlier date.

In the past, it was common for pension plans to contain "break-in-service" clauses whereby employees who left their employment for a period longer than one year for any reason other than an on-the-job injury lost valuable pension eligibility rights. Under the Retirement Equity Act of 1984,[23] which was designed to provide greater pension equity for women, an individual can leave the work force for up to five consecutive years and still retain eligibility for pension benefits.

(c) FUNDING. ERISA requires that contributions be made by employers to their pension funds on a basis that is actuarially determined so that the pension fund will be sufficiently large to make the payments that will be required of it. The Treasury Department is authorized to issue regulations, opinions, variances, and waivers pertaining to funding.[24]

(d) TERMINATION INSURANCE. ERISA establishes an insurance plan to protect employees when the employer goes out of business. To provide this protection, the statute creates a Pension Benefit Guaranty Corporation (PBGC). In effect, this corporation guarantees that the employee will receive benefits, much the same as the Federal Deposit Insurance Corporation protects bank depositors. The PBGC is financed by small payments made by employers for every employee covered by a pension plan.

(e) ENFORCEMENT. ERISA authorizes the Secretary of Labor and employees to bring court actions to compel the observance of the statutory requirements.

§ 45:7   ATTACHMENT AND GARNISHMENT OF WAGES

It is generally provided that a creditor may require a third person who owes money to

[22] PL 93-406, 88 Stat 829, 29 USC §§ 1001-1381. A number of subsequent acts have also affected private pensions, notably the Tax Equity and Fiscal Responsibility Act of 1982, the Tax Reform Act of 1984, and the Tax Reform Act of 1986.

[23] PL 98-397, 98 Stat 1426.
[24] Reorganization Plan No. 4 of 1978, 43 Fed Reg 47713, made effective December 28, 1978, by Executive Order No. 12108, 44 Fed Reg 1065, 29 USC § 1001 (1978).

a debtor of the creditor to pay such amount to the creditor to satisfy the creditor's claim against the debtor. That is, if *A* has a valid claim for $100 against *B*, and if *C* owes *B* $100, *A* can require *C* to pay the $100 to *A*, thereby satisfying both *C*'s debt to *B* and *B*'s debt to *A*. The necessary legal procedure generally requires the third person to pay the money into court or to the sheriff rather than directly to the original creditor. The original creditor may also, by this process, reach the debtor's tangible property that is in the custody or possession of a third person. This procedure is commonly called **attachment** and the third person is called a **garnishee.**

Under the federal Truth in Lending Act (Title I of the Federal Consumer Credit Protection Act), only a certain portion of an employee's pay can be garnisheed. Ordinarily, the amount that may be garnisheed may not exceed (a) 25 percent of the employee's weekly take-home pay or (b) the amount by which the weekly take-home pay exceeds 30 times the federal minimum hourly wage, whichever is less.[25] The federal statute also prohibits an employer from discharging an employee because wages have been garnisheed for any one indebtedness. The federal statute does not prevent the discharge of an employee because of several garnishments based on different debts.[26]

B.   UNEMPLOYMENT BENEFITS

Generally, when employees are without work through no fault of their own, they are eligible for unemployment compensation benefits.

§ 45:8   UNEMPLOYMENT COMPENSATION

Unemployment compensation today is provided primarily through a federal-state system under the unemployment insurance provisions of the Social Security Act of 1935. All of the states have laws that provide similar benefits, and the state agencies are loosely coordinated under the federal act. Agricultural employees, domestic employees, and state and local government employees are not covered by this federal-state system. Federal programs of unemployment compensation exist for federal civilian workers and former service personnel. A separate federal unemployment program applies to railroad workers.

§ 45:9   BENEFITS AND ELIGIBILITY

The states are largely free to prescribe the amount, and duration, of benefits and the conditions required for eligibility. In most states, the unemployed person must be available for placement in a similar job and be willing to take such employment at a comparable rate of pay. As the *Evjen* case illustrates, full-time students generally have difficulty proving that they are "available" for work once they become unemployed. If an employee quits a job without cause, or is fired for misconduct, or becomes unemployed because of a labor dispute in which the employee actively takes part, the employee is ordinarily disqualified from receiving unemployment compensation benefits.[27]

---

[25] Consumer Credit Protection Act § 303. Under the Uniform Consumer Credit Code, where adopted, this second alternative has been increased to 40 times the federal hourly minimum pay. UCCC § 5.105(2)(b). Prejudgment attachment of wages without notice and hearing is invalid. Sniadach v Family Finance Corp. 395 US 337 (1969).

[26] Cheatham v Virginia Alcoholic Beverage Control Board (CA4 Va) 501 F2d 1346 (1974).

[27] Only New York provides for payment of unemployment compensation to employees out of work because of participation in a strike. New York has concluded that the community interest in the security of persons directly affected by a strike outweighs the interest in avoiding any impact on a particular labor dispute. New York Telephone Co. v. New York Department of Labor, 440 US 519 (1979).

EVJEN V EMPLOYMENT AGENCY
22 Or App 372, 539 P2d 662 (1975)

Robert Evjen was a full-time employee of Boise Cascade. At the same time, he was a full-time student at the Chemeta Community College. He was laid off as part of a general economy move by the employer. He applied for unemployment compensation. The referee found that Evjen never missed work in order to go to classes, that Evjen could not afford to go to school without working, and that in case of any conflict between work and school, work came first. The referee held Evjen was entitled to unemployment compensation. The Appeals Board reversed this decision and Evjen appealed.

SCHWAB, C. J. . . . In order for an unemployed individual to obtain unemployment insurance benefits he must prove, among other things, that "he is able to work, available for work, and is actively seeking and unable to obtain suitable work." ORS 657.155. When such an individual files a claim for benefits ORS 657.265 provides that an authorized representative of the Administrator of the Employment Division shall compute and promptly notify claimant of his entitlement to benefits, if any. If the claimant or one of his affected employers does not agree with the determination he may ask for a hearing, ORS 657.265(4), before a referee, ORS 657.270.

If the administrator or any interested party is not satisfied with the referee's decision, he may have the matter reviewed by the Employment Appeals Board. ORS 657.275. . . .

In *Callaghan v Morgan*, 9 Or App 166, 496 P2d 55 (1972), in affirming an order denying benefits to an unemployed community college student we stated:

> All cases cited to us indicate that he who seeks to obtain unemployment compensation benefits while regularly attending school has a heavy burden to overcome. . . .

What has transpired since then is set forth in *Minniti v Employment Division*, 18 Or App 44, 523 P2d 1060 (1974).

> . . . On appeal, while reiterating that an individual's status as a student creates a substantial burden to be overcome in establishing eligibility under ORS 657.155, we clarified our earlier opinion by explicitly ruling that unequivocal testimony indicating a willingness on the part of a claimant to forego educational opportunities *together with* additional facts demonstrating that his education is "secondary" to employment might serve to meet that burden. . . . The Board's order was then reversed and remanded for a further determination of whether claimant was entitled to benefits.
>
> We did not . . . decide that an unequivocal statement of an intent to compromise one's educational interests in order to obtain employment would — in and of itself — be sufficient to overcome the burden imposed upon a student seeking unemployment benefits. As we noted in our previous opinion, citing *Couchman v Industrial Commission*, 33 Colo App 166, 515 P2d 636 (1973):
>
> "A determination of the availability for employment is one for which an all-inclusive rule cannot be stated, but rather must be made within the context of the factual situation presented by each case. . . ."

Although we have not so categorized school attendance in any of our opinions, both the referee and the Employment Appeals Board speak of enrollment in school as creating a "presumption" of nonavailability for work. There is authority for the proposition that evidence of this type creates an inference rather than a presumption . . . However, we need not consider that distinction here.

> Ordinarily whether an inference or presumption has been overcome is a question for the jury, but if the evidence is of such character that one reasonable deduction can be made therefrom the court may so declare as a matter of law. . . . *Judson v Bee Hive Auto Service Co.* 136 Or 1, 294 P 588 (1931).

> This is such a case. The only evidence presented at the hearing was claimant's testimony. Nothing in his testimony was in any way inconsistent with his statement that work came first. The referee found him credible. The Employment Appeals Board, in a review of the record only, has no basis for arriving at a different result on the issue of credibility. On the record here we find as a matter of law that the referee's decision was correct.
> [Judgment reversed]

QUESTIONS

1. What must an unemployed person prove in order to obtain unemployment benefits?
2. Why is it significant, under the eligibility requirements set forth in this case, whether an applicant for unemployment benefits is a student?
3. Did the court find that Evjen was entitled to benefits?

C.   EMPLOYEE'S HEALTH AND SAFETY

The Occupational Safety and Health Act of 1970 (OSHA) was passed in order to assure every worker, so far as possible, safe and healthful working conditions and to preserve the country's human resources.[28] OSHA provides for (a) establishing safety and health standards, and for (b) effective enforcement of these standards and the other employer duties required by OSHA.

§ 45:10   STANDARDS

The Secretary of Labor has been granted broad authority under OSHA to promulgate occupational safety and health standards. Except in emergency situations, public hearings and publication in the Federal Register are required before the secretary can issue a new standard. Thereafter, any person adversely affected may challenge the validity of the standard in a United States court of appeals. The secretary's standards will be upheld if they are reasonable and supported by substantial evidence. However, the secretary does not have unbridled discretion to adopt costly standards to create an absolutely risk-free work place. Rather the secretary must demonstrate a need for a new standard by showing that it is reasonably necessary to protect employees against a "significant risk" of material health impairment.[29] The cost of compliance with new standards

---

[28]   29 USC §§ 651 et seq.

[29]   Industrial Union Department, AFL-CIO v American Petroleum Institute, 448 US 607 (1980).

may run into billions of dollars. The secretary is not required to do a cost-benefit analysis for a new standard. However, the secretary must show that the standard is economically feasible.[30]

§ 45:11   EMPLOYER DUTIES

Employers have a "general duty" to furnish to each employee a place of employment that is free from recognized hazards that are likely to cause death or serious physical injuries.[31]

Employers are required by OSHA to maintain records of occupational illness and injuries if they result in death, loss of consciousness, medical treatment other than first aid, or one or more lost workdays. Such records have proven to be a valuable aid in recognizing areas of risk and have been especially helpful in identifying the presence of occupational illnesses.

§ 45:12   ENFORCEMENT

The Occupational Safety and Health Administration (also identified as OSHA), an agency within the Department of Labor, is the primary administrative agency under the act, having authority to conduct inspections and to seek enforcement action where there has been noncompliance. Work site inspections are conducted when employer records indicate incidents involving fatalities or serious injuries. Also, work site inspections may result from employee complaints. Employees making such complaints are protected by the act from possible employer retaliation.[32] Employers have the right to require that an OSHA inspector secure a warrant prior to inspection of the employer's plant.[33]

If OSHA issues a citation against an employer, the employer may challenge it before the Occupational Safety and Health Review Commission. The Commission is fully independent of OSHA; its sole function is to adjudicate contested enforcement actions. Judicial review of a commission ruling is obtained before the United States court of appeals.

The Secretary of Labor is empowered to seek injunctive and other appropriate relief in a United States district court against an employer who discriminates against an employee for testifying or exercising "any right" under the act. In the *Whirlpool* case the court was faced with the problems of whether two employees were exercising any right under the act when they refused to perform work that they considered dangerous and whether the employer's disciplinary action against the employees was discriminatory.

---

[30] American Textile Manufacturers Institute v Donovan, 452 US 490 (1981).
[31] 29 USC § 654(a). UAW v General Dynamics Land Systems Division (CA Dist Col) 815 F2d 1570 (1987).

[32] 29 USC § 660(C).
[33] Marshall v Barlow's, Inc. 436 US 307 (1978).

WHIRLPOOL CORPORATION V MARSHALL
445 US 1 (1980)

Virgil Deemer and Thomas Cornwell, employees at the Whirlpool Corporation's plant in Marion, Ohio, refused to comply with a supervisor's order that they perform maintenance work on certain mesh screens located some 20 feet above the plant floor. Twelve days before this incident a fellow employee had fallen to his death from the screens. After the refusal, the men were ordered to punch out and leave the plant. They were not paid for the remaining six hours of their shift, and written reprimands for insubordination were placed in their employment files. Section II(C)(1) of the Occupational Safety and Health Act provides that no employer shall discharge or in any manner discriminate against an employee because the employee filed a complaint with OSHA, or testified in any OSHA proceeding, or exercised any right afforded by the act. A regulation issued by the Secretary of Labor under the act provides that if an employee with no reasonable alternative refuses in good faith to expose himself to a dangerous condition, he will be protected against subsequent discrimination. The Secretary of Labor filed suit in U.S. district court against Whirlpool, contending that Whirlpool's actions against Deemer and Cornwell constituted "discrimination" under the secretary's regulation and Section II(C)(1) of the act. Whirlpool contended that the regulation encouraged workers to engage in "self-help" and unlawfully permitted a "strike with pay." The court held that the secretary's regulation was inconsistent with the act and denied relief. The U.S. court of appeals reversed this decision, and Whirlpool appealed.

STEWART, J. . . . The petitioner company maintains a manufacturing plant in Marion, Ohio, for the production of household appliances. Overhead conveyors transport appliance components throughout the plant. To protect employees from objects that occasionally fall from these conveyors, the petitioner has installed a horizontal wire mesh guard screen approximately 20 feet above the plant floor. This mesh screen is welded to angle-iron frames suspended from the building's structural steel skeleton.

Maintenance employees of the petitioner spend several hours each week removing objects from the screen, replacing paper spread on the screen to catch grease drippings from the material on the conveyors, and performing occasional maintenance work on the conveyors themselves. To perform these duties, maintenance employees usually are able to stand on the iron frames, but sometimes find it necessary to step onto the steel mesh screen itself.

In 1973 the company began to install heavier wire in the screen because its safety had been drawn into question. Several employees had fallen partly through the old screen, and on one occasion an employee had fallen completely through to the plant floor below but had survived. A number of maintenance employees had reacted to these incidents by bringing the unsafe screen conditions to the attention of their foremen. The petitioner company's contemporaneous safety instructions admonished employees to step only on the angle-iron frames.

On June 28, 1974, a maintenance employee fell to his death through the guard screen in an area where the newer, stronger mesh had not yet been installed. Following this incident, the petitioner effectuated some repairs and issued an order strictly forbidding maintenance employees from stepping on either the screens or the angle-iron supporting structure. An alternative but somewhat more cumbersome and less satisfactory method was developed for removing objects from the screen. This procedure required employees to stand on power raised mobile platforms and use hooks to recover the material.

On July 7, 1974, two of the petitioner's maintenance employees, Virgil Deemer and Thomas Cornwell, met with the plant maintenance superintendent to voice their concern about the safety of the screen. The superintendent disagreed with their view, but permitted the two men to inspect the screen with their foreman and to point out dangerous areas needing repair. Unsatisfied with the petitioner's response to the results of this inspection, Deemer and Cornwell met on July 9 with the plant safety director. At that meeting, they requested the name, address, and telephone number of a representative of the local office of the Occupational Safety and Health Administration (OSHA). Although the safety director told the men that they "had better stop and think about what [they] were doing," he furnished the men with the information they requested. Later that same day, Deemer contacted an official of the regional OSHA office and discussed the guard screen.

The next day, Deemer and Cornwell reported for the night shift at 10:45 p.m. Their foreman, after himself walking on some of the angle-iron frames, directed the two men to perform their usual maintenance duties on a section of the old screen. Claiming that the screen was unsafe, they refused to carry out this directive. The foreman then sent them to the personnel office, where they were ordered to punch out without working or being paid for the remaining six hours of the shift. The two men subsequently received written reprimands, which were placed in their employment files. . . .

As this case illustrates, however, circumstances may sometimes exist in which the employee justifiably believes that the express statutory arrangement does not sufficiently protect him from death or serious injury. Such circumstances will probably not often occur, but such a situation may arise when (1) the employee is ordered by his employer to work under conditions that the employee reasonably believes pose an imminent risk of death or serious bodily injury, and (2) the employee has reason to believe that there is not sufficient time or opportunity either to seek effective redress from his employer or to apprise OSHA of the danger.

Nothing in the Act suggests that those few employees who have to face this dilemma must rely exclusively on the remedies expressly set forth in the Act at the risk of their own safety. But nothing in the Act explicitly provides otherwise. Against this background of legislative silence, the Secretary has exercised his rulemaking power under 29 U S C § 657(g)(2) and has determined that, when an employee in good faith finds himself in such a predicament, he may refuse to expose himself to the dangerous condition, without being subjected to "subsequent discrimination" by the employer. . . .

The regulation clearly conforms to the fundamental objective of the Act — to prevent occupational deaths and serious injuries. The Act, in its preamble, declares that its purpose and policy is "to assure so far as possible every working man and woman in the Nation safe and healthful working conditions and to *preserve* our human resources." 29 U S C § 651(b). (Emphasis added.)

To accomplish this basic purpose, the legislation's remedial orientation is prophylactic in nature. The Act does not wait for an employee to die or become injured. It authorizes the promulgation of health and safety standards and the issuance of citations in the hope that these will act to prevent deaths or injuries from ever occurring. It would seem anomalous to construe an Act so directed and constructed as prohibiting an employee, with no other reasonable alternative, the freedom to withdraw from a workplace environment that he reasonably believes is highly dangerous.

Moreover, the Secretary's regulation can be viewed as an appropriate aid to the full effectuation of the Act's "general duty" clause. That clause provides that "[e]ach employer . . . shall furnish to each of his employees employment and a place of employment which are free from recognized hazards that are causing or are likely to cause death or serious physical harm to his employees." 29 U S C § 654(a)(1). As the legislative history of this provision reflects, it was intended itself to deter the occurrence of occupational deaths and serious injuries by placing on employers a mandatory obligation independent of the specific health and safety standards to be promulgated by the Secretary. Since OSHA inspectors cannot be present around the clock in every workplace, the Secretary's regulation ensures that employees will in all circumstances enjoy the rights afforded them by the "general duty" clause.

[The Court next considered and rejected Whirlpool's contention that the legislative history is contrary to the Secretary's regulation. The Court explained its view as follows:]

When it rejected the "strike with pay" concept, therefore, Congress very clearly meant to reject a law unconditionally imposing upon employers an obligation to continue to pay their employees their regular pay checks when they absented themselves from work for reasons of safety. But the regulation at issue here does not require employers to pay workers who refuse to perform their assigned tasks in the face of imminent danger. It simply provides that in such cases the employer may not "discriminate" against the employees involved. An employer "discriminates" against an employee only when he treats that employee less favorably than he treats others similarly situated.

[In a footnote to the decision, the Court applied the above principles to the situation of Mr. Deemer and Mr. Cornwell. The Court stated that the placing of reprimands in their personnel files clearly represents discrimination. The Court stated that whether the denial of work and pay for the six-hour period also represented discrimination was a question not before the Court.]

[Judgment of Court of Appeals affirmed]

QUESTIONS

1. Was the order of the foreman to perform maintenance duties on the old section of the screen contrary to the company's directive not to step on screens or the angle-iron supporting the structure?
2. Does the Secretary of Labor's regulation aid in giving full effect to OSHA's "general duty" clause?
3. Does the Secretary of Labor's regulation require the employer to pay employees who refuse to perform work in the face of imminent danger?

---

§ 45:13   STATE "RIGHT TO KNOW" LEGISLATION

Laws that guarantee individual workers the "right to know" if there are hazardous substances in their workplaces have been enacted by many states in recent years. These laws commonly require an employer to make known to an employee's physician the chemical composition of certain substances in the workplace in connection with the diagnosis and treatment of an employee by the physician. Further, local fire and public health officials as well as local neighborhood residents are granted the right to know if local employers are working with hazardous substances that could pose health or safety problems.

D.   COMPENSATION FOR EMPLOYEE'S INJURIES

For most kinds of employment, workers' compensation statutes govern compensation for injuries.[34] These statutes provide that the injured employee is entitled to compensation for accidents occurring in the course of employment from a risk involved in that employment.

§ 45:14   COMMON-LAW STATUS OF EMPLOYER

In some employment situations, the common-law principles apply. This application is so because workers' compensation statutes commonly do not apply to employers with less than a prescribed minimum number of employees or to agricultural, domestic, or casual employment. It is necessary, therefore, to consider the duties and defenses of employers apart from workers' compensation statutes.

(a) DUTIES. The employer is under the common-law duty to furnish an employee with a reasonably safe place in which to work, reasonably safe tools and appliances, and a sufficient number of competent fellow employees for the work involved. The employer is also under the common-law duty to warn the employee of any unusual dangers peculiar to the employer's business.

(b) DEFENSES. At common law, the employer is not liable to an injured employee if the employee was harmed by the act of a fellow employee, or if harmed by an ordi-nary hazard of the work because the employee assumed such risks. If the employee was guilty of contributory negligence, regardless of the employer's negligence, the employer is not liable to an injured employee at common law.

§ 45:15   STATUTORY CHANGES

The rising incidence of industrial accidents due to the increasing use of more powerful machinery and the growth of the industrial labor population led to a demand for statutory modification of common-law rules relating to liability of employers for industrial accidents.

(a) MODIFICATION OF EMPLOYER'S COMMON-LAW DEFENSES. One kind of change by statute was to modify the defenses that an employer could assert when sued by an employee for damages. For example, under the Federal Employer's Liability Act (FELA) which covers railroad workers, the injured employee must still bring an action in court and prove the negligence of the employer or other employees, but the burden of proving the case is made lighter by limitations on employers' defenses. Under FELA, contributory negligence is a defense only in mitigation of damages; assumption of the risk is not a defense.[35]

(b) WORKERS' COMPENSATION. A more sweeping development was made by the adoption of workers' compensation statutes in every state. In addition, civil employees of the United States government are covered by the Federal Employees' Compensation Act. When an employee is covered by a workers' compensation statute, and when the injury is job-connected, the employee's remedy is limited to that provided in the workers' compensation statute. The *Halliman* case illustrates the exclusivity of the Workers' Compensation Act remedy.

---

[34] Every state has some form of workers' compensation legislation, though the statutes vary widely from state to state. Some statutes apply only to employees engaged in manual or mechanical labor; others extend coverage to virtually all employees. Employer participation is voluntary to certain degrees in eighteen states.

[35] Federal Employer's Liability Act, 45 USC §§ 1 et seq.

HALLIMAN V LOS ANGELES UNIFIED SCHOOL DISTRICT

163 Cal App 3d 46, 209 Cal Rptr 175 (1984)

Robert Halliman was employed as a teacher by the Los Angeles Unified School District at Milliken Junior High School. On November 4, 1982, a minor student, Louis "R.," intentionally threw a rock at him, hitting him on the head and seriously injuring him. The same student had committed previous assaults on the school grounds, including an assault earlier that very day. Halliman and his wife brought suit against the Los Angeles Unified School District and the student's parents seeking damages. He contended that the defendants had the power and ability to prevent the student's conduct by appropriate disciplinary action but did not do so, ignoring their duty to protect students and teachers. The school district filed a motion for a summary judgment on the ground that the Workers' Compensation Act provided the exclusive remedy for Halliman's injury. From a summary judgment in favor of the school district, Halliman appealed.

ARGVELLES, A. J. . . . In this appeal from a judgment favoring a school district, we are called upon to determine whether workers' compensation is the exclusive remedy for a teacher's injuries caused by a student's unprovoked assault while the teacher is acting within the scope of his employment. . . .

. . . We find here, as we did in *Roberts v. Pup 'N' Taco Driveup*, 160 Cal. App. 3d 278, 206 Cal. Rptr. 533, that plaintiffs have failed to state facts negating application of the exclusive remedy provision of the workers' compensation laws in their complaint. . . .

We disagree with plaintiffs' contention that *Meyer v. Graphic Arts International Union* (1979) 88 Cal. App. 3d 176, 151 Cal. Rptr. 597, is dispositive of the issue in their favor. *Meyer* involved injury by a coemployee of plaintiff, and there had been reported prior acts of aggression by that person against the complaining employee followed by the employer's ratification or acquiescence in failing to discipline, censure, criticize, suspend or discharge the offending coemployee. Here, as defendant correctly points out, the assailant was not a coemployee but a student for whom the plaintiff teacher, among other employees at the school, was responsible. The record before us discloses no reports of prior assaults upon plaintiff teacher by the same student. Additionally, the student's school records indicated that he had, indeed, been previously suspended and otherwise disciplined for prior assaults.

In *Adler v. Los Angeles Unified School Dist.* (1979) 98 Cal. App. 3d 280, 288, 159 Cal. Rptr. 528, though the case was decided on other grounds, the court presumed that where a teacher was injured in a classroom attack by a student, the available workers' compensation remedy barred a civil lawsuit for damages against the employer by virtue of Labor Code section 3601. Under the facts of this case, we so hold.

Plaintiffs argue that a student in this context is akin to an employer's agent or a coemployee who is "under the control" of the employer; and, therefore, the school district "employer" comes within the statutory exception to the exclusive remedy provisions of the workers' compensation laws for intentional acts of agents and coemployees. But, teacher and student are not equals, standing shoulder to shoulder in the classroom or on the playground, with the same status, rights, duties, responsibilities, maturity, judgment, knowledge and skill. If an analogy is to be drawn, a more appropriate one would liken the student to raw material which must be wrought by the employee into a finished product.

Thus, we find it helpful in addressing plaintiff's contentions to refer to those cases where the alleged intentional misconduct of the employer does not go beyond failure to assure a safe working environment. The California Supreme Court in *Johns-Manville Products Corp. v. Superior Court* (1980) 27 Cal. 3d 465, 165 Cal. Rptr. 858, 612 P.2d 948, reviewed cases where the employer concealed inherent dangers in the material its employees were required to handle, or made false representations in that regard, or allowed an employee to use a machine without proper instruction. Workers' compensation was held to be the exclusive remedy for any injuries thus suffered. The Supreme Court concluded that the workers' compensation laws provided "the sole remedy for additional compensation against an employer whose employee is injured in the first instance as the result of a deliberate failure to assure that the physical environment of the work place is safe."

The facts of the present case do not justify a departure from such precedent. [Judgment affirmed]

QUESTIONS

1. State the issue before the court.
2. Why did the Hallimans bring an action for damages in a court of law when Halliman was clearly entitled to benefits under the workers' compensation law?
3. When an employee is injured as a result of an employer's deliberate failure to provide a safe workplace, may the employee sue the employer for damages in a court of law?
4. Is there an exception to the exclusive remedy provisions of the workers' compensation laws for intentional acts of agents or "coemployees"?

For injuries arising within the course of the employee's work from a risk involved in that work, the workers' compensation statutes usually provide: (1) immediate medical benefits, (2) prompt periodic wage replacement, very often computed as a percentage of weekly wages (ranging from 50 percent to 80 percent of the injured employee's wage), and (3) a death benefit of a limited amount. In such cases, compensation is paid without regard to whether the employer or the employee was negligent. However, generally no compensation is allowed for a willful, self-inflicted injury or one sustained while intoxicated.

There has been a gradual widening of the workers' compensation statutes so that compensation today is generally recoverable for both accident-inflicted injuries and occupational diseases. In some states compensation for occupational diseases is limited to those specified in the statute by name, such as silicosis, lead poisoning, or injury to health from radioactivity. In other states, any disease arising from an occupation is compensable.

Workers' compensation proceedings are brought before a special administrative agency or workers' compensation board. In contrast, a common-law action for damages or an action for damages under an employer's liability statute is brought in a court of law.

E. EMPLOYER-RELATED IMMIGRATION LAWS

The Immigration and Naturalization Act (INA) and the Immigration Reform and Control Act of 1986 (IRCA) are the principal employer-related immigration laws.

§ 45:16 IMMIGRATION REFORM

IRCA[36] granted amnesty to illegal aliens who had lived in the United States since before January 1, 1982. IRCA also established a system for the legalization of the residency of certain foreign, seasonal agricultural workers (SAWs). IRCA sets forth criminal and civil penalties against employers who knowingly hire illegal aliens. The Immigration Marriage Fraud Amendments[37] to the INA became law in 1986, allowing aliens married to U.S. citizens conditional permanent residence status. This status is reviewable at the end of a two-year period, at which time the condition will be lifted if the marriage has not been legally terminated. Criminal penalties of up to five years in prison and fines of up to $250,000 may be applied to those who knowingly arrange or participate in fraudulent marriage for immigration benefits.

[36] PL No 99-603, also known as the Simpson-Rodino Act.
[37] PL No 99-639.

§ 45:17 EMPLOYER SANCTIONS AND VERIFICATION RESPONSIBILITIES

The availability of jobs and the higher pay scales in the United States have been a principal factor in drawing illegal immigrants to the United States. The premise upon which the IRCA is structured is that if employer sanctions are applied and if employers are enlisted to help enforce the immigration laws, employment opportunities for illegal immigrants will be drastically diminished, and so will illegal immigration.

(a) EMPLOYER SANCTIONS. Section 101 of the IRCA makes it illegal to hire, recruit, or hire for a fee unauthorized aliens. The law also makes it illegal for an employer to employ a person in the United States knowing that person is (or has become) an unauthorized alien with respect to employment. An employer who violates the law is subject to pay civil penalties of $250 to $2,000 for each unauthorized alien. This penalty is increased to $2,000 to $5,000 for each alien for a second violation. Criminal penalties, when a "pattern or practice" of unlawful hiring exists, can include a fine of not more that $3,000 for each unauthorized alien and imprisonment for up to six months.

(b) EMPLOYER VERIFICATION. The law requires employers to verify that each new employee hired after November 6, 1986, is authorized to work in the United States. The INS has designated Form I-9, "Immigration Eligibility Verification Form," as the official verification form to comply with the IRCA. The prospective employee must complete the initial portion of Form I-9, attesting under the penalty of perjury that he or she is a U.S. citizen or is authorized to work in the U.S. by the INS and that the verification documents presented to the employer are genuine and relate to the signer. The employer must then review the documents that support the individual's right to work in the U.S. Documents that both identify and support an individual's eligibility to work are a U.S. passport, a certificate of U.S. citizenship, a certificate of nationalization, an unexpired foreign passport with attached visa authorizing U.S. employment, or an Alien Registration Card. If the individual does not have one of the above documents, he or she may provide an individual document evidencing his or her identity and another document evidencing his or her right to employment. Thus, a state driver's license is sufficient to provide identity and a social security card or official birth certificate issued by a municipal authority is sufficient to prove employment eligibility. Numerous other documents exist that will satisfy the identity and employment eligibility documentation requirements.

The employer, after examining all documents, signs the following certification:

> CERTIFICATION: I attest, under penalty of perjury, that I have examined the documents presented by the above individual, that they appear to be genuine, relate to the individual named, and that the individual, to the best of my knowledge, is authorized to work in the United States.

The employer has three days to complete the I-9s. I-9s must be completed for all employees hired after November 6, 1986, including employees who are U.S. citizens. The I-9s must be kept for three years after the date of hire.

Fines of between $100 and $1,000 may be assessed of the employer for each individual employee for failure to comply with the paperwork verification requirements.

(c) BURDEN OF PROOF AND AFFIRMATIVE DEFENSES. In an action against the employer under the IRCA, the government must establish that the employer had "actual knowledge" that the employee was unauthorized to work in the U.S. This standard is one of the highest standards of proof under law.

The IRCA provides an affirmative defense for an employer if the employer, in good faith, simply complies with the verification requirements of the act. This is ac-

complished "if the document reasonably appears on its face to be genuine."[38]

§ 45:18   BUSINESS VISAS

The IRCA does not effect business visas. Nonimmigrant "B-1" business visas are issued by a U.S. consular office abroad after it has been shown that, a) the visitor has a foreign residence that has not been abandoned, b) intends to enter the U.S. for a limited period of time, and c) will engage solely in legitimate business activities for which he or she will not be paid in the U.S.[39] Thus, aliens may qualify for a B-1 visa to perform after-sale warranty work on equipment sold by a foreign company to a U.S. purchaser.

Certain investors qualify for E-2 business visas. Principal foreign investors responsible for development and direction of an enterprise in the U.S. are granted such a visa. An E visa is very desirable because it is usually issued for extended periods of time, often four to five years, and may be renewed indefinitely, so long as the alien maintains his or her role with respect to the investment.

L-1 visas allow qualifying multinational businesses to make intracompany transfers of foreign persons to the United States, if the individuals are employed in management or have "specialized knowledge."[40] L-1 visas are good for an initial period of up to three years, with a possible extension not to exceed two years. The alien must then depart the country and live outside of it for a year before again being eligible for L-1 status.

H-1 classification visas allow aliens of "distinguished merit and ability" to enter and work in the United States for an initial period of up to three years, with extensions in increments of two years. These persons include architects, engineers, law-

---

[38] IRCA § 101(a)(1); 8 USC § 1324 A(b)(1)(A).
[39] Department of State, 9 Foreign Affairs Manual, § 41.25.
[40] Some 66,000 individuals were issued L-1 visas in 1986, up from 6,000 L-1 visas issued in 1972, AILA Capital Conference, Washington, D.C., November 21, 1986.

yers, physicians, surgeons, and teachers in elementary and secondary schools and in colleges.

Seasonal and temporary workers "performing skilled or unskilled labor" may obtain H-2 visas for an initial period of one year, with extensions allowing for a total length of stay not to exceed three years, if an employer demonstrates that qualified U.S. workers are not available.

SUMMARY

The relationship of employer and employee is created by the agreement of the parties and is subject to all of the principles applicable to contracts. If the employment contract sets forth a specific duration, the employer cannot terminate the contract at an earlier date, unless just cause exists. If no definite time period is set forth, the individual is an at-will employee. In those states where the employment-at-will doctrine is followed, an employer can terminate the contract of an at-will employee at any time for any reason or no reason. Courts in a majority of jurisdictions, however, have carved out exceptions to this doctrine when the discharge violates public policy or is contrary to good faith and fair dealing in the employment relationship. Also, federal laws prohibit termination of covered employees because of their union activities or because of their race, color, sex, religion, national origin, age, or handicap. However, employers may terminate employees for just cause.

The Employees Retirement Income Security Act (ERISA) was enacted to provide protection of the pension interests of employees by requiring: (a) high standards of those administering the funds; (b) reasonable vesting of benefits; (c) adequate funding; and (d) an insurance program to guarantee payments of earned benefits.

Unemployment compensation benefits are provided to persons for a limited period of time if they are out of work through no fault of their own and are available for placement in a similar job at a comparable rate of pay.

In order to assure every working person safe and healthful working conditions the Occupational Safety and Health Act provides for (a) the establishment of safety and health standards and (b) the effective enforcement of these standards. "Right-to-know" laws have been enacted by many states; these laws require employers to inform their employees of any hazardous substances present in the workplace.

Workers' compensation laws provide for the prompt payment of compensation and medical benefits to persons injured in the course of employment without regard to fault. The injured employee's remedy is generally limited to that provided by the workers' compensation statute.

The Immigration Reform and Control Act was designed to discourage aliens from illegally entering the United States, by eliminating job opportunities for them through employer sanctions. Business visas may be obtained from U.S. consular offices abroad by qualifying foreign persons.

QUESTIONS AND CASE PROBLEMS

1. What social forces are affected by the shop right rule applicable to inventions of an employee?
2. Compare the protection of trade secrets

and the protection given an unpublished literary or artistic work (common-law copyright).
3. What remedies does an employee who has

been wrongfully discharged have against an employer?

4. Michael Hauck claims that he was discharged by his employer, Sabine Pilot Service, Inc., because he refused his employer's direction to perform the illegal act of pumping the bilges of his employer's vessel into the waterways. Hauck was an employee at will, and Sabine contends that as such it had the right to discharge him without having to show cause. Hauck brought a wrongful discharge action against Sabine. Decide. [Sabine Pilot Service Inc v Hauck (Tex) 687 SW2d 733]

5. U.S. consular officers in West Germany issued B-1 visas to ten West Germans to perform technical bricklaying work in the installation of a new gold-ore processing system in California. The Bricklayers' Union challenged the validity of the instructions that allowed consular officers to issue the B-1 visas to these bricklayers, claiming that the proper visas should have been H-2 visas, which can only be issued where qualified U.S. workers are not available. The Bricklayers' Union stated that qualified U.S. bricklayers were available. Should the B-1 business visas have been issued to the foreign bricklayers? [International Union of Bricklayers v Meese (DC Cal) 616 F Supp 1387]

6. A teenage, female, high school student named Salazar was employed part-time at Church's Fried Chicken restaurant. Salazar was hired and supervised by Simon Garza, the assistant manager of the restaurant. Garza had complete supervisory powers when the restaurant's manager, Garza's roommate, was absent. Salazar alleged that while she worked at the restaurant, Garza would refer to her and all other females by a Spanish term that she found objectionable. According to Salazar, Garza once made a lecherous comment about her body and repeatedly asked her about her personal life. On another occasion, Garza allegedly physically removed eye shadow from Salazar's face because he felt it looked ugly. Salazar also claimed that one night, she was restrained in a back room of the restaurant while Garza and another employee fondled her. Later that night when Salazar told a customer what had happened, she was fired. Salazar filed an action under Title VII against Garza and Church's Fried Chicken, Inc. alleging sexual harassment. Church's, the corporate

defendant, maintains that it should not be held liable under Title VII for Garza's harassment. Church's bases its argument on the existence of a published "fair treatment policy." Decide. [Salazar v Church's Fried Chicken, Inc., 44 FEP 472 (SD Tex)]

7. Compare (a) an employee and (b) an independent contractor.

8. Juan Ortiz was regularly employed by Donegan Productions Co. as an actor on an afternoon television series. A dispute arose as to Donegan's financial obligations to Juan. Donegan claimed that the dispute must be resolved solely on the basis of the written individual employment contract that Juan and Donegan Productions had signed and that the past practice, usages of the profession, and an existing collective bargaining contract with AFTRA (American Federation of Television and Radio Artists) were not relevant. Is Donegan Productions correct?

9. Jane Richards was employed as the sole crane operator of the Gale Corporation. She also held the part-time union position of shop steward for the plant. On May 15, Richards complained to OSHA concerning what she contended were seven existing violations of the Occupational Safety and Health Act. These violations were brought to her attention by members of the bargaining unit. On May 21, she stated to the company's general manager at a negotiating session: "if we don't have a new contract by the time the present one expires on June 15, we will strike." On May 22, an OSHA inspector arrived at the plant and Richards told her supervisor that "I blew the whistle." On May 23, the company rented and later purchased two large electric forklifts that were utilized to do the work formerly performed by the crane; consequently, the crane operator's job was abolished. Under the existing collective bargaining contract, the company had the right to lay off for lack of work. The contract also provided for arbitration and prohibited discipline or discharge without "just cause." On May 23, Richards was notified that she was being laid off "for lack of work" within her classification of crane operator. She was also advised that the company was not planning on using the crane in the future and that, if she were smart, she would get another job. Richards claims that her layoff was in violation of the National Labor Relations Act,

the Occupational Safety and Health Act, and the collective bargaining agreement. Is she correct?

10. Samuel Sullivan, president of the Truck Drivers and Helpers International Union also holds the position of president of the union's pension fund. The fund consists of both employer and employee contributions that are forwarded quarterly to the fund's offices in New York City. Sullivan ordered Mark Gilbert, the treasurer of the fund, not to give out any information to anyone at any time concerning the fund, because it is union money and because the union is entitled to take care of its own internal affairs. Is Sullivan correct?

11. A Louisiana statute requires that when an employee hired for a fixed term is fired without cause, the employer must pay him the full "salary" for the contract term. Brasher was employed on a yearly basis by Chenille, Inc, and was fired by that company without cause. Had he worked the full year, Chenille would have made a contribution on his behalf to a retirement fund or pension plan. Brasher claimed that such a contribution was part of his "salary" and, therefore, that the statute requires Chenille to make that contribution. Was he correct? [Brasher v Chenille (La App) 251 So 2d 824]

12. Buffo was employed by the Baltimore & Ohio Railroad Co. Along with a number of other workers, he was removing old brakes from railroad cars and replacing them with new brakes. In the course of the work, rivet heads and scrap from the brakes accumulated on the tracks under the cars. This debris was removed only occasionally when the men had time. Buffo, while holding an air hammer in both arms, was crawling under a car when his foot slipped on scrap on the ground. This incident caused him to strike and injure his knee. He sued the railroad for damages under the Federal Employers' Liability

Act. Decide. [Buffo v Baltimore & Ohio Railroad Co. 364 Pa 437, 72 A2d 593]

13. Moore was an electronics engineer employed by the United States. While traveling under a work assignment from one air base to another, he ran into and injured Romitti, who then sued the United States. The United States raised the defense that Moore was not acting within the course of his employment while driving to the new job assignment. Was this defense valid? [United States v Romitti (CA9 Cal) 363 F2d 662]

14. Cream was an officer and employee of Leo Silfen, Inc. He was discharged and then went into business for himself, conducting a business similar to that of his former employer. He obtained lists of users of his products from enterprises publishing mailing and commercial lists. Out of the persons he solicited from these lists, forty-seven were customers of Silfen. Silfen brought an action to enjoin Cream from soliciting its customers. Cream showed that Silfen had approximately 1,100 customers. Decide. [Leo Silfen, Inc. v Cream, 29 NY2d 387, 328 NYS2d 423, 278 NE2d 636]

15. Michael Kittell, while operating a saw at the Vermont Weatherboard Company plant, was seriously injured when a splinter flew into his eye and penetrated his head. Kittell sued Vermont Weatherboard seeking damages on a common-law theory. His complaint alleged that he suffered severe injuries due solely to the employer's wanton and willful acts and omissions. The complaint stated that he was an inexperienced worker set to work without instructions or warning on a saw from which the employer had stripped away all safety devices. Vermont Weatherboard made a motion to dismiss the complaint on the ground that the Workers' Compensation Act provided the exclusive remedy for his injury. Decide. [Kittell v Vermont Weatherboard, Inc. 138 Vt 439, 417 A2d 926]

PART 8

——◆——

BUSINESS
ORGANIZATIONS

46

FORMS OF BUSINESS ORGANIZATIONS

Business ventures may be conducted under various forms of organization. The principal forms of business organizations are (1) individual or sole proprietorships, (2) partnerships, and (3) corporations. The particular form of business organization selected will be determined by the nature of the proposed business and considerations of control, tax liability, and liability for debts of (and claims against) the business.

Certain forms of special venture organizations have evolved to meet modern business and investment needs. These include franchises, limited partnerships, joint ventures, cooperatives, and unincorporated associations.

A. PRINCIPAL FORMS OF BUSINESS ORGANIZATIONS

The law of business organizations may be better understood if major advantages and disadvantages of proprietorships, partnerships, and corporations are first considered.

§ 46:1 INDIVIDUAL PROPRIETORSHIPS

A **sole** or **individual proprietorship** is a form of business ownership in which one individual owns a business. The owner may either be the sole worker of the business or may employ as many individuals as needed to run the concern. Individual proprietorships are commonly used in retail establishments, service businesses, and agriculture.

(a) ADVANTAGES. The proprietor or owner is not required to expend limited resources on organizational fees. The proprietor, as the sole owner, controls all of the decisions and receives all of the profits. The business's net earnings are not subject to the corporate income tax, but are taxed as personal income.

(b) DISADVANTAGES. The proprietor is subject to unlimited personal liability for the debts of the business, and the proprietor cannot effectively limit this risk. The investment capital in the business is limited by the resources of the sole proprietor, and this limitation very often impedes the growth of the business. With all contracts of the business being made by the owner or in the owner's name by agents of the owner, the authority to make contracts terminates upon the death of the owner, and the business is subject to disintegration.

§ 46:2   PARTNERSHIPS

While the individual proprietorship relies upon the capital investment and business skill of the sole owner, a **partnership** involves the pooling of capital resources and the business or professional talents of two or more individuals with the goal of making a profit. Law firms, medical associates, and architectural and engineering firms may operate under the partnership form, although there is a trend for such professional firms to incorporate. A wide range of retail and service businesses operate as partnerships.

(a) ADVANTAGES. The partnership form of business organization allows individuals to pool resources and then initiate and conduct their business without the requirement of a formal organizational structure and without the expense of organizational fees. As will be seen, partnership agreements are often informal and may even be unwritten.

(b) DISADVANTAGES. Major disadvantages of a partnership are the unlimited personal liability of each partner and the uncertain duration of the business because the partnership is dissolved by the death of a partner.

§ 46:3   CORPORATIONS

Business corporations exist primarily to make a profit. They are created by government grant, and the statute regulating the creation of corporations requires a corporate structure consisting of shareholders, directors, and officers. The shareholders, as the owners of the business, elect a board of directors who are responsible for the management of the business. The directors employ officers, who serve as the agents of the business and who run the day-to-day operations. Corporations range in size from incorporated one-owner enterprises to large multinational concerns.

(a) ADVANTAGES. The major advantage to the shareholder, or investor, is that the shareholder's risk of loss from the business is limited to the amount of capital that the shareholder invested in the business. This factor, coupled with the free transferability of corporate shares, makes the corporate form of business organization an acceptable mechanism for many investors to contribute the capital assets needed to finance large business enterprises. Indeed, as the capital needs of the business expand, the corporate form becomes more attractive.

A corporation is a separate legal entity capable of owning property, contracting, suing, and being sued in its own name. It may be established with a perpetual life, and unlike in a partnership or proprietorship, the death of an owner has no legal effect on the entity.

A corporation is also a separate taxable entity, which allows for certain tax savings (under particular circumstances) to the owners of the corporation. Also, executive employees of corporations have tax advantages.

(b) DISADVANTAGES. A corporation is required to pay corporate income taxes. Shareholders, when they receive a distribution of profits for the corporation, are required to pay personal income taxes on the amount received. This is a form of double taxation which may weigh against incorporation.

The limited liability of shareholders may result in a limitation of the credit available to the corporation. Also, incorporation involves the expenditure of funds for organizational and operational expenses. Documents necessary for the formation of a corporation, which are required by state law, must be prepared and certain filing fees must be paid. State corporation laws may also require the filing of an annual report and other reports.

B. SPECIALIZED BUSINESS RELATIONSHIPS AND FORMS OF ORGANIZATIONS

Specialized business relationships and forms of business organizations exist to meet modern business and investment needs. Thus a fast-food enterprise may choose to expand its business by the use of franchises, whereby it is paid royalties from the gross receipts of restaurants owned and operated by franchisees. Or, two construction companies may form a joint venture to construct a major project, when individually the companies lack sufficient resources to undertake the project. Each enterprise seeks to utilize the structure that will permit the attainment of its desired goals in the most efficient manner, while protecting the enterprise and the participants from the risks that may arise.

§ 46:4 FRANCHISES

The use of franchises has expanded rapidly in recent years as a method of controlling and financing operations by the franchisor and as a method of investment and participation by the franchisee.

(a) DEFINITIONS. A **franchise** has been defined by the Federal Trade Commission as "an arrangement in which the owner of a trademark, trade name, or copyright licenses others, under specified conditions or limitations, to use the trademark, trade name, or copyright in purveying goods or services." The **franchisor** is the party granting the franchise, and the **franchisee** is the person to whom the franchise is granted.

(b) THE FRANCHISOR AND THE FRANCHISEE. Theoretically the relationship between the franchisor and the franchisee is an arm's-length relationship between two independent contractors, their respective rights being determined by the contract existing between them. A franchise then is not a business entity *per se*, but rather is a business relationship between distinct business organizations, which relationship is governed by the franchise contract.

(1) Duration and Termination. The franchise may last for as long as the parties agree. Commonly, it runs for a short period of time, such as a year, so that the franchise holder is well aware that in order to stay in business the terms of the franchise contract must be followed. The *McDonald's Corp.* case is an example of the basic contractual nature of franchising. Moreover, it demonstrates that the parties may expect the courts to apply franchise agreements as written.

McDONALD'S CORP. V ROBERT A. MAKIN, INC.

(DC NY) 653 F Supp 401 (1986)

McDonald's Corporation entered into a contract with Robert A. Makin, Inc., to franchise a McDonald's restaurant in Clarence, New York. The franchise agreement required Makin, Inc., to make monthly payments of license and lease fees to McDonald's; and the agreement provided for the termination of the franchise if Makin, Inc., should fail to make all payments under the agreement. Makin, Inc., failed to make monthly payments from October 1985 through February 10, 1986. McDonald's gave notice that it had terminated the franchise. Makin, Inc., refused to terminate operations and surrender the premises. McDonald's brought suit for the amount due for the period, and sought a court order granting it the right to enter and take possession of the restaurant. Makin, Inc., defends that McDonald's engaged in a coercive pricing policy in violation of the Sherman Antitrust Act.

CURTIN, D.J. . . . The franchise agreement obligates the defendants to pay monthly fees to plaintiff for the franchise. Nowhere do the defendants deny their failure to pay these fees since October, 1985. Yet, defendants have maintained possession and operation of the franchise property. At oral argument, counsel for defendants contended that McDonald's conduct . . . caused defendants' inability to make the payments. Defendants' counterclaims do not allege that McDonald's conduct caused the non-payment; moreover, defendants contend that most of McDonald's alleged illegal conduct began 7-14 years ago, over which time defendants regularly made the monthly fee payments. In any event, it should be clear to all concerned that

> it is against the law as well as sound morals to permit a party to a contract to repudiate the contract or his obligation under it, and at the same time retain the consideration that he has received.

Defendants' counterclaims will, of course, be adjudicated in their own right; however, the alleged wrongs of plaintiff do not constitute affirmative defenses to defendants' non-payment of franchise fees. The defendants may not use their counterclaims to avoid judgment for the amounts already due under the franchise agreement. The failure of defendants to pay the monthly franchise fees is a breach of contract as to which there exists no genuine factual issue.

Accordingly, plaintiff's motion for summary judgment on Count III of the complaint is granted. . . .

[The] defendants' antitrust claim [will not] bar summary judgment with respect to the validity of the termination. In *Lewis v. Seanor Coal Company*, the United States Court of Appeals for the Third Circuit found that:

> [t]he company's claim that the agreement violates the Sherman Anti-Trust Act is not a defense to the trustees' action. It is now well established that the remedy for violation of the antitrust law is not avoidance of payments due under a contract, but rather the redress which the antitrust statute establishes, — a private treble damage action.

382 F.2d 437, 441 (3d Cir. 1967), cert. denied, 390 U.S. 947 (1968). . . .

Defendants have not alleged that the requirement that they pay fees for the use of the franchise is at all connected with the illegal price-fixing allegedly engaged in by McDonald's. The termination is a clear contractual result of the failure to pay the required fees. Thus, defendants' antitrust claim does not preclude summary judgment on this action.

. . . It is clear under basic contract principles that, absent an affirmative defense excusing the defendants' failure to pay, the Makins cannot refuse to meet their obligations under the contract while enjoying all of its benefits. Upon the Makins' refusal to pay the amounts owed, McDonald's had a clear contractual right to terminate the franchise agreement.

Accordingly, plaintiff's motion for summary judgment on Count I of the complaint is granted.

I find that the franchise contract, consisting of the license and lease documents referenced herein, has been lawfully terminated as of February 10, 1986. In accordance with the provisions of the agreement, McDonald's has an immediate right to enter and take possession of the North Transit Road McDonald's and to require defendants to forthwith return all material containing McDonald's trade secrets, operating instructions, or business practices and to discontinue the use of the McDonald's System. In accordance with the provisions of the contract, McDonald's is also awarded the reasonable expenses of litigation in this action, including attorney's fees, with interest thereon at the legal rate.

[So ordered]

QUESTIONS

1. On what basis did McDonald's contend that it had a right to receive monthly payments and, when the payments were not made, the right to terminate the franchise and take possession of the restaurant?
2. Is an alleged antitrust violation a defense for a franchisee's failure to make monthly payments under a franchise agreement?
3. What was the proper procedure for Makin, Inc., to follow if it believed McDonald's violated the Sherman Antitrust Act?

Franchise contracts generally specify the causes for which the franchisor may terminate the franchise, such as the franchisee's death, bankruptcy, failure to make payments, or failure to meet sales quotas. Franchise contracts frequently contain an arbitration provision under which a neutral party is to make a final and binding determination whether or not a breach of the contract has occurred that is sufficient to justify cancellation of the franchise. The arbitration provision may provide that the franchisor can appoint a trustee to run the business of the franchisee while the arbitration proceedings are pending.

Holders of automobile dealership franchises are protected from bad faith termination of their dealerships by the federal Automobile Dealers' Franchise Act.[1] When an automobile manufacturer makes arbitrary and unreasonable demands and thereafter terminates the dealer's franchise for failure to comply with the demands, the manufacturer is liable for the damages caused thereby. However, a manufacturer is justified in terminating an automobile dealership for failing to maintain the required sales quota when the manufacturer has given the dealer repeated warnings, when the quota is reasonable, and when the quota has been reduced to reflect local economic conditions.[2]

When the relationship between the

---

[1] 15 USC § 1222. Several states have similar statutes.
[2] Clifford Jacobs Motors, Inc. v Chrysler Corp. (DC Ohio) 357 F Supp 564 (1973).

franchisor and the franchisee is created primarily for the sale of products manufactured by the franchisor, the rights of the parties are governed by the law of sales of Article 2 of the UCC. Also, it should be remembered from Chapter 4, "Government Regulation," that vertical price-fixing agreements between a franchisor-manufacturer and its franchisee-distributor are a violation of the federal antitrust laws. Thus, when a manufacturer of winches terminated one of the distributorships for discounting prices contrary to the manufacturer's resale price maintenance policy, the manufacturer was in violation of section one of the Sherman Antitrust Act and was required to pay three times the actual damages caused by the termination.[3]

[3] Pierce v Ramsey Winch Co. (CA5 Tex) CCH Bus Fran Rptr, 8318 (1985).

(2) Regulation. There continue to be statutory reform movements, both at the federal and at the state levels, to provide general protection for the franchise holder. Protective regulation of franchisees generally relates to problems of fraud in the sale of the franchise and protecting the franchisee from unreasonable demands and termination by the franchisor.

The Petroleum Marketing Products Act (PMPA) gives a gasoline franchisee the opportunity to continue in business by purchasing the entire premises used in selling motor fuel when the franchisor determines to sell the property and not to renew a lease.

The *Roberts* case considered the question of whether the franchisor made a bona fide offer to sell, when the offer excluded the sale of the gasoline pumps and storage tanks.

ROBERTS V AMOCO OIL CO.
(CA8 Iowa) 740 F2d 602 (1985)

For fifteen years, Don Roberts operated an Amoco service station franchise in Des Moines, Iowa. Under the franchise agreement, he leased the service station premises from Amoco. His most recent lease had a five-year term, running from February 1, 1977, to January 31, 1982. On August 6, 1981, Amoco sent Roberts a letter notifying him that it did not intend to renew his lease upon expiration because Amoco intended to sell the premises. Amoco advised Roberts that it would shortly make an offer to sell the station to him. When Roberts received the letter, he got in contact with Amoco's area representative, Bob Williams, who informed him that Amoco's offer of sale would either contain a "petroleum exclusion clause" or exclude sale of the gasoline pumps and tanks. On September 4, 1981, Amoco sent Roberts an offer to sell the premises for $66,500. The offer specifically excluded "the gasoline pumps, dispensers, storage tanks, and piping or other equipment" from the sale. Roberts wrote Amoco a letter on September 28 stating that he intended to vacate the Penn Avenue station by October 1, 1981, and did so. Roberts then filed suit against Amoco, alleging that Amoco's conduct violated the Petroleum Marketing Practices Act (PMPA) in that Amoco had failed to make a "bona fide offer to sell, transfer or assign its interest" in the service station premises. Amoco filed a counterclaim seeking compensation for unpaid rent and gasoline. From a judgment for Amoco, Roberts appealed.

HEANEY, C. J. . . . The petroleum marketing franchise relationship has a history of tension and problems. In 1971, a leading commentator in the area of franchise law observed:

> In the Nation's second largest industry, the major oil firms have the gasoline station dealers in virtual bondage, hinged on the constant threat that their short-term contracts will not be renewed unless they submit to burdensome franchisor-imposed practices.
>
> . . . It is generally conceded that the gasoline station situation is almost hopeless and offers a prime example of the worst abuses in franchising.

The financial hardship imposed on franchisees by high minimum rent and "minimum gallonage" requirements, burdensome marketing requirements which benefit the franchisor but not the franchisee, and the ease of franchise termination have forced many franchisees out of business. The energy crisis has worsened the situation for franchisees; increasing supply costs have led oil companies to seek higher profits at the marketing level. As Senator Durkin observed during Senate debate of the PMPA, "[S]ince the embargo, there have been approximately 35,000 small-business people, hardworking gasoline dealers, gasoline station owners whose gasoline stations have been closed."

Congress enacted the PMPA after investigating and considering numerous allegations that petroleum franchisors used threats of termination or nonrenewal of the franchise to compel franchisees to comply with their marketing policies. There were also numerous complaints before Congress of unfair terminations and nonrenewals for arbitrary and discriminatory reasons. These practices thus posed a threat to the independence of the franchisee as a competitive influence in the marketplace. Congress intended the PMPA to address this disparity in bargaining power.

The statute seeks to protect and to effectuate the franchisee's reasonable expectations that the franchise relationship will be a continuing one. It regulates the conditions and grounds for which a franchisor may terminate or not renew a franchise. It requires that franchisors provide advance notice of termination or nonrenewal before taking action. The PMPA further provides franchisees with a cause of action against franchisors for violation of these provisions. Relief includes a preliminary injunction and other equitable relief, as well as actual and exemplary damages and attorney and expert witness fees.

Roberts argued below that Amoco violated the PMPA's requirements concerning nonrenewals by failing to make a bona fide offer to sell the Penn station to him when it decided to sell the premises. The district court determined that Amoco's offer of sale to Roberts was "bona fide," noting that "nothing in plaintiff's brief or the exhibits indicates that defendant's decision to sell the premises and not renew the lease was less than a good faith business decision." The court rejected Roberts' contention that the offer was not bona fide because the pumps and tanks were excluded. It accepted Amoco's suggestion that the company deducted the cost of replacing the equipment from the purchase price offered to Roberts. Finding that Roberts presented no evidence to show a genuine issue for trial on this point, the court granted summary judgment for Amoco. . . .

The PMPA provides that a franchisor may decide to sell a service station or otherwise withdraw from a particular market area so long as the franchisor makes that determination "in good faith and in the normal course of business." Specifically, the franchisor has "ground for nonrenewal of a franchise relationship" if it has made such a determination. But under § 2802(b)(3)(D)(iii):

> in the case of leased marketing premises such franchisor, during the 90-day period after notification [of nonrenewal to the franchisee] [must] either —
> (I) [have] made a bona fide offer to sell, transfer, or assign to the franchisee such franchisor's interests in such premises; or
> (II) if applicable, offered the franchisee a right of first refusal of at least 45-days duration of an offer, made by another, to purchase such franchisor's interest in such premises.

The term "leased marketing premises" is defined in § 2801(9) as "marketing premises owned, leased, or in any way controlled by a franchisor and which the franchisee is authorized or permitted, under the franchise, to employ in connection with the sale, consignment, or distribution of motor fuel."

The district court did not consider this statutory definition in its opinion. The language is quite clear, however, in its application to this case. Gasoline pumps, storage tanks, and dispensers are certainly "employed in connection with the sale, consignment, or distribution of motor fuel." When Congress required a franchisor to make a bona fide offer to sell the leased marketing premises to its franchisee, Congress certainly intended the offer to include more than the real property. It explicitly required that the offer include the property controlled by the franchisor and used by the franchisee to distribute motor fuel. . . .

We thus conclude that the district court erred in granting summary judgment for Amoco on Roberts' claim. We hold as a matter of law that a bona fide offer to sell the service station premises to a franchisee under the PMPA must include the property used in selling and distributing the gasoline, such as the pumps, storage tanks and dispensers.

We remand the case for trial so that Roberts may attempt to prove that Amoco's bad faith offer of sale caused him to vacate the premises out of practical business necessity. Roberts may also introduce evidence of actual damages pursuant to the statute. Amoco, of course, is free to present its defense concerning both whether it coerced Roberts into leaving the Penn Avenue station, and whether Roberts mitigated his damages, if any.

[Judgment reversed and remanded]

QUESTIONS

1. Why did Congress enact the PMPA?
2. What importance did the PMPA definition of *leased marketing premises* have in the court's decision?
3. Did the appellate court accept Amoco's position that it had made a bona fide offer to sell the premises because it had deducted the cost of replacing the equipment from the purchase price offered Roberts?

In order to protect a prospective franchisee from deception, the Federal Trade Commission adopted a rule that requires the franchisor to give a prospective franchisee a disclosure statement ten days before the franchisee signs a contract or pays any money for a franchise. Under the FTC disclosure rule a franchisor must pay a civil penalty up to $10,000 for each violation when it is shown that a "sale" relating to a franchise subject to the FTC rule was made, the franchisor "knew or should have known" of the disclosure rule, and no disclosure statement was given to the "buyer".[4]

(c) THE FRANCHISOR AND THIRD PERSONS. In theory, the franchisor is not liable to a third person dealing with or affected by the franchise holder. This freedom from liability is one of the reasons franchisors grant franchises. If the negligence of the franchisee causes harm to a third person, the franchisor is not liable, because the franchisee is an independent contractor.[5] However, franchisors continue to be subject to lawsuits based upon the wrongful conduct of their franchisees on an apparent authority theory. When plaintiffs have succeeded against franchisors, they have alleged and proven conduct or representations by the franchisor of control over the franchisee, and reliance upon such by the plaintiffs. In a recent case against the Shell Oil Company for damages for an injury caused by an employee of a franchisee, the plaintiff succeeded before the court, relying upon the following policy precedent:

> Public policy may require that an oil company ostensibly holding itself out to the public as the owner and operator of a service station and advertising special care and good service should bear the responsibility for seeing that the station's services are dispensed reasonably and appropriately.[6]

In another case against Shell Oil Company by a customer injured at a Shell gas station, the court rejected the plaintiff's apparent authority argument, noting that the oil company did not own or operate the station, but merely sold petroleum products to the station.[7]

In order to insulate themselves from liability, franchisors often require that individual franchisees take steps to publicly maintain their own individual identity as a business, including informing the public that the franchisee owns, supervises, and controls its own operations. Thus a gasoline service station may post a sign stating that it is "dealer owned and operated"; or a real estate franchisee may list on its business sign the franchise name and the name of the local owner, such as "Century 21, L & K Realty Co."

When the franchisee makes a contract with a third person, the franchisor is not liable on the contract. The franchisee is not the agent of the franchisor and does not have any authority to bind the franchisor by contract.

(1) Actual Control. A franchisor is liable to third persons when the franchisor exercises such actual control over the operations of the franchisee that the latter is not to be regarded as an independent contractor but rather as an employee or agent of the franchisor. Moreover, a franchisor is liable for its own negligence in inspecting and recommending fixtures and equipment to be used by its franchisees.[8]

(2) Product Liability. When the franchise involves the resale of goods manufactured or obtained by the franchisor and supplied to the franchisee and the product causes harm to the franchisee's customer the franchisor will be liable to the customer on theories of product liability.[9]

(d) THE FRANCHISEE AND THIRD PERSONS. When the franchise holder has any contract relationship or contact with a third person, the contract or tort liability of the franchisee is the same as though there were no franchise. The fact that there is a franchise does not add to or subtract from the liability that the franchisee would have in the same situation had there been no franchise. For example, if the franchise is to operate a restaurant, the franchise hold-

---

[4] US v TCI Inc. CCH Trade Cases, 62,058 (1987).
[5] McMullen v Georgia Girl Fashions Inc. 180 Ga App 228, 346 So 2d 748 (1986).
[6] Shadel v Shell Oil Co., CCH Bus Fran Rptr, 8211 at p 14, 623 (NJ Sup Ct 1984).
[7] Albright v Parr, CCH Bus Fran Rptr, 8228 (Ill Ct of App 1984).

[8] Papastathis v Southland Corp. (App) 150 Ariz 279, 723 P2d 97 (1986).
[9] UCC §§ 2-313, 2-314.

er is liable to a customer for breach of an implied warranty of the fitness of the food for human consumption to the same extent as though the franchise holder were running an independent restaurant. If the franchise holder negligently causes harm to a third person, as by running over that person with a truck used in the enterprise, the tort liability of the franchise holder is determined by the principles that would be applicable if no franchise existed. The franchise holder is liable on a contract made in the franchise holder's own name.

§ 46:5   LIMITED PARTNERSHIPS

A common form of modified partnership is the **limited partnership**. This form of partnership is solely a creature of statute — either the Uniform Limited Partnership Act (ULPA),[10] or the Revised Uniform Limited Partnership Act (RULPA), with the RULPA being amended in 1985.[11]

In a limited partnership certain members contribute capital without liability for firm debts beyond the loss of their investment. These members are known as **limited partners**. The partners who manage the business and are personally liable for the firm debts are **general partners**.[12] A limited partnership can be formed by "one or more general partners and one or more limited partners."[13]

(a) FORMATION. Unlike a general part-

nership, this special form can be created only by executing a certificate of limited partnership. Under the ULPA the certificate must set forth the name and business address of each partner specifying which partners are general partners and which are limited partners as well as the essential details of the partnership and the relative rights of the partners. The certificate, when executed, must be recorded locally in the office of the official in charge of public records, such as the Recorder of Deeds, of the county in which the principal place of business of the partnership is located.

Under the 1985 amendments to the RULPA the certificate need only include (1) the limited partnership's name; (2) the address of the partnership's registered office and the name and business address of its agent for service of process; (3) the name and business address of each general partner; (4) its mailing address; and (5) the latest date upon which the limited partnership is to dissolve. The names of the limited partners (the investors) are not required, which allows for the preservation of the confidentiality of the investors names from competitor syndicators. Moreover, new investors may be admitted as limited partners without the significant administrative burden involved in amending the certificate as is required under the ULPA. The RULPA provides for filing of the certificate with the office of the secretary of state as opposed to the local filing under the ULPA.

When there is no filing of the limited partnership certificate, the participants have the status and liability of general partners in a general partnership. However, technical defects in the certificate do not prevent formation of a limited partnership if there has been substantial, good-faith compliance with the filing requirements.[14] Under the 1985 amendments to the RULPA, the partnership agreement, and not the limited partnership certificate, is the operative agreement that defines the

---

[10] The ULPA governs limited partnerships in Alaska, Georgia, Hawaii, Indiana, Kentucky, Maine, Mississippi, New Hampshire, New Mexico, New York, North Carolina, Pennsylvania, Tennessee, Texas, Utah, and Vermont.

[11] The 1976 RULPA has been adopted by Alabama, Arizona, Arkansas, California, Colorado, Connecticut, Idaho, Iowa, Kansas, Maryland, Massachusetts, Michigan, Minnesota, Montana, Nebraska, Nevada, New Jersey, North Dakota, Ohio, Oklahoma, Oregon, Rhode Island, South Carolina, Virginia, Washington, and Wyoming. The RULPA with the 1985 amendments has been adopted by Delaware, the District of Columbia, Florida, Illinois, Minnesota, South Dakota, West Virginia, and Wisconsin. Louisiana has not enacted either the ULPA or RULPA.

[12] Brooke v Mt. Hood Meadows Ltd. 81 Or App 387, 725 P2d 925 (1986).

[13] ULPA § 1; RULPA § 101(7).

[14] ULPA § 2(2); RULPA § 201(b).

rights and duties of partners in a limited partnership.

(b) CAPITAL CONTRIBUTIONS. Under the ULPA the limited partner contributes cash or property, but not services. However, under the RULPA, the limited partner may contribute services.

(c) FIRM NAME. With certain exceptions, the limited partner's name cannot appear in the firm name. If improper use is made of the limited partner's name, giving the public the impression that the limited partner is an active partner, the limited partner loses the protection of limited liability and becomes liable without limit as a general partner. Under the Revised Act, the words

limited partnership must appear without abbreviation in the firm name.

(d) MANAGEMENT AND CONTROL OF THE FIRM. The general partners manage the business and are personally liable for firm debts. Limited partners (the investors) have the right to a share of the profits and a return of capital upon dissolution and have limited liability. This limited liability may be lost, however, should they participate in the control of the business.

In the *Holzman* case, the court was faced with the question of whether two limited partners had taken part in the control of the partnership business so as to be held liable for partnership debts as general partners.

HOLZMAN V DE ESCAMILLA
86 Cal App 2d 858, 195 P2d 833 (1948)

Hacienda Farms, Limited, was organized as a limited partnership with Ricardo de Escamilla as the general partner and James L. Russell and H. W. Andrews as limited partners. The partnership raised vegetables and truck crops that were marketed principally through a produce concern controlled by Mr. Andrews. All three individuals decided which crops were to be planted. The general partner had no power to withdraw money from the partnership's two bank accounts without the signature of one of the limited partners. After operating for some seven and one-half months under these procedures, the limited partners requested the general partner to resign as farm manager, which he did. Six weeks later the partnership went into bankruptcy. Laurance Holzman, as trustee in bankruptcy, brought an action against Russell and Andrews, claiming that they had become liable to the creditors of the partnership as general partners because they had taken part in the control of the partnership business. From a judgment against them, Russell and Andrews appealed.

MARKS, J. . . . De Escamilla was raising beans on farm lands near Escondido at the time the partnership was formed. The partnership continued raising vegetable and truck crops which were marketed principally through a produce concern controlled by Andrews.

The record shows the following testimony of de Escamilla:

A. We put in some tomatoes.
Q. Did you have a conversation or conversations with Mr. Andrews or Mr. Russell before planting the tomatoes?
A. We always conferred and agreed as to what crops we would put in. . . .
Q. Who determined that it was advisable to plant watermelons?
A. Mr. Andrews. . . .

Q. Who determined that string beans should be planted?

A. All of us. There was never any planting done — except the first crop that was put into the partnership as an asset by myself, there was never any crop that was planted or contemplated in planting that wasn't thoroughly discussed and agreed upon by the three of us; particularly Andrews and myself.

De Escamilla further testified that Russell and Andrews came to the farms about twice a week and consulted about the crops to be planted. He did not want to plant peppers or egg plant because, as he said, "I don't like that country for peppers or egg plant; no, sir," but he was overruled and those crops were planted. The same is true of the watermelons.

Shortly before October 15, 1943, Andrews and Russell requested de Escamilla to resign as manager, which he did, and Harry Miller was appointed in his place.

Hacienda Farms, Limited, maintained two bank accounts, one in a San Diego bank and another in an Escondido bank. It was provided that checks could be drawn on the signatures of any two of the three partners. It is stated in plaintiff's brief, without any contradiction (the checks are not before us) that money was withdrawn on twenty checks signed by Russell and Andrews and that all other checks except three bore the signatures of de Escamilla, the general partner, and one of the other defendants. The general partner had no power to withdraw money without the signature of one of the limited partners.

Section 2483 of the Civil Code provides as follows:

A limited partner shall not become liable as a general partner, unless, in addition to the exercise of his rights and powers as a limited partner, he takes part in the control of the business.

The foregoing illustrations sufficiently show that Russell and Andrews both took "part in the control of the business." The manner of withdrawing money from the bank accounts is particularly illuminating. The two men had absolute power to withdraw all the partnership funds in the banks without the knowledge or consent of the general partner. Either Russell or Andrews could take control of the business from de Escamilla by refusing to sign checks for bills contracted by him and thus limit his activities in the management of the business. They required him to resign as manager and selected his successor. They were active in dictating the crops to be planted, some of them against the wish of Escamilla. This clearly shows they took part in the control of the business of the partnership and thus became liable as general partners.

[Judgment affirmed]

QUESTIONS

1. State the rule of law applied by the court.
2. Did the manner in which money was withdrawn from the partnership bank accounts indicate that the limited partners took part in the control of the partnership business?
3. Did the partnership procedures for selection of which crops were to be planted prove that the limited partners took part in the control of the partnership business?

The RULPA lists a number of "safe harbor" activities in which limited partners may engage without losing their protection from liability. These activities include:

(1) being a contractor for or an agent or employee of the limited partnership or of a general partner;
(2) consulting with and advising a general partner regarding the partnership business;
(3) acting as a surety for the limited partnership; and
(4) voting on partnership matters such as dissolution and winding up the limited partnership or the removal of a general partner.

(e) RIGHT TO SUE. A limited partner may bring an action on behalf of the limited partnership against outsiders for economic injury to the firm, when the general partners refuse to do so. Also, the limited partners may sue the general partners to protect the limited partners' interests.

(f) DISSOLUTION. The dissolution and winding up of limited partnerships is governed by the same principles applicable to general partnerships, as will be discussed in Part B of Chapter 47.

	LIMITED PARTNERSHIP	GENERAL PARTNERSHIP
CREATION:	FILING A CERTIFICATE OF LIMITED PARTNERSHIP WITH APPROPRIATE STATE OFFICE	NO FORMALITY REQUIRED
LIABILITY:	GENERAL PARTNERS: UNLIMITED LIABILITY FOR FIRM DEBTS LIMITED PARTNERS: NO LIABILITY BEYOND LOSS OF INVESTMENT	UNLIMITED PERSONAL LIABILITY FOR EACH PARTNER
MANAGEMENT:	GENERAL PARTNERS ONLY	ALL PARTNERS ACCORDING TO THEIR PARTNERSHIP AGREEMENT OR UNIFORM PARTNERSHIP ACT (UPA)
DISSOLUTION:	IN MANY RESPECTS THE ULPA AND RULPA FOLLOW THE GENERAL PATTERN OF UPA	AS SET FORTH IN PARTNERSHIP AGREEMENT OR THE UPA

FIGURE 46-1
COMPARISON OF LIMITED PARTNERSHIP AND
GENERAL PARTNERSHIP

§ 46:6   JOINT VENTURES

A **joint venture**, or joint adventure, is a relationship in which two or more persons combine their labor or property for a single business undertaking and share profits and losses equally, or as otherwise agreed. When several contractors pool all their assets in order to construct one tunnel, the relationship is a joint venture.

A joint venture is similar in many respects to a partnership. It differs primarily in that the joint venture typically relates to the pursuit of a single enterprise or transaction, although its accomplishment may require several years, while a partnership is generally a continuing business or activity. The foregoing statement is not an exact definition because a partnership may be expressly created for a single transaction. Because this distinction is so insubstantial, many courts hold that joint ventures are subject to the same principles of law as partnerships.[15] Thus, the duties owed by the joint venturers to each other are the same as those partners owe to each other. For example, when the joint venturers agree to acquire and develop a certain tract of land but some of the venturers secretly purchase the land in their own names, the other joint venturers are entitled to damages for this breach of the duty of loyalty.

It is essential that there be a community of interest or purpose and that each co-adventurer have an equal right to control the operations or activities of the undertaking.[16] The actual control of the operations may be entrusted to one of the joint venturers. Thus, the fact that one joint adventurer is placed in control of the farming and livestock operations of the undertaking and appears to be the owner of the land does not destroy the joint adventure relationship.

(a) DURATION OF JOINT VENTURE. When a joint venture agreement states the time for which the venture is to last, such specification will be given effect. In the absence of a fixed duration provision, a joint venture is ordinarily terminable at the will of any participant, except that when the joint venture clearly relates to a particular transaction, such as the construction of a specified bridge, the joint venture ordinarily lasts until the particular transaction or project is completed or becomes impossible to complete.

The term *joint venture* is descriptive of a relationship rather than of a structure or organization. Thus, two joint venturers may organize a corporation for the purpose of carrying out their joint venture of constructing an apartment building. The relationship between the two is a joint venture even though the organization employed is a corporation.

(b) LIABILITY TO THIRD PERSONS. The conclusion that persons are joint venturers is important when a suit is brought by or against a third person for personal injuries or property damage. If there is a joint venture, the fault or negligence of one venturer will be imputed to the other venturer.[17]

§ 46:7   UNINCORPORATED ASSOCIATIONS

An **unincorporated association** is a combination of two or more persons for the furtherance of a common nonprofit purpose. No particular form of organization is required, and any conduct or agreement indicating an attempt to associate or work together for a common purpose is sufficient. Social clubs, fraternal associations, sororities, and political parties are common examples of unincorporated associations.

The authority of an unincorporated association over its members is governed by ordinary principles of contract law, and an association cannot expel a member for a ground that is not expressly authorized by

---

[15] Burruss v Green Auction & Realty Co. Inc. 228 Va 6, 319 SE2d 725 (1984).

[16] Milberg Factors Inc. v Hurwitz-Nordlight Joint Venture (Tex Civ App) 676 SW2d 613 (1984).

[17] Kim v Chamberlain (Ala App) 504 So 2d 1213 (1987).

the contract between the association and the member.[18]

Except when otherwise provided by statute, an unincorporated association does not have any legal existence apart from the members who compose it. Thus, an unincorporated association cannot sue or be sued in its own name.

Generally, the members of an unincorporated association are not liable for the

---

[18] Cunningham v Independent Soap & Chemical Workers, 207 Kan 812, 486 P2d 1316 (1971).

debts or liabilities of the association by the mere fact that they are members. It is generally required to show that they authorized or ratified the act in question. If either authorization or ratification by a particular member can be shown, that member has unlimited liability for the act.

In the *Perry* case the court, in order to determine liability for an individual's injury at a social event, was faced with the problem of determining whether each member of a voluntary association actively took part in planning the event.

LIBBY V PERRY
(Me) 311 A2d 527 (1973)

National Guard units based at the Augusta State Armory held an annual New Year's Eve dance. The dance was run and funds were handled by an Armory Committee that was composed of officers from the various guard units at the Armory. Willard Perry was a member of the Armory Committee. William Libby was a paying guest at the dance. Upon leaving, Libby fell on ice in the parking lot. He sued Perry and the other members of the Armory Committee. The evidence showed that every member of the committee, except Turner, had taken some part in planning or running the dance. Judgment was entered in favor of Libby against all defendants, who then appealed.

DUFRESNE, C. J. . . . The Armory Committee, [is] a voluntary unincorporated association and a nonentity at common law. . . .

Mr. Perry testified it was his opinion that on becoming an officer he automatically became a member of the Armory Committee. In the absence of any evidence that the official duties of an officer in the National Guard required participation in an association organized to conduct social activities, albeit for the benefit of the Guard, acceptance of membership in such association must be viewed as voluntary on the part of the accepting member, subjecting him to whatever liability the law applicable to voluntary unincorporated associations may impose.

A voluntary unincorporated association, formed to accomplish a common purpose, is duty bound to use the same care to avoid injury to others as natural persons are individually, but mere membership in the associate body does not make all the members liable for any and all unlawful or negligent acts of their associates.

In the case of a voluntary association such as the Armory Committee, dedicated by the mandate of its bylaws to promote social services for the immediate benefit of its members and the ultimate interest of the National Guard units located at the Augusta Armory, while at the same time enhancing good public relations between the Guard and the area residents through their sponsored social events, individual members of the association do not, merely by virtue of their membership in such association, subject themselves to liability for injuries sustained as a result of the negligent conduct of their associates or their agents in the running of the social event sponsored by the association. Liability attaches only to those members of the association who are shown to have actively participated in the affair resulting in plaintiff's injuries.

In the instant case, the evidence was sufficient to support the factual inference that the Armory Committee had assumed control of the premises . . . . The defect which caused the plaintiff's fall and consequential injuries was shown to have existed for a sufficient period of time to have permitted protective action such as salting and sanding and that the members of the Armory Committee or their agents, in charge of the affair, in the exercise of reasonable care should have known of, or discovered, the dangerous condition caused by the frozen ruts in the immediate approaches to the steps leading to the armory building where the dance was being held. The minutes of the meeting of the Committee in April 1966, indicating a unanimous vote of the attending members setting the charge of $2.00 per person for the New Year's Eve ball, establishes not only their presence at the meeting, but also, by justifiable inference, an active participation in the planned event by the defendants Pillsbury, Nichols, Bryant, Laflin, Perry, Fenderson, Quinn, Colford and Weymouth. The defendants Madore and Tondreau were shown to have approved the affair by the evidentiary records showing that they respectively held the office of treasurer during the period of planning and staging of the dance. The jury could have inferred active participation of the other defendants Musk, Lasso, Jacques, Hayes, Gagnon, Morang, Liscomb, Richards, and Drapeau, by reason of their attendance record immediately prior to the holding of the event. Defendant Storr's direct involvement was evidenced by the fact that he applied for the use of the Armory. The record, on the other hand, is silent respecting defendant Turner's participation in, or attendance at, the meeting of the Committee in April, 1966 and indicates that he was absent from the October, November, and December, 1966 meetings which preceded the dance. Under such circumstances, it was error as a matter of law for the jury to find the defendant Turner responsible to the plaintiff with the other defendants on the mere evidence that he was a member of the Armory committee. All the other defendants actively participated, aided, and abetted in the affair and are responsible to the plaintiff for the wrongful acts of omission of their associates or their agents in carrying out the social event duly authorized by the association. . . .

In the instant case, all the actively participating defendant members of the Armory Committee owed the plaintiff . . . the positive duty of exercising through their associates or agents in charge of the dance reasonable care to provide him with walkways or areaways reasonably safe from unreasonable risk of harm in the light of the totality of the existing circumstances. . . .

[Judgment reversed as to Turner but sustained as to other defendants]

QUESTIONS

1. Did Willard Perry's testimony that he thought upon becoming an officer he automatically became a member of the Armory Committee have any importance?

2. Does mere membership in a voluntary, unincorporated association make all members liable for the negligent conduct of their associates in the running of a social event sponsored by the association?

3. Was the judgment reversed as to Turner? Why or why not?

§ 46:8 COOPERATIVES

A **cooperative** consists of a group of two or more independent persons or enterprises that cooperate with respect to a common objective or function. Thus, farmers may pool their farm products and sell them as a group. Consumers may likewise pool their orders and purchase goods in bulk.

(a) INCORPORATED COOPERATIVES. Statutes commonly provide for the special incorporation of cooperative enterprises. Such statutes often provide that any excess of payments over cost of operation shall be refunded to each participant member in direct proportion to the volume of business that the member has done with the cooperative. This arrangement contrasts with the payment of a dividend by an ordinary business corporation in which the payment of dividends is proportional to the number of shares held by the shareholder and is unrelated to the extent of the shareholder's business activities with the enterprise.

(b) ANTITRUST LAW EXEMPTION. As the agreement by the members of sellers' cooperatives that all products shall be sold at a common price is an agreement to fix prices, the sellers' cooperative is basically an agreement in restraint of trade and a violation of antitrust laws. The Capper-Volstead Act of 1922 expressly exempts normal selling activities of farmers' and dairy farmers' cooperatives from the operation of the federal Sherman Antitrust Act as long as the cooperatives do not conspire with outsiders to fix prices.

SUMMARY

The three principal forms of business organizations are sole proprietorships, partnerships, and corporations. An individual proprietorship is a form of business organization in which one person owns the business, controls all decisions, receives all profits, and has unlimited liability for all obligations, liabilities, and losses, if any. A partnership involves the pooling of capital resources and talents of two or more persons with the goal of making a profit; the partners are subject to unlimited personal liability. A business corporation exists to make a profit. It is created by government grant, and its shareholders elect a board of directors who are responsible to manage the business. A shareholder's liability is limited to the capital the shareholder invested in the business. The corporation continues without regard to the death of shareholders or the transfer of stock by them.

The selection of the form of organization is often determined by the nature of the business, tax considerations, the financial risk involved and the importance of limited liability, and the extent of control of management desired.

A franchise is an agreement or a contract by which the owner of a trademark, trade name, or copyright licenses others to use such mark or copyright in the selling of goods or services. In order to protect against fraud, the FTC requires that franchisors provide prospective franchisees with a disclosure statement ten days prior to any transaction. The Automobile Dealers' Franchise Act and the Petroleum Marketing Products Act are national laws that provide covered franchisees with protection from bad faith terminations. State laws also provide protection to franchisees in a wide range of businesses. In theory the franchisor is not liable in any way to third persons dealing with the franchisee. However, litigation against franchisors for the torts of franchisees is common, with plaintiffs often alleging apparent authority. These suits are successful only if the plaintiffs can demonstrate actual or apparent control over the operations of the franchisee by the franchisor.

A limited partnership consists of one or more limited partners, who contribute cash, property, or services without liability for losses beyond their investment, and one or more general partners, who manage the business and have unlimited personal liability. Limited partnerships are created by statute. A certificate and public filing are required.

A joint venture exists when two or more persons combine their labor or property for a single business undertaking and share profits and losses as agreed. An unincorporated association is a combination of two or more persons for the pursuit of a common, nonprofit purpose.

A cooperative consists of two or more persons or enterprises, such as farmers, who cooperate with respect to a common objective, such as the distribution of farm products.

QUESTIONS AND CASE PROBLEMS

1. What social forces are affected by the federal Automobile Dealers' Franchise Act?
2. Golden Spike Little League was an unincorporated association of persons who joined together to promote a little league baseball team in Ogden, Utah. They sent one of their members to arrange for credit at Smith & Edwards, a local sporting goods store. After obtaining credit, various members went to the store and picked up and signed for different items of baseball equipment and uniforms at a total cost of $3,900. When Mr. Smith, the store owner, requested payment, the members arranged a fund-raising activity that produced only $149. Smith sued the Golden Spike Little League as an entity and the members who had picked up and signed for the equipment individually. The individual defendants denied that they had any personal liability, contending that only the Golden Spike Little League could be held responsible. Decide. [Smith & Edwards v Golden Spike Little League (Utah) 577 P2d 132]
3. When is a franchisor held liable to a third person dealing with or affected by the franchisee?
4. Elizabeth, Josephine, and Florence entered

into an agreement to purchase a tract of land, build houses on it, sell the houses, and then divide the net profit. What kind of business organization was intended?
5. Jerome, Sheila, Gary, and Ella agreed to purchase a tract of land and make it available for use as a free playground for neighborhood children. They called the enterprise the Meadowbrook Playground. One of the playground swings was improperly hung by Jerome and Gary, and a child was injured. Suit was brought against the Meadowbrook Playground. Can damages be recovered?
6. Compare and contrast a limited partnership and a general partnership with respect to (a) formality of creation, and (b) dissolution and winding up.
7. Compare and contrast a franchise and a contract.
8. Lauter and Domenick form a partnership. They find that they need more money. They induce Gerard to invest $50,000. He agrees to do so provided he is a limited partner. Lauter and Domenick agree to this, and Gerard contributes $50,000. Is Gerard a limited partner?
9. Professor Kerry Rhodes invented a filter for use in microwave telecommunications. She

desired to participate in the earnings that she anticipated would result from the manufacture and sale of her invention. Hal Jones, president of a venture capital firm, advised Rhodes of the tax advantages of a limited partnership, including the advantage of no liability for the firm's debts beyond the loss of her investment should the venture fail. A limited partnership was created in accordance with state law, and the certificate was properly filed. Henry Nickerson was named as the general partner, and Rhodes and Jones, both of whom contributed cash, were named as the limited partners in the certificate. Initially Rhodes and Jones advised Nickerson "to run all final employment candidates by us for a look see;" and only one candidate was rejected by them. When it was established at a weekly luncheon meeting of the three individuals that start-up expenses were greatly exceeding what had been anticipated, it was agreed that as a control feature all firm checks over $1,000 would require two signatures, one being Nickerson's and the other being that of either Rhodes or Jones. Later Rhodes found out at a professional meeting that a competitor had developed a new, lightweight filter with technical advantages superior to Rhodes' filter. She and Jones agreed to notify Nickerson to halt production and to lay off employees until Rhodes could improve the filter. The firm ran out of funds and could not pay its suppliers. General Suppliers Corp. sued Nickerson, Rhodes, and Jones as general partners for the money owed it for supplies delivered to the firm. Rhodes and Jones contend that as limited partners they are not liable beyond their investment. Decide.

10. Goodward, a newly hired newspaper reporter for the Cape Cod News, learned that the local cranberry growers had made an agreement under which they pooled their cranberry crops each year and sold the crops at what they determined to be a fair price. Goodward believes that such an agreement is in restraint of trade and a violation of the antitrust laws. Is he correct?

11. Food Caterers, Inc., of East Hartford, Connecticut, obtained a franchise from Chicken Delight, Inc., to use that name at its store and agreed to the product standards and controls specified by the franchisor. The franchise contract required the franchisee to maintain a free delivery service in order to deliver hot, freshly prepared food to customers. The franchisee used a delivery truck that bore no sign or name. Its employee Carfiro drove the truck in making a delivery of food. He negligently struck and killed McLaughlin. The victim's estate sued Chicken Delight on the theory that Carfiro was its agent because he was doing the work that Chicken Delight required to be done and that benefited Chicken Delight. Was Carfiro the agent of Chicken Delight? [McLaughlin's Estate v Chicken Delight, Inc. 164 Conn 317, 321 A2d 456]

12. A limited partnership owned and operated a marina under the name of West River Marina, Ltd. Radack was the general partner. McCully and others were limited partners. The partnership did not pay its debts and a foreclosure action was brought against it. McCully and other limited partners petitioned the court for permission to intervene in the foreclosure action on the theory that the action was a sham planned by Radack and others as a way of wiping out the interests of the limited partners and thus acquiring the property for themselves. Radack and the others objected to the intervention on the ground that limited partners have no voice in the management of a limited partnership and, therefore, could not take part in litigation. Should the intervention be allowed? [McCully v Radack, 27 Md App 350, 340 A2d 374]

13. Brenner was in the scrap iron business. Almost daily Plitt lent Brenner money with which to purchase scrap iron. The agreement of the parties was that when the scrap was sold, Plitt would be repaid and would receive an additional sum as compensation for making the loan. The loans were to be repaid in any case, without regard to whether Brenner made a profit. A dispute arose as to the relationship between the two men. Plitt claimed that it was a joint venture. Decide. [Brenner v Plitt, 182 Md 348, 34 A2d 853]

14. Donald Salisbury, William Roberts and others purchased property from Laurel Chapman, a partner of Chapman Realty, a franchisee of Realty World, Inc. The purchasers made payments directly to Laurel Chapman at the Realty World office, and

Chapman was supposed to make payments on the property's mortgage. Chapman, however, did not make the payments and absconded with the funds. Salisbury and Roberts sued the franchisor, Realty World, contending that Realty World was liable for the wrongful acts of the apparent agent, Chapman. Realty World and Chapman Realty are parties to a franchise agreement which states that the parties are franchisor/franchisee. The agreement contains a clause that required Chapman to prominently display a certificate in the office setting forth Chapman's status as an independent franchisee. Chapman displayed such a sign, but the plaintiffs do not recall seeing it. Chapman Realty hires, supervises, and sets the compensation for all of its employees. The plaintiffs point out that Chapman Realty used the service mark "Realty World" on its signs both outside and inside its offices. They point out that a Realty World manual sets forth the general standards by which franchisees must run their businesses and that such is clear control over the franchise.

They contend that, all things considered, Realty World held out Chapman Realty as having authority to bind Realty World. Realty World disagrees, stating both are independent businesses. Decide. [Salisbury v Chapman and Realty World, Inc. 124 Ill App 3d 1057, 65 NE2d 127]

15. H.C. Blackwell Co. held a franchise from the Kenworth Truck Co. to sell its trucks. After 12 years the franchise was nearing expiration. Kenworth notified Blackwell that the franchise would not be renewed unless Blackwell sold more trucks and improved its building and bookkeeping systems within the next 90 days. Blackwell spent $90,000 in attempting to meet the demands of Kenworth, but could not do so because a year was required to make the specified changes. Kenworth refused to renew the franchise. Blackwell sued Kenworth for damages under the Federal Automobile Dealers Franchise Act. Blackwell claimed that Kenworth had refused to renew in bad faith. Decide. [Blackwell v Kenworth Truck Co. (CA5 Ala) 620 F2d 104]

47

CREATION AND TERMINATION OF PARTNERSHIPS

Modern partnership law shows traces of Roman law, the law merchant, and the common law of England. A codification of partnership law is found in the Uniform Partnership Act (UPA), which has been adopted by forty-nine states.[1]

Partnerships are created by agreement; however, the agreements are often infor-mal and may be unwritten. The UPA contains a set of rules on the creation of partnerships; these rules deal with the wide range of issues that may develop from such an informal formation process.

Dissolution of a partnership may result from the acts of the partners; or may be by operation of law, as in the death of a partner; or may be by court decree, when the dissension among the partners is so serious that continuation of the business is impracticable.

---

[1] The UPA has been adopted in all states except Louisiana; and it is in force in the District of Columbia, Guam, and the Virgin Islands.

A.   NATURE AND
CREATION

A discussion of the creation of partnerships must be prefaced with a discussion of the nature of the partnership relation, including the characteristics of a partnership, the various classifications of partnerships and partners, and the nature of partnership property.

§ 47:1   DEFINITION

A **partnership** is a relationship created by the voluntary "association of two or more persons to carry on as co-owners a business for profit."[2] The persons so associated are called **partners**. A partner is the agent of the partnership and of each partner with respect to partnership matters. A partner, however, is not an employee of the partnership even when doing work that would ordinarily be done by an employee.

A partnership has many characteristics in common with a marriage; but, as the *Chocknok* decision demonstrates, a husband and wife are not necessarily partners.

[2]   Uniform Partnership Act, § 6(1); Miller v City Bank and Trust Co., 82 Mich App 120, 266 NW2d 687 (1978).

CHOCKNOK V COMMISSION
(Alaska) 696 P2d 669 (1985)

Under the Alaska Limited Entry Act the Commercial Fisheries Entry Commission (commission) issues limited entry permits for the Bristol Bay drift gill net fishery. Because of the limited number of fish and the large number of persons desiring to harvest those fish, the commission adopted regulations to rank entry permit applications on a point system. This system is based upon special "hardship standards," including the degree of economic dependence upon the fishery. Only those obtaining 17 points are granted a license, and all others are refused. It was held in a prior court decision that an applicant who had not held a gear license in his or her own name in 1971 or 1972, but who had fished as a business partner with a license holder, was entitled to up to 10 points. Katherine Chocknok and Elina Andrew claimed that they were entitled to points because they fished as business partners with their husbands during the years in question. The commission disagreed. These points, coupled with other points to which both were admittedly entitled, would have been sufficient to enable each to receive a permit. The superior court affirmed the commission's decision that Chocknok and Andrew did not qualify as partners, and the case was appealed.

MATTHEWS, J. . . . We turn now to the question of what factors validly can be considered to determine the existence of a business partnership between married persons. Alaska partnership law is governed by the Uniform Partnership Act, adopted by the Alaska legislature in AS 32.05. The U.P.A. defines a partnership as "an *association* of two or more persons to carry on as *co-owners* a *business* for *profit*." Contained in this definition are the key elements of a partnership.

The associational element requires the existence of an agreement to combine the spouses' property, money, effects, skill, and knowledge to carry out a business enterprise. Because of the mutual trust that exists in the typical marriage, this agreement might not be formalized and can be implied from the facts and circumstances of the case where the partnership is formed after the marriage. *Stephens v. Stephens,* 213 S.C. 525, 50 S.E.2d 577, 579 (1948) (no written agreement between husband and wife, but their actions evinced a contract "to place their money, effects, labor and skill or some or all of them in lawful commerce of business").

Co-ownership of the business has been described as the most important characteristics of a partnership. One aspect of co-ownership is the existence of a right in each partner to exercise authority in the management of the enterprise. "Although each venturer need not exercise actual physical control of the instrumentalities used in the enterprise each must have a legal right to some voice in the direction and control of the enterprise." Again, this power can be implied from the facts where the business co-exists with marriage. In this regard, the nature of the spouse's participation in the day to day operation and the long range planning of the business can be considered.

Profit-sharing is another component of the co-ownership requirement. Ordinarily, profit-sharing is prima facie evidence of a partnership, but some degree of profit-sharing is common in marriages whether or not a business partnership exists. Thus, it may be more appropriate for the Commission to focus on the actual ownership of the business property as evidence of partnership.

The U.P.A. provides that "[j]oint tenancy, tenancy in common, tenancy by the entireties, joint property, common property, or part ownership does not of itself establish a partnership, whether or not the co-owners share any profits made by the use of the property." This leads to the third element of the partnership definition: the partners must be in business. Co-ownership becomes business when a certain degree of activity is carried on or contemplated. Since commercial fishing is by definition a business activity, this criterion ordinarily will be met. But the extent of the spouse's participation in the fishing business also can be helpful in determining whether she is participating as a business partner. A spouse who works at another job or who keeps house ashore certainly is furthering the interests of the marriage, but is only indirectly putting her skill and efforts into the *fishing* partnership. Such a spouse fairly may be said not to be engaged in a business partnership; in terms of the statutory hardship standards she is less dependent on operating gear for her income than the fishing spouse.

We recognize that determinations of partnership between spouses will depend on the particular facts of each case. There is no single or conclusive test for a partnership that will suffice in every situation. The Commission must consider the traditional partnership factors and apply them evenhandedly to all applicants, making sure that the criteria used are not unjustly discriminatory in intent or impact.

[Judgment reversed and case remanded]

QUESTIONS

1. Is the UPA definition of a partnership applicable in Alaska?
2. Assess the validity of this statement: "A spouse who effectively manages a

home is furthering the interests of the family's business and is legally entitled to be considered a partner."
3. What elements are required for the existence of a partnership between a
husband and wife?

§ 47:2   CHARACTERISTICS OF A PARTNERSHIP

A partnership can be described in terms of
its characteristics:

(a) A partnership is a voluntary consensual relationship; it is not imposed by
law. Because of the intimate and confidential nature of the partnership relation, courts do not attempt to thrust a
partner upon anyone.
(b) A partnership usually involves partners' contributions of capital, services,
or a combination of these.
(c) The partners are associated as co-
owners and principals to transact the
business of the firm.
(d) A partnership is organized for the profit of its members. If profit is not its object, the group will commonly be an
unincorporated association.

The trend of the law is to treat a partnership as a separate legal person, although
historically and technically it is merely a
group of individuals with each partner being the owner of a fractional interest in the
common enterprise.[3] The Uniform Partnership Act does not make the partnership a
separate entity, and therefore, suit cannot
be brought by the firm in its name in the
absence of a special statute or procedural
rule so providing. Some courts regard a
partnership as distinct from the individual
partners, so that a partnership cannot
claim the benefit of a personal immunity
possessed by an individual partner.

As a partnership is based upon the
agreement of the parties, the characteris-

tics and attributes of the partnership relationship are initially a matter of the application of general principles of contract law,
to which the principles of partnership are
added.

§ 47:3   PURPOSES OF A PARTNERSHIP

A partnership, whether it relates to the
conduct of a business or a profession, may
be formed for any lawful purpose. A partnership cannot be formed to carry out immoral or illegal acts, or acts that are contrary to public policy.

§ 47:4   CLASSIFICATION OF PARTNERSHIPS

Ordinary partnerships are classified as
general and special partnerships, and as
trading and nontrading partnerships. The
ordinary partnership is distinguished from
the statutory limited partnership.[4]

(a) GENERAL AND SPECIAL PARTNERSHIPS.
A **general partnership** is created for the
general conduct of a particular kind of
business, such as a hardware business or a
manufacturing business. A **special partnership** is formed for a single transaction,
such as the purchase and resale of a certain
building.

(b) TRADING AND NONTRADING PART-
NERSHIPS. A **trading partnership** is organized for the purpose of buying and selling,
such as a firm engaged in the retail grocery
business. A **nontrading partnership** is one
organized for a purpose other than engag-

---

[3]   Decker Coal Co. v Commonwealth Edison Co.
(Mont) 714 P2d 155 (1986).

[4]   See Chapter 46.

ing in commerce, such as the practice of law or medicine.

§ 47:5 FIRM NAME

In the absence of a statutory requirement, a partnership need not have a firm name, although it is customary to have one. The partners may, as a general rule, adopt any firm name they desire. They may use a fictitious name or even the name of a stranger. There are, however, certain limitations upon the adoption of a firm name:

(a) The name cannot be the same as or be deceptively similar to the name of another firm for the purpose of attracting its patrons.
(b) Some states prohibit the use of the words "and company" unless they indicate an additional partner.
(c) Most states require the registration of a fictitious partnership name. For example, Ken and Steve Swain transact business under a partnership name *The Berkshire Dairy Farm*. Since such a name does not reveal the names of the partners, a certificate stating the names and addresses of the partners must be filed at the public office designated by state law, usually a city or town clerk's office.

§ 47:6 CLASSIFICATION OF PARTNERS

Partners may be general, nominal, silent, secret, or dormant.

(a) **General partners** are those who publicly and actively engage in the transaction of firm business.
(b) **Nominal partners** hold themselves out as partners or permit others to hold them out as such. They are not in fact partners, but in some instances they may be held liable as partners.
(c) **Silent partners** are those who, although they may be known to the public as partners, take no active part in the business.

(d) **Secret partners** are those who take an active part in the management of the firm but who are not known to the public as partners.
(e) **Dormant partners** are ones who take no active part in transacting the business and who remain unknown to the public.

§ 47:7 WHO MAY BE PARTNERS

In the absence of statutory provisions to the contrary, persons who are competent to contract may form a partnership. A minor may become a partner, but may avoid the contract of partnership and withdraw.

In general, the capacity of an insane person to be a partner is similar to that of a minor, except that an adjudication of insanity usually makes subsequent agreements void rather than merely voidable. An enemy alien may not be a partner, but other aliens may enter into partnerships. A corporation, unless expressly authorized by statute or its certificate of incorporation, may not act as a partner. The modern statutory trend, however, is to permit corporations to become partners.

§ 47:8 CREATION OF PARTNERSHIP

A partnership is a voluntary association, and it exists because the parties agree to be in partnership.[5] If there is no agreement, there is no partnership. If the parties agree that the legal relationship between them shall be such that they in fact operate a business for profit as co-owners, a partnership is created even though the parties may not have labeled their new relationship a partnership. The law is concerned with the substance of what is done rather than the name. Conversely, a partnership does not arise if the parties do not agree to the elements of a partnership, even though they call it a partnership.

The manner in which an enterprise is

---

5 Shain Investment Co., Inc. v Cohen, 15 Mass App 4, 443 NE2d 126 (1982).

described in a tax return or an application for a license is significant in determining whether it is a partnership as against a person making the return or the application.[6] The mere fact that the enterprise is described as a partnership is not controlling or binding, however, as to a person named as a partner in the return or in the application if that person did not know of its preparation, did not sign it, and did not know what it said. When the parties are in fact employer and employee, there is no partnership even though the employer files a partnership form of income tax return.

§ 47:9 PARTNERSHIP AGREEMENT

As a general rule, partnership agreements need not be in writing. A partnership agreement must be in writing, however, if it is within the provision of the statute of frauds that a contract that cannot be performed within one year must be in writing. In some situations the agreement may come under the provision of the statute that requires a transfer of interest in land to be in writing. Generally, however, the agreement need not be written solely because the partnership is formed to engage in the business of buying and selling real estate.

Even when unnecessary, it is always desirable to have the partnership agreement in writing to avoid subsequent controversies as to respective rights and duties. The formal document that is prepared to evidence the contract of the parties is termed a **partnership agreement, articles of partnership,** or **articles of copartnership.** The partnership agreement will govern the partnership during its existence and may also contain provisions relating to dissolution.[7] When matters arise that are not covered by the agreement, the rights of the parties will be determined by statute or court decision.

§ 47:10 DETERMINING EXISTENCE OF PARTNERSHIP

Whether a partnership exists is basically a matter of proving the intention of the parties.

As in the case of agency, the burden of proving the existence of a partnership is on the person who claims that one exists.

When the parties have not clearly indicated the nature of their relationship, the law has developed the following guidelines to aid in determining whether the parties have created a partnership:

(a) CONTROL. The presence or absence of control of a business enterprise is significant in determining whether there is a partnership and whether a particular person is a partner.

(b) SHARING PROFITS AND LOSSES. The fact that the parties share profits and losses is strong evidence of a partnership.[8]

(c) SHARING PROFITS. An agreement that does not provide for sharing losses but does provide for sharing profits is evidence that the parties are partners, as it is assumed that they will also share losses. Sharing profits is prima facie evidence of a partnership; but a partnership is not to be inferred when profits are received in payment of (1) a debt, (2) wages, (3) rent, (4) an annuity to a deceased partner's surviving spouse or representative, (5) interest, or (6) payment for the goodwill of the business. The fact that one doctor receives one-half of the net income does not establish that doctor as a partner of another doctor when the former was guaranteed a minimum annual amount and when the federal income tax and social security contributions were deducted from the payments to him or her, thus indicating that the relationship was employer and employee.[9] If there is no evidence of the reason for receiving the profits, a partnership of the parties involved exists.

---

[6]   Shinn v Vaughn, 83 Or App 251, 730 P2d 1290 (1986).
[7]   Bohn v Bohn Implement Co. (ND) 325 NW2d 281 (1982).

[8]   Boyarsky v Froccaro, 131 App Div 2d 710, 516 NYS2d 775 (1987).
[9]   UPA § 7(4).

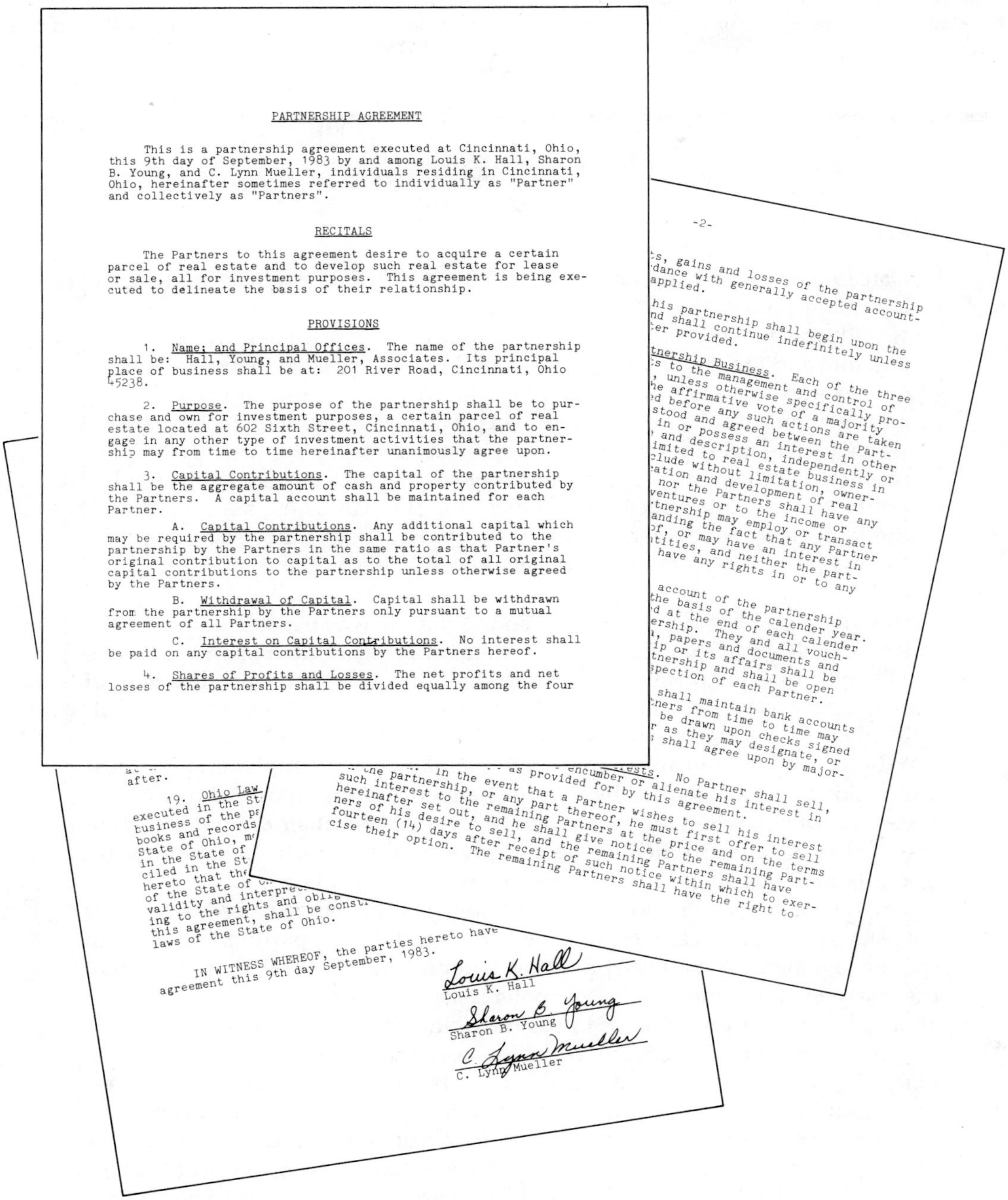

PARTNERSHIP AGREEMENT

This is a partnership agreement executed at Cincinnati, Ohio, this 9th day of September, 1983 by and among Louis K. Hall, Sharon B. Young, and C. Lynn Mueller, individuals residing in Cincinnati, Ohio, hereinafter sometimes referred to individually as "Partner" and collectively as "Partners".

RECITALS

The Partners to this agreement desire to acquire a certain parcel of real estate and to develop such real estate for lease or sale, all for investment purposes. This agreement is being executed to delineate the basis of their relationship.

PROVISIONS

1. Name; and Principal Offices. The name of the partnership shall be: Hall, Young, and Mueller, Associates. Its principal place of business shall be at: 201 River Road, Cincinnati, Ohio 45238.

2. Purpose. The purpose of the partnership shall be to purchase and own for investment purposes, a certain parcel of real estate located at 602 Sixth Street, Cincinnati, Ohio, and to engage in any other type of investment activities that the partnership may from time to time hereinafter unanimously agree upon.

3. Capital Contributions. The capital of the partnership shall be the aggregate amount of cash and property contributed by the Partners. A capital account shall be maintained for each Partner.

A. Capital Contributions. Any additional capital which may be required by the partnership shall be contributed to the partnership by the Partners in the same ratio as that Partner's original contribution to capital as to the total of all original capital contributions to the partnership unless otherwise agreed by the Partners.

B. Withdrawal of Capital. Capital shall be withdrawn from the partnership by the Partners only pursuant to a mutual agreement of all Partners.

C. Interest on Capital Contributions. No interest shall be paid on any capital contributions by the Partners hereof.

4. Shares of Profits and Losses. The net profits and net losses of the partnership shall be divided equally among the four

...

No Partner shall sell, encumber or alienate his interest in the partnership, except as provided for by this agreement. In the event that a Partner wishes to sell his interest or any part thereof, he must first offer to sell such interest to the remaining Partners at the price and on the terms hereinafter set out, and he shall give notice to the remaining Partners of his desire to sell, and the remaining Partners shall have fourteen (14) days after receipt of such notice within which to exercise their option. The remaining Partners shall have the right to

...

IN WITNESS WHEREOF, the parties hereto have ... agreement this 9th day September, 1983.

Louis K. Hall

Sharon B. Young

C. Lynn Mueller

FIGURE 47-1
PARTNERSHIP AGREEMENT
Ordinarily, the partnership agreement may be oral, but sound business practice requires that there be a detailed partnership agreement stating the rights and duties of all persons concerned.

In the *Cutler* case, the court was faced with the problem of determining whether a partnership existed between two persons, when one person owned all of the physical assets of the business, but both persons shared the net profits of the business equally.

CUTLER V BOWEN
(Utah) 543 P2d 1349 (1975)

Dale Bowen owned and operated the Havana Club in a rented building. He made an agreement with Frances Cutler, the bartender, that she would operate the club, purchase supplies, pay bills, keep the books, and hire and fire employees. Cutler and Bowen were each to receive $100 a week and to divide the net profits. The club was operated under this arrangement until the building was taken by the Redevelopment Agency. The agency paid the club $10,000 damages for disruption of business. The club was terminated because a suitable new location could not be found. Cutler then sued Bowen for one-half of the sum paid by the Redevelopment Agency on the theory that they had been partners. From a judgment in favor of Cutler, Bowen appealed.

CROCKETT, J. . . . The defendant contended that he was the sole owner of the entire business; and that the plaintiff's status was merely that of an employee. . . . Plaintiff took the position that, conceding the defendant was the owner of the physical assets of the business . . . insofar as the going concern and goodwill value, [she was] a partner in the business. . . .

When parties join in an enterprise, it is usually in contemplation of success and making profits, and is often without much concern about who will bear losses. However, when they so engage in a venture for their mutual benefit or profit, that is generally held to be a partnership, in which the law imposes upon them both liability for debts or losses that may occur. . . .

On the question whether profits shared should be regarded simply as wages, it is important to consider the degree to which a party participates in the management of the enterprise and whether the relationship is such that the party shares generally in the potential profits or advantages and thus should be held responsible for losses or liability incurred therein. . . .

It is not shown here that any occasion arose where the plaintiff's responsibility for debts or other liabilities of the business was tested. However, throughout the four years in which she operated and managed the Club, . . . it was her responsibility to see that all bills were paid, including the rental on the lease, employees' salaries, the costs of all purchases, licenses and other expenses of the business. During that time she saw the defendant Bowen only infrequently for the purpose of rendering an accounting and dividing the profits. It is further pertinent that the parties reported their income tax as a partnership.

Under the arrangement as shown and as found by the trial court, a good case can be made out that it was largely through the capability, experience, and efforts of the plaintiff that, in addition to the physical plant, there existed a separate asset in the value of the "going concern and goodwill" of the business, which was being lost by its displacement. On the basis of what has been said above, we see nothing to persuade us to disagree with the view taken by the trial court [that Cutler and Bowen were partners].

The failure of the parties to find another suitable location, and the cessation of operation of the Havana Club, was properly regarded as a termination of the partnership. The rule governing the rights of the parties in such circumstances is that after all debts and liabilities of the partnership have been satisfied, each partner should be repaid his contributions thereto, and any remainder allocated as their interests appear.

From the circumstances shown in evidence as discussed herein, there appears to be a reasonable basis for the trial court's view that, except for the physical assets, which belonged to the defendant and to which the plaintiff makes no claim, the further asset of the business: that is, the value of what is called going concern and goodwill belonged to the two of them as partners in the enterprise; and that when the business could not be relocated, the $10,000 should properly be regarded as compensation for the loss . . . of the business; and that the partners having lost their respective equal shares in the going business operation, they should also share equally in the compensation for its loss. . . .

[Judgment affirmed]

QUESTIONS

1. What defense was raised by the defendant, Bowen?
2. Did the court agree with the defendant?
3. Was the court influenced in its decision by the fact that Bowen and Cutler divided net profits equally?

(d) GROSS RETURNS. The sharing of gross returns is itself very slight, if any, evidence of partnership. To illustrate, in a case in which one party owned a show that was exhibited upon land owned by another under an agreement to divide the gross proceeds, no partnership was proven because there was no co-ownership or community of interest in the business. Similarly, it was not established that there was a partnership when it was shown that a farmer rented an airplane to a pilot to do aerial chemical spraying under an agreement by which the pilot would pay the farmer, as compensation for the use of the plane, a share of the fees that the pilot received.

(e) CO-OWNERSHIP. Neither the co-ownership of property nor the sharing of profits or rents from property that two or more persons own creates a partnership. Thus, the fact that a person acquires a 49 percent interest in a trailer park does not establish that such person is a partner. This in itself does not establish that the co-owners are together conducting the trailer park business for profit. Conversely, the mere fact that there is a sharing of the income from property by joint owners does not establish that they are partners.

(f) CONTRIBUTION OF PROPERTY. The fact that all persons have not contributed capital to the enterprise does not establish that the enterprise is not a partnership. A partnership may be formed even though some of its members furnish only skill or labor.

(g) FIXED PAYMENT. When a person who performs continuing services for another receives a fixed payment for such services, not dependent upon the existence of profit and not affected by losses, that person is not a partner.

§ 47:11   PARTNERS AS TO THIRD PERSONS

In some instances, persons who are in fact not partners may be held accountable to third persons as though they were partners. This liability arises when they conduct themselves in such a manner that others are reasonably led to believe that they are partners and to act in reliance upon that belief to their injury.[10] A person who is held liable as a partner under such circumstances is termed a nominal partner, a partner by estoppel, or an ostensible partner.

Partnership liability may arise by estoppel when a person who in fact is not a partner is described as a partner in a document filed with the government, provided the person so described has in some way participated in the filing of the document and the person claiming the benefit of the estoppel had knowledge of that document and relied upon the statement. For example, suppose that the partnership of *A* and *B*, in registering its fictitious name, specifies *A*, *B*, and *C* as partners and that the registration certificate is signed by all of them. If a creditor who sees this registration statement extends credit to the firm in reliance in part upon the fact that *C* is a partner, *C* has a partner's liability insofar as that creditor is concerned.

Conversely, no estoppel arises when the creditor does not know of the existence of the registration certificate and consequently does not rely thereon in extending credit to the partnership. Likewise, such liability does not arise when *C* does not know of the certificate.

§ 47:12   PARTNERSHIP PROPERTY

In general, partnership property consists of all the property contributed by the partners or acquired for the firm or with its funds.[11] There is usually no limitation upon the kind and amount of property that a partnership may acquire. The firm may own real as well as personal property, unless it is prohibited from doing so by statute or by the partnership agreement.

The parties may agree that real estate owned by one of the partners should become partnership property. When this intent exists, the particular property constitutes partnership property even though it is still in the name of the original owner.

§ 47:13   TENANCY IN PARTNERSHIP

Partners hold title to firm property by **tenancy in partnership**.[12] The characteristics of such a tenancy are:

(a) Each partner has an equal right to use firm property for partnership purposes in the absence of a contrary agreement.
(b) A partner possesses no interest in any specific item of partnership property that can be voluntarily sold, assigned, or mortgaged by a partner.[13]
(c) A creditor of a partner cannot proceed against any specific items of partnership property.[14] The creditor can only proceed against the partner's interest in the partnership. This is done by applying to a court for a **charging order.** By this procedure, the share of any profits that would be paid to the debtor-partner is paid to a receiver on behalf of the creditor or the court may direct the sale of the interest of the debtor-partner in the partnership.

---

[10]   UPA § 16(1): Johnson v Slusser, 33 Wash App 439, 655 P2d 261 (1982); Royal Bank and Trust Co. v Weintraub, Gold & Alper, 68 NY2d 124, 506 NYS2d 151 (1986).

[11]   UPA § 8. Rider's Estate, 487 Pa 373, 409 A2d 397 (1979).
[12]   UPA § 25(1): Smoot v Smoot (Tex Civ App) 568 SW2d 177 (1978).
[13]   Putnam v Shoaf (Tenn App) 620 SW2d 510 (1981).
[14]   UPA § 25(2)(c).

(d) On the death of a partner, the partnership property vests in the surviving partners for partnership purposes and is not subject to the rights of the surviving spouse of the deceased partner.

§ 47:14 ASSIGNMENT OF PARTNER'S INTEREST

Although a partner cannot transfer specific items of partnership property in the absence of authority to so act on behalf of the partnership, a partner's interest in the partnership may be voluntarily assigned by the partner. The assignee does not become a partner without the consent of the other partners.[15] Without this consent, the assignee is only entitled to receive the assignor's share of the profits during the continuance of the partnership and the assignor's interest upon the dissolution of the firm. The assignee has no right to participate in the management of the partnership; nor does the assignee have a right to inspect the books of the partnership.

B. DISSOLUTION AND TERMINATION

Partnerships may be dissolved by the acts of the partners, by order of a court, or by operation of law. Dissolution changes the legal status of both the partnership and the individual partners.

§ 47:15 EFFECT OF DISSOLUTION

Dissolution ends the right of the partnership to exist as a going concern, but it does not end the existence of the partnership.[16] It is followed by a winding-up period, upon the conclusion of which the partnership's legal existence is terminated.

Dissolution reduces the authority of the partners. From the moment of dissolution, the partners lose authority to act for the firm, "except so far as may be necessary to wind up partnership affairs or to complete transactions begun but not then finished."[17] The vested rights of the partners are not extinguished by dissolving the firm, and the existing liabilities remain. Thus, when the partnership is dissolved by the death of a partner, the estate of the deceased partner is liable to the same extent as the deceased partner.

§ 47:16 DISSOLUTION BY ACT OF PARTIES

A partnership may be dissolved by action of the parties.

(a) AGREEMENT. A partnership may be dissolved in accordance with the terms of the original agreement of the parties, as by the expiration of the period for which the relationship was to continue or by the performance of the object for which it was organized.[18] The relationship may also be dissolved by subsequent agreement, as when the partners agree to dissolve the firm before the lapse of the time specified in the articles of partnership or before the attainment of the object for which the firm was created.

(b) EXPULSION. A partnership is dissolved by the expulsion of any partner from the business in accordance with such a power conferred by the agreement between the partners.

(c) ALIENATION OF INTEREST. Neither a voluntary sale of a partner's interest nor an involuntary sale for the benefit of creditors works a dissolution of the partnership.

(d) WITHDRAWAL. A partner has the power to withdraw from the partnership at any time; but if the withdrawal violates the partnership agreement, the withdrawing partner becomes liable to the copartners for damages for breach of contract. When the relationship is for no definite purpose or time, a partner may withdraw without lia-

---

[15] Bourgeois v Medical Center of E. New Orleans (La App) 482 So 2d 795 (1986).
[16] Simmons v Quick-Stop Food Mart, Inc. 307 NC 33, 296 SE2d 275 (1982).

[17] UPA § 33.
[18] UPA § 31(1)(a).

bility at any time. Restrictive provisions on later employment are commonly found in partnership agreements, particularly in the accounting, legal, and medical professions and in marketing organizations.

The *Weeks* case raised the question of whether a partnership could be dissolved by a partner at any time because the partnership agreement did not state a definite period for its existence.

WEEKS V MCMILLAN
(SC App) 353 SE2d 289 (1987)

William Weeks joined an established public accounting firm known as Harris, McMillan, Hudgins & Co. in 1974. In 1980, Sara Penn joined the firm as a partner, and a new partnership agreement was executed by all of the partners. In 1983, Hudgins and Harris retired, and the partners agreed to admit Robert Cooper and Toni McKinley as partners, but no new partnership agreement was executed. Thereafter, Weeks became disgruntled and gave notice on July 31, 1984, that he elected to dissolve the partnership. After a short period of cooperation, the remaining partners denied Weeks access to the firm's records and files. Weeks commenced this action for a court-ordered confirmation of the dissolution and for an accounting. The partners counterclaimed for the enforcement of the 1980 partnership agreement that they claimed precluded dissolution. They also claimed that Weeks had violated the noncompetition clause in the 1980 agreement. From a judgment for Weeks, the partners appealed.

CURETON, J. . . .
Dissolution and the Noncompetition Provision

The threshold question in this appeal is whether the retirement of Hudgins and Harris and the admission of Cooper and McKinley effected a dissolution of the partnership. The master found that the change in the membership of the partnership resulted in a dissolution. We agree with the master. A dissolution is defined in [UPA § 29] as "the change in the relation of the partners caused by any partner ceasing to be associated in the carrying on as distinguished from the winding up of the business." The common law rule is that both the admission of a partner and the withdrawal of a partner will effect a dissolution. 60 Am.Jur.2d *Partnership* Sections 177 and 178 (1972).

While the authorities are not in total agreement on whether the Uniform Partnership Act changes the common law regarding the causes for dissolution, it is generally accepted that since the Uniform Act only incorporated in part the common law on dissolutions, other means of dissolution known to the common law are not precluded by the Act. We hold that the withdrawal of two partners and the admission of two other partners worked an ipso facto dissolution of the partnership represented by the 1980 agreement.

We agree with the master that after the change in membership of the partnership in 1983, there then existed between the parties to this action a partnership in fact of indefinite duration, and an at will partnership. A partnership at will is subject to dissolution by the act of one or more partners at any time.

The appellant partners also argue that the partnership existing after the change in membership adopted the provisions of the 1980 agreement and, thus, the partnership was not one at will. They further argue that because the partners adopted the 1980 agreement, Weeks is bound by the noncompetition clause in the agreement. We disagree. The 1980 agreement, even if adopted by the partners to this action, sets no definite time for termination of the partnership status and is, for all practical purposes, a partnership at will and subject to dissolution by Weeks. . . . Finally, we find that regardless of whether or not some portions of the agreement were adopted by all of the partners in the new partnership, the evidence is essentially uncontradicted that Weeks voiced objection to being bound by the noncompetition provision after the change in membership of the partnership, and never thereafter affirmatively agreed to be bound by the provision. Like any other contract, Weeks cannot be bound by partnership terms to which he did not agree. . . .

Accrual Method of Accounting

We find no abuse of discretion in the master's finding that the accounting should be accomplished by the accrual method. *Black's Law Dictionary* 18 (5th ed. 1979) defines the accrual method of keeping accounts as the method "which shows expenses incurred and income earned for a given period, although such expenses and income may not have been actually paid or received." Appellant partners claim that the accrual method of accounting would work an injustice to them because it would, among other things, cast upon them the total risk of uncollectible accounts. This contention is without merit since obvious adjustments can and should be made for uncollectible accounts and other contingencies. It is interesting to note that one of the appellants' exhibits reflects Weeks' interest in the partnership as of December 31, 1984 utilizing the accrual method.

[Judgment affirmed]

QUESTIONS

1. May a partnership of indefinite duration be dissolved by the act of one partner at any time?
2. Was the dissolution in this case by "act of the parties" or by "decree of court"?
3. Was Weeks bound by the noncompetition clause in the 1980 agreement?

---

§ 47:17 DISSOLUTION BY OPERATION OF LAW

A partnership is dissolved by operation of law in the following instances.

(a) DEATH. An ordinary partnership is dissolved immediately upon the death of any partner, even when the agreement provides for the continuance of the business. Thus, when the executor of a deceased partner carries on the business with the remaining partner, there is legally a new firm.

(b) BANKRUPTCY. Bankruptcy of the firm or of one of the partners causes the dissolution of the firm; insolvency alone does not.

(c) ILLEGALITY. A partnership is dissolved "by an event which makes it unlawful for the business of the partnership to be carried on or for the members to carry it on in partnership." To illustrate, when it is made unlawful by statute for judges to engage in the practice of law, a law firm is dissolved when one of its members becomes a judge.

(d) WAR. A partnership is ordinarily dissolved when there is war between the governments to which the different partners owe allegiance.

§ 47:18   DISSOLUTION BY DECREE OF COURT

When a partnership is to continue for a specified time, there are several situations in which one partner is permitted to obtain its dissolution through a decree of court. A court will not order the dissolution for trifling causes or temporary grievances that do not involve a permanent harm or injury to the partnership.

The filing of a complaint seeking a judicial dissolution does not in itself cause a dissolution of the partnership as it is the decree of the court that has that effect.

A partner may obtain a decree of dissolution for any of the following reasons:

(a) INSANITY. A partner has been judicially declared insane or of unsound mind.

(b) INCAPACITY. One of the partners has become incapable of performing the terms of the partnership agreement.

(c) MISCONDUCT. One of the partners has been guilty of conduct that substantially tends to affect prejudicially the continuance of the business. The habitual drunkenness of a partner is a sufficient cause for judicial dissolution.

(d) IMPRACTICABILITY. One of the partners persistently or willfully acts in such a way that it is not reasonably practicable to carry on the partnership business. Dissolution will be granted when dissensions are so serious and persistent as to make continuance impracticable, or when all confidence and cooperation between the parties have been destroyed.

(e) LACK OF SUCCESS. The partnership cannot continue in business except at a loss.

(f) EQUITABLE CIRCUMSTANCES. A decree of dissolution will be granted under any other circumstances that equitably call for a dissolution. Such a situation exists when one partner has been induced by fraud to enter into the partnership.

§ 47:19   NOTICE OF DISSOLUTION

The statement that dissolution terminates the authority of the partners to act for the firm requires some modification. Under some circumstances, one partner may continue to possess the power to make a binding contract.

(a) NOTICE TO PARTNERS. When the firm is dissolved by the act of a partner, notice must be given to the other partners unless that partner's act clearly shows an intent to withdraw from or to dissolve the firm. If the withdrawing partner acts without notice to the other partners, such partner is bound as between them upon contracts created for the firm.

> Where the dissolution is caused by the act, death, or bankruptcy of a partner, each partner is liable to his copartners for his share of any liability created by any partner acting for the partnership as if the partnership had not been dissolved unless (1) the dissolution being by act of any partner, the partner acting for the partnership had knowledge of the dissolution, or (2) the dissolution being by the death or bankruptcy of a partner, the partner acting for the partnership had knowledge or notice of the death or bankruptcy.[19]

(b) NOTICE TO THIRD PERSONS. When dissolution is caused by the act of a partner or of the partners, notice must be given to third parties. A notice should expressly state that the partnership has been dissolved.[20] Circumstances from which a termination may be inferred are generally not sufficient notice. Thus, the fact that the partnership checks added *Inc.* after the partnership name is not sufficient notice

---

[19]   UPA § 34.
[20]   Lemay Bank & Trust Co. v Lawrence (Mo App) 710 SW2d 318 (1986).

that the partnership does not exist and that the business has been incorporated.

Actual notice of dissolution must be given to persons who have dealt with the firm. To persons who have had no dealings with the firm, a publication of the fact is sufficient. Such notice may be by newspaper publication, by posting a placard in a public place, or by any similar method. Failure to give proper notice continues the power of each partner to bind the others in respect to third persons on contracts within the scope of the business.

When dissolution has been caused by operation of law, notice to third persons is not required. As between the partners, however, the UPA requires knowledge or notice of dissolution by death and bankruptcy. It has been held that when a third party dealing with the partnership is not informed of the death of a partner, the surviving partners and the firm are bound by a notice sent by the third person to the deceased partner.

§ 47:20   WINDING UP PARTNERSHIP AFFAIRS

In the absence of an express agreement permitting continuation of the business by the surviving partners, they must wind up the business and account for the share of any partner who has withdrawn, been expelled, or has died.[21] If the remaining partners continue the business and use the partner's distributive share in so doing, that partner is entitled to that share, together with interest or the profit earned thereon.

Although the partners have no authority after dissolution to create new obligations, they retain authority to do acts necessary to wind up the business.

The *King* decision illustrates the important distinction between the authority of a surviving partner to take actions appropriate for winding up the partnership business as opposed to the continuation of the partnership business as usual.

[21]   Ross v Walsh (Tex Civ App) 629 SW2d 823 (1982).

KING V STODDARD

28 Cal App 3d 708, 104 Cal Rptr 903 (1972)

The Stoddard family — father, mother, and son — formed a partnership that published a newspaper, the *Walnut Kernel*. The parents died, and the son continued to run the paper. King performed accounting services for the paper. When he was not paid, King sued the son and the executors of the estates of the deceased partners, claiming that his bill was a partnership liability for which each was liable. The executors defended on the ground that the son, as surviving partner, did not have authority to employ an accountant but was only authorized to wind up the partnership business. To this defense King answered that the newspaper was continued in order to preserve its asset value as a going concern, so that it could be sold, and that the running of the paper was, therefore, part of the winding-up process. If true, this would give the surviving partner the authority to employ the accountant. From a judgment in favor of the accountant, the executors appealed.

BROWN, A. J. . . . The estate's liability was predicated upon the court's finding that the services were rendered during the process of winding up the partnership operation of the Walnut Kernel newspaper. We have concluded that the trial court erred and that the continuation of the business was not a winding up of the affairs of the partnership.

The partnership was dissolved by operation of law upon the deaths of Alda and Lyman E. Stoddard, Sr. . . . "In general a dissolution operates only with respect to future transactions; as to everything past the partnership continues until all pre-existing matters are terminated." . . .

. . . [UPA § 35] provides that "[a]fter dissolution a partner can bind the partnership . . . (a) By any act appropriate for winding up partnership affairs. . . ."

It is this latter provision upon which the court based its decision that the estates of the deceased partners were liable for the accounting services performed after dissolution. The court found that "LYMAN STODDARD, JR.'S continuation of the WALNUT KERNEL business was an appropriate act for winding up the partnership, since the assets of the business would have substantial value only if it was a going business. . . .

We disagree with this finding. It is probably true that there might have been advantages to the partnership to sell the business as a going business, but the indefinite continuation of the partnership business is contrary to the requirement for winding up of the affairs upon dissolution. In *Harvey v Harvey*, 90 Cal App 2d 549, 203 P2d 112, the court disapproved a finding that the business and assets of a partnership were of such character as to render its liquidation impracticable and inadvisable until a purchaser could be found. The court stated: "In effect it [the finding] authorizes the indefinite continuation of the partnership after the death of a partner, a procedure not in accordance with section 571 of the Probate Code. Respondents counter with the argument that the business is such that it cannot be wound up profitably, and the estate given its share. But this argument overlooks the distinction between winding up a business and winding up the partnership interest in that business." . . .

Even if we assume that a situation might exist where continuation of the business for a period would be appropriate to winding up the partnership interest, such a situation did not exist here. The record reflects the fact that the surviving partner was not taking action to wind up the partnership as was his duty . . . nor did the estates consent in any way to a delay. Rather, their insistence on winding up took the form of an effort to sell the business and a suit to require an accounting. There is nothing in the record upon which to base the argument made by respondent that appellants consented to his continued employment. The fact that they did not object is of no relevance. They had no right to direct and did not participate in the operation of the business. Therefore, the determination that the acts of the accountants were rendered during a winding up process is not based upon substantial evidence. . . .

We conclude that the services of respondents were rendered after the dissolution resulting from the deaths of the partners, Lyman, Sr., and Alda Stoddard, and do not constitute services during the "winding up" processes of the partnership. . . .

[Judgment reversed]

QUESTIONS

1. What did King contend?
2. Did the court agree with King?

3. Based upon the first sentence of Section 47:20 of this text, when would it be possible for a surviving partner to temporarily continue a business during the winding up process?

When dissolution is obtained by court decree, the court may appoint a receiver to conduct the winding up of the partnership business. This may be done in the usual manner or the receiver may sell the business as a going concern to those partners who wish to continue its operation.

With a few exceptions, all partners have the right to participate in the winding up of the business.[22]

When the firm is dissolved by the death of one partner, the partnership property vests in the surviving partners for the purpose of administration. They must collect and preserve the assets, pay the debts, and with reasonable promptness, make an accounting to the representative of the deceased partner's estate. In connection with these duties, the law requires the highest degree of integrity. A partner cannot purchase any of the partnership property without the consent of the other partners.

§ 47:21 DISTRIBUTION OF ASSETS

Creditors of the firm have first claim on the assets of the partnership. Difficulty arises when there is a contest between the creditors of the firm and the creditors of the individual partners. The general rule is that firm creditors have first claim on assets of the firm, and the individual creditors share in the remaining assets, if any.

Conversely, creditors of the individual partners have priority in the distribution of the individual assets; the claims of the firm creditors may be satisfied out of the individual partner's assets only after claims of the creditors of the individuals are settled.

After the firm's liabilities to nonpartners

have been paid, the assets of the partnership are distributed as follows: (1) each partner is entitled to a refund of advances made to or for the firm; (2) contributions to the capital of the firm are then returned; (3) the remaining assets, if any, are divided equally as profits among the partners unless there is some other agreement. If the partnership has sustained a loss, the partners share it equally in the absence of a contrary agreement.

Distribution of partnership assets must be made on the basis of actual value when it is clear that the book values are merely nominal or arbitrary amounts.

A provision in a partnership agreement that upon the death of a partner the interest of the partner shall pass to that partner's surviving spouse is valid and takes effect as against the contention that it is not valid because it does not satisfy the requirements applicable to wills.

§ 47:22   CONTINUATION OF PARTNERSHIP BUSINESS

As a practical matter, the business of the partnership is commonly continued after dissolution and winding up. In all cases, however, there is a technical dissolution, winding up, and a termination of the life of the original partnership. If the business continues, either with the surviving partners, or with them and additional partners, it is a new partnership. Again, as a practical matter, the liquidation of the old partnership may in effect be merely a matter of bookkeeping entries with all parties in interest contributing again or relending to the new business any payment to which they would be entitled from the liquidation of the original partnership.

---

[22]   UPA § 37.

Summary

A partnership is a relationship created by the voluntary association of two or more persons to carry on as co-owners a business for profit. General partners are those who are publicly and actively engaged in the transaction of firm business. Nominal partners hold themselves out as partners or permit others to hold them out as such. Secret partners are those who take an active part in the management of the firm but who are not known to the public as partners.

A partnership agreement governs the partnership during its existence and may also contain provisions relating to dissolution. The agreement need not be in writing. Proof of the existence of a partnership may be found from the presence of an individual's actual control in the running of the business, and the fact that the parties share profits and losses. The sharing of gross returns, as opposed to profits, is very slight evidence of a partnership.

Partners hold title to firm property by tenancy in partnership. A creditor of a partner cannot proceed against any specific item of partnership property, but must obtain a charging order to seize the debtor-partner's share of the profits. An assignee of a partner's interest does not become a partner without the consent of the other partner, and is entitled only to a share of the profits and the assignor's interest upon dissolution.

Dissolution ends the right of the partnership to exist as a going concern and is followed by a winding-up period and the distribution of assets. A partnership may be dissolved by the parties themselves in accordance with the terms of the partnership agreement, by expulsion of a partner, by withdrawal of a partner, or by the bankruptcy of the firm or one of the partners. A court may order dissolution of a partnership on the petition of a partner because of the insanity, incapacity, or major misconduct of a partner. Lack of success is also a basis for dissolution, as well as impracticability or other circumstances that equitably call for dissolution. Notice of dissolution of the partnership must be given, except dissolution by operation of law, with actual notice being given to those who have dealt with the firm as a partnership. All partners generally have a right to participate in the winding up of the business. After the firm's liabilities to nonpartners have been paid, the assets are distributed among the partners as follows: (1) refund of advances, (2) return of contributions to capital, and (3) remaining assets are divided in accordance with the partnership agreement or, if no agreement is expressed, the net assets are divided equally among the partners.

Questions and Case Problems

1. What social forces are affected by the rule that distribution of partnership assets must be made on the basis of actual value when it is clear that the book values are merely nominal or arbitrary amounts?
2. What is the effect of dissolution on a partnership?
3. In proving that A and B are partners, compare the effect of proof that they (a) share gross returns, (b) are co-owners of proper-

ty used in or by a business, or (c) share profits.
4. Ray, Linda, and Nancy form a partnership. Ray and Linda contribute property and cash. Nancy contributes only services. Linda dies and the partnership is liquidated. After all debts are paid there is not sufficient surplus to pay back Linda's estate and to pay Ray for the property and cash originally contributed by Ray and Linda. Nancy claims that the bal-

ance should be divided equally between Ray, Linda's estate, and Nancy. Is she correct?

5. Compare the requirement of notice to third persons when (a) an agency is terminated, and (b) a partnership is dissolved.

6. Baxter, Bigelow, Owens, and Dailey were partners in a New York City advertising agency. Owens, who was in poor health and wanted to retire, advised the partners that she had assigned her full and complete interest in the partnership to her son Bartholomew, a highly qualified person with ten years of experience in the advertising business. Baxter, Bigelow, and Dailey refused to allow Bartholomew to attend management meetings and refused his request to inspect the books. Bartholomew points out that his mother had invested as much in the firm as any other partner. He believes, as assignee of his mother's full and complete partnership interest, that he is entitled to (a) inspect the books as he sees fit and (b) participate fully in the management of the firm. Is Bartholomew correct?

7. Amy Gargulo and Paula Frisken operated as a partnership "Kiddies Korner," an infants' and children's (to age 6) clothing store. They operated the business very successfully for three years, with both Paula and Amy doing the buying and Paula keeping the books and paying the bills. Amy and Paula decided to expand the business when an adjoining store became vacant. At the same time, they incorporated the business for protection against the business risks involved in the expansion. Children's Apparel, Inc., was a major supplier to the business before the expansion and allowed very liberal payment terms. Business did not increase after the expansion as anticipated and when a nationally known manufacturer of children's apparel opened a factory outlet nearby, the business could no longer pay its bills. Children's Apparel, Inc., which supplied most of the store's stock after expansion, sued Amy and Paula as partners for past due bills on expansion stock. Children's Apparel, Inc., did not know Amy and Paula had incorporated. Amy and Paula defend that the business was incorporated and, therefore, that they may not be held personally liable for business debts occurring after incorporation. Are Amy and Paula correct?

8. Bates and Huffman formed a partnership to run a shoe business. In a lawsuit between the partners, Huffman claimed that the partnership agreement was void because Bates was a minor. Was he correct? [Huffman v Bates (Mo App) 348 SW2d 363]

9. Williams owned and operated a bakery business. His two sons were employed in the business and from time to time received a share of the profits as a bonus. The father and one of the sons died. The administrator of the son's estate, the First National Bank, then sued the estate of the father for an accounting, claiming that the father and the two sons were a partnership and that the deceased son's estate was therefore entitled to a one-third share. Decide. [First National Bank v Williams, 142 Or 648, 20 P2d 222]

10. A suit was brought by the heirs of members of a partnership to determine the right to the proceeds of sale of certain real estate. The real estate had been purchased by the partnership with partnership money and in the partnership name. The real estate was not used in the partnership business but was held only for investment purposes. It was claimed by the heirs that this real estate was not subject to the provisions of the Uniform Partnership Act governing tenancy by partnership because it was not used in the business. Were they correct? [Brown v Brown, 45 Tenn App 78, 320 SW2d 721]

11. Langdon, Hurdle, and Hoffman formed a partnership to practice medicine. The agreement provided that if any partner withdrew from the firm within five years he could not practice within a specified geographic area for a specified time. Five years and one day later, Hoffman withdrew from the partnership. Langdon and Hurdle brought suit against Hoffman, claiming that Hoffman was liable for damages for withdrawing from the partnership. Decide. [Langdon v Hurdle, 17 NC App 530, 195 SE2d 71]

12. Simpson and Balaban, as partners, owned and operated the Desert Cab company. Simpson died. The administrator of his estate obtained a court order authorizing the sale of Simpson's interest in the partnership and in the physical assets of the partnership. Was this order proper? [Balban v Bank of Nevada, 86 Nev 826, 477 P2d 860]

13. Chaiken and two others ran a barber shop. The Delaware Employment Security Commission claimed that the other two persons

were employees of Chaiken and that Chaiken had failed to pay the unemployment compensation tax assessed against employers. He defended on the ground that he had not "employed" the other two and that all three were partners. The evidence showed that Chaiken owned the barber shop; he continued to do business in the same trade name as he had before he was joined by the two additional barbers; and he had a separate contract with each of the two, which specified the days for work and the days off. It was also shown that Chaiken had registered the partnership name and the names of the three partners and that federal tax returns used for partnership had been filed. Decide. [Chaiken v Employment Security Commission (Del Super) 274 A2d 707]

14. Gus Jebeles and his brother-in-law Gus Costellos entered into an oral partnership agreement on September 2, 1977, to conduct a business under the name of "Dino's Hot Dogs" at a location on the Montgomery Highway. Jebeles, who had expertise in this kind of business, arranged for the lease and furnished the logo used by the partnership. From the beginning, Costellos devoted himself to the business full-time, and Jebeles devoted relatively little time to the business. Marital difficulties developed between Jebeles and his wife, who was Costellos' sister. Divorce proceedings began in January of 1979; at that time Costellos ceased to remit any funds to Jebeles and changed the locks on the doors of the premises. Jebeles filed suit seeking a dissolution of the partnership and an accounting of all profits. As judge, you believe that it would be ill-advised to dissolve the partnership and lose the valuable lease to the business premises and the future profits of the business. Instead you are considering ordering that the partnership continue with Costellos as the sole active partner and Jebeles as a silent partner. You plan on ordering an accounting. Would your decision be upheld on appeal? [Jebeles v Costellos (Ala) 391 So 2d 1024]

15. On August 23, 1973, Friedman, the "O" Street Carpet Shop, Inc., and Langness formed a partnership know as NFL Associates. "O" Street Carpet's net contribution to capital was $5,004. Langness contributed $14,000 in cash. Friedman contributed his legal services, upon which no value was placed by the articles of partnership. The articles stated that Friedman was entitled to 10 percent of the profits. The articles provided that Langness was to receive payments of $116.66 per month. The partnership's accountant treated the payments to Langness as a return to Langness of her capital. In October of 1978, the partnership sold the rental property owned by the partnership and the partnership was wound up, whereupon Friedman claimed that he was entitled to 10 percent of the partnership capital upon dissolution. Langness claimed that Friedman was not entitled to a capital distribution and that the monthly payments to her should not have been treated as a return of capital. Decide. [Langness v "O" Street Carpet, Inc. 217 Neb 569, 353 NW2d 709]

48

POWERS AND DUTIES OF PARTNERS

The powers and duties of partners will be governed by the partnership agreement in those situations for which the partners had the foresight to make express provision in the partnership agreement. In all situations not covered by a partnership agreement, partnership law applies.

A partner's authority to act for the firm is similar to that of an agent's authority to act for a principal; however, unlike an agent, a partner is a co-owner who has rights in the partnership property and liability for partnership losses. As a result of each partner's power to make decisions that may bind the firm, high standards of fair dealing are necessary between the partners. Such high standards of conduct affect the duties, rights, and liabilities of the partners.

A. AUTHORITY OF PARTNERS

The scope of a partner's authority is determined by the partnership agreement and by the nature of the partnership.

§ 48:1 AUTHORITY OF MAJORITY OF PARTNERS

When there are more than two partners in a firm, the decision of the majority prevails in matters involving the manner in which the ordinary functions of the business will be conducted. To illustrate, a majority of the partners of a firm decide to increase the firm's advertising and subsequently enter into a contract for that purpose. The transaction is valid and binds the firm and all of the partners.

The act of the majority is not binding if it contravenes the partnership agreement. For such matters, unanimous action is required.[1] Thus, the majority of the members cannot change the nature of the business against the protests of the minority.

When there are an even number of partners, there is the possibility of an even division on a matter that requires majority approval. In such a case no action can be taken, and the partnership is deadlocked. When the partners are evenly divided on any question, one partner has no authority to act. If the division is over a basic issue and the partners persist in the deadlock so that it is impossible to continue the business, any one of the partners may petition the court to order the dissolution of the firm.

§ 48:2 EXPRESS AUTHORITY OF INDIVIDUAL PARTNERS

An individual partner may have express authority to perform certain acts, either because the partnership agreement so declares or because a sufficient number of partners have agreed thereto.

A partner's authority to act for the firm is similar to that of an agent to act for a principal. Thus, in addition to express authority, a partner has the authority to do those acts that are customary for a member of a partnership conducting the particular business of that partnership.[2] As in the case of an agent, the acts of a partner in ex-

cess of authority do not ordinarily bind the partnership.

§ 48:3 CUSTOMARY AUTHORITY OF INDIVIDUAL PARTNERS

A partner, by virtue of being a comanager of the business, customarily has certain powers necessary and proper to carrying out that business. In the absence of express limitation, the law therefore will imply that a partner has such powers. The scope of such power varies with the nature of the partnership and also with the business customs and usages of the area in which the partnership operates.

The following are the more common of the customary or implied powers of individual partners:

(a) CONTRACTS. A partner may make any contract necessary to the transaction of the firm business.[3]

When a plaintiff sues on a promissory note or other contract executed by a partner who does not possess express authority to enter into such transaction, the plaintiff has the burden of proving that the making of the contract or the giving of commercial paper was "usual" for a business of the character of the partnership.

(b) SALES. A partner may sell the firm's goods in the regular course of business and make the usual warranties incidental to such sales. This authority, however, is limited to the goods held for sale by the partnership.

(c) PURCHASES. A partner may purchase any kind of property within the scope of the business, and for this purpose may pledge the credit of the firm. This authority is not affected by the fact that the partner subsequently misuses or keeps the property instead of turning it over to the firm.

(d) LOANS. A partner in a trading firm may borrow money for partnership purposes. In doing so, the partner may execute commercial paper in the firm name or give security, such as a mortgage or a

---

[1] Uniform Partnership Act, § 18(h).
[2] Ball v Carlson (Colo App) 641 P2d 303 (1981).

[3] Barnes v Campbell Chain Co., Inc. 47 NC App 488, 267 SE2d 388 (1980).

pledge of the personal property of the firm. If the third person acts in good faith, the transaction is binding even though the partner misappropriates the money. A partner in a nontrading partnership does not ordinarily possess the power to borrow in the name of the firm.

(e) INSURANCE. A partner may insure the firm property, cancel a policy of insurance, or make proof of loss and accept a settlement for the loss.

(f) EMPLOYMENT. A partner may hire such employees and agents as are necessary to carry out the purpose of the enterprise.

(g) CLAIMS AGAINST FIRM. A partner has the authority to compromise, adjust, and pay bona fide claims against the partnership. A partner may pay debts out of the firm funds or may pay them by transferring firm property.

(h) CLAIMS OF FIRM. A partner may adjust, receive payment of, and release debts and other claims of the firm. In so doing, a partner may take money or commercial paper but, as a general rule, cannot accept goods in payment. One who makes a proper payment is protected even though the partner to whom the payment is made embezzles the money or fails to account to the firm for the payment.

(i) ADMISSIONS. A partner may bind the firm by admissions or statements that are adverse to the interests of the partnership if they are made in regard to firm affairs and in pursuance of firm business. For example, when a buyer takes a purchase back to the partnership's store, the admission by the partner then in the store that the product was defective binds the firm.

(j) NOTICE. A partner may receive notice of matters affecting the partnership affairs, and such notice, in the absence of fraud, is binding on the other partners.[4]

§ 48:4   LIMITATIONS ON AUTHORITY

The partners may agree to limit the normal powers of each partner. When a partner, contrary to such an agreement, negotiates a contract for the firm with a third person, the firm is bound if the third person was unaware of the agreement. In such a case, the partner violating the agreement is liable to the other partners for any loss caused by the breach of the limitation. If the third person knew of the limitation, the firm would not be bound.[5]

In the *Schnucks Markets* case the court was faced with the problem of deciding whether a partner whose authority was limited could nevertheless bind the partnership contrary to the limitation.

---

[4]   Grayson v Wolfsey, Rosen, Kweskin & Kuriansky, 40 Conn Supp 1, 478 A2d 629 (1984).
[5]   UPA § 9(4).

SCHNUCKS MARKETS INC. V CASSILLY

(Mo App) 724 SW2d 664 (1987)

David Cassilly and Joseph Mason, doing business as Glen Park Properties, were partners in the real estate development business. Schnucks Markets brought an action against the partners for breach of contract. Schnucks testified that Cassilly and Schnucks agreed that Glen Park and the Market would split the cost of extending a sewer line to the market, and that Glen Park did not pay its share of the $25,263.36 cost. Glen Park vigorously denied that Cassilly had authority to contract for Glen Park and to bind the partnership. From judgment for Schnucks, the partnership appealed.

PUDLOWSKI, P.J. . . . Glen Park . . . contend[s that] the court erred in not directing a verdict for them as the evidence conclusively established that Cassilly did not have the authority to bind the partnership and that the trial court failed to include an instruction on the issues of Cassilly's authority in the verdict director. In essence, Glen Park rests its defense on a statement made by Cassilly in a deposition that he did not have such authority. As it was "uncontradicted," Glen Park reasons that Schnuck's failed its burden of proving authority.

[UPA § 9(1)] states:

> 1. Every partner is an agent of the partnership for the purpose of its business, and the act of every partner, . . . for apparently carrying on in the usual way the business of the partnership of which he is a member binds the partnership, unless the partner so acting has in fact no authority to act for the partnership in the particular matter, and the person with whom he is dealing has knowledge of the fact that he has no such authority.

Cassilly and Mason conceded that Glen Park was a partnership, thus they are both agents of the partnership and of each other. As the statute notes, there are exceptions to this rule. First, the act of the partner must be "for the purpose of its business" and in "carrying on in the usual way the business of the partnership." Negotiating at conventions and elsewhere an oral contract to divide the costs of sewer installation necessary for development of property certainly fits these requirements. . . . Glen Park . . . contends that negotiating the installation of sewer lines is a one-time deal and thus not in the course of partnership business. This is clearly refuted by the record. Finally, Glen Park relies on *Boonville National Bank v. Thompson*, 99 S.W.2d 93, 102 (Mo.1936) which states that the doctrine of agency does not apply to a non-trading partnership. *Black's Law Dictionary* (5th ed.) defines "Trading partnership" as "[a] firm the nature of whose business, according to the usual modes of conducting it, imports the necessity of buying and selling." *Id.* at 1339. Thus, it appears that Glen Park qualifies as a trading partnership. More important, however, the Uniform Partnership Act, which Missouri adopted thirteen years after *Thompson*, defines "partnership" as "an association of two or more persons to carry on as co-owners of a business for profit." [UPA § 6(1)] This more expansive definition leads us to the conclusion that *Thompson's* distinction between trading and non-trading partnerships is no longer relevant to the issue of partner agency authority.

Glen Park urges error in the failure to include an instruction . . . on whether Cassilly served as Glen Park's agent. Glen Park argues that since Cassilly denied agency, there arose a disputed issue of material fact which required the court to give an instruction. . . . Cassilly's denial of agency did not elevate this to a legally material issue for even if Cassilly did not possess authority, Glen Park would still be bound. [UPA § 9(1)] requires that if the partner in fact has no authority, "the person with whom he is dealing must have knowledge that he has no such authority." Glen Park presented no evidence that Schnucks had knowledge of Cassilly's supposedly limited status. It thus became unnecessary for the trial court to submit on this issue. . . .

[Judgment affirmed]

Questions

1. Did Glen Park believe that the partnership was not liable because the plaintiff failed to prove that Cassilly had authority to bind the partnership?
2. How did the court dispose of Glen Park's contentions on the authority of Cassilly?
3. Can a partner whose authority is limited nevertheless bind the partnership contrary to the limitation?

A third person cannot assume that the partner has all the authority that the partner purports to have. If there is anything that would put a reasonable person on notice that the partner's powers are limited, the third person is bound by that limitation.

The third person must be on the alert for the following situations in particular, as they warn that the partner with whom the third person deals either has restricted authority or no authority at all:

(a) NATURE OF BUSINESS. A third person must take notice of limitations arising out of the nature of the business. A partnership may be organized for a particular kind of business, trade, or profession, and third persons are presumed to know the limitations commonly imposed on partners in such enterprises. Thus, an act of a partner that would ordinarily bind a commercial firm, such as the issuance of a note, would not bind a partnership engaged in a profession. A partner in a trading partnership has much greater powers than one in a nontrading firm.

(b) SCOPE OF BUSINESS. A third person must recognize and act in accordance with limitations that arise from the scope of the business. A partner cannot bind the firm to a third person in a transaction not within the scope of the firm's business unless the partner had express authority to do so. Thus, when a partner in a dental firm speculates in land or when a partner in a firm dealing in automobiles buys television sets for resale, the third person, in the absence of estoppel or express authority, cannot hold the other partners liable on such a contract. The scope of the business is a question of fact to be determined by the jury from the circumstances of each case. In general, such scope comprises the activities commonly recognized as a part of a given business at a given place and time. The usual scope, however, may be enlarged by agreement or by conduct.

(c) TERMINATION OF PARTNERSHIP. A third person should watch for the termination of the partnership, either when the partnership is terminated under conditions requiring no notice or when notice of the termination has been properly given.

(d) ADVERSE INTEREST. A third person should take notice of an act of a partner that is obviously against the interest of the firm. To illustrate, if a partner issues a promissory note in the firm name and delivers it to a creditor in payment of a personal obligation, the creditor risks nonpayment because such an act may be a fraud upon the firm.

§ 48:5   PROHIBITED TRANSACTIONS

There are certain transactions into which a partner cannot enter on behalf of the partnership unless the partner is expressly authorized to do so. A third person entering into such a transaction does so at the risk that the partner has not been so authorized.

The following are prohibited transactions:

(a) CESSATION OF BUSINESS. A partner cannot bind the firm by a contract that would make it impossible for the firm to conduct its usual business.

(b) SURETYSHIP. A partner has no implied authority to bind the firm by contracts of surety, guaranty, or indemnity for purposes other than the firm business.[6]

(c) ARBITRATION. A partner cannot submit controversies of the firm to arbitration "unless authorized by the other partners or unless they have abandoned the business."[7]

(d) CONFESSION OF JUDGMENT. A partner cannot confess judgment against the firm upon one of its obligations, because all partners should have an opportunity to defend in court, except when the other partners consent or when they have abandoned the business.

(e) ASSIGNMENT FOR CREDITORS. A partner cannot ordinarily make a general assignment of firm property for the benefit of creditors, unless authorized by the other partners or unless they have abandoned the business.

(f) PERSONAL OBLIGATIONS. A partner cannot discharge personal obligations or claims of the firm by interchanging them in any way.[8]

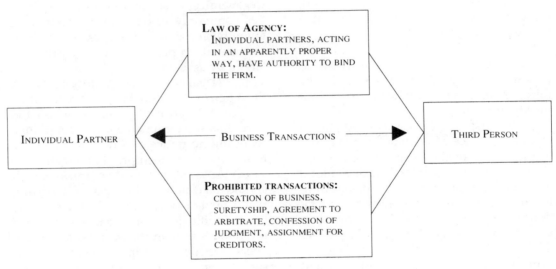

FIGURE 48-1
LIMITATIONS ON AUTHORITY OF INDIVIDUAL
PARTNER TO BIND PARTNERSHIP

B.   DUTIES, RIGHTS, REMEDIES, AND LIABILITIES OF PARTNERS

The duties, rights, remedies, and liabilities between the partners are influenced, to a large extent, by the high standards of fair dealing necessary for the successful operation of the partnership form of business.

§ 48:6   DUTIES OF PARTNERS

In many respects, the duties of a partner are the same as those of an agent.

---

[6]   First Interstate Bank of Oregon v Bergendahl, 80 Or App 479, 723 P2 1005 (1986).

[7]   UPA § 9(3)(e).

[8]   Slingerland v Hurley (Fla App) 288 So 2d 587 (1980).

(a) LOYALTY AND GOOD FAITH. Each partner must act in the highest good faith toward the other(s), and one must not take any advantage over the other(s) by the slightest misrepresentation or concealment. Each partner owes a duty of loyalty to the firm. This duty requires a partner's devotion to the firm's business and bars the making of any secret profit at the expense of the firm, the use of the firm's property for personal benefit, or the exploitation for personal gain of a business opportunity of the partnership.[9] A partner's duties to the firm must be observed above the furtherance of the partner's own personal interest. To illustrate, when one partner renewed a lease of the building occupied by the firm but the lease was renewed in the name of that partner alone, that partner was compelled to hold the lease for the firm on the ground that the failure to renew the lease in the name of the firm was a breach of the duties of good faith and loyalty owed to the firm.

A partner, in the absence of an agreement to the contrary, is required to give undivided time and energy to the furtherance of the business of the partnership. In any case, a partner cannot promote a competing business. If the partner does so, the partner is liable for damages sustained by the partnership.

In *Olivet v Frischling* some of the partners of a leasing company formed a competing partnership.

[9] Gilroy v Conway, 151 Mich App 628, 391 NW2d 419 (1986); Hooper v Yoder (Colo) 737 P2d 852 (1987).

OLIVET V FRISCHLING
104 Cal App 3d 831, 164 Cal Rptr 87 (1980)

The partners of the Whittier Leasing Company partnership consisted of the physicians on the staff of the Whittier Hospital and certain other individuals employed by the hospital. The Hospital's Board of Directors, including Frischling (the hospital's attorney), were also partners in Whittier Leasing. Whittier Leasing was formed to assist Whittier Hospital in its remodeling program. The partners received a financial gain in the form of favorable tax benefits and income tax shelters, while the hospital received funds. The partnership was formed for a term ending on June 30, 1990. Between 1975 and 1977 the partnership engaged in fifty-four sale and lease-back transactions with the hospital, whereby the partnership purchased certain pieces of medical equipment from the hospital and then leased these purchases back to the hospital. Sometime before February, 1977, Frischling and the eight other members of the Board formed a competing partnership known as Friendly Hills Leasing Company. Thereafter, all future lease-back transactions with the hospital were concluded with Friendly Hills Leasing to the total exclusion of Whittier Leasing. The excluded partners of Whittier Leasing — Olivet, Marcus and Lucidi — brought an action against the board members. They sought dissolution of the Whittier Leasing partnership, an accounting, and recovery of the profits lost by the Whittier Leasing partnership to the Friendly Hills Leasing Company. The trial court refused to grant relief to the plaintiffs, and they appealed.

KAUS, P. M. . . . [The Uniform Partnership Act, § 32] provides

(1) . . . On application by or for a partner the court shall decree a dissolution whenever: . . .

   (d) A partner willfully or persistently commits a breach of the partnership agreement, or otherwise so conducts himself in matters relating to the partnership business that it is not reasonably practicable to carry on the business in partnership with him, . . .

   (f) Other circumstances render a dissolution equitable. . . .

It is well settled that a partner who agrees to give his personal attention to the partnership business may not engage in any other business which gives him an interest adverse to that of the firm, or which prevents him from giving to the firm business all the attention which would be advantageous to it. Hence, a partner who does so act may reasonably be said to have breached his implicit agreement to refrain from undermining the partnership's best interests. Clearly, the facts here alleged reflect that certain of the partners of Whittier Leasing have elected to compete with the firm itself and to thus breach one of the partnership's basic underlying tenets. We think it therefore indisputable that plaintiffs, should they be able to prove their allegations, would be entitled to a court-ordered dissolution of Whittier Leasing pursuant to either subsection (d) or (f) of section [32]. Further, an accounting . . . would then follow as a matter of course, since "an account is a necessary incident to the dissolution. . . ."

[Judgment reversed]

QUESTIONS

1. What remedy did the plaintiffs seek?
2. Were the nine defendants still partners in the Whittier Leasing partnership when they formed their own competing partnership?
3. Did the court hold that partners have a right to form a competing partnership?

The obligation of a partner to refrain from competing with the partnership continues after the termination of the partnership if the partnership agreement contains a valid anticompetitive covenant.[10] In the absence of any such restriction, or if the restriction agreed upon is held invalid, a partner is free to compete with the remaining partners, even though they continue the partnership business.

(b) OBEDIENCE. Each partner is under the obligation to perform all duties and to obey all restrictions imposed by the partnership agreement or by the vote of the requisite number of partners. Consequently, each partner must observe any limitation imposed by a majority of the partners with respect to the ordinary details of the partnership business. If a majority of the partners operating a retail store decide that no sales shall be made on credit, a partner who is placed in charge of the store must obey this limitation. If a third person does not know of the limitation, the managing partner will have the power to make a binding sale on credit to such person. If the third person does not pay the bill and the firm thereby suffers loss, the partner who violated the no-credit limitation is li-

[10] Wright v Belt, 6 Kan App 2d 854, 636 P2d 188 (1981).

able to the firm for the loss caused by such disobedience.

(c) REASONABLE CARE. A partner must use reasonable care in transacting the business of the firm and is liable for any loss resulting from a failure to do so. A partner is not liable, however, for honest mistakes or errors of judgment.

(d) INFORMATION. A partner has the duty to inform the partnership of matters relating to the partnership and must "render on demand true and full information of all things affecting the partnership to any partner or the legal representative of any deceased partner or partner under legal disability." [11]

The obligation to inform embraces matters relating to the purchase by one partner of the interest of another and to matters relating to the liquidation of the partnership.

(e) ACCOUNTING. A partner transacting any business for the firm must make and keep, or turn over to the proper person, correct records thereof.

If the partners have delegated to one of the partners the task of keeping the books and accounts for all the business of the firm, that partner must keep proper records. If they are disputed, the record keeper has the burden of proving their accuracy, which means that if it is not shown that the records are correct, the record keeper will be held liable.

When an action is brought to compel a partner to account, the court may require the making of an audit by a disinterested third person.

When a partnership is organized for an illegal purpose or for conducting a lawful business in an unlawful manner, a wrongdoing partner cannot obtain an accounting by the partnership. For example, when the members of an engineering partnership did not have the license required for engineering work, one of the partners, an unlicensed engineer, could not require the other partners to account.

§ 48:7   RIGHTS OF PARTNERS AS OWNERS

Each partner, in the absence of a contrary agreement, has the following rights, which stem from the fact that the partner is a co-owner of the partnership business.

(a) MANAGEMENT. Each partner has a right to take an equal part in transacting the business of the firm. It is immaterial that one partner contributed more than another or that one contributed only services.

Incidental to the right to manage the partnership, each partner has the right to possession of the partnership property for the purposes of the partnership.

(b) INSPECTION OF BOOKS. All partners are equally entitled to inspect the books of the firm. "The partnership books shall be kept, subject to any agreement between the partners, at the principal place of business of the partnership, and every partner shall at all times have access to and may inspect and copy any of them."[12]

(c) SHARE OF PROFITS. Each partner is entitled to a share of the profits. The partners may provide, if they so wish, that profits shall be shared in unequal proportions. In the absence of such a provision in the partnership agreement, each partner is entitled to an equal share of the profits without regard to the amount of capital contributed or services performed for the partnership.

The right to profits is regarded as personal property regardless of the nature of the partnership business. Upon the death of a partner, the right to a share of the profits and an accounting passes to the dead partner's executor or administrator.

(d) COMPENSATION. In the absence of a contrary agreement, a partner is not entitled to compensation for services performed for the partnership.[13] There is no entitlement even though the services are unusual or more extensive than the services rendered by other partners. Consequently, when one partner becomes seri-

---

[11]   UPA § 20.

[12]   UPA § 19.
[13]   Altman v Altman (CA3 Pa) 653 F2d 755 (1981).

ously ill and the other partners transact all of the firm's business, they are not entitled to compensation for these services, because the sickness of a partner is considered a risk assumed in the relationship. No agreement can be inferred that the active partners are to be compensated, even though the services rendered by them are such that ordinarily they would be rendered in the expectation of receiving compensation. As an exception, "a surviving partner is entitled to reasonable compensation for services performed in winding up the partnership affairs."[14]

To illustrate the effect of an agreement of the partners, they may agree that one of the partners shall devote full time as manager of the business and that a salary shall be paid for such services in addition to the managing partner's share of the profits.

(e) REPAYMENT OF LOANS. A partner is entitled to the return of any money advanced to or for the firm. These amounts, however, must be separate and distinct from original or additional contributions to the capital of the firm.

(f) PAYMENT OF INTEREST. In the absence of an agreement to the contrary, contributions to capital do not draw interest. The theory is that the profits constitute sufficient compensation. Advances by a partner in the form of loans are treated as if they were made by a stranger and bear interest from the date the advance is made.

(g) CONTRIBUTION AND INDEMNITY. A partner who pays more than a proportionate share of the debts of the firm has a right to contribution from the other partners. Under this principle, if an employee of a partnership negligently injures a third person while acting within the scope of employment and if the injured party collects damages from one partner, the latter may enforce contribution from the other partners in order to divide the loss equally between them.

The partnership must indemnify every partner for payments made and personal liabilities reasonably incurred in the ordinary and proper conduct of its business or for the preservation of its business or property. A partner has no right, however, to indemnity or reimbursement if the partner has (1) acted in bad faith, (2) negligently caused the necessity for payment, or (3) previously agreed to bear the expense alone.

(h) DISTRIBUTION OF CAPITAL. After the payment of all creditors and the repayment of loans made to the firm by partners, every partner is entitled to receive a share of the firm property upon dissolution.[15] Unless otherwise stated in the partnership agreement, all partners are entitled to the return of their capital contributions.

After such distribution is made, each partner is the sole owner of the fractional part distributed to that partner, rather than a co-owner of all the property as during the existence of the partnership.

§ 48:8   LIABILITY OF PARTNERS AND PARTNERSHIP AS TO PARTICULAR ACTS

The liability of a partnership and of the partners for the acts of individual partners and of employees is governed by the same principles as apply to the liability of an employer or a principal for the acts of an employee or agent.

(a) CONTRACTS. All members of the firm are liable on contracts made by a partner for the partnership and in its name if such contracts were made within the scope of the partner's real or apparent authority. Members are liable even though the partners may be unknown to the third person. Thus, a dormant partner, when discovered, can be held liable with the others.

When a partner acting on behalf of the partnership makes an authorized, simple contract but does so in the partner's own name, the firm and the other partners are liable as undisclosed principals.

---

[14] UPA § 18(f).

[15] Mandell v Centrum Frontier Corp. 86 Ill App 3d 437, 41 Ill Dec 323, 407 NE2d 821 (1980).

When a partner with necessary authority executes commercial paper in the name of the firm, the firm and every partner is bound thereby, even though the individual partners did not sign the paper. If a partner signs commercial paper in the partner's own name, the partnership and the other partners cannot sue or be sued thereon as undisclosed principals. Although partnership law determines the authority of a partner to enter into transactions on behalf of the firm, the UCC governs how commercial paper is to be executed by a partner.

When a borrowing partner gives the lender a promissory note for the partner's personal obligation, the partnership and the other partners cannot be liable thereon, even though the borrowing partner used the money for the benefit of the partnership.

The fact that a partner has either express or implied authority to bind the partnership does not in itself establish that a contract made by the partner is a partnership contract, as distinguished from the individual contract of the partner. As in the case of agency situations generally, a contract between the third person and the principal, here the partnership, does not arise when that is not the intention of the parties. Consequently, where a third person and a partner make a contract intending to bind the partner individually, rather than the partnership, no contract liability of the partnership is created. Care must be taken to distinguish this situation from that in which the partnership is not disclosed and in which the third person has the intention of dealing with the partner only; in such cases the partnership and the other partners may be bound or have rights under the rules governing undisclosed principals who act through authorized agents.

(b) TORTS. All partners are liable for torts, such as fraud, trespass, negligence, and assaults committed by one partner while transacting firm business.[16] Accordingly, a partnership formed to manage real estate is liable for a battery inflicted by one partner upon a tenant in collecting the rent. Each partner in a partnership formed for the general practice of medicine is liable for an injury to a patient resulting from lack of skill or the negligence of any one of the partners.[17]

(c) CRIMES. The partners of a firm and the partnership itself are liable for certain crimes committed by a partner in the course of the business, such as selling goods without obtaining a necessary vendor's license or selling in violation of a statute prohibiting sale. A partnership, as distinct from the individual partners, may be fined for committing the crime of violating the federal law establishing regulations for the safe transportation in interstate commerce of explosives and other dangerous articles. If carrying on the firm business does not necessarily involve the commission of the act constituting a crime, the firm and the partners not participating in the commission of the crime or authorizing its commission generally are not criminally liable. This exception is not recognized in some cases, such as the making of prohibited sales to minors or sales of adulterated products.

§ 48:9 NATURE OF PARTNER'S LIABILITY

By virtue of the UPA, partners are jointly liable on all firm contracts.[18] They are jointly and severally liable for all torts committed by an employee or one of the partners in the scope of the partnership business. When partners are liable for the wrongful injury caused a third person, the latter may sue all or any of the members of the firm.

In the *Zuckerman* case, the issue was whether the court could render a judgment against a doctor for malpractice committed by his partner, even though the summons did not name the partnership or designate the doctor as a partner.

---

[16] UPA § 13.

[17] Martin v Barbour (Mo App) 588 SW2d 200 (1977).
[18] Holt v Owen Electric Supply Inc. (Tex Civ App) 722 SW2d 22 (1986).

ZUCKERMAN V ANTENUCCI

478 NYS2d 578 (1984)

Daniel Zuckerman, an infant, and Elaine Zuckerman, his mother, brought a medical malpractice action against Dr. Joseph Antenucci and Dr. Jose Pena. Both had treated the mother during pregnancy. Although the summons did not state that the two defendants were partners, the undisputed, unopposed, and uncontradicted evidence at the trial established that relationship and that the alleged acts of malpractice were done in the course of partnership business. The jury returned a verdict finding that Dr. Pena was guilty of malpractice, but that Dr. Antenucci was not guilty of malpractice. The amount of the verdict totalled $4 million. The Zuckermans made a posttrial motion for judgment against the defendants, Joseph Antenucci and Jose Pena, in the sum of $4 million. Dr. Antenucci contends that he should not be held liable on a partnership theory for the act of his partner when the plaintiffs had not named the partnership entity on the summons nor did it designate him as a partner.

LEVISS, J. . . . The issue is whether this court has jurisdiction to render a judgment against defendant Antenucci on the basis of a tort committed by his partner, even though the summons served did not designate defendant Antenucci as a partner. . . .

A party may be sued individually and directly for the tort of his partner. A partnership is liable for the tortious act of a partner, and a partner is jointly and severally liable for tortious acts chargeable to the partnership.

Thus, if a partner, while acting in the course of the partnership business injures a third person, such third person would have the right to sue all of the partners together in one lawsuit, or any one or all of the partners individually, including even one who did not cause the injury . . . .

If it is a joint and several obligation of the partnership (based on a tort), any one (or some or all) of the individual partners may be sued personally *without suing the partnership itself* . . . .

When a tort is committed by the firm, the wrong is imputable to all of the partners jointly and severally, and an action may be brought against all or any of them in their individual capacities . . . or against the partnership as an entity.

To illustrate how a plaintiff may proceed where a tort is chargeable to a partnership, Professor Beane supposes a partnership, the ABC Shoe Store, composed of Able, Baker, and Charles. A customer, Mrs. Jones, who is injured by Kit, an employee of the partnership, may elect to sue in several different ways:

For example, Mrs. Jones may commence an action listing as defendants: "Able, Baker, and Charles individually and as partners, doing business under the name of ABC Shoe Store"; or she could commence an action listing "ABC Shoe Store" as the defendant; or she could sue any of the individual partners directly (without naming the partnership) as they are each jointly and severally liable for the tort. Therefore, she could commence an action against "Able" or she could commence an action against "Able and Baker", or against "Able and Charles", or "Baker and Charles". Since a person is liable for one's own tort, Mrs. Jones could also sue Kit, the employee; Kit could be named as a defendant in any of the preceding suggested actions. (Beane, *The Essentials of Partnership Law,* p 63.)

It may thus be seen that the plaintiffs herein did not have to sue a partnership entity and did not have to write "Joseph Antenucci, a partner" on the summons in order to hold him liable on a partnership theory for the act of defendant Pena. Jurisdiction over defendant Antenucci individually is sufficient for a judgment against him based on a tort committed by his partner.

Therefore, even though the jury found that defendant Antenucci was not guilty of any malpractice in his treatment of the patient, but that defendant Pena (his partner) was guilty of malpractice in his treatment of the patient, they were then both jointly and severally liable for the malpractice committed by defendant Pena by operation of law.

[Motion granted]

QUESTIONS

1. Was Dr. Antenucci found guilty of malpractice?
2. Were Dr. Pena's acts of malpractice done in the course of the Pena-Antenucci partnership business?
3. Where the court had jurisdiction over Dr. Antenucci individually, could it render a judgment against him based on a tort committed by his partner?

§ 48:10   EXTENT OF PARTNER'S LIABILITY

Each member of the firm has individual and unlimited liability for the debts of the partnership regardless of the member's investment or interest in the firm.

In the *CCIC* case, the court considered the question of whether one partner of a three-partner firm could be held liable for the full amount of a judgment against the partnership.

CCIC v McELMURRY
102 Mich App 536, 302 NW2d 222 (1981)

The Inn Group, Inc., defaulted on a promissory note, loan agreement, and mortgage. MHS Enterprises, a Michigan partnership of which Leland McElmurry was one of three partners, guaranteed the Inn Group's performance to Commonwealth Capital Investment Corporation (CCIC). CCIC brought suit against both the partnership and the three partners for default on the loan agreement at a time when the partnership had been dissolved, and was in the winding up process. The court entered a judgment against the partnership. Five months later CCIC brought suit against Leland McElmurry in his capacity as a partner of MHS to satisfy the judgment against the partnership. Since McElmurry admitted that he was a partner of MHS, the court found him liable for the entire debt of $1,137,285. McElmurry appealed.

PER CURIAM. . . . Defendant first contends that since MHS was dissolved prior to the institution of plaintiff's suit, no judgment could be rendered against it and, as such, he could not be liable on the void judgment as a general partner. . . . section 30 of the Uniform Partnership Act, provides:

On dissolution the partnership is not terminated, but continues until the winding up of partnership affairs is completed.

In *Englestein v Mackie*, 35 Ill App 276, 182 NE2d 351 (1962), the Illinois Court of Appeals said the following about section 30 of the Uniform Partnership Act:

The terms "dissolution" and "termination", as employed in the Partnership Act are not synonyms and, as used, have different meanings. Dissolution does not terminate the partnership and does not end completely the authority of the partners. The order of events is: (1) dissolution; (2) winding up; and (3) termination. Termination extinguishes their authority. It is the ultimate result of the winding up and occurs at the conclusion of the wind up.

The "winding up of partnership affairs" includes the satisfaction of debts against it. Consequently, it is our opinion that a partnership may be sued in its own name following dissolution, but prior to termination. . . .

Plaintiff properly sued the partnership as an entity. Consequently, the judgment entered against the partnership was not void, and defendant could be held liable as a general partner of the partnership.

Defendant further contends that there is no right to proceed against an individual partner based upon a judgment against the partnership. We disagree. UPA § 15 provides that all partners are jointly liable for the debts and obligations of the partnership. Furthermore, UPA § 36(1) provides that the dissolution of the partnership does not discharge the existing liability of any partner.

We agree with defendant that the judgment creditor of a partnership must first bring execution against the partnership assets before seeking to reach a general partner's individual assets. See, UPA § 18(a); and UPA §40(d). However, defendant does not allege that partnership assets remain which might be used to satisfy the debt. An examination of the record suggests that, in fact, no such assets do continue to exist. Thus, the trial court's order was not improperly entered.

[Judgment affirmed]

QUESTIONS

1. Can a partnership be sued following dissolution of the partnership, when the partnership is in the winding up process?
2. Can one of three partners be held liable for the entire debt of a partnership?
3. Does dissolution of the partnership discharge the existing liability of the partners?

(a) LIABILITY FOR BREACH OF DUTY. When a partner violates a duty owed to the partnership, the partner's liability is determined by the general principles of contract, tort, or agency law that may be applicable to such conduct.

When one partner commits a fraud upon another partner, the injured partner may recover compensatory and sometimes exemplary damages from the wrongdoing partner.

(b) LIABILITY OF NEW PARTNERS. A person admitted as a partner into an existing partnership has limited liability for all the obligations of the partnership arising before such admission. This is a limited liability in that the preadmission claim may be satisfied only out of partnership property and does not extend to the individual property of the newly admitted partner.[19] The incoming partner does not become personally liable for preadmission claims unless the incoming partner expressly promises to pay such claims.

(c) EFFECT OF DISSOLUTION ON PARTNER'S LIABILITY. A partner remains liable after dissolution of the partnership unless expressly released by the creditors or unless all claims against the partnership have been satisfied.[20] The dissolution of the partnership does not of itself discharge the existing liability of any partner. The individual property of a deceased partner is liable for the obligations of the partnership that were incurred while the deceased partner was alive, but the individual creditors of the deceased partner have priority over the partnership creditors with respect to such property.[21]

[19] UPA § 17; see also UPA § 41(1), (7).
[20] Gjovik v Strope (Minn) 401 NW2d 664 (1987).
[21] UPA § 36.

§ 48:11   ENFORCEMENT OF PARTNER'S LIABILITY

The manner in which the civil liability of a partner may be enforced depends upon the form of the lawsuit brought by the creditor. The firm may have been sued in the name of all the individual partners doing business as the partnership, as "Plaintiff v A, B, and C, doing business as the Ajax Warehouse." In such a case, those partners named are bound by the judgment against the firm if they have been properly served in the suit. Partners either not named or not served are generally not bound by the judgment.

When a judgment is obtained against a partner, it may be enforced against the nonpartnership assets of that partner in the same way as a judgment would be enforced against any judgment debtor. The creditor may enforce judgment against the partner's interest in the partnership only by obtaining a charging order against that interest.

If the judgment binds an individual partner, the creditor may enforce the judgment against the partner before, at the same time, or after the creditor seeks to enforce the judgment against the firm or other partners who are also bound by the judgment. If a partner is not bound by a judgment, the creditor must bring another lawsuit against the partner in which the creditor establishes that the defendant is a partner in the particular partnership and that a judgment was entered against the partnership for a partnership liability. When this is established, a judgment is entered in favor of the creditor against the particular partner. The creditor may then have execution on this judgment against the property of the partner.

SUMMARY

When there are more than two partners in a firm, the decisions of the majority prevail on ordinary matters relating to the firm's business, unless they are contrary to the partnership agreement. A partner's authority to act for the firm is similar to that of an agent to act for a principal. A partner may have express authority to act as set forth in the partnership agreement or as agreed to by a sufficient number of partners. A partner has the customary or implied power to make contracts to transact the firm's business; to sell the firm's goods in the regular course of business; to make purchases within the scope of the business; and, in a trading partnership, to borrow money for firm purposes. Further, a partner may purchase insurance, hire employees, and adjust claims for and against the firm. A partner may not, however, bind the firm by a contract that would make it impossible for the firm to conduct its business. In the absence of express authority from the firm, an individual partner cannot enter into a suretyship contract or an agreement to submit a partnership dispute to arbitration, confess judgment against the firm, make an assignment of the firm's assets for the benefit of its creditors, or discharge personal obligations of the partner by paying them with obligations of the firm.

A partner's duties are the same as those of an agent, including the duties of loyalty and good faith, obedience, reasonable care, full information on all matters affecting the firm, and keeping proper and correct records. Absent a contrary agreement, each partner has the right to take an equal part in the management of the business, to inspect the books, to share in the profits, and after payment of all of the firm's debts and the return of capital, to share in the firm's property or surplus upon dissolution.

Partners are subject to unlimited personal liability to partnership claimants. Partners are jointly liable on all firm contracts. They are jointly and severally liable for all torts committed by one of the partners or a firm employee within the scope of the partnership's business. A partner remains liable after dissolution, unless expressly released by creditors. Absent assumption, an incoming partner is not personally liable for existing partnership debts.

QUESTIONS AND CASE PROBLEMS

1. What social forces are affected by the rule governing the authority of a majority of the partners?

2. The Acorn Hardware Store is owned and operated by a partnership consisting of five partners. They disagree as to whether they should have the building repainted. How many partners must agree to repaint?

3. John Summers and E. A. Dooley formed a partnership to collect trash. Summers became unable to work, and he hired a third man to do his work and paid him out of his personal funds. Summers suggested to Dooley that the third man be paid from the partnership funds but Dooley refused to do so, saying, "I'm voting no." Finally Summers sued Dooley for reimbursement of the money he had spent to pay the third man. Is Summers entitled to be reimbursed? [Summers v Dooley, 94 Idaho 87, 481 P2d 318]

4. Compare the right of a partner to engage in a business that competes with the firm (a) while still a partner, and (b) after leaving the partnership.

5. Ross, Marcos, and Albert are partners. Ross and Marcos each contributed $60,000 to the partnership. Albert contributed $30,000. At the end of the fiscal year, there are distributable profits totaling $150,000. Ross claims $60,000 as his share of the profits. Is he entitled thereto?

6. What is the effect of dissolution on a partner's liability?

7. Brenda and Stephen are partners owning and operating a paint store. Stephen opens another store in his own name. This second store competes with the partnership store. Brenda objects to Stephen's running his own store. Stephen replies that he can do so because there is nothing in the partnership agreement that prohibits such activity. Is Stephen entitled to run his own store in competition with the partnership store?

8. Compare the effect of a secret limitation on the authority of (a) an agent, and (b) a partner.

9. Elrod and Hansford were partners under the name of Walter Elrod & Co. Hansford purchased on credit from the firm of Dawson Blakemore & Co. certain merchandise

for the firm. Before the sale, Elrod had noti-fied Dawson Blakemore & Co. that he would not be bound to pay for any credit purchase for the firm made by Hansford. Thereafter, Dawson Blakemore & Co. brought an action against the members of Walter Elrod & Co. to recover the price of the goods. Elrod contended that he was not bound by the contract made by Hansford. Decide. [Dawson Blakemore & Co. v Elrod, 105 Ky 624, 49 SW 465]

10. Mason and Phyllis Ledbetter operated a business in Northbrook, Illinois as a part-nership. This partnership, called Ledbet-ters' Nurseries, specialized in the sale of garden lilies. The grounds of the nurseries were cultivated with the numerous species of garden lilies, and hundreds of people toured the Ledbetters' gardens each day. After a tour Mrs. Shelia Clark invited Mason to Chicago to discuss the possible sale of the facilities at a "top notch price." Mason felt he could not refuse the high of-fer made by Mrs. Clark on a take-it-or-leave-it basis, and he signed a contract to sell the entire facilities, including all flowers and the business name to Mrs. Clark. When Phyllis refused to go along with the con-tract, Mrs. Clark brought suit against the Ledbetters' Nurseries partnership seeking to obtain a decree of specific performance of the sales contract. Decide.

11. Holmes and Clay are partners in a medical partnership. Each had invested $25,000 in the practice; and the total market value of all firm assets was $50,000. Marsh, a former pa-tient of Holmes, sued Holmes and Clay for malpractice because of surgery performed by Holmes. Marsh's suit was successful, and a judgment was entered for $150,000 against the two partners. Holmes had suffered a prior financial setback, and he did not have funds or property other than partnership as-sets to pay the judgment. Arrangements were made by Holmes and Clay to pay $50,000 utilizing the firm assets. Marsh now seeks to collect $100,000 from Clay. Clay ob-jects that it is absurd to seek payment from her out of her own personal assets when she was not at fault and, indeed, was not even at the hospital on the day the surgery was per-formed. Is Clay liable to Marsh for the un-paid balance of the judgment?

12. The Port Richey Shopping Village was owned and operated by a partnership. Myrick and his wife were two of the part-ners. They owed money to the Second Na-tional Bank. The Second National Bank ob-tained a judgment against the Myricks that directed the sheriff to sell the Myricks' in-terest in the shopping village. Myrick and his wife filed a motion to prevent the sale. Will they succeed? [Myrick v Second Na-tional Bank (Fla App) 335 So 2d 343]

13. The St. John Transportation Co., a corpora-tion, made a contract with the partnership of Bilyeu & Herstel, contractors, by which the latter was to construct a ferryboat. Her-stel, a member of the firm of contractors, ex-ecuted a contract in the firm name with Ben-bow for certain materials and labor in con-nection with the construction of the ferry-boat. In an action brought by Benbow to en-force a lien against the ferryboat, the *James Johns*, it was contended that all members of the firm were bound by the contract made by Herstel. Do you agree? [Benbow v The James Johns, 56 Or 554, 108 P 634]

14. William and Charlotte Davis operated the Davis Nursing Home as a partnership. Wil-liam made a contract to sell the home and all its assets and goodwill to Feingold. Char-lotte refused to recognize the contract. Fein-gold sued William and Charlotte to obtain a decree of specific performance of the sales contract. Decide. [Feingold v Davis, 444 Pa 339, 282 A2d 291]

15. Zemelman and others did business as a part-nership under the name of Art Seating Com-pany. The partnership obtained a fire insur-ance policy from the Boston Insurance Com-pany. There was a fire loss, and a claim was filed under the policy. The claim was pre-pared by one of the partners, Irving Zemelman. The insurance company assert-ed that false statements were made by Zemelman and that consequently the insur-er was not liable on the policy. The policy contained an express provision stating that it was void if a false claim were made. The partnership replied that it was not bound by any fraudulent statement of Zemelman, as the making of fraudulent statements was not within the scope of his authority. Is the part-nership correct? [Zemelman v Boston Insur-ance Co. 4 Cal App 3d 15, 84 Cal Rptr 206]

49

NATURE, CREATION, AND TERMINATION OF CORPORATIONS

The corporation is one of the most important forms of business organization. To the large-scale enterprise the corporate form makes financing easier by dividing the entity's ownership into many small units that can be sold to a wide range of investors. In addition to assisting the financing of operations, the corporate device offers a limited liability to the owners and a perpetual succession not affected by the death of any particular owner or by the transfer of the shares of stock of any particular owner.

A. NATURE AND CLASSES

A corporation is an artificial person that is created by governmental action. A number of different kinds of corporations may be created.

§ 49:1 THE CORPORATION AS A PERSON

A **corporation** is an artificial being, created by government grant and endowed with certain powers. That is, the corporation exists in the eyes of the law as a person, separate and distinct from the persons who own the corporation.[1]

This concept means that property of the corporation is not owned by the persons who own shares in the corporation, but by the corporation. Debts of the corporation are debts of this artificial person and not of the persons running the corporation or owning shares of stock in it. The corporation can sue and be sued in its own name with respect to corporate rights and liabilities, but the shareholders cannot sue or be sued as to those rights and liabilities.

A corporation is formed by obtaining approval of a **certificate of incorporation, articles of incorporation,** or a **charter** from the state or national government.[2]

§ 49:2   CLASSIFICATIONS OF CORPORATIONS

Corporations may be classified in terms of their relationship to the public, the source of their authority, and the nature of their activities.

(a) PUBLIC, PRIVATE, AND QUASI-PUBLIC CORPORATIONS. A **public corporation** is one established for governmental purposes and for the administration of public affairs. A city is a public or municipal corporation acting under authority granted to it by the state.

A **private corporation** is one organized by persons, whether for charitable and be-

nevolent purposes or for purposes of finance, industry, and commerce. Private corporations are often called "public" in business circles when the stock is sold to the public, that is, publicly traded on the stock exchanges.

A **quasi-public corporation,** also known as a public-service corporation or a public utility, is a private corporation furnishing services upon which the public is particularly dependent, such as a railroad or a gas and electric company.

(b) PUBLIC AUTHORITIES. In the twentieth century, the public is increasingly demanding that government perform services. Some of these are performed directly by government. Others are performed by separate corporations or **authorities** that are created by government. For example, a city parking facility may be organized as a separate **municipal parking authority.** A public low-cost housing project may be operated as an independent **housing authority.**

(c) DOMESTIC AND FOREIGN CORPORATIONS. A corporation is called a **domestic corporation** with respect to the state or nation under whose law it has been incorporated. Any other corporation going into that state or nation is called a **foreign corporation.** Thus, a corporation holding a Texas charter is a domestic corporation in Texas but a foreign corporation in all other states and nations.

(d) SPECIAL SERVICE CORPORATIONS. Corporations formed for transportation, banking, insurance, savings and loan operations, and similar specialized functions, are subject to separate codes or statutes with regard to their organization. In addition, federal and state laws and administrative agencies regulate in detail the manner in which these businesses are conducted.

(e) CLOSE CORPORATIONS. A corporation whose shares are held by a single shareholder or a closely knit group of shareholders is known as a **close corporation.** The shares are not traded publicly. Many such corporations are small firms that in the past would have operated as proprietorships or

---

[1]   Macaluso v Jenkins, 96 Ill App 3d 254, 51 Ill Dec 743, 420 NE2d 251 (1981).

[2]   *Charter, certificate of incorporation,* and *articles of incorporation* are all terms used to refer to the documents that serve as evidence of a government's grant of corporate existence and powers. Most state incorporation statutes now provide for a certificate of incorporation issued by the secretary of state, but a Revised Model Business Corporation Act has done away with the certificate of incorporation in an attempt to reduce the volume of paperwork handled by the secretary of state. Under the RMBCA, corporate existence begins when articles of incorporation are filed with the secretary of state. An endorsed copy of the articles together with a fee, receipt, or acknowledgment replace the certificate of incorporation. See RMBCA §§ 1.25 and 2.03 and footnote 5 in this chapter.

partnerships but are incorporated either to obtain the advantages of limited liability or a tax benefit, or both.

Statutes have in many states liberalized the corporation law when close corporations are involved, such as permitting their incorporation by a smaller number of persons, allowing them to have a one-person board of directors, and eliminating the requirement of formal meetings.[3]

(f) PROFESSIONAL CORPORATIONS. A corporation may be organized for the purpose of conducting a profession.

(g) NONPROFIT CORPORATIONS. A **nonprofit corporation** (or an eleemosynary corporation) is one that is organized for charitable or benevolent purposes, such as certain hospitals, homes, and universities.[4] Special procedures for incorporation are sometimes prescribed, with provision being made for a detailed examination and hearing as to the purpose, function, and methods of raising money for the enterprise.

§ 49:3   CORPORATIONS AND GOVERNMENTS

Problems between governments and corporations arise with respect to the power of governments to create and regulate corporations.

(a) POWER TO CREATE. Since by definition a corporation is created by government grant, the right to be a corporation must be obtained from the proper government. The federal government may create

corporations whenever appropriate to carry out the powers granted to it.

Generally a state by virtue of its police power may create any kind of corporation for any purpose. Most states have a **general corporation code** that lists certain requirements, and anyone who satisfies the requirements and files the necessary papers with the government may automatically become a corporation. In 1950, the American Bar Association published a Model Business Corporation Act (ABA MBCA) to assist legislative bodies in the modernization of state corporation laws.[5] An updated version, incorporating numerous revisions made over the years was published in 1969. Statutory language similar to that contained in the 1969 version of the MBCA has been adopted in whole or in part by thirty-five states. A 1984 revision of the Model Act ,the RMBCA, represents the first complete revision in more than thirty years. Jurisdictions following the Model Act have made numerous modifications to reflect their differing views in the balancing of interests of public corporations, shareholders, and management. Caution must therefore be exercised in making generalizations about Model Act jurisdictions. There is no uniform corporation act.

(b) POWER TO REGULATE. The extent of the power of governments to regulate corporations is affected by whether a corporation is given the rights of a person and of a citizen.

(1) Protection of the Corporation as a Person. The Constitution of the United States prohibits the national government and the state governments from depriving any "person" of life, liberty, or property without due process of law. Many state

---

[3]   This distinction between large and small corporations is part of the same current of legal development that in the Uniform Commercial Code has given rise to the distinction between the merchant seller or buyer on the one hand, and the casual seller or buyer, on the other.

[4]   The Committee on Corporate Laws of the American Bar Association has prepared a Model Non-Profit Corporation Act as a comparison to the Model Business Association Act. The Non-Profit Corporation Act has formed the basis for nonprofit corporation statutes in Alabama, Iowa, Nebraska, North Carolina, North Dakota, Ohio, Oregon, Texas, Virginia, Washington, Wisconsin, and the District of Columbia.

[5]   The Revised Model Business Corporation Act (1984) was approved by the Committee on Corporate Laws of the Section of Corporation, Banking and Business Law of the American Bar Association. The Committee approved revisions to Sections 6.40 and 8.33 on March 27, 1987. Excerpts of the 1984 Act, as revised, are presented in the Appendix to this book. Model Act citations are to the 1984 Revised Model Business Corporation Act (RMBCA) unless specifically designated otherwise.

constitutions contain a similar limitation upon their respective state governments. A corporation is regarded as a "person" within the meaning of such provisions.

The federal Constitution prohibits a state from denying to any "person" within its jurisdiction the equal protection of the laws. No such express limitation is placed upon the federal government, although the due process clause binding the federal government is liberally interpreted so that it prohibits substantial inequality of treatment.

(2) Protection of the Corporation as a Citizen. For certain purposes, such as determining the right to bring a lawsuit in a federal court, a corporation today is deemed a citizen of any state in which it has been incorporated and of the state where it has its principal place of business, without regard to the actual citizenship of the individual persons owning the stock of the corporation. Thus, the corporation incorporated in New York is a New York corporation even though its shareholders are citizens of many other states. Likewise, a Delaware corporation having its principal place of business in New York is deemed to be a citizen of New York as well as of Delaware.[6] An environmental protection law authorizing any citizen to bring suit to prevent pollution permits a corporation to bring such a suit.

The federal Constitution prohibits states from abridging "the privileges or immunities of citizens of the United States." A corporation, however, is not regarded as a citizen within this clause. Thus, with one exception, a foreign corporation has no constitutional right to do business in another state if that other state wishes to exclude it. For example, Pennsylvania can deny a New York corporation the right to come into Pennsylvania to do business. As a practical matter, most states do not exclude foreign corporations but seize upon this power as justifying special regulation or taxation. On this basis it is commonly provided that a foreign corporation must register or even take out a domestic charter, file copies of its charter, pay certain taxes, or appoint a resident agent before it can do business within the state.

As an exception to the power of a state, a state cannot require a license or registration of a foreign interstate commerce corporation or impose a tax upon the right to engage in such a business.

§ 49:4   IGNORING THE
         CORPORATE ENTITY

Ordinarily, a corporation will be regarded and treated as a separate legal person and the law will not look behind a corporation to see who owns or controls it.

The fact that two corporations have identical shareholders does not justify a court in regarding the two corporations as being one. Likewise the fact that there is a close working relationship between two corporations does not in itself constitute any basis for ignoring their separate corporate entities when they in fact are separately run enterprises.[7]

(a) "PIERCING THE CORPORATE VEIL." A court may disregard the corporate entity, or figuratively "pierce the corporate veil," when exceptional circumstances warrant. The decision whether to disregard the corporate entity is made on a case-by-case basis, weighing all factors before the court. Factors that may lead to piercing the corporate veil and imposing liability upon its owners, the shareholders, are (1) failure to maintain adequate corporate records and the commingling of corporate and other funds, (2) grossly inadequate capitalization, (3) diversion by shareholders of corporate funds or assets, (4) the formation of the corporation to evade an existing obligation, (5) the formation of the corporation to perpetrate a fraud or conceal illegality,[8] and (6) injustice and inequitable conse-

---

[6]   28 United States Code § 1332(c).

[7]   Extra Energy Coal Co. v Diamond (Ind) 467 NE2d 439 (1984).

[8]   Brock Builders Inc. v Dahlbeck, 223 Neb 493, 391 NW2d 110 (1986).

quences would result if the corporate entity were recognized.[9] The corporate entity may sometimes be ignored and rights and liabilities determined as though there were no corporation.

The *Stap* case deals with whether the corporate entity should be ignored.

[9] Nebraska Engineering Co. v Gerstner, 212 Neb 440, 323 NW2d 84 (1982).

STAP V CHICAGO ACES TENNIS TEAM, INC.
63 Ill App 3d 23, 20 Ill Dec 230, 379 NE2d 1298 (1978)

Jordan and Walter Kaiser organized a corporation called The Chicago Aces Tennis Team, Inc. They made a contract with Susan Stap to play professional tennis. She was never paid the money called for by the contract, and she sued the Kaiser brothers. They raised the defense that they could not be sued individually because Susan's contract was with the corporation. She claimed that the corporate entity should be ignored and that the brothers should be held liable on the contract of the corporation. She based this claim on the fact that the brothers owned 100 percent of the stock of the corporation and had contributed 100 percent of the capital of a partnership that was a majority shareholder in another corporation that owned facilities used by The Chicago Aces corporation. She further claimed that the Kaiser brothers had handled the funds of the partnership and The Chicago Aces in disregard of the separate identity of the corporation. The lower court entered judgment in favor of the brothers, and Susan appealed.

SULLIVAN, P. J. . . . Plaintiff sought to have the corporate entity disregarded. She argues that because the Club was undercapitalized as the result of manipulation of funds through the other corporate interests controlled by the Kaisers and Kaiser Investments, there should be a piercing of the corporate veil and those defendants held liable.

A corporation is a legal entity that exists separate and distinct from its shareholders, officers, and directors, who are not as a general rule liable for the corporation's debts and obligations. . . . However, a corporate entity will be disregarded and the veil of limited liability pierced where it would otherwise present an obstacle to the protection of private rights or when the corporation is merely the alter ego or business conduit of a governing or dominating personality.

For the doctrine traditionally known as "piercing the corporate veil" to apply, two requirements must be met — (1) there must be such unity of interest and ownership that the separate personalities of the corporation and the individual no longer exist; and (2) circumstances must exist that adherence to the fiction of separate corporation existence would sanction a fraud or promote injustice. *Scott v Pintozzi* (1971), 50 Ill 2d 115, 277 NE2d 844. . . .

> The concept of disregarding the corporate existence and imposing liability personally upon the real parties to a transaction is well established . . . "[where the director or officer is the alter ego of the corporation, that is, where there is such unity of interest and ownership that the separateness of the individual and [the] corporation

has ceased to exist; and the facts are such that an adherence to the fiction of separate existence of the corporation would sanction a fraud or promote injustice, such director or officer will be held liable for obligations of the corporation." . . .

In *Ballantine on Corporations*, it is stated:

If a corporation is organized and carries on business without substantial capital in such a way that the corporation is likely to have no sufficient assets available to meet its debts, it is inequitable that shareholders should set up such a flimsy organization to escape personal liability. The attempt to do corporate business without providing any sufficient basis of financial responsibility to creditors is an abuse of the separate entity and will be ineffectual to exempt the shareholders from corporate debts. It is coming to be recognized as the policy of the law that shareholders should in good faith put at the risk of the business unencumbered capital reasonably adequate for its prospective liabilities. If the capital is illusory or trifling compared with the business to be done and the risks of loss, this is a ground for denying the separate entity privilege. *Ballantine on Corporations*, p. 302-03 (rev ed 1946).

The specific issue before us is whether the requirements of a cause of action founded upon a piercing of the corporate veil has been set forth. . . .

It is alleged that plaintiff entered into an agreement with the Club to play tennis for a salary and bonuses; that the Kaisers owned 100% of the Club stock; that they had contributed 100% of the capital in Kaiser Investments, a partnership; that the Kaisers were majority shareholders in four other corporations — one of which was the owner of the facilities used by the Club; that the Kaisers, through Kaiser Investments, manipulated the funds between the Club and the other corporation in disregard of the entities of each; that the Club was undercapitalized and, as a result, was unable to pay its debts and did not pay the salary and bonuses earned by plaintiff; that the Kaisers, through Kaiser Investments, failed to carry out the business of the Club and the other four corporations as separate interests; and that the observance of the fiction of separate corporate existence would sanction a fraud and permit injustice against the plaintiff. . . .

In the light of the foregoing, we are of the belief that the court improperly granted the motions to strike and dismiss . . . plaintiff's complaint.

[Judgment reversed and action remanded]

QUESTIONS

1. What factors led the court to ignore the separate entity of the tennis corporation?
2. Did the fact that the defendants had made the contract with the plaintiff on behalf of the corporation protect them from liability to her?
3. What is the basis for the court's decision?

Some courts use different terminology when disregarding the corporate entity. Thus when a person uses a corporation as a mask behind which to hide from a person being defrauded, the court will hold the wrongdoer liable for the acts of the corporation stating that it is the *alter ego* of the wrongdoer.

(b) FUNCTIONAL REALITY. When a corporation is in effect merely a department of a large enterprise, as when a large manufacturer incorporates its marketing department while continuing to hold itself out to the public as a single enterprise, it is likely that the separate corporate character of the incorporated department will be ignored.

(c)   OBTAINING   ADVANTAGES   OF CORPORATE EXISTENCE. The court will not go behind the corporate identity merely because the corporation has been formed to obtain tax savings or to obtain limited liability for its shareholders. Likewise, the corporate entity will not be ignored merely because the corporation does not have sufficient assets to pay the claims against it.

One-person, family, and other closely held corporations are permissible and fully entitled to all of the advantages of corporate existence. However, factors that lead to piercing the corporate veil more commonly exist in these kinds of corporations, such as grossly inadequate capitalization, commingling of assets, and failure to maintain separate corporate books and accounts.[10]

B.   CREATION OF THE CORPORATION

All states have general laws governing the creation of corporations by persons who comply with the provisions of the statutes.

§ 49:5   PROMOTERS

Corporations frequently come into existence as the result of the activities of one or more persons known as promoters, although there is no legal requirement for the services of a promoter in the formation of a corporation.

The **promoter** brings together persons interested in the enterprise, aids in obtaining subscriptions to stock, and sets in motion the machinery that leads to the formation of the corporation itself.

A corporation is not liable on a contract made by its promoter for its benefit unless it takes some affirmative action to adopt such contract. Such action may be express words of adoption, or the adoption of the contract may be inferred from the corporation's accepting the benefits thereof. A corporation may also become bound by such contracts by assignment or by novation.

The promoter is personally liable for all contracts made on behalf of the corporation before its existence unless exempted by the terms of the agreement or by the circumstances surrounding it.[11] When a promoter makes a contract on behalf of a corporation to be formed thereafter, the promoter is liable thereon if the corporation is not formed, in the absence of an agreement that the promoter should not be so liable.

A promoter is liable for all torts committed in connection with the promoter's activities. The corporation is not ordinarily liable for the torts of the promoter, but it may become liable by its conduct after incorporation. Thus, when a corporation, with actual or implied notice of the fraud of the promoter, assumes the promoter's contract, it is liable for the promoter's fraud that induced the other party to enter into the contract.

A promoter stands in a fiduciary relation to the corporation and to stock subscribers, and cannot make secret profits at their expense. Accordingly, if a promoter makes a secret profit on a sale of land to the corporation, the promoter must account to the corporation for this profit; that is, the promoter must surrender the profit to the corporation. The promoter may be held guilty of embezzlement if the promoter converts property that should have gone to the corporation.

The corporation is not liable in most states for the expenses and services of the

---

[10] Mac Chambers Co. v Iowa Tae Kwon Do Academy, Inc. (Iowa) 412 NW2d 593 (1987).

[11] Pierson v Coffey (Ky App) 706 SW2d 409 (1985). Company Store Development Corp. v Pottery Warehouse (Tenn App) 733 SW2d 886 (1987).

promoter unless it subsequently promises to pay for them or unless its charter or a statute imposes such liability upon it.

In the *Golden* case, the plaintiff claimed that the promoter was liable to the corporation because he had made a secret profit in purchasing shares from the corporation.

GOLDEN V OAHE ENTERPRISES, INC.
(SD) 295 NW2d 160 (1980)

Donald Emmick was a director and shareholder of Colonial Manors, Inc. (CM). He organized another corporation named Oahe Enterprises, Inc. In order to obtain shares of the Oahe stock, Emmick transferred CM shares to the new corporation. In making this exchange, the CM stock was valued at $19 a share. It had a book value of 47 cents a share. The figure of $19 had been arbitrarily selected because the CM directors had specified that price for certain option purchase contracts. Emmick also believed that eventually the stock would increase in value to $19. The board of directors of Oahe approved Emmick's payment for the Oahe shares with the CM shares valued at $19 share. Golden sued Donald Emmick on the ground that he had fraudulently deceived the corporation as to the value of the CM shares and thus had made a secret profit when he received the Oahe shares that had a much greater value than the CM shares that he gave in exchange. From a judgment against Golden, he appealed.

NOLLMAN, C. J. . . . In *Lloyd v Preston*, 146 US (1892), the Supreme Court held that the overvaluation of property exchanged for corporate stock, even though such valuation was ratified by the corporation's board of directors, established fraud and entitled complaining creditors to enforce full payment from the transferor for the stock issued him.

In *Donald v American Smelting & Refining Co.* 62 NJEq 729, 48 A 771 (1901), the court . . . stated:

> different estimates may be formed of the value of property [exchanged for stock]. When such differences are brought before judicial tribunals, the judgment of those who are by law entrusted with the power of issuing stock "to the amount of the value of the property," and on whom, therefore, is placed the first duty of valuing the property, must be accorded considerable weight. But it cannot be deemed conclusive when duly subjected to judicial scrutiny. Nor is it necessary that *conscious overvaluation or any other form of fraudulent conduct on the part of these primary valuers* should be shown, to justify judicial interposition. *Their honest judgment, if reached without due examination into the elements of value . . . or if plainly warped by self-interest,* may lead to a violation of this statutory rule, as surely as would corrupt motive. . . . It is the duty of the courts . . . to see that this standard is not violated, either intentionally or unintentionally.

(emphasis supplied). We believe that this approach should be applied to the case at bar. . . .

As a promoter of Oahe, Emmick stood in a fiduciary relationship to both the corporation and its stockholders and was bound to deal with them in the utmost good faith. "The obtaining of a secret profit by a promoter through the sale of property to a corporation is uniformly held to be a fraud on the corporation and stockholders, and the promoter may be required to account for such profit." . . .

The valuation of the CM stock was based on Emmick's self-serving estimate of matters well known to him as a CM insider and was warped by Emmick's self-interest. Emmick was not trading stock that had an easily ascertainable value; he was not dealing with people experienced in transactions of this type. He failed to make known facts of which he, as an insider of CM, was aware. It is true that Emmick was not the only member of the Oahe board of directors. He was, however, the controlling member and the one in possession of information pertinent to the value of his CM stock not generally available to the public or to the other Oahe board members. In addition to being an insider of CM, he was both a director of and the dominant and controlling force in Oahe. We hold, therefore, that he failed in his duty to the corporation to disclose information regarding stock he intended to transfer into Oahe for Oahe shares and is therefore liable for the shortfall to the corporation therefrom.

We conclude that the CM stock that Emmick transferred into Oahe was greatly overvalued at its $19.00 per share figure. We do not consider the $19.00 per share figure affixed by Emmick to be supported by credible evidence in the record, nor do we find it to be indicative of the true value of CM stock at the time of transfer, all factors considered. Nothing in the record indicates that Emmick knew at the time of the transfer whether any sales of CM stock in 1966 had actually occurred, nor did Jerry Jackson, a fellow CM associate, indicate that Emmick knew of any sales Jackson made in 1966. The certified public accountant who helped prepare the receiver's report advised the court that it should take judicial notice that the CM stock was watered or fictitiously increased at the time of the exchange. Further, the trial court found that valuation of the stock by the CM Board of Directors "was substantially based on future growth and profit." Article XVII, § 8 of the South Dakota Constitution prohibits the use of future or potential value for purposes of valuing property exchanged for corporate stock. Value based on future potential is speculative and arbitrary. Statutory authorization for the issuance of stock in exchange for property does not permit the issuance of stock for property that is overvalued or is worth substantially less than the par value of the stock. . . . It is the cash value of the exchanged property, not its future value or the hopes or expectations or the prospects of future value, that must be taken as the basis for exchange. . . . Accordingly, we conclude that the trial court erred insofar as it allowed future, potential or speculative value to determine the value assigned to the CM stock.

Because the total value of the CM stock Emmick transferred to Oahe was less than the value Emmick received in Oahe stock, the difference can be equalized by canceling the number of Oahe shares held by Emmick that is proportional to the overvaluation. . . .

[Judgment reversed and action remanded]

QUESTIONS

1. Did the court impose liability upon the defendant for the conduct in question?
2. What duty did Emmick owe to the Oahe corporation, its board of directors, and its shareholders?
3. What is the amount of the money judgment entered against Emmick?

§ 49:6   INCORPORATION

One or more natural persons or corporations may act as **incorporators** of a corporation by signing and filing articles of incorporation with the designated government official.[12] These articles are filed in duplicate. The designated official (usually the secretary of state) upon being satisfied that the articles conform to the statutory requirements, stamps *filed* and the date on each copy. The official then retains one copy and returns the other copy along with a filing fee receipt to the corporation.[13]

Statutes may require the incorporators to give some form of public notice, as by advertising in a newspaper, of the intention to form the corporation.

§ 49:7   APPLICATION FOR INCORPORATION

The instrument by which a private corporation is formed in most jurisdictions is called the **articles of incorporation**. The instrument is filed with the secretary of state and sets forth certain information about the new corporation. The articles of incorporation must contain (1) the name of the corporation, (2) the number of shares the corporation is authorized to issue, (3) the street address of the corporation's initial registered office and the name of its initial registered agent, and (4) the name and address of each incorporator.[14] The articles of incorporation may contain optional provisions such as the purpose or purposes for which the corporation is organized, but if it contains no "purpose clause," the corporation will automatically have the purpose of engaging in any lawful business.[15] Also, if no reference is made to the period of duration of the corporation in the articles of incorporation, it will automatically have perpetual duration.[16] If the articles of incorporation conform to the requirements of the state corporation law,

the secretary of state will issue a *certificate of incorporation* in most states.

§ 49:8   THE CERTIFICATE OF INCORPORATION

While most state incorporation statutes now provide for a certificate of incorporation issued by the secretary of state, the Revised Model Business Corporation Act has eliminated the certificate of incorporation in an effort to reduce the volume of paper work handled by the secretary of state. Under the Revised Act, corporate existence begins when the articles are filed with the secretary of state.[17] Under the older practice still followed by most states, corporate existence begins upon the issuance of the certificate of incorporation by the secretary of state.

§ 49:9   PROPER AND DEFECTIVE INCORPORATION

If the procedure for incorporation has been followed, the corporation has a perfect legal right to exist. It is then called a **corporation de jure,** meaning that it is a corporation by virtue of law.[18]

Assume that there is some defect in the corporation that is formed. If the defect is not a material one, the law usually will overlook the defect and hold that the corporation is a corporation de jure.

The RMBCA abolishes objections to irregularities and defects in incorporating. It provides that the "secretary of state's filing of the articles of incorporation is conclusive proof that the incorporators satisfied all conditions precedent to incorporation. . . ."[19] Many state statutes follow this pattern. Such an approach is based upon the practical consideration that when countless persons are purchasing shares of stock and entering into business transactions with thousands of corporations, it becomes

---

[12]   RMBCA § 2.01.
[13]   RMBCA § 1.25.
[14]   RMBCA § 2.02.
[15]   RMBCA § 3.01.
[16]   RMBCA § 3.02.

[17]   RMBCA § 2.03(a).
[18]   Kansas v Construction Enterprises, Inc. 6 Kan App 2d 627, 631 P2d 1240 (1981).
[19]   RMBCA § 2.03(b).

an absurdity to expect that anyone is going to make the detailed search that would be required to determine whether a given corporation is a de jure corporation.[20]

(a) DE FACTO CORPORATION. The defect in the incorporation may be so substantial that the law cannot ignore it and will not accept the corporation as a de jure corporation. Yet there may be sufficient compliance so that the law will recognize that there is a corporation. When this occurs, the association is called a **de facto corporation.**

Although there is conflict among the authorities, the traditional elements of a de facto corporation are that (1) a valid law exists under which the corporation could have been properly incorporated; (2) an attempt to organize the corporation has been made in good faith; (3) a genuine attempt to organize in compliance with the requirements of the statute has been made; and (4) there has been a use of the corporate powers.

(b) PARTNERSHIP VERSUS CORPORATION BY ESTOPPEL. The defect in incorporation may be so great that the law will not accept the association as a de facto corporation. In such a case, in the absence of a statute making the incorporation conclusive, there is no corporation. If the individuals proceed to run the business in spite of such irregularity, they may be held liable as partners.[21]

The partnership liability rule is sometimes not applied when the third person dealt with the business as though it were a corporation. In such instances, it is stated that the third person is estopped from denying that the "corporation" with which the business was transacted has legal existence. In effect, there is a corporation by estoppel with respect to that creditor.

Several jurisdictions that follow the 1969 MBCA have expressly retained the doctrines of corporation by estoppel and de facto corporations.[22] However, courts interpreting the language of the 1969 MBCA have determined that the de facto corporation doctrine and the corporation by estoppel doctrine no longer exist. The court in the *Thompson & Green* case deals with these doctrines.

The 1984 model act contains a more flexible standard than the 1969 version. The 1984 act imposes liability for preincorporation debts only upon persons who act as or on behalf of a corporation knowing that no corporation exists.[23]

---

[20] This trend and the reasons therefor may be compared to those involved in the concept of the negotiability of commercial paper. Note the similar protection from defenses given to the person purchasing shares for value and without notice. UCC § 8-202.

[21] In a minority of states the court will not hold the individuals liable as partners, but will hold liable the person who committed the act on behalf of the business on the theory that such person was an agent who acted without authority and is therefore liable for breach of the implied warranties of the existence of a principal possessing capacity and of proper authorization.

[22] See Ga. Bus. Corp. Code § 22-5103; Minn. Bus. Corp. Act § 301:08.

[23] RMBCA § 2.04.

THOMPSON & GREEN MACHINERY CO. V MUSIC CITY LUMBER CO.

(Tenn App) 683 SW2d 340 (1984)

On January 27, 1982, Joe Walker purchased a wheel loader machine from the Thompson & Green Machinery Co. (T-G). Walker signed a promissory note for $37,886.30 on behalf of "Music City Sawmill, Inc. by Joe Walker, President." When Sawmill was unable to make payments on the loader, the machine was returned to T-G and later sold for $17,925. T-G brought suit against Sawmill on May 5, 1983, and thereafter, discovered

> that Sawmill had not been incorporated on January 27, 1982 when the
> machine was sold, but rather had been incorporated on January 28, 1982.
> T-G then sued Walker individually. The lawsuit was Walker's first notice
> that Sawmill was not incorporated on the date of the sale. Walker insists
> that T-G dealt with Sawmill as a corporation and did not intend to bind
> him personally on the note and, therefore, is estopped to deny Sawmill's
> corporate existence. T-G responds that under language virtually identi-
> cal to Sections 56 and 146 of the 1969 MBCA the doctrines of de facto
> corporations and corporation by estoppel no longer are applicable in the
> state, and Walker is personally liable. From a judgment for Walker, T-G
> appealed.

LEWIS, J. . . . It is conceded that Sawmill did not have a corporate existence on
January 27th. It therefore follows that Mr. Walker could not and did not have
authority to act for Sawmill on January 27th when he executed the promissory
note to plaintiff.

It is a general rule that one who deals with an apparent corporation as such
and in such manner as to recognize its corporate existence de jure or de facto is
thereby estopped to deny the fact thus admitted. . . . The estoppel extends as
well to the privies as to the parties to such transactions. The general rule is
applied in actions brought by either of the contracting parties against the
other, and in actions by the persons dealing with the corporation, wherein the
existence of the corporation is assailed for the purpose of establishing individual partnership liability on the part of its members.

Tennessee has long recognized the foregoing rule. Our Supreme Court, in
Ingle System Co. v. Norris & Hall, 134 Tenn. 472, 178 S.W. 1113 (1915), stated:

> When a private person enters into a contract with a body purporting to be a corpora-
> tion, in which that body is described by the corporate name which it has assumed,
> such private person thereby admits the existence of the corporation for the purpose
> of the suit brought to enforce the obligations, and will not be permitted to deny the
> corporate existence of the plaintiff.

However, in 1968 the Tennessee General Assembly enacted the "Tennessee
General Corporations Act," Chapter 523, Pub. Acts of 1968.

Our research reveals no Tennessee decision which has addressed either de
facto corporation or corporation by estoppel since the passage of the act in
1968.

Courts in other jurisdictions which have considered the question of de facto
corporations under statutes similar to Tenn. Code Ann. §§ 48-1-204 and 48-1-
1405 have held that under the act, de facto corporations no longer exist. . . .

Corporate existence does not begin until such time as "the charter is filed by
the secretary of state." [See 1969 MBCA § 56]. . . .

[1969 MBCA § 146] mandates that "[a]ll persons who assume to act as a
corporation without authority so to do shall be jointly and severally liable for
all debts and liabilities incurred or arising as a result thereof."

The General Assembly, in enacting [MBCA § 146] saw fit to place statutory
liability upon those who assume to act as a corporation without authority.
[Section 146] does not contain an exception that one who assumes to act as a
corporation without authority shall be jointly and severally liable for debts and
liabilities *except* when the plaintiff thereafter dealt with the corporation as a
corporation or when the plaintiff did not intend to bind one who assumed to

act personally. No exceptions are contained in [§ 146]. For this Court to hold that under the circumstances here Mr. Walker is not liable, it would be necessary that this Court rewrite the Tennessee General Corporations Act and hold that the Act does not mean what it says. We are not at liberty to do so. We find nothing ambiguous in [§ 146]. It is clear that "[a]ll persons who assume to act as a corporation without authority so to do shall be jointly and severally liable for all debts and liabilities incurred or arising as a result thereof." We find no good faith exception in the act. To allow an estoppel would be to nullify [§ 146].

We are of the opinion that the doctrine of corporation by estoppel met its demise by the enactment of the Tennessee General Corporations Act of 1968.

[Judgment reversed and cause remanded]

QUESTIONS

1. Did Walker make the contract on behalf of Sawmill, Inc., in the good faith belief that it was a corporation?
2. Did T-G intend to hold Walker individually liable on the promissory note when it was signed?
3. State the rule of the case.

§ 49:10 INSOLVENCY, BANKRUPTCY, AND REORGANIZATION

When a corporation has financial troubles that are so serious that it is insolvent, the best thing may be to go through bankruptcy or reorganization proceedings. The law as to bankruptcy and reorganizations is discussed in Chapter 39.

§ 49:11 FORFEITURE OF CHARTER

Under the RMBCA the secretary of state may commence proceedings to administratively dissolve a corporation if (a) the corporation does not pay franchise taxes within 60 days after they are due, (b) the corporation does not file its annual report within 60 days after it is due, or (c) the corporation is without a registered agent or registered office for 60 days or more.[24]

§ 49:12 JUDICIAL DISSOLUTION

In some states, provision is made for the judicial dissolution of a corporation when its management is deadlocked and the deadlock cannot be broken by the shareholders.[25] In some states, a "custodian" may be appointed for a corporation when the shareholders are unable to break a deadlock in the board of directors and irreparable harm is threatened or sustained by the corporation because of the deadlock.

C. CONSOLIDATIONS, MERGERS, AND CONGLOMERATES

Two or more corporations may be combined to form a new structure or enter-

---

[24] RMBCA § 14.20.

[25] RMBCA § 14.30(2)(I).

prise. This combination may be a consolidation, a merger, or the formation of a conglomerate.[26]

§ 49:13   DEFINITIONS

The form through which the combination is accomplished will affect the identity of the resulting corporation.

(a) CONSOLIDATION. In a **consolidation** of two or more corporations, their separate existences cease, and a new corporation with the property and the assets of the old corporations comes into being.

When a consolidation is effected, the new corporation ordinarily succeeds to the rights, powers, and immunities of its component parts. Limitations, however, may be prescribed by certificate of incorporation, constitution, or statute.

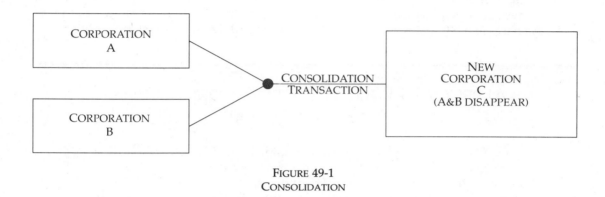

FIGURE 49-1
CONSOLIDATION

(b) MERGER. **Merger** differs from consolidation in that, when two corporations merge, one absorbs the other. One corporation preserves its original charter and identity and continues to exist; the other disappears, and its corporate existence terminates.

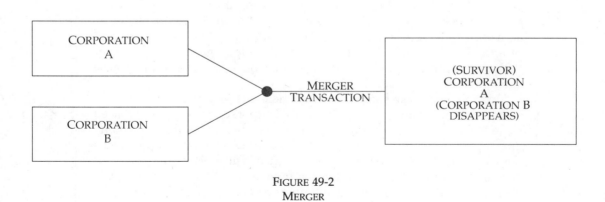

FIGURE 49-2
MERGER

Usually if a stockholder dissents from a proposed consolidation or merger, or if a stockholder fails to convert existing shares into stock of the new or continuing corporation, the dissenting stockholder or the corporation may make application to the courts to appraise the value of the stock

---

[26]   Federal law regulating tender offers is discussed in Chapter 51, § 13.

held. The new or continuing corporation is then required to pay the value of the stock to the stockholder, and the stockholder is required to transfer the stock to the new or continuing corporation. In effect, the court orders the new or continuing corporation to buy the stock from the dissenting stockholder.

Complex transactions are often involved in the elimination of the ownership interests of minority shareholders. A "two-step merger" may take place whereby (1) an outside investor purchases control of the majority shares of the target corporation by tender offer or through private negotiations; (2) this newly acquired control is used to arrange for the target and a second corporation controlled by the outside investor to merge, with one condition being the "freeze-out" of the minority shareholders of the target corporation by the forced cancellation of their shares, generally through a cash purchase. As set forth in *Alpert*, in reviewing a freeze-out merger the courts look to see if the merger was for a legitimate corporate purpose and, considering the transaction as a whole, whether it was fair to the minority shareholders.

ALPERT V 28 WILLIAMS STREET CORPORATION
63 NY2d 557, 473 NE2d 19 (1984)

Since 1955, a valuable 17-story office building located at 79 Madison Avenue in New York City had been owned by 79 Realty Corporation, which had no other substantial assets. About two-thirds of 79 Realty Corporation's outstanding shares were held by two couples, the Kimmelmans and the Zauderers, who were also the company's sole directors and officers. Jack Alpert and three others (the Alpert group) owned 26 percent of the outstanding shares. A consortium of investors formed a limited partnership known as Madison 28 Associates for the purpose of purchasing the building. In March of 1980, Madison Associates began negotiations with the Kimmelmans and Zauderers to purchase the controlling block of stock at a price equal to its proportion of the building's value — agreed in June 1980 to be $6,500,000. In addition, Madison Associates promised that it would offer to purchase the Alpert group's stock under the same terms within four months of the closing of the stock purchase agreement in September, 1980.

Upon selling their shares, the Kimmelmans and the Zauderers resigned their positions with the 79 Realty Corporation and were replaced by four partners of Madison Associates. Now acting as the controlling directors of 79 Realty Corporation on October 17, 1980, they approved a plan to merge the 79 Realty Corporation with Williams Street Realty Corporation, which Madison Associates owned. A shareholders meeting was called, and a statement of intention to merge was sent out to the shareholders prior to the meeting; the statement included the plan to dissolve 79 Realty Corporation after the merger. The merger was approved by two-thirds of the shareholders, and 79 Realty Corporation was thereafter dissolved. The Alpert group brought suit contending that the merger was unlawful because the sole purpose was to benefit the Madison Associates, which had a clear conflict of interest. The Madison Associates defended that the merger advanced certain proper business purposes such as the beneficial tax advantages through depreciation and the attraction of outside capital for needed renovations. From a judgment for the Madison Associates, the Alpert group appealed.

COOKE, C. J. . . . On this appeal, the principal task facing this court is to prescribe a standard for evaluating the validity of a corporate transaction that forcibly eliminates minority shareholders by means of a two-step merger. It is concluded that the analysis employed by the courts below was correct: the majority shareholders' exclusion of minority interests through a two-step merger does not violate the former's fiduciary obligations so long as the transaction viewed as a whole is fair to the minority shareholders and is justified by an independent corporate business purpose. Accordingly, this court now affirms.

In New York, two or more domestic corporations are authorized to "merge into a single corporation which shall be one of the constituent corporations", known as the "surviving corporation" (see Business Corporation Law, § 901). The statute does not delineate substantive justifications for mergers, but only requires compliance with certain procedures: the adoption by the boards of each corporation of a plan of merger setting forth, among other things, the terms and conditions of the merger, a statement of any changes in the certificate of incorporation of the surviving corporation; the submission of the plan to a vote of shareholders pursuant to notice to all shareholders; and adoption of the plan by a vote of two thirds of the shareholders entitled to vote on it.

Generally, the remedy of a shareholder dissenting from a merger and the offered "cash-out" price is to obtain the fair value of his or her stock through an appraisal proceeding. This protects the minority shareholder from being forced to sell at unfair prices imposed by those dominating the corporation while allowing the majority to proceed with its desired merger. . . . The pursuit of an appraisal proceeding generally constitutes the dissenting stockholder's exclusive remedy. An exception exists, however, when the merger is unlawful or fraudulent as to that shareholder, in which event an action for equitable relief is authorized. . . . Thus, technical compliance with the Business Corporation Law's requirements alone will not necessarily exempt a merger from further judicial review.

Because the power to manage the affairs of a corporation is vested in the directors and majority shareholders, they are cast in the fiduciary role of "guardians of the corporate welfare". . .In this position of trust, they have an obligation to all shareholders to adhere to fiduciary standards of conduct and to exercise their responsibilities in good faith when undertaking any corporate action, including a merger . . . .

[I]t has long been recognized in this State that, under certain circumstances, "the particular interest of the few must give way to the general interest of the many" . . . . Thus, "[d]eparture from precisely uniform treatment of stockholders may be justified, of course, where a bona fide business purpose indicates that the best interests of the corporation would be served by such departure". . . .

In the context of a freeze-out merger, variant treatment of the minority shareholders — i.e., causing their removal — will be justified when related to the advancement of a general corporate interest. The benefit need not be great, but it must be for the corporation. For example, if the sole purpose of the merger is reduction of the number of profit sharers—in contrast to increasing the corporation's capital or profits, or improving its management structure — there will exist no "independent corporate interest" . . . . All of these purposes ultimately seek to increase the individual wealth of the remaining shareholders. What distinguishes a proper corporate purpose from an improper one is that, with the former, removal of the minority shareholders furthers the objective of conferring some general gain upon the corporation. Only then will the fiduciary duty of good and prudent management of the corporation serve to override the concurrent duty to treat all shareholders fairly. . . .

In sum, in entertaining an equitable action to review a freeze-out merger, a court should view the transaction as a whole to determine whether it was tainted with fraud, illegality, or self-dealing, and whether the minority shareholders were dealt with fairly, and whether there exists any independent corporate purpose for the merger.

Noting that defendants had not employed any neutral committees in negotiating the merger, Supreme Court conducted its own objective review of the transaction. There is evidence in the record to support its conclusion that, viewed as a whole, the transaction was fair. Full disclosure of material information was made in the statement of intent mailed to plaintiffs who also had access to Realty Corporation's books. The stock price was tied to the fair market value of the office building, the corporation's only substantial asset, which was determined in arm's length negotiations.

Without passing on all of the business purposes cited by the Supreme Court as underlying the merger, it is sufficient to note that at least one justified the exclusion of plaintiffs' interests: attracting additional capital to effect needed repairs of the building. There is proof that there was a good-faith belief that additional, outside capital was required. Moreover, this record supports the conclusion that this capital would not have been available through the merger had not plaintiffs' interest in the corporation been eliminated. Thus, the approval of the merger, which would extinguish plaintiffs' stock, was supported by a bona fide business purpose to advance this general corporate interest of obtaining increased capital.

[Judgment affirmed]

QUESTIONS

1. What is a freeze-out merger?
2. Did the defendants follow the statutory procedures for the merger of the two domestic corporations?
3. What protection does state law provide shareholders dissenting from a merger?

(c) CONGLOMERATE. **Conglomerate** is the term describing the relationship of a parent corporation to subsidiary corporations engaged in diversified fields of activity unrelated to the field of activity of the parent corporation. For example, a wire manufacturing corporation that owns all the stock of a newspaper corporation and of a drug manufacturing corporation would be described as a conglomerate. In contrast, if the wire manufacturing company owned a mill to produce the metal used in making the wire and owned a mine which produced the ore that was used by the mill, the relationship would probably be described as an *integrated industry* rather than as a conglomerate. This term is merely a matter of usage, rather than of legal definition. Likewise, when the parent company is not engaged in production or the rendering of services, it is customary to call it a holding company.

Without regard to whether the enterprise is a holding company or whether the group of businesses constitute a conglomerate or an integrated industry, each part is a distinct corporation to which the ordinary corporation law applies. In some instances additional principles apply because of the nature of the relationship existing between the several corporations involved. In some instances the entity of one of the corporations in the conglomerate group may be ignored.

§ 49:14   LEGALITY

Consolidations, mergers, and asset acquisitions between enterprises are often prohibited by federal antitrust legislation on the ground that the effect is to lessen competition in interstate commerce. A business corporation may not merge with a charitable corporation because this combination would divert the assets of the respective corporations to purposes not intended by their shareholders.

§ 49:15   LIABILITY OF SUCCESSOR CORPORATIONS

When corporations are combined in any way, the question arises as to who is liable for the debts and obligations of the predecessor corporations.

(a) MERGERS. Generally, the enterprise engaging in or continuing the business after a merger or consolidation succeeds to all of the rights and property of the predecessor, or disappearing, corporations and is subject to all of the debts and liabilities of the predecessor corporations.[27] Thus, a successor corporation is liable for the contracts of a predecessor corporation, and it is no defense that the third party did not have a contract with the successor corporation.

(b) ASSET SALES. In contrast with a merger or consolidation, a corporation may merely purchase the assets of another business. In that case, the purchaser does not become liable for the obligations of the predecessor business.[28]

Successor firms may seek to avoid the predecessor firm's liabilities by casting the transaction in the form of an asset sale while in actuality (but not in form) structuring a merger.

In the *Marks* case the court was faced with deciding whether the transactions were asset sales, which insulated the purchaser from liability, or were *de facto* mergers, which made the purchaser liable for the obligations of the predecessor corporations.

---

[27]   Bernard v Kee Manufacturing Co. (Fla App) 394 So 2d 552 (1981).
[28]   Hamaker v Kenwel-Jackson Machine, Inc. (SD) 387 NW2d 515 (1986).

MARKS V MINNESOTA MINING AND MANUFACTURING CO.

187 Cal App 3d 1429, 232 Cal Rptr 594 (1986)

In June of 1977 McGhan/Cal. Inc., a manufacturer of prostheses used in breast augmentation surgery, was acquired by a wholly owned Delaware subsidiary of 3M, called McGhan/Del. Inc. In April 1977 Mary Marks had surgery; two McGhan implants were used. Because of defects in the McGhan implants, Marks underwent three additional operations, eventually having the McGhan products replaced with implants manufactured by another company. Since 1976 McGhan/Cal. and, later, McGhan/Del. received numerous complaints about their implants and received inquiries from the FDA. McGhan/Del. removed the product from the market in April of 1979. On January 1, 1981, 3M's wholly owned subsidiary McGhan/Del. Inc. was reorganized as a division of 3M and dissolved. In January 1982, following her fourth surgery, Marks brought a product liability suit against 3M. 3M contended that it was not liable for the actions of the predecessor corporation. The jury returned a verdict of $25,850 in compensatory damages and $75,000 in punitive damages. The trial judge deleted the punitive damages, and both parties appealed.

NEWSOM, A.J. . . . While it is the general rule that a purchaser of assets for cash does not assume the seller's liabilities, there are several exceptions to that rule, one of which — where a de facto merger has occurred — we find applicable here. This exception applies where the assets of one corporation are transferred without consideration which can be made available to satisfy claims or "where the consideration consists wholly of shares of the purchaser's stock which are promptly distributed to the seller's shareholders in conjunction with the seller's liquidation. (*Shannon v. Samuel Langston Company* (W.D. Mich. 1974) 379 F.Supp 797, 801)."

Our analysis of the McGhan/Cal. to McGhan/Del. transfer reveals that the first transaction was carried out pursuant to an agreement, dated May 11, 1977, between 3M and McGhan/Cal. entitled "Agreement and Plan of Reorganization." Pursuant to its terms, McGhan/Cal. was to receive shares of 3M stock in exchange for all of its business, assets and goodwill, including the corporate name and the shares of stock of its foreign subsidiary. McGhan/Cal. was required by the agreement to change its name, distribute the 3M stock to its shareholders and dissolve as soon as practicable. All McGhan/Cal. employees, including the seven shareholders, were requested to sign employment agreements with 3M. All five founders of McGhan/Cal. continued to work for McGhan/Del. in substantially the same capacity after the reorganization. Thus, as described by Donald McGhan, the "operating board" (if not the formal board of directors) remained the same. All McGhan/Cal. shareholders became shareholders of 3M.

The agreement also provided for the assumption by 3M of specified liabilities shown on the balance sheets. . . .

We find *Shannon, supra*, particularly persuasive. There, Harris Intertype Corporation entered into an agreement with Samuel M. Langston Company to purchase assets in exchange for Harris stock. (*Shannon, supra*, 379 F.Supp. at p. 799.) Langston was required to change its name. It was subsequently dissolved and the Harris stock distributed to its shareholders. Harris assumed all obligations which were "necessary for the uninterrupted continuation of normal business operations. . . ." A Harris subsidiary took over and continued the operations of Langston under the name The Langston Company. The subsidiary was merged into Harris the year after the plaintiff was injured by a product manufactured by the first Langston corporation. The court characterized this transaction as a de facto merger, and on that basis found Harris liable for the damages due to the defective product. Reasoning from the premise that "[a] purchaser of corporate assets will be liable for the debts and liabilities of the transferor when the transaction amounts to a consolidation or merger of the seller and purchaser", the court concluded: "Public policy requires that Harris Intertype, having received the benefits of a going concern, should also assume the costs which all other going concerns must ordinarily bear." The court added that "solvent corporations, going concerns, should not be permitted to discharge their liabilities to injured persons simply by shuffling paper and manipulating corporate entities."

Here, as in *Shannon, supra*, the result of the transaction was exactly that which would have occurred had a statutory merger taken place, and we are accordingly convinced of the necessity and the fairness of transferring liability from McGhan/Cal. to McGhan/Del. . . .

With respect to the second reorganization, McGhan/Del., the wholly owned subsidiary of 3M which manufactured the defective product at issue, was "reorganized" into its parent company 11 months before plaintiff's injury. Evidence of the nature of these transactions is sparse, consisting of the declaration of a 3M officer that effective January 1, 1981, McGhan/Del. was reorganized as a division of 3M and then dissolved. Counsel for 3M refers to the transaction as a "merger."

. . . . McGhan/Del. continued doing business after the reorganization as "McGhan/3M", a component of its corporate parent. And since 3M was the sole shareholder, it is highly unlikely that cash was paid for the business of McGhan/Del. We therefore find that the reorganization amounted to a continuation of a de facto merger. Thus, when McGhan/Del. became a part of its parent, as a matter of corporate law it carried with it all of its liabilities.

. . . . The critical fact is that while there was more than one merger or reorganization, an analysis of each transaction discloses to us that its intrinsic structure and nature, unlike a sale of assets for cash, was of a type in which the corporate entity was continued and all liability was transferred. All the indicia of a merger are present. We accordingly conclude that the second reorganization, like the first, transferred all liabilities to the surviving corporation. 3M is therefore liable for all liabilities of its subsidiary, including the punitive damages awarded to plaintiff.

The judgment notwithstanding the verdict is reversed with instructions to reinstate the judgment entered on the jury's verdict which included the award of punitive damages.

Appellant Marks is entitled to costs on this appeal.

[Judgment reversed]

QUESTIONS

1. Did the court find that the result of the transaction between McGhan/Cal. and McGhan/Del. was exactly what would have occurred had a statutory merger taken place?
2. What is the basis for holding a successor corporation liable for the debts of a predecessor corporation when there is a *de facto* merger?
3. If 3M had purchased all of the assets of McGhan/Cal. for cash and used the former McGhan/Cal. plant and equipment to make tapes, would it have been held liable to Marks?

SUMMARY

A corporation is an artificial person created by government action which exists as a separate and distinct entity and is endowed with certain powers. In most states the corporation comes into existence when the secretary of state issues a certificate of incorporation. The most common forms of corporations are private business corporations whose stock is sold to the public (publicly held), and close corporations, which are business firms whose shares are not traded publicly. Corporations may be formed for purposes other than conducting a business, such as nonprofit corporations, municipal corporations, and public authorities for governmental purposes.

Ordinarily, each corporation will be treated as a separate person, and the law will not look beyond the corporate identity merely because it has been formed to obtain tax savings or limited liability. The fact that two corporations have the same shareholders does not justify disregarding the separate corporate entities. However, when a corporation is formed to perpetrate a fraud, a court will ignore the corporate form or "pierce the corporate veil." The corporate form will also be ignored to prevent injustice or because of the functional reality that the two corporations in question are one.

A promoter is the person who brings together the persons interested in the enterprise and sets in motion all that must be done to form a corporation. A corporation is not liable on contracts made by its promoter for the corporation unless it adopts the contracts; the promoter is personally liable for contracts made for the corporation before its existence. A promoter stands in a fiduciary relation to the corporation and share subscribers.

The procedures for incorporation are set forth in the statutes of each state. The corporation comes into existence upon issuance of the certificate of incorporation. It is then called a corporation de jure. When compliance with all statutory procedures for incorporation is lacking, a de facto corporation may be found to exist. Or, when sufficient compliance for a de facto corporation does not exist, a third person may be estopped from denying the legal existence of the "corporation" with which it did business (corporation by estoppel). However, the ABA MBCA has been construed as having abolished the de facto and estoppel doctrines.

Two or more corporations may be combined to form a new enterprise. This combination may be a consolidation, with a new corporation coming into existence, or a merger, wherein one corporation absorbs the other.

QUESTIONS AND CASE PROBLEMS

1. What social forces are affected by the recognition of a corporation as a distinct legal entity?
2. The Karnak Chemical Company is incorporated in Utah. It wishes to do business in Oklahoma but is required to pay a tax assessed by Oklahoma against foreign corporations. Stephen owns shares in Karnak. He claims that it is not subject to the Oklahoma tax because Karnak is an American corpora-

tion and, therefore, is a domestic corporation to all states. Is he correct?
3. Susan sued the Mobile Construction Company. Philip was the only shareholder of the corporation. Susan obtained a judgment against the corporation. Philip then dissolved the corporation and took over all its assets. He agreed to pay all outstanding debts of the corporation except the judgment in favor of Susan. She sued Philip on the

ground that he was liable for the judgment against the corporation. He claimed that the judgment was only the liability of the corporation and that he was not liable because he was merely a shareholder and had not assumed the liability for the judgment. Is Philip liable on the judgment?

4. Edwin Edwards and Karen Davis owned EEE, Inc., which owned three convenience stores all of which sold gasoline. Reid Ellis delivered to the three convenience stores $26,675.02 of gasoline for which he was not paid. Ellis demonstrated that Edwards and Davis owned the business, ran it, and in fact personally ordered the gasoline. He contends that they are personally liable for the debt owed him by EEE, Inc. Decide. [Ellis v Edwards, 180 Ga App 301, 348 SE2d 764]

5. What are common grounds for forfeiture (administrative dissolution) of the corporate charter?

6. Compare and contrast consolidations, mergers, and conglomerates.

7. Norman was organizing a new corporation: the Collins Home Construction Company. Fairchild knew that the corporation was not yet formed but made a contract by which he agreed to sell certain goods to Collins. The corporation was later organized and ratified the contract that Norman had made with Fairchild. Fairchild, however, did not perform the contract and was sued by Collins. Fairchild raised the defense that he had never made any contract with Collins and that a corporation that did not exist could not have made a contract. Were these defenses valid?

8. Tilton and others, having formed a voluntary association called the Ottumwa Temperance Reform Club, were chosen to act as an executive committee. The committee made a contract with the Ottumwa Gas-Light Co. on behalf of the club. An action was later brought by the utility company to recover for the gas supplied. The members of the committee claimed that they were not individually liable because the club was a corporation. Was the group a corporation? [Lewis v Tilton, 64 Iowa 220, 19 NW 911]

9. An action was brought by Alabama Tank Lines and other carriers against the Martin Truck Line, Inc., claiming that the truck line was operating without the necessary certificate of the state Public Service Commission. It was shown that Martin Truck Line had ob-

tained a certificate at a time when all of its stock was owned by Thornbury, Cook, and Edwards. The stock was thereafter sold to Houghland and Page. No approval of the transfer of stock to them was obtained from the Public Service Commission. Was Martin Truck Line entitled to continue to do business under the certificate that had been originally issued? [Martin Truck Line v Alabama Tank Lines, 261 Ala 163, 73 So 2d 756]

10. The Branmar Theatre Co., a family corporation, leased a theater from Branmar, Inc. The lease prohibited it from assigning the lease. The holders of the stock of Branmar Theatre Co. sold their stock to the Schwartzes. The lessor, Branmar, Inc., claimed that this was a prohibited assignment and threatened to cancel the lease. Branmar Theatre Co. thereafter brought an action for a declaratory judgment to enjoin the cancellation of the lease. Should the court enjoin the cancellation of the lease? [Branmar Theatre Co. v Branmar, Inc. (Del Ch) 264 A2d 526]

11. Mulley was a promoter of a corporation not yet formed, Collier County Developers, Inc. He, as promoter, made a contract with Vodopich for services in selling certain real estate. Vodopich later sued Mulley for breach of the contract. Mulley claimed that he was not liable because Vodopich knew that the corporation had not yet been formed. Was he correct? [Vodopich v Collier County Developers, Inc. (Fla App) 319 So 2d 43]

12. Florence promoted a new corporation, the Kaskey Print Shop. She made contracts in the name of Kaskey with third persons. Thereafter, Kaskey was formed but soon went out of business. Suit was brought against Florence on the contracts that she had made for Kaskey. She claimed that she was not liable because she had made them on behalf of the corporation. Is she liable on the contracts?

13. Adams and two other persons were promoters for a new corporation, the Aldrehn Theaters Co. The promoters retained Kridelbaugh to perform legal services in connection with the incorporation of the new business and promised to pay him $1,500. Aldrehn was incorporated through Kridelbaugh's services, and the promoters became its only directors. Kridelbaugh attend-

ed a meeting of the board of directors at which he was told that he should obtain a permit for the corporation to sell stock because the directors wished to pay him for his prior services. The promoters failed to pay Kridelbaugh, and he sued the corporation. Was the corporation liable? [Kridelbaugh v Aldrehn Theaters Co. 195 Iowa 147, 191 NW 803]

14. On August 19, 1980, the plaintiff, Joan Ioviero, injured her hand when she slipped and fell while leaving the dining room at the Hotel Excelsior in Venice, Italy. This hotel was owned by the Italian corporation "Cigahotels, S.p.A." In 1973, a firm called "Ciga Hotels, Inc." was incorporated, in New York. Its certificate of incorporation was amended in 1979, changing its name to "Landia International Services, Inc." This New York corporation was employed by the Italian corporation, Cigahotels, S.p.A., to provide sales and promotional services in the United States and Canada. Ioviero seeks to hold the New York corporation liable for her hand injury at the Venice hotel. She points to the similarity of the first corporate name used by the New York firm to the name Cigahotels, S.p.A., and the fact the New York firm represents the interests of the Italian firm in the U.S., as clear evidence that the two firms are the same single legal entity. She asks that the court disregard the separate corporate entities. The New York corporation moves that the case be dismissed because it is duly incorporated in New York and does not own the Excelsior Hotel in which Ioviero was injured. Decide. [Ioviero v CigaHotel, Inc. aka Landia I.S. Inc. 475 NYS2d 830].

15. William Sullivan was ousted from the presidency of the New England Patriots Football Club, Inc. Later, he borrowed $5,348,000 to buy 100 percent control of the voting shares of the corporation. A condition of the loan was that he reorganize the Patriots so that the income from the corporation could be devoted to repayment of the personal loan and the team's assets could be used as collateral. Sullivan therefore arranged for a cash freeze-out merger of the holders of the 120,000 shares of nonvoting stock. David Coggins who owned 10 shares of nonvoting stock and took special pride in the fact that he was an owner of the team, refused the $15 a share buy out and challenged the merger in court. He contended that the merger was not for a legitimate corporate purpose but rather to enable Sullivan to satisfy his personal loan. Sullivan contends that legitimate business purposes were given in the merger proxy statement, such as the NFL policy of discouraging public ownership of teams. Coggins responded that before the merger Sullivan had 100 percent control of the voting stock and thus control of the franchise, and that no legal basis existed to eliminate public ownership. Decide. [Coggins v New England Patriots Football Club, 397 Mass 525, 492 NE2d 1112]

50

CORPORATE POWERS

Some of the powers possessed by a corporation, such as the right to own property, are the same as those powers held by a natural person. Others, such as the power of perpetual succession, are distinct powers not possessed by natural persons.

The articles of incorporation often contain a comprehensive and complicated *powers clause* setting forth in detail the corporation's powers. Where a corporation acts beyond the limits of its powers, the act is **ultra vires**. Modern statutes grant broad corporate powers, thus lessening the likelihood that a corporation will act beyond its powers.

§ 50:1 CORPORATE POWERS: NATURE AND LIMITATIONS

All corporations do not have the same powers. For example, those that operate banks, insurance companies, savings and loan associations, and railroads generally have special powers and are subject to special restrictions.

Except for limitations in the federal Constitution or the state's own constitution, a state legislature may give corporations any lawful powers. The Revised Model Business Corporation Act contains a general provision on corporate powers granting the corporation "the same powers as an individual to do all things necessary or convenient to carry out its business and affairs."[1] State statutes generally contain broad catchall grants of powers.

In some states, a corporation may not exercise its power until an organizational meeting has been held.[2]

[1] RMBCA § 3.02.
[2] Bostetter v Freestate Land Corp. 48 Md App 142, 426 A2d 404 (1981).

§ 50:2   PARTICULAR POWERS

Modern corporation codes give corporations a wide range of powers.

(a) PERPETUAL SUCCESSION. One of the distinctive features of a corporation is its perpetual succession or continuous life—the power to continue as a unit forever or for a stated period of time regardless of changes in stock ownership. If no period is fixed for its duration, the corporation will exist indefinitely unless it is legally dissolved. When the period is limited, the corporation may in many states extend the period by meeting additional requirements of the statute.

(b) CORPORATE NAME. A corporation must have a name to identify it. As a general rule, it may select any name for this purpose.

Most states require that the corporate name contain some word indicating the corporate character[3] and that it shall not be the same as or deceptively similar to the name of another corporation. Some statutes likewise prohibit the use of a name that is likely to mislead the public. The RMBCA states that the corporate name "may not contain language stating or implying that the corporation is organized for a purpose other than that permitted by . . . its articles of incorporation."[4]

(c) CORPORATE SEAL. A corporation may have a distinctive seal. However, a corporation need not use a seal in the transaction of business unless such is required by statute or unless a natural person in transacting that business would be required to use a seal. A corporation may use a different seal than the official corporate one unless the use of that official seal is required for the particular document that is being executed.

(d) BYLAWS. **Bylaws** are the rules and regulations enacted by a corporation to govern the affairs of the corporation and its shareholders, directors, and officers.

Bylaws are adopted by shareholders, although in some states it may be provided that they are to be adopted by the directors of the corporation. Action by the state or an amendment of the corporate charter is not required to make the bylaws effective.

The bylaws are subordinate to the general law of the state, including the statute under which the corporation is formed, as well as to the charter of the corporation.[5] Bylaws that conflict with such superior authority or that are in themselves unreasonable are invalid. Bylaws that are valid are binding upon all shareholders regardless of whether they know of the existence of those bylaws or were among the majority that consented to their adoption. Bylaws are not binding upon third persons, however, unless they have notice or knowledge of them.

(e) STOCK. A corporation may issue stock and certificates representing such stock.

(f) MAKING CONTRACTS. Corporation codes give corporations the power to make contracts. In addition, a corporation has the implied power to make any contract needed to conduct its business and accomplish its corporate purposes.[6]

(g) BORROWING MONEY. Corporations have the implied power to borrow money in carrying out their authorized business purposes. For example, a fire insurance company may borrow money to pay losses due on its policies. Statutes commonly prohibit corporations from raising the defense of usury.

(h) EXECUTING COMMERCIAL PAPER. The power to issue or indorse commercial paper, or to accept drafts, is implied when the corporation has the power to borrow money and when such means are appropriate and ordinarily used to further the authorized objectives of the corporation.

(i) ISSUING BONDS. A corporation may

---

[3]   RMBCA § 4.01(a) declares that the corporate name must contain the word "corporation," "company," "incorporated," "limited," or an abbreviation of one of such words.
[4]   RMBCA § 4.01(a)(2).

[5]   Roach v Bynum (Ala) 403 So 2d 187 (1981).
[6]   Bergy Brothers, Inc. v Zeeland Feeder Pig, Inc. 96 Mich App 111, 292 NW2d 493 (1980).

exercise its power to borrow money by issuing bonds.

The bonds issued by a corporation are subject to Article 8 of the UCC, "Investment Securities." If the bonds satisfy the requirements of UCC § 3-104, "Form of Negotiable Instruments," they are governed by Article 3 of the UCC, "Commercial Paper," as far as negotiation is concerned. Ordinarily, conditions inserted in the corporate bonds for the protection of the bondholders have the effect of making the bonds nonnegotiable. If this is the case, the bonds are not within the scope of Article 3 of the UCC, and only Article 8 applies to them.

(j) TRANSFERRING PROPERTY. The corpo-rate property may be leased, assigned for the benefit of creditors, or sold. In many states, however, a solvent corporation may not transfer all of its property without the consent of all or a substantial majority of its shareholders. In any case, the sale must be for a fair price.

The power to sell and transfer corporate property includes the power to assign accounts receivable and contracts with customers and to negotiate commercial paper received by the corporation.

The *Burnett's* case raised the question of whether a corporation transferring commercial paper of customers could agree to back the paper if the customers did not pay the paper.

BURNETT'S LUMBER & SUPPLY CO. V COMMERCIAL CREDIT CORP.

211 Miss 53, 51 So 2d 54 (1951)

Burnett's Lumber & Supply Company was incorporated to engage in the lumber business. It owned three trucks. It sold the trucks to three different buyers. The sales were made on credit, and each buyer executed a contract and a promissory note payable to Burnett's for the balance that was due on the sale. Burnett's then sold the contracts and the notes to the Commercial Credit Corp. The transaction was made "with recourse," which obligated Burnett's to pay the balances due if the customers of Burnett's did not. The customers did not pay, and Commercial sued Burnett's for the unpaid balances. Burnett's raised the defense that it had no authority to transfer the notes and contracts with recourse. Judgment was entered for Commercial Credit Corp., and Burnett's appealed.

HALL, J. . . . Appellant [Burnett's] is chartered under the laws of Mississippi and is authorized by its charter "to buy, own, hold, sell, and lease timber and timber lands; to buy, manufacture, and finish lumber and lumber products; to do a general wholesale and retail lumber and building material business, dealing in all building materials and supplies used in general lumber and supply business; to buy, hold, own, build, improve, sell, mortgage, lease, and rent real estate; and to buy, own, hold, sell, and assign notes and mortgages and other written evidence of indebtedness on real estate," . . .

It is here contended that the act of the corporation in acquiring and selling this equipment and in assigning and indorsing the paper with recourse is ultra vires and not binding upon it. Appellant was engaged in a general wholesale and retail lumber and supply business and under . . . its charter was fully authorized to transact any business which was incidental to its general corporate purposes. "A corporation may have implied power not only to acquire or purchase personal chattels, but also to take choses in action which are transferable by assignment; and it may itself become the payee of commercial paper, bonds, etc., for indebtedness owing to it, . . . " "A corporation has full power to alienate its property both real and personal, unless restricted by its charter, statute, or considerations of public policy. The implied power of a corporation to alienate its property extends to commercial paper and other choses in action which are transferable by indorsement or assignment." "An express grant is not necessary to confer upon a corporation the power, in the legitimate transaction of its business, to become a drawer, acceptor, or indorser of a bill of exchange or to become a party to any other negotiable paper. This power is generally implied in the case of a business corporation as a necessary incident of its express powers. Such power is, for example, incident to the power of a corporation to borrow money or incur indebtedness." "It is well settled that where a corporation acquires commercial paper or bonds in the legitimate transaction of its business it may sell them, and in furtherance of such a sale it may, in order to make them the more readily marketable, indorse or guarantee their payment." . . .

In the comparatively recent case of *Home Owners' Loan Corporation v Moore*, 184 Miss 283, 185 So 253, this Court . . . said: "The law looks with disfavor on the defense of ultra vires and will not allow it to prevail when it would defeat the ends of justice." . . . The doctrine should never be applied where it will defeat the ends of justice if such a result can be avoided.

. . . [W]e unhesitatingly hold that appellant corporation's participation in the transaction was not ultra vires but was within the implied powers granted under its corporate charter and it is bound thereby.

[Judgment affirmed]

QUESTIONS

1. Was Burnett's expressly authorized by its charter to transfer with recourse the contracts and promissory notes given to it by its customers?
2. Did the court examine the extent to which the selling of contracts and notes with recourse had been engaged in by Burnett's?
3. Compare the result reached in the *Burnett's* case with the law of commercial paper.

A corporation, having power to incur debts, may mortgage or pledge its property as security for those debts. This rule does not apply to franchises of public service companies, such as street transit systems and gas and electric companies.

(k) ACQUIRING PROPERTY. Although the power to acquire and hold property is usually given in the charter, a corporation always has the implied power to acquire and hold such property as is reasonably necessary for carrying out its express powers. In some states, the power of a corporation to hold property is restricted as to the method of acquiring it, or is limited as to the quantity or the value of the property or the period of time for which it may be held. Restrictions upon holding real estate are also imposed upon corporations by constitutions of some states.

(1) Investments. Modern corporation codes generally provide that a corporation may acquire the stock of other corporations.

(2) Holding Companies. A corporation owning stock in another corporation may own such a percentage of the stock of the other company that it controls the latter's operations. In such a case, the first company is commonly called a **holding company.** Sometimes a holding company is organized solely for the purpose of controlling other companies, which are called **operating** or **subsidiary companies.**

(l) BUYING BACK STOCK. Generally a corporation may purchase its own stock if it is solvent at the time and the purchase does not impair capital.[7] In a few states corporations are denied the implied power to purchase their own stock, but they are permitted to receive it as a gift, in payment of a debt, or as security for a debt.

Stock that is reacquired by the corporation that issued it is commonly called **treasury stock.** Ordinarily, the treasury stock is regarded as still being issued or outstanding stock.[8] As such, the shares are not subject to the rule that original shares cannot be issued for less than par. They can be sold by the corporation at any price.

The RMBCA eliminates the concept of par value and the technical distinctions between original shares and treasury shares that exist in conventional statutes. Thus under the Revised Model Act, authorized but unissued shares may be issued on the same basis as treasury shares.[9]

Although treasury stock retains the character of outstanding stock, it has an inactive status while it is held by the corporation. Thus, the treasury shares cannot be voted nor can dividends be declared on them.

(m) DOING BUSINESS IN ANOTHER STATE. A corporation has the inherent power, and generally is expressly authorized, to engage in business in other states. This grant of power by the incorporating state does not exempt the corporation, however, from satisfying the restrictions imposed by the foreign state in which it seeks to do business.

(n) PARTICIPATING IN ENTERPRISE. Corporations may generally participate in an enterprise to the same extent as individuals. They may enter into joint ventures. The modern statutory trend is to permit a corporation to be a member of a partnership. A corporation may be a limited partner. The RMBCA authorizes a corporation "to be a promoter, partner, member, associate, or manager of any partnership, joint venture, trust, or other entity."[10]

(o) PAYING EMPLOYEE BENEFITS. The RMBCA empowers a corporation "to pay pensions and establish pension plans, pension trusts, profit sharing plans, share bonus plans, share option plans, and benefit or incentive plans for any or all of its current or former directors, officers, employees, and agents."[11]

(p) MAKING CHARITABLE CONTRIBUTIONS. The RMBCA authorizes a corporation without any limitation "to make donations for the public welfare or for charitable, scientific, or educational purposes."[12] In some states limitation is imposed upon the amount that can be donated for charitable purposes.

§ 50:3   ULTRA VIRES ACTS

When a corporation acts in excess of or beyond the scope of the powers granted by its charter and the statute under which it was organized, the corporation's act is de-

---

[7]   See RMBCA § 6.31(a) subject to the limitations of § 6.40.

[8]   When a corporation reacquires its own shares, it has the choice of "retiring" them and thus restoring them to the status of authorized but unissued shares or of treating them as still issued and available for transfer. It is the latter that are described as treasury shares.

[9]   See Official Comments to RMBCA §§ 6.21 and 6.31.

[10]   RMBCA § 3.02(9).

[11]   RMBCA § 3.02(12).

[12]   RMBCA § 3.02(13).

scribed as ultra vires. Such an action is improper in the same way that it is improper for an agent to act beyond the scope of the authority given by the principal. It is also improper with respect to shareholders and creditors of the corporation because corporate funds have been diverted to unauthorized uses.

In the past, corporations were formed by obtaining a grant of a charter from the king or state legislature. Thus, a charter would be granted to build a turnpike or to run a bank. Typically, the application for a charter would concentrate on the main point and specifically grant the powers needed to attain the objective of the corporation. There was no general listing of corporate powers. In this century corporate existence begins by fulfilling the clerical matter of filing articles of incorporation that conform to the statute adopted by the legislature. Typically, this statute will state that every corporation formed under the statute will have certain powers unless the articles of incorporation expressly exclude some of the listed powers, and then the statute will list every possible power that is needed to run a business. In some states, the legislature makes a blanket grant of all the power that a natural person running the business would possess.[13] The net result is that the modern corporation possesses such a broad scope of powers that it is difficult to find an action that is ultra vires. If a mining corporation should begin to manufacture television sets, there might be an ultra vires transaction, but such an extreme departure rarely happens.

Nonprofit corporations have a more restricted range of powers than business corporations. Certain actions not authorized by the charters of nonprofit corporations may be found to be ultra vires.

In the *Lovering* case the court was faced with deciding whether a special assessment by a nonprofit corporation was an ultra vires act.

[13] Note the broad powers granted under the RMBCA § 3.02; *see also* Cal. Corp. Code §§ 202(ɔ), 207, 208 for all-purpose clause granting "all of the powers of a natural person in carrying out its business activities."

LOVERING V SEABROOK ISLAND PROPERTY OWNERS ASSOCIATION
(SC App) 344 SE2d 862 (1986)

The Seabrook Island Property Owners Association, Inc., (the Association) is a nonprofit corporation organized under state law to maintain streets and open spaces owned by property owners. The Seabrook Island Company is the developer of Seabrook Island and has majority control of the Board of Directors of the Association. The Association's bylaws empower the Board of Directors to levy an annual maintenance charge. Neither the Association's charter nor its bylaws authorized the Board to assess any other charges. When the Board levied, in addition to the annual maintenance charge, an "emergency budget assessment" on all members in order to rebuild certain bridges and to revitalize the beach, the Loverings and other property owners challenged in court the Association's power to impose the assessment. From a judgment for the Association, the property owners appealed.

BELL, J. . . . The main question presented by this appeal is whether the Association had authority to levy the emergency budget assessment. We hold that the levying of an emergency budget assessment was an *ultra vires* action by the Association.

A corporation may exercise only those powers which are granted to it by law, by its charter or articles of incorporation, and any by-laws made pursuant thereto. Acts beyond the scope of a corporation's powers as defined by law or its charter are *ultra vires*. In determining a corporation's powers, its charter is to be construed strictly; any ambiguity in the terms of a corporate charter must operate against the corporation. The specification of certain powers operates as a limitation on such objects as are embodied therein and is an implied prohibition of the exercise of other and distinct powers. . . .

As a matter of general law, a nonprofit corporation has the power to enforce the collection of dues and charges in accordance with the provisions of its by-laws. In this case, however, neither the protective covenants nor the by-laws give the Association power to levy special assessments. The protective covenants and the by-laws authorize the Association to impose only an annual maintenance charge. The annual maintenance charge must be based on the assessed value of the property for tax purposes. It may be adjusted from year to year, but still must be based on assessed value for taxation. The moneys collected are to be used only for the purposes enumerated in the by-laws.

Under the rules of construction outlined above, the specification of the power to levy an annual maintenance charge limits the power of the Association to impose other assessments on property owners within the Seabrook Island subdivision. It operates as an implied prohibition against the levying of special assessments. Therefore, the Association was without power to impose a special assessment, even if its object was to carry out a legitimate corporate purpose. A permissible purpose cannot be accomplished by a prohibited means. . . .

[Judgment reversed]

QUESTIONS

1. Summarize the facts of the case.
2. Did the corporation's charter authorize the emergency budget assessment to rebuild bridges and revitalize the beach?
3. Was the emergency budget assessment authorized under the corporation's bylaws?

(a) EFFECT OF ULTRA VIRES CONTRACTS. In most states, ultra vires cannot be raised to attack the validity of any act, contract, or transfer of property,[14] except as noted under § 50:3(b) in this book. Some states still follow the earlier rule that an ultra vires contract cannot have any effect be-cause it was not authorized and, therefore, was beyond the power of the corporation.

In most states if the ultra vires contract has been completely performed, neither party can rescind the contract on the ground that it was originally ultra vires. In contrast, if neither party to the ultra vires contract has performed, no court will enforce the contract or hold either party liable for its breach.

[14] RMBCA § 3.04; Re Terminal Moving and Storage Co. (CA8 Ark) 631 F2d 547 (1980).

(b) REMEDIES FOR ULTRA VIRES ACTS. In all states (1) a shareholder may obtain an injunction to stop the board of directors or other persons involved from entering into an ultra vires transaction; (2) the corporation, or a shareholder acting on behalf of the corporation, may sue the persons who made or approved the contract in order to recover damages for the loss caused the corporation by the ultra vires act; and (3) an action may be brought by the attorney general of the state to revoke the corporate charter on the ground of its serious or repeated violation.[15]

[15]   RMBCA § 3.04(b).

SUMMARY

A corporation has the power to continue as a unit forever or for a stated period of time, regardless of changes in the ownership of the stock. It may make contracts, issue stocks and bonds, borrow money, execute commercial paper, transfer and acquire property, acquire its own stock if it is solvent and the purchase does not impair capital, and make charitable contributions. Subject to limitations, a corporation has power to do business in other states. A corporation also may participate in a business enterprise to the same extent as an individual, that is, it may be a partner in a partnership or it may enter a joint venture or other enterprise. Special service corporations such as banks, insurance companies, and railroads are subject to separate statutes with regard to their organization and powers.

An ultra vires act occurs when a corporation acts beyond the scope of the powers granted by its charter and the statute under which it was organized. Because most states grant broad powers to corporations, it is unlikely that a modern corporation would act beyond the scope of its powers. Also, the modern statutory trend has been to restrict the use of the ultra vires doctrine. As a result, the doctrine's importance has been reduced. A shareholder may obtain an injunction against the corporation to stop an ultra vires transaction, and the corporation may recover damages from the persons who made the ultra vires contract. The state also has the right to bring an action to revoke the corporate charter because of ultra vires activity.

QUESTIONS AND CASE PROBLEMS

1. What social forces are affected by the rule of law permitting corporations to issue certificates representing shares of stock?
2. Do all corporations have the same powers?
3. The Mackelree Corporation owns 100 shares of its own stock. At a hotly contested shareholders' election, the board of directors voted these 100 shares. The vote of these shares provided the deciding margin, and the directors were reelected by a margin of 23 votes. Leon, who owns 10 shares of the corporate stock, had voted against reelecting the directors. Can he successfully challenge their reelection?
4. Super Electronics was a corporation. Its board of directors purchased a yacht for use by the executives of the corporation. Jill owned stock in Super Electronics. She brought a suit on behalf of the corporation and other shareholders against the directors to recover for the corporation the loss sustained by the purchase of the yacht. The directors raised the defense that no suit could be brought because the ultra vires contract had been performed. Is this a valid defense?
5. The Philadelphia Electric Company was incorporated "for the purpose of supplying heating, lighting, and power by electricity to

the public." The company supplied electricity but in addition began to sell to its customers household electrical appliances. The Attorney General claimed that the sale of appliances was not authorized by the company's charter's provision to produce and sell electricity. He brought a lawsuit to forfeit the charter of the Philadelphia Electric Company on the theory that it was acting beyond the scope of its charter. Was he correct? [Pennsylvania v Philadelphia Electric Co. 300 Pa 577, 151 A 344]

6. Compare the power of a corporation to (a) give a promissory note to represent a loan to the corporation, and (b) be an accommodation indorser on a note given in payment for the issue of its own corporate stock.

7. The Central Mutual Auto Insurance Co. was a Michigan corporation. A foreign corporation, the Central Mutual Insurance Co., was granted a license to do business in Michigan. Central Mutual Auto Insurance Co. brought an action to prevent the foreign corporation from doing business within Michigan under that name. Decide. [Central Mutual Auto Insurance Co. v Central Mutual Insurance Co. 275 Mich 554, 267 NW 733]

8. In an action by the Federal Savings State Bank, as the holder of a note, against Grimes, the maker of the note, the authority of the corporate payee, the Industrial Mutual Life Insurance Co., to accept the note from the maker was questioned. It was argued that the corporate payee possessed the power because there was no statute expressly prohibiting the exercise of that power. Was this argument valid? [Federal Savings State Bank v Grimes, 156 Kan 55, 131 P2d 894]

9. The Ohio Central Credit Union, Inc., (OCCU) made a loan to the Hamfab Credit Union (HCU). In borrowing this money HCU violated a state statute that prohibited a credit union from borrowing in excess of 25 percent of its unimpaired capital and surplus. Some time later, HCU became insolvent and Wagner was appointed the liquidator. Wagner admitted HCU's debt to OCCU but refused to pay it because the loan was made in excess of the 25 percent statutory limit, and was therefore ultra vires. A state statute abolished the defense of ultra vires as between corporations. Can Wagner use the defense of ultra vires to withhold payment? [Ohio Central Credit Union v Wagner, 67 Ohio App 2d 138, 426 NE2d 198]

10. The good faith of a director is a defense when sued for loss caused by an ultra vires act because there is no liability unless the director had the intent to defraud. Is this statement correct?

11. An employee of the Archer Pancoast Co., a corporation, was killed as the result of falling through a hatchway in the company's factory. Hoffman, superintendent of the factory, called Noll, an undertaker, and arranged for the funeral. Hoffman agreed to pay Noll $100 for his services. After performing the work, Noll brought an action against the Archer Pancoast Co. to recover the agreed sum. The defendant raised the defense that the contract with Noll was ultra vires. Decide. [Noll v Archer Pancoast Co. 60 App Div 414, 69 NYS 1007]

12. Porter owned stock in the Plymouth Gold Mining Company, a corporation. Porter made a contract with the corporation to sell his stock to the corporation. He later refused to perform the contract. The corporation sued him for breach of contract. He raised the defense that there was no valid contract because the corporate charter did not expressly give the corporation the power to purchase its own stock from stockholders. Was this defense valid? [Porter v Plymouth Gold Mining Co. 29 Mont 347, 74 P 983]

13. Connecticut General Life Insurance Co. is a Connecticut insurance company that obtained a license to write life insurance policies in New York. It thereafter proposed to acquire 80 percent or more of the common stock of the National Fire Insurance Co. of Hartford, a fire and casualty insurance company licensed to write policies in New York. The New York State Superintendent of Insurance brought an action for a declaratory judgment to have the Connecticut company prohibited from writing life policies in New York if it acquired such stock because, through its subsidiary, it would then also be writing fire and casualty insurance in New York. Was the superintendent correct? [Connecticut General Life Insurance Co. v Superintendent of Insurance, 10 NY2d 42, 217 NYS2d 39, 176 NE2d 631]

14. A husband, *H*, borrowed money from bank *B*. *B* promised to insure the loan so that if *H* died before the debt was repaid, the proceeds of the insurance policy would pay off

the debt. *B* failed to obtain the insurance, and *H* died owing a balance on the debt. On the theory that if *B* had obtained the insurance as it had promised to do there would not be any balance, *H*'s widow sued the bank to cancel the balance remaining. *B* defended on the ground that it could not have obtained the insurance because it would have been ultra vires for it to have done so. Was this defense valid?

15. Total Automation (Total), a corporation, had a checking account with the Illinois National Bank. Total owed money to the bank's travel department. The bank deducted the amount of the travel bill from the checking account balance. Creditors of Total brought an action on its behalf against the bank, claiming that the bank had no right to set off the agency debt because it was ultra vires for a national bank to operate a travel department. Decide. [Total Automation v Illinois National Bank & Trust Co. 40 Ill App 3d 266, 351 NE2d 879]

51

CORPORATE STOCK AND SHAREHOLDERS

The ownership of a corporation is divided among the shareholders, and the ownership is represented by share or stock certificates. Shares of stock may be acquired by subscription when the shares are originally issued or by transfer of existing shares from a shareholder or from the corporation.

After the stock market crash of 1929, Congress investigated the buying and selling practices that existed in the securities markets and determined that federal regulation was necessary to prevent the fraudulent, deceptive, and manipulative practices found to exist. Various federal statutes administered by the Securities and Exchange Commission were then enacted to regulate the sale of securities for the benefit of investors.

Shareholders have certain rights, including the right to vote in the election of directors and the right to receive dividends as they are declared. Shareholders are ordinarily exempt from liability for the acts of the corporation.

A.   CORPORATE STOCK

A shareholder owns a share or portion of the corporation. That fractional ownership is represented by a share or stock certificate. *Share* and *stock* are synonymous.

§ 51:1   NATURE OF STOCK

Membership in a corporation is based upon ownership of one or more shares of stock of the corporation. Each share represents a fractional interest in the total property possessed by the corporation. The shareholder does not own or have an interest in any specific property of the corporation; the corporation is the owner of all of its property.

(a) CAPITAL AND CAPITAL STOCK. **Capital** refers to the net assets of the corporation. Shares that have been issued to holders are said to be **outstanding**. **Capital stock** refers to the value received by the corporation for its outstanding stock.

(b) VALUATION OF STOCK. Corporate stock may have a specified **par value**. This means that the person subscribing to the stock and acquiring it from the corporation must pay that amount. When stock is issued by the corporation for a price greater than the par value, some statutes provide that only the par value amount is to be treated as stated capital, the excess being allocated to surplus.

Shares may be issued with no par value. In such a case no amount is stated in the certificate, and the amount that the subscriber pays the corporation is determined by the board of directors. The Revised Model Business Corporation Act eliminates the concept of par value; thus, stock issued by corporations in states following the RMBCA is always *no par*.

The value found by dividing the value of the corporate assets by the number of shares outstanding is the **book value** of the shares. The **market value** of a share of stock is the price at which that stock can be voluntarily bought or sold on the open market.

§ 51:2   CERTIFICATE OF STOCK

The corporation ordinarily issues a **certificate of stock** or **share certificate** as evidence of the shareholder's ownership of stock. The issuance of such certificates is not essential either to the existence of a corporation or to the ownership of its stock.[1] However, it is an almost universal practice since it is a convenient method of proving ownership and since it makes transfer of ownership easier.

§ 51:3   KINDS OF STOCK

The stock of a corporation may be divided into two or more classes.

(a) PREFERENCES. **Common stock** is ordinary stock that has no preferences. Each share usually entitles the holder to have one vote, to receive a share of the profits in the form of dividends when declared, and to participate in the distribution of capital upon dissolution of the corporation. **Preferred stock** has a priority over common stock. The priority may be with respect to dividends. Preferred stock may also have a priority over common stock in the distribution of capital upon dissolution of the corporation. Preferred stock is ordinarily nonvoting.

---

[1] Krosnar v Schmidt Krosnar McNaughton Garret Co. 282 Pa Super 526, 423 A2d 370 (1980). Amendments to Article 8 of the UCC adopted in 1977 give corporations the option of providing for the ownership of shares not represented by certificates. In substance, ownership is established by information stored in a data bank, but no share certificates are issued. These 1977 amendments have been adopted in Arkansas, California, Colorado, Connecticut, Delaware, Florida, Hawaii, Idaho, Indiana, Iowa, Kansas, Kentucky, Maryland, Massachusetts, Michigan, Minnesota, Montana, Nevada, New Hampshire, New Mexico, New York, North Dakota, Ohio, Oklahoma, Oregon, Rhode Island, South Dakota, Tennessee, Texas, Virginia, Washington, and West Virginia.

(1) Cumulative Preferred Stock. Ordinarily, the right to receive dividends is dependent upon the declaration of dividends by the board of directors for that particular period of time. If there is no fund from which the dividends may be declared or if the directors do not declare them from an available fund, the shareholder has no right to dividends. The fact that a shareholder has not received dividends for the current year does not in itself give the right to accumulate or carry over into the next year a claim for those dividends.

In the absence of a statement that the right to dividends is noncumulative, it is frequently held that preferred stock has the right to accumulate dividends for each year in which there was a surplus available for dividend payment but dividends were not declared.

(2) Participating Preferred Stock. Sometimes the preferred stock is given the right of participation. If so, after the common shares receive dividends or a capital distribution equal to that first received by the preferred stock, both kinds participate or share equally in the balance.

(b) DURATION OF SHARES. Ordinarily, shares continue to exist for the life of the corporation. However, any kind of shares, whether common or preferred, may be made terminable at an earlier date.

Convertible shares entitle the shareholder to exchange owned shares for a different kind of share or for bonds of the corporation.

(c) FRACTIONAL SHARES. A corporation may issue fractional shares or scrip or certificates representing such fractional shares that can be sold or combined for the acquisition of whole shares.

B. ACQUISITION OF SHARES

Shares of stock may be acquired by (1) subscription, either before or after the corporation is organized, or (2) transfer of existing shares from a shareholder or from the corporation.

§ 51:4 STATUTE OF FRAUDS

A contract for the sale of corporate shares must be evidenced by a writing or it cannot be enforced.[2] The writing must show that there has been a contract for the sale of a stated quantity of described securities at a defined or stated price. The writing must be signed in the manner required of a writing for the sale of goods. No writing is required for a contract by which a broker agrees with a customer to buy or sell securities for the customer.

§ 51:5 SUBSCRIPTION

A **stock subscription** is a contract or an agreement to buy a specific number and kind of shares when they are issued. As in the case of any other contract, the agreement to subscribe to shares of a corporation is subject to avoidance for fraud.

(a) SUBSCRIPTION BEFORE INCORPORATION. In many states a preincorporation subscription of shares is regarded as an offer to the corporation. By this view it is necessary for the corporation to accept the subscription offer either expressly or by conduct. A few states hold that such subscriptions automatically become binding contracts when the organization has been completed. In some states the preincorporation subscription is irrevocable for a stated period.[3] The RMBCA provides that "a subscription for shares entered into before incorporation is irrevocable for six months unless the subscription agreement provides a longer or shorter period or all the subscribers agree to revocation."[4]

(b) SUBSCRIPTION AFTER INCORPORATION. Subscriptions may be made after incorporation. In that event, the transaction is like any

---

[2] UCC, § 8-319(a). Smith v Baker (Ky App) 715 SW2d 890 (1986).
[3] Prejean v Commonwealth for Community Change, Inc. (La App) 503 So 2d 661 (1987).
[4] RMBCA § 6.20(a).

other contract with the corporation. The offer of the subscription may come from the subscriber or from the corporation. In either case there must be an acceptance. Upon acceptance the subscriber immediately becomes a shareholder with all the rights, privileges, and liabilities of a shareholder even though the subscriber has not paid any of the purchase price. The transaction, however, may only be a contract for the future issue of shares rather than a present subscription.

§ 51:6   TRANSFER OF SHARES

In the absence of a valid restriction, a shareholder may transfer shares to anyone.

(a) RESTRICTIONS ON TRANSFER. Restrictions on the transfer of stock are valid provided they are not unreasonable. In order to prevent its stock from going into the hands of strangers, it is lawful to require that the corporation or other stockholders be given the first right to purchase stock before a shareholder may sell it to an outsider. Also, a provision giving a corporation the right to purchase a shareholder's shares upon death is valid.

In the *Irwin* case, shares of stock were transferred in violation of the restriction imposed upon transfer, and the right of the transferee to keep the shares was attacked.

IRWIN V WEST END DEVELOPMENT CO.
(CA10 Colo) 481 F2d 34 (1973)

Ann and Ewing Taylor owned stock in the West End Development Company, a corporation. They sold their stock to Vroom, an officer of the corporation, in violation of a transfer restriction contained in the articles of incorporation. This restriction required that any stockholder selling shares must first offer to every existing stockholder a proportion of the shares being sold, the proportion being the same as the percentage of the stock that the other shareholder already owned. The other five stockholders in the corporation brought a lawsuit to compel Vroom to hold the stock as constructive trustee* for the benefit of all stockholders in order to give effect to the transfer restriction. Vroom raised the defense that the restriction was not binding. From a decision in favor of the plaintiffs, the corporation and Vroom appealed.

BARRETT, C. J. . . . Vroom contends that the Court erred in impressing a constructive trust on his stock purchased from the Taylors because Article IV, Paragraph 6 of the Articles of Incorporation is not enforceable. It states:

No shareholder shall sell or transfer any outstanding shares of the capital stock issued by the corporation to such shareholder, excepting to the other shareholders, in the proportion which the number of shares owned by each bears to the total shares outstanding, without the prior consent of the owners or at least two-thirds (2/3) of the shares entitled to vote at the shareholders' meeting . . .

Vroom alleges that the provision is unintelligible, unworkable, and too uncertain in its terms to be enforced or to give the appellees their pro rata rights

---

*   Authors' note: A **constructive trust** is a trust that the law implies, although none exists, when property has been wrongfully acquired, in order to compel the wrongdoer to hold such property for the benefit of the persons who should have received it. See § 56:10 of this book.

to the purchase of stock sold to Vroom by the Taylors. . . . Vroom argues that it is also an unreasonable restraint on the alienation of the corporation stock.

. . . The law prohibits an absolute restriction against transferability, but if a restriction does not amount to an effective prohibition against transferability, then the test is reasonableness. Thus, a "first refusal" provision is valid. . . . The trial court recognized that the provision contained ambiguities but it construed them against the drafter and gave the provision a reasonable meaning . . . to . . . provide a workable and equitable result. The trial court stated that instead of stating "in proportion which the number of shares owned by each bears to the total shares outstanding," the draftsman meant to state, "in the proportion which the number of shares owned by each bears to the total shares not offered for sale." Vroom was, or should have been, well aware of the provisions contained in the Articles of Incorporation. He should have offered the Taylors' stock to [other shareholders] on a pro rata basis before purchasing it entirely for himself . . . A constructive trust was imposed by the trial court because Vroom would be unjustly enriched by being permitted to keep the 30.76 shares. The trust arose because of unconscionable conduct by Vroom in obtaining the shares from the Taylors for his sole benefit.

Vroom contends that the provisions of Section 15 of the Uniform Stock Transfer Act barred the trial court's impression of a constructive trust upon the Taylor stock. It states:

> There shall be no lien in favor of a corporation upon the shares represented by a certificate issued by such corporation and there shall be no restriction upon the transfer of shares so represented by virtue of any bylaw of such corporation, or otherwise, unless the right of the corporation to such a lien or the restriction is stated upon the certificate. 1963 CRS 31-11-14.

Vroom alleges that the effect of the statute is to render ineffective the restrictive provisions of Article IV, Paragraph 6 of the Articles of Incorporation because the restrictions were not set forth upon the stock certificates sold by Taylors to Vroom.

Section 15 of the Uniform Stock Transfer Act was superseded by [UCC §] 8-204 which states:

> Unless noted conspicuously on the security, a restriction on transfer imposed by the issuer even though otherwise lawful is ineffective except against a person with actual knowledge of it.

The purpose of [this section] was to make ineffective restrictions on transfers to persons without notice. . . .

The failure to note the restriction on the certificates is no bar to its enforcement against Vroom who had actual notice of it. The trial court went further and stated that in any event, Vroom is estopped from setting up the absence of the restriction from the face of the stock certificate as a defense, inasmuch as he owed a fiduciary duty to the other stockholders. Vroom breached his contractual and fiduciary duties to the appellees when he purchased the Taylor stock without honoring the agreement he had previously made to permit the other stockholders to share in the purchase. The only equitable solution is the one the trial court arrived at, i.e., the imposition of a constructive trust on the 30.76 shares of stock purchased by Vroom from the Taylors. In this regard, we note that Vroom will share on a pro rata basis, notwithstanding his breach.

[Judgment imposing trust on purchased shares affirmed]

QUESTIONS

1. What defenses were raised by the defendant?
2. Did the court sustain the defenses of the defendant?
3. Did the defendant forfeit all right to the shares that were transferred to him in violation of the restriction?

A restriction upon the right to transfer is not effective as against the purchaser of the certificate unless the restriction is conspicuously noted on the certificate or unless the transferee has actual knowledge of the restriction.

A restriction on the transfer of stock is strictly interpreted. For example, a restriction on the sale of stock is not applicable to a gift of stock.

(b) INTEREST TRANSFERRED. The transfer of shares may be absolute, that is, it may divest all ownership and make the transferee the full owner, or it may be merely for security, as when stock is pledged to secure the repayment of a loan.

§ 51:7 MECHANICS OF TRANSFER

The ownership of shares is transferred by the delivery of the certificate of stock indorsed by its owner in blank or to a specified person. Ownership may also be transferred by the delivery of the certificate accompanied by a separate assignment or power of attorney executed by the owner.[5]

A delivery from the owner of the shares directly to the transferee is not required. It can be made to an intermediary. When there is no delivery of the share certificate to anyone, however, there is no transfer of ownership of the shares.

A physical transfer of the certificate without a necessary indorsement is effective as between the parties because indorsement is only necessary to make a transferee a bona fide purchaser as against third parties. Thus, a gift of shares is binding even though the above rules have not been satisfied.[6]

The owner of a security can prove continued ownership of a security by showing that what appears to be a proper indorsement on the security is actually unauthorized. Upon so doing, the owner recovers the security from the transferee of the security. The owner may not do so, however, if (1) the owner has ratified the unauthorized indorsement, or (2) the security was obtained by a purchaser for value without notice of any adverse claim and the purchaser in good faith surrendered the indorsed security to the issuer or its transfer agent and received a new, reissued, or reregistered security.

In the latter case, the remedy of the true owner is restricted to the issuer and its transfer agent. The owner may hold them liable for money damages for improper registration. As an alternative, the owner may require the issuance of a replacement security unless this would result in the overissue of outstanding stock, in which case the issuer must purchase a like security for the owner or pay the owner the value of the original security.

The transfer agent stands in the same

---

[5] UCC § 8-309. The second alternative of a delivery of an unindorsed certificate is designed to keep the certificate "clean," as when the transfer is for a temporary or special purpose as in the case of a pledge of the certificate as security for a loan.

[6] Ross' Estate (Utah) 626 P2d 489 (1981).

position as the corporation with respect to its stock and must make a formal transfer whenever the corporation would itself be required to recognize a transfer. When a corporation or its transfer agent wrongfully refuses to register a transfer of shares of stock, the new owner of the shares may bring suit for damages sustained and in some states may sue for the value of the shares on the theory of conversion.

§ 51:8 EFFECT OF TRANSFER

The transfer of existing shares of stock raises questions as to the validity and effect of the transfer as between the parties to the transfer and between them and the corporation.

(a) VALIDITY OF TRANSFER. As a transfer of shares is a transfer of ownership, the transfer must in general satisfy the requirements governing any other transfer of property or agreement to transfer property. As between the parties, a transfer may be set aside for any ground that would warrant similar relief under property law. If the transfer of stock has been obtained by duress, the transferor may obtain a rescission of the transfer.

(b) NEGOTIABILITY. Under the common law, the transferee of shares of stock had no greater right than the transferor because the certificate and the shares represented by the certificate were nonnegotiable. By statute, the common-law rule has been changed by imparting negotiability to the certificate. Just as various defenses cannot be asserted against the holder in due course of a commercial paper, it is provided that similar defenses cannot be raised against the person acquiring the certificate in good faith and for value. As against such a person, the defenses cannot be raised that the transferor did not own the shares, or did not have authority to deliver the certificate, or that the transfer was made in violation of a restriction upon transfer not known to such person

and not noted conspicuously on the certificate.

The fact that corporate stock has the quality of negotiability does not make it commercial paper within Article 3 of the UCC. Shares of stock are classified under the UCC as investment securities; and Article 8, as supplemented by the non-Code law which has not been displaced, is the source of the law governing the rights of the parties to the transaction involving such securities. Nevertheless, courts may look to Article 3 for guidance when a question regarding an investment security cannot be resolved on the basis of the language in Article 8 alone.

(c) SECURED TRANSACTION. Corporate stock is frequently delivered to a creditor as security for a debt owed by the shareholder. Thus, a debtor borrowing money from a bank may deliver shares of stock to the bank as collateral security for the repayment of the loan, or a broker's customer purchasing stock on margin may leave the stock in the possession of the broker as security for the payment of any balance due. The delivery of the security to the creditor gives rise to a perfected security interest without any filing by the creditor. In itself, the pledge does not make the pledgee of the corporate stock the owner of the stock.

(d) EFFECT OF TRANSFER ON CORPORATION. Until there is a transfer on its books, the corporation is entitled to treat as the owner the person whose name is on the books. The corporation may properly refuse to recognize the transferee when the corporation is given notice or has knowledge that the transfer is void or in breach of trust. In such a case, the corporation properly refuses to register a transfer until the rights of the parties have been determined.

The corporation may also refuse to register the transfer of shares when the outstanding certificate is not surrendered to it, in the absence of satisfactory proof that it has been lost, destroyed, or stolen.

§ 51:9   LOST, DESTROYED, AND STOLEN SECURITIES

The owner of a lost, destroyed, or stolen security is entitled to a replacement security if the owner files a sufficient indemnity bond and requests the new security within a reasonable time before the issuer has notice that the original certificate has been acquired by a bona fide purchaser. If, after the issue of the new security, a bona fide purchaser appears with the original security, the corporation must register a transfer of the security to that person and accept such person as the owner of the shares.[7]

§ 51:10   PROTECTION OF THE PUBLIC

State and federal laws have been adopted to protect investors.

(a) STATE REGULATION. In order to protect the public from the sale of fraudulent securities, many states have adopted regulations called **blue sky laws.** The term *blue sky* is derived from the purpose of such laws, which is the preventing of the sale of speculative schemes that have no more value than a small area of blue sky. The state statutes vary in detail. They commonly contain (1) an antifraud provision prohibiting fraudulent practices and imposing criminal penalties for violations; (2) broker-dealer licensing provisions regulating the persons engaged in the securities business; and (3) the registration of securities including disclosure requirements with a designated governmental official.

State blue sky laws are subject to the very important limitation that they can apply only to intrastate transactions and cannot apply to sales made in interstate commerce.

A Uniform Securities Act,[8] covering the foregoing three categories of regulations, exists to provide guidance to states in updating their securities laws. This act contains alternative regulations, which can be adopted by states with different regulatory philosophies.

(b) FEDERAL REGULATION. The stock market crash of 1929 and the Great Depression which followed led to the enactment of legislation to regulate the securities industry. Six federal securities regulation laws were passed in the period between 1933 and 1940. The two principal laws that provide the basic framework for the federal regulation of the sale of securities in interstate commerce are the Securities Act of 1933 and the Securities Exchange Act of 1934. The 1933 act deals with the original distribution of securities by the issuing corporations, while the 1934 act is concerned with the secondary distribution of securities in the national securities markets and in the over-the-counter markets.

Four other federal laws deal with more specific aspects of the securities industry. The Public Utility Holding Company Act of 1935[9] provides comprehensive regulation of holding companies and their subsidiaries in the interstate gas and electric utilities businesses. The Trust Indenture Act of 1939[10] was enacted to protect the interests of the holders of bonds and other debt securities offered to the public in interstate commerce through the required appointments of independent institutional trustees. The Investment Company Act of 1940[11] provides for the registration and comprehensive regulation of mutual funds and all other investment companies. The Investment Advisors Act of 1940[12] requires registration with the Securities and Exchange Commission of all persons engaged in the business of providing investment advice in interstate commerce.

§ 51:11   SECURITIES ACT OF 1933

The 1933 act deals with the original distribution of securities. It prohibits the offer

---

[7]   UCC § 8-405.
[8]   7B Uniform Laws Annotated 515.
[9]   15 USC §§ 79-792-6.
[10]   15 USC §§ 77aaa to 77bbb.
[11]   15 USC §§ 80a-1 to 80a-52.
[12]   15 USC §§ 80b-1 to 80-b21.

or sale of securities to the public in interstate commerce before a **registration statement** containing disclosure of specific financial information regarding the security, the issuer, and the underwriter has been filed with the Securities and Exchange Commission (SEC). The seller must also provide a prospectus to each potential purchaser of the securities. The **prospectus** sets forth the key information contained in the registration statement. The object is to provide the interested investor with detailed information about the security and the enterprise. The SEC does not approve or disapprove the securities as being good or bad investments but only reviews the form and content of the registration statement and the prospectus to assure full disclosure. The requirements of advance disclosure to the public through the filing of the registration statement with the SEC and the sending of a prospectus to each potential purchaser are commonly referred to as the **registration requirements** of the 1933 act.

(a) APPLICABILITY. The act applies to (1) stocks, (2) corporate bonds, and (3) any conceivable kind of corporate interest or instrument that has the characteristics of an investment security. A share of stock is an **equity security** and is an ownership interest in the corporation. A bond is a **debt security**, and holders of such a security are creditors of the corporation rather than owners. Numerous other instruments have been created to provide the capital structure of business, including convertible securities and variable annuities. The act applies to all such instruments that have investment characteristics.

(b) THE REGISTRATION PROCESS. Section 5 of the 1933 act provides for the division of the registration process into three time periods: (1) the *prefiling period*, which is that period prior to filing the registration statement with the SEC; (2) the *waiting period*, which applies from the date of filing with the SEC to the date the registration statement becomes effective (this period is a minimum of twenty days, but commonly

extends for additional twenty-day periods after each amendment by the issuer in compliance with SEC requirements for additional information); and (3) the *posteffective period*. The time divisions provide the public an opportunity to fully study the information disclosed in the registration process before a final sale can be consummated. Permissible, required, and prohibited activities during the time periods are set forth in Figure 51-1.

(c) REGISTRATION EXEMPTIONS. Certain private and limited offerings of securities are exempt from the registration requirements of the act.[13] Under SEC Regulation D offerings of any amount made solely to accredited investors, such as banks, insurance companies, investment companies, or directors and executive officers of the issuing corporation, are exempt from the registration requirements of the act. These accredited investors generally have access to the kinds of information disclosed in a registration statement and prospectus.

(1) Rule 505 Exemption. SEC Rule 505, promulgated under Regulation D, exempts from registration offerings of less than $5,000,000 to less than 35 nonaccredited purchasers (not offerees) over a 12-month period. No limit exists on the number of accredited investors who may participate. No general solicitation or general advertising is permitted under Rule 505. If any prospective investors are nonaccredited, the issuer must furnish all investors with specific information on the issuer, its business, and the securities offered for sale.

(2) Rule 504 Exemption. Under SEC Rule 504 of Regulation D an issuer is permitted to sell securities for an aggregate price up to $500,000 in a one-year period to any number of investors without furnishing any explanation to the purchasers. This rule was fashioned to provide an exception for small offerings by small issuers.

(3) Rule 506 Exemption. As opposed to Rules 505 and 504 which exempt offerings limited to $5,000,000 and $500,000 respec-

---

[13]   17 CFR §§ 239.501 to 506 (1982).

	Prohibited or Required Activities	Permitted Activities
Prefiling Period	Issuer must not sell or offer for sale a security before registration statement is filed.	Issuer may plan with underwriters the distribution of the security.
Waiting Period	No final sale of a security permitted during this period.	Preliminary prospectus* containing information from the registration statement being reviewed by the SEC may be distributed to investors, who may make offers. Advertisements may be placed in financial publications, identifying particulars of the security, from whom a prospectus can be obtained, and by whom orders will be executed.**
Post-effective Period	Must provide a copy of final prospectus with every written offer, confirmation of sale, or delivery of security. Must update prospectus whenever important new developments occur, or after nine months.	Sales of the security may be completed.

* The preliminary prospectus is commonly called the "red herring" prospectus because of the red ink caption required by the SEC, informing the public that a registration statement has been filed but is not yet effective, and that no final sale can be made until after the effective date.

** These advertisements are sometimes called "tombstone ads" because they are commonly framed by a black ink border.

Figure 51-1
Registration Periods

tively, SEC Rule 506, the so-called private placement exemption, has no limitation on the amount that may be raised by the offering. As in Rule 505, specific information must be provided to all buyers if any buyers are nonaccredited investors, and the number of nonaccredited investors is limited to less than thirty-five. Further, the rule requires that the issuer shall reasonably believe that each nonaccredited investor has sufficient experience in investments as to be capable of evaluating the merits and risks of the investment.

(4) Restrictions. Securities acquired under a Regulation D exemption from registration are considered **restricted securities,** and their resale may require registration. Rules requiring registration of Regulation D Securities prior to resale are promulgated to insure that investors purchase these securities as an investment rather than for public distribution. When there is no attempt to make public distributions, investors ordinarily fit within one of several exemptions to registration upon resale.

(d) Liability. The Securities Act of 1933 imposes civil liability under Section 11 for making materially false or misleading statements in a registration statement, and for the omission of any required material fact. Any investor who sustains a loss because of the false statements or omissions on the registration statement may sue to recover damages under Section 11. An issuing company has virtually no defense in such an action if there has been a false statement and a loss. However, individual defendants, such as accountants who helped prepare portions of the registration statement, may defend by proving they acted in good faith and with due diligence.

Section 12 of the 1933 act applies to those who "offer or sell" securities and employ any device or scheme to defraud or obtain money by means of untrue statements of material facts. This section makes such individuals or firms liable to purchasers for damages sustained.[14]

Section 24 of the 1933 act imposes criminal penalties upon anyone who willfully makes untrue statements of material facts or omits required material facts in a registration statement. Section 17 of the Securities Act makes it unlawful for any person to employ any device, scheme, or artifice to defraud in the offer or sale of securities. Law firms and public accounting firms who prepare fraudulent registration statements in conjunction with clients may be subject to civil liability as "aiders and abettors" under Section 12(2) of the act, and criminal liability under Section 17(a) of the act. Even though a security is exempt from registration, the civil and criminal liability discussed above still applies if interstate commerce or the mails are involved in the offer or sale of the security.

§ 51:12 SECURITIES EXCHANGE ACT OF 1934

The 1934 act deals with the secondary distribution of securities. It was designed to prevent fraudulent and manipulative practices on the security exchanges and in over-the-counter markets. The act also seeks to provide for fair and honest markets for securities by requiring disclosure of information to buyers and sellers of the securities. Furthermore, the act controls credit in these markets.

(a) REGISTRATION REQUIREMENTS. Exchanges, brokers, and dealers who deal in the securities traded in interstate commerce or on any national security exchange must register with the SEC unless exempted by it.

Companies whose securities are listed on a national securities exchange or unlisted companies that have assets in excess of $3 million and 500 or more shareholders

are subject to the reporting requirements of the act.[15]

Form 10-K is the principal annual report form used by commercial and industrial companies required to file under the 1934 act. The reports require nonfinancial information about the registrant's activities during the year, such as the nature of the firm's business, the property or businesses it owns, and a statement concerning legal proceedings by or against the company. The report requires the submission of financial statements, with management's analysis of the financial condition of the company, and a report and analysis of the performance of corporate shares. It requires a listing of all directors and executive officers and disclosure of executive compensation information.

Registrants who are required to file 10-K reports must also file quarterly reports, which are principally concerned with financial information relevant to the quarterly period.

Annual shareholder reports are required by the SEC to be submitted to shareholders in any proxy solicitation on behalf of management. These reports contain essentially the same information provided in the 10-K.

(b) ANTIFRAUD PROVISION. Section 10(b) of the 1934 act makes it unlawful for any person to use any manipulative or deceptive device in contravention of SEC rules.[16] Under the authority of Section 10(b) of the 1934 act, the SEC has promulgated Rule 10b-5. This rule is the principal antifraud rule relating to the secondary distribution of securities. The rule states:

> It shall be unlawful for any person, directly or indirectly, by use of any means or instrumentality of interstate commerce, or of the mails or of any facility of any national securities exchange,
>
> (a) To employ any device, scheme, or artifice to defraud.

---

[14] Securities Act of 1933, § 12(2).

[15] SEC Release No. 34-18647 (April 15, 1982).
[16] 15 USC § 78j(b).

(b) To make any untrue statement of a material fact or to omit to state a material fact necessary in order to make the statements made, in the light of the circumstances under which they were made, not misleading, or

(c) To engage in any act, practice, or course of business that operates or would operate as a fraud or deceit upon any person, in connection with the purchase or sale of any security.[17]

Rule 10b-5 applies to all securities, whether registered or not as long as use is made of the mails, interstate commerce, or a national stock exchange. Under this rule, a civil action for damages may be brought by any injured party who purchased or sold securities because of false, misleading, or undisclosed information.[18] Criminal penalties may also be imposed for willful violation of the act or SEC regulations promulgated under the act.

In some instances there is an overlap between the provisions of the 1933 act and the 1934 act. Thus, purchasers of registered securities who allege they were defrauded by misrepresentations in a registration statement filed under the 1933 act, may bring an action under the catchall antifraud provision of Section 10(b) of the 1934 act and SEC Rule 10b-5, notwithstanding the express remedy for misstatements in registration statements provided by Section 11 of the 1933 act.[19]

---

[17] 17 CFR § 240, 10b-5 (1982).
[18] Blue Chip Stamps v Manor Drug Store, 421 US 723 (1975).
[19] Herman & MacLean v Huddleston, 459 US 375 (1983).

(c) Insider Information. The SEC and the courts have relied upon Section 10(b) and Rule 10b-5 as the legal basis for imposing sanctions for trading on **insider information**. Under the Insider Trading Sanctions Act of 1984, which amended the 1934 act, the SEC may now bring an action against an individual purchasing or selling a security while in possession of material, inside information, and the court may impose a civil penalty of up to three times the profit gained or loss avoided as a result of the unlawful sale.[20] Persons who "aid or abet" in the violation may also be held liable under the act.

An **insider**, such as a director or corporate employee, or a **temporary insider** retained by the corporation for professional services, such as an attorney, accountant, or investment banker, is liable for inside trading when the insider fails to disclose material nonpublic information before trading on it and thus makes a secret profit. A **tippee**, that is, an individual who receives information from an insider or temporary insider, is subject to the insider's fiduciary duty to shareholders when the insider has breached the fiduciary duty to shareholders by improperly disclosing the information to the tippee and when the tippee knows or should know there has been a breach. Such a breach occurs when an insider benefits personally from his or her disclosure.

In the *Dirks* case, the court discussed the factors that subject a tippee to liability.

---

[20] PL 98-376, 58 Stat 1264, 15 USC § 780.

Dirks v Securities and Exchange Commission
463 US 646 (1983)

On March 6, 1973 Raymond Dirks, an investment analyst, received information from Ronald Secrist, a former officer of Equity Funding of America, alleging that the assets of Equity Funding were vastly overstated as the result of fraudulent corporate practices. Upon investigation

Dirks received only denials from senior management, but certain corporation employees corroborated the charges of fraud. Neither Dirks nor his firm owned or traded any Equity Funding stock, but throughout his investigation he openly discussed the information he had obtained with a number of clients and investors, causing liquidation of Equity Fund stock in excess of $16 million. Dirks urged *The Wall Street Journal* to publish a story on the fraud allegations. However, it declined because it feared that publishing damaging hearsay might be libelous. Dirks continued his investigation and spread word of Secrist's charges during the next two weeks. During this time, Equity Funding stock fell from $26 per share to less than $15 per share. On March 27, the NYSE halted trading of Equity Funding stock, and a subsequent investigation revealed the vast fraud that had taken place. The SEC, investigating Dirks' role in the exposure of the fraud, found that Dirks had aided and abetted violations of the Securities Act of 1933, the Securities Exchange Act of 1934, and SEC Rule 10b-5 by repeating the allegations of fraud to members of the investment community who later sold their Equity Funding stock. Upon appeal by Dirks, the decision of the lower court was upheld by the U.S. Court of Appeals. An appeal was taken to the Supreme Court.

POWELL, J. . . . In the seminal case of *In re Cady, Roberts & Co.*, 40 S.E.C. 907 (1961), the SEC recognized that the common law in some jurisdictions imposes on "corporate 'insiders', particularly officers, directors, or controlling stockholders" an "affirmative duty of disclosure . . . when dealing in securities." The SEC found that not only did breach of this common-law duty also establish the elements of a Rule 10b-5 violation, but that individuals other than corporate insiders could be obligated either to disclose material nonpublic information before trading or to abstain from trading altogether. In *Chiarella* [445 U.S. 222 (1980)], we accepted the two elements set out in *Cady, Roberts* for establishing a Rule 10b-5 violation: "(i) the existence of a relationship affording access to inside information intended to be available only for a corporate purpose, and (ii) the unfairness of allowing a corporate insider to take advantage of that information by trading without disclosure." In examining whether Chiarella had an obligation to disclose or abstain, the Court found that there is no general duty to disclose before trading on material nonpublic information, and held that "a duty to disclose under § 10(b) does not arise from the mere possession of nonpublic market information." Such a duty arises rather from the existence of a fiduciary relationship.

Not "all breaches of fiduciary duty in connection with a securities transaction," however, come within the ambit of Rule 10b-5. There must also be "manipulation or deception." In an inside-trading case this fraud derives from the "inherent unfairness involved where one takes advantage" of "information intended to be available only for a corporate purpose and not for the personal benefit of anyone." Thus, an insider will be liable under Rule 10b-5 for inside trading only where he fails to disclose material nonpublic information before trading on it and thus makes "secret profits."

We were explicit in *Chiarella* in saying that there can be no duty to disclose where the person who has traded on inside information "was not [the corporation's] agent, . . . was not a fiduciary, [or] was not a person in whom the sellers [of the securities] had placed their trust and confidence." Not to require such a fiduciary relationship, we recognized, would "depar[t] radically from the established doctrine that duty arises from a specific relationship between two parties" and would amount to "recognizing a general duty between all participants in market transactions to forgo actions based on material, nonpublic information." This requirement of a specific relationship between the shareholders and the individual trading on inside information has created analytical difficulties for the SEC and courts in policing tippees who trade on inside information. Unlike insiders who have independent fiduciary duties to both the corporation and its shareholders, the typical tippee has no such relationships.* In view of this absence, it has been unclear how a tippee acquires the *Cady, Roberts* duty to refrain from trading on inside information.

The SEC's position, as stated in its opinion in this case, is that a tippee "inherits" the *Cady, Roberts* obligation to shareholders whenever he receives inside information from an insider: . . .

In effect, the SEC's theory of tippee liability . . . appears rooted in the idea that the antifraud provisions required equal information among all traders. This conflicts with the principle set forth in *Chiarella* that only some persons, under some circumstances, will be barred from trading while in possession of material nonpublic information. . . .

Imposing a duty to disclose or abstain solely because a person knowingly receives material nonpublic information from an insider and trades on it could have an inhibiting influence on the role of market analysts, which the SEC itself recognizes is necessary to the preservation of a healthy market. It is commonplace for analysts to "ferret out and analyze information," and this often is done by meeting with and questioning corporate officers and others who are insiders. And information that the analysts obtain normally may be the basis for judgments as to the market worth of a corporation's securities. The analyst's judgment in this respect is made available in market letters or otherwise to clients of the firm. It is the nature of this type of information, and indeed of the markets themselves, that such information cannot be made simultaneously available to all of the corporation's stockholders or the public generally.

The conclusion that recipients of inside information do not invariably acquire a duty to disclose or abstain does not mean that such tippees always are free to trade on the information. The need for a ban on some tippee trading is clear. Not only are insiders forbidden by their fiduciary relationship from personally using undisclosed corporate information to their advantage, but they may not give such information to an outsider for the same improper purpose of exploiting the information for their personal gain. See 15 U.S.C. § 78t(b) (making it unlawful to do indirectly "by means of any other person" any act

---

*   Under certain circumstances, such as where corporate information is revealed legitimately to an underwriter, accountant, lawyer, or consultant working for the corporation, these outsiders may become fiduciaries of the shareholders. The basis for recognizing this fiduciary duty is not simply that such persons acquired nonpublic corporate information, but rather that they have entered into a special confidential relationship in the conduct of the business of the enterprise and are given access to information solely for corporate purposes. See *SEC v. Monarch Fund*, 608 F.2d 938 (CA2 1979); . . . When such a person breaches his fiduciary relationship, he may be treated more properly as a tipper than a tippee. See *Shapiro v. Merrill Lynch, Pierce, Fenner & Smith, Inc.*, 495 F.2d 228 (CA2 1974) (investment banker had access to material information when working on a proposed public offering for the corporation). For such a duty to be imposed, however, the corporation must expect the outsider to keep the disclosed nonpublic information confidential, and the relationship at least must imply such a duty.

made unlawful by the federal securities laws). Similarly, the transactions of those who knowingly participate with the fiduciary in such a breach are "as forbidden" as transactions "on behalf of the trustee himself." . . .

Thus, some tippees must assume an insider's duty to the shareholders not because they receive inside information, but rather because it has been made available to them *improperly*. And for Rule 10b-5 purposes, the insider's disclosure is improper only where it would violate his *Cady, Roberts* duty. Thus, a tippee assumes a fiduciary duty to the shareholders of a corporation not to trade on material nonpublic information only when the insider has breached his fiduciary duty to the shareholders by disclosing the information to the tippee and the tippee knows or should know that there has been a breach.

In determining whether a tippee is under an obligation to disclose or abstain, it thus is necessary to determine whether the insider's "tip" constituted a breach of the insider's fiduciary duty. All disclosures of confidential corporate information are not inconsistent with the duty insiders owe to shareholders. . . . Thus, the test is whether the insider personally will benefit, directly or indirectly, from his disclosure. Absent some personal gain, there has been no breach of duty to stockholders. And absent a breach by the insider, there is no derivative breach. . . .

Under the inside-trading and tipping rules set forth above, we find that there was no actionable violation by Dirks. It is undisputed that Dirks himself was a stranger to Equity Funding, with no pre-existing fiduciary duty to its shareholders. He took no action, directly or indirectly, that induced the shareholders or officers of Equity Funding to repose trust or confidence in him. There was no expectation by Dirks' sources that he would keep their information in confidence. Nor did Dirks misappropriate or illegally obtain the information about Equity Funding. Unless the insiders breached their *Cady, Roberts* duty to shareholders in disclosing the nonpublic information to Dirks, he breached no duty when he passed it on to investors as well as to [*T]he Wall Street Journal*.

It is clear that neither Secrist nor the other Equity Funding employees violated their *Cady, Roberts* duty to the corporation's shareholders by providing information to Dirks. The tippers received no monetary or personal benefit for revealing Equity Funding's secrets, nor was their purpose to make a gift of valuable information to Dirks. As the facts of this case clearly indicate, the tippers were motivated by a desire to expose the fraud.

[Judgment reversed]

BLACKMUN, J. (dissenting) . . . The Court today takes still another step to limit the protections provided investors by § 10(b) of the Securities Exchange Act of 1934. . . . The device employed in this case engrafts a special motivational requirement on the fiduciary duty doctrine. This innovation excuses a knowing and intentional violation of an insider's duty to shareholders if the insider does not act from a motive of personal gain. Even on the extraordinary facts of this case, such an innovation is not justified. . . .

In my view, Secrist violated his duty to Equity Funding shareholders by transmitting material nonpublic information to Dirks with the intention that Dirks would cause his clients to trade on that information. Dirks, therefore, was under a duty to make the information publicly available or to refrain from actions that he knew would lead to trading. Because Dirks caused his clients to trade, he violated § 10(b) and Rule 10b-5. Any other result is a disservice to this country's attempt to provide fair and efficient capital markets.

QUESTIONS

1. State the SEC's theory of tippee liability. Would such a theory have an inhibiting influence on the role of market analysts?
2. When is a tippee subject to a fiduciary duty to the shareholders not to trade on material nonpublic information?
3. Does the court establish a *constructive insider* rule in its footnote?

Individuals who misappropriate or steal valuable nonpublic information in breach of a fiduciary duty to their employer and trade in securities on that information are guilty of insider trading as so-called misappropriators. Thus, an employee working for a financial printing firm who, while proofreading a financial document being prepared for a client firm, was able to figure out the identity of certain tender offer targets and, soon thereafter, traded on such valuable nonpublic information to his advantage was found guilty of insider trading under § 10(b) and Rule 10b-5.[21]

It is no defense to a Section 10(b) and Rule 10b-5 criminal charge of participating in a "scheme to defraud" that the victim of the fraud had no economic interest in the securities traded. The convictions of a columnist for *The Wall Street Journal* and a stockbroker were upheld under Section 10(b) of the 1934 act when the columnist violated his fiduciary duty to his employer by revealing prepublication information about his column to the stockbroker who used it to trade in the securities identified in the column.[22] While it is argued that comprehensive new legislation is needed to deal with all aspects of insider trading, the SEC and federal prosecutors have been very successful in the courts under Section 10(b), Rule 10b-5, and the Insider Trading Sanctions Act, and Congress, thus, has not been disposed to adopt legislative changes.

Investors who lack inside information possessed by the insider and have sold their stock during the relevant time period, may recover damages from any insider who has made use of the undisclosed information. Recovery is through a civil action based on Rule 10b-5.

(d) DISCLOSURE OF OWNERSHIP AND SHORT-SWING PROFIT. Corporate directors and officers owning equity securities in their corporation and any shareholder owning more than 10 percent of any class of the corporation's equity securities must file a disclosure statement as to such ownership with the SEC under Section 16(a) of the 1934 act.

Section 16 is designed to prevent the unfair use of information available to these corporate insiders by preventing them from participating in short-term trading in their corporation's equity securities.

If such a person sells at a profit any of such securities in less than six months after their purchase, the profit is called a **short-swing profit**. Under Section 16(b) the corporation may sue the director, officer, or major stockholder for the short-swing profit and may recover that profit even though there was no fraudulent intent in acquiring and selling the securities.

§ 51:13   TENDER OFFERS

A corporation or group of investors may seek to acquire control of another corporation by making a general offer to all shareholders of the target corporation to pur-

---

21 SEC v Materia (CA2 NY) 745 F2d 197 (1984).
22 Carpenter v US, ___ US ___, 98 L Ed 2d 275 (1987).

chase their shares for cash at a specified price, subject to a minimum or maximum number of shares that the offeror will accept. Such is called a **cash tender offer.** The offer to purchase is usually contingent upon the tender of a fixed number of shares sufficient to assure takeover; the bid price is set at a premium over the prevailing market price. Should more shares be tendered than the offeror is willing to purchase, the tender offeror must purchase shares from each shareholder on a pro rata basis.

The Williams Act, which amended the 1934 act,[23] was passed in order to ensure that public shareholders who are confronted with a cash tender offer will not be required to respond without adequate information. Under Section 14(d) of the Williams Act a person making a tender offer must ordinarily file appropriate SEC forms providing information about the background and identity of the person filing, the source of funds used to make purchases of stock, the amount of stock beneficially owned, the purpose of the purchases, any plan the purchaser proposes to implement if it gains control over the target corporation, and any contracts or understandings that it has with other persons concerning the target corporation.[24]

Section 14(e) of the Williams Act is the antifraud section and prohibits fraudulent, deceptive, or manipulative practices. SEC Rule 14e-1 requires any tender offer to remain open for a minimum of twenty business days from the date it is first published or given to security holders. The SEC believes that tender offers that do not stay open for a reasonable length of time increase the likelihood of hasty, ill-considered decision making on the basis of inadequate or incomplete information, as well as the possibility for fraudulent, deceptive, or manipulative acts or practices by a bidder and others.

Corporations themselves have adopted antitakeover measures to ward off tender offers. Some states have enacted laws that make it more difficult for tender offers to succeed.[25]

The courts are not inclined to subject every tender offer to close judicial scrutiny, which could generally inhibit shareholders from taking advantage of favorable offerings. Fairness or unfairness of the offer may not be the basis of a Section 14(e) action, but rather it is essential to allege and prove misrepresentation.[26]

§ 51:14   REGULATION OF THE ACCOUNTING PROFESSION BY THE SEC

Accountants play a vital role in financial reporting under the federal securities laws administered by the SEC. Accountants are subject to liability under Sections 11, 12, 17, and 24 of the 1933 act and may also be liable under Section 10(b) of the 1934 act. An accountant who prepares any statement, opinion, or other legal paper filed with the SEC with the preparer's consent is deemed to be practicing before the SEC.[27] Because accountants are relied upon so heavily by the SEC, it has promulgated Rule 2(e) to regulate and discipline the many accountants (as well as attorneys and

---

[23]   PL90-439, 82 Stat 454, 15 USC §§ 78m(d)-(e).
[24]   Section 14(d) requires a filing by any person making a tender offer that, if successful, would result in the acquisition of 5 percent of any class of an equity security required to be registered under the 1934 act. Section 13(d) of the act requires disclosure to the issuer, the SEC, and the appropriate stock exchange when a person acquires 5 percent of a class of equity security through stock purchases on exchanges or through private purchases. The person may have acquired the stock for investment purpose and not for control, but must still file disclosure forms under Section 13(d). Section 14(d) applies only to shares to be acquired by tender offer.

[25]   See, for example, Indiana Control Share Acquisition Act, Ind Bus Corp Law § 23-1-17-1 (Supp 1986) that provides that acquisition of "control shares" in a corporation will not include voting rights unless a majority of preexisting disinterested shareholders so agree at a meeting to be held within 50 days. The constitutionality of this law, including the 50-day maximum period as compared to the 20-day waiting period of the Williams Act, was upheld by the U.S. Supreme Court in *CTS Corp. v Dynamics Corp. of America*, 107 S Ct 1637 (1987).
[26]   Data Probe Acquisition Corp. v Datatab, Inc. (CA2 NY), 722 F2d 1 (1983).
[27]   17 CFR § 201.2e (1979).

consultants) who practice before it. Under Rule 2(e) the SEC may suspend or disbar from practice before it those who are unqualified, unethical, or have violated federal securities laws or SEC rules.[28]

C.   RIGHTS OF SHAREHOLDERS

The control of the shareholders over the corporation is indirect. Periodically, ordinarily once a year, the shareholders elect directors and by this means can control the corporation. At other times, however, the shareholders have no right or power to control the corporate activity so long as it is conducted within lawful channels.

§ 51:15   OWNERSHIP RIGHTS

Ownership rights in a corporation are generally represented by shares of stock and are generally freely transferable.

(a) CERTIFICATES OF STOCK. A shareholder generally has the right to have a properly executed certificate as evidence of ownership of shares.[29]

(b) TRANSFER OF SHARES. Subject to certain valid restrictions, a shareholder has the right to transfer the shares and may sell the shares at any price or transfer them as a gift.

---

[28] Rule 2(e) provides in pertinent part: "*Suspension and disbarment.* (1) The Commission may deny, temporarily or permanently, the privilege of appearing or practicing before it in any way to any person who is found by the Commission after notice of an opportunity for hearing in the matter (i) not to possess the requisite qualifications to represent others, or (ii) to be lacking in character or integrity or to have engaged in unethical or improper professional conduct, or (iii) to have willfully violated, or willfully aided and abetted the violation of any provision of the Federal securities laws (15 U.S.C. 77a to 80B-20), or the rules and regulations thereunder. 17 CFR § 201.2(e) (1979)."
The authority of the SEC to promulgate the rule was upheld in *Touche Ross v SEC* (CA2 SEC) 609 F2d 570 (1979).
[29] As to shares without certificates under the 1977 version of the Uniform Commercial Code, see footnote 2 of this chapter.

§ 51:16   RIGHT TO VOTE

The right to vote means the right to vote at shareholders' meetings for the election of directors and on such other special matters as must be passed upon by the shareholders. As an illustration of the latter, a proposal to change the capital structure of the corporation or a proposal to sell all or substantially all the assets of the corporation must be approved by the shareholders.

(a) WHO MAY VOTE. Ordinarily, only **shareholders of record**, those common shareholders in whose name the stock appears on the books of the corporation, are entitled to vote. The board of directors may fix a date for closing the corporate books for this purpose.[30]

(b) NUMBER OF VOTES. Absent a provision to the contrary, for each share owned each shareholder is entitled to one vote on each matter to be voted. This procedure is called **straight voting,** and it is the normal method for shareholder voting on corporate matters. However, in the case of voting to elect directors only, cumulative voting is mandatory in nearly half of the states, being imposed by either constitution or statute; and it is permissive by law in other states, where cumulative voting rights are provided for in the articles of incorporation or bylaws. **Cumulative voting** is a form of voting that is designed to give proportional representation on the board of directors to minority shareholders. Under a cumulative voting plan, each shareholder has as many votes as the number of shares owned multiplied by the number of directors to be elected. Minority shareholders may then cast all of their votes for a candidate who will represent their interests on the board of directors. Under straight voting, minority shareholders would always be outvoted. Thus, if minority shareholder Susan Jones owned 350 shares of stock, and a majority interest controlled the remaining 650 shares of stock of the corporation, with nine directors to be elected to the board, Susan would be al-

---

[30]   RMBCA § 7.07.

lowed 3150 cumulative votes (350 shares X 9 directors). This number of votes would guarantee her being able to elect three directors to represent her interests on the board. (Susan who owns 35 percent of the stock is thus able to elect one-third of the board.) If straight voting were used for the election of directors, the majority shareholder with 650 shares would always outvote Susan's 350 shares.

(c) VOTING BY PROXY. A shareholder has the right to authorize another to vote the shares owned by the shareholder. This procedure is known as **voting by proxy.** In the absence of restrictions to the contrary, any person, even one not a shareholder, may act as a proxy. Ordinarily, authority to act as a proxy may be conferred by an informal written instrument.[31]

(d) VOTING AGREEMENTS AND TRUSTS. Shareholders, as a general rule, are allowed to enter into an agreement by which they concentrate their voting strength for the purpose of controlling the management.

A **voting trust** exists when by agreement a group of shareholders, or all of the shareholders, transfer their shares in trust to one or more persons as trustees who are authorized to vote the stock during the life of the trust agreement.[32] In general, such agreements have been upheld if their object is lawful. In some jurisdictions such trusts cannot run beyond a specific number of years. There are some signs of a relaxation as to this matter. Several states have abandoned any time limitations, several have extended the time limitation, and many states provide for an extension or renewal of the agreement.

§ 51:17   PREEMPTIVE OFFER OF SHARES

If the capital stock of a corporation is increased, shareholders ordinarily have the preemptive right to subscribe to such percentage of the new shares as their old shares bore to the former total of capital stock. This right is given in order to enable shareholders to maintain their relative interests in the corporation.

The existence of a preemptive right may make impossible the concluding of a transaction in which the corporation is to transfer a block of stock as consideration. Moreover, practical difficulties arise as to how stock should be allocated among shareholders of different classes.

The RMBCA provides that shareholders do not have preemptive rights unless the articles of incorporation so provide.[33] When the corporation elects to have preemptive rights by so stating in its articles of incorporation, the RMBCA sets forth rules dealing with most of the problems involving preemptive rights.[34] Under this model provision there is no preemptive right with respect to the transfer of a block of stock as consideration. Also the model provision deals with how stock should be allocated among shareholders of different classes.

§ 51:18   INSPECTION OF BOOKS

A shareholder has the right to inspect the books of the shareholder's corporation. The request for inspection must be made in good faith, for proper motives, and at a reasonable time and place. The RMBCA authorizes inspection of corporate records "if the demand is made in good faith and for proper purpose."[35]

The purpose of inspection must be reasonably related to the shareholder's interest as a shareholder. A shareholder is entitled to inspect the records to determine the financial condition of the corporation, the quality of its management, and any matters relating to rights or interests in

---

[31] See, for example, the regulations of the Securities and Exchange Commission, Rule X-14A-4.
[32] Bettner Trust v Bettner (Ind App) 495 NE2d 194 (1986).

[33] RMBCA § 6.30(a).
[34] RMBCA § 6.30(b).
[35] RMBCA § 16.02(c).

the corporate business, such as the value of stock.

Whether a stockholder who became part owner and employee of a competing business could inspect the books was the issue in the *Carter* case.

CARTER V WILSON CONSTRUCTION CO., INC.
(NC App) 348 SE2d 830 (1986)

William Carter, a former officer and employee of Wilson Construction Co. Inc., owned 317 shares of stock in the corporation. He left the Wilson corporation to become part owner and employee of C & L Contracting Co., which was a direct competitor of the Wilson corporation. Carter requested access to the Wilson corporate books in order to determine the value of his shares. The corporation refused, not wanting to divulge its business practices to a direct competitor. From a decision for Carter, which also assessed a $500 penalty against both the corporation's president and the corporation, the Wilson corporation and its president appealed.

JOHNSON, J. . . . Defendants contend in their first Assignment of Error that the court erred in finding that plaintiff had a proper purpose for obtaining access to the corporate information he requested. Defendants further contend that plaintiff's stated purpose was "a mask for more illegitimate purposes that would damage [defendant corporation's] ability to compete." Defendants characterize plaintiff as a "disgruntled minority shareholder" who "left his position without notice," leaving both companies "in pretty bad shape" in order to start his own competing business. . . .

The pertinent portion of G. S. § 55-38 provides as follows:

(b) A qualified shareholder, upon written demand stating the purpose thereof, shall have the right, in person, or by attorney, accountant or other agent, at any reasonable time or times, *for any proper purpose*, to examine at the place where they are kept and make extracts from, the books and records of account, minutes and record of shareholders of a domestic corporation or those of a foreign corporation actually or customarily kept by it within this State. . . . A shareholder's rights under this subsection may be enforced by an action in the nature of mandamus.

(Emphasis added.)

It is undisputed by the parties that plaintiff is a qualified shareholder. The issue is whether plaintiff's request to examine the corporate records was for "any proper purpose." Absent a statutory restriction, a shareholder has a common law right to inspect and examine the books and records of the corporation, given to him for the protection of his interests. G.S. § 55-38(b) does not give a qualified shareholder an absolute right of inspection and examination for a mere fishing expedition, or for a purpose not germane to the protection of his economic interest as a shareholder in the corporation. For a shareholder to have the right to actually visit a corporation's office and possibly disrupt its normal operation in order to inspect corporate books and records of account, our legislature has correctly decided that his motives must be "proper." Purposes which previously have been deemed proper are the shareholder's good faith desire to (1) determine the value of his stock; (2) investigate the conduct of the management; and (3) determine the financial condition of the corporation. The burden of proof rests upon the defendants, if they wish to defeat the shareholder's demand, to allege and show by facts, if they can, that the shareholder is motivated by some improper purpose. "In issuing the writ of mandamus the court will exercise a sound discretion, and grant the right under proper safeguards to protect the interests of all concerned." [*Cooke v. Outland*, 265 N.C. 601,] 613, 144 S.E.2d 843, *quoting Guthrie v. Harkness*, 199 U.S. 148, 156 (1905).

Here, plaintiff stated a proper purpose in his complaint. Defendants must overcome the presumption of good faith in plaintiff's favor by showing that plaintiff's purpose is improper. The evidence adduced at trial by plaintiff tended to show: that plaintiff tried to sell his stock in defendant corporation to defendant corporation, who declined plaintiff's offer to sell; . . . and that the net worth of defendant corporation decreased from August 1983 to August 1984. This evidence supports plaintiff's allegation of a proper purpose.

The evidence adduced at trial by defendants showed that plaintiff is currently part owner and employee of a business, C & L Contracting. According to the testimony of defendant Wilson, "[W]e are in direct competition on all work in the [P]iedmont, North Carolina, that is bridge work" and that to allow plaintiff access to the books and records of accounts of defendant corporation "would put us at a disadvantage."

This evidence is insufficient to override the presumption that plaintiff is acting in good faith. [T]he mere possibility that a shareholder may abuse his right to gain access to corporate information will not be held to justify a denial of a legal right, if such right exists in the shareholder. The trial court properly exercised its discretion in issuing a writ of mandamus. This Assignment of Error is overruled.

Next, defendants contend that the court erred in assessing total penalties of $1,000.00, that is $500.00 from each defendant. Defendants contend that the penalty is improper in the following regards: (1) the maximum total penalty allowed under G.S. 55-38(d) is $500.00; (2) the court erroneously failed to find mitigating circumstances which would allow for a decrease in the amount of the penalty; and (3) the penalty was based on a value of "at least $20,000.00" for plaintiff's shares in defendant corporation at the time of trial, a value that was insufficiently supported by the evidence. We disagree with each of these contentions . . . .

G.S. 55-38(d) provides, in pertinent part:

(d) Any officer or agent or corporation refusing to mail a statement as required by G.S. 55-37 or refusing to allow a qualified shareholder to examine and make extracts from the aforesaid books and records of account, minutes and record of shareholders, for any proper purpose, shall be liable to such shareholder in a penalty of ten percent (10%) of the value of the shares owned by such shareholder, but not to exceed five hundred dollars ($500.00), in addition to any other damages or remedy afforded him by law, but the court may decrease the amount of such penalty on a finding of mitigating circumstances.

The plain meaning of the disjunctive "or" indicates that the ceiling penalty of $500.00 may be assessed against each of "[a]ny officer or agent or corpora-tion." G.S. 55-38(d). . . .

We are unpersuaded by defendants' argument that the corporation's good faith interest in "wanting to protect its current business practices from being divulged to a direct competitor" requires finding a mitigating circumstance sufficient to compel a decrease in the penalty. . . .

[Judgment affirmed]

QUESTIONS

1. Is the applicable state statute similar to the RMBCA provision authorizing inspection of corporate records?
2. Did the court agree with the Wilson corporation that its refusal was justified because Carter, now a direct competitor for bridge work in the state, would gain an unfair competitive advantage?
3. Were the penalties reduced because of mitigating circumstances?

A shareholder is entitled to inspect the books to obtain information needed for a lawsuit against the corporation or its directors or officers, to organize the other shareholders into an "opposition" party to remove the board of directors at the next election, or to buy the shares of other shareholders.

Inspection has frequently been refused when it was sought merely from idle curiosity or for "speculative purposes." Inspection has sometimes been denied on the ground that it was merely sought to obtain a mailing list of persons who would be solicited to buy products of another enterprise. Inspection has also been refused when the object of the shareholder was to advance political or social beliefs without regard to the welfare of the corporation.

Many cases deny the right of inspection when it would be harmful to the corporation or is sought only for the purpose of annoying, harassing, or causing vexation, or for the purpose of aiding competitors of the corporation. In contrast, the right of inspection is so broadly recognized in some states that the fact that the shareholder may possibly make an improper use of the information obtained does not bar inspection.

(a) FORM OF BOOKS. There are generally no legal requirements as to the form of corporate books and records. The RMBCA recognizes that corporate books and records may be stored in modern data storage systems. "A corporation shall maintain its records in written form or in any other form capable of conversion into written form within a reasonable time."[36]

(b) FINANCIAL STATEMENTS. In recognition of the widespread practice of corporations' preparing formal financial statements, the RMBCA requires a corporation to furnish annual financial statements. These statements include a balance sheet as of the end of the fiscal year, an income statement for that year, and a statement of changes in shareholders' equity for that year.[37] A number of state statutes contain similar provisions.

§ 51:19   DIVIDENDS

A shareholder has the right to receive a proportion of dividends as they are declared, subject to the relative rights of other shareholders to preferences, accumulation of dividends, and participation. There is no

---

[36]   RMBCA § 16.01(d).
[37]   RMBCA § 16.20.

absolute right that dividends be declared but only that dividends, when declared, must be paid in the manner indicated.

(a) FUNDS AVAILABLE FOR DECLARATION OF DIVIDENDS. Statutes commonly provide that no dividends may be declared unless there is a "surplus" for their payment. This surplus is generally calculated as the amount of the corporate assets in excess of the outstanding liabilities and paid-in capital of the corporation.

As an exception to these rules, a wasting assets corporation may pay dividends out of current net profits without regard to the preservation of the corporate assets. **Wasting assets corporations** are those designed to exhaust or use up the assets of the corporation (as by extracting oil, coal, iron, and other ores), as compared with manufacturing plants wherein the object is to preserve the plant as well as to continue to manufacture. A wasting assets corporation may also be formed for the purpose of buying and liquidating a stock of merchandise from a company that has received a discharge in bankruptcy court.

In some states, statutes provide that dividends may be declared from current net profits, without regard to the existence of a deficit from former years, or from surplus.

(b) DISCRETION OF DIRECTORS. Assuming that a fund is available for the declaration of dividends, it is then a matter primarily within the discretion of the board of directors whether a dividend shall be declared. The fact that there is a surplus that could be used for dividends does not determine that they must be declared. This rule is not affected by the nature of the shares. Thus, the fact that the shareholders hold cumulative preferred shares does not give them any right to demand a declaration of dividends or to interfere with an honest exercise of discretion by the directors.

In general, a court will refuse to substitute its judgment for the judgment of the directors of the corporation and will interfere with their decision as to dividend declaration only when it is shown that their conduct is harmful to the welfare of the corporation or its shareholders.[38] The courts, however, will compel the declaration of a dividend when it is apparent that the directors have amassed a surplus beyond any practical business need.

(c) FORM OF DIVIDENDS. Customarily, a dividend is paid in money. However, it may be paid in property, such as a product manufactured by the corporation, in shares of other corporations held by the corporation, or in shares of the corporation itself.

(d) EFFECT OF TRANSFER OF SHARES. In determining who is entitled to dividends, it is immaterial when the surplus from which the distribution is made was earned. As between the transferor and the transferee, if the dividend is in cash or property other than the shares of the corporation declaring the dividend, the person who was the owner on the date the dividend was declared, the **record date**, is entitled to the dividend. Thus, if a cash dividend is declared before a transfer is made, the transferor is entitled to it. In applying this rule, it is immaterial when distribution of the dividend is made.

The rule that the date of declaration determines the right to cash dividend is subject to modification by the corporation. The board of directors in declaring the dividend may state that it will be payable to those who will be the holders of record on a later specified date, which then becomes the record date.

If the dividend consists of shares in the corporation declaring the dividend, ownership is determined by the date of distribution. Whichever party is the owner of the shares when the stock dividend is distributed is entitled to the stock dividend. The reason for this variation from the cash dividend rule lies in the fact that the declaration of a stock dividend has the effect of diluting the existing corporate assets among a large number of shares. The value of the holding represented by each share is

[38] Gabelli & Co. v Liggett Group, Inc. (Del Sup) 479 A2d 276 (1984).

accordingly diminished. Unless the person who owns the stock on the distribution date receives a proportionate share of the stock dividend, the net effect will be to lessen that person's holding.

The transferor and transferee may enter into any agreement they choose with respect to dividends.

These rules determine the right to dividends as between transferor and transferee. Regardless of what those rights may be, the corporation is generally entitled to continue to recognize the transferor as a shareholder until it has been notified that a transfer has been made and the corporate records are accordingly changed. If the corporation, believing that the transferor is still the owner of the shares, sends the transferor a dividend to which the transferee is entitled, the transferee cannot sue the corporation. In that case, the remedy of the transferee is to sue the transferor for the dividend that the latter has received.

§ 51:20 CAPITAL DISTRIBUTION

Upon the dissolution of the corporation, the shareholders are entitled to receive any balance of the corporate assets that remains after the payment of all creditors. Certain classes of stock may have a preference or priority in this distribution.

§ 51:21 SHAREHOLDERS' ACTIONS

When the corporation has the right to sue its directors or officers or third persons for damages caused by them to the corporation or for breach of contract, one or more shareholders may bring such action if the corporation refuses to do so. This is a **derivative** (secondary) **action** in that the shareholder enforces only the cause of action of the corporation, and any money recovery is paid into the corporate treasury.[39]

In a derivative action, when a corporation has failed to enforce a right, a shareholder bringing such a suit must show that a demand was made upon the directors to enforce the right in question and that the directors refused to do so. The Investment Company Act of 1940 (ICA) authorizes shareholders to sue investment advisors to recover excessive fees paid advisors by the corporation. The shareholders may bring such action without any prior demand upon the directors of the corporation.[40]

An action cannot be brought by minority shareholders, however, if the action of the corporate directors or officers has been ratified by a majority of the shareholders acting in good faith and if the matter is of such a nature that had such majority originally authorized the acts of the directors or officers there would not have been any wrong.

Shareholders may also intervene or join in an action brought against the corporation when the corporation refuses to defend the action against it or is not doing so in good faith. Otherwise, the shareholders may take no part in an action by or against the corporation.

Shareholders in a deadlocked corporation may bring an action to obtain a dissolution of the corporation.

D.   LIABILITY OF SHAREHOLDERS

The shareholder is ordinarily protected from liability for the acts of the corporation. Some exceptions are made by statute.

§ 51:22 LIMITED LIABILITY

The liability of a shareholder is generally limited. This means that the shareholder is not personally responsible for the debts and the liabilities of the corporation. The capital contributed by the shareholders may be exhausted by the claims of credi-

---

[39] Zapata Corporation v Maldonado (Del) 430 A2d 779 (1981).

[40] Daily Income Fund, Inc. v Fox, 464 US 523 (1984).

tors, but there is no personal liability for any unpaid balance.[41]

§ 51:23 EXCEPTIONS TO LIMITED LIABILITY

Liability may be imposed upon a shareholder as though there were no corporation when the court ignores the corporate entity either because of the particular circumstances of the case or because the corporation is so defectively organized that it is deemed not to exist.

(a) WAGE CLAIMS. Statutes sometimes provide that the shareholders shall be unlimitedly liable for the wage claims of corporate employees. This principle has been abandoned in some states in recent years or has been confined to the major shareholders of corporations of which the stock is not sold publicly.

(b) UNPAID SUBSCRIPTIONS. Most states prohibit the issuance of par value shares for less than par or except for "money, labor done, or property actually received." Whenever shares issued by a corporation are not fully paid for, the original subscriber receiving the shares or any transferee who does not give value, or who knows that the shares were not fully paid, may be liable for the unpaid balance if the corporation is insolvent and the money is required to pay the creditors.[42]

If the corporation has issued the shares as fully paid, or has given them as a bonus, or has agreed to release the subscriber for the unpaid balance, the corporation cannot recover that balance. The fact that the corporation is thus barred does not prevent the creditors of the corporation from bringing an action to compel payment of the balance. The same rules are applied when stock is issued as fully paid in return for property or services that were overvalued so that the stock is not actually paid for in full. There is a conflict of authority, however, as to whether the shareholder is liable from the mere fact that the property or service given for the shares was in fact overvalued by the directors or whether in addition it must be shown that the directors had acted in bad faith in making the erroneous valuation. The trend of modern statutes is, in the absence of proof of fraud to prohibit disputing the valuation placed by the corporation upon services or property.

If a statute makes void the shares issued for less than par, they may be canceled upon suit of the corporation.

(c) UNAUTHORIZED DIVIDENDS. If dividends are improperly paid out of capital, the shareholders generally are liable to creditors to the extent of such depletion of capital. In some states the liability of the shareholder depends upon whether the corporation was insolvent at the time, and whether debts were existing at the time.

§ 51:24 THE PROFESSIONAL CORPORATION

The liability of a shareholder in a professional corporation is limited to the same degree as that of a shareholder in an ordinary business corporation.[43] Several fact situations may arise.

(a) ACT OF SHAREHOLDER IN CREATING LIABILITY. The statutes that authorize the formation of professional corporations usually require that share ownership be limited to duly licensed professionals. If a shareholder in a professional corporation, such as a corporation of physicians, negligently drives the professional corporation's automobile in going to attend a patient, or is personally obligated on a contract made for the corporation, or is guilty of malpractice, the physician-shareholder is liable without limit for the liability that has been created. This is the same rule of law that applies in the case of the ordinary business corporation. Professional corporation statutes generally repeat

---

[41] Salem Tent & Awning Co. v Schmidt, 79 Or App 475, 719 P2d 899 (1986).
[42] Frasier v Trans-western Land Corp. 210 Neb 681, 316 NW2d 612 (1982).

[43] Jones v Teilberg (App) 151 Ariz 240, 727 P2d 18 (1986).

the rule with respect to malpractice liability by stating that the liability of shareholder for malpractice is not affected by the fact of incorporation.

(b) MALPRACTICE LIABILITY OF AN ASSOCIATE. The liability of a shareholder in a professional corporation for the malpractice of an associate varies from state to state depending upon the language of the professional corporation statute in effect and upon the court decisions under the statute.[44]

[44]   ABA Model Professional Corporation Supplement (1984) § 34 offers three alternative positions as to liability of shareholders: (1) limited liability as in a business corporation, (2) vicarious personal liability as in a partnership, and (3) personal liability limited in amount conditioned upon financial responsibility in the form of insurance or a surety bond.

If the statute provides for limited liability as in a business corporation, then where doctors *A*, *B*, and *C* are a professional corporation, *B* will not be liable for the malpractice of *C*. If the statute provides for vicarious personal liability as in a partnership, and doctors *A*, *B*, and *C* are a professional corporation, each will be unlimitedly liable for any malpractice liability incurred by the other. Often the statutory reference to malpractice liability is not very clear, and the courts are called upon to resolve the question of the liability of a shareholder-professional for the malpractice of an associate.

In the *Birt* case, the question was raised as to the extent of malpractice liability in the case of a professional corporation.

BIRT V ST. MARY MERCY HOSPITAL

175 Ind App 32, 370 NE2d (1977)

Eugene Birt was a patient in the hospital. The doctor who treated him was a shareholder of a professional corporation organized under the Indiana Medical Professional Corporation Act (IMPCA). Birt claimed that the doctor who treated him was guilty of malpractice. Birt then sued the doctor, the professional corporation, and all the officers, directors, and shareholders of the professional corporation. The lower court entered judgment in favor of Birt against the doctor who treated him and the professional corporation but entered judgment in favor of the shareholders, officers, and directors of the professional corporation. Birt appealed.

GARRARD, J. . . .   IMPCA . . . provides . . .

The Indiana General Corporation Act . . . Shall be applicable to professional corporations, *including their organization* and they shall enjoy the powers and privileges and be subject to the duties, restrictions and liabilities of other corporations, except where inconsistent with the provisions and purpose of this act. This act shall take precedence in the event of any conflict with provisions of the Indiana General Corporation Act. (emphasis added)

. . .

. . .[T]he General Corporation Act controls medical professional corporations absent a conflict with the purposes or provisions of the IMPCA . . . Thus, the act discloses legislative intent that the common law which supplements statutory corporations law shall also apply to medical professional corporations.

By statute, stockholder liability for corporate debts is limited to the extent of unpaid subscriptions or promised consideration for issued shares. . . . Under common law, a corporate stockholder, director, agent, or employee is not personally liable for the torts of the corporation, or of another agent, *merely* because of his office or holdings; some additional connection with the tort is required.

Is this general rule contrary to the provisions or purposes of IMPCA?. . .

We turn . . . to the express language of our statute. IC 1971, 23-1-14-14 provides:

> This act does not modify any law applicable to the *relationship between a person furnishing* professional medical service *and a person receiving* such a service, *including liability arising out of such* professional service. (emphasis added)

It is, thus, apparent that our legislature intended that the IMPCA should not destroy the traditional relationship between a professional and his patient through the creation of a corporate shield. . . . It has been argued that such provisions must be construed to preserve more than the personal liability of a corporate employee for his own negligent tort existing under general corporations law. We agree. However, it does not necessarily follow that the statute imports the vicarious liability of the Uniform Partnership Act to apply to associating physicians. Without deciding, we note that the statute may impose personal liability on contracts to cure and liability for the negligence of assistants acting under the physician's direction. . . .

In view of the provision that general corporation law applies except where contrary to the provisions or purpose of the IMPCA, vicarious liability due *solely* to association would appear to be beyond the purview of the explicit terms of 1C 1971, 23-1-14-14, which retains relationship and liability between "a person furnishing" and "a person receiving" professional medical service. . . .

At least one commentator has suggested that vicarious liability is necessary to protect patient expectations that an entire firm will be engaged in his behalf rather than merely the associate with whom he deals. It appear to us that this overstates the case. While a patient may well expect to have the organization's entire expertise *available* to him, experience dictates that the physician-patient relationship is generally intensely personal, rather than collective.

Apprehension has also been expressed concerning the ability of an injured patient to collect a damage award without the existence of vicarious liability. Again, however, we believe the fear is overstated. Of course, the malpracticing physician is liable to the extent of his personal assets and such malpractice insurance as he, or the corporation may possess. In addition, it is beyond question that the corporate entity is liable for malpractice committed by one of its members. . . .

Finally, it has been said that vicarious liability among associating professionals is necessary to insure the proper quality of services provided by professional corporations. However, the continuing supervision of professional status under the act [IC 1971, 23-1-14-8,15, and 16] and the penalties available for violations of professional ethics take most of the force from this argument. . . .

In addition we note that the rule of vicarious liability does not appear to have been imposed, historically, as a matter of public policy to guard against the effects of malpractice. The ancient prohibition against the practice of learned professions by corporations was primarily to prevent a lay intermediary from interfering with or controlling professional relationships, judgments and ethics. . . . Under this doctrine physicians and other professionals desiring to associate in practice were essentially limited to the device of partnership and its attendant rule of vicarious liability. Vicarious liability, however, was not limited to professionals. It is an effect of the rule, applicable to all general partnerships, that each partner is the agent of the others. . . . The rule of mutual agency, in turn, was an outgrowth of the "aggregate theory" of partnership under common law which refused recognition of the partnership as an entity distinct from its members. . . . This is reflected in the early case of *Hess v Lowery* (1889), 122 Ind 225, 23 NE 156, where our Supreme Court stated:

> That each partner is the agent of the firm while engaged in the prosecution of the partnership business, and that the firm is liable for the torts of each, if committed within the scope of his agency, appears to be well settled. It follows from the principles of agency, coupled with the doctrine that each partner is the agent of the firm, for the purpose of carrying on its business in the usual way, that an ordinary partnership is liable in damages for the negligence of any one of its members in conducting the business of the partnership. Thus in *Hyrne v Erwin*, 23 SC 226, 55 AmRep 15, which was an action against two physicians for an injury resulting from the negligent and unskillful setting of a broken arm, it was held that the act of one, within the scope of the partnership business, was the act of each and all, as fully as if each was present participating in all that was done, and that each partner guarantees that the one in charge shall display reasonable care, diligence and skill, and that the failure of one is the failure of all. . . .

The IMPCA manifests legislative intent that medical professional corporations be imbued with as many of the attributes of general corporations as may be, without destroying the traditional professional relationship between physician and patient. We conclude that neither the express language of the statute nor the qualification purpose of maintaining strong professional relationships require importation of the partnerships doctrine of vicarious liability into the professional corporate arena. Plainly general corporate concepts preclude it. Accordingly we hold that no vicarious liability arises solely from association under the IMPCA. . . .

[Judgment affirmed]

QUESTIONS

1. What was the holding of the case?
2. How does the decision of the court affect the prior law?
3. Does the court believe that vicarious liability of shareholders of a professional corporation is necessary to protect the public by encouraging adherence to proper medical standards?

SUMMARY

The ownership of a corporation is evidenced by a holder's shares of stock that have been issued by the corporation. Common stock is ordinary stock which has no preferences, but entitles the holder to (1) participate in the control of the corporation by having the right to exercise one vote per share of record, (2) share in the profits in the form of dividends, and (3) participate, upon dissolution, in the distribution of net assets, after the satisfaction of all creditors including bond holders. Other classes of stock exist, such as preferred stock, which has priority over common stock as to dividends and/or distributions of net assets upon dissolution. Shares may be acquired by subscription of an original issue or by transfer of existing shares.

State blue sky laws, which apply only to intrastate transactions, protect the public from the sale of fraudulent securities. The two principal laws providing the basic framework for federal regulation of the sale of securities in interstate commerce are the Securities Act of 1933, which deals with the original distribution of securities by the issuing corporations, and the Securities Exchange Act of 1934, which is concerned with the secondary distribution of securities on the exchanges. These acts are administered by the Securities and Exchange Commission. Except for certain private and limited offerings, the 1933 act requires that a registration statement be filed with the SEC and that a prospectus be provided to each potential purchaser. Criminal and civil penalties exist for fraudulent statements made in this process. The 1934 act provides reporting requirements for companies whose securities are listed on a national exchange, or unlisted companies that have assets in excess of $3 million and 500 or more shareholders. Rule 10b-5 is the principal antifraud rule under the 1934 act. Trading on "inside information" is unlawful and may subject those so involved to a civil penalty of three times the profit made on the improperly disclosed information. Cash tender offers are regulated by the SEC under authority of the Williams Act, which amended the 1934 act.

Shareholders control the corporation, but this control is indirect. Through their voting rights they elect directors, and by this means can control the corporation. Preemptive rights allow shareholders to maintain their voting percentage and control when the corporation issues additional shares of stock. Shareholders have the right to inspect the books of the corporation, unless it would be harmful to the corporation. Shareholders also have the right to receive dividends at the discretion of the directors. Shareholders may bring a derivative action on behalf of the corporation for damages to the corporation if, upon demand, the corporation refuses to do so. Shareholders are ordinarily protected from liability for the acts of the corporation.

QUESTIONS AND CASE PROBLEMS

1. What social forces are affected by the rule requiring that a transfer restriction be known to the transferee or conspicuously noted on the share certificate?
2. What is the distinction between capital and capital stock?
3. Barbara, Joel, and Edna each own less than 5 percent of the stock of the Enrico Storm Door Corporation. Individually their holdings are too small to be significant in any stockholders' election. Barbara suggests that they and other small shareholders combine their votes and that they do this by transferring their shares to trustees who will vote the aggregate of their shares as a block. Joel agrees with the idea but says he is afraid that this is an illegal conspiracy. Is he correct?
4. Compare the effect of an oral contract (a) by A to sell 100 shares of X corporation stock to B, and (b) by stockbroker C to sell A's stock in the X corporation when the market price reaches $10.00 a share.
5. The following transactions in Heritage Cosmetics Co., Inc. stock took place: On 1/21/90 John Jones the corporation's vice president of marketing purchased 1,000 shares of stock at $25 per share. On 1/24/90 J. Sylvan, a local banker and director of Heritage purchased 500 shares of stock at $26 per share. On 1/30/90 Mary McCarthy, a secretary at Heritage and the wife of a local dentist, purchased 300

shares of stock at $26 1/2. On 2/12/90 Endicott Winfried, a rich investor from New England purchased 25,000 shares at an average price of $26 per share. At that time, Heritage had a total of 200,000 shares of stock outstanding. On 6/14/90 Winfried sold his entire position in Heritage at an average price of $35 per share. In a local newspaper interview, Winfried was quoted regarding his reasons for selling the stock, "I have not had the pleasure of meeting any person from Heritage, but I have the highest regard for the Heritage Company. . . . I sold my stock simply because the market has gone too high and in my view is due for a correction." After independently reading Winfried's prediction on the stock market, Jones, Sylvan, and McCarthy sold their shares on June 15 for $33 per share. On June 20 Heritage Corp. demands that Jones, Sylvan, McCarthy, and Winfried remit to corporation the profits made on the sale of the stock. Is the corporation correct in making such a demand on each of these individuals?

6. Siebrecht organized a corporation called the Siebrecht Realty Co. and then transferred his building to the corporation in exchange for its stock. The corporation rented different parts of the building to different tenants. Elenkrieg, an employee of one of the tenants, fell and was injured because of the defective condition of a stairway. She sued Siebrecht individually on the ground that the corporation had been formed by him for the purpose of securing limited liability. Decide. [Elenkrieg v Siebrecht, 238 NY 254, 144 NE 519]

7. Dixon requested an inspection of the books of G. S. & M. Company. The objection was raised that he did not own 5 percent or more of the corporate stock. If this is true, is Dixon barred from inspecting the books?

8. Monroe owned 100 shares of stock in the Apex Corporation. On the certificates for the stock the following notation was conspicuously printed: "No shareholder shall transfer any shares of this corporation without first offering such shares for purchase by the other shareholders." Monroe died without a will and his entire estate was inherited by his wife Valenta. Some of the shareholders of Apex claimed that Valenta was not the owner of Monroe's shares because those shares had never been offered to them for purchase. Were they correct?

9. A owned corporate stock. He told B that he was going to give the stock to B and handed the stock certificate to B. B requested that A indorse the certificate. A refused to do so. Who was the owner of the stock? [Smith v Augustine, 82 Misc 2d 326, 368 NYS2d 675]

10. Shares of stock represent debts owed by the corporation to the shareholders. Is this statement correct?

11. K owned shares of stock in the J corporation. He left the shares of stock lying on top of his desk in his office. Many persons continually passed through the office, and one day K realized that someone had taken the shares of stock from the top of his desk. K applied to the J corporation for the issuance of a duplicate stock certificate. The corporation refused to issue a duplicate on the ground that it was K's own fault that the original certificate had been stolen. K claimed that he was entitled to a new certificate even though he had been at fault. Was he correct? [Ibanez v Farmers Underwriters Ass'n. 14 Cal 3d 390, 121 Cal Rptr 256, 534 P2d 1336]

12. Corporation A wished to employ B. Negotiations were conducted by telephone. In order to induce B to accept employment, the proper representative of Corporation A promised B that, in addition to a money salary, B would receive a specified number of shares of stock of Corporation A for each year of employment. B went to work for Corporation A and received his money salary but three years went by with no stock being delivered to him. B then sued Corporation A to compel it to issue the stock. It raised the defense that the agreement to give B stock could not be enforced because it was not evidenced by writing as required by UCC §-319. Was this a valid defense? [Bingham v Wells, Rich, Greene, Inc. 34 App Div 2d 924, 311 NYS2d 508; Butcher v United States Invest. Corp. 236 Pa Super 8, 344 A2d 583]

13. Linhart owned shares of stock in the First National Bank. She borrowed money from the bank and pledged the stock as security. She thereafter decided to transfer 70 head of cattle and the shares of stock to her son. She could not deliver the share certificate to him because it was held by the bank. She therefore executed a bill of sale reciting the trans-

fer of the cattle and the stock to the son. She gave him the bill of sale, and he had the bill recorded. After her death, the son brought an action to determine the ownership of the stock. Was the son the owner of the shares?

14. Texas International Speedway, Inc. (TIS), filed a registration statement and prospectus with the Securities and Exchange Commission offering a total of $4,398,900 in securities to the public. The proceeds of the sale were to be used to finance the construction of an automobile speedway. The entire issue was sold on the offering date. TIS did not meet with success, however, and the corporation filed a petition for bankruptcy. Huddleston and Bradley instituted a class action in the United States district court on behalf of themselves and other purchasers of TIS securities. The complaint alleged violations of Section 10(b) of the 1934 act. They sued most of the participants in the offering, including the accounting firm, Herman & MacLean, which had issued an opinion concerning certain financial statements and a pro forma balance sheet that were contained in the registration statement and prospectus. They claimed that the defendants had engaged in a fraudulent scheme to misrepresent or conceal material facts regarding the financial condition of TIS, including the costs incurred in building the speedway. Herman & MacLean defended that the case should be dismissed because Section 11 of the 1933 act provides an express remedy for a misrepresentation in a registration statement, and therefore an action under Section 10 (b) of the 1934 act is precluded. Decide. [Herman & MacLean v Huddleston, 459 US 375]

15. Ronald Naquin, an employee of Air Engineered Systems & Services, Inc., (Air Engineered), owned one third of its outstanding shares. After six years he was fired, and an offer was made to buy out his interest in Air Engineered at a price that Naquin thought inadequate. He then formed a competing business and made a written request to examine the corporate records of Air Engineered. This request was denied. Naquin filed suit to require Air Engineered to allow him to examine the books. Air Engineered raised the defense that he was a competitor seeking to gain unfair competitive advantage. Decide. [Naquin v Air Engineered Systems & Services, Inc. (La App) 463 So 2d 992]

52

⬥

MANAGEMENT OF CORPORATIONS

A corporation is managed, directly or indirectly, by its shareholders, board of directors, and officers.

In the large corporation it is common to find that the owners (the shareholders) are not to any appreciable extent the managers (directors and officers). In a closely held corporation, however, the owners commonly serve on the board of directors and hold corporate offices.

A. SHAREHOLDERS

Shareholders' management functions are usually very limited and take the form of voting at shareholders' meetings to elect directors whose management philosophies and interests best coincide with their own. In this sense shareholders indirectly determine the management policies of the business. Also, they may vote at shareholders' meetings to amend bylaws, approve shareholder resolutions, or vote on so-called extraordinary corporate matters. Extraordinary matters include the sale of corporate assets outside the regular course of the corporation's business or the merger or dissolution of the corporation.

§ 52:1   MEETINGS OF SHAREHOLDERS

To have legal effect, action by the shareholders must be taken at a regular or special meeting.

(a) REGULAR MEETINGS. The time and place of regular or stated meetings are usually prescribed by the articles of incorporation or bylaws. Notice to shareholders of such meetings is ordinarily not required, but it is usually given as a matter of good business practice. Some statutes require that notice be given of all meetings.

(b) SPECIAL MEETINGS. Generally, notice must be given specifying the subject matter when the meeting is of an unusual character. Unless otherwise prescribed, special meetings are called by the directors. It is sometimes provided that a special meeting may be called by a certain percentage of shareholders.[1] Notice of the day, hour, and the place of a special meeting must be given to all shareholders. The notice must also include a statement of the nature of the business to be transacted. No other business may be transacted at such a meeting.

(c) QUORUM. A valid meeting requires the presence of a quorum of the voting shareholders. In order to constitute a quorum, usually a specified number of shareholders or a number authorized to vote a stated proportion of the voting stock must attend. If a quorum is present, a majority of those present may act with respect to any matter, unless there is an express requirement of a greater affirmative vote.

When a meeting opens with a quorum, the quorum generally is not thereafter broken if shareholders leave the meeting and those remaining are not sufficient to constitute a quorum.

§ 52:2   ACTION WITHOUT MEETING

A number of statutes provide for corporate action by shareholders without holding a meeting. The RMBCA provides that "action required or permitted by this Act to be taken at a shareholder's meeting may be taken without a meeting if the action is taken by all shareholders entitled to vote on the action."[2] The action must be evidenced by a written consent describing the action taken, signed by all the shareholders entitled to vote on the action, and delivered to the corporation for inclusion in the minutes. Such provisions give flexibility of operation, which is needed by the small or close corporation.

B.   DIRECTORS

The management of a corporation is usually under the control of a board of directors elected by the shareholders. Most states now permit the number of directors to be fixed by the bylaws. Many specify that the board of directors shall consist of not less than three directors. A few authorize one or more directors.[3] Professional corporation legislation often authorizes or is interpreted as authorizing a one- or two-person board of directors.

§ 52:3   QUALIFICATIONS

Eligibility for membership on a board of directors is determined by statute, articles of incorporation, or bylaws. In the absence of a contrary provision, any person (including a nonresident, a minor, or even a per-

---

[1]   New York Business Corporation Law § 603.

[2]   RMBCA § 7.04 (a).
[3]   Delaware Ann § 141(b). See also ABA MBCA § 36.

son who is not a shareholder) is eligible for membership.

Bylaws may require that a director own stock in the corporation, although ordinarily this requirement is not imposed.

§ 52:4   POWERS OF DIRECTORS

The board of directors has authority to manage the corporation. The court will not interfere with the board's discretion in the absence of (a) illegal conduct or (b) fraud harming the rights of creditors, shareholders, or the corporation.[4]

[4] Iwasaki v Iwasaki Bros., Inc. 58 Or App 543, 649 P2d 598 (1982).

The board of directors may enter into any contract or transaction necessary to carry out the business for which the corporation was formed. The board may appoint officers and other agents to act for the company, or it may appoint several of its own members as an executive committee to act for the board between board meetings.

Broad delegation of authority to a single officer may, however, run the risk of being treated as an unlawful abdication of the board's management function.

In the *Boston Athletic Association* case the court considered whether the board improperly delegated authority to an individual officer.

BOSTON ATHLETIC ASSOCIATION V INTERNATIONAL MARATHON, INC.

(Mass) 467 NE2d 58 (1984)

On April 27, 1981, the board of the Boston Athletic Association (BAA), a nonprofit corporation whose principal activity is the presentation of an annual road race (the Boston Marathon), approved the following proposal:

That William T. Cloney, as President of the Association, be and hereby is authorized and directed to negotiate and to execute in the name of and in behalf of this Association such agreements as he deems in the best interest of the Association for the perpetuation, sponsorship, or underwriting of the Boston A.A. Marathon.

There was no mention at this meeting of hiring an exclusive promoter. In the past all sponsorship and broadcast coverage contracts were negotiated between Cloney and individual sponsors. On September 23, 1981, Cloney executed an agreement on behalf of the BAA with Marshall Medoff, an attorney and president of IMI (a business corporation headed by Medoff). The agreement designated Medoff as the exclusive promoter of the Marathon with the BAA transferring all right to the use of the Boston Marathon name and logos to IMI. The agreement's financial terms were extremely favorable to IMI. The agreement was automatically renewable year to year, at the option of IMI, with no way for the BAA to end the relationship. A majority of the Board members learned of the existence of the agreement in late February, 1982. By a vote taken on September 9, 1982, the board declared the agreement to be beyond the authorization vested in Cloney on April 27, 1981. The board brought an action to have the agreement set aside. IMI defended that Cloney had been given authority to make the contract with IMI, and therefore, the contract bound the corporation. From a judgment for the BAA, IMI (Medoff) appealed.

LYNCH, J. . . . Whether the board intended by its vote of April 27, 1981, to confer upon Cloney the authority to enter into the sponsorship agreement with IMI, that contract is void. The board of directors of a corporation cannot delegate total control of the corporation to an individual officer. . . . Neither can it delegate authority which is so broad that it enables the officer to bind the corporation to extraordinary commitments or significantly to encumber the principal asset or function of the corporation.

The contract seriously encumbers the manner in which the BAA may conduct the Marathon. The BAA is obliged to produce the race in its traditional form and to pay the entire bill. But it is not entitled to "present" the race. That right, as well as the right to use the name and logo of the BAA, belongs to IMI or its assignee. The BAA may not use its own logo in any way "inconsistent" with IMI's rights pursuant to the contract. The right to enter into sponsorship agreements belongs exclusively to IMI, although the BAA can reasonably withhold its approval. The BAA may not make independent agreements without written permission from IMI. Finally, the contract between IMI and the BAA is automatically renewable at the option of IMI. Under the plain language of the agreement, there is no way for the BAA to end the relationship.

In return for carrying out its obligations under the contract, the BAA is to be paid a $400,000 fee. Any revenues in excess of $400,000 are directly payable to IMI, and there is no limit to the number of sponsors who may be solicited or to the amount of money which may be raised. The annual fee is to be paid prior to the actual running of the race, but if the Marathon should not be run for some reason, the fee is to be returned to IMI.

According to the traditional principles of corporate governance, the board of governors of the BAA does not have the power to delegate to an individual officer authority to enter into a contract which so totally encumbers the most significant purpose of the BAA, the presentation of the Marathon. The by-laws of the BAA indicate that its organization and operation are, in all material respects, the same as those of a Massachusetts business corporation. Principles of corporate governance with respect to the power of the board of governors to delegate authority to individual officers are applicable to profit and nonprofit corporations alike. In fact, the powers of an officer of a charitable corporation to bind the corporation without specific ratification by the board of governors or directors are more strictly construed than would be similar powers of an officer of a business corporation. The validity of the board's purported delegation of authority to Cloney must be analyzed in this context.

Corporate officers are generally empowered, by delegation of authority of the board of directors, with general managerial functions. They are responsible for the day to day operation of the corporation. Courts are usually flexible and accommodating in allowing boards to delegate authority as necessary or expedient. But certain powers cannot be delegated generally. Certain transactions require specific authorization by the board in order to be valid. For example, in *Stoneman v. Fox Film Corp.*, 295 Mass. 419, 4 NE2d 63 (1936), the court found that the president, although authorized to act as a general manager on behalf of a film company, was not authorized to commit the company to the purchase of a theatre, an extraordinary transaction which involved a large financial commitment. The court indicated that delegation of authority to conduct such business was a "course of conduct manifestly . . . unusual and extraordinary in the management of a corporation." It was an abdication of "the entire control" of the corporation and "[t]he functions of directors may not be abdicated." . . .

The power of officers to bind charitable corporations is even more narrowly construed. . . .

In light of these principles, it is clear that if the delegation to Cloney was so broad as to enable him to commit the BAA to an extraordinary contract which encumbered substantially all its assets, the board would have delegated away control of the very essence of the BAA's corporate existence. . . . It is the obligation of the board of governors to oversee the presentation of the Marathon, not to surrender virtually complete control of the event to another organization. The fact that the agreement is automatically renewable and thus potentially perpetual demonstrates the pervasive nature of the limitation on the main purpose of the BAA. Authority to make such a contract was beyond the power of the board to delegate to Cloney.

Furthermore, the contract between IMI and the BAA is especially vulnerable because it is antithetical to the BAA's nature as a nonprofit corporation inasmuch as this agreement turns the solicitation of sponsors from a way to support the Marathon to a way for IMI to make a profit. It is entirely inconsistent with the nonprofit nature of the organization to permit such a substantial segment of the revenue earning capacity of the Marathon to be used as a vehicle for personal gain. . . .

For the foregoing reasons, the board of governors of the BAA was not empowered to delegate to Cloney the right to make this contract with IMI. . . .

Although the promotion contract between IMI and the BAA is unenforceable, nevertheless as the BAA concedes IMI is entitled to recover the fair value of its services. . . .

[Judgment affirmed]

QUESTIONS

1. Is there any difference between a business corporation and a nonprofit corporation with respect to the power of the board of directors to delegate authority to a corporate officer?
2. May a board of directors delegate control of a corporation to an individual officer?
3. Assess the September 23, 1981, contract negotiated by Cloney and Medoff as to its basic fairness.

---

§ 52:5 CONFLICT OF INTERESTS

A director is disqualified from taking part in corporate action with respect to a matter in which the director has a conflicting interest. Since it cannot be known how the other directors would have acted if they had known of the conflict of interest, the corporation generally may avoid any transaction because of the director's disqualification.

A number of states provide by statute that the conflict of interest of a director does not impair the transaction or contract entered into or authorized by the board of directors if the disqualified director disclosed the interest and if the contract or transaction is fair and reasonable with respect to the corporation.

§ 52:6 MEETINGS OF DIRECTORS

Theoretically, action by directors can only be taken at a proper meeting of the board. Bylaws sometimes require the meeting to be held at a particular place. Most states expressly provide that the directors may meet either in or out of the state of incorporation. Directors who participate without objection in a meeting irregularly held as to place or time other than as specified in the bylaws cannot object later. Generally, a director is not allowed to vote by proxy.

Most states permit action to be taken by the board of directors without the holding of an actual meeting. It is commonly provided when such action is taken that it be set forth in writing and signed by all the directors.

§ 52:7 LIABILITY OF DIRECTORS

In dealing with the corporation, the directors act in a fiduciary capacity, as it is to their care that the stockholders have entrusted the control of the corporate property and the management of the business.[5]

(a) THE BUSINESS JUDGMENT RULE. Courts recognize that the decisions of corporate directors often involve the weighing and balancing of legal, ethical, commercial, promotional, public relations, and other factors. Courts generally are reluctant to become involved in judicial second-guessing or enmeshed in complex corporate decision making, a task that they state they are ill-equipped to handle.[6] Some decisions of corporate directors, although made in good faith and in the best interest of the corporation when made, may eventually prove to be erroneous. The business judgment rule shields corporate directors from liability for informed business decisions made in good faith and in the best interest of the corporation.

(1) The Traditional Rule. Courts have applied the business judgment rule as a presumption that in making a business decision the directors acted (a) on an informed basis, (b) in good faith, and (c) in the honest belief that the action taken was in the best interest of the corporation.[7] Thus, the party challenging the directors' actions has the difficult initial burden of proving that the directors did not act on an informed basis or in good faith or that the directors acted in self-interest rather than in the interest of the corporation.[8]

(2) Application in Corporate Control Transactions. When a corporation receives a hostile or nonhostile takeover bid, the target board of directors may tend to take actions that are in their own self-interests and not in the interests of the shareholders (owners). Courts have recognized the potential for director self-interest in these situations and, in order to protect the interests of shareholders, have taken a more active role under the business judgment rule in reviewing control-related board decisions.

In the *Smith v. Van Gorkom* decision the directors relied upon the business judgment rule to shield themselves from individual liability in a lawsuit charging that the directors did not act on an "informed basis" in accepting and recommending a merger at a price per share that was less than the "intrinsic value" of the shares.

---

[5] Tillis v United Parts, Inc. (Fla App) 395 So 2d 518 (1981).

[6] Auerback v Bennett, 47 NY2d 619, 419 NYS2d 920 (1979).

[7] Alford v Shaw, 318 NC 289, 349 SE2d 41 (1986).

[8] Aronson v Lewis (Del) 473 A2d 805 (1984).

Smith v Van Gorkom

(Del) 488 A2d 858 (1985)

On September 13, Jerome Van Gorkom as chairman and chief executive officer of Trans Union Inc., a holding company in the railcar leasing business, arranged a meeting with Jay Pritzker, a well-known takeover specialist and a social acquaintance, to determine his interest in acquiring Trans Union. On Thursday, September 18, Pritzker made an offer of $55 per share (a price suggested by Van Gorkom) with a decision to be made by the Board no later than Sunday, September 21. On Friday, Van Gorkom called a special meeting of the board of directors for noon the following day; no agenda was announced. At the directors' meeting Van Gorkom made a 20-minute oral analysis of the merger transaction, showed that the company was having difficulty generating sufficient income to offset its increasingly large investment tax credits, and discussed his meeting with Pritzker and the reasons for the meeting. Copies of the proposed merger agreement were delivered too late to be studied before or during the meeting. No consultants or investment advisers were called upon to support the merger price of $55 per share. The merger was approved at the end of the two-hour meeting. Certain shareholders brought a class action suit against the directors, contending that the board's decision was not the product of informed business judgment. The directors responded that their good faith decision was shielded by the business judgment rule. From a decision for the directors, the shareholders appealed.

Horsey, J. . . . Under Delaware law, the business judgment rule is the offspring of the fundamental principle, codified in 8 *Del. C.* § 141(a), that the business and affairs of a Delaware corporation are managed by or under its board of directors. In carrying out their managerial roles, directors are charged with an unyielding fiduciary duty to the corporation and its shareholders. The business judgment rule exists to protect and promote the full and free exercise of the managerial power granted to Delaware directors. The rule itself "is a presumption that in making a business decision, the directors of a corporation acted on an informed basis, in good faith and in the honest belief that the action taken was in the best interests of the company." *Aronson [v. Lewis*, Del. Supr., 473 A2d 805,] 812. Thus, the party attacking a board decision as uninformed must rebut the presumption that its business judgment was an informed one.

The determination of whether a business judgment is an informed one turns on whether the directors have informed themselves "prior to making a business decision, of all material information reasonably available to them." *Id.* . . .

Thus, a director's duty to exercise an informed business judgment is in the nature of a duty of care, as distinguished from a duty of loyalty. . . .

The standard of care applicable to a director's duty of care has also been recently restated by this Court. In *Aronson, supra*, we stated:

> While the Delaware cases use a variety of terms to describe the applicable standard of care, our analysis satisfies us that under the business judgment rule director liability is predicated upon concepts of gross negligence.

473 A.2d at 812.

We again confirm that view. We think the concept of gross negligence is also the proper standard for determining whether a business judgment reached by a board of directors was an informed one.

In the specific context of a proposed merger of domestic corporations, a director has a duty under 8 *Del. C.* 251(b), along with his fellow directors, to act in an informed and deliberate manner in determining whether to approve an agreement of merger before submitting the proposal to the stockholders. Certainly in the merger context, a director may not abdicate that duty by leaving to the shareholders alone the decision to approve or disapprove the agreement. . . .

It is against those standards that the conduct of the directors of Trans Union must be tested, as a matter of law and as a matter of fact, regarding their exercise of an informed business judgment in voting to approve the Pritzker merger proposal.

. . . The issue of whether the directors reached an informed decision to "sell" the Company on September 20, 1980 must be determined only upon the basis of the information then reasonably available to the directors and relevant to their decision to accept the Pritzker merger proposal. . . .

On the record before us, we must conclude that the Board of Directors did not reach an informed business judgment on September 20, 1980 in voting to "sell" the Company for $55 per share pursuant to the Pritzker cash-out merger proposal. Our reasons, in summary, are as follows:

The directors (1) did not adequately inform themselves as to Van Gorkom's role in forcing the "sale" of the Company and in establishing the per share purchase price; (2) were uninformed as to the intrinsic value of the Company; and (3) given these circumstances, at a minimum, were grossly negligent in approving the "sale" of the Company upon two hours' consideration, without prior notice, and without the exigency of a crisis or emergency.

As has been noted, the Board based its September 20 decision to approve the cash-out merger primarily on Van Gorkom's representations. None of the directors, other than Van Gorkom and Chelberg, had any prior knowledge that the purpose of the meeting was to propose a cash-out merger of Trans Union. No members of Senior Management were present, other than Chelberg, Romans and Peterson; and the latter two had only learned of the proposed sale an hour earlier. Both general counsel Moore and former general counsel Browder attended the meeting, but were equally uninformed as to the purpose of the meeting and the documents to be acted upon.

Without any documents before them concerning the proposed transaction, the members of the Board were required to rely entirely upon Van Gorkom's 20-minute oral presentation of the proposal. No written summary of the terms of the merger was presented; the directors were given no documentation to support the adequacy of $55 price per share for sale of the Company; and the Board had before it nothing more than Van Gorkom's statement of his understanding of the substance of an agreement which he admittedly had never read, nor which any member of the Board had ever seen. . . .

In their brief, the defendants . . . mistake the business judgment rule's application to this case by erroneously invoking presumptions of good faith and "wide discretion":

> This is a case in which plaintiff challenged the exercise of business judgment by an independent Board of Directors. There were no allegations and no proof of fraud, bad faith, or self-dealing by the directors. . . .
>
> The business judgment rule, which was properly applied by the Chancellor, allows directors wide discretion in the matter of valuation and affords room for honest differences of opinion. In order to prevail, plaintiffs had the heavy burden of proving that the merger price was so grossly inadequate as to display itself as a badge of fraud. That is a burden which plaintiffs have not met.

However, plaintiffs have not claimed, nor did the Trial Court decide, that $55 was a grossly inadequate price per share for sale of the Company. That being so, the presumption that a board's judgment as to adequacy of price represents an honest exercise of business judgment (absent proof that the sale price was grossly inadequate) is irrelevant to the threshold question of whether an informed judgment was reached. . . .

We hold, therefore, that the Trial Court committed reversible error in applying the business judgment rule in favor of the director defendants in this case.

On remand, the Court of Chancery shall conduct an evidentiary hearing to determine the fair value of the shares represented by the plaintiffs' class, based on the intrinsic value of Trans Union on September 20, 1980. . . . Thereafter, an award of damages may be entered to the extent that the fair value of Trans Union exceeds $55 per share.

[Reversed and remanded]

QUESTIONS

1. Did the court hold that the business judgment rule shielded the directors from personal liability in this case?
2. Upon what facts did the court rely in reaching its decision in this case?
3. Describe the applicable standard of care for determining whether a board of directors' decision was an informed one?

In a takeover situation wherein an auction for control of the company develops, market forces must be allowed to operate freely to bring the target's shareholders the best price available for their shares.[9] Still, the business judgment rule will apply to shield board of directors' decisions on how to maximize the price of the shares once the auction has begun.

(3) Protection of Directors. In the wake of court decisions holding directors personally liable for damages for gross negligence and in the wake of the resulting general reluctance of individuals to serve as directors, states have passed laws modernizing the laws protecting directors. The aim of the various state laws is essen-

[9] Forbes Holding v Revlon Inc. (Del Ch) 501 A2d 1239 (1985); aff'd (Del) 506 A2d 173 (1986).

tially the same, to alleviate the risk of personal liability for directors who act in good faith, but whose decisions are retrospectively challenged. The laws permit a corporation, by a stockholder-approved amendment to its charter or certificate of incorporation, to protect its directors from monetary liability for duty of care violations (gross negligence) provided they have not acted in bad faith, breached their duty of loyalty, or gained an improper personal benefit.[10] The laws provide for indemnification and advancement of expenses.

(b) ACTION AGAINST DIRECTOR. Actions against directors should be brought by the corporation. If the corporation fails to act, as is the case when the directors alleged to be liable control the corporation, one or more shareholders may bring the action in a representative capacity for the corporation.

(c) REMOVAL OF DIRECTOR. Ordinarily directors are removed by the vote of the shareholders. In some states the board of directors may remove a director and elect a successor on the ground that the director removed (1) did not accept office; (2) failed to satisfy the qualifications for office; (3) was continually absent from the state without a leave of absence granted by the board, generally for a period of six months or more; (4) received a discharge in bankruptcy; (5) was convicted of a felony; (6) was unable to perform the duties of director because of any illness or disability, generally for a period of six months or more; or (7) has been judicially declared of unsound mind.[11]

The RMBCA provides for removal of directors "with or without cause" by a majority vote of the shareholders, unless the articles of incorporation provide that directors may be removed only for cause.[12]

C.   OFFICERS

Corporations will generally have a president, at least one vice-president, a secretary, and a treasurer. The duties of these officers are generally set forth in the corporation's bylaws. Commonly included is the duty of the secretary to keep minutes of the proceedings of shareholders and directors. Corporation codes generally expressly permit the same person to be both secretary and treasurer. In larger corporations there will often be a recording secretary and a corresponding secretary.

Sometimes the officers are elected by the shareholders but usually they are appointed by the board of directors. The RMBCA follows the general pattern of providing for the appointment of officers by the board of directors.[13] Ordinarily, no particular formality need be observed in making such appointments. Unless prohibited, a director may hold an executive office.

§ 52:8   POWERS OF OFFICERS

The officers of a corporation are its agents. Consequently, their powers are controlled by the laws of agency.[14] As in the case of any other agency, the third person has the burden of proving that a particular officer has the authority that such officer purports to have.

The fact that the officer or employee acting on behalf of the corporation is a major shareholder does not give the officer or employee any greater agency powers. Moreover, the person dealing with the officer or employee is charged with knowledge of any limitation upon authority contained in the recorded corporate charter.

When the nature of the transaction is unusual, that unusual nature should alert a third person to the necessity of specific authorization from the corporation.[15]

---

[10]   See Del. Code Anno tit. 8 § 102(b)(7) (1987); NY Bus Corp Law, § 721-723 (1987); Ohio Gen Corp Law § 1701.59 (1986); Ind Bus Corp Law, Ch 35, § 1(e)(1986); and Mo Gen Bus Corp Law 351.355 §,§ 2,7 (1986).
[11]   See California Corporations Code § 807, recognizing grounds (1), (2), (5), and (7).
[12]   RMBCA § 8.08(a).

[13]   RMBCA § 8.40(a).
[14]   Kuehn v Kuehn (Colo App) 642 P2d 524 (1982).
[15]   Kanavos v Hancock Bank & Trust Co. 14 Mass App 326, 439 NE2d 311 (1982).

(a) PRESIDENT. It is sometimes held that in the absence of some limitation upon authority, the president of a corporation has by virtue of that office the authority to act as agent on behalf of the corporation within the scope of the business in which the corporation is empowered to engage. It has also been held, however, that the president has such broad powers only when the president is the general manager of the corporation; and then, such powers stem from the office of general manager and not from that of president. In any event, the president does not have authority by virtue of that office to make a contract that, because of its unusual character, would require action by the board of directors.[16] The president, therefore, cannot make a contract to fix long-term or unusual contracts of employment, to bind the corporation as a guarantor, to release a claim of the corporation, or to promise that the corporation will later repurchase shares when issued to a subscriber.

It is ordinarily held that the president of a business corporation is not authorized to execute commercial paper in the name of the corporation although the president may do so when authorized by the board of directors to borrow money for the corporation.

(b) OTHER OFFICERS AND EMPLOYEES. The authority of corporate employees and other officers, such as secretary or treasurer, is generally limited to the duties of their offices. The authority may, however, be extended by the conduct of the corporation in accordance with the general principles governing apparent authority based upon the conduct of the principal. An unauthorized act may, of course, be ratified. The authority of the general manager of the corporation is determined by principles of ordinary agency law.

§ 52:9　LIABILITY OF OFFICERS

The relationship of the officers to the corporation, as with that of the directors, is a fiduciary one. For this reason, the officers are liable for secret profits made in connection with or at the expense of the business of the corporation.

If an officer diverts a corporate opportunity, the corporation may recover from the officer the profit of which the corporation has been thus deprived.

The *Klinicki* case was an action to recover lost profits caused by the diversion of a corporate business opportunity by an officer and majority shareholder.

---

[16] Molasky Enterprises, Inc. v Carps, Inc. (Mo App) 615 SW2d 83 (1981).

KLINICKI V LUNDGREN
298 Or 662, 695 P2d 906 (1985)

In April of 1977, F. R. Klinicki and Kim Lundgren incorporated Berlinair, Inc., a closely held Oregon corporation. Lundgren was president and was responsible for developing business. Klinicki was vice president and director and was responsible for operations and maintenance. Klinicki owned one-third of the stock, and Lundgren controlled the remaining stock. Both men were former Pan American pilots who had been laid off while stationed in West Germany. In November of 1977, they met with BFR, a consortium of Berlin travel agents that contract charter flights to warmer climates. The contract with BFR was considered a lucrative business opportunity. After the initial meeting all contacts with BFR were made by Lundgren. In early June, 1978, Lundgren learned that there was

a good chance that the BFR contract might be available. He informed a
BFR representative that he would make a proposal on behalf of a new
company. On July 7, 1978, he incorporated Air Berlin Charter Company
(ABC) and was its sole owner. On August 20, 1978, ABC presented BFR
with a contract proposal, and after a series of discussions, it was awarded
the contract on September 1, 1978. Lundgren effectively concealed from
Klinicki his negotiations with BFR and his diversion of the BFR contract
to ABC, even though he used Berlinair working time, staff, money, and
facilities. Klinicki, as a minority stockholder in Berlinair, brought a derivative action against ABC for diverting a corporate opportunity of Berlinair. ABC and Lundgren defend that there was no diversion of a corporate opportunity because Berlinair did not have the financial ability to
undertake the contract. The court ordered the defendants to hold the
profit made from the contract and return it to the plaintiff and also ordered that a computation be made of the amount of such profit. The defendants took this decision to the court of appeals, which affirmed the
trial court. The matter was thereafter appealed to the Supreme Court of
Oregon.

JONES, J. . . . There is no dispute that the corporate opportunity doctrine precludes corporate fiduciaries from diverting to themselves business opportunities in which the corporation has an expectancy, property interest or right, or
which in fairness should otherwise belong to the corporation. The doctrine
follows from a corporate fiduciary's duty of undivided loyalty to the corporation. ABC agrees that, unless Berlinair's financial inability to undertake the
contract makes a difference, the BFR contract was a corporate opportunity of
Berlinair.

We first address the issue, resolved by the Court of Appeals in Berlinair's
favor, of the relevance of a corporation's financial ability to undertake a business opportunity to proving a diversion of corporate opportunity claim. This
is an issue of first impression in Oregon.

The Court of Appeals held that a corporation's financial ability to undertake
a business opportunity is not a factor in determining the existence of a corporate opportunity unless the defendant demonstrates that the corporation is
technically or de facto insolvent. Without defining these terms, the Court of
Appeals specifically placed the burden of proof as to this issue on the fiduciary
by saying: "To avoid liability for usurping a corporate opportunity on the basis
that the corporation was insolvent, the fiduciary must prove insolvency." The
Court of Appeals then concluded "that ABC usurped a corporate opportunity
belonging to Berlinair when, acting through Lundgren, the BFR contract was
diverted" because nothing in Lundgren's testimony or otherwise in the record
suggested that Berlinair was insolvent or was no longer a viable corporate entity. Accordingly, the Court of Appeals held that the constructive trust, injunction, duty to account and other relief granted by the trial court against ABC
were appropriate remedies. . . .

One aspect of corporate fiduciary responsibility that has particularly troubled the courts in their search for a rule of thumb is that relating to so-called
corporate opportunities. *What are the legal rules to be applied in determining when a
corporate official, given an opportunity to make a profitable acquisition (business, lease,*

land, stock, whatever), can take it for himself rather than turning it over to the corporation? . . .

[A rule proposed by the American Law Institute in 1984 in a tentative draft concerning principles of corporate governance] permits a director or principal senior executive to deal with his corporation so long as he deals fairly with full disclosure and bears the burden of proving fairness unless the corporate opportunity was rejected by disinterested directors or shareholders. . . .

Where a director or principal senior executive of a close corporation wishes to take personal advantage of a "corporate opportunity," as defined by the proposed rule, the director or principal senior executive must comply strictly with the following procedure:

(1) the director or principal senior executive must promptly offer the opportunity and disclose all material facts known regarding the opportunity to the disinterested directors or, if there is no disinterested director, to the disinterested shareholders. If the director or principal senior executive learns of other material facts after such disclosure, the director or principal senior executive must disclose these additional facts in a like manner before personally taking the opportunity.

The director or principal senior executive may take advantage of the corporate opportunity only after full disclosure and only if the opportunity is rejected by a majority of the disinterested directors or, if there are no disinterested directors, by a majority of the disinterested shareholders. If, after full disclosure, the disinterested directors or shareholders unreasonably fail to reject the offer, the interested director or principal senior executive may proceed to take the opportunity if he can prove the taking was otherwise "fair" to the corporation. Full disclosure to the appropriate corporate body is, however, an absolute condition precedent to the validity of any forthcoming rejection as well as to the availability to the director or principal senior executive of the defense of fairness. . . .

Applying these rules to the facts in this case, we conclude:

1. Lundgren, as director and principal executive officer of Berlinair, owed a fiduciary duty to Berlinair.
2. The BFR contract was a "corporate opportunity" of Berlinair.
3. Lundgren formed ABC for the purpose of usurping the opportunity presented to Berlinair by the BFR contract.
4. Lundgren did not offer Berlinair the BFR contract.
5. Lundgren did not attempt to obtain the consent of Berlinair to his taking of the BFR corporate opportunity.
6. Lundgren did not fully disclose to Berlinair his intent to appropriate the opportunity for himself and ABC.
7. Berlinair never rejected the opportunity presented by the BFR contract.
8. Berlinair never ratified the appropriation of the BFR contract.
9. Lundgren, acting for ABC, misappropriated the BFR contract.

Because of the above, the defendant may not now contend that Berlinair did not have the financial ability to successfully pursue the BFR contract. As stated in proposed Section 5.12(c) of the Principles of Corporate Governance, *supra*, "If the challenging party satisfies the burden of proving that a corporate opportunity was taken without being offered to the corporation, the challenging party will prevail."

This specific conclusion is also backed by what some might call a legal platitude and others might call a legal classic. When placing special burdens on those in positions of trust, it is worthwhile to recall the well-known admonition of Chief Justice Cardozo speaking for the New York Court of Appeals:

> Joint adventurers, like copartners, owe to one another, while the enterprise continues, the duty of the finest loyalty. Many forms of conduct permissible in a workaday world for those acting at arm's length, are forbidden to those bound by fiduciary ties. A trustee is held to something stricter than the morals of the market place. Not honesty alone, but the punctilio of an honor the most sensitive, is then the standard of behavior. As to this there has developed a tradition that is unbending and inveterate. Uncompromising rigidity has been the attitude of courts of equity when petitioned to undermine the rule of undivided loyalty by the "disintegrating erosion" of particular exceptions. . . . Only thus has the level of conduct for fiduciaries been kept at a level higher than that trodden by the crowd. It will not consciously be lowered by any judgment of this court. *Meinhard v. Salmon*, 249 NY 458, 164 NE 545 (1928). . . .

[Judgment affirmed]

QUESTIONS

1. Was Lundgren a fiduciary to Berlinair in the period of time after he formed Air Berlin?
2. Outline the steps an officer must follow if wanting to take advantage of a corporate opportunity.
3. What remedy is available when a corporate officer improperly diverts a corporate opportunity?

Under some state statutes regulating the sale of corporate securities, an officer taking part in a sale that violates the statute is liable without regard to knowledge or lack of knowledge that the sale violated the statute. When the corporation has violated a statute designed to protect health or environment, corporate officers may be held liable for having failed to prevent the violation.

Officers are liable for willful or negligent acts that cause a loss to the corporation.[17] On the other hand, they are not liable for mere errors in judgment committed while exercising their discretion, provided they have acted with reasonable prudence and care.

D.   AGENTS AND EMPLOYEES

The authority, rights, and liabilities of an agent of a corporation are governed by the same rules applicable as when the principal is a natural person. The authority of corporate employees also is governed by general agency principles.

The fact that a person is acting on behalf of a corporation does not act as a shield from the liability that would be imposed

---

[17] Bellinzoni v Seland, 128 App Div 2d 583, 512 NYS2d 847 (1987).

for such acts if done on behalf of a natural person.

E.   LIABILITY

§ 52:10   LIABILITY OF MANAGEMENT TO THIRD PERSONS

Ordinarily, the management of a corporation, meaning its directors, officers, and executive employees, is not liable to third persons for the effect upon such third persons of their management or advice. The liability of a director or officer for misconduct ordinarily is a liability that may be enforced only by the corporation or by shareholders bringing a derivative action on behalf of the corporation. Ordinarily, directors or officers are not liable to a third person for loss caused by the negligent performance of their duties as directors or officers, even though because of such negligence the corporation is in turn liable to the third person to whom the corporation owed the duty to use care or was under a contract obligation to render a particular service.

Officers and managers of a corporation are not liable for the economic consequence of their advice upon third persons, even though they caused the corporation to refuse to deal with or to break its contract with such third persons, as long as the officers and managers acted in good faith to advance the interests of the corporation.

§ 52:11   CRIMINAL LIABILITY

Officers and directors, as in the case of agents generally, are personally responsible for any crimes committed by them even when they act in behalf of the corporation. At the local level they may be criminally responsible for violation of ordinances relating to sanitation, safety, and hours of clos-

ing. At the state level they may be criminally liable for conducting a business without obtaining necessary licenses or after the corporate certificate of incorporation was forfeited for failing to file reports or pay taxes.

Some statutes designed to regulate corporate activity provide specifically for fines and imprisonment of corporate officers and other individuals responsible for corporate violations. For example, the president of a national food chain corporation was held criminally liable under the federal Food, Drug, and Cosmetic Act on the ground that food in the corporation's warehouse had been exposed to rodent contamination.[18] Also, the Foreign Corrupt Practices Act makes it a crime to bribe a foreign official or political candidate to use influence to obtain business for an American corporation. The American corporation is subject to a fine, and officers and other individuals are subject to fine and imprisonment.[19]

A corporation itself may be convicted of a criminal offense if it is shown beyond a reasonable doubt that the offense was committed by its agent acting within the scope of the agent's authority. Thus an incorporated nursing home may be found guilty of criminal recklessness concerning the neglect of a patient.[20] Moreover, a corporation itself may be convicted of a crime involving specific intent, such as theft by swindle or forgery, when it is shown beyond a reasonable doubt (1) that the agent was acting at least in part in furtherance of the corporation's business interests and (2) that corporate management authorized, tolerated, or ratified the criminal activity. The requirements for imposing such criminal liability are discussed in the *Christy* case.

[18] United States v Park, 421 US 658 (1975).
[19] PL 95-213, 91 Stat 1494, 15 USC § 78m et seq.
[20] State v Monticello Developers Inc. (Ind App) 502 NE2d 927 (1987).

MINNESOTA V CHRISTY PONTIAC-GMC INC.
(Minn) 354 NW2d 17 (1984)

Christy Pontiac, a corporation, was indicted for theft by swindle and for forgery involving the GM cash rebate program in effect in 1981. Hesli, a middle-management employee of Christy Pontiac, had forged the cash rebate applications for two cars so that the rebate money was paid to Christy Pontiac instead of to its customers. In one case, a forged, back-dated rebate application was signed by an officer of Christy Pontiac. In the other case, the president of Christy, when confronted by the customer who should have received the rebate, attempted to negotiate a settlement. The corporation argued that it could not be held liable for a specific intent crime since only "natural" persons, as opposed to corporations, can form such intent. The corporation was found guilty and was fined $1,000 on each forgery conviction. The corporation appealed.

SIMONETT, J. . . . Christy Pontiac is a Minnesota corporation, doing business as a car dealership. It is owned by James Christy, a sole stockholder, who serves also as president and as director. In the spring of 1981, General Motors offered a cash rebate program for its dealers. A customer who purchased a new car delivered during the rebate period was entitled to a cash rebate, part paid by GM and part paid by the dealership.

At this time Phil Hesli was employed by Christy Pontiac as a salesman and fleet manager. On March 27, 1981, James Linden took delivery of a new Grand Prix for his employer, Snyder Brothers. Although the rebate period on this car had expired on March 19, the salesman told Linden that he would still try to get the $700 rebate for Linden. Later, Linden was told by a Christy Pontiac employee that GM had denied the rebate. Subsequently, it was discovered that Hesli had forged Linden's signature twice on the rebate application form submitted by Christy Pontiac to GM, and that the transaction date had been altered and backdated to March 19 on the buyer's order form. Hesli signed the order form as "Sales Manager or Officer of the Company."

On April 6, 1981, Ronald Gores purchased a new Le Mans, taking delivery the next day. The rebate period for this model car had expired on April 4, and apparently Gores was told he would not be eligible for a rebate. Subsequently, it was discovered that Christy Pontiac had submitted a $500 cash rebate application to GM and that Gores' signature had been forged twice by Hesli on the application. It was also discovered that the purchase order form had been backdated to April 3. This order form was signed by Gary Swandy, an officer of Christy Pontiac.

Both purchasers learned of the forged rebate applications when they received a copy of the application in the mail from Christy Pontiac. Both purchasers complained to James Christy, and in both instances the conversations ended in angry mutual recriminations. Christy did tell Gores that the rebate on his car was "a mistake" and offered half the rebate to "call it even." After the Attorney General's office made an inquiry, Christy Pontiac contacted GM and arranged for cancellation of the Gores rebate that had been allowed to Christy Pontiac. Subsequent investigation disclosed that of 50 rebate transactions, only the Linden and Gores sales involved irregularities.

In a separate trial, Phil Hesli was acquitted of three felony charges but found guilty on the count of theft for the Gores transaction and was given a misdemeanor disposition. An indictment against James Christy for theft by swindle was dismissed, as was a subsequent complaint for the same charge, for lack of probable cause. Christy Pontiac, the corporation, was also indicted, and the appeal here is from the four convictions on those indictments. Before trial, Mr. Christy was granted immunity and was then called as a prosecution witness. Phil Hesli did not testify at the corporation's trial.

Christy Pontiac argues on several grounds that a corporation cannot be held criminally liable for a specific intent crime. Minn. Stat. § 609.52, subd. 2 (1982), says "whoever" swindles by artifice, trick or other means commits theft. Minn. Stat. § 609.625, subd. 1 (182), says "whoever" falsely makes or alters a writing with intent to defraud, commits aggravated forgery. Christy Pontiac agrees that the term "whoever" refers to persons, and it agrees that the term "persons" *may* include corporations, but it argues that when the word "persons" is used here, it should be construed to mean only natural persons. This should be so, argues defendant, because the legislature has defined a crime as "conduct which is prohibited by statute and for which the actor may be sentenced to imprisonment, with or without a fine," and a corporation cannot be imprisoned. Neither, argues defendant, can an artificial person entertain a mental state, let alone have the specific intent required for theft or forgery.

. . . If a corporation can be liable in civil tort for both actual and punitive damages for libel, assault and battery, or fraud, it would seem it may also be criminally liable for conduct requiring specific intent. Most courts today recognize that corporations may be guilty of specific intent crimes. Particularly apt candidates for corporate criminality are types of crime, like theft by swindle and forgery, which often occur in a business setting.

We hold, therefore, that a corporation may be prosecuted and convicted for the crimes of theft and forgery.

There remains, however, the evidentiary basis on which criminal responsibility of a corporation is to be determined. Criminal liability, especially for more serious crimes, is thought of as a matter of personal, not vicarious, guilt. One should not be convicted for something one does not do. In what sense, then, does a corporation "do" something for which it can be convicted of a crime? The case law, as illustrated by the authorities above cited, takes differing approaches. If a corporation is to be criminally liable, it is clear that the crime must not be a personal aberration of an employee acting on his own; the criminal activity must, in some sense, reflect corporate policy so that it is fair to say that the activity was the activity of the corporation. There must be, as Judge Learned Hand put it, a "kinship of the act to the powers of the officials, who commit it."

We believe, first of all, the jury should be told that it must be satisfied beyond a reasonable doubt that the acts of the individual agent constitute the acts of the corporation. Secondly, as to the kind of proof required, we hold that a corporation may be guilty of a specific intent crime committed by its agent if: (1) the agent was acting within the course and scope of his or her employment, having the authority to act for the corporation with respect to the particular corporate business which was conducted criminally; (2) the agent was acting, at least in part, in furtherance of the corporation's business interests; and (3) the criminal acts were authorized, tolerated, or ratified by corporate management.

This test is not quite the same as the test for corporate vicarious liability for a civil tort of an agent. The burden of proof is different, and, unlike civil liability, criminal guilt requires that the agent be acting at least in part in furtherance of the corporation's business interests. Moreover, it must be shown that corporate management authorized, tolerated, or ratified the criminal activity. Ordinarily, this will be shown by circumstantial evidence, for it is not to be expected that management authorization of illegality would be expressly or openly stated. Indeed, there may be instances where the corporation is criminally liable even though the criminal activity has been expressly forbidden. What must be shown is that from all the facts and circumstances, those in positions of managerial authority or responsibility acted or failed to act in such a manner that the criminal activity reflects corporate policy, and it can be said, therefore, that the criminal act was authorized or tolerated or ratified by the corporation. . . .

This brings us, then, to the third issue, namely, whether under the proof requirements mentioned above, the evidence is sufficient to sustain the convictions. We hold that it is.

The evidence shows that Hesli, the forger, had authority and responsibility to handle new car sales and to process and sign cash rebate applications. Christy Pontiac, not Hesli, got the GM rebate money, so that Hesli was acting in furtherance of the corporation's business interests. Moreover, there was sufficient evidence of management authorization, toleration, and ratification. Hesli himself, though not an officer, had middle management responsibilities for cash rebate applications. When the customer Gores asked Mr. Benedict, a salesman, about the then discontinued rebate, Benedict referred Gores to Phil Hesli. Gary Swandy, a corporate officer, signed the backdated retail buyer's order form for the Linden sale. James Christy, the president, attempted to negotiate a settlement with Gores after Gores complained. Not until after the Attorney General's inquiry did Christy contact divisional GM headquarters. As the trial judge noted, the rebate money "was so obtained and accepted by Christy Pontiac and kept by Christy Pontiac until somebody blew the whistle . . . ." We conclude the evidence establishes that the theft by swindle and the forgeries constituted the acts of the corporation.

[Judgment affirmed]

QUESTIONS

1. Summarize the facts of this case.
2. May a corporation (as distinguished from employees and officers) be convicted of the crimes of theft by swindle and forgery?
3. State the rule of law set forth in this case.

§ 52:12   INDEMNIFICATION OF OFFICERS, DIRECTORS, EMPLOYEES, AND AGENTS

While performing what they believe to be their duty, officers, directors, employees, and agents of corporations may commit acts for which they are later sued or criminally prosecuted. The RMBCA broadly authorizes the corporation to indemnify such persons if they acted in good faith and in a manner reasonably believed to be in or not opposed to the interests of the corporation and had no reason to believe that their conduct was unlawful.

In some states statutory provision is made requiring the corporation to indemnify directors and officers for reasonable expenses incurred by them in defending unwarranted suits brought against them by shareholders. Such statutes have been adopted to induce responsible persons to accept positions of corporate responsibility.

§ 52:13   CORPORATE DEBTS

As the corporation is a separate legal person, debts owed by the corporation are ordinarily the obligations of the corporation only. Consequently, neither directors nor officers are individually liable for the corporate debts, even though it may have been their acts that gave rise to the debts.

In some states civil liability for corporate debts is imposed upon the officers and directors of the corporation when it improperly engages in business.

§ 52:14   PROTECTION OF SHAREHOLDERS

Various devices and limitations have developed to protect shareholders both from misconduct by management and from the action of the majority of the shareholders. Shareholders may protect themselves by voting at the next annual election for new directors and also for new officers, if the latter are elected; or they may take special remedial action at a special meeting of shareholders called for that purpose. In any case, the objecting shareholders may bring a legal action when the management misconduct complained of constitutes a legal wrong.

§ 52:15   CIVIL LIABILITY

A corporation is liable to third persons for the acts of its officers, employees, and agents to the same extent as a natural person is liable for the acts of agents and employees.[21] This means that the ordinary rules of agency law determine the extent to which the corporation is liable to a third person for a contract made or a tort committed by management personnel, employees, and agents.[22]

---

[21] Mercury Motors Express, Inc. v Smith (Fla) 393 So 2d 545 (1981).
[22] Jenson v Alaska Valuation Service, Inc. (Alaska) 688 P2d 161 (1984).

SUMMARY

To have legal effect, shareholder action must be taken at a regular meeting as specified in the bylaws or at a special meeting after due notice to shareholders. Also, the presence of a quorum of the voting shareholders is required.

Management of a corporation is under the control of a board of directors elected by the shareholders. The courts will not interfere with the board's discretion in the absence of unusual conduct such as fraud. A director is disqualified from taking part in corporate action where the director has a conflict of interests. Action by directors is usually taken at a properly called meeting of the board. Directors act in a fiduciary capacity in dealing with the corporation. Directors who act in good faith and have exercised reasonable care are not liable for losses resulting from their management decisions. Ordinarily, directors are removed by shareholders.

Officers of a corporation, including a president, vice president, secretary, and treasurer, are selected and removed by the board of directors. Officers are agents of the corporation and their powers are governed by the law of agency. Their relations with the corporation are fiduciary in nature, and they are liable for any secret profits and for diverting corporate opportunities to their own advantage.

Directors and officers, as in the case of agents generally, are personally responsible for any crimes they commit even though they act on behalf of the corporation. The corporation itself may be prosecuted for crimes and is subject to fines if convicted.

The ordinary rules of agency law determine the extent to which a corporation is liable for a contract made or tort committed by a director, officer, corporate agent, or employee.

QUESTIONS AND CASE PROBLEMS

1. What social forces are affected by the rule that a person dealing with a corporate officer is charged with knowledge of any limitation on the officer's authority contained in the recorded corporate charter?

2. What constitutes a quorum at a meeting of shareholders?

3. Roxanne owned 100 of the 10,000 outstanding shares of Microchip International Inc. She disagreed with the future plans of the board of directors. Should she bring a lawsuit against the directors?

4. Larry Phillips was hired for a two-year period as executive secretary of the Montana Education Association (MEA). Six months later he was fired. He then sued MEA for breach of contract and sued the directors and some of the other employees of MEA on the theory that they had caused MEA to break the contract with him and were, therefore, guilty of the tort of maliciously interfering with his contract with MEA. The evidence showed that the individual defendants, without malice, had induced the corporation to break the contract with Phillips but that this had been done in order to further the welfare of the corporation. Was MEA liable for breach of contract? Were the individual defendants shielded from personal liability? [Phillips v Montana Education Association, 187 Mont 419, 610 P2d 154]

5. Clara is the sales manager of Carmody Cosmetics, Inc. She plans and directs the advertising campaigns of the company. In a criminal prosecution brought by the attorney general of the state it is held that the ads of the corporation violate the state consumer protection law. By that statute, such a violation is a crime. Clara claims that she is not guilty of a crime because the advertising was run by the corporation. Is she correct?

6. Directors must always own stock of the corporation in order to insure that they will be attentive to their duties. Appraise this statement.

7. Discuss the power of a corporation president to employ a sales manager and to agree that the manager should be paid a stated amount per year plus a percentage of any increase in the dollar volume of sales that might take place.

8. Klockner and Combellick were directors and officers of K.M.S., a corporation engaged in the business of auctioning automobiles. The corporation sold some automobiles for Keser and gave him a check in payment of the proceeds. At the time the check was issued, Klockner and Combellick knew that the account of the corporation was overdrawn. When the check was dishonored by the bank, Keser sued them. They defended on the ground that the delivering of the bad check was the act of the corporation and that they, therefore, were not liable for the wrong done by the corporation. Were Klockner and Combellick liable? [Klockner v Keser (Colo App) 488 P2d 1135 (1971)]

9. Ponder was the president of the Long Beach Motel Hotel Corporation. He requested a quotation from General Electric on air conditioners for the hotel. He was sent a quotation, on the basis of which he sent in a purchase order on behalf of the corporation. General Electric rejected this order made in the name of the corporation and in effect stated that it would only sell to Ponder personally. Ponder was sent a new purchase order that showed him individually as the buyer. He signed his name but then added "Pres." When General Electric sued him for the purchase price, he claimed that he had signed on behalf of the corporation and that General Electric knew that it was dealing with the corporation. Was he bound by the contract? [General Electric Co. v Ponder (La App) 234 So 2d 786]

10. A director of a corporation cannot lend money to the corporation because that would create the danger of a conflict of interests between the director's status as a director and the status as a creditor. Appraise this statement.

11. AT&T had contracts with five subsidiary corporations by which AT&T furnished certain services for each subsidiary and by which each subsidiary was under contract to pay AT&T compensation of 2-1/2 percent of gross revenues of the subsidiary. Kutik owned shares in AT&T. He brought a lawsuit against Taylor and other directors of AT&T and the five subsidiaries. Kutik claimed that in the preceding six years AT&T had only collected 1 percent instead of 2-1/2 percent from each of the subsidiaries. Were the directors liable? [Kutik v Taylor, 364 NYS2d 387]

12. Anthony Yee was the president of the Waipahu Auto Exchange, a corporation. As part of his corporate duties, he arranged financing for the company. The Federal Services Finance Corporation drew twelve checks payable to the order of the Waipahu Auto Exchange. These were then endorsed by its president, "Waipahu Auto Exchange, Limited, by Anthony Yee, President," and were cashed at two different banks. The Bishop National Bank of Hawaii, on which the checks were drawn, charged its depositor, Federal Services, with the amount of these checks. Federal Services then sued Bishop National Bank to restore to its account the amount of these twelve checks on the theory that Bishop National Bank had improperly made payment on the checks because Anthony Yee had no authority to cash them. Did Yee have authority to endorse and cash the checks? [Federal Services Finance Corp. v Bishop National Bank of Hawaii (CA9 Hawaii) 190 F2d 442]

13. E. P. Fournier Co. is a closely held corporation engaged in the sale of new and used automobiles. The board of directors hired Paul Fournier and agreed that he "shall act as general manager with full authority to hire, approve sales, and contribute to policy decisions affecting the interests of the corporation." On the same date Roland Fournier was hired by the board to act as assistant general manager. Paul was president and treasurer of the corporation, and Roland was vice-president and secretary. Paul and Roland had a dispute about the roles of their respective sons who were also employed in the business. Soon thereafter, Paul informed Roland that "his services with the company were no longer required" and removed two vehicles from Roland's garage; these vehicles were owned by the corporation but used by Roland. Roland sued the corporation for back pay and benefits, claiming that Paul did not have authority to terminate him unilaterally without authorization from the board of directors. Paul defends that his employment agreement with the board clearly delegated to him all of the board's authority to manage the business, including the power to remove Roland. Decide. [Fournier v Fournier (RI) 479 A2d 708]

14. Rudolph Redmont was the president of Abbott Thinlite Corporation. He left that corporation to run the Circle Corporation in competition with his former employer. In so doing, it was claimed that he diverted contracts from his former employer to his new one, having gained the advantage of the specific information of the deals in progress while employed by Abbott. The former employer sued Redmont and Circle Corporation to recover lost profits. Redmont defends that all of the contracts in question were made after he left Abbott, at which time his fiduciary duty to Abbott had ceased. Decide. [Abbott Thinlite Corp. v Redmont (CA2 NY) 475 F2d 85]

15. William Gurtler was president and a board member of Unichem Corporation, which produced and sold chemical laundry products. While president of Unichem, he encouraged his plant manager to leave to join a rival business, which Gurtler was going to join in the near future. Moreover, Gurtler sold Unichem products to his son, G. B. Gurtler, in January of 1982 at a figure substantially below their normal price and on credit even though G. B. had no credit history. Gurtler made the sales with full knowledge that G. B. was going to start a rival business. Also at that time Gurtler was aware that his wife was soliciting Unichem employees to join the new Gurtler Chemical Co., and he helped her design Gurtler's label so that it would mirror Unichem's. On February 9, 1982, Gurtler guaranteed a $100,000 loan for Gurtler Chemical Co. with funds to be disbursed after he left Unichem, which occurred on March 12, 1982. On March 15, 1982, he became president of Gurtler Chemical Co. Unichem sued Gurtler for breach of fiduciary duty and for the loss of profits that resulted. Gurtler contends that his sales to G. B. guaranteed needed revenues to Unichem and constituted a sound business decision that should be applauded and that is protected under the "business judgment rule." Decide. [Unichem Corp v Gurtler, 148 Ill App 3d 284, 101 Ill Dec 400, 498 NE2d 724]

PART 9

REAL PROPERTY

53

NATURE AND OWNERSHIP OF REAL PROPERTY

The law of real property is technical and to a large extent uses a vocabulary drawn from the days of feudalism. Much of the earlier law of real property is no longer of practical importance in the modern business world. The following discussion is therefore a simplified presentation of the subject.

A.   NATURE OF REAL PROPERTY

Real property has special characteristics of permanence and uniqueness that have strongly influenced the rules that society has developed to resolve disputes concerning real property.

§ 53:1   DEFINITIONS

Real property includes (a) land, (b) buildings and fixtures, and (c) rights in the land of another.

(a) LAND. **Land** means more than the surface of the earth. It comprises the soil and all things of a permanent nature affixed to the ground, such as herbs, grass, or trees, and other growing, natural products. The term also includes the waters upon the ground and things that are embedded beneath the surface. For example, coal, oil, and marble embedded beneath the surface form part of the land.

Technically, land is considered as extending downward to the earth's center and upward indefinitely. The Uniform Aeronautics Act states that the owner of the land owns the space above, subject to the right of aircraft in flight that do not interfere with the use of the land and are not dangerous to persons or property lawfully on the land.[1]

(b) BUILDINGS AND FIXTURES. A **building** includes any structure placed on or beneath the surface of land, without regard to its purpose or use. A **fixture** is personal property that has been attached to the earth or placed in a building in such a way or under such circumstances that it is deemed part of the real property.

(c) RIGHTS IN LAND OF ANOTHER. These rights include easements, such as the right to cross another's land, and **profits**, such as the right to take coal from another's land.

§ 53:2   EASEMENTS

An **easement** is not only a right in the land of another, but it is a right that belongs to the land that is benefited. The benefited land is called the **dominant tenement,** and the land that is subject to the easement is called the **servient tenement**.

An easement is an interest in land and, therefore, an oral promise to create an easement is not binding because of the statute of frauds.

(a) CREATION OF EASEMENT. An easement may be created in several ways.

(1) An easement may be created by deed.
(2) An easement may be created by implication when one conveys part of the land that has been used as a dominant estate in relation to the part retained. To illustrate, if water or drain pipes run from the part conveyed through the part retained, there is an implied right to have such use continued. In order for an easement to be implied in such a case, the use must be apparent, continuous, and reasonably necessary.
(3) An easement may also be created by implication when it is necessary to the use of the land conveyed. This ordinarily arises when one subdivides land and sells a portion to which no entry can be made, except over the land retained or over the land of a stranger. The grantee's right to use the land retained by the grantor for the purpose of going to and from the land conveyed is known as a **way of necessity.**[2]

---

[1]   The Uniform Aeronautics Act (UAA) has been adopted in Arizona, Delaware, Georgia, Hawaii, Idaho, Indiana, Maryland, Minnesota, Missouri, Montana, Nevada, New Jersey, North Carolina, North Dakota, Pennsylvania, South Carolina, South Dakota, Tennessee, Utah, Vermont, and Wisconsin, but was withdrawn by the Commissioners on Uniform State Laws in 1943.

[2]   Joines v Herman (NC App) 366 SE2d 606 (1988).

(4) An easement may be created by estoppel, as when the grantor states that the plot conveyed is bounded by a street. If in such case, the grantor owns the adjoining land, the public cannot be denied the right to use the area that the owner has described as a street.

(5) An easement may be created by prescription by adverse use for a statutory period.[3] No easement is acquired if the use of the land is with the permission of the owner. This adverse use by which an easement is acquired is similar to the adverse possession by which title is acquired as is discussed in § 53:28.

(b) TERMINATION OF EASEMENT. Once an easement has been granted, it cannot be destroyed by the act of the grantor. A "revocation" attempted without the easement owner's consent has no effect.

An easement may be lost by nonuse when there are surrounding circumstances that show an intent to abandon the easement. For example, when a surface transit system had an easement to maintain trolley tracks, it could be found that there was an abandonment of the easement when the tracks were removed and when all surface transportation was discontinued. Likewise, when the owner of the easement planted a flower bed on the land across the end of the path of the easement, the intent to abandon the easement was evident.

§ 53:3   LICENSES

A **license** is a personal, revocable privilege to perform an act or series of acts upon the land of another. Unlike an easement, a license is not an interest in land. The person allowed to come into the house to use the telephone has a license. The advertising company that has permission to paint a sign on the side of a building also has a license.

A license may be terminated at the will

of the licensor and continues only as long as the licensor is the owner of the land.

§ 53:4   LIENS

Real property may be subject to liens that arise by the voluntary act of the owner of the land, such as the lien of a mortgage that is created when the owner voluntarily borrows money and when the land is made security for the repayment of the debt. Liens may also arise involuntarily as in the case of tax liens, judgment liens, and mechanics' liens. In the case of taxes and judgments, the liens provide a means for enforcing the obligations of the owner of the land to pay the taxes or the judgment.

Mechanics' liens give persons furnishing labor and materials in the improvement of real estate the right to proceed against the real estate for the collection of the amounts due them.

§ 53:5   DURATION AND EXTENT OF OWNERSHIP

A person's interest in real property may be defined in terms of the period of time for which such person will remain the owner, as (a) a fee simple estate or (b) a life estate. These estates are termed **freehold estates.** At the time of creation of a freehold estate, a termination date is not known. A life estate may be subject to a condition or may expire or terminate upon the happening of a specified contingency. Although a person may own property for a specified number of years this interest is not regarded as a freehold estate, but is a **leasehold estate** and is subject to special rules of law.

(a) FEE SIMPLE ESTATE. An **estate in fee, a fee simple,** or a **fee simple absolute** lasts forever. The owner of such fee has the absolute and entire interest in the land. The important characteristics of this estate are as follows: (1) it is alienable during life; (2) it is alienable by will; (3) it de-

---

[3]   Auxier v Holmes (Mo App) 605 SW2d 804 (1980).

scends to heirs generally if not devised (transferred by will); (4) it is subject to rights of the owner's surviving spouse; and (5) it is liable for debts of the owner before or after death.

(b) LIFE ESTATE. A **life estate** (or life tenancy), as its name indicates, lasts only during the life of a person, ordinarily its owner. Upon the death of the person by whose life the estate was measured, the owner of the life estate has no interest remaining to pass to heirs or by will.

B.   FIXTURES

By the concept of fixtures, personal property changes to real property, and third persons and creditors may acquire rights therein.

§ 53:6   DEFINITION

A **fixture** is personal property that is attached to the earth or placed in a building in such a way or under such circumstances that it is deemed part of the real property.

A person buys a refrigerator, an air-conditioner, or a furnace, or some other item that is used in a building, and then has the item installed. The question of whether the item is a fixture and, therefore, part of the building can arise in a variety of situations. (a) The real estate tax assessor assesses the building and adds in the value of the item on the theory that it is part of the building. (b) The buyer of the item owns the building and then sells the building, and the new owner of the building claims that the item stays with the building. (c) The buyer places the mortgage on the building, and the mortgagee claims that the item is bound by the mortgage. (d) The buyer is a tenant in the building in which the item is installed and the landlord claims that the item must stay in the building when the tenant leaves. (e) The buyer does not pay in full

for the item, and the seller of the item has a security interest that the seller asserts against the buyer of the item or against the landlord of the building in which the buyer installs the item. The seller of the item may also be asserting a claim against the mortgagee of the building or against the buyer of the building.

The determination of the rights of these parties depends upon the common law of fixtures, as occasionally modified by statute.

§ 53:7   TESTS OF A FIXTURE

In the absence of an agreement between the parties, the courts apply three tests to determine whether the personal property has become a fixture:

(a) ANNEXATION. Generally the personal property becomes a fixture if it is so attached to the realty that it cannot be removed without materially damaging the realty or destroying the personal property itself. If the property is so affixed as to lose its specific identity, such as bricks in a wall, it becomes part of the realty. When railroad tracks are so placed as to be immovable, they are fixtures.

(b) ADAPTATION. Personal property especially adapted or suited to the use made of the building may constitute a fixture.

(c) INTENT. The true test is the intention of the person affixing the property at the time it was affixed.[4]

In the absence of direct proof of such intent, it is necessary to resort to the nature of the property, the method of its attachment, and all the surrounding circumstances to determine what the intent was.

In the *Premonstratensian Fathers* case, the court considered all three tests in deciding if refrigeration equipment had become a fixture.

---

[4]   Harris v Rapke, 138 Misc 2d 429, 524 NYS2d 1005 (1988).

PREMONSTRATENSIAN FATHERS V BADGER MUTUAL FIRE INS. CO.

46 Wis 2d 362, 175 NW2d 337 (1970)

In 1958, a supermarket was constructed by Jacobs Realty Corporation and was owned by that corporation. The market contained five large walk-in coolers or refrigerators. Title to the market was thereafter transferred to the Premonstratensian Fathers and was insured against fire by Badger Mutual Insurance Company. The building was severely damaged by fire, and the insurer paid approximately $80,000 for the building damage. The Fathers claimed an additional $20,000 for the destruction of the coolers. The insurer refused to pay this amount and asserted that the coolers were not owned by the Fathers. From a judgment for the Fathers, the insurer appealed.

HANSE, N. J. . . . If the coolers are determined to be common-law fixtures, and were such at the time of the construction of the building and the installation of the coolers, then they would have passed to the Fathers under the warranty deed of March 7, 1960, and they would be insured under the terms of the policy. The issue then is whether these coolers constitute fixtures.

The rule which has developed . . . as to what constitutes a fixture is not really a comprehensive definition, but rather a statement of the factors which are to be applied to the facts and circumstances of a particular case to determine whether or not the property in question does constitute a fixture. . . .

Annexation

. . . An object will not acquire the status of a fixture unless it is in some manner or means . . . attached or affixed, either actually or constructively, to the realty. . . . The trial court ably pointed out the physical facts which led to its conclusion that there is indeed annexation in this case. The more important of these are as follows: (1) The exterior walls of the cooler, in four instances, constituted the interior wall of another room. (2) In the two meat coolers, a meat hanging and tracking system was built into the coolers. These tracks were used to move large cuts of meats from the cooler area into the meat preparation areas, and were suspended from the steel girders of the building structure by means of large steel bolts. These bolts penetrated through the roof of the cooler supporting wooden beams, which, in turn, supported the tracking system. The tracking in the coolers was a part of a system of tracking throughout the rear portion of the supermarket. (3) The coolers were attached to hardwood plank which was, in turn, attached to the concrete floor of the supermarket. The attachment of the plank to the floor was accomplished through the use of a ramsetting gun. The planks were laid on the floor, and the bolts were driven through them into the concrete floor, where they then exploded, firmly fixing the coolers into place. There was a material placed on the planks which served both as an adhesive and as an insulation. (4) The floor of the coolers was specially sloped during the construction of the building so that the slope would carry drainage into a specially constructed drain in the concrete. In addition, four of the coolers were coated with a protective coating to seal the floors. In the freezer, a special concrete buildup was constructed in the nature of a trough, the purpose of which was to carry away moisture as frozen chickens melted. (5) A refrigeration unit was built into each cooler. The unit was suspended from the ceiling of the cooler, and tubing was run through the wall of the cooler to compressors located elsewhere in the store. (6) Electric lights and power receptacles were built into each cooler and were connected by electrical wiring through the walls and the ceiling of the cooler to the store's electrical power supply. (7) The walls of the cooler were interlocked, and set into the splines, the hardwood planks ramset into the concrete floor, in tongue and groove fashion.

These factors adequately support the conclusion that the coolers were indeed physically annexed to the premises. The insurers argue that the coolers were removable without material injury to the premises, which detracts from the annexation. There was a dispute in the evidence introduced at the trial, with the insurers' expert testifying that this type of cooler was easily severable from the building, while one of the members of the Jacobs family testified that when he removed some of the bolts from the floor following the fire, large sections of concrete would crack on the floor. This was a conflict for resolution by the trial court. In any event, the element of removability without material damage to the building no longer enjoys the position of prominence in the law of fixtures which it once held. It is now only one of the factors which is to be considered by the trial court. . . .

Adaptation

Adaptation refers to the relationship between the chattel and the use which is made of the realty to which the chattel is annexed. The use of the realty was that of a retail grocery, commonly known as a supermarket. This was the intent of the parties at the time of the construction of the building, and the intent of the parties throughout the entire history of the business. The fact of operation has borne out this intent. In a business which carries fresh foods, frozen foods, produce, meats and butter, coolers used for storage and handling of these perishables are patently related to the use of the building. In fact, it would be hard to picture any equipment more closely related to the operation of a supermarket, where large quantities of perishables must, of necessity, be purchased for storage and processing.

The insurers raise a number of points to dispute this finding. They state: The coolers were not custom made; the coolers are useful not to the building, but to the use to which the building is put; the coolers could have been used anywhere; other coolers could have been used. There is no requirement that the coolers be custom made, but only that they be adapted to the use to which the building is put. The test here is not the adaptability to the building, but the adaptability to the use to which the building is put. The fact that other coolers could have been used, or that these coolers could have been used elsewhere, does not alter the fact that there was a close connection between these coolers and the retail grocery business conducted on the property. . . .

Intent

This court has repeatedly held that intent is the primary determinant of whether a certain piece of property has become a fixture. *Old Line Life Ins. Co. v Hawn* (1937) 225 Wis 627, 275 NW 542. The relevant intent is that of the party making the annexation. At the time of the construction of the supermarket and the installation of the coolers, both the Jacobs Realty Corporation and the

Jacobs Brothers Stores, Inc., were in existence as separate legal entities. The title to the land in question was registered in the name of the Jacobs Realty Corporation, but the exact status of Jacobs Brothers Stores, Inc., is unclear at that date. There is no definitive evidence which demonstrates whether it was the Jacobs Realty Corporation or the Jacobs Brothers Stores, Inc., which purchased the coolers and caused them to be installed on the premises. The invoice from the manufacturer was sent to the "Jacobs Bros. Super Market," a nonexistent legal entity. The evidence introduced at the trial as to who paid for the coolers consisted of the testimony of Henry Jacobs. He did not remember which of the corporations issued the check in payment of the coolers; many of their records were burned; John Norbert and Henry Jacobs paid for them through one of the corporations; and he was inclined to think it was Jacobs Realty Corporation that purchased them. Thus, there is no evidence from which it can be positively asserted that either Jacobs Realty Corporation or Jacobs Brothers Stores, Inc., purchased the coolers.

In its decision, the trial court found, as a reasonable and legitimate inference from all the facts and circumstances surrounding the placement of the coolers onto the realty, that there was an intention that the coolers become a permanent accession to the realty; that when Jacobs Realty Corporation conveyed the land together with all buildings and improvements thereon to Jacobs Brothers Stores, Inc., the intention still prevailed that the coolers were a permanent accession to the realty; and that the same intention still prevailed when Jacobs Brothers Stores, Inc., conveyed the building and improvements to the plaintiff, and when the plaintiff leased the premises (the land, with all buildings and improvements thereon) back to the corporation as lessee. . . .

The coolers were fixtures when installed; passed to Jacobs Brothers Stores, Inc., through the warranty deed; subsequently passed to the Fathers through that warranty deed; and are in fact fixtures within the meaning of the coverage clause of the insurance policy in this case. . . .

[Judgment affirmed]

QUESTIONS

1. Which party to the lawsuit had installed the coolers?
2. What difference would it make whether the coolers were or were not fixtures?
3. Does the adaptation test require that the goods be made especially for use in the particular building?

The fact that machinery installed in a plant would be very difficult and expensive to move and so delicate that the moving would cause damage and unbalancing is significant in reaching the conclusion that the owner of the plant had installed the equipment as a permanent addition and thus had the intent that would make the equipment become fixtures. When the floors in a large apartment house are of concrete that is covered with a thin sheet of plywood to which is stapled wall-to-wall carpeting, the carpeting constitutes a fixture that cannot be removed from the building. Removal would probably destroy the carpeting, since it was cut to size, and since the carpeting is necessary to make the building livable as an apartment.

§ 53:8   MOVABLE MACHINERY AND EQUIPMENT

Machinery and equipment that is movable is ordinarily held not to constitute fixtures, even though, in order to move it, it is necessary to unbolt it from the floor or to disconnect electrical wires or water pipes.

It is ordinarily held that refrigerators and freezers, and gas and electric ranges are not fixtures and do not lose their character as personal property when they are readily removable after disconnecting pipes or unplugging wires. A portable, window air-conditioner that rests on a rack that is affixed to the window sill by two screws and is connected directly to the building only by an electric cord plug is not a fixture.

The mere fact that an item may be unplugged, however, does not establish that it is not a fixture. For example, a computer and its related hardware constituted fixtures when there was such a mass of wires and cables under the floor that the installation gave the impression of permanence.

§ 53:9   TRADE FIXTURES

Equipment attached by a tenant to a rented building and used in a trade or business is ordinarily removable by the tenant when the tenant permanently leaves the premises. Such equipment is commonly called a **trade fixture**.[5]

C.   LIABILITY TO THIRD PERSONS FOR CONDITION OF REAL PROPERTY

In the case of real estate, liability is ordinarily based upon occupancy. That is, the person in possession may be liable for harm to the third person caused by a condition of the premises, even though the occupant is not the owner but is merely a tenant renting the premises.

§ 53:10   STATUS-OF-PLAINTIFF COMMON-LAW RULE

Under the common law, liability to a person injured on real estate was controlled by the status of the injured person, that is, whether the person injured was a trespasser, a licensee, or an invitee. A different duty was owed by the occupier of land to each of these three categories.[6]

(a) TRESPASSERS. As to **trespassers**, the occupier ordinarily owes only the duty of refraining from causing intentional harm once the presence of the trespasser is known; but the occupier is not under any duty to warn of dangers or to make the premises safe to protect the trespasser from harm. The most significant exception to this rule arises in the case of small children who, although trespassers, are generally afforded greater protection through the **attractive nuisance doctrine.** For example, the owner of a private residential swimming pool was liable for the drowning of a 5-year-old trespasser when the owner did not maintain adequate fencing around the pool, since the placing of such fencing would not have imposed a great burden.

(b) LICENSEES. As to **licensees**, who are on the premises with the permission of the occupier, the latter owes the duty of warning of nonobvious dangers that are known to the occupier. For example, a host must warn a guest of the dangers. Consequently, when a sliding glass door is "invisible" if the patio lights are on and the house lights are off, the host must warn guests of the presence of the glass and is liable if the guest is injured in shattering the glass.

---

[5]   B. Kreisman & Co. v First Arlington National Bank, 91 Ill App 3d 47, 47 Ill Dec 757, 415 NE2d 1070 (1981).

[6]   Huyck v Hecla Mining Co. 101 Idaho 299, 612 P2d 142 (1980).

In contrast, the occupier owes no duty to the licensee to take any steps to learn of the presence of unknown dangers.

(c) INVITEES. As to **invitees**, whose presence is sought to further the economic interest of the occupier, such as customers, there is a duty to take reasonable steps to discover any danger and a duty to warn the invitee or to correct the danger. For example, a store must make a reasonable inspection of the premises to determine that there is nothing on the floor that would be dangerous, such as a slippery substance that might cause a patron to fall, and must either correct the condition or appropriately rope off the danger area or give suitable warning. If the occupier of the premises fails to conform to the degree of care described and if harm results to an invitee on the premises, the occupier is liable for such harm.

In most states the courts have expanded the concept of invitees beyond the category of those persons whose presence will economically benefit the occupier. Invitees now usually include members of the public who are invited when it is apparent that such persons cannot be reasonably expected to make an inspection of the premises before making use of them and that they would not be making repairs to correct any dangerous condition. Some courts have also made inroads into the prior law by treating a recurring licensee, such as a letter carrier, as an invitee.

In the *Lucas* case, the court was asked to abolish the distinction between an invitee and a licensee.

LUCAS V B. JONES FORD LINCOLN MERCURY
(Miss App) 518 So 2d 646 (1988)

Joyce Lucas dropped her youngest son, Mark, at the Buddy Jones Ford dealership so that her husband, an employee of Ford, could babysit Mark while she kept an appointment with her doctor. After her appointment, Joyce returned for Mark. She parked her automobile and walked across the lot toward the service area of the dealership, where her husband worked. When she reached the freight ramp, she injured her arm by slipping and falling on ice that had accumulated because of a severe winter storm that had struck the area earlier in the day. Joyce charged Buddy Jones with the negligent maintenance of the entrances to its business. Jones argued that Joyce was a licensee and not an invitee as she contended. From a judgment in favor of Buddy Jones, Joyce appealed.

ZUCCARO, J. . . . Lucas argues that she was not a licensee, but was instead an invitee. The basis for this contention is the fact that Buddy Jones Ford had on occasion encouraged the relatives of employees to pick up payment checks, so that the employee would not have to leave the job site. Thus, as Lucas had an implied invitation, Buddy Jones Ford owed to her a duty of ordinary care to make the premises safe. . . .

In looking to the facts presented in the case, we must note that on the date in question, Lucas was not going to Buddy Jones Ford to pick up her husband's check. Instead, as she stated in her deposition, she was on her way to a doctor's appointment, and had dropped her son off so that her husband might "babysit." When the accident occurred, Lucas was simply in the process of picking up her son so that they could go home. Further, in her deposition,

Lucas admitted that there was no business purpose in her visit to Buddy Jones Ford, and that the business derived no benefit from her visit. The stop was made simply for her personal convenience.

In drawing the long standing, and traditional distinction between a "licensee" and an "invitee" it must be noted that a licensee is a person who enters upon the property of another for his own convenience, pleasure or benefit pursuant to the licenses or implied permission of the owner. *Kelley v. Sportmen's Speedway*, 224 Miss. 632, 80 So.2d 785 (1955). On the other hand, an invitee is a person who goes upon the premises of another in answer to an express or implied invitation of the owner or occupier for their *mutual advantage*. *Hoffman v. Planter's Gin Co., Inc.*, 358 So.2d 1008 (Miss.1978). From this distinction, and as can be seen from Lucas' own testimony, she clearly falls into the category of a "licensee."

The significance in drawing the above distinction can be found in the duty owed by the landowner, in the present case Buddy Jones Ford, to a licensee. A landowner owes a licensee the bare duty to refrain from willfully or wantonly injuring him. There is one recognized exception, in that ordinary reasonable care is required where the landowner engages in active conduct and the plaintiff's presence is known to him. This exception is not applicable where the licensee is injured as a result of the condition of the premises, or passive negligence. Conversely, a landowner always owes to a business invitee the duty to exercise reasonable care for said invitee's safety. As Lucas was a mere licensee, not falling within the above exception, Buddy Jones Ford owed to her only the duty not to willfully or wantonly harm her. The failure of Buddy Jones Ford to warn her of the open and obvious ice could hardly be said to rise to this level.

In *Graves v. Massey*, 227 Miss. 848, 87 So.2d 270 (1956), this Court stated that where the undisputed facts disclose that a plaintiff was a mere licensee, the court should not allow the jury to consider the question of whether or not his status was otherwise. The case presently at bar presents a similar situation, in that Lucas, in her own deposition, admitted that Buddy Jones Ford derived no advantage from her husband being allowed to babysit their son. As such, the lower court was correct in finding Lucas a licensee. Summary judgment was properly granted.

Additionally, we feel compelled to add that the views expressed in this opinion should not be construed as an indication that Buddy Jones Ford would be liable to Lucas if she were an invitee. Were appellant an invitee, (which as previously stated she obviously was not), Buddy Jones Ford would have only owed her the duty of exercising reasonable care to keep the premises safe, or of warning Lucas of *hidden or concealed perils* of which appellee knew or should have known in the exercise of reasonable care. The ice which caused Lucas to fall was in no way hidden or concealed.

Lucas next argues that if this Court cannot find her to be an invitee, that it should abolish the long-held distinction between an invitee and a licensee. In this context it must be noted that this Court has continuously and regularly adhered to the common law distinction between an invitee and a licensee since the world was young. Further, in very recent decisions, we have specifically refused to abandon our long-held recognition of the categories now in question.

Prosser and Keeton note that recently courts considering abandoning the distinction between an invitee and a licensee have refused to do so. *Prosser and*

Keeton on Torts, § 62 (5th ed. 1984). As such, this Court will not at this time do away with a legal principle so long held and thoroughly developed. The assignment of error is meritless.

It is readily apparent from the facts as presented that Mrs. Lucas was a licensee. She went to Buddy Jones Ford, by her own statement, to carry out no more than personal business. Buddy Jones Ford derived no advantage from her visit. As we decline at this time to abolish our traditional recognition of the distinction between a licensee and an invitee, the decision of the lower court should be and is affirmed.

[Judgment affirmed]

QUESTIONS

1. Was Lucas an invitee or a licensee?
2. Upon what basis did she allege she was an invitee?
3. Did the court abolish the distinction between an invitee and a licensee? Explain.

§ 53:11 NEGLIGENCE RULE

A number of courts have begun a trend in ignoring these common-law distinctions and holding the occupier liable according to ordinary negligence standards; that is, when the occupier as a reasonable person should foresee from the circumstances that harm would be caused a third person, the occupier has the duty to take reasonable steps to prevent such harm, without regard to whether the potential victim would be traditionally classified as a trespasser, a licensee, or an invitee.[7]

§ 53:12 INTERMEDIATE RULE

Some courts have taken an intermediate position and have merely abolished the distinction between licensees and invitees so that the occupier owes the same duty of care to all lawful visitors; and whether one is a licensee or an invitee is merely a circumstance to be considered by the jury in applying the ordinary rule of negligence.

In some states, the distinction between licensees and invitees has been retained in name but destroyed in fact by requiring an occupier to warn the licensee of unknown dangers of which the occupier in the exercise of reasonable care should have known, or by classifying a licensee as an invitee.[8]

D. CO-OWNERSHIP OF REAL PROPERTY

All interests in particular real property may be held in severalty, that is by one person alone. As explained in Chapter 24, ownership in severalty also exists when title is held in the form of "A or B."

§ 53:13 MULTIPLE OWNERSHIP

Several persons may have concurrent interests in the same real property. The forms of multiple ownership for real prop-

---

[7] Rowland v Christian, 69 Cal 2d 108, 70 Cal Rptr 97, 443 P2d 561 (1968).

[8] Caroff v Liberty Lumber Co. 146 NJ Super 353, 369 A2d 983 (1977) (holding that a public officer, such as a police officer or health inspector, who enters premises in the performance of official duties, has the same status as a business invitee when injured because of a condition of the premises).

erty are the same as those for personal property.[9]

When co-owners sell property, they hold the proceeds of sale by the same kind of tenancy as they held the original property.

§ 53:14   CONDOMINIUMS

A **condominium** is a combination of co-ownership and individual ownership. For example, persons owning an office building or an apartment house by condominium are co-owners of the land and of the halls, lobby, elevators, stairways, exits, surrounding land, incinerator, laundry rooms, and other areas used in common; but each apartment or office in the building is individually owned by its occupant.

(a) CONTROL AND EXPENSE. In some states, the owners of the various units in the condominium have equal voice in the management and share an equal part of its expenses. In others, control and liability for expenses are shared by a unit owner in the same ratio that the value of the unit bears to the value of the entire condominium project. In all states, the unit owners have an equal right to use the common areas.

The owner of each condominium unit makes such repairs as are required by the owner's deed or contract of ownership, and the owner is prohibited from making any major change that would impair or damage the safety or value of an adjoining unit.

(b) COLLECTION OF EXPENSES FROM UNIT OWNER. When a unit owner fails to pay the owner's share of taxes, operating expenses, and repairs, it is commonly provided that a lien may be entered against that owner's unit for the amount due.

(c) TORT LIABILITY. Most condominium projects fail to make provision as to the liability of unit owners for a tort occurring in the common areas. A few states expressly provide that when a third person is injured in the common areas a suit may only be brought against the condominium association, and any judgment recovered is a charge against the association to be paid off as a common expense. When the condominium association is incorporated, the same result should be obtained by applying ordinary principles of corporation law under which liability for torts occurring on the premises of the corporation are not the liability of the individual shareholders.

(d) COOPERATIVES DISTINGUISHED. Ownership in a condominium is to be distinguished from ownership in a **cooperative**. An apartment cooperative will typically be a corporation renting apartments to persons who are also owners of stock of the corporation. The apartment complex is owned only by the corporation and the only "ownership" interests of the stockholders are as tenants of their respective apartments or offices.

§ 53:15   ADVANTAGES OF CONDOMINIUM OWNERSHIP

The owner of a condominium unit has the benefits of limited liability, tax deductions, and the ownership of property that can be transferred or sold.

(a) FREEDOM FROM ENTERPRISE LIABILITY. The owner of a unit is not personally liable for an enterprise liability nor may the unit of the owner be taken to pay for such a liability.

(b) TRANSFERABILITY OF UNIT. The condominium unit is property that the unit owner can transfer as freely as any other kind of property.

(c) TAX DEDUCTIONS. A deduction for a share of the mortgage interest and property taxes paid may be claimed by the unit owners on their individual income tax returns. Over a period of time, the unit owner can thus enjoy a tax savings that in effect will lower the cost of the condominium unit.

---

[9]   See Chapter 24.

E.   TRANSFER OF REAL PROPERTY BY DEED

Although many of the technical limitations of the feudal and earlier common-law days have disappeared, much of the law relating to the modern deed originated in those days.

§ 53:16   DEFINITIONS

A **deed** is an instrument or writing by which an owner or **grantor** transfers or conveys an interest in land to a new owner called a **grantee** or transferee.

Unlike a contract, no consideration is required to make a deed effective.[10] Although consideration is not required to make a valid deed or transfer of title by deed, the absence of consideration may be evidence to show that the transfer is made by the owner in fraud of creditors who may then be able to set aside the transfer.

Real property may either be sold or given as a gift. However, a deed is necessary to transfer title to land, even if it is a gift.

§ 53:17   CLASSIFICATION OF DEEDS

Deeds may be classified in terms of the interest conveyed as (a) a **quitclaim deed,** which transfers merely whatever interest, if any, the grantor may have in the property, without specifying that interest in any way, and (b) a **warranty deed,** which purports to transfer a specified interest and which warrants or guarantees that such interest is transferred.

A deed may also be classified as a common-law deed or a statutory deed. The **common-law deed** is a long form that sets forth the details of the transaction. The statutory deed in substance merely recites that a named person is making a certain conveyance to a named grantee.

§ 53:18   EXECUTION OF DEEDS

Ordinarily, a deed must be signed, by signature or mark, or sealed by the grantor. In order to have the deed recorded, statutes generally require that two or more witnesses sign the deed and that the grantor then acknowledge the deed before a notary public or other officer. In the interest of legibility, it is frequently required that the signature of the parties be followed by their printed or typewritten names.

In many states the statute that authorizes a short or simplified form of deed also declares that no seal is required to make effective a writing that purports to convey an interest in land.

A deed must be executed and delivered by a person having capacity. It may be set aside by the grantor on the ground of the fraud of the grantee provided that innocent third persons have not acquired rights in the land.

The deed remains binding as between the grantor and the grantee even though it has not been acknowledged or recorded.

§ 53:19   DELIVERY OF DEEDS

A deed has no effect and title does not pass until the deed has been delivered. Delivery is a matter of intent as shown by words and conduct,[11] no particular form of ceremony is required. The essential intent in delivering a deed is not merely that the grantor intends to hand over physical control and possession of the paper upon which the deed is written, but that the grantor intends thereby to transfer the ownership of the property described in the deed. That is, the grantor must deliver the deed with the intent that it should take effect as a deed and convey an interest in the property.

A deed is ordinarily made effective by handing it to the grantee with the intention that the grantee should thenceforth be the owner of the property described in the

---

[10]   Robinson v Thompson, 192 Neb 428, 222 NW2d 123 (1974).

[11]   Smith v Smith (Tex Civ App) 607 SW2d 617 (1980).

deed. A delivery may also be made by placing the deed, addressed to the grantee, in the mail or by giving it to a third person with directions to hand it to the grantee.

When a deed is delivered to a third person for the purpose of delivery to the grantee upon the happening of some event or contingency, the transaction is called a **delivery in escrow.** No title passes until the fulfillment of the condition or the happening of the event or contingency.

An effective delivery of a deed may be made symbolically as by delivering to the grantee the key to a locked box and informing the grantee that the deed to the property is in the box.

In the *Green* case, it was claimed that the delivery of a safety deposit box key was a delivery of a deed that was in the box.

GREEN V STANFILL
(Mo App) 612 SW2d 435 (1981)

Charlsie Green and her husband executed a deed of property to their son Frankie Green. She put the deed in a safety deposit box. Attached to the deed was a slip of paper stating that Frankie was not to "bother" with the deed until his parents were dead. Thereafter, the mother rented a new safety deposit box, put the deed and other papers in it, and gave one of the two keys for the box to Frankie. Unknown to the mother, Frankie thereafter removed the deed from the box and recorded it. He then executed a deed transferring the property to himself and his wife. The mother was never told that the deed had been taken from the safety deposit box and recorded. Later Frankie was killed. His wife remarried and was then known as Violet Green Stanfill. The mother sued Violet to set aside the deed to Frankie on the ground that it had never been delivered. From a judgment against the mother, she appealed.

PREWITT, P. J. . . . Whether there is delivery of a deed depends upon the facts of each case and all relevant facts and circumstances should be considered in determining the question. "Whether or not a deed has been delivered is a mixed question of law and fact. The element which controls the resolution of that question is the intention of the parties, especially the intention of the grantor. The vital inquiry is whether the grantor intended a complete transfer — whether the grantor *parted with dominion over the instrument* with the intention of relinquishing *all* dominion over it and of making it presently operative as a conveyance of the title to the land." *Meadows v Brich,* 606 SW2d 258 (Mo App 1980). Intention of the parties may be manifested by words or acts or both. . . .

Defendant Stanfill contends that the trial court's determination of the effect of giving the key to Frankie was correct, citing *McBride v Mercantile-Commerce Bank & Trust Co.* 330 Mo 259, 48 SW2d 922 (banc 1932), and *Foley v Harrison,* 233 Mo 460, 136 SW 354 (1911). However, in those cases there was evidence that the donor intended to make a present gift of the contents of the box. Here there was contrary evidence as to plaintiff's intention. Plaintiff' acts, as described in her testimony, indicated that by giving

Frankie the key to the safety deposit box she did not then intend to deliver the deed and make a present conveyance of the property. She had the deed with her and deposited it in the box instead of giving it to her son. A note, apparently still attached to it, said he was not to take it until her death. It is essential to a valid delivery that the grantor part with the deed without reservation, with intention that it take effect at that time as a transfer of title. . . . Placing an executed and acknowledged deed in a place where the grantee has access and from which he can, without hindrance, transfer it to his possession, but with the intent that the grantee not take it and have it recorded until after the grantor's death, does not constitute a delivery. . . .

We hold that the delivery of the key to the safety deposit box did not constitute delivery of the deed as a matter of law and that plaintiff made a prima facie case. The judgment of dismissal is reversed and the cause remanded for a new trial.

[Judgment reversed and action remanded]

QUESTIONS

1. Does this case hold that there can never be a delivery of a deed by making a delivery of a key to a safety deposit box containing the deed?
2. What additional evidence would have changed the result in the *Green* case?
3. What was the significance of the fact that the mother was not told that the deed had been taken from the box and recorded?

§ 53:20 ACCEPTANCE OF DEEDS

Generally, there must be an acceptance by the grantee. In all cases an acceptance is presumed. However, the grantee may disclaim the transfer if the grantee acts within a reasonable time after learning that the transfer has been made.

§ 53:21 RECORDING OF DEEDS

The owner of land may record the deed in the office of a public official, sometimes called a recorder or commissioner of deeds. The recording is not required to make the deed effective to pass title but it is done so that the public will know that the grantee is the present owner and thereby prevent the former owner from making any other transaction relating to the property. The recording statutes provide that a person purchasing land from the last holder of record will take title free of any unrecorded claim to the land of which the purchaser does not have notice or knowledge.

The fact that a deed is recorded charges everyone with knowledge of its existence even though they in fact do not know of it because they have neglected to examine the record. The recording of a deed, however, is only such notice if the deed was properly executed. Likewise, the grantee of land cannot claim any protection by virtue of the recording of a deed when (a) a claim is made by one whose title is superior to that of the owner of record; (b) the grantee had notice or knowledge of the adverse claim when title was acquired; (c) a person acting under a hostile claim was then in possession of the land; (d) the grantee received the land as a gift; or (e) the transfer to the grantee was fraudulent.

§ 53:22   Additional Protection of Buyers

Apart from the protection given to buyers and third persons by the recorded title to property, a buyer may generally also be protected by procuring title insurance or an **abstract of title,** which is a summarized report of the title to the property as shown by the records, together with a report of all judgments, mortgages, and similar recorded claims against the property.

§ 53:23   Cancellation of Deeds

A deed, although delivered, acknowledged, and recorded, may be set aside or canceled by the grantor upon proof of such circumstances as would warrant the setting aside of a contract. For example, when a conveyance is made in consideration of a promise to support the grantor, the failure of the grantee to perform will ordinarily justify cancellation of the deed.

§ 53:24   Grantor's Warranties

The warranties of the grantor relate to the title transferred by the grantor and to the fitness of the property for use.

(a) Warranties of Title. In the common-law deed the grantor may expressly warrant or make certain covenants as to the title conveyed. The statutes authorizing a short form of deed provide that unless otherwise stated in the deed, the grantor shall be presumed to have made certain warranties of title.

The more important of the covenants or warranties of title that the grantor may make are (1) **covenant of seisin,** or guarantee that the grantor owns the estate conveyed; (2) **covenant of right to convey,** or guarantee that the grantor, if not the owner, as in the case of an agent, has the right or authority to make the conveyance; (3) **covenant against encum-**brances, or guarantee that the land is not subject to any right or interest of a third person, such as a lien or easement; (4) **covenant of quiet enjoyment,** or covenant by the grantor that the grantee's possession of the land shall not be disturbed either by the grantor, in the case of a limited covenant, or by the grantor or any person claiming title under the grantor, in the case of a general covenant; and (5) **covenant of further assurances,** or promise that the grantor will execute any additional documents that may be required to perfect the title of the grantee.

(b) Fitness for Use. In the absence of an express warranty in the deed, no warranty as to fitness arises under the common law in the sale or conveyance of real estate. Thus, by the common law there is no implied warranty that a house is reasonably fit for habitation, even though it is a new house sold by the builder.

In accord with a modern trend, however, courts in most states hold that when a builder or real estate developer sells a new house to a home buyer, an implied warranty that the house and foundation are fit for occupancy or use arises without regard to whether the house was purchased before, during, or after completion of construction.[12] This warranty will not be implied against the first buyer when the house is resold, but there is authority that the second buyer may sue the original contractor for breach of the implied warranty, even though there is no privity of contract.[13]

The *Blagg* case required the court to decide whether the implied warranty of habitability could be enforced by the second buyer of the house.

---

[12]   The buyer of a house should give notice to the seller of any defects within a reasonable time after the buyer learns or should have learned of the defects. Pollard v Saxe & Yolles Development Co. 12 Cal 3d 374, 115 Cal Rptr 648, 525 P2d 88 (1974) (extending the concept of UCC § 2-607(3), although recognizing that it was applicable only to the sale of goods).

[13]   Barnes v MacBrown and Co., Inc. 264 Ind 227, 342 NE2d 619 (1976).

THIS DEED, made the twentieth day of November, nineteen hundred and... between James K. Damron, residing at 132 Spring Street in the Borough of Manhattan, City and State of New York, party of the first part, and Terrence S. Bloemker, residing at 14 Steinway Street in the Borough of Queens, City and State of New York, party of the second part,

WITNESSETH, that the party of the first part, in consideration of the sum of one dollar ($1), lawful money of the United States, and other good and valuable consideration paid by the party of the second part, does hereby grant and release unto the party of the second part, his heirs and assigns forever,

ALL that certain lot, piece, and parcel of land situated in the Borough of Manhattan, City and County of New York, and State of New York, and bounded and described as follows:

Beginning at a point on the northerly side of Spring Street, distant two hundred (200) feet westerly from the corner formed by the intersection of the northerly side of Spring Street with the westerly side of 6th Avenue, running thence northerly parallel with 6th Avenue one hundred (100) feet, thence westerly and parallel with said Spring Street one hundred (100) feet; thence southerly, again parallel with said 6th Avenue one hundred (100) feet to the northerly side of Spring Street, and thence easterly along the said northerly side of Spring Street one hundred (100) feet to the point or place of beginning.

Together with the appurtenances and all the estate and rights of the party of the first part in and to said premises.

TO HAVE AND TO HOLD the premises herein granted unto the party of the second part, his heirs and assigns forever.

AND the party of the first part covenants as follows:

First. That the party of the first part is seised of the said premises in fee simple, and has good right to convey the same;

Second. That the party of the second part shall quietly enjoy the said premises;

Third. That the said premises are free from encumbrances except as expressly stated;

Fourth. That the party of the first part will execute or procure any further necessary assurance of the title to said premises;

IN WITNESS WHEREOF, the party of the first part has hereunto set his hand and seal the day and year first above written.

JAMES K. DAMRON (L.S.)

In presence of:

DIANA L. REILMAN

State of New York   } ss.:
County of New York }

On the twentieth day of November in the year nineteen hundred and ..., before me personally came James K. Damron, to me known and known to me to be the individual described in, and who executed, the foregoing instrument, and he acknowledged that he executed the same.

DIANA L. REILMAN
Notary Public, New York County

[AUTHORS' NOTE: ACKNOWLEDGEMENT BEFORE A NOTARY PUBLIC IS NOT ESSENTIAL TO THE EFFECTIVENESS OF A DEED, BUT IT IS TYPICALLY REQUIRED IN ORDER TO QUALIFY THE DEED FOR RECORDING.]

FIGURE 53-1
FORM OF WARRANTY DEED

BLAGG V FRED HUNT COMPANY, INC.
(Ark) 612 SW2d 321 (1981)

Fred Hunt Company was a building contractor. It purchased a tract of land on which it built a house that it sold to the Dentons in December,

1978. They sold it to the American Foundation Life Insurance Company which in June, 1979, sold the property to J. T. Blagg and his wife Kathye. Shortly after the Blaggs moved into the house, they smelled a strong odor coming from the carpeting. The Blaggs sued Fred Hunt. In the first part or count of their complaint, they claimed that Fred Hunt was liable for breach of the implied warranty of habitability. In the second part or count of their complaint, they asserted that Fred Hunt was liable for strict tort. The lower court dismissed the implied warranty claim and sustained the strict tort claim. The Blaggs appealed, and Fred Hunt filed a cross appeal.

Dudley, J. [The appellants, the Blaggs, purchased the house] . . . a few days less than 9 months after the date of the original sale. The appellants filed a two-count complaint alleging that after they purchased the home a strong odor and fumes from formaldehyde became apparent. They traced this defect to the carpet and pad which was installed by appellee. A motion to dismiss was filed by the appellee and the trial court granted the motion on count one of the complaint, the implied warranty count, on the basis of lack of privity. The court denied the motion on count two, which is framed in terms of strict liability.

Count one of the complaint is based upon an implied warranty. The trial judge dismissed this count because the appellants are not in privity with the appellee. This court, in *Wawak v Stewart*, 247 Ark 1093, 449 SW2d 922 (1970), abandoned the doctrine of caveat emptor and took the view that a builder-vendor impliedly warranted the home to the first purchaser. The issue of first impression in this case is whether the liability of the builder-vendor should be extended to a second or third purchaser.

Since *Wawak*, the original homebuyer has been able to place reliance on the builder-vendor's implied warranty. This has protected that investment which, in most instances, represents the family's largest single expenditure.

We find no reason that those same basic concepts should not be extended to subsequent purchasers of real estate. This is an area of the law being developed on a case by case basis. Our ruling is based on the complaint before us and involves a home which had a defect that became apparent to the third purchasers, the appellants, within 9 months of the original sale date. Obviously, there is a point in time beyond which the implied warranty will expire and that time should be based on a standard of reasonableness.

We hold that the builder-vendor's implied warranty of fitness for habitation runs not only in favor of the first owner, but extends to subsequent purchasers for a reasonable length of time where there is no substantial change or alteration in the condition of the building from the original sale. This implied warranty is limited to latent defects which are not discoverable by subsequent purchasers upon reasonable inspection and which become manifest only after the purchase. Wyoming adopted this rule in a well reasoned opinion. *Moxley v Laramie Builders, Inc.* 600 P2d 733 (Wyo 1979).

. . .

We hold that count one of the complaint should not have been dismissed.

Appellee, in its cross-appeal, contends that the trial judge committed error in not dismissing count two of the complaint, the claim for damages under strict liability. We affirm the trial judge's ruling.

Our strict liability statute, Ark Stat Ann § 85-2-318.2 (Supp 1979) is as follows:

Liability of Supplier — Conditions. — A supplier of a product is subject to liability in damages for harm to a person or to property if:

(a) the supplier is engaged in the business of manufacturing, assembling, selling, leasing or otherwise distributing such product;
(b) the product was supplied by him in a defective condition which rendered it unreasonably dangerous; and
(c) the defective condition was a proximate cause of the harm to person or to property. [Acts 1973, No 111, § 1, p 331]

This 1973 act broadens somewhat § 402A of the Restatement, Second, Torts (1965).

Our first issue is whether this strict liability statute encompasses count two of the complaint. . . . We must choose between the persuasive reasoning of two outstanding jurists — Chief Justice Traynor in *Seely v White Motor Company*, 63 Cal 2d 9, 403 P2d 145, 45 Cal Rptr 17 (1965), and Justice Francis in *Santor v A & M Karagheusian, Inc.* 44 NJ 52, 207 A2d 305 (1965). If the Traynor view is adopted, the implied warranty will be very much alive when a purchaser is suing for purely economic loss from a defective product. His view, as stated in *Seely*, supra, is that when economic losses result from commercial transactions, as here, the parties should be relegated to the law of sales:

Although the rules governing warranties complicated resolution of the problems of personal injuries, there is no reason to conclude that they do not meet the "needs of commercial transactions." The law of warranty "grew as a branch of the law of commercial transactions and was primarily aimed at controlling the commercial aspects of these transactions."

. . .

Although the rules of warranty frustrate rational compensation for physical injury, they function well in a commercial setting.

Justice Francis, in *Santor*, supra, prophetically extended the doctrine in a case involving carpeting that developed a defect, a purely economic loss, not a personal injury. In applying the doctrine of strict liability for purely economic loss he said:

The obligation of the manufacturer thus becomes what in justice it ought to be — an enterprise liability, and one which should not depend on the law of sales. . . .

Quoting further:

As we have indicated, the strict liability in tort formulation of the nature of the manufacturer's burden to expected consumers of his product represents a sound solution to an ever-growing problem, and we accept it as applicable in this jurisdiction. And, although the doctrine has been applied principally in connection with personal injuries sustained by expected users from products which are dangerous when defective, we reiterate our agreement with *Randy Knitwear, Inc. v American Cyanamid Company*, [11 NY2d 5, 226 NYS2d 363, 181 NE2d 399 (1962)] that the responsibility of the maker should be no different where damage to the article sold or to other property of the consumer is involved. . . . In this era of complex marketing practices and assembly line manufacturing conditions, restrictive notions of privity of contract between manufacturer and consumer must be put aside and the realistic view [adopted by which a remote purchaser may recover from the manufacturer of a product for loss sustained because of a defect in the product, even though privity of contract is lacking between the purchaser and the manufacturer].

[Judgment reversed as to warranty count and affirmed as to strict tort liability count]

QUESTIONS

1. What was the relationship between the Blaggs and the Fred Hunt Company?
2. What was the reason given by the court in support of its decision as to the defense of lack of privity?
3. What was the strategy of the plaintiff in asserting both an implied warranty and a strict tort claim?

§ 53:25 GRANTEE'S COVENANTS

In a deed, the grantee may agree to do or to refrain from doing certain acts. Such an agreement becomes a binding contract between the grantor and the grantee. The grantor may sue the grantee for its breach. When the covenant of the grantee relates directly to the property conveyed, such as an agreement to maintain fences on the property or that the property shall be used only for residential purposes, it is said not only that the covenant is binding between the grantor and the grantee but also that it **runs with the land.** This means that anyone acquiring the land from the grantee is also bound by the covenant of the grantee, even though this subsequent owner had not made any such agreement with anyone.

The right to enforce the covenant also runs with the land owned by the grantor to whom the promise was made. Thus, if *A* owns adjoining tracts of land and conveys one of them to *B* and if *B* covenants to maintain the surface drainage on the land so that it will not flood *A*'s land, the benefit of this covenant will run with the land retained by *A*. If *A* sells the remaining tract of land to *C*, *B* is bound to perform the covenant so as to benefit the neighboring tract even though it is now owned by *C*.

A covenant that provides that the grantee shall refrain from certain conduct is termed a **restrictive** (or negative) **covenant.** It runs with the land in the same manner as a covenant that calls for the performance of an act, that is, an **affirmative covenant.**

§ 53:26 SCOPE OF GRANTEE'S RESTRICTIVE COVENANTS

A **restrictive covenant** may impose a limitation on the kind of structure that can be erected on the land and may also impose a limitation on the use that may be made of the land.

(a) GENERAL BUILDING SCHEME. When a tract of land is developed and when individual lots or homes are sold to separate purchasers, it is common to use the same restrictive covenants in all deeds in order to impose uniform restrictions and patterns on the property. Any person acquiring a lot within the tract is bound by the restrictions if they are in the deed or a prior recorded deed, or if the grantee has notice or knowledge of such restrictions. Any person owning one of the lots in the tract may bring suit against another lot owner to enforce the restrictive covenant. The effect is to create a zoning code based upon the agreement of the parties in their deeds, as distinguished from one based upon government regulation.

(b) RESTRAINTS ON ALIENATION. The covenants may restrict the sale or transfer of the property. It is lawful to provide that the grantor shall have the option to repurchase the property, or that if the grantee offers to sell it to anyone, the grantor will be given an opportunity to match the price that a third person is willing to pay. Restrictions on the grantee's right to sell the property are not enforceable when the restriction discriminates against potential buyers because of race, color, creed, or national origin.

F.   OTHER METHODS OF TRANSFERRING REAL PROPERTY

Title to real property can also be acquired by eminent domain and by adverse possession.

§ 53:27   EMINENT DOMAIN

By **eminent domain** property is taken from its private owner and the title is acquired by the taking government or public authority. Two important questions arise: namely, whether there is a taking of property, and whether the property is taken for a public use. In respect to the first, it is not necessary that the owner be physically deprived of the property. It is sufficient that the normal use of the property has been impaired or lost. As to the second, it is not necessary that the public at large actually use the property. It is sufficient that it is appropriated for the public benefit.

§ 53:28   ADVERSE POSSESSION

Title to land may be acquired by holding it adversely to the true owner for a certain period of time. In such a case, the possessor gains title by **adverse possession.** If such possession is maintained, the possessor automatically becomes the owner of the property, even though the possessor admittedly had no lawful claim to the land.

In order to acquire title in this manner, possession must be (a) actual, (b) visible and notorious, (c) exclusive, (d) hostile, and (e) continuous for a required period of time.[14]

Commonly the period of time is 21 years, but state statutes may provide 10 to 20 years. Occupation of land in the mistaken belief that one is the owner is a "hostile" possession.

A claim of hostile possession was made in the *Meyers* case.

[14] Perivoliotis v Pierson, ___ Ill App 3d ___, ___ Ill Dec ___, 521 NE2d 254 (1988).

MEYERS V MEYERS
(Minn App) 368 NW2d 391 (1985)

Bernadine Meyers and Robert Meyers moved into the latter's house in 1947 after their marriage. In 1948, Robert enlisted in the army and moved to California while Bernadine remained in the home and cared for Robert's father until his death in 1950. When Robert returned for the funeral of his father, he and Bernadine had a violent argument. Robert was removed from the house by the police. He subsequently obtained a divorce from Bernadine in 1954. There was no mention in the divorce decree about the real estate. Numerous improvements were made to the house by Bernadine, and she paid taxes on the property for some time. When Robert instructed the taxing authorities to send property tax statements to his California address, Bernadine brought an action contending that she owned the property by adverse possession. From a judgment in favor of Bernadine, Robert appealed.

RANDALL, P. J. . . . Robert paid child support until 1957. In 1957 a dispute arose over the support. In a mediation attempt, a United States Army officer wrote Bernadine on Robert's behalf. He proposed that Robert pay $100 per month as child support, and deed the house to Bernadine. In exchange, she would return some personal property to Robert. Bernadine never replied to the offer. She testified that she made no reply on an attorney's advice.

Bernadine made significant improvements to the house in 1950. In addition, she has maintained the house and made minor repairs since that time. Robert paid the property taxes on the house through the first half of 1960, but Bernadine has paid the taxes since then.

Robert did not return to Minnesota from the time of his father's funeral in 1950 until 1979. In 1979 he indicated to Bernadine and the children that he thought he had deeded the house to the children. When informed otherwise, he told them he wanted the children to have it. When the children suggested he deed it to Bernadine instead, he said, "I'll burn it down first." Robert instructed local authorities to begin sending property tax statements to his California address, and Bernadine brought this action asking either for an equitable division of the property or reimbursement for improvements made, or for a declaration that she owned the property by virtue of adverse possession. The trial court ruled only on the adverse possession issue, finding that Bernadine owned the property.

Was the evidence sufficient to sustain the trial court's finding that Bernadine acquired ownership of appellant's house by adverse possession?

To establish title by adverse possession, the adverse possessor must show by clear and convincing evidence an actual, open, hostile, continuous, and exclusive possession for 15 years. *Wojahn v. Johnson*, 297 N.W.2d 298 (Minn.1980). At least from 1950 to 1979, Bernadine's possession was actual, open, continuous, and exclusive. All five elements are equally necessary, however, and if her possession was not hostile to Robert's title, her claim must fail.

Robert contends Bernadine's possession of the house throughout the more than 15 years was permissive. The *Wojahn* court said:

> The general rule of law is that the existence of a family relationship between the claimant of land and the record owner . . . creates the inference, if not the presumption, that the original possession by the claimant of the other's land was permissive and not adverse . . . ; and that when such original use was thus permissive, it would be presumed permissive, rather than hostile, until the contrary was affirmatively shown.

Here, the facts, as well as the "inference" referred to in *Wojahn*, establish that Bernadine's initial possession of the property was permissive. Once initial possession is permissive, proof of the inception of possession which is hostile to the record owner's title must be clear and unequivocal.

> Where the original entry is permissive, the statute does not begin to run against the legal owner until an adverse holding is declared and notice of such change is brought to the knowledge of the owner. . . . While it is true that assertion of adverse title need not be always expressly or affirmatively declared, but may be shown by circumstances, . . . proof of inception of hostility must in all cases be clear and unequivocal. *Johnson v. Raddohl*, 226 Minn. 343, 32 N.W.2d 860 (1948).

The trial court found that the 1950 argument after which Robert was removed from the house was a declaration of Bernadine's adverse holding, of which Robert had notice. We disagree. Because one spouse has the other removed from the home during a domestic dispute does not mean that the spouse who remains in the home now possesses the house adversely to the ejected spouse's title. Such a holding could substantially interfere in property rights between married couples. Courts could become reluctant to allow the legitimate temporary relief of ejectment that spouses are entitled to if they show domestic abuse because of concerns over alienating title.

Robert continuously paid all real estate taxes due until 1960, which period includes ten years after the argument in the home. During those ten years, there was neither oral nor written indication from Bernadine that she claimed the house as hers, and she allowed Robert to pay the real estate taxes while she and the children continued to live there. The 1950 incident simply did not rise to the level of a declaration of an adverse holding strong enough to commence the 15-year period needed to claim under adverse possession.

Bernadine argues that, even if the 1950 incident did not rise to that level, her failure to respond to the 1957 offer Robert made through a mediating army officer did. The *Johnson* court stated, however, the *notice* of a declaration of an adverse holding must be brought to the attention of the record owner. If Bernadine's silence was, in her own mind, a declaration that she held the property adversely to Robert's title, she never gave him notice of her intent. Again, for at least three years after Robert's offer he continuously paid the real estate taxes on the home with no indication by her that she claimed partial or full ownership adversely to Robert. The 1957 support and property settlement negotiations could not, therefore, start the running of the 15-year period.

After 1960, Robert stopped paying the property taxes. Bernadine never took any steps, however, to give him notice that she was claiming the property as her own. Although equitably a strong argument can be made that Robert abandoned the property, the law is clear that legal title to realty is never lost by abandonment.

At trial, Bernadine testified that she never told Robert prior to the commencement of this lawsuit that she felt she owned the house, and that she never told anyone else that she felt she owned the house. She testified that she, in fact, never claimed to have title to the property, and that neither while raising the children nor after they grew up did she do anything different with the house that might reasonably put Robert or anyone else on notice that she was asserting an ownership claim. Bernadine has failed to show that her permissive use of the property became hostile, and thus the finding of adverse possession cannot be sustained. . . .

[Judgment reversed and action remanded]

QUESTIONS

1. Were all the elements present to constitute adverse possession?
2. Can silence amount to a notice of a declaration of holding property adversely?
3. Did Robert abandon the property?

G.   MORTGAGES

An agreement that creates an interest in real property as security for an obligation and which is to cease upon the performance of the obligation is a **mortgage**. The person whose interest in the property is given as security is the **mortgagor**. The person who receives the security is the **mortgagee**.

§ 53:29   CHARACTERISTICS OF A MORTGAGE

There are three characteristics of a mortgage: (a) the termination of the mortgagee's interest upon the performance of the obligation secured by the mortgage; (b) the right of the mortgagee to enforce the mortgage by foreclosure upon the mortgagor's failure to perform; and (c) the mortgagor's right to redeem or regain the property. In any case, however, the intention of the parties determines whether there is a mortgage.

§ 53:30   PROPERTY SUBJECT TO MORTGAGE

In general, any form of property that may be sold or conveyed may be mortgaged. It is immaterial whether the right is a present right or a future interest, or merely a right in the land of another. It is not necessary that the mortgagor have complete or absolute ownership in the property. The mortgagor may mortgage any interest, legal or equitable, divided or undivided.

§ 53:31   FORM OF MORTGAGE

As a mortgage upon real property transfers an interest in the property, it must be in writing by virtue of the statute of frauds.

As a general rule, no particular form of language is required, provided the language used expresses the intent of the parties to create a mortgage. In many states, the substance of a mortgage is practically identical to that of a deed with the exception that a mortgage contains a defeasance clause, a description of the obligation secured, and sometimes a covenant to pay or perform the obligation. The **defeasance clause** states that the mortgage shall cease to have any effect when the obligation is performed, as when the debt of the mortgagor is paid. In many states, statutes provide a standardized form of mortgage that may be used.

§ 53:32   RECORDING OR FILING OF MORTGAGE

An unrecorded mortgage is valid and binding between the parties to it. The heirs or donees of a mortgagor cannot defend against the mortgage on the ground that it has not been recorded. Recording statutes in most states, however, provide that purchasers or creditors who give value and act in good faith in ignorance of an unrecorded mortgage may enforce their respective rights against the property without regard to the existence of the unrecorded mortgage. Accordingly, the purchaser of the land in good faith for value from the mortgagor holds the land free of the unrecorded mortgage, and the mortgagee's only remedy is against the mortgagor on the debt due the mortgagee. The mortgagee can proceed against the transferee only if the mortgagee can prove that the transferee of the land did not purchase it in good faith, for value, and in ignorance of the unrecorded mortgage.

§ 53:33   REPAIRS AND IMPROVEMENTS

In the absence of an agreement to the contrary, a mortgagor is under no duty to make improvements or to restore or repair parts of the premises that are destroyed or damaged through no fault of the mortgagor.

A mortgagee, when in possession, must make reasonable and necessary repairs in order to preserve the property. The mortgagee is entitled to reimbursement for such repairs. Ordinarily, however, the mortgagee may not charge to the mortgagor expenditures for valuable or enduring improvements.

§ 53:34 Taxes, Assessments, and Insurance

The duty to pay taxes and assessments rests upon the mortgagor. In the absence of an agreement, neither party is under a duty to insure the mortgaged property. Both parties, however, may insure their respective interests. It is common practice for the mortgagor to obtain a single policy of insurance on the property payable to the mortgagee and the mortgagor as their interests may appear.

§ 53:35 Impairment of Security

The mortgagor is liable to the mortgagee for any damage to the property, caused by the mortgagor's fault, that impairs the security of the mortgage by materially reducing the value of the property. Both the mortgagor and the mortgagee have a right of action against a third person who wrongfully injures the property.

§ 53:36 Transfer of Interest

Questions arise as to transfers by the mortgagor and the mortgagee of their respective interests and of the liability of a transferee of the mortgagor.

(a) Transfer by Mortgagor. The mortgagor may ordinarily transfer the land without the consent of the mortgagee. Such a transfer passes only the interest of the mortgagor and does not divest or impair the mortgage if properly recorded.

The transfer of the property by the mortgagor does not affect the liability of the mortgagor to the mortgagee. Unless the latter has agreed to substitute the mortgagor's grantee for the mortgagor, the latter remains liable for the mortgage debt as though no transfer had been made.

(b) Liability of Mortgagor's Transferee. The purchaser of mortgaged property does not become personally liable for the mortgage debt unless the purchaser expressly assumes that debt. Such an assumption of the debt does not release the mortgagor from liability to the mortgagee unless the mortgagee agrees to such substitution of parties.

(c) Transfer by Mortgagee. In most states, a mortgage may be transferred or assigned by the mortgagee.

§ 53:37 Rights of Mortgagee After Default

Upon the mortgagor's default, the mortgagee in some states is entitled to obtain possession of the property and collect the rents[15] or to have a receiver appointed for that purpose. In all states, the mortgagee may enforce the mortgage by **foreclosure** or sue to enforce the mortgage debt.

Generally, it is provided that upon any default under the terms of the mortgage agreement, the mortgagee has the right to declare that the entire mortgage debt is due even though the default related only to an installment or to the doing of some act, such as maintaining insurance on the property or producing receipts for taxes.

A sale on the foreclosure of the mortgage destroys the mortgage, and the property passes free of the mortgage to the buyer at the sale. But the extinction of the mortgage by foreclosure does not destroy the debt that was secured by the mortgage. The mortgagor remains liable for any unpaid balance or deficiency; although by statute, the mortgagor is generally given credit for the fair value of the property if it was purchased by the mortgagee.

§ 53:38 Rights of Mortgagor After Default

After default the mortgagor may seek to stop or stay foreclosure or to redeem the mortgaged land.

(a) Stay of Foreclosure. In certain

---

[15] Pine Lawn Bank and Trust Co. v M. H. & H. Inc. (Mo App) 607 SW2d 696 (1980).

cases, authorized by statute, a **stay** (or delay) **of foreclosure** may be obtained by the mortgagor to prevent undue hardship.

(b) REDEMPTION. The **right of redemption** means the right of the mortgagor to free the property of the mortgage lien after default. By statute in many states, the right may be exercised during a certain time following foreclosure and sale of the mortgaged land.

SUMMARY

Real property includes land, buildings and fixtures, and rights in the land of another such as easements.

The interest held by a person in real property may be defined in terms of the period of time for which such person will remain the owner. The interest may be a fee simple estate, which lasts forever, or a life estate, which lasts for the life of a person. These estates are known as freehold estates. If the ownership interest exists for a specified number of days, months, or years, the interest is a leasehold estate.

Personal property may be attached to or associated with real property in such a way that it becomes real property. In such a case it is called a fixture. To determine whether property has in fact become a fixture, the courts look to the method of attachment, to how the property is adapted to the realty, and to the intent of the person attaching the property.

Under common law, the liability of an occupier of land for injury to third persons on the premises is dependent upon the status of the third persons as trespassers, licensees, or invitees. Many jurisdictions are ignoring these common-law distinctions, however, in favor of an ordinary negligence standard.

Real property may be the subject of multiple ownership. The forms of multiple ownership are the same as for personal property. In addition, there are special forms of co-ownership for real property, such as condominiums and cooperatives.

A deed is an instrument transferring an interest in land by a grantor to a grantee. A deed can be a quitclaim deed, a warranty deed, or a statutory deed. A deed, to be effective, must be signed or sealed by the grantor and delivered to the grantee. Recording the deed is not required to make the deed effective to pass title but provides notice to the public that the grantee is the present owner. The warranties of the grantor relate to the title transferred by the grantor and to the fitness of the property for use. Absent any express warranty in the deed, no warranty of fitness arises under the common law in the sale or the conveyance of real estate. A substantial number of states today hold that when the builder or real estate developer sells a new home to a home buyer, an implied warranty of habitability arises. Title to real estate may also be acquired by eminent domain and adverse possession.

An agreement that creates an interest in real property as security for an obligation and that ends upon the performance of the obligation is a mortgage. A mortgage must be in writing under the statute of frauds. If the mortgage is unrecorded, it is valid between the parties. The mortgage should be recorded to put good faith purchasers on notice of the mortgage. A purchaser of the mortgaged property does not become liable for the mortgaged debt unless such purchaser assumes the mortgage. The mortgagor still remains liable unless the mortgagee agrees to a substitution of parties. If the mortgagor defaults, the mortgagee may enforce the mortgage by foreclosure. Such foreclosure may be delayed because of undue hardship.

QUESTIONS AND CASE PROBLEMS

1. What social forces are affected by recognizing the right of aircraft to fly over land at such a height that the flight does not interfere with the use of the land and is not dangerous to persons or property on the land?

2. Price sued Whisnant for cutting and removing trees from certain land. Price claimed title to the land by adverse possession. He proved that for over 20 years he had from time to time entered on the land and cut and removed trees. Was Price the owner of the land by adverse possession? [Price v Whisnant, 236 NC 381, 72 SE2d 851]

3. Cindy owned and operated a jewelry store. She moved the store into a new building in which she rented space for five years. She moved her showcases, chairs, lighting fixtures, and other equipment from her original store to the newly rented store. When the lease expired at the end of the five years, Cindy moved out and was about to take the showcases, chairs, lighting fixtures, and other equipment with her. The landlord objected and claimed that those items had become fixtures and that, therefore, Cindy was required to leave them when she left. Was the landlord correct?

4. Compare (a) an easement, (b) a profit, and (c) a fixture.

5. Compare the status of an "apartment owner" in (a) a condominium and (b) a cooperative.

6. What is the most important difference between a license and an easement?

7. Bradham and others, trustees of the Mount Olivet Church, brought an action to cancel a mortgage on the church property that had been executed by Davis and others as trustees of the church and given to Robinson as mortgagee. It was found by the court that the church was not indebted to the mortgagee for any amount. Should the mortgage be canceled? [Bradham v Robinson, 236 NC 589, 73 SE2d 555]

8. Miller executed a deed to real estate naming Mary Zieg as grantee. He placed the deed in an envelope upon which was written, "To be filed at my death," and put the envelope and deed in a safe deposit box in the National Bank. The box had been rented in the names of Miller and Mary Zieg. After Miller's death Mary removed the deed from the safe deposit box. Moseley, as executor under Miller's will, brought an action against Mary to declare the deed void. Decide. [Moseley v Zieg, 180 Neb 810, 146 NW2d 72]

9. Henry Lile owned a house. When the land on which it was situated was condemned for a highway, he removed the house to the land of his daughter, Sarah Crick. In the course of construction work, blasting damaged the house and Sarah Crick sued the contractors, Terry & Wright. They claimed that Henry should be joined in the action as a plaintiff and that Sarah could not sue by herself because it was Henry's house. Were the defendants correct? [Terry & Wright v Crick (Ky) 418 SW2d 217]

10. Sears, Roebuck and Co. supplied the Seven Palms Motor Inn with window curtains and rods and matching bedspreads. When payment was not made, Sears claimed that these were fixtures for which a mechanic's lien could be asserted. Were they fixtures?

11. Larry Wiersema was building a house for himself in the country. He made a contract with Workman Plumbing, Heating & Cooling, Inc., to do most of the plumbing and heating work in the new house. This work included the installation of a septic tank. Workman performed the contract correctly; however, because of the peculiar kind of clay surrounding the house, the drainage from the septic tank system was very poor, and the basement of Larry's house was frequently flooded. He sued Workman for breach of the implied warranty of habitability. Was Workman liable? [Wiersema v Workman Plumbing, Heating & Cooling, Inc. 87 Ill App 3d 535, 42 Ill Dec 664, 409 NE2d 159]

12. Davis Store Fixtures sold certain equipment on credit to Head, who installed it in a building that was later owned by the Cadillac Club. When payment was not made, Davis sought to repossess the equipment. If the equipment constituted fixtures, this could not be done. The equipment consisted of a bar for serving drinks, a bench, and a drain board. The first two were attached to

the floor or wall with screws, and the drain board was connected to water and drainage pipes. Did the equipment constitute fixtures?

13. Smikahl sold to Hansen a tract of land on which there were two houses and four trailer lots equipped with concrete patios and necessary connections for utility lines. The tract purchased by Hansen was completely surrounded by the land owned by Smikahl and third persons. In order to get onto the highway, it was necessary to cross the Smikahl tract. Several years later, Smikahl put a barbed wire fence around his land. Hansen sued to prevent obstruction to travel between his land and the highway over the Smikahl land. Smikahl defended on the ground that no such right of travel had been given to Hansen. Was he correct? [Hansen v Smikahl, 173 Neb 309, 113 NW2d 210]

14. Martin Manufacturing decided to raise additional long-term capital by mortgaging an industrial park that it owned. First National Loan Company agreed to lend Martin $1 million and to take a note and first mortgage on the land and building. The mortgage was duly recorded. Martin sold the property to Marshall, who took the property subject to the mortgage debt. Does Marshall have any personal liability on the mortgage indebtedness? Explain.

15. In 1980, Ortleb, Inc., a Delaware corporation, purchased certain land in Montana from the Alberts but neglected to record the deed. In 1988, the Alberts sold the same property to Bently, a resident of Montana, who purchased in good faith and recorded his deed. Ortleb sues Bently to resolve the title question. Who will win? Explain.

54

LEASES

A lease is an arrangement by which one person has for a time the possession and benefit of real property owned by another.

A. CREATION AND TERMINATION

Leases are governed by the common law of property as modified by judicial decisions and statutes.[1]

§ 54:1 DEFINITION AND NATURE

The agreement by which one person holds possession of the real property owned by

---

[1] A uniform act, the Uniform Residential Landlord and Tenant Act (URLTA), has been adopted in Alaska, Arizona, Florida, Hawaii, Iowa, Kansas, Kentucky, Montana, Nebraska, New Mexico, Oregon, Rhode Island, South Carolina, Tennessee, and Virginia.

another is a **lease**.

The person who owns the real property and permits the occupation of the premises is known as the **lessor**, or **landlord**. The **lessee**, or **tenant**, is the one who occupies the property. A **lease** establishes the relationship of landlord and tenant.

Basically, a lease parallels a bailment in which there is an agreement to make the bailment and a subsequent transfer of possession to carry out that agreement. In the case of a lease, there is the lease contract and the interest thereafter acquired by the tenant when possession is delivered under the lease contract. The common law looked at the transfer of possession and regarded the lease as merely the creation of an interest in land. The modern law looks at the contract and regards the lease as the same as the renting of an automobile. With this new approach, typical contract law concepts of unconscionability, mitigation of damages, and the implication of warranties are brought into the law of leases.

§ 54:2   CREATION OF THE LEASE RELATIONSHIP

The relationship of landlord and tenant is created by an express or implied contract. An oral lease is valid at common law, but statutes in most states require written leases for certain tenancies. Many states provide that a lease for a term exceeding three years must be in writing. Statutes in other states require written leases when the term exceeds one year.

(a) ANTIDISCRIMINATION. Statutes in many states prohibit an owner who rents property for profit from discriminating against prospective tenants on the basis of race, color, religion, or national origin. Enforcement of such statutes is generally entrusted to an administrative agency.

(b) COVENANTS AND CONDITIONS. Some obligations of the parties in the lease are described as covenants. Thus, a promise by the tenant to make repairs is called a **covenant to repair.** Sometimes it is provid-

ed that the lease shall be forfeited or terminated upon a breach of a promise, and that provision is then called a **condition** rather than a covenant.

(c) OTHER AGREEMENTS. The lease may be the only agreement between the parties. In contrast, there may also be a separate guaranty or a letter of credit to protect the landlord from breach by the tenant. The tenant, in addition to holding under the lease may also hold a franchise from the lessor.

(d) UNCONSCIONABILITY. At common law, the parties to a lease had relatively uncontrolled freedom to include such terms as they chose. As the lease is increasingly treated as a contract, some states require that leases conform to the concept of conscionability and follow the pattern of UCC § 2-302.[2] A provision in a residential lease stating that curtailment of services by the landlord will not constitute an eviction unless caused willfully or by gross negligence and that such interruption will not entitle the tenant to any compensation is unconscionable and does not bar the tenant from suing for breach of the implied warranty of habitability. Similarly, a provision in a lease declaring that the landlord is not responsible for interruptions in the various services provided tenants will not protect the landlord when the air-conditioning system is out of operation for six weeks in midsummer.

§ 54:3   ESSENTIAL ELEMENTS

The following elements are necessary to the establishment of the relation of landlord and tenant:

(a) The occupying of the land must be with the express or implied consent of the landlord.
(b) The tenant must occupy the premises in subordination to the rights of the landlord.

---

[2]   Flam v Herrmann, 90 Misc 2d 434, 395 NYS2d 136 (1977); URLTA § 1.303.

(c) A reversionary interest in the land must remain in the landlord. That is, the landlord must be entitled to retake the possession of the land upon the expiration of the lease.

(d) The tenant must have an estate of present possession in the land. This means a right to be in possession of the land now.

§ 54:4   CLASSIFICATION OF TENANCIES

Tenancies are classified by duration as tenancies for years, from year to year, at will, and by sufferance.

(a) TENANCY FOR YEARS. A **tenancy for years** is one under which the tenant has an estate of definite duration. The term "for years" is used to describe such a tenancy even though the duration of the tenancy is for only one year or for less than a year.

(b) TENANCY FROM YEAR TO YEAR. A **tenancy from year to year** is one under which a tenant, holding an estate in land for an indefinite duration, pays an annual, monthly, or weekly rent. A distinguishing feature of this tenancy is the fact that it does not terminate at the end of a year, month, or week except upon proper notice.

In almost all states a tenancy from year to year is implied if the tenant holds over after a tenancy for years with the consent of the landlord. This consent may be shown by an express statement or by conduct such as continuing to accept rent.[3] The lease will frequently state that a holding over shall give rise to a tenancy from year to year unless written notice to the contrary is given.

(c) TENANCY AT WILL. When land is held for an indefinite period, which may be ter-

minated at any time by the landlord or the tenant, a **tenancy at will** exists. A person who enters into possession of land for an indefinite period with the owner's permission but without any agreement as to rent is a tenant at will.

Statutes in some states and decisions in others require advance notice of termination of this kind of tenancy.

(d) TENANCY BY SUFFERANCE. When a tenant holds over without permission of the landlord, the latter may treat the tenant as a trespasser or as a tenant. Until the landlord elects to do one or the other, a **tenancy by sufferance** exists.

§ 54:5   TERMINATION OF LEASE

A lease is generally not terminated by the death, insanity, or bankruptcy of either party, except in the case of a tenancy at will. Provisions in a lease giving the landlord the right to terminate the lease under certain conditions are generally strictly construed.

Leases may be terminated in the following ways:

(a) TERMINATION BY NOTICE. A lease may give the landlord the power to terminate it by giving notice to the tenant. In states that follow the common law, it is immaterial why the landlord terminates the lease by notice.

(b) EXPIRATION OF TERM IN A TENANCY FOR YEARS. When a tenancy for years exists, the relation of landlord and tenant ceases upon the expiration of the term, without any requirement that one party give the other any notice of termination. Express notice to end the term may be required of either or both parties by provisions of the lease, except when a statute prohibits the landlord from imposing such a requirement.

(c) NOTICE IN A TENANCY FROM YEAR TO YEAR. In the absence of an agreement of the parties, notice is now usually governed by statute. It is common practice for the parties to require 30 or 60 days' notice to end a tenancy from year to year. As to ten-

---

[3]   In some jurisdictions, when rent is accepted from a tenant holding over after the expiration of the term of the lease and there is no agreement to the contrary, there results only a periodic tenancy from month to month rather than a tenancy from year to year. S.D.G. v Inventory Control Co. 178 NJ Super 411, 429 A2d 394 (1981).

ancies for periods of less than a year, the provisions of the statutes commonly require notice of only one week.

(d) RELEASE. The relation of landlord and tenant is terminated if the landlord makes a release or conveyance of the landlord's interest in the land to the tenant.

(e) MERGER. If the tenant acquires the landlord's interest in any manner, as by inheritance or purchase, the leasehold interest is said to disappear by merger into the title to the land now held by the former tenant.

The lease may give the tenant an option to purchase the property at any time or upon the expiration of the term of the lease, or may provide that the lessor shall offer to sell to the tenant before offering to sell the property to anyone else.[4]

(f) SURRENDER. A surrender or giving up of the tenant's estate to the landlord terminates the tenancy if the surrender is accepted by the landlord.[5] A surrender may be made expressly or may be implied. An express surrender must, under the statute of frauds, be in writing and be signed by the person making the surrender or by an authorized agent.

(g) FORFEITURE. The landlord may terminate the lease by forfeiting the relation because of the tenant's misconduct or breach of a condition, if a term of the lease or a statute so provides. In the absence of such a provision, the landlord may only claim damages for the breach. Terminating the relationship by forfeiture is not favored by the courts.

(h) DESTRUCTION OF PROPERTY. If a lot and building on it are leased, either an express provision in the lease or a statute generally releases the tenant from liability when the building is destroyed, or reduces the amount of rent in proportion to the loss sustained. Such statutes do not impose upon the landlord any duty to repair or restore the property to its former condition.

When the lease covers rooms or an apartment in a building, a destruction of the leased premises terminates the lease.

(i) FRAUD. As a lease is based upon a contract, a lease may be avoided when the circumstances are such that a contract could be avoided for fraud.

(j) TRANSFER OF THE TENANT. Residential leases may contain a provision for termination upon the tenant's being transferred by an employer to another city or upon the tenant's being called into military service. Such provisions are often strictly construed against the tenant; therefore, the tenant should exercise care to see that the provision is sufficiently broad to cover the situations that may arise.

§ 54:6   NOTICE OF TERMINATION

When notice of termination is required, no particular words are necessary to constitute a sufficient notice, provided the words used clearly indicate the intention of the party. The notice, whether given by the landlord or the tenant, must be definite. Statutes sometimes require that the notice be in writing. In the absence of such a provision, however, oral notice is generally held to be sufficient.

§ 54:7   RENEWAL OF LEASE

When a lease terminates for any reason, it is ordinarily a matter for the landlord and the tenant to enter into a new agreement if they wish to extend or renew the lease. The power to renew the lease may be stated negatively in the original lease by declaring that the lease runs indefinitely, as from year to year, subject to being terminated by either party by giving written notice a specified number of days or months before the termination date.

The lease may require the tenant to give written notice of the intention to renew the lease. In such case, there is no renewal if the tenant does not give the required no-

---

[4] Moore v Dodge (Tex Civ App) 603 SW2d 236 (1980).
[5] Roosen v Schaffer, 127 Ariz App 346, 621 P2d 33 (1980).

tice, but merely remains on the premises after the expiration of the original term.[6]

B. RIGHTS AND DUTIES OF PARTIES

The rights and duties of the landlord and tenant are based upon principles of real estate law and contract law. With the rising tide of consumer protectionism, the tendency is increasing to treat the relationship as merely a contract and to govern the rights and duties of the parties by general principles of contract law.

§ 54:8 POSSESSION

Possession involves both the right to acquire possession at the beginning of the lease and the right to retain possession until the lease is ended.

(a) TENANT'S RIGHT TO ACQUIRE POSSESSION. By making a lease, the lessor covenants by implication to give possession of the premises to the tenant at the agreed time. If the landlord rents a building that is being constructed, there is an implied covenant that it will be ready for occupancy at the commencement of the term of the lease.

(b) TENANT'S RIGHT TO RETAIN POSSESSION. After the tenant has entered into possession, the tenant has the exclusive possession and control of the premises as long as the lease continues and so long as there is no default under the lease, unless the lease otherwise provides. Thus, the tenant can refuse to allow the lessor to enter the property for the purpose of showing it to prospective customers, although today most leases expressly give this right to the landlord.

If the landlord interferes with this possession by evicting the tenant, the landlord commits a wrong for which the tenant is afforded legal redress. An **eviction** occurs when the tenant is deprived of the possession, use, and enjoyment of the premises by

the interference of the lessor or the lessor's agent. If the landlord wrongfully deprives the tenant of the use of one room when the tenant is entitled to use an entire apartment or building, there is a **partial eviction.**

(c) COVENANT OF QUIET ENJOYMENT. Most written leases today contain an express promise by the landlord to respect the possession of the tenant, called a **covenant of quiet enjoyment.** Such a provision protects the tenant from interference with possession by the landlord or the landlord's agent, but it does not impose liability upon the landlord for the unlawful acts of third persons.[7] Thus, such a covenant does not require the landlord to protect a tenant from damages by a rioting mob.

(d) CONSTRUCTIVE EVICTION. An eviction may be actual or constructive. It is a **constructive eviction** when some act or omission of the landlord substantially deprives the tenant of the use and enjoyment of the premises.

It is essential in a constructive eviction that the landlord intended to deprive the tenant of the use and enjoyment of the premises. This intent may, however, be inferred from conduct. There is no constructive eviction unless the tenant leaves the premises. If the tenant continues to occupy the premises for more than a reasonable time after the acts claimed to constitute a constructive eviction, the tenant waives or loses the right to object to the conduct of the landlord and cannot thereafter abandon the premises and claim to have been evicted.[8]

§ 54:9 USE OF PREMISES

The lease generally specifies the use to which the tenant may put the property and

---

[6] Ahmed v Scott, 65 Ohio App 2d 271, 418 NE2d 406 (1979).

[7] Rittenbert v Donohoe Construction Co. (Dist Col App) 426 A2d 338 (1981).

[8] Some states prohibit a landlord of residential property from "willfully" turning off the utilities of a tenant for the purpose of evicting the tenant. Kinney v Vaccari, 23 Cal 3d 348, 165 Cal Rptr 787, 612 P2d 877 (1980) (imposing civil penalty of $100 a day for every day utilities are shut off). Such conduct is also a violation of URLTA §§ 2.104, 4.105.

authorizes the landlord to adopt regulations with respect to the use of the premises that are binding upon the tenant as
long as they are reasonable, lawful, and
not in conflict with the terms of the lease.
In the absence of express or implied restrictions, a tenant is entitled to use the premises for any lawful purpose for which they
are adapted or for which they are ordinarily employed or in a manner contemplated
by the parties in executing the lease. A provision specifying the use to be made of the
property is strictly construed against the
tenant.

(a) CHANGE OF USE. The modern lease
will in substance make a change of use a
condition subsequent so that if the tenant
uses the property for any purpose other
than the one specified, the landlord has the
option of declaring the lease terminated.

(b) CONTINUED USE OF PROPERTY. With
the increased danger of damage to the
premises by vandalism or fire when the
building is vacant and because of the common insurance provision making a fire insurance policy void when a vacancy continues for a specified time, the modern
lease will ordinarily require the tenant to
give the landlord notice of nonuse or vacancy of the premises.

(c) RULES. The modern lease generally
contains a blanket agreement by the tenant
to abide by the provisions of rules and regulations adopted by the landlord. These
rules are generally binding on the tenant
whether they exist at the time the lease was
made or were thereafter adopted.

(d) PROHIBITION OF PETS. A restriction in
a lease prohibiting the keeping of pets is
valid.

§ 54:10   RENT

The tenant is under a duty to pay rent as
compensation to the landlord. The amount
of rent agreed to by the parties may be subject to governmental limitations establishing maximum amounts that can be
charged.

(a) TIME OF PAYMENT. The time of payment of rent is ordinarily fixed by the lease.
When the lease does not control, rent generally is not due until the end of the term. Statutes or custom, however, may require rent
to be paid in advance when the agreement of
the parties does not regulate the point. Rent
that is payable in crops is generally payable
at the end of the term.

(b) ASSIGNMENT. If the lease is assigned,
the assignee is liable to the landlord for the
rent. The assignment, however, does not
in itself discharge the tenant from the duty
to pay the rent. The landlord thus may
bring an action for the rent against either
the original tenant or the assignee, or both,
but is entitled to only one satisfaction. A
sublessee ordinarily is not liable to the original lessor for rent, unless that liability has
been expressly assumed or is imposed by
statute.

(c) RENT ESCALATION. When property is
rented for a long term, it is common to include some provision for the automatic increase of the rent at periodic intervals.
Such a provision is often tied to increases
in the cost of living or in the landlord's operating costs. Such a provision is called an
escalation clause.

In the *George Backer* case, the tenant
claimed that it was not bound by the escalation clause.

GEORGE BACKER MANAGEMENT CORP. V ACME QUILTING CO., INC.
413 NYS2d 135, 46 NY2d 211, 385 NE2d 1062 (1978)

George Backer Management owned an office building. It rented office
space to Acme Quilting Co. The lease contained a rent escalation clause
providing for the increase of rent when the wage scale fixed by the Realty

Advisory Board (RAB) rose. After the lease was executed, the wage scale was increased by RAB. George Backer did not belong to the group that was bound by the RAB wage scale and, in fact, paid its employees below the RAB scale. Nevertheless, George Backer demanded that Acme pay additional rent based upon the RAB scale. Acme refused to pay the increase in the rent. George Backer sued Acme for the amount of the increase in the rent. Judgment was entered in favor of George Backer, and Acme appealed.

FUCHSBERG, J. [The rent escalation clause in the Backer-Acme lease] was not a novel provision, but one commonly found in New York City commercial leases. . . .

The purpose . . . was to relate additional rent increases to a fluctuating factor beyond the control of either party, namely, the RAB wage rate. . . .

Significantly, the lease contains no requirement that rent escalations be measured by actual costs as opposed to the common industry-wide criterion chosen by the parties here. . . .

Nor was the operation of the clause unconscionable. Acme assumed the precise risk of which it now complains — that the RAB labor rate would rise so as to substantially increase its monthly rental payments. But parties are free to make their own contracts. Here Backer no doubt believed that it was to its economic advantage to tie the rent escalation clause to the RAB rate; though it needed no other reason, perhaps Backer also believed that if it were able to operate the building at lower than prevailing cost, it and not the tenants should be the beneficiary of its enterprise. Acme's view, fueled by its own self-interest, understandably would be the opposite.

Once a contract is made, only in unusual circumstances will a court relieve the parties of the duty of abiding by it. By no means did such circumstances exist here. Indeed, the indexing of rent or wage increases to outside factors, such as, for instance, the cost of living index which may or may not directly affect particular parties, is commonplace. So, a cost of living clause in a lease would certainly be enforceable. . . . Thus, the wage rate clause here contravened no principle of public policy nor is its effect so onerous as to shock the conscience. Hence, judicial interpretation will not relieve Acme of what it may now regard as a burdensome bargain.

We turn now to Acme's claim for reformation. . . .

Reformation is not granted for the purpose of alleviating a hard or oppressive bargain, but rather to restate the intended terms of an agreement when the writing that memorializes that agreement is at variance with the intent of both parties. . . .

. . . The history of the lease negotiations between Backer and Acme discloses continuing awareness on the prospective tenant's part that the wage rate escalation provision might be potentially disadvantageous. The negotiations were conducted in a most businesslike, meticulous and unhurried manner by both sides. These produced substantial economic modifications to Acme's advantage. And, only a month before the culmination of the negotiations, when [Acme advised Backer that it] was not satisfied with the clause, the latter remained steadfast and the lease containing the now objectionable provision was accepted by the tenant in unchanged form.

Furthermore, [Backer's] purported oral interpretation of the clause as limiting Acme's liability to about "four or five percent" of the actual wage rate sets forth no reasonable ground for reliance. The very indefiniteness of the figures confirms this statement as an expression of opinion rather than of fact. Above all, it did not relate to a concrete fact or a past or existing event. At best, it was no more than an expression of expectations as to labor agreements which had not yet been negotiated and the outcome of which, as both parties knew, could not be foretold. As a matter of law, then, it cannot form the basis for a claim of misrepresentation. . . .

[Judgment affirmed]

QUESTIONS

1. Was the rental due to George Backer fixed in amount?
2. Was the rent escalation clause limited to the wages paid by George Backer?
3. Was the escalation clause unconscionable because it employed the RAB wage scale rather than the wages actually paid by George Backer?

§ 54:11   REPAIRS AND CONDITION OF PREMISES

In the absence of an agreement to the contrary, the tenant has the duty to make those repairs that are necessary to prevent waste and decay of the premises, and is liable for **permissive waste** on failing to do so. When the landlord leases only a portion of the premises, or leases the premises to different tenants, the landlord is under a duty to make repairs to connecting parts, such as halls, basements, elevators, and stairways, that are under the landlord's control. When the landlord makes repairs, reasonable care must be exercised to make them in a proper manner; but the landlord is not automatically liable as an insurer if the tenant is injured after the landlord has made the repairs. The tenant is ordinarily liable for any damage to the premises caused by willful or negligent acts of the tenant.[9]

(a) INSPECTION OF PREMISES. Most states deny the landlord the right to enter the leased premises to inspect them for waste and need for repairs except when the right is expressly reserved in the lease. It is customary, however, for leases of apartments and commercial property to reserve to the landlord the right to enter to inspect the premises and to make repairs.

(b) HOUSING LAWS. Various laws protect tenants, as by requiring landlords to observe specified safety, health, and fire prevention standards. Some statutes require that a landlord who leases a building for dwelling purposes must keep it in a condition fit for habitation. Leases commonly require the tenant to obey local ordinances and laws relating to the care and use of the premises.

(c) WARRANTY OF HABITABILITY. At common law a landlord was not bound by any obligation that the premises be fit for use unless the lease contained an express warranty to that effect. Most jurisdictions now reject this view and infer from residential leases of furnished and unfurnished property a warranty that the premises are habitable. If the landlord breaches this warranty, the tenant is entitled to damages. These damages may be set off against the rent that is due, or if no rent is due, the tenant may bring an independent lawsuit to recover damages from the landlord.[10]

In the *Abram* case, a tenant whose per-

[9]   New Hampshire Ins. Co. v Hewins, 6 Kan App 2d 259, 627 P2d 1159 (1981); URLTA § 3.101.

[10]   Knight v Hallsthammar, 171 Cal Rptr 707, 623 P2d 268 (1981).

sonal property was destroyed in a fire, sued the landlord for property damage based upon a breach of the implied warranty of habitability.

ABRAM V LITMAN

___ Ill App 3d ___, ___ Ill Dec ___, 501 NE2d 370 (1986)

Abram lived at property owned and operated by Litman. A fire, resulting from faulty wiring, occurred on the premises. The tenant's personal possessions were destroyed. Abram sued Litman alleging a breach of the implied warranty of habitability. Litman argued that Abram did not show that Litman had notice of the alleged defects or dangerous condition nor had he received such notice. Litman also argued that the implied warranty of habitability cannot serve as a basis of recovery for property damage. From a judgment in favor of Litman, Abram appealed.

WEBER, J. . . . In *Jack Spring, Inc. v. Little* (1972), 50 Ill.2d 351, 280 N.E.2d 208, the Supreme Court of Illinois held that the implied warranty of habitability applied to leases, both oral and written, of multiple-unit dwellings. In *Jack Spring* the court stated that the warranty was fulfilled by substantial compliance with the pertinent provisions of the applicable building code. Subsequently several districts of the appellate court of Illinois interpreted the court's statement in *Jack Spring* to mean that the implied warranty of habitability is only fulfilled by substantial compliance with a building code. In *Glasoe [v. Trinkle* (1985)] our supreme court clarified this confusion by holding "that the implied warranty of habitability applies to all leases of residential real estate regardless of the existence of housing or building codes." (107 Ill.2d 1, 10, 88 Ill.Dec. 895, 898, 479 N.E.2d 915, 918.) The *Glasoe* court continued by examining the scope of the implied warranty of habitability. In so doing, the court stated:

> As did the Pennsylvania court, we decline to establish rigid standards for determining habitability and its breach. However, we think the guidelines above stated, which have been enunciated in other jurisdictions, will be helpful to the fact finder in determining the extent of the warranty of habitability and whether there has been a breach thereof in a particular case. *In addition to the guidelines stated, there, of course, must be notice of the alleged defects given by the tenant to the landlord and the landlord must have had a reasonable time within which to correct the alleged deficiencies.*

The trial court relied on the above-quoted statement in determining that plaintiff was required to plead and prove that she gave notice of the alleged defects to defendants.

Plaintiff argues that the above-quoted statement is mere dicta and that we should follow our holding in *Jarrell v. Hartman* (1977), 48 Ill.App.3d 985, 6 Ill.Dec. 812, 363 N.E.2d 626. In *Jarrell* we rejected the argument that a tenant seeking to establish a breach of the implied warranty of habitability is first required to give the landlord notice of the defect and an opportunity to repair. Our [principal] reason for rejecting defendants' argument was that no such requirement had been discussed in *Jack Spring*. This question was resolved in *Glasoe*.

In our opinion the trial court interpreted the statement of the supreme court in *Glasoe* concerning notice too broadly. *Glasoe* involved patent defects. Even in the case of such defects the court laid down no precise rule as to the nature of the required notice, only that some notice must be given. The court was not called upon to decide the matter of notice in the context of latent defects of the type involved in the instant case. If such defects were not apparent nor discoverable by either the landlord or the tenant until after the damage had occurred, it is at once apparent that notice of them would be logically impossible to give. We find that *Glasoe* is factually distinguishable from the instant case.

A short discussion of how other jurisdictions have treated the question of notice is in order.

. . . Some jurisdictions have stated that a landlord's knowledge may be either actual knowledge or constructive knowledge. . . .

We believe that one of the soundest approaches was that taken in *Old Town Development*. In *Old Town Development* the court held that the notice requirement may be satisfied in various ways depending upon the facts and circumstances of the case. Actual notice of the alleged defect given to the landlord by the tenant would always be sufficient. In addition, actual knowledge of the alleged defect on the part of the landlord would also be sufficient. In some instances the landlord could be charged with constructive knowledge of the alleged defect. For example, where the alleged defect is a latent defect and the landlord was also the builder of the premises, the landlord could properly be charged with constructive knowledge of the alleged defect. *(Old Town.)* However, defendants herein could not be charged with constructive knowledge of the faulty wiring since plaintiff did not allege that defendants were the builders of the premises leased to plaintiff. See *W.C. Haas Realty Management* (noting that liability could not be imposed on a nonbuilder landlord for a breach of the implied warranty of habitability which allegedly resulted from faulty wiring which had caused a fire on the premises).

Because the instant case concerns a latent defect about which the tenant knew nothing and because there is no allegation in the pleadings upon which the landlord could be charged with constructive notice of the defect, we find that the trial court properly dismissed the complaint. While its reliance upon the broad language in *Glasoe* was perhaps misplaced, its result was correct. As we have pointed out, the instant case differs from *Glasoe*, which was concerned with patent defects. An additional reason for the proper dismissal of the complaint is that the warranty of habitability cannot serve as a basis for recovery of property damage. *Auburn v. Amoco Oil Co.* (1982), 106 Ill.App.3d 60, 61 Ill.Dec. 939, 435 N.E.2d 780.

In *Auburn* the plaintiffs' complaint alleged that the defendant landlords breached the implied warranty of habitability by providing in the leased house a furnace which was neither in working order nor reasonably safe for its intended purpose. The complaint alleged further that as a result of the landlord's breach, an explosion occurred destroying the house and causing the plaintiffs to suffer personal injury and property damage. The complaint sought damages. Stating that no cause of action exists for personal injuries resulting from a breach of the implied warranty of habitability, the trial court dismissed the complaint. On appeal we affirmed, holding that the warranty of habitability implied in a lease of a dwelling does not give rise to a cause of action for personal injuries or property damage. We noted that although the implied warranty of habitability may be used as a sword as well as a shield and that an independent action for a landlord's breach of warranty may stand, such claims are "for a deterioration in the benefits from the lease rather than for personal injuries or property damage arising from a catastrophe." (106 Ill.App.3d 60, 63, 61 Ill.Dec. 939, 941, 435 N.E.2d 780, 782.). . . Because the complaint herein seeks recovery of damages for property damage, the court below properly dismissed the action. . . .

[Judgment affirmed]

QUESTIONS

1. How may notice of breach of implied warranty of habitability be satisfied?
2. Was proper notice given?
3. Why did the court refuse to give recovery for property damage?

(d) ABATEMENT AND ESCROW PAYMENT OF RENT. In order to protect tenants from unsound living conditions, statutes sometimes provide that a tenant is not required to pay rent as long as the premises are not fit to live in. As a compromise, some statutes require the tenant to continue to pay the rent but require that it be paid into an escrow or agency account from which it is paid to the landlord only upon proof that the necessary repairs have been made to the premises.

§ 54:12 IMPROVEMENTS

In the absence of special agreement, neither the tenant nor the landlord is under the duty to make improvements, as contrasted with repairs. Either party may, as a term of the original lease, agree or covenant to make improvements, in which case a failure to perform will result in liability in an action for damages for breach of contract brought by the other party. In the absence of an agreement to the contrary, improvements that are attached to the land become part of the realty and belong to the landlord.

§ 54:13 TAXES AND ASSESSMENTS

In the absence of an agreement to the contrary, the landlord, and not the tenant, is usually under a duty to pay taxes or assessments. The lease may provide for an increase in rent if taxes on the rented property are increased.[11]

If taxes or assessments are increased because of improvements made by the tenant, the landlord is liable for such increases if the improvements remain with the property. If the improvements can be removed by the tenant, the amount of the increase must be paid by the tenant.

§ 54:14 TENANT'S DEPOSIT

A landlord may require a tenant to make a deposit to protect the landlord from any default on the part of the tenant.

(a) CUSTODY. In some states, protection is given the tenant who is required to make a payment to the landlord as a deposit to insure compliance with the lease. It is sometimes provided that the landlord holds such payment as a trust fund and must inform the tenant of any bank in which the money is deposited and must be subject to a penalty if the money is used before the tenant has breached the lease.

(b) REFUND. Once paid by the tenant, it may happen that the landlord will keep the

---

[11] J. C. Penny Co., Inc. v 1700 Broadway Co. 104 Misc 2d 787, 429 NYS2d 369 (1980).

entire deposit, even though it is in excess of any claim against the tenant, and tenants will not bring suit because the amount involved is too small to justify an action. Tenant protection statutes sometimes remedy this situation by requiring the landlord to refund any part of the deposit in excess of the amount actually needed to compensate for the breach by the tenant.

§ 54:15   PROTECTION FROM RETALIATION

There is a modern trend to protect tenants from retaliation by the landlord for the tenants' exercising their lawful rights or reporting the landlord for violating a housing and sanitation code.[12] The retaliation of the lessor may take the form of refusing to renew a lease or evicting the tenant.

§ 54:16   REMEDIES OF LANDLORD

If a tenant fails to pay rent, the landlord may bring an ordinary lawsuit to collect the amount due and in some states may seize and hold the property of the tenant.

(a) LANDLORD'S LIEN. In the absence of an agreement or statute so providing, the landlord does not have a lien upon the personal property or crops of the tenant for money due for rent. The parties may create by express or implied contract a lien in favor of the landlord for rent and also for advances, taxes, or damages for failure to make repairs.

In the absence of a statutory provision, the lien of the landlord is superior to the claims of all other persons, except prior lienors and good faith purchasers without notice.

(b) SUIT FOR RENT. Whether or not the landlord has a lien for unpaid rent, the landlord may sue the tenant on the latter's obligation to pay rent as specified in the lease, or if payment of rent is not specified, the landlord may enforce a quasi-contractual obligation to pay the reasonable value of the use and occupation of the property. In some jurisdictions, the landlord is permitted to bring a combined action to recover the possession of the land and the overdue rent at the same time.

(c) DISTRESS. The common law devised a speedy remedy to aid the landlord in collecting rent. It permitted seizure of personal property found on the premises and allowed the landlord to hold such property until the arrears of rent were paid. This right was known as **distress**. It was not an action against the tenant for rent but merely a right to retain the property as security until the rent was paid. Statutes have generally either abolished or greatly modified the remedy of distress.[13]

(d) RECOVERY OF POSSESSION. The lease commonly provides that upon the breach of any of its provisions by the tenant, such as the failure to pay rent, the lease shall terminate or the landlord may exercise the option to declare the lease terminated. When the lease is terminated for any reason, the landlord then has the right to evict the tenant and retake possession of the property.

At common law, the landlord, when entitled to possession, could regain it without resorting to legal proceedings. This **right of reentry** is available in many states even when the employment of force is necessary. Other states deny the right to use force.

Modern cases hold that a landlord cannot lock out a tenant for overdue rent and must employ legal process to regain possession even though the lease expressly gives the landlord the right to self-help.

The landlord may resort to legal process to evict the tenant in order to enforce the right to possession of the premises. The action of ejectment is ordinarily used. In addition to the common-law remedies, statutes in many states provide a summary remedy to recover possession that is much

---

[12]   Mobil Oil Corp. v Handly, 76 Cal App 3d 956, 143 Cal Rptr 321 (1978). URLTA § 5.101.

[13]   It is abolished by the URLTA § 4.205(b). Callen v Sherman's, Inc. 182 NJ Super 438, 442 A2d 626 (1982).

more efficient than the slow common-law remedies.

(e) LANDLORD'S DUTY TO MITIGATE DAMAGES. If the tenant leaves the premises before the expiration of the lease, is the landlord under any duty to rent the premises again in order to reduce the rent or damages for which the departing tenant will be liable? By the common law and majority rule, a tenant owns an estate in land, and if the tenant abandons it, there is no duty upon the landlord to seek to find a new tenant for the premises. A growing minority view places greater emphasis upon the contractual aspects of a lease so that, when the tenant abandons the property and thereby defaults or breaks the contract, the landlord is under the duty to seek to mitigate the damages caused by the tenant's breach and must make a reasonable effort to rent the abandoned property.

SOMMER V KRIDEL
74 NJ 446, 378 A2d 767 (1977)

Abraham Sommer owned an apartment building. He rented one of the apartments to James Kridel for two years. Kridel intended to marry and move into the apartment with his bride. The engagement was broken. Kridel did not marry and never moved into the apartment. He never received any keys to the apartment. In May of 1972, he wrote to Sommer explaining the situation and requesting to be released from the obligations of the lease. Sommer never replied to this letter. Shortly thereafter, a stranger asked to rent the Kridel apartment. She was admittedly a proper applicant but the Kridel apartment was not rented to her because it was under the lease to Kridel. In October 1972, Sommer sued Kridel and claimed the rent for the entire two years that the lease would have run. Sommer had not showed the Kridel apartment to anyone until the next year when the apartment was relet to a tenant under a lease beginning September 1, 1973. In the lawsuit brought by Sommer, Kridel claimed that the amount due to Sommer should be reduced because Sommer had failed to mitigate the damages by attempting to relet the apartment. From a judgment against Kridel, he appealed.

PASHMAN, J. . . . The weight of authority in this State supports the rule that a landlord is under no duty to mitigate damages caused by a defaulting tenant. . . . This rule has been followed in a majority of states, and has been tentatively adopted in the American Law Institute's Restatement of Property, *Restatement (Second) of Property,* § 11.1(3) (Tent. Draft No 3, 1975).

Nevertheless, while there is still a split of authority over this question, the trend among recent cases appears to be in favor of a mitigation requirement.

. . .

The majority rule is based on principles of property law which equate a lease with a transfer of a property interest in the owner's estate. Under this rationale the lease conveys to a tenant an interest in the property which forecloses any control by the landlord; thus, it would be anomalous to require the landlord to concern himself with the tenant's abandonment of his own property.

For instance, in *Muller v Beck,* [94 NJL 311, 110 A 831 (Sup Ct 1920)] where essentially the same issue was posed, the court clearly treated the lease as governed by property, as opposed to contract, precepts. The court there observed that the "tenant had an estate for years, but it was an estate qualified by this right of the landlord to prevent its transfer," and that "the tenant has an estate with which the landlord may not interfere."

Yet the distinction between a lease for ordinary residential purposes and an ordinary contract can no longer be considered viable. As Professor Powell observed, evolving "social factors have exerted increasing influence on the law of estates for years." 2 *Powell on Real Property* (1977 ed), § 221 [1] at 180-81. The result has been that[:]

> the complexities of city life, and the proliferated problems of modern society in general, have created new problems for lessors and lessees and these have been commonly handled by specific clauses in leases. This growth in the number and detail of specific lease covenants has reintroduced into the law of estates for years a predominantly contractual ingredient.

Thus in 6 *Williston on Contracts* (3 ed 1962), § 890A at 592, it is stated:

> There is a clearly discernible tendency on the part of courts to cast aside technicalities in the interpretation of leases and to concentrate their attention, as in the case of other contracts, on the intention of the parties, . . .

Application of the contract rule requiring mitigation of damages to a residential lease may be justified as a matter of basic fairness. Professor McCormick first commented upon the inequity under the majority rule when he predicted in 1925 that eventually[:]

> the logic, inescapable according to the standards of a 'jurisprudence of conceptions' which permits the landlord to stand idly by the vacant, abandoned premises and treat them as the property of the tenant and recover full rent, [will] yield to the more realistic notions of social advantage which in other fields of the law have forbidden a recovery for damages which the plaintiff by reasonable efforts could have avoided. [McCormick, "The Rights of the Landlord Upon Abandonment of the Premises by the Tenant," 23 *MichLRev* 211 (1925)]

Various courts have adopted this position. . . .

We therefore hold that antiquated real property concepts which served as the basis for the pre-existing rule, shall no longer be controlling where there is a claim for damages under a residential lease. Such claims must be governed by more modern notions of fairness and equity. A landlord has a duty to mitigate damages where he seeks to recover rents due from a defaulting tenant.

If the landlord has other vacant apartments besides the one which the tenant has abandoned, the landlord's duty to mitigate consists of making reasonable efforts to re-let the apartment. In such cases he must treat the apartment in question as if it was one of his vacant stock.

As part of his cause of action, the landlord shall be required to carry the burden of proving that he used reasonable diligence in attempting to re-let the premises. We note that there has been a divergence of opinion concerning the allocation of the burden of proof on this issue.

. . .

The landlord will be in a better position to demonstrate whether he exercised reasonable diligence in attempting to re-let the premises.

. . .

The *Sommer v Kridel* case presents a classic example of the unfairness which occurs when a landlord has no responsibility to minimize damages. Sommer waited 15 months and allowed $4658.50 in damages to accrue before attempting to re-let the apartment. Despite the availability of a tenant who was ready, willing and able to rent the apartment, the landlord needlessly increased the damages by turning her away.

. . .

Here there has been no showing that the new tenant would not have been suitable. We therefore find that plaintiff could have avoided the damages which eventually accrued, and that the defendant was relieved of his duty to continue paying rent. Ordinarily we would require the tenant to bear the cost of any reasonable expenses incurred by a landlord in attempting to re-let the premises, but no such expenses were incurred in this case.

In assessing whether the landlord has satisfactorily carried his burden, the trial court shall consider, among other factors, whether the landlord, either personally or through an agency, offered or showed the apartment to any prospective tenants, or advertised it in local newspapers. Additionally, the tenant may attempt to rebut such evidence by showing that he proffered suitable tenants who were rejected. However, there is no standard formula for measuring whether the landlord has utilized satisfactory efforts in attempting to mitigate damages, and each case must be judged upon its own facts.

[Judgment reversed]

QUESTIONS

1. What did the plaintiff claim?
2. Was the landlord entitled to recover the agreed rental specified in the lease for the two-year term of the lease?
3. Did the lessor act in a reasonable manner?

C. LIABILITY FOR INJURY ON PREMISES

When the tenant, a member of the tenant's family, or a third person is injured by a condition of the premises, the question arises as to who is liable for the damages sustained by the injured person.

§ 54:17   LANDLORD'S LIABILITY TO TENANT

In the absence of a covenant to keep the premises in repair, the landlord is ordinarily not liable to the tenant for the latter's personal injuries caused by the defective condition of the premises that are placed under the control of the tenant by the lease. Likewise, the landlord is not liable for the harm caused by an obvious condition that was known to the tenant at the time the lease was made. For example, a landlord is not liable for the fatal burning of a tenant whose clothing was set on fire by an open-faced radiant gas heater.

The landlord is liable to the tenant for injuries caused by latent defects or defects that are not apparent of which the landlord has knowledge.[14] A new trend is beginning to appear that makes foreseeability of harm, rather than the mechanical test of whether the landlord had control of the part of the premises involved, the test of the landlord's liability.

[14] Alvarez v DeAguirre (Fla App) 395 So 2d 213 (1981).

In a number of states, by decision or statute, a landlord is liable to a tenant or a child or guest of the tenant when there is a defect that makes the premises dangerously defective, even though the landlord did not have any knowledge of the defect. Other states refuse to apply this strict tort liability concept.

(a) CRIMES OF THIRD PERSONS. Ordinarily, the landlord is not liable to the tenant for crimes committed on the premises by third persons, as when a third person enters the premises and commits larceny or murder. The landlord is not required to establish any security system to protect the tenant from crimes of third persons.

In contrast, when the criminal acts of third persons are reasonably foreseeable, the landlord may be held liable for the harm thereby caused a tenant. Consequently, when a tenant has repeatedly reported that the dead bolt on the apartment door was broken, the landlord is liable for the tenant's loss when a thief enters through the door, because such criminal conduct was foreseeable. Likewise, when the landlord of a large apartment complex does not take reasonable steps to prevent repeated criminal acts, the landlord is liable to the tenant for the harm caused by the foreseeable criminal act of a third person.[15]

In the *C. S.* case, the court takes up the issue of foreseeability as it relates to landlord liability.

[15] Lay v Dworman (Okla App) 732 P2d 455 (1986).

C. S. v SOPHIR
(Neb App) 368 NW2d 444 (1985)

C. S., a tenant in an apartment complex owned and operated by Sophir, was sexually assaulted in the parking lot provided for tenants. She alleged that the manager of the complex had actual knowledge of an earlier sexual assault and that the defendant should have warned the plaintiff of that assault. The tenant further alleged that that landlord was negligent for failure to provide proper lighting for security purposes. From a judgment in favor of the landlord, C. S. appealed.

HASTINGS, J. . . . We deal first with the failure to warn. In order to impose liability on the landlord, a duty must exist. "Whether a duty exists is ultimately a question of fairness."

Factors to consider in imposing a duty on a landlord include weighing the relationship of the parties against the nature of the risk and the public interest in the proposed solution, as well as the likelihood of injury, the magnitude of the burden of guarding against it, and the consequences of placing that burden on a defendant.

Under the facts as alleged in this case, it would be unfair to impose a duty upon the landlord based on a single prior assault at the complex.

First, landlords are not insurers that a tenant will be protected at all times.

Second, there is no duty to warn of a known danger. The ordinary, reasonable person is aware or should be aware that open parking lots provide an optimum place for crime to occur.

Third, there is no guarantee that if the duty to warn was imposed, a crime would be averted. As pointed out by the Illinois court in *Stelloh v. Cottage 83*, 52 Ill.App.2d 168, 201 N.E.2d 672 (1964), in affirming the dismissal of the plaintiff's case on facts similar to the present case, "[w]e doubt that the giving of [a] warning, under all the circumstances alleged, would have lessened the probability of the [rape], or that the failure so to notify plaintiff would have increased the hazard in any way." To impose liability over the mere possibility of a crime occurring is folly.

Plaintiff asks the court to invoke the minority rule which imposes liability upon a landlord with notice of a prior criminal act on the premises. However, even in cases where such liability was imposed, there was a history of criminal activity at the leased premises sufficient to create in the landlord constructive notice of the foreseeability that such activity would recur in the future.

No cases were found which impose liability on a landlord based on a *single* prior criminal act perpetrated upon a tenant. That none were found appears consistent with Nebraska's position with reference to a similar class of individuals, business invitees. A possessor of land who holds it open for public entry for business purposes is under a duty to exercise reasonable care to protect his patrons. Such care may require giving a warning or providing greater protection where there is a *likelihood* that third persons will endanger the safety of the visitors.

The rule, however, does not require the possessor to anticipate the unforeseeable independent acts of third persons. Only such acts as can be reasonably anticipated impose a duty on the landowner. In *Harvey* the court refused to impose liability on a tavern owner where a patron was assaulted by a third party who had become violent on the premises on a prior occasion. The foreseeability requirement necessary to impose liability was missing.

Likewise, in the present case there would be no foreseeability, based on one prior assault, upon which to predicate liability. . . .

[Judgment affirmed]

QUESTIONS

1. Does a landlord have a duty to warn of a danger known to the tenant?
2. Is a landlord an insurer of the tenant's safety?
3. What did the court decide?

(b) LIMITATION OF LIABILITY. A provision in a lease excusing or exonerating the landlord from liability is generally valid, regardless of the cause of the tenant's loss. A number of courts, however, have restricted the landlord's power to limit liability in the case of residential, as distinguished from commercial, leasing; so that a provision in a residential lease that the landlord shall not be liable for damage caused by water, snow, or ice is void. A modern trend holds that clauses limiting liability of the landlord are void with respect to harm caused by the negligence of the landlord when the tenant is a residential tenant generally or is in a government low-cost housing project.

Third persons on the premises, even with the consent of the tenant, are generally not bound by a clause exonerating the landlord and may therefore sue the landlord when they sustain injuries. Thus, it has been held that members of the tenant's family, employees, and guests, are not bound when they do not sign the lease; although, there is authority to the contrary.

(c) INDEMNIFICATION OF LANDLORD. The modern lease commonly contains a provision declaring that the tenant will indemnify the landlord for any liability (of the landlord to a third person) that arises in connection with the rented premises.

§ 54:18   LANDLORD'S LIABILITY TO THIRD PERSONS

The landlord is ordinarily not liable to third persons injured because of the condition of any part of the rented premises that is in the possession of a tenant by virtue of a lease.[16]

If the landlord retains control over a portion of the premises, such as hallways or stairways, however, liability exists for injuries to third persons caused by failure to exercise proper care in connection with that part of the premises. The modern trend of cases imposes liability upon the landlord when a third person is harmed by a condition that the landlord, under a contract with the tenant, was obligated to correct or when the landlord was obligated, under a contract with the tenant, to keep the premises in repair.

§ 54:19   TENANT'S LIABILITY TO THIRD PERSONS

A tenant in complete possession has control of the property and is therefore liable when the tenant's failure to use due care under the circumstances causes harm to (a) licensees, such as a person allowed to use a telephone, and (b) invitees, such as customers entering a store. With respect to both classes, the liability is the same as an owner in possession of property. It is likewise immaterial whether the property is used for residential or business purposes, provided the tenant has control of the area where the injury occurs.

The liability of the tenant to third persons is not affected by the fact that the landlord may have contracted in the lease to make repairs, which, if made, would have avoided the injury. The tenant can be protected, however, in the same manner that the landlord can, by procuring liability insurance for indemnity against loss from claims of third persons.

D.   TRANSFER OF RIGHTS

Both the landlord and the tenant have property and contract rights with respect to the lease. When either makes a transfer of them, questions arise as to the rights and liabilities of the transferee.

§ 54:20   TRANSFER OF LANDLORD'S REVERSIONARY INTEREST

The reversionary interest of the landlord may be transferred voluntarily by the landlord, or involuntarily by a judicial or execution sale. The tenant then becomes the tenant of the new owner of the reversionary interest, and the new owner is bound by the terms of the lease.

When the landlord assigns the reversion, the assignee is, in the absence of an agreement to the contrary, entitled to subsequent accruals of rent. The rent may, however, be reserved in an assignment or a reversion. The landlord also has the right to assign the lease independent of the reversion or to assign the rent independent of the lease.

§ 54:21   TENANT'S ASSIGNMENT OF LEASE AND SUBLEASE

An **assignment of a lease** is a transfer by the tenant of the tenant's entire interest in the premises to a third person.[17] A tenancy for years may be assigned by the tenant unless the latter is restricted from so doing

---

[16]   Gilbreath v J. H. Greenwalt, 88 Ill App 3d 265, 43 Ill Dec 533, 410 NE2d 539 (1980).

[17]   Weeks v Cal-Maine Foods, Inc. (Miss App) 522 So 2d 725 (1987).

by the terms of the lease or by a statute. A **sublease** is a transfer to a third person, the **sublessee**, of less than the tenant's entire interest.

Whether the transaction between the tenant and the third person is a sublease or an assignment is determined by the effect of the transaction. If the entire interest of the tenant is transferred to the third person, the transaction is an assignment of the lease, without regard to whether the parties have described the transaction as a sublease or as an assignment. In contrast, if there is some interest left over after the interest of the third person expires or if possession of only part of the premises is transferred, the relationship is a sublease.

(a) LIMITATIONS ON RIGHTS. The lease may contain provisions denying the right to assign or sublet or may contain provisions imposing specified restrictions upon the privilege of assigning or subletting. Such restrictions enable the landlord to obtain protection from new tenants who would damage the property or be financially irresponsible.

Restrictions in the lease are construed liberally in favor of the tenant. An ineffectual attempt to assign or sublet does not violate a provision prohibiting such acts. Equally, there is no violation when the tenant merely permits someone else to use the premises.

(b) EFFECT OF ASSIGNMENT OR SUBLEASE. An express covenant or promise by the sublessee is necessary to impose liability upon the sublessee for the obligations of the lease. In contrast, when the lease is assigned, the assignee becomes bound by the terms of the lease upon taking possession of the property. In any case, the rights of a sublessee and those of an assignee can rise no higher than the rights of the original lessee under the lease.[18]

Neither the act of subletting nor the landlord's agreement to it releases the original tenant from liability under the terms of the original lease.

When a lease is assigned, the original tenant remains liable for the rent that becomes due thereafter. If the assignee renews or extends the lease by virtue of an option contained therein, the original tenant is likewise liable for the rent for such extended period in the absence of a contrary agreement or novation by which the landlord agrees that the assignee shall be deemed substituted as tenant and that the original tenant shall be released from further liability.

It is customary and desirable for the tenant to require the sublessee to covenant or promise to perform all obligations under the original lease and to indemnify the tenant for any loss caused by the default of the sublessee. An express covenant or promise by the sublessee is necessary to impose such liability. The fact that the sublease is made "subject" to the terms of the original lease merely recognizes the superiority of the original lease but does not impose any duty upon the sublessee to perform the tenant's obligation under the original lease. If the sublessee promises to assume the obligations of the original lease, the landlord, as a third party beneficiary, may sue the sublessee for breach of the provisions of the original lease.

---

[18] Gulden v Newberry Wrecker Service, Inc. 154 Ga App 130, 267 SE2d 763 (1980).

SUMMARY

The agreement between a lessor and a lessee by which one person holds possession of real property owned by another is a lease. Statutes in many states prohibit discrimination by an owner who rents property and require that the lease may not be unconscionable. Tenancies are classified as to duration as tenancies for years, from year to year, at will, and by sufferance. A lease is generally not terminated by the death, insanity, or bankruptcy of either party except for a tenancy at will. Leases usually are terminated by notice, release, merger, surrender, forfeiture, destruction of the property, and because of fraud. A tenant has the right to acquire possession at the beginning of the lease and has the right to retain possession until the lease is ended. Evictions may be either actual or constructive. The tenant is under a duty to pay rent as compensation for the landlord. In the event the lease is assigned, the assignee is liable to the landlord for the rent. Such an assignment, however, does not discharge the tenant from the duty to pay rent. In a sublease, the sublessee ordinarily is not liable to the original lessor for rent unless that liability has been assumed or is imposed by statute. In long-term leases, rent escalation clauses are often included.

The tenant must make repairs to the premises absent agreement to the contrary. A warranty of habitability was not implied at common law. Many states now reject this view and infer from residential leases a warranty that the premises are fit for habitation.

A landlord is usually only liable to the tenant for injuries caused by latent defects or those that are not apparent of which the landlord had knowledge. Some states apply a strict tort liability, holding the landlord liable to a tenant or a child or guest of the tenant when there is a defect that makes the premises dangerously defective, even though the landlord does not have any knowledge of the defect. The landlord is not liable to the tenant for crimes of third persons unless they are reasonably foreseeable.

An assignment of a lease by the tenant is a transfer of the tenant's entire interest in the property to a third person; a sublease is a transfer of less than an entire interest — either in space or time. A lease may prohibit both an assignment and a sublease. In the event of an assignment, the assignee becomes bound by the terms of the lease upon taking possession of the property; a sublessee is not liable for the lease obligations unless there is a promise by the sublessee to assume such obligations.

QUESTIONS AND CASE PROBLEMS

1. What social forces are affected by the rule governing the duty of a landlord to relet premises wrongfully abandoned by a tenant?

2. Jacqueline rented a house from Harvey for two years. At the end of the two years, she remained in the house and offered to pay the next month's rent. Harvey refused to take the rent, told Jacqueline to leave, and stated that she was a trespasser and could be thrown out. She claimed that she was not a trespasser because she had lawfully entered the premises under the lease. Was she correct?

3. Must a landlord mitigate damages when a tenant breaches a lease?

4. Maralyn rented a farm from Dale for 20 years. She rented the south part of the land to Ching-ya for 5 of the 20 years. Was Ching-ya an assignee or a sublessee?

5. Compare (a) an actual eviction of the tenant, (b) a constructive eviction of the tenant, and (c) a breach of the warranty of habitability.

6. Clay owned a tract of land. Clay permitted Hartney to live in a cabin on the land. Nothing was said as to the length of time that it could be used by Hartney. Nothing was said as to paying anything for the use of the cabin. Hartney died. The next day Clay closed up the cabin and put Hartney's possessions outside the door. Paddock was appointed the executor of Hartney's will. Paddock claimed the right to use the cabin. Was he entitled to do so?

7. Phillips Petroleum, Inc., leased a service station to Prather. McWilliam was a customer at the service station. A rusted window fell from the wall, injuring her. She sued Phillips Petroleum. Was Phillips liable? [McWilliam v

Phillips Petroleum, Inc. 269 Or 526, 525 P2d 1011]

8. Morgan rented an apartment in the Melrose Apartments. A number of crimes were committed in the apartment house. Morgan notified Melrose that it was required to hire additional security guards in order to protect the lessees in the apartment house from crimes. Was Morgan correct?

9. The Old Dover Tavern, Inc., rented a building from Amershadian to conduct a "business under the style and trade name of 'Old Dover Tavern, Inc.' engaging in the serving and selling [of] cigars, tobacco and all kinds of drinks and beverages of any name, nature and description." Thereafter, the tenant claimed that it was entitled to sell cold foods, such as sandwiches, on the theory that such sale was "incidental to the sale of beverages." The corporation brought an action to establish that it was so entitled. Was it? [Old Dover Tavern, Inc. v Amershadian, 2 Mass App 882, 318 NE2d 191]

10. Cantanese leased a drugstore building from Saputa. Cantanese moved his store from the rented store to another location but continued to pay the rent to Saputa. Saputa, fearing that he was losing his tenant, entered the premises without the permission of Cantanese and made extensive alterations to the premises to suit two physicians who had agreed to rent the premises from Saputa. Cantanese informed Saputa that he regarded the making of the unauthorized repairs as ground for canceling the lease. Saputa then claimed that Cantanese was liable for the difference between the rent that Cantanese had agreed to pay and the rent that the doctors would pay for the remainder of the term of the Cantanese lease. Was Cantanese liable for such rent? [Saputa v Cantanese (La App) 182 So 2d 826]

11. Sargent rented a second-floor apartment in an apartment house owned by Ross. Anna, the four-year-old daughter of Sargent, fell from an outdoor stairway and was killed. Suit was brought against Ross for her death. Ross defended on the ground that she did not have control over the stairway and, therefore, was not liable for its condition. Was this defense valid? [Sargent v Ross, 113 NH 388, 308 A2d 528]

12. Lester obtained a twenty-year leasehold interest in an office building owned by Tess. Tess died a few months later. Her heirs claimed that her death terminated the lease. Decide.

13. Green rented an apartment from Stockton Realty. The three-story building had a washroom and clothesline on the roof for use by the tenants. The clothesline ran very near the skylight. There was no guardrail between the clothesline and the skylight. Mrs. Green's friend, who was fourteen years old, was helping her remove clothes from the line. Her friend tripped on an object and fell against the skylight. The glass was too weak to support her weight and she fell to the floor below sustaining serious injuries. Is the landlord responsible for damages for the injury sustained? Decide. [Reiman v Moore, 42 Cal 2d 130, 180 P2d 452]

14. Scott signed a two-year lease that contained a clause expressly prohibiting subletting. After six months, Scott asked the landlord for permission to sublet the apartment for one year. The landlord refused. This angered Scott, and he immediately assigned his rights under the lease to Wright. The landlord objected to the assignment. Can Scott assign the lease? Explain.

15. Williams rented an apartment in the Parker House. He was an elderly man who was sensitive to heat. His apartment was fully air-conditioned, which enabled him to stand the otherwise unbearable heat of the summer. The landlord was dissatisfied with the current rental and, although the lease had a year to run, insisted that Williams agree to an increase. Williams refused. The landlord attempted to force Williams to pay the increase by turning off the electricity and thereby stopping the apartment's air-conditioners. He also sent up heat on the hot days. After one week of such treatment Williams, claiming that he had been evicted, moved out. Has there been an eviction? Explain.

PART 10

ESTATES

55

DECEDENTS' ESTATES

Public policy dictates that, when an individual dies, the cost of proper burial and other expenses that may arise in connection with death be paid; that the just debts contracted before death be settled; that the property owned at the time of death be taken care of and applied to the payment of expenses and the debts mentioned; and that the remainder, if any, be distributed among those properly entitled to receive it.

The law of decedents' estates is governed by state statutes and court decisions. The general principles and the procedures that will be discussed herein may be considered typical. The statutory provisions of a particular jurisdiction, however, may differ from the principles and the procedures considered. A step toward national uniformity has been taken by the American Bar Association and the National Conference of Commissioners on Uniform Laws by approving a Uniform Probate Code (UPC) and submitting it to the states for adoption.[1]

A.   WILLS

After all of the debts of a decedent are paid, distribution is made of any balance of the estate to those entitled to receive it. If the decedent made a valid will, the will determines which persons are entitled to receive the property. If the decedent did not make a valid will, the distribution is determined by intestate law.

§ 55:1   DEFINITIONS

Testate distribution describes the distribution that is made when the decedent leaves a valid will. A **will** is ordinarily a writing that provides for a distribution of property upon the death of the writer but which confers no rights prior to that time. A man who makes a will is called a **testator**; a woman, a **testatrix**.

The person to whom property is left by a will is a **beneficiary**. A gift of personal property by will is a **legacy** or **bequest**, in which case the beneficiary may also be called a **legatee**. A gift of real property by will is a **devise**, in which case the beneficiary may be called a **devisee**.

§ 55:2   PARTIES TO WILL

Each state has a right to prescribe the qualifications of persons who wish to make a will. While there are some variations among the states, the following is typical.

(a) TESTATOR. Generally, the right to make a will is limited to persons 18 or older. The testator must always have **testamentary capacity**.[2] In order to have testamentary capacity, a person must have sufficient mental capacity to understand that the writing that is being executed is a will, that is, that it disposes of the person's property after death, and must also have a reasonable appreciation of the identity of relatives and friends and of the nature and extent of the property that may exist at death.

The excessive and continued use of alcohol, producing mental deterioration, may be sufficient to justify the conclusion that the decedent lacked testamentary capacity.

(b) BENEFICIARY. Generally, there is no restriction with respect to the capacity of the beneficiary. However, when part of a decedent's estate passes to a minor, it is ordinarily necessary to appoint a guardian to administer such interest for the minor. Two common exceptions are as follows: (1) If there is a will that directs that any share payable to a minor be held by a particular person as trustee for the minor, the minor's interest will be so held and a guardian is not required; (2) Statutes often provide that if the estate or interest of the minor is not large, it may be paid directly to the minor or to the parent or person by whom the minor is maintained.

§ 55:3   TESTAMENTARY INTENT

There cannot be a will unless the testator manifests an intention to make a provision that will be effective only upon death. This is called a **testamentary intent**.[3] Ordinarily, this is an intention that certain persons shall become the owners of certain property upon the death of the testator. But a writing also manifests a testamentary intent when the testator only designates an executor and does not make any disposition of property.

---

[1]   The Uniform Probate Code has been adopted in Alaska, Arizona, Colorado, Florida, Hawaii, Idaho, Maine, Michigan, Minnesota, Montana, Nebraska, New Mexico, North Dakota, South Carolina, and Utah. A number of minor amendments have since been made. Kentucky has adopted only Article VII, Part I, of the UPC.

[2]   Succession of Cahn (La App) 552 So 2d 1160 (1988).
[3]   Thomas v Copenhaver, ___ Va ___, 365 SE2d 760 (1988).

§ 55:4 FORM

Since the privilege of disposing of property by will is purely statutory, the will must be executed in the manner and with the formalities required by state statutes. Unless statutory requirements are met, the will is invalid and the testator is considered to have died intestate. In such a case the decedent's property will be distributed according to the laws of intestacy of the particular state.

(a) WRITING. Ordinarily, a will must be in writing. Some state statutes, however, permit oral wills made by soldiers and sailors.

(b) SIGNATURE. A written will must be signed by the testator. In the absence of a provision of the statute stating that the will must be signed "in writing," a rubber stamp signature has been held sufficient. It is common, however, to require a written signature.

Generally, a will must be signed at the bottom or end. The purpose of this requirement is to prevent unscrupulous persons from taking a will that has been validly signed and writing or typing additional provisions in the space below the signature.

(c) ATTESTATION AND PUBLICATION. **Attestation** is the act of witnessing the execution of a will.[4] Generally, it includes signing the will as a witness, after a clause that recites that the witness has observed either the execution of the will or the testator's acknowledgment of the writing as the testator's will. This clause is commonly called an **attestation clause.** Statutes often require that attestation be made by the witnesses in the presence of the testator and in the presence of each other.

Publication is the act of the testator of informing the attesting witnesses that the document that is signed before them or is shown to them is the testator's will. The law varies between states as to the necessity of publication.

In some states witnesses are not required. Most states require two witnesses, although in some states three are required.

(d) DATE. There is generally no requirement that a will be dated. It is advisable, however, to date a will, for when there are several wills, the most recent prevails with respect to conflicting provisions.

§ 55:5 MODIFICATION OF WILL

A will may be modified by executing a codicil. A **codicil** is a separate writing that amends a will. The will, except as changed by the codicil, remains the same. The result is as though the testator rewrote the will, substituting the provisions of the codicil for those provisions of the will that are inconsistent with the codicil. A codicil must be executed with all the formality of a will and is treated in all other respects the same as a will.

A will cannot be modified merely by crossing out a clause and writing in what the testator wishes. Such an interlineation is not operative unless it is executed with the same formality required of a will, or in some states unless the will is republished in its interlineated form. This was the problem in the *Currier* case.

---

[4] Weaver v Grant (Ala) 394 So 2d 15 (1981).

CURRIER GALLERY OF ART V PACKARD
—— Mass App ——, 504 NE2d 368 (1987)

The will of Marjorie T. Packard, dated September 4, 1969, and a first codicil thereto, dated December 1, 1970, were admitted to probate on May 4, 1978. In August, 1985, the Currier Gallery of Art offered a document for probate as a second codicil. It was typed on what appeared to be the decedent's personal stationery, was dated November 15, 1971, and was addressed "To whom it may concern."

Before an interlineation and addition, this document stated in part: "I give and bequeath — at my direction or if still in my possession at my death — to the Trustees of the Currier Gallery . . . my maple New Hampshire chest . . . in memory of my brother Donald Kingman Packard." The decedent had signed the instrument, and it was attested by two witnesses. On January 15, 1975, the decedent drew lines through the words "if still in my possession" and wrote by hand, in apparent substitution, the words "when I can no longer use it or." She initialed and dated the alterations but did not have the paper attested by witnesses. The executors of the will and first codicil argued that the instrument as altered could not qualify for probate because first, it was too informal to serve as a codicil, and second, it was not testamentary in content, but declared an intention to make an inter vivos gift of the piece. From a decision of the probate court admitting the second codicil, the executors appealed.

GREANEY, J. . . . As it stood on November 15, 1971, the instrument was in writing, signed by the decedent (whose capacity is not challenged), and attested by two witnesses. No more was required on the formal side to make an effective codicil (or will). It did not matter for this purpose that the paper was not labelled "codicil," did not refer to the will or first codicil, and generally lacked sophistication. Moreover, the substance was testamentary. "At my direction" may be read as the equivalent or, indeed, as a reinforcement of the expression "give and bequeath" (the will used "direct" repeatedly in such a testamentary sense). The words "if still in my possession" then merely note the possibility that the piece may pass from the testatrix and be unavailable for disposition at her death; the same would apply even if the bequest was in unqualified terms. Another, perhaps more difficult, way to read the text is that the testatrix may by her direction choose to give the piece to the Gallery before her death, but if it remains in her possession at her death it shall pass to the Gallery. In that view, too, testamentary character and intention are preserved.

We turn to the possible effects of the handwritten changes. Being unattested, they were not themselves effective. What would have been the testatrix's intention in that circumstance? That the attempt at change should have at least the result of cancelling (revoking) the crossed-out words, leaving the rest of the original instrument intact? Or that the original instrument should remain wholly intact, cancellation of the crossed-out words being desired only if the changes were effective.

We need not attempt a choice because the result in either case is testamentary. On the latter, we have a testamentary gift as explained above. On the former, we have the text "I give and bequeath — at my direction or at my death — to the Trustees." The executors, by evident mistake, elide or disregard the words "or at my death." Restoring those words, we have — giving the executors the benefit of a difficult reading — a statement that the testatrix may choose to "direct" the piece to the Gallery before she dies, otherwise it passes to the Gallery at her death. This is little different from the meaning of the original instrument, and is sufficiently testamentary. . . .

[Judgment affirmed]

QUESTIONS

1. What is the purpose of a codicil?
2. Were Packard's handwritten changes to the codicil admissible to probate?
3. Did the codicil qualify for probate?

---

§ 55:6   REVOCATION OF WILL

At any time during the testator's life, the testator may revoke the will made or make changes in its terms. It may be revoked by act of the testator or by operation of law.

(a) REVOCATION BY ACT OF TESTATOR. A will is revoked when the testator destroys, burns, or tears the will, or crosses out the provisions of the will with the intention to revoke it. The revocation may be in whole or in part.

A testator must have the same degree of mental capacity to revoke a will as is required to make a will.

(b) REVOCATION BY OPERATION OF LAW. In certain instances statutes provide that a change of circumstances has the effect of a revocation. Thus it may be provided that when a person marries after executing a will, the will is revoked or is presumed revoked, unless it was made in contemplation of marriage or unless it provided for the future spouse. In some states the revocation is not total but only to the extent of allowing the spouse to take such share of the estate as that to which the spouse would have been entitled had there been no will.

It is also commonly provided that the birth or adoption of a child after the execution of a will works a revocation or partial revocation of the will as to that child. In the case of a partial revocation, the child is entitled to receive the same share as though the testator had died intestate.

The divorce of the testator does not in itself work a revocation, but the majority of courts hold that if a property settlement is carried out on the basis of the divorce, a prior will of the testator is revoked, at least to the extent of the legacy given to the divorced spouse.

§ 55:7   PROBATE OF WILL

Probate is the act by which the proper court or official accepts a will and declares that the instrument satisfies the statutory requirements as the will of the testator. Until a will is probated, it has no legal effect.

When witnesses have signed a will, generally they must appear and state that they saw the testator sign the will. If those witnesses cannot be found, have died, or are outside the jurisdiction, the will may be probated nevertheless. When no witnesses are required, it is customary to require two or more persons to identify the signature of the testator at time of probate.

After the probate witnesses have made their statements under oath, the officer or court will ordinarily admit the will to probate in the absence of any particular circumstances indicating that the writing should not be probated. A certificate or decree that officially declares that the will is the will of the testator and has been admitted to probate is then issued.

Any qualified person wishing to object to the probate of the will on the ground that it is not a proper will may appear before the official or court prior to the entry of the decree of probate or may petition after probate to have the probate of the will set aside.

§ 55:8   WILL CONTEST

The probate of a will may be refused or set aside on the ground that the will is not the free expression of the intention of the testator. It may be attacked on the ground of (a) lack of mental capacity to execute a will; (b) undue influence, duress, fraud, or mistake existing at the time of the execution of the will that induced or led to its execution; or (c) forgery. With the exception of mental capacity, these concepts mean the same as they do in contract law.

If it is found that any one of these elements exists, the probate of the will is refused or set aside. The decedent's estate is then distributed as if there had been no will unless an earlier will can be probated.

The *Wall* case involved a will contest.

WALL V HODGES
(Ala App) 465 So 2d 359 (1984)

Jeanette Wall worked for D. J. Sharron for many years. Sharron executed a will leaving his entire estate to Jeanette. He re-executed the will some time thereafter with the same provisions. The contestants offered evidence that they claimed showed Sharron was a very sick man, physically as well as mentally, that Wall was active in Sharron's business as well as his personal life, and that she exerted undue influence over Sharron in both his earlier and later wills. From a judgment in favor of the contestants, Wall appealed.

PER CURIAM. . . . D. J. Sharron owned and operated a trucking business called Sharron Motor Lines. Jeanette T. Wall was first employed in the company's Birmingham office in 1970. In three years' time she became a vice-president, and, in 1977, was promoted to executive vice-president.

Sometime in late 1974 or early 1975, Sharron moved his residence to Birmingham, along with the main office of Sharron Motor Lines. After this move, Jeanette Wall began handling his personal business affairs — including writing his checks, paying his bills, doing his personal filing, and handling his mail. She also travelled with him to branch offices of the company, and even helped him buy some of his clothes. There was evidence adduced at trial tending to show that Wall did not like Sharron's children and might have had something to do with two of the children leaving their positions with the company.

Contestants produced evidence that D. J. Sharron was a very sick man, physically as well as mentally. Sharron had suffered two heart attacks and had been diagnosed as having various diseases late in his life. The majority of the testimony concerned Sharron's lack of mental capacity in the late 1970's and early 1980's. A review of the record reveals that Sharron had some problems maintaining control over his mental faculties. There was testimony from several witnesses (other than contestants) who had noticed drastic changes in Sharron's behavioral patterns.

The remainder of the testimony at trial offered by appellees concerned Wall's exercise of control over Sharron's life. On more than one occasion he voiced his apparent powerlessness to help his children when they had run-ins with Wall. By her testimony appellant attempted to show that she was Sharron's only real friend and the only real hope for the business to prosper after his death. Appellant also offered testimony that Sharron's children were interested only in his money, and caused many problems for Sharron, especially late in his life. There was even testimony at trial that Sharron did not believe that all of the children were actually his.

In December 1981, Sharron went to see his personal lawyer, Marvin B. Speed, in Meridian, Mississippi. While there, he executed a will on December 2 which left his entire estate to Jeanette Wall. Later, fearing that this will might not be valid in Alabama, Sharron contacted his corporate attorney, Donald B. Sweeney. After some consultation, Sharron was advised to re-execute the December 2, 1981, will in Alabama. Wanting to ensure that the provisions of this will would be followed, Sharron explored the possibility of having this will video-taped. Upon advice of counsel, he instead underwent a psychiatric examination in order to confirm his mental capacity to execute a will. On February 4, 1982, Sharron re-executed the December 1981 will, without revision. Sharron died approximately one month later.

On March 9, 1982, proponent Jeanette T. Wall filed a petition to probate the will of D. J. Sharron dated February 4, 1982, in the Probate Court of Jefferson County. Subsequently, four of Sharron's children filed four separate will contests and requests for transfer to circuit court, as well as filing three other purported wills of D. J. Sharron, dated December 2, 1981, September 25, 1980, and December 23, 1976. . . .

In *Pruitt v. Pruitt*, 343 So.2d 495 (Ala. 1977), this Court discussed what must be proven to establish the existence of undue influence:

> Our cases have consistently held that when undue influence is asserted in a will contest, the contestant has the burden, in order to raise a presumption of undue influence, to prove a *dominant* confidential relationship and *undue activity in the execution of the will* by or for a favored beneficiary. In other words, evidence must establish: (1) a confidential relationship between a favored beneficiary and testator; (2) that the influence of or for the beneficiary was dominant and controlling in that relationship; and (3) *undue* activity on the part of the dominant party in procuring the execution of the will.

Although the appellees may have proven the existence of the first two elements — a confidential relationship and a dominance or control over Sharron by Wall — they have failed to offer any proof of the third element. There is no evidence that Wall had any involvement in the procuring of either the December 1981 will or the February 1982 will of D. J. Sharron.

The appellees make much of the fact that Wall was active in Sharron's business as well as his personal affairs. This is not sufficient justification for the rejection of a will. "There must be evidence, in addition to the fact of relationship, of active interference in procuring the execution of the will." The appellees do not even offer a scintilla of evidence that Jeanette Wall had anything to do with either will, or that she knew either will existed until after J. D. Sharron died. To the contrary, Sharron's attorney testified that not only was Jeanette Wall never present when he and Sharron discussed the December 1981 will, but that she was not present on the day it was executed.

In fact, all of the evidence offered by the appellees concerning Wall's involvement in a will of J. D. Sharron was with regard to a will drawn up by a different attorney over five years earlier. We reject the appellees' argument that because Wall might have had some involvement in the 1976 will she must have exerted undue influence over Sharron five years later.

We agree with the appellees' statement that undue influence may be proven using circumstantial evidence. Further, all that is necessary for the issue to be submitted to the jury is a scintilla of evidence of each of the three elements. However, the evidence needed to take the case to the jury on the question of undue influence is a reasonable inference, rather than mere suspicion. In this case the appellees have failed to put forth one shred of evidence that Jeanette Wall had anything to do with the procurement of the December 1981 will or the re-execution of it in February 1982. Evidence proving that there was undue activity on the part of Jeanette Wall in procuring the execution of the will is crucial to the determination of the existence of undue influence. Since the appellees failed to offer even a scintilla of evidence regarding this issue, the question should not have been submitted to the jury. . . .

[Judgment reversed and action remanded]

QUESTIONS

1. In a will contest, who has the burden to establish the validity of the will?
2. In a will contest, who has the burden to establish undue influence?
3. Did the court find undue influence? What was the basis for its decision?

§ 55:9   SPECIAL KINDS OF WILLS

A **holographic will** is an unwitnessed will that is written by the testator entirely by hand. In some states no distinction is made between a holographic and other wills. In other states the general body of the law of wills applies, but certain variations are established. Thus, it may be required that a holographic will be dated.

A **nuncupative will** is an oral will made and declared by the testator in the presence of witnesses to be a will. Generally, it can be made only with respect to personal property during the last illness of the testator.

It is commonly provided that a nuncupative will cannot be probated unless the witnesses reduce it to writing and sign the writing within a certain period of time after the declaring of the will.

Soldiers and sailors generally may make an oral or a written will of their personal estates without complying with the formalities required of other wills. It is sufficient that testamentary intent be shown.

A will made by a soldier or sailor is not revoked by the termination of the testator's period of service. It remains in force upon returning to civilian life, and it can only be revoked in the same manner as any other will.

B.   DISTRIBUTION UNDER THE WILL

If the decedent died leaving a valid will, the last phase of the administration of the estate by the decedent's personal representative is the distribution of property remaining after the payment of all debts and taxes, in accordance with the provisions of the will.

§ 55:10   LEGACIES

The testator will ordinarily bequeath to named persons certain sums of money, called **general legacies** because no particular money is specified, or will bequeath identified property, called **specific legacies** or **specific devises.** Thus the testator may say, "$1,000 to *A;* $1,000 to *B;* my auto to *C.*" The first two bequests are general, the third is specific. After such bequests, the testator may make a bequest of everything remaining, called a **residuary bequest,** such as "the balance of my estate to *D.*"

(a) ABATEMENT OF LEGACIES. Assume in the preceding example that after all debts are paid, there remains only $1,500 and the auto. What disposition is to be made? Legacies abate or bear loss in the following order: (1) residuary, (2) general, (3) specific. The law also holds that legacies of the same class abate proportionately. Accordingly, in the hypothetical case, *C,* the specific legatee, would receive the auto; *A* and *B,* the general legatees, would each receive $750, and *D,* the residuary legatee would not receive anything.

(b) ADEMPTION OF PROPERTY. When specifically bequeathed property is sold or given away by the testator prior to death, the bequest is considered **adeemed** or canceled, and the specific legatee is not entitled to receive any property or money. Ademption has the same consequence as though the testator had formally canceled the bequest.

(c) ANTI-LAPSE STATUTES. If the beneficiary named in the testator's will has died before the testator and the testator did not make any alternate provision applicable in such case, the gift ordinarily does not lapse. **Anti-lapse** statutes commonly provide that the gift to the deceased beneficiary shall not lapse but that the children or heirs of that beneficiary may take the legacy in the place of the deceased beneficiary.[5] An anti-lapse statute does not apply if the testator specifies a disposition that should be made of the gift if the original legatee has died.

The *Murray* case involved the interpretation of an anti-lapse statute.

[5] Malecki's Estate, 79 App Div 2d 799, 435 NYS2d 112 (1980).

MURRAY V WILLETT

36 Md App 551, 373 A2d 1303 (1977)

Murray wrote a will by which he left all his property to his sisters Mary and Isabel. He further provided "in the event of the prior decease of Isabel, her share is to go to Mary. In the event of the prior decease [of] Mary, her share is to go to Isabel." Mary died in 1971 and was survived by a son. Isabel died in 1973 and was survived by a son. Murray died thereafter. The sons of the two sisters claimed that they were entitled to the estate of Murray. Other relatives of Murray claimed that the gifts to the named sisters had lapsed and that Murray's estate therefore passed to them. The lower court found in favor of the sons, and the relatives appealed.

GILBERT, C. J. . . . The difficulty . . . in the instant case is occasioned by the phrase "of the prior decease." Those words give rise to two distinct inferences. The phrase could be argued to mean, first, that each sister must survive the other in order to take under the will, or, second, that each sister must survive the testator before she may take under the will.

Had the testator been cognizant of and heeded the message in the "Minutes and Advices of the Yearly Meeting of Friends Held in London" (1802), that "[f]riends are earnestly recommended to employ persons skillful in law, and of good repute, to make their wills; as great inconvenience and loss, and sometimes the ruin of families, have happened through the unskillfulness of some who have taken upon them[selves] to make wills. . . .", it is likely that this litigation would never have arisen. . . .

We believe this case to be controlled by [Maryland Estate & Trust Code Annotated] § 4-403, which provides . . .

(a) *Death of legatee prior to testator.* Unless a contrary intent is expressly indicated in the will, a legacy may not lapse or fail because of the death of a legatee after the execution of the will but prior to the death of the testator if the legatee is:

(1) Actually and specifically named as legatee;

(2) Described or in any manner referred to, designated, or identified as legatee in the will; or

(3) A member of a class in whose favor a legacy is made.

(b) *Effect of death of legatee.* A legacy described in subsection (a) shall have the same effect and operation in law to direct the distribution of the property directly from the estate of the person who owned the property to those persons who would have taken the property if the legatee had died, testate or intestate, owning the property.

As we view the will in the case now before us, there is no "expressed" or "indicated" intent therein to demonstrate that the testator was desirous of having his estate, or any portion thereof, pass by way of intestacy. The clause can only reasonably be interpreted, therefore, to mean that Murray devised his estate to his two sisters, Mary and Isabel, in equal shares with the proviso that if either sister was not alive at his death, then the surviving sister would inherit the whole of the estate. Because both sisters predeceased Murray, it is safe to infer, in the light of the anti-lapse statute, § 4-403, that Murray intended for the children of Mary and Isabel to take by way of representation the share that the child's mother would have taken had she survived Murray. . . .

[Judgment affirmed]

QUESTIONS

1. What is the purpose of an anti-lapse statute?
2. What was the defect in Murray's will?
3. Could the court have made any other decision?

---

§ 55:11   ELECTION TO TAKE
AGAINST THE WILL

In order to protect the husband or wife of a testator, the surviving spouse may generally ignore the provisions of a will and elect to take against the will. In such a case the surviving spouse receives the share of the estate which that spouse would have received had the testator died without leaving a will, or a fractional share specified by statute.

The right to take against the will is generally barred by certain kinds of misconduct of the surviving spouse. Thus, if the spouse is guilty of such desertion or nonsupport as would have justified the decedent's obtaining a divorce, the surviving spouse usually cannot elect to take against the will.

§ 55:12 DISINHERITANCE

With two exceptions,[6] any person may be disinherited or excluded from sharing in the estate of a decedent.[7] A person who would inherit if there were no will is excluded from receiving any part of a decedent's estate if the decedent has left a will giving everything to other persons.

§ 55:13 CONSTRUCTION OF WILL

The will of a decedent is to be interpreted according to the ordinary or plain meaning evidenced by its words. The court will strive to give effect to every provision of the will in order to avoid concluding that any part of the decedent's estate was not disposed of by the will.[8]

C. INTESTACY

If the decedent does not effectively dispose of all property by will or does not have a will, the decedent's property is distributed to certain relatives. Since such persons acquire or succeed to the rights of the decedent and since the circumstances under which they do so is the absence of an effective will, it is said that they acquire title by **intestate succession.**

The right of intestate succession or inheritance is not a basic right of the citizen or an inalienable right but exists only because the state legislature so provides. It is within the power of the state legislature to modify or destroy the right to inherit property.

§ 55:14 PLAN OF INTESTATE DISTRIBUTION

Although wide variations exist among the statutory provisions of the states, a common pattern of intestate distribution can be observed:

(a) SPOUSES. The surviving spouse of the decedent, whether husband or wife, shares in the estate. Generally, the amount received is a fraction that varies with the number of children. If no children survive, the spouse is generally entitled to take the entire estate. Otherwise the surviving spouse ordinarily receives a one-half or one-third share of the estate.

(b) LINEALS. **Lineals** or **lineal descendants** are blood descendants of the decedent. That portion of the estate that is not distributed to the surviving spouse is generally distributed to lineals.

(c) PARENTS. If the estate has not been fully distributed by this time, the remainder is commonly distributed to the decedent's parents.

(d) COLLATERAL HEIRS. These are persons who are not descendants of the decedent but who are related through a common ancestor. Generally, brothers and sisters and their descendants share any part of the estate that has not already been distributed.

Statutes vary as to how far distribution will be made to the descendants of brothers and sisters. Under some statutes a degree of relationship is specified, such as first cousins, and no person more remotely related to the decedent is permitted to share in the estate. If the entire estate is not distributed within the permitted degree of relationship, the property that has not been distributed is given to the state government. This right of the state to take the property is the **right of escheat.** Under some statutes the right of escheat arises only when there is no relative of the decedent, however remotely related.

(e) DISTRIBUTION PER CAPITA AND PER STIRPES. The fact that different generations of distributees may be entitled to receive the estate creates a problem of determining the proportions in which distribution is to be made. When all the distributees stand in the same degree of relationship to the decedent, **distribution** is made **per capita,** each receiving the same share. Thus, if the

---

[6] The exceptions to this rule are based (a) upon the election of a spouse to take against the will and (b) in certain cases upon the partial revocation of a will by a subsequent marriage, birth, or adoption.

[7] Brown v Drake, 275 SC 299, 270 SE2d 130 (1980).

[8] Silverthorn v Jennings (Tex Civ App) 620 SW2d 894 (1981).

decedent is survived by three children, *A*, *B*, and *C*, each of them is entitled to receive one third of the estate.

If the distributees stand in different degrees of relationship, distribution is made in as many equal parts as there are family lines or stirpes represented in the nearest generation. Parents take to the exclusion of their children or subsequent descendants; and when members of the nearest generation have died, their descendants take by way of representation. This is called **distribution per stirpes** or **stipital distribution.**

(f) MURDER OF DECEDENT. Statutes generally provide that a person who murders the decedent cannot inherit from the victim by intestacy. In the absence of such a statute, some courts hold that the inheritance cannot be denied; however, others refuse to allow inheritance under such circumstances.

(g) DEATH OF DISTRIBUTEE AFTER DECEDENT. The persons entitled to distribution of a decedent's estate are determined as of the date of death. If a distributee dies thereafter, the rights of the distributee are not lost but pass from the original decedent's estate to the deceased distributee's estate.

(h) SIMULTANEOUS DEATH. The Uniform Simultaneous Death Act[9] provides that when survivorship cannot be established, "the property of each person shall be disposed of as if he had survived the other."[10]

D.   ADMINISTRATION OF DECEDENTS' ESTATES

A decedent's estate consists of the assets that a person owns at death. It must be determined who is entitled to receive that property. If the decedent owed debts, those debts must be paid first. After that, any balance is to be distributed according to the terms of any will, or by the intestate law if the decedent did not leave a will.

---

[9] This Act has been adopted for the District of Columbia and the Panama Canal Zone and in every state except Louisiana and Ohio.

[10] Special provision is made in the case of beneficiaries, joint tenants, tenants by entireties, community property, and insurance policies.

§ 55:15   DEFINITIONS

The decedent has the privilege of naming in the will the person who will administer the estate. A man named in a will to administer the estate of the decedent is an **executor**, a woman, an **executrix**. If the decedent failed to name an executor or did not leave a will, the law permits another person, usually a close relative, to obtain the appointment of someone to wind up the estate. This person is an **administrator** or **administratrix**.

In certain special instances a temporary administrator may be appointed. Thus, if there is a will contest, an **administrator pendente lite** may be appointed, that is, an administrator who serves during the litigation for the purpose of preserving the estate.

Administrators and executors are often referred to generally as **personal representatives** of the decedents since they represent the decedents or stand in their place.

§ 55:16   WHEN ADMINISTRATION IS NOT NECESSARY

No administration is required when the decedent did not own any property at the time of death or when all the property owned was jointly owned with another person who acquired the decedent's interest by right of survivorship. Thus, if all of the property of a husband and wife is held as tenants by the entireties, no administration is required upon the death of either of them because the other automatically acquires the entire estate free of any debts or liabilities of the decedent.

In some states special statutes provide for a simplified administration when the decedent leaves only a small estate.

§ 55:17   APPOINTMENT OF PERSONAL REPRESENTATIVE

Both executors and administrators must be appointed to act as such by a court or officer designated by law. The appointment is made by granting to the personal representative **letters testamentary,** in the case of an executor, or **letters of administration,** in the case of an administrator. For the appointment of a personal representative, an application or petition is filed with the court or officer setting forth the details of the decedent's death, stating that the decedent, if a resident of the state, lived within the county or, if a nonresident, that property of the decedent is within the county, and reciting the facts that justify the appointment of the personal representative.

(a) PERSON ENTITLED TO ACT AS PERSONAL REPRESENTATIVE. If the decedent has named an executor, that person has the right to act as personal representative or to decline to do so. If no executor has been named, an administrator is appointed.

The right to act as administrator is regulated by statutes, which generally give the right to administer to the surviving spouse; but if there is no surviving spouse or if the spouse declines, the right is given to the next of kin.

(b) OATH AND BOND. A personal representative who is appointed, is required to take an oath and to file a bond that the estate will be properly administered according to law. In some states an executor is not required to furnish a bond if a resident of the state and in sound financial condition or if the testator has expressly directed that no bond be required.

§ 55:18 PROOF OF CLAIMS AGAINST THE ESTATE

The statutes vary widely with respect to the presentation of claims against a decedent's estate. In very general terms the statutes provide for some form of public notice of the grant of letters, as by advertisement. Creditors are then required to give notice of their claims within a period specified either by statute or a court order, as within six months. In most states the failure to present the claim within the specified time bars the claim.

(a) NATURE OF CLAIMS. Claims against an estate can be grouped into one of four classifications. The classification of a particular claim will affect the order in which it is satisfied.

(1) Funeral Expenses. In most jurisdictions a personal representative either cannot or will not be appointed before the burial of the decedent. Accordingly, it is the surviving spouse or the next of kin who has the responsibility of arranging for the burial of the decedent.

(2) Administration Expenses. The estate is charged with the expenses of its administration. These include the cost of the personal representative's bond, if any; the fee charged by the court or clerk for the grant of the letters to the personal representative; the cost of advertising and giving notice when required; the cost of filing the account; the cost of any particular services, such as bringing suit against third persons; and the compensation of the personal representative and the estate's attorney.

(3) Family Allowance. Most states make some provision for the immediate necessities of a decedent's family during the period of administration. The widow or widower or the children are generally entitled to receive a certain portion of the estate for this purpose. In some states the granting of this allowance lies within the discretion of the court; while in others it is a matter of right. It most commonly takes the form of a specified sum of money, although in some states it is the right to take certain specified articles of property or to live in the house of the decedent for a specified time. It is immaterial whether the decedent left a will or, if there is a will, whether the claimant receives anything under the decedent's will.

The right of a spouse to receive this allowance is generally barred by conduct on the claimant's part that would have entitled the decedent to obtain a divorce. Thus, a wife who is guilty of deserting her husband is not entitled, upon his death, to receive the family allowance from his estate.

The family allowance is ordinarily not subject to the claim of creditors. This means that the person entitled to the allowance may receive it even though there will not be enough to pay creditors after the allowance has been deducted.

(4) Debts and Liabilities of the Decedent. Generally, any debt or liability of the decedent existing at the time of death may be asserted against the estate.

(b) PRIORITY OF CLAIMS. When the estate of a decedent is insolvent, that is, when it is not sufficiently large to pay all debts and taxes, the law generally provides that certain claims shall be paid first. Although there is great variation of detail, the most common pattern of priority provides for the payment of claims against the estate in the following order: (1) funeral expenses; (2) administration expenses; (3) family allowance; (4) claims due the United States;[11] (5) expenses of the last illness; (6) debts due state, county, and city governments; (7) claims for wages; (8) lien claims; (9) all other debts.

Assuming a state in which the priorities are as stated, the effect is that the decedent's estate is first used to pay claims listed in category (1). If any balance remains, claims in category (2) are paid. If any balance remains, claims in category (3) are paid, and so on. If there are several claimants within a particular class, but not enough money to pay each in full, they share proportionately the balance remaining, and creditors in lower priorities receive nothing.

§ 55:19 POWERS AND DUTIES OF PERSONAL REPRESENTATIVE

The powers and duties of the personal representative relate to the collection of the assets of the estate; the care and preservation of the assets; the management of the estate; the prosecution and defense of lawsuits to which the estate is a party; the payment of decedent's debts, administration expenses, federal estate taxes, and state taxes; accounting to the extent required by law; and distributing the estate to those entitled to it. Apart from special powers that a testator may confer upon an executor, the

[11] 31 USC § 191.

powers of an executor and administrator are the same.

(a) PERFORMANCE. A personal representative is under the duty to administer the estate according to law. An executor must also comply with directions contained in the will.

(b) DUE CARE AND LOYALTY. A personal representative has the duty of exercising due care and loyalty.

(c) POSSESSION AND PRESERVATION OF ESTATE. The personal representative has the task of collecting the assets of the estate and subsequently of distributing them to the persons entitled to them. An executor or administrator has the duty to defend the estate against adverse claims.

Checks and cash received by a personal representative will be deposited in a bank account opened in the representative's name, that is, as *Sally Jones, Administratrix of the Estate of Henry Brown, Deceased,* or in the name of the estate, as *Estate of Henry Brown, Deceased.* In either case checks on the account would be signed by Sally Jones as administratrix of the named estate.

(d) PAYMENT OF DEBTS. The personal representative has the duty to pay the decedent's debts, taxes, and the expenses of administering the estate.

(e) INVENTORY AND APPRAISAL. The personal representative must make a list or inventory of the assets of the decedent's estate. With this inventory must be an appraisal of the value of the various items so that the value of each bequest or distributive share and the total value of the estate can be determined.

Generally, the inventory and the appraisal are restricted to personal property, although some statutes require the listing of real estate as well. A number of states allow the omission of certain kinds of personal property, such as clothing, Bibles, and school books.

(f) MONUMENT OR TOMBSTONE. The personal representative has the duty to erect a tombstone or monument on the grave of the decedent.

(g) INVESTMENTS. Since the function of

the personal representative is to distribute the estate, the representative ordinarily has no authority to make investments. Sometimes the duty to do so will be implied when, because of litigation or the nature of the assets, there will be a long delay in the distribution of the estate.

(h) ADMINISTRATION OF REAL ESTATE. Whether the administrator has any duty or power with respect to real estate of the decedent depends upon the law of the particular state. At common law, only the personal property of a decedent was administered by a personal representative. Real estate of the decedent vested upon death in heirs or devisees.

In most states this rule has been modified to the extent that, when it is necessary to pay debts of the decedent, the personal representative may take control of the real estate and rent or sell it for that purpose. In some states the distinction between real and personal property is abolished, and the personal representative has the same administrative control over real estate of the decedent as over personal property.

In the absence of a statutory provision, generally the personal assets of the decedent must be consumed in the payment of debts before the real estate can be touched for that purpose.

Whether the personal representative is under a duty to insure the real estate depends upon whether, under the circumstances, a reasonable person would obtain insurance.

(i) CONTINUATION OF BUSINESS. In the absence of statute or an express direction in the will, an executor does not have the right to continue the business of the decedent.

(j) DETERMINATION OF PROPER DISTRIBUTEES. It is the duty of the personal representative to ascertain by the exercise of reasonable diligence the proper persons to whom distribution is to be made. For example, if an estate is to be divided among the brothers of the decedent, the personal representative should ascertain as far as can reasonably be done the identity and

whereabouts of all of the brothers. Or if a spouse is disqualified from sharing in the estate, the personal representative must make that fact known to the court.

After the rights of the parties who are entitled to the estate have been determined, the personal representative is under the duty to make distribution in accordance with those rights.

(k) ACCOUNTING. A personal representative is under the same duty to account as an agent.

(l) LIABILITY OF PERSONAL REPRESENTATIVE. If misconduct of the executor or the administrator or if failure to act causes loss to the estate, such representative may be required to indemnify the estate for the amount of the loss that has been caused.[12] The decree or order imposing liability is commonly called a **surcharge**.

§ 55:20   TERMINATION OF AUTHORITY OF PERSONAL REPRESENTATIVE

The termination of the authority of a personal representative ordinarily has no retroactive effect. The validity of transactions completed before the termination of authority is not affected.

(a) DISCHARGE OF THE REPRESENTATIVE. After the administration of the estate is completed, the personal representative applies to the court to be discharged. Once a discharge is entered, authority to act is terminated.

(b) REVOCATION OF GRANT OF LETTERS. The letters may have been erroneously granted. The letters will, in such a case, be revoked.

Letters will also be revoked when they have been granted in the wrong county, or when the person appointed was not qualified. Thus, letters of administration granted to the decedent's apparent widow will be revoked when it is shown that she had not been the decedent's wife.

Letters of administration will be revoked

[12]   Corbin's Estate (Fla App) 391 So 2d 731 (1980).

when it is later found that the decedent left a will and when the will is admitted to probate. Conversely, letters testamentary will be revoked when the will is set aside as being invalid.

(c) RESIGNATION. In most states the personal representative can resign if permission of the court is obtained. This request will ordinarily be granted if a good cause for resignation is shown and the estate will not be prejudiced thereby.

(d) REMOVAL. In most states, statutes have been adopted that specify the grounds for the removal of a personal representative. In general, these include any delinquency, misconduct, or personal incapacity of a nature sufficiently serious as to interfere with the administration of the estate. Thus, a personal representative may be removed for failure to file required papers, or for fraud, misappropriation of funds of the estate, or for a loss of personal competence or fitness to act as representative. A personal representative may also be removed for representing an interest adverse to the estate.

SUMMARY

A will is a disposition of property to take effect upon death. A man who makes a will is called a testator; a woman, a testatrix. The person to whom property is left by will is a beneficiary. A legacy is a gift of personal property by will; a gift of real property by will is known as a devise.

A testator must have testamentary capacity to make a will and must manifest some intention that the will be effective only upon death.

The will must ordinarily be in writing and must be signed by the testator and witnessed. Some states require publication, that is, some declaration that the document that is signed before the witnesses is the testator's will.

A will may be modified by a codicil or revoked by either the act of the testator or by operation of law.

Probate is the act by which a proper court official accepts a will. Probate may be refused or set aside on grounds that the will is not the free expression of the testator.

A holographic will is an unwitnessed will written entirely in the handwriting of the testator. A nuncupative will is an oral one.

If there is a valid will, the last phase of administration of the estate is the distribution of property after the payment of all debts and taxes. General legacies are bequests of money, while specific legacies or specific devises are gifts of identified personal or real property. Legacies abate in the following order: residuary, general, and specific. If a beneficiary named in the will has died before the testator and no alternate provision has been made for such beneficiary, anti-lapse statutes provide that the gift will not lapse. In that event, the children or heirs of the beneficiary may take the legacy in the place of the deceased beneficiary.

If the decedent does not dispose of all property by will or does not have a will, the property will be distributed according to state intestacy statutes. A surviving spouse may generally elect to take the statutory allocation instead of that provided in the will.

The estate of the testator will be administered by the person appointed in the will (the executor) or, if there is no will, by a person appointed by the court (an administrator). Creditors who have claims against the estate are required to give notice of their claim to the personal representative; otherwise, the claim will be barred. When the estate is insolvent, claims are generally paid in the following order of priority: funeral expenses; administration expenses; family allowance; claims due to the United States; expenses of the last illness; debts due state, county, and city governments; claims for wages; lien claims; and all other debts.

The personal representative must administer the estate according to law. If the misconduct of the executor or administrator or if failure to act causes loss to the estate, such representative may be required to indemnify the estate for the amount of the loss.

QUESTIONS AND CASE PROBLEMS

1. What social forces are affected by allowing a person to give property after death by means of leaving a will?

2. Jean repeatedly told her best friend, Dinah, and their neighbors, that Jean would leave her house to Dinah when she died. Jean died without having written any will. Dinah claimed the house, and the neighbors testified in court that Jean had repeatedly declared that she would leave the house to Dinah. Is Dinah entitled to the house?

3. Michael wrote his lawyer that he wanted the lawyer to prepare a will that would leave his property in the manner set forth in the letter. Michael signed and mailed this letter but died before the letter was received by his lawyer. Upon receiving the letter, the attorney offered the letter for probate as the will of Michael. Should it be probated?

4. Iona wrote her will. The following year she wrote another will that expressly revoked the earlier will. Later, while cleaning house, she came across the second will. She mistakenly thought that it was the first will and tore it up because the first will had been revoked. Iona died shortly thereafter. The beneficiaries named in the second will claimed that the second will should be probated. The beneficiaries named in the first will claimed that the second will had been revoked when it was torn up. Had the second will been revoked?

5. Gary died without any will or known relatives. During the last years of Gary's life, his neighbors had continually assisted him and taken care of him. The neighbors agreed that the proper thing to do since there were no relatives was for the neighbors to divide the property that was in Gary's house. Are they correct?

6. Lucille, by the terms of her will, gave and bequeathed her sterling silverware to her son, William, and the balance or residue of her estate to her daughter, Linda. Prior to the death of Lucille, she sold the sterling silverware and deposited the proceeds from the sale in the Eastern Bank. After the death of Lucille, William petitioned the court to award him the proceeds of the sterling silverware. What will the result be?

7. Contrast letters testamentary with letters of administration.

8. Logsdon, who had three children, disliked one of them without any reason. In his will he left only a small amount to the child he disliked and gave the bulk of his estate to the remaining two. Upon his death, the disliked child claimed that the will was void and had been obtained by undue influence. Do you agree? [Logsdon v Logsdon, 412 Ill 19, 104 NE2d 622]

9. Field executed a will. Upon her death the will was found in her safe deposit box, but the part of the will containing the fifth bequest was torn from the will. This torn fragment was also found in the box. There was no evidence that anyone other than Field had ever opened the box. A proceeding was brought to determine whether the will was entitled to be probated. Decide. [Flora v Hughes, 312 Ky 478, 228 SW2d 27]

10. Anna Miller wrote a will 11 pages long and enclosed it in an envelope, which she sealed. She then wrote on the envelope, "My last will & testament," and signed her name below this statement. This was the only place where she signed her name on any of the papers. Was this signature sufficient to allow this writing to be admitted to probate as her will? [Miller's Executor v Shannon (Ky) 299 SW2d 103]

11. *A* bequeathed the balance of her estate to *B* and *C* "if they both be living at the time of my demise and if one shall have predeceased me then all of my estate to the one remaining." Both *B* and *C* died before *A. B* was survived by a daughter, *D. C* was not survived by any children or grandchildren.

A was survived by *E*, a nephew, the child of a deceased brother. *E* and *D* each claimed the estate of *A*. The claim of *D* was based upon the anti-lapse statute. The claim of *E* was based upon the fact that he was the closest living relative of *A*. Who was entitled to *A*'s estate? [Kerr's Estate (CA Dist Col) 433 F2d 479]

12. E. J. White wrote by hand and signed the following: "To Whom It May concern. If anything should happen to me, I want all My Property & otherthing & Bonds divided between Marvin, Arlene & my sisters. Eight Thousand to Earl's children, the House 311 North 25 Ave. to Marvin, sell the property. I will finish this later." No change or addition was ever made to this writing. She died seven years later. This writing was offered for probate as her will. Objection was made to the probate on the ground that the last sentence showed that the writing had not been made with testamentary intent. Was this objection valid? [Maines v Davis (Miss) 227 So 2d 844]

13. Probate of the will of Vivian Lingenfelter was opposed. It was shown that the testatrix was sick, highly nervous, and extremely jealous and that she committed suicide a week after executing the will. In support of the will, it was shown that she understood the will when she discussed it with an attor-

ney; that her husband was seriously ill when she wrote the will; that he died the following day; and that she grieved his death. A proceeding was brought to determine whether the will was entitled to probate. Decide. [Lingenfelter's Estate, 38 Cal 2d 571, 241 P2d 990]

14. Brock made a will in which he bequeathed a legacy of $10,000 to his wife Mary. There then followed a clause stating "it is my express wish that no part of my estate shall go to my son Stewart." No further gift or testamentary provision was made in the will. When Brock died, Mary and Stewart survived him, and his net estate amounted to $30,000. Stewart claims that he is entitled to a share of $20,000. Is he correct?

15. By his original will, Leon bequeathed one third of his estate to Andrew. When the will was probated, it was found that the bequest to Andrew had been crossed out and at the bottom of the will was a typewritten statement: "Under no condition do I wish Andrew to be included in this will." There was no evidence as to where the will had been kept at any time, nor any evidence as to when or under what circumstances the changes had been made to the will. Was Andrew entitled to the legacy? Explain.

16. What is the distinction between a holographic will and a nuncupative will?

56

TRUSTS

A **trust** is a legal device by which property, real or personal, is held by one person for the benefit of another.

A. GENERAL PRINCIPLES

Legal problems in the area of trusts invariably require a determination as to the nature of the relationship created by the trust and the rights and obligations of the parties with respect to such relationship.

§ 56:1   DEFINITIONS

The property owner who creates the trust is the **settlor**. (The word *settlor* is taken from the old legal language of "settling the property in trust.") The settlor is sometimes called the donor or trustor. The person to whom the property is transferred in trust is the **trustee**. The person for whose benefit the trustee holds the property is the **beneficiary** (or **cestui que trust**).

Property held in trust is sometimes called the **trust corpus, trust fund, trust estate,** or **trust res.** A distinction is made between the **principal**, or the property in trust, and the **income** that is earned by the principal and distributed by the trustee.

Although an express trust is ordinarily created by a transfer of property, the settlor may retain the property as trustee for the beneficiary. The fact that there is a duty to make a payment does not create a trust.[1]

If the trust is created to take effect within the lifetime of the settlor, it is a **living trust** or an **inter vivos trust.** If the trust is provided for in the settlor's will and is to become effective only when the will takes effect after death, the trust is called a **testamentary trust.**

§ 56:2   CREATION OF TRUSTS

The requirements to create a trust are not uniform. The following, however, are typical of what is or is not required.

(a) CONSIDERATION. Since a trust is a transfer of property, consideration is not required, although the absence of consideration may show that the trust is a transfer in fraud of creditors.

(b) LEGALITY. A trust may generally be created for any lawful purpose. A trust is invalid when it is for an unlawful purpose or is in fraud of creditors.

(c) CAPACITY OF BENEFICIARY. The capacity of the beneficiary of the trust to hold property or to contract is immaterial. Many trusts are created because the beneficiary

---

[1]   Spicer v Wright, 215 Va 520, 211 SE2d 79 (1975).

lacks legal or actual capacity to manage the property.

(d) FORMALITY. In creating a trust, it is common practice to execute a writing, called a **trust agreement** or **deed of trust.** No particular form of language is necessary to create a trust so long as the property, the trust purpose, and the beneficiaries are designated. If an inter vivos trust relates to an interest in land, the statute of frauds requires that the trust be evidenced by a writing setting forth the details of the trust. A writing, signed by the trustee, that refers to a deed from the trustor can satisfy this requirement as the *McCaffrey* case illustrates. When the trust depends upon a transfer of title to land, there must be a valid transfer of the title to the trustee.

A trust in personal property may be declared orally without any writing. If a trust is created by the will of the settlor, there must be a writing that meets the requirements of a will. The same is true when the trust is not intended to come into existence until the death of the settlor.

In the absence of a specific requirement of the statute of frauds as to land or of the statutes setting forth the formal requirements for wills, any conduct or writing that shows an intent to create a trust will be given effect.

MCCAFFREY V LAURSEN

(Mont App) 697 P2d 103 (1985)

T. K. Laursen executed a deed that purported to convey his Lincoln County property to his son Orville. On the day the deed was executed, Orville Laursen executed an affidavit acknowledging a transfer of property from T. K. Laursen and agreeing that the property would be held in trust for T. K., that T. K. was to receive all rents and profits from the property, and that the property would be reconveyed upon trustor's request or death. Because of the father's mental and physical condition, a conservator was appointed to manage his affairs. McCaffrey, the conservator, sued Orville to recover title to the property. Orville contended that no trust existed. From a judgment in favor of the conservator of the father's estate, Orville appealed.

SHEEHY, J. . . . On July 21, 1981, T. K. executed a deed which purported to convey all title and interest in his Lincoln County property to his son Orville A. Laursen, defendant-appellant herein. On the same day, a separate document, defendant's Exhibit B, was executed and signed by Orville A. Laursen. The document provided:

> The undersigned acknowledges that as of this date his father, T. K. LAURSEN, did by written Deed convey certain property to him to be held by him in Trust for the said T. K. Laursen (a copy of said Deed is attached hereto). Undersigned covenants and agrees that all income from such properties shall belong to T. K. Laursen and that he, the affiant will re-convey the property to T. K. Laursen at anytime the said T. K. Laursen requests and that if the said T. K. Laursen should die while the property is still in the name of affiant such property shall be considered as an asset of T. K. Laursen's estate and be disposed of in accordance with T. K. Laursen's Will.

This document was delivered by appellant to Shelton R. Williams, T. K.'s attorney.

Based on these documents and the testimony of defendant, the District Court ruled that defendant holds the properties in trust for his father and by the terms of the trust, defendant is obligated to reconvey the property to T. K. and to account for all income from the properties. Appellant appeals this order and contends that there is no evidence that a trust existed. . . .

The creation of a voluntary trust as to the trustor is governed by § 72-20-107, MCA. Section 72-20-108, MCA, governs as to the trustee. They provide:

> 72-20-107. *Voluntary trust — how created as to trustor.* Subject to the provisions of 72-24-102, a voluntary trust is created, as to the trustor and beneficiary, by any words or acts of the trustor indicating with reasonable certainty:
> (1) an intention on the part of the trustor to create a trust; and
> (2) the subject, purpose, and beneficiary of the trust.

> 72-20-108. *Voluntary trust — how created as to trustee.* Subject to the provisions of 72-24-102, a voluntary trust is created, as to the trustee, by any words or acts of his indicating with reasonable certainty:
> (1) his acceptance of the trust or his acknowledgment, made upon sufficient consideration, of its existence; and
> (2) the subject, purpose, and beneficiary of the trust.

Section 72-24-102, MCA, refers to trusts concerning real property. It provides:

> No trust in relation to real property is valid unless created or declared by:
> (1) a written instrument subscribed by the trustee or his agent thereto authorized in writing;
> (2) the instrument under which the trustee claims the estate affected; or
> (3) operation of law.

The status of Orville A. Laursen, the appellant in this action, is that of trustee. He was entrusted with the property of T. K. Laursen. Exhibit B previously set forth herein and signed by appellant acknowledges that T. K. will receive all rents and profits from the properties and that appellant promises to reconvey the property on request. Together with the deed referred to therein, they satisfy the requirements of § 72-24-102, MCA. This instrument on its face conclusively proves that appellant accepted the deed from his father with the intent of holding the property for the benefit of his father. Appellant promised to convey the property to T. K. on request. He also promised to convey the property to T. K.'s estate if T. K. should die without demanding its return. These promises show appellant's intent to act as trustee for his father's property. Appellant's testimony concerning his intent was consistent with the document. He stated that the purpose of the transaction was estate planning. We hold appellant met the requirements of § 72-20-108, MCA.

T. K. Laursen did not sign Exhibit B, the aforementioned document. However, he was not required to sign the document to meet the requirements of § 72-24-102, MCA. Once those requirements are met by the actions of the trustee, the trustor, T. K., must by words or acts indicate with reasonable certainty: (1) an intention to create a trust; and (2) the subject, purpose, and beneficiary of the trust.

The fact that the document was given to T. K.'s now deceased attorney, Shelton Williams, for safekeeping is an act that tends to show T. K. intended a trust to be created. Appellant testified that he believed T. K. deeded the property to appellant because T. K. wanted someone to take care of the property and to take care of him; that T. K. wanted to make it more difficult for his wife to get the property in T. K.'s upcoming divorce action; and that T. K. deeded the property to appellant for estate planning purposes. Appellant's testimony taken with the circumstances of this case show with reasonable certainty that T. K.'s intention was to create a trust when he deeded his property to appellant. We hold the District Court's finding to be factually sound and legally correct.

[Judgment affirmed]

QUESTIONS

1. What are the essential elements that constitute a valid trust?
2. Was the father required to sign the affidavit executed by his son?
3. Did the court find a trust was created?

(e) INTENTION. An intention to impose a duty upon the trustee with respect to specific property must be expressed. It is not necessary, however, that the word *trust* or *trustee* be used. The settlor will ordinarily name a trustee, but failure to do so is not fatal to the trust because a trustee will be appointed by the court.

(f) ACTIVE DUTY. A trust does not exist unless an active duty is placed upon the trustee to manage the property in some manner or to exercise discretion or judgment. A bare direction to hold the property in trust without any direction as to its use or distribution is not sufficient for an active duty. Thus, when a decedent transferred $5,000 to a trustee to be held in trust for A, no trust was created. In such a case, the intended beneficiary is entitled to receive the property outright as though the decedent had not attempted to create a trust.

(g) IDENTITY OF BENEFICIARY. Every trust must have a beneficiary. In a private trust the beneficiaries must be identified by name, description, or designation of the class to which the beneficiaries belong. In a charitable trust it is sufficient that the beneficiaries be members of the public at large or a general class of the public.

Trusts for religious masses, for the maintenance of grave monuments, or for the care of particular animals are technically invalid because there is no human, identified beneficiary; but such trusts are nevertheless enforced because of the social interests that are involved.

(h) ACCEPTANCE OF TRUST. As the performance of a trust imposes duties upon the trustee, a trustee may renounce or reject the trust, but acceptance will be presumed in the absence of a disclaimer. A renunciation, however, does not affect the validity of the trust because a court will appoint a substitute trustee if the settlor does not do so.

§ 56:3   NATURE OF BENEFICIARY'S INTEREST

The effect of a transfer in trust is to divide the property so that the legal title is given to the trustee and the **equitable title** or beneficial interest is given to the beneficiary. The beneficiary may ordinarily transfer or assign such interest in the trust, and the beneficiary's creditors may reach that interest in satisfaction of their claims. An exception arises when the settlor has restricted the trust in such a way that the beneficiary cannot assign nor creditors reach the interest, creating what is commonly called a **spendthrift trust.**[2]

§ 56:4   POWERS OF TRUSTEE

A trustee can exercise only those powers that are given by law or the trust instrument or those that the court will construe as being given by implication. Modern trusts commonly give the trustee discretion to make decisions on matters that could not be foreseen by the settlor. For example, the trustee may be authorized to expend principal as well as income when, in the trustee's opinion, it is necessary for the education or medical care of a beneficiary. The trustee must exercise discretion in a reasonable manner.

§ 56:5   DUTIES OF TRUSTEE

The duty of a trustee is to administer the trust. The trustee who accepts the appointment must take all the necessary steps to carry out the trust in a proper manner.

(a) PERFORMANCE. A trustee is under a duty to carry out the trust according to its terms and is personally liable for any loss sustained from an unjustified failure to perform such duties. A trustee cannot delegate the performance of personal duties.[3]

(b) DUE CARE. The trustee is under a duty to use reasonable skill, prudence, and diligence in the performance of trust duties. More simply stated, the trustee must use the care that would be exercised by a reasonable person under the circumstances.

(c) LOYALTY. A trustee is not permitted to profit personally from the position of trustee, other than to receive the compensation allowed by contract or law.

(d) POSSESSION AND PRESERVATION OF TRUST PROPERTY. The trustee is under a duty to take possession of trust property and to preserve it from loss or damage. If the property includes accounts receivable or outstanding debts, the trustee is under the duty to collect them.

(e) DEFENSE OF TRUST. The trustee must defend the trust when its validity is disputed in court.

(f) PRODUCTION OF INCOME. Either by express or implied direction, the trustee is required to invest the money or property in enterprises or transactions that will yield an income to the estate.[4]

A trustee is generally permitted to invest in bonds of the United States, or of instrumentalities of the United States; bonds of states, cities, and counties, subject to certain restrictions; first mortgages on real estate when the mortgage does not repre-

---

[2]   Erickson v Bank of Cal, 25 Wash App 337, 623 P2d 721 (1981).

[3]   Shriners Hospitals v Gardner (App) __ Ariz __, 733 P2d 1102 (1986).
[4]   Witmer v Blair (Mo App) 588 SW2d 222 (1979).

sent more than a specified percentage of the value of the land; and mortgage bonds of certain kinds of corporations. Most states now permit a trustee to invest in corporate stocks. Court approval is generally required for investments in real estate.

(g) ACCOUNTING AND INFORMATION. A trustee must keep accurate records so that it can be determined whether the trust has been properly administered. Upon request by a beneficiary, the trustee must furnish information with respect to the trust. Periodically, or at certain times, as determined by the law in each state, a trustee must file an account in court at which time the court passes upon the stewardship of the trust.

§ 56:6   REMEDIES FOR BREACH OF TRUST

A breach of trust may occur in a variety of ways, which in turn affects the remedies available. These remedies include:

(a) money judgment against trustee for loss caused

(b) injunction or order to compel the trustee to do or refrain from doing an act

(c) criminal prosecution of the trustee for misconduct

(d) tracing and recovery of trust property that has been converted by the trustee,[5] unless the property had been acquired by a bona fide purchaser who gave value and purchased without notice of the breach of trust

(e) judgment against surety on the trustee's bond for loss caused the trust by the trustee's default

(f) removal of the trustee for misconduct, and

(g) suit against third persons who participated in a breach of trust.

---

[5] General Association of D.S.D.A., Inc. v General Association of D.S.D.A. (Tex Civ App) 410 SW2d 256 (1966).

§ 56:7   TERMINATION OF TRUST

A trust may be terminated (a) in accordance with its terms,[6] (b) because of the impossibility of attaining the object of the trust; (c) via revocation by the settlor, when allowed by the terms of the trust; (d) by merger of all interests in the same person; and (e) upon the request of all the beneficiaries when there is no express purpose that requires continuation of the trust.

B.   SPECIAL KINDS OF TRUSTS

In the preceding sections we examined the general principles related to express trusts. In the following sections we are concerned with the legal consequences and creation of tentative trusts, charitable trusts, and implied trusts.

§ 56:8   TENTATIVE TRUSTS

The law has developed a peculiar trust theory to govern a bank deposit made by *A* in an account marked "*A*, in trust for *B*." In the absence of any evidence showing an intention to create a formal trust by this method of deposit, a true trust is not created. Such a deposit is regarded as creating a **tentative trust**. The depositor and the depositor's creditors are permitted to treat a tentative trust as though there were no trust; but if the depositor dies, any money that remains in the account after creditors are paid belongs to the person named as the beneficiary. Some states refuse to recognize tentative trusts, while others have expressly authorized them by statute, or, as the *Wright* case illustrates, by judicial decision.

---

[6] Work v National Bank & Trust Company, 260 Iowa 898, 151 NW2d 490 (1967).

WRIGHT'S ESTATE
17 Ill App 3d 894, 308 NE2d 319 (1974)

Charles Wright opened a savings account in the Farmers State Bank. The account was marked "Charles Wright, Pay on Death to Mary Lowe." It was not intended that Mary should have any right to withdraw money from the account while Charles was alive. Charles thereafter died. By his will, he left his entire estate to his sons. Nothing was said in the will about the bank account. Both Mary and the sons claimed the balance on deposit in the account. The lower court entered judgment in favor of the sons, and Mary appealed.

ALLOY, J. . . . It is principally maintained by appellant that decedent, in opening and maintaining the account in question, established a so-called "Totten" or tentative trust, which device was recognized as valid in Illinois by our Supreme Court in the case of *In re Petralia*, 32 Ill2d 134, 204 NE2d 1 (1965) by the following language.

> We accept the position adopted by the American Law Institute in Section 58 of the *Restatement (second) of Trusts:* "Where a person makes a deposit in a savings account in a bank or other savings organization in his own name as trustee for another person intending to reserve a power to withdraw the whole or any part of the deposit at any time during his lifetime and to use as his own whatever he may withdraw, or otherwise revoke the trust, the intended trust is enforceable by the beneficiary upon the death of the depositor as to any part remaining on deposit on his death if he has not revoked the trust."

In support of the proposition that a recognized "Totten" or tentative trust was here created, appellant refers us to, *inter alia*, the following circumstances: at the time the account in question was opened, the decedent apparently withdrew $2,000 from his regular savings account (held in his name alone) and immediately used such money to fund the new account. Further, decedent continued to make significant deposits to the account in question throughout the rest of his life, while making only one withdrawal of $500, which withdrawal was "made up" with a deposit in the amount of $500 only 9 days later. Decedent and appellant were affectionate friends; their plans for marriage being thwarted, however, by the condition of the decedent's health.

Appellant points out that the primary object of all rules of construction in interpretation is to arrive at and give effect to the mutual intentions of the parties as expressed in the whole agreement and the circumstances surrounding the transaction.

> In the interpretation of any particular trust agreement, the Court is required to examine the entire agreement and it may also consider the relation of the parties, their connection with the subject matter of the agreement, the circumstances under which it was made, and the purpose for which it was made. . . .

Appellee, on the other hand, argues that "payable on death" accounts in banks are alien to the common law, and until rendered effective by affirmative legislative action, they must be held violative of public policy unless in compliance with the Statute of Wills (Ill. Rev. Stat. 1971, ch. 3, § 43). It is further maintained by appellee that the evidence adduced below failed to establish that decedent created a "present interest" in appellant in the purported trust *res* during the lifetime of decedent, a recognized requisite of a valid *inter vivos* trust. . . . In support of these conclusions, appellee relies heavily upon the case of *In re Estate of Gubala*, 81 Ill App2d 378, 225 NE2d 646 (1st Dist., 1967), where a "payable on death" account held in a savings and loan association was upheld, but only because of the existence of specific enabling legislation providing therefor (Ill.Rev.Stat., ch. 32, § 770(c)), which legislation is not applicable to accounts held in banks.

While the court in *Gubala* categorized "payable on death" accounts as pure testamentary dispositions, we do not think that is perforce true in all cases where the words "payable on death" or their equivalent appear in the title of an account. We believe, rather, that each case must be decided upon its own facts, and although it is true that the words "Pay upon Death" appear in the name of the account *sub judice*, it is also true that largely all of the indicia surrounding the creation of a "Totten" trust are equally in being. Thus, it was shown below that decedent and appellant had been close and affectionate friends; that, indeed, marriage had been contemplated, but rejected due to decedent's ill health. Decedent clearly established the account in question with an intent to benefit appellant, as he apparently transferred funds from an account held in his name alone in order to originally fund the new account, which named appellant a beneficiary thereof, and while it is true that he manifested an intent that appellant's possession and enjoyment of the account would not occur until his death, that is a feature of many *inter vivos* trusts given judicial sanction. . . .

> The Declaration of trust immediately creates an equitable interest in the beneficiaries although the enjoyment of the interest is postponed until the death of the settlor, and although the interest may be divested by the exercise of the power of revocation. The fact that the beneficiary's actual enjoyment of the trust is contingent on [the settlor's] death without having revoked the trust by withdrawing the balance in the account does not negate the existence of a present interest in the [beneficiary] during [the settlor's] lifetime, even though that interest may have been highly destructible.

Under the circumstances, we do not believe it may properly be said, as maintained by appellee, that appellant had no "present interest" in the account during the lifetime of decedent. On the contrary, she was a beneficiary named in the account and in our judgment thus held a present, although wholly defeasible, interest therein contemporaneous with decedent's superior rights. The latter's death, however, terminated his rights, and rendered appellant's indefeasible.

That we find, in accordance with the foregoing, that a tentative trust has been here established would seem to end our inquiry. However, a further argument advanced by appellant in our view serves as a basis for an alternate holding which we deem to be valid whether or not decedent established a trust in creating the account in question. We accordingly deem it wise to consider appellant's alternate theory, which maintains that the decedent in the case entered into a perfectly valid contract with the bank naming her as a third-party beneficiary thereto. As such, she is entitled to whatever funds were contained in the account at decedent's death, pursuant to the explicit terms of the contract. In support of this proposition, we are referred, *inter alia* to *4 Corbin on Contracts*, Sec. 783, at pages 89-90 (1951), where it is said as follows:

> Rarely has the third party been regarded as the beneficiary of a contract between A [the depositor] and the bank. This is due either to insufficient analysis or to the uncertainty and conflict that until recently existed in third party beneficiary law. In all cases, so long as there is no fraud on A's creditors, C [the named beneficiary] should get the money that A has not drawn out. . . as. . . beneficiary of the banking debtor's promise to the creditor [depositor]. . . .

We find appellant's third-party beneficiary contract theory quite compelling and entirely consistent with sound principles of jurisprudence. (See: *Dudley v Uptown National Bank of Moline*, 25 IllApp2d 514, 167 NE2d 257 (2d Dist., 1960) where the third-party beneficiary theory advanced herein was made, but was found by the court to be inapplicable under the facts before it.) It is absolutely clear that decedent named appellant as the death beneficiary of the account in question, and it is equally clear that he entered into a binding contractual arrangement with the bank in connection therewith. There being no rights of creditors or a surviving spouse here in question, we see no legally cogent reason for thwarting the decedent's clear dispositive intent concerning the sums held in the account at decedent's death.

In accordance with the foregoing, we find that decedent either established a valid "Totten" trust with respect to the account in question, or entered into a valid third-party beneficiary contract naming appellant as the beneficiary thereof. In either case, appellant is entitled to all sums in the account at the time of decedent's death.

[Judgment reversed and action remanded]

QUESTIONS

1. Why was it important to determine whether the account created a present interest in favor of Mary Lowe?
2. What theories did Mary Lowe raise to support her claim?
3. Why does the law recognize tentative trusts?

§ 56:9   CHARITABLE TRUSTS

Often a donor wishes to benefit society. This may be accomplished by the use of **charitable trusts.** They are administered and created in much the same manner as any other private trust.

(a) PURPOSE. **Charitable trusts** may be created for any purpose that advances the public welfare. These include trusts to (1) maintain or propagate religion, religious education, and missionary work; (2) further health and relieve human suffering by establishing institutions or by providing direct aid of food, clothing, shelter, and medical care to the needy; (3) found or maintain educational institutions, museums, libraries, or aid students or teachers;

(4) care for and maintain public cemeteries; (5) erect monuments to public figures or national heroes; (6) construct and maintain public buildings or improvements, such as an irrigation system or a playground; (7) further patriotism; and (8) prevent cruelty to animals.

(b) CY PRES DOCTRINE. In the absence of a contrary provision in the trust agreement, the law will not permit a charitable trust to end even though the original purpose has been accomplished or can no longer be achieved, or because the beneficiary no longer exists. In such a case the courts apply the **cy pres doctrine,** an abbreviation of the Norman French words "cy pres comme possible" or "as near as possible." By this doctrine the court directs that the trust fund be held for another purpose that will be as near as possible to that intended by the settlor.[7]

If, however, it is clear that the settlor intended the trust to be performed exactly as specified or not at all, the trust fails when it is not possible to follow its directions.

(c) LIMITATIONS. In most aspects a charitable trust is the same as a private trust. In some states additional limitations are imposed. Thus a maximum amount may be set on the property that a charitable corporation may own. In some states a decedent is limited as to the amount of property that can be left to charity when the decedent is survived by near relatives. When an absolute gift is made to a charity, the charity generally must hold it in trust for the purposes of the charity.

§ 56:10   IMPLIED TRUSTS

In certain instances trusts are implied in order to carry out the presumed intention of the parties or to protect the former owner of property from the fraud of the present owner. When the court implies a trust to carry out the presumed intent of the parties, the trust is called a **resulting trust;** when it implies a trust to correct or prevent a wrong, it is called a **constructive trust.**[8]

(a) PURCHASE MONEY RESULTING TRUST. The most common resulting trust arises when a person pays for the purchase of property but title to the property is taken in the name of another person. It is then presumed that the titleholder was intended to hold as trustee for the benefit of the person paying the money. To give effect to this presumption, a resulting trust is generally imposed upon the property and the titleholder. This means that the titleholder cannot use the property but must dispose of it as directed by the person paying the money. This presumption is not conclusive and may be overcome by evidence showing that it was the intention of the person paying the money to lend the money to the person taking title or to make a gift of the property. If the person paying the money is the husband or parent of the person taking title, there is a presumption that the payment was made as a gift, in which case a resulting trust does not arise unless the presumption of a gift is overcome by contrary evidence.

(b) CONSTRUCTIVE TRUST OF IMPROPERLY ACQUIRED PROPERTY. When a person has acquired title to property by unlawful or unfair means or in breach of a fiduciary duty as an agent or trustee, the law will make such person hold it as constructive trustee for the person who has been unjustly deprived of the property. Thus, if an agent privately purchases property that was to be purchased for the principal, the latter may hold the agent as constructive trustee of that property.

In the *Consolidated Bearing* case a corporation attempted to impose a constructive trust for a bank's breach of a fiduciary duty.

---

[7] Trammel v Elliott, 230 Ga 841, 199 SE2d 194 (1973).

[8] Metropulos v Chicago Art Glass, Inc. __ Ill App 3d __, __ Ill Dec __, 509 NE2d 1068 (1987).

CONSOLIDATED BEARING V FIRST NATIONAL BANK

(Tex App) 720 SW2d 647 (1986)

Consolidated Bearing issued 7,500 shares of stock to McWilliams, a director and employee. A bylaw restriction on transferability of the shares was noted on the certificate. This restriction required the shareholder to give the other shareholders or the corporation the right of first refusal on any "bona fide offer to sell." Sometime later, McWilliams, while still employed by Consolidated, borrowed $300,000 from the First National Bank and pledged the stock to the Bank to secure the loan. The money was to be used in a business venture similar to Consolidated. At the time of the loan, Consolidated had been a depositor and borrower at the bank for many years and was considered a valuable customer. The Bank did not notify Consolidated of the stock pledge because it had no reason to believe McWilliams was in competition with Consolidated. McWilliams told the loan officer that Consolidated was aware of McWilliams' outside business ventures. Consolidated's president said there was no knowledge of either the pledge or the outside ventures at the time of the loan. When Consolidated learned of the outside venture, McWilliams activity with Consolidated ended. McWilliams subsequently died leaving a substantial portion of the loan unpaid. The Bank instituted collection procedures and acquired, by a sheriff's sale, the 7,500 pledged shares. Consolidated then brought this action against the Bank to impose a constructive trust on the shares of the corporation held by the bank. From a judgment in favor of the bank, Consolidated appealed.

COUNTISS, J. . . . When attacking a transaction involving an alleged fiduciary, the attacking party must first establish that a confidential or fiduciary relationship existed, before the burden shifts to the confidant to show the fairness of the transaction. Thus, Consolidated had the burden of proving a fiduciary relationship and the trial court finding that there was no fiduciary relationship must be reviewed under the legal and factual sufficiency standards of *Holley v. Watts*, 629 S.W.2d 694 (Tex.1982) and *Parrish v. Hunt*, 160 Tex. 378, 331 S.W.2d 304 (1960). The legal sufficiency test requires us to review the entire record to determine (1) if there is any evidence to support the failure to impose a constructive trust, and, if not, (2) if the justification for such a trust is conclusively established. If the legal sufficiency attack is defeated, we must then test the factual sufficiency by examining the record for some probative evidence to support the finding, and, if we find supportive evidence, determine whether, in light of all the evidence, the finding is not manifestly unjust.

A constructive trust is an equitable remedy recognized . . . when one obtains legal title to property in violation of a confidence of fiduciary relations. As this Court has declared, it is imposed to prevent a person from holding something that he has gained "by reason of a fiduciary relation subsisting between him and those for whose benefit it is his duty to act."

Proving the necessary confidential relationship requires more, however, than evidence of prior dealings between the parties, and the subjective trust one party places in another does not establish a confidential relationship. Instead, it arises from formal fiduciary relations such as attorney-client, partnership, trustee-cestui que trust, and from informal social, moral or personal relationships. Proof of a confidential relationship outside the formal cases requires evidence that the dealings between the parties have continued for so long that one party is justified in relying on the other to act in his best interest. The Supreme Court recognizes that a fiduciary relationship can grow out of an informal relationship "when, over a long period of time, the parties had worked together for the joint acquisition and development of property previous to the particular agreement sought to be enforced."

Courts have been strict in applying this test, however, emphasizing the distinction between factual proof of a confidential relationship and mere subjective assertions by one party. Two cases factually compatible with this case are illustrative. In *Thigpen v. Locke*, the Supreme Court, while recognizing the principle that trust and confidence can arise informally from purely personal relationships, refused to find a confidential relationship between two parties to a deed when the grantee was a trust officer at a local bank. The evidence showed that the Lockes had a long-standing business and personal relationship with Thigpen, who was a director, officer and shareholder in their corporation, but the court held that there was no evidence to show that there existed anything more than a debtor-creditor relationship. *Thigpen v. Locke*, 363 S.W.2d at 253.

In contrast to *Thigpen*, the transaction in dispute in the present case is a loan between the bank and another of its customers; it involves Consolidated only indirectly. The corporation was not a party to the transaction it seeks to set aside.

In *Winston v. Lake Jackson Bank*, the endorsers of a promissory note failed to prove that a fiduciary relationship existed between them and the bank, requiring the bank to advise the endorsers of their potential individual liability before getting their signatures. The endorsers submitted as evidence to support their claim the following: (1) extensive prior dealings between the endorsers and the bank; (2) the fact that the bank president had been a financial advisor to one of the parties; and (3) the existence of prior notes entered into with the understanding that the liability would be limited. *Winston v. Lake Jackson Bank*, 574 S.W.2d at 628. The court concluded that evidence showing the existence of a debtor-creditor relationship for several years did not justify the endorser's assumption that the bank would act in their interest.

We reach the same conclusion here. However, Consolidated points to the testimony of a bank officer, Jim Cummings, to prove a confidential relationship. Cummings indicated that Consolidated was a substantial and valued customer of the Bank and he opined that the banker-customer relationship involves (1) a "kind of trust relationship" between the parties, (2) the disclosing of information about their business not shared with the public, and (3) the sharing of information that may be detrimental to either party. Those "admissions" of a relationship of trust and of a duty to disclose establish a confidential relationship, says Consolidated. However, we view the evidence only as proof of a long-standing banker-depositor relationship; Cummings admits to nothing more. Such a debtor-creditor relationship does not conclusively establish a relationship of trust and confidence.

. . . In the final analysis, we have evidence of a normal banking relationship between the Bank and a customer. We cannot conclude that, as a matter of law, the relationship carried a fiduciary label or that the finding of no fiduciary relationship is manifestly unjust. . . .

[Judgment affirmed]

QUESTIONS

1. Was there a fiduciary relationship between the bank and Consolidated?
2. What is required to establish a fiduciary relationship?
3. Did the court impose a constructive trust?

SUMMARY

A trust is a legal device by which property is held by one person for the benefit of another. The settlor creates the trust and the person for whose benefit the trustee holds the property is the beneficiary. Property held in trust is called the trust corpus, trust fund, trust estate, or res.

A trust is usually created by a writing called a trust agreement or deed of trust. No particular form or language is required. A trust will not exist unless an active duty is placed upon the trustee to manage the property in some manner. Acceptance of duties under a trust is presumed.

Legal title to trust property is given to the trustee while equitable title is held by the beneficiary. A beneficiary may transfer an interest in the trust except in the case of a spendthrift trust.

The trustee can only exercise those powers that are given by law or the trust instru-ment. The trustee must administer the trust and carry out the trust in a proper manner. A trustee may be sued for breach of the terms of the trust agreement. A trust comes to an end when its terms so provide or when it becomes impossible to attain the object of the trust.

Many states refuse to recognize tenta-tive trusts while others have expressly au-thorized them.

A charitable trust is created where a donor wishes to benefit society. By the cy pres doctrine, a court carries out the inten-tion of the settlor of a charitable trust as nearly as possible when the purpose can-not be accomplished in the manner specified.

A trust to carry out the presumed inten-tion of the parties is called a resulting trust. A trust established to right a wrong is called a constructive trust.

QUESTIONS AND CASE PROBLEMS

1. What social forces are affected by the rule of law authorizing the enforcement or applica-tion of constructive trusts?
2. Dolores states in her will, "I leave $10,000 to the First National Bank in trust for my niece, Clara." After the death of Dolores, the will is probated. Is the trust for Clara valid?

3. Robert is trustee under the will of his uncle. As trustee, he is holding $400,000. Because of the uncertainty of the stock market and the rising cost of living, Robert is uncertain as to how he should invest the money. He deposits it all in a checking account in the name of the trust estate. The checking ac-

count does not pay any interest. The beneficiaries of the trust complain that Robert will be liable to the trust for failing to earn income for the trust. Are they correct?

4. Rowena wrote a will that made a bequest of $1 million in trust to pay the income to the Ulan Free Public Library. She also stated that if for any reason the library ceased to exist or moved from the city, the money should be paid to her sister, Josephine, or, if the latter were deceased, to the lineal descendants of Josephine. Rowena died. Two years later Josephine died. Ten years later the Ulan Library moved to another city. A new library was formed by the "Friends of Learning." It rented the building formerly occupied by the Ulan Library and notified the trustee of Rowena's will that it claimed the money from the library bequest by virtue of the cy pres doctrine. Josephine's son, Milton, claimed the money. Decide.

5. What is the difference between an inter vivos trust and a testamentary trust?

6. State three ways a trust may be terminated.

7. Rachael conveyed certain land to Roland in trust for her daughter, Mary. Roland refused to accept the trust. What effect does this refusal have on the rights of her daughter, Mary?

8. Gerald, as agent for Victor, was authorized to purchase a certain tract of land for him. Gerald purchased the land but took title to the land in his own name instead of Victor's name. When Victor learned of this, he fired Gerald and demanded that Gerald convey the land to him. Gerald refused to do so, and Victor brought a lawsuit in which he claimed that Gerald held the land for him as constructive trustee and requested the court to order Gerald to convey the land to him. Gerald raised the defenses that he had never agreed to be a trustee on behalf of Victor and that he did not owe Victor any obligation as he was no longer Victor's agent. Are these defenses valid?

9. By her will, Hendricks provided: "I give, devise, and bequeath (the balance of my estate) to the City of Brookfield, Missouri, for the sole purpose of building and equipping and maintaining a city hospital. . . ." The city claimed that this was an absolute gift to the city subject to a condition as to its use. Do you agree? [Ramsey v City of Brookfield, 361 Mo 857, 237 SW2d 143]

10. The Pioneer Trust and Savings Bank was trustee of certain land for the benefit of Harmon. Under the terms of the trust, Harmon could require the trustee to sell the land as he directed. Schneider wrote Pioneer Trust, offering to buy the land. Harmon made a written notation on the letter that he accepted the offer and sent it back to Schneider. Schneider withdrew his offer and claimed that there was no contract. Harmon claimed that Schneider was bound by a contract. Decide. [Schneider v Pioneer Trust and Savings Bank, 26 Ill App 2d 463, 168 NE2d 808]

11. Fry was made trustee of approximately 880 acres of oil and gas land. The trust agreement gave him authority to execute "leases" of the land. He executed a lease of 80 acres to McCormick. Later Fry sued to set aside the lease on the ground that he had no authority to lease only a portion of the property. Decide. [Fry v McCormick, 170 Kan 741, 228 P2d 727]

12. Moulton executed and delivered a deed transferring property in trust to pay the income to his grandchild, Henry, and others for life, subject to spendthrift-trust limitations. Later, Henry was divorced and, as part of the property settlement with his wife, assigned to her a share of his interest in the income from the trust. The trustee refused to recognize the assignment. An action was brought to determine the validity of the assignment. Decide.

13. By his will, Biles directed that the balance of his estate be given to such charitable organization or organizations as his executors should select. Objection was made that this gave the executors authority to apply the cy pres doctrine. Was this correct? [Biles v Martin (Ala) 259 So 2d 258]

14. Laurens obtains a conveyance of property owned by Tomas, an illiterate person, by falsely representing that a document Tomas was to sign was a tax form. It was in fact a deed. What kind of trust, if any, arises in this situation.

15. Owens owned a 2,000-acre ranch that was very valuable. He decided that he wanted his daughter, Dorothy, to have this property after his death. He thereupon conveyed this land to Lockridge "in trust for my daughter, Dorothy, but Lockridge is to have no duties or burdens with respect to the land." Owens died sometime thereafter, and subsequently Dorothy contended that she was entitled to the possession, use, and enjoyment of the land. Is she correct? Explain.

APPENDICES

HOW TO FIND THE LAW

In order to determine what the law on a particular question or issue is, it may be necessary to examine (1) compilations of constitutions, treaties, statutes, executive orders, proclamations, and administrative regulations; (2) reports of state and federal court decisions; (3) digests of opinions; (4) treatises on the law; and (5) looseleaf services.

COMPILATIONS

In the consideration of a legal problem in business it is necessary to determine whether the matter is affected or controlled by the Constitution, national or state; by a national treaty; by an Act of Congress or a state legislature, or by a city ordinance; by a decree or proclamation of the President of the United States, a governor, or a mayor; or by a regulation of a federal, state, or local administrative agency.

Each body or person that makes laws, regulations, or ordinances usually will compile and publish at the end of each year or session all of the matter that it has adopted. In addition to the periodical or annual volumes, it is common to compile all the treaties, statutes, regulations, or ordinances in separate volumes. To illustrate, the federal Anti-Injunction Act may be cited as the Act of March 23, 1932, 47 Stat 70, 29 USC Sections 101 et seq. This means that this law was enacted on March 23, 1932, and that this law can be found at page 70 in Volume 47 of the reports that contain all of the statutes adopted by the Congress.

The second part of the citation, 29 USC Sections 101 et seq., means that in the collection of all of the federal statutes, which is known as the United States Code, the full text of the statute can be found in the sections of the 29th title beginning with Section 101.

COURT DECISIONS

For complicated or important legal cases or when an appeal is to be taken, a court will generally write an *opinion*, which explains why the court made the decision. Appellate courts as a rule write opinions. The great majority of these decisions, particularly in the case of the appellate courts, are collected and printed. In order to avoid confusion, the opinions of each court will ordinarily be printed in a separate set of reports, either by official reporters or private publishers.

In the reference "Pennoyer v Neff, 95 US 714, 24 LEd 565," the first part states the names of the parties. It does not necessarily tell who was the plaintiff and who was the defendant. When an action is begun in a lower court, the first name is that of the plaintiff and the second name that of the defendant. When the case is appealed, generally the name of the person taking the appeal appears on the records of the higher court as the first one and that of the adverse party as the second. Sometimes, therefore, the original order of the names of the parties is reversed.

The balance of the reference consists of two citations. The first citation, 95 US 714, means that the opinion which the court filed in the case of Pennoyer and Neff may be found on page 714 of the 95th volume of a series of books in which are printed officially the opinions of the United

States Supreme Court. Sometimes the same opinion is printed in two different sets of volumes. In the example, 24 LEd 565 means that in the 24th volume of another set of books, called *Lawyer's Edition*, of the United States Supreme Court Reports, the same opinion begins on page 565.

In opinions by a state court there are also generally two citations, as in the case of "Morrow v Corbin, 122 Tex 553, 62 SW2d 641." This means that the opinion in the lawsuit between Morrow and Corbin may be found in the 122d volume of the reports of the highest court of Texas, beginning on page 553; and also in Volume 62 of the *Southwestern Reporter*, Second Series, at page 641.

The West Publishing Company publishes a set of sectional reporters covering the entire United States. They are called sectional because each reporter, instead of being limited to a particular court or a particular state, covers the decisions of the courts of a particular section of the country. Thus the decisions of the courts of Arkansas, Kentucky, Missouri, Tennessee, and Texas are printed by the West Publishing company as a group in a sectional reporter called the *Southwestern Reporter*.[1] Because of the large number of decisions involved, generally only the opinions of the state appellate courts are printed. A number of states[2] have discontinued publication of the opinions of their courts, and those opinions are now found only in the West reporters.

The reason for the "Second Series" in the Southwestern citation is that when there were 300 volumes in the original series, instead of calling the next volume 301, the publisher called it Volume 1, Second Series. Thus 62 SW2d Series

really means the 362d volume of the *Southwestern Reporter*. Six to eight volumes appear in a year for each geographic section.

In addition to these state reporters, the West Publishing Company publishes a *Federal Supplement*, which primarily reports the opinions of the Federal District Courts; the *Federal Reporter*, which primarily reports the decisions of the United States Courts of Appeals; and the *Supreme Court Reporter*, which reports the decisions of the United States Supreme Court. The Supreme Court decisions are also reported in a separate set called the *Lawyers' Edition*, published by the Lawyers Co-operative Publishing Company.

The reports published by the West Publishing Company and Lawyers Co-operative Publishing Company are unofficial reports, while those bearing the name or abbreviation of the United States or of a state, such as "95 US 714" or "122 Tex 553" are official reports. This means that in the case of the latter, the particular court, such as the United States Supreme Court, has officially authorized that its decisions be printed and that by federal statute such official printing is made. In the case of the unofficial reporters, the publisher prints the decisions of a court on its own initiative. Such opinions are part of the public domain and not subject to any copyright or similar restriction.

DIGESTS OF OPINIONS

The reports of court decisions are useful only if one has the citation, that is, the name and volume number of the book and the page number of the opinion one is seeking. For this reason, digests of the decisions have been prepared. These digests organize the entire field of law under major headings, which are then arranged in alphabetic order. Under each heading, such as "Contracts," the subject is divided into the different questions that can arise with respect to that field. A master outline is thus created on the subject. This outline includes short paragraphs describing what each case holds and giving its citation.

TREATISES AND RESTATEMENTS

Very helpful in finding a case or a statute are the treatises on the law. These may be special

---

[1] The sectional reporters are: Atlantic—A. (Connecticut, Delaware, District of Columbia, Maine, Maryland, New Hampshire, New Jersey, Pennsylvania, Rhode Island, Vermont); Northeastern—N.E. (Illinois, Indiana, Massachusetts, New York, Ohio); Northwestern—N.W. (Iowa, Michigan, Minnesota, Nebraska, North Dakota, South Dakota, Wisconsin); Pacific—P. (Alaska, Arizona, California, Colorado, Hawaii, Idaho, Kansas, Montana, Nevada, New Mexico, Oklahoma, Oregon, Utah, Washington, Wyoming); Southeastern—S.E. (Georgia, North Carolina, South Carolina, Virginia, West Virginia); Southwestern—S.W. (Arkansas, Kentucky, Missouri, Tennessee, Texas); and Southern—So. (Alabama, Florida, Louisiana, Mississippi). There is also a special New York State reporter known as the New York Supplement and a special California State reporter known as the California Reporter.

[2] See, for example, Alaska, Florida, Iowa, Kentucky, Louisiana, Maine, Mississippi, Missouri, North Dakota, Oklahoma, Texas, and Wyoming.

books, each written by an author on a particular subject, such as *Williston on Contracts, Bogert on Trusts, Fletcher on Corporations,* or they may be general encyclopedias, as in the case of *American Jurisprudence, American Jurisprudence, Second,* and *Corpus Juris Secundum.*

Another type of treatise is found in the restatements of the law prepared by the American Law Institute. Each restatement consists of one or more volumes devoted to a particular phase of the law, such as the *Restatement of the Law of Contracts, Restatement of the Law of Agency,* and *Restatement of the Law of Property.* In each restatement the American Law Institute, acting through special committees of judges, lawyers, and professors of law, has set forth what the law is; and in many areas where there is no law or the present rule is regarded as unsatisfactory, the restatement specifies what the Institute deems to be the desirable rule.

Loose-Leaf Services

A number of private publishers, notably Commerce Clearing House and Prentice-Hall, publish loose-leaf books devoted to particular branches of the law. Periodically the publisher sends to the purchaser a number of pages that set forth any decision, regulation, or statute made or adopted since the prior set of pages was prepared. Such services are unofficial.

Computers and Legal Research

National and local computer services are providing constantly widening assistance for legal research. The database in such a system may be opinions, statutes, or administrative regulations stored word for word; or the later history of a particular case, giving its full citation and showing whether the case has been followed by other courts; or the text of forms and documents. By means of a terminal connected to the system, the user can retrieve the above information at a great saving of time and with the assurance that it is up-to-date.

There are three leading national systems for computer aid to research. Listed alphabetically, they are LEXIS, VERALEX, and WESTLAW.

A specialized service of legal forms for business is provided by Shepard's BUSINESS LAW CASE MANAGEMENT SYSTEM.

The computer field has expanded to such an extent that there is now a *Legal Software Review* of over 500 pages prepared by Lawyers Library, 12761 New Hall Ferry, Florissant, MO 63033.

THE CONSTITUTION
OF THE UNITED STATES

————◆————

We the people of the United States, in order to form a more perfect union, establish justice, insure domestic tranquillity, provide for the common defense, promote the general welfare, and secure the blessings of liberty to ourselves and our posterity, do ordain and establish this Constitution for the United States of America.

Article I

Section 1. All legislative powers herein granted shall be vested in a Congress of the United States, which shall consist of a Senate and House of Representatives.

Section 2. 1. The House of Representatives shall be composed of members chosen every second year by the people of the several States, and the electors in each State shall have the qualifications requisite for electors of the most numerous branch of the State legislature.

2. No person shall be a representative who shall not have attained to the age of twenty-five years, and been seven years a citizen of the United States, and who shall not, when elected, be an inhabitant of that State in which he shall be chosen.

3. Representatives and direct taxes[1] shall be apportioned among the several States which may be included within this Union, according to their respective numbers, which shall be determined by adding to the whole number of free persons, including those bound to service for a term of years, and excluding Indians not taxed, *three fifths of all other persons.*[2] The actual enumeration shall be made within three years after the first meeting of the Congress of the United States, and within every subsequent term of ten years, in such manner as they shall by law direct. The number of representatives shall not exceed one for every thirty thousand, but each State shall have at least one representative; and until such enumeration shall be made, the State of New Hampshire shall be entitled to choose three, Massachusetts eight, Rhode Island and Providence Plantations one, Connecticut five, New York six, New Jersey four, Pennsylvania eight, Delaware one, Maryland six, Virginia ten, North Carolina five, South Carolina five, and Georgia three.

4. When vacancies happen in the representation from any State, the executive authority thereof shall issue writs of election to fill such vacancies.

5. The House of Representatives shall choose their speaker and other officers; and shall have the sole power of impeachment.

Section 3. 1. The Senate of the United States shall be composed of two senators from each State, *chosen by the legislature thereof,*[1] for six years; and each senator shall have one vote.

2. Immediately after they shall be assembled in consequence of the first election, they shall be divided as equally as may be into three classes. The seats of the senators of the first class shall be vacated at the expiration of the second year, of the second class at the expiration of the fourth year, and of the third class at the expiration of the sixth year, so that one third may be chosen every second year; and if vacancies happen by resignation, or otherwise, during the recess of the legislature of any State, the executive thereof may make temporary appointments until the next meeting of the legislature, which shall then fill such vacancies.[3]

3. No person shall be a senator who shall not have attained to the age of thirty years, and been nine years a citizen of the United States, and who shall not, when elected, be an inhabitant of that State for which he shall be chosen.

4. The Vice President of the United States shall be President of the Senate, but shall have no vote, unless they be equally divided.

5. The Senate shall choose their other officers, and

---

[1] See the 16th Amendment.
[2] See the 14th Amendment.
[3] See the 17th Amendment.

also a president *pro tempore,* in the absence of the Vice President, or when he shall exercise the office of the President of the United States.

6. The Senate shall have the sole power to try all impeachments. When sitting for that purpose, they shall be on oath or affirmation. When the President of the United States is tried, the chief justice shall preside: and no person shall be convicted without the concurrence of two thirds of the members present.

7. Judgment in cases of impeachment shall not extend further than to removal from office, and disqualifications to hold and enjoy any office of honor, trust or profit under the United States: but the party convicted shall nevertheless be liable and subject to indictment, trial, judgment and punishment, according to law.

Section 4. 1. The times, places, and manner of holding elections for senators and representatives, shall be prescribed in each State by the legislature thereof; but the Congress may at any time by law make or alter such regulations, except as to the places of choosing senators.

2. The Congress shall assemble at least once in every year, and such meeting shall be on the first Monday in December, unless they shall by law appoint a different day.

Section 5. 1. Each House shall be the judge of the elections, returns and qualifications of its own members, and a majority of each shall constitute a quorum to do business; but a smaller number may adjourn from day to day, and may be authorized to compel the attendance of absent members, in such manner, and under such penalties as each House may provide.

2. Each House may determine the rules of its proceedings, punish its members for disorderly behavior, and, with the concurrence of two thirds, expel a member.

3. Each House shall keep a journal of its proceedings, and from time to time publish the same, excepting such parts as may in their judgment require secrecy; and the yeas and nays of the members of either House on any question shall, at the desire of one fifth of those present, be entered on the journal.

4. Neither House, during the session of Congress, shall, without the consent of the other, adjourn for more than three days, nor to any other place than that in which the two Houses shall be sitting.

Section 6. 1. The senators and representatives shall receive a compensation for their services, to be ascertained by law, and paid out of the Treasury of the United States. They shall in all cases, except treason, felony, and breach of the peace, be privileged from arrest during their attendance at the session of their respective Houses, and in going to and returning from the same; and for any speech or debate in either House, they shall not be questioned in any other place.

2. No senator or representative shall, during the time for which he was elected, be appointed to any civil office under the authority of the United States, which shall have been created, or the emoluments whereof shall have been increased during such time; and no person holding any office under the United States shall be a member of either House during his continuance in office.

Section 7. 1. All bills for raising revenue shall originate in the House of Representatives; but the Senate may propose or concur with amendments as on other bills.

2. Every bill which shall have passed the House of Representatives and the Senate, shall, before it becomes a law, be presented to the President of the United States; if he approves he shall sign it, but if not he shall return it, with his objections to that House in which it shall have originated, who shall enter the objections at large on their journal, and proceed to reconsider it. If after such reconsideration two thirds of that House shall agree to pass the bill, it shall be sent, together with the objections, to the other House, by which it shall likewise be reconsidered, and if approved by two thirds of that House, it shall become a law. But in all such cases the votes of both Houses shall be determined by yeas and nays, and the names of the persons voting for and against the bill shall be entered on the journal of each House respectively. If any bill shall not be returned by the President within ten days (Sundays excepted) after it shall have been presented to him, the same shall be a law, in like manner as if he had signed it, unless the Congress by their adjournment prevent its return, in which case it shall not be a law.

3. Every order, resolution, or vote to which the concurrence of the Senate and the House of Representatives may be necessary (except on a question of adjournment) shall be presented to the President of the United States; and before the same shall take effect, shall be approved by him, or being disapproved by him, shall be repassed by two thirds of the Senate and House of Representatives, according to the rules and limitations prescribed in the case of a bill.

Section 8. The Congress shall have the power

1. To lay and collect taxes, duties, imposts, and excises, to pay the debts and provide for the common defense and general welfare of the United States; but all duties, imposts, and excises shall be uniform throughout the United States;

2. To borrow money on the credit of the United States;

3. To regulate commerce with foreign nations, and among the several States, and with the Indian tribes;

4. To establish a uniform rule of naturalization, and uniform laws on the subject of bankruptcies throughout the United States;

5. To coin money, regulate the value thereof, and of foreign coin, and fix the standard of weights and measures;

6. To provide for the punishment of counterfeiting the securities and current coin of the United States;

7. To establish post offices and post roads;

8. To promote the progress of science and useful arts, by securing for limited times to authors and inventors the exclusive right to their respective writings and discoveries;

9. To constitute tribunals inferior to the Supreme Court;

10. To define and punish piracies and felonies committed on the high seas, and offenses against the law of nations;

11. To declare war, grant letters of marque and reprisal, and make rules concerning captures on land and water;

12. To raise and support armies, but no appropriation of money to that use shall be for a longer term than two years;

13. To provide and maintain a navy;

14. To make rules for the government and regulation of the land and naval forces;

15. To provide for calling forth the militia to execute the laws of the Union, suppress insurrections and repel invasions;

16. To provide for organizing, arming, and disciplining the militia, and for governing such part of them as may be employed in the service of the United States, reserving to the States respectively, the appointment of the officers, and the authority of training the militia according to the discipline prescribed by Congress.

17. To exercise exclusive legislation in all cases whatsoever, over such district (not exceeding ten miles square) as may, by cession of particular States, and the acceptance of Congress, become the seat of the government of the United States, and to exercise like authority over all places purchased by the consent of the legislature of the State in which the same shall be, for the erection of forts, magazines, arsenals, dockyards, and other needful buildings; and

18. To make all laws which shall be necessary and proper for carrying into execution the foregoing powers, and all other powers vested by this Constitution in the government of the United States, or in any department or officer thereof.

Section 9. 1. The migration or importation of such persons as any of the States now existing shall think proper to admit, shall not be prohibited by the Congress prior to the year one thousand eight hundred and eight, but a tax or duty may be imposed on such importation, not exceeding ten dollars for each person.

2. The privilege of the writ of *habeas corpus* shall not be suspended, unless when in cases of rebellion or invasion the public safety may require it.

3. No bill of attainder or *ex post facto* law shall be passed.

4. No capitation, or other direct, tax shall be laid, unless in proportion to the census or enumeration hereinbefore directed to be taken.[4]

[4]   See the 16th Amendment.

5. No tax or duty shall be laid on articles exported from any State.

6. No preference shall be given by any regulation of commerce or revenue to the ports of one State over those of another: nor shall vessels bound to, or from, one State be obliged to enter, clear, or pay duties in another.

7. No money shall be drawn from the treasury, but in consequence of appropriations made by law; and a regular statement and account of the receipts and expenditures of all public money shall be published from time to time.

8. No title of nobility shall be granted by the United States: and no person holding any office of profit or trust under them, shall, without the consent of the Congress, accept of any present, emolument, office, or title, of any kind whatever, from any king, prince, or foreign State.

Section 10. 1. No State shall enter into any treaty, alliance, or confederation; grant letters of marque and reprisal; coin money; emit bills of credit; make anything but gold and silver coin a tender in payment of debts; pass any bill of attainder, *ex post facto* law, or law impairing the obligation of contracts, or grant any title of nobility.

2. No State shall, without the consent of the Congress, lay any imposts or duties on imports or exports, except what may be absolutely necessary for executing its inspection laws: and the net produce of all duties and imposts laid by any State on imports or exports, shall be for the use of the treasury of the United States; and all such laws shall be subject to the revision and control of the Congress.

3. No State shall, without the consent of the Congress, lay any duty of tonnage, keep troops, or ships of war in time of peace, enter into any agreement or compact with another State, or with a foreign power, or engage in war, unless actually invaded, or in such imminent danger as will not admit of delay.

Article II

Section 1. 1. The executive power shall be vested in a President of the United States of America. He shall hold his office during the term of four years, and, together with the Vice President, chosen for the same term, be elected as follows:

2. Each State shall appoint, in such manner as the legislature thereof may direct, a number of electors, equal to the whole number of senators and representatives to which the State may be entitled in the Congress: but no senator or representative, or person holding an office of trust or profit under the United States, shall be appointed an elector.

The electors shall meet in their respective States, and vote by ballot for two persons, of whom one at least shall not be an inhabitant of the same State with themselves. And they shall make a list of all the persons voted for, and of the number of votes for each; which list they shall sign and certify, and transmit sealed to the seat of the government of the United States, directed to the president of the Senate. The president of the Senate shall, in the presence of the Senate and House of Representatives, open all the certificates, and the votes shall then be counted. The person having the greatest number of votes shall be the President, if such number be a majority of the whole number of electors appointed; and if there be more than one who have such majority, and have an equal number of votes, then the House of Representatives shall immediately choose by ballot one of them for President; and if no person have a majority, then from the five highest on the list the said House shall in like manner choose the President. But in choosing the President, the votes shall be taken by States, the representation from each State having one vote; a quorum for this purpose shall consist of a member or members from two thirds of the States, and a majority of all the States shall be necessary to a choice. In every case, after the choice of the President, the person having the greatest number of votes of the electors shall be the Vice President. But if there should remain two or more who have equal votes, the Senate shall choose from them by ballot the Vice President.[5]

3. The Congress may determine the time of choosing the electors, and the day on which they shall give their votes; which day shall be the same throughout the United States.

4. No person except a natural born citizen, or a citizen of the United States, at the time of the adoption of this Constitution, shall be eligible to the office of President; neither shall any person be eligible to that office who shall not have attained to the age of thirty-five years, and been fourteen years a resident within the United States.

5. In case of the removal of the President from office, or of his death, resignation, or inability to discharge the powers and duties of the said office, the same shall devolve on the Vice President, and the Congress may by law provide for the case of removal, death, resignation, or inability, both of the President and Vice President, declaring what officer shall then act as President, and such officer shall act accordingly, until the disability be removed, or a President shall be elected.

6. The President shall, at stated times, receive for his services a compensation, which shall neither be increased nor diminished during the period for which he shall have been elected, and he shall not receive within that period any other emolument from the United States, or any of them.

7. Before he enter on the execution of his office, he shall take the following oath or affirmation:—"I do solemnly swear (or affirm) that I will faithfully execute the office of President of the United States, and will to the best of my ability, preserve, protect and defend the Constitution of the United States."

Section 2. 1. The President shall be commander in chief of the army and navy of the United States, and of the militia of the several States, when called into the actual service of the United States; he may require the opinion, in writing, of the principal officer in each of the executive departments, upon any subject relating to the duties of their respective office, and he shall have power to grant reprieves and pardons for offenses against the United States, except in cases of impeachment.

2. He shall have power, by and with the advice and consent of the Senate, to make treaties, provided two thirds of the senators present concur; and he shall nominate, and by and with the advice and consent of the Senate, shall appoint ambassadors, other public ministers and consuls, judges of the Supreme Court, and all other officers of the United States, whose appointments are not herein otherwise provided for, and which shall be established by law: but the Congress may by law vest the appointment of such inferior officers, as they think proper, in the President alone, in the courts of law, or in the heads of departments.

3. The President shall have power to fill up all vacancies that may happen during the recess of the Senate, by granting commissions which shall expire at the end of their next session.

Section 3. He shall from time to time give to the Congress information of the state of the Union, and recommend to their consideration such measures as he shall judge necessary and expedient; he may, on extraordinary occasions, convene both Houses, or either of them, and in case of disagreement between them with respect to the time of adjournment, he may adjourn them to such time as he shall think proper; he shall receive ambassadors and other public ministers; he shall take care that the laws be faithfully executed, and shall commission all the officers of the United States.

Section 4. The President, Vice President, and all civil officers of the United States, shall be removed from office on impeachment for, and conviction of, treason, bribery, or other high crimes and misdemeanors.

Article III

Section 1. The judicial power of the United States shall be vested in one Supreme Court, and in such inferior courts as the Congress may from time to time ordain and establish. The judges, both of the Supreme and inferior courts, shall hold their offices during good behavior, and shall, at stated times, receive for their services, a compensation, which shall not be diminished during their continuance in office.

Section 2. 1. The judicial power shall extend to all cases, in law and equity, arising under this Consti-

[5] Superseded by the 12th Amendment.

tution, the laws of the United States, and treaties made, or which shall be made, under their authority;—to all cases affecting ambassadors, other public ministers and consuls;—to all cases of admiralty and maritime jurisdiction;—to controversies to which the United States shall be a party;—to controversies between two or more States; between a State and citizens of another State;[6]—between citizens of different States;—between citizens of the same State claiming lands under grants of different States, and between a State, or the citizens thereof, and foreign States citizens or subjects.

2. In all cases affecting ambassadors, other public ministers and consuls, and those in which a State shall be party, the Supreme Court shall have original jurisdiction. In all the other cases before mentioned, the Supreme Court shall have appellate jurisdiction, both as to law and to fact, with such exceptions, and under such regulations as the Congress shall make.

3. The trial of all crimes, except in cases of impeachment, shall be by jury; and such trial shall be held in the State where the said crimes shall have been committed; but when not committed within any State, the trial shall be at such place or places as the Congress may by law have directed.

Section 3. 1. Treason against the United States shall consist only in levying war against them, or in adhering to their enemies, giving them aid and comfort. No person shall be convicted of treason unless on the testimony of two witnesses to the same overt act, or on confession in open court.

2. The Congress shall have power to declare the punishment of treason, but no attainder of treason shall work corruption of blood, or forfeiture except during the life of the person attained.

Article IV

Section 1. Full faith and credit shall be given in each State to the public acts, records, and judicial proceedings of every other State. And the Congress may by general laws prescribe the manner in which such acts, records and proceedings shall be proved, and the effect thereof.

Section 2. 1. The citizens of each State shall be entitled to all privileges and immunities of citizens in the several States.[7]

2. A person charged in any State with treason, felony, or other crime, who shall flee from justice, and be found in another State, shall on demand of the executive authority of the State from which he fled, be delivered up to be removed to the State having jurisdiction of the crime.

3. No person held to service or labor in one State under the laws thereof, escaping into another, shall in consequence of any law or regulation therein, be discharged from such service or labor, but shall be delivered up on claim of the party to whom such service or labor may be due.[8]

Section 3. 1. New States may be admitted by the Congress into this Union; but no new State shall be formed or erected within the jurisdiction of any other State, nor any State be formed by the junction of two or more States, or parts of States, without the consent of the legislatures of the States concerned as well as of the Congress.

2. The Congress shall have power to dispose of and make all needful rules and regulations respecting the territory or other property belonging to the United States; and nothing in this Constitution shall be so construed as to prejudice any claims of the United States, or of any particular State.

Section 4. The United States shall guarantee to every State in this Union a republican form of government, and shall protect each of them against invasion; and on application of the legislature, or of the executive (when the legislature cannot be convened) against domestic violence.

Article V

The Congress, whenever two thirds of both Houses shall deem it necessary, shall propose amendments to this Constitution, or, on the application of the legislature of two thirds of the several States, shall call a convention for proposing amendments, which in either case, shall be valid to all intents and purposes, as part of this Constitution when ratified by the legislatures of three fourths of the several States, or by conventions in three fourths thereof, as the one or the other mode of ratification may be proposed by the Congress; Provided that no amendment which may be made prior to the year one thousand eight hundred and eight shall in any manner affect the first and fourth clauses in the ninth section of the first article; and that no State, without its consent, shall be deprived of its equal suffrage in the Senate.

Article VI

1. All debts contracted and engagements entered into, before the adoption of this Constitution, shall be as valid against the United States under this Constitution, as under the Confederation.[9]

2. This Constitution, and the laws of the United States which shall be made in pursuance thereof; and all treaties made, or which shall be made, under the authority of the United States, shall be the supreme law of the land; and the Judges in every State shall be bound thereby, anything in the Constitution or laws of any State to the contrary notwithstanding.

---

[6] See the 11th Amendment.
[7] See the 14th Amendment, Sec. 1.

[8] See the 13th Amendment.
[9] See the 14th Amendment, Sec. 4.

3. The senators and representatives before mentioned, and the members of the several State legislatures, and all executive and judicial officers, both of the United States and of the several States, shall be bound by oath or affirmation to support this Constitution; but no religious test shall ever be required as a qualification to any office or public trust under the United States.

Article VII

The ratification of the conventions of nine States shall be sufficient for the establishment of this Constitution between the States so ratifying the same.

Done in Convention by the unanimous consent of the States present the seventeenth day of September in the year of our Lord one thousand seven hundred and eighty-seven, and of the independence of the United States of America the twelfth. In witness whereof we have hereunto subscribed our names.

AMENDMENTS

First Ten Amendments passed by Congress Sept. 25, 1789.
Ratified by three-fourths of the States December 15, 1791.

Article I

Congress shall make no law respecting an establishment of religion, or prohibiting the free exercise thereof; or abridging the freedom of speech, or of the press; or the right of the people peaceably to assemble, and to petition the government for a redress of grievances.

Article II

A well regulated militia, being necessary to the security of a free State, the right of the people to keep and bear arms, shall not be infringed.

Article III

No soldier shall, in time of peace be quartered in any house, without the consent of the owner, nor in time of war, but in a manner to be prescribed by law.

Article IV

The right of the people to be secure in their persons, houses, papers, and effects, against unreasonable searches and seizures, shall not be violated, and no warrants shall issue, but upon probable cause, supported by oath or affirmation, and particularly describing the place to be searched, and the persons or things to be seized.

Article V

No person shall be held to answer for a capital, or otherwise infamous crime, unless on a presentment or indictment of a grand jury, except in cases arising in the land or naval forces, or in the militia, when in actual service in time of war or public danger; nor shall any person be subject for the same offense to be twice put in jeopardy of life or limb; nor shall be compelled in any criminal case to be a witness against himself, nor be deprived of life, liberty, or property, without due process of law; nor shall private property be taken for public use without just compensation.

Article VI

In all criminal prosecutions, the accused shall enjoy the right to a speedy and public trial, by an impartial jury of the State and district wherein the crime shall have been committed, which district shall have been previously ascertained by law, and to be informed of the nature and cause of the accusation; to be confronted with the witnesses against him; to have compulsory process for obtaining witnesses in his favor, and to have the assistance of counsel for his defense.

Article VII

In suits at common law, where the value in controversy shall exceed twenty dollars, the right of trial by jury shall be preserved, and no fact tried by a jury shall be otherwise reexamined in any court of the United States, than according to the rules of the common law.

Article VIII

Excessive bail shall not be required, nor excessive fines imposed, nor cruel and unusual punishments inflicted.

Article IX

The enumeration in the Constitution of certain rights shall not be construed to deny or disparage others retained by the people.

Article X

The powers not delegated to the United States by the Constitution, nor prohibited by it to the States, are reserved to the States respectively, or to the people.

Article XI

Passed by Congress March 5, 1794. Ratified January 8, 1798.

The judicial power of the United States shall not be construed to extend to any suit in law or equity, commenced or prosecuted against one of the United States by citizens of another State, or by citizens or subjects of any foreign State.

Article XII

Passed by Congress December 12, 1803. Ratified September 25, 1804.

The electors shall meet in their respective States, and vote by ballot for President and Vice President, one of whom, at least, shall not be an inhabitant of the same State with themselves; they shall name in their ballots the person voted for as President, and in distinct ballots, the person voted for as Vice President, and they shall make distinct lists of all persons voted for as President and of all persons voted for as Vice President, and of the number of votes for each, which lists they shall sign and certify, and transmit sealed to the seat of the government of the United States, directed to the President of the Senate; — The President of the Senate shall, in the presence of the Senate and House of Representatives, open all the certificates and the votes shall then be counted; — The person having the greatest number of votes for President, shall be the President, if such number be a majority of the whole number of electors appointed; and if no person have such majority, then from the persons having the highest numbers not exceeding three on the list of those voted for as President, the House of Representatives shall choose immediately, by ballot, the President. But in choosing the President, the votes shall be taken by States, the representation from each State having one vote; a quorum for this purpose shall consist of a member or members from two thirds of the States, and a majority of all the States shall be necessary to a choice. And if the House of Representatives shall not choose a President whenever the right of choice shall devolve upon them, before the fourth day of March next following, then the Vice President shall act as President, as in the case of the death or other constitutional disability of the President. The person having the greatest number of votes as Vice President shall be the Vice President, if such number be a majority of the whole number of electors appointed, and if no person have a majority, then from the two highest numbers on the list, the Senate shall choose the Vice President; a quorum for the purpose shall consist of two thirds of the whole number of Senators, and a majority of the whole number shall be necessary to a choice. But no person constitutionally ineligible to the office of President shall be eligible to that of Vice President of the United States.

Article XIII

Passed by Congress February 1, 1865. Ratified December 18, 1865.

Section 1. Neither slavery nor involuntary servitude, except as punishment for crime whereof the party shall have been duly convicted, shall exist within the United States, or any place subject to their jurisdiction.

Section 2. Congress shall have power to enforce this article by appropriate legislation.

Article XIV

Passed by Congress June 16, 1866. Ratified July 23, 1868.

Section 1. All persons born or naturalized in the United States, and subject to the jurisdiction thereof, are citizens of the United States and of the State wherein they reside. No State shall make or enforce any law which shall abridge the privileges or immunities of citizens of the United States; nor shall any State deprive any person of life, liberty, or property, without due process of law; nor deny to any person within its jurisdiction the equal protection of the laws.

Section 2. Representatives shall be apportioned among the several States according to their respective numbers, counting the whole number of persons in each State, excluding Indians not taxed. But when the right to vote at any election for the choice of electors for President and Vice President of the United States, representatives in Congress, the executive and judicial officers of a State, or the members of the legislature thereof, is denied to any of the male inhabitants of such State, being twenty-one years of age, and citizens of the United States, or in any way abridged, except for participation in rebellion, or other crime, the basis of representation therein shall be reduced in the proportion which the number of such male citizens shall bear to the whole number of male citizens twenty-one years of age in such State.

Section 3. No person shall be a senator or representative in Congress, or elector of President and Vice President, or hold any office, civil or military, under the United States, or under any State, who having previously taken an oath, as a member of Congress, or as an officer of the United States, or as a member of any State legislature, or as an executive or judicial officer of any State, to support the Constitution of the United States, shall have engaged in insurrection or rebellion against the same, or given aid or comfort to the enemies thereof. But Congress may by a vote of two thirds of each House, remove such disability.

Section 4. The validity of the public debt of the United States, authorized by law, including debts incurred for payment of pensions and bounties for services in suppressing insurrection or rebellion, shall not be questioned. But neither the United States nor any State shall assume or pay any debt or obligation incurred in aid of insurrection or rebellion against the United States, or any claim for the loss or emancipation of any slave; but all such debts, obligations, and claims shall be held illegal and void.

Section 5. The Congress shall have power to enforce, by appropriate legislation, the provisions of this article.

Article XV

Passed by Congress February 27, 1869. Ratified March 30, 1870.

Section 1. The right of citizens of the United States

to vote shall not be denied or abridged by the United States or by any State on account of race, color, or previous condition of servitude.

Section 2. The Congress shall have power to enforce this article by appropriate legislation.

Article XVI

Passed by Congress July 12, 1909. Ratified February 25, 1913.

The Congress shall have power to lay and collect taxes on incomes, from whatever source derived, without apportionment among the several States, and without regard to any census or enumeration.

Article XVII

Passed by Congress May 16, 1912. Ratified May 31, 1913.

The Senate of the United States shall be composed of two senators from each state, elected by the people thereof, for six years; and each senator shall have one vote. The electors in each State shall have the qualifications requisite for electors of the most numerous branch of the State legislature.

When vacancies happen in the representation of any State in the Senate, the executive authority of such State shall issue writs of election to fill such vacancies: *Provided,* That the legislature of any State may empower the executive thereof to make temporary appointments until the people fill the vacancies by election as the legislature may direct.

This amendment shall not be so construed as to affect the election or term of any senator chosen before it becomes valid as part of the Constitution.

Article XVIII

Passed by Congress December 17, 1917. Ratified January 29, 1919.

After one year from the ratification of this article, the manufacture, sale, or transportation of intoxicating liquors within, the importation thereof into, or the exportation thereof from the United States and all territory subject to the jurisdiction thereof for beverage purposes is hereby prohibited.

The Congress and the several States shall have concurrent power to enforce this article by appropriate legislation.

This article shall be inoperative unless it shall have been ratified as an amendment to the Constitution by the legislatures of the several States, as provided in the Constitution, within seven years from the date of the submission hereof to the states by Congress.

Article XIX

Passed by Congress June 5, 1919. Ratified August 26, 1920.

The right of citizens of the United States to vote shall not be denied or abridged by the United States or by any State on account of sex.

The Congress shall have power by appropriate legislation to enforce the provisions of this article.

Article XX

Passed by Congress March 3, 1932. Ratified January 23, 1933.

Section 1. The terms of the President and Vice President shall end at noon on the 20th day of January, and the terms of Senators and Representatives at noon on the 3d day of January, of the years in which such terms would have ended if this article had not been ratified; and the terms of their successors shall then begin.

Section 2. The Congress shall assemble at least once in every year, and such meeting shall begin at noon on the 3d day of January, unless they shall by law appoint a different day.

Section 3. If, at the time fixed for the beginning of the term of the President, the President-elect shall have died, the Vice President-elect shall become President. If a President shall not have been chosen before the time fixed for the beginning of his term, or if the President-elect shall have failed to qualify, then the Vice President-elect shall act as President until a President shall have qualified; and the Congress may by law provide for the case wherein neither a President-elect nor a Vice President-elect shall have qualified, declaring who shall then act as President, or the manner in which one who is to act shall be selected, and such person shall act accordingly until a President or Vice President shall have qualified.

Section 4. The Congress may by law provide for the case of the death of any of the persons from whom the House of Representatives may choose a President whenever the right of choice shall have devolved upon them, and for the case of the death of any of the persons from whom the Senate may choose a Vice President whenever the right of choice shall have devolved upon them.

Section 5. Sections 1 and 2 shall take effect on the 15th day of October following the ratification of this article.

Section 6. This article shall be inoperative unless it shall have been ratified as an amendment to the Constitution by the legislatures of three-fourths of the several States within seven years from the date of its submission.

Article XXI

Passed by Congress February 20, 1933. Ratified December 5, 1933.

Section 1. The Eighteenth Article of amendment to the Constitution of the United States is hereby repealed.

Section 2. The transportation or importation into any State, Territory, or possession of the United States for delivery or use therein of intoxicating liquors in violation of the laws thereof, is hereby prohibited.

Section 3. This article shall be inoperative unless it shall have been ratified as an amendment to the Constitution by conventions in the several States, as provided in the Constitution, within seven years from the date of the submission thereof to the States by the Congress.

Article XXII

Passed by Congress March 24, 1947. Ratified February 26, 1951.

Section 1. No person shall be elected to the office of the President more than twice, and no person who has held the office of President, or acted as President, for more than two years of a term to which some other person was elected President shall be elected to the office of the President more than once. But this article shall not apply to any person holding the office of President when this article was proposed by the Congress, and shall not prevent any person who may be holding the office of President, or acting as President, during the term within which this article becomes operative from holding the office of President or acting as President during the remainder of such term.

Section 2. This article shall be inoperative unless it shall have been ratified as an amendment to the Constitution by the legislatures of three-fourths of the several States within seven years from the date of its submission to the States by the Congress.

Amendment XXIII

Passed by Congress June 16, 1960. Ratified April 3, 1961.

Section 1 The District constituting the seat of Government of the United States shall appoint in such manner as the Congress may direct:

A number of electors of President and Vice President equal to the whole number of Senators and Representatives in Congress to which the District would be entitled if it were a State, but in no event more than the least populous State; they shall be in addition to those appointed by the States, but they shall be considered, for the purposes of the election of President and Vice President, to be electors appointed by a State; and they shall meet in the District and perform such duties as provided by the twelfth article of amendment.

Section 2 The Congress shall have power to enforce this article by appropriate legislation.

Amendment XXIV

Passed by Congress August 27, 1962. Ratified February 4, 1964.

Section 1 The right of citizens of the United States to vote in any primary or other election for President or Vice President, for electors for President or Vice President, or for Senator or Representative in Congress, shall not be denied or abridged by the United States or any State by reason of failure to pay any poll tax or other tax.

Section 2 The Congress shall have power to enforce this article by appropriate legislation.

Amendment XXV

Passed by Congress July 6, 1965. Ratified February 23, 1967.

Section 1 In case of the removal of the President from office or of his death or resignation, the Vice President shall become President.

Section 2 Whenever there is a vacancy in the office of the Vice President, the President shall nominate a Vice President who shall take office upon confirmation by a majority vote of both Houses of Congress.

Section 3 Whenever the President transmits to the President pro tempore of the Senate and the Speaker of the House of Representatives has written declaration that he is unable to discharge the powers and duties of his office, and until he transmits to them a written declaration to the contrary, such powers and duties shall be discharged by the Vice President as Acting President.

Section 4 Whenever the Vice President and a majority of either the principal officers of the executive departments or of such other body as Congress may by law provide, transmit to the President pro tempore of the Senate and the Speaker of the House of Representatives their written declaration that the President is unable to discharge the powers and duties of his office, the Vice President shall immediately assume the powers and duties of the office as Acting President.

Thereafter, when the President transmits to the President pro tempore of the Senate and the Speaker of the House of Representatives his written declaration that no inability exists, he shall resume the powers and duties of his office unless the Vice President and a majority of either the principal officers of the executive department or of such other body as Congress may by law provide, transmit within four days to the President pro tempore of the Senate and the Speaker of the House of Representatives their written declaration that the President is unable to discharge the powers and duties of his office. Thereupon Congress shall decide the issue, assembling within forty-eight hours for that purpose if not in session. If the Congress, within twenty-one days after receipt of the latter written declaration, or, if Congress is not in session, within twenty-one days after Congress is required to assemble, determines by two-thirds vote of both Houses that the President is unable to discharge the powers and duties of his office, the Vice President shall continue to discharge the same as Acting President; otherwise, the President shall resume the powers and duties of his office.

Amendment XXVI

Passed by Congress March 23, 1971. Ratified July 5, 1971.

Section 1 The right of citizens of the United States, who are eighteen years of age or older, to vote shall not be denied or abridged by the United States or by any State on account of age.

UNIFORM COMMERCIAL CODE

TITLE

AN ACT

To be known as the Uniform Commercial Code, Relating to Certain Commercial Trans-actions in or regarding Personal Property and Contracts and other Documents concerning them, including Sales, Commercial Paper, Bank Deposits and Collections, Letters of Credit, Bulk Transfers, Warehouse Receipts, Bills of Lading, other Documents of Title, Investment Securities, and Secured Transactions, including certain Sales of Accounts, Chattel Paper, and Contract Rights; Providing for Public Notice to Third Parties in Certain Circumstances; Regulating Procedure, Evidence and Damages in Certain Court Actions Involving such Transactions, Contracts or Documents; to Make Uniform the Law with Respect Thereto; and Repealing Inconsistent Legislation.

ARTICLE 1

GENERAL PROVISIONS

Part 1

SHORT TITLE, CONSTRUCTION, APPLICATION AND SUBJECT MATTER OF THE ACT

§ 1—101. Short Title

This Act shall be known and may be cited as Uniform Commercial Code.

§ 1—102. Purposes; Rules of Construction; Variation by Agreement

(1) This Act shall be liberally construed and applied to promote its underlying purposes and policies.

(2) Underlying purposes and policies of this Act are

  (a) to simplify, clarify and modernize the law governing commercial transactions;

  (b) to permit the continued expansion of commercial practices through custom, usage and agreement of the parties;

  (c) to make uniform the law among the various jurisdictions.

(3) The effect of provisions of this Act may be varied by agreement, except as otherwise provided in this Act and except that the obligations of good faith, diligence, reasonableness and care prescribed by this Act may not be disclaimed by agreement, but the parties may by agreement determine the standards by which the performance of such obligations is to be measured if such standards are not manifestly unreasonable.

(4) The presence in certain provisions of this Act of the words "unless otherwise agreed" or words of similar import does not imply

that the effect of other provisions may not be varied by agreement under subsection (3).

(5) In this Act unless the context otherwise requires

(a) words in the singular number include the plural, and in the plural include the singular;

(b) words of the masculine gender include the feminine and the neuter, and when the sense so indicates, words of the neuter gender may refer to any gender.

§ 1 — 103. Supplementary General Principles of Law Applicable

Unless displaced by the particular provisions of this Act, the principles of law and equity, including the law merchant and the law relative to capacity to contract, principal and agent, estoppel, fraud, misrepresentation, duress, coercion, mistake, bankruptcy, or other validating or invalidating cause shall supplement its provisions.

§ 1 — 104. Construction Against Implicit Repeal

This Act being a general act intended as a unified coverage of its subject matter, no part of it shall be deemed to be impliedly repealed by subsequent legislation if such construction can reasonably be avoided.

§ 1 — 105. Territorial Application of the Act; Parties' Power to Choose Applicable Law

(1) Except as provided hereafter in this section, when a transaction bears a reasonable relation to this state and also to another state or nation, the parties may agree that the law either of this state or of such other state or nation shall govern their rights and duties. Failing such agreement, this Act applies to transactions bearing an appropriate relation to this state.

(2) Where one of the following provisions of this Act specifies the applicable law, that provision governs and a contrary agreement is effective only to the extent permitted by the law (including the conflict of laws rules) so specified:

Rights of creditors against sold goods. Section 2 — 402.

Applicability of the Article on Bank Deposits and Collections. Section 4 — 102.

Bulk transfers subject to the Article on Bulk Transfers. Section 6 — 102.

Applicability of the Article on Investment Securities. Section 8 — 106.

Perfection provisions of the Article on Secured Transactions. Section 9 — 103.

§ 1 — 106. Remedies to Be Liberally Administered

(1) The remedies provided by this Act shall be liberally administered to the end that the aggrieved party may be put in as good a position as if the other party had fully performed, but neither consequential or special nor penal damages may be had except as specifically provided in this Act or by other rule of law.

(2) Any right or obligation declared by this Act is enforceable by action unless the provision declaring it specifies a different and limited effect.

§ 1 — 107. Waiver or Renunciation of Claim or Right After Breach

Any claim or right arising out of an alleged breach can be discharged in whole or in part without consideration by a written waiver or renunciation signed and delivered by the aggrieved party.

§ 1 — 108. Severability

If any provision or clause of this Act or application thereof to any person or circumstances is held invalid, such invalidity shall not affect other provisions or applications of the Act which can be given effect without the invalid provision or application, and to this end the provisions of this Act are declared to be severable.

§ 1 — 109. Section Captions

Section captions are parts of this Act.

Part 2

GENERAL DEFINITIONS AND PRINCIPLES OF INTERPRETATION

§ 1 — 201. General Definitions

Subject to additional definitions contained in the subsequent Articles of this Act which are applicable to specific Articles or Parts thereof, and unless the context otherwise requires, in this Act:

(1) "Action" in the sense of a judicial proceeding includes recoupment, counterclaim, set-off, suit in equity and any other proceedings in which rights are determined.

(2) "Aggrieved party" means a party entitled to resort to a remedy.

(3) "Agreement" means the bargain of the parties in fact as found in their language or by implication from other circumstances including course of dealing or usage of trade or course of performance as provided in this Act (Sections 1 — 205 and 2 — 208). Whether an agreement has legal consequences is determined by the provisions of this Act, if applicable; otherwise by the law of contracts (Section 1 — 103). (Compare "Contract.")

(4) "Bank" means any person engaged in the business of banking.

(5) "Bearer" means the person in possession of an instrument, document of title, or certificated security payable to bearer or indorsed in blank.

(6) "Bill of lading" means a document evidencing the receipt of goods for shipment issued by a person engaged in the business of transporting or forwarding goods, and includes an airbill. "Airbill" means

a document serving for air transportation as a bill of lading does for marine or rail transportation, and includes an air consignment note or air waybill.

(7) "Branch" includes a separately incorporated foreign branch of a bank.

(8) "Burden of establishing" a fact means the burden of persuading the triers of fact that the existence of the fact is more probable than its nonexistence.

(9) "Buyer in ordinary course of business" means a person who in good faith and without knowledge that the sale to him is in violation of the ownership rights or security interest of a third party in the goods buys in ordinary course from a person in the business of selling goods of that kind but does not include a pawnbroker. All persons who sell minerals or the like (including oil and gas) at wellhead or minehead shall be deemed to be persons in the business of selling goods of that kind. "Buying" may be for cash or by exchange of other property or on secured or unsecured credit and includes receiving goods or documents of title under a preexisting contract for sale but does not include a transfer in bulk or as security for or in total or partial satisfaction of a money debt.

(10) "Conspicuous": A term or clause is conspicuous when it is so written that a reasonable person against whom it is to operate ought to have noticed it. A printed heading in capitals (as: NON-NEGOTIABLE BILL OF LADING) is conspicuous. Language in the body of a form is "conspicuous" if it is in larger or other contrasting type or color. But in a telegram any stated term is "conspicuous." Whether a term or clause is "conspicuous" or not is for decision by the court.

(11) "Contract" means the total legal obligation which results from the parties' agreement as affected by this Act and any other applicable rules of law. (Compare "Agreement.")

(12) "Creditor" includes a general creditor, a secured creditor, a lien creditor and any representative of creditors, including an assignee for the benefit of creditors, a trustee in bankruptcy, a receiver in equity and an executor or administrator of an insolvent debtor's or assignor's estate.

(13) "Defendant" includes a person in the position of defendant in a cross-action or counterclaim.

(14) "Delivery" with respect to instruments, documents of title, chattel paper or certificated securities means voluntary transfer of possession.

(15) "Document of title" includes bill of lading, dock warrant, dock receipt, warehouse receipt or order for the delivery of goods, and also any other document which in the regular course of business or financing is treated as adequately evidencing that the person in possession of it is entitled to receive, hold and dispose of the document and the goods it covers. To be a document of title a document must purport to be issued by or addressed to a bailee and purport to cover goods in the bailee's possession which are either identified or are fungible portions of an identified mass.

(16) "Fault" means wrongful act, omission or breach.

(17) "Fungible" with respect to goods or securities means goods or securities of which any unit is, by nature or usage of trade, the equivalent of any other like unit. Goods which are not fungible shall be deemed fungible for the purposes of this Act to the extent that under a particular agreement or document unlike units are treated as equivalents.

(18) "Genuine" means free of forgery or counterfeiting.

(19) "Good faith" means honesty in fact in the conduct or transaction concerned.

(20) "Holder" means a person who is in possession of a document of title or an instrument or a certificated investment security drawn, issued or indorsed to him or to his order or to bearer or in blank.

(21) To "honor" is to pay or to accept and pay, or where a credit so engages, to purchase or discount a draft complying with the terms of the credit.

(22) "Insolvency proceedings" includes any assignment for the benefit of creditors or other proceedings intended to liquidate or rehabilitate the estate of the person involved.

(23) A person is "insolvent" who either has ceased to pay his debts in the ordinary course of business or cannot pay his debts as they become due or is insolvent within the meaning of the federal bankruptcy law.

(24) "Money" means a medium of exchange authorized or adopted by a domestic or foreign government as a part of its currency.

(25) A person has "notice" of a fact when
   (a) he has actual knowledge of it; or
   (b) he has received a notice or notification of it; or
   (c) from all the facts and circumstances known to him at the time in question he has reason to know that it exists.
A person "knows" or has "knowledge" of a fact when he has actual knowledge of it. "Discover" or "learn" or a word or phrase of similar import refers to knowledge rather than to reason to know. The time and circumstances under which a notice or notification may cease to be effective are not determined by this Act.

(26) A person "notifies" or "gives" a notice or notification to another by taking such steps as may be reasonably required to inform the other in ordinary course whether or not such other actually comes to know of it. A person "receives" a notice or notification when

   (a) it comes to his attention; or
   (b) it is duly delivered at the place of business through which the contract was made or at any other place held out by

him as the place for receipt of such communications.

(27) Notice, knowledge or a notice or notification received by an organization is effective for a particular transaction from the time when it is brought to the attention of the individual conducting that transaction, and in any event from the time when it would have been brought to his attention if the organization had exercised due diligence. An organization exercises due diligence if it maintains reasonable routines for communicating significant information to the person conducting the transaction and there is reasonable compliance with the routines. Due diligence does not require an individual acting for the organization to communicate information unless such communication is part of his regular duties or unless he has reason to know of the transaction and that the transaction would be materially affected by the information.

(28) "Organization" includes a corporation, government or governmental subdivision or agency, business trust, estate, trust, partnership or association, two or more persons having a joint or common interest, or any other legal or commercial entity.

(29) "Party," as distinct from "third party," means a person who has engaged in a transaction or made an agreement within this Act.

(30) "Person" includes an individual or an organization (See Section 1—102).

(31) "Presumption" or "presumed" means that the trier of fact must find the existence of the fact presumed unless and until evidence is introduced which would support a finding of its nonexistence.

(32) "Purchase" includes taking by sale, discount, negotiation, mortgage, pledge, lien, issue or reissue, gift or any other voluntary transaction creating an interest in property.

(33) "Purchaser" means a person who takes by purchase.

(34) "Remedy" means any remedial right to which an aggrieved party is entitled with or without resort to a tribunal.

(35) "Representative" includes an agent, an officer of a corporation or association, and a trustee, executor or administrator of an estate, or any other person empowered to act for another.

(36) "Rights" includes remedies.

(37) "Security interest" means an interest in personal property or fixtures which secures payment or performance of an obligation. The retention or reservation of title by a seller of goods notwithstanding shipment or delivery to the buyer (Section 2—401) is limited in effect to a reservation of a "security interest." The term also includes any interest of a buyer of accounts or chattel paper which is subject to Article 9. The special property interest of a buyer of goods on identification of such goods to a contract for sale under Section 2—401 is not a "security interest," but a buyer may also acquire a "security interest" by complying with Article 9. Unless a lease or consignment is intended as security, reservation of title thereunder is not a "security interest" but a consignment is in any event subject to the provisions on consignment sales (Section 2—326). Whether a lease is intended as security is to be determined by the facts of each case; however, (a) the inclusion of an option to purchase does not of itself make the lease one intended for security, and (b) an agreement that upon compliance with the terms of the lease the lessee shall become or has the option to become the owner of the property for no additional consideration or for a nominal consideration does make the lease one intended for security.

(38) "Send" in connection with any writing or notice means to deposit in the mail or deliver for transmission by any other usual means of communication with postage or cost of transmission provided for and properly addressed and in the case of an instrument to an address specified thereon or otherwise agreed, or if there be none to any address reasonable under the circumstances. The receipt of any writing or notice within the time at which it would have arrived if properly sent has the effect of a proper sending.

(39) "Signed" includes any symbol executed or adopted by a party with present intention to authenticate a writing.

(40) "Surety" includes guarantor.

(41) "Telegram" includes a message transmitted by radio, teletype, cable, any mechanical method of transmission, or the like.

(42) "Term" means that portion of an agreement which relates to a particular matter.

(43) "Unauthorized" signature or indorsement means one made without actual, implied or apparent authority and includes a forgery.

(44) "Value." Except as otherwise provided with respect to negotiable instruments and bank collections (Sections 3—303, 4—208 and 4—209) a person gives "value" for rights if he acquires them

(a) in return for a binding commitment to extend credit or for the extension of immediately available credit whether or not drawn upon and whether or not a charge-back is provided for in the event of difficulties in collection; or

(b) as security for or in total or partial satisfaction of a preexisting claim; or

(c) by accepting delivery pursuant to a preexisting contract for purchase; or

(d) generally, in return for any consideration sufficient to support a simple contract.

(45) "Warehouse receipt" means a receipt issued by a person engaged in the business of storing goods for hire.

(46) "Written" or "writing" includes printing,

typewriting or any other intentional reduction to tangible form.

§ 1—202. Prima Facie Evidence by Third Party Documents

A document in due form purporting to be a bill of lading, policy or certificate of insurance, official weigher's or inspector's certificate, consular invoice, or any other document authorized or required by the contract to be issued by a third party shall be prima facie evidence of its own authenticity and genuineness and of the facts stated in the document by the third party.

§ 1—203. Obligation of Good Faith

Every contract or duty within this Act imposes an obligation of good faith in its performance or enforcement.

§ 1—204. Time; Reasonable Time; "Seasonably"

(1) Whenever this Act requires any action to be taken within a reasonable time, any time which is not manifestly unreasonable may be fixed by agreement.

(2) What is a reasonable time for taking any action depends on the nature, purpose and circumstances of such action.

(3) An action is taken "seasonably" when it is taken at or within the time agreed or, if no time is agreed, at or within a reasonable time.

§ 1—205. Course of Dealing and Usage of Trade

(1) A course of dealing is a sequence of previous conduct between the parties to a particular transaction which is fairly to be regarded as establishing a common basis of understanding for interpreting their expressions and other conduct.

(2) A usage of trade is any practice or method of dealing having such regularity of observance in a place, vocation or trade as to justify an expectation that it will be observed with respect to the transaction in question. The existence and scope of such a usage are to be proved as facts. If it is established that such a usage is embodied in a written trade code or similar writing the interpretation of the writing is for the court.

(3) A course of dealing between parties and any usage of trade in the vocation or trade in which they are engaged or of which they are or should be aware give particular meaning to and supplement or qualify terms of an agreement.

(4) The express terms of an agreement and an applicable course of dealing or usage of trade shall be construed wherever reasonable as consistent with each other; but when such construction is unreasonable, express terms control both course of dealing and usage of trade and course of dealing controls usage of trade.

(5) An applicable usage of trade in the place where any part of performance is to occur shall be used in interpreting the agreement as to that part of the performance.

(6) Evidence of a relevant usage of trade offered by one party is not admissible unless and until he has given the other party such notice as the court finds sufficient to prevent unfair surprise to the latter.

§ 1—206. Statute of Frauds for Kinds of Personal Property Not Otherwise Covered

(1) Except in the cases described in subsection (2) of this section, a contract for the sale of personal property is not enforceable by way of action or defense beyond five thousand dollars in amount or value of remedy unless there is some writing which indicates that a contract for sale has been made between the parties at a defined or stated price, reasonably identifies the subject matter, and is signed by the party against whom enforcement is sought or by his authorized agent.

(2) Subsection (1) of this section does not apply to contracts for the sale of goods (Section 2—201) nor of securities (Section 8—319) nor to security agreements (Section 9—203).

§ 1—207. Performance or Acceptance Under Reservation of Rights

A party who with explicit reservation of rights performs or promises performance or assents to performance in a manner demanded or offered by the other party does not thereby prejudice the rights reserved. Such words as "without prejudice," "under protest" or the like are sufficient.

§ 1—208. Option to Accelerate at Will

A term providing that one party or his successor in interest may accelerate payment or performance or require collateral or additional collateral "at will" or "when he deems himself insecure" or in words of similar import shall be construed to mean that he shall have power to do so only if he in good faith believes that the prospect of payment or performance is impaired. The burden of establishing lack of good faith is on the party against whom the power has been exercised.

§ 1—209. Subordinated Obligations

An obligation may be issued as subordinated to payment of another obligation of the person obligated, or a creditor may subordinate his right to payment of an obligation by agreement with either the person obligated or another creditor of the person obligated. Such a subordination does not create a security interest as against either the common debtor or a subordinated creditor. This section shall be construed as declaring the law as it existed prior to the enactment of this section and not as modifying it.

ARTICLE 2

SALES

Part 1

Short Title, General Construction and Subject Matter

§ 2—101. Short Title

This Article shall be known and may be cited as Uniform Commercial Code—Sales.

§ 2—102. Scope; Certain Security and Other Transactions Excluded From This Article

Unless the context otherwise requires, this Article applies to transactions in goods; it does not apply to any transaction which although in the form of an unconditional contract to sell or present sale is intended to operate only as a security transaction nor does this Article impair or repeal any statute regulating sales to consumers, farmers or other specified classes of buyers.

§ 2—103. Definitions and Index of Definitions

(1) In this Article, unless the context otherwise requires,

    (a) "Buyer" means a person who buys or contracts to buy goods.

    (b) "Good faith" in the case of a merchant means honesty in fact and the observance of reasonable commercial standards of fair dealing in the trade.

    (c) "Receipt" of goods means taking physical possession of them.

    (d) "Seller" means a person who sells or contracts to sell goods.

(2) Other definitions applying to this Article or to specified Parts thereof, and the sections in which they appear are:

"Acceptance." Section 2—606.
"Banker's credit." Section 2—325.
"Between merchants." Section 2—104.
"Cancellation." Section 2—106(4).
"Confirmed credit." Section 2—325.
"Conforming to contract." Section 2—106.
"Contract for sale." Section 2—106.
"Cover." Section 2—712.
"Entrusting." Section 2—403.
"Financing agency." Section 2—104.
"Future goods." Section 2—105.
"Goods." Section 2—105.
"Identification." Section 2—501.
"Installment contract." Section 2—612.
"Letter of Credit." Section 2—325.
"Lot." Section 2—105.
"Merchant." Section 2—104.
"Overseas." Section 2—323.
"Person in position of seller." Section 2—707.
"Present sale." Section 2—106.
"Sale." Section 2—106.
"Sale on approval." Section 2—326.
"Sale or return." Section 2—326.
"Termination." Section 2—106.

(3) The following definitions in other Articles apply to this Article:

"Check." Section 3—104.
"Consignee." Section 7—102.
"Consignor." Section 7—102.
"Consumer goods." Section 9—109.
"Dishonor." Section 3—507.
"Draft." Section 3—104.

(4) In addition Article 1 contains general definitions and principles of construction and interpretation applicable throughout this Article.

§ 2—104. Definitions: "Merchant"; "Between Merchants"; "Financing Agency"

(1) "Merchant" means a person who deals in goods of the kind or otherwise by his occupation holds himself out as having knowledge or skill peculiar to the practices or goods involved in the transaction or to whom such knowledge or skill may be attributed by his employment of an agent or broker or other intermediary who by his occupation holds himself out as having such knowledge or skill.

(2) "Financing agency" means a bank, finance company or other person who in the ordinary course of business makes advances against goods or documents of title or who by arrangement with either the seller or the buyer intervenes in ordinary course to make or collect payment due or claimed under the contract for sale, as by purchasing or paying the seller's draft or making advances against it or by merely taking it for collection whether or not documents of title accompany the draft. "Financing agency" includes also a bank or other person who similarly intervenes between persons who are in the position of seller and buyer in respect to the goods (Section 2—707).

(3) "Between merchants" means in any transaction with respect to which both parties are chargeable with the knowledge or skill of merchants.

§ 2—105. Definitions: Transferability; "Goods"; "Future" Goods; "Lot"; "Commercial Unit"

(1) "Goods" means all things (including specially manufactured goods) which are movable at the time of identification to the contract for sale other than the money in which the price is to be paid, investment securities (Article 8) and things in action. "Goods" also includes the unborn young of animals and growing crops and other identified things attached to realty as

described in the section on goods to be severed from realty (Section 2—107).

(2) Goods must be both existing and identified before any interest in them can pass. Goods which are not both existing and identified are "future" goods. A purported present sale of future goods or of any interest therein operates as a contract to sell.

(3) There may be a sale of a part interest in existing identified goods.

(4) An undivided share in an identified bulk of fungible goods is sufficiently identified to be sold although the quantity of the bulk is not determined. Any agreed proportion of such a bulk or any quantity thereof agreed upon by number, weight or other measure may to the extent of the seller's interest in the bulk be sold to the buyer who then becomes an owner in common.

(5) "Lot" means a parcel or a single article which is the subject matter of a separate sale or delivery, whether or not it is sufficient to perform the contract.

(6) "Commercial unit" means such a unit of goods as by commercial usage is a single whole for purposes of sale and division of which materially impairs its character or value on the market or in use. A commercial unit may be a single article (as a machine) or a set of articles (as a suite of furniture or an assortment of sizes) or a quantity (as a bale, gross, or carload) or any other unit treated in use or in the relevant market as a single whole.

§ 2—106. Definitions: "Contract"; "Agreement"; "Contract for Sale"; "Sale"; "Present Sale"; "Conforming" to Contract; "Termination"; "Cancellation"

(1) In this Article unless the context otherwise requires, "contract" and "agreement" are limited to those relating to the present or future sale of goods. "Contract for sale" includes both a present sale of goods and a contract to sell goods at a future time. A "sale" consists in the passing of title from the seller to the buyer for a price (Section 2—401). A "present sale" means a sale which is accomplished by the making of the contract.

(2) Goods or conduct, including any part of a performance, are "conforming" or conform to the contract when they are in accordance with the obligations under the contract.

(3) "Termination" occurs when either party pursuant to a power created by agreement or law puts an end to the contract otherwise than for its breach. On "termination" all obligations which are still executory on both sides are discharged but any right based on prior breach or performance survives.

(4) "Cancellation" occurs when either party puts an end to the contract for breach by the other and its effect is the same as that of "termination" except that

the cancelling party also retains any remedy for breach of the whole contract or any unperformed balance.

§ 2—107. Goods to Be Severed From Realty: Recording

(1) A contract for the sale of minerals or the like (including oil and gas) or a structure or its materials to be removed from realty is a contract for the sale of goods within this Article if they are to be severed by the seller, but until severance a purported present sale thereof which is not effective as a transfer of an interest in land is effective only as a contract to sell.

(2) A contract for the sale apart from the land of growing crops or other things attached to realty and capable of severance without material harm thereto but not described in subsection (1) or of timber to be cut is a contract for the sale of goods within this Article whether the subject matter is to be severed by the buyer or by the seller even though it forms part of the realty at the time of contracting, and the parties can by identification effect a present sale before severance.

(3) The provisions of this section are subject to any third party rights provided by the law relating to realty records, and the contract for sale may be executed and recorded as a document transferring an interest in land and shall then constitute notice to third parties of the buyer's rights under the contract for sale.

Part 2

Form, Formation and Readjustment of Contract

§ 2—201. Formal Requirements; Statute of Frauds

(1) Except as otherwise provided in this section, a contract for the sale of goods for the price of $500 or more is not enforceable by way of action or defense unless there is some writing sufficient to indicate that a contract for sale has been made between the parties and signed by the party against whom enforcement is sought or by his authorized agent or broker. A writing is not insufficient because it omits or incorrectly states a term agreed upon but the contract is not enforceable under this paragraph beyond the quantity of goods shown in such writing.

(2) Between merchants, if within a reasonable time a writing in confirmation of the contract and sufficient against the sender is received and the party receiving it has reason to know its contents, it satisfies the requirements of subsection (1) against such party unless written notice of objection to its contents is given within 10 days after it is received.

(3) A contract which does not satisfy the requirements of subsection (1) but which is valid in other respects is enforceable

    (a) if the goods are to be specially manufactured for the buyer and are not suitable for sale to others in the ordinary course of the seller's business and the seller, before notice of repudiation is received and under circumstances which reasonably indicate that the goods are for the buyer, has made either a substantial beginning of their manufacture or commitments for their procurement; or

(b) if the party against whom enforcement is sought admits in his pleading, testimony or otherwise in court that a contract for sale was made, but the contract is not enforceable under this provision beyond the quantity of goods admitted; or

(c) with respect to goods for which payment has been made and accepted or which have been received and accepted (Sec. 2—606).

§ 2—202. Final Written Expression: Parol or Extrinsic Evidence

Terms with respect to which the confirmatory memoranda of the parties agree or which are otherwise set forth in a writing intended by the parties as a final expression of their agreement with respect to such terms as are included therein may not be contradicted by evidence of any prior agreement or of a contemporaneous oral agreement but may be explained or supplemented

(a) by course of dealing or usage of trade (Section 1—205) or by course of performance (Section 2—208); and

(b) by evidence of consistent additional terms unless the court finds the writing to have been intended also as a complete and exclusive statement of the terms of the agreement.

§ 2—203. Seals Inoperative

The affixing of a seal to a writing evidencing a contract for sale or an offer to buy or sell goods does not constitute the writing a sealed instrument and the law with respect to sealed instruments does not apply to such a contract or offer.

§ 2—204. Formation in General

(1) A contract for sale of goods may be made in any manner sufficient to show agreement, including conduct by both parties which recognizes the existence of such a contract.

(2) An agreement sufficient to constitute a contract for sale may be found even though the moment of its making is undetermined.

(3) Even though one or more terms are left open a contract for sale does not fail for indefiniteness if the parties have intended to make a contract and there is a reasonably certain basis for giving an appropriate remedy.

§ 2—205. Firm Offers

An offer by a merchant to buy or sell goods in a signed writing which by its terms gives assurance that it will be held open is not revocable, for lack of consideration, during the time stated or if no time is stated for a reasonable time, but in no event may such period of irrevocability exceed three months; but any such term of assurance on a form supplied by the offeree must be separately signed by the offeror.

§ 2—206. Offer and Acceptance in Formation of Contract

(1) Unless otherwise unambiguously indicated by the language or circumstances

(a) an offer to make a contract shall be construed as inviting acceptance in any manner and by any medium reasonable in the circumstances;

(b) an order or other offer to buy goods for prompt or current shipment shall be construed as inviting acceptance either by a prompt promise to ship or by the prompt or current shipment of conforming or non-conforming goods, but such a shipment of non-conforming goods does not constitute an acceptance if the seller seasonably notifies the buyer that the shipment is offered only as an accommodation to the buyer.

(2) Where the beginning of a requested performance is a reasonable mode of acceptance, an offeror who is not notified of acceptance within a reasonable time may treat the offer as having lapsed before acceptance.

§ 2—207. Additional Terms in Acceptance or Confirmation

(1) A definite and seasonable expression of acceptance or a written confirmation which is sent within a reasonable time operates as an acceptance even though it states terms additional to or different from those offered or agreed upon, unless acceptance is expressly made conditional on assent to the additional or different terms.

(2) The additional terms are to be construed as proposals for addition to the contract. Between merchants such terms become part of the contract unless:

(a) the offer expressly limits acceptance to the terms of the offer;

(b) they materially alter it; or

(c) notification of objection to them has already been given or is given within a reasonable time after notice of them is received.

(3) Conduct by both parties which recognizes the existence of a contract is sufficient to establish a contract for sale although the writings of the parties do not otherwise establish a contract. In such case the terms of the particular contract consist of those terms on which the writings of the parties agree, together with any supplementary terms incorporated under any other provisions of this Act.

§ 2—208. Course of Performance or Practical Construction

(1) Where the contract for sale involves repeated occasions for performance by either party with knowledge of the nature of the performance and opportunity for objection to it by the other, any course of performance accepted or acquiesced in without objection shall be relevant to determine the meaning of the agreement.

(2) The express terms of the agreement and any such course of performance, as well as any course of dealing and usage of trade, shall be construed whenever reasonable as consistent with each other; but when such construction is unreasonable, express terms shall control course of performance and course of performance shall control both course of dealing and usage of trade (Section 1—205).

(3) Subject to the provisions of the next section on modification and waiver, such course of performance shall be relevant to show a waiver or modification of any term inconsistent with such course of performance.

§ 2—209. Modification, Rescission and Waiver

(1) An agreement modifying a contract within this Article needs no consideration to be binding.

(2) A signed agreement which excludes modification or rescission except by a signed writing cannot be otherwise modified or rescinded, but except as between merchants such a requirement on a form supplied by the merchant must be separately signed by the other party.

(3) The requirements of the statute of frauds section of this Article (Section 2—201) must be satisfied if the contract as modified is within its provisions.

(4) Although an attempt at modification or rescission does not satisfy the requirements of subsection (2) or (3) it can operate as a waiver.

(5) A party who has made a waiver affecting an executory portion of the contract may retract the waiver by reasonable notification received by the other party that strict performance will be required of any term waived, unless the retraction would be unjust in view of a material change of position in reliance on the waiver.

§ 2—210. Delegation of Performance; Assignment of Rights

(1) A party may perform his duty through a delegate unless otherwise agreed or unless the other party has a substantial interest in having his original promisor perform or control the acts required by the contract. No delegation of performance relieves the party delegating of any duty to perform or any liability for breach.

(2) Unless otherwise agreed, all rights of either seller or buyer can be assigned except where the assignment would materially change the duty of the other party, or increase materially the burden or risk imposed on him by his contract, or impair materially his chance of obtaining return performance. A right to damages for breach of the whole contract or a right arising out of the assignor's due performance of his entire obligation can be assigned despite agreement otherwise.

(3) Unless the circumstances indicate the contrary, a prohibition of assignment of "the contract" is to be construed as barring only the delegation to the assignee of the assignor's performance.

(4) An assignment of "the contract" or of "all my rights under the contract" or an assignment in similar general terms is an assignment of rights and, unless the language or the circumstances (as in an assignment for security) indicate the contrary, it is a delegation of performance of the duties of the assignor, and its acceptance by the assignee constitutes a promise by him to perform those duties. This promise is enforceable by either the assignor or the other party to the original contract.

(5) The other party may treat any assignment which delegates performance as creating reasonable grounds for insecurity and may without prejudice to his rights against the assignor demand assurances from the assignee (Section 2—609).

Part 3
General Obligation and Construction of Contract

§ 2—301. General Obligations of Parties

The obligation of the seller is to transfer and deliver and that of the buyer is to accept and pay in accordance with the contract.

§ 2—302. Unconscionable Contract or Clause

(1) If the court as a matter of law finds the contract or any clause of the contract to have been unconscionable at the time it was made, the court may refuse to enforce the contract, or it may enforce the remainder of the contract without the unconscionable clause, or it may so limit the application of any unconscionable clause as to avoid any unconscionable result.

(2) When it is claimed or appears to the court that the contract or any clause thereof may be unconscionable, the parties shall be afforded a reasonable opportunity to present evidence as to its commercial setting, purpose and effect to aid the court in making the determination.

§ 2—303. Allocation or Division of Risks

Where this Article allocates a risk or a burden as between the parties "unless otherwise agreed," the agreement may not only shift the allocation but may also divide the risk or burden.

§ 2—304.   Price Payable in Money, Goods, Realty, or Otherwise

(1) The price can be made payable in money or otherwise. If it is payable in whole or in part in goods each party is a seller of the goods which he is to transfer.

(2) Even though all or part of the price is payable in an interest in realty the transfer of the goods and the seller's obligations with reference to them are subject to this Article, but not the transfer of the interest in realty or the transferor's obligations in connection therewith.

§ 2—305.   Open Price Term

(1) The parties, if they so intend, can conclude a contract for sale even though the price is not settled. In such a case, the price is a reasonable price at the time for delivery if
    (a) nothing is said as to price; or
    (b) the price is left to be agreed by the parties and they fail to agree; or
    (c) the price is to be fixed in terms of some agreed market or other standard as set or recorded by a third person or agency and it is not so set or recorded.

(2) A price to be fixed by the seller or by the buyer means a price for him to fix in good faith.

(3) When a price left to be fixed otherwise than by agreement of the parties fails to be fixed through fault of one party, the other may at his option treat the contract as cancelled or himself fix a reasonable price.

(4) Where, however, the parties intend not to be bound unless the price be fixed or agreed and it is not fixed or agreed, there is no contract. In such a case, the buyer must return any goods already received or if unable so to do must pay their reasonable value at the time of delivery and the seller must return any portion of the price paid on account.

§ 2—306.   Output, Requirements and Exclusive Dealings

(1) A term which measures the quantity by the output of the seller or the requirements of the buyer means such actual output or requirements as may occur in good faith, except that no quantity unreasonably disproportionate to any stated estimate or in the absence of a stated estimate to any normal or otherwise comparable prior output or requirements may be tendered or demanded.

(2) A lawful agreement by either the seller or the buyer for exclusive dealing in the kind of goods concerned imposes, unless otherwise agreed, an obligation by the seller to use best efforts to supply the goods and by the buyer to use best efforts to promote their sale.

§ 2—307.   Delivery in Single Lot or Several Lots

Unless otherwise agreed all goods called for by a contract for sale must be tendered in a single delivery and payment is due only on such tender; but where the circumstances give either party the right to make or demand delivery in lots, the price if it can be apportioned may be demanded for each lot.

§ 2—308.   Absence of Specified Place for Delivery

Unless otherwise agreed
    (a) the place for delivery of goods is the seller's place of business or, if he has none, his residence; but
    (b) in a contract for sale of identified goods which to the knowledge of the parties at the time of contracting are in some other place, that place is the place for their delivery; and
    (c) documents of title may be delivered through customary banking channels.

§ 2—309.   Absence of Specific Time Provisions; Notice of Termination

(1) The time for shipment or delivery or any other action under a contract if not provided in this Article or agreed upon shall be a reasonable time.

(2) Where the contract provides for successive performances but is indefinite in duration, it is valid for a reasonable time; but unless otherwise agreed may be terminated at any time by either party.

(3) Termination of a contract by one party, except on the happening of an agreed event, requires that reasonable notification be received by the other party and an agreement dispensing with notification is invalid if its operation would be unconscionable.

§ 2—310.   Open Time for Payment or Running of Credit; Authority to Ship Under Reservation

Unless otherwise agreed
    (a) payment is due at the time and place at which the buyer is to receive the goods even though the place of shipment is the place of delivery; and
    (b) if the seller is authorized to send the goods, he may ship them under reservation, and may tender the documents of title, but the buyer may inspect the goods after their arrival before payment is due unless such inspection is inconsistent with the terms of the contract (Section 2—513); and
    (c) if delivery is authorized and made by way of documents of title otherwise than by subsection (b), then payment is due at the time and place at which the buyer is to receive the documents regardless of where the goods are to be received; and
    (d) where the seller is required or authorized to ship the goods on credit, the credit period runs from the time of shipment but postdating the invoice or delaying its dispatch will correspondingly delay the starting of the credit period.

§ 2—311. Options and Cooperation Respecting Performance

(1) An agreement for sale which is otherwise sufficiently definite (subsection (3) of Section 2—204) to be a contract is not made invalid by the fact that it leaves particulars of performance to be specified by one of the parties. Any such specification must be made in good faith and within limits set by commercial reasonableness.

(2) Unless otherwise agreed, specifications relating to assortment of the goods are at the buyer's option and, except as otherwise provided in subsections (1) (c) and (3) of Section 2—319, specifications or arrangements relating to shipment are at the seller's option.

(3) Where such specification would materially affect the other party's performance but is not seasonably made or where one party's cooperation is necessary to the agreed performance of the other but is not seasonably forthcoming, the other party in addition to all other remedies

    (a) is excused for any resulting delay in his own performance; and

    (b) may also either proceed to perform in any reasonable manner or after the time for a material part of his own performance treat the failure to specify or to cooperate as a breach by failure to deliver or accept the goods.

§ 2—312. Warranty of Title and Against Infringement; Buyer's Obligation Against Infringement

(1) Subject to subsection (2), there is in a contract for sale a warranty by the seller that

    (a) the title conveyed shall be good, and its transfer rightful; and

    (b) the goods shall be delivered free from any security interest or other lien or encumbrance of which the buyer at the time of contracting has no knowledge.

(2) A warranty under subsection (1) will be excluded or modified only by specific language or by circumstances which give the buyer reason to know that the person selling does not claim title in himself or that he is purporting to sell only such right or title as he or a third person may have.

(3) Unless otherwise agreed a seller who is a merchant regularly dealing in goods of the kind warrants that the goods shall be delivered free of the rightful claim of any third person by way of infringement or the like but a buyer who furnishes specifications to the seller must hold the seller harmless against any such claim which arises out of compliance with the specifications.

§ 2—313. Express Warranties by Affirmation, Promise, Description, Sample

(1) Express warranties by the seller are created as follows:

    (a) Any affirmation of fact or promise made by the seller to the buyer which relates to the goods and becomes part of the basis of the bargain creates an express warranty that the goods shall conform to the affirmation or promise.

    (b) Any description of the goods which is made part of the basis of the bargain creates an express warranty that the goods shall conform to the description.

    (c) Any sample or model which is made part of the basis of the bargain creates an express warranty that the whole of the goods shall conform to the sample or model.

(2) It is not necessary to the creation of an express warranty that the seller use formal words such as "warrant" or "guarantee" or that he have a specific intention to make a warranty, but an affirmation merely of the value of the goods or a statement purporting to be merely the seller's opinion or commendation of the goods does not create a warranty.

§ 2—314. Implied Warranty; Merchantability; Usage of Trade

(1) Unless excluded or modified (Section 2—316), a warranty that the goods shall be merchantable is implied in a contract for their sale if the seller is a merchant with respect to goods of that kind. Under this section, the serving for value of food or drink to be consumed either on the premises or elsewhere is a sale.

(2) Goods to be merchantable must be at least such as

    (a) pass without objection in the trade under the contract description; and

    (b) in the case of fungible goods, are of fair average quality within the description; and

    (c) are fit for the ordinary purposes for which such goods are used; and

    (d) run, within the variations permitted by the agreement, of even kind, quality and quantity within each unit and among all units involved; and

    (e) are adequately contained, packaged, and labeled as the agreement may require; and

    (f) conform to the promises or affirmations of fact made on the container or label if any.

(3) Unless excluded or modified (Section 2—316), other implied warranties may arise from course of dealing or usage of trade.

§ 2—315. Implied Warranty: Fitness for Particular Purpose

Where the seller at the time of contracting has reason to know any particular purpose for which the goods are required and that the buyer is relying on the seller's skill or judgment to select or furnish suitable goods, there is unless excluded or modified under the next section an implied warranty that the goods shall be fit for such purpose.

§ 2—316. Exclusion or Modification of Warranties

(1) Words or conduct relevant to the creation of an express warranty and words or conduct tending to negate or limit warranty shall be construed wherever reasonable as consistent with each other; but, subject to the provisions of this Article on parol or extrinsic evidence (Section 2—202), negation or limitation is inoperative to the extent that such construction is unreasonable.

(2) Subject to subsection (3), to exclude or modify the implied warranty of merchantability or any part of it, the language must mention merchantability and in case of a writing must be conspicuous, and to exclude or modify any implied warranty of fitness the exclusion must be by a writing and conspicuous. Language to exclude all implied warranties of fitness is sufficient if it states, for example, that "There are no warranties which extend beyond the description on the face hereof."

(3) Notwithstanding subsection (2)

    (a) unless the circumstances indicate otherwise, all implied warranties are excluded by expressions like "as is," "with all faults" or other language which in common understanding calls the buyer's attention to the exclusion of warranties and makes plain that there is no implied warranty; and

    (b) when the buyer before entering into the contract has examined goods or the sample or model as fully as he desired or has refused to examine the goods, there is no implied warranty with regard to defects which an examination ought in the circumstances to have revealed to him; and

    (c) an implied warranty can also be excluded or modified by course of dealing or course of performance or usage of trade.

(4) Remedies for breach of warranty can be limited in accordance with the provisions of this Article on liquidation or limitation of damages and on contractual modification of remedy (Sections 2—718 and 2—719).

§ 2—317. Cumulation and Conflict of Warranties Express or Implied

Warranties whether express or implied shall be construed as consistent with each other and as cumulative, but if such construction is unreasonable the intention of the parties shall determine which warranty is dominant. In ascertaining that intention the following rules apply:

    (a) Exact or technical specifications displace an inconsistent sample or model or general language of description.

    (b) A sample from an existing bulk displaces inconsistent general language of description.

    (c) Express warranties displace inconsistent implied warranties other than an implied warranty of fitness for a particular purpose.

§ 2—318. Third Party Beneficiaries of Warranties Express or Implied

Note: *If this Act is introduced in the Congress of the United States this section should be omitted. (States to select one alternative.)*

Alternative A

A seller's warranty whether express or implied extends to any natural person who is in the family or household of his buyer or who is a guest in his home if it is reasonable to expect that such person may use, consume or be affected by the goods and who is injured in person by breach of the warranty. A seller may not exclude or limit the operation of this section.

Alternative B

A seller's warranty whether express or implied extends to any natural person who may reasonably be expected to use, consume or be affected by the goods and who is injured in person by breach of the warranty. A seller may not exclude or limit the operation of this section.

Alternative C

A seller's warranty whether express or implied extends to any person who may reasonably be expected to use, consume or be affected by the goods and who is injured by breach of the warranty. A seller may not exclude or limit the operation of this section with respect to injury to the person of an individual to whom the warranty extends.

§ 2—319. F.O.B. and F.A.S. Terms

(1) Unless otherwise agreed, the term F.O.B. (which means "free on board") at a named place, even though used only in connection with the stated price, is a delivery term under which

    (a) when the term is F.O.B. the place of shipment, the seller must at that place ship the goods in the manner provided in this Article (Section 2—504) and bear the expense and risk of putting them into the possession of the carrier; or

    (b) when the term is F.O.B. the place of destination, the seller must at his own expense and risk transport the goods to that place and there tender delivery of them in the manner provided in this Article (Section 2—503);

    (c) when under either (a) or (b) the term is also F.O.B. vessel, car or other vehicle, the seller must in addition at his own expense and risk load the goods on board. If the term is F.O.B. vessel, the buyer must name the vessel and, in an appropriate case, the seller must comply with the provisions of this Article on the form of bill of lading (Section 2—323).

(2) Unless otherwise agreed, the term F.A.S. vessel (which means "free alongside") at a named port, even though used only in connection with the stated price, is a delivery term under which the seller must

    (a) at his own expense and risk deliver the goods alongside the vessel in the manner usual in that port or on a dock designated and provided by the buyer; and

    (b) obtain and tender a receipt for the goods in exchange for which the carrier is under a duty to issue a bill of lading.

(3) Unless otherwise agreed in any case falling within subsection (1) (a) or (c) or subsection (2) the buyer must seasonably give any needed instructions for making delivery, including, when the term is F.A.S. or F.O.B., the loading berth of the vessel and, in an appropriate case, its name and sailing date. The seller may treat the failure of needed instructions as a failure of cooperation under this Article (Section 2—311). He may also at his option move the goods in any reasonable manner preparatory to delivery or shipment.

(4) Under the term F.O.B. vessel or F.A.S., unless otherwise agreed, the buyer must make payment against tender of the required documents and the seller may not tender nor the buyer demand delivery of the goods in substitution for the documents.

§ 2—320. C.I.F. and C. & F. Terms

(1) The term C.I.F. means that the price includes in a lump sum the cost of the goods and the insurance and freight to the named destination. The term C. & F. or C.F. means that the price so includes cost and freight to the named destination.

(2) Unless otherwise agreed and even though used only in connection with the stated price and destination, the term C.I.F. destination or its equivalent requires the seller at his own expense and risk to

    (a) put the goods into the possession of a carrier at the port for shipment and obtain a negotiable bill or bills of lading covering the entire transportation to the named destination; and

    (b) load the goods and obtain a receipt from the carrier (which may be contained in the bill of lading) showing that the freight has been paid or provided for; and

    (c) obtain a policy or certificate of insurance, including any war risk insurance, of a kind and on terms then current at the port of shipment in the usual amount, in the currency of the contract, shown to cover the same goods covered by the bill of lading and providing for payment of loss to the order of the buyer or for the account of whom it may concern; but the seller may add to the price the amount of the premium for any such war risk insurance; and

    (d) prepare an invoice of the goods and procure any other documents required to effect shipment or to comply with the contract; and

    (e) forward and tender with commercial promptness all the documents in due form and with any indorsement necessary to perfect the buyer's rights.

(3) Unless otherwise agreed, the term C. & F. or its equivalent has the same effect and imposes upon the seller the same obligations and risks as a C.I.F. term except the obligation as to insurance.

(4) Under the term C.I.F. or C. & F., unless otherwise agreed the buyer must make payment against tender of the required documents and the seller may not tender nor the buyer demand delivery of the goods in substitution for the documents.

§ 2—321. C.I.F. or C. & F.: "Net Landed Weights"; "Payment on Arrival"; Waranty of Condition on Arrival

Under a contract containing a term C.I.F. or C. & F.

(1) Where the price is based on or is to be adjusted according to "net landed weights," "delivered weights," "out turn" quantity or quality of the like, unless otherwise agreed the seller must reasonably estimate the price. The payment due on tender of the documents called for by the contract is the amount so estimated, but after final adjustment of the price a settlement must be made with commercial promptness.

(2) An agreement described in subsection (1) or any warranty of quality or condition of the goods on arrival places upon the seller the risk of ordinary deterioration, shrinkage and the like in transportation but has no effect on the place or time of identification to the contract for sale or delivery or on the passing of the risk of loss.

(3) Unless otherwise agreed, where the contract provides for payment on or after arrival of the goods the seller must before payment allow such preliminary inspection as is feasible; but if the goods are lost, delivery of the documents and payment are due when the goods should have arrived.

§ 2—322. Delivery "Ex-Ship"

(1) Unless otherwise agreed, a term for delivery of goods "ex-ship" (which means from the carrying vessel) or in equivalent language is not restricted to a particular ship and requires delivery from a ship which has reached a place at the named port of destination where goods of the kind are usually discharged.

(2) Under such a term, unless otherwise agreed

    (a) the seller must discharge all liens arising out of the carriage and furnish the buyer with a direction which puts the carrier under a duty to deliver the goods; and

    (b) the risk of loss does not pass to the buyer until the goods leave the ship's tackle or are otherwise properly unloaded.

§ 2—323.   Form of Bill of Lading Required in Overseas Shipment; "Overseas"

(1) Where the contract contemplates overseas shipment and contains a term C.I.F. or C. & F. or F.O.B. vessel, the seller unless otherwise agreed must obtain a negotiable bill of lading stating that the goods have been loaded on board or, in the case of a term C.I.F. or C. & F., received for shipment.

(2) Where in a case within subsection (1) a bill of lading has been issued in a set of parts, unless otherwise agreed, if the documents are not to be sent from abroad the buyer may demand tender of the full set; otherwise only one part of the bill of lading need be tendered. Even if the agreement expressly requires a full set

    (a) due tender of a single part is acceptable within the provisions of this Article on cure of improper delivery (subsection (1) of Section 2—508); and

    (b) even though the full set is demanded, if the documents are sent from abroad the person tendering an incomplete set may nevertheless require payment upon furnishing an indemnity which the buyer in good faith deems adequate.

(3) A shipment by water or by air or a contract contemplating such shipment is "overseas" insofar as by usage of trade or agreement it is subject to the commercial, financing or shipping practices characteristic of international deep water commerce.

§ 2—324.   "No Arrival, No Sale" Term

Under a term "no arrival, no sale" or terms of like meaning, unless otherwise agreed,

    (a) the seller must properly ship conforming goods and if they arrive by any means he must tender them on arrival, but he assumes no obligation that the goods will arrive unless he has caused the non-arrival; and

    (b) where without fault of the seller the goods are in part lost or have so deteriorated as no longer to conform to the contract or arrive after the contract time, the buyer may proceed as if there had been casualty to identified goods (Section 2—613).

§ 2—325.   "Letter of Credit" Term; "Confirmed Credit"

(1) Failure of the buyer seasonably to furnish an agreed letter of credit is a breach of the contract for sale.

(2) The delivery to seller of a proper letter of credit suspends the buyer's obligation to pay. If the letter of credit is dishonored, the seller may on seasonable notification to the buyer require payment directly from him.

(3) Unless otherwise agreed, the term "letter of credit" or "banker's credit" in a contract for sale means an irrevocable credit issued by a financing agency of good repute and, where the shipment is overseas, of good international repute. The term "confirmed credit" means that the credit must also carry the direct obligation of such an agency which does business in the seller's financial market.

§ 2—326.   Sale on Approval and Sale or Return; Consignment Sales and Rights of Creditors

(1) Unless otherwise agreed, if delivered goods may be returned by the buyer even though they conform to the contract, the transaction is

    (a) a "sale on approval" if the goods are delivered primarily for use, and

    (b) a "sale or return" if the goods are delivered primarily for resale.

(2) Except as provided in subsection (3), goods held on approval are not subject to the claims of the buyer's creditors until acceptance; goods held on sale or return are subject to such claims while in the buyer's possession.

(3) Where goods are delivered to a person for sale and such person maintains a place of business at which he deals in goods of the kind involved, under a name other than the name of the person making delivery, then with respect to claims of creditors of the person conducting the business the goods are deemed to be on sale or return. The provisions of this subsection are applicable even though an agreement purports to reserve title to the person making delivery until payment or resale or uses such words as "on consignment" or "on memorandum." However, this subsection is not applicable if the person making delivery

    (a) complies with an applicable law providing for a consignor's interest or the like to be evidenced by a sign, or

    (b) establishes that the person conducting the business is generally known by his creditors to be substantially engaged in selling the goods of others, or

    (c) complies with the filing provisions of the Article on secured Transactions (Article 9).

(4) Any "or return" term of a contract for sale is to be treated as a separate contract for sale within the statute of frauds section of this Article (Section 2—201) and as contradicting the sale aspect of the contract within the provisions of this Article on parol or extrinsic evidence (Section 2—202).

§ 2—327.   Special Incidents of Sale on Approval and Sale or Return

(1) Under a sale on approval, unless otherwise agreed

    (a) although the goods are identified to the contract, the risk of loss and the title do not pass to the buyer until acceptance; and

    (b) use of the goods consistent with the purpose of trial is not acceptance but failure seasonably to notify the seller of election to return the goods is acceptance, and if the goods conform to the contract acceptance of any part is acceptance of the whole; and

(c) after due notification of election to return, the return is at the seller's risk and expense but a merchant buyer must follow any reasonable instructions.

(2) Under a sale or return, unless otherwise agreed

(a) the option to return extends to the whole or any commercial unit of the goods while in substantially their original condition, but must be exercised seasonably; and

(b) the return is at the buyer's risk and expense.

§ 2—328.   Sale by Auction

(1) In a sale by auction, if goods are put up in lots each lot is the subject of a separate sale.

(2) A sale by auction is complete when the auctioneer so announces by the fall of the hammer or in other customary manner. Where a bid is made while the hammer is falling in acceptance of a prior bid, the auctioneer may in his discretion reopen the bidding or declare the goods sold under the bid on which the hammer was falling.

(3) Such a sale is with reserve unless the goods are in explicit terms put up without reserve. In an auction with reserve, the auctioneer may withdraw the goods at any time until he announces completion of the sale. In an auction without reserve, after the auctioneer calls for bids on an article or lot, that article or lot cannot be withdrawn unless no bid is made within a reasonable time. In either case a bidder may retract his bid until the auctioneer's announcement of completion of the sale, but a bidder's retraction does not revive any previous bid.

(4) If the auctioneer knowingly receives a bid on the seller's behalf or the seller makes or procures such a bid, and notice has not been given that liberty for such bidding is reserved, the buyer may at his option avoid the sale or take the goods at the price of the last good faith bid prior to the completion of the sale. This subsection shall not apply to any bid at a forced sale.

Part 4

Title, Creditors and Good Faith Purchasers

§ 2—401.   Passing of Title; Reservation for Security; Limited Application of This Section

Each provision of this Article with regard to the rights, obligations and remedies of the seller, the buyer, purchasers or other third parties applies irrespective of title to the goods except where the provision refers to such title. Insofar as situations are not covered by the other provisions of this Article and matters concerning title become material the following rules apply:

(1) Title to goods cannot pass under a contract for sale prior to their identification to the contract (Section 2—501), and unless otherwise explicitly agreed the buyer acquires by their identification a special property as limited by this Act. Any retention or reservation by the seller of the title (property) in goods shipped or delivered to the buyer is limited in effect to a reservation of a security interest. Subject to these provisions and to the provisions of the Article on Secured Transactions (Article 9), title to goods passes from the seller to the buyer in any manner and on any conditions explicitly agreed on by the parties.

(2) Unless otherwise explicitly agreed, title passes to the buyer at the time and place at which the seller completes his performance with reference to the physical delivery of the goods, despite any reservation of security interest and even though a document of title is to be delivered at a different time or place; and in particular and despite any reservation of a security interest by the bill of lading

(a) if the contract requires or authorizes the seller to send the goods to the buyer but does not require him to deliver them at destination, title passes to the buyer at the time and place of shipment; but

(b) if the contract requires delivery at destination, title passes on tender there.

(3) Unless otherwise explicitly agreed, where delivery is to be made without moving the goods,

(a) if the seller is to deliver a document of title, title passes at the time when and the place where he delivers such documents; or

(b) if the goods are at the time of contracting already identified and no documents are to be delivered, title passes at the time and place of contracting.

(4) A rejection or other refusal by the buyer to receive or retain the goods, whether or not justified, or a justified revocation of acceptance revests title to the goods in the seller. Such revesting occurs by operation of law and is not a "sale."

§ 2—402.   Rights of Seller's Creditors Against Sold Goods

(1) Except as provided in subsections (2) and (3), rights of unsecured creditors of the seller with respect to goods which have been identified to a contract for sale are subject to the buyer's rights to recover the goods under this Article (Sections 2—502 and 2—716).

(2) A creditor of the seller may treat a sale or an identification of goods to a contract for sale as void if as against him a retention of possession by the seller is fraudulent under any rule of law of the state where the goods are situated, except that retention of possession

in good faith and current course of trade by a merchant-seller for a commercially reasonable time after a sale or identification is not fraudulent.

(3) Nothing in this Article shall be deemed to impair the rights of creditors of the seller

(a) under the provisions of the Article on Secured Transactions (Article 9); or

(b) where identification to the contract or delivery is made not in current course of trade but in satisfaction of or as security for a preexisting claim for money, security or the like and is made under circumstances which under any rule of law of the state where the goods are situated would apart from this Article constitute the transaction a fraudulent transfer or voidable preference.

§ 2—403. Power to Transfer; Good Faith Purchase of Goods; "Entrusting"

(1) A purchaser of goods acquires all title which his transferor had or had power to transfer except that a purchaser of a limited interest acquires rights only to the extent of the interest purchased. A person with voidable title has power to transfer a good title to a good faith purchaser for value. When goods have been delivered under a transaction of purchase, the purchaser has such power even though

(a) the transferor was deceived as to the identity of the purchaser, or

(b) the delivery was in exchange for a check which is later dishonored, or

(c) it was agreed that the transaction was to be a "cash sale" or

(d) the delivery was procured through fraud punishable as larcenous under the criminal law.

(2) Any entrusting of possession of goods to a merchant who deals in goods of that kind gives him power to transfer all rights of the entruster to a buyer in ordinary course of business.

(3) "Entrusting" includes any delivery and any acquiescence in retention of possession regardless of any condition expressed between the parties to the delivery or acquiescence and regardless of whether the procurement of the entrusting or the possessor's disposition of the goods have been such as to be larcenous under the criminal law.

(4) The rights of other purchasers of goods and of lien creditors are governed by the Articles on Secured Transactions (Article 9), Bulk Transfers (Article 6) and Documents of Title (Article 7).

Part 5

Performance

§ 2—501. Insurable Interest in Goods; Manner of Identification of Goods

(1) The buyer obtains a special property and an insurable interest in goods by identification of existing goods as goods to which the contract refers even though the goods so identified are non-conforming and he has an option to return or reject them. Such identification can be made at any time and in any manner explicitly agreed to by the parties. In the absence of explicit agreement, identification occurs

(a) when the contract is made, if it is for the sale of goods already existing and identified;

(b) if the contract is for the sale of future goods other than those described in paragraph (c), when goods are shipped, marked or otherwise designated by the seller as goods to which the contract refers;

(c) when the crops are planted or otherwise become growing crops or the young are conceived, if the contract is for the sale of unborn young to be born within twelve months after contracting or for the sale of crops to be harvested within twelve months or the next normal harvest season after contracting whichever is longer.

(2) The seller retains an insurable interest in goods so long as title to or any security interest in the goods remains in him; and where the identification is by the seller alone, he may until default or insolvency or notification to the buyer that the identification is final substitute other goods for those identified.

(3) Nothing in this section impairs any insurable interest recognized under any other statute or rule of law.

§ 2—502. Buyer's Right to Goods on Seller's Insolvency

(1) Subject to subsection (2), and even though the goods have not been shipped, a buyer who has paid a part or all of the price of goods in which he has a special property under the provisions of the immediately preceding section may, on making and keeping good a tender of any unpaid portion of their price, recover them from the seller if the seller becomes insolvent within ten days after receipt of the first installment on their price.

(2) If the identification creating his special property has been made by the buyer, he acquires the right to recover the goods only if they conform to the contract for sale.

§ 2—503. Manner of Seller's Tender of Delivery

(1) Tender of delivery requires that the seller put and hold conforming goods at the buyer's disposition and give the buyer any notification reasonably necessary to enable him to take delivery. The manner, time and place for tender are determined by the agreement and this Article, and in particular

(a) tender must be at a reasonable hour, and, if it is of goods, they must be kept available for the period reasonably necessary to enable the buyer to take possession; but

(b) unless otherwise agreed, the buyer must furnish facilities reasonably suited to the receipt of the goods.

(2) Where the case is within the next section respecting shipment, tender requires that the seller comply with its provisions.

(3) Where the seller is required to deliver at a particular destination, tender requires that he comply with subsection (1) and also, in any appropriate case, tender documents as described in subsections (4) and (5) of this section.

(4) Where goods are in the possession of a bailee and are to be delivered without being moved

(a) tender requires that the seller either tender a negotiable document of title covering such goods or procure acknowledgment by the bailee of the buyer's right to possession of the goods; but

(b) tender to the buyer of a nonnegotiable document of title or of a written direction to the bailee to deliver is sufficient tender unless the buyer seasonably objects, and receipt by the bailee of notification of the buyer's rights fixes those rights as against the bailee and all third persons; but risk of loss of the goods and of any failure by the bailee to honor the nonnegotiable document of title or to obey the direction remains on the seller until the buyer has had a reasonable time to present the document or direction, and a refusal by the bailee to honor the document or to obey the direction defeats the tender.

(5) Where the contract requires the seller to deliver documents

(a) he must tender all such documents in correct form, except as provided in this Article with respect to bills of lading in a set (subsection (2) of Section 2—323); and

(b) tender through customary banking channels is sufficient and dishonor of a draft accompanying the documents constitutes nonacceptance or rejection.

§ 2—504. Shipment by Seller

Where the seller is required or authorized to send the goods to the buyer and the contract does not require him to deliver them at a particular destination, then, unless otherwise agreed, he must

(a) put the goods in the possession of such a carrier and make such a contract for their transportation as may be reasonable having regard to the nature of the goods and other circumstances of the case; and

(b) obtain and promptly deliver or tender in due form any document necessary to enable the buyer to obtain possession of the goods or otherwise required by the agreement or by usage of trade; and

(c) promptly notify the buyer of the shipment.

Failure to notify the buyer under paragraph (c) or to make a proper contract under paragraph (a) is a ground for rejection only if material delay or loss ensues.

§ 2—505. Seller's Shipment Under Reservation

(1) Where the seller has identified goods to the contract by or before shipment

(a) his procurement of a negotiable bill of lading to his own order or otherwise reserves in him a security interest in the goods. His procurement of the bill to the order of a financing agency or of the buyer indicates in addition only the seller's expectation of transferring that interest to the person named.

(b) a nonnegotiable bill of lading to himself or his nominee reserves possession of the goods as security but except in a case of conditional delivery (subsection (2) of Section 2—507) a nonnegotiable bill of lading naming the buyer as consignee reserves no security interest even though the seller retains possession of the bill of lading.

(2) When shipment by the seller with reservation of a security interest is in violation of the contract for sale it constitutes an improper contract for transportation within the preceding section but impairs neither the rights given to the buyer by shipment and identification of the goods to the contract nor the seller's powers as a holder of a negotiable document.

§ 2—506. Rights of Financing Agency

(1) A financing agency by paying or purchasing for value a draft which relates to a shipment of goods acquires to the extent of the payment or purchase, and in addition to its own rights under the draft and any document of title securing it, any rights of the shipper in the goods, including the right to stop delivery and the shipper's right to have the draft honored by the buyer.

(2) The right to reimbursement of a financing agency which has in good faith honored or purchased the draft under commitment to or authority from the buyer is not impaired by subsequent discovery of defects with reference to any relevant document which was apparently regular on its face.

§ 2—507. Effect of Seller's Tender; Delivery on Condition

(1) Tender of delivery is a condition to the buyer's duty to accept the goods and, unless otherwise agreed, to his duty to pay for them. Tender entitles the seller to acceptance of the goods and to payment according to the contract.

(2) Where payment is due and demanded on the delivery to the buyer of goods or documents of title, his

right as against the seller to retain or dispose of them is conditional upon his making the payment due.

§ 2—508. Cure by Seller of Improper Tender or Delivery; Replacement

(1) Where any tender or delivery by the seller is rejected because non-conforming and the time for performance has not yet expired, the seller may seasonably notify the buyer of his intention to cure and may then within the contract time make a conforming delivery.

(2) Where the buyer rejects a non-conforming tender which the seller had reasonable grounds to believe would be acceptable with or without money allowance, the seller may if he seasonably notifies the buyer have a further reasonable time to substitute a conforming tender.

§ 2—509. Risk of Loss in the Absence of Breach

(1) Where the contract requires or authorizes the seller to ship the goods by carrier

    (a) if it does not require him to deliver them at a particular destination, the risk of loss passes to the buyer when the goods are duly delivered to the carrier even though the shipment is under reservation (Section 2—505); but

    (b) if it does require him to deliver them at a particular destination and the goods are there duly tendered while in the possession of the carrier, the risk of loss passes to the buyer when the goods are there duly so tendered as to enable the buyer to take delivery.

(2) Where the goods are held by a bailee to be delivered without being moved, the risk of loss passes to the buyer

    (a) on his receipt of a negotiable document of title covering the goods; or

    (b) on acknowledgment by the bailee of the buyer's right to possession of the goods; or

    (c) after his receipt of a nonnegotiable document of title or other written direction to deliver, as provided in subsection (4)(b) of Section 2—503.

(3) In any case not within subsection (1) or (2), the risk of loss passes to the buyer on his receipt of the goods if the seller is a merchant; otherwise the risk passes to the buyer on tender of delivery.

(4) The provisions of this section are subject to contrary agreement of the parties and to the provisions of this Article on sale on approval (Section 2—327) and on effect of breach on risk of loss (Section 2—510).

§ 2—510. Effect of Breach on Risk of Loss

(1) Where a tender or delivery of goods so fails to conform to the contract as to give a right of rejection, the risk of their loss remains on the seller until cure or acceptance.

(2) Where the buyer rightfully revokes acceptance, he may to the extent of any deficiency in his effective insurance coverage treat the risk of loss as having rested on the seller from the beginning.

(3) Where the buyer, as to conforming goods already identified to the contract for sale, repudiates or is otherwise in breach before risk of their loss has passed to him, the seller may to the extent of any deficiency in his effective insurance coverage treat the risk of loss as resting on the buyer for a commercially reasonable time.

§ 2—511. Tender of Payment by Buyer; Payment by Check

(1) Unless otherwise agreed, tender of payment is a condition to the seller's duty to tender and complete any delivery.

(2) Tender of payment is sufficient when made by any means or in any manner current in the ordinary course of business unless the seller demands payment in legal tender and gives any extension of time reasonably necessary to procure it.

(3) Subject to the provisions of this Act on the effect of an instrument on an obligation (Section 3—802), payment by check is conditional and is defeated as between the parties by dishonor of the check on due presentment.

§ 2—512. Payment by Buyer Before Inspection

(1) Where the contract requires payment before inspection, non-conformity of the goods does not excuse the buyer from so making payment unless

    (a) the non-comformity appears without inspection; or

    (b) despite tender of the required documents, the circumstances would justify injunction against honor under the provisions of this Act (Section 5–114).

(2) Payment pursuant to subsection (1) does not constitute an acceptance of goods or impair the buyer's right to inspect or any of his remedies.

§ 2—513. Buyer's Right to Inspection of Goods

(1) Unless otherwise agreed and subject to subsection (3), where goods are tendered or delivered or identified to the contract for sale, the buyer has a right before payment or acceptance to inspect them at any reasonable place and time and in any reasonable manner. When the seller is required or authorized to send the goods to the buyer, the inspection may be after their arrival.

(2) Expenses of inspection must be borne by the buyer but may be recovered from the seller if the goods do not conform and are rejected.

(3) Unless otherwise agreed and subject to the provisions of this Article on C.I.F. contracts (subsection (3) of Section 2—321), the buyer is not entitled to inspect the goods before payment of the price when the contract provides

(a) for delivery "C.O.D." or on other like terms; or

(b) for payment against documents of title, except where such payment is due only after the goods are to become available for inspection.

(4) A place or method of inspection fixed by the parties is presumed to be exclusive but, unless otherwise expressly agreed, it does not postpone identification or shift the place for delivery or for passing the risk of loss. If compliance becomes impossible, inspection shall be as provided in this section unless the place or method fixed was clearly intended as an indispensable condition, failure of which avoids the contract.

§ 2—514. When Documents Deliverable on Acceptance; When on Payment

Unless otherwise agreed, documents against which a draft is drawn are to be delivered to the drawee on acceptance of the draft if it is payable more than three days after presentment; otherwise, only on payment.

§ 2—515. Preserving Evidence of Goods in Dispute

In furtherance of the adjustment of any claim or dispute

(a) either party on reasonable notification to the other, and for the purpose of ascertaining the facts and preserving evidence, has the right to inspect, test and sample the goods including such of them as may be in the possession or control of the other; and

(b) the parties may agree to a third party inspection or survey to determine the conformity or condition of the goods and may agree that the findings shall be binding upon them in any subsequent litigation or adjustment.

Part 6

Breach, Repudiation and Excuse

§ 2—601. Buyer's Rights on Improper Delivery

Subject to the provisions of this Article on breach in installment contracts (Section 2—612) and unless otherwise agreed under the sections on contractual limitations of remedy (Sections 2—718 and 2—719), if the goods or the tender of delivery fail in any respect to conform to the contract, the buyer may

(a) reject the whole; or

(b) accept the whole; or

(c) accept any commercial unit or units and reject the rest.

§ 2—602. Manner and Effect of Rightful Rejection

(1) Rejection of goods must be within a reason-able time after their delivery or tender. It is ineffective unless the buyer seasonably notifies the seller.

(2) Subject to the provisions of the two following sections on rejected goods (Sections 2—603 and 2—604),

(a) after rejection any exercise of ownership by the buyer with respect to any commercial unit is wrongful as against the seller; and

(b) if the buyer has before rejection taken physical possession of goods in which he does not have a security interest under the provisions of this Article (subsection (3) of Section 2—711), he is under a duty after rejection to hold them with reasonable care at the seller's disposition for a time sufficient to permit the seller to remove them; but

(c) the buyer has no further obligations with regard to goods rightfully rejected.

(3) The seller's rights with respect to goods wrongfully rejected are governed by the provisions of this Article on Seller's remedies in general (Section 2—703).

§ 2—603. Merchant Buyer's Duties as to Rightfully Rejected Goods

(1) Subject to any security interest in the buyer (subsection (3) of Section 2—711), when the seller has no agent or place of business at the market of rejection, a merchant buyer is under a duty after rejection of goods in his possession or control to follow any reasonable instructions received from the seller with respect to the goods and in the absence of such instructions to make reasonable efforts to sell them for the seller's account if they are perishable or threaten to decline in value speedily. Instructions are not reasonable if on demand indemnity for expenses is not forthcoming.

(2) When the buyer sells goods under subsection (1), he is entitled to reimbursement from the seller or out of the proceeds for reasonable expenses of caring for and selling them, and if the expenses include no selling commission then to such commission as is usual in the trade or, if there is none, to a reasonable sum not exceeding ten per cent on the gross proceeds.

(3) In complying with this section, the buyer is held only to good faith and good faith conduct hereunder is neither acceptance nor conversion nor the basis of an action for damages.

§ 2—604. Buyer's Options as to Salvage or Rightfully Rejected Goods

Subject to the provisions of the immediately preceding section on perishables, if the seller gives no instructions within a reasonable time after notification of rejection the buyer may store the rejected goods for the seller's account or reship them to him or resell them for the seller's account with reimbursement as provided in the preceding section. Such action is not acceptance or conversion.

§ 2—605. Waiver of Buyer's Objections by Failure to Particularize

(1) The buyer's failure to state in connection with rejection a particular defect which is ascertainable by reasonable inspection precludes him from relying on the unstated defect to justify rejection or to establish breach

    (a) where the seller could have cured it if stated seasonably; or

    (b) between merchants when the seller has after rejection made a request in writing for a full and final written statement of all defects on which the buyer proposes to rely.

(2) Payment against documents made without reservation of rights precludes recovery of the payment for defects apparent on the face of the documents.

§ 2—606. What Constitutes Acceptance of Goods

(1) Acceptance of goods occurs when the buyer

    (a) after a reasonable opportunity to inspect the goods signifies to the seller that the goods are conforming or that he will take or retain them in spite of their non-conformity; or

    (b) fails to make an effective rejection (subsection (1) of Section 2—602), but such acceptance does not occur until the buyer has had a reasonable opportunity to inspect them; or

    (c) does any act inconsistent with the seller's ownership; but if such act is wrongful as against the seller it is an acceptance only if ratified by him.

(2) Acceptance of a part of any commercial unit is acceptance of that entire unit.

§ 2—607. Effect of Acceptance; Notice of Breach; Burden of Establishing Breach After Acceptance; Notice of Claim or Litigation to Person Answerable Over

(1) The buyer must pay at the contract rate for any goods accepted.

(2) Acceptance of goods by the buyer precludes rejection of the goods accepted and if made with knowledge of a non-conformity cannot be revoked because of it unless the acceptance was on the reasonable assumption that the non-conformity would be seasonably cured but acceptance does not of itself impair any other remedy provided by this Article for non-conformity.

(3) Where a tender has been accepted

    (a) the buyer must within a reasonable time after he discovers or should have discovered any breach notify the seller of breach or be barred from any remedy; and

    (b) if the claim is one for infringement or the like (subsection (3) of Section 2—312) and the buyer is sued as a result of such a breach, he must so notify the seller within a reasonable time after he receives notice of the litigation or be barred from any remedy over for liability established by the litigation.

(4) The burden is on the buyer to establish any breach with respect to the goods accepted.

(5) Where the buyer is sued for breach of a warranty or other obligation for which his seller is answerable over

    (a) he may give his seller written notice of the litigation. If the notice states that the seller may come in and defend and that if the seller does not do so he will be bound in any action against him by his buyer by any determination of fact common to the two litigations, then unless the seller after seasonable receipt of the notice does come in and defend he is so bound.

    (b) if the claim is one for infringement or the like (subsection (3) of Section 2—312), the original seller may demand in writing that his buyer turn over to him control of the litigation including settlement or else be barred from any remedy over and if he also agrees to bear all expense and to satisfy any adverse judgment, then unless the buyer after seasonable receipt of the demand does turn over control the buyer is so barred.

(6) The provisions of subsections (3), (4) and (5) apply to any obligation of a buyer to hold the seller harmless against infringement or the like (subsection (3) of Section 2—312).

§ 2—608. Revocation of Acceptance in Whole or in Part

(1) The buyer may revoke his acceptance of a lot or commercial unit whose non-conformity substantially impairs its value to him if he has accepted it

    (a) on the reasonable assumption that its non-conformity would be cured and it has not been seasonably cured; or

    (b) without discovery of such non-conformity if his acceptance was reasonably induced either by the difficulty of discovery before acceptance or by the seller's assurances.

(2) Revocation of acceptance must occur within a reasonable time after the buyer discovers or should have discovered the ground for it and before any substantial change in condition of the goods which is not caused by their own defects. It is not effective until the buyer notifies the seller of it.

(3) A buyer who so revokes has the same rights and duties with regard to the goods involved as if he had rejected them.

§ 2 — 609. Right to Adequate Assurance of Performance

(1) A contract for sale imposes an obligation on each party that the other's expectation of receiving due performance will not be impaired. When reasonable grounds for insecurity arise with respect to the performance of either party, the other may in writing demand adequate assurance of due performance and until he receives such assurance may, if commercially reasonable, suspend any performance for which he has not already received the agreed return.

(2) Between merchants, the reasonableness of grounds for insecurity and the adequacy of any assurance offered shall be determined according to commercial standards.

(3) Acceptance of any improper delivery or payment does not prejudice the aggrieved party's right to demand adequate assurance of future performance.

(4) After receipt of a justified demand, failure to provide within a reasonable time, not exceeding thirty days, such assurance of due performance as is adequate under the circumstances of the particular case is a repudiation of the contract.

§ 2 — 610. Anticipatory Repudiation

When either party repudiates the contract with respect to a performance not yet due, the loss of which will substantially impair the value of the contract to the other, the aggrieved party may

(a) for a commercially reasonable time await performance by the repudiating party; or

(b) resort to any remedy for breach (Section 2 — 703 or Section 2 — 711), even though he has notified the repudiating party that he would await the latter's performance and has urged retraction; and

(c) in either case suspend his own performance or proceed in accordance with the provisions of this Article on the seller's right to identify goods to the contract notwithstanding breach or to salvage unfinished goods (Section 2 — 704).

§ 2 — 611. Retraction of Anticipatory Repudiation

(1) Until the repudiating party's next performance is due, he can retract his repudiation unless the aggrieved party has since the repudiation cancelled or materially changed his position or otherwise indicated that he considers the repudiation final.

(2) Retraction may be by any method which clearly indicates to the aggrieved party that the repudiating party intends to perform, but must include any assurance justifiably demanded under the provisions of this Article (Section 2 — 609).

(3) Retraction reinstates the repudiating party's rights under the contract with due excuse and allowance to the aggrieved party for any delay occasioned by the repudiation.

§ 2 — 612. "Installment Contract"; Breach

(1) An "installment contract" is one which requires or authorizes the delivery of goods in separate lots to be separately accepted, even though the contract contains a clause "each delivery is a separate contract" or its equivalent.

(2) The buyer may reject any installment which is non-conforming if the non-conformity substantially impairs the value of that installment and cannot be cured or if the non-conformity is a defect in the required documents; but if the non-conformity does not fall within subsection (3) and the seller gives adequate assurance of its cure, the buyer must accept that installment.

(3) Whenever non-conformity or default with respect to one or more installments substantially impairs the value of the whole contract, there is a breach of the whole. But the aggrieved party reinstates the contract if he accepts a non-conforming installment without seasonably notifying of cancellation or if he brings an action with respect only to past installments or demands performance as to future installments.

§ 2 — 613. Casualty to Identified Goods

Where the contract requires for its performance goods identified when the contract is made, and the goods suffer casualty without fault of either party before the risk of loss passes to the buyer, or in a proper case under a "no arrival, no sale" term (Section 2 — 324) then

(a) if the loss is total the contract is avoided; and

(b) if the loss is partial or the goods have so deteriorated as no longer to conform to the contract the buyer may nevertheless demand inspection and at his option either treat the contract as avoided or accept the goods with due allowance from the contract price for the deterioration or the deficiency in quantity but without further right against the seller.

§ 2 — 614. Substituted Performance

(1) Where without fault of either party the agreed berthing, loading, or unloading facilities fail or an agreed type of carrier becomes unavailable or the agreed manner of delivery otherwise becomes commercially impracticable but a commercially reasonable substitute is available, such substitute performance must be tendered and accepted.

(2) If the agreed means or manner of payment fails because of domestic or foreign governmental regulation, the seller may withhold or stop delivery unless the buyer provides a means or manner of payment which is commercially a substantial equivalent. If delivery has already been taken, payment by the means or in the manner provided by the regulation discharges the buyer's obligation unless the regulation is discriminatory, oppressive or predatory.

§ 2—615. Excuse by Failure of Presupposed Conditions

Except so far as a seller may have assumed a greater obligation and subject to the preceding section on substituted performance:

(a) Delay in delivery or nondelivery in whole or in part by a seller who complies with paragraphs (b) and (c) is not a breach of his duty under a contract for sale if performance as agreed has been made impracticable by the occurrence of a contingency the non-occurrence of which was a basic assumption on which the contract was made or by compliance in good faith with any applicable foreign or domestic governmental regulation or order whether or not it later proves to be invalid.

(b) Where the causes mentioned in paragraph (a) affect only a part of the seller's capacity to perform, he must allocate production and deliveries among his customers but may at his option include regular customers not then under contract as well as his own requirements for further manufacture. He may so allocate in any manner which is fair and reasonable.

(c) The seller must notify the buyer seasonably that there will be delay or nondelivery and, when allocation is required under paragraph (b), of the estimated quota thus made available for the buyer.

§ 2—616. Procedure on Notice Claiming Excuse

(1) Where the buyer receives notification of a material or indefinite delay or an allocation justified under the preceding section, he may by written notification to the seller as to any delivery concerned; and where the prospective deficiency substantially impairs the value of the whole contract under the provisions of this Article relating to breach of installment contracts (Section 2—612), then also as to the whole,

(a) terminate and thereby discharge any unexecuted portion of the contract; or

(b) modify the contract by agreeing to take his available quota in substitution.

(2) If, after receipt of such notification from the seller, the buyer fails so to modify the contract within a reasonable time not exceeding thirty days, the contract lapses with respect to any deliveries affected.

(3) The provisions of this section may not be negated by agreement except insofar as the seller has assumed a greater obligation under the preceding section.

Part 7

Remedies

§ 2—701. Remedies for Breach of Collateral Contracts Not Impaired

Remedies for breach of any obligation or promise collateral or ancillary to a contract for sale are not impaired by the provisions of this Article.

§ 2—702. Seller's Remedies on Discovery of Buyer's Insolvency

(1) Where the seller discovers the buyer to be insolvent, he may refuse delivery except for cash including payment for all goods theretofore delivered under the contract, and stop delivery under this Article (Section 2—705).

(2) Where the seller discovers that the buyer has received goods on credit while insolvent, he may reclaim the goods upon demand made within ten days after the receipt, but if misrepresentation of solvency has been made to the particular seller in writing within three months before delivery the ten day limitation does not apply. Except as provided in this subsection, the seller may not base a right to reclaim goods on the buyer's fraudulent or innocent misrepresentation of solvency or of intent to pay.

(3) The seller's right to reclaim under subsection (2) is subject to the rights of a buyer in ordinary course or other good faith purchaser under this Article (Section 2—403). Successful reclamation of goods excludes all other remedies with respect to them.

§ 2—703. Seller's Remedies in General

Where the buyer wrongfully rejects or revokes acceptance of goods or fails to make a payment due on or before delivery or repudiates with respect to a part or the whole, then with respect to any goods directly affected and, if the breach is of the whole contract (Section 2—612), then also with respect to the whole undelivered balance, the aggrieved seller may

(a) withhold delivery of such goods;

(b) stop delivery by any bailee as hereafter provided (Section 2—705);

(c) proceed under the next section respecting goods still unidentified to the contract;

(d) resell and recover damages as hereafter provided (Section 2—706);

(e) recover damages for non-acceptance (Section 2—708) or in a proper case the price (Section 2—709);

(f) cancel.

§ 2—704. Seller's Right to Identify Goods to the Contract Notwithstanding Breach or to Salvage Unfinished Goods

(1) An aggrieved seller under the preceding section may

(a) identify to the contract conforming goods not already identified if at the time he learned of the breach they are in his possession or control;

(b) treat as the subject of resale goods which have demonstrably been intended for the particular contract even though those goods are unfinished.

(2) Where the goods are unfinished an aggrieved seller may, in the exercise of reasonable commercial judgment for the purposes of avoiding loss and of effective realization, either complete the manufacture and wholly identify the goods to the contract or cease manufacture and resell for scrap or salvage value or proceed in any other reasonable manner.

§ 2—705. Seller's Stoppage of Delivery in Transit or Otherwise

(1) The seller may stop delivery of goods in the possession of a carrier or other bailee when he discovers the buyer to be insolvent (Section 2—702) and may stop delivery of carload, truckload, planeload or larger shipments of express or freight when the buyer repudiates or fails to make a payment due before delivery or if for any other reason the seller has a right to withhold or reclaim the goods.

(2) As against such buyer, the seller may stop delivery until

(a) receipt of the goods by the buyer; or

(b) acknowledgment to the buyer by any bailee of the goods except a carrier that the bailee holds the goods for the buyer; or

(c) such acknowledgment to the buyer by a carrier by reshipment or as warehouseman; or

(d) negotiation to the buyer of any negotiable document of title covering the goods.

(3) (a) To stop delivery the seller must so notify as to enable the bailee by reasonable diligence to prevent delivery of the goods.

(b) After such notification the bailee must hold and deliver the goods according to the directions of the seller, but the seller is liable to the bailee for any ensuing charges or damages.

(c) If a negotiable document of title has been issued for goods, the bailee is not obliged to obey a notification to stop until surrender of the document.

(d) A carrier who has issued a nonnegotiable bill of lading is not obliged to obey a notification to stop received from a person other than the consignor.

§ 2—706. Seller's Resale Including Contract for Resale

(1) Under the conditions stated in Section 2—703 on seller's remedies, the seller may resell the goods concerned or the undelivered balance thereof. Where the resale is made in good faith and in a commercially reasonable manner, the seller may recover the difference between the resale price and the contract price together with any incidental damages allowed under the provisions of this Article (Section 2—710), but less expenses saved in consequence of the buyer's breach.

(2) Except as otherwise provided in subsection (3) or unless otherwise agreed, resale may be at public or private sale including sale by way of one or more contracts to sell or of identification to an existing contract of the seller. Sale may be as a unit or in parcels and at any time and place and on any terms but every aspect of the sale including the method, manner, time, place and terms must be commercially reasonable. The resale must be reasonably identified as referring to the broken contract, but it is not necessary that the goods be in existence or that any or all of them have been identified to the contract before the breach.

(3) Where the resale is at private sale, the seller must give the buyer reasonable notification of his intention to resell.

(4) Where the resale is at public sale

(a) only identified goods can be sold except where there is a recognized market for a public sale of futures in goods of the kind; and

(b) it must be made at a usual place or market for public sale if one is reasonably available and except in the case of goods which are perishable or threaten to decline in value speedily the seller must give the buyer reasonable notice of the time and place of the resale; and

(c) if the goods are not to be within the view of those attending the sale, the notification of sale must state the place where the goods are located and provide for their reasonable inspection by prospective bidders; and

(d) the seller may buy.

(5) A purchaser who buys in good faith at a resale takes the goods free of any rights of the original buyer even though the seller fails to comply with one or more of the requirements of this section.

(6) The seller is not accountable to the buyer for any profit made on any resale. A person in the position of a seller (Section 2—707) or a buyer who has rightfully rejected or justifiably revoked acceptance must account for any excess over the amount of his security interest, as hereinafter defined (subsection (3) of Section 2—711.)

§ 2—707. "Person in the Position of a Seller"

(1) A "person in the position of a seller"

includes, as against a principal, an agent who has paid or become responsible for the price of goods on behalf of his principal or anyone who otherwise holds a security interest or other right in goods similar to that of a seller.

(2) A person in the position of a seller may as provided in this Article withhold or stop delivery (Section 2—705) and resell (Section 2—706) and recover incidental damages (Section 2—710).

§ 2—708. Seller's Damages for Nonacceptance or Repudiation

(1) Subject to subsection (2) and to the provisions of this Article with respect to proof of market price (Section 2—723), the measure of damages for nonacceptance or repudiation by the buyer is the difference between the market price at the time and place for tender and the unpaid contract price together with any incidental damages provided in this Article (Section 2—710), but less expenses saved in consequence of the buyer's breach.

(2) If the measure of damages provided in subsection (1) is inadequate to put the seller in as good a position as performance would have done, then the measure of damages is the profit (including reasonable overhead) which the seller would have made from full performance by the buyer, together with any incidental damages provided in this Article (Section 2—710), due allowance for costs reasonably incurred and due credit for payments or proceeds of resale.

§ 2—709. Action for the Price

(1) When the buyer fails to pay the price as it becomes due, the seller may recover, together with any incidental damages under the next section, the price
  (a) of goods accepted or of conforming goods lost or damaged within a commercially reasonable time after risk of their loss has passed to the buyer; and
  (b) of goods identified to the contract if the seller is unable after reasonable effort to resell them at a reasonable price or the circumstances reasonably indicate that such effort will be unavailing.

(2) Where the seller sues for the price, he must hold for the buyer any goods which have been identified to the contract and are still in his control except that if resale becomes possible he may resell them at any time prior to the collection of the judgment. The net proceeds of any such resale must be credited to the buyer and payment of the judgment entitles him to any goods not resold.

(3) After the buyer has wrongfully rejected or revoked acceptance of the goods or has failed to make a payment due or has repudiated (Section 2—610), a seller who is held not entitled to the price under this section shall nevertheless be awarded damages for nonacceptance under the preceding section.

§ 2—710. Seller's Incidental Damages

Incidental damages to an aggrieved seller include any commercially reasonable charges, expenses or commissions incurred in stopping delivery, in the transportation, care and custody of goods after the buyer's breach, in connection with return or resale of the goods or otherwise resulting from the breach.

§ 2—711. Buyer's Remedies in General; Buyer's Security Interest in Rejected Goods

(1) Where the seller fails to make delivery or repudiates or the buyer rightfully rejects or justifiably revokes acceptance, then with respect to any goods involved, and with respect to the whole if the breach goes to the whole contract (Section 2—612), the buyer may cancel and whether or not he has done so may in addition to recovering so much of the price as has been paid
  (a) "cover" and have damages under the next section as to all the goods affected whether or not they have been identified to the contract; or
  (b) recover damages for nondelivery as provided in this Article (Section 2—713).

(2) Where the seller fails to deliver or repudiates, the buyer may also
  (a) if the goods have been identified recover them as provided in this Article (Section 2—502); or
  (b) in a proper case obtain specific performance or replevy the goods as provided in this Article (Section 2—716).

(3) On rightful rejection or justifiable revocation of acceptance, a buyer has a security interest in goods in his possession or control for any payments made on their price and any expenses reasonably incurred in their inspection, receipt, transportation, care and custody and may hold such goods and resell them in like manner as an aggrieved seller (Section 2—706).

§ 2—712. "Cover"; Buyer's Procurement of Substitute Goods

(1) After a breach within the preceding section, the buyer may "cover" by making in good faith and without unreasonable delay any reasonable purchase of or contract to purchase goods in substitution for those due from the seller.

(2) The buyer may recover from the seller as damages the difference between the cost of cover and the contract price together with any incidental or consequential damages as hereinafter defined (Section 2—715), but less expenses saved in consequence of the seller's breach.

(3) Failure of the buyer to effect cover within this section does not bar him from any other remedy.

§ 2—713. Buyer's Damages for Nondelivery or Repudiation

(1) Subject to the provisions of this Article with respect to proof of market price (Section 2—723), the

measure of damages for nondelivery or repudiation by the seller is the difference between the market price at the time when the buyer learned of the breach and the contract price together with any incidental and consequential damages provided in this Article (Section 2—715), but less expenses saved in consequence of the seller's breach.

(2) Market price is to be determined as of the place for tender or, in cases of rejection after arrival or revocation of acceptance, as of the place of arrival.

§ 2—714. Buyer's Damages for Breach in Regard to Accepted Goods

(1) Where the buyer has accepted goods and given notification (subsection (3) of Section 2—607), he may recover as damages for any non-conformity of tender the loss resulting in the ordinary course of events from the seller's breach as determined in any manner which is reasonable.

(2) The measure of damages for breach of warranty is the difference at the time and place of acceptance between the value of the goods accepted and the value they would have had if they had been as warranted, unless special circumstances show proximate damages of a different amount.

(3) In a proper case any incidental and consequential damages under the next section may also be recovered.

§ 2—715. Buyer's Incidental and Consequential Damages

(1) Incidental damages resulting from the seller's breach include expenses reasonably incurred in inspection, receipt, transportation and care and custody of goods rightfully rejected, any commercially reasonable charges, expenses or commissions in connection with effecting cover and any other reasonable expense incident to the delay or other breach.

(2) Consequential damages resulting from the seller's breach include

(a) any loss resulting from general or particular requirements and needs of which the seller at the time of contracting had reason to know and which could not reasonably be prevented by cover or otherwise; and

(b) injury to person or property proximately resulting from any breach of warranty.

§ 2—716. Buyer's Right to Specific Performance or Replevin

(1) Specific performance may be decreed where the goods are unique or in other proper circumstances.

(2) The decree for specific performance may include such terms and conditions as to payment of the price, damages, or other relief as the court may deem just.

(3) The buyer has a right of replevin for goods identified to the contract if after reasonable effort he is unable to effect cover for such goods or the circumstances reasonably indicate that such effort will be unavailing or if the goods have been shipped under reservation and satisfaction of the security interest in them has been made or tendered.

§ 2—717. Deduction of Damages From the Price

The buyer on notifying the seller of his intention to do so may deduct all or any part of the damages resulting from any breach of the contract from any part of the price still due under the same contract.

§ 2—718. Liquidation or Limitation of Damages; Deposits

(1) Damages for breach by either party may be liquidated in the agreement but only at an amount which is reasonable in the light of the anticipated or actual harm caused by the breach, the difficulties of proof of loss, and the inconvenience or nonfeasibility of otherwise obtaining an adequate remedy. A term fixing unreasonably large liquidated damages is void as a penalty.

(2) Where the seller justifiably withholds delivery of goods because of the buyer's breach, the buyer is entitled to restitution of any amount by which the sum of his payments exceeds

(a) the amount to which the seller is entitled by virtue of terms liquidating the seller's damages in accordance with subsection (1), or

(b) in the absence of such terms, twenty percent of the value of the total performance for which the buyer is obligated under the contract or $500, whichever is smaller.

(3) The buyer's right to restitution under subsection (2) is subject to offset to the extent that the seller establishes

(a) a right to recover damages under the provisions of this Article other than subsection (1), and

(b) the amount or value of any benefits received by the buyer directly or indirectly by reason of the contract.

(4) Where a seller has received payment in goods, their reasonable value or the proceeds of their resale shall be treated as payments for the purposes of subsection (2); but if the seller has notice of the buyer's breach before reselling goods received in part performance, his resale is subject to the conditions laid down in this Article on resale by an aggrieved seller (Section 2—706).

§ 2—719. Contractual Modification or Limitation of Remedy

(1) Subject to the provisions of subsections (2) and (3) of this section and of the preceding section on liquidation and limitation of damages,

(a) the agreement may provide for remedies in addition to or in substitution for those provided in this Article and may limit or alter the measure of damages recoverable under this Article, as by limiting the buyer's remedies to return of the goods and repayment of the price or to repair and replacement of non-conforming goods or parts; and

(b) resort to a remedy as provided is optional unless the remedy is expressly agreed to be exclusive, in which case it is the sole remedy.

(2) Where circumstances cause an exclusive or limited remedy to fail of its essential purpose, remedy may be had as provided in this Act.

(3) Consequential damages may be limited or excluded unless the limitation or exclusion is unconscionable. Limitation of consequential damages for injury to the person in the case of consumer goods is prima facie unconscionable but limitation of damages where the loss is commercial is not.

§ 2 — 720. Effect of "Cancellation" or "Rescission" on Claims for Antecedent Breach

Unless the contrary intention clearly appears, expressions of "cancellation" or "rescission" of the contract or the like shall not be construed as a renunciation or discharge of any claim in damages for an antecedent breach.

§ 2 — 721. Remedies for Fraud

Remedies for material misrepresentation or fraud include all remedies available under this Article for non-fraudulent breach. Neither rescission or a claim for rescission of the contract for sale nor rejection or return of the goods shall bar or be deemed inconsistent with a claim for damages or other remedy.

§ 2 — 722. Who Can Sue Third Parties for Injury to Goods

Where a third party so deals with goods which have been identified to a contract for sale as to cause actionable injury to a party to that contract

(a) a right of action against the third party is in either party to the contract for sale who has title to or a security interest or a special property or an insurable interest in the goods; and if the goods have been destroyed or converted, a right of action is also in the party who either bore the risk of loss under the contract for sale or has since the injury assumed that risk as against the other;

(b) if at the time of the injury the party plaintiff did not bear the risk of loss as against the other party to the contract for sale and there is no arrangement between them for disposition of the recovery, his suit or settlement is, subject to his own interest, as a fiduciary for the other party to the contract;

(c) either party may with the consent of the other sue for the benefit of whom it may concern.

§ 2 — 723. Proof of Market Price: Time and Place

(1) If an action based on anticipatory repudiation comes to trial before the time for performance with respect to some or all of the goods, any damages based on market price (Section 2 — 708 or Section 2 — 713) shall be determined according to the price of such goods prevailing at the time when the aggrieved party learned of the repudiation.

(2) If evidence of a price prevailing at the times or places described in this Article is not readily available, the price prevailing within any reasonable time before or after the time described or at any other place which in commercial judgment or under usage of trade would serve as a reasonable substitute for the one described may be used, making any proper allowance for the cost of transporting the goods to or from such other place.

(3) Evidence of a relevant price prevailing at a time or place other than the one described in this Article offered by one party is not admissible unless and until he has given the other party such notice as the court finds sufficient to prevent unfair surprise.

§ 2 — 724. Admissibility of Market Quotations

Whenever the prevailing price or value of any goods regularly bought and sold in any established commodity market is in issue, reports in official publications or trade journals or in newspapers or periodicals of general circulation published as the reports of such market shall be admissible in evidence. The circumstances of the preparation of such a report may be shown to affect its weight but not its admissibility.

§ 2 — 725. Statute of Limitations in Contracts for Sale

(1) An action for breach of any contract for sale must be commenced within four years after the cause of action has accrued. By the original agreement, the parties may reduce the period of limitation to not less than one year but may not extend it.

(2) A cause of action accrues when the breach occurs, regardless of the aggrieved party's lack of knowledge of the breach. A breach of warranty occurs when tender of delivery is made, except that where a warranty explicitly extends to future performance of the goods and discovery of the breach must await the time of such performance the cause of action accrues when the breach is or should have been discovered.

(3) Where an action commenced within the time limited by subsection (1) is so terminated as to leave available a remedy by another action for the same breach, such other action may be commenced after the

expiration of the time limited and within six months after the termination of the first action unless the termination resulted from voluntary discontinuance or from dismissal for failure or neglect to prosecute.

(4) This section does not alter the law on tolling of the statute of limitations nor does it apply to causes of action which have accrued before this Act becomes effective.

See p1284 for Article 2A.

ARTICLE 3

COMMERCIAL PAPER

Part 1
Short Title, Form and Interpretation

§ 3—101.   Short Title

This Article shall be known and may be cited as Uniform Commercial Code—Commercial Paper.

§ 3—102.   Definitions and Index of Definitions

(1) In this Article unless the context otherwise requires

    (a) "Issue" means the first delivery of an instrument to a holder or a remitter.

    (b) An "order" is a direction to pay and must be more than an authorization or request. It must identify the person to pay with reasonable certainty. It may be addressed to one or more such persons jointly or in the alternative but not in succession.

    (c) A "promise" is an undertaking to pay and must be more than an acknowledgment of an obligation.

    (d) "Secondary party" means a drawer or indorser.

    (e) "Instrument" means a negotiable instrument.

(2) Other definitions applying to this Article and the sections in which they appear are:

"Acceptance." Section 3—410.
"Accommodation party." Section 3—415.
"Alteration." Section 3—407.
"Certificate of deposit." Section 3—104.
"Certification." Section 3—411.
"Check." Section 3—104.
"Definite time." Section 3—109.
"Dishonor." Section 3—507.
"Draft." Section 3—104.
"Holder in due course." Section 3—302.
"Negotiation." Section 3—202.
"Note." Section 3—104.
"Notice of dishonor." Section 3—508.
"On demand." Section 3—108.
"Presentment." Section 3—504.
"Protest." Section 3—509.

"Restrictive Indorsement." Section 3—205.
"Signature." Section 3—401.

(3) The following definitions in other Articles apply to this Article:

"Account." Section 4—104.
"Banking Day." Section 4—104.
"Clearing house." Section 4—104.
"Collecting bank." Section 4—105.
"Customer." Section 4—104.
"Depositary Bank." Section 4—105.
"Documentary Draft." Section 4—104.
"Intermediary Bank." Section 4—105.
"Item." Section 4—104.
"Midnight deadline." Section 4—104.
"Payor bank." Section 4—105.

(4) In addition Article 1 contains general definitions and principles of construction and interpretation applicable throughout this Article.

§ 3—103.   Limitations on Scope of Article

(1) This Article does not apply to money, documents of title or investment securities.

(2) The provisions of this Article are subject to the provisions of the Article on Bank Deposits and Collections (Article 4) and Secured Transactions (Article 9).

§ 3—104.   Form of Negotiable Instruments; "Draft"; "Check"; "Certificate of Deposit"; "Note"

(1) Any writing to be a negotiable instrument within this Article must

    (a) be signed by the maker or drawer; and

    (b) contain an unconditional promise or order to pay a sum certain in money and no other promise, order, obligation or power given by the maker or drawer except as authorized by this Article; and

    (c) be payable on demand or at a definite time; and

    (d) be payable to order or to bearer.

(2) A writing which complies with the requirements of this section is

    (a) a "draft" ("bill of exchange") if it is an order;

(b) a "check" if it is a draft drawn on a bank and payable on demand;

(c) a "certificate of deposit" if it is an acknowledgment by a bank of receipt of money with an engagement to repay it;

(d) a "note" if it is a promise other than a certificate of deposit.

(3) As used in other Articles of this Act, and as the context may require, the terms "draft," "check," "certificate of deposit" and "note" may refer to instruments which are not negotiable within this Article as well as to instruments which are so negotiable.

§ 3 — 105.   When Promise or Order Unconditional

(1) A promise or order otherwise unconditional is not made conditional by the fact that the instrument

(a) is subject to implied or constructive conditions; or

(b) states its consideration, whether performed or promised, or the transaction which gave rise to the instrument, or that the promise or order is made or the instrument matures in accordance with or "as per" such transaction; or

(c) refers to or states that it arises out of a separate agreement or refers to a separate agreement for rights as to prepayment or acceleration; or

(d) states that it is drawn under a letter of credit; or

(e) states that it is secured, whether by mortgage, reservation of title or otherwise; or

(f) indicates a particular account to be debited or any other fund or source from which reimbursement is expected; or

(g) is limited to payment out of a particular fund or the proceeds of a particular source, if the instrument is issued by a government or governmental agency or unit; or

(h) is limited to payment out of the entire assets of a partnership, unincorporated association, trust or estate by or on behalf of which the instrument is issued.

(2) A promise or order is not unconditional if the instrument

(a) states that it is subject to or governed by any other agreement; or

(b) states that it is to be paid only out of a particular fund or source except as provided in this section.

§ 3 — 106.   Sum Certain

(1) The sum payable is a sum certain even though it is to be paid

(a) with stated interest or by stated installments; or

(b) with stated different rates of interest before and after default or a specified date; or

(c) with a stated discount or addition if paid before or after the date fixed for payment; or

(d) with exchange or less exchange, whether at a fixed rate or at the current rate; or

(e) with costs of collection or an attorney's fee or both upon default.

(2) Nothing in this section shall validate any term which is otherwise illegal.

§ 3 — 107.   Money

(1) An instrument is payable in money if the medium of exchange in which it is payable is money at the time the instrument is made. An instrument payable in "currency" or "current funds" is payable in money.

(2) A promise or order to pay a sum stated in a foreign currency is for a sum certain in money and, unless a different medium of payment is specified in the instrument, may be satisfied by payment of that number of dollars which the stated foreign currency will purchase at the buying sight rate for that currency on the day on which the instrument is payable or, if payable on demand, on the day of demand. If such an instrument specifies a foreign currency as the medium of payment the instrument is payable in that currency.

§ 3 — 108.   Payable on Demand

Instruments payable on demand include those payable at sight or on presentation and those in which no time for payment is stated.

§ 3 — 109.   Definite Time

(1) An instrument is payable at a definite time if by its terms it is payable

(a) on or before a stated date or at a fixed period after a stated date; or

(b) at a fixed period after sight; or

(c) at a definite time subject to any acceleration; or

(d) at a definite time subject to extension at the option of the holder, or to extension to a further definite time at the option of the maker or acceptor or automatically upon or after a specified act or event.

(2) An instrument which by its terms is otherwise payable only upon an act or event uncertain as to time of occurrence is not payable at a definite time even though the act or event has occurred.

§ 3 — 110.   Payable to Order

(1) An instrument is payable to order when by its terms it is payable to the order or assigns of any person therein specified with reasonable certainty, or to him or his order, or when it is conspicuously designated on its face as "exchange" or the like and names a payee. It may be payable to the order of

(a) the maker or drawer; or

(b) the drawee; or

(c) a payee who is not maker, drawer or drawee; or

(d) two or more payees together or in the alternative; or

(e) an estate, trust or fund, in which case it is payable to the order of the representative of such estate, trust or fund or his successors; or

(f) an office, or an officer by his title as such in which case it is payable to the principal but the incumbent of the office or his successors may act as if he or they were the holder; or

(g) a partnership or unincorporated association, in which case it is payable to the partnership or association and may be indorsed or transferred by any person thereto authorized.

(2) An instrument not payable to order is not made so payable by such words as "payable upon return of this instrument properly indorsed."

(3) An instrument made payable both to order and to bearer is payable to order unless the bearer words are handwritten or typewritten.

§ 3 — 111. Payable to Bearer

An instrument is payable to bearer when by its terms it is payable to

(a) bearer or the order of bearer; or

(b) a specified person or bearer; or

(c) "cash" or the order of "cash," or any other indication which does not purport to designate a specific payee.

§ 3 — 112. Terms and Omissions Not Affecting Negotiability

(1) The negotiability of an instrument is not affected by

(a) the omission of a statement of any consideration or of the place where the instrument is drawn or payable; or

(b) a statement that collateral has been given to secure obligations either on the instrument or otherwise of an obligor on the instrument or that in case of default on those obligations the holder may realize on or dispose of the collateral; or

(c) a promise or power to maintain or protect collateral or to give additional collateral; or

(d) a term authorizing a confession of judgment on the instrument if it is not paid when due; or

(e) a term purporting to waive the benefit of any law intended for the advantage or protection of any obligor; or

(f) a term in a draft providing that the payee by indorsing or cashing it acknowledges full satisfaction of an obligation of the drawer; or

(g) a statement in a draft drawn in a set of parts (Section 3 — 801) to the effect that the order is effective only if no other part has been honored.

(2) Nothing in this section shall validate any term which is otherwise illegal.

§ 3 — 113. Seal

An instrument otherwise negotiable is within this Article even though it is under a seal.

§ 3 — 114. Date, Antedating, Postdating

(1) The negotiability of an instrument is not affected by the fact that it is undated, antedated or postdated.

(2) Where an instrument is antedated or postdated, the time when it is payable is determined by the stated date if the instrument is payable on demand or at a fixed period after date.

(3) Where the instrument or any signature thereon is dated, the date is presumed to be correct.

§ 3 — 115. Incomplete Instruments

(1) When a paper, whose contents at the time of signing show that it is intended to become an instrument, is signed while still incomplete in any necessary respect, it cannot be enforced until completed; but when it is completed in accordance with authority given, it is effective as completed.

(2) If the completion is unauthorized, the rules as to material alteration apply (Section 3 — 407), even though the paper was not delivered by the maker or drawer; but the burden of establishing that any completion is unauthorized is on the party so asserting.

§ 3 — 116. Instruments Payable to Two or More Persons

An instrument payable to the order of two or more persons,

(a) if in the alternative, is payable to any one of them and may be negotiated, discharged or enforced by any of them who has possession of it;

(b) if not in the alternative, is payable to all of them and may be negotiated, discharged or enforced only by all of them.

§ 3 — 117. Instruments Payable With Words of Description

An instrument made payable to a named person with the addition of words describing him

(a) as agent or officer of a specified person is payable to his principal but the agent or officer may act as if he were the holder;

(b) as any other fiduciary for a specified person or purpose is payable to the payee and may be negotiated, discharged or enforced by him;

(c) in any other manner is payable to the payee unconditionally and the additional words are without effect on subsequent parties.

§ 3—118. Ambiguous Terms and Rules of Construction

The following rules apply to every instrument:

(a) Where there is doubt whether the instrument is a draft or a note, the holder may treat it as either. A draft drawn on the drawer is effective as a note.

(b) Handwritten terms control typewritten and printed terms, and typewritten control printed.

(c) Words control figures except that if the words are ambiguous figures control.

(d) Unless otherwise specified, a provision for interest means interest at the judgment rate at the place of payment from the date of the instrument, or if it is undated from the date of issue.

(e) Unless the instrument otherwise specifies, two or more persons who sign as maker, acceptor or drawer or indorser and as a part of the same transaction are jointly and severally liable even though the instrument contains such words as "I promise to pay."

(f) Unless otherwise specified, consent to extension authorizes a single extension for not longer than the original period. A consent to extension, expressed in the instrument, is binding on secondary parties and accommodation makers. A holder may not exercise his option to extend an instrument over the objection of a maker or acceptor or other party who in accordance with Section 3—604 tenders full payment when the instrument is due.

§ 3—119. Other Writings Affecting Instrument

(1) As between the obligor and his immediate obligee or any transferee, the terms of an instrument may be modified or affected by any other written agreement executed as a part of the same transaction, except that a holder in due course is not affected by any limitation of his rights arising out of the separate written agreement if he had no notice of the limitation when he took the instrument.

(2) A separate agreement does not affect the negotiability of an instrument.

§ 3—120. Instruments "Payable Through" Bank

An instrument which states that it is "payable through" a bank or the like designates that bank as a collecting bank to make presentment but does not of itself authorize the bank to pay the instrument.

§ 3—121. Instruments Payable at Bank

Note: *If this Act is introduced in the Congress of the United States this section should be omitted. (States to select either alternative)*

Alternative A—

A note or acceptance which states that it is payable at a bank is the equivalent of a draft drawn on the bank payable when it falls due out of any funds of the maker or acceptor in current account or otherwise available for such payment.

Alternative B—

A note or acceptance which states that it is payable at a bank is not of itself an order or authorization to the bank to pay it.

§ 3—122. Accrual of Cause of Action

(1) A cause of action against a maker or an acceptor accrues,

(a) in the case of a time instrument, on the day after maturity;

(b) in the case of a demand instrument, upon its date or, if no date is stated, on the date of issue.

(2) A cause of action against the obligor of a demand or time certificate of deposit accrues upon demand, but demand on a time certificate may not be made until on or after the date of maturity.

(3) A cause of action against a drawer of a draft or an indorser of any instrument accrues upon demand following dishonor of the instrument. Notice of dishonor is a demand.

(4) Unless an instrument provides otherwise, interest runs at the rate provided by law for a judgment

(a) in the case of a maker, acceptor or other primary obligor of a demand instrument, from the date of demand;

(b) in all other cases from the date of accrual of the cause of action.

Part 2

Transfer and Negotiation

§ 3—201. Transfer: Right to Indorsement

(1) Transfer of an instrument vests in the transferee such rights as the transferor has therein, except that a transferee who has himself been a party to any fraud or illegality affecting the instrument or who as a prior holder had notice of a defense or claim against it cannot improve his position by taking from a later holder in due course.

(2) A transfer of a security interest in an instrument vests the foregoing rights in the transferee to the extent of the interest transferred.

(3) Unless otherwise agreed, any transfer for value of an instrument not then payable to bearer gives the transferee the specifically enforceable right to have the unqualified indorsement of the transferor. Negotiation takes effect only when the indorsement is made and until that time there is no presumption that the transferee is the owner.

§ 3 — 202. Negotiation

(1) Negotiation is the transfer of an instrument in such form that the transferee becomes a holder. If the instrument is payable to order, it is negotiated by delivery with any necessary indorsement; if payable to bearer, it is negotiated by delivery.

(2) An indorsement must be written by or on behalf of the holder and on the instrument or on a paper so firmly affixed thereto as to become a part thereof.

(3) An indorsement is effective for negotiation only when it conveys the entire instrument or any unpaid residue. If it purports to be of less, it operates only as a partial assignment.

(4) Words of assignment, condition, waiver, guaranty, limitation or disclaimer of liability and the like accompanying an indorsement do not affect its character as an indorsement.

§ 3 — 203. Wrong or Misspelled Name

Where an instrument is made payable to a person under a misspelled name or one other than his own, he may indorse in that name or his own or both; but signature in both names may be required by a person paying or giving value for the instrument.

§ 3 — 204. Special Indorsement; Blank Indorsement

(1) A special indorsement specifies the person to whom or to whose order it makes the instrument payable. Any instrument specially indorsed becomes payable to the order of the special indorsee and may be further negotiated only by his indorsement.

(2) An indorsement in blank specifies no particular indorsee and may consist of a mere signature. An instrument payable to order and indorsed in blank becomes payable to bearer and may be negotiated by delivery alone until specially indorsed.

(3) The holder may convert a blank indorsement into a special indorsement by writing over the signature of the indorser in blank any contract consistent with the character of the indorsement.

§ 3 — 205. Restrictive Indorsements

An indorsement is restrictive which either
- (a) is conditional; or
- (b) purports to prohibit further transfer of the instrument; or
- (c) includes the words "for collection," "for deposit," "pay any bank," or like terms signifying a purpose of deposit or collection; or
- (d) otherwise states that it is for the benefit or use of the indorser or of another person.

§ 3 — 206. Effect of Restrictive Indorsement

(1) No restrictive indorsement prevents further transfer or negotiation of the instrument.

(2) An intermediary bank, or a payor bank which is not the depositary bank, is neither given notice nor otherwise affected by a restrictive indorsement of any person except the bank's immediate transferor or the person presenting for payment.

(3) Except for an intermediary bank, any transferee under an indorsement which is conditional or includes the words "for collection," "for deposit," "pay any bank," or like terms (subparagraphs (a) and (c) of Section 3 — 205) must pay or apply any value given by him for or on the security of the instrument consistently with the indorsement and to the extent that he does so he becomes a holder for value. In addition, such transferee is a holder in due course if he otherwise complies with the requirements of Section 3 — 302 on what constitutes a holder in due course.

(4) The first taker under an indorsement for the benefit of the indorser or another person (subparagraph (d) of Section 3 — 205) must pay or apply any value given by him for or on the security of the instrument consistently with the indorsement and, to the extent that he does so, he becomes a holder for value. In addition, such taker is a holder in due course if he otherwise complies with the requirements of Section 3 — 302 on what constitutes a holder in due course. A later holder for value is neither given notice nor otherwise affected by such restrictive indorsement unless he has knowledge that a fiduciary or other person has negotiated the instrument in any transaction for his own benefit or otherwise in breach of duty (subsection (2) of Section 3 — 304).

§ 3 — 207. Negotiation Effective Although It May Be Rescinded

(1) Negotiation is effective to transfer the instrument although the negotiation is
- (a) made by an infant, a corporation exceeding its powers, or any other person without capacity; or
- (b) obtained by fraud, duress or mistake of any kind; or
- (c) part of an illegal transaction; or
- (d) made in breach of duty.

(2) Except as against a subsequent holder in due course, such negotiation is in an appropriate case subject to rescission, the declaration of a constructive trust or any other remedy permitted by law.

§ 3 — 208. Reacquisition

Where an instrument is returned to or reacquired by a prior party, he may cancel any indorsement which is not necessary to his title and reissue or further negotiate the instrument; but any intervening party is discharged as against the reacquiring party and subsequent holders not in due course and, if his indorsement has been cancelled, is discharged as against subsequent holders in due course as well.

Part 3
Rights of a Holder

§ 3—301. Rights of a Holder

The holder of an instrument whether or not he is the owner may transfer or negotiate it and, except as otherwise provided in Section 3—603 on payment or satisfaction, discharge it or enforce payment in his own name.

§ 3—302. Holder in Due Course

(1) A holder in due course is a holder who takes the instrument
   (a) for value; and
   (b) in good faith; and
   (c) without notice that it is overdue or has been dishonored or of any defense against or claim to it on the part of any person.

(2) A payee may be a holder in due course.

(3) A holder does not become a holder in due course of an instrument:
   (a) by purchase of it at judicial sale or by taking it under legal process; or
   (b) by acquiring it in taking over an estate; or
   (c) by purchasing it as part of a bulk transaction not in regular course of business of the transferor.

(4) A purchaser of a limited interest can be a holder in due course only to the extent of the interest purchased.

§ 3—303. Taking for Value

A holder takes the instrument for value
   (a) to the extent that the agreed consideration has been performed or that he acquires a security interest in or a lien on the instrument otherwise than by legal process; or
   (b) when he takes the instrument in payment of or as security for an antecedent claim against any person whether or not the claim is due; or
   (c) when he gives a negotiable instrument for it or makes an irrevocable commitment to a third person.

§ 3—304. Notice to Purchaser

(1) The purchaser has notice of a claim or defense if
   (a) the instrument is so incomplete, bears such visible evidence of forgery or alteration, or is otherwise so irregular as to call into question its validity, terms or ownership or to create an ambiguity as to the party to pay; or
   (b) the purchaser has notice that the obligation of any party is voidable in whole or in part, or that all parties have been discharged.

(2) The purchaser has notice of a claim against the instrument when he has knowledge that a fiduciary has negotiated the instrument in payment of or as security for his own debt or in any transaction for his own benefit or otherwise in breach of duty.

(3) The purchaser has notice that an instrument is overdue if he has reason to know
   (a) that any part of the principal amount is overdue or that there is an uncured default in payment of another instrument of the same series; or
   (b) that acceleration of the instrument has been made; or
   (c) that he is taking a demand instrument after demand has been made or more than a reasonable length of time after its issue. A reasonable time for a check drawn and payable within the states and territories of the United States and the District of Columbia is presumed to be thirty days.

(4) Knowledge of the following facts does not of itself give the purchaser notice of a defense or claim
   (a) that the instrument is antedated or postdated;
   (b) that it was issued or negotiated in return for an executory promise or accompanied by a separate agreement, unless the purchaser has notice that a defense or claim has arisen from the terms thereof;
   (c) that any party has signed for accommodation;
   (d) that an incomplete instrument has been completed, unless the purchaser has notice of any improper completion;
   (e) that any person negotiating the instrument is or was a fiduciary;
   (f) that there has been default in payment of interest on the instrument or in payment of any other instrument, except one of the same series.

(5) The filing or recording of a document does not of itself constitute notice within the provisions of this Article to a person who would otherwise be a holder in due course.

(6) To be effective, notice must be received at such time and in such manner as to give a reasonable opportunity to act on it.

§ 3—305. Rights of a Holder in Due Course

To the extent that a holder is a holder in due course, he takes the instrument free from
   (1) all claims to it on the part of any person; and
   (2) all defenses of any party to the instrument with whom the holder has not dealt except
      (a) infancy, to the extent that it is a defense to a simple contract; and
      (b) such other incapacity, or duress, or illegality of the transaction, as renders the obligation of the party a nullity; and
      (c) such misrepresentation as has induced the party to sign the instrument with neither knowledge nor reasonable opportunity to

obtain knowledge of its character or its essential terms; and

(d) discharge in insolvency proceedings; and

(e) any other discharge of which the holder has notice when he takes the instrument.

§ 3—306. Rights of One Not Holder in Due Course

Unless he has the rights of a holder in due course, any person takes the instrument subject to

(a) all valid claims to it on the part of any person; and

(b) all defenses of any party which would be available in an action on a simple contract; and

(c) the defenses of want or failure of consideration, nonperformance of any condition precedent, nondelivery, or delivery for a special purpose (Section 3—408); and

(d) the defense that he, or a person through whom he holds the instrument, acquired it by theft, or that payment or satisfaction to such holder would be inconsistent with the terms of a restrictive indorsement. The claim of any third person to the instrument is not otherwise available as a defense to any party liable thereon unless the third person himself defends the action for such party.

§ 3—307. Burden of Establishing Signatures, Defenses and Due Course

(1) Unless specifically denied in the pleadings, each signature on an instrument is admitted. When the effectiveness of a signature is put in issue

(a) the burden of establishing it is on the party claiming under the signature; but

(b) the signature is presumed to be genuine or authorized except where the action is to enforce the obligation of a purported signer who has died or become incompetent before proof is required.

(2) When signatures are admitted or established, production of the instrument entitles a holder to recover on it unless the defendant establishes a defense.

(3) After it is shown that a defense exists, a person claiming the rights of a holder in due course has the burden of establishing that he or some person under whom he claims is in all respects a holder in due course.

Part 4

Liability of Parties

§ 3—401. Signature

(1) No person is liable on an instrument unless his signature appears thereon.

(2) A signature is made by use of any name, including any trade or assumed name, upon an instru-

ment, or by any word or mark used in lieu of a written signature.

§ 3—402. Signature in Ambiguous Capacity

Unless the instrument clearly indicates that a signature is made in some other capacity, it is an indorsement.

§ 3—403. Signature by Authorized Representative

(1) A signature may be made by an agent or other representative, and his authority to make it may be established as in other cases of representation. No particular form of appointment is necessary to establish such authority.

(2) An authorized representative who signs his own name to an instrument

(a) is personally obligated if the instrument neither names the person represented nor shows that the representative signed in a representative capacity;

(b) except as otherwise established between the immediate parties, is personally obligated if the instrument names the person represented but does not show that the representative signed in a representative capacity, or if the instrument does not name the person represented but does show that the representative signed in a representative capacity.

(3) Except as otherwise established, the name of an organization preceded or followed by the name and office of an authorized individual is a signature made in a representative capacity.

§ 3—404. Unauthorized Signatures

(1) Any unauthorized signature is wholly inoperative as that of the person whose name is signed unless he ratifies it or is precluded from denying it; but it operates as the signature of the unauthorized signer in favor of any person who in good faith pays the instrument or takes it for value.

(2) Any unauthorized signature may be ratified for all purposes of this Article. Such ratification does not of itself affect any rights of the person ratifying against the actual signer.

§ 3—405. Impostors; Signature in Name of Payee

(1) An indorsement by any person in the name of a named payee is effective if

(a) an impostor by use of the mails or otherwise has induced the maker or drawer to issue the instrument to him or his confederate in the name of the payee; or

(b) a person signing as or on behalf of a maker or drawer intends the payee to have no interest in the instrument; or

(c) an agent or employee of the maker or drawer has supplied him with the name of the payee intending the latter to have no such interest.

(2) Nothing in this section shall affect the criminal or civil liability of the person so indorsing.

§ 3 — 406. Negligence Contributing to Alteration or Unauthorized Signature

Any person who by his negligence substantially contributes to a material alteration of the instrument or to the making of an unauthorized signature is precluded from asserting the alteration or lack of authority against a holder in due course or against a drawee or other payor who pays the instrument in good faith and in accordance with the reasonable commercial standards of the drawee's or payor's business.

§ 3 — 407. Alteration

(1) Any alteration of an instrument is material which changes the contract of any party thereto in any respect, including any such change in

(a) the number or relations of the parties; or

(b) an incomplete instrument, by completing it otherwise than as authorized; or

(c) the writing as signed, by adding to it or by removing any part of it.

(2) As against any person other than a subsequent holder in due course.

(a) alteration by the holder which is both fraudulent and material discharges any party whose contract is thereby changed unless that party assents or is precluded from asserting the defense;

(b) no other alteration discharges any party and the instrument may be enforced according to its original tenor, or as to incomplete instruments, according to the authority given.

(3) A subsequent holder in due course may in all cases enforce the instrument according to its original tenor, and when an incomplete instrument has been completed, he may enforce it as completed.

§ 3 — 408. Consideration

Want or failure of consideration is a defense as against any person not having the rights of a holder in due course (Section 3 — 305), except that no consideration is necessary for an instrument or obligation thereon given in payment of or as security for an antecedent obligation of any kind. Nothing in this section shall be taken to displace any statute outside this Act under which a promise is enforceable notwithstanding lack or failure of consideration. Partial failure of consideration is a defense pro tanto whether or not the failure is in an ascertained or liquidated amount.

§ 3 — 409. Draft Not an Assignment

(1) A check or other draft does not of itself operate as an assignment of any funds in the hands of the drawee available for its payment, and the drawee is not liable on the instrument until he accepts it.

(2) Nothing in this section shall affect any liability in contract, tort or otherwise arising from any letter of credit or other obligation or representation which is not an acceptance.

§ 3 — 410. Definition and Operation of Acceptance

(1) Acceptance is the drawee's signed engagement to honor the draft as presented. It must be written on the draft, and may consist of his signature alone. It becomes operative when completed by delivery or notification.

(2) A draft may be accepted although it has not been signed by the drawer or is otherwise incomplete or is overdue or has been dishonored.

(3) Where the draft is payable at a fixed period after sight and the acceptor fails to date his acceptance, the holder may complete it by supplying a date in good faith.

§ 3 — 411. Certification of a Check

(1) Certification of a check is acceptance. Where a holder procures certification, the drawer and all prior indorsers are discharged.

(2) Unless otherwise agreed, a bank has no obligation to certify a check.

(3) A bank may certify a check before returning it for lack of proper indorsement. If it does so, the drawer is discharged.

§ 3 — 412. Acceptance Varying Draft

(1) Where the drawee's proffered acceptance in any manner varies the draft as presented, the holder may refuse the acceptance and treat the draft as dishonored in which case the drawee is entitled to have his acceptance cancelled.

(2) The terms of the draft are not varied by an acceptance to pay at any particular bank or place in the United States, unless the acceptance states that the draft is to be paid only at such bank or place.

(3) Where the holder assents to an acceptance varying the terms of the draft, each drawer and indorser who does not affirmatively assent is discharged.

§ 3 — 413. Contract of Maker, Drawer and Acceptor

(1) The maker or acceptor engages that he will pay the instrument according to its tenor at the time of his engagement or as completed pursuant to Section 3 — 115 on incomplete instruments.

(2) The drawer engages that upon dishonor of the draft and any necessary notice of dishonor or protest he will pay the amount of the draft to the holder or to any indorser who takes it up. The drawer may disclaim this liability by drawing without recourse.

(3) By making, drawing or accepting, the party admits as against all subsequent parties including the drawee the existence of the payee and his then capacity to indorse.

§ 3—414. Contract of Indorser; Order of Liability

(1) Unless the indorsement otherwise specifies (as by such words as "without recourse"), every indorser engages that upon dishonor and any necessary notice of dishonor and protest he will pay the instrument according to its tenor at the time of his indorsement to the holder or to any subsequent indorser who takes it up, even though the indorser who takes it up was not obligated to do so.

(2) Unless they otherwise agree, indorsers are liable to one another in the order in which they indorse, which is presumed to be the order in which their signatures appear on the instrument.

§ 3—415. Contract of Accommodation Party

(1) An accommodation party is one who signs the instrument in any capacity for the purpose of lending his name to another party to it.

(2) When the instrument has been taken for value before it is due, the accommodation party is liable in the capacity in which he has signed even though the taker knows of the accommodation.

(3) As against a holder in due course and without notice of the accommodation, oral proof of the accommodation is not admissible to give the accommodation party the benefit of discharges dependent on his character as such. In other cases, the accommodation character may be shown by oral proof.

(4) An indorsement which shows that it is not in the chain of title is notice of its accommodation character.

(5) An accommodation party is not liable to the party accommodated, and if he pays the instrument has a right of recourse on the instrument against such party.

§ 3—416. Contract of Guarantor

(1) "Payment guaranteed" or equivalent words added to a signature mean that the signer engages that if the instrument is not paid when due he will pay it according to its tenor without resort by the holder to any other party.

(2) "Collection guaranteed" or equivalent words added to a signature mean that the signer engages that if the instrument is not paid when due he will pay it according to its tenor, but only after the holder has reduced his claim against the maker or acceptor to judgment and execution has been returned unsatisfied, or after the maker or acceptor has become insolvent or it is otherwise apparent that it is useless to proceed against him.

(3) Words of guaranty which do not otherwise specify guarantee payment.

(4) No words of guaranty added to the signature of a sole maker or acceptor affect his liability on the instrument. Such words added to the signature of one of two or more makers or acceptors create a presumption that the signature is for the accommodation of the others.

(5) When words of guaranty are used, presentment, notice of dishonor and protest are not necessary to charge the user.

(6) Any guaranty written on the instrument is enforceable notwithstanding any statute of frauds.

§ 3—417. Warranties on Presentment and Transfer

(1) Any person who obtains payment or acceptance and any prior transferor warrants to a person who in good faith pays or accepts that

(a) he has a good title to the instrument or is authorized to obtain payment or acceptance on behalf of one who has a good title; and

(b) he has no knowledge that the signature of the maker or drawer is unauthorized, except that this warranty is not given by a holder in due course acting in good faith
  (i) to a maker with respect to the maker's own signature; or
  (ii) to a drawer with respect to the drawer's own signature, whether or not the drawer is also the drawee; or
  (iii) to an acceptor of a draft if the holder in due course took the draft after the acceptance or obtained the acceptance without knowledge that the drawer's signature was unauthorized; and

(c) the instrument has not been materially altered, except that this warranty is not given by a holder in due course acting in good faith
  (i) to the maker of a note; or
  (ii) to the drawer of a draft whether or not the drawer is also the drawee; or
  (iii) to the acceptor of a draft with respect to an alteration made prior to the acceptance if the holder in due course took the draft after the acceptance, even though the acceptance provided "payable as originally drawn" or equivalent terms; or
  (iv) to the acceptor of a draft with respect to an alteration made after the acceptance.

(2) Any person who transfers an instrument and receives consideration warrants to his transferee and if the transfer is by indorsement to any subsequent holder who takes the instrument in good faith that

(a) he has a good title to the instrument or is authorized to obtain payment or acceptance on behalf of one who has a good title and the transfer is otherwise rightful; and

(b) all signatures are genuine or authorized; and

(c) the instrument has not been materially altered; and

(d) no defense of any party is good against him; and

(e) he has no knowledge of any insolvency proceeding instituted with respect to the maker or acceptor or the drawer of an unaccepted instrument.

(3) By transferring "without recourse," the transferor limits the obligation stated in subsection (2) (d) to a warranty that he has no knowledge of such a defense.

(4) A selling agent or broker who does not disclose the fact that he is acting only as such gives the warranties provided in this section, but if he makes such disclosure warrants only his good faith and authority.

§ 3—418. Finality of Payment or Acceptance

Except for recovery of bank payments as provided in the Article on Bank Deposits and Collections (Article 4) and except for liability for breach of warranty on presentment under the preceding section, payment or acceptance of any instrument is final in favor of a holder in due course, or a person who has in good faith changed his position in reliance on the payment.

§ 3—419. Conversion of Instrument; Innocent Representative

(1) An instrument is converted when

(a) a drawee to whom it is delivered for acceptance refuses to return it on demand; or

(b) any person to whom it is delivered for payment refuses on demand either to pay or to return it; or

(c) it is paid on a forged indorsement.

(2) In an action against a drawee under subsection (1), the measure of the drawee's liability is the face amount of the instrument. In any other action under subsection (1), the measure of liability is presumed to be the face amount of the instrument.

(3) Subject to the provisions of this Act concerning restrictive indorsements, a representative, including a depositary or collecting bank, who has in good faith and in accordance with the reasonable commercial standards applicable to the business of such representative dealt with an instrument or its proceeds on behalf of one who was not the true owner, is not liable in conversion or otherwise to the true owner beyond the amount of any proceeds remaining in his hands.

(4) An intermediary bank or payor bank which is not a depositary bank is not liable in conversion solely by reason of the fact that proceeds of an item indorsed restrictively (Sections 3—205 and 3—206) are not paid or applied consistently with the restrictive indorsement of an indorser other than its immediate transferor.

Part 5

Presentment, Notice of Dishonor and Protest

§ 3—501. When Presentment, Notice of Dishonor, and Protest Necessary or Permissible

(1) Unless excused (Section 3—511), presentment is necessary to charge secondary parties as follows:

(a) presentment for acceptance is necessary to charge the drawer and indorsers of a draft where the draft so provides, or is payable elsewhere than at the residence or place of business of the drawee, or its date of payment depends upon such presentment. The holder may at his option present for acceptance any other draft payable at a stated date;

(b) presentment for payment is necessary to charge any indorser;

(c) in the case of any drawer, the acceptor of a draft payable at a bank or the maker of a note payable at a bank, presentment for payment is necessary, but failure to make presentment discharges such drawer, acceptor, or maker only as stated in Section 3—502(1) (b).

(2) Unless excused (Section 3—511)

(a) notice of any dishonor is necessary to charge any indorser;

(b) in the case of any drawer, the acceptor of a draft payable at a bank or the maker of a note payable at a bank, notice of any dishonor is necessary, but failure to give such notice discharges such drawer, acceptor or maker only as stated in Section 3—502(1) (b).

(3) Unless excused (Section 3—511), protest of any dishonor is necessary to charge the drawer and indorsers of any draft which on its face appears to be drawn or payable outside of the states, territories, dependencies and possessions of the Unites States, the District of Columbia and the Commonwealth of Puerto Rico. The holder may at his option make protest of any dishonor of any other instrument and in the case of a foreign draft may on insolvency of the acceptor before maturity make protest for better security.

(4) Notwithstanding any provision of this section, neither presentment nor notice of dishonor nor protest is necessary to charge an indorser who has indorsed an instrument after maturity.

§ 3—502. Unexcused Delay; Discharge

(1) Where without excuse any necessary presentment or notice of dishonor is delayed beyond the time when it is due

(a) any indorser is discharged; and

(b) any drawer or the acceptor of a draft payable at a bank or the maker of a note payable at a bank who because the drawee or payor bank becomes insolvent during the delay is deprived of funds maintained with the drawee or payor bank to cover the instrument may discharge his liability by written assignment to the holder of his rights against the drawee or payor bank in respect of such funds, but such drawer, acceptor or maker is not otherwise discharged.

(2) Where without excuse a necessary protest is delayed beyond the time when it is due, any drawer or indorser is discharged.

§ 3—503.   Time of Presentment

(1) Unless a different time is expressed in the instrument, the time for any presentment is determined as follows:
- (a) where an instrument is payable at or a fixed period after a stated date, any presentment for acceptance must be made on or before the date it is payable;
- (b) where an instrument is payable after sight, it must either be presented for acceptance or negotiated within a reasonable time after date or issue whichever is later;
- (c) where an instrument shows the date on which it is payable, presentment for payment is due on that date;
- (d) where an instrument is accelerated, presentment for payment is due within a reasonable time after the acceleration;
- (e) with respect to the liability of any secondary party, presentment for acceptance or payment of any other instrument is due within a reasonable time after such party becomes liable thereon.

(2) A reasonable time for presentment is determined by the nature of the instrument, any usage of banking or trade and the facts of the particular case. In the case of an uncertified check which is drawn and payable within the United States and which is not a draft drawn by a bank, the following are presumed to be reasonable periods within which to present for payment or to initiate bank collection:
- (a) with respect to the liability of the drawer, thirty days after date or issue whichever is later; and
- (b) with respect to the liability of an indorser, seven days after his indorsement.

(3) Where any presentment is due on a day which is not a full business day for either the person making presentment or the party to pay or accept, presentment is due on the next following day which is a full business day for both parties.

(4) Presentment to be sufficient must be made at a reasonable hour, and, if at a bank, during its banking day.

§ 3—504.   How Presentment Made

(1) Presentment is a demand for acceptance or payment made upon the maker, acceptor, drawee or other payor by or on behalf of the holder.

(2) Presentment may be made
- (a) by mail, in which event the time of presentment is determined by the time of receipt of the mail; or
- (b) through a clearing house; or
- (c) at the place of acceptance or payment specified in the instrument or, if there be none, at the place of business or residence of the party to accept or pay. If neither the party to accept or pay nor anyone authorized to act for him is present or accessible at such place, presentment is excused.

(3) It may be made
- (a) to any one of two or more makers, acceptors, drawees or other payors; or
- (b) to any person who has authority to make or refuse the acceptance or payment.

(4) A draft accepted or a note made payable at a bank in the United States must be presented at such bank.

(5) In the cases described in Section 4—210 presentment may be made in the manner and with the result stated in that section.

§ 3—505.   Rights of Party to Whom Presentment Is Made

(1) The party to whom presentment is made may without dishonor require
- (a) exhibition of the instrument; and
- (b) reasonable identification of the person making presentment and evidence of his authority to make it if made for another; and
- (c) that the instrument be produced for acceptance or payment at a place specified in it, or if there be none at any place reasonable in the circumstances; and
- (d) a signed receipt on the instrument for any partial or full payment and its surrender upon full payment.

(2) Failure to comply with any such requirement invalidates the presentment, but the person presenting has a reasonable time in which to comply and the time for acceptance or payment runs from the time of compliance.

§ 3—506.   Time Allowed for Acceptance or Payment

(1) Acceptance may be deferred without dishonor until the close of the next business day following presentment. The holder may also in a good faith effort to obtain acceptance, and without either dishonor

of the instrument or discharge of secondary parties, allow postponement of acceptance for an additional business day.

(2) Except as a longer time is allowed in the case of documentary drafts drawn under a letter of credit, and unless an earlier time is agreed to by the party to pay, payment of an instrument may be deferred without dishonor pending reasonable examination to determine whether it is properly payable, but payment must be made in any event before the close of business on the day of presentment.

§ 3—507. Dishonor; Holder's Right of Recourse; Term Allowing Re-Presentment

(1) An instrument is dishonored when

    (a) a necessary or optional presentment is duly made and due acceptance or payment is refused or cannot be obtained within the prescribed time or in case of bank collections the instrument is seasonably returned by the midnight deadline (Section 4—301); or

    (b) presentment is excused and the instrument is not duly accepted or paid.

(2) Subject to any necessary notice of dishonor and protest, the holder has upon dishonor an immediate right of recourse against the drawers and indorsers.

(3) Return of an instrument for lack of proper indorsement is not dishonor.

(4) A term in a draft or an indorsement thereof allowing a stated time for re-presentment in the event of any dishonor of the draft by nonacceptance if a time draft or by nonpayment if a sight draft gives the holder as against any secondary party bound by the term an option to waive the dishonor without affecting the liability of the secondary party and he may present again up to the end of the stated time.

§ 3—508. Notice of Dishonor

(1) Notice of dishonor may be given to any person who may be liable on the instrument by or on behalf of the holder or any party who has himself received notice, or any other party who can be compelled to pay the instrument. In addition, an agent or bank in whose hands the instrument is dishonored may give notice to his principal or customer or to another agent or bank from which the instrument was received.

(2) Any necessary notice must be given by a bank before its midnight deadline and by any other person before midnight of the third business day after dishonor or receipt of notice of dishonor.

(3) Notice may be given in any reasonable manner. It may be oral or written and in any terms which identify the instrument and state that it has been dishonored. A misdescription which does not mislead the party notified does not vitiate the notice. Sending the instrument bearing a stamp, ticket or writing stating that acceptance or payment has been refused or sending a notice of debit with respect to the instrument is sufficient.

(4) Written notice is given when sent although it is not received.

(5) Notice to one partner is notice to each although the firm has been dissolved.

(6) When any party is in insolvency proceedings instituted after the issue of the instrument, notice may be given either to the party or to the representative of his estate.

(7) When any party is dead or incompetent, notice may be sent to his last known address or given to his personal representative.

(8) Notice operates for the benefit of all parties who have rights on the instrument against the party notified.

§ 3—509. Protest; Noting for Protest

(1) A protest is a certificate of dishonor made under the hand and seal of a United States consul or vice consul or a notary public or other person authorized to certify dishonor by the law of the place where dishonor occurs. It may be made upon information satisfactory to such person.

(2) The protest must identify the instrument and certify either that due presentment has been made or the reason why it is excused and that the instrument has been dishonored by nonacceptance or nonpayment.

(3) The protest may also certify that notice of dishonor has been given to all parties or to specified parties.

(4) Subject to subsection (5), any necessary protest is due by the time that notice of dishonor is due.

(5) If, before protest is due, an instrument has been noted for protest by the officer to make protest, the protest may be made at any time thereafter as of the date of the noting.

§ 3—510. Evidence of Dishonor and Notice of Dishonor

The following are admissible as evidence and create a presumption of dishonor and of any notice of dishonor therein shown:

    (a) a document regular in form as provided in the preceding section which purports to be a protest;

    (b) the purported stamp or writing of the drawee, payor bank or presenting bank on the instrument or accompanying it stating that acceptance or payment has been refused for reasons consistent with dishonor;

    (c) any book or record of the drawee, payor bank, or any collecting bank kept in the usual course of business which shows dishonor, even though there is no evidence of who made the entry.

§ 3—511. Waived or Excused Presentment, Protest or Notice of Dishonor or Delay Therein

(1) Delay in presentment, protest or notice of dishonor is excused when the party is without notice

that it is due or when the delay is caused by circumstances beyond his control and he exercises reasonable diligence after the cause of the delay ceases to operate.

(2) Presentment or notice or protest as the case may be is entirely excused when

(a) the party to be charged has waived it expressly or by implication either before or after it is due; or

(b) such party has himself dishonored the instrument or has countermanded payment or otherwise has no reason to expect or right to require that the instrument be accepted or paid; or

(c) by reasonable diligence the presentment or protest cannot be made or the notice given.

(3) Presentment is also entirely excused when

(a) the maker, acceptor or drawee of any instrument except a documentary draft is dead or in insolvency proceedings instituted after the issue of the instrument; or

(b) acceptance or payment is refused but not for want of proper presentment.

(4) Where a draft has been dishonored by nonacceptance, a later presentment for payment and any notice of dishonor and protest for nonpayment are excused unless in the meantime the instrument has been accepted.

(5) A waiver of protest is also a waiver of presentment and of notice of dishonor even though protest is not required.

(6) Where a waiver of presentment or notice or protest is embodied in the instrument itself, it is binding upon all parties; but where it is written above the signature of an indorser, it binds him only.

Part 6

Discharge

§ 3 — 601.　Discharge of Parties

(1) The extent of the discharge of any party from liability on an instrument is governed by the sections on

(a) payment or satisfaction (Section 3 — 603); or

(b) tender of payment (Section 3 — 604); or

(c) cancellation or renunciation (Section 3 — 605); or

(d) impairment of right of recourse or of collateral (Section 3 — 606); or

(e) reacquisition of the instrument by a prior party (Section 3 — 208); or

(f) fraudulent and material alteration (Section 3 — 407); or

(g) certification of a check (Section 3 — 411); or

(h) acceptance varying a draft (Section 3 — 412); or

(i) unexcused delay in presentment or notice of dishonor or protest (Section 3 — 502).

(2) Any party is also discharged from his liability on an instrument to another party by any other act or agreement with such party which would discharge his simple contract for the payment of money.

(3) The liability of all parties is discharged when any party who has himself no right of action or recourse on the instrument

(a) reacquires the instrument in his own right; or

(b) is discharged under any provision of this Article, except as otherwise provided with respect to discharge for impairment of recourse or of collateral (Section 3 — 606).

§ 3 — 602.　Effect of Discharge Against Holder in Due Course

No discharge of any party provided by this Article is effective against a subsequent holder in due course unless he has notice thereof when he takes the instrument.

§ 3 — 603.　Payment or Satisfaction

(1) The liability of any party is discharged to the extent of his payment or satisfaction to the holder even though it is made with knowledge of a claim of another person to the instrument unless prior to such payment or satisfaction the person making the claim either supplies indemnity deemed adequate by the party seeking the discharge or enjoins payment or satisfaction by order of a court of competent jurisdiction in an action in which the adverse claimant and the holder are parties. This subsection does not, however, result in the discharge of the liability

(a) of a party who in bad faith pays or satisfies a holder who acquired the instrument by theft or who (unless having the rights of a holder in due course) holds through one who so acquired it; or

(b) of a party (other than an intermediary bank or a payor bank which is not a depositary bank) who pays or satisfies the holder of an instrument which has been restrictively indorsed in a manner not consistent with the terms of such restrictive indorsement.

(2) Payment or satisfaction may be made with the consent of the holder by any person including a stranger to the instrument. Surrender of the instrument to such a person gives him the rights of a transferee (Section 3 — 201).

§ 3 — 604.　Tender of Payment

(1) Any party making tender of full payment to a holder when or after it is due is discharged to the extent

of all subsequent liability for interest, costs and attorney's fees.

(2) The holder's refusal of such tender wholly discharges any party who has a right of recourse against the party making the tender.

(3) Where the maker or acceptor of an instrument payable otherwise than on demand is able and ready to pay at every place of payment specified in the instrument when it is due, it is equivalent to tender.

§ 3 — 605. Cancellation and Renunciation

(1) The holder of an instrument may even without consideration discharge any party

    (a) in any manner apparent on the face of the instrument or the indorsement, as by intentionally cancelling the instrument or the party's signature by destruction or mutilation, or by striking out the party's signature; or

    (b) by renouncing his rights by a writing signed and delivered or by surrender of the instrument to the party to be discharged.

(2) Neither cancellation nor renunciation without surrender of the instrument affects the title thereto.

§ 3 — 606. Impairment of Recourse or of Collateral

(1) The holder discharges any party to the instrument to the extent that, without such party's consent, the holder

    (a) without express reservation of rights releases or agrees not to sue any person against whom the party has to the knowledge of the holder a right of recourse or agrees to suspend the right to enforce against such person the instrument or collateral or otherwise discharges such person, except that failure or delay in effecting any required presentment, protest or notice of dishonor with respect to any such person does not discharge any party as to whom presentment, protest or notice of dishonor is effective or unnecessary; or

    (b) unjustifiably impairs any collateral for the instrument given by or on behalf of the party or any person against whom he has a right of recourse.

(2) By express reservation of rights against a party with a right of recourse, the holder preserves

    (a) all his rights against such party as of the time when the instrument was originally due; and

    (b) the right of the party to pay the instrument as of that time; and

    (c) all rights of such party to recourse against others.

Part 7

Advice of International Sight Draft

§ 3 — 701. Letter of Advice of International Sight Draft

(1) A "letter of advice" is a drawer's communication to the drawee that a described draft has been drawn.

(2) Unless otherwise agreed, when a bank receives from another bank a letter of advice of an international sight draft the drawee bank may immediately debit the drawer's account and stop the running of interest pro tanto. Such a debit and any resulting credit to any account covering outstanding drafts leaves in the drawer full power to stop payment or otherwise dispose of the amount and creates no trust or interest in favor of the holder.

(3) Unless otherwise agreed and except where a draft is drawn under a credit issued by the drawee, the drawee of an international sight draft owes the drawer no duty to pay an unadvised draft but if it does so and the draft is genuine, may appropriately debit the drawer's account.

Part 8

Miscellaneous

§ 3 — 801. Drafts in a Set

(1) Where a draft is drawn in a set of parts, each of which is numbered and expressed to be an order only if no other part has been honored, the whole of the parts constitutes one draft but a taker of any part may become a holder in due course of the draft.

(2) Any person who negotiates, indorses or accepts a single part of a draft drawn in a set thereby becomes liable to any holder in due course of that part as if it were the whole set, but as between different holders in due course to whom different parts have been negotiated, the holder whose title first accrues has all rights to the draft and its proceeds.

(3) As against the drawee, the first presented part of a draft drawn in a set is the part entitled to payment, or if a time draft to acceptance and payment. Acceptance of any subsequently presented part renders the drawee liable thereon under subsection (2). With respect both to a holder and to the drawer, payment of a subsequently presented part of a draft payable at sight has the same effect as payment of a check notwithstanding an effective stop order (Section 4 — 407).

(4) Except as otherwise provided in this section, where any part of a draft in a set is discharged by payment or otherwise the whole draft is discharged.

§ 3 — 802. Effect of Instrument on Obligation for Which It Is Given

(1) Unless otherwise agreed, where an instrument is taken for an underlying obligation

(a) the obligation is pro tanto discharged if a bank is drawer, maker or acceptor of the instrument and there is no recourse on the instrument against the underlying obligor; and

(b) in any other case the obligation is suspended pro tanto until the instrument is due or, if it is payable on demand, until its presentment. If the instrument is dishonored, action may be maintained on either the instrument or the obligation; discharge of the underlying obligor on the instrument also discharges him on the obligation.

(2) The taking in good faith of a check which is not postdated does not of itself so extend the time on the original obligation as to discharge a surety.

§ 3 — 803. Notice to Third Party

Where a defendant is sued for breach of an obligation for which a third person is answerable over under this Article, he may give the third person written notice of the litigation, and the person notified may then give similar notice to any other person who is answerable over to him under this Article. If the notice states that the person notified may come in and defend and that if the person notified does not do so, he will in any action against him by the person giving the notice be bound by any determination of fact common to the two litigations, then unless after seasonable receipt of the notice, the person notified does come in and defend he is so bound.

§ 3 — 804. Lost, Destroyed or Stolen Instruments

The owner of an instrument which is lost, whether by destruction, theft or otherwise, may maintain an action in his own name and recover from any party liable thereon upon due proof of his ownership, the facts which prevent his production of the instrument and its terms. The court may require security indemnifying the defendant against loss by reason of further claims on the instrument.

§ 3 — 805. Instruments Not Payable to Order or to Bearer

This Article applies to any instrument whose terms do not preclude transfer which is otherwise negotiable within this Article but which is not payable to order or to bearer, except that there can be no holder in due course of such an instrument.

ARTICLE 4

BANK DEPOSITS AND COLLECTIONS

Part 1

General Provisions and Definitions

§ 4 — 101. Short Title

This Article shall be known and may be cited as Uniform Commercial Code — Bank Deposits and Collections.

§ 4 — 102. Applicability

(1) To the extent that items within this Article are also within the scope of Articles 3 and 8, they are subject to the provisions of those Articles. In the event of conflict the provisions of this Article govern those of Article 3 but the provisions of Article 8 govern those of this Article.

(2) The liability of a bank for action or nonaction with respect to any item handled by it for purposes of presentment, payment or collection is governed by the law of the place where the bank is located. In the case of action or nonaction by or at a branch or separate office of a bank, its liability is governed by the law of the place where the branch or separate office is located.

§ 4 — 103. Variation by Agreement; Measure of Damages; Certain Action Constituting Ordinary Care

(1) The effect of the provisions of this Article may be varied by agreement except that no agreement can disclaim a bank's responsibility for its own lack of good faith or failure to exercise ordinary care or can limit the measure of damages for such lack or failure; but the parties may by agreement determine the standards by which such responsibility is to be measured if such standards are not manifestly unreasonable.

(2) Federal Reserve regulations and operating letters, clearing house rules, and the like, have the effect of agreements under subsection (1), whether or not specifically assented to by all parties interested in items handled.

(3) Action or nonaction approved by this Article or pursuant to Federal Reserve regulations or operating letters constitutes the exercise of ordinary care and, in the absence of special instructions, action or nonaction consistent with clearing house rules and the like or with a general banking usage not disapproved by this Article, prima facie constitutes the exercise of ordinary care.

(4) The specification or approval of certain procedures by this Article does not constitute disapproval of other procedures which may be reasonable under the circumstances.

(5) The measure of damages for failure to exercise ordinary care in handling an item is the amount of the item reduced by an amount which could not have been realized by the use of ordinary care, and where

there is bad faith it includes other damages, if any, suffered by the party as a proximate consequence.

§ 4–104.   Definitions and Index of Definitions

(1) In this Article unless the context otherwise requires

(a) "Account" means any account with a bank and includes a checking, time, interest or savings account;

(b) "Afternoon" means the period of a day between noon and midnight;

(c) "Banking day" means that part of any day on which a bank is open to the public for carrying on substantially all of its banking functions;

(d) "Clearing house" means any association of banks or other payors regularly clearing items;

(e) "Customer" means any person having an account with a bank or for whom a bank has agreed to collect items and includes a bank carrying an account with another bank;

(f) "Documentary draft" means any negotiable or nonnegotiable draft with accompanying documents, securities or other papers to be delivered against honor of the draft;

(g) "Item" means any instrument for the payment of money even though it is not negotiable but does not include money;

(h) "Midnight deadline" with respect to a bank is midnight on its next banking day following the banking day on which it receives the relevant item or notice or from which the time for taking action commences to run, whichever is later;

(i) "Property payable" includes the availability of funds for payment at the time of decision to pay or dishonor;

(j) "Settle" means to pay in cash, by clearing house settlement, in a charge or credit or by remittance, or otherwise as instructed. A settlement may be either provisional or final;

(k) "Suspends payments" with respect to a bank means that it has been closed by order of the supervisory authorities, that a public officer has been appointed to take it over or that it ceases or refuses to make payments in the ordinary course of business.

(2) Other definitions applying to this Article and the sections in which they appear are:

"Collecting bank" Section 4—105.
"Depositary bank" Section 4—105.
"Intermediary bank" Section 4—105.
"Payor bank" Section 4—105.
"Presenting bank" Section 4—105.
"Remitting bank" Section 4—105.

(3) The following definitions in other Articles apply to this Article:

"Acceptance" Section 3—410.
"Certificate of Deposit" Section 3—104.
"Certification" Section 3—411.
"Check" Section 3—104.
"Draft" Section 3—104.
"Holder in due course" Section 3—302.
"Notice of dishonor" Section 3—508.
"Presentment" Section 3—504.
"Protest" Section 3—509.
"Secondary party" Section 3—102.

(4) In addition Article 1 contains general definitions and principles of construction and interpretation applicable throughout this Article.

§ 4—105.   "Depositary Bank"; "Intermediary Bank"; "Collecting Bank"; "Payor Bank"; "Presenting Bank"; "Remitting Bank"

In this Article unless the context otherwise requires:

(a) "Depositary bank" means the first bank to which an item is transferred for collection even though it is also the payor bank;

(b) "Payor bank" means a bank by which an item is payable as drawn or accepted;

(c) "Intermediary bank" means any bank to which an item is transferred in course of collection except the depositary or payor bank;

(d) "Collecting bank" means any bank handling the item for collection except the payor bank;

(e) "Presenting bank" means any bank presenting an item except a payor bank;

(f) "Remitting bank" means any payor or intermediary bank remitting for an item.

§ 4—106.   Separate Office of a Bank

A branch or separate office of a bank [maintaining its own deposit ledgers] is a separate bank for the purpose of computing the time within which and determining the place at or to which action may be taken or notices or orders shall be given under this Article and under Article 3.

Note: *The brackets are to make it optional with the several states whether to require a branch to maintain its own deposit ledgers in order to be considered to be a separate bank for certain purposes under Article 4. In some states, "maintaining its own deposit ledgers" is a satisfactory test. In others, branch banking practices are such that this test would not be suitable.*

§ 4—107.   Time of Receipt of Items

(1) For the purpose of allowing time to process items, prove balances and make the necessary entries on its books to determine its position for the day, a bank may fix an afternoon hour of 2 p.m. or later as a cutoff hour for the handling of money and items and the making of entries on its books.

(2) Any item or deposit of money received on any day after a cutoff hour so fixed or after the close of the banking day may be treated as being received at the opening of the next banking day.

§ 4—108. Delays

(1) Unless otherwise instructed, a collecting bank in a good faith effort to secure payment may, in the case of specific items and with or without the approval of any person involved, waive, modify or extend time limits imposed or permitted by this Act for a period not in excess of an additional banking day without discharge of secondary parties and without liability to its transferor or any prior party.

(2) Delay by a collecting bank or payor bank beyond time limits prescribed or permitted by this Act or by instructions is excused if caused by interruption of communication facilities, suspension of payments by another bank, war, emergency conditions or other circumstances beyond the control of the bank provided it exercises such diligence as the circumstances require.

§ 4—109. Process of Posting

The "process of posting" means the usual procedure followed by a payor bank in determining to pay an item and in recording the payment including one or more of the following or other steps as determined by the bank:

(a) verification of any signature;
(b) ascertaining that sufficient funds are available;
(c) affixing a "paid" or other stamp;
(d) entering a charge or entry to a customer's account;
(e) correcting or reversing an entry or erroneous action with respect to the item.

Part 2

Collection of Items: Depositary and Collecting Banks

§ 4—201. Presumption and Duration of Agency Status of Collecting Banks and Provisional Status of Credits; Applicability of Article; Item Indorsed "Pay Any Bank"

(1) Unless a contrary intent clearly appears and prior to the time that a settlement given by a collecting bank for an item is or becomes final (subsection (3) of Section 4—211 and Sections 4—212 and 4—213), the bank is an agent or subagent of the owner of the item and any settlement given for the item is provisional. This provision applies regardless of the form of indorsement or lack of indorsement and even though credit given for the item is subject to immediate withdrawal as of right or is in fact withdrawn; but the continuance of ownership of an item by its owner and any rights of the owner to proceeds of the item are subject to rights of a collecting bank such as those resulting

from outstanding advances on the item and valid rights of setoff. When an item is handled by banks for purposes of presentment, payment and collection, the relevant provisions of this Article apply even though action of parties clearly establishes that a particular bank has purchased the item and is the owner of it.

(2) After an item has been indorsed with the words "pay any bank" or the like, only a bank may acquire the rights of a holder

(a) until the item has been returned to the customer initiating collection; or
(b) until the item has been specifically indorsed by a bank to a person who is not a bank.

§ 4—202. Responsibility for Collection; When Action Seasonable

(1) A collecting bank must use ordinary care in
(a) presenting an item or sending it for presentment; and
(b) sending notice of dishonor or nonpayment or returning an item other than a documentary draft to the bank's transferor [or directly to the depositary bank under subsection (2) of Section 4—212] (see note to Section 4—212) after learning that the item has not been paid or accepted, as the case may be; and
(c) settling for an item when the bank receives final settlement; and
(d) making or providing for any necessary protest; and
(e) notifying its transferor of any loss or delay in transit within a reasonable time after discovery thereof.

(2) A collecting bank taking proper action before its midnight deadline following receipt of an item, notice or payment acts seasonably; taking proper action within a reasonably longer time may be seasonable but the bank has the burden of so establishing.

(3) Subject to subsection (1) (a), a bank is not liable for the insolvency, neglect, misconduct, mistake or default of another bank or person or for loss or destruction of an item in transit or in the possession of others.

§ 4—203. Effect of Instructions

Subject to the provisions of Article 3 concerning conversion of instruments (Section 3—419) and the provisions of both Article 3 and this Article concerning restrictive indorsements, only a collecting bank's transferor can give instructions which affect the bank or constitute notice to it; and a collecting bank is not liable to prior parties for any action taken pursuant to such instructions or in accordance with any agreement with its transferor.

§ 4—204. Methods of Sending and Presenting; Sending Direct to Payor Bank

(1) A collecting bank must send items by reason-

ably prompt method taking into consideration any relevant instructions, the nature of the item, the number of such items on hand, and the cost of collection involved and the method generally used by it or others to present such items.

(2) A collecting bank may send
   (a) any item direct to the payor bank;
   (b) any item to any nonbank payor if authorized by its transferor; and
   (c) any item other than documentary drafts to any nonbank payor, if authorized by Federal Reserve regulation or operating letter, clearing house rule or the like.

(3) Presentment may be made by a presenting bank at a place where the payor bank has requested that presentment be made.

§ 4—205. Supplying Missing Indorsement; No Notice from Prior Indorsement

(1) A depositary bank which has taken an item for collection may supply any indorsement of the customer which is necessary to title unless the item contains the words "payee's indorsement required" or the like. In the absence of such a requirement, a statement placed on the item by the depositary bank to the effect that the item was deposited by a customer or credited to his account is effective as the customer's indorsement of.

(2) An intermediary bank, or payor bank which is not a depositary bank, is neither given notice nor otherwise affected by a restrictive indorsement of any person except the bank's immediate transferor.

§ 4—206. Transfer Between Banks

Any agreed method which identifies the transferor bank is sufficient for the item's further transfer to another bank.

§ 4—207. Warranties of Customer and Collecting Bank on Transfer or Presentment of Items; Time for Claims

(1) Each customer or collecting bank who obtains payment or acceptance of an item and each prior customer and collecting bank warrants to the payor bank or other payor who in good faith pays or accepts the item that
   (a) he has a good title to the item or is authorized to obtain payment or acceptance on behalf of one who has a good title; and
   (b) he has no knowledge that the signature of the maker or drawer is unauthorized, except that this warranty is not given by any customer or collecting bank that is a holder in due course and acts in good faith
      (i) to a maker, with respect to the maker's own signature; or
      (ii) to a drawer, with respect to the drawer's own signature, whether or not the drawer is also the drawee; or

      (iii) to an acceptor of an item, if the holder in due course took the item after the acceptance or obtained the acceptance without knowledge that the drawer's signature was unauthorized; and
   (c) the item has not been materially altered, except that this warranty is not given by any customer or collecting bank that is a holder in due course and acts in good faith
      (i) to the maker of a note; or
      (ii) to the drawer of a draft whether or not the drawer is also the drawee; or
      (iii) to the acceptor of an item with respect to an alteration made prior to the acceptance if the holder in due course took the item after the acceptance, even though the acceptance provided "payable as originally drawn" or equivalent terms; or
      (iv) to the acceptor of an item with respect to an alteration made after the acceptance.

(2) Each customer and collecting bank who transfers an item and receives a settlement or other consideration for it warrants to his transferee and to any subsequent collecting bank who takes the item in good faith that
   (a) he has a good title to the item or is authorized to obtain payment or acceptance on behalf of one who has a good title and the transfer is otherwise rightful; and
   (b) all signatures are genuine or authorized; and
   (c) the item has not been materially altered; and
   (d) no defense of any party is good against him; and
   (e) he has no knowledge of any insolvency proceeding instituted with respect to the maker or acceptor or the drawer of an unaccepted item.

In addition, each customer and collecting bank so transferring an item and receiving a settlement or other consideration engages that upon dishonor and any necessary notice of dishonor and protest he will take up the item.

(3) The warranties and the engagement to honor set forth in the two preceding subsections arise notwithstanding the absence of indorsement or words of guaranty or warranty in the transfer or presentment and a collecting bank remains liable for their breach despite remittance to its transferor. Damages for breach of such warranties or engagement to honor shall not exceed the consideration received by the customer or collecting bank responsible plus finance charges and expenses related to the item, if any.

(4) Unless a claim for breach of warranty under this section is made within a reasonable time after the person claiming learns of the breach, the person liable

is discharged to the extent of any loss caused by the delay in making claim.

§ 4 — 208. Security Interest of Collecting Bank in Items, Accompanying Documents and Proceeds

(1) A bank has a security interest in an item and any accompanying documents or the proceeds of either

    (a) in case of an item deposited in an account, to the extent to which credit given for the item has been withdrawn or applied;

    (b) in case of an item for which it has given credit available for withdrawal as of right, to the extent of the credit given whether or not the credit is drawn upon and whether or not there is a right of charge-back; or

    (c) if it makes an advance on or against the item.

(2) When credit which has been given for several items received at one time or pursuant to a single agreement is withdrawn or applied in part, the security interest remains upon all the items, any accompanying documents or the proceeds of either. For the purpose of this section, credits first given are first withdrawn.

(3) Receipt by a collecting bank of a final settlement for an item is a realization on its security interest in the item, accompanying documents and proceeds. To the extent and so long as the bank does not receive final settlement for the item or give up possession of the item or accompanying documents for purposes other than collection, the security interest continues and is subject to the provisions of Article 9 except that

    (a) no security agreement is necessary to make the security interest enforceable (subsection (1) (b) of Section 9 — 203); and

    (b) no filing is required to perfect the security interest; and

    (c) the security interest has priority over conflicting perfected security interests in the item, accompanying documents or proceeds.

§ 4 — 209. When Bank Gives Value for Purposes of Holder in Due Course

For purposes of determining its status as a holder in due course, the bank has given value to the extent that it has a security interest in an item provided that the bank otherwise complies with the requirements of Section 3 — 302 on what constitutes a holder in due course.

§ 4 — 210. Presentment by Notice of Item Not Payable by, Through or at a Bank; Liability of Secondary Parties

(1) Unless otherwise instructed, a collecting bank may present an item not payable by, through or at a bank by sending to the party to accept or pay a written notice that the bank holds the item for acceptance or payment. The notice must be sent in time to be received on or before the day when presentment is due, and the bank must meet any requirement of the party to accept or pay under Section 3 — 505 by the close of the bank's next banking day after it knows of the requirement.

(2) Where presentment is made by notice and neither honor nor request for compliance with a requirement under Section 3 — 505 is received by the close of business on the day after maturity or in the case of demand items by the close of business on the third banking day after notice was sent, the presenting bank may treat the item as dishonored and charge any secondary party by sending him notice of the facts.

§ 4 — 211. Media of Remittance; Provisional and Final Settlement in Remittance Cases

(1) A collecting bank may take in settlement of an item

    (a) a check of the remitting bank or of another bank on any bank except the remitting bank; or

    (b) a cashier's check or similar primary obligation of a remitting bank which is a member of or clears through a member of the same clearing house or group as the collecting bank; or

    (c) appropriate authority to charge an account of the remitting bank or of another bank with the collecting bank; or

    (d) if the item is drawn upon or payable by a person other than a bank, a cashier's check, certified check or other bank check or obligation.

(2) If before its midnight deadline the collecting bank properly dishonors a remittance check or authorization to charge on itself or presents or forwards for collection a remittance instrument of or on another bank which is of a kind approved by subsection (1) or has not been authorized by it, the collecting bank is not liable to prior parties in the event of the dishonor of such check, instrument or authorization.

(3) A settlement for an item by means of a remittance instrument or authorization to charge is or becomes a final settlement as to both the person making and the person receiving the settlement

    (a) if the remittance instrument or authorization to charge is of a kind approved by subsection (1) or has not been authorized by the person receiving the settlement and in either case the person receiving the settlement acts seasonably before its midnight deadline in presenting, forwarding for collection or paying the instrument or authorization, — at the time the remittance instrument or authorization is finally paid by the payor by which it is payable;

    (b) if the person receiving the settlement has authorized remittance by a nonbank check or obligation or by a cashier's check or similar primary obligation of or a check upon the payor or other remitting bank which is not of a kind approved by subsection (1) (b), — at the time of the receipt of such remittance check or obligation; or

(c) if in a case not covered by sub-paragraphs (a) or (b) the person receiving the settlement fails to seasonably present, forward for collection, pay or return remittance instrument or authorization to it to charge before its midnight deadline, — at such midnight deadline.

§ 4 — 212. Right of Charge-Back or Refund

(1) If a collecting bank has made provisional settlement with its customer for an item and itself fails by reason of dishonor, suspension of payments by a bank or otherwise to receive a settlement for the item which is or becomes final, the bank may revoke the settlement given by it, charge back the amount of any credit given for the item to its customer's account or obtain refund from its customer whether or not it is able to return the items, if by its midnight deadline or within a longer reasonable time after it learns the facts it returns the item or sends notification of the facts. These rights to revoke, charge-back and obtain refund terminate if and when a settlement for the item received by the bank is or becomes final (subsection (3) of Section 4 — 211 and subsections (2) and (3) of Section 4 — 213).

[(2) Within the time and manner prescribed by this section and Section 4 — 301, an intermediary or payor bank, as the case may be, may return an unpaid item directly to the depositary bank and may send for collection a draft on the depositary bank and obtain reimbursement. In such case, if the depositary bank has received provisional settlement for the item, it must reimburse the bank drawing the draft and any provisional credits for the item between banks shall become and remain final.]

> **Note:** *Direct returns is recognized as an innovation that is not yet established bank practice, and therefore, Paragraph 2 has been bracketed. Some lawyers have doubts whether it should be included in legislation or left to development by agreement.*

(3) A depositary bank which is also the payor may charge-back the amount of an item to its customer's account or obtain refund in accordance with the section governing return of an item received by a payor bank for credit on its books. (Section 4 — 301)

(4) The right to charge-back is not affected by

(a) prior use of the credit given for the item; or

(b) failure by any bank to exercise ordinary care with respect to the item but any bank so failing remains liable.

(5) A failure to charge-back or claim refund does not affect other rights of the bank against the customer or any other party.

(6) If credit is given in dollars, as the equivalent of the value of an item payable in a foreign currency, the dollar amount of any charge-back or refund shall be calculated on the basis of the buying sight rate for the foreign currency prevailing on the day when the person entitled to the charge-back or refund learns that it will not receive payment in ordinary course.

§ 4 — 213. Final Payment of Item for Payor Bank; When Provisional Debits and Credits Become Final; When Certain Credits Become Available for Withdrawal

(1) An item is finally paid by a payor bank when the bank has done any of the following, whichever happens first:

(a) paid the item in cash; or

(b) settled for the item without reserving a right to revoke the settlement and without having such right under statute, clearing house rule or agreement; or

(c) completed the process of posting the item to the indicated account of the drawer, maker or other person to be charged therewith; or

(d) made a provisional settlement for the item and failed to revoke the settlement in the time and manner permitted by statute, clearing house rule or agreement.

Upon a final payment under subparagraphs (b), (c) or (d), the payor bank shall be accountable for the amount of the item.

(2) If provisional settlement for an item between the presenting and payor banks is made through a clearing house or by debits or credits in an account between them, then to the extent that provisional debits or credits for the item are entered in accounts between the presenting and payor banks or between the presenting and successive prior collecting banks seriatim, they become final upon final payment of the item by the payor bank.

(3) If a collecting bank receives a settlement for an item which is or becomes final (subsection (3) of Section 4 — 211, subsection (2) of Section 4 — 213), the bank is accountable to its customer for the amount of the item and any provisional credit given for the item in an account with its customer becomes final.

(4) Subject to any right of the bank to apply the credit to an obligation of the customer, credit given by a bank for an item in an account with its customer becomes available for withdrawal as of right

(a) in any case where the bank has received a provisional settlement for the item, — when such settlement becomes final and the bank has had a reasonable time to learn that the settlement is final;

(b) in any case where the bank is both a depositary bank and a payor bank and the item is finally paid, — at the opening of the bank's second banking day following receipt of the item.

(5) A deposit of money in a bank is final when made but, subject to any right of the bank to apply the deposit to an obligation of the customer, the deposit becomes available for withdrawal as of right at the

opening of the bank's next banking day following receipt of the deposit.

§ 4—214. Insolvency and Preference

(1) Any item in or coming into the possession of a payor or collecting bank which suspends payment and which item is not finally paid shall be returned by the receiver, trustee or agent in charge of the closed bank to the presenting bank or the closed bank's customer.

(2) If a payor bank finally pays an item and suspends payments without making a settlement for the item with its customer or the presenting bank which settlement is or becomes final, the owner of the item has a preferred claim against the payor bank.

(3) If a payor bank gives or a collecting bank gives or receives a provisional settlement for an item and thereafter suspends payments, the suspension does not prevent or interfere with the settlement becoming final if such finality occurs automatically upon the lapse of certain time or the happening of certain events (subsection (3) of Section 4—211, subsections (1) (d), (2) and (3) of Section 4—213).

(4) If a collecting bank receives from subsequent parties settlement for an item which settlement is or becomes final and suspends payments without making a settlement for the item with its customer which is or becomes final, the owner of the item has a preferred claim against such collecting bank.

Part 3

Collection of Items: Payor Banks

§ 4—301. Deferred Posting; Recovery of Payment by Return of Items; Time of Dishonor

(1) Where an authorized settlement for a demand item (other than a documentary draft) received by a payor bank otherwise than for immediate payment over the counter has been made before midnight of the banking day of receipt, the payor bank may revoke the settlement and recover any payment if before it has made final payment (subsection (1) of Section 4—213) and before its midnight deadline it

    (a) returns the item; or

    (b) sends written notice of dishonor or nonpayment if the item is held for protest or is otherwise unavailable for return.

(2) If a demand item is received by a payor bank for credit on its books, it may return such item or send notice of dishonor and may revoke any credit given or recover the amount thereof withdrawn by its customer, if it acts within the time limit and in the manner specified in the preceding subsection.

(3) Unless previous notice of dishonor has been sent, an item is dishonored at the time when for purposes of dishonor it is returned or notice sent in accordance with this section.

(4) An item is returned:

    (a) as to an item received through a clearing house, when it is delivered to the presenting or last collecting bank or to the clearing house or is sent or delivered in accordance with its rules; or

    (b) in all other cases, when it is sent or delivered to the bank's customer or transferor or pursuant to his instructions.

§ 4—302. Payor Bank's Responsibility for Late Return of Item

In the absence of a valid defense such as breach of a presentment warranty (subsection (1) of Section 4—207), settlement effected or the like, if an item is presented on and received by a payor bank the bank is accountable for the amount of

    (a) a demand item other than a documentary draft whether properly payable or not if the bank, in any case where it is not also the depositary bank, retains the item beyond midnight of the banking day of receipt without settling for it or, regardless of whether it is also the depositary bank, does not pay or return the item or send notice of dishonor until after its midnight deadline; or

    (b) any other properly payable item unless within the time allowed for acceptance or payment of that item the bank either accepts or pays the item or returns it and accompanying documents.

§ 4—303. When Items Subject to Notice, Stop-Order, Legal Process or Setoff; Order in Which Items May Be Charged or Certified

(1) Any knowledge, notice or stop-order received by, legal process served upon or setoff exercised by a payor bank, whether or not effective under other rules of law to terminate, suspend or modify the bank's right or duty to pay an item or to charge its customer's account for the item, comes too late to so terminate, suspend or modify such right or duty if the knowledge, notice, stop-order or legal process is received or served and a reasonable time for the bank to act thereon expires or the setoff is exercised after the bank has done any of the following:

    (a) accepted or certified the item;

    (b) paid the item in cash;

    (c) settled for the item without reserving a right to revoke the settlement and without having such right under statute, clearing house rule or agreement;

    (d) completed the process of posting the item to the indicated account of the drawer, maker or other person to be charged therewith or otherwise has evidenced by examination of such indicated account and by action its decision to pay the item; or

    (e) become accountable for the amount of the item under subsection (1) (d) of

Section 4—213 and Section 4—302 dealing with the payor bank's responsibility for late return of items.

(2) Subject to the provisions of subsection (1), items may be accepted, paid, certified or charged to the indicated account of its customer in any order convenient to the bank.

Part 4

Relationship Between Payor Bank and Its Customer

§ 4—401.   When Bank May Charge Customer's Account

(1) As against its customer, a bank may charge against his account any item which is otherwise properly payable from that account even though the charge creates an overdraft.

(2) A bank which in good faith makes payment to a holder may charge the indicated account of its customer according to

    (a) the original tenor of his altered item; or

    (b) the tenor of his completed item, even though the bank knows the item has been completed unless the bank has notice that the completion was improper.

§ 4—402.   Bank's Liability to Customer for Wrongful Dishonor

A payor bank is liable to its customer for damages proximately caused by the wrongful dishonor of an item. When the dishonor occurs through mistake, liability is limited to actual damages proved. If so proximately caused and proved, damages may include damages for an arrest or prosecution of the customer or other consequential damages. Whether any consequential damages are proximately caused by the wrongful dishonor is a question of fact to be determined in each case.

§ 4—403.   Customer's Right to Stop Payment; Burden of Proof of Loss

(1) A customer may by order to his bank stop payment of any item payable for his account but the order must be received at such time and in such manner as to afford the bank a reasonable opportunity to act on it prior to any action by the bank with respect to the item described in Section 4—303.

(2) An oral order is binding upon the bank only for fourteen calendar days unless confirmed in writing within that period. A written order is effective for only six months unless renewed in writing.

(3) The burden of establishing the fact and amount of loss resulting from the payment of an item

contrary to a binding stop payment order is on the customer.

§ 4—404.   Bank Not Obligated to Pay Check More Than Six Months Old

A bank is under no obligation to a customer having a checking account to pay a check, other than a certified check, which is presented more than six months after its date, but it may charge its customer's account for a payment made thereafter in good faith.

§ 4—405.   Death or Incompetence of Customer

(1) A payor or collecting bank's authority to accept, pay or collect an item or to account for proceeds of its collection if otherwise effective is not rendered ineffective by incompetence of a customer of either bank existing at the time the item is issued or its collection is undertaken if the bank does not know of an adjudication of incompetence. Neither death nor incompetence of a customer revokes such authority to accept, pay, collect or account until the bank knows of the fact of death or of an adjudication of incompetence and has reasonable opportunity to act on it.

(2) Even with knowledge a bank may for 10 days after the date of death pay or certify checks drawn on or prior to that date unless ordered to stop payment by a person claiming an interest in the account.

§ 4—406.   Customer's Duty to Discover and Report Unauthorized Signature or Alteration

(1) When a bank sends to its customer a statement of account accompanied by items paid in good faith in support of the debit entries or holds the statement and items pursuant to a request or instructions of its customer or otherwise in a reasonable manner makes the statement and items available to the customer, the customer must exercise reasonable care and promptness to examine the statement and items to discover his unauthorized signature or any alteration on an item and must notify the bank promptly after discovery thereof.

(2) If the bank establishes that the customer failed with respect to an item to comply with the duties imposed on the customer by subsection (1), the customer is precluded from asserting against the bank

    (a) his unauthorized signature or any alteration on the item if the bank also establishes that it suffered a loss by reason of such failure; and

    (b) an unauthorized signature or alteration by the same wrongdoer on any other item paid in good faith by the bank after the first item and statement was available to the customer for a reasonable period not exceeding fourteen calendar days and before the bank receives notification from the customer of any such unauthorized signature or alteration.

(3) The preclusion under subsection (2) does not apply if the customer establishes lack of ordinary care on the part of the bank in paying the item(s).

(4) Without regard to care or lack of care of either the customer or the bank, a customer who does not within one year from the time the statement and items are made available to the customer (subsection (1)) discover and report his unauthorized signature or any alteration on the face or back of the item or does not within 3 years from that time discover and report any unauthorized indorsement is precluded from asserting against the bank such unauthorized signature or indorsement or such alteration.

(5) If under this section a payor bank has a valid defense against a claim of a customer upon or resulting from payment of an item and waives or fails upon request to assert the defense, the bank may not assert against any collecting bank or other prior party presenting or transferring the item a claim based upon the unauthorized signature or alteration giving rise to the customer's claim.

§ 4—407. Payor Bank's Right to Subrogation on Improper Payment

If a payor bank has paid an item over the stop payment order of the drawer or maker or otherwise under circumstances giving a basis for objection by the drawer or maker, to prevent unjust enrichment and only to the extent necessary to prevent loss to the bank by reason of its payment of the item, the payor bank shall be subrogated to the rights

(a) of any holder in due course on the item against the drawer or maker; and

(b) of the payee or any other holder of the item against the drawer or maker either on the item or under the transaction out of which the item arose; and

(c) of the drawer or maker against the payee or any other holder of the item with respect to the transaction out of which the item arose.

Part 5

Collection of Documentary Drafts

§ 4—501. Handling of Documentary Drafts; Duty to Send for Presentment and to Notify Customer of Dishonor

A bank which takes a documentary draft for collection must present or send the draft and accompanying documents for presentment and, upon learning that the draft has not been paid or accepted in due course, must seasonably notify its customer of

such fact even though it may have discounted or bought the draft or extended credit available for withdrawal as of right.

§ 4—502. Presentment of "On Arrival" Drafts

When a draft or the relevant instructions require presentment "on arrival," "when goods arrive" or the like, the collecting bank need not present until in its judgment a reasonable time for arrival of the goods has expired. Refusal to pay or accept because the goods have not arrived is not dishonor; the bank must notify its transferor of such refusal but need not present the draft again until it is instructed to do so or learns of the arrival of the goods.

§ 4—503. Responsibility of Presenting Bank for Documents and Goods; Report of Reasons for Dishonor; Referee in Case of Need

Unless otherwise instructed and except as provided in Article 5, a bank presenting a documentary draft

(a) must deliver the documents to the drawee on acceptance of the draft if it is payable more than three days after presentment; otherwise, only on payment; and

(b) upon dishonor, either in the case of presentment for acceptance or presentment for payment, may seek and follow instructions from any referee in case of need designated in the draft or if the presenting bank does not choose to utilize his services it must use diligence and good faith to ascertain the reason for dishonor, must notify its transferor of the dishonor and of the results of its effort to ascertain the reasons therefor and must request instructions.

But the presenting bank is under no obligation with respect to goods represented by the documents except to follow any reasonable instructions seasonably received; it has a right to reimbursement for any expense incurred in following instructions and to prepayment of or indemnity for such expenses.

§ 4—504. Privilege of Presenting Bank to Deal With Goods; Security Interest for Expenses

(1) A presenting bank which, following the dishonor of a documentary draft, has seasonably requested instructions but does not receive them within a reasonable time may store, sell, or otherwise deal with the goods in any reasonable manner.

(2) For its reasonable expenses incurred by action under subsection (1), the presenting bank has a lien upon the goods or their proceeds, which may be foreclosed in the same manner as an unpaid seller's lien.

ARTICLE 5

LETTERS OF CREDIT

§ 5 — 101.   Short Title

This Article shall be known and may be cited as Uniform Commercial Code — Letters of Credit.

§ 5 — 102.   Scope

(1) This Article applies

    (a) to a credit issued by a bank, if the credit requires a documentary draft or a documentary demand for payment; and

    (b) to a credit issued by a person other than a bank, if the credit requires that the draft or demand for payment be accompanied by a document of title; and

    (c) to a credit issued by a bank or other person, if the credit is not within subparagraphs (a) or (b) but conspicuously states that it is a letter of credit or is conspicuously so entitled.

(2) Unless the engagement meets the requirements of subsection (1), this Article does not apply to engagements to make advances or to honor drafts or demands for payment, to authorities to pay or purchase to guarantees or to general agreements.

(3) This Article deals with some but not all of the rules and concepts of letters of credit as such rules or concepts have developed prior to this act or may hereafter develop. The fact that this Article states a rule does not by itself require, imply or negate application of the same or a converse rule to a situation not provided for or to a person not specified by this Article.

§ 5 — 103.   Definitions

(1) In this Article unless the context otherwise requires

    (a) "Credit" or "letter of credit" means an engagement by a bank or other person, made at the request of a customer and of a kind within the scope of this Article (Section 5 — 102), that the issuer will honor drafts or other demands for payment upon compliance with the conditions specified in the credit. A credit may be either revocable or irrevocable. The engagement may be either an agreement to honor or a statement that the bank or other person is authorized to honor.

    (b) A "documentary draft" or a "documentary demand for payment" is one honor of which is conditioned upon the presentation of a document or documents. "Document" means any paper including document of title, security, invoice, certificate, notice of default and the like.

    (c) An "issuer" is a bank or other person issuing a credit.

    (d) A "beneficiary" of a credit is a person who is entitled under its terms to draw or demand payment.

    (e) An "advising bank" is a bank which gives notification of the issuance of a credit by another bank.

    (f) A "confirming bank" is a bank which engages either that it will itself honor a credit already issued by another bank or that such a credit will be honored by the issuer or a third bank.

    (g) A "customer" is a buyer or other person who causes an issuer to issue a credit. The term also includes a bank which procures issuance or confirmation on behalf of that bank's customer.

(2) Other definitions applying to this Article and the sections in which they appear are:

    "Notation of Credit." Section 5 — 108.

    "Presenter." Section 5 — 112(3).

(3) Definitions in other Articles applying to this Article and the sections in which they appear are:

    "Accept" or "Acceptance." Section 3 — 410.

    "Contract for sale." Section 2 — 106.

    "Draft." Section 3 — 104.

    "Holder in due course." Section 3 — 302.

    "Midnight deadline." Section 4 — 104.

    "Security." Section 8 — 102.

(4) In addition, Article 1 contains general definitions and principles of construction and interpretation applicable throughout this Article.

§ 5 — 104.   Formal Requirements; Signing

(1) Except as otherwise required in subsection (1) (c) of Section 5 — 102 on scope, no particular form of phrasing is required for a credit. A credit must be in writing and signed by the issuer, and a confirmation must be in writing and signed by the confirming bank. A modification of the terms of a credit or confirmation must be signed by the issuer or confirming bank.

(2) A telegram may be a sufficient signed writing if it identifies its sender by an authorized authentication. The authentication may be in code and the authorized naming of the issuer in an advice of credit is a sufficient signing.

§ 5 — 105.   Consideration

No consideration is necessary to establish a credit or to enlarge or otherwise modify its terms.

§ 5 — 106.   Time and Effect of Establishment of Credit

(1) Unless otherwise agreed, a credit is established

(a) as regards the customer, as soon as a letter of credit is sent to him or the letter of credit or an authorized written advice of its issuance is sent to the beneficiary; and

(b) as regards the beneficiary, when he receives a letter of credit or an authorized written advice of its issuance.

(2) Unless otherwise agreed, once an irrevocable credit is established as regards the customer, it can be modified or revoked only with the consent of the customer; and once it is established as regards the beneficiary, it can be modified or revoked only with his consent.

(3) Unless otherwise agreed after a revocable credit is established, it may be modified or revoked by the issuer without notice to or consent from the customer or beneficiary.

(4) Notwithstanding any modification or revocation of a revocable credit, any person authorized to honor or negotiate under the terms of the original credit is entitled to reimbursement for or honor of any draft or demand for payment duly honored or negotiated before receipt of notice of the modification or revocation and the issuer in turn is entitled to reimbursement from its customer.

§ 5 — 107. Advice of Credit; Confirmation; Error in Statement of Terms

(1) Unless otherwise specified, an advising bank by advising a credit issued by another bank does not assume any obligation to honor drafts drawn or demands for payment made under the credit, but it does assume obligation for the accuracy of its own statement.

(2) A confirming bank by confirming a credit becomes directly obligated on the credit to the extent of its confirmation as though it were its issuer and acquires the rights of an issuer.

(3) Even though an advising bank incorrectly advises the terms of a credit it has been authorized to advise, the credit is established as against the issuer to the extent of its original terms.

(4) Unless otherwise specified, the customer bears as against the issuer all risks of transmission and reasonable translation or interpretation of any message relating to a credit.

§ 5 — 108. "Notation Credit"; Exhaustion of Credit

(1) A credit which specifies that any person purchasing or paying drafts drawn or demands for payment made under it must note the amount of the draft or demand on the letter or advice of credit is a "notation credit."

(2) Under a notation credit

(a) a person paying the beneficiary or purchasing a draft or demand for payment from him acquires a right to honor only if the appropriate notation is made; and by transferring or forwarding for honor the documents under the credit, such a person warrants to the issuer that the notation has been made; and

(b) unless the credit or a signed statement that an appropriate notation has been made accompanies the draft or demand for payment, the issuer may delay honor until evidence of notation has been procured which is satisfactory to it; but its obligation and that of its customer continue for a reasonable time not exceeding thirty days to obtain such evidence.

(3) If the credit is not a notation credit

(a) the issuer may honor complying drafts or demands for payment presented to it in the order in which they are presented and is discharged pro tanto by honor of any such draft or demand;

(b) as between competing good faith purchasers of complying drafts or demands, the person first purchasing has priority over a subsequent purchaser even though the later purchased draft or demand has been first honored.

§ 5 — 109. Issuer's Obligation to Its Customer

(1) An issuer's obligation to its customer includes good faith and observance of any general banking usage but, unless otherwise agreed, does not include liability or responsibility

(a) for performance of the underlying contract for sale or other transaction between the customer and the beneficiary; or

(b) for any act or omission of any person other than itself or its own branch or for loss or destruction of a draft, demand or document in transit or in the possession of others; or

(c) based on knowledge or lack of knowledge of any usage of any particular trade.

(2) An issuer must examine documents with care so as to ascertain that on their face they appear to comply with the terms of the credit but, unless otherwise agreed, assumes no liability or responsibility for the genuineness, falsification or effect of any document which appears on such examination to be regular on its face.

(3) A nonbank issuer is not bound by any banking usage of which it has no knowledge.

§ 5 — 110. Availability of Credit in Portions; Presenter's Reservation of Lien or Claim

(1) Unless otherwise specified, a credit may be used in portions in the discretion of the beneficiary.

(2) Unless otherwise specified, a person by presenting a documentary draft or demand for payment under a credit relinquishes upon its honor all

claims to the documents and a person by transferring such draft or demand or causing such presentment authorizes such relinquishment. An explicit reservation of claim makes the draft or demand non-complying.

§ 5—111. Warranties on Transfer and Presentment

(1) Unless otherwise agreed, the beneficiary, by transferring or presenting a documentary draft or demand for payment, warrants to all interested parties that the necessary conditions of the credit have been complied with. This is in addition to any warranties arising under Articles 3, 4, 7 and 8.

(2) Unless otherwise agreed, a negotiating, advising, confirming, collecting or issuing bank presenting or transferring a draft or demand for payment under a credit warrants only the matters warranted by a collecting bank under Article 4 and any such bank transferring a document warrants only the matters warranted by an intermediary under Articles 7 and 8.

§ 5—112. Time Allowed for Honor or Rejection; Withholding Honor or Rejection by Consent; "Presenter"

(1) A bank to which a documentary draft or demand for payment is presented under a credit may without dishonor of the draft, demand or credit

    (a) defer honor until the close of the third banking day following receipt of the documents; and

    (b) further defer honor if the presenter has expressly or impliedly consented thereto.

Failure to honor within the time here specified constitutes dishonor of the draft or demand and of the credit [except as otherwise provided in subsection (4) of Section 5—114 on conditional payment].

    Note: *The bracketed language in the last sentence of subsection (1) should be included only if the optional provisions of Section 5—114(4) and (5) are included.*

(2) Upon dishonor the bank may unless otherwise instructed fulfill its duty to return the draft or demand and the documents by holding them at the disposal of the presenter and sending him an advice to that effect.

(3) "Presenter" means any person presenting a draft or demand for payment for honor under a credit even though that person is a confirming bank or other correspondent which is acting under an issuer's authorization.

§ 5—113. Indemnities

(1) A bank seeking to obtain (whether for itself or another) honor, negotiation or reimbursement under a credit may give an indemnity to induce such honor, negotiation or reimbursement.

    (2) An indemnity agreement inducing honor, negotiation or reimbursement

    (a) unless otherwise explicitly agreed applies to defects in the documents but not in the goods; and

    (b) unless a longer time is explicitly agreed expires at the end of ten business days following receipt of the documents by the ultimate customer unless notice of objection is sent before such expiration date. The ultimate customer may send notice of objection to the person from whom he received the documents and any bank receiving such notice is under a duty to send notice to its transferor before its midnight deadline.

§ 5—114. Issuer's Duty and Privilege to Honor; Right to Reimbursement

(1) An issuer must honor a draft or demand for payment which complies with the terms of the relevant credit regardless of whether the goods or documents conform to the underlying contract for sale or other contract between the customer and the beneficiary. The issuer is not excused from honor of such a draft or demand by reason of an additional general term that all documents must be satisfactory to the issuer, but an issuer may require that specified documents must be satisfactory to it.

(2) Unless otherwise agreed, when documents appear on their face to comply with the terms of a credit but a required document does not in fact conform to the warranties made on negotiation or transfer of a document of title (Section 7—507) or of a certificated security (Section 8—306) or is forged or fraudulent or there is fraud in the transaction

    (a) the issuer must honor the draft or demand for payment, if honor is demanded by a negotiating bank or other holder of the draft or demand which has taken the draft or demand under the credit and under circumstances which would make it a holder in due course (Section 3—302) and in an appropriate case would make it a person to whom a document of title has been duly negotiated (Section 7—502) or a bona fide purchaser of a certificated security (Section 8—302); and

    (b) in all other cases, as against its customer, an issuer acting in good faith may honor the draft or demand for payment despite notification from the customer of fraud, forgery or other defect not apparent on the face of the documents but a court of appropriate jurisdiction may enjoin such honor.

(3) Unless otherwise agreed, an issuer which has duly honored a draft or demand for payment is entitled to immediate reimbursement of any payment made under the credit and to be put in effectively available funds not later than the day before maturity of any acceptance made under the credit.

[(4) When a credit provides for payment by the issuer on receipt of notice that the required documents are in the possession of a correspondent or other agent of the issuer

 (a) any payment made on receipt of such notice is conditional; and

 (b) the issuer may reject documents which do not comply with the credit, if it does so within three banking days following its receipt of the documents; and

 (c) in the event of such rejection, the issuer is entitled by charge-back or otherwise to return of the payment made.]

[(5) In the case covered by subsection (4), failure to reject documents within the time specified in subparagraph (b) constitutes acceptance of the documents and makes the payment final in favor of the beneficiary.]

Note: *Subsections (4) and (5) are bracketed as optional. If they are included the bracketed language in the last sentence of Section 5—112(1) should also be included.*

§ 5 — 115.   Remedy for Improper Dishonor or Anticipatory Repudiation

(1) When an issuer wrongfully dishonors a draft or demand for payment presented under a credit, the person entitled to honor has, with respect to any documents, the rights of a person in the position of a seller (Section 2—707) and may recover from the issuer the face amount of the draft or demand, together with incidental damages under Section 2—710 on seller's incidental damages and interest but less any amount realized by resale or other use or disposition of the subject matter of the transaction. In the event no resale or other utilization is made the documents, goods or other subject matter involved in the transaction must be turned over to the issuer on payment of judgment.

(2) When an issuer wrongfully cancels or otherwise repudiates a credit before presentment of a draft or demand for payment drawn under it, the beneficiary has the rights of a seller after anticipatory repudiation by the buyer under Section 2—610 if he learns of the repudiation in time reasonably to avoid procurement of the required documents. Otherwise the beneficiary has an immediate right of action for wrongful dishonor.

§ 5 — 116.   Transfer and Assignment

(1) The right to draw under a credit can be transferred or assigned only when the credit is expressly designated as transferable or assignable.

 (2) Even though the credit specifically states that it is nontransferable or nonassignable, the beneficiary may, before performance of the conditions of the credit, assign his right to proceeds. Such an assignment is an assignment of an account under Article 9 on Secured Transactions and is governed by that Article except that

 (a) the assignment is ineffective until the letter of credit or advice of credit is delivered to the assignee which delivery constitutes perfection of the security interest under Article 9; and

 (b) the issuer may honor drafts or demands for payment drawn under the credit until it receives a notification of the assignment signed by the beneficiary which reasonably identifies the credit involved in the assignment and contains a request to pay the assignee; and

 (c) after what reasonably appears to be such a notification has been received the issuer may without dishonor refuse to accept or pay even to a person otherwise entitled to honor until the letter of credit or advice of credit is exhibited to the issuer.

(3) Except where the beneficiary has effectively assigned his right to draw or his right to proceeds, nothing in this section limits his right to transfer or negotiate drafts or demands drawn under the credit.

§ 5 — 117.   Insolvency of Bank Holding Funds for Documentary Credit

(1) Where an issuer or an advising or confirming bank or a bank which has for a customer procured issuance of a credit by another bank becomes insolvent before final payment under the credit and the credit is one to which this Article is made applicable by paragraphs (a) or (b) of Section 5—102(1) on scope, the receipt or allocation of funds or collateral to secure or meet obligations under the credit shall have the following results:

 (a) to the extent of any funds or collateral turned over after or before the insolvency as indemnity against or specifically for the purpose of payment of drafts or demands for payment drawn under the designated credit, the drafts or demands are entitled to payment in preference over depositors or other general creditors of the issuer or bank; and

 (b) on expiration of the credit or surrender of the beneficiary's rights under it unused any person who has given such funds or collateral is similarly entitled to return thereof; and

 (c) a charge to a general or current account with a bank if specifically consented to for the purpose of indemnity against or payment of drafts or demands for payment drawn under the designated credit falls under the same rules as if the funds had been drawn out in cash and then turned over with specific instructions.

(2) After honor or reimbursement under this section, the customer or other person for whose account the insolvent bank has acted is entitled to receive the documents involved.

ARTICLE 6

BULK TRANSFERS

§ 6—101. Short Title

This Article shall be known and may be cited as Uniform Commercial Code—Bulk Transfers.

§ 6—102. "Bulk Transfers"; Transfers of Equipment; Enterprises Subject to This Article; Bulk Transfers Subject to This Article

(1) A "bulk transfer" is any transfer in bulk and not in the ordinary course of the transferor's business of a major part of the materials, supplies, merchandise or other inventory (Section 9—109) of an enterprise subject to this Article.

(2) A transfer of a substantial part of the equipment (Section 9—109) of such an enterprise is a bulk transfer if it is made in connection with a bulk transfer of inventory, but not otherwise.

(3) The enterprises subject to this Article are all those whose principal business is the sale of merchandise from stock, including those who manufacture what they sell.

(4) Except as limited by the following section, all bulk transfers of goods located within this state are subject to this Article.

§ 6—103. Transfers Excepted From This Article

The following transfers are not subject to this Article:

(1) Those made to give security for the performance of an obligation;

(2) General assignments for the benefit of all the creditors of the transferor, and subsequent transfers by the assignee thereunder;

(3) Transfers in settlement or realization of a lien or other security interests;

(4) Sales by executors, administrators, receivers, trustees in bankruptcy, or any public officer under judicial process;

(5) Sales made in the course of judicial or administrative proceedings for the dissolution or reorganization of a corporation and of which notice is sent to the creditors of the corporation pursuant to order of the court or administrative agency;

(6) Transfers to a person maintaining a known place of business in this State who becomes bound to pay the debts of the transferor in full and gives public notice of that fact, and who is solvent after becoming so bound;

(7) A transfer to a new business enterprise organized to take over and continue the business, if public notice of the transaction is given and the new enterprise assumes the debts of the transferor and he receives nothing from the transaction except an interest in the new enterprise junior to the claims of creditors;

(8) Transfers of property which is exempt from execution.

Public notice under subsection (6) or subsection (7) may be given by publishing once a week for two consecutive weeks in a newspaper of general circulation where the transferor had its principal place of business in this state an advertisement including the names and addresses of the transferor and transferee and the effective date of the transfer.

§ 6—104. Schedule of Property, List of Creditors

(1) Except as provided with respect to auction sales (Section 6—108), a bulk transfer subject to this Article is ineffective against any creditor of the transferor unless:

(a) The transferee requires the transferor to furnish a list of his existing creditors prepared as stated in this section; and

(b) The parties prepare a schedule of the property transferred sufficient to identify it; and

(c) The transferee preserves the list and schedule for six months next following the transfer and permits inspection of either or both and copying therefrom at all reasonable hours by any creditor of the transferor, or files the list and schedule in (a public office to be here identified).

(2) The list of creditors must be signed and sworn to or affirmed by the transferor or his agent. It must contain the names and business addresses of all creditors of the transferor, with the amounts when known, and also the names of all persons who are known to the transferor to assert claims against him even though such claims are disputed. If the transferor is the obligor of an outstanding issue of bonds, debentures or the like as to which there is an indenture trustee, the list of creditors need include only the name and address of the indenture trustee and the aggregate outstanding principal amount of the issue.

(3) Responsibility for the completeness and accuracy of the list of creditors rests on the transferor, and the transfer is not rendered ineffective by errors or omissions therein unless the transferee is shown to have had knowledge.

§ 6—105. Notice to Creditors

In addition to the requirements of the preceding section, any bulk transfer subject to this Article, except one made by auction sale (Section 6—108), is ineffective against any creditor of the transferor unless at least ten days before he takes possession of the goods or pays for them, whichever happens first, the transferee gives notice of the transfer in the manner and to the persons hereafter provided (Section 6—107).

[§ 6—106. Application of the Proceeds

In addition to the requirements of the two preceding sections:

(1) Upon every bulk transfer subject to this Article for which new consideration becomes payable except those made by sale at auction, it is the duty of the transferee to assure that such consideration is applied so far as necessary to pay those debts of the transferor which are either shown on the list furnished by the transferor (Section 6—104) or filed in writing in the place stated in the notice (Section 6—107) within thirty days after the mailing of such notice. This duty of the transferee runs to all the holders of such debts, and may be enforced by any of them for the benefit of all.

(2) If any of said debts are in dispute, the necessary sum may be withheld from distribution until the dispute is settled or adjudicated.

(3) If the consideration payable is not enough to pay all of the said debts in full, distribution shall be made pro rata.]

Note: *This section is bracketed to indicate division of opinion as to whether or not it is a wise provision, and to suggest that this is a point on which State enactments may differ without serious damage to the principle of uniformity.*

In any State where this section is omitted, the following parts of sections, also bracketed in the text, should also be omitted, namely:

Section 6—107(2)(e).
6—108(3)(c).
6—109(2).

In any State where this section is enacted, these other provisions should be also.

Optional Subsection (4)

[(4) The transferee may within ten days after he takes possession of the goods pay the consideration into the (specify court) in the county where the transferor had its principal place of business in this state and thereafter may discharge his duty under this section by giving notice by registered or certified mail to all the persons to whom the duty runs that the consideration has been paid into that court and that they should file their claims there. On motion of any interested party, the court may order the distribution of the consideration to the persons entitled to it.]

Note: *Optional subsection (4) is recommended for those states which do not have a general statute providing for payment of money into court.*

§ 6—107. The Notice

(1) The notice to creditors (Section 6—105) shall state:

(a) that a bulk transfer is about to be made; and

(b) the names and business addresses of the transferor and transferee, and all other business names and addresses used by the transferor within three years last past so far as known to the transferee; and

(c) whether or not all the debts of the transferor are to be paid in full as they fall due as a result of the transaction, and if so, the

address to which creditors should send their bills.

(2) If the debts of the transferor are not to be paid in full as they fall due or if the transferee is in doubt on that point, then the notice shall state further:

(a) the location and general description of the property to be transferred and the estimated total of the transferor's debts;

(b) the address where the schedule of property and list of creditors (Section 6—104) may be inspected;

(c) whether the transfer is to pay existing debts and if so, the amount of such debts and to whom owing;

(d) whether the transfer is for new consideration and if so, the amount of such consideration and the time and place of payment; [and]

[(e) if for new consideration, the time and place where creditors of the transferor are to file their claims.]

(3) The notice in any case shall be delivered personally or sent by registered or certified mail to all the persons shown on the list of creditors furnished by the transferor (Section 6—104) and to all other persons who are known to the transferee to hold or assert claims against the transferor.

Note: *The words in brackets are optional. See Note under § 6—106.*

§ 6—108. Auction Sales; "Auctioneer"

(1) A bulk transfer is subject to this Article even though it is by sale at auction, but only in the manner and with the results stated in this section.

(2) The transferor shall furnish a list of his creditors and assist in the preparation of a schedule of the property to be sold, both prepared as before stated (Section 6—104).

(3) The person or persons other than the transferor who direct, control or are responsible for the auction are collectively called the "auctioneer." The auctioneer shall:

(a) receive and retain the list of creditors and prepare and retain the schedule of property for the period stated in this Article (Section 6—104);

(b) give notice of the auction personally or by registered or certified mail at least ten days before it occurs to all persons shown on the list of creditors and to all other persons who are known to him to hold or assert claims against the transferor; [and]

[(c) assure that the net proceeds of the auction are applied as provided in this Article (Section 6—106).]

(4) Failure of the auctioneer to perform any of these duties does not affect the validity of the sale or the title of the purchasers; but if the auctioneer knows that the auction constitutes a bulk transfer, such failure

renders the auctioneer liable to the creditors of the transferor as a class for the sums owing to them from the transferor up to but not exceeding the net proceeds of the auction. If the auctioneer consists of several persons their liability is joint and several.

Note: *The words in brackets are optional. See Note under § 6 — 106.*

§ 6 — 109. What Creditors Protected; [Credit for Payment to Particular Creditors]

(1) The creditors of the transferor mentioned in this Article are those holding claims based on transactions or events occurring before the bulk transfer, but creditors who become such after notice to creditors is given (Sections 6 — 105 and 6 — 107) are not entitled to notice.

[(2) Against the aggregate obligation imposed by the provisions of this Article concerning the application of the proceeds (Section 6 — 106 and subsection (3) (c) of 6 — 108), the transferee or auctioneer is entitled to credit for sums paid to particular creditors of the transferor, not exceeding the sums believed in good faith at the time of the payment to be properly payable to such creditors.]

Note: *The words in brackets are optional. See Note under § 6 — 106.*

§ 6 — 110. Subsequent Transfers

When the title of a transferee to property is subject to a defect by reason of his noncompliance with the requirements of this Article, then:

(1) a purchaser of any of such property from such transferee who pays no value or who takes with notice of such noncompliance takes subject to such defect, but

(2) a purchaser for value in good faith and without such notice takes free of such defect.

§ 6 — 111. Limitation of Actions and Levies

No action under this Article shall be brought nor levy made more than six months after the date on which the transferee took possession of the goods unless the transfer has been concealed. If the transfer has been concealed, actions may be brought or levies made within six months after its discovery.

Note to Article 6: *Section 6 — 106 is bracketed to indicate division of opinion as to whether or not it is a wise provision, and to suggest that this a point on which State enactments may differ without serious damage to the principle of uniformity.*

In any State where Section 6 — 106 is not enacted, the following parts of sections, also bracketed in the text, should also be omitted, namely:

Sec. 6 — 107(2) (e).

6 — 108(3) (c).

6 — 109(2).

In any State where Section 6 — 106 is enacted, these other provisions should be also.

ARTICLE 7

WAREHOUSE RECEIPTS, BILLS OF LADING AND OTHER DOCUMENTS OF TITLE

Part 1

General

§ 7 — 101. Short Title

This Article shall be known and may be cited as Uniform Commercial Code — Documents of Title.

§ 7 — 102. Definitions and Index of Definitions

(1) In this Article, unless the context otherwise requires:

(a) "Bailee" means the person who by a warehouse receipt, bill of lading or other document of title acknowledges possession of goods and contracts to deliver them.

(b) "Consignee" means the person named in a bill to whom or to whose order the bill promises delivery.

(c) "Consignor" means the person named in a bill as the person from whom the goods have been received for shipment.

(d) "Delivery order" means a written order to deliver goods directed to a warehouseman, carrier or other person who in the ordinary course of business issues warehouse receipts or bills of lading.

(e) "Document" means document of title as defined in the general definitions in Article 1 (Section 1 — 201).

(f) "Goods" means all things which are treated as movable for the purposes of a contract of storage or transportation.

(g) "Issuer" means a bailee who issues a document except that in relation to an unaccepted delivery order it means the person who orders the possessor of goods to deliver. Issuer includes any person for whom an agent or employee purports to act in issuing a document if the agent or employee has real or apparent authority to issue documents, notwithstanding that the issuer received no goods or that the goods were misdescribed or that in any other respect the agent or employee violated his instructions.

(h) "Warehouseman" is a person engaged in the business of storing goods for hire.

(2) Other definitions applying to this Article or to specified Parts thereof, and the sections in which they appear are:

"Duly negotiate." Section 7—501.

"Person entitled under the document." Section 7—403(4).

(3) Definitions in other Articles applying to this Article and the sections in which they appear are:

"Contract for sale." Section 2—106.

"Overseas." Section 2—323.

"Receipt" of goods. Section 2—103.

(4) In addition, Article 1 contains general definitions and principles of construction and interpretation applicable throughout this Article.

§ 7—103. Relation of Article to Treaty, Statute, Tariff, Classification or Regulation

To the extent that any treaty or statute of the United States, regulatory statute of this State or tariff, classification or regulation filed or issued pursuant thereto is applicable, the provisions of this Article are subject thereto.

§ 7—104. Negotiable and Nonnegotiable Warehouse Receipt, Bill of Lading or Other Document of Title

(1) A warehouse receipt, bill of lading or other document of title is negotiable

(a) if by its terms the goods are to be delivered to bearer or to the order of a named person; or

(b) where recognized in overseas trade, if it runs to a named person or assigns.

(2) Any other document is nonnegotiable. A bill of lading in which it is stated that the goods are consigned to a named person is not made negotiable by a provision that the goods are to be delivered only against a written order signed by the same or another named person.

§ 7—105. Construction Against Negative Implication

The omission from either Part 2 or Part 3 of this Article of a provision corresponding to a provision made in the other Part does not imply that a corresponding rule of law is not applicable.

Part 2

Warehouse Receipts: Special Provisions

§ 7—201. Who May Issue a Warehouse Receipt; Storage Under Government Bond

(1) A warehouse receipt may be issued by any warehouseman.

(2) Where goods including distilled spirits and agricultural commodities are stored under a statute requiring a bond against withdrawal or a license for the issuance of receipts in the nature of warehouse receipts, a receipt issued for the goods has like effect as a warehouse receipt even though issued by a person who is the owner of the goods and is not a warehouseman.

§ 7—202. Form of Warehouse Receipt; Essential Terms; Optional Terms

(1) A warehouse receipt need not be in any particular form.

(2) Unless a warehouse receipt embodies within its written or printed terms each of the following, the warehouseman is liable for damages caused by the omission to a person injured thereby:

(a) the location of the warehouse where the goods are stored;

(b) the date of issue of the receipt;

(c) the consecutive number of the receipt;

(d) a statement whether the goods received will be delivered to the bearer, to a specified person, or to a specified person or his order;

(e) the rate of storage and handling charges, except that where goods are stored under a field warehousing arrangement a statement of that fact is sufficient on a nonnegotiable receipt;

(f) a description of the goods or of the packages containing them;

(g) the signature of the warehouseman, which may be made by his authorized agent;

(h) if the receipt is issued for goods of which the warehouseman is owner, either solely or jointly or in common with others, the fact of such ownership; and

(i) a statement of the amount of advances made and of liabilities incurred for which the warehouseman claims a lien or security interest (Section 7—209). If the precise amount of such advances made or of such liabilities incurred is, at the time of the issue of the receipt, unknown to the warehouseman or to his agent who issues it, a statement of the fact that advances have been made or liabilities incurred and the purpose thereof is sufficient.

(3) A warehouseman may insert in his receipt any other terms which are not contrary to the provisions of this Act and do not impair his obligation of delivery (Section 7—403) or his duty of care (Section 7—204). Any contrary provisions shall be ineffective.

§ 7—203. Liability for Non-Receipt or Misdescription

A party to or purchaser for value in good faith of a document of title other than a bill of lading relying in either case upon the description therein of the goods may recover from the issuer damages caused by the non-receipt or misdescription of the goods, except to the extent that the document conspicuously indicates that the issuer does not know whether any part or all of the goods in fact were received or conform to the description, as where the description is in terms of marks or labels or kind, quantity or condition, or the receipt or description is qualified by "contents, condition and quality unknown," "said to contain" or the like, if such indication be true, or the party or purchaser otherwise has notice.

§ 7—204. Duty of Care; Contractual Limitation of Warehouseman's Liability

(1) A warehouseman is liable for damages for loss of or injury to the goods caused by his failure to exercise such care in regard to them as a reasonably careful man would exercise under like circumstances but, unless otherwise agreed, he is not liable for damages which could not have been avoided by the exercise of such care.

(2) Damages may be limited by a term in the warehouse receipt or storage agreement limiting the amount of liability in case of loss or damage, and setting forth a specific liability per article or item, or value per unit of weight, beyond which the warehouseman shall not be liable; provided, however, that such liability may on written request of the bailor at the time of signing such storage agreement or within a reasonable time after receipt of the warehouse receipt be increased on part or all of the goods thereunder, in which event increased rates may be charged based on such increased valuation, but that no such increase shall be permitted contrary to a lawful limitation of liability contained in the warehouseman's tariff, if any. No such limitation is effective with respect to the warehouseman's liability for conversion to his own use.

(3) Reasonable provisions as to the time and manner of presenting claims and instituting actions based on the bailment may be included in the warehouse receipt or tariff.

(4) This section does not impair or repeal . . .

Note: *Insert in subsection (4) a reference to any statute which imposes a higher responsibility upon the warehouseman or invalidates contractual limitations which would be permissible under this Article.*

§ 7—205. Title Under Warehouse Receipt Defeated in Certain Cases

A buyer in the ordinary course of business of fungible goods sold and delivered by a warehouseman who is also in the business of buying and selling such goods takes free of any claim under a warehouse receipt even though it has been duly negotiated.

§ 7—206. Termination of Storage at Warehouseman's Option

(1) A warehouseman may, on notifying the person on whose account the goods are held and any other person known to claim an interest in the goods, require payment of any charges and removal of the goods from the warehouse at the termination of the period of storage fixed by the document, or, if no period is fixed, within a stated period not less than thirty days after the notification. If the goods are not removed before the date specified in the notification, the warehouseman may sell them in accordance with the provisions of the section on enforcement of a warehouseman's lien (Section 7—210).

(2) If a warehouseman in good faith believes that the goods are about to deteriorate or decline in value to less than the amount of his lien within the time prescribed in subsection (1) for notification, advertisement and sale, the warehouseman may specify in the notification any reasonable shorter time for removal of the goods and in case the goods are not removed, may sell them at public sale held not less than one week after a single advertisement or posting.

(3) If as a result of a quality or condition of the goods of which the warehouseman had no notice at the time of deposit, the goods are a hazard to other property or to the warehouse or to persons, the warehouseman may sell the goods at public or private sale without advertisement on reasonable notification to all persons known to claim an interest in the goods. If the warehouseman after a reasonable effort is unable to sell the goods, he may dispose of them in any lawful manner and shall incur no liability by reason of such disposition.

(4) The warehouseman must deliver the goods to any person entitled to them under this Article upon due demand made at any time prior to sale or other disposition under this section.

(5) The warehouseman may satisfy his lien from the proceeds of any sale or disposition under this section but must hold the balance for delivery on the demand of any person to whom he would have been bound to deliver the goods.

§ 7—207. Goods Must Be Kept Separate; Fungible Goods

(1) Unless the warehouse receipt otherwise provides, a warehouseman must keep separate the goods covered by each receipt so as to permit at all times identification and delivery of those goods, except that different lots of fungible goods may be commingled.

(2) Fungible goods so commingled are owned in common by the persons entitled thereto, and the warehouseman is severally liable to each owner for that owner's share. Where because of overissue a mass of fungible goods is insufficient to meet all the receipts which the warehouseman has issued against it, the persons entitled include all holders to whom overissued receipts have been duly negotiated.

§ 7—208. Altered Warehouse Receipts

Where a blank in a negotiable warehouse receipt has been filled in without authority, a purchaser for value and without notice of the want of authority may treat the insertion as authorized. Any other unauthorized alteration leaves any receipt enforceable against the issuer according to its original tenor.

§ 7 — 209.   Lien of Warehouseman

(1) A warehouseman has a lien against the bailor on the goods covered by a warehouse receipt or on the proceeds thereof in his possession for charges for storage or transportation (including demurrage and terminal charges), insurance, labor, or charges present or future in relation to the goods, and for expenses necessary for preservation of the goods or reasonably incurred in their sale pursuant to law. If the person on whose account the goods are held is liable for like charges or expenses in relation to other goods whenever deposited and it is stated in the receipt that a lien is claimed for charges and expenses in relation to other goods, the warehouseman also has a lien against him for such charges and expenses whether or not the other goods have been delivered by the warehouseman. But against a person to whom a negotiable warehouse receipt is duly negotiated, a warehouseman's lien is limited to charges in an amount or at a rate specified on the receipt or if no charges are so specified then to a reasonable charge for storage of the goods covered by the receipt subsequent to the date of the receipt.

(2) The warehouseman may also reserve a security interest against the bailor for a maximum amount specified on the receipt for charges other than those specified in subsection (1), such as for money advanced and interest. Such a security interest is governed by the Article on Secured Transactions (Article 9).

(3) (a) A warehouseman's lien for charges and expenses under subsection (1) or a security interest under subsection (2) is also effective against any person who so entrusted the bailor with possession of the goods that a pledge of them by him to a good faith purchaser for value would have been valid but is not effective against a person as to whom the document confers no right in the goods covered by it under Section 7 — 503.

(b) A warehouseman's lien on household goods for charges and expenses in relation to the goods under subsection (1) is also effective against all persons if the depositor was the legal possessor of the goods at the time of deposit. "Household goods" means furniture, furnishings and personal effects used by the depositor in a dwelling.

(4) A warehouseman loses his lien on any goods which he voluntarily delivers or which he unjustifiably refuses to deliver.

§ 7 — 210.   Enforcement of Warehouseman's Lien

(1) Except as provided in subsection (2), a warehouseman's lien may be enforced by public or private sale of the goods in block or in parcels, at any time or place and on any terms which are commercially reasonable, after notifying all persons known to claim an interest in the goods. Such notification must include a statement of the amount due, the nature of the proposed sale and the time and place of any public sale. The fact that a better price could have been obtained by a sale at a different time or in a different method from that selected by the warehouseman is not of itself sufficient to establish that the sale was not made in a commercially reasonable manner. If the warehouseman either sells the goods in the usual manner in any recognized market therefor, or if he sells at the price current in such market at the time of his sale, or if he has otherwise sold in conformity with commercially reasonable practices among dealers in the type of goods sold, he has sold in a commercially reasonable manner. A sale of more goods than apparently necessary to be offered to insure satisfaction of the obligation is not commercially reasonable except in cases covered by the preceding sentence.

(2) A warehouseman's lien on goods other than goods stored by a merchant in the course of his business may be enforced only as follows:

(a) All persons known to claim an interest in the goods must be notified.

(b) The notification must be delivered in person or sent by registered or certified letter to the last known address of any person to be notified.

(c) The notification must include an itemized statement of the claim, a description of the goods subject to the lien, a demand for payment within a specified time not less than ten days after receipt of the notification, and a conspicuous statement that unless the claim is paid within that time the goods will be advertised for sale and sold by auction at a specified time and place.

(d) The sale must conform to the terms of the notification.

(e) The sale must be held at the nearest suitable place to that where the goods are held or stored.

(f) After the expiration of the time given in the notification, an advertisement of the sale must be published once a week for two weeks consecutively in a newspaper of general circulation where the sale is to be held. The advertisement must include a description of the goods, the name of the person on whose account they are being held, and the time and place of the sale. The sale must take place at least fifteen days after the first publication. If there is no newspaper of general circulation where the sale is to be held, the advertisement must be posted at least ten days before the sale in not less than six conspicuous places in the neighborhood of the proposed sale.

(3) Before any sale pursuant to this section, any person claiming a right in the goods may pay the amount necessary to satisfy the lien and the reasonable expenses incurred under this section. In that event, the goods must not be sold but must be retained by the warehouseman subject to the terms of the receipt and this Article.

(4) The warehouseman may buy at any public sale pursuant to this section.

(5) A purchaser in good faith of goods sold to enforce a warehouseman's lien takes the goods free of any rights of persons against whom the lien was valid, despite noncompliance by the warehouseman with the requirements of this section.

(6) The warehouseman may satisfy his lien from the proceeds of any sale pursuant to this section but must hold the balance, if any, for delivery on demand to any person to whom he would have been bound to deliver the goods.

(7) The rights provided by this section shall be in addition to all other rights allowed by law to a creditor against his debtor.

(8) Where a lien is on goods stored by a merchant in the course of his business, the lien may be enforced in accordance with either subsection (1) or (2).

(9) The warehouseman is liable for damages caused by failure to comply with the requirements for sale under this section and, in case of willful violation, is liable for conversion.

Part 3

Bills of Lading: Special Provisions

§ 7—301. Liability for Non-Receipt or Misdescription; "Said to Contain"; "Shipper's Load and Count"; Improper Handling

(1) A consignee of a nonnegotiable bill who has given value in good faith or a holder to whom a negotiable bill has been duly negotiated relying in either case upon the description therein of the goods, or upon the date therein shown, may recover from the issuer damages caused by the misdating of the bill or the nonreceipt or misdescription of the goods, except to the extent that the document indicates that the issuer does not know whether any part or all of the goods in fact were received or conform to the description, as where the description is in terms of marks or labels or kind, quantity, or condition or the receipt or description is qualified by "contents or condition of contents of packages unknown," "said to contain," "shipper's weight, load and count" or the like, if such indication be true.

(2) When goods are loaded by an issuer who is a common carrier, the issuer must count the packages of goods if package freight and ascertain the kind and quantity if bulk freight. In such cases, "shipper's weight, load and count" or other words indicating that the description was made by the shipper are ineffective except as to freight concealed by packages.

(3) When bulk freight is loaded by a shipper who makes available to the issuer adequate facilities for weighing such freight, an issuer who is a common carrier must ascertain the kind and quantity within a reasonable time after receiving the written request of the shipper to do so. In such cases, "shipper's weight" or other words of like purport are ineffective.

(4) The issuer may by inserting in the bill the words "shipper's weight, load and count" or other words of like purport indicate that the goods were loaded by the shipper; and if such statement be true, the issuer shall not be liable for damages caused by the improper loading. But their omission does not imply liability for such damages.

(5) The shipper shall be deemed to have guaranteed to the issuer the accuracy at the time of shipment of the description, marks, labels, number, kind, quantity, condition and weight, as furnished by him; and the shipper shall indemnify the issuer against damage caused by inaccuracies in such particulars. The right of the issuer to such indemnity shall in no way limit his responsibility and liability under the contract of carriage to any person other than the shipper.

§ 7—302. Through Bills of Lading and Similar Documents

(1) The issuer of a through bill of lading or other document embodying an undertaking to be performed in part by persons acting as its agents or by connecting carriers is liable to anyone entitled to recover on the document for any breach by such other persons or by a connecting carrier of its obligation under the document but, to the extent that the bill covers an undertaking to be performed overseas or in territory not contiguous to the continental United States or an undertaking including matters other than transportation, this liability may be varied by agreement of the parties.

(2) Where goods covered by a through bill of lading or other document embodying an undertaking to be performed in part by persons other than the issuer are received by any such person, he is subject with respect to his own performance while the goods are in his possession to the obligation of the issuer. His obligation is discharged by delivery of the goods to another such person pursuant to the document, and does not include liability for breach by any other such persons or by the issuer.

(3) The issuer of such through bill of lading or other document shall be entitled to recover from the connecting carrier or such other person in possession of the goods when the breach of the obligation under the document occurred, the amount it may be required to pay to anyone entitled to recover on the document therefor, as may be evidenced by any receipt, judgment, or transcript thereof, and the amount of any expense reasonably incurred by it in defending any action brought by anyone entitled to recover on the document therefor.

§ 7—303. Diversion; Reconsignment; Change of Instructions

(1) Unless the bill of lading otherwise provides, the carrier may deliver the goods to a person or destination other than that stated in the bill or may otherwise dispose of the goods on instructions from

(a) the holder of a negotiable bill; or

(b) the consignor on a nonnegotiable bill notwithstanding contrary instructions from the consignee; or

(c) the consignee on a nonnegotiable bill in the absence of contrary instructions from the consignor, if the goods have arrived at the billed destination or if the consignee is in possession of the bill; or

(d) the consignee on a nonnegotiable bill if he is entitled as against the consignor to dispose of them.

(2) Unless such instructions are noted on a negotiable bill of lading, a person to whom the bill is duly negotiated can hold the bailee according to the original terms.

§ 7—304. Bills of Lading in a Set

(1) Except where customary in overseas transportation, a bill of lading must not be issued in a set of parts. The issuer is liable for damages caused by violation of this subsection.

(2) Where a bill of lading is lawfully drawn in a set of parts, each of which is numbered and expressed to be valid only if the goods have not been delivered against any other part, the whole of the parts constitute one bill.

(3) Where a bill of lading is lawfully issued in a set of parts and different parts are negotiated to different persons, the title of the holder to whom the first due negotiation is made prevails as to both the document and the goods, even though any later holder may have received the goods from the carrier in good faith and discharged the carrier's obligation by surrender of his part.

(4) Any person who negotiates or transfers a single part of a bill of lading drawn in a set is liable to holders of that part as if it were the whole set.

(5) The bailee is obliged to deliver in accordance with Part 4 of this Article against the first presented part of a bill of lading lawfully drawn in a set. Such delivery discharges the bailee's obligation on the whole bill.

§ 7—305. Destination Bills

(1) Instead of issuing a bill of lading to the consignor at the place of shipment, a carrier may at the request of the consignor procure the bill to be issued at destination or at any other place designated in the request.

(2) Upon request of anyone entitled as against the carrier to control the goods while in transit and on surrender of any outstanding bill of lading or other receipt covering such goods, the issuer may procure a substitute bill to be issued at any place designated in the request.

§ 7—306. Altered Bills of Lading

An unauthorized alteration or filling in of a blank in a bill of lading leaves the bill enforceable according to its original tenor.

§ 7—307. Lien of Carrier

(1) A carrier has a lien on the goods covered by a bill of lading for charges subsequent to the date of its receipt of the goods for storage or transportation (including demurrage and terminal charges) and for expenses necessary for preservation of the goods incident to their transportation or reasonably incurred in their sale pursuant to law. But against a purchaser for value of a negotiable bill of lading, a carrier's lien is limited to charges stated in the bill or the applicable tariffs, or if no charges are stated then to a reasonable charge.

(2) A lien for charges and expenses under subsection (1) on goods which the carrier was required by law to receive for transportation is effective against the consignor or any person entitled to the goods unless the carrier had notice that the consignor lacked authority to subject the goods to such charges and expenses. Any other lien under subsection (1) is effective against the consignor and any person who permitted the bailor to have control or possession of the goods unless the carrier had notice that the bailor lacked such authority.

(3) A carrier loses his lien on any goods which he voluntarily delivers or which he unjustifiably refuses to deliver.

§ 7—308. Enforcement of Carrier's Lien

(1) A carrier's lien may be enforced by public or private sale of the goods, in block or in parcels, at any time or place and on any terms which are commercially reasonable, after notifying all persons known to claim an interest in the goods. Such notification must include a statement of the amount due, the nature of the proposed sale and the time and place of any public sale. The fact that a better price could have been obtained by a sale at a different time or in a different method from

that selected by the carrier is not of itself sufficient to establish that the sale was not made in a commercially reasonable manner. If the carrier either sells the goods in the usual manner in any recognized market therefor or if he sells at the price current in such market at the time of his sale or if he has otherwise sold in conformity with commercially reasonable practices among dealers in the type of goods sold, he has sold in a commercially reasonable manner. A sale of more goods than apparently necessary to be offered to ensure satisfaction of the obligation is not commercially reasonable except in cases covered by the preceding sentence.

(2) Before any sale pursuant to this section, any person claiming a right in the goods may pay the amount necessary to satisfy the lien and the reasonable expenses incurred under this section. In that event the goods must not be sold, but must be retained by the carrier subject to the terms of the bill and this Article.

(3) The carrier may buy at any public sale pursuant to this section.

(4) A purchaser in good faith of goods sold to enforce a carrier's lien takes the goods free of any rights of persons against whom the lien was valid, despite noncompliance by the carrier with the requirements of this section.

(5) The carrier may satisfy his lien from the proceeds of any sale pursuant to this section but must hold the balance, if any, for delivery on demand to any person to whom he would have been bound to deliver the goods.

(6) The rights provided by this section shall be in addition to all other rights allowed by law to a creditor against his debtor.

(7) A carrier's lien may be enforced in accordance with either subsection (1) or the procedure set forth in subsection (2) of Section 7—210.

(8) The carrier is liable for damages caused by failure to comply with the requirements for sale under this section and in case of willful violation is liable for conversion.

§ 7—309. Duty of Care; Contractual Limitation of Carrier's Liability

(1) A carrier who issues a bill of lading, whether negotiable or nonnegotiable, must exercise the degree of care in relation to the goods which a reasonably careful man would exercise under like circumstances. This subsection does not repeal or change any law or rule of law which imposes liability upon a common carrier for damages not caused by its negligence.

(2) Damages may be limited by a provision that the carrier's liability shall not exceed a value stated in the document if the carrier's rates are dependent upon value and the consignor by the carrier's tariff is afforded an opportunity to declare a higher value or a value as lawfully provided in the tariff, or, where no tariff is filed, he is otherwise advised of such oppor-

tunity; but no such limitation is effective with respect to the carrier's liability for conversion to its own use.

(3) Reasonable provisions as to the time and manner of presenting claims and instituting actions based on the shipment may be included in a bill of lading or tariff.

Part 4

Warehouse Receipts and Bills of Lading: General Obligations

§ 7—401. Irregularities in Issue of Receipt or Bill or Conduct or Issuer

The obligations imposed by this Article on an issuer apply to a document of title regardless of the fact that

(a) the document may not comply with the requirements of this Article or of any other law or regulation regarding its issue, form or content; or

(b) the issuer may have violated laws regulating the conduct of his business; or

(c) the goods covered by the document were owned by the bailee at the time the document was issued; or

(d) the person issuing the document does not come within the definition of warehouseman, if it purports to be a warehouse receipt.

§ 7—402. Duplicate Receipt or Bill; Overissue

Neither a duplicate nor any other document of title purporting to cover goods already represented by an outstanding document of the same issuer confers any right in the goods, except as provided in the case of bills in a set, overissue of documents for fungible goods and substitutes for lost, stolen or destroyed documents. But the issuer is liable for damages caused by his overissue or failure to identify a duplicate document as such by conspicuous notation on its face.

§ 7—403. Obligation of Warehouseman or Carrier to Deliver; Excuse

(1) The bailee must deliver the goods to a person entitled under the document who complies with subsections (2) and (3), unless and to the extent that the bailee establishes any of the following.

(a) delivery of the goods to a person whose receipt was rightful as against the claimant;

(b) damage to or delay, loss or destruction of the goods for which the bailee is not liable [, but the burden of establishing negligence in such cases is on the person entitled under the document];

Note: *The brackets in (1)(b) indicate that State enactments may differ on this point without serious damage to the principle of uniformity.*

    (c) previous sale or other disposition of the goods in lawful enforcement of a lien or on warehouseman's lawful termination of storage;

    (d) the exercise by a seller of his right to stop delivery pursuant to the provisions of the Article on Sales (Section 2—705);

    (e) a diversion, reconsignment or other disposition pursuant to the provisions of this Article (Section 7—303) or tariff regulating such right;

    (f) release, satisfaction or any other fact affording a personal defense against the claimant;

    (g) any other lawful excuse.

(2) A person claiming goods covered by a document of title must satisfy the bailee's lien where the bailee so requests or where the bailee is prohibited by law from delivering the goods until the charges are paid.

(3) Unless the person claiming is one against whom the document confers no right under Sec. 7—503(1), he must surrender for cancellation or notation of partial deliveries any outstanding negotiable document covering the goods, and the bailee must cancel the document or conspicuously note the partial delivery thereon or be liable to any person to whom the document is duly negotiated.

(4) "Person entitled under the document" means holder in the case of a negotiable document, or the person to whom delivery is to be made by the terms of or pursuant to written instructions under a nonnegotiable document.

§ 7—404. No Liability for Good Faith Delivery Pursuant to Receipt or Bill

A bailee who in good faith, including observance of reasonable commercial standards, has received goods and delivered or otherwise disposed of them according to the terms of the document of title or pursuant to this Article is not liable therefor. This rule applies even though the person from whom he received the goods had no authority to procure the document or to dispose of the goods and even though the person to whom he delivered the goods had no authority to receive them.

Part 5

Warehouse Receipts and Bills of Lading: Negotiation and Transfer

§ 7—501. Form of Negotiation and Requirements of "Due Negotiation"

(1) A negotiable document of title running to the order of a named person is negotiated by his indorsement and delivery. After his indorsement in blank or to bearer, any person can negotiate it by delivery alone.

    (2) (a) A negotiable document of title is also negotiated by delivery alone when by its original terms it runs to bearer.

       (b) When a document running to the order of a named person is delivered to him, the effect is the same as if the document had been negotiated.

(3) Negotiation of a negotiable document of title after it has been indorsed to a specified person requires indorsement by the special indorsee as well as delivery.

(4) A negotiable document of title is "duly negotiated" when it is negotiated in the manner stated in this section to a holder who purchases it in good faith without notice of any defense against or claim to it on the part of any person and for value, unless it is established that the negotiation is not in the regular course of business or financing or involves receiving the document in settlement or payment of a money obligation.

(5) Indorsement of a nonnegotiable document neither makes it negotiable nor adds to the transferee's rights.

(6) The naming in a negotiable bill of a person to be notified of the arrival of the goods does not limit the negotiability of the bill nor constitute notice to a purchaser thereof of any interest of such person in the goods.

§ 7—502. Rights Acquired by Due Negotiation

(1) Subject to the following section and to the provisions of Section 7—205 on fungible goods, a holder to whom a negotiable document of title has been duly negotiated acquires thereby:

    (a) title to the document;

    (b) title to the goods;

    (c) all rights accruing under the law of agency or estoppel, including rights to goods delivered to the bailee after the document was issued; and

    (d) the direct obligation of the issuer to hold or deliver the goods according to the terms of the document free of any defense or claim by him except those arising under the terms of the document or under this Article. In the case of a delivery order, the bailee's obligation accrues only upon acceptance and the obligation acquired by the holder is that the issuer and any indorser will procure the acceptance of the bailee.

(2) Subject to the following section, title and rights so acquired are not defeated by any stoppage of the goods represented by the document or by surrender of such goods by the bailee, and are not impaired even though the negotiation or any prior negotiation constituted a breach of duty or even though any person has been deprived of possession of the

document by misrepresentation, fraud, accident, mistake, duress, loss, theft or conversion, or even though a previous sale or other transfer of the goods or document has been made to a third person.

§ 7—503. Document of Title to Goods Defeated in Certain Cases

(1) A document of title confers no right in goods against a person who before issuance of the document had a legal interest or a perfected security interest in them and who neither

    (a) delivered or entrusted them or any document of title covering them to the bailor or his nominee with actual or apparent authority to ship, store or sell or with power to obtain delivery under this Article (Section 7—403) or with power of disposition under this Act (Sections 2—403 and 9–307) or other statute or rule of law; nor

    (b) acquiesced in the procurement by the bailor or his nominee of any document of title.

(2) Title to goods based upon an unaccepted delivery order is subject to the rights of anyone to whom a negotiable warehouse receipt or bill of lading covering the goods has been duly negotiated. Such a title may be defeated under the next section to the same extent as the rights of the issuer or a transferee from the issuer.

(3) Title to goods based upon a bill of lading issued to a freight forwarder is subject to the rights of anyone to whom a bill issued by the freight forwarder is duly negotiated; but delivery by the carrier in accordance with Part 4 of this Article pursuant to its own bill of lading discharges the carrier's obligation to deliver.

§ 7—504. Rights Acquired in the Absence of Due Negotiation; Effect of Diversion; Seller's Stoppage of Delivery

(1) A transferee of a document, whether negotiable or nonnegotiable, to whom the document has been delivered but not duly negotiated, acquires the title and rights which his transferor had or had actual authority to convey.

(2) In the case of a nonnegotiable document, until but not after the bailee receives notification of the transfer, the rights of the transferee may be defeated

    (a) by those creditors of the transferor who could treat the sale as void under Section 2—402; or

    (b) by a buyer from the transferor in ordinary course of business if the bailee has delivered the goods to the buyer or received notification of his rights; or

    (c) as against the bailee by good faith dealings of the bailee with the transferor.

(3) A diversion or other change of shipping instructions by the consignor in a nonnegotiable bill of lading which causes the bailee not to deliver to the consignee defeats the consignee's title to the goods if they have been delivered to a buyer in ordinary course of business and in any event defeats the consignee's rights against the bailee.

(4) Delivery pursuant to a nonnegotiable document may be stopped by a seller under Section 2—705, and subject to the requirement of due notification there provided. A bailee honoring the seller's instructions is entitled to be indemnified by the seller against any resulting loss or expense.

§ 7—505. Indorser Not a Guarantor for Other Parties

The indorsement of a document of title issued by a bailee does not make the indorser liable for any default by the bailee or by previous indorsers.

§ 7—506. Delivery Without Indorsement: Right to Compel Indorsement

The transferee of a negotiable document of title has a specifically enforceable right to have his transferor supply any necessary indorsement, but the transfer becomes a negotiation only as of the time the indorsement is supplied.

§ 7—507. Warranties on Negotiation or Transfer of Receipt or Bill

Where a person negotiates or transfers a document of title for value otherwise than as a mere intermediary under the next following section, then unless otherwise agreed he warrants to his immediate purchaser only, in addition to any warranty made in selling the goods,

    (a) that the document is genuine; and

    (b) that he has no knowledge of any fact which would impair its validity or worth; and

    (c) that his negotiation or transfer is rightful and fully effective with respect to the title to the document and the goods it represents.

§ 7—508. Warranties of Collecting Bank as to Documents

A collecting bank or other intermediary known to be entrusted with documents on behalf of another or with collection of a draft or other claim against delivery of documents warrants by such delivery of the documents only its own good faith and authority. This rule applies even though the intermediary has purchased or made advances against the claim or draft to be collected.

§ 7—509. Receipt or Bill: When Adequate Compliance With Commercial Contract

The question whether a document is adequate to fulfill the obligations of a contract for sale or the conditions of a credit is governed by the Articles on Sales (Article 2) and on Letters of Credit (Article 5).

Part 6
Warehouse Receipts and Bills of Lading: Miscellaneous Provisions

§ 7—601.   Lost and Missing Documents

(1) If a document has been lost, stolen or destroyed, a court may order delivery of the goods or issuance of a substitute document and the bailee may without liability to any person comply with such order. If the document was negotiable, the claimant must post security approved by the court to indemnify any person who may suffer loss as a result of non-surrender of the document. If the document was not negotiable, such security may be required at the discretion of the court. The court may also in its discretion order payment of the bailee's reasonable costs and counsel fees.

(2) A bailee who without court order delivers goods to a person claiming under a missing negotiable document is liable to any person injured thereby, and if the delivery is not in good faith becomes liable for conversion. Delivery in good faith is not conversion if made in accordance with a filed classification or tariff or, where no classification or tariff is filed, if the claimant posts security with the bailee in an amount at least double the value of the goods at the time of posting to indemnify any person injured by the delivery who files a notice of claim within one year after the delivery.

§ 7—602.   Attachment of Goods Covered by a Negotiable Document

Except where the document was originally issued upon delivery of the goods by a person who had no power to dispose of them, no lien attaches by virtue of any judicial process to goods in the possession of a bailee for which a negotiable document of title is outstanding unless the document be first surrendered to the bailee or its negotiation enjoined, and the bailee shall not be compelled to deliver the goods pursuant to process until the document is surrendered to him or impounded by the court. One who purchases the document for value without notice of the process or injunction takes free of the lien imposed by judicial process.

§ 7—603.   Conflicting Claims; Interpleader

If more than one person claims title or possession of the goods, the bailee is excused from delivery until he has had a reasonable time to ascertain the validity of the adverse claims or to bring an action to compel all claimants to interplead and may compel such interpleader, either in defending an action for non-delivery of the goods, or by original action, whichever is appropriate.

ARTICLE 8
INVESTMENT SECURITIES

Part 1
Short Title and General Matters

§ 8—101.   Short Title

This Article shall be known and may be cited as Uniform Commercial Code—Investment Securities.

§ 8—102.   Definitions and Index of Definitions

(1) In this Article, unless the context otherwise requires:

(a) A "certificated security" is a share, participation, or other interest in property of or an enterprise of the issuer or an obligation of the issuer which is
  (i) represented by an instrument issued in bearer or registered form;
  (ii) of a type commonly dealt in on securities exchanges or markets or commonly recognized in any area in which it is issued or dealt in as a medium for investment; and
  (iii) either one of a class or series or by its terms divisible into a class or series of shares, participations, interests, or obligations.

(b) An "uncertificated security" is a share, participation, or other interest in property or an enterprise of the issuer or an obligation of the issuer which is
  (i) not represented by an instrument and the transfer of which is registered upon books maintained for that purpose by or on behalf of the issuer;
  (ii) of a type commonly dealt in on securities exchanges or markets; and
  (iii) either one of a class or series or by its terms divisible into a class or series of shares, participations, interests, or obligations.

(c) A "security" is either a certificated or an uncertificated security. If a security is certificated, the terms "security" and "certificated security" may mean either the intangible interest, the instrument representing that interest, or both, as the context requires. A writing that is a certificated security is governed by this Article and not by Article 3, even though it also meets the requirements of that Article. This Article does not apply to money. If a certificated security has been retained by or surrendered to the issuer or its transfer agent for reasons other than registration of transfer, other temporary purpose, payment, exchange, or acquisition by the issuer, that security shall be treated as an uncertificated security for purposes of this Article.

(d) A certificated security is in "registered form" if
  (i) it specifies a person entitled to the security or the rights it represents; and
  (ii) its transfer may be registered upon books maintained for that purpose by or on behalf of the issuer, or the security so states.

(e) A certificated security is in "bearer form" if it runs to bearer according to its terms and not by reason of any indorsement.

(2) A "subsequent purchaser" is a person who takes other than by original issue.

(3) A "clearing corporation" is a corporation registered as a "clearing agency" under the federal securities laws or a corporation:

(a) at least 90 percent of whose capital stock is held by or for one or more organizations, none of which, other than a national securities exchange or association, holds in excess of 20 percent of the capital stock of the corporation, and each of which is
  (i) subject to supervision or regulation pursuant to the provisions of federal or state banking laws or state insurance laws,
  (ii) a broker or dealer or investment company registered under the federal securities laws, or
  (iii) a national securities exchange or association registered under the federal securities laws; and

(b) any remaining capital stock of which is held by individuals who have purchased it at or prior to the time of their taking office as directors of the corporation and who have purchased only so much of the capital stock as is necessary to permit them to qualify as directors.

(4) A "custodian bank" is a bank or trust company that is supervised and examined by state or federal authority having supervision over banks and is acting as custodian for a clearing corporation.

(5) Other definitions applying to this Article or to specified Parts thereof and the sections in which they appear are:
  "Adverse claim." Section 8—302.
  "Bona fide purchaser." Section 8—302.
  "Broker." Section 8—303.
  "Debtor." Section 9—105.
  "Financial intermediary." Section 8—313.
  "Guarantee of the signature." Section 8—402.
  "Initial transaction statement." Section 8—408.
  "Instruction." Section 8—308.
  "Intermediary bank." Section 4—105.
  "Issuer." Section 8—201.
  "Overissue." Section 8—104.
  "Secured Party." Section 9—105.
  "Security Agreement." Section 9—105.

(6) In addition, Article 1 contains general definitions and principles of construction and interpretation applicable throughout this Article.

§ 8—103. Issuer's Lien

A lien upon a security in favor of an issuer thereof is valid against a purchaser only if:
  (a) the security is certificated and the right of the issuer to the lien is noted conspicuously thereon; or
  (b) the security is uncertificated and a notation of the right of the issuer to the lien is contained in the initial transaction statement sent to the purchaser or, if his interest is transferred to him other than by registration of transfer, pledge, or release, the initial transaction statement sent to the registered owner or the registered pledgee.

§ 8—104. Effect of Overissue; "Overissue"

(1) The provisions of this Article which validate a security or compel its issue or reissue do not apply to the extent that validation, issue, or reissue would result in overissue; but if:
  (a) an identical security which does not constitute an overissue is reasonably available for purchase, the person entitled to issue or validation may compel the issuer to purchase the security for him and either to deliver a certificated security or to register the transfer of an uncertificated security to him, against surrender of any certificated security he holds; or
  (b) a security is not so available for purchase, the person entitled to issue or validation may recover from the issuer the price he or the last purchaser for value paid for it with interest from the date of his demand.

(2) "Overissue" means the issue of securities in excess of the amount the issuer has corporate power to issue.

§ 8—105. Certificated Securities Negotiable; Statements and Instructions Not Negotiable; Presumptions

(1) Certificated securities governed by this Article are negotiable instruments.

(2) Statements (Section 8—408), notices, or the like, sent by the issuer of uncertificated securities and instructions (Section 8—308) are neither negotiable instruments nor certificated securities.

(3) In any action on a security:

(a) unless specifically denied in the pleadings, each signature on a certificated security, in a necessary indorsement, on an initial transaction statement, or on an instruction, is admitted;

(b) if the effectiveness of a signature is put in issue, the burden of establishing it is on the party claiming under the signature, but the signature is presumed to be genuine or authorized;

(c) if signatures on a certificated security are admitted or established, production of the security entitles a holder to recover on it unless the defendant establishes a defense or a defect going to the validity of the security;

(d) if signatures on an initial transaction statement are admitted or established, the facts stated in the statement are presumed to be true as of the time of its issuance; and

(e) after it is shown that a defense or defect exists, the plaintiff has the burden of establishing that he or some person under whom he claims is a person against whom the defense or defect is ineffective (Section 8—202).

§ 8—106. Applicability

The law (including the conflict of laws rules) of the jurisdiction of organization of the issuer governs the validity of a security, the effectiveness of registration by the issuer, and the rights and duties of the issuer with respect to:

(a) registration of transfer of a certificated security;

(b) registration of transfer, pledge, or release of an uncertificated security; and,

(c) sending of statements of uncertificated securities.

§ 8—107. Securities Transferable; Action for Price

(1) Unless otherwise agreed and subject to any applicable law or regulation respecting short sales, a person obligated to transfer securities may transfer any certificated security of the specified issue in bearer form or registered in the name of the transferee, or indorsed to him or in blank, or he may transfer an equivalent uncertificated security to the transferee or a person designated by the transferee.

(2) If the buyer fails to pay the price as it comes due under a contract of sale, the seller may recover the price of:

(a) certificated securities accepted by the buyer;

(b) uncertificated securities that have been transferred to the buyer or a person designated by the buyer; and

(c) other securities if efforts at their resale would be unduly burdensome or if there is no readily available market for their resale.

§ 8—108. Registration of Pledge and Release of Uncertificated Securities

A security interest in an uncertificated security may be evidenced by the registration of pledge to the secured party or a person designated by him. There can be no more than one registered pledge of an uncertificated security at any time. The registered owner of an uncertificated security is the person in whose name the security is registered, even if the security is subject to a registered pledge. The rights of a registered pledgee of an uncertificated security under this Article are terminated by the registration of release.

Part 2

Issue—Issuer

§ 8—201. "Issuer"

(1) With respect to obligations on or defenses to a security, "issuer" includes a person who:

(a) places or authorizes the placing of his name on a certificated security (otherwise than as authenticating trustee, registrar, transfer agent, or the like) to evidence that it represents a share, participation, or other interest in his property or in an enterprise, or to evidence his duty to perform an obligation represented by the certificated security;

(b) creates shares, participations, or other interests in his property or in an enterprise or undertakes obligations, which shares, participations, interests, or obligations are uncertificated securities;

(c) directly or indirectly creates fractional interests in his rights or property, which fractional interests are represented by certificated securities; or

(d) becomes responsible for or in place of any other person described as an issuer in this section.

(2) With respect to obligations on or defenses to a security, a guarantor is an issuer to the extent of his guaranty, whether or not his obligation is noted on a certificated security or on statements of uncertificated securities sent pursuant to Section 8—408.

(3) With respect to registration of transfer, pledge, or release (Part 4 of this Article), "issuer" means a person on whose behalf transfer books are maintained.

§ 8 — 202. Issuer's Responsibility and Defenses; Notice of Defect or Defense

(1) Even against a purchaser for value and without notice, the terms of a security include:

(a) if the security is certificated, those stated on the security;

(b) if the security is uncertificated, those contained in the initial transaction statement sent to such purchaser or, if his interest is transferred to him other than by registration of transfer, pledge, or release, the initial transaction statement sent to the registered owner or registered pledgee; and

(c) those made part of the security by reference, on the certificated security or in the initial transaction statement, to another instrument, indenture, or document or to a constitution, statute, ordinance, rule, regulation, order or the like, to the extent that the terms referred to do not conflict with the terms stated on the certificated security or contained in the statement. A reference under this paragraph does not of itself charge a purchaser for value with notice of a defect going to the validity of the security, even though the certificated security or statement expressly states that a person accepting it admits notice.

(2) A certificated security in the hands of a purchaser for value or an uncertificated security as to which an initial transaction statement has been sent to a purchaser for value, other than a security issued by a government or governmental agency or unit, even though issued with a defect going to its validity, is valid with respect to the purchaser if he is without notice of the particular defect unless the defect involves a violation of constitutional provisions, in which case the security is valid with respect to a subsequent purchaser for value and without notice of the defect. This subsection applies to an issuer that is a government or governmental agency or unit only if either there has been substantial compliance with the legal requirements governing the issue or the issuer has received a substantial consideration for the issue as a whole or for the particular security and a stated purpose of the issue is one for which the issuer has power to borrow money or issue the security.

(3) Except as provided in the case of certain unauthorized signatures (Section 8 — 205), lack of genuineness of a certificated security or an initial transaction statement is a complete defense, even against a purchaser for value and without notice.

(4) All other defenses of the issuer of a certificated or uncertificated security, including nondelivery and conditional delivery of a certificated security, are ineffective against a purchaser for value who has taken without notice of the particular defense.

(5) Nothing in this section shall be construed to affect the right of a party to a "when, as and if issued" or a "when distributed" contract to cancel the contract in the event of a material change in the character of the security that is the subject of the contract or in the plan or arrangement pursuant to which the security is to be issued or distributed.

§ 8 — 203. Staleness as Notice of Defects or Defenses

(1) After an act or event creating a right to immediate performance of the principal obligation represented by a certificated security or that sets a date on or after which the security is to be presented or surrendered for redemption or exchange, a purchaser is charged with notice of any defect in its issue or defense of the issuer if:

(a) the act or event is one requiring the payment of money, the delivery of certificated securities, the registration of transfer of uncertificated securities, or any of these on presentation or surrender of the certificated security, the funds or securities are available on the date set for payment or exchange, and he takes the security more than one year after that date; and

(b) the act or event is not covered by paragraph (a) and he takes the security more than 2 years after the date set for surrender or presentation or the date on which performance became due.

(2) A call that has been revoked is not within subsection (1).

§ 8 — 204. Effect of Issuer's Restrictions on Transfer

A restriction on transfer of a security imposed by the issuer, even if otherwise lawful, is ineffective against any person without actual knowledge of it unless:

(a) the security is certificated and the restriction is noted conspicuously thereon; or

(b) the security is uncertificated and a notation of the restriction is contained in the initial transaction statement sent to the person or, if his interest is transferred to him other than by registration of transfer, pledge, or release, the initial transaction statement sent to the registered owner or the registered pledgee.

§ 8 — 205. Effect of Unauthorized Signature on Certificated Security or Initial Transaction Statement

An unauthorized signature placed on a certificated security prior to or in the course of issue or placed on an initial transaction statement is ineffective, but the signature is effective in favor of a purchaser for value of the certificated security or a purchaser for value of an uncertificated security to whom the initial transaction statement has been sent, if the purchaser is without notice of the lack of authority and the signing has been done by:

(a) an authenticating trustee, registrar, transfer agent, or other person entrusted by the issuer with the signing of the security, or similar securities, or of initial transaction statements or the immediate preparation for signing of any of them; or

(b) an employee of the issuer, or of any of the foregoing, entrusted with responsible handling of the security or initial transaction statement.

§ 8—206. Completion or Alteration of Certificated Security or Initial Transaction Statement

(1) If a certificated security contains the signatures necessary to its issue or transfer but is incomplete in any other respect:

(a) any person may complete it by filling in the blanks as authorized; and

(b) even though the blanks are incorrectly filled in, the security as completed is enforceable by a purchaser who took it for value and without notice of the incorrectness.

(2) A complete certificated security that has been improperly altered, even though fraudulently, remains enforceable, but only according to its original terms.

(3) If an initial transaction statement contains the signatures necessary to its validity, but is incomplete in any other respect:

(a) any person may complete it by filling in the blanks as authorized; and

(b) even though the blanks are incorrectly filled in, the statement as completed is effective in favor of the person to whom it is sent if he purchased the security referred to therein for value and without notice of the incorrectness.

(4) A complete initial transaction statement that has been improperly altered, even though fraudulently, is effective in favor of a purchaser to whom it has been sent, but only according to its original terms.

§ 8—207. Rights and Duties of Issuer With Respect to Registered Owners and Registered Pledgees

(1) Prior to due presentment for registration of transfer of a certificated security in registered form, the issuer or indenture trustee may treat the registered owner as the person exclusively entitled to vote, to receive notifications, and otherwise to exercise all the rights and powers of an owner.

(2) Subject to the provisions of subsections (3), (4), and (6), the issuer or indenture trustee may treat the registered owner of an uncertificated security as the person exclusively entitled to vote, to receive notifications, and otherwise to exercise all the rights and powers of an owner.

(3) The registered owner of an uncertificated security that is subject to a registered pledge is not entitled to registration of transfer prior to the due presentment to the issuer of a release instruction. The exercise of conversion rights with respect to a convertible uncertificated security is a transfer within the meaning of this section.

(4) Upon due presentment of a transfer instruction from the registered pledgee of an uncertificated security, the issuer shall:

(a) register the transfer of the security to the new owner free of pledge, if the instruction specifies a new owner (who may be the registered pledgee) and does not specify a pledgee;

(b) register the transfer of the security to the new owner subject to the interest of the existing pledgee, if the instruction specifies a new owner and the existing pledgee; or

(c) register the release of the security from the existing pledge and register the pledge of the security to the other pledgee, if the instruction specifies the existing owner and another pledgee.

(5) Continuity of perfection of a security interest is not broken by registration of transfer under subsection (4) (b) or by registration of release and pledge under subsection (4) (c), if the security interest is assigned.

(6) If an uncertificated security is subject to a registered pledge:

(a) any uncertificated securities issued in exchange for or distributed with respect to the pledged security shall be registered subject to the pledge;

(b) any certificated securities issued in exchange for or distributed with respect to the pledged security shall be delivered to the registered pledgee; and

(c) any money paid in exchange for or in redemption of part or all of the security shall be paid to the registered pledgee.

(7) Nothing in this Article shall be construed to affect the liability of the registered owner of a security for calls, assessments, or the like.

§ 8—208. Effect of Signature of Authenticating Trustee, Registrar, or Transfer Agent

(1) A person placing his signature upon a certificated security or an initial transaction statement as authenticating trustee, registrar, transfer agent, or the like, warrants to a purchaser for value of the certificated security or a purchaser for value of an uncertificated security to whom the initial transaction statement has been sent, if the purchaser is without notice of the particular defect, that:

(a) the certificated security or initial transaction statement is genuine;

(b) his own participation in the issue or registration of the transfer, pledge, or release of the security is within his capacity and within the scope of the authority received by him from the issuer; and

(c) he has reasonable grounds to believe the security is in the form and within the amount the issuer is authorized to issue.

(2) Unless otherwise agreed, a person by so placing his signature does not assume responsibility for the validity of the security in other respects.

Part 3

Transfer

§ 8—301.   Rights Acquired by Purchaser

(1) Upon transfer of a security to a purchaser (Section 8—313), the purchaser acquires the rights in the security which his transferor had or had actual authority to convey unless the purchaser's rights are limited by Section 3—302(4).

(2) A transferee of a limited interest acquires rights only to the extent of the interest transferred. The creation or release of a security interest in a security is the transfer of a limited interest in that security.

§ 8—302.   "Bona Fide Purchaser"; "Adverse Claim"; Title Acquired by Bona Fide Purchaser

(1) A "bona fide purchaser" is a purchaser for value in good faith and without notice of any adverse claim:

(a) who takes delivery of a certificated security in bearer form or in registered form, issued or indorsed to him or in blank;

(b) to whom the transfer, pledge, or release of an uncertificated security is registered on the books of the issuer; or

(c) to whom a security is transferred under the provisions of paragraph (c), (d), (i), or (g) of Section 8—313(1).

(2) "Adverse claim" includes a claim that a transfer was or would be wrongful or that a particular adverse person is the owner of or has an interest in the security.

(3) A bona fide purchaser in addition to acquiring the rights of a purchaser (Section 8—301) also acquires his interest in the security free of any adverse claim.

(4) Notwithstanding Section 8—301(1), the transferee of a particular certificated security who has been a party to any fraud or illegality affecting the security, or who as a prior holder of that certificated security had notice of an adverse claim, cannot improve his position by taking from a bona fide purchaser.

§ 8—303.   "Broker"

"Broker" means a person engaged for all or part of his time in the business of buying and selling securities, who in the transaction concerned acts for, buys a security from, or sells a security to, a customer. Nothing in this Article determines the capacity in which a person acts for purposes of any other statute or rule to which the person is subject.

§ 8—304.   Notice to Purchaser of Adverse Claims

(1) A purchaser (including a broker for the seller or buyer, but excluding an intermediary bank) of a certificated security is charged with notice of adverse claims if:

(a) the security, whether in bearer or registered form, has been indorsed "for collection" or "for surrender" or for some other purpose not involving transfer; or

(b) the security is in bearer form and has on it an unambiguous statement that it is the property of a person other than the transferor. The mere writing of a name on a security is not such a statement.

(2) A purchaser (including a broker for the seller or buyer, but excluding an intermediary bank) to whom the transfer, pledge, or release of an uncertificated security is registered is charged with notice of adverse claims as to which the issuer has a duty under Section 8—403(4) at the time of registration and which are noted in the initial transaction statement sent to the purchaser or, if his interest is transferred to him other than by registration of transfer, pledge, or release, the initial transaction statement sent to the registered owner or the registered pledgee.

(3) The fact that the purchaser (including a broker for the seller or buyer) of a certificated or uncertificated security has notice that the security is held for a third person or is registered in the name of or indorsed by a fiduciary does not create a duty of inquiry into the rightfulness of the transfer or constitute constructive notice of adverse claims. However, if the purchaser (excluding an intermediary bank) has knowledge that the proceeds are being used or the transaction is for the individual benefit of the fiduciary or otherwise in breach of duty, the purchaser is charged with notice of adverse claims.

§ 8—305.   Staleness as Notice of Adverse Claims

An act or event that creates a right to immediate performance of the principal obligation represented by a certificated security or sets a date on or after which a certificated security is to be presented or surrendered for redemption or exchange does not itself constitute any notice of adverse claims except in the case of a transfer;

(a) after one year from any date set for presentment or surrender for redemption or exchange; or

(b) after 6 months from any date set for payment of money against presentation or surrender of the security if funds are available for payment on that date.

§ 8—306. Warranties on Presentment and Transfer of Certificated Securities; Warranties of Originators of Instructions

(1) A person who presents a certificated security for registration of transfer or for payment or exchange warrants to the issuer that he is entitled to the registration, payment, or exchange. But, a purchaser for value and without notice of adverse claims who receives a new, reissued, or re-registered certificated security on registration of transfer or receives an initial transaction statement confirming the registration of transfer of an equivalent uncertificated security to him warrants only that he has no knowledge of any unauthorized signature (Section 8—311) in a necessary indorsement.

(2) A person by transferring a certificated security to a purchaser for value warrants only that:

(a) his transfer is effective and rightful;

(b) the security is genuine and has not been materially altered; and

(c) he knows of no fact which might impair the validity of the security.

(3) If a certificated security is delivered by an intermediary known to be entrusted with delivery of the security on behalf of another or with collection of a draft or other claim against delivery, the intermediary by delivery warrants only his own good faith and authority, even though he has purchased or made advances against the claim to be collected against the delivery.

(4) A pledgee or other holder for security who redelivers a certificated security received, or after payment and on order of the debtor delivers that security to a third person, makes only the warranties of an intermediary under subsection (3).

(5) A person who originates an instruction warrants to the issuer that:

(a) he is an appropriate person to originate the instruction; and

(b) at the time the instruction is presented to the issuer he will be entitled to the registration of transfer, pledge, or release.

(6) A person who originates an instruction warrants to any person specially guaranteeing his signature (subsection 8—312(3)) that:

(a) he is an appropriate person to originate the instruction; and

(b) at the time the instruction is presented to the issuer

(i) he will be entitled to the registration of transfer, pledge, or release; and

(ii) the transfer, pledge, or release requested in the instruction will be registered by the issuer free from all liens, security interests, restrictions, and claims other than those specified in the instruction.

(7) A person who originates an instruction warrants to a purchaser for value and to any person guaranteeing the instruction (Section 8—312(6)) that:

(a) he is an appropriate person to originate the instruction;

(b) the uncertificated security referred to therein is valid; and

(c) at the time the instruction is presented to the issuer

(i) the transferor will be entitled to the registration of transfer, pledge, or release;

(ii) the transfer, pledge, or release requested in the instruction will be registered by the issuer free from all liens, security interests, restrictions, and claims other than those specified in the instruction; and

(iii) the requested transfer, pledge, or release will be rightful.

(8) If a security party is the registered pledgee or the registered owner of an uncertificated security, a person who originates an instruction of release or transfer to the debtor or, after payment and on order of the debtor, a transfer instruction to a third person, warrants to the debtor or the third person only that he is an appropriate person to originate the instruction and, at the time the instruction is presented to the issuer, the transferor will be entitled to the registration of release or transfer. If a transfer instruction to a third person who is a purchaser for value is originated on order of the debtor, the debtor makes to the purchaser the warranties of paragraphs (b), (c)(ii) and (c)(iii) of subsection (7).

(9) A person who transfers an uncertificated security to a purchaser for value and does not originate an instruction in connection with the transfer warrants only that:

(a) his transfer is effective and rightful; and

(b) the uncertificated security is valid.

(10) A broker gives to his customer and to the issuer and a purchaser the applicable warranties provided in this section and has the rights and privileges of a purchaser under this section. The warranties of and in favor of the broker, acting as an agent are in addition to applicable warranties given by and in favor of his customer.

§ 8—307. Effect of Delivery Without Indorsement; Right to Compel Indorsement

If a certificated security in registered form has been delivered to a purchaser without a necessary indorsement he may become a bona fide purchaser only as of the time the indorsement is supplied; but against the transferor, the transfer is complete upon delivery and the purchaser has a specifically enforceable right to have any necessary indorsement supplied.

§ 8—308. Indorsements; Instructions

(1) An indorsement of a certificated security in

registered form is made when an appropriate person signs on it or on a separate document an assignment or transfer of the security or a power to assign or transfer it or his signature is written without more upon the back of the security.

(2) An indorsement may be in blank or special. An indorsement in blank includes an indorsement to bearer. A special indorsement specifies to whom the security is to be transferred, or who has power to transfer it. A holder may convert a blank indorsement into a special indorsement.

(3) An indorsement purporting to be only of part of a certificated security representing units intended by the issuer to be separately transferable is effective to the extent of the indorsement.

(4) An "instruction" is an order to the issuer of an uncertificated security requesting that the transfer, pledge, or release from pledge of the uncertificated security specified therein be registered.

(5) An instruction originated by an appropriate person is:

(a) a writing signed by an appropriate person; or

(b) a communication to the issuer in any form agreed upon in a writing signed by the issuer and an appropriate person.

If an instruction has been originated by an appropriate person but is incomplete in any other respect, any person may complete it as authorized and the issuer may rely on it as completed even though it has been completed incorrectly.

(6) "An appropriate person" in subsection (1) means the person specified by the certificated security or by special indorsement to be entitled to the security.

(7) "An appropriate person" in subsection (5) means:

(a) for an instruction to transfer or pledge an uncertificated security which is then not subject to a registered pledge, the registered owner; or

(b) for an instruction to transfer or release an uncertificated security which is then subject to a registered pledge, the registered pledgee.

(8) In addition to the persons designated in subsections (6) and (7), "an appropriate person" in subsections (1) and (5) includes:

(a) if the person designated is described as a fiduciary but is no longer serving in the described capacity, either that person or his successor;

(b) if the persons designated are described as more than one person as fiduciaries and one or more are no longer serving in the described capacity, the remaining fiduciary or fiduciaries, whether or not a successor has been appointed or qualified;

(c) if the person designated is an individual and is without capacity to act by virtue of

death, incompetence, infancy, or otherwise, his executor, administrator, guardian, or like fiduciary;

(d) if the persons designated are described as more than one person as tenants by the entirety or with right of survivorship and by reason of death all cannot sign, the survivor or survivors;

(e) a person having power to sign under applicable law or controlling instrument; and

(f) to the extent that the person designated or any of the foregoing persons may act through an agent, his authorized agent.

(9) Unless otherwise agreed, the indorser of a certificated security by his indorsement or the originator of an instruction by his origination assumes no obligation that the security will be honored by the issuer but only the obligations provided in Section 8—306.

(10) Whether the person signing is appropriate is determined as of the date of signing and an indorsement made by or an instruction originated by him does not become unauthorized for the purposes of this Article by virtue of any subsequent change of circumstances.

(11) Failure of a fiduciary to comply with a controlling instrument or with the law of the state having jurisdiction of the fiduciary relationship, including any law requiring the fiduciary to obtain court approval of the transfer, pledge, or release, does not render his indorsement or an instruction originated by him unauthorized for the purposes of this Article.

§ 8—309. Effect of Indorsement Without Delivery

An indorsement of a certificated security, whether special or in blank, does not constitute a transfer until delivery of the certificated security on which it appears or, if the indorsement is on a separate document, until delivery of both the document and the certificated security.

§ 8—310. Indorsement of Certificated Security in Bearer Form

An indorsement of a certificated security in bearer form may give notice of adverse claims (Section 8—304) but does not otherwise affect any right to registration the holder possesses.

§ 8—311. Effect of Unauthorized Indorsement or Instruction

Unless the owner or pledgee has ratified an unauthorized indorsement or instruction or is otherwise precluded from asserting its effectiveness:

(a) he may assert its ineffectiveness against the issuer or any purchaser, other than a purchaser for value and without notice of adverse claims, who has in good faith received a new, reissued, or re-registered certificated security on registration of transfer or received an initial transaction statement confirming the registration of transfer, pledge, or release of an equivalent uncertificated security to him; and

(b) an issuer who registers the transfer of a certificated security upon the unauthorized indorsement or who registers the transfer, pledge, or release of an uncertificated security upon the unauthorized instruction is subject to liability for improper registration (Section 8—404).

§ 8—312. Effect of Guaranteeing Signature, Indorsement or Instruction

(1) Any person guaranteeing a signature of an indorser of a certificated security warrants that at the time of signing:

(a) the signature was genuine;

(b) the signer was an appropriate person to indorse (Section 8—308); and

(c) the signer had legal capacity to sign.

(2) Any person guaranteeing a signature of the originator of an instruction warrants that at the time of signing:

(a) the signature was genuine;

(b) the signer was an appropriate person to originate the instruction (Section 8—308) if the person specified in the instruction as the registered owner or registered pledgee of the uncertificated security was, in fact, the registered owner or registered pledgee of the security, as to which fact the signature guarantor makes no warranty;

(c) the signer had legal capacity to sign; and

(d) the taxpayer identification number, if any, appearing on the instruction as that of the registered owner or registered pledgee was the taxpayer identification number of the signer or of the owner or pledgee for whom the signer was acting.

(3) Any person specially guaranteeing the signature of the originator of an instruction makes not only the warranties of a signature guarantor (subsection (2)) but also warrants that at the time the instruction is presented to the issuer;

(a) the person specified in the instruction as the registered owner or registered pledgee of the uncertificated security will be the registered owner or registered pledgee; and

(b) the transfer, pledge, or release of the uncertificated security requested in the instruction will be registered by the issuer free from all liens, security interests, restrictions, and claims other than those specified in the instruction.

(4) The guarantor under subsections (1) and (2) or the special guarantor under subsection (3) does not

otherwise warrant the rightfulness of the particular transfer, pledge, or release.

(5) Any person guaranteeing an indorsement of a certificated security makes not only the warranties of a signature guarantor under subsection (1) but also warrants the rightfulness of the particular transfer in all respects.

(6) Any person guaranteeing an instruction requesting the transfer, pledge, or release of an uncertificated security makes not only the warranties of a special signature guarantor under subsection (3) but also warrants the rightfulness of the particular transfer, pledge, or release in all respects.

(7) No issuer may require a special guarantee of signature (subsection (3)), a guarantee of indorsement (subsection (5)), or a guarantee of instruction (subsection (6)) as a condition to registration of transfer, pledge, or release.

(8) The foregoing warranties are made to any person taking or dealing with the security in reliance on the guarantee, and the guarantor is liable to the person for any loss resulting from breach of the warranties.

§ 8—313. When Transfer to Purchaser Occurs; Financial Intermediary as Bona Fide Purchaser; "Financial Intermediary"

(1) Transfer of a security or a limited interest (including a security interest) therein to a purchaser occurs only:

(a) at the time he or a person designated by him acquires possession of a certificated security;

(b) at the time the transfer, pledge, or release of an uncertificated security is registered to him or a person designated by him;

(c) at the time his financial intermediary acquires possession of a certificated security specially indorsed to or issued in the name of the purchaser;

(d) at the time a financial intermediary, not a clearing corporation, sends him confirmation of the purchase and also by book entry or otherwise identifies as belonging to the purchaser

(i) a specific certificated security in the financial intermediary's possession;

(ii) a quantity of securities that constitute or are part of a fungible bulk of certificated securities in the financial intermediary's possession or of uncertificated securities registered in the name of the financial intermediary; or

(iii) a quantity of securities that constitute or are part of a fungible bulk of securities shown on the account of the financial intermediary on the books of another financial intermediary;

(e) with respect to an identified certificated security to be delivered while still in the possession of a third person, not a financial intermediary, at the time that person acknowledges that he holds for the purchaser;

(f) with respect to a specific uncertificated security the pledge or transfer of which has been registered to a third person, not a financial intermediary, at the time that person acknowledges that he holds for the purchaser;

(g) at the time appropriate entries to the account of the purchaser or a person designated by him on the books of a clearing corporation are made under Section 8—320;

(h) with respect to the transfer of a security interest where the debtor has signed a security agreement containing a description of the security, at the time a written notification, which, in the case of the creation of the security interest, is signed by the debtor (which may be a copy of the security agreement) or which, in the case of the release or assignment of the security interest created pursuant to this paragraph, is signed by the secured party, is received by

    (i) a financial intermediary on whose books the interest of the transferor in the security appears;

    (ii) a third person, not a financial intermediary, in possession of the security, if it is certificated;

    (iii) a third person, not a financial intermediary, who is the registered owner of the security, if it is uncertificated and not subject to a registered pledge; or

    (iv) a third person, not a financial intermediary, who is the registered pledgee of the security, if it is uncertificated and subject to a registered pledge;

(i) with respect to the transfer of a security interest where the transferor has signed a security agreement containing a description of the security, at the time new value is given by the secured party; or

(j) with respect to the transfer of a security interest where the secured party is a financial intermediary and the security has already been transferred to the financial intermediary under paragraphs (a), (b), (c), (d), or (g), at the time the transferor has signed a security agreement containing a description of the security and value is given by the secured party.

(2) The purchaser is the owner of a security held for him by a financial intermediary, but cannot be a bona fide purchaser of a security so held except in the circumstances specified in paragraphs (c), (d)(i), and (g) of subsection (1). If a security so held is part of a fungible bulk, as in the circumstances specified in paragraphs (d)(ii) and (d)(iii) of subsection (1), the purchaser is the owner of aproportionate property interest in the fungible bulk.

(3) Notice of an adverse claim received by the financial intermediary or by the purchaser after the financial intermediary takes delivery of a certificated security as a holder for value or after the transfer, pledge, or release of an uncertificated security has been registered free of the claim to a financial intermediary who has given value is not effective either as to the financial intermediary or as to the purchaser. However, as between the financial intermediary and the purchaser the purchaser may demand transfer of an equivalent security as to which no notice of adverse claim has been received.

(4) A "financial intermediary" is a bank, broker, clearing corporation, or other person (or the nominee of any of them) which in the ordinary course of its business maintains security accounts for its customers and is acting in that capacity. A financial intermediary may have a security interest in securities held in account for its customer.

§ 8—314. Duty to Transfer, When Completed

(1) Unless otherwise agreed, if a sale of a security is made on an exchange or otherwise through brokers:

(a) the selling customer fulfills his duty to transfer at the time he:

    (i) places a certificated security in the possession of the selling broker or a person designated by the broker;

    (ii) causes an uncertificated security to be registered in the name of the selling broker or a person designated by the broker;

    (iii) if requested, causes an acknowledgment to be made to the selling broker that a certificated or uncertificated security is held for the broker; or

    (iv) places in the possession of the selling broker or of a person designated by the broker a transfer instruction for an uncertificated security, providing the issuer does not refuse to register the requested transfer if the instruction is presented to the issuer for registration within 30 days thereafter; and

(b) the selling broker, including a correspondent broker acting for a selling customer, fulfills his duty to transfer at the time he:

    (i) places a certificated security in the possession of the buying broker or a person designated by the buying broker;

(ii) causes an uncertificated security to be registered in the name of the buying broker or a person designated by the buying broker;

(iii) places in the possession of the buying broker or of a person designated by the buying broker a transfer instruction for an uncertificated security, providing the issuer does not refuse to register the requested transfer if the instruction is presented to the issuer for registration within 30 days thereafter; or

(iv) effects clearance of the sale in accordance with the rules of the exchange on which the transaction took place.

(2) Except as provided in this section or unless otherwise agreed, a transferor's duty to transfer a security under a contract of purchase is not fulfilled until he:

(a) places a certificated security in form to be negotiated by the purchaser in the possession of the purchaser or of a person designated by the purchaser;

(b) causes an uncertificated security to be registered in the name of the purchaser or a person designated by the purchaser; or

(c) if the purchaser requests, causes an acknowledgment to be made to the purchaser that a certificated or uncertificated security is held for the purchaser.

(3) Unless made on an exchange, a sale to a broker purchasing for his own account is within subsection (2) and not within subsection (1).

§ 8 — 315. Action Against Transferee Based Upon Wrongful Transfer

(1) Any person against whom the transfer of a security is wrongful for any reason, including his incapacity, as against anyone except a bona fide purchaser, may:

(a) reclaim possession of the certificated security wrongfully transferred;

(b) obtain possession of any new certificated security representing all or part of the same rights;

(c) compel the origination of an instruction to transfer to him or a person designated by him an uncertificated security constituting all or part of the same rights; or

(d) have damages.

(2) If the transfer is wrongful because of an unauthorized indorsement of a certificated security, the owner may also reclaim or obtain possession of the security or a new certificated security, even from a bona fide purchaser, if the ineffectiveness of the purported indorsement can be asserted against him under the provisions of this Article on unauthorized indorsements (Section 8 — 311).

(3) The right to obtain or reclaim possession of a certificated security or to compel the origination of a transfer instruction may be specifically enforced and the transfer of a certificated or uncertificated security enjoined and a certificated security impounded pending the litigation.

§ 8 — 316. Purchaser's Right to Requisites for Registration of Transfer, Pledge, or Release on Books

Unless otherwise agreed, the transferor of a certificated security or the transferor, pledgor, or pledgee of an uncertificated security on due demand must supply his purchaser with any proof of his authority to transfer, pledge, or release or with any other requisite necessary to obtain registration of the transfer, pledge, or release of the security; but if the transfer, pledge, or release is not for value, a transferor, pledgor, or pledgee need not do so unless the purchaser furnishes the necessary expenses. Failure within a reasonable time to comply with a demand made gives the purchaser the right to reject or rescind the transfer, pledge, or release.

§ 8 — 317. Creditors' Rights

(1) Subject to the exceptions in subsections (3) and (4), no attachment or levy upon a certificated security or any share or other interest represented thereby which is outstanding is valid until the security is actually seized by the officer making the attachment or levy, but a certificated security which has been surrendered to the issuer may be reached by a creditor by legal process at the issuer's chief executive office in the United States.

(2) An uncertificated security registered in the name of the debtor may not be reached by a creditor except by legal process at the issuer's chief executive office in the United States.

(3) The interest of a debtor in a certificated security that is in the possession of a secured party not a financial intermediary or in an uncertificated security registered in the name of a secured party not a financial intermediary (or in the name of a nominee of the secured party) may be reached by a creditor by legal process upon the secured party.

(4) The interest of a debtor in a certificated security that is in the possession of or registered in the name of a financial intermediary or in an uncertificated security registered in the name of a financial intermediary may be reached by a creditor by legal process upon the financial intermediary on whose books the interest of the debtor appears.

(5) Unless otherwise provided by law, a creditor's lien upon the interest of a debtor in a security obtained pursuant to subsection (3) or (4) is not a restraint on the transfer of the security, free of the lien, to a third party for new value; but in the event of a transfer, the lien applies to the proceeds of the transfer in the hands of the secured party or financial intermediary, subject to any claims having priority.

(6) A creditor whose debtor is the owner of a security is entitled to aid from courts of appropriate jurisdiction, by injunction or otherwise, in reaching the

security or in satisfying the claim by means allowed at law or in equity in regard to property that cannot readily be reached by ordinary legal process.

§ 8—318.   No Conversion by Good Faith Conduct

An agent or bailee who in good faith (including observance of reasonable commercial standards if he is in the business of buying, selling, or otherwise dealing with securities) has received certificated securities and sold, pledged, or delivered them or has sold or caused the transfer or pledge of uncertificated securities over which he had control according to the instructions of his principal, is not liable for conversion or for participation in breach of fiduciary duty although the principal had no right so to deal with the securities.

§ 8—319.   Statute of Frauds

A contract for the sale of securities is not enforceable by way of action or defense unless:

    (a) there is some writing signed by the party against whom enforcement is sought or by his authorized agent or broker, sufficient to indicate that a contract has been made for sale of a stated quantity of described securities at a defined or stated price;

    (b) delivery of a certificated security or transfer instruction has been accepted, or transfer of an uncertificated security has been registered and the transferee has failed to send written objection to the issuer within 10 days after receipt of the initial transaction statement confirming the registration, or payment has been made, but the contract is enforceable under this provision only to the extent of the delivery, registration, or payment;

    (c) within a reasonable time a writing in confirmation of the sale or purchase and sufficient against the sender under paragraph (a) has been received by the party against whom enforcement is sought and he has failed to send written objection to its contents within 10 days after its receipt; or

    (d) the party against whom enforcement is sought admits in his pleading, testimony, or otherwise in court that a contract was made for the sale of a stated quantity of described securities at a defined or stated price.

§ 8—320.   Transfer or Pledge Within Central Depository System

(1) In addition to other methods, a transfer, pledge, or release of a security or any interest therein may be effected by the making of appropriate entries on the books of a clearing corporation reducing the account of the transferor, pledgor, or pledgee and increasing the account of the transferee, pledgee, or pledgor by the amount of the obligation or the number of shares or rights transferred, pledged, or released, if the security is shown on the account of a transferor, pledgor, or pledgee on the books of the clearing corporation; is subject to the control of the clearing corporation; and

    (a) if certificated,

        (i) is in the custody of the clearing corporation, another clearing corporation, a custodian bank, or a nominee of any of them; and

        (ii) is in bearer form or indorsed in blank by an appropriate person or registered in the name of the clearing corporation, a custodian bank, or a nominee of any of them; or

    (b) if uncertificated, is registered in the name of the clearing corporation, another clearing corporation, a custodian bank, or a nominee of any of them.

(2) Under this section entries may be made with respect to like securities or interests therein as a part of a fungible bulk and may refer merely to a quantity of a particular security without reference to the name of the registered owner, certificate or bond number, or the like, and, in appropriate cases, may be on a net basis taking into account other transfers, pledges, or releasee of the same security.

(3) A transfer under this section is effective (Section 8—313) and the purchaser acquires the rights of the transferor (Section 8—301). A pledge or release under this section is the transfer of a limited interest. If a pledge or the creation of a security interest is intended, the security interest is perfected at the time when both value is given by the pledgee and the appropriate entries are made (Section 8—321). A transferee or pledgee under this section may be a bona fide purchaser (Section 8—302).

(4) A transfer or pledge under this section is not a registration of transfer under Part 4.

(5) That entries made on the books of the clearing corporation as provided in subsection (1) are not appropriate does not affect the validity of effect of the entries or the liabilities or obligations of the clearing corporation to any person adversely affected thereby.

§ 8—321.   Enforceability, Attachment, Perfection and Termination of Security Interests

(1) A security interest in a security is enforceable and can attach only if it is transferred to the secured party or a person designated by him pursuant to a provision of Section 8—313(1).

(2) A security interest so transferred pursuant to agreement by a transferor who has rights in the security to a transferee who has given value is a perfected security interest, but a security interest that has been transferred solely under paragraph (i) of Section

8—313(1) becomes unperfected after 21 days unless, within that time, the requirements for transfer under any other provision of Section 8—313(1) are satisfied.

(3) A security interest in a security is subject to the provisions of Article 9, but:

    (a) no filing is required to perfect the security interest; and

    (b) no written security agreement signed by the debtor is necessary to make the security interest enforceable, except as provided in paragraph (h), (i), or (j) of Section 8—313(1). The secured party has the rights and duties provided under Section 9—207, to the extent they are applicable, whether or not the security is certificated, and, if certificated, whether or not it is in his possession.

(4) Unless otherwise agreed, a security interest in a security is terminated by transfer to the debtor or a person designated by him pursuant to a provision of Section 8—313(1). If a security is thus transferred, the security interest, if not terminated, becomes unperfected unless the security is certificated and is delivered to the debtor for the purpose of ultimate sale or exchange or presentation, collection, renewal, or registration of transfer. In that case, the security interest becomes unperfected after 21 days unless, within that time, the security (or securities for which it has been exchanged) is transferred to the secured party or a person designated by him pursuant to a provision of Section 8—313(1).

Part 4
Registration

§ 8—401. Duty of Issuer to Register Transfer, Pledge, or Release

(1) If a certificated security in registered form is presented to the issuer with a request to register transfer or an instruction is presented to the issuer with a request to register transfer, pledge, or release, the issuer shall register the transfer, pledge, or release as requested if:

    (a) the security is indorsed or the instruction was originated by the appropriate person or persons (Section 8—308);

    (b) reasonable assurance is given that those indorsements or instructions are genuine and effective (Section 8—402);

    (c) the issuer has no duty as to adverse claims or has discharged the duty (Section 8—403);

    (b) any applicable law relating to the collection of taxes has been complied with; and

    (e) the transfer, pledge, or release is in fact rightful or is to a bona fide purchaser.

(2) If an issuer is under a duty to register a transfer, pledge, or release of a security, the issuer is also liable to the person presenting a certificated security or an instruction for registration or his principal for loss resulting from any unreasonable delay in registration or from failure or refusal to register the transfer, pledge, or release.

§ 8—402. Assurance that Indorsements and Instructions Are Effective

(1) The issuer may require the following assurance that each necessary indorsement of a certificated security or each instruction (Section 8—308) is genuine and effective:

    (a) in all cases, a guarantee of the signature (Section 8—312(1) or (2)) of the person indorsing a certificated security or originating an instruction including, in the case of an instruction, a warranty of the taxpayer identification number or, in the absence thereof, other reasonable assurance of identity;

    (b) if the indorsement is made or the instruction is originated by an agent, appropriate assurance of authority to sign;

    (c) if the indorsement is made or the instruction is originated by a fiduciary, appropriate evidence of appointment or incumbency;

    (d) if there is more than one fiduciary, reasonable assurance that all who are required to sign have done so; and

    (e) if the indorsement is made or the instruction is originated by a person not covered by any of the foregoing, assurance appropriate to the case corresponding as nearly as may be to the foregoing.

(2) A "guarantee of the signature" in subsection (1) means a guarantee signed by or on behalf of a person reasonably believed by the issuer to be responsible. The issuer may adopt standards with respect to responsibility if they are not manifestly unreasonable.

(3) "Appropriate evidence of appointment or incumbency" in subsection (1) means;

    (a) in the case of a fiduciary appointed or qualified by a court, a certificate issued by or under the direction or supervision of that court or an officer thereof and dated within 60 days before the date of presentation for transfer, pledge, or release; or

    (b) in any other case, a copy of a document showing the appointment or a certificate issued by or on behalf of a person reasonably believed by the issuer to be responsible or, in the absence of that document or certificate, other evidence reasonably deemed by the issuer to be appropriate. The issuer may adopt standards with respect to the evidence if they are not manifestly unreasonable. The issuer is not charged with notice of the contents of any document obtained pursuant to this paragraph (b) except to the extent that the contents relate directly to the appointment or incumbency.

(4) The issuer may elect to require reasonable assurance beyond that specified in this section, but if it does so and, for a purpose other than that specified in subsection (3) (b), both requires and obtains a copy of a will, trust, indenture, articles of co-partnership, by-laws, or other controlling instrument, it is charged with notice of all matters contained therein affecting the transfer, pledge, or release.

§ 8—403. Issuer's Duty as to Adverse Claims

(1) An issuer to whom a certificated security is presented for registration shall inquire into adverse claims if:

    (a) a written notification of an adverse claim is received at a time and in a manner affording the issuer a reasonable opportunity to act on it prior to the issuance of a new, reissued, or re-registered certificated security, and the notification identifies the claimant, the registered owner, and the issue of which the security is a part, and provides an address for communications directed to the claimant; or

    (b) the issuer is charged with notice of an adverse claim from a controlling instrument it has elected to require under Section 8—402(4).

(2) The issuer may discharge any duty of inquiry by any reasonable means, including notifying an adverse claimant by registered or certified mail at the address furnished by him or, if there be no such address, at his residence or regular place of business that the certificated security has been presented for registration of transfer by a named person, and that the transfer will be registered unless within 30 days from the date of mailing the notification, either:

    (a) an appropriate restraining order, injunction, or other process issues from a court of competent jurisdiction; or

    (b) there is filed with the issuer an indemnity bond, sufficient in the issuer's judgment to protect the issuer and any transfer agent, registrar, or other agent of the issuer involved from any loss it or they may suffer by complying with the adverse claim.

(3) Unless an issuer is charged with notice of an adverse claim from a controlling instrument which it has elected to require under Section 8—402(4) or receives notification of an adverse claim under sub-section (1), if a certificated security presented for registration is indorsed by the appropriate person or persons the issuer is under no duty to inquire into adverse claims. In particular:

    (a) an issuer registering a certificated security in the name of a person who is a fiduciary or who is described as a fiduciary is not bound to inquire into the existence, extent, or correct description of the fiduciary relationship; and thereafter the issuer may assume without inquiry that the newly registered owner continues to be the fiduciary until the issuer receives written notice that the fiduciary is no longer acting as such with respect to the particular security;

    (b) an issuer registering transfer on an indorsement by a fiduciary is not bound to inquire whether the transfer is made in compliance with a controlling instrument or with the law of the state having jurisdiction of the fiduciary relationship, including any law requiring the fiduciary to obtain court approval of the transfer; and

    (c) the issuer is not charged with notice of the contents of any court record or file or other recorded or unrecorded document even though the document is in its possession and even though the transfer is made on the indorsement of a fiduciary to the fiduciary himself or to his nominee.

(4) An issuer is under no duty as to adverse claims with respect to an uncertificated security except:

    (a) claims embodied in a restraining order, injunction, or other legal process served upon the issuer if the process was served at a time and in a manner affording the issuer a reasonable opportunity to act on it in accordance with the requirements of subsection (5);

    (b) claims of which the issuer has received a written notification from the registered owner or the registered pledgee if the notification was received at a time and in a manner affording the issuer a reasonable opportunity to act on it in accordance with the requirements of subsection (5);

    (c) claims (including restrictions on transfer not imposed by the issuer) to which the registration of transfer to the present registered owner was subject and were so noted in the initial transaction statement sent to him; and

    (d) claims as to which an issuer is charged with notice from a controlling instrument it has elected to require under Section 8—402(4).

(5) If the issuer of an uncertificated security is under a duty as to an adverse claim, he discharges that duty by:

(a) including a notation of the claim in any statements sent with respect to the security under Sections 8—408(3), (6), and (7); and

(b) refusing to register the transfer or pledge of the security unless the nature of the claim does not preclude transfer or pledge subject thereto.

(6) If the transfer or pledge of the security is registered subject to an adverse claim, a notation of the claim must be included in the initial transaction statement and all subsequent statements sent to the transferee and pledgee under Section 8—408.

(7) Notwithstanding subsections (4) and (5), if an uncertificated security was subject to a registered pledge at the time the issuer first came under a duty as to a particular adverse claim, the issuer has no duty as to that claim if transfer of the security is requested by the registered pledgee or an appropriate person acting for the registered pledgee unless:

(a) the claim was embodied in legal process which expressly provides otherwise;

(b) the claim was asserted in a written notification from the registered pledgee;

(c) the claim was one as to which the issuer was charged with notice from a controlling instrument it required under Section 8—402(4) in connection with the pledgee's request for transfer; or

(d) the transfer requested is to the registered owner.

§ 8—404. Liability and Non-Liability for Registration

(1) Except as provided in any law relating to the collection of taxes, the issuer is not liable to the owner, pledgee, or any other person suffering loss as a result of the registration of a transfer, pledge, or release of a security if:

(a) there were on or with a certificated security the necessary indorsements or the issuer had received an instruction originated by an appropriate person (Section 8—308); and

(b) the issuer had no duty as to adverse claims or has discharged the duty (Section 8—403).

(2) If an issuer has registered a transfer of a certificated security to a person not entitled to it, the issuer on demand shall deliver a like security to the true owner unless:

(a) the registration was pursuant to subsection (1);

(b) the owner is precluded from asserting any claim for registering the transfer under Section 8—405(1); or

(c) the delivery would result in overissue, in which case the issuer's liability is governed by Section 8—104.

(3) If an issuer has improperly registered a transfer, pledge, or release of an uncertificated security, the issuer on demand from the injured party shall restore the records as to the injured party to the condition that would have obtained if the improper registration had not been made unless:

(a) the registration was pursuant to subsection (1); or

(b) the registration would result in overissue, in which case the issuer's liability is governed by Section 8—104.

§ 8—405. Lost, Destroyed, and Stolen Certificated Securities

(1) If a certificated security has been lost, apparently destroyed, or wrongfully taken, and the owner fails to notify the issuer of that fact within a reasonable time after he has notice of it and the issuer registers a transfer of the security before receiving notification, the owner is precluded from asserting against the issuer any claim for registering the transfer under Section 8—404 or any claim to a new security under this section.

(2) If the owner of a certificated security claims that the security has been lost, destroyed, or wrongfully taken, the issuer shall issue a new certificated security or, at the option of the issuer, an equivalent uncertificated security in place of the original security if the owner:

(a) so requests before the issuer has notice that the security has been acquired by a bona fide purchaser;

(b) files with the issuer a sufficient indemnity bond; and

(c) satisfies any other reasonable requirements imposed by the issuer.

(3) If, after the issue of a new certificated or uncertificated security, a bona fide purchaser of the original certificated security presents it for registration of transfer, the issuer shall register the transfer unless registration would result in overissue, in which event the issuer's liability is governed by Section 8—104. In addition to any rights on the indemnity bond, the issuer may recover the new certificated security from the person to whom it was issued or any person taking under him except a bona fide purchaser or may cancel the uncertificated security unless a bona fide purchaser or any person taking under a bona fide purchaser is then the registered owner or registered pledgee thereof.

§ 8—406. Duty of Authenticating Trustee, Transfer Agent, or Registrar

(1) If a person acts as authenticating trustee, transfer agent, registrar, or other agent for an issuer in the registration of transfers of its certificated securities or in the registration of transfers, pledges, and releases of its uncertificated securities, in the issue of new securities, or in the cancellation of surrendered securities:

(a) he is under a duty to the issuer to exercise good faith and due diligence in performing his functions; and

(b) with regard to the particular functions he performs, he has the same obligation to the holder or owner of a certificated security or to the owner or pledgee of an uncertificated security and has the same rights and privileges as the issuer has in regard to those functions.

(2) Notice to an authenticating trustee, transfer agent, registrar or other agent is notice to the issuer with respect to the functions performed by the agent.

§ 8—407. Exchangeability of Securities

(1) No issuer is subject to the requirements of this section unless it regularly maintains a system for issuing the class of securities involved under which both certificated and uncertificated securities are regularly issued to the category of owners, which includes the person in whose name the new security is to be registered.

(2) Upon surrender of a certificated security with all necessary indorsements and presentation of a written request by the person surrendering the security, the issuer, if he has no duty as to adverse claims or has discharged the duty (Section 8—403), shall issue to the person or a person designated by him an equivalent uncertificated security subject to all liens, restrictions, and claims that were noted on the certificated security.

(3) Upon receipt of a transfer instruction originated by an appropriate person who so requests, the issuer of an uncertificated security shall cancel the uncertificated security and issue an equivalent certificated security on which must be noted conspicuously any liens and restrictions of the issuer and any adverse claims (as to which the issuer has a duty under Section 8—403(4)) to which the uncertificated security was subject. The certificated security shall be registered in the name of and delivered to:

(a) the registered owner, if the uncertificated security was not subject to a registered pledge; or

(b) the registered pledgee, if the uncertificated security was subject to a registered pledge.

§ 8—408. Statements of Uncertificated Securities

(1) Within 2 business days after the transfer of an uncertificated security has been registered, the issuer shall send to the new registered owner and, if the security has been transferred subject to a registered pledge, to the registered pledgee a written statement containing:

(a) a description of the issue of which the uncertificated security is a part;

(b) the number of shares or units transferred;

(c) the name and address and any taxpayer identification number of the new registered owner and, if the security has been transferred subject to a registered pledge, the name and address and any taxpayer identification number of the registered pledgee;

(d) a notation of any liens and restrictions of the issuer and any adverse claims (as to which the issuer has a duty under Section 8—403(4)) to which the uncertificated security is or may be subject at the time of registration or a statement that there are none of those liens, restrictions, or adverse claims; and

(e) the date the transfer was registered.

(2) Within 2 business days after the pledge of an uncertificated security has been registered, the issuer shall send to the registered owner and the registered pledgee a written statement containing:

(a) a description of the issue of which the uncertificated security is a part;

(b) the number of shares or units pledged;

(c) the name and address and any taxpayer identification number of the registered owner and the registered pledgee;

(d) a notation of any liens and restrictions of the issuer and any adverse claims (as to which the issuer has a duty under Section 8—403(4) to which the uncertificated security is or may be subject at the time of registration or a statement that there are none of those liens, restrictions, or adverse claims; and

(e) the date the pledge was registered.

(3) Within 2 business days after the release from pledge of an uncertificated security has been registered, the issuer shall send to the registered owner and the pledgee whose interest was released a written statement containing:

(a) a description of the issue of which the uncertificated security is a part;

(b) the number of shares or units released from pledge;

(c) the name and address and any taxpayer identification number of the registered owner and the pledgee whose interest was released;

(d) a notation of any liens and restrictions of the issuer and any adverse claims (as to which the issuer has a duty under Section 8—403(4)) to which the uncertificated security is or may be subject at the time of registration or a statement that there are none of those liens, restrictions, or adverse claims; and

(e) the date the release was registered.

(4) An "initial transaction statement" is the statement sent to:

(a) the new registered owner and, if applicable, to the registered pledgee pursuant to subsection (1);

(b) the registered pledgee pursuant to subsection (2); or

(c) the registered owner pursuant to subsection (3).

Each initial transaction statement shall be signed by or on behalf of the issuer and must be identified as "Initial Transaction Statement."

(5) Within 2 business days after the transfer of an uncertificated security has been registered, the issuer shall send to the former registered owner and the former registered pledgee, if any, a written statement containing:

(a) a description of the issue of which the uncertificated security is a part;

(b) the number of shares or units transferred;

(c) the name and address and any taxpayer identification number of the former registered owner and of any former registered pledgee; and

(d) the date the transfer was registered.

(6) At periodic intervals no less frequent than annually and at any time upon the reasonable written request of the registered owner, the issuer shall send to the registered owner of each uncertificated security a dated written statement containing:

(a) a description of the issue of which the uncertificated security is a part;

(b) the name and address and any taxpayer identification number of the registered owner;

(c) the number of shares or units of the uncertificated security registered in the name of the registered owner on the date of the statement;

(d) the name and address and any taxpayer identification number of any registered pledgee and the number of shares or units subject to the pledge; and

(e) a notation of any liens and restrictions of the issuer and any adverse claims (as

to which the issuer has a duty under Section 8—403(4)) to which the uncertificated security is or may be subject or a statement that there are none of those liens, restrictions, or adverse claims.

(7) At periodic intervals no less frequent than annually and at any time upon the reasonable written request of the registered pledgee, the issuer shall send to the registered pledgee of each uncertificated security a dated written statement containing:

(a) a description of the issue of which the uncertificated security is a part;

(b) the name and address and any taxpayer identification number of the registered owner;

(c) the name and address and any taxpayer identification number of the registered pledgee;

(d) the number of shares or units subject to the pledge; and

(e) a notation of any liens and restrictions of the issuer and any adverse claims (as to which the issuer has a duty under Section 8—403(4)) to which the uncertificated security is or may be subject or a statement that there are none of those liens, restrictions, or adverse claims.

(8) If the issuer sends the statements described in subsections (6) and (7) at periodic intervals no less frequent than quarterly, the issuer is not obliged to send additional statements upon request unless the owner or pledgee requesting them pays to the issuer the reasonable cost of furnishing them.

(9) Each statement sent pursuant to this section must bear a conspicuous legend reading substantially as follows: "This statement is merely a record of the rights of the addressee as of the time of its issuance. Delivery of this statement, of itself, confers no rights on the recipient. This statement is neither a negotiable instrument nor a security."

ARTICLE 9

SECURED TRANSACTIONS; SALES OF ACCOUNTS AND CHATTEL PAPER

Part 1

Short Title, Applicability and Definitions

§ 9—101. Short Title

This Article shall be known and may be cited as Uniform Commercial Code—Secured Transactions.

§ 9—102. Policy and Subject Matter of Article

(1) Except as otherwise provided in Section 9—104 on excluded transactions, this Article applies

(a) to any transaction (regardless of its form) which is intended to create a security interest in personal property or fixtures including goods, documents, instruments, general intangibles, chattel paper or accounts; and also

(b) to any sale of accounts or chattel paper.

(2) This Article applies to security interests created by contract including pledge, assignment, chattel mortgage, chattel trust, trust deed, factor's lien, equipment trust, conditional sale, trust receipt, other lien or title retention contract and lease or consignment in-

tended as security. This Article does not apply to statutory liens except as provided in Section 9—310.

(3) The application of this Article to a security interest in a secured obligation is not affected by the fact that the obligation is itself secured by a transaction or interest to which this Article does not apply.

Note: *The adoption of this article should be accompanied by the repeal of existing statutes dealing with conditional sales, trust receipts, factor's liens where the factor is given a nonpossessory lien, chattel mortgages, crop mortgages, mortgages on railroad equipment, assignment of accounts and generally statutes regulating security interests in personal property.*

Where the state has a retail installment selling act or small loan act, that legislation should be carefully examined to determine what changes in those acts are needed to conform them to this Article. This Article primarily sets out rules defining rights of a secured party against persons dealing with the debtor; it does not prescribe regulations and controls which may be necessary to curb abuses arising in the small loan business or in the financing of consumer purchases on credit. Accordingly there is no intention to repeal existing regulatory acts in those fields by enactment or re-enactment of Article 9. See Section 9—203(4) and the Note thereto.

§ 9—103. Perfection of Security Interests in Multiple State Transactions

(1) Documents, instruments and ordinary goods.

(a) This subsection applies to documents and instruments and to goods other than those covered by a certificate of title described in subsection (2), mobile goods described in subsection (3), and minerals described in subsection (5).

(b) Except as otherwise provided in this subsection, perfection and the effect of perfection or non-perfection of a security interest in collateral are governed by the law of the jurisdiction where the collateral is when the last event occurs on which is based the assertion that the security interest is perfected or unperfected.

(c) If the parties to a transaction creating a purchase money security interest in goods in one jurisdiction understand at the time that the security interest attaches that the goods will be kept in another jurisdiction, then the law of the other jurisdiction governs the perfection and the effect of perfection or non-perfection of the security interest from the time it attaches until thirty days after the debtor receives possession of the goods and thereafter if the goods are taken to the other jurisdiction before the end of the thirty-day period.

(d) When collateral is brought into and kept in this state while subject to a security interest perfected under the law of the jurisdiction from which the collateral was removed, the security interest remains perfected, but if action is required by Part 3 of this Article to perfect the security interest,

(i) if the action is not taken before the expiration of the period of perfection in the other jurisdiction or the end of four months after the collateral is brought into this state, whichever period first expires, the security interest becomes unperfected at the end of that period and is thereafter deemed to have been unperfected as against a person who became a purchaser after removal;

(ii) if the action is taken before the expiration of the period specified in subparagraph (i), the security interest continues perfected thereafter;

(iii) for the purpose of priority over a buyer of consumer goods (subsection (2) of Section 9—307), the period of the effectiveness of a filing in the jurisdiction from which the collateral is removed is governed by the rules with respect to perfection in subparagraphs (i) and (ii).

(2) Certificate of title.

(a) This subsection applies to goods covered by a certificate of title issued under a statute of this state or of another jurisdiction under the law of which indication of a security interest on the certificate is required as a condition of perfection.

(b) Except as otherwise provided in this subsection, perfection and the effect of perfection or non-perfection of the security interest are governed by the law (including the conflict of laws rules) of the jurisdiction issuing the certificate until four months after the goods are removed from that jurisdiction and thereafter until the goods are registered in another jurisdiction, but in any event not beyond surrender of the certificate. After the expiration of that period, the goods are not covered by the certificate of title within the meaning of this section.

(c) Except with respect to the rights of a buyer described in the next paragraph, a security interest, perfected in another jurisdiction otherwise than by notation on a certificate of title, in goods brought into this state and thereafter covered by a certificate of title issued by this state is subject to the rules stated in paragraph (d) of subsection (1).

(d) If goods are brought into this state while a security interest therein is perfected in any manner under the law of the jurisdiction from which the goods are removed and a certificate of title is issued by this state and the certificate does not show that the goods are subject to the security interest or that they may be subject to security interests not shown on the certificate, the security interest is subordinate to the rights of a buyer of the goods who is not in the business of selling goods of that kind to the extent that he gives value and receives delivery of the goods after issuance of the certificate and without knowledge of the security interest.

(3) Accounts, general intangibles and mobile goods.

(a) This subsection applies to accounts (other than an account described in subsection (5) on minerals) and general intangibles (other than uncertificated securities) and to goods which are mobile and which are of a type normally used in more than one jurisdiction, such as motor vehicles, trailers, rolling stock, airplanes, shipping containers, road building and construction machinery and commercial harvesting machinery and the like, if the goods are equipment or are inventory leased or held for lease by the debtor to others, and are not covered by a certificate of title described in subsection (2).

(b) The law (including the conflict of laws rules) of the jurisdiction in which the debtor is located governs the perfection and the effect of perfection or non-perfection of the security interest.

(c) If, however, the debtor is located in a jurisdiction which is not a part of the United States, and which does not provide for perfection of the security interest by filing or recording in that jurisdiction, the law of the jurisdiction in the United States in which the debtor has its major executive office in the United States governs the perfection and the effect of perfection or non-perfection of the security interest through filing. In the alternative, if the debtor is located in a jurisdiction which is not a part of the United States or Canada and the collateral is accounts or general intangibles for money due or to become due, the security interest may be perfected by notification to the account debtor. As used in this paragraph, "United States" includes its territories and possessions and the Commonwealth of Puerto Rico.

(d) A debtor shall be deemed located at his place of business if he has one, at his chief executive office if he has more than one place of business, otherwise at his residence. If, however, the debtor is a foreign air carrier under the Federal Aviation Act of 1958, as amended, it shall be deemed located at the designated office of the agent upon whom service of process may be made on behalf of the foreign air carrier.

(e) A security interest perfected under the law of the jurisdiction of the location of the debtor is perfected until the expiration of four months after a change of the debtor's location to another jurisdiction, or until perfection would have ceased by the law of the first jurisdiction, whichever period first expires. Unless perfected in the new jurisdiction before the end of that period, it becomes unperfected thereafter and is deemed to have been unperfected as against a person who became a purchaser after the change.

(4) Chattel paper.

The rules stated for goods in subsection (1) apply to a possessory security interest in chattel paper. The rules stated for accounts in subsection (3) apply to a non-possessory security interest in chattel paper, but the security interest may not be perfected by notification to the account debtor.

(5) Minerals.

Perfection and the effect of perfection or non-perfection of a security interest which is created by a debtor who has an interest in minerals or the like (including oil and gas) before extraction and which attaches thereto as extracted, or which attaches to an account resulting from the sale thereof at the wellhead or minehead are governed by the law (including the conflict of laws rules) of the jurisdiction wherein the wellhead or minehead is located.

(6) Uncertificated securities.

The law (including the conflict of laws rules) of the jurisdiction of organization of the issuer governs the perfection and the effect of perfection or non-perfection of a security interest in uncertificated securities.

§ 9—104.   Transactions Excluded from Article

This Article does not apply

(a) to a security interest subject to any statute of the United States, to the extent that such statute governs the rights of parties to and third parties affected by transactions in particular types of property; or

(b) to a landlord's lien; or

(c) to a lien given by statute or other rule of law for services or materials except as provided in Section 9—310 on priority of such liens; or

(d) to a transfer of a claim for wages, salary or other compensation of an employee; or

(e) to a transfer by a government or governmental subdivision or agency; or

(f) to a sale of accounts or chattel paper as part of a sale of the business out of which they arose, or an assignment of accounts or chattel paper which is for the purpose of collection only, or a transfer of a right to payment under a contract to an assignee who is also to do the performance under the contract or a transfer of a single account to an assignee in whole or partial satisfaction of a preexisting indebtedness; or

(g) to a transfer of an interest in or claim in or under any policy of insurance, except as provided with respect to proceeds (Section 9—306) and priorities in proceeds (Section 9—312); or

(h) to a right represented by a judgment (other than a judgment taken on a right to payment which was collateral); or

(i) to any right of setoff; or

(j) except to the extent that provision is made for fixtures in Section 9—313, to the creation or transfer of an interest in or lien on real estate, including a lease or rents thereunder; or

(k) to a transfer in whole or in part of any claim arising out of tort; or

(l) to a transfer of an interest in any deposit account (subsection (1) of Section 9—105), except as provided with respect to proceeds (Section 9—306) and priorities in proceeds (Section 9—312).

§ 9—105. Definitions and Index of Definitions

(1) In this Article unless the context otherwise requires:

(a) "Account debtor" means the person who is obligated on an account, chattel paper or general intangible;

(b) "Chattel paper" means a writing or writings which evidence both a monetary obligation and a security interest in or a lease of specific goods, but a charter or other contract involving the use or hire of a vessel is not chattel paper. When a transaction is evidenced both by such a security agreement or a lease and by an instrument or a series of instruments, the group of writings taken together constitutes chattel paper;

(c) "Collateral" means the property subject to a security interest, and includes accounts and chattel paper which have been sold;

(d) "Debtor" means the person who owes payment or other performance of the obligation secured, whether or not he owns or has rights in the collateral, and includes the seller of accounts or chattel paper. Where the debtor and the owner of the collateral are not the same person, the term "debtor" means the owner of the collateral in any provision of the article dealing with the collateral, the obligor in any provision dealing with the obligation, and may include both where the context so requires;

(e) "Deposit account" means a demand, time, savings, passbook or like account maintained with a bank, savings and loan association, credit union or like organization, other than an account evidenced by a certificate of deposit;

(f) "Document" means document of title as defined in the general definitions of Article 1 (Section 1—201), and a receipt of the kind described in subsection (2) of Section 7—201;

(g) "Encumbrance" includes real estate mortgages and other liens on real estate and all other rights in real estate that are not ownership interests;

(h) "Goods" includes all things which are movable at the time the security interest attaches or which are fixtures (Section 9—313), but does not include money, documents, instruments, accounts, chattel paper, general intangibles, or minerals or the like (including oil and gas) before extraction. "Goods" also includes standing timber which is to be cut and removed under a conveyance or contract for sale, the unborn young of animals, and growing crops;

(i) "Instrument" means a negotiable instrument (defined in Section 3—104), or a certificated security (defined in Section 8—102) or any other writing which evidences a right to the payment of money and is not itself a security agreement or lease and is of a type which is in ordinary course of business transferred by delivery with any necessary indorsement or assignment;

(j) "Mortgage" means a consensual interest created by a real estate mortgage, a trust deed on real estate, or the like;

(k) An advance is made "pursuant to commitment" if the secured party has bound himself to make it, whether or not a subsequent event of default or other event not within his control has relieved or may relieve him from his obligation;

(l) "Security agreement" means an agreement which creates or provides for a security interest;

(m) "Secured party" means a lender, seller or other person in whose favor there is a security interest, including a person to whom accounts or chattel paper have been sold. When the holders of obligations issued under an indenture of trust, equipment trust agreement or the like are represented by a trustee or other person, the representative is the secured party;

(n) "Transmitting utility" means any person primarily engaged in the railroad, street railway or trolley bus business, the electric or electronics communications transmission business, the transmission of goods by pipeline, or the transmission or the production and transmission of electricity, steam, gas or water, or the provision of sewer service.

(2) Other definitions applying to this Article and the sections in which they appear are:

"Account."	Section 9—106.
"Attach."	Section 9—203.
"Construction mortgage."	Section 9—313(1).
"Consumer goods."	Section 9—109(1).
"Equipment."	Section 9—109(2).
"Farm products."	Section 9—109(3).
"Fixture."	Section 9—313(1).
"Fixture filing."	Section 9—313(1).
"General intangibles."	Section 9—106.
"Inventory."	Section 9—109(4).
"Lien creditor."	Section 9—301(3).
"Proceeds."	Section 9—306(1).
"Purchase money security interest."	Section 9—107.
"United States."	Section 9—103.

(3) The following definitions in other Articles apply to this Article:

"Check."	Section 3—104.
"Contract for sale."	Section 2—106.
"Holder in due course."	Section 3—302.
"Note."	Section 3—104.
"Sale."	Section 2—106.

(4) In addition Article 1 contains general definitions and principles of construction and interpretation applicable throughout this Article.

§ 9—106. Definitions: "Account"; "General Intangibles"

"Account" means any right to payment for goods sold or leased or for services rendered which is not evidenced by an instrument or chattel paper, whether or not it has been earned by performance. "General intangibles" means any personal property (including things in action) other than goods, accounts, chattel paper, documents, instruments, and money. All rights to payment earned or unearned under a charter or other contract involving the use or hire of a vessel and all rights incident to the charter or contract are accounts.

§ 9—107. Definitions: "Purchase Money Security Interest"

A security interest is a "purchase money security interest" to the extent that it is

(a) taken or retained by the seller of the collateral to secure all or part of its price; or

(b) taken by a person who, by making advances or incurring an obligation, gives value to enable the debtor to acquire rights in or the use of collateral, if such value is in fact so used.

§ 9—108. When After-Acquired Collateral Not Security for Antecedent Debt

Where a secured party makes an advance, incurs an obligation, releases a perfected security interest, or otherwise gives new value which is to be secured in whole or in part by after-acquired property, his security interest in the after-acquired collateral shall be deemed to be taken for new value and not as security for an antecedent debt if the debtor acquires his rights in such collateral either in the ordinary course of his business or under a contract of purchase made pursuant to the security agreement within a reasonable time after new value is given.

§ 9—109. Classification of Goods; "Consumer Goods"; "Farm Products"; "Inventory"

Goods are

(1) "consumer goods" if they are used or bought for use primarily for personal, family or household purposes;

(2) "equipment" if they are used or bought for use primarily in business (including farming or a profession) or by a debtor who is a non-profit organization or a governmental subdivision or agency or if the goods are not included in the definitions of inventory, farm products or consumer goods;

(3) "farm products" if they are crops or livestock or supplies used or produced in farming operations or if they are products of crops or livestock in their unmanufactured states (such as ginned cotton, wool-clip, maple syrup, milk and eggs) and if they are in the possession of a debtor engaged in raising, fattening, grazing or other farming operations. If goods are farm products, they are neither equipment nor inventory;

(4) "inventory" if they are held by a person who holds them for sale or lease or to be furnished under

contracts of service or if he has so furnished them, or if they are raw materials, work in process or materials used or consumed in a business. Inventory of a person is not to be classified as his equipment.

§ 9 — 110. Sufficiency of Description

For the purposes of this Article, any description of personal property or real estate is sufficient whether or not it is specific if it reasonably identifies what is described.

§ 9 — 111. Applicability of Bulk Transfer Laws

The creation of a security interest is not a bulk transfer under Article 6 (see Section 6 — 103).

§ 9 — 112. Where Collateral Is Not Owned by Debtor

Unless otherwise agreed, when a secured party knows that collateral is owned by a person who is not the debtor, the owner of the collateral is entitled to receive from the secured party any surplus under Section 9 — 502(2) or under Section 9 — 504(1), and is not liable for the debt or for any deficiency after resale, and he has the same right as the debtor

    (a) to receive statements under Section 9 — 208;
    (b) to receive notice of and to object to a secured party's proposal to retain the collateral in satisfaction of the indebtedness under Section 9 — 505;
    (c) to redeem the collateral under Section 9 — 506;
    (d) to obtain injunctive or other relief under Section 9 — 507(1); and
    (e) to recover losses caused to him under Section 9 — 208(2).

§ 9 — 113. Security Interests Arising Under Article on Sales

A security interest arising solely under the Article on Sales (Article 2) is subject to the provisions of this Article except that to the extent that and so long as the debtor does not have or does not lawfully obtain possession of the goods

    (a) no security agreement is necessary to make the security interest enforceable; and
    (b) no filing is required to perfect the security interest; and
    (c) the rights of the secured party on default by the debtor are governed by the Article on Sales (Article 2).

§ 9 — 114. Consignment

(1) A person who delivers goods under a consignment which is not a security interest and who would be required to file under this Article by paragraph (3) (c) of Section 2 — 326 has priority over a secured party who is or becomes a creditor of the consignee and who would have a perfected security interest in the goods if they were the property of the

consignee, and also has priority with respect to identifiable cash proceeds received on or before delivery of the goods to a buyer, if

    (a) the consignor complies with the filing provision of the Article on Sales with respect to consignments (paragraph (3) (c) of Section 2 — 326) before the consignee receives possession of the goods; and
    (b) the consignor gives notification in writing to the holder of the security interest, if the holder has filed a financing statement covering the same types of goods before the date of the filing made by the consignor; and
    (c) the holder of the security interest receives the notification within five years before the consignee receives possession of the goods; and
    (d) the notification states that the consignor expects to deliver goods on consignment to the consignee, describing the goods by item or type.

(2) In the case of a consignment which is not a security interest and in which the requirements of the preceding subsection have not been met, a person who delivers goods to another is subordinate to a person who would have a perfected security interest in the goods if they were the property of the debtor.

Part 2

Validity of Security Agreement and Rights of Parties Thereto

§ 9 — 201. General Validity of Security Agreement

Except as otherwise provided by this Act, a security agreement is effective according to its terms between the parties, against purchasers of the collateral and against creditors. Nothing in this Article validates any charge or practice illegal under any statute or regulation thereunder governing usury, small loans, retail installment sales, or the like, or extends the application of any such statute or regulation to any transaction not otherwise subject thereto.

§ 9 — 202. Title to Collateral Immaterial

Each provision of this Article wtih regard to rights, obligations and remedies applies whether title to collateral is in the secured party or in the debtor.

§ 9 — 203. Attachment and Enforceability of Security Interest; Proceeds; Formal Requisites

(1) Subject to the provisions of Section 4 — 208 on the security interest of a collecting bank, Section 8 — 321 on security interests in securities and Section 9 — 113 on a security interest arising under the Article of Sales, a security interest is not enforceable against the debtor or third parties with respect to the collateral and does not attach unless

(a) the collateral is in the possession of the secured party pursuant to agreement, or the debtor has signed a security agreement which contains a description of the collateral and in addition, when the security interest covers crops growing or to be grown or timber to be cut, a description of the land concerned; and

(b) value has been given; and

(c) the debtor has rights in the collateral.

(2) A security interest attaches when it becomes enforceable against the debtor with respect to the collateral. Attachment occurs as soon as all of the events specified in subsection (1) have taken place unless explicit agreement postpones the time of attaching.

(3) Unless otherwise agreed, a security agreement gives the secured party the rights to proceeds provided by Section 9—306.

(4) A transaction, although subject to this Article, is also subject to . . . . *, and in the case of conflict between the provisions of this Article and any such statute, the provisions of such statute control. Failure to comply with any applicable statute has only the effect which is specified therein.

Note: *At * in subsection (4) insert reference to any local statute regulating small loans, retail installment sales and the like.*

The foregoing subsection (4) is designed to make it clear that certain transactions, although subject to this Article, must also comply with other applicable legislation.

This Article is designed to regulate all the "security" aspects of transactions within its scope. There is, however, much regulatory legislation, particularly in the consumer field, which supplements this Article and should not be repealed by its enactment. Examples are small loan acts, retail installment selling acts and the like. Such acts may provide for licensing and rate regulation and may prescribe particular forms of contract. Such provisions should remain in force despite the enactment of this Article. On the other hand if a retail installment selling act contains provisions on filing, rights on default, etc., such provisions should be repealed as inconsistent with this Article except that inconsistent provisions as to deficiencies, penalties, etc., in the Uniform Consumer Credit Code and other recent related legislation should remain because those statutes were drafted after the substantial enactment of the Article and with the intention of modifying certain provisions of this Article as to consumer credit.

§ 9—204. After-Acquired Property; Future Advances

(1) Except as provided in subsection (2), a security agreement may provide that any or all obligations covered by the security agreement are to be secured by after-acquired collateral.

(2) No security interest attaches under an after-acquired property clause to consumer goods other than accessions (Section 9—314) when given as additional security unless the debtor acquires rights in them within ten days after the secured party gives value.

(3) Obligations covered by a security agreement may include future advances or other value whether or not the advances or value are given pursuant to commitment (subsection (1) of Section 9—105).

§ 9—205. Use or Disposition of Collateral Without Accounting Permissible

A security interest is not invalid or fraudulent against creditors by reason of liberty in the debtor to use, commingle or dispose of all or part of the collateral (including returned or repossessed goods) or to collect or compromise accounts or chattel paper, or to accept the return of goods or make repossessions, or to use, commingle or dispose of proceeds or by reason of the failure of the secured party to require the debtor to account for proceeds or replace collateral. This section does not relax the requirements of possession where perfection of a security interest depends upon possession of the collateral by the secured party or by a bailee.

§ 9—206. Agreement Not to Assert Defenses Against Assignee; Modification of Sales Warranties Where Security Agreement Exists

(1) Subject to any statute or decision which establishes a different rule for buyers or lessees of consumer goods, an agreement by a buyer or lessee that he will not assert against an assignee any claim or defense which he may have against the seller or lessor is enforceable by an assignee who takes his assignment for value, in good faith and without notice of a claim or defense, except as to defenses of a type which may be asserted against a holder in due course of a negotiable instrument under the Article on Commercial Paper (Article 3). A buyer who as part of one transaction signs both a negotiable instrument and a security agreement makes such an agreement.

(2) When a seller retains a purchase money security interest in goods, the Article on Sales (Article 2) governs the sale and any disclaimer, limitation or modification of the seller's warranties.

§ 9—207. Rights and Duties When Collateral is in Secured Party's Possession

(1) A secured party must use reasonable care in the custody and preservation of collateral in his possession. In the case of an instrument or chattel paper, reasonable care includes taking necessary steps to preserve rights against prior parties unless otherwise agreed.

(2) Unless otherwise agreed, when collateral is in the secured party's possession

(a) reasonable expenses (including the cost of any insurance and payment of taxes or other charges) incurred in the custody, preservation, use or operation of the collateral are chargeable to the debtor and are secured by the collateral;

(b) the risk of accidental loss or damage is on the debtor to the extent of any deficiency in any effective insurance coverage;

(c) the secured party may hold as additional security any increase or profits (except money) received from the collateral, but money so received, unless remitted to the debtor, shall be applied in reduction of the secured obligation;

(d) the secured party must keep the collateral identifiable but fungible collateral may be commingled;

(e) the secured party may repledge the collateral upon terms which do not impair the debtor's right to redeem it.

(3) A secured party is liable for any loss caused by his failure to meet any obligation imposed by the preceding subsections but does not lose his security interest.

(4) A secured party may use or operate the collateral for the purpose of preserving the collateral or its value or pursuant to the order of a court of appropriate jurisdiction or, except in the case of consumer goods, in the manner and to the extent provided in the security agreement.

§ 9—208. Request for Statement of Account or List of Collateral

(1) A debtor may sign a statement indicating what he believes to be the aggregate amount of unpaid indebtedness as of a specified date and may send it to the secured party with a request that the statement be approved or corrected and returned to the debtor. When the security agreement or any other record kept by the secured party identifies the collateral, a debtor may similarly request the secured party to approve or correct a list of the collateral.

(2) The secured party must comply with such a request within two weeks after receipt by sending a written correction or approval. If the secured party claims a security interest in all of a particular type of collateral owned by the debtor, he may indicate that fact in his reply and need not approve or correct an itemized list of such collateral. If the secured party without reasonable excuse fails to comply, he is liable for any loss caused to the debtor thereby; and if the debtor has properly included in his request a good faith statement of the obligation or a list of the collateral or both, the secured party may claim a security interest only as shown in the statement against persons misled by his failure to comply. If he no longer has an interest in the obligation or collateral at the time the request is received, he must disclose the name and address of any successor in interest known to him; and he is liable for any loss caused to the debtor as a result of failure to disclose. A successor in interest is not subject to this section until a request is received by him.

(3) A debtor is entitled to such a statement once every six months without charge. The secured party may require payment of a charge not exceeding $10 for each additional statement furnished.

Part 3

Rights of Third Parties; Perfected and Unperfected Security Interests; Rules of Priority

§ 9—301. Persons Who Take Priority Over Unperfected Security Interests; Rights of "Lien Creditor"

(1) Except as otherwise provided in subsection (2), an unperfected security interest is subordinate to the rights of

(a) persons entitled to priority under Section 9—312;

(b) a person who becomes a lien creditor before the security interest is perfected;

(c) in the case of goods, instruments, documents, and chattel paper, a person who is not a secured party and who is a transferee in bulk or other buyer not in ordinary course of business or is a buyer of farm products in ordinary course of business, to the extent that he gives value and receives delivery of the collateral without knowledge of the security interest and before it is perfected;

(d) in the case of accounts and general intangibles, a person who is not a secured party and who is a transferee, to the extent that he gives value without knowledge of the security interest and before it is perfected.

(2) If the secured party files with respect to a purchase money security interest before or within ten days after the debtor receives possession of the collateral, he takes priority over the rights of a transferee in bulk or of a lien creditor which arise between the time the security interest attaches and the time of filing.

(3) A "lien creditor" means a creditor who has acquired a lien on the property involved by attachment, levy or the like and includes an assignee for benefit of creditors from the time of assignment, and a trustee in bankruptcy from the date of the filing of the petition or a receiver in equity from the time of appointment.

(4) A person who becomes a lien creditor while a security interest is perfected takes subject to the security interest only to the extent that it secures advances made before he becomes a lien creditor or within 45 days thereafter or made without knowledge of the lien or pursuant to a commitment entered into without knowledge of the lien.

§ 9—302. When Filing Is Required to Perfect Security Interest; Security Interests to Which Filing Provisions of This Article Do Not Apply

(1) A financing statement must be filed to perfect all security interests except the following:

(a) a security interest in collateral in possession of the secured party under Section 9—305;

(b) a security interest temporarily perfected in instruments or documents without delivery under Section 9—304 or in proceeds for a 10 day period under Section 9—306;

(c) a security interest created by an assignment of a beneficial interest in a trust or a decedent's estate;

(d) a purchase money security interest in consumer goods; but filing is required for a motor vehicle required to be registered; and fixture filing is required for priority over conflicting interests in fixtures to the extent provided in Section 9—313;

(e) an assignment of accounts which does not alone or in conjunction with other assignments to the same assignee transfer a significant part of the outstanding accounts of the assignor;

(f) a security interest of a collecting bank (Section 4—208) or in securities (Section 8—321) or arising under the Article on Sales (see Section 9—313) or covered in subsection (3) of this section;

(g) an assignment for the benefit of all the creditors of the transferor, and subsequent transfers by the assignee thereunder.

(2) If a secured party assigns a perfected security interest, no filing under this Article is required in order to continue the perfected status of the security interest against creditors of and transferees from the original debtor.

(3) The filing of a financing statement otherwise required by this Article is not necessary or effective to perfect a security interest in property subject to

(a) a statute or treaty of the United States which provides for a national or international registration or a national or international certificate of title or which specifies a place of filing different from that specified in this Article for filing of the security interest; or

(b) the following statutes of this state; [list any certificate of title statute covering automobiles, trailers, mobile homes, boats, farm tractors, or the like, and any central filing statute*.]; but during any period in which collateral is inventory held for sale by a person who is in the business of selling goods of that kind, the filing provisions of this Article (Part 4) apply to a security interest in that collateral created by him as debtor; or

(c) a certificate of title statute of another jurisdiction under the law of which indication of a security interest on the certificate is required as a condition of perfection (subsection (2) of Section 9—103).

(4) Compliance with a statute or treaty described in subsection (3) is equivalent to the filing of a financing statement under this Article, and a security interest in property subject to the statute or treaty can be perfected only by compliance therewith except as provided in Section 9—103 on multiple state transactions. Duration and renewal of perfection of a security interest perfected by compliance with the statute or treaty are governed by the provisions of the statute or treaty; in other respects the security interest is subject to this Article.

*Note: It is recommended that the provisions of certificate of title acts for perfection of security interests by notation on the certificates should be amended to exclude coverge of inventory held for sale.

§ 9—303. When Security Interest Is Perfected; Continuity of Perfection

(1) A security interest is perfected when it has attached and when all of the applicable steps required for perfection have been taken. Such steps are specified in Section 9—302, 9—304, 9—305 and 9—306. If such steps are taken before the security interest attaches, it is perfected at the time when it attaches.

(2) If a security interest is originally perfected in any way permitted under this Article and is subsequently perfected in some other way under this Article, without an intermediate period when it was unperfected, the security interest shall be deemed to be perfected continuously for the purposes of this Article.

§ 9—304. Perfection of Security Interest in Instruments, Documents, and Goods Covered by Documents; Perfection by Permissive Filing; Temporary Perfection Without Filing or Transfer of Possession

(1) A security interest in chattel paper or negotiable documents may be perfected by filing. A security interest in money or instruments (other than certificated securities or instruments which constitute part of chattel paper) can be perfected only by the secured party's taking possession, except as provided in subsections (4) and (5) of this section and subsections (2) and (3) of Section 9—306 on proceeds.

(2) During the period that goods are in the possession of the issuer of a negotiable document therefor, a security interest in the goods is perfected by perfecting a security interest in the document, and any security interest in the goods otherwise perfected during such period is subject thereto.

(3) A security interest in goods in the possession of a bailee other than one who has issued a negotiable document therefor is perfected by issuance of a document in the name of the secured party or by the bailee's receipt of notification of the secured party's interest or by filing as to the goods.

(4) A security interest in instruments (other than certificated securities) or negotiable documents is perfected without filing or the taking of possession for a period of 21 days from the time it attaches to the extent that it arises for new value given under a written security agreement.

(5) A security interest remains perfected for a period of 21 days without filing where a secured party having a perfected security interest in an instrument (other than a certificated security), a negotiable document or goods in possession of a bailee other than one who has issued a negotiable document therefor

    (a) makes available to the debtor the goods or documents representing the goods for the purpose of ultimate sale or exchange or for the purpose of loading, unloading, storing, shipping, transshipping, manufacturing, processing or otherwise dealing with them in a manner preliminary to their sale or exchange, but priority between conflicting security interests in the goods is subject to subsection (3) of Section 9—312; or

    (b) delivers the instrument to the debtor for the purpose of ultimate sale or exchange or of presentation, collection, renewal or registration of transfer.

(6) After the 21 day period in subsections (4) and (5), perfection depends upon compliance with applicable provisions of this Article.

§ 9—305. When Possession by Secured Party Perfects Security Interest Without Filing

A security interest in letters of credit and advices of credit (subsection (2) (a) of Section 5—116), goods, instruments (other than certificated securities), money, negotiable documents or chattel paper may be perfected by the secured party's taking possession of the collateral. If such collateral other than goods covered by a negotiable document is held by a bailee, the secured party is deemed to have possession from the time the bailee receives notification of the secured party's interest. A security interest is perfected by possession from the time possession is taken without relation back and continues only so long as possession is retained, unless otherwise specified in this Article. The security interest may be otherwise perfected as provided in this Article before or after the period of possession by the secured party.

§ 9—306. "Proceeds"; Secured Party's Rights on Disposition of Collateral

(1) "Proceeds" includes whatever is received upon the sale, exchange, collection or other disposition of collateral or proceeds. Insurance payable by reason of loss or damage to the collateral is proceeds, except to the extent that it is payable to a person other than a party to the security agreement. Money, checks, deposit accounts, and the like are "cash proceeds." All other proceeds are "noncash proceeds."

(2) Except where this Article otherwise provides, a security interest continues in collateral notwithstanding sale, exchange or other disposition thereof unless the disposition was authorized by the secured party in the security agreement or otherwise, and also continues in any identifiable proceeds including collections received by the debtor.

(3) The security interest in proceeds is a continuously perfected security interest if the interest in the original collateral was perfected, but it ceases to be a perfected security interest and becomes unperfected ten days after receipt of the proceeds by the debtor unless

    (a) a filed financing statement covers the original collateral and the proceeds are collateral in which a security interest may be perfected by filing in the office or offices where the financing statement has been filed and, if the proceeds are acquired with cash proceeds, the description of collateral in the financing statement indicates the types of property constituting the proceeds; or

    (b) a filed financing statement covers the original collateral and the proceeds are identifiable cash proceeds; or

    (c) the security interest in the proceeds is perfected before the expiration of the ten day period.

Except as provided in this section, a security interest in proceeds can be perfected only by the methods or under the circumstances permitted in this Article for original collateral of the same type.

(4) In the event of insolvency proceedings instituted by or against a debtor, a secured party with a perfected security interest in proceeds has a perfected security interest only in the following proceeds:

    (a) in identifiable noncash proceeds and in separate deposit accounts containing only proceeds;

    (b) in identifiable cash proceeds in the form of money which is neither commingled with other money nor deposited in a deposit account prior to the insolvency proceedings;

    (c) in identifiable cash proceeds in the form of checks and the like which are not deposited in a deposit account prior to the insolvency proceedings; and

    (d) in all cash and deposit accounts of the debtor in which proceeds have been commingled with other funds, but the perfected security interest under this paragraph (d) is

(i) subject to any right to setoff; and

(ii) limited to an amount not greater than the amount of any cash proceeds received by the debtor within ten days before the institution of the insolvency proceedings, less the sum of (I) the payments to the secured party on account of cash proceeds received by the debtor during such period and (II) the cash proceeds received by the debtor during such period to which the secured party is entitled under paragraphs (a) through (c) of this subsection (4).

(5) If a sale of goods results in an account or chattel paper which is transferred by the seller to a secured party and if the goods are returned to or are repossessed by the seller or the secured party, the following rules determine priorities:

(a) If the goods were collateral at the time of sale, for an indebtedness of the seller which is still unpaid, the original security interest attaches again to the goods and continues as a perfected security interest if it was perfected at the time when the goods were sold. If the security interest was originally perfected by a filing which is still effective, nothing further is required to continue the perfected status; in any other case, the secured party must take possession of the returned or repossessed goods or must file.

(b) An unpaid transferee of the chattel paper has a security interest in the goods against the transferor. Such security interest is prior to a security interest asserted under paragraph (a) to the extent that the transferee of the chattel paper was entitled to priority under Section 9—308.

(c) An unpaid transferee of the account has a security interest in the goods against the transferor. Such security interest is subordinate to a security interest asserted under paragraph (a).

(d) A security interest of an unpaid transferee asserted under paragraph (b) or (c) must be perfected for protection against creditors of the transferor and purchasers of the returned or repossessed goods.

§ 9—307.   Protection of Buyers of Goods

(1) A buyer in ordinary course of business (subsection (9) of Section 1—201), other than a person buying farm products from a person engaged in farming operations, takes free of a security interest created by his seller even though the security interest is perfected and even though the buyer knows of its existence.

(2) In the case of consumer goods, a buyer takes free of a security interest even though perfected if he buys without knowledge of the security interest, for value and for his own personal, family or household purposes unless prior to the purchase the secured party has filed a financing statement covering such goods.

(3) A buyer other than a buyer in ordinary course of business (subsection (1) of this section) takes free of a security interest to the extent that it secures future advances made after the secured party acquires knowledge of the purchase, or more than 45 days after the purchase, whichever first occurs, unless made pursuant to a commitment entered into without knowledge of the purchase and before the expiration of the 45 day period.

§ 9—308.   Purchase of Chattel Paper and Instruments

A purchaser of chattel paper or an instrument who gives new value and takes possession of it in the ordinary course of his business has priority over a security interest in the chattel paper or instrument

(a) which is perfected under Section 9—304 (permissive filing and temporary perfection) or under Section 9—306 (perfection as to proceeds) if he acts without knowledge that the specific paper or instrument is subject to a security interest; or

(b) which is claimed merely as proceeds of inventory subject to a security interest (Section 9—306) even though he knows that the specific paper or instrument is subject to the security interest.

§ 9—309.   Protection of Purchasers of Instruments, Documents and Securities

Nothing in this Article limits the rights of a holder in due course of a negotiable instrument (Section 3—302) or a holder to whom a negotiable document of title has been duly negotiated (Section 7—501) or a bona fide purchaser of a security (Section 8—302), and such holders or purchasers take priority over an earlier security interest even though perfected. Filing under this Article does not constitute notice of the security interest to such holders or purchasers.

§ 9—310.   Priority of Certain Liens Arising by Operation of Law

When a person in the ordinary course of his business furnishes services or materials with respect to goods subject to a security interest, a lien upon goods in the possession of such person given by statute or rule of law for such materials or services takes priority over a perfected security interest unless the lien is statutory and the statute expressly provides otherwise.

§ 9—311.   Alienability of Debtor's Rights: Judicial Process

The debtor's rights in collateral may be voluntarily or involuntarily transferred (by way of sale, creation of a security interest, attachment, levy, garnishment or other judicial process) notwithstanding a provision in the security agreement prohibiting any transfer or making the transfer constitute a default.

§ 9—312. Priorities Among Conflicting Security Interests in the Same Collateral

(1) The rules of priority stated in other sections of this Part and in the following sections shall govern when applicable: Section 4—208 with respect to the security interests of collecting banks in items being collected, accompanying documents and proceeds; Section 9—103 on security interests related to other jurisdictions; Section 9—114 on consignments.

(2) A perfected security interest in crops for new value given to enable the debtor to produce the crops during the production season, and given not more than three months before the crops become growing crops by planting or otherwise, takes priority over an earlier perfected security interest to the extent that such earlier interest secures obligations due more than six months before the crops become growing crops by planting or otherwise, even though the person giving new value had knowledge of the earlier security interest.

(3) A perfected purchase money security interest in inventory has priority over a conflicting security interest in the same inventory and also has priority in identifiable cash proceeds received on or before the delivery of the inventory to a buyer if

   (a) the purchase money security interest is perfected at the time the debtor receives possession of the inventory; and
   (b) the purchase money secured party gives notification in writing to the holder of the conflicting security interest if the holder had filed a financing statement covering the same types of inventory (i) before the date of the filing made by the purchase money secured party, or (ii) before the beginning of the 21 day period where the purchase money security interest is temporarily perfected without filing or possession (subsection (5) of Section 9—304); and
   (c) the holder of the conflicting security interest receives the notification within five years before the debtor receives possession of the inventory; and
   (d) the notification states that the person giving the notice has or expects to acquire a purchase money security interest in inventory of the debtor, describing such inventory by item or type.

(4) A purchase money security interest in collateral other than inventory has priority over a conflicting security interest in the same collateral or its proceeds if the purchase money security interest is perfected at the time the debtor receives possession of the collateral or within ten days thereafter.

(5) In all cases not governed by other rules stated in this section (including cases of purchase money security interests which do not qualify for the special priorities set forth in subsections (3) and (4) of this sec-tion), priority between conflicting security interests in the same collateral shall be determined according to the following rules:

   (a) Conflicting security interests rank according to priority in time of filing or perfection. Priority dates from the time a filing is first made covering the collateral or the time the security interest is first perfected, whichever is earlier, provided that there is no period thereafter when there is neither filing nor perfection.
   (b) So long as conflicting security interests are unperfected, the first to attach has priority.

(6) For the purposes of subsection (5), a date of filing or perfection as to collateral is also a date of filing or perfection as to proceeds.

(7) If future advances are made while a security interest is perfected by filing or the taking of possession, or under Section 8—321 on securities, the security interest has the same priority for the purposes of subsection (5) with respect to the future advances as it does with respect to the first advance. If a commitment is made before or while the security interest is so perfected, the security interest has the same priority with respect to advances made pursuant thereto. In other cases, a perfected security interest has priority from the date the advance is made.

§ 9—313. Priority of Security Interests in Fixtures

(1) In this section and in the provisions of Part 4 of this Article referring to fixture filing, unless the context otherwise requires

   (a) goods are "fixtures" when they become so related to particular real estate that an interest in them arises under a real estate law
   (b) a "fixture filing" is the filing in the office where a mortgage on the real estate would be filed or recorded of a financing statement covering goods which are or are to become fixtures and conforming to the requirements of subsection (5) of Section 9—402
   (c) a mortgage is a "construction mortgage" to the extent that it secures an obligation incurred for the construction of an improvement on land including the acquisition cost of the land, if the recorded writing so indicates.

(2) A security interest under this Article may be created in goods which are fixtures or may continue in goods which become fixtures, but no security interest exists under this Article in ordinary building materials incorporated into an improvement on land.

(3) This Article does not prevent creation of an encumbrance upon fixtures pursuant to real estate law.

(4) A perfected security interest in fixtures has

priority over the conflicting interest of an encumbrancer or owner of the real estate where

> (a) the security interest is a purchase money security interest, the interest of the encumbrancer or owner arises before the goods become fixtures, the security interest is perfected by a fixture filing before the goods become fixtures or within ten days thereafter, and the debtor has an interest of record in the real estate or is in possession of the real estate; or
>
> (b) the security interest is perfected by a fixture filing before the interest of the encumbrancer or owner is of record, the security interest has priority over any conflicting interest of a predecessor in title of the encumbrancer or owner, and the debtor has an interest of record in the real estate or is in possession of the real estate; or
>
> (c) the fixtures are readily removable factory or office machines or readily removable replacements of domestic appliances which are consumer goods, and before the goods become fixtures the security interest is perfected by any method permitted by this Article; or
>
> (d) the conflicting interest is a lien on the real estate obtained by legal or equitable proceedings after the security interest was perfected by any method permitted by this Article.

(5) A security interest in fixtures, whether or not perfected, has priority over the conflicting interest of an encumbrancer or owner of the real estate where

> (a) the encumbrancer or owner has consented in writing to the security interest or has disclaimed an interest in the goods as fixtures; or
>
> (b) the debtor has a right to remove the goods as against the encumbrancer or owner. If the debtor's right terminates, the priority of the security interest continues for a reasonable time.

(6) Notwithstanding paragraph (a) of subsection (4) but otherwise subject to subsections (4) and (5), a security interest in fixtures is subordinate to a construction mortgage recorded before the goods become fixtures if the goods become fixtures before the completion of the construction. To the extent that it is given to refinance a construction mortgage, a mortgage has this priority to the same extent as the construction mortgage.

(7) In cases not within the preceding subsections, a security interest in fixtures is subordinate to the conflicting interest of an encumbrancer or owner of the related real estate who is not the debtor.

(8) When the secured party has priority over all owners and encumbrancers of the real estate, he may, on default, subject to the provisions of Part 5, remove his collateral from the real estate but he must reimburse any encumbrancer or owner of the real estate who is not the debtor, and who has not otherwise agreed, for the cost of repair of any physical injury, but not for any diminution in value of the real estate caused by the absence of the goods removed or by any necessity of replacing them. A person entitled to reimbursement may refuse permission to remove until the secured party gives adequate security for the performance of this obligation.

§ 9—314. Accessions

(1) A security interest in goods which attaches before they are installed in or affixed to other goods takes priority as to the goods installed or affixed (called in this section "accessions") over the claims of all persons to the whole except as stated in subsection (3) and subject to Section 9—315(1).

(2) A security interest which attaches to goods after they become part of a whole is valid against all persons subsequently acquiring interests in the whole except as stated in subsection (3) but is invalid against any person with an interest in the whole at the time the security interest attaches to the goods who has not in writing consented to the security interest or disclaimed an interest in the goods as part of the whole.

(3) The security interests described in subsections (1) and (2) do not take priority over

> (a) a subsequent purchaser for value of any interest in the whole; or
>
> (b) a creditor with a lien on the whole subsequently obtained by judicial proceedings; or
>
> (c) a creditor with a prior perfected security interest in the whole to the extent that he makes subsequent advances.

If in the subsequent purchase is made, the lien by judicial proceedings obtained or the subsequent advance under the prior perfected security interest is made or contracted for without knowledge of the security interest and before it is perfected. A purchaser of the whole at a foreclosure sale other than the holder of a perfected security interest purchasing at his own foreclosure sale is a subsequent purchaser within this section.

(4) When under subsections (1) or (2) and (3), a secured party has an interest in accessions which has priority over the claims of all persons who have interests in the whole, he may, on default, subject to the provisions of Part 5, remove his collateral from the whole but he must reimburse any encumbrancer or owner of the whole who is not the debtor and who has not otherwise agreed for the cost of repair of any physical injury but not for any diminution in value of the whole caused by the absence of the goods removed or by any necessity for replacing them. A person entitled to reimbursement may refuse permission to remove

until the secured party gives adequate security for the performance of this obligation.

§ 9—315. Priority When Goods Are Commingled or Processed

(1) If a security interest in goods was perfected and subsequently the goods or a part thereof have become part of a product or mass, the security interest continues in the product or mass if

(a) the goods are so manufactured, processed, assembled or commingled that their identity is lost in the product or mass; or

(b) a financing statement covering the original goods also covers the product into which the goods have been manufactured, processed or assembled.

In a case to which paragraph (b) applies, no separate security interest in that part of the original goods which has been manufactured, processed or assembled into the product may be claimed under Section 9—314.

(2) When under subsection (1) more than one security interest attaches to the product or mass, they rank equally according to the ratio that the cost of the goods to which each interest originally attached bears to the cost of the total product or mass.

§ 9—316. Priority Subject to Subordination

Nothing in this Article prevents subordination by agreement by any person entitled to priority.

§ 9—317. Secured Party Not Obligated on Contract of Debtor

The mere existence of a security interest or authority given to the debtor to dispose of or use collateral does not impose contract or tort liability upon the secured party for the debtor's acts or omissions.

§ 9—318. Defenses Against Assignee; Modification of Contract After Notification of Assignment; Term Prohibiting Assignment Ineffective; Identification and Proof of Assignment

(1) Unless an account debtor has made an enforceable agreement not to assert defenses or claims arising out of a sale as provided in Section 9—206, the rights of an assignee are subject to

(a) all the terms of the contract between the account debtor and assignor and any defense or claim arising therefrom; and

(b) any other defense or claim of the account debtor against the assignor which accrues before the account debtor receives notification of the assignment.

(2) So far as the right to payment or a part thereof under an assigned contract has not been fully earned by performance, and notwithstanding notification of the assignment, any modification of or substitution for the contract made in good faith and in accordance with reasonable commercial standards is effective against an assignee unless the account debtor has otherwise agreed, but the assignee acquires corresponding rights under the modified or substituted contract. The assignment may provide that such modification or substitution is a breach by the assignor.

(3) The account debtor is authorized to pay the assignor until the account debtor receives notification that the amount due or to become due has been assigned and that payment is to be made to the assignee. A notification which does not reasonably identify the rights assigned is ineffective. If requested by the account debtor, the assignee must seasonably furnish reasonable proof that the assignment has been made; and unless he does so, the account debtor may pay the assignor.

(4) A term in any contract between an account debtor and an assignor is ineffective if it prohibits assignment of an account or prohibits creation of a security interest in a general intangible for money due or to become due or requires the account debtor's consent to such assignment or security interest.

Part 4

Filing

§ 9—401. Place of Filing; Erroneous Filing; Removal of Collateral

First Alternative Subsection (1)

(1) The proper place to file in order to perfect a security interest is as follows:

(a) when the collateral is timber to be cut or is minerals or the like (including oil and gas) or accounts subject to subsection (5) of Section 9—103, or when the financing statement is filed as a fixture filing (Section 9—313) and the collateral is goods which are or are to become fixtures, then in the office where a mortgage on the real estate would be filed or recorded;

(b) in all other cases, in the office of the [Secretary of State].

Second Alternative Subsection (1)

(1) The proper place to file in order to perfect a security interest is as follows:

(a) when the collateral is equipment used in farming operations, or farm products, or accounts or general intangibles arising from or relating to the sale of farm products by a farmer, or consumer goods, then in the office of the .... in the county of the debtor's residence or if the debtor is not a resident of this state then in the office of the .... in the county where the goods are kept, and in addition when the collateral is crops growing or to be grown in the office of the .... in the county where the land is located;

(b) when the collateral is timber to be cut or is minerals or the like (including oil and gas) or accounts subject to subsection (5) of Section 9—103, or when the financing statement is filed as a fixture filing (Section 9—313) and the collateral is goods which are or are to become fixtures, then in the office where a mortgage on the real estate would be filed or recorded;

(c) in all other cases, in the office of the [Secretary of State].

Third Alternative Subsection (1)

(1) The proper place to file in order to perfect a security interest is as follows:

(a) when the collateral is equipment used in farming operations, or farm products, or accounts or general intangibles arising from or relating to the sale of farm products by a farmer, or consumer goods, then in the office of the . . . . in the county of the debtor's residence or if the debtor is not a resident of this state then in the office of the . . . . in the county where the goods are kept, and in addition when the collateral is crops growing or to be grown in the office of the . . . . in the county where the land is located;

(b) when the collateral is timber to be cut or is minerals or the like (including oil and gas) or accounts subject to subsection (5) of Section 9—103, or when the financing statement is filed as a fixture filing (Section 9—313) and the collateral is goods which are or are to become fixtures, then in the office where a mortgage on the real estate would be filed or recorded;

(c) in all other cases, in the office of the [Secretary of State] and in addition, if the debtor has a place of business in only one county of this state, also in the office of . . . . of such county, or, if the debtor has no place of business in this state, but resides in the state, also in the office of . . . . of the county in which he resides.

Note: *One of the three alternatives should be selected as subsection (1).*

(2) A filing which is made in good faith in an improper place or not in all of the places required by this section is nevertheless effective with regard to any collateral as to which the filing complied with the requirements of this Article and is also effective with regard to collateral covered by the financing statement against any person who has knowledge of the contents of such financing statement.

(3) A filing which is made in the proper place in this state continues effective even though the debtor's

residence or place of business or the location of the collateral or its use, whichever controlled the original filing, is thereafter changed.

Alternative Subsection (3)

[(3) A filing which is made in the proper county continues effective for four months after a change to another county of the debtor's residence or place of business or the location of the collateral, whichever controlled the original filing. It becomes ineffective thereafter unless a copy of the financing statement signed by the secured party is filed in the new county within said period. The security interest may also be perfected in the new county after the expiration of the four-month period; in such case, perfection dates from the time of perfection in the new county. A change in the use of the collateral does not impair the effectiveness of the original filing.]

(4) The rules stated in Section 9—103 determine whether filing is necessary in this state.

(5) Notwithstanding the preceding subsections, and subject to subsection (3) of Section 9–302, the proper place to file in order to perfect a security interest in collateral, including fixtures, of a transmitting utility is the office of the [Secretary of State]. This filing constitutes a fixture filing (Section 9—313) as to the collateral described therein which is or is to become fixtures.

(6) For the purposes of this section, the residence of an organization is its place of business if it has one or its chief executive office if it has more than one place of business.

Note: *Subsection (6) should be used only if the state chooses the Second or Third Alternative Subsection (1).*

§ 9—402. Formal Requisites of Financing Statement; Amendments; Mortgage as Financing Statement

(1) A financing statement is sufficient if it gives the names of the debtor and the secured party, is signed by the debtor, gives an address of the secured party from which information concerning the security interest may be obtained, gives a mailing address of the debtor and contains a statement indicating the types, or describing the items, of collateral. A financing statement may be filed before a security agreement is made or a security interest otherwise attaches. When the financing statement covers crops growing or to be grown, the statement must also contain a description of the real estate concerned. When the financing statement covers timber to be cut or covers minerals or the like (including oil and gas) or accounts subject to subsection (5) of Section 9—103, or when the financing statement is filed as a fixture filing (Section 9—313) and the collateral is goods which are or are to become fixtures, the statement must also comply with subsection (5). A copy of the security agreement is sufficient as a financing statement if it contains the above information and is signed by the debtor. A car-

bon, photographic or other reproduction of a security agreement or a financing statement is sufficient as a financing statement if the security agreement so provides or if the original has been filed in this state.

(2) A financing statement which otherwise complies with subsection (1) is sufficient when it is signed by the secured party instead of the debtor if it is filed to perfect a security interest in

  (a) collateral already subject to a security interest in another jurisdiction when it is brought into this state, or when the debtor's location is changed to this state. Such a financing statement must state that the collateral was brought into this state or that the debtor's location was changed to this state under such circumstances; or

  (b) proceeds under Section 9—306 if the security interest in the original collateral was perfected. Such a financing statement must describe the original collateral; or

  (c) collateral as to which the filing has lapsed; or

  (d) collateral acquired after a change of name, identity or corporate structure of the debtor (subsection (7)).

(3) A form substantially as follows is sufficient to comply with subsection (1):

Name of debtor (or assignor) . . . .
Address . . . .
Name of secured party (or assignee). . . . . . .
Address . . . .

1. This financing statement covers the following types (or items) of property:
    (Describe). . . . .
2. (If collateral is crops) The above described crops are growing or are to be grown on:
    (Describe Real Estate) . . . .
3. (If applicable) The above goods are to become fixtures on*
    (Describe Real Estate) . . . .
    and this financing statement is to be filed [for record] in the real estate records. (If the debtor does not have an interest of record) The name of a record owner is. . . . .
4. (If products of collateral are claimed) Products of the collateral are also covered.

| (use whichever is applicable) | . . . . Signature of Debtor (or Assignor) |
| | . . . . Signature of Secured Party (or Assignee) |

---

* Where appropriate substitute either "The above timber is standing on . . . ." or "The above minerals or the like (including oil and gas) or accounts will be financed at the wellhead or minehead of the well or mine located on . . . ."

(4) A financing statement may be amended by filing a writing signed by both the debtor and the secured party. An amendment does not extend the period of effectiveness of a financing statement. If any amendment adds collateral, it is effective as to the added collateral only from the filing date of the amendment. In this Article, unless the context otherwise requires, the term "financing statement" means the original financing statement and any amendments.

(5) A financing statement covering timber to be cut or covering minerals or the like (including oil and gas) or accounts subject to subsection (5) of Section 9—103, or a financing statement filed as a fixture filing (Section 9—313) where the debtor is not a transmitting utility, must show that it covers this type of collateral, must recite that it is to be filed [for record] in the real estate records, and the financing statement must contain a description of the real estate [sufficient if it were contained in a mortgage of the real estate to give constructive notice of the mortgage under the law of this state]. If the debtor does not have an interest of record in the real estate, the financing statement must show the name of a record owner.

(6) A mortgage is effective as a financing statement filed as a fixture filing from the date of its recording if

  (a) the goods are described in the mortgage by item or type; and

  (b) the goods are or are to become fixtures related to the real estate described in the mortgage; and

  (c) the mortgage complies with the requirements for a financing statement in this section other than a recital that it is to be filed in the real estate records; and

  (d) the mortgage is duly recorded.

No fee with reference to the financing statement is required other than the regular recording and satisfaction fees with respect to the mortgage.

(7) A financing statement sufficiently shows the name of the debtor if it gives the individual, partnership or corporate name of the debtor, whether or not it adds other trade names or names of partners. Where the debtor so changes his name or, in the case of an organization, its name, identity or corporate structure that a filed financing statement becomes seriously misleading, the filing is not effective to perfect a security interest in collateral acquired by the debtor more than four months after the change, unless a new appropriate financing statement is filed before the expiration of that time. A filed financing statement remains effective with respect to collateral transferred by the debtor even though the secured party knows of or consents to the transfer.

(8) A financing statement substantially complying with the requirements of this section is effective even though it contains minor errors which are not seriously misleading.

Note: *Language in brackets is optional.*

Note: *Where the state has any special recording system for real estate other than the usual grantor-grantee index (as, for instance, a tract system or a title registration or Torrens system) local adaptations of subsection (5) and Section 9—403(7) may be necessary. See Mass. Gen. Laws Chapter 106, Section 9—409.*

§ 9—403. What Constitutes Filing; Duration of Filing; Effect of Lapsed Filing; Duties of Filing Officer

(1) Presentation for filing of a financing statement and tender of the filing fee or acceptance of the statement by the filing officer constitutes filing under this Article.

(2) Except as provided in subsection (6), a filed financing statement is effective for a period of five years from the date of filing. The effectiveness of a filed financing statement lapses on the expiration of the five-year period unless a continuation statement is filed prior to the lapse. If a security interest perfected by filing exists at the time insolvency proceedings are commenced by or against the debtor, the security interest remains perfected until termination of the insolvency proceedings and thereafter for a period of sixty days or until expiration of the five-year period, whichever occurs later. Upon lapse, the security interest becomes unperfected, unless it is perfected without filing. If the security interest becomes unperfected upon lapse, it is deemed to have been unperfected as against a person who became a purchaser or lien creditor before lapse.

(3) A continuation statement may be filed by the secured party within six months prior to the expiration of the five year period specified in subsection (2). Any such continuation statement must be signed by the secured party, identify the original statement by file number and state that the original statement is still effective. A continuation statement signed by a person other than the secured party of record must be accompanied by a separate written statement of assignment signed by the secured party of record and complying with subsection (2) of Section 9—405, including payment of the required fee. Upon timely filing of the continuation statement, the effectiveness of the original statement is continued for five years after the last date to which the filing was effective whereupon it lapses in the same manner as provided in subsection (2) unless another continuation statement is filed prior to such lapse. Succeeding continuation statements may be filed in the same manner to continue the effectiveness of the original statement. Unless a statute on disposition of public records provides otherwise, the filing officer may remove a lapsed statement from the files and destroy it immediately if he has retained a microfilm or other photographic record, or in other cases after one year after the lapse. The filing officer shall so arrange matters by physical annexation of

financing statements to continuation statements or other related filings, or by other means, that if he physically destroys the financing statements of a period more than five years past, those which have been continued by a continuation statement or which are still effective under subsection (6) shall be retained.

(4) Except as provided in subsection (7), a filing officer shall mark each statement with a file number and with the date and hour of filing and shall hold the statement or a microfilm or other photographic copy thereof for public inspection. In addition, the filing officer shall index the statement according to the name of the debtor and shall note in the index the file number and the address of the debtor given in the statement.

(5) The uniform fee for filing and indexing and for stamping a copy furnished by the secured party to show the date and place of filing for an original financing statement or for a continuation statement shall be $........ if the statement is in the standard form prescribed by the [Secretary of State] and otherwise shall be $........, plus in each case, if the financing statement is subject to subsection (5) of Section 9—402, $........ The uniform fee for each name more than one required to be indexed shall be $....... The secured party may at his option show a trade name for any person and an extra uniform indexing fee of $....... shall be paid with respect thereto.

(6) If the debtor is a transmitting utility (subsection (5) of Section 9—401) and a filed financing statement so states, it is effective until a termination statement is filed. A real estate mortgage which is effective as a fixture filing under subsection (6) of Section 9—402 remains effective as a fixture filing until the mortgage is released or satisfied of record or its effectiveness otherwise terminates as to the real estate.

(7) When a financing statement covers timber to be cut or covers minerals or the like (including oil and gas) or accounts subject to subsection (5) of Section 9—103, or is filed as a fixture filing, [it shall be filed for record and] the filing officer shall index it under the names of the debtor and any owner of record shown on the financing statement in the same fashion as if they were the mortgagors in a mortgage of the real estate described, and, to the extent that the law of this state provides for indexing of mortgages under the name of the mortgagee, under the name of the secured party as if he were the mortgagee thereunder, or where indexing is by description in the same fashion as if the financing statement were a mortgage of the real estate described.

Note: *In states in which writings will not appear in the real estate records and indices unless actually recorded, the bracketed language in subsection (7) should be used.*

§ 9—404. Termination Statement

If a financing statement covering consumer goods is filed on or after.............., then within one month or within ten days following written demand by the debtor after there is no outstanding secured obligation and no commitment to make advances, incur obligations or otherwise give value, the secured party must file with each filing officer with whom the financing statement was filed, a termination statement to the effect that he no longer claims a security interest under the financing statement, which shall be identified by file number. In other cases whenever there is no outstanding secured obligation and no commitment to make advances, incur obligations or otherwise give value, the secured party must on written demand by the debtor send the debtor, for each filing officer with whom the financing statement was filed, a termination statement to the effect that he no longer claims a security interest under the financing statement, which shall be identified by file number. A termination statement signed by a person other than the secured party of record must be accompanied by a separate written statement of assignment signed by the secured party of record complying with subsection (2) of Section 9—405, including payment of the required fee. If the affected secured party fails to file such a termination statement as required by this subsection, or to send such a termination statement within ten days after proper demand therefor, he shall be liable to the debtor for one hundred dollars, and in addition for any loss caused to the debtor by such failure.

(2) On presentation to the filing officer of such a termination statement, he must note it in the index. If he has received the termination statement in duplicate, he shall return one copy of the termination statement to the secured party stamped to show the time of receipt thereof. If the filing officer has a microfilm or other photographic record of the financing statement, and of any related continuation statement, statement of assignment and statement of release, he may remove the originals from the files at any time after receipt of the termination statement, or if he has no such record, he may remove them from the files at any time after one year after receipt of the termination statement.

(3) If the termination statement is in the standard form prescribed by the [Secretary of State], the uniform fee for filing and indexing the termination statement shall be $......, and otherwise shall be $........, plus in each case an additional fee of $....... for each name more than one against which the termination statement is required to be indexed.

Note: *The date to be inserted should be the effective date of the revised Article 9.*

§ 9—405.   Assignment of Security Interest; Duties of Filing Officer; Fees

(1) A financing statement may disclose an assignment of a security interest in the collateral described in the financing statement by indication in the financing statement of the name and address of the assignee or by an assignment itself or a copy thereof on the face or back of the statement. On presentation to the filing officer of such a financing statement the filing officer shall mark the same as provided in Section 9—403(4). The uniform fee for filing, indexing and furnishing filing data for a financing statement so indicating an assignment shall be $....... if the statement is in the standard form prescribed by the [Secretary of State] and otherwise shall be $........., plus in each case an additional fee of $....... for each name more than one against which the financing statement is required to be indexed.

(2) A secured party may assign of record all or part of his rights under a financing statement by the filing in the place where the original financing statement was filed of a separate written statement of assignment signed by the secured party of record and setting forth the name of the secured party of record and the debtor, the file number and the date of filing of the financing statement and the name and address of the assignee and containing a description of the collateral assigned. A copy of the assignment is sufficient as a separate statement if it complies with the preceding sentence. On presentation to the filing officer of such a separate statement, the filing officer shall mark such separate statement with the date and hour of the filing. He shall note the assignment on the index of the financing statement, or in the case of a fixture filing, or a filing covering timber to be cut, or covering minerals or the like (including oil and gas) or accounts subject to subsection (5) of Section 9—103, he shall index the assignment under the name of the assignor as grantor and, to the extent that the law of this state provides for indexing the assignment of a mortgage under the name of the assignee, he shall index the assignment of the financing statement under the name of the assignee. The uniform fee for filing, indexing and furnishing filing data about such a separate statement of assignment shall be $....... if the statement is in the standard form prescribed by the [Secretary of State] and otherwise shall be $........, plus in each case an additional fee of $....... for each name more than one against which the statement of assignment is required to be indexed. Notwithstanding the provisions of this subsection, an assignment of record of a security interest in a fixture contained in a mortgage effective as a fixture filing (subsection (6) of Section 9—402) may be made only by an assignment of the mortgage in the manner provided by the law of this state other than this Act.

(3) After the disclosure or filing of an assignment under this section, the assignee is the secured party of record.

§ 9—406.   Release of Collateral; Duties of Filing Officer; Fees

A secured party of record may by his signed statement release all or a part of any collateral described in a filed financing statement. The statement of release is sufficient if it contains a description of the collateral being released, the name and address of the debtor, the name and address of the secured party, and the file number of the financing statement. A statement of release signed by a person other than the secured party of record must be accompanied by a separate written statement of assignment signed by the secured party of record and complying with subsection (2) of Section 9—405, including payment of the required fee. Upon presentation of such a statement of release to the filing officer, he shall mark the statement with the hour and date of filing and shall note the same upon the margin of the index of the filing of the financing statement. The uniform fee for filing and noting such a statement of release shall be $. . . . . . . if the statement is in the standard form prescribed by the [Secretary of State] and otherwise shall be $. . . . . . . , plus in each case an additional fee of $. . . . . . . for each name more than one against which the statement of release is required to be indexed.

[§ 9—407. Information From Filing Officer]

[(1) If the person filing any financing statement, termination statement, statement of assignment, or statement of release, furnishes the filing officer a copy thereof, the filing officer shall upon request note upon the copy the file number and date and hour of the filing of the original and deliver or send the copy to such person.]

[(2) Upon request of any person, the filing officer shall issue his certificate showing whether there is on file on the date and hour stated therein, any presently effective financing statement naming a particular debtor and any statement of assignment thereof and if there is, giving the date and hour of filing of each such statement and the names and addresses of each secured party therein. The uniform fee for such a certificate shall be $. . . . . . . if the request for the certificate is in the standard form prescribed by the [Secretary of State] and otherwise shall be $. . . . . . . Upon request the filing officer shall furnish a copy of any filed financing statement or statement of assignment for a uniform fee of $. . . . . . . per page.]

Note: *This section is proposed as an optional provision to require filing officers to furnish certificates. Local law and practices should be consulted with regard to the advisability of adoption.*

§ 9—408. Financing Statements Covering Consigned or Leased Goods

A consignor or lessor of goods may file a financing statement using the terms "consignor," "consignee," "lessor," "lessee" or the like instead of the terms specified in Section 9—402. The provisions of this Part shall apply as appropriate to such a financing statement but its filing shall not of itself be a factor in determining whether or not the consignment or lease is intended as security (Section 1—201(37)). However, if

it is determined for other reasons that the consignment or lease is so intended, a security interest of the consignor or lessor which attaches to the consigned or leased goods is perfected by such filing.

Part 5

Default

§ 9—501. Default; Procedure When Security Agreement Covers Both Real and Personal Property

(1) When a debtor is in default under a security agreement, a secured party has the rights and remedies provided in this Part and, except as limited by subsection (3), those provided in the security agreement. He may reduce his claim to judgment, foreclose or otherwise enforce the security interest by any available judicial procedure. If the collateral is documents, the secured party may proceed either as to the documents or as to the goods covered thereby. A secured party in possession has the rights, remedies and duties provided in Section 9—207. The rights and remedies referred to in this subsection are cumulative.

(2) After default, the debtor has the rights and remedies provided in this Part, those provided in the security agreement and those provided in Section 9—207.

(3) To the extent that they give rights to the debtor and impose duties on the secured party, the rules stated in the subsections referred to below may not be waived or varied except as provided with respect to compulsory disposition of collateral (subsection (3) of Section 9—504 and Section 9—505) and with respect to redemption of collateral (Section 9—506) but the parties may by agreement determine the standards by which the fulfillment of these rights and duties is to be measured if such standards are not manifestly unreasonable:

    (a) subsection (2) of Section 9—502 and subsection (2) of Section 9—504 insofar as they require accounting for surplus proceeds of collateral;

    (b) subsection (3) of Section 9—504 and subsection (1) of Section 9—505 which deal with disposition of collateral;

    (c) subsection (2) of Section 9—505 which deals with acceptance of collateral as discharge of obligation;

    (d) Section 9—506 which deals with redemption of collateral; and

    (e) subsection (1) of Section 9—507 which deals with the secured party's liability for failure to comply with this Part.

(4) If the security agreement covers both real and personal property, the secured party may proceed under this Part as to the personal property or he may proceed as to both the real and the personal property in

accordance with his rights and remedies in respect of the real property, in which case the provisions of this Part do not apply.

(5) When a secured party has reduced his claim to judgment, the lien of any levy which may be made upon his collateral by virture of any execution based upon the judgment shall relate back to the date of the perfection of the security interest in such collateral. A judicial sale, pursuant to such execution, is a foreclosure of the security interest by judicial procedure within the meaning of this section, and the secured party may purchase at the sale and thereafter hold the collateral free of any other requirements of this Article.

§ 9—502. Collection Rights of Secured Party

(1) When so agreed, and in any event on default, the secured party is entitled to notify an account debtor or the obligor on an instrument to make payment to him whether or not the assignor was theretofore making collections on the collateral, and also to take control of any proceeds to which he is entitled under Section 9—306.

(2) A secured party who by agreement is entitled to charge back uncollected collateral or otherwise to full or limited recourse against the debtor and who undertakes to collect from the account debtors or obligors must proceed in a commercially reasonable manner and may deduct his reasonable expenses of realization from the collections. If the security agreement secures an indebtedness, the secured party must account to the debtor for any surplus, and unless otherwise agreed, the debtor is liable for any deficiency. But, if the underlying transaction was a sale of accounts or chattel paper, the debtor is entitled to any surplus or is liable for any deficiency only if the security agreement so provides.

§ 9—503. Secured Party's Right to Take Possession After Default

Unless otherwise agreed, a secured party has on default the right to take possession of the collateral. In taking possession, a secured party may proceed without judicial process if this can be done without breach of the peace or may proceed by action. If the security agreement so provides, the secured party may require the debtor to assemble the collateral and make it available to the secured party at a place to be designated by the secured party which is reasonably convenient to both parties. Without removal, a secured party may render equipment unusable and may dispose of collateral on the debtor's premises under Section 9—504.

§9—504. Secured Party's Right to Dispose of Collateral After Default; Effect of Disposition

(1) A secured party after default may sell, lease or otherwise dispose of any or all of the collateral in its then condition or following any commercially reasonable preparation or processing. Any sale of goods is subject to the Article on Sales (Article 2). The proceeds of disposition shall be applied in the order following to

(a) the reasonable expenses of retaking, holding, preparing for sale or lease, selling, leasing and the like and, to the extent provided for in the agreement and not prohibited by law, the reasonable attorneys' fees and legal expenses incurred by the secured party;

(b) the satisfaction of indebtedness secured by the security interest under which the disposition is made;

(c) the satisfaction of indebtedness secured by any subordinate security interest in the collateral if written notification of demand therefor is received before distribution of the proceeds is completed. If requested by the secured party, the holder of a subordinate security interest must seasonably furnish reasonable proof of his interest, and unless he does so, the secured party need not comply with his demand.

(2) If the security interest secures an indebtedness, the secured party must account to the debtor for any surplus, and, unless otherwise agreed, the debtor is liable for any deficiency. But if the underlying transaction was a sale of accounts or chattel paper, the debtor is entitled to any surplus or is liable for any deficiency only if the security agreement so provides.

(3) Disposition of the collateral may be by public or private proceedings and may be made by way of one or more contracts. Sale or other disposition may be as a unit or in parcels and at any time and place and on any terms but every aspect of the disposition including the method, manner, time, place and terms must be commercially reasonable. Unless collateral is perishable or threatens to decline speedily in value or is of a type customarily sold on a recognized market, reasonable notification of the time and place of any public sale or reasonable notification of the time after which any private sale or other intended disposition is to be made shall be sent by the secured party to the debtor, if he has not signed after default a statement renouncing or modifying his right to notification of sale. In the case of consumer goods, no other notification need be sent. In other cases, notification shall be sent to any other secured party from whom the secured party has received (before sending his notification to the debtor or before the debtor's renunciation of his rights) written notice of a claim of an interest in the collateral. The secured party may buy at any public sale; and if the collateral is of a type customarily sold in a recognized market or is of a type which is the subject of widely distributed standard price quotations, he may buy at private sale.

(4) When collateral is disposed of by a secured party after default, the disposition transfers to a pur-

chaser for value all of the debtor's rights therein, discharges the security interest under which it is made and any security interest or lien subordinate thereto. The purchaser takes free of all such rights and interests even though the secured party fails to comply with the requirements of this Part or of any judicial proceedings

> (a) in the case of a public sale, if the purchaser has no knowledge of any defects in the sale and if he does not buy in collusion with the secured party, other bidders or the person conducting the sale; or
> (b) in any other case, if the purchaser acts in good faith.

(5) A person who is liable to a secured party under a guaranty, indorsement, repurchase agreement or the like and who receives a transfer of collateral from the secured party or is subrogated to his rights thereafter the rights and duties of the secured party. Such a transfer of collateral is not a sale or disposition of the collateral under this Article.

§ 9—505. Compulsory Disposition of Collateral; Acceptance of the Collateral as Discharge of Obligation

(1) If the debtor has paid sixty percent of the cash price in the case of a purchase money security interest in consumer goods or sixty percent of the loan in the case of another security interest in consumer goods and has not signed after default a statement renouncing or modifying his rights under this Part, a secured party who has taken possession of collateral must dispose of it under Section 9—504; and if he fails to do so within ninety days after he takes possession, the debtor at his option may recover in conversion or under section 9—507(1) on secured party's liability.

(2) In any other case involving consumer goods or any other collateral, a secured party in possession may, after default, propose to retain the collateral in satisfaction of the obligation. Written notice of such proposal shall be sent to the debtor if he has not signed after default a statement renouncing or modifying his rights under this subsection. In the case of consumer goods, no other notice need be given. In other cases, notice shall be sent to any other secured party from whom the secured party has received (before sending his notice to the debtor or before the debtor's renunciation of his rights) written notice of a claim of an interest in the collateral. If the secured party receives objection in writing from a person entitled to receive notification within twenty-one days after the notice was sent, the secured party must dispose of the collateral under Section 9—504. In the absence of such written objection, the secured party may retain the collateral in satisfaction of the debtor's obligation.

§ 9—506. Debtor's Right to Redeem Collateral

At any time before the secured party has disposed of collateral or entered into a contract for its disposition under Section 9—504 or before the obligation has been discharged under Section 9—505(2), the debtor or any other secured party may, unless otherwise agreed in writing after default, redeem the collateral by tendering fulfillment of all obligations secured by the collateral as well as the expenses reasonably incurred by the secured party in retaking, holding and preparing the collateral for disposition, in arranging for the sale, and to the extent provided in the agreement and not prohibited by law, his reasonable attorneys' fees and legal expenses.

§ 9—507. Secured Party's Liability for Failure to Comply With This Part

(1) If it is established that the secured party is not proceeding in accordance with the provisions of this Part, disposition may be ordered or restrained on appropriate terms and conditions. If the disposition has occurred, the debtor or any person entitled to notification or whose security interest has been made known to the secured party prior to the disposition has a right to recover from the secured party any loss caused by a failure to comply with the provisions of this Part. If the collateral is consumer goods, the debtor has a right to recover in any event an amount not less than the credit service charge plus ten percent of the principal amount of the debt or the time price differential plus 10 percent of the cash price.

(2) The fact that a better price could have been obtained by a sale at a different time or in a different method from that selected by the secured party is not of itself sufficient to establish that the sale was not made in a commercially reasonable manner. If the secured party either sells the collateral in the usual manner in any recognized market therefor, or if he sells at the price current in such market at the time of his sale, or if he has otherwise sold in conformity with reasonable commercial practices among dealers in the type of property sold, he has sold in a commercially reasonable manner. The principles stated in the two preceding sentences with respect to sales also apply as may be appropriate to other types of disposition. A disposition which has been approved in any judicial proceeding or by any bona fide creditors' committee or representative of creditors shall conclusively be deemed to be commercially reasonable, but this sentence does not indicate that any such approval must be obtained in any case nor does it indicate that any disposition not so approved is not commercially reasonable.

ARTICLE 10

EFFECTIVE DATE AND REPEALER

See Article 11 for Transition Provisions for those juris-dictions adopting the 1972 amendments.

§ 10 — 101.   Effective Date

This Act shall become effective at midnight on December 31st following its enactment. It applies to transactions entered into and events occurring after that date.

§ 10 — 102.   Specific Repealer; Provision for Transition

(1) The following acts and all other acts and parts of acts inconsistent herewith are hereby repealed:

(Here should follow the acts to be specifically repealed including the following:

    Uniform Negotiable Instruments Act
    Uniform Warehouse Receipts Act
    Uniform Sales Act
    Uniform Bills of Lading Act
    Uniform Stock Transfer Act
    Uniform Conditional Sales Act
    Uniform Trust Receipts Act
    Also any acts regulating:
      Bank collections
      Bulk sales
      Chattel mortgages
      Conditional sales
      Factor's lien acts
      Farm storage of grain and similar acts
      Assignment of accounts receivable)

(2) Transactions validly entered into before the effective date specified in Section 10 — 101 and the rights, duties and interests flowing from them remain valid thereafter and may be terminated, completed, consummated or enforced as required or permitted by any statute or other law amended or repealed by this Act as though such repeal or amendment had not occurred.

Note: *Subsection (1) should be separately prepared for each state. The foregoing is a list of statutes to be checked.*

§ 10 — 103.   General Repealer

Except as provided in the following section, all acts and parts of acts inconsistent with this Act are hereby repealed.

§ 10 — 104.   Laws Not Repealed

[(1)] The Article on Documents of Title (Article 7) does not repeal or modify any laws prescribing the form or contents of documents of title or the services or facilities to be afforded by bailees, or otherwise regulating bailees' businesses in respects not specifically dealt with herein; but the fact that such laws are violated does not affect the status of a document of title which otherwise complies with the definition of a document of title (Section 1 — 201).

[(2) This act does not repeal . . . .
. . . .*, cited as the Uniform Act for the Simplification of Fiduciary Security Transfers, and if in any respect there is any inconsistency between that Act and the Article of this Act on investment securities (Article 8) the provisions of the former Act shall control.]

Note: *At * in subsection (2) insert the statutory reference to the Uniform Act for the Simplification of Fiduciary Security Transfers if such Act has previously been enacted. If it has not been enacted, omit subsection (2).*

ARTICLE 11

EFFECTIVE DATE AND TRANSITION PROVISIONS

This material has been numbered Article 11 to distinguish it from Article 10, the transition provision of the 1962 Code, which may still remain in effect in some states to cover transition problems from pre-Code law to the original Uniform Commercial Code. Adaptation may be necessary in particular states. The terms "[old Code]" and "[new Code]" and "[old U.C.C.]" and "[new U.C.C.]" are used herein and should be suitably changed in each state.

This draft was prepared by the Reporters and has not been passed upon by the Review Committee, the Permanent Editorial Board, the American Law Institute, or the National Conference of Commissioners or Uniform State Laws. It is submitted as a working draft which may be adapted as appropriate in each state.

§ 11 — 101.   Effective Date

This Act shall become effective at 12:01 A.M. on ____, 19__.

§ 11 — 102.   Preservation of Old Transition Provision

The provisions of [here insert reference to the original transition provision in the particular state] shall continue to apply to [the new U.C.C.] and for this purpose the [old U.C.C. and new U.C.C.] shall be considered one continuous statute.

§ 11 — 103.   Transition to [New Code] — General Rule

Transactions validly entered into after [effective date of old U.C.C.] and before [effective date of new U.C.C.], and which were subject to the provisions of [old U.C.C.] and which would be subject to this Act as amended if they had been entered into after the effective date of [new U.C.C.] and the rights, duties and interests flowing from such transactions remain valid after the latter date and may be terminated, completed, consummated or enforced as required or permitted by the [new U.C.C.]. Security interests arising out of such transactions which are perfected when [new U.C.C.] becomes effective shall remain perfected until they lapse as provided in [new U.C.C.], and may be continued as permitted by [new U.C.C.], except as stated in Section 11 — 105.

§ 11 — 104. Transition Provision on Change of Requirement of Filing

A security interest for the perfection of which filing or the taking of possession was required under [old U.C.C.] and which attached prior to the effective date of [new U.C.C.] but was not perfected shall be deemed perfected on the effective date of [new U.C.C.] if [new U.C.C.] permits perfection without filing or authorizes filing in the office or offices where a prior ineffective filing was made.

§ 11 — 105. Transition Provision on Change of Place of Filing

(1) A financing statement or continuation statement filed prior to [effective date of new U.C.C.] which shall not have lapsed prior to [the effective date of new U.C.C.] shall remain effective for the period provided in the [old Code], but not less than five years after the filing.

(2) With respect to any collateral acquired by the debtor subsequent to the effective date of [new U.C.C.], any effective financing statement or continuation statement described in this section shall apply only if the filing or filings are in the office or offices that would be appropriate to perfect the security interests in the new collateral under [new U.C.C.].

(3) The effectiveness of any financing statement or continuation statement filed prior to [effective date of new U.C.C.] may be continued by a continuation statement as permitted by [new U.C.C.], except that if [new U.C.C.] requires a filing in an office where there was no previous financing statement, a new financing statement conforming to Section 11 — 106 shall be filed in that office.

(4) If the record of a mortgage of real estate would have been effective as a fixture filing of goods described therein if [new U.C.C.] had been in effect on the date of recording the mortgage, the mortgage shall be deemed effective as a fixture filing as to such goods under subsection (6) of Section 9 — 402 of the [new U.C.C.] on the effective date of [new U.C.C.].

§ 11 — 106. Required Refilings

(1) If a security interest is perfected or has priority when this Act takes effect as to all persons or as to certain persons without any filing or recording, and if the filing of a financing statement would be required for the perfection or priority of the security interest

against those persons under [new U.C.C.], the perfection and priority rights of the security interest continue until 3 years after the effective date of [new U.C.C.]. The perfection will then lapse unless a financing statement is filed as provided in subsection (4) or unless the security interest is perfected otherwise than by filing.

(2) If a security interest is perfected when [new U.C.C.] takes effect under a law other than [U.C.C.] which requires no further filing, refiling or recording to continue its perfection, perfection continues until and will lapse 3 years after [new U.C.C.] takes effect, unless a financing statement is filed as provided in subsection (4) or unless the security interest is perfected otherwise than by filing, or unless under subsection (3) of Section 9 — 302 the other law continues to govern filing.

(3) If a security interest is perfected by a filing, refiling or recording under a law repealed by this Act which required further filing, refiling or recording to continue its perfection, perfection continues and will lapse on the date provided by the law so repealed for such further filing, refiling or recording unless a financing statement is filed as provided in subsection (4) or unless the security interest is perfected otherwise than by filing.

(4) A financing statement may be filed within six months before the perfection of a security interest would otherwise lapse. Any such financing statement may be signed by either the debtor or the secured party. It must identify the security agreement, statement or notice (however denominated in any statute or other law repealed or modified by this Act), state the office where and the date when the last filing, refiling or recording, if any, was made with respect thereto, and the filing number, if any, or book and page, if any, of recording and further state that the security agreement, statement or notice, however denominated, in another filing office under the [U.C.C.] or under any statute or other law repealed or modified by this Act is still effective. Section 9 — 401 and Section 9 — 103 determine the proper place to file such a financing statement. Except as specified in this subsection, the provisions of Section 9 — 403(3) for continuation statements apply to such a financing statement.

§ 11 — 107. Transition Provisions as to Priorities

Except as otherwise provided in [Article 11], [old U.C.C.] shall apply to any questions of priority if the positions of the parties were fixed prior to the effective date of [new U.C.C.]. In other cases questions of priority shall be determined by [new U.C.C.].

§ 11 — 108. Presumption that Rule of Law Continues Unchanged

Unless a change in law has clearly been made, the provisions of [new U.C.C.] shall be deemed declaratory of the meaning of the [old U.C.C.].

ARTICLE 2A

LEASES

Part 1
General Provisions

§ 2A-101. Short Title
This Article shall be known and may be cited as the Uniform Commercial Code—Leases.

§ 2A-102. Scope
This Article applies to any transaction, regardless of form, that creates a lease.

§ 2A-103. Definitions and Index of Definitions
(1) In this Article unless the context otherwise requires:

(a) "Buyer in ordinary course of business" means a person who in good faith and without knowledge that the sale to him [or her] is in violation of the ownership rights or security interest or leasehold interest of a third party in the goods buys in ordinary course from a person in the business of selling goods of that kind but does not include a pawnbroker. "Buying" may be for cash or by exchange of other property or on secured or unsecured credit and includes receiving goods or documents of title under a pre-existing contract for sale but does not include a transfer in bulk or as security for or in total or partial satisfaction of a money debt.

(b) "Cancellation" occurs when either party puts an end to the lease contract for default by the other party.

(c) "Commercial unit" means such a unit of goods as by commercial usage is a single whole for purposes of lease and division of which materially impairs its character or value on the market or in use. A commercial unit may be a single article, as a machine, or a set of articles, as a suite of furniture or a line of machinery, or a quantity, as a gross or carload, or any other unit treated in use or in the relevant market as a single whole.

(d) "Conforming" goods or performance under a lease contract means goods or performance that are in accordance with the obligations under the lease contract.

(e) "Consumer lease" means a lease that a lessor regularly engaged in the business of leasing or selling makes to a lessee, except an organization, who takes under the lease primarily for a personal, family, or household purpose, if the total payments to be made under the lease contract, excluding payments for options to renew or buy, do not exceed $25,000.

(f) "Fault" means wrongful act, omission, breach, or default.

(g) "Finance lease" means a lease in which (i) the lessor does not select, manufacture or supply the goods, (ii) the lessor acquires the goods or the right to possession and use of the goods in connection with the lease, and (iii) either the lessee receives a copy of the contract evidencing the lessor's purchase of the goods on or before signing the lease contract, or the lessee's approval of the contract evidencing the lessor's purchase of the goods is a condition to effectiveness of the lease contract.

(h) "Goods" means all things that are movable at the time of identification to the lease contract, or are fixtures (Section 2A-309), but the term does not include money, documents, instruments, accounts, chattel paper, general intangibles, or minerals or the like, including oil and gas, before extraction. The term also includes the unborn young of animals.

(i) "Installment lease contract" means a lease contract that authorizes or requires the delivery of goods in separate lots to be separately accepted, even though the lease contract contains a clause "each delivery is a separate lease" or its equivalent.

(j) "Lease" means a transfer of the right to possession and use of goods for a term in return for consideration, but a sale, including a sale on approval or a sale or return, or retention or creation of a security interest is not a lease. Unless the context clearly indicates otherwise, the term includes a sublease.

(k) "Lease agreement" means the bargain, with respect to the lease, of the lessor and the lessee in fact as found in their language or by implication from other circumstances including course of dealing or usage of trade or course of performance as provided in this Article. Unless the context clearly indicates otherwise, the term includes a sublease agreement.

(l) "Lease contract" means the total legal obligation that results from the lease agreement as affected by this Article and any other applicable rules of law. Unless the context clearly indicates otherwise, the term includes a sublease contract.

(m) "Leasehold interest" means the interest of the lessor or the lessee under a lease contract.

(n) "Lessee" means a person who acquires the right to possession and use of goods under a lease. Unless the context clearly indicates otherwise, the term includes a sublessee.

(o) "Lessee in ordinary course of business" means a person who in good faith and without knowledge that the lease to him [or her] is in violation of the ownership rights or security interest or leasehold interest of a third party in the goods leases in ordinary course from a person in the business of selling or leasing goods of that kind but does not include a pawnbroker. "Leasing" may be for cash or by exchange of other property or on secured or unsecured credit and includes receiving goods or documents of title under a pre-existing lease contract but does not include a transfer in bulk or as security for or in total or partial satisfaction of a money debt.

(p) "Lessor" means a person who transfers the right to possession and use of goods under a lease. Unless the context clearly indicates otherwise, the term includes a sublessor.

(q) "Lessor's residual interest" means the lessor's interest in the goods after expiration, termination, or cancellation of the lease contract.

(r) "Lien" means a charge against or interest in goods to secure payment of a debt or performance of an obligation, but the term does not include a security interest.

(s) "Lot" means a parcel or a single article that is the subject matter of a separate lease or delivery, whether or not it is sufficient to perform the lease contract.

(t) "Merchant lessee" means a lessee that is a merchant with respect to goods of the kind subject to the lease.

(u) "Present value" means the amount as of a date certain of one or more sums payable in the future, discounted to the date certain. The discount is determined by the interest rate specified by the parties if the rate was not manifestly unreasonable at the time the transaction was entered into; otherwise, the discount is determined by a commercially reasonable rate that takes into account the facts and circumstances of each case at the time the transaction was entered into.

(v) "Purchase" includes taking by sale, lease, mortgage, security interest, pledge, gift, or any other voluntary transaction creating an interest in goods.

(w) "Sublease" means a lease of goods the right to possession and use of which was acquired by the lessor as a lessee under an existing lease.

(x) "Supplier" means a person from whom a lessor buys or leases goods to be leased under a finance lease.

(y) "Supply contract" means a contract under which a lessor buys or leases goods to be leased.

(z) "Termination" occurs when either party pursuant to a power created by agreement or law puts an end to the lease contract otherwise than for default.

(2) Other definitions applying to this Article and the sections in which they appear are:

"Accessions". Section 2A-310(1).

"Construction mortgage". Section 2A-309(1)(d).

"Encumbrance". Section 2A-309(1)(e).

"Fixtures". Section 2A-309(1)(a).

"Fixture filing". Section 2A-309(1)(b).

"Purchase money lease". Section 2A-309(1)(c).

(3) The following definitions in other Articles apply to this Article:

"Accounts". Section 9-106.

"Between merchants". Section 2-104(3).

"Buyer". Section 2-103(1)(a).

"Chattel paper". Section 9-105(1)(b).

"Consumer goods". Section 9-109 (1).

"Documents". Section 9-105(1)(f).

"Entrusting". Section 2-403(3).

"General intangibles". Section 9-106.

"Good faith". Section 2-103(1)(b).

"Instruments". Section 9-105(1)(i).

"Merchant". Section 2-104(1).

"Mortgage". Section 9-105(1)(j).

"Pursuant to commitment". Section 9-105(1)(k).

"Receipt". Section 2-103(1)(c).

"Sale". Section 2-106(1).

"Sale on Approval". Section 2-326.

"Sale or Return". Section 2-326.
"Seller". Section 2-103(1)(d).

(4) In addition Article 1 contains general definitions and principles of construction and interpretation applicable throughout this Article.

§ 2A-104. Leases Subject to Other Statutes

(1) A lease, although subject to this Article, is also subject to any applicable:

    (a) statute of the United States;

    (b) certificate of title statute of this State: (list any certificate of title statutes covering automobiles, trailers, mobile homes, boats, farm tractors, and the like);

    (c) certificate of title statute of another jurisdiction (Section 2A-105); or

    (d) consumer protection statute of this State.

(2) In case of conflict between the provisions of this Article, other than Section 2A-105, 2A-304(3) and 2A-305(3), and any statute referred to in subsection (1), the provisions of that statute control.

(3) Failure to comply with any applicable statute has only the effect specified therein.

§ 2A-105. Territorial Application of Article to Goods Covered by Certificate of Title

Subject to the provisions of Sections 2A-304(3) and 2A-305(3), with respect to goods covered by a certificate of title issued under a statute of this State or of another jurisdiction, compliance and the effect of compliance or noncompliance with a certificate of title statute are governed by the law (including the conflict of laws rules) of the jurisdiction issuing the certificate until the earlier of (a) surrender of the certificate, or (b) four months after the goods are removed from that jurisdiction and thereafter until a new certificate of title is issued by another jurisdiction.

§ 2A-106. Limitation on Power of Parties to Consumer Lease to Choose Applicable Law and Judicial Forum

(1) If the law chosen by the parties to a consumer lease is that of a jurisdiction other than a jurisdiction in which the lessee resides at the time the lease agreement becomes enforceable or within 30 days thereafter or in which the goods are to be used, the choice is not enforceable.

(2) If the judicial forum chosen by the parties to a consumer lease is a forum that would not otherwise have jurisdiction over the lessee, the choice is not enforceable.

§ 2A-107. Waiver or Renunciation of Claim or Right After Default

Any claim or right arising out of an alleged default or breach of warranty may be discharged in whole or in part without consideration by a written waiver or renunciation signed and delivered by the aggrieved party.

§ 2A-108. Unconscionability

(1) If the court as a matter of law finds a lease contract or any clause of a lease contract to have been unconscionable at the time it was made the court may refuse to enforce the lease contract, or it may enforce the remainder of the lease contract without the unconscionable clause, or it may so limit the application of any unconscionable clause as to avoid any unconscionable result.

(2) With respect to a consumer lease, if the court as a matter of law finds that a lease contract or any clause of a lease contract has been induced by unconscionable conduct or that unconscionable conduct has occurred in the collection of a claim arising from a lease contract, the court may grant appropriate relief.

(3) Before making a finding of unconscionability under subsection (1) or (2), the court, on its own motion or that of a party, shall afford the parties a reasonable opportunity to present evidence as to the setting, purpose, and effect of the lease contract or clause thereof, or of the conduct.

(4) In an action in which the lessee claims unconscionability with respect to a consumer lease:

    (a) If the court finds unconscionability under subsection (1) or (2), the court shall award reasonable attorney's fees to the lessee.

    (b) If the court does not find unconscionability and the lessee claiming unconscionability has brought or maintained an action he [or she] knew to be groundless, the court shall award reasonable attorney's fees to the party against whom the claim is made.

    (c) In determining attorney's fees, the amount of the recovery on behalf of the claimant under subsections (1) and (2) is not controlling.

§ 2A-109. Option to Accelerate At Will

(1) A term providing that one party or his [or her] successor in interest may accelerate payment of performance or require collateral or additional collateral "at will" or "when he [or she] deems himself [or herself] insecure" or in words of similar import must be construed to mean that he [or she] has power to do so only if he [or she] in good faith believes that the prospect of payment or performance is impaired.

(2) With respect to a consumer lease, the burden of establishing good faith under subsection (1) is on the party who exercised the power; otherwise the burden of establishing lack of good faith is on the party against whom the power has been exercised.

Part 2
Formation and Construction of Lease Contract

§ 2A-201. Statute of Frauds

(1) A lease contract is not enforceable by way of action or defense unless:

    (a) the total payments to be made under the lease contract, excluding payments for options to renew or buy, are less than $1,000; or

    (b) there is a writing, signed by the party against whom enforcement is sought or by that party's authorized agent, sufficient to indicate that a lease contract has been made between the parties and to describe the goods leased and the lease term.

(2) Any description of leased goods or of the lease term is sufficient and satisfies subsection (1)(b), whether or not it is specific, if it reasonably identifies what is described.

(3) A writing is not insufficient because it omits or incorrectly states a term agreed upon, but the lease contract is not enforceable under subsection (1)(b) beyond the lease term and the quantity of goods shown in the writing.

(4) A lease contract that does not satisfy the requirements of subsection (1), but which is valid in other respects, is enforceable:

    (a) if the goods are to be specially manufactured or obtained for the lessee and are not suitable for lease or sale to others in the ordinary course of the lessor's business, and the lessor, before notice of repudiation is received and under circumstances that reasonably indicate that the goods are for the lessee, has made either a substantial beginning of their manufacture or commitments for their procurement;

    (b) if the party against whom enforcement is sought admits in that party's pleading, testimony or otherwise in court that a lease contract was made, but the lease contract is not enforceable under this provision beyond the quantity of goods admitted; or

    (c) with respect to goods that have been received and accepted by the lessee.

(5) The lease term under a lease contract referred to in subsection (4) is:

    (a) if there is a writing signed by the party against whom enforcement is sought or by that party's authorized agent specifying the lease term, the term so specified;

    (b) if the party against whom enforcement is sought admits in that party's pleading, testimony, or otherwise in court a lease term, the term so admitted; or

    (c) a reasonable lease term.

§ 2A-202. Final Written Expressions: Parol or Extrinsic Evidence

Terms with respect to which the confirmatory memoranda of the parties agree or which are otherwise set forth in a writing intended by the parties as a final expression of the agreement with respect to such terms as are included therein may not be contradicted by evidence of any prior agreement or of a contemporaneous oral agreement but may be explained or supplemented.

    (a) by course of dealing or usage of trade or by course of performance; and

    (b) by evidence of consistent additional terms unless the court finds the writing to have been intended also as a complete and exclusive statement of the terms of the agreement.

§ 2A-203. Seals Inoperative

The affixing of a seal to a writing evidencing a lease contract or an offer to enter into a lease contract does not render the writing a sealed instrument and the law with respect to sealed instruments does not apply to the lease contract or offer.

§ 2A-204. Formation in General

(1) A lease contract may be made in any manner sufficient to show agreement, including conduct by both parties which recognizes the existence of a lease contract.

(2) An agreement sufficient to constitute a lease contract may be found although the moment of its making is undetermined.

(3) Although one or more terms are left open, a lease contract does not fail for indefiniteness if the parties have intended to make a lease contract and there is a reasonably certain basis for giving an appropriate remedy.

§ 2A-205. Firm Offers

An offer by a merchant to lease goods to or from another person in a signed writing that by its terms gives assurance it will be held open is not revocable, for lack of consideration, during the time stated or, if no time is stated, for a reasonable time, but in no event may the period of irrevocability exceed 3 months. Any such term of assurance on a form supplied by the offeree must be separately signed by the offeror.

§ 2A-206. Offer and Acceptance in Formation of Lease Contract

(1) Unless otherwise unambiguously indicated by the language or circumstances, an offer to make a lease contract must be construed as inviting acceptance in any manner and by any medium reasonable in the circumstances.

(2) If the beginning of a requested performance

is a reasonable mode of acceptance, an offeror who is not notified of acceptance within a reasonable time may treat the offer as having lapsed before acceptance.

§ 2A-207. Course of Performance or Practical Construction

(1) If a lease contract involves repeated occasions for performance by either party with knowledge of the nature of the performance and opportunity for objection to it by the other, any course of performance accepted or acquiesced in without objection is relevant to determine the meaning of the lease agreement.

(2) The express terms of a lease agreement and any course of performance, as well as any course of dealing and usage of trade, must be construed whenever reasonable as consistent with each other; but if that construction is unreasonable, express terms control course of performance, course of performance controls both course of dealing and usage of trade, and course of dealing controls usage of trade.

(3) Subject to the provisions of Section 2A-208 on modification and waiver, course of performance is relevant to show a waiver or modification of any term inconsistent with the course of performance.

§ 2A-208. Modification, Rescission and Waiver

(1) An agreement modifying a lease contract needs no consideration to be binding.

(2) A signed lease agreement that excludes modification or rescission except by a signed writing may not be otherwise modified or rescinded, but, except as between merchants, such a requirement on a form supplied by a merchant must be separately signed by the other party.

(3) Although an attempt at modification or rescission does not satisfy the requirements of subsection (2), it may operate as a waiver.

(4) A party who has made a waiver affecting an executory portion of a lease contract may retract the waiver by reasonable notification received by the other party that strict performance will be required of any term waived, unless the retraction would be unjust in view of a material change of position in reliance on the waiver.

§ 2A-209. Lessee Under Finance Lease as Beneficiary of Supply Contract

(1) The benefit of the supplier's promises to the lessor under the supply contract and of all warranties, whether express or implied, under the supply contract, extends to the lessee to the extent of the lessee's leasehold interest under a finance lease related to the supply contract, but subject to the terms of the supply contract and all of the supplier's defenses or claims arising therefrom.

(2) The extension of the benefit of the supplier's promises and warranties to the lessee (Section 2A-209(1)) does not: (a) modify the rights and obliga-

tions of the parties to the supply contract, whether arising therefrom or otherwise, or (b) impose any duty or liability under the supply contract on the lessee.

(3) Any modification or rescission of the supply contract by the supplier and the lessor is effective against the lessee unless, prior to the modification or rescission, the supplier has received notice that the lessee has entered into a finance lease related to the supply contract. If the supply contract is modified or rescinded after the lessee enters the finance lease, the lessee has a cause of action against the lessor, and against the supplier if the supplier has notice of the lessee's entering the finance lease when the supply contract is modified or rescinded. The lessee's recovery from such action shall put the lessee in as good a position as if the modification or rescission had not occurred.

§ 2A-210. Express Warranties

(1) Express warranties by the lessor are created as follows:

(a) Any affirmation of fact or promise made by the lessor to the lessee which relates to the goods and becomes part of the basis of the bargain creates an express warranty that the goods will conform to the affirmation or promise.

(b) Any description of the goods which is made part of the basis of the bargain creates an express warranty that the goods will conform to the description.

(c) Any sample or model that is made part of the basis of the bargain creates an express warranty that the whole of the goods will conform to the sample or model.

(2) It is not necessary to the creation of an express warranty that the lessor use formal words, such as "warrant" or "guarantee," or that the lessor have a specific intention to make a warranty, but an affirmation merely of the value of the goods or a statement purporting to be merely the lessor's opinion or commendation of the goods does not create a warranty.

§ 2A-211. Warranties Against Interference and Against Infringement; Lessee's Obligation Against Infringement

(1) There is in a lease contract a warranty that for the lease term no person holds a claim to or interest in the goods that arose from an act or omission of the lessor, other than a claim by way of infringement or the like, which will interfere with the lessee's enjoyment of its leasehold interest.

(2) Except in a finance lease there is in a lease contract by a lessor who is a merchant regularly dealing in goods of the kind a warranty that the goods are delivered free of the rightful claim of any person by way of infringement or the like.

(3) A lessee who furnishes specifications to a

lessor or a supplier shall hold the lessor and the supplier harmless against any claim by way of infringement or the like that arises out of compliance with the specifications.

§ 2A-212.　Implied Warranty of Merchantability

(1) Except in a finance lease, a warranty that the goods will be merchantable is implied in a lease contract if the lessor is a merchant with respect to goods of that kind.

(2) Goods to be merchantable must be at least such as

(a) pass without objection in the trade under the description in the lease agreement;

(b) in the case of fungible goods, are of fair average quality within the description;

(c) are fit for the ordinary purposes for which goods of that type are used;

(d) run, within the variation permitted by the lease agreement, of even kind, quality, and quantity within each unit and among all units involved;

(e) are adequately contained, packaged, and labeled as the lease agreement may require; and

(f) conform to any promises or affirmations of fact made on the container or label.

(3) Other implied warranties may arise from course of dealing or usage of trade.

§ 2A-213.　Implied Warranty of Fitness for Particular Purpose

Except in a finance lease, if the lessor at the time the lease contract is made has reason to know of any particular purpose for which the goods are required and that the lessee is relying on the lessor's skill or judgment to select or furnish suitable goods, there is in the lease contract an implied warranty that the goods will be fit for that purpose.

§ 2A-214.　Exclusion or Modification of Warranties

(1) Words or conduct relevant to the creation of an express warranty and words or conduct tending to negate or limit a warranty must be construed wherever reasonable as consistent with each other; but, subject to the provisions of Section 2A-202 on parol or extrinsic evidence, negation or limitation is inoperative to the extent that the construction is unreasonable.

(2) Subject to subsection (3), to exclude or modify the implied warranty of merchantability or any part of it the language must mention "merchantability", be by a writing, and be conspicuous. Subject to subsection (3), to exclude or modify any implied warranty of fitness the exclusion must be by a writing and be conspicuous. Language to exclude all implied warranties of fitness is sufficient if it is in writing, is conspicuous and states, for example, "There is no

warranty that the goods will be fit for a particular purpose".

(3) Notwithstanding subsection (2), but subject to subsection (4),

(a) unless the circumstances indicate otherwise, all implied warranties are excluded by expressions like "as is," or "with all faults," or by other language that in common understanding calls the lessee's attention to the exclusion of warranties and makes plain that there is no implied warranty, if in writing and conspicuous;

(b) if the lessee before entering into the lease contract has examined the goods or the sample or model as fully as desired or has refused to examine the goods, there is no implied warranty with regard to defects that an examination ought in the circumstances to have revealed; and

(c) an implied warranty may also be excluded or modified by course of dealing, course of performance, or usage of trade.

(4) To exclude or modify a warranty against interference or against infringement (Section 2A-211) or any part of it, the language must be specific, be by a writing, and be conspicuous, unless the circumstances, including course of performance, course of dealing, or usage of trade, give the lessee reason to know that the goods are being leased subject to a claim or interest of any person.

§ 2A-215.　Cumulation and Conflict of Warranties Express or Implied

Warranties, whether express or implied, must be construed as consistent with each other and as cumulative, but if that construction is unreasonable, the intention of the parties determines which warranty is dominant. In ascertaining that intention the following rules apply:

(a) Exact or technical specifications displace an inconsistent sample or model or general language of description.

(b) A sample from an existing bulk displaces inconsistent general language of description.

(c) Express warranties displace inconsistent implied warranties other than an implied warranty of fitness for a particular purpose.

§ 2A-216.　Third-Party Beneficiaries of Express and Implied Warranties

ALTERNATIVE A

A warranty to or for the benefit of a lessee under this Article, whether express or implied, extends to any natural person who is in the family or household of the lessee or who is a guest in the lessee's home if it is reasonable to expect that such person may use, consume, or be affected by the goods and who is injured in person by breach of the warranty. This section does not displace principles of law and equity that extend a warranty to or for the benefit of a lessee to other persons. The operation of this section may not be excluded, modified, or limited, but an exclusion, modification, or limitation of the warranty, including any with respect to rights and remedies, effective against the lessee is also effective against any beneficiary designated under this section.

ALTERNATIVE B

A warranty to or for the benefit of a lessee under this Article, whether express or implied, extends to any natural person who may reasonably be expected to use, consume, or be affected by the goods and who is injured in person by breach of the warranty. This section does not displace principles of law and equity that extend a warranty to or for the benefit of a lessee to other persons. The operation of this section may not be excluded, modified, or limited, but an exclusion, modification, or limitation of the warranty, including any with respect to rights and remedies, effective against the lessee is also effective against the beneficiary designated under this section.

ALTERNATIVE C

A warranty to or for the benefit of a lessee under this Article, whether express or implied, extends to any person who may reasonably be expected to use, consume, or be affected by the goods and who is injured by breach of the warranty. The operation of this section may not be excluded, modified, or limited with respect to injury to the person of an individual to whom the warranty extends, but an exclusion, modification, or limitation of the warranty, including any with respect to rights and remedies, effective against the lessee is also effective against the beneficiary designated under this section.

§ 2A-217.   Identification

Identification of goods as goods to which a lease contract refers may be made at any time and in any manner explicitly agreed to by the parties. In the absence of explicit agreement, identification occurs:

(a) when the lease contract is made if the lease contract is for a lease of goods that are existing and identified;

(b) when the goods are shipped, marked, or otherwise designated by the lessor as goods to which the lease contract refers, if the lease contract is for a lease of goods that are not existing and identified; or

(c) when the young are conceived, if the lease contract is for a lease of unborn young of animals.

§ 2A-218.   Insurance and Proceeds

(1) A lessee obtains an insurable interest when existing goods are identified to the lease contract even though the goods identified are nonconforming and the lessee has an option to reject them.

(2) If a lessee has an insurable interest only by reason of the lessor's identification of the goods, the lessor, until default or insolvency or notification to the lessee that identification is final, may substitute other goods for those identified.

(3) Notwithstanding a lessee's insurable interest under subsections (1) and (2), the lessor retains an insurable interest until an option to buy has been exercised by the lessee and risk of loss has passed to the lessee.

(4) Nothing in this section impairs any insurable interest recognized under any other statute or rule of law.

(5) The parties by agreement may determine that one or more parties have an obligation to obtain and pay for insurance covering the goods and by agreement may determine the beneficiary of the proceeds of the insurance.

§ 2A-219.   Risk of Loss

(1) Except in the case of a finance lease, risk of loss is retained by the lessor and does not pass to the lessee. In the case of a finance lease, risk of loss passes to the lessee.

(2) Subject to the provisions of this Article on the effect of default on risk of loss (Section 2A-220), if risk of loss is to pass to the lessee and the time of passage is not stated the following rules apply:

(a) If the lease contract requires or authorizes the goods to be shipped by carrier

(i) and it does not require delivery at a particular destination, the risk of loss passes to the lessee when the goods are duly delivered to the carrier; but

(ii) if it does require delivery at a particular destination and the goods are there duly tendered while in the possession of the carrier, the risk of loss passes to the lessee when the goods are there duly so tendered as to enable the lessee to take delivery.

(b) If the goods are held by a bailee to be delivered without being moved, the risk of loss passes to the lessee on acknowledgment by the bailee of the lessee's right to possession of the goods.

(c) In any case not within subsection (a) or (b), the risk of loss passes to the lessee on the lessee's receipt of the goods if the lessor, or, in the case of a finance lease, the supplier, is a merchant: otherwise the risk passes to the lessee on tender of delivery.

§ 2A-220.   Effect of Default on Risk of Loss

(1) Where risk of loss is to pass to the lessee and the time of passage is not stated:

(a) If a tender or delivery of goods so fails to conform to the lease contract as to give a right of rejection, the risk of their loss remains with the lessor, or, in the case of a finance lease, the supplier, until cure or acceptance.

(b) If the lessee rightfully revokes acceptance, he [or she], to the extent of any deficiency in his [or her] effective insurance coverage, may treat the risk of loss as having remained with the lessor from the beginning.

(2) Whether or not risk of loss is to pass to the lessee, if the lessee as to conforming goods already identified to a lease contract repudiates or is otherwise in default under the lease contract, the lessor, or, in the case of a finance lease, the supplier, to the extent of any deficiency in his [or her] effective insurance coverage may treat the risk of loss as resting on the lessee for a commercially reasonable time.

§ 2A-221.   Casualty to Identified Goods

If a lease contract requires goods identified when the lease contract is made, and the goods suffer casualty without fault of the lessee, the lessor or the supplier before delivery, or the goods suffer casualty before risk of loss passes to the lessee pursuant to the lease agreement or Section 2A-219, then:

(a) if the loss is total, the lease contract is avoided; and

(b) if the loss is partial or the goods have so deteriorated as to no longer conform to the lease contract, the lessee may nevertheless demand inspection and at his [or her] option either treat the lease contract as avoided or, except in a finance lease that is not a consumer lease, accept the goods with due allowance from the rent payable for the balance of the lease term for the deterioration or the deficiency in quantity but without further right against the lessor.

Part 3
Effect of Lease Contract

§ 2A-301.   Enforceability of Lease Contract

Except as otherwise provided in this Article, a lease contract is effective and enforceable according to its terms between the parties, against purchasers of the goods, and against creditors of the parties.

§ 2A-302.   Title to and Possession of Goods

Except as otherwise provided in this Article, each provision of this Article applies whether the lessor or a third party has title to the goods, and whether the lessor, the lessee, or a third party has possession of the goods, notwithstanding any statute or rule of law that possession or the absence of possession is fraudulent.

§ 2A-303.   Alienability of Party's Interest Under Lease Contract or of Lessor's Residual Interest in Goods; Delegation of Performance; Assignment of Rights

(1) Any interest of a party under a lease contract and the lessor's residual interest in the goods may be transferred unless

(a) the transfer is voluntary and the lease contract prohibits the transfer; or

(b) the transfer materially changes the duty of or materially increases the burden or risk imposed on the other party to the lease contract, and within a reasonable time after notice of the transfer the other party demands that the transferee comply with subsection (2) and the transferee fails to comply.

(2) Within a reasonable time after demand pursuant to subsection (1)(b), the transferee shall:

(a) cure or provide adequate assurance that he [or she] will promptly cure any default other than one arising from the transfer;

(b) compensate or provide adequate assurance that he [or she] will promptly compensate the other party to the lease contract and any other person holding an interest in the lease contract, except the party whose interest is being transferred, for any loss to that party resulting from the transfer;

(c) Provide adequate assurance of future due performance under the lease contract; and

(d) assume the lease contract.

(3) Demand pursuant to subsection (1)(b) is without prejudice to the other party's rights against the transferee and the party whose interest is transferred.

(4) An assignment of "the lease" or of "all my rights under the lease" or an assignment in similar general terms is a transfer of rights, and unless the language or the circumstances, as in an assignment for security, indicate the contrary, the assignment is a delegation of duties by the assignor to the assignee and acceptance by the assignee constitutes a promise by him [or her] to perform those duties. This promise is enforceable by either the assignor or the other party to the lease contract.

(5) Unless otherwise agreed by the lessor and the lessee, no delegation of performance relieves the assignor as against the other party of any duty to perform or any liability for default.

(6) A right to damages for default with respect to the whole lease contract or a right arising out of the assignor's due performance of his [or her] entire obligation can be assigned despite agreement otherwise.

(7) To prohibit the transfer of an interest of a party under a lease contract, the language of prohibition must be specific, by a writing, and conspicuous.

§ 2A-304.   Subsequent Lease of Goods by Lessor

(1) Subject to the provisions of Section 2A-303, a subsequent lessee from a lessor of goods under an existing lease contract obtains, to the extent of the leasehold interest transferred, the leasehold interest in the goods that the lessor had or had power to transfer, and except as provided in subsection (2) and Sec-

tion 2A-527(4), takes subject to the existing lease contract. A lessor with voidable title has power to transfer a good leasehold interest to a good faith subsequent lessee for value, but only to the extent set forth in the preceding sentence. When goods have been delivered under a transaction of purchase the lessor has that power even though:

    (a) the lessor's transferor was deceived as to the identity of the lessor;

    (b) the delivery was in exchange for a check which is later dishonored;

    (c) it was agreed that the transaction was to be a "cash sale"; or

    (d) the delivery was procured through fraud punishable as larcenous under the criminal law.

(2) A subsequent lessee in the ordinary course of business from a lessor who is a merchant dealing in goods of that kind to whom the goods were entrusted by the existing lessee before the interest of the subsequent lessee became enforceable against the lessor obtains, to the extent of the leasehold interest transferred, all of the lessor's and the existing lessee's rights to the goods, and takes free of the existing lease contract.

(3) A subsequent lessee from the lessor of goods that are subject to an existing lease contract and are covered by a certificate of title issued under a statute of this State or of another jurisdiction takes no greater rights than those provided both by this section and by the certificate of title statute.

§ 2A-305. Sale or Sublease of Goods by Lessee

(1) Subject to the provisions of Section 2A-303, a buyer or sublessee from the lessee of goods under an existing lease contract obtains, to the extent of the interest transferred, the leasehold interest in the goods that the lessee had or had power to transfer, and except as provided in subsection (2) and Section 2A-511(4), takes subject to the existing lease contract. A lessee with a voidable leasehold interest has power to transfer a good leasehold interest to a good faith buyer for value or a good faith sublessee for value, but only to the extent set forth in the preceding sentence. When goods have been delivered under a transaction of lease the lessee has that power even though:

    (a) the lessor was deceived as to the identity of the lessee;

    (b) the delivery was in exchange for a check which is later dishonored; or

    (c) the delivery was procured through fraud punishable as larcenous under the criminal law.

(2) A buyer in the ordinary course of business or a sublessee in the ordinary course of business from a lessee who is a merchant dealing in goods of that kind to whom the goods were entrusted by the lessor obtains, to the extent of the interest transferred, all of the lessor's and lessee's rights to the goods, and takes free of the existing lease contract.

(3) A buyer or sublessee from the lessee of goods that are subject to an existing lease contract and are covered by a certificate of title issued under a statute of this State or of another jurisdiction takes no greater rights than those provided both by this section and by the certificate of title statute.

§ 2A-306. Priority of Certain Liens Arising by Operation of Law

If a person in the ordinary course of his [or her] business furnishes services or materials with respect to goods subject to a lease contract, a lien upon those goods in the possession of that person given by statute or rule of law for those materials or services takes priority over any interest of the lessor or lessee under the lease contract or this Article unless the lien is created by statute and the statute provides otherwise or unless the lien is created by rule of law and the rule of law provides otherwise.

§ 2A-307. Priority of Liens Arising by Attachment or Levy on, Security Interest in, and Other Claims to Goods

(1) Except as otherwise provided in Section 2A-306, a creditor of a lessee takes subject to the lease contract.

(2) Except as otherwise provided in subsections (3) and (4) of this section and in Sections 2A-306 and 2A-308, a creditor of a lessor takes subject to the lease contract:

    (a) unless the creditor holds a lien that attached to the goods before the lease contract became enforceable, or

    (b) unless the creditor holds a security interest in the goods that under the Article on Secured Transactions (Article 9) would have priority over any other security interest in the goods perfected by a filing covering the goods and made at the time the lease contract became enforceable, whether or not any other security interest existed.

(3) A lessee in the ordinary course of business takes the leasehold interest free of a security interest in the goods created by the lessor even though the security interest is perfected and the lessee knows of its existence.

(4) A lessee other than a lessee in the ordinary course of business takes the leasehold interest free of a security interest to the extent that it secures future advances made after the secured party acquires knowledge of the lease or more than 45 days after the lease contract becomes enforceable, whichever first occurs, unless the future advances are made pursuant to a commitment entered into without knowledge of the lease and before the expiration of the 45-day period.

§ 2A-308. Special Rights of Creditors

(1) A creditor of a lessor in possession of goods subject to a lease contract may treat the lease contract

as void if as against the creditor retention of possession by the lessor is fraudulent under any statute or rule of law, but retention of possession in good faith and current course of trade by the lessor for a commercially reasonable time after the lease contract becomes enforceable is not fraudulent.

(2) Nothing in this Article impairs the rights of creditors of a lessor if the lease contract (a) becomes enforceable, not in current course of trade but in satisfaction of or as security for a pre-existing claim for money, security, or the like, and (b) is made under circumstances which under any statute or rule of law apart from this Article would constitute the transaction a fraudulent transfer or voidable preference.

(3) A creditor of a seller may treat a sale or an identification of goods to a contract for sale as void if as against the creditor retention of possession by the seller is fraudulent under any statute or rule of law, but retention of possession of the goods pursuant to a lease contract entered into by the seller as lessee and the buyer as lessor in connection with the sale or identification of the goods is not fraudulent if the buyer bought for value and in good faith.

§ 2A-309. Lessor's and Lessee's Rights When Goods Become Fixtures

(1) In this section:

(a) goods are "fixtures" when they become so related to particular real estate that an interest in them arises under real estate law;

(b) a "fixture filing" is the filing, in the office where a mortgage on the real estate would be recorded or registered, of a financing statement concerning goods that are or are to become fixtures and conforming to the requirements of subsection (5) of Section 9-402;

(c) a lease is a "purchase money lease" unless the lessee has possession or use of the goods or the right to possession or use of the goods before the lease agreement is enforceable;

(d) a mortgage is a "construction mortgage" to the extent it secures an obligation incurred for the construction of an improvement on land including the acquisition cost of the land, if the recorded writing so indicates; and

(e) "encumbrance" includes real estate mortgages and other liens on real estate and all other rights in real estate that are not ownership interests.

(2) Under this Article a lease may be of goods that are fixtures or may continue in goods that become fixtures, but no lease exists under this Article of ordinary building materials incorporated into an improvement on land.

(3) This Article does not prevent creation of a lease of fixtures pursuant to real estate law.

(4) The perfected interest of a lessor of fixtures has priority over a conflicting interest of an encumbrancer or owner of the real estate if:

(a) the lease is a purchase money lease, the conflicting interest of the encumbrancer or owner arises before the goods become fixtures, the interest of the lessor is perfected by a fixture filing before the goods become fixtures or within ten days thereafter, and the lessee has an interest of record in the real estate or is in possession of the real estate; or

(b) the interest of the lessor is perfected by a fixture filing before the interest of the encumbrancer or owner is of record, the lessor's interest has priority over any conflicting interest of a predecessor in title of the encumbrancer or owner, and the lessee has an interest of record in the real estate or is in possession of the real estate.

(5) The interest of a lessor of fixtures, whether or not perfected, has priority over the conflicting interest of an encumbrancer or owner of the real estate if:

(a) the fixtures are readily removable factory or office machines, readily removable equipment that is not primarily used or leased for use in the operation of the real estate. . .

§ 2A-310. Lessor's and Lessee's Rights When Goods Become Accessions

(1) Goods are "accessions" when they are installed in or affixed to other goods.

(2) The interest of a lessor or a lessee under a lease contract entered into before the goods became accessions is superior to all interests in the whole except as stated in subsection (4).

(3) The interest of a lessor or a lessee under a lease contract entered into at the time or after the goods became accessions is superior to all subsequently acquired interests in the whole except as stated in subsection (4) but is subordinate to interest in the whole existing at the time the lease contract was made unless the holders of such interests in the whole have in writing consented to the lease or disclaimed an interest in the goods as part of the whole.

(4) The interest of a lessor or a lessee under a lease contract described in subsection (2) or (3) is subordinate to the interest of

(a) a buyer in the ordinary course of business or a lessee in the ordinary course of business of any interest in the whole acquired after the goods became accessions; or

(b) a creditor with a security interest in the whole perfected before the lease contract was made to the extent that the creditor makes subsequent advances without knowledge of the lease contract.

(5) When under subsections (2) or (3) and (4) a lessor or a lessee of accessions holds an interest that is superior to all interests in the whole, the lessor or the lessee may (a) on default, expiration, termination, or cancellation of the lease contract by the other party but subject to the provisions of the lease contract and this Article, or (b) if necessary to enforce his [or her] other rights and remedies under this Article, remove the goods from the whole, free and clear of all interests in the whole, but he [or she] must reimburse any holder of an interest in the whole who is not the lessee and who has not otherwise agreed for the cost of repair of any physical injury but not for any diminution in value of the whole caused by the absence of the goods removed or by any necessity for replacing them. A person entitled to reimbursement may refuse permission to remove until the party seeking removal gives adequate security for the performance of this obligation.

Part 4
Performance of Lease Contract: Repudiated, Substituted and Excused

§ 2A-401. Insecurity: Adequate Assurance of Performance

(1) A lease contract imposes an obligation on each party that the other's expectation of receiving due performance will not be impaired.

(2) If reasonable grounds for insecurity arise with respect to the performance of either party, the insecure party may demand in writing adequate assurance of due performance. Until the insecure party receives that assurance, if commercially reasonable the insecure party may suspend any performance for which he [or she] has not already received the agreed return.

(3) A repudiation of the lease contract occurs if assurance of due performance adequate under the circumstances of the particular case is not provided to the insecure party within a reasonable time, not to exceed 30 days after receipt of a demand by the other party.

(4) Between merchants, the reasonableness of grounds for insecurity and the adequacy of any assurance offered must be determined according to commercial standards.

(5) Acceptance of any nonconforming delivery or payment does not prejudice the aggrieved party's right to demand adequate assurance of future performance.

§ 2A-402. Anticipatory Repudiation

If either party repudiates a lease contract with respect to a performance not yet due under the lease contract, the loss of which performance will substan-

tially impair the value of the lease contract to the other, the aggrieved party may:

(a) for a commercially reasonable time, await retraction of repudiation and performance by the repudiating party;

(b) make demand pursuant to Section 2A-401 and await assurance of future performance adequate under the circumstances of the particular case; or

(c) resort to any right or remedy upon default under the lease contract or this Article, even though the aggrieved party has notified the repudiating party that the aggrieved party would await the repudiating party's performance and assurance and has urged retraction. In addition, whether or not the aggrieved party is pursuing one of the foregoing remedies, the aggrieved party may suspend performance or, if the aggrieved party is the lessor, proceed in accordance with the provisions of this Article on the lessor's right to identify goods to the lease contract notwithstanding default or to salvage unfinished goods (Section 2A-524).

§ 2A-403. Retraction of Anticipatory Repudiation

(1) Until the repudiating party's next performance is due, the repudiating party can retract the repudiation unless, since the repudiation, the aggrieved party has cancelled the lease contract or materially changed the aggrieved party's position or otherwise indicated that the aggrieved party considers the repudiation final.

(2) Retraction may be by any method that clearly indicates to the aggrieved party that the repudiating party intends to perform under the lease contract and includes any assurance demanded under Section 2A-401.

(3) Retraction reinstates a repudiating party's rights under a lease contract with due excuse and allowance to the aggrieved party for any delay occasioned by the repudiation.

§ 2A-404. Substituted Performance

(1) If without fault of the lessee, the lessor and the supplier, the agreed berthing, loading, or unloading facilities fail or the agreed type of carrier becomes unavailable or the agreed manner of delivery otherwise becomes commercially impracticable, but a commercially reasonable substitute is available, the substitute performance must be tendered and accepted.

(2) If the agreed means or manner of payment fails because of domestic or foreign governmental regulation:

(a) the lessor may withhold or stop delivery or cause the supplier to withhold or stop delivery unless the lessee provides a means or manner of payment that is commercially a substantial equivalent; and

(b) if delivery has already been taken, payment by the means or in the manner provided by the regulation discharges the lessee's obligation unless the regulation is discriminatory, oppressive, or predatory.

§ 2A-405.   Excused Performance

Subject to Section 2A-404 on substituted performance, the following rules apply:

(a) Delay in delivery or nondelivery in whole or in part by a lessor or a supplier who complies with paragraphs (b) and (c) is not a default under the lease contract if performance as agreed has been made impracticable by the occurrence of a contingency the nonoccurrence of which was a basic assumption on which the lease contract was made or by compliance in good faith with any applicable foreign or domestic governmental regulation or order, whether or not the regulation or order later proves to be invalid.

(b) If the causes mentioned in paragraph (a) affect only part of the lessor's or the supplier's capacity to perform, he [or she] shall allocate production and deliveries among his [or her] customers but at his [or her] option may include regular customers not then under contract for sale or lease as well as his [or her] own requirements for further manufacture. He [or she] may so allocate in any manner that is fair and reasonable.

(c) The lessor seasonably shall notify the lessee and in the case of a finance lease the supplier seasonably shall notify the lessor and the lessee, if known, that there will be delay or nondelivery and, if allocation is required under paragraph (b), of the estimated quota thus made available for the lessee.

§ 2A-406.   Procedure on Excused Performance

(1) If the lessee receives notification of a material or indefinite delay or an allocation justified under Section 2A-405, the lessee may by written notification to the lessor as to any goods involved, and with respect to all of the goods if under an installment lease contract the value of the whole lease contract is substantially impaired (Section 2A-510):

(a) terminate the lease contract (Section 2A-505(2)); or

(b) except in a finance lease that is not a consumer lease, modify the lease contract by accepting the available quota in substitution, with due allowance from the rent payable for the balance of the lease term for the deficiency but without further right against the lessor.

(2) If, after receipt of a notification from the lessor under Section 2A-405, the lessee fails so to modify the lease agreement within a reasonable time not exceeding 30 days, the lease contract lapses with respect to any deliveries affected.

§ 2A-407.   Irrevocable Promises: Finance Leases

(1) In the case of a finance lease that is not a consumer lease the lessee's promises under the lease contract become irrevocable and independent upon the lessee's acceptance of the goods.

(2) A promise that has become irrevocable and independent under subsection (1):

(a) is effective and enforceable between the parties, and by or against third parties including assignees of the parties, and

(b) is not subject to cancellation, termination, modification, repudiation, excuse, or substitution without the consent of the party to whom the promise runs.

Part 5
Default

A. In General

§ 2A-501.   Default: Procedure

(1) Whether the lessor or the lessee is in default under a lease contract is determined by the lease agreement and this Article.

(2) If the lessor or the lessee is in default under the lease contract, the party seeking enforcement has rights and remedies as provided in this Article and, except as limited by this Article, as provided in the lease agreement.

(3) If the lessor or the lessee is in default under the lease contract, the party seeking enforcement may reduce the party's claim to judgment, or otherwise enforce the lease contract by self-help or any available judicial procedure or nonjudicial procedure, including administrative proceeding, arbitration, or the like, in accordance with this Article.

(4) Except as otherwise provided in this Article or the lease Agreement, the rights and remedies referred to in subsections (2) and (3) are cumulative.

(5) If the lease agreement covers both real property and goods, the party seeking enforcement may proceed under this Part as to the goods, or under other applicable law as to both the real property and the goods in accordance with his [or her] rights and remedies in respect of the real property, in which case this Part does not apply.

§ 2A-502.   Notice After Default

Except as otherwise provided in this Article or the lease agreement, the lessor or lessee in default under the lease contract is not entitled to notice of default or notice of enforcement from the other party to the lease agreement.

§ 2A-503.   Modification or Impairment of Rights and Remedies

(1) Except as otherwise provided in this Article, the lease agreement may include rights and remedies for default in addition to or in substitution for

those provided in this Article and may limit or alter the measure of damages recoverable under this Article.

(2) Resort to a remedy provided under this Article or in the lease agreement is optional unless the remedy is expressly agreed to be exclusive. If circumstances cause an exclusive or limited remedy to fail of its essential purpose, or provision for an exclusive remedy is unconscionable, remedy may be had as provided in this Article.

(3) Consequential damages may be liquidated under Section 2A-504, or may otherwise be limited, altered, or excluded unless the limitation, alteration, or exclusion is unconscionable. Limitation of consequential damages for injury to the person in the case of consumer goods is prima facie unconscionable but limitation of damages where the loss is commercial is not.

(4) Rights and remedies on default by the lessor or the lessee with respect to any obligation or promise collateral or ancillary to the lease contract are not impaired by this Article.

§ 2A-504.   Liquidation of Damages

(1) Damages payable by either party for default, or any other act or omission, including indemnity for loss or diminution of anticipated tax benefits or loss or damage to lessor's residual interest, may be liquidated in the lease agreement but only at an amount or by a formula that is reasonable in light of the then anticipated harm caused by the default or other act or omission.

(2) If the lease agreement provides for liquidation of damages, and such provision does not comply with subsection (1), or such provision is an exclusive or limited remedy that circumstances cause to fail of its essential purpose, remedy may be had as provided in this Article.

(3) If the lessor justifiably withholds or stops delivery of goods because of the lessee's default or insolvency (Section 2A-525 or 2A-526), the lessee is entitled to restitution of any amount by which the sum of his [or her] payments exceeds:

   (a) the amount to which the lessor is entitled by virtue of terms liquidating the lessor's damages in accordance with subsection (1); or

   (b) in the absence of those terms, 20 percent of the then present value of the total rent the lessee was obligated to pay for the balance of the lease term, or, in the case of a consumer lease, the lesser of such amount or $500.

(4) A lessee's right to restitution under subsection (3) is subject to offset to the extent the lessor establishes:

   (a) a right to recover damages under the provisions of this Article other than subsection (1); and

   (b) the amount or value of any benefits received by the lessee directly or indirectly by reason of the lease contract.

§ 2A-505.   Cancellation and Termination and Effect of Cancellation, Termination, Rescission, or Fraud on Rights and Remedies

(1) On cancellation of the lease contract, all obligations that are still executory on both sides are discharged, but any right based on prior default or performance survives, and the cancelling party also retains any remedy for default of the whole lease contract or any unperformed balance.

(2) On termination of the lease contract, all obligations that are still executory on both sides are discharged but any right based on prior default or performance survives.

(3) Unless the contrary intention clearly appears, expressions of "cancellation," "rescission," or the like of the lease contract may not be construed as a renunciation or discharge of any claim in damages for an antecedent default.

(4) Rights and remedies for material misrepresentation or fraud include all rights and remedies available under this Article for default.

(5) Neither rescission nor a claim for rescission of the lease contract nor rejection or return of the goods may bar or be deemed inconsistent with a claim for damages or other right or remedy.

§ 2A-506.   Statute of Limitations

(1) An action for default under a lease contract, including breach of warranty or indemnity, must be commenced within 4 years after the cause of action accrued. By the original lease contract the parties may reduce the period of limitation to not less that one year.

(2) A cause of action for default accrues when the act or omission on which the default or breach of warranty is based is or should have been discovered by the aggrieved party, or when the default occurs, whichever is later. A cause of action for indemnity accrues when the act or omission on which the claim for indemnity is based is or should have been discovered by the indemnified party, whichever is later.

(3) If an action commenced within the time limited by subsection (1) is so terminated as to leave available a remedy by another action for the same default or breach of warranty or indemnity, the other action may be commenced after the expiration of the time limited and within 6 months after the termination of the first action unless the termination resulted from voluntary discontinuance or from dismissal for failure or neglect to prosecute.

(4) This section does not alter the law on tolling of the statute of limitations nor does it apply to causes of action that have accrued before this Article becomes effective.

§ 2A-507. Proof of Market Rent: Time and Place

(1) Damages based on market rent (Section 2A-519 or 2A-528) are determined according to the rent for the use of the goods concerned for a lease term identical to the remaining lease term of the original lease agreement and prevailing at the time of the default.

(2) If evidence of rent for the use of the goods concerned for a lease term identical to the remaining lease term of the original lease agreement and prevailing at the times or places described in this Article is not readily available, the rent prevailing within any reasonable time before or after the time described or at any other place or for a different lease term which in commercial judgment or under usage of trade would serve as a reasonable substitute for the one described may be used, making any proper allowance for the difference, including the cost of transporting the goods to or from the other place.

(3) Evidence of a relevant rent prevailing at a time or place or for a lease term other than the one described in this Article offered by one party is not admissible unless and until he [or she] has given the other party notice the court finds sufficient to prevent unfair surprise.

(4) If the prevailing rent or value of any goods regularly leased in any established market is in issue, reports in official publications or trade journals or in newspapers or periodicals of general circulation published as the reports of that market are admissible in evidence. The circumstances of the preparation of the report may be shown to affect its weight but not its admissibility.

B. Default by Lessor

§ 2A-508. Lessee's Remedies

(1) If a lessor fails to deliver the goods in conformity to the lease contract (Section 2A-509) or repudiates the lease contract (Section 2A-402), or a lessee rightfully rejects the goods (Section 2A-509) or justifiably revokes acceptance of the goods (Section 2A-517), then with respect to any goods involved, and with respect to all of the goods if under an installment lease contract the value of the whole lease contract is substantially impaired (Section 2A-510), the lessor is in default under the lease contract and the lessee may:

    (a) cancel the lease contract (Section 2A-505(1));

    (b) recover so much of the rent and security as has been paid, but in the case of an installment lease contract the recovery is that which is just under the circumstances;

    (c) cover and recover damages as to all goods affected whether or not they have been identified to the lease contract (Sections 2A-518 and 2A-520), or

recover damages for nondelivery (Sections 2A-519 and 2A-520).

(2) If a lessor fails to deliver the goods in conformity to the lease contract or repudiates the lease contract, the lessee may also:

    (a) if the goods have been identified, recover them (Section 2A-522); or

    (b) in a proper case, obtain specific performance or replevy the goods (Section 2A-521).

(3) If a lessor is otherwise in default under a lease contract, the lessee may exercise the rights and remedies provided in the lease contract and this Article.

(4) If a lessor has breached a warranty, whether express or implied, the lessee may recover damages (Section 2A-519(4)).

(5) On rightful rejection or justifiable revocation of acceptance, a lessee has a security interest in goods in the lessee's possession or control for any rent and security that has been paid and any expenses reasonably incurred in their inspection, receipt, transportation, and care and custody and may hold those goods and dispose of them in good faith and in a commercially reasonable manner, subject to the provisions of Section 2A-527(5).

(6) Subject to the provisions of Section 2A-407, a lessee, on notifying the lessor of the lessee's intention to do so, may deduct all or any part of the damages resulting from any default under the lease contract from any part of the rent still due under the same lease contract.

§ 2A-509. Lessee's Rights on Improper Delivery; Rightful Rejection

(1) Subject to the provisions of Section 2A-510 on default in installment lease contracts, if the goods or the tender or delivery fail in any respect to conform to the lease contract, the lessee may reject or accept the goods or accept any commercial unit or units and reject the rest of the goods.

(2) Rejection of goods is ineffective unless it is within a reasonable time after tender or delivery of the goods and the lessee seasonably notifies the lessor.

§ 2A-510. Installment Lease Contracts: Rejection and Default

(1) Under an installment lease contract a lessee may reject any delivery that is nonconforming if the nonconformity substantially impairs the value of that delivery and cannot be cured or the nonconformity is a defect in the required documents; but if the nonconformity does not fall within subsection (2) and the lessor or the supplier gives adequate assurance of its cure, the lessee must accept that delivery.

(2) Whenever nonconformity or default with respect to one or more deliveries substantially impairs the value of the installment lease contract as a whole there is a default with respect to the whole. But, the aggrieved party reinstates the installment lease con-

tract as a whole if the aggrieved party accepts a non-conforming delivery without seasonably notifying of cancellation or brings an action with respect only to past deliveries or demands performance as to future deliveries.

§ 2A-511. Merchant Lessee's Duties as to Rightfully Rejected Goods

(1) Subject to any security interest of a lessee (Section 2A-508(5)), if a lessor or a supplier has no agent or place of business at the market of rejection, a merchant lessee, after rejection of goods in his [or her] possession or control, shall follow any reasonable instructions received from the lessor or the supplier with respect to the goods. In the absence of those instructions a merchant lessee shall make reasonable efforts to sell, lease, or otherwise dispose of the goods for the lessor's account if they threaten to decline in value speedily. Instructions are not reasonable if on demand indemnity for expenses is not forthcoming.

(2) If a merchant lessee (subsection (1)) or any other lessee (Section 2A-512) disposes of goods, he [or she] is entitled to reimbursement either from the lessor or the supplier or out of the proceeds for reasonable expenses of caring for and disposing of the goods and, if the expenses include no disposition commission, to such commission as is usual in the trade, or if there is none, to a reasonable sum not exceeding 10 percent of the gross proceeds.

(3) In complying with this section or Section 2A-512, the lessee is held only to good faith. Good faith conduct hereunder is neither acceptance or conversion nor the basis of an action for damages.

(4) A purchaser who purchases in good faith from a lessee pursuant to this section or Section 2A-512 takes the goods free of any rights of the lessor and the supplier even though the lessee fails to comply with one or more of the requirements of this Article.

§ 2A-512. Lessee's Duties as to Rightfully Rejected Goods

(1) Except as otherwise provided with respect to goods that threaten to decline in value speedily (Section 2A-511) and subject to any security interest of a lessee (Section 2A-508(5)):

(a) the lessee, after rejection of goods in the lessee's possession, shall hold them with reasonable care at the lessor's or supplier's disposition for a reasonable time after the lessee's seasonable notification of rejection;

(b) if the lessor or the supplier gives no instructions within a reasonable time after notification of rejection, the lessee may store the rejected goods for the lessor's or the supplier's account or ship them to the lessor or the supplier or dispose of them for the lessor's or the supplier's account with reimbursement in the manner provided in Section 2A-511; but

(c) the lessee has no further obligations with regard to goods rightfully rejected.

(2) Action by the lessee pursuant to subsection (1) is not acceptance or conversion.

§ 2A-513. Cure by Lessor of Improper Tender or Delivery; Replacement

(1) If any tender or delivery by the lessor or the supplier is rejected because nonconforming and the time for performance has not yet expired, the lessor or the supplier may seasonably notify the lessee of the lessor's or the supplier's intention to cure and may then make a conforming delivery within the time provided in the lease contract.

(2) If the lessee rejects a nonconforming tender that the lessor or the supplier had reasonable grounds to believe would be acceptable with or without money allowance, the lessor or the supplier may have a further reasonable time to substitute a conforming tender if he [or she] seasonably notifies the lessee.

§ 2A-514. Waiver of Lessee's Objections

(1) In rejecting goods, a lessee's failure to state a particular defect that is ascertainable by reasonable inspection precludes the lessee from relying on the defect to justify rejection or to establish default:

(a) if, states seasonably, the lessor or the supplier could have cured it (Section 2A-513); or

(b) between merchants if the lessor or the supplier after rejection has made a request in writing for a full and final written statement of all defects on which the lessee proposes to rely.

(2) A lessee's failure to reserve rights when paying rent or other consideration against documents precludes recovery of the payment for defects apparent on the face of the documents.

§ 2A-515. Acceptance of Goods

(1) Acceptance of goods occurs after the lessee has had a reasonable opportunity to inspect the goods and

(a) the lessee signifies or acts with respect to the goods in a manner that signifies to the lessor or the supplier that the goods are conforming or that the lessee will take or retain them in spite of their nonconformity; or

(b) the lessee fails to make an effective rejection of the goods (Section 2A-509(2)).

(2) Acceptance of a part of any commercial unit is acceptance of that entire unit.

§ 2A-516. Effect of Acceptance of Goods; Notice of Default; Burden of Establishing Default After Acceptance; Notice of Claim or Litigation to Person Answerable Over

(1) A lessee must pay rent for any goods accepted in accordance with the lease contract, with due

allowance for goods rightfully rejected or not delivered.

(2) A lessee's acceptance of goods precludes rejection of the goods accepted. In the case of a finance lease, if made with knowledge of a nonconformity, acceptance cannot be revoked because of it. In any other case, if made with knowledge of a nonconformity, acceptance cannot be revoked because of it unless the acceptance was on the reasonable assumption that the nonconformity would be seasonably cured. Acceptance does not of itself impair any other remedy provided by this Article or the lease agreement for nonconformity.

(3) If a tender has been accepted:

    (a) within a reasonable time after the lessee discovers or should have discovered any default, the lessee shall notify the lessor and the supplier, or be barred from any remedy;

    (b) except in the case of a consumer lease, within a reasonable time after the lessee receives notice of litigation for infringement or the like (Section 2A-211) the lessee shall notify the lessor or be barred from any remedy over for liability established by the litigation; and

    (c) the burden is on the lessee to establish any default.

(4) If a lessee is sued for breach of a warranty or other obligation for which a lessor or a supplier is answerable over:

    (a) The lessee may give the lessor or the supplier written notice of the litigation. If the notice states that the lessor or the supplier may come in and defend and that if the lessor or the supplier does not do so he [or she] will be bound in any action against him [or her] by the lessee by any determination of fact common to the two litigations, then unless the lessor or the supplier after seasonable receipt of the notice does come in and defend he [or she] is so bound.

    (b) The lessor or the supplier may demand in writing that the lessee turn over control of the litigation including settlement if the claim is one for infringement or the like (Section 2A-211) or else be barred from any remedy over. If the demand states that the lessor or the supplier agrees to bear all expense and to satisfy any adverse judgment, then unless the lessee after seasonable receipt of the demand does turn over control the lessee is so barred.

(5) The provisions of subsections (3) and (4) apply to any obligation of a lessee to hold the lessor or the supplier harmless against infringement or the like (Section 2A-211).

§ 2A-517. Revocation of Acceptance of Goods

(1) A lessee may revoke acceptance of a lot or commercial unit whose nonconformity substantially impairs its value to the lessee if he [or she] has accepted it:

    (a) except in the case of a finance lease, on the reasonable assumption that its nonconformity would be cured and it has not been seasonably cured; or

    (b) without discovery of the nonconformity if the lessee's acceptance was reasonably induced either by the lessor's assurance or, except in the case of a finance lease, by the difficulty of discovery before acceptance.

(2) Revocation of acceptance must occur within a reasonable time after the lessee discovers or should have discovered the ground for it and before any substantial change in condition of the goods which is not caused by the nonconformity. Revocation is not effective until the lessee notifies the lessor.

(3) A lessee who so revokes has the same rights and duties with regard to the goods involved as if the lessee had rejected them.

§ 2A-518. Cover; Substitute Goods

(1) After default by a lessor under the lease contract (Section 2A-508(1)), the lessee may cover by making any purchase or lease of or contract to purchase or lease goods in substitution for those due from the lessor.

(2) Except as otherwise provided with respect to damages liquidated in the lease agreement (Section 2A-504) or determined by agreement of the parties (Section 1-102(3)), if a lessee's cover is by lease agreement substantially similar to the original lease agreement and the lease agreement is made in good faith and in a commercially reasonable manner, the lessee may recover from the lessor as damages (a) the present value, as of the date of default, of the difference between the total rent for the lease term of the new lease agreement and the total rent for the remaining lease term of the original lease agreement and (b) any incidental or consequential damages less expenses saved in consequence of the lessor's default.

(3) If a lessee's cover is by lease agreement that for any reason does not qualify for treatment under subsection (2), or is by purchase or otherwise, the lessee may recover from the lessor as if the lessee had elected not to cover and Section 2A-519 governs.

§ 2A-519. Lessee's Damages for Nondelivery, Repudiation, Default and Breach of Warranty in Regard to Accepted Goods

(1) Except as otherwise provided with respect to damages liquidated in the lease agreement (Section 2A-504) or determined by agreement of the parties (Section 1-102(3)), if a lessee elects not to cover or a lessee elects to cover and the cover is by lease agree-

ment that for any reason does not qualify for treatment under Section 2A-518(2), or is by purchase or otherwise, the measure of damages for non-delivery or repudiation by the lessor or for rejection or revocation of acceptance by the lessee is the present value as of the date of the default of the difference between the then market rent and the original rent, computed for the remaining lease term of the original lease agreement together with incidental and consequential damages, less expenses saved in consequence of the lessor's default.

(2) Market rent is to be determined as of the place for tender or, in cases of rejection after arrival or revocation of acceptance, as of the place of arrival.

(3) If the lessee has accepted goods and given notification (Section 2A-516(3)), the measure of damages for non-conforming tender or delivery by a lessor is the loss resulting in the ordinary course of events from the lessor's default as determined in any manner that is reasonable together with incidental and consequential damages, less expenses saved in consequence of the lessor's default.

(4) The measure of damages for breach of warranty is the present value at the time and place of acceptance of the difference between the value of the use of the goods accepted and the value if they had been as warranted for the lease term, unless special circumstances show proximate damages of a different amount, together with incidental and consequential damages, less expenses saved in consequence of the lessor's default or breach of warranty.

§ 2A-520. Lessee's Incidental and Consequential Damages

(1) Incidental damages resulting from a lessor's default include expenses reasonably incurred in inspection, receipt, transportation, and care and custody of goods rightfully rejected or goods the acceptance of which is justifiably revoked, any commercially reasonable charges, expenses or commissions in connection with effecting cover, and any other reasonable expense incident to the default.

(2) Consequential damages resulting from a lessor's default include:

    (a) any loss resulting from general or particular requirements and needs of which the lessor at the time of contracting had reason to know and which could not reasonably be prevented by cover or otherwise; and

    (b) injury to person or property proximately resulting from any breach of warranty.

§ 2A-521. Lessee's Right to Specific Performance or Replevin

(1) Specific performance may be decreed if the goods are unique or in other proper circumstances.

(2) A decree for specific performance may include any terms and conditions as to payment of the rent, damages, or other relief that the court deems just.

(3) A lessee has a right of replevin, detinue, sequestration, claim and delivery, or the like for goods identified to the lease contract if after reasonable effort the lessee is unable to effect cover for those goods or the circumstances reasonably indicate that the effort will be unavailing.

§ 2A-522. Lessee's Right to Goods on Lessor's Insolvency

(1) Subject to subsection (2) and even though the goods have not been shipped, a lessee who has paid a part or all of the rent and security for goods identified to a lease contract (Section 2A-217) on making and keeping good a tender of any unpaid portion of the rent and security due under the lease contract may recover the goods identified from the lessor if the lessor becomes insolvent within 10 days after receipt of the first installment of rent and security.

(2) A lessee acquires the right to recover goods identified to a lease contract only if they conform to the lease contract.

C. Default by Lessee

§ 2A-523. Lessor's Remedies

(1) If a lessee wrongfully rejects or revokes acceptance of goods or fails to make a payment when due or repudiates with respect to a part or the whole, then, with respect to any goods involved, and with respect to all of the goods if under an installment lease contract the value of the whole lease contract is substantially impaired (Section 2A-510), the lessee is in default under the lease contract and the lessor may:

    (a) cancel the lease contract (Section 2A-505(1));

    (b) proceed respecting goods not identified to the lease contract (Section 2A-524);

    (c) withhold delivery of the goods and take possession of goods previously delivered (Section 2A-525);

    (d) stop delivery of the goods by any bailee (Section 2A-526);

    (e) dispose of the goods and recover damages (Section 2A-527), or retain the goods and recover damages (Section 2A-528), or in a proper case recover rent (Section 2A-529).

(2) If a lessee is otherwise in default under a lease contract, the lessor may exercise the rights and remedies provided in the lease contract and this Article.

§ 2A-524. Lessor's Right to Identify Goods to Lease Contract

(1) A lessor aggrieved under Section 2A-523(1) may:

    (a) identify to the lease contract conforming goods not already identified if at the time the lessor learned of the default they were in the lessor's or the supplier's possession or control; and

    (b) dispose of goods (Section 2A-527(1)) that demonstrably have been intended for the particular lease contract even though those goods are unfinished.

(2) If the goods are unfinished, in the exercise of reasonable commercial judgment for the purposes of avoiding loss and of effective realization, an aggrieved lessor or the supplier may either complete manufacture and wholly identify the goods to the lease contract or cease manufacture and lease, sell, or otherwise dispose of the goods for scrap or salvage value or proceed in any other reasonable manner.

§ 2A-525. Lessor's Right to Possession of Goods

(1) If a lessor discovers the lessee to be insolvent, the lessor may refuse to deliver the goods.

(2) The lessor has on default by the lessee under the lease contract the right to take possession of the goods. If the lease contract so provides, the lessor may require the lessee to assemble the goods and make them available to the lessor at a place to be designated by the lessor which is reasonably convenient to both parties. Without removal, the lessor may render unusable any goods employed in trade or business, and may dispose of goods on the lessee's premises (Section 2A-527).

(3) The lessor may proceed under subsection (2) without judicial process if that can be done without breach of the peace or the lessor may proceed by action.

§ 2A-526. Lessor's Stoppage of Delivery in Transit or Otherwise

(1) A lessor may stop delivery of goods in the possession of a carrier or other bailee if the lessor discovers the lessee to be insolvent and may stop delivery of carload, truckload, planeload, or larger shipments of express or freight if the lessee repudiates or fails to make a payment due before delivery, whether for rent, security or otherwise under the lease contract, or for any other reason the lessor has a right to withhold or take possession of the goods.

(2) In pursuing its remedies under subsection (1), the lessor may stop delivery until

    (a) receipt of the goods by the lessee;

    (b) acknowledgment to the lessee by any bailee of the goods, except a carrier, that the bailee holds the goods for the lessee; or

    (c) such an acknowledgment to the lessee by a carrier via reshipment or as warehouseman.

(3) (a) To stop delivery, a lessor shall so notify as to enable the bailee by reasonable diligence to prevent delivery of the goods.

    (b) After notification, the bailee shall hold and deliver the goods according to the directions of the lessor, but the lessor is liable to the bailee for any ensuing charges or damages.

    (c) A carrier who has issued a nonnegotiable bill of lading is not obliged to obey a notification to stop received from a person other than the consignor.

§ 2A-527. Lessor's Rights to Dispose of Goods

(1) After a default by a lessee under the lease contract (Section 2A-523(1)) or after the lessor refuses to deliver or takes possession of goods (Section 2A-525 or 2A-526), the lessor may dispose of the goods concerned or the undelivered balance thereof by lease, sale or otherwise.

(2) Except as otherwise provided with respect to damages liquidated in the lease agreement (Section 2A-504) or determined by agreement of the parties (Section 1-102(3)), if the disposition is by lease agreement substantially similar to the original lease agreement and the lease agreement is made in good faith and in a commercially reasonable manner, the lessor may recover from the lessee as damages (a) accrued and unpaid rent as of the date of default, (b) the present value as of the date of default of the difference between the total rent for the remaining lease term of the original lease agreement and the total rent for the lease term of the new lease agreement, and (c) any incidental damages allowed under Section 2A-530, less expenses saved in consequence of the lessee's default.

(3) If the lessor's disposition is by lease agreement that for any reason does not qualify for treatment under subsection (2), or is by sale or otherwise, the lessor may recover from the lessee as if the lessor had elected not to dispose of the goods and Section 2A-528 governs.

(4) A subsequent buyer or lessee who buys or leases from the lessor in good faith for value as a result of a disposition under this section takes the goods free of the original lease contract and any rights of the original lessee even though the lessor fails to comply with one or more of the requirements of this Article.

(5) The lessor is not accountable to the lessee for any profit made on any disposition. A lessee who has rightfully rejected or justifiably revoked acceptance shall account to the lessor for any excess over the amount of the lessee's security interest (Section 2A-508(5)).

§ 2A-528.   Lessor's Damages for Non-Acceptance or Repudiation

(1) Except as otherwise provided with respect to damages liquidated in the lease agreement (Section 2A-504) or determined by agreement of the parties (Section 1-102(3)), if a lessor elects to retain the goods or a lessor elects to dispose of the goods and disposition is by lease agreement that for any reason does not qualify for treatment under Section 2A-527(2), or is by sale or otherwise, the lessor may recover from the lessee as damages for non-acceptance or repudiation by the lessee (a) accrued and unpaid rent as of the date of default, (b) the present value as of the date of default of the difference between the total rent for the remaining lease term of the original lease agreement and the market rent at the time and place for tender computed for the same lease term, and (c) any incidental damages allowed under Section 2A-530, less expenses saved in consequence of the lessee's default.

(2) If the measure of damages provided in subsection (1) is inadequate to put a lessor in as good a position as performance would have, the measure of damages is the profit, including reasonable overhead, the lessor would have made from full performance by the lessee, together with any incidental damages allowed under Section 2A-530, due allowance for costs reasonably incurred and due credit for payments or proceeds of disposition.

§ 2A-529.   Lessor's Action for the Rent

(1) After default by the lessee under the lease contract (Section 2A-523(1)), if the lessor complies with subsection (2), the lessor may recover from the lessee as damages:

(a) for goods accepted by the lessee and for conforming goods lost or damaged within a commercially reasonable time after risk of loss passes to the lessee (Section 2A-219), (i) accrued and unpaid rent as of the date of default, (ii) the present value as of the date of default of the rent for the remaining lease term of the lease agreement, and (iii) any incidental damages allowed under Section 2A-530, less expenses saved in consequence of the lessee's default; and

(b) for goods identified to the lease contract if the lessor is unable after reasonable effort to dispose of them at a reasonable price or the circumstances reasonably indicate that effort will be unavailing, (i) accrued and unpaid rent as of the date of default, (ii) the present value as of the date of default of the rent for the remaining lease term of the lease agreement, and (iii) any incidental damages allowed under Section 2A-530, less expenses saved in consequence of the lessee's default.

(2) Except as provided in subsection (3), the lessor shall hold for the lessee for the remaining lease term of the lease agreement any goods that have been identified to the lease contract and are in the lessor's control.

(3) The lessor may dispose of the goods at any time before collection of the judgment for damages obtained pursuant to subsection (1). If the disposition is before the end of the remaining lease term of the lease agreement, the lessor's recovery against the lessee for damages will be governed by Section 2A-527 or Section 2A-528.

(4) Payment of the judgment for damages obtained pursuant to subsection (1) entitles the lessee to use and possession of the goods not then disposed of for the remaining lease term of the lease agreement.

(5) After a lessee has wrongfully rejected or revoked acceptance of goods, has failed to pay rent then due, or has repudiated (Section 2A-402), a lessor who is held not entitled to rent under this section must nevertheless be awarded damages for non-acceptance under Sections 2A-527 and 2A-528.

§ 2A-530.   Lessor's Incidental Damages

Incidental damages to an aggrieved lessor include any commercially reasonable charges, expenses, or commissions incurred in stopping delivery, in the transportation, care and custody of goods after the lessee's default, in connection with return or disposition of the goods, or otherwise resulting from the default.

§ 2A-531.   Standing to Sue Third Parties for Injury to Goods

(1) If a third party so deals with goods that have been identified to a lease contract as to cause actionable injury to a party to the lease contract (a) the lessor has a right of action against the third party, and (b) the lessee also has a right of action against the third party if the lessee:

(i)   has a security interest in the goods;

(ii) has an insurable interest in the goods; or

(iii) bears the risk of loss under the lease contract or has since the injury assumed that risk as against the lessor and the goods have been converted or destroyed.

(2) If at the time of the injury the party plaintiff did not bear the risk of loss as against the other party to the lease contract and there is no arrangement between them for disposition of the recovery, his [or her] suit or settlement, subject to his [or her] own interest, is as a fiduciary for the other party to the lease contract.

(3) Either party with the consent of the other may sue for the benefit of whom it may concern.

ARTICLE 1 AND ARTICLE 9:

CONFORMING AMENDMENTS TO ARTICLE 2A

§ 1-105.   Territorial Application of the Act; Parties' Power to Choose Applicable Law

(1) Except as provided hereafter in this section, when a transaction bears a reasonable relation to this state and also to another state or nation the parties may agree that the law either of this state or of such other state or nation shall govern their rights and duties. Failing such agreement this Act applies to transactions bearing an appropriate relation to this state.

(2) Where one of the following provisions of this Act specifies the applicable law, that provision governs and a contrary agreement is effective only to the extent permitted by the law (including the conflict of laws rules) so specified:

> Rights of creditors against sold goods. Section 2-402.
> Applicability of the Article on Leases. Sections 2A-105 and 2A-106.
> Applicability of the Article on Bank Deposits and Collections. Section 4-102.
> Bulk transfers subject to the Article on Bulk Transfers. Section 6-102.
> Applicability of the Article on Investment Securities. Section 8-106.
> Perfection provisions of the Article on Secured Transactions. Section 9-103.

§ 1-201(37).   General Definitions: "Security Interest"

(37) "Security interest" means an interest in personal property or fixtures which secures payment of performance of an obligation. The retention or reservation of title by a seller of goods notwithstanding shipment or delivery to the buyer (Section 2-401) is limited in effect to a reservation of a "security interest". The term also includes any interest of a buyer of accounts or chattel paper which is subject to Article 9. The special property interest of a buyer of goods on identification of those goods to a contract for sale under Section 2-401 is not a "security interest", but a buyer may also acquire a "security interest" by complying with Article 9. Unless a consignment is intended as security, reservation of title thereunder is not a "security interest", but a consignment in any event is subject to the provisions on consignment sales (Section 2-326).

Whether a transaction creates a lease or security interest is determined by the facts of each case; however, a transaction creates a security interest if the consideration the lessee is to pay the lessor for the right to possession and use of the goods is an obligation for the term of the lease not subject to termination by the lessee, and

  (a) the original term of the lease is equal to or greater than the remaining economic life of the goods,

  (b) the lessee is bound to renew the lease for the remaining economic life of the goods or is bound to become the owner of the goods,

  (c) the lessee has an option to renew the lease for the remaining economic life of the goods for no additional consideration or nominal additional consideration upon compliance with the lease agreement, or

  (d) the lessee has an option to become the owner of the goods for no additional consideration or nominal additional consideration upon compliance with the lease agreement.

A transaction does not create a security interest merely because it provides that

  (a) the present value of the consideration the lessee is obligated to pay the lessor for the right to possession and use of the goods is substantially equal to or is greater than the fair market value of the goods at the time the lease is entered into,

  (b) the lessee assumes risk of loss of the goods, or agrees to pay taxes, insurance, filing, recording, or registration fees, or service or maintenance costs with respect to the goods,

  (c) the lessee has an option to renew the lease or to become the owner of the goods,

  (d) the lessee has an option to renew the lease for a fixed rent that is equal to or greater than the reasonably predictable fair market rent for the use of the goods for the term of the renewal at the time the option is to be performed, or

  (e) the lessee has an option to become the owner of the goods for a fixed price that is equal to or greater than the reasonably predictable fair market value of the goods at the time the option is to be performed.

For purposes of this subsection (37):

  (x) Additional consideration is not nominal if (i) when the option to renew the lease is granted to the lessee the rent is stated to be the fair market rent for the use of the goods for the term of the renewal determined at the time the option is to be performed, or (ii) when the option to become the owner of the goods is granted to the lessee the price is stated to be the fair market value of the goods determined at the time the option is to be performed. Additional consideration is nominal if it is less than the lessee's reasonably predictable cost of performing under the lease agreement if the option is not exercised;

(y) "Reasonably predictable" and "remaining economic life of the goods" are to be determined with reference to the facts and circumstances at the time the transaction is entered into; and

(z) "Present value" means the amount as of a date certain of one or more sums payable in the future, discounted to the date certain. The discount is determined by the interest rate specified by the parties if the rate is not manifestly unreasonable at the time the transaction is entered into; otherwise, the discount is determined by a commercially reasonable rate that takes into account the facts and circumstances of each case at the time the transaction was entered into.

§ 9-113. Security Interests Arising Under Article on Sales or Under Article on Leases

A security interest arising solely under the Article on Sales (Article 2) or the Article on Leases (Article 2A) is subject to the provisions of this Article except that to the extent that and so long as the debtor does not have or does not lawfully obtain possession of the goods

(a) no security agreement is necessary to make the security interest enforceable; and

(b) no filing is required to perfect the security interest; and

(c) the rights of the secured party on default by the debtor are governed (i) by the Article on Sales (Article 2) in the case of a security interest arising solely under such Article or (ii) by the Article on Leases (Article 2A) in the case of a security interest arising solely under such Article.

LEASES UNDER ARTICLE 2A OF THE UNIFORM COMMERCIAL CODE

A. General Principles

In 1987, a new Article 2A, leases, was added to the Uniform Commercial Code to regulate the widespread modern practice of leasing personal property. At the date of publication of this book, Article 2A has only been adopted by Oklahoma, but it is highly probable that the new article will soon be widely adopted and that courts will apply its principles by analogy even before it is adopted.

§ 1. Subject of lease. The Article 2A lease is a lease of goods or of goods that are or become fixtures. Goods are defined in the same manner as in Article 2 as property that is movable. Whether property is a fixture is determined by the local non-Code law of real estate.

§ 2. Kinds of leases. Article 2A regulates the widely varied fact situations involved in leasing and makes special provision for (1) consumer leases, (2) nonconsumer or commercial leases, (3) finance leases, (4) nonfinance leases, and (5) subleases. These categories may overlap in some cases, as when there is a nonconsumer finance lease. There could also be a consumer finance lease.

In this Appendix, consideration will first be given to principles applicable to all kinds of leases, and then special consideration will be given to consumer leases and finance leases.[1]

§ 3. Lease defined. A lease, for the purpose of Article 2A of the UCC, is "a transfer of the right to possession and use of goods [or fixtures] for a term in return for consideration . . ."[2] A gratuitous bailment is thus excluded from the definition of *lease*. Also excluded are absolute sales and sales on approval or return. A lease that creates a security interest is also excluded.[3]

B. Formation and Effect of Lease

§ 4. Formation of the lease. A lease is formed when the parties reach an agreement to lease. The process specified by Article 2A is in substance a copy of the process described by Article 2 on the sale of goods. Article 2A repeats the firm offer provision as to merchants. It also nullifies the common-law effect of a seal. Offer and acceptance under Article 2A is the same as under Article 2 except that there is no provision for acceptance by shipment of goods nor for additional terms in an acceptance or confirmation. The subject of modification, rescission, and waiver is treated by Article 2A in the same manner as Article 2.[4]

§ 5. Validity of lease. A lease is subject to the general rules of law that determine the validity of a contract. Article 2A repeats the prohibition against unconscionability[5] that is found in UCC § 2-302.

Article 2A recognizes that a lease may also be subject to a law of the United States, a title certificate statute of the local state or of a foreign state, and to consumer protection laws.[6]

§ 6. Interest of parties. As long as the lease continues, the lessor and the lessee both have property interests in the goods involved. As between the two of them, the lessor has a residual or reversionary interest that entitles the lessor to possession of the goods upon termination of the lease for any reason, and the lessee has the right to possess and use the goods while the lease continues.

Each party to the lease has an insurable interest in the goods and has standing to sue a third person for injury done to the goods.

§ 7. Assignment. Either party to a lease may make a voluntary transfer of that party's interest under the lease unless the lease contains an express prohibition against such transfer. However, even when a transfer is permitted it may be nullified by a condition subsequent declared by the UCC. If the transfer will change the duty, burden, or risk imposed upon the other party to the lease, that party may demand protection against such harm. If such a protective demand is not satisfied, the transfer made has no effect.[7]

It is not expressly stated whether duties may be delegated but references to "duty" in the UCC[8] may be construed as including the delegation of duties. In any event, as there is no displacement by the UCC of the pre-Code law relating to the delegation of duties, it should be concluded that duties under a lease may be delegated subject to the pre-Code limitations on delegation.

§ 8. Involuntary transfer. An involuntary transfer of the interest of any party to a lease may occur without regard to whether the lease contains a prohi-

---

[1] Those wishing to go beyond the scope of this Appendix will find an exhaustive, professional-level analysis of Article 2A in the 1989 Annotation to Volume 5 of *Anderson on the Uniform Commercial Code*, 3rd edition, Lawyers Cooperative Publishing Company, Rochester, New York, beginning with the 1989 annotation.

[2] UCC § 2A-103(1)(j).

[3] States adopting Article 2A will also adopt a 1987 Amendment to UCC § 1-103(37), redefining security interest in order to clarify the problem of when a lease is to be regarded as a secured transaction.

[4] UCC § 2A-208. No provision is made as to whether a lease as modified is required to satisfy the statute of frauds.

[5] UCC § 2A-108.

[6] UCC § 2A-104(1).

[7] UCC § 2A-303.

[8] UCC § 2A-303(1)(b),(4).

bition against transfer. Thus, the interest of a party under a lease may, in an otherwise proper case, be sold in execution on a creditor's judgment against that party. Likewise, if a party to a lease files a petition in bankruptcy court, the trustee in bankruptcy acquires the interest of the debtor.

The involuntary transfer of the interest of a party to a lease is subject to the same condition subsequent as discussed in § 7. That is, if the transfer will change the duty, burden, or risk imposed upon the other party to the lease, that party may make a protective demand and, if that demand is not satisfied, the transfer is nullified or canceled.

§ 9. **Filing or recording.** No filing or recording is required in the case of a lease in order to protect the rights of the parties thereto. An exception is made to this statement when the goods involved are or will become fixtures.[9]

The fact that a lease results in one person owning title to goods that are in the possession of another person is not fraudulent but is the very nature of a lease. Some jurisdictions have local statutes declaring the split of possession and title to be fraudulent or evidence of fraud. These statutes are overridden by Article 2A in states in which 2A is adopted.[10]

§ 10. **Parol evidence.** Article 2A repeats the parol evidence rule provision of Article 2 and permits a written lease to be supplemented or explained by evidence of a course of dealings, usage of trade, and course of performance.

§ 11. **Statute of frauds.** An oral lease is valid when the rental payments are less than $1,000. If $1,000 or more, the lease must be evidenced by a writing. If there is not a sufficient writing, the lease cannot be enforced by way of action or defense, although the lease is not in itself illegal and when voluntarily performed cannot be canceled on the claim that it was illegal.

The writing that is offered to satisfy the statute of frauds must be signed by the party against whom enforcement is sought. The content of the writing need only be "sufficient to indicate" that a lease contract has been made and to describe the goods and state the term or duration of the lease.[11]

As in the case of transactions in goods under Article 2, the absence of a writing that satisfies the statute of frauds is excused when the goods cannot be disposed of by sale or lease, or there is a judicial admission of the existence of the oral lease, or the goods have been received and accepted by the lessee. The fact that the lessee makes payments under the lease does not excuse the absence of a writing.

§ 12. **Identification of goods to lease.** Article 2A follows the pattern of identification of goods made by Article 2.

§ 13. **Insurable interest.** The lease article follows the pattern of the sales article with respect to identification's giving rise to an insurable interest of the lessee. The lease article goes further and makes a more detailed regulation of insurable interest. The lessor, whether purchasing or leasing goods from the supplier, has an insurable interest in the goods that continues and is only terminated should the lessee purchase the goods. The lessee acquires an insurable interest in the leased goods when they are both existing and identified to the lease, even though the goods are so nonconforming that the lessee has the power to reject them.[12]

§ 14. **Express and implied warranties.** The express and implied warranty provisions of Article 2A parallel those of Article 2 except that the implied warranty of title is replaced under Article 2A by an implied warranty of quiet possession. This is a warranty that "for the lease term no person holds a claim to or interest in the goods that arose from an act or omission of the lessor . . . which will interfere with the lessee's enjoyment of its leasehold interest."[13]

When warranties are excluded by words, there must in all cases be a writing in which the exclusion is conspicuous, and "merchantability" must be expressly mentioned in order to exclude the implied warranty of merchantability.[14]

The subject of third party beneficiaries of warranties is regulated by UCC § 2A-216 in the same manner as in UCC § 2-318. In addition, the lessee of a finance lease is a beneficiary of the warranties of the supplier.[15]

§ 15. **Performance of lease contract.** Article 2A sets forth provisions paralleling those of Article 2 relating to insecurity and demand for assurance, the making and retracting of an anticipatory repudiation, and substituted and excused performance.[16]

C. Rights of Third Persons

§ 16. **Effect of lease.** A lease passes to the lessee no greater interest than it purports to transfer. Thus, a lease for one year passes only the right to possession for one year. At the same time it ordinarily passes no greater right to the goods than possessed by the lessor. To illustrate, assume that *A* holds possession under a lease for 6 months. A sublease by *A* to *B* for 12 months could not have effect beyond 6 months. Ordinarily, third persons, such as purchasers from and creditors of the lessor and lessee, can acquire no greater right than possessed by the party to the lease.[17]

---

[9]   UCC § 2A-309.
[10] UCC § 2A-302.
[11] UCC § 2A-201(b).

[12] UCC § 2A-219(1).
[13] UCC § 2A-211(1).
[14] UCC § 2A-214(20).
[15] See this Appendix, § 43.
[16] UCC § 2A-401 to § 2A-406.
[17] UCC § 2A-301.

§ 17. Voidable title of lessor. When the lessee acts in good faith and gives value in entering into the lease, it is immaterial that the lessor had only a voidable title. The lessee then acquires "a good leasehold interest," meaning that the lessee's interest is not subject to avoidance on the ground on which the lessor's interest could have been avoided had there not been such a subsequent good faith lessee for value.

Whether the lessor's title is voidable will depend upon continuing pre-Code law as Article 2A does not define the term. It does, however, indicate that there is a voidable title when there was an impersonation, a dishonored check, a cash sale, or criminal fraud.[18]

§ 18. Entrustment to lessor merchant. If the lessee entrusts the leased goods to the lessor from whom the goods had been leased and that lessor is a merchant who deals in goods of that kind, a lease of those goods made by the entrustee to a third person who leases in the ordinary course of business transfers the goods to such subsequent lessee free of the leasehold interest of the original lessee in the entrusted goods.[19]

If any element of this entrustment provision is not satisfied, a subsequent lease by the person in possession of the goods, whether or not an entrustee, passes merely the rights of that person and the rights of the original lessee remain unchanged. Moreover, if the goods are covered by a certificate of title, the rights of the subsequent lessee are governed both by the Article 2A provision above noted and by the certificate of title statute.[20]

§ 19. Sale or lease by merchant lessee. If the lessee is a merchant dealing in goods of that kind, the lessee has the power to pass the title or interest of the lessor by a lease of the goods to a lessee in the ordinary course of business or by a sale of the goods to a buyer in the ordinary course of business. If the goods are subject to a certificate of title statute, the effect of the sale or lease by the lessee is governed by both Article 2A and by such statute.[21]

§ 20. Rights of creditors of the parties. The general creditors of either party to the lease must recognize the limited right of their debtor and the rights of the other party to the lease.

The claim of a creditor of the lessor is superior to the lease if the creditor holds a lien on or security interest in the goods that was perfected before the lease became binding or is able to avoid the lease as fraudulent under non-Code rules of law. The interest of a secured creditor that would otherwise be superior may be defeated if the entrustment provisions are applicable.[22]

§ 21. — Fraudulent lease. If the creditor of the lessor can establish that the lease to the lessee was made to defraud creditors, the lease can be set aside. The mere fact that the lease gives possession of the goods to a person who is not its owner is not fraudulent. Likewise, the fact that the lessee in a given case allows the seller to retain possession of the leased goods for a commercially reasonable time does not constitute fraud, or as stated by the UCC, when goods are so left "in good faith and current course of trade." It is also declared that fraud is not established by showing that there was a sale of goods to a buyer who then made a lease back (a leaseback) to the seller.[23]

§ 22. — Priority over hypothetical perfected secured creditor. In the absence of a contrary local non-Code consumer protection statute, a creditor of the lessor will prevail over the rights of the lessee if the creditor would have priority over a perfected hypothetical creditor. In order to satisfy this requirement, the creditor of the lessor must hold an Article 9 security interest in the leased goods, and by virtue of UCC § 9-312 that interest would have priority over a hypothetical secured creditor who perfected his interest by filing at the time when the lease became enforceable. When these conditions are met, the creditor of the lessor may ignore the lease, even though it is a consumer lease, and treat the goods as belonging, without any limitation, to the lessor.[24]

§ 23. — Bailee's lien for services and materials. Non-Code law in many jurisdictions gives a bailee for hire a lien upon goods for services or materials supplied in connection with the goods. When any party to the lease delivers the goods to a bailee who furnishes services or materials and this gives rise to a lien, that lien is binding on all parties to the lease unless the law declaring the existence of the lease expressly makes the lien inferior or subordinate to the leasehold interests.[25]

To illustrate, when the lessee takes the leased truck to a shop for repairs, the lien for repairs is superior to the right of both the lessee and the lessor in the truck. This means that the truck cannot be obtained from the repairer without making payment of the amount due for repairs and, under most statutes, that the repairer, after giving statutory notice, may sell the truck in spite of the lease in order to obtain payment of the amount due.

---

[18] UCC § 2A-304. The "cash sale" provision was apparently inadvertently included in Article 2A in disregard of the fact that UCC § 2-403 had abolished the view that a "cash sale" was a transaction subject to a condition subsequent of nonpayment.

[19] UCC § 2A-304(2).

[20] UCC § 2A-304(3).

[21] UCC § 2A-305.

[22] See this Appendix, § § 18 et seq.

[23] UCC § 2A-308. See Official Code Comment to that section, 4.

[24] UCC § 2A-307(2)(b).

[25] UCC § 2A-306.

D. Remedies on Default

§ 24. Generally. Part 5 of Article 2A of UCC specifies in detail the remedies available to a party to a lease upon breach by the other party. In addition to the remedies specified by the UCC, the parties in their lease may provide for other remedies. Such other remedies are to be regarded as cumulative with those provided by the UCC unless expressly stated to be exclusive.

The power to provide for remedies in the lease includes the power to modify the UCC remedies and to liquidate or limit damages. When a limited remedy fails of its intended purpose, the aggrieved party, as under Article 2, may pursue any remedy authorized by the UCC or by the contract of the parties.[26]

When there is a default, the aggrieved party is not required to give the defaulting party any notice of the fact that there is a default nor of the steps that the aggrieved party will take to enforce the obligations of the lease.[27]

§ 25. Statute of Limitations. An action for breach of a lease must be brought within 4 years after the breach "was or should have been discovered by the aggrieved party or when the default occurs whichever is later."[28]

The same limitations period applies to a suit by a defendant against a third person, such as a suit by a lessor against a supplier, to obtain indemnity for the liability of the defendant to the plaintiff.

§ 26. Refund of payments to lessee. When the lessee is in default or when delivery of the goods to the lessee has been withheld or stopped because of the lessee's insolvency, the lessor must make a refund of part of the payments already made by the lessee to the lessor. If there is a valid limitation or liquidation of damages, the refund that must be made to the lessee is the difference between the amount of the payments made and the amount of the limitation. If there is no valid limitation or liquidation of damages, the refund is the difference between the total payments made by the lessee and 20 percent of the "then present value of the total rent the lessee was obligated to pay for the balance of the lease term."[29]

§ 27. Lessor's default. The default of the lessor may consist of a failure to deliver any goods under the lease, a repudiation of the lease, or delivery of nonconforming goods that were rightfully rejected by the lessee or the acceptance of which was rightfully revoked by the lessee.

§ 28. — Lessee's remedies. When the lessor has defaulted under the provisions of the UCC or the lease contract, the lessee may employ the following remedies: (1) rejection of improper tender of goods, (2) revocation of acceptance of improper goods, (3) cancellation of the lease, (4) recovery of payments made to the lessor, (5) cover and recovery of damages from the lessor, (6) recovery of damages for nondelivery or breach of warranty, (7) recovery of identified goods in case of nondelivery or repudiation by the lessor, (8) specific performance, replevin, or other action to obtain the goods, and (9) employment of the remedies provided by the lease contract or any collateral contract.

The above remedies are cumulative and the use of one does not bar use of another as long as the facts are such as to permit the use of the remedy in question.[30]

Although not strictly defined as a remedy, a lessee who has possession of nonconforming goods that have been rejected or as to which acceptance has been revoked has a security interest in such goods equal to any payments that should be refunded and any expenses reasonably incurred in the inspection of the goods, and in their receipt, transportation, custody, and care.[31]

§ 29. Lessee's default. The default of the lessee may be an improper rejection or an improper revocation of the acceptance of conforming goods or nonpayment of the rent or a repudiation of the lease contract.[32]

§ 30. — Lessor's remedies. When the lessee is in default, the lessor may (1) employ the remedies specified in the lease, (2) cancel the lease, (3) identify to the lease goods in the lessor's possession and dispose of the goods, (4) withhold delivery or stop delivery by a bailee or carrier, (5) repossess the goods, (6) retain the goods and recover damages, (7) dispose of the goods and recover damages, and (8) recover rent.[33]

As in the case of a lessee, the foregoing remedies of the lessor are cumulative and the lessor has the option to employ any remedy that is supported by the facts of the case. However, the lessor cannot be required to select one remedy and give up the others.

E. Consumer Lease

§ 31. Consumer lease defined. A consumer lease is defined in terms of the character of the parties, the nature of the lessee's use of the goods, and the total rental payments due under the lease. The lessor must be a merchant who customarily sells or leases the kind of goods involved. The lessee must be a natural person and must obtain the goods "primarily for a personal, family, or household use." Finally, the total

---

[26]   UCC § 2A-503(2).
[27]   Official Code Comment to UCC § 2A-501.
[28]   UCC § 2A-506(2). This may be described as a modified discovery rule and abandons the breach-on-tender rule of UCC § 2-725.
[29]   UCC § 2A-504(3)(b).

[30]   UCC § 2A-508 to § 2A-522.
[31]   UCC § 2A-508(5).
[32]   UCC § 2A-523(1). As to installment leases, see UCC § 2A-510.
[33]   UCC § 2A-523 to § 2A-530.

rental payments required by the lease must be under $25,000.[34]

A consumer lease arises when a person leases a car from a car rental agency to take a vacation trip or to make daily trips to and from work or school. A consumer lease is, in general, subject to the provisions noted in the preceding parts of this Appendix.[35] Article 2A makes certain exceptions or substitute provisions with respect to consumer leasing, and these are set forth in the following sections of this Appendix.[36]

§ 32. Consumer protection laws. Article 2A does not displace or repeal any consumer protection law applicable to consumer leases. If there is no conflict between the provisions of such statutes and the provisions of Article 2A, the statutes and Article 2A will apply concurrently to a given consumer lease. In the event of an inconsistency, the consumer protection statute will prevail and displace the provisions of Article 2A.

§ 33. Choice of law. When the lease is a consumer lease, the parties do not have the full freedom given by UCC § 1-105 to designate the jurisdiction whose law is to govern. Instead, it must be a jurisdiction in which the goods are to be used or in which the lessee resides at the time the lease becomes binding or within 30 days thereafter.[37]

§ 34. Specification of forum. When the consumer lease specifies a forum in which suit may be brought against the lessee, that forum must be one that would have jurisdiction over the consumer even in the absence of such provision.[38] No provision is made as to the designation of the forum in which the consumer lessee is required to bring a suit against the lessor. If the effect of such a limitation is to place an unreasonable barrier that will bar a suit by the consumer lessee, it is likely that it will be held invalid as unconscionable.

§ 35. Statute of frauds. The statute of frauds provision applicable to leases,[39] is equally applicable to consumer leases.

UCC § 2A-201 does not alter or affect a consumer protection statute that may require a more detailed writing than is required to satisfy the Article 2A statute of frauds. If the consumer protection statute is not satisfied, the consumer lease cannot be enforced even though the UCC provision is satisfied. This supremacy of the consumer protection statute is expressly declared by the UCC.[40]

§ 36. Unconscionability. Article 2A restates the protection against unconscionability made by UCC § 2-302 and, in the case of consumer leases, expands it to authorize judicial examination of preleasing and postleasing conduct and to provide for the award of attorney's fees. If the consumer lease was induced by "unconscionable conduct" the court may also grant appropriate relief when "unconscionable conduct has occurred in the collection of a claim arising from the lease contract." If the court finds that the lessee has been the victim of unconscionability, it shall award reasonable attorney's fees to the lessee. However, if the claim of unconscionability was groundless, the court shall award such fees to the lessor.[41]

§ 37. Acceleration of rent. When the lease permits the lessor to accelerate the balance of rent due for the remainder of the lease term when the lessee defaults, the lessor must act in the good faith belief that the default has made the lessor insecure. In the case of a consumer lease, the lessor has the burden of proving that the acceleration was made in good faith, as against the general rule that the lessee has the burden of proving that the lessor acted in bad faith.[42]

F. Nonconsumer or Commercial Lease

§ 38. Nonconsumer or commercial lease defined. When a lease does not satisfy the definition of a consumer lease, it may be called a nonconsumer or commercial lease. For example, a contractor rents a truck for a year for the purpose of hauling building materials.

§ 39. Commercial nonfinance lease. When a lease is a commercial nonfinance lease, the provisions set forth in this Appendix in the first four parts will govern the rights of the parties.[43]

G. Finance Lease

1. General principles

§ 40. Finance lease defined. In a finance lease, the customer knows exactly what is wanted and who makes or distributes it. Instead of going directly to the supplier, the customer goes to a financer and tells the financer where and what to obtain. The financer then purchases the goods from the supplier and leases the goods to the customer. As a variation of this pattern, the financer might lease the goods from the supplier and then sublet the goods to the customer. In either case, the financer is in effect merely a paper channel, or conduit, between the supplier and the customer; the supplier and the customer are the real parties in interest. Article 2A emphasizes this character of the financer of a finance lease by defining a finance lease as a lease in which (1) the lessor does not select, manufacture, or supply the goods, (2) the financer acquires the goods in order to fill the lease to the customer, and (3) the lessee must approve the terms of

---

[34] UCC § 2A-103(1)(e).
[35] Parts A to D, inclusive.
[36] See this Appendix, § § 33 et seq.
[37] UCC § 2A-106.
[38] UCC § 2A-106.
[39] See this Appendix, § 11.
[40] UCC § 2A-104(1)(d).
[41] UCC § 2A-108.
[42] UCC § 2A-109(2).
[43] Parts A to D, inclusive.

the transaction between the supplier and the financer.[44]

§ 41. Independence-irrevocability concept. When the lessee of a nonconsumer finance lease accepts the goods, the lessee's obligations under the lease become irrevocable and independent from the obligations of the finance lessor.[45] This independence and irrevocability requires the lessee to perform under the lease without regard to whether the finance lessor performs. This reverses the ordinary rule of contract law by which the obligations of the lessee and lessor would be mutually dependent so that a default by the lessor would entitle the lessee to assert remedies for breach of contract. By virtue of the UCC provision, the lessee cannot claim nonliability for a breach on the ground that the lessor had failed to perform its obligation under the lease. When suit is brought against the lessee by the finance lessor's assignee, the lessee is also barred from asserting that the finance lessor had not performed the lease.[46]

The waiver that the finance lessee makes by accepting the goods is irrevocable.[47] However, this finality does not bar avoiding the lease on such grounds as fraud, duress, or any other factor that by principles of contract law warrant avoiding a contract. The waiver that the lessee makes by accepting the goods is also canceled if the lessee makes a proper revocation of acceptance.

The independence-irrevocability concept is not applicable to a consumer finance lease and, therefore, does not bar the assertion by the consumer lessee of any defenses that would otherwise be available.

§ 42. Formation of supply contract. The finance lessor and the supplier of the lessor may make the supply contract on such terms as they decide. They may include in the supply contract any provision that is valid in a sales contract. In the making of the supply contract, the parties can ignore the fact that there will be a lessee who will ultimately receive the goods supplied to the lessor. If the supply contract is a sale, as distinguished from a lease, any exclusion of warranties, any limitation of damages or remedies, and any modification of the statute of limitations that is valid under Article 2 may be properly included in the supply contract; and the lessee is bound thereby when asserting a claim against the supplier. This arrangement does not give the finance lessor and the supplier the power to impose upon the finance lessee a transaction that is not acceptable to the finance lessee. The finance lessee will not enter into the finance lease without first approving a copy of the supply contract, or a finance lease executed in advance of seeing the

supply contract will include a provision that it shall be void if the lessee does not approve the supply contract. That is, the economic reality of the situation gives the finance lessee a control over the supply contract that does not exist as a matter of law.

§ 43. Lessee as beneficiary of supply contract. Article 2A in effect makes the finance lessee the third party beneficiary of the supply contract. The lessee may bring suit in the lessee's own name directly against the supplier for breach by the supplier of any obligation of the supplier under the supply contract that would benefit the lessee if performed. This provision enables the finance lessee to sue the supplier directly for breach of any express or implied warranty of the supply contract.[48] As in the case of a third party beneficiary contract, the finance lessee is bound by the terms of the supply contract. Likewise, the fact that the lessee acquires rights under the supply contract does not constitute a delegation of any duties to the lessee.[49]

2. Particular applications of status of finance lessee

§ 44. Generally. The effect of the independence-irrevocability concept[50] and the conferring on the lessee of the status of beneficiary of the supply contract[51] have the practical effect of making the finance lessee the other contracting party to the supply contract as far as the obligations of the supplier are concerned. This treatment of the parties to the finance lease is also seen in the following sections of this Appendix.

§ 45. Exemption of finance lessor from implied warranties. The finance lessor does not make any implied warranty of freedom from infringement claims, merchantability, or fitness for a particular purpose.[52] Any warranty of a finance lessor must, therefore, rest on an express warranty made by the lessor.

§ 46. Restriction of revocation of acceptance. The finance lessee may only revoke acceptance when the lessee has accepted the goods because the lessor's assurance of conformity induced the lessee to accept the goods without discovering their nonconformity. Thus, the finance lessee is deprived of the right to revoke acceptance for the two other grounds that can be asserted by a nonfinance lessee: (1) acceptance was made without knowledge of the nonconformity because of the difficulty of discovering the nonconformity before acceptance, or (2) although the nonconformity was known by the lessee at the time of acceptance, the lessee accepted the goods on the reasonable assumption that the nonconformity would be seasonably cured, but it was not so cured.[53] The nonconformity upon which the finance lessee's revocation is

---

[44] UCC § 2A-103(1)(g). This third element is important because the lessee is in effect a third party beneficiary of the contract between the supplier and the financer. See this Appendix, § 43.
[45] UCC § 2A-407(1).
[46] UCC § 2A-307(2)(a).
[47] UCC § 2A-407(2)(b).

[48] UCC § 2A-209(1).
[49] Official Code Comment to UCC § 2A-209, 3.
[50] See this Appendix, § 41.
[51] See this Appendix, § 43.
[52] UCC § 2A-211(2), § 2A-212(1), and § 2A-213.
[53] UCC § 2A-517(1).

based is a nonconformity with respect to the finance lease as distinguished from the supply contract.[54]

§ 47. **Transfer of risk of loss.** In a nonfinance lease, the risk of loss remains with the lessor and does not pass to the lessee. In contrast, in a finance lease the risk of loss passes to the lessee, and Article 2A makes detailed provisions similar to UCC § 2-509 as to when such risk of loss passes to the lessee when not specified in the finance lease.[55]

§ 48. **Procedure on reduced performance.** Article 2A follows the pattern of UCC § § 2-615 and 2-616 when complete performance cannot be made because of the failure of a presupposed condition. When the lease is a nonfinance lease, the lessee, upon being offered a partial performance, may elect to take such performance; but the acceptance thereof is a waiver of any claim for a deficiency. This procedure does not apply to a nonconsumer finance lessee.[56] The net result is that such finance lessee may accept the reduced performance but reserve the right to damages for the deficiency.

§ 49. **Modification and rescission of supply contract.** The finance lessor and the supplier may as between themselves make any modification of the supply contract they choose. However, the making of a change that is harmful to the finance lessee imposes liability upon the party to the supply contract to the finance lessee for the amount of the loss caused thereby. With respect to the supplier, this liability arises as to any harmful change made after the supplier has received notice that the finance lease has been entered into. In the case of the finance lessor, the liability for harmful change arises as soon as the finance lease is entered into. In applying the above provisions, it is immaterial that as a practical matter the finance lessor and the supplier had reason to know and contemplated that a finance lease would in fact be entered into.[57]

§ 50. **Nondeduction of damage claims from rent due.** If a nonfinance lessee has a right to recover damages from the lessor, the lessee may deduct all or part of such damage claim from any part of the rent "still due under the same lease contract."[58] In the case of a nonconsumer finance lessee, this deduction cannot be made if the lessee has already accepted the goods. This result follows from application of the independence-irrevocability concept.[59]

If the finance lease is a consumer lease, the lessee has the same right of setoff of a damage claim as in the case of a nonfinance lease.

---

[54] Official Code Comment to § 2A-516, 1.
[55] UCC § 2A-219.
[56] UCC § 2A-406.

[57] UCC § 2A-209(3).
[58] UCC § 2A-508(6).
[59] See this Appendix, § 41.

UNIFORM PARTNERSHIP ACT

Part 1

Preliminary Provisions

§ 1. Name of Act

This act may be cited as Uniform Partnership Act.

§ 2. Definition of Terms

In this act, "Court" includes every court and judge having jurisdiction in the case.

"Business" includes every trade, occupation, or profession.

"Person" includes individuals, partnerships, corporations, and other associations.

"Bankrupt" includes bankrupt under the Federal Bankruptcy Act or insolvent under any state insolvent act.

"Conveyance" includes every assignment, lease, mortgage, or encumbrance.

"Real property" includes land and any interest or estate in land.

§ 3. Interpretation of Knowledge and Notice

(1) A person has "knowledge" of a fact within the meaning of this act not only when he has actual knowledge thereof, but also when he has knowledge of such other facts as in the circumstances shows bad faith.

(2) A person has "notice" of a fact within the meaning of this act when the person who claims the benefit of the notice

    (a) States the fact to such person, or

    (b) Delivers through the mail, or by other means of communication, a written statement of the fact to such person or to a proper person at his place of business or residence.

§ 4. Rules of Construction

(1) The rule that statutes in derogation of the common law are to be strictly construed shall have no application to this act.

(2) The law of estoppel shall apply under this act.

(3) The law of agency shall apply under this act.

(4) This act shall be so interpreted and construed as to effect its general purpose to make uniform the law of those states which enact it.

(5) This act shall not be construed so as to impair the obligations of any contract existing when the act goes into effect, nor to affect any action or proceedings begun or right accrued before this act takes effect.

§ 5. Rules for Cases Not Provided for in this Act

In any case not provided for in this act the rules of law and equity, including the law merchant, shall govern.

Part II

Nature of Partnership

§ 6. Partnership Defined

(1) A partnership is an association of two or more persons to carry on as co-owners a business for profit.

(2) But any association formed under any other statute of this state, or any statute adopted by authority, other than the authority of this state, is not a partnership under this act, unless such association would have been a partnership in this state prior to the adoption of this act; but this act shall apply to limited partnerships except in so far as the statutes relating to such partnerships are inconsistent herewith.

§ 7. Rules for Determining the Existence of a Partnership

In determining whether a partnership exists, these rules shall apply:

(1) Except as provided by Section 16 persons who are not partners as to each other are not partners as to third persons.

(2) Joint tenancy, tenancy in common, tenancy by the entireties, joint property, common property, or part ownership does not of itself establish a partnership, whether such co-owners do or do not share any profits made by the use of the property.

(3) The sharing of gross returns does not of itself establish a partnership, whether or not the persons sharing them have a joint or common right or interest in any property from which the returns are derived.

(4) The receipt by a person of a share of the profits of a business is prima facie evidence that he is a partner

in the business, but no such inference shall be drawn if such profits were received in payment:

    (a) As a debt by installments or otherwise,

    (b) As wages of an employee or rent to a landlord,

    (c) As an annuity to a widow or representative of a deceased partner,

    (d) As interest on a loan, though the amount of payment vary with the profits of the business,

    (e) As the consideration for the sale of a goodwill of a business or other property by installments or otherwise.

§ 8. Partnership Property

(1) All property originally brought into the partnership stock or subsequently acquired by purchase or otherwise, on account of the partnership, is partnership property.

(2) Unless the contrary intention appears, property acquired with partnership funds is partnership property.

(3) Any estate in real property may be acquired in the partnership name. Title so acquired can be conveyed only in the partnership name.

(4) A conveyance to a partnership in the partnership name, though without words of inheritance, passes the entire estate of the grantor unless a contrary intent appears.

Part III

Relations of Partners to Persons Dealing with the Partnership

§ 9. Partner Agent of Partnership as to Partnership Business

(1) Every partner is an agent of the partnership for the purpose of its business, and the act of every partner, including the execution in the partnership name of any instrument, for apparently carrying on in the usual way the business of the partnership of which he is a member binds the partnership, unless the partner so acting has in fact no authority to act for the partnership in the particular matter, and the person with whom he is dealing has knowledge of the fact that he has no such authority.

(2) An act of a partner which is not apparently for the carrying on of the business of the partnership in the usual way does not bind the partnership unless authorized by the other partners.

(3) Unless authorized by the other partners or unless they have abandoned the business, one or more but less than all the partners have no authority to:

    (a) Assign the partnership property in trust for creditors or on the assignee's promise to pay the debts of the partnership,

    (b) Dispose of the goodwill of the business,

    (c) Do any other act which would make it impossible to carry on the ordinary business of a partnership,

    (d) Confess a judgment,

    (e) Submit a partnership claim or liability to arbitration or reference.

(4) No act of a partner in contravention of a restriction on authority shall bind the partnership to persons having knowledge of the restriction.

§ 10. Conveyance of Real Property of the Partnership

(1) Where title to real property is in the partnership name, any partner may convey title to such property by a conveyance executed in the partnership name; but the partnership may recover such property unless the partner's act binds the partnership under the provisions of paragraph (1) of section 9 or unless such property has been conveyed by the grantee or a person claiming through such grantee to a holder for value without knowledge that the partner, in making the conveyance, has exceeded his authority.

(2) Where title to real property is in the name of the partnership, a conveyance executed by a partner, in his own name, passes the equitable interest of the partnership, provided the act is one within the authority of the partner under the provisions of paragraph (1) of Section 9.

(3) Where title to real property is in the name of one or more but not all the partners, and the record does not disclose the right of the partnership, the partners in whose name the title stands may convey title to such property, but the partnership may recover such property if the partners' act does not bind the partnership under the provisions of paragraph (1) of section 9, unless the purchaser or his assignee, is a holder for value, without knowledge.

(4) Where the title to real property is in the name of one or more or all the partners, or in a third person in trust for the partnership, a conveyance executed by a partner in the partnership name, or in his own name, passes the equitable interest of the partnership, provided the act is one within the authority of the partner under the provisions of paragraph (1) of section 9.

(5) Where the title to real property is in the names of all the partners a conveyance executed by all the partners passes all their rights in such property.

§ 11. Partnership Bound by Admission of Partner

An admission or representation made by any partner concerning partnership affairs within the scope of his authority as conferred by this act is evidence against the partnership.

§ 12. Partnership Charged with Knowledge of or Notice to Partner

Notice to any partner of any matter relating to partnership affairs, and the knowledge of the partner acting in the particular matter, acquired while a partner or then present to his mind, and the knowledge of any other partner who reasonably could and should have communicated it to the acting partner, operate as notice to or knowledge of the partnership, except in the case of a fraud on the partnership committed by or with the consent of that partner.

§ 13. Partnership Bound by Partner's Wrongful Act

Where, by any wrongful act or omission of any partner acting in the ordinary course of the business of the partnership or with the authority of his co-partners, loss or injury is caused to any person, not being a partner in the partnership, or any penalty is incurred, the partnership is liable therefor to the same extent as the partner so acting or omitting to act.

§ 14. Partnership Bound by Partner's Breach of Trust

The partnership is bound to make good the loss:

(a) Where one partner acting within the scope of his apparent authority receives money or property of a third person and misapplies it; and

(b) Where the partnership in the course of its business receives money or property of a third person and the money or property so received is misapplied by any partner while it is in the custody of the partnership.

§ 15. Nature of Partner's Liability

All partners are liable

(a) Jointly and severally for everything chargeable to the partnership under sections 13 and 14.

(b) Jointly for all other debts and obligations of the partnership; but any partner may enter into a separate obligation to perform a partnership contract.

§ 16. Partner by Estoppel

(1) When a person, by words spoken or written or by conduct, represents himself, or consents to another representing him to any one, as a partner in an existing partnership or with one or more persons not actual partners, he is liable to any such person to whom such representation has been made, who has, on the faith of such representation, given credit to the actual or apparent partnership, and if he has made such representation or consented to its being made in a public manner he is liable to such person, whether the representation has or has not been made or communicated to such person so giving credit by or with the knowledge of the apparent partner making the representation or consenting to its being made.

(a) When a partnership liability results, he is liable as though he were an actual member of the partnership.

(b) When no partnership liability results, he is liable jointly with the other persons, if any, so consenting to the contract or representation as to incur liability, otherwise separately.

(2) When a person has been thus represented to be a partner in an existing partnership, or with one or more persons not actual partners, he is an agent of the persons consenting to such representation to bind them to the same extent and in the same manner as though he were a partner in fact, with respect to persons who rely upon the representation. Where all the members of the existing partnership consent to the representation, a partnership act or obligation results; but in all other cases it is the joint act or obligation of the person acting and the persons consenting to the representation.

§ 17. Liability of Incoming Partner

A person admitted as a partner into an existing partnership is liable for all the obligations of the partnership arising before his admission as though he had been a partner when such obligations were incurred, except that this liability shall be satisfied only out of partnership property.

Part IV

Relations of Partners to One Another

§ 18. Rules Determining Rights and Duties of Partners

The rights and duties of the partners in relation to the partnership shall be determined, subject to any agreement between them, by the following rules:

(a) Each partner shall be repaid his contributions, whether by way of capital or advances to the partnership property and share equally in the profits and surplus remaining after all liabilities, including those to partners, are satisfied; and must contribute toward the losses, whether of capital or otherwise, sustained by the partnership according to his share in the profits.

(b) The partnership must indemnify every partner in respect of payments made and personal liabilities reasonably incurred by him in the ordinary and proper conduct of its business, or for the preservation of its business or property.

(c) A partner, who in aid of the partnership makes any payment or advance beyond the amount of capital which he agreed to contribute, shall be paid interest from the date of the payment or advance.

(d) A partner shall receive interest on the capital contributed by him only from the date when repayment should be made.

(e) All partners have equal rights in the management and conduct of the partnership business.

(f) No partner is entitled to remuneration for acting in the partnership business, except that a surviving partner is entitled to reasonable compensation for his services in winding up the partnership affairs.

(g) No person can become a member of a partnership without the consent of all the partners.

(h) Any difference arising as to ordinary matters connected with the partnership business may be decided by a majority of the partners; but no act in contravention of any agreement between the partners may be done rightfully without the consent of all the partners.

§ 19. Partnership Books

The partnership books shall be kept, subject to any agreement between the partners, at the principal place of business of the partnership, and every partner shall at all times have access to and may inspect and copy any of them.

§ 20. Duty of Partners to Render Information

Partners shall render on demand true and full information of all things affecting the partnership to any partner or the legal representative of any deceased partner or partner under legal disability.

§ 21. Partner Accountable as a Fiduciary

(1) Every partner must account to the partnership for any benefit, and hold as trustee for it any profits derived by him without the consent of the other partners from any transaction connected with the formation, conduct, or liquidation of the partnership or from any use by him of its property.

(2) This section applies also to the representatives of a deceased partner engaged in the liquidation of the affairs of the partnership as the personal representatives of the last surviving partner.

§ 22. Right to an Account

Any partner shall have the right to a formal account as to partnership affairs:

(a) If he is wrongfully excluded from the partnership business or possession of its property by his co-partners,

(b) If the right exists under the terms of any agreement,

(c) As provided by Section 21,

(d) Whenever other circumstances render it just and reasonable.

§ 23. Continuation of Partnership Beyond Fixed Term

(1) When a partnership for a fixed term or particular undertaking is continued after the termination of such term or particular undertaking without any express agreement, the rights and duties of the partners remain the same as they were at such termination, so far as is consistent with a partnership at will.

(2) A continuation of the business by the partners or such of them as habitually acted therein during the term, without any settlement or liquidation of the partnership affairs, is prima facie evidence of a continuation of the partnership.

Part V
Property Rights of a Partner

§ 24. Extent of Property Rights of a Partner

The property rights of a partner are (1) his rights in specific partnership property, (2) his interest in the partnership, and (3) his right to participate in the management.

§ 25. Nature of a Partner's Right in Specific Partnership Property

(1) A partner is co-owner with his partners of specific partnership property holding as a tenant in partnership.

(2) The incidents of this tenancy are such that:

(a) A partner, subject to the provisions of this act and to any agreement between the partners, has an equal right with his partners to possess specific partnership property for partnership purposes; but he has no right to possess such property for any other purpose without the consent of his partners.

(b) A partner's right in specific partnership property is not assignable except in connection with the assignment of rights of all the partners in the same property.

(c) A partner's right in specific partnership property is not subject to attachment or execution, except on a claim against the partnership. When partnership property is attached for a partnership debt the partners, or any of them, or the representatives of a deceased partner, cannot claim any right under the homestead or exemption laws.

(d) On the death of a partner his right in specific partnership property vests in the surviving partner or partners, except where the deceased was the last surviving partner or partners, or the legal representative of the last surviving partner, has no right to possess the partnership property for any but a partnership purpose.

    (e) A partner's right in specific partnership property is not subject to dower, courtesy, or allowances to widows, heirs, or next of kin.

§ 26. Nature of Partner's Interest in the Partnership

A partner's interest in the partnership is his share of the profits and surplus, and the same is personal property.

§ 27. Assignment of Partner's Interest

(1) A conveyance by a partner of his interest in the partnership does not of itself dissolve the partnership, nor, as against the other partners in the absence of agreement, entitle the assignee, during the continuance of the partnership to interfere in the management or administration of the partnership business or affairs, or to require an information or account of partnership transactions, or to inspect the partnership books; but it merely entitles the assignee to receive in accordance with his contract the profits to which the assigning partner would otherwise be entitled.

(2) In case of a dissolution of the partnership, the assignee is entitled to receive his assignor's interest and may require an account from the date only of the last account agreed to by all the partners.

§ 28. Partner's Interest Subject to Charging Order

(1) On due application to a competent court by any judgment creditor of a partner, the court which entered the judgment, order, or decree, or any other court, may charge the interest of the debtor partner with payment of the unsatisfied amount of such judgment debt with interest thereon; and may then or later appoint a receiver of his share of the profits, and of any other money due or to fall due to him in respect of the partnership, and make all other orders, directions, accounts and inquiries which the debtor partner might have made, or which the circumstances of the case may require.

(2) The interest charged may be redeemed at any time before foreclosure, or in case of a sale being directed by the court may be purchased without thereby causing a dissolution:

    (a) With separate property, by any one or more of the partners, or

    (b) With partnership property, by any one or more of the partners with the consent of all the partners whose interests are not so charged or sold.

(3) Nothing in this act shall be held to deprive a partner of his right, if any, under the exemption laws, as regards his interest in the partnership.

Part VI

Dissolution and Winding Up

§ 29. Dissolution Defined

The dissolution of a partnership is the change in the relation of the partners caused by any partner ceasing to be associated in the carrying on as distinguished from the winding up of the business.

§ 30. Partnership Not Terminated by Dissolution

On dissolution the partnership is not terminated, but continues until the winding up of partnership affairs is completed.

§ 31. Causes of Dissolution

Dissolution is caused: (1) Without violation of the agreement between the partners,

    (a) By the termination of the definite term or particular undertaking specified in the agreement,

    (b) By the express will of any partner when no definite term or particular undertaking is specified,

    (c) By the express will of all the partners who have not assigned their interests or suffered them to be charged for their separate debts, either before or after the termination of any specified term or particular undertaking,

    (d) By the expulsion of any partner from the business bona fide in accordance with such a power conferred by the agreement between the partners;

(2) In contravention of the agreement between the partners, where the circumstances do not permit a dissolution under any other provision of this section, by the express will of any partner at any time;

(3) By any event which makes it unlawful for the business of the partnership to be carried on or for the members to carry it on in partnership;

(4) By the death of any partner;

(5) By the bankruptcy of any partner or the partnership;

(6) By decree of court under Section 32.

§ 32. Dissolution by Decree of Court

(1) On application by or for a partner the court shall decree a dissolution whenever:

    (a) A partner has been declared a lunatic in any judicial proceeding or is shown to be of unsound mind,

    (b) A partner becomes in any other way incapable of performing his part of the partnership contract,

    (c) A partner has been guilty of such conduct as tends to affect prejudicially the carrying on of the business,

    (d) A partner willfully or persistently commits a breach of the partnership agreement, or otherwise so conducts himself in matters relating to the partnership business that it is not reasonably practicable to carry on the business in partnership with him,

(e) The business of the partnership can only be carried on at a loss,

(f) Other circumstances render a dissolution equitable.

(2) On the application of the purchaser of a partner's interest under Sections 27 or 28:

(a) After the termination of the specified term or particular undertaking,

(b) At any time if the partnership was a partnership at will when the interest was assigned or when the charging order was issued.

§ 33. General Effect of Dissolution on Authority of Partner

Except so far as may be necessary to wind up partnership affairs or to complete transactions begun but not then finished, dissolution terminates all authority of any partner to act for the partnership,

(1) With respect to the partners,

(a) When the dissolution is not by the act, bankruptcy or death of a partner, or

(b) When the dissolution is by such act, bankruptcy or death of a partner, in cases where Section 34 so requires.

(2) With respect to persons not partners, as declared in Section 35.

§ 34. Right of Partner to Contribution from Copartners After Dissolution

Where the dissolution is caused by the act, death or bankruptcy of a partner, each partner is liable to his copartners for his share of any liability created by any partner acting for the partnership as if the partnership had not been dissolved unless

(a) The dissolution being by act of any partner, the partner acting for the partnership had knowledge of the dissolution, or

(b) The dissolution being by the death or bankruptcy of a partner, the partner acting for the partnership had knowledge or notice of the death or bankruptcy.

§ 35. Power of Partner to Bind Partnership to Third Persons After Dissolution

(1) After dissolution a partner can bind the partnership except as provided in Paragraph (3)

(a) By any act appropriate for winding up partnership affairs or completing transactions unfinished by dissolution;

(b) By any transaction which would bind the partnership if dissolution had not taken place, provided the other party to the transaction

(I) Had extended credit to the partnership prior to dissolution and had no knowledge or notice of the dissolution; or

(II) Though he had not so extended credit, had nevertheless known of the partnership prior to dissolution, and, having no knowledge or notice of dissolution, the fact of dissolution had not been advertised in a newspaper of general circulation in the place (or in each place if more than one) at which the partnership business was regularly carried on.

(2) The liability of a partner under paragraph (1b) shall be satisfied out of partnership assets alone when such partner had been prior to dissolution.

(a) Unknown as a partner to the person with whom the contract is made; and

(b) So far unknown and inactive in partnership affairs that the business reputation of the partnership could not be said to have been in any degree due to his connection with it.

(3) The partnership is in no case bound by any act of a partner after dissolution.

(a) Where the partnership is dissolved because it is unlawful to carry on the business, unless the act is appropriate for winding up partnership affairs; or

(b) Where the partner has become bankrupt; or

(c) Where the partner has no authority to wind up partnership affairs; except by a transaction with one who

(I) Had extended credit to the partnership prior to dissolution and had no knowledge or notice of his want of authority; or

(II) Had not extended credit to the partnership prior to dissolution, and, having no knowledge or notice of his want of authority, the fact of his want of authority has not been advertised in the manner provided for advertising the fact of dissolution in paragraph (1bII).

(4) Nothing in this section shall affect the liability under section 16 of any person who after dissolution represents himself or consents to another representing him as a partner in a partnership engaged in carrying on business.

§ 36. Effect of Dissolution on Partner's Existing Liability

(1) The dissolution of the partnership does not of itself discharge the existing liability of any partner.

(2) A partner is discharged from any existing liability upon dissolution of the partnership by an agree-

ment to that effect between himself, the partnership creditor and the person or partnership continuing the business; and such agreement may be inferred from the course of dealing between the creditor having knowledge of the dissolution and the person or partnership continuing the business.

(3) Where a person agrees to assume the existing obligations of a dissolved partnership, the partners whose obligations have been assumed shall be discharged from any liability to any creditor of the partnership who, knowing of the agreement, consents to a material alteration in the nature or time of payment of such obligations.

(4) The individual property of a deceased partner shall be liable for all obligations of the partnership incurred while he was a partner but subject to the prior payment of his separate debts.

§ 37.   Right to Wind Up

Unless otherwise agreed the partners who have not wrongfully dissolved the partnership or the legal representative of the last surviving partner, not bankrupt, has the right to wind up the partnership affairs; provided, however, that any partner, his legal representative or his assignee, upon cause shown, may obtain winding up by the court.

§ 38.   Rights of Partners to Application of Partnership Property

(1) When dissolution is caused in any way, except in contravention of the partnership agreement, each partner as against his co-partners and all persons claiming through them in respect of their interests in the partnership, unless otherwise agreed, may have the partnership property applied to discharge its liabilities, and the surplus applied to pay in cash the net amount owing to the respective partners. But if dissolution is caused by expulsion of a partner, bona fide under the partnership agreement and if the expelled partner is discharged from all partnership liabilities, either by payment or agreement under Section 36(2), he shall receive in cash only the net amount due him from the partnership.

(2) When dissolution is caused in contravention of the partnership agreement the rights of the partners shall be as follows:

(a) Each partner who has not caused dissolution wrongfully shall have,
   (I) All the rights specified in paragraph (1) of this section, and
   (II) The right, as against each partner who has caused the dissolution wrongfully, to damages for breach of the agreement.
(b) The partners who have not caused the dissolution wrongfully, if they all desire to continue the business in the same name, either by themselves or jointly with others, may do so, during the agreed term for the partnership and for that purpose may possess the partnership property, provided they secure the payment by bond approved by the court, or pay to any partner who has caused the dissolution wrongfully, the value of his interest in the partnership at the dissolution, less any damages recoverable under clause (2aII) of the section, and in like manner indemnify him against all present or future partnership liabilities.
(c) A partner who has caused the dissolution wrongfully shall have:
   (I) If the business is not continued under the provisions of paragraph (2b) all the rights of a partner under paragraph (1), subject to clause (2aII), of this section,
   (II) If the business is continued under paragraph (2b) of this section the right as against his co-partners and all claiming through them in respect of their interests in the partnership, less any damages caused to his copartners by the dissolution, ascertained and paid to him in cash, or the payment secured by bond approved by the court, and to be released from all existing liabilities of the partnership; but in ascertaining the value of the partner's interest the value of the goodwill of the business shall not be considered.

§ 39.   Rights Where Partnership is Dissolved for Fraud or Misrepresentation

Where a partnership contract is rescinded on the ground of the fraud or misrepresentation of one of the parties thereto, the party entitled to rescind is, without prejudice to any other right, entitled,

(a) To a lien on, or right of retention of, the surplus of the partnership property after satisfying the partnership liabilities to third persons for any sum of money paid by him for the purchase of an interest in the partnership and for any capital or advances contributed by him; and
(b) To stand, after all liabilities to third persons have been satisfied, in the place of the creditors of the partnership for any payments made by him in respect of the partnership liabilities; and
(c) To be indemnified by the person guilty of the fraud or making the representation against all debts and liabilities of the partnership.

§ 40.   Rules for Distribution

In settling accounts between the partners after dissolution, the following rules shall be observed, subject to any agreement to the contrary:

(a) The assets of the partnership are:
  (I) The partnership property,
  (II) The contributions of the partners necessary for the payment of all the liabilities specified in clause (b) of this paragraph.
(b) The liabilities of the partnership shall rank in order of payment, as follows:
  (I) Those owing to creditors other than partners,
  (II) Those owing to partners other than for capital and profits,
  (III) Those owing to partners in respect of capital,
  (IV) Those owing to partners in respect of profits.
(c) The assets shall be applied in the order of their declaration in clause (a) of this paragraph to the satisfaction of the liabilities.
(d) The partners shall contribute, as provided by Section 18(a) the amount necessary to satisfy the liabilities; but if any, but not all, of the partners are insolvent, or, not being subject to process, refuse to contribute, the other parties shall contribute their share of the liabilities, and, in the relative proportions in which they share the profits, the additional amount necessary to pay the liabilities.
(e) An assignee for the benefit of creditors or any person appointed by the court shall have the right to enforce the contributions specified in clause (d) of this paragraph.
(f) Any partner or his legal representative shall have the right to enforce the contributions specified in clause (d) of this paragraph, to the extent of the amount which he has paid in excess of his share of the liability.
(g) The individual property of a deceased partner shall be liable for the contributions specified in clause (d) of this paragraph.
(h) When partnership property and the individual properties of the partners are in possession of a court for distribution, partnership creditors shall have priority on partnership property and separate creditors on individual property, saving the rights of lien or secured creditors as heretofore.
(i) Where a partner has become bankrupt or his estate is insolvent the claims against his separate property shall rank in the following order:
  (I) Those owing to separate creditors,
  (II) Those owing to partnership creditors,
  (III) Those owing to partners by way of contribution.

§ 41. Liability of Persons Continuing the Business in Certain Cases

(1) When any new partner is admitted into an existing partnership, or when any partner retires and assigns (or the representative of the deceased partner assigns) his rights in partnership property to two or more of the partners, or to one or more of the partners and one or more third persons, if the business is continued without liquidation of the partnership affairs, creditors of the first or dissolved partnership are also creditors of the partnership so continuing the business.

(2) When all but one partner retire and assign (or the representative of a deceased partner assigns) their rights in partnership property to the remaining partner, who continues the business without liquidation of partnership affairs, either alone or with others, creditors of the dissolved partnership are also creditors of the person or partnership so continuing the business.

(3) When any partner retires or dies and the business of the dissolved partnership is continued as set forth in paragraphs (1) and (2) of this section, with the consent of the retired partners or the representative of the deceased partner, but without any assignment of his right in partnership property, rights of creditors of the dissolved partnership and of the creditors of the person or partnership and of the creditors of the person or partnership continuing the business shall be as if such assignment had been made.

(4) When all the partners or their representatives assign their rights in partnership property to one or more third persons who promise to pay the debts and who continue the business of the dissolved partnership, creditors of the dissolved partnership are also creditors of the person or partnership continuing the business.

(5) When any partner wrongfully causes a dissolution and the remaining partners continue the business under the provisions of Section 38(2b), either alone or with others, and without liquidation of the partnership affairs, creditors of the dissolved partnership are also creditors of the person or partnership continuing the business.

(6) When a partner is expelled and the remaining partners continue the business either alone or with others, without liquidation of the partnership affairs, creditors of the dissolved partnership are also creditors of the person or partnership continuing the business.

(7) The liability of a third person becoming a partner in the partnership continuing the business, under this section, to the creditors of the dissolved partnership shall be satisfied out of partnership property only.

(8) When the business of a partnership after dissolution is continued under any conditions set forth in

this section the creditors of the dissolved partnership, as against the separate creditors of the retiring or deceased partner or the representative of the deceased partner, have a prior right to any claim of the retired partner or the representative of the deceased partner against the person or partnership continuing the business, on account of the retired partner or the representative of the deceased partner against the person or partnership continuing the business, on account of the retired or deceased partner's interest in the dissolved partnership or on account of any consideration promised for such interest or for his right in partnership property.

(9) Nothing in this section shall be held to modify any right of creditors to set aside any assignment on the ground of fraud.

(10) The use by the person or partnership continuing the business of the partnership name, or the name of a deceased partner as part thereof, shall not of itself make the individual property of the deceased partner liable for any debts contracted by such person or partnership.

§ 42. Rights of Retiring or Estate of Deceased Partner When the Business Is Continued

When any partner retires or dies, and the business is continued under any of the conditions set forth in Section 41(1, 2, 3, 5, 6), or Section 38(2b), without any settlement of accounts as between him or his estate and the person or partnership continuing the business, unless otherwise agreed, he or his legal representative as against such persons or partnership may have the value of his interest at the date of dissolution ascertained, and shall receive as an ordinary creditor an amount equal to the value of his interest in the dissolved partnership with interest, or, at his option or at the option of his legal representative, in lieu of interest, the profits attributable to the use of his right in the property of the dissolved partnership as against the separate creditors, or the representative of the retired or deceased partner, shall have priority on any claim arising under this section, as provided by Section 41(8) of this act.

§ 43. Accrual of Actions

The right to an account of his interest shall accrue to any partner, or his legal representative, as against the winding up partners or the surviving partners or the person or partnership continuing the business, at the date of dissolution, in the absence of any agreement to the contrary.

Part VII

Miscellaneous Provisions

§ 44. When Act Takes Effect

This act shall take effect on the _____ day of _____ one thousand nine hundred and _____.

§ 45. Legislation Repealed

All acts or parts of acts inconsistent with this act are hereby repealed.

REVISED MODEL BUSINESS CORPORATION ACT

As Amended in 1986 and 1987
(EXCERPTS)

---

§ 1.20. FILING REQUIREMENTS

(a) A document must satisfy the requirements of this section, and of any other section that adds to or varies from these requirements, to be entitled to filing by the secretary of state.

(b) This Act must require or permit filing the document in the office of the secretary of state.

(c) The document must contain the information required by this Act. It may contain other information as well.

(d) The document must be typewritten or printed.

(e) The document must be in the English language. A corporate name need not be in English if written in English letters or Arabic or Roman numerals, and the certificate of existence required of foreign corporations need not be in English if accompanied by a reasonably authenticated English translation.

(f) The document must be executed:
   (1) by the chairman of the board of directors of a domestic or foreign corporation, by its president, or by another of its officers;
   (2) if directors have not been selected or the corporation has not been formed, by an incorporator; or
   (3) if the corporation is in the hands of a receiver, trustee, or other court-appointed fiduciary, by that fiduciary.

(g) The person executing the document shall sign it and state beneath or opposite his signature his name and the capacity in which he signs. The document may but need not contain: (1) the corporate seal, (2) an attestation by the secretary or an assistant secretary, (3) an acknowledgment, verification, or proof.

(h) If the secretary of state has prescribed a mandatory form for the document under section 1.21, the document must be in or on the prescribed form.

(i) The document must be delivered to the office of the secretary of state for filing and must be accompanied by one exact or conformed copy (except as provided in sections 5.03 and 15.09), the correct filing fee, and any franchise tax, license fee, or penalty required by this Act or other law.

§ 1.21. FORMS

(a) The secretary of state may prescribe and furnish on request forms for: (1) an application for a certificate of existence, (2) a foreign corporation's application for a certificate of authority to transact business in this state, (3) a foreign corporation's application for a certificate of withdrawal, and (4) the annual report. If the secretary of state so requires, use of these forms is mandatory.

(b) The secretary of state may prescribe and furnish on request forms for other documents required or permitted to be filed by this Act but their use is not mandatory.

§ 1.23. EFFECTIVE TIME AND DATE OF DOCUMENT

(a) Except as provided in subsection (b) and section 1.24(c), a document accepted for filing is effective:
   (1) at the time of filing on the date it is filed, as evidenced by the secretary of state's date and time endorsement on the original document; or
   (2) at the time specified in the document as its effective time on the date it is filed.

(b) A document may specify a delayed effective time and date, and if it does so the document becomes effective at the time and date specified. If a delayed effective date but no time is specified, the document is effective at the close of business on that date. A delayed effective date for a document may not be later than the 90th day after the date it is filed.

§ 1.25. FILING DUTY OF SECRETARY OF STATE

(a) If a document delivered to the office of the secretary of state for filing satisfies the requirements of section 1.20, the secretary of state shall file it.

(b) The secretary of state files a document by stamping or otherwise endorsing "Filed," together with his name and official title and the date and time of receipt, on both the original and the document copy and on the receipt for the filing fee. After filing a document, except as provided in sections 5.03 and 15.10, the secretary of state shall deliver the document copy, with the filing fee receipt (or acknowledgment of receipt if no fee is required) attached, to the domestic or foreign corporation or its representative.

(c) If the secretary of state refuses to file a document, he shall return it to the domestic or foreign corporation or its representative within five days after the document was delivered, together with a brief, written explanation of the reason for his refusal.

(d) The secretary of state's duty to file documents under this section is ministerial. His filing or refusing to file a document does not:

(1) affect the validity or invalidity of the document in whole or part;

(2) relate to the correctness or incorrectness of information contained in the document;

(3) create a presumption that the document is valid or invalid or that information contained in the document is correct or incorrect.

§ 1.40. ACT DEFINITIONS

In this Act:

(1) "Articles of incorporation" include amended and restated articles of incorporation and the articles of merger.

(2) "Authorized shares" means the shares of all classes a domestic or foreign corporation is authorized to issue.

(3) "Conspicuous" means so written that a reasonable person against whom the writing is to operate should have noticed it. For example, printing in italics or boldface or contrasting color, or typing in capitals or underlined, is conspicuous.

(4) "Corporation" or "domestic corporation" means a corporation for profit, which is not a foreign corporation, incorporated under or subject to the provisions of this Act.

(5) "Deliver" includes mail.

(6) "Distribution" means a direct or indirect transfer of money or other property (except its own shares) or incurrence of indebtedness by a corporation to or for the benefit of its shareholders in respect of any of its shares. A distribution may be in the form of a declaration or payment of a dividend; a purchase, redemption, or other acquisition of shares; a distribution of indebtedness; or otherwise.

(7) "Effective date of notice" is defined in section 1.41.

(8) "Employee" includes an officer but not a director. A director may accept duties that make him also an employee.

(9) "Entity" includes corporation and foreign corporation; not-for-profit corporation; profit and not-for-profit unincorporated association; business trust, estate, partnership, trust, and two or more persons having a joint or common economic interest; and state, United States, and foreign government.

(10) "Foreign corporation" means a corporation for profit incorporated under a law other than the law of this state.

(11) "Governmental subdivision" includes authority, county, district, and municipality.

(12) "Includes" denotes a partial definition.

(13) "Individual" includes the estate of an incompetent or deceased individual.

(14) "Means" denotes an exhaustive definition.

(15) "Notice" is defined in section 1.41.

(16) "Person" includes individual and entity.

(17) "Principal office" means the office (in or out of this state) so designated in the annual report where the principal executive offices of a domestic or foreign corporation are located.

(18) "Proceeding" includes civil suit and criminal, administrative, and investigatory action.

(19) "Record date" means the date established under chapter 6 or 7 on which a corporation determines the identity of its shareholders and their shareholdings for purposes of this Act. The determinations shall be made as of the close of business on the record date unless another time for doing so is specified when the record date is fixed.

(20) "Secretary" means the corporate officer to whom the board of directors has delegated responsibility under section 8.40(c) for custody of the minutes of the meetings of the board of directors and of the shareholders and for authenticating records of the corporation.

(21) "Shares" means the units into which the proprietary interests in a corporation are divided.

(22) "Shareholder" means the person in whose name shares are registered in the records of a corporation or the beneficial owner of shares to the extent of the rights granted by a nominee certificate on file with a corporation.

(23) "State," when referring to a part of the United States, includes a state and commonwealth (and their agencies and governmental subdivisions) and a territory and insular possession (and their agencies and governmental subdivisions) of the United States.

(24) "Subscriber" means a person who sub-

scribes for shares in a corporation, whether before or after incorporation.

(25) "United States" includes district, authority, bureau, commission, department, and any other agency of the United States.

(26) "Voting group" means all shares of one or more classes or series that under the articles of incorporation or this Act are entitled to vote and be counted together collectively on a matter at a meeting of shareholders. All shares entitled by the articles of incorporation of this Act to vote generally on the matter are for that purpose a single voting group.

§ 1.41. NOTICE

(a) Notice under this Act must be in writing unless oral notice is reasonable under the circumstances.

(b) Notice may be communicated in person; by telephone, telegraph, teletype, or other form of wire or wireless communication; or by mail or private carrier. If these forms of personal notice are impracticable, notice may be communicated by a newspaper of general circulation in the area where published; or by radio, television, or other form of public broadcast communication.

(c) Written notice by a domestic or foreign corporation to its shareholder, if in a comprehensible form, is effective when mailed, if mailed postpaid and correctly addressed to the shareholder's address shown in the corporation's current record of shareholders.

(d) Written notice to a domestic or foreign corporation (authorized to transact business in this state) may be addressed to its registered agent at its registered office or to the corporation or its secretary at its principal office shown in its most recent annual report or, in the case of a foreign corporation that has not yet delivered an annual report, in its application for a certificate of authority.

(e) Except as provided in subsection (c), written notice, if in a comprehensible form, is effective at the earliest of the following:

(1) when received;

(2) five days after its deposit in the United States Mail, as evidenced by the postmark, if mailed postpaid and correctly addressed;

(3) on the date shown on the return receipt, if sent by registered or certified mail, return receipt requested, and the receipt is signed by or on behalf of the addressee.

(f) Oral notice is effective when communicated if communicated in a comprehensible manner.

(g) If this Act prescribes notice requirements for particular circumstances, those requirements govern. If articles of incorporation or bylaws prescribe notice requirements, not inconsistent with this section or other provisions of this Act, those requirements govern.

§ 1.42. NUMBER OF SHAREHOLDERS

(a) For purposes of this Act, the following identified as a shareholder in a corporation's current record of shareholders constitutes one shareholder:

(1) three or fewer co-owners;

(2) a corporation, partnership, trust, estate, or other entity;

(3) the trustees, guardians, custodians, or other fiduciaries of a single trust, estate, or account.

(b) For purposes of this Act, shareholdings registered in substantially similar names constitute one shareholder if it is reasonable to believe that the names represent the same person.

§ 2.01. INCORPORATIONS

One or more persons may act as the incorporator or incorporators of a corporation by delivering articles of incorporation to the secretary of state for filing.

§ 2.02. ARTICLES OF INCORPORATION

(a) The articles of incorporation must set forth:

(1) a corporate name for the corporation that satisfies the requirements of section 4.01;

(2) the number of shares the corporation is authorized to issue;

(3) the street address of the corporation's initial registered office and the name of its initial registered agent at that office; and

(4) the name and address of each incorporator.

(b) The articles of incorporation may set forth:

(1) the names and addresses of the individuals who are to serve as the initial directors;

(2) provisions not inconsistent with law regarding:

(i) the purpose or purposes for which the corporation is organized;

(ii) managing the business and regulating the affairs of the corporation;

(iii) defining, limiting, and regulating the powers of the corporation, its board of directors, and shareholders;

(iv) a par value for authorized shares or classes of shares;

(v) the imposition of personal liability on shareholders for the debts of the corporation to a specified extent and upon specified conditions; and

(3) any provision that under this Act is required or permitted to be set forth in the bylaws.

(c) The articles of incorporation need not set

forth any of the corporate powers enumerated in this Act.

§ 2.03.   INCORPORATION

(a)   Unless a delayed effective date is specified, the corporate existence begins when the articles of incorporation are filed.

(b)   The secretary of state's filing of the articles of incorporation is conclusive proof that the incorporators satisfied all conditions precedent to incorporation except in a proceeding by the state to cancel or revoke the incorporation or involuntarily dissolve the corporation.

§ 2.04.   LIABILITY FOR PREINCORPORATION TRANSACTIONS

All persons purporting to act as or on behalf of a corporation, knowing there was no incorporation under this Act, are jointly and severally liable for all liabilities created while so acting.

§ 2.05.   ORGANIZATION OF CORPORATION

(a)   After incorporation:

(1)   if initial directors are named in the articles of incorporation, the initial directors shall hold an organizational meeting, at the call of a majority of the directors, to complete the organization of the corporation by appointing officers, adopting bylaws, and carrying on any other business brought before the meeting;

(2)   if initial directors are not named in the articles, the incorporator or incorporators shall hold an organizational meeting at the call of a majority of the incorporators:

(i)   to elect directors and complete the organization of the corporation; or

(ii)   to elect a board of directors who shall complete the organization of the corporation.

(b)   Action required or permitted by this Act to be taken by incorporators at an organizational meeting may be taken without a meeting if the action taken is evidenced by one or more written consents describing the action taken and signed by each incorporator.

(c)   An organizational meeting may be held in or out of this state.

§ 2.06.   BYLAWS

(a)   The incorporators or board of directors of a corporation shall adopt initial bylaws for the corporation.

(b)   The bylaws of a corporation may contain any provision for managing the business and regulating the affairs of the corporation that is not inconsistent with law or the articles of incorporation.

§ 2.07.   EMERGENCY BYLAWS

(a)   Unless the articles of incorporation provide otherwise, the board of directors of a corporation may adopt bylaws to be effective only in an emergency defined in subsection (d). The emergency bylaws, which are subject to amendment or repeal by the shareholders, may make all provisions necessary for managing the corporation during the emergency, including:

(1)   procedures for calling a meeting of the board of directors;

(2)   quorum requirements for the meeting; and

(3)   designation of additional or substitute directors.

(b)   All provisions of the regular bylaws consistent with the emergency bylaws remain effective during the emergency. The emergency bylaws are not effective after the emergency ends.

(c)   Corporate action taken in good faith in accordance with the emergency bylaws:

(1)   binds the corporation; and

(2)   may not be used to impose liability on a corporate director, officer, employee, or agent.

(d)   An emergency exists for purposes of this section if a quorum of the corporation's directors cannot readily be assembled because of some catastrophic event.

§ 3.01.   PURPOSES

(a)   Every corporation incorporated under this Act has the purpose of engaging in any lawful business unless a more limited purpose is set forth in the articles of incorporation.

(b)   A corporation engaging in a business that is subject to regulation under another statute of this state may incorporate under this Act only if permitted by, and subject to all limitations of, the other statute.

§ 3.02.   GENERAL POWERS

Unless its articles of incorporation provide otherwise, every corporation has perpetual duration and succession in its corporate name and has the same powers as an individual to do all things necessary or convenient to carry out its business and affairs, including without limitation power:

(1)   to sue and be sued, complain and defend in its corporate name;

(2)   to have a corporate seal, which may be altered at will, and to use it, or a facsimile of it, by impressing or affixing it or in any other manner reproducing it;

(3)   to make and amend bylaws, not inconsistent with its articles of incorporation or with the laws of this state, for managing the business and regulating the affairs of the corporation;

(4)   to purchase, receive, lease, or otherwise acquire, and own, hold, improve, use, and otherwise deal with, real or personal property, or any legal or equitable interest in property, wherever located;

(5)   to sell, convey, mortgage, pledge, lease,

exchange, and otherwise dispose of all or any part of its property;

(6) to purchase, receive, subscribe for, or otherwise acquire; own, hold, vote, use, sell, mortgage, lend, pledge, or otherwise dispose of; and deal in and with shares or other interests in, or obligations of, any other entity;

(7) to make contracts and guarantees, incur liabilities, borrow money, issue its notes, bonds, and other obligations (which may be convertible into or include the option to purchase other securities of the corporation), and secure any of its obligations by mortgage or pledge of any of its property, franchises, or income;

(8) to lend money, invest and reinvest its funds, and receive and hold real and personal property as security for repayment;

(9) to be a promoter, partner, member, associate, or manager of any partnership, joint venture, trust, or other entity;

(10) to conduct its business, locate offices, and exercise the powers granted by this Act within or without this state;

(11) to elect directors and appoint officers, employees, and agents of the corporation, define their duties, fix their compensation, and lend them money and credit;

(12) to pay pensions and establish pension plans, pension trusts, profit sharing plans, share bonus plans, share option plans, and benefit or incentive plans for any or all of its current or former directors, officers, employees, and agents;

(13) to make donations for the public welfare or for charitable, scientific, or educational purposes;

(14) to transact any lawful business that will aid governmental policy;

(15) to make payments or donations, or do any other act, not inconsistent with law, that furthers the business and affairs of the corporation.

§ 3.03. EMERGENCY POWERS

(a) In anticipation of or during an emergency defined in subsection (d), the board of directors of a corporation may:

    (1) modify lines of succession to accommodate the incapacity of any director, officer, employee, or agent; and

    (2) relocate the principal office, designate alternative principal offices or regional offices, or authorize the officers to do so.

(b) During an emergency defined in subsection (d), unless emergency bylaws provide otherwise:

    (1) notice of a meeting of the board of directors need be given only to those directors whom it is practicable to reach and may be given in any practicable manner, including by publication and radio; and

    (2) one or more officers of the corporation present at a meeting of the board of directors may be deemed to be directors for the meeting, in order of rank and within the same rank in order of seniority, as necessary to achieve a quorum.

(c) Corporate action taken in good faith during an emergency under this section to further the ordinary business affairs of the corporation:

    (1) binds the corporation; and

    (2) may not be used to impose liability on a corporate director, officer, employee, or agent.

(d) An emergency exists for purposes of this section if a quorum of the corporation's directors cannot readily be assembled because of some catastrophic event.

§ 3.04. ULTRA VIRES

(a) Except as provided in subsection (b), the validity of corporate action may not be challenged on the ground that the corporation lacks or lacked power to act.

(b) A corporation's power to act may be challenged:

    (1) in a proceeding by a shareholder against the corporation to enjoin the act;

    (2) in a proceeding by the corporation, directly, derivatively, or through a receiver, trustee, or other legal representative, against an incumbent or former director, officer, employee, or agent of the corporation; or

    (3) in a proceeding by the Attorney General under section 14.30.

(c) In a shareholder's proceeding under subsection (b)(1) to enjoin an unauthorized corporate act, the court may enjoin or set aside the act, if equitable and if all affected persons are parties to the proceeding, and may award damages for loss (other than anticipated profits) suffered by the corporation or another party because of enjoining the unauthorized act.

§ 4.01. CORPORATE NAME

(a) A corporate name:

    (1) must contain the word "corporation," "incorporated," "company," or "limited," or the abbreviation "corp.," "inc.," "co.," or "ltd.," or words or abbreviations of like import in another language; and

    (2) may not contain language stating or implying that the corporation is organized for a purpose other than that permitted by section 3.01 and its articles of incorporation.

(b) Except as authorized by subsections (c) and (d), a corporate name must be distinguishable upon the records of the secretary of state from:

    (1) the corporate name of a corporation in-

corporated or authorized to transact business in this state;

(2) a corporate name reserved or registered under section 4.02 or 4.03;

(3) the fictitious name adopted by a foreign corporation authorized to transact business in this state because its real name is unavailable; and

(4) the corporate name of a not-for-profit corporation incorporated or authorized to transact business in this state.

(c) A corporation may apply to the secretary of state for authorization to use a name that is not distinguishable upon his records from one or more of the names described in subsection (b). The secretary of state shall authorize use of the name applied for if:

(1) the other corporation consents to the use in writing and submits an undertaking in form satisfactory to the secretary of state to change its name to a name that is distinguishable upon the records of the secretary of state from the name of the applying corporation; or

(2) the applicant delivers to the secretary of state a certified copy of the final judgment of a court of competent jurisdiction establishing the applicant's right to use the name applied for in this state.

(d) A corporation may use the name (including the fictitious name) of another domestic or foreign corporation that is used in this state if the other corporation is incorporated or authorized to transact business in this state and the proposed user corporation:

(1) has merged with the other corporation;

(2) has been formed by reorganization of the other corporation; or

(3) has acquired all or substantially all of the assets, including the corporate name, of the other corporation.

(e) This Act does not control the use of fictitious names.

§ 5.01. REGISTERED OFFICE AND REGISTERED AGENT

Each corporation must continuously maintain in this state:

(1) a registered office that may be the same as any of its places of business; and

(2) a registered agent, who may be:

(i) an individual who resides in this state and whose business office is identical with the registered office;

(ii) a domestic corporation or not-for-profit domestic corporation whose business office is identical with the registered office; or

(iii) a foreign corporation or not-for-profit foreign corporation authorized to transact business in this state whose business office is identical with the registered office.

§ 6.03. ISSUED AND OUTSTANDING SHARES

(a) A corporation may issue the number of shares of each class or series authorized by the articles of incorporation. Shares that are issued are outstanding shares until they are reacquired, redeemed, converted, or canceled.

(b) The reacquisition, redemption, or conversion of outstanding shares is subject to the limitations of subsection (c) of this section and to section 6.40.

(c) At all times that shares of the corporation are outstanding, one or more shares that together have unlimited voting rights and one or more shares that together are entitled to receive the net assets of the corporation upon dissolution must be outstanding.

§ 6.20. SUBSCRIPTION FOR SHARES BEFORE INCORPORATION

(a) A subscription for shares entered into before incorporation is irrevocable for six months unless the subscription agreement provides a longer or shorter period or all the subscribers agree to revocation.

(b) The board of directors may determine the payment terms of subscriptions for shares that were entered into before incorporation, unless the subscription agreement specifies them. A call for payment by the board of directors must be uniform so far as practicable as to all shares of the same class or series, unless the subscription agreement specifies otherwise.

(c) Shares issued pursuant to subscriptions entered into before incorporation are fully paid and nonassessable when the corporation receives the consideration specified in the subscription agreement.

(d) If a subscriber defaults in payment of money or property under a subscription agreement entered into before incorporation, the corporation may collect the amount owed as any other debt. Alternatively, unless the subscription agreement provides otherwise, the corporation may rescind the agreement and may sell the shares if the debt remains unpaid more than 20 days after the corporation sends written demand for payment to the subscriber.

(e) A subscription agreement entered into after incorporation is a contract between the subscriber and the corporation subject to section 6.21.

§ 6.22. LIABILITY OF SHAREHOLDERS

(a) A purchaser from a corporation of its own shares is not liable to the corporation or its creditors with respect to the shares except to pay the consideration for which the shares were authorized to be issued (section 6.21) or specified in the subscription agreement (section 6.20).

(b) Unless otherwise provided in the articles of

incorporation, a shareholder of a corporation is not personally liable for the acts or debts of the corporation except that he may become personally liable by reason of his own acts or conduct.

§ 7.01. ANNUAL MEETING

(a) A corporation shall hold a meeting of shareholders annually at a time stated in or fixed in accordance with the bylaws.

(b) Annual shareholders' meetings may be held in or out of this state at the place stated in or fixed in accordance with the bylaws. If no place is stated in or fixed in accordance with the bylaws, annual meetings shall be held at the corporation's principal office.

(c) The failure to hold an annual meeting at the time stated in or fixed in accordance with a corporation's bylaws does not affect the validity of any corporate action.

§ 7.04. ACTION WITHOUT MEETING

(a) Action required or permitted by this Act to be taken at a shareholders' meeting may be taken without a meeting if the action is taken by all the shareholders entitled to vote on the action. The action must be evidenced by one or more written consents describing the action taken, signed by all the shareholders entitled to vote on the action, and delivered to the corporation for inclusion in the minutes or filing with the corporate records.

(b) If not otherwise fixed under section 7.03 or 7.07, the record date for determining shareholders entitled to take action without a meeting is the date the first shareholder signs the consent under subsection (a).

(c) A consent signed under this section has the effect of a meeting vote and may be described as such in any document.

(d) If this Act requires that notice of proposed action be given to nonvoting shareholders and the action is to be taken by unanimous consent of the voting shareholders, the corporation must give its nonvoting shareholders written notice of the proposed action at least 10 days before the action is taken. The notice must contain or be accompanied by the same material that, under this Act, would have been required to be sent to nonvoting shareholders in a notice of meeting at which the proposed action would have been submitted to the shareholders for action.

§ 7.05. NOTICE OF MEETING

(a) A corporation shall notify shareholders of the date, time, and place of each annual and special shareholders' meeting no fewer than 10 nor more than 60 days before the meeting date. Unless this Act or the articles of incorporation require otherwise, the corporation is required to give notice only to shareholders entitled to vote at the meeting.

(b) Unless this Act or the articles of incorporation require otherwise, notice of an annual meeting need not include a description of the purpose or purposes for which the meeting is called.

(c) Notice of a special meeting must include a description of the purpose or purposes for which the meeting is called.

(d) If not otherwise fixed under section 7.03 or 7.07, the record date for determining shareholders entitled to notice of and to vote at an annual or special shareholders' meeting is the day before the first notice is delivered to shareholders.

(e) Unless the bylaws require otherwise, if an annual or special shareholders' meeting is adjourned to a different date, time, or place, notice need not be given of the new date, time, or place if the new date, time, or place is announced at the meeting before adjournment. If a new record date for the adjourned meeting is or must be fixed under section 7.07, however, notice of the adjourned meeting must be given under this section to persons who are shareholders as of the new record date.

§ 7.06. WAIVER OF NOTICE

(a) A shareholder may waive any notice required by this Act, the articles of incorporation, or bylaws before or after the date and time stated in the notice. The waiver must be in writing, be signed by the shareholder entitled to the notice, and be delivered to the corporation for inclusion in the minutes or filing with the corporate records.

(b) A shareholder's attendance at a meeting:

    (1) waives objection to lack of notice or defective notice of the meeting, unless the shareholder at the beginning of the meeting objects to holding the meeting or transacting business at the meeting;

    (2) waives objection to consideration of a particular matter at the meeting that is not within the purpose or purposes described in the meeting notice, unless the shareholder objects to considering the matter when it is presented.

§ 7.07. RECORD DATE

(a) The bylaws may fix or provide the manner of fixing the record date for one or more voting groups in order to determine the shareholders entitled to notice of a shareholders' meeting, to demand a special meeting, to vote, or to take any other action. If the bylaws do not fix or provide for fixing a record date, the board of directors of the corporation may fix a future date as the record date.

(b) A record date fixed under this section may not be more than 70 days before the meeting or action requiring a determination of shareholders.

(c) A determination of shareholders entitled to notice of or to vote at a shareholders' meeting is effective for any adjournment of the meeting unless the board of directors fixes a new record date, which it must do if the meeting is adjourned to a date more than 120 days after the date fixed for the original meeting.

(d) If a court orders a meeting adjourned to a date more than 120 days after the date fixed for the original meeting, it may provide that the original record date continues in effect or it may fix a new record date.

§ 7.21. VOTING ENTITLEMENT OF SHARES

(a) Except as provided in subsections (b) and (c) or unless the articles of incorporation provide otherwise, each outstanding share, regardless of class, is entitled to one vote on each matter voted on at a shareholders' meeting. Only shares are entitled to vote.

(b) Absent special circumstances, the shares of a corporation are not entitled to vote if they are owned, directly or indirectly, by a second corporation, domestic or foreign, and the first corporation owns, directly or indirectly, a majority of the shares entitled to vote for directors of the second corporation.

(c) Subsection (b) does not limit the power of a corporation to vote any shares, including its own shares, held by it in a fiduciary capacity.

(d) Redeemable shares are not entitled to vote after notice of redemption is mailed to the holders and a sum sufficient to redeem the shares has been deposited with a bank, trust company, or other financial institution under an irrevocable obligation to pay the holders the redemption price on surrender of the shares.

§ 7.22. PROXIES

(a) A shareholder may vote his shares in person or by proxy.

(b) A shareholder may appoint a proxy to vote or otherwise act for him by signing an appointment form, either personally or by his attorney-in-fact.

(c) An appointment of a proxy is effective when received by the secretary or other officer of agent authorized to tabulate votes. An appointment is valid for 11 months unless a longer period is expressly provided in the appointment form.

(d) An appointment of a proxy is revocable by the shareholder unless the appointment form conspicuously states that it is irrevocable and the appointment is coupled with an interest. Appointments coupled with an interest include the appointment of:

(1) a pledgee;
(2) a person who purchased or agreed to purchase the shares;
(3) a creditor of the corporation who extended it credit under terms requiring the appointment;
(4) an employee of the corporation whose employment contract requires the appointment; or
(5) a party to a voting agreement created under section 7.31.

(e) The death or incapacity of the shareholder appointing a proxy does not affect the right of the corporation to accept the proxy's authority unless notice of the death or incapacity is received by the secretary or other officer or agent authorized to tabulate votes before the proxy exercises his authority under the appointment.

(f) An appointment made irrevocable under subsection (d) is revoked when the interest with which it is coupled is extinguished.

(g) A transferee for value of shares subject to an irrevocable appointment may revoke the appointment if he did not know of its existence when he acquired the shares and the existence of the irrevocable appointment was not noted conspicuously on the certificate representing the shares or on the information statement for shares without certificates.

(h) Subject to section 7.24 and to any express limitation on the proxy's authority appearing on the face of the appointment form, a corporation is entitled to accept the proxy's vote or other action as that of the shareholder making the appointment.

§ 8.01. REQUIREMENT FOR AND DUTIES OF BOARD OF DIRECTORS

(a) Except as provided in subsection (c), each corporation must have a board of directors.

(b) All corporate powers shall be exercised by or under the authority of, and the business and affairs of the corporation managed under the direction of, its board of directors, subject to any limitation set forth in the articles of incorporation.

(c) A corporation having 50 or fewer shareholders may dispense with or limit the authority of a board of directors by describing in its articles of incorporation who will perform some or all of the duties of a board of directors.

§ 8.03. NUMBER AND ELECTION OF DIRECTORS

(a) A board of directors must consist of one or more individuals, with the number specified in or fixed in accordance with the articles of incorporation or bylaws.

(b) If a board of directors has power to fix or change the number of directors, the board may increase or decrease by 30 percent or less the number of directors last approved by the shareholders, but only the shareholders may increase or decrease by more than 30 percent the number of directors last approved by the shareholders.

(c) The articles of incorporation or bylaws may establish a variable range for the size of the board of directors by fixing a minimum and maximum number of directors. If a variable range is established, the number of directors may be fixed or changed from time to time, within the minimum and maximum, by the shareholders or the board of directors. After shares are issued, only the shareholders may change the range for the size of the board or change from a fixed to a variable-range size board or vice versa.

(d) Directors are elected at the first annual shareholders' meeting and at each annual meeting thereafter unless their terms are staggered under section 8.06.

§ 8.04. ELECTION OF DIRECTORS BY CERTAIN CLASSES OF SHAREHOLDERS

If the articles of incorporation authorize dividing the shares into classes, the articles may also authorize the election of all or a specified number of directors by the holders of one or more authorized classes of shares. A class (or classes) of shares entitled to elect one or more directors is a separate voting group for purposes of the election of directors.

§ 8.05. TERMS OF DIRECTORS GENERALLY

(a) The terms of the initial directors of a corporation expire at the first shareholders' meeting at which directors are elected.

(b) The terms of all other directors expire at the next annual shareholders' meeting following their election unless their terms are staggered under section 8.06.

(c) A decrease in the number of directors does not shorten an incumbent director's term.

(d) The term of a director elected to fill a vacancy expires at the next shareholders' meeting at which directors are elected.

(e) Despite the expiration of a director's term, he continues to serve until his successor is elected and qualifies or until there is a decrease in the number of directors.

§ 8.06. STAGGERED TERMS FOR DIRECTORS

If there are nine or more directors, the articles of incorporation may provide for staggering their terms by dividing the total number of directors into two or three groups, with each group containing one half or one-third of the total, as near as may be. In that event, the terms of directors in the first group expire at the first annual shareholders' meeting after their election, the terms of the second group expire at the second annual shareholders' meeting after their election, and the terms of the third group, if any, expire at the third annual shareholders' meeting after their election. At each annual shareholders' meeting held thereafter, directors shall be chosen for a term of two years or three years, as the case may be, to succeed those whose terms expire.

§ 8.08. REMOVAL OF DIRECTORS BY SHAREHOLDERS

(a) The shareholders may remove one or more directors with or without cause unless the articles of incorporation provide that directors may be removed only for cause.

(b) If a director is elected by a voting group of shareholders, only the shareholders of that voting group may participate in the vote to remove him.

(c) If cumulative voting is authorized, a director may not be removed if the number of votes sufficient to elect him under cumulative voting is voted against his removal. If cumulative voting is not authorized, a director may be removed only if the number of votes cast to remove him exceeds the number of votes cast not to remove him.

(d) A director may be removed by the shareholders only at a meeting called for the purpose of removing him and the meeting notice must state that the purpose, or one of the purposes, of the meeting is removal of the director.

§ 8.20. MEETINGS

(a) The board of directors may hold regular or special meetings in or out of state.

(b) Unless the articles of incorporation or bylaws provide otherwise, the board of directors may permit any or all directors to participate in a regular or special meeting by, or conduct the meeting through the use of, any means of communication by which all directors participating may simultaneously hear each other during the meeting. A director participating in a meeting by this means is deemed to be present in person at the meeting.

§ 8.30. GENERAL STANDARDS FOR DIRECTORS

(a) A director shall discharge his duties as a director, including his duties as a member on a committee:

(1) in good faith;

(2) with the care an ordinarily prudent person in a like position would exercise under similar circumstances; and

(3) in a manner he reasonably believes to be in the best interests of the corporation.

(b) In discharging his duties a director is entitled to rely on information, opinions, reports, or statements, including financial statements and other financial data, if prepared or presented by:

(1) one or more officers or employees of the corporation whom the director reasonably believes to be reliable and competent in the matters presented;

(2) legal counsel, public accountants, or other persons as to matters the director reasonably believes are within the person's professional or expert competence; or

(3) a committee of the board of directors of which he is not a member if the director reasonably believes the committee merits confidence.

(c) A director is not acting in good faith if he has knowledge concerning the matter in question that makes reliance otherwise permitted by subsection (b) unwarranted.

(d) A director is not liable for any action taken as a director, or any failure to take any action, if he performed the duties of his office in compliance with this section.

§ 8.31.   DIRECTOR CONFLICT OF INTEREST

(a) A conflict of interest transaction is a transaction with the corporation in which a director of the corporation has a direct or indirect interest. A conflict of interest transaction is not voidable by the corporation solely because of the director's interest in the transaction if any one of the following is true:

(1) the material facts of the transaction and the director's interest were disclosed or known to the board of directors or a committee of the board of directors and the board of directors or committee authorized, approved, or ratified the transaction;

(2) the material facts of the transaction and the director's interest were disclosed or known to the shareholders entitled to vote and they authorized, approved, or ratified the transaction; or

(3) the transaction was fair to the corporation.

(b) For the purposes of this section, a director of the corporation has an indirect interest in a transaction if (1) another entity in which he has a material financial interest or in which he is a general partner is a party to the transaction or (2) another entity of which he is a director, officer, or trustee is a party to the transaction and the transaction is or should be considered by the board of directions of the corporation.

(c) For purposes of subsection (a)(1), a conflict of interest transaction is authorized, approved, or ratified if it receives the affirmative vote of a majority of the directors on the board of directors (or on the committee) who have no direct or indirect interest in the transaction, but a transaction may not be authorized, approved, or ratified under this section by a single director. If a majority of the directors who have no direct or indirect interest in the transaction vote to authorize, approve, or ratify the transaction, a quorum is present for the purpose of taking action under this section. The presence of, or a vote cast by, a director with a direct or indirect interest in the transaction does not affect the validity of any action taken under subsection (a)(1) if the transaction is otherwise authorized, approved, or ratified as provided in that subsection.

(d) For purposes of subsection (a)(2), a conflict of interest transaction is authorized, approved, or ratified if it receives the vote of a majority of the shares entitled to be counted under this subsection. Shares owned by or voted under the control of a director who has a direct or indirect interest in the transaction, and shares owned by or voted under the control of an entity described in subsection (b)(1), may not be counted in a vote of shareholders to determine whether to authorize, approve, or ratify a conflict of interest transaction under subsection (a)(2). The vote of those shares, however, is counted in determining whether the transaction is approved under other sections of this Act. A majority of the shares, whether or not present, that are entitled to be counted in a vote on the transaction under this subsection constituted a quorum for the purpose of taking action under this section.

§ 8.33.   LIABILITY FOR UNLAWFUL DISTRIBUTIONS

(a) A director who votes for or assents to a distribution made in violation of section 6.40 or the articles of incorporation is personally liable to the corporation for the amount of the distribution that exceeds what could have been distributed without violating section 6.40 or the articles of incorporation if it is established that he did not perform his duties in compliance with section 8.30. In any proceeding commenced under this section, a director has all of the defenses ordinarily available to a director.

(b) A director held liable under subsection (a) for an unlawful distribution is entitled to contribution:

(1) from every other director who could be held liable under subsection (a) for the unlawful distribution; and

(2) from each shareholder for the amount the shareholder accepted knowing the distribution was made in violation of section 6.40 or the articles of incorporation.

(c) A proceeding under this section is barred unless it is commenced within two years after the date on which the effect of the distribution was measured under section 6.40(e) or (g).

§ 8.40.   REQUIRED OFFICERS

(a) A corporation has the officers described in its bylaws or appointed by the board of directors in accordance with the bylaws.

(b) A duly appointed officer may appoint one or more officers or assistant officers if authorized by the bylaws or the board of directors.

(c) The bylaws or the board of directors shall delegate to one of the officers responsibility for preparing minutes of the directors' and shareholders' meetings and for authenticating records of the corporation.

(d) The same individual may simultaneously hold more than one office in a corporation.

§ 8.41.   DUTIES OF OFFICERS

Each officer has the authority and shall perform the duties set forth in the bylaws or, to the extent consistent with the bylaws, the duties prescribed by the board of directors or by direction of an officer authorized by the board of directors to prescribe the duties of other officers.

§ 8.42. STANDARDS OF CONDUCT FOR OFFICERS

(a) An officer with discretionary authority shall discharge his duties under that authority:

(1) in good faith;

(2) with the care an ordinarily prudent person in a like position would exercise under similar circumstances; and

(3) in a manner he reasonably believes to be in the best interests of the corporation.

(b) In discharging his duties an officer is entitled to rely on information, opinions, reports, or statements, including financial statements and other financial data, if prepared or presented by:

(1) one or more officers or employees of the corporation whom the officer reasonably believes to be reliable and competent in the matters presented; or

(2) legal counsel, public accountants, or other persons as to matters the officer reasonably believes are within the person's professional or expert competence.

(c) An officer is not acting in good faith if he has knowledge concerning the matter in question that makes reliance otherwise permitted by subsection (b) unwarranted.

(d) An officer is not liable for an action taken as an officer, or any failure to take any action, if he performed the duties of his office in compliance with this section.

§ 11.01. MERGER

(a) One or more corporations may merge into another corporation if the board of directors of each corporation adopts and its shareholders (if required by section 11.03) approve a plan of merger.

(b) The plan of merger must set forth:

(1) the name of each corporation planning to merge and the name of the surviving corporation into which each other corporation plans to merge;

(2) the terms and conditions of the merger; and

(3) the manner and basis of converting the shares of each corporation into shares, obligations, or other securities of the surviving or any other corporation or into cash or other property in whole or part.

(c) The plan of merger may set forth:

(1) amendments to the articles of incorporation of the surviving corporation; and

(2) other provisions relating to the merger.

§ 13.02. RIGHT TO DISSENT

(a) A shareholder is entitled to dissent from and obtain payment of the fair value of his shares in the event of, any of the following corporate actions:

(1) consummation of a plan of merger to which the corporation is a party (i) if shareholder approval is required for the merger by section 11.03 or the articles of incorporation and the shareholder is entitled to vote on the merger or (ii) if the corporation is a subsidiary that is merged with its parent under section 11.04;

(2) consummation of a plan of share exchange to which the corporation is a party as the corporation whose shares will be acquired, if the shareholder is entitled to vote on the plan;

(3) consummation of a sale or exchange of all, or substantially all, of the property of the corporation other than in the usual and regular course of business, if the shareholder is entitled to vote on the sale or exchange, including a sale in dissolution, but not including a sale pursuant to court order or a sale for cash pursuant to a plan by which all or substantially all of the net proceeds of the sale will be distributed to the shareholders within one year after the date of sale;

(4) an amendment of the articles of incorporation that materially and adversely affects rights in respect of a dissenter's shares because it:

(i) alters or abolishes a preferential right of the shares;

(ii) creates, alters, or abolishes a right in respect of redemption, including a provision respecting a sinking fund for the redemption or repurchase, of the shares;

(iii) alters or abolishes a preemptive right of the holder of the shares to acquire shares or other securities;

(iv) excludes or limits the right of the shares to vote on any matter, or to cumulate votes, other than a limitation by dilution through issuance of shares or other securities with similar voting rights; or

(v) reduces the number of shares owned by the shareholder to a fraction of a share if the fractional share so created is to be acquired for cash under section 6.04; or

(5) any corporate action taken pursuant to a shareholder vote to the extent the articles of incorporation, bylaws, or a resolution of the board of directors provides

that voting or nonvoting shareholders are entitled to dissent and obtain payment for their shares.

(b) A shareholder entitled to dissent and obtain payment for his shares under this chapter may not challenge the corporate action creating his entitlement unless the action is unlawful or fraudulent with respect to the shareholder or the corporation.

§ 16.01.   CORPORATE RECORDS

(a) A corporation shall keep as permanent records minutes of all meetings of its shareholders and board of directors, a record of all actions taken by the shareholders or board of directors without a meeting, and a record of all actions taken by a committee of the board of directors in place of the board of directors on behalf of the corporation.

(b) A corporation shall maintain appropriate accounting records.

(c) A corporation or its agent shall maintain a record of its shareholders, in a form that permits preparation of a list of the names and addresses of all shareholders, in alphabetical order by class of shares showing the number and class of shares held by each.

(d) A corporation shall maintain its records in written form or in another form capable of conversion into written form within a reasonable time.

(e) A corporation shall keep a copy of the following records at its principal office:

(1) its articles or restated articles of incorporation and all amendments to them currently in effect;

(2) its bylaws or restated bylaws and all amendments to them currently in effect;

(3) resolutions adopted by its board of directors creating one or more classes or series of shares, and fixing their relative rights, preferences, and limitations, if shares issued pursuant to those resolutions are outstanding;

(4) the minutes of all shareholders' meetings, and records of all action taken by shareholders without a meeting, for the past three years;

(5) all written communications to shareholders generally within the past three years, including the financial statements furnished for the past three years under section 16.20;

(6) a list of the names and business addresses of its current directors and officers; and

(7) its most recent annual report delivered to the secretary of state under section 16.22.

§ 16.02.   INSPECTION OF RECORDS BY SHAREHOLDERS

(a) A shareholder of a corporation is entitled to inspect and copy, during regular business hours at the corporation's principal office, any of the records of the corporation described in section 16.01(e) if he gives the corporation written notice of his demand at least five business days before the date on which he wishes to inspect and copy.

(b) A shareholder of a corporation is entitled to inspect and copy, during regular business hours at a reasonable location specified by the corporation, any of the following records of the corporation if the shareholder meets the requirements of subsection (c) and gives the corporation written notice of his demand at least five business days before the date on which he wishes to inspect and copy:

(1) excerpts from minutes of any meeting of the board of directors, records of any action of a committee of the board of directors while acting in place of the board of directors on behalf of the corporation, minutes of any meeting of the shareholders, and records of action taken by the shareholders or board of directors without a meeting, to the extent not subject to inspection under section 16.02(a);

(2) accounting records of the corporation; and

(3) the record of shareholders.

(c) A shareholder may inspect and copy the records described in subsection (b) only if:

(1) his demand is made in good faith and for a proper purpose;

(2) he describes with reasonable particularity his purpose and the records he desires to inspect; and

(3) the records are directly connected with his purpose.

(d) The right of inspection granted by this section may not be abolished or limited by a corporation's articles of incorporation or bylaws.

(e) This section does not affect:

(1) the right of a shareholder to inspect records under section 7.20 or, if the shareholder is in litigation with the corporation, to the same extent as any other litigant;

(2) the power of a court, independently of this Act, to compel the production of corporate records for examination.

(f) For purposes of this section, "shareholder" includes a beneficial owner whose shares are held in a voting trust or by a nominee on his behalf.

§ 16.20.   FINANCIAL STATEMENTS FOR SHAREHOLDERS

(a) A corporation shall furnish its shareholders annual financial statements, which may be consolidated or combined statements of the corporation and one or more of its subsidiaries, as appropriate, that include a balance sheet as of the end of the fiscal year, an income statement for that year, and a statement of changes in shareholders' equity for the year unless that information appears elsewhere in the financial statements. If financial statements are prepared for the corporation on the basis of generally accepted accounting principles, the annual financial statements must also be prepared on that basis.

(b) If the annual financial statements are reported upon by a public accountant, his report must accompany them. If not, the statements must be accompanied by a statement of the president or the person responsible for the corporation's accounting records:

(1) stating his reasonable belief whether the statements were prepared on the basis of generally accepted accounting principles and, if not, describing the basis of preparation; and

(2) describing any respects in which the statements were not prepared on a basis of accounting consistent with the statements prepared for the preceding year.

(c) A corporation shall mail the annual financial statements to each shareholder within 120 days after the close of each fiscal year. Thereafter, on written request from a shareholder who was not mailed the statements, the corporation shall mail him the latest financial statements.

GLOSSARY

A

abandon: give up or leave employment; relinquish possession of personal property with intent to disclaim title.

abate: put a stop to a nuisance; reduce or cancel a legacy because the estate of the decedent is insufficient to make payment in full.

ab initio: from the beginning.

abrogate: recall or repeal; make void or inoperative.

absolute liability: liability for an act that causes harm even though the actor was not at fault.

absolute privilege: protection from liability for slander or libel given under certain circumstances regardless of the fact that the statements are false or maliciously made.

abstract of title: history of the transfers of title to a given piece of land, briefly stating the parties to and the effect of all deeds, wills, and judicial proceedings relating to the land.

acceleration clause: provision in a contract or any legal instrument that upon a certain event the time for the performance of specified obligations shall be advanced; for example, a provision making the balance due upon debtor's default.

acceptance: unqualified assent to the act or proposal of another; as the acceptance of a draft (bill of exchange), of an offer to make a contract, of goods delivered by the seller, or of a gift or deed.

accession: acquisition of title to personal property by virtue of the fact that it has been attached to property already owned or was the offspring of an owned animal.

accessory after the fact: one who after the commission of a felony knowingly assists the felon.

accessory before the fact: one who is absent at the commission of the crime but who aided and abetted its commission.

accident: an event that occurs even though a reasonable person would not have foreseen its occurrence, because of which the law holds no one responsible for the harm caused.

accommodation party: a person who signs a commercial paper to lend credit to another party to the paper.

accord and satisfaction: an agreement to substitute a different performance for that called for in the contract and the performance of that substitute agreement.

accretion: the acquisition of title to additional land when the owner's land is built up by gradual deposits made by the natural action of water.

acknowledgment: an admission or confirmation, generally of an instrument and usually made before a person authorized to administer oaths, such as a notary public; the purpose being to declare that the instrument was executed by the person making the instrument, or that it was a voluntary act or that that person desires that it be recorded.

action: a proceeding to enforce any right.

action in personam: an action brought to impose liability upon a person, such as a money judgment.

action in rem: an action brought to declare the status of a thing, such as an action to declare the title to property to be forfeited because of its illegal use.

action of assumpsit: a common-law action brought to recover damages for breach of a contract.

action of ejectment: a common-law action brought to recover the possession of land.

action of mandamus: a common-law action brought to compel the performance of a ministerial or clerical act by an officer.

action of quo warranto: a common-law action

brought to challenge the authority of an officer to act or to hold office.

action of replevin: a common-law action brought to recover the possession of personal property.

action of trespass: a common-law action brought to recover damages for a tort.

Act of God: a natural phenomenon that is not reasonable foreseeable.

administrative agency: a governmental commission or board given authority to regulate particular matters.

administrator-administratrix: the person (man-woman) appointed to wind up and settle the estate of a person who has died without a will.

adverse possession: the hostile possession of real estate, which when actual, visible, notorious, exclusive, and continued for the required time, will vest the title to the land in the person in such adverse possession.

advisory opinion: an opinion that may be rendered in a few states when there is no actual controversy before the court and the matter is submitted by private persons, or in some instances by the governor of the state, to obtain the court's opinion.

affidavit: a statement of facts set forth in written form and supported by the oath or affirmation of the person making the statement setting forth that such facts are true on the basis of actual knowledge or on information and belief. The affidavit is executed before a notary public or other person authorized to administer oaths.

affinity: the relationship that exists by virtue of marriage.

affirmative covenant: an express undertaking or promise in a contract or deed to do an act.

agency: the relationship that exists between a person identified as a principal and another by virtue of which the latter may make contracts with third persons on behalf of the principal. (Parties — principal, agent, third person)

agency coupled with an interest in the authority: an agency in which the agent has given a consideration or has paid for the right to exercise the authority granted.

agency coupled with an interest in the subject matter: an agency in which for a consideration the agent is given an interest in the property to which the agency relates.

agency shop: a union contract provision requiring that nonunion employees pay to the union the equivalent of union dues in order to retain their employment.

agent: one who is authorized by the principal or by operation of law to make contracts with third persons on behalf of the principal.

allonge: a paper securely fastened to a commercial paper in order to provide additional space for endorsements.

alluvion: the additions made to land by accretion.

alteration: any material change of the terms of a writing fraudulently made by a party thereto.

ambulatory: not effective and therefore may be changed, as in the case of a will that is not final until its maker has died.

amicable action: an action that all parties agree should be brought and one that is begun by the filing of such an agreement, rather than by serving the adverse parties with process. Although the parties agree to litigate, the dispute is real, and the decision is not an advisory opinion.

amicus curiae: literally, a friend of the court; one who is appointed by the court to take part in litigation and to assist the court by furnishing an opinion in the matter.

annexation: attachment of personal property to realty in such a way as to make it become real property and part of the realty.

annuity: a contract by which the insured pays a lump sum to the insurer and later receives fixed annual payments.

anomalous indorser: a person who signs a commercial paper but is not otherwise a party to the instrument.

anticipatory breach: the repudiation by a promisor of the contract prior to the time that performance is required when such repudiation is accepted by the promisee as a breach of the contract.

anti-injunction acts: statutes prohibiting the use of injunctions in labor disputes except under exceptional circumstances; notably the federal Norris-La Guardia Act of 1932.

Anti-Pertrillo Act: a federal statute that makes it a crime to compel a radio broadcasting station to hire musicians not needed, to pay for services not performed, or to refrain from broadcasting music of school children or from foreign countries.

antitrust acts: statutes prohibiting combinations and contracts in restraint of trade, notably the federal

Sherman Antitrust Act of 1890, now generally inapplicable to labor union activity.

appeal: taking a case to a reviewing court to determine whether the judgment of the lower court or administrative agency was correct. (Parties — appellant, appellee)

appellate jurisdiction: the power of a court to hear and decide a given class of cases on appeal from another court or administrative agency.

arbitration: the settlement of disputed questions, whether of law or fact, by one or more arbitrators by whose decision the parties agree to be bound. Increasingly used as a procedure for labor dispute settlement.

assignment: transfer of a right. Generally used in connection with personal property rights, as rights under a contract, commercial paper, an insurance policy, a mortgage, or a lease. (Parties — assignor, assignee)

assumption of risk: the common-law rule that an employee could not sue the employer for injuries caused by the ordinary risks of employment on the theory that the employee assumed such risks by undertaking the work. The rule has been abolished in those areas governed by workers' compensation laws and most employers' liability statutes.

attachment: the seizure of property of a debtor to secure satisfaction of a judgment.

attractive nuisance doctrine: a rule imposing liability upon a landowner for injuries sustained by small children playing on the land when the landowner permits a condition to exist or maintains equipment that a reasonable person should realize would attract small children who could not realize the danger. The rule does not apply if an unreasonable burden would be imposed upon the landowner in taking steps to protect the children.

authenticate: make or establish as genuine, official, or final, such as by signing, countersigning, sealing, or performing any other act indicating approval.

B

bad check laws: laws making it a criminal offense to issue a bad check with intent to defraud.

baggage: such articles of necessity or personal convenience as are usually carried for personal use by passengers of common carriers.

bail: variously used in connection with the release of a person or property from the custody of the law,

referring (a) to the act of releasing or bailing, (b) to the persons who assume liability in the event that the released person does not appear or that it is held that the property should not be released, and (c) to the bond or sum of money that is furnished the court or other official as indemnity for nonperformance of the obligation.

bailee's lien: a specific, possessory lien of the bailee upon the goods for work done to them. Commonly extended by statute to any bailee's claim for compensation and eliminating the necessity of retention of possession.

bailment: the relationship that exists when personal property is delivered into the possession of another under an agreement, express or implied, that the identical property will be returned or will be delivered in accordance with the agreement. (Parties — bailor, bailee)

bankruptcy: a procedure by which one unable to pay debts may surrender to the court for administration and distribution to creditors all assets in excess of any exemption claim, and the debtor is given a discharge that releases from the unpaid balance due on most debts.

bearer: the person in physical possession of commercial paper payable to bearer, a document of title directing delivery to bearer, or an investment security in bearer form.

beneficiary: the person to whom the proceeds of a life insurance policy are payable, a person for whose benefit property is held in trust, or a person given property by a will.

bequest: a gift of personal property by will.

bill of exchange (draft): an unconditional order in writing by one person upon another, signed by the person giving it, and ordering the person to whom it is directed to pay upon demand or at a definite time a sum certain in money to order or to bearer.

bill of lading: a document issued by a carrier reciting the receipt of goods and the terms of the contract of transportation. Regulated by the federal Bills of Lading Act or the UCC.

bill of sale: a writing signed by the seller reciting that the personal property therein described has been sold to the buyer.

binder: a memorandum delivered to the insured stating the essential terms of a policy to be executed in the future, when it is agreed that the contract of insurance is to be effective before the written policy is executed.

blank indorsement: an indorsement that does not

name the person to whom the paper, document of title, or investment security is negotiated.

blue sky laws: state statutes designed to protect the public from the sale of worthless stocks and bonds.

boardinghouse keeper: one regularly engaged in the business of offering living accommodations to permanent lodgers or boarders.

bona fide: in good faith; without any fraud or deceit.

bond: an obligation or promise in writing and sealed, generally of corporations, personal representatives, and trustees; fidelity bonds.

boycott: a combination of two or more persons to cause harm to another by refraining from patronizing or dealing with such other person in any way or inducing others to so refrain; commonly an incident of labor disputes.

bulk sales acts: statutes to protect creditors of a bulk seller. Notice must be given creditors, and the bulk sale buyer is liable to the seller's creditors if the statute is not satisfied. Expanded to *bulk transfers* under the UCC.

business trust: a form of business organization in which the owners of the property to be devoted to the business transfer the title of the property to trustees with full power to operate the business.

C

cancellation: a crossing-out of a part of an instrument or a destruction of all legal effect of the instrument, whether by act of party, upon breach by the other party, or pursuant to agreement or decree of court.

capital: net assets of a corporation.

capital stock: the declared money value of the outstanding stock of the corporation.

cash surrender value: the sum paid the insured upon the surrender of a policy to the insurer.

cause of action: the right to damages or other judicial relief when a legally protected right of the plaintiff is violated by an unlawful act of the defendant.

caveat emptor: let the buyer beware. This maxim has been nearly abolished by warranty and strict tort liability concepts.

certificate of protest: a written statement by a notary public setting forth the fact that the holder had presented the commercial paper to the primary party and that the latter had failed to make payment.

certiorari: a review by a higher court of the regularity of proceedings before a lower court. Originally

granted within the discretion of the reviewing court. The name is derived from the language of the writ, which was in Latin and directed the lower court to certify its record and transfer it to the higher court. In modern practice, the scope of review has often been expanded to include a review of the merits of the case and, also, to review the action of administrative agencies.

cestui que trust: the beneficiary or person for whose benefit the property is held in trust.

charter: the grant of authority from a government to exist as a corporation. Generally replaced today by a certificate of incorporation approving the articles of incorporation.

chattels personal: tangible personal property.

chattels real: leases of land and buildings.

check: an order by a depositor on a bank to pay a sum of money to a payee; a bill of exchange drawn on a bank and payable on demand.

chose in action: intangible personal property in the nature of claims against another, such as a claim for accounts receivable or wages.

chose in possession: tangible personal property.

circumstantial evidence: relates to circumstances surrounding the facts in dispute from which the trier of fact may deduce what has happened.

civil action: in many states a simplified form of action combining all or many of the former common-law actions.

civil court: a court with jurisdiction to hear and determine controversies relating to private rights and duties.

closed shop: a place of employment in which only union members may be employed. Now prohibited.

codicil: a testator's or testatrix's writing executed with all the formality of a will and treated as an addition to or modification of the will.

coinsurance: a clause requiring the insured to maintain insurance on property up to a stated amount and providing that to the extent that this is not done the insured is to be deemed a coinsurer with the insurer, so that the latter is liable only for its proportionate share of the amount of insurance required to be carried.

collateral note: a note accompanied by collateral security.

collective bargaining: the process by which the terms of employment are agreed upon through negotiations between the employer or employers within a given industry or industrial area and the union or the bargaining representative of the employees.

collective bargaining unit: the employment area within which employees are by statute authorized to select a bargaining representative, who is then to represent all the employees in bargaining with the employer.

collusion: an agreement between two or more persons to defraud the government or the courts, as by obtaining a divorce by collusion when no grounds for a divorce exist, or to defraud third persons of their rights.

color of title: circumstances that make a person appear to be the owner when in fact not the owner, as the existence of a deed appearing to convey the property to a given person gives color of title although the deed is worthless because it is in fact a forgery.

commission merchant: a bailee to whom goods are consigned for sale.

common carrier: a carrier that holds out its facilities to serve the general public for compensation without discrimination.

common law: the body of unwritten principles originally based upon the usages and customs of the community that were recognized and enforced by the courts.

common stock: stock that has no right or priority over any other stock of the corporation as to dividends or distribution of assets upon dissolution.

common trust fund: a plan by which the assets of small trust estates are pooled into a common fund, each trust being given certificates representing its proportionate ownership of the fund, and the pooled fund is then invested in investments of large size.

community property: the cotenancy held by husband and wife in property acquired during their marriage under the law of some of the states, principally in the southwestern United States.

complaint: the initial pleading filed by the plaintiff in many actions, which in many states may be served as original process to acquire jurisdiction over the defendant.

composition of creditors: an agreement among creditors that each shall accept a part payment as full payment in consideration of the other creditors doing the same.

concealment: the failure to volunteer information not requested.

conditional estate: an estate that will come into being upon the satisfaction of a condition precedent or that will be terminated upon the satisfaction of a condition subsequent.

confidential relationship: a relationship in which, because of the legal status of the parties or their respective physical or mental conditions or knowledge, one party places full confidence and trust in the other.

conflict of laws: the body of law that determines the law of which state is to apply when two or more states are involved in the facts of a given case.

confusion of goods: the mixing of goods of different owners that under certain circumstances results in one of the owners becoming the owner of all the goods.

consanguinity: relationship by blood.

consideration: the promise or performance that the promisor demands as the price of the promise.

consignment: a bailment made for the purpose of sale by the bailee. (Parties — consignor, consignee)

consolidation of corporations: a combining of two or more corporations in which the corporate existence of each one ceases and a new corporation is created.

constructive: an adjective employed to indicate that the instrument, described by the noun that is modified by the adjective, does not exist but the law disposes of the matter as though it did; as a constructive bailment or a constructive trust.

contingent beneficiary: the person to whom the proceeds of a life insurance policy are payable in the event that the primary beneficiary dies before the insured.

contract: a binding agreement based upon the genuine assent of the parties, made for a lawful object, between competent parties, in the form required by law, and generally supported by consideration.

contract carrier: a carrier that transports on the basis of individual contracts that it makes with each shipper.

contract to sell: a contract to make a transfer of title in the future as contrasted with a present transfer.

contribution: the right of a co-obligor who has paid more than a proportionate share to demand that the other obligor pay the amount of the excess payment made.

contributory negligence: negligence of the plaintiff that contributes to injury and at common law bars from recovery from the defendant although the defendant may have been more negligent than the plaintiff.

conveyance: a transfer of an interest in land, ordinarily by the execution and delivery of a deed.

cooling-off period: a procedure designed to avoid strikes by requiring a specified period of delay before the strike may begin during which negotiations for a settlement must continue.

cooperative: a group of two or more persons or enterprises that acts through a common agent with respect to a common objective, such as buying or selling.

copyright: a grant to an author or artist of an exclusive right to publish and sell the copyrighted work for the life of the author or artist and fifty years thereafter. For a "work made for hire," a grant of an exclusive right to publish and sell the copyrighted work for 100 years from its creation or 75 years from its publication, whichever is shorter.

corporation: an artificial being created by government grant, which for many purposes is treated as a natural person.

cost plus: a method of determining the purchase price or contract price by providing for the payment of an amount equal to the costs of the seller or contractor to which is added a stated percentage as the profit.

costs: the expenses of suing or being sued, recoverable in some actions by the successful party, and in others, subject to allocation by the court. Ordinarily, costs do not include attorney's fees or compensation for loss of time.

counterclaim: a claim that the defendant in an action may make against the plaintiff.

covenants of title: covenants of the grantor in a deed that guarantee such matters as the right to make the conveyance, to ownership of the property, to freedom of the property from encumbrances, or that the grantee will not be disturbed in the quiet enjoyment of the land.

crime: a violation of the law that is punished as an offense against the state or government.

cross complaint: a claim that the defendant may make against the plaintiff.

cross-examination: the examination made of a witness by the attorney for the adverse party.

cumulative voting: a system of voting for directors in which each shareholder has as many votes as the number of voting shares owned multiplied by the number of directors to be elected and such votes can be distributed for the various candidates as desired.

cy pres doctrine: the rule under which a charitable trust will be carried out as nearly as possible in the way the settlor desired, when for any reason it cannot be carried out exactly in the way or for the purposes expressed.

D

damages: a sum of money recovered to redress or make amends for the legal wrong or injury done.

damnum absque injuria: loss or damage without the violation of a legal right, or the mere fact that a person sustains a loss does not mean that legal rights have been violated.

declaratory judgment: a procedure for obtaining the decision of a court on a question before any action has been taken or loss sustained. It differs from an advisory opinion in that there must be an actual, imminent controversy.

dedication: acquisition by the public or a government of title to land when it is given over by its owner to use by the public and such gift is accepted.

deed: an instrument by which the grantor (owner of land) conveys or transfers the title to a grantee.

de facto: existing in fact as distinguished from as of right, as in the case of an officer or a corporation purporting to act as such without being elected to the office or having been properly incorporated.

deficiency judgment: a personal judgment entered against any person liable on the mortgage debt for the amount still remaining due on the mortgage after foreclosure. Statutes generally require the mortgagee to credit the fair value of the property against the balance due when the mortgagee has purchased the property. Also, a similar judgment entered by a creditor against a debtor in a secured transaction under Article 9 of the UCC.

del credere agent: an agent who sells goods for the principal and who guarantees to the principal that the buyer will pay for the goods.

delegation: the transfer to another of the right and power to do an act.

de minimis non curat lex: a maxim that the law is not concerned with trifles. Not always applied, as in the case of the encroachment of a building over the property line, in which case the law will protect the landowner regardless of the extent of the encroachment.

demonstrative evidence: evidence that consists of visible, physical objects, such as a sample taken from the wheat in controversy or a photograph of the subject matter involved.

demonstrative legacy: a legacy to be paid or distributed from a specified fund or property.

demurrage: a charge made by the carrier for the unreasonable detention of cars by the consignor or consignee.

demurrer: a pleading that may be filed to attack the sufficiency of the adverse party's pleading as not stating a cause of action or a defense.

dependent relative revocation: the doctrine recognized in some states that if a testator revokes or cancels a will in order to replace it with a later will, the earlier will is to be deemed revived if for any reason the later will does not take effect or no later will is executed.

deposition: the testimony of a witness taken out of court before a person authorized to administer oaths.

detrimental reliance: see *reliance* and *promissory estoppel*.

devise: a gift of real estate made by will.

directed verdict: a direction by the trial judge to the jury to return a verdict in favor of a specified party to the action.

directors: the persons vested with control of the corporation, subject to the elective power of the shareholders.

discharge in bankruptcy: an order of the bankruptcy court discharging the debtor from the unpaid balance of most claims.

discharge of contract: termination of a contract by performance, agreement, impossibility, acceptance of breach, or operation of law.

discovery: procedures for ascertaining facts prior to the time of trial in order to eliminate the element of surprise in litigation.

dishonor by nonacceptance: the refusal of the drawee to accept a draft (bill of exchange).

dishonor by nonpayment: the refusal to pay a commercial paper when properly presented for payment.

dismiss: a procedure to terminate an action by moving to dismiss on the ground that the plaintiff has not pleaded a cause of action entitling the plaintiff to relief.

disparagement of goods: the making of malicious, false statements as to the quality of the goods of another.

distress for rent: the common-law right of the lessor to enter the premises when the rent has not been paid and to seize all personal property found on the premises. Statutes have modified or abolished this right in many states.

distributive share: the proportionate part of the estate of the decedent that will be distributed to an heir or legatee, and also as devisee in those jurisdictions in which real estate is administered as part of the decedent's estate.

domestic bill of exchange: a draft drawn in one state and payable in the same or another state.

domestic corporation: a corporation that has been incorporated by the state in question as opposed to incorporation by another state.

domicile: the home of a person or the state of incorporation, to be distinguished from a place where a person lives but does not regard as home, or a state in which a corporation does business but in which it was not incorporated.

double indemnity: a provision for payment of double the amount specified by the insurance contract if death is caused by an accident and occurs under specified circumstances.

double jeopardy: the principle that a person who has once been placed in jeopardy by being brought to trial at which the proceedings progressed at least as far as having the jury sworn cannot thereafter be tried a second time for the same offense.

draft: see *bill of exchange*.

draft-varying acceptance: one in which the acceptor's agreement to pay is not exactly in conformity with the order of the instrument.

due care: the degree of care that a reasonable person would exercise to prevent the realization of harm, which under all the circumstances was reasonably foreseeable in the event that such care was not taken.

due process of law: the guarantee by the 5th and 14th Amendments to the U.S. Constitution and the guarantee of many state constitutions that no person shall be deprived of life, liberty, or property without due process of law. As currently interpreted, this process prohibits any law, either state or federal, that sets up an unfair procedure or the substance of which is arbitrary or capricious.

duress: conduct that deprives the victim of free will

and that generally gives the victim the right to set aside any transaction entered into under such circumstances.

E

easement: a permanent right that one has in the land of another, as the right to cross another's land or an easement of way.

eleemosynary corporation: a corporation organized for a charitable or benevolent purpose.

embezzlement: a statutory offense consisting of the unlawful conversion of property entrusted to the wrongdoer.

eminent domain: the power of government and certain kinds of corporations to take private property against the objection of the owner, provided the taking is for a public purpose and just compensation is made therefor.

encumbrance: a right held by a third person in or a lien or charge against property, such as a mortgage or judgment lien on land.

equity: the body of principles that originally developed because of the inadequacy of the rules then applied by the common-law courts of England.

erosion: the loss of land through a gradual washing away by tides or currents, with the owner losing title to the lost land.

escheat: the transfer to the state of the title to a decedent's property when the owner of the property dies intestate not survived by anyone capable of taking the property as heir.

escrow: a conditional delivery of property or of a deed to a custodian or escrow holder, who in turn makes final delivery to the grantee or transferee when a specified condition has been satisfied.

estate: the extent and nature of one's interest in land; the assets constituting a decedent's property at the time of death; the assets of a debtor in bankruptcy proceedings.

estate in fee simple: the largest estate possible, in which the owner has absolute and entire property in the land.

estoppel: the principle by which a person is barred from pursuing a certain course of action or of disputing the truth of certain matters.

evidence: that which is presented to the trier of fact as the basis upon which the trier is to determine what happened.

exception: an objection, such as an exception to the admission of evidence on the ground that it is hearsay; a clause excluding particular property from the operation of a deed.

ex contractu: a claim or matter that is founded upon or arises out of a contract.

ex delicto: a claim or matter that is founded upon or arises out of a tort.

execution: the carrying out of a judgment of a court, generally directing that property owned by the defendant be sold and the proceeds first be used to pay the execution or judgment creditor.

exemplary damages: damages, in excess of the amount needed to compensate for the plaintiff's injury, that are awarded in order to punish the defendant for malicious or wanton conduct; also called punitive damages.

exoneration: an agreement or provision in an agreement that one party shall not be held liable for loss; the right of the surety to demand that those primarily liable pay the claim for which the surety is secondarily liable.

expert witness: one who has acquired special knowledge in a particular field as through practical experience or study, or both, whose opinion is admissible as an aid to the trier of fact.

ex post facto law: a law making criminal an act that was lawful when done or that increases the penalty when done. Such laws are generally prohibited by constitutional provisions.

extraordinary bailment: a bailment in which the bailee is subject to unusual duties and liabilities, such as a hotel keeper or common carrier.

F

factor: a bailee to whom goods are consigned for sale.

factors' acts: statutes protecting persons who buy in good faith for value from a factor although the goods had not been delivered to the factor with the consent or authorization of their owner.

fair employment practice acts: statutes designed to eliminate discrimination in employment on the basis of race, religion, national origin, or sex.

fair labor standards acts: statutes, particularly the federal statute, designed to prevent excessive hours of employment and low pay, the employment of young children, and other unsound practices.

featherbedding: the exaction of money for services not performed, which is made an unfair labor practice generally and a criminal offense in connection with radio broadcasting.

Federal Securities Act: a statute designed to protect the public from fraudulent securities.

Federal Securities Exchange Act: a statute prohibiting improper practices at and regulating security exchanges.

Federal Trade Commission Act: a statute prohibiting unfair methods of competition in interstate commerce.

fellow-servant rule: a common-law defense of the employer that barred an employee from suing an employer for injuries caused by a fellow employee.

felony: a criminal offense that is punishable by confinement in prison or by death, or that is expressly stated by statute to be a felony.

financial responsibility laws: statutes that require a driver involved in an automobile accident to prove financial responsibility in order to retain a license, such responsibility may be shown by procuring public liability insurance in a specified minimum amount.

financing factor: one who lends money to manufacturers on the security of goods to be manufactured thereafter.

firm offer: an offer stated to be held open for a specified time, which must be so held in some states even in the absence of an option contract, or under the UCC, with respect to merchants.

fixture: personal property that has become so attached to or adapted to real estate that it has lost its character as personal property and is part of the real estate.

Food, Drug, and Cosmetic Act: a federal statute prohibiting the interstate shipment of misbranded or adulterated foods, drugs, cosmetics, and therapeutic devices.

forbearance: refraining from doing an act.

foreclosure: procedure for enforcing a mortgage resulting in the public sale of the mortgaged property and, less commonly, in merely barring the right of the mortgagor to redeem the property from the mortgage.

foreign (international) bill of exchange: a bill of exchange made in one nation and payable in another.

foreign corporation: a corporation incorporated under the laws of another state.

forgery: the fraudulent making or altering of an instrument that apparently creates or alters a legal liability of another.

franchise: (a) a privilege or authorization, generally exclusive, to engage in a particular activity within a particular geographic area, such as a government franchise to operate a taxi company within a specified city, or a private franchise as the grant by a manufacturer of a right to sell products within a particular territory or for a particular number of years; (b) the right to vote.

fraud: the making of a false statement of a past or existing fact, with knowledge of its falsity or with reckless indifference as to its truth, with the intent to cause another to rely thereon, and such person does rely thereon and is harmed thereby.

freight forwarder: one who contracts to have goods transported and, in turn, contracts with carriers for such transportation.

fructus industriales: crops that are annually planted and raised.

fructus naturales: fruits from trees, bushes, and grasses growing from perennial roots.

fungible goods: goods of a homogeneous nature of which any unit is the equivalent of any other unit or is treated as such by mercantile usage.

future advance mortgage: a mortgage given to secure additional loans to be made in the future as well as to secure an original loan.

G

garnishment: the name given in some states to attachment proceedings.

general creditor: a creditor who has a claim against a debtor but does not have any lien on any of the debtor's property, whether as security for the debt or by way of a judgment or execution upon a judgment.

general damages: damages that in the ordinary course of events follow naturally and probably from the injury caused by the defendant.

general legacy: a legacy to be paid out of the decedent's assets generally without specifying any particular fund or source from which the payment is to be made.

general partnership: a partnership in which the partners conduct as co-owners a business for profit, and each partner has a right to take part in the management of the business and has unlimited liability.

gift causa mortis: a gift, made by the donor in the

belief that death was immediate and impending, that is revoked or is revocable under certain circumstances.

grace period: a period generally of 30 or 31 days after the due date of a life insurance premium in which the payment may be made.

grand jury: a jury not exceeding 23 in number that considers evidence of the commission of crime and prepares indictments to bring offenders to trial before a petty jury.

grant: convey real property; an instrument by which such property has been conveyed, particularly in the case of a government.

gratuitous bailment: a bailment in which the bailee does not receive any compensation or advantage.

grievance settlement: the adjustment of disputes relating to the administration or application of existing contracts as compared with disputes over new terms of employment.

guarantor: one who undertakes the obligation of guaranty.

guaranty: an undertaking to pay the debt of another if the creditor first sues the debtor and is unable to recover the debt from the debtor or principal. (In some instances the liability is primary, in which case it is the same as suretyship.)

H

hearsay evidence: statements made out of court that are offered in court as proof of the information contained in the statements, and that, subject to many exceptions, are not admissible in evidence.

hedging: the making of simultaneous contracts to purchase and to sell a particular commodity at a future date with the intention that the loss on one transaction will be offset by the gain on the other.

heirs: those persons specified by statute to receive the estate of a decedent not disposed of by will.

holder: the person in possession of a commercial paper payable to that person as payee or indorsee, or the person in possession of a commercial paper payable to bearer.

holder in due course: a holder of a commercial paper who is favored and is given an immunity from certain defenses.

holder through a holder in due course: a person who is not a holder in due course but is a holder of the paper after it was held by some prior party who was

a holder in due course, and who is given the same rights as a holder in due course.

holographic will: an unwitnessed will written by hand.

hotel keeper: one regularly engaged in the business of offering living accommodations to all transient persons.

hung jury: a petty jury that has been unable to agree upon a verdict.

I

ignorantia legis neminem excusat: ignorance of the law excuses no one.

implied contract: a contract expressed by conduct or implied or deduced from the facts. Also used to refer to a quasi contract.

imputed: vicariously attributed to or charged to another; for instance the knowledge of an agent obtained while acting in the scope of authority is imputed to the principal.

incidental authority: authority of an agent that is reasonably necessary to execute express authority.

incontestability clause: a provision that after the lapse of a specified time the insurer cannot dispute the policy on the ground of misrepresentation or fraud of the insured or similar wrongful conduct.

in custodia legis: in the custody of the law.

indemnity: the right of a person secondarily liable to require that a person primarily liable pay for loss sustained when the secondary party discharges the obligation that the primary party should have discharged; the right of an agent to be paid the amount of any loss or damage sustained without fault because of obedience to the principal's instructions; an undertaking by one person for a consideration to pay another person a sum of money to indemnify that person when a specified loss is incurred.

independent contractor: a contractor who undertakes to perform a specified task according to the terms of a contract but over whom the other contracting party has no control except as provided for by the contract.

indictment: a grand jury's formal accusation of crime, from which the accused is then tried by a petty or trial jury.

inheritance: the interest that passes from the decedent to the decedent's heirs.

injunction: an order of a court of equity to refrain from doing (negative injunction) or to do (affirmative or mandatory injunction) a specified act. Its use in labor disputes has been greatly restricted by statute.

in pari delicto: equally guilty; used in reference to a transaction as to which relief will not be granted to either party because both are equally guilty of wrongdoing.

insolvency: an excess of debts and liabilities over assets; or inability to pay debts as they mature.

insurable interest: an interest in the nonoccurrence of the risk insured against, generally because such occurrence would cause financial loss, although sometimes merely because of the close relationship between the insured and the beneficiary.

insurance: a plan of security against risks by charging the loss against a fund created by the payments made by policyholders.

intangible personal property: an interest in an enterprise, such as an interest in a partnership or stock of a corporation, and claims against other persons, whether based upon contract or tort.

interlineation: a writing between the lines or adding to the provisions of a document, the effect thereof depending upon the nature of the document.

interlocutory: an intermediate step or proceeding that does not make a final disposition of the action and from which ordinarily no appeal may be made.

international bill of exchange: a bill or draft made in one nation and payable in another.

interpleader: a form of action or proceeding by which a person against whom conflicting claims are made may bring the claimants into court to litigate their claims between themselves, as in the case of a bailee when two persons each claim to be the owner of the bailed property, or an insurer when two persons each claim to be the beneficiary.

inter se: among or between themselves, such as the rights of partners inter se or as between themselves.

inter vivos: any transaction which takes place between living persons and creates rights prior to the death of any of them.

intestate: the condition of dying without a will as to any property.

intestate succession: the distribution, made as directed by statute, of a decedent's property not effectively disposed of by will.

ipso facto: by the very act or fact in itself without any further action by any one.

irrebuttable presumption: a presumption that cannot be rebutted by proving that the facts are to the contrary; not a true presumption but merely a rule of law described in terms of a presumption.

irreparable injury to property: an injury that would be of such a nature or inflicted upon such an interest that it would not be reasonably possible to compensate the injured party by the payment of money damages because the property in question could not be purchased in the open market with the money damages that the defendant could be required to pay.

J

joint and several contract: a contract in which two or more persons are jointly and separately obligated or under which they are jointly and separately entitled to recover.

joint contract: a contract in which two or more persons are jointly liable or jointly entitled to performance under the contract.

joint stock company: an association in which the shares of the members are transferable and control is delegated to a group or board.

joint tenancy: the estate held by two or more jointly with the right of survivorship as between them, unless modified by statute.

joint venture: a relationship in which two or more persons combine their labor or property for a single undertaking and share profits and losses equally unless otherwise agreed.

judgment: the final sentence, order, or decision entered into at the conclusion of the action.

judgment note: a promissory note containing a clause authorizing the holder of the note to enter judgment against the maker of the note if it is not paid when due; also called a cognovit note.

judgment n.o.v.: a judgment that may be entered after verdict upon the motion of the losing party on the ground that the verdict is so wrong that a judgment should be entered the opposite of the verdict, or non obstante veredicto (notwithstanding the verdict).

judgment on the pleadings: a judgment that may be entered after all the pleadings are filed when it is clear from the pleadings that a particular party is entitled to win the action without proceeding any further.

judicial sale: a sale made under order of court by an officer appointed to make the sale or by an officer having such authority as incident to the office. The sale may have the effect of divesting liens on the property.

jurisdiction: the power of a court to hear and determine a given class of cases; the power to act over a particular defendant.

jurisdictional dispute: a dispute between rival labor unions that may take the form of each claiming that particular work should be assigned to it.

justifiable abandonment by employee: the right of an employee to abandon employment because of nonpayment of wages, wrongful assault, the demand for the performance of services not contemplated, or injurious working conditions.

justifiable discharge of employee: the right of an employer to discharge an employee for nonperformance of duties, fraud, disobedience, disloyalty, or incompetence.

L

laches: the rule that the enforcement of equitable rights will be denied when the party has delayed so long that rights of third persons have intervened or the death or disappearance of witnesses would prejudice any party through the loss of evidence.

land: earth, including all things embedded in or attached thereto, whether naturally or by the act of man.

last clear chance: the rule that a defendant who had the last clear chance to have avoided injuring the plaintiff is liable even though the plaintiff had also been contributorily negligent. In some states also called the humanitarian doctrine.

law of the case: matters decided in the course of litigation that are binding on the parties in the subsequent phases of litigation.

leading questions: questions that suggest the desired answer to the witness, or assume the existence of a fact that is in dispute.

lease: an agreement between the owner of property and a tenant by which the former agrees to give possession of the property to the latter in consideration of the payment of rent. (Parties — landlord or lessor, tenant or lessee)

leasehold: the estate or interest of a tenant in rented land.

legacy: a gift of personal property made by will.

legal tender: such form of money as the law recognizes as lawful and declares that a tender

thereof in the proper amount is a proper tender that the creditor cannot refuse.

letter of credit: a written agreement by which the issuer of the letter, usually a bank, agrees with the other contracting party, its customer, that the issuer will honor drafts drawn upon it by the person named in the letter as the beneficiary. Domestic letters are regulated by the UCC, Article 5; international letters by the Customs and Practices for Commercial Documentary Credits. Commercial or payment letter: the customer is the buyer of goods sold by the beneficiary and the letter covers the purchase price of the goods. Standby letter: a letter obtained instead of a suretyship or guaranty contract requiring the issuer to honor drafts drawn by the beneficiary upon the issuer when the customer of the issuer fails to perform a contract between the customer and the beneficiary. Documentary letter: a letter of credit that does not obligate the issuer to honor drafts unless they are accompanied by the documents specified in the letter.

letters of administration: the written authorization given to an administrator of an estate as evidence of appointment and authority.

letters testamentary: the written authorization given to an executor of an estate as evidence of appointment and authority.

levy: a seizure of property by an officer of the court in execution of a judgment of the court, although in many states it is sufficient if the officer is physically in the presence of the property and announces the fact that it is "seized," but then allows the property to remain where it was found.

lex loci: the law of the place where the material facts occurred as governing the rights and liabilities of the parties.

lex loci contractus: the law of the place where the contract was made as governing the rights and liabilities of the parties to a contract with respect to certain matters.

lex loci fori: the law of the state in which the action is brought as determining the rules of procedure applicable to the action.

lex loci sitae rei: the law of the place where land is located as determining the validity of acts done relating thereto.

libel: written or visual defamation without legal justification.

license: a personal privilege to do some act or series of acts upon the land of another, as the placing of a sign thereon, not amounting to an easement or a right of possession.

lien: a claim or right, against property, existing by virtue of the entry of a judgment against its owner or by the entry of a judgment and a levy thereunder on the property, or because of the relationship of the claimant to the particular property, such as an unpaid seller.

life estate: an estate for the duration of a life.

limited jurisdiction: a court's power to hear and determine cases within certain restricted categories.

limited liability: loss of contributed capital or investment as maximum liability.

limited partnership: a partnership in which at least one partner has a liability limited to the loss of the capital contribution made to the partnership, and such a partner neither takes part in the management of the partnership nor appears to the public to be a general partner.

lineal consanguinity: the relationship that exists when one person is a direct descendant of the other.

liquidated damages: a provision stipulating the amount of damages to be paid in the event of default or breach of contract.

liquidation: the process of converting property into money whether of particular items of property or of all the assets of a business or an estate.

lis pendens: the doctrine that certain kinds of pending action are notice to everyone so that if any right is acquired from a party to such action, the transferee takes that right subject to the outcome of the pending action.

lobbying contract (illegal): a contract by which one party agrees to attempt to influence the action of a legislature or Congress, or any members thereof, by improper means.

lottery: any plan by which a consideration is given for a chance to win a prize.

lucri causa: with the motive of obtaining gain or pecuniary advantage.

M

majority: of age, as contrasted with being a minor; more than half of any group, as a majority of stockholders.

malice in fact: an intention to injure or cause harm.

malice in law: a presumed intention to injure or cause harm when there is no privilege or right to do

the act in question, such presumption cannot be contradicted or rebutted.

maliciously inducing breach of contract: the wrong of inducing the breach of any kind of contract with knowledge of its existence and without justification.

malum in se: an offense that is criminal because it is contrary to the fundamental sense of a civilized community, such as murder.

malum prohibitum: an offense that is criminal not because inherently wrong but is prohibited for the convenience of society, such as overtime parking.

marshalling assets: the distribution of a debtor's assets in such a way as to give the greatest benefit to all creditors.

martial law: government exercised by a military commander over property and persons not in the armed forces, as contrasted with military law which governs military personnel.

mechanic's lien: protection afforded by statute to various kinds of laborers and persons supplying materials, by giving them a lien on the building and land that has been improved or added to by them.

mens rea: the mental state that must accompany an act to make the act a crime. Sometimes described as the guilty mind, although appreciation of guilt is not required.

merger by judgment: the discharge of a contract through being merged into a judgment that is entered in a suit on the contract.

merger of corporations: a combining of corporations by which one absorbs the other and continues to exist, preserving its original charter and identity while the other corporation ceases to exist.

misdemeanor: a criminal offense that is neither treason nor a felony.

misrepresentation: a false statement of fact although made innocently without any intent to deceive.

mobilia sequuntur personam: the maxim that personal property follows the owner and in the eyes of the law is located at the owner's domicile.

moratorium: a temporary suspension by statute of the enforcement of debts or the foreclosure of mortgages.

mortgage: an interest in land given by the owner to a creditor as security for the payment of the creditor for a debt, the nature of the interest depending upon the law of the state where the land is located. (Parties — mortgagor, mortgagee)

multiple insurers: insurers who agree to divide a risk so that each is only liable for a specified portion.

N

National Labor Management Relations Act: the federal statute, also known as the Taft-Hartley Act, designed to protect the organizational rights of labor and to prevent unfair labor practices by management or labor.

natural and probable consequences: those ordinary consequences of an act that a reasonable person would foresee.

negative covenant: an undertaking in a deed to refrain from doing an act.

negligence: the failure to exercise due care under the circumstances in consequence of which harm is proximately caused to one to whom the defendant owed a duty to exercise due care.

negligence per se: an action that is regarded as so improper that it is declared by law to be negligent in itself without regard to whether due care was otherwise exercised.

negotiable instruments: drafts, promissory notes, checks, and certificates of deposit in such form that greater rights may be acquired thereunder than by taking an assignment of a contract right; called negotiable commercial paper by the UCC.

negotiation: the transfer of a commercial paper by indorsement and delivery by the person to whom then payable in the case of order paper and by physical transfer in the case of bearer paper.

nominal damages: a nominal sum awarded the plaintiff in order to establish that legal rights have been violated although the plaintiff in fact has not sustained any actual loss or damages.

Norris-La Guardia Anti-Injunction Act: a federal statute prohibiting the use of the injunction in labor disputes, except in particular cases.

notice of dishonor: notice given to parties secondarily liable that the primary party to the instrument has refused to accept the instrument or to make payment when it was properly presented for that purpose.

novation: the discharge of a contract between two parties by their agreeing with a third person that such third person shall be substituted for one of the original parties to the contract, who shall thereupon be released.

nudum pactum: a mere promise for which there is not consideration given and which, therefore, is ordinarily not enforceable.

nuisance: any conduct that harms or prejudices another in the use of land or which harms or prejudices the public.

nuisance per se: an activity that is in itself a nuisance regardless of the time and place involved.

nuncupative will: an oral will made and declared to be a will by the testator in the presence of witnesses; generally made during the testator's last illness.

O

obiter dictum: that which is said in the opinion of a court in passing or by the way, but which is not necessary to the determination of the case and is therefore not regarded as authoritative as though it were actually involved in the decision.

obliteration: any erasing, writing upon, or crossing out that makes all or part of a will impossible to read, and which has the effect of revoking such part when done by the maker of the will with the intent of effecting a revocation.

occupation: taking and holding possession of property; a method of acquiring title to personal property after it has been abandoned.

open-end mortgage: a mortgage given to secure additional loans to be made in the future as well as to secure the original loan.

operation of law: the attaching of certain consequences to certain facts because of legal principles that operate automatically, as contrasted with consequences that arise because of the voluntary action of a party designed to create those consequences.

opinion evidence: evidence not of what the witness observed but the conclusion drawn from what the witness has observed; in the case of expert witnesses, what has been observed in tests or experiments or what has been heard in court.

option contract: a contract to hold an offer to make a contract open for a fixed period of time.

P

paper title: the title of a person evidenced only by deeds or matter appearing of record under the recording statutes.

parol evidence rule: the rule that prohibits the introduction in evidence of oral or written statements made prior to or contemporaneously with the execution of a complete written contract, deed, or instrument, in the absence of clear proof of fraud, accident, or mistake causing the omission of the statement in question.

passive trust: a trust that is created without imposing any duty to be performed by the trustee and is therefore treated as an absolute transfer of the title to the trust beneficiary.

past consideration: something that has been performed in the past and which, therefore, cannot be consideration for a promise made in the present.

patent: the grant to an inventor of an exclusive right to make and sell an invention for a nonrenewable period of 17 years; a deed to land given by a government to a private person.

pawn: a pledge of tangible personal property rather than of documents representing property rights.

pecuniary legacy: a general legacy of a specified amount of money without indicating the source from which payment is to be made.

per autre vie: limitation of an estate. An estate held by A during the lifetime of B is an estate of A per autre vie.

per curiam opinion: an opinion written by the court rather than by a named judge when all the judges of the court are in such agreement on the matter that it is not deemed to merit any discussion and may be simply disposed of.

perpetual succession: a phrase describing the continuing life of the corporation unaffected by the death of any stockholder or the transfer by stockholders of their stock.

perpetuities, rule against: a rule of law that prohibits the creation of an interest in property that will not become definite or vested until a date further away than 21 years after the death of persons alive at the time the owner of the property attempts to create the interest.

per se: in, through, or by itself.

person: a term that includes both natural persons, or living persons, and artificial persons, such as corporations which are created by act of government.

personal defenses: limited defenses that cannot be asserted by the defendant against a holder in due course. This term is not expressly used in UCC.

per stirpes: according to the root or by way of representation. Distribution among heirs related to the decedent in different degrees, the property being divided into lines of descent from the descendent and the share of each line then divided within the line by way of representation.

petit larceny: more commonly, petty larceny. At common law, the larceny of property having the value of 12 pence or less. When the property had a greater value, the crime was grand larceny and the punishment was death. In many states, degrees of larceny have replaced the common-law classification.

petty jury: the trial jury. Also, petit jury.

picketing: the placing of persons outside of places of employment or distribution so that by words or banners they may inform the public of the existence of a labor dispute or may influence employees or customers.

pleadings: the papers filed by the parties in an action in order to set forth the facts and frame the issues to be tried, although under some systems, the pleadings merely give notice or a general indication of the nature of the issues.

pledge: a bailment given as security for the payment of a debt or the performance of an obligation owed to the pledgee. (Parties — pledgor, pledgee)

police power: the power to govern; the power to adopt laws for the protection of the public heath, welfare, safety, and morals.

policy: the paper evidencing the contract of insurance.

polling the jury: the process of inquiring of each juror individually in open court as to whether the verdict announced in court was agreed to.

possession: exclusive dominion and control of property.

possessory lien: a right to retain possession of property of another as security for some debt or obligation owed the lienor, such right continues only as long as possession is retained.

possibility of reverter: the nature of the interest held by the grantor after conveying land outright but subject to a condition or provision that may cause the grantee's interest to become forfeited and the interest to revert to the grantor or heirs.

postdate: to insert or place on an instrument a later date than the actual date on which it was executed.

power of appointment: a power given to another, commonly a beneficiary of a trust, to designate or appoint who shall be beneficiary or receive the fund after the death of the grantor.

power of attorney: a written authorization to an agent by the principal.

precatory words: words indicating merely a desire or a wish that another use property for a particular purpose but which in law will not be enforced in the absence of an express declaration that the property shall be used for the specified purpose.

preemptive offer of shares: shareholder's right upon the increase of a corporation's capital stock to be allowed to subscribe to such a percentage of the new shares as the shareholder's old shares bore to the former total capital stock.

preferred creditor: a creditor who by some statute is given the right to be paid first or before other creditors.

preferred stock: stock that has a priority or preference as to payment of dividends or upon liquidation, or both.

preponderance of evidence: the degree or quantum of evidence in favor of the existence of a certain fact when from a review of all the evidence it appears more probable that the fact exists than that it does not. The actual number of witnesses involved is not material nor is the fact that the margin of probability is very slight.

prescription: the acquisition of a right to use the land of another, as an easement, through the making of hostile, visible, and notorious use of the land, continuing for the period specified by the local law.

presumption: a rule of proof that permits the existence of a fact to be assumed from the proof that another fact exists when there is a logical relationship between the two or when the means of disproving the assumed fact are more readily within the control or knowledge of the adverse party against whom the presumption operates.

presumption of death: the rebuttable presumption that a person has died when that person has been continuously absent and unheard of for a period of 7 years.

presumption of innocence: the presumption of fact that a person accused of crime is innocent until shown guilty of the offense charged.

presumption of payment: a rebuttable presumption that one performing continuing services that would normally be paid periodically, such as weekly or monthly, has in fact been paid when a number of years have passed without any objection or demand for payment having been made.

presumptive heir: a person who would be the heir if the ancestor should die at that moment.

pretrial conference: a conference, held prior to the trial, at which the court and the attorney seek to simplify the issues in controversy and eliminate matters not in dispute.

price: the consideration for sale of goods.

prima facie: evidence that, if believed, is sufficient by itself to lead to a particular conclusion.

primary beneficiary: the person designated as the first one to receive the proceeds of a life insurance policy, as distinguished from a contingent beneficiary who will receive the proceeds only if the primary beneficiary dies before the insured.

primary liability: the liability of a person whose act or omission gave rise to the cause of action and who in all fairness should, therefore, be the one to pay the victim even though others may also be liable for misconduct.

principal: one who employs an agent; the person who, with respect to a surety, is primarily liable to the third person or creditor.

principal in the first degree: one who actually engages in the commission or perpetration of a crime.

principal in the second degree: one who is actually or constructively present at the commission of the crime and who aids and abets in its commission.

private carrier: a carrier owned by the shipper, such as a company's own fleet of trucks.

privileged communication: information that the witness may refuse to testify to because of the relationship with the person furnishing the information, such as husband-wife or attorney-client.

privilege from arrest: the immunity from arrest of parties, witnesses, and attorneys while present within the jurisdiction for the purpose of taking part in other litigation.

privity: a succession or chain of relationship to the same thing or right, such as privity of contract, privity of estate, privity of possession.

probate: the procedure for formally establishing or proving that a given writing is the last will and testament of the person who purportedly signed it.

product liability: liability imposed upon the manufacturer or seller of goods for harm caused by a defect in the goods, comprising liability for (a) negligence, (b) fraud, (c) breach of warranty, and (d) strict tort.

profit à prendre: the right to take a part of the soil or produce of another's land, such as timber or water.

promissory estoppel: the doctrine that a promise will be enforced although it is not supported by consideration when the promisor should have reasonably expected that the promise would induce action or forbearance of a definite and substantial character on the part of the promisee, and injustice can only be avoided by enforcement of the promise.

promissory note: an unconditional promise in writing made by one person to another, signed by the maker engaging to pay on demand, or at a definite time, a sum certain in money to order or to bearer. (Parties — maker, payee)

promissory representation: a representation made by the applicant to the insurer as to what is to occur in the future.

promissory warranty: a representation made by the applicant to the insurer as to what is to occur in the future that the applicant warrants will occur.

promoters: the persons who plan the formation of the corporation and sell or promote the idea to others.

proof: the probative effect of the evidence; the conclusion drawn from the evidence as to the existence of particular facts.

property: the rights and interests one has in anything subject to ownership.

pro rata: proportionately, or divided according to a rate or standard.

protest: the formal certificate by a notary public or other authorized person that proper presentment of a commercial paper was made to the primary party and that such party defaulted, the certificate commonly also including a recital that notice was given to secondary parties.

proximate cause: the act that is the natural and reasonably foreseeable cause of the harm or event that occurs and injures the plaintiff.

proximate damages: damages that in the ordinary course of events are the natural and reasonably foreseeable result of the defendant's violation of the plaintiff's rights.

proxy: a written authorization by a shareholder to another person to vote the stock owned by the shareholder; the person who is the holder of such a written authorization.

public charge: a person who because of personal disability or lack of means of support is dependent upon public charity or relief for sustenance.

public domain: public or government-owned lands.

public easement: a right of way for use by members of the public at large.

public policy: certain objectives relating to health, morals, and integrity of government that the law seeks to advance by declaring invalid any contract that conflicts with those objectives even though there

is no statute expressly declaring such a contract illegal.

punitive damages: damages, in excess of those required to compensate the plaintiff for the wrong done, that are imposed in order to punish the defendant because of the particularly wanton or willful character of wrongdoing; also called exemplary damages.

purchase-money mortgage: a mortgage given by the purchaser of land to the seller to secure the seller for the payment of the unpaid balance of the purchase price, which the seller purports to lend the purchaser.

purchaser in good faith: a person who purchases without any notice or knowledge of any defect of title, misconduct, or defense.

Q

qualified acceptance: An acceptance of a draft that varies the order of the draft in some way.

qualified indorsement: an indorsement that includes words such as *without recourse* evidencing the intent that the indorser shall not be held liable for the failure of the primary party to pay the instrument.

quantum meruit: an action brought for the value of the services rendered the defendant when there was no express contract as to the purchase price.

quantum valebant: an action brought for the value of goods sold the defendant when there was no express contract as to the purchase price.

quasi: as if, as though it were, having the characteristics of; a modifier employed to indicate that the subject is to be treated as though it were in fact the noun that follows the word *quasi*, as in quasi contract, quasi corporation, quasi public corporation.

quid pro quo: literally "what for what." An early form of the concept of consideration by which an action for debt could not be brought unless the defendant had obtained something in return for the obligation sued upon.

quitclaim deed: a deed by which the grantor purports only to give up whatever right or title the grantor may have in the property without specifying or warranting transfer of any particular interest.

quorum: the minimum number of persons, shares represented, or directors who must be present at a meeting in order that business may be lawfully transacted.

R

ratification by minor: a minor's approval of a contract after the minor attains majority.

ratification of agency: the approval of the unauthorized act of an agent or of a person who is not an agent for any purpose. The approval occurs after the act has been done and has the same effect as though the act had been authorized before it was done.

ratio decidendi: the reason or basis for deciding the case in a particular way.

ratio legis: the reason for a principle or rule of law.

real defenses: certain defenses (universal) that are available against any holder of a commercial paper, although this term is not expressly used by the UCC.

real evidence: tangible objects that are presented in the courtroom for the observation of the trier of fact as proof of the facts in dispute or in support of the theory of a party.

real property: land and all rights in land.

reasonable care: the degree of care that a reasonable person would take under all the circumstances then known.

rebate: a refund, made by the seller or the carrier, of part of the purchase price or freight bill.

rebuttable presumption: a presumption that may be overcome or rebutted by proof that the actual facts were different from those presumed.

receiver: an impartial person appointed by a court to take possession of and manage property for the protection of all concerned.

recognizance: an obligation entered into before a court to do some act, such as to appear at a later date for a hearing. Also called a contract of record.

redemption: the buying back of one's property, which has been sold because of a default, upon paying the amount that had been originally due together with interest and costs.

referee: an impartial person selected by the parties or appointed by a court to determine facts or decide matters in dispute.

referee in bankruptcy: a referee appointed by a bankruptcy court to hear and determine various matters relating to bankruptcy proceedings.

reformation: a remedy by which a written instrument is corrected when it fails to express the actual intent of both parties because of fraud, accident, or mistake.

registration of titles: a system generally known as the

Torrens system of permanent registration of title to all land within the state.

reimbursement: the right of one paying money on behalf of another, which such other person should have paid, to recover the amount of the payment from such other person.

release of liens: an agreement or instrument by which the holder of a lien of property such as a mortgage lien, releases the property from the lien although the debt itself is not discharged.

reliance: action taken or not taken by a person in the belief that the facts as stated by another are true or that the promise of another will be performed. Detrimental reliance: a term generally used to refer to reliance of such a degree that the person relying would sustain substantial damages that could not be compensated for by the payment of money; the same concept that underlies part performance as taking an oral contract out of the statute of frauds. In some cases, loosely used when merely reliance was present. See *promissory estoppel*.

remedy: the action or procedure that is followed in order to enforce a right or to obtain damages for injury to a right.

remote damages: damages that were in fact caused by the defendant's act but the possibility that such damages should occur seemed so improbable and unlikely to a reasonable person that the law does not impose liability for such damages.

renunciation of duty: the repudiation of one's contractual duty in advance of the time for performance.

renunciation of right: the surrender of a right or privilege, such as the right to act as administrator or the right to receive a legacy under the will of a decedent.

reorganization of corporation: procedure devised to restore insolvent corporations to financial stability through readjustment of debt and capital structure either under the supervision of a court of equity or of bankruptcy.

repossession: any taking again of possession although generally used in connection with the act of a secured seller in taking back the property upon the default of the credit buyer.

representations: any statements, whether oral or written, made to give the insurer the information that it needs in writing the insurance, and which if false and relating to a material fact will entitle the insurer to avoid the contract.

representative capacity: action taken by one on behalf

of another, as the act of a personal representative on behalf of a decedent's estate, or action taken both on one's behalf and on behalf of others, as a shareholder bringing a representative action.

rescission upon agreement: the setting aside of a contract by the action of the parties as though the contract had never been made.

rescission upon breach: the action of one party to a contract to set the contract aside when the other party is guilty of a breach of the contract.

residuary estate: the balance of the decedent's estate available for distribution after all administrative expenses, exemptions, debts, taxes, and legacies have been paid.

res inter alios acta: the rule that transactions and declarations between strangers having no connection with the ending action are not admissible in evidence.

res ipsa loquitur: the permissible inference that the defendant was negligent in that the thing speaks for itself when the circumstances are such that ordinarily the plaintiff could not have been injured had the defendant not been at fault.

res judicata: the principle that once a final judgment is entered in an action between the parties, it is binding upon them and the matter cannot be litigated again by bringing a second action.

respondeat superior: the doctrine that the principal or employer is vicariously liable for the unauthorized torts committed by an agent or employee while acting within the scope of the agency or the course of the employment, respectively.

restraints on alienation: limitations on the ability of the owner to convey freely as the owner chooses. Such limitations are generally regarded as invalid.

restrictive covenants: covenants in a deed by which the grantee agrees to refrain from doing specified acts.

restrictive indorsement: an indorsement that prohibits the further transfer, constitutes the indorsee the agent of the indorser, vests the title in the indorsee in trust for or to the use of some other person, is conditional, or is for collection or deposit.

resulting trust: a trust that is created by implication of law to carry out the presumed intent of the parties.

retaliatory statute: a statute that provides that when a corporation of another state enters the state it shall be subject to the same taxes and restrictions as would be imposed upon a corporation from the retaliating state

if it had entered the other state. Also known as reciprocity statutes.

reversible error: an error or defect in court proceedings of so serious a nature that on appeal the appellate court will set aside the proceedings of the lower court.

reversionary interest: the interest that a lessor has in property that is subject to an outstanding lease.

revival of judgment: the taking of appropriate action to preserve a judgment, in most instances to continue the lien of the judgment that would otherwise expire after a specified number of years.

revival of will: the restoration, by the writer, of a will that had previously been revoked.

rider: a slip of paper executed by the insurer and intended to be attached to the insurance policy for the purpose of changing it in some respect.

riparian rights: the right of a person through whose land runs a natural watercourse to use the water free from unreasonable pollution or diversion by upper riparian owners and blocking by lower riparian owners.

risk: the peril or contingency against which the insured is protected by the contract of insurance.

Robinson-Patman Act: a federal statute designed to eliminate price discrimination in interstate commerce.

run with the land: the concept that certain covenants in a deed to land are deemed to "run" or pass with the land so that whoever owns the land is bound by or entitled to the benefit of the covenants.

S

sale or return: a sale in which the title to the property passes to the buyer at the time of the transaction but the buyer is given the option of returning the property and restoring the title to the seller.

scienter: knowledge, referring to those wrongs or crimes that require a knowledge of wrong in order to constitute the offense.

scope of employment: the area within which the employee is authorized to act with the consequence that a tort committed while so acting imposes liability upon the employer.

seal: at common law an impression on wax or other tenacious material attached to the instrument. Under modern law, any mark not ordinarily part of the signature is a seal when so intended, including the letters *L.S.* and the word *seal*, or a pictorial representation of a seal, without regard to whether they had been printed or typed on the instrument before its signing.

sealed verdict: a verdict that is rendered when the jury returns to the courtroom during an adjournment of the court, the verdict then being written down and sealed and later affirmed before the court when the court is in session.

secondary evidence: copies of original writings or testimony as to the contents of such writings that are admissible when the original cannot be produced and the inability to do so is reasonably explained.

secured transaction: a credit sale of goods or a secured loan that provides special protection for the creditor.

securities: stock and bonds issued by a corporation. Under some investor protection laws, the term includes any interest in an enterprise that provides unearned income to its owner. Investment securities: under the UCC, Article 8, this term also includes any instrument representing an interest in property or an enterprise that is commonly dealt in or recognized as a medium of investment. Uncertificated securities: under the 1977 version of the UCC rights to securities that are not represented by a certificate but only by a record on a computer of the issuing enterprise.

settlor: one who settles property in trust or creates a trust estate.

severable contract: a contract the terms of which are such that one part may be separated or severed from the other so that a default as to one part is not necessarily a default as to the entire contract.

several contracts: separate or independent contracts made by different persons undertaking to perform the same obligation.

severalty: ownership of property by one person.

severed realty: real property that has been cut off and made movable, as by cutting down a tree, and which thereby loses its character as real property and becomes personal property.

shareholder's action: an action brought by one or more shareholders on behalf of themselves and on behalf of all shareholders generally and of the corporation to enforce a cause of action of the corporation against third persons.

sheriff's deed: the deed executed and delivered by the sheriff to the purchaser at a sale conducted by the sheriff.

Sherman Antitrust Act: a federal statute prohibiting combinations and contracts in restraint of interstate

trade, now generally inapplicable to labor union activity.

shop right: the right of an employer to use in business without charge an invention discovered by an employee during working hours and with the employer's material and equipment.

sight draft: a draft or bill of exchange payable on sight or when presented for payment.

sit-down strike: a strike in which the employees remain in the plant and refuse to allow the employer to operate it.

slander: defamation of character by spoken words or gestures.

slander of title: the malicious making of false statements as to a seller's title.

slowdown: a slowing down of production by employees without actual stopping work.

social security acts: statutes providing for assistance for the aged, blind, unemployed, and similar classes of persons in need.

special agent: an agent authorized to transact a specific transaction or to do a specific act.

special damages: damages that do not necessarily result from the injury to the plaintiff but at the same time are not so remote that the defendant should not be held liable therefor provided that the claim for special damages is properly made in the action.

special indorsement: an indorsement that specifies the person to whom the instrument is indorsed.

special jurisdiction: a court with power to hear and determine cases within certain restricted categories.

specific (identified) goods: goods that are so identified to the contract that no other goods may be delivered in performance of the contract.

specific lien: the right of a creditor to hold particular property or assert a lien on particular property of the debtor because of the creditor's having done work on or having some other association with the property, as distinguished from having a lien generally against the assets of the debtor merely because the debtor is indebted to the lien holder.

specific performance: an action brought to compel the adverse party to perform a contract on the theory that merely suing for damages for its breach will not be an adequate remedy.

spendthrift trust: a trust that, to varying degrees, provides that creditors of the beneficiary shall not be able to reach the principal or income held by the trustee and that the beneficiary shall not be able to assign any interest in the trust.

spoliation: an alteration or change made to a written instrument by a person who has no relationship to or interest in the writing. It has no effect as long as the terms of the instrument can still be ascertained.

stare decisis: the principle that the decision of a court should serve as a guide or precedent and control the decision of a similar case in the future.

status quo ante: the original positions of the parties to a contract prior to the making of the contract or the doing of some other act.

Statute of Frauds: a statute that, in order to prevent fraud through the use of perjured testimony, requires that certain kinds of transactions be evidenced in writing in order to be binding or enforceable.

Statute of Limitations: a statute that restricts the period of time within which an action may be brought.

stop delivery: the right of an unpaid seller under certain conditions to prevent a carrier or a bailee from delivering goods to the buyer.

stop payment: an order by a depositor to the bank to refuse to make payment of a check when presented for payment.

strict tort liability: a product liability theory that imposes liability upon the manufacturer, seller, or distributor of goods for harm caused by defective goods.

sublease: a transfer of the premises by the lessee to a third person, the sublessee or subtenant, for a period of less than the term of the original lease.

subpoena: a court order directing a person to appear as a witness. In some states it is also the original process that is to be served on the defendant in order to give the court jurisdiction over the defendant.

subrogation: the right of a party secondarily liable to stand in the place of the creditor after making payment to the creditor and to enforce the creditor's right against the party primarily liable in order to obtain indemnity from such primary party.

subsidiary corporation: a corporation that is controlled by another corporation through the ownership by the latter of a controlling amount of the voting stock of the former.

subsidiary term: a provision of a contract that is not fundamental or does not go to the root of the contract.

substantial performance: the equitable doctrine that a contractor substantially performing a contract in good faith is entitled to recover the contract price less damages for noncompletion or defective work.

substantive law: the law that defines rights and liabilities.

substitution: discharge of a contract by substituting another in its place.

subtenant: one who rents the leased premises from the original tenant for a period of time less than the balance of the lease to the original tenant.

sui generis: in a class by itself, or its own kind.

sui juris: legally competent, possessing capacity.

summary judgment: a judgment entered by the court when no substantial dispute of fact is present, the court acting on the basis of affidavits or depositions that show that the claim or defense of a party is a sham.

summons: a writ by which an action was commenced under the common law.

supersedeas: a stay of proceedings pending the taking of an appeal or an order entered for the purpose of effecting such a stay.

suretyship: an undertaking to pay the debt or be liable for the default of another.

surrender: the yielding up of the tenant's leasehold estate to the lessor in consequence of which the lease terminates.

survival acts: statutes that provide that causes of action shall not terminate on death but shall survive and may be enforced by or against a decedent's estate.

survivorship: the right by which a surviving joint tenant or tenant by the entireties acquires the interest of the predeceasing tenant automatically upon the death of such tenant.

symbolic delivery: the delivery of goods by delivery of the means of control, such as a key or a relevant document of title, such as a negotiable bill of lading.

syndicate: an association of individuals formed to conduct a particular business transaction, generally of a financial nature.

T

tacking: adding together successive periods of adverse possession of persons in privity with each other in order to constitute a sufficient period of continuous adverse possession to vest title thereby.

Taft-Hartley Act: popular name for the Labor Management Relations Act of 1947.

tariff: domestically — a government-approved schedule of charges that may be made by a regulated business, such as a common carrier or warehouser. Internationally — a tax imposed by a country on goods crossing its borders, without regard to whether the purpose is to raise revenue or to discourage the traffic in the taxed goods.

tenancy at sufferance: a tenant's holding over of the rented land after a lease has expired without the permission of the landlord and prior to the time that the landlord has elected to treat such possessor as a trespasser or a tenant.

tenancy at will: the holding of land for an indefinite period that may be terminated at any time by the landlord or by the landlord and tenant acting together.

tenancy for years: a tenancy for a fixed period of time, even though the time is less than a year.

tenancy from year to year: a tenancy that continues indefinitely from year to year until terminated.

tenancy in common: the relationship that exists when two or more persons own undivided interests in property.

tenancy in partnership: the ownership relationship that exists between partners under the Uniform Partnership Act.

tender of payment: an unconditional offer to pay the exact amount of money due at the time and place specified by the contract.

tender of performance: an unconditional offer to perform at the time and in the manner specified by the contract.

tentative trust: a trust that arises when money is deposited in a bank account in the name of the depositor "in trust for" a named person.

terminable fee: an estate that terminates upon the happening of a contingency without any entry by the grantor or heirs, as a conveyance for "so long as" the land is used for a specified purpose.

testamentary: designed to take effect at death, as by

disposing of property or appointing a personal representative.

testate: the condition of leaving a will upon death.

testate succession: the distribution of an estate in accordance with the will of the decedent.

testator-testatrix: a man-woman who makes a will.

testimonium clause: a concluding paragraph in a deed, contract, or other instrument, reciting that the instrument has been executed on a specified date by the parties.

testimony: the answers of witnesses under oath to questions given at the time of the trial in the presence of the trier of fact.

theory of the case: the rule that, when a case is tried on the basis of one theory, the appellant in taking an appeal cannot argue a different theory to the appellate court.

third party beneficiary: a third person whom the parties to a contract intend to benefit by the making of the contract and to confer upon such person the right to sue for breach of contract.

tie-in sale: the requirement imposed by the seller that the buyer of particular goods or equipment also purchase certain other goods from the seller in order to obtain the original property desired.

time draft: a bill of exchange payable at a stated time after sight or at a definite time.

title insurance: a form of insurance by which the insurer insures the buyer of real property against the risk of loss should the title acquired from the seller be defective in any way.

toll the statute: stop the running of the period of the Statute of Limitations by the doing of some act by the debtor.

Torrens system: see *registration of titles.*

tort: a private injury or wrong arising from a breach of a duty created by law.

trade acceptance: a draft or bill of exchange drawn by the seller of goods on the purchase at the time of sale and accepted by the purchaser.

trade fixtures: articles of personal property that have been attached to the freehold by a tenant and that are used for or are necessary to the carrying on of the tenant's trade.

trademark: a name, device, or symbol used by a

manufacturer or seller to distinguish goods from those of other persons.

trade name: a name under which a business is carried on and, if fictitious, it must be registered.

trade secrets: secrets of any character peculiar and important to the business of the employer that have been communicated to the employee in the course of confidential employment.

treason: an attempt to overthrow or betray the government to which one owes allegiance.

treasury stock: corporate stock that the corporation has reacquired.

trier of fact: in most cases a jury, although it may be the judge alone in certain classes of cases (as in equity) or in any case when jury trial is waived, or when an administrative agency or commission is involved.

trust: a transfer of property by one person to another with the understanding or declaration that such property be held for the benefit of another; the holding of property by the owner in trust for another, upon a declaration of trust, without a transfer to another person. (Parties — settlor, trustee, beneficiary.)

trust corpus: the fund or property that is transferred to the trustee or held by the settlor as the body or subject matter of the trust.

trust deed: a form of deed that transfers the trust property to the trustee for the purposes therein stated, particularly used when the trustee is to hold the title to the mortgagor's land in trust for the benefit of the mortgage bondholders.

trustee de son tort: a person who is not a trustee but who has wrongly intermeddled with property of another and who is required to account for the property as though an actual trustee.

trustee in bankruptcy: an impartial person elected to administer the debtor's estate.

U

uberrima fides: utmost good faith, a duty to exercise the utmost good faith that arises in certain relationships, such as that between an insurer and the applicant for insurance.

ultra vires: an act or contract that the corporation does not have authority to do or make.

underwriter: an insurer.

undisclosed principal: a principal on whose behalf an agent acts without disclosing to the third person the fact of agency or the identity of the principal.

undue influence: the influence that is asserted upon another person by one who dominates that person.

unfair competition: the wrong of employing competitive methods that have been declared unfair by statute or an administrative agency.

unfair labor practice acts: statutes that prohibit certain labor practices and declare them to be unfair.

unincorporated association: a combination of two or more persons for the furtherance of a common nonprofit purpose.

union contract: a contract between a labor union and an employer or group of employers prescribing the general terms of employment of workers by the latter.

union shop: under present unfair labor practice statutes, a place of employment where nonunion workers may be employed for a trial period of not more than 30 days after which the nonunion workers must join the union or be discharged.

universal agent: an agent authorized by the principal to do all acts that can lawfully be delegated to a representative.

usury: the lending of money at greater than the maximum rate of interest allowed by law.

V

vacating of judgment: the setting aside of a judgment.

valid: legal.

verdict: the decision of the trial or petty jury.

void: of no legal effect and not binding on anyone.

voidable: a transaction that may be set aside by one party thereto because of fraud or similar reason but which is binding on the other party until the injured party elects to avoid.

voidable preference: a preference given by the debtor in bankruptcy to a creditor, but which may be set aside by the trustee in bankruptcy.

voir dire examination: the preliminary examination of a juror or a witness to ascertain fitness to act as such.

volenti non fit injuria: the maxim that the

defendant's act cannot constitute a tort if the plaintiff has consented thereto.

voluntary nonsuit: a means of a plaintiff's stopping a trial at any time by moving for a voluntary nonsuit.

voting trust: the transfer by two or more persons of their shares of stock of a corporation to a trustee who is to vote the shares and act for such shareholders.

W

waiver: the release or relinquishment of a known right or objection.

warehouse receipt: a receipt issued by the warehouser for stored goods. Regulated by the UCC, which clothes the receipt with some degree of negotiability.

warranties of indorser of commercial paper: the implied covenants made by an indorser of a commercial paper distinct from any undertaking to pay upon the default of the primary party.

warranties of insured: statements or promises made by the applicant for insurance that, if false, will entitle the insurer to avoid the contract of insurance in many jurisdictions.

warranties of seller of goods: warranties consisting of express warranties that relate to matters forming part of the basis of the bargain; warranties as to title and right to sell; and the implied warranties that the law adds to a sale depending upon the nature of the transaction.

warranty deed: a deed by which the grantor conveys a specific estate or interest to the grantee and makes one or more of the covenants of title.

warranty of authority: an implied warranty of an agent of the authority exercised by the agent.

warranty of principal: an implied warranty of an

agent that the agent is acting for an existing principal who has capacity to contract.

watered stock: stock issued by a corporation as fully paid when in fact it is not.

will: an instrument executed with the formality required by law, by which a person makes a disposition of property to take effect upon death or appoints a personal representative.

willful: intentional, as distinguished from accidental or involuntary. In penal statutes, with evil intent or legal malice, or without reasonable ground for believing one's act to be lawful.

Wool Products Labeling Act: a federal statute prohibiting the misbranding of woolen fabrics.

workers' compensation: a system providing for payments to workers because they have been injured from a risk arising out of the course of their employment while they were employed at their employment or who have contracted an occupational disease in that manner, payment being made without consideration of the negligence or lack of negligence of any party.

Y

year and a day: the common-law requirement that death result within a year and a day in order to impose criminal liability for homicide.

Z

zoning restrictions: restrictions imposed by government on the use of property for the advancement of the general welfare.

CASE INDEX

Principal cases are in boldface type; cases cited are in roman type.

A

A & M Karagheusian, Inc., Santor v, 630, 1103

A & M Pest Control Service Co., Inc., Melancon v, 857-858

Abbott Thinlite Corp. v Redmont, 1080

Abram v Litman, 1121-1123

A, C & Y Ry. Co., Betsy Ross Foods v, 566

Acey Oldsmobile, Inc., Umlas v, 617-618

Acme Quilting Co., Inc., George Backer Management Corp. v, 1118-1120

Adams, Mennonite Board of Missions v, 58

Addressograph Multigraph Corp., Danjee, Inc. v, 623

Aderholdt, Lewis v, 555

Adkins v Sky Blue, Inc., 38-40

Adler, H. Rosenblum, Inc. v, 495, 500

Adler v Los Angeles Unified School Dist., 929

Advanced Alloys, Inc. v Sergeant Steel Corp., 750

Advanced Appliance Service, Panko v, 279

A. E. Investment Corp. v Link Builders, Inc., 490-491

Aetna Cas. & Sun., Virginia Capital Bank v, 711

Aetna Cas. Co., Hammond's Estate v, 304

Aetna Casualty and Surety Co., Funding Consultants, Inc. v, 707

Aetna Casualty & Surety Co., Leverette v, 844

Aetna Casualty & Surety Co. v Traders Nat. Bank & Trust Co., 887

Aetna Chemical Co. v Spaulding & Kimball Co., 627

Aetna Life and Casualty, Behrens v, 829, 845

Aetna Life Ins. Co., Boston v, 155

A. F. Murch Co., West Cent. Packing, Inc. v, 592

Agricultural Marketing and Bargaining Board, Michigan Canners and Freezers Ass'n., Inc. v, 46

Ahmed v Scott, 1117

Air Engineered Systems & Services, Inc., Naquin v, 1059

Air-Speed, Inc., Rae v, 504-505

Aivagedis, Rodman v, 383

Akins, Holsombach v, 722

Alabama Football, Inc. v Stabler, 483

Alabama Tank Lines, Martin Truck Line v, 1017

Aladdin Products Div., Nat. Service Industries, Inc., Avery v, 650-651

Alamo Hotel, Hanover Ins. Co. v, 570

Alaska Packers' Ass'n v Domenico, 340

Alaska Valuation Service, Inc., Jenson v, 1078

Albany Med. Center Hosp. v Purcell, 893

Alberts, Turner v, 467

Alber v Standard Heating and Air Conditioning, Inc., 336

Albion, Stika v, 406

Albright v Parr, 947

Alcoa, United States v, 97

Aldrehn Theaters Co., Kridelbaugh v, 1017-1018

Alessi v Raybestos-Manhattan, Inc., 82

Alexander, McLean v, 503

Alexander & Alexander, Field v, 285

Alexander Grant & Co., Equitable Life Assur. Soc. v, 503

Alexander Grant & Co., Spherex, Inc. v, 495-498

Alexander Proudfoot Co., Sanitary Linen Service Co. v, 353

Alexander v Brown Builders Inc., 919

Alexandria Scrap Corp., Hughes v, 83

Alford v Shaw, 1065

Algoma Lumber Co., Federal Trade Comm'n v, 161

All America Export-Import Corp., A. M. Knitwear Corp. v, 615

Allard, Foley v, 855

Allen, Andrews v, 539

Allen, Ingle v, 499

Allen Industries Inc. v Sheldon Good Co., 880-881

Allied Polymers, Wright Waterproofing Co. v, 873

Allright, Inc. v Elledge, 546

Allright, Inc. v Pearson, 205

Allright, Inc. v Schroeder, 545-548

Allstate Ins. Co., Kraus v, 831

Allstate Ins. Co., Root v, 449

C

E

F

G

I

M

O

P

S

U

V

W

Y

Z

SUBJECT INDEX

A

absolute guaranty, 772

absolute liability, 206-207

absolute ownership, 510

abstract of title, 1100

acceptance: defined, 722; of an offer, 285-294; revocation of, by buyer, 655

acceptor, 674, 676

accommodation party, 676-677

accord, 447

accord and satisfaction, 447

account, revolving charge, 373

accountants: fraud liability of, 501-502; liability for malpractice, 492-503; limitations on liability for malpractice, 487-488; standard of conduct for, 492

action: choses in, 510; derivative, 1052

act of state doctrine, 95

actual delivery, 536

addresses, opening, 17

adeemed, 1145

adhesion, contract of, 326

administration, letters of, 1149

administrative agencies: and the Constitution, 50-51; defined, 116-117; establishment of, 8-9; executive power of, 123-124; importance of, 117; judicial power of, 124-133; legislative power of, 121-123; nature of, 116-121; uniqueness of, 117

administrative law, 117

administrative regulations, 3

administrator, 1148; pendente lite, 1148

administratrix, 1148

adventure, joint. See joint venture

adverse possession, 1105

advertising, 159-161; corrective, 161; retractive, 161

affirmative covenant, 1104

after-acquired goods, 754

Age Discrimination in Employment Act (ADEA), 916

agencies, administrative. See administrative agencies

agency: authorization by appointment, 854-855; authorization by conduct, 855; creation of, 854-859; defined, 850; by operation of law, 859; purpose of, 853; by ratification, 857; termination of, 859-865

agent: authority of, 870-878; classifications of, 854; corporate, 1073-1074; coupled with an interest, 854; defined, 850; delegation of authority by, 875-878; duties and liabilities of, 878-882; enforcement of liability of, 883-884; general, 854; who may be, 854; insurance, 806; liability to third persons, 889-894; limitations of authority of, 875; scope of authority, 870; special, 854; universal, 854. See also agency; principal

agreement: affecting public welfare, 365-367; contrary to public policy, 365-366; effect of illegality on, 356; effect of partial illegality on, 361; evading statutory protection, 365-366; exceptions to effect of illegality on, 358-359; illegal lobbying, 366; injuring public service, 366; involving conflicts of interests, 366; noncompetition, 370-371; 528; nondisclosure, 528; obstructing legal processes, 366; partnership, 964; security, 754; trust, 1156; usurious, 371; void, 263. See also contract

airbill, 565

Aktiengesellschaft (A.G.), 92

alteration, 714

alternate payees, 689

ambiguity: in contracts, 409; and parol evidence, 394-395

amendments: to the Constitution, 49-50: express, 49-50; by judicial interpretation, 50; by practice, 50

anatomical gift, 516

annuity policies, 836

answer, 15

anticipatory repudiation, 464, 618; by conduct, 464; remedies upon, 467

anti-lapse statutes, 1145

anti-modification clause, 466

antitrust laws, 68-74; exceptions to, 74; in international trade, 94-102; jurisdiction of, 94-95

apparent authority, 855

appeals, courts of, 14

appellate jurisdiction, 8

approval, sale on, 605

Q

R

S